MW00489345

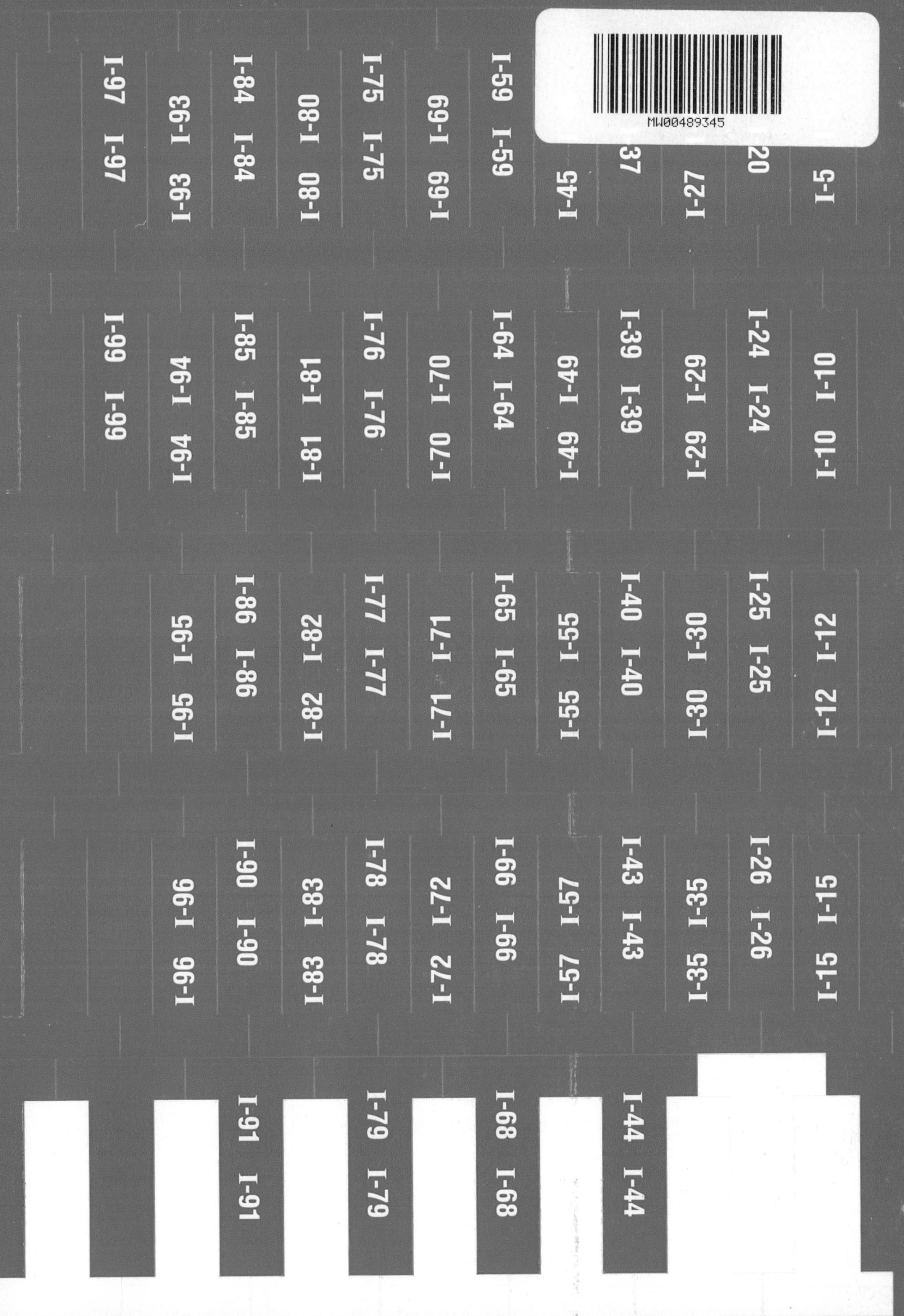

Exit Now Interstate Sticker Tabs

(Note: The Interstates listed here are the most requested and is not a complete list of all main Interstate Highways.)

Sticker Tabs courtesy of Exit Now: Interstate Exit Directory, a publication of Trailer Life Books.

Visit www.TrailerLifeDirectory.com for more information.

HOW TO APPLY TABS

This set of self-adhesive tabs is designed for simplicity and ease of use. The unique T-shape grabs the page better, and makes applying the tabs a breeze.

There are tabs for flagging Interstates, as well as blank tabs to use any way you wish. You can use them to flag favorite exits, index other Interstates or key content.

To apply tabs, follow these easy instructions:

(1) Remove the tab from the backing sheet. (For blank tabs, it is best to write on them before removing them from the backing sheet.)

(2) Open Exit Now to the page you wish to index.

(3) Apply the top of the T-shape to the page you are flagging, being careful not to cover any Exit Now copy. The tab will extend outward from the page, with sticky side down. (See Figure 1.)

(4) Turn the page you are flagging so the sticky side of the tab is now facing up. (See Figure 2.) Double-check the page number to make sure you haven't turned more than one page.

(5) Fold the tab along the scored line, and apply the other end of the tab to the back of the page you are flagging, again taking care not to cover any Exit Now copy. (See Figure 3.) The applied tab should extend about 1/2 inch outward from the Exit Now page.

Repeat the steps above for each Interstate you want to flag. You can set up the tabs in your new Exit Now before you start your trip or as you travel. Either way, with your custom-tabbed Exit Now you'll always know what's at every Interstate exit, making your trip planning safer, smarter and easier than ever!

Figure 1

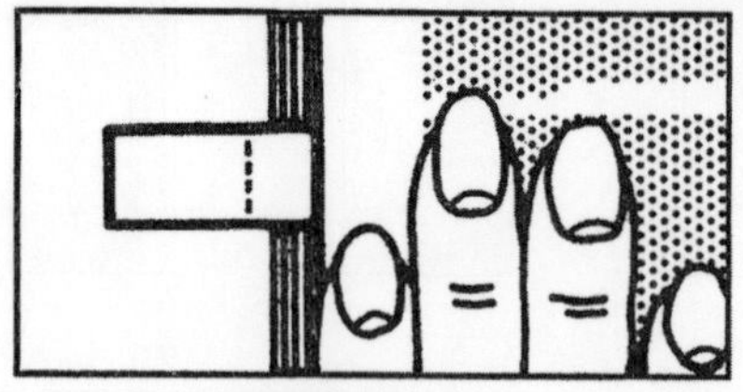
Figure 2

Figure 3

EXIT NOW
Interstate Exit Directory

CONTENTS

How to Read a Map

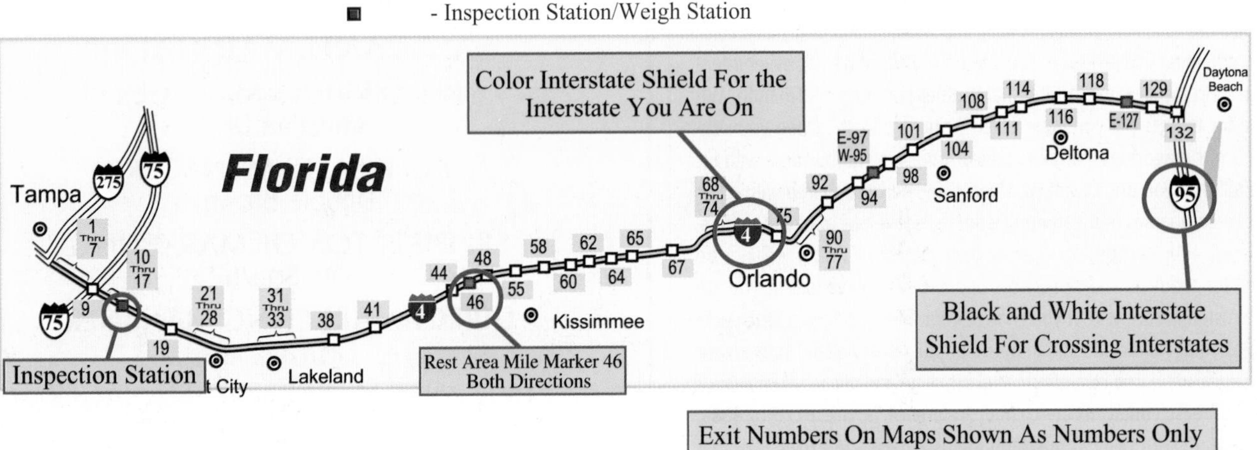

2575 Vista Del Mar Drive, Ventura, California 93001-2575

www.trailerlifedirectory.com

If you would like to provide us with updated information, or would like to be included in this publication, please email us at:

directory@TL.com

To make comments, ask questions, or to place an order please call:

(800)685-6246

Distributed to the book trade by:

Publishers Group West,

1700 Fourth Street, Berkeley, CA 94710

(800) 788-3123

ISBN 0-934798-92-3

Published in the United States of America.

PRIVACY PROMISE

We recognize that your privacy is very important to you and we're committed to helping you protect it. You should know that we will never intentionally share your name, address, and other personal information with anyone for their use if you have asked us not to do so. When you subscribe to our magazines, join our clubs or otherwise do business with us, please tell us if you don't want your name and address shared with other reputable companies or if you don't want to receive our marketing offers. We'll mark your account for a three-year period so that it will not be selected for products and/or services offers which you've told us you are not interested in receiving. If you change your mind, just get in touch with us and ask that we include you in future offerings. Obviously, you can ask to not be included in future offerings at any time and it'll be taken care of promptly. Please contact us at AGI Mail Preference Service, P.O. Box 6888, Englewood, CO 80155-6888 or telephone us at 1-800-766-1674.

Please note that this policy does not apply to e-mail marketing. We will not send you commercial emails unless you have authorized us to do so.

affinity

recreation in motion

EXIT NOW

INTERSTATE EXIT DIRECTORY

Published by Affinity Media
2575 Vista del Mar Dr., Ventura, CA 93001
(800) 234-3450

HOW TO USE EXIT NOW

SERVICE LEGEND

TStop	Diesel/Gas Centers, Travel Centers with services available:Large vehicle access, parking, restaurants and/or fast food, services
FStop	Diesel/Gas location: Large vehicle access, fast food, other services may be available
Gas	Gas stations (locations listed in red may be large vehicle [RV] accessible) Food Restaurants and fast food
Lodg	Lodging services: Hotel, motel, and B&B (bed & breakfast)
AServ	Automotive services, tires
TServ	Diesel engine service, commercial vehicle services, tires
TWash	Large vehicle wash, trailer wash
Med	Hospitals, emergency service, other medical services
Other	Services and attractions near the exit, including but not limited to auto services, attractions, airports, banking, campgrounds, carwashes, colleges, convention centers, entertainment, golf courses, malls, RV parks, RV sales and services, racetracks, shopping, stadiums, and universities

COLOR-CODED EXIT NUMBERS

GREEN	Exit numbers
RED	Rest areas
BLUE	Inspection/weigh stations
BLACK	Interstate junctions, toll roads

COLOR-CODED TEXT

BOLD RED	Rest areas, Med: + medical services
RED	Large vehicle parking on site or nearby, pharmacies, TStop/FStop Diesel/gas for all size vehicles
BLUE	Inspection/weigh stations, highway patrol, police stations, and border crossings
BOLD GREEN	Casinos
BOLD BROWN	Campgrounds/RV parks/RV resorts, RV sales and services, RV dumps, and propane/LP

SYMBOL	LOCATION	MEANING
◈	Next to gas station	Diesel available (Large vehicle parking and/or maneuvering large vehicles may not be possible)
◈	Next to gas station	Bio-diesel and/or ethanol available
♥	Next to listing	Pet services, pet friendly lodging
▲	Next to RV parks/campgrounds	RV park and/or campground
▲	Walmart or business	RV parking permitted overnight
✈	Next to airports	Airport
DAD	Next to TStop/FStop	Difficult access diesel vehicles (RVers)
DAND	Next to TStop/FStop	Difficult access non-diesel vehicles (RVers)
MIL	Before campground listing	RV parks/campgrounds accessible to military personnel
COE	Before campground listing	Corps of Engineers campground
BLM	Before campground listing	Bureau of Land Management campground

REST AREA & WELCOME CENTER ABBREVIATIONS

RR..........Rest rooms
Phone..........Pay phone
Pic..........Designated picnic area
Playgr..........Playground
Vend..........Vending machines on site
WiFi..........Wireless internet
Info..........Traveler information
RVDump..........Sanitary waste dump
RVWater..........RV water
WB, EB, NB & SB..........Direction of rest area/welcome center (Westbound, Eastbound, Northbound, Southbound)
(Both dir)Services available on both sides of interstate

Scenic INTERSTATES

I-95 North/South from Maine to Florida

Interstate 95 is the longest north/south Interstate and passes through fifteen states. The Interstate's northernmost point is at the eastern Canadian border of New Brunswick. It reaches the Atlantic coast at Portland and travels through urban areas such as Boston; Providence, Rhode Island; Hartford, Connecticut; New York City; Philadelphia; Baltimore; Washington; Savannah; Jacksonville, and finally Ft. Lauderdale and Miami.

I-95 crosses the George Washington Bridge in New York City. From Baltimore past Washington, D.C. to Richmond, Virginia, I-95 follows the fall line, where the Atlantic Coastal Plain meets the Appalachian Piedmont. At Richmond, I-64 takes travelers east to Norfolk and Virginia Beach, passing Colonial Williamsburg and Colonial National Historic Park, a National Park Service site encompassing Jamestown Island, Yorktown Battlefield, Greensprings, the Colonial Parkway, and Cape Henry National Memorial.

I-93 South/North from Canton, Massachusetts to St. Johnsbury, Vermont

The largest cities along this route are Boston, Massachusetts, and Manchester and Concord, New Hampshire. Beginning south of Boston, Interstate 93 travels through the city and its suburbs and crosses the state line into New Hampshire. Passing through Manchester and Concord, it travels north to Plymouth, where it enters the scenic White Mountain region.

At the north end of White Mountain National Forest, Franconia Notch is a spectacular mountain pass traversed by a unique parkway, which extends from the Flume Gorge at the south to

Echo Lake at the north. For eight miles, I-93 winds between the high peaks of the Kinsman and Franconia mountain ranges.

I-87 from Albany, New York, to Montreal, Quebec

North of Albany, Interstate 87 is known as the Adirondack Northway (or simply the Northway) and continues all the way to the Canada/United States border at Champlain.

The Adirondacks is a six-million-acre wilderness, the largest wilderness in the east, featuring 2,000 mountains, 3,000 ponds and lakes, 30,000 miles of rivers, streams and brooks as well as the largest hiking trail system in the nation. In fact, there are 2,000 miles of marked hiking trails guiding travelers past ponds, waterfalls and spectacular mountain vistas.

In Lake George, the road parallels the shore of Lake Champlain, which becomes visible near Plattsburgh.

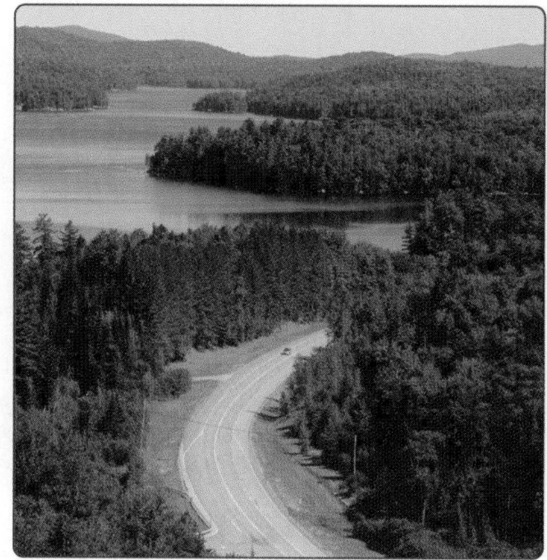

In Clinton County, exit signs from exit 34 to 43 are bilingual in English and French due to its proximity to Quebec. Also, signs for Quebec Autoroute 15 are posted on I-87 North as the Northway approaches the Canadian border.

The southern section of A-15 connects the south shore suburbs of Montreal, linking Quebec Autoroute 15 to Interstate 87 at the Canada-United States border.

I-81 Through the Blue Ridge Mountains in Virginia

Interstate 81 runs for 325 miles along Virginia's northwest spine from West Virginia to Tennessee. This increasingly busy highway opened up mountainous, and formerly remote, parts of the state to a burgeoning national economy.

Interstate 81 does not enter major metropolitan areas; it instead serves smaller cities such as Bristol, Marion, Wytheville, Christiansburg, Roanoke, Lexington, Staunton, Harrisonburg, and Winchester along its 324.92-mile northeast-southwest route in Virginia. It parallels the Blue Ridge Parkway most of the way, providing outstanding mountain vistas.

For some, spring is the best season in the Blue Ridge as a wealth of flowering trees, bushes, and wildflowers appear. The area's strikingly different vegetative life zones, successive floral displays, autumn foliage, geological features, and animals are major attractions each year for visitors.

I-40 – Smoky Mountains, North Carolina

In southwestern North Carolina, Interstate 40 crosses the Great Smoky Mountains, the southern section of the Appalachian Range, and provides access to Great Smoky Mountains National Park.

Dominated by plant-covered, gently contoured mountains, the crest of the Great Smokies forms the boundary between Tennessee and North Carolina, bisecting the park from northeast to southwest in an unbroken chain that rises more than 5,000 feet for over 36 miles.

Some 100 species of native trees find homes in the Smokies, more than in any other North American national park. Almost 95% of the park is forested, and about 25% of that area is old-growth forest — one of the largest blocks of deciduous, temperate, old-growth forest remaining in North America.

More than 1,500 additional flowering plant species have been identified in the park. It is also home to lungless salamanders and more than 200 species of birds, 66 types of mammals, 50 native fish species, 39 varieties of reptiles, and 43 species of amphibians.

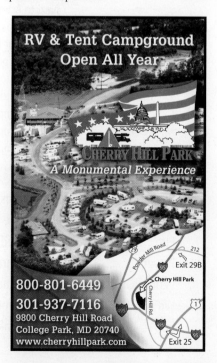

I-77 from South Carolina to North Carolina

Interstate 77 begins in the far southeastern part of the Columbia, South Carolina, metropolitan area. Much of the interstate's path through Fairfield and Chester County (north of Columbia) is uphill. This marks the changing terrain from the Midlands to the Piedmont as the road climbs the Fall Line.

Interstate 77 through North Carolina begins at the South Carolina state line at Pineville. North of Charlotte, it skirts Lake Norman.

Nestled on the banks of beautiful Lake Norman are the towns of Cornelius, Davidson and Huntersville. These unique towns present a wide array of leisure amenities for visitors and guests including upscale shopping, year-round golfing, fishing and other water activities. Lake Norman is the largest man-made lake in the Carolinas — 34 miles long with 520 miles of shoreline.

I-26 from Asheville, North Carolina to Johnson City, Tennessee

North of Asheville, Interstate 26 crosses the French Broad River, and turns north towards Weaverville and Mars Hill. It enters first the Blue Ridge and then the Great Smoky mountains of the Appalachian range, passing through the Pisgah and Cherokee National Forests.

About 1 mile south of Sam's Gap, as it approaches the North Carolina and Tennessee state line, I-26 reaches its highest elevation at 4,000 feet.

In Tennessee, I-26 continues in a northeast direction past Erwin. As it approaches Johnson City in the Tri-Cities area, it leaves the Cherokee National Forest.

I-75 from Mackinaw City to Sault Ste. Marie, Michigan

Near its northernmost section, Interstate 75 connects Michigan's Upper and Lower Peninsulas via the 5-mile-long Mackinac Bridge (pronounced MACK-in-aw). The "Mighty Mac" is a suspension bridge spanning the Straits of Mackinac to connect the separate Upper and Lower peninsulas of the state. The straits link Lake Michigan and Lake Huron. Envisioned since the 1880s, the bridge was completed in 1957 after decades of controversy over the construction.

Designed by engineer David B. Steinman, the bridge connects the village of Mackinaw on the south end with the city of St. Ignace on the north.

It is the longest suspension bridge between anchorages in the Western hemisphere. The bridge's main span is 3,800 feet long, making it the third-longest suspension span in the country and the twelfth longest worldwide.

For drivers who are squeamish about driving across the bridge, The Mackinac Bridge Authority has a Drivers Assistance Program that provides drivers. Anyone interested can arrange to have their vehicle or motorcycle driven to the other end at no additional fee.

As travelers cross the Mackinac Bridge they can listen to an AM radio broadcast that tells the history of the bridge and provides updates on driving conditions.

Proceeding north, I-75 passes through the east unit of the Hiawatha National Forest, which features stands of northern hardwoods, jack pine and other conifers. The forest provides abundantly unique habitats for wildlife, plant species, recreation opportunities, and outstanding scenery, wildlife viewing and scenic vegetation.

At the northern end of I-75, at Sault Ste. Marie, Michigan, the Sault Ste. Marie International Bridge crosses into Sault Ste. Marie, Ontario.

The "Soo" Locks allow ships to travel between Lake Superior and Lake Huron and beyond to Lake Erie and Lake Ontario. The locks are closed from January through March, when ice shuts down shipping. During the remaining months, the locks pass an average of 10,000 ships per year.

I-90 from Sheridan, Wyoming to Billings, Montana

Interstate 90 turns north leaving Sheridan and crosses the Wyoming/Montana state line. South of Hardin, Montana, it passes the site of The Battle of the Little Bighorn (Custer's Last Stand).

Little Bighorn Battlefield National Monument memorializes one of the last armed efforts of the Northern Plains Indians to preserve their way of life. Here in 1876, 263 soldiers and attached personnel of the U.S. Army, including Lt. Col. George A. Custer, met death at the hands of several thousand Lakota and Cheyenne warriors.

White crosses on the hillsides and in the gullies mark the location where each man died. Originally buried where they fell, they were later disinterred and reburied in a mass grave on top of the hill, around an obelisk-shaped monument with their names inscribed upon it. A tribute to the estimated 60 to 100 Indian warriors, The Indian Memorial stands 75 yards northeast of the cavalry monument in the form of a circular earthwork carved gently into the prairie.

At the visitor center, rangers give information-packed talks and answer questions. Outside, tepees represent the Indian camp where more than 3,000 Lakota Sioux, Arapahoe and Cheyenne warriors gathered, led by Crazy Horse, Sitting Bull and other chiefs. Nearby is a military cemetery where veterans of other American wars are buried.

Visitors may tour the battleground by car — motorhomes can navigate the two-lane roadway, but it's not always easy to pull off at vantage points — or on foot. The logical way to experience the sequence of events to drive or walk 5 1/2 miles to the far end of the roadway and work your way back to the visitor center, stopping at the frequent pullouts and historical markers.

In June, Hardin celebrates Little Big Horn Days, featuring the Custer's Last Stand Reenactment, the Grand Ball, a Little Big Horn symposium, a historical field trip and parades.

I-80 from San Francisco, California, to Cheyenne, Wyoming

Interstate 80 begins in San Francisco and heads northeast through Oakland, Vallejo, Sacramento and the Sierra Nevada mountains before crossing into Nevada.

In the state of Nevada, Interstate 80 runs northeast from the Lake Tahoe region near Reno to Battle Mountain. Here it turns east via Elko, following the Truckee and Humboldt rivers.

The stretch of I-80 through Nevada is largely desolate and mountainous. Services are limited compared to I-80 in other states.

After crossing Utah's western border, I-80 crosses the Bonneville Salt Flats west of the Great Salt Lake. The longest stretch between exits on an interstate highway is between Wendover and Knolls — 37.1 miles. This portion of I-80, crossing the Great Salt Desert, is extremely flat and straight. Signs warn drivers about fatigue and drowsiness.

East of the salt flats, I-80 passes through Salt Lake City before entering the Wasatch Mountains east of the city. It ascends Parley's

Canyon and passes within a few miles of Park City as it follows a route through the mountains towards Wyoming.

I-80 roughly traces the Oregon Trail across Wyoming, passing through the dry Red Desert and over the Continental Divide. The highway actually crosses the Divide twice, since two ridges of the Rocky Mountains split in Wyoming, forming the Great Divide Basin — from which no surface water escapes.

I-70 – West of Denver, Colorado

Eastbound I-70 enters Colorado from Utah on a plateau between the north rim of Ruby Canyon of the Colorado River and the south rim of the Book Cliffs. The plateau ends just past the state line and the highway descends into the Grand Valley formed by the Colorado River and its tributaries.

The Grand Valley is home to several towns and small cities. Grand Junction is the largest city between Denver and Salt Lake City and serves as the economic hub of the area.

I-70 exits the valley through De Beque Canyon, a path carved by the Colorado River that separates the Book Cliffs from Battlement Mesa. The river and its tributaries provide the course for the ascent up the Rocky Mountains. In the canyon, I-70 enters the Beavertail Mountain Tunnel, the first of several tunnels built to route the freeway across the Rockies. This tunnel design features a curved sidewall to give added strength. After the canyon winds past the Book Cliffs, the highway follows the Colorado River through a valley containing the communities of Parachute and Rifle.

Approaching the city of Glenwood Springs, the highway enters Glenwood Canyon. Both the federal and state departments of transportation have praised the engineering achievement required to build the freeway through the narrow gorge while preserving the natural beauty of the canyon. A 12-mile section of roadway features the No Name Tunnel, Hanging Lake Tunnel, Reverse Curve Tunnel, 40 bridges and viaducts, and miles of retaining walls. Through a significant portion of the canyon, the freeway hugs the north bank of the Colorado River.

To minimize the hazards along this portion, a command center staffed with emergency response vehicles and tow trucks on standby monitors cameras along the tunnels and viaducts in the canyon. Traffic signals have been placed at strategic locations to stop traffic in the event of an accident, and variable message signs equipped with radar guns will automatically warn motorists exceeding the design speed. Usually prohibited along Interstate Highways, the USDOT has provisions for bicycles along the freeway corridor in Glenwood Canyon.

The highway departs the Colorado River near Dotsero. From here, I-70 follows the Eagle River towards Vail Pass. Along the ascent, I-70 serves the ski resort town of Vail and the ski areas of Beaver Creek Resort, Vail Ski Resort and Copper Mountain.

The construction of the freeway over Vail Pass is also listed as an engineering marvel. One of the challenges of this portion is the management of the wildlife that roams this area. Several parts of the approach to the pass feature large fences that prevent wildlife from crossing the freeway and direct the animals to one of several underpasses. At least one underpass is located along a natural migratory path and has been landscaped to encourage deer to cross.

The highway descends to Dillon Reservoir, near the town of Frisco, and begins one final ascent to the Eisenhower Tunnel, where the freeway crosses the Continental Divide. The Eisenhower Tunnel is noted as both the longest mountain tunnel and highest point on the Interstate Highway System. The tunnel has a command center, staffed with 52 full-time employees, to monitor traffic, remove stranded vehicles, and maintain generators to keep the tunnel's lighting and ventilation systems running in the event of a power failure. Signals are placed at each entrance and at various points inside the tunnel to close lanes or stop traffic in an emergency.

The last geographic feature of the Rocky Mountains traversed before the highway reaches the Great Plains is the Dakota Hogback. The path through the hogback features a massive cut that exposes various layers of rock millions of years old. The site includes a nature study area for visitors.

As the freeway passes from the Rocky Mountains to the Great Plains, I-70 enters the Denver metropolitan area, part of a larger urban area called the Front Range. The freeway arcs around the northern edge of the LoDo district, the common name of the downtown area of Denver.

I-25 Albuquerque, New Mexico to Trinidad, Colorado

Coming from the south, as Interstate 25 nears Albuquerque it meets up with State Road 6, the original U.S. Route 66, in Los Lunas.

In Albuquerque, there is an interchange with Interstate 40. Named the Big I, it was given an honorable mention by the United States Department of Transportation and the Federal Highway Administration for excellence in urban highway design in 2002.

Leaving Albuquerque, I-25 starts to curve into an east–west orientation as it heads toward Santa Fe. I-25 retains that orientation until Las Vegas, where it starts to revert back into its usual north–south orientation. The highway stays this way as it leaves New Mexico to enter Colorado.

Trinidad, a city near the Trinidad Lake, is the last major city that lies along I-25.

I-15 from Mesquite, Nevada to St. George, Utah

After Interstate 15 leaves North Las Vegas, the route travels northeast, crosses the Muddy River at Glendale and then climbs up onto the Mormon Mesa. At Mesquite, the freeway then crosses the Nevada/Arizona state line and cuts through the extreme northwestern corner of Arizona, passing through the Beaver Dam Wilderness Area and the Virgin River Gorge before entering Utah just south of St. George.

The Virgin River Gorge is a long canyon that has been carved out by the Virgin River. As I-15 runs through the canyon, it crosses the Virgin River several times. The Virgin River Gorge section of Interstate 15 is one of the most expensive parts of interstate highway ever constructed. Due to the winding of the interstate, the canyon is noted for tricky driving conditions.

Take the Cedar Pockets Interchange and find yourself in the middle of a wilderness wonderland. The Virgin River Canyon Recreation Area is the only developed campground on the Arizona Strip. Whether you are having a picnic or spending the night, hike the short trails leading to the Virgin River, and to a hilltop site where geology and history are explained.

Keep a lookout for bighorn sheep that live on the rocky crags above the gorge. Flora and fauna in the canyon are typical of the Mojave Desert. The vegetation is primarily Mohave Desert shrub such as creosote bush and Joshua tree in the Virgin River Gorge and Beaver Dam Slope.

Higher elevations are dominated by blackbrush merging into piñon-juniper woodlands.

Nestled in a pocket of the spectacular Virgin River Gorge, this recreation area is surrounded by colorful cliffs and rocky canyons. The canyon is popular among outdoor recreationalists such as rock climbers, hikers and campers. Its climate is typical of the Mojave Desert with hot summers and mild winters.

Photo by Mark Nielsen

The Virgin River Canyon Recreation Area offers a developed campground, picnic/day use area, hiking trails and access to the Virgin River and two wilderness areas.

The Recreation Area is located off of Interstate 15 about 20 miles southwest of St. George Utah and about 20 miles northeast of Mesquite, Nevada. The Cedar Pockets exit is located halfway through the Virgin River Gorge. Fees are charged for overnight camping and group use.

I-84 from Portland to Boardman, Oregon through the Columbia Gorge; Detour to Multnomah Falls

Interstate 84 travels west-east, following the Columbia River and the rough path of the old Oregon Trail from Portland east as far as Boardman before it leaves the river.

As the only sea-level route from the Great Basin to the Pacific Ocean, the Gorge is a land of contrasts. The western Gorge, with an average annual rainfall of 75 inches, is a place of misty mountains, rich forestlands and more waterfalls than any area in the country. The eastern Gorge, with an annual rainfall of less than 15 inches, is a scenic place of rim-rock bluffs, rolling hills, farm and ranchlands.

As you work your way through the Columbia River Gorge, there are many attractions, places to stay overnight and dine and a world of recreational opportunities

Plummeting 620 feet from its origins on Larch Mountain, Multnomah Falls is the second highest year-round waterfall in the United States. Nearly two million visitors a year come to see this ancient waterfall.

Fed by underground springs from Larch Mountain, the flow over the falls varies; usually it's highest during winter and spring.

Multnomah Falls offers one of the best places in the Columbia River Gorge National Scenic Area to study geology exposed by floods. Five flows of Yakima basalt are visible in the fall's cliff face.

Benson Bridge, crafted by Italian stonemasons, allows visitors to cross the falls between its lower and upper cataracts. In 1914, Simon Benson, a prominent businessman and owner of the falls at that time, erected the bridge. The trail continues to a platform at the top of the upper falls, the Larch Mountain Lookout, where visitors get a bird's-eye view of the Columbia Gorge and also of "Little Multnomah," a small cascade slightly upstream from the "upper" falls, which is not visible from ground level.

The Lodge was built in 1925 and is on the National Register of Historic Places. Inside the lower level of the Lodge are a USDA Forest Service Information Center, a snack bar, and a gift shop. In the upper portion of the lodge is a restaurant accessible by elevator.

In the town of Hood River, "the Aspen of windsurfing," windsurfers from around the world congregate on an idyllic stretch of river, their concentration broken only by winds that often exceed 30 mph. If water sports aren't your speed, more leisurely options abound: Enjoy the jaw-dropping scenery aboard the Sternwheeler Columbia Gorge or the historic Mt. Hood Railroad; or play a round of golf at Indian Creek or Skamania Lodge.

Head east from Hood River to take in fishing and white-water rafting. Close by, The Dalles is the location of the Columbia Gorge Discovery Center. Listen to early river explorers weave stories of discovery, learn about the geologic forces that created the gorge, or ride the waves on a windsurfing simulator.

I-280 San Jose to San Francisco, California

Traveling northward from San Jose to San Francisco, Interstate 280 passes through the cities and towns of Santa Clara, Cupertino, Los Altos and Los Altos Hills before it reaches its scenic section west of the communities of the San Francisco Peninsula east of the Santa Cruz Mountains. I-280 then becomes an urban highway in San Bruno, passing through South San Francisco and Daly City before it traverses the southeastern part of the city of San Francisco.

Most of Interstate 280 from San Jose to Daly City is designated as the Junipero Serra Freeway in honor of the Spanish missionary who founded many of California's missions in the 18th century. Drivers can see a 26-foot statue of Father Serra kneeling and pointing over the freeway in Hillsborough.

The segment of the Junipero Serra Freeway between Cupertino and Daly City has been called the "World's Most Beautiful Freeway" since its dedication in the 1960s. Travelers enjoy scenic views of the Santa Cruz Mountains to the west and San Francisco Bay to the east, and are shielded by hills from the cities to the east. Crystal Springs Reservoir fills the bottom of a canyon between Hillsborough and Belmont.

I-5 Red Bluff to Weed, California

At Red Bluff, Interstate 5 enters the volcanic Shasta Cascade region. Passing northward through Anderson and Redding, it continues through the city of Shasta Lake before crossing over the lake on a causeway and climbing upward near the foot of Mount Shasta. In Siskiyou County, I-5 passes through Dunsmuir before passing near Lake Siskiyou and entering the city of Mount Shasta. The interstate then continues to Weed and eventually to Yreka before crossing the Klamath River and reaching Siskiyou Pass and the Oregon border.

I-10 from Santa Monica, California, to Jacksonville, Florida

Interstate 10 is the southernmost west-east, coast-to-coast interstate highway in the United States. It stretches from the Pacific Ocean at State Route 1 (Pacific Coast Highway) in Santa Monica, California, to Interstate 95 in Jacksonville, Florida.

Major cities along the route are Tucson, Arizona, Las Cruces, New Mexico, El Paso, San Antonio and Houston, Texas; Baton Rouge and New Orleans, Louisiana; Biloxi, Mississippi; Mobile, Alabama; and Tallahassee, Florida.

INTERSTATE LOW CLEARANCE OVERPASSES

HIGHWAY	LOCATION	HEIGHT
ALABAMA		
AL 1/ US 31	Seale	13'0"
AL 2/ US43/72	Florence- 5 miles east at Shoals Creek bridge	12'0"
AL 10	Greenville	10'0"
US 31 SB	Montgomery- at Coosa River	13'4"
AL 51	Opelika- South of jct. I-85	13'4"
AL 53	Ardmore- West, East of jct I-65	10'8"
US 90	Mobile- Bankhead Tunnel	12'0"
US 98 WB	Spanish Fort-0.3 miles west	13'6"
AL 111	Wetumpka-at Coosa River Bridge	12'6"
AL 251	Ardmore	11'0"
Swan Bridge Rd	Cleveland- 1 mile west at Locust Fork River bridge	13'0"
Local Road	Nectar- 1 mile east, Locust Fork River, covered bridge	9'0"
ARIZONA		
AZ 80	Douglas- mile point 366.10	12'10"
AZ 84 EB	Casa Grande- mile point 177.66	13'6"
AZ 188	4 miles north of jct. AZ 88 at Salt River mile point 262.44	12'3"
US 191	Morenci- tunnel at mile point 169.90	12'10"
6th Ave	Tuscon- mile point 66.73	10'11"
ARKANSAS		
AR 7	Camden- North, 0.8 mi. nortwest of US 79	13'1"
AR 42	Turrell- 0.01 miles east of AR 77	11'9"
AR 43	Siloam Springs- jct. US 12	13'6"
AR 51	Arkadelphia- 0.59 miles east of US 67	12'6"
AR 69	Moorefield	12'6"
AR 69	Trumann-0.82 miles east of US 63	9'0"
AR 69	Trumann- 0.19 miles northeast of US 63	12'0"
AR 75	Parkin	12'1"
AR 106	Batesville- west, 2.43 miles west of AR 69	10'6"
AR 127	Beavertown- between US Hwy 62 and AR Hwy 23, the Beaver Bridge at the White River/Tablerock Lake	11'6"
AR 134	Garland- jct. US 82	13'5"
AR 247	Pottsville- 0.11 miles south of US 64	11'1"
AR 282	Mountainburg- approx. 4.5 miles southwest	13'1"
AR 296	Mandeville- approx. 0.5 miles southwest	11'0"
AR 307	Briggsville- 2.5 miles south of Fourche LaFave River	13'0"
AR 365	North Little Rock- 0.4 miles west of US 70	13'0"
CALIFORNIA		
CA 2	Angeles National Forest- west of CA 39 at Angeles Crest tunnels	13'6"
CA 33 NB, SB	Ventura- Matilija Tunnels	13'0"
CA 41	Atascadero-1.3 mile northeast of US 101	13'2"
CA 70 WB	Belden- east of North Fork at Feather Ridge bridge	13'3"
CA 70	Marysville- 0.7 miles north of CA 20	14'0"
CA 70 EB, WB	Spanish Creek Tunne south of Camp Alexander at milepost 35.55	13'0"

HIGHWAY	LOCATION	HEIGHT
I-80	San Francisco- San Francisco Oakland Bay Tunnel	13'10"
CA 48 NB, SB	Rio Vista- 12 miles northwest of Yolo County line	13'1"
US 101	Thousand Oaks- 3.9 miles west of CA 23	14'0"
CA 110 NB	Los Angeles- College Street overpass	13'6"
CA 110 NB	Los Angeles- Hill Street overpass	14'0"
CA 110 NB	Los Angeles- Tunnel 0.5 miles southwest of I-5	13'0"
CA 110 SB	Los Angeles- I-5 overpass	14'0"
CA 110 SB	Los Angeles- 0.2 miles northeast of I-5	14'0"
CA 129 WB	River Oaks- 2.8 miles west of US 101	14'0"
CA 151 EB, WB	Summit City- Coram overpass	13'9"
CA 160 NB (16 St.)	Sacremento- 0.6 miles south of American River	13'10"
CA 238 SB	Fremont- 2.2 miles north of I-680	14'0"
COLORADO		
US 6 EB (6th Ave)	Denver- 0.4 miles west of CO 88 (Federal Ave.) at Knox Ct. overpass, milepost 283.58	14'4"
US 6 WB (6th Ave)	Denver- 0.4 miles west of CO 88 (Federal Ave.) at Knox Ct. overpass, milepost 283.58	14'6"
US 6 EB (6th Ave)	Denver- CO 88 (Federal Blvd) overpass, milepost 283.66	14'3"
US 6 WB (6th Ave)	Denver- CO 88 (Federal Blvd) overpass, milepost 283.66	14'2"
US 6	Eagle- 0.67 miles east of Eagle River, milepost 150.24	14'4"
CO 14	Poudre Park- tunnel 4.7 miles west, milepost 107.25	14'5"
Bus. CO 24	Manitou Springs- milepost 3.14	13'10"
US 36	Westminster- W. 80 Ave. overpass, milepost 53.93	14'4"
US 40/I-70	Deer Trail- 4.92 miles west at milepost 346.25	14'3"
BR US 50 EB (Santa Fe Ave)	Pueblo- just south of I-25/US 85/87 at Arkansas River	13'10"
I-70 EB	Idaho Springs- milepost 238.689	14'4"
I-70 EB	Palisade- Beaver Tunnel, milepost 50.38	14'1"
CO 95 SB (Sheridan Blvd)	Denver- at I-70, milepost 9.013	14'1"
CO 144	Fort Morgan- at I-76 overpass, milepost 0.01	13'5"
CO 265 (Brighton Blvd)	Denver- 1.2 miles north of I-70, milepost 1.198	11'7"
US 550/CO 789	Ouray- tunnel 1.17 miles south at milepost 90.86	13'9"
CONNECTICUT		
US 1 (Boston Post Rd)	Branford- west between CT 142 and Branford Connector to I-95, Exit 53	13'1"
US 1	Darien- 0.1 mile southwest of CT 124	11'1"
US 1	Madison- 2.1 miles west of CT 79	12'7"
US 1 SB	Milford- Milford Parkway overpass	13'6"
US 1	Stamford- 1.2 miles east of CT 137	13'1"
US 5	Wallingford- CT 15 overpass	13'5"
US 6	Bristol- 0.5 miles west of CT 69	13'6"
US 6	Newtown- 0.3 miles southwest of I-84	12'7"
CT 8	Derby- 1 mile north of CT 34	13'6"
CT 10	Farmington- US 6 overpass	13'4"

HIGHWAY	LOCATION	HEIGHT
CT 10	Hamden	13'6"
CT 10	Hamden- CT 15 overpass	13'6"
CT 12	Groton- CT 184 overpass	12'2"
CT 53	Bethel- 1.3 miles south of CT 302	11'1"
CT 53	Norwalk- CT 15 overpass	12'0"
CT 58	Fairfield- CT 15 overpass	11'8"
CT 67	Seymour	12'6"
CT 71	Wallingford	10'0"
CT 72	Pequabuck- 1 mile southeast of US 6	13'3"
CT 81	Clinton- 0.1 miles north of US 1	11'10"
I-95	Darien- 1.1 mile northeast of Exit 9	13'6"
I-95	Milford- 0.2 miles west of Exit 38	13'6"
CT 104	Stamford- CT 15 overpass	11'10"
CT 106	New Canaan- 0.4 miles north of CT 15	11'7"
CT 110	Stratford- 0.2 miles north of I-95	11'2"
CT 113	Stratford- 0.1 miles north of I-95	13'4"
CT 115	Seymour- 0.2 miles east of CT 8	12'8"
CT 123	Norwalk- northwest at CT 15 (Merritt Parkway)	12'4"
CT 130	Bridgeport- I-95 overpass	13'6"
CT 130	Bridgeport- 0.1 mile north of I-95	11'1"
CT 133	Brookfield- 0.2 miles east of US 1	12'1"
CT 135	Fairfield- 0.1 miles south of I-95	10'4"
CT 136	Westport- 0.1 miles south of I-95	10'8"
CT 137	Stamford- CT 15 overpa	
CT 146	Branford	9'9"
CT 146	Guilford- 1.25 miles southwest	11'3"
CT 146	Leetes Island	13'6"
CT 159	Windsor- 0.1 miles northeast of CT 305	12'9"
CT 190	Stafford Springs- 1.4 miles northwest	13'6"
CT 243	New Haven- CT 15 overpass	12'8"
CT 275	Eagleville- 0.2 miles west of CT 33	12'0"
CT 322	Milldale- CT 10 overpass	12'7"
CT 372	Berlin- 1.5 miles west of US 5	11'2"
CT 533	Vernon	12'7"
CT 598	Hartford- Main Streeet overpass	12'1"
CT 598	Hartford- Columbus Blvd overpass	13'6"
CT 649	Groton- 1.2 miles east of CT 349	10'6"
CT 719	Norwalk- CT 15 overpass	13'4"
CT 796 (Milford Pkwy)	Milford- 0.2 miles north of I-95	13'6"
CT 847	Waterbury	12'8"
CT 847	Waterbury Lake Ave	12'10"
	Danbury- A RailRoad Bridge Just off I-84 west bound on Lake Ave.	10'

DELAWARE

HIGHWAY	LOCATION	HEIGHT
US 13A	Laurel	12'11"
DE 100 (Mountchannin Rd)	Guyencourt	13'0"
Local Rd. 018C	Ogletown	10'8"
Local Rd 258	Ashland- covered bridge at Red Clay Creek	7'6"
Local Rd 35A	Kirkwood- 0.75 miles north, west of DE 71	11'4"
Local Rd 356D (North Chapel St.)	Newark- at Paper Mill Rd.	12'3"
Casho Mill Rd	Newark- between DE 2 and DE 273, west of junction	8'11"
James Street	Newport- 0.1 mile south of jct DE 4	13'2"
Local Rd 336D	Stanton- 1 mile south	11'1"
Local Rd 338 (Telegraph Rd)	Stanton- 0.5 mile west	10'10"
18th Street	Wilmington- just south of Augustine cut-off	13'0"
Rising Sun Rd	Wilmington- between DE 52 (Pennsylvania Ave) and DE 141 (New Bridge Rd) east of the junction	12'4"
Rising Sun Rd	Wilmington- between DE 52 (Pennsylvania Ave) and DE 141 (New Bridge Rd) at Brandywine River bridge	13'6"
Local Rd 263A	Wooddale- Between DE 48 (Lancaster Pike) and Barley Mill Rd., west of Centerville Rd. at Red Clay Creek bridge	9'6"

DISTRICT OF COLUMBIA

HIGHWAY	LOCATION	HEIGHT
3rd Street	I-395 Mall tunnel	13'0"
Connecticut Ave	Q Street underpass, near jct of Connecticut and New Hampshire Ave	13'5"
Massachusetts Ave	underpass at Thomas Circle- jct of 14 St., M St. and Vermont Ave"	12'6"
Potomac River Fwy	US 50 (Theodore Roosevelt Memorial Bridge) overpass- between 23 St. and the Rock Creek & Potomac Pkwy	12'6"
Potomac River Fwy	27th Street underpass	12'11"
Potomac River Fwy	Whitehurst Fwy ramp overpass	12'6"
8th Street	Franklin Street viaduct, north of US 1	13'0"
Florida Ave	1 block south of US 50 (New York Ave)	13'0"
L Street	east of 1st Street, under Washington Terminal Yards"	13'6"
M Street	east of 1st Street, under Washington Terminal Yards"	13'5"
2nd Street	underpass at Virginia Ave	13'5"
3rd Sreet	underpass at Virginia Ave	13'6"
7th Street	underpass at Virginia Ave	13'6"
Anacostia Drive	South Capital Street overpass	13'4"
Canal Street	overpass near I-395	13'3"
South Capital St.	underpass north of I-395	13'4"
Suitland Pkwy	Anacostia Freeway overpass	12'6"

FLORIDA

HIGHWAY	LOCATION	HEIGHT
US 92 W	Lakeland- 1.5 mile east of Wabash Ave	12'6"
Alton Road (FL 945)	Miami Beach- FL A1A/US 41 overpass	11'11"
Barth Road	Jacksonville- US 1 / 23 overpass	12'4"
Bloxam Street	Tallahassee- FL 61 overpass	12'6"
College Street	Jacksonville- I-95 overpass	12'8"
Gadsden Street	Tallahassee- US 27 overpass	13'0"
Palm Ave	Jacksonville- I-95 overpass	8'6"
Sea World Drive	Orlando-southwest, I-4 overpass"	13'1"
Washington St.	Lake City- US 41 overpass	12'9"

IDAHO

HIGHWAY	LOCATION	HEIGHT
US 26 SB	Idaho Falls- milepost 333.48	13'10"
US 30	Pocatello- milepost 334.14	13'6"
US 30 B	Pocatello- milepost 0.16	13'6"
US 30 B	Pocatello- milepost 0.24	13'11"
I-84B (11th Ave)	Nampa- milepost 58.89	13'10"
I-84B (11th Ave)	Nampa- Front Street overpass, milepost 58.88	13'9"
US 95 Spur SB	Weiser- milepost 0.15	13'11"

ILLINOIS

HIGHWAY	LOCATION	HEIGHT
IL 1 NB, SB	Crete- 4.78 miles north of jct. IL394	13'5"
US 6 EB, WB	Joliet- 0.5 mile north of IL 53	12'2"
IL 7, NB, SB (Southwest Hwy)	Palos Park- 86 Ave overpass	13'2"
IL 7 NB, SB (Southwest Hwy)	Palos Park- 123 Street overpass	13'2"
US 12/ 20 EB, WB (95th Street)	Chicago- 1.7 to 3.4 miles east of I-94	13'1"
US 12/ 20 EB, WB (95th Street)	Chicago- just east of Chicago Skyway	13'5"

HIGHWAY	LOCATION	HEIGHT
US 14/ 41 EB, WB (Foster Ave)	Chicago- just east of Broadway	11'11"
US 14 EB, WB (Peterson Ave)	Chicago- 0.75 miles east of Western Ave	13'0"
IL 19 EB, WB (Irving Park Rd)	Chicago- 0.25 miles west of Ashland Ave., 1800 west	13'5"
IL 19 EB,WB	Chicago- just west of I-90/94, 4200 west	13'0"
IL 25 SB (Broadway)	Aurora- 0.3 miles south of New York St.	13'0"
IL 25 NB	Montgomery- 0.5 mile south of US 30	13'0"
OS 30 EB (Jefferson St)	Joliet- at Broadway, west of Des Plaines River	12'7"
US 30 EB	Joliet- 0.6 mile east of IL 53	13'6"
US 30 WB	Joliet- 0.6 mile east of IL 53	13'4"
US 41 EB, WB (Foster Ave)	Chicago- 0.25 west of Ashland Ave	11'10"
IL 43 NB (Harlem Ave)	East Forest- 0.5 mile north of Madison St.	13'0"
IL 43 SB (Harlem Ave)	River Forest- 0.5 mile south of MAdison St.	13'1"
US 45/ 150 NB (Springfield Ave)	Champaign- 0.1 mile east of Neil St.	12'8"
US 45/ 150 SB (Springfield Ave)	Champaign- 0.1 mile east of Neil St.	12'7"
US 45/52 NB, SB (Water St)	Kankakee- 0.1 mile east of Washington Ave.	12'9"
IL 50 NB, SB (Cicero Ave)	Chicago- just south of I-90	13'2"
US 52 EB, WB	Kankakee- 0.1 mile east of Il 115	12'8"
IL 53 NB, SB (Chicago St)	Joliet- just south of Washington Street	13'2"
IL 64 EB, WB (North Ave)	Chicago- 0.3 mile east of Pulaski Road	13'2"
IL 64 EB, WB (North Ave)	Chicago- just east of I-90/94	12'10"
IL 64 EB, WB (North Ave)	Chicago- east of I-94 at Chicago River	11'6"
IL 62 NB, SB	Geneseo- 0.5 mile north of US 6	10'0"
US 150 (Springfield Ave)	Champaign- US 45/150 entry	12'7"

INDIANA

HIGHWAY	LOCATION	HEIGHT
IN 1	Connersville- 0.47 mile north of IN 44	11'2"
IN 17	Plymouth- 1.7 miles south of US 30	11'0"
IN 43 NB	Solsberry- 4.13 miles north of IN 54	11'2"
IN 43 SB	Solsberry- 4.13 miles north of IN 54	11'3"
US 136 EB	Clermont- 1.5 miles west of IN 134	12'5"
US 136 EB	Clermont- 1.5 miles west of IN 134	12'4"
US 150	Ferguson Hill- 1.94 miles north of US 40	13'0"
US 231	Lake City- 0.23 mile south of jct. US 41	13'6"
IN 450 EB, WB	Williams- 8.3 miles west of IN 158	12'11"

IOWA

HIGHWAY	LOCATION	HEIGHT
IA 14	Corydon- north	13'6" & 13'3"
US 61 NB (Brady St)	Davenport- 0.1 mile north of 4th Street	12'2" & 11'8"
US 61 SB (Harrison Ave)	Davenport- 0.3 mile north of US 61/67 (River Drive)	12"1" & 11'8"
IA 83	Atlantic- 0.5 mile west	14'6" & 13'4"
IA 146	Grinnell- 2 miles north	13'9" & 13'6"
IA 415 NB (2nd Ave)	Des Moines- 0.9 mile south of I-35/80	13'7" & 13'4"
IA 415 SB (2nd Ave)	Des Moines- 0.9 mile south of I-35/80	13'6" & 13'4"

KANSAS

HIGHWAY	LOCATION	HEIGHT
KS 31/ US 59	Garnett- 1.0 mile south	14'0"
KS 34	Bucklin- 0.1 mile north of jct. US 54	13'9"
US 40/ 59	Lawrence- 1 mile south of jct. I-70	14'0"
KS 53	Mulvane- 0.3 mile west of KS 15	14'0"
US 56	Herington- 3.3 miles east of US 77	13'6"
US 59	Garnett- at KS 31/ US 59 entry	
US 147	Spillway at Cedars Bluff Reservoir	14'0"
US 166	Arkansas City- 0.3 mile east of US 77	13'6"
Turner Diagonal EB overpass	Kansas City- 0.3 mile south of I-70 exit 415, Riverview Ave.	14'0"

KENTUCKY

HIGHWAY	LOCATION	HEIGHT
KY 7	Colson- 3 miles east	12'10"
KY 7	Garrett- at KY 80 overpass	12'2"
KY 8 (4th St.)	Newport-Covington-Licking River Bridge	13'6"
KY 8 (Elm St.)	Ludlow	13'6"
KY 9	Newport- south of 12th Street	13'2"
KY 17 (Scott St)	Covington- 17th Street	12'3"
KY 17 (Greenup St)	Covington- near 17th Street	13'6"
US 25 (W. 12th St)	Covington- I-71/75 overpass, 0.3 mile north of Jefferson St. ramp	13'5"
US 25 (Dixie Hwy)	Erlanger- 0.1 mile northeast at jct KY 236	13'6"
US 25 W	Corbin- 0.5 mile north of KY 312	12'0"
KY 26	Woodbine- 3 miles southwest	13'6"
US 27 (Manmouth St)	Newport- south of 11th Street	13'6"
US 27 (Broadway)	Lexington- 0.1 mile southeast of KY 4, northern intersection	13'2"
US 31 W (Main St)	Louisville- at 14th Street	13'0"
US 31 W (22nd St)	Louisville- 0.25 miles south of Woodland	12'6"
KY 40	Paintsville- 0.75 mile east of US 23/460	13'5"
US 45	Paducak- Ohio River bridge	13'1"
Bus US 45	Fulton	13'6"
KY 52	Beattyville- 0.3 mile west of KY 11	13'4"
KY 57	2.3 miles west of KY 627	13'4"
US 60	Owensboro- 0.5 mile east of US 431 at US 231 Ohio River bridge underpass	13'0"
US 60	east of Paducah at Tennessee River	12'11"
Alt. US 60 (3rd St)	Louisville- at Eastern Parkway	12'2"
Alt. US 60 (3rd St)	Louisville- 0.2 mile south of Eastern Parkway	12'2"
KY 70	Eubank- 1.2 mile west of US 27	11'0"
KY 94	Fulton- north, 0.1 mile west of KY 307	11'6"
KY 139 & KY 293	Princeton- 0.1 mile west of KY 91	12'1"
KY 177	Butler- 1.1 mile west of US 27	10'3"
KY 254	Madisonville- 0.2 mile south of KY 892	13'3"
KY 282	Kentucky Dam Village State Resort Park	13'2"
KY 307	Fulton-0.3 mile north of Tennessee state line	10'0"
KY 307	Fulton- 1.1 mile north of Fulton County line	12'9"
US 421	Fayette County- 1 mile east of Scott County line	13'6"
US 431	Central City- 0.1 mile south of KY 70	11'9"
KY 867 EB	Royalton- 1.5 miles west	8'0"
KY 867 WB	Royalton- 1.5 miles west	13'3"
KY 1120 (W. 12th St)	Covington- I-71/75 overpass, 0.3 miles north of Jefferson ramp	13'5"
KY 2513 (2nd St)	Maysville- 100 feet east of KY 8	12'4"

LOUISIANA

HIGHWAY	LOCATION	HEIGHT
Bus. LA 1	Natchitoches	13'1"

HIGHWAY	LOCATION	HEIGHT
LA 8	Sabine River bridge	12'1"
LA 15	Alto- Boeuf River bridge (curb)	13'1"
LA 23	Belle Chase- 1 mile north of Belle Chase Tunnel	13'4"
LA 48 SB	Norco- 2 miles north of LA 627	13'2"
US 71	Alexandria- Allen bridge	13'6"
US 90	New Orleans- 0.2 mile south of I-610	13'4"
Bus. US 165	Pineville	11'10"
US 171 NB	Leesville	13'0"
LA 385	Lake Charles- under I-10 Calcasieu River bridge	12'6"
LA 538	Mooringsport- 4.75 miles southeast	13'1"
LA 546	Cheniere- 0.5 mile south of I-20	12'6"
LA 729	Lafayette- just west of US 90, near Lafayette Regional Airport"	12'7"

MAINE

HIGHWAY	LOCATION	HEIGHT
ME 9	Saco- mile marker 39.9	12'6" & 12'1"
ME 24	Richmond- mile marker 34.9	12'6" & 11'2"
ME 197	Richmond- at Kennebec River, mile marker 16.5	15'4" & 11'2"

MARYLAND

HIGHWAY	LOCATION	HEIGHT
MD 7	North East	12'0"
MD 7	Perryville	13'0"
MD 7	Parryville	13'0"
MD 36	Frostburg	10'4"
MD 51	Northwest of Paw Paw WV	13'4"
MD 75	Monrovia	12'6"
MD 109	Barnesville	13'0"
MD 117	Boyds	12'0"
MD 117	Bucklodge- 1.5 miles northwest of Boyds	13'0"
MD 135	Cumberland- south of US 220 overpass	12'0"
MD 269	Colora	11'0"
MD 303	Cardova- northeast at MD 309	12'6"
MD831A	Homewood- bypasses jct. of US 40 and MD 36	11'3"

MASSACHUSETTS

HIGHWAY	LOCATION	HEIGHT
US 1 (Lafayette Rd)	Salisbury- 0.75 mile north of MA 110	13'3"
MA 1A (Dodge St)	Beverly- at jct MA 128	13'5"
MA 1A NB	Boston- at jct of road to Logan Int'l Airport	12'2"
MA 1A	Boston- at Porter St., west of airport	13'5"
MA 2 (Commonwealth Ave)	Boston- express underpass at jct MA 2A	13'1"
MA 2/US 3 (Memorial Drive)	Cambridge- 0.4 mile south of River Street	11'10"
MA 3 NB	Boston- 0.4 mile south of jct. MA 28	11'6"
MA 3 (Memorial Dr)	Cambridge- express underpass at jct. MA 2A	9'2"
MA 3A/113 (Kendall Rd)	Tyngsboro- at Merrimack River bridge	12'11"
US 5/ MA 10	Greenfield- 0.2 mile south of MA 2A, Main Street	12'10"
US 6 WB	West Barnstable- 0.7 mile southwest at MA 149 overpass	13'4"
MA 6A (Main St)	Barnstable- approx 1 mile west	12'2"
MA 9 (Huntington Ave)	Boston- MA 2A (Massachusetts Ave) overpass	13'4"
MA 9 (Main St)	Northampton- just east of US 5	12'3"
MA 10/ US 202 (Elm St)	Westfield- 0.25 mile south of Westfield River	13'5"
MA 13 (Main St)	Leonminster	13'6"
MA 10/ US 202 (N. Elm St)	Westfield- just north of Westfield River	11'5"
MA 19 (Maple St)	Warren- just south of MA 67	13'0"
MA 21 (Parker St)	Springfield	12'5"
MA 27 (Crescent St)	Brockton- just east of MA 28	12'8"
MA 28 (McGrath Hwy)	Somerville- 0.4 mile south of I-93	13'4"
MA 31 (Depot St)	Fitchburg- 0.2 mile north of MA12	12'6"
MA 31 (Princeton Rd)	Fitchburg- 1.6 miles north of MA 2	13'2"
MA 32A (Barre Rd/ Old MA 32)	Hardwick- 0.2 mile west of MA 32	12'0"
MA 35 (High St)	Danvers	13'5"
MA 62/70 (Main St)	Clinton	11'0"
MA 62 (Main St)	Concord	12'2"
MA 68 (Gardner St)	Baldwinville- just east of US 202	13'6"
MA 85 (River St)	Cordaville- 0.8 mile south of I-90	11'0"
I-93/ MA 3	Boston- 1.5 mnile south of I-90	13'6"
MA 101 (Parker St)	Gardner- 0.75 mile west of MA 68	13'3"
MA 116 (Cabot St)	Holyoke	12'0"
MA 116 (Lyman St)	Holyoke- at Lyman and Main Streets	11'5"
MA 117 (Lancaster St)	Leominster- 0.3 mile east of MA 12	13'3"
MA 122A	Holden	13'6"
MA 122 (Madison St)	Worcester- 0.4 mile west of I-290	12'0"
MA 146	Uxbridge	13'6"
MA 202A (Union Ave)	Westfield	13'4"
MA 203 (Morton St)	Boston- American Legion Highway overpass	12'11"
Belmont	Belmont-Train Bridge at Common St/Concord Ave and Leonard St.	10'3"

MICHIGAN

HIGHWAY	LOCATION	HEIGHT
MI 1 EB (Woodward Ave)	Highland Park- Davidson Ave	13'1"
MI 1 WB (Woodward Ave)	Highland Park- Davidson Ave.	13'3"

MINNESOTA

HIGHWAY	LOCATION	HEIGHT
Bus. US 2	East Grand Forks- Red River bridge at North Dakota state line, mile point 0.00	13'0"
MN 36	Stillwater- St. Croix River bridge at Wisconsin state line, mile point 205.25	13'2"
MN 39	Duluth- 0.9 mile east of MN 23, St. Louis River bridge, mile point 0.90	11'0"
MN 70	Pine City- 4.5 miles south at mile point 20.06	13'6"
MN 72	Baudette- Rainey River bridge, mile point 76.90	11'8"
MN 93	0.7 mile east of jct. US 169, mile point 0.05	12'8"

MISSISSIPPI

HIGHWAY	LOCATION	HEIGHT
MS 12	Columbus- approx. 3.8 miles north of US 82	12'9"

MISSOURI

HIGHWAY	LOCATION	HEIGHT
MO 5	Laclede- 0.5 mile north of US 36	13'10"
MO 5	Marceline- 2.4 miles south of US 36	13'11"
MO 5	Syracuse- 0.1 mile north of US 50	13'9"
MO 12 EB (Truman Rd.)	Independence- 0.4 mile west of Sterling Ave	13'11"
MO 12 WB (Truman Ave)	Independence- 0.4 mile west of Sterling Ave.	13'5"
MO 13	Higginsville- 0.5 mile south of US 24	13'8"
MO 13	Polo- 0.3 mile south of MO 116	13'8"
MO 19	Cuba- 0.7 mile north of I-44	13'10"
MO 19	New Florence- 2 miles north of I-70	13'9"

HIGHWAY	LOCATION	HEIGHT
MO 21	Paulina Hills- east of Meramec River bridge	13'9"
US 24	Kansas City- 0.2 mile west of jct. I-435	12'3"
US 24 EB	West Quincy- at Mississippi River	13'10"
MO 28	Dixon- 0.2 mile south of County Road C	13'10"
MO 30	Affton- 0.3 mile east of jct MO 21	13'9"
US 36 EB	Bucklin- 0.8 mile west of MO 129	13'9"
US 40	Kansas City- just south of I-70 at Blue Ridge Blvd overpass	13'4"
US 40	Kansas City- Topping Ave overpass	13'6"
US 50	Sedalia- 1.3 miles east of US 65	13'9"
US 61 NB	Frontenac- at I-64 overpass	13'10"
US 61/67	Arnold- north at Meramec River bridge	13'9"
US 63	Clark- 0.3 mile south of Bus US 63	13'11"
US 63B SB	Moberly- 1.5 miles south of US 24	13'10"
US 69 NB	Claycomo	13'8"
US 69B	Excelsior Springs- 0.5 mile west of jct. County Road H	13'6"
I-70BL	Columbia- at Paris Road overpass	14'0"
MO 94	West Alton- 0.1 mile west of US 67	12'9"
MO 94	West Alton- 0.5 mile wst of US 67	12'7"
MO 100	Gasconade- Gasconade River bridge	13'10"
US 159	Missouri River bridge	12'10"
MO 168	Palmyra- 1.1 mile west of jct. County Road C at North River bridge	13'9"
MO Spur 180	Pagedale- 0.2 mile north of jct. Rte. D (Page Ave)	13'8"
MO 350 EB	Raytown- 1.7 miles southeast of I-435 at Blue Ridge Blvd overpass	13'7"
MO 350 WB	Raytown- 1.7 miles southeast of I-435 at Blue Ridge Blvd overpass	14'0"

MONTANA

HIGHWAY	LOCATION	HEIGHT
MT 7	Wibaux- milepost 79.9	13'6"
MT 13W	Wolf Point- milepost 52.7	14'0"
MT 49	East Glacier Park- just west of US 2 at milepost 209.3	13'6"
US 87 SB	Black Eagle- 15th Street, milepost 3.70	14'0"
US 87	Great Falls- Smelter Ave., milepost 3.77	14'0"
US 191	Big Timber- milepost 0.79	13'8"
US 191	Malta- just south of US 2 at milepost 157.5	13'5"
US 212/310	Laurel- 0.5 mile north of I-90 at milepost 54.5	13'3"

NEBRASKA

HIGHWAY	LOCATION	HEIGHT
NE 2/ US 385	Alliance	13'11"
US 6/ NE 31	Elkhorn- 1 mile south, Link 28B	14'4"
US 6	Emerald	14'5"
US 6	Lincoln- 2 miles west	13'10"
US 30 SB	Columbus- 1 mile south at Loup River bridge	14'4"
NE 31	Gretna- at US 6 and Dodge Street	14'4"
NE 71	Kimball- 0.2 mile north of US 30	13'6"
US 81 SB	Columbus- Loup River bridge, 1 mile south	14'4"
US 81	York- at 14th Street and 15th Street	13'11"
NE 133 (90th St)	Omaha- 0.2 mile south of NE 64 (Maple St) at Lake Street	13'7"
US 275	at jct. US 6 and NE 31	14'0"

NEVADA

HIGHWAY	LOCATION	HEIGHT
US 50	Cave Rock tunnel- Lake Tahoe	12'4"
US 50	Cave Rock tunnel- Lake Tahoe	13'7"
NV 738	Las Vegas- south, Jean underpass	14'0"
NV 794 (Winnemucca Blvd)	Winnemucca	14'0"
Bonanza Road	Las Vegas- Bonanza underpass	14'0"
(F.A.U. 579)		
2nd St & Kuenzil Ln (F.A.U. 648)	Reno- 2nd Street underpass	14'0"
Wells Ave (F.A.U. 663)	Reno- 0.2 mile north of E 2nd Street	13'10"

NEW HAMPSHIRE

HIGHWAY	LOCATION	HEIGHT
NH 9	Chesterfield- Connecticut River bridge	13'6"
NH 16A	Jackson- Ellis River bridge	12'3"
NH 16B	Rochester	12'2"
NH 25	Piermont- 1.7 miles west, Conecticut River bridge	12'0"
NH 63	Hinsdale- 2.3 miles south	12'8"
NH 85	Exeter	11'8"
NH 110	Berlin	10'4"
NH 110A	Milan	13'6"
NH 119	Hinsdale- 7.3 miles north, Connecticut River bridge	12'0"
NH 135	Dalton	10'3"
NH 135	Woodsville- just north of US 302	10'11"

NEW JERSEY

HIGHWAY	LOCATION	HEIGHT
US 1/9	Elizabeth- mile marker 44.6	13'3"
US 1/9	Elizabeth- Elizabeth River viaduct (Elizabeth St), mile marker 43.94	12'10"
US 1/9/46	Palisades Park- Oakdene Ave overpass, mile marker 63.86	13'5"
NJ 4	Englewood- Jones Rd. overpass, mile marker 9.62	13'4"
NJ 5	Cliffside Park- Delia Blvd overpass, mile marker 0.5	10'6"
NJ 24 WB	Madison, mile marker 4.81	13'0"
NJ 28	Plainfield- mile marker 14.42	11'11"
US 30	Camden- Baird Blvd overpass, mile marker 2.49	13'4"
NJ 53	Denville- mile marker 4.2	13'2"
I-80	Columbia- mile marker 3.62	12'3"
I-80	Columbia- Decatur St. overpass, mile marker 4.18	13'2"
NJ 93 (Grand Ave)	Palisades Park- US 46 overpass, mile marker 0.61	13'5"
NJ 94	Hainesburg- Scranton Branch overpass, mile marker 2.20	13'6"
US 130	Brooklawn (south of Gloucester City)- mile marker 25.61	13'6"
NJ 173	Bloomsbury- mile marker 4.35	12'4"
US 202	Morris Plains- mile marker 46.96	13'6"
I-278	Linden- mile marker 0.66	12'0"
NJ 439	Elizabeth- mile marker 1.93	12'1"
I-495	Union City- Hudson Ave overpass, mile marker 1.85	13'3"
Access Road	Elmwood Park- I-80 underpass, mile marker 60.59	10'10"
Main Street	Ft. Lee- US 1/9/46 overpass, mile marker 64.51	13'4"
Cemetary Road	River Edge- NJ 4 overpass, mile marker 5.5	13'0"
Bordentown Ave	South Amboy- NJ 35 overpass, mile marker 49.1	13'5"

NEW MEXICO

HIGHWAY	LOCATION	HEIGHT
US 54	Logan- 0.4 mile east of jct NM 39	14'0"
US 56	Springer- 0.1 mile east of jct I-25	13'8"
US 70	Lordsburg- 29.6 miles east of Arizona state line	14'0"
US 84	Fort Sumner- 0.4 mile north of jct. US 60	13'11"
NM 118	Gallup- 12.7 miles east of Arizona state line at I-40	14'0"
NM 118	Mentmore- 8.4 miles east of Arizona state line at I-40	13'11"
NM 124	Grants- 1.2 miles east if NM 117/124 at I-40	13'6"
NM 152	Kingston- 1.2 miles east	12'8"
NM 152	Kingston- 3.2 miles east	12'5"
NM 161	Watrous- at I-25 overpass at Exit 364	13'11"

HIGHWAY	LOCATION	HEIGHT
NM 320 NB	Dona Ana- 3.7 miles north of US 70	13'10"
NM 395	Hondo- 0.2 mile south of jct US 70/380 at Rio Hondo	12'9"
NM 423 Paseo del Norte	Albuquerque- 0.8 mile west of jct 2nd Street	13'11"
NM 423	Albuquerque- jct. Rio Grande Blvd	13'11"
NM 567	Pilar- 6.1 mile north of jct. NM 68 at Rio Grande	12'10"
FR 4184	Aztec- 0.1 mile east of US 550	11'3"
FR 4221	Belen- 0.5 mile east of Loop 13/ NM 309	13'6"
Central Ave	Albuquerque- 0.1 mile east of 1st Street	13'11"

NEW YORK

HIGHWAY	LOCATION	HEIGHT
US 1	Pelham Manor- at Hutchinson River Pkwy overpass	13'8"
US 1	Port Chester	12'11"
US 1	Port Chester	12'8"
NY 3/26	Carthage- 0.4 mile north of jct NY 3 & NY 26	12'6"
US 4	Fort Edward- 0.5 mile north of NY 197	13'11"
US 4	Schuylerville- 0.2 mile north of NY 32	12'10"
NY 5/US 20	Canandaigua- 0.1 mile southwest of NY 332	11'7"
NY 5	Scotia- 2.5 miles west of NY 147	13'11"
NY 5	Syracuse- 1.4 miles west of US 11	12'2"
US 6	Port Jervis- 0.5 mile north of I-84 at Neversink River bridge	13'4"
US 6	Shrub Oak- at jct US 6 and Taconic State Pkwy	13'0"
NY 7	Binghampton- 0.1 mile north of US 11	12'4"
NY 7	Cobleskill	13'10"
NY 7	Cobleskill	13'9"
NY 7	Rotterdam- 1.7 miles northwest of NY 146	13'9"
NY 7	Sanitaria Springs- 5.5 miles east of NY 369	13'7"
US 9 SB	Albany- ramp to EB I-90	13'5"
US 9 NB	Albany- at ramp to I-90 WB	13'9"
US 9	New York City- 2.3 miles north of I-95 at Harlem River	13'6"
US 9	Peekskill- at US 6 overpass	11'1"
US 9	South Glens Falls- at Hudson River bridge	12'10"
US 9	Underwood- at I-87 overpass, Exit 30	13'9"
US 9A	New York City- at Harlem River	12'8"
NY 9A	Ossining- 0.2 miles north of NY 133	12'6"
NY 9A	Ossining- 1.4 miles north of NY 133	11'9"
NY 9A/100	Briarcliffe Manor- 1.5 miles north of jct NY 117	12'2"
NY 9A/100	Hawthorne- north, at NY 117 overpass	13'3"
NY 9J	Rensselaer- at jct. with US 9/20	13'10"
NY 9J	Stuyvesant- 1.6 miles north	13'9"
NY 9L	Lake George- 0.3 mile northeast of US 9	13'5"
US 9W	Cementon- 1.1 mile north	13'4"
US 9W	West Camp	13'1"
US 11	Binghamton- 6 miles north at I-81 overpass	13'11"
US 11	Binghamton- 0.4 mile north of NY 17C	13'11"
US 11	Binghamton- 0.25 mile south of jct. NY 7	13'2"
US 11	Champlain- 2.5 miles east	13'10"
US 11	Evans Mills- 0.8 mile south of NY 342	13'8"
US 11 (Wolf St)	Syracuse- 0.4 mile south of I-90	12'11"
NY 11A	Cardiff- US 20 overpass	13'6"
NY 12	Waterville- 0.5 mile north of US 20	13'9"
NY 12E	Watertown	13'9"
NY 13	Chittenango	13'11"
NY 14A	Reading Center- 0.7 mile northwest of NY 14	13'10"
NY 15	Lakeville- 2 miles north of Alt US 20	13'8"
NY 16 WB	Buffalo- 0.5 mile west of Fillmore Ave	12'7"
NY 16	East Aurora	13'10"
NY 16	Machias- 0.1 mile north of NY 242	13'11"

HIGHWAY	LOCATION	HEIGHT
NY 16	West Seneca- at I-90 overpass	13'11"
NY 17	Corning- 1.2 mile northwest of jct. US 15	13'11"
NY 17	Harriman- 0.9 mile west of I087	13'11"
NY 19	Brockport- 0.5 mile south of Nwe York State Barge Canal	11'8"
NY 19	Rock Glen- 0.7 mile south	13'6"
NY 19A	Silver Springs- 1.6 mile southeast of NY 19	13'0"
US 20	Border City- 0.2 mile west of NY 96A	13'10"
US 20	Cherry Valley- 0.2 miles east of NY 166	13'10"
US 20	Duanesburg- 0.7 mile northwest of NY 7	13'9"
US 20	McCormack Corners- 0.2 mile northwest of NY 146	13'11"
US 20	Sangerfield- 0.2 miles west of NY 12	13'8"
US 20/NY 78	West Seneca- 0.25 mile north of NY 400	13'6"
Alt. US 20	Warsaw- 0.3 miles east of NY 19	13'6"
NY 22	North Hoosick- 0.1 mile south of NY 67	13'11"
NY 22 SB	Petersburg- at jct. NY 2 and NY 22	13'1"
NY 22A	Granville- 2.6 miles northeast of NY 22	11'10"
NY 23	Catskill- 0.5 mile east of NY 385	12'11"
NY 25	Mineola- at Northern State Pkwy overpass	13'5"
NY 25	New York City- Queensboro Bridge over East River	8'5"
NY 25	New York City- 0.1 mile east of I-278	13'10"
NY 25	New York City- 0.1 mile east of I-495	13'8"
NY 25	Smithtown- 0.5 mile west	13'10"
NY 25	Smithtown- 1 mile west	13'8"
NY 25A	New York City- 1.5 mile west of I-295	13'6"
NY 25A	St. James- 1.5 miles northeast of NY 25	13'9"
NY 26	Endicott- 0.2 mile north of NY 17C	13'0"
NY 27	Amityville- at NY 110 overpass	13'10"
NY 27	Freeport- Meadowbrook State Pkwy overpass	13'3"
NY 27	Lynbrook	13'5"
NY 27	Lynbrook- 1.5 mile west	13'6"
NY 27	New York City- 0.5 mile east of Rockaway Pkwy	12'4"
NY 28	Kingston	13'10"
NY 28	Thendara- 1 mile northeast	13'5"
NY 30	Esperance- 1.2 miles south of US 20	13'10"
NY 30A	Central Bridge- 0.5 mile north of NY 7	13'11"
NY 31	Niagra Falls- 0.4 miles east of NY 104	13'7"
NY 31	Rochester- 0.7 miles northwest of I-490	12'9"
NY 31F	Macedon- 0.9 mile north of NY 31	13'7"
NY 32	Albany- 1.4 mile north of I-90	13'11"
NY 32	Albany- 0.6 mile south of I-90	11'4"
NY 33	Rochester- 1 mile east of New York State Barge Canal	12'0"
NY 33A	Rochester- 0.1 mile east of New York State Barge Canal	13'0"
NY 33B	Buffalo- 0.4 mile west of US 62	13'8"
NY 34	Spencer- 4.3 miles north	12'6"
NY 37	Malone- 0.5 mile north of US 11	13'7"
NY 38	Owego	13'7"
NY 38/96	Owego- south at NY 17 overpass	9'6"
NY 41	Afton	13'11"
NY 42	Lexington	12'3"
NY 46	Oneida- 0.2 mile north of NY 5	13'8"
NY 49	Utica- 1 mile west of NY 12	13'11"
NY 55	Billings- 1.3 miles west at Taconic St. Pkwy overpass	13'9"
NY 59	Nanuet- at NY 304 overpass	13'10"
US 62	Buffalo- 0.6 mile north of NY 354	13'7"
US 62	Eden- 1.5 mile south	13'9"
US 62	Lackawanna- 2.9 mile north of NY 179	13'7"
NY 63	Griegsville- 0.2 mile west of NY 36	13'10"

HIGHWAY	LOCATION	HEIGHT
I-78	New York City- Holland Tunnel	12'6"
Co. 80 (Mantauk Hwy)	East Port	11'11"
Co. 80 (Montauk Hwy)	Hampton Bays- 1 mile west	13'9"
Co. 80 (Montauk Hwy)	Moriches	12'6"
NY 85	New Scotland- 0.7 mile west of NY 85A	13'9"
Co. 85 (Montauk Hwy)	Sayville	13'7"
NY 85	Slingerlands- 0.7 miles southwest of NY 140	12'2"
NY 85A	Voorheesville- 0.2 mile west of NY 155	12'1"
I-90	Albany- at US 9 overpass	13'5"
I-90	Clifton- 8.8 miles east of I-490, Exit 47	13'11"
I-95	New York City- 0.7 mile east of I-87	13'10"
NY 102	East Meadow- at Meadowbrook State Park overpass	13'11"
NY 104	Niagra Falls- 0.1 mile north of NY 182	12'1"
NY 104	Rochester- 0.1 mile east of St. Paul Blvd	13'10"
NY 107	Massapequa- north at Southern State Pkwy	13'3"
NY 110	Huntington Station- 1.3 miles north of NY 25	13'10"
NY 110	Melville- at Northern State Pkwy overpass	13'4"
NY 112	Medford- 0.5 mile south of I-495	13'9"
NY 114	East Hampton- 1 mile northwest	12'0"
NY 115	Poughkeepsie- 1.1 mile northeast	11'0"
NY 120	Rye- just south of I-95	11'9"
NY 120A	Port Chester	11'2"
NY 120A	Port Chester- 0.1 mile north of US 1	12'0"
NY 129	Croton on Hudson- 4.6 miles northeast	12'4"
NY 130	Depew- 1.4 miles west of US 20	13'11"
NY 146	Schenectady- 3.5 miles north of NY 7	13'11"
NY 158	Rotterdam- 0.7 mile south of NY 7	13'8"
NY 164	Towners	12'5"
NY 164	Towners	12'4"
NY 164	Towners	12'0"
NY 173	Syracuse- 3 miles south of I-81 overpass	13'11"
NY 182	Niagra Falls- at Niagra River	13'10"
I-190	Buffalo- 0.8 mile east of NY 5	12'6"
I-190	Tonawanda- 2 miles north of I-290	13'10"
NY 198	Buffalo- 1.7 mile east of I-190	13'11"
NY 201	Johnson City- 0.7 mile south of Exit 70 on NY 17	11'11"
US 202	Suffern- 0.4 mile north of NY 59	12'3"
NY 208	Washingtonville- 2.5 miles north	9'2"
NY 211	Otisville	12'6"
NY 237	Holley- 0.4 miles southwest of NY 31	12'11"
NY 249	Farnham- 0.3 mile east of NY 5	11'0"
NY 251	Scottsville	13'9"
NY 253	East Rochester	13'11"
NY 259	Spencerport- 0.2 mile south of New York State Barge Canal	12'6"
NY 265	Buffalo- 2.7 mile south of NY 324	13'8"
NY 266	Buffalo- 0.3 mile north of NY 198	12'4"
NY 266	Tonawanda- 0.5 mile north of NY 325	13'11"
I-278	New York City- Brooklyn Bridge overpass	13'2"
I-278 WB	New York City- 0.1 mile east of Brooklyn Bridge	13'4"
I-278	New York City- 2.4 miles southwest of I-495	13'11"
I-278	New York City- at 31st Street overpass	13'8"
I-278	New York City- at NY 25 overpass	13'7"
I-278	New York City- 0.2 mile north of NY 25	13'10"
I-278	New York City- 0.6 mile north of NY 25	13'10"
I-278	New York City- 0.3 mile north of NY 25A	13'4"

HIGHWAY	LOCATION	HEIGHT
I-278	New York City- 0.2 mile south of NY 25A	13'10"
I-278	New York City- 0.2 mile north of Exit 25, 26	13'10"
I-278	New York City- 0.2 mile south of Exit 32	13'11"
I-278	New York City- 1.9 mile west of jct. I-95 and I-678	13'9"
NY 286	Macedon- 0.75 mile north of NY 31	13'4"
NY 291	Stittsville- 2 miles south of NY 365	13'11"
I-295	New York City- 0.6 miles southeaast of I-95	13'7"
NY 308	Rhineback- 1.8 miles east at NY 9G overpass	13'11"
NY 311	Lake Carmel- 0.34 mile north of NY 164	11'9"
NY 329	Watkins Glen- 2 miles southwest	12'5"
NY 334	Fonda- 0.6 mile northwest of NY 5	13'0"
NY 335	Elsmere	13'6"
NY 352 WB	Elmira- east of NY 14	13'6"
NY 354	Buffalo- 0.7 mile west of US 62	12'3"
NY 354	Buffalo- 1 mile west of US 62	13'6"
NY 354	Buffalo- 1.4 miles west of US 62	12'10"
NY 356	Tonawanda- 0.3 mile east of NY 384	13'0"
NY 362	Bliss- 0.4 mile north of jct. NY 39	13'5"
NY 366	Varna	13'8"
NY 370	Liverpool- 1.3 mile northwest of I-81	10'9"
NY 370	Syracuse- at jct. I-81	10'6"
NY 370	Syracuse- 0.5 mile northwest of US 11	12'3"
NY 372	Greenwich	11'11"
NY 383	Scottsville- 1 mile west	13'10"
NY 384	Buffalo- at jct. NY 198	13'3"
NY 384	Niagra Falls- 0.6 miles east of NY 61	13'7"
NY 385	Coxsackie- 0.8 miles east of US 9W	13'5"
NY 417	Portville- 0.4 miles east of NY 305	13'3"
NY 443	Delmar- 2.4 miles southwest	13'6"
NY 443	Elsmere	13'6"
NY 470	Cohoes- 0.8 miles southwest of NY 32	10'10"
I-478	New York City- Brooklyn Battery Tunnel	12'9"
I-490	Rochester- 0.2 miles northwest of NY 33	13'8"
I-495	Locust Grove- at NY 135 overpass	13'10"
NY 495	New York City- Queens Midtown Tunnel	12'9"
NY 495	New York City- east end of Lincoln Tunnel access	13'11"
NY 495	New York City- Lincoln Tunnel	13'0"
I-678	New York City- at 14th Ave overpass	13'7"
I-678	New York City- at NY 25 overpass	13'8"
I-678	New York City 0.8 mile south of NY 25	11'0"
I-678	New York City- 0.1 mile north of Exit 5 and Atlantic Ave	11'1"
I-678	New York City- at Kennedy Int'l Airport	13'8"
I-678	New York City- at Cross Island Pkwy	13'7"
I-787	Albany- onramp to northbound I-787 over Hudson River	13'7"
Rte 951R	Vandalia- 0.3 miles southeast at Allegheny River	11'3"
Brooklyn Battery Terminal	New York City- Exit 25 NB to I-278	13'8"
Brooklyn-Queens Expwy. NB	New York City- at Astoria Blvd overpass	13'6"
F.D. Roosevelt Dr.	New York City- at Battery Pl overpass	13'9"
F.D. Roosevelt Dr. Ramp SB	New York City- 60th Street overpass	12'10"
F.D. Roosevelt Dr.	New York City- at Williamsburg Bridge	10'6"
F.D. Roosevelt Dr.	New York City- 0.25 mile south of Williamsburg Bridge	13'8"
F.D. Roosevelt Dr.	New York City- just north of NY 25	13'0"
F.D. Roosevelt Dr.	New York City- 0.2 mile northeast of NY 25	13'8"
F.D. Roosevelt Dr.	New York City- 0.9 miles northeast of NY 25	13'8"
F.D. Roosevelt Dr.	New York City- 1.3 miles northeast of NY 25	12'8"

HIGHWAY	LOCATION	HEIGHT
F.D. Roosevelt Dr.	New York City- 0.5 miles south of Triborough bridge	12'6"
F.D. Roosevelt Dr. Access Rd	New York City- at 78th Street, 0.9 miles northeast of NY 25	13'0"
Harlem River Dr.	New York City- at Willis Ave overpass	11'4"
Harlem River Dr.	New York City- at 3rd Ave overpass	13'8"
Harlem River Dr.	New York City- at 145th Street overpass	13'7"
Harlem River Dr.	New York City- 0.75 miles south of I-95	13'9"

NORTH CAROLINA

HIGHWAY	LOCATION	HEIGHT
Bus US 15/501 EB (Chapel Hill Blvd)	Durham- at NC 1127 (Chapel Hill Road) & Cornwallis overpass	13'1"
Bus US 15/70/501 (Roxboro St.)	Durham- 0.25 mile north of NC 147	12'0"
Bypass US 15/501	Chapel Hill- 2.8 miles northeast of NC 86, Bus 15/501 overpass	13'2"
NC 16	Crumpler- southwest, before jct. US 221	13'1"
NC 54 (Nelson Chapel Hill Hwy)	Durham- 0.1 mile west of NC 1959 (Miami Blvd)	13'6"
NC 55	Durham- 0.1 mile north of jct. NC 147	13'6"
NC 55 (Alston Ave)	Durham- 0.2 mile north of NC 147	13'2"
NC 94	Fairfield- 3.6 miles north at the Intracoastal Waterway	13'6"
Bus. I-95/US 301	Fayetteville- Bus. I-95/US 301 underpass before jct. I-95	11'10"
US 157 (Guess Rd)	Durham- I-85 underpass 0.6 mile north of jct. I-85 & NC 1321	13'6"
US 155 EB	Welden- 0.5 mile west of jct. US 301	13'6"
NC 215	Beach Gap- Blue Ridge Pkwy underpass	13'0"
NC 1603	Stoneville- 1 mile north of NC 770	13'5"
NC 1603	Stoneville- 0.8 mile south of NC 770	13'6"
NC 581	just south of Alt. US 264	9'0"
SR 3841 (E. Market St)	Greensboro- just west of Alt. US 29	8'0"

NORTH DAKOTA

HIGHWAY	LOCATION	HEIGHT
Bus US 2 (Demers Ave)	Grand Forks- at Red River Bridge	13'0"
ND 8	Stanley- 0.9 mile north of US 2	14'0"
ND 14	Towner- 0.4 mile north of US 2	13'7"
ND 22	Dickinson- 1.2 miles south of I-94	13'10"
US 10/52/I-94	Casselton- 0.5 mile west of ND 18	13'9"
Bus US 81 (Main Ave)	Fargo	13'9"
Bus US 81 NB (10th St)	Fargo- 0.1 mile north of Main Ave	14'0"
BUS 81 SB (University Dr)	Fargo- 0.1 mile north of Main Ave	13'7"
Bus US 83 SB (7th St)	Bismark- 0.1 mile south of Main Ave	13'9"
Bus 83 NB (9th St)	Bismark- 0.1 mile south of Main Ave	13'11"

OHIO

HIGHWAY	LOCATION	HEIGHT
OH 7	Bellaire- 0.4 mile north of OH 147	12'6"
OH 7	Bellaire- 0.5 mile north of jct. OH 149	13'2"
OH 14	2.5 miles southeast of OH 165	13'6"
OH 17	In Brook Park and Cleveland- .054 mile west of I-71	13'6"
OH 18	Hicksville- 0.5 mile northwest of jct. OH 2 and OH 49	12'6"
OH 19	Republic- 0.6 mile south of jct. OH 162	11'7"
US 20 (Euclid Ave)	Cleveland- 0.4 miles east of jct. US 322 (Mayfield Road)	13'6"
US 33 WB	Columbus- 0.6 mile east of Olentangy River on Spring St	13'3"
US 36	Piqua- 0.5 mile west of OH 185	13'0"
OH 37	Delaware- 1 mile west of US 23	12'8"
OH 39	Mansfield- 0.3 mile west of US 42	13'2"
US 42	Delaware- 1.2 mile northeast of US 36	13'6"
US 42	Mansfield- 0.2 mile east of OH 430	12'1"
OH 48	Covington- 0.1 mile north of US 36	12'9"
OH 61	New Haven- 0.2 mile north of OH 103	10'10"
US 62 (Rich St)	Columbus- 0.1 mile west of Scioto River	12'10"
US 62	Columbus- 0.4 mile southwest of I-71	13'6"
OH 66	Defiance- 0.5 mile south of OH 15/18	13'0"
OH 82	Macedonia- 0.2 mile east of I-271	13'6"
OH 100	Tiffin- 0.3 mile north of OH 18	11'7"
OH 103	Willard- 1.4 mile north of US 224	13'4"
OH 111 NB	Defiance- 0.7 mile south of OH 424	11'11"
OH 111 SB	Defiance- 0.7 mile south of OH 424	11'10"
OH 126	The Village of Indian Hills- 1.7 miles east of US 22	12'9"
OH 148	Armstrong Mills- Captina Creek bridge, 0.1 mile west of OH 9	13'5"
OH 175 (Richmond Rd)	Solon- 0.6 mile north of jct. OH 43 (Aurora Rd)	10'0"
OH 183	Alliance- 1.5 miles north of US 62	11'8"
OH 212	Bolivar- 0.3 mile west	12'6"
OH 245	West Liberty- 0.8 mile west of US 68	13'0"
OH 303	Hudson- 0.2 mile west of OH 91	13'5"
US 322 (Mayfield Rd)	Cleveland- 0.3 mile east of US 20 (Euclid Ave)	12'8"
OH 335	Omega- approx 2.7 miles east	12'0"
OH 335	Portsmouth- 3.8 miles north of US 52	12'8"
OH 508	DeGraff- 0.3 mile south of OH 235	12'7"
OH 521	Delaware- 1.4 mile northeast of US 36	12'9"
OH 558	East Fairfield- 1.5 mile west of OH 517	13'0"
OH 611	Lorain- 2.1 mile east of OH 58	13'4"
OH 646	Germano- 0.8 mile east of OH 9	12'11"
OH 666	Zanesville- 0.8 mile north	10'7"
OH 762	Orient- 1 mile southeast of US 62	13'3"

OKLAHOMA

HIGHWAY	LOCATION	HEIGHT
US 51 (Broken Arrow Expressway)	Tulsa, 31st, as it goes under the expressway	13'4"
US 70	Mead	13'6"
Alt. US 75	Beggs- 0.9 mile north of OK 16	13'6"

OREGON

HIGHWAY	LOCATION	HEIGHT
OR 99W NB	Corvallis- 0.6 mile south of US 20 at Mary's River bridge	12'9"
OR 180 (Eddyville-Blodgett Hwy)	Eddyville- approx 6 mile east of jct US 20	12'5"
OR 260 (Rogue River Loop Hwy)	Merlin- approx 4 miles southwest of Robertson Bridge	12'6"

PENNSYLVANIA

HIGHWAY	LOCATION	HEIGHT
US 6	Mill Village- west at French Creek bridge	13'6"
PA 8 (Washington Blvd)	Pittsburg- 0.3 mile north of PA 380	13'4"
PA 8 NB	Wilkinsburg- at I-376	13'2"
PA 8 NB	Wilkinsburg- at I-376	13'2"
US 13 (Highland Ave)	Chester- 0.7 mile west of US 322	13'0"
US 13	Norwood- 0.5 mile north at South Ave	12'9"

HIGHWAY	LOCATION	HEIGHT
US 13	Philadelphia- 0.15 mile south of Wissahickon Ave	13'4"
US 13 NB (Chester Pike)	Ridley Park- 0.35 mile east of Fairview Rd	13'5"
US 19	Fairview- 2 miles south	13'5"
US 19	Mercer- 2.6 miles south of I-80	12'6"
PA 27	Pittsfield- 0.2 mile west of jct 6	12'9"
US 29	Phoenixville- 1.1 mile northeast of PA 23	13'6"
US 30 (Girard Ave)	Philadelphia- just west of Belmont Ave	13'2"
US 30	Stoystown- PA 281 overpass	13'5"
US 30 WB	Chambersburg- 0.35 mile east of US 11	13'5"
PA 36	Altoona- 0.2 mile northwest of PA 764 (7th Ave)	13'6"
PA 36	Punxsutawney- 0.5 mile west of US 119	13'4"
PA 38	Hooker- .0.3 mile south	13'6"
PA 45	Spruce Creek- just south of Little Juniata River	8'2"
PA 50	Woodrow- 0.5 mile east	12'8"
PA 51 SB (Carson St)	Pittsburgh- just northwest of jct. PA 51/US 19	13'5"
PA 53	Jamestown	13'1"
PA 53	Wilmore- 0.4 mile west of PA 160	13'0"
PA 54	Danville-at Susquehanna River bridge	13'2"
PA 56/711	Seward- just north of Conemaugh River	13'4"
PA 58	Jamestown- just southwest of jct. PA 56 and US 322	10'8"
PA 59	Ornsby- 1.5 mile west of jct. PA 646	13'3"
PA 61	Sunbury- east at Shamokin Creek bridge	13'6"
US 62	Mercer- 1.5 mile northeast of jct. US 19	12'3"
US 62	Tionesta- 3 miles southwest at Allegheny River bridge	13'1"
PA 87	Mehoopany- 0.5 mile south	12'6"
PA 89	Northeast- 0.4 mile south of US 20	13'4"
PA 98	Fairview- 0.8 mile north of US 20	13'3"
PA 100	Chadds Ford- 0.3 mile south of US 1	10'10"
PA 108	New Castle- at Mahoning River bridge	11'6"
PA 168	Moravia- between PA 18 and Beaver River	12'6"
PA 173	Cochranton- west at French Creek Bridge	13'6"
PA 183	Cressona- 1 mile west of PA 61	11'11"
PA 214	Seven Valleys	11'3"
PA 217	Blairsville- 0.4 mile south of US 22/119	13'3"
PA 220	Hughesville- northeast at Muncy Creek bridge	13'4"
US 220 BUS	Tyrone	12'9"
PA 221	Taylorstown- 0.9 mile north of US 40	13'2"
US 222	Quarryville- 0.5 mile north of PA 372	10'0"
PA 225	Dornsife- at Mahanoy Creek bridge	12'8"
PA 249	Cowanesque- at Cowanesque River bridge	12'10"
PA 259	Bolivar	9'4"
PA 284	English Center- 2.1 mmiles east of PA 287	11'1"
PA 288	Chewton	11'1"
PA 288	Wampum	13'4"
US 322	Downingtown- 0.25 mile south of BR 20	10'3"
PA 324	Martic Forge- 0.8 mile east of Pequea Creek	12'0"
PA 329	Northampton- at Lehigh River bridge	12'10"
PA 339	Mahanoy City- just north of PA 54	11'6"
PA 340	Bird in Hand- west of town	13'5"
PA 352	Frazer- 0.25 mile south of US 30	10'3"
PA 372	Atglen- 1.2 mile west of PA 41	11'2"
PA 412	Bethlehem- 1.5 mile east of PA 378	13'3"
PA 413	West Bristol- just south of US 13 (Bristol Pike)	13'4"
PA 420	Prospect Park- 0.4 mile north of US 13	12'8"
PA 438	La Plume- 0.5 mile east of US 6/11	12'1"
PA 441	Middletown- 0.45 mile south of jct. PA 320	11'3"
PA 488	Ellport- 1.3 mile east of PA 65	12'2"
PA 488	Wurtemburg- 1.6 mile north of Slippery Rock Creek	11'3"
PA 501	Myerstown- 1 mile south of jct. US 422	13'6"
PA 532 NB	Holland- 0.2 mile south	9'8"
PA 532 SB	Holland- 0.2 mile south	9'11"
PA 532 SB	Newtown- 2.2 miles south	13'5"
PA 568	Gibralter- just south of PA 724	13'6"
PA 611 NB	Easton- 0.2 mile south	12'11"
PA 616	Railroad- 0.4 mile north of PA 851	8'1"
PA 616	Seitzland	10'0"
PA 641	Carlisle- just west of US 11	12'10"
PA 690 EB	Moscow- just east of PA 435	12'10"
PA 690 WB	Moscow- just eats of PA 435	12'5"
PA 849	Duncannon- just west of Juniata River	13'6"
PA 866	Ganister- 1.7 mile east of US 22	12'4"
PA 885 (2nd Ave)	Pittsburg- 0.2 mile south of I-376	12'1"
PA 981	Latrobe	9'10"

RHODE ISLAND

HIGHWAY	LOCATION	HEIGHT
High Street	Central Falls- approx. 0.75 mile south of RI 123 and 0.1 mile east of RI 114 (Broad Street)	11'3"
High Street	Central Falls- approx. 1.5 mile south of RI 123 and 0.25 mile east of RI 114 (Broad Street)	9'9"
Lincoln Ave	Lincoln Park- 0.3 mile south of RI 37, between I-95 and US1 (Boston Post Rd)	10'3"
Blackstone Ave	Pawtucket	9'3"
Church Street	Valley Falls	12'7"
West Street	Westerly	11'5"
Main Street	Woonsocket	12'7"

SOUTH CAROLINA

HIGHWAY	LOCATION	HEIGHT
SC 10	McCormick- 2 miles northwest	10'6"
US 25	Edgefield- 0.6 mile south of SC 23	13'6"
SC 86	Piedmont- 0.09 mile east of jct SC 20	11'6"
SC 86	Piedmont- 0.13 mile east of jct. SC 20	11'8"
SC 146 (Woodruff Rd)	Greenville- 0.25 mile east of US 276	13'6"
SC 177	5 miles north of SC 9, north of Cheraw	13'6"
SC 183 NB (Cedar Ln)	Greenville- 1 mile west of Bus. US 25	13'4"
SC 823	Little River bridge- approx 3 miles north of Mt. Carmel	12'7"

SOUTH DAKOTA

HIGHWAY	LOCATION	HEIGHT
US 14	Pierre- downtown	11'1"
Alt. US 16	Keystone- 2.8 miles southeast at mile marker 54.09	9'7"
Alt. US 16	Keystone- tunnel 3.3 miles southeast at mile marker 53.68	12'7"
Alt. US 16	Keystone- tunnel 4 miles southeast at mile marker 53.00	12'4"
Alt. US 16	Keystone- 4 miles southeast at mile marker 53.02	12'6"
Alt. US 16	Keystone- tunnel 6.5 miles southeast at mile marker 50.49	12'1"
SD 53	White River bridge- 13.8 miles south at I-90 at mile marker 69.70	11'7"
SD 79 NB	Rapid City- west of I-90 interchange 51 at mile marker 87.08	13'10"
US 81	Yankton- 12 miles north at James River Bridge at mile marker 13.61	12'4"
SD 87	Sylvan Lake- tunnel 1 mile southeast in Custer State Park, mile marker 74.65	10'7"
SD 87	Sylvan Lake- tunnel 2 mile southeast in	

Driving Distances Betw

	Albany NY	Albuquerque NM	Atlanta GA	Baltimore MD	Billings MT	Birmingham AL	Boise ID	Boston MA	Buffalo NY	Charleston SC	Charlotte NC	Cheyenne WY	Chicago IL	Cleveland OH	Dallas TX	Denver CO	Des Moines IA	Detroit MI	El Paso TX	Houston TX	Indi
Albany NY	**000**	2040	1016	340	2076	1070	2507	170	302	890	768	1773	828	480	1680	1830	1180	648	2222	1770	810
Albuquerque NM	2040	**000**	1400	1890	994	1250	965	2220	1774	1727	1634	539	1310	1590	640	440	970	1560	270	850	127
Atlanta GA	1016	1400	**000**	650	1890	152	2184	1112	910	321	240	1450	710	730	820	1430	960	730	1444	790	530
Baltimore MD	340	1890	650	**000**	1960	770	2391	432	373	563	420	1657	718	355	1364	1638	1040	510	1980	1394	570
Billings MT	2076	994	1890	1960	**000**	1839	621	2242	1787	2196	2055	455	1247	1598	1429	555	997	1534	1178	1676	143
Birmingham AL	1070	1250	152	770	1839	**000**	2133	1230	900	469	390	1399	660	730	640	1330	830	760	1270	700	480
Boise ID	2507	965	2184	2391	621	2133	**000**	2690	2210	2490	2349	735	1702	2029	1704	830	1367	1965	1207	1951	185
Boston MA	170	2220	1112	432	2242	1230	2690	**000**	470	966	848	1939	1000	660	1750	2000	1340	798	2380	1830	930
Buffalo NY	302	1774	910	373	1787	900	2210	470	**000**	864	710	1484	540	190	1360	1550	850	360	1970	1490	510
Charleston SC	890	1727	321	563	2196	469	2490	966	864	**000**	207	1756	911	721	1112	1721	1208	850	1747	1113	730
Charlotte NC	768	1634	240	420	2055	390	2349	848	710	207	**000**	1615	740	520	1060	1580	1060	630	1650	1030	550
Cheyenne WY	1773	539	1450	1657	455	1399	735	1939	1484	1756	1615	**000**	968	1295	974	100	633	1231	723	1221	1118
Chicago IL	828	1310	710	718	1247	660	1702	1000	540	911	740	968	**000**	350	922	1020	340	280	1460	1090	190
Cleveland OH	480	1590	730	355	1598	730	2029	660	190	721	520	1295	350	**000**	1190	1360	660	170	1740	1310	320
Dallas TX	1680	640	820	1364	1429	640	1704	1750	1360	1112	1060	974	922	1190	**000**	780	700	1160	620	250	890
Denver CO	1830	440	1430	1638	555	1330	830	2000	1550	1721	1580	100	1020	1360	780	**000**	670	1280	690	1030	106
Des Moines IA	1180	970	960	1040	997	830	1367	1340	850	1208	1060	633	340	660	700	670	**000**	590	1130	940	480
Detroit MI	648	1560	730	510	1534	760	1965	798	360	850	630	1231	280	170	1160	1280	590	**000**	1670	1280	280
El Paso TX	2222	270	1444	1980	1178	1270	1207	2380	1970	1747	1650	723	1460	1740	620	690	1130	1670	**000**	740	142
Houston TX	1770	850	790	1394	1676	700	1951	1830	1490	1113	1030	1221	1090	1310	250	1030	940	1280	740	**000**	100
Indiannapolis IN	810	1270	530	570	1433	480	1852	930	510	730	550	1118	190	320	890	1060	480	280	1420	1000	**000**
Kansas City MO	1300	780	820	1070	1078	730	1372	1440	1010	1116	970	638	540	820	510	610	200	770	940	740	500
Las Vegas NV	2630	590	1980	2400	966	1830	361	2750	2280	2305	2200	829	1780	2090	1230	760	1430	2020	720	1470	184
Little Rock AR	1360	886	555	1040	1513	430	1788	1440	1060	852	780	1058	660	870	320	940	560	880	940	430	610
Memphis TN	1230	1010	380	910	1606	260	1900	1340	920	744	630	1166	540	730	450	1040	620	720	1070	570	470
Nashville TN	1030	1230	250	706	1650	190	1944	1090	720	548	420	1210	470	530	660	1180	690	540	1280	780	280
New Orleans LA	1440	1200	480	1140	1954	350	2229	1510	1260	784	720	1499	920	1060	520	1280	980	1070	1100	350	800
New York NY	160	1998	850	202	2067	980	2498	210	370	762	620	1765	810	470	1560	1790	1120	650	2150	1610	730
Norfolk VA	510	1890	560	230	2147	710	2550	580	600	431	310	1816	870	510	1350	1770	1150	730	1950	1350	710
Oklahoma City OK	1500	540	830	1310	1221	720	1496	1690	1220	1183	1100	766	830	1030	210	630	550	1030	680	460	740
Orlando FL	1230	1740	430	890	2330	550	2624	1300	1198	381	530	1890	1150	1050	1100	1880	1360	1170	1680	980	970
Philadelphia PA	260	1948	750	100	2017	870	2448	320	360	661	510	1714	790	430	1440	1740	1090	610	2070	1510	660
Phoenix AZ	2490	460	1830	3210	1206	1680	995	2670	2220	2183	2030	906	1740	2030	1000	810	1430	2010	440	1160	173
Pittsburgh PA	472	1649	686	251	1716	753	2147	586	216	654	449	1413	460	135	1228	1460	778	288	1796	1347	359
Portland OR	2920	1370	2660	2806	891	2590	425	3140	2670	2910	2780	1155	2120	2430	2040	1260	1820	2380	1630	2240	224
Reno NV	2720	1021	2406	2613	955	2355	424	2895	2440	2712	2571	957	1924	2251	1665	1052	1589	2187	1171	1911	207
San Diego CA	2850	810	2150	2680	1299	1990	938	2880	2530	2475	2410	1162	2090	2390	1350	1100	1770	2370	730	1490	208
Seattle WA	2899	1456	2675	2783	821	2624	496	3065	2610	2981	2840	1226	2070	2421	2195	1321	1820	2357	1698	2442	225
St. Louis MO	1040	1041	556	841	1333	505	1627	1206	750	862	721	893	360	565	633	858	350	550	1188	837	249
Washington DC	365	1886	635	38	1961	743	2392	441	388	525	398	1658	705	380	1326	1694	1023	533	1959	1414	593

een Major U.S. Cities

nnapolis IN

Kansas City MO	Las Vegas NV	Little Rock AR	Memphis TN	Nashville TN	New Orleans LA	New York NY	Norfolk VA	Oklahoma City OK	Orlando FL	Philadelphia PA	Phoenix AZ	Pittsburgh PA	Portland OR	Reno NV	San Diego CA	Seattle WA	St. Louis MO	Washington DC	
1300	2630	1360	1230	1030	1440	160	510	1500	1230	260	2490	472	2920	2720	2850	2899	1040	365	**Albany NY**
780	590	886	1010	1230	1200	1998	1890	540	1740	1948	460	1649	1370	1021	810	1456	1041	1886	**Albuquerque NM**
820	1980	555	380	250	480	850	560	830	430	750	1830	686	2660	2406	2150	2675	556	635	**Atlanta GA**
1070	2400	1040	910	706	1140	202	230	1310	890	100	3210	251	2806	2613	2680	2783	841	38	**Baltimore MD**
1078	966	1513	1606	1650	1954	2067	2147	1221	2330	2017	1206	1716	891	955	1299	821	1333	1961	**Billings MT**
730	1830	430	260	190	350	980	710	720	550	870	1680	753	2590	2355	1990	2624	505	743	**Birmingham AL**
1372	361	1788	1900	1944	2229	2498	2550	1496	2624	2448	995	2147	425	424	938	496	1627	2392	**Boise ID**
1440	2750	1440	1340	1090	1510	210	580	1690	1300	320	2670	586	3140	2895	2880	3065	1206	441	**Boston MA**
1010	2280	1060	920	720	1260	370	600	1220	1198	360	2220	216	2670	2440	2530	2610	750	388	**Buffalo NY**
1116	2305	852	744	548	784	762	431	1183	381	661	2183	654	2910	2712	2475	2981	862	525	**Charleston SC**
970	2200	780	630	420	720	620	310	1100	530	510	2030	449	2780	2571	2410	2840	721	398	**Charlotte NC**
638	829	1058	1166	1210	1499	1765	1816	766	1890	1714	906	1413	1155	957	1162	1226	893	1658	**Cheyenne WY**
540	1780	660	540	470	920	810	870	830	1150	790	1740	460	2120	1924	2090	2070	360	705	**Chicago IL**
820	2090	870	730	530	1060	470	510	1030	1050	430	2030	135	2430	2251	2390	2421	565	380	**Cleveland OH**
510	1230	320	450	660	520	1560	1350	210	1100	1440	1000	1228	2040	1665	1350	2195	633	1326	**Dallas TX**
610	760	940	1040	1180	1280	1790	1770	630	1880	1740	810	1460	1260	1052	1100	1321	858	1694	**Denver CO**
200	1430	560	620	690	980	1120	1150	550	1360	1090	1430	778	1820	1589	1770	1820	350	1023	**Des Moines IA**
770	2020	880	720	540	1070	650	730	1030	1170	610	2010	288	2380	2187	2370	2357	550	533	**Detroit MI**
940	720	940	1070	1280	1100	2150	1950	680	1680	2070	440	1796	1630	1171	730	1698	1188	1959	**El Paso TX**
740	1470	430	570	780	350	1610	1350	460	980	1510	1160	1347	2240	1911	1490	2442	837	1414	**Houston TX**
500	1840	610	470	280	800	730	710	740	970	660	1730	359	2240	2074	2080	2256	249	593	**Indiannapolis IN**
000	1370	420	480	580	840	1230	1160	350	1250	1170	1240	855	1820	1594	1590	1863	253	1089	**Kansas City MO**
1370	**000**	1460	1600	1810	1730	2570	2480	1110	2350	2480	290	2208	1000	445	340	1122	1606	2464	**Las Vegas NV**
420	1460	**000**	140	350	420	1250	1020	340	960	1140	1330	913	1140	2010	1990	2279	403	1011	**Little Rock AR**
480	1600	140	**000**	210	410	1100	880	480	780	1010	1470	776	2310	2122	1810	2391	284	874	**Memphis TN**
580	1810	350	210	**000**	530	900	670	680	690	790	1670	568	2370	2166	2000	2435	316	664	**Nashville TN**
840	1730	420	410	530	**000**	1340	1040	690	650	1230	1500	1095	2540	2193	1840	2720	675	1085	**New Orleans LA**
1230	2570	1250	1100	900	1340	**000**	370	1480	1090	110	2450	368	2910	2720	2800	2890	978	237	**New York NY**
1160	2480	1020	880	670	1040	370	**000**	1370	770	270	2350	438	2970	2772	2680	3041	922	196	**Norfolk VA**
350	1110	340	480	680	690	1480	1370	**000**	1230	1390	980	1104	1870	1565	1330	1987	496	1342	**Oklahoma City OK**
1250	2350	960	780	690	650	1090	770	1230	**000**	990	2080	972	3070	2846	2410	3115	996	843	**Orlando FL**
1170	2480	1140	1010	790	1230	110	270	1390	990	**000**	2370	308	2860	2670	2770	2840	898	136	**Philadelphia PA**
1240	290	1330	1470	1670	1500	2450	2350	980	2080	2370	**000**	2112	1270	735	350	1486	1504	2349	**Phoenix AZ**
855	2208	913	776	568	1095	368	438	1104	972	308	2112	**000**	2567	2369	2466	2539	608	252	**Pittsburgh PA**
1820	1000	1140	2310	2370	2540	2910	2970	1870	3070	2860	1270	2567	**000**	578	1090	174	2047	2812	**Portland OR**
1594	445	2010	2122	2166	2193	2720	2772	1565	2846	2670	735	2369	578	**000**	565	752	1849	2614	**Reno NV**
1590	340	1990	1810	2000	1840	2800	2680	1330	2410	2770	350	2466	1090	565	**000**	1265	1858	2703	**San Diego CA**
1863	1122	2279	2391	2435	2720	2890	3041	1987	3115	2840	1486	2539	174	752	1265	**000**	2118	2785	**Seattle WA**
253	1606	403	284	316	675	978	922	496	996	898	1504	608	2047	1849	1858	2118	**000**	878	**St. Louis MO**
1089	2464	1011	874	664	1085	237	196	1342	843	136	2349	252	2812	2614	2703	2785	878	**000**	**Washington DC**

HIGHWAY	LOCATION	HEIGHT
	Custer State Park, mile marker 72.85	11'9"
SD 87	Sylvan Lake- tunnel 6 mile southeast in Custer State Park, mile marker 66.85	12'5"
SD 248	Reliance- I-90 underpass at Interchange 248	13'5"
SD 271	Java- 1.1 mile northeast of SD 130 at mile marker 167.65	12'1"

TENNESSEE

HIGHWAY	LOCATION	HEIGHT
TN 17	Chattanooga- near Lookout Mountain, Mile marker 2.05	8'6"
US 25 W/ TN 9	Clinton0 0.15 mile north of TN 61, mile marker 9.94	13'5"
US 27	Chattanooga- southeast of jct I-124 at McCallie Tunnel	12'4"
US 31/ TN 6 (8th Ave S)	Nashville- 0.2 miles north of I-40, mile marker 8.24	12'10"
TN 33 (Maryville Pike)	Knoxville- 0.8 miles southwest of US 441, mile marker 4.76	10'2"
TN 33 (Maryville Pike)	Mt. Olive- 0.3 miles north, mile marker 3.00	12'9"
TN 39	Riceville- 0.2 mile east of US 11, mile marker 1.77	13'3"
TN 40/ US 64	Cleveland- 0.9 mile east of Byp. US 11, mile marker 0.93	11'1"
US 41/ 64/ 72	Chattanooga- wset of I-24, mile marker 5.75	13'6"
US 41/ 64/ 72	Chattanooga- 1.2 mile west of I-24, mile marker 3.33	12'7"
US 41/ 76/ TN 8 NB	Chattanooga- Bachman Tubes (tunnel), mile marker 5.04	12'7"
US 41/ 76/ TN 8 SB	Chattanooga- Bachman Tubes (tunnel), mile marker 5.04	12'7"
TN 47	White Bluff- 2 miles south of US 70, mile marker 8.57	11'10"
TN 58	Chattanooga- 1 mile south of I-24, mile marker 3.25	10'11"
TN 87	Henning- 0.5 mile east of TN 209, mile marker 20.79	8'0"
TN 116	Disney- 1.27 miles north of I-75, mile marker 0.97	13'5"
TN 131	Ball Camp- 1.1 mile north, mile marker 5.93	10'7"
TN 241	Center- 6.9 miles north, Natchez Trace Pkwy overpass, mile marker 1.20	11'6"
TN 246	Columbia- 3.4 miles north of jct. US 31 and TN 99, mile marker 0.79	11'1"
TN 252	Clovercroft- 1.7 miles southeast, mile marker 3.59	10'7"
TN 252	Clovercroft- mile marker 5.26	10'9"
TN 252	Clovercroft- 2 miles north, mile marker 7.37	10'5"
TN 299	Oakdale- 1.0 mile west of TN 328, mile marker 9.89	10'6"
TN 346	Church Hill- 0.3 miles north of US 11W, mile marker 8.21	10'2"
US 441	Great Smokey Mountains National Park-1 mile north of North Carolina state line, mile marker 1.07	11'4"
US 441	Great Smokey Mountains National Park-tunnel north of North Carolina state libne, mile marker 6.40	11'0"

TEXAS

HIGHWAY	LOCATION	HEIGHT
US283	3/4 mile south of BI20, Baird	14'
FM2047	at IH20, Baird	14'
FM604	at IH20, Clyde	14'
FM18	1 mile west of BI20, Baird	14'
FM821	IH20, east of Coahoma	13'
FM820	at IH20, Coahoma	13'6"
FM818	at IH20, west of Big Spring	13'6"
FM700 SB	at IH20, Big Spring	14'
E.BI20	at E.IH20, Westbrook	13'6"
W.BI20	IH20, Loraine	13'6"
BI20	between W.IH20 and FM644, Loraine	14'
E.SH208	at IH20, Colorado City	14'
SH163	1/8 mile south of BI20, Colorado City	14'
FM3525	at IH20, Colorado City	14'
FM2836	at IH20, west of Colorado City	13'6"
FM1899	at IH20, Colorado City	13'6"
FM1229	at IH20, west of Colorado City	13'6"
W.FM670	at IH20, Westbrook	14'
W.FM644	at IH20, Loraine	13'6"
W.BI20	at IH20, Roscoe	14'
BS70	between BI20 and S.SH70, Sweetwater	14'
FM608	at IH20, Roscoe	14'
LP170	at IH20, Sweetwater	13'
US84	FM1673, Snyder, WB NFR, EB SFR, WB ML	14'
US84 WB	at US180, Snyder	14'
N.BU84	1/4 mile south of N.US84, Snyder	14'
FM1673	at US84, Snyder	14'
E.BI20 WB	at IH20, Trent	13'6"
W.BI20 WB	at IH20, Merkel	13'6"
BI20/FM1235	at E.IH20, Merkel	13'
US83	atIH20, Abilene	14'
BU83 SB	SB, at BI20, Abilene	14'
FM3438	at BI20, Abilene	14'
FM1085	at IH20, Trent	13'6"
FM126	at IH20, Merkel	13'6"
SH207	1/10 mile north of US60, Panhandle	13'6"
US87	SB, between US54 and N.US385, Dalhart	13'
US87	NB, between US54 and N.US385, Dalhart	13'6"
US385	mile south of US60, Hereford	14', 1/4"
SH70	between US60 and N.SH152, Pampa	14'
FM809	at IH40, Wildorado	14'
BI40/US60	between SH136 and E.LP335, Amarillo	14'
US287/US87/US60	between SP279 and BI40, Amarill	13'6"
SP279	1 mile west of US287/US87/US60, Amarillo	13'6"
US87	NB to WB, at S.US60, Canyon	13'6"
US87	SB to WB, at S.US60, Canyon	14'
SH217	1/4 mile south of US60, Canyon	14'
FM1541	at IH27, Amarillo	14'
IH30 NFR	between FM559 and FM1397, Texarkana	14'
US82	between SH93 and SP14, Texarkana	14'
US67	between SH93 and US82, Texarkana	13'6"
FM1997	1/8 mile north of US80, Marshall	11'
SH49	1/2 mile north of FM1969, Lassate	14'
SH49	1/2 mile east of FM134, Jefferson	13'6"
US259/SH49/SH11	between E.SH11 and W.SH11, Daingerfiel	13'6"
BU271	1/8 mile north of SH49, Mount Pleasant	14'
FM12/SH80	WB at IH35, San Marcos	14'
FM12/SH80	EB at IH35, San Marcos	13'6"
N.LP82 EB	at IH35, San Marcos	13'6"
IH35 SB	at Ceasar Chavez, Austin	14'
IH35 Lower Level	at Manor, Austin	13'6"
IH35 Lower Level	at 32nd, Austin	13'6"
IH35 Lower Level	at 38 1/2, Austin	13'6"
US290 SFR	EB on-ramp from Industrial Oaks, Austin	13'6
SH71 WB	at US183, Austin	14'
N.FM487	at IH35, Jarrell	13'6"
SH61	at IH10, Hankamer	14'
FM563	at IH10, Hankamer	14'
US287/US96/US69	1/4 mile north of SH87, Port Arthur	14'
US287/US96/US69 SB	at W.IH10, Beaumont	14'

HIGHWAY	LOCATION	HEIGHT
SH347 SB	SB, at SH73, Groves	14'
SH63	at Sabine River Truss Bridge, east of Burkeville	12'3"
SH87 SB	at IH10, Orange	14'
US183/US84	between FM2126 and FM1467, Brownwood	14'
US377/US67	between FM3100 and FM1467, Blanket	14'
SH206	1/2 mile north of W.SH153, Coleman	13'
US377/US67	1/3 mile west of W.SH36, Comanche	14'
US183	between FM574 and US84, Goldthwaite	14'
SH16	1/4 mile north of US190, San Sab	13' 6"
SH16	at Colorado River Truss Bridge, north of San Saba	13'9"
SH6 FR's	1 mile north of FM974, Bryan	14'
SH36	3/4 mile south of FM166, Caldwel	14'
FM166	1/3 mile east of SH36, Caldwell	11'6"
FM60	1/4 mile north of FM111, Deanville	13'
SH75	1/8 mile east of W.LP262, Streetman	14'
SH75	at IH45, north of Madisonville	14'
US190/US77/SH36	1/2 mile east of FM1600, Cameron	13'
SH36	1/10 mile south of E.US190/US79, Milano	13'6"
IH45 NB	at S.SH75, Huntsville	14'
PR40	at IH45, south of Huntsville	14'
FM390	1 mile west of SH36, Gay Hill	10'6"
US83 NB	at Salt Fork of the Red River Truss Bridge, north of Wellington	13'
SH203	at Salt Fork of the Red River Truss Bridge east of Wellington	13'6"
SH6	at Brazos River Truss Bridge, north of Knox City	13'
IH37 WFR	at RR & SH234, south of Mathis	13'
US181	NB to SB turnaround at S.FM2986, Portland	13'6"
SH358	NB to SB turnaround at BS286, Corpus Christi	13'6"
SH359	between SP459 and FM666, Mathis	14'
US380	EB to NB and WB to NB, at SH78, Farmersville	13'6"
US380	3/4 mile east of SH78, Farmersville	13'6"
SH121 WB	WB and WB to SB at SH5, Melissa	14'
SH5	or less, 1/4 mile south of FM1378, Allen	12'
SH78	NB/SB, SB to WB, SB to EB, at US380, Farmersville	13'6"
SP339 WB	WB to US75 SB, McKinney	14'
IH30	at NW.19th, Grand Prairie	14'
IH30 EB	1/4 mile east of W.LP12, Dallas	14'
IH30 WB	at N.Hampton Road, Dallas	14'
IH30 WB	at Fort Worth Avenue, Dallas	14'
IH30/IH35E	between W.IH30 and E.IH30, Dallas	14'
IH30	between E.IH35E and IH45, Dallas	14'
IH30 EB	at Dolphin Road, Dallas	14'
IH30	at Jim Miller Road, Dallas	14'
IH30	at St Francis Avenue, Dallas	14'
IH35E SB	SB to SP354, Carrollton	14'
IH35E	between SH356 and SH183, Dallas	14'
IH35E SB	at SH180, Dallas	14'
IH35E	between South Marsalis Avenue and South Beckley Avenue, Dallas	14'
IH635 EB	at MacArthur Blvd, Irving	14'
IH635 EB	EB to SB, at SH78, Garland	14'
IH635 SB	SB to WB, at US80, Dallas	14'
US175 SB	at Martin Luther King Blvd, Dallas	13'6"
US175 FR's	at South Prairie Creek Road, Dallas	14'
US80 EB	at Big Town Blvd, Mesquite	14'
US80	at Town East Blvd, Mesquite	14'
US80	at IH635, Mesquite	14'
SH352	at US80, Mesquite	13'6"
SH352	at E.LP12, Dallas	14'

HIGHWAY	LOCATION	HEIGHT
SH183 EB	EB to NB, at W.LP12, Irving	14'
SH114 FR	EB, between SH161 and SP348, Irving	14'
SH78	SB at IH30, Dallas	14'
SH78	NB at IH30, Dallas	13'
SH78	between SP244 and IH635, Dallas	14'
SH78	SB to EB, NB to EB, at IH635, Dallas	14'
BS66	1/4 mile south of W.SH66, Rowlett	12'
W.LP12 NB	NB, at Old Irving Blvd, Irving	14'
W.LP12 FR	FR NB, south of SH356, Irving Blvd., Dallas	14'
W.LP12 NB	at NB exit ramp to SH356, Irving	14'
N.LP12	at Skillman Street, Dallas	14'
N.LP12	1/4 mile east of SP354, Dallas	14'
FM1382	at IH35E, Dallas	14'
SP366 WB	WB on-ramp from Maple and Routh, Dallas	13'6"
US380	1/8 mile west of IH35, Denton	14'
US377	1/2 mile south of IH35E, Denton	14'
SH114	EB/WB, WB to SB, and WB to NB, at FM156, Justin	13'6"
BS114	85' west of US377, Roanoke	13'6"
BS114	at US377, Roanoke	13'6"
FM3524	1/8 mile south of US377, Aubrey	13'6"
FM156	NB to EB and SB to EB, at SH114, Justin	13'6"
IH35E WFR	at Red Oak Road, Red Oak	14'
BU287	1/2 mile south of N.IH35E, Waxahachie	14'
US80	3-1/3 miles east of E.FM429, east of Terrell	13'6"
SH34	NB, at US175, Kaufman	14'
FM1641/FM548	at US80, Forney	14'
IH45 NB	NB to S.IH45 NB, Corsicana	14'
SH14	2-1/2 miles south of Richland	14'
IH30 NFR	EB/WB, WB to SB, WB to NB, at FM549, Rockwall	13'
IH30 NFR	EB/WB, EB to SB, EB to NB, at FM551, Fate	13'6"
US90/US67	1/3 mile west of FM1703, Alpine	13'6"
US90	7 miles south of IH10, Van Horn	14'
SH20 SB	at Mesa Street/IH10, El Paso	14'
E.BI10	3/4 mile west of E.IH10, Sierra Blanca	13'
US377	1/2 mile north of N.FM56, Tolar	14'
IH35W WFR	at Bethesda Road, Burleson	14'
N.BI35 SB	at N.IH35W, Alvarado	13'6"
BI35	at BU67, Alvarado	13'6"
SP50	at IH35W, Burleson	14'
US281	4-1/2 miles north of IH20, Brazos	13'6"
US281	at Brazos River Truss Bridge, Brazos	12'
IH35W NB	NB and NB to WB, at N.IH820, Fort Worth	14'
IH35W	1/4 mile south of SH180, Fort Worth	14'
IH30/US377	EB, at Merrick Street, Fort Worth	14'
IH30	at Ridgmar Road/Ridglea Avenue, Fort Worth	14'
IH30	EB to NB, and WB to SB, at SH183, Fort Worth	14'
IH30 EB	1/4 mile east of SH360, Arlington	13'6"
IH30 EB	at Fielder, Arlington	13'6"
E.IH820	NB to EB, NB to WB, and WB to EB at SH180, Fort Worth"	14'
E.IH820 FR's	SB/13'6"" NB at SH180, Fort Worth	14'
E.IH820 FR's	between SH180 and SP303, Fort Worth	14'
SH360	at SH180, Arlington	14'
SH360	less than 600' south of SH180, Arlington	14'
SH183	between BU287 and IH35W, Fort Worth	13'6"
SH183	SB to EB/13'6"" NB to WB, at IH30, Fort Worth	14'
SH183 EB	EB to NB, at SE.IH820, Fort Worth	14'
SH180	EB to NB, at E.IH820, Fort Worth	13'6"
SH180	WB to SB and EB to SB/	14'
SH121	at Sylvania, Fort Worth"	13'6"
SH10 WB	WB to SB, at E.IH820, Fort Worth	14'

HIGHWAY	LOCATION	HEIGHT
FM157	at IH30, Arlington”	14’
FM156 SB	at US287/US81, Fort Worth	14’
SP465 NB	NB to WB, at SH183, Fort Worth	14’
SP341	SB, 1/4 of a mile south of state maint., Fort Worth	13’6”
SP341	NB, 1/4 of a mile south of state maint., Fort Worth	14’
LP303 WB	WB and WB to NB, at E.IH820, Fort Worth	14’
SH332	350 feet east of FM521, Brazoria	14’
SH332	at FM521, Brazoria	14’
SH6	at SH35, Alvin	14’
US90A	at W.SH36, Rosenberg	13’6"
US90A	1/4 mile west of FM3155, Richmond	14’
SH36	200 feet north of W.US90A, Rosenberg	13’6"
IH45 NB	NB to NB, at SH6, Texas City	14’
SH146 SB	SB to SB, at IH45, Texas City	13’
SH146/SH3 SB	SB, 1/4 mile north of IH45, Texas City	14’
SH146/SH3 SB	SB to NB, at SH6, Texas City	14’
IH45	SB to WB and NB to WB, at N.IH610, Houston	14’
IH45	at West Dallast Street, Houston	14’
IH45	at Quitman Street, Houston	13’
IH45	NB, at North Main Street, Houston	14’
IH45	SB, at North Main Street, Houston	13’6”
IH45	at Cottage Street, Houston	14’
IH45/IH10	between E.IH10 and W.IH10, Houston	13’6”
IH10	at E.IH610, Houston	14’
IH10 EB	EB to NB, at US59, Houston	14’
IH10 WB	at SE.IH45, Houston	14’
IH10 WB	at NW.IH45, Houston	14’
IH10	at Sawyer Street, Houston	14’
IH10	at W.IH610, Houston	14’
N.IH610	WB to SB, at N.IH45, Houston	14’
W. IH610 SB	WB to EB, at W.IH10, Houston	14’
US90A	1 1/3 miles northwest of IH45, Houston	14’
US90A	1 1/4 miles southwest of IH45, Houston	14’
US59 SB	SB to SB, at SW.IH610, Houston	14’
SH225 EB	EB to NB, at SE.IH610, Houston	14’
SH225 FR	WB to SB, at SH146, La Porte	14’
SH146 FR	1/4 mile south of SH225, La Porte	14’
SH146 FR	NB to WB, at SH225, La Porte	14’
SH35 SB	at S.IH610, Houston	14’
SH225 FR	EB to SB, at SH46, La Porte	14’
SH6	at IH10, Houston	13’6"
SP261	at N.IH610, Houston	14’
SH75	1/4 mile south of FM2854, Conroe	13’6”
FM1572	4 miles west of US90, Brackettville	13’
FM469	at IH35, Millet	14’
IH35	1 mile north of N.US83, Webb	14’
FM1472	at IH35, Laredo	14’
SP369	at IH27, Abernathy	14’
IH27 FR’s	at N.LP289, Lubbock	14’
US82	1/2 mile west of IH27, Lubbock	14’
US62	1/4 mile east of BU87, Lubbock	14’
BU87	1/2 mile north of US62, Lubbock	14’
PR18	at US82, Lubbock	13’6"
FM597	power lines at SP369, Abernathy	14’
SP369	power lines north side of FM579, Abernathy	14’
SH86	between US60 and W.FM173, Bovina	14’
FM145	1/10 mile east of US84/US70, Farwell	12’
US87	at S.SH86, Tulia	14’
US87/SH86	between S.SH86 and N.SH86, railroad, Tulia	14’
US59	between FM3439 and FM3521, Lufkin	13’6”

HIGHWAY	LOCATION	HEIGHT
BU69/S103	WB, 1/8 mile west of N.BU59, Lufkin	13’6”
BU69/S103	EB, 1/8 mile west of N.BU59, Lufkin	14’
N.BU59	1/4 mile south of US69, Lufkin	13’6”
SH94	1/8 mile west of SP266, Lufkin	13’6”
SH21/7	between SH19 and FM229, Crockett	13’6"
FM1	1 mile north of N.FM83, Magasco	13’6"
US59	1/10 mile south of S.LP424, Shepherd	13’6"
SH7	1/2 mile north of SH87, Center	13’6"
SH349	at BI20, Midland	14’
US75 FR	NB to SB turnaround at SH56, Sherman	13’6"
US69	1/8 mile north of SH56, Bells	13’6"
US69	at Spruce Street, Whitewright	14’
US69	1/4 mile south of FM898, Whitewright	14’
BU377	1/10 mile north of S.US377, Whitesboro	13’
SH91	to/from SP503, Denison	14’
SH91	at SH75, Sherman	14’
SH56	at US377, Whitesboro	13’
SH56	1/8 mile east of US69, Bells	14’
SP503	at SH91, Denison	14’
SP503	to/from SH91, Denison	14’
BU271 NB	at N.LP286, Paris	14’
US82/N.LP286	1/4 mile west of N.US271, Paris	14’
FM499	1/8 mile north of E.IH30, Cumby	14’
IH30 EB	at SH34, Greenville	13’6"
SH11	at SH224, Commerce	14’
FM2642	at IH30, west of Greenville	13’6"
FM1903	at IH30, west of Greenville	13’6"
FM1570	at IH30, Greenville	13’6"
E.FM1565	at IH30, west of Greenville	13’6"
W.FM36	at IH30, 8 1/2 miles west of Greenville	14’
S.BU77	SB, at US83/US77, San Benito	13’6”
FM801	atUS83/US77, Harlinge	14’
FM1479	atUS83/US77, Harlingen	14’
SP486	at US83/US77, San Benito	14’
US281	at US83, Pharr	14’
SH336	at US83, McAllen	14’
IH10 NFR	at Johnson Fork Creek Truss Bridge, Segovia	14’
LP481	at South Llano River Truss Bridge, Junction	10’
BU67	between E.LP306 and US277, San Angelo	14’
S.LP306	EB to WB and WB to EB turnarounds at Ben Ficklin, San Angelo	13’6’
IH35	SB, 1/2 mile north of SP422, San Antonio	14’
IH37/US281 NB	at Hot Wells Blvd, San Antonio	14’
IH37/US281	at New Braunfels Avenue, San Antonio	13’6"
IH10	at New Braunfels Avenue, San Antonio	14’
IH10	at Gevers, San Antonio	14’
IH10 WB	at Walters Street, San Antonio	14’
N.IH410 WB	at NW.IH10, San Antonio	14’
N.IH410 EB	at Airport Blvd, San Antonio	14’
N.IH410	at Starcrest Drive, San Antonio	14’
US281 SB	at S.IH410, San Antonio	14’
W.US90	3/4 mile west of W.LP13, detourable, San Antonio	14’
SH218	EB, at E.LP1604, Converse	14’
SH16	NB, at W.IH410, San Antonio	14’
FM2790	1/4 mile south of S.LP1604, Somerset	13’6"
FM2790	at S.IH410, San Antonio	13’6"
FM2252 SB	SB to EB, at N.IH410, San Antonio	14’
FM1346	at E.IH410, San Antonio	14’
SP537	at N.IH410, San Antonio	13’6"
SP371	1 mile south of US90, San Antonio	14’

HIGHWAY	LOCATION	HEIGHT
SP368	at IH35, San Antonio	14'
SP117	at E.IH410, San Antonio	13'6"
LP13 EB	at IH37, San Antonio	14'
IH35 FR's	NB/SB and SB to WB at FM1102, Hunter	14'
IH35 WFR	atKohlenberg Road-Conrads Lane, New Braunfels	13'6"
IH35 FR's	SB to NB and NB to SB turnarounds, at Guadalupe River, New Braunfels	14'
BS46	1/2 mile west of IH35, New Braunfels	14'
BS46	1-1/4 mile north of BI35, New Braunfels	12'
N.BI35	1/2 mile south of N.IH35, Pearsall	14'
FM775	at IH10, Seguin	14'
FM725	1/4 mile north of FM78, McQueeney	14'
LP534	at IH10, Kerrville	14'
SH132	1 mile north of SH173, Devine	14'
SH294	1/10 mile east of US84/US79, Tucker	14'
SH135	NB, 3/4 mile south of SH31, Kilgore	13'6"
SH135	SB, 3/4 mile south of SH31, Kilgore	14'
SP63 SB	1/10 mile south of US80, Longview	14'
SH323	1/2 mile south of SH135, Overton	13'6"
FM1513	1/2 mile east of SH42, New London	14'
US69/SH110/SH64	1/8 mile south of SH31, Tyler	14'
SH135	at SH64, Arp	13'6"
SH31	EB, 1/8 mile east of US69/SH110/SH64, Tyler	14'
SH31	WB, 1/8 mile east of US69/SH110/SH64, Tyler	13'6"
W.LP323	NB, 1/4 mile south of SH31, Tyler	14'
W.LP323	SB, 1/4 mile south of SH31, Tyler	13'6"
IH35	at FM935, Troy	13'6"
IH35	at US190/SH36/S.LP363, Temple	14'
IH35 NB	at Stagecoach Rd, Salado	14'
FM817	1-1/2 miles south of IH35, Belton	13'6"
FM817	1/3 mile north of FM93, Belton	14'
US190/SH36/ S.LP363 WB	1-1/4 mile west of E.LP363, Temple	14'
FM56	1/10 mile southeast of FM1859, Kopperl	13'6"
BS6	1 mile south of SH7, Marlin	14'
BS6	3/4 mile north of SH7, Marlin	13'6"
IH35 SB	at County Line Road, south of Abbott	14'
SH81	1 mile south of SP579, Hillsboro	14'
US77/SP579 SB	at IH35, Hillsboro	14'
IH35 NB	at Old Dallas Road, Elm Mott	14'
IH35 NB	NB, at FM3148, Lorena	14'
IH35	at FM2063, south of Waco	14'
IH35	at N.FM2837, Lorena	14"
IH35	at S.FM2837, Lorena	14"
IH35 NB FR	NB to SB turnaround at BU77/SP299, Waco	14'
IH35 FR's	3/4 mile south of FM3149, north of Elm Mott	14'
BU77	at US84, Waco	14'
BU77	NB to SB and SB to NB turnarounds at IH35/SP299, Waco	13'6"
SH6	at SP412, Woodway	14'
FM2114	WB at IH35, West	13'6"
FM2114	EB, at IH35, West	14'
FM2417	at IH35, north of Waco	14'
FM308	at IH35, Elm Mott	14'
LP2	at IH35, Waco	14'
SP484 NB	NB to BU77 SB, Waco	14'
SP510	1/8 mile north of US287, Henrietta	14'
FM922	at IH35, Valley View	14'
FM372	at IH35, Gainesville	14'
FM51	at IH35, Gainesville	14'

HIGHWAY	LOCATION	HEIGHT
US82	3/4 mile west of US81, Ringgold	13'6"
FM1125	1/10 mile south of US81, Bowie	14'
US287	at Rifle Range Road, Iowa Park	14'
US287 NB	at SP11, Wichita Falls	13'6"
US287	SB, at Wellington Lane, Wichita Falls	14'
US287	NB, at Wellington Lane, Wichita Falls	13'6"
US287	at Huntington Lane, Wichita Falls	13'6"
BU287	1/2 mile north of SH240, Wichita Falls	13'6"
FM369	at US287, Wichita Falls	14'
FM171	between BU287 and S.SH240, Wichita Falls	14'
SP325	SE to N, at US287, Wichita Falls	13'
SP325 WB	WB to US287 SB, Wichita Falls	14'
US183/S.LP145	at S.US287, Oklaunion	14'
SH36	at US90, Sealy	14'
US90	3-1/3 miles east of E.FM155, Weimar	14'
BS71	1/10 mile north of US90, Columbus	13'6"
SH111	1/4 mile east of S.BU77, Yoakum	14'
US90	between FM2762 and W.SH95, Flatonia	14'
US77	between US90 and SP222, Schulenburg	13'6"
W.US90	1-1/2 miles west of FM794, Harwood	13'6"
FM1686	at US59, Victoria	14'

VERMONT

HIGHWAY	LOCATION	HEIGHT
US 2	Bolton- 6.5 miles west of VT 100N	13'9" & 13'6"
US 2	Danville- 4 miles east, 3.5 miles west of US 5	13'3" & 13'0"
US 2	Waterbury- 0.2 miles west of VT 100 at Winooski River	11'0"
US 4	Hartford- 0.1 mile east of jct. US 4, US 5 & VT 14	13'8" & 13'6"
Bus. US 7	Bennington- 0.2 miles north of VT 67A	12'6" & 12'2"
VT 12 NB	Berlin- 2.7 miles south of US 2	13'2"
Alt. VT 12	Roxbury- 4 miles south	13'6" & 13'4"
VT 14	Royalton- northwest to jct. VT 107	12'2"
VT 15	Walden- 5.7 miles northwest of US 2	13'6" & 13'3"
Alt. VT 22	Vergennes- north 0.3 miles south of US 7	13'6" & 13'0"
VT 102	Bloomfield- 0.1 mile south of VT 105	12'9" & 12'6"
Alt. VT 105	Stevens Mill- 0.1 mile north of VT 105	12'8" & 12'5"
VT 123	Westminster- 0.1 mile east of US 5	12'2" & 11'11"
VT 346	North Pownal- 4.7 miles west of US 7 at Hoosick River, New York state line	11'8" & 11'5"

VIRGINIA

HIGHWAY	LOCATION	HEIGHT
US 1	Alberta- 0.7 miles northwest of VA 46	13'6"
US 1	Woodbridge- 4.5 miles north	13'3"
VA 2/ Bus. US 17 NB, SB	Fredericksburg- 0.5 miles south of VA 3	13'6"
VA 5	Richmond- 0.8 miles south of US 80	12'11"
VA 7	Alexandria- 0.6 miles west of US 1	13'0"
US 11 SB	Staunton- 0.5 miles south of jct. VA 254	9'9"
US 13	Chesapeake Bay Bridge Tunnel- 7 miles north of US 60	13'3"
US 13	Kiptopeke	13'3"
US 13	Kiptopeke- 1 mile south	13'3"
US 15	Orange	13'6"
Bus. US 23	Appalachia- 0.4 miles southwest	13'3"
VA 24 WB	Vinton- east of Blueridge Parkway overpass	13'0"
VA 27 WB	Arlington- at US 50 (Arlington Blvd)	13'0"
Bus. US 29	Charlottesville- 0.4 miles south of Bus. US 250	12'7"
Bus. US 29	Charlottesville- 0.1 miles north of Bus. US 250	13'3"
VA 31	Scotland- at James River erry, both banks	12'3"
VA 39	Goshen- 0.1 mile south of VA 42	11'10"

HIGHWAY	LOCATION	HEIGHT
VA 57	Martinsville- 0.9 miles west of Bus. US 220	9'9"
US 58/VA 337	Portsmouth- Midtown Toll Tunnel, both ends	13'3"
US 60	Covington- 0.8 miles west of jct. US 220	13'5"
US 60/I-64 WB	Hampton Roads Bridge Tunnel	13'3"
VA 102	Bluefield- 0.2 miles north of US 19	8'9"
VA 110	Arlington- 0.5 miles southeast of US 50	13'4"
VA 113	Bristol	12'9"
VA 130	Glasgow- east at Blue Ridge Pkwy overpass	13'6"
VA 166	Chesapeake- at jct. US 13/460	13'5"
VA 218	Ferry Farms- 0.6 miles east of VA 3	13'5"
VA 240	Crozet	11'6"
US 250	Yancey Mills- 7.3 miles east of jct. I-64	13'3"
Bus. US 250	Charlottesville- 0.6 miles east of Bus. US 29	10'8"
VA 254	Staunton- just east of US 11 overpass	13'1"
I-264 Alt. US 460 WB	Portsmouth- Norfolk Downtown Tunnel, both ends	13'3"
VA 311 SB	Crows- 3.5 miles north	12'11"
VA 360	Danville- 1.7 miles north of US 58/360	12'3"
US 501	Rustburg- 0.2 miles north of VA 24	13'3"

WASHINGTON

HIGHWAY	LOCATION	HEIGHT
US 2	Skykomish- tunnel 2.7 miles northwest, milepost 45.98	19'6" & 13'6"
US 2/395 NB (Browne St)	Spokane- 0.2 miles north of I-90, US 2 milepost 287.18	14'6" & 14'
US 2/395 SB (Division St)	Spokane- 0.2 miles north of I-90, US 2 milepost 287.18	14' & 13'6"
I-5 NB	Seattle- ramp northbound on I-5 to WA 522 (Lake City Way)	13'8"
I-5 NB	Vader- ramp northbound on I-5 to westbound on WA 506	13'8"
WA 14 EB	five tunnels between Cook & Underwood, mileposts 58.08, 58.45, 58.92, 59.61, & 60.23	14'6" & 12'9"
WA 14 EB	Lyle- two tunnels approx. 1 mile east, mileposts 76.77 and 76.86	13'10"" & 12'6"
WA 24 NB	Othello- 1 mile south of WA 26 underpass, milepost 79.63	13'10"
WA 99 SB, NB	Seattle- pedestrian overpass, 0.4 miles south of N 45 St	16'9" & 13'7"
WA 99 SB	Seattle- at Columbia St. entrance ramp southbound	14'
WA 99 SB (Alaskan Way Viaduct)	Seattle- 3.8 miles north of jct. WA 509, milepost 29.84	14'3" & 14'
WA 125 NB (Pine St)	Walla Walla- north of Oregon state line, milepost 5.93	14'3" & 14'
WA 167 NB	Renton- 0.6 miles north of I-405, milepost 26.90	13'9" & 13'8"
US 395 SB Lewis St)	Pasco- westbound on Lewis St. to southbound on US 395	14'5" & 13'10"
WA 506 WB	Vader-ramp westbound on WA 506 to northbound I-5	12'9"
WA 509 SB (East 11th St.)	Tacoma- 1.6 miles north of I-5 over City Waterway, milepost 0.22	17'9" & 13'11"
WA 513 SB	Seattle- 0.6 miles north of WA 520 at Univ of WA, milepost 0.61	15'2" & 12'8"
WA 536	Mt Vernon- 2 St underpass, milepost 4.98	14' & 13'11"
WA 538 EB	Mt Vernon- east of jct. I-5	15' & 14'

WEST VIRGINIA

HIGHWAY	LOCATION	HEIGHT
Alt. WV 10	Huntington- between 7th Ave and 8th Ave	13'4"
WV 16	War- approximately 1 mile north	13'5"
WV 16	Welch- 0.27 miles south of WV 7	10'6"
WV 17	Logan- 0.02 miles north of WV 10	9'4"
US 19	Kegley- 0.5 miles south of WV 10	12'9"
County 21	0.2 miles south of US 50	13'4"
WV 28	0.16 miles south of Maryland state line	12'8"
Alt. WV 37	Wayne- 0.15 miles south of US 52 at Twelvepole Creek	13'4"
US 40	Wheeling- just north of I-70	11'0"
WV 49	Matewan	11'8"
WV 63	Caldwell- 0.23 miles south of US 60	9'11"
Wv 88	Bethany- 0.9 miles south of WV 67 at Buffalo Creek bridge	11'9"
Alt. US 119	Mitchell Heights- 0.64 miles north of US 119	12'0"
US 119	Williamson- 0.02 miles south of US 52	13'5"
US 250	Philippi- south of US 119 at Tygart Valley River bridge	12'0"

WISCONSIN

HIGHWAY	LOCATION	HEIGHT
WI 32 NB (Kinnickinnic Rd.)	Milwaukee- 1 mile south of jct. WI 15/59 (National Ave)	13'
WI 32 SB (Kinnickinnic Rd.)	Milwaukee- 1 mile south of jct. WI 15/59 (National Ave)	13'3"
WI 32 NB (Kinnickinnic Rd.)	Milwaukee- 2.1 mile north of WI 62	13'5"
WI 32 SB (Kinnickinnic Rd.)	Milwaukee- 2.1 mile north of jct. WI 62	13'3"
WI 32 SB (Kinnickinnic Rd.)	Milwaukee- 1.2 mile south of jct. WI 15/59 (National Ave)	13'3"
WI 32 NB, SB (South 1st Street)	Milwaukee- 0.3 miles north of jct. WI 15/59 (National Ave)	13'6"
WI 32 NB (S 1 St)	Milwaukee- 0.3 miles north of jct. WI 15/59 (National Ave.)	13'6"
WI 32 SB (S 1 St)	Milwaukee- 0.3 miles north of jct. WI 15/59 (National Ave.)	11'
WI 32 NB, SB	South Milwaukee- 2.6 miles north of jct. WI 100	13'1"
WI 51 NB, SB	Plover- 4.5 miles north of jct. WI 54	13'6"
WI 64 EB, WB	Houlton- St. Croix River bridge, 0.7 miles west of WI 95 at Minnesota State line	13'2"
WI 73 NB, SB	0.3 miles south of southern jct. WI 64	13'1"
WI 105 EB	Oliver- St. Louis River bridge at Minnesota state line	11'9"
WI 145 NB, SB (Fond Du Lac Ave)	Milwaukee- 1.1 miles northwest of WI 57 at W. Locust	13'6"
WI 145 NB (Fond Du Lac Ave)	Milwaukee- 0.2 miles northwest of jct. I-43 at 12 St	13'6"

WYOMING

HIGHWAY	LOCATION	HEIGHT
Bus. I-25	Casper- 0.2 miles south of I-25 Center Street. Int., milepost 0.44	13'5"
WY 96	La Prelle Int.- jct. I-25, 5 miles west of Douglas at milepost 3.11	13'
XR I-25	at milepost 131.59	13'8"
XR I-25	Barber Int.- at milepost 154.24	13'7"
XR I-25	Powder River Int.- at milepost 246.56	14'
XR I-80	Coal Int.- at milepost 21.75	13'9"
XR I-80	Bar Hat Int.- at milepost 23.12	13'11"
XR I-80	French Int.- at milepost 28.71	13'8"
XR I-80	Union Int.- at milepost 33.18	13'8"
XR I-80	BLM Rd Int.- at milepost 154.06	13'10"
XR I-80	GL Road Int.-at milepost 156.03	13'11"
XR I-80	Tipton Int.- at milepost 158.55	13'10"
XR I-80	Red Desert Int.- at milepost 165.58	13'6"
XR I-80	Booster Road Int.- at milepost 166.92	13'11"
XR I-80	Frewen Road Int.- at milepost 168.94	13'10"
XR I-80	Rasmussen Road Int.- at milepost 170.68	13'11"
XR I-80	Daley Int.- at milepost 201.16	13'7"
XR I-80	Hadsell Int.- at milepost 206.18	13'9"
XR I-90	County Road- at milepost 23.54	13'11"
XR I-90	Inyan Kara Int.- at milepost 172.09	14'

FUN *Festivals*

Lou Henry

MARCH

March dates TBD: Wings & Wildlife Festival of Southern Nevada, Laughlin, Nevada

The Wings & Wildlife Festival of Southern Nevada was created to showcase the wide varieties of birds and animals that make the Mohave Desert and Colorado River Valley their home. This event allows attendees to experience four different ecological systems and the wildlife that thrive in the desert's springtime splendor. Optional tours, including kayaking, canoeing, rafting, and river boat trips, provide the perfect opportunity to spot more than 400 species of birds, from bald eagles to mallards, that live along the Colorado River. This four-day event also provides opportunities for land excursions by RV. Tours, educational seminars, live and static exhibits, a nature art show with wine reception, and a host of other activities make this event the perfect venue to explore the beautiful Mohave Desert. Nearest Interstates: I-15, I-515 and I-40. For more information: Laughlin Visitor Information Center, 800-4LAUGHLIN; www.lvcva.com

March 5–6: La Grand Boucherie and Mardi Gras Newcomer's Parade, St. Martinville, Louisiana

Saturday: Butchering of the Pig, Squeal Like a Pig Contest, Cracklin' Throwing Contest, Acadiana Puller "Battle on the Teche" Arm-Wrestling Competition. Cajun food, music and Zydeco dancing. Sunday: Parade travels down Main Street; be sure to watch from the balcony of La Maison Restaurant on the church square. Nearest Interstate: I-10. For more information: St. Martin Parish Tourism Commission, (337) 298-3556; cajuncountry.org

APRIL

April 6–10: North Carolina Azalea Festival, Wilmington, North Carolina

The 64th annual festival will be held in the greater Wilmington area, celebrating the city's exceptional artwork, gardens, rich history and culture during its five days of entertainment that includes: a parade, street fair, circus, concerts, pageantry, and all that is Southern. Nearest Interstate: I-40. For more information: North Carolina Azalea Festival, (910) 794-4650; www.ncazaleafestival.org

MAY

May 5–7: Pella Tulip Time Festival, Pella, Iowa

Celebrate the Dutch Heritage of Pella. Nearly one-half million tulips are planted to provide tulip lanes along the streets, as well as gardens full of color. Highlights of the festival are the parades; each day features two: an afternoon parade and a lighted evening parade. No Dutch

Lou Henry

celebration would be complete without the Street Scrubbers to ensure the parade route is Dutch clean. The authentic Dutch working windmill and the Historical Village fascinate all who visit. Dozens of food stands provide a meal with a touch of Dutch and churches provide indoor sit-down meals. Nearest Interstates: I-80 and I-35. For more information: Pella Historical Village, (641) 628-4311; www.pellatuliptime.com

May 13–22: Rochester Lilac Festival, Rochester, New York

Each May, this festival signals spring as the park's 1,200 lilac bushes display a floral rainbow of more than 500 varieties creating brilliant floral colors, and a truly "living rainbow." Visitors come from nearly every continent creating an exotic spectacle of languages, customs and costumes. The festival features a grand opening parade, arts and crafts, international food court, live entertainment, and wine tasting. Flowering trees and bushes enhance the floral experience as well as the elaborate tulip and pansy displays. Lamberton Botanical Garden on the grounds features colorful tropical floral and foliage plants. The festival offers visitors a beautiful way to welcome spring. Nearest Interstate: I-90. For more information: Rochester Lilac Festival, (800) 677-7282, (585) 279-8305; www.lilacfestival.com

May 31–October 1: Quilt Gardens Tour of Amish Country, Elkhart, Indiana

Nothing says Amish Country of Northern Indiana like an exquisitely handcrafted quilt. A tour of 16 vibrant quilt patterned gardens bursting with colorful annuals and 16 outdoor quilt art murals create a colorful patchwork "sewn" across seven welcoming communities in Northern Indiana including Nappanee, Middlebury, and Shipshewana. The tour, inspired by quilt designs, celebrates the heritage and artistry of Northern Indiana Amish Country. There are specialty hands-on programs, gardening seminars, quilt exhibits and quilt shop hops. Nearest Interstate: I-80/I-90. For more information: Elkhart County Visitor Center, (800) 250-4827; www.quiltgardenstour.com

JUNE

June dates TBD: 20th Annual Grand Celebration Pow Wow, Hinckley, Minnesota

Native Americans of all ages in colorful regalia come from around the country to honor their traditions and heritage through song, dance, and drums. Men, women, teens and children compete for prizes in several categories throughout this event sponsored by Grand Casino Hinckley. Stroll the grounds and enjoy a variety of food and crafts. The event is free, and grandstand seating is available. Nearest Interstate: I-35.For more information: (800) 472-6321; www.grandcasinomn.com

June 10–12, 2011: Festevents –Harborfest, Norfolk, Virginia

Tall ships from all over the world frequently call on the City of Norfolk, and nearly half a million visitors gather on the waterfront each year for a celebration of the region's nautical heritage. Harborfest is three days of free entertainment, fireworks, and the biggest outdoor dock party in Hampton Roads. Celebrate the grand opening of the newly renovated Town Point Park and enjoy the annual 4th of July Great American Picnic and Fireworks all in one spectacular weekend. Nearest Interstate: I-64. For more information: (757) 441-2345; www.festevents.org

June 29–July 4, 2011: 30th Boston Harborfest, Boston, Massachusetts

Boston's rich colonial and maritime history of America's Revolutionary birthplace is celebrated annually by the six-day celebration of Boston Harborfest. It features more than 200 events, including historical reenactments, walking tours, sunset harbor cruises and Chowderfest. Nearest Interstate: I-93. For more information: Greater Boston Convention & Visitors Bureau, (888) SEE-BOSTON; www.bostonusa.com

JULY

July 16–17: Vectren Dayton Air Show, Vandalia, Ohio

Dayton, the Birthplace of Aviation, is home to the fabulous Vectren Dayton Air Show. Dayton is conveniently located at the "Crossroads of America," the intersection of I-70 and I-75, making it easily accessible. The Dayton Air Show offers something to please everyone. The U.S. Navy Blue Angels dazzle crowds with their breathtaking performances. Also see world-class civilian aerobatic pilots. Thrilling military single-ship fighter jet demonstrations along with spectacular flyovers also round out a blockbuster line-up. While most of the action takes place up in the air, there are plenty of interesting displays and aircraft on the ground available for touring. Nearest Interstates: I-70 and I-75. For more information: Vectren Dayton Air Show, (937) 898-5901; www.daytonairshow.com

July 1–4: National Tom Sawyer Days, Hannibal, Missouri

A Hannibal tradition for more than 50 years, National Tom Sawyer Days are about wholesome family fun, while celebrating Missouri's famous native son, Mark Twain. Visitors of all ages can watch and join in the many activities during this unforgettable festival in America's Hometown. Some events are pulled straight from the pages of Twain's novels, like the National Fence Painting Competition, which invites kids from around the country to try their hand at whitewashing a fence just like Tom Sawyer. Nearest Interstate: I-72. For more information: Hannibal Convention & Visitors Bureau, (866) 263-4825; www.visithannibal.com

AUGUST

August 10–16: Elvis Week, Memphis, Tennessee

Elvis Week features a week of activities, including concerts, the semifinal and final rounds of the Ultimate Elvis Tribute Artist Contest, special events with those who knew and worked with Elvis and live musical entertainment. In addition, while at Elvis Week, guests can enjoy tours of Graceland mansion and other Graceland attractions and special exhibits. One of the highlights of Elvis Week is the annual Candlelight Vigil, which begins on August 15 and lasts until the early morning hours of August 16. After an opening ceremony at the gates of Graceland, fans are invited to walk up the driveway to Meditation Garden carrying a candle in quiet remembrance of Elvis Presley. Nearest Interstates: I-40 and I-55. For more information: www.elvisweek.com NOTE: NO PHONE FOR Elvis Week

SEPTEMBER

September 2–5:Gold Rush Days, Sacramento, California

Each Labor Day weekend, Gold Rush days is a four-day celebration of California's rich gold rush history. Modern-day sights like cars and parking meters are eliminated from Sacramento's Historic Old Town and the streets are covered with 200 tons of dirt for an authentic Old West look. Plus, a colorful cast of Old West living history players are set loose on the streets to entertain the crowds, including miners, bandits, pony express riders, and an "ethnic village" celebrating the cultures which came together to shape the West. There's entertainment, music, delicious food, and excellent history lessons, and, best of all, no admission fee. Nearest Interstates: I-5 and I-80. For more information: Sacramento Convention & Visitors Bureau, (916) 808-7777; www.discovergold.org/goldrush

September dates TBD: National Buffalo Wing Festival, Buffalo, New York

The National Buffalo Wing Festival features more than 100 different flavors of chicken wings from restaurants throughout the country, live music, and contests, including the U.S. Chicken Wing Eating Championship. Founder Drew Cerza says the National Buffalo Wing Festival paved the way for the Chicken Wing Hall of Fame, which will further solidify Buffalo as the birthplace of America's most popular finger food. In 2008, more than 78,000 people attended the festival, with 560,000 wings served. Nearest Interstate: I-90. For more information: National Buffalo Wing Festival, (716) 565-4141; www.buffalowing.com

September dates TBD: Navajo Nation Fair, Window Rock, Arizona

As the largest Indian fair in the country, Navajo Nation Fair offers cultural experiences with the Contest Pow-Wow, traditional songs, and dances performed in the arena by various Indian tribes. The Navajo Nation Fair is similar to a county fair in that it has a rodeo, a parade, concerts, dances, exhibits, competitions and amusement rides. Navajo arts and crafts, known for their beauty and quality, are abundant at fair time. Nearest Interstate: I-40. For more information: Navajo Tourism, (928) 810-8501; www.discovernavajo.com

September dates TBD: Biloxi Seafood Festival, Gulfport, Mississippi

The festival focuses on the rich seafood heritage of Biloxi, which was once known as the "Seafood Capital of the World." Culinary highlights include boiled shrimp, fried shrimp, fried fish, seafood po-boys, shrimp salad, seafood jambalaya, shrimp spaghetti, and even alligator sausage. The gumbo competition invites the public to sample many delicious recipes of seafood gumbo. In addition to fabulous food, the Biloxi Seafood Festival features continuous live entertainment from jazz, blues, zydeco, country, and contemporary bands, and arts and crafts booths. Nearest Interstate: I-10. For more information: Harrison County Tourism Commission, (888) 467-4853; www.gulfcoast.org

September dates TBD: World War II History Weekend at Eisenhower National Historic Site, Gettysburg, Pennsylvania

This World War II history weekend features an authentic re-creation of both Allied and German army camps, complete with original World War II vehicles. More than 200 living history enthusiasts will portray military personnel from the European Theater in 1944 and present programs

on World War II medical services, weapons and equipment, communications, military vehicles, and the life of the common G.I. Exhibits about life on the home front, 1940s fashions and Civil Defense air raid wardens are also presented. A highlight of the weekend is the Saturday night World War II style "USO" dance held at the US Army Reserve Center featuring 1940s big band music by the Gettysburg Big Band. Admission to the Eisenhower National Historic Site is by shuttle bus departing every 15 minutes from the National Park Service Visitor Center. Nearest Interstate: I-81. For more information: Eisenhower National Historic Site, (717) 338-9114; www.nps.gov/eise

Lou Henry

September dates TBD: Buffalo Roundup and Arts Festival Custer, South Dakota

Feel the thunder, and join the fun at the annual Buffalo Roundup and Arts Festival at Custer State Park in the Black Hills of South Dakota. On Saturday and Sunday enjoy two days of Arts in the Park where regional artisans display and sell Western and Native American items, enjoy the ongoing entertainment under the big top and buffalo burgers hot off the grill. Check out the annual Buffalo Wallow Chili Cook-Off on the festival grounds. On Monday, watch as park staff, cowboys, and cowgirls round up the park's 1,500 head of buffalo and drive them into the corrals. Following the Buffalo Roundup, view the branding and sorting of the herd in preparation for the annual buffalo auction in November. Last year, more than 11,000 guests from around the world came to watch this event. Nearest Interstate: I-90. For more information: South Dakota Tourism, (800) S-DAKOTA; www.travelsd.com

Road & Weather Condition Phone Numbers

	Road Conditions	Weather Conditions
Alabama	888-588-2848	205-664-3010
Alaska	907-273-6037	907-936-2525
Arizona	888-411-7623	602-265-5550
Arkansas	800-245-1672	501-376-4400
California	800-427-7623	661-393-2340
Colorado	303-639-1111	303-337-2500
Connecticut	508-822-0634	
Delaware	866-492-6299	
Florida	800-475-0044	305-229-4550
Georgia	404-635-6800	770-603-3333
Idaho	888-432-7623	208-342-6569
Illinois	800-452-4368	217-522-0642
Indiana	800-261-7623	317-635-5959
Iowa	800-288-1047	515-270-2614
Kansas	866-511-5368	785-234-2592
Kentucky	866-737-3767	502-968-6025
Louisiana	888-762-3511	504-522-7330
Maine	866-282-7578	207-688-3210
Maryland	800-327-3125	703-996-2200
Massachusetts	617-374-1234	508-822-0634
Michigan	800-381-8477	616-949-4253
Minnesota	800-542-0220	218-729-6697
Mississippi	800-843-5352	601-936-2189
Missouri	800-222-6400	816-540-6021
Montana	800-226-7623	406-652-1916
Nebraska	800-906-9069	402-359-5166
Nevada	877-687-6237	702-263-9744
New Hampshire	866-282-7579	603-225-5191
New Jersey	866-511-6538	609-261-6600
New Mexico	800-432-4269	
New York	800-847-8929	716-565-0802
North Carolina	877-511-4662	877-511-4662
North Dakota	866-696-3511	701-223-3700
Ohio	888-876-7453	Tpk 513-241-1010
Oklahoma	405-425-2385	405-478-3377
Oregon	800-977-6368	541-276-0103
Pennsylvania	888-783-6783	814-231-2408
Rhode Island	800-354-9595	508-822-0634
South Carolina	803-896-9621	St Pol 843-744-3207
South Dakota	866-697-3511	605-341-7531
Tennessee	877-244-0065	877-244-0065
Texas	800-452-9292	800-452-9292
Utah	866-511-8824	866-511-8824
Vermont	802-828-2648	802-828-2648
Virginia	800-367-7623	866-695-1182
Washington	800-695-7623	206-526-6087
West Virginia	304-558-2889	304-746-0180
Wisconsin	800-762-3947	608-249-6645
Wyoming	888-996-7623	307-635-9901

Fir0002, flagstaffotos.com.au

Area Code Listings by State

States listed in alphabetical order, followed by area codes listed in numerical order.

State	Area Codes
Alabama	205, 251, 256, 334
Alaska	907
Arizona	480, 520, 602, 623, 928
Arkansas	479, 501, 870
California	209, 213, 310, 323, 408, 415, 424, 510, 530, 559, 562, 619, 626, 650, 661, 707, 714, 747, 760, 805, 818, 831, 858, 909, 916, 925, 949
Colorado	303, 719, 720, 970
Connecticut	203, 475, 860, 959
Delaware	302
Florida	239, 305, 321, 352, 386, 407, 561, 727, 754, 772, 786, 813, 850, 863, 904, 941, 954
Georgia	229, 404, 470, 478, 678, 706, 770, 912
Hawaii	808
Idaho	208
Illinois	217, 224, 309, 312, 331, 464, 618, 630, 708, 773, 815, 847, 872
Indiana	219, 260, 317, 574, 765, 812
Iowa	319, 515, 563, 641, 712
Kansas	316, 620, 785, 913
Kentucky	270, 502, 606, 859
Louisiana	225, 318, 337, 504, 985
Maine	207
Maryland	227, 240, 301, 410, 443, 667
Massachusetts	339, 351, 413, 508, 617, 774, 781, 857, 978
Michigan	231, 248, 269, 313, 517, 586, 616, 734, 810, 906, 947, 989
Minnesota	218, 320, 507, 612, 651, 763, 952
Mississippi	228, 601, 662
Missouri	314, 417, 557, 573, 636, 660, 816, 975
Montana	406
Nebraska	308, 402
Nevada	702, 775
New Hampshire	603
New Jersey	201, 551, 609, 732, 848, 856, 862, 908, 973
New Mexico	505
New York	212, 315, 347, 516, 518, 585, 607, 631, 646, 716, 718, 845, 914, 917
North Carolina	252, 336, 704, 828, 910, 919, 980, 984
North Dakota	701
Ohio	216, 234, 283, 330, 419, 440, 513, 567, 614, 740, 937
Oklahoma	405, 580, 918
Oregon	503, 541, 971
Pennsylvania	215, 267, 412, 445, 484, 570, 610, 717, 724, 814, 835, 878
Rhode Island	401
South Carolina	803, 843, 864
South Dakota	605
Tennessee	423, 615, 731, 865, 901, 931
Texas	210, 214, 254, 281, 361, 409, 469, 512, 682, 713, 737, 806, 817, 830, 832, 903, 915, 936, 940, 956, 972, 979
Utah	435, 801
Vermont	802
Virginia	276, 434, 540, 571, 703, 757, 804
Washington	206, 253, 360, 425, 509, 564
Washington, DC	202
West Virginia	304
Wisconsin	262, 414, 608, 715, 920
Wyoming	307

USEFUL PHONE NUMBERS

Airlines:

American	800-433-7300
Continental	800-525-0280
Delta	800-221-1212
United	800-241-6522
US Air	800-428-4322

Auto Rentals:

Alamo	800-462-5266
Avis	800-331-1212
Budget	800-527-0700
Dollar	800-800-4000
Enterprise	800-325-8007
Hertz	800-654-3131
National	800-227-7368
Rent-A-Wreck	800-421-7253
Thrifty	800-367-2277
Penske	888-996-5415
U-Haul	800-468-4285

Credit Card Co:

American Express	800-528-4000
Capital One	800-955-7070
Chase	800-935-9915
Citi Bank	800-374-9700
Discover	800-347-2683
Mastercard	800-626-8372
Visa	800-847-2911

Insurance:

Allstate	866-621-6900
Geico	800-861-8380
Mercury	877-263-7287
Progressive	800-776-4737

Hotels/Motels:

Adams Mark Hotels	800-444-2326
Baymont Inns & Suites	877-229-6668
Best Western	800-528-1234
Clarion Hotels	800-424-6423
Comfort Inns	800-424-6423
Country Inns & Suites	888-201-1746
Days Inns	800-329-7466
Doubletree Hotels	800-222-8733
Econolodge	877-424-6423
Embassy Suites	800-362-2779
Extended Stay America	800-804-3724
Fairfield Inn	800-228-2800
Fairmont Hotels	800-527-4727
Four Seasons	800-332-3442
Hilton Hotels	800-445-8667
Holiday Inns	800-465-4329
Howard Johnson	800-654-2000
Hyatt Hotels	800-233-1234
Jameson Inns	800-526-3766
La Quinta Inns	800-531-5900
Marriott Hotels	800-228-9290
Microtel	800-222-2142
Quality Inns	800-228-5151
Radisson Hotels	800-333-3333
Ramada Inns	800-228-2828
Red Roof Inns	800-733-7663
Sheraton	800-325-3535
Signature Inns	800-526-3766
Super 8	800-800-8000
Travelodge	800-578-7878
Westin	800-228-3000
Wingate	800-228-1000

TOWING LAWS BY STATE

See Footnotes xxx–xxxi

State	Height	Width	Combined Length	Trailer Length	Trailer Width	Trailer Height	Two Vehicle Length	Triple Tow	Safety Chains	Breakaway
Alabama	13 1/2'	8 1/2'	65'	57' [41]	8'0"	13'6"	65'	no	yes	yes [2]
Alaska	14'	8 1/2'	75'	40'	8'6"	14'0"	75'	yes	yes	yes [2]
Arizona	13 1/2'	8'	65'	40'	8'0"	13'6"	65'	yes [43]	Not Stated	yes [2]
Arkansas	13 1/2'	8 1/2'	65'	43 1/2'	8'6"	13'6"	2 Unit Limit (No max given)	yes	yes	yes [2]
California	14'	8 1/2'	65'	NS	8'6"	14'0"	65'	yes [41]	yes	yes
Colorado	13'	8 1/2'	70'	NS [42]	8'6"	13'0"	70'	yes [42]	yes	yes
Connecticut	13 1/2'	8 1/2'	60' [1] max length = 48'	53' [19]	8'6"	13'6"	60' [1, 13]	no	yes	yes
Delaware	13 1/2'	8 1/2'	60'	NS [19]	8'6"	13'6"	65'	no	Not Stated	Not Stated
DC	13 1/2'	8 1/2'	60'	NS	8'0"	13'0"	55'	no	yes	yes
Flordia	13 1/2'	8 1/2'	65'	40'	8'6"	13'6"	65'	no	yes	yes
Georgia	13 1/2'	8 1/2'	60'	NS [19]	8'0"	13'6"	None	no	yes	Not Stated
Hawaii	14'	9'	65'	40'	9'0"	13'6"	65'	no	yes	yes [2]
Idaho	14'	8 1/2'	75'	48'	8'6"	14'0"	75'	yes [41]	Not Stated	yes
Illinois	13 1/2'	8 1/2'	60'	53' [19]	8'0"	13'6"	60'	yes [19,43]	yes [1]	yes [5]
Indiana	13 1/2'	8 1/2'	60'	40'	8'0"	13'6"	60'	yes [41]	yes	yes
Iowa	13 1/2'	8 1/2'	60'	NS [19]	8'6"	13'6"	65'	yes	yes	yes
Kansas	14'	8 1/2'	65'	NS [41]	9'0"	14'0"	65'	yes [41]	yes [37]	yes
Kentucky	13 1/2'	8'	65'	NS [41]	8'0"	13'6"	65'	yes [42]	yes	yes
Lousiana	13 1/2'	8 1/2'	65'	30'	8'0"	13'6"	70'	yes [42]	yes [7]	yes [2]
Maine	13 1/2'	8 1/2'	65'	48'	8'6"	13'6"	65'	no	yes	Not Stated
Maryland	13 1/2'	8'	55'	NS	8'0"	13'6"	60' total; 55' on desig. Routes	yes	yes	yes [6]
Massachusetts	13 1/2'	8 1/2'	60'	33'	8'6"	13'6"	60'	no	yes	Not Stated
Michigan	13 1/2'	8'	59'	53 [45]	8'0"	13'6"	65'	yes [43]	yes	yes
Minnesota	13 1/2'	8 1/2'	75'	45'	8'6"	13'6"	75' [19]	yes [43]	yes	yes [7]
Mississippi	13 1/2'	8 1/2'	none	NS	8'6"	13'6"	99'	yes	yes	yes
Missouri	14'	8 1/2'	65'	NS [41]	8'6"	13'6"	65'	yes [41]	yes [37]	Not Stated
Montana	14'	8 1/2'	75'	NS [40]	8'6"	13'6"	75'	yes [42]	yes	yes
Nebraska	14 1/2'	8 1/2'	65'	40'	8'6"	14'6"	65'	yes [41]	yes	yes [2]

TOWING LAWS BY STATE

Fire Extinguisher	Flare Signs	Brake Laws Trailers	Brake Laws Towed Cars	Overnight Parking	Max Tow Speed	Ride In 5th Wheel	Ride in Travel Trailer	Axle	License Required
yes [36]	Not Stated	3000	Brakes not required.	P	70			20,000 lbs	Class D
Not Stated	yes	5000	Brake hook-up required if towed object over 3,000 pounds.	yes	55			N/A	Class D
Not Stated	Not Stated	3000 [17]	Brakes not required.	yes [3]	75	yes	yes	20,000 lbs	Class D
Not Stated	yes	3000	No laws regarding.	yes	70			20,000 lbs	Class D
yes	yes	1500 [17]	Brakes must be sufficient to stop within a specified distance according to weight, at 20 mph.	P	55	yes [10,20]		20,000 lbs	<40ft. - Class C >= - non-com. < 40ft. - Class C >= 40ft. Non-comm. Class B w/ med. Questionnaire
Not Stated	Not Stated	3000 [17]	No laws regarding.	Not Stated	75	yes		20,000 lbs	Class R
yes	yes	3000 [17]	No laws regarding.	P	65			18,000 lbs	Class 2
Not Stated	yes	4000	If towed vehicle over 4,000 pounds, brakes must connected to those of towing vehicle.	P	55			20,000 lbs	Class D
Not Stated	Not Stated	3000 [17]	No laws regarding.	Not Stated	55			20,000 lbs	Class C
yes	yes	3000 [17]	If towed vehicle weight exceeds 3,000 pounds, brake hook-ups required as well as breakaway system.	P	70			20,000 lbs	Class D
yes	yes	1500	No laws regarding.	Not Stated	55			20,340 lbs	Class C
Not Stated	Not Stated	3000 [17]	Brake hook-ups required.	Not Stated	55			22,500 lbs	Type 4 (Non-CDL)
Not Stated	Not Stated	1500	No laws regarding.	P	65			20,000 lbs	Class D
Not Stated	yes	3000 [17]	Brake hook-up required if towed vehicle is over 3,000 pounds.	Not Stated	55			20,000 lbs on interstates & hwys;18,000 lbs others	Class D
Not Stated	yes	3000 [17]	No laws regarding.	yes	65	yes	yes	20,000 lbs	Class C
Not Stated	yes	3000	No laws regarding.	Not Stated	65	yes	yes	20,000 lbs	Class C
yes [36]	yes	yes [24]	No laws regarding..	yes	70	yes [33]	yes [33]	20,000 lbs	26,000 lbs Class C >= 26,000 lbs Class B
yes	yes	3000 [6]	No laws regarding.	Not Stated	65			20,000 lbs	Class D
Not Stated	yes	3000	No laws regarding.	P	70			20,000 lbs	Class E
Not Stated	Not Stated	3000	No laws regarding.	P	55			22,400 lbs	Class C
yes	yes	3000 [17]	No laws regarding.	P	65	yes	yes	22,400 lbs	Non-com. B>= 26,001 lbs; Non-com. C <=26,000 lbs
Not Stated	Not Stated	10,000	No laws regarding.	P	65			22,400 lbs	Class D
Not Stated	Not Stated	3000	No laws regarding.	P	55	yes	yes	18,000 lbs	Class B
Not Stated	yes	3000 [17]	Brake hook-up required except where brakes on towing vehicle are adequate to stop both vehicles within distance required by law.	P	70	yes	yes	20,000 lbs	Class D
Not Stated	yes	2000 [17]	Brake hook-up required.	Not Stated	55			20,000 lbs	Class R
Not Stated	Not Stated	NS	Both vehicles require brakes.	yes	70	yes	yes	20,000 lbs	Non-Commercial Class F
Not Stated	yes	3000	No laws regarding.	P	65	yes		20,000 lbs	Class D
Not Stated	yes	3000	No laws regarding.	Not Stated	75	yes	yes	20,000 lbs	Class O

TOWING LAWS BY STATE

State	Height	Width	Combined Length	Trailer Length	Trailer Width	Trailer Height	Two Vehicle Length	Triple Tow	Safety Chains	Breakaway
Nevada	14'	8 1/2'	70'	NS	8'6"	143'0"	70'	yes [42]	yes	yes [2]
New Hampshire	13 1/2'	8'	none	48'	8'0"	13'6"	45'	no	yes	Not Stated
New Jersey	13 1/2'	8'	62'	40'	8'0"	13'6"	53'	no	yes	yes
New Mexico	14' [1]	8 1/2'	65'	NS [41]	8'0"	14'0"	65'	yes	yes	Not Stated
New York	13 1/2'	8 1/2' some exceptions	65'	NS [41]	8'6"	13'6"	65'	no	yes	Not Stated
North Carolina	13 1/2'	8 1/2' [25]	60'	NS [19]	8'6"	13'6"	60'	no	yes	Not Stated
North Dakota	14'	8 1/2'	75'	53'	8'6"	14'0"	75'	yes [40]	yes	yes
Ohio	13 1/2'	8 1/2'	65'	NS [41]	8'6"	13'6"	65'	yes [41]	yes	yes
Oklahoma	13 1/2'	8 1/2'	70'	NS [41]	8'6"	13'6"	65'	yes [41]	yes	yes
Oregon	14'	8' some exceptions	50' max length =60', special permit	NS [41]	8'6"	14'0"	65' [19]	no	yes	Not Stated
Pennsylvania	13 1/2'	8 1/2'	60'	NS [19]	8'6"	13'6"	65'	no	yes	yes
Rhode Island	13 1/2'	8 1/2'	60'	NS	8'6"	13'6"	60'	no	Not Stated	yes
South Carolina	13 1/2'	8 1/2'	none	35'	8'6"	13'6"	N/A	no	yes	yes
South Dakota	14'	8 1/2'	75'	53	8'6"	14'0"	80'	yes [40]	yes	yes
Tennessee	13 1/2'	8 1/2'	65'	40' [41]	8'0"	13'6"	65'	yes [41]	yes	yes [2]
Texas	14'	8 1/2'	65'	NS [41]	8'6"	14'0"	65'	yes [41]	yes	yes [2]
Utah	14'	8 1/2'	65'	NS [41]	8'6"	14'0"	65'	yes [41]	yes	yes [2]
Vermont	13 1/2'	8 1/2'	65'	NS	8'6"	13'6"	68'	no	yes	yes [2]
Virginia	13 1/2'	8'	60'	NS [41]	8'6"	13'6"	65'	no	yes	yes [34]
Washington	14'	8 1/2'	75'	NS [40]	8'6"	14'0"	75'	no	yes	yes 2
West Virginia	13 1/2'	8 1/2'	55' max length =60'	48'	8'0"	13'6"	55' [19]	no	yes	yes
Wisconsin	13 1/2'	8 1/2'	65'	45'	8'6"	13'6"	65'	yes [43]	yes	Not Stated
Wyoming	14'	8 1/2'	85'	60'	8'6"	14'0"	85'	yes	yes	Not Stated

FOOTNOTES

1. On designated rural interstates; some exceptions.
2. Required on trailers over 3000 lbs
3. Prohibited where posted.
4. Required on trailers over 3000 lbs. Or if gross weight of trailer exceeds empty weight of tow vehicle.
5. Required on trucks over 3700 kgs.
6. Required if weight of trailer exceeds 40% of tow-vehicle weight.
7. Required on trailers over 6000 lbs.
8. Required if gross weight is over 2500 kgs.
9. Required on trailers over 1000 lbs. unladen, or 3000 lbs. laden.
10. Riding in fifth-wheel with audible or visual device with tow vehicle and safety glass.
11. 24-hour limit
12. Required if trailer exceeds 50% of tow-vehicle weight. BC: laden.
13. Trailer limited to 48' in a 60' combination.
14. Eight-hour limit.
15. Only if required by CSA at time of manufacture.
16. 8 1/2 ft. on certain federal road systems.
17. Gross weight requiring brakes.
18. Must have free access to drive compartment
19. Maximum combined length 60 ft. on selected highways. Special permit in Oregon, Wisconsin
20. At least one exit that can be opened from outside and inside
21. Not to exceed 18 hours in any two-week period.
22. Headlights or daytime running lights required at all times.
23. 12-hour limit
24. Must be able to stop in 40 feet and 20 mph.
25. On interstate highways; secondary roads still 8 ft.
26. 8 1/2' on all state routes. On some other roads 8' limits are posted.

TOWING LAWS BY STATE

Fire Extinguisher	Flare Signs	Brake Laws Trailers	Brake Laws Towed Cars	Overnight Parking	Max Tow Speed	Ride In 5th Wheel	Ride in Travel Trailer	Axle	License Required
Not Stated	Not Stated	1500	Braking system required when gross weight of towed object exceeds 3,000 pounds, 1,500 pounds if 1975 or newer model.	yes [21]	75			20,000 lbs	Class A or B non-comm. W/ "R" endorsement for RV, a "J" endorsement for towing vehicles >= 10,000 lbs
Not Stated	Not Stated	3000	No laws regarding.	Not Stated	55			18,000 lbs	Class D
Not Stated	yes	3000	Brake hookup required.	P	65	yes		22,400 lbs	Class D
Not Stated	yes	3000 [17]	Brake hookup required.	P	75			21,600 lbs	Class D
Not Stated	Not Stated	1000 [9]	No laws regarding.	P	65			22,400 lbs w/ a GVWR of 10,000 lbs	Non-CDL C may tow vehicles
Not Stated	Not Stated	1000	No laws regarding.	Not Stated	55	yes	yes	20,000 lbs	Class A traveling w/>= 10,001 lbs Class B traveling w/>=26,001 lbs non towing
Not Stated	yes	3000	No laws regarding.	yes	70	yes		20,000 lbs	Class D non-CDL
yes	yes	2000 [17]	No laws regarding.	Not Stated	55			20,000 lbs	Class D
Not Stated	yes	3000	No laws regarding.	yes	65			20,000 lbs	Class D
Not Stated	Not Stated	Not Stated	No laws regarding.	yes [1,23]	55	yes [35]		20,000 lbs	Class C
yes	yes	yes [4,6]	No laws regarding.	Not Stated	55	yes [10]		20,000 lbs	Non-commercial Class A or B
Not Stated	yes	4000	No laws regarding.	yes	65			22,400 lbs	Class B > 26,000 lbs; Reg. Operators < 26,000 lbs; air brake endorsement required if > 26,000 lbs w/ air brakes
yes	yes	3000 [17]	Brakes required if combined vehicle weight exceeds 3,000 pounds.	P	55			20,000 lbs	Class E >= 26,000 lbs Class F if towing
yes	yes	3000	Brakes, turn signals, and near lights required.	P	75	yes [10]		20,000 lbs	Non-commercial Class 1
yes	yes	1500	Brake hookup required.	yes	70			20,000 lbs	Class D<= 26,000 lbs
Not Stated	yes	4500	No laws regarding.	P [11]	70			20,000 lbs	Class B non-CDL >=26,000 lbs
yes	yes	2000	No laws regarding.	P [23]	75			20,000 lbs	Class D
yes	yes	3000	No laws regarding.	Not Stated	65			20,000 lbs	Class B
Not Stated	Not Stated	3000	No laws regarding.	P	55			20,000 lbs	Class B
yes	yes	3000	No laws regarding.	yes [14]	65			20,000 lbs	Regular Operator License
Not Stated	yes	3000 [6,17]	No laws regarding.	Not Stated	65	yes		20,000 lbs	Class E
Not Stated	Not Stated	3000 [17]	Brake hook-up required on vehicle over 3,000 pounds.	Not Stated	65	yes [27]		20,000 lbs	Class D
Not Stated	Not Stated	Not Stated	No laws regarding.	yes	75			20,000 lbs	Class B if GVWR>26,000 lbs; Class C if GVWR < 26,000 lbs.

27. Some exceptions or restrictions.
28. Special wide-body regulations.
29. Two safety chains or breakaway switch required on trailers.
30. Required if RV is wider than 2 meters.
31. Not recommended.
32. Seats must be equipped with safety belts.
33. 14 years of age and older.
34. Required on trailers 3000 lbs. and over
35. If passenger can communicate with driver, and exit can be opened from both interior and exterior. CA: Seat belts required.
36. Suggested, but not required.
37. Required on bumper hitches only.
38. Required if gross weight is more than 1350 kgs.
39. Headlights must be used when visibility is less than 500 ft. Yukon: always, outside of city.
40. Total maximum combined length of 75 ft.
41. Total maximum combined length of 65 ft.
42. Total maximum combined length of 70 ft.
43. With certain qualifications. Only with fifth-wheel trailer in Arizona, Illinois, Michigan, Minnesota, Manitoba (maximum length 23m.) and Saskatchewan.44. Total maximum length of 72 ft.
44. Total maximum length of 72 ft.
45. See state and provincial regulations. L. Indicates legislation pending to increase length allowance.NS. Indicates not specified. NS. Indicates not specified.
47. Total maximum combined length of 80 ft.
48. Total maximum combined length of 21m.
49. Total maximum combined length of 23m.
50. Total maximum combined length of 20m.

2011 EXIT NOW Interstate Index

EXIT		FLORIDA

Begin Eastbound I-4 from Tampa, FL to Daytona Beach, FL

FLORIDA

NOTE: I-4 begins/ends on I-95, Exit #260B, I-4 begins/ends on I-275, Exit #45B

EASTERN TIME ZONE

(0) **Jct I-275S, Tampa Airport, St Petersburg, Gulf Beaches Jct I-275N, to I-75N, to Ocala**

1 **FL 585, 21st St, 22nd St, Port of Tampa, Ybor City**
- **Gas** S: BP
- **Food** S: Burger King, Hardee's, McDonald's
- **Lodg** S: Hampton Inn, Hilton Garden Inn
- **Other** S: Ybor City Shops, Brewery, Cigar Shops, Museum

3 **US 41, 50th St, Columbus Dr**
- **TStop** S: Sunoco #2595
- **Gas** N: Shell, Chevron
  S: BP, Speedway
- **Food** S: Burger King, Checkers, Church's Chicken, IHOP, McDonald's, Pizza Hut, Subway, Taco Bell, Waffle House, Wendy's
- **Lodg** N: Days Inn♥, Quality Inn, USA Inn♥
  S: Best Value Inn, Howard Johnson Express
- **Other** S: Advance Auto, Family Dollar

5 **FL 574, FL 583, ML King Jr Blvd**
- **Gas** S: BP, Shell, Sunoco
- **Food** N: McDonald's, Sunshine Cafe
  S: Subway/Shell, Wendy's
- **Lodg** S: Fairfield Inn, Holiday Inn Express, Masters Inn
- **TServ** N: Tampa Bay Truck Repairs & Wash
  S: Great Dane Trailers, Kenworth

6 **Orient Rd (EB)**
- **Other** N: Seminole Hard Rock **Casino** & Hotel
  S: **Holiday RV Superstore**

7 **US 92, to US 301, Hillsborough Ave (WB), US 301, US 92E, Riverview, Zephyrhills Ave (EB)**
- **FStop** S: Petro Mart #627/Marathon
- **TStop** N: 301Truck Stop/Citgo (Scales)
- **Gas** N: Chevron, Circle K
  S: BP, Citgo, RaceTrac
- **Food** N: Waffle House
  S: Denny's, Kettle Restaurant
- **Lodg** N: Motel 6♥
  S: Baymont Inn, Holiday Inn Express, La Quinta Inn, Red Roof Inn♥
- **Other** N: **RVDump**/301 TS, FL St Fairgrounds, Vandenburg Airport✈
  S: **Holiday RV Superstore, Foretravel of Florida**

(9) **Jct I-75, N - Ocala, S - Naples**

10 **CR 579, Seffner, Tampa, Mango, Thonotosassa**
- **TStop** N: Flying J Travel Plaza #5081 (Scales), Travel Center of America #158/BP (Scales)
- **Gas** N: Marathon, Racetrac◈
  S: Shell◈
- **Food** N: CountryMkt/FastFood/FJ TP, Arby's/ Popeye's/TA TC, Bob Evans, **Cracker Barrel**
  S: Hardee's, Wendy's
- **Lodg** N: Country Inn, Hampton Inn
  S: Masters Inn, Quality Motel
- **TServ** N: TA TC/Tires
- **Other** N: Laundry/WiFi/**RVDump/LP**/FJ TP, Laundry/WiFi/**RVDump**/TA TC, **Lazy Days RV Center/Rally RV Park ▲**, **McCormick Lakes RV Park▲**, Auto Dealer, Mamoofs, **Camping World**, U-Haul, **Hillsborough River State Park▲**

(12) **WIM Weigh Station (Both dir)**

14 **McIntosh Rd, Dover, Seffner**
- **Gas** N: BP◈
  S: 7-11◈, BP, Hess, RaceWay◈
- **Food** S: Burger King, McDonald's
- **Other** N: **Longview Motorhomes & RV Superstore**, to appr 2mi: **Windward Knoll RV Park▲**
  S: **Encore RV Park▲**, **Green Acres RV Travel Park▲**, **Tampa East RV Resort ▲**, **Bates RV**

17 **Branch Forbes Rd, Plant City**
- **Gas** N: Shell◈, Marathon◈
  S: BP◈, Chevron, Citgo
- **Food** S: Subway
- **Other** N: Dinosaur World, Keel Farms Winery

19 **FL 566, Thonotosassa Rd**
- **Gas** N: BP
  S: RaceTrac
- **Food** S: Applebee's, Carrabba's, McDonald's, Outback Steak House, Sonny's BBQ, Starbucks, Waffle House
- **Med** S: + Hospital
- **Other** S: Dollar General, Publix

21 **FL 39, Alexander St, Buchman Hwy, Zephyrhills, Plant City (EB)**
- **Gas** S: BP◈, Shell
- **Food** S: Red Rose Diner, Tony's Pizza, Rest/Ramada Inn
- **Lodg** S: Days Inn, Ramada Inn, Red Rose Inn
- **Med** S: + Hospital, + Urgent Care
- **Other** N: to appr 5 mi: **Sundial RV Park▲**

21AB **FL 39, Buchman Hwy, Alexander St, Zephyrhills, Plant City (WB)**

22 **FL 553, Park Rd, Plant City**
- **Gas** S: Shell, Texaco
- **Food** N: Chancy's
  S: Arby's, Burger King, Denny's, Taco Bell/Subway/Shell
- **Lodg** S: Comfort Inn, Days Inn, Holiday Inn Exp
- **Other** S: **Turning Wheel RV Center**, Plant City Stadium, Hillsborough Community College, Strawberry Festival Fairgrounds, Tourist Info

25 **County Line Rd, Lakeland, Plant City**
- **FStop** S: Speedlane Citgo
- **Gas** S: Shell
- **Food** S: McDonald's, Wendy's, Subway/Shell
- **Lodg** S: Fairfield Inn
- **Other** N: FL Air Museum, Lakeland Linder Reg'l Airport✈
  S: **Florida RV World & Rentals**

27 **US 92, FL 570E (TOLL), Polk Pkwy, Lakeland, Winter Haven, Bartow**

28 **Memorial Blvd, FL 546, to US 92, N Galloway Rd, Lakeland (EB)**
- **TServ** S: to Truck PM Plus

31 **FL 539, Kathleen Rd, Lakeland**

32 **US 98, Lakeland, Dade City**
- **Gas** N: BP◈, Chevron◈, Shell, Sam's, Murphy
  S: 7-11, BP, RaceTrac, Sunoco◈
- **Food** N: Checkers, Chili's, Chuck E Cheese, CiCi's Pizza, Denny's, Don Pablo, Dunkin Donuts, Golden Corral, Hooters, IHOP, KFC, Lonestar Steak House, McDonald's, Olive Garden, Outback Steakhouse, Panera Bread, Red Lobster, Ruby Tuesday, Smokey Bones BBQ, Steak 'n Shake, Taco Bell, TGI Friday, Whataburger, Zaxby's
  S: Bob Evans, Burger King, Denny's, Long John Silver, McDonald's, Roadhouse Grill, Waffle House, Wendy's
- **Lodg** N: Comfort Inn, La Quinta Inn♥, Royalty Inn, Suburban Extended Stay, Wellesley Inn
  S: Best Western, Crossroads Motor Lodge, Days Inn, Holiday Inn, Motel 6♥, Ramada Inn, Value Place
- **Med** S: + Hospital

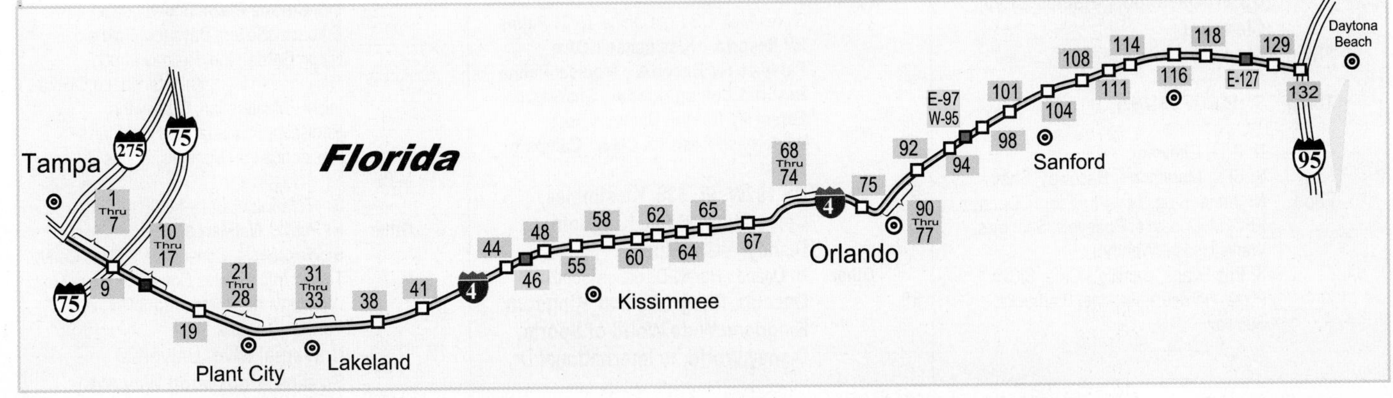

◈= Regular Gas Stations with Diesel ▲ = RV Friendly Locations ♥= Pet Friendly Locations
Red print shows large vehicle parking / access on site or nearby Brown Print = Campgrounds / RV PARKS

EXIT **FLORIDA**

Other N: ATMs, B&N, Best Buy, Carwash, CVS, Dollar General, Goodyear Auto & Truck Tire, Kash n Karry, Lakeland Square Mall, Lowe's, Northside Animal Clinic♥, Polk Co Animal Hospital♥, Publix, Sam's Club, Staples, Target, Tires Plus, Tire Kingdom, Walgreen's, **WalMart SC▲**, **Lazy Dazy Retreat**, **RV World of Lakeland, Tiki Village Resort▲**, **to Scenic View RV Park▲**, **to Gator Creek Campground▲**
S: Auto Zone, Family Dollar, Home Depot, Office Depot, Radio Shack, U-Haul, Winn Dixie, **Sanlan RV Park▲**, Bramble Ridge Golf Course

33 **FL 33, Lakeland (EB), CR 582, to FL 33, Lakeland (WB)**
Gas N: 7-11, Exxon
S: BP◈
Food N: Applebee's, Cracker Barrel, Five Guys Burgers & Fries, Hungry Howie's, McDonald's, Starbucks, Subway, Wendy's
S: Waffle House
Lodg N: Country Inn, Crestwood Suites, Days Inn, Hampton Inn, Jameson Inn♥, Quality Inn, Sleep Inn
S: Howard Johnson, Ramada, Relax Inn, Value Place
Med S: + Hospital
Other N: CVS, Publix/Pharmacy, UPS Store, Carwash/Exxon
S: Harley Davidson Lakeland, Lakeland Animal Clinic♥, Veterinary Emergency Care♥, **to Lakeland RV Resort▲**

38 **FL 33, USA Int'l Speedway, Lakeland, Polk City**
Other N: USA Speedway, **Ken Robertson RV Center**

41 **FL 570W (TOLL), Polk Pkwy, Lakeland (EB), FL 570W, Polk Pkwy, Auburndale, Lakeland (WB)**

44 **FL 559, Polk City, Auburndale**
TStop S: Love's Travel Stop #228(Scales), Polk City Truck Stop/BP (Scales)
Food S: Arby's/TJCinn/Love's TS, Rest/Polk City TS
Other N: WiFi/RVDump/Love's TS, **Le Lynn RV Resort▲**
S: Fantasy of Flight, **Bay Lake Motorcoach Resort▲**

(46) **Rest Area (Both dir)**
(RR, Fam RR, Phone, Picnic, Vend, Pet, Sec24/7)

48 **CR 557, Lake Alfred , Winter Haven**
Gas S: BP◈

55 **US 27, Davenport, Haines City, Clermont**
FStop N: Kangaroo Express #2125, Speedway Sunoco
TStop S: (10 mi to US17/92) Commercial Truck Terminal/Citgo (Scales)
Gas N: 7-11, Chevron◈
S: BP◈, Marathon◈, Raceway, Shell◈
Food N: Burger King, Cracker Barrel, Denny's, KFC, McDonald's, Popeye's, Shoney's, Waffle House, Wendy's
S: Bob Evans, Camille's Cafe, CiCi's Pizza, Hardee's, Perkins, Starbucks, Subway

EXIT **FLORIDA**

Lodg N: Comfort Inn, Fairfield Inn, Hampton Inn, Holiday Inn Express, Home Suites, Super 8
S: Americas Best Value Inn, Best Western, Days Inn, Microtel, Quality Inn
TServ S: CTT/Tires
TWash S: CTT
Med S: + Hospital
Other S: Laundry/CTT
S: Best Buy, BooksAMillion, Dick's Sporting Goods, Dollar Tree, Michael's, PetSmart♥, Staples, Target, Walgreens, **Deer Creek RV Golf Resort/RVDump▲**, **Orlando SW Fort Summit KOA/RVDump▲**, **Theme World RV Resort/RVDump▲**

58 **FL 532, Osceola Polk Line Rd, Davenport, Kissimmee, Poinciana**
Gas N: 7-11, BP
Food N: China One, Chili's, McDonald's, Subway
Other N: Publix/Pharmacy, Walgreen's
S: **Lakewood RV Resort▲**, **Mouse Mountain RV & MH Resort▲**, **21 Palms RV Resort /RVDump▲**, **Rainbow Chase RV Resort▲**

60 **FL 429 (TOLL), Apopka**

62 **FL 417N (TOLL) (EB), World Dr, Disney World, Celebration, Epcot, MGM, Cape Canaveral, Kennedy Space Center, Int'l Airport, Sanford**
Other N: to Disney World
S: to Orlando Int'l Airport✈, Celebration Station

64A **US 192E, FL 536, to FL 417 (TOLL), Kissimmee, Celebration Station, Magic Kingdom, Disney, MGM Studios**
Gas S: Mobil◈, RaceTrac
Food S: Arby's, Bob Evans, Charlie's Steak House & Seafood, Checkers, ChickFilA, Chili's, CiCi's Pizza, Cracker Barrel, Denny's, IHOP, Joe's Crab Shack, KFC, Kobe Japanese Rest, Logan's Roadhouse, McDonald's, Olive Garden,
Food S: Red Lobster, Shoney's, Starbucks, Subway, Waffle House, Wendy's, Western Sizzlin
Lodg S: Best Western, Comfort Suites, Days Inn, Econo Lodge, Hampton Inn, Holiday Inn, Homewood Suites, Howard Johnson, Hyatt Hotel, Knights Inn, Masters Inn, Motel 6, Quality Suites, Radisson, Ramada, Red Roof Inn♥, Rodeway Inn, Suites at Ole Town, Super 8, Travelodge♥
Med S: + Med-Plus Family Medical Center
Other S: CVS, Publix, Walgreen's, Factory Outlet Stores Mall, US Post Office, **to 21 Palms RV Resort▲**, **Kissimmee KOA▲**, **Paradise RV Resort▲**, **Tropical Palms Resort & Campground▲**, **Sherwood Forest RV Resort, Disney's Fort Wilderness Resort & CG▲**, **Camping World**

64B **US 192W, FL 536, Kissimmee, Celebration, Magic Kingdom, Disney, MGM Studios**
Other N: Orlando Harley Davidson South

65 **Osceola Pkwy, Animal Kingdom, Kingdom, Wide World of Sports, Disney World, to International Dr.**

EXIT **FLORIDA**

67 **FL 536, to FL 417 (TOLL), World Center Pkwy, to Epcot, Disney, International Dr**
Gas S: 7-11/Citgo
Food S: Restaurant, Starbucks
Lodg S: Holiday Inn, Marriott, Radisson
Other N: to Disney, Attractions
S: CVS, Prime Outlet Mall, Arabian Nights,

68 **FL 535, S Apopka Vineland Rd, Lake Buena Vista, Kissimmee**
Gas N: Chevron, Shell◈
S: 7-11, Chevron
Food N: Black Angus Steaks, Chili's, China Buffet, Denny's, Dunkin Donuts, Hooters, IHOP, Joe's Crab Shack, Kobe, Macaroni Grill, McDonald's, Olive Garden, Perkins, Pizza Hut, Qdoba Mexican, Red Lobster, Shoney's, Steak 'n Shake, Subway, Taco Bell, TGI Friday, Tony Roma, Waffle House
S: Carrabba's, CiCi's Pizza, ChickFilA, Golden Corral, Landry's Seafood, Lone Star Steakhouse, Starbucks, Wendy's
Lodg N: Best Western, Comfort Inn, Days Inn, DoubleTree, Fairfield Inn, Hampton Inn, Holiday Inn, Marriott, Radisson, Springhill Suites, Wyndham
S: Country Inn, Crowne Plaza, Fairfield Inn, Holiday Inn, Marriott, Sheraton
Other N: Grocery, Walgreen's, US Post Office
S: CVS, Premium Outlets Mall, **to Aloha RV Park▲**, **Kissimmee/ Orlando KOA▲**

71 **Central Florida Pkwy, Sea World, International Dr (EB, no EB rentry)**
Gas S: Chevron
Food S: Wendy's
Lodg S: Extended Stay Inn, Hilton Garden Inn, Marriott, Residence Inn, Westgate Leisure Resort
Other S: Sea World

72 **FL 528E (TOLL-Beeline Expwy), Int'l Airport, Cape Canaveral**

74A **FL 482, Sand Lake Rd, International Drive**
Gas N: Chevron, 7-11
S: BP, Chevron, Mobil◈, Shell
Food N: ChickFilA, McDonald's, Wendy's
S: Burger King, Chili's, Denny's, Don Pablo, Fishbones, Golden Corral, IHOP, McDonald's, Olive Garden, Perkins, Po Folks, Sizzler, Starbucks,Tony Roma
Lodg N: Comfort Suites, Courtyard, Days Inn, Hampton Inn, Hawthorne Suites, Quality Suites
Lodg S: Baymont Inn♥, Best Western, Comfort Inn, Crowne Plaza, Econo Lodge, Embassy Suites, Days Inn, Fairfield Inn, Hilton Garden Inn, Holiday InnX2, Howard Johnson, Knights Inn, La Quinta Inn♥, Masters Inn, Quality Inn, Radisson, Ramada, Red Roof Inn♥, Residence Inn, Springhill Suites
Med N: + Hospital
S: + Walk-In Family Medical Center
Other N: Publix, **WalMart SC**
S: Walgreen's, Convention & Civic Center, Tourist Info, Pirates Cove Adventure Golf, Wonderworks, **International World RV Park/RVDump▲**

74B **Universal Blvd, Universal Studios, Hollywood Way (WB)**

◈= Regular Gas Stations with Diesel ▲ = RV Friendly Locations ♥= Pet Friendly Locations
Red print shows large vehicle parking / access on site or nearby Brown Print = Campgrounds / RV PARKS

EXIT **FLORIDA**

75A **FL 435S (WB, Left Exit), Universal, International Dr, to FL 435S (WB)**
Gas S: 7-11, Chevron
Food S: Bill Wong's, Burger King, China Café, El Patio, IHOP, Panera Bread, Red Lobster, Starbucks, Steak 'n Shake, Sweet Tomatoes, Rest/Bass Pro Shop
Lodg S: Best Western, Clarion, Days Inn, Econo Lodge, Hampton Inn, Hilton Garden Inn, Howard Johnson, Homewood Suites, Motel 6♥, Orlando Grand Plaza, Ramada Inn, Rodeway Inn, Sheraton, Super 8, Travelodge
Other N: Universal Orlando, Attractions
S: Bass Pro Shop, Belz Factory Outlet World, Festival Bay Mall, Office Depot, Wet N Wild, Walgreen's

75B **FL 435N, Kirkman Rd (EB, Left exit)**
Gas N: Chevron, Mobil
Food N: Cracker Barrel, Denny's, Hard Rock Cafe, McDonald's, TGI Friday, Waffle House
Lodg N: AmeriSuites, Best Western, Days Inn, Fairfield Inn, Hard Rock Hotel, Holiday Inn, Motel 6♥, Quality Inn

(77) **Jct FL Turnpike (TOLL), N - Ocala, S - Miami**

78 **Conroy Rd**
Gas N: 7-11/Citgo
S: Chevron, Shell, BJ's
Food N: IHOP
S: ChickFilA, Chinatown, Kelly's Cajun Grill, McDonald's, Mimi's Cafe, Olive Garden, Panda Express, Pollo Tropical, Seafood Rest, Starbucks, TGI Friday, Tuscan Bistro, Wendy's, Zaxby's
Other N: Orlando Harley Davidson, Holy Land Experience, Historic District, Golf Course
S: BJ's, Home Depot, Petco♥, Publix, Super Target, Mall at Millenia, Golf Course

79 **FL 423, John Young Pkwy, 33rd St, Orlando**
Gas N: Citgo, Chevron
S: 7-11, RaceTrac, Shell◈
Food N: McDonald's
S: Burger King, IHOP, KFC, McDonald's, Rest/Days Inn
Lodg N: Extended Stay America, Ramada Inn
S: Days Inn♥, Super 8
Other N: Harley Davidson, El Monte RV Rentals & Sales
S: Cedars RV Park▲

80 **US 441, US 17, US 92 (WB)**
Gas N: 7-11
S: BP, Chevron, Mobil, RaceTrac, Texaco
Food N: China Palace
S: Denny's, Dunkin Donuts, Krystal's,, McDonald's, Subway, Waffle House, Wendy's
Lodg N: Super 8, Sands Motel
S: Days Inn, Melody Motel, Regency Inn
Other N: Auto & Tire Services, Orlando Int'l Airport✈
S: Auto Services & Repairs, Gator Tire Store, Food Lion, Grocery

80A **US 441S, US 17S, US 92W, Orlando International Airport (EB)**

80B **US 441N, US 17N, US 92E (EB)**

81A **Michigan St (WB)**
Gas N: Citgo◈

Personal Notes

EXIT **FLORIDA**

Food N: Shoney's
Lodg N: Budget Motel, Sands Motel

81B **Kaley Ave East (WB)**

81C **Kaley Ave West (WB)**

81BC **Kaley Ave East/West (EB)**
Gas S: Citgo, Marathon, Mobil, Sunoco
Food S: Burger King, Starbucks, Wendy's
Med S: + Hospital
Other S: Amtrak (auto train at x101C)

82B **South St (EB)**

82A **FL 408, Jct East – West Expy (TOLL), to FL 526, Univ of Centr FL**

82C **Anderson St. East, Downtown, Church St Station (diff reacc)**

83 **South St, to Church St Station, to Downtown (WB)**

83B **FL 50, Colonial Dr, US 17, US 92, Amelia St (EB)**

84 **FL 50, Colonial Dr (WB), Ivanhoe Blvd, Orlando**
Gas S: Chevron, Citgo, Marathon
Food S: IHOP
Lodg N: Holiday Inn, Howard Vernon Motel
S: Courtyard, Knights Inn, Radisson, Sheraton
Other S: to Orlando Executive Airport✈

85 **Princeton St, Orlando**
Gas N: Hess◈
S: Chevron◈
Food N: Godfather's Pizza/Hess
S: Giant Subs, Wendy's, White Wolf Cafe

EXIT **FLORIDA**

Lodg S: Comfort Suites
Med S: + Florida Hospital - Orlando

86 **Par St, College Park (EB, No Rentry)**
Gas S: Shell

87 **FL 426, Fairbanks Ave, Winter Park**
Gas N: Hess◈
S: Chevron, Shell
Food N: Blimpie Subs, Dunkin Donuts
S: Burger King, Poco's Mexican, Popeye's Chicken, Steak 'n Shake, Subway, Wendy's, Winter Park Diner
Lodg S: Quality Inn
Other S: Rollins College, to Lake Breeze RV Park▲

88 **FL 423, Lee Rd, Winter Park**
Gas N: Citgo, Texaco, 5-Star
S: Chevron◈, Mobil◈
Food N: Arby's, Bombay Kitchen Indian Rest, Burger King, Del Frisco's Prime Steak & Lobster, Dunkin Donuts, IHOP, Long John Silver's, McDonald's, Shoney's, Subway, Taco Bell, Waffle House
S: Denny's, Little Caesar's Pizza
Lodg N: Comfort Inn, Days Inn, InTown Suites, Knights Inn, La Quinta Inn♥, Motel 6♥
S: Fairfield Inn, Park Inn, Ramada
Med S: + Hospital
Other N: Home Depot, West Marine, Everest Univ

90A **FL 414E, Maitland Blvd East (EB)**

90B **FL 414W, Maitland Blvd West (EB)**

90 **FL 414, Maitland Blvd (WB)**
Gas N: 7-11
Food N: Applebee's, ChickFilA
Lodg N: Courtyard, Extended Stay America, Homewood Suites, Sheraton, Studio +, VIP Suites
S: Best Value Inn
Other N: Sportsplex
S: Art Center, Jai Alai, Seminole Harley Davidson, to Green Acres RV Park of Orlando▲

92 **FL 436, Altamonte Springs, Semoran Blvd, Apopka**
Gas N: 7-11, Circle K/Shell◈, Shell◈
S: BP, Citgo, Hess, Mobil, Shell
Food N: ChickFilA, Checkers, Chipolte Mexican Grill, Chuck E Cheese's, Cracker Barrel, Dominos Pizza, ,Kobe Japanese Rest, Longhorn Steakhouse, McDonald's, Olive Garden, Perkins, Pizza Hut, Red Lobster, Sweet Tomatoes, TGI Friday, Taco Bell, Waffle House
Food S: A&W, Chili's, Denny's, MiMi's Cafe, Panda Express, Steak 'n Shake
Lodg N: Best Western, Clarion Inn, Days Inn♥, La Quinta Inn♥, Holiday Inn♥, Hampton Inn, Quality Inn, Ramada, Residence Inn, Remington Inn, Springhill Suites, Travelodge
S: Embassy Suites, Hilton, Homestead Suites, Marriott
Med N: + Central Care Urgent Care
S: + Florida Hospital
Other N: ATMs, Banks, CVS, Firestone, U-Haul, Walgreen's, Carwash/Circle K
S: Altamonte Mall, B&N, CVS, CompUSA, Office Depot, PetCo♥, Tourist Info, to Weikiwa Springs State Park▲

◈ = Regular Gas Stations with Diesel ▲ = RV Friendly Locations ♥ = Pet Friendly Locations
Red print shows large vehicle parking / access on site or nearby **Brown Print = Campgrounds / RV PARKS**

EXIT	FLORIDA

94 — **FL 434, Longwood, Winter Springs**
- **Gas** — **N:** Mobil, Hess◈
  S: 7-11, Chevron, Maverick, Mobil◈, Shell
- **Food** — **N:** Burger King, Denny's, Kobe Japanese Rest, Miami Subs, Panera Bread, Pizza Hut, Roadhouse Grill, Starbucks, Wendy's
  S: Arby's, Bonefish Grill, Boston Market, Calypso Grill, Taco Bell
- **Lodg** — **N:** Comfort Inn♥, Rodeway Inn
  S: Candlewood Suites
- **Med** — **S:** + Orlando Reg'l S Seminole Hospital
- **Other** — **N:** CVS

(94) — **Richey Green Rest Area (WB)**
(RR/Fam, Phone, Pic, Vend, Sec 247, Pet)

(96) — **Rest Area (EB) (Last Rest Area on I-4)**
(RR/Fam, Phone, Pic, Vend, Sec 247, Pet)

98 — **Lake Mary Blvd, Lake Mary, Heathrow**
- **Gas** — **N:** Citgo, Exxon, Kangaroo Exp, Shell
  S: 7-11, BP, Chevron, Citgo, Mobil◈
- **Food** — **N:** Burger King, Luigino's Pasta & Steakhouse, McDonald's, Panera Bread, Samurai Sushi, Subway, Wendy's
  S: Arby's, Bob Evans, Boston Market, Chili's, ChickFilA, Checkers, KFC, Krystal, Longhorn Steakhouse, McDonald's, Quiznos, Romano's Macaroni Grill, Steak 'n Shake, Starbucks, Taco Bell, TGI Friday, Wendy's
- **Lodg** — **N:** Courtyard, Hyatt Place, Omni One Executive Suites
  S: Candlewood Suites, Extended Stay America, Hilton Garden Inn, Homewood Studio Suites, Homestead Orlando, La Quinta Inn♥, Mainstay Suites
- **Other** — **N:** CVS, Walgreen's, Winn Dixie
  S: Albertson's/Pharmacy, Auto Services, Goodyear, Home Depot, Gander Mountain, Kmart, Mall, Office Depot, PetSmart♥, Publix/Pharmacy, Staples, Target/Pharm, Tires Plus, US Post Office, UPS Store, Vets♥, Walgreen's, **to Appr 7 mi:** Orlando-Sanford Int'l Airport✈

101A — **CR 46A, Lake Mary, Sanford, Heathrow, Mt Dora (EB)**

101BC — **FL 417, CR 46, Central FL Greenway (TOLL), Int'l Airport (EB)**

101AB — **CR 46A, FL 417 (TOLL) (WB)**

EXIT	FLORIDA

101C — **FL 46, W 1st St, Sanford, Mt Dora (WB)**
- **FStop** — **N:** BP #5089
- **Gas** — **N:** 7-11
  S: Chevron, Mobil, RaceTrac, Sunoco, BJ's
- **Food** — **N:** Pizza Hut/BP
  S: Baskin Robbins/Dunkin Donuts, Burger King, Cracker Barrel, Don Pablo's, Denny's, IHOP, Grill & Bar, Logan's Roadhouse, McDonald's, Olive Garden, Outback Steakhouse, Pollo Tropical, Red Lobster, Ruby Tuesday, Steak 'n Shake, Waffle House, Wendy's
- **Lodg** — **S:** Comfort Inn, Days Inn, Hampton Inn, Holiday Inn, Marriott, Springhill Suites, Super 8
- **Other** — **N: to appr 3mi: Town & Country RV Resort▲, Wekiva Falls RV Resort▲**
  S: Best Buy, Big 10 Tire, BJ's Whsl, Books A-Million, CVS, Publix, Sam's Club, Super Target, **WalMart SC**, Seminole Towne Center Mall, Various Stores, Seminole Harley Davidson, **to** Amtrak, Amtrak Auto Service, **Twelve Oaks RV Resort▲**

104 — **Orange Blvd, Zoological Park, Sanford (EB)**
US 17, US 92, Sanford (WB)
- **FStop** — **S:** Kangaroo Express #2406/Citgo
- **Food** — **S:** Subway/Citgo
- **Med** — **S:** + Hospital
- **Other** — **N: La Mesa RV Center, Florida Luxury Coach, to Lake Monroe Park▲**
  S: Bates Motorhomes & Rentals, Central FL Zoo, US Post Office, Port of Sanford

108 — **Dirksen Dr, DeBary Dr, DeBary, Deltona, Enterprise**
- **Gas** — **N:** Chevron, Citgo◈
- **Gas** — **S:** Shell, Kangaroo
- **Food** — **N:** Burger King, IHOP
  S: McDonald's, Subway, Waffle House
- **Lodg** — **N:** Hampton Inn
  S: Best Western♥
- **Other** — **N:** Publix, **to appr 5.5 mi Highbanks Marina & Camp Resort▲**

111 — **Saxon Blvd, Deltona, Debary. Orange City (WB)**
- **Gas** — **N:** Circle K/Shell, Hess◈, RaceTrac
  S: Chevron
- **Food** — **N:** Bob Evans, ChickFilA, Chili's, Denny's, Fazoli's, KFC, McDonald's, Perkins, Pizza Hut, Ruby Tuesday, Sonic, Sonny's BBQ, Steak 'n Shake, Zaxby's
  S: Wendy's

EXIT	FLORIDA

- **Lodg** — **N:** Country Inn, Holiday Inn Express
- **Med** — **N:** + Hospital
- **Other** — **N:** Home Depot, Lowe's, Office Depot, Publix, Walgreen's, **WalMart SC, to Highbanks Marina & Camp Resort▲**
  S: Albertson's, Auto Services, Family Dollar, Publix, Walgreen's, **to appr 3.5 mi Paradise Lakes Travel Trailer Park▲**

111A — **Saxon Blvd East (EB)**
- **Other** — **S:** Deltona Hills Golf & Country Club

111B — **Saxon Blvd West (EB)**
- **Med** — **N:** + Hospital

114 — **FL 472, Deltona, Orange City, Deland, Cassadaga**
- **Other** — **N: to appr 2 mi: Clark Family Campground▲, to appr 2.5 mi Orange City RV Resort▲, Blue Spring State Park▲, Lake Monroe Park▲**

116 — **W Main St, Lake Helen, Orange Camp Rd, Deland**

118AB — **FL 44, E New York Ave, Deland, New Smyrna Beach (Addtl Serv appr 3.5 mi N in Deland)**
- **Gas** — **N:** BP, Shell◈
- **Food** — **N:** Rest/Howard Johnson, Subway
- **Lodg** — **N:** Howard Johnson Express♥
- **Med** — **N:** + Hospital
- **Other** — **N:** Daytona Beach Comm College-Deland, Stetson Univ, **to appr 8 mi: Lakeside Village RV Park▲**
  S: Volusia Co Fairgrounds▲

129 — **US 92E, Daytona Beach (EB, Left exit)**
- **Other** — **E: Town & Country RV Park▲**, Daytona Beach Int'l Airport✈, Daytona Int'l Speedway, Daytona Flea Market, **to appr 2 mi: Int'l RV Park & Campground/ RVDump▲**

(132) — **Jct I-95, N - Jacksonville, S - Miami, FL 400E, Daytona Beach (EB)**
- **Other** — **E: FL 400E to DB Int'l Airport✈**

EASTERN TIME ZONE

NOTE: **I-4 begins/ends on I-275, Exit #45B**
I-4 begins/ends on I-95, Exit #260B

ⓘ FLORIDA

Begin Westbound I-4 from Daytona Beach, FL to Tampa, FL

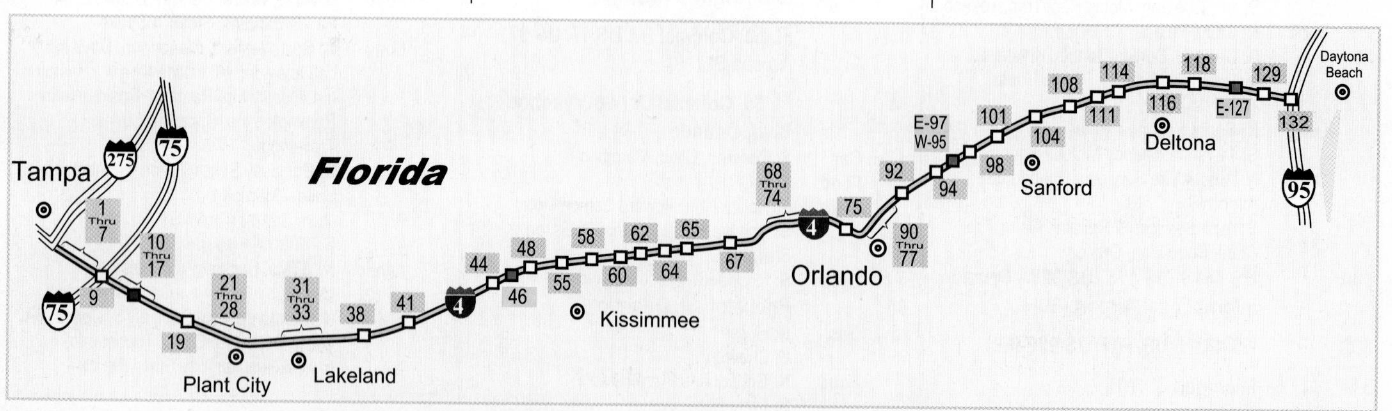

◈= Regular Gas Stations with Diesel ▲ = RV Friendly Locations ♥= Pet Friendly Locations
Red print shows large vehicle parking / access on site or nearby **Brown Print = Campgrounds / RV PARKS**

EXIT		WASHINGTON

Begin Southbound I-5 from US / Canada border to US / Mexico border.

CANADA
WASHINGTON

NOTE: I-5 begins/ends CA/ MX Border

PACIFIC TIME ZONE

(277) **US Customs & Immigration Port of Entry, USA/Canada Border**

276 **WA 548S, D St, Peace Portal Dr, Blaine**
- Gas: **E:** MP◈, Shell◈, Topline, USA◈, Amex Border Fuel Stop; **W:** Chevron
- Food: **E:** Denny's; **W:** Cafe/ Motel International, Paso Del Norte Mexican, Pizza Factory,Subway
- Lodg: **E:** Northwoods Motel; **W:** Anchor Inn Motel, Bayside Motor Inn, Motel International
- AServ: **W:** Chevron
- Other: **E:** **Peace Arch State Park**, Amex DutyFree Shopping; **W:** Coast Hardware, NAPA, Visitor Info Center

275 **WA 543N, Blaine, Port of Entry Truck Customs (NB, No Rentry) (All Comm'l Vehicles MUST Exit)**
- TStop: **E:** Yorky's Market #7/Exxon (Scales)
- Gas: **E:** Chevron◈, Shell◈
- Food: **E:** Deli/Yorky's, Burger King
- TServ: **E:** Yorky's TS
- Other: **E:** Laundry/**LP**/Yorky's, Rite Aid, Blaine Muni Airport✈, Dollar Tree, Greyhound

274 **Peace Portal Dr, Portal Way, to Blaine (NB, No Rentry)**
- Gas: **W:** Star Power/Shell
- Food: **W:** Niki's Diner
- Other: **W:** **Semiahmoo Resort Camping▲**

270 **Birch Bay-Lynden Rd, to Birch Bay, Lynden, Blaine**
- Gas: **W:** Shell◈
- Food: **W:** Subway/Shell
- Lodg: **W:** Semiahmoo Resort
- Other: **W:** **to Lighthouse by the Bay RV Resort▲**, Grandview Golf Course, **to Beachside RV Park▲**, Birch Bay Outlet Mall, Vet♥

(269) **Custer Welcome Center (SB) (RR, Phone, Picnic, Vend)**

(267) **Custer Rest Area (NB) (RR, Phone, Picnic, Vend, Info, Pet)**

266 **WA 548N, Custer, Grandview Rd**
- Gas: **W:** ArcoAmPm
- Other: **W:** **Birch Bay State Park**

263 **Portal Way, Ferndale**
- Gas: **E:** Shell◈
- Other: **E:** **The Cedars RV Resort▲**

262 **Main St, Ferndale, Bellingham**
- FStop: **E:** Starvin' Sam's #4/76
- TStop: **E:** Ferndale Truck Stop/AmBest/Tesoro (Scales)
- Gas: **W:** 76, Citgo, Exxon◈, Shell◈
- Food: **E:** Denny's, McDonald's, Subway; **W:** Bob's Burgers, DQ, Papa Murphy's Take 'n Bake, Thai Garden

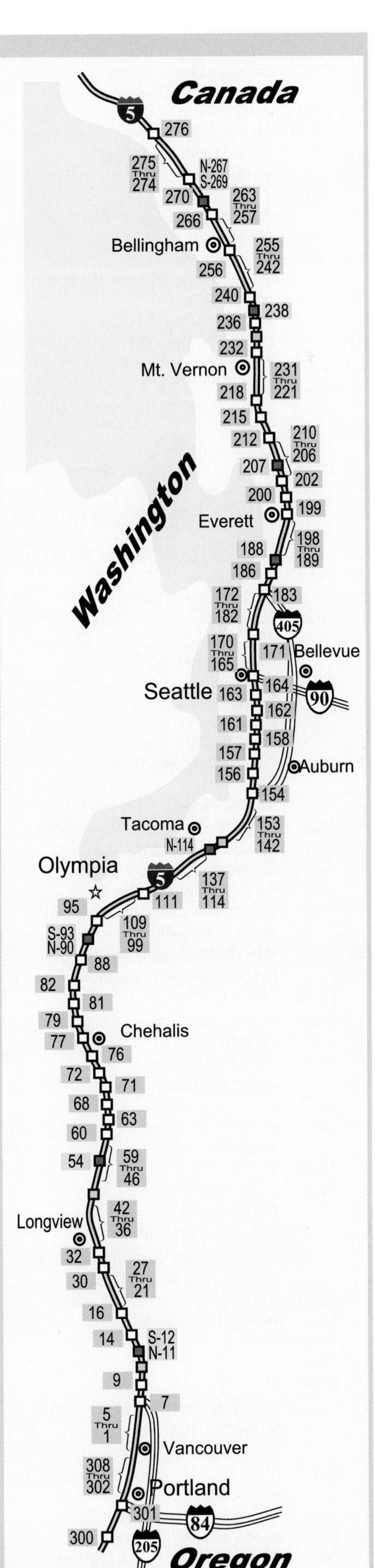

EXIT		WASHINGTON

- Lodg: **E:** Motel/Ferndale TS, Super 8♥; **W:** Scottish Lodge Motel
- Other: **E:** Laundry/Ferndale TS, **LP**/76, U-Haul, **Norwest RV Park▲**; **W:** Grocery, NAPA, Schwab Tire, Riverside Golf Course, Walgreen's

260 **Slater Rd, Bellingham, to Lummi Island**
- Gas: **E:** ArcoAmPm; **W:** to 76, Shell◈
- Other: **E:** **El Monte RV Sales**; **W:** **to Eagle Haven RV Park▲**, Lummi Indian Reservation

258 **Maplewood Ave, Bakerview Rd, Bellingham Int'l Airport**
- FStop: **W:** Yorky's Market #6/Exxon (Scales)
- Gas: **W:** 76, ArcoAmPm
- Food: **E:** Papa Murphys Take n Bake, Starbucks; **W:** Rest/Hampton Inn, Cruisin Coffee Airport 24hr, Mykonos Greek Rest
- Lodg: **W:** Hampton Inn, Shamrock Motel
- Other: **E:** to Whatcom Comm College, UPS Store, Bellis Fair Mall; **W:** **Bellingham RV Park▲**, Bellingham Int'l Airport✈, **LP/RVDump**/Yorky's, **WA State Hwy Patrol Post**

257 **Northwest Ave, Bellingham, to Lynden**
- Gas: **W:** Shell

256 **Meridian Rd (SB)**

256B **Bellis Fair-Mall Pkwy, WA 539N, Meridian Rd (NB)**
- FStop: **E:** (5mi on 539N) Pacific Pride
- Other: **E:** Bellis Fair Mall, Target

256A **WA 539N, Meridian St (NB)**
- Gas: **E:** Exxon◈, Chevron, Shell◈, Costco
- Food: **E:** Arby's, Burger King, DQ, Denny's, Godfather's, McDonald's, Olive Garden, Pizza Hut, Red Robin, Shari's, Starbucks, Taco Bell, Taco Time, Wendy;s; **W:** Eleni's Family Rest
- Lodg: **E:** Best Western, Comfort Inn, Days Inn, Holiday Inn Express♥, La Quinta Inn, Quality Inn; **W:** Rodeway Inn
- Med: **E:** + Hospital
- Other: **E:** Bellis Fair Mall, B&N, Best Buy, Costco, Dollar Tree, Grocery, Home Depot, Office Depot, Petco♥, RiteAid, Safeway, Target, Walgreen's, **WalMart**, U-Haul, **WA State Hwy Patrol Post**, **RVDump**/Carwash/Shell

255 **WA 542E, to Mt Baker (SB), Sunset Dr, Bellingham (NB)**
- Gas: **E:** Chevron◈, Exxon, Shell◈
- Food: **E:** Subway/Shell, Applebee's, Dominos Pizza, Jack in the Box, Panda Express, Round Table Pizza, Taco Bell
- Med: **W:** + St Joseph Hospital
- Other: **E:** Grocery, Kmart, Lowe's, RiteAid, Walgreen's, US Post Office

254 **Ohio St, State St, to City Center, Iowa St, Bellingham**
- FStop: **W:** Pacific Pride
- Gas: **E:** Starvin Sam's/Conoco, Valero; **W:** 76, Chevron, Shell
- Food: **W:** DQ, McDonald's, Skipper's Seafood, Subway
- AServ: **W:** Chevron

◈= Regular Gas Stations with Diesel ▲ = RV Friendly Locations ♥= Pet Friendly Locations
Red print shows large vehicle parking / access on site or nearby Brown Print = Campgrounds / RV PARKS

EXIT		WASHINGTON
	Other	E: **Vacationland RV Sales**, Auto Dealers W: Auto Dealers, NAPA, Schwab Tire **RVDump**/Chevron
253		**Lakeway Dr, Bellingham** **(W Services same as Ex #252)**
	Gas	E: USA W: Chevron
	Food	E: Lakeway Teriyaki, Little Caesar's Pizza, Subway
	Lodg	E: Best Western, ValuInn Motel, A Secret Garden B&B
	Other	E: Discount Tire, Grocery, Radio Shack, Tires, Laundromat
252		**Samish Way, Bellingham, West Washington University** **(E Services same as Ex #253)**
	Gas	W: 76, Chevron, Mobil, Shell◊, Tesoro◊
	Food	W: Arby's, Black Angus Steakhouse, Burger King, Boomer's Drive In, IHOP, Denny's, Kyoto's, McDonald's, Pizza Hut, Popeye's Chicken, Quiznos, Starbucks, Subway
	Lodg	W: Aloha Motel, Bay City Motor Inn, Coachman Inn, Mac's Motel,Motel 6♥, Ramada Inn, Travelodge, Villa Inn
	Other	W: Grocery, RiteAid, **to** W WA Univ
250		**WA 11, Old Fairhaven Pkwy, S Bellingham, to Chuckanut Dr**
	Gas	W: ArcoAmPm, Chevron
	Food	W: Dos Padres Mexican, Tony's Cafe
	AServ	W: Chevron
	Other	W: Albertson's
246		**Samish Way, North Lake Samish**
	Gas	W: Shell◊
	Other	W: **Lake Samish Terrace Park▲**
242		**Nulle Rd, South Lake Samish**
240		**Lake Samish Rd, to Alger**
	FStop	E: Alger Food Mart/Shell
	Food	E: Alger Grille
	Lodg	E: Whispering Firs Motel & **RV Park▲**
	Other	E: **RVDump**/**LP**/Shell, **Wildwood Resort▲**
(238)		**Bow Hill Rest Area (Both dir)** **(RR, Phone, Pic, Vend, WiFi, Info, Pet)**
236		**Bow Hill Rd, Bow, Belfast, Edison**
	Gas	E: Chevron◊
	Food	E: Rest/Skagit Resort
	Lodg	E: Skagit Valley Casino Resort
	Other	E: **LP**/Skagit Valley Resort, **Burlington KOA▲**, **1000 Trails Mt Vernon▲**
(235)		**Inspection Station (SB)**
232		**Cook Rd, Burlington, to Sedro Woolley**
	FStop	E: Cook Rd Shell, Pacific Pride
	Gas	E: 76◊, Gas 'n Go
	Food	E: Bob's Burgers, DQ, Iron Skillet, Jack in The Box, Subway/76
	Med	E: + Hospital
	Other	E: **Burlington KOA▲**, **Foley's RV/LP**, **RVDump**/Shell W: **Action RV Service**
231		**WA 11N, Chuckanut Dr, to Burlington, to Bow, Edison, Larrabee**
	Other	E: **Camping World/RVDump▲** W: **WA State Hwy Patrol Post**
230		**WA 20, Anacortes, Burlington**
	FStop	W: Pacific Pride

EXIT		WASHINGTON
	Gas	E: Exxon, Shell◊, Tesoro W: ArcomPm◊, Chevron◊
	Food	E: Berry Patch Rest, Burger King, Jack in the Box, Pizza Factory, Outback Steak house, Red Robin, Subway W: McDonald's
	Lodg	E: Cocusa Motel W: Holiday Inn Express, Mark II Motel
	Med	E: + Hospital
	Other	E: Grocery, Mall, Pharmacy, Target, Schwab Tire, **to RV Parts Outlet**, **to JR's RV Repair** W: Skagit Harley Davidson
229		**George Hopper Rd**
	Gas	E: ArcoAmPm, Chevron, USA◊, Costco
	Food	E: McDonald's, Olive Garden, Pizza Hut, Shari's, Starbucks, Subway, Taco Bell, Wendy's
	Lodg	E: Hampton Inn
	Other	E: Costco, Discount Tire, Home Depot, PetSmart♥, Sportmans Warehouse W: NAPA, Prime Outlets/Famous Brands Auto Dealers, **RV Center**
227		**WA 538E, College Way, Mt Vernon**
	Gas	E: 76, Safeway W: Gas Express, Shell◊
	Food	E: Big Scoop, Denny's, Jack in the Box, KFC, McDonald's, Skipper's Seafood, Starbucks, Subway, Taco Bell W: Arby's, Burger King, Buzz In Steak House, Cranberry Tree, Drummond's, Mitzel's Kitchen, Royal Fork Buffet, Taco Time, Rest/BW
	Lodg	E: Best Western♥, Days Inn W: Best Western, Comfort Inn, Quality Inn, Travelodge
	Other	E: Ace Hardware, Albertson's, ATMs, Auto Repair, Auto Zone, Dollar Tree, Goodyear, Office Depot, PetCo♥, RiteAid, Safeway, **WalMart▲** W: Firestone, Lowe's, **Riverbend RV Park▲**, **Valley RV**
226		**WA 536W, Kincaid St, Broad St, City Center, Mt. Vernon**
	FStop	W: Pacific Pride
	Food	W: Old Towne Grainery, Skagit River Brewing Co
	Med	E: + Hospital
225		**Anderson Road**
	FStop	W: Gasco Truck Stop
	Gas	E: 76◊ W: Chevron, Valero
	TServ	W: Freightliner
	Other	E: **Lifestyle RV Center** W: **Poulsbo RV**
224		**Cedardale Rd, Old Hwy 99S, Hickox Rd, Mt Vernon (NB, no reacc)** **(NB Use #224, SB Use#225)**
	TStop	W: Truck City Truck Stop (Scales)
	Food	W: Rest/Truck City TS
	TWash	W: Truck City TS
	TServ	W: Truck City TS
	Other	W: Laundry/Truck City TS
221		**WA 534E, Pioneer Hwy, to Lake McMurray, to Conway, Stanwood**
	Gas	E: Shell◊ W: 76◊, Shell◊
	Food	W: Channel Lodge, Conway Deli
	Lodg	W: Ridgway B&B, Wild Iris B&B
	Other	W: **to Blake's RV Park & Marina▲**

EXIT		WASHINGTON
218		**Starbird Road, Milltown Rd**
	Gas	W: Foodmart
	Lodg	W: Hillside Motel
215		**300th Ave NW**
(214)		**Inspection Station (NB)**
212		**WA 532W, 268th St NE, Bryant, Stanwood, Camano Island**
	Gas	W: 76◊, Shell, Shell◊
	Food	W: Burger King, McDonald's
210		**236th St NE**
208		**WA 530, Pioneer Hwy, Silvana, to Arlington, to Stanwood**
	FStop	E: Island Crossing Tesoro W: Arlington Fuel Stop/76
	Gas	E: 76, Chevron, Shell
	Food	E: Denny's, O'Brien's Turkey House, Wallers Family Rest
	Lodg	E: Arlington Motor Inn
	Med	E: + Hospital
(207)		**Smokey Pt Rest Area (Both dir)** **(RR, Phone, Picnic, Vend, Pet, WiFi, Coffee, Info, RVDump)**
206		**WA 531, Smokey Point, 172nd St NE, to Lakewood**
	Gas	E: 7-11, 76◊, ArcoAmPm, Mobil, Shell, Safeway W: Chevron, Costco
	Food	E: Alfy's Pizza, Buzz Inn Steakhouse, Jack in the Box, KFC, McDonald's, Quiznos, Red Robin, Starbucks, Wendy's W: IHOP, Nick's, Pizza Hut, Porky's, Village Inn
	Lodg	E: Crossroads Inn♥, Hawthorn Inn & Suites, Quality Inn W: Smokey Point Motor Inn
	Other	E: **LP**/**RVDump**/76, Grocery, Lowe's, Harley Davidson, RiteAid, Schwab Tire, Safeway, Arlington Muni Airport✈ W: Best Buy, Costco, Discount Tire, Office Depot, Target, **Cedar Grove Shores RV Park▲**, **Lake Kl RV Resort▲**,
202		**116th St NE, Tulalip, Marysville**
	TStop	W: PTP/Donna's Truck Plaza/Chev (Scales)
	Gas	E: Shell, Texaco
	Food	E: Carl's Jr, Papa John's, Starbucks, Subway, Taco Bell W: FastFood/Donna's TS, McDonald's, Starbucks, Subway, Rest/Tulalip Resort
	Lodg	W: Tulalip Resort
	Other	E: PetCo♥, RiteAid W: Albertson's/Pharmacy, Seattle Premium Outlets Mall, **WA State Hwy Patrol Post**, **Tulalip Resort Casino/RV Park▲**
200		**88th St NE, Marysville**
	Gas	E: 7-11, 76, Shell◊ W: Miirastar, Murphy
	Food	E: Applebee's, Quiznos, Starbucks
	Lodg	E: Holiday Inn Express
	Other	E: **LP**/Shell, Grocery W: Home Depot, **WalMart SC▲**
199		**WA 528E, 66th St. NE, to Marysville, to Tulalip**
	Gas	E: 76, ArcoAmPm, Chevron, Shell◊ W: 76
	Food	E: Burger King, DQ, Don's, Jack in the Box, Starbucks, Subway/Shell, Village Inn W: Rest/Best Western, Arby's, Golden Corral, McDonald's, Wendy's

◊= Regular Gas Stations with Diesel ▲ = RV Friendly Locations ♥= Pet Friendly Locations
Red print shows large vehicle parking / access on site or nearby Brown Print = Campgrounds / RV PARKS

EXIT		WASHINGTON
	Lodg	**E:** Village Motor Inn **W:** Best Western, Comfort Inn, Holiday Inn Express, Tulalip Inn
	Other	**E:** Albertson's, Big O Tire, Costco, RiteAid, Schwab Tire, Staples, Marysville Towne Center Mall, **All RV Repair**, **RV** & Marine Supply **W: RV Super Mall▲** , **to** Tulalip Indian Res
198		**WA 529S, Pacific Hwy, Everett, N Broadway, Port of Everett, to Marysville (SB)**
	Other	**W: WA State Hwy Patrol Post**
195		**E Grand Ave, Port of Everett, Marine View Dr (NB)**
	Med	**W: + Hospital**
194		**US 2E, to WA 529W, Everett Ave**
	Gas	**W:** 76, Shell◈
	Food	**W:** Denny's, Best BBQ
	Lodg	**W:** Best Western, Holiday Inn
	TServ	**W:** Schwab Tires
193		**WA 529, Pacific Ave, Everett (NB) (Access to Ex #194 Serv)**
	Gas	**W:** 76, Chevron, Shell
	Food	**W:** Denny's, Grand Roaster, Hardee's,
	Lodg	**W:** Best Western, Howard Johnson♥, Travelodge
	Med	**W: + Hospital**
	Other	**W:** Lowe's
192		**Broadway (NB Left exit), City Center, Naval Station, Port of Everett**
	Gas	**W:** 76, ArcoAmPm, Chevron, Exxon, Shell
	Food	**W:** Alfy's Pizza, IHOP, Jack in the Box, Kings Table, McDonald's, Taco Bell
	Lodg	**W:** Days Inn, Super 8, Travelodge
189		**WA 526W, Everett, WA 99, to Lynnwood, WA 527, Mill Creek**
	Gas	**E:** ArcoAmPm, Chevron, Shell◈, Costco **W:** 7-11, Chevron, Shell
	Food	**E:** Burger King, Buzz Inn Steakhouse, McDonald's, Wendy's **W:** Denny's, Jack in the Box, Olive Garden, Red Robin, Starbucks, Taco Bell, Village Inn
	Lodg	**E:** Travelodge **W:** Best Western, Comfort Inn, Days Inn, Extended Stay America, Motel 6♥, Rodeway Inn
	Other	**E:** Costco **W:** Discount Tire, Kmart, Everett Mall, Animal Hospital♥, Boeing Co
(188)		**Inspection Station (Both dir)**
(188)		**Silver Lake Rest Area (SB) (RR, Phone, Picnic, Vend, WiFi, Info, Info, Coffee, RVDump)**
186		**WA 96E, 128th St**
	Gas	**E:** 76, Chevron, Shell◈ **W:** 7-11, ArcoAmPm, Chevron, Shell, Texaco
	Food	**W:** Alfy's Pizza, Burger King, Denny's, KFC, McDonald's, Mitzel's Kitchen, Papa John's, Pizza Hut, Skipper's Seafood, Starbucks, Subway, Taco Bell, Taco Time
	Lodg	**E:** Comfort Inn, Holiday Inn, Quality Inn **W:** Best Western, Cypress Inn, Everett Inn, Holiday Inn Express, La Quinta Inn & Suites♥ , Motel 6♥
	Other	**E: Lakeside RV Park▲** , **Silver Lake RV Park▲** , McCollum Co Park

EXIT		WASHINGTON
	Other	**W:** Albertson's/Pharmacy, Dollar Tree, Goodyear, **Maple GroveRV Resort▲** , **Great American Casino**, **to** Snohomish Co Airport✈
183		**164th St, to Mill Creek**
	Gas	**E:** ArcoAmPm, Shell◈ **W:** Shell◈
	Food	**E:** Jack in the Box, Panda Express, Taco Time, Shari's, Starbucks, Subway
	Other	**E:** Radio Shack, **WalMart**, Walgreen's, Martha Lake Co Park **W:** Airport✈, **Lakeside RV Park▲** , **Silver Lake RV Park▲**
(182)		**Jct I-405S, to Bellevue, to I-90, WA 525, to WA99, Mukilteo, Alderwood Mall Blvd**
	Other	**W:** to **Maple Grove RV Resort▲**
181		**196th St SW (SB), Lynnwood, to WA 524, 44th Ave W (NB)**
	Gas	**E:** 76, ArcoAmPm, Shell, Texaco **W:** 7-11, 76◈, Chevron, Shell
	Food	**E:** Litte Caesar's Pizza, McDonald's **W:** Applebee's, Arby's, Black Angus Steakhouse, Burger King, Chipolte Mexican Grill, Chuck E Cheese, Country Harvest, Denny's, Hooters, IHOP, Jack in the Box, KFC, McDonald's, Olive Garden, Panda Express, Red Lobster, Starbucks, Subway, Taco Time, Tony Roma's, Wendy's
	Lodg	**E:** Embassy Suites, Extended Stay America, Hampton Inn **W:** Best Western, Comfort Inn, Courtyard, Holiday Inn Express, La Quinta Inn♥
	Med	**W: + Chec Medical Clinic**
	Other	**E:** Albertson's, B&N, Best Buy, Lowe's, Staples, PetCo♥, Carwash/76 **W:** CompUSA, Firestone, Goodyear, Radio Shack, Schwab Tire, Target, Alderwood Mall, Convention Center, US Post Office
181B		**196th St SW, Poplar Way (NB)**
181A		**44th Ave W (NB), Lynnwood**
179		**220th St SW, Mountlake Terrace**
	Gas	**W:** 7-11, Shell, Shell◈
	Food	**W:** Azteca Mex Rest, Starbucks, Subway, Teriyaki Bowl
	Lodg	**W:** Andy's Motel, Travelers Inn
	Med	**W: + Hospital, + Mt Lake Medical Immediate Care**
	Other	**W:** Fantasia Family Fun Park, Silver Dollar Casino
178		**236th St SW, Mountlake Terr (NB)**
	Gas	**E:** Shell
177		**Lakeview Dr, 236th St, 205th St (SB) 244th St SW, WA 104, (NB) to Edmonds, Lake Forest Park (Most West Serv on WA 99)**
	Gas	**E:** Arco AmPm, Chevron**x2**, Shell◈ **W:** 76**x2**◈, Shell
	Food	**E:** McDonald's, Starbucks, Subway **W:** Arby's, Denny's, Godfather Pizza, Starbucks
	Lodg	**E:** Motel 6 **W:** Days Inn, Golden West Motel, Harbor Inn, K&E Motor Inn, St Frances Motel, Travelodge
	Med	**E: + Ballinger Clinic**
	Other	**E:** CompUSA, Grocery, Office Depot, RiteAid

EXIT		WASHINGTON
	Other	**W:** Auto Dealers, Costco, Discount Tire, Home Depot, Les Schwab Tire, PetCo♥, Radio Shack
176		**NE 175th St, Seattle, to Shoreline**
	Other	**W: Evergreen RV Supply/RVDump**
175		**WA 523, NE 145th, 5th Ave NE (Serv W to WA 99)**
	Lodg	**W:** Extended Stay America
	Other	**W: Golden Nugget Casino, Goldie's Shoreline Casino**
174		**NE 125th, N 130th St, Roosevelt Way, to WA 99, Seattle (NB) (Serv W to WA 99)**
	Gas	**W:** Texaco
	Food	**W:** Burger King, Outback Steakhouse
	Lodg	**W:** Best Western, Rodeside Lodge
	Other	**W:** Alberson's, Firestone, Office Depot, RiteAid, Sam's Club
173		**NE Northgate Way, 1st Ave NE**
	Gas	**E:** 76, ArcoAmPm **W:** 7-11, 76, Chevron, Shell◈
	Food	**E:** Chipolte Mexican Grill, Ivar's Seafood Bar, Olive Garden, Panera Bread, Red Robin, Romano's Macaroni Grill, Starbucks, Subway, Tony Roma's, Taco del Mar **W:** Arby's, Berkshire Grill, McDonald's, Starbucks
	Lodg	**W:** Ramada Inn
	Med	**W: + Northwest Hospital**
	Other	**E:** B&N, Best Buy, Discount Tire, FedEx Office, Office Depot, Target, Northgate Mall
172		**N 85th St, N 80th St, Banner Way NE, Seattle**
171		**NE 71st St, NE 70th St, WA 522, Lake City Way, Bothell**
170		**NE Ravenna Blvd, Seattle (NB)**
169		**NE 50th St (SB), NE 45th St (NB)**
	Gas	**E:** 76, Shell **W:** 7-11/Citgo
	Food	**E:** Burger King, Godfather's Pizza, Subway **W:** Café, Dino's Pizza
	Lodg	**E:** University Inn, Watertown Hotel **W:** University Plaza Hotel
	Med	**E: + University of Washington Medical Center**
	Other	**E:** Petco♥, **to** Univ of WA **W:** RiteAid, **to** Zoo
168B		**WA 520E, Boylston Ave, Roanoke St, to Bellevue, Kirkland**
168A		**Lakeview Blvd, Downtown Seattle**
	Food	**W:** Sam's Steakhouse
167		**Eastlake Ave, Mercer St, Fairview Ave, Downtown Seattle (NB, Left exit)**
	Gas	**W:** 76, Shell
	Food	**W:** Chandler Crab House, Hooters
	Lodg	**W:** Residence Inn, Silver Cloud Inn
166		**Denny Way, Olive Way (NB), Stewart St (SB), Seattle**
	Food	**E:** Starbucks, Timberline Rest
	Lodg	**E:** Capitol Hill Inn, Garden Hotel **W:** SpringHill Suites
	Other	**W:** Greyhound, Key Arena, Visitor Center
165C		**Union St (SB)**
	Food	**W:** Ruth Chris Steakhouse
	Lodg	**W:** Sheraton♥

◈= Regular Gas Stations with Diesel ▲ = RV Friendly Locations ♥= Pet Friendly Locations
Red print shows large vehicle parking / access on site or nearby **Brown Print = Campgrounds / RV PARKS**

165B Seneca St, Madison St, 6th Ave, Ave, Downtown Seattle (SB)
Food W: Ruth Chris Steakhouse
Lodg E: Wyndham Hotel
Med E: + Swedish Medical
W: Sheraton ♥
Other W: Convention Center

165A University St, Seneca St, Downtown
Lodg W: Crowne Plaza, Hilton
Med E: + Virginia Medical Center
Other E: to Seattle Univ
W: Harlequin Cellar, Market Cellar Winery

165 Seneca St, Downtown (NB, Left Exit)

164 Spring St, Madison St, 6th Ave (SB)

164B 4th Ave S, 8th Ave S, Dearborn St, to Kingdome
Other W: to Qwest Field, Safeco Field

(164A) Jct I-90E, to Spokane

163B 6th Ave S, S Forest St, Airport Way S (SB)
Other W: Rainier Brewery Tour

163A W Seattle Fwy, S Spokane St, S Columbian Way (SB)
TServ W: Cummins NW
Med E: + Hospital

163 S Spokane St, S Columbian Way, W Seattle Fwy (NB)

162 Corson Ave, Michigan St (NB Left Exit)
Gas W: Shell
Lodg W: Georgetown Inn

161 S Albro Place, Swift Ave S
Gas W: Shell◈
Food W: Starbucks
Other W: Boeing Field/King Co Int'l Airport✈

158 Boeing Access Rd, MLK Jr Way S, E Marginal Way, Pacific Hwy S
Gas W: Chevron
Food W: Randy's
Lodg W: Hilton
TServ E: Sea-Tac Ford, TEC of Seattle
W: GMC Trucks, Kenworth
Other W: NAPA, Boeing Field/King Co Int'l Airport✈

157 M L King Jr Way, WA 900

156 Interurban Ave S, to WA 599N, Tukwila (SB, diff reacc)
FStop E: Pacific Express #160
W: Tukwila Shell
Gas W: 76◈
Food E: Gordy's Steak & BBQ Smokehouse
W: Denny's, Jack in the Box, Quiznos, Starbucks
Lodg W: Days Inn, Quality Inn
Other E: Golden Nugget Casino, Silver Dollar Casino, Grand Central Casino, Great American Casino
W: Downtown Harley Davidson

154B 154th St, Southcenter Blvd, to WA 518 to Burien (SB)
Gas E: Arco AmPm
Food E: Denny's
Other E: Westfield Southcenter Mall

154A Southcenter Pkwy, to I-405N, to I-90, to Bellevue
Lodg W: Extended Stay America
TServ E: Cummins NW

EXIT WASHINGTON

(154) Jct I-405N, WA 518, to Bellevue (NB)

153 Southcenter Pkwy, Seattle (NB) (Addt'l Serv E to Valley Hwy)
Gas E: ArcoAmPm, Chevron◈
W: ArcoAmPm
Food E: Applebee's, Azteca Mexican, Chipolte Mexican Grilll, Claim Jumper, Denny's, Famous Dave's, Godfather's Pizza, IHOP, Jack in the Box, McDonald's, Olive Garden, Outback Steakhouse, Panda Express, Rainforest Cafe, Red Robin, Starbucks, Subway, Taco Bell, Taco del Mar, Wendy's
Lodg E: Doubletree Inn
Med E: + Hospital
Other E: Best Buy, Borders, PetSmart♥, RiteAid, Schwab Tire, Target, World Market, Westfield Southcenter Mall

152 S 188th St, Orillia Rd S, Airport
Gas W: 76◈
Food W: Dave's Diner, Denny's, Jack in the Box, Spencer's Steak & Chops, Taco Bell
Lodg W: Comfort Inn, Days Inn, Doubletree Hotel, Econo Lodge, Hampton Inn, La Quinta Inn♥, Motel 6♥, Quality Inn, Red Lion Hotel, Super 8♥, Sea Tac Inn, Travelodge
Other W: Seattle Tacoma Int'l Airport✈, Silver Dollar Casino, Seattle/Tacoma KOA▲

151 S 200th St, Military Road S, Kent
Gas E: Shell◈
W: 7-11, 76, Chevron
Food W: Bob's Burgers, Godfather's Pizza, IHOP
Lodg E: Motel 6♥
W: Best Value Inn, Best Western, Econo Lodge, Fairfield Inn, Hampton Inn, Howard Johnson, Holiday Inn♥, Sleep Inn, Seatac Skyway Inn
TServ W: Kenworth NW
Other W: NAPA, U-Haul

149 WA 516, Kent-Des Moines Rd, to Des Moines, Kent (SB)
Gas W: 7-11, 76, ArcoAmPm, Shell, Shell◈
Food W: Burger King, Dunkin Donuts, McDonald's, Pizza Hut, Subway, Taco Bell, Wendy's
Lodg E: Century Motel
W: Best Western, Garden Suites, Kings Arms Motel
Other E: Poulsbo RV, Golf Course
W: Albertson's, Dollar Tree, Radio Shack, Walgreen's, US Post Office

149AB WA 516, Kent-DesMoines Rd, to Des Moines, to Kent (NB)

147 272nd St, Kent (Serv on Pacific Hwy)
Gas E: 76
W: 7-11, ArcoAmPm, Shell◈
Food W: Jack in the Box, McDonald's, Papa Murphy's Take 'n Bake, Quiznos, Subway, Taco Bell
Lodg W: Travel Inn
Other W: Auto Zone, Firestone, RiteAid, Safeway

143 320th St, Federal Way
Gas W: 76, ArcoAmPm, BP, Shell◈
Food W: Applebee's, Arby's, Azteca Mexican, Black Angus Steakhouse, Black Bear Diner, Burger King, Chipolte Mexican, Church's Chicken, CoCo's, Denny's,

EXIT WASHINGTON

Food W: Dunkin Donuts, Ivar's Seafood Bar, KFC, Marie Callendar's, McDonald's, Old Country Buffet, Outback Steakhouse, Panda Express, Panera Bread, Pizza Hut, Qdoba Mexican Grill, Red Lobster, Red Robin, Starbucks, Subway, Taco Bell, TCBY, Tokyo Japanese Steakhouse, Tony Roma's, Wendy's
Lodg W: Best Western, Clarion, Comfort Inn, Courtyard, East Wind Motel, Extended Stay America, La Quinta Inn♥, Ridgecrest Motel, Stevenson Motel
Other W: ATMs, AT&T, B&N, Banks, Best Buy, Big Lots, Borders, Cascade Veterinary Services♥, Discount Tire, FedEx Office, Firestone, Goodyear, Kmart, Office Max, PetCo♥, PetSmart♥, Radio Shack, RiteAid, Safeway, Starplex Gateway Movies 8, Target/Pharmacy, Trader Joe's, UPS Store, **Walmart sc**, The Commons At Federal Way, Golf Course

142A WA 18E, Federal Way, to Auburn

142B S 348th St, to WA 161

142AB WA 18E, to Auburn, S 348th St, Enchanted Pkwy, Pacific Hwy S, Federal Way
TStop W: Ernie's Federal Way Fuel Stop #3/76
Gas W: Chevron, Shell, Costco
Food W: Arby's, Burger King, DQ, Del Taco, Denny's, Jack in the Box, Long John Silver, Olive Garden, McDonald's, Panda Express, Popeye's, Shari's, Starbucks, Taco Bell
Lodg W: Days Inn, Holiday Inn Express, Quality Inn, Super 8
Med W: + St Francis Hospital, + Sound Medical
Other E: SuperMall, Wild Waves & Enchanted Village
W: Laundry/Ernie's FS, Costco, Home Depot, Lowe's, NAPA, Office Depot, Schwab Tire, **WalMart sc**, Vets For Less♥

(140) SeaTac Rest Area (NB) (RR, Phone, Picnic, Vend, WiFi, Pet, Info, RVDump)

(140) Inspection Station (Both dir)

137 54th Ave E, Fife, WA 99N, Pacific Hwy, Tacoma, Milton
TStop W: Pacific Xpress/Gulf
Gas E: ArcoAmPm, Chevron◈, Shell
W: 76, ArcoAmPm
Food E: BBQ, DQ, Johnny's
W: FastFood/Pac Xpr, Arby's, Burger King, Denny's, Los Cabos, KFC, McDonald's, Mitzel's, Pizza Experience, Pizza Hut/TacoBell, Subway, Starbucks, Taco Bell, Wendy's,
Lodg E: Motel 6♥
W: Best Value Inn, Best Western, Comfort Inn, Fife Motel, Kings Motor Inn, Quality Inn, Royal Coachman Inn
Other E: Auto Dealers, Baydo's RV, Tacoma RV
W: Costco, Les Schwab Tires, NAPA, Pharmacy, Camping World, Great American RV Center, Emerald Queen Casino

136 20th St E, Port of Tacoma Rd (SB)

◈= Regular Gas Stations with Diesel ▲ = RV Friendly Locations ♥= Pet Friendly Locations
Red print shows large vehicle parking / access on site or nearby Brown Print = Campgrounds / RV PARKS

EXIT		WASHINGTON
136AB		**20th St E, Port of Tacoma Rd (NB)**
	TStop	**W:** Love's Travel Stop #448 (Scales)
	Gas	**W:** Chevron, Shell◈
	Food	**W:** Subway/Love's TS, Jack in the Box
	Lodg	**W:** Days Inn, Econo Lodge, Extended Stay America, Hometel Inn, Howard Johnson, Ramada Ltd, Travelodge
	TServ	**E:** Western Peterbilt
	Other	**E:** Auto Dealers, Sam's Club, Costco **W:** Laundry/WiFi/**LP**/**RVDump**/Love's TS, Auto Dealers, Destination Harley Davidson, **Wescraft RV**, **to** Port of Tacoma
135		**E 28th, Bay St, WA 167S, Tacoma, to Puyallup**
	Gas	**E:** Shell **W:** 76, ArcoAmPm
	Food	**W:** Café/LQ, Ports of Call Rest
	Lodg	**W:** Bay Motel, La Quinta Inn♥
	Other	**E: River Lane RV Park▲** **W:** Amtrak, **to** Tacoma Dome
134		**E "L" St, E 27th, Portland Ave (NB)**
	Gas	**E:** Shell **W:** ArcoAmPm
	Food	**W:** Pegasus Rest
	Lodg	**W:** La Quinta Inn♥
	Other	**W:** Button Vet Hospital♥
(133)		**Jct I-705N, Ruston, WA 7S, Mt. Rainier, Tacoma**
	Lodg	**E:** Corporate Suites **W:** Best Western, Courtyard, Ramada Inn, Travel Inn
	Other	**W:** Tacoma Dome/Civic Center, **to** Univ of WA/Tacoma
132		**S 38th St, WA 16W, to Bremerton**
	Gas	**E:** Shell, Safeway **W:** Circle K, Tesoro, Costco
	Food	**W:** Arby's, Burger King, McDonald's, Outback Steakhouse, Quiznos, Red Robin, Starbucks, Subway, TGI Friday's, Taco del Mar, Wendy's
	Med	**W: + Medical Center**
	Other	**E:** Safeway **W:** Auto Dealers, Auto Services, Tacoma Mall, Best Buy, Borders, CompUSA, Costco, Dollar Tree, Firestone, PetCo♥, Car Wash
130		**56th St, Tacoma Mall Blvd, Tacoma**
	Gas	**W:** Shell
	Food	**W:** Chuck E Cheese, El Torito, Jack in the Box, Pizza Hut, Subway, Tony Roma's, Wendy's
	Lodg	**W:** Extended Stay America
	Other	**W:** Home Depot, **to** S Tacoma Univ Place
129		**74th St, 72nd St, to Steilacoom**
	Gas	**E:** Chevron, Exxon, Valero **W:** Arco
	Food	**E:** Applebee's, Burger King, DQ, Elmer's, Famous Dave's, IHOP, Jack in the Box, Mitzel's Kitchen, Olive Garden, Red Lobster, Shari's, Starbucks, Taco Bell **W:** Hooter's, Quizno's, Yankee Diner
	Lodg	**E:** Best Western, Hampton Inn, Howard Johnson, Motel 6♥, Shilo Inn, Travelodge **W:** Days Inn
	Other	**E:** Lowe's **W:** Auto & **RV** Country Store, Home Depot, Qwest Auto Service, Sports Authority
128		**84th St, Hosmer St, Tacoma (NB) (Access to Exit # 129 Services)**
	Gas	**E:** 76, Shell◈ **W:** Tesoro
	Food	**E:** Rest/BW, Denny's, Great Wall Chinese, Round Table Pizza, Subway **W:** Ruby Tuesday
	Lodg	**E:** Best Western, Comfort Inn, Crossland Economy Studios, Econo Lodge, Hampton Inn, Holiday Inn Express, King Oscar Tacoma Inn, Motel 6♥, Red Lion Hotel, Rodeway Inn, Rothem Inn
	Other	**E:** Carwash/76, Hertz RAC, Laundromat **W:** Regal Lakewood Stadium 15 Cinema, Discount Tire, Chips Casino Lakewood
127		**S Tacoma Way, Lakewood, WA 512E, to Puyallup, Mt Rainier**
	Gas	**E:** 76 **W:** 7-11, ArcoAmPm, Chevron, Shell◈
	Food	**W:** Burger King, DQ, Denny's, IHOP, Ivar's Seafood, Korean Buffet, Los Panchos Mexican, McDonald's, Sizzler, Starbucks, Subway, Wendy's
	Lodg	**W:** Americas Best Value Inn, Best Night Inn, Candlewood Suites, Golden Lion Motor Inn, Vagabond Motel, Western Inn
	Med	**W: + to Hospital**
	Other	**E:** McChord AFB, Dirk's Truck Repair, **W:** Auto Services, Schucks Auto Supply, Fleet Truck Wash, **Oaknoll RV Park▲**, **Great American Casino**, **Macau Casino**, Lakewood Pharmacy
125		**Bridgeport Way, Lakewood, Pacific Hwy, McChord AFB, Tacoma**
	FStop	**W:** 76
	Gas	**E:** Exxon **W:** Chevron, Shell◈
	Food	**W:** Black Angus Steakhouse, Carr's Rest, Church's Chicken, Denny's, KFC, Pizza Hut, Wendy's
	Lodg	**W:** Best Western, Colonial Motel, Fort Lewis Motel, Home Motel, La Quinta Inn, Madigan Motel
	Med	**W: + St Clare Hospital**
	Other	**E: MIL**/McChord AFB/**RV Park▲** **W: LP**/76, Auto Services, Goodyear, Laundromat, Mall, U-Haul
124		**Gravelly Lake Dr, Nyanza Rd SW (Access to Ex #125 Serv)**
	Gas	**W:** 76, ArcoAmPm
	Food	**W:** El Toro, Pizza Casa
	Lodg	**W:** Ft Clarke Motel, La Casa Motel
	AServ	**W:** Arco
	Med	**W: + to** American Lake Vets Hospital
123		**Thorn Lane, Tillicum, Fort Lewis (Acc to Exits #124 & #122)**
	Food	**W:** House of Teriyaki
	Lodg	**W:** Thornewood Castle Inn **(Reserv only)**
122		**Jackson Ave, Berkeley St SW, Blaine Ave, Madigan Hospital, Camp Murray**
	Gas	**W:** 7-11, Chevron
	Food	**W:** BBQ Inn, Coffee Strong, Dominos Pizza, Galloping Gertie's Rest, House of Teriyaki, KFC, McDonald's, Papa John's Pizza, Pizza Hut, Subway, Taco Bell, Wok Inn Express
	AServ	**W:** Chevron
	Other	**W:** AutoZone, Laundromat, Grocery, Camp Murray National Guard
120		**41st Division Dr, Fort Lewis**
	Other	**E:** Ft Lewis Military Museum **W: Travel Campground▲**
119		**Steilacoom-Dupont Rd, Clark Rd, Barksdale Ave, Fort Lewis, Dupont, to Steilacoom**
	Gas	**W:** 76
	Food	**W:** Happy Teriyaki, Jack in the Box, Subway, Starbucks
	Other	**W:** Museum
118		**Center Dr, DuPont**
	Food	**W:** Bruceskis Buffalo Wings, Dominos Pizza, McNamara's, Starbucks, Subway, Super Buffet, Viva Mexico
	Lodg	**W:** GuestHouse Inn, Liberty Inn
	Other	**W:** ATMs, Banks, Jiffy Lube, US Post Office
(117)		**Inspection Station (NB)**
116		**Mounts Rd, to Nisqually**
114		**Martin Way, Olympia, Nisqually**
	Gas	**E:** Chevron, Exxon◈, Shell◈
	Food	**E:** Nisqually Grill, Norma's Burgers
	AServ	**E:** Chevron
	Other	**E: LP**/Shell, Nisqually Auto & Towing, **Lost Lake RV Resort▲**, **Nisqually Plaza RV Park▲**
111		**Marvin Rd NE, WA 510E, Olympia, to Yelm, to Mt Rainer**
	FStop	**E:** Hawks Prairie Grocery & Deli **W:** Pacific Pride
	Gas	**E:** 76, Chevron, Shell◈, Tesoro, Safeway, Costco
	Food	**E:** Burger King, DQ, Fuji Japanese Steakhouse, Godfather's Pizza, Hawk's Prairie, Jack in the Box, McDonald's, Papa Murphy's Take 'n Bake Pizza, Panda Express, Panera Bread, Ram Bighorn Brewery, Ruby Tuesday, Starbucks, Subway, Sushi Go Round, Taco Time **W:** Country Junction, Mayan Mexican
	Lodg	**E:** King Oscar Motel, Hawks Prairie Inn
	Other	**E:** ATMs, Banks, Best Buy, Big Lots, Big 5 Sporting Goods, Car Wash, Costco, Dollar Tree, Home Depot, Les Schwab Tire, Office Max, Radio Shack, RiteAid, Safeway, Sportsmans Warehouse, UPS Store, Walgreen's, **Walmart sc**, Vet♥, Northwest Harley Davidson, **Martinway MH & RV Park ▲**, **RV** Hitches & Welding, **Hawks Prairie Casino** **W:** Cabela's, Ferrellgas/**LP**, Marvin Rd Mini Golf
109		**Martin Way, Olympia, Lacey**
	Gas	**W:** 76, ArcoAmPm, Exxon◈, Shell◈, Safeway
	Food	**E:** Chinese Buffet, Pizza Hut/Taco Bell
	Food	**W:** Burger King, Casa Mia, Denny's, IHOP, Jack in the Box, Panda Express, Red Lobster, Shari's, Starbucks, Subway
	Lodg	**E:** Candlewood Suites, Holiday Inn Express **W:** Comfort Inn, La Quinta Inn♥, Quality Inn, Super 8
	Med	**W: + Hospital**
	Other	**E:** Grocery, Discount Tire, ShopKO, St Martins Univ **W:** ATMs, Banks, Firestone, Lowe's, NAPA, Safeway

◈ = Regular Gas Stations with Diesel ▲ = RV Friendly Locations ♥ = Pet Friendly Locations
Red print shows large vehicle parking / access on site or nearby Brown Print = Campgrounds / RV PARKS

EXIT	WASHINGTON

108 **Sleater-Kinney Rd, S College St, Lacey, Olympia (Acc to Ex #109)**
- **Gas** E: Shell◈ / W: ArcoAmPm
- **Food** E: Applebee's, Arby's, Carl's Jr, Jack in the Box, McDonald's, Passage to India, Skippers Seafood 'n Chowder, Starbucks, Subway, Taco Bell, Taco Del Mar, Wendy's
- **Lodg** W: Quality Inn, Super 8
- **Med** E : + Pacific Walk-in Clinic / W: + Providence St Peter Hospital
- **Other** E: ATMs, Banks, Dollar Tree, Firestone, Jiffy Lube, Midas, Office Depot, PetSmart♥, Radio Shack, RiteAid, Safeway, Target, Tire Dogs, Verizon / W: Gary's Tire Factory, Kmart, Lowe's, Randy's Compunding Pharmacy, Safeway, Super Supplements, WA Wine Warehouse

107 **Pacific Ave, Olympia (Acc to #108)**
- **Gas** E: Shell◈
- **Food** E: DQ, Izzy's Pizza, Shari's, Sizzler, Skipper' Seafood 'n Chowder, Taco Time / W: IHOP
- **Med** W: + Hospital
- **Other** E: Albertson's, Animal Care Veterinary Clinic♥, FedEx Office, Home Depot, J-Vee's Health Foods & Cafe, NAPA, Rick's Auto Repair, Schucks Auto Supplies / W: Auto Dealer, Aztec Lanes, Interstate Battery, Olympia Food Co-op, U-Haul, **Coumbs RV Sales & Accessories/LP**

105 **14th Ave, Henderson Blvd, E Bay Dr, State Capitol, City Center, Port of Olympia**
- **Gas** W: Chevron, Shell◈
- **Food** W: Casa Miia, Jack in the Box, McDonald's, Starbucks
- **Lodg** W: Capitol Plaza Olympia Hotel, Carriage Inn Motel, Fertile Ground Guesthouse B&B, Quality Inn♥, Ramada Inn, ShortStay Lodgings, Swantown Inn B&B
- **Other** E: Grocery, Mall, **Sundance RV Center** / W: WA State Capitol, Attractions, Museums

105AB **Plum St, E Bay Dr (SB)**

104 **Deschutes Pkwy, W Olympia, US 101N, to Aberdeen**
- **FStop** W: (to US 101, 1st Ex R) Pacific Pride
- **Gas** W: 7-11, ArcoAmPm, Chevron, Shell◈
- **Food** W: Jack in the Box
- **Lodg** W: Extended Stay America, Red Lion Hotel
- **Other** W: to appr 4 mi: **Columbus Park at Black Lake▲**

103 **2nd Ave, Custer Way, Capitol Blvd, Olympia, Tumwater (NB)**
- **Other** E: Safeway, Tumwater Falls Park, Tumwater Valley Golf Course / W: to State Capitol, Museums

102 **Trosper Rd, Black Lake, Olympia**
- **Gas** E: Shell◈ / W: 76, Chevron, Albertson's, Costco
- **Food** E: Arby's, Burger King, Cattin's, Dominos Pizza, El Sarape 4, Happy Teriyaki, Jack in the Box, KFC, McDonald's, Pizza Hut, Starbucks, Subway, Taco Bell / W: Panda Express, Papa Murphy's Take 'n Bake Pizza, Quiznos, Starbucks
- **Lodg** E: Best Western♥, Motel 6♥, Tumwater Inn

Personal Notes

EXIT	WASHINGTON

- **Med** E: + Hospital
- **Other** E: ATMs, Banks, Dollar Store, Goodyear, Jiffy Lube, Laundromat, Les Schwab Tire, Martin's Southgate Drug, Southgate Ace Hardware, Schucks Auto Supply, Tumwater Lanes / W: ATMs, Banks, Albertson's, AutoZone, Costco, Fred Meyer, Grocery, Home Depot, Radio Shack, **Alderbrook Estates RV Park▲**

101 **Tumwater Blvd, Olympia Airport**
- **Gas** E: Chevron, Shell
- **Food** E: Quiznos
- **Lodg** E: Best Western, Comfort Inn, Guesthouse Int'l, Super 8
- **Other** E: Olympia Muni Airport & Museum✈, **Olympia Campground▲**

99 **93rd Ave SW, WA 121S, Olympia, Tumwater, to Tenino, Scott Lake**
- **TStop** E: **Pilot** Travel Center #151 (Scales) / W: Restover Truck Stop/Shell (Scales)
- **Gas** E: Texaco◈/Amer Her CG/Olympia CG / W: Exxon◈
- **Food** E: McDonald's/Subway/Pilot TC / W: Rest/Restover TS
- **Lodg** W: Motel/Restover TS
- **TServ** W: Restover TS
- **Other** E: Laundry/WiFi/Pilot TC, **American Heritage Campground▲**, **Olympia Campground▲**, US Post Office **Millersylvania State Park▲** / W: Laundry/**LP/RVDump**/Restover TS

95 **Maytown Rd SW, WA 121N, to Littlerock Rd, to Tenino**
- **Food** W: Farm Boy Drive In Rest

EXIT	WASHINGTON

- **Other** E: to appr 3 mi: **Deep Lake Resort Adult RV Park▲**

(93) **Maytown Rest Area (SB)** (RR, Phone, Picnic, Vend, WiFi, Info)

(90) **Scatter Creek Rest Area (NB)** (RR, Phone, Picnic, Vend, WiFi, Info)

88 **US 12W, Rochester, Aberdeen, Tenino, Old Hwy 99 SW (SB)**
- **FStop** W: Pacific Pride, Short Stop 76
- **Gas** W: ArcoAmPm, End of the Trail III◈, Shell◈
- **Food** W: Rest/PacPride, DQ, Grand Mound Espresso, McDonald's/Shell, Little Red Barr
- **Lodg** W: Great Wolf Lodge
- **Other** E: **I-5 RV's**, **Frank's RV Repair**, Trailer Town / W: True Value Hardware, **to appr 2.5 mi: Outback RV Park▲**, **to appr 12 mi:** Lucky Eagle Casino & Hotel/**RVParking**

88B **US 12W, Old Hwy 99SW, Rochester, Aberdeen, Tenino (NB)**

88A **Tenino Grand Mpund Rd SW (NB)**

82 **Harrison Ave, Centralia**
- **Gas** E: ArcoAmPm, Shell◈ / W: Chevron, Circle K, Texaco, Safeway
- **Food** E: Burger King, Burgerville USA, Casa Ramos, DQ, Godfather's Pizza, Pizza Hut, Panda Inn, Quiznos, Shari's, Wendy's / W: Arby's, Country Cousin, Denny's, Dominos Pizza, Jack in the Box, McDonald's, Quiznos, Starbucks, Taco Bell
- **Lodg** E: Ferryman's Inn, King Oscar Motel, Econo Lodge / W: Motel 6♥
- **Other** E: Dollar Store, Pharmacy, Jiffy Lube, VF Outlet, Auto & Diesel Repair / W: Centralia Factory Outlet Mall, Centralia Tire, Safeway, Schwab Tire, RiteAid, **Fort Borst Park**, **Mid-Way RV Park▲**, **Harrison RV Park▲**,

81 **WA 507N, Mellen St, Centralia**
- **Gas** E: Chevron, Shell
- **Food** E: PJ's Pizza, The Oasis Rest, Subway/Chevron
- **Lodg** E: Americas Best Value Inn, Peppermill Empress Inn, Peppertree West Motor Inn & **RV Park▲**, Travel Inn Express
- **Med** W: + Providence Centralia Hospital
- **Other** E: Greyhound

79 **Chamber Way, Chehalis**
- **Gas** E: Shell◈ / W: Airport Depot 76◈
- **Food** W: Burger King/76, Applebee's, Buckaroos Pizza, McDonald's, Starbucks, Subway, Taco del Mar, Wendy's
- **TServ** W: Cummins NW
- **Other** E: Auto Dealers, Goodyear, Staples, Tires, Museum, Vet♥ / W: Home Depot, Kmart, Walgreen's, **WalMart sc**, Chehalis Centralia Airport✈, Riverside Golf Course

77 **WA 6W, Main St (Acc to Ex #79)**
- **Gas** E: Cenex◈, Shell
- **Food** E: Dairy Bar / W: McDonald's, Sowerby's
- **Lodg** E: Holiday Inn Express
- **Other** E: Ace Hardware, Auto Services, Chehalis Bowling, Les Schwab Tire, NAPA, RiteAid, Safeway/Pharmacy, U-Haul, US Post Office, Museum,

◈= Regular Gas Stations with Diesel ▲ = RV Friendly Locations ♥= Pet Friendly Locations
Red print shows large vehicle parking / access on site or nearby Brown Print = Campgrounds / RV PARKS

EXIT		WASHINGTON
	Other	E: Police Dept, Laundromat
		W: Veterans Memorial Museum, WA State Hwy Patrol Post
76		**13th St, Chehalis**
	Gas	E: Chevron
	Food	E: Denny's, Jack in the Box, Kit Carson, Subway
	Lodg	E: Best Western, Chehalis Inn, Relax Inn
	Other	E: Bowling, Laundromat, Safeway, **Baydo's RV Sales & Service**
		W: **Stan Hedwell Park▲**
72		**Rush Road, Chehalis, Napavine**
	FStop	W: Rush Road Travel Center/Chevron, Pacific Pride
	TStop	E: Now Truck Stop/Shell (Scales)
	Gas	W: Shell◈
	Food	E: FastFood/Now TS, McDonald's, Beck's Rib Eye, Burger King, Subway
		W: Hot Stuff Pizza/RR TC
	TServ	W: Cummins Northwest
	Other	E: LP/Shell, **Country Canopy & RV Center, Carson Trailer Sales**
		W: **Poulsbo RV Clearance Center, J&D RV Sales, Uhlmann RV**
71		**Forest-Napavine Rd, WA 508E, Napavine, Onalaska**
	FStop	E: Eagle Truck Plaza/76 (Scales)
	Food	E: FastFood/Eagle TP
	TServ	E: KC's Truck Parts
	Other	E: to appr 6 mi: **Chehalis Thousand Trails Campground▲**
68		**Avery Rd, US 12E, Chehalis, to Morton, Yakima**
	Gas	E: ArcoAmPm, Shell◈
		W: Shell◈
	Food	E: Spiffy's Rest
		W: Mustard Seed Rest
	Lodg	E: to Country Cabins Motel & **RV Park▲**
	Other	E: Jackson Hwy Vet Clinic♥, to appr 5mi: **Lewis & Clark State Park▲**, **Mayfield RV Park▲**, to appr 20 mi: **Harmony Lakeside RV Park▲**
63		**WA 505, Winlock, Toledo**
	Gas	W: Shell◈
	Other	E: LP/Shell, to **Frost Road RV Park▲** Mt St Helens Nat'l Volcanic Monument
60		**WA 506, Toledo Vader Rd, Toledo, Vader**
59		**WA 506W, to Vader, Ryderwood**
	Gas	E: Shell◈
		W: Chevron◈
	Food	E: Mrs Beesley's Burgers
		W: Subway/Chevron, Country House Rest, Riverside Rest, Rick's Place
	Other	W: **River Oaks RV Park & CG▲**
57		**Jackson Hwy, Barnes Dr, Toledo**
	TStop	W: Gee Cee's Truck Stop (Scales)
	Food	W: Rest/FastFood/Gee Cee's TS
	TServ	W: Gee Cee's TS/Tires, Western Star Trucks, Jarvis Truck Sales
	Other	W: Laundry/Gee Cee's TS, **Barnes State Park**
(54)		**Toutle River Rest Area (Both dir) (RR, Phone, Pic, Pet, WiFi, Info)**
52		**Barnes Dr, Old Pacific Hwy, Castle Rock**
	Other	E: **Paradise Resort & RV Park▲**
		W: **Toutle River RV Park Resort▲**

EXIT		WASHINGTON
49		**WA 411S, WA 504E, Castle Rock**
	FStop	E: Pac Pride/Gateway Fuel & Food/Shell
	Gas	E: 76, Chevron, Texaco◈
	Food	E: Rest/Gateway F&F, Burger King, C&L Burger Bar, El Compadre Rest, Peper's 49er Diner, Papa Pete's Pizza, Rose Tree Rest, Subway
	Lodg	E: Mt St Helens Motel, Motel 7 West, Timberland Motor Inn♥
	Other	E: LP/Texaco, to Mt St Helens Visitor Center, Mt St Helens Nat'l Volcanic Monument, to appr 2mi: **Mt St Helens RV Park▲**, to appr 5mi: **Silver Cove RV Resort▲**
48		**Huntington Ave, Castle Rock**
	Other	W: **RVDump/City Park**
46		**Headquarters Rd, Pleasant Hill Rd, Pacific Ave N**
	Other	E: **Cedars RV Park▲**
(44)		**Inspection Station (SB)**
42		**Sparks Dr, Kelso**
	Gas	W: Chevron
	Other	W: to **Riverside Co Park**
40		**N Kelso Ave, WA 431, to WA 4 (Access to Ex #39 Serv)**
	FStop	W: Pacific Pride
	Gas	W: 76, Texaco
	Lodg	W: Best Western, Budget Inn, Best Value Inn, Econo Lodge
	Med	W: + Hospital
39		**WA 4, Allen St, Kelso, Longview**
	Gas	E: ArcoAmPm, Shell
		W: Chevron◈
	Food	E: Denny's, McDonald's, Shari's, Subway, Taco Time
		W: Azteca Mexican Rest, Burger King, DQ, Izzy's Pizza Bar, Red Lobster, Starbucks, Taco Bell
	Lodg	E: Motel 6♥, Red Lion Hotel, Super 8♥
		W: Best Western, Comfort Inn, Guesthouse Inn, to Town House Motel
	Med	W: + Hospital
	Other	E: Grocery, RiteAid, DMV, Greyhound Terminal, Tourist Info, **Brookhollow RV Park▲**
		W: Auto Services, Jiffy Lube, Safeway, Tires, Three Rivers Mall, Target/Pharmacy, Riverside Animal Hospital♥, Amtrak, Museum, Police Dept, River Casino, to Lower Columbia College, Long Beach, Ocean Beaches
36B		**WA 432, Tennant Way (SB)**
36A		**WA 432, Old Hwy 99S (SB)**
36		**Old Hwy 99S, WA 432W, Tennant Way, to WA 4, Kelso, Longview (NB)**
	FStop	E: Industrial Way Chevron
		W: Pacific Pride
	Gas	W: ArcoAmPm, Chevron, Texaco◈
	Food	W: Burger King, Pancake House
	Lodg	W: Hudson Manor Inn♥, Quality Inn♥, Rodeway Inn, Travelodge♥
	Med	W: + St John Medical Center
	TServ	W: Peterbilt
	Other	E: **U-Neek RV Center**
		W: Auto Dealers, CarWash/Texaco, Home Depot, Longview Tire Sales, **Longview RV Center, McCord's Truck & RV Center**, National Auto Parts, Superior Tire, **Valley RV Parts & Services**, Vet♥,

EXIT		WASHINGTON
	Other	E: Kelso Longview Airport✈, WA State Hwy Patrol Post
32		**Kalama River Rd, Kelso**
	Food	E: Fireside Cafe/**CG**
	Other	E: **Camp Kalama Campground▲**
30		**Oak St (SB), Elm St (NB), Kalama**
	Gas	E: Chevron
		W: Spirit
	Food	E: Antique Deli & Pastry Shoppe, Burger Bar, Burger King, Columbia Inn Rest, Lucky Dragon, Subway,
	Lodg	E: Kalama River Inn, Montgomery House B&B
	Other	E: Kalama Auto Supply & Repair, Pharmacy
		W: Port of Kalama
27		**Robb Rd, Hwy 99, Old Pacific Hwy, Port of Kalama, Kalama**
	TStop	E: Pacific Pride/ Rebel Truck Stop/Shell
	Food	E: Rest/Rebel Truck Stop
	Other	E: LP/Rebel TS
		W: to Port of Kalama
22		**Dike Access Rd, Woodland**
	FStop	W: CFN/Wilson Oil
	Other	E: **Woodland Shores RV Park▲**
		W: to appr 3mi: **Columbia Riverfront RV Park▲**
21		**WA 503E, Scott Ave, Lewis River Rd, Woodland, Cougar**
	FStop	E: Pacific Pride
	Gas	E: ArcoAmPm, Chevron, Shell◈
		W: Shell, Astro, Safeway
	Food	E: Burgerville USA, Casa Maria's, DQ, Oak Tree, Quiznos, Rosie's, South China, Subway
		W: McDonald's, Quiznos, Starbucks, Subway, Whimpy's
	Lodg	E: Best Western/Woodland Inn, Lewis River Inn, Woodland Cedars Inn Express
		W: Hansen's Motel, Lakeside Motel, Scandia Motel
	TServ	W: A-1 Truck Repair
	Other	E: LP/Shell, Ace Hardware, Car Quest, Laundromat, Hi-School Pharmacy, Radio Shack, U-Haul, Woodland State Airport✈, to **Woodland Shores RV Park▲**, **Lewis River RV Park▲**
		W: ATMs, Banks, NAPA, Safeway, Timberland Pet Clinic♥, Woodland Veterinary Hospital♥, Police Dept, **Horseshoe Lake Park**
16		**NW 319th St, NW La Center Rd, Ridgefield, to La Center**
	FStop	E: Paradise Truck Stop/Shell
	Other	E: LP/Paradise TS, **Paradise Point State Park▲**
(15)		**Inspection Station / Port of Entry (NB)**
14		**WA 501W, Pioneer St, NW 269th Ridgefield, to CityW Center**
	Gas	E: ArcoAmPm, Circle K◈
		W: Chevron◈
	Food	E: Country Café, Subway
	Other	E: **Tri-Mountain RV Park▲**, to appr 4mi: **Big Fir RV Park▲**, to **Battleground Lake State Park▲**
(12)		**Gee Creek Rest Area (SB) (RR, Phone, Picnic, Vend, Pet, WiFi, Info, RVDump)**

◈= Regular Gas Stations with Diesel ▲ = RV Friendly Locations ♥= Pet Friendly Locations

Red print shows large vehicle parking / access on site or nearby Brown Print = Campgrounds / RV PARKS

EXIT		WASHINGTON
(11)		**Gee Creek Rest Area (NB)** (RR, Phone, Picnic, Vend, Pet, WiFi, Info, RVDump)
9		**WA 502E, NE 179th St, Ridgefield, to Battle Ground**
	Gas	W: Chevron◈
	Food	E: Jollie's Restaurant
	Other	E: Poulsbo RV
		W: U-Haul, Clark Co Fairgounds, Clark Co Amphitheater,
7		**NE Tenney Rd, NE 134th St, to Jct I-205S, to I-84, WA-14, Portland Airport, Vancouver**
	Gas	E: 7-11, 76, ArcoAmPm, Safeway, Trail Mart◈
		W: Mobil◈
	Food	E: Applebee's, Burger King, Burgerville USA, Billygan's Roadhouse, Jack in the Box, McDonald's, Panda Express, Round Table Pizza, Starbucks, Subway, Taco Bell
	Food	W: Bamboo Hut, El Tapatio, Garlic Jim's, Plane Thai, Quiznos, Starbucks
	Lodg	E: Comfort Inn♥, Days Inn, Holiday Inn Express, Shilo Inn
		W: La Quinta Inn, Red Lion Hotel, University Inn
	Med	E: + Salmon Creek Hospital
		W: + Urgent Care
	Other	E: ATMs, Auto Services, Albertson's/Pharmacy, Banks, Long Drug, Safeway, Salmon Creek Veterinary Clinic♥, 99 RV Park▲
		W: ATMs, AT&T, Budget Truck Rental, Mtn View Animal Hospital♥,
5		**NE 99th St, Vancouver**
	Gas	E: 7-11, 76, ArcoAmPm, Foodmart, Miirastar, Murphy
		W: ArcoAmPm, Chevron
	Food	E: Burgerville, Carl's Jr, Del Taco, Domino's Pizza, Fat Dave's, Quiznos
		W: Applebee's, McDonald's, Papa John's Pizza, Subway
	Other	E: Auto Center, Advanced RV, Custom RV Interiors, Enterprise RAC, Four Seasons Auto Repair & Tire Center, Grocery, Harley Davidson, Regal Cinemas Walgreen's, Walmart, Winco Foods,
		W: Albertson's, Dollar Tree, Office Depot, PetCo♥, Target
4		**78th St, Vancouver, Hazel Dell**
	Gas	E: 7-11, Exxon
		W: Shell◈
	Food	E: Baja Fresh, Burger King, Canton Chinese Rest, Del Taco, Dragon King, Izzy's Pizza, KFC, McDonald's, Pizza Hut, Skipper's Seafood, Starbucks, Subway, Sushi Umi, Taco Bell
		W: Five Guys Burgers & Fries, Jack in the Box, Panda Express, Round Table Pizza, Wendy's
	Lodg	E: Best Inn, Quality Inn
		W: Best Western
	Other	E: Auto Dealers, Auto Services, Banks, Big 5 Sporting Goods, Car Quest, Evergreen Animal Hospital♥, Firestone, Fred Meyer, Grocery, Hazel Dell CarWash, Jiffy Lube, Radio Shack, Schuck's Auto Supply, U-Haul, Vanover RV Park▲ , Good Sam RV Park▲

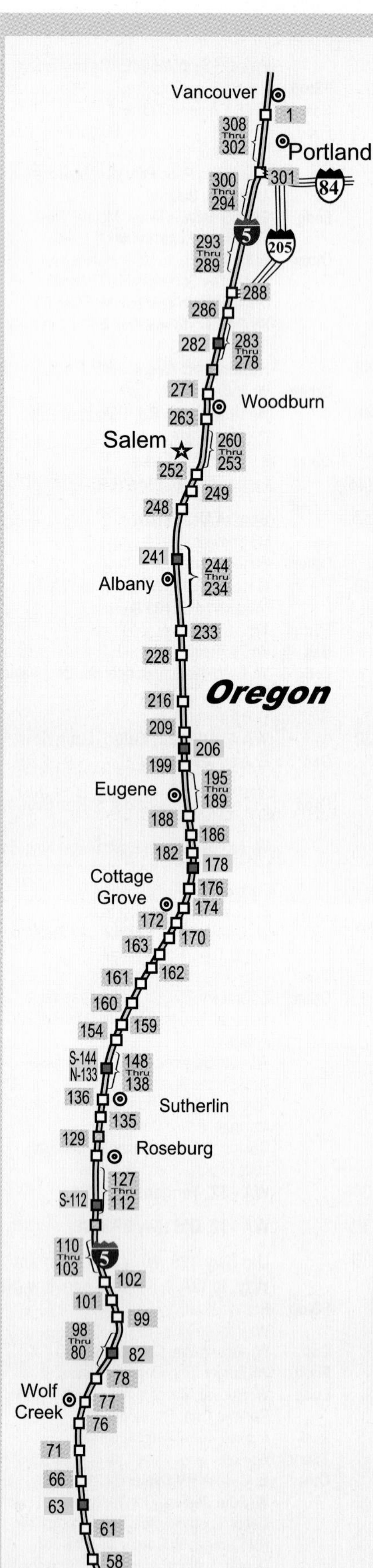

EXIT		WA / OR
	Other	W: ATMs, Banks, Avis RAC, Office Depot, PetSmart♥, RiteAid, Safeway, Target, LP/Shell
3		**NE Hwy 99, Main St, Vancouver (Access to Ex #4 Serv-both dir)**
	Gas	W: ArcoAmPm
	Food	E: Don Pedro, El Tapapito, Muchos Gracias Mexican Rest, Pizza Hut, Skippers Seafood 'n Chowder, Subway
	Med	E: + Hospital
	Other	E: Jiffy Lub, Les Schwab Tires, Hazeldell Animal Hospital♥, Hazeldell Lanes, Hazeldell Tire Factory, Auto Services, NW RV Specialities
		W: U-Haul
2		**39th St, WA 500E, Vancouver**
	FStop	W: Pacific Pride
	Other	E: Leverich Park, Arnold Park
		W: Auto Services, Safeway
1D		**Fourth Plain Blvd, Mill Plain Blvd, McLoughlin Blvd, Vancouver, Port of Vancouver**
	Food	W: DQ, Starbucks, Subway
	Lodg	W: Comfort Inn
	Other	W: Penske Truck Rental, Tire Place, Walgreen's
1C		**WA 501,t Mill Plain Blvd, 15th St, 14th St, Downtown Vancouver**
	Gas	W: Chevron
	Food	W: Burgerville USA, Black Angus Steak House, Denny's,
	Lodg	W: Comfort Inn, Shilo Inn
	Other	E: Pearson Airpark✈
		W: Auto Dealers, FedEx Office, Grocery, Auto Services, Museum WA State Hwy Patrol Post
1B		**6th St, C St, Downtown Vancouver**
	Food	E: Joe's Crab Shack
		W: Jerusalem Rest & Cafe, Starbucks, Woody's Tacos
	Lodg	W: Econo Lodge, Hilton
	Other	W: Regal Cinema 12, Vancouver Farmers Market, Ester Short Park
1A		**WA 14E, to Camas**
	Med	E: + Hospital

PACIFIC TIME ZONE

⬆ WASHINGTON
⬇ OREGON

PACIFIC TIME ZONE

NOTE: MM 308.5: Washington State Line

308		**Hayden Island, Jantzen Beach**
	Gas	E: Chevron
		W: 76◈, ArcoAmPm
	Food	E: Burger King, Hayden Island Steak house/DblTree, Starbucks, Taco Bell
		W: BJ's, Denny's, Original Joe's Café, Hooters, Homestead Rest, McDonald's, Newport Bay Seafood, Subway
	Lodg	E: Doubletree Hotel, Oxford Suites, Red Lion Hotel
		W: Holiday Inn Express
	Other	E: Carwash, Safeway/Pharmacy
		W: B&N, CompUSA, Firestone, Home Depot, Kmart, Office Depot, Staples, Target, Jantzen Beach Mall, Jantzen Beach RV Park▲

◈= Regular Gas Stations with Diesel ▲ = RV Friendly Locations ♥= Pet Friendly Locations
Red print shows large vehicle parking / access on site or nearby Brown Print = Campgrounds / RV PARKS

EXIT	OREGON
307	**OR 99E S, Martin Luther King Jr Blvd, Marine Dr, N Vancouver Wy**
TStop	E: Jubitz Travel Center/PacPr/AmBest (Scales), TEC Equipment
Food	E: Rest/FastFood/Jubitz TC, Chompers Burgers, Elmer's Rest, Pizza Mia
Lodg	E: Portlander Inn/Jubitz TC, Courtyard, Fairfield Inn, Residence Inn
TServ	E: Jubitz TC/Tires, Selectrucks of Portland, Portland Freightliner, Diesel Repair, North Pacific Truck Repair
TWash	E: Blue Beacon TW/Jubitz TC
Other	E: Laundry/Cinema/Chiro/Jacuzzi/ BarbBtySh/RVDump/Jubitz TC, Laundry/TEC, **Columbia River RV Park▲**, Portland Meadows Racetrack, Portland Int'l Airport✈, Harley Davidson, GCR Tire Center, **Delta Park East** W: Portland Expo Center, **Delta Park West**
306B	**US 30 ByP, Lombard St, Interstate Ave (SB), Delta Park (NB)**
Gas	E: 76
Food	E: Burger King, Burrito House, Elmer's, Mar's Meadows Chinese, Shari's
Lodg	E: Best Western, Days Inn, Delta Inn
Other	E: Baxter Auto Parts, Grocery, Fisherman's Marine & Outdoor, Lowe's, PetCo♥, West Marine, Pet Clinic♥, Portland Meadows Golf Course, Portland Meadows Racetrack W: Portland Int'l Raceway
306A	**Columbia Blvd (NB)**
FStop	E: E to MLK Jr Blvd, Left: Pacific Pride
Gas	W: 7-11, 76, Shell
Food	E: Chopsticks III, Jack in the Box W: Wendy's
Other	E: Ryder Truck,
306	**N Denver Ave, Columbiana Blvd (SB)**
305B	**US 30 ByP, Lombard St W (NB)**
Food	E: Little Caesar's Pizza, Pizza Hut, Taco Bell W: Starbucks, Subway, Wendy's
Lodg	E: Econo Lodge
Other	E: Lombard Animal Hospital♥, W: ATMs, Banks, Laundry, Radio Shack, RiteAid, Walgreen's, North Portland Veterinary Hospital♥,
305A	**US 30 ByP, Lombard St E (NB)**
Food	E: Pizza Hut, Taco Express
Other	E: Auto Services, Laundromat,
304	**Portland Blvd, Univ of Portland**
Gas	W: ArcoAmPm
Food	W: Japanese Rest, Nite Hawk Café, Thai Ginger Rest
Lodg	W: Viking Motel
Other	E: **Peninsula City Park**
303	**Alberta St, Going St, Portland**
FStop	W: Pacific Pride
Gas	W: 76
Food	E: Big City Burritos, Golden Chopsticks, Cascade Café House, Vinny's Pizza W: Atomic Pizza, Fish & Chip Shop, Subway, Taco Bell, Taco Time,
Lodg	W: Budget Motel, Economy Inn, Monticello Motel, Palms Motor Hotel, Super Value Inn, Westerner Motel
TServ	W: Cummins NW, Peterbilt/GMC
Med	E: + Legacy Emanuel Hospital
Other	W: Auto Services, Peninsular Dog & Cat Clinic♥, CarQuest, Harbor Freight

EXIT	OREGON
302C	**Greeley Ave (NB)**
(302B)	**Jct I-405, US 30W, Beaverton, St. Helens**
FStop	W: to Exit #3: Pacific Pride
302A	**Coliseum, Broadway, Weidler St**
Gas	E: Circle K◈, Shell◈
Food	E: Burgerville, Chipolte Mexican Grill, McDonald's, Red Robin, Starbucks, Wendy's
Lodg	E: Crowne Plaza, Courtyard, Holiday Inn, La Quinta Inn, Red Lion Inn, Shilo Inn W: Econo Lodge, Ramada Inn
Med	E: + Emmanuel Hospital
Other	E: AT&T, FedEx Office, Radio Shack, Safeway, US Post Office W: Coliseum, Rose Garden Arena, Portland Farmers Market
(301)	**Jct I-84E (SB)**
(300B)	**Jct I-84E, US 30E, Portland Airport**
300	**Water Ave, Morrison St (NB), OR 99ES, US 26E, ML King Jr Blvd, Morrison St, Downtown (SB)**
(299B)	**Jct I-405W, Portland**
299A	**OR 43S, Macadam Ave (SB), US 26E, Ross Island Bridge, Powell Blvd (NB)**
298	**Corbett Ave (NB)**
FStop	E: (approx 10 blks) Pacific Pride
297	**Terwilliger Blvd (NB), to OR 10, Bertha Blvd, Terwilliger Blvd (SB)**
Food	W: Burger King, KFC, Starbucks
Med	W: + VA Hospital
296B	**Multnomah Blvd (SB)**
296A	**OR 99W S, Barbur Blvd (SB)**
Gas	W: 7-11, 76◈, Chevron, Shell
Food	W: Indian Cuisine, Old Barn, Original Pancake House, Subway, Wendy's
Lodg	W: Aladdin Motor Inn, Capitol Hill Motel, King's Row Motel, Portland Rose Motel
Other	W: AT&T, Jiffy Lube, Les Schwab Tire, Safeway
295	**Capitol Hwy (SB), Taylors Ferry Rd (NB)**
FStop	E: Pacific Pride (DAD)
Gas	E: Shell◈
Food	E: Dunkin Donuts, McDonald's, Round Table Pizza, Starbucks
Lodg	E: Hospitality Motel, Ranch Inn Motel
294	**OR 99W, Barbur Blvd (NB) OR 99W, Tigard, Newburg (SB)**
FStop	E: Pacific Pride (DAD)
Gas	W: BP, Texaco
Food	W: Arby's, Burger King, Buster's Texas BBQ, Carrow's, KFC, Newport Bay, Subway, Starbucks, Taco Bell
Lodg	E: Comfort Suites W: Days Inn, Howard Johnson, Quality Inn, Value Inn
Other	E: Portland Comm College W: Baxter Auto Parts, Costco, PetCo♥, Laundromat, Les Schwab Tire, PetSmart♥, U-Haul
293	**Dartmouth St, Haines St (SB) Haines St (NB)**
Other	W: Costco, Lowe's, PetSmart♥, Tigard Bowl, Regal Cinema 11, Vet♥,

EXIT	OREGON
292B	**Kruse Way, Lake Oswego (NB)**
Gas	E: Shell
Food	E: Rest/Residence Inn, Rest/Crowne Pl, Applebee's, Chili's, Classic Café, Olive Garden, Taco Bell, Starbucks
Lodg	E: Crowne Plaza, Fairfield Inn, Hilton Garden Inn, Phoenix Inn, Residence Inn
Other	E: Grocery
292A	**Jct OR 217W, Tigard, Beaverton**
291	**Carman Dr, Lake Oswego**
Gas	W: Chevron, Shell
Food	W: Burgerville USA, Starbucks, Sweet Tomatoes, Subway
Lodg	W: Courtyard, Holiday Inn Express, Travelodge
Other	E: Trader Joe's, W: Home Depot, Office Depot
290	**Lower Boones Ferry Rd, Lake Oswego (NB), Durham (SB)**
Gas	E: 76, Chevron W: 76, Arco
Food	E: Arby's, Baha Fresh Mex Grill, Baskin Robbins, Burger King, Carl's Jr, Fuddrucker's, Skipper's Seafood 'N Chowder, Starbucks, Taco Bell W: CA Pizza Kitchen, Claim Jumper Rest, PF Chang's, Romano's Macaroni Grill, Royal Panda, Village Inn
Lodg	E: Motel 6♥, Red Roof Inn♥ W: Best Western, Bridgeport Value Inn, Grand Hotel, Quality Inn
Other	E: Auto Services, Carwash, Safeway, UPS Store, Walgreen's W: Apple Store, Borders, CarQuest, Regal Cinema 18, Verizon, Whole Foods Market, Wild Oats Market, Bridgeport Village Mall, To RVDump/Durham Wastewater Treatment Plant **(16580 SW 85th Ave)**
289	**Nyberg St, Tualatin-Sherwood Rd**
Gas	E: 76, Jackson's FS/Shell W: Arco, Chevron
Food	E: Chipolte Mexican Grill, Famous Dave's, McDonald's, Panera Bread, Starbucks, Subway, The Sweetbrier Inn W: Jack in the Box, McDonald's, Outback Steakhouse, Quiznos, Subway, Taco Bell, Wendy's
Lodg	E: The Sweetbrier Inn W: Century Hotel, Comfort Inn
Med	E: + Hospital
Other	E: Best Buy, Carwash/Shell, Meridian Park Veterinary Hospital♥, **RV Park of Portland▲** W: ATMs, Banks, FedEx Office, Grocery, Emergency Vet Clinic♥, Kmart, Laundromat, Radio Shack, Safeway, Staples, Auto Services
(288)	**Jct I-205, Oregon City**
286	**Elligsen Rd, Wilsonville, Stafford**
Gas	E: 76◈, Costco W: Chevron, Exxon
Food	E: Burger King, Moe's SW Grill, Panda Express, Starbucks, Subway W: Rest/Hol Inn
Lodg	E: La Quinta Inn♥, Super 8 W: Holiday Inn
Other	E: Costco, PetSmart♥, Office Depot, Target, **Pheasant Ridge RV Resort▲**, W: **Camping World**

◈ = Regular Gas Stations with Diesel ▲ = RV Friendly Locations ♥ = Pet Friendly Locations
Red print shows large vehicle parking / access on site or nearby Brown Print = Campgrounds / RV PARKS

EXIT — OREGON

283 Wilsonville Rd, Wilsonville
- Gas: E: 76◊, W: Chevron
- Food: E: Applebee's, Arby's, Bullwinkle's, DQ, Denny's, Izzy's Pizza, McDonald's, Shari's, Starbucks, Subway, Taco Bell, Wendy's. W: Burger King, Chili's, Hunan Kitchen, Starbucks
- Lodg: E: Best Western, Comfort Inn, Snooz Inn. W: Phoenix Inn
- Med: E: + Wilsonville Medical Clinic
- Other: E: NAPA, RiteAid, Schwab Tire, US Post Office, Animal Care Clinic♥, W: Albertson's, Walgreen's, Penske Truck Rental, **Camping World**

282B Miley Rd (SB)

282A Canby, Hubbard (SB)

282 Miley Rd (NB)

(281.6) Baldock Rest Area (Both dir) (RR, Phone, Pic, Vend, Pet, Info)

278 Ehlen Rd, Aurora, Donald
- FStop: E: Pac Pride/Fuel 'n' Mart
- TStop: W: Travel Center of America #56/Shell (Scales), Leathers Truck Stop/Shell
- Food: W: CountryPr/Popeyes/TA TC, Deli/Leathers, Salt & Pepper Rest
- TWash: W: Truck Wash
- TServ: W: TA TC/Tires, Speedco
- Other: E: FuelnMart/**RVPark ▲**, **Aurora Acres RV Resort ▲**, to Aurora State Airport✈. W: Laundry/WiFi/TA TC, LP/Leathers,

(275) Inspection Station (SB)

(274) Inspection Station (NB)

271 OR 214, Woodburn
- Gas: E: 76, ArcoAmPm, Chevron, Conoco◊. W: Shell◊
- Food: E: Burger King, DQ, Denny's, KFC, McDonald's, Shari's, Subway, Taco Bell. W: Arby's, Elmer's, Jack in the Box, Quiznos, Starbucks
- Lodg: E: Best Western, Fairway Inn & **RV Park▲**, Super 8. W: La Quinta Inn♥
- AServ: E: 76
- Other: E: ATMs, Banks, Pharmacy, **Walmart sc** Woodburn Pet Hospital♥, W: Auto Dealers, Enterprise RAC, Winco Foods, Woodburn Co Stores/ Famous Brands Outlet, **Portland-Woodburn RV Park▲**

263 Brooklake Rd, Salem, Brooks
- TStop: W: Pilot Travel Center #386 (Scales)
- Food: W: Subway/Taco Bell/Pilot TC, Chalet Rest
- TServ: W: Freightliner
- Other: W: Laundry/WiFi/LP/Pilot TC, Antique Powerland Museums

260B Lockhaven Dr, Keizer (SB)

260A OR 99E, Salem Pkwy, Salem (SB)

260 Lockhaven Dr, Keizer (NB)

Note: MM 259: 45th Parallel - Halfway between Equator & North Pole

258 Portland Rd (SB), OR 99E, Salem, Pacific Hwy E (NB)
- FStop: W: Pacific Pride
- Gas: E: Circle K/76. W: 76, Chevron, Shell◊
- Food: E: Guesthouse, Italian, McDonald's, The Original Pancake House. W: Jack in the Box
- Lodg: E: Best Western, Crossland Economy Studios, Rodeway Inn. W: Budget Lodge, Travelers Inn
- Med: W: + OR State Hospital
- Other: E: Auto Repair, Flea Market, Grocery, Food 4 Less, Salem Harley Davidson, PetSmart♥, Radio Shack, **Walmart sc**, **Hee Hee Illahee RV Resort▲**, **Salem RV Park▲**, **Highway RV Center**. W: OR State Hwy Patrol Post

256 OR 213, Market St, State Capitol
- FStop: W: Pacific Pride
- Gas: E: Shell. W: ArcoAmPm, Chevron, Shell◊
- Food: E: Carl's Jr, Denny's, Elmer's, Italian, Mexican, Jack in the Box, Olive Garden, Outback Steakhouse, Skipper's Seafood, Sizzler, Starbucks, Subway, Taco Bell. W: Almost Home, DQ, McDonald's, Newport Bay Seafood, Roger's 50's Diner, Tony Roma's, Village Inn
- Lodg: E: Best Western, Crossland Economy Inn, Tiki Lodge. W: Comfort Inn, Holiday Lodge, Motel 6♥, Quality Inn, Phoenix Inn, Red Lion Hotel, Shilo Inn, Super 8
- TServ: W: Brattaiin International
- Med: W: + to OR State Hospital
- Other: E: Albertson's, America's Tire, Best Buy, Big Lots, Borders, Car Wash, Fred Meyer, Goodyear, Les Schwab Tires, NAPA, Target, UPS Store, Verizon, Walgreen's,
- Other: W: Auto Dealers, Grocery, OR State Fairgrounds

253 OR 22, OR 99E, Salem, Stayton
- FStop: W: Pacific Pride
- Gas: E: Chevron, Shell◊. W: Shell, Costco
- Food: E: Arby's, Burger King, Carl's Jr, McDonald's, Red Robin, Shari's, Subway. W: DQ, Denny's, Jack in the Box, Panda Express, Teriyaki Diner
- Lodg: W: Best Western, Comfort Suites, Motel 6♥, Holiday Inn Express♥, Howard Johnson, La Quinta Inn, Residence Inn
- AServ: E: Chevron
- Med: W: + Salem Hospital
- Other: E: Auto Services, AutoZone, Dollar Tree, Grocery, Home Depot, Office Depot, RiteAid, Regal Stadium 11 Cinema, ShopKO, Sportmans Warehouse, U-Haul, Meadowlawn Golf Course. W: AAA, Auto Dealers, Costco, Kmart, Lowe's, Les Schwab Tires, **Walmart sc**, **Roberson RV Center**, McNaray Field Airport✈, Salem Muni Airport✈, OR State Hwy Patrol Post, US Post Office

252 Kuebler Blvd, Salem
- FStop: W: (3.5 mi Rt on Comm St) Pacific Pride
- Gas: W: 76, ArcoAmPm
- Food: W: Burger King, Jack in the Box, McDonald's, Shari's
- Lodg: W: Phoenix Inn
- Med: W: + Salem Hospital
- Other: E: U-Haul. W: **Roberson RV Center**

249 Commercial St, Salem (NB)
- FStop: W: (3.5 mi) Pacific Pride
- Other: W: to appr 12 mi: **Premier RV Resort of Salem▲**

248 Sunnyside
- FStop: W: Pacific Pride
- Other: E: **Forest Glen Resort▲**, Enchanted Forest Theme Park, Thrillville Fun Park

244 Jefferson Hwy

243 Ankeny Hill Rd

242 Talbot Rd

(240.9) Santiam River Rest Area (Both dir) (RR, Phone, Pic, Vend, Pet, Info-NB)

240 Hoefer Dr

239 Dever-Conner Rd

238 OR 99E, Jefferson (NB)
- Other: E: McKay Truck & **RV Center/RVDump**

237 Viewcrest, Century Dr, Albany (SB)

235 Millersburg (SB), Viewcrest (NB)
- Other: E: AMC Harley Davidson

234B OR 99E S, Albany (SB)

234A Knox Butte Rd (SB)

234 OR 99E, Knox Butte Dr, Albany (NB)
- Gas: W: 76, ArcoAmPm, Shell◊, Costco
- Food: W: Rest/BW, Arby's, Burger King, DQ, China Buffet, McDonald's, Pizza Hut, Skippers Seafood, Subway, Taco Bell
- Lodg: E: Comfort Suites, Holiday Inn Express. W: Best Western, Budget Inn, Days Inn, La Quinta Inn, Motel 6♥, Super 8
- TServ: W: Lee's Diesel & Mobile Repair
- Med: W: + Hospital
- Other: E: **Knox Butte RV Park/RVDump▲**, Albany Muni Airport✈, Linn Co Expo Fairgrounds. W: Auto Dealers, Auto Services, Big Lots, Costco, Kmart, Tires

233 US 20, Santiam Hwy, Albany, Bend
- FStop: E: (4175 Santiam Hwy SE) Carson Chevron Food Mart
- TStop: E: Jack's Truck Stop/76 (Scales)
- Gas: W: ArcoAmPm, Shell, Leathers
- Food: E: FastFood/Jacks TS, FastFood/Carson, Burgundy's, Chinese, Denny's. W: AppleTree, Burgerville USA, Carl's Jr, Elmer's, McDonald's, Mexican, Original Breakfast, Skipper's Seafood & Chowder, Starbucks
- Lodg: E: Best Inn Suites, Econo Lodge♥, Motel Orleans, Relax Inn, Phoenix Inn Suites♥, Quality Inn. W: Valu Inn
- Med: W: + Hospital
- Other: E: LP/Carson's, OR State Hwy Patrol Post, Home Depot, Albany Muni Airport✈, **Lassen RV Center**, **Blue Ox RV Park▲**. W: Albertson's, Goodyear, Les Schwab Tires, NAPA, RiteAid, Staples, Target, Walgreen's, Auto Dealers, To Heritage Mall, UPS Store

228 OR 34, Lebanon, Corvallis
- FStop: E: I-5 76 Food Mart. W: CFN/Younger Oil Co/Chevron

◊= Regular Gas Stations with Diesel ▲ = RV Friendly Locations ♥= Pet Friendly Locations

Red print shows large vehicle parking / access on site or nearby Brown Print = Campgrounds / RV PARKS

EXIT		OREGON
	Gas	W: ArcoAmPm, Shell
	Food	E: Pine Cone Café
	TServ	W: 24hr Towing & Auto/Truck Repair
	Other	E: to Mallard Creek Golf Course & RV Park▲ , W: Albany/Corvallis KOA▲ , Benton Oaks RV & Camp▲ , to Oregon St Univ
216		**OR 228, Brownsville, Halsey**
	TStop	E: Pioneer Villa Truck Plaza/76
	Gas	W: Halsey Shell◈
	Food	E: Rest/FastFood/Pioneer TP, Rest/BW W: Subway/Taco Bell/Shell
	Lodg	E: Best Western/Pioneer Villa TP
	TServ	E: Pioneer Villa TP/Tires
	TWash	E: Pioneer Villa TP
	Other	E: Laundry/BarberSh/WiFi/Pioneer Villa TP
209		**Harrisburg, Junction City**
	Food	W: The Hungry Farmer Cafe
	TServ	W: Diamond Hill Trailer Repair
	Other	W: Diamond Hill RV Park▲
(206)		**Oak Grove Rest Area (Both dir) (RR, Phone, Pic, Pet, Vend, Info -SB)**
199		**C E Pearl St, Coburg, Eugene**
	TStop	E: Fuel n Go/PacPride W: Travel Center of America #78/Truck n Travel/CFN/Shell
	Gas	W: Shell, Star Mart
	Food	W: CountryFare/FastFood/TA TC/TnT, The Hillside Grill, La Perla Pizzeria
	Lodg	W: Truck n Travel Motel/TA TC/TnT, Coburg Inn
	TServ	W: TA TC/TnT, Cummins NW, Farwest Truck Center, Pacific Detroit Diesel, Freightliner/GMC
	TWash	W: TA TC/TnT
	Other	E: Laundry/LP/FuelnGo, Premier RV Resort of Eugene▲ W: Laundry/WiFi/LP/RVDump/TA TC/TnT, La Mesa RV Center, Guaranty RV Center, Marathon Coach, Paradise RV, Eugene Kamping World RV Park ▲
195B		**Beltline Hwy W, Eugene (SB)**
195A		**Beltline Hwy E, N Springfield (SB)**
195AB		**Beltline Hwy E, N Springfield**
	Gas	E: 76/Circle K, ArcoAmPm, Chevron
	Food	E: Rest/Gateway Inn, Rest/Doubletree Hotel, Rest/Shilo Inn, Applebee's, Chuck E Cheese, Carl's Jr, Denny's, Elmer's, Hometown Buffet, IHOP, Jack in the Box KFC, McDonald's, Outback Steakhouse, Shari's, Sizzler, Starbucks, Taco Bell
	Lodg	E: Best Western, Comfort Suites, Clarion Inn, Crossland, Courtyard, Extended Stay, Holiday Inn Express, Motel 6♥, Quality Inn, Shilo Inn, Super 8
	TServ	E: Stalick International Trucks
	Med	E: + Sacred Heart Medical Hospital
	Other	E: Best Buy, Big 5 Sporting Goods, Office Max, Radio Shack, Ross, Sears, Staples, Target/Pharmacy, Walgreen's, Gateway Mall, Cinema, US Post Office, OR State Hwy Patrol Post W: Costco
(194B)		**Jct I-105W, Eugene**
	Lodg	W: Best Value Inn♥, Campus Inn, Red Lion Hotel
(194A)		**Jct I-105E, OR 126, Springfield**

EXIT		OREGON
192		**OR 99N, Franklin Blvd, Eugene, Univ of Oregon (NB)**
	Food	W: Burger King, McDonald's, Wendy's
	Lodg	W: Best Western, Days Inn, Quality Inn
	Med	W: + Hospital
	Other	W: Pharmacy
191		**Glenwood Blvd**
	Gas	W: 76◈, Shell◈
	Food	W: Denny's
	Lodg	W: Motel 6♥
	Other	E: CAT
190		**30th Ave (SB)**
189		**30th Ave (NB)**
	Gas	E: Shell◈ W: Exxon, SeQuential◈◈
	Other	E: Doyle's Harley Davidson, Doris Ranch Living History Farm W: Shamrock Village RV Park▲ , Eugene RV Center
188		**OR 58E, Oakridge, Klamath Falls, OR 99S, Goshen (SB)**
188B		**Franklin Blvd, Goshen (NB)**
188A		**OR 58E, Oakridge (NB)**
	FStop	W: Pacific Pride
	Food	W: Café/PacPr
	TServ	W: PacPr, Superior Tire Truck & Service
	Other	E: Deerwood RV Park▲ W: Big Boy's RV Center
186		**Dillard Rd, Goshen (NB)**
182		**Creswell**
	Gas	W: 76◈, ArcoAmPm, Shell
	Food	W: Creswell Café, Pizza, TJ's
	Lodg	W: Best Western, Creswell Inn
	Other	W: Pharmacy, Grocery, Sherwood Forest KOA▲ , Airport✈
(178)		**Gettings Creek Rest Area (Both dir) (RR, Phone, Picnic, Vend, Info-NB)**
176		**Saginaw**
174		**Cottage Grove, Dorena Lake**
	FStop	E: Market Express/Chevron (Scales), Pacific Pride
	Gas	E: Shell W: 76◈, Shell◈
	Food	E: FastFood/MktExpress, Rest/B W, Subway, Taco Bell W: Arby's, Burger King, Carl's Jr, KFC, McDonald's, Subway, Vintage Inn
	Lodg	E: Best Western, Village Green Resort♥ W: Comfort Inn, Holiday Inn Express, Relax Inn
	Med	E: + Hospital
	Other	E: Laundry/Mkt Expr, WalMart, Auto Dealers, Cottage Grove State Airport✈ W: Village Green RV Park▲ , Dollar Tree, Safeway
172		**6th St, Cottage Grove Lake (SB)**
170		**OR 99N, Cottage Grove (NB)**
	Other	E: Cottage Grove RV Park▲
163		**Curtin**
	Gas	W: 76
	Lodg	E: Stardust Motel
	Other	E: US Post Office, Lucky Duck RV Park▲ , Pass Creek RV Park▲
162		**OR 99S, to OR 38, Drain, Reedsport**
161		**Buck Creek Rd, Anlauf (NB)**

EXIT		OREGON
160		**Salt Springs Rd**
159		**Elk Creek, Cox Rd**
154		**Scotts Valley Rd, Yoncalla (SB), Elkhead Rd (NB)**
150		**Yoncalla, Red Hill (SB) OR 99, Yoncalla, Drain (NB)**
	Other	W: Trees of Oregon RV Park▲
148		**Rice Hill**
	TStop	E: Pilot Travel Center #233/CFN (Scales), Rice Hill Truck Plaza/Pacific Pr (Scales)
	Gas	E: Chevron
	Food	E: Rest/FastFood/Pilot TC, Rest/Ranch Motel, K-R Drive Inn
	Lodg	E: Best Western♥, Ranch Motel
	TServ	E: Bridgestone Tire & Auto, Pro Fleet Diesel Service, NW Diesel Service
	Other	E: Laundry/WiFi/Pilot TC, Rice Hill RV Park▲ , Economy Truck, Auto & RV Towing & Repair, CAT, Tires
146		**Rice Valley**
(142.8)		**Cabin Creek Rest Area (Both dir) (RR, Phone, Picnic, Vend)**
142		**Metz Hill Rd**
140		**OR 99S, Oakland (SB)**
138		**Oakland (NB)**
136		**OR 138W, Elkton-Sutherlin Hwy, Sutherlin, Elkton**
	Gas	E: 76◈ Chevron◈, W: Shell◈
	Food	E: Apple Peddler, Bronx Bagel, Burger King, Dominos Pizza, Dutch Bros Coffee,
	Food	E: McDonald's, Papa Murphy's Take n Bake Pizza, Pedotti's Italian, Subway/76 W: DQ, Taco Bell, Subway
	Lodg	E: Best Western♥, Microtel♥ W: Budget Inn
	TServ	W: Mobile Diesel Repair & Towing
	Other	E: RVDump/BP, I-5 RV Sales & Service, Sutherlin Visitor Info Center, Sutherlin Muni Airport✈ W: RVDump/LP/Shell, U-Haul, Hi-Way Haven RV Park▲ , Umpqua Golf Resort & RV Park▲ Umpqua Golf, Henry Winery
135		**Sutherlin, Wilbur (Access to Ex #136 via E)**
	FStop	E: CFN
	Other	E: A&W Auto Repair
(130)		**Inspection Station (SB)**
129		**Del Rio Rd, Winchester, N Roseburg**
	Other	E: Kamper Korner RV Center/RVDump
127		**Edenbower Blvd, N Roseburg**
	Gas	E: Shell W: Taco Maker/Texaco◈, Albertson's
	Food	E: Shari's Rest, Western Wings W: Applebee's, Carl's Jr, IHOP, McDonald's, Red Robin, Subway, Taco Bell
	Lodg	E: Motel 6♥, Super 8 W: Sleep Inn♥
	Med	W: + Mercy Medical Center
	Other	E: Home Depot, Lowe's, Mt Nebo RV Park▲ , Roseburg Reg'l Airport✈ W: Albertson's, Big 5 Sporting Goods, Big O Tires, Doyle's Harley Davidson,

◈= Regular Gas Stations with Diesel ▲ = RV Friendly Locations ♥= Pet Friendly Locations
Red print shows large vehicle parking / access on site or nearby Brown Print = Campgrounds / RV PARKS

Other — E: Kmart, Office Depot, Pharmacy, Staples, **Walmart**, UPS Store

125 Garden Valley Blvd (Acc #127 via W)
Gas — E: Chevron, Shell◈, Texaco
W: 76, Chevron◈, Shell,
Food — E: Rest/Windmill Inn, Casey's, Brutke's Wagon Wheel, Elmer's, Jack in the Box, KFC, McDonald's, Taco Bell
W: Arby's Booster Juice, Burger King, Carl's Jr, IHOP, Izzy's Pizza, La Hacienda, Quiznos, Rodeo Steakhouse & Grill, Round Table Pizza, Sizzler, Wendy's
Lodg — E: Comfort Inn, Quality Inn, Windmill Inn♥
W: Americas Best Value Inn, Best Western, Econo Lodge, Howard Johnson Express
Med — W: + Mercy Urgent Care, Roseburg Oregon Medical Center, VA Hospital
Other — E: Albertson's, Ace Home Center, Auto Dealers, Big Lots, Car Quest, Jiffy Lube, Laundromat, NAPA, RiteAid, Safeway, Waldron Outdoor Sports, Bailey Veterinary Clinic♥, Carwash/Texaco, **Police Dept**, **OR State Hwy Patrol Post**, Roseburg Reg'l Airport✈
W: Roseburg Valley Mall, Auto Repair, Cinema 7, Fred Meyer/Pharmacy, RiteAid ,Schuck's Auto Supply, Staples, **Walmart**, Waldenbooks, Auto Services, Auto Service/Shell, Roseburg Skate Park

124 OR 138E, Roseburg, Crater Lake National Park
Gas — E: 76◈, Mobil◈
W: Chevron, Shell
Food — E: Anthony's Italian Cafe, Ami Japanese Rest, Chi's Chinese Garden Rest, Denny's
W: Subway/Shell, Gay 90's Deli, KFC, Taco Time
Lodg — E: Best Western, Dunes Motel♥, Holiday Inn Express♥, Travelodge♥
Med — W: + Douglas Community Hospital
Other — W: Safeway, RiteAid

123 Douglas Co Fairgrounds
Other — W: Fairgrounds/**RVDump**/**RVPark▲**

121 McLain Ave

120 OR 99N, Green, S Roseburg
Lodg — E: Shady Oaks Motel
W: Best Western

119 OR 99S, OR 42, Roseburg, Winston, Coos Bay
TStop — W: Love's Travel Stop #312 (Scales) Pacific Pride/Chevron
Gas — W: Shell◈
Food — W: Arby's/TJCinn/Love's TS, Rest/PacPr, McDonald's, Papa Murphy's, Subway
Other — W: WiFi/**RVDump**/Love's TS, **Western Star RV Park▲**

NOTE: MM 116.5 SB: 6% Steep Grade

113 Clarks Branch Rd
Lodge — W: Quikstop Motel/Market
TServ — W: Diesel Repair
Other — W: **to On the River Golf & RV Resort▲**

112 Dillard (SB), OR 99N, to OR 42, Winston, Coos Bay (NB)
Other — E: **Rivers West RV Park▲**

(111.6) S Umpqua Rest Area (Both dir)
(RR, Phone, Picnic)

(111) Inspection Station (NB)

110 Boomer Hill Rd

108 OR 99S, Myrtle Creek
Other — E: **Myrtle Creek RV Park▲**, City Park/**RVDump**

106 Weaver

103 Tri-City, Riddle (SB), Myrtle Creek, OR 99N, Tri City (NB) (Addt'l serv 3 mi E in Tri City)
FStop — W: Pacific Pride/Chevron
Gas — W: Chevron
Food — E: Diner
W: McDonald's
Other — E: **Tri City RV Park▲**, **South Country RV Center/LP**, Bowling, Myrtle Creek Muni Airport✈

102 Gazley Rd, Surprise Valley
Other — E: **Surprise Valley RV Park▲**

101 OR 99S, Riddle, Stanton Park (SB), Riddle (NB)

99 Main St, North Canyonville
TStop — W: 7 Feathers Travel Plaza (Scales)
Food — E: Burger King, Cow Creek Café
W: Rest/FastFood/7 Feathers TP
Lodg — E: Riverside Motel, Valley View Motel, **7 Feathers Casino & Hotel**
W: Best Western
TServ — W: 7 Feathers TP/Tires
Other — W: Laundry/**RVDump**/7 Feathers TP, **7 Feathers RV Resort▲ /LP**, Stanton Co Park/**RVDump**

98 OR 99N, Canyonville, to OR 227, Days Creek
Gas — E: 76◈, BP◈, Shell◈
Food — E: Bob's Country Junction
Lodg — E: Leisure Inn
Med — E: + Pioneer Healthcare Clinic
W: + Mercy Health Clinic
Other — E: Ace Hardware, Grocery, Laundromat, NAPA, Promise Natural Foods & Bakery, US Post Office
W: Bill's Tire & Auto Repair, Canyonville Feed & Ranch Supply, U-Haul

95 Canyon Creek

NOTE: MM 90 SB: 4% Steep Grade for 2 mi

88 Azalea

86 Quines Creek Rd, Barton Rd (Acc to Ex #83 via W to Azalea Glen Rd)
Gas — E: Shell◈
Food — E: Heaven On Earth Rest & **RVCamping**
Other — E: **Meadow Wood RV Park▲ /RVDump**

83 Barton Rd

(82) Cow Creek Rest Area (Both dir)
(RR, Phone, Picnic, Vend, Info-NB)

80 Junction Rd, Glendale (Acc thru #86 via W to Azalea Glen Rd)
Gas — W: Country Junction/Chevron
Food — W: Village Inn
Other — W: LP/Country Junction

NOTE: MM 79.5 SB: 5% Steep Grade, Next 3 mi

78 Speaker Rd, Glendale

77 Speaker Rd (SB)

76 Wolf Creek (NB Diff reaccess)
TStop — W: Pacific Pride/Wolf Creek Bio◈
Gas — W: 76◈, Exxon◈
Food — W: Hungry Wolf Rest
Lodg — W: Wolf Creek Historic Inn
Other — W: **Creekside RV Park▲**

NOTE: MM 73.5 SB: 6% Steep Grade next 2 mi

71 Sunny Valley Lp, Wolf Creek
Gas — E: Covered Bridge Gas & Country Store
Lodg — E: Sunny Valley Motel & **RV Parking▲**
Other — W: **Grants Pass/Sunny Valley KOA▲**

NOTE: MM 69: 6% Steep Grade next 3 mi

66 Hugo
Other — W: **Joe Creek Waterfalls RV CG▲**

(62.8) Manzanita Rest Area (Both dir)
(RR, Phone, Picnic, Vend, Info-SB)

61 Merlin Rd, Grants Pass
Gas — W: Shell◈
Other — E: **Beaver Creek RV Resort▲**, **Twin Pines RV Park▲**
W: **Rogue Valley RV Center & Repair**, **OR RV Outlet**, Grants Pass Airport✈

58 OR 99, to OR 199, Grants Pass
Gas — W: 76◈, ArcoAmPm, BP, Chevron, Shell◈
Food — W: Angela's Mexican, Burger King, China Hut, Della's, Denny's, Pizza Hut, McDonald's, Sizzler, Subway, Skipper's Seafood, Taco Bell, Wendy's
Lodg — W: Best Way Inn, Comfort Inn♥, Hawk's Inn, Hawthorne Suites, La Quinta Inn♥, Royal Vue Motor Lodge, Shilo Inn, Super 8♥, Sunset Inn♥, Travelodge♥
Med — W: + Hospital
Other — W: 76/**RVDump**, AutoZone, Auto Dealers, **OR State Hwy Patrol Post**, **Rogue Valley Overniter RV Park▲**, **Jack's Landing RV Resort▲**

55 OR 199, Grants Pass, Crescent City, Siskiyou, Jason
Gas — W: ArcoAmPm, Exxon◈
Food — W: Applebee's, Arby's, Burger King, Carl's Jr, Elmer's, McDonald's, JJ North's Grand Buffet, Shari's, Subway, Taco Bell
Lodg — W: Best Western, Holiday Inn Express
Med — W: + Hospital
Other — W: **Walmart sc**, Albertson's, Big O Tires, Big Lots, Dollar Tree, RiteAid, Staples, Visitor Info, Fairgrounds, Rogue College, **Siskiyou RV World**, **Moon Mountain RV Resort▲**, **Riverfront RV Park▲**, **Caveman RV**

48 Rogue River, Savage
Gas — E: Chevron◈, Exxon, Shell◈
Food — E: Abby's Pizza Inn
W: Aunt Betty's Family Kitchen , Karen's Kitchen, Mexican Rest
Lodg — W: Best Western, Bella Rosa Inn, Rogue River Inn
Other — W: **Chinook Winds RV Park▲**, **Bridgeview RV Resort▲**, Grocery, Info Center, Savage Rapids Dams

45B Valley of the Rogue State Park Rest Area (Both dir)
(RR, Phone, Picnic, **RVDump**)
Other — W: **to State Park▲**

45A Rogue River Hwy (SB), OR 99, Rogue River Hwy (NB)
Other — E: **Cypress Grove RV Park▲**

43 OR 99, OR 234, Gold Hill (SB), OR 99, Rogue River Hwy (NB)
Food — E: Café

◈= Regular Gas Stations with Diesel ▲ = RV Friendly Locations ♥= Pet Friendly Locations
Red print shows large vehicle parking / access on site or nearby Brown Print = Campgrounds / RV PARKS

EXIT		OREGON
	Lodg	E: Rock Point Motel & **RV Park▲**
40		**Gold Hill (SB), OR 99, OR 234, Gold Hill (NB)**
	Other	E: **Medford/Gold Hill KOA/RVDump▲**, Lazy Acres Motel & **RV Park▲** W: **Dardanell's Trailer & RV Park▲**
35		**OR 99S, Central Point (SB), OR 99S, Blackwell Rd (NB)**
33		**Pine St, Central Point**
	FStop	E: Pilot Travel Center #391 (Scales)
	Gas	E: Chevron W: 76◈, Shell◈, Texaco
	Food	E: Subway/Taco Bell/Pilot TC, Burger King, KFC, Shari's W: Bee Gee's, Pappy's Pizza, Mazaltan Grill, McDonald's
	Lodg	E: Fairfield Inn, Holiday Inn Express W: Courtyard, Grand Hotel, Super 8
	Other	E: Laundry/WiFi/Pilot TC, Fairgrounds Expo Park, Rogue Valley Int'l Airport✈, Fun Park, **RV Camping, Triple A RV Center▲** W: **RVDump**/76, Albertson's, **Central Point RV Center, RV Camping ▲**
30		**OR 62, Crater Lake Hwy, Medford, Crater Lake Nat'l Park**
	TStop	E: Witham Truck Stop/76 (Scales)
	Gas	E: ArcoAmPm◈, Chevron◈, Shell◈, Gas4Less W: 76◈, Chevron, Shell◈
	Food	E: Rest/Witham TS, Arby's, Applebee's, Asian Grill, Denny's, DQ, Elmers, IHOP, Marie Callendar's, Pizza Hut, Olive Garden, Red Robin, Starbucks, Subway, Sushi, Taco Delight W: Burger King, Jack in the Box, KFC, Red Lobster, King Wah Chinese, Skipper's Seafood, Starbucks, Wendy's
	Lodg	E: Best Western, Cedar Lodge, Comfort Inn, Hampton Inn, Medford North, Motel 6♥, Quality Inn, Rogue Regency Inn, Ramada, Shilo Inn, Windmill Inn♥ W: Cedar Lodge, Red Lion Hotel, Shilo Inn♥, Tiki Lodge Motel
	TServ	E: Witham TS/Tires, CAT Truck Engines Parts & Service, Cummins NW, Oregon Tire, Freightliner, Western Star Trucks
	Med	E: + Providence Medford Medical Ctr W: + Rogue Valley Manor Medical Hospital
	Other	E: **LP**/Witham TS, US Post Office, **OR State Hwy Patrol Post**, Aamco Repair, Ace Hardware, Albertsons, B&N, Big Lots, Cinemark Tinseltown USA,FedEx Office, NAPA, Tires, Bowling, **WalMart**, Rogue Valley Int'l Medford Airport✈, **Mike's RV Service**, **Ferrell Gas Propane/LP**, **Medford Oaks RV Park▲**, **River City RV Center**, **Southern OR RV, RV Consignment**
	Other	W: Rogue Valley Mall, Target, Tires, U-Haul, Auto Parts, Auto Services, Carwash/Shell, CarQuest, Jiffy Lube, Quality Tire
27		**Barnett Rd, Medford**
	FStop	W: 936 S Central Ave: Pacific Pride
	Gas	E: Exxon◈, Shell◈ W: 76/Circle K◈, Chevron, Exxon, Shell◈, Texaco
	Food	E: Black Bear Diner, DQ, Kopper Kitchen, Rest/Days Inn

EXIT		OREGON
	Food	W: Abby's Pizza, Apple Annie's, Burger King, Jack in the Box, KFC, McGrath's Fish House, McDonald's, Hometown Buffet, Pizza Hut, Senor Sam, Shari's, Starbucks, Subway, Taco Bell, Wendy's
	Lodg	E: Best Western, Days Inn, Homewood Suites, Motel 6♥, Travelodge♥ W: Best Inn, Budget Inn, Cedar Lodge Motel, City Center Motel, Comfort Inn, Holiday Inn Express, Knights Inn, Medford Inn, Red Carpet Inn, Red Lion Hotel, Rodeway Inn, Royal Crest Motel, Springhill Suites, TownePlace Suites
	Med	E: + Rogue Valley Manor Medical Hospital, Walk in Medical Center W: + Valley Immediate Care
	Other	E: AAA, ATMs, Banks, **Bear Creek Park** W: ATMs, Banks, Ace Hardware, Big 5 Sporting Goods, Grocery, Harbor Freight, Harry & David, Kmart, Les Schwab Tire, Siskiyou Veterinary Hospital♥, Radio Shack, Staples, Southern OR Ice Arena, Bear Creek Golf Course, Roxy Ann Bowling Lanes, Greyhound Terminal, **RVDump**/Shell,
24		**Fern Valley Rd, Phoenix**
	TStop	E: Petro Stopping Center #324 (Scales)
	Gas	E: Texaco◈ W: Exxon, 76/Circle K◈
	Food	E: IronSkillet/Petro SC, Rest/Super 8 W: Angelo's Pizza, Courtyard Café, Jack in the Box, Luigi's Cafe, McDonald's, Randy's Café, Subway
	Lodg	E: Super 8♥ & **Pear Tree RV Park▲** W: Bavarian Inn Motel, Phoenix Motel
	TServ	E: Petro SC/Tires, Pear Tree Center, Peterbilt/GMC, Cummins
	Other	E: Laundry/BarbSh/WiFi/**RVDump/LP**/Petro SC W: **Holiday RV Park▲**, Pear Tree Factory Outlet Stores, Car Quest, D&S Harley Davidson, Hansens BMW, Triumph, Ducati Motorcycles, Grocery, Home Depot, Phoenix Pharmacy, Visitor Info, Roxy Ann Winery, Affordable Truck & **RV**, **Jackson RV Parts & Service**, Phoenix Animal Hospital♥
(22)		**Suncrest Rest Area (SB) (RR, Phone, Picnic, Vend)**
21		**W Valley View Rd, Talent**
	TStop	W: Talent Truck Stop
	Gas	W: Gas 4 Less, Chevron◈
	Food	E: Figaro's Pizza W: Rest/Talent TS, Expresso Café, Italian, Senor Sam's Mexican
	Lodg	W: Good Nite Inn
	TServ	E: T&T Repair
	Other	W: Pharmacy, **Walmart**, **OR RV Round Up**, **American RV Resort▲**, Paschal Winery
19		**Valley View Rd, Ashland**
	FStop	W: Pacific Pride
	Gas	W: 76◈, Shell◈
	Food	W: Burger King
	Lodg	W: Best Western, Econo Lodge, Lithia Springs Inn, La Quinta Inn♥& **RV Park▲**
	Med	W: + Ashland Comm Hospital
	Other	W: **OR State Welcome Center**, Auto Services, Animal Medical Hospital♥, Enterprise RAC, Siskiyou Auto Care,

EXIT		OR / CA
	Other	W: Valley View Auto Repair, U-Haul, Dick's Towing, **to** Jackson Wellsprings▲
(18)		**Inspection Station (Both dir)**
14		**OR 66, Ashland St, Ashland, Klamath Falls**
	Gas	E: 76◈, Chevron, Shell◈ W: 76, ArcoAmPm, Mobil, Texaco
	Food	E: Rest/Ashland Hills Inn, Denny's, KFC, Oak Tree Rest W: Rest/Knights Inn, McDonald's, DQ, Pizza Hut, Starbucks, Subway, Taco Bell, Wendy's
	Lodg	E: Ashland Hills Inn, Best Western, Holiday Inn Express, Relax Inn, Rodeway Inn, Village Suites, Windmill Inn♥ W: Knights Inn, Super 8
	Med	W: + Hospital
	Other	E: **RVDump**/Shell, Enterprise RAC, Ashland Towing & Repair, Ashland Muni Airport✈, Oak Knoll Golf Course, **Klamath Falls KOA▲**, **to Emigrant Lake Rec Area▲**, **Glenyan RV Park & Campground▲**, **to Howard Prairie Lake Rec Area & Resort▲** W: Albertson's, Les Schwab Tire, NAPA, Radio Shack, RiteAid, U-Haul, S OR Univ, Bear Creek Animal Clinic♥
NOTE:		**MM 13.8 SB: Chain-Up Area**
11		**OR 99, Siskiyou Blvd, Ashland (NB) (Access to Ex #13 via W OR 99)**
	Gas	W: Shell
	Food	W: Italian, Little Caesar's Pizza, Senor Sam's, Subway, Wendy's
	Lodg	W: Best Western, Hillside Inn, Rodeway Inn, Stratford Inn
	Other	E: Ashland Muni Airport✈ W: Weisinger Brewery
(9)		**RunAway Truck Ramp (NB)**
(7)		**RunAway Truck Ramp (NB)**
6		**OR 273, Mount Ashland**
	Food	E: Callahans Siskiyou Lodge
	Lodg	E: Callahans Siskiyou Lodge
	Other	E: Ski Area
NOTE:		**MM 4.5: 6% Steep Grade next 7 mi**
(4)		**Brake Inspection (Both dir) Siskiyou Summit**
NOTE:		**Elev 4310 Highest Elevation on I-5**
1		**OR 273, Windemar Rd, Siskiyou Summit (NB)**

PACIFIC TIME ZONE

⬆OREGON
⬇CALIFORNIA

PACIFIC TIME ZONE

EXIT		OR / CA
NOTE:		**MM 797: OR State Line**
NOTE:		**SB: 4% Steep Grade next 2 mi**
796		**Hilt Rd, Hornbrook, Hilt**
	Gas	W: Shell
	Food	W: Café/Shell
793		**Bailey Hill Rd**
(791)		**Agricultural Insp Station (SB)**

EXIT		CALIFORNIA
790		**Hornbrook Hwy, Ditch Creek Rd**
789		**CR A-28, Henley, Hornbrook**
	Gas	E: Chevron◈
	Other	W: **Blue Heron RV Park▲**, **Robert Johnson Trailer & RV**
786		**CA 96, Klamath River Rd**
	W:	Randolph E Collier Rest Area (Both dir) (RR, Phone, Pic, Vend, Pet)
	NOTE:	**MM 782: Elevation 3067'**
	NOTE:	**MM 781: SB: 5% Steep Grade next 3 mi**
(780)		Vista Point (SB)
776		**CA 3, Montague Rd, Yreka, Montague**
	Gas	W: USA◈
	Food	W: Casa Ramos Mex Rest, Grandma's House Rest, Ma & Pa's, KFC
	Lodg	E: Holiday Inn Express W: Budget Inn, Mountain View Inn, Super 8♥, Third St Inn
	Other	E: **Yreka RV Park▲**, to Montague Yreka Airfield✈ W: AmeriGas Propane/LP, ATMs, Laundromat, Grocery
775		**Center St, Central Yreka**
	FStop	E: Pacific Pride
	Gas	W: 76, Chevron, Texaco◈, Valero◈
	Food	W: Capps Speakeasy, Classic 50's Diner, China Dragon, Denny's, Grandma's House Rest, Purple Plum, Lalo's Mexican Rest, Ming's Chinese Rest, Nature's Kitchen, Round Table Pizza
	Lodg	W: Best Western, Budget Inn, Comfort Inn, Econo Lodge, Relax Inn, Rodeway Inn, Yreka Motel
	Med	W: + Siskiyou Gen'l Hospital
	Other	E: Vet♥ W: ATMs, Banks, Baxter Auto Parts, Car Quest, **Co Sheriff Dept**, Enterprise RAC, Grocery, **Police Dept**, Radio Shack, RiteAid, Yreka Hardware, US Post Office, Clayton Tire Service, Littrell's Auto & **RV Service**
773		**CA 3, Yreka, Fort Jones, Etna**
	FStop	E: CFN
	Gas	W: Exxon, Shell◈
	Food	W: Black Bear Diner, Burger King, Carl's Jr, KFC, McDonald's, Papa Murphy's Take n Bake, Pizza Hut, Subway, Taco Bell
	Lodg	W: Amerihost Inn, Baymont Inn, Comfort Inn, Days Inn, Motel 6♥
	Med	W: + Hospital
	Other	E: Les Schwab Tires, U-Haul, Siskiyou Co Fairgrounds W: AT&T, Carwash, Grocery, NAPA, RiteAid, Schucks Auto Supply, **WalMart**, **CA State Hwy Patrol Post**
770		**Shamrock Rd, Easy St, Yreka**
	FStop	W: Easy Mart Fuel 247◈
	Food	W: Grandma's House
	Other	W: LP/Easy Mart
766		**CR A12, Grenada, Montague, Gazelle**
	FStop	E: Three J's Mini Mart/76
	Gas	W: Fergie's Qwik Stop/Shell, Texaco
759		**Louie Rd, Weed**

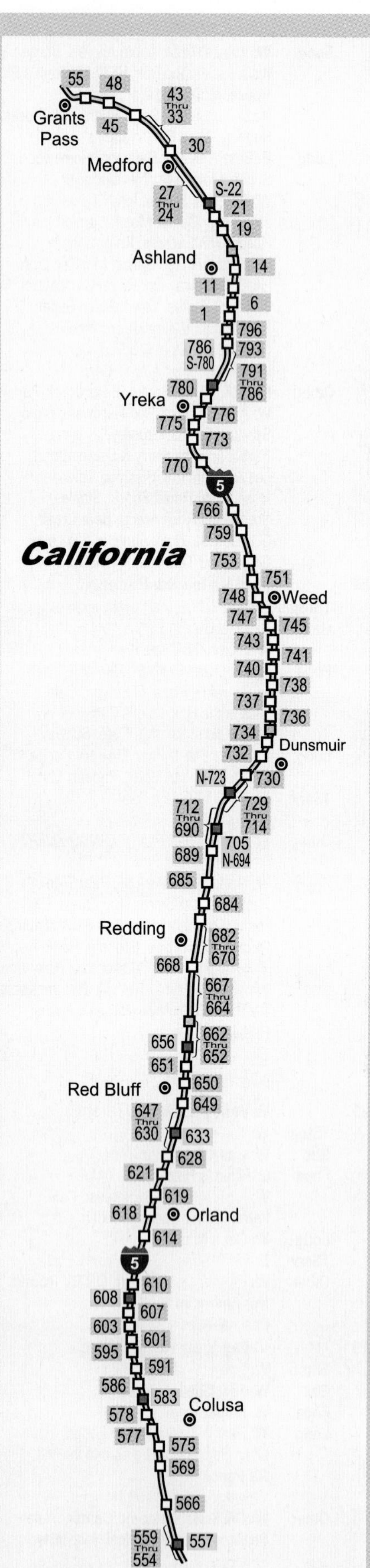

EXIT		CALIFORNIA
753		**Weed Airport Rd**
	W:	Weed Rest Area (Both dir) (RR, Phone, Pic, Pet)
	Other	E: Weed Airport✈
751		**Stewart Springs Rd, Weed, Edgewood, Gazelle**
	Other	E: to **Lake Shasta Rec Area▲** W: to Stewart Mineral Springs Resort
748		**CA 265, to US 97, Central Weed, Klamath Falls, N Weed Blvd**
	Gas	E: Shell◈, Spirit◈
	Food	E: Rest/Summit Inn, Pizza Factory
	Lodg	E: Motel 6♥, Summit Inn
	Other	E: Weed Golf Club, **Trailer Lane RV Park▲**
747		**Weed Blvd, Central Weed, College of Siskiyous (SB), US 97, Klamath Falls (NB) (Acc to #748)**
	Gas	E: Sports & Spirits/Chevron, Miner St Station/Shell◈, Spirit Food Mart◈
	Food	E: Expresso Bakery, Café/Hi-Lo Motel, Pizza Factory, Rest/Summit Inn
	Lodg	E: Hi-Lo Motel Cafe & **RV Park▲**, Motel 6♥, Summit Inn, Townhouse Motel
	Other	E: NAPA, Laundromat, Grocery, Auto Repair W: College of the Siskiyous
745		**S Weed Blvd, Weed**
	TStop	E: Travelers Travel Plaza/PacPr (Scales)
	Gas	E: CFN, Chevron◈, Shell
	Food	E: Subway/Trav TP, McDonald's, Silva's Family Rest, Burger King, Taco Bell
	Lodg	E: Comfort Inn♥, Quality Inn♥, Sis-Q-Inn Motel
	TServ	E: Trav TP
	Other	E: Laundry/LP/TravTP, Carwash/Chevron, **Friendly RV Park▲**
743		**Summit Dr, Truck Village Dr**
	FStop	E: CFN
741		**Abrams Lake Rd, Mt Shasta**
	Lodg	W: Mt Shasta Shastao B&B
	Other	E: Bill Ackerman Tire Center W: Jack Trout Fly Fishing & Guide, Siskiyou Co Visitor Center, **Abrams Lake RV Park▲**
740		**Mt Shasta City (SB) (NO reaccess, reacc via Ex #738)**
	Gas	E: Pacific Pride
	Lodg	E: Cold Creek Inn
	Other	E: **Mt Shasta City KOA▲**
738		**Central Mt Shasta**
	Gas	E: 76◈, Chevron◈, Shell, Spirit◈
	Food	E: Rest/Best Western, Black Bear Diner, Burger King, KFC/Taco Bell, Lalo's Mexican Rest, Organic Japanese, Papa Murphy Take 'n Bake, Round Table Pizza, Say Cheese Pizza, Subway W: Rest/Mt Shasta Resort
	Lodg	E: Best Western, Choice Inn, Cold Creek Inn, Dream Inn B&B, Econo Lodge, Mt Shasta Inn, Travel Inn, W: Mt Shasta Resort, Mt Shasta Ranch B&B
	TServ	E: Skinner's Roadside Truck Repair
	Med	E: + Mercy Medical Center
	Other	E: ATMS, Banks, Ace Hardware, Grocery, Mt Shasta Laundromat & Carwash, NAPA, Radio Shack, RiteAid, Mt Shasta Animal Hospital♥, US Post Office, Visitor Info, **Mt Shasta City Park, Surburban Propane/LP, Mt Shasta City KOA/RVDump/LP▲**

◈= Regular Gas Stations with Diesel ▲ = RV Friendly Locations ♥ = Pet Friendly Locations
Red print shows large vehicle parking / access on site or nearby Brown Print = Campgrounds / RV PARKS

EXIT		CALIFORNIA
	Other	W: Museum, Lake Siskiyou RV Park▲, Chateau Shasta MH & RV Park▲
737		**Mt Shasta City (NB) (Acc to #738 E Serv)**
	Food	E: Liliy's, Mike & Tony's
	Lodg	E: A-1 Choice Inn, Econo Lodge, Evergreen Lodge, Finlandia Motel, Strawberry Valley Inn, Swiss Holiday Lodge, Woodsman Cabins& Lodge
	Other	E: U-Haul, Mt Shasta Lavendar Farm
736		**CA 89, McCloud, Lassen Natl Park**
	Other	E: to appr 9mi McCloud Dance Country RV Resort▲
(735)		**Inspection Station (SB)**
	NOTE:	MM 734: 5% Steep Grade next 3 mi
734		**Mott Rd, Mt Shasta, to Dunsmuir**
	Other	E: Dunsmuir Mott Muni Airport✈
732		**Dunsmuir Ave, Siskiyou Ave, Dunsmuir**
	Gas	W: Chevron◈, Shell◈
	Food	E: House of Glass Rest, Penny's Diner W: Subway/Chevron
	Lodg	E: Best Choice Inn, Oak Tree Inn W: Acorn Inn, Cedar Lodge
730		**Dunsmuir Ave, Central Dunsmuir**
	Gas	W: Chevron
	Food	E: Brown Trout Cafe & Gallery, Burger Barn, Cafe Maddalena, Cornerstone Bakery & Cafe, Dunsmuir Brewery Works, Pizza Factory W: Subway/Chevron, Hitching Post, Micki's Better Burger
	Lodg	E: Dunsmuir Inn, Travelodge W: Cave Springs Resort
	Other	E: ATMs, Banks, Amtrak, Dunsmuir Hardware, Fisher Auto Parts, Grocery, US Post Office
729		**Dunsmuir Ave, Hist District**
728		**Crag View Dr, Railroad Park Rd Castella (SB), Castle Crags Dr (NB)**
	Gas	E: Manfredi's Food & Gas Depot◈
	Food	E: Burger Barn, Pizza Factory, River Café, Salt H20 Cafe
	Lodg	E: Dunsmuir Lodge, W: Railroad Park Resort RV Park▲ & Caboose Motel,
	Other	E: Cedar Pines RV Resort▲, Rustic Trailer Park▲
727		**Crag View Dr (NB)**
726		**Soda Creek Rd, Castella (Acc to #724 via E Frontage Rd)**
724		**Castle Creek Rd, Castella**
	Gas	W: Chevron◈
	Lodg	E: Castle Stone Cottage Inn Rentals
	Other	W: to Castle Crags State Park▲
(723)		**Vista Point (NB)**
723		**Sweetbrier Ave, Castella**
721		**Conant Rd**
720		**Flume Creek Rd**
718		**Sims Rd, Castella**
	Lodg	E: Best in the West Resort & RV Park▲
714		**Gibson Rd**
712		**Pollard Flat, Lakehead**
	FStop	E: Pollard Flat USA/Exxon
	Food	E: Rest/PF USA

EXIT		CALIFORNIA
	Other	E: LP/Pollard Flat
710		**La Moine Rd, Slate Creek Rd, Lakehead**
707		**Vollmers, Dog Creek Rd, Delta Rd**
	Lodg	E: to Delta Lodge
(705)		**Lakehead Rest Area (SB) (RR, Phone, Picnic)**
704		**Riverview Dr, Lakehead (Acc to #702 via W to Lakeshore Dr)**
	Food	E: Basshole Bar & Grill, Camp Shasta Coffee Co, Klub Klondike Bar & Rest,
	Lodg	E: Lakehead Lodge♥
	Other	E: Grocery
702		**Lakeshore Dr, Antlers Rd (Acc to #704 via W to Lakeshore Dr)**
	Gas	E: Shell◈ W: 76
	Food	E: Brewster's, Top Hat Café, Café/New Lodge Motel, Subway/Shell, W: Allyson's Rest, Basshole Bar & Grill, Canyon Kettle
	Lodg	E: Neu Lodge Motel W: Lakeshore Inn & RV Park▲, Shasta Lake Motel
	AServ	E: Auto Repair, Towing
	Other	E: US Post Office, Antlers RV Park & CG▲, Lakehead RV Park & CG▲ W: Lakeshore Villa RV Park▲, Shasta Lake RV Resort & CG▲, Rancheria RV Park▲, Whiskeytown Shasta Trinity Nat'l Rec Area, to appr 2mi: Tsasdi Resort Cabins, appr 3mi: Sugarloaf Cottages Resort
	NOTE:	MM 698: 5% Steep Grade next 2 mi
698		**Salt Creek Rd, Gilman Rd**
	Other	W: Salt Creek Resort & RV▲, Trail In RV CG▲, Oak Grove Campground▲
695		**Shasta Caverns Rd, Lakehead, to O'Brien**
	Lodg	W: Shasta Marina Resort/Houseboats, O'Brien Mountain Inn B&B
(694)		**(Closed indefinite per CA DOT) O'Brien Rest Area (NB) (RR, Phone, Picnic)**
693		**Packers Bay Rd (SB, no NB reacc)**
692		**Turntable Bay Rd, Lakehead**
	Other	Whiskeytown Shasta Trinity Nat'l Rec Area
690		**Bridge Bay Rd, Redding**
	Food	W: Tail O'the Whale/Br Bay Resort
	Lodg	W: Bridge Bay Resort♥ & RV Park▲
	Other	W: Boat Rentals/BrBayResort
689		**Fawndale Rd, Wonderland Blvd**
	Lodg	E: Fawndale Lodge & RV Resort▲
	Other	E: Fawndale Oaks RV Park▲ W: Wonderland RV Park▲
687		**Mountain Gate, Wonderland Blvd**
	FStop	E: CFN/Chevron/KC's Corner Mart (DAND)
	Gas	W: Shell◈
	Other	E: LP/KC's, Mountain Gate RV Park & CG▲, Bear Mountain RV Resort▲, Shasta Lake Visitor Info Center
685		**CA 151, Shasta Dam Blvd, Shasta Dam, Shasta Lake, Central Valley**
	Gas	W: Circle K/76, Chevron◈, Valero◈

EXIT		CALIFORNIA
	Food	W: Black Oak Rest, Burger King/Chevron, Latinos Rest, McDonald's, Olde Mill Eatery, Oriental Express, Pizza Factory, Taco Shop
	Lodg	W: Shasta Dam Motel
	Med	W: + Shasta Dam Medical Clinic
	Other	W: Shasta Dam Visitor Info Center, Hardware Express, NAPA, RiteAid, US Post Office, Auto Repair/Valero
684		**Pine Grove Ave, Shasta Lake**
	Gas	W: 76◈,
	Food	W: Giant Orange Café, RC's BBQ & Steakhouse
	Other	E: Safari RV Parts & Service, Cousin Gary RV Supermart W: Oasis Fun Center
682		**Oasis Rd, Redding**
	Gas	W: ArcoAmPm, Shell
	Food	W: McDonald's, Subway/Shell
	TServ	W: Truck Repair
	Other	E: Myers Marine & RV Center, CA Trailer & RV Sales W: Redding RV Center & Repair, Shasta Lake RV, CA State Hwy Patrol Post, Budget Truck Rental, Oasis & I-5 Rentals: Auto Service/UHaul/LP,
681B		**CA 273, to Market St, Lake Blvd (SB, No re-entry)**
	FStop	W: CFN/SST Oil #893
	Gas	W: Exxon
	Med	W: + Hospital
	TServ	E: Redding Freightliner W: Redding Truck Center, Shasta Valley Ford Truck, Towing & Repair
681A		**Twin View Blvd, Redding (SB)**
	FStop	W: Pacific Pride
	Gas	E: 76◈
	Lodg	E: Motel 6♥, Ramada Ltd♥ W: Best Western, Fairfield Inn
	Other	E: Redding Harley Davidson, Tractor Supply W: Auto Services, CC RV & Auto Repair, Cummins West,
681		**Twin View Blvd, Redding (NB)**
680		**CA 299, Lake Blvd**
	Gas	W: ArcoAmPm, Chevron, Fast Stop Mini Mart
	Food	W: Arby's, Carl's Jr, Cattleman's Steak House, Giant Burger, KFC, Giant Burger, McDonald's, Starbucks, Subway, Rest/ River Inn Motel
	Lodg	W: River Inn Motel, Travelodge
	Other	E: to appr 34 mi: Mt Lassen/ Shingletown KOA▲ W: AutoZone, Carwash, Dollar Tree, Grocery, Kragen Auto Parts, ShopKO/Pharmacy, Shasta Lanes, Vet♥, Walgreen's, Waterworks Park, Premier RV Resort-Redding▲, Redding RV Park▲, to appr 30 mi: Trinity Lake KOA▲
678B		**CA 44W (SB)**
678A		**CA 44, Hilltop Dr, Lassen NP (SB)**
678		**CA 44, Eureka, Lassen NP (NB) (Acc #677 via E to Hilltop Dr)**
	FStop	W: CFN/SST Oil #1472
	Gas	E: ArcoAmPm, Chevron◈, Shell, Tesoro, Valero

◈= Regular Gas Stations with Diesel ▲ = RV Friendly Locations ♥= Pet Friendly Locations

Red print shows large vehicle parking / access on site or nearby Brown Print = Campgrounds / RV PARKS

EXIT		CALIFORNIA
	Food	E: Applebee's, BurgerKing/Valero, Carl's Jr, Chevy's Fresh Mexican, Chuck E Cheese's, Far East Cafe, In 'n Out Burger, Italian Cottage, Jack in the Box, Logan's Roadhouse, McDonald's, Olive Garden, Outback Steakhouse, Panda Express, Pasta Pronto, Pizza Hut, Quiznos, Red Lobster, Red Robin, Starbucks, Waters Seafood Grill
	Food	W: Dominos Pizza, Starbucks
	Lodg	E: Holiday Inn, Hilton, Motel 6♥, Red Lion Hotel W: Americas Best Inn, Americana Lodge, River Inn Motor Hotel, Stardust Motel, Thunderbird Lodge
	MED	W: + Shasta Reg'l Medical Center
	Other	E: Albertson's, B&N, Best Buy, Big Lots, Cinemark Movies 10, Costco, Cost Plus World Market, Food Max, Home Depot, Kragen Auto Parts, Les Schwab Tires, Office Depot, Office Max, PetCo♥, PetSmart♥, Redding Sports, Sports Authority, Target, Trader Joe's, Verizon, **WalMart**, Grocery, Mt Shasta Mall, Laundromat, Dana Park Veterinary Hospital♥, W: to Benton Field Airport✈, Amtrak, Redding Convention Center
677	**Cypress Ave, Hilltop Dr, Redding (Acc #678 via E to Hilltop Dr)**	
	FStop	E: CFN/Hilltop Circle K/76 W: CFN/SST Oil #555
	Gas	E: Circle K/76, Chevron, Exxon, Shell, Spirit, Valero, Safeway W: 76, Beacon, Shell, USA◈
	Food	E: Applebee's, Black Bear Diner, Carl's Jr, Del Taco/Circle K, Denny's, IHOP, Jack In the Box, KFC, Little Caesar's Pizza, McDonald's, Starbucks, Taco Bell W: Big Red's BBQ, CA Cattle Co, Denny's, Fat Burrito, Guadalajara Mexican Rest, Jack in the Box, Lumberjacks, Round Table Pizza, Subway
	Lodg	E: Best Western, Baymont Inn, Comfort Inn, Hampton Inn, Hilltop Lodge, Holiday Inn Express, La Quinta Inn♥, Oxford Suites, Quality Inn, Red Lion Hotel, Ramada
	Lodg	W: Americas Best Value Inn, Howard Johnson Express, Motel 6♥, Vagabond Inn
	Med	W: + Mercy Medical Center
	Other	E: ATMs, AutoZone, Auto Services, Big 5 Sporting Goods, Costco, FedEx Office, Grocery, Grocery Outlet, Golf USA, Harbor Freight, Kmart, Les Schwab Tires, Lowe's, **Northern Trailer & RV Supply**, PetSmart♥, Safeway, Walgreen's, **Walmart**, US Post Office, VCA Asher Animal Hospital♥, W: America's Tire, Big O Tire, Auto Dealers, AutoZone, Cinemark Movies 8, Enterprise RAC, Grocery, Jiffy Lube, Les Schwab Tire, Midas, Office Depot, Radio Shack, U-Haul, **Marina RV RV Park▲**, **Cousin Gary's RV Center**, **to appr 4mi Green Acres RV Park▲**, **Redding RV Center**
675	**S Bonnyview Rd, Churn Creek Rd (SB), Bechelli Lane (NB), Redding**	
	Gas	E: Chevron◈, Valero W: Texaco◈

EXIT		CALIFORNIA
	Food	E: Taco Bell W: Burger King/Texaco
	Lodg	E: Super 8 W: Hilton Garden Inn,
	TServ	E: Redding Kenworth
	Other	E: Chevron/LP, AmeriGas/LP
673	**Knighton Rd, Redding Airport**	
	FStop	E: CFN/SST Oil #345
	TStop	E: Travel Center of America #57 (Scales)
	Food	E: CountryPr/PHut/Popeye's/TA TC
	TServ	E: TA TC
	Other	E: Laundry/WiFi/LP/TA TC, Redding Muni Airport✈, Churn Creek Golf Course **W: to JGW RV Park▲, Sacramento River RV Park▲**,
670	**Riverside Ave, Anderson**	
	FStop	W: Mike's Fuel & Food
	Food	E: Woodside Grill/Gaia Hotel
	Lodg	E: Gaia Hotel & Spa♥
	Other	W: Premier Towing, **Anderson Campers, Anderson RV Sales & Rentals**
668	**Central Anderson, Lassen NP**	
	Gas	E: 76◈, Beacon, USA, Valero, Safeway W: Chevron, Sarco◈
	Food	E: Burger King, McDonald's, Round Table Pizza, Subway, Taco Bell W: Giant Burger, KFC, Pizza
	Lodg	E: Best Western, Valley Inn
	Med	E: + Anderson Walk-In Medical Clinic
	Other	E: Ace Hardware, Dollar Tree, Kragen Auto Parts. Les Schwab Tire, NAPA, Radio Shack, RiteAid x2, Safeway, W: Auto Repairs,
667	**Deschutes Rd, Factory Outlet Blvd, Anderson, Cottonwood**	
	Gas	E: Shell◈ W: Tower Mart
	Food	W: Arby's, Cascade Beef, Jack in the Box, Ca Expresso, Long John Silver, Luigi's Pizza, Sonic, Subway
	Lodg	W: AmeriHost
	Other	E: LP/Shell, Gateway Animal Hospital♥, W: Ace Hardware, Prime 11 Cinemas, Prime Factory Outlets, 4G Wireless, **Walmart sc**, CA Welcome Center
665	**Cottonwood (SB, NB re-entry)**	
	Lodg	E: Alamo Motel & **RV Park▲**
664	**Balls Ferry Rd, Gas Point Rd**	
	FStop	W: CFN/SST/CircleB/Beacon
	Gas	E: Payless, Gas 4 Less W: Holiday◈, Valero◈
	Lodg	E: Travelers Motel, Alamo Motel & **RV Park▲**
	Other	E: Pharmacy, Grocery, **to Drakesbad Guest Ranch** W: Laundromat
662	**Bowman Rd, Cottonwood**	
	FStop	E: Cross Country Travel Center/PacPride/Shell
	Food	E: Rest/PacPr
(660)	**Inspection Station (Both dir)**	
659	**Sunset Hills Dr, Auction Yard Rd**	
657	**Auction Yard Rd, Hooker Creek Rd**	
	Other	E: Truck & Trailer Repair
(656)	**Herbert S Miles Rest Area (Both dir) (RR, Phone, Picnic, Pet)**	
653	**Jellys Ferry Rd, Red Bluff**	
	Other	**E: Bend RV Park▲**

EXIT		CALIFORNIA
652	**Wilcox Golf Rd**	
651	**Red Bluff, CA 36W, Fortuna (SB, no re-entry) (Acc to #650)**	
650	**Adobe Rd, Red Bluff**	
	Gas	W: Chevron◈
	Food	W: Casa Ramos Mexican Rest
	Lodg	W: Hampton Inn
	Other	W: Auto Dealer, Home Depot
649	**CA 36E Chico, CA 99, Lassen NP, Antelope Blvd, CA 36W Red Bluff**	
	FStop	E: to 22678 Antelope Blvd CFN/Sunshine Market
	Gas	E: Exxon, Chevron, Red Buff Gas, Shell◈, Valero◈, Rest/Sunshine Mkt W: Gas 4 Less, USA◈
	Food	E: Applebee's, Burger King, Del Taco, Green Barn Steakhouse, KFC, McDonald's W: Carl's Jr, Denny's, Egg Roll King, Pizza, Shari's, Subway
	Lodg	E: Best Inn, Best Western♥, Comfort Inn, Motel 6♥, 2 mi: Sportsmans Lodge♥ W: Best Value Inn, Cinderella Riverview Motel, Super 8, Travelodge
	Other	E: LP/Red Buff Gas, LP/Sunshine Mkt, **Red Bluff RV Park▲, Campers Corral**, Greyhound, Les Schwab Tires, Tehama Co Fairgrounds, **CA State Hwy Patrol Post**, W: Laundromat, Grocery, CVS, **Durango RV Resort▲, Idle Wheels RV Park▲, O'Nite Park▲, Rivers Edge RV Resort▲**
647B	**Diamond Ave (SB)**	
647A	**S Main St (SB)**	
647	**Red Bluff, Diamond Ave (NB)**	
	Gas	E: 76◈, Exxon, Valero W: ArcoAmPm◈, Chevron
	Food	E: Mexican Rest W: Arby's, Jack in the Box, Italian, Pizza Hut, Starbucks, Taco Bell, Yogurt Alley
	Lodg	E: Days Inn W: Sky Terrace Motel, Triangle Motel
	Med	E: + Hospital
	Other	W: Grocery, Kragen Auto Parts, Radio Shack, Staples, Walgreen's, **WalMart**, Red Bluff Muni Airport✈
642	**Flores Ave, Proberta, Gerber** **NOTE: Trucks & RV's NOT ADVISED**	
636	**CR A11, Gyle Rd, Gerber, to Tehama, Los Molinos**	
	Other	**E: to Los Molinos RV Camping▲**
633	**Finnell Ave, Corning, Richfield**	
(633)	**Lt JC Helmick Rest Area (Both dir) (RR, Phone, Picnic, Vend)**	
631	**Corning Rd, Corning**	
	Gas	E: 76◈, 7-11, Chevron, Shell◈, Spirit
	Food	E: Burger King, Marco's Pizza, Olive Pit, Quiznos, Starbucks, Taco Bell W: Bartell's Giant Burger
	Lodge	E: 7 Inn, American Inn, Best Western, Economy Inn
	Other	E: Auto Services, Bob's Tires, Dollar Tree, Laundromat, NAPA, RiteAid, Safeway, Les Schwab Tire, **Heritage RV Park▲**, to Corning Muni Airport✈, **to Woodson Bridge State Rec Area/RV Park▲** **W: Corning RV Park▲**

◈= Regular Gas Stations with Diesel ▲ = RV Friendly Locations ♥ = Pet Friendly Locations
Red print shows large vehicle parking / access on site or nearby Brown Print = Campgrounds / RV PARKS

630 South Ave, Corning
- TStop E: Petro Stopping Center #309 (Scales), Travel Center of America #40/Arco (Scales) Love's Travel Stop #410 (Scales)
- Food E: Buckhorn/Arby/Subw/TA TC, Rest/ Petro SC, Denny's/HotColdDeli/Love's TS, McDonald's, Jack in the Box
- Gas E: Chevron, Spirit
- Lodg E: Days Inn♥, Holiday Inn Express♥
- TServ E: TA TC, Petro SC/Tires, Speedco, Corning Truck & Radiator Service
- TWash E: Blue Beacon TW/Petro SC, Royal Truck Wash
- Other E: Laundry/WiFi/Petro SC, Laundry/WiFi/ RVDump/TA TC, Laundry/LP/RVDump/ Love's TS, U-Haul, Corning Truck & RV Center

628 CA 99W (NB), Liberal Ave (SB)
- FStop E: Pacific Pride
- Gas W: CFN/RoadysTS/Rolling Hills Chevron◈
- Food W: Rest/PacPr, Rest/Ramada Inn/RHC
- Lodg W: The Lodge/Ramada Inn/RHC
- Other W: Rolling Hills Casino/RV Parking

621 CR 7, Orland

619 CA 32E, Orland, Chico
- Gas E: 76◈, Orland Stop 'n Shop◈ W: Tesoro, Sportsman's Market & Gas◈
- Food E: Berry Patch, Burger King, Dutch Bros Coffee, Subway W: City Gates Cafe & Rest, Taco Bell
- Lodg E: Amber Light Inn Motel, Orlanda Inn
- Other E: LP/76, ATMs, Banks, Longs Drugs, NAPA, Orland Carwash, Radio Shack, Walker St Veterinary Clinic♥, Best Buy RV Parts & Supplies, John's Mobile RV Repair, to Haigh Field✈ W: Old Orchard RV Park▲, The Parkway RV Resort & Campground▲, North State RV Services Center, Performance Speciality Trailer,

618 CR 16, Orland
- FStop E: CFN/USA Fuel Stop
- Food E: Pizza Factory
- Lodg E: Orland Inn
- Other E: Laundromat, Grocery, Les Schwab Tire Center, Pharmacy, Towing, Orland MH & RV Park▲

614 CR 27

610 CR 33, Artois
- Other E: US Post Office

(608) Willows Rest Area (Both dir) (RR, Ph, Pic, Vend, Pet, RVDump/Water)

607 CR 39, Willows
- Lodg E: Blue Gum Motel♥

603 CA 162, Wood St, Willows, Oroville
- FStop E: Pacific Pride
- Gas E: ArcoAmPm, Chevron, Shell◈ W: 76
- Food E: Rest/Best Western, Black Bear Diner, Burger King, Casa Ramos Mexican Rest, Common Grounds Coffee, Denny's, KFC, McDonald's, Round Table Pizza, Starbucks, Subway, Taco Bell W: Nancy's 24hr Airport Café
- Lodg E: AmeriHost, Baymont Inn, Days Inn♥, Economy Inn♥, Holiday Inn Express, Motel 6, Super 8♥, Travelodge
- Med E: + Glynn Medical Center
- Other E: ATMs, Banks, Carwash, NAPA, Pharmacy, Radio Shack, US Post Office, Vet♥, Willows Hardware, Sheriff 's Dept, CA State Hwy Patrol Post W: Walmart/Pharmacy, Willows-Glenn Co Airport✈, Willow Glenn RV & MH Park▲, to appr 7mi: Thunderhill Raceway Park

601 CR 57, Willows
- FStop E: to CA99W, N: CFN/ValleyPetro, to 1481 Hwy 99W: Willow TP/76

595 Norman Rd, Rd 68, Princeton
- Other E: Sacramento Wildlife Refuge

591 Delevan Rd

588 Maxwell Rd (SB) (Acc #586 W to 99W)

586 Maxwell Rd
- Gas W: CFN/Chevron, Caldwell's Mini Mart
- Food W: Rest/Maxwell Inn
- Lodg W: Maxwell Inn
- Other E: to Colusa Casino W: US Post Office

(583) Maxwell Rest Area (Both dir) (RR, Phone, Picnic, Pet)

578 CA 20, Colusa, Clear Lake
- Gas W: 76, Chevron, Orv's Cnty Store & Deli/Sh
- Food E: Baskin Robbins, Carl's Jr, Taco Bell W: Burger King, Denny's, Granzella's Rest, McDonald's
- Lodg E: Holiday Inn Express, Ramada W: Capri Williams, Granzella's Inn, Motel 6, Quality Inn, Stage Stop Inn, Travelers Motel
- Med W: + Urgent Care Med Center
- Other E: Amerigas/LP, Ace Hardware, Grocery, Museum, Williams Airport✈ W: CA Hwy Patrol Post

577 E Street, Williams
- FStop E: Pacific Pride
- Gas E: Shell W: 76, ArcoAmPm ◈, Chevron, Shell◈
- Food E: Baskin Robbins, Carl's Jr, Subway, Taco Bell W: Burger King, Casa Lupe, Denny's, Granzella's Bakery & Rest, McDonald's, Subway, Wendy's
- Lodg E: Holiday Inn Express♥, Ramada♥ W: Granzella's Inn♥, Motel 6, Quality Inn♥, Stage Stop Inn
- Med W: + Hospital
- Other W: Pharmacy, NAPA, US Post Office, U-Haul, CA State Hwy Patrol Post, I-5 RV Park▲

575 Husted Rd, to Williams (Acc to # 577 via W to 7th St/Old 99W)

569 Hahn Rd, Grimes

567 Putnam Lateral, Arbuckle
- FStop E: Pacific Pride
- Gas E: Exxon W: CFN

566 Arbuckle, College City
- FStop E: Pacific Pride
- Gas E: Shell

NOTE: MM 559: SB: Begin Call Boxes

559 County Line Rd

(557) Dunnigan Rest Area (Both dir) (RR, Phone, Picnic, Pet)

556 CR E4, CR 6, Dunnigan
- Gas E: BP, Chevron◈, Valero◈ W: 76, Shell
- Food E: Bill & Kathy's, BBQ, Jack in the Box
- Lodg E: Best Value Inn
- Other W: Campers Inn & RV Golf Resort▲

554 CR 8, Chula Vista, Dunnigan
- TStop E: Pilot Travel Center #168 (Scales) W: United (Scales)
- Food E: Wendy's/Pilot TC, Oasis Grill W: FastFood/United
- Lodg E: Budget 8, Horizon Motel, Sands Motel
- TWash E: Pilot TC
- TServ E: Bob's Truck Repair W: United
- Other E: Laundry/WiFi/Pilot TC, Happy Time RV Park▲ W: Laundry/Wifi/United

(553) Jct I-505S, Winters, to San Francisco (SB) (Begin NB Call Boxes)

548 CR 13, CR E10, Zamora
- FStop E: Pacific Pride/Shell
- Food E: Rest/PacPr, Zamora Mini Mart & Deli
- TServ W: Peterson Power Systems

542 Yolo

541 CR E7, to CA 16, Woodland
- Med W: + to Hospital

540 CR 99, West St
- Food W: Denny's
- Lodg W: Cache Creek Lodge

538 CA 113N, East St, Woodland, to Yuba City
- FStop W: Pacific Pride
- Gas W: Chevron◈
- Food W: Denny's
- Lodg E: Valley Oaks Inn W: Best Western
- Med W: to + Yolo Co General Hospital

537 Main St, CA 113S, Woodland, Davis
- FStop W: Valero Food Stop, Pacific Pride
- Gas W: 76
- Food W: Burger King, Denny's, McDonald's, Starbucks, Subway, Taco Bell, Wendy's
- Lodg W: Days Inn♥, Motel 6♥, Quality Inn
- Med W: to + Yolo Co General Hospital
- Other E: CA State Hwy Patrol Post W: Carwash, Food4Less, Longs Drugs, Office Depot, to County Fair Mall, Target/Pharmacy, UPS Store, Yolo Co Fairgrounds

536 CR 102, Woodland
- Gas E: ArcoAmPm, Shell, Murphy W: Chevron
- Food E: Applebee's, Burger King, Cold Stone Creamery, Jack in the Box, McDonald's, Quiznos, Starbucks, Subway
- Lodg E: Hampton Inn, Holiday Inn Express
- Other E: ATMs, America's Tire, Costco, Home Depot, Staples, Target, Walmart W: Best Buy, Food4Less, Carwash, CA State Hwy Patrol Post, to County Fair Mall, Yolo Co Fairgrounds, Woodland Comm College

531 CR 22, Sacramento, Elkhorn

(529) Elkhorn Rest Area (SB) (RR, Phone, Picnic, Pet)

528 Airport Blvd, Sacramento
- Gas E: ArcoAmPm
- Food E: Foods/Airport, Jim's Tacos
- Lodg E: Host Airport Hotel
- Other E: Sacramento Metro Airport✈

◈= Regular Gas Stations with Diesel ▲ = RV Friendly Locations ♥= Pet Friendly Locations
Red print shows large vehicle parking / access on site or nearby Brown Print = Campgrounds / RV PARKS

EXIT		CALIFORNIA
525B		**CA 99N, Yuba City, CA 70, Marysville** (diff reacc) (begin run w/I-99)
525A		**Del Paso Rd, Sacramento**
	Gas	E: Chevron, Safeway, Shell
	Food	E: IHOP, In 'n Out Burger, Jack in the Box, KFC, Malabar American Cooking, Panda Express, Panera Bread, Quiznos, Sizzler, Starbucks, Straw Hat Pizza, Taco Bell, Teriyaki to Go
		W: Subway
	Lodg	E: Hampton Inn, Holiday Inn Express, Homewood Suites
		W: Four Points Sheraton
	Med	E: + Med 7 Urgent Care Center
	Other	E: Arco Arena, Grocery, RiteAid, Safeway, UPS Store, Carwash/Chevron, Scotty's Carwash, Natomas Veterinary Hospital ♥
524		**Arena Blvd** (Addtl Serv E to Truxel Rd)
	Food	E: Papa John's Pizza, Subway
		W: Bangkok Garden, Mandarin Express, Round Table Pizza, Starbucks
	Lodg	W: Four Points Sheraton, Marriott Executsay
	Other	E: Arco Arena, Natomas Field
(522		**Jct I-80, E-Reno, W-San Francisco**
	TServ	W: Cummins West
521		**Garden Hwy** (SB)
521B		**W El Camino Ave** (NB)
	Food	W: Carl's Jr, Jack in the Box, Sushi King
	Lodg	E: Best Western
		W: Guest Suites Hotel, Hilton Garden Inn, Residence Inn, Springhill Suites
521A		**Garden Hwy** (NB)
	Food	E: Chipolte Mexican Grill
	Food	W: HungryHunter/Courtyard, Chevy's Fresh Mex Rest, Crawdad's River Cantina, Virgin Sturgeon Rest
	Lodg	W: Courtyard
	Other	E: Walgreen's
520		**Richards Blvd, Sacramento**
	FStop	E: Pacific Pride
	Gas	E: Chevron
		W: Shell◈, Valero
	Food	E: Burger King, Carl's Jr, Hungry Hunter, Lyon's, Memphis BBQ, McDonald's, Monterrey Bay Canners, Stonebrooks Rest, The Rusty Duck
		W:
	Lodg	E: Governors Inn, Hawthorne Inn, Ramada Inn, Super 8
		W: Best Western, Comfort Inn, Days Inn, La Quinta Inn♥, Motel 6♥, Super 8
	Other	E: Convention Center, State Capitol, CA Hwy Patrol Post
519B		**J St, Old Sacramento**
	Food	E: Cyprus Grille, Denny's, Tandoori Wok, Zokku Rest, Grange Rest/Citizen Hotel
		W: Annabelle's Pizza & Pasta, Cafe New Orleans, Fats Rest, Firehouse Rest
	Lodg	E: Citizen Hotel, Holiday Inn, Vagabond Inn
		W: Delta King Hotel, Embassy Suites, Sacramento Suites
	Other	E: Amtrak, Sacramento Valley Rail System, To CA State Capitol, Convention Center, City Hall, IMAX, Cesar Chavez Park
		W: CA Railroad Museum, Museums, Riverboat Cruises, Old Town
519A		**Q St, Downtown Sacramento**
	Lodg	E: The Inn & Spa at Parkside
	Other	E: to State Capitol, City Hall

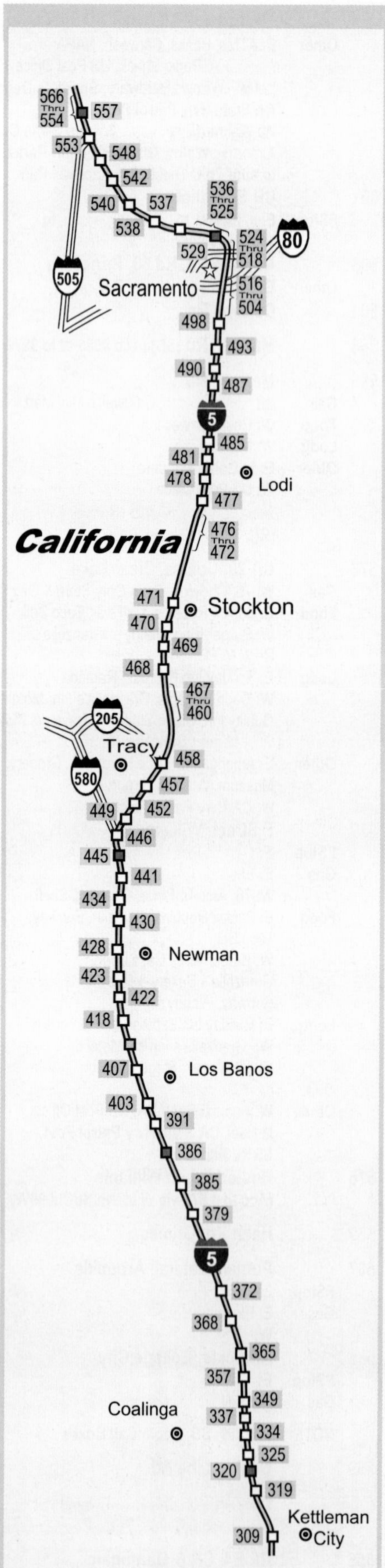

EXIT		CALIFORNIA
518		**to US 50, I-80W Bus, San Francisco, CA 99S, Fresno** (NB) (End run w/I-99)
516		**Sutterville Rd**
	Other	E: Sacramento Zoo, William Land Muni Golf Course, Sacramento City College
515/B		**Seamas Ave, Fruitridge Rd**
514		**43rd Ave, Riverside Blvd** (SB)
	Gas	E: 76
	Other	E: Sacramento Exec Airport✈
		W: Greenhaven Animal Hospital♥
513		**Florin Rd**
	Gas	E: ArcoAmPm, Chevron
	Food	E: Rosalinda's Mexican Rest, Round Table Pizza
		W: Cold Stone Creamery, Panda Garden, Shari's Rest, Starbucks, Subway, Wendy's
	Other	E: ATMs, Banks, CVS, Dollar Tree, Grocery, Laundry Kragen Auto Parts, Pharmacy, to Big O Tires
		W: Big 5 Sporting Goods, Grocery, RiteAid
512		**Pocket Rd, Meadowview Rd, Sacramento, Freeport**
	Gas	E: Shell, Valero
	Food	E: Baskin Robbins, IHOP, Long John Silver McDonald's, Starbucks, Wendy's
	Other	E: Carwash/Shell, Home Depot, Staples
508		**Laguna Blvd, Elk Grove**
	Gas	E: Chevron, Shell
	Food	E: KFC/A&W, McDonald's/Chevron, Starbucks, Subway, Wendy's
	Lodg	E: Extended Stay America♥, Hampton Inn
	Other	E: Auto Services, Goodyear, Jiffy Lube, Bowling, Abel Pet Clinic♥
506		**Elk Grove Blvd**
	Gas	E: ArcoAmPm, Chevron, Shell
	Food	E: Carl's Jr, Original Pete's Pizza, Quiznos, Wasabi Japanese Sushi Seafood
	Lodg	E: Holiday Inn Express
	Other	E: Just for Cats Vet Hospital♥
504		**Hood Franklin Rd, Elk Grove**
	NOTE:	**SB: Gusty Wind Area next 3 mi**
498		**Twin Cities Rd, Walnut Grove**
	Other	E: to Franklin Field✈
493		**Walnut Grove Rd, N Thornton Rd, Thornton, Lodi**
	Gas	E: Chevron◈
	Food	E: Subway/Pizza/Chevron
	Other	E: Grocery, US Post Office
490		**Peltier Rd**
487		**Turner Rd, Lodi, to CA 99**
485		**CA 12, S - Lodi, N - Fairfield**
	FStop	E: Flag City Chevron Shell
	TStop	E: PacPride/3 B's Truck & Auto Plaza/ RoadysTS/76 (Scales), Flying J Travel Plaza #5079 (Scale)
	Gas	E: ArcoAmPm◈
	Food	E: Rocky's Rest/Subway/3B's TP, CountryMkt/FastFood/FJ TP, Burger King, Carl's Jr/Starbucks/Flag City Chevron, McDonald's/ Taco Bell/Wendy's/Flag City Shell, Subway/Arco
	Lodg	E: Best Western/Microtel♥/Flag City
	TServ	E: 3 B's TP/Tires, ProFleet Truck Lube
	TWash	E: Blue Beacon TW/FJ TP

◈= Regular Gas Stations with Diesel ▲ = RV Friendly Locations ♥= Pet Friendly Locations
Red print shows large vehicle parking / access on site or nearby Brown Print = Campgrounds / RV PARKS

EXIT		CALIFORNIA
	Other	E: Laundry/3B's TP, Laundry/WiFi/ LP/RVDump/FJ TP, LP/Flag City Chevron & Shell, Michael-David Winery, Flag City RV Resort/LP▲, to Lodi RV Center, Addt'l RV Services N on CA 99, W: to 5mi: Tower Park Resort & Marina▲
481		**Eight Mile Rd, Stockton**
	Gas	W: Chevron◈
	Food	W: Hawaiian BBQ, Jack in the Box, Italian Café, Moo Moo's Burger Barn, Panera Bread, Panda Express, Qdoba Mexican, Raw Sushi Bistro, Starbucks, Subway, Taco Bell, Wing Stop
	Lodg	W: Vagabond Inn
	Med	W: + Trinity Urgent Care
	Other	E: Oak Grove Reg'l Park, to Kingdon Airpark✈ W: Banks, Borders, Lowe's, Office Depot, PetSmart♥, Radio Shack, Sports Authority Target, Verizon
478		**Hammer Lane, Stockton (NO Trucks)**
	Gas	E: ArcoAmPm, 76◈ W: Chevron◈, Quik Stop
	Food	E: Japanese Sushi, KFC, Little Caesar's Pizza, McDonald's,Subway W: Burger King, Jack in the Box, Lupe's Mexican Rest, Subway, Taco Bell
	Lodg	W: Americas Best Value Inn
	Other	E: ATMs, AutoZone, Carwash, Laundromat, Park & Ride, Radio Shack, Smart Foods Grocery/Pharmacy, W: ATMs, Launderland
477		**Benjamin Holt Dr, Stockton (NO Trucks)**
	Gas	E: ArcoAmPm, Chevron◈ W: Shell◈
	Food	E: Pizza Guys W: Lyon's, McDonald's, Subway
	Lodg	E: Motel 6♥
	Other	W: Ace Hardware, Village Veterinary Hospital♥,
476		**March Lane, Stockton**
	Gas	E: 7-11 W: 76◈, Safeway
	Food	E: Applebee's, Black Angus, Carl's Jr, Denny's, Jack in the Box, McDonald's, Red Lobster, Taco Bell, Tony Roma, Wendy's W: Carrow's, In N Out Burger, Old Spaghetti Factory, Round Table Pizza, Starbucks, Subway, Wong's Chinese
	Lodg	E: Comfort Inn, Hilton♥ W: Best Western, Courtyard, Extended Stay America, La Quinta Inn♥, Quality Inn, Residence Inn
	Med	E: + Medical Center
	Other	E: Grocery, Longs Drugs, Office Depot, Pharmacy, Target, Stores, Malls W: Big Lots, Home Depot, Office Max, Safeway
475		**Alpine Ave, Country Club Blvd**
474B		**Country Club Blvd, Alpine Ave**
	Gas	E: Shell W: 7-11, USA, Safeway
	Food	W: Round Table Pizza, Subway
	Other	W: Big Lots, Safeway, Pharmacy, Univ of the Pacific
474A		**Monte Diablo**
473		**Pershing Ave, Stockton**
	Gas	E: ArcoAmPm
	Food	E: Catfish Café
	Lodg	W: Red Roof Inn♥

EXIT		CALIFORNIA
	Med	E: + Dameron Hospital, + SOS Medical Clinic
	Other	E: Laundromat, CalState Univ W: West Marine
472		**CA 4E, Fresno Ave, Downtown**
471		**CA 4E, Charter Way**
	TStop	W: PacPr/Vanco Truck & Auto Plaza/76 (Scales)
	Gas	E: Chevron, Shell, United W: ArcoAmPm◈, Valero
	Food	E: Burger King, Church's Chicken, Denny's, Little Caesar's Pizza, McDonald's, Quiznos W: Jack in the Box, Taco Bell
	Lodg	E: Budget Inn, Days Inn♥ W: Motel 6♥
	TWash	E: Truck Tub Truck Wash
	TServ	W: Holt Bros, International Trucks, Peterbilt, Vanco TP, Interstate Truck Center, Central Valley Trailer Repair
	Other	E: ATMs, Banks, Amtrak, AutoZone, Auto Repairs, Carwash, Grocery, Kragen Auto Parts, Pharmacy, Tires, U-Haul, Vet♥, US Post Office W: Laundry/Vanco TP, Les Schwab Tires
470		**8th St, Stockton**
	Gas	W: Shell
	Food	W: Subway/Shell
	Lodg	W: Econo Lodge
469		**Downing Ave**
	Food	W: Mountain Mike's Pizza, Subway
	Lodg	E: Motel 6
468		**French Camp Turnpike**
	FStop	E: PacPr/Togo's/TigerExpr/76
	Food	E: FastFood/Rest/PacPr/TigerExp
	Med	W: + San Joaquin Hospital
	Other	E: Pan Pacific RV Center
467B		**Mathews Rd, French Camp**
	FStop	E: CFN/Exxon
	Med	W: + San Joaquin Hospital
	Other	E: to Stockton Metro Airport✈, to French Camp RV Park Resort & Golf Course▲
467A		**El Dorado St, French Camp (NB)**
	Other	E: Bennett's RV Sales & Service
465		**Roth Rd, Lathrop**
	TServ	E: Arrow Truck Sales, Peterbilt, Kenworth, Freightliner, Repairs
	Other	E: MIL/Sharp RV Park▲
463		**Lathrop Rd, to CA 99, Lathrop**
	FStop	E: Joe's Travel Plaza (Scales)
	Gas	E: Chevron, Valero, Tower Mart, United Food & Fuel/Citgo
	Food	E: Subway/Joe's TP, Applebee's, Carl's Jr, Country Kitchen/Days Inn, Denny's, Isadores Rest, Jack in the Box, Japanese Bistro, Little Caesars Pizza, Royal Pizza Cafe, Starbucks, Subway
	Lodg	E: Best Western, Comfort Inn, Days Inn♥, Hampton Inn, Holiday Inn Express
	Other	E: ATM's, Banks, Walgreen's, to Best RV Center
462		**Louise Ave, Lathrop**
	Gas	E: 76, ArcoAmPm, Circle K
	Food	E: Carl's Jr, Jack in the Box, McDonald's, Quiznos, Taco Bell
	Lodg	E: Hampton Inn, Holiday Inn Express
461		**CA 120E, S - Manteca, N - Sonora**
	Other	E: to Oakwood Lake Resort Camping▲, to Yosemite
460		**Manthey Rd (SB), Mossdale Rd(NB)**
	Gas	E: ArcoAmPm◈

EXIT		CALIFORNIA
(458B)		**Jct I-205W, to I-580 (SB)**
458A		**11th St, Tracy (SB)**
	FStop	W: Pacific Pride
	Other	W: to Tracy Defense Depot, The Orchard Campground▲
457		**Kasson Rd, Tracy**
	FStop	W: CFN/Valley Pacific #151
452		**CA 33S, S Ahern Rd, Patterson, Vernalis**
449B		**CA 132W, W Vernalis Rd, to San Francisco**
	Other	W: to The Orchard Campground▲
449A		**CA 132E, W Vernalis Rd, Modesto**
(446)		**Jct I-580W, Tracy, San Francisco (NB, Left Exit)**
(445)		**Westley Rest Area (Both dir) (RR, Ph, Pic, Vend, RV Water/Dump NB)**
441		**Howard Rd, Ingram Creek, Westley**
	TStop	E: Westley Triangle Travel Plaza (Scales), Joe's Travel Plaza (Scales)
	Gas	E: 76◈, Chevron◈ W: Shell◈, Valero◈
	Food	E: Rest/Westley TP, Quiznos/Joe TP, McDonald's, Carls Jr W: Ingram Creek Rest
	Lodg	E: America's Best Value Inn♥, Days Inn, Econo Lodge, Holiday Inn Express
	TServ	W: Westley TP/Tires, Joes TP/Tires, Cummins West
	TWash	E: Westley TP, Joes TP, A-1 Quality Truck Wash, G & S Truck Wash
	Other	E: Laundry/Westley TP, Laundry/WiFi/Joes TP,
434		**Sperry Ave, Diablo Grand Pkwy, Patterson, Modesto**
	Gas	E: 76◈, ArcoAmPm
	Food	E: Subway/76, Carl's Jr, Denny's, Del Lago Steakhouse, Jack in the Box, KFC, Quiznos, Starbucks, Wendy's
	Lodg	E: Best Western♥
	Other	E: Kit Fox RV Park▲, CarWash, Grocery
(430)		**Vista Point (NB)**
428		**Fink Rd, Crows Landing**
	Other	E: Naval Aux Landing Field✈
423		**Stuhr Rd, Newman**
	Med	E: + Hospital
(422)		**Vista Point (SB)**
418		**CA 140E, Gustine, Merced**
	Gas	E: 76◈, Shell
(417)		**Picnic Area**
(409)		**Inspection Station (Both dir)**
407		**CA 33, Gilroy, Santa Nell Blvd Santa Nella, Gustine**
	TStop	E: Travel Center of America #163/76 (Scales), Love's Travel Stop #441 (Scales) W: Pac Pr/Rotten Robbie #59 Truck & Auto Plaza (Scales)
	Gas	E: ArcoAmPm, Chevron, Shell◈ W: Shell◈, Valero◈
	Food	E: Rest/FastFood/TA TC, Del Taco/Love's TS, Anderson's Pea Soup Rest, Burger King, Carl's Jr, Jack in the Box/Shell W: Denny's, McDonald's, Quiznos, Starbucks, Taco Bell

◈= Regular Gas Stations with Diesel ▲ = RV Friendly Locations ♥= Pet Friendly Locations
Red print shows large vehicle parking / access on site or nearby Brown Print = Campgrounds / RV PARKS

EXIT		CALIFORNIA
	Lodg	**E:** Best Western, Holiday Inn Express♥ **W:** Motel 6♥, Ramada Inn
	TServ	**E:** TA TC
	TWash	**E:** TA TC
	Other	**E:** Laundry/WiFi/**RVDump**/TA TC, WiFi/Pilot TC **W: Santa Nella RV Park ▲**, Golf Course, Los Banos Muni Airport✈
403B		**CA 152W, Monterey, Hollister Gustine, San Jose, Gilroy**
	TStop	**W:** Petro 2 #46 (Scales)
	Food	**W:** PetroDiner/Petro2
	TServ	**W:** Petro2 SC/Tires
	Other	**W:** Laundry/WiFi/Petro SC, **to San Luis RV Resort▲**
403A		**CA 152E, Los Banos (SB), CA 33S (NB)**
	FStop	**W: (5 mi on CA 152E)** Pacific Pride
	Med	**E: + Hospital**
391		**CA 165N, Mercy Springs Rd**
	Gas	**W:** Shell
(386)		**Rest Area (Both dir) (RR, Ph, Pic, Pet, RVDump/Water-NB)**
385		**Nees Ave, Firebaugh**
	FStop	**W:** MBP Firebaugh Travel Plaza (Scales)
	Food	**W:** FastFood/MBP/Firebaugh TP
379		**Shields Ave, Mendota**
372		**Russell Ave**
368		**Panoche Rd, Mendota**
	FStop	**W:** Shell
	Gas	**W:** 76◈, Chevron, Mobil
	Food	**W:** Rest/BW, McDonald's/Chevron, TacoBell/Mobil, Apricot Tree Rest
	Lodg	**W:** Best Western
	Other	**E:** Cardella Winery
365		**Manning Ave, San Joaquin**
357		**Kamm Ave, Mendota**
349		**CA 33N, Derrick Ave**
337		**CA 33S, CA 145N, Coalinga**
334		**CA 198, Doris Ave, Coalinga, Lemoore, Hanford, Huron**
	FStop	**E:** Harris Ranch Shell, CFN/WHillsOil
	Gas	**W:** 76/Circle K, Chevron, Mobil◈
	Food	**E:** Rest/Subway/Harris Ranch Inn **W:** Burger King, Carls Jr, Denny's, McDonald's, Oriental Express, Red Robin, Taco Bell
	Lodg	**E:** Harris Ranch Inn **W:** Best Western♥, Motel 6♥, Travelodge♥
	Med	**W: + Coalinga Reg'l Med Center**
	Other	**E:** Harris Ranch Airport✈
325		**Jayne Ave, Coalinga, Huron**
	TStop	**W:** Jayne Travel Center/Shell
	Gas	**W:** ArcoAmPm
	Med	**W: + Coalinga State Hospital**
	TServ	**W:** Jayne TC/Tires
	Other	**W: CA Hwy Patrol Post**, State Prison, **Sommerville Almond Tree RV Park▲**
(320)		**Coalinga Rest Area (Both dir) (RR, Phone, Pic, Vend, Pet, RV Water)**
319		**CA 269, Lassen Ave, Avenal**
	FStop	**E:** Valero
	TStop	**W:** Hillcrest Travel Plaza/76 (Scales)
	Food	**W:** Rest/FF/Hillcrest TP
	Other	**W:** Laundry/WiFi/Hillcrest TP

Personal Notes

EXIT		CALIFORNIA
309		**CA 41, Avenal, Kettleman City**
	FStop	**E:** Valero Truck Stop (Scales), CFN/W Hills
	Gas	**E:** Chevron, Exxon◈, Mobil◈, Shell◈
	Food	**E:** Burger King, Carl's Jr, In 'n Out Burger, Jack in the Box, McDonald's/Chevron, Mike's Roadhouse Café, PizzaHut/Taco Bell, Quiznos, Subway/Exxon
	Lodg	**E:** Best Western♥, Super 8♥
	TServ	**E:** Kettleman City Tire & Repair Service
	Med	**W: + Hospital**
	Other	**E: Travelers RV Park▲**
305		**Utica Ave**
288		**Twissleman Rd, Lost Hills**
278		**CA 46, Paso Robles Hwy, Lost Hills, Lemore, Stanford, Wasco**
	FStop	**E:** Buford Star Mart **W:** Lost Hills Travel Center/Arco
	TStop	**W:** Pilot Travel Center #154 (Scales), Love's Travel Stop #230 (Scales)
	Gas	**W:** 76◈, Chevron◈, Mobil◈, Shell, Valero◈
	Food	**E:** Subway/Buford Star Mart **W:** Wendy's/Pilot TC, Arby's/Love's TS, Rest/Lost Hills TC, Carl's Jr, Denny's, Jack in the Box, McDonald's/Mobil, Quiznos/76
	Lodg	**W:** Days Inn, Motel 6♥
	TServ	**W:** Lost Hills TC
	Other	**W:** Laundry/WiFi/Pilot TC, Laundry/ WiFi/**RVDump**/Love's TS, **Lost Hills RV Park▲**
268		**Lerdo Hwy, Shafter**
	Other	**W:** Buttonwillow Raceway Park ▲

EXIT		CALIFORNIA
263		**Buttonwillow, McKittrick (SB)**
	Lodg	**W:** Buena Vista Motel
262		**7th Standard Rd (NB)**
(259)		**Buttonwillow Rest Area (Both dir) (RR, Phone, Picnic, Pet)**
	NOTE:	**Severe Dust Area next 40 miles.**
257		**CA 58, Blue Star Memorial Hwy, McKittrick Hwy, Rosedale Hwy, to Bakersfield, McKittrick**
	FStop	**E:** Chevron (Scales), Speedy Fuel (Scales)
	TStop	**E:** Travel Center of America #160 (Scales)
	Gas	**E:** ArcoAmPm, Chevron, Mobil, Shell◈
	Food	**E:** CntryPr/PHut/TBell/TA TC, Carl's Jr, Denny's, McDonald's, Starbucks, Taste of India, Titas Pupuseria, Subway, Willow Ranch BBQ
	Lodg	**E:** Econo Lodge, Motel 6♥, Red Roof Inn♥, Super 8♥
	TServ	**E:** TA TC/Tires, Cummins West
	TWash	**E:** TA TC, Chevron FS, Castro Tire & Truck Wash
	Other	**E:** Laundry/Med/WiFi/**RVDump**/TA TC
253		**Stockdale Hwy, Kern City**
	TStop	**E:** EZ Trip Auto Truck Stop/Shell
	Food	**E:** IHOP, Jack in the Box, Rest/EZ Trip
	Lodg	**E:** Americas Best Inn, Best Western, Rodeway Inn♥
	Other	**E: CA State Hwy Patrol Post**
246		**CA 43, Taft, Maricopa**
244		**CA 119, Taft Hwy, Bakersfield, Pumpkin Center, Lamont**
	Gas	**E:** Mobil◈ **W:** Chevron◈
239		**CA 223, Bear Mountain Blvd**
234		**Old River Rd**
228		**Copus Rd, Bakersfield**
225		**CA 166, Maricopa Hwy, Mettler, Maricopa (Services approx 5mi E in Mettler)**
221		**CA 99N, Bakersfield, Fresno (NB, Left Exit)**
219B		**Laval Rd West**
	TStop	**W:** Petro Stopping Center #27/Mobil(Scales)
	Food	**W:** IronSkillet/PHut/Subw/Wend/BskRob/ Petro SC, In N Out Burger, McDonald's, Panda Express, Starbucks
	Lodg	**W:** Best Western
	TServ	**W:** Petro SC/Tires
	TWash	**W:** Blue Beacon TW/Petro SC
	Other	**W:** BarbrSh/Laundry/WiFi/Petro SC
219A		**Laval Rd East, Wheeler Ridge**
	TStop	**E:** Travel Center of America #38/Chevron (Scales)
	Gas	**E:** BP
	Food	**E:** BKing/Subw/TBell/TA TC,
	TServ	**E:** TA TC
	Other	**E:** Laundry/WiFi/**RVDump**/TA TC
(218)		**Inspection Station (SB)**
215		**Grapevine Rd, Lebec, Bakersfield**
	FStop	**W:** Shell
	Gas	**E:** Mobil **W:** Circle K/76◈
	Food	**E:** Denny's, Jack in the Box **W:** Don Perico Rest, Taco Bell/Shell
	Lodg	**W:** Ramada Ltd

◈= Regular Gas Stations with Diesel ▲ = RV Friendly Locations ♥= Pet Friendly Locations
Red print shows large vehicle parking / access on site or nearby Brown Print = Campgrounds / RV PARKS

EXIT	CALIFORNIA
210	**Fort Tejon Rd**
TServ	W: B & J Heavy Duty Towing
(209)	**Brake Inspection** (Both dir)
(208)	**Rest Area** (SB) (RR, Ph, Pic, Vend, RVDump/Water)
207	**Lebec Rd, Lebec**
Other	E: CA State Hwy Patrol Post W: US Post Office
(206)	**Rest Area** (NB) (RR, Ph, Pic, Vend, RVDump/Water)
205	**Frazier Mountain Park Rd, Lebec**
FStop	W: Frazier Park Chevron/CFN
TStop	W: Flying J Travel Plaza #5055 (Scales)
Gas	W: ArcoAmPm, Shell
Food	W: Cookery/FF/FJ TP, Subway/Chevron, Quiznos/Shell, Jack in the Box, Los Pinos Mexican Rest, Rocky's Rest
Lodg	W: BestRestInn/FJ TP, Holiday Inn Express
TServ	W: Bell Automotive & Diesel Repair, FJ TP
Other	W: Laundry/BarbSh/WiFi/LP/RVDump/ FJ TP, Auto Services, Towing, CA State Hwy Patrol Post
(204)	**Truck Break Off Ramp** (SB)
202	**Gorman Rd, to Hungry Valley**
Gas	E: 76, Chevron◈ W: Valero
Food	E: Carl's Jr, Sizzler W: McDonald's
Lodg	E: Econo Lodge♥
199	**CA 138E, Lancaster Rd, Lancaster, Palmdale** (SB)
198	**Quail Lake Rd, Coalinga** (SB)
198B	**Quail Lake Rd** (NB)
198A	**CA 138E** (NB)
195	**Smoky Bear Rd, Pyramid Lake**
Other	W: Pyramid Lake RV Park▲
191	**Vista Del Lago Rd**
(186)	**Brake Inspection** (SB)
NOTE:	SB: Begin Motorist Call Boxes
(185)	**Truck Break Off Ramp** (SB)
183	**Templin Hwy**
176	**Lake Hughes Rd, Castaic** (SB)
TStop	E: NB Access via Ex #176B: Pilot Travel Center #372 (Scales), NB Access via Ex #176A: Castaic Truck Stop
Gas	E: 7-11, Alliance W: 76/Circle K, Mobil
Food	E: Wendy's/Pilot TC, Burger King, Carl's Jr, Denny's, Domino's Pizza, Del Taco, Foster's, McDonald's, Quzinos, Starbucks W: Jack in the Box, PizzaHut/TacoBell/76
Lodg	E: Castaic Inn, Comfort Inn, Days Inn, Econo Lodge, Rodeway Inn♥ W: Comfort Suites
TServ	E: Benny's Tire Service,Canyon Comm'l Tire & Towing, Castaic Truck Repair
TWash	E: Castaic TW
Other	E: Laundry/WiFi/Pilot TC, Castaic Animal Hospital♥, Grocery, Kragen's Auto Parts, RiteAid, US Post Office W: Auto Repair, Carwash, Ralph's, Tires, Towing, Walgreen's

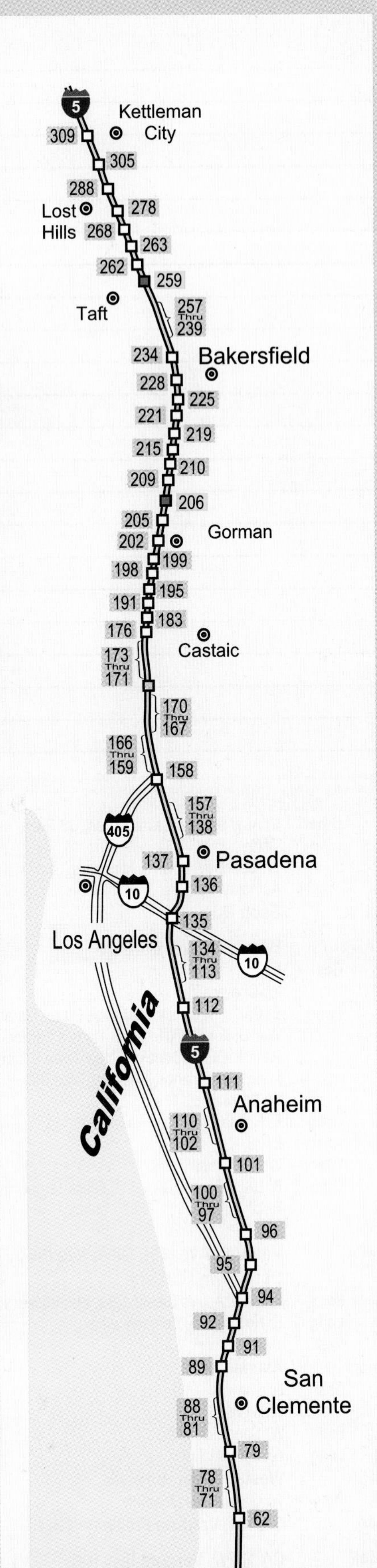

EXIT	CALIFORNIA
176B	**Lake Hughes Rd** (NB)
TStop	E: Pilot Travel Center #372 (Scales)
176A	**Parker Rd, Castaic** (NB)
TStop	E: Castaic Truck Stop
173	**Hasley Canyon Rd**
172	**CA 126W, Ventura**
Lodg	E: Courtyard, Embassy Suites
171	**Rye Canyon Rd** (SB)
FStop	W: Valencia Chevron
Gas	W: Shell
Food	W: Del Taco, Jack in the Box, Starbucks/ Subway/Shell
Other	W: Carwash/Shell, Six Flags Magic Mtn
(171)	**Inspection Station** (NB)
170	**CA 126, Magic Mountain Pkwy**
Gas	W: Chevron
Food	E: Rest/Best Western, Denny's, Wendy's
Food	W: El Torito Mexican, Marie Callendar's, Red Lobster, Wendy's
Lodg	E: Best Western, Holiday Inn Express W: Hilton Garden Inn
Other	E: to Target, W: CA State Hwy Patrol Post, Six Flags of California
169	**Valencia Blvd**
Food	W: Nick & Willy's Pizza, Panda Express, Starbucks, Subway, Sushi
Other	W: Albertson's/Pharmacy
168	**McBean Pkwy, Stevenson Ranch**
Gas	E: Shell
Food	W: Chili's, Chuck E Cheese, Claim Jumper, Pick Up Stix, Starbucks, Subway, Wood Ranch BBQ & Grill
Med	E: + Henry Mayo Newhall Memorila Hospital
Other	E: Staples
Other	W: Von's/Pharmacy, World Market
167	**Lyons Ave, Pico Canyon Rd**
Gas	E: 76/Circle K, Chevron, Exxon, Shell◈ W: ArcoAmPm, Mobil, Shell
Food	E: Pizza, Burger King W: Carl's Jr, Chuys, CoCo's, Denny's, El Pollo Loco , IHOP, In N Out Burger, Jack in the Box, McDonald's, Outback Steakhouse, Subway, Taco Bell, Yamato Japanese
Lodg	W: Comfort Inn, Fairfield Inn, Hampton Inn, La Quinta Inn♥, Residence Inn
Other	W: Carwash, FedEx Office, PetSmart♥, Jiffy Lube, Ralph's/Pharmacy, Walmart, RV Service, Camping World, Stier's RV
166	**Calgrove Blvd, Stevenson Ranch**
163	**CA 14, Truck Route** (SB)
162	**CA 14N, Palmdale, Lancaster**
161B	**Balboa Blvd** (SB), **Jct I-210, Pasadena, San Fernando** (NB)
(161A)	**Jct I-210, Pasadena** (SB), **Truck Lane Off Ramp** (NB)
(160A)	**Jct I-210, San Francisco, Pasadena**
159	**Roxford St** (SB)
Gas	E: Chevron◈, Mobil◈
Food	E: Denny's, McDonald's
Lodg	E: Motel 6♥
159B	**Roxford St West** (NB)
159A	**Roxford St East** (NB)

◈= Regular Gas Stations with Diesel ▲ = RV Friendly Locations ♥= Pet Friendly Locations
Red print shows large vehicle parking / access on site or nearby Brown Print = Campgrounds / RV PARKS

EXIT	CALIFORNIA

(158) **Jct I-405S, San Diego Freeway (SB)**
Truck Lane Off Ramp (NB)

157 **San Fernando Mission Blvd (SB)**

157A **Brand Blvd (NB)**

157B **SF Mission Blvd (NB)**
- Gas: E: 76, Chevron, Mobil
- Food: E: Ameci Pizza, Carl's Jr, In N Out Burger, Popeye's
- Med: E: + Hospital, Mission Park Medical Center
- Other: E: Laundromat, Auto Zone, RiteAid

156B **CA 118E (SB), Paxton St (NB)**

156A **Paxton St (SB), CA 118 (NB)**

155B **Van Nuys Blvd (NB, diff reaccess)**
- Gas: E: 76, Mobil
- Food: E: KFC, McDonald's, Pizza Hut
- Other: E: Auto Zone

155A **Terra Bella St (NB)**
- Gas: E: ArcoAmPm, Citgo

154 **Osborne St, Arleta**
- Gas: E: 76, ArcoAmPm
  W: 7-11, ArcoAmPm, Exxon, Mobil
- Food: W: CA Deli Mart, NY Giant Pizza
- Other: E: Big Lots, Grocery, Target
  W: Laundry, Pharmacy, US Post Office

153B **CA 170, Hollywood Freeway (SB), Branford St (NB)**

153A **Sheldon St**
- Med: E: + Pacifica Hospital of the Valley

152 **Lankershim Blvd, Sun Valley**
- FStop: W: Super Fine Truck Stop
- Food: W: FastFood/Superfine TS

151 **Penrose St**

150 **Sunland Blvd (SB)**

150B **Sunland Blvd (NB)**
- Gas: E: 7-11, 76, Mobil
  W: Shell
- Food: E: Acapulco Mexican, Carl's Jr, El Pollo Loco, Golden Wok Chinese, Quiznos, Subway, Taco Bell
  W: Dimion's, Domino's, McDonald's
- Lodg: E: Scottish Inns
- Med: W: + Med-Cal Clinic
- Other: W: Laundromat

150A **Glen Oaks Blvd (NB)**
- Gas: E: ArcoAmPm

149 **Hollywood Way, Burbank**
- Gas: W: Shell◈
- Other: W: U-Haul, Bob Hope Airport

148 **Buena Vista St**
- Gas: E: Arco
  W: Exxon◈, World Gas
- Food: W: Jack in the Box
- Lodg: E: Bel Vista Motel
  W: Quality Inn, Ramada Inn

147C **San Fernando, Empire Ave (NB)**

147B **San Fernando Blvd, Empire Ave (SB), Lincoln St (NB)**
- Gas: E: Sevan◈
- Food: W: Home Town Buffet, Olive Garden, Outback Steakhouse, Sharkie's Woodfire Mexican Rest, Sbarros, Starbucks, Subway, Wendy's
- Lodg: E: Scott Motel
  W: Courtyard, Extended Stay America

Personal Notes

EXIT	CALIFORNIA

- Other: E: Auto Service/Sevan, Tires, US Post Office
  W: Best Buy, Lowe's, Michael's, Sports Authority, Staples, Target/Pharmacy

147A **Scott Rd**

146B **Burbank Blvd, Burbank**
- Gas: E: 76
  W: Chevron
- Food: E: Carl's Jr, Chuck E Cheese Pizza, Great Wall Buffet, El Pollo Loco, Harry's Family Rest, IHOP,McDonald's, New Town Buffet, Popeye's, Quiznos, Subway, Taco Bell
  W: Subway
- Lodg: E: Holiday Inn
- AServ: E: 76
- TServ: W: Fitzpatrick Trailer
- Other: E: B&N, CompUSA, CVS, Office Depot, Ralph's/Pharmacy, Radio Shack, Von's/Pharmacy

146A **Verdugo Ave (SB), Olive Ave (NB) Downtown Burbank**
- Food: E: Black Angus Steakhouse, Fuddrucker's
- Lodg: E: Holiday Inn, Residence Inn
- Med: E: + Hospital

145B **Alameda Ave**
- Gas: E: Chevron
  W: Mobil, Shell
- Food: W: Sandwich Shop
- Lodg: W: Burbank Inn

145A **Western Ave, Burbank**
- Other: W: Gene Autry Museum

144 **CA 134, Ventura Freeway (SB)**

144B **CA 134W, Ventura Fwy (NB)**

144A **CA 134E, Ventura Fwy (NB)**

EXIT	CALIFORNIA

142 **Colorado St, Glendale**

141 **Los Feliz Blvd, Griffith Park Dr (SB)**

141B **Griffith Park Dr (NB)**

141A **Los Feliz Blvd (NB)**
- Gas: E: 76, Arco, Shell
- Food: E: Del Taco, Kathy's Kitchen
- Lodg: E: Los Feliz Motel
- Med: E: + Hospital
- Other: W: Griffith Park, Zoo

140B **Glendale Blvd (SB)**

140A **Fletcher Dr (SB)**

140 **Glendale Blvd (NB)**
- Gas: E: 76, Shell
  W: ArcoAmPm, Chevron
- Food: E: McDonald's
  W: KFC

139 **CA 2, Glendale Freeway (SB)**

139B **CA 2W, Echo Park (NB)**

139A **CA 2, Glendale Freeway E (NB)**

138 **Stadium Way Connections**
- Other: E: Home Depot
  W: Dodger Stadium

137B **CA-110, Pasadena Freeway S (SB)**
CA-110, Pasadena Frwy N (NB)

137A **CA-110, Pasadena Frwy N (SB), Figueroa St (NB)**

136 **Main St (SB)**

136B **Broadway (NB)**

136A **Main St (NB)**
- Gas: E: 76, Chevron
- Food: E: McDonald's, Mr Pizza

135C **Mission Rd (SB), Jct I-10E, San Bernardino Fwy (NB, end run w/I-10)**
- Gas: E: 76, Chevron
- Food: E: McDonald's, Jack in the Box
- Lodg: E: Howard Johnson
- Med: E: + Hospital

(135B) **Jct I-10E, San Bernardino Freeway, (SB), Caesar Chavez Ave (NB)**
- Med: W: + Hospital

135A **4th St (SB, Begin run with I-10WB)**

134E **CA 60E, Pomona, Golden State Freeway (SB)**

134D **CA 60E, Soto St (SB)**

134C **Soto St (SB), 7th St (NB Left Exit)**

134B **CA 60E (SB, End with I-10 WB)**
Soto St (NB, Begin run with I-10 WB)

134A **Soto St (SB), CA 60W, Santa Monica Freeway (NB)**

133 **Euclid Ave (SB), Grand Vista Ave (NB), Los Angeles**
- FStop: E: Speedy Fuel
- Gas: E: ArcoAmPm
  W: Mobil, Shell
- Med: W: + Hospital

132 **Indiana St (SB), Calzona St**
- Gas: E: ArcoAmPm

131B **Ditman Ave (SB)**

131A **Olympic Blvd (SB)**

EXIT — CALIFORNIA

131 — Indiana St (NB)

(130C) — Jct I-710N, Pasadena (NB, Left Exit)

(130B) — Jct I-710, Long Beach Freeway (SB), Eastern Ave (NB)

130A — Triggs St (SB), Atlantic Blvd S (NB)
- Gas — W: 76
- Food — W: Denny's

129 — Atlantic Blvd (NB), Eastern Ave
- Gas — W: Chevron
- Food — W: Denny's, Steven's Steakhouse
- Other — E: Outlet Mall

128B — Washington Blvd, Commerce
- FStop — E: Unified Gas, Valero (Scales) Commerce Truck Stop (Scales)
- Gas — E: Chevron
- Food — E: Gibbs Coffee Shop, McDonald's
- Lodg — E: Commerce Hotel, Radisson
- AServ — E: Chevron
- TServ — E: Westrux Int'l; W: CA Transport Refrigeration
- Other — E: Mall, **Commerce Casino**, Firestone, Office Depot

128A — Garfield Ave (NB), Bandini Blvd
- Other — E: Home Depot, Office Depot; W: Staples

126B — Slauson Ave, Montebello
- FStop — E: DeWitt Petroleum (Scales)
- Gas — E: Shell◈, Valero◈; W: ArcoAmPm
- Food — E: Burger King, Ozzie's Diner, Starbucks; W: Denny's, Jack in the Box, Mexican Rest
- Lodg — E: Best Western, Best Star Inn, Super 8; W: Best Value Inn, Ramada Inn
- TServ — E: ENGS Motor Truck; W: Cummins Cal Pacific
- TWash — E: Calivas Truck Wash/DeWitt Petro
- Other — E: Auto Service/Valero

126A — Paramount Blvd, Downey
- Gas — E: Shell
- Food — E: China Kitchen, Jack in the Box
- Lodg — E: Super 8

125 — Lakewood Blvd, Rosemead Blvd CA 19, Downey
- Gas — E: Mobil, Thrifty; W: 76
- Food — E: Arthur's Rest, Starbucks, Taco Bell; W: Jack in the Box, Little Caesar's Pizza, McDonald's, Golden Wok, Chris & Pitts BBQ, Subway
- Lodg — E: Econo Lodge, GuestHouse Inn
- Med — W: + Downey Reg'l Med Center
- Other — E: Auto Service, Grocery, Tires

(124) — Jct I-605, San Gabriel River Frwy

123 — Florence Ave

122 — Imperial Hwy, Pioneer Blvd, Norwalk
- Gas — E: Chevron; W: Shell
- Food — E: IHOP, McDonald's, Red Lobster, Subway, Wendy's; W: Denny's, Pizza Hut, Sizzler
- Lodg — E: Best Western; W: Anchor Inn, Comfort Inn, Rodeway Inn
- Other — E: Grocery, RiteAid, Target; W: **Walmart SC**

121 — Norwalk Blvd, San Antonio Dr
- Gas — E: Chevron, Shell; W: 76

EXIT — CALIFORNIA

- Food — E: Jack in the Box, KFC, McDonald's, Outback Steakhouse
- Lodg — E: Sheraton; W: Marriott

120 — Rosecrans Ave, La Mirada (SB)

120B — Firestone Blvd, CA 42 (NB Left Exit)

120A — Rosecrans Ave, La Mirada (NB)
- Gas — E: Valero◈; W: ArcoAmPm
- Food — E: Burger King, Jim's Burgers,KFC, Pizza Hut/TacoBell,Renu Nakorn Thai Rest, Starbucks; W: El Pollo Loco
- Other — E: Carwash; W: Auto Services, Budget RAC, **El Monte RV Center**

119 — Carmenita Rd, Buena Park
- Gas — E: 76◈; W: ArcoAmPm, Mobil
- Food — E: Burger King, Carrow's, Jack in the Box; W: Carl's Jr, China Express
- Lodg — E: Motel 6♥; W: Budget Inn, Dynasty Suites
- TServ — E: Carmenita Truck Service; W: Ryan's Truck Collision Repair Center
- Other — E: Lowe's

118 — Valley View Blvd, La Mirada
- Gas — E: ArcoAmPm◈; W: Chevron, Shell◈
- Food — E: Carl's Jr, In 'n Out Burger, Red Robin, Starbucks, Subway; W: Denny's, El Pollo Loco, Taco Tio
- Lodg — E: Holiday Inn, Residence Inn; W: Residence Inn
- Other — E: Staples; W: Chevron/LP, **Thompson's RV Center, Camping World**

117 — Artesia Blvd (NB), Knott Ave
- Gas — E: 76, Shell◈
- Lodg — E: Extended Stay America
- Med — E: + Buena Park Doctors Hospital

116 — CA 39 (SB), Beach Blvd (NB)
- Gas — E: Chevron; W: Chevron, Mobil, Valero
- Food — E: McDonald's; W: Arby's, Black Angus Steakhouse, Denny's, KFC, Pizza Hut, Subway
- Lodg — W: Hampton Inn, Red Roof Inn♥
- Med — E: + Hospital
- Other — E: Auto Dealers; W: Laundromat, Target, to Knotts Berry Farm

115 — Manchester Bvd, Auto Ctr Dr (NB)

114B — CA 91E, Riverside Hwy, to Airport (SB)

114A — Magnolia (SB)

114 — Magnolia Ave, CA 91E (NB)
- Gas — E: Mobil◈; W: 76
- Food — E: Taco Bell; W: Del Taco
- Other — E: Laundromat, Harley Davidson, to Fullerton Muni Airport✈

113 — Brookhurst St, La Palma Ave (SB)

113C — CA 91W (NB)

113B — La Palma Ave East (NB)

EXIT — CALIFORNIA

113A — Brookhurst St, La Palma Ave (NB)
- Gas — E: Chevron◈; W: ArcoAmPm, Shell
- Food — E: Donut Shop, Subway; W: Carl's Jr, Mexi Casa Rest, Quiznos
- Lodg — W: Kettle Motor Hotel
- Other — W: Buena Park Mall, Home Depot, Staples, Target/Pharmacy

112 — Euclid St, Anaheim
- Gas — E: 7-11, Mobil; W: 76, ArcoAmPm
- Food — E: Chris & Pitts BBQ, IHOP, Marie Callendar's, McDonald's, Quiznos, Rubio's Fresh Mexican Grill, Starbucks, Subway, Ten Ten Chinese Rest, Wendy's; W: Arby's, Burger King, Denny's
- Other — E: Pharmacy, Petco♥, **Walmart**; W: Laundromat, Pharmacy, Radio Shack, Target

111 — Lincoln Ave, Downtown Anaheim
- FStop — E: (E to Manchester) Buena Park Mart/Shell
- Gas — E: 76
- Food — E: FastFood/Shell, Mexican Rest, Starbucks, Subway

110B — Disneyland Dr, Ball Rd (SB)

110A — Harbor Blvd (SB)

110 — Harbor Blvd, Ball Rd (NB)
- Gas — E: Chevron◈, Shell; W: ArcoAmPm, Shell◈, Valero
- Food — E: Burger King, El Pollo Loco, KFC, McDonald's, MiMi's Cafe, Subway, Taco Bell, Tony Roma's; W: Carl's Jr, Denny's, IHOP, McDonald's, Mamoof's Cafe, Spaghetti Station
- Lodg — E: Anaheim Best Inn, Best Value Inn, Days Inn, Holiday Inn, Hotel Menage♥, Ramada; W: Best Western, Carousel Inn, Carriage Inn, Comfort Inn, Days Inn, Desert Inn, Doubletree Hotel, Fairfield Inn, Holiday Inn, Howard Johnson, Quality Inn, Ramada, Rodeway Inn, Sheraton, Travelodge, Tropicana Inn, Super 8
- Med — E: + Western Medical Center-Anaheim
- Other — E: **Anaheim Harbor RV Park▲ , Anaheim Resort RV Park▲ , Anaheim RV Village▲ Travelers World RV Park▲**; W: to Convention Center, **Camping World**, DisneyLand, **Anaheim Overnight Trailer Park, CC Camperland RV Park**

109B — Disney Way, Anaheim Blvd (SB)

109A — Katella Ave, Orangewood Ave (SB)

109 — Katella Ave, Disney Way (NB), Disneyland Resort
- Gas — E: 76, ArcoAmPm; W: 7-11
- Food — E: Denny's, El Torito, McDonald's; W: Café, CoCo's, Country Kitchen, Del Taco, Tony Roma
- Lodg — E: Ramada Inn, Travelodge; W: Best Western, Comfort Inn, Hampton Inn, Hilton, Howard Johnson, Marriott, Radisson, Red Roof Inn♥, Super 8
- AServ — E: 76
- Other — E: to **OC RV Rentals**, Honda Center, Angel Stadium; W: to Disneyland, Convention Center

◈= Regular Gas Stations with Diesel ▲ = RV Friendly Locations ♥= Pet Friendly Locations
Red print shows large vehicle parking / access on site or nearby Brown Print = Campgrounds / RV PARKS

EXIT — CALIFORNIA

107C **State College Blvd, The City Drive, Chapman Ave, Anaheim**
Gas W: Chevron, Shell
Food W: El Torrito Mexican Rest, Starbucks, Taco Bell, Wendy's, Whataburger
Lodg E: Hilton Suites, Home Stay Suites
W: Ayers Inn, Doubletree Hotel
Med E: to + St Joseph Hospital, + Children's Hospital of Orange Co
W: + U C Irvine Medical Center, to + Garden Grove Hospital & Medical Center
Other E: UPS Store
W: Best Buy, CVS, Target/Pharmacy, Von's, Walgreen's, Ponderosa RV Park▲, The Block at Orange, CC Camperland RV Park▲

107B **CA 22W, Bristol St, LaVeta Ave, Long Beach (SB), Chapman Ave (NB)**
Food E: Burger King, Del Taco
W: El Torito, Krispy Kreme
Med E: + St Joseph Hospital, + Children's Hospital of Orange Co

107A **CA 22E, Orange, La Veta Ave, Bristol St (SB) CA 57N, Pomona (NB)**

106 **CA 22W, Long Beach (NB)**

105B **Main St, Broadway**
Gas E: 76
Food E: Carl's Jr, Polly's Café, Starbucks
Lodg E: Red Roof Inn♥
Other E: B&N, Mall, Pharmacy

105A **17th St, Santa Ana College**
Gas E: 76◈
W: Chevron
Food E: Home Town Buffet, IHOP, McDonald's
W: Ruby Tuesday, Seafood Rest
Lodg E: Howard Johnson
Other E: CVS, Food4Less, Target

104B **Santa Ana Blvd, Grand Ave, Downtown (SB) (Serv E on Grand Ave)**

104A **1st St, 4th St (SB)**
Gas E: Chevron

104 **Grand Ave, Santa Ana Blvd (NB)**
Gas E: Chevron
Food E: Denny's, Marie Callendar, McDonald's, Starbucks, Subway
Lodg E: Howard Johnson
Other E: Big O Tire, CVS, Dollar Tree, Food4Less, Goodyear, Target, Grand Pet Care Animal Hospital♥

103 **CA 55S, Newport Beach (SB)**

103C **1st St, 4th St (NB)**
Gas W: Chevron, Gas Right, Shell
Food W: Del Taco, Pizza
Other W: Laundromat, Santa Anna Zoo

103B **CA 55S, Newport Beach (NB)**

103A **CA 55N, Riverside (NB)**

102 **Newport Ave (SB)**

101B **Red Hill Ave, Tustin**
Gas E: 76, ArcoAmPm, Mobil◈, Shell
W: 76, Chevron, Valero◈
Food E: BBQ Buffet, Del Taco, Denny's, Starbucks, Subway, Wendy's
W: Burger King, Taco Bell
Lodg E: Key Inn
AServ E: Arco, Shell

EXIT — CALIFORNIA

Med W: + Tustin Hospital
Other E: Laundromat, Grocery, Pharmacy, U-Haul
W: to Tustin Marine Air Corp Station

101A **Tustin Ranch Rd**
Other E: Auto Dealers, Costco

100 **Jamboree Rd**
Gas E: 76, Shell
Food E: BJ's, Baja Fresh Mexican Rest, Black Angus Steakhouse, Burger King, El Pollo Loco, IHOP, On the Border, Panda Express, Quiznos, Red Robin, Romano's Macaroni Grill, Rubio's, Starbucks, Taco Bell, Taco Rosa
Other E: B&N, Best Buy, CompUSA, Costco, Lowe's, Petsmart♥, Ralph's, RiteAid, Sports Authority, Target, Tires, Carwash/Shell
W: Just Tires, Midas, to Sam's Club

99 **Culver Dr, Irvine**
Gas E: Shell
W: Chevron
Food E: Starbucks
W: Curry House, Denny's, Pizza Hut, Quiznos, Super Mex Rest, Sizzler, Starbucks, Wendy's
Lodg E: Comfort Suites
Other E: Best Buy, Vet♥
W: Police, Pharmacy, UPS Store, Vet♥

97 **Jeffrey Rd**
Gas E: Arco
W: 76
Food E: Fatburger, Quiznos, Starbucks
W: A&J Rest, Chen Chen's, Clay Oven of India, SW Seafood & BBQ, Taiko Japanese Rest, Tomikawa Sushi Bar Rest
Other W: Albertson's, Kohl's, Laundromat, Irvine Valley College, Oak Creek Golf Course, Animal Hospital♥

96B **CA 133N, Santa Margarita (SB)**

96A **Sand Canyon Ave (SB)**

96 **Sand Canyon Ave (NB)**
Gas W: 76
Food W: Burrell's BBQ, Denny's, Jack in the Box, Knowlwood Rest, TiaJuana's Long Bar & Grill
Lodg W: La Quinta Inn♥
TServ W: CAT Truck Service
Med W: + Irvine Reg'l Hospital
Other W: Traveland USA Multiple Dealerships & RV Park▲, El Toro RV Service

95 **CA 133S, Laguna Beach (SB), CA 133N, Riverside (NB)**

94 **Alton Pkwy (SB)**

94B **Alton Pkwy (NB)**
Gas E: Shell
Food E: Carl's Jr, Starbucks, Taco Bell
W: Cheesecake Factory, Dave & Busters, Maki Maki Sushi, PF Chang's, Panda Express, Red Robin, Rubio's Mexican, Starbucks, Subway/Shell
Lodg E: Homestead Suites
W: Doubletree Hotel
Other E: Costco
W: B&N, Target, Enterprise RAC

(94A) **Jct I-405N, Santa Ana Fwy (NB)**

92 **Bake Pkwy, I-5 Truck Bypass, Lake Forest Dr (SB)**

EXIT — CALIFORNIA

92B **Bake Pkwy (NB), I-5 Truck Bypass**

92A **Lake Forest Dr (NB)**
Gas E: Chevron, Shell◈
W: Chevron, Shell
Food E: Black Angus, Burger King, Chinese, IHOP, Mimi's Cafe, Panera Bread, Pizza Hut, Round Table Pizza, Subway, Taco Bell
W: Carl's Jr, Coco's, Del Taco, McDonald's
Lodg E: Best Western, Travelodge
W: Comfort Inn, Courtyard, Quality Suites, Travelodge
Other E: Auto Dealers, Americas Tire, Staples
W: Auto Dealer, Best Buy, to Wild Rivers Water Park, Verizon Wireless Amphitheatre

91 **El Toro Rd, Laguna Hills, Lk Forest**
Gas E: ArcoAmPm, Chevron, Mobil, Shell◈, USA
W: Circle K/76, Chevron◈, Shell◈
Food E: Arby's, Carino's, Carl's Jr, Denny's, Jack in the Box, KFC, McDonald's, Quiznos, Red Lobster, Starbucks, Subway, Wendy's
W: BJ's Rest, Carrow's, Coco's, CA Pizza, In N Out Burger, Lonestar Steakhouse, Monterey Seafood
Lodg W: Ayers Hotel, Laguna Hills Lodge
Med W: + Saddleback Memorial Hospital
Other E: 99 Store, CVS, Home Depot, Office Depot, Petco♥, Ralph's, Smart n Final, Staples, Pharmacy
W: Firestone, Longs Drugs, Walgreen's, Trader Joe's, Von's, Laguna Hills Mall

90 **Alicia Pkwy, Mission Viejo**
Gas W: 76◈, Chevron
Food E: Carl's Jr, Denny's, Del Taco, Subway
W: Togo's, Wendy's
Other E: Albertson's, Americas Tire, Auto Dealers CVS, Firestone, Kragen Auto Parts, Target, Tires
W: Big Lots, Auto Dealers

89 **La Paz Rd, Laguna Hills (Acc to Ex #88 via W to Cabot Rd)**
Gas E: ArcoAmPm, Mobil
W: 76◈, Chevron
Food E: Chronic Tacos, KFC/Pizza Hut, Paradise Donuts & Deli, Starbucks, Taco Bell, Wendy's
W: Claim Jumper, DQ, Jack in the Box, Italian Rest, McDonald's, Outback Steakhouse, Quiznos, Spasso's Italian Grill, Yamato Japanese
Lodg W: Holiday Inn, The Hills Hotel
Other E: Albertson's, CVS, Animal & Bird Clinic♥, Big Lots, Ralph's, Trader Joe's, UPS Store, Saddleback Lanes
W: Best Buy, Borders, CompUSA, Goodyear, Petco♥

88 **Oso Pkwy, Pacific Park Dr**
Gas E: 76, Chevron
Food E: Carl's Jr, Starbucks, Subway
W: DQ, Jack in the Box, Krispy Kreme,
Lodg E: Fairfield Inn
Other E: Mission Viejo Golf Course, Mission Viejo Animal Hospital♥,

86 **Crown Valley Pkwy, Mission Viejo**
Gas E: 76, ArcoAmPm, Chevron
W: Chevron◈
Food E: Baja Fresh Mexican, Cheesecake Factory, CoCo's, Crown Chinese, Islands Rest, McDonald's, Panda Express, PF Chang's, Ruby's Diner

◈ = Regular Gas Stations with Diesel ▲ = RV Friendly Locations ♥ = Pet Friendly Locations
Red print shows large vehicle parking / access on site or nearby Brown Print = Campgrounds / RV PARKS

EXIT		CALIFORNIA
	Med	E: + Mission Regional Medical Center + Mission Medical Urgent Care
	Other	E: Apple Store, CVS, Cost Plus World Market,Complete Care Auto & Tire, Office Max, Regal Stadium 10, Sir Speedy Printing, UPS Store, US Post Office, Animal Urgent Care of S Orange♥, The Shoppes @ Mission Viejo W: Amtrak, Auto Dealers, Auto Services, Carwash, Costco, Tucker Tires, On Target Indoor Shooting Range
85		**Avery Pkwy (SB)**
85B		**Avery Pkwy (NB)**
	Gas	E: Shell◈ W: Shell◈, ArcoAmPm
	Food	E: Alberto's Mexican, Big Grill Mongolian BBQ, Billy's Pizza, Del Taco, Carrow's, Jack in the Box, Sheesh Kabob, McDonald's, Starbucks W: Buffy's, Carl's Jr, In 'n Out Burger
	Lodg	W: Amercas Best Value Inn, Laguna Inn
	Other	E: America's Tire, Avery Animal Clinic♥, Burlington Coat Factory, Goodyear, Staples, World Market, Saddleback College W: Amtrak, Firestone
85A		**CA 73N (TOLL), Long Beach (NB)**
	Other	W: Restaurants, Grocery at 1st Exit L
83		**Junipero Serra Rd**
	Gas	W: Shell
	Other	W: Budget Truck Rental
82		**CA 74, Ortega Hwy E, San Juan Capistrano**
	Gas	E: 76, Chevron◈, Shell W: ArcoAmPm, Chevron
	Food	E: Ball Park Pizza, Denny's, Key West Fish Market & Grill, Starbucks, Tannins Rest & Wine Bar W: Arby's, Carl's Jr, Del Taco, Jack in the Box, Marie Callendar's, McDonald's, Pizza Hut, Sizzler, Starbucks, Subway
	Lodg	E: Best Western W: Mission Inn
	Other	E: ATMs, Banks, Carwash, Pharmacy, Ortega Animal Hospital♥, W: ATMs, Banks, Amtrak, Big Lots, Capistrano Animal Clinic♥, FedEx Office, PetCo♥, Ralph's, UPS Store, Zoomar's Petting Zoo,
81		**San Juan Creek Rd, Valle Rd, Camino Capistrano**
	Gas	W: Chevron
	Food	W: KFC, Pick Up Stix, Starbucks
	Other	W: Goodyear, Grocery, Harley Davidson, Petco♥, Radio Shack, RiteAid, **San Juan RV Services & Rentals, CA Hwy Patrol Post**
79		**CA 1, Pacific Coast Hwy, Dana Pt, Camino Las Ramblas, Beach Cities**
	Gas	W: 76◈, 76, ArcoAmPm, Shell
	Food	W: Carl's Jr, Del Taco, Denny's, El Pollo Loco, Jack in the Box, McDonald's, Patio Cafe, Subway
	Lodg	W: DoubleTree Hotel, Hilton, Ramada Inn
	Other	W: Auto Dealers, Big 5 Sporting Goods, Carwash, Enterprise RAC, Smart n Final, Staples, US Post Office, U-Haul,
78		**Camino Estrella (SB), Camino de Estrella (NB), San Clemente**
	Gas	E: 76◈ W: ArcoAmPm◈

EXIT		CALIFORNIA
	Food	E: Carl's Jr, China Well, Crispins Comfort Food, Melting Pot, Rose Donuts & Cafe, Rubio's Fresh Mexican, Round Table Pizza, Starbucks, Subway, Wahoo's Fish Taco W: Little Caesar's Pizza, Taco Bell
	Med	E: + Saddleback Memorial Medical Ctr + San Clemente Hospital
	Other	E: CVS, Laundry, Grocery, Pharmacy, Ralph's, Trader Joe's W: Big Lots, Grocery, Kragen Auto Parts, Estrella Veterinary Hospital♥, Dr Sears Family Pediatrics
77		**Avenida Vista Hermosa**
	Gas	E: Mobil W: Chevron, Texaco
	Food	E: Carrow's, McDonald's W: Burger Stop, Del Taco, Denny's
	Other	W: Grocery, Pharmacy, US Post Office
76		**Avenida Pico, San Clemente**
	Gas	E: Mobil W: Chevron, Exxon, Shell◈
	Food	E: Carrow's, Juice it Up, McDonald's, Panda Express, Starbucks W: Bad to the Bone BBQ, Burger Stop, Chronic Tacos, Del Taco, Denny's, Pick Up Stix, Pizza Hut, Subway, Waffle Lady Internet Cafe
	Lodg	W: Best Western, Country Plaza Inn, Days Inn
	Other	E: Albertson's, Jimmy's Tire Center W: Auto Repairs & Services, Discount Tire, Carwash, Staples, Pharmacy, Towing, U-Haul, US Post Office
75		**Avenida Palizada (SB), Avenida Presedio, San Clemente (NB)**
	Gas	W: 7-11, ArcoAmPm, Valero
	Food	W: Dominos Pizza, KFC, Pizza Port, Starbucks, Subway, Japanese Rest
	Lodg	W: Always Inn, Best Western, Days Inn, Holiday Inn
	Other	W: Albertson's, AutoZone, Big O Tire, CVS, FedEx Office, RiteAid,
74		**El Camino Real, San Clemente**
	Gas	E: Chevron◈ W: 76◈, Exxon
	Food	E: Burrito Basket, El Mariachi Rest, Hapa J's Rest, San Clemente Café, Wild Flower Café, W: Fat Burger, KFC, Little Caesa's Pizza, Love Burger, Rib Trader, Taco Bell, Taste of China, Tommy's Family Rest, The Bagel Shack
	Lodg	E: Budget Lodge♥, San Clemente Little Inn by the Beach, San Clemente Motel W: Welcome Inn
	Med	W: + San Clemente Medi-Center
	Other	E: Laundromat, San Clemente Veterinary Hospital♥, W: 7-11, Grocery, Kragen Auto Parts, Radio Shack, Ralph's
73		**Ave Calafia, Coastal Hwy (SB), Avenida Magdelena (NB)**
	Gas	E: 7-11, 76, Shell
	Food	E: Bob's Big Boy, CoCo's, Jack in the Box, Pedro's Tacos, Sugar Shack
	Lodg	E: Hampton Inn, Quality Suites, The Inn At Calafia Beach, Travelodge W: San Clemente Inn
	Other	E: Auto Service, San Clemente Muni Golf Course, Trap & Skeet Range W: San Clemente State Beach▲ San Mateo State Beach▲

EXIT		CALIFORNIA
72		**Cristianitos Rd**
	Food	E: Carl's Jr, Cafe del Sol
	Lodg	E: Carmelo Motel, Comfort Suites, Garden Cottage at the Green B&B,
71		**Basilone Rd, San Onofre**
	Other	E: Mil/San Onofre Rec Beach RV Park▲ W: San Clemente State Park
(69)		**Border Patrol Check Point**
(67)		**Inspection Station (Both dir)**
(63)		**Vista Point (SB)**
62		**Las Pulgas Rd**
(60)		**Aliso Creek Rest Area (SB) (RR, Phone, Pic, Vend, Pet, RVDump)**
(59)		**Aliso Creek Rest Area (NB) (RR, Phone, Pic, Vend, Pet, RVDump)**
54C		**Oceanside Harbor Dr, Camp Pendleton**
	Gas	W: Chevron, Mobil
	Food	W: Burger King, Del Taco, Denny's
	Lodg	W: Comfort Inn, Sandman Motel, Travelodge
54B		**Coast Hwy, Oceanside (SB), Camp Pendleton (NB)**
	Gas	E: Arco, Shell, Texaco W: Mobil
	Food	E: Angelo's, Hamburger Heaven W: Carrow's, Flying Bridge
	Lodg	W: Comfort Inn
54A		**CA 76E (SB), Coast Hwy (NB)**
	Gas	W: Chevron
	Food	E: Davina's Mexican Rest
	Food	W: Alfredo's Mexican Food, Angelo's Burgers, Harbor House Cafe, Veneto's Italian
	Lodg	E: Super 8 W: Americas Best Inn, Comfort Suites, Coast Inn, GuestHouse Inn, La Quinta Inn, Motel 6, Motel 9, The Blue Whale
	Other	E: Auto Repairs & Services, Budget Truck Rental, **Funday RV Services**, Mission Animal & Bird Hospital♥, Oceanside Animal Hospital♥, Oceanside Muni Airport✈ W: CA Welcome Center, Grocery, Thrifty Car Rental, U-Haul
53		**Mission Ave, Downtown Oceanside**
	Gas	E: 76, ArcoAmPm, Mobil◈
	Food	E: Burger King, China Star Super Buffet, Jack in the Box, Jimmy's, KFC, McDonald', Mission Donut House W: Carrow's, DQ, El Pollo Loco, Long John Silver's, Panda Express, Sushi, Wendy's
	Lodg	E: Comfort Inn, Econo Lodge, Motel 6♥, Quality Inn, Ramada Ltd W: Wyndham Oceanside Pier Resort
	Other	E: Auto Services, CarQuest, Grocery, Oceans Eleven Casino, Pep Boys, US Post Office W: Auto Zone, Grocery, Harbor Freight, Laundromat, Museums, Office Depot, Radio Shack, UPS Store, US Post Office
52		**Oceanside Blvd, Oceanside**
	Gas	E: ArcoAmPm W: 76, Shell
	Food	E: Bakers Square, Dominos Pizza, IHOP, Hooligan's, McDonald's, Pizza Hut, Starbucks, Subway, Taco Bell

◈= Regular Gas Stations with Diesel ▲ = RV Friendly Locations ♥= Pet Friendly Locations
Red print shows large vehicle parking / access on site or nearby **Brown Print = Campgrounds / RV PARKS**

EXIT — **CALIFORNIA**

Food — **W:** Angelo's Burgers, Baskin Robbins, Diego's Mexican Food, Port of Subs
Lodg — **W:** Best Western,
Other — **E:** CVS, **Cruise America MH Rental**, Jiffy Lube, Laundromat, Longs Drugs, NAPA, Oceanside Truck & **RV Repair**, Pacific Animal Hospital♥, Pharmacy, Ralph's, Smart 'n Final, Von's, West Marine, **CA State Hwy Patrol Post**
W: Discount Tire, **Oceanside RV Park▲**

51C **Cassidy St (SB), Oceanside, Vista Way (NB)**
Gas — **W:** 7-11, Mobil
Lodg — **W:** Oceanside Inn
Other — **W: NB Acc via 51B : Paradise by the Sea RV Resort▲**

51B **CA 78E, Vista Way, Escondido**
Gas — **E:** 76, Chevron◈
Food — **E:** Applebee's, Burger King, Chili's, Chuck E Cheese, Fuddrucker's, Hooters, McDonald's, Mimi'sCafé, Olive Garden, Romano's Macaroni Grill, Rubio's Fresh Mexican, Starbucks, Wendy's
W: Hungry Hunter Steakhouse
Lodg — **E:** Extended Stay America, Holiday Inn
Other — **E:** B&N, Best Buy, Big 5 Sporting Goods, CVS, Discount Tire, Dollar Tree, FedEx Office, Petco♥, Sports Authority, Staples, Target, Toys R Us, Trader Joe's, **Walmart,** World Market, Verizon, Vet♥, Carwash/76,

51A **Las Flores Dr**

50 **Carlsbad Village Dr, Elm Ave (SB) Downtown Carlsbad (NB)**
Gas — **E:** Shell
W: Chevron, Carlsbad Gas, Valero
Food — **E:** Shari's
W: Carl's Jr, Denny's, Jack in the Box, Mikko Japanese Rest
Lodg — **W:** Extended Stay America, Motel 6♥, Carlsbad Inn Beach Resort, Ocean Palms Beach Resort
Other — **E:** Laundromat, Von's
W: Albertson's, Pharmacy, LP/Gas

49 **Tamarack Ave, Carlsbad**
Gas — **E:** 76, Chevron, Exxon◈
W: 76 , ArcoAmPm
Food — **E:** Village Kitchen
W: Koko Palms
Lodg — **E:** Comfort Inn, Rodeway Inn, Travel Inn
Other — **E:** Laundromat, Von's Grocery/Pharmacy

48 **Cannon Rd, Legoland**
Gas — **W:** West Mart
Food — **W:** Bistro West, West Steak Seafood
Lodg — **E:** Inns of America, West Inn, Sheraton Carlsbad Resort, Grand Pacific Marbrisa
Other — **E:** Auto Dealers, Legoland, McClellan-Palomar Airport

47 **Palomar Airport Rd, Carlsbad Blvd**
FStop — **W:** Palomar Shell
Gas — **E:** 7-11, Chevron, Mobil◈
Food — **E:** Carl's Jr, Denny's, Panda Express, TGI Friday, Taco Bell, Subway, Anderson's Dutch Cooking
W: Claim Jumper, In N Out Burger, Kings Fish House, Marie Callendar's, McDonald's, Panda Express, Starbucks, TGI Friday

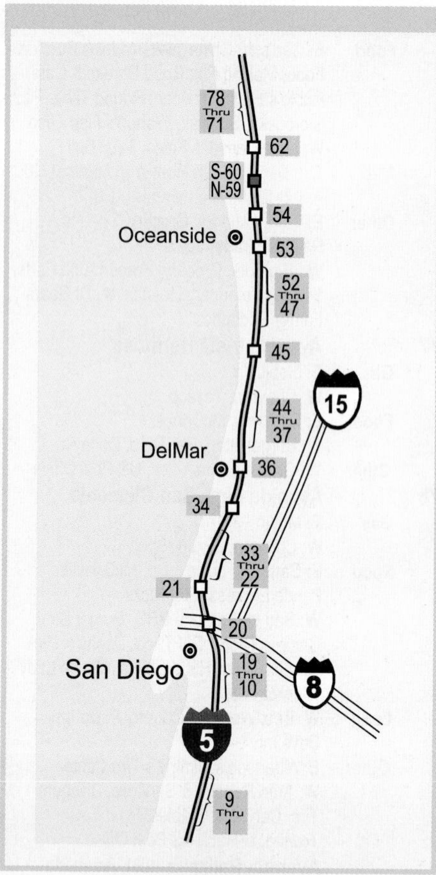

EXIT — **CALIFORNIA**

Lodg — **E:** Best Western, Courtyard, Grand Pacific Palisades Resort & Hotel, Hampton Inn, Homewood Suites, Holiday Inn, Motel 6♥,
W: Hilton Garden Inn
Other — **E:** Costco, Carlsbad Premium Outlet Mall, Legoland, Museum, McClellan-Palomar Airport✈,
W: LP/Shell

45 **Poinsettia Lane, Aviara Pkwy**
Food — **W:** Chinese Cuisine, El Pollo Loco, Jack in the Box, Panda Buffet, Starbucks, Subway
Lodg — **W:** Inns of America, Motel 6♥, Ramada
Other — **E:** Albertson's, CVS
W: RiteAid, Ralph's

44 **La Costa Ave**
Gas — **W:** Chevron◈

43 **Leucadia Blvd, Encinitas**
Gas — **W:** Shell
Lodg — **E:** Howard Johnson

41B **Encinitas Blvd**
Gas — **E:** Chevron, Exxon, O'Brien's
W: Shell
Food — **E:** Coco's, Del Taco, Oggi's Pizza, Roxy Rest
W: Rest/Best Western, Denny's, Tomiku Japanese Rest, Wendy's
Lodg — **W:** Best Western♥, Days Inn, Inn at Moonlight Beach B&B, Moonlight Beach Motel
Med — **W: + Hospital**
Other — **E:** LP/Exxon, CVS, Smart N Final, Carwash/Chevron, Quail Botanical Gardens, Animal Clinic♥
W: Petco♥, Laundromat, Carwash/Shell

EXIT — **CALIFORNIA**

41A **Santa Fe Dr, to Encinitas (NB)**
Gas — **E:** Shell
Food — **E:** Carl's Jr, El Nopalito
W: Santa Fe Cafe, Today's Pizza
Med — **W: + Scripps Memorial Hospital**
Other — **E:** Shell/Carwash
W: Laundromat, RiteAid, Von's

40 **Birmingham Dr, Cardiff by the Sea**
Gas — **E:** Chevron, Valero◈
W: ArcoAmPm
Food — **E:** Glenn's, Taco Bell
Lodg — **E:** Countryside Inn, Comfort Inn
Other — **E:** Carwash/Valero

(39B) **Vista Point (SB)**

39A **Manchester Ave (SB)**

39 **Manchester Ave**
Gas — **E:** 76
Food — **E:** Kava Coffee Shop
Other — **E:** Miira Costa College

37 **Lomas Santa Fe Dr, Solana Beach**
Gas — **W:** Mobil
Food — **E:** Jolly Roger, Round Table Pizza
W: Carl's Jr, Chinese, Panera Bread, Round Table Pizza, Starbucks
Other — **E:** Von's/Pharmacy
W: CVS, Discount Tire, Staples

36 **Via De La Valle, Del Mar**
Gas — **E:** Chevron, Mobil
W: ArcoAmPm, Shell◈
Food — **E:** Burger King, Chevy's, McDonald's, Milton's Deli, Pasta Pronto, Starbucks
W: Denny's, The Fish Market
Lodg — **W:** Hilton
Other — **E:** Albertson's, Pharmacy, Petco♥, Radio Shack, Carwash/Chevron
W: Del Mar Fairgrounds, Del Mar Racetrack

34 **Del Mar Heights Rd**
Gas — **E:** Shell◈
W: 7-11
Food — **W:** Jack in the Box
Other — **W:** Von's, Longs Drugs

33 **Carmel Valley Rd, CA 56E (SB)**

33B **Carmel Valley Rd (NB)**
Gas — **E:** ArcoAmPm, Chevron, Shell
Food — **E:** Bakers Square, Taco Bell
Lodg — **E:** Doubletree Hotel, Hampton Inn

33A **CA 56E (NB)**

32 **Carmel Mountain Rd**

(31) **Jct I-805S, National City, Chula Vista (SB, Left Exit)**

30 **Sorrento Valley Rd (NB)**

29 **Genesee Ave, La Jolla**
Med — **E: + Scripps Memorial Hospital**
W: + Scripps Green Hospital

28 **La Jolla Village Dr (SB)**

28B **La Jolla Village Dr (NB)**
Gas — **W:** Mobil◈
Food — **E:** Donovan's Steak & Chop House, Einstein Bros Bagels, Fleming's Prime Steakhouse, Cafe Japengo, La Salsa Rest, L&L Hawaiian BBQ, Nozomi, Roy's Rest, Starbucks, Trophy's Rest, Trulock's Rest
W: BJ's Rest, CA Pizza, El Torito, Islands Rest, Pasta Bravo, Rubio's, TGI Friday
Lodg — **E:** Embassy Suites, Hyatt, Marriott♥
W: Residence Inn, Sheraton

◈= Regular Gas Stations with Diesel ▲ = RV Friendly Locations ♥= Pet Friendly Locations
Red print shows large vehicle parking / access on site or nearby Brown Print = Campgrounds / RV PARKS

EXIT		CALIFORNIA
	Med	W: + VA Hospital
	Other	E: Mall, Miramar Marine Air Corp Station W: Grocery, Trader Joe's, CVS, PetSmart♥, Radio Shack, Ralph's
28A		**Nobel Dr (NB) (Access to 28B Serv)**
27		**Gilman Dr, La Jolla Colony Dr**
26		**CA 52E, Santee (SB)**
26B		**CA 52E (NB)**
26A		**W La Jolla Pkwy (NB) (Former Ardath Rd)**
23		**Balboa Ave, Garnet Ave (SB)**
23B		**Balboa Ave E (NB)**
	Gas	E: Shell W: 76, 7-11, Mobil
	Food	E: Del Taco W: Arby's, In 'n Out Burger, McDonald's
	Lodg	W: Comfort Inn, Days Inn, Holiday Inn Express
	Med	W: + Hospital
	Other	W: Auto Dealers, Auto Services, Discount Tire
23A		**Grand Ave, Garnet Ave (NB)**
22		**Clairemont Dr, Mission Bay Dr**
	Gas	E: 76, ArcoAmPm, Shell
	Food	E: Jack in the Box, McDonald's, Subway
	Lodg	E: Best Western
	Other	E: RiteAid
21		**Sea World Dr, Tecolote Rd**
	Gas	E: ArcoAmPm, Shell
	Lodg	W: Hilton Resort
	Other	E: Univ of San Diego W: CA Hwy Patrol Post, SeaWorld
(20)		**Jct I-8, E - El Centro, W - Beaches, CA 209S, Rosecrans St, Beaches**
19		**Old Town Ave**
	Gas	E: ArcoAmPm, Shell
	Food	E: Old Town Deli
	Lodg	E: Courtyard, La Quinta Inn♥
18B		**Washington St, San Diego**
	Lodg	E: Comfort Inn
18A		**Kettner St, S Diego Airport, Vine UC, Sassafras St (SB), Pacific Hwy Viaduct (NB)**
17		**Front St, Civic Center (SB)**
17B		**India St, Sassafras St (NB)**
	Gas	E: Gas, Mobil W: Exxon
	Lodg	W: Holiday Inn Express, Super 8
17A		**Hawthorne St, SD Airport (NB)**
	Gas	W: Exxon◊
	Lodg	W: Holiday Inn Express, Motel 6, Super 8
	Med	W: + Hospital
16		**CA 163N, Escondido, 10th Ave (SB)**
16B		**6th Ave, Downtown San Diego (NB)**
16A		**CA 163N, Escondido (NB)**
	Gas	W: Shell

EXIT		CALIFORNIA
	Food	W: Jack in the Box, McDonald's
	Lodg	W: Days Inn, Holiday Inn, Marriott, Super 8
	Med	W: + Hospital
	Other	E: Aerospace Museum
15C		**Pershing Dr, B St (SB)**
15B		**CA 94E, ML King Jr Fwy (SB), Civic Center, Pershing Dr (NB)**
15A		**Imperial Ave (SB), CA 94E, J St (NB)**
14B		**Cesar E Chavez Pkwy (Formerly Crosby St)**
14A		**CA 75S, (TOLL), Coronado**
13B		**National Ave, 28th St**
	Gas	W: Shell
	Food	E: Starbucks, Subway W: Alberto's Mexican, Burger King, El Pollo Loco, Long John Silver's, McDonald's
13A		**CA 15N, Riverside, Wabash Blvd**
12		**Main St, National City Blvd (SB), Division St (NB)**
	Gas	E: Mobil, Shell
	Food	E: Keith's
	Lodg	E: Suncoast Inn
11B		**8th St, National City (SB), Plaza Blvd, Downtown (NB)**
	Gas	E: ArcoAmPm, Shell W: Chevron◊
	Food	E: Jack in the Box
	Lodg	E: Holiday Inn, Howard Johnson, Radisson, Ramada Inn, Super 8
11A		**Civic Center Dr (SB), Harbor Dr**
10		**Bay Marina Dr, Mile of Cars (Formerly 24th St)**
	TStop	W: So Cal Truck Stop
	Food	W: Denny's, In 'n Out Burger
	Other	W: LP/SC TS
9		**CA 54E, Lemon Grove**
8B		**E St, Chula Vista**
	Gas	E: 76, Arco, Mobil, Shell
	Food	E: Aunt Emma's, Black Angus Steak House, Mary Kaye's, McDonald's, Pizza, Taco Bell, Wendy's W: Anthony's Fish Grotto
	Lodg	E: Best Western, Motel 6♥ W: Days Inn, Good Nite Inn
	Other	E: Grocery, Laundromat
8A		**H St**
	Gas	E: 7-11, Arco, Chevron
	Food	E: Alberto's Mexican, El Pollo Loco
	Lodg	E: Early CA Motel
	Med	E: + Hospital
	Other	E: Goodyear
7B		**J St, Marina Pkwy, to Chula Vista Harbor**
7A		**L St**
	Gas	E: 7-11, 76, Shell◊
	Food	E: Golden Pagoda
	Lodg	E: Best Western
	Other	E: AutoZone, Grocery, Office Depot
6		**Palomar St**
	Gas	E: ArcoAmPm, Costco

EXIT		CALIFORNIA
	Food	E: Del Taco, DQ, Home Town Buffet, KFC, McDonald's, Subway
	Lodg	E: Palomar Inn
	Other	E: Costco, Office Depot, Target, Grocery, Walmart
5B		**Main St, Imperial Beach**
	Gas	E: ArcoAmPm
5A		**CA 75, Palm Ave, Imperial Beach**
	Gas	E: ArcoAmPm W: ArcoAmPm, Mobil, Shell
	Food	W: Burger King, Carl's Jr, Carrow's,El Chili Chinese, El Pollo Loco, McDonald's, Roberto's, Subway
	Lodg	W: Super 8
	Other	E: Discount Tire W: Auto Zone, CVS, Grocery, Home Depot, Pharmacy, Shops,Von's
4		**Coronado Ave**
	Gas	E: Chevron, Shell W: ArcoAmPm, Shell
	Food	E: Bakery, Denny's, Dos Panchos
	Lodg	E: Travelers Motel, Eazy 8 Motel W: Days Inn
	Other	E: Auto Services
3		**CA 905, Tocayo Ave**
2		**Dairy Mart Rd, San Ysidro Blvd**
	Gas	E: ArcoAmPm, Circle K
	Food	E: Burger King, Carl's Jr, CoCo's, Maty's Seafood, McDonald's
	Lodg	E: Americana Inn, Motel 6♥, Super 8
	Other	E: Pacifica RV Resort▲, CarQuest, Radio Shack
1B		**Via de San Ysidro**
	Gas	E: 76, Exxon, Mobil W: Chevron
	Food	E: Santa Fe Chinese W: Denny's, KFC, Outback Steakhouse
	Lodg	W: Economy Inn, Motel 6♥, Motel 8 & RV Park▲, Old Mill Hotel
	Other	W: International Inn & RV Park▲
(1A)		**Jct I-805N, San Ysidro Blvd (NB), Camino de la Plaza (SB)**
	Food	E: Burger King, El Pollo Loco, KFC, IHOP, Jack in the Box, McDonald's, Subway W: IHOP, McDonald's, Pizza Hut/Taco Bell
	Lodg	E: Flamingo Motel, Holiday Lodge, Travelodge
	Other	E: AutoZone, Greyhound, Customs Station W: Tourist Info, Kmart, Factory Outlets
(0)		**US / Mexico Border, CA State Line, Mexican Customs**

PACIFIC TIME ZONE

↑ CALIFORNIA
↓ MEXICO

Above lists Northbound I-5 from US / Mexico border to US / Canada border.

◊= Regular Gas Stations with Diesel ▲ = RV Friendly Locations ♥= Pet Friendly Locations
Red print shows large vehicle parking / access on site or nearby Brown Print = Campgrounds / RV PARKS

EXIT | CALIFORNIA

Begin Eastbound I-8 from Jct I-5 in San Diego, CA to Jct I-10 in AZ.

CALIFORNIA

PACIFIC TIME ZONE

NOTE: I-8 begins/ends Jct I-10, Ex #199 AZ

(0) **Sunset Cliffs Blvd, Nimitz Blvd, San Diego**
- Gas: N: Shell
- Food: N: Deli, Jack in the Box

1 **W Mission Bay Blvd, (WB) Sports Arena Blvd**
- Gas: S: 76, ArcoAmPm, Shell, Shell
- Food: S: Arby's, Coco's, Denny's, Jack in the Box, Kobe, McDonald's, Red Lobster
- Lodg: S: EZ 8 Motel, Holiday Inn Express, Holiday Inn, Marriott, Ramada Ltd
- Other: N: to Sea World
  S: Home Depot, Ralph's, Von's, U-Haul

(2) **Jct I-5S, Downtown (EB)**

(2A) **Jct I-5N, Los Angeles (WB)**
- Gas: S: Chevron
- Food: S: Burger King, Denny's, Jack in the Box, McDonald's, Perry's Cafe
- Lodg: S: Best Western, Days Inn, Holiday Inn, Howard Johnson, Quality Inn, Super 8
- Other: S: Grocery, Goodyear, Staples, Pharmacy

(2B) **Jct I-5, N - LA, S - San Diego (EB) Rosecrans St (WB)**

2C **Morena Blvd (WB)**

3 **Taylor St, Hotel Circle**
- Gas: N: Chevron
  S: Chevron
- Food: N: DW Ranch, Hunter Steaks
  S: Rest/Kings Inn, Albie's, Valley Kitchen
- Lodg: N: Best Western, Comfort Inn, Motel 6♥, Premier Inn, Red Lion Hotel, Town & Country Suites
  S: Best Western, Comfort Inn, Doubletree Hotel, Econo Lodge, Extended Stay America, Hawthorne Suites, Holiday Inn Express, Howard Johnson, Kings Inn, Ramada Plaza, Residence Inn, Travelodge
- Other: N: Cinema, Golf Course

4A **Hotel Circle Dr (EB), CA 163S, Downtown (WB)**
- Lodg: S: Best Western, Days Inn, Extended Stay America, Hotel Circle Inn, Quality Inn, Ramada Plaza, Super 8, Vagabond Inn

EXIT | CALIFORNIA

4B **CA 163S, Downtown (EB) CA 163N, Hotel Circle (WB)**

4C **CA 163N, Escondido (EB)**

5 **Mission Center Rd**
- Gas: N: Chevron, Mobil, Shell
  S: ArcoAmPm
- Food: N: Applebee's, Fuddrucker's, Hooters, Outback Steakhouse, Quiznos, Taco Bell
  S: Benihana, Denny's, TGI Friday, Wendy's
- Lodg: N: Marriott
  S: Comfort Inn, Fairfield Inn, Hilton, La Quinta Inn, Radisson, Sheraton
- Other: N: Mall, Best Buy, Borders, Staples, Target
  S: Auto Dealers

6A **Texas St, Qualcomm Way (Access to Ex #5 Services)**
- Gas: N: Chevron
  S: Valero

(6B) **Jct I-805, N - LA, S - Chula Vista**

7 **CA 15S, to 40th St, Fairmont Ave, Mission Gorge Rd (EB)**
- FStop: N: CFN/Cosby Oil #7

7A **CA 15S (WB)**

(7B) **Jct I-15N, to Riverside (WB)**

(8) **Jct I-15, Mission Gorge Rd, San Diego (EB), Fairmont Ave (WB)**
- Gas: N: 7-11, ArcoAmPm, Mobil◈, Shell, Valero◈
- Food: N: Arby's, Burger King, Chili's, Coco's, El Pollo Loco, Jack in the Box, KFC, McDonald's, Starbucks, Subway, Taco Bell
- Lodg: N: Super 8, Travelodge
- Med: N: + Hospital
- Other: N: Home Depot, NAPA, Von's, RiteAid

9 **Waring Rd, San Diego**
- Gas: N: 76, Shell
- Food: N: Italian
- Lodg: N: Good Nite Inn, Days Inn, Quality Inn
- Other: N: Albertson's

10 **College Ave**
- Gas: N: Chevron◈
  S: ArcoAmPm
- Food: S: Jack in the Box, McDonald's, Pita Pit
- Med: S: + Alvarado Hospital
- Other: N: US Post Office
  S: San Diego St Univ

EXIT | CALIFORNIA

11 **70th St, Lake Murray Bvd, Alvarado Rd, La Mesa**
- Gas: N: Shell
  S: 7-11, Shell◈
- Food: N: Mexican, Subway
  S: Deli, Denny's, Marie Callendar's, Mexican Rest
- AServ: N: Chevron
  S: Shell
- Med: S: + Hospital
- Other: S: San Diego RV Resort▲

12 **Fletcher Pkwy, La Mesa**
- Gas: N: 7-11, Shell
- Food: N: Bakers Square, Boston Market, Carl's Jr, Chili's, McDonald's, Red Oak Steak House, Starbucks
  S: Mexican
- Lodg: N: EZ 8 Motel, Comfort Inn
  S: Motel 6♥
- Other: N: Albertson's, Costco

13A **Spring St (EB), El Cajon Blvd (WB)**
- Lodg: S: Travelodge

13B **Jackson Dr, Grossmont Blvd**
- Gas: N: 7-11, ArcoAmPm, Chevron, Mobil, Shell
- Food: N: Arby's, Burger King, Chili's, Chuck E Cheese Piza, Fuddrucker's, KFC, Olive Garden, McDonald's, Panda Express, Red Lobster, Starbucks, Taco Bell
  S: Jack in the Box
- Other: N: Barnes & Noble, Longs Drug, Mall, Staples, Target, US Post Office
  S: Discount Tire, Firestone, Ralph's, Walmart

14A **CA 125(EB), Grossmont Ctr Dr (WB)**

14B **La Mesa Blvd (EB), CA 125 (WB)**

14C **Severin Dr, Fuerte Dr**
- Gas: N: 7-11, ArcoAmPm, Mobil
- Food: N: Anthony's Fish, Charcoal House
  S: Seafood Rest
- Lodg: N: Holiday Inn Express

15 **El Cajon Blvd (EB)**
- Gas: S: Mobil, Shell
- Food: S: BBQ
- Lodg: N: Days Inn, Quality Inn
  S: Cottage Motel, Villa Serena Motel

16 **Main St**
- Gas: N: 7-11, ArcoAmPm
  S: 76, Chevron
- Food: N: Denny's, Papa's Pizza, Sombrero's
- Lodg: N: Relax Inn, Thriftlodge
- Other: S: Greyhound Terminal, 76/RVDump

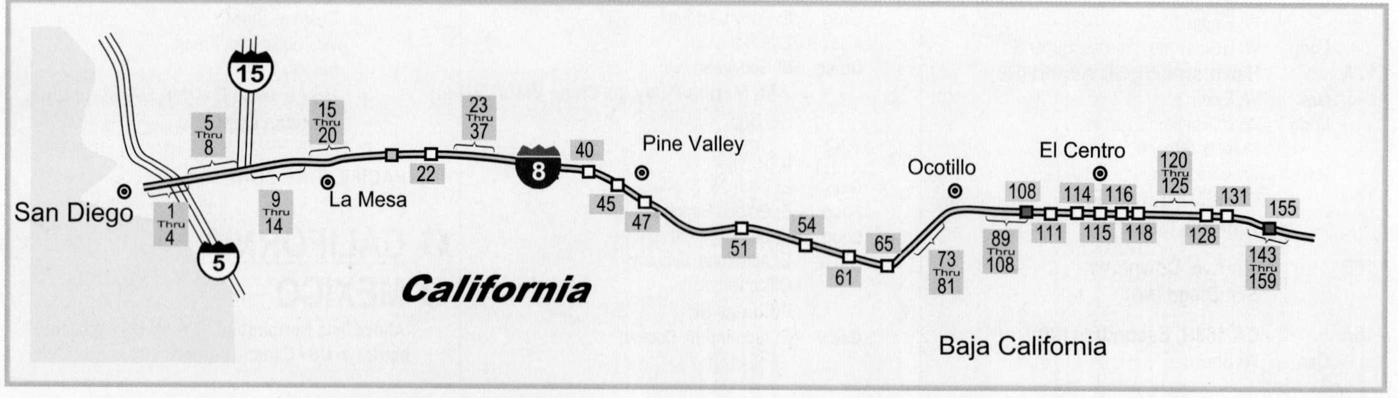

◈= Regular Gas Stations with Diesel ▲ = RV Friendly Locations ♥ = Pet Friendly Locations
Red print shows large vehicle parking / access on site or nearby Brown Print = Campgrounds / RV PARKS

EXIT		CALIFORNIA
17A		**Johnson Ave, El Cajon (EB)**
	Food	N: Applebee's, Boston Market, Burger King, Carl's Jr, Coco's, KFC, Long John Silver's, Panda Express, Rubio's, Sizzler, Starbucks, Subway
	Other	N: Albertson's, Best Buy, Home Depot, Long Drugs, Office Depot, PetSmart♥, RiteAid, **Walmart**, Mall S: Cummins Cal Pacific, Auto Dealers
17B		**CA 67N (EB)**
	Other	N: Mall, Stores
17C		**Magnolia Ave (EB)**
	Gas	N: ArcoAmPm S: Shell
	Food	N: Applebee's, China King, Jack in the Box, Long John Silver's, On the Border, Panda Express
	Food	S: Mexican, Perry's Café
	Lodg	S: El Cajon Inn, Motel 6♥, Travelodge
	Other	N: Best Buy, Food4Less, Mall, Shopping S: Auto Services
17		**Magnolia Ave, CA 67N (WB)**
18		**Mollison Ave**
	Gas	N: ArcoAmPm, Chevron, Citgo, Exxon S: ArcoAmPm, QT◈
	Food	N: Arby's, Denny's, Starbucks, Wendy's S: Taco Bell
	Lodg	N: Best Western, Days Inn S: Super 8, Valley Motel
19		**2nd St, El Cajon**
	Gas	N: ArcoAmPm, Chevron, Exxon◈ S: 76, Gas Depot, Shellx2
	Food	N: Taco Shop S: Arby's, Burger King, Carl's Jr, Jack in the Box, Golden Corral, IHOP, Pizza Hut, McDonald's, Subway, Taco Bell
	Lodg	S: Parkside Inn, Royal Inn
	Other	N: Grocery, CVS, Von's S: Firestone, Grocery, PetCo♥, Ralph's, Walgreen's
20		**Greenfield Dr (EB)**
20A		**E Main St (WB) (Diff reaccess)**
	Gas	S: ArcoAmPm
	Food	N: Buffy's, Coco's, Italian Rest, Main St Grill, Starbucks
	Lodg	N: Best Western, Budget Inn, Fabulous 7 Motel
	Other	N: **Vacationer RV Resort▲**
20B		**Greenfield Dr, to Crest (WB)**
	Gas	N: 7-11, Chevron◈, Exxon◈, Shell S: Mobil
	Food	N: Janet's Café, McDonald's
	Med	N: **+ Hospital**
	Other	N: Albertson's, AutoZone, O'Reilly, Von's, **Circle RV Resort▲**, **CA State Highway Patrol Post**, Auto Repair
22		**Los Coches Rd Interchange (EB) Camino Canada, Lakeside**
	Gas	N: 7-11, Mobil, Valero S: Shell◈
	Food	N: Mexican, Pizza S: Denny's, McDonald's, Panda Express, Subway, Taco Bell
	Other	N: Pharmacy, **Rancho Los Coches RV Park▲** S: Grocery, Midas, Radio Shack, Von's, **Walmart**
23		**Lake Jennings Park Rd**
	Gas	N: ArcoAmPm◈ S: 7-11

EXIT		CALIFORNIA
	Food	N: Jack in the Box/Arco S: Burger King, Marechiaro's
27		**Harbison Canyon Ln, Dunbar Ln**
	Other	N: **Oak Creek RV Resort▲**
30		**Tavern Rd, to Alpine**
	FStop	N: Alpine Valero, Tavern Rd Alliance
	Gas	S: 76/Circle K, Shell
	Food	S: Breadbasket, Carl's Jr, La Carretta, Long John Silver's, Ramos BBQ
	Lodg	S: Country Inn, Harris Inn
	Other	N: **LP**/Tav Rd Alliance S: Grocery, RiteAid, Radio Shack
	NOTE:	**MM 31: Elev 2000'**
33		**W Willows Rd, Alpine Blvd**
	Other	N: **Viejas Casino & Outlet Center, Lodge & Restaurants**, **Alpine Springs RV Resort▲**
36		**E Willows Rd**
	Other	N: **Alpine Springs RV Park▲**, Viejas Casino/Lodge/Rest/Outlet Center
(38)		**Vista Point (EB) (Elev 3000')**
40		**CA 79N, Japatul Valley Rd, Alpine, to Descanso**
	Other	N: **to KQ Ranch RV Resort▲**
	NOTE:	**MM 42: Elev 4000'**
45		**Pine Valley Rd, Campo, Pine Valley, Julian**
	Food	N: Diner, Frosty Burger, Major's Coffee Shop, Pine Valley House Rest & Store
	Lodg	N: Pine Valley Inn Motel
	Other	N: **Cuyamaca Ranch State Park**
47		**Sunrise Hwy, Campo, CR S1**
(48)		**Inspection Station (WB)**
(51)		**Buckman Springs Rd, CR S1, to Lake Morena** **Buckman Springs Rest Area (Both dir) (CLOSED ReConstr ETA 1/11) (RR, Phone, Pic, Vend, Pet, RVDump)**
	Other	S: **to RV Camping▲**
54		**Cameron Stn, Kitchen Creek Rd**
61		**Crestwood Rd, Boulevard, Live Oak Springs, Campo**
	TStop	S: Golden Acorn **Casino** & Travel Center
	Food	S: Rest/FastFood/Golden Acorn TC
	Lodg	S: Live Oak Springs Country Inn
	Other	S: Laundry/**Casino**/GA TC, **Outdoor World RV Park▲**, Campo Indian Res
	NOTE:	**MM 62: Crestwood Summit Elev 4190'**
	NOTE:	**MM 63: Tecate Divide-Elev 4140'**
65		**CA 94S, Boulevard, Campo**
	Gas	S: Mountain Top◈
	Food	S: Burning Tree
	Lodg	S: Buena Vista Motel, Lux Inn S: Grocery, **Outdoor World Retreat▲**
73		**Carrizo Gorge Rd, Jacumba**
	Gas	S: Shell◈, Valero◈
	Food	S: Subway/Shell
	AServ	S: Towing/Shell
	Other	N: **DeAnza Springs Nudist Resort▲** S: NAPA, **RV Camping▲**
(75)		**Brake Inspection Area (EB)**
77		**In-Ko-Pah Park Rd**
	Other	N: Towing Service, Phone
80		**Mountain Springs Rd**

EXIT		CALIFORNIA
(81)		**Runaway Truck Ramp (EB)**
87		**CA 98, Calexico (EB)**
89		**Imperial Hwy, CA 98, Ocotillco**
	FStop	N: OTU Fuel Mart S: Desert Fuel Stop/76
	Gas	N: Shell
	Food	S: Desert Kitchen/Desert FS
	Lodg	N: Ocotillo Motel & **RV Park▲**
	TServ	S: 76
	Other	S: **RV Camping▲**, US Post Office
101		**Dunaway Rd, Imperial Valley**
107		**Drew Rd, El Centro, Seeley**
	Other	N: **Sunbeam Lake RV Resort▲**, El Centro Naval Air Facility S: **Rio Bend RV Golf Resort▲**
(108)		**Sunbeam Rest Area (Both dir) (RR, Phone, Pic, Vend, Pet, RVDump) (CLOSED for ReConstr early 2011)**
111		**Forrester Rd, to Westmorland**
114		**Imperial Ave, El Centro, Imperial**
	Gas	N: Citgo/7-11◈, ArcoAmPm, Chevron, Shell, USA◈
	Food	N: 4 Seasons Buffet, Applebee's, Burger King, Carrow's, Del Taco, Denny's, El Pollo Loco, Golden Corral, Jack in the Box, KFC, McDonald's, Sizzler, Subway, Starbucks, Taco Bell, Wendy's
	Lodg	N: Clarion Inn, Days Inn, Howard Johnson, Knights Inn, Laguana Inn, Ramada Inn, Super 8, Vacation Inn
	Other	N: Albertson's, America's Tire, Big Lots, Costco, Food4Less, Goodyear, Lowe's, Pep Boys, RiteAid, Staples, Target, Von's, **Walmart SC**, Walgreen's, **Vacation Inn RV Park▲**, **Ca State Hwy Patrol Post**, Imperial Co Airport✈
115		**CA 86, 4th St, El Centro**
	TStop	N: 7-11 Food Store S: On the Go Travel Center/Mobil (Scales)
	Gas	N: ArcoAmPm, Chevron, Shell◈, USA
	Food	N: Carl's Jr, Chiba Express, Jack in the Box, McDonald's, Mexicali Taco S: Subway/Pizza Hut/Rest/OTG TC, Chili's, IHOP, Starbucks, Taco Bell
	Lodg	N: Holiday Inn Express, Motel 6♥ S: Best Western, Comfort Inn, EZ 8 Motel, Rodeway Inn♥, Value Inn
	TServ	N: Kennedy's for Tires
	Other	N: Auto Dealers, Goodyear, Grocery, U-Haul S: Laundry/**LP**/**RVDump**/OTG TC, Auto Dealers, Home Depot, Staples, **Desert Trails RV Park & Golf Course▲**
116		**Dogwood Rd**
	FStop	N: Pacific Pride
	Gas	S: ArcoAmPm
	Food	S: Carino's, Chili's, Chuck E Cheese, Denny's, Famous Dave's BBQ, Jack in The Box, Johnny Carino's, Starbucks
	Lodg	S: Fairfield Inn, Towneplace Suites
	Other	N: **RV Camping▲** S: Best Buy, Petco♥, Radio Shack, Staples, Imperial Valley Mall, Cinema, Carwash/Arco
118A		**CA 111S, Calexico (EB)**
118B		**CA 111N, Brawley (EB)**
	TStop	N: Truck Stop 111/Shell (Scales)
	Food	N: Subway/TS 111

EXIT **CA / AZ**

TWash N: TS 111
TServ N: TS 111/Tires
Other N: Laundry/RVDump/LP/TS 111, **Country Life RV & MH Park▲**

120 **Bowker Rd**

125 **Orchard Rd, CR S32, Holtville** (Serv 5 mi N in Holtville)

128 **Bonds Corner Rd** (Serv 5 mi N)

131 **CA 115N, Vanderlinden Rd, Holtville** (Serv 5 mi N)

143 **CA 98W, to Calexico**

146 **Brock Center Rd, Winterhaven**

151 **Gordons Well Rd**
Other N: **Gordons Well RV Park▲**

(155) **Sand Hills Rest Area** (L Ex, Both dir) (RR, Picnic)

156 **Grays Well Rd**

159 **Ogilby Rd, to Blythe**

164 **Sidewinder Rd**
Gas S: Shell
Other N: CA State Hwy Patrol Post
S: **Pilot Knob RV Park▲**

(165) **Inspection Station** (WB)

166 **CA 186S (EB), Algondones Rd**
Other Fort Yuma-Quechan Indian Reservation, S to Mexico

170 **Winterhaven Dr, Winterhaven**
Other S: **Rivers Edge RV Park▲**

172 **4th Ave, Yuma, Winterhaven**
Gas S: Barney's, Circle K, Chevron, Shell
Food S: Domino's Pizza, Jack in the Box, Mexican, Yuma Landing Bar & Grill
Lodg S: Best Western, Desert Sands Motel, Yuma Inn
Other N: Fort Yuma Paradise Casino
S: Family Dollar, Carwash, **Rivers Edge RV Resort▲**, **Friendly Acres RV Park▲**, **Yuma State Park**

NOTE: MM# 178.5: Arizona State Line

PACIFIC TIME ZONE

⬆ CALIFORNIA
⬇ ARIZONA

MOUNTAIN TIME ZONE

NOTE: AZ does NOT observe D S T

NOTE: I-8 begins/ends on I-10, Ex #199

1 **Giss Pkwy, 4th Ave, Redondo Center Dr, Yuma** (Serv S on 4th Ave)
Gas S: 76, Barney's, Circle K, Chevron, Shell
Food S: Filiberto's, Jack in the Box, Taco Bell
Lodg S: Best Western, Lee Hotel, Rodeway Inn, Yuma Inn

Personal Notes

EXIT **ARIZONA**

Other N: **Yuma Territorial Prison State Historical Park**
Other S: Amtrak, Auto Services, Grocery, 99 Store, Big Lots, IGA, Radio Shack, Main St Cinema, **Yuma Quartermaster Depot State Historical Park**, to appr 4mi: **Cocopah RV & Golf Resort▲**, to **Friendly Acres RV Park▲**, **Lazy S & Roadrunner RV Park▲**, **Shady Acres MH & RV Park▲**,

(1.5) **Inspection Station** (Both dir)

2 **US 95, 16th St, Yuma, Yuma Proving Grounds, Quartzite** (Addt'l Services-Gas, Food, Lodging, Shopping on 4th Ave S, Pacific Ave S)
Gas N: 76, ArcoAmpm, Circle K, Chevron, Murphy◈, Sam's
S: ArcoAmPm◈, Chevron◈, Mobil, Shell
Food N: Ah-So Sushi & Steak, Applebee's, Carl's Jr, Chili's, Chuck E Cheese, Cracker Barrel, Del Taco, Denny's, Famous Dave's BBQ, In N Out Burger, Logan's Roadhouse, McDonald's, Mimi's Cafe, Musick's, Panda Express, Penny's Diner, Quiznos, Red Lobster, Starbucks, Subway, Taylor's Taste of TX
S: Burger King, Carl's Jr, Carino's, Golden Corral, IHOP, Jack in the Box, McDonald's, Outback Steakhouse, Wendy's
Lodg N: Best Western♥, Candlewood Suites, Days Inn, Fairfield Inn, Hampton Inn, Holiday Inn♥, La Fuente Inn, Motel 6♥, Oak Tree Inn, Shilo Inn, Springhill Suites, Towneplace Suites
S: Comfort Inn♥, Motel 6, Radisson, Super 8

EXIT **ARIZONA**

Med S: **+ Yuma Reg'l Medical Center, + Northside Medical Walk-In Clinic**
Other N: Auto/Tire Repair, Best Buy, NAPA, PetSmart♥, Sam's Club, Target, Tires, **Walmart** sc, Yuma Palms Mall, to appr 4 mi: **Yuma Lakes RV Resort/Col River Adv/KOA▲**
S: Big Lots, Family Dollar, FedEx Office, Grocery, Home Depot, Harbor Freight Tools, Radio Shack, Staples, UPS Store, U-Haul, Vets & Animal Clinics♥, Towing,
Other N: Camel Farm, Desert Hills Muni Golf Course, Discount Tire, Yuma Civic Center/RVDump, Yuma Int'l Airport✈

3 **AZ 280S, Ave 3E, Yuma, Int'l Airport, Marine Corps Air Station**
TStop S: Love's Travel Stop #349 (Scales), To 3200 E US 80: Barney's #30
Food N: Burger King
S: Chesters/Subway/Love's TS, KFC, Pizza Hut
Lodg N: Candlewood Suites, Holiday Inn Express♥, Homewood Suites♥
TServ S: Diesel Injection Service
Other S: Laundry/WiFi/RVDump/Love's TS, Purcell Tires, Auto Dealers, Auto Services, **Walmart** sc, Yuma Co Fairgrounds, US Marine Corps Air Station, Yuma Airport, **Az West RV Park▲**, **Sun Vista RV Resort▲**, **Araby Acres RV Resort▲**, **Guaranty RV**, to appr 4mi-**Del Pueblo RV Park & Tennis Resort▲**, to **Southern Mesa RV Park▲**

7 **Araby Rd, 32nd St, Yuma**
FStop S: Circle K Truxtop #1948/Unocal 76
TServ S: Yuma Diesel Service
Other S: **Windhaven RV Park▲**, **Westwind RV & Golf Resort▲**, **La Mesa RV**, **AZ Sands RV Park▲**, **Country Roads RV Village▲**, **RV Connection**, **RV World**, **Blue Diamond Home & RV**, to **Villa Alameda RV Resort▲**, **Suni Sands RV Resort/Encore▲**, **Araby Acres RV Resort▲**, Northern AZ Univ, AZ Western College

9 **I-8 Bus Lp, 32nd St, 4th Ave, Ave 8½ E, to Yuma** (WB, diff reaccess)
Gas S: 76, Chevron, Circle K
Food S: Carl's Jr, Carrow's, Domino's Pizza, Jack in the Box, Pizza Hut, Taco Bell
Lodg S: Holiday Inn Express, Quality Inn, Ramada Inn, Travelodge
Other N: **Bonita Mesa RV Park▲**, **Sun Vista RV Park▲**, **Desert Paradise RV Resort▲**
S: Albertson's, Auto Dealers, Lowe's, Pep Boys, Target, Walgreen's

12 **Fortuna Rd, to US 95N**
FStop S: Shell #10
TStop N: Barney's Auto Truck Plaza/FJ TP (Scales)
Gas N: Chevron, Shell
S: 76
Food N: DaybreakersCafe/Barney's ATP, Jack in the Box, Pizza Hut, Tyler's BBQ
S: Burger King/Shell, Applebee's, DQ, Subway
Lodg N: Courtesy Inn, Comfort Inn
S: Microtel♥
TServ N: Barney's TP/Tires
Med S: **+ Walk In Medical Care & Urgent Care**

◈= Regular Gas Stations with Diesel ▲ = RV Friendly Locations ♥= Pet Friendly Locations
Red print shows large vehicle parking / access on site or nearby Brown Print = Campgrounds / RV PARKS

EXIT		ARIZONA
	Other	N: Laundry/**RVDump**/Barney's ATP, Ace Hardware, Grocery, **Caravan Oasis RV Park▲**, **Shangri La RV Park▲**, **Las Quintas Oasis RV Park▲**, **Cactus Gardens RV Resort▲** **MIL/Lake Martinez Rec Facility**, **MIL/Desert Breeze Travel Camp▲** S: **LP**/Shell, Dollar General, Fry's, Radio Shack, **Blue Sky RV Park▲**, **Western Sands RV Park▲**, **Sunset Palm RV Park▲**, **Sun Ridge RV Park▲**, **Adobe Village RV Park▲**
14		**Foothills Blvd, Yuma**
	Food	S: Domino's, Foothills Rest, Kountry Kitchen Café, Mi Fajita
	Other	N: **Sundance RV Resort▲**, Yuma Proving Ground, National Guard Rifle Range, **Fortuna De Oro RV Park▲**, S: **Sun Ridge RV Park▲**, **Foothills Village RV Park▲**, **Gila Mtn RV Park▲**, Barry M Goldwater Air Force Base
(17)		**Inspection Station/Border Patrol (EB)**
21		**Los Angeles Ave, Welton, Dome Valley Rd, Dome Valley**
	Food	N: Café
	Other	N: **Coach Stop RV Park▲**, **Arrowhead RV Park▲**
(22)		**Parking Area** (Both dir)
30		**Ave 29E, Wellton**
	Gas	N: 76, Circle K S: Chevron
	Food	S: Jack in the Box
	Lodg	S: Microtel
	Other	N: **Tier Drop RV Park▲**, **Pioneer RV Park▲**, **to Desert Rose RV Park▲**, **M & M RV Village▲**, **Sun Country RV Park▲**, **Desert Sands RV Park▲** S: Chevron/**RVDump**, Golf Course
37		**Ave 36E, Welton, to Roll**
	Other	S: Wellton Airport✈
42		**Ave 40E, Tacna, Wellton**
	Gas	N: Chevron◈
	Lodg	N: Chaparral Motel
	Other	S: Colfred Airport✈
54		**Ave 52E, Roll, Mt Mohawk Valley**
(56)		**Mohawk Rest Area** (Both dir) (RR, Phone, Pic, Vend)
67		**Ave 64E, Roll, Dateland**
	Gas	S: Dateland Palms Village/Exxon◈
	Food	S: Dateland Palms Village Restaurant (FYI: Kennels available for your pets while u eat)
	Other	N: Harley's Tire Service, Dateland Airfield✈ S: **Dateland Palms Village Gift Shop/ LP/RV Park▲**, **to Oasis RV Park at Aztec Hills▲**
73		**Aztec Rd**
78		**Spot Rd, Ave 75E, Dateland**
(84)		**Rest Area (EB)** (RR, Phone, Picnic, Vend, Pet)
(85)		**Rest Area (WB)** (RR, Phone, Picnic, Vend, Pet)
87		**Sentinel, Hyder, Aqua Caliente**
102		**Painted Rock Rd, Gila Bend**
106		**Paloma Rd, Gila Bend**
111		**Citrus Valley Rd**
115		**AZ 85, Ajo, (EB, Left Exit) Bus Lp 8, Gila Bend, to Phoenix, Ajo, Mexico**
	TStop	N: Love's Travel Stop #296 (Scales), Bill Henry's Food Mart/Texaco
	Gas	N: Circle K
	Food	N: Taco Bell/Love's TS, Burger King, McDonald's, Sofia's Mexican Food, Rest/BW
	Lodg	N: Best Western, Knights Inn, Yucca Motel
	TServ	N: Bill Henry's FM/Tires/Towing
	Med	N: + Hospital
	Other	N: WiFi/**RVDump**/Love's TS, **RVDump/LP**/Bill Henry's, NAPA, Gila Bend Muni Airport✈ S: Gila Bend Air Force Aux Field
119		**Bus 8, Gila Bend, Butterfield Trail (EB), AZ 85N, to I-10, Gila Bend**
	TStop	N: Holt Interstate Services/Shell (Scales)
	Gas	N: Chevron
	Food	N: Subway/CafeCharro/Holt's TS, Rest/BW, DQ, Café
	Lodg	N: America'sChoiceInn/Holt's TS, Best Western, Super 8
	Other	N: WiFi/**RV Dump**/**RVPark**/Holts Shell, **Augie's Quail Trail RV Park▲**, Gila Bend Muni Airport✈
140		**Freeman Rd, Gila Bend**
144		**Vekol Rd**
(149)		**Picnic Area** (Both dir)
151		**AZ 84E, Maricopa Rd, to AZ 347N, Stanfield**
	Other	N: **to John Wayne RV Ranch▲**, Harrah's Casino Resort S: **Saguaro RV Park▲**
161		**Stanfield Rd, Stanfield**
	Gas	N: Circle K
167		**Montgomery Rd, Casa Grande (Serv appr 5 mi N)**
	Lodg	N: to Francisco Grand Hotel & Golf Resort
	Other	N: **to Sierra Vista RV Park▲**, **Casa Grande Golf & RV Resort▲**
169		**Bianco Rd**
172		**Thornton Rd, Casa Grande (Serv appr 5 mi N)**
	Food	N: Sizzler
	Lodg	N: to Best Western, Holiday Inn, Super 8
	Other	N: **to Sundance RV Resort▲**, Casa Grande Muni Airport✈, **to Arizona Motel & RV Park▲**
174		**Trekell Rd, Casa Grande**
	Med	N: + Hospital
	Other	S: Casa Grande Military Reservation
(178A)		**Jct I-10, E - Tucson**
(178B)		**Jct I-10, W - Phoenix (EB, Left exit)**
	Other	N: **Buena Tierra Family Campground & RV Park▲**

MOUNTAIN TIME ZONE

NOTE: I-8 begins/ends on Sunset Cliff Blvd

NOTE: AZ does not observe D S T

ARIZONA

Begin Westbound I-8 from Jct I-10 in AZ to Jct I-5 in San Diego, CA.

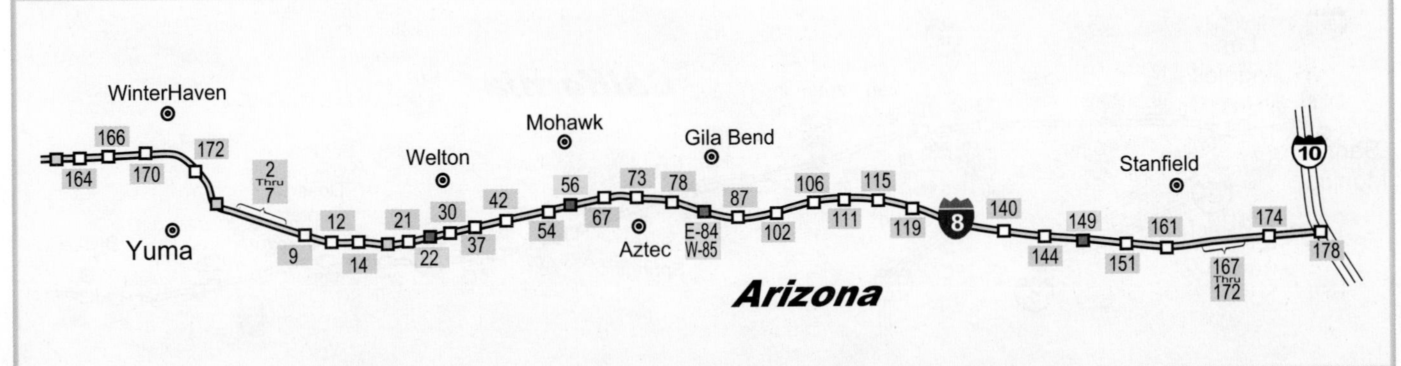

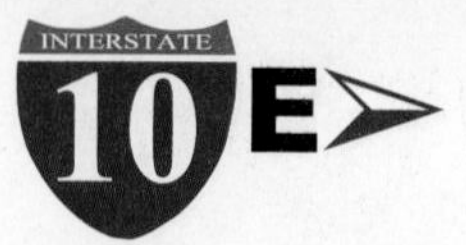

EXIT		CALIFORNIA

Below lists Eastbound I-10 from Santa Monica, CA to Jct I-95 in Jacksonville, FL.

CALIFORNIA

PACIFIC TIME ZONE

NOTE: I-10 begin/ends in FL on I-95, Ex #351B

(0) **CA 1N, Oxnard, Santa Monica Blvd, to Beaches**

1A **4th St, 5th St**

1B **20th St (EB), CA 1S, Lincoln Blvd (WB)**
Gas S: Chevron, Exxon, Shell
Food N: Denny's, El Pollo Loco, Norm's Rest, Subway
S: Jack in the Box
Lodg N: Holiday Inn
Other N: Mall, Auto Repair, Von's
S: Firestone, U-Haul

1C **Cloverfield Blvd (WB)**
Gas N: ArcoAmPm, Shell
AServ N: Shell
Med N: + Hospital

2 **Centinela Ave (EB)**

2A **Centinela Ave, Pico Blvd (WB)**
Food N: Mexican, Taco Bell
S: McDonald's, KFC
Lodg S: Santa Monica Hotel
Other S: Trader Joe's

2B **Bundy Dr S (WB)**
Food S: Taco Bell
Other S: Santa Monica Airport✈

2C **Bundy Dr N (WB)**
Gas N: 76, Chevron, Shell◈
Food N: Pizza Hut, Taco Bell

(3A) **Jct I-405N, to Sacramento**

(3B) **Jct I-405S, to Long Beach**

4 **Overland Ave (WB), National Blvd**
Gas S: Mobil
Other S: Jiffy Lube

5 **National Blvd (WB)**
Gas N: 76
S: ArcoAmPm
Food N: Papa John's, Subway, Starbucks
S: KFC
Other N: RiteAid, Von's

6 **Robertson Blvd, Culver City**
Gas N: Chevron, Mobil, Valero
Food N: Del Taco, Dominos Pizza, Starbucks, Taco Bell, Wendy's

EXIT		CALIFORNIA

Other N: Goodyear
S: Albertson's/Pharmacy

7A **La Cienega Blvd (EB), Venice Blvd**
Gas N: Chevron, Mobil
S: ArcoAmPm, Mobil
Food S: Carl's Jr, McDonald's, Subway
Med S: + Kaiser Permamente Hospital
Other S: Auto Services

7B **Fairfax Ave (EB), Washington Blvd**

8 **La Brea Ave, Englewood**
Gas N: Chevron, Shell◈
S: Chevron
AServ N: Shell
Other N: Walgreen's
S: Auto Zone, Ralph's, Auto Services

9 **Crenshaw Blvd, Englewood**
Gas N: Mobil
S: Chevron, Mobil, Shell, Thrifty
Food N: Jack in the Box
S: El Pollo Loco, McDonald's, Taco Bell
Other S: U-Haul

10 **Arlington Ave, Los Angeles**
Gas N: 76, Chevron, Mobil
Other N: Auto & Tire Services

11 **Western Ave, Normandie Ave**
Gas N: Chevron, Mobil
S: Chevron, Texaco
Food N: McDonald's
Other N: Auto Zone, Food 4 Less, Pharmacy
S: Auto Repair

12 **Vermont Ave (EB), Hoover St**
Gas N: Mobil, Texaco
S: ArcoAmPm, Chevron, Valero◈
Food N: Burger King, McDonald's
S: Jack in the Box
Other N: Auto Services, Pep Boys, Thrifty Drug
S: Staples, Office Depot, Univ of S Cal, Expo Center, LA Memorial Sports Arena, LA Memorial Coliseum

(13A) **Jct I-110S, Harbor Fwy, San Pedro CA 110N, Pasadena, Harbor Fwy (EB, Left Exit)**
Other N: Staples Center/Conv Center

(13) **Jct I-110, CA 110, Harbor Fwy, Downtown, San Pedro**

14A **Maple Ave (EB), Los Angeles St**
Gas S: 76
Other S: Auto Services, Radio Shack, RiteAid

14B **San Pedro St**
Gas S: Chevron
Other S: Auto & Tire Services

15A **Central Ave, Los Angeles**
Gas N: Shell
Lodg S: Eastside Motel

EXIT		CALIFORNIA

AServ N: Shell

15B **Alameda St, Downtown LA**
FStop S: Pacific Pride
TStop N: Superfine Texaco II (Scales)
TServ N: Superfine Texaco TS
TWash N: Superfine Texaco TS

16A **Santa Fe Ave**
Gas S: Shell

16B **CA 60E, Pomona, I-5S, Santa Ana (WB, Left Exit)**

(17) **Jct I-5N, to Sacramento**

19 **State St, Soto St (EB)**

19A **State St (WB, Left exit)**
Gas N: Shell
Med N: + USC Medical Center

19B **US 101, Los Angeles, I-5N, Sacramento (WB, Left exit)**

19C **Soto St (WB)**
Gas N: Shell
S: Mobil, Pronto, Shell
Lodg S: Vista Motel
Med N: + USC Medical Center
Other S: Auto Services

20A **City Terrace Dr, Herbert Ave (EB)**

20B **Eastern Ave (EB)**

20 **Eastern Ave, City Terrace Dr**
Gas S: Chevron, Mobil
Food S: Burger King, McDonald's
TServ N: L&S Diesel Service

(21) **Jct I-710, Long Beach Fwy (EB), Eastern Ave (WB)**

22 **Fremont Ave, Alahambra (All Serv N to N Valley Blvd)**
Gas S: 7-11
Med N: + Hospital

23A **Atlantic Blvd, Monterey Park**
Gas N: Mobil
Food N: Del Taco, Pizza Hut, Popeye's
Lodg S: Best Western
Med N: + Hospital
Other S: Firestone, Ralph's

23B **Garfield Ave, Alhambra, Monterey Park**
Gas S: Shell◈
Med N: + Garfield Medical Center

24 **New Ave, to Monterey Park**
Gas N: Mobil

25A **Del Mar Ave, to San Gabriel**
Gas N: 76
S: Arco, Chevron◈
Lodg S: Best Value Inn

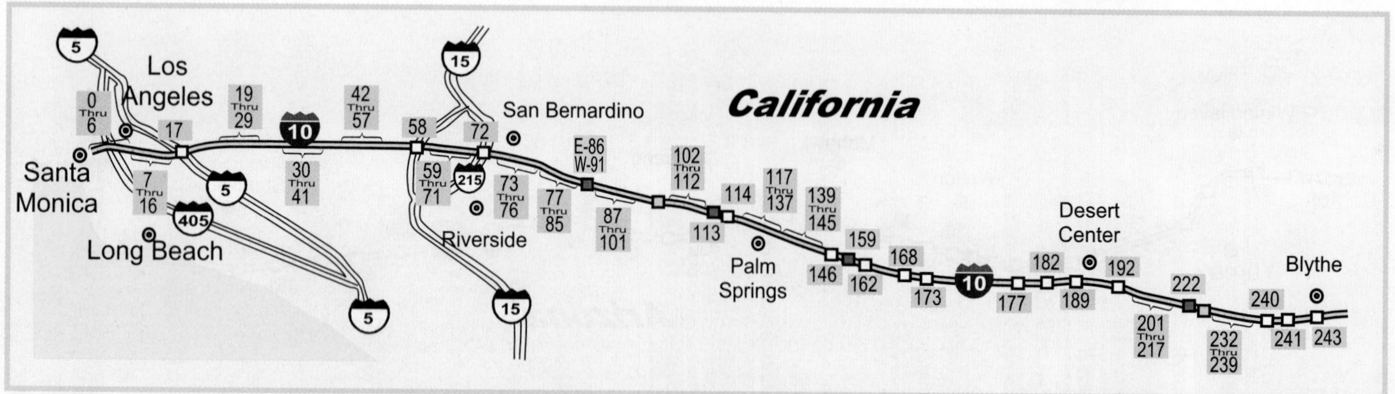

◈= Regular Gas Stations with Diesel ▲ = RV Friendly Locations ♥= Pet Friendly Locations
Red print shows large vehicle parking / access on site or nearby Brown Print = Campgrounds / RV PARKS

EXIT		CALIFORNIA
25B		**San Gabriel Blvd, San Gabriel**
	Gas	N: Arco, Mobil Shell
		S: 7-11/Citgo
	Food	N: Carl's Jr, Popeye's, Taco Bell
		S: Burger King
	Lodg	N: Budget Inn
	AServ	N: Shell
26A		**Walnut Grove Ave, Rosemead**
26B		**CA 164, Rosemead Blvd (EB), CA 19 (WB)**
	Food	N: Denny's, IHOP
		S: Jack in the Box, Starbucks
	Lodg	N: Ramada Inn, Rosemead Inn, Vagabond Inn
	Other	N: Office Depot, Radio Shack, Target, U-Haul
27B		**Temple City Blvd, Rosemead**
27		**Baldwin Ave (EB), Temple City Blvd, Rosemead**
	Gas	S: ArcoAmPm, USA
	Food	S: Denny's, Edwards Steakhouse
28		**Santa Anita Ave, El Monte**
	Gas	N: Shell
		S: 76
	Other	N: El Monte Airport✈
29A		**Peck Rd S, El Monte**
29B		**Peck Rd N (EB), Valley Blvd, El Monte**
	Gas	N: Chevron
		S: 76, Mobil, Shell
	Food	N: Burger King, Carl's Jr, Denny's , KFC
		S: Del Taco, McDonald's
	Lodg	N: Motel 6♥
	Other	N: Auto Dealers
		S: El Monte RV Rentals & Sales
29C		**Peck Rd N (WB)**
30		**Garvey Ave, El Monte (WB)**
(31)		**Jct I-605S, to Long Beach, N to Baldwin Park (WB)**
(31A)		**Jct I-605S, to Long Beach (EB)**
(31B)		**Jct I-605N, to Baldwin Park (EB) Frazier St (WB)**
31C		**Frazier St (EB)**
32A		**Baldwin Park Blvd, Baldwin Park**
	Gas	N: ArcoAmPm, Chevron, Shell
	Food	N: Burger King, IHOP, In 'n Out Burger, Jack in the Box, McDonald's/Chevron
	Lodg	N: Angel Motel, Aristocrat Motel
	Med	N: + Hospital
	Other	N: CVS, Office Max, Target, Food 4 Less, CA RV
		S: Altman RV Center
32B		**Francisquito Ave, La Puente**
	Gas	S: Chevron
	Food	N: In 'n Out
		S: Carl's Jr
	Lodg	S: Grand Park Inn
	Other	N: CA State Hwy Patrol Post
33		**Puente Ave, Baldwin Park**
	Gas	N: Chevron
		S: Valero◈
	Food	N: China Palace, Denny's, McDonald's, Panda Express, Sizzler, Starbucks
		S: Jack in the Box

EXIT		CALIFORNIA
	Lodg	N: Courtyard, Motel 6♥, Plaza Motel, Radisson
		S: Baldwin Motor Lodge, Regency Inn
	Other	N: Home Depot, Staples, Walmart sc
		S: Laidlaw's Harley Davidson, U-Haul
34		**Pacific Ave, Covina Pkwy (EB)**
	Gas	S: Mobil, Shell
	Food	S: Chevy's Mex Rest
	Lodg	N: Covina Motel
	Med	S: + Dr's Hospital of W Covina
	Other	N: Laundromat, Grocery
		S: Goodyear, Westfield Mall
34B		**Sunset Ave, West Covina (WB)**
	Lodg	N: Wayside Motel
34A		**Pacific Ave, W Covina Pkwy (WB)**
35		**Vincent Ave, Glendora Ave**
	Gas	N: Chevron, Mobil
		S: 76
	Food	N: KFC, Pizza Hut
		S: Applebees, CA Steak & Fries, Chevy's Mexican, Red Robin, Starbucks, Subway
	Other	S: Best Buy, Barnes & Noble, Big O Tire, Cinema, Greyhound, Mall
36		**CA 39, Azusa Ave, West Covina**
	Gas	N: 76, ArcoAmPm, Chevron
		S: Mobil, Shell
	Food	N: Black Angus Steakhouse, Subway McDonald's, Red Lobster, Steak Corral
		S: Carrow's
	Lodg	N: El Dorado Motor Inn, Ramada
	Other	N: Auto Dealers
		S: Auto Dealers, Hertz RAC
37A		**Citrus St, W Covina**
	Gas	N: Chevron, Shell
		S: 76, Valero
	Food	N: Burger King, IHOP, TGI Friday
	Lodg	S: Comfort Inn, Courtyard, Five Star Inn
	Med	S: + Hospital
	Other	N: Grocery, Target, Office Depot
		S: Trader Joe's
37B		**Barranca St**
	Gas	N: Shell
	Food	N: Coco's, El Torito, Monterrey
		S: McDonald's, In 'n Out Burger
	Lodg	N: Best Western, Hampton Inn, Holiday Inn
		S: Comfort Inn
38A		**Grand Ave, W Covina**
	Gas	N: Arco
	Food	N: Chinese, Denny's
		S: McDonald's
	Lodg	N: Best Western
		S: Holiday Inn
38B		**Holt Ave, Garvey Ave**
	Lodg	N: Embassy Suites, Radisson
40		**Via Verde, Covina**
41		**Kellogg Dr, Cal Poly University**
42		**CA 57, Santa Ana, I-210W (WB)**
42A		**CA 57, Santa Ana, I-210W**
42B		**CA 71S, Corona**
43		**Fairplex Dr, La Verne (EB)**
44		**Dudley St (EB), Fairplex Dr (WB), Pomona, La Verne**
	Gas	N: 76, ArcoAmPm◈
		S: Chevron, Mobil
	Food	N: Denny's
		S: McDonald's, Jack in the Box

EXIT		CALIFORNIA
	Lodg	N: Lemon Tree Motel, Fairplex Sheraton
45		**Garey Ave, Pomona (WB)**
45A		**White Ave, Pomona (EB)**
45B		**Garey Ave, Pomona (EB)**
	Gas	S: Chevron, Shell◈ (DAD)
	Other	S: Carwash/Shell
46		**Towne Ave, Pomona**
	Gas	N: 7-11
	Food	N: Jack in the Box, Subway
47		**Indian Hill Blvd, Claremont**
	Gas	N: Mobil
		S: 76◈, Chevron, Shell
	Food	N: Baker's Square, Tony Roma
		S: Burger King, Carl's Jr, Denny's, In N Out Burger, McDonald's/Chevron, Starbucks
	Lodg	N: Howard Johnson, Travelodge♥
		S: Ramada Inn♥
	Other	S: Albertson's, America's Tire, AutoZone, Radio Shack, Greyhound
48		**Monte Vista Ave, Montclair (Access to Ex #49)**
	Gas	N: Shell
	Food	N: Applebee's, Black Angus Steakhouse, Chili's, Olive Garden, Red Lobster, Tony Roma
	Med	S: + Dr's Hospital of Montclair
	Other	N: Mall
49		**Central Ave, Montclair (acc to #48)**
	Gas	N: 7-11, Chevron, Mobil, Shell
		S: 76, Costco
	Food	N: El Pollo Loco, McDonald's
		S: Jack in the Box, Long John Silver's
	Other	N: Best Buy, Borders, Firestone, Goodyear, Harbor Freight Tools, Office Depot, Pep Boys, PetSmart♥, Mall, Vet♥, Animal Hospital♥, to Cable Airport✈
		S: Costco, Target, Giant RV
50		**Mountain Ave, Upland, Ontario**
	Gas	N: ArcoAmPm, Chevron, Mobil, Shell◈
		S: 76◈
	Food	N: BBQ, Carrow's, Denny's, El Torito, Happy Wok, Mimi's Café, Subway, Wendy's
		S: Carl's Jr, Starbucks
	Lodg	N: Super 8
		S: Comfort Inn♥, Motel 6♥
	Other	N: Home Depot, Staples, Pharmacy, Trader Joe's
		S: Albertson's, RiteAid, Target, US Post Office, UPS Store
51		**CA 83, Euclid Ave**
	Food	N: Coco's
53		**4th St, to Ontario**
	Gas	N: ArcoAmPm, Chevron, Shell
		S: 76, ArcoAmPm, Exxon
	Food	N: Carl's Jr, Jack in the Box, Popeye's, Sizzler, Taco Bell
		S: Denny's, KFC, Mexican, McDonald's, Pizza Hut
	Lodg	N: Motel 6♥, Quality Inn
		S: CA Inn, Days Inn, Travelodge
	Other	N: Radio Shack, Pharmacy, Ralph's
54		**Vineyard Ave, Ontario**
	Gas	N: Shell
		S: ArcoAmPm, Mobil, Shell, USA
	Food	N: Del Taco, Sizzler, Taco Bell
		S: Denny's, In 'n Out Burger, Indian Rest, Japanese Rest, Mexican Rest

◈= Regular Gas Stations with Diesel ▲ = RV Friendly Locations ♥= Pet Friendly Locations
Red print shows large vehicle parking / access on site or nearby Brown Print = Campgrounds / RV PARKS

Lodg **S:** Best Western, Comfort Suites, Country Suites, Ontario Airport Inn, Ramada, Red Roof Inn♥, Sheraton x2, Super 8
Other **N:** Grocery, Auto Zone, RiteAid, Ralph's

55 Archibald Ave, Ontario Airport

55A Holt Blvd, Ontario (WB)
Gas **N:** Mobil◈
Food **N:** Subway
Med **N:** + Family Urgent Care
Lodg **S:** Holiday Inn
Other **S:** Auto Dealers, Convention Center

55B Archibald Ave, Ontario Int'l Airport
Other **S:** Ontario Int'l Airport✈

56 Haven Ave, Rancho Cucamonga
Gas **N:** Mobil
Food **N:** Black Angus Steakhouse, El Torito, Benihana, Tony Roma
S: Panda Chinese, TGI Friday
Lodg **N:** Best Western♥, Extended Stay America, Hilton, Holiday Inn, La Quinta Inn♥
S: Fairfield Inn
Other **N:** Best Buy, Target

57 Milliken Ave, Ontario
TStop **N:** Travel Center of America #162/76 (Scales)
S: Travel Center of America #26 (Scales)
Gas **N:** ArcoAmPm, Chevron, Mobil◈, Shell, Sam's, Costco
Food **N:** Rest/PHut/Subw/TB/TA TC, Applebee's, Arby's, Burger King, BJ's Rest, Carl's Jr, ChickFilA, Chipolte Grill, Coco's Rest, Dave & Busters, Daphne's Greek Cafe, El Pollo Loco, Fuddruckers, Hooters, IHOP, Iron Chef Cafe, Market Broiler Rest, McDonald's, Olive Garden, Red Lobster, Rubio's Mexican Grill, Starbucks, Subway/Mobil, Wendy's
S: Rest/BKing/TB/ChesterFrChkn/TA TC
Lodg **N:** Ayers Inn, Ayers Suite Hotel, Baymont Inn, Country Suites, Extended Stay America, Hampton Inn, Hilton Garden Inn, Hyatt Place, Towneplace Suites
S: Rodeway Inn
TWash **N:** TA TC
TServ **N:** TA TC/Tires
S: TA TC/Tires
Other **N:** Laundry/BarbSh/WiFi/TA TC, Ontario Mills Mall, Americas Tire, Best Buy, Big O Tires, Costco, Sam's Club, Staples, Target, UPS Store, Pharmacy
S: Laundry/WiFi/TA TC, **Affordable RV Center▲**

(58) Jct I-15N, to Barstow, Las Vegas Jct I-15S, to San Diego (WB)

(58A) Jct I-15N, to Barstow, Las Vegas

(58B) Jct I-15S, to San Diego (EB)

59 Etiwanda Ave, Ontario, Fontana

61 Cherry Ave, Fontana
FStop **N:** A-Z Fuel Stop, Fontana Chevron
S: BTE Gas Stop (Scales)
TStop **N:** Truck Town Truck & Travel Plaza (Scales), to 10002 Almond Ave: Fontana Truck Stop (Scales)
S: Three Sisters Truck Stop (Scales), North American Truck Stop
Gas **N:** ArcoAmPm, Valero
S: 76/Circle K

EXIT CALIFORNIA

Food **N:** Rest/TT TS, FastFood/Fontana Chev, Cozy Corner Café, Carl's Jr, Del Taco, Jack in the Box
S: Farmer Boys Rest
Lodg **N:** Circle Inn Motel
TWash **S:** 3S TS
TServ **N:** TT TP, Big Rig Truck Repair, N Amer TS, Peterbilt, Rene's Tire Service, Trans West Truck Center, Ford Trucks
S: 3S TS
Other **N:** Laundry/TT TP, CA Speedway
S: Laundry/3S TS, **California RV Sales**

63 Citrus Ave, Fontana
FStop **N:** EZ Truck Stop/76
Gas **N:** Beacon
S: 7-11/Citgo, ArcoAmPm
Food **N:** Bakers Burgers, D/T, Mexican Rest
Other **N:** LP/EZ TS, Auto Dealer

64 Sierra Ave, Fontana
Gas **N:** ArcoAmPm, Mobil,Valero
S: Circle K
Food **N:** Applebee's, Arby's, Burger King, China Buffet, DQ, Chuck E Cheese, Del Taco, Denny's, In N Out Burger, Jack in the Box, KFC, Millie's Kitchen, McDonald's, Papa John's, Popeye's, Sizzler, Taco Bell, Wendy's
S: China Buffet, Mexican Rest, Rest/HGI
Lodg **N:** Americas Best Value Inn, Econo Lodge, Motel 6, Skyview Motel, Valley Motel
S: Hilton Garden Inn
Med **N:** + Hospital
Other **N:** Albertson's/Pharmacy, Big Lots, Dollar Tree, Cinema, Food4Less, Goodyear, Kragen Auto Parts, Pep Boys, Radio Shack, RiteAid, Tires, Auto Services
S: Target/Pharmacy

66 Cedar Ave, Bloomington
Gas **N:** ArcoAmPm, Mobil
S: 7-11
Food **N:** Baker's D/T, Burger King
Lodg **N:** Sierra Crossing Motel
Other **N:** Auto Services

68 Riverside Ave, Bloomington, to Rialto, Colton
FStop **S:** PacPride/Poma
TStop **N:** I-10 Truck Stop (Scales)
Gas **N:** Chevron
S: 76/Circle K
Food **N:** Rest/I-10 TS, Burger King, China Place, Coco's, El Pollo Loo, Hometown Buffet, Jack in the Box, McDonald's, Starbucks, Taco Joe's, Subway
Lodg **N:** American Inn, Best Western, Empire Inn, Rialto Motel, Rodeway Inn,Valley View Inn
TWash **N:** I-10 TS
TServ **N:** I-10 TS
Other **N:** Laundry/I-10 TS, **Walmart**

69 Pepper Ave, Colton
Gas **N:** Valero
Food **N:** Baker's D/T
Lodg **N:** Lido Motel
Med **N:** + Arrowhead Reg'l Medical Center
Other **N:** **California RV Sales**

70A Rancho Ave, Colton
Food **N:** Del Taco, El Rancho, Jack in the Box, KFC/TacoBell

70B 9th St, La Cadena Dr, Downtown, Colton
Gas **N:** Mobil

EXIT CALIFORNIA

Food **N:** Burger King, Denny's, KFC, McDonald's, Mexican Rest, Subway, Taco Bell
Lodg **N:** Hampton Inn
Other **N:** Carwash/Mobil

71 Mt Vernon Ave, Sperry Dr, Colton
FStop **N:** Pacific Pride
S: CFN/Poma #26
TStop **N:** Valley Colton Truck Stop (Scales)
Gas **N:** Arco
Food **N:** Rest/Valley Colton TS, Pepito's
Lodg **N:** Colony Inn, Colton Motel
TWash **N:** Valley Colton TS
TServ **N:** Valley Colton TS
Other **N:** Laundry/LP/Valley Colton TS

(72) Jct I-215, N - San Bernardino, S - Riverside
TServ **S:** Cummins Cal Pacific

73A Waterman Ave S (EB)

73B Waterman Ave N (EB)
Other **N:** America's Tire
S: **Walmart sc**

73 Waterman Ave (WB)
FStop **N:** 1055 N-CFN/Ultramar Food 'n Fuel #82
S: 2649 S-CFN/Ultramar Food 'n Fuel #81
TStop **S:** Royal Truck Stop (Scales)
Gas **N:** 76, Shell◈
S: ArcoAmPm
Food **N:** Black Angus Steakhouse, Bobby McGee's, Chili's, Chuck E Cheese, Claim Jumper Rest, Coco's, El Torito, Guadalajara Harry's, IHOP, MiMi's Cafe, Olive Garden, Panda Express, Red Lobster, Sizzler, Starbucks, TGI Friday, Tony Roma, Yamazato Japanese Rest
S: Rest/Royal TS, Burger King, Carl's Jr, Del Taco, Donut Factory, KFC, McDonald's, Popeye's, Starbucks, Taco Bell
Lodg **N:** Best Western♥, Days Inn, Hilton Garden Inn, Hilton, La Quinta Inn♥, Quality Inn♥, Super 8♥
S: Motel 6♥
TServ **S:** Royal TS/Tires
Other **N:** Best Buy, Home Depot, Office Depot, Office Max, PetSmart♥, Sam's Club, Vet♥
S: Laundry/Beacon TS, Auto Services, **La Mesa RV Center, Camping World, El Monte RV Rentals & Sales, Cruise America RV Rental, RV Services**

74 Tippecanoe Ave, Anderson St
Gas **N:** ArcoAmPm, Thrifty
S: 76◈
Food **N:** BJ's Rest, Denny's, Jack in the Box, Subway, Wendy's
S: Baker's, Del Taco, Hometown Buffet, KFC, Napoli's Italian Rest, Taco Bell
Lodg **N:** American Inn, Fairfield Inn, Loma Linda Lodge, Residence Inn
S: Dutch Motel
Med **S:** + Loma Linda University Medical Center
Other **N:** Best Buy, Costco, Home Depot, PetSmart♥, Office Depot, Sam's Club, Staples, Sports Authority, Walgreen's
S: Carwash, Harley Davidson, to Loma Linda Univ

75 Mountain View Ave, Loma Linda
Gas **N:** Valero◈
Food **S:** Farmer's Boy, Lupe's, Subway
Med **S:** + Veterans Medical Center

◈ = Regular Gas Stations with Diesel ▲ = RV Friendly Locations ♥ = Pet Friendly Locations
Red print shows large vehicle parking / access on site or nearby Brown Print = Campgrounds / RV PARKS

EXIT		CALIFORNIA
76		**California St, Redlands**
	Gas	S: ArcoAmPm, Shell
	Food	N: Mill Creek Cattle Co
		S: Applebee's, Jack in the Box, Mexican Rest, Panda Express, Subway, Wendy's
	Other	S: Food4Less, Radio Shack, **Walmart ▲**, **El Monte RV**, **Mission RV Park▲**
77A		**Alabama St (reaccess via #77C)**
	Gas	N: Chevron
		S: ArcoAmPm, Chevron, Shell
	Food	N: Denny's, Chili's, Red Robin, Romano's Macaroni Grill, Starbucks
		S: Burger King, El Pollo Loco, IHOP, Little Caesar's Pizza, Marie Callendar's, McDonald's, Papa John's, Starbucks
	Lodg	N: Amer Best Value Inn, Motel 7, Super 8
		S: Ayers Hotel, Best Western, Comfort Suites, Country Inn, Dynasty Suites, Good Night Inn
	Other	N: Barnes & Noble, Petco♥, Target, U-Haul, **RV Center**
		S: Auto Dealers, Grocery, Home Depot, Long Drugs, **RV Center**
77B		**CA 210 W to CA 330 N, Pasadena, Running Springs**
77C		**Tennessee St (EB), CA 30, Highland (WB)**
	Gas	S: Shell
	Food	S: Arby's, Burger King, Coco's, El Pollo Loco, Pizza, Subway, Taco Bell
	Lodg	S: Ayers Hotel, Best Western, Comfort Suites, Dynasty Suites
	Other	N: Home Depot, Mall
		S: US Post Office
79		**CA 38, 6th St, Redlands (WB)**
	Gas	N: Chevron
		S: 76, Shell
	Food	N: Redlands Rest
		S: Boston Market, Denny's, Rubio's, Starbucks,
	Lodg	N: Budget Inn Motel, Stardust Motel
	Other	N: Goodyear
		S: Albertson's, Office Depot, Von's/ Pharmacy, to Redlands Mall
79AB		**CA 38, Orange St (EB)**
80		**University St (EB), Cypress Ave, Citrus Ave (WB)**
	Med	N: + Hospital
	Other	N: to University of Redlands
81		**Ford St (EB), Redlands Blvd**
	Gas	S: 76
82		**Wabash Ave (WB)**
83		**Yucaipa Blvd, Redlands, Yucaipa**
	FStop	N: appr 2mi CFN/Valero #1611
	Gas	N: ArcoAmPm◈, Chevron
		S: Conv Store/Gas
	Food	N: Bakers D/T
	Lodg	S: Vincent St George Motel
85		**Live Oak Canyon Rd, Oak Glen Rd**
(86)		**Wildwood Rest Area (EB)** (RR, Phone, Picnic)
87		**County Line Rd, Calimesa**
	Gas	N: Shell◈
	Food	N: Del Taco
	Lodg	N: America's Best Value Inn, Calimesa Inn

EXIT		CALIFORNIA
	Other	N: Laundromat, Auto & Tire Services
88		**Calimesa Blvd, Calimesa**
	Gas	N: ArcoAmPm, Chevron◈, Shell
	Food	N: Burger King, Jack in the Box, McDonald's, Subway, Taco Bell
	Lodg	N: Calimesa Motor Inn
89		**Singleton Rd, Calimesa (WB)**
90		**Cherry Valley Blvd, Desert Lawn Dr**
(91)		**Brooksdie Rest Area (WB)** (RR, Phone, Picnic, Vend, Pet)
92		**San Timoteo Canyon Rd, Oak Valley Parkway, Beaumont**
	Lodg	N: Holiday Inn Express
	Other	N: Premium Outlet Mall, RiteAid
93		**CA 60W, Sixth St, Riverside (WB, Left exit)**
	Other	S: **Banning RV Discount Center**
94		**CA 79S, Beaumont Ave, Beaumont**
	Gas	N: 76, ArcoAmPm
	Food	N: Baker's, McDonald's, El Rancho Steaks
		S: Denny's, Del Taco
	Lodg	N: Best Western♥, Americas Best Value Inn♥
	Other	N: NAPA
		S: **Country Hills RV Park▲**, **Golden Village Palms RV Resort▲**
95		**Pennsylvania Ave, Beaumont (WB)**
	Gas	N: 76/Circle K
	Food	N: ABC, Rusty Lantern
	Lodg	N: Hampton Inn, Mountain Vista Hotel, Windsor Motel
	Other	N: Home Depot, **Tom's RV & Trailer Sales**
		S: **Country Hills RV Park▲**
96		**Highland Springs Ave, Banning**
	TStop	N: Banning Truck Stop
	Gas	N: ArcoAmPm, Chevron◈, Valero◈
		S: Mobil
	Food	N: Applebee's, Burger King, Denny's, Farmhouse Rest, Jack in the Box, Little Caesar's Pizza, Subway, Wendy's
		S: Carl's Jr, Chili's, McDonald's, Starbucks
	Lodg	N: Hampton Inn, Super 8
	TWash	N: Banning TS
	TServ	N: Banning TS
	Med	N: + San Gorgonio Memorial Hospital
	Other	N: Auto Services, Kragen Auto Parts, Grocery, Radio Shack, Walgreen's, **Ray's RV**
		S: ATMs, Banks, Albertson's, Best Buy, Home Depot, RiteAid, Staples, **Walmart SC**, **CA Hwy Patrol Post**
98		**Sunset Ave, Banning**
	Gas	N: Chevron◈
	Food	N: Domino's Pizza, Donut Factory, Gus's, Gramma's Country Kitchen, Roman's Chicken Palace & Mexican Food
	Lodg	N: Banning Suites, Holiday Inn Express, Sunset Motel
	Other	N: Auto Zone, Big Lots, Grocery, RiteAid, **RV Center**
		S: **Camper Corral**
99		**22nd St, Downtown, Banning**
	Gas	N: ArcoAmPm, Mobil, Shell
	Food	N: BJ's BBQ, Carl's Jr, Carrow's, KFC, McDonald's, Sizzler, Starbucks, Subway, Taco Bell, Wendy's
	Lodg	N: Days Inn, Margarita Motel, Super 8, Sunset Motel, Travelodge

EXIT		CALIFORNIA
	Other	N: Auto Dealer, Goodyear, **Banning Discount RV Center**
100		**CA 243S, 8th St, Banning**
	Gas	N: Chevron
	Food	N: IHOP, Jack in the Box, Rest/SG Inn
	Lodg	N: PeachTree Motel, Hacienda Inn, San Gorgonio Inn
	Other	N: RiteAid, Visitor Info Center, Airport✈
		S: **Stagecoach RV Park▲**
101		**Hargrave St, Banning**
	Gas	N: 76, Shell, Valero
	Food	N: Consuelo's Mexican Rest
	Lodg	N: Country Inn
	Other	N: LP/Valero, Carwash/Shell, Towing, Tires
		S: Banning Muni Airport✈
102		**Ramsey St (WB)**
	Lodg	N: 5 Star Motel, Stagecoach Motor Inn
	Other	N: Morongo Indian Res
(102)		**Inspection Station / Truck Scales** (Both dir)
103		**Fields Rd, Ramsey St, Banning**
	Gas	N: Chevron
	Food	N: McDonald's
	Other	N: Desert Hills Factory Stores, Cabazon Outlets
104		**Apache Trail, Cabazon**
	FStop	N: Morongo Travel Center
	Gas	N: Shell
	Food	N: A&W, Coco's, Hadley's, Ruby's Diner
	TServ	N: Charles Truck Repair
	Other	N: **RVDump/LP/**Morongo TC, Morongo Indian Res Hotel & **Casino/RVParking**, Bowling, Desert Hills Factory Stores, Cabazon Outlets
106		**Main St, Cabazon**
	TStop	N: Cabazon Truck & Auto Stop/Shell
	Gas	S: ArcoAmPm◈
	Food	N: Rest/Cabazon TS, Burger King, Spanky's BBQ, Wheel Inn Rest
110		**Haugen Lehmann Way**
111		**Verbenia Ave, Haugen-Lehmann Way, Whitewater**
112		**CA 111, to Palm Springs (EB)**
(113)		**Whitewater Rest Area (Both dir)** (RR, Phone, Picnic, Vend, Pet)
114		**Whitewater, Windmill Farms**
117		**CA 62N, Twenty Nine Palms, Yucca Valley, to Joshua Tree**
120		**Indian Ave, N Palm Springs**
	FStop	S: Pilot Travel Center #307 (Scales)
	Gas	N: 76, Shell
		S: Chevron
	Food	N: Denny's
		S: DQ/Wendy's/Pilot TC
	Lodg	N: Motel 6♥
	Med	S: + Hospital
	Other	S: WiFi/Pilot TC, Amtrak
123		**Palm Dr, Gene Autry Trail, to Desert Hot Springs**
	Gas	N: ArcoAmPm, Chevron
	Food	N: Jack in the Box/Chevron
	Other	N: **Sands RV Resort & Golf▲**, to **Caliente Springs RV Resort▲**, **Sky Valley Resort▲**, **Desert Pools RV Resort▲**
		S: Palm Springs Int'l Airport✈, to Gene Autry Trail

◈= Regular Gas Stations with Diesel ▲ = RV Friendly Locations ♥ = Pet Friendly Locations
Red print shows large vehicle parking / access on site or nearby Brown Print = Campgrounds / RV PARKS

EXIT — CALLIFORNIA

126 Date Palm Dr, Cathedral City to Palm Springs, Rancho Mirage
- Gas S: ArcoAmPm, Mobil, Shell
- Food S: McDonald's/Shell, Round Table Pizza, Taco Bell
- Other S: Walmart sc, to Desert Shadows RV Resort▲, Palm Springs Oasis RV Resort▲, Cathedral Palms RV Resort▲

130 Ramon Rd, Varner Rd, Bob Hope Dr, Thousand Palms, Rancho Mirage, to Palm Springs, Cathedral City
- TStop N: Flying J Travel Plaza #5020 (Scales) (DAND)
- Gas N: Chevron, Ultramar, Valero
- Food N: Carl's Jr, Del Taco, Denny's, In 'n Out Burger, McDonald's
- Lodg N: Red Roof Inn♥
  S: Westin Hotel
- TServ N: Flying J TP, Parkhouse Tire, Little Sister Truck Wash
- Other N: Laundry/WiFi/LP/RVDump/Flying J TP
  S: Desert Shadows RV Resort▲, Agua Caliente Indian Reservation & Casino Resort & Spa

131 Monterey Ave, Thousand Palms, Palm Desert, Rancho Mirage
- Gas N: ArcoAmPm, Chevron
  S: Costco, Sam's
- Food N: Jack in the Box/Chevron
  S: El Pollo Loco, IHOP, McDonald's, Panda Express, Subway, Taco Bell
- Other S: America's Tire, Costco, Home Depot, PetSmart♥, Sam's Club, Walmart sc

134 Cook St, to Indian Wells
- Gas S: ArcoAmPm, Mobil
- Food S: Applebee's, Jack in the Box, Starbucks
- Lodg S: Courtyard, Hampton Inn, Residence Inn
- Med S: + Hospital
- Other S: Emerald Desert Golf & RV Resort▲, CA State Univ, Animal Clinic♥

137 Washington St, Country Club Dr, Varner Rd, to Indian Wells
- Gas N: ArcoAmPm, Chevron
  S: 76, Mobil
- Food N: Burger King, Coco's, Del Taco, Starbucks
  S: Carl's Jr, Subway
- Lodg N: Comfort Suites, Motel 6♥
  S: Embassy Suites
- Other N: Auto Dealers, Mailbox Etc, RiteAid, Walgreen's, Thousand Trails RV Park▲, Sky Valley Resort▲, Giant RV

139 Jefferson St, Indio Blvd, Indio (Addt'l Serv appr 3mi S)
- TStop N: Clark's Truck Stop/PacPride
- Food N: Rest/Clark's TS
- TWash N: Clark's TS
- Other N: CarWash/Laundry/Clark's TS, CA State Hwy Patrol Post, Shadow Hills RV Resort▲, Sunnyside RV Park▲
  S: Bermuda Dunes Airport✈, to County Fairgrounds, Augustine Casino

142 Monroe St, Central Indio
- Gas S: 76, Shell◈
- Food S: Carrow's, Denny's
- Lodg S: Best Western, Comfort Inn, Motel 6♥, Quality Inn, to Super 8
- Med S: + Hospital
- Other N: Bob's RV Roundup▲
- Other S: Target, Indian Waters RV Resort▲, to Augustine Casino

143 Jackson St, Indio
- Gas S: Circle K
- Food N: McDonald's
- Other N: CVS, Home Depot, Super Target, Bob's RV Roundup
  S: Amtrak, to Augustine Casino

144 CA 111N, Auto Center Dr, Golf Center Pkwy, Indio
- Food N: Big America Home Cooking, Mexican Restaurant
- Lodg N: Holiday Inn Express
- Other N: Classis RV Park▲, Rancho Casa Blanca Resort▲, Fantasy Springs Casino/Hotel/Rest
  S: Auto Dealers, Fairgrounds, US Post Office

145 CA 86S, Brawley, El Centro (EB)

146 Dillon Rd, to CA 86 Expy, to CA 111S, Coachella
- TStop N: Love's Travel Stop #207 (Scales)
  S: Travel Center of America #41/Arco (Scales)
- Gas N: Chevron, Valley Gas
- Food N: Carl's Jr/Love's TS, Del Taco
  S: Rest/Arby/TB/ChestFrChkn/TA TC
- TServ S: TA TC
- TWash S: Eagle TW/TA TC
- Other N: Laundry/WiFi/RVDump/Love TS, to appr 19 mi Sky Valley Resort▲, Caliente Springs Resort▲
  S: Laundry/BarbSh/WiFi/LP/TA TC, Spotlight 20 Casino, B&K RV Sales, Coachella Valley RV Rentals

NOTE: MM 158: WB: Steep Grade

(159) Rest Area (Both dir) (RR, Phone, Picnic, RVDump/Water)

162 Frontage Rd

168 Cottonwood Springs Rd, Desert Center, to Mecca, Twenty Nine Palms
- Other N: 29 Palms Resort▲, Joshua Tree National Park

173 Summit Rd, Chiriaco Summit
- FStop N: Chevron
- Food N: Café, Chiriaco Summit Coffee Shop
- Other N: Truck & Tire Repair, Airport

177 Hayfield Rd, Desert Center

182 Red Cloud Mine Rd

189 Eagle Mountain Rd

192 CA 177N, Desert Center Rice Rd, Desert Center, to Lake Tamarisk
- Gas N: Stanco
- Food N: Family Café

201 Chuckwalla Valley, Corn Springs Rd, Desert Center

217 Ford Dry Lake Rd

(222) Wiley Well Rd, State Prison, Desert Center
- N: Rest Area (Both dir) (RR, Phone, Picnic)

(231) Inspection Station (WB)

232 Mesa Dr, Airport, Blythe
- FStop S: Valero
- TStop N: BB Travel Center/Roady's/76 (Scales)
- Food N: Rest/FastFood/BB TC
- TWash N: BB TC
- TServ N: BB TC
- Other N: Laundry/BB TC, Blythe Airport✈

236 CA 78S, Neighbors Blvd, Blythe, to Ripley, Brawley
- FStop N: CFN/COPA #1373
- Gas N: Shell, Valero

239 Lovekin Blvd, Blythe
- FStop S: CFN/COPA #590, Pacific Pride
- Gas N: ArcoAmPm, Mobil◈, Shell
  S: 76◈, ArcoAmPm, Chevron, Shell◈
- Food N: Carl's Jr, Del Taco, Jack in the Box, McDonald's, Pizza Hut, Popeye's, Sizzler, Starbucks
- Food S: Burger King, Denny's, KFC, Towne Square Café, Taco Bell
- Lodg N: Best Value Inn, Best Western, Comfort Inn, Days Inn, EZ 8 Motel, Hampton Inn, Willard Inn
  S: Holiday Inn Express, Motel 6♥, Super 8
- TServ S: Triple A Refrigeration
- Med N: + Hospital
- Other N: Ace Hardware, Dollar Tree, Goodyear, Radio Shack, Auto & Tire Services, Carwash, Ca Hwy Patrol Post
  S: RVDump/Water/City Park

240 7th St, Blythe
- Gas N: Chevron
- Food N: Blimpie, Subway, Starbucks
- Lodg N: Blue Line Motel, Blythe Inn, Budget Inn, Comfort Suites, Dunes Motel, Paradise Inn
- Med N: + Hospital
- Other N: Albertson's/Starbucks/Pharmacy, Auto Zone, Laundromat, Carwash, Dollar Tree, RiteAid, LP, RV Repair, Auto Repair, Hwy Patrol Post, Fairgrounds, to Banks, Kmart

241 US 95N, Intake Blvd, Blythe, Needles
- FStop N: CFN/QuikChek Mobil COPA #2989
- Gas N: Shell
- Food N: Steaks & Cakes
- Lodg N: Best Western, Travelers Inn Express, Willow Inn
- TServ N: Ramsey Int'l/CAT/Cummins, Detroit Diesel Truck & Trailer Repair
- Other N: Burton's MH & RV Park▲, Valley Palms RV Park▲

243 Riveria Dr, Blythe, Hobsonway
- Gas N: Mobil, Shell
- Lodge N: Desert Inn, Dunes Motel, Economy Inn Express
- Other N: Fairgrounds
  S: Riviera RV Campground▲, to Destiny McIntyre Campground▲

(244) Inspection Station (WB)

NOTE: MM 245: Arizona State Line

PACIFIC TIME ZONE

CALIFORNIA

◈ = Regular Gas Stations with Diesel ▲ = RV Friendly Locations ♥ = Pet Friendly Locations
Red print shows large vehicle parking / access on site or nearby Brown Print = Campgrounds / RV PARKS

EXIT		CA / AZ

ARIZONA

MOUNTAIN TIME ZONE

1 — **Posten Rd, Cibola, to Ehrenberg, Parker**
- TStop S: Flying J Travel Plaza #5250 (Scales)
- Food S: Cookery/Wendy's/FJ TP
- Lodg S: Best Western/FJ TP
- TWash S: Flying J TP
- TServ S: Flying J TP, Two Way CB Shop
- Other N: Villa Verde RV & MH Park▲, River Breeze RV Park▲
  S: Laundry/CB/WiFi/RVDump/LP/FJ TP

(2) — **Port of Entry / Insp Station (EB)**

(3) — **Inspection Station (WB)**

(4) — **Ehrensburg Rest Area (Both dir) (RR, Phone, Pic, Vend) (TEMP CLOSED)**

5 — **Tom Wells Rd, Cibola**
- TStop N: Sunmart #640/Texaco (Scales)
- Food N: Quiznos/Texaco

11 — **Dome Rock Rd, Parker**

17 — **I-10 Bus, Quartzsite, US 95S to Yuma, AZ 95N to Parker**
- TStop N: Pilot Travel Center #328 (Scales)
  S: Love's Travel Store #286 (Scales), QuikChek Shell
- Gas N: Mobil◈
- Food N: Subway/DQ/Pilot TS, Burger King/ Mobil, Carl's Jr, McDonald's, Best Chinese Rest, BBQ, Taco Mio Mexican Rest
  S: ChestersChkn/Subway/Loves TS
- Lodg N: Best Western
  S: Super 8
- TServ N: Amer Custom Tire Truck/Auto/RV
- Med N: + Medical Center
- Other N: WiFi/Pilot TC, Big Market, US Post Office, LP/Mobil,NAPA, Auto & RV Service & Tires, Radio Shack, Hardware Store, Laundromat, Desert Oasis RV Park▲, 88 Shades RV Park▲, B I-10 Campground▲, Holiday Palms RV Park▲, La Mirage RV Park▲, Hasslers RV Park▲
  S: WiFi/RVDump/Love's TS, Laundromat, Tyson Wells RV Park▲, Desert Sands RV Park▲, Paul Everts RV Sales, Guaranty RV Center, RV Lifestyles

19 — **Bus 10, Quartzsite, to US 95S to Yuma, AZ 95N to Parker**
- FStop S: QuikChek Shell

EXIT		ARIZONA

- TStop N: Park Place Travel Center
- Gas N: Chevron◈, Shell
- Food N: Grill/Park Place TC, Taco Miio, Bakery
- Other N: Grocery, Family Dollar, Radio Shack, Laundromat, US Post Office, LP, La Mirage RV Park▲, Welcome Friends RV Park▲, La Mesa RV Center, RV Lifestyles, RV Pit Stop/RVDump, RV Corral, Park Plaza RV Resort▲

26 — **Gold Nugget Rd, Parker**

31 — **US 60E, to Wickenburg, Prescott**

45 — **Vicksburg Rd, to AZ 72N, Parker**
- TStop N: Zip's Travel Plaza/Roady's (Scales)
  S: PTP/Tomahawk Auto Truck Plaza/ Valero (Scales)
- Food S: Rest/FastFood/Tomahawk TP
- TServ S: Jobski's Diesel Repair & Towing, C&S Tires
- Other N: LP/Zip's TP, to Black Rock RV Village▲
  S: Laundry/LP/RVDump/TomahawkTP, RV Park▲

(52) — **Bouse Wash Rest Area (Both dir) (RR, Phone, Pic, Vend) (TEMP CLOSED)**

53 — **Hovatter Rd, Roll**

69 — **Ave 75E, Roll**

81 — **Salome Rd, Tonopah, Harquahala Valley Rd**

(86) — **Burnt Well Rest Area (Both dir) (RR, Phone, Picnic, Vend)**

94 — **411th Ave, Tonopah, El Dorado Hot Springs**
- TStop S: Miinute Mart #42/Shell
- Gas S: Chevron◈, Mobil◈
- Food S: Tonapah Family Rest, Subw/NRPizza/ Chester's/Shell
- Lodg S: Mineral Wells Motel
- Other S: Laundry/LP/MM TS, US Post Office, El Dorado Hot Springs/RVDump, Saddle Mountain RV Park▲

98 — **Wintersburg Rd**

103 — **339th Ave, Tonopah**
- TStop S: Travel Center of America #225/Shell
- Food S: CountryFare/PHut/Subw/TBell/TA TC
- TWash S: TA TC
- TServ S: TA TC/Tires
- Other S: Laundry/WiFi/TA TC

109 — **Sun Valley Pkwy, Palo Verde Rd Buckeye**
- Other S: Buckeye Muni Airport✈

EXIT		ARIZONA

112 — **AZ 85, to I-8, Gila Bend, Phoenix ByPass, I-10E Alt (EB), Yuma, to San Diego, Mexico (WB)**

114 — **Miller Rd, Buckeye**
- FStop S: to 825 Monroe: CFN/Mustang Conoco #6901/Firebird Fuel Co #2214
- TStop S: Love's Travel Stop #280 (Scales)
- Gas S: Chevron
- Food S: Subway/ChestFrChkn/Love's TS, Burger King
- Lodg S: Days Inn
- Other N: Buckeye Military Reservation
  S: Laundry/WiFi/RVDump/Love's TS, Leaf Verde RV Resort▲

117 — **Watson Rd, Buckeye (EB)**
- Food S: Cracker Barrel
- Other S: ATM's, Banks, Fry's, Lowe's, Office Max, Walmart

120 — **Verrado Way (EB)**

121 — **Jackrabbit Trail, N 195th Ave**
- Gas N: Chevron, Phillips 66◈
  S: Circle K◈

124 — **Cotton Lane, to Lp 303, Goodyear**
- Other N: State Prison
  S: PetSmart♥, Sports Authority, Super Target, Destiny Phoenix RV Resort▲, Cotton Lane RV Resort▲

126 — **Pebblecreek Pkwy, Estrella Pkwy, to Estrella Park, Goodyear**
- Gas S: Safeway
- Food S: Jack in the Box, McDonald's, Panda Express, Subway
- Other N: PetCo♥,
  S: Safeway/Pharmacy, Walmart sc, Walgreen's

128 — **Litchfield Rd, Litchfield Park, Goodyear, Luke Air Force Base**
- Gas N: Mobil◈
  S: Chevron, Mobil
- Food N: Applebee's, Arby's, Bennett's BBQ, Black Angus Steakhouse, Carl's Jr, Chili's, Chipolte Mexican Rest, Cracker Barrel, Denny's, Fazoli's, McDonald's, On the Border, Starbucks, TGI Friday, Wendy's
  S: Arby's, Burger King, Taco Bell
- Lodg N: Hampton Inn, Holiday Inn Express, Residence Inn
  S: Best Western
- Med S: + Samaritan W Valley Health Center
- Other N: B&N, Best Buy, Super Target/Pharmacy, Wildlife World Zoo, to Luke Air Force Base

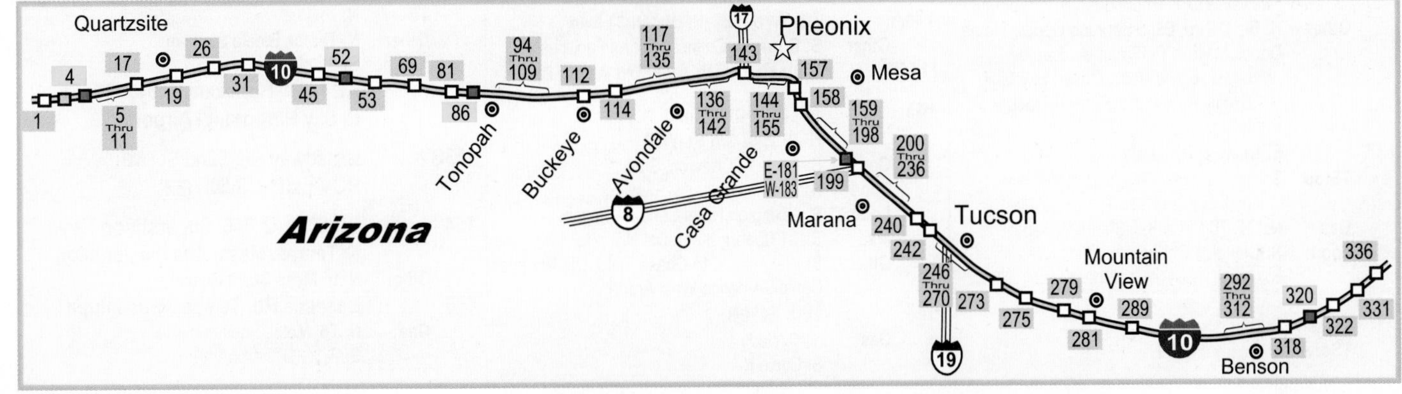

◈ = Regular Gas Stations with Diesel ▲ = RV Friendly Locations ♥ = Pet Friendly Locations
Red print shows large vehicle parking / access on site or nearby Brown Print = Campgrounds / RV PARKS

EXIT — ARIZONA

S: Albertson's, Fry's/Pharmacy, Osco, Radio Shack, Carwash, Phoenix Goodyear Muni Airport✈

129 Dysart Rd, Goodyear, Avondale
Gas N: Chevron, Shell◈
S: QT, Sam's Club
Food N: Carino's, ChickFilA, In N Out Burger, Jack in the Box, Mimi's Cafe, Panda Express, Taco Bell
S: Del Taco, Golden Corral, IHOP, KFC, McDonald's, Waffle House, Whataburger
Lodg N: Wingate Inn
S: Best Value Inn, Comfort Inn, Holiday Inn, Quality Inn, Ramada Inn, Super 8
Other N: Auto Zone, Discount Tire, Dollar Tree, Fry's/Pharmacy, Lowe's, PetSmart♥, **Walmart sc**
S: Auto Services, Home Depot, Sam's Club, Walgreen's

131 115th Ave, Avondale Blvd, Phoenix Int'l Raceway, to Cashion
Gas N: Mobil
Lodg S: Hilton Garden Inn
Other S: Phoenix Int'l Raceway

132 107th Ave (EB)
Other S: Auto Dealers

133A 99th Ave (EB), 107th Ave, Avondale
TStop S: Pilot Travel Center #459 (Scales)
Gas N: Chevron◈
S: Costco
Food N: Carrabba's, McDonald's, Subway
S: Subway/Wendys/Pilot TC
TServ S: Freightliner
Other N: Best Buy, Borders, Costco, PetCo♥, + West Valley Naturopathic Center, Walgreen's
S: Laundry/WiFi/Pilot TC, **Earnhardt's RV Center**, Auto Dealers

133B AZ 101N Loop

134 91st Ave, Tolleson

NOTE: MM 134: Begin HOV Lane (EB) End (WB)

135 83rd Ave, Phoenix
Gas N: Circle K
Food N: Arby's, Burger King, Jack in the Box, Waffle House
Lodg N: Comfort Suites, Econo Lodge
Other N: Sam's Club

(136A) HOV Exit-79th Ave (WB)

136B 75th Ave, Phoenix
Gas N: Circle K, Chevron
S: ArcoAmPm
Food N: CiCi's Pizza, Denny's, IHOP, Olive Garden, PizzaHut/Taco Bell, Starbucks, Subway, Texas Roadhouse, Whataburger
Other N: Big O Tire, Big 5 Sporting Goods, Home Depot, Lowe's, PetSmart♥, Staples, **Walmart sc**, CarWash, Desert Sky Mall
S: O'Reilly Auto Parts, Penske Truck Rental

137 67th Ave, Phoenix
TStop S: Flying J Travel Plaza #5006 (Scales), Danny's Big Rig Resort
Gas N: QT, 76/Circle K◈, Shell◈
Food N: Church's Chicken
S: CountryMarket/FastFood/FJ TP, Diner/ Danny's BRR
TWash S: Danny's BRR
TServ S: Danny's BRR/Tires
Other S: Laundry/WiFi/BarbSh/**LP/RVDump**/ FJ TP, CB/Chrome/Danny's BRR, Carwash/Shell

138 59th Ave, Phoenix
FStop S: Quik Trip #444 (Scales), **to 5821 W Buckeye Rd:** CFN/Firebird Fuel #2427
TStop S: PTP/Liberty Fuel (Scales)
Gas N: 7-11, Circle K
Food N: Mexican
S: Waffle House, Whataburger
TWash S: Blue Beacon TW (Scales)
Other N: Auto Zone, Family Dollar, Walgreen's
S: Laundry/WiFi/Liberty Fuel

139 51st Ave, Phoenix
FStop **S: to 5049 W Buckeye Rd:** Valero #6652, **To 1001 N 53rd Ave:** CFN/Firebird Fuel#321 Quik Trip #444 (Scales)
Gas N: Circle K, Chevron◈
Food N: Burger King, El Pollo Loco, Chinese, McDonald's, Waffle House
S: Carl's Jr, IHOP, Taco Bell
Lodg N: Budget Inn, Days Inn, Holiday Inn, Motel 6♥, Red Roof Inn♥, Travelodge
S: Fairfield Inn, Hampton Inn, Super 8
Other N: 7-11, Auto Services, Laundromat, Discount Tire, Food City

140 43rd Ave
FStop **N: to 4333 W Glenrosa Ave:** CFN/Firebird Fuel #1248
Gas N: 7-11, Circle K◈, Shell
S: 7-11, Chevron, Circle K
Food N: KFC, Subway, Wendy's
Med N: + Priority Medical Center
Other N: AutoZone, Fry's, Radio Shack, Walgreen's

141 35th Ave, Phoenix
FStop N: Bair's Gas Stop
S: to 3618 W Buckeye Rd: Circle K #2885
Gas N: Circle K
S: Shell
Food N: Jack in the Box

142 27th Ave, State Capitol (EB)
FStop N: AFCO Gas, **to 2343 N 27th Ave:** CFN/ Firebird Fuel #304
Gas N: 7-11, ArcoAmPm,Circle K
S: Pacific Pride
Lodg N: Comfort Inn♥

(143A) Jct I-17N, to Flagstaff

(143B) Jct I-17S, US 60E, I-10 Trk Rte (EB) Jct I-17S (WB), Phoenix

143C 19th Ave, State Capitol, Fairgrounds, Coliseum (WB)

144 7th Ave (WB)
Other S: Downtown Cultural, Sports Facilities

144A 7th Ave (EB) (HazMat MUST Exit)
Other S: Downtwn Cultural, Sports Facilities

(144B) HOV Exit - 5th Ave, 3rd Ave (EB)

145 7th St, Downtown HOV Exit-3rd St (WB)
Gas S: Circle K, Chevron, Shell
Food N: McDonald's
Lodg S: Lexington Hotel Central Phoenix
Med S: + Phoenix Memorial Hospital
Other S: Walgreen's, **to** Chase Field, US Airways Center, America West Arena

146 16th St (EB)
Gas N: Circle K
S: Circle K
Food N: KFC
S: Church's Chicken, Jack in the Box
Med N: + Banner Good Sam Medical Center
S: + St Luke's Medical Center

147A AZ 202E Loop, to Mesa HOV Exit - 202E (EB), HOV Exit- AZ 51N (WB)

147B AZ 51N, to Paradise Valley

148 Washington St, Jefferson St
Gas N: Chevron, Exxon
S: Circle K
Food N: Carl's Jr, McDonald's, Rally's
Lodg N: Motel 6♥, Rodeway Inn
Med S: + Hospital
Other N: Airport Rental Car Return

149 Sky Harbor Int'l Airport (EB), Buckeye Rd, Sky Harbor Center, Int'l Airport (WB)
Lodg N: Howard Johnson, Motel 6♥
Other N: Airport, Greyhound

(150) Jct I-17N, to Flagstaff (EB)

(150A) Jct I-17N to Flagstaff, US 60W to Wickenburg, I-10 Truck Rte (WB)

150B 24th St E (WB)
Gas N: Exxon
Food N: Durados, Rest/Golden 9
S: Rest/BW
Lodg N: Golden 9 Motel, Knights Inn, Motel 6♥, Rodeway Inn
S: Best Western
TServ N: Purcell Western States Tire

151 32nd St, University Dr (EB)

151AB 32nd St, University Dr, AZ State University
Gas S: Circle K
Lodg N: Extended Stay America, Hilton Garden Inn, Holiday Inn Express, La Quinta Inn♥, Radisson
Other N: Univ of Phoenix

152 40th St, Univ of Phoenix
Gas N: Shell◈
S: Circle K/Shell
Food S: Burger King

153 AZ 143, 48th St, Broadway Rd (EB)
Gas S: Shell
Food N: Denny's
S: JB's Rest, Del Taco, George & Dragon II English Pub & Rest, Panda Express, Papa John's, Pizza Hut, Whataburger
Lodg N: Comfort Suites, Courtyard, Fairfield Inn, Hilton, La Quinta Inn♥, Quality Inn, Red Roof Inn♥, Sheraton
S: Hampton Inn, Homewood Suites
TServ N: Purcell Western States Tire
Other N: Tempe Diablo Stadium
S: Staples

153A AZ 143N, Hohokam Expy, 48th St, to Sky Harbor Int'l Airport (WB)

153B Broadway Rd, 52nd St (WB) HOV Exit - US 60E (EB)

154 US 60E, AZ 360, Superstition Fwy, to Tempe, Mesa, Apache Junction
Other **N: to Mesa Spirit Resort▲**

155 Baseline Rd, Tempe, Guadalupe
Gas N: 76, Mobil, Shell◈
S: 7-11, QT, ArcoAmPm

◈= Regular Gas Stations with Diesel ▲ = RV Friendly Locations ♥= Pet Friendly Locations
Red print shows large vehicle parking / access on site or nearby Brown Print = Campgrounds / RV PARKS

EXIT		ARIZONA
	Food	**N:** Carl's Jr, Claim Jumper Rest, El Pollo Loco, Garcia's Mexican Rest, Jack in the Box, Joe's Crab Shack, Johnny Rockets, McDonald's, Panda Express, Rainforest Cafe, Shoney's, Waffle House, Wendy's **S:** Aunt Chilada's Mexican Rest, Denny's, Sonic, Subway
	Lodg	**N:** Best Western♥, Candlewood Suites♥, Holiday Inn Express, Inn Suites, Ramada ♥, Residence Inn, Towneplace Suites **S:** Arizona Grand Resort, Studio 6♥
	Other	**N:** Auto Zone, CVS, Walgreen's, AZ Mills Mall, AZ Mills Cinema, Tourist Info **S:** Fry's/Pharmacy, South Point Animal Clinic♥
157		**Elliot Rd, Guadalupe, Tempe**
	Gas	**N:** Circle K/Shell, Chevron **S:** Circle K/Shell, Mobil◊
	Food	**N:** Applebee's, Arby's, Baja Fresh, Black Eyed Pea, Burger King, Chili's, Coco's, Fuddrucker's, Honey Bears BBQ, Kobe Japanese Rest, Kyoto's Japanese Rest, Olive Garden, Panda Express, Red Robin, Subway, Taco Bell, Wendy's **S:** KFC, McDonald's, Pizza Hut
	Lodg	**N:** Country Inn & Suites♥ **S:** Clarion♥, Grace Inn
	Other	**N:** Auto Services, Costco, Discount Tire, Dollar Tree, Midas, Office Max, PetSmart♥, Staples, Vet♥, **Walmart**, U-Haul **S:** Safeway, Walgreen's, Auto Dealers, Vet♥
158		**Warner Rd, Tempe**
	Gas	**N:** 76 , Circle K **S:** ArcoAmPm, Circle K◊
	Food	**S:** Burger King, Chuck E Cheese, DQ, McDonald's, Quiznos, Taco Bell
	Other	**N:** Firestone, Vet♥ **S:** Advance Auto, Basha's, Big O Tires, Osco, U-Haul, Tempe Auto Plex, Vet♥
159		**Ray Rd, Phoenix, Chandler**
	Gas	**N:** 76, Shell◊ **S:** Circle K◊, Exxon
	Food	**N:** Carrabba's Italian, Chipolte Mexican Grill, Charleston's Rest, El Pollo Loco, Fleming's Prime Steakhouse, 5 & Diner, In N Out Burger, McDonald's, Outback Steakhouse, Paradise Bakery, Red Lobster, TGI Friday's, Z"Tejas, Rest/Courtyard **S:** Boston Market, El Paso BBQ, IHOP, Jack in the Box, Mimi's Café, On the Border, RA Sushi Bar, Rock Bottom Brewery & Rest, Romano's Macaroni Grill, Sweet Tomatoes, Valle Luna Mexican Rest, Wendy's
	Lodg	**N:** Courtyard **S:** Extended Stay America♥
	Med	**S:** + Thomas Davis Medical Center
	Other	**N:** Borders, CompUSA, Home Depot, Lowe's, PetSmart♥,Sam's Club, Auto Services, Auto Dealers **S:** Albertson's/Pharmacy, B&N, Best Buy, FedEx Office, Osco, Target, UPS Store, AMC Theatre, Auto Dealers, Auto Services, Carwash
160		**Chandler Blvd, Pecos Rd, Phoenix, Chandler**
	Gas	**N:** Circle K, Chevron, Circle K

Personal Notes

EXIT		ARIZONA
	Gas	**S:** 7-11, Chevron, Circle K
	Food	**N:** Burger King, Damon's, Denny's, Marie Callendar's, Perkins, Sizzler, Whataburger, Rest/Radisoon **S:** Applebee's, Chili's, Cracker Barrel, Del Taco, Hooters, Waffle House, Wendy's
	Lodg	**N:** Fairfield Inn, Hampton Inn, Homewood Suites♥, Motel 6♥, Radisson Inn, Red Roof Inn♥, Super 8♥ **S:** Extended Stay America, La Quinta Inn♥, Holiday Inn Express, Intown Suites
	Med	**N:** to + Chandler Regional Hospital **S:** + Hospital, + Awhatukee Foothills Medical Center
	Other	**N:** Basha's/Pharmacy, Big O Tire, CVS, Firestone, Chandler Harley Davidson, Carwash/Chevron, **to** Stellar Airpark✈, **S:** Auto Zone, CVS, Discount Tire, Fletcher Tire & Auto Service
	NOTE:	**MM 160: HOV Lane Ends EB, Begin WB**
161		**Loop 202E, Pecos Rd, Chandler**
162		**Wild Horse Pass Blvd, Sundust Rd, Firebird Sports Park (SB)**
	TStop	**N:** Love's Travel Stop #328 (Scales)
	Food	**N:** Arby's/TJCinn/Love's TS **S:** Rest/Wild Horse Pass, to Rawhide Western Town & Steakhouse
	Lodg	**S:** Wild Horse Pass Resort & Spa
	TServ	**N:** Freightliner
	Other	**N:** WiFi/Love's TS, **Beaudry RV Center/** RVDump

EXIT		ARIZONA
	Other	**S:** Firebird Sports Park, Firebird Int'l Raceway, **Gila Bend Casino**, **Lone Butte Casino**, **Wild Horse Pass Casino**, Gila River Indian Reservation
162A		**Wild Horse Pass Blvd, Maricopa Rd, Chandler (EB)**
162B		**S Maricopa Rd, Chandler (EB)**
164		**Queen Creek Rd , AZ 347S, Maricopa, Ak-Chin Indian Comm**
	Other	**N:** to **Harrah's Casino** **S:** Ak Chin Indian Comm
167		**Riggs Rd, Sun Lakes**
	FStop	**N:** Chevron
	Other	**N:** to **1320 E Riggs Rd:** Kelley Family Car, RV & Truck Wash/RVDump
175		**AZ 587, Casa Blanca Rd, Sacaton, Chandler, Gilbert**
	Gas	**S:** Shell◊
	Other	**S:** **Casa Blanca RV Park▲** , Gila Indian Center
(181)		**Sacaton Rest Area (EB)** (RR, Ph, Pic, Vend, Info) **(TEMP CLOSED)**
(183)		**Sacaton Rest Area (WB)** (RR, Ph, Pic, Vend) **(TEMP CLOSED)**
185		**AZ 187, AZ 387, Bus Loop 10, to Casa Grande, Sacaton, Florence**
	Lodg	**S:** Francisco Grand Hotel & Golf Resort
	Other	**S:** **Val Vista RV Village▲** , **Foothills RV Resort▲** , **Leisure Valley RV Resort▲** , AZ State Hwy Patrol, Casa Grande Muni Airport✈
190		**McCartney Rd, Central AZ Coll**
	Other	**N:** to Central AZ College **S:** **Casita Verde RV Resort▲** , **Desert Shadows RV Resort▲** , Casa Grande Airport✈
194		**AZ 287, Florence Blvd, Coolidge, Bus 10, Casa Grande**
	Gas	**S:** ArcoAmPm◊, Chevron
	Food	**N:** In N Out Burger, Mimi's Cafe, Olive Garden, Subway **S:** Burger King, Cracker Barrel, Del Taco, Denny's, DQ/Chevron, Golden Corral, IHOP,JB's Rest, Panda Express, Wendy's
	Lodg	**S:** Best Western♥, Comfort Inn, Francisco Grand Hotel & Golf Resort, Mainstay Suites, Super 8
	Med	**S:** + Hospital
	Other	**N:** Best Buy, PetSmart♥, Radio Shack, Staples, Target, World Market, Pinal Co Fairgrounds, **to appr 7mi: Sunscape RV Resort▲** , **S:** Albertson's, CVS, Fry's, Walgreen's, **Walmart sc**, Factory Stores Of America Outlet Center, **to** Casa Grande Mall, **to Palm Creek Golf & RV Resort▲** , **Fiesta Grande RV Resort▲**
198		**Jimmie Kerr Blvd, AZ 84, AZ 93, Casa Grande, to Eloy**
	Food	**S:** Wendy's
	Other	**S:** **Buena Tierra RV Park & CG ▲** , Outlets at Casa Grande, Dobson Ranch Golf Course
(199)		**Jct I-8W, to Yuma, San Diego (Phoenix ByPass)**

◊= Regular Gas Stations with Diesel ▲ = RV Friendly Locations ♥= Pet Friendly Locations
Red print shows large vehicle parking / access on site or nearby **Brown Print = Campgrounds / RV PARKS**

EXIT — ARIZONA

200 Sunland Gin Rd, Arizona City
- **TStop** N: Petro Stopping Center #6 (Scales), Pride Travel Center; S: Love's Travel Stop #265
- **Food** N: Rest/Sunland Inn, Subway/Pride TC, IronSkillet/Petro SC, Burger King, Mex Rest; S: Golden 9 Family Rest, Arby's/Love's TS, Starbucks
- **Lodg** N: Days Inn, Sunland Inn; S: Motel 6♥
- **TServ** N: Petro SC/Tires, Southwest Towing, Rocha's Truck Tire & Diesel Service; S: Speedco
- **TWash** N: Blue Beacon TW/Petro SC, Eagle Truck Wash
- **Other** N: Laundry/WiFi/Petro SC, **LP**/Pride TC, **Las Colinas RV Park▲**; S: WiFi/Love's TS, **High Chaparral RV Park▲**, **Quail Run RV Resort▲**, AZ City Golf Course, Eddie's Auto & RV Service

203 Toltec Rd, to Eloy
- **TStop** S: Travel Center of America/Exxon (Scales)
- **FStop** S: Circle K Truxtop #2947
- **Gas** N: Chevron
- **Food** N: Carl's Jr, Mexican, Waffle House, McDonald's/Chevron; S: Rest/TBell/TA TC, Pizza Hut
- **Lodg** N: Best Value Inn, Red Roof Inn♥
- **TWash** S: TA TC, Blue Beacon TW/Circle K TS
- **TServ** N: West's I-10 Diesel; S: TA TC/Tires
- **Other** N: **Golden Corridor RV Park▲**, **Desert Valley RV Resort▲**; S: Laundry/WiFi/**RVDump**/TA TC

208 Sunshine Blvd, Eloy
- **TStop** N: Pilot Travel Center #458 (Scales) (DAD) (DAND); S: Flying J Travel Plaza #5310/Conoco (Scales)
- **Food** N: DQ/Subway/Pilot TC; S: Cookery/FastFood/FJ TP
- **TWash** S: Blue Beacon TW/FJ TP
- **TServ** N: Diesel Service, M&M Truck Polishing
- **Other** N: Laundry/WiFi/Pilot TC; S: Laundry/WiFi/**LP**/**RVDump**/FJ TP

211A Picacho, State Prison (EB)
- **Other** S: **Picacho RV Park▲**, State Prison

211B AZ 87N, to Coolidge

212 Picacho (WB)
- **Other** S: State Prison

219 Picacho Peak Rd, Picacho
- **Gas** N: Picacho Plaza/Citgo, Mobil
- **Food** N: DQ/PP, Eddie's Bar & Grill
- **Other** S: **Picacho Peak RV Resort▲**, **Picacho Peak State Park▲**, Ostrich Ranch

226 Sasco Rd, Red Rock

(228) WB pull off, to Frontage Rd, APS Power Plant

232 Pinal Air Park Rd, Army National Guard Aviation Training Site
- **Other** S: Pinal Airpark✈

236 Marana Rd, Marana
- **Gas** S: Circle K, Chevron◈
- **Other** S: **Valley of the Sun RV Park▲**

240 Tangerine Rd, Oro Valley, Marana, to Rillito
- **Other** N: **A Bar A Campground▲**

242 Avra Valley Rd, Marana
- **Other** S: Marana Reg'l Airport✈

245 Twin Peaks Rd

246 Cortaro Rd, Tucson
- **Gas** N: Circle K◈, Chevron◈; S: Shell◈
- **Food** N: Arby's, IHOP, Wendy's; S: Burger King, Chili's, **Cracker Barrel**, Hot Dog Heaven, In N Out Burger, KFC, McDonald's, Panda Express, Starbucks, Subway, Taco Bell, Texas Roadhouse
- **Lodg** S: Best Western, Days Inn, Holiday Inn Express, La Quinta Inn♥, Quality Inn, Super 8
- **Other** S: Ace Hardware, **Walmart sc▲**, Auto Services, US Post Office, **to Saguaro Nat'l Park, RV Camping▲**

248 Ina Rd, Tucson, Marana
- **Gas** N: Circle K, Chevron◈, Conoco◈, Quik Mart◈; S: Circle K, Exxon
- **Food** N: Arby's, Burger King, Carl's Jr, DQ, El Pollo Loco, Hooters, Jack in the Box, Long John Silver, McDonald's, Peter Piper Pizza, Pizza Hut, Taco Bell, Waffle House; S: Denny's
- **Lodg** N: InTowne Suites, Motel 6♥; S: Comfort Inn♥, Park Inn, Red Roof Inn♥, Travelodge
- **Other** N: Auto Zone, Big Lots, Checker Auto Parts CVS, Discount Tire, Fry's, Goodyear, Lowe's, Midas, Office Depot, Radio Shack, Target, Walgreen's, 99 Store, Jiffy Lube, Carwash/Chevron, Carwash/**LP**/Conoco, U-Haul, to Foothills Mall; S: **LP**/Circle K, Sports Parks of America, Purcell Tire Center

250 Orange Grove Rd, Marana
- **Gas** N: ArcoAmPm, Circle K
- **Food** N: Wendy's
- **Other** N: Costco, Home Depot, PetSmart♥, **National RV Central**

251 Sunset Rd, Frontage Rd, Tucson El Camino Del Cerro (EB)
- **Other** N: **National RV Central**

252 El Camino Del Cerro, Ruthrauff Rd, Frontage Rd, Tucson (WB)
- **FStop** N: **to 4703 N Parkway St:** CFN/Firebird Fuel #306
- **Gas** N: ArcoAmPm; S: Chevron◈
- **Food** S: Jack in the Box/Chevron
- **Other** S: Big Tex Trailers

254 Prince Rd, Tucson
- **Gas** N: Circle K, Diamond Shamrock
- **Lodg** S: Best Western
- **TServ** N: Cummins SW, Thermo King Service; S: Inland Kenworth
- **Other** N: U-Haul, **to 4324 N Flowing Wells Rd: Merrigan's AZ Roadrunner RV Service/RVDump**; S: **Prince of Tucson RV Park/RVDump▲**, Silverbell Golf Course

255 AZ 77N, Miracle Mile

256 Grant Rd, Tucson
- **Gas** S: 76, Circle K, Exxon, Shell, Shamrock
- **Food** N: Sonic; S: Del Taco, IHOP, Subway, Waffle House
- **Lodg** S: Comfort Inn, Hampton Inn, Holiday Inn Express, La Quinta Inn♥, Motel 6, Quality Inn, Super 8
- **Other** S: Office Max, Walgreen's, Animal Hospital♥, Auto Services

- **Lodg** S: Comfort Inn, Hampton Inn, Holiday Inn Express, La Quinta Inn♥, Motel 6, Quality Inn, Super 8
- **Other** S: Office Max, Walgreen's, Animal Hospital♥, Auto Services

257 Speedway Blvd, St Mary's Rd, Univ of AZ, Pima Comm College
- **Gas** N: 7-11; S: ArcoAmPm◈
- **Lodg** N: Best Western
- **Med** N: + Hospital; S: to + St Mary's Hospital
- **Other** N: Office Depot, AZ Victory Motorcylces, Old Town Tucson, **to** Univ of AZ; S: **to** Pima Comm College West

257A St. Mary's Rd
- **Gas** N: 76◈; S: Shell
- **Food** S: Burger King, Denny's, Jack in the Box
- **Lodg** N: Inn Suites; S: La Quinta Inn♥, Ramada
- **Med** N: + Hospital
- **Other** N: U-Haul

258 Congress St, Broadway Blvd, Conv Center, Downtown Tucson
- **Gas** N: Circle K
- **Food** N: Garcia's Mexican Rest, Sizzler; S: Carl's Jr, Whataburger
- **Lodg** N: Holiday Inn, Motel 6♥, Ramada Inn; S: Days Inn, Riverpark Inn
- **Other** S: Amtrak

259 22nd St, 20th St, Starr Pass Blvd
- **Gas** N: Circle K◈; S: 76
- **Food** S: Kettle, Waffle House
- **Lodg** S: Comfort Inn, Holiday Inn Express, Howard Johnson, La Quinta♥, Motel 6♥, Super 8, Travel Inn

(260) Jct I-19S, to Nogales

261 Bus Loop 19, 4th Ave-6th Ave
- **Gas** N: Chevron
- **Food** S: Burger King, Silver Saddle Steakhouse
- **Lodg** N: Budget Inn, Econo Lodge, Star Motel, Quality Inn, Super Inn Motel; S: Economy Inn, Lazy 8 Motel, Rodeway Inn
- **TServ** S: Peterbilt
- **Other** N: Discount Tire, Food City; S: Family Dollar

262 Bus Lp 10, Benson Hwy, Park Ave
- **Gas** S: ArcoAmPm, Chevron, Shell
- **Food** S: McDonald's, Waffle House, Rest/QI
- **Lodg** S: Best Value Inn, Howard Johnson, Motel 6♥, Quality Inn, Rodeway Inn, Western Inn
- **TServ** S: Peterbilt

263 Ajo Way, Kino Pkwy (WB)
- **Gas** N: Chevron
- **Med** N: + University Physicians Hospital
- **Other** S: **Oasis RV Center**, Tucson Int'l Airport✈

263A Kino Pkwy S (EB)

263B Kino Pkwy N, Ajo Way (EB)

◈= Regular Gas Stations with Diesel ▲ = RV Friendly Locations ♥= Pet Friendly Locations
Red print shows large vehicle parking / access on site or nearby Brown Print = Campgrounds / RV PARKS

EXIT		ARIZONA
264		**Irvington Rd, Palo Verde Rd (WB)**
	Gas	N: Chevron◈
		S: Quik Mart
	Food	N: Carl's Jr, Denny's, Waffle House, Wendy's/Chevron
		S: Arby's, McDonald's
	Lodg	N: Days Inn, Fairfield Inn, Holiday Inn, Red Roof Inn♥
		S: Motel 6♥, Ramada Inn♥
	Med	N: + University Physicians Hospital
	Other	N: **Freedom RV**, **Ed Hannon RV Center**, Tucson Expo Center
		S: Fry's, Food City, Factory Outlet Mall, **Beaudry RV**, **Camping World**, **La Mesa RV Center**, **Pedata RV & Rentals**, **Beaudry RV Resort/RVDump▲**
264A		**Palo Verde Rd S (EB)**
	Other	S: to **Apollo RV Park▲**
264B		**Palo Verde Rd N, Irvington Rd (EB)**
	Other	N: Kino Sports Complex
265		**Alvernon Way, Davis-Monthan Air Force Base**
	Other	N: **Freedom RV**
267		**Valencia Rd, Tucson International Airport (EB), Valencia Rd, I-10 Bus Lp, Benson Hwy, Airport (WB)**
	Gas	N: ArcoAmPm
	Food	N: Jack in the Box/Arco
	Lodg	S: Apache Tears Motel
	Other	N: Davis-Monthan Air Force Base
		S: Tucson Int'l Airport✈
268		**Craycroft Rd, Tucson**
	TStop	N: Triple T/Tucson Truck Terminal/Roady's TS, Mr T's Conoco (Scales)
	Gas	N: 76/Circle K
	Food	N: Rest/FastFood/Triple T TS
	Lodg	N: Motel/Triple T TS
	TWash	N: Tucson Truck & RV Wash/Triple T TS
	TServ	N: Triple T TS
		S: Interstate Diesel Service
	Other	N: Laundry/CB/PostOffice/RVDump/LP/Triple T TS, **Crazy Horse Campground & RV Park/LP/RVDump▲**
269		**Wilmot Rd, Tucson**
	Gas	N: Chevron◈
		S: Shell
	Food	N: A&W/Chevron
		S: Quiznos/Shell
	Lodg	N: Travel Inn
	Other	N: to Pima Air Museum
270		**Kolb Rd, Tucson**
	FStop	N: to Gas City, Diamond Shamrock◈
	Gas	N: Chevron
	Other	N: RVDump/Carwash/Gas City, to 6mi **Rincon Country East RV Resort▲**
		S: **Voyager RV Resort & Rentals▲**
273		**Rita Rd**
	FStop	N: Rita Ranch Fuels
	Gas	N: Shell
	Other	S: to Pima Co Fairgrounds/RVDump
275		**Houghton Rd, Tucson**
	Other	N: **ABTucson/Cactus Country RV Resort/RVDump▲**, to Saguaro Natl Park
		S: Pima Co Fairgrounds/RVDump
279		**Vail Rd, Wentworth Rd, Vail**
	Other	N: to Colossal Caves
281		**AZ 83S, to Sonoita, Patagonia**
289		**Marsh Station Rd, Mt Lemmon**

EXIT		ARIZONA
292		**Empirita Rd**
297		**Mescal Rd, J-Six Ranch Rd**
	Gas	N: Quick Pic◈
	Food	N: Deli/QP
299		**Skyline Rd, Benson**
302		**AZ 90S, Benson, to Ft. Huachuca, Sierra Vista**
	TStop	S: AmBest/Gas City #90/Coastal
	Gas	S: Shell◈
	Food	S: KFC/Taco Bell, McDonald's, Subway/Shell, Pizza Hut/Gas City TS
	Lodg	S: Holiday Inn Express, Motel 6♥
	Twash	S: Gas City TS
	Other	S: **Cochise Terrace RV Resort▲**, LP/RVDump/Gas City TS, RV/Car Wash, **Arizona Legends RV Resort ▲ (See AD Page 40)** to Karchner Caverns, to Fort Huachuca Nat'l Historic Site
303		**W 4th St, Benson, Bus 10, AZ 80, to Bisbee, Tombstone (EB)**
	Gas	S: Mobil◈, Shell◈
	Food	S: Chinese, Mexican, Wendy's
	Lodg	S: Cavern Garden Motel, Quarter Horse **RV Park▲** & Motel
	Other	S: **Pardner's RV Park▲**, **Butterfield RV Resort & Observatory▲**, Safeway, NAPA, **Walmart sc**
304		**Ocotillo St, Benson**
	Gas	S: Chevron, Texaco
	Food	N: Denny's, Jack in the Box
		S: Apple Farm Rest, Burger King, Country Folks, Wendy's
	Lodg	N: Baymont Inn, Days Inn, Motel 6♥, Super 8♥
		S: Best Western, Quail Hollow Inn
	Med	S: + Hospital
	Other	N: **Benson KOA▲**, **Benson I-10 RV Park▲**, **Red Barn Campground▲**,
		S: **Pardner's RV Park▲**, **Dillons RV Sales**, Dollar General, Family Dollar, Laundry, Radio Shack, Safeway, US Post Office
306		**Pomerene Rd, Benson (EB), AZ 80, Bus Loop 10 (WB)**
	Gas	S: Mobil◈
	Food	S: Pizza
	Other	S: **San Pedro RV Park▲**, **Pata Blanco Lakes RV Park▲**, Amtrak
312		**Sibyl Rd, Benson**
318		**Dragoon Rd, Benson**
	Other	S: to **Camping▲**
(320)		**Texas Canyon Rest Area (Both dir) (RR, Phone, Picnic, Vend)**
322		**Johnson Rd, Benson**
	FStop	S: Citgo◈
	Food	S: DQ/Citgo
331		**US 191S, Sun Sites, Douglas**
336		**Bus Loop 10, Willcox**
	FStop	S: Freeway Chevron
	Food	S: KFC
	Lodge	S: to Desert Inn Motel
	Other	N: Cochise Co Airport✈
		S: LP/Frwy Chevron, **Ft Willcox RV Park▲**, **Lifestyle RV Resort▲**

EXIT		AZ / NM
340		**AZ 186, Rex Allen Dr, S Fort Grant Rd, Willcox**
	FStop	S: Mobil
	TStop	N: Travel Center of America/Shell(Scales)
		S: Wilcox Travel Plaza/Chevron
	Gas	S: 76/Circle K
	Food	N: CountryFare/Subway/Popeye/TA TC
		S: Rest/Wilcox TC, Burger King, KFC, Mexican, Pizza Hut, McDonald's
	Lodg	N: Holiday Inn Express, Super 8
		S: Best Western, Days Inn, Motel 6
	TWash	N: 340 Truck Wash
	TServ	N: TA TC, Freightliner
	Med	S: + N Cochise Comm Hospital
	Other	N: Laundry/WiFi/LP/RVDump/TA TC, **Magic Circle RV Park▲**, Crop Circle Winery
		S: Laundry/Wilcox TC, Auto Zone, Big O Tire, Family Dollar, Food City, IGA, Safeway, Dicks Tire & Auto, RV & Truck, Chiricahua Nat'l Monument, **Grande Vista RV Park▲**, **Lifestyle RV Resort▲**
344		**I-10 Bus Lp, Wilcox**
	Gas	S: Chevron◈
	TServ	S: Wilcox Diesel Service
	Other	S: LP/Chevron, Coronado Vineyards, **Lifestyle RV Resort▲**
352		**US 191N, to Safford**
	Other	N: **Roper Lake St Park**
355		**US 191N, to Safford**
362		**I-10 Bus Lp, Bowie**
	Other	N: **Mountain View RV Park▲**
366		**I-10 Bus Lp, Bowie**
	FStop	N: PJ's Travel Center/Shell
	Food	N: Bella's Cafe/Shell
	Other	N: **PJ's RV Park▲**, Ft Bowie Nat'l Historic Site
378		**I-10 Bus Loop, San Simon**
	Tstop	N: CFN/Sunmart #605/Chevron (Scales)
	Gas	N: Shell
	Food	N: Rest/Chester Fr Chicken/Sunmart, Kactus Kafe/Shell
	TServ	N: Sunmart/Tires, Car/Diesel/RV Repair, CAT
	Other	N: LP/Sunmart
382		**I-10 Bus Lp, Portal Rd, San Simon (access to Ex #378 Serv)**
(383)		**Weigh Station (EB) Inspection Station (WB)**
(389)		**San Simon Rest Area (Both dir) (RR, Ph, Pic, Vend)**
390		**Cavot Rd, San Simon**
	NOTE:	**MM 391: NM State Line**

MOUNTAIN TIME ZONE, NO DST

⬆ ARIZONA
⬇ NEW MEXICO

MOUNTAIN TIME ZONE

EXIT		
3		**CR A12, Steins Rd, Steins, Lordsburg**
5		**NM 80S, Lordsburg, to Road Forks Douglas, AZ, to Agua Prieta, MX**
	TStop	S:Tesoro/USA Travel Plaza #802 (Scales)

◈= Regular Gas Stations with Diesel ▲ = RV Friendly Locations ♥= Pet Friendly Locations
Red print shows large vehicle parking / access on site or nearby Brown Print = Campgrounds / RV PARKS

EXIT — NEW MEXICO

Food S: Rest/USA TP
TServ S: USA TP/Tires
Other S: Laundry/USA TP

11 NM 338S, to Animas

15 to Gary

20A W Motel Dr, Lordsburg (EB)

20B W Motel Dr, Lordsburg (EB)

20 W Motel Dr, Lordsburg
NM Welcome Center (Both dir)
S: (RR, Phone, Picnic, WiFi, Info)
FStop S: Chevron
TStop N: Love's Travel Stop #276 (Scales)
(EB Access via Exit #20B)
Food N: Subway/Pizza/Love's TS
S: GreenChiliGrill/Chevron
Lodg N: Days Inn
Other N: WiFi/RVDump/Love's TS

22 NM 494, US 70, Main St, Lordsburg, Silver City, Globe Az
(FYI: Access thru town to Ex 20 & 24)
Gas S: Diamond Shamrock◈, Texaco◈
Food N: DQ, McDonald's
S: KFC/Taco Bell, Kranberry's Rest
Lodg N: Comfort Inn
S: America Best Value Inn, Best Western, Motel 10, Super 8♥
TServ N: Oscar's Truck Service
Other N: Family Dollar, Carwash
S: Lordsburg KOA▲, Lordsburg Muni Airport✈, Amtrak, Greyhound, Laundromat

(23) Weigh Station (Both dir)

24 US 70W, I-10 Bus Loop, E Motel Dr, Lordsburg (acc to Ex #22 Serv)
TStop N: Pilot Travel Center #163 (Scales), Flying J Travel Plaza #5129 (Scales)
Gas N: Chevron
Food N: Arby's/TJCinn/Pilot TC, Rest/Fast Food/FJ TP
Lodg N: Budget Motel
TServ N: Great Western Truck Service, Towing, Tires
Other N: Laundry/WiFi/Pilot TC, Laundry/WiFi/RVDump/LP/FJ TP, Range RV Park▲, Amtrak
S: Lordsburg Muni Airport✈

29 Ulmoris, Turbin

34 NM 113, Hurley, Playas, Muir, Lisbon

42 Separ Rd, Separ, Hurley
Gas S: Bowlin's Continental Divide
Other S: Truck & Tire Repair

EXIT — NEW MEXICO

49 NM 146, Hachita, Antelope Wells

NOTE: MM 51: Continental Divide (Elev 4585')

(53) Rest Area (EB)
(RR, Picnic, Vend)

55 Frontage Rd, Quincy, Deming

(61) Rest Area (WB)
(RR, Picnic, Vend)

62 CR D094, to Gage
FStop S: Butterfield Station/Exxon
Food S: DQ/Exxon
Other S: Butterfield Station RV Park▲

68 NM 418, CR D006, Deming
TStop S: PTP/RoadysTS/Savoy Travel Center
Food S: Rest/Savoy TC
TWash S: Savoy TC
TServ S: Savoy TC/Tires
Other S: Laundry/Savoy TC

81 I-10 Bus, Pine St, W Motel Dr, Deming
TStop S: Deming Truck Terminal/USA Petroleum #801/Tesoro (Scales)
Gas S: Chevron, Shamrock◈
Food S: Rest/Deming TT, Arby's, Burger King, Burger Time, Cano's Mexican Rest, McDonald's, Si Senor Mexican Rest, Sonic, Taco Bell
Lodg S: Best Western♥, Comfort Inn, Deluxe Inn, Executive Inn, Super 8, Western Motel♥
Tires S: Deming TT
TWash S: Truck & RV Wash/Deming TT
Med S: + Hospital
Other N: City of Rocks State Park
S: Laundry/LP/Deming TT, Pic Quik Food Store, 81 Palms RV Park▲, Hitchin' Post RV Park▲, to Pancho Villa State Park, Rock Hound State Park▲

82A US 180, NM 26, Cedar St, Gold Ave, To E Motel Dr, Deming, Silver City
(Shortcut to I-25)
Gas N: Chevron◈
S: Exxon, Phillips 66, Shell◈
Food N: Blake's Lotaburger
S: Burger King, Cactus Café, Chinese Rest, Denny's, K-Bob's Steakhouse, KFC, Long John Silver's, McDonald's, Pizza Hut, Ranchers Rest, Si Senor Mexican Rest, Subway
Lodg S: ALL Lodging S to Pine St /Motel Dr (Access same as Ex 81 - 85)
Starlight Village Motel & RV Park▲
TServ S: Great Western Truck Service, Truck & Tire Repair

EXIT — NEW MEXICO

Other N: Amtrak, to appr 11 mi: Hidden Valley Resort RV Ranch▲, to appr 45 mi Silver City KOA▲
S: Auto Zone, Auto Services, CarQuest, Grocery, Kmart, Radio Shack, Walmart sc, Propane/LP, to appr 4 mi: LoW Hi RV Ranch▲, to Pancho Villa State Park, Rock Hound State Park▲

82B Cedar St, Pearl St, Deming
Gas S: Chevron, Fina, Phillips 66, Shell◈
Food S: DQ, KFC, Pizza Hut, Rancher's Rest
Lodg S: ALL Lodging S to Pine St /Motel Dr (Access same as Ex 81 - 85)
Other S: Auto Dealers, Auto Services, Carquest, Goodyear, Laundromat, Little Vineyard RV Park▲, A Deming Roadrunner RV Park▲, Wagon Wheel RV Park▲

85 I-10 Bus Lp, US 70, to E Motel Dr, East Deming
Gas S: Chevron◈, Sandis SaveGas◈
Lodg S: Days Inn, Holiday Inn, La Quinta Inn♥, Motel 6♥
Other S: NM St Hwy Patrol, Deming Muni Airport✈, Dream Catchers RV Park▲, to appr 4 mi: LoW Hi RV Ranch▲, to appr 11 mi: El Rancho Lobo RV Park▲

102 CR B049, Akela
Gas N: Bowlin's Exxon
Other S: To El Rancho Lobo RV Park▲

116 NM 549, Las Cruces

(120) US Border Patrol Checkpoint Inspection Station (WB)
Parking Area (EB)

127 Corralones Rd, Las Cruces
Gas N: Bowlin's Old West Trading Post/Exxon
Other S: Fairgrounds, NM Corr Facility

132 Las Cruces Int'l Airport
TStop S: Love's Travel Stop #259 (Scales)
Food S: Subway/Love's TS
Other N: Airport✈
S: WiFi/Love's TS, to Fairgrounds

135 I-10 Bus, US 70E, Las Cruces, Alamo Gordo, Roswell
Other N: Las Cruces KOA▲
S: Best View RV Park▲

(135) Rest Area (EB)
(RR, Phone, Picnic, RVDump)

139 NM 292, Motel Blvd, Las Cruces Amador Ave, Mesilla
FStop S: Pacific Pride/Porter Oil Co
TStop N: Pilot Travel Center #226 (Scales), Travel Center of America #14/Shell (Scales)

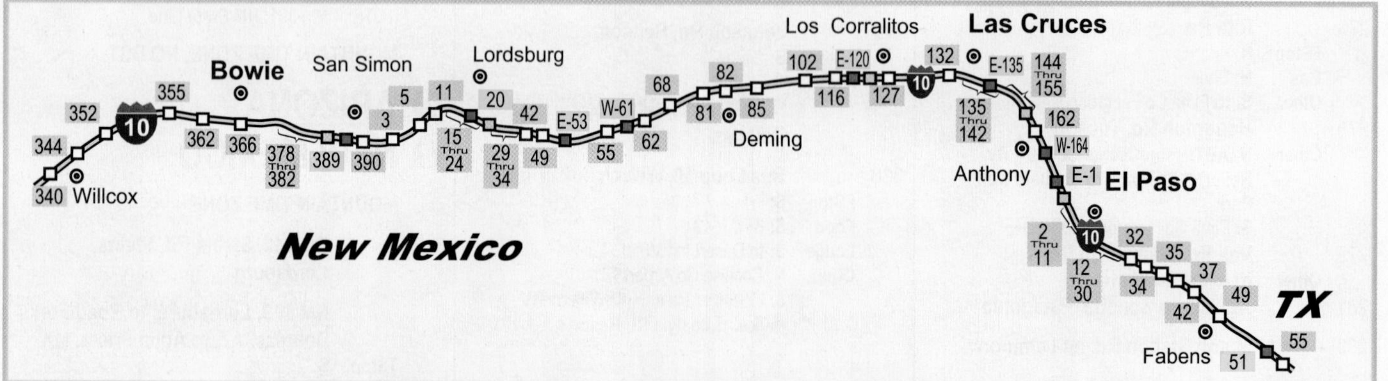

◈= Regular Gas Stations with Diesel ▲ = RV Friendly Locations ♥= Pet Friendly Locations
Red print shows large vehicle parking / access on site or nearby Brown Print = Campgrounds / RV PARKS

EXIT — NEW MEXICO

Food N: Subway/Pilot TC, Rest/BKing/PHut/TBell/TA TC, Pit Stop Cafe
S: Mexican Rest
Lodg S: Coach Light Inn & **RV Park▲**
TWash N: TA TC
TServ N: Peterbilt, TA TC
Other N: WiFi/Pilot TC, Laundry/WiFi/**RVDump**/TA TC, to **Sunny Acres RV Park▲**, **Fun City RV's**

140 NM 28, Avenida de Mesilla, Historic Mesilla Plaza, Las Cruces
Gas N: Phillips 66◈, Shell◈, Fina◈
S: Shell
Food N: Applebee's, Blake's Lotaburger, It's Burger Time, Cracker Barrel, McDonald's, Quiznos, Santa Fe Grill, Starbucks
S: DQ, Domino's Pizza, Old Town
Lodg N: Best Western, Comfort Inn, Drury Inn, Hampton Inn, La Quinta Inn♥, La Quinta Inn - Mesilla Valley♥, Springhill Suites
S: Comfort Inn
TServ N: International
Other N: **Walmart sc**, to **Sunny Acres RV Park▲**, to NM State Univ, (Addt'l serv N to El Paseo Rd, then right)
S: Barnett Harley Davidson, **Hacienda RV Resort▲**, **RV Doc's RV Park & Service▲**, **Siesta RV Park▲**, **Sunland RV Center**, **Leasburg Dam State Park**

142 NM 478, Main St, Las Cruces, University Ave, NM St Univ
Gas N: Chevron◈
S: Fina
Food N: Blimpie, Denny's, Dick's Cafe, Taco Bell, Village Inn, Whataburger
S: Bravo's Cafe, La Cocina
Lodg N: Best Western, Comfort Inn, Days Inn, Holiday Inn, Holiday Inn Express, Motel 6♥, Plaza Suites, Quality Inn, Ramada, Sands Motel, Super 8, Teakwood Inn & Suites
Med N: + Hospital
Other N: **Dalmonts RV Park▲**, Auto Dealers, to NM State Univ
S: Family Dollar, US Post Office

(144) Jct I-25N, to Albuquerque

151 NM 228, Mesquite, San Miguel

155 NM 227, Vado Dr, Vado, Berino
TStop S: National Truck Stop #305/Fina, Sunmart #675/Texaco
Food S: Rest/FastFood/SunMart, Rest/FastFood/National TS, Ernesto's, Golden West, Your Place, Simon's Café
TServ S: National TS/Tires
Other N: **Vado RV Park▲**, **Aguirre Springs Nat'l Rec Area**
S: Laundry/BarbSh/Vado TC, Laundry/WiFi/**RVDump**/National TS

(159) Weigh / Inspection Station (EB)

(160) Weigh / Inspection Station (WB)

162 NM 404, O'Hara Rd, Anthony, Chaparral
Other S: **El Paso West RV Park▲**

(164) NM Welcome Center (WB)
(RR, Phone, Picnic, WiFi, Info, Coffee)

EXIT — NM / TX

NOTE: **MM 164.5: Texas State Line**

MOUNTAIN TIME ZONE

NEW MEXICO
TEXAS

MOUNTAIN TIME ZONE

(0) New Mexico Border, FM 1905, Anthony
Rest Area (WB)
N: (RR, Phone, Picnic)
TStop N: Flying J Travel Plaza #5460/Conoco (Scales)
S: Pilot Travel Center #435 (Scales)
Gas S: Chevron◈, Exxon◈, 7-11/Fina◈
Food N: Cookery/FastFood/FJ TP
S: Wendy's/Subway/Pilot TC, Burger King/Exxon, KFC
Lodg N: Super 8
S: Best Western
TWash S: Horizon Truck Wash
TServ N: Southwest Refrigeration, TLC Trucks/Great Dane Trailers
S: Pilot TC/Tires
Other N: Laundry/Wifi/**RVDump/LP**/FJ TP, **American RV & Marine Resort▲** / **Camping World**
S: Laundry/**RVDump**/Pilot TC, **Anthony RV Center**, Anthony Animal Clinic♥, AutoZone, Big 8 Grocery, Dollar General, Walgreen's, Wet & Wild Waterworld, **Sun Country RV & Marine**

(1) Welcome Center (EB)
(RR, Phone, Picnic, Info, Pet, Sec)
Inspection Station (WB)

2 Vinton Rd, Canutillo, Westway, Vinton, El Paso
TStop N: Petro 2 #50/Mobil (Scales) **(DAND)**
Gas S: Piggy Bank, Circle N
Food N: FastFood/Petro SC, Maria's, El Taco Rico, Natalie's Kitchen, El Rincon Mexican Cafe
S: Burger King/Piggy Bank, Great American Land & Cattle Steakhouse
TServ N: Petro SC/Tires
S: Westside Trucks/Tires
Other N: Laundry/WiFi/Petro SC, **Camping World/American RV Park▲**

(5) Inspection Station (EB)

NOTE: **8% Steep Grade**

6 Lp 375, Trans Mountain Rd, Canutillo Rd
FStop N: Howdy's Shell
Gas S: Chevron◈, Shorty's Food Mart◈
Food N: DQ/Howdy's
S: McDonald's/Chevron, Subway/Shell
Other N: Hoover Co, **Franklin Mountain State Park▲**
S: Xpress Lube & Repair, Outlet Shops of El Paso, El Paso Comm College NW, **ADDTL SERV S to TX 20:** AutoZone, Checker Auto Parts, Family Dollar, Pharmacy, Tires, Restaurants

8 TX 178, Artcraft Rd, Port of Entry
Gas S: Shell◈
Food S: Carl's Jr, Rudy's Country Store & BBQ, Subway

EXIT — TEXAS

Lodg S: Hampton Inn, Holiday Inn Express
Other S: to Santa Teresa Airport✈, War Eagles Air Museum

9 Redd Rd, El Paso
Gas N: Valero, Albertson's
S: 7-11/Fina, Diamond Shamrock, Phillips 66◈, Albertson's
Food N: Applebee's, Burger King, Double Dave's Pizzaworks, Pizza Hut, Starbucks
Lodg S: Microtel
Med S: + **Upper Valley Urgent Care Center**
Other N: Auto Dealers, Albertson's, Checker Auto Parts, Lowe's, Pet's Barn♥
S: Adventure Zone Funpark, Auto Dealers, Budget RAC, Enterprise RAC, 84 Lumber, Country Club Animal Clinic♥,

11 TX 20, Mesa St, El Paso
Gas N: Chevron◈, Circle K, Phillips 66◈,
S: Chevron, Valero◈, Sam's
Food N: Baskin Robbins, Carrow's, Chili's, CiCi's Pizza, Cracker Barrel, Denny's, Famous Dave's BBQ, Fuddruckers, Golden Corral, Leo's Mexican Rest, Long John Silver's, McDonald's, Olive Garden, Popeye's Chicken, Rancher's Grill, Red Lobster, Split Peas Soup Cafe, Subway, Taco Bell, Texas Roadhouse, Wendy's, Whataburger
S: Burger King, Church's Chicken, Dominos Pizza, Golden China, Jack in the Box, KFC, Luby's, McDonald's, Peter Piper Pizza, Pizza Hut, Starbucks, Subway, Taco Cabana, Village Inn
Lodg N: Comfort Inn, Comfort Suites, Econo Lodge, Fairfield Inn, La Quinta Inn♥, La Quinta Inn West♥, Red Roof Inn♥, Springhill Suites
S: Days Inn, Super 8, Travelodge
Other N: Albertson's/Pharmacy, Big 5 Sporting Goods, Big Lots, Checker Auto Parts, Cinemark West, Desert Hills Carwash, Discount Tire, Firestone, Goodyear, Grocery, Home Depot, Pep Boys, Radio Shack, UPS Store, US Post Office, **Walmart sc**,
S: Auto Zone, Cars Plus Auto Services, Crossroads Animal Clinic♥, Dollar Tree, Hobby Lobby, Lowes Big 8 Grocery, Martin Tire Co, Radio Shack, Sam's Club, Walgreen's

12 Resler Dr, Mesa St (WB)
(Acc to Ex #11 Serv)

13 US 85, Sunland Park Dr, Paisano Dr, El Paso
Gas N: Shamrock
S: Shamrock◈, Shell
Food N: ChickFilA, Chuck E Cheese, Grand China, Great American Land & Cattle, IHOP, Johnny Carinos Italian, Olive Garden, PF Changs, Red Lobster, Whataburger
S: McDonald's, Sonic, Subway
Lodg S: Best Western, Comfort Suites, Holiday Inn♥, Sleep Inn, Studio Plus
Other N: Sunland Park Mall, B&N, Best Buy, Fiesta Lanes Bowling, Office Depot, PetSmart♥, Target, Verizon
S: Family Dollar, Sunland Park Race Track & Casino

16 Executive Center Blvd, El Paso
Gas N: Shamrock

EXIT | TEXAS

Food N: Burger King
Lodg N: Howard Johnson, Mesa Inn, Ramada Inn, Rio Casino & Suites

18A Shuster Ave, UT El Paso
Med N: + Providence Memorial Hospital, + Las Palmas Medical Center
Other N: Sun Bowl
S: Univ of Texas El Paso

18B Porfirio Diaz St, Franklin Ave

19 TX 20, Downtown El Paso, to Conv Center, to Juarez MX (EB)
Gas N: Chevron
S: Texaco
Lodg N: Holiday Inn
S: Holiday Inn Express, International Hotel, Travel Lodge
Med N: + Hospital
Other S: Amtrak

19A Mesa St, TX 20 (WB)

19B TX 20, Mesa St, Downtown El Paso, to Conv Center, Juarez MX

20 Dallas St, Cotton St, Gatway Blvd,
Gas N: Exxon
Lodg N: Ramada

21 Piedras St, El Paso
Gas N: Exxon
Food N: Burger King, McDonald's
Other N: Family Dollar, Palms Mexican Insurance

22A Lp 478, Copia St
Gas N: Fina, Shamrock
Food N: KFC

22B US 54, to I-110, Patriot Fwy, Ft Bliss, to Juarez, Mexico
Gas N: Diamond Shamrock
Food N: KFC
Other N: Coliseum, **Mil/Fort Bliss RV Park▲**

23A Reynolds St, El Paso
Food S: Arby's
Lodg S: Motel 6♥, Super 8
Med S: + Thomason Hospital, + Texas Tech Medical Center

23B US 62, US 180, Paisano Dr, El Paso, Carlsbad
Food N: Jack in the Box, McDonald's
Lodg N: Budget Inn
Other N: U-Haul, El Paso Int'l Airport✈, Ft Bliss Military Reservation
S: El Paso Zoo

24A Trowbridge Dr, El Paso
Gas N: Fina
Food N: Luby's, Steak & Ale, McDonald's
Lodg N: Budget Inn
S: Embassy Suites, La Quinta Inn♥
Med S: + Gateway Medical Clinic

24B Geronimo Dr, Surety Dr
Gas N: Chevron
S: 7-11, Phillips 66
Food N: El Taco Torte, Seafood Galley
S: Denny's, Rest/Travelodge
Lodg N: El Rancho, Quality Inn, Residence Inn, Wingate Inn
S: AmeriSuites, Embassy Suites, Hyatt, Homewood Suites, La Quinta Inn♥, Travelodge
Other N: Mall, Banks, Target, Walgreen's, to El Paso Int'l Airport✈, Ft Bliss Mil Res

24 Geronimo Dr, Trowbridge Dr (WB)

EXIT | TEXAS

25 Airway Blvd, El Paso Airport (Access to Exit #26 Serv)
TStop S: El Paso Truck Terminal/Chevron Airway Truck Terminal
Gas N: Exxon, Shell◈
Food N: Hooters, Jack in the Box, Landry's Seafood, Starbucks
S: Rest/El Paso TT
Lodg N: Courtyard, Hampton Inn, Holiday Inn, Radisson
TServ S: El Paso TT, WhiteGMC
Other S: Goodyear, El Paso Saddle Blanket

26 Hawkins Blvd, El Paso
Gas N: Chevron, Shamrock, Shell, Sam's
S: Shamrock
Food N: Arby's, Burger King, Chili's, Country Kitchen, IHOP, Golden Corral, Landry's Seafood, Luby's, Olive Garden, Wyatt's
S: China King, McDonald's, Village Inn
Lodg N: Holiday Inn, Howard Johnson
S: Best Western
TServ N: Kenworth
Med S: + Rio Grande Medical Center
Other N: B&N, Cinema, Office Depot, Sam's Club, Pennzoil, **Walmart sc**, Cielo Vista Mall, Ft Bliss Mil Rest, Int'l Airport✈

27 Hunter Dr, Viscount Blvd (EB)
Gas N: 7-11, Shamrock
S: Exxon◈, Shell
Food N: Carrow's, Red Lobster, Taco Bell
S: Whataburger, Subway/Exxon
Lodg N: La Quinta Inn♥
Other N: Best Buy, Firestone, Fort Bliss
S: Food City, El Paso Comm College

28A McRae Blvd, FM 2316, Viscount Blvd
Gas N: Chevron
S: 7-11, Chevron, Phillips 66
Food N: Chico's Tacos, Jack in the Box, KFC
S: Gabriel's
Lodg N: InTown Suites
Med N: + Hospital
Other N: ATMs, Best Buy, Big Lots, Big O Tire, Firestone, Goodyear, Office Depot, Walgreen's

28B Yarbrough Dr, Sumac Dr
Gas N: Chevron, Murphy
S: Shamrock, Shell
Food N: Burger King, Long John Silver, McDonald's, Subway, Wendy's
S: Applebee's, Fuddrucker's, Pizza Hut
Lodg N: Days Inn
S: Baymont Inn, Comfort Inn
Med N: + Columbia Medical Center
Other N: PetSmart♥, Pharmacy, **Walmart sc**,
S: **Roadrunner RV Park▲**

29 Lomaland Dr (EB)
Gas N: Exxon
S: 7-11
Food N: Denny's, Whataburger
S: Dot's BBQ, Café, Tony Roma
Lodg N: La Quinta Inn♥, Motel 6♥, Studio 6
S: Ramada
TServ N: Kenworth
Other N: Auto Dealers, Discount Tire
S: Barnett Harley Davidson

30 Lee Trevino Dr, Lomand Dr
Gas N: Exxon
S: Shamrock
Food N: TGI Friday
Lodg N: Motel 6, Ramada Inn♥, Red Roof Inn♥, Studio 6

EXIT | TEXAS

Med N: + Hospital
Other N: Firestone, Home Depot, Mall

32 FM 659, Zaragosa Rd, George Dieter Rd, El Paso
Gas N: 7-11/Fina, Chevron◈, Phillips 66
S: Chevron, Fina, Shamrock◈
Food N: Famous Dave's BBQ, Furr's, IHOP, Logan's Roadhouse, Macaroni Grill, McDonald's, Outback Steakhouse, Peter Piper Pizza, Whataburger, Village Inn
Lodg N: Holiday Inn Express, Microtel
TServ N: Border Int'l Truck Service
Med N: + Hospital
Other N: Lowe's, Office Depot

34 Lp 375, Americas Ave, Joe Battle Blvd, El Paso
Gas N: Chevron◈, Shamrock◈, Texaco
Lodg N: Microtel, ValuePlace
TServ N: Western Star Trucks, Rush GMC Commercial Truck Center/Peterbilt
Other S: El Paso Museum of History, **Mission RV Park▲**

35 Eastlake Blvd

37 FM 1281, Horizon Blvd, El Paso
TStop N: Flying J Travel Plaza (Scales), Love's Travel Stop #214 (Scales)
S: Petro Stopping Center #1/Mobil (Scales)
Gas N: Exxon
Food N: Rest/FastFood/FJ TP, Subway/Chesters/Love's TS
S: IronSkillet/Blimpie/Petro SC, McDonald's
Lodg N: Americana Inn
S: Deluxe Inn
TServ N: Flying J TP, Cummins SW, El Paso Thermo King, Truck Center of El Paso
S: Petro SC, El Paso Freightliner, Speedco, Peterbilt, Expert Trailer Repair
TWash S: Blue Beacon TW/Petro SC, Texas TW
Other N: WiFi/Love's TS, Laundry/WiFi/LP/FJ TP, Vet♥, El Paso Connection
S: Laundry/CB/BarbSh/WiFi/Petro SC, Laundry/El Paso TP, **Samson RV Park▲**

42 FM 1110, Clint, San Elizario
Gas S: Exxon◈
Food S: Rest/Cotton Valley Motel
Lodg S: Cotton Valley Motel & **RV Park▲**, Super 8

49 FM 793, Clint, Fabens
TStop S: Texas 49 Truck Stop
Gas S: Phillips 66◈
Food S: Rest/TX 49 TS, Church's Chicken, McDonald's, Lower Valley Café, Subway
Lodg S: Fabens Inn
TServ S: Faben's Tire Co
Other S: Fabens Airport✈

(51) El Paso Co Rest Area (Both dir) (RR, Picnic) (EB: Next Rest Area 95 mi)

55 Tornillo

68 Acala Rd

72 Spur 148, Knox Ave, Ft Hancock
Gas S: Shell◈
Food S: Rest/Shell
Lodge S: Ft Hancock Motel

(77) TRUCK Parking Area (WB)

78 TX 20W, McNary

81 FM 2217, Ft Hancock

85 Esperanza Rd

◈= Regular Gas Stations with Diesel ▲ = RV Friendly Locations ♥= Pet Friendly Locations
Red print shows large vehicle parking / access on site or nearby **Brown Print = Campgrounds / RV PARKS**

EXIT		TEXAS
87		**FM 34, Esperanza**
	TStop	**S:** Drivers Travel Mart **(Diesel Avail ONLY)**
95		**Frontage Rd (EB)**
(98)		**Picnic Area (EB)**
99		**Lasca Rd, Ft Hancock**
		N: Picnic Area (Both dir)
(102)		**Inspection / Border Patrol (EB)**
105		**I-10 Bus Lp, Sierra Blanca (EB)**
106		**I-10 Bus Lp, Sierra Blanca (WB)**
107		**RM 1111, Sierra Blanca Ave**
	FStop	**N:** Sierra Blanca Exxon **(EB Use Ex #106)**
	Gas	**S:** Chevron
	Food	**N:** Café, Michael's Rest
		S: Cafe
	Lodg	**N:** Sierra Motel
	TServ	**N:** Truck Tire Repair
	Other	**N: Sierra Blanca RV Park▲**
108		**I-10 Bus, Sierra Blanca**
129		**Old Hwy 80, Allamore, Hot Wells**
133		**Frontage Rd (WB)**
	NOTE:	**MM 135: Mountain / Central Time Zone**
(136)		**Weigh Station (EB)**
(136)		**Scenic Overlook (WB)**
138		**Golf Course Dr, Lp 10, Van Horn** **(Note Access Serv Ex 138-140B to the N Via Broadway or S via Frontage Rd)**
	TStop	**S:** Chevron Truck Stop/RoadysTS
	Gas	**N:** Shell◊
	Food	**N:** Cattle Co Steakhouse, Chuey's, DQ, Pizza Hut
		S: CountryGrill/Chevron TS, McDonald's
	Lodg	**N:** America Best Value Inn, Budget Inn, Econo Lodge, Knights Inn, Motel 6♥
		S: Hampton Inn, Holiday Inn Express, Ramada♥, Super 8
	TServ	**S:** Bud's Diesel
	Other	**N:** Goodyear, Grocery, US Post Office, Municipal Golf Course, **Country Inn RV Park▲**, **Eagles Nest RV Park▲**, **LP**
		S: Mountain View Golf Course
140A		**US 90, TX 54, Van Horn St, Harfa**
	TStop	**S:** Pilot Travel Center #209 (Scales) **(DAND)**
	Gas	**N:** Phillips 66◊, Shell◊
		S: Exxon
	Food	**N:** Leslie's BBQ
		S: Papa's Café, Wendy's/Pilot TC
	Lodg	**N:** Days Inn, Desert Inn, Village Inn Motel
	Med	**N: + Hospital**

EXIT		TEXAS
	Other	**N:** NAPA, US Post Office, Mike's Tire Service, **El Campo RV Park▲**
		S: WiFi/Pilot TC, **Van Horn KOA▲**, **Mountain View RV Park▲**, McDonald Observatory, Visitor Center
140B		**I-10 Bus, Ross Dr, Van Horn (Note Access Serv Ex 140B-138 to the N Via Broadway or S via Frontage Rd)**
	TStop	**N:** Love's Travel Stop #256
	Gas	**N:** Chevron, Exxon◊
	Food	**N:** Pizza Palace, Subway/Love's TS, Chevy's Mexican Rest, Rest/Days Inn, Rest/Sands Motel
	Lodg	**N:** Bells Motel, Days Inn, Motel 6♥, Sands Motel
	Other	**N:** WiFi/Love's TS, **Van Horn Propane**, Pharmacy, Auto/Truck Repair, **El Campo RV Park▲**, Culberson Co Airport✈
		S: Mountain View RV Park▲
(145)		**Culberson Co Rest Area (Both dir) (RR, Picnic)**
(146)		**Weigh Station (WB)**
146		**Wild Horse Rd, Van Horn**
153		**Evergreen Rd, Salt Flat, Michigan Flat**
159		**Moon Rd, Salt Flat, Plateau**
	TStop	**N:** Plateau Truck & Auto Center/Roadys TS/Fina
	Food	**N:** Rest/FastFood/Plateau TAC
	TServ	**N:** Plateau TAC/Tires
	Other	**N:** Laundry/Plateau TAC
166		**Boracho Rd, Salt Flat**
173		**Hurds Draw Rd**
176		**TX 118, FM 2424, Kent, Ft Davis**
	Gas	**N:** Chevron◊
	Other	**S: to Davis Mountains State Park**
181		**Cherry Creek Rd, Fort Davis**
	FStop	**S:** Chevron
184		**Stocks Ranch Rd, Springhills**
(185)		**Picnic Area (Both dir)**
(186)		**Jct I-20E, to Dallas, Ft Worth (WB, LEFT exit)**
(187)		**Jct I-20E, to Pecos (WB)**
188		**Griffin Rd, Balmorhea**
192		**FM 3078E, to Toyahvale**
206		**FM 2903, Balmorhea, Toyah**
209		**I-10W Bus, TX 17S, Balmorhea**
	Other	**S: to Davis Mountains State Park**

EXIT		TEXAS
212		**TX 17, Balmorhea, to Saragosa, Pecos**
	FStop	**S:** I-10 Travel Stop/Fina
	Food	**S:** Rest/Fina FS
	Other	**S:** **RVDump**/Fina
214		**FM 2448 (WB)**
222		**Hoefs Rd**
229		**Hovey Rd, Fort Stockton**
(233)		**Pecos West Co Rest Area (Both dir) (RR, Phone, Picnic, Vend)**
235		**Mendel Rd, Ft Stockton**
241		**Kennedy Rd**
246		**Firestone Rd, Fort Stockton**
248		**US 67S, FM 1776, to Alpine, Big Bend National Park**
253		**FM 2037, to Belding**
256		**I-10 Bus, Dickinson Blvd, US 285, Fort Stockton**
	Gas	**S:** Valero◊, Shell◊
	Food	**S:** China Inn, DQ, K-Bob's Steak House, KFC, Pizza, Sonic, Subway
	Lodg	**S:** Best Western, Comfort Inn, Econo Lodge, Motel 6♥, Sleep Inn, Super 8
	Med	**S: + Hospital**
	Other	**S:** SW Vet Clinic♥, Animal Medical Clinic♥, Pharmacy, **Walmart▲**
257		**US 285, Fort Stockton, to Pecos, Sanderson**
	FStop	**S:** Town & Country #113/Chevron
	TStop	**S:** Comanche Springs Truck Terminal/ RoadysTS/Exxon
	Gas	**S:** Valero◊
	Food	**S:** Rest/Comanche Springs TT, BBQ, IHOP, KFC/Taco Bell, McDonald's, Pizza Hut, Sonic, Subway
	Lodg	**S:** Best Western, Comfort Inn, Days Inn, Hampton Inn, Holiday Inn Express, Knights Inn, La Quinta Inn♥, Motel 6♥, Quality Inn
	TWash	**S:** Chaparral Truck Wash
	TServ	**N:** I-10 Garage
		S: Comanche Sp TT
	Other	**N: Comanche Land RV Park▲**, Fort Stockton-Pecos Co Airport✈, Desert Pines Golf Course, Fort Stockton Golf Course
		S: Laundry/WiFi/Comanche Sp TT, **Walmart▲**, Auto Zone, Goodyear
259B		**TX 18, Ft Stockton, Monahans (WB)**
259A		**FM 1053 (WB)**

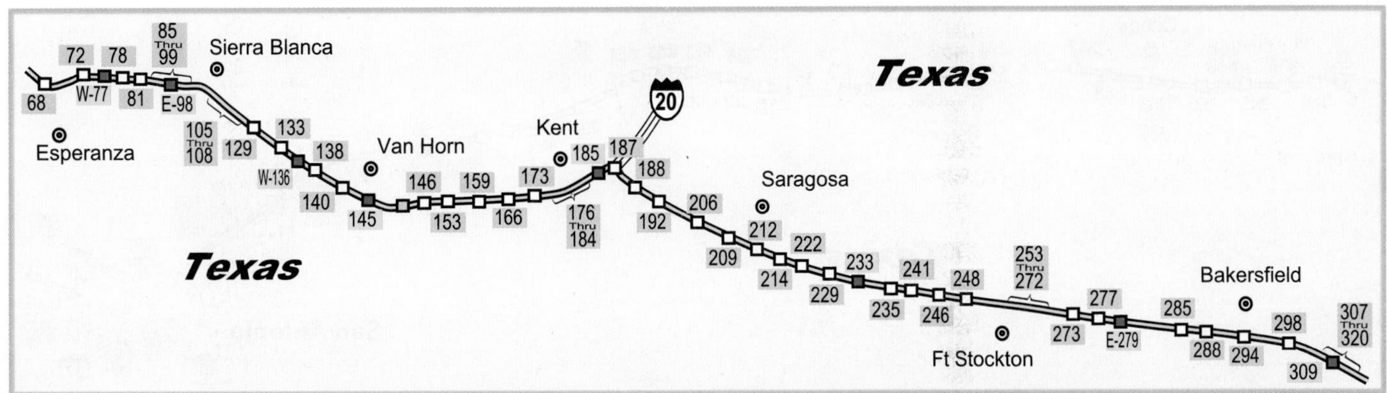

◊= Regular Gas Stations with Diesel ▲ = RV Friendly Locations ♥= Pet Friendly Locations
Red print shows large vehicle parking / access on site or nearby **Brown Print = Campgrounds / RV PARKS**

EXIT — TEXAS

259 **TX 18, Monahan's, FM 1053 (EB)**
FStop N: Oasis Travel /Shell
TStop N: Johnny's Circle n Food Store/Fina
Gas N: Apache Liquors & Fuel Center
Food N: Burger King/Shell, FastFood/Johnny's
TServ N: Johnny's TS/Tires
Med S: + Pecos Co Memorial Hospital
Other N: I-10 RV Park▲ , Laundry/Johnny's

261 **US 10, US 385, Marathon, Fort Stockton**
FStop N: 7-D Exxon
Lodg S: Best Value Inn, Econo Lodge
Med S: + Pecos Co Memorial Hospital

264 **Warnock Rd**
Other N: Fort Stockton KOA▲

272 **University Rd, Fort Stockton**

273 **US 67, US 385, Fort Stockton, to McCamey, San Angelo**
N: Picnic Area (WB)

277 **FM 2023, Fort Stockton**

(279) **Picnic Area (EB)**

285 **McKenzie Rd**

288 **Ligon Rd, Fort Stockton**

294 **FM 11, Bakersfield**
Gas N: Exxon
S: Chevron◈
Food S: Café/Chevron

298 **RM 2886**

307 **US 190, Iraan, to FM 305, to McCamey, Sheffield**

(309) **Pecos East Co Rest Area (Both dir)**
(RR, Phone, Picnic)

314 **Frontage Rd**

320 **Frontage Rd, Iraan**

325 **TX 290, TX 349, Iraan, Sheffield**
Med N: + Iraan General Hospital

328 **River Rd, Ozona, to Sheffield**

337 **Live Oak Rd, Ozona**

343 **TX 290W, Sheffield**

(346) **Parking Area (EB)**

(349) **Parking Area (WB)**

350 **RM 2398, Howard Draw Rd**

361 **RM 2083, Pandale Rd, Ozona**

363 **Loop 466, RM 2398, Ozona**

EXIT — TEXAS

365 **TX 163, Ozona, Sterling City, Comstock**
FStop N: Town & Country #219
Gas N: Chevron◈, Exxon
S: Chevron, Shell
Food N: FastFood/T&C, Burger King, DQ, Café Next Door, Subway
Lodg N: Best Western, Economy Inn ♥ & RV Park▲ , Holiday Inn Express, Super 8, Travelodge
Med N: + Crockett Co Care Center

368 **Loop 466, Ozona**
Med N: + Crockett Co Care Center

372 **Taylor Box Rd, Ozona**
TStop N: AmBest/Circle Bar Auto & Truck Plaza/ Exxon (Scales)
Food N: Deli/Rest/Circle Bar TP
Lodg N: Super 8
TWash N: Circle Bar TP
TServ N: Circle Bar TP/Tires
Other N: Laundry/RVDump/Circle Bar TP, Circle Bar RV Park▲ , Auto Museum

381 **FM 1312 (EB)**

388 **FM 1312 (WB)**

392 **FM 1312, RM 1989, Caverns of Sonora Rd, Sonora**

(394) **Sutton Co Rest Area (Both dir)**
(EB: Next RA 119 mi)
(RR, Phone, Picnic, WiFi, RVDump)

399 **Lp 467, Sonora (EB) (Acc to Ex #404)**

400 **US 277, Loop 467, Sonora, to San Angelo, Del Rio**
FStop S: Skinny's Conv Store #407/7-11/Fina
Gas N: Shell◈
S: T&C/Chevron◈, Exxon◈, Shell
Food N: Sutton County Steak House
S: Country Cookin Café, DQ, La Mexicana, Pizza Hut, Sonic, Subway
Lodg N: Days Inn♥
S: Best Value Inn, Best Western, Comfort Inn♥
Med S: + Hudspeth Memorial Hospital
Other N: Sonora Muni Airport✈, Sonora Golf Club
S: LP, Busters RV Park▲ , Animal Hospital♥

404 **Lp 467, RM 864, RM 3130, Sonora (Acc to #400-399 S via Lp 467)**

412 **RM 3130, Allison Rd**

420 **RM 3130, Baker Rd**

EXIT — TEXAS

(423) **Parking Area (Both dir)**

429 **RM 3130, Harrell Rd**

437 **Lp 291, Roosevelt (EB, Diff reacc)**

438 **Lp 291, Roosevelt (WB)**

442 **Lp 291, RM 1674, Ft. McKavatt**

445 **RM 1674, Roosevelt (EB)**

451 **RM 2291, Cleo Rd**

456 **US 83N, US 377, Junction, London, Rocksprings, Menard, Mason**
FStop N: Joy's Conoco
S: Harold's Food Mart/Shell, Junction Country Store/RoadysTS/Valero
TStop N: Gene's Go Truck Stop Chevron
Gas S: Exxon◈
Food N: FastFood/Gene's TS, BBQ, JR's,
S: McDonald's/Valero, Junction Rest, DQ, Git-It, Sonic, Rest/Slumber Inn
Lodg N: Comfort Inn, Motel 6
S: Best Western, Days Inn♥, Lazy T Motel, Hills Motel, Legends Inn, Slumber Inn, Sun Valley Motel
Med S: + Kimble Hospital
Other N: Laundry/Gene's TS, Kimble Co Airport✈
S: WiFi/Jct CS, Lakeview RV Park▲ , Lazy Daze RV Park▲ , Junction KOA▲ , Morgan Shady Park▲ , to S Llano River State Park▲ , TX Tech Univ

457 **FM 2169, Junction, Martinez St**
FStop N: Grandad's Corner Store/Shell
Food S: Rest/Days Inn
Lodg S: Days Inn
Other S: S Llano River State Park▲

(459) **Picnic Area (WB)**

460 **Bus Loop, Junction (WB)**

(461) **Picnic Area (EB)**

462 **US 83S, to Uvalde**

465 **FM 2169, Junction, Segovia**
TStop S: Segovia Truck Stop/P66
Food S: Rest/Segovia TS
Lodg S: Econo Lodge/Segovia TS
TServ S: Segovia TS/Tires
Other S: Laundry/Segovia TS, Pecan Valley RV Park▲

472 **Old Segovia Rd, CR 450, FM 479, FM 2169, Junction**

477 **US 290E, to Fredericksburg**

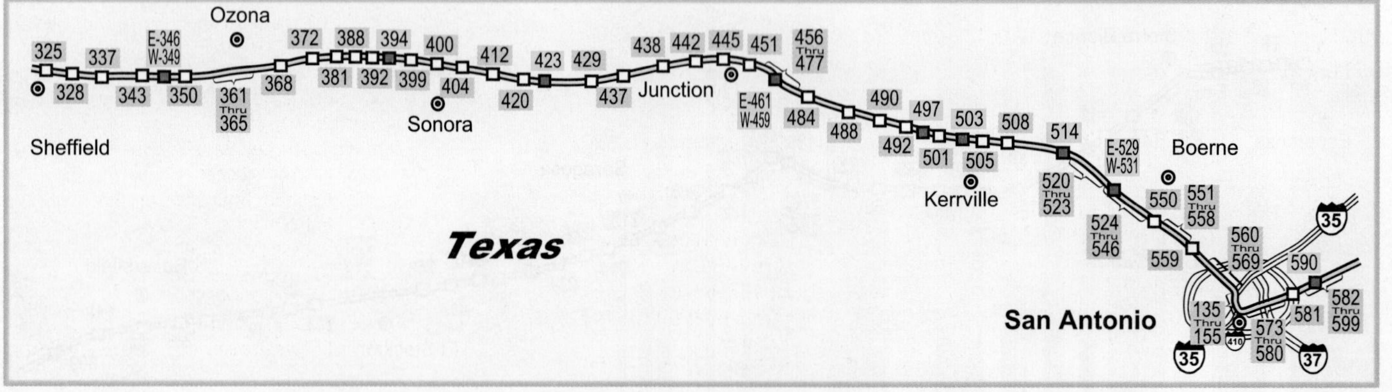

◈= Regular Gas Stations with Diesel ▲ = RV Friendly Locations ♥= Pet Friendly Locations
Red print shows large vehicle parking / access on site or nearby Brown Print = Campgrounds / RV PARKS

EXIT	TEXAS
484	**Midway Rd**
488	**TX 27, Mountain Home, Ingram**
Other	N: to 9mi **Johnson Creek RV Resort▲**
490	**TX 41, Mountain Home, Rock Springs**
492	**FM 479, Mountain Home**
(497)	Picnic Area (Both dir)
NOTE:	MM 501: EB: 7% Steep Grade
501	**FM 1338, Goat Creek Rd, Kerrville**
Other	N: **Buckhorn Lake RV Resort▲** S: **Kerrville KOA▲**
(503)	Scenic View (Both dir)
NOTE:	MM 504: EB: 7% Steep Grade
505	**FM 783, Harper Rd, Kerrville, to Harper, Ingram (Serv S to TX 27)**
Gas	S: Exxon◈
Lodg	S: Inn of the Hills
Food	S: Chili's, CiCi's Pizza, McDonald's, Pizza Hut, Starbucks, Wendy's
Other	S: **Walmart sc▲**, to appr 2mi: **Take-It-Easy Adult RV Park▲**, to appr 5 mi **Guadalupe River RV Resort▲**, Classic Car Museum
508	**TX 16, Fredericksburg Rd, Kerrville**
Gas	N: Exxon◈ S: Chevron◈, Valero◈, Shell◈
Food	S: Subway/Chevron, McDonald's/Shell, Burger King, Cracker Barrel, Denny's, IHOP, Jack in the Box, Luby's, Sonic
Lodg	S: Americas Best Value Inn, Best Western, Big Texas Inn, Comfort Inn, Days Inn, Hampton Inn, Holiday Inn Express, La Quinta Inn♥, Motel 6♥, Super 8, Y.O. Ranch Resort Hotel & Conf Center
Med	S: + Hospital
Other	N: **Johnson Creek RV Resort▲** S: AutoZone, Home Depot, Lowe's, Grocery, Walgreen's, **Kerrville RV Center**, **Kerrville Schreiner State Park**
NOTE:	MM 514: EB: 7% Steep Grade
(514)	Kerr Co Rest Area (Both dir) (RR, Ph, Pic, Vend, WiFi, RVDump/Water)
520	**FM 1341, Cypress Creek Rd, Kerrville**
523	**US 87, Bus 87, Comfort, to San Angelo, Fredericksburg**
Gas	N: Chevron S: Exxon◈, Texaco
Food	N: McDonald's/Chevron S: DQ
Lodg	S: Executive Inn
Other	N: Golf Course S: **USA RV Park/LP▲**
524	**US 87 Bus, FM 1621, Comfort, Waring**
Gas	S: Chevron◈, Shell
Food	S: Double D Family Rest
Other	N: Lindner Animal Hospital♥
527	**FM 1621, Comfort, Waring (WB)**
(529)	Picnic Area (EB)
(531)	Picnic Area (WB)

Personal Notes

EXIT	TEXAS
533	**FM 289, Boerne, Welfare**
Food	N: PoPo Family Rest
Other	N: **Top of the Hill RV Park▲**
537	**US 87 Bus, Ranger Creek Rd, Boerne (Serv appr 3mi)** **(Acc to Ex #537-542 N to Main St)**
Gas	N: Chevron, Shamrock
Food	N: La Hacienda, Pete's Place, Subway
Lodg	N: Best Western, Holiday Inn, Key to the Hills Motel
538	**Ranger Creek Rd, Boerne (WB)**
539	**Johns Rd, Boerne**
Gas	S: Valero◈
Lodg	N: La Quinta Inn♥
Other	S: LP/Valero, **Boerne RV Service**
540	**TX 46, to New Braunfels, Bandera**
Gas	N: Exxon, Shamrock, Shell◈, Murphy, HEB
Food	N: Burger King, DQ, Denny's, Wendy's, Margarita's Café, Pizza Hut, Sonic, Starbucks, Taco Cabana S: Chili's, Whataburger
Lodg	N: Americas Best Value Inn, Best Western, Holiday Inn Express S: Hampton Inn, La Quinta Inn♥
Med	S: + Medical Center
Other	N: Auto Services, HEB/Pharmacy, Radio Shack, Walgreen's, **Explore USA RV Sales**, to Bus 87: **Walmart sc▲** S: Home Depot
542	**Bus 87, Boerne (WB)** **(Acc to Ex #542-537 N to Main St)**
Food	N: Wendy's
Other	N: Tires,

EXIT	TEXAS
543	**Boerne Stage Rd, Cascade Caverns Rd, Scenic Loop Rd**
FStop	N: Kwik Pantry/Citgo
Gas	N: Chevron, Exxon, Valero◈
Food	N: Café/Chevron, Café/Exxon, Copeland's Seafood & Steaks, Rest/Cavern Inn
Lodg	N: Cavern Inn
Other	N: Auto Dealers, Enterprise RAC, Lester's Auto Center Cars/Trucks/**RV**, **Walmart sc**, **Alamo Fiesta RV Park▲**, **American Dream Vacations RV Center**, Cascade Caverns
546	**Fair Oaks Pkwy, Tarpon Dr, Fair Oaks Ranch**
Gas	S: Chevron◈, Exxon◈
Food	S: Café/Chevron, FlagstopCafé/Exxon
Other	N: Javalina Harley Davidson, Vet♥, **American Dream RV Sales & Rentals** S: Auto Services, Ancira Auto & **RV Center**, **Ron Hoover RV & Marine Centers**, **C & S RV Center**, Boerne Stage Airport✈, **Explore USA RV Center**, to **Tejas Valley RV Park▲**
550	**FM 3351, Ralph Fair Rd, Boerne Stage Rd, Camp Stanley**
FStop	N: Pico #10/Valero Travel Center
Gas	N: Exxon S: Shell◈, HEB
Food	N: FastFood/Pico, McDonald's/Exxon, Mexican Rest, Romano's Macaroni Grill, Starbucks S: Domino's/Shell
Lodg	N: La Quinta Inn♥
Other	N: Bank, Camp Stanley Military Res S: HEB
551	**Boerne Stage Rd, San Antonio, to Leon Springs (WB)**
Gas	S: HEB
Food	S: Longhorn Steakhouse, Starbucks
Med	S: + Texas Medical Clinic
Other	S: HEB, UPS Store
554	**Camp Bullis Rd**
Gas	N: Citgo S: Shell
Food	N: ChickFilA, Habaneros Grill, Mimi's Cafe, Quiznos, Red Robin, TGI Friday
Lodg	N: Motel 6♥ S: Rodeway Inn
Other	N: Bass Pro Shop, Best Buy, Dick's Sporting Goods, Palladium IMAX, Lowe's, Staples, Auto Services S: Shell/Carwash
555	**La Cantera Pkwy, Fiesta**
Other	S: Univ of Texas San Antonio
556A	**Lp 1604, Anderson Loop**
Food	S: Olive Garden
Lodg	S: Comfort Inn, Drury Inn, La Quinta Inn♥, Motel 6♥
Other	S: to Sea World
556B	**Frontage Rd, San Antonio**
Lodg	S: Motel 6♥
Other	S: Best Buy, Bass Pro Shop, Lowe's, Palladium, Target
557	**Spur 53, Univ of Texas SA**
Gas	N: Exxon S: Costco
Lodg	N: Best Western, Econo Lodge, Howard Johnson, Super 8 S: La Quinta Inn♥
Other	N: Auto Dealers

EXIT		TEXAS
	Other	S: Auto Dealers, Costco, Discount Tire, Sam's Club
558		**De Zavala Rd, San Antonio**
	Gas	N: Chevron, Exxon◈, Shell
	Food	N: BBQ, Carrabba's, Chili's, Joe's Crab Shack, Jim's Rest, Logan's, McDonald's, Outback Steakhouse, Subway S: IHOP, TGI Friday, Whataburger
	Lodg	N: Best Western, Econo Lodge, Howard Johnson, Holiday Inn Express, Super 8 S: Days Inn
	Other	N: Bank, Home Depot, HEB, Office Max, PetSmart♥, Target S: Sam's Club, **Walmart sc**, Bowling
559		**Loop 335, Fredericksburg Rd, US 87, Woodstone Dr**
	Gas	S: Texaco
	Food	N: Barnacle Bill's Seafood, Carrabba's, Joe's Crab Shack, Outback Steakhouse, Starbucks
	Lodg	S: Econo Lodge, Studio 6
	Other	N: FedEx Office
560A		**Huebner Rd, San Antonio (EB)**
	Gas	N: Chevron, Valero S: Exxon, Shell
	Food	N: BBQ, Golden Corral, On the Border, Romano's Macaroni Grill, Saltgrass Steakhouse S: Burger King, **Cracker Barrel**, Jim's Rest, McDonald's
	Lodg	S: AmeriSuites, Days Inn, Hampton Inn
	Other	N: AMC24 Cinema, Borders
560B		**Frontage Rd (EB) (Access to #560A)**
560C		**Medical Dr, Callaghan Rd**
561		**Huebner Rd, Wurzbach Rd**
	Gas	N: Mobil◈, Phillips 66 S: Shell
	Food	N: Fuddruckers, Golden Corral, Jason's Deli, Popeye's, Sea Island Shrimphouse, Pappasito's, TX Land & Cattle Co Rest S: Alamo Café, Benihana, Co Line BBQ, Denny's, Jack in the Box, IHOP, Luby's, Mamacita's, McDonald's, Pizza Hut, Sombrero Rosa Cafe, Taco Bell, Wendy's, Village Inn
	Lodg	N: AmeriSuites, Ramada, Wyndham S: Best Western, Drury Inn, Holiday Inn Express, La Quinta Inn♥, Motel 6♥, Residence Inn, Sleep Inn
	Med	S: + Hospital
	Other	N: Albertson's
562		**Frontage Rd, Wurzbach Rd (EB)**
563		**Callaghan Rd, San Antonio**
	Gas	N: Mobil S: Exxon
	Food	N: Las Palapas, Subway S: Mama's
	Lodg	N: Embassy Suites, Marriott
	Other	N: Auto Dealers S: Lowe's
(564AB)		**Jct I-410, to Airport, Connally Lp**
565A		**Crossroads Blvd, Dewhurst Rd, Balcones Heights Rd**
	Gas	N: Exxon, Shell
	Food	N: Denny's, WhataBurger S: El Pollo Loco, McDonald's
	Lodg	N: Comfort Suites, Howard Johnson, Rodeway Inn, Marriott, Springhill Suites

EXIT		TEXAS
	Lodg	S: La Quinta Inn♥, Super 8
	Other	N: Animal Hospital♥ S: Firestone, Mall, Super Target
565B		**Vance Jackson Rd, West Ave (EB), First Park Ten Blvd (WB)**
	Gas	S: Exxon, Shell
	Food	N: Bill Miller BBQ
	Lodg	N: Econo Lodge, Quality Inn S: La Quinta Inn♥
	Other	N: **Walmart sc**▲
565C		**Vance Jackson Rd (WB)**
	Lodg	N: Quality Inn S: La Quinta Inn♥
566A		**Fresno Dr (EB), West Ave (WB)**
	Gas	N: Exxon, Shamrock
566B		**Fresno Dr, Hildebrand Ave, Fulton Ave, San Antonio**
	Gas	S: 7-11, Exxon
567		**Loop 345, Fredericksburg Rd, Woodlawn Ave (EB)** **(EB-Upper Level-to I-35S, I-10E, US 87S) (Lower Level to I-35N)**
567A		**Fulton Ave, Hildebrand Ave (WB)**
567B		**Loop 345, Woodlawn Ave (WB)**
568		**Spur 421, Culebra, Bandera (EB)**
	Other	S: to St Mary's Univ
568A		**Cincinnati Ave (WB)**
568B		**Spur 421, Culebra Rd**
569		**Santa Rosa St, Downtown (EB), Colorado St (WB)**
569A		**N Colorado St (EB)**
569B		**N Frio St (EB)**
	NOTE:	**I-10 follows I-35 below for next 3 mi, Exit #'s follow I-35.**
(570/ 156)		**Jct I-35N, to Austin**
155C		**W Houston St, Commerce St, Market Square (EB)**
155B		**Frio St, Durango Blvd (EB), Durango Blvd, Downtown (WB)**
	Food	E: Jim Miller BBQ
	Lodg	E: Holiday Inn W: Radisson
155A		**Spur 536, Alamo St (EB)**
	Lodg	E: Microtel
154B		**S Laredo St, Cevallos St**
	FStop	E: Conoco (Scales)
	Gas	E: Exxon, Shell
	Food	E: McDonald's, Wendy's
	Lodg	E: Days Inn
154A		**San Marcos St, Nogalios St (EB), Loop 353, Nogalitos St (WB)**
	Gas	E: Conoco
	Lodg	E: Scottish Inn
(572/ 153)		**Jct I-10E, US 90W, I-35S to Laredo, US 87, to I-37**
	NOTE:	**I-10 follows I-35 Above for next 3 mi. Exit #'s follow I-35.**
573		**Probandt St, TX 536, Roosevelt Ave, Steves Ave, San Antonio**
	Gas	S: Conoco, Valero
	Food	N: Bill Miller BBQ

EXIT		TEXAS
(574)		**Jct I-37, US 281, S - Corpus Christi, N - Johnson City**
575		**Pine St, Hackberry St**
	Food	S: Little Red Barn Steakhouse
576		**New Braunfels Ave, Gevers St**
	Gas	S: Valero
	Food	S: McDonald's
577		**US 87S, Roland Ave, Victoria**
	Food	S: Whataburger
	Lodg	S: Super 8
578		**Pecan Valley Dr, M L King Dr**
	Gas	N: Phillips 66
579		**Houston St, Commerce St**
	Gas	N: Valero S: Chevron
	Lodg	N: Best Value Inn, Ramada, Travelodge S: Days Inn, Passport Inn
	Other	N: Coliseum
580		**Lp 13, WW White Rd, San Antonio**
	Gas	N: Chevron, Fina S: Exxon
	Food	N: Wendy's, Rest/Comfort Inn S: Bill Miller BBQ, McDonald's, Pizza Hut
	Lodg	N: Comfort Inn, Motel 6♥, Red Roof Inn, Rodeway Inn S: Econo Lodge, Quality Inn, Super 8, Spur Motel
	TServ	N: Bonanza Tire Sales S: Sterling, Grande Truck Sales, Davis Truck Service, Ford, WhiteGMC, Freightliner
	Other	N: **Dixie Campground▲**, **San Antonio KOA▲**
(581)		**Jct I-410, Connally Loop**
582		**Ackerman Rd, Kirby**
	TStop	N: Pilot Travel Center #306 (Scales) S: Petro Stopping Center #5/Mobil (Scales)
	Food	N: Wendys/PizzaHut/Pilot TC S: IronSkillet/Petro SC, KFC/TacoBell
	Lodg	N: Bonita Inn Motel S: Rest Inn
	TWash	S: Blue Beacon TW/Petro SC
	TServ	N: Petro SC, Fruehauf, International, Thermo King Service S: Petro SC
	Other	N: WiFi/Pilot TC S: Laundry/CB/WiFi/Petro SC, Martindale Army Air Field ✈
583		**Foster Rd, San Antonio**
	TStop	N: Flying J Travel Plaza #5410/Conoco (Scales) S: Travel Center of America/Chevron
	Gas	N: Valero◈
	Food	N: Rest/FastFood/FJ TP, Jack in the Box S: Rest/BKing/PHut/Popeye/TA TC
	Lodg	N: Holiday Inn Express, La Quinta Inn♥
	TServ	N: Charlie's Truck Wash S: TA TC/Tires
	Other	N: Laundry/BarbSh/WiFi/**RVDump**/FJ TP S: Laundry/WiFi/**RVDump**/TA TC
585		**FM 1516, Converse**
	TStop	N: San Antonio Travel Center/Shell (Scales)
	Food	N: FastFood/SA TC, Rest/Windfield's
	Lodg	N: La Quinta Inn♥, Rest Inn, Ramada, Windfield's Motel

◈ = Regular Gas Stations with Diesel ▲ = RV Friendly Locations ♥ = Pet Friendly Locations
Red print shows large vehicle parking / access on site or nearby Brown Print = Campgrounds / RV PARKS

EXIT		TEXAS
	TServ	N: Arrow Truck Sales, Rush Truck Center S: Peterbilt/Freightliner, Kenworth, CB Sales & Svc, Werts Welding & Tank Svc
	Other	N: Laundry/San Antonio TC, **Alamo City RV Center**
587		**Loop 1604, Anderson Loop, Randolph AFB, Universal City**
	Other	N: to appr 13mi: **Blazing Star Luxury RV Resort▲**
589		**Graytown Rd, Pfeil Rd**
(590)		**Rest Area** (Both dir) (RR, Phone, Picnic, **RVDump**)
591		**FM 1518, Converse, Schertz**
	Gas	N: Shell
	Other	S: Riske Fleet Service, to appr 9mi: **Easy Acres RV Park▲**
593		**FM 2538, Trainer Hale Rd**
	FStop	N: Citgo
	Gas	N: Texaco◈ S: Exxon◈
	Food	N: DQ/Citgo, Mexican Rest
	Lodg	S: Stay Inn
	Other	N: Auto Repair S: Auto Repair, **RV Rentals**
595		**Zuehl Rd, Marion**
597		**Santa Clara Rd, Seguin**
	Other	N: Rivercity Raceway
599		**FM 465, Linne Rd, to Marion**
600		**Schwab Rd**
601		**FM 775, Seguin, New Berlin, La Vernia**
	TStop	N: Sunmart #167/Chevron (Scales)
	Food	N: Subway/Sunmart
603		**US 90E, Alt 90, Seguin (EB)**
	Other	N: **D & A RV Resort▲ , Explore USA RV Center**
604		**FM 725, Seguin, to Lake McQueeney**
	Other	N: **D & A RV Resort▲ , Twin Palms RV Park▲ , America Go RV Sales, Explore USA RV Center** S: **to Brian's Country RV Park▲**
605		**FM 464, Seguin**
	Other	N: **Twin Pines RV Park▲** S: **On the River RV Park▲ , ABC RV Park▲**
607		**TX 46, FM 78, New Braunfels, to Lake McQueeney**
	FStop	S: Pacific Pride
	Gas	N: Texaco S: Chevron, Exxon◈
	Food	N: Jack in the Box/Texaco, Huddle House S: Bill Miller BBQ, Chili's, IHOP, McDonald's, Kettle Rest, Mexican Rest
	Lodg	N: Alamo Country Inn S: Best Western, La Quinta Inn♥, Super 8♥
	Other	N: Geronimo Field, Texas Lutheran Univ
609		**TX 123 Bus, Austin St, Seguin**
	Gas	S: Mobil◈, Phillips 66◈
	TServ	S: Seguin Diesel Service
	Other	S: Home Depot, Ryder
610		**TX 123, Seguin, San Marcos, Stockdale**
	TStop	N: Jud's Food & Fuel #5/RoadysTS/ Chevron
	Gas	N: Exxon◈ S: Valero◈
	Food	N: FastFood/Jud's F&F, IHOP, K&G Steak House, Chili's, Mexican Rest, Luby's S: Taco Cabana
	Lodg	N: Comfort Inn, Hampton Inn, Holiday Inn, Quality Inn
	Med	S: **+ Guadalupe Valley Hospital**
	Other	N: D&D Trailer Sales, Tires, **Dusty Oaks RV Park & Campground▲** S: **River Shade RV Park▲**
612		**US 90, Seguin**
(615)		**Weigh Station** (Both dir)
617		**FM 2438, to Kingsbury**
(619)		**Guadalupe Co Rest Area** (Both dir) (RR, Picnic, Vend, Pet)
620		**FM 1104, Kingsbury**
625		**CR 217, Darst Field Rd**
628		**TX 80, to US 183N, Luling, Nixon, San Marcos**
	TStop	N: to Luling Mini Mart/Shamrock
	Gas	N: Valero
	Food	N: FastFood/Luling Mini Mart
	Lodg	N: to Luling Inn, Coachway Inn
	Med	N: + Hospital
	Other	N: **River Bend RV Park▲** S: **Rivershade RV Park▲**
632		**US 90, US 183, Gonzales, Luling, Cuero, Lockhart**
	FStop	S: Buc-ee's/Shell (NO TRUCKS)
	TStop	N: Love's Travel Stop #264 (DAND)
	Gas	S: Shell
	Food	N: Subway/Love's TS
	AServ	N: G&K Auto Repair
	TServ	N: Ballard Diesel Service
	Other	N: WiFi/**RVDump**/Love's TS S: **to Palmetto State Park**
637		**FM 794, Harwood**
642		**TX 304, Bastrop, Gonzales**
	Other	N: **Kactus Korral RV Park▲** S: **to Palmetto State Park**
649		**TX 97, Waelder, Gonzales**
653		**US 90, Waelder**
	Gas	N: Shell◈
(657)		**Picnic Area** (Both dir)
661		**TX 95, FM 409, Flatonia, Moulton, Smithville, Shiner**
	FStop	N: Joel's/Mobil S: CJ's Country Juction
	TStop	S: Stockman's Travel Center/Exxon, Flatonia Travel Center/RoadysTS/Shell S: Valero
	Food	N: Joel's BBQ
	Food	S: FastFood/Flatonia CS, DQ, Jamie's Café, McDonald's/Shell, Thumper's Road House Grill, Two Sisters Rest
	Lodg	S: Carefree Inn, Grumpy's Motor Inn
	TServ	S: Tire & Lube
	Other	N: **Flatonia RV Ranch**, Flatonia Airfield✈ S: Laundry/Flatonia CS, Carwash
668		**FM 2238, Schulenburg, to Engle**
674		**US 77, Kessler Ave, Schulenburg, La Grange, Halletsville**
	FStop	N: Speedy Stop #68/Exxon
	Gas	N: Chevron◈ S: Citgo◈, Exxon, Shell◈, Valero
	Food	N: FastFood/Speedy Stop, Oakridge Smokehouse, McDonald's S: FastFood/Andy's FM, Subway/Valero, Burger King, DQ, Express BBQ Depot, Frank's Rest, Sonic, Whataburger
	Lodg	N: Oak Ridge Motor Inn, Executive Inn S: Best Western
	TServ	N: Auto & Diesel Repair S: International Cummins Truck Service
	Other	N: Potter's Country Store/Pecans, Chevron/ Carwash, **to Sun Catchers RV Park▲** S: Potter's Country Store/Pecans, **to Schulenburg RV Park▲**
677		**US 90, Schulenburg**
682		**FM 155, Eagle St, Weimar**
	FStop	N: Fishbeck Shell
	Gas	N: Chevron, Exxon◈
	Food	N: Fishbeck BBQ, Subway, Tx Burger
	Lodg	N: Czech Inn, Super 8

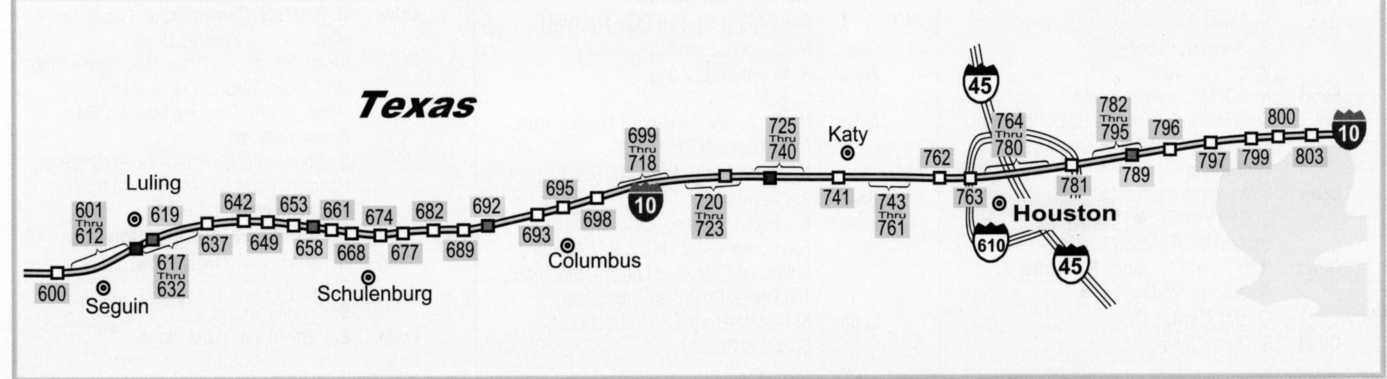

◈ = Regular Gas Stations with Diesel ▲ = RV Friendly Locations ♥ = Pet Friendly Locations
Red print shows large vehicle parking / access on site or nearby Brown Print = Campgrounds / RV PARKS

EXIT — TEXAS

Med N: + Hospital
Other N: LP/Shell

689 US 90, CR 210, CR 219, Columbus, Hattermann Lane
Other N: Columbus KOA▲

(692) Colorado Co Rest Area (Both dir) (RR, Phone, Picnic, Vend, WiFi, RVDump)

693 FM 2434, to W Tx 71, Columbus, to Glidden

695 TX 71W, LaGrange, Austin (WB)

696 TX 71S, Bus TX 71E, Columbus, El Campo
Gas N: Chevron◈, Shell◈
S: Citgo, Valero◈
Food N: Burger King, Denny's, Jack in the Box, Pizza Hut/TacoBell, McDonald's
S: Church's/Citgo, Subway/Mobil, Nancy's Steak House, McDonalds, Sonic, Whataburger
Lodg N: Columbus Inn, Holiday Inn Express
S: Country Hearth Inn, Hotel
Med N: + Columbus Comm Hospital
Other N: HEB, Walmart
S: Columbus RV Park & Campground▲

698 US 90, Alleyton Rd, Columbus
FStop S: Columbus Travel Center/Shell
Food N: Jerry Mikeska BBQ
S: Taco Bell/Col TC
Lodg N: Passport Inn Motel

699 FM 102, Eagle Lake
Other N: Columbus Cycle Shop/Yamaha, Happy Oaks RV Park▲
S: to Eagle Lake St ate Park

(701) Picnic Area (WB)

704 FM 949

709 FM 2761, Bernardo Rd

713 Beckendorff Rd

716 Pyka Rd, Mound Rd, Sealy
TStop N: Sealy Truck Stop/RoadysTS/Exxon
Food N: Rest/Sealy TS
Lodg N: Ranch Motel
S: Holiday Inn Express, Sealy Inn
TServ N: Sealy TS/Tires
Other N: Laundry/Sealy TS

718 US 90, Sealy, FM 3538, Rosenberg (EB)

720 TX 36, Meyer St, Sealy, to Bellville, Wallace
FStop S: Sunmart #123/Mobil
Gas N: Shell◈
S: Chevron◈, Shell◈, Valero◈, Murphy◈
Food N: DQ, McDonald's, Sonic, Tony's
S: China Buffet, Hinze's BBQ, Pizza Hut, KFC/Taco Bell, Omar's, Subway, Whataburger
Lodg N: Austin Motel, Ranch Motel
S: Best Western♥, Holiday Inn Express♥, Rodeway Inn, Super 8
Other N: Walgreen's, Jones RV Center▲
S: Grocery, Walmart sc▲

720A Outlet Center Dr
Other S: Outlet Center

721 US 90, Outlet Center Dr (WB)
Gas N: Shell
Other S: to Outlet Center

723 FM 1458, Sealy, to San Felipe, Frydek
TStop N: Sunmart #121/ Mobil (Scales)
Food N: Subway/Sunmart
TServ N: Peterbilt, Brown Bros Discount Truck Tire Center
Other N: Goodyear Riverside Tire Center, Stephen F Austin State Park

725 Micak Rd (WB)

(729) Weigh Station (WB)

726 Chew Rd

729 Peach Ridge Rd, Donigan Rd (EB)

(729) Weigh Station (EB)

730 Donigan Rd (WB)

731 FM 1489, Koomey Rd, Brookshire, Simonton
Gas N: Exxon◈, Shell
Food N: Mexican, Pizza West
Lodg N: Brookshire Motel, Carefree Inn, Travelers Inn
S: La Quinta Inn♥
TServ S: Bayou City Ford Truck Sales
Other N: Houston West KOA▲

732 FM 359, Brookshire
FStop N: US Truxtop/Exxon
S: Citgo
TStop N: Flying J Travel Plaza (Scales) (DAND)
Gas N: Shell
S: Chevron◈
Food N: CountryMkt/FastFood/FJ TP BBQ, Orlando's Pizza
S: Rest/Houston WTC, BurgerKing/Exxon, Jack in the Box, Charlie's
Lodg N: Executive Inn, Travelers Inn
S: Super 8
TWash S: 10 Star Truck Wash
TServ S: Houston W TC/Tires, Brookshire Truck & Trailer Service, Diesel Chaser
Other N: Laundry/LP/RVDump/FJ TP, Houston West KOA▲ , CarQuest
S: Laundry/Houston WTC, LP

735 Igloo Rd
Other N: Igloo

737 Pederson Rd, Katy
TStop N: Love's Travel Stop #234 (Scales)
Food N: Arby's/Love's TS
TServ N: Bridgestone Tire & Auto
Other N: WiFi/RVDump/Love's TS
S: Holiday World RV Center, Camping World RV Supercenter

740 FM 1463 (EB), Pin Oak Rd (WB)
Gas N: Chevron, Exxon
Food N: McDonald's, Sonic
Med N: + Hospital
Other N: Adventure Yamaha & Marine, Auto & RV World of Texas

741 US 90W, Katy, Pin Oak Rd (EB)
Gas S: Chevron
Food S: Chuck E Cheese, CiCi's Pizza, Fuddrucker's, Jack in the Box, Quiznos, Rainforest Cafe, Red Lobster, Starbucks, TGI Friday, Rest/Bass Pros Shop
Lodg S: Best Western, Comfort Suites, SpringHill Suites
Med S: + Hospital
Other S: Bass Pro Shop, Katy Mills Outlet Mall, Discount Tire, AMC 20, Walmart sc▲

742 US 90W, Katy (WB) (Acc to #741 Serv)
TStop S: Sunmart #131/Texaco
Food S: FastFood/SunMart

743 TX 99, Grand Pkwy
Gas S: Exxon, Shell◈
Food S: Chili's, Hooters, McDonald's, Popeye's, On the Bayou, Swampy's Cajun Shack
Lodg S: Best Western, Comfort Inn, Hampton Inn, Holiday Inn Express, La Quinta Inn♥, Super 8
Med N: + Hospital
Other S: Kroger

745 Mason Rd, Katy
Gas S: Chevron◈, Exxon, Diamond Shamrock, Shell
Food S: Black Eyed Pea, Burger King, Chili's, Carrabba's, CiCi's Pizza, DQ, KFC, Landry's Seafood Rest, Luby's Cafeteria, McDonald's, Monterey Rest, Pizza Hut, Salt Grass Steak House, Subway, Taco Bell
Lodg S: Comfort Inn, Hampton Inn, Holiday Inn Express, La Quinta Inn♥, Sleep Inn, Super 8
Other S: Auto Dealers, Car Quest, Discount Tire, Enterprise RAC, FedEx Office, Firestone, Goodyear, Kroger/Pharmacy, PetCo♥, UPS Store, Walgreen's

746 Westgreen Blvd
Gas N: Chevron◈, Valero◈
Food N: Chang's Chinese, Cheddars, Jack in the Box/Chevron, NY Pizza, Spring Creek Rest, Texas Roadhouse, Wild Wing Cafe
Lodg N: Holiday Inn Express
Other S: CVS

747A Fry Rd, Katy, Houston (EB)

747B Greenhouse Rd, Katy, Houston (EB)

747AB Fry Rd, Katy, Houston
Gas N: Chevron, Mobil◈, Shamrock◈, Shell, Sam's, Kroger, HEB, Murphy
S: Chevron, Citgo, Shell
Food N: Aloha Hawaiian BBQ, Applebee's, Arby's, Burger King, Chipolte Mexican Grill, Church's, DQ, Denny's, McDonald's, Pizza Hut, Panda Express, Souper Salad, Sonic, Subway, Taco Bell, Texas Borders Bar & Grill, Whataburger
S: Capt Tom's Seafood, Jack in the Box, IHOP, Omar's Mexican, Orient Express, Outback Steakhouse, Quiznos, Texas Racks, Wendy's, Willie's Grill & Icehouse
Lodg N: Candlewood Suites
Med S: + Christus St Catherine Hospital
Other N: Best Buy, Garden Ridge, Goodyear, HEB/Pharmacy, Home Depot, Kroger/Pharmacy, Office Max, Sam's Club, UPS Store, Walmart sc, Walgreen's, Vet♥, Fry Rd Crossing Mall, Fry Rd Animal Clinic♥
S: Albertson's, CVS, Lowe's, PetSmart♥, Randall's Food & Pharmacy, TJ Maxx, Target/Pharmacy, U-Haul

748 Barker Cypress Rd, W Houston
Food N: Applebee's, Panera Bread, Ruby Tuesday
S: Cracker Barrel
Lodg S: Fairfield Inn, Value Place
Med N: + Texas Children's Hospital

◈= Regular Gas Stations with Diesel ▲ = RV Friendly Locations ♥= Pet Friendly Locations
Red print shows large vehicle parking / access on site or nearby Brown Print = Campgrounds / RV PARKS

EXIT — TEXAS

Other N: Garden Ridge
S: Enterprise RAC, Lowe's, **Hoover RV Center▲**

750 Park Ten Blvd (EB)
Med N: + Texas Children's Hospital
Other S: Auto Dealers, Hertz RAC

751 TX 6, FM 1960, to Addicks
Gas N: Shell, Sam's Club
S: Chevron, Conoco◈, Exxon, Texaco
Food N: Brothers Pizzeria, Cattle Guard, Mexican Rest, Waffle House
S: Blimpie, Denny's, El Yucatan, Jack in the Box, Wendy's
Lodg N: Crowne Plaza, Drury Inn♥, Holiday Inn, Homewood Suites, Red Roof Inn♥, Studio 6
S: AmeriHost, Extended Stay, Fairfield Inn, La Quinta Inn♥, Motel 6♥, Super 8, TownePlace Suites
Other N: Sam's Club, Greyhound, **to** West Houston Airport✈
S: Bank, US Post Office, Auto Dealers, Enterprise RAC, **Ron Hoover RV & Marine Center**

753A Eldridge Pkwy, Houston
Gas N: Conoco◈
S: Valero
Lodg N: Omni Hotel
S: Marriott
Other S: Pennzoil

753B Dairy-Ashford Rd
Gas S: Exxon, Shamrock
Food S: Beck's Prime, Shoney's, TX Land & Cattle Steakhouse, Whataburger
Lodg S: Courtyard, Guesthouse Inn, Holiday Inn Express, Shoney's Inn
Med S: + Urgent Care
Other N: Auto Dealers
S: Auto Dealers, Discount Tire, FedEx Office, Hertz RAC, Stadium

754 Kirkwood Rd, Houston
Gas S: Chevron◈, Shell
Food N: Taco Bell
S: Carrabba's, IHOP, Subway
Lodg S: Extended Stay America, Hampton Inn
Other N: Auto Dealers, Discount Tire
S: Auto Dealers

755 Beltway 8, Wilcrest Dr, Houston
FStop S: Citgo Gas Stop
Gas S: Exxon, Thrifty
Food S: Denny's, IHOP, McDonald's/Exxon, Steak & Ale, Dimassi's Mediterranean Buffet
Lodg S: Hampton Inn, La Quinta Inn♥

756 Sam Houston Toll Way (EB)

756B Sam Houston Toll Way (WB)

757 Gessner Rd
Gas N: Exxon
S: Shell, Texaco
Food N: BBQ, Chili's, CiCi's Pizza, McDonald's, Taco Bell, Wendy's, Whataburger
S: Fuddrucker's, Goode Co Seafood Rest, Jack in the Box, Jason's Deli, Olive Garden, Pappadeaux Seafood, Pappasito's, Papa Joe's BBQ, Romano's Macaroni Grill, Taste of Texas Rest
Lodg S: Candlewood Suites, Four Points, Radisson, Sheraton♥
Med S: + Memorial City Hospital

EXIT — TEXAS

Other N: Best Buy, Home Depot, Kroger, NAPA, PetSmart♥, Radio Shack, Sam's Club, **Walmart**, U-Haul
S: Firestone, Goodyear, Office Depot, Office Max, Target, Memorial City Mall

758 Bunker Hill Rd (EB)

758A Bunker Hill Rd
Gas N: Exxon, Costco
S: Texaco◈
Food N: CiCi's Pizza
S: Charlie's Burger, Mexican Rest, Subway, Texas BBQ
Lodg S: Days Inn, Howard Johnson, Quality Inn, Super 8
Other N: Bank, Lowe's, Costco, HEB/Pharmacy, PepBoys
S: Firestone, Goodyear, Target/Pharmacy

758B Blalock Rd, Echo Lane
Gas N: Phillips 66
S: Chevron◈
Food N: Sonic, McDonald's
Other N: Pharmacy
S: Kroger, Target/Pharmacy, Walgreen's

759 Campbell Rd, Blalock Rd, Echo Lane, (WB) (Acc to #758BA Serv)
Gas S: Chevron, Exxon, Texaco
Food N: Ciro's Italian, Fiesta Foods
Med S: + Hospital
Other N: Bank, Costco
S: Kroger, Walgreen's

760 Bingle Rd, Voss Rd
Gas S: Citgo, Exxon, Mobil◈
Food S: Café, Mason Jar, Pappy's Café, Sweet Tomatoes, Salt Grass Steak House, Starbucks, Subway, Texas BBQ
Med S: + Hospital
Other N: Home Depot
S: CVS

761A Chimney Rock Rd, Wirt Rd, Antoine Dr
Gas S: Chevron, Exxon, Shell
Food N: Capt Benny's Oyster Bar, Starbucks
S: 59 Diner, Denny's, Dixie's Roadhouse, McDonald's, Mexican Rest, Steak & Ale
Lodg S: La Quinta Inn♥
Other N: Home Depot

761B Antoine Dr
Gas S: Exxon, Shell, Citgo
Food N: Country Harvest Buffet, Chinese Rest
S: Blue Oyster Bar, McDonald's
Lodg S: La Quinta Inn♥, Wellesley Inn
Other S: Cingular, CVS, UPS Store

762 Silber Rd, Antoine Dr, Houston
Gas S: Shell
Food N: Aubrey's Ribs
S: Jack in the Box
Lodg S: Best Western, Holiday Inn Express♥, Ramada♥
Other N: US Post Office

(763) Jct I-610

764 Westcott St, Washington Ave
Gas S: Chevron
Food N: Denny's
S: McDonald's, IHOP
Lodg N: Comfort Inn, Rodeway Inn
S: Scottish Inn
Other S: Memorial Park Muni Golf Course

765A TC Jester Blvd, Houston
Gas S: Exxon, Texaco

EXIT — TEXAS

765B N Shepherd Dr, Patterson St, N Durham Dr
Gas N: Shamrock
S: Valero
Food N: Wendy's
Lodg N: Howard Johnson Express
Other N: Vet♥

766 Studemont St, Heights Blvd, Yale St (WB)
Gas N: Chevron
S: Exxon
Food S: Chili's
Other S: PetSmart♥, Staples, Target

767A Yale St, Heights Blvd, Studemont St (EB)
Gas S: Shell◈

767B Taylor St
Food S: Chili's
Other S: Bank, Target

(768A) Jct I-45, N to Dallas (EB, Left Exit)

(768B) Jct I-45, S to Galveston (Left Exit)

769A Downtown, Smith St (EB)

769B San Jacinto St, Main St

769C McKee St, Hardy St, Nance St

770A US 59S, Downtown, to Victoria

770C US 59N, Cleveland

770B Jensen Dr, Gregg St, Meadow St (EB Left Exit)

771A Waco St
Food N: Frenchy's Fried Chicken
Lodg N: Waco Motel

771B Lockwood Dr
Gas N: Chevron
S: Phillips 66, Shell◈
Food N: McDonald's, Subway/Chevron
Other N: Family Dollar

772 Kress St, Lathrop St
Gas N: Conoco
Food S: Burger King

773A US 90 Alt, N Wayside Dr
FStop S: Sunmart #314/Chevron (Scales), Wayside Coastal/Texaco
Gas N: Chevron◈, Exxon, Mystik
S: Shell
Food N: Jack in the Box, Whataburger
S: BBQ, Church's Chicken/Shell, Quiznos
Other S: Houston Truck Parts, Wayside Auto & Truck Parts, NAPA

773B McCarty Dr, Houston
FStop N: Conners Gas & Diesel, Fleet Fuel Management/Citgo
Gas N: Mobil◈, Shell
Food S: Don Chile Mexican
TServ N: Stewart & Stevenson Truck & Trailer Service
S: Nick's Diesel Service Mustang Truck Sales

774 Gellhorn Dr, Houston (EB)
FStop S: Texas Truck Stop
Food S: FastFood/Texas TS
Other S: Anheuser Busch Brewery, Arrow Truck Sales

(775AB) Jct I-610
TServ N: Lone Star White GMC, Cummins Southern Plains

◈= Regular Gas Stations with Diesel ▲ = RV Friendly Locations ♥= Pet Friendly Locations
Red print shows large vehicle parking / access on site or nearby Brown Print = Campgrounds / RV PARKS

EXIT	TEXAS
776A	**Mercury Dr, Jacinto City, Galena Park**
Gas	**N:** Conoco, Shamrock◊, Texaco **S:** Shell◊, Valero
Food	**N:** Burger King, McDonald's, Pizza Inn **S:** Steak & Ale, Tony's Seafood
Lodg	**N:** Best Western, Days Inn, Fairfield Inn, Hampton Inn, Quality Inn
TServ	**N:** WhiteGMC, Volvo
Other	**N:** Family Dollar, Kroger, NTB **S:** Banks
776B	**John Ralston Rd, Holland Ave, Jacinto City, Galena Park**
Gas	**N:** Citgo, Mobil
Food	**N:** Checker's, Long John Silver's, Luby's
Lodg	**N:** Best Western, Comfort Inn
Other	**N:** Kroger, Walgreen's
778A	**FM 526, Federal Rd, Normandy St, Houston, Pasadena**
FStop	**N:** Sunmart #150/Mobil
Gas	**N:** Chevron, Shell, Kroger **S:** Shell, Valero
Food	**N:** BBQ, Blimpie, Denny's, Jack in the Box, KFC, Pizza Hut, Pappasito's, Popeye's, Taco Bell, Wendy's, Zomo's Buffet **S:** Chili's, Joe's Crab Shack, McDonald's, Mexican Rest, Pappas Seafood
Lodg	**N:** Comfort Inn, La Quinta Inn♥ **S:** Holiday Inn Express, Super 8
Med	**N: + North Shore Hospital**
Other	**N:** CVS, Discount Tire, HEB, Kroger, Target **S:** Auto Zone, Discount Tire, Family Dollar
778B	**Normandy St (EB)**
FStop	**N:** Normandy Truck Stop/Conoco /Texaco
Gas	**N:** Shell **S:** Citgo
Food	**N:** Golden Corral, Jack in the Box/Shell
Lodg	**N:** La Quinta Inn♥ **S:** Bayou Motel, Mainstay Suites, Scottish Inn♥
778	**Normandy St (EB)**
779A	**Westmont Dr (WB, EB U-Turn Req)**
Lodg	**N:** Interstate Motor Lodge
Med	**N: + E Houston Reg'l Medical Center**
779B	**Uvalde Rd, Freeport St, Market St (WB, EB U-Turn Req'd)**
Gas	**N:** Chevron◊, Texaco
Food	**N:** Cracker Barrel, IHOP, Jack in the Box, KFC, Taco Cabana, Subway, Sonic
Lodg	**N:** Interstate Motor Lodge
TServ	**S:** Diesel Repair
Med	**N: + Sunbelt Regional Medical Center**
Other	**S: Walmart**

EXIT	TEXAS
780	**Market St, Uvalde Rd, Freeport St, Frances**
Gas	**N:** Chevron◊, Mobil **S:** Sam's
Food	**N:** Cracker Barrel, IHOP, Jack in the Box, KFC, Mexican, Subway, Taco Bell **S:** BlackEyed Pea, Thomas Steak & BBQ
Med	**N: + Hospital**
Other	**N:** FedEx Kinko's, Office Depot **S:** Home Depot, Sam's Club, **Walmart**
781A	**Redmond St, Beltway 8**
TStop	**S:** Sunmart #149/Mobil
Food	**S:** FastFood/SunMart
781B	**Beltway 8, Houston**
Lodg	**N:** Holiday Inn
Med	**N: + Hospital**
782	**Dell Dale Ave, Grand Ave**
Gas	**N:** Exxon **S:** Conoco, Texaco◊
Lodg	**N:** Best Value Inn, Days Inn, Dell Dale Motel, I-10 Motel, Palace Inn, Super 8 **S:** Glen Shady Motel
Med	**S: + Hospital**
783	**Sheldon Rd, Channelview**
FStop	**N:** Texaco Mart
Gas	**N:** Coastal, Shell
Food	**N:** Burger King, Jack in the Box, KFC, Pizza Hut, Subway, Taco Bell, Whataburger **S:** Captain D's, McDonald's, Wendy's
Lodg	**N:** Americas Best Value Inn, Days Inn, Economy Inn, I-10 Motel, Super 8, Travelodge♥ **S:** Scottish Inn
Other	**N:** Advance Auto Parts, Auto Zone, CVS, Discount Tire, Family Dollar, Goodyear, Pharmacy, Radio Shack, Carwash/Shell
784	**Cedar Lane, Market St (EB) River Rd, Bayou Dr (WB)**
FStop	**N:** Texaco Mart
Gas	**N:** Valero◊
Lodg	**N:** Budget Lodge, Knights Inn, Magnolia Motel
785	**River Rd (EB), Magnolia Ave (WB), Channelview**
FStop	**S:** USA Truck Stop
TStop	**N:** Cobra Truck Stop/Shell (Scales) **(DAND)** **S:** Key Truck Stop/P66 (Scales)
Food	**N:** FastFood/Cobra TS, Restaurant Flores **S:** Rest/FastFood/Key TS, FastFood/USA TS
Lodg	**N:** Budget Lodge, Knights Inn, Magnolia
TWash	**S:** Truck Wash
TServ	**S:** Key TS, Trak-ta Lube, Southern Truck Sales
Other	**S:** Laundry/Key TS

EXIT	TEXAS
786	**Monmouth Dr**
787	**Spur 330, Crosby-Lynchburg Rd, FM 2100, Highlands, Baytown**
FStop	**N:** Sunmart #136/Texaco
Gas	**S:** Phillips 66◊
Food	**N:** Domino's/Sunmart **S:** 4 Corners BBQ
Lodg	**S:** to Bays Inn, Days Inn♥
Other	**N: to Houston Leisure RV Resort▲, Hunters RV Park ▲, River Front RV Park▲, San Jacinto River Front RV Park▲**
788	**Spur 330, Baytown (EB)**
(789)	**Rest Area (Both dir) (RR, Phone, Picnic, Pet)**
789	**Thompson Rd, Baytown, McNair**
TStop	**N:** Love's Travel Stop #401 (Scales), Baytown Express Travel Plaza/Valero (Scales) **S:** Flying J Travel Plaza #725 (Scales), Travel Center of America #17 (Scales)
Food	**N:** McDonald's/Love's TS **S:** Country Market Rest/FastFood/FJ TP, Country Pride Rest/FastFood/TA TC
Lodg	**N:** Super 8♥
TWash	**S:** Blue Beacon Truck Wash
TServ	**N:** Four G's CB Shop **S:** TA TC/Tires, Speedco, Truck King Truck Lube
Other	**N:** Laundry/WiFi/Love's TS, Laundry/CB/ Baytown TP, Greyhound **S:** Laundry/WiFi/**RVDump**/TA TC, Laundry/WiFi/**LP/RVDump**/FJ TP
790	**Ellis School Rd (WB), John Martin Rd, Wade Rd, Baytown (EB) (Acc to Serv at #789 - #792)**
791	**John Martin Rd, Wade Rd (EB)**
Lodg	**S:** Value Place
Other	**N:** Auto Dealers **S:** Auto Dealers
792	**Garth Rd, Baytown**
Gas	**N:** Chevron **S:** Raceway◊, Shell◊
Food	**N:** Burger King, Cracker Barrel, Denny's, Jack in the Box, Red Lobster, Richard's Cajun Rest, Waffle House, Whataburger **S:** Bravo's Mexican Rest, ChickFilA, Chili's, El Toro Mexican Rest, Johnny Carino's, McDonald's, Outback Steakhouse, Pancho's Mexican, Popeye's, Seafood Corner, Taco Bell, Tortuga Mexican Kitchen, Wendy's
Lodg	**N:** Best Western, Comfort Suites♥, La Quinta Inn♥, Hampton Inn♥ **S:** Sleep Inn♥, Value Place

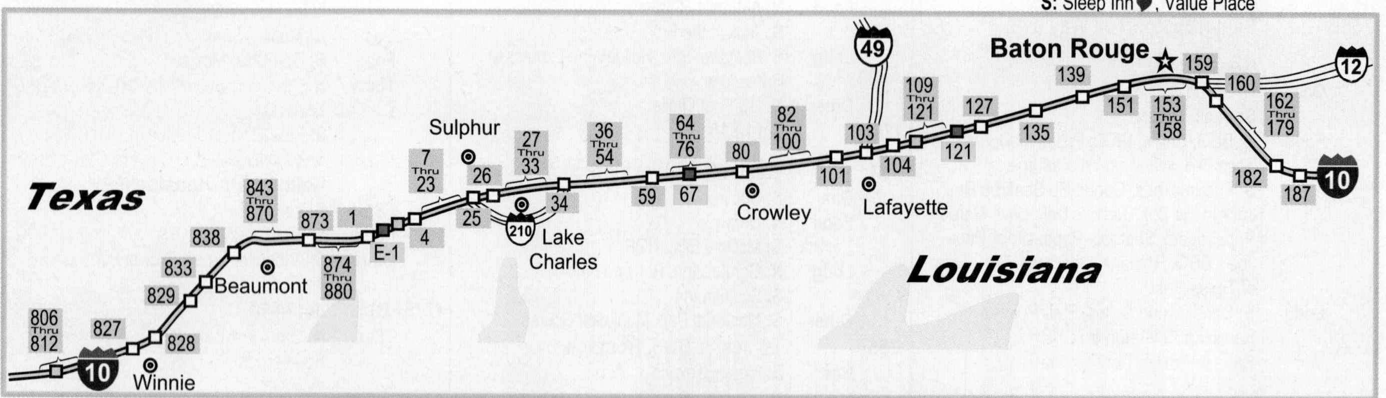

◊= Regular Gas Stations with Diesel ▲ = RV Friendly Locations ♥= Pet Friendly Locations
Red print shows large vehicle parking / access on site or nearby Brown Print = Campgrounds / RV PARKS

EXIT		TEXAS
	Med	S: + Hospital
	Other	N: Auto Dealers, Walgreen's
		S: San Jacinto Mall, Dollar General, Office Max, **Vaughn RV Center▲** ,**NOTE: Appr 2.5 mi S: Grocery Stores, Target, Walmart SC, etc**
793		**N Main St, Baytown**
	TStop	S: Baytown Travel Center (Scales)
	Food	S: FastFood/Baytown TC
	Other	S: Laundry/Baytown TC, Baytown Airport✈
795		**Sjolander Rd (WB)**
796AB		**Frontage Rd, Baytown (WB)**
796		**Frontage Rd, Refineries (EB)**
797		**TX 146, Baytown, to Mont Belvieu, Dayton**
	TStop	N: Conoco Travel Center (Scales)
		S: Sunmart Truck Stop #400/Texaco (Scales)
	Gas	N: Chevron, Shell◈
		S: Exxon
	Food	N: DQ, IHOP, McDonald's, Pizza Inn, Waffle House, FastFood/Conoco TC
		S: Popeye's/Sunmart, Jack in he Box, Sonic
	Lodg	N: Motel 6♥, Super 8♥, Value Inn & **RV Park▲**
	TServ	S: Sunmart TS/Tires
	Med	S: + Hospital
	Other	N: Laundry/Conoco TC, Carwash/Shell, LP, **L&R RV Park▲ , A & J RV Park▲**
		S: to Pinelakes RV Resort▲ , Shady Oaks RV Park▲ , Houston East RV Resort/RVDump▲
799		**Frontage Rd (EB)**
	Other	N: Yamaha, Polaris, Artic Cat Dealer
		S: Able LP, to Houston Raceway Park
800		**FM 3180, Eagle Dr**
	Gas	N: Exxon◈
	Other	**N: Houston East RV Resort▲**
803		**FM 565, Baytown (EB)**
	Gas	S: Valero◈
	Other	**N: Lost River RV Park▲**
806		**Frontage Rd, Anahuac**
	Other	**S: Trinity River Island Rec Area**
807		**Wallisville Liberty Rd, Anahuac, Wallisville**
810		**FM 563, TX 73, Anahuac, Liberty**
	Gas	S: Chevron◈, Shell◈
	Food	S: Blimpie/Chevron, JackintheBox/Shell
	Other	**S: WB: Turtle Bayou RV Park▲** ,
811		**Turtle Bayou TurnAround (EB)**
	Gas	S: Gator Jct◈
	Food	S: Grandma's Diner, Gator Jct BBQ
	Other	**S: EB:Turtle Bayou RV Park▲** , Auto Dealers
(812)		**Inspection Station (Both dir) (Commercial Vehicles Only MUST Exit)**
812A		**Frontage Rd, Indian Trail (WB)**
812		**TX 61, Anahuac. Hankamer (EB)**
	FStop	N: Country Boys Country Store/Shell
	Gas	S: Exxon◈
	Food	N: FastFood/Country Boys CS
		S: DJ's Diner, McDonald's
	Lodg	N: America Best Value Inn
813		**TX 61, Hankamer, Anahuac (WB)**
	FStop	N: Country Boys Country Store/Shell

EXIT		TEXAS
	Gas	S: Exxon◈
	Food	N: FastFood/Country Boys CS
		S: McDonald's
	Lodg	N: America Best Value Inn
(815)		**Weigh Station (Both dir)**
817		**FM 1724, Anahuac**
819		**Jenkins Rd**
	Gas	S: Gas
	Food	S: Stuckey's
822		**FM 1410, Oak Island Rd**
	Other	S: Chamber Co Winnie Stowell Airport✈
827		**FM 1406, Winnie**
828		**TX 73, TX124, Winnie, Port Arthur (EB) (Acc to #829 Serv)**
829		**FM 1663, Anahuac, Winnie, TX 73, TX 124, Galveston, Beaches**
	FStop	S: Speedy Stop #15/Exxon
	TStop	S: Bingo Truck Stop/Chevron, Sunmart #111/Mobil (Scales), JP's Truck Stop/Mobil
	Gas	N: Exxon◈, Shell◈, Texaco◈
	Food	N: Burger King/Texaco, McDonald's, Taco Bell, Whataburger
		S: Rest/Bingo TS, Subway/Sunmart, Al-T's Seafood & Steakhouse, Jack in the Box, Pizza Inn, Waffle House, Rest/Riceland Motel
	Lodg	N: Days Inn
		S: Comfort Inn♥, Holiday Inn Express, La Quinta Inn, Quality Inn♥, Riceland Motel, Studio 6, Winnie Inn♥ & **RV Park▲**
	Med	**S: + Winnie Community Hospital**
	Other	N: Old Time Trade Days Flea Market▲ ,
	Other	S: Laundry/Bingo TS, Auto Dealers, Auto Services, Clinic/Vet♥, Family Dollar, NAPA, True Value, Grocery, **Tri County RV Mobile Services**, to Beaches
833		**Hamshire Rd, Hamshire**
(837)		**Picnic Area (Both dir)**
838		**FM 365, Beaumont, Hamshire**
	Gas	S: Country Store/Gas
	Food	N: Rest/Gator Country
		S: Homestyle Cafe,
	Other	N: Gator Country
		S: to appr 7 mi: End of the Road RV Park▲ , appr 8 mi: In the Middle RV Park▲ , appr 9 mi: La Belle RV Park▲ ,
843		**Smith Rd**
845		**FM 364, Major Dr, Brooks Rd, Beaumont**
	Other	S: Ford Park, Ford Arena, Fairgrounds, Tourist Info, **Gulf Coast RV Resort▲** , **Hidden Lake RV Resort ▲**
846		**Brooks Rd, Major Dr (EB)**
847		**to TX 364, Major Dr (WB)**
	Other	**S: Gulf Coast RV Resort▲** , Visitor Center, Baseball Fields, **Hidden Lake RV Resort ▲**
848		**Walden Rd, to TX 124, Beaumont**
	TStop	S: Petro Stopping Center #4/Mobil (Scales)
	Gas	N: Shell
	Food	N: Pappadeaux Seafood Rest, Sonic, Rest/Holiday Inn
		S: Iron Skillet/Petro SC, Subway/Chevron, Carino's, Cheddars Cracker Barrel, Jack in the Box, Joe's Crab Shack, Waffle House
	Lodg	N: Comfort Suites, Holiday Inn♥, La Quinta Inn♥

EXIT		TEXAS
	Lodg	S: Candlewood Suites, Hampton Inn, Hilton Garden Inn, Knights Inn, Residence Inn, Super 8
	TWash	S: Blue Beacon TW/Petro SC
	TServ	N: Kenworth/Mack
		S: Petro SC
	Other	N: US Post Office
		S: Laundry/CB/WiFi/Petro SC, Tinseltown USA, **Mobile Manor RV Park & Parts▲** ,
849		**US 69S, US 96, US 287, Washington Blvd, Pt Arthur, Airport, Beaumont**
	FStop	S: appr 1-2 mi: Exxon, 1.5 mi to: Super Foodmart/Valero
850		**Washington Blvd (WB) (Acc to Ex #851 Serv)**
851		**US 90, College St**
	Gas	N: Exxon◈, RaceWay
		S: Exxon, Mobil, Shell, Texaco, Sam's
	Food	N: Burger King, Cajun Cafe, Carrabba's, China Border, Golden Corral, Hooters, Japanese Rest, Outback Steakhouse, Waffle House
		S: DQ, IHOP, Jason's Deli, KFC, Pizza Hut, Sonic, Taco Bell, Wendy's
	Lodg	N: Best Western, Comfort Inn, Ramada Inn
		S: Econo Lodge♥, Motel 6♥, Premier Inn
	TServ	N: Smart GM Trucks, GMC, Volvo
		S: Kinsel Ford
	Med	**S: + Hospital**
	Other	N: Auto Zone, Advanced Auto, Carwash, Hertz RAT, Pennzoil Lube & Wash, O'Reilly Auto Parts, Harley Davidson
	Other	S: Auto Dealers, CVS, Discount Tire, Firestone, HEB/Pharmacy, Office Depot, Radio Shack, Sam's Club, Walgreen's, U-Haul, Auto Service/Mobil
852A		**Laurel St, Phelan Blvd (EB)**
	Gas	N: Chevron◈, Shell, Valero◈
		S: Chevron◈, Texaco
	Food	N: Chili's, Olive Garden, Steak & Ale, Willy Ray's BBQ
		S: Church's Chicken, McDonald's
	Lodg	S: Americas Best Value Inn, Best Western, Castle Motel, Days Inn, Econo Lodge, Holiday Inn, La Quinta Inn♥
	Med	**S: + Stat Care**
	Other	N: Carwash/Shell, Copy Right
852B		**Harrison Ave, Calder Ave, Phelan Blvd (WB)**
	Gas	S: Gas, Market Basket
	Food	S: Sonic
	Other	S: CVS, Market Basket/Pharmacy
853A		**US 69N, US 287, Beaumont, to Lufkin**
853B		**11th St, Harrison Ave, Calder Ave**
	Gas	S: Texaco
	Food	N: Ninfa's Mexican, Red Lobster, Waffle House, Rest/HI
		S: Jack in the Box, Luby's
	Lodg	N: Americas Best Value Inn, Best Western, Holiday Inn, Ramada Inn, Red Carpet Inn, Studio 6
		S: Best Western, Howard Johnson, Motel 6♥, Quality Inn, Rodeway Inn, Super 8
	Med	**S: + St Elizabeth Hospital**
	Other	N: Kroger/Pharmacy,
		S: Bank, Staples
853C		**8th St, 7th St (EB)**
	Gas	N: Exxon◈

EXIT TEXAS

Gas S: Shell◈
Food N: Burger King, McDonald's, Mexican Rest, Red Lobster, Waffle House
S: Rest/MCM
Lodg N: Holiday Inn, Scottish Inn, Super 8
S: Courtyard, Fairfield Inn, MCM Elegante Hotel

854 **Spur 380, Gulf St, ML King Pkwy, Magnolia Ave, Beaumont**
Gas S: Exxon, Shamrock, Russell's Service Center
Food N: Burger King, Carrabba's
S: Café Del Rio, McDonald's
Lodg N: Super 8
S: Comfort Inn

855A **US 90W, Downtown, Civic Center, Port of Beaumont (EB)**

855B **US 90, Pine St, Magnolia Ave (WB)**

856 **Old Hwy 90, Rose City (EB)**
Lodg S: Holiday Inn Express

857A **Rose City West (EB)**
FStop S: EZ Mart

857B **Workman Turn Around (WB)**

858 **Asher Turn Around (EB)**

858A **Rose City East (EB)**
FStop S: I-10 Fuel Mart (Scales)

858B **Asher Turn Around, Beaumont, Vidor (WB)**
TStop S: Gateway Truck Plaza/RoadysTS/Chevron (Scales)
Food S: Rest/FastFood/Gateway TP, Denny's
TServ S: Gateway TP/Tires
Lodg S: Holiday Inn Express
Other N: Boomtown USA Resort & RV Park▲
S: Laundry/Gateway TP

859 **Bonner Turn Around, Dewitt Rd (EB)**
Other N: Boomtown USA Resort & RV Park▲ ,

860A **Dewitt Rd (WB)**

860B **West Vidor (WB)**

860 **FM 105, N Main St, Vidor(EB)**

861A **FM 105, N Main St, Vidor**
Gas N: Chevron◈, Shell, Valero
S: Exxon, Texaco
Food N: Burger King, Church's Chicken, DQ, Domino's Pizza, Gary's Cafe & Family Rest, Jack in the Box, Little Caesars Pizza, McDonald's, Mings Buffet, Popeye's Chicken, Waffle House, Wrights BBQ
S: KFC, Pizza Hut, Sonic, Subway, Taco Bell, Whataburger
Lodg S: Holiday Inn Express, La Quinta Inn♥
Med S: + Vidor Family Medical Center
Other N: AutoZone, Auto Repairs & Services, Banks, CVS, Grocery Stores, Laundromat, O'Reilly Auto Parts, Pharmacy, Radio Shack, Superior Tire, McGowan Veterinary Hospital♥, Walgreens, Walmart , to Smith Lake RV Park▲ , Pine Haven RV & MH Park▲ ,
S: Auto Repairs & Services, Family Dollar, Laundromat, Pharmacy, US Post Office

861B **Lamar St (WB)**
Gas N: Conoco◈

EXIT TEXAS

861C **Denver St (EB)**
Gas N: Conoco◈

861D **TX 12, Deweyville (WB)**

862A **Railroad Ave (EB)**

862B **Old Hwy 90, Vidor (WB)**

862C **Lexington Dr, Timberlane Dr (EB)**

864 **FM 1132, FM 1135**
Gas N: 2745 Evangeline Dr: Super Stop
Food N: Burr's BBQ
Lodg N: Budget Inn
Other N: Texas Star RV Park▲ ,

865 **Doty Rd, Frontage Rd (WB)**

867 **Frontage Rd (EB)**

(867) **Orange Co Rest Area (Both dir)**
(RR, Picnic, Vend, WiFi)

869 **FM 1442, Orange, Bridge City**
Other S: Lloyd's RV Center

870 **FM 1136**

873 **TX 62, TX 73, Orange, Bridge City, Port Arthur**
TStop N: Flying J Travel Plaza #5026/Conoco (Scales) (DAD)
S: Pilot Travel Center #431 (Scales)
Gas N: Exxon◈
S: Shell◈, Valero◈
Food N: Rest/FastFood/FJ TP
S: Wendy's/Subway/Pilot TC, Burger King, Church's/Shell, Jack in the Box, McDonald's, Sonic, Waffle House, Whataburger
Lodg S: Comfort Suites, La Quinta Inn♥, Sleep Inn
Other N: Laundry/BarbSh/WiFi/RVDump/LP/FJ TP, Oak Leaf Park RV Park▲ , Greyhound/Exxon
S: WiFi/Pilot TC, to Orange Co Airport✈

874A **US 90 Bus, to Orange (EB)**
Med S: + Hospital
Other N: Oak Leaf Park RV Park▲

874B **Womack Rd (WB)**

875 **FM 3247, ML King Jr Dr**
Food N: Richard's Cafeteria & Grill

876 **Frontage Rd, Adams Bayou**
Gas N: Exxon, Mobil◈
S: Chevron◈
Food N: Gary's Cafe, Luby's, Richard's Cafeteria & Grill, Waffle House, Rest/Ramada
Lodg N: Best Western, Best Value Inn, Days Inn, Executive Inn, Hampton Inn, Motel 6♥ Ramada Inn, Super 8
S: Holiday Inn Express
Other N: Auto Dealer

877 **TX 87, 16th St, Port Arthur, Pinehurst, Orange, Newton**
FStop N: Diamond Shamrock
Gas N: Chevron◈, Exxon
S: Chevron◈, Shell◈
Food N: Cajun Cookery, Pizza Hut, Subway, Waffle House
S: Burger King, Church's, DQ, Jack in the Box, McDonald's, Sonic, Taco Bell
Lodg N: Americas Best Value Inn, Days Inn, Econo Lodge, Executive Inn, Hampton Inn, Motel 6♥, Ramada Inn, Super 8♥

EXIT TX / LA

Other N: CVS, Dollar General, Grocery, Tractor Supply
S: CVS, HEB, Kroger, O'Reilly Auto Parts, Tires, Walgreen's

(878) **Livestock Inspection Station**

878 **US 90 Bus, Simmons Dr, Orange**
TStop N: Sunmart #363/Mobil
Food N: FastFood/SunMart
Other N: Cypress Lakes RV Park▲

(879) **TX Welcome Center (WB)**
Rest Area (Both dir)
(RR, Phone, Picnic, Vend, Pet, Info)

(880) **Sabine River Turn Around (EB)**

NOTE: **MM 880.5: LA State Line**

TEXAS

LOUISIANA

CENTRAL TIME ZONE

(1) **Sabine River Turn Around (WB)**

(1) **LA Welcome Center (EB)**
Rest Area (Next Rest Area 121 mi)
(RR, Phone, Vend, Sec)

(2) **Port of Entry / Weigh Station (Both dir)**

4 **US 90E, LA 109, Toomey Rd, Vinton, to Toomey, Starks**
TStop N: Bayou Gold Truck Stop #3120/Exxon, Longhorn Truck & Car Plaza/Chevron (Scales), Cash Magic Truck Stop
S: Delta Town Truck Stop/Shell, Delta Truck Plaza, Tobacco Plus #5/Exxon
Food N: Rest/Bayou Gold TS, Rest/FastFood/Longhorn TCP, Rest/FastFood/Cash Magic, Texas Longhorn, Waffle Shoppe
S: Rest/Delta Town TS, Rest/Delta Truck Plaza, FastFood/Tobacco Plus, Pelican Palace
Lodg N: Motel/Longhorn TCP
S: Cash Magic Casino & Hotel, Delta Down Motor Inn
TServ N: Longhorn TCP/Tires, State Line Truck S\
Other N: Laundry/Bayou Gold TS, Laundry/Casino/Longhorn TCP, Laundry/Cash Magic TS, Delta Downs Racetrack, Casino & Hotel
S: Laundry/Delta Down TS, Laundry/Delta TP, Laundry/Tobacco Plus, Vinton KOA▲ , Texas Pelican RV Park▲ , Starz Casino, Pelican Palace

7 **LA 3063, West St, Vinton**
TStop N: CFN/Delta Fuel Stop/Exxon
S: Love's Travel Stop #362 (Scales)
Food N: Lucky Delta Café/Delta FS, Burger King, Sonic, Subway
S: Arby's/Love's TS
Other N: Goodrich, Lucky Delta Casino
S: WiFi/Love's TS

8 **LA 108, Vinton**
FStop N: Tiger EZ Mart/Exxon
Gas N: Chevron, Citgo◈
Food N: Pizza Inn
Lodg N: to Vinton Motel
Other N: Vinton RV Park▲

20 **to LA 27, Ruth St, LA 1256, Sulphur, Cameron**
TStop S: Pilot Travel Center #85

◈= Regular Gas Stations with Diesel ▲ = RV Friendly Locations ♥= Pet Friendly Locations
Red print shows large vehicle parking / access on site or nearby Brown Print = Campgrounds / RV PARKS

Gas N: Circle K, Chevron, Exxon, Shell
S: Shell◈
Food N: Rest/Hol Inn, Burger King, Bonanza, Cajun Charlie's Seafood, Casa Ole, Checkers, Hollier's Cajun Kitchen, Hong Kong Rest, Guadalajara Rest, McDonald's, Mr Gatti's Pizza, Pitt Grill, Popeye's, Subway, Taco Bell, Wendy's
S: Pizza Hut, Sonic, Waffle House
Lodg N: Americas Best Value Inn, Econo Lodge, Hampton Inn
S: Baymont Inn, Candlewood Suites, Fairfield Inn, La Quinta Inn♥, Microtel, Wingate Inn♥
Med N: + W Calcasieu Cameron Hospital
Other N: Pro Tire Care, Firestone, Family Dollar, Goodyear, Grocery, Pennzoil Jiffy Lube, Carwash, Historical Museum, **Southern MH & RV Supply**
S: WiFi/**RVDump**/Pilot TC, to **Grand Acadian RV Resort & Campground▲**, To Southland Field✈

21 LA 3077, LA 27, Arizona St, Beglis Pky, Sulphur, DeQuincy
FStop S: Super Saver Express/Valero, To 500 N Beglis Pky: Conoco
Gas N: Citgo◈, Exxon, Kroger
S: Chevron, USA Super Shop/Citgo◈
Food N: Boiling Point, China Taste, KFC, Papa John's Pizza
S: FastFood/Super Saver Exp,Cajun Deli/U:
Med N: + W Calcasieu Cameron Hospital
Other N: AT&T, CVS, Dollar General, Kroger, NAPA, Walgreen's, to **Royal Palace Casino**
S: **Wagin Cajun$**, to **Hidden Ponds RV Park▲**

23 LA 108, S Cities Service Hwy, Sulphur. Industries
TStop N: CFN/Winners Choice Truck Stop/ Citgo
Gas N: Exxon, Murphy
S: Circle K, Citgo, Conoco◈
Food N: Rest/FastFood/Winners Choice TS, Subway/Exxon, Blimpie, Chili's, China Wok, Hollier's Cajun Diner, Little Caesar Pizza, McDonald's/WalMart, Sonic, Taco Bell, Wendy's
S: **Cracker Barrel**, Jack in the Box, Waffle House
Lodg N: Comfort Suites, Quality Inn
S: Best Western, Crossland Economy Studio♥, Fairfield Inn, Holiday Inn Express, Super 8
Other N: Dollar General, Lowe's, Radio Shack, **Walmart sc**

(25) Jct I-210E, Lake Charles Loop

26 US 90W, Columbia Southern Rd, PPG Dr, Sulphur, to Westlake
Gas N: Circle K

27 LA 378, LA 379, Westlake (Difficult reaccess)
Gas N: Circle K, Fina, Shell
S: Conoco
Food N: Burger King, DQ, Pizza Hut
Lodg S: Isle of Capri Hotel & **Casino**
Other N: to **Big Oaks RV Park▲**, **Tall Pines RV Park▲**, **Whispering Meadow RV Park▲**, to **Sam Houston Jones State Park▲**
S: **Riverboat Casinos**, to Westlake **Casino** Area

EXIT LOUISIANA

29 LA 385, Broad St, Lakeshore Dr, Business Dist, Civic Ctr (EB)
Gas N: Exxon
S: Citgo
Food N: Waffle House
S: LA Café, Renee's
Lodg N: Days Inn, Lakeview Inn, Players Island Hotel & **Casino**
S: Best Suites, Harrah's **Casino** & Hotel
Other S: Tourist Info

30A LA 385, Broad St, Lakeshore Dr, Business Dist, Civic Center (WB)
Gas N: Exxon
S: Citgo
Food N: Waffle House
S: Popeye's, Steamboat Bill's
Lodg N: Players Island Hotel & **Casino**, Days Inn
S: America's Best Inn, Harrah's **Casino** & Hotel
Other S: Tourist Info

30B Ryan St, Bus District (WB)
Food S: Barolo's, Cajun Café, Montana's Smokehouse
Lodg S: Holiday Inn, Lakeview Motel
Other N: Amtrak

31A US 90 Bus, Enterprise Blvd Lake Charles (Serv S to Broad St)
Gas S: BP◈, Exxon
Food S: Captain Seafood, Jim's Seafood, Popeye's Chicken
Lodg S: Howard Johnson

31B Prater St, Shattuck St, US 90E, to US 171, LA 14, Lake Charles (Difficult reaccess)
TStop N: Road King Truck Stop/Shell (Scales)
S: Gas
Food N: Rest/Road King TS
S: McDonald's
Lodg S: Econo Lodge, Motel 6♥, Sunrise Inn
TServ N: Road King TS/Tires

32 Opelousas St, Lake Charles
Gas N: Exxon
Lodg N: Motel 6♥
S: Holiday Inn Express, Treasure Inn

33 US 171N, to LA 14, DeRidder
Gas N: Chevron, RaceWay, Shamrock
Food N: Burger King, McDonald's, Taco Bell
Lodg N: Baymont Inn, Best Western, Comfort Inn, Days Inn, La Quinta Inn♥,
S: Holiday Inn Express, Motel 6♥
Other N: AutoZone, CVS, **Walmart sc**, Walgreen's, **Sam Houston Jones State Park**, **Yogi Bear's Jellystone Camp▲**

(34) Jct I-210W, Lake Charles Loop
Other N: Pine Shadows Golf Course
S: Chennault Int'l Airport✈

36 LA 397, Ward Line Rd, Lake Charles, to Creole, Cameron
TStop N: Fuel Stop 36/Conoco (Scales)
S: Chardele Auto & Truck Plaza/Chevron
Food S: FastFood/Chardele ATP, J Wesley
Lodg S: Red Roof Inn
TWash N: FS 36
TServ N: FS 36/Tires
Other N: to **Jean LaFitte RV Park▲**, to **Yogi Bear's Jellystone Park▲**, to **I-10 MH Village, RV Park & Campground▲**
S: Laundry/**RVDump**/Chardele ATP, **Casino**, to Chennault Int'l Airport✈, Mallard Cove Golf Course

EXIT LOUISIANA

43 LA 383, Thompson Ave, Lake Charles, Iowa
TStop N: Love's Travel Stop #243 (Scales), King's Travel Plaza/RoadysTS/Exxon (Scales)
S: Speedy Stop/Conoco
Gas S: Citgo◈, Shell, Valero
Food N: Burger King, Hardee's/Love's TS, Rest/FF/King's TP
S: McDonald's/Speedy Stop, Big Daddy's Cajun Seafood & Steaks, Fausto's Rest, Subway
Lodg N: Howard Johnson Express, La Quinta Inn♥
S: Deluxe Inn, Sunrise Inn
TServ N: King's TP/Tires
Other N: Laundry/**Casino**/WiFi/**RVDump**/Love's TS, Laundry/**Casino**/**RVDump**/King's TP, **Jean Lafitte RV Park▲**
S: Laundry/Speedy Stop, Factory Outlet Stores, **Cypress Bend RV Park▲**

44 LA 165, Iowa, Alexandria, Kinder
Other N: to 12mi: **Quiet Oaks RV Park▲**, to Appr 23 mi: Coushatta **Casino** Resort/ **Red Shoes RV Park▲**

48 LA 101, Iowa, Lacassine, Kinder
Gas S: Exxon

54 LA 99, Adams St, Welsh
Gas S: Circle R Mini Mart, Cajun Lunch Box◈, Exxon◈
Food S: Cajun Tales Seafood Rest, DQ,

59 LA 395, Roanoke

64 LA 26, Lake Arthur Ave, Jennings, to Elton, Lake Arthur
TStop S: Jennings Travel Center/Shop Rite #82 (Scales)
Gas S: Citgo, Chevron, Exxon◈, EZ Mart, Fina, Valero, Murphy◈
Food N: Mike's Seafood Rest
S: Rest/Jennings TC, Burger King, DQ, Denny's, General Wok, McDonald's, Pizza Hut, Shoney's, Sonic, Subway, Taco Bell, Waffle House, Walker's Cajun Dining, Wendy's
Lodg N: Boudreax Inn, Budget Inn
S: Comfort Inn, Holiday Inn, Quality Inn
Med S: + Jennings Hospital, + American Legion Hospital
Other S: Laundry/**RVDump**/Jennings TP, Auto Zone, Auto Dealers, Dollar Tree, Dollar General, Bank, Goodyear, O'Reilly Auto Parts, Radio Shack, RiteAid, Walgreen's, **Walmart sc▲**, Tourist Info, Jennings Airport✈, **La Maison RV Park▲**

65 LA 97, Evangeline Rd, Jennings
FStop S: Gottson Oi/Spur
TStop S: CFN/Road Master Travel Plaza/Shell
Food S: Rest/FF/Road Master TP
Lodg S: Americas Best Value Inn♥
Other S: Laundry/**Casino**/Road Master TP

72 Egan Hwy, Trumps Rd, Egan
Other N: **Cajun Haven RV Park▲**

76 LA 91, Crowley, Iota, Estherwood
TStop S: Petro 2 Mobil (Scales)
Food S: PetroDiner/Subway/Petro 2
Other S: Laundry/Petro 2

80 LA 13, Parkerson Ave, Crowley
TStop N: CFN/Exit 80 Travel Plaza/Conoco (Scales)
Gas S: Chevron◈, Exxon◈, RaceWay◈, Tobacco Plus, Valero◈

◈= Regular Gas Stations with Diesel ▲ = RV Friendly Locations ♥= Pet Friendly Locations
Red print shows large vehicle parking / access on site or nearby Brown Print = Campgrounds / RV PARKS

EXIT LOUISIANA

Food N: RicePalace/Ex 80 TP, Fezzo's Seafood & Steakhouse, Waffle House
S: Burger King, El Dorado Mexican Rest, KFC, Lucky Wok, McDonald's, Mr Gatti's, Pizza Hut, Popeye's Chicken, PJ's Grill, Sonic, Subway, Taco Bell, Wendy's
Lodg N: Crowley Inn♥, Days Inn, La Quinta Inn♥
TServ N: Dubus Engine Co
S: Lee's Auto & Truck Repair
Other N: Laundry/**Casino**/Ex 80 TP, **Muscrat Haven Campground▲**
S: Auto Dealers, Dollar General, O'Reilly Auto, Radio Shack, RiteAid, Winn Dixie, U-Haul, Carwash/Exxon

82 LA 1111, Tower Rd, E Crowley
Gas S: Chevron, Murphy
Food S: Chili's, Subway, Wendy's
Med S: **+ American Legion Hospital**
Other S: Dollar Tree, Lowe's, Radio Shack, Walgreen's, **Walmart sc▲**, Tourist Info

87 LA 35, LA 98, Rayne
FStop S: Econo-Mart/Mobil
TStop S: Frog City AmBest Travel Plaza/Citgo (Scales) **(DAND)**
Gas N: Chevron, Exxon◈, Shell
S: Valero◈
Food N: Burger King, Chef Roy's Frog City Café, McDonald's, Subway/Exxon
S: Rest/FastFood/Frog City TP, Gabe's Cajun, Great Wall Chinese, Popeye's, DQ, McDonald's, Subway
Lodg N: Days Inn
S: Best Western
TWash S: Frog City TP
TServ S: Frog City TP, Young's Trucking Svc, Raymond's Truck & Trailer Repair
Med S: **+ Hospital**
Other N: **Casino**/Days Inn, **Casino**/Exxon, Dollar General
S: **Casino**/Laundry/CB/**LP/RVDump**/Frog City TP, Advance Auto Parts, CVS, Family Dollar, NAPA, O'Reilly Auto Parts, Walgreen's, Winn Dixie

92 LA 95, Rayne, to Duson
TStop N: Studebaker Texaco Travel Plaza (Scales)
S: I-10/Duson Travel Center/Chevron, Big D Truck Stop/BP, Four Deuces Truck Stop/RoadysTS/Exxon
Food N: Rest/FastFood/Studebaker TP
S: FastFood/Duson TC, FastFood/Big D TS, Rest/Four Deuces TS, Thibodeaux's
Lodg S: Super 8
Other N: Laundry/**Casino**/WiFi/**RVDump**/Studebaker Texaco TP
S: Laundry/Duson TC, Laundry/4 Deuces TS, Laundry/Big D TS, **Frog City RV Park▲**

97 LA 93, LA 3168, Scott, Cankton
Gas S: Chevron, Cracker Barrel Convenience, Shell◈
Food S: Fezzo's Seafood & Steakhouse III, McDonald's/Chevron, Subway
Lodg N: Howard Johnson Express
S: Holiday Inn Express
Other S: **Lafayette KOA▲**, Cajun Harley Davidson

100 LA 3184, Ambassador Caffery Pkwy, Scott
Gas N: Chevron◈, Exxon◈
S: BP, Chevron◈, Exxon◈, RaceTrac◈,

Personal Notes

EXIT LOUISIANA

Gas S: Shell◈
Food N: Subway/Exxon
S: Burger King, **Cracker Barrel**, Sonic, Taco Bell/Pizza Hut, Waffle House, Wendy's
Lodg S: Ambassador Inn, Hampton Inn, Microtel, Sleep Inn
TWash N: Pit Stop Truck Wash
TServ S: Peterbilt
Med S: **+ University Medical Center, + Southwest Medical Center**
Other N: **Gauthier RV Center**
S: Family Dollar, Carwash/Chevron, **to** Cajun Dome

101 LA 182, University Ave, Lafayette
FStop N: Jubilee Express #4627/Ride USA
TStop N: Travel Center of America #161 (Scales)
Gas N: Chevron
S: Chevron, Exxon, RaceTrac◈, Shell◈, Texaco
Food N: CountryPride/Arby's/PizzaHut/TA TC, McDonald's/Chevron, Burger King, Waffle House, Whataburger
S: **Cracker Barrel**, McDonald's, Subway, Taco Torro, Toddle House Diner
Lodg N: Red Roof Inn♥
S: Americas Best Value Inn, Days Inn♥, Drury Inn, Hilton Garden Inn, Pear Tree Inn, St Francis Motel
TServ N: TA TC
Med N: **+ Vermilion Hospital**
S: **+ Our Lady of Lourdes Med Ctr**
Other N: Laundry/WiFi/**RVDump**/TA TC, Wetlands Golf Course
S: Auto Service, Tires, Family Dollar, Laundromat, O'Reilly Auto, Carwash/Shell,

EXIT LOUISIANA

Other S: Carwash/Exxon, Carwash, **to** Univ of LA/Lafayette

103A US 167S, Lafayette, to US 90
Gas S: Chevron◈, Racetrac, Shell, Shell◈, Murphy, Albertson's
Food S: Buster's Rest, Checker's, Chopsticks Chinese Rest, KFC, McDonald's, Pizza Hut, Popeye's, Shoney's, Starbucks, Subway, Taco Bell, Waffle House
Lodg S: Baymont Inn, Comfort Inn, Econo Lodge♥, Fairfield Inn, Hawthorne Suites, Holiday Inn♥, Howard Johnson, Jameson Inn, La Quinta Inn♥, Quality Inn, Royal Inn, Super 8, Travel Host Inn
Med S: **+ Hospital**
Other S: Albertson's/Pharmacy, Allied Discount Tire & Brake, CVS, CarQuest, Dollar General, Firestone, Grocery, Home Depot, **Walmart sc▲**, Northgate Mall, Northgate Cinema, US Post Office, Visitor Center, **to** Univ of LA - Lafayette, Lafayette Reg'l Airport✈

(103B) Jct I-49N, US 167, to Opelousas

104 Louisiana Ave, to Johnston St, to US 167, Lafayette (Acc #103 Serv)
Gas N: Exxon◈, Shell, Valero
Food N: Burger King, Crawfish Time, Church's Chicken, Little Caesar's Pizza
S: ChickFilA, Subway, Taco Bell
Lodg N: Plantation Motor Inn
Other N: Advance Auto, Auto Zone, CVS, Dollar Tree, Family Dollar, Walgreen's, **to** Flea Market, **RV Center**
S: AT&T, Hibbett Sports, JC Penney, Office Depot, Petco♥, Ross, Target, Stirling Shopping Center

(108) WIM Weigh Station (Both dir) (In Motion - NO Lane Changes)

109 LA 328, Rees St, Breaux Bridge
TStop N: Silver's Travel Center/RoadysTS/Texaco
S: Pilot Travel Center #274 (Scales)
Gas S: Chevron, Mobil◈, Mapco Express
Food N: Hardee's/Silver's TC, Crawdaddy's Seafood Boilers
S: Arby's/TJCinn/Pilot TC, Burger King/Mobil, Popeye's/Chevron, Cajun Cafe, Domino's, McDonald's, Pizza Hut, Sonic, Taco Bell, Waffle House, Wendy's
Lodg N: Microtel
S: Sona Inn♥, Super 8
Other N: Laundry/BarbSh/Silver's TC, **Campers Unlimited**, Tourist Info, **Poche's Fish-N-Camp▲**
S: Laundry/**Casino**/WiFi/Pilot TC, **LP**, Walgreen's, **Walmart sc**, Auto Dealers, Breaux Bridge Veterinary Clinic♥, **Pioneer Campground▲**

115 LA 347, Grandpoint Hwy, Breaux Bridge, Henderson, Cecilia
FStop N: Little Capital Exxon
S: I-10 Travel Center/Valero
TStop N: Diesi's Lucky Capital/BP
S: PTP/Bayou Belle Truck Stop & **Casino**, Henderson Travel Plaza/Citgo (Scales)
Gas N: Texaco◈
S: Chevron◈, Shell, Valero
Food N: FastFood/Little Capital Exxon, Rest/FastFood/Diesi's BP, Boudin's Rest, Landry's Seafood,

◈= Regular Gas Stations with Diesel ▲ = RV Friendly Locations ♥= Pet Friendly Locations
Red print shows large vehicle parking / access on site or nearby Brown Print = Campgrounds / RV PARKS

Food S: FastFood/Bayou Belle TS, FastFood/Henderson TP, FastFood/I-10 TC, Crawfish Town USA, McDonald's/Shell, Subway, Waffle House
Lodg N: Holiday Inn Express, Cajun Country Cottages
S: Best Western,
Other N: **Cajun Palms RV Resort▲**
S: Laundry/WiFi/Bayou Belle TS, Laundry/**Casino**/Henderson TP, **to Pioneer Campground▲**, Boat City USA,

NOTE: MM 115: Begin EB, End WB Call Boxes

121 LA 3177, Butte La Rose
LA Welcome Center (Both dir) (RR, Vend, Sec, WiFi, **RVDump**)
Other N: **to Frenchmens Wilderness CG▲**

127 LA 975, Grosse Tete, Whiskey Bay

135 LA 3000, Ramah, Maringouin

NOTE: MM 136: Begin WB, End EB Call Boxes

139 LA 77, Bayou Rd, Grosse Tete, Rosedale, Maringouin
TStop N: Bayou Shell Truck Stop
S: Tiger Truck Stop/RoadysTS/Conoco
Food N: Subway/Shell
S: Rest/FastFood/Tiger TS
TServ N: Bayou TS/Tires
S: Tiger TS/Tires
Other N: Laundry/**Casino**/Bayou TS
S: Laundry/LiveTigerExhibit/Tiger TS

151 LA 415, Lobdell Hwy, to US 190, Port Allen, Alexandria, Westport, Opelousas
TStop N: Pilot Travel Center #426 (Scales), Port Allen Truck Stop & **Casino**, Cash's Truck Plaza (Scales), H&R Truck Stop, Minnow's II Truck Stop, **6mi W on US 190:** Cajun Circus Truck Stop
S: River Port Truck Stop/Shell, Love's Travel Stop #240 (Scales)
Gas N: Chevron◈, RaceTrac
Food N: FastFood/Pilot TC, Rest/FastFood/Cash's TP, Rest/H&R TS, Rest/Port Allen TS, Rest/Cajun Circus TS, Burger King, Domino's, McDonald's, Kajun BBQ & Tamales, Popeye's, Shoney's, Subway, Taco Bell/KFC, Waffle House, Wendy's
S: Rest/FastFood/River Port TS, Arby's/Love's TS
Lodg N: Best Western, Comfort Suites, Days Inn, Holiday Inn Express, Quality Inn
S: Audubon Inn, Motel 6♥, Super 8
Other N: Laundry/**Casino**/Cash's TP, Laundry/**Casino**/Cajun Circus TS, Nino's Casino Truck Plaza, **Goldmine Casino, Cajun Country Campground▲**
Dollar General, Tourist Info Center
S: Laundry/WiFi/**RVDump**/**Casino**/Love's TS, Truck Service Center

153 LA 1, Port Allen, Plaquemine, Port of Baton Rouge
TStop N: **N to US 190 appr 7mi:** Lucky Louie's Truck Stop, TMI Fuel Stop (Scales)
S: LA 1 South Casino Truck Plaza/BP
Gas N: Circle K/Shell, Chevron, Spirit
S: RaceTrac, Chevron, Texaco◈

Food N: FastFood/Louie's TS, Rest/TMI FS, Best Lil PoBoy House, PicAPac Fried Chicken, River Queen Drive In, Church's Chicken, Sonic
S: FastFood/LA 1S TS, Waffle House
Lodg N: Ed's Motel
S: Port Allen Inn
Other N: Laundry/TMI FS, Auto Zone, Family Dollar, Grocery, NAPA, Port Allen Tire & Automotive, Carwash/Circle K, Tires/Spirit, **to** Southern Univ, A&M College
S: Laundry/LA 1S TS, Dollar General, Spillway Sportsman, **Walmart sc**

155A LA 30, Nicholson Dr, Highland Rd, Baton Rouge, Downtown
Gas N: Chevron
Food S: Chinese Inn
Lodg N: Sheraton
Med N: **+ Baton Rouge Medical Center**
Other N: FedEx Office, UPS Store, Belle of Baton Rouge **Casino**, Conv Center, Museums, **Police Dept**
S: Enterprise RAC, LA State Univ

(155B) Jct I-110N, to Baton Rouge Bus District, Airport (EB-Left Exit)
Other N: **to** Southern Univ, A&M College, Memorial Stadium, Baton Rouge Metro Airport✈

155C Louise St, Baton Rouge (WB)

156A Washington St (EB ex, WB reacc)

156B Dalrymple Dr
Other S: to LA State Univ

157A Perkins Rd (EB ex, WB reacc)
Gas S: Circle K/Shell, Cracker Barrel/Freedom Fuel
Food S: Jimmy John's, Oyster House, Parrain's Seafood, Zippy's Burritos
Other N: City Park Golf Course

157B Acadian Thruway, Stanford Ave
Gas N: Chevron◈, Circle K/Shell
S: Exxon, Shell
Food N: Denny's, TJ Rib's Rest
S: Coyote Blues Fresh Mex, Outback Steakhouse, Sonic,
Lodg N: La Quinta Inn♥, Radisson Hotel
S: Courtyard
Other S: Budget Truck Rental, CVS

158 College Dr, Baton Rouge
Gas N: Jubilee Express/RideUSA
S: Chevron, Exxon◈, Circle K/Shell
Food N: Albasha Greek & Lebanese Rest, CiCi's Pizza, Damon's, Flemings Prime Steak House, Fuddrucker's, Hooters, Jason's Deli, Mansur's on the Blvd, Melting Pot Rest, On the Border Mexican Rest, Romano's Macaroni Grill, Ruby Tuesday, Starbucks, Subway, Sullivan's Steakhouse, Waffle House, Wendy's
S: Burger King, Casa Maria Mexican Rest, Chili's, IHOP, Gino's Rest, Koto Sushi Bar, McDonald's, Quiznos, Ruth's Chris Steak House, Sarita's Mexican Buffet, Starbucks, Subway, Taco Bell
Lodg N: Best Western, Chase Suites, Extended Stay America, Homewood Suites, Marriott
S: Cambria Suites, Comfort Inn, Comfort Suites, Crown Plaza♥, Embassy Suites, Hampton Inn, Holiday Inn♥
Med N: **+ US Vets Outpatient Clinic, + Synergy Hospital**

Other N: AT&T, B&N, Cinema, UPS Store
S: Albertson's/Pharmacy, Dollar Tree, FedEx Office, Hobby Lobby, Office Depot Radio Shack, RiteAid, Walgreen's, **Walmart sc▲**, Carwash/Exxon, Carwash/Shell, Carwash/Chevron

(159) Jct I-12E, to Hammond (EB, Left exit)
TServ N: **N US 61/US 190:** Timmons Int'l

160 LA 3064, Essen Lane, N to I-12
Gas S: Chevron, Exxon◈, Racetrac, Albertson's
Food S: Baskin Robbins, Burger King, Copeland's, Dominos Pizza, Heads & Tails Seafood, Ichiban Sushi, India's Rest, McDonald's, Piccadilly Cafeteria, Popeye's Chicken, Starbucks, Taco Bell, Wendy's
Lodg S: Drury Inn, Fairfield Inn, SpringHill Suites
Med S: **+ Our Lady of the Lake Regional Medical Center**
Other S: Albertson's, Allied Discount Tire & Brake Dick's Sporting Goods, Dollar General, O'Reilly Auto Parts, RiteAid, Tire Kingdom, Walgreen's, Winners Circle Car Care, Carwash, SE LA Nursing School

162 Bluebonnet Blvd, Baton Rouge
Gas N: Cracker Barrel/Chevron◈,
S: RaceWay
Food S: Arzi's Lebanese Rest, BJ's Rest & Brewhouse, Boutin's Rest, Bravo Cucina Italia, Burger King, CA Pizza Kitchen, ChickFilA, Coffee House, Copeland's Cheesecake Bistro, J Alexander's, King Buffet, Logan's Roadhouse, Ralph & Kacoo's Seafood Rest
Lodg N: Quality Suites
S: AmeriSuites, Hyatt Place, TownePlace Suites
Med S: **+ Health Center, + CPC Meadow Wood Hospital**
Other S: Mall of Louisiana, Apple Store, All Pets Hospital♥, Best Buy, Borders, CompUSA, Cost Plus World Market, Grocery, US Post Office, Jimmy Swaggart Bible College

163 Siegen Lane, Baton Rouge, N to I-12
Gas N: Chevron, Circle K/Shell, RaceTrac
S: Exxon, Sam's
Food N: Arby's, Burger King, Cane's, CiCi's Pizza, Hooters, IHOP, McDonald's, Olive Garden, Shoney's, Smoky Bones BBQ, Subway, Taco Bell/Pizza Hut, Waffle House, Whataburger
S: Backyard Burger, Chili's, Chuck E Cheese, Jack in the Box, Joe's Crab Shack, Subway, Texas Roadhouse, Wendy's
Lodg N: Crestwood Suites, Days Inn , Hampton Inn, Holiday Inn Express, La Quinta Inn♥, Microtel, Motel 6♥
S: Courtyard, Residence Inn
Other N: Advance Auto, Auto Dealers, Auto Zone, AT&T, Big Lots, Dollar Tree, Firestone, Harley Davidson, Hummer, PetCo♥, Precision Firearm Indoor Range,Office Depot, O'Reilly Auto Parts, Radio Shack, Target, Verizon, Carwash/Chevron, Carwash/Shell
S: BooksAMillion, Carwash/Exxon, Grocery, Lowe's, PetSmart♥, RiteAid, Sam's Club, Siegen Ln Animal Clinic♥, **Walmart sc**, Walgreen's, Winn Dixie/Pharmacy

EXIT — LOUISIANA

166 — LA 42, LA 427, Highland Rd
(Acc to #163 N 42 to LA 61)
Gas: N: Chevron◈, Exxon◈
S: Shell, Texaco◈
Food: N: Church's Chicken, Las Palmas Mexican Rest, Popeye's Chicken, Serop's Middle Eastern Cafe, Sonic, Starbucks, Waffle House
S: Subway
Other: N: Home Depot, Carwash/Exxon, Blue Bayou Water Park, Dixie Landin Amusement Park, Santa Maria Golf Course

173 — LA 73, Geismar, Prairieville
Gas: N: Shell◈
S: Exxon◈, Mobil◈
Food: S: Burger King, McDonald's/Mobil, Popeye's Chicken, Sonic, Subway, TCBY/Exxon
Med: N: + Ascension Urgent Care
Other: S: U-Haul, **Twin Lakes RV Park▲**

177 — LA 30, Gonzales, St Gabriel
Gas: N: Freedom◈, Shell
S: Chevron, Shell◈
Food: N: Burger King, Jack in the Box, McDonald's, Outback Steakhouse, Taco Bell, Waffle House, Mike Anderson's Seafood/Hol Inn
S: Chili's, Cracker Barrel, KFC, Popeye's Chicken, Sonic, Starbucks, Wendy's
Lodg: N: America's Best Suites, Best Western, Budget Inn, Days Inn, Highland Inn, Holiday Inn, Western Inn
S: Hampton Inn, Supreme Inn
Med: N: + St Elizabeth Hospital
Other: N: Auto Dealer, Cabela's, Fred's Pharmacy, Home Depot, Tractor Supply, Yamaha ATV Center, Carwash/Shell
S: Tanger Factory Outlet Mall, Carwash/Shell, Lamar Dixon Expo Center, **Vesta MH & RV Park▲**,

179 — LA 44, Burnside Ave, to LA 30, Gonzales, Burnside (Acc to #177)
Gas: N: Exxon

182 — LA 22, John Leblanc Blvd, to US 61, Sorrento, Donaldsonville
FStop: S: Speedy Junction
TStop: S: Sorrento Super Stop/Chevron (Scales)
Gas: N: Chevron◈, Texaco◈
Food: S: FastFood/Sorrento SS, McDonald's, Waffle House
Other: S: Laundry/Sorrento SS

187 — US 61, Airline Hwy, S - Gramercy, N - Sorrento (Serv appr 10mi S)

194 — LA 641S, LA 3213, to Gramercy, Lutcher (Serv appr 5mi S)

EXIT — LOUISIANA

206 — LA 3188S, Belle Terre Blvd, to US 61, LaPlace, Reserve
TStop: S: S appr 8mi to US 61W: Riverbend Truck Stop
Gas: S: Exxon, Shell◈, Texaco◈
Food: S: KFC, McDonald's - **Addt'l food S to W Airline Hwy**
Lodg: S: Millett Motel
Med: S: to + River Parishes Hospital
Other: S: Carwash, **to** St John the Baptist Parish Airport✈

(207) — Weigh Station (Both dir)

209 — US 51, to I-55N (EB), La Place, Hammond, to Jackson
(Many Serv S to US 61)
TStop: N: LaPlace Travel Center/RoadysTS/Shell (Scales)
S: Pilot Travel Center #82 (Scales),
Gas: S: Chevron, Shell
Food: N: Rest/LaPlace TC,
S: Subway/Pilot TC, Basile's, McDonald's, 51 Seafood Rest, Shoney's, Waffle House, Wendy's
Lodg: N: Suburban Extended Stay
S: Best Western♥, Days Inn, Hampton Inn, Holiday Inn Express, Quality Inn
TServ: N: LaPlace TC/Tires
Med: S: + to River Parishes Hospital
Other: N: Laundry/LaPlace TC,
S: Laundry/WiFi/RVDump/Pilot TC, Auto Zone, Hibbett Sports, Office Depot, Radio Shack, Verizon, U-Haul, **La Place Trailer Park & Camp▲**, **R&S MH & RV Park▲**, **Uncle Sam's RV & Trailer Park▲**, **Cruise America RV Rentals, Riverside RV Park▲**

(210) — Jct I-55N, Hammond (WB)

(220) — Jct 310S, Boutte, to Houma

221 — Loyola Dr, Veterans Memorial Hwy, Kenner
Gas: N: Circle K, Exxon◈, Shell◈, Loyola One Stop, Sam's
S: BP◈, Discount Zone
Food: N: Church's Chicken, McDonald's, Popeye's Chicken, Rally's, Starbucks, Taco Bell
S: Rick's Famous Café, Wendy's
Lodg: S: Motel 6♥,
Med: N: to + Kenner Regional Medical Center
Other: N: Advance Auto, Pharmacy, Sam's Club, Carwash/Shell, Chateau Veterinary Hospital♥, Radio Shack, **Walmart sc**
S: Family Dollar, Motorhome Rentals of LA, NO Int'l Airport✈

EXIT — LOUISIANA

223AB — LA 49, Williams Blvd, New Orleans Intl Airport (EB)

223B — New Orleans Int'l Airport (WB)

223A — LA 49, Williams Blvd, 32nd St (WB)
(Addtl Serv N to Esplanade Ave & S to Veterans Memorial Blvd)
Gas: N: Exxon, Shell
S: BP, Discount Zone,
Food: N: Asian Super Buffet, Baskin Robbins, Burger King, ChickFilA, Canes, El Patio, Fisherman's Cove Harbor Seafood, Golden Corral, IHOP, Jade Palace, Pizza Hut, Saki Sushi Hibachi House, Taco Bell
S: Denny's, McDonald's, Prime Time Seafood & Steakhouse, Subway
Lodg: N: Fairfield Inn, Hilton Garden Inn
S: Airport Inn♥, Americas Best Inn, Comfort Inn, Days Inn, Extended Stay America♥, Holiday Inn, La Quinta Inn♥, Radisson, Travelodge, Wingate Inn
Other: N: AutoZone, Dollar Tree, Office Depot, PetCo♥, RiteAid, UPS Store, Walmart Market, Winn Dixie, Esplanade Mall
S: CVS, Carwash, CompUSA, Dollar General, Firestone, Goodyear, Home Depot, NAPA, PetSmart♥, U-Haul, Verizon, **Walmart**,
New Orleans West KOA▲

224 — Power Blvd, David Dr, S to Veterans Memorial Blvd (WB) (Acc to #223/225)

225 — Veterans Memorial Blvd, Metairie
Gas: N: Chevron, Discount Zone, Shell
S: Shell, Speedway
Food: N: Burger King, Celebration Station, Denny's, Donut Den, Hooters, Italian Pie, McDonald's, Subway, Taco Bell
S: Godfather's Pizza, Popeye's Chicken, Wendy's, New Orleans Seafood
Lodg: N: La Quinta Inn♥
S: Holiday Inn, Four Points Sheraton
Med: N: + Ochsner Hospital, + Doctors After Hours Urgent Care & Walk-In Clinic
Other: N: Auto Services, Celebration Station, CVS, Carwash, Grocery, Hobby Hut, Laundromat, Radio Shack, RiteAid
S: Auto Dealers, Best Buy, Big Lots, Home Depot, Jiffy Lube, Kmart, Office Depot, PetSmart♥, **Walmart**, Walgreen's, US Post Office

226 — LA 3152, Clearview Pky, Huey Long Bridge, Metairie
(Addtl Serv N to Veterans Mem'l Blvd)
Gas: N: Chevron, Exxon
S: Chevron, Circle K

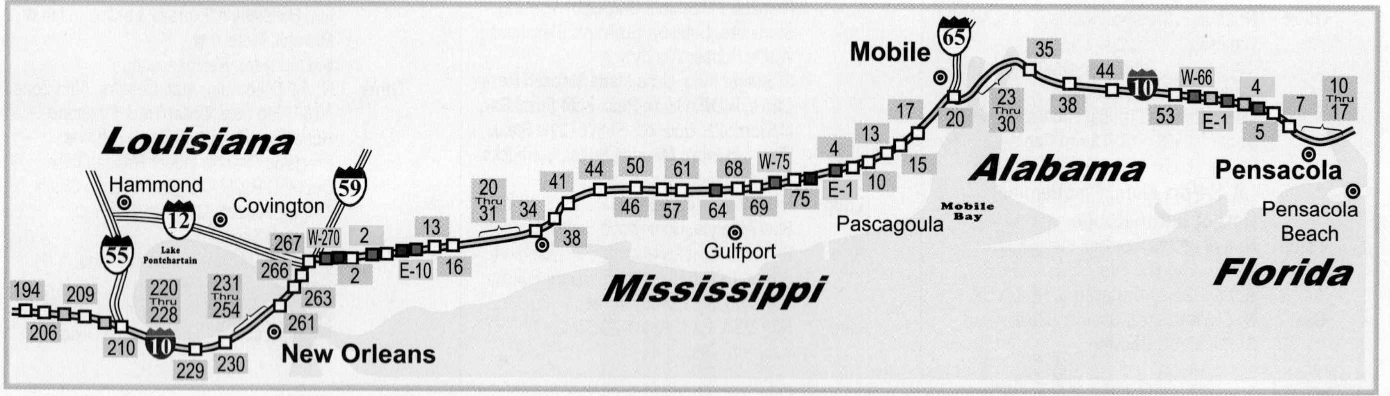

◈= Regular Gas Stations with Diesel ▲ = RV Friendly Locations ♥ = Pet Friendly Locations
Red print shows large vehicle parking / access on site or nearby Brown Print = Campgrounds / RV PARKS

EXIT		LOUISIANA
	Food	N: Café East, Chili's, Hooters, Popeye's Chicken, Ruby Tuesday, Webster's
		S: Bud's Broiler Burger King, Piccadilly's, Subway, Wing Zone
	Lodg	N: Sleep Inn
		S: Super 8, Sun Suites
	AServ	S: Green Acres Towing & Repair
	Med	N: + E Jefferson General Hospital
		S: + After Hours Urgent Care
		Tulane Lakeside Hospital
	Other	N: Target, Clearview Mall, AMC 12
		S: Auto Dealers, Firestone
228		**Causeway Blvd, Downtown Metairie, Mandeville**
	Gas	N: Exxon, Shell
		S: BP, Exxon, Phillips 66, Discount Zone
	Food	N: Acme Oysterhouse, Bravo Cucina Italian, Burger King, Causeway Grill, Chevy's Fresh Mex, ChickFilA, Cuco's Mexican, IHOP, KFC, Outback Steakhouse, Ruth's Chris Steak House,Shogun Japanese, Steak Escape
	Food	S: Rest/Days Hotel, Rest/Wyndham, Cajun Grill & Bar, Café Fresca, Denny's, IHOP, NO Hamburger & Seafood, Subway
	Lodg	N: Best Western, Hampton Inn, Ramada Inn
		S: Courtyard, Days Hotel, Extended Stay, Holiday Inn, La Quinta Inn♥, Plaza Suite, Quality Inn, Sheraton, Wyndham
	Med	N: + Omega Hospital
	Other	N: Apple Store, Auto Dealers, Borders, Cat Hospital♥, CVS, CarQuest, Grocery, Laundromat, Lowe's, NAPA, Radio Shack, Target, US Post Office, West Esplanade Veterinary Clinic♥, UPS Store
		S: to Sam's Club
229		**Bonnabel Blvd, Metairie**
(230)		**Jct I-610E, to Slidell (EB)**
(231B)		**Jct I-610E, Florida Blvd, W End Blvd (WB)**
231A		**LA 611, Metairie Rd, City Park Ave, New Orleans**
	Other	N: Degado Comm College, Tad Gormley Stadium
		S: New Orleans Museum of Art
232		**US 61, Airline Hwy, Tulane Ave, Howard Ave, Carrollton Ave**
	Gas	N: Amoco
		S: Exxon
	Food	N: Burger King
		S: McDonald's, Piccadilly
	Lodg	N: Crystal Inn, Quality Inn
		S: Keystone Motel
	Other	N: Fairgrounds Race Course
		S: Xavier Univ of LA
234A		**US 90W, Claiborne Ave, Poydras St, Superdome (EB)**
234B		**Poydras St, Claiborne Ave, Superdome (EB, Left exit)**
	Lodg	S: Hyatt, Holiday Inn, Ramada Inn
	Med	N: + Medical Center of LA West
	Other	N: Best Western
		S: Downtown, Superdome, NO Arena, Amtrak, Greyhound, LA State Univ, NO Centre

EXIT		LOUISIANA
234C		**Poydras St, Howard Ave, US 90 Bus, LA 3139, Claiborne Ave, Earhart Blvd (WB, Left exit)**
	Med	S: + Tulane Univ Medical Center
	Other	S: Greyhound, Amtrak, Tulane Univ
235C		**Poydras St, Superdome (WB)**
235B		**Canal St, Superdome (WB)**
	Food	S: Rest/Days Inn
	Lodg	N: NO Grand Palace Hotel, Ramada, Rodeway Inn
		S: Clarion, Days Inn, Radisson, Warwick Hotel
235A		**Orleans Ave, Vieux Carre French Quarter, Superdome**
	Gas	S: Chevron
	Food	S: Café, Mama Rosa's
	Lodg	N: Rainbow Inn Hotel
		S: Creole House, Maison Dupry Hotel
	Other	S: French Quarter RV Resort▲
236A		**Esplanade Ave, Downtown (EB)**
	Gas	S: Gas
236B		**LA 39, N Claiborne Ave (EB)**
	TStop	N: PTP/Mardi Gras Truck Stop (Scales)
	Food	N: Burger King, McDonald's
	Other	N: Laundry/RVDump/Mardi Gras TS
236C		**St Bernard Ave, Downtown (WB)**
237		**LA 3021, Elysian Fields Ave**
	TStop	N: Mardi Gras Truck Stop (Scales)
	Gas	S: Chevron
	Other	N: Laundry/RVDump/Mardi Gras TS, Dillard Univ, Univ of New Orleans
(238A)		**Jct I-610W, Baton Rouge, New Orleans Int'l Airport (WB)**
238A		**Franklin Ave (WB)**
(238B)		**Jct I-610W (WB)**
239		**Louisa St, Almonaster Blvd (WB)**
239AB		**Louisa St, Almonaster Blvd (EB)**
	TStop	N: PTP/Big Easy Travel Plaza (Scales)
	Gas	N: Chevron, Exxon
	Food	N: Rest/FastFood/Big Easy TP, Burger King, McDonald's, Pizza Hut, Popeye's, Sonic, Wendy's
	Lodg	N: Econo Lodge, Friendly Inn, Howard Johnson, Knights Inn, Royal Inn
	TServ	N: Big Easy TP
	Other	N: Laundry/RVDump/Big Easy TP, Goodyear, Walgreen's, Winn Dixie, Mall Mardi Gras RV Park▲, Riverboat Travel Park▲
240A		**Jourdan Rd, Downman Rd, US 90 LA 3021, New Orleans (EB)**
	Gas	N: Shell, Spur
		S: Chevron
	Food	N: Church's, McDonald's, Popeye's
	Lodg	N: Red Carpet Inn, Super 8
	Other	N: Mardi Gras RV Park▲, Riverboat Travel Park▲
240B		**US 90, Chef Hwy**
	Gas	N: Chevron, Exxon, Shell
	Food	N: Church's Chicken, Pizza Hut, Subway
	Lodg	N: Econo Lodge, Howard Johnson, Monte Carlo Hotel, Knights Inn, Red Carpet Inn, Royal Inn, Super 8

EXIT		LOUISIANA
241		**LA 3021, Morrison Rd**
	Gas	N: Shell
	Food	N: Burger King
	AServ	N: Shell
	Other	N: NO Lakefront Airport✈
242		**Crowder Blvd**
	Gas	S: Gas
244		**Read Blvd, New Orleans**
	Gas	N: Shell
		S: EZ Fuel Stop◈
	Food	N: McDonald's
		S: Popeye's
	Lodg	S: Best Western, Comfort Suites, Days Inn, Holiday Inn Express, Studio 6
	Med	S: + East Lake Hospital, + Pendleton Memorial Methodist Hospital
	Other	N: Sam's Club,
		S: Goodyear, Mall, Walgreen's
245		**Bullard Ave**
	Gas	N: Chevron, Shell
		S: Shell
	Food	N: IHOP, Pizza Hut, Sonic, Wendy's
		S: Burger King, KFCl
	Lodg	N: Comfort Suites, Fairfield Inn, Holiday Inn Express, La Quinta Inn♥
		S: Best Western, Studio 6
	Med	S: + Hospital
	Other	S: Home Depot, Pep Boys, Rite Aid, Walgreen's
(246AB)		**Jct I-510S, LA 47, S to Chalmette, Michoud (EB), N to Little Woods**
	TStop	S: to EX 2C: The Palace Truckstop, Paradise Truck Stop
	Other	S: to Six Flags of New Orleans, NASA Michoud Assembly Factory
248		**LA 68, Michoud Blvd**
251		**LA 72, Bayou Sauvage National Wildlife Refuge**
254		**US 11, Irish Bayou, N Shore Dr**
	TStop	S: Irish Bayou Travel Center/BP
	Food	S: FastFood/Irish Bayou TS
	Other	S: Laundry/Irish Bayou TS
261		**Oak Harbor Blvd, Eden Isles**
	Gas	N: Exxon
		S: BP
	Food	N: Café
	Lodg	S: Sleep Inn
263		**LA 433, Slidell**
	FStop	S: Kanagaroo Express #3474/Texaco
	TStop	S: Fleet Travel Center #601 (Scales)
	Gas	N: BP, Exxon
	Food	N: China Buffet, Waffle House
		S: Subway/Fleet TC, Rest/Holiday Inn, McDonald's, Wendy's
	Lodg	N: Hampton Inn
		S: Holiday Inn
	Other	S: Auto Dealers, Factory Outlet Mall, New Orleans East KOA▲, Pinecrest RV Park▲
(265)		**Weigh Station (Both dir)**
266		**US 190, Slidell**
	TStop	N: Travel Center of America #180 (Scales)
	Gas	N: Danny's, Jubilee, Magnolia's◈, Shell
		S: Chevron◈, Racetrac◈, Murphy

◈= Regular Gas Stations with Diesel ▲ = RV Friendly Locations ♥= Pet Friendly Locations
Red print shows large vehicle parking / access on site or nearby Brown Print = Campgrounds / RV PARKS

EXIT		LA / MS
	Food	N: Rest/TA TC, Arby's, Burger King, Cane's, Denny's, KFC, McDonald's, Pizza Hut, Shoney's, Taco Bell, Wendy's S: Applebee's, Big Easy Diner, Cracker Barrel, OsakaGrill, Outback Steakhouse, Starbucks, Texas Roadkhouse, Waffle Hous Subway/Chevron
	Lodg	N: Best Western, Days Inn, Deluxe Inn, Motel 6♥, Super 8 S: Americas Best Value Inn, La Quinta Inn♥, Regency Inn
	TServ	N: TA TC
	Med	S: + Northshore Reg'l Med Center
	Other	N: Laundry/WiFi/**RVDump**/TA TC, Cinema 8, Carwash, Firestone, Hobby Lobby, Harley Davidson, Office Depot, O'Reilly Auto Parts, Grocery, Radio Shack, Pep Boys, U-Haul S: Casino, Craig's Automotive Center, Home Depot, Lowe's, **Walmart sc ▲**
(267A)		**Jct I-59N, to Meridian**
(267B)		**Jct I-12W, to Baton Rouge**
(270)		**LA Slidell Welcome Center** (WB) **(RR, Ph, Pic, Vend, Sec, Pet, RVDump)**

CENTRAL TIME ZONE

NOTE: MM 274: Mississippi State Line

LOUISIANA
MISSISSIPPI

CENTRAL TIME ZONE

EXIT		MISSISSIPPI
(1)		**Weigh Station** (Both dir)
2		**MS 607, Bay St Louis, to US 90, Waveland, NASA Stennis Space Center** **MS Hancock Co Welcome Center** **(NO Trucks / Buses)** **S: (Both dir)** **(RR, Phone, Picnic, RVDump, Sec247)**
	Other	N: John C Stennis Space Center S: **Buccaneer State Park/Closed, Bay St Louis/Gulfport KOA▲**
(10)		**Weigh Station** (Both dir)
13		**MS 43, MS 603, Kiln Rd, Bay St Louis, Kiln, Picayune, Waveland** **(Addt'l Ser 4-5 mi S to US 90)**
	Gas	S: Exxon◈, Pure
	Lodg	S: Knights Inn
	Med	S: to + Hancock Medical Center
	Other	N: **McLeod State Park/Closed**, Stennis Int'l Airport✈, **Nella's RV Park▲** S: **to Bay Marina & RV Park▲, Bay St Louis/Gulfport KOA▲, Bay St Louis RV Park▲**, Hollywood Casino **& RV Park▲**, Silver Slipper Casino **& RV Park▲, Buccaneer State Park▲, to** Amtrak, Auto Dealers, U-Haul, **Walmart sc**, Casinos
16		**Interchange St, Diamondhead**
	Gas	N: BP, Kangaroo Express #3752/Chevron◈
	Food	N: Bigg E Grill & Bar, Burger King, DQ, Domino's/BP, Subway, Waffle House
	Lodg	N: Diamondhead Resort S: Econo Lodge
	Med	N: + Hancock Medical Center, + Urgent Medical Care
	Other	N: Carwash/KE Chevron, Ace Hardware, U-Haul S: Diamondhead Airport✈
20		**Kiln DeLisle Rd, Pass Christian**
	Gas	N: Spur
24		**Menge Ave, Pass Christian**
	TStop	N: MS Fuel Center #17/Chevron (Scales)
	Gas	S: I-10 Quick Stop/Texaco
	Food	N: FastFood/MS FC
	TServ	N: MS FC
	TWash	N: MS FC
	Other	N: Laundry/**RVDump**/MS FC S: **Flea Market & RV Park▲**, Oaks Golf Club, **to** Beaches
28		**County Farm Rd, Gulfport, to Long Beach, Pass Christian**
	Gas	S: Chevron, Shell◈
	Other	S: Coastal Tire, **to Magic River Resort▲, Plantation Pines Park▲**
31		**Canal Rd, Gulfport**
	TStop	N: Love's Travel Stop #212 (Scales)**(DAND)** S: Flying J Travel Plaza #5065/Conoco (Scales)
	Gas	S: Shell◈
	Food	N: Arby's/Love's TS S: Cookery/FastFood/FJ TP, Waffle House, Wendy's, McDonald's/Shell
	Lodg	S: Crystal Inn, Econo Lodge, Legacy Inn
	TServ	N: Dee's 24 Hr Tire Service, Tires
	Other	N: Laundry/WiFi/**RVDump**/Love's TS, **Bay Berry RV Park▲, RV Repair**, Southern Tire Mart S: Laundry/BarbSh/WiFi/**LP/RVDump**/FJ TP, Carwash/Shell, **Plantation Pines RV Park▲**, Univ of S MS Reg'l Campus, US Naval Reserve Station
34A		**US 49S, Gulfport, Hattiesburg**
	FStop	S: Hwy 49 Shell #33, Kangaroo Express
	Gas	S: Chevron, RaceWay, Shell
	Food	S: Applebee's, Arby's, China Garden Express, Great Steak & Potato, Hooters, IHOP, Krispy Kreme, Los Tres Amigos, McDonald's, Montana's Rest, Shoney's, Sonic, Subway, Waffle House, Wendy's, Zaxby's
	Lodg	S: Best Value Inn, Best Western, Comfort Inn, Days Inn, Fairfield Inn, Hampton Inn, Holiday Inn Express, Holiday Inn, Motel 6♥, Quality Inn, Studio Inn, Shoney's Inn
	TServ	S: Empire Truck Sales
	Med	S: + Memorial Hospital Gulfport
	Other	S: Auto Dealers, Home Depot, **Walmart sc**, Verizon, Prime Outlets at Gulfport, Sam's Club, Budget RAC, Gulfport-Biloxi Reg'l Airport✈, Amtrak, US Naval Reserve Station, Navy Seabee Center, **to** South Wind Motel **& RV Park▲**, Gulfport Biloxi Int'l Airport ✈
34B		**US 49N, Gulfport, to Hattiesburg**
	FStop	N: Interstate 49/Chevron
	Gas	N: Kangaroo Express/Texaco◈
	Food	N: Backyard Burger, Burger King, Cane's, ChickFilA, Chili's, Chuck E Cheese's Pizza, CiCi'sPizza, Cracker Barrel, Hardee's, Logan's Roadhouse, McDonald's, O'Charley's, Papa John's Pizza, Pizza Hut, Starbucks, TGI Friday, Waffle House, Wendy's, Whataburger
	Lodg	N: Deer Run Resort
	Med	N: + Garden Park Medical Center
	Other	N: Auto Dealers, Advance Auto Parts, Albertson's, Barnes & Noble, CVS, Fred's, Dollar General, Grocery, Kroger, Office Depot, PetSmart♥, Radio Shack, RiteAid, Tire Kingdom, Crossroads Outlet Mall, Tinseltown Movie Theater, Waterpark, US Post Office, **Southern Oaks MH & RV Community▲, Campgrounds of the South RV Park▲, RV Park▲**
38		**MS 605, Lorraine Rd**
	Gas	N: Exxon, Fina, Kangaroo Express◈ S: Pure Country
	Food	N: Captain Al's cafe, KFC, McDonald's, Subway
	Lodg	S: Econo Lodge, Ramada Ltd
	Other	S: **to** William Carey College, Gulf Coast Comm College, Beaches, **Sand Beach RV Park▲, appr 3mi: Baywood Campground & RV Park▲, Fox's RV Park▲**
41		**MS 67N, Biloxi, Woolmarket**
	Gas	N: BP, Chevron◈, Texaco
	Other	S: **Parker's Landing Campground▲, Mazalea Travel Park▲, Oaklawn RV Park▲, Reliable RV Sales & Service Center**
44		**Cedar Lake Rd, Coast Coliseum, Biloxi**
	FStop	S: Interstate Shell
	TStop	N: Love's Travel Stop #402 (Scales)
	Gas	S: BP, Chevron◈
	Food	N: Subway/Love's TS S: FastFood/Interstate Shell, Waffle House, McDonald's, Sonic
	Lodg	S: La Quinta Inn♥
	Med	S: + Gulf Coast Medical Center
	Other	N: Laundry/WiFi/**RVDump**/Love's TS S: **RVDump**/Shell, **Motorhome** & Truck Service, Biloxi National Cemetery, Harley Davidson, Home Depot
(46A)		**Jct 110S, MS 15N, D'Iberville, Biloxi, Keesler AFB** **(South Serv on I-110, Exit #2)**
	Other	S: **to** Beaches, Keesler AFB, Boomtown Casinos, **Majestic Oaks RV Resort▲, Fox RV Park▲**
(46B)		**MS 15N**
	Gas	N: Chevron◈, Kangaroo◈
	Food	N: Chili's, CiCi's Pizza, McDonald's, Outback Steakhouse, Ruby Tuesday, Subway, Sonic, Waffle House, Wendy's
	Lodg	N: Best Western, Travel Inn, Wingate Inn
	Other	N: Lowe's, Radio Shack, **Walmart sc, to Southern Comfort Camping Resort▲, Lakeview RV Resort▲, to DeSoto National Forest**
50		**MS 609S, Tucker Rd, Biloxi, Ocean Springs**
	TStop	S: Fleet Travel Center #504/Pilot Travel Center (Scales)
	Gas	N: Shell S: BP, Chevron
	Food	N: Domino's/Shell, Rest/Super 8 S: FastFood/Fleet TC, Denny's, McDonald's/Chevron, Waffle House, Wendy's
	Lodg	N: Best Western, Comfort Inn, Ramada, Super 8 S: Country Inn, Days Inn, Hampton Inn, Howard Johnson, Quality Inn

◈= Regular Gas Stations with Diesel ▲ = RV Friendly Locations ♥= Pet Friendly Locations
Red print shows large vehicle parking / access on site or nearby **Brown Print = Campgrounds / RV PARKS**

EXIT		MS / AL
	Other	N: Martin's Lake ▲ S: Vet♥, Paradise Camper Sales
57		**MS 57, Ocean Springs, Gautier, Fontainbleau, Vancleve**
	Gas	N: Shell◈ S: Exxon, Kangaroo
	Food	N: Shed BBQ & Blues Joint
	Lodg	N: Wilson House Inn B&B
	Med	S: + Hospital
	Other	N: Camp Journey's End RV Park & Campground▲, Bluff Creek Camping▲ S: Gulf Island National Seashore, Naval Facilities
61		**Vancleve Rd, Gautier, Vancleve**
	Gas	S: BP◈
	Food	S: McDonald's, Pizza Hut, Wendy's
	Lodg	S: Best Western, Suburban Lodge
	Other	N: Bluff Creek Camping▲ S: to Wonderland Campground▲, Indian Pt RV Resort▲, Gulf Coast Comm College, Jackson Co Campus, Sand Hill Crane Wildlife Refuge Area/ CLOSED, to Shepard State Park▲
(64)		**Moss Point Rest Area (Both dir)** (RR, Phone, Picnic, RVDump, Sec247)
68		**MS 613, Main St, Moss Point, Pascagoula, Escatawpa**
	Gas	N: BP, Chevron◈ S: BP◈
	Lodg	N: Super 8
	Med	S: + Hospital
	Other	N: Riverbend Park Resort▲
69		**MS 63, E Moss Point, Escatawpa, E Pascagoula, Lucedale**
	FStop	S: Moss Point Chevron #2
	TStop	S: Cone Auto/Truck Plaza #230 (Scales)
	Gas	N: KangarooExpress/Texaco◈ S: Exxon
	Food	S: Rest/Cone ATP, Domino's Pizza/KE Texaco, Barnhill's, Burger King, Cracker Barrel, Hardee's, McDonald's, Ruby Tuesday, Waffle House, Wendy's, Subway/Exxon, Rest/BW
	Lodg	N: Americas Best Value Inn, Deluxe Inn, La Quinta Inn♥, Super 8 S: Best Western, Comfort Inn, Days Inn, Hampton Inn, Holiday Inn Express, Quality Inn, Ramada, Shular Inn
	TServ	S: Chevron
	Med	S: + Hospital
	Other	N: Trent Lott Int'l Airport✈ S: Laundry/Cone ATP, Ingalls Ship Building
(75)		**Weigh Station (EB)**
(75)		**MS Jackson Co Welcome Center** (WB) (RR, Phone, Picnic, RVDump)
75		**Franklin Creek Rd, to US 90**
(77)		**Weigh Station (WB)**
	NOTE:	MM 77.2: Alabama State Line

MISSISSIPPI
ALABAMA

EXIT		ALABAMA
(1)		**AL Welcome Center (EB) Grand Bay** (RR, Ph, Pic, Sec247, Vend, RVDump)
4		**AL 188E, CR 11, Grand Bay, Dauphin Island**
	TStop	N: Travel Center of America #54/BP(Scales)
	Gas	N: Citgo◈, Shell S: Chevron
	Food	N: Rest/TA TC, Subway/Shell, McDonald's, Waffle House S: Hardee's
	TServ	N: TA TC, Kenworth
	Other	N: Laundry/Clinic/WiFi/TA TC S: Trav-L-Kamp
10		**CR 39, McDonald Rd**
	Other	S: St Elmo Airport✈
13		**CR 30, Theodore Dawes Rd, Theodore, Irvington** (Gas/Food/Lodg S to US 90)
	TStop	N: Pilot Travel Center #302 (Scales)
	Gas	N: Conoco, Shell, Texaco
	Food	N: Wendy's/Pilot TC, McDonald's, Subway, Waffle House
	Lodg	N: Spanish Oak Inn
	Other	N: Laundry/WiFi/Pilot TC, Mobile Greyhound Park, Azalea RV Park▲, To Mobile Reg'l Airport✈ S: I-10 Kampground▲, Shady Grove Campground▲, Bellingrath RV Park▲, Payne's RV Park▲, Johnny's RV Resort▲
15A		**US 90S, AL 16, Government Blvd, Mobile, Theodore, Historic Mobile Pkwy, Tillman's Corner**
	TStop	S: Shell
	Gas	S: BP◈, Conoco, Raceway
	Food	S: McDonald's, Hardee's, Waffle House
	Lodg	S: Knights Inn♥, Red Roof Inn♥
	TServ	S: Peterbilt
	Other	S: Nestled Away RV Park▲, Bellingrath RV Park▲, Cruise America RV Rentals, Johnny's RV Center
15B		**US 90N, AL 16, Government Blvd, Mobile, Theodore, Historic Mobile Pkwy, Tillman's Corner**
	Gas	N: BP, Raceway, Shell
	Food	N: Arby's, Burger King, Checkers, CiCi's, Dick Russell's BBQ, El Toro Mexican, Hooters, IHOP, KFC, McDonald's, Papa John's, Pizza Hut, Popeye's, Subway, Waffle House
	Lodg	N: Best Western, Comfort Suites, Days Inn, Econo Lodge, Hampton Inn, Holiday Inn, La Quinta Inn♥, Motel 6♥, Quality Inn, Red Roof Inn♥, Rodeway Inn, Ramada Inn, Super 8, Suite One
	Other	N: Auto Zone, CarQuest, Dollar Tree, Family Dollar, Firestone, Goodyear, Grocery, O'Reilly Auto Parts, RiteAid, Radio Shack, Walgreen's, Winn Dixie, S AL Bus Sales, Dog Track, Azalea RV Park▲, Pala Verde Mobile Home and RV Park▲
17A		**AL 193, Rangeline Rd, Higgins Rd, Mobile, to Tillman's Corner, Dauphin Island**
	FStop	S: Stop N Shop #2/Shell
17B		**AL 193N, Higgins Rd, to AL 90, Mobile, to Tillman's Corner, Dauphin Island**
	Gas	N: Chevron, Citgo

EXIT		ALABAMA
	Food	N: Boiling Pot, Burger King, CiCi's Pizza, Dick's BBQ, McDonald's, IHOP, Ruby Tuesday, Sonny's BBQ, Zaxby's
	Med	N: + Hospital
	Other	N: Big Lots, Big 10 Tire, Family Dollar, Lowe's, Radio Shack, Walmart sc▲, Christmas Town & Village
(20)		**Jct I-65N, Montgomery (EB, Left exit)**
	TServ	N: Empire Truck Sales
22		**AL 163, Dauphin Island Pkwy (EB)**
22B		**AL 163S, Dauphin Island Pkwy (WB, Left Exit)**
	Gas	S: Exxon, Shell◈
	Food	S: Checker's, Waffle House
	Lodg	S: Heritage Inn
	TServ	S: Volvo Kenworth
	Other	S: Dollar General
22A		**AL 163N, Dauphin Island Pkwy (WB)**
	Gas	N: BP
	Lodg	N: Villager Lodge
	Other	N: Family Dollar
23		**Michigan Ave, Ladd Stadium**
	Gas	N: Exxon
	Other	S: Mobile Downtown Airport✈
24		**Broad St, Duval St, Mobile**
	Gas	N: Chevron
25A		**Virginia St (EB), Texas St (WB)**
25B		**Virginia St (WB)**
	Gas	N: Shell◈
26A		**Canal St, Civic Center, Cruise Terminal (EB)**
26B		**Water St, Downtown, Mobile Conv Center, Historic District**
	Food	N: Restaurants, Sports Bar
	Lodg	N: Holiday Inn, Hampton Inn, Radisson, Ramada
	Note:	MM 27: George C Wallace Tunnel (runs under Mobile River)
27		**US 90, US 98, Government St, Battleship Pkwy, Mobile** (HAZMAT, Trucks Use US 90/98)
	Food	S: Captains Table Seafood
	Lodg	S: Best Western, Ramada Inn
	Tserv	N: Dixie Nationwide Truck Service
	Other	S: to USS Alabama, Meaher State Park
	Note:	MM 27-35: 8 mi bridge over Mobile Bay
30		**US 90, US 98, Battleship Pkwy, Battleship Park, Spanish Fort**
	Gas	S: Shell
	Food	S: Oysterella's
35A		**US 98, 90W, Daphne, Fairhope, Spanish Fort (EB)**
35B		**US 90E (EB)**
35		**US 98, 90, Daphne, Fairhope (WB)**
	Gas	N: BP, Shell S: Exxon◈, Shell, Oil
	Food	S: Arby's, Burger King, Checkers, Hooters, IHOP, Mexican Rest, McDonald's, Krystal, O'Charley's, Shoney's, Subway, Starbucks, Taco Bell, Waffle House, Wendy's

◈ = Regular Gas Stations with Diesel ▲ = RV Friendly Locations ♥ = Pet Friendly Locations
Red print shows large vehicle parking / access on site or nearby Brown Print = Campgrounds / RV PARKS

EXIT — ALABAMA

- **Lodg** S: Comfort Inn, Eastern Shore Motel, Hampton Inn, Hilton Garden Inn, Homewood Suites, Quality Inn, Microtel
- **Med** S: + Hospital
- **Other** N: Bass Pro Shop, US Post Office
  S: Home Depot, Office Depot, US Sports Academy, **Blakely State Park**

38 — AL 181, Daphne, Malbis

- **Gas** N: BP
  S: Chevron◊, Shell, Texaco
- **Food** N: David's Catfish House, ChickFilA, Cracker Barrel, Logan's Roadhouse, McDonald's, Olive Garden, Panera Bread, Ryan's Grill, Wendy's
  S: Plantation Restaurant
- **Lodg** N: Comfort Suites, Country Inn, Holiday Inn Express, La Quinta Inn♥
  S: Value Place Inn
- **TServ** N: CAT
- **Other** N: B&N, Best Buy, Dollar Tree, PetSmart♥, Walgreen's
  S: Lowe's, Sam's Club

44 — AL 59, Loxley, Bay Minette, to Gulf Shores, Beaches

- **FStop** N: Love's Travel Stop #206 (Scales)
  S: Khan Food Mart
- **TStop** N: Econ Travel Center/Shell (Scales)
- **Gas** S: Chevron, RaceWay
- **Food** N: Arby's/Love's TS, Rest/Econ TC
  S: Rest/Wind Chase Inn, Firehouse Café, Hardee's, McDonald's, Waffle House
- **Lodg** N: Bay Inn
  S: Wind Chase Inn, Days Inn
- **Other** N: Laundry/WiFi/**RVDump**/Love's TS, **RVDump**/Econ TC
  S: Auto & Truck Repair, Gulf Shore Beaches, **Gulf Breeze RV Resort▲**, **Gulf State Park**

53 — CR 64, Wilcox Rd, Robertsdale

- **TStop** N: AmBest/Oasis Travel Center/BP (Scales)
- **Gas** S: Chevron, Outpost◊
- **Food** N: Rest/FastFood/Oasis TC
  S: Café 64
- **Lodg** N: Styx River Resort
- **TWash** N: Oasis TC
- **TServ** N: Oasis TC
- **Other** N: Laundry/CB/**RVDump**/**LP**/Oasis TC
  S: **to Hilltop RV Park▲**, **Wilderness RV Park▲**

(66) — Weigh Station (WB)

(66) — AL Welcome Center (WB)
Baldwin Rest Area
(RR, Phone, Picnic, Vend)

Personal Notes

EXIT — AL / FL

NOTE: MM 66.5: Florida State Line

CENTRAL TIME ZONE

↑ ALABAMA

↓ FLORIDA

CENTRAL TIME ZONE

(1) — Inspection Station (EB)

(3) — WIM Weigh Station (Both dir)

(4) — FL Welcome Center (EB)
(RR/Fam, Ph, Pic, Vend, Pet, Info, Sec)

5 — US 90 Alt, Pensacola

- **TStop** N: Fleet Travel Center #320/Shell (Scales)
- **Gas** N: Shell, Albertson's

EXIT — FLORIDA

- **Food** N: Subway/Fleet TC
- **Other** N: Albertson's/Pharmacy, Walgreen's, **To appr 3.5mi: Drifters RV Park▲**
  S: **Leisure Lakes RV Park▲**

7 — FL 297, Pine Forest Rd, Pensacola Naval Air Station (WB)

- **Gas** N: Exxon
  S: BP, Citgo, Shell, Texaco◊
- **Food** S: Burger King, Carnley's Diner, Cracker Barrel, Figaro's Pizza, Hardee's, McDonald's, Ruby Tuesday, Sonny's BBQ, Subway, Waffle House
- **Lodg** N: Best Western, Comfort Inn, Rodeway Inn, Value Place♥
  S: Country Inn, Holiday Inn Express, Microtel, Quality Inn, Sleep Inn
- **Med** S: + Hospital
- **Other** N: **Tall Oaks RV Park▲**
  S: Carwash, Grocery, Fun Station USA, Fairgrounds, **Pensacola RV Park▲**, US Naval Air Base, **to MIL/Blue Angel Naval Rec Area▲**, **MIL/Oak Grove Park & Cottages▲**, **Leisure Lakes RV Park▲**

7A — FL 297S, Pine Forest Rd (EB)

7B — FL 297N, Pensacola (EB)

10A — US 29S, FL 95, Pensacola Blvd

- **Gas** S: RaceWay, Shell◊
- **Food** S: Burger King, Denny's, IHOP, McDonald's, Subway, Waffle House, Wendy's
- **Lodg** S: Americas Best Value Inn, Comfort Inn, Days Inn, Hospitality Inn, Howard Johnson Express♥, Palm Court, Quality Inn, Ramada Inn, Travelodge♥
- **Med** S: + Pensacola Blvd Family Care Center, + US Vets Outpatient Clinic
- **Other** S: **Lazy Days RV Campground▲**, **Hill Kelly RV Center**, **Turning Wheel RV Center**, **Leisure Time RV**, Harley Davidson of Pensacola, Greyhound, Auto Dealers

10B — US 29, FL 95, Pensacola

- **TStop** N: Fleet Travel Center #319 (Scales)
- **Gas** N: Williams, Murphy
- **Food** N: Hardee's, Sonic, Waffle House
- **Other** N: Dollar Tree, Office Depot, Tires Plus, **Walmart sc▲ to appr 2..5 mi: Drifters RV Park▲**, **Cruise America RV Rentals**

(12) — Jct I-110, Pensacola

- **Other** S: **Gulf Islands Nat'l Seashore▲**, **to MIL/Mid Bay Shores Maxwell/Gunter Recreation Area▲**

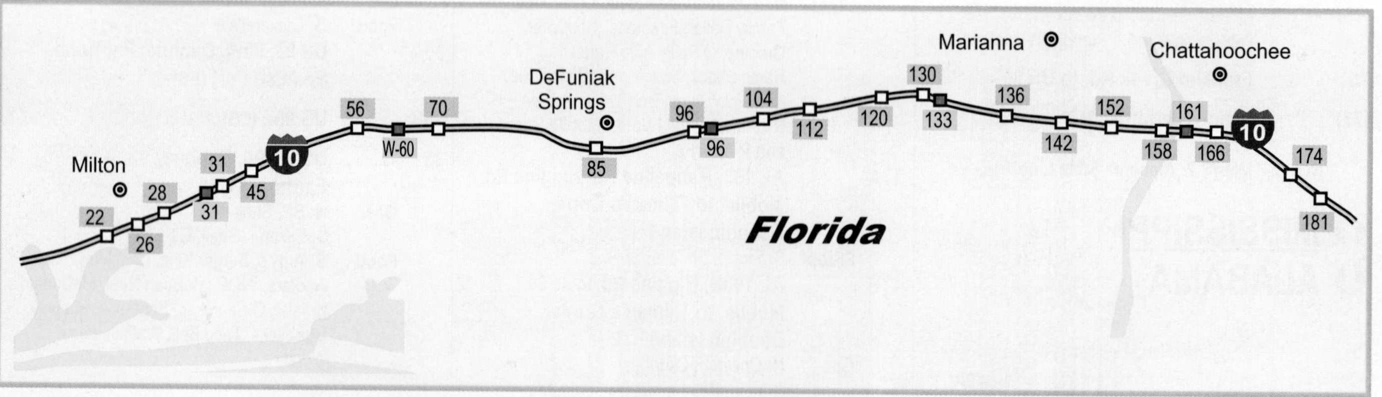

◊= Regular Gas Stations with Diesel ▲ = RV Friendly Locations ♥= Pet Friendly Locations
Red print shows large vehicle parking / access on site or nearby **Brown Print = Campgrounds / RV PARKS**

EXIT FLORIDA

13 FL 291, N Davis Hwy, to US 90, Pensacola, Univ of West Florida

Gas N: Happy Store/BP, Shell◈
Food N: Arby's, Barnhill's Buffet, Burger King, Captain D's, Denny's, McDonald's, La Hacienda Mexican Rest, Montana's BBQ, Subway, Taco Bell, Waffle House
S: Chuck E Cheese, Steak & Ale, Waffle House
Lodg N: Best Western, Comfort Inn, La Quinta Inn♥
S: Baymont Inn, Clarion Hotel, Extended Stay, Fairfield Inn, Hampton Inn, Holiday Inn Express, Motel 6♥, Red Roof Inn♥, Residence Inn, Super 8
Med N: + West Florida Hospital, + Medical Center Clinic
Other N: Albertson's, Auto Zone, CVS, Food World, **Brookhaven RV Park ▲**
S: Big 10 Tire, Firestone, Grand Slam Food & Fun, Time Out Family Rec Center, University Mall, University Mall Cinema, Pensacola Reg'l Airport ✈

17 US 90, FL 10A, Pensacola

Gas N: BP◈
S: Exxon
Food S: DQ/Exxon, Rest/Ramada Inn
Lodg S: Ramada Inn
Med N: + Scenic Hwy Family Med Center

22 FL 281, Avalon Blvd, Milton

Gas N: Tom Thumb Food Store/BP◈
S: Circle K/Shell◈
Food N: McDonald's
S: Subway/Shell, Waffle House
Lodg S: Red Roof Inn♥
Med N: + Hospital
Other **S: Avalon Landing RV Park▲, By the Bay RV Park▲**

26 CR 191, Garcon Pt Rd, Milton

FStop S: Mike's
Gas N: Circle K/Shell
S: Chevron, Citgo, Shell
Food S: DQ, Stuckey's/Chevron
Tires S: Mike's
Med N: + Hospital
Other **S: Pelican Palms RV Park▲**

28 CR 89, Ward Basin Rd, Milton

Med N: + Hospital
Other **S: to Cedar Lakes RV Park & CG▲**

(29) Santa Rosa Co Rest Area (Both dir)
(RR/Fam, Ph, Pic, Vend, Pet, Sec247)

31 FL 87, Milton, Navarre, Ft Walton Beach

TStop S: Rolling Thunder Truck Stop
FStop N: Exxon Fuel Express
Gas S: BP, Shell
Food N: Waffle House
S: Rest/FastFood/RT TS
Lodg N: Holiday Inn Express
S: Comfort Inn♥, Red Carpet Inn ♥
Other **N: Gulf Pines/Milton KOA/RVDump▲, Blackwater River State Park**, to Peter Prince Airport✈
S: Santa Rosa Naval Field ✈, Laundry/WiFi/Rolling Thunder TS

45 CR 189, Log Lake Rd, Holt

FStop N: Exprezit #743/Chevron
Other **N: Eagle's Landing RV Park▲, Blackwater River State Park**
S: to Rivers Edge RV Campground▲

EXIT FLORIDA

56 FL 85, Crestview, Niceville

FStop N: CJ Food Mart #2 Chevron
Gas N: BP◈, Mobil◈, Shell◈
S: Citgo, Exxon
Food N: Applebee's, Asian Garden, Burger King, McDonald's, Ryan's Grill, Sonny's BBQ, Starbucks
S: Arby's, **Cracker Barrel**, Hardee's, Hooters, Shoney's, Subway, Taco Bell, Waffle House, Wendy's, Whataburger
Lodg N: Country Inn, Econo Lodge
S: Best Western, Comfort Inn, Days Inn, Hampton Inn, Holiday Inn, Jameson Inn♥, Quality Inn, Super 8
Med N: + Gateway Medical Clinic
Other N: Advance Auto, Auto Zone, ATMs, Big Lots, Banks, Carwash, Days Tire & Service, Dollar General, Lowe's, Publix/Pharmacy, **Walmart sc**, Walgreen's, Carwash/Mobil, **To** Bob Sikes Airport✈
S: Auto Dealers, **to MIL**/Eglin AFB/ **FamCamp▲**

(58) Okaloosa Co Rest Area (EB)
(RR/Fam, Phone, Picnic, Vend, Pet, Sec)

(61) Okaloosa Co Rest Area (WB)
(RR/Fam, Phone, Picnic, Vend, Pet, Sec)

70 FL 285, Mossy Head, DeFuniak, to Ft Walton Beach, Niceville, Eglin Air Force Base

Gas N: Raceway
Lodg S: Rodeway Inn

85 US 331, DeFuniak Springs, Freeport

FStop S: Emerald Express #515
Gas N: Chevron, Texaco, Murphy
S: BP, Exprezit, Shell
Food N: Arby's, Burger King, McLain Family Steak House, Waffle House
S: Hardee's, KFC, McDonald's, Whataburger
Lodg N: Americas Best Value Inn, Days Inn, Sundown Inn, Super 8♥, Travelodge♥
S: Best Western♥, Comfort Inn
AServ N: Rockman's Auto Service
Med N: + Hospital, +Gateway Medical Clinic
Other N: Lowe's, Walgreen's, **Walmart sc▲**, Winn Dixie/Pharmacy, Laundromat, DeFuniak Springs Airport✈, Chautauqua Vineyard and Winery, **to 8 mi: Sunset Lake Resort, to Juniper Lake RV Campground▲, to Bass Haven Campground▲**
S: Longleaf RV Park▲, to Lazy Days RV Park▲, to Red Bay RV Park▲

96 FL 81, Ponce de Leon
Holmes Co Rest Area (FL 81, 1st Left)
S: (Both dir)
(RR/Fam, Phone, Picnic, Vend, Pet, Sec247)

FStop S: Exprezit #604
Gas N: Exxon◈
S: BP◈
Food N: Sally's Seafood Kitchen
S: FastFood/Exprezit
Lodg N: Ponce De Leon Motor Lodge & **RV Park▲**
Other N: Dollar General
S: Ponce De Leon Springs State Rec Area

104 CR 279, Caryville

EXIT FLORIDA

112 FL 79, Bonifay, Panama City Beach

Gas N: Chevron, Exxon◈, Tom Thumb/Citgo◈
Food N: Burger King, Hardee's, McDonald's, Pizza Hut, Waffle House
Lodg N: Bonifay Inn, Economy Lodge, Tivoli Inn
Med N: + Dr's Memorial Hospital
Other N: Fred's, Carwash, **LP**, Eastern Diesel & Auto Wrecker Towing & Repair Service, **Florida Springs RV Resort▲**
S: to appr 16 mi Southern Trails RV Park▲

120 FL 77, Chipley, to Panama City

Gas N: Exxon◈, Exprezit, Murphy◈
S: Exprezit, Shell
Food N: Arby's, Burger King/Exxon, KFC, McDonald's,Taco Bell, Wendy's, Waffle House, Rest/Days Inn,
Lodg N: Comfort Inn, Days Inn, Executive Inn, Holiday Inn Express, Super 8
Med N: + Hospital
Other N: CVS, Carwash, **Walmart sc▲**, **NW Florida Campground▲**, Baptist College of FL
S: Falling Waters State Rec Area▲

130 US 231, FL 75, Cottondale, Panama City

FStop N: Exprezit #702/BP
Gas N: Chevron
S: BP, Raceway
Food N: Hardee's, Subway
Other **S: Sunny Oaks RV Park▲, to appr 15mi: Pine Lake RV Park▲**

(133) Jackson Co Rest Area (Both dir)
(RR, Phone, Pic, Vend, Pet, Sec247)

136 FL 276, CR 167, Marianna

Gas N: Exprezit◈
Lodg N: Days Inn, Executive Inn
Med N: + Hospital
Other **N: to Fort Caverns State Park**
S: Sunny Oaks RV Park▲

142 FL 71, Marianna, Blountstown

FStop S: Waco #18/Sunoco, Exprezit #601
TStop N: Pilot Travel Center #374 (Scales),
S: Travel Center of America #178/BP (Scales)
Gas N: Murphy◈
S: Chevron◈
Food N: Arby's/TJCinn/Pilot TC, Burger King, Firehouse Subs, KFC/Long John Silver's, Po Folks, Ruby Tuesday, San Marcos Mexican Rest, Shoney's, Sonny's BBQ, Waffle House, **to appr 4 mi** Madison's Warehouse Rest
S: CourtesyHouseRest/PizzaHut/Popeyes/ TacoBell/TA TC, FastFood/Waco/Sunoco, FastFood/Exprezit, McDonald's,
Lodg N: Comfort Inn, Country Inn♥, Fairfield Inn, Hampton Inn, Holiday Inn, Microtel, Quality Inn♥, Super 8
S: Amer Best Value Inn♥
TServ S: TA TC/Tires
Other N: WiFi/Pilot TC, Lowe's, **Walmart sc▲**, **To appr 4mi:** Big Lots, CVS, Dollar General, Family Dollar, Fred's, Radio Shack, Winn Dixie/Pharmacy, Greyhound, **to** Marianna Muni Airport✈, **FL Caverns State Park▲, to Arrowhead Campsites & RV Sales▲**
S: Laundry/WiFi/TA TC, **Dove Rest RV & MH Park▲**

◈= Regular Gas Stations with Diesel ▲ = RV Friendly Locations ♥= Pet Friendly Locations
Red print shows large vehicle parking / access on site or nearby Brown Print = Campgrounds / RV PARKS

EXIT		FLORIDA
152		**FL 69, Grand Ridge, Blountstown**
	FStop	**N:** Golden Lariat, **5miN:** Blondie's Food & Fuel
	Gas	**N:** BP, Exxon
	Food	**N:** Rest/Golden Lariat
(155)		**WIM Weigh Station** (Both dir)
158		**CR 286, Blueberry Dr, Sneads**
	Other	**N: to appr 8 mi: Three Rivers State Park**
	Note:	**MM 160: Central / Eastern Time Zone**
(162)		**Gadsden Co Rest Area** (Both dir) (RR/Fam, Phone, Pic, Vend, Pet, Sec247)
166		**CR 270A, Chattahoochee**
	Gas	**S:** Shell◈
	Other	**S: Chattahoochee/Tallahassee W KOA▲**
174		**FL 12, Quincy, Greensboro**
	FStop	**N:** Johnson & Johnson #18/Shell
	Gas	**N:** BP
	Food	**N:** BurgerKing/J&J
	Other	**N: Beaver Lake Campground▲**
181		**FL 267, Pat Thomas Pky, Robert St, Quincy, to Tallahassee**
	Gas	**N:** Exprezit, Murphy◈ **S:** BP◈
	Lodg	**S:** Hampton Inn, Holiday Inn Express, Parkway Inn
	Med	**N:** + Hospital
	Other	**N: Walmart sc▲** **S: to Bear Creek State Park**
192		**US 90, Blue Star Hwy, Midway, Havana, to Quincy, Tallahassee**
	TStop	**N:** Flying J Travel Plaza #5054/Conoco (Scales) **S:** Pilot Travel Center #425 (Scales)
	Gas	**N:** BP
	Food	**N:** CountryMkt/FastFood/Flying J TP, **S:** Subway/Pilot TC, Waffle House
	Lodg	**N:** Comfort Suites, Howard Johnson♥ **S:** Best Western
	Other	**N:** Laundry/BarbSh/WiFi/**LP/RVDump**/FJ TP, **Camping World RV Sales/RVDump**
	Other	**S:** Laundry/WiFi/**RVDump**/Pilot TC, Midway Tire, **to Lakeside Travel RV Park▲**, **Coe Landing RV Park▲**, **Eagles Nest MH & RV Park▲**, **Williams Landing Campground▲**
(194)		**Leon Co Rest Area** (Both dir) (RR, Phone, Pic, Vend, Pet, Sec247)
196		**FL 263, Capital Circle, Tallahassee**
	Gas	**S:** Chevron◈, Shell◈, Stop N Save
	Food	**S:** Firehouse Subs, Sonic, Steak 'n Shake, Subway, Waffle House, Wendy's
	Lodg	**S:** Sleep Inn
	TServ	**S:** Seminole Truck & **RV** Service
	Other	**N: to** Tallahassee Commercial Airport✈ **S:** Capital City Harley Davidson, Home Depot, Lowe's, Museum, Winn Dixie, Zoo, Auto Dealers, Tallahassee Regional Airport✈, **S to 90: Walmart sc**
199		**US 27, FL 63, Monroe St, Tallahassee**
	Gas	**N:** Chevron, McKenzie Market◈ **S:** BP, Chevron◈, Circle K/Shell, USA
	Food	**N:** Burger King, Marie Livingston's Steak House, Taco Bell, Waffle House **S:** ChickFilA, **Cracker Barrel**, Crystal River Seafood, El Chico Rest, Long John Silver, Longhorn Steakhouse, McDonald's, Melting Pot Rest, Qdoba Mexican Rest, Red Lobster, Roadhouse Grill, Shoney's, Sonny's BBQ, Steak & Ale, Starbucks, Subway, Village Inn, Whataburger, Wendy's, Zaxby's, Rest/DI, Rest/La QI, Rest/Ramada
	Lodg	**N:** Best Inn, Comfort Inn, Fairfield Inn, Hampton Inn, Holiday Inn, Microtel, Quality Inn, Villager Inn **S:** America's Best Value Inn, Country Inn, Days Inn, Econo Lodge, Hilton Garden Inn, Howard Johnson Express, La Quinta Inn♥, Motel 6♥, Ramada Inn, Red Roof Inn♥, Super 8, Wingate Inn
	Other	**N:** Food Lion, Sam's Club, Winn Dixie, **to appr 3 mi: Big Oak RV Park▲**, **to Indian Mounds State Park** **S:** Albertson's, AutoZone, Big O Tire, B&N, CompUSA, Dollar Tree, Firestone, Publix, Petland♥, Staples, Sun Tire, Walgreen's, Tallahassee Mall, Movies 8, Capital Cinemas, AMC 20/Tall Mall, Fairgrounds & Civic Center, Northwood Animal Hospital♥
203		**US 319, FL 61, FL 261, Thomasville Rd, Tallahassee, Thomasville**
	Gas	**N:** BP◈, Chevron, Circle K/Shell, Shell, USA Gas **S:** Citgo
	Food	**N:** Applebee's, Bonefish Grill, Checker's, Georgio's Rest, McDonald's, Pizza Hut, Popeye's, Sonny's BBQ, Starbucks, Subway, Taco Bell, Waffle House, Wendy's **S:** Boston Market, Carrabba's Italian Rest, Calico Jack's Seafood Rest, ChickFilA, Italian Deli, Outback Steakhouse, Osaka Japanese Steakhouse, Outback Steakhouse, Reangthai Thai Rest, Smokey Bones BBQ, Steak 'n Shake, TGI Friday's, Ted's Montana Grill
	Lodg	**N:** Motel 6♥ **S:** Cabot Lodge, Courtyard, Hilton Garden Inn, Hampton Inn, Residence Inn, Studio Plus
	Med	**S: + Tallahassee Memorial Hospital**
	Other	**N:** Albertson's, CVS, Discount Tire, FedEx Office, Publix, Radio Shack, Walgreen's, **Walmart sc▲**, Winn Dixie, Northeast Animal Hospital♥ **S:** Advance Auto Parts, Home Depot, Newman's Auto Service, Office Depot, PetSmart♥, UPS Store
209A		**US 90W, Mahan Dr, Tallahassee**
	Gas	**S:** Circle K◈, Shell◈
	Food	**S:** Cross Creek Creekside Grill, Waffle House, Wendy's
	Lodg	**S:** Best Western, Country Inn
	Other	**S:** Cross Creek Driving Range & Par 3 Golf, **Tallahassee RV Park▲**, **Pepco RV Center**, **to appr 3 mi:** Costco, Publix,
209B		**US 90E, Mahan Dr, Monticello**
217		**FL 59, Gamble Rd, Monticello, Lloyd**
	TStop	**S:** PTP/Big Bend Travel Plaza/BP (Scales)
	Gas	**S:** Shell◈
	Food	**S:** Rest/Pizza/Big Bend TP, Subway/Shell
	Lodg	**S:** Quality Inn♥/Big Bend TP
	Other	**S:** TServ/Tires/AutoServ/Laundry/BarbSh/Big Bend TP, Lloyd CB Sales & Service
225		**US 19, FL 57, Monticello (Addt'l serv 5 mi N in Monticello)**
	TStop	**S:** Fast Track #427/Mobil
	Gas	**S:** BP, Chevron, Exxon
	Food	**S:** Arby's/Mobil, Huddle House, McDonald's/Chevron, Wendy's/Exxon
	Lodge	**S:** Days Inn, Super 8
	TServ	**S:** Interstate Towing & Repair
	Other	**N: A Camper's World▲** **S: Tallahassee East/Monticello KOA▲**
233		**CR 257, Salt Rd, Lamont, Aucilla**
	Gas	**N:** Shell◈
(233)		**Jefferson Co Rest Area** (Both dir) (RR/Fam, Phone, Pic, Pet, Vend, Sec)
241		**US 221, Greenville, Perry**
	Gas	**N:** Mobil

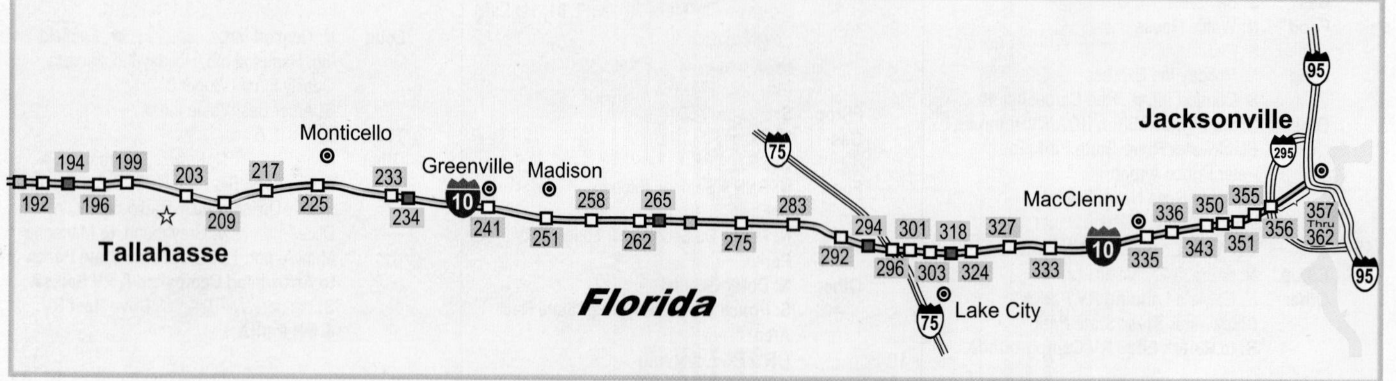

◈= Regular Gas Stations with Diesel ▲ = RV Friendly Locations ♥= Pet Friendly Locations
Red print shows large vehicle parking / access on site or nearby **Brown Print = Campgrounds / RV PARKS**

EXIT		FLORIDA
	Food	N: DQ/Mobil
251		**FL 14, Madison, Perry (Addt'l Serv 2.5 mi N in Madison)**
	Gas	N: Mobil
	Food	N: Arby's/Mobil
	Med	N: + Madison Co Memorial Hospital
	Other	N: North FL Comm College
258		**FL 53, Madison (Addt'l Serv 5 mi N in Madison)**
	TStop	N: Madison Travel Plaza/Mobil, Johnson & Johnson #5/Shell
	Food	N: Wendy's/Subway/DQ/, Burger King/ J&J TP, Denny's, Waffle House
	Lodg	N: Days Inn♥, Holiday Inn Express, Super 8 S: Deerwood Inn Resort Motel & Madison Campground▲
	TServ	N: J&J TP/Tires
	Med	N: + Madison Co Memorial Hospital
	Other	N: Laundry/WiFi/Madison TP, Laundry/BarbSh/Jimmie's TS S: Laundry/J&J, Yogi Bear's Jellystone Park & RV Resort/RVDump▲
262		**CR 255, Lee**
	TStop	S: Jimmie's Auto & Truck Plaza/Chevron, Love's Travel Stop #379
	Gas	N: Exxon◈ S: Texaco
	Food	S: Rest/Jimmie's ATP, Arby's/Love's TS, Kountry Kitchen, Red Onion Grill
	TServ	S: Jimmie's ATP
	Other	N: to Suwannee River State Park
(264)		**WIM Weigh Station (Both dir)**
(265)		**Madison Co Rest Area (Both dir) (RR/Fam, Phone, Pic, Pet, Vend, Sec)**
(271)		**Weigh Station / Agricultural Inspection Station (Both dir)**
275		**US 90, Live Oak, Lee**
	Med	S: + Hospital
	Other	N: to Suwannee State Park▲
283		**US 129, Live Oak, Jasper**
	FStop	N: Penn Oil Co, Johnson & Johnson #25
	Gas	S: BP, Chevron, Shell◈, Murphy,
	Food	S: China Buffet, Huddle House, Krystal, McDonald's, Subway, Taco Bell, Waffle House, Wendy's
	Lodg	S: Best Western, Econo Lodge, Holiday Inn Express, Royal Inn
	Med	S: + Hospital
	Other	N: to appr 4.5 mi: Spirit of the Suwannee Music Park & Campground▲ S: Lowe's, Walmart sc▲, appr 1.5 mi: CVS, Dollar General, Family Dollar, Fred's, Publix, Walgreen's, Auto Services, Duncan Tire & Auto, Vet♥
292		**CR 137, Live Oak, to Wellborn**
(294)		**Rest Area (EB) (RR, Phone, Pic, Pet, Vend, Sec)**
(295)		**Rest Area (WB) (RR/Fam, Phone, Pic, Pet, Vend, Sec)**
(296A)		**Jct I-75S, to Tampa**
(296B)		**Jct I-75N, to Valdosta, Ga**
301		**US 41, FL 100, Lake City, White Springs**
	FStop	N: Exxon

EXIT		FLORIDA
	Gas	N: BP S: Shell
	Med	S: + Hospital
	Other	N: to appr 6 mi: Kelly's RV Park▲
303		**US 441, Lake City, Fargo**
	FStop	S: S&S Food Store #37/Shell
	Gas	N: Chevron◈, Citgo, Exxon
	Lodg	S: Days Inn♥
	Med	S: + Hospital
	Other	N: Oaks 'n Pines RV Campground▲, Lake City KOA Campground/RVDump▲ S: to Lake City Muni Airport✈
(318)		**Baker Co Rest Area (Both dir) (RR/Fam, Phone, Pic, Pet, Vend, Sec)**
324		**US 90, Sanderson, Olustee**
	Gas	S: Citgo◈
327		**CR 229, Sanderson, Raiford**
333		**CR 125, Glen St Mary**
	FStop	N: Glen Fuel Stop/Citgo
335		**FL 121, MacClenny, Lake Butler**
	FStop	N: S&S Food Store #34/BP S: Exxon #454
	Gas	N: Citgo, Shell S: Raceway
	Food	N: KFC, Hardee's, McDonald's, Pizza Hut, Subway, Taco Bell, Waffle House, Wendy's, Woody's BBQ S: Burger King, China Garden
	Lodg	N: American Inn S: Econo Lodge, Travelodge
	Med	N: + MacClenny Family Care Center, S: + Northeast FL Hospital
	Other	N: Advance Auto, Food Lion, Jiffy Lube, Radio Shack, Winn Dixie, Laundromat
336		**FL 228, MacClenny, Maxville**
	Med	N: + Hospital
	Other	N: Walmart sc▲, Fireworks
343		**US 301, Baldwin, to Starke**
	TStop	S: Travel Center of America #125/Amoco (Scales), Pilot Travel Center #87 (Scales)
	Gas	S: Chevron, Citgo, Exxon
	Food	N: BBQ S: T&C Rest/Arby's/TA TC, Subway/Pilot TC, McDonald's, Waffle House,
	Lodg	S: Best Western
	TWash	S: TA TC
	TServ	S: TA TC/Tires
	Other	S: Laundry/TA TC , WiFi/Pilot TC ,
	NOTE:	**EB: On-going construction over next several years. Please refer to: www.i10northflorida.com Or call 511 to check conditions & updates.**
(350)		**FUTURE - Branan Field-Chaffee Rd Expresswayy, FL 23**
351		**FL 115C, Chaffee Rd, to Cecil Field Naval Air Station**
	FStop	N: Kangaroo Express #6032
	Gas	S: Kangaroo Express/Chevron, Kwik Chek Gas, Shell◈
	Food	N: FastFood/Kangaroo #6032 S: Cracker Barrel, King Wok Chinese, McDonald's, Perard's Pizza, Quiznos, Subway/Shell, Wendy's
	Lodg	S: Best Western, Hampton Inn, Holiday Inn Express

EXIT		FLORIDA
	Other	N: Rivers RV Service & Park▲, to Whitehouse Field NAS✈ S: Winn Dixie/Pharmacy, Carwash/Shell, to Golf Course, Herlong Airport✈, Cecil Field NAS Airport✈
	NOTE:	**MM 355: WB: Begin Call Boxes**
355		**Greeland Rd, Calhoun Rd, to Marietta**
	NOTE:	**2013-2016: Construction to relocate exit West to new Hammond Blvd & Devoe St**
	Gas	N: Exxon, Gate◈ S: Shell◈
	Food	S: Bill's Diner, Domino's Pizza,, Godfather Pizza
(356)		**Jct I-295, N to Savannah, GA; S to St Augustine**
357		**FL 103, Lane Ave, Jacksonville**
	FStop	N: Fuel Man
	Gas	N: Hess◈ S: BP◈, Shell◈
	Food	N: Andy's, Krispy Kreme/Hess, Rest/Days Inn S: Applebee's, Bono's Pit BBQ, Burger King, Denny's, Cross Creek BBQ & Steaks, Hardee's, KFC, McDonald's, Piccadilly, Shoney's
	Lodg	N: Days Inn♥, Ramada Ltd♥ S: Budget Inn, Executive Inn, Super 8
	Other	N: Blvd Tire Center, Sun Tires S: CVS, Firestone, Home Depot, Office Depot, Pep Boys Auto, Tire Kingdom, Winn Dixie, Carwash/Shell, Flea Market, Animal Hospital♥
358		**FL 111, Cassat Ave, Edgewood Ave**
	FStop	N: First Coast Energy/Amoco
	Gas	N: BP/Lil Champ, Chevron, Hess◈, Shell◈ S: RaceTrac, Sunoco
	Food	N: Burger King, Blimpie's, McDonald's, Popeye's S: Dunkin Donuts, Krispy Kreme, Taco Bell
	Other	N: AutoZone S: Discount Tire, Lowe's, Walgreen's,
359		**Lenox Ave, Edgewood Ave (WB, difficult reaccess)**
360		**FL 129, McDuff Ave, Waller St**
	Gas	S: BP, Chevron
	Food	S: Popeye's Chicken
361		**US 17S, Roosevelt Blvd (WB)**
362		**Stockton St, Riverside, Russell St**
	Gas	S: BP, Gate◈
	Med	S: + Hospital
(363)		**I-10 Begins/Ends on I-95, Ex #351B**
(364)		**Jct I-95N, to Savannah GA, Jct I-95S, to St Augustine FL**
	NOTE:	**WB: On-going construction over next several years. Please refer to: www.i10northflorida.com Or call 511 to check conditions & updates.**

FLORIDA

Begin Westbound I-10 from Jct I-95 in Jacksonville, FL to Santa Monica, CA.

◈= Regular Gas Stations with Diesel ▲ = RV Friendly Locations ♥= Pet Friendly Locations
Red print shows large vehicle parking / access on site or nearby Brown Print = Campgrounds / RV PARKS

EXIT	LOUISIANA

Begin Eastbound I-12 from Baton Rouge, LA to Jct I-10 near New Orleans, LA.

LOUISIANA

CENTRAL TIME ZONE

NOTE: I-12 Begins/Ends on I-10, Exit #159

(1A) Jct I -10E, New Orleans (WB)

1B LA 3064, Essen Ln, Baton Rouge (EB, no immed WB re-entry)
- Gas — S: RaceTrac
- Food — N: McDonald's, Subway; S: Copelands, Fast Track Hamburgers, Vincent's Italian
- Med — N: + Hospital, + E-Med Walk-in Clinic; S: + Our Lady of the Lake Med Center, LSU Medical Center
- Other — N: Albertson's, Auto Services, Carwash, Dick's Sporting Goods, Family Dollar, Jefferson Animal Hospital♥, Jiffy Lube, Plantation Tire & Auto Care, Radio Shack; S: Grocery, Walgreen's

1B to LA 73, Jefferson Hwy, Drusilla Lane (WB)
- Gas — N: Shell◈
- Food — N: Cane's, Drusilla Seafood Rest, McDonald's; S: Mr Gatti's
- Med — N: + Lake After Hours Clinic
- Other — S: Grocery, CVS

2A US 61S, Airline Hwy, to La Place
- FStop — S: S on US 61: Express 1 Stop/Shell
- Gas — S: Chevron, Circle K, Exxon◈, Airline Super Express
- Food — S: Dominos Pizza, McDonald's, Waffle House
- Lodg — S: Holiday Inn
- Other — S: Budget Truck Rental, Home Depot, Harley Davidson of Baton Rouge, Ryder Truck, UPS Store, Auto Dealers, to **Courtney's MH & RV Park▲**

2B US 61N, Airline Hwy, Baton Rouge
- FStop — N: N on US 190: Mobil Truck Stop
- Gas — N: Amoco, Chevron, Exxon◈, Shell, Albertson's
- Food — N: Applebees, **Cracker Barrel**, McDonald's, Pizza Hut/TacoBell, Shoney's, Subway, Wendy's
- Lodg — N: Days Inn, Hampton Inn, Holiday Inn, Microtel, Motel 6♥, Ramada, Sleep Inn
- Other — N: Auto Dealers, Auto Services, Albertson's, Carwash/Exxon, Dollar Tree, FedEx Office, Pep Boys, Walgreen's, Walmart Market, to Uncle Sam's Hotel, **RV & Trailer Park▲**

4 Sherwood Forest Blvd
- Gas — N: Exxon, Shell◈; S: Chevron, RaceTrac, Shell
- Food — N: Bamboo House, Burger King, Chuck E Cheese, Denny's, Jack in the Box, KFC, McDonald's, Popeye's Chicken, Sonic, Subway, Waffle House; S: Applebee's, Bayou Cajun Seafood, Pasta Garden, Piccadilly Cafeteria, Pizza Hut, Starbucks, Taco Bell, Wingstop
- Lodg — N: Crossland Inn, Red Roof Inn♥, Super 8; S: Calloway Inn, Crestwood Suites
- Other — N: Grocery, Harbor Freight, RiteAid, US Post Office; S: AT&T, CVS, Harley Davidson of Baton Rouge, Sherwood South Animal Hospital & Boarding Resort♥, Vet♥,

6 Millerville Rd
- Gas — N: Chevron◈
- Food — N: ChickFilA, Chili's, Dominos Pizza
- Other — N: Best Buy, Jiffy Lube, Lowe's, Office Depot, PetSmart♥, RiteAid, Super Target, Winn Dixie; S: Brothers Ace Hardware

NOTE: EB: Expect construction delays Exits #7 - 10, thru Nov 2011

7 LA 3245, O'Neal Ln, Baton Rouge
- Gas — N: Mobil; S: BP◈, Chevron◈, RaceTrac, Texaco
- Food — S: Subway/BP, Burger King, China King, Las Palmas Mexican, Lone Star Steak house, McDonald's, Popeye's, Pizza Hut/Taco Bell, Sonic, Subway, Waffle House, Wendy's
- Lodg — N: Comfort Suites
- TServ — N: Peterbilt
- Med — S: + Ochsner Summit Hospital, + Med Center, + Urgent Care
- Other — N: Auto Dealers, Best Buy, Hobby Lobby, Lowe's, Office Depot, Penske Truck Rental, Target, **to appr 2 mi: Night RV Park▲, Reliable RV Services & Repairs**; S: AutoZone, Cinema, Dollar General, Dollar Tree, Grocery, Radio Shack, **Walmart sc**, Walgreen's, White Oak Animal Hospital♥,

10 LA 3002, S Range Ave, LA 1034, LA 16, Denham Springs
- TStop — N: Magnolia Plaza; S: Pilot Travel Center #79 (Scales)
- Gas — N: Chevron, Cricle K, Circle K Express/Shell◈, RaceTrac, Murphy◈; S: Shell
- Food — N: Arby's, Brew-Bacher's Grill, Burger King, Cane's Rest, Cactus Café, Chili's, Dominos Pizza, Don's Seafood Hut, Fernando's Mexican Grill, IHOP, KFC, McDonald's, Mamoof's Cafe, Popeye's Chicken, Ryan's Grill, Sakura Sushi House, Sonic, Starbucks, Subway, Super Buffet, Waffle House, Wendy's; S: Subway/Pilot TC, Longhorn Steakhouse, Piccadilly's, Shoney's
- Lodg — N: Best Western, Candlewood Suites♥, Hampton Inn, Homegate Inn, Quality Inn, Travel Inn; S: Days Inn, Highland Inn♥
- Med — N: + Urgent Care Clinic
- Other — N: Advance Auto Parts, Auto Services, AutoZone, CVS, Dollar General, Dollar Tree, Family Dollar, Firestone, Grocery, Home Depot, Mobil Lube Express/Carwash, Office Depot, O'Reilly Auto Parts, Petco♥, Radio Shack, RiteAid, Stage, Tire Kingdom, **Walmart sc**, Carwash, Carwash/Chevron, Carwash/CircleK/Shell Avis RAC, Enterprise RAC, **Gulf Coast RV Rentals & Repairs, Millers RV Center Sales & Service**; S: Bass Pro Shop, Performance Tire & Automotive, Skate Heaven, Verizon, **Baton Rouge East KOA/RVDump▲**

NOTE: WB: Expect construction delays Exits #7 - 10, thru Nov 2011

12 LA 1026, Juban Rd

15 LA 447, Walker South Rd, Walker, Port Vincent
- FStop — S: Swifty's #16/Chevron
- Gas — N: Circle K/Shell, Chevron, Shell, Texaco◈, Murphy USA Express◈
- Food — N: Burger King, Dominos Pizza, Jack in the Box, La Fleurs, McDonald's, Popeye's Chicken, Sonic, Subway/Shell, Waffle House, Wendy's
- Lodg — N: La Quinta Inn
- Med — N: + Med Walk In Clinic
- Other — N: AutoZone, Pharmacy, Carwash/Shell, Dollar Tree, **Walmart sc▲**, Winn Dixie/

19 Satsuma Rd, LA 1024, Satsuma, to Livingston

22 LA 63, Frost Rd, Livingston, Frost
- Gas — N: Chevron◈, Conoco◈, Exxon,
- Food — N: Subway/Chevron, to Wayne's BBQ
- Other — N: Family Dollar, Firestone, Fireworks, Laundromat, NAPA; S: **to appr 1.5 mi: Lakeside RV Park/RVDump▲**

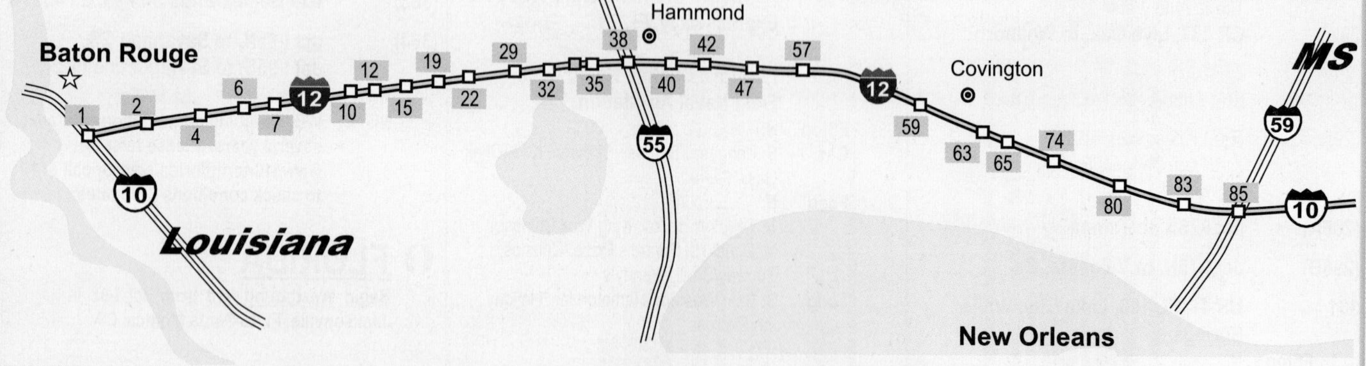

◈= Regular Gas Stations with Diesel ▲ = RV Friendly Locations ♥= Pet Friendly Locations
Red print shows large vehicle parking / access on site or nearby Brown Print = Campgrounds / RV PARKS

EXIT LOUISIANA

(28) **Rest Area** (Both dir)
(RR, Phone, Picnic)

29 **LA 441, Holden**
Other N: Berryland Campers Outlet

32 **LA 43, Hammond, to Albany, Springfield**
Gas N: Chevron, Exxon◇
S: to Citgo
Food N: Subway/Chevron
Other N: Family Dollar, Addt Serv N to US 90
S: Tickfaw State Park▲

35 **Baptist Pumpkin Center, LA 1249, Pumpkin Center Rd, Hammond**
FStop N: Jemworks Texaco
Gas N: Exxon◇
S: Chevron◇
Other N: Dollar General, Camping World SC & & Nat'l Clearance Outlet, Punkin Park Campground▲ , J&W Campground▲ ,
S: Grocery, to SavALot, U-Haul

(37) **Weigh Station** (Both dir)

(38A) **Jct I-55, S to New Orleans** (Serv x28)

(38B) **Jct I-55, N to Jackson** (Serv at x31)

40 **US 51 Bus, Railroad Ave, Veterans Ave, Hammond, Ponchatoula**
TStop S: Petro Stopping Center #19/Mobil (Scales), Pilot Travel Center #300 (Scales)
Gas N: RaceTrac◇, Circle K/Shell
S: Shell◇
Food N: Albasha Greek & Lebanese Rest, Burger King, Cane's, ChickFilA, China Garden, Church's Chicken, Don's Seafood & Steak House, IHOP, McDonald's, Pizza Hut, Ryan's Grill, Santa Fe Cattle Co, Subway, Taco Bell, Wendy's
S: IronSkilletRest/Petro SC, Arby's/TJCinn/ Pilot TC, Waffle House
Lodg N: Best Western, Motel 6, Quality Inn, Supreme Inn
S: Colonial Inn, Days Inn
TWash S: Blue Beacon Truck Wash/Petro SC
TServ S: Petro SC/Tires, Speedco
Med S: + Hospital
Other N: AMC Theatre, Amtrak, AT&T, Best Buy, BooksAMillion, Hammond Harley Davidson, Hammond Square Mall, RiteAid, Sears, TJ Maxx, Target, U-Haul, Verizon, Walgreen's, Sandy Springs Campground▲ , SE LA Univ, to Hammond Northshore Reg'l Airport✈
S: Laundry/Petro SC, Laundry/WiFi/Pilot TC, CB Radio Service, CarWash/Shell, Dollar General, Calloway Campground & RV Park▲ , to I-55 x26

42 **LA 3158, Airport Rd, to Airport, Hammond**
FStop N: PT Self Service Auto Truck Stop/ Chevron
Lodg N: Friendly Inn
TWash N: Truck Wash
Other N: to Hammond Northshore Reg'l Airport✈
S: Berryland Campers/LP

47 **LA 445, Ponchatoula, Roberts**
Other N: to appr 3 mi: Hidden Oaks Family Campground▲ , Yogi Bear Jellystone Campground▲

Personal Notes

EXIT LOUISIANA

57 **LA 1077, Covington, Goodbee, Madisonville**
Other S: T Family Campground, to Fairview Riverside State Park▲

59 **LA 21, to LA 1077, Covington, Madisonville**
Gas N: Good to Go, Kangaroo, Shell
S: Shell, Texaco
Food N: Jerks Island Grill, Lee's Hamburgers, McDonald's, Pelican Market Cafe, Subway
S: ChickFilA, Chopsticks, Cold Stone Creamery, Dominos Pizza, Longhorn Steakhouse, Quiznos, Taco Bell, Wendy's
Lodg N: Hampton Inn, La Quinta Inn♥
Med N: + Regency Hospital, + St Tammany Parrish Hospital
Other N: Carwash/Shell, CVS
S: Best Buy, Cinema, Marshall's, Ross, Target, Carwash/Texaco

60 **Pinnacle Pkwy, E Brewster Rd**

63A **New Orleans via Causeway Toll Bridge, US 190S, Covington, Mandeville, Bogalusa**
Med S: + Lakeview Reg'l Hospital
Other S: Winn Dixie/Pharmacy, LA State Hwy Patrol Post

63B **US 190N Fwy/Expy, Covington, Mandeville, Bogalusa**
Gas N: Circle K/Shell x2, Exxon◇, RaceTrac◇,
Food N: Acme Oyster House, Applebee's, Burger King, ChickFilA, Coffee Rani, Copeland's of New Orleans, Dakota Rest, IHOP, KFC, Osaka West Japanese Rest, Outback Steakhouse, Piccadilly, Romano's Macaroni Grill, Sonic, Starbucks, Subway, TGI Friday, Voodoo BBQ & Grill, Waffle House, Wendy's
Lodg N: Best Western, Comfort Inn, Country Inn, Courtyard, Hampton Inn, Holiday Inn, Residence Inn, Staybridge Suites, uper 8
Med N: + SE LA Hospital
Other N: Albertson's, Auto Dealers, ATMs, Banks, BooksAMillion, Carwash/QuikLube, CVS, FedEx Office, Home Depot, Lowe's, Office Depot, PetSmart♥, Walmart sc▲, Carwash/CircleK/Shell, Addtl Serv N to Boston St, to appr 11mi: Land-O-Pines Family Campground▲ ,

65 **LA 59, Mandeville, Abita Springs**
Gas N: Chevron◇, Shell, Danny & Clyde's
S: Kangaroo◇, Texaco◇
Food N: Sonic, Waffle House, Cafe/D&C
S: FastFood/Kangaroo, Dominos/Texaco
Other N: Tourist Info, Carwash/Shell, Carwash/ Chevron
S: Carwash/Texaco, Winn Dixie, to appr 5 mi: Fontainebleau State Park▲

74 **LA 434, Lacombe, St Tammany**
FStop S: Lacombe Chevron Travel Center
Food S: Subway/Lacombe TC
Med N: + LA Medical Center & Heart Hospital

80 **Airport Dr, Northshore Blvd**
Gas N: Kangaroo
S: Chevron, Shell◇, Sam's
Food N: IHOP, Sonic
S: Burger King, ChickFilA, Chili's, CC's Seafood, Chuck E Cheese's, McDonald's, Olive Garden, Starbucks, Subway, Taco Bell, Uni Sushi Bar, Wendy's
Lodg N: Comfort Inn
S: La Quinta Inn♥
Other N: PetSmart♥, Target, to Camp Villere Nat'l Guard Center, Slidell Airport✈
S: Advance Auto, Best Buy, Dollar Tree, Goodyear, Grand Theatres 16, Home Depot, Office Depot, Sam's Club, Walmart sc, North Shore Square Mall

83 **US 11, Pearl River, Slidell**
FStop N: Kangaroo Express #3744/Chevron
S: Ride USA/Jubilee Express #4815/ Speedway Truck Stop #9063
Gas N: Cracker Barrel Gas, Exxon◇
S: Shell◇
Food N: Bad to the Bone BBQ, Burger King, CiCi's Pizza, McDonald's, Waffle House
S: Subway/Ride USA
Lodg N: Best Western
Med S: + Hospital
Other N: Bowling USA, Dollar General, Mike's Hardware, Winn Dixie
S: U-Haul/Ride USA

(85A) **Jct I-10W, to New Orleans**

(85B) **Jct I-59N, to Hattiesburg**

(85C) **Jct I-10E, to Bay St Louis** (Left Exit)

NOTE: **I-12 Begins / Ends on I-10, Exit #267**

CENTRAL TIME ZONE

LOUISIANA

Begin Westbound I-12 from Jct I-10 in Slidell, LA to Jct I-10, in Baton Rouge, LA.

◇= Regular Gas Stations with Diesel ▲ = RV Friendly Locations ♥= Pet Friendly Locations
Red print shows large vehicle parking / access on site or nearby Brown Print = Campgrounds / RV PARKS

EXIT	MONTANA

Begin Southbound I-15 from the Canada / MT border, to Jct I-8 in San Diego, CA.

CANADA

(1) **in Canada, MT Weigh Station (Both dir)**

MONTANA

MOUNTAIN TIME ZONE

(398) **MT / US / CANADA BORDER**

397 **Loop Rd, 3rd Ave, Sweetgrass**
Rest Area (SB) (Open All Yr)
W: (RR, Phone, Picnic, RVDump)
- Gas: W: Sinclair
- Other: W: Duty Free Americas Shops, US Post Office, Ross Int'l Airport✈,

394 **McVey Rd, Ranch Acc, Sunburst**

389 **MT 552, 9 Mile Rd, Sunburst**
- Gas: W: Gas◈
- Other: W: Laundromat, Prairie Market, US Post Office, **Sunburst RV Park▲**, Sunburst Airport✈,

385 **Swayze Rd, Sunburst**

379 **MT 215, MT 343, Kevin, Oilmont**
- Food: W: 4 Corner's Café

373 **Potter Rd, Kevin**

369 **Bronken Rd, Shelby**

(367) **Weigh Station (SB)**

364 **Bus Loop 15, Shelby**
- Lodg: E: Shelby Motel, Totem Motel
- Med: **E: + Marius Medical Center**
- Other: E: Acc to #363 E Serv, **Lewis & Clark RV Park/RVDump▲**, **Lake Shel-Oole Park/RVDump▲**
  W: Shelby Airport✈

363 **US 2, I-15 Bus, Shelby, Cut Bank, Port of Shelby**
- TStop: E: Town Pump Travel Plaza #8926/ Pilot #909/Exxon (Scales)
- Gas: E: Conoco, Main St Conv, Noon's
- Food: E: Subway/CountrySkillet/Deli/Town Pump, Dixie Inn, Dash Inn, Pizza Hut, South of the Border Café, The Griddle
  W: McDonald's
- Lodg: E: Comfort Inn♥, Crossroads Inn♥, Glacier Motel, Sherlock Motel, Shelby Motel, Totem Motel
- Med: **E: + Marias Heathcare Clinic**
- Other: E: Laundry/WiFi/**Casino**/**RVDump**/Town Pump TP, Marias Museum of History & Art, Albertson's, Amtrak, CarQuest, Radio Shack, Taylor's True Value Hardware, U-Haul, US Post Office, **Lake Shel-Oole Park/RVDump▲**, **Glacier RV Park/RVDump▲**, **to Williamson Park Campground▲**,
  W: Pamida Pharmacy, Shelby Airport✈, **to Glacier Natl'l Park, to appr 23mi: Riverview RV Park▲**

(361) **Parking Area (NB)**

358 **Lincoln Rd, to Marias Valley Rd, Golf Course Rd, Shelby**

352 **Bullhead Rd, Conrad**
- Other: W: Zoomer Trucks

348 **MT 44, Valier Hwy, Conrad**

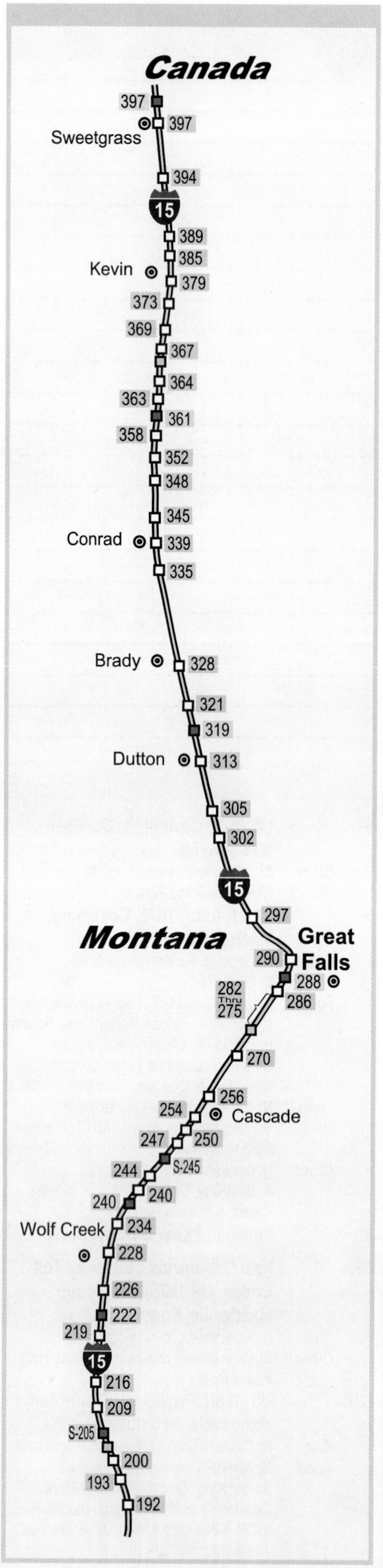

Canada
397 Sweetgrass 397 394 389 385 Kevin 379 373 369 367 364 363 361 358 352 348 345 Conrad 339 335 Brady 328 321 319 Dutton 313 305 302 297
Montana
Great Falls 290 288 282 Thru 275 286 270 256 254 Cascade 247 250 244 S-245 240 240 Wolf Creek 234 228 226 222 219 216 209 S-205 200 193 192

EXIT	MONTANA

345 **MT 366, Ledger Rd, to US 91, Conrad, to Tiber Dam**

339 **I-15 Bus Lp, US 91, MT 218, Solid Rd, Conrad**
- TStop: W: Town Pump #8929/Exxon
- Gas: W: Cenex◈, Dan's Gas & Tire Service, MRC
- Food: W: Deli/Subway/Town Pump, Arby's, A&W, Home Café, Home Cafe, House of Pizza, Joe's Family Steakhouse, Keg Family Rest
- Lodg: W: Super 8/Town Pump, Conrad Motel, Northgate Motel
- TWash: W: Robo TW
- Med: **W: + Pondera Medical Center**
- Other: W: Laundry/**Casino**/Town Pump, IGA, Pharmacy, U-Haul/Dan's Tire Service, Conrad Tire Co, Conrad Airport✈, Pondera Golf Club, **Pondera RV Park▲**

335 **Midway Rd, to Bus Lp 15, US 91, Conrad (Use 15Bus to access serv for Exit #339, approx 5 mi)**

328 **MT 365, Central Ave, Brady**
- Other: W: US Post Office

321 **Collins Rd, 24th Rd NE, Dutton**

(319) **Teton River Rest Area (Both dir) (RR, Phone, Picnic, Pet) (Open All Yr)**

313 **MT 221, MT 379, Main St, Dutton, to Choteau**
- Gas: W: Johnson's Conoco & Conv Store
- Food: W: Café Dutton
- Other: W: MVC/Tires, **to 20mi: Choteau KOA▲**

305 **Bozeman**

302 **MT 431, Power**
- Gas: W: Mountain View Co-Op

297 **Anderson Rd, Vaugh S Frontage Rd, Power, Gordon**

290 **US 89N, MT 200W, Power, Vaugh, Vaugh S Frontage Rd, to Missoula, Choteau**
- FStop: W: Valley Country Store/Sinclair
- Gas: W: Exxon◈,
- Food: W: Smoke Haus Grill & Deli
- Other: W: **RVDump/LP**/Valley CS

(288) **Parking Area (Both dir)**

286 **Manchester Rd, Vaughn Frontage Rd, Power**
- Food: W: Cattlemen's Cut Supper Club, Mary's Midway **Casino** & Rest

282 **NW ByP, to US 87N, Great Falls (SB, No rentry) (Serv 3-4mi E)**
- Gas: E: Holiday Station Store, On Your Way, Town Pump, Albertson's, Sam's Club
- Food: E: Arby's, 3D Int'l Rest, Burger King, Dante's, McDonald's, Peking Garden West, Pizza Hut, Subway, Taco Bell
- Lodg: E: Days Inn♥
- TServ: E: Bouma Truck Sales, I State Truck Center/Freightliner, Swain's Spring Service
- TWash: E: Big Sky TW
- Other: E: Albertson's, Ace Hardware, Checker Auto Parts, Dollar Tree, Fireworks, Kmart, O'Reilly Auto Parts, Sam's Club, ShopKO, Staples, Tire-Rama, Walgreen's, **Walmart sc**, Westgate Mall, **Northern Energy PropaneLP**

◈= Regular Gas Stations with Diesel ▲ = RV Friendly Locations ♥= Pet Friendly Locations
Red print shows large vehicle parking / access on site or nearby Brown Print = Campgrounds / RV PARKS

EXIT		MONTANA
280		**Central Ave W, I-15Bus, to US 87N, Great Falls**
	Gas	E: Conoco, Mini Mart
	Food	E: Double Barrel Cafe, Ford's Drive In, Hardee's, KFC, Papa John's
	Lodg	E: Alberta Motel, Best Western, Central Motel, Days Inn, Quality Inn♥, Starlit Motel, Staybridge Suites, Triple Crown Motor Inn♥
	Other	E: Bridgestone Tire, NAPA, Auto Dealers, U-Haul, Formula Fun Raceway, Great Falls Vet Service♥, **to** Electric City Speedway, Malmstrom AFB, Great Falls Civic Center, Childrens Museum,
278		**US 89S, MT 200E, I-15 Bus, 10th Ave S, Great Falls (Loads over 12' wide not permitted)**
	Gas	E: Cenex◈, Conoco, Exxon, Holiday Station, Sinclair◈
	Food	E: Applebee's, Arby's, Burger King, China Town, Classic 50's Diner, Country Kitchen, Elmer's Pancake & Steak House, DQ, Fuddrucker's, Golden Corral, Hardee's, Howard's Pizza, JB's Rest, KFC, McDonald's, On the Border, Papa John's, Perkins, Pizza Hut, Prime Cut Rest, Romano's Macaroni Grill, Starbucks, Subway, Taco Bell, Taco del Mar, Tony Roma's, TGI Friday's, Willow Creek Steakhouse, Wendy's
	Lodg	E: Best Western, Budget Inn, Comfort Inn, Collins Mansion B&B, Extended Stay America♥, Fairfield Inn, Hampton Inn♥, Hilton Garden Inn, Holiday Inn Express, Holiday Inn♥, La Quinta Inn♥, Motel 6♥, O'Haire Motor Inn, Super 8, Town House Inn♥
	Med	E: **+ Central MT Hospital, + Great Falls Immed Care Center**
	Other	E: Albertson's, Ace Hardware, Auto Dealer, B&N, Big O Tires, Carmike 10, Checker Auto Parts, Dollar Tree, Enterprise RAC, Firestone, Home Depot, Kmart, NAPA, Osco Drug, PetCo♥, Smith Food & Drug, Target/Pharmacy, Tire Rama, UPS Store, US Post Office, Verizon, Walgreen's, Holiday Village Mall, College of Great Falls, Fleet Maintenance Service-Trucks, Cars & **RV, Dick's RV Park▲, Travel Time RV Center, McCollum Modern RV's, RVDump**/Sinclair, **RVDump**/Holiday, **to MIL/Gateway FamCamp**/Malmstrom AFB▲, **to Giant Springs Heritage State Park, to Great Falls KOA▲**, W: Great Falls Int'l Airport✈
277		**31st St, Great Falls Int'l Airport**
	TStop	E: Flying J Travel Plaza #5203 (Scales), Town Pump/Pilot #917/Conoco (Scales)
	Food	E: Rest/FJ TP, Subway/TP
	Lodg	E: Crystal Inn
	Other	E: Laundry/**Casino**/WiFi/**LP/RVDump**/ FJ TP, Laundry/**Casino**/TP/Pilot W: Great Falls Int'l Airport✈
(275)		**Weigh Station (NB)**
270		**Center St, MT 330, Cascade, Ulm**
	Gas	E: Conoco◈
256		**MT 68, Simms Cascade Rd, 1st St N, Cascade**
	Gas	E: Sinclair
	Food	E: Pizza, Café/Badger Motel
	Lodg	E: A&C Motel, Badger Motel
254		**MT 68, 1st St S, Cascade (Access to Ex #256 Serv)**
250		**Local Access**
247		**Old US 91, Frontage Rd, Hardy Creek, Cascade**
(245)		**Scenic View (SB)**
244		**Old US 91, Frontage Rd, Canyon Access, Cascade**
	Other	W: **Rosie's Missouri Inn RV Park▲**
240		**Bald Eagle Dr, Cascade, Dearborn**
	Food	W: Dearborn Country Inn
	Lodg	W: Dearborn Country Inn & Resort & **RV Park▲**
(240)		**Dearborn Rest Area (Both dir) (RR, Phone, Picnic, Pet) (Open All Year)**
234		**Bridge St, Wolf Creek, Craig**
	Gas	E: O'Connell's Store
	Food	E: Izaak's, Trout Shop Cafe
	Lodg	E: Flyway Ranch, Trout Shop Lodge
	Other	E: Choteau Dinosaur Museum
228		**US 287N, Wolf Creek, to Augusta, Choteau**
	Lodg	W: Bungalow Bed & Breakfast
226		**MT 434, Frontage Rd, Wolf Creek**
	Gas	E: Canyon Store/Exxon◈
	Food	E: Oasis Cafe W: Frenchman Café & Saloon
	Lodg	E: Frenchy's Motel & Trailer/RV
	Other	E: Montana River Outfitters/FishTrips/ Tours/FlyShop/Lodging/**RVSites▲**, US Post Office
(222)		**Lyons Creek Parking Area (Both dir)**
219		**Recreation Rd, Canyon Creek, Spring Creek (NB, no re-ntry)**
216		**Chevallier Dr, Canyon Cr, Sieben**
209		**Gates of the Mountains Rd, Wolf Creek, Gates of the Mtn Rec Area**
(205)		**Helena Turn Out (SB)**
(202)		**Weigh Station (SB)**
200		**MT 279, MT 453, Lincoln Rd, Helena**
	Gas	W: Sinclair◈
	Food	E: Grub Stake
	Other	E: Erickson Veterinary Service♥ W: Montana Hams, **Preferred RV Center, Lincoln Rd RV Park/RVDump▲, to appr 4 mi: Helena Campground & RV Park▲**
193		**I-15 Bus, Cedar St, to Washington St, Custer Ave, Helena**
	Gas	W: Conoco◈, Exxon◈, Sinclair◈, Jolly O's Gas n Go
	Food	E: Hardee's, IHOP, Romano's Macaroni Grill W: Applebee's, Arby's, Godfather's Pizza, Jade Garden, McDonald's, Perkins, Pizza Hut, Subway, Taco Bell, Taco John's
	Lodg	W: Quality Inn, Wingate Inn♥
	Other	E: Costco, Home Depot, Hertz RAC, Verizon, Whalen Tire, Avis RAC, Helena Reg'l Airport✈ W: Albertson's, Auto Zone, Budget Truck Rental, CarQuest, Checker Auto Parts, Dollar Tree, Helena Veterinary Service♥, Jiffy Lube, Kmart, NAPA, O'Reilly Auto Parts, PetCo♥, **Preferred Auto & RV Center**, ShopKO, Target, Tire-Rama, UPS Store, US Post Office, Verizon, Auto Service/Exxon, Carwash, Bill RobertsMuni Golf Course
192B		**US 12W, US 287W, Prospect Ave, Helena, Capitol Area, (NB)**
192A		**US 12E, US 287E, Prospect Ave, Helena, Capitol Area (NB)**
192		**US 12, US 287, Prospect Ave, Helena, Capitol Area (SB)**
	TStop	E: High Country Travel Plaza/Conoco
	Gas	W: TownPump/Exxon◈, Sinclair, Albertson's, Safeway
	Food	E: Rest/High Country TP, Burger King, Golden Corral, Pizza Hut, Subway W: DQ, KFC, JB's Rest, McDonald's, Overland Express, Romano's Macaroni Grill, Starbucks, Taco Treat, Village Inn Pizza, Wendy's
	Lodg	E: Hampton Inn W: Comfort Inn, Days Inn♥, Fairfield Inn, Guest House Inn, Holiday Inn Express, Howard Johnson, Jorgensen's Inn, Motel 6♥, Red Lion Hotel, Shilo Inn, Super 8, to The Barrister B&B, Sanders B&B
	TWash	E: High Country TP
	TServ	E: R&R Diesel Repair, J&D Truck Repair
	Med	W: **+ St Peter's Hospital, + Shodair Children's Hospital**
	Other	E: Laundry/**Casino/RVDump/LP**/High Country TP, J&D Truck & Auto Repair & Service/**RVDump,** Auto Dealers, Enterprise RAC, Home Depot, J&D Truck/NAPA, Les Schwab Tires, Safeway, Staples, **Walmart sc**, Rocky Mtn RV & Auto Glass, **Montana RV Center, D&D RV Center, Buzz Inn RV Park & Campground▲**, **MT State Hwy Patrol Post**, Casinos, **to Kim's Marina & RV Resort▲** W: Albertson's, CVS, Goodyear, Osco, Capital Hill Mall, Safeway/Pharmacy, Tire Factory, U-Haul, Walgreen's, Carwash, Last Chance Gulch Tour, State Capitol, **Capital RV Center, to** Fort William Henry Harrison
190		**Stirrup Dr**
187		**MT 518, Frontage Rd, Clancy, Montana City**
	Gas	W: Elk Horn Mtn Inn/Cenex◈
	Food	E: Hugo's Pizza W: Hardware Cafe, Montana City Grill & Saloon
	Lodg	W: Elk Horn Mountain Inn♥
	Other	W: Carwash, Casinos
182		**Legal Tender Ln, Clancy**
	Food	W: Legal Tender Restaurant
	Other	E: **Alhambra RV Park▲**
(178)		**Jefferson City Rest Area (Both dir) (RR, Phone, Pic, Pet) (Open 4/15-11/15)**
176		**Main St, Clancy, Jefferson City**
	Other	E: Tizer Botanic Gardens
(174)		**Chain Up Area (Both dir)**
(168)		**Chain Up Area (Both dir)**
164		**MT 69, Main St, Boulder**
	FStop	E: Town Pump #310/Exxon

◈ = **Regular Gas Stations with Diesel** ▲ = **RV Friendly Locations** ♥ = **Pet Friendly Locations**
Red print shows large vehicle parking / access on site or nearby **Brown Print = Campgrounds / RV PARKS**

EXIT — MONTANA

Food E: Deli/Town Pump, Elkhorn Café & Supper Club, Bear Claw, DQ, Mountain Good Rest, Gator's Pizza
Lodg E: Castoria Inn, O-Z Motel
Other E: Lucky Lil's Casino/TP, **RC RV Park▲**, **RVDump**/Boulder City Park, Ace Hardware, Grocery, US Post Office, **To appr 3 mi:** Boulder Airport✈, Boulder Hot Springs Inn & Spa

(161) Boulder Parking Area (NB)

160 **Galena Gulch Rd, Boulder**

156 **Basin, Cataract Creek Rd, Clancy**
Other E: Earth Angel Health Radon Mine, Merry Widow Health Mine/**RVCamping▲**, Basin Creek Pottery & Gallery & Guest House

151 **Boulder River Rd, Boulder, Bernice, Bear Gulch Access**

(148) **Chain Up Area** (Both dir)

(143) **Chain Up Area** (Both dir)

138 **Lowland Rd, Boulder, Elk Park**

134 **Woodville**

NOTE: MM 133: Continental Divide, Elev 6368'

(130) Scenic Overlook (SB)

NOTE: I-15N below runs with I-90 for 8 mi.. Exit #'s follow I-15.

(129/227) **Jct I-90E to Billings, Jct I-15S / I-90W to Butte**

127A **I-15 Bus S, Harrison Ave, Butte (NB)**

127B **I-15 Bus N, Harrison Ave, Butte (NB)**

127 **I-15 Bus, Harrison Ave, Butte (SB)**
Gas E: Thriftway/Conoco◈, TownPump/Exxon◈, Sinclair
W: Cenex◈, Thriftway/Conoco, Town Pump/Exxon◈
Food E: 4 B's Rest, Arbys, Burger King, DQ, Godfather's, KFC, MacKenzie River Pizza McDonald's, Perkins, Taco Bell, Wendy's
W: Denny's, DQ, Dominos Pizza, Hanging 5 Family Rest, L&D Chinese Buffet, Papa John's Pizza, Papa Murphy's Take n Bake, Pork Chop John's, Quiznos
Lodg E: Best Western, Comfort Inn, Hampton Inn, Super 8
W: Butte War Bonnet Hotel, Comfort Inn, Days Inn, Holiday Inn Express, Red Lion Hotel
TServ W: Milo's Auto Truck & RV Repair
Other E: **RVDump**/Town Pump, Casinos, Auto Dealers, American Car Care Center/Tires, Animal Medical Clinic♥, Budget RAC, Bugs n Bullets Sports Shop, Dollar Tree, Enterprise RAC, Grocery, Highland View Golf Course, Kmart, Staples, St Francis Veterinary Hospital♥, **Walmart sc**, Our Lady of the Rockies, Butte Plaza Mall, Bert Mooney Airport✈, **Rocky Mountain RV Sales & Service, Al's RV Center**
W: Ace Hardware, Albertson's, Amherst Animal Hospital♥, Casinos, Butte Civic Center, CVS, Checker Auto Parts, NAPA, O'Reilly Auto Parts, Safeway/Pharmacy, Tires, The Stone Fly Fly Shop, UPS Store, U-Haul, Whalen Tire, Animal Hospital♥, Carwash/Cenex, Carwash, Laundromat

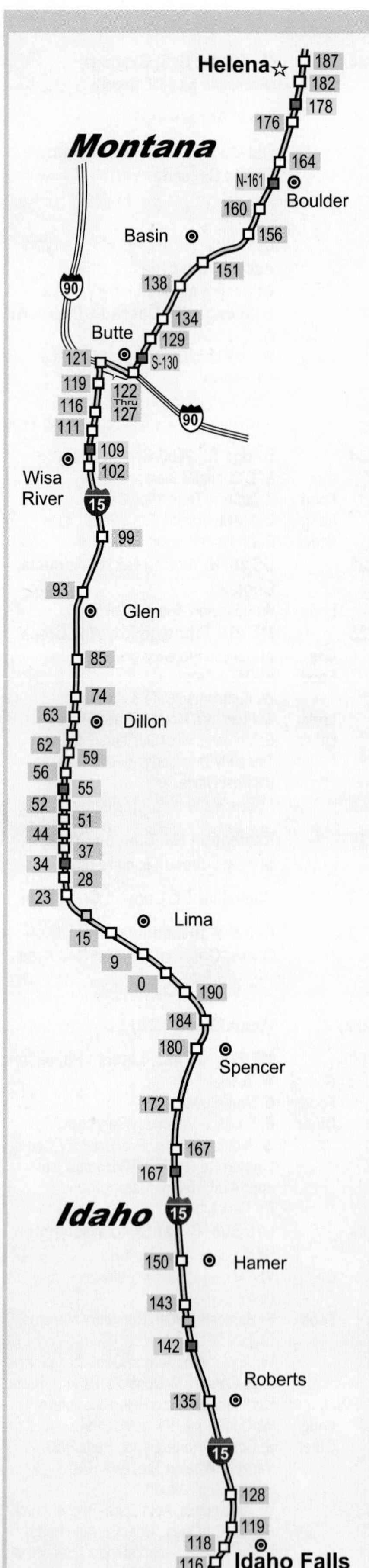

EXIT — MONTANA

126 **Montana St, Butte**
Gas W: Thriftway/Conoco, Town Pump/Exxon◈
Food W: Bonanza Steakhouse, Jokers Wild Casino & Restaurant
Lodg W: Eddy's Motel
Med W: + St James Healthcare
Other W: **Butte KOA/RVDump▲**, Budget Truck Rental, Les Schwab Tires, Safeway, Auto Services, U-Haul

(124) **Jct I-115, Butte City Center, Harrison Ave, Montana St (NB)**

122 **MT 276, Butte, Rocker**
TStop E: Flying J Travel Plaza #5130 (Scales)
W: Town Pump Travel Plaza#560/ Pilot #908/Conoco
Food E: Thad'sRest/FJ TP
W: Arby's/Subway/McDonald's/TP Pilot
Lodg E: Rocker Inn
W: Motel 6♥
TServ E: Rocker Repair
Other E: **Casino**/Laundry/WiFi/FJ TP
W: Laundry/**Casino**/**LP**/WiFi/TP Pilot TP, **2 Bar Lazy H RV Park▲**,

(122) **Weigh Station** (Both dir)

(121/219) **Jct I-90W to Missoula, I-15S to Idaho Falls, I-15N/I-90E to Butte**

NOTE: I-15 above runs with I-90 for 8 mi. Exit #'s follow I-15.

119 **German Gulch Rd, Butte, Silver Bow, Port of MT Hub Access**
Other W: Silver Bow Drive-In

116 **Buxton Rd, Butte, Buxton**

NOTE: MM 112: Continental Divide, Elev 5879'

111 **Divide Creek Rd, Divide, Feely**

(109) **Divide Rest Area (Both dir)** (RR, Phone, Pic, Pet) (Open All Year)

102 **MT 43, Divide, Wisdom**
Other W: US Post Office

99 **Moose Creek Rd, Divide**

93 **Frontage Rd, Twin Bridges, to MT 361, Melrose**
Gas W: Gas◈/Melrose Bar & Cafe
Food W: Hitching Post, Melrose Bar & Café
Lodg W: Pioneer Mtn Cabins/Melrose B&C, Sportman Motel♥, Cabins & **RV Park▲**

85 **Rock Creek Rd, Dillon, Glen**

74 **Birch Creek Rd, Dillon, Apex**

63 **MT 41, I-15 Bus Lp, US 91, Montana St, Dillon, Twin Bridges**
FStop E: Rocky Mtn Supply/Cenex
TStop E: Town Pump #360/Exxon
Gas E: Phillips 66◈, Safeway
Food E: KFC/TP, McDonald's, Pizza Hut, Subway
Lodg E: Best Western, Comfort Inn♥, Guest House Inn♥, Motel 6♥, Sundowner Motel♥, Super 8
Med E: + to Hospital
Other E: **RVDump/LP**/Casino/Cenex, American Car Care Center, Auto Dealers, CarQuest, Cinema, Les Schwab Tire, O'Reilly Auto Parts, Safeway/Pharmacy, Yamaha, Carwash, Museums, Carwash/P66, Dillon Animal Hospital♥,
W: Dillon KOA/**RVDump▲**

◈= Regular Gas Stations with Diesel ▲ = RV Friendly Locations ♥= Pet Friendly Locations
Red print shows large vehicle parking / access on site or nearby Brown Print = Campgrounds / RV PARKS

EXIT		MT / ID
62		**Bus Lp 15, S Atlantic St, Dillon** (Acc to Ex #63 Serv)
	Gas	E: Exxon
	Food	E: Rest/Crosswinds Motel, Artic Circle, Sparky's, Taco John
	Lodg	E: Crosswinds Motel, Creston Motel, Quality Inn, Rusty Duck
	Med	E: + Barrett Memorial Hospital
	Other	E: Southside RV Park/RVDump▲ W: Dillon KOA/RVDump▲
59		**MT 278, Dillon, Jackson, Wisdom**
	Other	W: Countryside RV Park/RVDump▲ , To appr 21 mi: Bannack State Park▲
56		**Rebich Lane, Dillon, Barretts**
52		**Grasshopper Creek**
51		**Dalys** (SB) (No reaccess)
44		**MT 324, Dillon, Clark Canyon Reservoir**
	Other	E: to appr 1 mi: Armstead RV Park/ RVDump▲ , to Beaverhead Marina & RV Park/RVDump▲ , Clark Canyon Reservoir Park
37		**Red Rock Rd, Dillon**
(34)		**Parking Area** (Both dir) (RR)
29		**Kidd**
23		**Old US 91, Main St, Lima, Dell**
	Gas	E: Cenex◈
	Food	E: Yesterday's Cafe
	Lodg	E: Stockyard Inn
	Other	W: Dell Flight Strip
(16)		**Weigh Station** (Both dir)
15		**Bailey St, Lima**
	Gas	E: Exxon◈
	Food	E: Jan's Cafe & Cabins
	Lodg	E: Mountain View Motel & RV Park▲
	Med	E: + Ambulance Service
	Other	E: Auto Repair, Tire Repair, US Post Office
9		**Snowline**
0		**MT 509, Lima, Monida**
	NOTE:	MM 0: Monida Pass - Elev 6870'

MOUNTAIN TIME ZONE

⬆ MONTANA
⬇ IDAHO

MOUNTAIN TIME ZONE

EXIT		IDAHO
	NOTE:	MM 196: Montana State Line
190		**Old Hwy 91, Spencer, Humphrey**
184		**W Camas Creek Rd, Spencer, Stoddard Creek Area, Old Beaver**
	Other	E: Camping▲ W: Stoddard Creek Camping▲
180		**Old Hwy 91, Spencer**
	Food	E: Cafe W: Spencer Bar & Grill
	Lodg	W: Spencer Camping Cabins
	Other	W: Spencer RV Park▲
172		**Modoc Rd, US Sheep Experiment Station, Dubois**
167		**ID 22, CR A2, Dubois, Arco** Rest Area (Both dir) (CLOSED in Winter) E: (RR, Phones, Picnic)
	FStop	E: Clark Co True Value/P66, Ike's 66
	TStop	E: Scoggins Exxon
	Food	E: Opal Mine Café, Tacos Tamazula
	Lodg	E: Crossroads Motel, Hernandez Motel
	TServ	E: Scoggins
	Other	E: LP/Exxon, LP/P66, Scoggins RV Park/RVDump▲ , US Post Office, Dubois Muni Airport✈
150		**2100 North Rd, Hamer, Camas**
	Food	E: Corner Bar & Cafe
143		**ID 33, ID 28N, Terreton, to Mud Lake, to US 20, Rexburg**
(143)		**Weigh Station** (Both dir)
(142)		**Parking Area/Hist Site** (Both dir)
135		**ID 48E, Roberts**
	TStop	E: Teton Truck Stop/Tesoro
	Food	E: Rest/Teton TS
	Other	E: LP/Tesoro, Western Wings RV Park▲
128		**County Line Rd, Osgood Area**
	Gas	E: Sinclair◈
119		**US 20E, Idaho Falls, Rigby, W Yellowstone, Rexburg, Yellowstone National Park**
	FStop	E: Gas N Grub Fuel Stop/Sinclair (Scales)
	Gas	W: Shell
	Food	E: Chili's, Denny's, JB's Rest, Jaker's Rest, Outback Steakhouse, Rutabaga's Rest, Sandpiper Rest, Rest/QI, Rest/Shilo Inn
	Lodg	E: Best Western (2), Comfort Inn, Days Inn, Guest House Inn, Motel 6♥, Quality Inn, Shilo Inn, Super 8
	TServ	E: Rumble's Diesel
	Other	E: LP/GasNGrub, Idaho Falls KOA▲ , Snake River RV Park & Campground/ KOA▲ , ID State Hwy Patrol Post W: Fanning Field, Idaho Falls Reg'l Airport✈
118		**US 20W, Broadway St, Idaho Falls Arco, Mountain Home, US 91S**
	TStop	E: CFN/KJ's Kicks66/P66
	Gas	W: Chevron◈, Exxon, Shaka's/Flying J◈, Phillips 66◈, Sinclair◈
	Food	E: FastFood/KJ's, Artic Circle, Chili's, Applebee's, Domino's Pizza, Hometown Kitchen, Jack in the Box, Smitty's Pancake & Steak House, Starbucks, Wendy's W: Burger King, DQ, Jack in the Box, McDonald's/Sinclair, Pizza Hut, Subway
	Lodg	E: Fairfield Inn, Hilton Garden Inn, Le Ritz Hotel W: Comfort Inn, Motel West
	Med	E: + Hospital
	Other	E: American RV & Marine, Auto Dealers, Harley Davidson, Walmart sc, Idaho Falls KOA/RVDump▲ W: Albertson's, Auto Zone, Checker Auto Parts, RiteAid, Carwash/P66
116		**I-15 Bus N, US 26E, Sunnyside Rd, S Idaho Falls, Ammon, Jackson**
	Other	E: to appr 2 mi: Sunnyside Acres MHC & RV Park▲
113		**US 26E, Idaho Falls, Shelley, Grand Teton National Park**
	TStop	E: Yellowstone Truck Stop/Exxon (Scales), Dad's 113 Travel Center/Sinclair
	Food	E: Rest/FastFood/Yellowstone TS, Rest/FastFood/Dad's TC
	Lodg	E: Targee Inn & RV Park/RVDump▲
	TWash	E: Dad's TC
	TServ	E: Yellowstone TS/Tires, Lake City Trucks, Lindsay Truck & Automotive & Towing, Peterbilt, Schow's Truck Center, Dad's Truck & Trailer Sales/Dad's
	Med	E: + Hospital
	Other	E: Laundry/LP/RVDump/Yellowstone TS, Laundry/WiFi/RVDump/Dad's TC, Army Surplus Warehouse, Sunnyside Acres Park/RVDump▲
108		**1250 North Rd, Shelley**
	Other	E: N Bingham Co Park/RVDump
(101)		**Blackfoot Rest Area** (Both dir) (RR, Phones, Picnic, Vend, Pet)
98		**River Rd, Rose-Firth Area**
93		**US 26W, W Blackfoot, Arco** (NB), **Snoshone, I-15, Blackfoot** (SB)
	TStop	E: Flying J Travel Plaza #11182 (Scales)
	Gas	E: Chevron, Maverik W: Phillips 66
	Food	E: FastFood/FJ TP, Arby's, Artic Circle, Domino's Pizza, Little Caesar's Pizza, McDonald's, Pizza Hut, Rolberto's Mexican Food, Subway, Taco Bell, Wendy's
	Lodg	E: Best Western♥, Super 8♥
	Med	E: + Bingham Memorial Hospital, + Blackfoot Medical Center Urgent Care
	Other	E: WiFi/LP/RVDump/FJ TP, RVDump/Chevron, Albertson's, AutoZone, Checker Auto Parts, Kesler's Market, Les Schwab Tire, Ogden Tire Factory, Radio Shack, RiteAid, Walmart sc▲, Muni Golf Course
89		**US 91, I-15 Bus, S Blackfoot**
	TStop	W: Sage Hill Travel Center & Casino
	Food	W: Rest/FastFood/Sage Hill TC
	Lodg	W: Sage Hill TC
	Other	W: Wifi/Sage Hill TC
80		**Ross Fork Rd, Fort Hall**
	TStop	W: TP Truck Stop/Sinclair
	Food	W: FastFood/TP TS
	Other	W: Casino/TP TS, Shoshone Tribal Museum, Ft Hall Casino/Buffalo Meadows RV Park▲
(72/63AB)		**Jct I-86W, to Twin Falls, Boise**
	TServ	W: Cummins Intermountain, Western States Equipment
	Other	W: to Pocatello Reg'l Airport✈
71		**Pocatello Creek Rd, Pocatello**
	Gas	E: Chevron◈, Jacksons/Shell◈, Phillips66◈ W: Exxon, Maverick◈
	Food	E: Applebee's, Burger King/Chevron, Hardee's, Jack in the Box, Perkins, Sandpiper Rest, Subway, W: DQ, Sizzler, Pier 49 SF Pizza, Senor Iguanas Rest, Starbucks
	Lodg	E: Ameritel Inn, Best Western♥, Comfort Inn, Holiday Inn, Quality Inn, Red Lion Hotel♥, Super 8♥
	Med	E: + Hospital
	Other	E: Golf Course, Carwash/P66, Pocatello KOA/RVDump▲ , Bannock Co Fairgrounds/RVDump W: Albertson's, Auto Zone, Checker Auto Parts, Eagle Rock Harley Davidson, Fred Meyer, Radio Shack, Walgreen's, WinCo Foods, Pocatello Mall, Vet♥, Alameda Pet Hospital♥

◈= Regular Gas Stations with Diesel ▲ = RV Friendly Locations ♥= Pet Friendly Locations
Red print shows large vehicle parking / access on site or nearby Brown Print = Campgrounds / RV PARKS

EXIT		IDAHO
69		**Center St, Clark St, Pocatello** (NO Trucks)
	Gas	E: Maverick, Shell◈, Sinclair◈
	Food	E: Artic Circle/Sinclair, Blimpie/Shell
	Lodg	E: Hampton Inn, Towneplace Suites
	Med	E: + Pocatello Reg'l Medical Center, + US Vets Outpatient Clinic W: + Bannock Regional Medical Center, Portneuf Medical Center
	Other	E: Carwash/Shell W: Holt Arena, ID State Univ, Pocatello Zoo
67		**US 30W, US 91N, I-15 Bus (NB), S 5th Ave (SB), Pocatello**
	TStop	W: Forde Johnson Truck Service/P66 (Scales)
	Gas	E: Common Cents Exxon◈ W: Shell, Sinclair◈
	Food	W: Rest/Forde TS, Elmer's, McDonald's, Pizza Hut, Subway, Taco Bell
	Lodg	W: Best Western, Econo Lodge, Executive Inn, Sundial Inn, Thunderbird Motel
	Med	W: + Hospital
	Other	E: Bailey Truck & Auto Supply, ID State Hwy Patrol Post W: Laundry/Forde TS, Grocery, Harbor Freight Tools, ID State Univ, Museum, Pharmacy, Cowboy RV Park/RVDump▲, Sullivans MH & RV Park/RVDump▲
63		**Portneuf Rd, Mink Creek Rec Area**
(59)		**Inkom Rest Area (Both dir)** (RR, Phones, Picnic, Vend, Pet)
(59)		**Weigh Station (Both dir)**
58		**I-15 Bus, Inkom (SB)**
	Gas	W: Sinclair◈
	Food	W: El Rancho Café
	Other	W: to Pebble Creek Ski Area
57		**Inkom (NB) (Acc to Ex #58 Serv)**
47		**US 30E, McCammon, Montpelier Lava Hot Springs, Soda Springs, to Jackson, WY**
	TStop	E: Flying J Travel Plaza #50023/ Conoco (Scales), McCammon Chevron
	Food	E: Rest/FJ TP, Taco Time/Chevron
	Other	E: Laundry/WiFi/LP/RVDump/FJ TP, Laundry/RVDump/McCammon Chevron, McCammon RV Park▲
44		**I-15 Bus, Jensen Rd, McCammon**
40		**Arimo**
	Gas	E: Sinclair◈
	Food	E: Cafe
36		**US 91S, Virginia, Preston**
31		**ID 40E, to US 91S, Downey, Preston**
	TStop	E: PTP/Flags West Truck Stop/Shell
	Food	E: Rest/FW TS
	Lodg	E: Motel/FW TS
	Other	E: Laundry/LP/RVDump/FW TS, Downata Hot Springs▲, Hot Springs RV Campground▲
(25)		**Downey Rest Area (SB)** (RR, Phones, Picnic, Vend, Pet)
	NOTE:	**MM 24.5: Malad Summit (Elev 5574')**
22		**Malad Valley Rd, Devils Creek Rd, Devil Creek Reservoir**
	Other	E: Devil Creek Reservoir RV Park▲

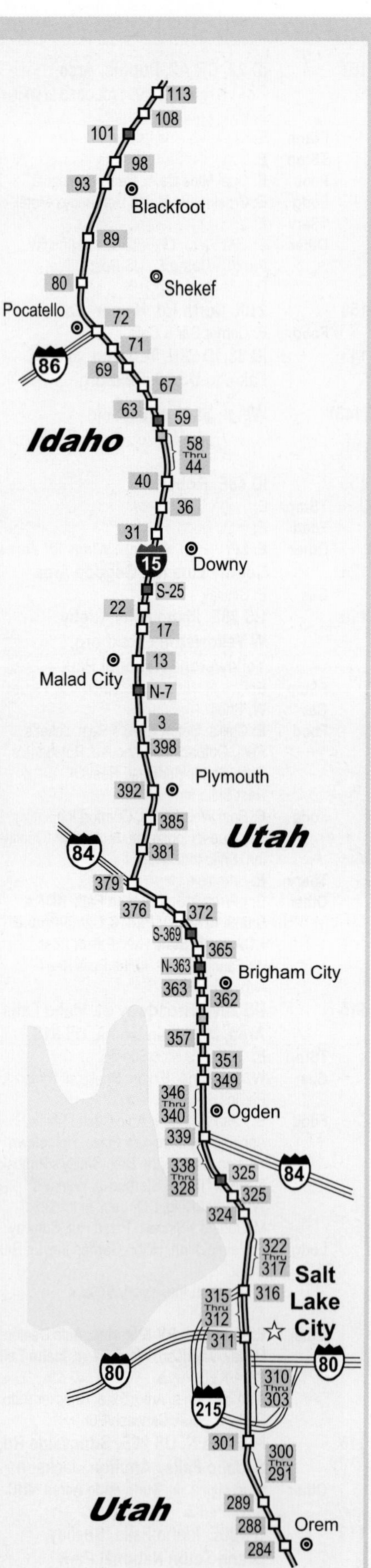

EXIT		ID / UT
17		**ID 36E, Weston, Preston**
	Food	W: Jim's Deep Creek Inn
13		**ID 38, Malad City**
	Gas	W: Chevron, Phillips 66◈
	Food	W: Burger King/Chevron, Café/Taco Time/P66, Pizza, Restaurant
	Lodg	W: Village Inn Motel
	TServ	W: 3 R's Country Tire
	Med	W: + Hospital
	Other	W: Grocery, Auto Repair, True Value, Carwash
(7)		**ID Welcome Center (NB)** (RR, Picnic, Vend, Pet, Info)
3		**Woodruff, to Samaria**

MOUNTAIN TIME ZONE

⬆ IDAHO

⬇ UTAH

MOUNTAIN TIME ZONE

EXIT		ID / UT
	NOTE:	**MM 403: Idaho State Line**
398		**Portage**
392		**20800 Rd N, to UT 13S, Portage, Plymouth**
	TStop	E: Fast-Stop/Sinclair
	Food	E: Subway/Fast Stop
	Other	E: Camperworld Hot Springs▲, Camperworld Hot Springs Golf Course
385		**15200 Rd N, UT 30E, Garland, Riverside, Logan, Fielding**
	Gas	E: Sinclair◈
	Food	E: Riverside Grill/Sinclair
	Lodg	E: Jay's Motel
381		**1000N, to UT 102, Tremonton, Garland (Serv S to Main St) (Access to Serv I-84, Exit #40)**
	FStop	E: Jim & Dave's Sinclair, Archibald & Sons/P66
	TStop	W: RJ's Fuel Stop/Sinclair (Scales), CFN/Golden Spike Travel Plaza/Chevron
	Gas	E: Maverick◈, Sinclair
	Food	E: Coachman Café, Crossroads Family Rest, Mack's Family D/I Rest, Pizza Plus, Subway, Taco Time W: Burger King/RJ's FS, Rest/Quiznos/ Golden Spike TP, Denny's, McDonald's, Wendy's
	Lodg	E: Marble Motel, Sandman Motel W: Hampton Inn, Western Inn♥
	TWash	W: RJ's FS, Golden Spike TP
	TServ	W: RJ's FS/Tires, Golden Spike TP/Tires, Transport Diesel Service, Archibald & Sons/Tires
	Med	E: + Bear River Valley Hospital
	Other	E: Police Dept, Tremonton Muni Airport✈, Auto Dealers, Auto Services, Grocery, Family Dollar, Jiffy Lube, Kent's Market, Bear River Animal Hospital♥, Pharmacy, AmeriGas LP, Carwash/Sinclair W: Laundry/RVDump/RJ's FS, Laundry/ BarbSh/WiFi/RVDump/LP/ Golden Spike TP, WiFi/LP/Archibald & Sons, Interstate Auto & Truck Center, Jack's RV Sales & Repair,

◈ = Regular Gas Stations with Diesel ▲ = RV Friendly Locations ♥ = Pet Friendly Locations
Red print shows large vehicle parking / access on site or nearby Brown Print = Campgrounds / RV PARKS

EXIT	UTAH
NOTE:	**I-15N below runs with I-84 for 39 mi. Exit #'s follow I-15.**
(379/ 41)	**Jct I-84W, to Boise, Tremonton (NB, Left exit)**
376	**UT 13, N 5200 St W, Tremonton, to UT 102, Garland, Bear River (lodging N to UT 102W/)**
FStop	**E:** Sunmart Texaco
Gas	**E:** Chevron, Conoco◈
Food	**E:** Arby's/Sunmart, JC's Country Diner
Lodg	**E:** Marble Motel, Sandman Motel **W:** Hampton Inn, Western Inn♥
372	**UT 240, Honeyville, to UT 13, UT 38, Bear River**
(369)	**UT Welcome Center (SB) (RR, Phones, Pic, Pet, Vend, Info, WiFi)**
365	**UT 13, I-15 Bus, I-84 Bus, 900 North St, Brigham City, Corinne**
Other	**E:** Brigham City Airport✈
363	**Forest St, Brigham City**
Other	**E:** Parson's Service Center, Auto & Truck Repair, Towing, U-Haul
362	**US 91, to US 89, 1100 South St, Brigham City, Logan**
FStop	**E:** Flying J Travel Plaza #1188 **W:** LW's Travel Plaza/FJ TP (Scales)
Gas	**E:** 7-11/Citgo, Chevron◈, Mirastar◈, Sinclair
Food	**E:** Rest/FJ TP, Arby's, Aspen Grill, Burger King, Hunan Chinese, KFC/Taco Bell, McDonald's, Pizza Hut, Sonic, Subway, Taco Time, Wendy's
Lodg	**E:** Crystal Inn, Galaxie Motel, Howard Johnson Express **W:** Comfort Inn, Days Inn
TServ	**E:** Willard Auto & Diesel Service **W:** S&M Diesel Service
Med	**E:** + **Brigham City Comm Hospital**
Other	**E:** WiFi/**LP/RVDump**/FJ TP, **Golden Spike RV Park▲**, Walker Cinema, Auto Dealers, Auto Zone, Checkers Auto Parts, Radio Shack, ShopKO, Chevron/Carwash, **Walmart sc**, Eagle Mountain Golf Course **W:** Laundry/WiFi/**RVDump/LP**/LW/FJ TP
(363)	**Perry Rest Area (NB) (RR, Phones, Picnic, Vend, Info)**
(361)	**Port of Entry / Weigh Station (Both dir)**
357	**750N, UT 360, UT 15, N Willard, Perry, Willard Bay**
TStop	**E:** Flying J Travel Plaza #1125 (Scales)
Food	**E:** Rest/FastFood/FJ TP
Other	**E:** Laundry/WiFi/**RVDump/LP**/FJ TP, **Brigham City/Perry South KOA▲**, **Police Dept** **W: Willard Bay State Park▲**
351	**UT 126, to US 89, S Willard, Pleasant View, Willard Bay**
Other	**W: Willard Bay State Park▲**
349	**2700 N, UT 134, to US 89, Ogden, Farr West, Pleasant View**
Gas	**E:** 7-11, Chevron, Exxon, Maverik◈, **W:** Conoco◈

EXIT	UTAH
Food	**E:** Arby's, Dominos Pizza, McDonald's, Bellas Fresh Mexican Grill, Subway, Wendy's/Exxon **W:** Deli/Conoco
Lodg	**E:** Comfort Inn♥
Other	**E:** Auto Repair, Carwash/Exxon, Kwik Lube Fort Carson Army Res Center, UT Truck & Trailer Repair, Carwash/Chevron, **to** US 89S appr 3.5mi: **Walmart sc**,
346	**Pioneer Rd, Ogden, Harrisville, Defense Depot**
Gas	**W:** Excel Conv Store◈
TServ	**W:** Diesel Service, Rush Truck Center
Other	**E:** Mulligan's Golf Course, Toad's Fun Zone, Fort Carson Army Res Center, Weber Co Fairgrounds **W:** C-A-L Ranch Stores
344	**UT 39, 1200S, 12th St, Ogden**
TStop	**W:** Pilot Travel Center #294 (Scales) **(DAND)**
Gas	**E:** Chevron, Phillips 66, Shell◈
Food	**E:** Carl's Jr, Deny's, Golden Corral, Hogi Yogi, IHOP, Jeremiah's Rest, Panda Express, Sizzler, Subway, Taco Bell, Wendy's **W:** DQ/Subway/TacoBell/Pilot TC, CJ's Rest & Bakery
Lodg	**E:** Best Western♥ **W:** Sleep Inn♥
TServ	**W:** Big Bubba's Trailer Sales, General Diesel Services
Other	**E:** AmeriGas, Big 5 Sporting Goods, Cinepointe 6 Theaters, Family Dollar, Home Depot, Les Schwab Tires, NAPA, Office Max, ShopKO, U-Haul, V-1 Propane, **W:** WiFi/Pilot TC, Steve's Car Care
343	**UT 104, 21st St, Wilson Lane (Acc to 344 via W to UT 126, E to UT204)**
FStop	**W:** Super Stop/Shell
TStop	**E:** Flying J Travel Plaza #50001/Conoco (Scales), Wilson Lane/Chevron
Gas	**W:** Phillips 66
Food	**E:** Rest/FastFood/FJ TP, Arby's/ Wilson Lane, Cactus Red's, McDonald's, Mi Rancho Rest, Rest/ComfSts, Rest/HI **W:** FastFood/Texaco, Café/Super 8, Blimpie
Lodg	**E:** Flying J Inn/FJ TP, Big Z Motel, Best Rest Inn♥, Comfort Suites, Holiday Inn Express **W:** Super 8♥
Tires	**E:** J-Care Truck Service, Wilson Lane
TWash	**E:** J-Care Truck Wash, Wilson Lane Service
TServ	**E:** J-Care Truck Service, Ogden Diesel Sales & Service
Other	**E:** Laundry/CB/WiFi/**RVDump/LP**/ FJ TP, **RVDump**/Wilson Lane, **Century MH & RV Park▲** **W:** Auto Repair, Diesel Services
342	**UT 53, Pennsylvania Ave, 24th St, Ogden (NB Only)**
FStop	**E:** Sinclair
Food	**W:** Sunrise Cafe
Other	**E:** Animal Hospital♥, Auto Repair, **Fort Buenaventura State Park** **W:** Diesel Service, Welding Service, **All Seasons RV Center**, TJ Trailers (Trailers, RV & Marine)
341	**UT 79W, 31st St WB, Ogden**
341B	**UT 79W, 31st St WB, Ogden**
Other	**W:** Ogden Hinckley Airport✈, U-Haul

EXIT	UTAH
341A	**UT 79W, 31st St EB, Hinckley, to UT 204, US 89, Ogden (Serv E to Wall Ave/UT204 &US 89)**
Gas	**E:** 7-11/Citgo, Sinclair, Maverik
Food	**E:** Arby's, Golden Corral, Skippers
Lodg	**E:** Days Inn♥
Med	**E:** + **McKay-Dee Hospital**
Other	**E: to** AutoZone, Auto Dealers, Avis RAC, Budget Truck Rental, CarQuest, Checker Auto Parts, Costco, Family Dollar, Firestone, Newgate Mall, U-Haul, **to** Weber St Univ
(340)	**Jct I-84E, to Cheyenne, WY (SB)**
NOTE:	**I-15N above runs with I-84 for 39mi. Exit #'s Follow I-15.**
339	**Riverdale Rd, UT 241, UT 26, to I-84E, Riverdale (NB) (acc to 341 serv)**
Gas	**E:** Conoco◈, Sinclair, Sam's
Food	**E:** Applebee's, Arby's, Boston Market, Carl's Jr, Chili's, IHOP, La Salsa Mexican Rest, McDonald's
Lodg	**E:** Motel 6♥, Red Roof Inn♥ **W:** Circle R Motel
Other	**E:** Auto Dealers, Costco, Harley Davidson, Home Depot, Sam's Club, Target, **Walmart sc**, **RV Center**, Banks, Museum, Newcastle Mall, to Coleman's Motor-Vu Drive-In **W:** Auto Repair, Big O Tires, **Police Dept**
338	**UT 97, 5600S, Roy, Sunset, Hill Air Force Base**
Gas	**W:** 7-11, Exxon◈, Phillips 66, Sinclair, Smith's
Food	**W:** Arby's, Artic Circle, Blimpie's, KFC, Burger King, DQ, Denny's, McDonald's, Pizza Hut, Sonic, Taco Bell, Village Inn
Lodg	**W:** Quality Inn, Motel 6♥
Med	**E:** + **Now Care Immediate Medical**
Other	**E:** Aerospace Museum, **MIL/Hill AFB FamCamp▲** **W:** Albertson's, Auto Zone, Banks, Checker Auto Parts, Discount Tire, Goodyear, Les Schwab Tires, Radio Shack, RiteAid, Smith's Drug & Food, Tires, Walgreen's
335	**UT 103, 650N, N Clearfield, Sunset, Hill Air Force Base**
Gas	**W:** 7-11, Chevron, Conoco, Petro Mart, Texaco
Food	**W:** Arby's, Carl's Jr, KFC, McDonald's, Skipper's, Subway, Taco Bell
Lodg	**W:** Crystal Cottage Inn, Super 8
Other	**E:** Hill AFB **W:** Big O Tires, **Sierra RV Center**
334	**UT 193, Bernard Fisher Hwy, S Clearfield, Hill Air Force Base**
Gas	**E:** Circle K, Chevron◈, Maverik, Tesoro
Food	**E:** Arby's
Other	**E:** American Car Care Center **W:** Banks, Smith's Food & Drug, Banks
332	**UT 108, Antelope Dr, Layton, Freeport, Antelope Island, Syracuse**
FStop	**E:** Phillips 66
Gas	**E:** Chevron, Circle K **W:** 7-11, Conoco◈
Food	**E:** Applebee's, Carl's Jr, **Cracker Barrel**, Chili's, Golden Corral, JB's Rest, Outback Steakhouse, Pier 49 SF Pizza, Sonic, Timberlodge Steaks, Tony Roma's

EXIT		UTAH
		W: Arby's, Burger King, McDonald's, Quiznos, Outback Steakhouse
	Lodg	E: Courtyard, Fairfield Inn, Hampton Inn, Hilton Garden Inn, Holiday Inn Express, La Quinta Inn♥, Towneplace Suites W: Marriott
	Med	E: + IHC Healthcare W: + Davis Hospital & Med Center
	Other	E: ATMs, Anderson's Auto & Tire Service, Banks, B&N, Office Depot, Target, Layton Hills Mall, Lowe's, Tires, Tinseltown USA, Cinema W: Albertson's, Auto Repair, Banks, Checker Auto Parts, Kmart, Univ of Utah, **RV Dealer**
331		**UT 232, Hill Field Rd, to UT 126, N Layton**
	Gas	E: Phillips 66, Mobil W: Flying J
	Food	E: Denny's, Garcia's, McDonald's, Olive Garden, Red Lobster, Sizzler, Tony Roma W: Arizona Big Salad, Blimpie's, Burger King, China Buffet, Einstein Bros Bagel, Fuddrucker's, IHOP, KFC, Lone Star Steakhouse, Taco Bell
	Lodg	E: Comfort Inn, Hilton Garden Inn
	Med	W: + Hospital
	Other	E: Layton Hills Mall, Tinseltown USA, Cinema, Hill AFB, Banks W: Discount Tire, Home Depot, NTB, PetSmart♥, Sam's Club, ShopKO, Staples, **Walmart sc**, Weber St Univ, Banks, Auto Dealers, **RV Dealer**
330		**to UT 126, Main St, to UT 109, S Layton (NB)**
	Gas	W: Texaco
	Food	E: Little Orient Chinese W: Doug & Emmy's Family Rest, Sills Cafe
	Other	E: American Car Care Center, Banks W: Auto Repair, Banks, **RV Center**
328		**UT 273, 200 North, Kaysville**
	Gas	E: Chevron, 7-11/Citgo, Phillips 66◈, Sinclair
	Food	E: Cutler's Sandwiches, Joanie's, KFC, McDonald's/Chevron, Subway, Taco Time, Wendy's
	Lodg	W: West Motel
	Other	E: Albertson's, Checker Auto Parts, Les Scwab Tires, Walgreen's, Auto Repair, Banks, **Police Dept** W: **Camping World/Blaine Jensen & Sons RV Center/RVDump**, Auto Repair
(325)		**Parking Area (Both dir)**
325		**UT 225, US 89, to UT 106, Lagoon Dr, Farmington (SB)**
	Gas	E: Maverick
	Food	E: Arby's, Burger King, Pizza Hut, Subway
	Other	E: Pioneer Village, Banks
324		**UT 225, US 89, to UT 106, Lagoon Dr, Farmington (NB)**
	Gas	E: Maverick, Smith's F&D◈
	Food	E: Arby's, Burger King, Little Caesars Pizza Pizza Hut, Subway
	Other	E: Smith's Food & Drug, Pioneer Village, **Lagoon RV Park & Campground▲**, **Cherry Hill Camping Resort▲**
322		**UT 227, 200W, Lagoon Dr, Farmington (NB, NO reaccess)**
	Other	E: Banks, Pioneer Village, **Lagoon RV Park & Campground▲**, **Police Dept**

Personal Notes

EXIT		UTAH
319		**UT 105, Parrish Ln, Centerville**
	Gas	E: Chevron◈, Phillips 66◈
	Food	E: Arby's, Artic Circle, Carl's Jr, DQ, Hardee's, IHOP, Lone Star Steakhouse, McDonald's, Subway, Taco Bell, Wendy's
	Other	E: Albertson's, Big O Tires, Banks, checker Auto Parts, Home Depot, Les Schwab Tire, Radio Shack, Target, **Walmart sc**, **Police Dept** W: Auto Repairs, **RV Center**
317		**UT 131, 400 North (NB) Bountiful, US 89S, 500W (SB, Left exit) Woods Cross (Reaccess both dir via US 89)**
	Gas	E: Chevron, Exxon◈, Sinclair◈
	Food	E: Café Alicia, Starbucks
	Lodg	E: Country Inn
	Other	E: Goodyear, Office Depot, Petco♥, Auto, Truck & Marine Repair, Banks W: **Police Dept**
316		**UT 68, 500S, Woods Cross**
	TStop	W: RB's One Stop/P66
	Gas	E: Exxon, Tesoro W: Chevron
	Food	E: Applebee's, Burger King, Carl's Jr, Christopher's Seafood & Steakhouse, Del Taco, Hogi Yogi, JB's Rest, KFC, McDonald's, Mexican Rest, Panda Express, Pizza Hut, Sizzler, Subway, Taco Bell W: FastFood/RB's
	Lodg	E: Bear River Lodge, Country Inn Suites W: InTowne Suites
	Med	E: + Benchmark Regional Hospital

EXIT		UTAH
	Other	E: Albertson's, Auto Zone, Auto Repair, Banks, B&N, Big O Tires, Checker Auto Parts, Costco, Firestone, Radio Shack, ShopKO, TJ Maxx, Walgreen's, Univ of Utah, **RV Service Center**, **Police Dept** W: Laundry/**RVDump**/RB's, Diesel Service, Auto Repair, Skypark Airport✈
315		**1100N, to US 89, Woods Cross**
	FStop	E: Slim Olson's #2/Chevron
	Gas	E: Chevron◈, Sinclair, Texaco W: Conoco
	Food	E: Arby's, Apollo Burger, Burger King, Empire Chinese, KFC, McDonald's, Mexican, Pappas Steak House, Skipper's, Village Inn, Wendy's W: Denny's, Lorena's Mexican Rest
	Lodg	E: Best Western, Comfort Inn W: Hampton Inn, Motel 6♥
	Other	E: **RVDump/LP**/Slim Olson's, Ace Hardware, Auto Dealers, BF Goodrich Tires, Cinema, Banks, Discount Tire, Enterprise RAC, Hertz RAC, Grocery Stores, Les Schwab Tires, Smith Food & Drug, U-Haul W: **Colonial Woods RV & MH Park▲**, Skypark Airport✈
314		**Center St, N Salt Lake (SB no reacc)**
	Tstop	W: **(I-215, 1st Exit)** Flying J Travel Plaza/Scales/FastFood/**LP**/**RVDump**
	Gas	E: Walker's W: Maverick
	Food	E: Quiznos, Puerto Vallarta
	Other	E: Diesel Repair & Service, **Police Dept** W: I-215, 1st Exit **Pony Express RV Resort▲**
(313)		**Jct I-215W, Belt Route, to Salt Lake City Int'l Airport (SB)**
312		**US 89, Center St, N Salt Lake (NB), US 89, Beck St (SB) (NB access Exit #314 services)**
311		**2200N, to UT 68, Redwood Rd, Warm Springs Rd**
310		**900W, 1000N (SB)**
	Lodg	W: Salt City Inn, Mamoof's
309		**UT 268, 600N, Salt Lake City (Addt'l Serv E to US 89) (Many Serv S on 900W to UT 186)**
	Gas	W: Neil's Pro Service/Conoco
	Food	W: Papa John's Pizza
	Med	E: + Hospital, to + SLC VA Med Hospital
	Other	E: Univ of UT W: Smith's Food & Drug, Bank, to UT State Fairgrounds
	NOTE:	**I-15N below runs with I-80 for 5 mi Exit #'s Follow I-15**
(308)		**Jct I-80W, SL Int'l Airport, to Reno**
307		**400 South , UT 186 (SB), 400 South HOV Exit (NB)**
	Gas	E: Chevron, Food Mart
	Food	E: Various
	Lodg	E: Courtyard, Hampton Inn, Rio Grande Hotel, Renaissance Suites, Residence Inn
	Other	E: Amtrak, Enterprise RAC, Aquarium, Museum, Auto Repair, Grocery, Banks W: Grocery
306		**600 South, UT 269 (NB)**
	Gas	E: Chevron, Maverick, Sinclair

◈= Regular Gas Stations with Diesel ▲ = RV Friendly Locations ♥= Pet Friendly Locations
Red print shows large vehicle parking / access on site or nearby Brown Print = Campgrounds / RV PARKS

EXIT		UTAH
	Food	E: Denny's, McDonald's, Rest/Hilton, Salty Dogs, Rest/Quality Inn, Rest/ Ramada, Rest/Travelodge
	Lodg	E: Ameritel Inn, Best Western, Embassy Suites, Hilton Garden Inn, Little America Hotel, Motel 6♥, Quality Inn, Ramada, Red Lion Hotel, Sheraton, Super 8, Travelodge♥
	Other	E: Amtrak, Enterprise RAC, Aquarium, Museum, Auto Repair, Grocery, Banks
305C-A		**Exit to SB Collector (SB)**
305D		**900 South (NB)**
	Gas	E: Chevron, Sinclair
	Food	E: Artic Circle, Chinese Rest, Mexican Rest
	Lodg	E: Best Inns, Holiday Inn
	Other	E: Auto Repairs, Tires
305C		**1300S, Salt Lake City**
	Gas	E: Maverik
	Food	E: Various
	Other	E: Auto Repairs, Tires, Banks
305B		**2100S, UT 201, Salt Lake City (Addt'l Serv W to UT 68)**
	FStop	E: Premium Oil/Chevron
	Gas	E: 7-11, Petro Mart, Costco
	Food	E: FastFood/Prem Oil, Burger King, Carl Jr's, IHOP, McDonald's, Subway
	Lodg	E: Marriott
	Other	E: LP/Prem Oil, Costco, Home Depot, Pep Boys, PetSmart♥, Bank, U-Haul, **Walmart sc**
305A		**UT 201W, 900W, Salt Lake City (Addt'l Serv W to UT 68)**
	TStop	W: Flying J Travel Plaza #50007(Scales)
	Food	W: Rest/FJ TP, Wendy's
	TServ	W: Diesel Repair
	TWash	W: Blue Beacon/FJ TP
	Other	W: Laundry/WiFi/RVDump/LP/FJ TP, Best Buy, Goodyear, NAPA, Repair
305A-D		**Exit to NB Collector (NB)**
(304)		**Jct I-80E, to Cheyenne, Denver (Gas & Lodging at 1st Exit on I-80E)**
	TServ	E: Cummins Intermountain
	NOTE:	**I-15N above runs with I-80 for 5 mi Exit #'s Follow I-15**
303		**UT 171, 3300S, S Salt Lake**
	Gas	E: 7-11/Citgo W: Maverick, Sam's
	Food	E: Burger King, McDonald's, Taco Bell
	Lodg	E: Days Inn♥, InTown Suites, Marriott
	Other	E: Banks, Cinema, Safeway, Repairs W: Sam's Club, Salt Valley GMC Trucks
301		**UT 266, 4500S, Murray, Kearns**
	Gas	E: Chevron, Oil W: Chevron, Conoco, Shell◈, Sinclair◈, Texaco
	Food	E: McDonald's W: Burger King, Denny's, Wendy's
	Lodg	E: Skyline Mtn Resort W: Fairfield Inn, Hampton Inn, Holiday Inn Express, Marriott, Quality Inn
	Other	E: Banks, Auto Repairs W: Lowe's, Bank, **RV Center**
300		**UT 173, 5300S, Murray, Kearns**
	Gas	W: 7-11, Chevron, Conoco, Sinclair
	Food	E: Café Delights, Pizza Hut W: KFC, Hogi Yogi
	Lodg	W: Reston Hotel

EXIT		UTAH
	Med	E: + Hospital
	Other	E: UT State Hwy Patrol Post W: Banks, Smith Food & Drug, Fun Dome
(298)		**Jct I-215, Belt Route**
297		**UT 48, 7200S, Midvale**
	Gas	E: Chevron, Conoco, Sinclair, Texaco W: BP, Maverik
	Food	E: Chili's, Denny's, Furr's, KFC, Hooters, McDonald's, Midvale Mining Café, Sizzler, Taco Bell, Village Inn,
	Lodg	E: Best Western, Days Inn, Discovery Inn, La Quinta Inn♥, Motel 6♥
	Other	E: Hertz RAC, Enterprise RAC, Walgreen's
295		**UT 209, 9000S, Sandy, W Jordan**
	Gas	E: Chevron, Sinclair W: Maverik, Tesoro
	Food	E: Arby's, Burger King, Fuddrucker's, Hardee's, Sweet Tomatoes, Subway, Sizzler W: KFC, Village Inn
	Lodg	E: Comfort Inn
	Med	E: + Hospital
	Other	E: Discount Tire, Lowe's, NAPA, Carwash, to Alta & Snowbird Ski Areas W: Grocery
293		**UT 151, 10600S, Sandy, S Jordan**
	Gas	E: Conoco, Phillips 66, Tesoro, Costco
	Food	E: Bennett's BBQ, Black Angus, Chili's, Carver's, HomeTown Buffet, Shoney's, Starbucks, Subway, TGI Friday, Taco Bell, Village Inn, Wendy's W: Denny's
	Lodg	E: Best Western, Courtyard, Extended Stay American, Hampton Inn, Quality Inn W: Country Inn, Sleep Inn, Super 8
	Other	E: Auto Dealers, Mall, Banks, Best Buy, Costco, Target W: Auto Dealers, **Walmart sc**
291		**UT 71, 12300S, Draper, Riverton**
	Gas	E: Flying J◈, Holiday◈, 7-11/P66◈ W: 7-11/P66, to Holiday◈, Tesoro
	Food	E: Arby's, Artic Circle, Carl's Jr, Café Rio Mexican Rest, Del Taco, Fazoli's, KFC, Guadalahonky's Mexican Rest, Quiznos, McDonald's, Panda Express, Ruby Tuesday, Wendy's, Wingers
	Lodg	E: Comfort Inn, Fairfield Inn, Holiday Inn Express, Ramada ♥, Travelodge
	TServ	E: Jake's Auto & Truck Repair
	Other	E: Banks, Discount Tire, Goodyear, Outlet Mall, Smith's Food & Drug, **Walmart sc**, Carwash/7-11, **Mountain Shadows RV Park▲**, **Camping World▲**, W: to Carwash/Tesoro, Riverbend Gof Course
289		**UT 154, 10600 S, Bangerter Hwy**
	Gas	W: 7-11, Exxon◈
	Other	E: **Mountain Shadows RV Park▲**
288		**UT 140, 14600S, Higland Dr, Draper, Bluffdale, State Prison** NOTE: Low Clearance 2 mi West
	Gas	E: to Chevron◈
	Other	W: State Prison
284		**UT 92, 11000 N Lehi, Highland, Alpine**
	Gas	W: Chevron◈, Maverick◈
	Food	W: Iceberg Drive In/Chevron
	Lodg	W: Hampton Inn, Springhill Suites
	Other	E: Cabela's Outfitters/RVDump, W: **Lone Peak Trailers & RV's**, to Timpanogos Cave Nat'l Monument

EXIT		UTAH
282		**US 89S, 1200W, Lehi**
	Gas	W: Chevron
	Food	W: Huckleberry's Rest
279		**UT 73, E Main St, State Rd, Lehi (Acc to Ex #278 Serv via E to State Rd)**
	Gas	E: Conoco ◈, Texaco◈, Chevron◈ W: Chevron◈, Phillips 66◈
	Food	E: One Man Band Diner, Starbucks W: Artic Circle, KFC/Pizza Hut, McDonald's, Subway, Wendy's/P66, Wingers
	Lodg	E: Motel 6♥ W: Best Western, Days Inn, Super 8♥
	TServ	E: Rex's Diesel Service
	Other	E: Lowe's, PetSmart♥, Walgreen's, **Walmart sc** W: Albertson's, Big O Tire, Carwash/LP/ Jiffy Lube/Chevron, US Post Office, Banks, Repairs, **Police Dept**
278		**UT 145, W Main St, State Rd, American Fork, Lehi**
	FStop	E: Harts Fuel Stop/P66
	Gas	E: Chevron, Sinclair
	Food	E: FastFood/Harts, Arby's, China Isle, Del Taco, Hogi Yogi, McDonald's, Skipper Seafood, Subway
	Lodg	E: Quality Inn
	TServ	E: Rex Diesel, Vern's Towing
	Other	E: Albertson's, Auto Dealers, Banks, Big 5 Sporting Goods, Cinema, Dollar Tree, Kmart, Home Depot, Office Depot, PetSmart♥, Smith Food & Drug, Target, **Walmart sc**, **Police Dept**
276		**UT 180, 500E, American Fork Pleasant Grove**
	Gas	E: Conoco, Phillips 66, Texaco
	Food	E: Arby's, Carl's Jr, Del Taco, Denny's, Golden Corral, Hogi Yogi, McDonald's, Subway, Wendy's
	Lodg	E: Park Place Inn
	Med	E: + Glass Hospital, + American Fork Hospital
	Other	E: Big Lots, Big O Tires, Carwash, **American Campground▲**, **RV Dealer**
275		**S Pleasant Grove Blvd, Pleasant Grove, American Fork, Lindon**
	Gas	E: Gas, Texaco
	Food	E: Panda Express, Quiznos, Sonic, Weinerschnitzel's
	Other	E: Macey's Food & Drug, Walgreen's
273		**W1600N, to UT 114, Orem, Lindon, Pleasant Grove**
	FStop	E: Pirate Petroleum/Sinclair
	Gas	E: Exxon◈, Holiday
	Food	E: Quiznos, Hogi Yogi/Holiday
	TServ	W: Mickelson Diesel Service, Utah Diesel Center
	Med	E: + American Fork Hospital, + Glass Hospital
	Other	E: Discount Tire, Home Depot, Les Schwab Tire, Carwash/Holiday W: Harley Davidson
272		**UT 52, 800N, to US 89, Orem (Addt'l Serv E to US 89)**
	Gas	E: Phillips 66
	Food	E: Arby's, Denny's, Sonic
	Lodg	E: La Quinta Inn♥
	Other	E: **All Coach RV Repair**
271		**Center St, Orem, to US 89**
	Gas	E: 7-11, Conoco, GasNGo W: Tesoro

◈ = Regular Gas Stations with Diesel ▲ = RV Friendly Locations ♥ = Pet Friendly Locations

Red print shows large vehicle parking / access on site or nearby **Brown Print = Campgrounds / RV PARKS**

EXIT **UTAH**

Food E: Artic Circle, Burger King, Hardee's, Panda Express, Taco Bell, Wendy's
Lodg W: Econo Lodge
Med E: + Orem Comm Hospital

269 UT 265, University Pkwy, to US 89, BYU, 1200S, Orem (Addtl Serv- US 89)
Gas E: Phillips 66◊, Sinclair, Texaco
W: Chevron, Express
Food E: Applebee's, Black Angus, Carrabba's, Chili's, Fuddrucker's, Golden Corral, IHOP, McDonald's, Outback Steakhouse, Red Lobster, Subway, Village Inn
W: Hogi Yogi
Lodg E: Best Western, Fairfield Inn, Hampton Inn, La Quinta Inn♥
Other E: B&N, Best Buy, Lowe's, Office Depot, PetSmart♥, **Walmart sc**, University Mall, UT Valley State College
W: Carwash/Chevron

265 UT 114W, Center St, Provo (SB)
Gas E: 7-11, Conoco, Shell, Sinclair
W: Chevron, Conoco
Food E: Lotus Garden, Osaka Japanese
W: Taco Bell
Lodg E: Marriott, Travelers Inn, Travelodge
W: Econo Lodge
Other E: Albertson's, UT Co Visitor Info Center
W: **Provo KOA▲**, **Utah Lake State Park**, **Lakeside Campground▲**

265B UT 114W, Center St, Airport (NB)
Other W: **Provo KOA▲**, **Utah Lake State Park**, **Lakeside Campground▲**, Provo Municipal Airport✈, Grocery

265A UT 114, Center St, Provo (NB)

263 US 189N, University Ave, 1860S, Provo
Gas E: Chevron, Conoco◊, P66, Maverick, Sinclair, Sam's Club
Food E: Arby's, Blimpie's, Burger King, KFC, McDonald's, Red Robin, Ruby River Steakhouse, Shoney's, Sizzler, Taco Bell, Village Inn, Wendy's
Lodg E: Best Western, Colony Inn, Fairfield Inn, Hampton Inn, Holiday Inn, Motel 6♥, Sleep Inn, Super 8
Other E: Good Earth Foods, Home Depot, Kmart, Les Schwab Tires, NAPA, Banks, Mall, Sam's Club, Staples, East Bay Golf Course, Amtrak, Repairs, to Brigham Young University, Visitor Info, **Silver Fox Campground▲**
W: **Provo KOA▲**, **Lakeside Camp ground▲**, **UT Lake State Park**

261 UT 75, 1500N, N Springville, Provo
TStop E: Flying J Travel Plaza #11105 (Scales) (Springville Rest Stop - Both dir)
Gas E: Maverick◊, Chevron
Food E: CountryMarket/FJ TP, McDonald's/Chevron
Lodg E: Best Western
Other E: Laundry/WiFi/LP/FJ TP, **East Bay RV Park Campground▲**, Suntana Raceway
W: Spanish Fork-Springville Airport✈, Sheriff's Dept, **Canyon View RV Park/RVDump▲**, **Quality RV**

260 UT 77, 3900S, S Springville
Gas E: Maverick, Phillips 66◊, Mirastar
W: Chevron, Sinclair
Food E: Burger King, DQ, Del Taco, IHOP, Pier 49 SF Pizza, Mongolian Grill, Pizza Hut, Quiznos, Subway, Wendy's

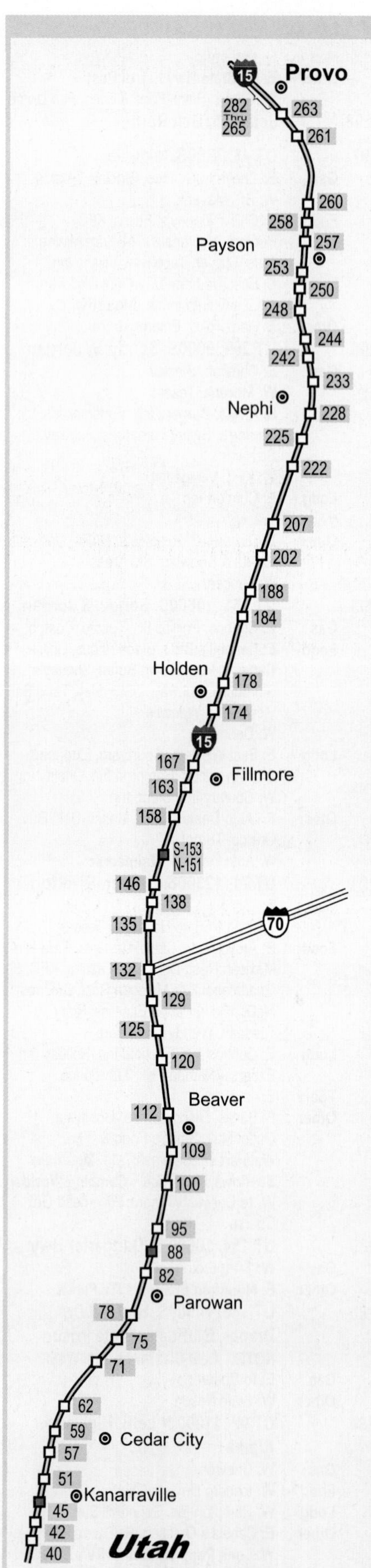

EXIT **UTAH**

W: Cracker Barrel
Lodg W: Days Inn♥
Other E: Big O Tires, Carwash, Jiffy Lube, **Walmart sc**, Banks, **East Bay RV Park & Campground▲**
W: Spanish Fork-Springville Airport✈, **Quality RV**, **Canyon View RV Park/RVDump▲**

258 US 6, UT 156, Moark Connection, to US 89S, Price, Manti (SB)
Gas E: Chevron◊, Phillips 66, S&S Texaco◊, Albertson's
Food E: Arby's, Burger King, Carl's Jr, McDonald' Pizza, Taco Bell, Wendy's
W: Papa Murphy's Take n Bake
Lodg E: Holiday Inn Express
Other E: Albertson's, Auto Zone, Checker Auto Parts, Food4Less, Kmart, UPS Store, Carwash Express, Cinema, Expressway Lube, **RV Center**

257 US 6E, UT 156, Spanish Fork, Price (SB, Right Lane Exit Only)
Gas E: Chevron, Conoco◊, Texaco◊, Pit Stop
W: Conoco◊, Phillips 66
Food E: Arby's, Amber Family Rest, Artic Circle, Burger King, Hogi Yogi, JB's, KFC, Little Caesar's Pizza, McDonald's, Pizza Factory, Sonic, Spanish Fork, Subway, Taco Bell, Wendy's
Other E: Albertson's, Dollar Tree, Kmart, Macey Food & Drug, Pharmacy, **Police**, Cinema 8
W: Auto Dealers, Bank, Laundromat, ShopKO

253 UT 164, Spanish Fork, Benjamin

250 UT 115, 3200W, N Payson, Salem, Benjamin
TStop E: Flying J Travel Plaza #11198 (Scales
Gas E: Gas 'n' Dash, Sinclair
Food E: Rest/FastFood/FJ TP, McDonald's, Subway
Lodg E: Comfort Inn
Med E: + Mountain View Hospital
Other E: Laundry/WiFi/**RVDump/LP**/FJ TP, Checker Auto Parts, Grocery, RiteAid

248 UT 178, to UT 198, Payson, Salem
Gas E: Chevron◊, Sinclair◊
W: Walker's Phillips 66◊
Food E: Arby's/Sinclair, Hunan City, Little Caesar's, Subway
W: Wendy's/P66
Other E: LP/Carwash/Chevron, **Walmart sc**

244 US 6, UT 198, Main St, Santaquin, Delta, Ely
Gas W: Chevron◊, Sinclair
Food W: 5 Buck Pizza, Family Tree Rest, Main St Pizza, Subway

242 South Santaquin

233 UT 54, Mona (Gas & Food W to UT 91)

228 I-15 Bus, UT 41, Nephi, Delta (Addt'l Serv W to UT 41S)
Lodg W: Economy Lodge

225 UT 132, Nephi, Manti (W to UT 41S, Acc to Ex 222 Serv)
FStop W: TopStop/Sinclair
Gas E: Tesoro◊
W: Chevron◊, Walker's P66◊
Food E: One Man Band Diner, Taco Time, Salt Creek Steak House
W: Arby's/Chevron, Wendy's/P66

◊= Regular Gas Stations with Diesel ▲ = RV Friendly Locations ♥= Pet Friendly Locations
Red print shows large vehicle parking / access on site or nearby Brown Print = Campgrounds / RV PARKS

EXIT		UTAH
	Lodg	W: Economy Inn
	Med	W: + Central Valley Medical Center
	Other	W: Auto Repair & Towing, Big O Tires, Bank, to Laundry/CarWash/Sinclair, **High Country RV Campground▲**
222		**UT 28, I-15 Bus Loop, Nephi, UT 41, to I-70, Salina, Richfield**
	FStop	W: Sunmart #903/Texaco, Top Stop Truck Plaza/AmBest/Sinclair (Scales)
	TStop	W: Flying J Travel Plaza #11196/Conoco (Scales)
	Gas	W: Sinclair
	Food	W: FastFood/Sunmart, HogiYogi/ KrispyKreme/Top Stop TP, Rest/Fast Food/Flying J TP, Burger King, Denny's, JC Mickelson's, Lisa's Country Kitchen, Mi Racherito Mexican Rest, Subway,
	Lodg	W: Best Western, Motel 6♥, Super 8, Roberta's Cove Motor Inn, Safari Motel
	TServ	W: Doyle's Diesel
	Other	W: RVDump/Sunmart, Laundry/Carwash / Sinclair, Laundry/RVDump/LP/WiFi/ Flying J TP, **High Country RV Camp▲** . Carwash/LP/Sinclair
207		**UT 78, Nephi, Mills, Levan**
202		**Old US 90, Nephi, Yuba Lake State Park**
	Other	E: **Yuba Lake State Park▲**
188		**US 50E, to I-70, Scipio, Fillmore, Salina**
	TStop	W: Eagles Landing/Flying J TP (Scipio Rest Stop - Both dir)
	Gas	E: Sinclair◈, Texaco◈
	Food	E: DQ/Eagles Landing
	Lodg	E: Super 8
	Other	E: Diesel, Auto & Tire Service W: Tires/LP/Eagles Landing
184		**Ranch Exit, Fillmore**
178		**US 50W, to Delta, Holden**
	Other	W: to Great Basin Nat'l Park
174		**UT 64, to US 50W, Ely, Holden, Delta**
	Other	W: to Great Basin Nat'l Park
167		**Bus Loop I-15, Fillmore** W: Fillmore Rest Stop (Both dir)
	FStop	E: Steve's Tire & Oil/Sinclair, Fillmore Shell, Miller Chevron
	Gas	E: Chevron x2 W: Texaco
	Food	E: Rest/Best Western, Burger King, Garden of Eat'n, 5 Buck Pizza W: Subway
	Lodg	E: Best Western
	TServ	E: Steve's Tire
	Med	E: + Fillmore Comm Medical Center
	Other	E: LP/Steve's, **Wagons West RV Park & Campground▲** , Paradise Golf Resort, Auto Repair, Grocery, Bank W: Territorial Statehouse State Park
163		**I-15 Bus Loop, to UT 100, UT 99**
	FStop	E: First Capital Chevron W: Sunmart #807/Texaco
	TStop	E: Sinclair #43041
	Gas	E: Maverick◈
	Food	E: FastFood/Sinclair, Arby's/Chevron, Larry's Drive-In W: Burger King/Sunmart
	Lodg	E: Comfort Inn♥, to Country Garden Inn B&B, Spinning Wheel Motel
	Other	E: **Fillmore KOA▲** , **Wagons West RV Park▲** , Bank, Grocery W: Fillmore Airport✈

EXIT		UTAH
158		**UT 133, Main St, Fillmore, Meadow, Kanosh, Green River**
	FStop	E: Meadow Chevron
	Gas	E: Shell◈
	Food	E: FastFood/Chevron
146		**UT 133, Fillmore, Kanosh (Access same serv E as Ex #158)**
138		**Ranch Exit**
135		**Historic Cove Fort, UT 161, Paiute Indian Res, to I-70E**
	FStop	E: Cove Fort Chevron (Rest Stop - Both dir)
	Food	E: FastFood/Cove Ft Chevron
(132)		**Jct I-70E, Richfield, Denver**
129		**UT 161, to I-70E, Beaver, Sulphurdale** (NB: Chain Up Area)
125		**Ranch Exit, Beaver**
120		**Old US 91, Beaver, Manderfield** NOTE: NB Chain Up Area
112		**to UT 21, Bus Lp 15, UT 153, UT 160, Beaver, Milford** (acc to #109 Serv)
	FStop	E: High Country Shell
	TStop	E: Ernie's Truck Plaza/Sinclair W: Eagles Landing Truck Plaza/Flying J (Beaver Rest Stop - Both dir)
	Gas	E: Conoco, Phillips 66, Sinclair
	Food	E: FastFood/Ernie's TP, Rest/BW, Arby's, El Bambi Cafe, Hunan Garden Chinese, McDonald's, Sportman Paradise Steakhouse, Subway W: MrGrumpy's/Pizza/Wendy's/EL TP
	Lodg	E: Best Western♥, Country Inn Motel♥/Sinclair, Days Inn, De Lano Motel & RV W: Eagles Landing Motel/EL TP
	Other	E: Mike's Foodtown, **Beaver KOA▲** , **Beaver Canyon Campground▲** , Anytime Road Service & Repair, Southcreek Beaver Towing & Tire/RVDump W: Laundry/Eagles Landing TP
109		**to UT 21, I-15 Bus Loop, UT 160, Beaver, Milford** (acc to #112 Serv)
	FStop	E: Southcreek Shell
	Gas	E: Chevron◈, Phillips 66
	Food	E: Burger King/Shell, Cindy's Pizza, Mel's Drive In, Rest/Best Western
	Lodg	E: Aspen Lodge Motel, Best Western♥, Comfort Inn, De Lano Motel & RV, Eagles Roost Inn, Elk Meadows Resort, Mansfield Motel, Sleepy Lagoon Motel
	TServ	E: Anytime Road Svc & Repair, Southcreek Beaver Towing & Tire/
	Med	E: + Beaver Valley Hospital
	Other	E: Evan's Garage, **Beaver Canyon Campground▲** , **United Beaver Camperland▲**
100		**Ranch Exit, Freemont Rd**
95		**UT 20, Paragonah, to US 89, Panguitch, Kanab, Circleville**
	Other	E: to **Bryce Canyon National Park**, Lake Powell
(88)		**Lunt Park Rest Area** (Both dir) (RR, Phones, Picnic, Vend, Info)
82		**UT 271, Paragonah**

EXIT		UTAH
78		**I-15 Bus, UT 271, Main St, to UT 143, Parowan, Paragonah**
	TStop	W: Travel Center of America #186
	Food	W: Subway/Taco Bell/TA TC
	Lodg	E: Ace Motel, Days Inn
	TServ	W: TA TC
	Other	E: Banks, Auto Service, to Brian Head & Cedar Breaks Ski Resorts W: WiFi/RVDump/LP/TA TC
75		**I-15 Loop, UT 143, Parowan (Access to Ex #178 Serv E to UT 143N)**
	Food	E: Pizza, Mexican
	Lodg	E: Days Inn
	Other	E: to Brian Head, Cedar Breaks Ski Resorts
71		**Old US 91, Main St, Summit, Cedar City, Paraowan, Enoch (Acc to Ex #62 via Old US 91S)**
	TStop	E: Sunshine Truck Stop
	Food	E: Rest/Sunshine TS
	Tires	E: Sunshine TS
	Other	E: Laundry/Sunshine TS W: to Riverside Motel & **RV Park▲**
62		**I-15 Bus Loop, Cedar City, UT 130, to UT 14, Enoch, Minersville**
	TStop	E: Love's Travel Stop #335 (Scales) W: JR's Truck Stop/Shell (Scales)
	Gas	E: Phillips 66◈ W: Maverick, Sinclair
	Food	E: Carl's Jr/Subway/Love's TS, Fast Food/JR's TS, La Villa Mexican Rest W: Steaks n Stuff Rest
	Lodg	E: Best Western, Holiday Inn W: Travelodge, to Riverside Motel & **RV Park▲**
	TServ	W: JR's TS
	Other	E: WiFi/RVDump/Love's TS, **Country Aire RV Park▲** , **Cedar City KOA/RVDump▲** , UT State Hwy Patrol Post
59		**UT 56, 200N, Cedar City**
	Gas	E: Maverick, Phillips 66◈, Shell◈, Shell, Texaco W: Sinclair◈
	Food	E: Arby's, Denny's, Burger King, KFC, McDonald's, Shoney's, Taco Bell, Wendy's W: Subway, Rest/HolidayInn
	Lodg	E: Abbey Inn, Best Western, Comfort Inn, Econo Lodge, Rodeway Inn W: Holiday Inn, Motel 6♥, Super 8
	Other	E: **Cedar City KOA/RVDump▲** , Southern UT Univ, Coliseum, Auto Repairs, Auto Dealers W: Cedar City Muni Airport✈
57		**I-15 Bus Lp, UT 130, to UT 14, Cedar City**
	Gas	E: Chevron, Phillips 66◈, Sinclair◈, Shell, Smith's W: Chevron◈, Mirastar, Murphy
	Food	E: DQ, Hunan Chinese, JB's, Subway W: Applebee's, Chili's, Del Taco, McDonald's, Panda Express, Starbucks
	Lodg	E: Best Value Inn, Days Inn, Holiday Inn Express, Rodeway Inn W: Hampton Inn
	Med	E: + Hospital
	Other	E: Albertson's, Auto Zone, Banks, Big O Tire, Radio Shack, Smith's Food & Drug, **Cedar City KOA/RVDump▲** , **Town & Country RV Park▲** , W: Cinema, Home Depot, **Walmart sc**

◈ = Regular Gas Stations with Diesel ▲ = RV Friendly Locations ♥ = Pet Friendly Locations
Red print shows large vehicle parking / access on site or nearby Brown Print = Campgrounds / RV PARKS

EXIT		UTAH
51		**5300W, 4000S, UT 130, Cedar City, Hamilton Fort, Kanarraville**
(45)		Kanarraville Rest Area (Both dir) (RR, Phones, Picnic, Vend, Info) **(SB : Next Rest Area 196 mi)**
42		**UT 144, Cedar City, Kanarraville, New Harmony**
40		**Kolob Carqua Rd, Hurricane, Kolob Canyons, Zion Nat'l Park (Info / Scenic Drive)**
	Other	E: Zion National Park
36		**Ranch Exit, Hurricane**
33		**Ranch Exit**
31		**Pintura**
30		**Browse**
27		**UT 17, Hurricane, Tocquerville, Zion National Park**
	Other	E: Add'l Serv appr 10 mi E, Willowind RV Park▲, to US Air Force Proving Grounds, Silver Springs RV Resort▲, Virgin Territories RV Park▲
23		**Silver Reef Rd, Hurricane, Leeds, Silver Reef (SB)**
	Lodg	E: to Leeds Motel & RV Park▲
22		**UT 228, UT 212, Red Cliff Rd, Hurricane, Leeds, Silver Reef (NB)**
	Lodg	E: Cottam's Leeds Motel & RV Park▲
	Other	E: Zion West RV Park▲, St George RV Resort▲ W: BLM/Red Cliffs Campground▲
16		**UT 9, Hurricane, Kanab, Grand Canyon, Zion Nat'l Park, Lk Powell**
	Gas	E: Shell◈
	Food	E: Blimpie's, DQ, Ernesto's Mexican, McDonald's, Wendy's
	Lodg	E: Best Western, Days Inn, Motel 6♥, Holiday Inn Express, Super 8, Travelodge
	Other	E: Brentwood RV Resort▲, The Canyons RV Resort▲, Harrisburg RV Resort▲, Silver Springs RV Resort▲, Willowind RV Park▲, Quail Creek State Park Campground▲, Zions Gate RV Resort▲, To Zion Nat'l Park
13		**Washington**
10		**UT 212, Middleton Dr, Green Springs Rd, Washington**
	TStop	W: Freeway Chevron
	Gas	E: Phillips 66◈, Sinclair, Costco W: Shell
	Food	E: FastFood/Frwy Chevron, Arby's, Artic Circle, Burger King, IHOP, Jack in the Box, Little Caesar's Pizza, Ruby Tuesday, St Helens of Washington, Texas Roadhouse, Wendy's
	Lodg	E: Country Inn, Red Cliffs Inn W: La Quinta Inn♥
	Tires	W: Freeway Chevron
	Other	E: Albertson's, Auto Zone, Banks, Best Buy, Big Lots, Costco, Discount Tire, Home Depot, Jiffy Lube, PetCo♥, Walmart sc, Red Cliffs Mall, Auto Repairs, Mamoof's, Redlands RV Park▲, Valley View Trailer Park▲ W: Tri City Auto & RV Repair, St George Campground▲

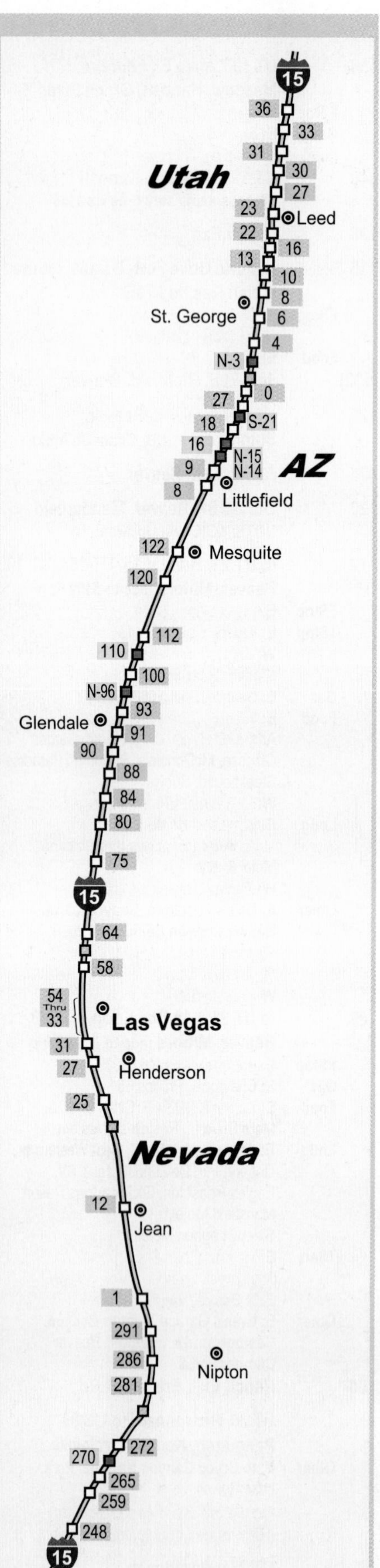

EXIT		UTAH
8		**UT 100N, UT 34, St George Blvd, Bus 15, to UT 18, St George (Acc Ex 10 & 8 via Red Cliffs Dr on E & and Highland Dr on W)**
	FStop	W: Premium Oil/Sinclair
	Gas	E: Chevron◈, Texaco W: Conoco◈, Maverick, Shell◈, Texaco◈
	Food	E: Applebee's, Arby's, Bodacious Rib & BBQ, Carl's Jr, Chili's, Chuck-A-Rama Buffet, Durango's Mex Grill, Famous Dave's BBQ, Golden Corral, Mongolian BBQ, Outback Steakhouse, Panda Express, Quiznos, Red Lobster, Shoney's, Starbucks, Subway/Chevron, Village Inn, Winger's W: Burger King, Bear Paw Cafe, Cafe Rio Mexican Grill, Denny's, Ernesto's Mexican Rest, KFC, McDonald's, Pizza Hut, Taco Bell, Wendy's
	Lodg	E: America's Best Inn, Courtyard, Hampton Inn, Ramada Inn, Red Cliffs Inn W: Best Westernx2, Chalet Motel, Comfort Inn, Coronada Inn, Days Inn, Economy Inn, Econo Lodge, Motel 6♥, Park Inn, Rodeway Inn, Sunbird Inn, Super 8, Travelodge♥
	TServ	W: Dixie Diesel Service
	Med	E: + Dixie Reg'l Medical Center W: + VA Outpatient Clinic
	Other	E: Auto Repair, Banks, Grocery, Lowe's, Staples, Target, Factory Outlet Stores, Red Clffs Mall, St George Campground & RV Park▲ W: RVDump/LP/Premium Oil, Canyonland RV Rentals, Hillside Palms RV & MH Park, Big O Tires, Checker Auto Parts, NAPA, RiteAid, Auto Repairs, Banks, Carwash, Enterprise RAC, Grocery, LP/Shell, Animal Hospital♥, Twin Lakes Golf Course, St George Muni Airport✈
6		**UT 18, Bus 15, Bluff St, St George**
	Gas	E: CFN, Chevron◈, Sunmart, Texaco◈ W: Chevron, Maverick◈, Shell, Texaco◈
	Food	E: Chili's, Cracker Barrel, Jack in the Box, Players Sports Grill W: Burger King, Claimjumper Rest, DQ, Denny's, JB's Rest, McDonald's, Pizza Hut, Tony Roma, Wendy's
	Lodg	E: Ambassador Inn, Comfort Inn, Fairfield Inn, Hilton Garden Inn W: America's Best Value Inn, Best Western, Budget Inn, Claridge Inn, Comfort Suites, Holiday Inn, Howard Johnson, Knights Inn, Quality Inn, Ridgeview Inn, Super 8
	TServ	E: Transport Tire Service W: Zion Motors Truck Service
	Med	W: + Dixie Reg'l Medical Center
	Other	E: Firestone, U-Haul, Auto Dealers, to Rio Virgin RV Park▲ W: Albertson's, Auto Zone, Big O Tires, Firestone, Goodyear, Kmart, Radio Shack, Staples, Auto Dealers, Kwik Lube & Carwash, U-Haul, St George Muni Airport✈, Animal Hospital/Vet♥, Vacation World RV Center Service & Sales, Sun Country RV Center, Desert Coach RV, McArthur's Temple View RV Resort▲, St George Resort▲, Snow Canyon State Park Campground▲

◈= Regular Gas Stations with Diesel ▲ = RV Friendly Locations ♥= Pet Friendly Locations
Red print shows large vehicle parking / access on site or nearby **Brown Print = Campgrounds / RV PARKS**

EXIT — UT / AZ / NV

4 — **Brigham Rd, St George, Bloomington**
- TStop — E: Flying J Travel Plaza #5101 (Scales) (DAD)
- Gas — W: Chevron, Mirastar
- Food — E: FastFood/Flying J TP
  W: 2 Fat Guys Pizza, Arby's, Hunan City, Subway/Taco Bell/Chevron, Wendy's
- Lodg — W: La Quinta Inn♥
- Other — E: WiFi/**LP**/Flying J TP
  W: **Walmart sc**

(3) — UT Welcome Center (NB) (RR, Phone, Picnic, RVDump)

(0) — Port of Entry / Weigh Station (Both dir)

MOUNTAIN TIME ZONE

↑ UTAH
↓ ARIZONA

MOUNTAIN TIME ZONE, NO DST

NOTE: MM 29: Utah State Line

27 — **Black Rock Rd, Littlefield**

(21) — TurnOut (SB)

(16) — TurnOut (TRUCK PARKING)

(15) — TurnOut (Truck Parking) (NB)

(14) — TurnOut (Truck Parking) (NB)

18 — **Cedar Pocket Rd, Littlefield**
- Other — S: **BLM/Virgin River Campground▲**, Virgin River Gorge

(10) — TurnOut (Truck Parking) (NB)

9 — **Farm Rd, Littlefield**

8 — **CR 91, Cane Beds Rd, Littlefield, Beaver Dam**
- Other — E: **Chief Sleep Easy RV Park▲**
  W: **Beaver Dam Resort & RV Park▲**

NOTE: AZ does *not* observe DST

MOUNTAIN TIME ZONE

↑ ARIZONA
↓ NEVADA

PACIFIC TIME ZONE

NOTE: MM 123: Arizona State Line

PACIFIC / MOUNTAIN TIME ZONE

122 — **NV 144, I-15 Bus, Pioneer Blvd, Mesquite, to Bunkerville**
- E: NV Welcome Center (Both dir)
- FStop — W: Virgin River Food Mart/76
- Gas — E: Chevron◈, Maverick◈, Shell, Sinclair
- Food — E: Subway/Chevron, Arby's/Sinclair, Burger King, Chinese Buffet, Golden West Rest & Casino, Jack in the Box, KFC, Taco Time
  W: McDonald's, Rest/Eureka Hotel, Rest/Virgin River Hotel
- Lodg — E: Budget Inn, Desert Palms Motel, Executive Suites, MV Motel
  W: Eureka Casino Hotel, Virgin River Hotel & Casino & RV Park▲, Mesquite Springs Suites
- Other — E: Auto Parts, Banks, Cinema, Museum, US Post Office, Diesel & Auto Repair, Smith's Food & Drug, RiteAid, **Police**, **Desert Skies RV Resort & Park▲**
  W: **LP**/Virgin River FM, Int'l Sports Hall of Fame, Golf Courses, Mesquite Airport✈

EXIT — NEVADA

120 — **Mesquite Blvd, to Pioneer Blvd, UT 170, Mesquite, to Bunkerville**
- Gas — E: C-Mart/Chevron◈, Shell◈, Terrible Herbst
- Food — E: McDonald's, Rest/Casablanca Resort, Rest/Oasis Resort, Rest/Stateline Motel
- Lodg — E: Casablanca Resort & Casino & RV Park/RVDump▲, Oasis Resort Golf Spa Casino & RV Park▲, Stateline Motel & Casino, Valley Inn Motel
  W: Best Western, Falcon Ridge Hotel
- Other — E: **Desert Skies RV Resort▲**, Auto Repair, Auto Parts, Banks, Carwash, Family Dollar, Mesquite Casino
  W: Walgreen's, **Walmart sc**

112 — **NV 170, Mesquite, to Riverside, Bunkerville**

(110) — Parking Area (Both dir)

100 — **Carp Elgin Rd, Bunkerville**

(96) — Parking Area (NB)

93 — **NV 169, Moapa Valley Blvd, to Logandale, Overton**
- Other — E: to appr 11 mi: gas, Clark Co Fairgrounds, Lost City Museum, Overton Muni Airport✈, **Fun n Sun MH & RV Park▲**, **Robbins Nest MH & RV Park▲**

91 — **NV 168, Glendale Blvd, Moapa, Glendale**
- Gas — W: Sinclair◈
- Lodg — W: Motel/Sinclair

90 — **NV 168, Glendale, Moapa (NB) (Access to same serv as Ex #91)**
- Other — W: to appr 8 mi: **Palm Creek Gardens RV Park▲**, Moapa Indian Reservation, Grocery

88 — **NV 78, Hidden Valley Rd, to NV 168, Moapa**

84 — **Byron**

80 — **Ute, Moapa River Indian Res**

75 — **NV 169E, Valley of Fire State Park, Lake Mead**
- TStop — E: Moapa Paiute Travel Plaza/Sinclair/Rest/Casino/Laundry/Fireworks
- Other — E: **Valley of Fire State Park**

64 — **US 93N, NV 604, Great Basin Hwy, Moapa, Pioche, Ely**

(61) — Check Station (SB)

58 — **NV 604, US 93, N Las Vegas, Nellis Air Force Base**
- Other — E: **American Campgrounds▲**, to **Hitchin Post RV Park▲**, Las Vegas Speedway, Nellis AFB/**FamCamp▲**

EXIT — NEVADA

54 — **Speedway Blvd, Hollywood Blvd**
- TStop — E: Petro Stopping Center #31/Mobil (Scales)
- Food — E: IronSkilletRest/Petro SC, Fast Lane Cafe
- TServ — E: Petro SC/Tires
- Other — E: Laundry/**RVDump**/Petro SC, Las Vegas Speedway, Richard Petty Driving Experience

(52) — **Jct I-215W, Las Vegas Beltway**

50 — **Lamb Blvd, NV 610 (SB)**

48 — **NV 573, Craig Rd, N Las Vegas**
- TStop — E: Pilot Travel Center #341 (Scales)
- Gas — E: ArcoAMPM, Chevron, Mobil, Shell. Sinclair◈
  W: 7-11
- Food — E: Burger King, DQ/KFC/PH/Pilot TC, Subway/Chevron, Speedway Grill
- Lodg — E: Barcelona Motel & Casino, Best Western, Hampton Inn, La Quinta Inn♥
  W: Cannery Casino Hotel, Holiday Inn Express
- TWash — E: Fleet Wash
- TServ — E: Diesel Specialist
  W: Truck Parts & Equipment, Cashman Equipment Co, Ford Trucks, McCandless International, Peterbilt, Freightliner
- Other — E: Laundry/Pilot TC, to Nellis AFB, Grocery, Tire & Auto Center, **Walmart sc** **to Hitchin Post RV Park▲**, **American Campground▲**
  W: Grocery, Auto Repair, Sam's Club

46 — **Cheyenne Ave, NV 574, Las Vegas**
- TStop — E: (E to NV604) Maverick Truck Stop/76
  W: Hallmark Truck Center/Sinclair (Scales), Flying J Travel Plaza #10010 (Scales)
- Gas — E: 7-11, ArcoAmPm, Chevron, Exxon
  W: 7-11◈◈
- Food — E: Rest/Maverick TS, Panda Express, Popeye's, Starbucks, Wing's Rest
  W: Rest/JackintheBox/Hallmark TC, CookeryRest/Pizza/FJ TP, Denny's, McDonald's
- Lodg — E: Ramada Inn & Casino, Lucky Club Casino & Hotel
  W: Comfort Inn
- TWash — W: ADC Truck Wash, Hallmark TC, Blue Beacon/FJ TP
- TServ — W: Hallmark TC, FJ TP/Tires, SpeedCo, Purcell Tires, Kenworth
- Other — E: **LP**/Maverick TP, NAPA, Auto Repair, Comm College of S Nevada, **Hitchin Post RV Park▲**
  W: Laundry/WiFi/**RVDump**/FJ TP, **RVDump**/Hallmark TC, N Las Vegas Air Terminal✈, N Las Vegas Golf Course

45 — **NV 147, Lake Mead Blvd (SB) (Addt'l Serv E to NV 604)**
- Gas — E: 7-11, Terrible Herbst
  W: Chevron, Terrible Herbst
- Food — E: Carl's Jr, McDonald's, Wendy's
  W: Domino's Pizza, Long John Silver
- Med — E: + Lake Mead Hospital Med Center
- Other — E: NLV Police Dept, Banks
  W: Auto Repairs

45B — **Lake Mead Blvd W (NB)**

45A — **NV 147E, Lake Mead Blvd E (NB)**

44 — **Washington Ave, D St (SB)**
- Food — E: Rest/Best Western

EXIT		NEVADA
	Lodg	E: Best Western
	Other	E: Casinos $, Shopping, Convention Center, Cashman Field, Museum, Visitor Center
43		**D St, F St, to NV 579, Washington Ave (NB)**
	Gas	E: Gas
	Food	E: Rest/Best Western
	Lodg	E: Best Western♥, Main St Station Hotel & Casino W: Moulin Rouge Hotel & Casino
	Other	E: **Main St Station RV Park▲**, Bank, Museum
(42)		**Jct I-515S, US 93S, US 95, Phoenix, US 95N to Reno, MLK Jr Blvd (SB)**
	Gas	E: 76 W: ArcoAmPm, Shell
	TServ	W: Cummins Intermountain
	Other	E: Casinos $
(42B)		**Jct I-515. US 93, US 95 (NB)**
42A		**Las Vegas Expwy, US 95 (NB)**
41		**NV 159, Charleston Blvd, MLK King Blvd, Las Vegas (SB)**
	Gas	E: 7-11, ArcoAmPm◈ W: 76, Shell, Rebel
	Food	W: Carl's Jr, Del Taco, McDonald's
	Med	W: + University Medical Center, + Valley Hospital Medical Center
	Lodg	W: Marriott
	Other	E: Las Vegas Premium Outlets, Ca Hotel Casino & **RV Park▲**, **Western RV Park▲** W: Costco, CVS, Banks, Univ of NV/Reno, Auto Services & Repairs
41B		**NV 159, Charleston Blvd W, Grand Central Pkwy, Las Vegas**
	Gas	W: 76, Shell
	Food	W: Carl's Jr, Del Taco, McDonald's
	Med	W: + University Medical Center
41A		**NV 159, Charleston Blvd E, to NV 604, Main St, (NB) (Addt'l Serv E to Main St, NV 604)**
	Gas	E: 7-11, ArcoAmPm
	Lodg	E: Bridger Inn Hotel, Travel Inn
40		**Sahara Ave, Las Vegas**
	TStop	E: Maverick Truck Stop/76
	Gas	E: 76, Texaco W: 7-11, Rebel, Texaco
	Food	E: Rest/Maverick TS, Arby's, Golden Steer, Lunch Stop, Steak House, Southern Seafood, Vegas Pizza
	Food	W: Blimpie, Denny's, In N Out Burger, McDonald's, Rest/Palace Station Hotel, Landry's Seafood, Romano's Macaroni Grill, Starbuck's
	Lodg	E: Artesian Hotel & Spa, Bluemoon Resort, Las Vegas Inn & Casino, Sahara Hotel & Casino, Stratosphere Hotel & Casino & Tower, Travelodge W: Palace Station Hotel & Casino, Town Palms Hotel
	TServ	E: Nevada RV & Truck Service
	Other	E: to The Strip, Casinos, Las Vegas Convention Center, Big O Tire, Goodyear, Adventure Dome, Wet 'N Wild, Banks, **CircusCircus KOA/RVDump▲**, **Sahara RV Center** W: Banks, Auto Repairs, Food

EXIT		NEVADA
39		**Desert Inn Rd, Spring Mountain Rd (SB), Flamingo Rd, Twain Ave, Spring Mountain Rd (NB)**
	Gas	W: ArcoAmPm, Circle K, Shell, United◈
	Food	E: Deli, Port of Subs, Hawaiian BBQ, W: Deli
	Lodg	E: Budget Suites, New Frontier Hotel & Casino, Stardust Hotel & Casino, Treasure Island Hotel & Casino, Mirage Hotel & Casino, Harrah's LV Hotel & Casino
	Other	E: Fashion Show Mall, Budget, Banks, Auto Repairs, Hotels, Casinos, Food W: Auto Repair, Discount Tire, Firestone, Goodyear, Sam's Club
38A		**W Flamingo Rd (SB)**
	Gas	W: ArcoAmPm, Chevron, Texaco
	Food	W: Burger King, Outback Steakhouse, Rest/Gold Coast Hotel, Rest/Rio Hotel
	Lodg	W: Gold Coast Hotel & Casino, Rio Hotel & Casino, Palms Hotel & Casino
	Other	W: Banks, Cinema, Food
38B		**E Flamingo Rd (SB)**
	Gas	E: ArcoAmPm
	Food	E: Bally's, Barbary Coast, Bellagio Hotel, Caesars Palace, Hilton, McDonald's
	Lodg	E: Atrium Suites Hotel, Bally Hotel & Casino, Barbary Hotel & Casino, Bellagio Hotel & Casino, Caesars Palace Hotel & Casino, Crest Budget Motel, Days Inn, Flamingo Hilton Hotel & Casino, Holiday Inn, Paris Resort & Casino, Residence Inn,Super 8
38		**Flamingo Rd (NB)**
37		**Tropicana Ave, NV 593**
	TStop	W: Wild Wild West Travel Plaza/King 8 Truck Plaza (Scales)
	FStop	E: 76/The Bus Stop
	Gas	W: 76, ArcoAmPm, Chevron, Shell
	Food	E: Excalibur Hotel, Luxor Hotel, MGM Grand Hotel, Mandalay Bay, Motel 6♥, Tropicana Hotel, CoCo's W: Harley Davidson Cafe, Howard Johnson Hotel, IHOP, In N Out Burgers, Jack in the Box, KFC, King 8 Hotel, McDonald's, Pizza Hut, Taco Bell, Wendy's
	Lodg	E: America's Best Value Inn♥, Comfort Inn, Excalibur Hotel & Casino, Hawthorn Suites, Luxor Resort & Casino, La Quinta Inn♥, MGM Grand Hotel & Casino, Motel 6♥, Monte Carlo Resort & Casino, New York New York Hotel & Casino, Tropicana Resort & Casino, Tropicana Inn, Travelodge W: American 5, Best Western, Budget Suites, Motel 6, Hampton Inn, Howard Johnson Hotel & Casino, King 8 Hotel /WildWildWest & Casino, Motel 6♥
	Other	E: Cinema, Casinos $, Airport✈ W: Cinema, Casinos $
36		**Russell Rd, Las Vegas**
	Gas	E: Shell W: Terrible Herbst/Chevron
	Food	E: McDonald's, Panda Express
	Lodg	E: Diamond Inn Motel, Four Seasons Hotel, Klondike Hotel & Casino, Royal Oasis Motel, Mandalay Bay Resort & Casino
	Lodg	W: Interstate Hotel, Holiday Inn Express

EXIT		NEVADA
	Other	E: McCarran Int'l Airport✈ W: Tourist Info
(34)		**Jct I-215E to Henderson, NV 604 Las Vegas Blvd, Las Vegas Beltway**
33		**NV 160, Blue Diamond Rd, to NV 604, Las Vegas, Pahrump, to Blue Diamond, Death Valley**
	TStop	W: Travel Center of America /76 (Scales)
	Gas	E: 7-11◈, ArcoAmPm, Terrible Herbst/ Chevron, Mobil◈ W: Chevron◈
	Food	E: Dickey's BBQ Pit, Canes, IHOP, Joe's NY Pizza, Panda Express, Samurai Sam's W: BK/Subway/TacoTime/TA TC, Jack in the Box
	Lodg	E: Budget Suites, Emerald Suites, Hilton Garden Inn, Hampton Inn, Malibu Bay Suites, Microtel, Residence Inn W: Firebird Motel/TA TC, Silverton Hotel & Casino & **RV Parking▲**
	TServ	W: TA TC, D&D Tire
	TWash	W: Truck Wash, TA TC
	Other	E: **Oasis LV RV Resort/RVDump▲** U-Haul, CVS, Food4Less, UPS Store, Belz Factory Outlet World, **Cancun Casino Resort** W: Laundry/**RVDump**/HealthCl/TA TC, **LP**, Bass Pro Shop, Factory Outlet Mall, Office Depot, Petco♥, **Outdoor Resorts LV Motorcoach Resort▲**
31		**Silverado Ranch Blvd**
	Gas	E: 7-11, Shell
	Lodg	E: South Point Hotel, Casino & Spa
	Other	E: to Albertson's, Walmart Neighborhood Market, CVS, Walgreen's
27		**NV 146, Lake Mead Dr, NV 604, St Rose Pkwy, Southern Highlands Pkwy, Henderson, to Lake Mead, Hoover Dam**
	TStop	E: Vegas Valley Travel Center
	Food	E: Rest/FastFood/VV TC
	Other	E: Laundry/**RVDump/LP**/VV TC, Factory Outlet Stores, LV-Henderson Sky Harbor Airport✈, **Wheelers LV RV**, **Las Vegas RV/Camping World**
25		**Sloan Rd, Las Vegas**
	Other	E: **Camping World Wheeler's LV RV/LP**
(24)		**Check Station (NB)**
12		**NV 161, Jean, to Goodsprings NV Welcome Center (NB) (RR, Phone, Picnic, Vend, Info)**
	TStop	E: Gold Strike Auto Truck Plaza/Mobil
	Gas	W: Shell◈ /Nevada Landing Hotel & Casino
	Food	E: Burger King/Gold Strike Hotel
	Lodg	E: Gold Strike Hotel & Casino
	Other	E: Jean Airport✈, Visitor Center, US Post Office
1		**Primm Blvd, Jean, Stateline**
	Tstop	W: Whiskey Pete's Casino Truck Stop/ Shell (Scales)
	Gas	E: 76◈, Chevron
	Food	E: Carl's Jr, Denny's, McDonald's, Starbucks W: Rest/Whiskey Pete's TS
	Lodg	E: Buffalo Bill's Resort & Casino & **RV▲**, Primm Valley Resort & Casino & **RV▲** W: Whiskey Pete's Hotel & Casino

◈= Regular Gas Stations with Diesel ▲ = RV Friendly Locations ♥= Pet Friendly Locations
Red print shows large vehicle parking / access on site or nearby Brown Print = Campgrounds / RV PARKS

EXIT		NV / CA
	Other	E: Fashion Outlet of LV, **Prima Donna RV Park▲**, Laundry/Whiskey Pete's

PACIFIC TIME ZONE

⬆ NEVADA
⬇ CALIFORNIA

PACIFIC TIME ZONE

	NOTE:	**MM 298: Nevada State Line**
291		**Yates Well Rd, Nipton**
286		**Nipton Rd, Nipton, to Searchlight**
	Other	E: Mojave Nat'l Preserve
281		**Bailey Rd, Nipton**
	Other	E: Mojave Nat'l Preserve
(276)		**Brake Inspection Area (NB)**
272		**Cima Rd, Nipton**
	Gas	E: Stateline Service/Shell◈
	Other	E: Repairs/Tires/Towing/Stateline Shell Mojave Nat'l Preserve
(270)		**Valley Wells Rest Area (Both dir) (RR, Phones, Pic, Vend, Pet)**
	NOTE:	**MM 265: SB: Steep downgrade 17mi**
265		**Halloran Summit Rd, Baker**
259		**Halloran Springs Rd, Baker**
248		**Baker Blvd (SB) (Access to Exit #246 Serv)**
246		**CA 127, Kelbaker Rd, Baker, Death Valley**
	FStop	W: Bandit Valero, CFN/Shell
	Gas	W: 76◈, ArcoAmPm, Chevron, Mobil◈, Valero◈
	Food	W: Arby's, Bob's Big Boy, Burger King, Coco's Rest, Del Taco, Jack in the Box/ Shell, Mr Wok Chinese, Starbucks, The Mad Greek, Taco Bell/Chevron, Subway/PHut/A&W/Valero, DQ/Quiznos/ Valero
	Lodg	W: Bun Boy Motel, Royal Hawaiian Motel, Motel Wills Fargo, Microtel
	Other	W: Alien Fresh Jerky, Auto Repair, ATM/Bank, Baker Market, Baker Garage Auto Parts, Ken's Towing & Tire Car/Truck/ RV, Lucky 7 Market, NAPA, US Post Office, RVDump/Valero, A-1 LP
245		**Baker Blvd (NB) (Acc Ex #246 Serv)**
239		**Zzyzx Rd, Baker**
233		**Rasor Rd, Arrowhead Tr, Baker**
	FStop	E: Rasor Road Services
	TServ	E: Rasor Rd Service & Towing
230		**Basin Rd, Cronese Lake Rd, Ludlow, Cronese Valley**
221		**Afton Rd, Ludlow, Dunn**
	Other	W: Mini Market
(217)		**Clyde Kane Rest Area (Both dir) (RR, Phones, Picnic, Pet)**
213		**Field Rd, Ludlow**
206		**Harvard Rd, Newberry Springs**
	Other	E: to appr 7.5 mi: **Twin Lakes RV Park▲**, to I-40
198		**Minneola Rd, Newberry Springs**
	Gas	W: Valero◈
	Other	E: to Barstow-Daggett Airport✈, to I-40

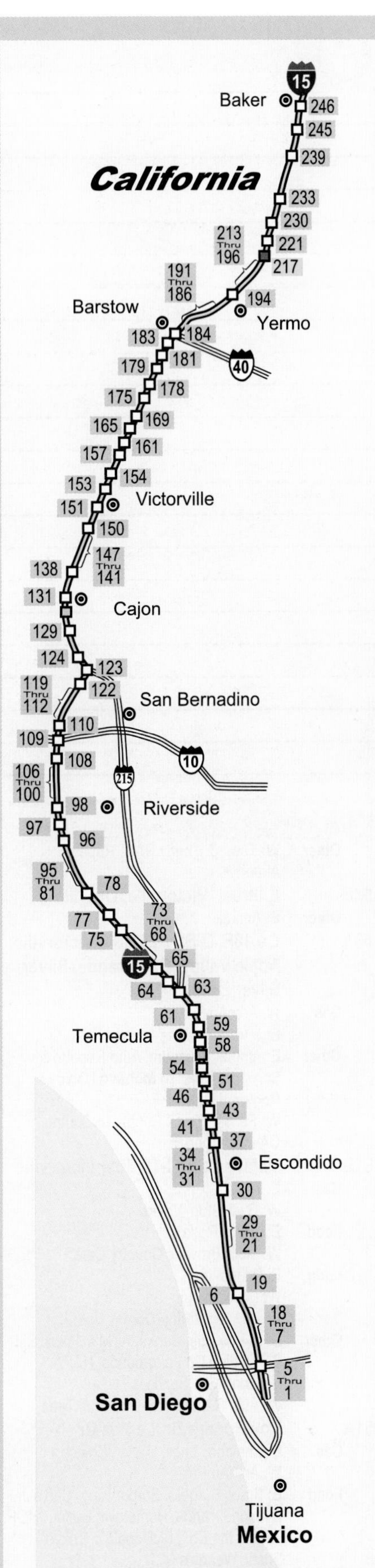

EXIT		CALIFORNIA
(197)		**Agricultural Insp Station (SB)**
196		**Yermo Rd, Newberry Springs**
194		**Calico Rd, Newberry Springs, Yermo, Bismarck**
	Other	E: **Barstow/Calico KOA▲**
191		**Ghost Town Rd, Daggett Yermo Rd, Yermo Rd, Newberry Springs, Daggett, E to I-40**
	TStop	E: Vegas Truck Stop/Mohsen Oil Truck & Travel W: Ghost Town Mini Mart/Shell
	Gas	E: ArcoAmPm W: 76
	Food	E: FastFood/Mohsen, Jack in the Box, Peggy Sue's 50's Diner, Penny's Diner W: Jenny Rose Rest, Old Miners Cafe
	Lodg	E: Oak Tree Inn
	Other	E: **Desert Springs RV Park▲**, W: **Barstow/Calico KOA▲**, to appr 3.5mi **Calico Ghost Town Campground▲**
189		**Fort Irwin Rd, Meridian Rd, Yermo Rd, Barstow**
186		**Old Hwy 58, Barstow, Bakersfield**
	Other	W: Skyline Drive-In Theater, **Shady Lane RV Camp▲**, to BLM/Rainbow Basin Natural Area/**Owl Canyon Campground▲**
184		**E Main St, to I-40E, Needles (SB)**
	Gas	E: Barstow Station/Shell, 76◈, Chevron, Mobil◈ W:ArcoAmPm, Chevron, Circle K, Shell◈, Thrifty, Valero
	Food	E: Barstow Station/BJ's BBQ/Ice Cream Shoppe/McDonald's/Panda Express/ Popeye's Chicken/Quiznos, Donut Star Chinese Food, Starbucks, Straw Hat Pizza, Tom's Burgers W: Arby's, Burger King, Carl's Jr, China Gourmet, Carrow's, COCO's, Denny's, Dinapolis Fire House Italian Rest, IHOP, KFC, Little Caesars Pizza, Long John Silver's, Sizzler, Taco Bell, Weinerschnitzel, Rest/Qual Inn
	Lodg	E: Best Western, Travelodge♥ W: Astro Budget Motel, Best Motel, Brant's Motel, Budget Inn, California Inn, Cactus Motel, Desert Inn, Days Inn, Econo Lodge, Economy Inn, Motel 6, Quality Inn, Ramada Inn♥, Rodeway Inn, Stardust Inn Motel, Super 8
	Med	W: + Meridian Urgent Care
	Other	E: Ace Hardware, Barstow Station/Liquor Store/Shopping/Greyhound, S of I-40: **Walmart** W: AutoZone, BJ's Health Foods, Car wash/Valero, Diane's Laundromat, Food4Less, Kragen Auto Parts, Radio Shack, Ruby's Nightclub, SavALot, U-Haul, Von's Food & Drug,
184B		**I-15 Bus, E Main St, to I-40E (NB)**
(184A)		**Jct I-40E, Needles (NB) (Begin/End I-40) (Acc to #184 Serv)**
183		**CA 247S, Barstow Rd, Barstow (Addt'l Serv W/N to I-15 Bus)**
	Gas	E: 76, UltraMar/Beacon, Valero W: Chevron
	Food	E: Pizza Hut/Valero, Casa Jimenez Mex Rest, Red Baron Pizza, Subway W: Little Caesars Pizza, Steak Your Way

◈= Regular Gas Stations with Diesel ▲ = RV Friendly Locations ♥= Pet Friendly Locations

Red print shows large vehicle parking / access on site or nearby Brown Print = Campgrounds / RV PARKS

EXIT CALIFORNIA

Med W: + Barstow Comm Hospital
Other E: Lube Express, RiteAid, Stater Bros Market, to Barstow College
W: Auto Repair, Auto Dealers, Amtrak, ATM's, Banks, Food 4 Less, Food Depot, Pharmacy, U-Haul, **Police Dept, CA Hwy Patrol Post, Addtl Serv W to Main St**

181 L St, W Main St, Barstow (F/Tstops W Main/L St)
FStop W: Heartland Truck Stop (Scales)
TStop W: American Travel Center
Gas W: ArcoAmPm, Chevron, Thrifty
Food W: Rest/ATC, Rest/HTS, Bun Boy Rest, Pizza Palace, Mexican Rest
Lodg W: Americas Best Value Inn, Holiday Inn Express, Motel 66, Motel 7, Nites Inn,
TWash W: Heartland TS, Vernon TW
TServ W: CB Service, Heartland TS, Barstow Truck Parts & Equipment
Other W: Avis RAC, Auto Repairs, Banks, Enterprise RAC, Firestone, Grocery, Home Depot, Laundromat, Penske Truck Rental, Tire Services, Towing

179 CA 58W, to Bakersfield

178 Lenwood Rd, Barstow
TStop E: Flying J Travel Plaza #5090 (Scales),
W: Pilot Travel Center #282 (Scales), Travel Center of America/Shell (Scales), Love's Travel Stop #374 (Scales)
Gas E: 76, Chevron◈, Shell, Valero
W: Mobil
Food E: CountryMkt/Pizza/Chinese/FJ TP, Arby's, Baja Fresh Mex Grill, Burger King, Big Boy, Carl's Jr, Chili's, Chipolte Mexican Grill, Del Taco, El Pollo Loco, In N Out Burger, Jack in the Box, KFC, Panda Express, Quigley's Rest, Starbucks, Taco Bell, Tommy's Hamburgers
W: Subway/Pilot TC, CountryFareRest/ Subway/TA TC, ChestersFrCh/ Godfathers Pizza/Love's TS, Denny's, KFC, McDonald's, Wendy's
Lodg E: Comfort Suites, Country Inn, Hampton Inn♥, Holiday Inn Express♥
W: Days Inn♥,
TWash E: Blue Beacon Truck Wash
W: Truck Wash AmPm, Little Sisters Truck Wash, Today Truck Wash Tires & Restaurant
TServ W: TA TC
Other E: Laundry/BarbSh/WiFi/RVDump/LP/ FJ TP, Tanger Outlet Mall, Barstow Outlets
W: Laundry/WiFi/Pilot TC, Laundry/WiFi/ RVDump/TA TC

175 Outlet Center Dr, Sidewinder Rd

169 Hodge Rd, Stoddard Mtn Rd

165 Wild Wash Rd, Sorrel Trail, Helendale

161 Dale Evans Pkwy, Apple Valley

157 Stoddard Wells Rd, Bell Mountain Rd, Apple Valley, Victorville

154 Stoddard Wells Rd, Victorville
Gas W: 76, Mobil
Food W: Denny's
Lodg W: Motel 6♥
Med E: + St Mary Hospital
Other **E: Shady Oasis Kampground▲ /LP/ RVDump**

Personal Notes

EXIT CALIFORNIA

Other W: Towing, Thrifty RAC, Repairs, Airport✈

153B E Street, Victorville, Oroville
Other E: Amtrak

153A CA 18E, D St, I-15 Bus, Victorville, Apple Valley, Oro Grande, Silver Silver Lakes
Gas W: ArcoAmPm
Med E: + Victor Valley Comm Hospital
Other E: Amtrak, Museum, Auto Repairs & Services, Tires, **to Mohave Narrows Regional Park▲**
W: Penske Truck Rental, **to** Southern CA Int'l Airport✈

151B Mojave Dr, to I-15 Bus, Victorville
Gas E: 76◈
W: Qwik Stop, Valero
Food E: Mama Rosa's
W: Molly Brown's Country Cafe
Lodg E: Budget Inn
W: Economy Inn, Sunset Inn
Med E: + Victor Valley Comm Hospital
Other E: **to** I-15 Bus, Banks, ATM's, Food, San Bernardino Co Fairgrounds, NAPA, Verizon, Auto Services
W: Auto Repair, Transmission, Tires

151A Roy Rogers Dr, La Paz Dr
Gas E: Chevron, Shell, USA◈, Costco
W: ArcoAmPm
Food E: Bravo Burgers, Burger King, Carl's Jr, Diamond Panda, Hometown Buffet, IHOP, Jack in the Box, McDonald's, Tokyo Sushi, Wendy's
W: Dominos Pizza, Starbucks
Lodg E: New Corral Motel

EXIT CALIFORNIA

Other E: **to** I-15 Bus, ATM's, Banks, Auto Zone, Big Lots, Budget RAC, Costco, Food4Less, Goodyear, Kragen Auto Parts, RiteAid, San Bernardino Co Fairgrounds, Smart 'n Final, U-Haul, US Post Office, Victor Valley Harley Davidson, Von's Food & Drug,
W: America's Tire, Auto Dealers, Enterprise RAC

150 CA 18W, Palmdale Rd, 7th St, Victorville, Palmdale (Acc to #151)
TStop W: **to US 395N:** High Desert Travel Center
Gas W: ArcoAmPm, Chevron, Shell, Valero
Food E: Rest/Best Western, Burger King, Carl's Jr, Denny's, El Pollo Loco, Jack in the Box, KFC, Richie's Diner, Starbucks
W: Coco's, Del Taco, La Casita Mexican, Long John Silver, McDonald's, Pizza Hut, Starbucks, Subway, Taco Bell, Yoshi Sushi
Lodg E: Quality Inn, Red Roof Inn
W: Ambassador Hotel, Budget Inn, Days Inn
Other E: Auto Dealers, Avis RAC, Victorville Muni Golf Course
W: Auto Dealers, Auto Zone, Park Center Shopping Center, Budget Truck Rental, Enterprise RAC, Holiday Skate World, Mesa Animal Hospital♥, Ralph's, Target, Mall of Victor Valley, **Police Dept, CA Hwy Patrol Post, Cruise America RV Rentals, Kampers Korner RV Sales & Service/LP, Victor Valley RV Discount Center/El Monte RV Rentals & Sales**

147 Bear Valley Rd, Victorville, Lucerne Valley, Apple Valley
Gas E: 76, ArcoAmPm, BP, Mobil, Shell
W: Chevron, Valero
Food E: Baker's Burgers, Burger King, Carl's Jr, Del Taco, Dragon Express, KFC, Long John Silver's, McDonald's, Panda Express, Quiznos, Red Robin, Starbucks, Stein & Steer, TNT Cafe
W: Applebee's, California Fresh, Chuck E Cheese's, Chili's, El Tio Pepe, El Pollo Loco, Carino's, Jack in the Box, Little Caesars Pizza, Mimi's Cafe, Olive Garden, On the Border, Outback Steakhouse, Red Lobster, Roadhouse Grill, Starbucks, Subway, Tony Roma, Wendy's
Lodg E: Comfort Suites, Days Inn, Econo Lodge, Extended Stay, Hampton Inn, Hilton Garden Inn, La Quinta Inn♥, Super 8, Travelodge
W: Hawthorne Suites
Med E: + Desert Valley Hospital
Other E: Auto Zone, America's Tire, American Tire Depot, Bear Valley Car Wash, BJ's Health Foods, Cinemark Movies 10, Firestone, High Desert Veterinary Care♥, Home Depot, Jiffy Lube, Kragen Auto Parts, Penske Truck Rental, RiteAid, Smart 'n Final, Staples, Scandia Family Fun Center, Tires, Victor Bowl, **WalMart**/Pharmacy, Budget RAC, Hertz RAC, **Affordable RV Center, Range RV Rentals, Victor Valley Discount RV Center**
W: Albertson's, Avis RAC, Banks, B&N, Best Buy, Big 5 Sporting Goods, CVS, Cinemark Bear Valley 10, Cost Plus World Market, Lowe's, Mall of Victor Valley, Office Max, PetSmart♥, Stater Bros Market, Tires, UPS Store, Walgreen's,

◈= Regular Gas Stations with Diesel ▲ = RV Friendly Locations ♥= Pet Friendly Locations
Red print shows large vehicle parking / access on site or nearby Brown Print = Campgrounds / RV PARKS

EXIT		CALIFORNIA
143		**Main St, to US 395, Hesperia**
	Gas	E: ArcoAmPm, Chevron, Shell◈, Valero W: 76◈, ArcoAmPm◈
	Food	E: Arby's, Burger King, DQ/Valero, Denny's, El Pollo Loco, In 'N Out Burger, IHOP, Jack in the Box, Main St Grill & Bakery, Pizza, Popeye's Chicken/Shell, Starbucks, Wood Grill Buffet W: Bakers Burgers, Subway, Valentino Pizzeria, FastFood/76
	Lodg	E: Courtyard, Springhill Suites W: Country Hearth Inn, Holiday Inn Express, Motel 6
	Other	E: **Police Dept**, Major RV & Auto Sales, to Hesperia Airport✈, **Hesperia Lake Park & Campground▲** , W: Super Target, Verizon, LP/76, **Desert Willow RV Resort▲** , to US 395,
141		**US 395N (NB), Joshua St, Palm Ave, US 395N (SB)**
	TStop	W: Pilot Travel Center #381 (Scales) Newton's Outpost Café & Truck N Travel
	Food	E: Summit Inn Rest W: Wendy's/Pilot TC
	TWash	W: Newton's Outpost Café & Truck N Travel, Little Sisters Truck Wash
	TServ	W: CAT/Cummins, Goodyear, Zippy Lube
	Other	W: Laundry/WiFi/Pilot TC, **RVDump**/ Newton's Outpost Café & Truck N Travel, **RV Supply Center Repairs & Rentals, Adelanto RV Park▲**
138		**Oak Hill Rd, Hesperia**
	Gas	E: Shell◈
	Food	E: Summit Inn Rest
	Other	W: **Oak Hills RV Village▲**
	NOTE:	**MM 132: Cajon Summit (Elev 4260)**
	NOTE:	**MM 137: SB: 6% Steep Grade next 12mi**
(133)		**RunAWay Truck Ramp (SB)**
131		**CA 138, San Bernardino, Palmdale, Silverwood Lake**
	Gas	E: Chevron W: 76/Circle K◈, Shell◈,
	Food	E: McDonald's W: Del Taco/76, Subway/Shell
	Lodg	W: Best Western
	Other	E: to Silverwood Lake, **Silverwood Lake State Rec Area**
(131)		**Weigh Station (Both dir)**
129		**Cajon Blvd, Cleghorn Rd**
	Other	W: to **San Bernardino Nat'l Forest▲**
124		**Kenwood Ave, Historic Rte 66, San Bernardino**
(123)		**Jct I-215S, to San Bernardino (SB Exit Left) (Gas,Food at 1st Exit)**
122		**Devore Rd, Glen Helen Pkwy (E to I-215, Acc #119 W via Devore Rd)**
	Food	E: Country Corner Rest
	Other	E: **RVDump/Glen Helen Reg'l Park**, Glen Helen Off Hwy Vehicle Park, Bank, Hyundai Pavilion, San Manuel Amphitheater
119		**Sierra Ave, Riverside Ave, to I-210 Lytle Creek Rd, Fontana, Rialto**
	TStop	E: (S Riverside Ave) Rialto Shell Travel Center (Scales)
	Gas	W: ArcoAmPm◈, Shell◈

EXIT		CALIFORNIA
	Food	E: FastFood/Rialto TC W: Blimpie, Del Taco/Shell, Dominos Pizza, Jack in the Box/Arco, McDonald's
	Other	E: Laundry/**LP/RVDump**/Rialto TC
116		**Beech Ave, Summit Ave, to I-210**
	Gas	E: 7-11, Chevron
	Food	E: Chili's, El Ranchero Rest, Jack in the Box, Ono Hawaiian BBQ, Panera Bread, Starbucks, Subway, Taco Bell, Wendy's
	Other	E: CVS, Longs Drug, PetSmart♥, Sports Authority, Staples, Stater Bros Market, Target/Pharmacy
115B		**CA 210E, to San Bernardino (SB), CA 210W, to Pasadena (NB)**
115A		**CA 210W, to Pasadena (SB), CA 210E, to San Bernardino (NB)**
113		**Baseline Rd, Fontana**
	Gas	E: Shell, USA W: Chevron, Speedway
	Food	E: Denny's, Jack in the Box, KFC, Rosa Maria's, Logan's Roadhouse, Pizza Hut, Starbucks, Wendy's W: Pizza
	Lodg	E: Comfort Inn
	Other	E: ATM, Grocery, Mountain View Tire & Service, to Rialto Muni Airport✈ W: Winery, to PetCo♥
112		**CA 66, Foothill Blvd, Fontana, Rancho Cucaomonga, Hist Rte 66**
	Gas	E: Circle K, Chevron W: ArcoAmPm, Mobil
	Food	E: Arby's, Claim Jumper, Coco's, Golden Spoon, Hungry Howie's, In N Out Burger, McDonald's, Melting Pot, Panda Express, Pizza Hut, Starbucks, Subway, Stuffed Bagel, Taco Bell W: Carl's Jr, Carino's, ChickFilA, Denny's, Farmer Boys, Red Robin, Starbucks, Wendy's
	Lodg	W: Best Western
	Med	W: + **Rancho San Antonio Med Center**
	Other	E: Auto Repairs, ATM, Grocery, Costco, Food 4 Less, Office Depot, Radio Shack, Target, **Walmart**, U-Haul, J & J Diesel Repair W: Auto Zone, ATM's, Banks, Best Buy, Bass Pro Shop, Lowe's, Globe Theatres, Home Depot, PetSmart♥, Tires, U-Haul, **Police Station**
110		**4th St, Ontario**
	Gas	W: ArcoAmPm◈, Mobil◈, Costco
	Food	W: Applebee's, Baja Fresh, Carl's Jr, Chevy's Mexican Rest, Chipolte Grill, Coco's, Dave & Buster's, Del Taco, Denny's, El Pollo Loco, Fuddrucker's, IHOP, Jack in the Box, KFC, McDonald's, Japanese Rest, Olive Garden, Outback Steakhouse, Panda Express, Red Lobster, Rainforest Café, Starbucks, Subway
	Lodg	W: Amerisuites, Country Suites, Hilton, Extended Stay America, Holiday Inn, La Quinta Inn♥
	Other	E: California Speedway, Fontana Diesel Service, Auto Repairs, Mamoof's W: AMC 30, America's Tire, Big O Tires, Costco, Sam's Club, Staples, Ontario Mills Mall, IMAX, Empire Lakes Golf Course, Plaza Continental Factory Stores, Banks, ATM's, Tires
(109B)		**Jct I-10E, to San Bernardino (SB)**

EXIT		CALIFORNIA
(109A)		**Jct I-10W, to Los Angeles (SB)**
	Other	W: to Ontario Int'l Airport✈
(109)		**Jct I-10 (NB)**
108		**Jurupa Ave, Ontario, Fontana**
	Gas	W: ArcoAmPm
	Food	E: Starbucks W: Carl's Jr
	Other	E: Auto Dealers, U-Haul W: Auto Dealers, Auto Repairs, Ontario Int'l Airport✈, Rental Car Companies, Scandia Amusement Park
106		**CA 60, W - LA, E - Riverside (SB)**
106B		**CA 60W, to Los Angeles (NB)**
106A		**CA 60E, to Riverside (NB)**
103		**Limonite Ave, Mira Loma**
	Gas	E: to appr 1.5 mi: Circle K, Valero
	Food	E: Carl's Jr, Del Taco, Jack in the Box, Jamba Juice, Philly's Best, Wabi Sabi W: Applebee's, Buffalo Wild Wings, Carino's Italian Grill, El Gran Burrito, Farmer Boys, Figaro Pizza, Johnny Rockets, L&L Hawaiian BBQ, On the Border, Pick Up Stix, Pita Pit, Starbucks, Wendy's
	Other	E: BevMo, Kirkland's, Lowe's, Michael's, Petco♥, Rosas W: Best Buy, Home Depot, PetSmart♥, Ralph's, Staples, Target, UPS Store, Von's
100		**Sixth St, Norco Dr, Bus 15, Norco**
	Gas	E: ArcoAmPm, Chevron W: Valero
	Food	E: Jack in the Box, McDonald's W: Country Junction Rest
	Other	W: Auto Service, Diesel Service, Banks, Jiffy Lube, Vet♥
98		**2nd St, Bus 15 Norco, Corona**
	Gas	W: 7-11, Shell◈, Shell, Spirit
	Food	W: Burger King, Chipolte Mexican Grill, Denny's, Domino's, In N Out Burgers, Marie Callendar's, Sizzler
	Lodg	W: Howard Johnson Express
	Other	W: Auto Dealers, Auto Service, America's Tire, Auto Zone, Big O Tire, Staples, Stater Bros, Target, Diesel Service, Banks, Truck Repair, Riverside Comm College
97		**Mountain Ave, Hidden Valley Pkwy**
	Gas	W: 76, Chevron, Shell◈
	Food	E: ChickFilA W: Arby's, Carl's Jr, Chipolte Mexican Grill, DQ, Denny's, Fazoli's, Hong Kong Express, Jack in the Box, McDonald's, Papa John's, Pizza Hut, Quiznos, Rubio's, Starbucks, Taco Bell, Wendy's
	Lodg	W: Hampton Inn
	Other	W: Albertson's/Pharmacy, Big Lots, Staples, Target, UPS Store, Walgreen's, to Corona Muni Airport✈
96B		**CA 91W, Corona, Beach Cities, to Anaheim, Long Beach (SB)**
	Other	W: to Corona Muni Airport✈
96A		**CA 91E, to Riverside (SB)**
96		**CA 91, Beach Cities, Riverside (NB)**
95		**Magnolia Ave, Corona**
	Gas	E: CFN, Chevron W: Mobil, Shell

◈= Regular Gas Stations with Diesel ▲ = RV Friendly Locations ♥= Pet Friendly Locations
Red print shows large vehicle parking / access on site or nearby **Brown Print = Campgrounds / RV PARKS**

EXIT	CALIFORNIA
Food	E: Blackwood American Grill, Chili's, Chuy's Mesquite Rest, Islands Rest, Jack in the Box, Outback Steakhouse, Quiznos, Romano's Macaroni Grill W: Burger King, Carl's Jr, Chinese Rest, CoCo's, Donut Star, Little Caesars Pizza, Pizza Hut, McDonald's, Sizzler, Subway
Lodg	E: Residence Inn♥ W: Holiday Inn Express
Med	W: + Corona Reg'l Medical Center
Other	E: Lowe's, Office Depot, Auto Repair W: Banks, Auto Repair, Grocery, CVS, Dollar Tree, Kragen Auto Parts, Ralph's, RiteAid, Stater Bros
93	**Ontario Ave, Corona**
Gas	E: Shell W: Chevron, Sam's
Food	E: Starbucks W: Denny's, In N Out Burger, Jack in the Box, KFC, McDonald's, Quiznos, Tommy's Orig'l WF Hamburgers
Other	E: Auto Repair, Diesel Repair W: Albertson's, Home Depot, Longs Drug, Radio Shack, Sam's Club, **Walmart**, US Post Office, Banks
92	**El Cerrito Rd, Corona, El Cerrito**
Gas	E: Circle K
91	**Cajalco Rd, Corona**
Food	E: Chili's, ChickFilA, On the Border Mexican Rest, Romano's Macaroni Grill, Starbucks, Wendy's
Other	E: B&N, Best Buy, Michael's, Petco♥, Ross, Staples, Target
90	**Weirick Rd, Corona**
88	**Temescal Canyon Rd, Corona, Glen Ivy**
Gas	E: Shell W: ArcoAmPm
Food	W: Carl's Jr
Other	**W: to Glen Ivy RV Park▲**, Glen Ivy Hot Springs
85	**Indian Truck Trail, Corona**
81	**Lake St, Lake Elsinore, Alberthill**
78	**Nichols Rd**
Gas	W: ArcoAmPm
Food	W: Carl's Jr
Other	W: Lake Elsinore Outlet Center
77	**CA 74, Central Ave, Perris, San Juan Capistrano, Lake Elsinore**
Gas	E: ArcoAmPm, Chevron, Mobil, Costco
Food	E: Burger King, Chili's, Del Taco, Douglas Burgers, Panda Express, Off-Ramp Cafe, Wendy's W: El Pollo Loco, Farmer Boys, Starbucks
Lodg	W: to Bedrock Motel & **Campground**
Other	E: Costco, Lowe's, PetSmart♥, Staples, **Elsinore Hills RV Park▲** W: Albertson's, Auto Repair, Home Depot, Petco♥, Target, Walgreen's, **Lake Elsinore West Marina & RV Resort▲**, **Weekend Paradise▲**, **Lake Elsinore Campground▲**
75	**Main St, Lake Elsinore**
Gas	W: 76, Circle K
Food	W: Family Basket Rest
Lodg	W: Lake Elsinore Hot Spring Motel
Other	W: Lake Elsinore Tire & Auto
73	**Diamond Dr, Railroad Canyon Rd**
Gas	E: Circle K, Shell W: ArcoAmPm, Mobil◈

EXIT	CALIFORNIA
Food	E: El Pollo Loco, Denny's, In n Out Burger, KFC, McDonald's, Latte Express, Quiznos, Starbucks W: Burger King, Carl's Jr, CoCo's, Del Taco, McDonald's, Pizza Hut, Sizzler, Subway, Taco Bell
Lodg	E: Holiday Inn Express, Lake Elsinore Inn W: Lake Elsinore Resort & Casino, Lake View Inn, Travel Inn
Other	E: Banks, Kragen Auto Parts, Jiffy Lube, Von's Grocery, **Walmart sc**, **to Pepper Tree RV Park▲** W: Auto Dealers, Albertson's/Pharmacy, Auto Zone, Big Lots, Big O Tire, CVS, Firestone, Goodyear, NAPA, Radio Shack,
71	**Bundy Canyon Rd, Wildomar**
Gas	W: ArcoAmPm
Food	W: Jack in the Box
Other	**W: to Pepper Tree RV Park▲**, to Skylark Airport✈, **Casa De Mobile RV Park▲**
69	**Baxter Rd**
68	**Clinton Keith Rd, Wildomar**
Gas	E: Chevron◈, USA W: 7-11◈, ArcoAmPm
Food	E: Arby's, Denny's, La Cresta Mexican Rest, McDonald's, Panda Express, Starbucks, Subway W: D'Canters Wine Bar & Grill, Del Taco, Jack in the Box, Starbucks
Med	E: + Inland Valley Reg Med Center
Other	E: Albertson's/Pharmacy, Ace Hardware W: Stater Bros Market
65	**California Oaks Rd, Kalmia St, Murietta**
Gas	E: 76, Chevron, Mobil◈, Shell◈ W: ArcoAmPm, Chevron
Food	E: Burger King, Carl's Jr, DQ, KFC, McDonald's W: Applebee's, Carrow's, ChickFilA, Farmer Boys, Jack in the Box
Other	E: Albertson's/Pharmacy, Auto Zone, Big O Tire, Kragen Auto Parts, Radio Shack RiteAid, Target, Walgreen's, **Police Dept** W: America's Tire, Lowe's, Office Depot, Petco♥, **Giant RV**
64	**Murrieta Hot Springs Rd, to I-215, Murrieta** (Addtl Serv E past I-215)
Gas	E: 7-11, Shell◈ W: Citgo, Shell◈
Food	E: Carl's Jr, El Pollo Loco, Richie's Diner, Starbucks, Wendy's W: Arby's, Bella's Pizza, China Inn, Chuy's, IHOP, McDonald's, Panda Express, Quiznos, Starbucks, Subway
Med	E: + Rancho Springs Medical Center
Other	E: Ralph's, RiteAid, Sam's Club, Walgreen's, **Temecula Valley RV/RVDump** W: Best Buy, Big Lots, CompUSA, Grocery, Home Depot, PetSmart♥, Staples, **Walmart sc**, **El Monte RV Sales & Rentals**
(63)	**Jct I-215N, to San Bernardino, Riverside (NB)**
61	**CA 79N, Winchester Ave, Hemet, Temecula**
FStop	E: Jefferson Chevron
Gas	E: Costco W: ArcoAmPm, Chevron, Mobil

EXIT	CALIFORNIA
Food	E: Baja Fresh, Burger King, Carino's, Carl's Jr, CoCo's, El Torito, Great Steak & Potato Co, McDonald's, Mimi's Café, On the Border, Panda Express, Roadhouse Grill, Quiznos, Starbucks, TGI Friday, Taco Bell W: Arby's, CA Grill, DQ, El Pollo Loco, Farmer Boys, Hungry Hunter Steakhouse, Hooters, Jack in the Box, Richie's Diner, Sizzler, Starbucks, Tecate Grill, Taco Factory, Tony Roma's
Lodg	W: Best Western♥, Comfort Inn♥, Extended Stay America, Fairfield Inn
Other	E: Auto Dealers, ATM's, America's Tire, Banks, B&N, Big O Tire, Costco, FedEx Office, Food4Less, Kragen Auto Parts, Longs Drug, Lowe's, Office Depot, Pep Boys, PetSmart♥, World Market, Stadium Cinemas 15, The Promenade W: ATM's, Auto Dealers, Banks, NAPA, Hertz, **RV Super Center**, **CA State Hwy Patrol Post**, **Richardson's RV Center**
59	**Rancho California Rd, Temecula**
FStop	W: Temecula 76/Bill's Unocal 76
Gas	E: Mobil◈, Shell◈ W: Chevron, Circle K◈
Food	E: Aloha Joe's, Black Angus, Chili's, Claim Jumper, Panda Express, Rockin Baja Lobster, Oscar's Rest, Round Table Pizza, Rubio's Mexican Grill, Starbucks, Rest/Embassy Suites
Food	W: Denny's, Domino's, KFC, Penfold's Café, Rosa's Cantina, Steak Ranch Rest, Taco Grill, Texas Lil's Rest
Lodg	E: Embassy Suites W: Hampton Inn, Motel 6♥
Other	E: Albertson's, ATM's, Banks, Big Lots, CVS, Kroger, Target, Von's, Auto Repair W: Auto Service/Chevron, US Post Office, **CA Hwy Patrol Post**
58	**CA 79S, Old Town Front Rd, Temecula, Indio**
Gas	E: 7-11, Mobil, Valero◈ W: Shell◈
Food	E: Carl's Jr, In N Out Burger, Italian Rest, Molina's, Pizza, Pedro's Tacos, Starbucks
Lodg	E: Temecula Creek Inn & Golf Resort W: Hans Motel, Ramada Inn
Other	E: America's Tire, Long Drugs, Harley Davidson, Pechanga Indian Reservation, **Pechanga RV Resort▲**, **to Woodchuck Campground & RV Park▲** W: Firestone, Goodyear, **RV Service**
(55)	**Inspection Station (NB)**
54	**Rainbow Valley Blvd, to US 395, Fallbrook**
Other	E: Phillips Diesel Repair **W: CA Inspection Station**
51	**Mission Rd, US 395, to Fallbrook**
Med	W: + Hospital
Other	**E: Rancho Corrido Campground▲**
46	**CA 76, Pala Rd, Pala, Oceanside**
Gas	W: Mobil
Lodg	W: Comfort Inn, La Estancia Inn, Pala Mesa Resort
Other	**E: La Jolla Band of Indians Camping▲**, to 5mi: Pala Casino Resort Spa
43	**Old Hwy 395, US 95, W Lilac Rd**
41	**Gopher Canyon Rd, US 395, Old Castle Rd, Escondido**
Gas	E: Texaco

◈ = Regular Gas Stations with Diesel ▲ = RV Friendly Locations ♥ = Pet Friendly Locations
Red print shows large vehicle parking / access on site or nearby Brown Print = Campgrounds / RV PARKS

EXIT		CALIFORNIA
	Lodg	E: Castle Creek Inn Resort & Spa
	Other	E: **Lilac Oaks Campground▲** , **All Seasons RV Park & Campground▲** , **Champagne Lakes RV Resort▲** , Deer Park Auto Museum, Lawrence Welk Museum, **Lawrence Welk Resort▲**
37		**Deer Springs Rd, Mtn Meadow Rd, Escondido, San Marcos**
	Gas	W: ArcoAmPm
34		**Centre City Pkwy, Escondido (SB)**
33		**El Norte Pkwy, Escondido**
	Gas	E: ArcoAmPm, Shell◈, Texaco W: 76◈, Circle K
	Food	E: Arby's, IHOP, Taco Bell W: Jack in the Box, Wendy's
	Lodg	E: Best Western
	Other	E: **Escondido RV Resort▲** W: Longs Drug, Von's, Bank, ATM
32		**CA 78, W to San Marcos, E to Ramona, to Oceanside** **(Serv E to Centre City Pkwy & Mission Ave)**
	Other	E: **Freeway Trailer Sales/RVDump**
31		**Valley Pkwy, Downtown Escondido** **(Addt'l Serv E to Centre City Pkwy)**
	Gas	E: ArcoAmPm W: 7-11
	Food	E: Chili's, McDonald's, Olive Garden, Panda Express, Subway W: Applebee's, Burger King, Carl's Jr, Coco's, Del Taco, La Salsa, Starbucks, Wendy's
	Lodg	W: Comfort Inn, Holiday Inn Express♥
	Med	E: **+ Palomar Medical Center**
	Other	E: Barnes & Noble, PetCo♥, Winery, Rental Cars, **Police Dept**, **CA State Hwy Patrol Post** W: Albertson's, Hertz RAC, Home Depot, Staples, Target, World Market, Carwash, Mall
30		**9th Ave, Auto Park Way** **(Access to Ex #31 via Auto Park Way)**
	Gas	W: Shell
	Food	W: Applebee's, Subway, Taco Bell
	Other	W: Auto Dealers, Home Depot, Target,
29		**Felicita Rd, Citricado Pkwy**
28		**Centre City Pkwy (NB)**
27		**Via Rancho Parkway**
	Gas	E: Chevron, Shell W: Shell◈
	Food	E: Big Jim's Old South BBQ, DQ, La Salsa, McDonald's, Red Lobster, Red Robin, Romano's Macaroni Grill, Starbucks, Taco Bell W: McDonald's, Panda King, Tony's Spunky Steer Rest, Starbucks
	Other	E: Zoo, Shopping, Mall, Vineyard & Winery
26		**W Bernardo Dr, Pomerado Rd, Highlands Valley Rd, San Diego, Escondido**
24		**Rancho Bernardo Rd, San Diego** **(Addt'l Serv E to Bernardo Ctr Dr)**
	Gas	E: ArcoAmPm, Mobil W: 76, Shell
	Food	E: Dominos Pizza, Roberto's Taco Shop W: Elephant Bar & Rest, Denny's, Hooters, Wendy's
	Lodg	E: Hilton Garden Inn W: Best Western, Holiday Inn, Radisson, Travelodge

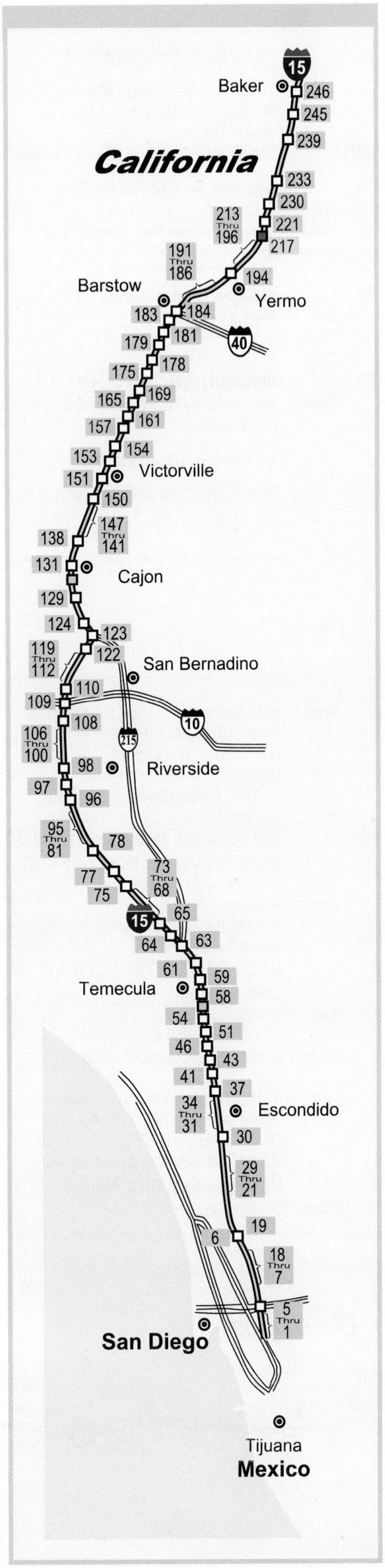

EXIT		CALIFORNIA
	AServ	W: Shell
	Other	E: ATMs, Banks, Von's Grocery,
23		**Bernardo Center Dr, San Diego**
	Gas	E: 7-11, Chevron
	Food	E: Burger King, Carl's Jr, Denny's, Hunan Chinese, Jack in the Box, Quizno's, Rubio's Grilll, Taco Bell
	Other	E: ATM's, Banks, Avis RAC, CVS, Firestone
22		**Camino del Norte**
	Med	E: **+ Hospital**
21		**Carmel Mountain Rd, San Diego**
	Gas	E: Chevron, Shell, Texaco W: 7-11, Chevron
	Food	E: Boston Market, CA Pizza, Carl's Jr, Chevy's Mexican, Claim Jumper Rest, El Pollo Loco, In N Out Burger, McDonald's, Olive Garden, Rubio's Grill, Subway, Taco Bell, TGI Friday's, Wendy's W: Jack in the Box, Starbucks
	Lodg	E: Residence Inn W: Doubletree Golf Resort
	Other	E: Banks, Barnes & Noble, Borders, Costco, Grocery, Home Depot, PetCo ♥, Ralph's, RiteAid, Staples, Trader Joe's, US Post Office W: Albertson's, Big O Tires, Office Depot
19		**Ted Williams Pkwy, CA 56W**
18		**Poway Rd, Rancho Penasquitos Blvd, San Diego**
	Gas	E: ArcoAmPm W: 7-11, 76◈, Exxon◈, Mobil◈
	Food	E: Deli W: Burger King, IHOP, Little Caesar's Pizza, McDonald's, Starbucks, Subway, Sushi USA, Taco Bell
	Lodg	W: La Quinta Inn♥
17		**Scripps Poway Pkwy, Mercy Rd**
	FStop	W: Pacific Pride
	Gas	E: USA◈
	Food	E: Carl's Jr, Chili's, El Pollo Loco, Jack in The Box, Panda Express, Taco Bell W: Starbucks
	Lodg	E: Springhill Suites
	Other	E: ATM, Auto Service, Bank, Carwash, Grocery
16		**Mira Mesa Blvd, San Diego**
	Gas	W: Shell
	Food	E: Chuck E Cheese, Denny's, Pizza Hut, Golden Crown Chinese W: Applebee's, Arby's, DQ, In N Out Burger, Jack in the Box, Mimi's Café, On the Border, Rubio's, Starbucks, Subway, Taco Bell, Togo's, Wendy's
	Lodg	E: Holiday Inn Express, Quality Suites
	Other	E: ATMs, Banks, US Post Office W: Albertson's, Bank, Barnes & Noble, Best Buy, Home Depot, Longs Drug, Ralph's, RiteAid, US Post Office, Grocery, Stadium 18, **to** Mira Mesa Mall
15		**Carroll Canyon Rd**
	Food	E: Carl Jr's
	Other	E: Bank, ATM, Grocery
14		**Pomerado Rd, Miramar Rd**
	Gas	W: Arco, Chevron, Mobil, Shell, Texaco
	Food	W: Carl's Jr, Keith's Family Rest, Pizza Hut, Subway, Indian, Mexican Rest
	Lodg	E: Marriott W: Best Western, Budget Inn, Hampton Inn, Holiday Inn

◈ = Regular Gas Stations with Diesel ▲ = RV Friendly Locations ♥ = Pet Friendly Locations
Red print shows large vehicle parking / access on site or nearby **Brown Print = Campgrounds / RV PARKS**

EXIT		CALIFORNIA
	Other	W: RVDump/Texaco, Auto Service, Banks, ATMs, Miramar Marine Corps Air Station, Alliant Int'l Univ
13		**Miramar Way, US Naval Air Station**
12		**CA 163, Downtown San Diego (SB)**
11		**Jct CA 52, Clairemont Mesa Blvd, W to La Jolla, E to Santee**
10		**Clairemont Mesa Blvd (NB) (Gas, Food, Serv appr 2 mi W)**
9		**CA 274, Balboa Ave, Tierrasanta Blvd, San Diego**
8		**Aero Dr, San Diego**
	Gas	W: ArcoAmPm, Chevron, Shell
	Food	W: Baja Fresh, Chinese, Jack in the Box, McDonalds, Sizzler, Starbucks, Taco Bell
	Lodg	W: Extended Stay America, Holiday Inn
	Other	W: ATMs, Bank, Radio Shack, Von's, **Walmart**, Montgomery Field Airport✈
7B		**Friars Rd W, San Diego (NB)**
	Other	W: Costco, Lowe's, Stadium
7A		**Friars Rd E, San Diego (NB)**
7		**Friars Rd, San Diego Stadium (SB)**
	Other	W: Qualcomm Stadium, Costco, Lowe's, Bank, ATM
(6B)		**Jct I-8, W - Beaches, E - El Centro**
6A		**Adams Ave, Camino del Rio**
	Gas	E: Chevron
	Food	E: KFC, Mexican Rest, Starbucks
	Other	E: Diesel Service W: Bank, ATM
5B		**El Cajon Blvd**
	Gas	E: Pearson Fuel
	Food	E: Pizza Hut
	Other	E: Bank, ATM
5A		**University Ave, San Diego**
	Other	Both: Restaurants, Auto Repair, Grocery
3		**to CA 94E (SB)**
(3)		**Jct I-805, to Chula Vista**
2C		**CA 94, ML King Jr Fwy, Dwtn (SB)**
2B		**CA 94W, MLK Jr Fwy, Dwtn (SB) CA 94E, ML King Jr Frwy, Home Ave (NB)**
2A		**Market St, San Diego**
1D		**National Ave, Ocean View Blvd (SB)**
	Gas	E: Save
(1C)		**Jct I-5S, National City, Chula Vista (SB, Left Exit)**
(1B)		**Jct I-5N, to Downtown (SB)**
1A		**Main St, Wabash Blvd (SB)**
	Other	W: US Naval Station
1		**Ocean View Blvd (NB)**
(1)		**CA Welcome Center (NB) (RR, Phones, Vend)**

PACIFIC TIME ZONE

CALIFORNIA

Begin Northbound I-15 from Jct I-5 in San Diego, CA to Canada/ MT border.

Begin Eastbound I-16 from Jct I-75 at Macon, GA to Savannah, GA.

GEORGIA

EASTERN TIME ZONE

NOTE: I-16 Begins/Ends on I-75, Exit #165

EXIT		GEORGIA
(1)		**Jct I-75, N - Atlanta, S - Valdosta (NB Exits Left)**
1A		**Spring St, GA 19, Gray Hwy, GA 11, GA 49, US 129, US 23, Macon (EB)**
	Gas	N: BP, Citgo, Marathon, Speedway S: Exxon, Marathon, Spectrum
	Food	N: Arby's, Burger King, El Sombrero, DQ, Golden Corral, Hong Kong Express, Huddle House, McDonalds, Papa John's Pizza, Pizza Hut, Subway, Taco Bell S: Burger King, Checkers, KFC, Krystal, Pizza Hut, Waffle House, Zaxby's, Rest/Crowne Plaza
	Lodg	S: Ramada Plaza, Macon Inn
	Med	S: + Medical Center of Central GA
	Other	N: ATM, Banks, Advance Auto Parts, CVS, Dollar Tree, Jiffy Lube, Kroger/Pharmacy Midas, O'Reilly Auto Parts, Pharmacy, Radio Shack, **Walmart SC**, Walgreen's, U-Haul S: ATM, Banks, Greyhound Terminal, Grocery, Museum, Olson Tires, Tires +
1B		**2nd St, GA 22, Macon, to US 129, to GA 49 (WB) (Acc Ex 1A Serv N&S)**
	Med	N: + Coliseum Medical Center
	Other	N: Macon Coliseum S: ATM, Banks, GA State Fairgrounds, Police Dept
2		**US 80, GA 87, ML King Jr Blvd, Coliseum Dr**
	Gas	S: Marathon
	Med	N: + Coliseum Medical Center
	Other	N: Auto Repair, Convention Center, Macon Coliseum S: Theatres, Museums, Truck Repair, Tourist Info, Auto Repair, Banks, ATM, GA State Fairgrounds, to Robins AFB
6		**US 23, Alt 129, Golden Isles Hwy, Ocmulgee East Blvd, Macon**
	TStop	S: Ocmulgee Chevron #419
	Gas	N: BP, Spectrum
	Food	N: DQ/Spectrum S: HuddleHouse/Ocmulgee TS, Subway
	Lodg	S: Days Inn
	TServ	S: Ocmulgee TS
	Other	N: Herbert Smart Downtown Airport✈ S: to appr 35mi Hillside Bluegrass RV Park▲
12		**CR 193, Sgoda Rd, Dry Branch, Huber, to US 23, US 129, Macon**
	FStop	N: Quick Way Foods/Marathon
18		**Alton White Blvd, Dry Branch, CR 189, Bullard, Jeffersonville**
24		**GA 96, Jeffersonville, Tarversville**
	FStop	N: Citgo Food Mart #16
	TStop	S: 96 Truck Plaza/BP
	Food	S: 96 TP, Huddle House
	Lodg	S: Best Value Inn
	Other	S: Laundry/96 TP, to Robins AFB
27		**GA 358, Homer Chance Hwy, Danville, to US 80, to US 129**
	Other	N: to appr 2.5mi: Back to Nature Campground▲

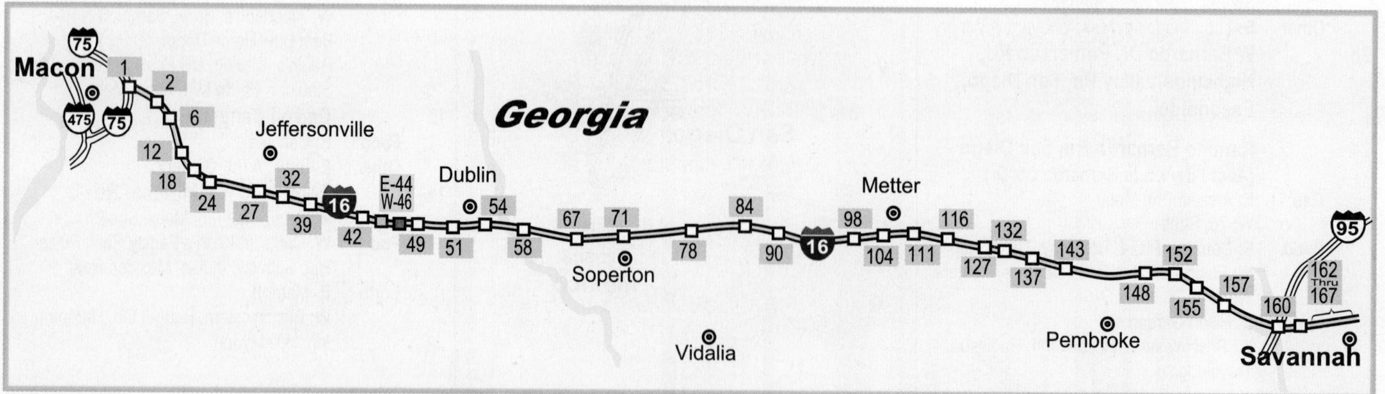

◈ = Regular Gas Stations with Diesel ▲ = RV Friendly Locations ♥ = Pet Friendly Locations
Red print shows large vehicle parking / access on site or nearby Brown Print = Campgrounds / RV PARKS

EXIT — GEORGIA

32 GA 112, Montrose, Allentown
Gas: S: Chevron◊

39 GA 26, Montrose, Cochran

42 GA 338, CR 348, Dudley, Dexter
Other: N: to 6mi: T&T Farms U-Pick

(44) Rest Area (EB)
(RR, Phone, Pic, Pet, Vend, RVDump)

(46) Rest Area (WB)
(RR, Phone, Pic, Pet, Vend, RVDump)

49 GA 257, Dublin, Dexter
TStop: S: Dublin 257 Truck Plaza, Love's Travel Stop #320 (Scales)
Gas: N: Chevron
Food: S: 257 TP, Chesters/Subway/Love's TS
TServ: S: 257 Truck Tire Service
Med: N: + Hospital
Other: N: to Barron Airport✈
S: Laundry/257 TS, WiFi/RVDump/Love's TS

51 US 319, US 441, Dublin, McRae
FStop: N: Pilot Travel Center #68 (Scales), Neighbor's Express/Exxon, Jet Food Store #73/Shell
Gas: N: BP◊, Flash
S: Chevron
Food: N: Arby's, Buffalo's Café, Burger King, KFC, McDonald's, Ruby Tuesday, Taco Bell, Waffle House, Wendy's, Subway/BP
S: Cracker Barrel, Longhorn Steakhouse
Lodg: N: Days Inn♥, Econo Lodge, Hampton Inn Holiday Inn Express, Jameson Inn, Quality Inn, Super 8, Travelodge
S: La Quinta Inn♥
Med: N: + Hospital
Other: N: Ace Hardware, GA State Patrol Post, Appr 41mi: Scenic Mountain RV Park▲
S: to appr 2 mi: Pinetucky Campground▲
To Little Ocmulgee State Golf Course, appr 27mi: Little Ocmulgee State Park▲
Appr 24mi: Hillside Bluegrass RV Park▲

54 GA 19, Dublin
TStop: N: Friendly Gus #23/Chevron (Scales)
Food: N: FastFood/Friendly Gus
Other: N: Laundry/Friendly Gus

58 GA 199, Old River Rd, E Dublin

67 GA 29, Soperton
Gas: S: Chevron◊, Citgo◊
Food: S: Huddle House

71 GA 15, GA 78, Soperton, Adrian
Gas: N: Chevron◊

78 US 221, GA 56, to Swainsboro
Gas: N: BP◊

84 GA 297, Vidalia
TServ: N: I-16 Truck Sales & Equip, Towing

90 US 1, GA 4, Oak Park, Swainsboro, Lyons
TStop: N: Ed's Truck Stop/Pure, Red Roof Express/Citgo
Gas: N: BP
Food: N: Rest/Ed's TS, FastFood/Red Roof
Lodg: N: Days Inn
TServ: N: Red Roof Express TS
Other: N: LP/Red Roof Express

EXIT — GEORGIA

98 GA 57, GA 46, Metter, Swainsboro, Stillmore, Altamaha State Park
FStop: S: Metter BP
Gas: S: Chevron◊
Other: S: to Gordonia Altamaha State Park▲

104 GA 23, GA 121, Metter, Reidsville
FStop: S: Marathon
TStop: N: Jay's Fuel Stop/BP
Gas: N: Chevron◊, Exxon, Pure, Shell◊
S: Phillips 66◊
Food: N: Bevrick's Char House Grill Rest, Burger King, DQ, Hardeee's, Huddle House, Jomax BBQ, KFC, McDonald's, Subway, Village Piza, Waffle House, Wendy's, Zaxby's
Lodg: N: American Inn, Comfort Inn♥, Econo Lodge, Holiday Inn Express, Scottish Inn
Med: N: + to Candler Co Hospital
Other: N: ATM's, Banks, Auto Dealer, RiteAid, Randy's Wrecker & Service Center, Tires, Guido Gardens, to George Smith State Park▲
S: Auto Dealer, Metter Muni Airport✈, to Gordonia Altamaha State Park▲, to Altamaha State Golf Course

111 CR 49, Pulaski Excelsior Rd, Pulaski
TStop: S: PTP/Grady's Truck Stop/Citgo
Food: S: Grady's Grill
Lodg: S: Motel/Grady's
TServ: S: Grady's TS
Other: S: Laundry/Grady's, Beaver Run RV Park▲

116 GA 73, US 25, US 301, Statesboro, Claxton, Register
TStop: N: Po Jo's Gas 'N Go/Chevron (Scales),
S: El Cheapo#89/Sunoco
Food: N: Po Jo's TS
S: El Cheapo TS, Huddle House
Lodg: S: Scottish Inn
Other: N: Laundry/Po Jo's, to appr 9mi: Parkwood RV Park & Cottages▲, to appr 10mi: GA Southern Univ, to Statesboro Muni Airport✈, to appr 45mi: Magnolia Springs State Park▲

127 GA 67, GA46, Brooklet, Statesboro, Pembroke, Fort Stewart
FStop: N: Time Saver
Gas: N: Shell◊
S: Chevron◊
Food: N: Barnard's BBQ, Morgan's Creek
Other: N: to Magnolia Springs State Park▲
S: 67 Antique Mall, 24th Infantry Museum

132 Arcola Rd, Ash Branch Church Rd, CR 582, Pembroke
Other: S: to Fort Stewart Military Reservation

137 GA 119, Pembroke, Ft Stewart
Other: N: Historic Guyton

143 US 280, GA 30, to US 80, GA 26, Ellabell, Pembroke
Gas: S: BP, El Cheapo◊
Food: S: Subs/BP
Other: S: Black Creek Golf Course

(144) Weigh Station (Both dir)

148 CR 310, Old River Rd, to US 80
Other: S: to Fort Stewart Military Reservation, to Bellaire Woods Campground▲

EXIT — GEORGIA

152 GA 17, Bloomingdale Rd, Bloomingdale

155 Pooler Pkwy, Savannah, Pooler (N to US 80, to I-95)
Food: N: Jalapenos Mex Rest, Meijia Chinese Rest, Papa John's Pizza
Other: N: Lowe's, to Savannah Hilton Head Intl Airport✈

(157A) Jct I-95, S to Brunswick, to Jacksonville, FL (Serv @ x94)

(157B) Jct I-95, N to Florence, SC (Serv@ X102)
Other: N: to Savannah Hilton Head Intl Airport✈

160 GA 307, Dean Forest Rd, N to US 80, S to US 17, Savannah
FStop: N: Pilot Travel Center #72 (Scales)
Gas: N: Chevron, Shell◊
Food: N: Subway/Pilot TC, Ronnie's Rest, Waffle House, Rest/Days Inn
Lodg: N: Days Inn, Quality Lodge
S: Quality Inn
TServ: N: Truck & Tire Repair, Mack Trucks, Lil Truck Center
Other: N: BarbSh/Pilot TC, Auto Repair & Towing, to Savannah Int'l Airport✈, Transmissions
S: Food Lion, Sunshine RV Park▲, GA State Hwy Patrol Post, to Waterway RV Park▲

162 Chatham Pkwy, Savannah, N to US 80, I-516, S to US 17, GA 25
Gas: S: Shell◊
Other: N: Chatham Truck Center
S: Auto Dealers, Bank, to Biltmore Gardens RV Park▲

(164AB) Jct I-516, Lynes Pkwy, US 80, US 17, GA 21

165 GA 204, 37th St (EB)

166 US 17 Alt, GA 25, Gwinnett St, Louisville Rd, Savannah

167AB ML King Jr Blvd, Gaston St, Montgomery St, Savannah
Gas: N: BP◊, Chevron, Enmark, Parkers
Food: N: Just Cuzzin's, Teaser's Café, Asst'd
S: Burger King, KFC, Popeye's
Lodg: N: Best Western, Comfort Suites, Country Inn, Courtyard, DoubleTree Hotel, Four Points Sheraton, Hampton Inn, Hilton Garden Inn, Quality Inn, Radisson, Residence Inn, Springhill Suites
S: Garden Inn, Paradise Inn, B&B's
Other: N: Savannah Civic Center, Visitor Center, Carriage Tours of Atlanta, Gallery, Museums, Riverboat Cruises, Greyhound, Tourist Info, Assorted Tours, to Convention Center
S: Amtrak, Auto Repairs, Carwash

EASTERN TIME ZONE

NOTE: I-16 Begins/Ends on I-75, Exit #165

GEORGIA

Begin Westbound I-16 from Savannah, GA to to Jct I-75 at Macon, GA.

EXIT	ARIZONA

Begin Southbound I-17 at Jct I-40 near Flagstaff, AZ to Junction I-10 in Phoenix, AZ.

ARIZONA

MOUNTAIN TIME ZONE

NOTE: AZ does NOT observe DST

NOTE: I-17 Begins/Ends on Jct I-10, Exit #143

341 McConnell Dr, Milton Rd, to US 180, to I-40 Bus, I-40, US 66, Flagstaff, Grand Canyon (NB) (AZ 89A North continues to Flagstaff, Grand Canyon)
- **Gas** W: 76, Chevron, Circle K, Conoco◈, Exxon◈, Gasser◈, Giant◈, Mobil, Shell
- **Food** W: Arby's, Burger King, Carl's Jr, Chli's, China Garden Coco's, DQ, Denny's, Del Taco, Fazoli's, Fuddrucker's, Himalayan Grill, IHOP, Jack in the Box, KFC, McDonald's, Olive Garden, Perkins, Pizza Hut, Quiznos, Red Lobster, Sizzler, Souper Salad, Stromboli Rest, Taco Bell, TCBY, Village Inn, Wendy's
- **Lodg** W: Auto Lodge Motel, Budget Inn, Comfort Inn, Days Inn, Econo Lodge, Embassy Suites, Fairfield Inn, Flagstaff Suites♥, Hampton Inn, Hilton Garden Inn, La Quinta Inn♥, Motel 6♥, Quality Inn,
- **Lodg** W:Ramada Ltd, Rodeway Inn, Sleep Inn, Travelodge
- **Med** W: + Flagstaff Comm Hospital, + Urgent Care
- **Other** W: ATM's, Banks, B&N, Basha's, Big 5 Sporting Goods, Cinema, CarQuest, Checker Auto Parts, Discount Tire, FedEx Office, Jiffy Lube, Kmart, Laundromats x4, Michael's, Office Max, Osco Drug, Paws For Pastries Treats & Wash♥, Petland♥, PetSmart♥, Safeway, Staples, Target, UPS Store, Walgreen's, New Frontiers Natural Foods Store, **Walmart**, Canyon Pet Hospital♥, Vets♥, **to** Sam's Club, Lowell Observatory, **N to US 66: to Camping World, Woody Mountain Campground & RV Park▲, Kit Carson RV Park▲, Flagstaff KOA▲, Meteor Crater RV Park▲, Ponderosa Forest RV Park▲, Kaibab Camper Village▲**, Rt 66 RV & Auto Service Center

(340B) Jct I-40, W to Kingman, to LA

(340A) Jct I-40, E to Albuquerque, NM

339 Lake Mary Rd, Mormon Lake (NB) (Access to Exit #341 Services)
- **Gas** E: Mobil◈
- **Food** E: Belgium Bistro
- **Lodg** E: AZ Mountain Inn & Cabin Rentals
- **Other** E: Carwash/Mobil, **Lake Mary Country Store & RV Park▲**

337 AZ 89A S, Flagstaff Airport, Pulliam Airport, Sedona, Oak Creek Canyon
- **Other** E: Flagstaff Pulliam Airport✈
  W: **Fort Tuthill/Coconino Co Park/ RVDump, MIL/Fort Tuthill Rec Area/** Luke Air Force Base

333 Kachina Blvd, Mountainaire Rd
- **Gas** W: Pic-N-Run◈
- **Food** W: Subway

331 Kelly Canyon Rd, Flagstaff

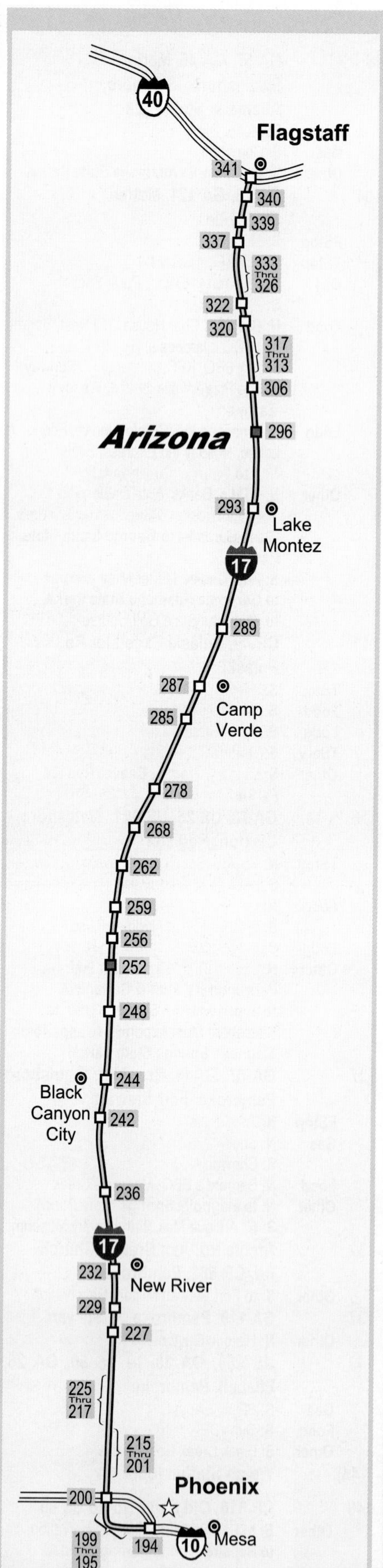

EXIT	ARIZONA

328 Newman Park Rd

326 Willard Springs Rd, Flagstaff

322 Pinewood Rd, Mormon Lake Rd, Frontage Rd, Munds Park
- **FStop** E: Woody's/Chevron
- **Gas** W: Exxon◈
- **Food** E: Lone Pines Restaurant
- **Lodg** E: Motel in the Pines
- **Other** E: **Pines RV Camping▲**
  W: **Munds Park RV Resort/RVDump▲**

320 Schnebly Hill Rd, Sedona

317 Fox Ranch Rd, Sedona

315 Rocky Park Rd

(313) Scenic View / Safety Pullout (SB)

306 Stoneman Lake Rd, Sedona

(300) Runaway Truck Ramp (SB)

298 AZ 179, Rimrock, to Sedona, Oak Creek Canyon (Serv NW in Sedona)

(296) McGuireville Rest Area (Both dir) (RR, Phone, Pic, Vend)

293 CR 30, Cornville Rd, McGuireville, Montezuma Well, Cornville, Rimrock, Lake Montezuma
- **Gas** E: Xpress Gas
  W: 76◈
- **Food** E: McGuireville Café
- **Other** E: Rimrock Airport✈, Montezuma Well National Monument, Auto Service Center

289 Middle Verde Rd, Camp Verde
- **FStop** E: Texaco Star Mart
- **Gas** E: Mobil◈, Shell
- **Food** E: Café, Sonic
- **Lodg** E: Cliff Castle Lodge & Casino
- **Other** E: Montezuma Castle Nat'l Monument, **Krazy K RV Park▲, RVDump**/Texaco
  W: Camp Verde RV Resort▲, Distant Drums RV Resort▲, Camp Verde Indian Reservation

287 AZ 260, AZ 279, to AZ 89A, Camp Verde, to Cottonwood, Payson, Jerome, Clarkdale
- **TStop** E: Camp Verde Shell #48
- **Gas** E: ArcoAmPm, Chevron
  W: Chevron◈
- **Food** E: Subway/Shell, Burger King, Denny's, McDonald's, Starbucks, Taco Bell,
  W: Wendy's/Chevron
- **Lodg** E: Comfort Inn, Days Inn, Territorial Town Inn, Microtel
- **Other** E: Basha's, Banks, **LP/RVDump**/Shell, **Trails End RV Park▲, Clear Creek RV Park▲, to Zane Grey RV Park▲**
  W: Dead Horse Ranch State Park▲, Slide Rock State Park, Camp Verde RV Resort▲, Out of Africa Wildlife Park

285 General Crook Trail, Camp Verde
- **Other** **E: Fort Verde State Park▲, Trail End RV Park▲, to Zane Grey RV Park▲**

(283) Runaway Truck Ramp (NB, Left Exit)

(280) Safety Pullout (NB)

278 AZ 169, Cherry Rd, Mayer, to Prescott, Dewey

◈ = Regular Gas Stations with Diesel ▲ = RV Friendly Locations ♥ = Pet Friendly Locations
Red print shows large vehicle parking / access on site or nearby Brown Print = Campgrounds / RV PARKS

EXIT — ARIZONA

268 — Dugas Rd, Orme Rd, Mayer
Other: E: Agua Fria Nat'l Monument

262B — AZ 69N, Prescott (SB)

262A — AZ 69N, Cordes Lake Rd, Prescott, Arcosanti (SB)

262 — AZ 69N, Cordes Junction, Cordes Lake Rd, Arcosanti, Prescott (NB)
FStop: E: Shell Travel Center #323
Gas: E: Chevron
Food: E:Subway/Shell, CJ Diner, McDonald's, Papa's Place
W: Blondie's Kitchen
Lodg: E: Cordes Junction Motel & **RV Park▲**
W: Teskey's T Tumble 7 Motel

259 — Bloody Basin Rd, to Crown King
Other: W: **Horse Thief Basin Rec Area**

256 — Badger Springs Rd, Mayer

(252) — Sunset Point Rest Area (Both dir) (RR, Phone, Picnic, Vend, View)

248 — Bumble Bee Rd, Crown King Rd, Black Canyon City

244 — AZ 17 Bus, Black Canyon City, Clearwater Canyon Rd
Gas: E: Chevron◈, Shell
Food: E: Medicine Horse Café, School Peak Steak House
Other: W: **Bradshaw Mountain RV Resort▲**

242 — AZ 17 Bus, Rock Springs Rd, Black Canyon City, Rock Springs
Gas: W: Chevron◈
Food: W: Rock Springs Café
Other: E: **Black Canyon City KOA▲**
W: **Bradshaw Mountain RV Resort▲**

236 — Table Mesa Rd, New River

232 — New River Rd, New River

229 — Anthem Way, Phoenix
Gas: E: Mobil◈
W: Chevron◈, Mobil◈
Food: E: McDonald's, Pizza Hut, Quiznos, Starbucks, Subway, Taco del Mar
W: Burger King, Blimpie, Denny's, Del Taco, Fresca's Mex Grill, Papa John's Pizza, Taco Bell, Villa Pizza
Lodg: W: Hampton Inn♥
Other: E: Ace Hardware, Banks, CVS, Safeway, Osco, Walgreen's
W: Anthem Outlets Mall, Anthem Pet Medical Center♥, Auto Zone, Buddy Stubbs Anthem Harley Davidson, Checker Auto Parts, Discount Tire, Econo Lube 'n Tune, Tires, U-Haul, **Walmart sc**,

227 — Daisy Mountain Dr, Phoenix
Food: E: Ebisu Sushi & Grill, Jack in the Box, Peter Piper Pizza, Roberto's Mexican Food, Starbucks, Streets of NY Rest,
Other: E: Bank, CVS,

225 — Pioneer Rd, Phoenix
Other: W: Pioneer Living History Museum, **Pioneer RV Park▲**

223B — AZ 74, Carefree Hwy, Wickenburg

223A — AZ 74, Carefree Hwy

223 — AZ 74, Carefree Hwy, Phoenix, to Carefree, Wickenburg (SB)
Gas: E: Circle K, Chevron◈

EXIT — ARIZONA

Food: E: Applebee's, Azooi Grill, Burger King/ Circle K, Chili's, Good Egg, In 'N Out Burge Krispy Kreme, McDonald's, Subway, Taco Bell
Other: E: Albertson's, Banks, Home Depot, Pharmacy, Staples, **to Cave Creek Rec Area/Maricopa Co Park▲** ,
W: Cowtown Paintball Park, Ben Avery Shooting Facility, **to Pleasant Harbor RV Resort▲** , **to Lake Pleasant Regional Park/Maricopa Co Park▲**

222 — Dove Valley Pky

221B — AZ Loop 303

221 — Lone Mountain Drive

220 — Dixileta Drive (NB exit, SB entr)

219 — Jomax Rd

218 — Happy Valley Rd, Phoenix
Gas: E: Shell
W: **appr 1.5mi:** Circle K/Shell
Food: E: Applebee's, Carl's Jr, Chipolte Mexican Grill, Dickey's BBQ Pit, Jack in the Box, Johnny Rockets, L& L Hawaiian BBQ, Logan's Roadhouse, Olive Garden, PF Chang's, Panda Express, Paradise Bakery & Cafe, Red Robin, Starbucks, TGI Friday
Lodg: E: Courtyard, Hampton Inn, Homewood Suites♥, Residence Inn
Other: E: B&N, Best Buy, Checker Auto Parts, Harkins 14 Theater, Lowe's, PetCo♥, Sport Chalet, Staples, World Market, **Walmart sc**

217 — Pinnacle Peak Rd, Phoenix
Food: E: Olive Tree Mediterranian Market & Grill, Rest/Drury, Rest/HG Inn
W: Blimpie, KFC, McDonald's, Subway
Lodg: E: Drury Inn, Hilton Garden Inn
Other: E:
W: Banks, ATM's, **Adobe Dam Rec Area**, Gray Mobile Tire Service, Thunderbird Park, Golf Course

215B — Deer Valley Rd, Rose Garden Ln, Phoenix, Deer Valley Airport
Gas: E: Circle K, Exxon◈, Texaco
W: ArcoAmPm, Circle K, Texaco
Food: E: Arby's, Burger King, Jack in the Box, McDonald's, Sonic, Taco Bell, Wendy's
W: Black Angus Steakhouse, Cracker Barrel, Denny's, Waffle House
Lodg: W: Country Inn, Days Inn, Extended Stay America
Other: E: **Deserts Edge RV Village▲** , **Phoenix Metro RV Park▲** , Phoenix Deer Valley Muni Airport✈, Auto Repair Services
W: Ace Hardware, Auto Repairs, AutoZone NAPA, Target, Walgreen's, U-Haul, **Desert Sands RV Park▲** , **N Phoenix RV Park▲**

215A — Rose Garden Lane (NB) (SB Access via Exit #215B)
Food: W: Baskin Robbins, Black Angus, 5 & Diner, Wendy's
Lodg: E: Sea Castle Resort
W: Country Inn, Extended Stay America
Med: W: + John Lincoln Hospital
Other: W: ATM, Bank

214C — AZ Loop 101, Phoenix By-Pass

214B — Yorkshire Dr
Gas: E: 7-11, Circle K/Shell, Shamrock

EXIT — ARIZONA

Gas: W: Circle K, Mobil, Costco
Food: E: Four Bros Pizza, In 'N Out Burger, Jack In the Box, KFC, Subway, Taco Bell
W: 19th Hole, Bamboo Grill, Charley's, Chili's, Jack in the Box, Panda Express, McDonald's, Souper Salad, Subway
Lodg: W: Best Western, Budget Suites, Country Inn, Days Inn, Marriott, Sleep Inn, Wyndham
Med: W: + John C Lincoln Hospital
Other: E: Frye's, Safeway
W: AMC Theatres Deer Valley 30, Univ of Phoenix, Costco, NAPA, PetSmart♥, Target, Walgreen's, **Desert Shadows RV Resort▲**

214A — Union Hills Dr

212 — W Bell Rd, Phoenix, Glendale, Scottsdale, to Surprise, Sun City
Gas: E: Chevron◈, Exxon, Mobil, QT, Sam's
W: 76, Chevron◈, Mobil
Food: E: Black Bear Diner, Burger Mania, Coco's, Jack in the Box, Long John Silver, McDonalds, Quiznos, Waffle House, Wendy's
W: Applebee's, Burger King, Carl's Jr, Denny's, Good Egg, Garden of Eden, Hooters, Hometown Buffet, Pizza Hut, Kyoto Bowl, Native New Yorker, Thai, Sizzler, Subway, Village Inn
Lodg: E: Best Western, Comfort Inn, Fairfield Inn, Motel 6♥
W: Red Roof Inn♥, Studio 6
Other: E: Auto Dealers, Big O Tire, Checker Auto Parts, Osco, Sam's Club, U-Haul, **Walmart sc**, Turf Paradise Racetrack, Rental Cars,
Other: W: Albertson's, Firestone, Fry's, Cinema 8, Banks, ATM's, Rental Cars, Bell Canyon Pavilion

211 — Greenway Rd, to Surprise
Gas: E: Circle K
W: FastGas
Food: E: Domino's, Rest/LQ Inn
W: Cousins Subs, Famous Sam's Rest, Deli, Wendy's
Lodg: E: Embassy Suites, La Quinta Inn♥
Other: E: Cave Creek Muni Golf Course, Turf Paradise Race Track
W: Grocery, AZ State Univ W, Univ of Phx, Penske Auto Center

210 — Thunderbird Rd
Gas: E: Circle K, Exxon
W: QT
Food: E: Jack in the Box, Pizza Hut, Wendy's
W: Fazoli's, McDonald's, Mamoof's Cafe
Lodg: W: Hawthorne Suites
Other: E: CVS, Home Depot, Jiffy Lube, Safeway, Walgreen's
W: Best Buy, Banks, ATM, Fry's, Diesel Express, Lowe's

209 — Cactus Rd, Phoenix, Sun City
Gas: W: 7-11, Chevron
Food: W: Denny's, Stackers, Rest/RL Hotel
Lodg: W: Ramada Plaza, Red Lion Hotel
Other: W: Basha's, Food City, Bank, ATM

208 — Peoria Ave
Gas: W: 76, Chevron, Exxon, Mobil
Food: E: Fajita's, Garden Fresh Rest, Lone Star Steakhouse, Outback Steakhouse, Pappadeaux Seafood, TGI Friday

◈= Regular Gas Stations with Diesel ▲ = RV Friendly Locations ♥= Pet Friendly Locations
Red print shows large vehicle parking / access on site or nearby Brown Print = Campgrounds / RV PARKS

EXIT		ARIZONA
		W: Burger King, Black Angus Steakhouse, Chipolte Mexican Grill, Coco's, Dominos Pizza, El Torito, Garcia's Mexican Rest, MiMi's Cafe, Olive Garden, Red Lobster, Sizzler, Starbucks, Souper Salad, Wendy's
	Lodg	E: AmeriSuites, Candlewood Suites, Comfort Suites, Crowne Plaza, Extended Stay America, Homewood Suites, Hyatt Place, Wellesley Inn
		W: Premier Inn, Four Points Sheraton,
	Other	E: FedEx Office, **Cave Creek Park**
		W: B&N, Castles N' Coasters Theme Park, CVS, Dollar Tree, Enterprise RAC, Firestone, Fry's Grocery, Laser Quest, Metro Center Mall, Michael's, Staples, Trader Joe's
207		**Dunlap Ave, Black Canyon Hwy (Acc to #208 Serv both dir)**
	Gas	E: 76, Shell◈
		W: Circle K, Exxon, Chevron
	Food	E: Cousins Subs, Dominos Pizza, Fuddrucker's, Jack in the Box, Lone Star Steakhouse, Outback Steakhouse, Sweet Tomato, Sushi Q, Taco Bell
		W: Denny's, Subway
	Lodg	E: Comfort Suites, Courtyard, Homewood Suites, Mainstay Suites, Parkway Inn, Sheraton Crescent, Springhill Suites, Towneplace Suites
		W: ValuePlace
	Med	E: + Advanced Urgent Care, to + Joseph C Lincoln N Mountain Hospital
	Other	E: ATM, Bank, Auto Repair, CVS, Firestone, Fletcher's Tire & Auto Service, U-Haul, **Royal Palm Campground▲**
	Other	W: ATM, Banks, Auto Repairs & Services, Checker Auto Parts, Cortez Animal Hospital♥, Fry's Grocery, Office Max, Sports Authority, Toys R Us, U-Haul, Walgreen's
206		**Northern Ave**
	Gas	E: Circle K, Mobil, Shell◈
		W: ArcoAmPm, Circle K
	Food	E: Burger King, Denny's, El Pollo Loco, McDonald's, Mr Sushi, Pizza Hut, Subway, Starbucks, Yesterday's
		W: Bobby Q BBQ, Furr's Cafeteria, DQ, Village Inn
	Lodg	E: Best Western, Hampton Inn
		W: Motel 6♥, Residence Inn, Super 8
	Other	E: Albertson's, Checker Auto Parts, **Sun City RV**, US Post Office, Walgreen's,
		W: Dinner Theatre, Vet♥

EXIT		ARIZONA
205		**Glendale Ave, Luke AFB**
	Gas	W: Circle K◈, Exxon, Grand Serv Stn
	Food	W: Jack in the Box, Pancho Villa, Lenny's
	Med	E: + Community Hospital Med Center
	Other	W: RVDump/Giant Grand Serv Station, Auto Repairs, Greyhound, Walgreen's, **Covered Wagon RV Park▲**
204		**Bethany Home Rd**
	Gas	E: ArcoAmPm, Circle K, Shell◈
		W: Chevron◈, Exxon
	Food	E: McDonald's, Subway, Whataburger
	Med	E: + Community Hospital Med Center, + Phoenix Baptist Hospital
	Other	E: Big Lots, Banks, ATMs, Cinemas
		W: Food City, Bank, ATM, Jiffy Lube, Auto Repair, **Welcome Home RV Park▲**
203		**Camelback Rd, Phoenix**
	Gas	E: ArcoAmPm, Circle K
		W: Mobil, QT
	Food	E: Burger King, Country Boys, Denny's, Pizza Hut
		W: Bistro, Denny's, Jack in the Box, McDonald's, Taco Bell, Steakhouse,
	Lodg	W: Comfort Inn♥
	Other	E: Auto Dealers, Auto Repairs, ATMs, Banks, Budget RAC, Checker Auto Parts, Discount Tire, Firestone, Walgreen's, Grand Canyon Univ,
		W: ATM, Auto Zone, Flea Market, Enterprise RAC, Northwest Village
202		**Indian School Rd**
	Gas	E: ArcoAmPm
		W: Circle K, Exxon, Shell, Valero
	Food	E: Filiberto's, Jimmy's, Pizza Hut, Subway
		W: JB's Rest, Wendy's
	Lodg	W: Motel 6♥, Super 8
	Med	E: + VA Hospital
	Other	E: ATMs, Banks, Albertson's, Ace Hardware, CVS, Family Dollar, Food City
		W: ATM, Banks, Grocery, **Desert Shadows Travel Trailer Resort▲**
201		**US 60W, Thomas Rd, Grand Ave**
	Gas	E: Circle K
		W: QT
	Food	E: Arby's, Denny's, Jack in the Box, McDonald's, Starbucks, Taco Bell
		W: Burger King, Carl's Jr, Subway
	Lodg	E: Days Inn, La Quinta Inn♥
	Med	E: + St Joseph's Hospital
	Other	E: Coliseum, Municipal Golf Course, Ryder, State Fairgrounds, to Park Central Mall

EXIT		ARIZONA
	Other	W: CarWash, Hertz RAC, Bank, Auto Repairs
200B		**McDowell Rd, Van Buren St; Adams St, Van Buren St (SB)**
	Gas	W: Circle K, ArcoAmPm
	Food	W: Subs
	Lodg	W: Travelodge
	Other	W: Truck & Trailer Repair, Diesel Service
(200A)		**Jct I-10, Central Phoenix, W to Los Angeles, CA**
199B		**Adams St, Van Buren St (NB) (SB Exit via Exit #200B)**
199B		**Jefferson St, State Capitol (SB Exit, NB Entr)**
	Gas	E: Circle K
		W: Circle K
	Food	E: Jack in the Box, McDonald's
		W: Mexican Rest
	Lodg	E: Sandman Motel
199A		**Grant St, Buckeye Rd**
	Gas	E: Circle K
198		**Buckeye Rd (NB) (SB exit via #199A)**
197		**19th Ave, Durango St, State Capitol**
	Gas	E: Circle K
	Food	E: Jack in the Box, Whataburger
196		**7th Ave, Central Ave, Phoenix**
	Med	E: + Phoenix Memorial Hospital
	Other	E: Amtrak Station
195B		**7th St, Central Ave**
	Gas	E: Circle K, Exxon, Trailside Gas◈
		W: Total
	Food	E: McDonald's, Lebanese Rest, Taco Bell, Rest/EZ8
	Lodg	E: EZ 8 Motel
	Med	E: + Phoenix Memorial Hospital
195A		**16th St (SB ex, NB entr) (Diff reaccess)**
(194)		**Jct I-10W, to Sky Harbor Int'l Airport, I-10E to US 60E, to Globe, Tucson (SB exit, NB entr)**

NOTE: AZ does NOT observe DST

MOUNTAIN TIME ZONE

ARIZONA

Begin Northbound I-17 at Phoenix, AZ to Junction I-40 at Flagstaff, AZ.

EXIT		ARIZONA

Begin Southbound I-19 at Jct I-10 in Tucson, AZ to Nogales, AZ @ AZ / MX Border

ARIZONA

MOUNTAIN TIME ZONE

NOTE: AZ *does NOT* observe DST

NOTE: I-19 Begins/Ends at Jct I-10, Exit #260
I-19 Begins/Ends at Nogales, AZ

NOTE: I-19 mileposts signed in km

EXIT		ARIZONA
(101B)		**Jct I-10W, to Phoenix (NB)**
(101A)		**Jct I-10E, to El Paso, Tx (NB)**
99		**AZ 86, Ajo Way, Old Tucson, Desert Museum, Tucson**
	FStop	W: to appr 7 mi: Superstop #619/Mobil
	Gas	E: Circle K, Star Mart
		W: Circle K, Chevron◈, Conoco◈, Whiting
	Food	E: Buffalo Bell, Long John Silver, La Bella China, Pizza Hut, Subway, Taco Bell, Weinerschnitzel

EXIT		ARIZONA
	Food	W: Bamboo Terrace, Burger King, Church's Chicken
	Med	E: + Pueblo Medical Clinic, + US Vets Hospital, + Golden West Med Center, + Madera Med Center
	Other	E: ATMs, Banks, Auto Repairs, Fry's, IGA, Walgreen's, U-Haul
		W: ATMs, Auto Repairs, Banks, Food City, Fry's, Jiffy Lube, **Desert Pueblo MH Park▲ Tucson Mountain RV Park▲**, **Rincon Country West RV Resort▲**

◈= Regular Gas Stations with Diesel ▲ = RV Friendly Locations ♥= Pet Friendly Locations
Red print shows large vehicle parking / access on site or nearby Brown Print = Campgrounds / RV PARKS

EXIT		ARIZONA
98		**Irvington Rd, Tucson**
	Gas	E: ArcoAmPm, Circle K, Chevron W: Chevron
	Food	E: Little Mexico Rest, Vida Rock Cafe W: China Olive Buffet, El Presidente Family Rest, McDonald's, Panda Express, Starbucks
	Med	E: + El Rio Health Center
	Other	E: Bus Station, ATM, Auto Repairs, Bank, Fry's Grocery, Rodeo Grounds, Tires, to Oasis RV Center W: Auto Repairs, Food City, Home Depot, PetSmart♥, Target
95		**Valencia Rd, Tucson Airport, Pascula Yaqui Pueblo**
	Gas	E: Whiting Conoco W: Chevron, Circle K
	Food	E: China Bay, Church's Chicken, DQ, Diego's, Jack in the Box, McDonald's, Peter Piper Pizza, Whataburger W: Applebee's, Arby's, Burger Kings, Carl's Jr, Chli's, Chuy's, Denny's, Dunkin Donuts, IHOP, Papa John's Pizza, McDonald's, Pizza Hut, Taco Bell, Wendy's
	Other	E: Auto Service, Auto Zone, Checker Auto Parts, Bank, Grocery, Jiffy Lube, to Tucson Int'l Airport✈
	Other	W: ATMs, Banks, Auto Repairs, Big O Tires, CVS, Grocery, Lowe's, Radio Shack, Walgreen's, Walmart sc,Enterprise RAC, Tohono O'odham Indian Reservation
92		**San Xavier Rd, San Xavier Mission**
	Other	E: to Mission View RV Resort▲, to Desert Diamond Casino W: San Xavier Indian Reservation, San Xavier Del Bac Mission
87		**Papago Rd, Sahuarita**
80		**Pima Mine Rd, Sahuarita**
	Other	E: Desert Diamond Casino
75		**Helmut Peak Rd, Sahuarita Rd, Sahuarita, to I-19 Bus**
69		**Bus 19N, Duval Mine Rd, US 89N, Green Valley**
	Gas	W: Circle K, Safeway
	Food	E: Denny's, Pizza Hut, Popeye's Chicken, Quiznos, Subway W: Burger King, Manuel's Mexican Rest, Taco Bell
	Lodg	W: Holiday Inn Express
	Other	E: Bank, Basha's Grocery, Radio Shack, Walgreen's, Walmart sc W: Auto Repairs, Auto Dealers, Big O Tires, Safeway, Cinema, Carwash, Green Valley RV Resort▲, Titan Missile Silo-Natl Historic Landmark & Museum
65		**Esperanza Blvd, Green Valley**
	Gas	E: Texaco W: Exxon
	Food	W: AZ Family Rest, Diner, Rest/BW
	Lodg	W: Best Western
	Other	W: ATM, Banks, Family Dollar, Green Valley Mall, Walgreen's
63		**Continental Rd, Madera Canyon Rec Area, Green Valley**
	Gas	W: Super Center
	Food	W: Mama's Kitchen, McDonald's, Mesquite Willy's Rib & Steakhouse, KFC, Starbucks, Taco Bell

EXIT		ARIZONA
	Other	W: Auto Repairs, ATMs, Banks, CVS, Firestone, Safeway, Walgreen's
56		**Canoa Rd, Green Valley**
(53)		**Canoa Ranch Rest Area** (Both dir) (RR, Phone, Picnic, Vend)
48		**Arivaca Rd, Frontage Rd, Amado**
	Other	E: De Anza Trails RV Resort▲, Mountain View RV Ranch▲
42		**Agua Linda Rd, Frontage Rd**
	Other	E: De Anza Trails RV Resort▲, Mountain View RV Ranch▲
40		**Chavez Siding Rd, Amado, to Tubac** (Addt'l Serv appr 4mi E)
	Other	E: Tubac Golf Resort
34		**Aliso Spring Rd, Tubac, Tubac Presidio State Park**
	Other	E: Tubac Presidio Hist State Park
29		**Santa Gertrudis Lane, Tumacacori, Carmen**
	Other	E: Tumacacori National Hist Park
25		**Palo Parado Rd, Rio Rico**
22		**Peck Canyon Rd**
17		**Rio Rico Dr, Yavapi Dr, Rio Rico**
	Gas	W: Chevron
	Other	W: IGA, US Post Office, Rio Rico Resort & Country Club

EXIT		ARIZONA
12		**AZ 289, Ruby Rd, Nogales Ranger Station, Rio Rico, Pena Blanca Lake Rec Area**
	TStop	E: Pilot Travel Center #279 (Scales) (DAND)
	Food	E: Wendy's/Pilot TC
	Other	E: Laundry/WiFi/Pilot TC W: to Pena Blanca Rec Area
8		**Bus 19, S Grand Ave, to AZ 82E, Patagonia** (SB, Left Exit)
	TStop	E: Ace's Truck Stop, Nogales Truck Stop (Scales)
	Gas	E: Circle K, Mac Mini Market/Texaco, Pronto Market
	Food	E: Pizza, Mexican Rest
	TServ	E: 51 Diesel Truck Repair, Nogales Diesel Service
	Other	E: Auto Service Center, Carwash, Mexico Insurance, Tires, Mi Casa RV Travel Park▲
4		**AZ 189S, Mariposa Rd** (SB, Border Truck Route)
	TStop	E: Nogales Truck Stop (Scales)
	Gas	E: Chevron
	Food	E: Rest/Nogales TS, Arby's, Chinese, DQ/Chevron, HomeTown Buffet, Jack in the Box, KFC, McDonald's, Samurai Japanese Steakhouse, Sonic, Taco Bell, Yokohama Rice Bowl W: Carl's Jr, Famous Sam's Rest, IHOP
	Lodg	E: Motel 6♥, Super 8 W: Best Western, Candlewood Suites, Holiday Inn Express
	TServ	E: Nogales TS/Tires
	Other	E: Laundry/Nogales TS, Auto Repairs, ATMs, Auto Dealers, AutoZone, Banks, Batteries Plus, Big Lots, Dollar General, Dollar Tree, Hibbett Sports, Home Depot, NAPA, Radio Shack, Safeway, U-Haul, Walgreen's, Walmart sc W: Auto Dealers, Enterprise RAC
1B		**Western Ave, Target Range Rd, Nogales** (Serv E to Bus 19, US 89)
	Gas	E: Circle K
	Med	W: + Holy Cross Hospital
	Other	E: Galen's Auto & Truck Repair
1A		**International St** (SB)
(0)		**Bus I-19, US 89, Downtown, Int'l Border, Frwy Ends, to US 82** (SB)
	Gas	E: Circle K, Shell
	Food	E: Jack in the Box, McDonald's,
	Lodg	E: Dos Marias
	Other	E: ATMs, Auto Repairs, Auto Zone, Banks, Checker Auto Parts, Family Dollar, Grocery, NAPA, Museum, Walgreen's, Vet♥, to Patagonia RV Park▲

NOTE: I-19 mileposts signed in km

NOTE: I-19 Begins/Ends in Nogales, AZ Near the MX Border or Jct I-10, Ex #260

NOTE: AZ *does NOT* observe DST

MOUNTAIN TIME ZONE

ARIZONA

Begin Northbound I-19 @ AZ / MX Border to Junction of I-10 in Tucson, AZ

◈= Regular Gas Stations with Diesel ▲ = RV Friendly Locations ♥= Pet Friendly Locations
Red print shows large vehicle parking / access on site or nearby Brown Print = Campgrounds / RV PARKS

EXIT		TEXAS
		Begin Eastbound I-20 from Jct I-10 near Van Horn, TX to Jct I-55 in Jackson, MS.

TEXAS

CENTRAL TIME ZONE

NOTE: I-20 Begins/Ends I-10, Exit #186

(Recommendation - Keep Fueled Up!)

Exit		
3		**Stocks Rd, Pecos**
7		**Johnson Rd, Pecos**
13		**McAlpine Rd, Pecos**
22		**FM 2903, Centre St, Pecos, Toyah**
(25)		**Picnic Area (EB), Parking Area (WB)**
29		**CR 211, Shaw Rd, Pecos**
33		**FM 869, Pecos**
37		**I-20E Bus, US 80, Pecos**
	Lodg	N: Budget Inn
39		**TX 17, Bickley Ave, Pecos, Ft Davis, Balmorhea**
	Food	S: DQ
	Lodg	S: Best Western
40		**Country Club Dr, Pecos**
	Gas	S: T&C Chevron
	Food	S: Subway/Chevron, Rest/BW
	Lodg	S: Best Western
	Other	N: TX State Hwy Patrol S: Auto Dealers, Pecos Muni Airport✈, **Trapark RV Park▲**
42		**US 285, Pecos, to Bus 20, Carlsbad, Ft Stockton, Pecos**
	TStop	N: Flying J Travel Plaza #5260/Conoco (Scales)
	Gas	N: Chevron, Exxon, Shell◈
	Food	N: Cookery/FastFood/FJ TP, McDonald's, Rest/QI, Pizza Hut
	Lodg	N: Motel 6♥, Oak Tree Inn, Quality Inn
	Other	N: Laund/BarbSh/WiFi/**LP**/**RVDump**/FJ TP, Auto Zone, **Walmart**
44		**Collie Rd, Pecos**
49		**FM 516, Barstow**
52		**20 Bus, Barstow (WB)**
58		**Frontage Rd, Barstow**
66		**FM 1927, TX 115, Barstow, to Pyote, Kermit**
(69)		**Ward Co Rest Area (Both dir)** (RR, Phone, Picnic, WiFi) (EB: Next Rest Area 122 mi)
70		**Spur 65, CR 415, Monahans**
73		**FM 1219, Monahans, Wickett**
	FStop	N: Allsup's #283/Shell
	TStop	S: SunMart #112/Mobil
	Food	S: Subway/SunMart
	Other	S: **RVDump**/SunMart
76		**20E Bus, Spur 57, Monahans**
	Other	N: Million Barrel Museum
79		**Loop 464, Monahans**
	Gas	N: Exxon
	Other	N: Ray Hurd Memorial Airport✈
80		**TX 18, Stockton Ave, Monahans, to Kermit, Fort Stockton**
	TStop	S: Town & Country #82/Fina
	Gas	N: Chevron◈, Exxon S: Kent Kwik
	Food	N: Bar H Steaks, DQ, McDonald's, Sonic S: FastFood/T&C, Taco Bell
	Lodg	N: Sunset Motel & **RV Park▲** S: Best Value Inn
	Other	N: ATMs, Banks, CarQuest, Dollar General, Family Dollar, Grocery, **Country Club RV Resort▲** S: Auto Dealers
83		**20W Bus, Monahans**
86		**TX 41, Monahans**
	Other	N: **Monahans Sandhills State Park▲**
93		**FM 1053, Odessa, Fort Stockton**
101		**FM 1601, Odessa, Penwell**
(103)		**Parking Area (Both dir)**
(104)		**Weigh Station (EB)**
104		**FM 866, FM 1936, Meteor Crater Rd, Odessa, Goldsmith**
108		**Moss Ave, Meteor Crater**
	Other	S: Meteor Crater, Meteor & Crater Museum
112		**FM 1936, Odessa**
	TStop	N: Odessa Truck Stop/Drivers Travel Mart #405/Citgo (Scales)
	Food	N: FastFood/Drivers TM
	TServ	S: Kenworth, Tires/Drivers TM
	Other	N: Laundry/Driver TM, Auto Repairs, Grocery
113		**TX 302, Lp 338, Odessa, Kermit, Meteor Crater Rd**
115		**FM 1882, County Rd W, Frontage Rd, Odessa**
	TStop	N: Town & Country #105 S: Love's Travel Stop #339 (Scales)
	Food	N: Country Cookin'/T&C S: McDonald's/Subway/Love's TS
	Med	N: + Tx Tech Univ Health Center
	Other	S: Laundry/WiFi/**RVDump**/Love's TS
116		**US 385, Andrews, Crane**
	Gas	N: Town & Country/Chevron S: Fina◈, Shell◈
	Food	N: DQ
	Lodg	N: Best Western, Delux Inn, Villa West Inn S: Motel 6♥
	Med	N: + Hospital
	Other	N: **Billy Sims Trailer Town**
118		**FM 3503, Grandview Ave**
	Gas	N: Fina◈
	TServ	N: Cummins Southern Plains, Goodyear Truck Tire Center, Freightliner/Peterbilt, W TX Volvo, Mack, Warren CAT S: Diesel Service, Truck & Tire Repair
120		**JBS Pkwy (WB)**
121		**Loop 338, Odessa**
	Gas	N: 7-11, Chevron, Sam's
	Food	N: Denny's, McDonald's
	Lodg	N: Days Inn, Elegante Hotel, Holiday Inn Express, La Quinta Inn♥, Motel 6♥, Super 8
	Other	N: Presidential Museum, Univ of Tx/ Permian Basin **(Services on TX 191—3 mi N)**
	Food	Chili's, Logan's, On the Border, Quiznos, Whataburger
	Lodg	Fairfield Inn, Hampton Inn
	Other	Albertson's, Home Depot, Sam's Club, Staples, Target, **Walmart sc**
126		**FM 1788, Midland Int'l Airport, Warfield**
	FStop	N: SB: x131: Flying J Cardlock #982
	TStop	N: Pilot Travel Center #257 (Scales), Warfield Truck Terminal/SunMart #109/ Mobil (Scales)
	Food	N: McDonald's/Pilot TC, Rest/Subway/ SunMart
	Lodg	N: Ramada Inn
	TWash	N: SunMart
	TServ	N: SunMart/Tires, Warren CAT
	Other	N: Laundry/WiFi/Pilot TC, Laundry/BarbSh/ SunMart, Western Auto, Midland Airport✈, Museum, Rental Cars, Water Wonderland, **Midessa Oil Patch RV Park▲**
131		**TX 158, Lp 250, Midland**
	FStop	N: NB: x126: Flying J Cardlock #982
	Lodg	N: Travelodge
	Other	N: Auto Repairs, Sports Complex, **Midland RV Campground▲**, **Pecan Grove RV Park▲**

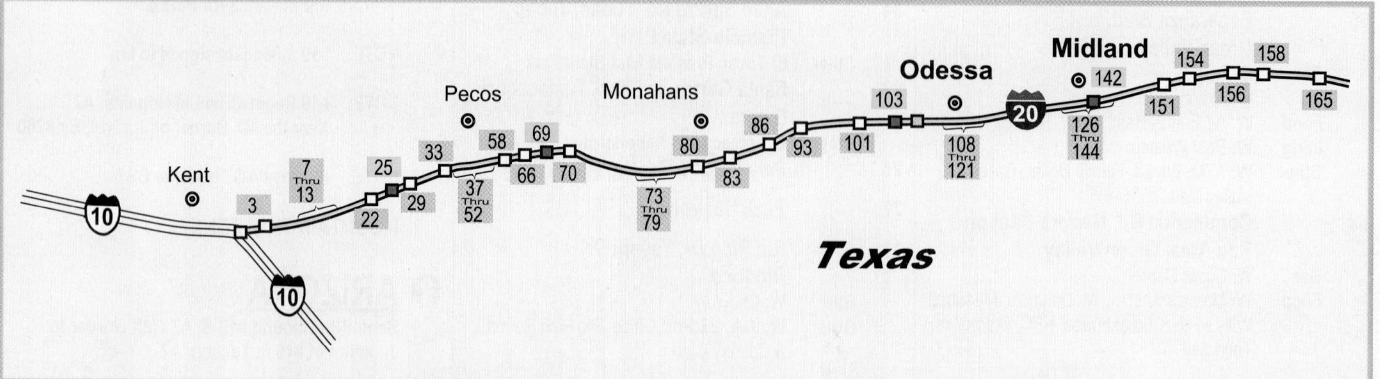

◈ = Regular Gas Stations with Diesel ▲ = RV Friendly Locations ♥ = Pet Friendly Locations
Red print shows large vehicle parking / access on site or nearby Brown Print = Campgrounds / RV PARKS

EXIT		TEXAS
134		**Midkiff Rd, Midland**
	FStop	N: Town & Country #122/Chevron
	Gas	N: 7-11/Fina, Exxon◈
	Food	N: Subway/T&C, DQ, Denny's
	Lodg	N: Americas Best Value Inn, Clarion, Days Inn, Executive Inn, La Quinta Inn♥, Midtown Hotel, Sleep Inn, Studio 6, Super 8
	Med	N: + to Midland Memorial Hospital, Midland Memorial Hospital West
	Other	N: Auto Dealers, **Bo's RV Center**, **To appr 4.5 mi TX 250:** Mall, Addtl Serv
136		**TX 349, Midland, Rankin, Lamesa**
	TStop	S: Travel Mart #10/Exxon
	Gas	N: Phillips 66◈, NAPA Gas, Murphy◈ S: Texaco◈, Town & Country◈
	Food	N: McDonald's, IHOP, Sonic, Starbucks S: Burger King/Exxon
	Lodg	N: Comfort Inn, Howard Johnson, Super 8
	AServ	N: Harold Logan Auto Service
	Other	N: Auto & Tire Services, Advance Auto, CarWash, Convention Center, Discount Tire, Dollar Tree, Family Dollar, IGA, Museum, **Walmart sc**, Greyhound Bus Terminal S: Laundry/Travel Mart
137		**Old Lamesa Rd**
138		**TX 158, FM 715, Midland, Greenwood, Garden City**
	FStop	S: Town & Country #107
	Gas	N: Shell◈, Conv Store/Gas
	Food	N: KD's BBQ, Whataburger S: Subway/T&C
	Other	N: Big 3 Tire & Automotive Center
140		**FM 307 (EB)**
(142)		**Picnic Area (Both dir)**
143		**Frontage Rd (EB)**
144		**20 Bus, TX 250 Lp, Midland**
151		**FM 829 (WB)**
154		**20E Bus, US 80, Stanton (Access to Exit #156 Serv)**
156		**TX 137, Stanton, Lamesa**
	TStop	S: Town & Country #209/P66 (DAND)
	Gas	S: Rita's Conv Store/Shell
	Food	S: CountryCookin/Subway/TC, DQ, Pizza Pro, Sonic
	Other	S: IGA
158		**Bus 20W, Lp 154, Stanton**
165		**FM 818, Big Spring**
(168)		**Picnic Area (Both dir)**

EXIT		TEXAS
169		**FM 2599, Big Spring**
171		**Moore Field Rd**
172		**Cauble Rd, Big Spring**
174		**20E Bus, US 80, Big Spring**
	Gas	S: Shell◈
	Food	S: IHOP
	Med	S: + Scenic Mountain Medical Center
	Other	S: Big Spring McMahon-Wrinkle Air port✈, **to Big Spring State Park▲**
176		**Andrews Hwy, TX 176, Big Spring (Access to Ex #177 Services)**
	FStop	S: Town & Country #103/Chevron
	Food	S: FastFood/T&C
	Lodg	N: Advantage Inn, Whitten Inn
	Other	S: RVDump/T&C
177		**US 87, San Angelo, Lamesa**
	TStop	N: Travel Center of America/P66 (Scales)
	Gas	N: Exxon◈ S: Fina◈, HEB
	Food	N: CountryFare/Popeye's/Subway/TA TC S: Country Kitchen, DQ, McDonald's, Wendy's
	Lodg	N: Econo Lodge♥, Motel 6♥ S: Days Inn, Holiday Inn Express
	TServ	N: TA TC/Tires S: Texas Truck Tire
	Med	N: + Big Spring State Hospital
	Other	N: Laundry/WiFi/TA TC S: Big Spring Harley Davidson, Banks, Grocery, Museum, **to appr 4 mi: Texas RV Park of Big Spring▲**
178		**TX 350, Snyder**
	Gas	N: Shell◈
	Other	N: Don's Truck & Tire Service
179		**20 Bus, US 80, Big Spring**
	Gas	S: Fina, Texaco
	Food	S: DQ, Denny's, Café, TNT BBQ
	Lodg	S: Comfort Inn, Inn at Big Spring, Quality Inn
	Other	S: Bowling Alley, Auto Dealers, Dollar General
181A		**FM 700, Airport, Big Spring**
	Med	S: + Hospital
	Other	S: **Big Spring State Park▲**
181B		**Refinery Rd**
182		**Midway Rd, Big Spring**
	Other	S: **Suburban East RV & Mobile Park▲**
184		**Moss Lake Rd, Sand Springs**
	Gas	N: Phillips 66, Fina◈
	Other	N: **Pioneer RV Park▲** S: **Whip In RV Park▲, Suburban East RV & Mobile Park▲**, Big Spring Mall

EXIT		TEXAS
186		**Salem Rd, Sand Spring**
188		**FM 820, Coahoma Rd, Coahoma**
	Gas	N: Town & Country◈
	Food	N: DQ, Country Cookin'
	Other	N: US Post Office
189		**McGregor Rd**
190		**Snyder Field Rd**
(191)		**Howard Co Rest Area (EB) (RR, Phone, Picnic, WiFi)**
192		**FM 821**
194		**E Howard Field Rd (WB)**
194A		**E Howard Field Rd**
194B		**Frontage Rd, Coahoma**
195		**Frontage Rd**
199		**Latan Rd, Westbrook**
200		**Conway Rd, CR 270**
(204)		**Mitchell Co Rest Area (WB) (RR, Phone, Picnic, Pet, WiFi)**
206		**FM 670, 20 Bus, Westbrook**
	FStop	N: Citgo
207		**20 Bus, Westbrook**
209		**Dorn Rd**
210		**FM 2836**
	Gas	S: T & C/Fina◈
	Other	S: **to appr 11 mi: Lake Colorado City State Park▲/RVDump, Coopers Cove Marine▲**
212		**FM 1229, Westbrook**
213		**20E Bus, CR 204, Enderly Rd, Colorado City (Serv S 3-4 mi)**
	Other	S: **to SpeakEasy RV Park▲**
215		**FM 3525, Rogers Rd**
	Med	N: + Hospital
216		**TX 208, Hickory St, Colorado City, N to Snyder**
	FStop	N: Chevron, Exxon S: T & C/Chevron
	Food	N: DQ, Subway/Chevron S: Pizza Hut, Sonic
	Lodg	N: Days Inn♥ S: American Inn♥
	Med	S: + Hospital
	Other	N: Auto & Truck Services, Cooper Tires, to Colorado City Airport✈, **to appr 20mi: Key RV Park▲, appr 22 mi: Trailertopia RV Park▲**

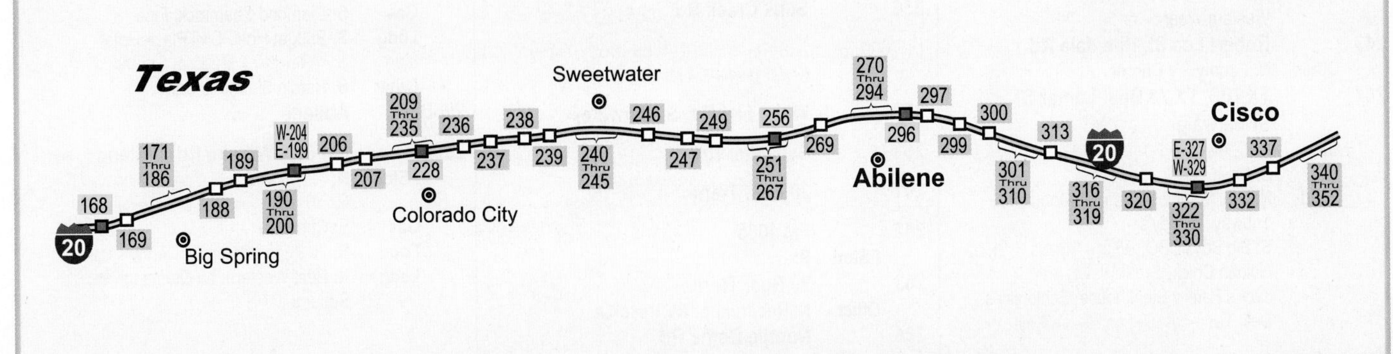

◈= Regular Gas Stations with Diesel ▲ = RV Friendly Locations ♥ = Pet Friendly Locations
Red print shows large vehicle parking / access on site or nearby **Brown Print = Campgrounds / RV PARKS**

EXIT — TEXAS

Other — S: U-Haul, to app 2.5mi: SpeakEasy RV Park▲, Lake Colorado City State Park▲/RVDump,

217 — **TX 208S, San Angelo**

219 — **20 Bus, Colorado City (EB)**

219A — **Country Club Rd (WB)**

219B — **20 Bus W, Colorado City (WB)**

220 — **FM 1899**

221 — **Lasky Rd**

223 — **Lucas Rd**

224 — **20 Bus, TX 316 Spur, Loraine**

225 — **FM 644S**

226A — **FM 644N**

226B — **CR 438, Loraine**

227 — **Narrell Rd, Loraine**

(228) — **Picnic Area (Both dir)**

230 — **FM 1230, Roscoe**

235 — **20 Bus, Roscoe**
- TStop — S: 235 Travel Stop
- Food — S: Rest/235 TS

236 — **FM 608, Roscoe**
- FStop — N: Town & Country #226
- Gas — N: Shell
- Food — N: FastFood/T&C; S: DQ
- Other — N: to appr 22mi: Key RV Park▲, Trailertopia RV Park▲; S: CB Shop

237 — **Cemetery Rd**

238A — **US 84W, Roscoe, Lubbock, Snyder**
- Other — N: to Snyder: Beacon Lodge Motel♥ & Campground▲

238B — **Blackland Rd**

238C — **Frontage Rd**

239 — **May Rd, CR 256**

240 — **TX 170, Lp 170, City Airport**
- Other — N: Museum, Avenger Field Airport✈; S: Sweetwater RV Park▲

241 — **20 Bus, TX 432 Lp, Sweetwater**
- Other — S: Chaparrel RV Park▲, Rolling Plains RV Park▲

242 — **Hopkins Rd, Sweetwater**
- TStop — S: Travel Center of America #/Conoco (Scales) (DAND)
- Food — S: Rest/Popeye's/PHut/TA TC
- TServ — S: TA TC/Tires, B Line Lube
- Other — S: Laundry/ChromeSh/WiFi/TA TC, Western Wear

243 — **Robert Lee St, Hillsdale Rd**
- Other — N: Family RV Center

244 — **TX 70S, TX 70 Bus, Lamar St, Sweetwater**
- Gas — N: Chevron◈, 7-11/Fina◈ x2, Murphy◈; S: Shell
- Food — N: DQ, Dominos Pizza, McDonald's, Subway, Wendy's; S: Big Boys BBQ, Buck's Steaks & BBQ, Golden Chick, Great Wall Buffet, Jack's Family Steakhouse, Schlotsky's Deli, Taco Bell, Ranch House Rest

Personal Notes

EXIT — TEXAS

- Lodg — N: Best Western, La Quinta Inn♥, Motel 6♥; S: Country Hearth Inn♥, Days Inn♥, Hampton Inn, Holiday Inn Express, Ranch House Motel
- Med — N: + Rolling Plains Memorial Hospital
- Other — N: A-1 Auto Parts, Auto Zone, Lowe's, Pharmacy, Tractor Supply, Walmart sc▲, Family RV Center; S: Bowling, Carwash, Grocery, Kmart, Sweetwater RV Park▲, Chaparrel RV Park▲, Rolling Plains RV Park▲

245 — **Arizona Ave (Acc #244 Serv)**

246 — **Alabama Ave, CR 304**

247 — **20 Bus, TX 70N, Sweetwater, Roby**

249 — **FM 1856, Sweetwater**

251 — **Eskota Rd, CR 277**

255 — **Adrian Rd**

256 — **Stink Creek Rd**

(256) — **Nolan Co Rest Area (Both dir) (RR, Phone, Picnic, Vend, WiFi)**

258 — **White Flat Rd, Sweetwater**

259 — **Sylvester Rd**

261 — **20 Bus, Trent**

262 — **FM 1085**
- FStop — S: Fina/7-11

263 — **20 Bus, Trent**
- Other — N: Roadrunner RV Resort▲

264 — **Noodle Dome Rd**

EXIT — TEXAS

266 — **Derstine Rd**

267 — **20 Bus, N 1st St, Merkel**

269 — **FM 126, Kent St, Merkel**
- FStop — S: Skinny's Fina
- Food — N: Subway; S: DQ, Rest/Merkel Motel, Mesquite Bean BBQ, Pizza Pro
- Lodg — N: Scottish Inn♥; S: Merkel Motel

270 — **20 Bus, FM 1235, Merkel**
- TStop — S: Big Country Truck Stop/Shell
- Gas — N: Conoco
- Food — S: Rest/Big Country TS; S: Holliday's Kitchen
- Other — S: Laundry/Big Country TS

272 — **Wimberley Rd**

274 — **Wells Lane**

277 — **FM 707, I-20 Bus, Scott St, Abilene, Tye**
- TStop — N: Flying J Travel Plaza #5064/Shell (Scales)
- Gas — S: Fina
- Food — N: Country Market/FastFood/FJ TP
- TServ — N: Peterbilt, Big Rig Lube
- Other — N: Tye RV Park▲; N: Laundry/BarbSh/WiFi/RVDump/LP/FJ TP

278 — **20 Bus, Spinks Rd, Market St, Tye**
- FStop — S: Top #18/Conoco
- TStop — S: AmBest/Wes-T-Go Truck Stop/Conoco (Scales)
- Food — S: Rest/FastFood/Wes-T-Go TS
- Tires — S: Wes-T-Go TS
- TServ — N: Volvo Mack
- Other — N: Trailer Sales & Service; S: Laundry/Wes-T-Go TS, Tye RV Park▲

279 — **US 84E, to Abilene**

280 — **Fulwiler Rd**

282 — **FM 3438, Shirley Rd, Dyess AFB**
- Lodg — S: Motel 6♥
- Other — S: Abilene KOA/RVDump▲, Kent's Harley Davidson

283A — **US 83, 277S, Ballinger, San Angelo (WB Exit Left, Diff reaccess)**

283B — **US 83, 277N, Anson**

285 — **Old Anson Rd, Impact**
- Gas — N: Texaco◈; S: Texaco◈
- Lodg — N: Travel Inn; S: Econo Lodge

286A — **83 Bus, Pine St, Abilene**
- Gas — S: Diamond Shamrock, Fina
- Lodg — S: Budget Host, Civil Plaza Hotel
- Med — S: + Hendrick Medical Center
- Other — S: Hardin Simmons Univ

286B — **Abilene**

286C — **FM 600, W Lake Rd, Abilene**
- FStop — N: Allsup's #331/Exxon, Skinny's #77/Fina/7-11
- Gas — S: Chevron◈
- Food — N: FastFood/Skinny's, Denny's
- Lodg — N: Best Western, La Quinta Inn♥, Super 8

◈= Regular Gas Stations with Diesel ▲ = RV Friendly Locations ♥= Pet Friendly Locations
Red print shows large vehicle parking / access on site or nearby Brown Print = Campgrounds / RV PARKS

EXIT		TEXAS
288		**TX 351, Abilene, Albany**
	Gas	N: Allsup's ◈, Chevron, Murphy, Skinny's Fina◈
	Food	N: Cracker Barrel, DQ, Oscar's, Skillets, Subway
	Lodg	N: Comfort Inn, Days Inn, Executive Inn, Holiday Inn Express, Whitten Inn
	Med	S: + Hendrick Medical Center
	Other	N: Dollar Tree, Lowe's, **Walmart sc** S: Abilene Christian College
290		**TX 36, to Loop 322, Cross Plains, to Abilene Regional Airport**
	Other	S: Abilene Reg'l Airport✈, Zoo, Taylor Co Expo Center
292A		**20 Bus, Abilene (WB, Left Exit)**
	TServ	S: Young's Truck Service
292B		**Elmdale Rd**
	Other	N: **Big Country RV/RVDump** S: **Abilene RV Park▲**, **W Texas RV**, **Duke's RV Repair**
294		**Buck Creek Rd, Clyde**
	Other	N: **Buck Creek RV Park/RVDump▲**
(296)		**Callahan Co Rest Area (Both dir) (RR, Phone, Picnic, WiFi)**
297		**FM 603**
299		**FM 1707, S Hays Rd, CR 112N**
300		**FM 604N, Spur 189N, Clyde**
	Gas	S: Conoco, Shell
	Food	S: Little Pit BBQ
	Other	S: Laundromat, **Arrowhead Campground▲**, **White's RV Park▲**
301		**FM 604S, Spur 189S, Clyde, Cherry Lane**
	Gas	N: Exxon S: Fina◈, Shell◈
	Food	N: DQ, Little Pit BBQ, Sonic S: Pizza House, Subway, Whataburger
	TWash	S: 301 TW
	Other	N: U-Haul S: Auto Repairs, Bank, Family Dollar, Golf Course, IGA, **Franklin RV Center**
303		**Union Hill Rd, CR 279, Clyde**
306		**20 Bus, FM 2047, Baird**
	Other	N: Auto Dealers
307		**US 283, Albany, Coleman**
	Gas	S: Conoco◈
	Food	N: DQ
	Lodg	N: Baird Motor Inn & **RV Park▲**
	Other	N: **Hanner RV**
308		**Bus Loop 20, Baird**
310		**Finley Rd**
313		**FM 2228**
316		**Brushy Creek Rd, Baird**
319		**FM 880S, Putnam, Cross Plains**
320		**FM 880N, FM 2945N, Moran**
322		**Cooper Creek Rd**
324		**Scranton Rd**
(327)		**Picnic Area (EB)**
(329)		**Picnic Area (WB)**
330		**TX 206, Cross Plains, Cisco**
	FStop	N: Chevron
	Food	N: White Elephant
	Lodg	N: Best Western, Best Value Inn
	Med	N: + Hospital
332		**US 183, Cisco, Brownwood, Breckenridge, Albany**
	FStop	N: Allsup's Exxon, Cowpokes
	Food	N: DQ, Pizza Heaven, Sonic, Subway,
	Lodg	N: Knights Inn
	TServ	N: Lee's Truck Service
	Other	N: **Everett's RV Park▲**
337		**Spur 490, Cisco**
	Other	N: **Wild Country RV Resort▲**
340		**TX 6, Eastland, Gorman, Breckenridge**
	TStop	S: Red Star Truck Terminal/Shell
	Gas	N: Chevron◈
	Food	S: Red Star Café/Red Star TS
	Med	N: + Hospital
	Other	N: Eastland Muni Airport✈
343		**TX 112, FM 570, Eastland, Lake Leon**
	Gas	N: Conoco, Fina, Shell, Murphy S: Exxon
	Food	N: DQ, McDonald's, Rafter BBQ, Taco Bell, Sonic, Starbucks, Subway/Fina S: Pulido's Mexican, Burger King/Exxon
	Lodg	N: La Quinta Inn♥, Super 8 & **RV Park▲** S: Budget Host Inn, Ramada Inn
	Med	N: + Hospital
	Other	N: Auto Dealers, **Walmart sc** S: Auto Dealers
345		**FM 3363, Olden (EB)**
347		**FM 3363, Olden (WB)**
349		**FM 2461, Lp 254, US 80, Ranger College, Lake Leon**
	TStop	N: Love's Travel Stop #270 (Scales) **(DAND)**
	Gas	S: Shell
	Food	N: Cattle Barron Rest, DQ, Godfather's/ Subway/Godfathers/Love's TS S: Diner
	Lodg	N: Best Value Inn, Days Inn, Relax Inn
	Other	N: WiFi/Love's TS, **RL RV Park▲**, Ranger Muni Airport✈, ATMs, Banks, Auto Repairs, Grocery S: **to appr 5mi: North Shore RV Park ▲**
351		**Desdemona Blvd (EB)**
352		**Blundell St (WB)**
354		**Lp 254W, Ranger**
358		**Frontage Rd**
361		**TX 16, Ranger, Strawn, DeLeon**
(362)		**Parking Area (Both dir)**
363		**Tudor Rd** **Picnic Area (Both dir)**
367		**TX 108, FM 919, Mingus, Gordon, Bluff Dale, Stephenville**
	Food	N: Smoke Stack S: New York Hill
370		**TX 108, FM 919, Gordon, Stephenville**
	FStop	N: Bar-B Travel Plaza/Citgo
	Gas	S: Exxon
	Food	N: Rest/FastFood/Bar-B TP
	Lodg	N: Longhorn Inn Motel
	TServ	N: Bar-B TP/Tires
373		**TX 193, Gordon**
376		**Panama Rd, Blue Flat Rd**
380		**FM 4, Palo Pinto, Lipan-Santo**
	Food	S: Sunday Creek Rest
	Other	S: **Windmill Acres RV Park & Cafe▲**
386		**US 281, Stephenville, Mineral Wells**
	FStop	N: Circle H Shell
	Gas	N: Fina
	Food	N: Subway/Shell
(390)		**Palo Pinto Co Rest Area (Both dir) (RR, Phone, Picnic, Vend, WiFi)**
391		**Gilbert Pit Rd**
394		**FM 113, Millsap**
	Other	N: **Hillbilly Haven Campground▲**, **to 13mi Back Acre RV Park/RVDump▲**
397		**FM 1189, MillsapBrock**
	Other	S: **Oak Creek RV Park▲**
402		**Spur 312E, Weatherford (EB)**
	Other	S: **Buxton's Diamond B RV Park▲**
403		**Dennis Rd (WB)**
	Other	N: Auto, Truck & Trailer Repair S: **Buxton's Diamond B RV Park▲**
406		**Old Dennis Rd, S Bowie Dr, Weatherford**
	TStop	N: Truck & Travel/Conoco (Scales) S: Pilot Travel Center #206 (Scales)
	Food	N: Rest/FastFood/Truck & Travel, Rest/Days Inn S: Wendy's/Pilot TC
	Lodg	N: Quality One Motel/Truck & Travel, Econo Lodge
	TServ	N: Truck & Travel/Tires S: Pilot TC/Tires
	Other	N: CB/**RVDump**/Truck&Travel S: Laundry/WiFi/Pilot TC
407		**TX 171, FM 1884, Tin Top Rd (EB) (Access Ex #408 Services)**
408		**TX 171, FM 51, FM 1884, Tin Top Rd, Weatherford, Granbury, Cleburne**
	Gas	N: Exxon◈, Mobil, Murphy S: Exxon◈, Shell◈
	Food	N: Applebee's, Bakers Ribs, Braum's Ice, Cream, Cracker Barrel, CiCi's Pizza, Golden Corral, IHOP, McDonald's, Subway, Starbucks, Taco Bueno, Taco Bell S: Burger King/Shell, ChickFilA, Chili's, Waffle House
	Lodg	N: La Quinta Inn♥, Sleep Inn, Super 8♥ S: Best Value Inn, Comfort Suites, Hampton Inn, Holiday Inn Express, Motel 6♥
	Med	N: + Campbell Memorial Hospital
	Other	N: Albertson's, ATMs, Auto Zone, Banks, CVS, Discount Tire, Dollar Tree, Greyhound Bus Terminal, Home Depot, Kroger, Museum,Radio Shack, **Walmart sc**, Weatherford College S: Best Buy, Lowe's, Office Depot, PetSmart♥, Target, **Weatherford Fort Worth Kamp▲**, **Serenity Ranch RV Park▲**, **Hooves 'N Wheels RV Park▲**
409		**FM 2552, Clear Lake Rd, Santa Fe Rd, Weatherford**
	TStop	N: Petro Stopping Center #2/Mobil (Scales)
	Gas	S: Chevron◈, Shell
	Food	N: IronSkillet/Petro SC, Antonio's, Jack in the Box, La Fiesta
	Lodg	N: Best Western/Petro SC

◈= Regular Gas Stations with Diesel ▲ = RV Friendly Locations ♥= Pet Friendly Locations
Red print shows large vehicle parking / access on site or nearby Brown Print = Campgrounds / RV PARKS

EXIT		TEXAS
	TWash	N: Blue Beacon TW/Petro SC
	TServ	N: Petro SC/Tires
	Med	N: + Weatherford Reg'l Medical Center
	Other	N: Laundry/WiFi/CB/BarbSh/Petro SC, Pharmacy, Grote Veterinary Clinic♥, US Post Office
410		**Bankhead Hwy, Weatherford**
	TStop	S: Love's Travel Stop #273 (Scales) (DAND)
	Food	S: Subway/Love's TS
	Other	S: WiFi/Love's TS
413		**Lakeshore Dr (EB)**
	Gas	N: Texaco
	Food	N: Sonic, Steaks Plus
414		**US 180, Weatherford, Mineral Wells, Hudson Oaks (WB)**
	Gas	N: RaceTrac, Texaco◈, Murphy USA S: Chevron◈
	Food	N: DQ, Jack's Family Rest, R&K Café, Sonic, Steaks Plus
	Other	N: Auto Dealers, **Walmart sc**,
415		**Mikus Rd, Annetta Rd, Willow Park**
	FStop	S: Drivers Travel Mart #402/Chevron
	Gas	S: Shell
	Food	S: Rest/FastFood/Drivers TM
	Other	S: **Exit 415 RV Center**, Parker Co Airport✈
(417)		**Weigh Station (WB)**
418		**Ranch House Rd, Willow Park**
	FStop	N: Sprint #103/Gateway Shell
	Gas	N: Exxon S: Shell◈
	Food	N: FastFood/Gateway, Burger King, Pizza Hut, Subway, Taco Casa S: McDonald's, FastFood/Shell
	Lodg	S: Ramada Inn
	Other	N: Bank, ATM S: **Fun Time RV Outlet**
(419)		**Weigh Station (EB)**
420		**FM 1187, Aledo, Farmer Rd**
	Other	S: **Cowtown RV Park▲**
(421)		**Jct I-30E, Downtown Ft Worth (EB, Left Exit)**
425		**Markham Ranch Rd, Ft Worth**
426		**FM 2871, Chapin School Rd**
(428)		**Jct I-820N, Ft Worth ByPass**
429A		**US 377, Benbrook Hwy, Benbrook, (Access N to #429B)**
	Gas	S: Express Stop/Fina, RaceTrac, Valero, Quick Way/Shell
	Food	S: Braum's, Burger King, Chicken Express, Dominos Pizza, Jack in the Box, Little Caesars Pizza, McDonald's, Riscky's BBQ,

EXIT		TEXAS
	Food	N: Starbucks, Taco Bell/KFC, Waffle House Whataburger,
	Lodg	S: Motel 6
	Other	S: Albertson's, Auto Zone, Auto Repairs & Services, Banks, Brookshires Grocery, CVS Dollar General, Mercedes Place Animal Hospital♥, Tractor Supply, U-Haul, US Post Office, Walgreen's, Carwash/Valero
429B		**Winscott Rd, Benbrook (Access S to #429A)**
	FStop	N: Circle K
	Gas	S: Shell, Shamrock
	Food	N: Cracker Barrel
	Lodg	N: Best Western, Comfort Suites♥
431		**Bryant-Irving Rd, Ft Worth (Acc N #432 Serv/S #433 Serv)**
	Gas	N: Sam's S: Chevron, Costco, Tom Thumb, Shell, QT
	Food	N: Chipolte Mex Grill, Edohana Hibachi Sushi, Genghis Grill, Keg Steakhouse & Bar, Mimi's Café, On the Border, Taste of Asia S: Chicken Express, Cousins BBQ, IHOP, Fuddrucker's, Jason's Deli, Loafin Joe's Hot Subs, Outback Steakhouse, Pei Wei Asian Diner, Razzoo's Cajun Cafe, Rio Mambo Tex Mex, Rosa's Cafe & Tortilla Factory, Saltgrass Steak House, Wingstop
	Lodg	S: Courtyard, Extended Stay Deluxe♥, Hampton Inn, Holiday Inn Express, Hyatt Place, La Quinta Inn,
	Med	S: + Lifecare Hospital of Ft Worth, to + Kindred Hospital, + Baylor Medical Center SW Ft Worth, + Harris Methodist SW Hospital
	Other	N: Banks, Best Buy, Cavendar's Boot City, FedEx Office, Garden Ridge, Golf Etc, Lowe's, PetSmart♥, Sam's Club, S: ATMs, Banks, Auto Dealers, AT&T, Albertson's, CVS, Cityview Carwash & Lube, Cityview Animal Hospital♥, Costco, Goodyear/Auto, Hulen Mall, Hulen Movie Tavern, Pack 'n Mail, PetCo♥, Staples, Super Target, Tom Thumb Food & Pharmacy, Verizon, Walgreen's,
432		**TX 183, Southwest Blvd (WB) (Access to #431 N Services)**
	Gas	N: Sam's
	Food	N: Bonnell's Fine Texas Cuisine, Hooters, Perrotti's Pizza, Pizza Hut, Plaza Cafe

EXIT		TEXAS
	Lodg	N: Towneplace Suites
	Other	N: ATMs, Banks, Best Buy, Garden Ridge, Lowe's, NTB, Sam's Club
433		**Hulen St, Fort Worth (Acc to #431 S Serv)**
	Gas	N: Shell◈ S: Valero, Costco
	Food	N: Chef Chen, Chuck E Cheese's Pizza, Grady's, Hooters, Olive Garden, Red Lobster, Souper Salad, Starbucks, Subway, TGI Friday S: Applebee's, Carino's Italian Grill, Chili's, ChickFilA, Colter's BBQ, Denny's, Dixie House Cafe, Jack in the Box, KFC, Kincaid's, Maharaja Indian Rest, McDonald's, Papa John's Pizza, Potbelly Sandwich Shop, Red Lobster, Starbucks, Steak 'n Shake, Taco Bell, Wendy's, Whataburger
	Lodg	N: TownePlace Suites S: Hampton Inn
	Med	N: + Hulen Medical Clinic
	Other	N: Albertson's/Pharmacy, Home Depot, NTB, Office Depot, PetSmart♥, Sports Authority, TJ Maxx, S: ATMs, Aldi, Banks, Barnes & Noble, Borders, Burlington Coat Factory, Colonial Carwash & Lube, Dollar General, Dollar Tree, Enterprise RAC, FedEx Office, Firestone Auto, Half Price Books, Hobby Lobby, Hulen Mall, Hulen 10 Cinema, Michael's, Office Max, Play it Again Sports, Ross, Starplex Hulen 10, UPS Store, Vitamin Shoppe, **Walmart sc**, Walgreen's,
434A		**Granbury Dr, Ft Worth**
	Gas	S: Gas
	Food	N: Charley's Old Fashioned Hamburger S: DQ, Pancho's Mexican Rest,
	Other	S: Auto Service, Dollar General, Firestone, Goodyear, Harbor Freight, O'Reilly Auto Parts, Wedgewood Tire & Auto Center, Wedgwood Animal Hospital♥, **to Hulen St: Acc #433 Services**
434B		**Trail Lake Dr, Woodway Dr**
	Gas	S: Shell
	Food	S: Coffee Urn Cafe, Dominos Pizza, Sonic, Starbucks, Subway, Wendy's
	Lodg	N: Days Inn
	Other	N: ATMs, Bank, Auto Services S: Auto Repairs, CVS
435		**McCart Ave, West Creek Dr (Most 1-2 mi / Addt'l S to Altamesa Blvd)**
	Gas	N: Shell S: Mobil◈, Fina
	Food	S: Braum's, Church's Chicken, Cousin's BBQ, Italian Express, Jack in the Box,

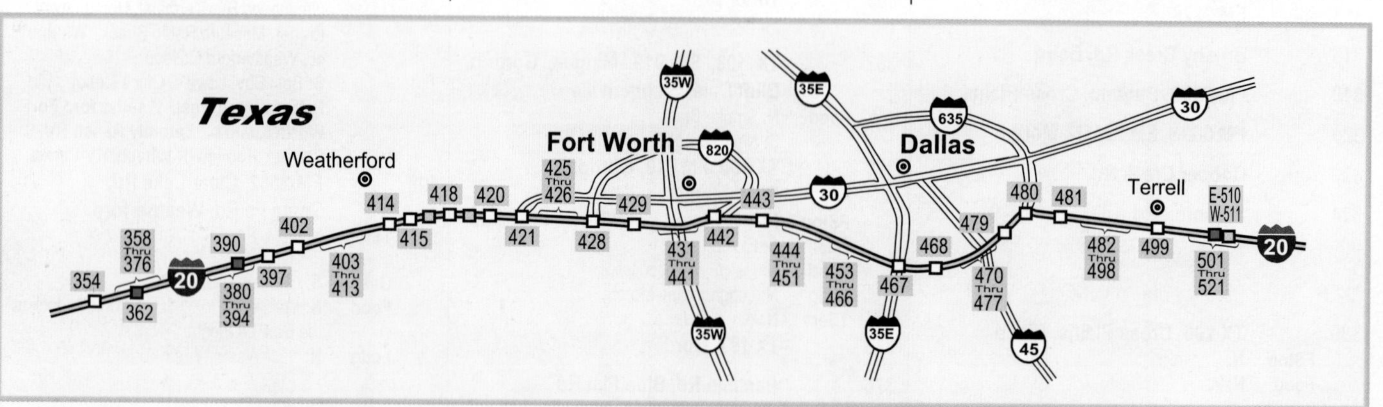

◈= Regular Gas Stations with Diesel ▲ = RV Friendly Locations ♥= Pet Friendly Locations
Red print shows large vehicle parking / access on site or nearby Brown Print = Campgrounds / RV PARKS

EXIT		TEXAS
		McDonald's, Mexico Real, Popeye's Chicken
	Other	N: South Hills Animal Hospital♥, S: ATMs, Banks, Avis RAC, CVS, Discount Tire, Jiffy Lube, Kroger, NAPA, Speedclean Carwash, U-Haul, Walgreen's, Westcreek Animal Clinic♥,
436A		**FM 731, Crowley Rd, James Ave**
	Gas	N: Conoco◈, Valero◈ S: to Altamesa Blvd QT, Valero
	Food	S: DQ, Pizza Hut, Taco Bell
	Other	N: Dollar General, SavALot
436B		**Hemphill St**
	Gas	N: Shell
(437)		**Jct I-35W, N to Fort Worth, S to Waco (Serv at 1st Exits N&S)**
438		**Oak Grove Rd, Fort Worth**
	Gas	N: Shell S: Conoco, Shamrock
	Food	N: Burger King, Denny's, McDonald's
	Lodg	N: Days Inn
	Other	N: Enterprise RAC
439		**Campus Dr**
	Gas	S: Sam's Club
	Other	N: Auto Dealers S: Sam's Club
440A		**Wichita St, Forest Hill**
	Gas	N: Chevron S: Texaco◈, Valero
	Food	N: Taco Bueno, Wendy's S: Bavarian Bakery & Cafe, Chicken Express, Dominos Pizza, McDonald's, Pizza Hut, Taco Bueno, Whataburger,
	Lodg	S: Hampton Inn
	Other	N: Bank
440B		**Forest Hill Dr**
	Gas	N: Chevron◈, S: Conoco, Shell◈
	Food	S: Captain D's, CiCi's Pizza, DQ, Denny's, Jack in the Box, Luby's Cafeteria, Sonic, Starbucks, Subway, Taco Bell
	Lodg	N: ValuePlace S: Comfort Inn
	Other	S: CVS, Discount Tire, Dollar Tree, Dollar General, Grocery, Walgreen's,
441		**Anglin Dr, Hartman Lane**
	Gas	S: Conoco◈
442A		**287 Bus, Mansfield Hwy, Kennedale**
	Gas	N: Texaco◈, Valero◈ S: Chevron
	Food	N: Mexican Food/Texaco, Off the Bone BBQ
	Lodg	N: Great Western Inn, Super 8
(442B)		**Jct I-820, 287N, Downtown Fort Worth**
443		**Bowman Springs Rd (WB)**
444		**US 287S, to Waxahachie**
445		**Green Oaks Blvd, Little Rd, Arlington, Kennedale**
	Gas	N: 7-11, Conoco, Shell S: 7-11, Valero
	Food	N: Arby's, Braums', Burger King, Colter's Tx BBQ, Grandys, Hooters, Iris Bagel & Coffee House, Jack in the Box, KFC, Mac's Bar & Grill, Pizza Hut, Starbucks, Taco Bell, Taco Cabana, Taisho Japanese Rest, Whataburger

EXIT		TEXAS
	Food	S: Cheddar's Cafe, IHOP, McDonald's, Molly's Burgers & Shakes, Pancho's Mex Buffet, Steak & Ale, Sake Japanese Steak House, Salut Italian Bistro, Taco Bueno, Waffle House
	Other	N: Albertson's, Ace Hardware, CVS, Carwash, Firestone, Kroger, Little Road Animal Clinic♥, Meineke Car Care, Pharmacy, Office Depot, Radio Shack, S: ATMs, Bank, Auto Zone, Discount Tire, Dollar General, Dog Wash, Jiffy Lube, Laundromat, O'Reilly Auto Parts, Winn Dixie, I-20 Animal Medical Center♥,
447		**Park Springs Rd, Kelly-Elliott Rd**
	Gas	N: 7-11 S: Exxon, Fina
	Food	N: Church's Chicken S: Blimpie's/Fina, Dominos Pizza, Little Caesar's Pizza, Subway
	Other	S: CVS, Walgreen's, U-Haul, US Post Office
448		**Bowen Rd, Arlington**
	Gas	N: QT, RaceTrac, Shell, Valero S: Shell
	Food	N: **Cracker Barrel**, Bobby V's Sports Gallery Cafe, Sonic
	Other	N: Grocery, Bowen 8 Theatre S: Creature Comfort Animal Clinic♥
449		**FM 157, Cooper St, Arlington (WB)**
	Gas	N: 7-11, Fina, Mobil, Shell S: Chevron, Citgo, Conoco, QT
	Food	N: BlackEyed Pea, ChickFilA, Chili's, CiCi's Pizza, China Cafe, Don Pablo, Golden Corral, Grady's, IHOP, Jack in the Box, KFC, Long John Silver, McDonald's, Nagoya Japanese, On the Border Mexican Rest, Outback Steakhouse, Pei Wei Asian Diner, Razzoo's Cajun Cafe, Red Lobster, Saltgrass Steak House, Souper Salad, Spring Creek BBQ, Starbucks, Subway, Thai House, Wendy's, Whataburger S: Applebee's, Arby's, Boston Market, Burger King, Burger Street, ChickFilA, Denny's, Dickey's BBQ Pit, El Fenix Mexican Rest, HomeTown Buffet, Long John Silver's, Luby's Cafeteria, Old Country Buffet, Olive Garden, Panda Express, Papa John's Pizza, Pizza Hut, Romano's Macaroni Grill, Ryan's Grill, Shoney's, Sonic, Starbucks, Taco Bueno, TGI Friday's, Whataburger,
	Lodg	N: Best Western♥, Comfort Inn, Days Inn, Holiday Inn Express, La Quinta Inn♥, Studio 6, Super 8♥ S: InTowne Suites, Microtel♥,
	Med	N: + Arlington Urgent Care S: + Care Now Medical Center
	Other	N: AMC 18 Theatres, ATMs, Academy Sports & Outdoors, Animal Healthcare Center♥, Auto Repairs & Services, Banks, Barnes & Noble, Batteries Plus, Best Buy, Carwash, Dick's Sporting Goods, Discount Tire, Enterprise RAC, FedEx Office, Lowe's, Michael's, Office Depot, Parks at Arlington Mall, Putt-Putt Fun Center, Radio Shack, Super Target, US Post Office, Verizon, **Treetops RV Village▲**, **Dallas Metro KOA▲**

EXIT		TEXAS
	Other	S: Albertson's, Auto Zone, Auto Services, Auto Dealers, Burlington Coat Factory, Carwash/Conoco, Discount Tire, Dollar General, Firestone Auto, Gully Animal Hospital♥, Harold Patterson Sports Center, Hobby Lobby, Home Depot, Kroger, Pharmacy, Sports Authority, South Cooper Animal Hospital♥, Tom Thumb Food & Pharmacy, UPS Store, **Walmart sc**,
449A		**FM 157S, Cooper St, Arlington (EB)**
449B		**FM 157N, Cooper St, Arlington (EB)**
450		**Matlock Rd**
	Gas	N: Citgo, Fina◈, QT S: Citgo, Diamond Shamrock, E-Z Mart, RaceTrac, Shell
	Food	N: America's Best Coffee, BJ's Rest & Brewhouse, Bravo Cucina, Burger King, Chuy's, IHOP, Melting Pot, MiMi's Cafe, PF Chang's, Red Robin, Saltgrass Steak House, Sonic, Steak 'n Shake, Sweet Tomatos, Sushi Domo, Taco Bell, The Keg Steakhouse & Bar, Tony Roma, Wendy's S: China King Super Buffet, Dominos Pizza, Joe's Pizza, Pasta & Subs, Panda Delite, Potbelly Sandwich Shop, Starbucks
	Lodg	N: Comfort Inn, Courtyard, Hampton Inn, La Quinta Inn♥, Quality Inn,
	Med	N: + Columbia Medical Center + USMD Hospital + Medical Center of Arlington
	Other	N: ATMs, Banks, AT&T, CVS, Costco, Lowe's, U-Haul, Walgreen's, S: Auto Dealer, NTB, O'Reilly Auto Parts, Arlington Muni Airport✈
451		**Collins St, New York Ave**
	Gas	N: Exxon, Mobil, RaceTrac S: Diamond Shamrock, QT, Shell
	Food	N: IHOP, Jack in the Box, Tony Roma's, Wendy's, Whataburger S: Chicken Express, McDonald's, Romano's Macaroni Grill, Sonic, Subway, Taco Bueno
	Lodg	S: La Quinta Inn
	Other	N: Traders Village Flea Market, **Traders Village RV Park▲** S: Arlington Muni Airport✈
453AB		**TX 360, Dallas-Ft Worth Airport, Watson Rd (Serv at first exits)**
454		**Great Southwest Pkwy, Grand Prairie**
	FStop	N: Golden Express #2/Conoco
	Gas	N: Chevron S: Exxon, Shell◈, Shamrock
	Food	N: Carino's Italian Grill, Chuck E Cheese, Golden Corral, McDonald's, Taco Bell, Texas Roadhouse, Waffle House, Wendy's S: Burger King/Shamrock, Subway/Shell Applebee's, Arby's, Buffalo Wild Wings, Sonic
	Lodg	N: Comfort Suites, Quality Inn S: Super 8
	Med	N: + Hospital
	Other	N: Avis RAC, Garden Ridge, Harley Davidson, U-Haul, Grand Prairie Muni Airport✈ S: ATMs, Banks, Discount Tire, Kroger/ Pharmacy, Office Depot, PetSmart♥, Pharmacy, Sam's Club, **Walmart sc**, Walgreen's,

EXIT		TEXAS
456		**Carrier Pkwy, Grand Prairie**
	Gas	S: Fina
	Food	N: ChickFilA, Don Pablo, Starbucks, Whataburger S: Chili's, Denny's, IHOP, McDonald's, Soulman's BBQ, Mongolian BBQ, Cafe
	Other	N: ATM, Banks, Home Depot, Target S: Albertson's, ATM, Cinemark 16, CVS, Grand Prairie 10, Walgreen's
457		**FM 1382, Grand Prairie, Cedar Hill**
	Gas	N: Diamond Shamrock◈, Shell◈ S: RaceTrac
	Food	N: Taco Bell, Waffle House S: Jack in the Box
	Other	N: Bank, **Mtn Creek Lake State Park** S: **to Cedar Hill State Park▲**
458		**Mountain Creek Pkwy, Dallas**
460		**Spur 408 (diff reaccess)**
461		**Cedar Ridge Dr, Duncanville**
	Gas	S: RaceTrac, Shamrock
462		**Duncanville Rd, Main St**
462A		**N Duncanville Rd (EB)**
	Gas	S: Exxon, Shell
	Food	S: Arby's, Whataburger
	Lodg	S: Motel 6♥
	Other	N: Auto Service, Museum, U-Haul S: ATMs, Banks, Budget RAC, Family Dollar, Harbor Freight, Kroger, Radio Shack
462B		**N Main St (WB)**
	Gas	S: Conoco, Exxon, Kroger, Shell◈, QT
	Food	S: Arby's, Captain D's, Cesar's Taco, Church's Chicken, Jack In the Box, KFC, Odom's BBQ, Whataburger
	Lodg	S: Hilton Garden Inn
	Other	S: ATM, Banks, Dollar General, Firestone Auto, Laundromat,
463		**Cockrell Hill Rd, Camp Wisdom Rd, Duncanville, Dallas**
	Gas	N: Chevron◈, Exxon◈ S: Fina, Texaco
	Food	N: Catfish King, Denny's, Long John Silver/Taco Bell, Taco Cabana S: Blimpie's, Burger King, Chubby's Rest, Jack in the Box, McDonald's, Olive Garden, Red Lobster, Subway, Wendy's
	Lodg	N: America's Best Value Inn, Holiday Inn, Lexington Hotel Suites, Motel 6♥, Ramada Inn, Royal Inn, Suburban Extended Stay
	Other	N: Auto Dealers, ATMs, Banks, Midas, Southwest Center Mall S: Advance Auto Parts, Best Buy, CVS, Enterprise RAC, Kmart, NTB, Pep Boys, Target
464AB		**US 67, Dallas, Cleburne**
465		**Hampton Rd, Wheatland Rd**
	Gas	N: Shell◈ S: Chevron, RaceWay, Sam's, Murphy
	Food	N: ChickFilA, Chili's S: Arby's, Cheddar's, Jack in the Box, Popeye's Chicken, Sonic, Spring Creek BBQ, Taco Bell, Wendy's
	Lodg	S: Comfort Inn, Super 8♥
	Med	S: + Hospital
	Other	N: Target S: Auto Dealers, Hertz RAC, Home Depot, Lowe's, Office Max, PetSmart♥, Sam's Club, **Walmart sc**
466		**S Polk St, Dallas**
	TStop	S: Love's Travel Stop #294 (Scales)
	Gas	N: Exxon, Quick Track, Texaco
	Food	N: DQ, Dean Seafood, Sonic, Western BBQ, Subway/Exxon, S: Carl'sJr/Love's TS
	Tires	S: Love's TS
	Other	N: ATM, Bank S: WiFi/**RV Dump**/Love's TS, Greyhound
(467AB/ 418AB)		**Jct I-35E, N to Dallas, S to Waco (Gas/Food/Lodg at 1st Ex S)**
468		**Houston School Rd, Lancaster**
	Gas	S: Tiger Mart/Exxon◈
	Food	S: Whataburger
470		**TX 342, Lancaster Rd, Dallas**
	TStop	N: USA Travel Center/Texaco (Scales) S: Pilot Travel Center #433 (Scales)
	Gas	N: Chevron◈ S: Shell
	Food	N: Popeye's Chicken/USA TC, Big Bruce's BBQ, S: DQ/Wendy's/Pilot TC, McDonald's, Sonic, Subway, Taco Bell, Whataburger, Williams Chicken
	Lodg	S: Days Inn
	TWash	S: Galaxy TW, Dallas Super TW
	Other	N: ATM, Bank, Univ of N Tx/Dallas S: Chrome Shop, Laundry/WiFi/Pilot TC, CarQuest, Goodyear, Cedar Valley College
472		**Bonnie View Rd, Dallas**
	TStop	N: Flying J Travel Plaza #5520/Conoco (Scales) S: Travel Center of America/Exxon (Scales)
	Gas	N: Shell◈
	Food	N: Cookery/FastFood/FJ TP, Jack in the Box/Shell S: BK/TBell/PHut/TA TC
	Lodg	N: Ramada Ltd
	TServ	N: Flying J TP/Tires, Speedco, Kenworth, Utility Trailer of Dallas, Boss Truck Shop/ FJ TP, Chrome Shop S: TA TC/Tires
	TWash	N: Blue Beacon TW, Eagle TW
	Other	N: Laundry/BarbSh/WiFi/**RVDump/LP**/ FJ TP S: Laundry/WiFi/**RVDump**/TA TC, Great Dane Trailers, NTB,
473A		**JJ Lemmon Rd, Dallas (EB)**
(473A/ 276AB)		**Jct 45N, to Dallas (WB)**
(473B)		**Jct 45N, to Dallas**
(473C)		**Jct 45S, to Houston**
474		**TX 310N, S Central Expy (WB)**
476		**Dowdy Ferry Rd, Dallas**
	Other	S: Carl's Auto & Truck Repair
477		**St Augustine Rd**
	Gas	S: Shell◈
	Food	S: Sonic/Shell
479AB		**US 175, Kaufman, Dallas**
	FStop	S: Marlow's Fuel Center/Shell
	Food	S: FastFood/Marlow's, Fat Bean BBQ
(480)		**Jct I-635N, ByPass, to Mesquite**
	TServ	N: Cummins Southern Plains
481		**Seagoville Rd, Balch Springs, Dallas**
	Gas	N: Fina, Shell, Valero
	Food	N: Deli/Valero, Taco Bell S: Lindy's Rest, Kiss My Ribs BBQ
	Lodg	N: La Quinta Inn♥
482		**Belt Line Rd**
	Gas	S: Shell◈
	Food	S: KFC/PizzaHut/Shell
483		**Lawson Rd, Lasater Rd, Mesquite**
487		**FM 740, Forney**
	Other	S: **Lakeside RV Park▲**
490		**FM 741, Forney**
491		**FM 2932, Helms Trail Rd**
493		**FM 1641, Forney**
	Gas	S: Exxon◈
	Food	S: Sonic
	Other	S: Carwash/Exxon
498		**TX 148, Terrell**
	FStop	N: Tiger Mart #30/Exxon
	Gas	S: Shell◈
	Food	N: Dennys/Subway/Exxon, Soulman's BBQ
	Other	S: **Terrell RV Park▲**
499A		**to US 80W, to Dallas, Forney, Mesquite (No reaccess)**
499B		**Rose Hill Rd**
501		**TX 34, Terrell, Kaufman**
	FStop	S: Valero #4532
	Gas	N: Chevron, Exxon◈ S: Circle K, Phillips 66
	Food	N: DQ, Double T Steak & Grill, Sonic, Subway, Starbucks, Waffle House S: Carmona's Tex Mex, McDonald's, IHOP, Wendy's, FastFood/Valero
	Lodg	N: Americas Best Value Inn♥, Best Western, Comfort Inn, Days Inn♥, La Quinta Inn♥, Motel 6♥
	Lodg	S: Holiday Inn Express, Super 8♥
	Med	N: + Hospital
	Other	N: Home Depot, Museum, Terrell Muni Airport✈ S: Tanger Outlet Mall, Equine Veterinary Service♥
503		**Wilson Rd, Terrell**
	TStop	S: Travel Center of America/Shell (Scales)
	Food	S: Rest/PHut/Subway/TA TC
	TServ	S: TA TC/Tires
	Other	S: Laundry/WiFi/**RVDump**/**LP**/TA TC
506		**FM 429, FM 2728, College Mound Rd, Terrell**
	Other	N: **Bluebonnet Ridge RV Park▲**
509		**Hiram Rd, Terrell**
	TStop	S: McDonald's Phillips 66
	Food	S: FastFood/P66
(512)		**Weigh Station (Both dir)**
512		**FM 2965, Hiram-Wills Point Rd**
516		**FM 47, Lake Tawakoni, Wills Pt**
	Gas	S: Diamond Shamrock, Robertson's
	Food	N: Four Winds Steakhouse S: Robertson's Cafe
	Lodg	S: Interstate Motel
519		**Turner-Hayden Rd**
	Other	S: **Canton I-20 RV Park▲**
521		**Myrtle Cemetery Rd (WB), Myrtle Springs Rd (EB), Canton**
523		**TX 64, Canton, Wills Point**
	Other	N: **Canton Campground/RV & Horse Park▲**, Sundown Trailers
526		**FM 859, Edgewood**

◈= Regular Gas Stations with Diesel ▲ = RV Friendly Locations ♥= Pet Friendly Locations
Red print shows large vehicle parking / access on site or nearby **Brown Print = Campgrounds / RV PARKS**

EXIT		TEXAS
527		**TX 19, Emory, Canton, Athens**
	FStop	S: Kick 66/Circle K/P66
	Gas	N: Exxon, Texaco◈
		S: Chevron◈, Shell◈
	Food	N: Little Jewel's, Ranchero Rest, Subway, Whataburger
		S: DQ, Jerry's Pizza, McDonald's, KFC, Taco Bell
	Lodg	N: Comfort Inn, Holiday Inn Express, Super 8
		S: Best Western & **RV Park▲**, Days Inn
	Other	N: **Fish & Jog RV Park▲**
		S: **Hide-A-Way RV Ranch▲**, **Ford RV Sales & Service**
528		**FM 17, Canton**
530		**FM 1255, Canton**
533		**Colfax Oakland Rd, Canton**
	TStop	S: Canton Travel Plaza/Shamrock
	Food	S: Rest/Canton TP
	TServ	S: Canton TP
	Other	S: Laundry/WiFi/Canton TP
536		**Tank Farm Rd**
537		**FM 773, FM 16, Ben Wheeler, Van**
(538)		**Van Zandt Co Rest Area (Both dir) (RR, Ph, Pic, Vend, Pet, WiFi, RVDump)**
540		**FM 314, Van**
	TStop	N: Love's Travel Stop #287 (Scales)
	Food	N: DQ, Carl's Jr/Love's TS
	Lodg	N: Van Inn
	Other	N: RVDump/WiFi/Love's TS, CB, Tires
544		**Willow Branch Rd, Van**
	TStop	N: Running W Truck Stop/Conoco
	Food	N: Rest/Running W TS
	TServ	N: Running W TS/Tires
	Other	N: **Willow Branch RV Park▲**
(546)		**Inspection Station (Both dir)**
548		**TX 110, Grand Saline, Carol, Van, Lindale**
	FStop	S: Oasis/Valero
	Gas	N: Exxon◈
552		**FM 849, Lindale**
	Gas	N: Chevron
	Other	N: Bank, Pharmacy
554		**Harvey Rd**
556		**US 69, Lindale, Tyler, Mineola**
	FStop	N: Tyler Fuel Plaza/Shamrock
	Gas	N: RaceWay, Murphy
		S: Chevron, Exxon, Texaco
	Food	N: Burger King, Chili's, Dominos Pizza, KFC/Long John Silver, Juanita's Mexican, Lone Star Steakhouse, McDonald's, Pizza Hut, Pizza Inn, Subway, Taco Bell
		S: Cracker Barrel, Wendy's
	Lodg	N: Best Western, Comfort Suites, Days Inn, Hampton Inn
		S: Americas Best Value Inn♥
	Med	S: + Hospital
	Other	N: Animal Hospital of Lindale♥, AutoZone, Dollar General, Family Dollar, Lowe's, O'Reilly Auto Parts, U-Haul, **Walmart sc**
		S: appr 3mi: **Southern RV Supercenter**
557		**Jim Hogg Rd, Tyler**
	Gas	N: Shell◈
	Other	N: Santa Land Amusement Park
560		**Lavender Rd**
	Other	N: to **Tyler State Park▲**
		S: appr 2.3mi: **5 Star RV Park/RVDump▲**

EXIT		TEXAS
562		**TX 14, Tyler, State Park, Hawkins**
	TStop	S: Pilot Travel Center #486 (Scales)
	Food	N: Bodacious BBQ
		S: McDonald's/Pilot TC,
	Other	N: appr 2mi: **Tyler State Park▲**, **Lions RV Park▲**, to appr 6mi: **Whispering Pines Resort & Campground▲**
		S: Laundry/WiFi/Pilot TC, appr 4 mi: **Northgate RV Park▲**, appr 4.5 mi: **Tyler RV Center Sales & Service/LP/RVDump**,
565		**FM 2015, Driskill, Lake Rd**
567		**TX 155, E Texas Center, Tyler, Gilmer, Winona, Big Sandy**
	FStop	N: Wilco Travel Stop/Citgo
	Food	N: FastFood/Wilco TS
	Lodg	S: Days Inn
	Med	S: + E TX TB Hospital
	Other	N: Laundry/Wilco TS
		S: CB Shop
571A		**US 271, Tyler, Gladewater**
	Gas	S: Chevron
	Med	S: + E TX TB Hospital
	Other	S: Budget Diesel & RV Repair
571B		**FM 757, Starrville, Oman Rd**
(573)		**Picnic Area (Both dir)**
575		**Barber Rd, Winona**
579		**CR 3111, Joy-Wright Mountain Rd, Gladewater**
582		**FM 3053, Liberty City, Overton**
	Gas	N: Exxon◈, Chevron◈,
	Food	N: BBQ, DQ, Java Shop, Sonic, Subway/Exxon, Whataburger/Chevron
	Lodg	S: Thrifty Inn
	Other	N: Carwash, Quik Lube
583		**TX 135, Kilgore, Gladewater, Overton, to US 271**
	Gas	N: EZ Mart◈
		S: Exxon
	Other	N: Dollar General, appr 1.5mi: **Shallow Creek RV Resort▲**
587		**TX 42, Kilgore, White Oak**
	FStop	S: Gateway Travel Plaza Exxon
	Gas	N: Diamond Shamrock
	Food	N: Bodacious BBQ, Country Kitchen
	Med	S: + Hospital
	Other	S: to **Walmart sc**, Museum
589A		**US 259, TX 31, Kilgore, Longview, Henderson (EB)**
589B		**US 259, TX 31, Kilgore (EB Left Exit)**
589		**US 259, TX 31, Kilgore (WB Left Exit)**
	FStop	S: Rudy's #3/Exxon
	Gas	S: Conoco
	Food	S: Rudy's #3/Exxon
	Lodg	S: Days Inn♥, Hampton Inn, Holiday Inn Express, Ramada♥
	Other	N: to appr 10mi: **Secluded Acres RV Park▲**
		S: Kilgore College, Addtl Serv
591		**FM 2087, FM 2011, Old Kilgore Hwy, Longview**
	Other	N: **Pine Ridge RV Park▲**
		S: Kilgore Airport✈, appr 2mi: **Fernbrook RV Park▲**

EXIT		TEXAS
595A		**TX 322S, Estes Pkwy, to TX149, Longview (EB)**
595B		**TX 281N, Estes Pkwy, Longview (EB)**
595		**TX 322, FM 1845, Lp 281, Estes Parkway, Longview (WB)**
	Gas	N: E-Z Mart, Exxon, Texaco◈
		S: Fina◈, Mobil, Murphy
	Food	N: DQ, Jack in the Box, KFC, Lupe's, McDonald's, Pizza Hut, Subway, Waffle House
		S: KFC/Taco Bell
	Lodg	N: Americas Best Value Inn, Days Inn, Express Inn, Guest Inn♥
		S: Baymont Inn, Hampton Inn, Motel 6♥
	Other	N: Kilgore College, LeTourneau Univ, Tx Baptist College
		S: AT&T, **Walmart sc**, to appr 3.5 mi: **349 West RV Park▲**
596		**US 259N, TX 149, Eastman Rd, Carthidge**
	FStop	N: Fastop Foods/Exxon, Howie's Get & Go #22/Shell
	Gas	S: Valero◈
	Food	N: Grandys/Exxon, Burger King, Whataburger
		S: Arby's
	Lodg	N: Best Western, Comfort Suites, La Quinta Inn, Microtel, Super 8
		S: Holiday Inn Express
	Other	N: Carwash
599		**Loop 281, FM 968, Longview**
	TStop	S: PTP/ National Truck Stop/Chevron (Scales)
	Gas	S: Exxon◈
	Food	S: Rest/National TS
	Lodg	N: Best Western, Comfort Inn, to Fairfield Inn, Wingate Inn
	TServ	S: National TS, Bridgestone Tire & Auto, Detroit Diesel, E Texas Truck Equip, TX Kenworth, Truck Parts World
	Other	N: appr 1mi: **Camp Coles RV Park▲**, Appr 2 mi: **Shady Pines RV Park▲**
		S: Laundromat/Exxon
604		**FM 450, Hallsville**
	Gas	N: Shamrock◈
	Other	N: **450 Hitching Post RV Park▲**
(608)		**Harrison Co Rest Area (Both dir) (RR, Phone, Picnic, Vend, WiFi)**
610		**FM 3251, Marshall**
614		**TX 43, Marshall, Kado Lake, Henderson**
	Other	S: **Martin Creek Lake State Park**
617		**US 59, SE End Blvd, Marshall, Carthage**
	FStop	S: Pump & Pantry #15/Shamrock
	TStop	S: Pony Express Travel Center/Conoco (Scales)
	Gas	N: Exxon◈, Texaco
		S: Chevron◈,
	Food	N: Applebee's, Catfish Express, Golden Corral, IHOP, McDonald's, Subway, Waffle House, Wendy's, Whataburger
		S: Rest/Pony Express TC, The Hungry Maverick
	Lodg	N: Best Western, Comfort Suites, Days Inn♥, Fairfield Inn, Hampton Inn,

◈ = Regular Gas Stations with Diesel ▲ = RV Friendly Locations ♥ = Pet Friendly Locations
Red print shows large vehicle parking / access on site or nearby Brown Print = Campgrounds / RV PARKS

EXIT		TX / LA
	Lodg	N: La Quinta Inn ♥, Quality Inn S: Days Inn, Econo Lodge, Holiday Inn Express, Motel 6 ♥, Super 8
	TServ	S: Pony Express TC/Tires
	Other	N: Auto Dealers, Auto Repairs, to Country Pines RV Park▲, Holiday Springs RV, S: Laundry/Pony Express TC, to 7mi: Circle M RV Park▲,
620		**FM 31, Marshall, Elysian Fields**
	Other	N: appr 1.7mi: Marshall RV Park & Cabin Rentals▲
624		**FM 2199, Scottsville**
628		**to US 80, Frontage Rd, Waskom**
633		**FM 9, FM 134, Caddo Lake**
	Gas	N: Texaco
	Food	N: Catfish Village
	Other	S: Miss Ellie's RV Park▲
635		**TX 156, TX 9, Spur 156, Waskom**
	Gas	N: Chevron◈, Exxon◈
	Food	N: Burger King, DQ, Jim's BBQ, Sub Express
(636)		**TX Welcome Center (WB)** (RR, Phone, Picnic, WiFi) **Parking Area (EB)**

NOTE: MM 636: Louisiana State Line

CENTRAL TIME ZONE

⇧ TEXAS
⇩ LOUISIANA

EXIT		LOUISIANA
(1)		**Weigh Station (Both dir)**
(3)		**Greenwood Welcome Center (EB)** (RR, Ph, Vend, Pet, Sec, WiFi, RV Water/RVDump)
3		**US 79S, LA 169, Greenwood, to Shreveport**
	TStop	S: Flying J Travel Plaza #5048/Conoco (Scales) (DAND), Love's Travel Stop #209 (Scales)
	Food	S: Rest/FF/FJ TP, Arby's/Love's TS, Sonic
	Lodg	S: to Country Suites, MidContinent Inn
	TServ	S: Flying J TP, Speedco
	Other	S: Laundry/BarbSh/Casino/RVDump/LP/WiFi/FJ TP, Laundry/RVDump/WiFi/Casino/Love's TS, Zoo
5		**US 79N, US 80, Greenwood**
	FStop	S: Derrick Truck Stop
	TStop	N: Travel Center of America #237 (Scales)
	Food	N: FamilyRest/Subway/TA TC S: Angelina's Italian Rest
	Lodg	N: Country Inn S: Mid Continent Inn
	TWash	N: TA TC
	TServ	N: TA TC/Tires
	Other	N: Laundry/BarbSh/WiFi/RVDump/TA TC, Greenwood Flea Market S: B&D Truck & Gear, Auto Repairs, Rose Cottage Animal Hotel & Holistic Pet Care Center ♥, Greenwood Flea Market, Watertown USA
8		**US 80, LA 526E, Industrial Loop**
	TStop	S: Petro Stopping Center #8/Mobil (Scales), J&S Citgo
	Gas	S: Chevron◈
	Food	N: Greenwood Rd Smoke House S: IronSkillet/Wendy's/Petro SC, Jan's River Rest
	Lodg	N: Motel 6 ♥ S: Motel California
	TWash	S: Blue Beacon TW/Petro SC
	TServ	N: Detroit Diesel, Shreveport Truck Center, United Engines, Auto & Diesel Repair, Freightliner S: Petro SC
	Other	S: Laundry/WiFi/Petro SC, Tall Pines RV Park▲, Campers RV Center Powersports & RV Park▲,
10		**Pines Rd, Shreveport**
	Gas	N: BP◈ S: Exxon◈, Shell, Murphy
	Food	N: DQ, Pizza Hut, Popeye's, Subway, Western Sizzlin S: Burrito Stand, Burger King, CiCi's Pizza, Cracker Barrel, IHOP, KFC, Sonic, Starbucks, Taco Bell, Waffle House, Wendy's, Whataburger
	Lodg	S: Comfort Suites, Courtyard, Fairfield Inn, Hilton Garden Inn, Holiday Inn, Jameson Inn, La Quinta Inn ♥
	Other	N: Grocery, Auto Repairs, S: ATM, Bank, CVS, Dollar General, Dollar Tree, Family Dollar, Home Depot, Kroger, O'Reilly Auto Parts, Radio Shack, RiteAid, Walgreen's, Walmart sc, US Post Office, Diesel Service, Auto Dealers, Shreveport/Bossier KOA▲, American RV Parts & Service
(11)		**Jct I-220E, LA 3132E, to I-49S, Inner Loop Expwy**
13		**Monkhouse Dr, Shreveport**
	Gas	S: Chevron, Exxon◈,
	Food	N: Denny's, Kettle, Leona's Smokehouse S: Kings BBQ, Waffle House
	Lodg	N: Best Value Inn, Days Inn, Holiday Inn Express, Residence Inn S: Best Western, Candlewood Suites, Hampton Inn, Ramada Inn, Super 8
	Other	N: Bank, Tires, Westwood Golf Course S: Airport✈ Casino, Rental Cars, Shreveport Reg'l Airport✈
14		**Jewella Ave, Shreveport**
	Gas	N: Texaco◈, Valero
	Food	N: Burger King, Church's Chicken, McDonald's, Subway, Taco Bell, Whataburger
	Other	N: Advance Auto Parts, Auto Zone, Family Dollar, Grocery, O'Reilly Auto Parts, RiteAid, Walgreen's, Independence Stadium, ATM, Bank
16A		**US 171, Hearne Ave**
	Gas	N: Citgo◈ S: Exxon, Raceway, Texaco◈
	Food	N: Subway S: KFC, Krystal's
	Lodg	S: Cajun Inn, Howard Johnson
	Med	N: + Hospital
	Other	N: Museum
16B		**US 79, US 80, Greenwood Rd**
	Gas	S: Citgo◈
	Food	S: Burger King, El Chico
	Lodg	S: Travelodge
	Med	N: + Medical Center
17A		**Lakeshore Dr, Linwood Ave**
	Gas	N: Circle K
	Lodg	N: Lakeshore Inn
	Med	N: + LSU Medical Center
(17B)		**Jct I-49S, to Alexandria**
18A		**Common St, Line Ave (EB)**
	Med	S: + Doctors Hospital
18C		**Fairfield Ave (WB, diff reaccess)**
	Gas	S: Circle K
	Food	S: Bears,
	Med	S: + Hospital, + Promise Hospital
	Other	S: Auto Services, B&N, Medic Compounding Pharmacy
18D		**Fairfield Ave, Louisiana Ave, Common St, Line Ave**
	Gas	S: Citgo
19A		**US 71N, LA 1, Spring St**
	Food	N: Rest/Holiday Inn
	Lodg	N: Best Western, Holiday Inn, Hollywood Casino & Hotel, Sam's Town Hotel & Casino
	Other	N: Shreveport Riverfront Conv Center, Expo Hall, IMAX, Museums, Harrah's Casino
19B		**Traffic St, Riverside Dr**
	Gas	S: Exxon
	Food	S: Circle B Ranch Steakhouse, Sundance Cantina, Cattleman's Buffet

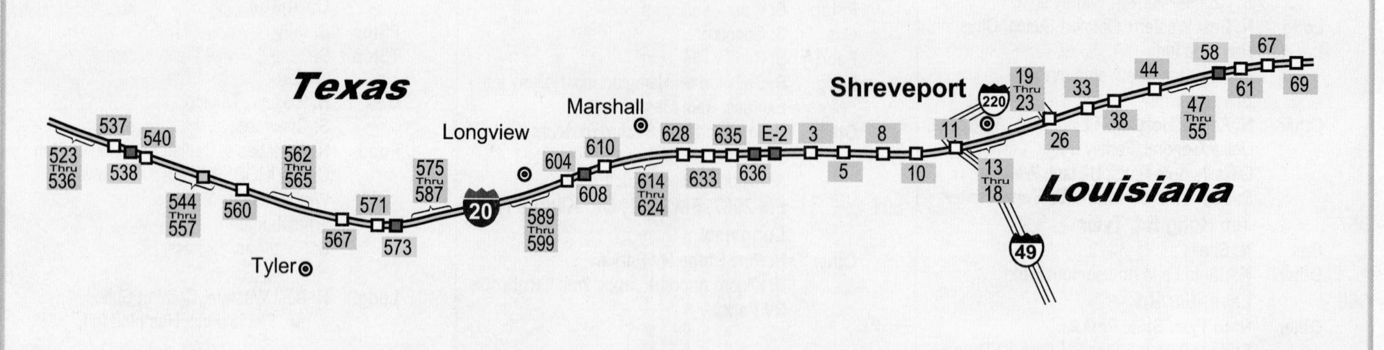

◈= Regular Gas Stations with Diesel ▲ = RV Friendly Locations ♥= Pet Friendly Locations
Red print shows large vehicle parking / access on site or nearby Brown Print = Campgrounds / RV PARKS

EXIT		LOUISIANA
	Lodg	**N:** Horseshoe Casino $ & Hotel **S:** Boomtown Hotel & Casino $
	Other	**S:** Bass Pro Shop
20A		**Hamilton Rd, Isle of Capri Blvd**
	Gas	**N:** Circle K, Ride USA, Texaco **S:** Chevron, Exxon
	Food	**N:** Cobb Joe Bossier BBQ **S:** Calypso Buffet, Lucky Palace
	Lodg	**N:** Comfort Inn **S:** Isle of Capri Casino$ Resort, Diamond Jacks Hotel, Casino Resort & **Campground▲** , Ramada
	Other	**N:** Auto Repairs, Bank **S: Isle of Capri RV Park▲**
20B		**LA 3, Benton Spur Rd (EB)** **(Access Same Serv as Ex #21 N)**
	Other	**N:** Bossier Civic Center
20C		**US 71S, Barksdale Blvd (EB)**
	Gas	**S:** Clark, Exxon◈,
	Other	**S:** Advance Auto, Dollar General, Just Tires
21		**LA 72, Old Minden Rd, to US 71S**
	Gas	**N:** Circle K, Exxon, Valero **S:** RaceWay
	Food	**N:** Burger King, Cowboys, El Chico Cafe, Kobe Steakhouse & Sushi Bar, McDonald's Posados, Ralph & Kacoo's, **S:** Dragon Ho, Waffle House, Wendy's
	Lodg	**N:** Americas Best Value Inn, Hampton Inn, Holiday Inn, InnPlace Suites Extended Stay, La Quinta Inn♥, Residence Inn, **S:** Days Inn, Motel 6♥, Value Place
	Other	**N:** Auto Repairs, Auto Dealers, AutoZone, Advance Auto, Dollar General, Enterprise RAC, O'Reilly Auto Parts, Bayou Outdoor Supercenter **RV**, Marine & **RV Rentals**, Sales & Service, US Post Office **S:** Visitor Center, **to appr 10 mi:** Red River South Marina & **Campground▲**
22		**LA 3105, Airline Dr, Barksdale AFB, Bossier City**
	Gas	**N:** Citgo◈, KangarooExp/Chevron◈, Shell, Valero◈, Albertson's **S:** Exxon◈, Texaco◈
	Food	**N:** Applebee's, Arby's, BackYard Burgers, Captain D's, ChickFilA, Chili's, Chuck E Cheese's Pizza, CiCi's Pizza, Grandy's Rest, IHOP, Luby's Cafeteria, McDonald's/ Chevron, Pizza Hut, Red Lobster, Starbucks, Sonic, Taco Bell, Waffle House **S:** Catfish King, Darryl's Grill & Family Rest, Outback Steakhouse, Popeye's Chicken
	Lodg	**N:** Best Western, Crossland Economy Studios♥, Grand Isle Hotel, Howard Johnson♥, Rodeway Inn♥, Super 8 **S:** Baymont Inn, Microtel♥, Quality Inn♥, Red Carpet Inn
	Med	**N:** + Hospital
	Other	**N:** Albertson's, Big Lots, BooksAMillion, CVS, Cinema 9, Firestone Auto, Goodyear Auto, Kmart, Office Depot, Pierre Bossier Mall, Pep Boys, Twin Cities Carwash, UPS Store, Verizon, **Walmart sc**, Walgreen's **S:** ATM, Auto Service, Auto Zone, Bank, Grocery, Holiday Lanes Bowling, to Barksdale AFB, Air Force Museum
23		**Industrial Dr, Barksdale AFB, to US 79, US 80, Bossier City** **(Acc to #22-N to E Texas St)**
	FStop	**S:** Industrial Dr Exxon

Personal Notes

EXIT		LOUISIANA
	TStop	**N: I-220 Ex #17A:** I-220 Travel Plaza/ Chevron
	Gas	**N:** Circle K, Exxon, Texaco **S:** Chevron◈
	Food	**N:** Burger King, Country Kitchen, Great American Steak & Buffet, McDonald's, Popeye's Chicken, Shane's Seafood & BBQ, Taco Bell, Rest/I-220 TP **S:** Subway/Ind Dr Exxon
	Lodg	**N:** Econo Lodge, Economy Inn **S:** Ramada Inn
	TServ	**S:** Peterbilt of Shreveport
	Other	**N:** Laundry/I-220 TP, Auto Services **S:** Barksdale AFB, **Southern RV Super Center**, **LA State Hwy Patrol Post**
(26)		**Jct I-220W ByPass**
	Other	**N: to Exit #17A:** I-220 Travel Plaza, Harrah's LA Downs/Rest/Springhill Suites/Casino,
33		**LA 157, Haughton, Fillmore**
	TStop	**S:** Pilot Travel Center #199 (Scales)
	Gas	**N:** Texaco **S:** Exxon
	Food	**S:** Arby's/TJCinn/Pilot TC, Waffle House
	Other	**N: Hilltop Campground▲** **S:** Laundry/**Casino**/WiFi/**RVDump**/Pilot TC, Dollar General, Barksdale AFB, **MIL/ Barksdale AFB FamCamp▲**
38		**LA 117, Goodwill Rd, Minden**
	TStop	**S:** Fillmore Express/BP
	Food	**S:** RainbowDiner/Fillmore Express,
	Tires	**S:** BP
	Other	**S: Interstate RV Park▲** , LA Army Ammu Plant, **to appr 12mi: Green Park Resort▲** , **Lake Bistineau State Park▲** ,

EXIT		LOUISIANA
44		**US 371N, LA 7, to US 80, US 79, Minden, Cotton Valley** **(Addtl Serv E on US 80)**
	FStop	**N:** Dixie Inn Travel Center/Buzz By #24/ Exxon
	Gas	**N:** Chevron
	Food	**N:** Huddle House/Exxon, Crawfish Hole #2, Nicky's Mexican Rest, Sonic
	Lodg	**N:** Minden Motel
	Other	**N:** Family Dollar, **Cinnamon Creek RV Park▲** , **to appr 2 mi: Lakeside RV Park▲** , **appr 2.5mi: Farmers Branch MH RV Park▲**
47		**US 371S, LA 159N, Sibley Rd, Minden, Sibley**
	Gas	**N:** Chevron◈, Citgo◈, Mobil◈,
	Food	**N:** Domino's Pizza, Golden Biscuit Rest, Williams Chicken, Rest/Exacta Inn,
	Lodg	**N:** Best Western♥, Exacta Inn, Holiday Inn Express, Southern Inn
	Med	**N: + to Minden Medical Center**
	Other	**N:** ATM, Bank, Auto Dealer, Greyhound, **To appr 2.5mi: Woods Ranch RV Park▲** **S: to Lake Bastineau State Park▲** , **Madden Circle RV Park▲**
49		**LA 531, Industrial Dr, to US 79, US 80, Minden, Dubberly**
	TStop	**N:** Truckers Paradise, Love's Travel Stop #289 (Scales), Minden Truck Stop/Shell, QuickDraw
	Gas	**N:** to Murphy
	Food	**N:** Rest/Truckers Paradise, Arby's/Love's TS, Subway/Shell, Pepe's Mex Rest
	Other	**N: Casino**/Minden TS, Truckers Paradise, WiFi/**RVDump**/Love's TS, **to appr 3mi: Walmart sc**
52		**LA 532, Minden, Dubberly, to US 80**
	FStop	**N:** Valero **S:** Clark
	TStop	**N:** Triple C Truck Travel Plaza/Exxon (Scales)
	Food	**N:** Mom's Diner/BBQ/Triple C
	Other	**N:** Laundry/WiFi/**Casino**/Triple C
55		**US 80, Gibsland, to Ada, Taylor**
(58)		**Rest Area (Both dir) (CLOSED)** **(RR, Phone, Vend, Sec, RVDump)**
61		**LA 154, Gibsland, Athens**
	Other	**N: to Lake Claiborne State Park▲**
67		**LA 9, Homer Arcadia Hwy, 6th St, Arcadia, Homer** **(Addtl Serv S on US 80 in Arcadia)**
	Gas	**S:** Rogers Shell, addtl gas 2-3 mi in town
	Food	**S:** J&J Express
	Lodg	**S: appr 3mi:** Days Inn♥
	Other	**N: to appr 11mi: Lake Claiborne State Park▲** **S:** Auto Service/Tires/**LP**/Rogers
69		**LA 151, Hazel St, to US 80, Arcadia, Dubach**
	FStop	**N:** Gap Farms Travel Center/Mobil **S:** Get 'n Geaux #83/BP
	Gas	**S:** Citgo, Shell◈
	Food	**N:** BurgerKing/Deli/BBQ/Gap Farms TC **S:** Country Folks Kitchen, El Jarrito Mex Rest, McDonald's, Sonic, Subway

◈ = **Regular Gas Stations with Diesel** ▲ = **RV Friendly Locations** ♥ = **Pet Friendly Locations**
Red print shows large vehicle parking / access on site or nearby **Brown Print = Campgrounds / RV PARKS**

Lodg S: Days Inn, Nob Hill Inn
Other N: RV Park ▲ /Gap Farms TC
S: Auto Repairs, Brookshire Grocery, Carwash, Dollar General, Diesel Repairs, Factory Outlet Mall, Fred's, NAPA, Pharmacy, U-Haul, **to appr 4 mi:** Bonnie & Clyde Trade Days Flea Market **& RV Park▲ , to appr 7 mi: Creekwood Gardens RV Park▲**

77 LA 507, Martha St, Simsboro
Food S: JR's Place Restaurant
Other S: US Post Office, **Antique Village RV Park▲**

78 LA 563, Simsboro, Industry
FStop S: Magnolia Corner Gen'l Store/Texaco

81 LA 149, Grambling
Gas S: Exxon
Other S: to Grambling State Univ

(New) Proposed LA 818, Tarbutton Rd

84 LA 544, Cooktown Rd, Ruston, LA Tech, to Tarbutton Rd
Gas N: Mobil◈
S: Chevron◈, Chevron, Exxon,
Food N: Dowling's Smokehouse
S: DQ, Dominos Pizza, Johnny's Pizza, Pizza Inn, Quiznos, Starbucks, Subway, TCBY, Waffle House, Wendy's
Lodg S: Super 8, Travel Inn
Med S: + Lincoln General Hospital
Other S: Auto Service/Chevron, FastLube/ Carwash/Chevron, Grambling Univ

85 US 167, LA 146, Ruston, Dubach
Gas N: Chevron, Circle K/Shell
S: BP◈, Tobacco House, Valero◈
Food N: Applebee's, Burger King, Captain D's, Huddle House, McDonald's, Old Mexico Rest, Peking
Chinese Rest, SubwayChevron, Wendy's
S: Crescent City Coffee, Pizza Hut, Starbucks
Lodg N: Budget Lodge, Econo Lodge, Hampton Inn, Holiday Inn, Howard Johnson, Ramada Inn, Relax Inn
S: Americas Best Value Inn♥, Sleep Inn
Med S: + Lincoln General Hospital
Other N: ATMs, AT&T, Banks, Dollar General, Grocery, Office Depot, Radio Shack, SpeeDee Oil, Sterling Pharmacy,
S: ATMs, Banks, Advance Auto Parts, Jiffy Lube, O'Reilly Auto Parts, UPS Store

86 LA 33, Farmerville Hwy, Ruston, Farmerville
Gas N: Circle K/Shell◈ , Citgo, RaceWay, Texaco◈

Food N: Cajun Café, Cane's Chicken, Chili's, Hot Rod BBQ, Log Cabin Smokehouse, McDonald's, Ryan's Grill, Sonic
Lodg N: Comfort Inn, Days Inn♥,
S: Fairfield Inn, Holiday Inn Express♥, Lincoln Motel
Other N: Auto Dealers, Best Hardware, Carwash, Lowe's, Sexton Animal Health Center♥, **Walmart SC**, U-Haul, Tri Lake Marine & **RV, to appr 4 mi: Lincoln Parish Park▲**
S: Enterprise RAC, Museums, US Post Office

93 LA 145, Elm St, Choudrant, Sibley
FStop N: Spillers I-20 Texaco
Gas S: Chevron
Other **S: Jimmie Davis State Park▲**

(95) Tremont Rest Area (EB)
(RR, Phone, Vend, Pet, Sec, RVDump)

(97) Tremont Rest Area (WB) (CLOSED)
(RR, Phone, Vend, Pet, Sec, RVDump)
(Per LA DOT: to reopen 3/15/11)

101 LA 151, Calhoun, Downsville
FStop S: 101 Travel Plaza
Gas N: Texaco
S: Chevron
Food S: Subway/Huddle House/101 TP,
Other S: Auto Service/Chevron, Dollar General

103 US 80, Calhoun
TStop N: USA Truck Stop/103 TS/Shell (Scales)
Gas N: Stop 'n Shop◈
Food N: 103Rest/USA TS, Subway, Johnny's Pizza
Lodge N: Avant Motel West
TWash N: Truck Wash
TServ N: Ogden's Tire & Diesel, CB Shops
Other N: Laundry/WiFi/**LP**/USA TS

107 Camp Rd, Cheniere
Other **N: Sunset Cove RV Park▲**

108 to US 80, LA 546, Cheniere
Gas N: Shell◈
Other **N: Carter's Camping Center,** Excalibur Family Fun Center,

112 Well Rd, LA 3429, W Monroe
TStop S: Pilot Travel Center #428 (Scales)
Gas N: Circle K/Shell◈, Texaco◈, Conoco
Food N: DQ, Dominos Pizza, Flapjacks Rest, Hob Nob Steak & Seafood, Johnny's Pizza House, McDonald's, Sonic, Subway, Taco Bell, Waffle House
S: Subway/Wendy's/Pilot TC
TServ S: Frost Trailer Parts
Med N: + Cornerstone Hospital

Other N: Auto & Tire Service, Carwash, Coopers Veterinary Service♥, Dollar General, Shell Rapid Lube, Walgreen's,
S: Laundry/**RVDump**/Pilot TC,
Pavilion RV Park▲ , to Cheniere Lake Park▲

113 Mane St, Downing Pines Rd (EB)
Food S: Rest/HG Inn
Lodg S: Hilton Garden Inn, Holiday Inn Express
Other S: Ike Hamilton Expo Center, Mane St Mini Golf

114 LA 617, Thomas Rd, W Monroe
FStop S: Circle K #8773/Exxon
Gas N: RaceWay, Murphy, Brookshire's, Circle K◈, Exxon◈,
S: Chevron
Food N: Burger King, Cane's, Captain D's, ChickFilA, El Chico Cafe, Grandy's, IHOP, KFC, Little Caesars Pizza, McAlister's Deli, McDonald's, Pizza Hut, Popeye's Chicken, Scott's Catfish & Seafood, Shoney's, Subway, Taco Bell, Waffle House, Wendy's
S: Chili's, China Garden Buffet, Cracker Barrel, Hooters, Logan's Roadhouse, Lone Star Steakhouse, Outback Steakhouse, Peking Chinese Rest, Sonic, Waffle House
Lodg N: Shoney's Inn, Super 8, Wingate Inn
S: Best Western, Holiday Inn Express♥, Jameson Inn, Motel 6♥, Quality Inn♥, Red Roof Inn♥
Med N: + Ouachita Memorial Hospital, + Glenwood Reg'l Medical Center
Other N: ATMs, Auto Zone Parts, Banks, Big Lots, Brookshire's Grocery, Budget Truck Rental, CVS, Cinemark Tinseltown 17, Office Depot, O'Reilly Auto Parts, UPS Store, Verizon, Walgreen's, **Walmart SC**, West Monroe Convention Center,
S: ATMs, Advance Auto Parts, Banks, **Clay's RV Center**, Dollar General, Firestone Auto, Ike Hamilton Expo Center, Radio Shack,

115 LA 34, Stella St, Mill St
Gas N: Citgo
Food N: Curl's Cupcakes, Fire & Ice Grill, McDonald's, Roly Poly Sandwiches,
Med N: + Ouachita Memorial Hospital
TServ S: Diesel Truck Repair Co
Other N: Auto Repairs
S: Auto Repairs, **Clays RV Center**, Dan's Diesel Truck Repair, U-Haul, **to appr 5 mi: Bayou D'Arbonne Camping▲**

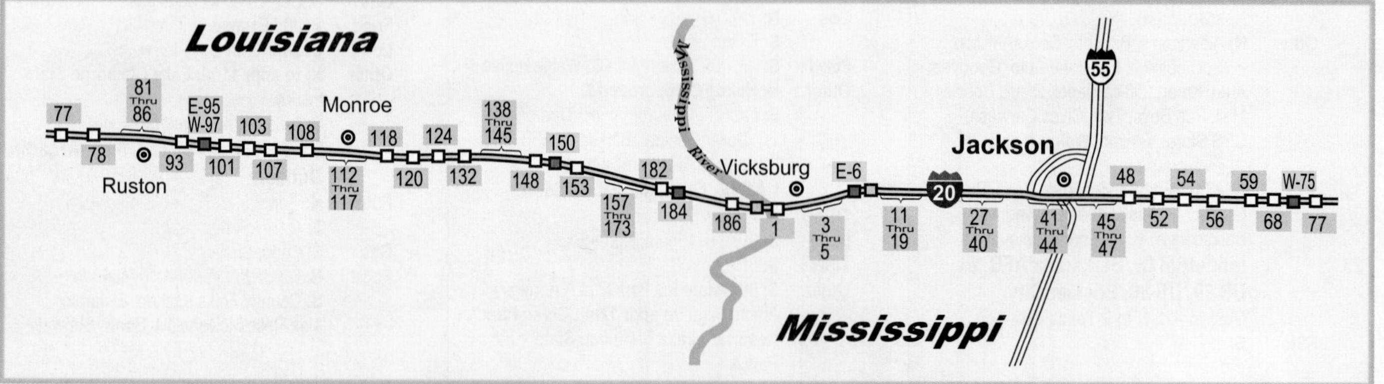

◈= Regular Gas Stations with Diesel ▲ = RV Friendly Locations ♥= Pet Friendly Locations
Red print shows large vehicle parking / access on site or nearby Brown Print = Campgrounds / RV PARKS

EXIT	LOUISIANA
116A	**Fifth St, Coleman Ave**
Gas	N: Circle K, Phillips 66
Other	N: Museum
116B	**Jackson St, 2nd St, LA 15, to US US 165 Bus, Monroe (EB)**
117A	**Hall St, Monroe (EB)**
Other	N: Civic Center
Med	N: + St Francis Medical Center
117B	**LA 594, Texas Ave**
117C	**US 165 Bus, LA 15 (WB)**
Med	N: + Hospital
Other	N: NE La Childrens Museum
117D	**Hall St, Catalpa St (WB)**
118	**US 165, ML King Dr, N-Bastrop, S-Columbia (EB)**
Gas	S: Chevron, Citgo, Exxon, Shell
Food	S: Burger King, BBQ, Captain D's Seafood, KFC, McDonald's, Sonic, Subway, Wendy's
Lodg	N: La Quinta Inn♥ S: Comfort Suites,Motel 6♥, Ramada Inn♥, Super 8♥
Med	N: + St Francis Hospital
Other	N: Consolidated Truck Parts, Greyhound, Home Depot, Southern Tire Mart, Monroe Reg'l Airport✈, to Univ of LA/Monroe S: Advance Auto, AutoZone, Budget Truck Rental, Dollar General, Grocery, to appr 2mi: Louisiana Purchase Gardens & Zoo
118A	**US 165S, Columbia (WB)**
118B	**US 165N, Bastrop (WB)**
120	**Garrett Rd, Pecanland Mall Dr**
Gas	N: Chevron◈, Shell S: Kangaroo Express◈
Food	N: Applebee's, Gators, IHOP, McAlister's Deli, Olive Garden, Red Lobster, Ronin Steak House & Sushi, Zipps, The Bistro/Courtyard
Lodg	N: Comfort Inn, Courtyard, Holiday Inn, Residence Inn♥ S: Best Western♥, Days Inn♥
Other	N: Best Buy, Cinema 10, Firestone, Home Depot, PetCo♥, Target, Tilt, Pecanland Ma Monroe Regional Airport✈ S: Bleu Bayou Harley Davidson, Lowe's, Sam's Club, Hope's Camper Corner, Freightliner, Cooper Truck Center, Moore's Truck Tire Center, Pecanland Estates & RV Park▲, Monroe Shilo RV & Travel Resort▲
124	**LA 594, Russell Sage Rd, Millhaven, R Sage Wildlife Area**
FStop	N: E-Z Mart #114
Other	N: LA State Hwy Patrol, to Wildlife Area
132	**LA 133, to US 80, Rayville, to Columbia, Start**
Gas	N: Exxon
138	**LA 137, Rayville, Archibald**
FStop	S: Rayville Travel Center/Citgo
TStop	N: Pilot Travel Center #335 (Scales),
Gas	N: BP S: Chevron◈, CircleK/Exxon◈, Raceway
Food	N: Wendy's/Pilot TC, Burger King, McDonald's, Quiznos, Huddle House, Waffle House S: Big John's Steak & Seafood, Subway/ Rayville TC, Popeye's Chicken, Quiznos/ Exxon, Waffle House

EXIT	LOUISIANA
Lodg	N: Days Inn♥, Rayville Motel S: Ramada Ltd♥, Super 8
TServ	N: USA Truck Repair, Lee's Truck Srv S: Goodyear
Med	N: + Richland Parish Hospital, + Richardson Medical Center
Other	N: Auto Dealers, AutoZone, Dollar General, Family Dollar, Firestone, Shell Rapid Lube S: Cottonland RV Park▲
141	**LA 583, Bee Bayou Rd, Rayville**
TStop	N: Bee Bayou Truck Stop/BP
Food	N: Rest/Bee Bayou TS
TServ	N: Bee Bayou TS
Other	N: Laundry/Bee Bayou TS
145	**LA 183, Holly Ridge, Richland Parish 202**
148	**LA 609, Delhi, Dunn**
(150)	**Rest Area (Both dir) (CLOSED) (RR, Phone, Vend, Sec, RVWtr/RVDump)**
153	**LA 17, Broadway St, Delhi, Winnsboro**
TStop	N: Nielsen's I-20 Texaco/Jubilee Truck Stop #1201/Texaco
Gas	N: Chevron◈, Loyd's S: Valero◈
Food	N: DQ, Burger King, Pizza Hut, Sonic, Subway/Chevron, S: Handy House Rest
Lodg	S: Best Western♥, Days Inn♥
TWash	N: The Truck Wash
Med	N: + Richland Parish Hospital
Other	N: Brookshires Grocery, Carwash, Dollar General, Fred's, NAPA, Pharmacy, 247 Auto Spa S: to Delhil Muni Airport✈
157	**LA 577, Waverly**
TStop	N: Waverly Truck Stop/Tiger Truck Stop S: Madison Auto Truck Plaza/Shell, Big Top Travel Center & Casino/Chevron
Food	N: Rest/Waverly TS S: Rest/Madison TP, Subway
Other	N: Laundry/Lucky's Casino/Waverly TS, S: Lucky Dollar Casino
171	**US 65, Tallulah, Vidalia, Newellton**
FStop	N: U-Pak-It/Chevron, Kangaroo #3450
TStop	S: Love's Travel Stop #237 (Scales), (DAND) Tallulah Truck Stop/Conoco (Scales), Travel Center of America #46/Mobil (Scales)
Gas	N: Shell◈ S: Texaco
Food	N: KFC, McDonald's, Subway/Chevron, Wendy's S: Arby's/Love's TS, Rest/Tallulah TS, CountryPr/BurgerKing/Popeye's/Starbucks/ TA TC,
Lodg	N: Days Inn♥, to Holiday Capri Motel, Super 8♥
TServ	S: TA TC/Tires, Tallulah Truck & Tire Shop
Med	N: + Madison Parish Hospital
Other	S: Kings Treasure, Laundry/Casino/WiFi/ RVDump/Love's TS, Laundry/Casino/ Tallulah TS, Laundry/WiFi/TA TC
173	**LA 602, to US 80, Tallulah, Richmond**
182	**LA 602, to US 80, Tallulah, Mound**
Other	N: Vicksburg Tallulah Reg'l Airport✈
(184)	**Mound Rest Area (Both dir) (RR, Ph, Pic, Vend, Pet, Sec, RVDump)**

EXIT	LA / MS
186	**US 80W, LA 193, Tallulah, Delta**
TStop	S: Interstate Station #7/Chevron
Food	S: FastFood/Chevron
Other	S: Laundry/Interstate Stn, Delta Discount Wine & Spirits
(187)	**Weigh Station (Both Dir)**
NOTE:	**MM 189: Mississippi State Line**

CENTRAL TIME ZONE

⇑ LOUISIANA
⇓ MISSISSIPPI

CENTRAL TIME ZONE

EXIT	LA / MS
1A	**Washington St, Warrenton Rd** **N: MS Welcome Center (Both dir) (RR, Phone, Pic) (TO RE-OPEN 4/11)**
Gas	N: Kangaroo Express◈, Ameristar Shell◈
Food	N: Ameristar Casino Hotel/Restaurants, Delta Point River, Diamond Jacks Casino Hotel/Rest, Goldie's Trail BBQ, Subway/ Shell S: Dominos Pizza, Waffle House
Lodg	N: Ameristar Casino Hotel & RV Park▲, Days Inn, Delta Point Inn, Diamond Jacks Casino & Hotel, Dixieana Motel S: Americas Best Value Inn, Days Inn, La Quinta Inn♥, Ridgeland Suites, Rainbow Hotel Casino♥, Riverwalk Casino Hotel,
Other	N: Auto Service, Tires, Towing, Isle of Capri RV Park▲, Isle of Capri Casino, Harrah's Casino, Ameristar Casino to appr 14mi N-Hwy 465: Sunset View RV Park▲ S: Rainbow Casino, to Vicksburg Muni Airport✈
1B	**US 61S, to Pemberton Blvd, Vicksburg, Natchez (WB Exits LEFT) (Access to #1-C via Pemberton Blvd)**
Gas	S: BP, Chevron, Kangaroo Express
Food	S: McDonald's
Other	S: Auto Service, Dollar Tree, Office Max, Walmart sc, Magnolia RV Park Resort▲, to appr 6mi: River Town Campground▲
1C	**Halls Ferry Rd, Vicksburg**
Gas	N: Chevron, Exxon S: FastLane, Kangaroo Express◈
Food	N: Burger King, Sonic, Whataburger S: Café Latte, Captain D's, DQ, Wok, El Sombrero Mex Rest, Hardee's, Pizza Hut, Ryan's Grill, Shoney's, Taco Bell, Wendy's
Lodg	N: Econo Lodge, Travel Inn S: Candlewood Suites, Fairfield Inn, Rodeway Inn♥, Super 8
Med	N: + Vicksburg Medical Center
Other	N: Pharmacy, Vicksburg Cycles S: ATMs, AT&T, Auto Service, Banks, Advance Auto Parts, Big Lots, Cinema 4, Family Dollar, Fred's, Home Depot, Kroger, Tires, True Value Hardware, UPS Store, US Post Office, Mall, Walgreen's
3	**Indiana Ave, Vicksburg**
Gas	N: Kangaroo Express, Texaco◈ S: BP
Food	N: Subway/Texaco, Krystal, McDonald's, Pizza Hut, Sun Garden, Waffle House S: Goldie's BBQ, Heavenly Ham, KFC

◈ = Regular Gas Stations with Diesel ▲ = RV Friendly Locations ♥ = Pet Friendly Locations
Red print shows large vehicle parking / access on site or nearby **Brown Print = Campgrounds / RV PARKS**

Lodg N: Best Western, Deluxe Inn
S: Americas Best Inn, Battlefield Inn
Other N: ATM, Auto Dealers, Bank, Grocery, IGA, RiteAid, **Vicksburg Nat'l Military Park**
S: Auto Dealers

4A Clay St, US 80, to MS 27, Downtown Vicksburg
Gas S: Texaco◈,
Food S: Billy's Italian Rest, China Buffet, Cracker Barrel, McAlister's Deli, Pizza Inn, Waffle House, The Bistro/Courtyard
Lodg S: Battlefield Inn, Comfort Suites, Courtyard, Econo Lodge♥, Holiday Inn Express, Jameson Inn, La Quinta Inn♥, Scottish Inn♥
Other S: Auto Dealers, Dollar General, Sun-Up Laundry, Vicksburg Factory Outlet Mall,

4B N Clay St, Village St, Vicksburg
Gas N: Chevron, Kangaroo Express
Food N: Bumper Drive-In, Cappes Steakhouse, KFC, Pizza Hut, Rowdy's Family Catfish Shack, Subway, Wendy's
Lodg N: Hampton Inn, Motel 6
Other N: Auto Zone, **Battlefield Campground▲**, Firestone, Goodyear, Museum, O'Reilly Auto Parts, Red Carpet Lanes Bowling Alley, RiteAid, **to Sunset View RV Park▲** & Motel, Vicksburg Animal Hospital♥, Vicksburg National Military Park, Visitor Center

5B MS 27S, to US 80, Vicksburg, Beechwood, Utica
(Appr 1 mi S on US 80 to Ex 4 S Serv)
Gas S: Kangaroo Express/Texaco◈
Food S: Domino's/KE Texaco, Beechwood Rest
Lodg S: Beechwood Inn, Hillcrest Inn
Other S: Laundromat, Stevens Service Center, Shorters Towing

5A US 61N, to Rolling Fork
FStop N: Zips, Kangaroo Express #3445
Food N: Gregory's Kitchen, Grill Depot/Kangaroo Expr, Sonic
Med N: + River Region Medical Center

(6) Parking Area (EB)

(8) Weigh Station (EB)

(10) Weigh Station (WB)

11 Tiffintown Rd, Bovina
TStop N: Bovina Truckstop
Food N: Bovina Café
Other N: RVDump/Bovina TS

15 Brabston Rd, Flowers

19 MS 22, to MS 467, US 80, Anderson Rd, Jackson Ave, Edwards, Flora
Gas S: BP◈, Phillips 66◈
Other N: to appr 2.5 mi: **Askew's Landing Campground▲**, Petrified Forest
S: Grocery, **Police**, Cactus Plantation

27 Bolton Brownsville Rd, Bolton
Gas N: Chevron
S: BP◈
Other S: Farr Animal Hospital, Grocery/Deli/Gas, US Post Office

31 Norrell Rd, Bolton

34 Natchez Trace Pkwy, Clinton
(Access to Ex #35 & 36 Serv via Access Rd, Frontage Rd, & US 80)
Other S: to John Bell Williams Airport✈, Raymond Airport✈

EXIT MISSISSIPPI

35 Clinton-Raymond Rd, to US 80
Gas N: Chevron◈, Phillips 66◈, Texaco◈
Other N: Auto Service/Chevron, Carwash/Texaco, MS College
S: Eagle Ridge RV Park▲, to Springridgev Mobile Estates & RV Park▲,

36 Springridge Rd, to US 80, Clinton
(Many Services N to US 80)
Gas N: Chevron◈, Shell◈, Kroger, Murphy, Orbit
S: Exxon, Texaco◈
Food N: Backyard Burger, Burger King/Chevron, Captain D's, ChickFilA, China Garden, DQ, Danny's Seafood, Jade Buffet, KFC, Little Caesars Pizza, Los Amigos Rest, Mazzios, McDonald's, Petra Cafe, Sonic, Starbucks, Subway, Waffle House, Wendy's, Zaxby's
S: Applebee's, El Sombrero Mexican Rest, Froghead Grill, Pizza Hut, Popeye's Chicken, Quiznos, Shoney's, Taco Bell, Thai Garden, Waffle House
Lodg N: Clinton Inn, Comfort Inn, Days Inn
S: Best Western♥, Comfort Inn, Hampton Inn, Holiday Inn Express, Quality Inn, Super 8
Other N: Ace Hardware, Advance Auto Parts, ATMs, Avis RAC, Dollar Tree, Enterprise RAC, Family Dollar, Fred's, Hibbett Sporting Goods, Home Depot, Kroger, Midas, NAPA, O'Reilly Auto Parts, Radio Shack, Surplus City Shooting Range, Tires, Walgreen's, U-Haul, UPS Store, US Post Office, **Walmart sc▲**, Wilson's Tire & Auto Care, Ms College, **Police Dept**
Other S: ATM, Animal Hospital of Clinton♥, Bank, Carwash/Texaco, Davis Tire & Auto, Regal Clinton Cinema, **Springridge Mobile Estates & RV Park▲**

40 MS 18W, Robinson St, to US 80, to I-220, Jackson (EB)
Gas N: BP, Phillips 66, Shell◈, Spur
S: Chevron, Shell, Murphy,
Food N: Arby's, El Chico, Krystal, Mazzio's Pizza, McDonald's, Piccadilly, Pizza Hut, Morrison's, Popeye's Chicken, Wendy's
S: Church's Chicken, IHOP, McDonald's, Subway, Waffle House, Wendy's
Lodg N: Days Inn, Sleep Inn
S: Comfort Inn
Med S: + Central MS Medical Center
Other N: ATMs, AT&T, Auto Services, Avis RAC, Bank, Burlington Coat Factory, Car Care Clinic, Dollar General, Hinds Comm College, Home Depot, Metrocenter Mall, Office Depot, Pineview Animal Hospital♥, US Post Office
S: Auto Services, Dollar Tree, Lowe's, Radio Shack, **Walmart sc**

40B MS 18E, Raymond, Robinson Rd

40A MS 18W, Raymond, Robinson Rd

(41) Jct I-220, US 49N, N Jackson, to Yazoo City (EB, Left exit & entrance)

42A Ellis Ave S, Jackson
Gas S: Exxon◈, Save, Shell
Food S: DQ, IHOP, Po Folks, Pizza Hut
Med S: + MEA Medical Clinic
Other S: Big Lots, Fred's, Grocery

EXIT MISSISSIPPI

42B Ellis Ave N, Jackson
Gas N: BP, Conoco, Shell
Food N: Arby's, Burger King, Captain D's, Church's Chicken, Country Kitchen, Denny's, McDonald's, Pizza Hut, Popeye's Chicken, Sonny's BBQ, Waffle House, Wendy's
Lodg N: Best Western, Budget Inn, Days Inn♥, Econo Lodge, Ramada Inn, Sleep Inn, Super 8
Other N: Auto Zone, Advance Auto Parts, Budget Truck Rental, Cotton Bowl Lanes, Family Dollar, Firestone, Grocery, NAPA, O'Reilly Auto Parts, Radio Shack, U-Haul, Zoo

43A Terry Rd S, to I-55, to Jackson, New Orleans, La
(Access to #42A via Raymond Rd)
Gas S: Exxon
Lodg S: La Quinta Inn♥
Other S: Grocery, Fred's

43B Terry Rd N, to I-55, to Jackson., New Orleans, La
Gas N: Exxon◈, Shell
Food N: Collins Dream Kitchen, Kim's Seafood, Krystal, Lumpkins BBQ, Rally's, T&A BBQ
Lodg N: Regency Inn, Tarrymore Hotel
Other N: ATMs, Auto Repairs, Banks, **S & S Apache Camping Center**, U-Haul

NOTE: I-20 below runs with I-55 to Birmingham, AL. Exit #'s follow I-20

(44/92C) Jct I-55S, to New Orleans, McComb (WB, Left Exit)

45 US 51N, State St, Gallatin St (EB, Left exit)

45A Gallatin St, Jackson (WB)
TStop N: Petro Stopping Center #28/Mobil (Scales)
S: Pilot Travel Center #77 (Scales)
Gas N: BP, Chevron, D&E Food & Gas
Food N: IronSkillet/Petro SC
S: McDonald's/Pilot TC
Lodg S: Knights Inn
TWash N: Blue Beacon TW/Petro SC
TServ N: Petro SC/Tires
Other N: Laundry/BarbSh/RVDump/Petro SC, Amtrak, Auto Repairs, Jackson Animal Clinic♥, U-Haul, Tires
S: Laundry/WiFi/Pilot TC

45B US 51, State St (WB)
Gas N: Chevron
S: Speedway◈
Other N: Big 10 Tire, Enterprise RAC, **Police**, to Coliseum, Fairgrounds

(46/94) Jct I-55N, to Grenada, Memphis (EB, Left exit)

NOTE: I-20 above runs with I-55 to Birmingham, AL. Exit #'s follow I-20

47 US 49S, Hattiesburg, Flowood (WB)

47AB US 49, Hattiesburg, Flowood (EB)
(Serv N to US 80, S to US 49)
FStop S: Capital Fuel Center #2
TStop N: Flying J Travel Plaza #678/Conoco (Scales), Love's Travel Stop #420 (Scales)
S: Delta Travel Center (Scales)
Food N: Rest/FastFood/FJ TP, Subway/Love's TS, Western Sizzlin' Wood Grill
S: DQ, Waffle House

◈ = Regular Gas Stations with Diesel ▲ = RV Friendly Locations ♥ = Pet Friendly Locations
Red print shows large vehicle parking / access on site or nearby Brown Print = Campgrounds / RV PARKS

EXIT		MISSISSIPPI
	Lodg	N: Airport Inn♥, Holiday Inn S: Days Inn♥, Super 8♥
	TServ	N: Speedco S: Empire Truck Sales, Freightliner, Kenworth
	Other	N: Laundry/BarbSh/WiFi/LP/RVDump/FJ TP, Laundry/BarbSh/WiFi/RVDump/Pilot TC, Bass Pro Shop, Auto Repairs, Sutherland Lumber, Tires, to Swinging Bridge RV Park▲ S: Laundry/Delta TC, Truck-Man RV Center, to appr 4 mi: Walmart sc, Addtl Gas, Food, Lodging Services
48		**MS 468, Pearson Rd, Pearl**
	FStop	N: Speedway S: Kangaroo Express
	Gas	N: BP, Exxon, Shell◈, Super Saver S: Huff Texaco Food Shop
	Food	N: Arby's, Baskin Robbins, Bumpers Drive-In, Burger King, Cracker Barrel, Domino's Pizza, El Charro Mexican Rest, KFC, Lone Star Steakhouse, McDonald's, O'Charley's, Pizza Hut, Popeye's Chicken, Ruby Tuesday, Ryan's Grill, Shoney's, Sonic, Starbucks, Waffle House
	Lodg	N: Best Western, Comfort Inn, Fairfield Inn, Econo Lodge, Hampton Inn, Hilton Garden Inn, Holiday Inn Express, Motel 6♥, Jameson Inn S: Country Inn, Days Inn, La Quinta Inn♥
	Other	N: ATM, Bank, Budget RAC, Budget Truck Rental, Donald's Truck & Auto Repair, Jerry's Tire Service, Kroger, Police, Quality Trailer Service , Tinseltown USA, Travel America RV Center, S: Dollar General
52		**MS 475, Airport Rd, Pearl, Int'l Airport, Whitfield**
	Gas	N: Kangaroo Express/Chevron◈, Texaco◈
	Food	N: BBQ2Go/Chevron, Waffle House, Wendy's
	Lodg	N: Quality Inn, Ramada Ltd♥, Sleep Inn, Super 8
	TServ	N: Peterbilt, White/GMC Volvo, S: Buddy's Truck Repair
	Med	N: + MEA Medical Clinic, + Baptist Medical Clinic
	Other	N: Carwash/Chevron, Rental Cars, Jackson Int'l Airport✈, S: Central MS Correction Facility
54		**MS 18, Crossgates Blvd, US 80, Greenfield Rd, West Brandon**
	Gas	N: BP, Exxon, Phillips 66, Murphy S: Chevron, Texaco
	Food	N: Applebee's, Burger King, Domino's Pizza, El Sombrero Mexican, Kismet's, KFC, Little Caesar's Pizza, Mazzio's, McAlister's Deli, McDonald's, Papa John's Pizza, Pig Shak BBQ, Pizza Hut, Popeye's Chicken, Quiznos, Subway, Waffle House, Wendy's S: Domino's Pizza, Wendy's
	Lodg	N: Ridgeland Inn S: La Quinta Inn
	Med	N: + Rankin Medical Center, + Crossgates River Oaks Hospital
	Other	N: ATMs, Banks, Auto Dealers, Big Lots, Brandon Animal Hospital♥, CVS, Crossgates Veterinary Clinic♥, Dollar General, Enterprise RAC, Firestone Auto, Fred's, Goodyear, Hibbett Sports,

EXIT		MISSISSIPPI
	Other	N: Kroger/Pharmacy, Office Depot, Piggly Wiggly, Radio Shack, Tires, Walmart sc S: Home Depot, Upton Tires
56		**US 80, Government St, Downtown Brandon**
	Gas	N: Texaco S: Exxon, Mac's Gas, Texaco
	Food	N: Bonkers, Burger King, CiCi's Pizza, Krystal, McDonald's, Popeye's Chicken, Sonny's BBQ, Taco Bell
	Food	S: DQ, McDonald's, Sonic, Smoke House BBQ, Waffle House
	Lodg	N: Microtel♥ S: Days Inn♥, Red Roof Inn♥
	Med	N: + Rankin Medical Center
	Other	N: Auto Zone Parts, ATM, Bank, Grocery, Police, to Barnett Reservoir, Barnett Reservoir Campground▲ S: Luckett Animal Clinic♥,
59		**US 80, East Brandon (Serv 2 mi S)**
	Gas	S: D's One Stop Food & Gas
	Other	S: Police
68		**MS 43, to US 80, Pelahatchie, to Puckett**
	FStop	N: Chevron, Super Stop #21/Conoco S: BP Fuel Center
	Food	N: Subway/Chevron, Rest/Conoco
	Other	N: RV Dump/Conoco, Pelatchie Lake Campground▲ , Police, to Vaiden Campground▲ , on US 80: Dollar General, NAPA, US Post Office
(75)		**Morton Rest Area (WB) (ReOpen 8/11) (RR, Phone, Pic, Pet, Sec247, RVDump)**
77		**MS 13, to US 80, Morton, Puckett**
	FStop	N: Phillips 66
	Med	N: + Hospital
	Other	N: Roosevelt State Park▲
80		**MS 481, Morton, Raleigh**
88		**MS 35, Forest, Raleigh**
	FStop	N: BP, to 1mi N: Forest Red Apple Texaco S: Chevron Express Line
	Gas	N: Shell, Murphy◈
	Food	N: Subway/BP, McDonald's, KFC, Wendy's S: Santa Fe Steak House & Grill
	Lodg	N: Apple Tree Inn, Best Value Inn, Comfort Inn♥, Days Inn, Holiday Inn Express
	Med	N: + Hospital
	Other	N: Forest Muni Airport✈, J&J Tire, Auto Dealers, Grocery, Walmart sc
(91)		**Forest Rest Area (EB) (ReOpen 8/11) (RR, Phone, Picnic, Sec247, RVDump)**
96		**Lake Norris Rd, to US 80, Lake (Addtl Serv approx 3mi N)**
	Food	N: Back Forty Seafood Rest
	Other	S: to Bienville National Forest▲
100		**US 80, Lake, Lawrence**
	TStop	N: 100 Travel Center/BP
	Food	N: Rest/100 TC
	Tires	N: 100 TC
109		**MS 15, to US 80, Newton, Union, Decatur, Philadelphia**
	FStop	N: Newton Junction Shell S: Conoco, Spanky's Food Mart
	Gas	S: BP, Chevron◈, Texaco
	Food	N: Wendy's/Shell, Boro Family Rest, S: Hardee's, KFC/TacoBell, McDonald's, Pizza Hut, Quiznos/Chevron, Sonic, Subway, Zack Garvin's Steak House

EXIT		MISSISSIPPI
	Lodg	N: Thrifty Inn S: Days Inn
	Other	N: S&S Auto & Truck Repair, U-Haul, to Turkey Creek Water Park▲ S: Advance Auto Parts, Auto Zone, Dollar General, Fred's, JR's Auto Repair, Newton Co Animal Clinic♥, Piggly Wiggly, Walmart sc
115		**MS 503, Hickory, Decatur**
	FStop	S: Hickory Quik Stop
	Other	S: Hickory Tire, Pharmacy, US Post Office
121		**Chunky**
129		**US 80W, Lost Gap, Meehan Jct**
	TStop	S: Spaceway Truck Stop/Conoco (Scales)
	Food	S: Rest/Spaceway TS
	Other	S: Laundry/WiFi/RVDump/Spaceway TS
	NOTE:	**I-20 runs below with I-59 to Birmingham, AL. Exit #'s follow I-20.**
(130/149)		**Jct I-59S, to Laurel, New Orleans**
150		**US 11S, MS 19N, Philadelphia, Meridian Airport**
	FStop	S: Stuckey's Express #653/Chevron, SuperStop #10/Shell
	TStop	N: Queen City Truck Stop (Scales)
	Food	N: Rest/Queen City TS S: Subway/Stuckey's
	Other	N: Okitibbee Lake, Meridian Community College, LP/Tires/QC TS S: Key Field Airport✈
151		**49th Ave, Valley Rd, Meridian**
	FStop	S: Pilot Travel Center #388 (Scales)
	Food	S: Subway/Pilot TC
	Other	S: Laundry/WiFi/Pilot TC
152		**29th Ave, MLK Jr Blvd, Meridian**
	Gas	N: Chevron◈
	Lodg	N: Ramada S: Royal Inn
153		**MS 145S, 22nd Ave, Quitman, Downtown Meridian**
	Gas	N: BP, Shell, Super Stop S:Chevron◈, Exxon◈, Texaco, Murphy
	Food	N: Arby's, Barnhill Buffet, Burger King, Captain D's, China Buffet, Hardee's, KFC, McDonald's, Pizza Hut, Subway, Wendy's, Western Sizzlin S: Depot Rest, Waffle House
	Lodg	N: Relax Inn S: Astro Motel, Best Western♥, Budget 8 Motel, Econo Lodge, Holiday Inn Express, Motel 6♥, Quality Inn♥, Sleep Inn
	Med	N: + Hospital
	Other	N: ATMs, Banks, Amtrak, Dollar General, Firestone, Fred's, Goodyear, Grocery, Museums, Pharmacy S: Auto Dealers, Budget Truck Rental, Bonita Lakes Mall, Lowe's, Walmart sc
154		**MS 19S, MS 39N, US 11N, US 80E, to Butler, DeKalb (WB)**
	Gas	N: BP◈, Shell, Texaco S: Chevron, Conoco, Texaco
	Food	N: Applebee's, Back Yard Burgers, Cracker Barrel, Krystal's, Logan's Road House, Waffle House, Rest/Hol Inn
	Food	S: ChickFilA, CiCi's Pizza, Crescent City Grill, McDonald's, O'Charley's, Outback Steakhouse, Red Lobster, Ryan's Grill, Taco Bell

◈ = Regular Gas Stations with Diesel ▲ = RV Friendly Locations ♥ = Pet Friendly Locations
Red print shows large vehicle parking / access on site or nearby Brown Print = Campgrounds / RV PARKS

EXIT	MISSISSIPPI
Lodg	N: Days Inn♥, Drury Inn, Econo Lodge, Hampton Inn, Hilton Garden Inn, Holiday Inn, Northeast Inn, Relax Inn, Rodeway Inn, Super 8, Western Motel
	S: Comfort Inn, Country Inn, Jameson Inn, Microtel
Other	N: Animal Hospital♥, Auto Dealers, **Back Country RV Center Sales & Service**, Grocery, Penske Truck Rental, U-Haul, Vet♥, Winn Dixie
	S: ATMs, AT&T, Best Buy, Bonita Lakes Mall, BooksAMillion, Chunky River Harley Davidson, Cinema, Dollar Tree, Fred's, Office Max, PetCo♥, Radio Shack, Sam's Club, TJ Maxx, Truckers Supply Co, United Artists Theatre, **Bonita Lakes RV Park▲**
154AB	**MS19S, MS 39N, US 11N, US 80E, Butler AL, DeKalb, Naval Air Station (EB) (Acc to #153 Serv)**
157B	**US 45N, to Macon**
Other	N: to appr 4 mi: **Benchmark Coach & RV Park▲**
157A	**US 45S, to Quitman**
160	**Russell Mt Gilead Rd, Meridian**
TStop	N: Travel Center of America #47/BP (Scales) (DAND)
	S: Russell Shell #21
Food	N: CountryPride/TA TC
TServ	N: TA TC/Tires
Other	N: Laundry/TA TC, **Nanabe Creek Campground▲**
	S: Laundry/Russell Shell
(164)	**MS Welcome Center (WB) Lauderdale Co Rest Area (RR, Ph, Pic, Vend, Pet, Sec24, RVDump)**
165	**Garrett Rd, Toomsuba**
TStop	S: Love's Travel Stop #343 (Scales)
Gas	N: Shell, Texaco◈
Food	N: Subway/Shell, Chesters/BBQ/Texaco
	S: Arby's/Love's TS
Other	N: Carwash/Texaco
	S: WiFi/Love's TS, **Meridian East/ Toomsuba KOA▲**
169	**Kewanee**
FStop	S: Kewanee One Stop
Food	S: Rest/Kewanee One Stop
(170)	**Weigh Station (Both dir)**

NOTE: **I-20W & I-59S above run together to Meridian, MS. Exit #'s follow I-20.**

EXIT	MS / AL

NOTE: **MM 172: Alabama State Line**

CENTRAL TIME ZONE

MISSISSIPPI

ALABAMA

CENTRAL TIME ZONE

NOTE: **I-20E & I-59N below run together from Meridian, MS to Birminham, AL.**

EXIT	MS / AL
(0)	**AL Welcome Center (EB) (RR, Phone, Pic, Pet, Vend, RVDump)**
1	**AL 8, to US 80E, Cuba, Demopolis**
TStop	S: Rocking Chair/P66
Gas	S: Chevron, Dixie
Food	S: Diner/Rocking Chair
8	**AL 17, York**
TStop	S: PTP/York Truck Plaza/BP (Scales)
Food	S: Briar Patch Rest
Lodg	S: Days Inn
TServ	S: York TP/Tires
TWash	S: York TP
Med	S: + Hospital
Other	S: ATM, Bank, Dollar General
17	**AL 28, Livingston, Boyd**
FStop	S: Interstate BP
TStop	S: Noble Truck Stop/Citgo (Scales)
Gas	S: Chevron
Food	S: Rest/Noble TS, Burger King, GM Steak Corral, Pizza Hut, Subway/Chevron
Lodg	S: Comfort Inn
Med	S: + Hospital
TServ	S: Noble TS/Tires, Bullocks Truck Service
Other	S: Laundry/Noble TS, Univ of W AL
23	**CR 20, Main St, Epes, to Gainesville**
32	**CR 20, Boligee**
TStop	N: Boligee Truck Stop/BP
Gas	S: Chevron◈
Food	N: Rest/Boligee TS
	S: Subway/Chevron
(38)	**Rest Area (EB) (RR, Phone, Pic, Pet, Vend, RVDump)**
(39)	**Rest Area (WB) (RR, Phones, Pic, Pet, Vend, RVDump)**
40	**AL 14, Eutaw, Aliceville**
Med	S: + Hospital
Other	N: Tom Bevil Lock & Dam

EXIT	ALABAMA
45	**CR 208, to Union**
TStop	S: Trackside BP
Food	N: Cotton Patch Restaurant
	S: Hardee's, Southfork, Western Inn,
Lodg	S: Western Inn
TServ	S: Trackside BP/Tires, Southfork Auto & Truck Center
Other	S: Greene Co Greyhound Park
52	**US 11, US 43, Knoxville**
FStop	N: Speedmart Fuel Center/Exxon
Food	N: FastFood/Speedmart FC
62	**CR10, CR 51, Holly Springs Ln, Fosters**
Gas	N: Chevron
68	**Tuscaloosa Western By-Pass (Gas 2 mi N in Tuscaloosa)**
Gas	N: Chevron, Citgo, Exxon
Food	N: Nick's Filet House
Other	N: U-Haul
71A	**AL 69S, to US 11, LA 7, Moundville**
Gas	N: Citgo, Shell
	S: Chevron, Exxon◈, Mapco Mart, Shell
Food	S: Arby's, Country Hic Café & BBQ, Dominos Pizza, Hooters, IHOP, Lone Star Steakhouse, Outback Steakhouse, Pizza Hut, Ryan's Grill, Tokyo Japanese Steak & Sushi, Waffle House, Wendy's, Zaxby's
Lodg	S: Ambassador Inn, Candlewood Suites, Courtyard, Fairfield Inn, Hilton Garden Inn, Jameson Inn
Other	N: Taylor's Automotive Services
	S: Academy Sports & Outdoors, Advance Auto, AT&T, Auto Services, Big 10 Tires, Firestone, Foodworld, Hollywood 16 Theatres, Kmart, L&H Truck Service, Lowe's, O'Reilly Auto Parts, Penske Truck Rental, RiteAid, Town & Country Veterinary Hospital♥, Tuscaloosa Tire, Tires, U-Haul, **Police Dept**
(71B)	**Jct I-359, AL 69N, Tuscaloosa**
Other	N: Univ of AL, Amtrak, Bryant-Denny Stadium, Coleman Coliseum, Stillman College
73	**US 82, AL 6, McFarland Blvd, Tuscaloosa, Centreville**
Gas	N: BP, Chevron◈ **x2**, Exxon, RaceWay, Shell◈
	S: Amoco, Exxon, Shell, Sam's
Food	N: Arby's, Burger King, Captain D's, Checkers, ChickFilA, Five Guys Burger & Fries, Krystal's, Long John Silver, Moe's SW Grill, O'Charley's, Olive Garden,

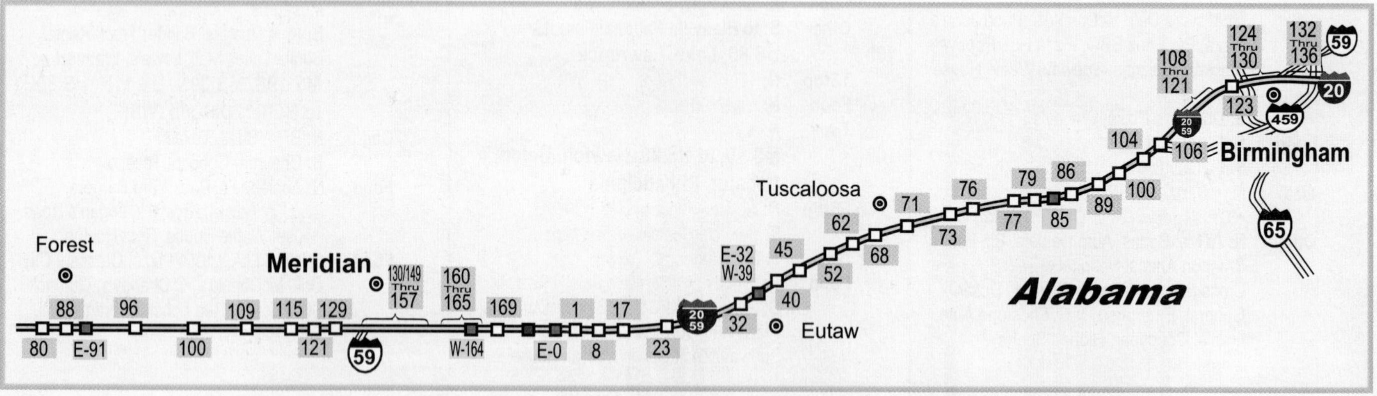

◈= Regular Gas Stations with Diesel ▲ = RV Friendly Locations ♥= Pet Friendly Locations
Red print shows large vehicle parking / access on site or nearby **Brown Print = Campgrounds / RV PARKS**

EXIT — ALABAMA

Food N: Panera Bread, Pizza Hut, Popeye's Chicken, Red Lobster, Waffle House
S: Chili's, Hardee's, Huddle House, KFC, Logan's Roadhouse, Lone Star Steakhouse, McDonalds, Piccadilly, Subway, Taco Cabana, Taco Bell, Waffle House, Wendy's, Western Sizzlin,
Lodg N: America's Best Value Inn, Best Western, Comfort Suites, Holiday Inn Express, Master's Inn, Shoney's
S: Country Inn, Econo Lodge, Days Inn, La Quinta Inn♥, Motel 6♥, Quality Inn, Ramada Inn, Super 8
Med N: + **DCH Reg'l Medical Center**
Other N: ATMs, Banks, Advance Auto Parts, Big 10 Tire, B&N, Big Lots, CVS, Firestone, Goodyear, Hobby Lobby, Tide Clean Car Wash, U-Haul, University Mall, **Lake Lurleen State Park**
S: ATMs, Auto Dealers, Banks, Books A Million, Dollar General, Dollar Tree, Enterprise RAC, FoodWorld, NAPA, Office Depot, RiteAid, Sam's Club, **Walmart sc**, Winn Dixie, McFarland Mall, Fox 12 Cinema, **AL State Hwy Patrol Post**

76 — US 11, Skyland Blvd E, Tuscaloosa, Cottondale (Acc to #73 S Serv)
TStop S: Pilot Travel Center #76 (Scales)
Gas N: Citgo◈, Kang Expr/Exxon, Shell◈ Kangaroo Expr/Exxon◈, Chevron◈,
S: Shell◈
Food N: Burger King, **Cracker Barrel**, Waffle House
S: Subway/Pilot TC, Dominos Pizza
Lodg N: Comfort Inn, Scottish Inn, Super Inn, Value Place, Wingate♥
S: Sleep Inn
TServ N: McLeod Truck Parts
S: Southland Int'l Trucks
Med N: **to + Tuscaloosa Veterans Med Center**
Other N: ATM, **AL MH & Camper Service/LP**, Bank, **Sunset II Travel Park▲**,
to University Blvd: Advance Auto Parts, Bi-Lo, CVS, Gas, RiteAid, Walgreen's, Winn Dixie, **Country Roads RV Sales & Service,**
S: Laundry/WiFi/Pilot TC, Auto Service, Auto Dealers, **AL State Hwy Patrol Post**, Kwik Kopy Printing

77 — CR 85, Buttermilk Rd, Cottondale
TStop N: Travel Center of America /BP (Scales) **(DAND)**, WilcoHess Travel Plaza #5501 (Scales)
Gas N: Chevron
Food N: McDonald's/Chevron, CountryPride/ Subway/Taco Bell/TA TC, Wendy's/ WilcoHess TP, Pizza Hut, Ruby Tuesday
Lodg N: Hampton Inn, Microtel Inn
TWash N: Blue Beacon TW, Eagle TW/TA TC
TServ N: TA TC/Tires, Speedco
Other N: Laundry/WiFi/**RVDump**/TA TC, Laundry/WilcoHess TP, US PostOffice
S: Tuscaloosa Chevrolet

79 — US 11, University Blvd, Coaling
Gas S: Chevron◈
Food S: Pottery Grill

(85) — Cottondale Rest Area (Both dir) (RR, Phones, Pic, Pet, RVDump)

86 — CR 59, Covered Bridge Rd, Cottondale, Brookwood, Vance
TStop N: Brookwood Shell Truck Stop,

EXIT — ALABAMA

TStop N: Mary's Travel Center/BP
Food N: Rest/Brookwood TS, Subway/Mary's TC

89 — Mercedes Dr, Vance, Tuscaloosa
Lodg N: Greystone Inn
Other S: Mercedes Benz Auto Plant

97 — US 11, AL 5, AL 7, McCalla
FStop S: Caffe Junction BP, Package 97 Truck Stop
Gas S: Exxon◈, Shell◈,
Food S: Jack's Rest, KFC/BP, Subway/Shell,

100 — AL 216, McCalla, Abernant, Bucksville
TStop N: Love's Travel Stop #227 (Scales)
S: Petro Stopping Center #19/ Chevron (Scales)
Gas N: Citgo
S: BP, Exxon
Food N: McDonald's/Subway/Love's TS
S: Rest/Petro SC, Shenanigan's BBQ
TServ N: Tires/Love's TS
S: Petro SC/Tires
Other N: **RVDump**/Love's TS, **McCalla RV Park▲**
S: Laundry/WiFi/**RVDump**/Petro SC, Auto Repair, Dollar General, **Sheriff Dept**, Tannehill Nat'l Golf Course, Museum, **Tannehill Ironworks Historic State Park▲**

104 — McAshen Dr, Rock Mountain Lakes, McCalla
TStop S: Flying J Travel Plaza #5042/Conoco (Scales)
Food S: Rest/FastFood/FJ TP
Other S: Laundry/BarbSh/WiFi/**LP**/**RVDump**/ FJ TP

(106) — Jct I-459N, Montgomery, to Gadsden, Atlanta (South ByPass of Birmingham)

108 — US 11, AL 5N, Academy Dr
Gas N: Exxon
S: BP, Citgo◈
Food N: Applebee's, **Cracker Barrel**, Santa Fe Steakhouse, Waffle House
S: Burger King, Cajun Landing Seafood, Dominos Pizza, Little Caesars Pizza, Milo's, McDonald's, Omelet Shop, Ruby Tuesday, Sonic, Wendy's
Lodg N: Best Western, Comfort Inn♥, Fairfield Inn, Holiday Inn Express, Jameson Inn♥
S: Country Inn, Days Inn, Hampton Inn, Motel 6♥, Scottish Inn
Med S: + **UAB Medical West Medical Center**
Other N: ATM, Auto Dealers, Aamco, Bank, **Holiday Coach & RV Center**, Visionland Theme Park, Watermark Place
S: ATMs, Banks, Big 10 Tire, Bessemer Muni Golf Course, Bessemer State Tech College, Bessemer Civic Center, Carwash/ BP, Dollar Tree, Enterprise RAC, Grocery, Hibbett Sports, Pharmacy, Radio Shack, Verizon, **Walmart sc**, Winn Dixie, West Lake Outlet Mall

110 — Visionland Pkwy

112 — 18th St, 19th St, Bessemer
Gas N: RaceWay, Shell
S: Chevron
Food N: Jack's Hamburgers
S: Arby's, Bob Sykes BBQ, Burger King, Krystal, McDonald's
Other N: Auto Repairs, Budget Truck Rental, Tires, White's Hardware

EXIT — ALABAMA

Other S: ATM, Auto & Tire Services, Advance Auto Parts, Auto Zone, Banks, Bessemer Pet Clinic♥, Carwash/Chevron, Food Giant Grocery, Greyhound, Lowe's, Museum, Pharmacy, Walgreen's

113 — 18th Ave, Brighton, Lipscomb
FStop S: I-20/59 Travel Center/Chevron
Gas S: Shell
Food S: McDonald's
Other S: **Police Dept, to Central Camper**, Penske Truck Rental

115 — Jaybird Rd, 15th St, Pleasant Grove Rd, Birmingham, Allison Bonnett Memorial Dr
Gas N: RaceWay, Shell◈
S: S to Woodward Rd: Shell, Texaco
Food N: Church's Chicken, Green Acres Cafe, Hardee's, Subway
Lodg S: Best Western
Med S: + **St Vincents Hospital**
Other N: Advance Auto Parts, Auto Services, Carwash, O'Reilly Auto Parts, U-Haul, **to appr 4.5mi: RV Repair & Sales**
S: to M & J RV Park▲, Addtl Serv S To US 11/Bessemer Super Hwy

118 — Valley Rd, Fairfield
Food S: Papa Johns Pizza
Lodg S: Fairfield Inn, Villager Lodge
Med S: + **Metro West Hospital**
Other S: Home Depot, Radio Shack, Winn Dixie, Auto & Tire Services, **to** Fairfield Civic Center, Western Hills Mall, Radio Museum, **Police Dept**

119A — RM Schrushy Pkwy, Ave F, Gary Ave, Lloyd Nolan Pkwy
Gas N: BP, Chevron◈
S: Mobil, Texaco
Food N: Burger King, McDonald's, Seafood Delite, Subway, Taco Bell
S: Omelete Shoppe,
TServ S: Big Moe Spring & Alignment
Med S: + **Metro West Hospital**
Other N: Auto Repairs, Family Dollar

119B — Ave I, 34th St (WB, reacc via #119A)

120 — AL 269, 20th St, Ensley Ave, AL State Fair Complex (diff reaccess)
Gas S: BP, Crown
Food N: KFC, Taco Bell
TServ N: Wayne Gargus GMC
Med S: + **Hospital**
Other N: **Police Dept**
S: AL State Fairgrounds, Birmingham International Raceway, Auto Dealers

121 — 19th St, Bush Blvd, Ave V, Ensley (WB, no re-entry)
Gas N: BP, Exxon
S: Chevron
Food N: Wings & Waffles

123 — US 78, AL 4, Arkadelphia Rd, Birmingham, Jasper
TStop N: Pilot Travel Center #369 (Scales)
Gas N: BP, Chevron
Food N: Wendy's/Pilot TC, Popeye's Chicken
S: Pizza Hut
Lodg N: Days Inn, La Quinta Inn♥
Med S: + **Princeton Baptist Med Center**
Other N: Laundry/WiFi/Pilot TC, Birmingham Southern College
S: Battle Coliseum, to Legion Field

EXIT — ALABAMA

(124A) **Jct I-65S, Montgomery, Huntsville (WB, Left Exit)**

(124B) **Jct I-65N, Nashville (EB, Left Exit)**

125A **17th St, Dwntwn Birmingham (EB)**
- Other — S: Jazz Hall of Fame, Museum of Art, Civic Center

125B **22nd St, Dwtwn Birmingham (WB)**

125 **22nd St, Downtown Birmingham (WB, Left Exit)**
- Lodg — N: Best Western, Starwood Hotel, Sheraton
- Other — N: B'ham Jefferson Convention Complex, Sports Hall of Fame, Sheriff's Dept

126A **US 31S, US 280E, Carraway Blvd**
- Med — S: + Cooper Green Hospital, + Children's Hospital of AL

126B **31st St, Sloss Furnaces**
- Gas — N: Citgo, Shell
- Food — S: McDonald's
- TServ — S: Freightliner Trucks, Mack Trucks, K Diamond Truck Service
- Med — N: + Carraway Methodist Med Center
- Other — N: Family Dollar; S: Laundromat, W AL Tire Service, Various Truck & Tire Services

128 **AL 79, Tallapoosa St, Tarrant**
- TStop — N: Kangaroo Express #3672 (Scales)
- Gas — N: Exxon◈
- Food — N: Subway/Kang Exp
- TServ — S: Cummins Alabama
- Other — N: Carwash/Laundromat/Exxon

129 **Messer Airport Hwy, Birmingham**
- Gas — S: BP, Shell
- Food — N: Rest/Ramada Inn; S: Hardee's, Rest/Holiday Inn, Sammy's Sandwich Shop
- Lodg — N: Clarion; S: Americas Best Inn, Holiday Inn
- Other — N: Birmingham Int'l Airport✈, Rental Cars

NOTE: I-20 above runs with with I-59. Exit #'s follow I-20.

(130) **Jct I-20E, Atlanta, Jct I-59N, Gadsden, Chattanooga, Jct 20W, Jct 59S**

(130A) **Jct I-59N, to Gadsden, Chattanooga**

130B **US 11S, 1st Ave (EB) (diff reacc) 1st Ave S (WB)**
- Gas — N: Chevron, Conoco◈, Crown, Shell; S: Exxon
- Food — S: McDonald's, Pacific Seafood
- Lodg — N: Bama Motel; S: Interstate Motel, Relax Inn, Sky Inn
- Med — N: to + Hillcrest Hospital
- Other — N: Auto Zone, Martin Animal Hospital♥, Piggly Wiggly; S: ATM, Bank,

132A **Oporto Rd, to US 78 (EB)**
- Gas — S: Crown, Shell
- Food — S: Arby's, Burger King, Captain D's, Chili's, China Garden, Denny's, Golden Palace, Hooters, IHOP, KFC, Long John Silver's/Taco Bell, Logan's Roadhouse, Mrs Winner's, McDonald's, O'Charley's, Olive Garden, Pizza Hut, Ryan's Grilll, Red Lobster, Ruby Tuesday, Wendy's
- Lodg — S: Comfort Inn, Delux Inn, Park Inn, USA Economy Lodge
- Other — S: ATMs, Banks, Century Plaza Mall, Cobb Theatres, Eastwood Mall, Enterprise RAC, Firestone, Grocery, Home Depot, Kmart, Office Depot, Penske Auto Center, Radio Shack, TJ Maxx, Waldenbooks

132B **to US 78, Montevallo Rd (EB)**
- Gas — N: Exxon
- Food — N: Arby's, Barnhill's Buffet, Green Acres Cafe, Hamburger Heaven, Jack's Hamburgers, Krystal, Villa Fiesta, Waffle House
- Lodg — N: Americas Best Value Inn, Eastwood Inn
- Other — N: Aamco, Burlington Coat Factory, Jiffy Lube, O'Reilly Auto Parts, Lawson Field Stadium, Super Petz

132 **AL 4, Montevallo Rd, to US 78, Oporto Rd (WB)**

133 **Kilgore Memorial Dr, to US 78, (EB), US 78, AL 4 (WB)**
- FStop — N: Pacific Pride
- Gas — N: Chevron, Kangaroo Express/Exxon◈; S: BP, Sam's
- Food — N: Arby's, Golden Rule BBQ, Jack's Rest, Krystal, Waffle House; S: Arby's, Subway
- Lodg — N: Americas Best Value Inn; S: Hampton Inn, Holiday Inn Express, Quality Inn, Rime Garden Inn♥
- Other — N: ATMs, Banks, 84 Lumber, Grocery, Penske Truck Rental, US Post Office, Acc #132B Serv; S: Dollar Tree, Sam's Club, Tire Pros, Walmart

135 **Old Leeds Rd, to US 78**
- Gas — N: Shell
- Other — N: Birmingham Race Track, Eastwood Animal Clinic♥

(136) **Jct I-459S, to Montgomery, Tuscaloosa, Gadsden**

140 **US 78, AL 4, Leeds**
- Gas — S: Chevron, Exxon
- Food — S: to appr 1.5 mi: Huck's Rib Shack, Old Smokey BBQ, Rusty's BBQ
- Lodg — S: Americas Best Value Inn♥, Hampton Inn
- Other — S: Bass Pro Shop, Carwash/Exxon, Leeds Civic Center,

144AB **US 411, Ashville Rd, Moody Pkwy, Leeds, Moody (EB)**
- FStop — S: Speedway #0119
- Gas — N: BP◈, RaceWay, Shell◈; S: Chevron, RaceWay
- Food — N: Arby's, Burger King, Cracker Barrel, Krystal's, Pizza Hut, Milo's Cafe, Ruby Tuesday, Subway/Shell, Waffle House, Wendy's; S: Burger King, Captain D's, ChickFilA, Hardee's, KFC, Little Caesars Pizza, Mexican Rest, McDonald's, Papa John's Pizza, Santa Fe Steak House, Taco Bell
- Lodg — N: Best Western, Comfort Inn, Super 8; S: Days Inn♥
- Other — N: Auto Repairs, Crossroads Animal Hospital♥, Food Giant Grocery, Carwash/Shell, Holiday Trav-L-Park▲; S: Advance Auto Parts, Auto Zone, Dollar General, Dollar Tree, Express Oil Change, Lowe's, NAPA, Radio Shack, Walgreen's, Walmart sc, Carwash/Chevron, S to #140 Serv

147 **Kelly Creek Rd, Pell City, to Brompton**
- Gas — N: Citgo; S: Chevron◈

152 **Cook Springs Rd, Pell City**

153 **US 78W, Chula Vista**

156 **US 78E, Pell City, Eden, Odenville**
- Gas — S: Chevron◈, Exxon◈, Shell

158 **US 231, Ashville, Pell City (EB)**
- FStop — S: Henson's Service
- Gas — N: Exxon◈, Murphy; S: BP, Chevron, Citgo◈
- Food — N: Arby's, Golden Rule BBQ, Krystal, Wendy's, Western Sizzlin, Zaxby's; S: Burger King, Hardee's, KFC, Pizza Hut, McDonald's, Waffle House
- Lodg — N: Comfort Suites, Hampton Inn, Holiday Inn Express; S: Quality Inn♥
- Med — S: + St Claire Reg'l Hospital

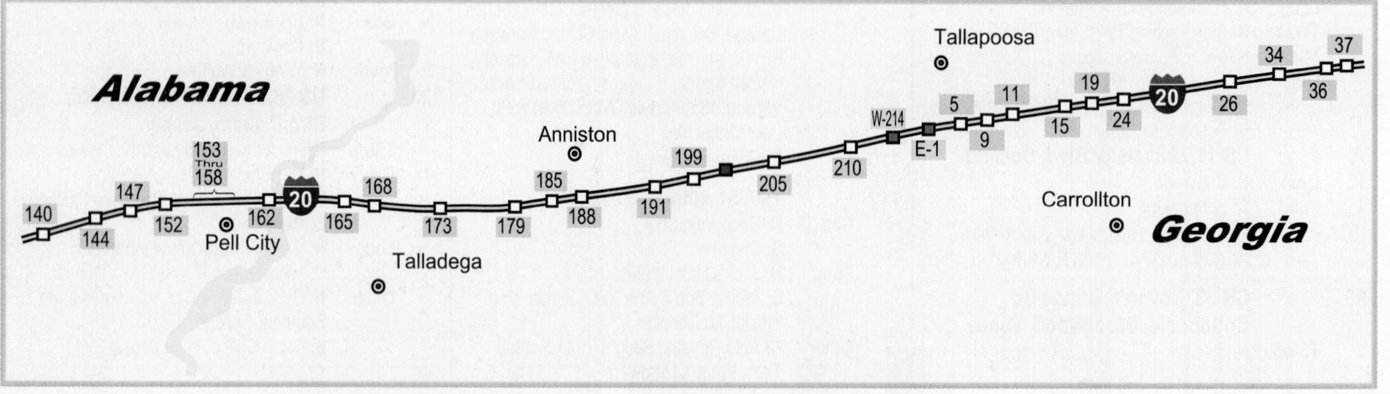

◈= Regular Gas Stations with Diesel ▲ = RV Friendly Locations ♥= Pet Friendly Locations
Red print shows large vehicle parking / access on site or nearby Brown Print = Campgrounds / RV PARKS

EXIT	ALABAMA
Other	N: Dollar Tree, Hibbett Sports, Home Depot, Radio Shack, Walgreen's, **Walmart sc**
	S: Auto Dealers, Auto Zone, CVS, Fred's, Food World, Logan Martin Vet Clinic ♥, Walgreen's, Winn Dixie/Pharmacy, **to Lakeside Landing RV Park & Marina▲**
158B	**US 231S, Ashville, Pell City (WB)**
158A	**US 231N, Ashville, Pell City (WB)**
162	**US 78, AL 4, Riverside, Pell City**
Gas	S: BP◈, Chevron
Food	S: Rest/ABVI
Lodg	S: Americas Best Value Inn♥
Other	N: **to Safe Harbor Camping▲**
165	**CR 207, Stemley Rd, Lincoln, Embry Cross Roads**
TStop	N: Pilot Travel Center #496 (Scales)
	S: RoadysTS/I-20 Truck Stop/Shell (Scales), 165 Auto & Truck Plaza/Chevron
Food	N: Subway/Pilot TC
	S: HuddleHouse/165 TP, Rest/Subway/ I-20 TS, Carter's BBQ
Lodg	S: I-20 TS
TWash	S: TW
TServ	S: Bobby Orr Tire Shop & Garage, I-20 TS/Tires
Other	N: Laundry/WiFi/Pilot TC, **to** Honda Mfg Plant
	S: Laundry/WiFi/CB/**LP**/I-20 TS, Repair Services, **Turner's Outdoor Center, to Safe Harbor RV Park▲** ,
168	**AL 77, CR 5, Talladega, Lincoln**
TStop	N: 77 Fuel Mart/Citgo
	S: RoadysTS/ Race City Travel Center/ Shell
Gas	N: QV Gas, Chevron
	S: Shop n Fill
Food	N: Jack's Hamburger's, KFC,
	S: Rest/Race City TC, Burger King, Double E Family Rest, McDonald's, Pace Car Diner
Lodg	S: Comfort Inn, Days Inn♥, McCaig's Motel
TServ	N: 77 FM/Tires
Other	N: Laundry/**LP**/77 FM
	S: Talladega Speedway▲ , Int'l Motorsports Hall of Fame, Talladega Muni Airfield✈ , **Dry Valley Junction RV Park▲** , **Talladega Taz RV Park & Campground▲** **Wazoo Campground & RV Park▲**
173	**AL 5, Lincoln, Eastaboga**
Gas	S: Texaco
Food	S: Stuckey's/DQ/Texaco
Lodg	S: Speedway Lodging

EXIT	ALABAMA
Other	S: Talladega Speedway▲ , Int'l Motor Sports Hall of Fame, **Talladega Taz RV Park & Campground▲** , Talladega Muni Airfield✈, **Wazoo Campground & RV Park▲**
179	**CR 467, Oxford, to Munford, Coldwater (Serv N to US 78)**
FStop	N: Chevron
Gas	S: Texaco
Food	N: China King, Jack's Family Rest, Pizza
Other	N: Carwash/Chevron, Dollar General, G&J Truck Repair, Grocery, RiteAid, Anniston Army Depot,
185	**AL 21, US 431N, Oxford, Anniston**
FStop	S: Texaco Food Mart #155
TStop	S: Kangaroo Express #3667 (Scales)
Gas	N: BP◈, Chevron,
	S: Exxon, Shell◈, Murphy◈
Food	N: Arby's, Applebee's, Burger King, CiCi's Pizza, Captain D's, Dominos Pizza, Hardee's, Krystal, Logan's Roadhouse, Los Mexicanos, McDonald's, O'Charley's, Pizza Hut, Red Lobster, Shoney's, Sonic, Starbucks, Taco Bell, Waffle House
	S: ChickFilA, El Pablano Mex, Firehouse Sub, Jazz Cajun, McDonalds, Outback Steakhouse, Panda Express TakeOut, Pizza Express, Wendy's, Subway/Texaco
Lodg	N: Days Inn♥, Liberty Inn, Oxford Inn♥, Red Carpet Inn
	S: Americas Best Value Inn♥, Baymont Inn♥, Comfort Inn, Econo Lodge♥, Key West Inn, Motel 6, Travelodge
Med	N: **+ Stringfellow Memorial Hospital**
Other	N: Auto & Diesel Service, ATMs, Auto Dealers, Ace Hardware/Oxford Lumber, Anniston Museum of Natural History, Banks, Bi-Lo/Pharmacy, BooksAMillion, Cheahea Harley Davidson, Cinema 12, Dollar General, Express Oil Change, Firestone Auto, Lowe's, Martin's Pharmacy, Office Max, Quintard Mall, RiteAid, Verizon, **to** Amtrak, Fort McClellan Military Reservation
	S: **LP**/Kang Exp, Auto Dealers, Best Buy, Dollar Tree, Home Depot, Sunshine Skate Center, Target, **Walmart sc**, Auto & Tire Center, Vet♥, Anniston Metro Airport✈
188	**Morgan Rd, to US 78, Oxford, Anniston**
Gas	N: Exxon, Shell, Texaco
Food	N: Brad's BBQ, **Cracker Barrel**, Fuji Japanese Cuisine, KFC, IHOP, Lone Star Steakhouse, Mellow Mushroom, Sonny's BBQ, Waffle House, Wendy's, Zaxby's

EXIT	AL / GA
Food	S: Arby's, Longhorn Steakhouse, Olive Garden
Lodg	N: Comfort Suites, Country Inn, Fairfield Inn, Hampton Inn♥, Hilton Garden Inn, Holiday Inn Express, Jameson Inn, Sleep Inn, to Budget Inn
Other	N: ATVs & Golf Carts Sales & Service, **Calhoun Campers, Camping World/ Dandy RV Sales, Country Court RV Park▲** , Fred's, Grocery, Lowe's, O'Reilly Auto Parts, Oxford Tire, T&L Outdoor Superstore, U-Haul,
	S: Best Buy, Dick's Sporting Goods, Home Depot, PetSmart♥, Target, TJ Maxx
191	**US 431, to US 78, Talladega Scenic Hwy**
Other	S: **Cheaha State Park▲**
199	**AL 9, Heflin, Hollis**
FStop	N: I-20 Texaco Food Mart #185
	S: Super Mart #225/BP
Gas	S: Chevron
Food	N: Subway/TacoBell/Texaco, Hardee's, Pop's Burgers, Marie's BBQ House
	S: Huddle House
Lodg	N: Americas Best Value Inn♥
Other	N: Auto Dealer, US Post Office
205	**AL 46, Ranburne, to Heflin**
TStop	N: State Line Fuel Center/BP
	S: 205 Shell Truck Center
Food	N: FastFood/StateLine FC
	S: 205 Shell TC
Tires	N: State Line FC
	S: 205 Shell TC
Other	N: **to appr 1.5mi: Cane 9 Creek RV Park & Campground▲**
	S: Laundry/205 STC
(208)	**Weigh Station (WB)**
210	**AL 49, Abernathy**
(214)	**AL Heflin Welcome Center (WB) (RR, Ph, Pic, Vend, Pet, Sec24, RVDump)**
NOTE:	**MM 215: Georgia State Line**

MM 215: CENTRAL / EASTERN TIME ZONE

CENTRAL TIME ZONE

ALABAMA
GEORGIA

EASTERN / CENTRAL TIME ZONE

(1)	**GA Cuba Welcome Center (EB) (RR, Phone, Picnic, Vend)**

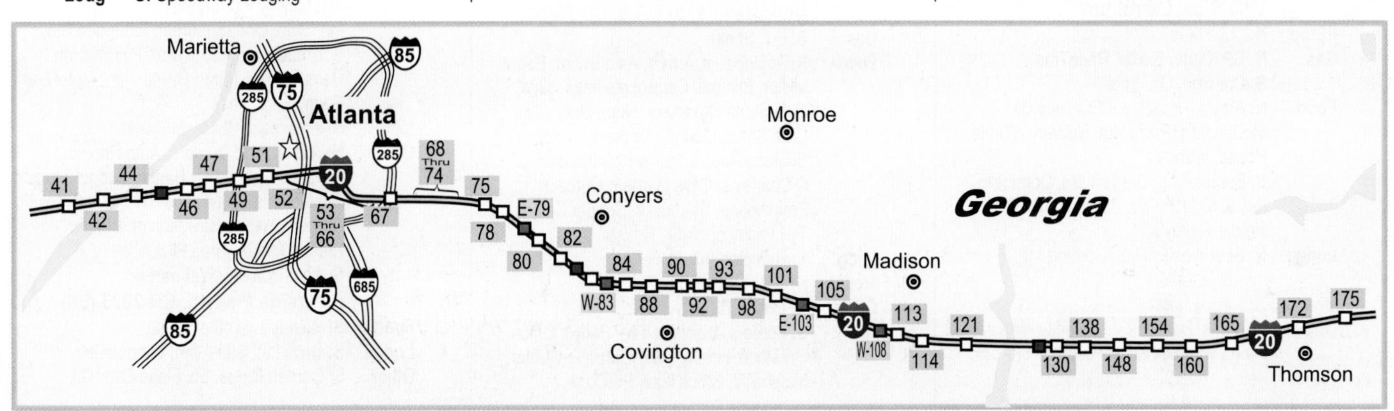

◈= Regular Gas Stations with Diesel ▲ = RV Friendly Locations ♥= Pet Friendly Locations
Red print shows large vehicle parking / access on site or nearby Brown Print = Campgrounds / RV PARKS

5 GA 100, Veterans Memorial Hwy, Tallapoosa, Bowdon

FStop N: Citgo Food Mart
TStop S: Noble Auto/Truck Plaza/Citgo (Scales), Pilot Travel Center #312 (Scales)
Food N: Waffle House
S: Rest/DQ/Noble ATP, KFC/TacoBell/ Pilot TC, Huddle House
TWash S: Noble ATP
TServ S: Noble ATP/Tires
Other S: Laundry/Noble ATP, Laundry/WiFi/ Pilot TC
N: **Big Oak RV Park▲**

9 Waco Rd, CR 348, Atlantic Ave, Waco

TStop N: Love's Travel Stop #311 (Scales)
Food N: Chesters/Subway/Love's TS
Other N: Laundry/WiFi/**RVDump**/Love's TS, Univ of GA Tech College, **to Yogi Bear Jellystone Park▲**

11 GA 1, US 27, Martha Berry Hwy, North Park St, Bremen, Carrollton

FStop N: Swifti Food Store #7/Shell, Kangaroo Express/Texaco
S: Cowboys Food Mart #3687
Gas N: Chevron, Murphy
S: BP◈
Food N: Arby's, Captain D's, Checkers, **Cracker Barrel**, KFC, McDonald's, Pizza Hut, Waffle House, Wendy's
S: Waffle House
Lodg N: Days Inn, Hampton Inn, Holiday Inn, Micotel♥, Quality Inn, Travelodge
Other N: Advance Auto Parts, CVS, Carwash, Dollar General, Ingles, Publix, **Walmart sc**,
S: U-Haul, Tires, Truck/Diesel Services, US Post Office

(15) Weigh Station (WB)

19 GA 113, Temple-Carrollton Rd, Temple, Carrollton, W Atlanta

TStop N: Flying J Travel Plaza #5045/Conoco (Scales), Pilot Travel Center #417 (Scales)
Gas S: Shell
Food N: Rest/FastFood/FJ TP, Subway/ Wendy's/Pilot TC, Hardee's, Waffle House
S: Captain D's, Philly Connection, Waffle House
TWash N: Truckomat
Other N: Laundry/BarbSh/**LP**/FJ TP, Laundry/WiFi/Pilot TC, Auto Zone, Ingles
S: to W GA Reg'l Airport✈

24 GA 61, Industrial Blvd, GA 101, Villa Rica, Carrollton

FStop N: Shell Mart
Gas N: BP, Citgo, Exxon, RaceTrac
S: Chevron, QT, Shell◈
Food N: Arby's, Hardee's, KFC/Taco Bell, McDonald's, Pizza Hut, Subway, Waffle House, Wendy's
S: Burger King, Captain D's, Domino's Pizza, McDonald's, Papa John's, Waffle House, Zaxby's
Lodg N: Best Western Inn, Comfort Inn, Days Inn, Super 8
Med N: + Hospital
Other N: ATMs, Banks, CVS, Ingles, Walgreen's, Winn Dixie, **GA State Hwy Patrol Post**
S: Dollar Tree, U-Haul, **Walmart sc**, West GA College

26 CR 939, Liberty Rd, Villa Rica

TStop S: WilcoHess Travel Plaza #3010 (Scales)
Gas N: Shell◈
Food N: Mexican Rest, Waffle House
S: FastFood/Godfather Pizza/WilcoHess
Lodg S: American Inn
TWash S: WilcoHess TP
TServ S: WilcoHess TP/Tires
Other N: Auto Repairs, Grocery, **to Sweetwater RV Park▲**
S: Laundry/WilcoHess TP, Auto Repairs, U-Haul

30 CR 808, Post Rd, Winston

Gas S: Shell◈

34 GA 5, Bill Arp Rd, Douglasville

Gas N: RaceTrac, Shell
S: Circle K, Chevron, Shell
Food N: China East, **Cracker Barrel**, Hooters, Huddle House, Waffle House, Williamson Bros BBQ, Zaxby's
S: Applebee's, Burger King, ChickFilA, Chili's, China King, Chinese Pagoda, Chuck E Cheese Pizza, CiCi's Pizza, DQ, Dominos Pizza, Dunkin Donuts, El Rodeo Mexican Rest, IHOP, Iron Horse BBQ, Krystal, La Fiesta Mexican, Long John Silver, McDonald's, Mellow Mushroom, Monterrey Mexican, Papa John's Pizza, Pizza Hut, Red Lobster, Ruby Tuesday, Ryan's Grill, Sea Breeze Seafood, Smokey Bones BBQ, Sonny's BBQ, Taco Bell, Tokyo Steakhouse, Waffle House, Wasabi Steakhouse & Sushi Bar, Wendy's,
Lodg N: Holiday Inn Express, La Quinta Inn♥, Lee's Motel, Sleep Inn
S: InTowne Suites
Other N: Auto Repair, Dollar Tree, Kaufmann Tire, Sam's Club, **Walmart sc, Sheriff Dept**
S: ATMs, Advance Auto Parts, Auto Dealers, Avis RAC, Banks, Best Buy, Big 10 Tires, Discount Tire, Dollar RAC, Douglas Co Animal Hospital♥, Douglas Oaks Animal Hospital♥, Enterprise RAC, Exchange Cinema 3, Garden Ridge, Goodyear, Home Depot, J&J Tire, J&J Welding, Kmart, Kroger/Pharmacy, Lowe's, NTB, Office Depot, Pep Boys, PetCo♥, Publix, Radio Shack, Regal Arbor Place Mall 18, RiteAid, Splash 'n Go Auto Spa, U-Haul, US Post Office, UPS Store, Walgreen's,

36 Chapel Hill Rd, Campbellton St, Douglasville, to GA 5, US 78

Gas S: QT, Shell◈
Food S: Applebee's, Arby's, Asia Buffet, Bagel Mister, Blimpie, Carrabba's Italian Grill, Cold Stone Creamery, Hops Grill, Joe's Crab Shack, Johnny Rockets, Landry's Seafood Rest, Logan's Roadhouse, O'Charley's, Olive Garden, Outback Steakhouse, Starbucks, Souper Salad, TGI Friday's, Waffle House
Lodg S: Hampton Inn, Super 8
Med N: + Douglas Hospital
Other N: Police Dept
S: Borders, Discount Tire, FedEx Office, Firestone, Hobby Lobby, Mailing Center, Marshall's, Office Max, PetCo♥, PetSmart♥, Radio Shack, RiteAid, Ross, Sears, Target/Pharmacy, Arbor Place Mall, Arbor 18, UPS Store, **to** Seven Flags Speedway

37 GA 92, Fairburn Rd, Douglasville

Gas N: BP, Chevron, Citgo, RaceTrac
S: Chevron, QT, RaceTrac, Shell
Food N: Arby's, Burger King, **Cracker Barrel**, Checkers, KFC, Krystal, McDonald's, Monterey Mex Rest, Mrs Winner's, Pagoda Express, Pizza Hut, Shoney's, Subway, Taco Bell, Waffle House, Wendy's
S: Dominos Pizza, Mexican Rest, Waffle House
Lodg N: Americas Best Value Inn, Best Western, Comfort Inn, Days Inn. Holiday Inn Express, Ramada Inn, Royal Inn, Sun Suites, Super 8
Med N: + Promina Douglas Gen'l Hospital
Other N: ATMs, Advance Auto Parts, Auto Repairs & Services, Auto Zone, Banks, Big Lots, CVS, Checker Auto Parts, Dollar General, Douglas Cinema 3, Douglasville Veterinary Hospital♥, Enterprise RAC, Hertz, **John Bleakley Motorhomes**, Kroger, Midas, NAPA, O'Reilly Auto Parts, RiteAid, U-Haul, U Tire Center,
S: Auto Repairs & Services, Dazzles Skating Rink, Ingles, Winn Dixie, Your Bowling Center

41 CR 817, Lee Rd, Lithia Springs

FStop N: Econo Flash #5/Citgo
S: Spedway Truck Stop #72/Chevron, Shell
Food N: Hardee's, Courtni's Iron Skillet, Pizza Hut
S: Waffle House/Chevron, Subway/Shell
Other N: Auto Service, Tires, ATM, Banks, Ace Hardware, Dependable Tire,
S: Auto Service, Fleet Service, Grocery, **Sweetwater Creek State Park▲**

(42) Weigh Station (EB)

44 GA 6, Thornton Rd, Austell, Atlanta Int'l Airport, Powder Springs, Lithia Springs

Gas N: BP, RaceTrac, Shell, Kroger
Food N: BBQ House, Burger King, ChickFilA, **Cracker Barrel**, Chilito's, Domino's Pizza, El Pollo Loco, Hardee's, IHOP, KFC, La Fiesta Mexican Rest, McDonald's, New China, Olive Tree, Ruby Tuesday, Sonic, Subway, Taco Bell, Waffle House, Wendy's
Lodg N: Budget Inn, Comfort Inn, InTowne Suites, Hampton Inn, Holiday Inn, Knights Inn, Quality Inn, Shoney's Inn, Suite One, Suburban Extended Stay,
S: Country Inn, Courtyard, Fairfield Inn, Hampton Inn, Hilton Garden Inn, Motel 6♥, SpringHill Suites,
Med N: + Parkway Medical Center
Other N: ATMs, Auto Dealers, Auto Repairs, Advance Auto Parts, Banks, Budget Truck Rental, CVS, Enterprise RAC, Goodyear, Grocery, Harley Davidson of Atlanta, Kroger, Midas, Tires Plus, Walgreen's,
S: Auto Dealers, **Walmart sc**

46 Riverside Pkwy S, CR 2623 (EB)

Food S: Wendy's, Waffle House
Lodg S: Days Inn, Sleep Inn, Wingate Inn
Other S: Garden Ridge, Six Flags Over GA

◈ = Regular Gas Stations with Diesel ▲ = RV Friendly Locations ♥ = Pet Friendly Locations
Red print shows large vehicle parking / access on site or nearby Brown Print = Campgrounds / RV PARKS

EXIT		GEORGIA
46A		**Riverside Pkwy SW, CR 2623, Six Flags Dr, Austell (WB) (Access Same as Exit #46)**
46B		**Six Flags Dr, CR 2633 (WB)**
	Gas	N: BP, Citgo, Marathon, QT
	Food	N: Church's Chicken, Waffle House
	Lodg	N: Baymont Inn♥
47		**Six Flags Pkwy, CR 4408, Six Flags Park (WB)**
	Gas	N: BP
	Food	N: Waffle House S: McDonald's
	Lodg	N: Baymont Inn♥, S: Days Inn, Wingate Inn
	Other	S: Sam's Club, Six Flags Over GA Amusement Park
49		**GA 70, Fulton Industrial Blvd, Fulton Co Airport, Atlanta**
	FStop	S: Citgo Truck Stop
	TStop	S: to appr 4mi: QT #777 (Scales)
	Gas	N: Shell S: BP, Chevron, Fleet Pride, Shell,
	Food	N: Captain D's, Checkers, DQ, EJ's Soul Food, Hardee's Krystal, McDonald's, Mrs Winners Chicken, Shoney's, Subway, Waffle House, Wendy's, FastFood/QT, FastFood/Citgo S: Arby's, Blimpie, Burger King, Grand Buffet, McDonald's, Pizza Pizza, Waffle House
	Lodg	N: Days Inn, Efficiency Lodge, Masters Economy Inn, Majestic Lodge & Extended Stay, Ramada♥, Super 7 Inn S: Comfort Inn, Executive Inn, Parkview Inn, Quality Inn, Red Roof Inn♥, Rodeway Inn, Super 8, Travelodge
	Other	N: ATMs, Banks, Greyhound, Fulton Co Brown Airport✈, to I-285 S: Carwash/Chevron, Grocery, Hurricane Truck Parts, NAPA, Office Depot, Penske Truck Rental, U-Haul
(51A)		**Jct I-285S, GA 407, to Macon, Montgomery (fr WB, LEFT exit) (Serv at 1st Exits both dir)**
(51B)		**Jct I-285N, GA 407, to Chattanooga, Greenville**
52		**GA 280, Burton Rd, Holmes Dr, Hightower Rd, Atlanta (EB) (Gas & Food S to ML King Dr)**
52AB		**GA 280, HE Holmes Dr, Hightower Rd, Atlanta (WB)**
53		**to GA 139, M L King Jr Dr, Anderson Ave (Diff reaccess)**
	Gas	N: Chevron, Shell S: BP
54		**Langhorn St, Cascade Rd, Westview Dr, Sells Ave (WB)**
	Gas	S: Shell
55A		**Lowery Blvd, Ashby St**
	Gas	N: Chevronl S: BP, Exxon◈
	Food	S: American Deli, Church's Chicken, Popeye's Chicken, Taco Bell, Taste of Tropical
	Med	S: + West End Medical Center
	Other	S: ATMs, Banks, CVS, Family Dollar, Grocery, Museum, Radio Shack, SavALot, Tires, US Post Office, Westend Ace Hardware, West End Mall
55B		**Lee St, Park St, to US 29 (WB) (Access to Ex #55A Services)**
56A		**McDaniel St, to US 19, US 29, US 41, Whitehall St (EB)**
	Gas	N: Chevron, Texaco
	Food	N: Burgers R Us, Wing House
	Other	N: U-Haul
56B		**Windsor St, Spring St, Turner Field, Central Ave, Pryor St,**
	Other	N: CNN Studio Tour, GA State Univ, GA Dome, GA World Congress Center, Greyhound Bus Terminal, Loudermilk Convention Center, Philips Arena, The Omni, Underground Atlanta, S: Atlanta Fulton Co Stadium, Turner Field, Atlanta Braves, US Post Office
(57)		**Jct I-75S, to Macon, I-85S to Montgomery, Jct I-75N to Chattanooga, I-85N, to Greenville**
58A		**Capitol Ave, Downtown (WB)**
58B		**Hill St, Turner Field (WB)**
	Gas	N: BP, Marathon
	Food	N: Mrs Winner's Chicken
	Lodg	S: Holiday Inn Select, Hill St B&B
	Other	S: U-Haul
59A		**Boulevard SE, to Confederate Ave**
	Gas	N: BP, Chevron◈ S: BP
	Food	N: Blimpie, Bucc's BBQ, Stone Soup Kitchen S: Factory BBQ
	Other	S: Art Exchange, Atlanta Fulton Co Zoo, CVS, Cyclorama, Grant Park, Stockade, Youngblood Galleries,
59B		**GA 154 Conn, RR Ave, Glenwood Conn, Memorial Dr (EB)**
60		**US 23, GA 42, Moreland Ave (WB)**
	Gas	N: Exxon, Texaco S: BP, Phillips 66◈, Shell
	Food	S: Big Wok, Checker's, KFC, Krystal, Long John Silver's, McDonald's, Wendy's
	Lodg	N: Atlanta Motel
	Other	N: Auto Services, Advance Auto Parts, S: ATMs, Banks, Hardware Store, US Post Office
60AB		**US 23, GA 42, Moreland Ave (EB)**
61A		**Maynard Terrace SE, to Memorial Dr, Atlanta (EB, No Re-Entry)**
	Gas	N: BP, Citgo
	Food	N: Ann's Snack Bar, Checkers, Wyatt's Diner
	Other	N: Advance Auto Parts, Walgreen's,
61B		**GA 260, Glenwood Ave**
	Gas	N: BP, Chevron
62		**Flat Shoals Rd SE (EB, No reaccess)**
	Gas	N: Citgo, Exxon, Shell
	Other	N: Family Dollar
63		**Gresham Rd, Flat Shoals Rd, Brannen Rd, Cook Rd (diff reaccess)**
	Gas	N: Chevron, Citgo S: AmocoBP, Citgo, Phillips 66, Shell
	Food	N: Subway/Walmart S: Church's Chicken, G&G BBQ, Hot Spot,
	Med	S: + Southside Healthcare Family Medical Clinic
	Med	S: + Southside Healthcare Family Medical Clinic
	Other	N: Walmart sc S: Carwash, U-Haul
65		**GA 155, Candler Rd, Decatur**
	Gas	N: Amoco, Citgo, Hess, Marathon S: Amoco, Chevron, Conoco, Shell
	Food	N: Blimpie, Checkers, Dundee's Café, Little Caesars Pizza, Long John Silver, Mrs Winners Chicken, Panda Kitcchen, Pizza Hut, Red Lobster, Wendy's S: Arby's, Burger King, Checkers, China Cafeteria, ChickFilA, Church's Chicken, DQ, KFC, McDonald's, Taco Bell
	Lodg	N: Americas Best Value Inn, Best Western, Discover Inn, Howard Johnson, Motel 6 S: Candler Inn, Sunset Lodge
	Other	N: Advance Auto, Auto Zone, CVS, Carwash, Family Dollar, Laundromat, O'Reilly Auto Parts, Piggly Wiggly, U-Haul, Walgreen's, S: ATMs, Banks, Big Lots, Carwash, Firestone Auto, Goodyear Auto, Jiffy Lube, Kroger, Mitchell Tire, Pep Boys, South Dekalb Mall, **S to I-285**
66		**Columbia Dr, CR 5154, Decatur (EB, No Re-Entry)**
	Gas	N: Chevron, Citgo, Phillips 66 S: Fina
	Food	S: Subway
	Other	N: Auto Repair
(67)		**Jct I-285 By-Pass, S to Macon, N to Greenville (EB)**
(67A)		**Jct I-285S ByPass, to Atlanta Int'l Airport, Macon (WB)**
(67B)		**Jct I-285N ByPass, to Greenville, Chattanooga (WB)**
68		**Wesley Chapel Rd, CR 5196, Snapfinger Woods Dr, Decatur**
	Gas	N: Conoco, Exxon, Shell S: BP, Chevron, Crown, Mobil, QT, Shell
	Food	N: Blimpie, Captain D's, Checkers, Chick-Fil-A, Church's Chicken, Hardee's, Hong Kong Buffet, KFC, Long John Silvers, Popeye's Chicken, Subway, Taco Bell, 3 Dollar Café, Waffle House, Wendy's, Uncle Mack's BBQ
	Food	S: Burger King, DQ, McDonald's, J&J Fish, Popeye's Chicken
	Lodg	N: Holiday Inn Express, Motel 6♥ S: Days Inn
	Other	N: AAA Truck Rental, Coral Sands Animal Hospital♥, CVS, Grocery, Goodyear, Home Depot, Ingles, Kroger, Laundromat, NTB, Snapfinger Woods Golf Course S: ATM, Bank, Auto Services, Enterprise RAC, Precision Tire Auto Care, Truck Service, US Post Office
71		**Panola Rd, CR 5150, Lithonia**
	Gas	N: Quik Trip◈, Shell◈ S: BP◈, Citgo, Exxon◈, Shell, Murphy
	Food	N: Burger King, Checkers, Cajun, Cracker Barrel, KFC, McDonald's, Mrs Winner's, Waffle House, Wendy's S: American Deli, IHOP, New China, Popeye's Chicken, Ruby Tuesday, Wendy's

◈= Regular Gas Stations with Diesel ▲ = RV Friendly Locations ♥= Pet Friendly Locations
Red print shows large vehicle parking / access on site or nearby Brown Print = Campgrounds / RV PARKS

EXIT		GEORGIA
	Lodg	**N:** Holiday Inn Express, La Quinta Inn♥, Motel 6, Super 8 **S:** Red Roof Inn, Sleep Inn
	Med	**N: + DeKalb Medical Hospital**
	Other	**N:** 8 Cinemas, Cartopia Car Care, Family Dollar,
	Other	**S:** Auto Services, Bank, FedEx Office, Lowe's, Publix, NAPA, Radio Shack, Tires +, Walgreen's, **Walmart sc**
74		**Evans Mills Rd, CR 6305, Lithonia, N to Stone Mountain**
	FStop	**S:** Citgo Truck Stop, Speedway
	Gas	**N:** BP, Chevron◈, Phillips 66, Shell◈
	Food	**N:** Captain D's, KFC/TacoBell, McDonald's, Mamie's Kitchen, Roberts Rest, Shoney's, Waffle House, Wendy's **S:** DQ, Krystal, Waffle House,
	Lodg	**S:** Econo Lodge, Microtel
	Med	**N: + DeKalb Medical Hospital**
	Other	**N:** Advance Auto Parts, American Hardware, Evans Mill Animal Hospital♥, Family Dollar, O'Reilly Auto Parts, Martin Tire, US Post Office **S:** CVS, Dollar General, Grocery, Radio Shack, **to** Stonecrest Mall
75		**GA 124, US 278, Turner Hill Rd**
	FStop	**N:** Buddy's Fuel Stop #5/Citgo
	Gas	**N:** BP◈, **S:** Sam's
	Food	**S:** Applebee's, Atlanta Steaks, Bourbon St Café, Bugaboo Creek Steakhouse, ChickFilA, Firehouse Subs, Grand China, Great Steak & Potato, Kampai Sushi & Steak, McDonald's, La Costa, Olive Garden, Panera Bread, Ruby Tuesday, Smokey Bones BBQ, Steak N Shake, Subway, This is it BBQ & Seafood, Wendy's, Zaxby's
	Lodg	**S:** AmeriSuites, Comfort Suites, Fairfield Inn, Hilton Garden Inn, Hyatt Place
	Other	**N:** Rockdale Truck Repair **S:** Stonecrest Mall, ATMs, AMC Theatres, Bank, Best Buy, Borders, Marshall's, RiteAid, Ross, Sam's Club, Staples, Target, Tires Plus+, UPS Store, World Market, Strayer Univ
78		**Sigman Rd, CR 66, Conyers**
	Gas	**N:** Shell, BP
	Food	**N:** Waffle House, Bradley's Real Pit BBQ
	Other	**N:** Auto Service, Tires, Diesel Service, **Sheriff Dept** **S:** Auto Dealers, **Crown RV Center Sales/ Service/Rentals**, **GA State Hwy Patrol Post**
(79)		**Parking Area (EB)**
80		**West Ave, Klondike Rd, CR 437, Conyers**
	Gas	**N:** Exxon, Shell◈, Speedway◈ **S:** Exxon◈
	Food	**N:** Atantla Bread Co, Burger King, DQ, Dominos Pizza, Don Pablo's, Golden Palace, IHOP, Mrs Winner's, O'Charley's, On the Border, Outback Steakhouse, Red Lobster, Up the Creek Fish Camp & Grill, Subway, Waffle House
	Food	**S:** Longhorn Steakhouse, McDonald's
	Lodg	**N:** Holiday Inn, Richfield Lodge **S:** Comfort Inn
	Med	**N: + Rockdale Hospital, + Concentra Urgent Care**
	Other	**N:** Auto Services, Carmike Cinemas,

Personal Notes

EXIT		GEORGIA
	Other	**N:** Family Dollar, Laundromat, Piggly Wiggly, Rockdale Plaza, **S:** Auto Dealers, Conyers Animal Hospital♥, Laundromat, Truck Repair, **Suncoast RV Center**, Super 1 Trailer Sales, **GA State Hwy Patrol Post**
82		**GA 20, GA 138, Stockbridge Hwy, Conyers, Monroe**
	FStop	**N:** Joy Food Mart
	Gas	**N:** BP, Speedway, BJ's, QT **S:** Chevron, Shell◈, Kroger
	Food	**N:** Chuck E Cheese, **Cracker Barrel**, Don Pablo's, Golden Corral, IHOP, McDonald's, O'Charley's, Outback Steak House, Red Lobster, Roadhouse Grill, Sonic, Waffle House, Woody's BBQ **S:** Arby's, Applebee's, Billy Bob's Pizza & Skating Rink, Burger King, Captain D's, Checkers, Chili's, ChickFilA, CiCi's Pizza, DJ's Country Kitchen, Folks Southern Kitchen, Glenn's BBQ, Hardee's, Hooters, Huddle House, Jim & Nick's BBQ, KFC, Krystal, Long John Silver, Los Charros Mexican, McDonald's, Mellow Mushroom, Nagoya Japanese Seafood, Papa John's Pizza, Piccadilly, Popeye's Chicken, Ryan's Grill, Ruby Tuesday, Shoney's, Starbucks, Taco Bell, Waffle House, Wendy's
	Lodg	**N:** Country Inn, Days Inn, Hampton Inn♥, Holiday Inn Express, Jameson Inn, La Quinta Inn♥, Super 8♥ **S:** Horizon Extended Stay♥, Intown Suites, Microtel♥,
	Med	**N: + Hospital**

EXIT		GEORGIA
	Other	**N:** Auto Services, Auto Dealers, ATM, AT&T, Avis RAC, BJ's, Carmike Cinema 16, Cowan Ace Hardware, Granite Mountain Harley Davidson, Home Depot, Hertz, Horizons Motorsports, Kmart, Laundromat, Mountain Motorsports, NAPA, Office Depot PetSmart♥, Staples, Tires +, U-Haul, **Walmart sc**, Reid Stadium, **Police Dept**, **to JTF Mobile Services** **S:** AMF Bowling Center, Aldi, ATMs, Auto Dealers, Auto Services, Big Lots, Big 10 Tires, Burlington Coat Factory, Budget Truck Rental, Dollar General, FedEx Office, Firestone Auto, Food Depot, Goodyear Auto, Grocery, Hobby Lobby, Jiffy Lube, Kroger, NTB, Pep Boys, Publix, Radio Shack, RiteAid, Target, Mall, Shopping Center, US Post Office
(83)		**Parking Area (WB)**
84		**GA 162, Salem Rd**
	Gas	**N:** BJ's **S:** BP, Chevron, Liberty, RaceTrac
	Food	**S:** Burger King, China Kitchen, ChickFilA, Subway, Smokehouse BBQ, Waffle House
	Other	**N:** BJ's Club **S:** ATMs, Auto Service, Bank, Dollar General, Ingles, Winn Dixie, Pharmacy, Golf Courses, **Crown RV**, **Super 1 RV Center**
88		**Almon Rd, CR 46, Crowell Rd, Covington, to Porterdale**
	Gas	**N:** Chevron◈ **S:** BP
	Food	**S:** McDonald's
	Other	**N: Riverside Estates RV Park▲, RV Rentals of GA**
90		**US 278E, GA 12, to GA 81, Turner Lk Rd NW, Covington, Oxford**
	Gas	**S:** BP, Citgo, RaceTrac, Shell
	Food	**S:** Arby's, Bojangles Chicken, Burger King, Captain D's, Checkers, ChickFilA, Dominos Pizza, Hardee's, KFC, Longhorn Steakhouse, Japanese Rest, Papa John's Pizza, Rib House, Shoney's, Taco Bell, Town Center Breads Coffee House, Waffle House, Zaxby's
	Lodg	**S:** Holiday Inn Express
	Med	**S: + Newton Medical Center, + Alliance Family Care**
	Other	**N:** Troy State Univ, Oxford College of Emory Univ, US Post Office **S:** Auto Service, ATMs, Advance Auto Parts, Auto Dealer, AutoZone, Banks, Big Lots, Bulldog Tire, Dollar General, Grocery, Hertz, Ingles, Kmart, Kroger, O'Reilly Auto Parts, Sundowner of GA Trailer, Tire Depot, U-Haul, VetMed Animal Clinic♥,
92		**Alcovy Rd, CR 660, Covington (Addtl Serv S to US 278)**
	FStop	**N:** Circle K #2284
	Gas	**N:** Chevron◈
	Food	**S:** ChickFilA, Dunkin Donuts, Krystal, McDonald's, Pippin's BBQ, Pizza Hut, Waffle House, Wendy's
	Lodg	**N:** Baymont Inn♥, Covington Lodge, Days Inn♥, Super 8♥, **S:** Americas Best Value Inn
	Med	**S: + Newton Medical Center**

◈ = Regular Gas Stations with Diesel ▲ = RV Friendly Locations ♥ = Pet Friendly Locations
Red print shows large vehicle parking / access on site or nearby **Brown Print = Campgrounds / RV PARKS**

EXIT	GEORGIA
	Other N: to Covington Muni Airport✈ S: Big Lots, Kroger, NAPA, Newton Co Fairgrounds, **Acc to Ex #90/#93 Serv**
93	**GA 142, John R Williams Hwy, Covington, Hazelbrand, (Serv South to US 278/Acc to #92/#90)**
	FStop S: Flash Foods #259/Exxon
	Gas S: Shell
	Food S: Waffle House
	Lodg S: Hampton Inn, Quality Inn♥
	Med S: + Newton Medical Center
	Other N: Home Depot S: Animal Medical of Covington♥, Dollar General, Midas, Penske Truck Rental, Tractor Supply, U-Haul, **Walmart sc**
98	**GA 11, Social Circle, to Monroe, Monticello (Addtl Serv 4mi N in Soc Cir)**
	Gas N: to BP S: Chevron◈, Citgo
	Food S: Blimpie,
	Other S: Fox Vineyards & Winery
101	**US 278, GA 12, Social Circle**
(103)	**Rest Area-Morgan Co #52 (EB) (RR, Phone, Pic, Vend, Pet, RVDump)**
105	**Newborn Rd, CR 240, Rutledge**
	Gas N: BP◈
	Food N: Carol's Wing Shack, Classic Rock Café, Yesterday's Cafe
	Other N: Grocery, Bank, **to** appr 6 mi: **Hard Labor Creek State Park▲**
(108)	**Rest Area-Morgan Co #53 (WB) (RR, Phone, Pic, Vend, Pet, RVDump)**
113	**GA 83, Monticello Hwy, Madison**
	FStop N: BP
	Gas S: Liberty
	Med N: + Hospital
	Other S: GA State Hwy Patrol Post
114	**US 441, US 129, GA 24, Eatonton Hwy, Madison, Eatonton**
	TStop N: Pilot Travel Center #420 (Scales) S: Travel Center of America #45/BP (Scales), Fuel Mart #786
	Gas N: Chevron, Citgo, RaceTrac S: Shell, Texaco
	Food N: FastFood/Pilot TC, Arby's, Burger King, **Cracker Barrel**, KFC, Krystal, McDonald's, Open Air BBQ, Pizza Hut, Subway/Chevron, Taco Bell, Waffle House, Wendy's, Zaxby's, Rest/Days Inn S: CountryPride/Popeyes/TA TC, Waffle House
	Lodg N: Comfort Inn, Hampton Inn, Quality Inn♥, Red Roof Inn♥, S: Super 8, Wingate Inn
	TWash S: TA TC
	TServ S: TA TC/Tires, Towing & Truck Repair
	Med N: + Morgan Memorial Hospital
	Other N: Laundry/WiFi/**RVDump**/Pilot TC, Advance Auto Parts, Auto Dealers, Auto Repairs, ATMs, Bi-Lo, Dollar General, Enterprise RAC, Family Dollar, Ingles, Lowe's, Madison Mall & Flea Market, O'Reilly Auto Parts, Radio Shack, RiteAid, **Walmart sc**, to Madison Muni Airport✈, S: Laundry/WiFi/TA TC, **Country Boy RV Park▲**, Tractor Supply, **to** Southern Cross Guest Ranch B&B

EXIT	GEORGIA
121	**CR 251, 7 Islands Rd, Buckhead. to Lake Oconee**
	Gas S: Chevron
	Food S: Bonner's Triple B Rest
130	**GA 44, Eatonton Rd, Greensboro**
	Gas N: BP, Exxon S: Chevron◈
	Food N: McDonald's, Pizza Hut, Subway, Wendy's, Waffle House, Zaxby's
	Lodg N: Jameson Inn, Microtel♥
	Other N: Auto Dealer, Dollar General, Durham Veterinary Clinic♥, Tires S: **to appr 10-11 mi: Parks Ferry Park/ GA Power▲, Northshore at Lake Oconee▲, Old Salem Public Rec Area▲**
138	**GA 77, GA 15, Siloam, Union Point, Sparta**
	TStop N: Flying J Travel Plaza # (Scales)
	Gas S: BP◈
	Food N: CountryMkt/FastFood/FJ TP
	Med N: + to Minnie G Boswell Memorial Hospital
	Other N: Laundry/WiFi/**LP**/**RVDump**/FJ TP
148	**GA 22, Crawfordville, Sparta**
	TStop S: Midway Truck Stop/Pure
	Gas N: BP◈
	Food S: FastFood/Midway TS
	Tires S: Midway TS
	Other N: **AH Stephens Hist Memorial State Park▲**
154	**US 278, GA 12, Norwood, to Warrenton, Washington**
160	**Cadley Norwood Rd, CR 185**
165	**GA 80, Washington Hwy, Camak**
172	**US 78, GA 10, GA 17, Thomson, to Washington**
	TStop N: Love's Travel Stop #354 (Scales) S: Circle K #5367/76 (Scales), M&A Food & Gas
	Gas N: Chevron◈ S:BP◈, RaceWay◈, Shell, Murphy USA
	Food N: ChestersChkn/Subway/Love's TS, Waffle House S: Amigos Rest, Arby's, Burger King, Checkers, Denny's, Domino's Pizza, Hardee's, Krystal, Long John Silver's, McDonald's, Pizza Hut, Taco Bell, Shoney's, Waffle House, Wendy's, Western Sizzlin', Zaxby's, FastFood/Circle K
	Lodg S: Best Western, Econo Lodge, Holiday Inn Express, Scottish Inn
	Med S: + Hospital
	Other N: WiFi/**RVDump**/Love's TS, **GA State Patrol Post**, Auto Dealers, Thomson McDuffie Co Airport✈, **to appr 11 mi: Big Hart Camp Area▲, appr 8 mi: Raysville Bridge Camp Area▲** S: Auto Zone, Auto Repairs, ATMs, Advance Auto Parts, Banks, Bi-Lo, Food Lion, CVS, Kmart, Lowe's, Twin Cinema, **Walmart SC**
175	**GA 150, Cobbham Rd, Thomson**
	TStop N: USA Truck Stop/BP
	Food N: Rest/USA TS
	Lodg N: Days Inn
	TServ N: USA TS
	Other N: **to appr 11 mi: Mistletoe State Park▲**

EXIT	GEORGIA
(181)	**Rest Areas (Both dir) (RR, Phone, Picnic, Vend, RVDump) Columbia Co EB #62 / WB: #63**
183	**GA 47, US 221, Appling Harlem Rd,**
	Gas N: 76 S: BP◈
	Other N: **to MIL/Pointes West Rec Area▲, MIL/Fort Gordon Rec Area▲, to Ridge Road Camp Area▲, to Petersburg Camp Area▲, to appr 13 mi: Wildwood Park▲**
(187)	**Weigh Station (Both dir)**
190	**GA 388, Lewiston Rd, Grovetown (Gas/Food/Serv appr 2mi S)**
	TStop N: BP Pumping Station #8
	Food N: FastFood/BP PS, Waffle House
	Other S: Fort Gordon Military Res
194	**GA 383, Belair Rd, Dyess Pkwy, Augusta, Evans**
	FStop N: Circle K #5382
	TStop S: Pilot Travel Center #65 (Scales)
	Gas N: Citgo, Circle K/Shell, Sprint S: BP◈,
	Food N: FastFood/Circle K, Burger King, Popeye's, Waffle House, Wendy's
	Food S: Subway/Pilot TC, **Cracker Barrel**, Huddle House, Waffle House,
	Lodg N: Georgia Inn, Villager Lodge S: America's Best Inn, Best Western, Hampton Inn, Holiday Inn, Quality Inn, Ramada Ltd, Wingate
	Other N: ATM, Banks, Food Lion, Funsville Amusement Park S: Laundry/WiFi/Pilot TC, Goodyear
195	**Wheeler Rd, CR 601, Augusta**
	Gas N: Sprint S: BP◈, Circle K/Shell◈, Circle K/Shell◈
	Food N: O'Charley's, Waffle House
	Lodg S: Days Inn, Howard Johnson, Red Roof Inn♥, Ramada Inn
	Med S: + Doctors Hospital
	Other N: Auto Service, Tires S: ATMs, Banks, Auto Services, Augusta Harley Davidson, Augusta Triumph/Ducati, RiteAid, **to I-520:** Food/Lodg/Shopping,
(196A)	**Jct I-520E, GA 415, Bobby Jones Expwy (Access All Serv 1st Exit S)**
196B	**GA 232W, GA 415, Bobby Jones Expwy (Access All Serv 1st Exit N)**
197	**Pleasant Home Rd (WB) (Acc to #199 & #195 Serv)**
	Gas N: Circle K/Shell, Kangaroo Express/BP S: BP, Chevron
	Food N: Cadwallader's Cafe, California Dreamin, Checkers, Golden Corral, KFC, Longhorn Steakhouse, McDonald's, Ruby Tuesday, Shangri-La Gourmet Buffet, Snug Steak & Grill, Wife Saver S: Atlanta Bread, Back Yard Burger, Cheddar Cafe, ChickFilA, Chili's, Logan's Roadhouse, O'Charley's, Panera Bread, Romano's Macaroni Grill, Souper Salad, Starbucks, Sticky Fingers Ribhouse, Subway,
	Lodg N: Baymont Inn, Suburban Lodge, S: Doubletree Hotel, **Acc to #195 Serv**
	Other N: ATMs, Auto Dealers, Auto Services, Banks, Bonaventure Discount Golf, CVS,

EXIT — GEORGIA

Other N: Discount Tire, Dollar General, Enterprise RAC, Hertz, K-Mart, Lowe's, NAPA, Radio Shack, Sam's Club, Tire Kingdom, Tractor Supply, US Golf, Walgreen's, **Walmart SC**, West Marine
S: ATMs, Best Buy, Borders, FedEx Office, Hobby Lobby, Michael's, PetSmart♥, Regal Augusta Exchange 20 Cinema, Sprint, Staples, Target, Tires Plus, T-Mobile

199 — GA 28, Washington Rd, Augusta

FStop S: Circle K #5582/76
Gas N: BP, RaceWay
S: BP, Circle K/Shell, Crown,
Food N: Applebee's, Burger King, Captain D's, California Dreaming, Checkers, ChickFilA, Damon's, Denny's, DQ, Huddle House, KFC, Krystal, Longhorn Steakhouse, Pizza Hut, McDonald's, Shogun Japanese Rest, Piccadilly, Rhinehart's Seafood, Sonic, Shoney's, Sho-Gun, Starbucks, Waffle House
S: Bojangles, BoneFish Rest, Carrabba's Italian Grill, Cane's, ChickFilA, Church's Chicken, Famous Dave's BBQ, Hooters, Hardee's, Krispy Kreme, Long John Silver, Lone Star Steakhouse, McDonald's, Malley's Bagel, Olive Garden, Outback Steakhouse, Red Lobster, Subway, TGI Fridays, T-Bonz Rest, Waffle House, Wendy's
Lodg N: America's Best Value Inn, Candlewood Suites, Clarion Suites, Courtyard, Days Inn, Hampton Inn, Hilton Garden Inn, Homewood Suites, Jameson Inn, La Quinta Inn♥, Masters Inn, National Inn, Quality Inn, Ramada Ltd, Scottish Inn, Sunset Inn, Sleep Inn, Travelodge
S: Best Western, Country Inn, Fairfield Inn, Guest Inn, Knights Inn, Parkway Inn, Ramada, Staybridge Suites, Super 8, Westbank Inn
TServ S: Cummins South
Med S: + Hospital
Other N: ATM, Banks, Auto Service, Auto Dealers, Auto Zone, CVS, Enterprise RAC, Economy RAC, NAPA, Quick Lube,
S: ATMs, Augusta National Golf Club, Banks, Books A Million, Carwash/Oil Change, Dollar Tree, Firestone, Fred's, Goodyear, Jiffy Lube, Kroger, Laundromat, Master 7 Cinema, Midas, Pep Boys, Publix, RiteAid, Tire Kingdom, Walgreen's

200 — GA 104, River Watch Pkwy, Augusta

TStop N: Pilot Travel Center #144 (Scales)

EXIT — GA / SC

Food N: Wendy's/Pilot TC
Lodg N: Baymont Inn, Comfort Suites, Microtel, Quality Inn, Sleep Inn, Value Place
Other N: Laundry/WiFi/Pilot TC

(201) — GA Augusta Welcome Center (WB)
(RR, Phone, Pic, Pet, Vend)

NOTE: MM 202: South Carolina State Line

EASTERN TIME ZONE

GEORGIA
SOUTH CAROLINA

EASTERN TIME ZONE

(1) — SC Welcome Center (EB)
(RR, Phone, Pic, Pet, Vend)

1 — SC 230, Martintown Rd, N Augusta
(Addt'l Serv 4mi S in N Augusta)

FStop S: Circle K #5588/76
Food S: Blimpie/Circle K, Waffle House
Other S: Carwash/76

5 — US 25, SC 121, Edgefield Rd, N Augusta, Belvedere, Edgefield, Johnston

FStop N: Greg's Gas Plus
TStop N: Circle K #5350/76 (Scales), S & S Truck Stop
Gas N: BP◇, Circle K/Shell, Circle K
S: Kangaroo Express/Citgo◇, **Gas◇**
Food N: Rest/S&S TS, Blimpie/Circle K, Bojangles/Circle K, Burger King, Checkers, Catfish One, DQ/Circle K, Hardee's, Huddle House, Sonic, Subway
S: Waffle House, Little Mexico Mexica Rest, Edmunds BBQ
Lodg S: Sleep Inn
Tires N: S&S TS
TWash N: S&S TS
Other N: Laundry/S&S TS, Advance Auto Parts, Dollar General, Food Lion/Pharmacy, Carwash/Circle K
S: Appr 4-5 mi S: Walmart sc

(6) — Jct I-520W, Palmetto Pkwy, N Augusta, Augusta

11 — SC 144, Graniteville

TStop N: Kent's Corner #24/BP (Scales)
Food N: Rest/Kent's
TWash N: Kent's
Other N: Laundry/Kent's

18 — SC 19, Aiken, Johnston

FStop S: Kent's Corner #15/BP

EXIT — SOUTH CAROLINA

Gas S: Shell◇
Food S: FastFood/Kent's, Blimpie/Shell, Waffle House
Lodg S: Deluxe Inn, GuestHouse Inn
Med S: + Hospital
Other N: C&E Truck & Auto Repair, Auto & Cycle Shop

(20) — TRUCK Parking Area (Both dir)

22 — US 1, Columbia Hwy, Aiken, to Ridge Spring

TStop S: Circle K #5377
Gas S: BP◇, RaceWay, Shell◇
Food S: FastFood/Circle K, Baynham Family Rest, Hardee's, McDonald's, Waffle House
Lodg S: Days Inn, Inn of Aiken
Other S: Auto & Truck Services, **Aiken RV Park▲**, **Pineacres Park**, **Palmetto Lake RV Park▲**, Aiken Muni Airport✈, **to** USC/Aiken

29 — SC 49, Wire Rd, Aiken

33 — SC 39, Batesburg, Wagener, Moneta

TStop S: Kent's Corner #18/BP
Gas N: El Cheapo◇
Food S: Rest/Kent's

(35) — Weigh Station (EB)

39 — US 178, Orangeburg Rd, Batesburg, Leesville

FStop N: Mr B's Exxon
TStop S: Hill View Truck Stop/BP
Food N: Mr B's Grill
S: Rest/FastFood/Hill View TS
TServ S: Hill View TS/Tires
Other S: **Cedar Pond Campground▲**

44 — SC 34, Gilbert

TStop N: 44 Truck Stop/Citgo
Food N: Rest/44 TS
TServ N: 44 TS/Tires

51 — SC 204, Lexington, Gilbert

FStop S: Pitt Stop #38/Mobil
TStop N: Pitt Stop #15/Shell
Gas N: Exxon◇
Food N: FastFood/Pitt Stop
S: Subway, Gertie's

(53) — Weigh Station (WB)

55A — SC 6, E to Swansea

55B — SC 6, W to Lexington

55 — SC 6, Lexington, Swansea (EB)

FStop S: Kangaroo Express #3254/BP
Gas N: Shell

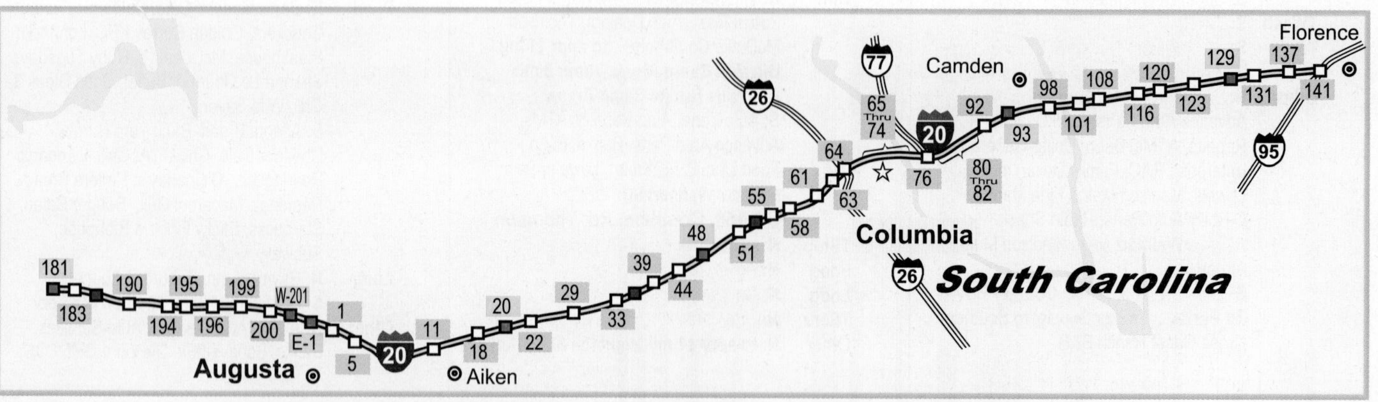

◇= Regular Gas Stations with Diesel ▲ = RV Friendly Locations ♥ = Pet Friendly Locations
Red print shows large vehicle parking / access on site or nearby Brown Print = Campgrounds / RV PARKS

EXIT		SOUTH CAROLINA
	Gas	S: Citgo, Kangaroo◈
	Food	N: Hardee's S: McDonald's, Subway, Waffle House, Wendy's
	Lodg	N: Comfort Inn, Hampton Inn S: Ramada Inn
	Other	S: ATM, Auto Repairs, Bank, CVS, Piggly Wiggly Grocery, Day Star Truck & Trailer Repair, Lexington Comm'l Tire, **John's RV Sales & Service, Ken's Bus Repair, Tony's RV Parts & Services to appr 6mi: Edmund RV Park▲**,
58		**US 1, Augusta Rd, Lexington**
	TStop	N: Pitt Stop #6/Shell S: The 1 Truck Stop
	Gas	N: Exxon
	Food	N: FastFood/Pitt Stop, Waffle House S: Burger King, McDonald's, KFC
	Lodg	N: to appr 3 mi: Comfort Suites, Hampton Inn, Quality Inn S: Value Place
	Other	N: Auto Repairs, 84 Lumber, Bowling, Franks Discount Tire, Millcreek Animal Hospital♥, **Police Dept, Sheriff Dept** S: Auto Repair, Auto Rental, County Tire, Four Oaks Farm Old Timey Country Store, to Columbia Airport✈, Univ of SC, Barnyard Flea Market, **Barnyard RV Park▲**, **S to I-26**
61		**US 378, Sunset Blvd, Lexington, (Most Serv N 2-3mi on US 378)**
	Gas	N: Exxon S: 76, AmocoBP◈
	Food	N: Bellacino's Pizza & Grinders, Chili's, ChickFilA, Dominos Pizza, Hardee's/Exxon, Hudson's Smokehouse BBQ, IHOP, Papa John's Pizza, Ruby Tuesday, Taco Bell, Travinia Italian Kitchen, Wings & Ale S: Waffle House
	Med	S: + Lexington Medical Center
	Other	N: ATMs, AT&T, Auto Dealers, Auto Services, Banks, Best Buy, BooksAMillion, CVS, Cherokee Trail Veterinary Hospital♥, Food Lion, Honda, Hope Ferry Pet Hospital♥, Lowe's, Mountain Top **RV** & Marine, Office Depot, PakMail, **Sunset RV's**, Target, **Walmart** sc, World Market S: Lexington Automotive & Truck
63		**SC 273, Bush River Rd, Columbia**
	Gas	N: Circle K/76◈ S: Kangaroo Express/Citgo, Raceway
	Food	N: Burger King, **Cracker Barrel**, Subway, Wings & Ale, S: El Chico Cafe Mexican, Fuddrucker's, Waffle House
	Lodg	N: Travelodge, Wingate S: Best Western, Courtyard, Knights Inn♥, Radisson, Sleep Inn
	Other	N: CVS, Carwash/Circle K, S: Advance Auto Parts, AMF Bowling Center, Bush River Mall, CVS, Carwash/ Citgo, **Walmart** SC, **to I-26**
(64A)		**Jct I-26, US 76E, to Columbia**
(64B)		**Jct I-26, US 76W, to Greenville, Spartanburg**
65		**US 176, Broad River Rd, Columbia**
	Gas	N: Circle K/76, Exxon S: Hess, RaceWay
	Food	N: Applebee's, Bojangles, Monterey Mex Rest, Subway, Waffle House

EXIT		SOUTH CAROLINA
	Food	S: Arby's, ChickFilA, Church's Chicken, Cracker Jack's, Captain Tom's Seafood, Dunkin Donuts, Golden Corral, Godfathers Pizza, Hooters, KFC, Lizard's Thicket, McDonald's, Pizza Hut, Ruby Tuesday, Touch Of India, Wendy's
	Lodg	N: Economy Inn, Rodeway Inn S: American Inn, Homewood Suites, InTowne Suites, Quality Inn♥, Ramada Ltd, Royal Inn
	Other	N: Aamco, Auto & Tire Services, Carwash, CVS, Family Dollar, Jiffy Lube, Laundromat, O'Reilly Auto Parts, US Post Office, U-Haul, Walgreen's, S: ATMs, Advance Auto Parts, Bank, Budget Truck Rental, CVS, Dutch Square Mall, Family Dollar, Food Lion, Jiffy Lube, Pep Boys, Radio Shack, RiteAid, **S to I-126**
68		**SC 215, Monticello Rd, Columbia, to Jenkinsville**
	FStop	N: Pitt Stop #10/Shell
	Gas	N: Exxon◈ S: Shell
	Food	N: Sunrise Rest & Cafe
	Other	N: A-1 Diesel Repair, Auto Repair, Jimmy's General Repairs/Tires, to Columbia Int'l Univ
70		**US 321, Fairfield Rd, Columbia, Winnsboro**
	TStop	S: Flying J Travel Plaza #5031/Conoco (Scales)
	Gas	S: Exxon
	Food	S: Rest/FastFood/FJ TP, Hardee's
	Lodg	S: Super 8♥
	TWash	S: Frontier Truck Wash
	Other	S: Laundry/BarbSh/WiFi/**LP/RVDump**/ FJ TP
71		**US 21, N Main St, Columbia**
	TStop	N: PTP/Columbia Travel Center/Exxon (Scales)
	Gas	N: BP◈ S: Shell
	Food	N: Rest/PizzaHut/Subway/Col TC, McDonald's
	Lodg	N: Days Inn
	TWash	N: Col TC
	TServ	N: Col TC/Tires
	Other	N: Laundry/WiFi/**LP**/Col TC
72		**SC 555, Farrow Rd**
73A		**SC 277S, Columbia**
73B		**SC 277N, to I-77N, to Charlotte**
74		**US 1, Two Notch Rd, to I-77, Columbia, to Ft Jackson**
	Gas	N: BP, Exxon◈, Kangaroo, Shell S: ArcoAmPm, Hess◈, Exxon, Shell◈
	Food	N: Arby's, Burger King, Chili's, Denny's, Hops Grill, IHOP, Outback Steakhouse, Waffle House S: Applebee's, Bojangles, Captain D's, Charleston Crabhouse, ChickFilA, Hardee's, McDonald's, Monterrey Mexican, O'Charley's, Santa Fe Mexican, Shoney's, Texas Roadhouse Grill, Wendy's, Western Sizzlin
	Lodg	N: Comfort Suites, Econo Lodge, Fairfield Inn, Hampton Inn, Holiday Inn, InTowne Suites, Jameson Inn, La Quinta Inn♥,

EXIT		SOUTH CAROLINA
	Lodg	N: Microtel, Motel 6♥, Quality Inn, Ramada Plaza, Red Roof Inn♥, Travelodge, Wingate Inn S: Days Inn♥
	Med	N: + Richland Memorial Hospital
	Other	N: ATMs, Banks, Bowling, Home Depot, U-Haul, US Post Office, Big Lots, RiteAid, Walgreen's, **to Sesquicentennial State Park▲, to I-77** S: ATMs, Banks, Advance Auto Parts, Auto Services, Auto Zone, Best Buy, Columbia Place Mall, Dollar Tree, Family Dollar, FedEx Office, Firestone, Fred's, Kmart/Pharmacy, Lowe's, Marshall's, NAPA, O'Reilly Auto Parts, Radio Shack, Sears, Staples, Theatres, U-Haul, Verizon,
(76)		**Jct I-77, Charlotte, Charleston (EB)**
(76A)		**Jct I-77, N-Charlotte, S-Charleston**
76B		**SC 63, Alpine Rd, to Fort Jackson**
	Food	S: Little Pig BBQ, Pizza Hut
	Other	N: **Sesquicentennial State Park▲** S: BBQ, Fort Jackson Mil Res
80		**Clemson Rd, Columbia**
	Gas	N: 76/Circle K, Exxon◈, Shell◈ S: Circle K
	Food	N: McDonald, San Jose Mexican, Solstice Kitchen, Sumo Japanese Steakhouse, Travinia Italian Kitchen, Waffle House, Zaxby's S: Bojangles Chicken, Wendy's
	Lodg	N: Hampton Inn, Holiday Inn Express
	Other	N: CVS S: U-Haul
82		**SC 53, Pierce Rd, Elgin, Pontiac**
	Gas	N: Shell
	Food	N: Piccadilly Pizza
	Lodg	N: Value Place
87		**SC 47, White Pond Rd, Elgin**
	FStop	N: BP
	Gas	N: Texaco◈
92		**US 601, to Lugoff, Camden**
	TStop	N: Pilot Travel Center #346 (Scales)
	Gas	N: Shell◈
	Food	N: DQ/Subway/Pilot TC, Hardee's, Waffle House
	Lodg	N: Days Inn, Econo Lodge♥, Ramada Ltd♥,
	Other	N: WiFi/Pilot TC, Auto Dealers, **Addtl Food & Services N to US 601** **S: Columbia/Camden RV Park▲**
(93)		**Rest Area (Both dir) (RR, Phone, Vend, Pet)**
98		**US 521, to Camden, Sumter**
	Gas	N: BP, Citgo, Shell
	Lodg	N: Comfort Inn, Holiday Inn Express
	Med	N: + Hospital
101		**SC 329, to Camden**
108		**SC 31, to SC 34, Bishopville, to Manville, Jamestown**
	Gas	N: BP S: Citgo◈
116		**US 15, Sumter Hwy, Bishopville, Sumter, to Hartsville**
	TStop	N: Interstate Shell S: WilcoHess Travel Plaza #935 (Scales)
	Food	N: FastFood/Shell, McDonald's, Pizza Hut, Subway, Waffle House, Zaxby's

◈= Regular Gas Stations with Diesel ▲ = RV Friendly Locations ♥= Pet Friendly Locations
Red print shows large vehicle parking / access on site or nearby **Brown Print = Campgrounds / RV PARKS**

EXIT		SOUTH CAROLINA
		S: DQ/Wendy's/WilcoHess
	Lodg	N: Econo Lodge
	Other	N: Laundry/Interstate Shell
120		**SC 341, Bishopville, Lynchburg, Lake City, Elliot**
	FStop	S: A&T Quik Stop/Exxon
	Food	S: A Taste of Country/A&T QS
	Lodg	S: Best Value Inn
	Other	S: LP/A&T QS

EXIT		SOUTH CAROLINA
123		**SC 22, Lamar, Lee State Park**
	Other	N: Lee State Park▲
(129)		Parking Area (Both dir)
131		**US 401, SC 403, Timmonsville, to Darlington, Lamar**
	Gas	N: Exxon◈
	Other	N: to Darlington Int'l Raceway
137		**SC 340, to Darlington**
	Gas	S: Marathon

EXIT	SOUTH CAROLINA
(141AB)	**Jct I-95, N - Fayetteville (LEFT Exit), S - Savannah**

NOTE: I-20 starts/ends on I-95, Exit #160

EASTERN TIME ZONE

⬆ SOUTH CAROLINA

Begin I-20 Westbound from Jct I-95 in Florence, SC to Jct I-55 at Jackson, MS.

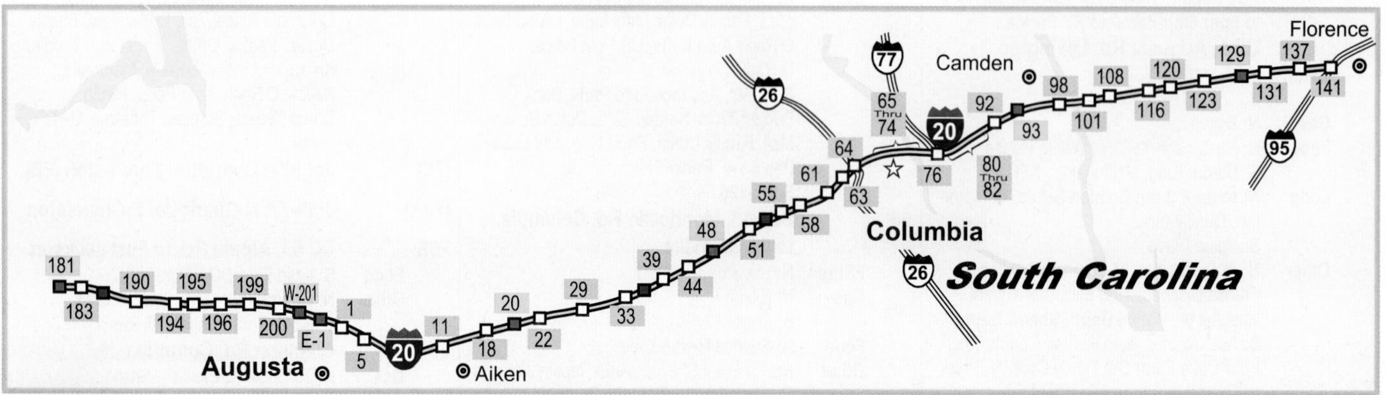

EXIT		TENNESSEE

Begin FUTURE I-22 from US 78 near Memphis, TN to Jct I -65 near Birmingham, AL.

⬇ TENNESSEE

CENTRAL TIME ZONE

FUTURE I-22 / US 78 / Corridor X is slated to begin at either I-55/I-69, Future I-269, or I-240 to the S/SE of Memphis, TN and continue to I-65 N of Birmingham, AL. When completed, I-22 will follow the US 78 Corridor from Memphis, TN to Birmingham, AL. Construction is expected Thru 2014.

EXIT		TENNESSEE
NA		**TN 175, E Shelby Dr, to I-55/I-69**
	TStop	N: Circle K Truck Stop/BP S: Pilot Travel Center #363 (Scales), Pilot Travel Center #405 (Scales), Coastal Truck Stop/Citgo
	Food	N: Wendy's S: Arby's/Pilot TC, Subway/Pilot TC, Church's/Citgo,
	Lodg	N: Best Western♥

EXIT		TN / MS
	Other	S: Custom Springs, U-Haul, to approx 5 mi: Memphis Int'l Airport✈, Jct I-55/I-69
NA		**E Holmes Rd, Memphis**
	TServ	N: Crow's Truck Service
NA		**Old US 78, Davidson Rd, Lamar Ave**
	Other	N: Southern Tire Mart

CENTRAL TIME ZONE

NOTE: MM : MS State Line

⬆ TENNESSEE

⬇ MISSISSIPPI

CENTRAL TIME ZONE

NOTE: Expect construction thru 2012. Most construction complete in MS, with the exception of the Future I-269 Connection to I-55.

EXIT		MISSISSIPPI

NOTE: MM 0: MS/TN State Line, Begin/End I-22. WB continues as US 78.

EXIT		MISSISSIPPI
1		**Craft Rd, Olive Branch, to MS 178 (Acc to #2 Serv)**
	Other	N: American RV Sales & Service,
2		**MS 302, Goodman Rd, MS 305, Olive Branch, to Southaven**
	Gas	N: to Chevron, Kangaroo/Shell S: Chevron, Circle K/Shell, Kroger
	Food	N: Abbay's Buffalo Wild Wings, ChickFilA, Chili's, Colton's Steakhouse, Dominos Pizza, IHOP, Krystal, McAlister's Deli, Mi Pueblo Mexican, O'Charley's, Old Towne Bakery, Quiznos, Sonic, Starbucks, wendys S: Applebees, Backyard Burger, BBQ Pit, Burger King, Casa Mexicana, Kyoto Steak House, McDonald's, Subway, Taco Bell, Waffle House, Zaxby's
	Lodg	N: Candlewood Suites♥, Comfort Suites, to Fairfield Inn, Whispering Woods Hotel S: Comfort Inn, Hampton Inn, Magnolia Inn/Olive Branch♥,

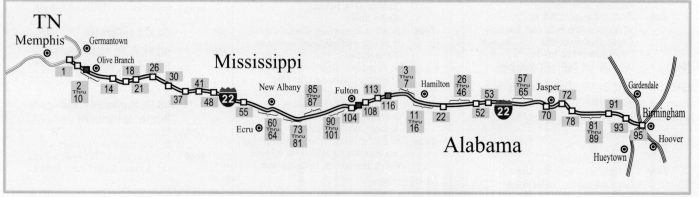

TN
Memphis
Germantown
Olive Branch
Mississippi
New Albany
Ecru
Fulton
Hamilton
Jasper
Alabama
Gardendale
Birmingham
Hoover
Hueytown

◈= Regular Gas Stations with Diesel ▲ = RV Friendly Locations ♥= Pet Friendly Locations
Red print shows large vehicle parking / access on site or nearby Brown Print = Campgrounds / RV PARKS

EXIT		MISSISSIPPI
	Other	N: Auto Dealers, Dollar Tree, Home Depot, to Holiday Golf Course, Jiffy Lube, Lowe's, To Olive Branch Airport✈, Penske Truck Rental, Radio Shack, **South Haven RV Center**, **Walmart sc**,
	Other	S: Advance Auto Parts, All Animal Hospital♥, AT&T, Auto Zone, Enterprise RAC, Goodyear, Kroger, NAPA, O'Reilly Auto Parts, Raleigh Tire & Auto Service Center, Super D Drug Store, Target, UPS Store, Walgreen's,
(3)		**Weigh Station** (Both dir)
4		**MS 305, Cockrum Rd, Olive Branch, Independence**
	Gas	N: BP◈, Circle K/Shell, Mobil, S: BP
	Food	N: Huddle House/Mobil, Old Style BBQ, Pizza Hut, Red Sun Chinese, Sweet Pea's Table, Wray's Fins & Feathers S: Quiznos/BP
	Lodg	N: Holiday Inn Express♥,
	Other	N: Dollar General, Piggly Wiggly Grocery, U-Haul, US Post Office
6		**Hacks Cross Rd, Bethel Rd, to MS 302, TN 385, E Memphis**
	TStop	N: Flying J Travel Plaza #677/Conoco (Scales)
	Gas	N: BP, GAS
	Food	N: FastFood/Flying J TP, Baskin Robbins/ GAS, Tops BBQ
	Lodg	N: Best Western, Super 8, **to** Fairfield Inn, Whispering Woods Hotel
	TServ	N: Angel's Truck Service,
	Other	N: Laundry/WiFi/**RVDump/LP**/Flying J TP, Southern States Utility Trailer Sales, Tires, **To appr 2.5 mi:** Olive Branch Animal Clinic♥ S: **to appr 1.5 mi:** Cat & Cow Veterinary Clinic♥
10		**Ingrams Mill, West Byhalia**
	Gas	N: Taylor's Conv Store/Chevron
14		**MS 309, Byhalia**
	TStop	N: Shell Truck Stop
	Gas	N: Gas Mart #,
	Food	N: Chesters/Pizza/Gas Mart, Pattycakes, Seafood Junction Too, Whistle Stop
	Lodg	N: Americas Best Value Inn♥
	Other	N: Carwash/Gas Mart,
18		**Victoria Rd, East Byhalia**
	Gas	N: BP
	Other	N: US Post Office
21		**Red Banks Rd, Red Banks**
	TStop	N: Dee's Express
	Gas	N: Texaco
	Other	N: **to** Holly Springs Marshall Co Airport✈
26		**West Holly Springs**
	Other	N: **to** Holly Springs Marshall Co Airport✈
30		**MS 4, MS 7, Holly Springs, Oxford To Senatobia via MS 7**
	Gas	N: Exxon◈, Shell, S: Exxon
	Food	N: Chesters/BBQ/Shell, El Nopalito Mex, Good Fellas Bar&Grill, Huddle House, JB's Rest, KFC, McDonald's, Michael's Country Creole, Panda Buffet, Pizza Hut, Popeye's Chicken, Subway, Victor's Pizza
	Lodg	N: Court Square Inn B&B, Magnolia Inn S: Days Inn♥, Le Brooks Inn♥
	Other	N: Banks, Hibbett Sports, Shell Rapid Lube, **to** Rust College

EXIT		MISSISSIPPI
	Other	S: Bank, Carwash/Exxon, Holly Springs Motor Sports Dragstrip, **Walmart sc**, **to appr 5 mi: Wall Doxey State Park ▲**
37		**CCC Rd, to MS 178, Lake Center**
41		**to MS 178, MS 349, Potts Camp**
	FStop	S: Flick's Amoco/BP
	Gas	S: Corner Quick Stop, Potts Camp OneStop
	Other	S: Bank, Carwash/BP, NAPA, US Post Office
48		**MS 178, Hickory Flat, to MS 2, MS 5**
	TStop	S: C & T Truck Stop/Hwy 78 TS (Scales)
	Food	S: Rest/C&T TS
	Other	N: US Post Office, **to appr 12 mi:** Yesteryear Lodge, **Little Snow Creek RV Park ▲** S: Laundry/C&T TS
55		**CR 515, Willow Dr, Myrtle**
60		**Munsford Dr, to MS 178, MS 30, Glenfield, New Albany** (acc to #61)
	Gas	N: Dave's One Stop/Pure, Tony's Quik Mart
	Lodg	N: Budget Inn♥
	Other	N: Friendly City Tire & Auto Service Center, Union Co Fairgrounds & Arena, **to appr 2.5 mi:** New Albany Union Co Airport✈,
61		**MS 30W, West New Albany, Oxford**
	TStop	S: **to 926 MS 30:** Regal Truck Stop
	Gas	N: Exxon S: Exxon, Shell, Murphy USA,
	Food	N: Betty's, McAlister's Deli, McDonald's, Pizza Hut, Subway, Wendy's S: Rest/Regal TS, Baskin Robbins/Shell, Burger King, Captain D's, China Buffet, Dominos Pizza, Huddle House, KFC, Mi Pueblo, Taco Bell, Western Sizzlin
	Lodg	N: Hampton Inn♥ S: Comfort Inn♥, Economy Inn♥, Hallmarc Inn, Holiday Inn Express♥
	Med	N: + **Baptist Memorial Hospital**
	Other	N: Action Lanes Bowling, Banks, Carwash, Dollar General, RiteAid, Walgreen's, S: Laundry/WiFi/TrlrWash/Regal TS, Dollar Tree, **Walmart sc**,
63		**Bratton Rd (EB), Central Ave, Carter Ave, Downtown Albany (WB)**
	Other	N: Auto Dealers, U-Haul S: Dollar Tree, Hibbett Sports, Lowe's, **MS State Hwy Patrol Post**, **Acc to #61**
64		**MS 15, MS 30E, to MS 178, New Albany, to Pontotoc, Ripley**
	TStop	S: Pilot Travel Center #174 (Scales), Kangaroo Express/Shell
	Gas	N: BP, Chevron◈
	Food	N: George's Rest, Westside BBQ S: Arby's/TJCinn/Pilot TC,
	Lodg	N: Hallmarc Inn
	Other	N: Dollar General, US Post Office S: Laundry/WiFi/Pilot TC, Greyhound
73		**MS 9N, Blue Springs, Toyota Plant**
76		**MS 9S, MS 178, Sherman, Pontotoc, Toyota Plant**
	FStop	N: Wild Bill's Truck Stop (DAND)
	Food	N: Rest/Wild Bill's TS, Cravin Catfish,
	Other	N: **Sherman RV Center**, US Post Office S: **to Trace State Park▲**
81		**MS 178, McCullough Blvd, W Tupelo**
	NOTE:	NB: Low Clearance 13'4
	TStop	N: Love's Travel Stop #398 S: Express Stop Travel Center/Exxon
	Gas	S: Endville Gen'l Store, NT's/Fina, GAS

EXIT		MISSISSIPPI
	Food	N: McDonald's/Subway/Love's TS S: Rest/Express Stop TC,
	Lodg	S: Super 8♥
	Other	S: Laundry/Express Stop TC, **to** Tupelo Buffalo Park & Zoo, Tupelo Reg'l Airport✈
85		**Natchez Trace Pkwy**
86A		**US 45S, Corridor V West, MLK Dr, To MS 145/178, Tupelo, to Shannon (Acc Serv S to McCullough Blvd/MS178 & on MS 145/Gloster St)**
	Gas	S: Exxon, Sprint/Shell, Texaco
	Food	S: Outback Steakhouse, Shogun Japanese, Shoney's, Vanelli's Rest, Waffle House
	Lodg	S: Baymont Inn, Comfort Inn♥, Comfort Suites, Clarion Inn, Courtyard, Days Inn, Economy Inn, Hampton Inn, Howard Johnson Express♥, La Quinta Inn♥, Microtel, Motel 6♥, Quality Inn, Ramada, Sleep Inn, Travelodge, Travelers Motel
	Other	S: Banks, UPS Store, to Noble Stadium, **to** Tupelo Buffalo Park & Zoo, Tupelo Reg'l Airport✈, **Natchez Trace RV Park▲**
86B		**US 45N, MLK Dr, Corridor V West, MS 145, Tupelo, to Corinth (Acc Most Serv 1st Ex N to N Gloster St)**
	FStop	NE: T-Mart #3/Texaco,
	Gas	NW: BP, Shell, Kroger, Sam's
	Food	NE: **Cracker Barrel**, NW: Abner's, Applebee's, Burger King, Captain D's, ChickFilA, Chili's, Chuck E E Cheese's Pizza, CiCi's Pizza, Food Court, Kyoto Japanese Rest, Logan's Roadhouse, McDonald's, Newk's Express Cafe, O'Charley's, Olive Garden, Pizza Hut, Red Lobster, Ryan's Grill, Subway, Taco Bell, Wendy's
	Lodg	N: Americas Best Inn♥,
	Med	NE: **+ Urgent Care Clinic**
	Other	NE: Home Depot, PetSmart♥, Staples, NW: AT&T, Auto Dealers, Banks, Barnes & Noble, Best Buy, BooksAMillion, carwash, Shell, Dick's Sporting Goods, Dollar Tree, Hobby Lobby, Kohl's, Kroger/Pharmacy, Lowe's, Mall at Barnes Crossing, Midas, NAPA, Office Max, Ross, Sam's Club, TJ Maxx, Verizon, Walgreen's, **Walmart sc**, **Campground at Barnes Crossing▲**
87		**Veterans Blvd, to MS 178, Tupelo (Addt'l Serv S to MS 178/Main St)**
	TStop	N: Sprint Mart #47/Shell, One Stop
	Food	N: Huddle House,
	Lodg	N: Wingate Inn
	Other	S: to Elvis's Birthplace/Museum
90		**Auburn Rd, Tupelo (Addt'l Serv S to MS 178)**
	Gas	S: Kirby's BP◈
	Other	S: **to Tombigbee State Park▲**
94		**MS 371, to MS 178, Mantachie, Mooreville**
	Gas	N: **Woco**◈ S: Mooreville One Stop, Short Stop,
	Other	S: US Post Office, **to Tombigbee State Park▲**
97		**Fawn Grove Rd, Dorsey**
101		**MS 178, MS 363, Peppertown, Mantachie**
	Gas	N: BP, Exxon S: **to appr 2mi:** Dorsey Food Mart◈
	Other	N: Midway Marine

EXIT		MS / AL
104		**MS 25S, Adams St, Fulton, Amory**
	TStop	N: Sprint Mart #9/Shell (Scales)
	Gas	N: Pit Stop◈
		S: Murphy USA◈,
	Food	N: Rest/Sprint Mart, Burger Kings, Hardees Huddle House, McDonald's, Sonic, Subway
		S: Mexican Rest, Pizza Hut, Wendy's,
	Lodg	N: Days Inn
	Other	N: Auto Zone, Fred's, O'Reilly Auto Parts, **to appr 4 mi: COE/Jamie L Whitten Historical Center Park/Whitten Park Campground/RVDump▲**
		S: Walmart sc,
(107)		**Weigh Station** (Both dir)
108		**MS 25N, Corridor V East, Fulton, Belmont, Iuka**
113		**MS 23, Tremont, Smithville**
(116)		**MS Welcome Center** (WB) (RR, Phone, Pic, Vend, **RVDump**)

CENTRAL TIME ZONE

NOTE: MM 118: AL State Line

MISSISSIPPI

ALABAMA

CENTRAL TIME ZONE

EXIT		ALABAMA
3		**CR 33, Bexar**
7		**CR 94, to AL 74, US 278E, AL 19, Hamilton** (acc #11-16 via N to AL 74)
	Lodg	N: to appr 3mi: Hamilton Holiday Motel
11		**AL 17, to AL 19, Hamilton, Sulligent**
	TStop	N: K&A Citgo/Martin Food Mart #5
	Gas	N: to Chevron, Shell
	Food	S: Oh Bryan's Family Steakhouse
14		**CR 35, to AL 171, US 43, US 278, Hamilton** (Acc to #16 N Serv)
	FStop	**N: to US 278/4677 Bexar Ave appr 6.5 mi:** Moore's Sugarbend Shell
	TStop	N: WOCO
	Food	N: Huddle House
	Lodg	N: Key West Inn, to Days Inn♥,
	Other	N: to Marion Co Rankin Fite Airport✈,
16		**Military St, US 43, US 278, AL 171, Hamilton, Guin**
	FStop	N: to 195 1st St SE: Watha's, **N appr 5mi** To 26211 US 43/AL 187: Harpers Junction
	TStop	S: Moore's Shell Super Store (Scales)
	Food	N: Burger King,
		S: Rest/Moore's Shell
	Lodg	N: Days Inn♥, Econo Lodge
	Other	**N: AL State Hwy Patrol Post,** To Auto Zone, Pharmacy, **Walmart sc,**
		S: Laundry/**LP**/Moore's Shell
22		**CR 45, to AL 253, to US 278**
26		**AL 44, Brilliant, Guin, Twin**
30		**AL 129, Winfield, Brilliant**
	TStop	S: Token #19/Texaco
	Gas	S: Shell
34		**AL 233, Glen Allen, Natural Bridge**
39		**AL 13, Natural Bridge, Eldridge via AL 13S to Fayette, Tuscaloosa**
	Gas	S: to Parade/Barbara Ann's Place◈
	Food	S: Cafe/Parade
46		**CR 11, Nauvoo Rd, to AL 118, Carbon Hill** (Addt'l Serv appr 2 mi S to AL 118)
	Gas	S: Mill Creek Grocery/Pure, Shell
52		**AL 118, Carbon Hill** (acc #46)
53		**Future AL 102, to AL 118**
57		**AL 118E, Jasper** (Many Serv on AL 118 appr 4mi)
	Gas	N: Chevron, Exxon
61		**AL 69, Jasper, Tuscaloosa**
	Gas	N: 69 Superstop
	Other	S: to Area Head Golf Course
63		**AL 269, Jasper, Parrish**
	Gas	N: Chevron◈, Star Mart
65		**Industrial Parkway Rd, to AL 5**
	Other	S: Auto Dealer
70		**CR 22, Cordova, to Parrish, Jasper**
72		**CR 61, Cordova**
78		**CR 81, Flat Creek Rd, Dora, Sumiton**
81		**CR 45, West Jefferson, Access to AL Power Miller Steam Plant**
85		**US 78, Birmingham, Adamsville, Graysville, AL 5, Sumiton, Dora**
87		**CR 112, Graysville**
89		**CR 65, Hillcrest Rd, Minor Pkwy, Adamsville, Graysville**
91		**CR 105, Cherry Ave, to US 78, AL 4, To Brookside, Forestdale**
93		**CR 77, N to Coalburg, S to Birmingham**

NOTE: EB: Expect construction thru Fall 2014

(95)		**Jct I-65, Birmingham, Huntsville**

NOTE: WB: Expect construction thru 2014

ALABAMA

Begin I-22 from Jct I-65 near Birmingham, AL to US 78 near Memphis, TN.

EXIT		ILLINOIS

Begin I-24 Eastbound at Jct I-57 near Marion, IL to Chattanooga, TN

ILLINOIS

CENTRAL TIME ZONE

NOTE: I-24 begins/ends on I-57, Exit #44

EXIT		ILLINOIS
(1)		**Jct I-57, N - Chicago, S - Memphis**
7		**CR 12, Tunnel Hill Rd, Goreville, Tunnel Hill**
	FStop	N: Citgo
	Other	N: to Bella Terra Winery
		S: Ferne Clyffe State Park▲
14		**US 45, N 1st St, to IL 146,Vienna, To Harrisburg** (Acc to Ex #16 S Serv)
	Gas	S: Casey's, Citgo
	Food	S: Pizza/Casey's
	Other	**N: to Shawnee Nat'l Forest, Cedar Lake Campground▲**
		S: Family Dollar, IGA, Carwash
16		**IL 146, Vienna, Golconda**
	Gas	S: BP◈, Citgo, Gas & Go◈
	Food	N: Gambit Steakhouse
		S: DQ, McDonald's, Subway
	Lodg	N: Gambit Inn
		S: Limited Inn
	Other	N: Gambit Golf Course
		S: Carwash, Shawnee Winery Co-Op, U-Haul
27		**CR 10, Metropolis, New Columbia Big Bay**
37		**US 45, Metropolis, Brookport**
	FStop	N: Short Stop #4/Citgo
	TStop	S: Metropolis Truck & Travel Plaza/BP
	Food	S: Rest/Metropolis TTP, Huddle House, Pizza Hut, Quiznos
	Lodg	S: Comfort Inn, Holiday Inn Express, Metropolis Inn, Super 8
	TServ	N: Short Stop
		S: Metropolis T&TP
	Med	S: + Hospital
	Other	S: Auto Dealers, ATMs, Banks, Carwash, Dayton Tire, O'Reilly Auto Parts, Metropolis Muni Airport✈, **to** Museum, Attractions, **Casinos, Fort Massac State Park▲**
(37)		**IL Welcome Center** (Both dir) (RR, Phone, Picnic, Vend, Info)

CENTRAL TIME ZONE

ILLINOIS

KENTUCKY

CENTRAL TIME ZONE

EXIT		IL / KY
3		**KY 305, Cairo Rd, Paducah**
	FStop	S: Cheers Food & Fuel #136
	TStop	N: Max Fuel Express #33/Exit 3 Travel Plaza/BP (Scales)
		S: Pilot Travel Center #358 (Scales)
	Food	N: Rest/FastFood/Exit 3 TP
		S: Subway/Pilot TC, VariousRest/Cheers,

◈ = Regular Gas Stations with Diesel ▲ = RV Friendly Locations ♥ = Pet Friendly Locations
Red print shows large vehicle parking / access on site or nearby Brown Print = Campgrounds / RV PARKS

EXIT	KENTUCKY
	Waffle Hut, Yu's Kitchen
Lodg	N: America's Best Value Inn♥, Comfort Inn, Econo Lodge♥
	S: Baymont Inn♥
TWash	N: MFE/Exit 3 TP
TServ	N: MFE/Exit 3 TP/Tires, A & K Truck Repair
	S: Whayne Power System
Other	N: Laundry/WiFi/Exit 3 TP
	S: Laundry/WiFi/Pilot TC, **Fern Lake Campground▲**
4	**US 60, Bus Lp 24, Hinkleville Rd, Paducah, Wickliffe**
Gas	N: Shell◈, Gas
	S: BP, Citgo, Exxon, Shell, Sam's, Murphy USA
Food	N: Applebee's, Bob Evans, Burger King, Denny's, McDonald's, O'Charley's, Outback Steakhouse, Rafferty's Rest
	S: Arby's, Backwoods BBQ, Captain D's, ChickFilA, Chong's Chinese Rest, Chuck E Cheese's Pizza, **Cracker Barrel**, Dominos Pizza, El Chico Mexican Rest, Hananoki Japanese Steakhouse, Hardee's, Logan's Roadhouse, McAlister's Deli, Olive Garden, Pasta House, Pizza Hut, Red Lobster, Ryan's Grill, Shoney's, Starbucks, Steak 'n Shake, Subway, Texas Roadhouse, TGI Friday, Wendy's
Lodg	N: Candlewood Suites, Courtyard, Days Inn, Drury Inn, Holiday Inn Express, Hampton Inn, Residence Inn
	S: Best Inns, Comfort Suites, Country Inn, Drury Suites, Motel 6♥, Pear Tree Inn/Drury, Thrifty Inn, Travelodge
TServ	S: McBridge Mack Truck Sales
Med	N: + to Hospital
	S: + Baptist Prime Care Walk-in Clinic
Other	N: Advance Auto Parts, Auto Dealers, Auto Repairs, Dollar General, Enterprise RAC, Hoopers Outdoor Center, Kroger/Pharmacy, US Post Office
	S: Advance Auto Parts, Aldi, ATMs, AT&T, Auto Services, Best Buy, Books A Million, Cinemark, Gander Mountain, Goodyear Auto, Hobby Lobby, Home Depot, Hibbett Sporting Goods, Kohl's, Kentucky Oaks Mall, Lowe's, Michael's, Office Depot, Office Max, PetSmart♥, Pharmacy, Purcell Tire, Radio Shack, Sam's Club, Verizon, Vet♥, **Walmart sc**, Mill Springs Fun Park, Barkley Reg'l Airport✈
(7)	**US 62, Alben Barkley Dr, Paducah, US 45, Lone Oak Rd**

EXIT	KENTUCKY
	KY Whitehaven Welcome Center
	S: (RR, Phones, Vend, Info)
Gas	N: BP◈, Citgo, Petro2, Shell◈
	S: BP◈, Shell◈, Supervalu, Supermax
Food	N: Burger King, Subway, Taco Bell
	S: Arby's, Backyard Burger, Golden Corral, Hardee's, McDonald's, Popeye's Chicken, Sonic, Waffle House
Lodg	N: Quality Inn
	S: Comfort Suites, Denton Motel
Med	N: + Lourdes Hospital, to + Western Baptist Hospital
Other	S: CVS, Gores IGA, Kmart, O'Reilly Auto Parts, Pharmacy, SuperValu Foods,
11	**KY 1954, Husband Rd, Paducah (Addtl Gas/Food/Lodg N to US 62)**
TStop	N: Exit 11 Exxon
Food	N: FastFood/Ex 11
Lodg	N: Best Western
TServ	N: Thurston Truck Parts
Other	N: Laundry/Ex 11, **Duck Creek RV Park▲**, Sportsmans Edge
	S: Four Rivers Harley Davidson, **to appr 2mi: Victory RV Park & Campground▲**
16	**US 68, Benton Rd, Paducah**
TStop	S: Max Fuel Express #35/Southern Pride Travel Plaza/BP (Scales)
Food	S: FastFood/Southern Pride TP
TWash	S: Southern Pride ATP
TServ	S: Southern Pride ATP/Tires
Other	N: Flanary Veterinary Clinic♥,
	S: Laundry/WiFi/CB/LP/SP ATP, Traders Flea Market, U-Haul
25AB	**Purchase Pkwy (TOLL), Fulton, Calvert City (Acc Serv 1mi N)**
27	**US 62, Calvert City, KY Dam**
TStop	S: Love's Travel Stop #348 (Scales)
Gas	N: Max Fuel #41/BP,
Food	N: Cracker Barrel, DQ, KFC, McDonald's, Waffle House
	S: Arby's/Love's TS
Lodg	N: Days Inn, Fox Fire Motor Inn, Super 8
	S: Ramada Inn Resort KY Dam
TServ	N: Duckett Truck Center, Freightliner
Other	N: Calvert Drive-In Theatre, **Cypress Lakes RV Park▲, Paducah/I-24 Ky Lake KOA▲, to LazyDaz RV Park▲**
	S: **Ky Dam Village State Resort Park▲**, Ky Dam State Airport✈
31	**KY 453, Grand Rivers, Smithland**
FStop	S: Cheers Food & Fuel #102
Gas	N: BP◈
Food	S: Diana's Family Rest, Miss Scarlett's Rest

EXIT	KENTUCKY
Lodg	N: Microtel
	S: Americas Best Value Inn
Other	S: **Exit 31 RV Park▲, to Lake Barkley Canal Rec Area▲**
(36)	**Lyon Co Weigh Station (Both dir)**
40	**US 62, US 641, Kuttawa, Eddyville**
FStop	S: Max Fuel Express #10/BP
TStop	S: AmBest/Huck's Travel Center #52 (Scales)
Gas	S: Shell
Food	N: Blue Grass Grill, Scoops Diner
	S: Rest/FastFood/Hucks TC, Wendy's/BP, Huddle House, Oasis Southwest Grill
Lodg	N: Country Hearth Inn, Relax Inn, Regency Inn
	S: Days Inn, Hampton Inn
Other	N: Bank, Dollar General, Food Giant, US Post Office, Venture River Water Park, Lake Barkley
	S: Laundry/WiFi/LP/RVDump/Huck's TC
42	**West KY Pkwy East, Eddyville, Princeton, Elizabethtown**
45	**KY 293, Eddyville, Princeton**
FStop	S: Max Fuel #122/Chevron
Lodg	S: Regency Inn
Other	**S: appr 1mi: Murphy RV, Murphy's Outback RV Resort▲, to Cedar Hill RV Park▲, Indian Point RV Park▲, Lake Barkley RV Resort▲, appr 2mi: Holiday Hills Resort▲, appr 4mi: Eddy Creek Marina Resort▲,**
56	**KY 139, Princeton, Cadiz**
FStop	S: Blue Spring Chevron
Other	**S: to Lake Barkley Hurricane Creek Rec Area▲, to Goose Hollow Campground▲, to appr 9mi: Ky Lakes/Prizer Point Marina & Resort KOA▲**
65	**US 68, KY 80, Hopkinsville Rd, Cadiz, Hopkinsville**
FStop	S: Max Fuel Express #9/Chevron,
Gas	S: Max Fuel Express #40/BP◈, Shell◈
Food	S: Cracker Barrel, KFC, Ky Smokehouse, McDonald's, Taco Bell, Wendy's
Lodg	S: Broadbent Inn & Suites♥, Knights Inn, Super 7 Inn,
Med	S: + Hospital
Other	S: Broadbent's B&B Foods, U-Haul, **Traveln Time RV Center, to Lake Barkley State Park Resort▲**
73	**KY 117, Hopkinsville, to Newstead, Gracey**

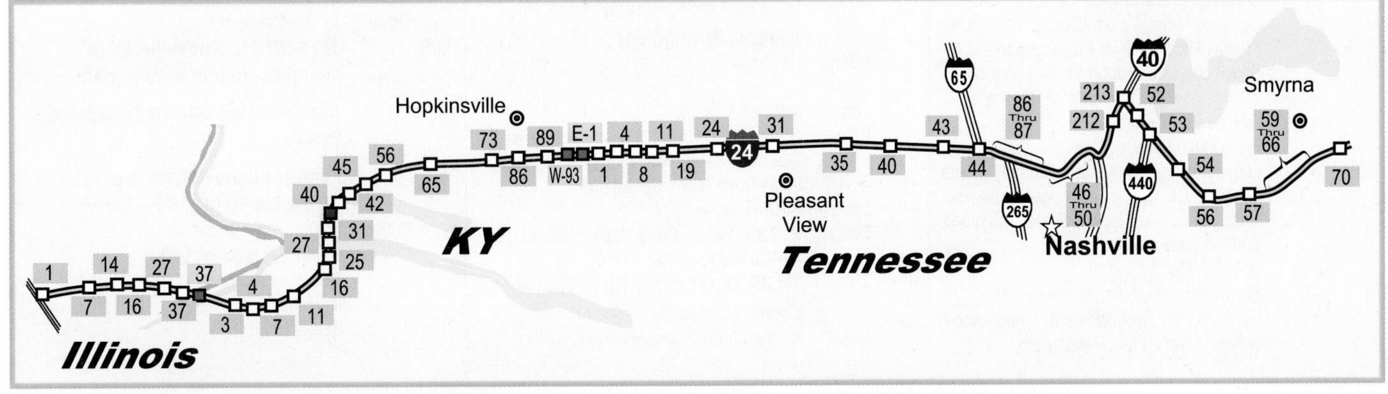

◈= Regular Gas Stations with Diesel ▲ = RV Friendly Locations ♥ = Pet Friendly Locations
Red print shows large vehicle parking / access on site or nearby Brown Print = Campgrounds / RV PARKS

EXIT		KY / TN
86		**US 41 Alt, Oak Grove, Hopkinsville, Fort Campbell**
	TStop	N: Max Fuel Express #24/I-24 Chevron Fuel Express (Scales) S: Flying J Travel Plaza #5058/Conoco (Scales), Pilot Travel Center #439
	Gas	S: BP◈
	Food	N: Chesters/I-24 Chevron FE S: CountryMkt/FastFood/FJ TP, Subway/Wendys/Pilot TC, Burger King, Great American Buffet, McDonald's, Waffle House
	Lodg	S: Days Inn, Holiday Inn Express, Quality Inn♥,
	Med	S: + Hospital
	Other	S: Laundry/WiFi/**LP/RVDump**/FJ TP, Laundry/WiFi/Pilot TC, Tourist Info, ATMs, Banks, Ft Campbell Mil Res, Ft Campbell Airfield✈
89		**KY 115, Pembroke, Oak Grove**
	TStop	S: Pilot Travel Center #49 (Scales)
	Gas	S: Shell◈
	Food	S: McDonald's/Pilot TC
	TWash	S: Pilot TC
	Other	S: Laundry/WiFi/Pilot TC, **to** Outlaw Field ✈
(93)		**KY Welcome Center (WB) (RR, Phone, Picnic, Pet, Vend)**

NOTE: MM 93.5: Tennessee State Line

CENTRAL TIME ZONE

⬆ KENTUCKY
⬇ TENNESSEE

CENTRAL TIME ZONE

EXIT		TENNESSEE
(1)		**TN Welcome Center (EB) (RR, Phone, Picnic, Vend)**
1		**TN 48, Clarksville, Trenton**
	Gas	N: Shell◈ S: BP, Mystic
	Food	S: El Tapito Cafe, Sonic
	Other	N: **Clarksville RV Park & Campground▲** S: Carwash, Dollar General, Shell Rapid Lube, Walgreen's, **to** Outlaw Field✈
4		**US 79, TN 13, Clarksville, Guthrie**
	Gas	N: BP◈, Sam's S: BP◈, Citgo◈, Shell◈, Murphy
	Food	N: **Cracker Barrel** S: Applebee's, Arby's, Baskin Robbins, Burger King, Captain D's, Chili's, Chuck E Cheese's Pizza, Church's Chicken, DQ, Dominos Pizza, Golden Corral, IHOP, KFC, Krystal, Little Caesars Pizza, Logan's Roadhouse, Long John Silver, Longhorn Steakhouse, McDonalds's, O'Charley's, Olive Garden, Outback Steakhouse, Pizza Hut, Quiznos, Rafferty's, Red Lobster, Ryan's Grill, Ruby Tuesday, Santa Fe Cattle Co, Shoney's, Shogun Japanese Rest, Starbucks, Steak N Shake, Taco Bell, Waffle House, Wendy's
	Lodg	N: Hilton Garden Inn S: Americas Best Inn, Americas Best Value Inn♥, Best Western, Candlewood Suites, Comfort Inn, Country Inn, Courtyard, Days Inn♥, Econo Lodge, Fairfield Inn, Guest House Inn, Hampton Inn, HomeTowne Suites♥, MainStay Suites, Microtel, Quality Inn♥, Ramada Ltd, Red Roof Inn♥, Super 8, Value Place, Wingate Inn
	Med	S: + Gateway Medical Center
	Other	N: Beachaven Vineyards & Winery, Sam's Club, Tractor Supply, **Clarksville RV Super Center, Spring Creek Campground▲** S: Advance Auto Parts, Auto Dealers, Auto Services, ATMs, AT&T, Banks, BA Wolfe Motorsports, Best Buy, Batteries Plus, BooksAMillion, Borders, Carmike Cinemas, Clarksville Tire, Enterprise RAC, Fabric Outlet, FedEx Office, Goodyear, Governors Square Mall, Hobby Lobby, Home Depot, Kmart, Kroger, Lowe's, Office Depot, O'Reilly Auto Parts, Putterz Golf & Games, PetSmart♥, Sprint, Target, Truck Repair, Tourist Center, U-Haul, US Post Office, Walgreen's, **Walmart sc**,
8		**TN 237, Rossview Rd (Acc to #8 and #4 N to Int'l Blvd)**
11		**TN 76, Dr MLK Jr Pky, Clarksville, Adams (Addtl Serv S to US 41)**
	FStop	N: Sudden Service/Shell S: BP
	Food	S: McDonald's, Michael's Pizza, Waffle House
	Lodge	S: Days Inn, Holiday Inn Express, Quality Inn, Super 8♥
	Med	S: + Hospital
	Other	S: Family Pet Hospital ♥, Mid-South Motoplex, Reliable Truck & Diesel, **Red River Campground▲**, **to** appr 3mi **US 41/Madison St:** Addtl Serv, **Walmart sc**
19		**TN 256, Maxey Rd, Cedar Hill, Springfield, Adams**
	Gas	N: BP◈ S: Shell◈
24		**TN 49, US 41A, Pleasant View, to Springfield, Ashland City**
	TStop	N: Mapco Express #1007
	Gas	N: BP◈, Phillips 66◈ S: Sudden Service Travel Plaza, Shell◈
	Food	S: BJ's Family Rest, Sonic, Subway, Wendy's/SS TP
	Other	S: CJ's Garage/P66, Dollar General, Grocery Store, Animal Hospital♥
31		**TN 249, New Hope Rd, Joelton**
	FStop	S: Daily's/Shell
	Gas	S: BP◈
	Food	S: FastFood/Shell, Taste of N'Awlins
	Other	S: Carwash, Sycamore Animal Hospital♥
35		**US 431, TN 65, Whites Creek Pike, Joelton, Springfield**
	FStop	S: Chip's Quik Stop/BP, Heritage Travel Center
	Gas	S: Shell
	Food	S: FastFood/Chips, Country Jct Rest, DQ, McDonald's, Mazatlan Mexican Rest, Pizza Done Right, Subway/BP
	Lodg	S: Days Inn♥
	Other	S: Bank, Family Dollar, US Post Office, **OK Campground▲**,
40		**TN 45, Old Hickory Blvd, Whites Creek, Nashville**
	Gas	N: Shell◈, Shell, Phillips 66◈
	Food	N: Subway/Shell
	Lodg	N: Super 8♥
	Other	N: Carwash/P66, **Addt'l Serv appr 3 mi N To Dickerson Rd, to** A Cowboy Town
43		**TN 155, Briley Pkwy, to Brick Church Pike, Dickerson Pike, US 41, US 31, Nashville**
(44AB)		**Jct I-65, to Nashville, Louisville**

NOTE: I-24 below runs w/I-65 thru Nashville. Exit #'s follow I-65.

EXIT		TENNESSEE
87		**US 431, Trinity Lane, Nashville**
	TStop	E: Love's Travel Stop #429 (Scales)
	Gas	E: Circle K, Phillips 66 W: BP, Chevron, Exxon, Shell, Texaco
	Food	E: Subway/Love's TS, Arby's, Krystal, White Castle W: Burger King, Captain D's, Denny's, Fatmo's Burgers, Jack in the Box, Jack's BBQ, McDonald's, Shoney's, Subway, Taco Bell, Waffle House
	Lodg	E: Cumberland Inn, Deluxe Inn, Trinity Inn, Scottish Inn W: Americas Best Value Inn, Days Inn, Econo Lodge♥, Hallmark Inn, Liberty Inn, Quality Inn♥, Regency Inn, Rodeway Inn♥,
	Med	W: + FHC Nashville
	Other	E: Laundry/WiFi/Pilot TC, Auto Service, Tires, **Holiday Mobile Village▲** W: Auto Services, American Baptist College, Family Dollar
(86)		**Jct I-24E, to I-40E, to Memphis**

NOTE: I-24 above runs w/I-65 thru Nashville, Exit #'s follow I-65.

EXIT		TENNESSEE
(46B)		**Jct I-65S, Nashville (Left Exit)**
47		**Jefferson St, Spring St, US 41**
	FStop	N: Pacific Pride
	Gas	N: Express◈ S: Citgo◈, Larry's Quick Stop◈
	Lodg	S: Days Inn, Knights Inn
	Other	S: U-Haul, Budget Truck Rental
47A		**US 41, US 431, Ellington Pkwy, Spring St (WB)**
48		**James Robertson Pkwy, Nashville**
	TStop	S: Travel Center of America #34 (Scales)
	Gas	N: Citgo, Shell
	Food	S: Buckhorn/TA TC, Shoney's
	Lodg	S: Ramada Inn, Stadium Inn
	TServ	S: TA TC/Tires
	Other	S: Laundry/WiFi/TA TC, ATM, Banks, **to** State Capitol, Titan Stadium
49		**Shelby Ave, Nashville**
	Gas	S: Exxon
	Other	S: The Coliseum
(50B)		**Jct I-40, E to Knoxville, W to Memphis, to I-65 Birmingham**

NOTE: I-24 below runs w/I-40 thru Nashville, Exit #'s follow I-40.

EXIT		TENNESSEE
212		**Fesslers Lane (EB, No re-entry) TN 24, US 70 (WB, No re-entry)**
	TStop	S: Daly's #604/Shell
	Food	N: Harley Davidson Grill S: Burger King, McDonald's, Wendy's
	Other	N: Harley Davidson S: Laundry/Daly's

◈= Regular Gas Stations with Diesel ▲ = RV Friendly Locations ♥= Pet Friendly Locations
Red print shows large vehicle parking / access on site or nearby Brown Print = Campgrounds / RV PARKS

213 **US 41 (WB), Spence Lane**
Gas N: Phillips 66◈
S: Shell
Food S: Denny's, Red Lobster, Shoney's

(213A) **Jct I-24E, Jct I-440E**

(213B) **Jct I-24W, Jct I-40W**

NOTE: **I-24 above runs w/I-40 thru Nashville, Exit #'s follow I-40.**

(52AB) **Jct I-40, E-Knoxville, W-Memphis**

52 **US 41, Murfreesboro Rd**
Gas N: BP, Shell, Texaco
Food N: Denny's, Golden Corral, Pizza Hut, Red Lobster, Taco Bell, Waffle House
Lodg N: Days Inn, Holiday Inn Express,Quality Inn, Ramada Inn, Scottish Inn
Other N: ATM, Bank, Office Depot, State Fairgrounds
S: Total Truck & Trailer Service, Auto Repairs, ATM, Auto Dealers, Bank

(53) **Jct I-440W, to Memphis**

54 **TN 155, Briley Pkwy**
Other N: Nashville Metro Airport✈, to Opryland

56 **TN 255, Harding Place**
Gas N: Amoco, Mobil◈, Mapco Express
S: Mapco Express, Shell◈
Food N: Applebee's, Arby's, City Café, East Café, McDonald's, Japanese Rest, KFC, Subway, Taco Bell, Wendy's, Waffle House
S: Burger King, Hooters, Jack in the Box, Waffle House
Lodg N: Drury Inn, Executive Inn, Howard Johnson Express, Motel 6♥, Super 8
S: Best Value Inn, Economy Inn, Motel 6♥
Med S: + Southern Hills Medical Center
Other N: ATMs, Banks, to Tn Natl Guard, Nashville Airport✈
S: Repairs/Shell, Harding Mall

57 **Haywood Lane, Antioch (WB)**
Gas N: Marathon, Speedway
S: Phillips 66◈
Food N: Hardee's, Pizza Hut, Waffle House, Whitts BBQ
Other N: Auto Services, Food Lion, Walgreen's

57AB **Haywood Lane, Antioch (EB)**

59 **TN 254, Bell Rd, Antioch, Nashville**
FStop S: Daily's Shell
Gas N: BP, Chevron, Mapco Express◈, Shell, Murphy
S: BP◈,
Food N: Applebee's, Arby's, Burger King, ChickFilA, Chuck E Cheese Pizza, **Cracker Barrel**, KFC, Logan's Roadhouse, Long John Silver/KFC, O'Charley's, Olive Garden, Pizza Hut, Panda Express, Red Lobster, Starbucks, TGI Friday, Taj Mahal Indian, Wendy's
S: Camino Real Mexican Rest, Casa Fiesta Mexican Rest, Evergreen Rest, IHOP, Olive Garden, Shoney's, Steak 'n Shake, Waffle House, Dunkin Donuts/Shell
Lodg N: Country Inn, Days Inn, Holiday Inn, Hampton Inn
S: Knights Inn, Quarters Inn, Super 8, Vista Inn, to InTowne Suites
Other N: ATMs, Auto Dealer, Auto Repairs, Banks, Best Buy, Carmike Cinemas, Enterprise RAC, FedEx Office, Firestone, Harbor Freight Tools, Hickory Hollow Mall, Kroger, NTB, Office Depot, **to Walmart sc**
S: Goodyear, Home Depot, IGA, Target, Carwash, **Appr 2.5 mi S to** Nolensville Pk: **Walmart sc**, Shopping, Food, Etc

60 **Hickory Hollow Pkwy**
(Access to Exit #59 Services)

62 **TN 171, Old Hickory Blvd**
FStop N: Antioch Food Mart/Citgo
TStop N: Travel Center of America/BP (Scales)
Gas N: Chevron, Shell◈
Food N: CountryPride/BurgerKing/Popeyes/TA TC, Subway/Citgo, Mexican Rest, Waffle House
Lodg N: Best Western
TWash N: TA TC
TServ N: TA TC/Tires
Other N: Laundry/WiFi/TA TC, Carwash/Chevron, to **Music City Campground▲**

64 **Waldron Rd, La Vergne**
TStop N: Pilot Travel Center #52 (Scales)
Gas N: Chevron, Exxon, Kangaroo, Mapco, Marathon, Speedway,
S: Mapco Express◈
Food N: Subway/Pilot TC, Arby's, Hardee's, Krystal, Las Canoas Mexican Rest, McDonald's, Rice Bowl II, Waffle House
Lodg N: Comfort Inn, Holiday Inn, Super 8
S: Driftwood Inn
Other N: **RVDump**/WiFi/Pilot TC, to Starwood Amphitheatre, **Music City Campground▲ Nashville Easy Livin' Country RV Sales & Service**

66 **TN 266, Sam Ridley Pkwy, Smyrna**
Gas N: Citgo◈, Shell, Scot Market, Kroger
Food N: Chili's, Logan's, Sonic, Starbucks, Subway, Wendy's
S: **Cracker Barrel**, Ruby Tuesday
Lodg N: Days Inn
S: Comfort Suites, Fairfield Inn, Hampton Inn, Hilton Garden Inn, Holiday Inn Express, Sleep Inn
Med N: + Hospital Medical Center
Other N: **Nashville I-24 Campground▲**, CVS, Food Lion, Kroger/Pharmacy, PetSmart♥, Publix/Pharmacy, Staples, Target, Tires, Smyrna Airport✈
S: I-24 Expo Center

66AB **TN 266, Sam Ridley Pkwy (EB)**

70 **TN 102, Lee Victory Pkwy, Smyrna**
FStop S: Kangaroo Express #3631, Mapco Express #3316
TStop N: Daly's Travel Center #6130/Shell
Gas S: BP,
Food N: Bar-B-Cutie Rest
S: Legends Rest, Malee Asian Rest, McDonald's, Oishii Steak & Sushi, Sonic, Subway, Grill Depot/Quiznos/KE
Lodg S: Deerfield Inn
Med N: + to Smyrna Hospital
Other N: **Nashville I-24 Campground▲**, **N to Lowry St:** Nissan Plant, Kroger/Pharmacy, RiteAid, **Walmart sc**

74A **TN 840W, Franklin**

74B **TN 840E, Lebanon, Knoxville**

76 **Medical Center Pkwy, Manson Pike**

78A **TN 96S, Old Fort Pkwy, Franklin**
Gas S: BP◈, Chevron, Kangaroo Express◈, Mapco Express, Sam's
Food S: Camino Real Mexican Rest, Captain D's, DQ, Hardee's, Little Caesars Pizza, O'Charley's, Papa John's Pizza, Sonic, Subway, Taco Bell, Waffle House
Lodg S: Value Place
Other S: ATMs, Auto Zone, Banks, Animal Medical Center♥, Carmike 16 Cinema, Carwash, CVS, Dollar General, Duds 'n Suds Laundromat, Express Oil Change, Kroger, Old Time Pottery, Quality Tire & Auto, RiteAid, Sam's Club, Tractor Supply, UPS Store, Walgreen's, River Rock Outlet Mall,

78B **TN 96N, Old Fort Pkwy, Franklin Rd, Murfreesboro, Franklin**
Gas N: Phillips 66◈, Shell◈, Texaco, Murphy
Food N: Arby's, Bonefish Grill, Chop House, ChickFilA, CiCi's Pizza, Coconut Bay Cafe, **Cracker Barrel**, IHOP, Jack in the Box/ Shell, Jim & Nick's BBQ, KFC, McDonald's, Outback Steakhouse, Puleo's Grill, Ryan's Grill, Santa Fe Cattle Co, Steak 'n Shake, Starbucks, Subway, Waffle House, Wendy's, White Castle
Lodg N: Baymont Inn♥, Best Western, Clarion Inn♥, Comfort Suites, Country Inn, Crestwood Suites♥, Days Inn, DoubleTree Hotel♥, Embassy Suites, Econo Lodge, Fairfield Inn, Hampton Inn♥, Holiday Inn Express, Microtel, Motel 6♥, Quality Inn♥, Red Roof Inn♥, Sleep Inn, Super 8,
Med N: + Hospital
Other N: ATMs, AT&T, Banks, Discount Tire, FedEx Office, Go USA Fun Park, Hobby Lobby, Home Depot, Lowe's, Middle TN State Univ, Office Depot, Old Fort Golf Course, Petland♥, PetSmart♥, Staples, Stones River Mall, Target, **Walmart sc**, Williams Animal Hospital♥,

81A **US 231S, TN 10, Murfreesboro (EB)**

81B **US 231N, TN 10, Murfreesboro (EB)**

81 **US 231, TN 10, Shelbyville Hwy, Church St, Murfreesboro, to Shelbyville (WB)**
FStop N: Uncle Sandy's Auto Truck Plaza/BP **(EB: Use Exit #81B)**
S: Mapco Express
TStop S: Pilot Travel Center #404 (Scales) **(DAND) (EB: Use Exit #81A)**
Gas N: Exxon, Mapco, RaceWay, Shell
S: Citgo, Kangaroo,
Food N: Arby's, Burger King,**Cracker Barrel**, Krystal, Ponderosa, Parthenon Steak House, Shoney's, Waffle House, Wendy's
S: Arby's/Pilot TC, La Siesta, Sonic McDonald's, Subway, Taco Bell/PizzaHut Waffle House
Lodg N: Americas Best Value Inn, Baymont Inn, GuestHouse Inn, Knights Inn, Quality Inn, Ramada Inn, Regal Inn, Scottish Inn
S: Howard Johnson, Safari Inn, Vista Inn
TWash S: Pilot TC
Tires S: Pilot TC
Med N: + Hospital
Other N: Auto Dealers, Carwash, Fireworks, U-Haul

◈= Regular Gas Stations with Diesel ▲ = RV Friendly Locations ♥= Pet Friendly Locations
Red print shows large vehicle parking / access on site or nearby Brown Print = Campgrounds / RV PARKS

EXIT		TENNESSEE
	Other	S: Laundry/Wifi/Pilot TC, ATMs, Auto Dealer, Auto Services, Advance Auto Parts, Discount Tire, Food Lion, Gateway Tire, Jiffy Lube, Kroger/Pharmacy, Pharmacy, RiteAid, Trailer Sales, Indian Hills Golf Course, **to Candy's Campers**
84A		**Joe B Jackson Pkwy S (WB)**
84B		**Joe B Jackson Pkwy N (WB)**
84		**Joe B Jackson Pkwy (EB)**
89		**Epps Mill Rd, to US 41, Christiana**
	TStop	N: Love's Travel Stop #314 (Scales), Danny's Food & Fuel/Shell
	Gas	N: The Outpost General Store & Rest/ Texaco◈
	Food	N: McDonald's/Love's TS, Huddle House
	Other	N: Laundry/WiFi/Love's TS S: I-24 Truck Repair, **A & L RV Sales**
97		**TN 64, Beechgrove Rd, Bell Buckle, Manchester, Shelbyville**
	Gas	S: Beech Grove Market & Grill/Citgo
105		**US 41, TN 2, Murfreesboro Hwy, Manchester, Beechgrove**
	FStop	N: Busy Corner Travel Center/BP
	Gas	N: Shell◈
	Food	N: Busy Corner TC, Ranch House Rest
	Other	N: Auto Services S: Best Auto & Tire
110		**TN 53, Woodbury Hwy, Paradise St, Manchester, Woodbury**
	FStop	S: Hullett Shell #4140
	Gas	N: BP, Kangaroo Express, Shell◈
	Food	N: Cracker Barrel, Crockett's Roadhouse Rest, Floyd's Family Rest, Oak Rest, Waffle House S: Mexican Rest, Waffle House
	Lodg	N: Ambassador Inn, Economy Inn, Hampton Inn S: Econo Lodge
	Med	N: + Hospital
	Other	N: Auto & Truck Repairs **S: Old Stone Fort State Park▲**
111		**TN 55, McMinnville Hwy, Manchester, to Tullahoma**
	TStop	N: K & K Top Stop
	Gas	N: BP◈, Chevron, Kangaroo Express/ Citgo◈ S: BP
	Food	N: Rest/K&K TS S: Hardee's, J&G Pizza & Steakhouse
	Med	S: + to United Regional Medical Center
	Other	S: Gateway Tire & Repair Services, to RiteAid, Walgreen's, **Old Stone Fort Campground ▲ , Outback Kamping▲**
114		**US 41, TN 2, Hillsboro Blvd, Manchester**
	TStop	N: I-24 Truck Plaza/BP (Scales)
	Gas	N: Marathon, Shell◈, Murphy S: Golden Gallon, Raceway
	Food	N: FastFood/I-24 TP, Huddle House, O'Charley's, Panda Express, Starbucks S: Arby's, Burger King, Krystal, KFC, McDonald's, Papa John's Pizza, Pizza Hut, Shoney's, Taco Bell, Subway, Waffle House, Wendy's
	Lodg	N: Comfort Inn, Holiday Inn Express, Ramada, Scottish Inn, Sleep Inn, Super 8, Truckers Inn S: Americas Best Value Inn, Country Inn, Days Inn, Knights Inn, Microtel, Royal Inn
	TServ	N: I-24 TP
	Med	S: + to United Regional Medical Center
	Other	N: Home Depot, **Walmart sc**, Auto Dealers, Aerospace Museum, **Manchester KOA▲ , to TN Hills Campground▲** S: ATMs, Banks, Advance Auto Parts, Auto Zone, Animal Health Clinic♥, Bi-Lo, CarQuest, Family Dollar, Food Lion, Fred's, Goodyear, NAPA, O'Reilly Auto Parts, Manchester Tire & Brake, **Scenic Roads RV Center**, US Post Office, **Whispering Oaks Campground▲ , to Old Stone Fort Campground▲**
(116)		**Weigh Station (Both dir)**
117		**US Air Force, Arnold Center, Tullahoma, UT Space Institute**
(119)		**TRUCK Parking Area (Both dir)**
127		**US 64, TN 50, Pelham, Winchester**
	Gas	N: BP, Phillips 66, Texaco S: Exxon◈
	Food	N: Stuckey's/Texaco
	Other	**S: Fairview Devil Step Campground▲**
(133)		**Grundry Rest Area (Both dir) (RR, Phone, Picnic, Vend)**
	NOTE:	**MM 134: WB: 5% Steep Grade next 4 mi**
134		**US 41 Alt, US 64, Monteagle, to Sewanee**
	Gas	N: BP, Mapco Express S: Kangaroo/Citgo, Shell◈
	Food	N: High Point Rest, McDonald's/BP S: Hardee's, Jim Oliver's Smokehouse Rest, Monteagle Diner, Papa Ron's Italian Steakhouse, Pizza Hut, Waffle House
	Lodg	N: American Eagle Inn, Budget Host Inn. Monteagle Inn B&B, Monteagle Motel S: Best Western♥, Regency Inn
	Med	S: + Hospital
	Other	N: CVS, I-24 Flea Market, Monteagle Winery, U-Haul, US Post Office, **The Cottages at Bear Hollow, to appr 3mi: South Cumberland State Park▲** S: Auto Parts & Service, Dollar General, Firestone, Fred's, Piggly Wiggly Grocery, **Tims Ford State Park▲ , Holiday Hills Campground▲**
135		**TN 2, Dixie Lee Hwy, to US 41, US US 64, Monteagle, Tracy City (Acc to #134 via Dixie Hwy)**
	TStop	N: Monteagle Truck Plaza/Citgo (Scales) Sam's Travel Center/Mystik◈
	Gas	S: Kangaroo Express
	Food	N: Rest/Monteagle TP, Smokin B's BBQ & Deli/Sam's TC, High Point Rest
	Lodg	S: Days Inn♥
	TServ	N: Monteagle TP/Tires, Monteagle Truck & Tire/Towing
	TWash	N: Monteagle TP
	Other	N: Laundry/Monteagle TP, to CVS, **Laurel Trails Campground▲ , to appr 3mi: South Cumberland State Park▲**
143		**TN 2, US 64, Martin Springs Rd**
	FStop	N: Chevron
152		**US 72, TN 150, TN 27, US 64, Kimball, S Pittsburg, Jasper,**
	Gas	N: BP, RaceWay, Scot Market◈
	Food	N: Arby's, Cracker Barrel, Domino's Pizza, Hardee's, KFC, Krystal, Long John Silver's/A&W, McDonald's, Pizza Hut, Shoney's, Subway, Taco Bell, Waffle House, Wendy's
	Lodg	N: Americas Best Value Inn♥, Comfort Inn Country Hearth Inn, Holiday Inn Express♥, Super 8♥
	Med	N: + Hospital
	Other	N: Dollar Tree, Enterprise RAC, Goody's, Hibbett Sporting Goods, Lowe's, Radio Shack, Tractor Supply, **Walmart sc**
155		**TN 28, Jasper, Dunlap**
	FStop	N: Interstate Exxon
	Gas	N: BP◈
	Food	N: DQ, Hardee's, Western Sizzlin'
	Lodg	N: Acuff Country Inn
	Med	S: + Grandview Medical Center
158		**TN 27, to US 41, US 64, Dunlap**
	Gas	N: Shell S: BP◈
	Other	**S: to appr 2.5mi: TVA Shellmound Campground▲**
(160)		**TN Welcome Center (WB) Marion Rest Area (EB) (RR, Phone, Picnic, Vend, Pet)**

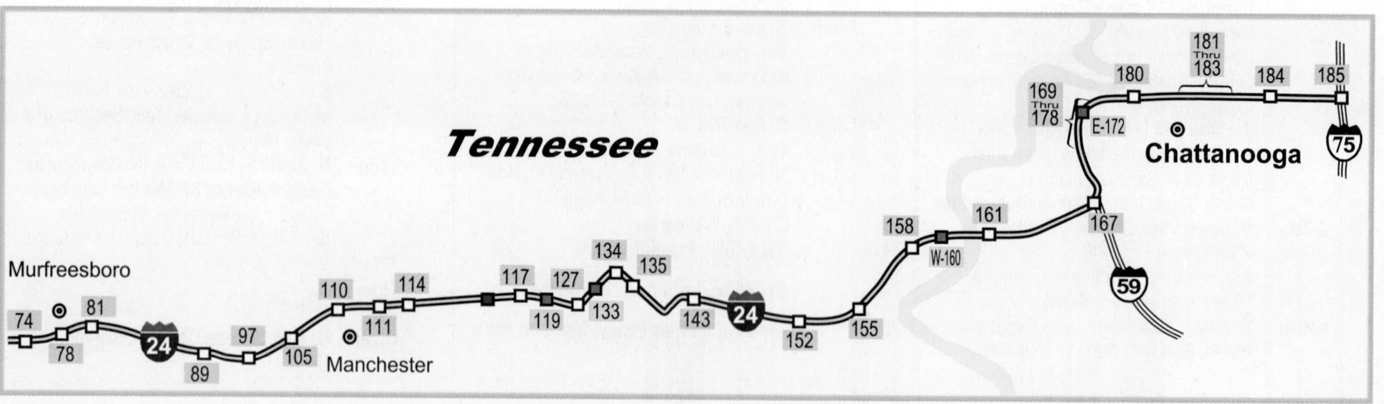

◈= Regular Gas Stations with Diesel ▲ = RV Friendly Locations ♥= Pet Friendly Locations
Red print shows large vehicle parking / access on site or nearby **Brown Print = Campgrounds / RV PARKS**

EXIT	TENNESSEE
161	**TN 156, Shellmound Rd, Guild, to Haletown, New Hope**
Gas	S: Chevron
Other	N: to Hales Bar Marina Resort & RV Park▲
	S: Camp on the Lake Campground▲
NOTE:	MM 167: TN / GA STATE LINE Exits #167 & #169 run thru GA
NOTE:	MM 167: Central/Eastern Time Zone
(167)	**Jct I-59S, to Birmingham** (WB, LEFT Exit)
169	**GA 299, to US 11, Hooker Rd, Wildwood, GA**
TStop	N: Fast Food & Fuel #166/Exxon
	S: Pilot Travel Center #254 (Scales), Fast Travel #190/BP (Scales)
Gas	S: RaceWay
Food	S: Subway/Pilot TC, Rest/FastTravel
Med	S: + to Wildwood Hospital
Other	S: WiFi/Pilot TC
NOTE:	Exits #167 & #169 run thru GA MM 171: GA / TN Border
(172)	**TN Welcome Center (EB)** (RR, Phone, Picnic, Vend, Pet)
174	**US 64, US 11, US 41, Lookout Mountain, Chattanooga**
FStop	S: Fast Food & Fuel #3538/BP
Gas	S: Kangaroo Express
Food	N: Waffle House
	S: Circle C BBQ & Steak House, Cracker Barrel, Hillbilly Willy's BBQ, New China Buffet & Grill, Sonic, Taco Bell, Waffle House, Wendy's
Lodg	N: Days Inn
	S: Baymont Inn, Best Western, Comfort Inn, Country Inn, Days Inn, Fairfield Inn,

EXIT	TENNESSEE
Lodg	Hampton Inn, Holiday Inn Express, Knights Inn, Quality Inn, Ramada Ltd, Super 8
Other	N: to appr 2 mi: Chattanooga's Racoon Mountain Caverns & Campground▲
	S: Circle C Truck & Trailer Repair, ATM, Ace Hardware, Banks, O'Reilly Auto Parts, Town & Country ATV's, Walmart sc, TN State Hwy Patrol Post
175	**Browns Ferry Rd, Lookout Mtn**
FStop	S: Conoco Favorite Market #3686
Gas	N: Kangaroo Express/BP, Exxon◈
	S: Shell◈
Food	S: Hardee's, McDonald's, Subway
Lodg	N: Americas Best Value Inn
	S: Comfort Inn, Econo Lodge, Quality Inn
Other	N: CVS, Food Lion, Lookout Valley Pet Hospital♥, Moccasin Bend Public Golf Course
	S: Bi-Lo, Ruby Falls, Lookout Mtn Attractions
178	**US 27N, US 41, Market St, to Lookout Mtn, Chattanooga** (Difficult reaccess)
FStop	N: Fast Food & Fuel #206/BP
Gas	N: Citgo
Food	N: Rest/Ramada, BBQ
	S: KFC, Soups On, Subway, Sweeney's Pit BBQ, Taco Bell, Wendy's
Lodg	N: Days Inn, Knights Inn, Ramada Inn, Staybridge Suites
	S: Comfort Inn, Hampton Inn, La Quinta Inn, Motel 6♥
Med	N: + Hospitals
Other	N: Moccasin Bend Public Golf Course, Finley Stadium, Auto Repairs, Conv Center, Exhibit Hall, Prime Outlet Mall, U-Haul
Other	S: Ace Hardware, Enterprise RAC, Lookout Mountain Attractions, Museum
180A	**Rossville Blvd** (diff reaccess)

EXIT	TENNESSEE
180B	**US 27S, Rossville Blvd**
FStop	S: Fast Food & Fuel #219/Exxon
Gas	S: Raceway◈
Food	S: KFC, Long John Silver's
Lodg	S: Hamilton Inn
181	**Fourth Ave, Chattanooga**
Gas	N: Citgo◈, Conoco, Exxon◈
	S: Citgo
Food	N: Bojangle's, Burger King, Captain D's, Hardee's, Krystal, Subway, Waffle House
	S: McDonald's, Wendy's
Lodg	N: Villager Lodge
	S: Kings Lodge
TServ	N: CAT Truck Service, Cummins South, Mack Trucks, Freightliner
Med	N: + Hospital
Other	N: Bi-Lo, Dollar General, Family Dollar, O'Reilly Auto Parts
181A	**US 41S, to US 76, East Ridge** (EB: difficult reaccess)
Gas	N: Citgo
Food	S: Rest/Kings Lodge
Lodg	S: Kings Lodge
TServ	N: Doug Yates Diesel Repair
	S: Ace Truck & Trailer Repair
183	**Germantown Rd** (EB)
183A	**Belvoir Avenue** (WB)
184	**Moore Rd, Chattanooga** (All Serv N to US 11/64, S to US 76)
Other	N: Eastgate Mall
(185AB)	**Jct I-75, N-Knoxville, S-Atlanta**
NOTE:	I-24 beings/ends on I-75, Exit #2

EASTERN TIME ZONE

⇑ TENNESSEE

Begin Westbound I-24 from Chattanooga, TN to Jct I-57 near Marion, IL.

EXIT	WYOMING

Begin Southbound I-25 from Buffalo, WY to Jct I-10 in Las Cruces, NM.

⇓ WYOMING

MOUNTAIN TIME ZONE

NOTE:	I-25 begins/ends on I-90, Exit #56
(300)	**Jct I-90, E - Gillette, W - Billings**
299	**US 16, I-25 Bus, I-90 Bus, Buffalo**
TStop	W: Big Horn Travel Plaza, Kum & Go #943/Cenex
Gas	E: Cenex, Conoco, Exxon, Shell
Food	W: Rest/Big Horn TP, Bozeman Trail Steak House, Dash Inn, Hardee's, Pizza Hut, McDonald's, Taco John's, Silver Dollar Steakhouse, Subway
Lodg	E: Motel 6♥
	W: Best Western, Big Horn Motel, Comfort Inn, Crossroads Inn, Econo

EXIT	WYOMING
Lodg	W: Lodge, Mansion House Inn, Mountain View Motel & Campground▲, Super 8 Occidental Hotel, Wyoming Motel
Med	W: + Family Medical Center
Other	E: NAPA, Deer Park Campground▲, Buffalo KOA▲
	W: Laundry/WiFi/RVDump/Big Horn TP, Jim's Auto & Tire, Auto Services, ATMs, Banks, Familly Dollar, Grocery, Carousel Park, Museum, Indian Campground▲, Big Horn Mountains Campground▲
298	**25 Bus, US 87 Bus, Buffalo** (Access to Exit #299 Services)
291	**Trabing Rd, CR 13**
280	**Middle Fork Rd, Buffalo**
(274)	**Parking Area** (Both dir)
265	**Reno Rd, CR 208, Kaycee**

EXIT	WYOMING
254	**WY 191, Kaycee**
W:	Rest Area (Both dir) (RR, Phone, Picnic, RVDump)
TStop	W: Kaycee Sinclair
Gas	E: Exxon◈, Shell◈
Food	E: Diner/Country Inn
	W: FastFood/Sinclair
Lodg	E: Country Inn, Cassidy Inn
	W: Kaycee Bunkhouse
Other	E: Powder River Campground▲
	W: LP/Sinclair, KC RV Park▲
249	**TTT Rd, Lone Bear Rd**
246	**Powder River Rd, WY 196N**
235	**Tisdale Mountain Rd, CR 210S**
227	**WY 387E, CR 115, Midwest, to Edgerton**
223	**Ranch Access, to Kaycee**
(219)	**Parking Area** (Both dir)

◈= Regular Gas Stations with Diesel ▲ = RV Friendly Locations ♥= Pet Friendly Locations
Red print shows large vehicle parking / access on site or nearby Brown Print = Campgrounds / RV PARKS

EXIT WYOMING

216 South Castle Creek Rd

210 WY 259, Horse Ranch Creek Rd

197 Ormsby Rd, CR 705, Casper

191 Wardwell Rd, to WY 254,Casper, to Bar Nunn
- Gas W: MiniMart◈
- Other W: **Casper KOA▲**

189 US 20, US 26, Salt Creek Hwy, to Shoshone, Airport, Port of Entry
- FStop W: **5 mi SW:** Ghost Town Fuel Stop/Conoco

188B WY 220, Poplar St, Walnut St, to CY Ave, Casper
- Gas E: Conoco, Shell
  W: Exxon
- Food E: El Jarro Rest, JB's Family Rest
  W: Burger King, Caspers Good Cooking, DQ
- Lodg E: Best Western, Econo Lodge, Hampton Inn, Holiday Inn, Radisson, Super 8
- TServ W: Casper Truck Center
- Other W: Albertson's, Deluxe Harley Davidosn Buell, Safeway, **Fort Casper Campground▲** , **to Alcova Dam RV & Trailer Park▲**

188A I-25 Bus, US 87 Bus, Center St, Central & Downtown Casper
- Gas E: Conoco◈, Shell◈
  W: Cenex, Kum&Go
- Food E: JB's, Taco John's
  W: Fish Factory, Poor Boy's Steakhouse, Platte River Rest
- Lodg E: National 9 Inn, Holiday Inn
  W: Days Inn, Parkway Plaza Hotel
- Other E: Auto Services
  W: Auto Services, ATMs, Banks, Visitor Info, Cinemas

187 McKinley St, to US 20/26, Casper
- Gas E: Mini Mart
- Lodg E: Ranch House Motel
- Med W: **+ WY Medical Center**

186 US 20, US 26, N Beverly St, Bryan Scott Stock Trail, Yellowstone Hwy, Casper
- Gas W: Conoco
- Food W: Highway Café Home Cooking, Plow's Diner, Rest/BW
- Lodg W: Best Western
- TServ E: Central Truck & Diesel
- Med W: **+ WY Medical Center**
- Other E: Auto Dealers, **Casper East RV Park & Campground▲**
  W: Albertson's, Auto Dealers, **Smith RV Sales & Service**

185 WY 258, Curtis St, E Casper, Wyoming Blvd, to Evansville
- FStop W: Loaf N Jug #127/Conoco, Mini Market/Conoco
- TStop W: Flying J Travel Plaza #5029 (Scales)
- Gas E: Kum&Go◈, Mini Mart
  W: Exxon◈, Sam's
- Food E: Applebee's, Golden Dragon Chinese, IHOP, Kindler's Rest, Outback Steakhouse
  W: Cookery/FastFood/FJ TP, Arby's, Burger King, Flaming Wok, Hardee's, Hometown Buffet, McDonald's, Perkins, Red Lobster, Subway, Taco John's, Wendy's, Village Inn
- Lodg E: Comfort Inn, Shiloh Inn, Super 8

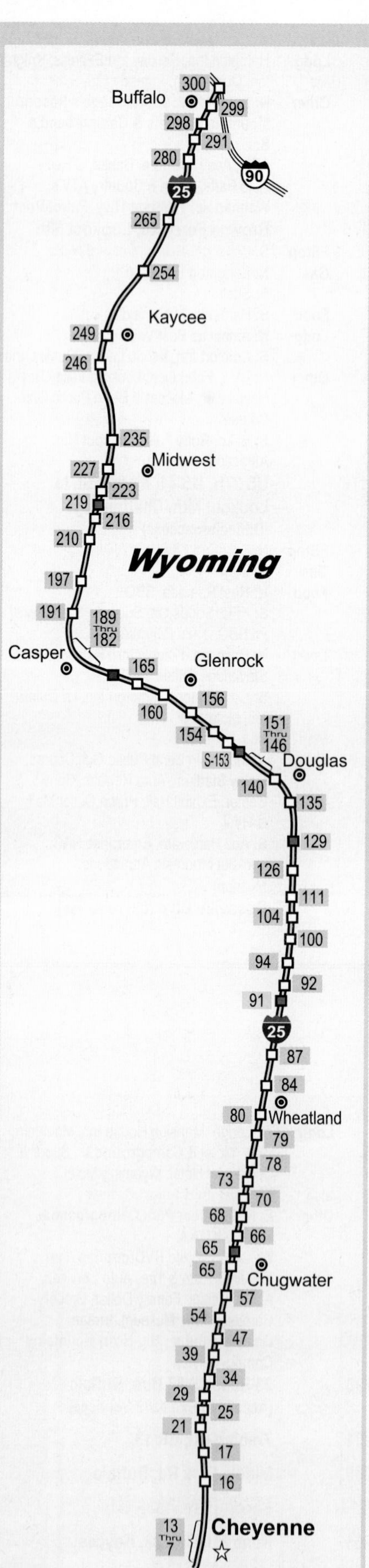

EXIT WYOMING

- Lodg W: Holiday Inn Express, Red Stone Motel
- Med W: **+ Wyoming Medical Center**
- Other E: **Sonny's RV**
  W: Laundry/WiFi/**RV Dump**/**LP**/FJ TP, ATMs, Banks, Auto Dealers, Auto Repair, American Tire, Auto Zone, Eastridge Mall, Eastridge Theatre, Enterprise RAC, Hobby Lobby, Home Depot, Kmart, O'Reilly Auto Parts, PetCo♥, Plains Tire, Radio Shack, Sam's Club, Safeway, Sportsmans Warehouse, Staples, Target, **Walmart sc**, Walgreen's, Vet♥, Verizon

182 WY 253, CR 606, Hat Six Rd, Cole Creek Rd, Evansville
- TStop E: AmBest/Eastgate Travel Plaza/ Sinclair (Scales)
- Food E: Rest/FastFood/Eastgate TP
  W: Fire Rock Steak House
- Lodg E: Sleep Inn
- Other E: Laundry/**RVDump**/**LP**/Eastgate TP
  W: **Rivers Edge RV & Cabins Resort▲**

(171) Parking Area (Both dir)

165 WY 95, I-25 Bus, Deer Creek Rd, Glenrock
- Gas E: General Store
- Food E: Grandma's Kitchen, Noble Romans, Subway, Rest/Hotel Higgins
- Lodg E: Glenrock Motel, Hotel Higgins
- Other E: **Deer Creek RV Park▲**

160 US 87, US 20, US 26, Glenrock (Access to Ex #165 Services)

156 Bixby Rd, Glenrock

154 Barber Rd, Douglas

(153) Parking Area (SB)

151 Natural Bridge Rd, CR 13

150 Inez Rd

146 WY 96, CR 30, La Prele Rd, to Cold Springs Rd
- Other W: **to Douglas KOA▲**

140 WY 59, Douglas Esterbrook Rd, Douglas, Gillette
- Gas E: Conoco◈, Maverick◈
- Food E: Arby's, La Costa Mexican Rest, McDonald's, Subway/Conoco
- Lodg E: Best Western♥, Holiday Inn Express♥, Super 8♥
- Med E: **+ Memorial Hospital**
- Other E: **LP**, Auto Dealers, Pioneer Museum, State Fairgrounds, Converse Co Airport✈, Vet♥, **Lone Tree Village MH & RV Park▲**
  W: Douglas KOA▲

135 US 20, 26, 87, Douglas, to WY 59
- TStop E: Broken Wheel Truck Stop/Sinclair (Scales)
- Food E: Rest/Broken Wheel, Clementine's Cattle Co, KFC/Taco Bell, Pizza Hut, Village Inn
- Lodg E: Alpine Inn, First Interstate Inn
- TServ E: Bud's Field Service & Truck Repair
- Med E: **+ Memorial Hospital**
- Other E: Laundry/BW TS, **Four Winds Campground▲** , Auto Dealer, Auto Services, Pamida/Pharmacy, Safeway, Towing, Douglas Int'l Raceway
  W: Douglas Comm Golf Course

(129) Parking Area (Both dir)

◈= Regular Gas Stations with Diesel ▲ = RV Friendly Locations ♥= Pet Friendly Locations
Red print shows large vehicle parking / access on site or nearby **Brown Print = Campgrounds / RV PARKS**

EXIT — WYOMING

(126) US 18, US 20, Douglas, Orin
E: Rest Area (Both dir)
(RR, Phones, Pet, RVDump)
TStop E: Orin Junction Truck Stop/Sinclair
Food E: Rest/Orin Jct TS
Other E: Laundry/RVDump/Orin Jct TS

111 A St, CR 59, Horseshoe Creek Rd, Glendo
FStop E: Howard's General Store/Sinclair
Food E: FastFood/Howard's GS, Glendo Café, Rest/Howard's Motel
Lodg E: Lakeview Motel, Howard's Motel,
Other E: US Post Office, **Glendo Lakeside RV Park▲**, **Glendo State Park▲**

104 Middle Bear Creek Rd

100 Cassa Rd, WY 319N

94 El Rancho Rd, Fish Creek Rd, Pepper Rd, Wheatland

92 US 26E, to WY 319, Wheatland, Guernsey, Torrington
Other E: to Guernsey State Park

(91) Rest Area (Both dir)
(RR, Picnic, Pet, RVDump)

87 Johnson Rd

84 Laramie River Rd, CR 47

80 I-25 Bus, US 87, to WY 320N, Wheatland
TStop E: Wheatland Travel Plaza/Sinclair
Food E: FastFood/Wheatland TP, Casey's Timber Haus, Pizza Hut
Lodg E: Best Western, Super 8, WY Motel
Med E: + Platte Co Memorial Hospital
Other E: Laundry/WiFi/LP/Wheatland TP, Auto Dealers, ATMs, Bank, Auto Repairs, Museum, Pamida, Platte Co Fairgrounds, Safeway, **Arrowhead RV Campground▲**

78 I-25 Bus, US 87, to WY 312S
FStop W: Common Cents/Exxon
TStop E: Wheatland Co-Op/Cenex (Scales)
W: I-25 Pit Stop
Gas E: Cenex◊
Food E: Arby's, Burger King, China Garden, El Gringo's, Pizza Hut, Subway, Taco John's, Vimbo's Rest
W: West Winds Motel
Lodg E: Best Western, Motel 6♥, Parkway Motel, Plains Motel, Vimbo's Motel♥
Tires E: Co-Op
Med E: + Platte Co Memorial Hospital
Other E: ATMs, Banks, Repairs, Cinema West, Grocery, Platte Co Fairgrounds, Museum, Phifer Airfield ✈, Tires, Sheriff Dept
W: Laundry/I-25, LP/Co-Op, **Mountain View RV Park▲**, Radio Shack

73 WY 34W, Wheatland, to Laramie

70 Bordeaux Rd, WY 34, Wheatland

68 Antelope Rd, CR 264

66 Hunton Rd

(65) Parking Area (Both dir)

65 WY 314E, Slater Rd, Wheatland

57 WY 321, Ty Basin Rd, Chugwater

NOTE: SB: Check Fuel!!

EXIT — WYOMING

(54) WY 211, Lp 25, Chugwater, to WY 322E, WY 321, WY 313
E: Rest Area (Both dir)
(RR, Phone, Picnic, Pet, RVDump)
FStop E: Sinclair
Food E: Buffalo Grill, Chugwater Soda Ftn
Lodg E: Super 8
Other W: Diamond Guest Ranch

47 Bear Creek Rd, to Little Bear Rd, CR 245, Chugwater

39 Little Bear Community Rd, CR 245, to Hirsig Rd, Moffett Rd, Dayton Rd, Cheyenne

34 Nimmo Rd, True Rd, to CR 232

29 CR 228, Whitaker Rd, Cheyenne

25 CR 224, Atlas Rd

21 Ridley Rd, CR 220, Little Bear Rd

17 US 85N, Yellowstone Rd, Cheyenne, to Torrington (SB L ex)

16 WY 211, Horse Creek Rd, Iron Mountain Rd, Cheyenne
Food W: Little Bear Inn 2mi N via Service Rd

13 Vandehei Ave, Cheyenne
Gas E: Loaf 'n Jug
W: Diamond Shamrock◊

12 US 87 Bus, US 85, Central Ave, Bus 25, WY 224, Cheyenne (Addtl Serv Yellowstone Rd, Dell Range Blvd)
Gas E: Exxon
Food E: Arby's, DQ, Double Eagle Diner, Godfathers Pizza, McDonald's, Starbucks, Taco John's
Lodg E: Rodeway Inn♥
Med E: + United Medical Center West
Other E: ATMs, Bank, Albertson's, Cheyenne Muni Airport ✈, Airport Golf Course, Avenues Pet Clinic II, Big O Tires, to Frontier Mall, Frontier Days Museum
W: FE Warren AFB, Visitor Info, WY State Hwy Patrol Post

11 Randall Ave, Warren AFB-Gate 1
Gas E: Loaf 'n Jug
Other E: to WY State Capitol, Museum
W: MIL/FE Warren AFB Fam Camp▲

10B Plant Rd, Missile Dr, Warren AFB-Gate 2

10D Missile Dr, Happy Jack Rd
Acc All Serv: E to US 30, I-80 Bus, Ex #9
Other E: Police Dept, Sheriff Dept

9 US 30, I-80 Bus, W Lincolnway, Otto Rd, Cheyenne
TStop W: AmBest/Little America Travel Plaza/ Sinclair
E: Big D Truck Stop/Exxon
Gas E: Conoco
Food E: Rest/FastFood/Big D TS, Denny's, Crossroads Café, Outback Steakhouse
W: Rest/Little America
Lodg E: Atlas Motel, Candlewood Suites, Days Inn♥, Express Inn♥, Hampton Inn, Holiday Inn, La Quinta Inn♥, Luxury Inn, Microtel, Motel 6♥, Ramada, Super 8,
W: Little America Hotel & Resort/Little America TP

EXIT — WY / CO

TServ E: Conoco FS, Wyoming Caterpillar
W: Little America TP/Tires
Other E: Auto Dealers, Auto Services, ATMs, **Adventure RV**, Banks, Convention Center, Home Depot, Museums, Train Station, Theatres, Laundry/LP/Big D TS
W: LP/Little America, Little America Golf Course

NOTE: NB: Check Fuel!!

(8B) Jct I-80,W to Laramie

(8D) Jct I-80, E to Omaha, NE

(7) US 87, Bus 25, WY 212, College Dr
WY Welcome Center (Both dir)
W: (RR, Phone, Picnic, Pet, Info)
TStop E: Love's Travel Stop #220 (Scales), Valero #4545
W: Flying J Travel Plaza #5018/ Conoco (Scales)
Food E: Wendy's/Love's TS, Subway/Valero
W: Rest/FastFood/FJ TP, McDonald's
Lodg W: Comfort Inn/FJ TP
Other E: Laundry/WiFi/RVDump/Love's TS, Laundry/WiFi/Valero, **to AB RV Park & Campground▲**, Art's Truck Repair
W: Laundry/WiFi/LP/RVDump/FJ TP, Info Center

(6) Weigh / Check Station
WY Port of Entry (NB)

2 Terry Ranch Rd, WY 223E, to US 85, Cheyenne
Other E: Terry Bison Ranch/Rest/Hotel, Wine Cellars, & **RV Park▲**

MOUNTAIN TIME ZONE

⬆ WYOMING
⬇ COLORADO

MOUNTAIN TIME ZONE

NOTE: MM 299: Wyoming State Line

(296) Parking Area (Both dir)

293 CR 126, to Carr, Norfolk

288 CR 82, Buckeye Rd, Carr

281 CR 70, Wellington
Other E: Ft Collins North/Wellington KOA/RVDump▲

278 CO 1S, Cleveland Ave, Wellington
Gas W: Loaf 'n Jug, Shell
Food W: Burger King, Subway
Lodg W: Comfort Inn
Other W: ATM, Bank, Auto Repair

271 CR 50, Mtn Vista Dr, Ft Collins
Other W: Anheiser Busch Brewery

269B CO 14W, Mulberry St, to US 287, Fort Collins, to Laramie
FStop W: Phillips 66
Gas W: Conoco
Food W: BBQ, Burger King, Denny's, Italian, Sundance Steak House & Saloon, Waffle House
Lodg E: Guest House Inn
W: Best Western♥, Comfort Inn, Days Inn, Econo Lodge, Holiday Inn, La Quinta Inn♥,

◊= Regular Gas Stations with Diesel ▲ = RV Friendly Locations ♥= Pet Friendly Locations
Red print shows large vehicle parking / access on site or nearby Brown Print = Campgrounds / RV PARKS

EXIT	COLORADO
Lodg	E: Motel 6♥, Ramada Inn♥, Sleep Inn, Super 8
Med	W: + Poudre Valley Hospital
Other	W: Albertson's, Auto Service, Diesel Services of N CO, Fort Fun, Front Range Veterinary Clinic♥, Link 'n Green Golf Course, NAPA, Paws 'n Claws Veterinary Clinic♥, Radio Shack, Rollerland Skate Center, Towing, U-Haul, UPS Store, **Walmart SC**, to Colorado State Univ,
T	Fort Collins Downtown Airpark✈, **Fort Collins/Lakeside KOA▲**
269A	**CO 14E, to Ault, Sterling**
Food	E: McDonald's
Lodg	E: Mulberry Inn
(268)	**CR 44, Prospect Rd, Fort Collins (Gas & Food W to Lemay Ave/Acc #269)**
W:	Rest Area (Both dir) (RR, Picnic, Pet, Info)
Med	W: + Concerta Urgent Care, + Poudre Valley Hospital
Other	E: Ft Collins Motorsports, Max-Air Trailer Sales, Mannon Truck & Auto Repair, RV World/LP/U-Haul, W: CO State Univ, Hughes Stadium,
(267)	**Weigh / Check Station (Both dir)**
265	**CO 68W, Harmony Rd, Ft Collins Timnath, (Serv appr 4 mi W)**
Gas	W: Shell◈
Food	W: Austin's American Grill, Buffalo Wild Wings, Carrabba's, DQ, Dominos Pizza, Golden Corral, IHOP, Jason's Deli, Noodle & Co, Outback Steakhouse, Red Robin, Romanos Macaroni Grill, Starbucks, Subway, Texas Roadhouse, Village Inn
Lodg	W: Cambria Suites, Courtyard, Comfort Suites, Hampton Inn, Hilton Garden Inn, Holiday Inn, Homewood Suites, Marriott, Residence Inn
Other	E: **Walmart SC** W: ATMs, Auto Dealers, Auto Services, AT&T, Banks, Best Buy, Cinema, FedEx Office, Friendship Hospital for Animals♥, Hobby Lobby, Home Depot, Island Lake Marine & Sports, King Soopers/Pharmacy, Peloton Cycles, Safeway, Sam's Club, **Sheriff Dept**, Sports Authority, Staples, T-Mobile, Target, ToysRUs, UPS Store, Verizon, Walgreen's, **to Foothills Mall, Horsetooth Reservoir**
262	**CO 392E, CR 32, Windsor**
Gas	E: Conoco, Phillips 66
Food	E: Arby's, McDonald's, Subway
Lodg	E: AmericInn, Super 8
Other	E: Highland Meadows Golf Course
259	**CO 26, Crossroads Blvd**
Gas	E: Phillips 66
Food	E: Carl's Jr, Hardee's, Nordy's BBQ, Qdoba Mexican Grill, Subway W: Hooters
Lodg	E: Candlewood Suites, Embassy Suites, Holiday Inn Express, Value Place
Other	W: Auto Dealers, Hertz RAC, Thunder Mountain Harley Davidson, Budweiser Events Center, County Fairgrounds, Fort Collins-Loveland Muni Airport✈,
257	**US 34, Loveland, Greeley**
257B	**US 34W, Loveland, Rocky Mtn NP**
Gas	W: Conoco◈

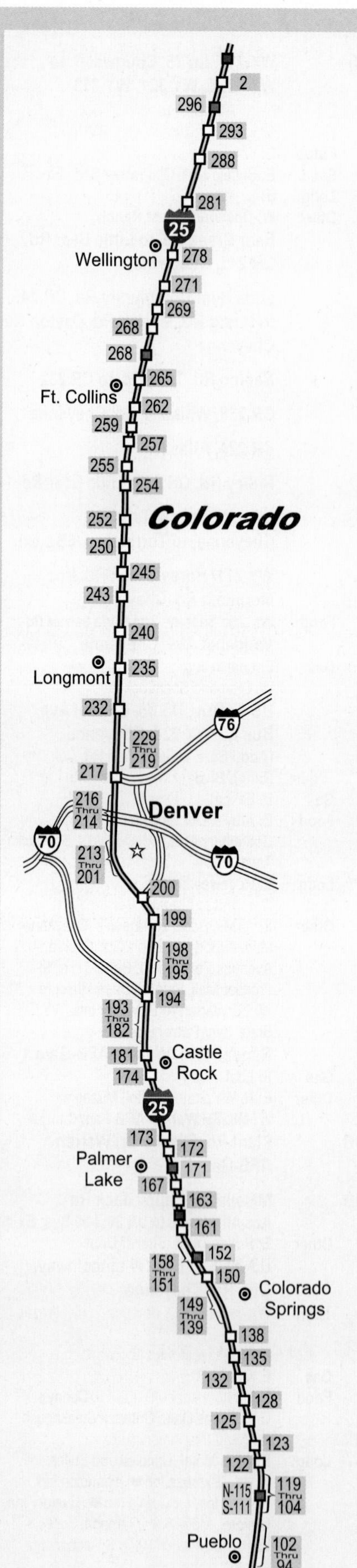

EXIT	COLORADO
Food	W: Burger King, ChickFilA, Chili's, Cracker Barrel, DQ, Dominos Pizza, IHOP, Lone Star Steakhouse, McDonald's, MiMi's Cafe, Old Chicago Pizza & Pasta, Panera Bread, Souper Salad, Subway, Waffle House, Wendy's
Lodg	W: Best Western, Comfort Inn, Fairfield Inn, Hampton Inn, Holiday Inn, Quality Inn, Residence Inn, Super 8
Med	W: + McKee Medical Center, + Medical Center of the Rockies
Other	W: Albertson's, ATMs, Banks, Boyd Lake Veterinary Center♥, Crystal Rapids Waterpark, Discount Tire, Enterprise RAC, Family Member Animal Hospital♥, Home Depot, Mountain Rentals, **Mountain Vista RV**, Museum, Peloton Cycles, PetSmart♥, Prime Outlets at Loveland, Sam's Club, Sportsmens Warehouse, Target, UPS Store, **Walmart sc**, **Visitor Center**, Police, **Loveland RV Village Campground▲**, **to Boyd Lake State Park▲**, **Rocky Mountain National Park, to appr 10mi: Riverview RV Park & Campground▲**
257A	**US 34E, Loveland, to Greeley**
Gas	E: Diamond Shamrock◈
Food	E: Bent Fork Grill, Biaggi's Ristorante, Bonefish Grille, Charlie's Grilled Subs, On the Border Mexican Grill, PF Chang's, Red Robin, Rock Bottom Rest & Brewery, Spicy Pickle, Starbucks
Lodg	E: Clarion Hotel♥, Country Inn Suites
Other	E: B&N, Best Buy, Dick's Sporting Goods, Metrolux 14 Theatres, **Loveland Station Campground▲**
255	**CO 402W, Johnstown, Loveland**
Other	E: **Loveland Station Campground▲** W: **to appr 3.5 mi: Loveland RV Sales & Service**
254	**CR 16, to CO 60W, to Campion (NB/SB reaccess via Ex #255)**
TStop	E: AmBest/Johnson's Corner Truck Stop (Scales)
Food	E: Johnson's Corner Rest
Lodg	E: Budget Host Inn
Other	E: Laundry/WiFi/**LP/RVDump**/ Johnson's Corner TS, **Johnson's Corner RV Retreat/RVDump/RV Service▲**, **RV America**
252	**CO 60E, CR 48, Berthoud, to Johnstown, Milliken**
Gas	W: Loaf 'n Jug
Food	W: Subway
250	**CO 56W, Berthoud, Carter Lake**
245	**CR 34, to Mead**
243	**CO 66, CR 30, Longmont, Lyons, to Platteville**
FStop	E: Boulder Gas/Shell
Gas	E: Conoco◈
Food	E: Blimpie/Shell, Scott's on 66, Pizza Plus
Other	E: **Camping World/K&C RV Center**, **J & D Marine & RV** W: **to Rocky Mountain Nat'l Park**
240	**CO 119W, Longmont, Firestone**
FStop	E: Get on the Go/P66 W: Alpine Station #1/Conoco (Scales)
TStop	W: Shell Gas Stop (Scales)
Food	E: Carl's Jr, Del Taco, Morning Star Rest, Quiznos, Starbucks, Wendy's

◈ = Regular Gas Stations with Diesel ▲ = RV Friendly Locations ♥ = Pet Friendly Locations
Red print shows large vehicle parking / access on site or nearby Brown Print = Campgrounds / RV PARKS

EXIT		COLORADO
	Food	W: Subway/Conoco, Arby's, Burger King, McDonald's, Pizza Hut, Taco Bell, Waffle House
	Lodg	E: Best Western, Comfort Suites♥, Value Place W: 1st Inn, Americas Best Value Inn♥, Comfort Inn, Days Inn♥, Quality Inn, Super 8♥,
	TWash	W: Del Camino Truck Wash
	TServ	W: Del Camino Truck Wash/Tires
	Med	W: + Hospital
	Other	E: Auto Zone, **Century RV**, Firestone W: Laundry/Shell FS, Auto Repair, **Discount RV & Big John's RV Sales & Service, Windish RV Center, to appr 7 mi: Countrywood Inn & RV Park▲**, Boulder Co Fairgrounds & **Campground▲**, **Vrain State Park▲**, Vance Brand Airport✈
235		**CO 52, Erie, Dacono, Fort Lupton, Frederick, Firestone, Eldora**
	TStop	W: 25-52 AutoTruck Plaza/Conoco
	Food	W: Rest/Pepper Jack's/McDonalds/ 25-52 ATP, Starbucks, Subway
	Other	E: Grocery, **Police Dept** W: **LP/RVDump**/25-52 ATP, High Country Harley Davidson/Buell
232		**CR 8, Erie, Dacono**
	Other	E: CO Nat'l Speedway
229		**CO 7, Baseline Rd, Broomfield, Thornton, to Lafayette, Brighton**
	Gas	E: Costco
	Food	E: ChickFilA, Chili's, Famous Dave's BBQ, Good Times Burgers, Starbucks, Subway, Village Inn
	Med	W: + Childrens Hospital North Campus
	Other	E: ATMs, Banks, Costco, Dick's Sporting Goods, Home Depot, Office Max, PetSmart♥, Sears Grand, Verizon W: Erie Muni Airport✈, Vista Ridge Golf Course
(228)		**Jct E-470 Toll Way S, to Limon, Colo Spgs, NW Pky, (TOLL), Boulder**
226		**144th Ave, Broomfield**
	Food	W: Crepes des Paris, Happy Sumo at the Orchard, Mexico Cantina, Mimi'sCafe, Red Robin, Rock Bottom Rest & Brewery, Starbucks
	Other	W: AMC Theatres, AT&T, Staples, Super Target/Pharmacy, Verizon, Asstd Retail Shopping
225		**136th Ave, Westminster, Denver**
	Food	W: Big City Burrito, Carl's Jr, Long John Silver/KFC, McDonald's, Starbucks, Subway
	Other	W: Advance Auto Parts, ATMs, Banks, Lowe's, **Walmart sc**
223		**CO 128W, 120th Ave, Broomfield, Westminster, Northglenn**
	Gas	E: Conoco, Sinclair, Shamrock◈ W: Circle K/Shell◈, Conoco◈, Shamrock◈
	Food	E: Applebee's, Burger King, Chipolte Mexican Grill, Café Mexico, ChickFilA, Damon's, Fuddrucker's, Lone Star Steakhouse, McDonald's, Olive Garden, Outback Steakhouse, Panda Express, Popeye's Chicken, Sonic, Souper Salad, Starbucks, TGI Friday W: Chili's, **Cracker Barrel**, DQ, Hooters, Jade City Chinese, Kabob Station, Perkins, Starbucks, Subway, Tokyo Joe's, Village Inn, Wendy's,

EXIT		COLORADO
	Lodg	E: Castle Hotel, Days Inn, Hampton Inn, Ramada♥, Sleep Inn W: Comfort Suites, Extended Stay, Fairfield Inn, La Quinta Inn♥, Savannah Suites, Super 8♥
	Other	E: ATMs, Albertson's/Pharmacy, Animal Clinic North♥, Auto Services, Auto Repairs, Avis RAC, B&N, Big 5 Sporting Goods, Big Lots, Big O Tire, Brakes Plus, Budget RAC, CarQuest, Checker Auto Parts, Community Pet Hospital & Emergency Service♥, Discount Tire, Meineke, NAPA, O'Reilly Auto Parts, PetCo♥, **Police**, Super Target, Tires Plus, U-Haul, Walgreen's, Washtime Laundry, World Market W: ATMs, Banks, Brakes Plus, FedEx Office, Northside Emergency Pet Clinic♥, Skate City
221		**104th Ave, Denver, Northglenn, Thornton**
	Gas	E: Conoco, Phillips 66, Shamrock W: 7-11, Circle K/Conoco, Circle K/Shell◈
	Food	E: Backdraft BBQ, Buffalo Wild Wings, Burger King, CiCi's Pizza, Culver's, Dennys, IHOP, Panda Garden, Sonic, Starbucks, Subway, Taco Bell, Texas Roadhouse, W: Applebee's, Armadillo Rest, Atlanta Bread, Black Eyed Pea, CoCo's, Furr's, Gunther Toody's Diner, Hop's Grill, McDonald's, Red Lobster, Subway, Taco Bell, Wingman
	Lodg	W: La Quinta Inn♥, Ramada Ltd
	Med	E: + North Suburban Medical Center
	Other	E: ATMs, Banks, Advance Auto Parts, Auto Zone, Carwash, Cinema 10, Gander Mountain, Grocery, Home Depot, K-Mart, King Sooper's/Pharmacy, Midas, Safeway/Pharmacy, Target, Thornton Town Center Mall, Tires Plus, T-Mobile, **Walmart sc, to** American Auto, Truck & RV Service W: ATMs, Ace Hardware, Albertson's, AMF Bowling Center, Auto Dealers, Batteries Plus, Best Buy, Borders, Carson Trailer of CO, Enterprise RAC, Firestone Auto, Goodyear, Golf Courses, Lowe's, NAPA, Northglenn Mall, Office Depot, Paris Tire & Service, PetSmart♥, Radio Shack, Ross, RiteAid, Safeway/Pharmacy, Shepler's, Tool Zone, UPS Store
220		**Thornton Pkwy, 92nd Ave, Denver (Access Ex #221 via E to Grant St or W to Huron St, or Washington St S to 88th)**
	Gas	E: Sam's W: Conoco, Valero
	Food	E: Egg & I, Golden Corral, Starbucks
	Med	E: + North Suburban Medical Center
	Other	E: Hobby Lobby, Sam's Club, Safeway/ Pharmacy, Thornton Civic Center, UPS Store, **Walmart sc, Police Dept** W: Hyland Hills Water World
219		**84th Ave, Federal Heights (Acc E 88th Ave via N on Washington St)**
	Gas	E: 7+11, Diamond Shamrock W: Gas, Diamond Shamrock
	Food	E: Arby's, Chubby's, Good Times Grill, Long John Silver, McDonald's, Quiznos, Sonic, Starbucks, Taco Bell, Waffle House W: Burger King, DQ, Lotus Chinese, Pizza Hut, Popeye's Chicken, Village Inn, 5 J's Italian Dining

EXIT		COLORADO
	Lodg	E: Crossland Economy Studios W: Motel 6♥,
	Med	E: + North Valley Hospital W: + St Anthony's Hospital
	Other	E: Auto Services, Advance Auto Parts, Checker Auto Parts, Family Dollar, Laundromat, North Valley Mall, Office Depot, O'Reilly Auto Parts, Sir Speedy, Sun Harley Davidson, Walgreen's, W: CarQuest, Carwash, Discount Tire, Hyland Hills Water World, King Soopers/ Pharmacy, Meineke Car Care, Sportsmans Warehouse, Vets Animal Hospital♥, Walgreen's,
(217B)		**Jct I-270E, to Aurora, Limon, I-25S, to Denver (SB)**
	Other	E: to Denver Int'l Airport✈
217A		**US 36W, Boulder, CO 224, Broadway (SB)**
217		**US 36W, to Boulder, I-25N, to Fort Collins (NB, LEFT exit)**
(216)		**Jct I-76, W-Grand Junction, E to Ft Morgan, 70th Ave, CO 224 (NB)**
(216A)		**Jct I-76E, to Ft Morgan (SB)**
(216B)		**Jct I-76W, to Grand Junction (SB)**
215		**CO 53, 58th Ave, Denver**
	FStop	W: Diamond Shamrock #4095
	Food	E: Burger King, Coffee World, McDonald's, Papa John's, Steak Escape, Wendy's W: Colorado Café
	Lodg	E: Comfort Inn♥, Quality Inn W: Super 8
	Med	E: + Concentra Urgent Care
	Other	E: Auto & Truck Repair, Coyote Yamaha, Hammonds Candies, W: LP/Shamrock
(214A)		**Jct I-70, E to Limon, Kansas City, W to Grand Junction**
	Other	E: to Denver Coliseum, Denver Int'l Airport✈
(214B)		**48th Ave, to Pecos St, to I-70 (SB)**
	Food	W: Village Inn,
	Lodg	W: Holiday Inn, Quality Inn
	Other	**E: Acc to I-70, x276A Serv via 47th or 46th Ave to Washington St** W: Family Dollar, Diversified Truck & RV Repair, Safeway, True Value, **Access to I-70, x 273 Services**
213		**38th Ave, Park Ave W, Fox St, Downtown, Coors Field**
	Gas	E: BP, 7-11, Shell
	Food	E: Burger King, Denny's, McDonald's
	Lodg	E: La Quinta Inn♥ W: Regency Hotel, Town & Country Motel, Travelodge
212C		**20th St, Downtown Denver, Coors Field, Amtrak**
212B		**North Speer Blvd (NB)**
212A		**Speer Blvd, Downtown (NB)**
	Gas	W: Conoco, Shell
	Lodg	W: Continental Hotel, Residence Inn, Super 8
	Other	E: Amtrak, Columbine Cellars, Convention Center, Elitch Garden, Ocean Journey, Pepsi Center, Performing Arts Center, Six Flags, Union Station,

◈ = Regular Gas Stations with Diesel ▲ = RV Friendly Locations ♥ = Pet Friendly Locations
Red print shows large vehicle parking / access on site or nearby Brown Print = Campgrounds / RV PARKS

EXIT	COLORADO
212	**Speer Blvd, Denver (SB)**
211	**23rd Ave, Water St, Denver**
Other	W: Invesco Field/Mile High Stadium
210C	**US 287, US 40, CO 33, 17th Ave, Denver (NB)**
Other	W: Broncos Stadium
210B	**US 40W, Colfax Ave, Auraria Pkwy, Aquarium Pkwy (NB)**
Food	W: Denny's, KFC, Rest/Ramada Inn, Rest/Red Lion
Lodg	W: Ramada Inn, Red Lion Hotel ♥
Other	E: Pepsi Center, Downtown W: Broncos Stadium
210A	**US 40, US 287, US 70 Bus, Colfax Ave, Downtown**
Med	W: + St Anthony's Hospital
Other	W: Invesco Field/Broncos Stadium, Downtown, Civic Center, State Capitol
209C	**8th Ave, Wyandot St (NB), Zuni St (SB), Downtown**
Lodg	E: Motel 7
Other	E: Auto Repair
209B	**US 6W, 6th Ave, Lakewood**
Lodg	W: Candlewood Suites ♥, Days Inn
209A	**6th Ave East, Downtown**
Med	E: + St Joseph Hospital
NOTE:	**Bridge Construction x208 thru 9/12**
208	**CO 26W, Alameda Ave (SB)**
Gas	W: BP, Shamrock
Food	W: Burger King, Denny's
Lodg	W: Motel 5
Other	W: ATMs, Auto Repair, Shopping Center
207B	**US 85S, Santa Fe Dr, Edgewood, Littleton (SB), to CO 26W, US 85S, Alameda Ave (NB)**
Gas	E: BP, Shamrock W: Conoco
Food	E: Burger King, Denny's, Subway
Other	E: Albertson's, ATMs, Banks, Home Depot, Pharmacy, Safeway W: Auto Services
207A	**Broadway (SB), Lincoln St (NB)**
Food	E: Griff's Burger Bar
Other	E: Amtrak, Auto Repairs
206	**Washington St, Emerson St, Louisiana Ave (SB), Downing St (NB)**
206B	**Washington St, Louisiana Ave (SB) Louisiana Ave (NB)**
206A	**Downing St (NB, reenter Buchtel Blvd)**
205	**University Blvd, Denver**
Gas	W: Conoco
Food	W: Domino's Pizza, Dunkin Donuts, Pita Jungle, Starbucks, Treehouse Cafe
Lodg	W: Comfort Inn, Days Inn ♥
Med	W: + University Park Medical Clinic
Other	E: Police Dept W: Univ of Denver
204	**CO 2, Colorado Blvd, Glendale**
Gas	E: 7-11, BP, Conoco, Shell W: Conoco
Food	E: Arby's, Black Eyed Pea, Boston Market, Grisanti Italian, Good Times Grill, Hooters, KFC, McDonald's, Noodles & Co, Little Caesars Pizza, Pizza Hut, Quiznos, Starbucks, Subway, Village Inn W: Crown Burgers, Dave & Buster's, Denny's, KFC, Japanese Rest, Middle Eastern Rest, Perkins, Taco Stop, Wok USA
Lodg	E: Days Inn, Fairfield Inn, Hampton Inn, Ramada W: La Quinta Inn ♥, Metropolitan Suites
Other	E: ATMs, Auto Dealers, Banks, Barnes & Noble, Best Buy, Enterprise RAC, Safeway, Walgreen's, Wild Oats W: ATMs, Banks, Albertson's, Auto Repairs, Colorado Center 9, Middle East Grocery,
203	**Evans Ave**
Gas	E: Shell
Food	E: Denny's, KFC, McDonald's, Quiznos, Rest/Holiday Inn
Lodg	E: Holiday Inn ♥, Ramada Ltd ♥, Rockies Inn W: Cameron Motel
Other	E: Auto Services, Auto Zone, Discount Tire, Hertz RAC, NAPA, Walgreen's **W: W to CO 2, Access Exit #204 Serv**
202	**Yale Ave, Denver, Englewood**
Gas	E: Valero W: Valero
201	**US 285S, CO 30E, Hampden Ave, Englewood, Aurora**
Gas	E: BP, Conoco, Phillips 66, Shell W: Conoco, Shell
Food	E: Bagel Deli, Benihana, Black Eyed Pea, Chili's, Domino's Pizza, Jason's Deli, McDonald's, On the Border, Noodles & Co, Qdoba Mexican Grill, Skillet's Rest, Starbucks, Subway, Sushi Train, Wahoo's Fish Taco W: Burger King, Starbuckss
Lodg	E: Embassy Suites, Marriott, Quality Inn, Sheraton, Towneplace Suites ♥
Med	E: + Rocky Mountain Health Center
Other	E: ATMs, Banks, Carwash, Cinema 6, Discount Tire, King Soopers Grocery, Regal Cinema 10, Staples, Tamarac Square Mall, Walgreen's,
(200)	**Jct I-225N, Aurora, to I-70, Limon**
Other	E: to Denver Int'l Airport ✈
199	**CO 88W, Belleview Ave, Cherry Hills Village, Greenwood Village, Littleton**
Gas	E: BP, Phillips 66, Sinclair W: Conoco, Valero ◈
Food	E: Bonefish Grille, Compari's, Cool River Cafe, Garcia's Mexican Rest, Harvest Grill, Original Pancake House, Paradise Bakery & Cafe, Shanahan's, Sandwiches +, Starbucks, Wendy's, Yia Yia's Bistro W: McDonald's, La Fondue, Pappadeaux, Pizza Hut, Taco Bell,
Lodg	E: Hampton Inn, Hilton Garden Inn, Hyatt Place, Hyatt Regency, Marriott, Residence Inn, Wyndham W: Extended Stay, Holiday Inn Express, Homestead Suites, Wellesley Inn
Other	E: ATMs, Banks, FedEx Office, Hertz RAC, King Soopers/Pharmacy, National RAC, Radio Shack, Staples W: Mountain View Golf Course
198	**Orchard Rd, Greenwood Village**
Gas	W: Shell
Food	E: Black Cow Deli, Double Eagle Steak House, Mama Mia's Italian, Starbucks W: Quizno's, Le Peep's Café, Starbucks, Venice Italian, Zink Kitchen & Bar,
Lodg	W: Hilton
Other	W: Coors Amphitheater, Denver Tech Center, Museum, **Police Dept**,
197	**CO 88E, Arapahoe Rd, Greenwood Village, Centennial**
Gas	E: BP, Conoco W: 7-11, Phillips 66 ◈, Valero
Food	E: Arby's, Black Jack Pizza, Black Eye Pea, Boston Market, Burger King, Brook's Steak House, Brothers BBQ, Carrabba's, Denny's, Dickey's BBQ, Fire Bowl Cafe, IHOP, Landry's Seafood, Outback Steakhouse, Papa John's Pizza, Pizza Hut, Qdoba, Red Lobster, Red Robin, Romano Macaroni Grill, Sahara Middle Eastern Rest Starbucks, Subway, Sushi Wave, Taco Bell, Wendy's W: Arby's, Bakery, Boston Market, Black Eyed Pea, Chevy Fresh Mex, DQ, IHOP, KFC, La Monica's Steak & Chop House, McDonald's, Mongolian BBQ, Quiznos, Red Robin, Romano's Macaroni Grill, Ruby Tuesday, Sakura, Souper Salad, Taco Bell
Lodg	E: Candlewood Suites ♥, Courtyard, Embassy Suites, Hampton Inn, Holiday Inn ♥, Hyatt, La Quinta Inn ♥, Radisson, Sheraton ♥, Sleep Inn, Wingate W: Executive Suites, Residence Inn
Med	E: + Concentra Urgent Care
Other	E: Auto Dealers, Auto Repairs, Avis RAC, ATMs, Banks, Budget RAC, Centennial Airport ✈, Discount Tire, Enterprise RAC, Home Depot, Lowe's, Pak-Mail, Southshore Water Amusement Park, Target, Thrifty RAC, US Post Office, **Walmart sc**,
Other	W: Albertson's/Pharmacy, ATMs, Banks, Barnes & Noble, Big O Tire, Brakes Plus, Coors Amphitheater, District 9 Cinema, Firestone Auto, Goodyear Auto, Greenwood Plaza 12 Cinema, Office Depot, Safeway
196	**Dry Creek Rd, Havana St, Centennial, Englewood**
Gas	W: Pride Auto Care/Conoco
Food	E: Big Bowl, IHOP, Jimmy's John's Gourme Sandwiches, Landry's Seafood House, Maggiano's Little Italy, Maxwell's, Trail Dust Steak House W: Bono's Pit BBQ,
Lodg	E: Best Western, Comfort Suites, Days Inn, Extended Stay America, Holiday Inn Express, Homestead Studio Suites, La Quinta Inn ♥, Quality Inn ♥, Staybridge Suites W: Drury Inn ♥,
Other	E: Pak-Mail Center W: Auto & Tire Services/Pride, Walgreen's,
195	**County Line Rd, Centennial**
Gas	W: Conoco, Costco
Food	E: Fleming's Prime Steakhouse & Wine Bar W: Burger King, J Alexander's, Champ's CA Pizza, DQ, High Tide Grill, Panda Express, McDonald's, PF Chang's, Red Robin, Starbucks, Steak Escape, That Basil
Lodg	E: Courtyard, Homewood Suites, Inverness Hotel, Residence Inn W: Hyatt Place, Towneplace Suites ♥
Other	W: Auto Services, Barnes & Noble, Best Buy, Costco, Goodyear, Home Depot, PetCo ♥, Park Meadows Mall, Sam's Club, UPS Store
194AB	**CO 470W, E470 N Toll Way, Limon, Grand Junction**

◈ = Regular Gas Stations with Diesel ▲ = RV Friendly Locations ♥ = Pet Friendly Locations
Red print shows large vehicle parking / access on site or nearby Brown Print = Campgrounds / RV PARKS

EXIT		COLORADO
194		**CO 470 (TOLL), Grand Junction (Access Serv W to Quebec St)**
	Gas	**W:** Love's, Texaco, Murphy
	Food	**W:** Arby's, ClaimJumper, Lone Star Steakhouse, On the Border, TGI Friday's
	Lodg	**W:** Comfort Suites, Extended Stay America, Fairfield Inn
	Other	**W:** Barnes & Noble, Firestone, Home Depot, Sam's Club, **Walmart sc**
193		**Lincoln Ave, Parker, Lone Tree, Highlands Ranch**
	Gas	**E:** Shamrock **W:** Conoco◈
	Food	**E:** Carrabba's, Great Beginnings Cafe, Hacienda Colorado, Rest/Hilton GI **W:** Chili's, McDonald's, Noodles & Co, Papa John's Pizza, Pizza Hut/Taco Bell, Starbucks, Subway
	Lodg	**E:** Candlewood Suites, Hilton Garden Inn **W:** Marriott
	Med	**W: + Sky Ridge Medical Center, + Lone Tree Urgent Care**
	Other	**E:** Meridian Golf Course, Wildlife Experience Museum **W:** Discount Tire, Lone Tree Veterinary Center♥, Safeway, Super Target, Univ of Phoenix, US Post Office, Walgreen's,
191		**Ridgegate Pkwy, Surrey Ridge, (Acc to #193 via W Ridgegate Pkwy)**
189		**Clydesdale Rd, Surrey Ridge**
188		**Castle Pines Pkwy, Castle Rock, Beverly Hills**
	Gas	**W:** BP, Conoco, Shell
	Food	**W:** Little Italy Pizzeria, Papa John's Pizza, Popeye's Chicken, Starbucks, Subway, Wendy's, Wild Bean Cafe
	Other	**W:** Big O Tire, Discount Tire, King Soopers/ Pharmacy, Safeway
187		**Happy Canyon Rd, CR 33**
184		**US 85N, CO 86E, Meadows Pkwy, Founders Pkwy, Castle Rock, to Sedalia, Littleton, Franktown**
	Gas	**E:** Conoco◈, Texaco◈ **W:** Loaf 'n Jug/Conoco◈
	Food	**E:** Applebee's, Carl's Jr, ChickFilA, Java Guru, Outback Steakhouse, Qdoba Mexican Grill, Quiznos, Red Robin, Starbucks, Sonic, Taco Bell, Wendy's **W:** Arby's, Black Eyed Pea, Burger King, Chili's, Duke's Steakhouse, Great Steak & Potato, IHOP, McDonald's, Rockyard Brewing Co, Subway, Taco Bell
	Lodg	**W:** Best Western, Comfort Suites♥, Days Inn♥, Hampton Inn
	Other	**E:** ATMs, Banks, Auto Services, Big 5 Sporting Goods, Cherished Companion Animal Clinic♥, Cost Cutters, Home Depot, King Sooper/Pharmacy, MotoSpa Carwash & Lube, Office Depot, O'Reilly Auto Parts, PetSmart♥, Radio Shack, Tires, Target/Pharmacy, UPS Store, Walgreen's, **Walmart sc** **W:** Bank, Auto Services, CarQuest, Castle Pines Golf Course, CO Cinema, Discount Tire, Midas, Prime Outlets at Castle Rock, Safeway/Pharmacy,

EXIT		COLORADO
182		**Wolfensberger Rd, Wilcox St, Castle Rock, to CO 83E, CO 86**
	FStop	**W:** Circle K/Shell Fuel Stop #1416
	Gas	**E:** Conoco, Phillips 66, Save O Mat **W:** Gas, Diamond Shamrock
	Food	**E:** Augustine Grill, Mexicali Café, Nick & Willie's, Skadoodles Baked Goods, **W:** Burger King, Domino's Pizza, KFC, Margarita's, McDonald's, Santiago's, Shari's, Taco Bell, Village Inn, Waffle House, Wendy's
	Lodg	**E:** Castle Pines Motel **W:** Comfort Inn, Holiday Inn Express, Quality Inn, Super 8
	Other	**E: CO State Hwy Patrol Post**, Douglas Co Animal Hospital♥, Greyhound, Museum, **Police Dept, Acc to #181 via E to Wilcox St, then S** **W:** Auto Dealer, Auto Services, Boyer Tire, Budget Truck Rental, Carstar Towing, Castle Rock Veterinary Clinic♥, Double D Auto Repair, Golf Course, Harley Davidson, NAPA,
181		**Wilcox St, Plum Creek Pkwy (SB), Castle Rock, to CO 86E (NB)**
	FStop	**E:** Western
	Gas	**E:** 7-11, BP, Gas 4 Less, Shamrock◈
	Food	**E:** China Cafe, New Rock Café, Pizza Hut, Subway, Union American Bistro
	Lodg	**E:** Castle Rock Motel
	Med	**E: + Swedish Health Park**
	Other	**E:** Auto Dealers, Auto Zone, Big O Tires, Douglas Co Fairgrounds, Meineke Car Care Safeway/Pharmacy, **Sheriff Dept**, South Street Auto & 4x4 Repair, US Post Office, Walgreen's, **Acc #182 N on Wilcox St**
174		**Bear Dance Dr, Tomah Rd**
	Other	**W: Castle Rock Campground/Jellystone Park at Larkspur▲**
173		**CR 53, Spruce Mountain Rd, Larkspur, Palmer Lake (SB, reaccess NB only)**
	Gas	**W:** Conoco◈
172		**Upper Lake Gulch Rd, Larkspur**
	Gas	**W:** Conoco◈
(171)		**Chain-Up Area (Both dir)**
167		**Greenland Rd, Larkspur**
	NOTE:	**MM 163: Area Prone to Severe Weather**
163		**County Line Rd, Palmer Lake**
	NOTE:	**MM 162.5: Elev 7352'**
(162)		**Weigh Station (Both dir)**
161		**CO 105, Monument, Palmer Lake, Woodmoor Dr, Second St**
	TStop	**W:** Conoco Truck Stop #6507
	Gas	**E:** BP **W:** 7-11, Texaco
	Food	**E:** Rest/Falcon Inn **W:** Boston Market, Burger King, DQ, Domino's Pizza, McDonald's, Pizza Hut, Rosie's Diner, Starbucks, Subway, Taco Bell, Village Inn
	Lodg	**E:** Falcon Inn
	Other	**E:** ATM, Bank, **Colorado Heights Campground/RVDump▲** **W:** ATMs, Banks, Auto Services, Big O Tires, RiteAid, Safeway, **Police Dept**

EXIT		COLORADO
158		**Baptist Rd, Colorado Springs**
	FStop	**W:** Diamond Shamrock #4136 (Scales)
	Gas	**E:** Shell◈
	Food	**E:** Chili's, Chinese, Popeye's/Shell, Subway **W:** FastFood/DS
	Other	**E:** King Sooper Grocery, Home Depot, **Walmart sc** **W:** Laundry/DS
156B		**North Gate Blvd West, US Air Force Academy, Visitor Center**
	Other	**W:** US Air Force Academy, Falcon Stadium, Golf Course
156A		**North Gate Road East (NB), Gleneagle Dr (SB) , USAF Academy**
153		**Interquest Pkwy, Colorado Springs**
	Lodg	**E:** Hampton Inn, Residence Inn, Renaissance Inn
	Other	**E:** Pikes Peak Comm College
(152)		**Scenic View-Pikes Pike View (SB)**
151		**Briargate Pkwy, to CO 83, Black Forest, Colo Springs**
	Gas	**E:** Conoco
	Food	**E:** Panera Bread, PF Changs, Qdoba Mexican Grill, Starbucks
	Lodg	**E:** Hilton Garden Inn, Homewood Suites
	Other	**E:** Focus on the Family Visitor Center
150AB		**CO 83, Academy Blvd**
150		**CO 83, Academy Blvd**
	Gas	**E:** Conoco, Diamond Shamrock, Shell
	Food	**E:** Applebee's, Burger King, Captain D's Chevy's Mexican, Cracker Barrel, IHOP, Denny's, KFC, Joe's Crab Shack, Mimi's Café, McDonald's, Olive Garden, Pizza Hut, On the Border, Red Robin, Souper Salad, Starbucks, Wendy's, Village Inn
	Lodg	**E:** Comfort Inn, Days Inn, Drury Inn, Howard Johnson♥, Marriott, Radisson, Red Roof Inn♥, Sleep Inn, Super 8
	Other	**E:** ATMs, Advance Auto Parts, Auto Services, Banks, Barnes & Noble, Big O Tire, Best Buy, Borders, Carmike Cinema, Chapel Hills Mall, Checker Auto Parts, Dollar Tree, Firestone Auto, Home Depot, King Sooper/Pharmacy, Office Depot, NAPA, Pep Boys, Pharmacy, Rental Cars, Sam's Club, US Post Office, **Walmart sc**, **W:** South Entr - Air Force Academy
149		**Woodmen Rd, Colo Springs, to CO 83, Academy Blvd**
	Gas	**E:** Loaf 'n Jug/Conoco◈ **W:** Shell
	Food	**E:** Carrabba's, Carl's Jr, Subway/Conoco **W:** Old Chicago Pasta & Pizza, Hooters, TGI Friday's, Outback Steakhouse
	Lodg	**W:** Comfort Inn, Embassy Suites, Extended Stay America, Fairfield Inn, Hampton Inn, Holiday Inn Express, Microtel♥, Staybridge Suites
148B		**Corporate Center Dr (SB)**
	Food	**W:** New South Wales Rest
	Lodg	**W:** Comfort Inn, Crestwood Suites, Hearthside, Extended Stay America
148A		**Bus 25S, Nevada Ave, Colorado Springs (SB LEFT Exit)**
	Lodg	**E:** Howard Johnson Express
148		**Bus 25S, Nevada Ave (NB)**

◈= Regular Gas Stations with Diesel ▲ = RV Friendly Locations ♥= Pet Friendly Locations
Red print shows large vehicle parking / access on site or nearby **Brown Print = Campgrounds / RV PARKS**

EXIT COLORADO

147 Rockrimmon Blvd
Gas W: Shell
Lodg W: Bradford Home Suites, Wyndham
Other W: Auto Repairs, Enterprise, Pro Rodeo Hall of Fame, Cowboy Museum, Safeway

146 Garden of the Gods Rd, Colo Spgs (Addt'l Serv East to US 85)
FStop E: K&G #63/Shell
Gas E: BP
W: 7-11, Conoco, Phillips 66, Shamrock
Food E: Carl's Jr, Denny's, McDonald's
W: Applebee's, Arby's, BlackEyed Pea, Hungry Farmer Rest, Quiznos, Taco Bell, Subway, Village Inn, Wendy's
Lodg E: Econo Lodge, La Quinta Inn♥
W: Days Inn, Holiday Inn, Quality Inn, Towneplace Suites♥
Other E: Rocky Mtn Greyhound Park, Auto Repair, High Country Truck Specialist, Hertz RAC, Enterprise RAC, Transmissions
W: Albertson's, ATMs, Banks, Discount Tire, Tire World, to Garden of the Gods

145 CO 38E, Fillmore St (Addt'l Serv East to US 85)
Gas E: 7-11, Shamrock
W: Conoco◈, Shell◈
Food E: DQ, Burger King
W: County Line BBQ, Waffle House, Rest/BW
Lodg E: Budget Host Inn, Ramada Inn
W: Best Western♥, Motel 6♥, Super 8
Med E: + Penrose Hospital
Other E: Auto Services, to Univ of Co
W: Auto Repairs

144 Fontanero St, Colo Springs

143 Uintah St
Gas E: 7-11
Other E: CO College

142 Bijou St, Kiowa St, Central Bus Distr, Dwntwn Colo Spgs
Gas W: Gas
Food E: Rest/BW, Rest/Clarion
W: Denny's
Lodg E: Best Western, Clarion Hotel♥, Doubletree Hotel
W: Red Lion Hotel
Med E: + Memorial Hospital
Other E: ATMs, Auto Services, Banks, Firestone, Museums, Monument Valley Park, US Olympic Complex

141 US 24W, Cimarron St, Manitou Spgs, Woodland Park (Addt'l Serv W to S 8th St)
Gas W: Conoco, Phillips 66
Food W: Arby's, Burger King, Captain D's, Dunkin Donuts, McDonald's, Papa John's Pizza, Popeye's Chicken, Subway, Texas Roadhouse, Taco John's, Waffle House
Lodg W: Express Inn, Holiday Inn Express, Old Town Guesthouse B&B, Travelodge
Other E: Costco, Greyhound, Museum, Sheriff Dept
W: to Adventure Camper Rentals, Auto Dealers, Auto Services, Auto Zone, CO Ave Veterinary Clinic♥, appr 3.5 mi: Crystal Kangaroo CG▲, Dee'Sales/Service/RV Rentals, Discount Tire, Enterprise RAC, Foot of the Rockies RV Resort▲, Fountain Creek RV Park▲, Appr 3 mi: Garden of the Gods Campground▲, Gateway RV,

EXIT COLORADO

Other W: Hobby Lobby, Just Brakes, Meineke Car Care, NAPA, Office Depot, Walmart sc, Pike's Peak RV Park & CG▲, Radio Shack, appr 2mi: Garden of the Gods, Goldfield RV Campground/RVDump▲, Ghost Town Museum,

140 Bus 25N, US 85S, Nevada Ave, Tejon St (NB), Bus 25N, US 85S, to CO 115, Tejon St, Nevada Ave, Canon City (SB) (Acc to Ex #141/#138)
Gas W: Circle K, Conoco, Shamrock, Shell
Food W: Burger King, El Miridor, KFC, McDonald's, Panera Bread, Pizza Hut, Shogun, Subway, Taco Bell, Wendy's
Lodg E: Bent Fort Inn, Chateau Motel, Howard Johnson, Nevada Motel, Travel Inn
W: Chief Motel♥, Circle S Motel, Rodeway Inn♥, Sun Springs Motel, Stagecoach Motel♥, Travelodge♥
Other E: Auto & Truck Repair, Tires, Police Dept
W: ATMs, Banks, Auto Dealers, Auto Repairs, Big O Tires, Cheyenne Mountain Zoo, Motorcycle Museum, Walgreen's,

139 US 24E, E Fountain Blvd, Colorado Springs Airport, Limon
Other E: to Peterson AFB, Colo Spgs Airport✈

138 CO 29, Circle Dr, Lake Ave
Gas E: Conoco, Circle K/Shell◈,
W: 7-11
Food E: McDonald's
W: Arby's, Baskin Robbins, Burger King, Carl's Jr, Carrabba's, Chili's, Denny's, Fazoli's, Flatiron's, IHOP, Olde World Bagel, On the Border, Outback Steakhouse, Red Robin, Romano's Macaroni Grill, Subway, Village Inn
Lodg E: Crowne Plaza, Days Inn♥/Super 8♥,
W: Best Western♥, Broadmoor Hotel, Comfort Inn♥, DoubleTree Hotel, Fairfield Inn, Hampton Inn, La Quinta Inn♥, Residence Inn,
TServ W: Colorado Kenworth
Other E: Pikes Peaks Vineyards
W: AT&T, Auto Services, Batteries Plus, Broadmoor Golf Course, Cheyenne Mountain Zoo, Colo Springs World Arena, Home Depot, Michael's, Office Max, PetCo♥, Tinseltown Movies 20,

135 CO 83, Academy Blvd, Colorado Springs Airport, Fort Carson
TServ E: to One Stop Truck Shop Truck & RV
Other E: High Country Veterinary Hospital♥
W: Pike's Peak Comm College

132 CO 16E, Mesa Ridge Pkwy, Magrath Ave, Fountain (Serv E 1.5mi to Fountain Mesa Rd, Addtl Serv: to US 85, 3 mi North)
Gas E: Love's Country Store #357◈, 7-11
Food E: Subway/Love's CS, Carl's Jr
Other E: Colorado Springs South KOA▲, Camping World, Camping Country RV Sales & Service, Gateway RV, Advance Auto Parts, Carwash/Love's CS, Fountain Creek Veterinary Clinic♥, Lowe's, Safeway, Walgreen's,
W: Fort Carson Military Res

128 US 85N, Santa Fe Ave, Fountain
TStop W: PTP/ Tomahawk Auto Truck Plaza/ Shell (Scales)
Gas E: 7-11, Loaf n Jug◈, Texaco
Food E: El Rodeo Mexican Rest, Subway/Loaf 'N Jug

EXIT COLORADO

Food W: Rest/Tomahawk ATP
Lodg E: Ute Motel
W: Motel/Tomahawk ATP, Super 8♥
TWash W: Tomahawk ATP
TServ W: Tomahawk ATP, Ace Diesel Repair
Other E: Auto Service & Tires, Laundromat
W: Laundry/WiFi/Tomahawk ATP

125 Ray Nixon Rd

123 Midway Ranch Rd

122 Pikes Peak Int'l Raceway Buttes
Other W: Pikes Peak Int'l Raceway

119 Rancho Colorado Blvd, Midway

116 County Line Rd, Henkel

(115) Pueblo Rest Area (NB) (RR, Picnic, Pet, RVDump)

114 Young Hollow Rd

(111) Pueblo Rest Area (SB) (RR, Picnic, Pet, RVDump)

110 Pace Rd, CR 501, Pinon
TStop W: AmBest/Rocky Mountain Travel Center/ Sinclair (Scales)
Food W: Rest/FastFood/Rocky Mtn TC
Lodg W: Motel/Rocky Mtn TC, Pinon Tree Inn
TServ W: Rocky Mtn TC/Tires
Other W: Laundry/Rocky Mtn TC

108 Purcell Blvd, Pueblo West , Bragdon
Other E: I-25 Speedway
W: Pueblo KOA▲

106 Porter Draw (Frontage Rd Acc Only)

104 Dillon Dr W, N Elizabeth St, to Platteville Blvd, Pueblo West, Eden (Acc #102 via Elizabeth St)
Food E: Buffalo Wild Wings, Cactus Flower, Chili's, Johnny Carino's Rest,
Other E: Bed Bath & Beyond, Kohl's, Old Navy, Office Depot, PetCo♥

102 Eagleridge Blvd, Pueblo (Frontage Rd Access to Ex #101 & #104)
Gas E: Loaf n Jug◈, Sam's Club
W: JR's Country Store/Shell◈
Food E: Burger King, IHOP, Starbucks, Texas Roadhouse
W: Cracker Barrel, DJ's Steakhouse, IHOP, Starbucks, Village Inn
Lodg E: Holiday Inn♥,
W: Best Western♥, Comfort Inn, Econo Lodge, Hampton Inn, La Quinta Inn♥, Wingate Inn
TServ W: Kenworth Dealer
Other E: Big O Tire, Cinemark Tinseltown USA, Home Depot, Sam's Club
W: Outpost Harley Davidson, Tires Plus,

101 US 50W, CO 47E, to US 50E Pueblo West, Canon City, Royal Gorge, La Junta (Acc to #102 & 104)
FStop W: Diamond Shamrock #4138
Gas E: Conoco, Loaf 'n Jug◈, Sam's
W: 7-11, Diamond Shamrock, JR's Country Store/Shell, Loaf 'n Jug, Phillips 66◈, Albertson's
Food E: Captain D's, Country Buffet, Denny's, Ruby Tuesday, Souper Salad, Starbucks, Texas Roadhouse, Three Margarita's,
W: Applebee's, Arby's, Black Eyed Pea, Boston Market, Burger King, Carl's Jr, Country Kitchen, Domino's Pizza, Fazoli's, Golden Corral, Little Caesar's Pizza,

◈= Regular Gas Stations with Diesel ▲ = RV Friendly Locations ♥= Pet Friendly Locations
Red print shows large vehicle parking / access on site or nearby Brown Print = Campgrounds / RV PARKS

EXIT — COLORADO

- **Food** E: McDonald's, Olive Garden, Papa John's Pizza, Pizza Hut, Popeye's Chicken, Planet Smoothie, Quiznos, Red Lobster, Ruby Tuesday, Santa Fe Café, Starbucks, Taco Bell, Wendy's, Blimpie/Cafe/JR's Shell
- **Lodg** E: Sleep Inn♥
  W: Clarion, Days Inn, Quality Inn♥, Super 8♥,
- **Med** W: + Emergicare Medical Clinic
- **Other** E: ATMs, Banks, Barnes & Noble, Big 5 Sporting Goods, Big Lots, Big O Tire, Carwash/Loaf 'n Jug, CO State Univ/Pueblo CO Tire, Home Depot, Pueblo Mall, Pueblo Mem'l Airport✈, Radio Shack, Sam's Club, Sports Authority, Target, Tinseltown USA, U-Haul, **Walmart sc**, Walking Stick Golf Course
  W: Advance Auto Parts, Auto Zone, Auto Services, Auto Dealers, ATMs, Banks, Albertson's/Pharmacy, Batteries Plus+, Carwash/P66, Carwash, Checker Auto Parts, Discount Tire, Goodyear, Kmart, **Appr 8 mi: Lake Pueblo State Park▲**, Lowe's, Midas, NAPA, PetSmart♥, Pueblo Motor Sports Park, **appr 9 mi: Pueblo West Campground & Arena▲**, **Rocky Mountain Greyhound Park**, Staples, Topper Factory & **RV Center**, Walgreen's, **Appr 6mi: Walmart sc**,

100B — 29th St, Pueblo (E Frontage Rd Access to Ex #101)
- **Gas** W: P66
- **Food** E: Country Buffet, KFC, Peter Piper Pizza, Panda Buffet
  W: Sonic, Tony's Chop House
- **Lodg** W: USA Motel
- **Other** E: Bank, Dollar Tree, Hobby Lobby, King Soopers/Pharmacy, Natural Grocery
  W: Grease Monkey, Safeway/Pharmacy,

100A — US 50E, to La Junta (E Frontage Rd Access to Ex #101)
- **FStop** E: 1st Stop/P66
- **Gas** E: Loaf n Jug
- **Food** E: McDonald's, Pizza Hut, Wendy's
- **Lodg** E: Val U Stay Inn
- **Other** E: AT&T, Big R Stores, Freeway Truck & Auto Repair, Goodyear, Greyhound Bus, Pueblo Memorial Airport✈, SavAlot, Skate City, Walgreen's,

99B — US 50 Bus, 13th St, Santa Fe Ave
- **Gas** W: Amoco
- **Food** W: Wendy's
- **Lodg** W: Best Western, Travelers Motel
- **Med** W: + Parkview Medical Center

99A — 6th St, to CO 96, Downtown Pueblo, State Fairgrounds (SB) (Access to Exit #99B Serv)

98B — 1st St, 4th St, CO 96, Downtown
- **Gas** W: Loaf 'n Jug
- **Food** W: Bingo Burger, Carl's Jr, Conway's Red Top, Rojas Mexican Rest, Shamrock Brewing Co
- **Lodg** W: Cambria Suites, Marriott
- **Other** E: Animal Emergency Room, Enterprise RAC,
  W: Family Dollar, Great Divide Ski, Bike, Hike Store, Museums, Pueblo Convention Center, to Pueblo Zoo

98A — US 50E Bus, La Junta (SB), US 50W Bus, Santa Fe Ave, Pueblo
- **FStop** E: Cliff Brice Station/Sinclair
  W: Acorn Petroleum/P66

Colorado
Colorado City
Walsenburg
Trinidad
Raton
Maxwell
New Mexico
Wagon Mount
Watros
Las Vegas
Pecos
Glorieta

EXIT — COLORADO

- **Food** W: Sonic
- **Other** E: Runyan Field

97B — Abriendo Ave
- **Gas** W: Diamond Shamrock, Texaco
- **Lodg** W: Abriendo Inn B&B
- **Other** W: to Pueblo Comm College, Pueblo Zoo & City Park, **Blue Mountain Village RV Park▲**,

97A — Central Ave, to Northern Ave
- **Gas** W: Shamrock,
- **Food** W: McDonald's, Mexican Restaurants
- **Other** W: Auto & Tire Services, CO State Fairgrounds, to Pueblo Zoo

96 — Minnequa Ave (SB, no reaccess), Indiana Ave (NB)
- **Gas** W: Gas◈
- **Lodg** W: motels W to Lake Ave
- **Med** W: + St Mary Corwin Medical Center

95 — Illinois Ave (SB, no re-entry)

94 — CO 45N, Pueblo Blvd, to US 50W, Pueblo, Canon City
- **Gas** W: Loaf 'n Jug◈, Western◈
- **Food** W: Pizza Hut/Taco Bell
- **Lodg** W: Hampton Inn, Kozy Motel, Microtel♥, Minnequa Motel
- **Other** W: Budget Truck Rental, **Fort's MH & RV Park▲**, **JDL Trailer Sales**, **to Lake Pueblo State Park▲**,

91 — CR 308, Lime Rd, Stem Beach
- **Lodg** W: Country Bunk Inn & **RV Park▲**

88 — CR 246, Burnt Mill Rd

87 — CR 337, Verde Rd, Pueblo

83 — Verde Rd, Brezell

77 — CR 345, Abbey Rd, Beulah, to Cedarwood

(74) — CO 165W, Colorado City, Rye, San Isabel
W: Rest Area (Both dir) (RR, Picnic, Vend, Pet, RVDump)
- **FStop** E: Diamond Shamrock #4062
- **Gas** W: Shell◈
- **Food** E: Hot Deli/Shamrock
  W: Ice Cream Shoppe/Subway/Noble Romans Pizza/Shell, Max's Rest
- **Lodg** W: Days Inn
- **Other** E: **Pueblo South/Colorado City KOA▲**

71 — CR 344, Graneros Rd, Thacker Rd, Colorado City

NOTE: SB: Exits 67 - 50 High Wind Area

67 — CR 660, CR 670, Apache City

64 — CR 110, CR 650, Lascar Rd

60 — CR 104, Huerfano River Crossing

(59) — Scenic Area-Huerfano Butte (NB)

59 — CR 103, Butte Rd

56 — CR 610, Red Rock Rd, to CO 69W, Gardner

55 — CR 101, Airport Rd
- **Other** E: Johnson Field Airport✈

52 — Bus 25S, to CO 69W, Walsenburg, Gardner (NB), to US 160, CO 69, Alamosa (SB)
- **TStop** W: Acorn Travel Plaza/P66

◈ = Regular Gas Stations with Diesel ▲ = RV Friendly Locations ♥ = Pet Friendly Locations
Red print shows large vehicle parking / access on site or nearby **Brown Print = Campgrounds / RV PARKS**

EXIT — COLORADO

Gas — W: Western
Food — W: George's Drive Inn, Pizza Hut, Subway
Lodg — W: Best Western, Budget Host Inn♥ & **RV Park▲**
Other — W: Laundry/Acorn TP, Auto Services, **Dakota Campground▲**, **Lathrop State Park▲**

50 — US 160W, Walsenburg, Alamosa, CO 10E, Hawley, La Junta
Gas — W: 7-11, Standard
Food — W: Alpine Rose Café, BJ's, Blue Rooster Saloon, Corine's Mex Rest, Donuts & Deli, Carl's Jr, Fireside Cafe, La Plaza Rest
Lodg — W: Anchor Motel, Knights Inn♥, La Plaza Inn B&B,
Med — W: + Hospital
Other — W: Auto Services, Dollar General, Mining Museum, NAPA, Safeway, US Post Office, U-Haul, Walsenburg Wildwaters Water Park, **to Lathrop State Park▲**

NOTE: NB: Exits 50 - 67 High Wind Area

49 — US 87, US 85, Bus 25N, to US 160W, Alamosa, Walsenburg (Access to Ex #50 Services)

42 — CR 310, Rouse Rd, Pryor

41 — CR 240, CR 310, Rugby Rd

34 — Spur 25, CR 60, Aguilar
TStop — E: Amato Truck Stop/BP
Food — E: Rest/Amato TS

30 — CR 63, Aguilar Rd

27 — CR 44, Ludlow
Other — W: Ludlow Monument

NOTE: SB: Construction thru x13 to end 7/11

23 — CR 42, Hoehne Rd

(18) — CR 32, El Moro Rd
W: El Morro Rest Area (Both dir) (RR, Picnic, Pet)

15 — US 160E, to US 350, CO 239, Kit Carson Trail, La Junta
Gas — W: Five Points Super Service, Texaco
Food — E: Burger King
W: Frontier Café, Lee's Drive-In
Lodg — E: Super 8
W: Frontier Motel

(14) — Colorado Ave, Commercial St, Trinidad (NB)
E: CO Welcome Center (NB) (RR, Phone, Picnic, Info, Free Coffee)
Gas — E: BP, Shell, JR's
W: Conoco, Phillips 66, Shamrock
Food — E: McDonald's, Pizza Hut, Subway
W: DQ, Chinese Rest, Domino's Pizza, El Capitan Rest, McDonald's
Lodg — E: Inn on the Santa Fe Trail
W: Prospect Plaza Motel
Other — E: Amtrak, Auto Repair, ATM, Bank, Museums
W: ATM, Auto Repair,

14B — Colorado Ave, Trinidad (SB)

13 — CO 12W, Main St, Trinidad (SB) University St, N Animas St
Gas — E: Jrs/Shamrock◈
W: Shamrock◈

EXIT — CO / NM

Food — E: Belle West Rest, KFC, McDonald's, Sonic, Subway
W: DQ
Lodg — E: Best Western, Blackjack's Saloon, Steakhouse & Inn, Cawthon Motel & **Campground▲**, Downtown Motel, Silver Dollar Inn, Stone Mansion B&B, Tarabino Inn B&B, Trail's End Motel, Villager Lodge
Med — E: + Mt San Rafael Hospital
Other — E: ATM, Bank, Auto Services, Auto Dealers, CarQuest, Family Dollar, Fox Theatre, Goodyear, Hometown Pharmacy, Museums, Safeway, Trinidad Lanes,

13B — CO 12W, S 160E, Main St, US 350 Trinidad (NB)

13A — Country Club Dr, Trinidad (NB)

NOTE: NB: Construction thru x 23 to end 7/11

(12) — NEW Exit

(11) — Santa Fe Trail, Trinidad, Starkville
E: Weigh / Check Station (NB)
TStop — E: Trinidad Fuel Stop/Shell
Gas — W: Tesoro
Food — E: Wendy's/Trinidad FS, 3 Margaritas
W: Country Kitchen, Rest/Qual Inn
Lodg — E: Budget Host Derrick Motel & **RV Park▲**
Budget Summit Inn♥ & **RV Park▲**, Holiday Inn
W: La Quinta Inn♥, Quality Inn
Other — E: CO State Patrol Post
W: Auto Dealer, Auto Services, Checker Auto Parts, Big O Tires, **Walmart sc**, **Trinidad Lake State Park▲**

8 — Frontage Rd, Spring Creek

6 — Frontage Rd, Gallinas

2 — Morley, Wootton

(0) — Weigh Station (SB)

NOTE: MM 460: Raton Pass - Elev 7834 ft

MOUNTAIN TIME ZONE

⬆ COLORADO
⬇ NEW MEXICO

MOUNTAIN TIME ZONE

NOTE: MM 460.5: Colorado State Line

NOTE: MM 460: Raton Pass - Elev 7834 ft

(460) — Port of Entry / Weigh Station (SB)
Other — E: Cedar Rail Campground & RV Park▲

454 — I-25 Bus, US 87, Raton (Serv appr 2mi/Access to Ex 452 Serv)
Gas — W: Shell
Lodg — W: Budget Host, Capri Motel, El Portal Hotel, Pass Inn
Med — W: + Hospital

452 — NM 72, Cook Ave, to US 87, Raton, Folsom
Gas — W: Conoco
Lodg — W: Mesa Vista Motel, Hearts Desire Inn B&B
Other — W: Amtrak, ATMs, Banks, Auto Repairs, Auto Dealers, Museum, **to Climax Canyon Park**

EXIT — NEW MEXICO

451 — US 64E, US 87, Clayton Rd, Raton, Clayton (Addt'l serv W to Bus 25)
FStop — E: Raton Truck Stop/Shell
TStop — E: 87 Express
Gas — E: Chevron◈
W: Chevron◈, Conoco◈, Phillips 66, Shell◈
Food — E: Rest/Hooter Brown TS, Subway,
W: All Seasons Family Rest, Arby's, DQ, Denny's, El Matador Rest, Icehouse Rest, KFC, K-Bob's Steakhouse, McDonald's, Pappas Sweet Shop Rest, Shanghai Rest
Lodg — W: Americas Best Value Inn, Best Western, Colt Motel, El Kapp Motel, Microtel♥, Motel 6♥, Quality Inn, Robin Hood Motel♥ Super 8, Travel Motel
TServ — W: Raton Auto & Truck Service
Med — W: + Hospital
Other — E: Laundry/Hooter Brown TS, Auto Service/Chevron, **Kickback RV Park▲**
W: ATMs, Banks, Ace Hardware, Auto Zone, Big Kmart, Carwash, Dollar General, Family Dollar, Hesters Motorsports, Laundromat, NAPA, **Raton KOA▲**, **Raton RV Park▲**, **Summerlan RV Park▲**, Vermejo Park Ranch & Lodge

450 — I-25 Bus, US 64, S 2nd St, Raton
FStop — W: Pendleton's 66
Gas — W: Conoco, Shamrock◈
Food — W: China Kitchen, K-Bob's, Rainmaker Café, Sonic, Sweet Shop
Lodg — W: Holiday Inn Express, Maverick Motel, Robin Hood Motel
Med — W: + Hospital
Other — W: **Raton KOA▲**, LP/Pendleton's 66, Auto & Tire Services, La Mesa Airport✈, Grocery, Drive In Theatre, La Mesa Park Racetrack & Casino, **Acc #451 Serv**

446 — US 64W, to Taos, Cimarron
Other — W: Raton Muni Airport✈

435 — CR A9, Raton, to Tinaja

(434) — Rest Area (Both dir) (RR, Picnic, Weather)

426 — NM 505, Maxwell Ave, Maxwell, to Maxwell Lakes
Gas — W: Gas◈
Food — W: Simple Simon's Pizza
Other — W: US Post Office

419 — NM 58, Springer, to Cimarron, Eagle Nest
TStop — E: Russell Truck & Travel/Shell (Scales)
Food — E: Rest/Russell T&T
Tires — E: Russell T&T
TWash — E: Russell T&T
Other — E: Laundry/Russell T&T

414 — US 85, Railroad Ave, Springer
Gas — E: Conoco◈, Shell
Food — E: Dairy Delite
Lodg — E: Oasis Motel

412 — US 56, US 412, NM 21, NM 468 S Springer, Clayton
Gas — E: Fina
Food — E: Brown Hotel & Cafe
Lodg — E: Brown Hotel & Cafe
Other — W: Springer Muni Airport✈

404 — NM 569, Colmor, Charette Lakes

393 — Levy, Wagon Mound

◈= Regular Gas Stations with Diesel ▲ = RV Friendly Locations ♥= Pet Friendly Locations
Red print shows large vehicle parking / access on site or nearby Brown Print = Campgrounds / RV PARKS

EXIT	NEW MEXICO
387	**NM 120, Wagon Mound, to Roy, Ocate**
Gas	E: Chevron◈, Phillips 66◈
(375)	Rest Area (SB) (RR, Picnic, RVDump)
(374)	Rest Area (NB) (RR, Picnic, RVDump)
366	**NM 161, to NM 97, Fort Union, to Watrous, Valmora**
364	**NM 161, NM 97, Watrous**
361	**Warren Ranch Rd, Las Vegas**
(360)	Parking Area (Both dir)
356	**Onava**
352	**Airport, Las Vegas**
Other	E: Duke RV Park▲ , Las Vegas Muni Airport✈
347	**Bus 25, to NM 518, N Las Vegas, to Taos**
FStop	W: Texaco
TStop	W: Pino's Travel Center/Fina
Gas	W: Phillips 66, SavOMat
Food	W: Rest/Pino's TS, Burger King, DQ, Great Wall Chinese, Mexican Kitchen, McDonald's, Taco Bell
Lodg	W: Budget Inn, Comfort Inn, Days Inn, El Camino Motel, Inn of Las Vegas, Inn on the Santa Fe Trail, Regal Motel, Super 8 Town House Motel, Sunshine Motel
Med	W: + Las Vegas Medical Center
Other	W: LP/Pino's TC, ATMs, Banks, Big O Tire, Firestone, Pinos Wrecker Service, Kiva Theatre, Museums, Auto Dealers, Amtrak, Vegas Truck & Automotive, Vegas RV Park▲ , Storrie Lake State Park▲
345	**NM 65, NM 104, University Ave**
Gas	W: Allsup's, Fina◈, Shell◈, SavOMat
Food	W: Arby's, DQ, Mexican Kitchen, KFC, Pizza Hut, Wendy's, Rest/El Camino Motel
Lodg	W: Budget Inn, El Fidel Motel
Med	W: + Las Vegas Medical Center
Other	W: ATMs, Banks, Museums, Theatre, Auto Services, Tires
343	**I-25 Bus, Grand Ave, to NM 518, S Las Vegas**
Gas	W: Chevron, Citgo, Fina, Phillips 66
Food	W: Burger King, McDonald's, Maryann's Famous Burrito Kitchen, Pizza Palace
Lodg	W: Plaza Motel, Thunderbird Lodge
339	**US 84, Las Vegas, to Romeroville, Santa Rosa, Historic Rte 66**
FStop	W: Tenorio's Travel Center/Texaco
Food	W: FastFood/Tesorio's TC
Other	E: Las Vegas/New Mexico KOA▲
335	**Tecolote, San Jose**
330	**Bernal**
(325)	Parking Area (Both dir)
323	**NM 3S, Ribera, Villanueva**
Gas	E: Shell
Other	E: to Pecos River Campground▲
319	**San Juan, San Jose, Sands**
307	**NM 63, Rowe, Pecos**

Personal Notes

EXIT	NEW MEXICO
299	**NM 50, Glorieta, Pecos**
Other	E: Pecos National Hist Park
297	**Valencia**
294	**Canoncito at Apache Canyon**
Other	E: Santa Fe KOA▲ , Pecos National Historic State Park
290	**US 285, Clines Corners, Lamy, Eldorado**
Other	E: to Santa Fe KOA▲ , Rancheros de Santa Fe Campground▲
284	**NM 466, Old Pecos Trail, Santa Fe**
Gas	W: Chevron◈, Fina
Food	W: Bobcat Bite, India Palace, Italian Bisto, Rest/BW, Steaksmith
Lodg	W: Bobcat Inn, Best Western, Pecos Trail Inn
Med	W: + St Vincent Hospital
Other	W: Quail Run Golf Course, Police Dept, Museums, Santa Fe Vineyards
282	**US 84, US 285, St Francis Dr, Santa Fe Plaza, to NM 14, Los Alamos, Taos (MANY Serv W 3mi+)**
FStop	W: Giant Travel Center #6046
Gas	W: QuickStop/Conoco
Food	W: Wendy's/Conoco, Church's Chicken, Mexican Rest
Lodg	W: to Cities of Gold Casino & Hotel, Camel Rock Casino & Suites, Ohkay Casino Resort W: Residence Inn, Santa Fe Suites, Travelodge,
Med	W: + St Vincent Hospital
Other	W: ATMs, Banks, Auto Services, FedEx Office, Grocery

EXIT	NEW MEXICO
282AB	**US 84, US 285, St Francis Dr (SB)**
278	**I-25 Bus, NM 14, Cerrillos Rd, Santa Fe, Madrid**
FStop	W: NM 14 3mi: Polk Oil/Shamrock
Gas	W: 1-3 mi: Chevron◈, Conoco, Phillips 66◈, Shell◈
Food	W: Applebee's, Arby's, Burger King, Blue Corn Café & Brewery, CiCi's Pizza, Bobby Rubino's Ribs, CoCo's, Denny's, IHOP, Horseman's Haven Café, KFC, Long John Silver, McDonald's, Olive Garden, Outback Steakhouse, Panda Express, Pizza Hut, Red Lobster, Taco Bell, Village Inn
Lodg	W: Inn at Santa Fe, Santa Fe Lodge, 2-3 mi: Best Western♥, Comfort Inn♥, Comfort Suites, Courtyard, Days Inn♥, El Rey Inn, Fairfield Inn, Hampton Inn, Holiday Inn, Holiday Inn Express, La Quinta Inn♥, Luxury Inn, Motel 6♥, Park Inn♥, Ramada Inn, Red Roof Inn, Super 8
Other	E: Santa Fe Skies RV Park▲ , to Santa Fe Comm College W: Santa Fe Premium Outlets, Villa Linda Mall, ATMs, Auto Dealers, Auto Services, Albertson's/Pharmacy, Animal Hospital♥, Banks, Best Buy, Cinemas, Discount Tire, Enterprise RAC, Firestone, Pep Boys, PetSmart♥, Sam's Club, Smith Food & Drug, Target/Pharmacy, Tires, Walgreen's, Walmart, Police Dept, Los Campos de Santa Fe RV Resort▲ , to Trailer Ranch RV Resort▲
278B	**Cerillos Rd, NM 14N, Santa Fe (SB)**
278A	**Cerillos Rd, NM 14S, Santa Fe (SB)**
276	**NM 599, NM 14, Madrid (SB)**
Gas	E: Phillips 66◈ W: Conoco, Shell◈
Lodg	W: Sunrise Springs Inn
Other	E: Land of Enchantment MH & RV Supply, Santa Fe Skies RV Park▲ , National Guard Armory W: Downs at Santa Fe, Santa Fe County Muni Airport✈, Avis RAC, Hertz RAC, Pinon RV Park▲
276B	**NM 599N, Airport, to Madrid (NB)**
276A	**NM 599S, to NM 14, Madrid (NB)**
271	**CR 50F, La Cienega**
Other	W: to appr 4 mi via Frontage Rd: Pinon RV Park▲ , Access to x276 serv
(268)	Rest Area (NB) (RR, Phone, Picnic)
267	**Waldo Canyon Rd, Waldo**
264	**NM 16, Cochiti, Pueblo, Pena Blanco**
259	**NM 22, Santo Domingo Pueblo**
FStop	W: Santa Domingo Tribal Gas Station/ P66
257	**Budagher**
252	**San Felipe, Pueblo**
TStop	E: San Felipe Travel Center/66
Food	E: Rest/Grill/San Felipe TC
Other	E: Laundry/RVDump/RVPark/Casino Hollywood/Speedway/San Felipe TC

◈= Regular Gas Stations with Diesel ▲ = RV Friendly Locations ♥= Pet Friendly Locations
Red print shows large vehicle parking / access on site or nearby Brown Print = Campgrounds / RV PARKS

EXIT | NEW MEXICO

248 NM 474, Bernalillo, Algodones

242 NM 44W, NM 165E, US 550, Rio Rancho, Bernalillo, Placitas
- Gas: **W:** Chevron◈, Conoco◈, Phillips 66, Shell◈
- Food: **W:** Burger King/Shell, Denny's, Dunkin Donuts, KFC, La Hacienda Express, Lotaburger, McDonald's, Pizza Hut, Sonic, Starbucks, Subway, Taco Bell, Wendy's
- Lodg: **W:** Days Inn, Holiday Inn Express, Quality Inn, Super 8, Santa Ana Star Hotel & Casino
- Other: **W:** **Albuquerque North KOA▲**, **Stagecoach Stop Resort RV Park▲**, **Coronado Campground▲**, ATMs, Banks, Auto Services, Auto Zone, Dollar General, Walgreen's, **Sheriff Dept**

240 NM 473, Bernalillo, Albuquerque (Access to Exit #242 Serv)
- Gas: **W:** Allsups, Conoco◈, M&R Gas
- Food: **W:** Range Café
- Other: **W:** True Value Hardware, **Albuquerque North/Bernalillo KOA▲**

234 NM 556, Tramway Rd
- Gas: **E:** Shamrock◈
  W: Phillips 66◈
- Other: **W:** **Casino Sandia**

233 Alameda Blvd, Albuquerque
- Gas: **E:** Chevron
  W: Phillips 66◈
- Food: **E:** Burger King, Long John Silver
  W: Carl's Jr, Marlene's Mexican
- Lodg: **E:** Comfort Inn, Motel 6♥
  W: Holiday Inn, Ramada Inn
- Other: **E:** Coronado Airport✈, Auto Dealers, Towing, Winery
  W: Balloon Fiesta Park

232 NM 423, Paseo del Norte NE
- Gas: **W:** Circle K/Shell◈
- Food: **E:** Starbucks, Subway
  W: Arby's/TJ Cinnamon/Shell
- Lodg: **E:** Country Inn, Howard Johnson, Motel 6♥
  W: Courtyard, Embassy Suites, Marriott
- Other: **E:** Kohl's, Lowe's, Office Depot, Target, Walgreen's

231 San Antonia Ave, Ellison Rd
- Gas: **E:** 7-11/Fina◈, Circle K/Phillips 66◈
- Food: **E:** Blake's Lotaburger, **Cracker Barrel**, Kettle Rest
- Lodg: **E:** Hilton Garden Inn, Homewood Suites, La Quinta Inn♥, Quality Inn
  W: Crossland Economy Suites, Hampton Inn, La Quinta Inn♥
- Med: **E:** **+ Hospital**
- Other: **E:** Family Dollar, Carwash/P66
  W: Auto Dealers, Century 10, Auto Serv

230 San Mateo Blvd, Osuna Rd
- FStop: **W:** Shamrock◈
- Gas: **E:** Chevron, Conoco◈, Giant◈, Shell, Star Mart
  W: Circle K/Chevron
- Food: **E:** Applebee's, Arby's, Burger King, DQ, Chili's, Hooters, KFC, Long John Silver, McDonald's, Olive Garden, Pizza Hut/ Taco Bell, Starbucks, Sweet Tomato, Subway, Taco Cabana, Texas Roadhouse, Village Inn, Wendy's, Weinershnitzel
  W: Cajun Kitchen, McDonald's/Chevron, Quiznos, SW Deli, Whataburger
- Lodg: **E:** Nativo Lodge, Wyndham Garden Suites
  W: Studio 6♥
- Other: **E:** ATMs, Bank, Auto Dealers, Auto Services, Dollar Tree, Firestone, Grocery, NAPA, Pep Boys, Tires, Towing, Cinema, Cliff's Amusement Park, Golf Course
  W: to Balloon View Homes & RV Park▲

229 Jefferson St, Albuquerque
- Food: **E:** Carrabba's Italian Rest, Landry's Seafood, Outback Steakhouse, Pappadeaux Seafood
  W: Boston Gourmet Pizza, Fuddrucker's, Genghis Grill, Jersey Jack's Eatery, Mimi's Café, Red Robin, Texas Land & & Cattle, Rockfish Café
- Lodg: **E:** Holiday Inn
  W: Drury Inn, Residence Inn, Wyndham Garden Suites
- Med: **E:** **+ St Joseph's NE Heights Hospital**
- Other: **E:** Cliff's Amusement Park

228 Montgomery Blvd, Montano Rd
- Gas: **E:** Chevron, Shell
  W: Circle K/Shell◈, Costco, Sam's Club
- Food: **E:** Blake's Lotaburger
  W: Arby's, IHOP, McDonald's, Panda Express, Starbucks, Subway, Wendy's
- Lodg: **E:** Best Western
  W: InTowne Suites
- Med: **E:** **+ Lovelace Womens Hospital**
- Other: **E:** Albertson's/Pharmacy, Walgreen's
  W: Auto Dealers, Costco, Home Depot, Office Depot, PetSmart♥, Sam's Club, Sports Authority, FedEx Depot

227B Comanche Blvd, Griegos

227A Candelaria Rd, Menaul Blvd
- TStop: **E:** Travel Center of America/Chevron (Scales) **(NB Access via Ex #225)**
- Gas: **E:** Circle K◈, Fina◈, Shell
- Food: **E:** CountryPrideRest/TA TC, JB's Rest, IHOP, Little Anita's Mexican Rest, Mesa Grill, Ranchers Club, Subway, Twisters, Village Inn
  W: Domino's Pizza, Waffle House
- Lodg: **E:** Comfort Inn, Days Inn, Elegante Hotel, Fairfield Inn, Hilton, Holiday Inn, La Quinta Inn♥, Quality Inn♥, Rodeway Inn, Super 8,
  W: Red Roof Inn♥, Travelodge
- TServ: **E:** TA TC /Tires
- Other: **E:** Laundry/WiFi/**RVDump**/TA TC, Utility Trailer, Auto Services
  W: Auto Services & Repairs

(226) Jct I-40, E-Amarillo, W-Flagstaff, Santa Rosa, Grants

225 Lomas Blvd, Albuquerque (NB: Access to Ex #227A)
- Gas: **E:** 7-11/Chevron
- Food: **E:** JB's Rest, Rest/Plaza Inn
- Lodg: **E:** Plaza Inn, Quality Inn♥, Rodeway Inn
  W: Embassy Suites
- Med: **E:** **+ Carrie Tingley Hospital**

224B Dr Martin Luther King Jr Ave, Central Ave, Albuquerque
- Gas: **W:** Chevron
- Food: **W:** Milton's, Rest/Econo Lodge
- Lodg: **W:** Crossroads Motel, Econo Lodge♥
- Med: **E:** **+ Presbyterian Hospital**
  W: **+ St Joseph Medical Center**

224A Lead Ave, Coal Ave, Central Ave
- Gas: **E:** Texaco
- Lodg: **E:** Crossroads Motel, Econo Lodge
- Med: **E:** **+ Presbyterian Hospital**

223 Avenida Caesar Chavez
- Gas: **W:** Chevron
- Lodg: **E:** Motel 6♥
- Other: **E:** Univ of NM Arena, Athletic Fields

222AB Gibson Blvd, Kirtland AFB, Airport (SB)

222 Gibson Blvd, Kirtland AFB, Int'l Airport (NB)
- FStop: **W:** to NM 47: Duke City/CFN
- Gas: **E:** Phillips 66
  W: 7-11/Fina
- Food: **E:** Applebee's, Burger King, Subway, Waffle House
  W: Blake's Lotaburger, Church's Chicken
- Lodg: **E:** Country Inn Suites, Comfort Inn, Fairfield Inn, Hampton Inn, Holiday Inn Express, La Quinta Inn♥, Quality Suites, Radisson, Sleep Inn
- Med: **E:** **+ Lovelace Hospital & Med Ctr**
- Other: **E:** Albuquerque Int'l Airport✈, Kirtland AFB, **MIL/Kirtland AFB FamCamp▲**

221 Sunport Blvd SE, Albuquerque
- Lodg: **E:** AmeriSuites, Holiday Inn Select, Wyndham

220 NM 500, Rio Bravo Blvd (Addtl Serv W to Isleta Blvd)
- Gas: **W:** Giant, Conoco
- Food: **W:** Burger King, McDonald's, Pizza Hut, Subway, Taco Bell
- Other: **E:** Albertson's, Auto Services, Diesel Service, Walgreen's, **RVDump**/Giant

215 NM 47, S Broadway
- Gas: **E:** Conoco◈
- Other: **E:** Isleta Gaming Palace & **Casino Resort**, **Isleta Lakes & Rec Area▲**, Isleta Eagle Golf Course

213 NM 314, Isleta Blvd
- Gas: **W:** Chevron◈
- Food: **W:** Subway/Chevron

209 NM 317, to NM 45, NM 314, Isleta Pueblo

203 NM 6, Main St, Los Lunas
- Gas: **E:** Chevron◈, Diamond Shamrock, Shell◈
  W: Phillips 66◈
- Food: **E:** Arby's, McDonald's, Popeye's Chicken, Quiznos, Ragin Cajun, Starbucks, Sonic, Village Inn, Wendy's
  W: Carino's, Chili's, KFC
- Lodg: **E:** Comfort Inn, Days Inn
  W: Western Skies Inn
- Other: **E:** ATMs, Banks, Albertson's, Auto Service, Auto Zone, Home Depot, **Police Dept**
  W: Walmart sc

195 Bus 25, Belen North, Los Chavez
- Gas: **E:** Murphy
- Food: **E:** McDonald's, Pizza Hut, Taco Bell
- Other: **E: Walmart sc**

191 Camino del Llano Rd, Sosimo Padilla, Belen
- Gas: **E:** Conoco◈
- Food: **E:** Carlos Cantina & Grill, KFC, McDonald's, Deli, Golden Corral, Montano's, Pizza Hut, Subway, TJ's Mex Rest
  W: Rio Grande Diner

◈= Regular Gas Stations with Diesel ▲ = RV Friendly Locations ♥= Pet Friendly Locations
Red print shows large vehicle parking / access on site or nearby Brown Print = Campgrounds / RV PARKS

EXIT — NEW MEXICO

Lodg E: Super 8♥
W: Best Western, Holiday Inn Express, La Mirada B&B & **RV Park▲**,

Other E: ATMs, Auto Zone, Banks, Big O Tires, Dollar General, Grocery, IGA, US Post Office
W: Alexander Muni Airport✈

190 — I-25 Bus, NM 314, S Belen (NB) (Access to #191 Services)

Gas E: Akins◈, Mustang, Nice n Fresh, Phillips 66◈

Food E: A&W/LongJohnSilver/P66, Arby's, Casa Pizza,

Lodg E: Chavez Estate B&B♥

Other E: Auto Service/Akins, Auto Services, Auto Zone, Big O Tires, Tourist Info,

175 — US 60E, Bernardo, Mountainair

Other W: **Kiva RV Park & Horse Motel▲**

169 — La Joya State Game Refuge

Other W: Wildlife Refuge

(167) — San Acacia Rest Area (Both dir)
NB: (RR, Pic, Vend, Pet, **RVDump**)
SB: (RR, Picnic, Pet)

(165) — Weigh Station (Both dir)

163 — Alamillo Rd, Magdalena, San Acacia, Polvadera

156 — NM 408, Lemitar

FStop W: RoadysTS/Roadrunner Travel Center/P66

Food W: Café/Roadrunner TC

Other W: Laundry/**RVDump**/Roadrunner TC

152 — Escondida

150 — I-25 Bus, US 60W, N Socorro, Escondido Ln, Magdalena

Gas W: Chevron, Exxon◈, Phillips 66◈, Shamrock◈,

Food E: Frank & Lupe's Mexican Rest
W: Blake's Lotaburger, Burger King, Denny's, Domino's Pizza, KFC, McDonald's, Pizza Hut, Sonic, Subway, Taco Bell

Lodg W: Best Western, Comfort Inn♥, Days Inn♥, Econo Lodge♥, Economy Inn, Holiday Inn Express, Howard Johnson♥, Prickly Pear Inn B&B, Rodeway Inn, Socorro Old Town B&B, Super 8

Other W: Ace Hardware, Auto Dealers, Auto Service, Carwash/Chevron, Dollar General, Family Dollar, NAPA, Radio Shack, Smith Food & Drug, **Walmart sc**,

147 — I-25 Bus, US 60W, US 85, S Socorro, Magdalena (Acc to #150 via N US 60/California St)

FStop W: Chevron,

Gas W: Conoco, Shell◈

Food W: Arby's, Denny's, McDonald's, Pizza Hut

Lodg W: Motel 6♥, San Miguel Inn

Med W: + Socorro General Hospital

Other W: **RVDump**/Chevron, Radio Shack, **Socorro RV Park▲**, Socorro Muni Airport✈

139 — US 380E, San Antonio, Carrizozo

Other E: **Bosque Bird Watchers RV Park▲**

124 — NM 178, Magdalena, to San Marcial

115 — NM 107, Magdalena, Socorro

TStop E: Santa Fe Diner & Truck Stop

Food E: Rest/FastFood/Santa Fe TS

EXIT — NEW MEXICO

Tires E: Santa Fe TS

Other E: Laundry/**RVDump**/Santa Fe TS

(114) — Rest Area (Both dir) (RR, Vend, Picnic)

100 — Red Rock

92 — Monticello Pt Rd, Mitchell Point

89 — NM 181, US 85, NM 52, T or C, to Cuchillo, Monticello

Other E: to appr 4mi: **Monticello RV Park▲**, **Elephant Butte State Park**

83 — US 85, NM 181, NM 195, NM 52, Hot Springs Landing, Cuchillo, Monticello

Other E: to appr 6mi: **Cedar Cove RV Park▲**, **Enchanted View RV Park▲**, **Lakeside RV Park▲**, **Cozy Cove RV Park▲**, **Elephant Butte Lake State Park▲**
W: Truth or Consequences Airport✈

(82) — Inspection Station (NB)

79 — I-25 Bus, N Truth or Consequences

FStop E: Chevron

Gas E: Circle K, Phillips 66◈

Food E: DQ, K-Bobs Steakhouse, Los Arcos Steak & Lobster House, McDonald's, Pizza Hut, Sonic, Subway

Lodg E: Ace Lodge, Charles Motel & Hot Springs Comfort Inn♥, Desert View Inn♥, Hot Springs Inn♥, La Paloma Hot Springs & Spa♥, Motel 6♥, Oasis Motel, Pelican Spa & Lodging, Red Haven Motel♥, Riverbend Hot Springs Lodging & Mineral Baths, Sierra Grand Lodge & Spa, Super 8, Trail Motel,

Med E: to + Sierra Vista Hospital

Other E: Auto Services, Auto Zone, IGA, NAPA, T or C Golf Course, True Value, US Post Office, **Walmart sc**

76 — I-25 Bus, South Truth or Consequences, Williamsburg (SB)

75 — US 85, S Broadway, I-25 Bus, Williamsburg, South Truth or Consequences (NB) (Acc to #79)

FStop E: Fast Stop/Shell

Gas E: Chevron, Conoco◈

Food E: Café Rio, Hacienda Mexican Rest, La Pinata Mexican Rest

Lodg E: Rio Grande Motel

Med E: + NM Vets Center Hospital

Other E: Laundry/FastStop, **Cielo Vista RV Resort▲**, **Monticello RV Park▲**, **RJ RV Park▲**, **Desert Skies RV Park▲**, **Cottonwood RV Park▲**, **Palmos RV Park▲**, Hyde Ave/**RVDump**, Auto Repair & Service, ATMs, Banks, Auto Dealer, Grocery, Museums, US Post Office, Fairgrounds, Police Dept

71 — Las Palomas

63 — NM 152, Caballo, Hillsboro

Other E: Caballo Emergency Truck Repair, **Lakeview RV Park▲** /LP/Gas◈, Lil Abner's Store & **RV Park▲**, US Post Office, U-Haul,

59 — NM 187, Arrey, Caballo-Percha State Parks, Caballo Lake

Other E: **Caballo Lake State Park/RVDump▲**
W: to **Percha Dam State Park▲**, **Arrey RV Park▲**

51 — NM 546, Arrey, Garfield, Derry

◈= Regular Gas Stations with Diesel ▲ = RV Friendly Locations ♥ = Pet Friendly Locations
Red print shows large vehicle parking / access on site or nearby Brown Print = Campgrounds / RV PARKS

EXIT NEW MEXICO

41 NM 26, Hatch, to Deming
Gas W: Conoco
Food W: DQ, B&E Burritos, Pepper Pot
Lodg W: Village Plaza Motel
Other E: Space Port
W: ATMs, Banks, Hatch Muni Airport✈, **Franciscan RV**, Grocery, **Happy Trails RV Park▲**, Hatch Chile Express

35 NM 140W, Rincon

32 Upham

(27) Scenic View (NB)

(26) Inspection Station (NB)

(23) Rincon Rest Area (Both dir) (RR, Picnic, Vend)

19 NM 157, Radium Springs
Other W: to appr 1.5mi: **Leasburg Dam State Park▲, Rio Grande River Resort▲**

9 NM 320, Dona Ana, Las Cruces
Gas W: Chevron◈, Conoco◈
Food W: Alejandro's Rest, Pizza Inn
Other W: Auto Services, Family Dollar, US Post Office

6AB US 70, US 82E, Alamagordo,
Gas E: Phillips 66◈, Texaco
W: Chevron, Conoco, Shamrock, Shell
Food E: Cattleman's Steakhouse, Coldstone Creamery, IHOP, Outback Steakhouse, Papa John's Pizza, Peter Piper Pizza, Ruby Tuesday, Santa Fe Grill, Starbucks,
W: Blake's Lotaburger, Burger Time, DQ, Domino's Pizza, KFC, McDonald's, Sonic, Spanish Kitchen, Subway, Taco Bell
Lodg E: Fairfield Inn, Motel 6♥, Super 8, Staybridge Suites, Towneplace Suites
Med E: + Mesilla Valley Hospital
Other E: AT&T, Jornada Veterinary Clinic♥, Kmart, Sam's Club, Theatre, US Post Office
W: Albertson's, Animal Hospital of Las Cruces♥, Auto Zone, Checker Auto Parts, Cinemas, Family Dollar, Golf Course, IGA, Lowe's, Radio Shack, **Sunny Acres RV Park▲**, Walgreen's,

3 NM 342, Lohman Ave, Las Cruces
Gas E: Shamrock, Shell
W: Conoco◈, Shell, Valero
Food E: Applebee's, Aqua Reef, Burger King, Cattle Baron Steak & Seafood, Chili's, Carino's Italian, Chuck E Cheese, Dion's Pizza, Golden Corral, Hooters, Jack in the Box, KFC, Luby's Cafeteria, Pecan Grill, Pizza Hut, Popeye's Chicken, Red Lobster, Sonic, Starbucks, Tiffany's Pizza & Deli, Twisters, Village Inn, Whataburger
W: Arby's, Carl's Jr, Delicias Cafe, El Sombrero Patio Cafe, Furr's Family Rest, Los Compas Mexican, McDonald's, Mesilla Valley Kitchen, Quiznos, Roberto's Mexican Food, Shem's Moroccan Rest, Si Senor Mexican, Subway, Taco Bell, Texas Road house, Wendy's,
Lodg E: Fairfield Inn, Hilton Inn, Hotel Encanto ♥ Motel 6
W: Hampton Inn
Med E: + Mountain View Reg'l Medical Center
W: + Concentra Urgent Care
Other E: ATMs, Albertson's, Barnes & Noble, Big 5 Sporting Goods, Discount Tire, Home Depot, Mesilla Valley Mall, Museums, Office Max, PetCo♥, Sportsmans Warehouse, Target,
W: 10 Pin Alley, Arroyo Veterinary Clinic♥, Best Buy, Big Lots, Brake Masters, East Lohman Veterinary Clinic♥, Enterprise RAC, Jiffy Lube, Martin Tire, NAPA, Pep Boys, PetSmart♥, Solano Animal Clinic♥, Staples, Suds Carwash, Tires, Toys R Us, UPS Store, US Post Office, Walgreen's, **Walmart sc**

1 University Ave, Las Cruces (Access Ex #3 Serv E to Telshor Blvd)
Gas W: Conoco
Food W: DQ, McDonald's
Lodg W: Comfort Suites
Med E: + Memorial Medical Hospital
Other W: FedEx Office, NM State Univ

(0) Jct I-10, E to El Paso, TX; W to Tucson, AZ

(0) Weigh Station (NB)

CENTRAL TIME ZONE

NEW MEXICO

Begin Northbound I-25 from Jct I-10 Exit #144 in Las Cruces, NM to Jct I-90 in Buffalo, WY

EXIT TENNESSEE

Begin Eastbound I-26 from VA Border to Jct I-17, near Charleston, SC

TENNESSEE

EASTERN TIME ZONE

NOTE: Former US 23, Last exit # remains

57 TN 36S, Lynn Garden Dr, Kingsport (WB exit, EB entr) (End US 23)

1 US 11W, TN 1, W Stone Dr
Gas N: Exxon, Shell, Sunoco, Valero
S: KenJo, Murphy USA, KarKorner
Food N: Bamboo Garden, KFC, Little Caesar's Pizza, Paradise Café, Pizza Plus, Wendy's
S: Bojangles, Burger King, Fatz Cafe, McDonald's, Papa John's Pizza, Pizza Hut, Waffle House
Lodg N: Days Inn, Super 8♥, Westside Inn
Med N: + Holston Valley Hospital, + Valley Medical Center
Other N: ATMs, Auto & Tire Services, Animal Hospital♥, Banks, CVS, Dollar General, Grocery, Penske Truck, **Tri City Travel Trailers**, U-Haul, Walgreen's
S: Auto Service, Auto Zone, Budget Truck Rental, CVS, Lowe's, O'Reilly Auto Parts, Stadium, Towing, Tractor Supply, **Walmart sc**

3 Meadow View Pkwy
Lodg N: Marriott Meadowview Conference Resort
Other N: Meadowview Golf Course, **Acc to #4**

4 TN 93, John B Dennis Hwy, Wilcox Dr, Sullivan Gardens Pky (WB)

4A TN 93S, Kingsport (EB)
Gas S: BP, Exxon
Food S: Arby's/Exxon, Little Caesar's Pizza, Pizza Plus
Other S: ATMs, Auto Services, Tires

4B TN 93N, Wilcox Dr (EB)
FStop N: Roadrunner #110/BP
Gas N: Shell
Food N: Subway/RR, McDonald's/Shell, Burger King, Hardee's, La Carreta Mexican Rest, Wendy's
Lodg N: Hampton Inn, Holiday Inn Express, Jameson Inn♥, Marriott
Other N: ATMs, Auto Services, Banks, Dollar General, Food City/Pharmacy, Golf Course, Pharmacy, Tires, **to 2-3 mi Ft Henry Dr:** Ft Henry Mall, **Walmart sc**, Asst Serv

6 TN 347, Rock Spring Rd
Other S: Eric's Truck & Trailer Repair

(8B/57B) Jct I-81, N to Bristol

(8A/57A) Jct I-81, S to Knoxville

10 Eastern Star Rd, Kingsport
Food N: Phil's Dream Pit BBQ
TServ N: Smoky Mountain Truck Center
Other N: Free Service Tire Co Auto & Truck

13 TN 75, Suncrest Dr, Bobby Hicks Hwy, Johnson City
Gas N: BP◈, Shell◈, Food City
S: Appco
Food N: Burger King, DQ, McDonald's, Pal's, Papa John's Pizza, Pizza Hut, Japanese Rest, Subway, TCBY,
Other N: Advance Auto, Firestone, Food City, RiteAid, Robinson Animal Hospital♥, Walgreen's, US Post Office, **to** Washington Co Fairgrounds, **appr 5 mi:** Tri-Cities Airport✈

17 TN 354, Boones Creek Rd, to Jonesborough
Gas N: BP
S: Appco, Shell◈
Food N: Beef O'Brady's, Bob Evans, Giovanni's, Kemosabee's Roadhouse
S: Burger King, **Cracker Barrel**, Dominos Pizza, El Matador Rest, Subway, Waffle House, Wendy's, Rest/HI Exp
Lodg S: Holiday Inn Express, Jameson Inn, Value Place
Other N: Boone's Creek Animal Hospital♥, Boone's Creek Pharmacy, Budget Truck Rental, Ingles, U-Haul

19 TN 381, State of Franklin Rd, Oakland Ave, to US 321, Bristol
Gas N: Appco, Murphy

◈ = Regular Gas Stations with Diesel ▲ = RV Friendly Locations ♥ = Pet Friendly Locations
Red print shows large vehicle parking / access on site or nearby Brown Print = Campgrounds / RV PARKS

EXIT		TENNESSEE
	Gas	**S:** Exxon
	Food	**N:** McDonald's/Appco, Dixie BBQ, Golden Corral, Logan's Roadhouse, Outback Steakhouse, Quiznos, Subway, Sonic **S:** Atlanta Bread, Cafe Pacific, Carrabba's, ChickFilA, CiCi's Pizza, Chili's, Chuck E Cheese, Fuddrucker's, IHOP, Mellow Mushroom, Panera Bread, Stir Fry Cafe, Wendy's
	Lodg	**N:** Comfort Suites **S:** Courtyard, Hampton Inn, Sleep Inn
	Other	**N:** ATMs, Advance Auto, Auto Dealers, Auto Services, Big Lots, Carwash, Fred's, Hobbytown USA, Office Max, Penske Truck Rental, Radio Shack, Tires, UPS Store, **Walmart sc,** **S:** AT&T, Barnes & Noble, Best Buy, Home Depot, Kmart/Pharmacy, Lowe's, Natural Foods Market, PetSmart ♥, Verizon
20		**US 11E, US 19W, TN 34, N Roan St, Johnson City, Bluff City (EB)**
20A		**US 11E, US 19W, TN 34, to Bluff City (WB)**
	Gas	**S:** BP, Sunoco
	Food	**S:** Applebee's, Burger King, Cafe Lola Bistro, Cafe 111, ChickFilA, Five Guys Burgers & Fries, Gourmet & Co, Hooters, McDonald's, Nascar Cafe, O'Charley's, Red Pig BBQ, Red Lobster, Ryan's Grill, Shoney's, Smokey Bones BBQ, Starbucks, Subway, Taco Bell, Texas Roadhouse
	Lodg	**S:** Days Inn, Doubletree Hotel, Quality Inn♥, Red Roof Inn
	Other	**S:** ATMs, Banks, Cinemas, CVS, Dick's Sporting Goods, Dollar General, Dollar Tree, Food City, Johnson City Mall, Kroger/Pharmacy, Midas, Office Depot, Target/Pharmacy, Walgreen's
20B		**N Roan St, Johnson City (WB)**
	Gas	**N:** Citgo, Phillips 66
	Food	**N:** Arby's, Cootie Brown's, Crazy Tomato, Empire Chinese Buffet, Hardee's, Harbor House Seafood, Little Caesars Pizza, Perkins, Sagebrush Steakhouse, Waffle House
	Lodg	**N:** Best Western, Holiday Inn, Ramada, Super 8
	Med	**N: + Northside Hospital**
	Other	**N:** Auto Dealers, Auto Zone, Advance Auto Parts, Banks, Grocery, Tri City's Fun Expedition
22		**TN 400, Unaka Ave, Watauga Ave, Johnson City, Airport**
	Food	**S:** Scratch Brick Oven Pizza,
	Med	**S: + Johnson City Speciality Hospital**

EXIT		TENNESSEE
	Other	**S:** Auto Services, Pharmacy, Robinson Animal Hospital ♥
23		**TN 91, Market St, Main St, to 11E, Johnson City**
	Gas	**N:** Appco **S:** BP
	Food	**N:** DQ, McDonald's **S:** Dominos Pizza, Freiberg's German Rest, Mid City Grill, Pizza Hut, Zaxby's
	Med	**S: + Johnson City Medical Center**
	Other	**N:** Food Lion, Meineke Car Care, US Post Office **S:** Auto Services, E TN State Univ, Kroger, Museum
24		**US 321, TN 67, University Pkwy, to TN 381, to Elizabethton**
	Gas	**N:** Shell◈ **S:** BP◈
	Food	**N:** Deli **S:** Arby's, Burger King, Jerry's Café, Little Caesars Pizza, Subway
	Lodg	**S:** Comfort Inn
	Med	**S: + US Veterans Medical Center**
	Other	**S:** Advance Auto Parts, Cherokee Animal Hospital♥, Food City, Pine Oaks Golf Course, **Roan Mountain State Park,** to E TN State Univ
27		**TN 359N, Okolona Rd**
	Gas	**N:** BP
	Lodg	**N:** Budget Inn
	Other	**N:** Milligan College
32		**TN 173, Unicoi Rd**
	Gas	**N:** Phillips 66
	Food	**N:** Maple Grove Cafe
	Lodg	**N:** Budget Inn
	Other	**N: to Grand View Ranch RV Campground▲ , appr 3.5 mi: North Indian Creek Campground▲ , to appr 5.5mi: Blackberry Blossom Farm & Campground** **S: Woodsmoke Campground▲**
34		**Tinker Rd, Unicoi**
	Gas	**N:** Murphy USA
	Other	**N: Walmart sc,**
36		**Harris Hollow Rd, to Main St, Erwin (Acc to #37 via Main St/TN 107)**
	Gas	**N:** Appco, BP◈,
	Food	**N:** Azteca Mexican Rest, Backwood BBQ, Hardee's, KFC, Little Caesar's Pizza, Pizza Hut, Rocky's Pizza, Subway, Taco Bell, Wendy's/Appco
	Other	**N:** ATMs, Bank, Advance Auto Parts, Dollar General, Garland Tires, Grocery, RiteAid
37		**TN 81, TN 107, Jonesborough Rd**
	Gas	**N:** Shell◈

EXIT		TN / NC
	Food	**N:** Huddle House, McDonald's, Sonic, Taco Bell **S:** River's Edge
	Lodg	**S:** Super 8♥
	Med	**N: + Hospital**
	Other	**N:** CVS, Liberty Ace Hardware, Walgreen's, **Cherokee Nat'l Forest** **S: Cherokee Nat'l Forest▲ , to appr 3mi: Riverpark Campground▲ , Riverview Campground▲ , to appr 22 mi: Pebble Mountain Family Campground▲**
40		**Jackson-Love Hwy, Erwin**
	FStop	**N:** Appco #69
	Gas	**N:** BP, Exxon, Valero
	Food	**N:** Pizza Plus, A&W/LJ, Silver/Appco
	Lodg	**N:** Holiday Inn Express, Southern Motel
	Other	**N:** Auto & Tire Services/Exxon, Auto & Tire Services, Carwash, Dollar General, U-Haul, **to** Uncle Johnny's Nolichucky Hostel & Outfitters, White's Grocery, **appr 2.5 mi: Nolichucky Gorge Campground▲**
43		**US 19W, to TN 352, Temple Hill Rd**
	Gas	**N: to appr 2mi:** Exxon
	Other	**N: Double D Roost Campsites▲**
46		**Clear Branch Rd, Flag Pond Rd**
	Other	**N: Acorn RV Park▲**
(48)		**Scenic Overlook (WB) (NO Trucks)**
50		**Higgins Creek Rd, Flag Pond**
(54)		**Scenic Overlook (EB) (NO Trucks)**

EASTERN TIME ZONE

⬆ TENNESSEE
⬇ NORTH CAROLINA

EASTERN TIME ZONE

EXIT		TN / NC
(0)		**Brake Check Area**
(2)		**Runaway Truck Ramp (EB)**
3		**Mars Hill, US 23 Alt, Wolf Laurel**
	Gas	**N:** Wolf Creek Market/Exxon◈
	Food	**N:** Little Creek Cafe
	Lodg	**N: to appr 5 mi:** Scenic Wolf Resort at Wolf Ridge
(5)		**Runaway Truck Ramp (EB)**
(6)		**NC Welcome Center (EB) (RR, Phone, Picnic)**
(7)		**Runaway Truck Ramp (EB)**
(8)		**Scenic View (WB)**

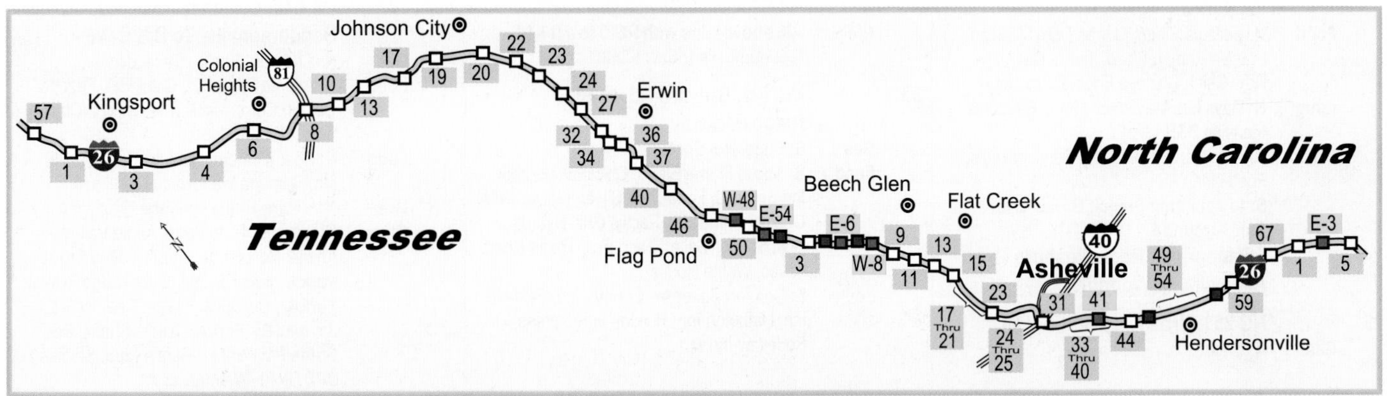

◈= Regular Gas Stations with Diesel ▲ = RV Friendly Locations ♥= Pet Friendly Locations
Red print shows large vehicle parking / access on site or nearby Brown Print = Campgrounds / RV PARKS

EXIT		NORTH CAROLINA
9		**US 19N, Burnsville, Spruce Pine**
11		**NC 213, Carl Eller Rd, Mars Hill, To Marshall**
	Gas	**S:** Chevron◈, Exxon◈, Shell◈
	Food	**S:** Hardee's/Exxon, Osake Japanese Rest, Subway, Waffle House
	Lodg	**S:** Comfort Inn♥
	Other	**S:** Banks, CVS, Dollar General, Ingles, Mars College, NAPA, Radio Shack,
13		**Forks of Ivy, Weaverville**
	FStop	**N:** Payless Food Mart/BP
	Gas	**S:** Exxon◈
15		**NC 197, Barnardsville Hwy, to Jupiter, Barnardsville**
	Gas	**N:** to Stockton Farms Country Store/Valero
	Food	**N:** Cafe/Valero
	Other	**N:** Mountain Animal Hospital♥
17		**Flat Creek, Weaverville**
18		**US 19 Bus, Monticello Rd, (Diff Reacc EB-S on US19, reacc via #19) (Acc to #19 Serv)**
	Gas	**N:** Corner Store, Handi Mart
	Food	**N:** Athens Rest
	Other	**N:** NAPA, Tractor Supply, US Post Office
19		**US 25N, US 70W, Weaver Blvd, Weaverville, to Marshall (EB)**
19A		**US 25N, US 70W, Marshall (WB)**
	FStop	**S:** Mountain Energy/Shell, Mountain Energy/BP
	Other	**S:** NAPA, U-Haul
19B		**US 25N, US 70W, Weaverville (WB)**
	Gas	**N:** Shell◈, Ingles
	Food	**N:** Arby's, Bojangles, Burger King, KFC, McDonald's, Subway, Waffle House, **S on US 23:** Well Bread Bakery & Cafe, Blue Mountain Pizza
	Med	**N: + Sisters of Mercy Urgent Care**
	Lodg	**N:** Dry Ridge Inn B&B, Inn on Main St B&B
	Other	**N:** Ace Hardware, Advance Auto Parts, Ingles, Kerr Drug **S:** Lowe's, U-Haul, **Walmart sc**,
21		**New Stock Rd, Aiken Rd, Asheville to US 19 Bus, US 23 Bus**
	Gas	**N:** BP, Citgo, Ingles
	Food	**N:** Granny's Kitchen, Pizza Hut, Stoney Knob Rest
	Other	**N:** Ingles
23		**Merrimon Ave, US 25, N Ashville, New Bridge, Weaverville Hwy**
	Gas	**N:** BP, Exxon◈, Hot Spot, Red's Service Center/P66
	Food	**N:** Bellagio Bistro, Curras Dom Mexican, Frank's Roman Pizza, Ilene's Café, New China Chinese Food, Pizza Hut
	Lodg	**N:** Days Inn, Mayflower Motel, Reynolds Mansion B&B
	Other	**N:** Auto Service/BP, Auto Service/Red's, Food Lion **S:** to appr 4mi: **French Broad River Campground▲**
24		**Elk Mountain Rd, Lakeshore Dr, Asheville, to Woodfin**
25		**NC 251, Broadway St, Univ NC,**
	Gas	**N:** Citgo

EXIT		NORTH CAROLINA
	Lodg	**N:** 1899 Wright Inn & Carriage House B&B, 1900 Inn on Montford B&B, Abbington Green B&B♥, Applewood Manor Inn B&B♥, Asheville Seasons B&B, A Hill House B&B, At Cumberland Falls B&B, Lion & Rose B&B, **S:** Richmond Hill Inn B&B,
	Other	**N:** Univ of NC/Asheville, **to I-240 Addtl Services**
(*)		**Hill St (WB exit, EB entr)**
	NOTE:	**I-26 below runs with I-240 to Jct I-40. Exit numbers follow I-240.**
(31)		**Jct I-240E, US 70E, US 74 Alt E (EB)**
4B		**Patton Ave, Downtown Asheville**
(4A)		**I-26W, US 19N, US 23N, US 70W**
3B		**Resort Dr, Westgate Pkwy**
	Gas	**N:** Sam's Club
	Lodg	**N:** Crowne Plaza
	Other	**N:** CVS, Earth Fare Healthy Supermarket, Sam's Club
3A		**US 19S, US 23S, US 74 Alt W, Patton Ave**
	Gas	**N:** BP
	Food	**N:** Arby's, Bojangles, Denny's, Green Tea Japanese Rest, Little Caesars Pizza, Long John Silvers, McDonald's, Pizza Hut,
	Other	**N:** Advance Auto Parts, Auto Dealers, Auto Zone, Aldi, Banks, Family Dollar, Hertz RAC, Ingles, Kerr Drug, Mountain View Tire & Services, Pet Vet on Patton♥, Radio Shack, RiteAid, Sam's Club, US Post Office, Verizon,
2		**US 19 Bus, US 23 Bus**
	Gas	**N:** Shell **S:** BJ's Food Mart, Gas Up,
	Food	**N:** Lucky Otter Rest, Sunny Pointe Cafe, Tastee Diner
	Other	**N:** Ingles, Laundromat, O'Reilly Auto Parts, **Addt'l Serv on Patton Ave** **S:** B&B Pharmacy, Auto Services
1C		**Amboy Rd (WB exit, EB entr)**
	Gas	**S:** Citgo
	Food	**S:** Pizza Hut
	Other	**S:** Asheville Outdoor Center, **Wilson's Riverfront RV Park▲**, **Wilson's RV Service**
1B		**NC 191, Brevard Rd, to I-40E**
	Other	**S:** to **Bear Creek RV Park▲**
(31B)		**Jct I-240W, US 74W, to Canton, Knoxville, TN**
(31A)		**Jct I-40E, to Hickory (WB exit, EB entr)**
	NOTE:	**I-26 above runs with I-240 to Jct I-40. Exit numbers follow I-240.**
33		**NC 191, Brevard Rd, to Blue Ridge Parkway**
	Gas	**S:** Citgo, Hot Spot
	Food	**S:** Apollo Flame Bistro, ChickFilA, Harbor Inn Seafood, Long John Silver, McDonald's, Original Prime Rib, Pacific Grill, Ryan's Grill, Souper Salad, Taco Bell, Texas Road house, Waffle House
	Lodg	**S:** Comfort Suites♥, Country Inn, Fairfield Inn, Hampton Inn, Holiday Inn Express, Rodeway Inn♥,

EXIT		NORTH CAROLINA
	Other	**N:** Auto Dealer, Reach Emergency Veterinary Hospital♥, **to Ashville Bear Creek RV Park & Campground▲**, **S:** Biltmore Square Mall, Cinema, Ingles Grocery, Kmart, ToysRUs, **to appr 2mi: Lake Powhatan Rec Area▲**
37		**NC 146, Long Shoals Rd, Arden, to Skyland**
	Gas	**N:** Exxon, Shell◈
	Food	**N:** Arby's, McDonald's, Shoney's, Waffle House
	Lodg	**N:** Quality Inn
	Other	**N:** CVS **S:** Avery Creek Pet Hospital♥
40		**NC 280, Airport Rd, Fletcher, Arden, Asheville Reg'l Airport**
	Gas	**N:** Exxon◈, Shell◈ **S:** BP◈
	Food	**N:** Arby's/Shell, Carrabba's, **Cracker Barrel**, Lone Star Steakhouse, McDonald's, Pizza Hut, Ruby Tuesday, Waffle House, **S:** Circle B Ranch BBQ, J & S Cafeteria
	Lodg	**N:** Budget Inn, Comfort Inn♥, Days Inn, Econo Lodge, Hampton Inn, Holiday Inn Express **S:** Fairfield Inn
	Med	**N: + Sisters of Mercy Urgent Care**
	Other	**N:** Arden Animal Hospital♥, Auto Dealer, Best Buy, CarQuest, Dollar Depot, Jim Campen Trailer Sales, Lowe's, Michael's, PetSmart ♥, Target, UPS Store, US Post Office, Walgreen's, **Walmart sc**, **S:** Asheville Reg'l Airport✈, **Rutledge Lake RV Park▲**
(41)		**Rest Area (Both dir) (RR, Phone, Picnic)**
44		**US 25, Hendersonville Rd, Fletcher, Mountain Home**
	TStop	**S:** Mountain Energy Travel Center #26/ Shell (Scales)
	Gas	**N:** Exxon◈ **S:** Citgo◈
	Food	**N:** Hardee's, Subway **S:** Mtn Energy TC, Burger King, Huddle House
	Lodg	**S:** Mountain Inn♥
	TServ	**S:** Mountain Energy TC
	Med	**N: + Park Ridge Urgent Care**
	Other	**N:** Auto & Tire Services, Fletcher Animal Hospital♥, Jim Campen Trailer Sales, Smiley's Flea Market, Snider Tire, U-Haul, US Post Office **S:** Laundry/Mountain Energy TC, **Todd's RV & Marine**
(46)		**Weigh Station (Both dir)**
49A		**US 64E, Chimney Rock Rd, Hendersonville, to Bat Cave**
	Gas	**N:** Chevron, Shell◈, Texaco◈
	Food	**N:** Atlanta Bread Co, ChickFilA, Fazoli's, Golden Corral, Jack in the Box, O'Charley's, Sonic, Waffle House
	Lodg	**N:** Best Western, Hampton Inn, Quality Inn, Ramada Inn
	Med	**N: + Park Ridge Hospital**
	Other	**N:** Advance Auto Parts, Apple Valley Animal Hospital♥, **Apple Valley Travel Park▲**, **to appr 5mi: Blue Ridge Travel Park▲**, CarQuest, Dollar Tree, Ingles, **Jaymar RV Park▲**, Radio Shack, **Red Gates RV Park▲**, Sam's Club, Staples, UPS Store, **Walmart sc**,

◈ = Regular Gas Stations with Diesel ▲ = RV Friendly Locations ♥ = Pet Friendly Locations
Red print shows large vehicle parking / access on site or nearby Brown Print = Campgrounds / RV PARKS

EXIT NC / SC

49B **US 64W, 4 Seasons Blvd**
Gas S: Chevron◈, Exxon◈, Shell◈
Food S: Applebee's, Arby's, Bojangles, Burger King, CiCi's Pizza, Denny's, Fatz Cafe, Hardee's, KFC, Krispy Kreme, Long John Silver, McDonald's, Outback Steakhouse, Ryan's Grill, Shoney's, Taco Bell, Wendy's
Lodg S: Comfort Inn, Days Inn, Red Roof Inn♥
Med S: + Margaret Pardee Memorial Hospital
Other S: ATMs, Banks, Aldi's, Auto Dealers, Bi-Lo, Big Lots, Blue Ridge Mall, CVS, Four Seasons Cinema, Home Depot, Jiffy Lube, Kmart, Lowe's, Mountain View Tire, U-Haul, Verizon, **to Phil & Ann's RV Sales & Service & RV Park▲** ,

53 **Upward Rd, Hendersonville**
Gas N: Texaco◈
S: Exxon◈, Shell◈
Food N: Zaxby's
S: Pizza Inn/Shell, Burger King, Cracker Barrel, McDonald's/Exxon, Subway, Waffle House
Lodg N: Mountain Inn & Suites, Mountain Lodge
S: Holiday Inn Express
Other N: **Lakewood RV Resort▲**
S: Auto Dealer, **Park Place RV Park▲** , **Town Mountain Travel Park▲** , Blue Ridge Comm College, **to** Hendersonville-Winkler Airport✈

54 **US 25, to US 176, NC 225, to Greenville, E Flat Rock**

NOTE: **MM 55: EB: 6% Steep Grade**

59 **Saluda**
TStop S: Saluda Truck Plaza/BP
Gas S: Texaco
Food S: Apple Mill Rest
Lodg N: Heaven's View Motel, Saluda Mountain Motel
Other N: **to appr 5.5 mi: Orchard Lake CG▲**

NOTE: **MM 62: EB: 6% Steep Grade**

67 **US 74E, NC 108, Columbus, Tryon, Rutherfordton, Shelby**
Gas N: BP◈
S: Exxon◈, Shell
Food N: Burger King/BP, Hardee's, McDonald's, Subway, Waffle House, Wendy's
S: KFC, Mountain View BBQ & Deli
Lodg S: Days Inn
Med N: + St Lukes Hospital
Other N: Advance Auto Parts, CVS, Family Dollar, Food Lion, US Post Office
S: Bi-Lo, Dollar General,

(68) **NC Welcome Center (WB)**
(RR, Phone, Picnic)

NOTE: **MM 71: South Carolina State Line**

EASTERN TIME ZONE

⬆NORTH CAROLINA
⬇SOUTH CAROLINA

EASTERN TIME ZONE

1 **SC 14, SC 128, Landrum**
Gas S: BP◈, Hot Spot, Ingles
Food S: Burger King/BP, Bojangles, Denny's, Pizza Hut, Subway
Other S: Bi-Lo, Dollar General, Ingles, Vet♥

EXIT SOUTH CAROLINA

(3) **SC Welcome Center (EB)**
(RR, Phones, Pic, Vend, Pet, Info)

5 **SC 11, Cherokee Foothills Scenic Hwy, Campobello, Chesnee, to Coopers Battlefield**
TStop N: Kangaroo #3439 (Scales)
Gas S: Phillips 66
Food N: Aunt M's Café/Kangaroo
Other N: Carolina Trailers
S: U-Haul

(9) **Parking Area (Both dir)**

10 **SC 292, Inman, New Prospect**
TStop N: Hot Spot Travel Center #2013/Shell (Scales)
Food N: Subway/Hot Spot TC

15 **US 176, Asheville Hwy, to I-585, N Inman, Spartanburg**
FStop S: Corner Mart/Mystik
TStop N: Circle K #5370/76 (Scales)
Gas N: Breakers, to RaceTrac
Food N: FastFood/Circle K, Waffle House
S: FastFood/CornerMart, Burger King,
Med N: + Hospital
Other N: Auto Service/Tires/Brakes

16 **John Dodd Rd, to Wellford**
FStop N: Kangaroo Express #3415/Citgo
Gas N: to Valero
Food N: FastFood/AuntieM's/Kangaroo
Other N: **Camping World**
S: **to Cunningham RV Park▲**

17 **New Cut Rd, Sigsbee, Cunningham,**
Gas S: Chevron◈, Sunoco◈
Food N: Southern Diner
S: Burger King, Fatz Café, Hardee's, McDonald's, Waffle House
Lodg S: Days Inn♥, Econo Lodge♥, Howard Johnson Express, Red Roof Inn♥
Other N: Spartanburg Tech College
S: **to appr 1.5mi: Cunningham RV Park▲**
Spartanburg Expo Center

(18B) **Jct I-85, N - Charlotte**

(18A) **Jct I-85, S - Greenville**

(19B) **I-85N Lp, Spartanburg**
Gas N: Fast Fuel◈
Food N: Cracker Barrel, Rest/Clarion
Lodg N: Country Hearth Inn♥, Residence Inn, Roberts Vista Hotel Clarion,
Other N: Goodyear, Spartanburg Comm College

(19A) **I-85S Lp, to Greenville**
Lodg S: Brookwood Inn
Other S: Lowe's, **Walmart sc**

21A **US 29S, Abernathy Hwy, to Greer**
Gas S: Kangaroo Express/Citgo◈, Texaco◈, Sam's, Ingle's
Food S: Applebee's, Blimpie Subs, IHOP, McDonald's, Piccadilly Cafeteria, Pizza Inn, Prime Sirloin, Shogun Japanese Steak house & Sushi Bar, Taco Bell, Taste of Thai, Waffle House
Other S: ATMs, Academy Sports & Outdoors, Advance Auto Parts, CarQuest, Dollar Tree, Great Escape Bikes & Hobbies, Hobby Lobby, Ingles, Lowe's, RiteAid, Sam's Club, Target, True Value Hardware, U-Haul,

21B **US 29N, Ezell Blvd, Spartanburg**
Gas N: BP, Exxon, Costco
Food N: Burger King, Checkers, ChickFilA, CiCi's Pizza, City Range Steakhouse Grill,

EXIT SOUTH CAROLINA

Food N: Corona Mexican, DQ, Dunkin Donuts, Fuji, Golden Corral, Hardee's, Hooters, Hops Grill, Jack in the Box, Kanpai of Tokyo, Lone Star Steakhouse, Long John Silver/A&W, Moe's SW Grill, Monterey Mexican, O'Charley's, Papa John's Pizza, Pizza Hut, Red Lobster, Rock Ola Café, Ruby Tuesday, Souper Salad, Subway, Wendy's
Lodg N: Comfort Suites, Hampton Inn, Holiday Inn Express
Other N: ATMs, Banks, Barnes & Noble, Best Buy, Budget RAC, Cinema 8, Costco, Dick's Sporting Goods, Discount Tire, Dollar General, Firestone Auto, Goodyear, Home Depot, Lowe's, Michael's, Office Depot, Office Max, PetSmart♥, Regal Cinema 16, RiteAid, UPS Store, **Walmart sc**, Westgate Mall, **to** Methodist College

22 **SC 296, Reidville Rd, Spartanburg, Roebuck, Reidville**
Gas N: BP◈, Exxon
S: BP◈
Food N: Arby's, Carolina BBQ, Fatz Cafe, Fuddrucker's, Hong Kong Express, Little Caesars Pizza, McDonald's, Outback Steak house, Ryan's Grill, Waffle House, Wasabi Japanese, Zaxby's
S: Burger King, Denny's, Dominos Pizza, Hardee's, Papa John's Pizza, Subway, TCBY, Waffle House
Lodg S: Sleep Inn, Southern Suites, Super 8♥
Med N: + Doctors Care
Other N: ATMs, Banks, Advance Auto Parts, Auto Services, Carmike Cinemas, Enterprise RAC, Grocery, Paradise Lanes, Play it Again Sports, Reidville Rd Animal Hospital♥, RiteAid, Thrifty RAC, Tirerama, U-Haul, Spartanburg Downtown Memorial Airport✈
S: Auto Dealers, Auto Services, ATMs, Bi-Lo, CVS, Dollar General, Food Lion, Midas, Pet Vac Animal Hospital♥, RiteAid, Walgreen's, Westside Veterinary Clinic♥,

28 **US 221, Roebuck, Spartanburg, Moore, Woodruff**
FStop N: Kangaroo Express #3416/Citgo
Gas N: Hot Spot #2017/Shell◈
Food N: Bojangles, Burger King, Hardee's, Waffle House, Walnut Grove Seafood Rest, Subway/Shell, Quiznos/AuntM's/Kang Exp
Other N: **to appr 2.5 mi Pine Ridge Campground▲** , **to** Walnut Grove Plantation, **to approx 8 mi: Croft State Park▲**

35 **SC 50, Walnut Grove Rd, Woodruff**
FStop S: BP Truck Auto Plaza
Food S: Rest/BP
Med S: + Hospital

38 **SC 146, Cross Anchor, Woodruff**
TStop N: Hot Spot #6004/Shell
Food N: Hardee's/Hot Spot, Big Country Rest
Other N: Laundry/Hot Spot

41 **SC 92, Enoree**
Gas N: Valero
Other S: to U-Haul, US Post Office

44 **SC 49, Union Hwy, Laurens, Cross Anchor, Union**

(51) **Jct I-385, Greenville, Laurens**
(WB exit, EB entr)

◈= **Regular Gas Stations with Diesel** ▲ = **RV Friendly Locations** ♥= **Pet Friendly Locations**
Red print shows large vehicle parking / access on site or nearby **Brown Print = Campgrounds / RV PARKS**

EXIT	SOUTH CAROLINA

52 **SC 56, Clinton, Cross Anchor**
TStop N: Pilot Travel Center #61 (Scales)
Gas S: Citgo, Phillips 66, Shell
Food N: Subway/Pilot TC, McDonald's, Waffle House
S: Hardee's, Waffle House, Wendy's
Lodg N: Comfort Inn♥, Quality Inn
S: Days Inn, Howard Johnson,

54 **SC 72, Clinton, Whitmire**
FStop N: BP
S: Corner Mart #49/Citgo
Food S: FastFood/Corner Mart
Lodg S: Hampton Inn
Other N: to **Cane Creek Resort▲**

60 **SC 66, Joanna, Whitmire**
Gas S: BP
Food S: Country Kitchen, Joanna Cafe
Other S: **Magnolia Family Campground▲**

(63) **Rest Area (Both dir)**
(RR, Phone, Pic, Pet, Vend)

66 **SC 32, Jalapa Rd, Kinards, Jalapa**

72 **SC 121, to US 76, Newberry, Whitemire, Union**
FStop S: Corner Mart #44/Citgo
Gas S: to Buddy's◈
Other S: to Ace Hardware, Newberry Muni Airport✈

74 **SC 34, Winnsboro Rd, to US 76, Newberry, Winnsboro (Addt'l Serv S to US 76)**
FStop N: Pop's Pantry Express/Shell
S: I-26 Citgo
Gas N: BP
Food N: Bill & Fran's Cafe
S: Arby's, Captain D's, Waffle House, **to** Hardee's, McDonald's,
Lodg N: Americas Best Value Inn♥
S: Days Inn♥, **to** Comfort Inn, Holiday Inn Express
Med S: to + Newberry Co Memorial Hospital
Other N: Enoree River Vineyards

76 **SC 219, Main St, Newberry, to Pomaria (Addtl Serv S to US 76)**
TStop N: Love's Travel Stop #396 (Scales)
Gas S: BP, **to** Murphy USA
Food N: ChestersChkn/McDonald's/Love's TS
S: **to** Burger King, Chinatown Rest, Pizza Hut, Waffle House, Wendy's, Zaxby's
Lodg S: Holiday Inn Express, to Quality Inn
Med S: to + Newberry Co Memorial Hospital
Other N: WiFi/Love's TS
S: **to appr 2.5mi:** Advance Auto Parts, Auto Zone, CVS, Hibbett Sports, RiteAid, Tractor Supply, **Walmart sc, to appr 12mi: Saluda River Resort▲**

(81) **Weigh Station (EB)**

82 **SC 773, Pomaria, Prosperity**
TStop N: Kangaroo #3441/BP (Scales), Wilco Hess (Scales),
Food N: Subway/Kangaroo, Wendy's/WilcoHess
TServ N: Kangaroo/Tires

85 **SC 202, Pomaria, Little Mountain**
Other S: to **Dreher Island State Park▲**

91 **SC 48, Columbia Ave, Chapin**
FStop S: Pitt Stop #7/Shell, Rainbow Gas Garden #12/Exxon
Gas S: BP◈
Food S: Farm Boys BBQ, Hardee's, McDonald's, Subway, Taco Bell, Waffle House

EXIT	SOUTH CAROLINA

Other N: to **Glenn's Campground▲**
S: **to** NAPA, RiteAid, **Dreher Lake State Park▲**

(94) **Weigh Station (WB)**

97 **US 176, Ballentine, White Rock, Peak**
FStop S: Exxon
Food N: Little Pigs BBQ, Subway
Other N: **Woodsmoke Family Campground▲**
S: Plex Indoor Sports & Ice, U-Haul, **to US 76: Walmart sc, Many Services**

101A **US 76, 176, Broad River Rd**
Gas S: BP, Mobil
Food S: Burger King, Crabs in the Pot Rest, Monterrey Mexican, Waffle House
Other S: Auto Dealers, Discount Tire, Laundromat

101B **US 176, Broad River Rd (Acc #102)**
Gas N: Exxon◈
Food N: Blimpie, Fatz Cafe, Subway/Exxon

102A **SC 60S, Lake Murray Blvd, Irmo**
Gas S: 76, Exxon, Shell
Food S: Arby's, Catch 22 Seafood, Domino's Pizza, Maurice's BBQ, McDonald's, Moe's SW Grill, Papa John's Pizza, Zaxby's
Med S: + Lexington Medical Center
Other S: ATMs, Advance Auto Parts, Anchor Lanes, Banks, CVS, **Carolina RV**, Kroger/Pharmacy, **Police Dept**, Publix/Pharmacy, Tires, Walgreen's, **Acc to #103**

102B **SC 60N, Lake Murray Blvd (Acc #103)**
Food N: **Cracker Barrel**, Fatz Cafe, Subway
Lodg N: Extended Stay Deluxe, Hyatt Place,
Other N: AutoZone, Banks, Dollar General, Food Lion, Publix/Pharmacy, RiteAid, Walgreen's

103 **Harbison Blvd, Columbia**
Gas S: BP, Exxon, Hess◈, Shell
Food N: Applebee's, HOPS Grill, Hooters, Wendy's
S: Bojangles, Bonefish Grill, ChickFilA, Chili's, Carrabba's Italian, Cajun Café, DQ, Denny's, McDonald's, Monterey Mexican, Myabi Kyoto Japanese Steakhouse, O'Charley's, Outback Steakhouse, Olive Garden, Panera Bread, Popeye's Chicken/BP, Romano's Macaroni Grill, Ruby Tuesday, Smokey Bones BBQ, Sesame Inn Chinese Rest, Shoney's, Sonic, Starbucks, Subway, Texas Roadhouse, Taco Bell, Yamato Steakhouse
Lodg N: Hampton Inn
S: Comfort Suites, Country Inn, Fairfield Inn, Hilton Garden Inn, Holiday Inn Express, InTowne Suites, Towneplace Suites, Wingate Inn
Med S: + Baptist Medical Center
Other N: Auto Dealers, Frankie's Fun Park, Grocery, Home Depot, Hummer, Lowe's,
S: ATMs, AT&T, Auto Services, Banks, Barnes & Noble, Best Buy, BooksAMillion, Carmike Cinema 10, Columbiana Centre Mall, Dick's Sporting Goods, FedEx Office, Goodyear Auto, Grocery, Midas, Office Depot, PetSmart♥, Publix, Radio Shack, Regal Cinema 14, RiteAid, Sam's Club, **Sheriff Dept**, Speedee Oil Change, Staples, Target/Pharmacy, Tire Kingdom, Triangle RAC, **Walmart sc**,

104 **Piney Grove Rd, W Columbia**
FStop N: Sunoco #2634
Gas S: Exxon◈, Shell

EXIT	SOUTH CAROLINA

Food N: Hardee's, McDonald's, Quincy's, San Jose Mexican Rest, Waffle House
Lodg N: Knights Inn♥, Quality Inn
S: Country Inn, **to** Microtel
Med S: to + Doctors Care
Other N: Conference Center, Green's Beverage Warehouse, Hertz RAC, Home Depot, Walgreen's, SC Veterinary Emergency Care♥
S: Auto Dealer, **to** Sportsmans Warehouse, Aldi, Auto Services, Auto Zone, Banks Animal Hospital♥, Bi-Lo, NAPA,

106A **SC 36W, St Andrews Rd (WB)**
Gas S: BP, Hess◈, Shell
Food S: Domino's Pizza, Maurice's BBQ, McDonald's, Old Country Buffet, Pizza Hut, Ryan's Grill, Steak Out, Waffle House, Wendy's, WG's Wings, Zaxby's
Lodg S: Econo Lodge♥, Red Roof Inn♥
Other S: ATMs, Banks, Cinema, Dollar General, Food Lion, Fred's, Harbor Freight, Seven Oaks Animal Hospital♥, Tire Kingdom, UPS Store,

106B **SC 36E, St Andrews Rd (WB)**
Gas N: Exxon◈
Food N: Blimpie's/Exxon, BB's Steak & Ribs, Burger King, ChickFilA, Chuck E Cheese's, Elie's Mediterranean Cuisine,IHOP, Sonic
Lodg N: Motel 6♥
Other N: Auto Dealers, CVS, Carwash/BP, **Camping World**, Dollar General, Grocery, Kroger, Laundromat, **Outdoor RV & Marine World**, O'Reilly Auto Parts, Walgreen's, Wash World

106 **St Andrews Rd, Columbia (EB)**

(107A) **Jct I-20, W to Augusta, GA**

(107B) **Jct I-20, E to Florence**

(108A) **Bush River Rd (EB Access #108 Serv)**
Gas S: City Gas, RaceWay, Sunoco◈, Murphy USA, **to** Kangaroo Express/Citgo
Food S: **Cracker Barrel**, El Chico Cafe, Fuddrucker's, Key West Grill, Punjabi Daba Indian, Pizza Hut, Waffle House
Lodg S: Americas Best Inn, Courtyard, Days Inn, to Best Western, Knights Inn, Radisson Inn, Sleep Inn
Other S: Bush River Shopping Mall, AMF Bowling Center, **Walmart sc, Acc to I-20, x63 Serv**

(108B) **Jct I-126, Downtown Columbia**

(108) **Jct I-126, Bush River Rd, Columbia**
Gas N: Citgo, Shell◈
Food N: Blimpie, Captain D's, ChickFilA, Hardee's, KFC, Piccadilly, Ruby Tuesday, Shoney's, Subway, Super China Buffet, Wendy's, Zaxby's
Lodg N: Comfort Inn, Ramada Ltd, Scottish Inn, Western Inn,
Other N: AMC Cinema, ATMs, Auto Services, Advance Auto Parts, Banks, Burlington Coat Factory, Carwash, Dollar Tree, Dutch Square Mall, Firestone Auto, Hibbett Sporting Goods, Kmart, Midas, Office Depot, Radio Shack, RiteAid, Vet♥, West Marine, **Acc to I-20, x65 Serv**

110 **US 378, Sunset Blvd, W Columbia**
Gas N: Hess, Kangaroo Express/BP
S: Circle K/76, Lil Cricket◈
Food N: Burger King, McDonald's, Pizza Hut, Subway, Waffle House
S: Atlanta Bread Co, Bojangles, Hardee's, Pizza Hut

◈= Regular Gas Stations with Diesel ▲ = RV Friendly Locations ♥= Pet Friendly Locations
Red print shows large vehicle parking / access on site or nearby Brown Print = Campgrounds / RV PARKS

EXIT		SOUTH CAROLINA
	Lodg	**N:** Americas Best Value Inn, Hampton Inn, Holiday Inn **S:** Executive Inn, Springhill Suites
	Med	**S:** + Lexington Medical Center
	Other	**N:** ATMs, Banks, Laundromat, CVS, Food Lion, Fred's, RiteAid, U-Haul, Vet♥ **S:** ATM, Banks, Franks Discount Tire
111A		**US 1S, Augusta Rd, to Lexington**
	Gas	**S:** Hess
	Food	**S:** Applebee's, Gilbert Rib, Popeye's Chicken, Wendy's
	Lodg	**S:** Super 8
	Other	**S:** Auto Service, Big Lots, CVS, Dollar General, Family Dollar, Grocery, Lowe's, U-Haul, to Barnyard Flea Market & RV Park▲
111B		**US 1N, Augusta Rd, Columbia**
	Gas	**N:** Circle K/Shell, RaceTrac◈, Murphy USA
	Food	**N:** #1 Chinese Rest, Applebee's, Carolina Wings & Rib House, Domino's Pizza, Hardee's, Little Caesar's Pizza, Maurice's BBQ, McDonald's, Ruby Tuesday, Sonic, Subway, Waffle House, Zaxby's
	Lodg	**N:** Clarion Inn, Delta Motel, Quality Inn♥
	TServ	**N:** Williams Truck Service
	Other	**N:** ATMs, AT&T, Banks, Bi-Lo/Pharmacy, Dollar General, Dollar Tree, Hobby Lobby, Kroger, Oriental Grocery, Radio Shack, Van Crest Animal Hospital♥, Walgreen's, Walmart sc
113		**SC 302, Airport Blvd, Columbia Airport, W Columbia, to Cayce**
	Gas	**N:** Pitt Stop/Mobil, Texaco◈ **S:** BP, Circle K/Shell, RaceWay
	Food	**N:** BK/Mobil, Waffle House **S:** Burger King, Denny's, Don Pedro, Fat Boy, Lizard's Thicket, Shoney's, Subway, Waffle House, Wendy's
	Lodg	**N:** Airport Inn, Cambridge Plaza Hotel, Knights Inn, Masters Inn♥ **S:** Carolina Lodge, Comfort Inn, Country Inn, Days Inn♥, Sleep Inn
	TServ	**N:** Cherokee Kenworth
	Other	**N:** Auto & Diesel Repair & Services, Truck & Trailer Repair, O'Reilly Auto Parts **S:** ATM, Bank, Midlands Tech College, NAPA, Columbia Metro Airport✈
115		**US 21, US 176, US 321, Charleston Hwy, to Gaston, Cayce**
	TStop	**S:** Pilot Travel Center #338 (Scales), Corner Pantry #127/Shell
	Gas	**N:** BP, RaceWay, Texaco
	Food	**N:** Waffle House **S:** DQ/Wendy's/Pilot TC, Bojangles, Great China Rest, Hardee's, McDonald's, Subway
	Lodg	**S:** Country Hearth Inn
	Med	**S:** + Doctors Care
	Other	**N:** ATM, Bank, Bi-Lo, Carwash, Carwash/Shell, Dollar General, Farmers Market, Harley Davidson Harley Haven, Laundromat **S:** Firestone, Piggly Wiggly Grocery, to Home Depot, Palmetto Falls Mini Golf
(116)		**Jct I-77N, to Charlotte, NC, to US 76, US 378, to Ft Jackson**
119		**US 21, US 176, W Columbia, to St Matthews, Dixiana**
	FStop	**S:** Kangaroo Express #3272/BP

Personal Notes

EXIT		SOUTH CAROLINA
	TStop	**S:** Pitt Stop #36/Exxon (Scales)
	Gas	**S:** Shell
	Food	**S:** Rest/Pitt Stop, Subway/Shell
	TServ	**S:** SC Truck & Trailer
(122)		**Rest Area (Both dir)** **(RR, Phones, Pic, Pet, Vend)**
125		**SC 31, Old Sandy Run Rd, Gaston**
129		**US 21, Columbia Rd, Swansea, to Orangeburg**
	Gas	**N:** Shell◈
136		**SC 6, Caw Caw Rd, St Matthews**
	TStop	**N:** Brakefield's Exxon
	Gas	**N:** Palmetto Petro
	Food	**N:** Deli/Pizza/Brakefield's
	Tires	**N:** Brakefield's
	Other	**N:** LP/Brakefield's
139		**SC 22, Burke Rd, St Matthews**
	TStop	**S:** WilcoHess Travel Plaza #933 (Scales)
	Gas	**S:** Lil Cricket,
	Food	**S:** Arby's/WilcoHess TP
	Other	**N:** Tire Country **S:** to appr 2.5mi: Sweetwater Lake Campground▲
145B		**US 601N, to St Matthews**
145A		**US 601S, St Matthews Rd, Orangeburg**
	FStop	**S:** Sunoco #2679, Speedway #0284, Shell #121
	Gas	**S:** BP, Exxon
	Food	**S:** Burger King/Shell, Cracker Barrel, Fatz Café, Hardee's, KFC, McDonald's, Ruby Tuesday, Subway, Waffle House, Wendy's

EXIT		SOUTH CAROLINA
	Lodg	**S:** Best Western, Carolina Lodge, Comfort Inn♥, Country Inn♥, Fairfield Inn, Hampton Inn, Holiday Inn Express, Howard Johnson Express, Sleep Inn, Southern Lodge, Travelers Inn♥
	Med	**S:** + Hospital
	Other	**S:** Auto Dealers, CVS, Pharmacy, Orangeburg Calhoun Tech College, SC State Univ, **Many Serv S appr 4mi to US 21/US178**
149		**SC 33, Orangeburg, Cameron** **(All Serv 4-5mi S in Orangeburg)**
	Other	**S:** to SC State Univ
(150)		**Rest Area (EB)** **(RR, Phones, Pic, Pet, Vend)**
(152)		**Rest Area (WB)** **(RR, Phones, Pic, Pet, Vend)**
154B		**US 301N, to Santee**
	Lodg	**N:** Days Inn♥
154A		**US 301S, to Orangeburg**
	FStop	**S:** Shell #116
	TStop	**S:** Love's Travel Stop #326 (Scales)
	Gas	**S:** Exxon◈,
	Food	**S:** Chesters/Subway/Love's TS, Blimpie/Exxon, Waffle House
	Other	**S:** WiFi/Love's TS, Auto & Truck Service, Honda, Kawasaki, Suzuki, Yamaha of Orangeburg, to SC State Univ
159		**SC 36, Homestead Rd, Bowman**
	FStop	**S:** Lil Cricket
	TStop	**N:** Pilot Travel Center #60 (Scales)
	Food	**N:** McDonald's/Pilot TC
	TServ	**N:** Pilot TC/Wingfoot Truck Care
	Other	**N:** Laundry/WiFi/Pilot TC
165		**SC 210, Vance Rd, Bowman, Vance**
	FStop	**N:** Exxon **S:** Quick C Mart/BP
(169A)		**Jct I-95, S to Savannah, GA** **(All Serv Available at 1st Exit S)**
(169B)		**Jct I-95, N to Florence**
172A		**US 15S, to St George**
	TStop	**S:** EZ Shop Horizon Travel Center #27 (Scales)
	Food	**S:** Subway/Horizon EZ Shop
	Other	**S:** Laundry/Horizon EZ Shop
172B		**US 15N, to Holly Hill**
(173)		**Weigh Station (EB)**
(174)		**Weigh Station (WB)**
177		**SC 453, Harleyville, Holly Hill**
	FStop	**S:** Ronnie's Shell
	TStop	**S:** Harleyville Truck Stop
	Food	**S:** Derrick's Country Kitchen
	Lodg	**S:** Ashley Inn, RV Park & Campground▲
	Other	**S:** LP/RVDump/Ronnie's, to US 178/Main St: Ace Hardware, Banks, Consolidated Tires, Harleyville Custom Cycles, US Post Office
187		**SC 27, Ridgeville, St George**
	Gas	**N:** Shell **S:** BP◈
194		**SC 16, Summerville, to Jedburg, Pinopolis**
199A		**Alt US 17S, Main St, Summerville**
	Gas	**S:** Circle K/Shell, Kangaroo Express/BP,

◈= Regular Gas Stations with Diesel ▲ = RV Friendly Locations ♥= Pet Friendly Locations
Red print shows large vehicle parking / access on site or nearby Brown Print = Campgrounds / RV PARKS

EXIT — SOUTH CAROLINA

Food S: Applebee's, Atlanta Bread, Bojangles, Burger King, ChickFilA, China Town, Domino's Pizza, Fazoli's, Firewater Grille, Hardee's, Huddle House, IHOP, La Hacienda Mexican Rest, Papa John's Pizza Perkins, Quincy's, Ruby Tuesday, Ryan's Grill, Shoney's, Sticky Fingers Rest, Taco Bell, Waffle House, Wendy's

Lodg S: Comfort Inn, Country Inn, Econo Lodge, Economy Inn, Hampton Inn, Holiday Inn Express, Sleep Inn

Other S: ATMs, Banks, Auto Dealers, Auto & Truck Service, Best Buy, Carolina Tire, Dick's Sporting Goods, Home Depot, Jiffy Lube, Kohl's, Lowe's, Meineke, Parks Auto Parts, PetSmart♥, Radio Shack, Regal 16 Cinema, Staples, TJ Maxx, Target, Tire Kingdom, Walgreen's, **Walmart sc,**

199B — Alt US 17N, to Monck's Corner

TStop N: Pilot Travel Center #64 (Scales), Kangaroo Express #3871/Texaco (Scales)

Gas N: Kangaroo Express/BP, Hess◊, Shell

Food N: McDonald's/Pilot TC, Blimpie/Dunkin Donuts/GodfathersPizza/Hess, Boston Billy's, China Wok, Hardee's, KFC, Pizza Hut, Subway, Waffle House

TServ N: Blanchard CAT, Carolina Diesel

Other N: LP/Laundromat/Shell, Advance Auto Parts, ATP Gun Shop & Range, Auto Zone, Auto Dealers, Auto Repairs, Bi-Lo, CVS, Carwash, Carwash/Hess, Diesel Service, Dollar General, Food Lion, Music in Motion Skate Center, Penske Truck Rental, Sangaree Homes & **RV Center**, Sangaree Animal Hospital♥, Tractor Supply

(202) — Rest Area (WB)
(RR, Phones, Picnic, Vend)

203 — College Park Rd, Ladson, Goose Creek (Most S Serv S to US 78)

FStop N: Sunoco

Gas N: BP
S: Exxon, Hess, Sunoco

Food N: McDonald's, Waffle House, Wendy's
S: Burger King, KFC

Lodg N: Best Western, Days Inn

Other N: Food Lion, Carwash/BP
S: ATMs, Banks, Advance Auto Parts, CVS, Flea Market, Grocery, **to Charleston/ Mt Pleasant KOA▲**

(204) — Rest Area (EB)
(RR, Phones, Picnic, Vend)

205A — US 78S, University Blvd, Charleston Summerville

Gas S: BP, Exxon, Hess, Sunoco◊,

Food S: KFC, Ladson Seafood, Mama Mia's

EXIT — SOUTH CAROLINA

Other S: Charleston/Mt Pleasant KOA▲

205B — US 78N, University Blvd, to US 52, N Charleston, to Goose Creek

Gas N: Kangaroo Express/BP, Hess◊

Food N: Arby's, Atlanta Bread, Chinese Rest, Dunkin Donuts, Subway, Waffle House, Wendy's, Zaxby's

Lodg N: Fairfield Inn, Hampton Inn, Holiday Inn Express, Wingate

Med N: + Hospital

Other N: Baptist College, Charleston Southern Univ, Whirlin Waters Adventure Waterpark

208 — US 52W, US 78W, to Moncks Corner Goose Crk, Kingstree (WB)

209A — Ashley Phosphate Rd (EB),

Gas S: BP, Hess, RaceWay

Food S: Bojangles, China Palace, Cracker Barrel, Domino's Pizza, IHOP, Kobe Japanese Rest, McDonald's, Ruby Tuesday, Shoney's, Waffle House

Lodg S: Best Western, Comfort Suites, Hampton Inn, Hyatt, InTowne Suites, La Quinta Inn♥, Motel 6♥, Quality Inn♥, Relax Inn, Sleep Inn, Springhill Suites, Staybridge Suites, Value Place

Other S: Carwash/Citgo, Snider Tire, Tire Kingdom

209A — to US 52, US 78, Goose Creek (WB)

Gas N: Lil Cricket, Raceway

Food N: Arby's, McDonald's, Texas Roadhouse

Lodg N: N on US 78 to access #205B

Med N: + Doctors Care

Other N: Auto Dealers, Camping World, K-Mart/ Pharmacy, Piggly Wiggly,

209B — Ashley Phosphate Rd, to US 52, US 78, N Charleston

Gas N: Exxon, Kangaroo

Food N: Applebee's, Carrabba's, ChickFilA, Chuck E Cheese, DQ, Denny's, Don Pablo, Hardee's, Hooters, Hops Grill, Longhorn Steakhouse, McDonald's, K& W Cafeteria, Noisy Oyster, O'Charley's, Olive Garden, Outback Steakhouse, Perkins, Pizza Hut, Ryan's Grill, Smokey Bones BBQ, Subway, Taco Bell, Waffle House, Wendy's

Lodg N: Candlewood Suites♥, Country Hearth Inn♥, Country Inn, Holiday Inn Express, Ramada♥, Red Roof Inn, Residence Inn♥, Studio Plus, Suburban Extended Stay

Other N: ATMs, Banks, AT&T, AMC Cinema, Auto Dealers, Auto Repair & Services, B&N, Best Buy, BooksAMillion, Carolina Ice Palace, Dollar General, Dollar Tree, Kmart/ Pharmacy, Firestone Auto, Home Depot,

EXIT — SOUTH CAROLINA

Other N: Lowe's, Northwoods Mall, Office Depot, Target/Pharmacy, Tire Kingdom, Verizon, **Walmart sc,**

211A — Aviation Ave, to Remont Rd, Air Force Base

TStop S: Charleston Travel Plaza/Citgo (Scales)

Food S: Rest/Charleston TP, Waffle House, Rest/Budget, Rest/BW

Lodg S: Best Western, Budget Inn, Seagrass Inn, Travelodge

Other S: Laundry/Charleston TP, Charleston AFB

211B — to US 52, US 78, Rivers Rd (Most Serv N to US 52/78)

Gas N: Exxon, Fuel Express

Food N: Arby's, Burger King, C&W Super Buffet, Captain D's, Hickory Hawg, Huddle House, KFC, McDonald's, Old Country Buffet, Popeye's Chicken, Shoney's, Sonic, Subway, Wendy's

Lodg N: Masters Inn, Radisson

Other N: Big Lots, Goodyear, Pep Boys, Radio Shack, Sam's Club, Stardust Skate Center, U-Haul,

212A — Remount Rd, Hanahan (WB, diff reacc (Reaccess via N on US52/78 to #211) (Many Serv N on US 52/78, S to I-526)

Gas N: Exxon, Hess◊, Speedway

Food N: Burger King, Cajun Country Kitchen Cafe, China Wok, KFC, PizzaHut/Taco Bell

Other N: Auto & Tire Services, Auto Zone, Dollar General, Food Lion, Hanahan Veterinary Clinic♥, Office Depot, RiteAid,

(212) — Jct I-526, W to Savannah, GA; E to Mount Pleasant (EB)

(212B) — Jct I-526, W to Savannah, GA;

(212C) — Jct I-526, E to Mount Pleasant

213A — Montague Ave West, Mall Dr, Coliseum Dr (EB)

FStop S: Kangaroo Express #3692/BP

Gas S: Hess◊, Mobil

Food S: Bojangles/Hess, Buffalo Wild Wings, Chili's, Graby's Ribs, McDonald's, Waffle House, Rest/HG Inn,

Lodg S: Comfort Inn♥, Days Inn♥, Embassy Suites, Hampton Inn, Hilton Garden Inn, Holiday Inn, Homestead Studio Suites, Homeplace Suites, Homewood Suites, Hyatt Place, Quality Inn, Residence Inn, Wingate Inn

TServ S: Cummins

Other S: ATMs, Banks, Auto Services, Charleston Convention Center, Sam's Club, Staples, Tanger Outlet, **Walmart sc,** to Charleston Int'l Airport via N on Int'l Blvd

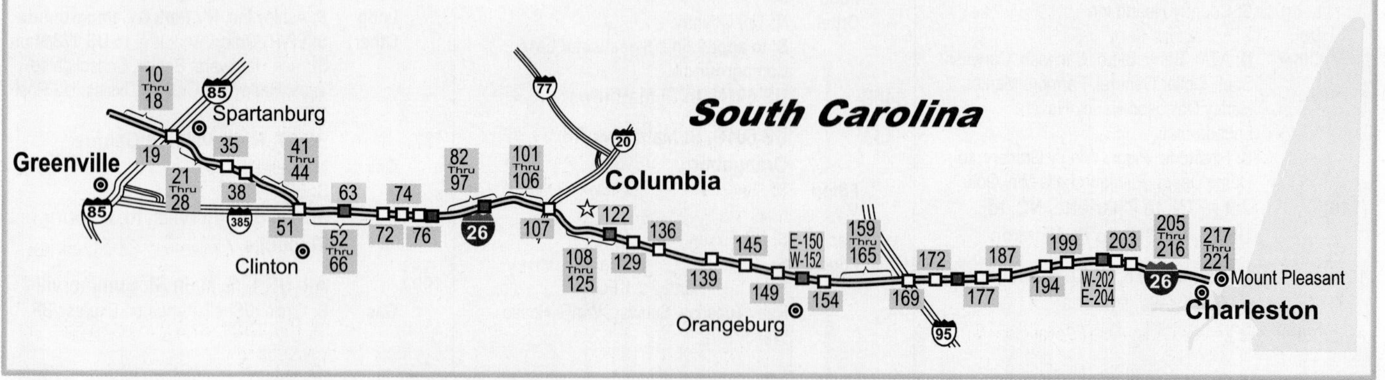

◊ = Regular Gas Stations with Diesel ▲ = RV Friendly Locations ♥ = Pet Friendly Locations
Red print shows large vehicle parking / access on site or nearby Brown Print = Campgrounds / RV PARKS

EXIT	SOUTH CAROLINA
213B	**Montague Ave E, Mall Dr (EB)**
Gas	N: Exxon
Food	N: Dunkin Donuts, Piccadilly, Red Lobster
Lodg	N: Courtyard, Sheraton, Value Place
Other	N: ATM, Amtrak, Auto Services, Bank, Charles Towne Square, Police Dept, Regal Cinema 18, N on US 78 to I-526
213	**Montague Ave, Mall Dr (WB)**
215	**SC 642, Dorchester Rd**
FStop	N: El Cheapo
Gas	N: Hess◈ S: Kangaroo Express/BP◈,
Food	N: Hardee's, Old Town Family Rest S: Alex's
Lodg	N: Clarion Inn S: Charleston Inn, Rodeway Inn
Med	N: + to US Naval Hospital
Other	N: Greyhound, Laundromat, S: Auto Services, ATM

EXIT	SOUTH CAROLINA
216A	**SC 7S, to US 17S, Naval Base**
Other	S: to restaurants, grocery store, mall
216B	**SC 7N, Cosgrove Ave**
217	**N Meeting St, Charleston (EB exit, WB entr)**
FStop	N: Kangaroo #3355
218	**Spruill Ave, Naval Base (WB ex, EB entr)**
Other	N: Bishops Towing, Jennings Towing, Jones Truck Service, Pressley's Gen'l Store & Rest, Tire Service
219A	**Rutledge Ave, The Citadel (EB exit, WB entr)**
Other	S: Diesel Service
219B	**Mt Pleasant St to Morrison Dr, E Bay St (EB ex, WB entr) Meeting St (WB entr)**
Other	S: Oaks Service Station

EXIT	SOUTH CAROLINA
220	**US 17N, Mt Pleasant, Georgetown (EB exit, WB entr) Cypress St, Brigade St (EB entr)**
220A	**Romney St (WB exit only)**
220B	**US 17N, Mt Pleasant, Georgetown (WB exit, EB entr)**
221B	**Meeting St, Visitor Ctr (EB exit)**
221A	**US 17S, Savannah, GA (EB exit, WB entr) King St, Downtown Charleston (EB exit)**

EASTERN TIME ZONE

SOUTH CAROLINA

Begin Westbound I-26 from Jct I-17 near Charleston to VA Border.

EXIT	TEXAS

Begin Southbound I-27 from Amarillo, TX to Lubbock, TX.

TEXAS

CENTRAL TIME ZONE

NOTE: I-27 begins/ends on I-40, Exit #70

EXIT	TEXAS
(123B)	**Jct I-40, US 287, US 87, Amarillo, W to Tucumcari, NM, E to Oklahoma City, OK**
123	**26th - 29th Ave, Amarillo (SB)**
123A	**26th - 29th Ave, Amarillo**
Gas	E: Fina
122C	**34th Ave, Tyler St (SB ex, NB entr)**
122B	**FM 1541, Washington St, 34th Ave**
122A	**Parker St, Moss Lane**
Gas	E: Shamrock W: Texaco
Food	E: Sonic W: Taco Bell
121B	**Hawthorne Dr, Austin St (SB)**
Gas	W: Texaco
Lodg	E: Amarillo Motel
121A	**Georgia St, Amarillo (SB)**
Gas	E: Phillips 66◈, Walmart W: Texaco
Food	E: Waffle House
Lodg	W: Traveler Motel
TServ	W: Ford/Kenworth
Other	E: Auto Dealers, Sizemore RV, Walmart sc
121	**Georgia St (NB)**
120B	**45th Ave, Amarillo (SB)**
Gas	E: Fina W: Shamrock
Food	E: Waffle House W: Burger King, Hardee's, McDonald's, Whataburger
Other	W: Advance Auto Parts, Dollar General, Pharmacy

EXIT	TEXAS
120A	**Republic Ave, Western St (SB)**
120	**45th Ave (NB)**
119B	**Western St, 58th Ave (SB)**
Gas	W: Shamrock, Shell◈
Food	W: Arby's, Braum's, Long John Silver, Pizza Hut, Wendy's
Other	W: U-Haul, US Post Office
119A	**Hillside Rd (SB)**
119	**Hillside Rd, 58th Ave (NB)**
117	**Arden Rd (SB), Bell St (NB)**
Gas	W: Fina, Shell
Food	W: Long John Silver, Sonic
Other	E: Auto Repair Services W: Dollar General, Camper RoundUp RV
116	**Lp 335, Hollywood Rd, Amarillo**
TStop	E: Love's Travel Stop #261
Gas	E: Phillips 66◈
Food	E: Subway/Love's TS, McDonald's, Waffle House, Whataburger
Lodg	E: Days Inn
Other	E: WiFi/Love's TS
115	**Sundown Lane**
113	**McCormick Rd, Amarillo**
Gas	E: J's Country Corner
Other	W: Cinema 16, Family Camping RV▲
112	**FM 2219, Lair Rd, Amarillo**
111	**Rockwell Rd, Canyon**
110	**US 87S, US 60W, Canyon, Hereford (SB)**
Other	W: West TX State Univ
109	**Buffalo Stadium Rd**
108	**FM 3331, Hunsley Rd, Canyon**
106	**TX 217, 4th Ave, Canyon**
Gas	W: Pak-A-Sak
Lodg	W: to Holiday Inn Express
Other	E: Palo Duro Trailer & RV Park▲
103	**FM 1541N, Washington St, Cemetery Rd, Canyon**

EXIT	TEXAS
99	**Hungate Rd, Canyon**
(98)	**Parking Area (Both dir)**
96	**Dowlen Rd**
94	**FM 285, Wayside Dr, Canyon**
92	**Haley Rd**
90	**FM 1075, Happy Rd, to US 87, Canyon**
Gas	W: Phillips 66
88	**US 87, FM 1881 (SB)**
88B	**US 87N, Happy**
88A	**FM 1881, Happy**
83	**FM 2698**
82	**FM 214, Tulia**
77	**US 87, Tulia**
75	**NW 6th St (SB) (Gas & Food E in Tulia)**
74	**TX 86, to US 87, Tulia**
TStop	W: AmBest/Rip Griffin Travel Center (Scales)
Food	W: Rest/Subway/RipGriffin
Lodg	W: Select Inn
Other	W: Laundry/WiFi/Rip Griffin
(69)	**Parking Area (Both dir)**
68	**FM 928, Tulia**
63	**FM 145, Kress**
61	**US 87, County Rd, Kress**
56	**FM 788, Plainview**
54	**FM 3183**
53	**Lp 27 Bus, Columbia St, Plainview**
51	**Quincy St, Industrial Blvd**
50	**TX 194, Dimmitt Rd, Plainview**
Gas	E: Phillips 66

◈ = Regular Gas Stations with Diesel ▲ = RV Friendly Locations ♥ = Pet Friendly Locations

Red print shows large vehicle parking / access on site or nearby Brown Print = Campgrounds / RV PARKS

EXIT		TEXAS
	Food	W: Burger King, New China Buffet, Rice Steakhouse, Kettle Rest, Subway
	Med	E: + Hospital
	Other	W: Cinema 6
49		**US 70, Olton Rd, Plainview**
	FStop	E: Uncles #82/Shamrock, Taylor's/Shell
	Gas	E: Phillips 66 W: Chevron, Phillips 66◈, Murphy USA
	Food	E: FastFood/Taylor's, Domino's Pizza, Far East Rest, Furr's, KFC, Kettle Rest, Long John Silver, Pizza Hut, Taco Bell W: Burger King, Chili's, IHOP, Mexican, McDonald's, Monterey, Sonic, Starbucks, Subway, Taco Bell, Wendy's
	Lodg	E: Best Western, Days Inn W: Best Value Inn, Holiday Inn
	Other	E: Auto Dealers, Dollar Tree, Grocery, NAPA, O'Reilly Auto Parts, Radio Shack W: **Walmart sc**
48		**FM 3466 (NB)**
45		**I-27 Bus, Plainview**
43		**FM 2337, Plainview**
41		**CR-R, Hale Center**
38		**Ave E, Main St, Hale Center (SB)**
37		**FM 1914, 4th St, Cleveland St**
	Gas	E: Co-Op
	Food	E: DQ
	Med	W: + Hospital
36		**FM 1424, Ave E, Hale Center**
32		**FM 37W, Abernathy**
31		**FM 37E**
(28)		**Rest Area (Both dir)** (RR, Phone, Picnic)
27		**CR 275, Abernathy**
24		**FM 54**
22		**Lp 369, 16th St, Abernathy**
	Gas	W: Phillips 66◈
	Other	E: to Abernathy Muni Airport✈
21		**FM 597, FM 2060, Main St, Abernathy**
	Gas	W: Conoco◈, Co-Op
	Food	W: DQ, Restaurant
20		**FM 597, 1st (NB)**
17		**CR 54, CR 53, Lubbock**
15		**Lp 461, FM 1729, Main St, Lubbock, to New Deal**
14		**FM 1729, Main St, Lubbock**
	TStop	E: New Deal Truck Stop/Fina (Scales)
	Food	E: Rest/FastFood/New Deal TS
	Other	E: Laundry/WiFi/**RVDump**/New Deal TS
13		**Lp 461, CR 57, Lubbock, New Deal**
12		**Access Rd, Auburn Ave (NB)**
11		**FM 1294, CR 6, Lubbock to Shallowater**
10		**CR 6, Keuka St, Lubbock**
9		**Airport Rd, Lubbock Int'l Airport**
	Other	E: Lubbock Int'l Airport✈ W: **Lubbock RV Park▲**
8		**FM 2641, Regis St**

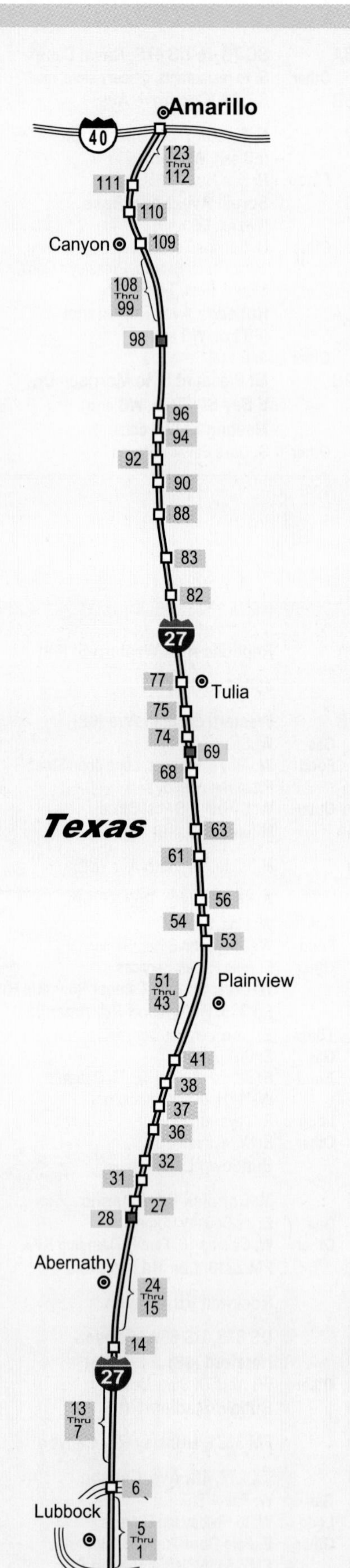

EXIT		TEXAS
7		**Yucca Lane, Amarillo Rd, Ash Ave**
6B		**Loop 289 (SB)**
6A		**Spur 326, Ave Q, Amarillo Rd (SB)**
	Lodg	E: Texas Motel
	Other	W: **Pharr RV Park▲**
6		**Loop 289, Amarillo Rd (NB)**
	Other	E: **Pharr RV Park▲**
5		**Ave H, Municipal Dr, Buddy Holly Ave, to US 82, Lubbock (SB)**
4		**US 82, Bus 87, 4th St, Parkway Dr, Lubbock, to Crosbyton**
	TStop	W: Flying J Travel Plaza #5155/Shell
	Food	W: Rest/FastFood/FJ TP
	Other	E: **MacKenzie State Park** W: Laundry/**LP/RVDump**/FJ TP, Auto Service, Texas Tech Univ
3		**US 62, TX 114, 19th St, 23rd St, Floydada, Leveland, Depot Distr**
	Other	W: Auto Services, **to Ann's RV Park▲**, **Buffalo Lake Springs Campground▲**, **I-27 Marine & RV, Bigham Auto & RV Service Center**
3A		**13th St, Buddy Holly Ave, to US 62, Broadway St (NB)**
2		**34th St, Ave H, to US 84, Bus 87**
	Gas	E: Phillips 66
	Food	W: Mr Lee's Burgers, La Fiesta Rest
	Lodg	E: Budget Motel
	Other	W: Auto Services, **to Loop 289 RV Park▲**, **Camelot Village RV & CG▲**
1C		**50th St, Ave H, Lubbock (SB)**
	TStop	E: (E to US 87N) AmBest/Rip Griffin TC
	Gas	E: Fina W: Conoco, Fina, Shamrock
	Food	E: Rest/RG TC, DQ, JoJo's, Café W: Bryan's Steaks, Burger King, China Star, Carrows Rest, DQ, KFC, Long John Silver, McDonald's, Pizza Hut, Subway, Whataburger
	TServ	E: RG TC/Tires
	Other	E: Laundry/WiFi/RG TC W: Auto & Tire Service, US Post Office, Dollar General, O'Reilly Auto Parts, Walgreen's
1B		**US 84E, Lp 289, US 87S, Slaton, Post, Tahoka (SB)**
	Gas	W: Skillet's
	Food	W: 50th St Caboose Rest, Carrow's, Country Plate Diner, KFC, Long John Silver, Skillet's Burgers
	Lodg	E: Days Inn W: Best Western, Comfort Inn, Econo Lodge, Holiday Inn Express
	Other	W: **Lubbock KOA▲**
1A		**50th St (NB), Loop 289 (SB)**
	Lodg	W: Motel 6♥
	Other	W: **Sims RV Center▲**
1		**82nd St (SB), Lp 289 (NB), Lubbock (Gas, Food, Serv W to University)**
	Other	E: Benson Auto, Truck & **RV** Repair W: Auto Services

CENTRAL TIME ZONE

⬆ TEXAS

Begin Northbound I-27 from Lubbock, TX to Amarillo, TX.

◈ = Regular Gas Stations with Diesel ▲ = RV Friendly Locations ♥ = Pet Friendly Locations

Red print shows large vehicle parking / access on site or nearby Brown Print = Campgrounds / RV PARKS

EXIT — **NORTH DAKOTA**

Begin Southbound I-29 from Canada Border
Jct I-70, Kansas City, MO.

NORTH DAKOTA

CENTRAL TIME ZONE

NOTE: MM 218: North Dakota State Line/ US / CANADA Border

(217) **US Customs (SB)**

(215) **US Customs (NB)**

215 **ND 59, CR 55, Pembina, Neche**
- TStop E: Gastrak (Scales)
- Gas E: Citgo◈
- Food E: FastFood/Gastrak, The Depot Café, Subway
- Lodg E: Gateway Motel, Red Roost Motel
- Other E: LP/Gastrak, Duty Free Store, Museum

212 **Pembina**

208 **CR 1, Pembina, to Bathgate**

203 **US 81, ND 5, Hamilton, Cavalier**
- TStop W: Joliette Express Truck Stop (Scales)
- Food W: FastFood/JE TS
- Other W: WiFi/JE TS

(203) **Weigh Station / Port of Entry (Both dir)**

200 **93rd St NE, Pembina**

196 **CR 3, 89th St NE, Drayton**

193 **86th St NE**

191 **CR 11, Drayton, to St Thomas**

187 **ND 66, 80th St NE, Drayton**
- Gas E: Cenex◈
- Food E: Andy's Drive In, DQ, Rte 66 Cafe
- Lodg E: Motel 6♥, Red River Resort

184 **160th Ave, SD 44, Drayton**

180 **CR 9, 73rd St NE, Grafton**

(179) **Rest Area (Both dir, Left Exit) (RR, Phones, Picnic, Vend)**

176 **ND 17, Grafton (All Serv 10 mi W in Grafton)**
- Med W: + Unity Medical Center

172 **65th St, Minto**

168 **61st St, CR 15, Minto, Warsaw**

164 **57th St NE, Minto**

161 **ND 54, CR 19, to Oslo, Ardoch**

157 **CR 1, 32nd Ave NE, Manvel**

152 **CR 33, 28th Ave, US 81, Manvel**

145 **N Washington St, US 81 Bus, CR 11, Grand Forks**

141 **US 2, Gateway Dr, 18th Ave, Grand Forks, Emerado**
- FStop E: Loaf'n Jug/Cenex
- TStop W: PTP/Simonson Travel Center (Scales), StaMart Travel Plaza #13/Tesoro (Scales)
- Gas E: AmocoBP◈, Conoco
- Food E: Burger King, Chuck House Ranch Rest, China Buffet, DQ, Hardee's, McDonald's, Rest/Holiday Inn

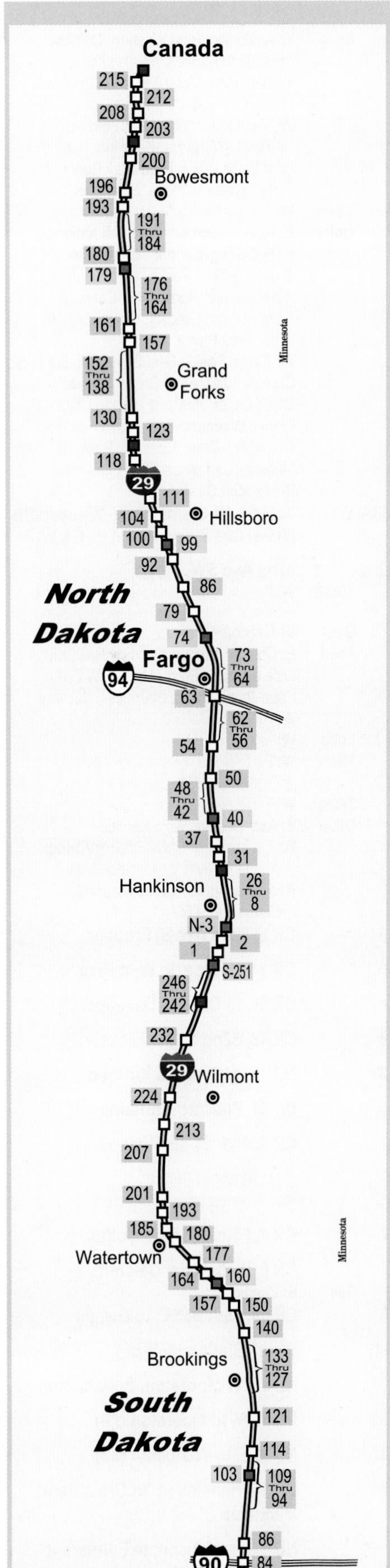

EXIT — **NORTH DAKOTA**

- Food W: Rest/Simonson TC, Rest/FastFood/StaMart TP, Emerald Grill, Perkins
- Lodg E: Budget Inn Express, Holiday Inn, Super 8, Westward Ho Motel
  W: Motel/Simonson TC, Prairie Inn
- AServ E: Gateway Amoco
- TWash W: Simonson TC
- TServ E: Forks Freightliner, Dempsey Truck Service, Grand Forks Diesel Injection Service
  W: Simonson TC/Tires, StaMart TC/Tires, Cummins Scott's Express
- Other E: ATMs, Auto Dealers, Auto Services, Advance Auto Parts, Checker Auto Parts, Banks, Goodyear, U-Haul, Engelstad Arena Museum, Randy's Repair & Towing, Univ of ND
  W: WiFi/Laundry/Simonson TC, Laundry/WiFi/RV Dump/LP/StaMart TP, Grand Forks Int'l Airport✈, to Grand Forks AFB, to 20 mi: Turtle River State Park▲

140 **SD 297, CR 4, Demers Ave, City Center, Grand Forks**
- Gas E: BP, Conoco
- Food E: Subway
- Lodg E: Hilton Garden Inn
- AServ E: Demers Interstate Amoco
- TServ E: Interstate Detroit Diesel
- Other E: ATMs, Banks
  W: Amtrak

138 **US 81 Bus, 32nd Ave S**
- TStop W: AmBest/Big Sioux Travel Plaza/Conoco, SuperPumper
- Gas E: Amoco, Tesoro, Sam's
- Food E: Applebee's, Burger King, Buffalo Wild Wings, China Garden, Domino's Pizza, Ground Round, McDonald's, Qdoba, Quiznos, Red Lobster, Starbucks, Taco Bell, Village Inn, Wendy's
  W: Subway/Big Sioux TP
- Lodg E: Comfort Inn, Country Suites, C'Mon Inn, Days Inn, Fairfield Inn, Holiday Inn Express, Lakeview Inn, Road King Inn
- TWash W: Big Sioux TP
- TServ W: Big Sioux TP/Tires
- Other E: ATMs, Banks, Auto Dealers, Best Buy, Carmike Cinemas, CVS, Grocery, Lowe's, PetCo♥, Sam's Club, Target, Tires Plus+, Mall, Walmart SC, Grand Forks Campground & RV Park▲, Wagon Train RV Park▲
  W: Laundry/WiFi/LP/RVDump/Big Sioux TP, RVDump/SuperPumper

130 **US 81, ND 15, Thompson**
- Gas W: Tim's Quick Stop
- Food W: Fireside Grill

123 **CR 25, Reynolds**

(119) **Inspection Station (Both dir)**

118 **CR 21, Hillsboro, to Buxton**

111 **ND 200W, Mayville, Cummings**
- Other W: Mayville State Univ

104 **CR 11, Hillsboro**
- FStop E: Cenex
- Gas E: Tesoro◈
- Food E: Burger King/Cenex, Country Hearth Inn
- Lodg E: Hillsboro Inn
- Med E: + Hillsboro Medical Center
- Other E: Hillsboro Campground & RV Park▲

◈= Regular Gas Stations with Diesel ▲ = RV Friendly Locations ♥= Pet Friendly Locations
Red print shows large vehicle parking / access on site or nearby Brown Print = Campgrounds / RV PARKS

EXIT — NORTH DAKOTA

100 **ND 200E, ND 200W Alt, Hillsboro, Halstead, Blanchard**

(99) Rest Area (Both dir)
(RR, Phones, Picnic, Vend)

92 **CR 11, Hillsboro, Grandin**
- FStop — W: Nepstad's Stop N Shop/Citgo
- Gas — E: Co-Op
- Food — W: Rest/Deli/Nepstad's

86 **CR 26, Gardner**

79 **CR 4, 1st St, Argusville**

(74) Rest Area (Both dir)
(RR, Phones, Picnic)

73 **CR 17, CR 22, Harwood**
- TStop — E: Cenex
- Food — E: Café/Cenex

69 **CR 20, Fargo**

67 **US 81 Bus, 19th Ave N**
- Lodg — E: Days Inn
- Med — E: + Vets Medical Center
- Other — E: Hector Field Airport✈, Fargo Dome, The Coliseum, Dakotah Field, Bison Sports Arena

66 **12th Ave NW**
- TStop — E: StaMart Travel Center #5/Tesoro◈ (Scales)
- Gas — E: Stop 'N Go
  W: Cenex◈
- Food — E: Rest/FastFood/StaMart TC, North Town Grill
  W: Arby's, Freshway Cafe
- Lodg — W: Microtel
- TServ — W: Interstate Detroit Diesel, NW Truck & Trailer
- Med — E: + MeritCare Medical Center
- Other — E: Laundry/WiFi/RVDump/LP/StaMart, Auto Repairs, ND State Univ

65 **US 10, Main Ave, W Fargo**
- TStop — E: StaMart Conv Ctr #14/Tesoro
- Gas — E: Amoco, Simonson
  W: Cenex◈, Simonson◈
- Food — E: Rest/FastFood/StaMart, Burger Time, China Buffet, Kroll's Café, Valley Kitchen
  W: Hardee's, Outback Steakhouse, Subway
- Lodg — W: Best Western
- TServ — W: Nelson International, Cummins
- Med — E: + Dakota Heartland Hospital
- Other — E: Civic Mem'l Auditorium, Grocery, Greyhound, Amtrak, NAPA, Auto Service, McLaughlin's RV & Marine
  W: CarQuest, Auto Dealers, Adventure RV Sales, ND State Hwy Patrol Post, Auto Services

64 **13th Ave SW, Downtown Fargo**
- Gas — E: BP, Cenex, Conoco, StaMart◈
  W: BP, Cenex, Tesoro
- Food — E: Applebee's, Arby's, Acapulco Mexican Rest, Burger King, Chuck E Cheese's Pizza, DQ, Ground Round, Hardee's, Mr Steak, Quiznos, Perkins, Starbucks, Subway, Wendy's
  W: Arby's, Chili's, Denny's, Hooters, McDonald's, Fuddrucker's, Lone Star Steakhouse, Olive Garden, Red Lobster, TGI Friday, Taco Bell, Timberlodge Steak House
- Lodg — E: AmericInn, Best Western, Comfort Inn, Country Suites, Econo Lodge, Hampton Inn, Motel 6♥, Red Roof Inn, Super 8
  W: Comfort Inn, Days Inn, Fairfield Inn, Holiday Inn Express, Kelly Inn, Red Roof Inn♥, Long Term Stay Rooms & Suites, Ramada Plaza, Select Inn
- TServ — W: Midwest Mack
- Other — E: I-29 Amusement Park, Lindenwood Park Campground▲, Cactus Jack's Casino, ATMs, Banks, Auto Services, Advance Auto Parts, CVS, Carwash, Family Dollar, Grocery, Goodyear, Jiffy Lube, Tires Plus +
  W: ATMs, Banks, Best Buy, B&N, Big Lots, Century 10 Cinema, Grocery, Lowe's, Office Depot, PetCo♥, Sam's Club, Target, Walmart sc, Walgreen's, West Acres Mall, West Acres 14, Baseball Museum, Jail House Rock Casino, Brass Mint Casino

(63AB) **Jct I-94, W-Bismarck, E-Minneapolis (Travel Ctrs & Serv loc 1st Ex E & W)**

62 **32nd Ave SW, Fargo**
- TStop — W: Flying J Travel Plaza #5009/Conoco (Scales)
- Gas — E: AmocoBP, Tesoro
- Food — E: Country Kitchen, Culver's Rest, KFC, Little Caesar's Pizza, Moe's SW Grill, Papa John's Pizza, Starbucks, Subway
  W: Rest/FJ TP
- Lodg — W: Motel/FJ TP
- TServ — W: FJ TP/Tires, Goodyear, Peterbilt, Johnson Trailer, Isuzu Diesel
- TWash — W: FJ TP
- Other — E: Auto Dealers, Auto Service
  W: Laundry/BarbSh/WiFi/LP/RVDump/FJ TP, Red River Valley Speedway, Red River Valley Campground▲, Pleasure Land RV

60 **CR 6, 52nd Ave S, Frontier**

56 **CR 14, Horace, to Wild Rice**

54 **CR 16, to Oxbow, Davenport**

50 **CR 18, 52nd St SE, Hickson**

48 **ND 46, Walcott, to Kindred**

44 **US 81, Walcott, Christine**

42 **CR 2, 60th St SE, Walcott**

(40) Rest Area (Both dir)
(RR, Phones, Picnic, Vend)

37 **CR 4, 65th St SE, to Colfax**

31 **CR 8, Wahpeton, Galchutt**
- Gas — E: Cenex

26 **CR 10, 76th St SE, to Dwight**

(24) Weigh Station (Both dir)

23 **ND 13, W-Mooreton, E-Wahpeton**

23B **ND 13W, to Mooreton (SB)**

23A **ND 13E, to Wahpeton (SB)**

15 **CR 16, Hankinson, to Great Bend, Mantador**

8 **ND 11, Hankinson, to Fairmount (Addt'l Serv 4mi W in Hankinson)**
- TStop — E: MGS Oil/Mobil
- Food — E: FastFood/MGS

EXIT — ND / SD

(3) ND Welcome Center (NB)
(RR, Phones, Vend, Info)

2 **CR 22, 100th St SE, Hankinson**

1 **CR 1E, 102nd St SE**
- Other — E: Dakota Magic Casino & Hotel/Gas/ConvStore/Restaurants/RVPark▲, Sisseton Indian Reservation

CENTRAL TIME ZONE

⬆NORTH DAKOTA
⬇SOUTH DAKOTA

CENTRAL TIME ZONE

NOTE: MM 253: North Dakota State Line

(251) SD Welcome Center (SB)
(RR, Phone, Picnic, Info, RVDump)

246 **SD 127, Rosholt, New Effington**

242 **CR 8, CR 23, Sisseton**

(235) Weigh Station / Port of Entry (SB)

232 **SD 10, 119th St, Sisseton, Browns Valley (W Serv Approx 3.5 mi)**
- TStop — E: Dakota Travel Center Connection Casino/Phillips 66
- Gas — W: BP, Cenex, Sinclair
- Food — W: American Hearth Rest, Country Kitchen, DQ, Dairy Freeze
- Lodg — W: I-29 Motel, Holiday Motel, Super 8
- Med — W: + Coteau des Prairies Hospital
- Other — E: Sisseton Indian Reservation, Dakota Connection Casino/Restaurants
  W: Camp Dakotah▲, Sisseton Muni Airport✈, to 20mi: Roy Lake State Park▲

224 **CR 5, 127th St, Peever**
- Gas — E: Cenex

(213) **SD 15, SD 109, Summitt, to Wilmot**
E: Rest Area
(RR, Ph, Picnic, RVDump)
- Other — E: Servs 10mi, SD State Hwy Patrol

207 **US 12, Summit, Aberdeen**
- TStop — W: PTP/Coffee Cup Fuel Stop #1/Conoco (Scales)
- Food — E: High Plains Café, County Line
  W: Rest/Deli/CC FS
- Other — E: Bank, Grocery, Auto Service

201 **CR 8, 149th St, Twin Brooks, to Milbank**

193 **SD 20, South Shore, Stockholm**

185 **CR 6, 164th St, Watertown, Waverly**
- Other — W: to 5 mi: Dakota Sioux Casino & Hotel/Gas/ConvStore/Restaurant/RVPark▲, Sisseton Indian Reservation

180 **US 81S, CR 10, 169th St, Bramble Park Zoo, Watertown**
- Med — W: + Prairie Lakes Care Center
- Other — W: Zoo, Watertown Muni Airport✈

177 **US 212, 172nd St, Watertown, to Kranzburg**
- FStop — W: P&L Conv/Shell
- TStop — E: Stone's Truck Stop/Sinclair (Scales)

◈= Regular Gas Stations with Diesel ▲ = RV Friendly Locations ♥= Pet Friendly Locations
Red print shows large vehicle parking / access on site or nearby Brown Print = Campgrounds / RV PARKS

EXIT		SOUTH DAKOTA
	Gas	W: AmocoBP◈, Cenex◈, Conoco◈, Sinclair
	Food	E: Rest/Subway/Stone's TS W: FastFood/P&L, Applebee's, Arby's, Burger King, Domino's Pizza, Hardee's, Little Caesar's Pizza, McDonald's, New Kitchen, Perkins, Pizza Hut, Kings Buffet, Coffeyville Cafe, Starbucks, Subway
	Lodg	E: Holiday Inn Express, Stone's Inn W: Comfort Inn, Days Inn, Drake Motor Inn, Budget Host Inn, Travelers Inn
	Med	W: + Prairie Lakes Care Center
	TServ	E: R&H Repairs & Service, Wheelco Brakes
	Other	E: RVDump/Stone's TS W: Advance Auto Parts, Auto Dealers, Carwash, Firestone, Goodyear, Grocery, KMart, NAPA, ShopKO, Target, Tires Plus, Vet♥, **Walmart sc**, Mall, **to Sandy Shores Rec Area▲**
164		**SD 22, Castlewood, Clear Lake (Serv & Hosp 10 mi E to Clear Lake)**
(160)		**Rest Area (Both dir) (RR, Phone, Picnic, Vend, RVDump)**
157		**CR 313, Toronto, to Brandt**
150		**SD 15, SD 28, Toronto, Estelline (Serv 7-10 mi W)**
	Other	W: to Lake Poinsett State Rec Area▲
140		**SD 30, CR 6, White, Bruce (Gas, Food, Repairs 4mi E to White)**
	Other	W: to appr 12mi: **Oakwood Lakes State Park▲**
133		**US 14 ByP, Brookings, Arlington**
	Other	W: to SD State Univ, Laura Ingalls Wilder Home
132		**I-29 Bus, US 14, Brookings, Huron**
	FStop	E: Kum & Go #623/Cenex W: Lloyd's Amoco
	Gas	W: Casey's Gen'l Store, Gas N More, Citgo, Shell
	Food	E: Burger King/Cenex, Applebee's W: Burger King, Country Kitchen, DQ, Hardee's, KFC, McDonald's, Mad Jack's Brown Baggers, King Wok's Chinese, Pizza Ranch, Perkins, Subway, Rest/Qual Inn, Rest/Brookings Inn,
	Lodg	E: Fairfield Inn, Super 8 W: Brookings Inn, Comfort Inn, Quality Inn, Wayside Motel
	Med	W: + Brookings Health System
	Other	W: Auto Dealers, ATMs, Banks, Auto Services, Advance Auto Parts, Big O Tires, Grocery, Lowe's, Radio Shack, Brookings Muni Airport✈
127		**SD 324, Brookings, to Elkton, Sinai**
121		**CR 4, Flandreau, Nunda, Ward** **E: Rest Area (Both dir) (RR, Phones, Picnic, Vend, RVDump)**
	Other	E: SD Hwy Patrol Post
114		**SD 32, Flandreau (All Serv 7-10 mi E in Flandreau)**
109		**SD 34, Madison, Colman, Egan**
	TStop	W: Crossroads Truck Stop/Shell, Prairie Junction Truck Stop/BP
	Food	W: Rest/Crossroads TS, FastFood/Prairie Junction TS
	Other	W: Eich Trucking Repair

EXIT		SOUTH DAKOTA
104		**CR 14, Trent, Chester**
(103)		**Parking Area (Both dir)**
98		**SD 115S, Dell Rapids, Chester (Serv 3-5mi E in Dell Rapids)**
	Gas	E: Mobil, Kum & Go
	Food	E: DQ, Subway/TCBY, Pizza Ranch, Prairie View Steakhouse
	TServ	E: Dell's Diesel Service
	Med	E: + Dells Area Health Center
94		**SD 114, Baltic, Lyons, Colton**
	Gas	E: Citgo
	Other	E: ATM, Auto Repairs, Bank, EROS Data Center, Grocery
86		**CR 130, Sioux Falls, to Renner, Crooks**
(84AB)		**Jct I-90, W to Pierre, E to Albert Lea**
83		**SD 38W, 60th St N, Sioux Falls, Airport (Addtl Serv E to N Cliff Ave)**
	TStop	E: Flying J Travel Plaza #5035/Conoco (Scales)
	Food	E: Country Market/FastFood/FJ TP
	Lodg	E: Quality Inn
	TServ	E: Flying J TP, Holcomb Freightliner
	Other	E: Laundry/WiFi/RVDump/LP//FJ TP, J & L Harley Davidson, **Yogi Bear's Jellystone Campground▲**, **Sioux Falls KOA▲**, Sioux Falls Reg'l Airport✈, ATM, Banks, Graham Tire, Catfish Bay Water Ski Park
82		**Benson Rd, Sioux Falls**
81		**CR 140, SD 38E, Maple St, Russell St, Airport, Sioux Falls**
	Gas	E: BP, Citgo, Gas Barrel
	Food	E: Burger King, Country Kitchen, Roll'n Pin Rest, Front Porch Grill, Rest/Oaks Hotel
	Lodg	E: Arena Motel, Best Western, Kelly Inn, Oaks Hotel, Motel 6♥, Ramada Inn, Sleep Inn, Sheraton, Super 8
	TServ	E: Becks Truck Repair
	Other	E: **SD Hwy Patrol Post**, Sioux Falls Convention Center, Sioux Falls Arena, Sioux Falls Stadium, Sioux Falls Reg'l Airport✈, Auto Services, Avis RAC, Budget RAC, Hertz RAC, National RAC, **Schaap's RV Traveland**
80		**Madison St**
	Other	E: Turner Co Fairgrounds
79		**I-29 Bus, SD 42, 12th St**
	FStop	W: Kum & Go #619/Cenex
	Gas	E: Amoco, Cenex W: Citgo, Phillips 66
	Food	E: Burger King, Burger Time, Fryin Pan Family Rest, KFC, McDonald's, Golden Harvest Chinese, Pizza Hut, Taco Bell, Wendy's W: FastFood/K&G, Hardee's
	Lodg	E: Ramada W: Pinecrest Motel, Westwick Motel
	TServ	E: Graham Tire
	Med	E: + Sioux Valley Hospital
	Other	E: Kmart, Walgreen's, Auto Dealers, ATMs, Banks, Fairgrounds, Greyhound, Grocery, Museums, Great Plains Zoo, Thunder Road Amusement Park, USS SD Mem'l W: **Tower Campground▲**, **Westwick RV Park▲**, **Jack's Campers**, Kmart, Grocery, SF Tire, Auto Repairs

EXIT		SOUTH DAKOTA
78		**26th St, Sioux Falls**
	Gas	E: Phillips 66◈, Sam's
	Food	E: Carino's Italian Rest, Chevy's Mexican Rest, Cracker Barrel, Chuck E Cheese, Culver's Rest, Domino's Pizza, Foley's Fish Chop & Steak House, Granite City Food & Brewery, Hibachi, Outback Steak House, Rio Bravo Mexican Rest, Ruby Tuesday, Rue 41 W: Dynasty Chinese, Papa John's, Quiznos, Spaghetti Shop, Starbucks, Westwinds Rest
	Lodg	E: Hampton Inn, Holiday Inn Express, Microtel, Staybridge Suites W: Settle Inn, TownePlace Suites
	Other	E: Century Stadium 14, Grocery, Home Depot, Sam's Club, World Market, USPS
77		**41st St, Sioux Falls**
	Gas	E: AmocoBP◈, Shell, Sinclair◈ W: Citgo, Shell◈
	Food	E: Applebee's, Arby's, Burger King, Chili's, China Buffet, Fryin Pan Family Rest, Fuddrucker's, Ground Round, Inca Mexican Rest, KFC, La Fiesta Mexican Rest, Lone Star Steakhouse, McDonald's, Naps Southern BBQ, Olive Garden, Pizza Hut, Perkins, Qdoba Mexican Grill, Quiznos Red Lobster, Royal Fork Buffet, Starbucks, Subway, TGI Friday, Texas Roadhouse, Timber Lodge Steak House, Wendy's W: Burger King, Godfather's Pizza, Little Caesar's Pizza, IHOP, Perkins, Subway
	Lodg	E: Best Western, Comfort Suites, Empire Inn, Fairfield Inn, Radisson, Residence Inn, Microtel, Super 8 W: AmericInn, Baymont Inn, Days Inn, Select Inn
	Other	E: ATMs, Banks, Auto Services, Advance Auto Parts, Barnes & Noble, Best Buy, Big O Tires, Carwash, Checker Auto Parts, FedEx Office, Grocery, Jiffy Lube, PetCo♥, Radio Shack, ShopKO, Sam's Club, Target, Tires Plus+, Walgreen's, **Walmart sc**, Empire Mall, Western Mall, Visitor Info W: Carmike Cinema, ATM, Banks, Pharmacy, US Post Office
(75)		**Jct I-229N, to I-90E**
73		**CR 106, Sioux Falls, Tea**
	TStop	E: Larry's I-29 Truck Plaza/Texaco
	Food	E: Rest/Larry's TP, I-29 Bar & Grill
	Other	W: Auto Services, Larson Truck Sales, **Red Barn RV Park▲**
71		**CR 110, Harrisburg, Tea**
	Other	W: **Red Barn RV Park▲**
68		**CR 116, Lennox, Parker**
64		**SD 44, Worthing, Lennox**
	Gas	E: Shell
	Food	E: Old Towne Dinner Theatre
62		**US 18E, Worthing, Canton**
	TStop	E: Countryside Convenience/Shell
	Gas	E: Phillips 66
	Food	E: FastFood/Countryside
	Lodg	E: Charlie's Motel
59		**US 18W, CR 134, to Davis, Hurley**
56		**CR 140, Beresford, Fairview**

◈= Regular Gas Stations with Diesel ▲ = RV Friendly Locations ♥= Pet Friendly Locations
Red print shows large vehicle parking / access on site or nearby Brown Print = Campgrounds / RV PARKS

EXIT — SD / IA

53 **CR 146, Beresford, to Viborg**

50 **CR 152, to Centerville, Hudson**

47 **SD 46, W Cedar St, Beresford**
- TStop — E: Jet Truck Plaza/Sinclair; W: Truck Towne/Cenex
- Gas — E: Cenex, Casey's Gen'l Store, Conoco
- Food — E: Rest/FastFood/Jet TP, Burger King, Emily's Cafe, Good Times Pizza, Subway; W: Rest/Truck Towne, Silver Dollar Rest
- Lodg — E: Crossroads Motel, Super 8, Starlite Motel
- TServ — E: Jet TP/Tires
- Other — E: Grocery, Auto Services, ATMs, Bank, **Windmill Campground▲**; W: LP/Laundry/TT, Radio Shack

42 **CR 13, to Alcester, Wakonda**

(40) **Parking Area (SB)**

38 **CR 15, Beresford, to Volin**
- Other — E: to **Union Grove State Park▲**

31 **SD 48, Burbank, to Spink, Akron**

(26) **SD 50, to Vermillion, Yankton**
(Addt'l serv 7 mi W)
E: SD Welcome Center (Both dir)
(RR, Phone, Picnic, Vend, RVDump)
- TStop — W: PTP/Coffee Cup Fuel Stop #6/Conoco (Scales)
- Food — W: Rest/Deli/Coffee Cup FS
- Other — W: Laundry/CC FS

18 **Bus Lp 29, Elk Point, Burbank**
- Gas — E: AmocoBP◊, Phillips 66
- Food — E: Cody's Homestead, DQ
- Lodg — E: Home Towne Inn, Sun Motel
- Other — E: ATM, Bank, Grocery, Auto Repairs

15 **29 Bus, Elk Point**
(Access Same Serv as Ex #18)

9 **SD 105, Jefferson**
- FStop — E: Amoco
- Food — E: Choice Cut/Amoco

4 **CR 23, to SD 105, N Sioux City, to McCook**
- Other — W: **Sioux City North KOA▲**

(3) **Weigh Station / Port of Entry (NB)**

2 **SD 105N, N Sioux City**
- FStop — E: Connie's AmPride
- Gas — E: Cenex; W: Casey's Gen'l Store, Citgo
- Food — E: Rest/AmPride, McDonald's, Taco John's, Razz's Pizza, Subway
- Lodg — E: Comfort Inn, Super 8; W: Hampton Inn♥, Red Carpet Inn
- Other — E: Fireworks, to **Stone State Park▲**; W: **Sioux City North KOA▲**

1 **Dakota Dunes, N Sioux City**
- Gas — W: Dune's General Store◊
- Food — W: Graham's Grill
- Lodg — W: Country Inn
- Med — W: + Medical Center
- Other — E: Elmwood Golf Course

CENTRAL TIME ZONE

⬆ SOUTH DAKOTA
⬇ IOWA

CENTRAL TIME ZONE

EXIT — IOWA

NOTE: MM 152: South Dakota State Line

NOTE: WiFi Access in All Rest Areas

(151) **IA 12N, Riverside Blvd, Sioux City**
- Gas — E: Casey's Gen'l Store
- Other — E: ATMs, Dollar General, Grocery, **to Stone State Park, Dorothy Pecaut Nature Center**

(149) **Hamilton Blvd, Sioux City**
US 77S, Wesley Pky, So Sioux City
W: IA Welcome Center (SB)
(RR, Phone, Picnic, Vend, RVDump)
- Gas — E: Conoco
- Food — E: Rest/Qual Inn
- Lodg — E: Hamilton Inn, Quality Inn
- Other — E: Jiffy Lube; W: Museum, Briar Cliff Univ, Belle of Sioux City Casino

148 **US 77S, US 20 Bus, Wesley Way, to S Sioux City, NE (NB)**
- Gas — W: Conoco◊, Phillips 66
- Food — W: McDonald's, Pizza Hut, Taco Bell
- Lodg — W: Regency Inn
- Other — W: Advance Auto Parts, O'Reilly Auto Parts, to **Scenic Park Campground▲**

147B **US 20 Bus, IA 12S, Gordon Dr, Nebraska St, Bus Distr, Downtown**
- Gas — E: Heritage Express
- Food — E: Arby's, Burger King, Chili's, IHOP, Hardee's, KFC, Perkins, Rest/Hol Inn
- Lodg — E: Best Western, Hilton Garden Inn, Holiday Inn, Super 8♥
- Other — E: Auto Dealer, Staples, Walgreen's, US Post Office, Gateway Arena, Sioux City Auditorium, Sioux City Convention Center

147A **Floyd Blvd, Stockyards, Sioux City**
- Gas — E: Ivy's EZ Stop
- Med — E: + Mercy Medical Hospital
- Other — E: Sioux City Convention Center; W: Home Depot, Museum, River Front, to Riverboat Casino

144B **I-129, US 20W, US 75S, South Sioux City (NB)**

144A **US 20E, US 75N, to Ft Dodge Le Mars (Serv 1mi E on Lakeport St)**

144 **US 20, US 75, to Ft Dodge, Le Mars, I-129, to NE (SB) (Appr 1mi E to Lakeport St: Gas/Food/Lodg/Retail)**

143 **US 75 Bus, Industrial Rd, Singing Hills Blvd, Sioux City**
(Addt'l Serv appr 1 mi E to Lakeport St)
- TStop — E: Truck Haven Auto Truck Plaza/Shell (Scales); W: Sioux Harbor Travel Plaza/BP (Scales)
- Gas — E: Kum & Go/Cenex, Murphy, Sam's
- Food — E: Cafe/Truck Haven, China Super Buffet, Culver's, Hunan Palace Chinese Rest, KFC, McDonald's, Monterrey Mexican Rest, Pizza Hut, Quiznos, Taco John's; W: Rest/FastFood/SH TP, Wendy's
- Lodg — E: Motel/TruckHaven, AmericInn, Baymont Inn♥, Days Inn♥, Holiday Inn Express; W: Super 8♥
- TWash — E: Green Light Truck Wash, Truck Haven
- TServ — E: Truck Haven/Tires, Kenworth White GMC Volvo, Peterbilt, Pomp's Tire Services; W: Diesel Specialties, Sioux City Truck & Trailer
- Other — E: Laundry/WiFi/LP/Truck Haven, Auto Dealers, Batteries Plus, Sam's Club, Tuffy Auto Services, **Walmart sc**, Green Valley Golf Course; W: Laundry/WiFi/SH TP

141 **CR D38, 1st St, Sioux Gateway Airport, Sergeant Bluff**
- Gas — E: Casey's Gen'l Store, Phillips 66◊, Shell◊; W: Amoco
- Food — E: Aggies Smoked Rest, China Taste, Godfather's Pizza, Olie's Lunch Box, Pizza Ranch, Subway; W: Jerry's Rib House
- Lodg — E: Econo Lodge; W: Motel 6♥
- Other — W: Sioux Gateway Airport✈

(139) **Rest Area (Both dir)**
(RR, Phones, Picnic, RVDump)

135 **CR D51, Port Neal Landing**

134 **CR K25, 275th St, Salix**
- Gas — E: Citgo, Total
- Other — E: Grocery; W: to **Snyder Bend Park▲**

(132) **Weigh Station (SB)**
TRUCK Parking Area (NB)

127 **IA 141 E, 330th St, Sloan**
- Gas — E: Casey's Gen'l Store, Shell◊
- Food — E: Italian Rest, Sloan Cafe
- Lodg — E: Rip Van Winkle Motel
- Other — E: Sloan Golf Course; W: **Winnavegas▲**, to Winnebago Indian Reservation/Casino

120 **CR E24, 160th St, Whiting**
- Other — W: **Lighthouse Marina & Campground▲**

112 **IA 175, Onawa, to Decatur, NE**
- FStop — E: Onawa 66
- TStop — E: Dave's World/Conoco (Scales)
- Food — E: Subway/Dave's, Oehler Bros Rest, Bamboo Village Chinese, Denise's Family Rest, DQ, McDonald's, Pizza Hut
- Lodg — E: Super 8
- Med — E: + Burgess Hospital, + Family Medicine Clinic
- Other — E: LP/Dave's, ATMs, Auto Dealer, Auto & Truck Repairs, NAPA, **On-Ur-Wa RV Park▲**, **Interchange RV Campground▲**, to Onawa Muni Airport✈; W: **Onawa/Blue Lake KOA▲**, **Lewis & Clark State Park▲**

(110) **Onawa Rest Area (Both dir)**
(RR, Phones, Picnic, Vend, RVDump)

105 **E60, Blencoe**

95 **IA 301, CR F20, Little Sioux**
- Gas — E: to River Mart
- Other — E: to Auto Repairs; W: **Woodland RV Campground▲**

(92) **Parking Area (Both dir)**

89 **IA 127 E, Mondamin**
- Gas — E: Jiffy Mart◊

82 **CR F50, Modale**
- Gas — W: Cenex

(80) **MO Valley Rest Area (SB)**
(RR, Phones, Picnic, RVDump)

(79) **MO Valley Rest Area (NB)**
(RR, Phones, Picnic, RVDump)

◊ = Regular Gas Stations with Diesel ▲ = RV Friendly Locations ♥ = Pet Friendly Locations
Red print shows large vehicle parking / access on site or nearby Brown Print = Campgrounds / RV PARKS

EXIT	IOWA
75	**US 30, Erie St, Missouri Valley, to Blair, NE**
FStop	E: Taylor Quick Pik/Shell W: Petro Mart Travel Plaza/P66
Gas	E: to Casey's General Store, Shell, BP, Kum & Go W: I-29 Country Store/BP
Food	E: FastFood/T QP, Arby's, Bluegrass Cafe, McDonald's, Penny's Diner, Subway, to Casey's C/O Pizza, Dairy Den, Pizza Ranch W: Junction Cafe/PetroMart TP, Burger King, The Edge Bar & Grill
Lodg	E: Oak Tree Inn W: Rath Inn, Super 8
Med	E: + to Hospital
Other	E: ATMs, to Bank, Grocery, Carwash, Auto Repairs & Services, Family Dollar W: Auto Dealer
(74)	**Weigh Station (SB)**
(73)	**Weigh Station (NB)**
72	**G12W (Former IA 362), G14E, DeSota Ave, to Loveland**
FStop	E: DeSoto Bend Mini Mart/Conoco
Other	W: to Wilson Island State Park▲
NOTE:	**I-29 below runs with I-680 exits #71-61. Exit #'s follow I-29.**
(71)	**Jct I-680E, to Des Moines**
66	**Rosewood Rd, Crescent, to Honey Creek**
FStop	W: IA Feed & Grain/Sinclair & Rest
(61B)	**Jct I-680W, to North Omaha**
NOTE:	**I-29 above runs with I-680 exits 61-71. Exit #'s follow I-29.**
61A	**G37E (Former IA 988), to Crescent**
Gas	E: Phillips 66
Other	E: to Crescent Ski Area
56	**IA 192S, N 16th St, Bus District, Council Bluffs (SB, LEFT Exit)**
55	**N 25th St, Council Bluffs**
Gas	E: Sinclair, Pump n Munch
Lodg	E: Ramada Inn
54B	**N 35th St, G Ave (NB)**
54A	**G Ave, Council Bluffs (SB)**
Gas	W: WestEnd Service
(53B)	**Jct I-480W, US 6W, to Omaha (NB, LEFT Exit - No Access to US 6E)**
53A	**9th Ave, S 37th St, Harrah's Blvd**
Gas	E: Conoco, Phillips 66, Shell, Shamrock
Food	E: Country Kitchen
Lodg	E: Days Inn
Other	W: Harrah's Casino & Hotel, Riverboat Casino
52	**Nebraska Ave, Council Bluffs**
Gas	E: Conoco◈
Lodg	E: Comfort Suites, Bluffs Run Casino, Hotel & RV Park▲ W: AmeriStar Casino & Hotel, Hampton Inn, Holiday Inn, Harrah's Casino & Hotel & Rest
Other	E: Mid America Center W: Dodge Park Golf Course, Dog Track

EXIT	IOWA
NOTE:	**I-29 & I-80 run together for 3 mi below. Exit #'s follows I-80.**
(51/1A)	**Jct I-80W, to Omaha (NB, Left Exit)**
1B	**S 24th St, Council Bluffs**
TStop	N: Pilot Travel Center #329 (Scales), Sapp Bros Oasis/Shell (Scales)
Gas	N: Casey's, Conoco, Sinclair
Food	N: Arby's/Pilot TC, Rest/BK/Sapp Bros
Lodg	N: AmericInn, Best Western, Country Inn, Interstate Inn, Super 8
TWash	N: Sapp Bros/Blue Beacon TW
TServ	N: Sapps Bros/Tires, Goodyear, Peterbilt, Speedco, Boyers Diesel
Other	N: Laundry/WiFi/Pilot TC, Laundry/WiFi/LP/RVDump/Sapp Bros, to Bluff's Run Casino Hotel & RV Park▲
3	**IA 192N, Council Bluffs, Bus Distr, Lake Manawa**
TStop	S: Travel Center of America (Scales)
Gas	N: Casey's Gen'l Store S: Phillips 66◈, Shell◈
Food	S: CountryPride/Pizza Hut/TA TC, DQ, Applebee's, Burger King, Golden Corral, Cracker Barrel, Hardee's, McDonald's, Perkins, Red Lobster, Subway, Taco Bell
Lodg	S: Comfort Inn, Days Inn, Fairfield Inn
TServ	N: Whitehill Trailer Repair S: TA TC/Tires, Larry's Diesel Repair, CAT, Peterbilt, Cummins, V&Y Truck & Trailer
Other	S: Laundry/WiFi/TA TC, Advance Auto, ATMs, Auto Dealers, Auto Repairs, Auto Rentals, Banks, Grocery, Home Depot, Sam's Club, U-Haul, Walmart sc,
(48/4)	**Jct I-80E, to Des Moines (SB, LEFT Exit)**
NOTE:	**I-29 & I-80 run together above for 3 mi. Exit #'s follow I-80.**
47	**US 275 N, IA 92, Lake Manawa**
Gas	E: Phillips 66 W: Gas Mart, Oil
Other	W: Tomes Country Club Acres RV Park▲ , Lake Manawa State Park▲ , T & K Truck Repair
42	**IA 370W, Pacific Jct, to Bellevue, NE**
Food	W: K&B Steakhouse
Other	W: to Offutt AFB, Haworth Park▲
(38)	**Pacific Jct Rest Area (Both dir) (RR, Ph, Pic, Vend, Weather, RVDump)**
35	**US 34E, US 275S, Pacific Jct, to Glenwood, Red Oak (All Serv E 3-5mi in Glenwood)**
Gas	W: BP◈
Food	W: Bluff View Cafe
Lodg	W: Bluff View Motel
Other	W: Walker's Harley Davidson
32	**US 34W, L35E, Plattsmouth, Pacific Junction**
24	**CR L31, to J10, Waubonsie Ave, Thurman, Bartlett, Tabor**
20	**J24, (Former IA 145), CR J34, McPaul, Thurman**
15	**J26, Percival**
Gas	E: Percival Farm Service/BP◈
(11)	**Weigh Station (NB)**

EXIT	IA / MO
10	**IA 2, Percival to Sidney, Nebraska City, NE**
FStop	W: The Junction/Conoco
TStop	W: Crossroads Travel Center/Shell (Scales), Sapp Bros/BP (Scales)
Food	W: FastFood/The Jctn, FastFood/Cr Rds TC, Rest/FastFood/SappBros, Arby's, Burger King, McDonald's, Subway, Wendy's
Lodg	W: Best Value Inn, Best Western, Days Inn, Super 8
Other	E: to Waubonsie State Park▲ W: RVDump/CR TC, Laundry/WiFi/ RVDump/SappBros, to Victorian Acres RV Park & Campground▲ , Riverview Marina State Rec Area▲
1	**IA 333E, CR J64, Hamburg**
Gas	E: Casey's Gen'l Store◈
Food	E: Pizza Hut
Lodg	E: Hamburg Motel
Other	E: Auto Repairs, Grocery
NOTE:	**WiFi Access in All Rest Areas**

CENTRAL TIME ZONE

⬆ IOWA
⬇ MISSOURI

CENTRAL TIME ZONE

EXIT	IA / MO
NOTE:	**MM 124: Iowa State Line**
(121)	**Weigh Station (Both dir)**
116	**CR A, CR B, to Watson**
110	**US 136, Rock Port, Phelps City**
FStop	E: Rockport Shell
TStop	W: Trails End Truck Stop/P66, Dominator Fuel/BP (Scales)
Gas	E: to Casey's General Store
Food	W: Rest/Tr End TS, FastFood/RP TP, McDonald's
Lodg	E: Rockport Inn, to White Rock Motel W: Motel/Trails End, Super 8
TServ	W: Watson Auto & Truck Repair
Other	E: Auto Services, Towing W: Laundry/RP TP, Rock Port KOA▲
(110)	**Rest Area (SB) (RR, Phones, Vend, Picnic)**
107	**MO 111, Rock Port, Langdon**
Lodg	W: Elk Inn/Cafe & RV Park▲
99	**CR W, Fairfax, Corning**
92	**US 59, Craig, Fairfax**
Gas	W: Sinclair◈
Other	W: Peters RV Lots▲
84	**MO 118, Mound City, Bigelow**
FStop	W: Mound City Shell
Gas	E: Phillips 66◈, Shamrock◈, Sinclair
Food	E: Dick's Diner, Hardee's, Quacker's Steakhouse, McDonald's, Subway/P66 W: Taco Bell/Shell
Lodg	E: Audrey's Motel, Super 8
Other	E: Auto Dealer, Dollar General, Grocery W: to Big Lake State Park▲
(82)	**Rest Area (Both dir) (RR, Phones, Vend, Picnic)**
79	**US 159, Mound City, to Rulo**
TStop	E: Squaw Creek Eagle Nest Plaza

◈= Regular Gas Stations with Diesel ▲ = RV Friendly Locations ♥= Pet Friendly Locations
Red print shows large vehicle parking / access on site or nearby Brown Print = Campgrounds / RV PARKS

EXIT — MISSOURI

Food E: Rest/FastFood/Squaw Crk
TServ E: Sqauw Crk
Other E: Laundry/WiFi/**RVDump**/Squaw Crk

75 — US 59, Oregon

67 — US 59N, Oregon

65 — US 59, Amazonia, Fillmore
FStop E: Trip Stop/Conoco
Food E: FastFood/Trip Stop

60 — MO CC, MO K, Amazonia

56A — Jct US 59N, US 71, Savannah
FStop E: to Finish Line

(56B) — Jct I-229S, St Joseph

53 — I-71 Bus, Savannah, US 59S, I-29S Bus, St Joseph
Gas W: Phillips 66◊
Other E: **AOK Campground & RV Park▲**, **Walnut Grove Campground▲**
W: **Antique Mall, Fireworks World, Appr 4-5 mi:** Gas/Food/Walmartsc/HomeDepot **Asstd Retail Shops--Acc Ex #50 W Serv**

50 — US 169, Rochester Rd, to US 59, N Belt Hwy, Bus 29, St Joseph
Gas W: GasMart USA/Conoco, Phillips 66◊, Shell, Sinclair◊
Food W: Bob Evans, Captain D's, Cheddars Cafe, Chili's, Chipolte Mexican, CiCi's Pizza, Culver's Rest, Famous Daves, Hardee's, Long John Silver, McDonald's, Panara Bread, Panda Express, Papa John's, Pizza Hut, Quiznos, Ryan's Grill, Sonic, Subway, Taco Bell, Taco John's, Wendy's
Med W: + **Heartland Clinic Urgent Care**
Other W: ATMs, Banks, Advance Auto Parts, Auto Bath, Auto Services, Auto Dealers, Best Buy, Big Lots, **Bill's Camper Sales**, Borders, Carwashes, Hobby Lobby, Home Depot, Kmart, Lowe's, Office Max, Sam's Club, Target, Tires Plus, Walgreen's, **Walmart sc**

47 — MO 6, Frederick Blvd, St Joseph
Gas E: Conoco
W: Sinclair, Phillips 66◊
Food E: Bandana's BBQ, Country Kitchen
W: Applebee's, Cracker Barrel, Carlos O'Kelly's, Denny's, Dunkin Donuts, Ground Round, Hunan Rest, KFC, McDonald's, Perkins, Red Lobster, Rib Crib, Sonic, Subway, Starbucks, Taco Bell, Taste of China, Village Steakhouse & Buffet, Whiskey Creek Steakhouse
Lodg E: Days Inn, Drury Inn
W: Budget Inn, Comfort Suites, Hampton Inn, Motel 6♥, Ramada Inn, Stoney Creek Inn, Super 8
Med E: + **Heartland Reg'l Medical Center**
W: + **Heartland Health Hospital**
Other E: to MO Western State College
W: Auto Dealers, ATMs, Banks, CVS, Firestone, Food 4 Less, Midas, Museums, Office Depot, Office Max, Walgreen's, Plaza 8 Cinema, UPS Store, Vet♥, U-Haul, Visitor Info Center, **Beacon RV Park▲**

46AB — US 36, to US 169, St. Joseph, Cameron (Serv West to US 169 N&S)
FStop E: to 1310 Riverside Rd: Speedy's Convenience/Sinclair (Scales)
Gas W: to BP◊

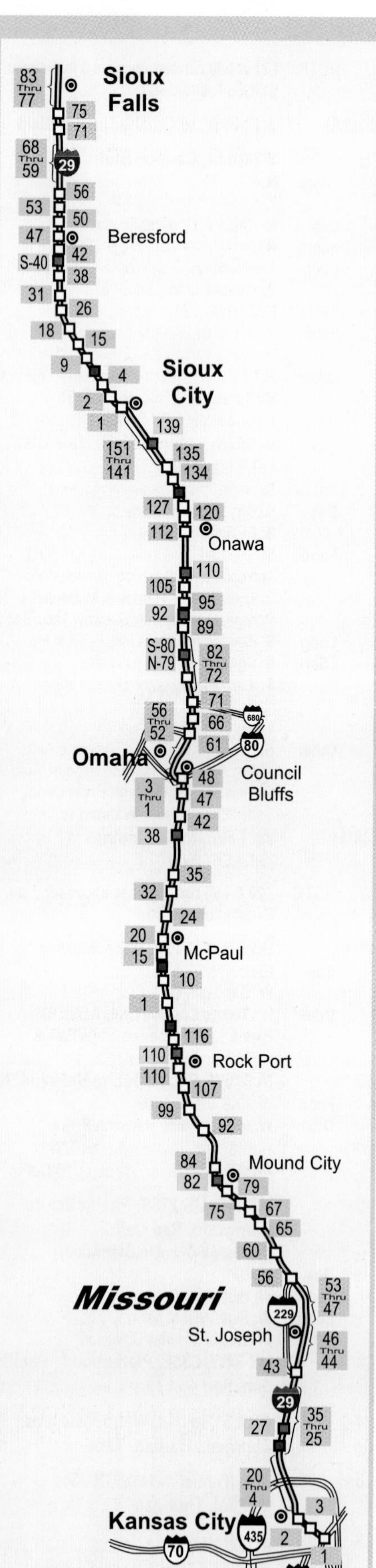

EXIT — MISSOURI

Other E: to Mo Western College
W: to Walgreen's, **Beacon RV Park▲**

44 — I-29 Bus, US 169, St. Joseph
TStop E: Love's Travel Stop #235 (Scales)
W: AmBest/ Wiedmaier Truck Stop/Shell (Scales)
Gas E: Phillips 66◊
Food E: Subway/Love's TS, Mexican Rest
W: Rest/Wiedmaier's TS, McDonald's, Taco Bell
Lodg E: Best Western
TServ E: Love's TS/Tires/Twash, Dave's Diesel
W: Wiedmaier TS/Tires
Other E: Laundry/WiFi/**RVDump**/Love's TS
W: Laundry/WiFi/Wiedmaier's TS, Dollar General, Dollar Tree, Goodyear, Price Chopper Grocery, **Walmart sc**, Auto Dealers & Services

(43) — Jct I-229N, Downtown St Joseph
Other W: **River View Retreat & RV Park▲**

35 — CR DD, Faucett
TStop W: Farris Truck Stop/66 (Scales)
Food W: Rest/Subway/Farris TS
Lodg W: Motel/Farris TS
TWash W: Farris TS
TServ W: Farris TS/Tires
Other W: Laundry/Farris TS

30 — CR Z, CR H, Dearborn
FStop E: Trex Mart Tank nTummy #1/Conoco
Food E: Tank 'n Tummy

(27) — Rest Area (Both dir) (RR, Vending, Picnic)

25 — CR U, CR E, Camden Point
Gas E: Phillips 66◊
Food E: Merle's Country Café

(24) — Weigh Station (Both dir)

20 — MO 92, MO 371N, Atchison, Weston, Leavenworth
Gas W: Phillips 66
Other W: Vaughn Orchard & Store, Weston Red Barn Farm, **to Weston Bend State Park▲**

19 — CR HH, Platte City
Gas W: Amoco, Conoco, Phillips 66◊
Food W: Branch St Café, DQ, Maria's Mex, Pizza Hut, Red Dragon Rest,
Lodg W: Comfort Inn, Super 8, Travelodge Motel & **RV Park▲**
Other W: ATMs, Auto Services, CVS, Grocery, Laundromat, Museum, **Police Dept**, **Sheriff Dept**, US Post Office

18 — MO 92, Platte City, Leavenworth, Weston
FStop W: QT #236 (Scales)
Gas W: Conoco
Food W: Burger King, McDonald's, Ma & Pa's Kettle Rest, Subway, Taco Bell, Waffle House, Wendy's, KFC/Conoco
Lodg W: AmericInn, Comfort Inn, Super 8
Other E: **to Basswood Country Inn & RV Resort▲**

(17) — Jct I-435S, to Topeka

15 — Mexico City Ave, Ks City
Lodg W: Marriott
Other W: Auto Rentals/KC Int'l Airport✈

(14) — Jct I-435E, to St Louis (SB)

◊ = Regular Gas Stations with Diesel ▲ = RV Friendly Locations ♥ = Pet Friendly Locations
Red print shows large vehicle parking / access on site or nearby Brown Print = Campgrounds / RV PARKS

EXIT		MISSOURI
13		**CR D, to I-435E, KC Int'l Airport**
	Lodg	**E:** Best Western, Clarion, Comfort Suites, Extended Stay America, Fairfield Inn, Hampton Inn, Holiday Inn, Microtel, Radisson
		W: Marriott
	Other	**E:** KCI Expo Center
		W: KC Int'l Airport✈
12		**NW 112th St, Ks City**
	Gas	**E:** BP, Conoco◈
	Food	**E:** Allie's
	Lodg	**E:** Days Inn, DoubleTree Hotel, Hampton Inn, Hilton
		W: Econo Lodge
	Other	**E:** ATMs. Banks, Harley Davidson, Visitor Center
10		**Tiffany Springs Pkwy, Ks City**
	Gas	**E:** Shell
	Food	**E:** Del & More, Jade Garden Chinese, Mamoof Cafe, Smokebox BBQ Café, Tiffany Grill
		W: Cracker Barrel, Ruby Tuesday, Waffle House, Wendy's
	Lodg	**E:** Embassy Suites, Homewood Suites
		W: AmeriSuites, Chase Suites, Courtyard, Drury Inn, Homestead Studio Suites, Hyatt, MainStay Suites, Ramada Inn, Residence Inn, Sleep Inn
	Other	**W:** US Post Office, Auto Dealers
9AB		**MO 152, to Liberty, Topeka**
8		**NW Barry Rd, Ks City**
	Gas	**E:** Valero◈
		W: Phillips 66, QT◈
	Food	**E:** Applebee's, Bob Evans, Boston Market, Chili's, China Wok, Einstein Bros, Golden Corral, Hooters, Lone Star Steak House, On the Border, Panera Bread, Panda Express, Starbucks, Subway, Taco Bell, Wendy's
	Food	**W:** Arby's, Barry BBQ, Dirk's Bar & Grill, Hardee's, JoToGo Coffee, Long John Silver, McDonald's, Mimi's Cafe, Mr Goodcents Subs,Outback Steakhouse, Smokehouse BBQ, Taco John's, Taco Bueno,
	Lodg	**W:** La Quinta Inn♥, Motel 6♥, Quality Inn, Super 8
	Med	**E:** + St Luke's Northland Hospital
	Other	**E:** AMC, ATMs, Auto Dealers, Auto Services, Banks, HyVee Grocery, Lowe's, **Walmart sc**
		W: Auto Services, Barnes & Noble, CVS, Carwash/P66, Fast Lane Carwash, Jiffy Lube, Staples, Tires Plus,
6		**NW 72nd St, to Platte Woods**
	Gas	**E:** Sinclair◈
		W: BP, QuikTrip
	Food	**W:** DQ, KFC, Pizza Hut
	Other	**W:** IGA, Sears Grand, Police Dept
5		**MO 45N, NW 64th St, Kansas City**
	Gas	**W:** Shell
	Food	**W:** Blimpie's/Texaco, Colonial Bakery, IIHOP, Little Caesar's Pizza, McDonald's, Pizza Hut, Paradise Grill, Pete's Inn, Subway, Thai Place
	Other	**W:** CVS, Dollar General, Goodyear, Radio Shack
4		**NW 56th St (NB)**
	Gas	**W:** Phillips 66
3C		**CR A, to US 69, Riverside (SB)**
	Gas	**W:** QT◈
	Food	**W:** Corner Cafe, Sonic, Sorrento's Italian Rest, U Gene's Deli & Pizza
	Other	**W:** Auto & Tire Services
(3B)		**Jct I-635S, to Kansas (NB, LEFT exit)**
3A		**CR AA, Waukomis Dr (NB)**
	Other	**E:** Museum
2B		**US 169S, N Kansas City**
2A		**US 169N, Smithville**
1E		**US 69, Vivion Rd**
	Gas	**E:** Shell◈
		W: QuikTrip
	Food	**E:** Deli Depot, Steak n Shake
		W: McDonald's, Subway
	Other	**E:** Auto Service, Auto Dealer, Grocery, Home Depot, Sam's Club
1D		**MO 283S, Oak Trafficway (SB)**
1C		**MO 283N, US 69, Gladstone**
(1B)		**Jct I-35N, Des Moines (SB)**
1A		**Davidson Rd**
	Gas	**E:** Shell
	NOTE:	**I-29 & I-35 run together below for 6 mi (End of I-29) Exit #'s follow I-35.**
(8B)		**Jct I-35N, to Des Moines**
8A		**NE Parvin Rd, Kansas City**
	Gas	**E:** Shell
	Lodg	**W:** Super Inn Motel
6AB		**MO 210, Armour Rd, N Ks City**
	FStop	**E:** Apple Trails Truck Stop/P66
	Gas	**W:** QT, Phillips 66, Texaco
	Food	**E:** Arby's, Big Boy's, Burger King, Captain D's, Denny's, McDonald's
		W: Long John Silver, Pizza Hut, Taco Bell, Wendy's
	Lodg	**E:** Americas Best Value Inn, La Quinta Inn♥
		W: American Inn, Quality Inn
	Med	**E:** + North KC Hospital
	Other	**E:** ATMs, Banks, to Harrah's Casino,
		W: Auto Services, ATMs, Banks, Conv Center, Police Dept
5B		**16th Ave (NB)**
5A		**Levee Rd, Bedford St**
4B		**Front St, Ks City (NB)**
	Other	**E:** Isle of Capri Casino & Rest
4A		**US 24, Independence Ave (SB)**
	Lodg	**E:** Capri Motel, Royale Inn Motel
	Other	**E:** Auto Services, Grocery
(3)		**Jct I-70W, to Topeka**

CENTRAL TIME ZONE

MISSOURI

Begin Northbound I-29 from Jct I-70 in Kansas City, MO to Canada Border.

Begin Eastbound I-30 from Ft Worth, TX to Jct I-40 in Little Rock, AR.

TEXAS

CENTRAL TIME ZONE

EXIT		TEXAS
	NOTE:	I-30 begins/ends on I-20, Exit #421
(1A)		**Jct I-20W, Weatherford, Abilene**
1B		**Linkcrest Dr, Aledo, Ft Worth**
	FStop	**S:** SunMart #401/Mobil
	Gas	**S:** Chevron, Fina◈, Shamrock
2		**Spur 580E**
	Lodg	**S:** El Dorado Motel
	Other	**S:** Lost Creek Golf Course
3		**RM 2871, Chapel Creek Blvd**
5A		**Alemeda St (EB, diff reaccess)**
(5B)		**Jct I-820N**
(5C)		**Jct I-820S**
6		**Las Vegas Trail, Ft Worth**
	Gas	**N:** Chevron
		S: Citgo, Shell◈, Valero◈
	Food	**N:** McDonald's/Chevron, Waffle House
		S: Mex Rest, Pancake House, Wendy's
	Lodg	**N:** Best Western, Days Inn, Super 8
		S: Comfort Inn, Motel 6♥
	Other	**N:** Auto Dealer, Cinema
		S: Auto Zone, Winn Dixie
7A		**Cherry Lane, TX 183**
	Gas	**N:** Conoco, Shell, Sam's
	Food	**N:** CiCi's Pizza, IHOP, Luby's, Popeye's Chicken, Ryan's Grill, Subway, Taco Bell, Wendy's
		S: Parton's Pizza, Whataburger
	Lodg	**N:** La Quinta Inn♥, Super 8
		S: Best Western, Hampton Inn, Holiday Inn Express, Quality Inn
	Other	**N:** Home Depot, Sam's Club, U-Haul **Walmart**, Westridge Mall, Auto Services, **White Settlement RV Park▲**
		S: Target, Auto Dealers
7B		**TX 183, Spur 341, Green Oaks Rd**
	Gas	**S:** Diamond Shamrock
	Food	**N:** Don Pablo's, Jack in the Box, Olive Garden, Subway, Taco Bueno
	Lodg	**S:** American Inn, Green Oaks Hotel
	Other	**N:** Firestone, U-Haul, Ridgmar Mall, Naval Air Station Ft Worth
		S: Auto Services
8A		**Green Oaks Rd (WB)**
	Food	**N:** Applebee's, Chili's, Jack in the Box,

◈= Regular Gas Stations with Diesel ▲ = RV Friendly Locations ♥= Pet Friendly Locations
Red print shows large vehicle parking / access on site or nearby Brown Print = Campgrounds / RV PARKS

EXIT		TEXAS
	Food	N: Olive Garden, Old Country Buffet, Taco Bueno, Subway, TGI Friday
	Lodg	N: Hawthorne Suites
	Other	N: ATMs, Banks, Albertson's, Best Buy, Firestone, Office Depot, NTB, Ridgmar Mall
8B		**Ridgmar Blvd, Ridglea Ave (Access to #8A Serv)**
	Gas	N: Citgo, Texaco, Valero
9A		**Bryant-Irvin Rd, Ft Worth**
	Gas	S: Shell
9B		**US 377S, Camp Bowie Blvd**
	Gas	N: Texaco S: 7-11, Exxon, Fina, Shell, Texaco
	Food	N: Tommy's Hamburgers, Uncle Julio's Mex Rest, Tokyo Café S: Burger King, Jack in the Box, Purple Cow Diner, Starbucks, Souper Salad, Subway, Wendy's, Whataburger
	Lodg	S: Embassy Suites
	Other	S: ATMs, Banks, Grocery, Auto Service, CarWash, UPS Store
10		**Hulen St, Ft Worth**
	Food	S: ChickFilA, Mamoof Cafe, Purple Cow Diner, Subway, Starbucks
11		**Montgomery St, Ft Worth**
	Gas	S: Texaco◈
	Food	S: Flying Fish, Railhead Smokehouse, Whataburger
	Other	N: Ft Worth Botanic Gardens, Will Rogers Memorial Center
12		**Forest Park Blvd (WB)**
	Food	N: Pappasito's, Pappadeaux
12A		**Montgomery St, University Dr**
	Food	N: Pap S: Chili's, Hoffbrau Steaks, McKinley's Fine Bakery & Cafe, Ole South Pancake House, Panera Bread
	Lodg	S: Courtyard, Days Inn, Fairfield Inn, Homestead Studio Suites, Residence Inn, Springhill Suites, Travelodge
	Other	S: AT&T, Barnes & Noble, Carwash & Lube
12B		**Vickery Blvd, Rosedale St (EB)**
12C		**Forest Park Blvd, Ft Worth (EB)**
	Food	N: Pappasito's, Pappadeaux
	Med	S: + Columbia Medical Center FW
13		**Summit Ave, 8th Ave, TX 199, Henderson St, Downtown**
13A		**8th Ave, Downtown**
	Gas	S: Texaco
	Food	S: Pappa Chang Asia Bistro
	Med	S: + Kindred Hospital, + Baylor Surgical Hospital
13B		**TX 199, Henderson St**
	Lodg	N: Holiday Inn Express
	Med	S: + Cooks Children's Medical Center, + Harris Methodist Hospital
	Other	N: Budget RAC, Walgreen's
14		**Cherry St, Lancaster Ave, Downtown Fort Worth (EB)**
(15)		**Jct I-35W, US 81, N to Denton, S to Waco (EB)**
(15A)		**Jct I-35W, US 81 (WB)**
15B		**Jct US 287S, Lancaster Ave (EB)**
(15C)		**Jct US 287N, I-35, Downtown (WB)**
16		**Riverside Dr S**
16A		**Riverside Dr S (WB)**
	Food	S: Gladys Soul Food
	Lodg	S: Great Western Inn, Luxury Inn, Valley View Motel
	Other	S: Auto Services, East Lancaster Animal Hospital♥
16B		**Riverside Dr N (WB)**
16C		**Beach St, Ft Worth**
	Gas	S: 7-11, Chevron
	Food	S: Ft Worth Cattle Drive Rest
	Lodg	S: Quality Inn♥
	Other	S: ATM, Bank
18		**Oakland Blvd, Bridge St (South Serv to Lancaster Ave)**
	Gas	N: Circle K, Shell S: Citgo, Phillips 66
	Food	N: Burger King, Taco Bell, Waffle House S: McDonald's, Pizza Hut, Subway
	Lodg	N: Motel 6♥
	Other	S: Auto Zone, CVS, Dollar General, Dollar Tree, Family Dollar, Pep Boys, Walgreen's
19		**Brentwood Stair Rd, Woodhaven Blvd, Bridge St (EB)**
	Gas	N: Chevron, Shell◈ S: Shamrock
	Food	N: China Grill, Italy Pasta & Pizza, Steak & Ale, Stroud's Rest
	Other	N: ATM, Bank, Bridge St Animal Clinic♥, Kroger, Laundromat S: Auto Services, Family Dollar, Meadowbrook Golf Course
(21A)		**Jct I-820S (WB) (Serv at 1st Exit)**
(21B)		**Jct I-820N (WB) (Serv at 1st Exit)**
21C		**Bridgewood Dr, Bridge St, Ft Worth**
	Gas	N: Mobil, Shell S: Fina, Shell◈
	Food	N: Dan's Seafood & Chicken, Luby's, KFC, Subway, Wendy's S: Burger King, McDonald's
	Other	N: Albertson's, Firestone, Home Depot, Kroger, U-Haul
23		**Cooks Lane**
	Gas	S: Mobil
24		**Eastchase Pkwy, Ft Worth**
	Gas	S: Chevron, RaceTrac, Shell, Shamrock
	Food	N: Jack in the Box, Panda Express S: Burger King, Chicken Express, IHOP, McDonald's, Steak & More, Subway, Taco Bell, Wendy's, Whataburger
	Other	N: Lowe's, Sam's Club, **Walmart sc** S: Cinema, Office Depot, Radio Shack, Target
26		**Fielder Rd, Arlington**
	Other	S: to Six Flags
27		**Lamar Blvd, Cooper St**
	Gas	N: Mobil, Kroger S: 7-11, Shell
	Food	N: Hong Kong II, Jack in the Box, Subway S: Burger King, Denny's, Tom's Burger
	Med	S: + Arlington Memorial Hospital
	Other	N: Banks, Big Lots, Family Dollar, Kroger/Pharmacy, Pet Clinic & Boarding♥, Walgreen's S: ATM, Arlington North Animal Clinic♥, Banks, Cost Plus, **Dallas Metro KOA▲**, to Univ of TX/Arlington
28		**FM 157, Collins St (WB)**
	Food	N: Boston Market, Pei Wei Asian, Waffle House, Whataburger
	Lodg	N: Econo Lodge, Holiday Inn
	Other	N: Albertson's, Carwash, UPS Store, Whole Foods Market
28A		**FM 157, Collins St (EB)**
	Food	S: BlackEyed Pea, Chili's, ChickFilA, Cici's Pizza, Country Kitchen, Colter's BBQ & Grill Harrigan's, Hooters, Jason's Deli, Joe's Crab Shack, Landry Seafood, Olive Garden Pappadeaux,Red Hot & Blue Memphis BBQ,Souper Salad, TGI Friday, Taco Cabana, Tony Roma, Wendy's
	Lodg	S: Courtyard, Days Inn, Howard Johnson Express, Wyndham
	Other	S: Arlington Conv Center, Ameriquest Field, Baseball Museum, Best Buy, Costco, Discount Tire, FedEx Office, Home Depot, Pep Boys, PetSmart♥, Radio Shack, Six Flags Fun Park, TX Stadium, Walgreen's, **Walmart sc**, Vet♥, Visitor Info Center,
28B		**Nolan Ryan Expressway (EB)**
	Gas	N: Mobil

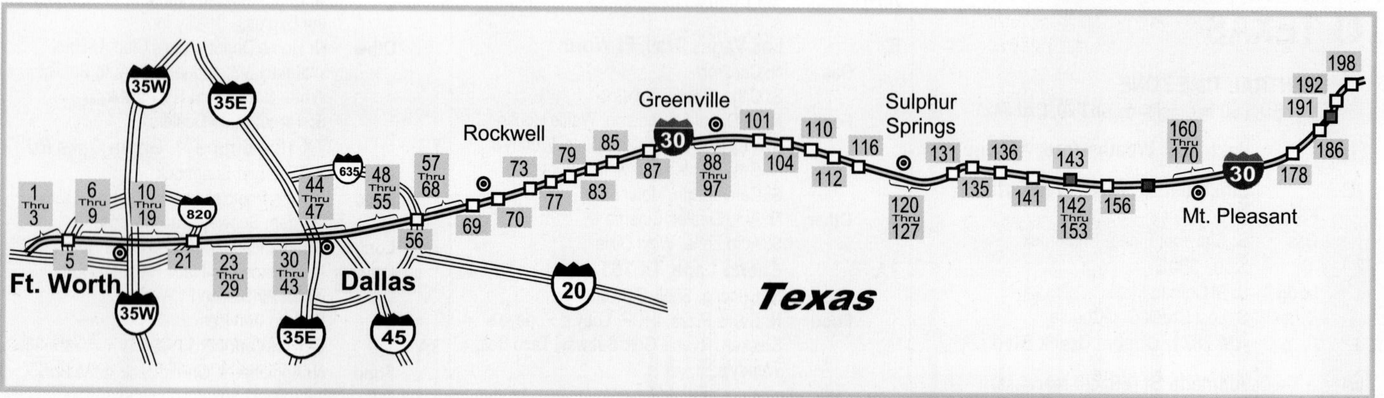

◈ = Regular Gas Stations with Diesel ▲ = RV Friendly Locations ♥ = Pet Friendly Locations
Red print shows large vehicle parking / access on site or nearby Brown Print = Campgrounds / RV PARKS

EXIT — TEXAS

Food N: Waffle House, Whataburger
Lodg N: Country Inn, Ramada Inn

29 Ballpark Way, Arlington
Gas N: Chevron, Citgo, Valero
S: Fina
Food N: Frijoles Café, Romano's Macaroni Grill, Manhattan's, Saltgrass Steakhouse, Trail Dust Steak House
S: On the Border, Texas Land & Cattle
Lodg N: Candlewood Suites, Fairfield Inn, Hawthorn Suites, Hilton Garden Inn, Residence Inn, Springhill Suites, Studio Plus, Towneplace Suites, Wingate Inn
S: Homewood Suites, Howard Johnson, Marriott, Stadium Inn, Wyndham Hotel
Other N: ATMs, Banks, AMF Bowling Center,
S: Six Flags Fun Park, Arlington Conv Center, Ameriquest Field, Legends of the Game Baseball Museum, Visitor Center

30 TX 360, Six Flags Dr, Airport
Gas N: Shell, Star Mart
S: Conoco, Shell◊, Total
Food N: **Cracker Barrel**, Grand Buffet, Salt Grass Steakhouse, McDonald's
S: Denny's, Jack in the Box, Luby's Cafeteria, Ninfa's Mex Express, Pancho's Mexican Buffet, Steak & Ale, Subway
Lodg N: Crowne Plaza, Days Inn, Fairfield Inn, Flagship Inn, Homestead Studio, Park Inn, Studio Plus, Super 8, Travelodge, Wingate Inn
S: Amerisuites, Baymont Inn, Holiday Inn Express, Homewood Suites, Hyatt Place, La Quinta Inn♥, Motel 6♥, Ranger Inn, Sleep Inn, Value Inn
Med S: + Dallas FW Medical Center
Other N: Great SW Golf Course, to Dallas FW Int'l Airport✈
S: ATMs, Banks, Arlington Motorsports, Cinemark Tinseltown 9, Auto Services & Repairs, Firestone, Greyhound, Kmart, Office Depot, Six Flags Mall, Six Flags Fun Park, General Motors Plant, U-Haul

32 NW 19th St, TX 161, Grand Prairie
Gas N: Exxon, Shamrock
S: Fina, Mobil
Food S: Denny's, Long John Silver, Taco Bell, McDonald's, Pizza Hut, Whataburger
Lodg S: La Quinta Inn♥
Other S: Banks, ATMs, Auto Service, U-Haul

34 Belt Line Rd, NE 8th St
Gas N: Chevron, RaceTrac
S: Fina, RaceTrac◊, Shell, Shamrock
Food S: Burger King, McDonald's, Popeye's Chicken, Starbucks, Subway
Lodg N: Days Inn, Motel 6♥, Ramada Inn, Studio 6, Super 8
Other N: Enterprise RAC, Museum, Ripley's Enchanted Mirror Maze, Skate Park
S: Auto Services, CVS,

36 MacArthur Blvd, Grand Prairie
Other N: Starbuck Trucking & Auto
S: to Dallas Millenium Airport✈

38 Loop 12, Dallas
Gas N: Exxon
Food N: Burger King, Popeye's Chicken

39 Cockrell Hill Rd
Gas S: Murphy USA
Food S: Chili's, Golden Corrral, IHOP, McDonald's, Starbucks
Lodg N: Comfort Suites
S: Holiday Inn Express

EXIT — TEXAS

Other N: Conn's, Staples
S: AT&T, Best Buy, Dollar Tree, Lowe's, Radio Shack, **Walmart sc**,

41 Westmoreland Rd, to Bus 180 (EB)
Gas S: to Conoco, Valero
Food S: Jack in the Box, Luby's, Pizza Hut, Taco Bell, Wendy's
Other S: Auto Services, Grocery, Goodyeair, Auto Zone, O'Reilly Auto Parts

42 Hampton Rd N, Westmoreland Rd
Gas S: Exxon, Shell
Lodg N: Galaxy Inn, Ranch Motel, Shady Oaks Motel
S: Miramar Motor Hotel
Other N: Auto Zone
S: O'Reilly Auto Parts, Stevens Park Golf Course

42A Hampton Rd S (EB)

42B Hampton Rd N (EB)

43A Sylvan Ave, to Beckley Ave (WB)
Gas N: Dairy Mart, Valero◊
Food N: Quiznos/Valero, Pitt Grill
Lodg N: Alamo Plaza Hotel, Avalon Motel, Belmont Hotel, Budget Travel Inn
Med S: + Methodist Medical Center
Other N: ATMs, Banks, Auto Services, Family Dollar, **Dallas West MH & RV Park▲**

43B Sylvan Ave, to Beckley Ave (WB)

44A Beckley Ave (EB exi, WB entr)

44B Riverfront Blvd, Industrial Blvd (EB exit, WB entr)
Gas N: Kwik Stop
S: Red E Martt
Food S: Hickory House BBQ

(44A) Jct I-35E N, US 77N, Denton (WB)

(45A) Jct I-35E N, US 77N, Denton (EB)

(44B) Jct I-35E S, US 77S, US 67S, Waco (WB)

45B Lamar St (EB exit, WB ent)
Other N: Amtrak, Downtown, Dallas Convention Center, Museums, Tourist & Visitor Info

45B Griffin St, Cadiz St (EB ex, WB ent)
Food N: Starbucks
Other N: Dallas Convention Center

45 Ervay St (WB exit, EB entr)

46A Central Expressway (WB)
Other N: Dallas Farmers Market, Lodging, Restaurants, Museums, Galleries
S: Restaurants, Lodging, Auto Services

46B Central Expwy, to Jct I-45, US 75, to Houston (EB)

(46) Jct I-45S, US 75, to Houston, McKinney (EB)

47 2nd Ave, 1st Ave, Fair Park (EB)

(47B) Jct I-45S, US 75, to Houston, McKinney (WB)
Other S: Cotton Bowl, Tx Vietnam Vets Mem'l, Aquarium, Science Place/IMAX, Planetarium, Various Museums

47C 2nd Ave, 1st Ave, Fair Park (WB)

48A Haskell Ave, Peak St, Carroll Ave
Gas N: Shamrock
S: Exxon

EXIT — TEXAS

48B Barry Ave, Munger Blvd, to Grand Ave, to TX 78E, Dallas
Gas N: Saks Food & Gas, Texaco
Other N: ATMs, Banks, Repairs, Samuel Grand Amphitheater, Restaurants, Grocery

49A Winslow St, fr WB: TX 78E, Grand Ave
Gas N: Fina, Phillips 66
S: Phillips 66, Shell
Food N: Furr's, Chicken & Rice
Lodg N: Welcome Inn, Eastern Hills Hotel
Other N: Laundromat/Fina

49B Dolphin Rd, Samuell Blvd
Gas N: Diamond Shamrock, Texaco
Lodg N: Americas Best Value Inn, Palace Motel
S: Lawnview Motel
Other N: Tenison Golf Course
S: **Woodshire MH & RV Park▲**

50 Ferguson Rd, to Samuell Ave (WB)
Gas N: Gas, Mobil, Texaco
Other N: Auto Repair, Tires
S: Budget Truck Rental, U-Haul

50A Lawnview Ave (EB)

50B Ferguson Rd, to Samuell Ave (EB)

52A Jim Miller Rd, to Highland Rd, to Samuell Blvd, Dallas
Gas N: Exxon
S: RaceWay◊, Shell◊
Food N: Country China Super Bufffet, Denny's, Kettle Rest, Luby's, McDonald's
S: Burger King, Captain D's, CiCi's Pizza, Furr's Rest, Grandy's, KFC/WingWorks, Lupita's Seafood Rest, Popeye's Chicken, Subway, Wendy's
Lodg N: La Quinta Inn♥
S: Motel 6♥
Other S: Auto Zone, CVS, Carwash/Shell, Family Dollar, Laundromat, O'Reilly Auto Parts, The Mail Center, Tribe Auto Repairs,

52B St Francis Ave, to Samuell Blvd
Gas S: WalMart
Food N: Luby's
Lodg N: Holiday Inn Express, Super 8
Other N: Enterprise RAC
S: ATMs, Bank, Auto Services,
Other N: Buckner Terrace Animal Clinic♥, Kwik Kar Lube & Auto Repairs, Radio Shack, to Sam's Club, Staples, **Walmart sc**

53A Loop 12, Buckner Blvd
Gas N: RaceTrac, Texaco, Exxon
S: 7-11
Food N: Burger King, Circle C Grill, Dominos Pizza, Jack in the Box, John's Seafood & Chicken
S: CiCi's Pizza, Taco Cabana, Whataburger
Lodg S: Holiday Inn Express
Other N: Auto Services, Auto Zone, Grocery, Loop 12 Animal Hospital♥, U-Haul
S: Big Town Bowl Lanes, Big Town Mall, Dollar Tree, Sam's Club, Staples, **Walmart sc**,

53B US 80E, to Terrell (EB ex, WB ent)

54 Big Town Blvd, Mesquite
Gas N: Texaco◊, Valero◊
Lodg N: Mesquite Inn
S: Big Town Inn, to Tejas Motel
Other N: DFW Camper Corral Truck Accessories, Laundromat, to Eastfield Comm College

EXIT		TEXAS
	Other	**S:** Cummins Southern Plains, CB Shop, **Holiday World of Dallas RV Center, to** Big Town Mall, Thrifty RAC,
55		**Motley Dr, Mesquite**
	Gas	**N:** Fina, Shell◈
		S: Chevron
	Food	**N:** Castillo Mexican Rest
	Lodg	**N:** Executive Inn
		S: Microtel
	Med	**S: + Mesquite Community Hospital**
	Other	**N: to** Eastfield Comm College
56A		**Gus Thomasson Rd, Galloway Ave (EB), Jct I-635N (WB)**
	Gas	**N:** Shamrock, Supertrac
		S: 7-11
	Food	**N:** KFC, McDonald's, Sonic
		S: Arby's, Celebration Station, Checkers, Dickey's BBQ Pit, Hooters, Horny Toad Cantina, Luby's, Olive Garden, Outback Steakhouse, Red Lobster, Southern Maid Donut, Subway, Wendy's
	Lodg	**S:** Delux Inn, Crossland, Fairfield Inn
	Other	**S:** Auto Services, Big Lots, Firestone, Grocery, Midas, NTB, **Nichols RV Center, to** Town East Mall
(56B)		**Jct I-635N (EB), I-635S (WB)**
(56C)		**Jct I-635S (EB)**
57		**Galloway Ave, Gus Thomasson Rd,**
	Gas	**N:** Texaco◈, Valero
		S: Exxon
	Food	**N:** Burger King, **Cracker Barrel**, TC's BBQ Express
		S: Slabs BBQ, **to** BlackEyed Pea, Boston Market, Chili's, Colter's BBQ, Denny's, Don Pueblo's, El Fenix Mexican Rest, Grady's, Hogi Yogi, Long John Silver, McDonald's, Outback Steakhouse, Salt grass Steak House, Spaghetti Warehouse, Souper Salad, Starbucks, Subway, Wing Zone, Whataburger
	Lodg	**S:** Crossland, Courtyard, Delux Inn, Extended Stay America, Fairfield Inn
	Other	**N:** Albertson's, Auto Repairs, Auto Dealer
		S: ATMs, Food Lion, **to** Town East Mall, Auto Services, Auto Zone, ATMs, Banks, Best Buy, Carwash, Firestone, Kroger, **Nichols RV Center**
58		**Northwest Dr, Mesquite**
	Gas	**N:** Valero◈
		S: Fina
	Food	**S:** Jack in the Box/Fina
	Other	**N:** Enterprise RAC, Mesquite Muni Golf Course
		S: ExploreUSA RV Supercenter, Lowe's,
59		**Broadway Blvd, N Belt Line Rd, Rowlett Rd, Frontage Rd, Garland**
	Gas	**N:** 7-11, Conoco, QT, Albertson's
		S: Exxon
	Food	**N:** Chili's, China City, Church's Chicken, Denny's, KFC, Long John Silver, Papa John's Pizza, Starbucks, Taco Bueno, Wendy's, Whataburger,
		S: Bakers Ribs, Burger King, Chinese Buffet King, Sonic, Waffle House
	Lodg	**S:** Americas Best Value Inn, Motel 6♥, Super 8
	Med	**N: + CARE NOW Medical Center**
	Other	**N:** Albertson's, Auto Repairs, ATMs, Banks, Discount Tire, Dollar General, Grocery, Radio Shack, Walgreen's, **Walmart sc**
		S: Kroger, **Tx State Hwy Patrol Post**

EXIT		TEXAS
60A		**Rose Hill Rd, Garland**
60B		**Roan Rd, Bobtown Rd, Frontage Rd**
	Gas	**N:** Pit Stop/Texaco◈
		S: Shell, EZ Mart/Shell
	Food	**N:** Jack in the Box, Wendy's
		S: Kettle Rest, Old Whiskers Catfish Rest, Subway/Shell
	Lodg	**S:** La Quinta Inn♥
61		**Zion Rd, Bobtown Rd, Garland**
	FStop	**N:** I-30 Truck Stop/Golden Express Travel Center/Conoco
	Food	**S:** China Cafe
	Lodg	**N:** Discovery Inn
62		**Bass Pro Dr, Garland**
	Gas	**S:** Shell, Texaco, Valero
	Food	**N:** Mexican Rest
		S: CiCi's Pizza, Sonic, Whataburger, Islamorada Rest/BPS
	Lodg	**N:** Best Western
	Other	**N:** Dick's Sporting Goods
		S: Bass Pro Shop, Carwash/Shell
64		**Dalrock Rd, Rowlett**
	Gas	**N:** Exxon◈, Valero◈
	Food	**N:** Dickie's BBQ, Alejandro's Grill & Cantina
	Lodg	**N:** Comfort Suites
	Med	**N: + Hospital**
	Other	**N:** Carwash/Exxon, Pharmacy, Dalrock Marina
		S: Tx Queen Riverboat, Bayview Marina & Restaurants
67		**FM 740, Ridge Rd (WB)**
	Gas	**N:** Chevron
	Food	**N:** Burger King, Chiloso Mexican Bistro, Grandy's, IHOP, McDonald's, Popeye's, Waffle House, Wendy's
		S: ChickFilA, Quiznos, Starbucks
	Other	**N:** Auto Services, Goodyear, **Walmart sc**
		S: Albertson's, Home Depot, Lowe's, Radio Shack, Walgreen's
67A		**Horizon Rd, Village Dr, Rockwall (EB ex, WB entr) (Acc to #67B Serv)**
	Gas	**N:** Shamrock
		S: Exxon, Shell
	Food	**N:** Culpepper Steak House, Ghengis Grill, Kyoto Japanese Steak House, Saltgrass Steakhouse, Snuffers Rockwall
	Food	**S:** Jack in the Box, Linebackers, Oar House, Rockwall Coutry Café, Subway
	Lodg	**S:** Hilton
	Other	**S:** ATMs, AT&T, Banks, Cinema 8, Kroger,
67B		**FM 740, Ridge Rd (EB)**
	Gas	**N:** Chevron, Mobil, Murphy USA
		S: Chevron, Exxon, Shamrock◈, Shell
	Food	**N:** Arby's, Burger King, Carrabba's, IHOP, Edohana Japanese Rest, Grandy's, Island Kitchen Chinese Buffet, Logan's Road house, McDonald's, Popeye's Chicken, Steak n Shake, Taco Cabana, Waffle House, Wendy's
		S: Applebee's, Black Eyed Pea, Carino's, Chili's, CiCi's Pizza, El Chico Mexican Rest, Jack in the Box, Johnny Carino's Italian McDonald's, On the Border Mexican Grill, Soulman's BBQ, Starbucks, Subway, Taco Bell, TCBY
	Lodg	**S:** Country Inn Suites
	Med	**N: + Care United Urgent Care**
	Other	**N:** Goodyear, Radio Shack, **Walmart sc**
		S: Albertson's, ATMs, Banks, CVS, Discount Tire, Dollar Tree, Hobby Lobby,

EXIT		TEXAS
	Other	**N:** Home Depot, Lowe's, Petco♥, Radio Shack, Sports Authority, Staples, Target, Vet♥, Walgreen's
67C		**Frontage Rd (EB ex, WB entr)**
68		**TX 205, Goliad St, Rockwall, to Terrell**
	TStop	**S:** Travel Center of America #49/Exxon (Scales)
	Gas	**N:** RaceWay, Shell
		S: Valero◈
	Food	**N:** Braum's, Donna's Kitchen, DQ, Joe Willy's, KFC, Luigi's Italian Cafe, Pizza Hut, Richards BBQ, Shirley's BBQ, Subway, Whataburger
		S: BKing/Starbucks/TA TC, Taco Bell
	Lodg	**N:** Holiday Inn Express, Super 8, Value Place
	TServ	**S:** TA TC
	Other	**N:** Auto Dealers, Auto Zone, Carwash, Enterprise RAC, Honda, Hobby Lobby, Rockwall Veterinary Hospital♥,
		S: Laundry/WiFi/**RVDump**/TA TC, Costco
69		**Frontage Rd (WB ex, EB entr)**
	Food	**N:** Buffalo Wild Wings Grill, Chipolte Mexican Grill, Cotton Patch Cafe, Double Dave's Pizza, TGI Friday
	Other	**N:** Best Buy, Dick's Sporting Goods, Dollar Tree, FedEx Office, Kirkland's, PetSmart♥, TJ Maxx, Staples, Hacienda Carwash
		S: Repair Services, **All Season RV**
70		**FM 549, Rockwall**
	TStop	**S:** Love's Travel Stop #283 (Scales)
	Food	**S:** Carl'sJr/Love's TS
	Other	**N: to** Rockwall Muni Airport✈
		S: Laundry/WiFi/**RVDump**/Love's TS
73		**FM 551, W Crawford Rd, Royse City, to Fate**
	Gas	**N:** Shell◈
	Other	**N: Happy Trails RV Center, McClain's RV**
		S: u-Haul, **Walkabout RV**
77A		**FM 548, Royse City**
	Gas	**N:** Shell◈
		S: Exxon
	Food	**N:** Jack in the Box, McDonald's
		S: KFC/Exxon, Sonic
	Lodg	**N:** Sun Royse Inn
	Other	**N:** Auto Zone, Carwash, Grocery, Johnson's Wrecker & Auto Service, Scooters Oil & Lube, **Police Dept**
77B		**FM 35, CR 36, Royse City**
	FStop	**N:** Exxon Prime Stop
	TStop	**N:** SunMart #106/Texaco (Scales)
	Food	**N:** Subway/Texaco, Soulman's BBQ
	Other	**N:** Family Dollar
79		**FM 2642, FM 1565**
	Other	**N: Budget RV's of Texas**
		S: Country Friends Veterinary Clinic♥, N Texas Motor Speedway
83		**FM 1565**
	Gas	**N:** Exxon◈
	Other	**N:** Caddo Mills Muni Airport✈
85		**FM 36, Caddo Mills**
	Other	**N: Dallas NE/Caddo Mills KOA▲**
87		**FM 1903, Caddo Mills (EB)**
	FStop	**S:** Greenville Exxon Truck Stop
	TStop	**S:** Pilot Travel Center #367 (Scales)
	Gas	**N:** Chevron◈
	Food	**N:** Pizza Inn/Chevron
		S: McDonalds/Pilot TC, Pancake House/ Greenville TS

◈= Regular Gas Stations with Diesel ▲ = RV Friendly Locations ♥= Pet Friendly Locations

Red print shows large vehicle parking / access on site or nearby **Brown Print = Campgrounds / RV PARKS**

EXIT		TEXAS
	TServ	S: Diesel & Tire Repair
	Other	S: Laundry/WiFi/Pilot TC
88		**FM 1903 (WB) (Access Ex #87 Serv)**
89		**FM 1570, Greenville**
	Lodg	S: Luxury Inn
93A		**Bus 67S, TX 34S, Wesley St (EB)**
93B		**Bus 67N, TX 34N, Wesley St (EB)**
93		**TX 34, Wesley St , Greenville, Terrell (WB)**
	NOTE:	**Overpass Low Clearance 13' 10"**
	Gas	N: Chevron◈, Exxon, Texaco S: Chevron◈, Exxon◈, Valero, Murphy
	Food	N: Applebee's, CiCi's Pizza, IHOP, Jack in the Box, KFC, Long John Silver, Pizza Hut, Ryan's Grill, Sonic, Starbucks, Taco Bell, Taco Bueno, Taco Casa/Chevron, Wendy's Whataburger S: Chili's, Cracker Barrel, Dickey's BBQ Pit, Red Lobster, Ta Molly's Mexican Rest
	Lodg	N: Hampton Inn S: Holiday Inn Express, La Quinta Inn♥
	Med	N: + Presbyterian Hospital
	Other	N: ATMs, AT&T, Auto Services, Banks, Big Lots, Brookshire's Grocery, CVS, Carwash, Crossroads Mall, Enterprise, Greenville Hardware, Lowe's, O'Reilly Auto Parts, Rolling Hills Cinema 4, Staples, Vet♥, Walgreen's, S: ATMs, Auto Dealers, Auto Services, Carwash/Exxon, Carwash/Valero,Dollar Tree, Enterprise RAC, Home Depot, NTB, Radio Shack, Tractor Supply, Uniroyal, **Walmart sc**, to Majors Airport✈
94A		**US 69, US 380, Joe Ramsey Blvd, to Denison, McKinney, Emory**
	Gas	S: Exxon
	Lodg	S: Motel 6
	Other	S: Auto Dealers, Turtle Creek Veterinary Center♥,
94B		**US 69 Bus, Moulton St, Greenville**
	Gas	N: Valero◈ S: Exxon, Fina◈
	Food	N: Kettle Rest, McDonald's, Mexican S: Arby's, McDonald's
	Lodg	N: American Inn, Royal Inn S: Economy Inn, Econo Lodge, Motel 6♥, Quality Inn, Super 8
	Other	S: Skate Safari Family Fun Center
95		**Division St**
	Med	S: + Glen Oaks Hospital
	Other	N: Greenville Animal Hospital♥
96		**Bus 67, Loop 302**
97A		**Frontage Rd (WB exit, EB entr)**
97		**Lamar St, Greenville**
	Gas	S: Exxon◈
	Lodg	N: Dream Lodge Motel S: Sunrise Motel
	Other	S: Animal Hospital♥
101		**TX 24, TX 50, FM 1737, Campbell, to Commerce, Paris**
	FStop	N: Valero◈
	Food	N: Cafe/Deli/Valero
	Other	N: to E Tx State Univ
104		**FM 513, FM 2649, Campbell, Lone Oak**
110		**FM 275, FM 2649, S Mill St, Cumby**

EXIT		TEXAS
112		**FM 499 (WB exit, EB entr)**
116		**US 67, FM 2653, Brashear**
120		**US 67 Bus N, Sulphur Springs**
122		**TX 19, Hillcrest Rd, to Emory, Paris**
	TStop	S: Crossroads Travel Center/66, Pilot Travel Center #157 (Scales)
	Gas	N: Chevron
	Food	S: Rest/Crossroads TC, Arby's/Pilot TC
	Med	N: + Hospital
	Other	N: to Sulphur Springs Muni Airport✈ S: WiFi/Pilot TC, **Shady Lake RV Park▲**
123		**FM 2297, League St**
	Gas	N: Shell, to Exxon
124		**TX 11, TX 154, Sulphur Springs, Quitman**
	Gas	N: Chevron◈, Exxon, Brookshire's S: Exxon◈, Shell◈, Shell, Murphy
	Food	N: Bodacious BBQ, Catfish King, Domino's, Hal's Diner, KFC, Pitt Grill, Pizza Hut, Popeye's, Sonic, Subway S: Braum's Burger King, Chili's, CiCi's Pizza, Domino's Pizza, Furr's Cafeteria, Grandy's, Jack in the Box, McDonald's, Pizza Inn, Quiznos, Taco Bell/Long John Silver, Wendy's, Whataburger
	Lodg	N: Royal Inn, Holiday Inn Express S: Holiday King Motel
	Med	N: + Hospital
	Other	N: Auto Zone, Auto Dealers, Brookshire's Food, CVS, Classic Lanes, Dollar General, Family Dollar, Ferrell Gas/LP, O'Reilly Auto Parts, US Post Office S: ATMs, Banks, Broadway Veterinary Hospital ♥, Classic Carwash, Discount Wheel & Tire, Fred's, Kwik Kar Auto Service Lowe's, Radio Shack, Starplex Cinema 6, Verizon, **Walmart sc**
125		**Frontage Rd (Access to Ex #124)**
126		**FM 1870, College St (acc to x127)**
127		**US 67 Bus S, Loop 301**
	Gas	S: Shell
	Food	N: Burton's Rest/Qual Inn S: Rest/Best Western
	Lodg	N: Budget Inn, Comfort Suites, Holiday Inn, Quality Inn S: Best Western
131		**FM 69, Sulphur Springs**
135		**US 67N, Como**
136		**FM 269, Weaver Rd, Como**
141		**FM 900, Saltillo Rd**
142		**County Line Rd, Mt Vernon (EB exit, WB entr)**
(143)		**Rest Area (Both dir) (RR, Phones, Pic, Pet, Vend, WiFi)**
146		**TX 37, Frontage Rd, Mt Vernon, Clarksvillle, Winnsboro**
	TStop	S: Fina Food Fast #50
	Gas	N: Shell◈ S: Chevron◈
	Food	S: FastFood/Fina, Burger King, DQ, Hubbard's Café, La Cabana, Sonic, Texas BBQ Corral

EXIT		TEXAS
	Lodg	S: Mt Vernon Motel, Super 8
	Med	N: + E Tx Medical Center
	Other	N: to Franklin Co Airport✈ S: to appr 2 mi: **Still Meadow RV Park▲**, Appr 15 mi: **Trails End RV Park▲**
147		**Spur 423, Frontage Rd, Mt Vernon**
	TStop	N: Love's Travel Stop #279 (Scales)
	Food	N: Subway/Chesters/Love's TS S: TX BBQ Corral
	Lodg	N: American Inn, Economy Inn
	Other	N: WiFi/Love's TS, Lucky 7 Truck & **RV** Wash, Preston's CB Shop, Tires, Shelton's Propane/LP
150		**Ripley Rd**
153		**Spur 185, Winfield, Millers Cove**
	Gas	N: BP◈, Chevron, Winfield Travel Center◈ S: Shamrock◈
	Food	N: Pizza/WTC, Shrimp Shack, Chinese Express
	Other	N: **Paradise RV Park▲**, Pay Trk Parking
156		**Frontage Rd**
(157)		**Weigh Station (Both dir)**
160		**US 271, to US 67, TX 49, FM 1734, Mt Pleasant, Pittsburg, Paris**
	FStop	S: Gateway #11/Shell (WB: Acc via #162)
	Gas	N: Texaco◈ S: Exxon◈
	Food	S: El Chico, Elmwood Café, Sally's Café, Western Sizzlin
	Lodg	S: Comfort Inn, Days Inn, Executive Inn, Hampton Inn
	Other	N: Lowe's, to appr 2 mi: **Ramblin Fever RV Park▲** S: to **Momentum Motorsports & RV**
162		**US 271 Bus, FM 1402, FM 2152, Mount Pleasant**
	FStop	S: Total Stop #2/Valero
	Gas	N: Exxon◈ S: Shell◈, Shell◈
	Food	N: Applebee's, Blalock BBQ, Pizza Hut, Pitt Grill, Subway S: Subway/Total, Burger King, DQ, McDonald's
	Lodg	N: Best Western, Holiday Inn Express, Super 8 S: Best Western
	Med	S: + Titus Co Memorial Hospital
	Other	N: Greyhound, **Mt Pleasant KOA▲** S: ATMs, Banks, Auto Dealer, Auto Services, Carwash, Civic Center, Family Dollar, Laundromat, Pharmacy, Tires, Animal Hospital♥
162A		**US 271 Bus, FM 2152 (WB)**
162B		**FM 1402 (WB)**
165		**FM 1001, Cookville**
	FStop	S: Big Tex Fuel Stop/Exxon
	Food	S: FastFood/BT FS
170		**FM 1993, Cookville**
178		**US 259, Omaha, DeKalb**
	FStop	S: Armadillo's #23/Exxon
	Food	S: FastFood/Armadillo's
	Other	S: Laundry/Armadillo's
186		**FM 561**
(191)		**Rest Area (Both dir) (RR, Phones, Picnic, Vend, WiFi)**

◈= Regular Gas Stations with Diesel ▲ = RV Friendly Locations ♥= Pet Friendly Locations
Red print shows large vehicle parking / access on site or nearby Brown Print = Campgrounds / RV PARKS

EXIT		TEXAS
192		**FM 990, DeKalb**
	TStop	**N:** Texas 192 Truck Stop
	Food	**N:** Rest/TX 192 TS
	TServ	**N:** TX 192 TS/Tires
198		**TX 98, New Boston, De Kalb**
	Gas	**N:** Shell
199		**US 82, New Boston, DeKalb**
	Gas	**N:** Shell
201		**TX 8, N McCoy Blvd, New Boston**
	FStop	**S:** Valero #4522, Shell
	Gas	**S:** Shell, Brookshire's, Murphy◈
	Food	**N:** Pitt Grill **S:** Burger King, Catfish King, Church's Chicken, China Cafe, DQ, McDonald's, Nana's Family Diner, Pizza Hut, Subway, Taco Bell/KFC
	Lodg	**N:** Tex-Inn♥ **S:** Americas Best Value Inn♥, Bostonian Inn, Holiday Inn Express
	Med	**S:** + Hospital
	Other	**N:** Auto Dealers **S:** Auto Dealers, Brookshire's Grocery Pharmacy, CVS, **Walmart sc**
206		**Spur 86, Red River Army Depot**
	Other	**S:** Red River Army Depot, **to MIL/Elliot Lake Rec Area▲**
208		**FM 560, Main St, Hooks**
	TStop	**N:** Quick Go **S:** SunMart #105/Texaco (Scales) **(DAND)**
	Food	**N:** TX BBQ **S:** Subway/SunMart, DQ, Hooks Pizza Place, Sonic, Tastee House Rest
	Other	**N: Hooks Camper Center** **S:** Cooper Tire, Carwash, Family Dollar
212		**Spur 74, Lone Star Army Ammo Plant, Hooks**
	Gas	**S:** Shell
213		**FM 2253, Leary Rd**
	Other	**N: Palma Family RV Center**
218		**FM 989, N Kings Hwy, Texarkana, Nash**
	Gas	**N:** Road Runner◈ **S:** Exxon◈
	Food	**N:** Deli/Grill/RR, Dixie Diner, Mimi & Poppa's Burgers **S:** Burger King/Exxon
	Other	**N:** Carwash/RR, **McKinnon RV & Marine** **S:** Peterbilt Truck Center, Holt CAT, State Line Speedway, US Post Office
220A		**US 59S, Jarvis Pkwy, Texarkana, Atlanta, Houston**
	Gas	**S:** Exxon, Murphy's
	Food	**S:** Wendy's/Exxon, DQ
	Other	**S:** Carwash, Dollar General, Doolin's Harley Davidson, Honda, Lowe's, Sam's Club, Yamaha, Radio Shack, **Walmart sc** to Pratt's Truck Towing Services & **RV, to Shady Pines RV Center & RV Park▲**
220B		**FM 559, Richmond Rd, Texarkana**
	Gas	**N:** Chevron, Exxon, Shell, Sam's **S:** Shell
	Food	**N:** Burger King, ChickFilA, CiCi's Pizza, **Cracker Barrel**, Domino's Pizza, DQ, Johnny Carino's Italian Grill, Little Caesars Pizza, On the Border, Poncho's Mexican, Pizza Hut, Popeye's, Randy's Smokehouse & BBQ, Red Lobster, Ruby Tuesday, Sonic, Starbucks, Texas Roadhouse, Wendy's **S:** Arby's, Bryce's Cafeteria, Chili's, Chuck E Cheese 's Pizza, El Chico, Golden Corral, Luby's Cafeteria

EXIT		TX / AR
		McDonald's, Outback Steakhouse, Subway
	Lodg	**N:** Comfort Suites, Courtyard, Hampton Inn, Holiday Inn Express, Towneplace Suites **S:** Candlewood Suites♥, Fairfield Inn, Ramada Inn
	Med	**N: + Christus St Michael Health**
	Other	**N:** ATMs, Banks, Auto Dealers, Auto Services, Best Buy, Carwash, Discount Tire, Gander Mountain, Home Depot, Post Pharmacy, Super 1 Foods, Staples, Sam's Club, Target
	Other	**S:** Auto Zone, Albertson's, Auto Dealers, Carwash, Central Mall, Office Depot, PetSmart♥, Shelby's Service & Tires, Walgreen's, **to** Texarkana College
222		**TX 93, FM 1397, Summerhill Rd**
	Gas	**N:** Shell, Valero◈, E-Z Mart **S:** Shell
	Food	**N:** Amigo Juan Rest, Applebee's, Shogun Steak House & Sushi, McDonald's, Waffle House **S:** Bryce's Cafeteria
	Lodg	**N:** Motel 6♥
	Med	**N: + Christus St Michael Health**
	Other	**N:** ATMs, Banks, Heintschel Truck Tire Center, Pharmacy, Texarkana Truck Center **S:** Auto Dealers, Car Wash, Grocery
(223)		**TX Welcome Center (WB)** **(RR, Phone, Pic, Pet, Vend, Info)**
223A		**US 71S, State Line Ave, Texarkana**
	TStop	**S:** 76 Auto/Truck Stop (Scales)
	Gas	**S:** EZ Mart, Exxon, RaceWay, Shell
	Food	**S:** Arby's, Burger King, Cattleman's Steak House, El Chico Mexican, Hooters, KFC, La Carreta Mexican, Long John Silver, Pizza Hut, Popeye's Chicken, Quiznos, Subway, Taco Bell, Whataburger, Wendy's
	Lodg	**S:** Ambassador Inn, Americas Best Value Inn♥, Country Host Inn, Days Inn♥, Econo Lodge, Economy Inn, La Quinta Inn♥, Rodeway Inn
	Other	**S:** ATMs, Advance Auto Parts, Auto Zone, Auto Services, Albertson's/Pharmacy, **Four States RV Sales**, Holiday Bowl, Midas, Tractor Supply, Walgreen's, **Walmart sc**,
223B		**US 59N, US 71N, State Line Ave, Ashdown**
	Gas	**N:** Citgo◈, Mobil, Mobil, Shell, Speedway
	Food	**N:** Denny's, IHOP, Pizza Inn, Red Lobster, Waffle House,
	Lodg	**N:** Baymont Inn, Best Western, Budget Host Inn♥, Clarion, Holiday Inn Express, La Quinta Inn♥, Quality Inn♥, Super 8
	Other	**N:** ATMs, Firestone, Greyhound, **Texarkana KOA▲**

NOTE: MM 223: Arkansas State Line

CENTRAL TIME ZONE

TEXAS

ARKANSAS

CENTRAL TIME ZONE

EXIT		
1		**Jefferson Ave, Texarkana**
	Lodg	**S:** Country Host Inn

EXIT		ARKANSAS
	Other	**N: Texarkana KOA▲**
2		**AR 245, US 67, Texarkana**
	FStop	**N:** Circle K/Phillips 66 Fuel Stop, Road Runner **S:** Camp I-30 Truck Stop/BP
	Food	**S:** Rest/Camp I-30 TS
	Other	**S:** Truck & Trailer Repair, Four States Fairgrounds & **RV Park▲**, Texarkana Reg'l Webb Airport✈
7		**AR 108, Texarkana, Mandeville**
	TStop	**N:** Flying J Travel Plaza #5021/Conoco (Scales)
	Food	**N:** Cookery/FastFood/FJ TP, T-Town Diner
	TWash	**N:** TWA Truck Wash
	Other	**N:** Laundry/BarbSh/WiFi/**RVDump**/**LP**/FJ TP, **Sunrise RV Park▲**,
(8)		**AR Welcome Center (EB)** **Rest Area (WB)** **(RR, Phone, Picnic, Vend, Info)**
12		**US 67, Fulton (EB exit, WB entr)**
18		**Red Lake Rd, Fulton**
	TStop	**N:** Red River Truck Stop
	Food	**N:** Red River TS
	TServ	**N:** Red River TS/Tires
(25)		**Weigh Station (Both dir)**
30		**AR 4, US 278, Hervey St, Hope, to Nashville**
	Gas	**N:** Valero, Murphy◈ **S:** Exxon, Shell
	Food	**N:** Western Sizzlin **S:** Amigo Juan, Burger King, McDonald's, Pizza Hut, Subway, Taco Bell, Waffle House, Wendy's/Exxon
	Lodg	**N:** Best Western, Holiday Inn Express, Super 8 **S:** Days Inn
	Med	**S: + Medical Park Hospital**
	Other	**N:** ATMs, **Walmart sc**, **to** Hope Muni Airport✈, **to Crater of Diamonds State Park▲** **S:** Advance Auto Parts, Auto Dealers, Auto Zone, Banks, Carwash, Museum, O'Reilly Auto Parts, Super 1 Foods, Walgreen's, **RVDump/Hope City Park, to Fair City RV Park▲**
31		**AR 29, AR 32, Hazel St, Hope**
	FStop	**N:** Triple J Fuel Stop #7/Shell
	Gas	**S:** Exxon◈, Valero◈
	Food	**N:** Uncle Henry's Smokehouse BBQ **S:** Catfish Den, KFC, Pitt Grill
	Lodg	**N:** Relax Inn **S:** America's Best Value Inn, Hope Village Inn & **RV Park▲**,
36		**AR 299, Hope, to Emmet**
44		**AR 24, US 371, Blevins Rd, Prescott**
	TStop	**N:** Travel Center of America #224 (Scales) **S:** Exit 44 Truck Stop (Scales)
	Food	**N:** CountryFare/Subway/TacoBell/TA TC **S:** Rest/FastFood/Exit 44 TS, Sonic
	Lodg	**S:** AmericasBestValueInn/Exit 44 TS
	TWash	**S:** Exit 44 TS
	TServ	**N:** TA TC/Tires **S:** Exit 44 TS/Tires
	Other	**N:** Laundry/WiFi/**RVDump**/**LP**/TA TC **S:** Laundry/Exit 44 TS
46		**AR 19, Delight Hwy, Prescott, Magnolia**
	TStop	**N:** J&J Fuels/Fina **S:** Love's Travel Stop #277 (Scales)

◈= Regular Gas Stations with Diesel ▲ = RV Friendly Locations ♥= Pet Friendly Locations
Red print shows large vehicle parking / access on site or nearby Brown Print = Campgrounds / RV PARKS

Food N: Deli/Fina
S: Hardee's/Love's TS, Pizza Hut, Fly Wheel Pies
TServ N: Fina/Tires
Other N: to appr 25mi: Crater of Diamonds State Park▲
S: Laundry/WiFi/RVDump/Love's TS, ByPass Diesel & Wrecker Service

54 **AR 51, Okolona, Gurdon**

(56) **Rest Area (Both dir) (RR, Vend, Picnic)**

63 **AR 53, Gurdon**
FStop S: Dillard's Shell Superstop
TStop N: Southfork Truck Stop/Citgo
Food N: Rest/Southfork TS
S: Rest/Shell SS
Lodg N: Americas Best Value Inn♥
TServ N: Southfork TS/Tires/CBShop

69 **AR 26E, Arkadelphia, Gum Springs**

73 **AR 8, AR 26, AR 51, Arkadelphia**
Gas N: Citgo◈, Shell
S: Exxon◈, Shell
Food N: Domino's/Citgo, McDonald's, Western Sizzlin
S: Ardy's, Burger King, Cancun Mexican Rest, Pizza Shack, Subway, Taco Tico
Med S: + Baptist Health Medical Center
Other N: ATMs, Dollar Tree, Hibbett Sports, Walmart sc, to appr 35 mi:Crater of Diamonds State Park▲
S: Auto Zone, Auto Services, Amtrak, ATMs, Banks, Brookshire's Grocery, Fred's, O'Reilly Auto Parts, Pharmacy, Tires, UPS Store, US Post Office, to Henderson State Univ,

78 **AR 7, Caddo Valley, Arkadelphia, to Hot Springs**
FStop N: Jordan's Kwik Stop/Valero
TStop N: Mid-Ark Auto/Truck Plaza #2/Fina (Scales), Superstop #81/Shell
Gas S: Exxon, Phillips 66
Food N: Cracker Barrel, O'Keefe's Fish Net Family Rest
S: FastFood/Mid Ark TP, Subway/Exxon, McDonald's, Pig Pit BBQ, Shoney's, Taco Bell, Ta Molly's, Waffle House, Wendy's
Lodg S: Americas Best Value Inn♥, Best Western, Comfort Inn♥, Days Inn♥, Hampton Inn, Motel 6♥, Quality Inn, Super 8♥
TServ N: Mid-Ark ATP/Tires
Other N: Arkadelphia Campground ▲, to appr 6 mi: COE/De Gray State Park▲

83 **AR 283, Friendship**
Gas S: Shell◈

91 **AR 84, Old Military Rd, Malvern, Social Hill**

(93) **Rest Area (Both dir, Left Exit) (RR, Phones, Vend, Picnic)**

97 **AR 84, AR 171, Malvern**
Other N: to Lake Catherine State Park▲

98AB **US 270, AR 51, Malvern, to Hot Springs**
TStop S: Winner's Circle/Fina, Superstop #80/Shell
Gas S: Valero, Murphy◈
Food S: Burger King, McDonald's, Pizza Hut, Sonic, Subway, Taco Bell, Waffle House, Western Sizzlin, Wendy's

Lodg N: Super 8
S: Americas Best Value Inn, Holiday Inn Express
Med S: + Hospital
Other N: to Pearson's Landing RV Park▲
S: ATMs, Advance Auto Parts, Auto Zone, Auto Dealers, Dollar Tree, Dollar General, O'Reilly Auto Parts, Pharmacy, Radio Shack, Walmart sc, US Post Office, Beason Tire & Wrecker Service

99 **US 270S, Malvern**

106 **Old Military Rd, to US 67, Benton**
TStop N: AmBest/JJ's Truck Stop/Fina (Scales)
Food N: Rest/JJ's TS
Lodg N: Motel 106
TServ N: JJ's TS/Tires
Other N: LP/JJ's, to Pathway Campground▲
S: JB's RV Park & Campground▲

111 **US 70W, Hot Springs**
Other N: to Cloud 9 RV Park▲

(112) **Inspection Station (Both dir)**

114 **US 67S, Hwy 229, to W South St, Benton**

116 **Sevier St, W South St, Benton**
Gas N: Bullock's SuperStop, Shell◈
S: BP, Shell
Food N: Ed & Kay's, Chinese Rest, Granny's Grill
S: Arby's, El Cena Casa Rest, KFC, No Name Orig'l BBQ, Smokey Joe's
Lodg N: Trout Motel
S: Capri Inn Motel, Days Inn
Other S: ATMs, Banks, Auto Services, Grocery, Museums, Saline Co Fairgrounds

117 **AR 35, AR 5W, Benton (S Serv on Military Rd)**
Gas N: Citgo, Shell
Food N: Bo's BBQ, Denny's, Firehouse Subs, IHOP, Pizza Hut, Waffle House
S: Arby's, KFC, McDonald's, Smokey Joe's, Subway
Lodg N: America's Best Inn, Best Western, Cedarwood Motel, Econo Lodge, Ramada
Med S: + Saline Memorial Hospital
Other S: ATMs, Banks, Carwash, Grocery, Auto Services

118 **Congo Rd (EB)**
Gas N: Big Red, Shell◈
S: Citgo, Exxon, Shell, Murphy
Food N: Applebee's, Benton Family Rest, CiCi's Pizza, Santa Fe Grill, Weng's Chinese
S: Burger King, Colton's Steakhouse, Mexican, Shoney's, Sonic, Taco Bell, Waffle House, Western Sizzlin, Wendy's
Lodg N: Relax Inn
S: Best Western, Days Inn
Other N: ATMs, Auto Dealers, Home Depot, Whitfield Tire
S: Advance Auto, ATMs, Banks, Auto Zone, Firestone, Kroger, O'Reilly Auto Parts, Radio Shack, RV City II, Tire Town, US Post Office, Walmart sc

121 **Alcoa Rd, Benton**
TStop N: Pilot Travel Center #118 (Scales)
Gas N: Citgo
S: Texaco
Food N: Subway/Pilot TC, McDonald's, Pizza Hut, Sonic, Starbucks
Food S: Chili's, Moe's SW Grill, McAlister's Deli, Sakura Japanese Steakhouse, Starbucks, Subway

TWash S: Superior Truck Wash & Lube
Other N: Laundry/WiFi/Pilot TC, Auto Dealers,
S: Auto Dealers, Kirkland's, Kohl, Target, I-30 Travel Park▲

123 **AR 183, Reynolds Rd, Bryant**
FStop S: Speedzone/Conoco
Gas N: Phillips 66, Shell, Murphy◈
S: Exxon◈, Phillips 66◈
Food N: Arby's, Backyard Burgers, Burger King, Catfish Barn, Cracker Barrel, Domino's Pizza, KFC, Pizza Hut, Ruby Tuesday, Subway, Ta Molly's, Taste of D-Light, Waffle House
S: FastFood/Speedzone, ChickFilA, Little Caesar's Pizza, McDonald's, Ole South Pancake House, Sonic, Subway, Taco Bell, Wendy's
Lodg N: Americas Best Value Inn♥, Comfort Inn♥, Hampton Inn, Holiday Inn Express, HomeTown Hotel, Vista Inn♥
S: Super 8♥
Med N: + Bryant Medical Clinic
Other N: ATMs, Banks, Auto Zone, Bryant Veterinary Clinic♥, Dollar Tree, Fought Tire Center, Kwik Kopy, Radio Shack, Walgreen's, Walmart sc
S: ATMs, Banks, Auto Service/Exxon, Carwash, Dollar General, Lowe's, Pharmacy, Quaker State Lube

126 **AR 111, Alexander Rd, Alexander**
FStop N: County Line Superstop/Shell
Gas N: US Fuel◈
S: Mapco Express◈
Other N: RVDump/Fred & Jack's Trailer Sales
S: Moix RV

128 **Mabelvale West Rd, Otter Creek Rd**
Gas S: Exxon◈
Food S: Rest/La Quinta Inn♥
Lodg S: La Quinta Inn♥
TServ S: Purcell Tire/Goodyear
Med S: + SW Regional Hospital

(129) **Jct I-430N, to Fort Smith**

130 **AR 338, Baseline Rd, Mabelvale Pike, Mabelvale**
Gas N: Mapco Express◈
S: Phillips 66, Shell
Food N: The Hawg Diner, Frontier Diner
S: Dixie Cafe, El Rancho Rest, Luby's, McDonald's, Pizza Hut, Popeye's/Shell, Sonic, Subway, Taco Bueno, Wendy's
Lodg N: Americas Best Inn, Cimarron Inn
S: Knights Inn
Other N: Jones Harley Davidson
S: ATMs, Banks, Dollar Tree, Crain RV, United Engines, Walmart sc,

131 **Frontage Rd, S Chicot Rd (EB) Frontage Rd, McDaniel Dr (WB)**
Gas S: Shell, Sinclair
Food S: Popeye's/Shell, McDonald's
Lodg S: Knights Inn, Plantation Inn, Super 7 Inn
Other N: U-Haul
S: ATMs, Auto Services, Firestone, Grocery, Riggs CAT, Walmart sc,

132 **US 70B, University Ave (EB), Frontage Rd, W Baseline (WB)**

133 **Geyer Springs Rd, Little Rock**
Gas N: Exxon, Hess
S: Conoco, Exxon, Phillips 66, Shell
Food N: Church's, Fat Boys BBQ, Mama B's Big Burgers, Sim's BBQ, Subway, Whataburger

EXIT		ARKANSAS
	Food	S: Arby's, Backyard Burgers, Burger King, Dixie Cafe, El Chico Mexican, KFC, McDonald's, Pizza Inn, Taco Bell, Waffle House, Wendy's
	Lodg	S: Best Western, Comfort Inn, Hampton Inn, Rest Inn, Super 8
	TServ	N: Looney Truck & Tire Service
	Other	S: ATMs, Banks, Auto Services, Advance Auto Parts, Family Dollar, Kroger, Radio Shack, Walgreen's
134		**Scott Hamilton Dr, Stanton Rd**
	Gas	S: Exxon◈
	Food	S: Waffle House
	Lodg	S: Americas Best Value Inn, Motel 6♥
135		**65th St, Little Rock**
	FStop	N: Exxon
	Gas	N: Mapco Express, Shell◈
	Lodg	N: Executive Inn♥
		S: Rodeway Inn
(138A)		**Jct I-440E, Little Rock Nat'l Airport, LR River Port, Memphis (EB)**

EXIT		ARKANSAS
(138B)		**Jct I-530S, US 167S, US 65S, Pine Bluff, El Dorado, LR Airport**
(138)		**Jct I-440E, Little Rock Nat'l Airport, LR River Port, Memphis (WB)**
139A		**AR 365, Roosevelt Rd**
	Gas	N: Citgo, Exxon
		S: Shell
	Other	N: Auto Zone
		S: Family Dollar, Kroger, Adams Field✈
(139B)		**Jct I-630W**
140		**9th St, 6th St, Little Rock (EB)**
	Gas	N: Exxon, Shell
		S: Phillips 66
	Food	N: Pizza Hut
		S: Waffle House
	Lodg	N: Best Western, Holiday Inn
		S: Comfort Inn, Masters Inn
140B		**6th St (WB)**
140A		**9th St (WB)**

EXIT		ARKANSAS
141A		**E 2nd St, to AR 10, Cantrell Rd**
141B		**US 70E, US 67, Broadway**
	Gas	N: Exxon, US Fuel
		S: Citgo, Superstop
	Food	N: Burger King, Wendy's
		S: Arby's, KFC, McDonald's, Popeye's, Taco Bell, Wendy's
	Other	N: Alltel Arena, Kroger
142		**15th St, N Little Rock**
	Gas	S: Phillips 66, Super Stop◈
(143AB)		**Jct I-40, W-Ft Smith, E-Memphis**

NOTE: I-30 begins/ends on I-40, Exit #153B

CENTRAL TIME ZONE

ARKANSAS

Begin Westbound I-30 from Jct I-40 in Little Rock, AR to Ft Worth, TX.

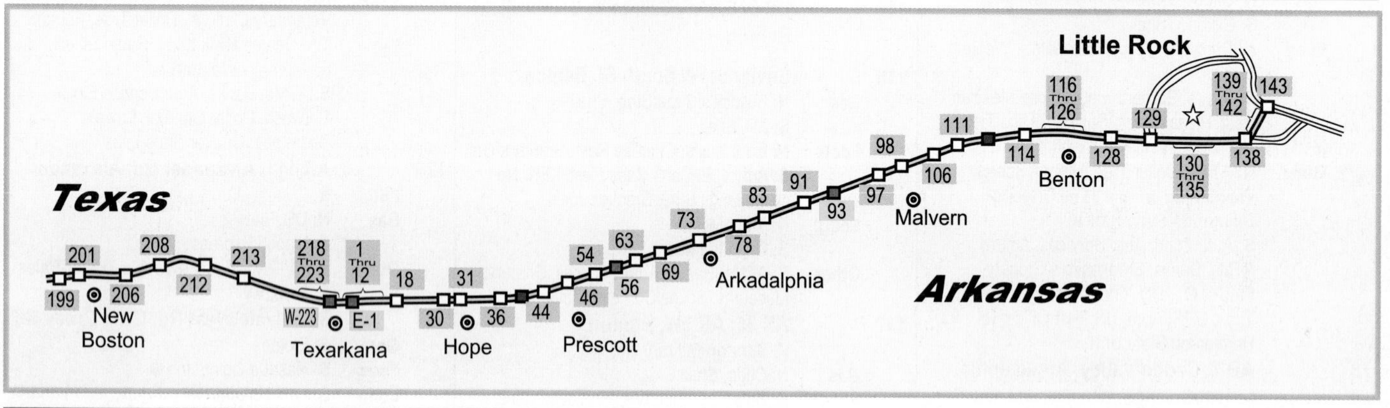

EXIT		MINNESOTA
		Begin Southbound I-35 from Duluth, MN to Laredo, TX.
		MINNESOTA
	NOTE:	I-35 begins/ends in Duluth, MN
		CENTRAL TIME ZONE
259		**Jct MN 61, London Rd, 26th Ave, N Shore Dr, to Two Harbors**
	Gas	W: Holiday◈, ICO◈, Spur◈, Speedway
	Food	W: Blackwood Grill, Burger King, KFC, McDonald's, Perkins, Pizza Hut, Taco John's, Wendy's, Rest/BW
	Lodg	W: Best Western, Edgewater Motel
	NOTE:	MM 258 - 256: Tunnel
258		**21st Ave, Duluth (NB) (Acc to #259)**
	Other	E: to Univ of MN/Duluth
256B		**Lake Ave, 5th Ave, Mesaba Ave, Superior St**
	Food	E: Angie's Cantina & Grill, Burger King, DQ, Red Lobster
	Lodg	E: Comfort Suites, Hampton Inn, Inn on Lake Superior, Park Inn,

EXIT		MINNESOTA
	Lodg	W: Holiday Inn, Radisson
	Other	E: Omnimax Theater
		W: Grocery, Galleries, Museums
256A		**MN 194W, MN 23, Mesaba Ave, Michigan St, Superior St, Downtown Duluth (NB)**
	Med	W: + Hospital
(255B)		**Jct I-535S, US 53, to Wisconsin (SB, LEFT Exit)**
255A		**US 53N, Piedmont Ave, 21st Ave Duluth Intl Airport (NB, LEFT Exit)**
254		**27th Ave W, Truck Center Dr**
	TStop	W: W to Truck Ctr Dr: Lincoln Park Travel Plaza (Scales)
	Gas	W: BP, Holiday◈, Spur◈
	Food	W: FastFood/Lincoln Park TP, Embers, Burger King/Holiday, Quiznos, Subway
	Lodg	W: Motel 6♥
	TServ	W: Lincoln Park TP
	Other	W: Laundry/Lincoln Park TP
253B		**40th Ave**
	TStop	to W 1st St: Lakehead Travel Plaza/BP
	Food	W: FastFood/Lakehead TP, Perkins
	Lodg	W: Comfort Inn, Super 8

EXIT		MINNESOTA
253A		**46th Ave, US 2E, Superior**
	Gas	W: ICO◈
	Food	W: Grandma's Saloon, Taco John's
252		**Central Ave, Duluth**
	Gas	W: Conoco◈, Holiday◈
	Food	W: Giant Panda, KFC, McDonald's, Pizza Hut, Subway, Taco Bell
	Other	W: ATMs, Auto Services, Advance Auto Parts, Grocery, Walgreen's
251B		**MN 23S, Grand Ave (SB, LEFT exit)**
	Other	E: Zoo, to Indian Point Campground▲
251A		**Cody St (NB)**
	Lodg	W: Allyndale Motel
	Other	E: Zoo, to Indian Point Campground▲
250		**US 2W, Proctor (SB)**
		MN Welcome Center (Both dir) Thompson Hill Rest Area (RR, Phone, Picnic, Vend, Info)
	Gas	W: Holiday◈, Mobil◈
	Food	W: Blackwoods Grill, Country Kitchen
	Lodg	W: AmericInn
249		**CR 14, to US 2W (NB), Boundary Ave (SB), Duluth, to Proctor**
	Gas	E: Holiday◈
		W: Phillips 66◈

◈= Regular Gas Stations with Diesel ▲ = RV Friendly Locations ♥= Pet Friendly Locations
Red print shows large vehicle parking / access on site or nearby Brown Print = Campgrounds / RV PARKS

EXIT		MINNESOTA
	Food	E: Country Kitchen, McDonald's/Holiday
		W: Blackwoods Grill
	Lodg	E: Country Inn Suites, Sundown Motel
		W: Travelodge
	Other	E: to Spirit Mountain Ski Resort & CG▲
	NOTE:	MM 249 - 251: NB: 6% Steep Grade
246		**CR 13, Midway Rd, Duluth**
	Food	W: Dry Dock Rest
245		**CR 61, CR 3, Esko**
	Food	E: Buffalo House Rest
	Other	E: Buffalo Valley Camping▲
		W: Knife Island Campground▲
242		**CR 1, Esko, to Thomson**
	Gas	E: BP
	Other	E: to Jay Cook State Park▲
239		**MN 45S, Cloquet, to CR 61, CR 16, Scanlon, Carlton**
	Gas	W: Conoco
	Food	W: River Inn Bar & Grilll, Wood City Grill
	Lodg	W: Golden Gate Motel
	Med	W: + Hospital
	Other	E: to Cloquet/Duluth KOA▲ , to Jay Cook State Park▲
		W: Auto Dealers
237		**MN 33, Cloquet**
	Gas	W: BP, Conoco, Spur, Murphy
	Food	W: Applebee's, Arby's, Country Kitchen, DQ, Hardee's, McDonald's, Perkins, Pizza Hut, Subway, Taco Bell, Wendy's
	Lodg	W: American Motel, Super 8
	Med	W: + Fond du Lac Hospital
	Other	W: Auto Dealer, Family Dollar, Pharmacy, NAPA, Walmart SC, Cloquet Carlton Co Airport✈
(236)		**Weigh Station (SB)**
235		**MN 210, Carlton, Cromwell**
	TStop	E: Carlton Travel Center/BP, Junction Oasis #34/Spur (Scales)
	Food	E: Rest/Carlton TC, Rest/Jct Oasis
	Lodg	E: Royal Pines Motel, AmericInn
		W: Black Bear Casino, Hotel & Grill
	TWash	E: Carlton TC
	TServ	E: Junction Oasis
	Other	E: Laundry/Carlton TC, LP/Jct Oasis
		W: Fond du Lac Indian Reservation
227		**CR 4, Barnum, Mahtowa**
	Gas	W: Conoco
	Other	E: Bent Trout Lake Campground▲
(226)		**Culkin Rest Area (NB)** (RR, Phones, Pic, Vend, Playgr)
220		**CR 6, Main St, Barnum**
	Gas	W: BP◈
	Food	W: Café/BP
	Lodg	W: Northwoods Motel
	Other	W: Auto Repairs
216		**MN 27W, CR 8, Moose Lake (SB)**
	Gas	W: BP, Holiday◈, Phillips 66
	Food	W: Café, Wyndtree
	Lodg	W: Moose Lake Motel
	Med	W: + Hospital
	Other	W: Auto Dealer, Auto Services, Moose Lake City Park▲
214		**MN 73N, Moose Lake**
	FStop	W: Little Store/Conoco
	Gas	W: BP, Holiday◈
	Food	W: Subway/Little Store
	Lodg	W: AmericInn
	Other	E: Moose Lake State Park▲
		W: Red Fox Campground & RV Park▲ , to Moose Lake Carlton Co Airport✈,

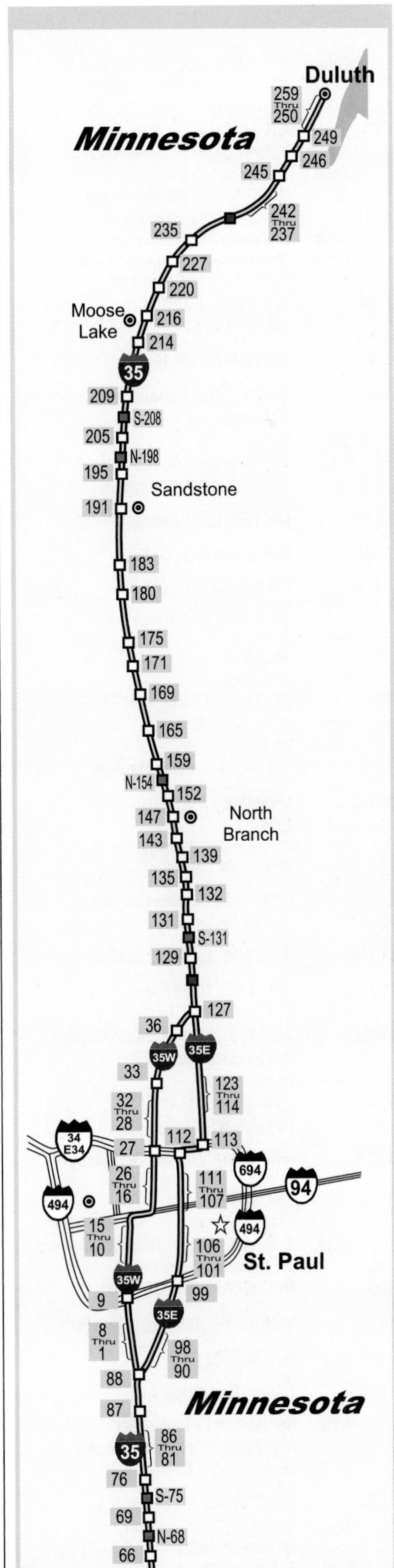

EXIT		MINNESOTA
209		**CR 46, Sturgeon Lake**
	Gas	E: Phillips 66
(208)		**Gen'l Andrews Rest Area (SB)** (RR, Phones, Picnic, Vend)
205		**CR 43, Willow River**
	Gas	W: Citgo◈
	Other	W: to Gen'l CC Andrews State Forest Willow River Campground▲
(198)		**Kettle River Rest Area (NB)** (RR, Phones, Picnic, Vend)
195		**MN 23, MN 18W, Finlayson**
	Gas	E: Banning Junction/Shell◈
	Food	E: Cafe/BJ Shell
	Lodg	E: Americas Best Value Inn
	Other	E: Banning State Park▲
191		**MN 23E, to MN 123, Sandstone**
	Gas	E: BP◈, Conoco◈
	Other	E: Sandstone Muni Airport✈
183		**MN 23W, MN 48E, Hinckley**
	FStop	W: W to MN 61: Slim's Service/BP
	Gas	E: Conoco, Holiday◈
		W: Mobil, Phillips 66◈
	Food	E: Burger King, Hardee's/Holiday, Subway
		W: Cassidy's
	Lodg	E: Days Inn
		W: Gold Pine Inn, Travelodge
	Other	E: Grand Casino Hinckley RV Resort▲ , Grand Casino Hinckley
		W: LP/Slim's
180		**MN 23, CR 61, Mora**
175		**CR 14, Beroun**
	Gas	E: BP◈
171		**CR 11, Pine City**
	FStop	E: SuperAmerica #4500
	Food	E: McDonald's
	Other	E: Auto Dealers, Pine City Muni Airport✈
169		**MN 324, CR 7, Pine City**
	Gas	E: BP◈, Holiday◈
	Food	E: DQ, Domino's Pizza, Grizzly's Grill, KFC, Pizza Hut, Subway
	Other	E: Radio Shack, Walmart sc
165		**MN 70, Rock Creek, Grantsburg**
	FStop	W: Rock Creek Motor Stop/BP
	Gas	E: Citgo◈
	Food	W: Rest/Rock Creek MS
	Lodg	E: Chalet Motel
159		**MN 361, CR 1, Rush City**
	TStop	E: Holiday/Rush City Travel Plaza
	Food	E: Burger King/Holiday TP
	Med	E: + Hospital
	Other	E: Laundry/Holiday TP, Auto Service, to Rush City Muni Airport✈
		W: to Rush Lake Resort & Campground▲
(154)		**Goose Creek Rest Area (NB)** (RR, Phones, Picnic, Vend)
152		**CR 10, Harris**
147		**MN 95, North Branch, Cambridge**
	FStop	E: Gas Plus #8
	Gas	E: BP, Holiday Station Store◈
	Food	E: DQ, KFC/Taco Bell, McDonald's, Perkins, Pizza Hut, Subway, Oak Inn
		W: Burger King, Denny's, McDonald's
	Lodg	E: AmericInn, Super 8
	Other	E: ATMs, Auto Services, Grocery, NAPA, Radio Shack, Tires, Golf Course
		W: Tanger Outlet Mall, Auto Dealers

EXIT — MINNESOTA

(143) CR 17, New Exit

139 CR 19, Stacy Trail, Stacy
- Gas: E: BP, Phillips 66; W: Conoco◈
- Food: E: Rustic Restaurant, Subway

135 US 61S, CR 22, Wyoming
- FStop: E: Wyoming BP Food Shop; W: Wyoming Shell
- Food: E: FastFood/WY FS, Cornerstone Café, Pizza Zone, Subway; W: FastFood/WY Citgo, McDonald's, Village Inn, Rest/Exec Inn
- Lodg: W: Executive Inn♥
- Med: E: + Hospital
- Other: E: ATMs, Auto Services, IGA; W: LP/WY Citgo

132 US 8E, to US 61, Forest Lake, Taylors Falls (NB)

131 CR 2, Broadway Ave, Forest Lake
- Gas: E: AmocoBP, Holiday◈, SuperAmerica◈; W: Holiday◈
- Food: E: Applebee's, Arby's, Perkins, Quack's; W: Famous Dave's BBQ, Quiznos, Starbucks, Wendy's
- Lodg: E: AmericInn; W: Country Inn Suites
- Med: E: + Fairview Lakes Hospital
- Other: E: ATMs, Checker Parts, Grocery, Target, Tires Plus+, Walgreen's, **Walmart**, **American RV Repair & Services**; W: ATMs, Auto Dealers, Auto Services, Grocery, Home Depot

(131) Forest Lake Rest Area (SB)
(RR, Phone, Picnic, Vend)

129 MN 97, CR 23, Forest Lake
- FStop: W: Forest Lake BP
- Food: W: FastFood/FL BP
- Other: E: Auto & Truck Repair, **to** Forest Lake Airport✈; W: **Coates RV Center**, Gander Mountain

(128) Weigh Station (SB)

35E S — Listings below are for I-35E thru St Paul, MN.

(127) Jct I-35W, to Minneapolis, I-35E to St Paul

123 CR 14, Main St, Centerville, Hugo
- Gas: E: Kwik Trip; W: Marathon, Shell, Bobby & Steve's Auto World/Mobil
- Food: E: American & Asian Bistro, Blue Heron Grille, Dunn Bros Grill & Cafe, Sertino's Cafe, Savoy Pizza; W: DQ, Embers, Wiseguys Pizza, Rest/B&S AW
- Other: E: Carwash/KT, Festival Foods, Otter Lake Animal Care Center♥, **Otter Lake RV Center**; W: ATMs, Carwash/Shell, Carwash/Serv/B&S AW, U-Haul

120 CR 81, CR J, Hugo (NB ex, SB entr)

117 Ramsey CR 96, St Paul
- Gas: E: Marathon, Super America◈; W: BP, Holiday, PDQ, Shell
- Food: E: Burger King; W: Applebee's, Arby's, Boston Market, McDonald's, Subway
- Lodg: E: AmericInn
- Med: W: + Northeast Medical & Dental
- Other: E: ATMs, Banks, Auto Services, NAPA; W: ATMs, Auto Dealers, Cub Foods, Tires Plus+, Walgreen's

115 CR 15, CR E, St Paul
- Gas: E: BP, Conoco, Super America
- Food: E: Perkins; W: KFC/Pizza Hut, McDonald's, Panera Bread, Quiznos, Wendy's
- Lodg: E: Country Inn, Holiday Inn Express
- Other: W: ATMs, Banks, Auto Services, Festival Foods, Target, **Walmart SC**

(114) Jct I-694E, Eau Claire (SB LEFT exit)

(113) Jct I-694W, US 10W

112 CR 21, Little Canada Rd, Little Canada
- Gas: E: BP
- Food: W: Porterhouse Steak & Seafood

111B MN 36W, to Minneapolis

111A MN 36E, to Stillwater

110B Roselawn Ave, St Paul

110A CR 30, Larpentur Ave, Wheelock Pkwy
- Gas: E: BP, Mobil; W: Sinclair
- Food: E: Subway

109 CR 31, Maryland Ave
- Gas: E: 76, Super America
- Other: W: Kmart

108 CR 33, Pennsylvania Ave

107C University Ave (SB)
- Gas: E: BP
- Med: W: + Regions Hospital
- Other: W: to State Capitol

NOTE: I-35E & I-94 run together below. Exit #'s follow I-35E.

(107B) Jct I-94W, to Minneapolis

(107A) Jct I-94E, to St Paul
- Med: E: + St Joseph's Hospital

(106C) Jct I-94E, 11th St, State Capitol (NB exit, SB reentry)
- Lodg: E: Holiday Inn

106B Kellogg Blvd, to I-94W (NB exit, SB reentry)

106A Grand Ave (NB exit, SB reentry)
- Gas: E: Mobil
- Med: E: + United Hospital, + Children's Healthcare
- Other: E: SP Civic Center, Theatres, Museums; W: Theatres, Museums

105 St Clair Ave, St Paul (SB)

104C Victoria St, Jefferson Ave (SB)

104B Ayd Mill Rd (NB)

104A CR 38, Randolph Ave

NOTE: NB: All Trucks Over 9000# GVW MUST exit. Trucks over not allowed between MN 5 & I-94.

103B MN 5, W 7th St, St Paul
- Gas: E: Mobil; W: Super America◈
- Food: E: Burger King
- Lodg: W: Crosby Lake Inn

103A Shepard Rd (NB)

102 MN 13, Sibley Hwy
- Gas: W: BP, Holiday

101B Mendota Rd W (SB)

101A Mendota Rd E (SB)

101AB MN 110, Mendota Rd (NB)
- Gas: W: Super America
- Other: W: Police Dept

(99B) Jct I-494W, to Bloomington, Airport, Mall of America

(99A) Jct I-494E, to Maplewood (SB)

99AB MN 55, Jct I-494 (NB)

98 CR 26, Lone Oak Rd
- Gas: E: Sam's; W: BP, Fina, Marathon
- Food: W: Joe's Grill, Thai Cafe
- Lodg: E: Homestead Suites, Microtel; W: Hampton Inn, Residence Inn
- Other: E: Sam's Club

97AB CR 31, CR 28, Pilot Knob Rd, Yankee Doodle Rd (NB)
- Gas: E: Holiday, Phillips 66, Super America◈; W: BP, Shell, Super America◈
- Food: E: Applebee's, Arby's, Black Angus, Chili's, Don Pablo's, KFC, McDonald's, Hunan Rest, Houlihan's, Grand India, Perkins, Red Robin, Taco Bell, Wendy's; W: Boston Market, Dragon Palace, El Loro Mex Rest, Chipolte, Steakhouse
- Lodg: E: Marriott, Residence Inn, Springhill Suites, Towneplace Suites; W: Best Western, Extended Stay America
- Med: E: + Eagan Medical Center
- Other: E: ATMs, Banks, Auto Services, B&N, Best Buy, Checker Auto Parts, Cinema, FedEx Office, Firestone, Grocery, Home Depot, Office Depot, PetSmart♥, Tires Plus, **Walmart sc**, Walgreen's, Mall

97A CR 28, Yankee Doodle Rd (SB)

97B CR 31, Pilot Knob Rd (SB)

94 CR 30, Diffley Rd, St Paul
- Gas: E: Holiday
- Food: E: Starbucks
- Other: E: CVS; W: to Difley Square Mall

93 CR 32, Cliff Rd
- Gas: E: Shell; W: Holiday◈, Mobil, Total
- Food: W: Bakers Square, Boston Market, Burger King, Denny's, Greenmill Rest, KFC, McDonald's, Quiznos, Starbucks, Subway, Taco Bell, Wendy's
- Lodg: W: Hilton Garden Inn, Holiday Inn Express♥, Staybridge Suites
- Med: E: + Park Medical Center; W: + Medical Center
- Other: E: to Lebanon Hills Park▲; W: ATMs, Banks, Cinema 16, Grocery, Radio Shack, Target, Walgreen's

92 MN 77, Cedar Ave, to Cliff Rd
- Gas: W: BP, Holiday
- Other: W: Access to Ex #93 W Serv

90 CR 11, St Paul
- Gas: E: Kwik Trip; W: Freedom Valu Center/SuperAmerica◈

◈ = Regular Gas Stations with Diesel ▲ = RV Friendly Locations ♥ = Pet Friendly Locations
Red print shows large vehicle parking / access on site or nearby Brown Print = Campgrounds / RV PARKS

EXIT — MINNESOTA

88B **CR 42, Burnsville**
Gas W: BP, Holiday, PDQ, Super America
Food E: Ciatti's Italian Rest, Roadhouse Grill
W: Arby's, Applebee's, Burger King, Chili's, Chipolte Mex Grill, KFC, TGI Friday, Fuddrucker's, McDonald's, Old Country Buffet, Outback Steakhouse, Panda Express, Romano's Macaroni Grill, Roadhouse Grill, Tin Alley Grill
Lodg W: Days Inn, Fairfield Inn, Holiday Inn, Hampton Inn
Med W: + Fairview Ridges Hospital
Other E: Grocery, ATM, Bank
W: ATMs, Banks, Auto Services, Cinema, Discount Tire, Firestone Auto, Goodyear Auto, Home Depot, Target, Tires Plus, Burnsville Center,

(88A) **Jct I-35W (NB) to Minneapolis, Jct I-35, to Duluth**

NOTE: I-35W begins/ends on I-35, Exit #127

35E N — Above listings are for I-35E thru St Paul.

35W S — Below listings are for I-35W thru Minneapolis, MN.

36 **MN 49, County 23, Circle Pines**
FStop E: Oasis Market #557/BP
Gas W: Phillips 66◊
Food E: FastFood/Oasis
W: McDonald's, Subway
Other W: ATMs, Discount Tire, Super Target

33 **County 17, Lexington Ave**
Gas E: BP
Food E: Burger King, McDonald's
W: Applebee's, Green Mill, Wendy's
Other W: ATMs, Cub Foods, Home Depot, Radio Shack, **Walmart**, Walgreen's

32 **County 52, 95th Ave NE**
Other W: Anoka Co Blaine Airport✈

31B **County 23, Lake Dr**
Gas E: Shell◊

31A **County 1, 85th Ave NE, County J (NB exit, diff reacc)**

30 **US 10W, to MN 65, Anoka**

29 **CR 3, County I**
Gas W: Fina

28C **CR 5, to Co 10W, CR H (SB)**
Gas W: BP
Food W: KFC, McDonald's, Perkins, Taco Bell, RJ Riches, Subway
Lodg W: Days Inn

28B **US 10E, St. Paul (SB), MN 10W, County H, Anoka (NB)**
Lodg W: Skyline Motel

28A **MN 96**

(27AB) **Jct I-694, to St Cloud, Eau Claire**

26 **CR 73, County E2, 5th St NW**
Gas W: Phillips 66◊

25B **CR 88, New Brighton Blvd (SB, difficult reaccess)**
Gas E: Super America◊
W: Mobil, PDQ

EXIT — MINNESOTA

Food W: Jake's Cafe, KFC, Main Event, Perkins, McDonald's, Subway
Lodg E: Courtyard, Fairfield Inn, Residence Inn

25A **CR 19, County D, St Paul**

24 **CR 23, County C, St Paul**
FStop W: Gas Discount
TStop W: Cleanco Truck Wash & Fuel Stop
Food E: Burger King
Lodg E: Holiday Inn
W: Comfort Inn
TWash W: Cleanco TW & FS
TServ W: Freightliner Trucks
Other E: Enterprise RAC
W: Auto Dealers

23B **MN 36, Cleveland Ave, Stillwater (fr SB, LEFT Exit)**
Food E: Burger King, India Palace
Lodg E: Days Inn, Motel 6♥, Ramada
Other E: to Rosedale Shopping Center

23A **MN 280S, to Industrial Blvd (SB)**

22 **to MN 280 (NB), St Anthony Blvd, Industrial Blvd (SB)**
Lodg E: Sheraton Inn

21A **CR 88, Stinson Blvd (SB)**
Food W: Country Kitchen, McDonald's, Pizza Hut/Taco Bell
Other W: Grocery, Home Depot, Target

21B **Johnson St NE (NB)**

21A **CR 88, Stinson Blvd, New Brighton Blvd**
Food W: Burger King, Country Kitchen, McDonald's
Other W: ATMs, Grocery, Home Depot, Target, **to Lowry Grove Campground▲**

19 **E Hennepin Ave (NB)**
Gas W: EZ Stop
Other E: Auto Services, Food, Museums

18 **4th St SE, University Ave**
Gas E: BP
Food E: Hardee's
W: The Fish Basket
Lodg E: Gopher Campus Motor Lodge
Other E: Univ of MN
W: Laundromat

17C **CR 152, Washington Ave (SB)**
Other W: to MetroDome

(17B) **Jct I-94W, 11th Ave (SB)**

17A **MN 55E, Hiawatha Ave (SB)**

17C **Washington Ave, 3rd St, U of M**
Gas W: Mobil
Lodg E: Holiday Inn♥
Med W: + Hennepin Co Med Center
Other E: Univ of MN

(16B) **Jct I-94E, to St Paul (NB)**
Other E: to + Fairview Riverside Med Center

16A **MN 65N, I-94W, Downtown (NB, LEFT Exit)**

15 **CR 3, 31st St, Lake St (NB)**
Gas W: Food 'n Fuel
Food E: McDonald's, Taco Bell
W: Subway, Wendy's
Med E: + Abbott NW Hospital, + Childrens Healthcare
Other E: Auto Services, ATMs, Bank, Grocery
W: Grocery, **Police Dept**, Banks, ATMs

14 **35th St, 36th St**

EXIT — MINNESOTA

13 **CR 46, 46th St, Minneapolis**

12B **Diamond Lake Rd**
Food W: Ja Mama's BBQ, Best Steak House

12A **60th St (SB exit, NB reentry)**
Gas W: Mobil
Other W: Grocery, Auto Services

11B **MN 62E, to Airport (SB, LEFT exit)**

11A **Lyndale Ave (SB)**
Gas E: Shell

10B **MN 62W (SB), MN 121N, 58th St, Lyndale Ave (NB, LEFT Exit)**

10A **CR 53, 66th St**
Gas E: SuperAmerica

9C **76th St (SB exit, NB reentry)**
Other W to Penn Ave: Food, Services at Southtown Center, Target, Best Buy

(9AB) **Jct I-494, MN 5, to Airport**
Other E: to Mall of America, MSP Intl Airport✈

8 **82nd St**
Other W to Penn Ave: Food, Services at Southtown Ctr, Best Buy, Target

7B **90th St**

7A **94th St (Addt'l Serv E to Lyndale Ave)**
Gas E: BP
Lodg W: Holiday Inn
Other E: Auto Services, Goodyear

6 **CR 1, 98th St, Bloomington**
FStop W: Super America #4180
Gas E: E-Z Stop
Food E: Bakers Square, Deli, Burger King, New China Buffet, Starbucks, Wendy's
W: Burger King, Denny's, Subway
Other E: ATMs, Banks, Checker Auto Parts, Festival Foods, Radio Shack, Walgreen's

5 **106th St, Minneapolis**

4B **Black Dog Rd**

4A **CR 32, Cliff Rd**
Other E: Zoo

3AB **MN 13, Shakopee, Mendota Heights**

2 **Burnsville Pkwy, Burnsville**
Gas E: Citgo, Marathon
W: BP, Holiday
Food E: Denny's, Hardee's
W: Hooters, Perkins, Timber Lodge Steak House
Lodg W: Americas Best Value Inn, Red Roof Inn♥, Super 8
Other E: Mall
W: Best Buy

(1/88B) **CR 42, Crystal Lake Blvd (SB)**
Gas E: BP, PDQ
W: Amoco, Sinclair
Food E: Arby's, Burger King, McDonald's, Old Country Buffet
W: Applebee's, Bakers Square, Chili's, Green Mill, Red Lobster
Lodg E: Country Inn, Holiday Inn
Med E: + Fairview Ridges Hospital
Other W: Target, UPS Store, **Mystic Lake Casino & Hotel**

35W N — Above listings are for I-35W thru Minneapolis, MN & I-35E thru St Paul, MN. I-35 SB listed below.

(88A) **Jct I-35E to St Paul, Jct I-35W to Minneapolis**

◊ = Regular Gas Stations with Diesel ▲ = RV Friendly Locations ♥ = Pet Friendly Locations
Red print shows large vehicle parking / access on site or nearby Brown Print = Campgrounds / RV PARKS

EXIT	MINNESOTA
87	**Crystal Lake Rd, Burnsville (NB)**
Gas	**W:** KwikTrip
Other	**W:** Auto Dealers, Auto Services, Buck Hill Ski Area
86	**CR 46, 162nd St, Lakeville, Apple Valley (NB)**
Gas	**E:** KwikTrip, Super America◈
Food	**E:** Starbucks
Other	**E:** ATM, Bank, Auto Services, Twin Cities Harley Davidson **W:** O'Reilly Auto Parts
85	**CR 50, CR 5, Kenwood Trail, Lakeville**
Gas	**E:** BP, Super America◈ **W:** Holiday◈
Food	**E:** Burger King, DQ, Lakeville Chinese, Pizza Hut, Taco Bell, Wendy's **W:** Cracker Barrel, Perkins
Lodg	**E:** Americas Best Value Inn, Comfort Inn, Lakeville Inn **W:** AmericInn
Med	**E:** + Family Convenience Care
Other	**E:** Goodyear, Grocery, Heartland Tire & Service, Pharmacy, Walgreen's **W:** ATMs, Banks, Gander Mountain
84	**CR 60, 185th St W, Prior Lake**
Other	**W:** Mystic Lake Casino & Hotel
81	**CR 70, Lakeville, Farmington**
TStop	**E:** PTP/Mega Stop Holiday
Food	**E:** Rest/FastFood/Mega Stop, Jordan's Steak House, McDonald's, Subway, Tacoville
Lodg	**E:** Motel 6♥, Super 8
TServ	**E:** Repairs, Towing
Other	**E:** Laundry/BarbSh/Mega Stop, Airlake AirField✈, Fairgrounds
76	**CR 2, 260th St, Elko, New Market**
FStop	**E:** Phillips 66
Other	**W:** Elko Speedway, **to** Sky Harbor Residential Airpark✈
(75)	**New Market Rest Area (SB)** **(RR, Phones, Pic, Vend, Playgr)**
69	**MN 19, Northfield, Little Chicago, Lonsdale, New Prague**
FStop	**W:** PTP/Big Steer Travel Center (Scales)
Gas	**E:** Gas Mart, Kwik Trip
Food	**W:** Rest/FastFood/Big Steer TC
Other	**E:** to St Olaf College, Carlton College **W:** Laundry/**RVDump**/Big Steer TC
(68)	**Heath Creek Rest Area (NB)** **(RR, Phones, Pic, Vend, Playgr)**
66	**CR 1, Dundas, to Millersburg, Montgomery**
59	**MN 21, Bus 35, to MN 3, Faribault, Le Center**
TStop	**E:** Truckers Inn #4/BP (Scales)
Gas	**E:** Mobil, Super America
Food	**E:** Rest/Truckers Inn, Burger King, Hardee's, Peppermill Grill, Pizza Hut
Lodg	**E:** AmericInn, Days Inn, Super 8
Other	**E:** Laundry/WiFi/Truckers Inn **W:** Faribault Muni Airport✈, **Roberds Lake Resort & Campground▲**
56	**MN 60, Faribault, Morristown**
FStop	**W:** Petro Wash
Gas	**E:** BP, Mobil
Food	**E:** Burger King, Hardee's, Perkins, Starbucks, Subway

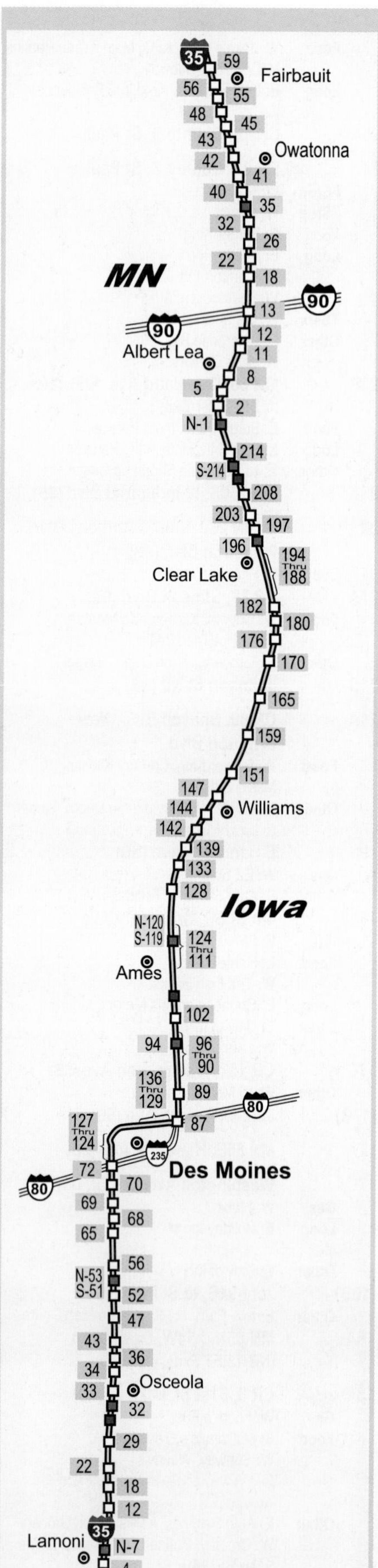

EXIT	MINNESOTA
Food	**W:** DQ, Happy Chef
Lodg	**E:** Galaxie Inn, Lyndale Motel **W:** Select Inn
TServ	**W:** Cummins
Med	**E:** + District One Hospital
Other	**E:** Auto Dealers, Cinema 6, Goodyear, Grocery, Farbo West Mall, Tires Plus+, **Walmart SC**, Auto Services & Repairs **W: Camp Faribo▲ , to Sakatah Lake State Park▲ , Camp Maiden Rock West▲**
55	**CR 48, Faribault (NB, no re-entry)**
Lodg	**E:** Budget Inn **(Acc to Ex #56 Serv)**
48	**CR 12, CR 23, Medford**
Gas	**E:** Anhorn's Gas & Tire
Food	**W:** McDonald's
Other	**W:** Outlet Mall
45	**CR 9, CR 23, Owatonna, Clinton Falls**
FStop	**W:** Kwik Trip #403
Food	**W:** FastFood/KwikTrip, Famous Dave's BBQ, Green Mill Rest, Timberlodge Steaks, Wendy's
Lodg	**W:** Comfort Inn, Holiday Inn
Other	**W:** Cabela Sporting Goods
43	**CR 34, 26th St, Airport Rd**
Other	**W:** Owatonna Muni Airport✈
42B	**US 14W, Waseca (SB)**
42A	**CR 45, Owatonna (SB)**
42AB	**US 14W, CR 45, Owatonna, Waseca, Mankato (NB)**
TStop	**W:** AmBest/Petrol Pumper #65/BP (Scales)
Gas	**E:** Sinclair **W:** Kwik Trip, Murphy
Food	**E:** Grace's Mex & Amer Rest, Kernel Rest **W:** FastFood/Petrol Pumper, Happy Chef, Culver's Family Rest, McDonald's, Perkins, Subway
Lodg	**E:** AmericInn, Budget Host Inn **W:** Best Budget Inn, Super 8
Other	**E:** Grocery, Auto Services, Auto Zone, Auto Dealers, **to Rice Lake State Park▲** **W:** Laundry/**LP**/Petrol Pumper, Auto Dealers, Auto Service, Dollar Tree, Lowe's, Radio Shack, **Walmart SC**,
41	**CR 25, Bridge St, Owatonna**
Gas	**E:** Holiday◈ **W:** Mobil◈
Food	**E:** Applebee's, Arby's, Burger King, KFC, Quiznos, Starbucks, Subway, Taco Bell
Lodg	**E:** Country Inn & Suites, AmericInn **W:** Microtel
Med	**E:** + Hospital
Other	**W:** Target
40	**US 218S, US 14E, Owatonna, to Rochester, Austin**
Gas	**E:** Shell
Food	**E:** Hardee's, Pizza Hut, Taco John
Lodg	**E:** Oakdale Motel
Med	**E:** + Hospital
Other	**E:** ATMs, Auto Dealers, Auto Service, Grocery, Tires, Walgreen's, **to Rice Lake State Park▲** **W: Riverview Campground▲**
(35)	**Straight River Rest Area (Both dir)** **(RR, Phone, Pic, Vend, Playgr)**
32	**CR 4, Owatonna, Hope**
Other	**E: Hope Oak Knoll Campground▲**

◈ = Regular Gas Stations with Diesel ▲ = RV Friendly Locations ♥ = Pet Friendly Locations
Red print shows large vehicle parking / access on site or nearby **Brown Print = Campgrounds / RV PARKS**

EXIT	MN / IA

26 — **MN 30, 5th Ave, Blooming Prairie, Ellendale, New Richland**
- TStop W: Roki's/BP (Scales)
- Gas E: Conoco
- Food E: Rest/Conoco; W: Rest/FastFood/Roki's

22 — **CR 35, Geneva, Hartland**

18 — **MN 251E, CR 31, Hollandale, Clarks Grove**
- FStop W: BP

(13B) — **Jct I-90W, Blue Earth, Sioux Falls**

(13A) — **Jct I-90E, Austin, La Crosse**

12 — **US 65, Albert Lea (SB) (Access to Ex #11 Serv)**

11 — **CR 46, Albert Lea, Hayward**
- TStop E: Travel Center of America #134/Shell (Scales); W: Love's Travel Stop #337 (Scales)
- Gas W: KwikTrip, Shell, Murphy
- Food E: TrailsRest/McDonald's/PHut/TA TC; W: CountryMarket/FastFood/FJ TP, Chesters/Godfathers/Wendy's/Loves TS, Burger King, China Buffet, Golden Corral, Green Mill Rest, Perkins, Pizza Hut, Starbucks, Subway, Wendy's
- Lodg E: Comfort Inn; W: Country Inn, Countryside Motel, Days Inn♥, Guest House Inn, Super 8
- TServ E: TA TC/Tires
- Med W: + Hospital
- Other E: Laundry/WiFi/RV Dump/LP/TA TC, to appr 7 mi: Albert Lea/Austin KOA▲, to Myre Big Island State Park▲; W: Laundry/WiFi/LP/FJ TP, WiFi/RVDump/Love's TS, ATMs, Auto Zone, Auto Dealers, Banks, Dollar Tree, Grocery, Home Depot, NAPA, Radio Shack, Walmart sc

8 — **I-35 Bus (NB), US 65, Albert Lea, Glenville (W to Access Ex #11 Serv)**
- Gas W: Freeborn Co Co-Op◊
- Food W: Hardee's, KFC
- Lodg W: Motel 65

5 — **CR 13, to Twin Lakes, Glenville**
- Other W: to Hickory Hills Campground▲

2 — **CR 5, CR 18, Twin Lakes**

(1) — **MN Welcome Center (NB)** Albert Lea Rest Area (RR, Phone, Picnic, Vend, Info)

CENTRAL TIME ZONE

⬆ MINNESOTA
⬇ IOWA

CENTRAL TIME ZONE

NOTE: MM 219: Minnesota State Line

NOTE: WiFi Access Available at Rest Areas

(214) — **CR 105, Northwood, Lake Mills** IA Welcome Center (SB) W: (RR, Ph, Pic, Vend, Info, RVDump)
- FStop W: Jo Stop/BP
- Food W: FastFood/BP
- Lodg W: Country Inn

EXIT	IOWA

(212) — **Weigh Station (Both dir)**

208 — **CR A38, Hanlontown, to Joice, Kensett**

203 — **IA 9, Hanlontown, to Manly, Forest City**
- FStop W: Food-n-Fuel/BPAmoco
- Med W: + Hospital
- Other W: Pilot Knob State Park▲

197 — **CR B20, Clear Lake**

(196) — **Parking Area (Both dir)**

194 — **US 18, Clear Lake, Mason City**
- FStop E: Horizon Truck & Travel Plaza/ Conoco (Scales)
- TStop W: Pilot Travel Center #407 (Scales)
- Gas W: Casey's, Shell◊
- Food E: Taco John's/Conoco; W: Subway/Denny's/Pilot TC, Burger King, McDonald's, Perkins, Wendy's/Shell, Rest/Best Western
- Lodg W: AmericInn, Best Western, Budget Inn, Microtel, Lake Country Inn
- Med E: + Mercy Medical Center
- Other E: Laundry/Horizon TP, Mason City Muni Airport✈, Interstate Motor Trucks; W: WiFi/Pilot TC, Meyer's Wrecker & Repair, to Clear Lake State Park▲, Oakwood RV Park▲, McIntosh Woods State Park▲

193 — **255th St, CR B35, Clear Lake, to Mason City**
- FStop E: I-35 BP
- Gas W: Phillips 66
- Food E: Happy Chef
- Lodg E: Heartland Inn
- Other W: Clear Lake State Park▲

190 — **US 18, IA 27, to Mason City**

188 — **CR B43, Rockwell, Burchinal**
- Other W: to Twin Oaks Campgrounds▲, Clear Lake State Park▲, Oakwood RV Park▲, McIntosh Woods State Park▲

182 — **CR B60, Swaledale, to Rockwell**

180 — **CR B65, 125th St, Thornton**
- Gas E: Cenex

176 — **CR C13, Sheffield, Belmond**

170 — **CR C25, Alexander**

165 — **IA 3, Hampton, Clarion (All Serv 7-10 mi E in Hampton)**
- TStop E: Dudley's Corner/Shell
- Food E: Rest/Dudley's Corner
- Med E: + Hospital
- Other E: to Beeds Lake State Park▲

(159) — **CR C47, Dows** IA Welcome Center (Both dir) W: (RR, Phone, Picnic, Vend, RVDump)
- Other W: Restored Railroad Depot, Historic Blacksmith Shop

151 — **CR R75, to C70, Woolstock**

147 — **CR D20, to US 20E**

144 — **220th St, CR R75, D25, CR 928, Williams**
- TStop E: Boondocks USA Truck Stop/66; W: Broadway Flying J Travel Plaza/ Conoco (Scales)

EXIT	IOWA

- Food E: Rest/Boondocks TS; W: Rest/Flying J TP
- Lodg E: Best Western/Boondocks TS
- TWash E: Boondocks TS
- TServ E: Boondocks TS/Tires
- Other E: Laundry/Boondocks TS; W: WiFi/BarbSh/LP/Flying J TP

142B — **US 20W, to Fort Dodge**

142A — **US 20E, to Waterloo**

139 — **CR D41, to Kamrar, Buckeye**

133 — **IA 175, Ellsworth, to Jewell**
- FStop W: Kum&Go
- Food W: Subway/K&G
- Other W: to Little Wall Lake Campground▲

128 — **CR D65, to Randall, Stanhope**
- Other W: to Little Wall Lake Campground▲

124 — **115th St, CR E15, Story City**
- FStop W: Kum & Go #124
- Gas W: Casey's, Texaco
- Food W: DQ, Godfather's Pizza, McDonald's, Happy Chef, Subway, Valhalla Rest
- Lodg W: Comfort Inn, Super 8, Viking Motor Inn
- Other W: ATM, Bank, Auto Services, VF Factory Outlet Stores, Whispering Oaks RV Park▲, Gookin RV Center

123 — **IA 221, CR E18, to Roland, McCallsburg**

(120) — **Story City Rest Area (NB)** (RR, Phone, Pic, Vend, RVDump)

(119) — **Story City Rest Area (SB)** (RR, Phone, Vend, RVDump)

116 — **CR E29, Ames, to Story**
- Other W: to Story Co Conservation Center

113 — **13th St, Ames**
- Gas W: BP◊, Kum & Go◊
- Food W: Arby's/BP, Burger King/Kum&Go, Starlite Village Rest, Rest/Best Western
- Lodg W: Best Western, Holiday Inn Express, Quality Inn
- Med W: + Mary Greeley Medical Center
- Other W: Towing, Zylstra Harley Davidson, IA State Univ

111B — **US 30W, to Ames**
- FStop W: Fuel Right, Kum & Go #227
- TStop W: Cyclone Truck Stop/Shell
- Food W: Rest/FastFood/Cyclone TS, Happy Chef, El Azteca Rest
- Lodg W: AmericInn, Comfort Inn, Hampton Inn, Heartland Inn, Super 8♥
- TWash W: Cyclone TS
- TServ W: Cyclone TS/Tires
- Other W: Laundry/Cyclone TS, to IA State Univ, Ames Muni Airport✈

111A — **US 30E, to Nevada**

(106) — **Weigh Station (Both dir)**

102 — **IA 210, Maxwell, Slater**

96 — **IA 87, NE 126th Ave, Elkhart, to Polk City**
- Other W: to Big Creek State Park, Saylorville Lake

(94) — **Ankeny Rest Area (Both dir)** (RR, Phones, Picnic, Vend)

92 — **1st St, IA 941, Ankeny**
- Gas W: BP, Casey's, Kum & Go, QT

◊ = Regular Gas Stations with Diesel ▲ = RV Friendly Locations ♥ = Pet Friendly Locations
Red print shows large vehicle parking / access on site or nearby Brown Print = Campgrounds / RV PARKS

EXIT IOWA

Food W: Applebee's, Arby's, Burger King, Cazador, Golden Corral, Happy Chef, KFC, Long John Silver, McDonald's, Pizza Hut, Subway, Taco John's, Village Inn, Rest/BW
Lodg W: Best Western♥, Days Inn♥, Super 8 Fairfield Inn, Heartland Inn
Other W: Auto Services, Goodyear, Grocery, Museum, NAPA, O'Reilly Parts, **Police Dept**, Staples, Tires Plus, John Deere Assembly Plant, **Cherry Glen Campground▲**, Saylorville Lake

90 IA 160W, Oralabor Rd, Ankeny, to Bondurant
Gas W: Casey's◈, Phillips 66
Food E: Chip's Diner
W: Amana Steaks & Chops, Burger King, Chili's, Culver's, IHOP, McDonald's, Panchero's Mexican Grill, Starbucks
Lodg E: AmericInn, Country Inn, Holiday Inn Express
W: Super 8
Other E: Ankeny Reg'l Airport✈
W: ATMs, Banks, Auto Dealers, Big O Tires, Grocery, Home Depot, Radio Shack, Springwood 9, Target, Walgreen's, **Walmart sc**

89 Corporate Woods Dr
Lodg W: Value Place

(87BA) Jct I-80W, to Council Bluffs, I-235W

(87A) Jct I-80E, to Davenport

NOTE: **I-35 runs with I-80 below to bypass Des Moines. Exit #'s follow I-80.**

136/85 US 69, NE 14th St, Des Moines
TStop S: QT #562 (Scales)
Gas N: BP, Phillips 66, Sinclair
S: Casey's, Citgo
Food N: Bonanza Steak House, Country Kitchen, Rest/Best Western
S: Burger King/QT, KFC, Long John Silver's, McDonald's, Pizza Hut
Lodg N: Best Western, Bavarian Inn, Red Roof Inn♥
S: 14th St Inn, Motel 6♥, Ramada
TServ N: GMC Trucks
S: Mack Trucks, Auto & Truck Service
Other N: **Sheriff Dept**
S: Advance Auto Parts, Kmart, Auto Services, Hitch Service, **Mid State RV Center**

135/84 IA 415, NW 2nd St, to Polk City
Gas S: QT
TServ N: Interstate Detroit Diesel
S: Freightliner Trucks
Med S: + Broadlawns Medical Center, + VA Medical Center
Other N: **IA State Hwy Patrol Post**
S: ATMs, Auto Service, Banks, Park Fair Mall

131/79 IA 28, Merle Hay Rd, NW 58th St, Des Moines, Urbandale
Gas N: Casey's, QT
S: BP◈, QT, Sinclair◈
Food N: North End Diner, Quiznos, Sonic
S: Arby's, Burger King, Denny's, KFC, Famous Dave's BBQ, Ground Round, McDonald's, Perkins, Texas Cattle Co, Taco John's, Village Inn
Lodg N: Best Inn, Best Western♥, Ramada
S: Comfort Inn♥, Days Inn, Holiday Inn, Quality Inn, Sheraton, Super 8
Med S: + VA Medical Center
Other N: Auto Dealer, Goodyear, Grocery
S: Auto Dealers, Firestone, Goodyear, Grocery, Walgreen's, Merle Hay Mall,
Other S: ATMs, Banks, Best Buy, Enterprise RAC, Office Depot, Nova 10 Cinemas,

129/77 NW 86th St, Urbandale
Gas N: Kum & Go
S: BP, Phillips 66
Food N: Burger King, McDonald's, Village Inn
S: Arby's, Culver's, Embers, Pizza
Lodg N: Birchwood Creek Inn, Stoney Creek Inn
S: Microtel♥

127/75 IA 141, Urbandale, Grimes, Perry
FStop N: Swift Stop/66
Gas N: BP
Food N: Subway/P66, Blimpie/BP
Other N: Vehicle Services
S: Target

126/74 Douglas Ave, Urbandale
TStop N: Pilot Travel Center #373 (Scales)
Gas S: Kum & Go◈, QT
Food N: Grandma Max's Rest/Pilot TC
S: Blimpie, Dragon House, Happy Chef
Lodg S: Days Inn, Econo Lodge
TWash N: Pilot TC
TServ N: Pilot TC/Tires, Bar B Truck Repair
Other N: Laundry/WiFi/**RVDump**/Pilot TC

125/73 US 6, Hickman Rd, Clive
TStop N: Love's Travel Stop #411 (Scales)
Food N: Denny's/Subway/Love's TS
S: IA Machine Shed Rest
Lodg S: Comfort Suites, Clarion, Sleep Inn
Other N: Laundry/WiFi/**LP/RVDump**/Love's TS
S: Auto Dealers, Living History Farms, Metro Ice Sports Arena, Tire & Auto Center, Auto Services

124/72C University Ave, W Des Moines
FStop N: Kum & Go #124
Gas N: BP, QT
S: Phillips 66
Food N: Biaggi's Italian Rest, Burger King, **Cracker Barrel**, Mustard's Rest
S: Applebee's, Bakers Square, Burger King, Chili's, Damon's, Don Pablo's, KFC, McDonald's, Outback Steakhouse, Ocean Grill, Romano's Macaroni Grill
Lodg N: Baymont Inn, Best Western, Country Inn, La Quinta Inn♥
S: Courtyard, Chase Suites, Fairfield Inn, Heartland Inn, Holiday Inn, Inn at University, Wildwood Lodge
Med S: + Mercy West Health Center, + Iowa Clinic
Other S: ATMs, Banks, Barnes & Noble, Best Buy, Carmike Cinema, Grocery, Lowe's, Valley West Mall

(72B) Jct I-80W

(72A) Jct I-235E, to Des Moines

NOTE: **I-35 & I-80 above runs together around Des Moines. Exit #'s follow I-80. I-35 SB continues below.**

70 Mills Civic Pkwy, W Des Moines
Gas E: Kum & Go, HyVee
Food E: McDonald's
Lodg E: Residence Inn
W: Holiday Inn
Other E: HyVee, Walgreen's
W: Best Buy, Jordan Creek Town Center, PetCo♥, Super Target, **Walmart sc**

69AB Grand Ave, W Des Moines
Other E: **to Walnut Woods State Park▲**

68 IA 5E, Des Moines Airport

65 CR G14, Cumming, to Norwalk
Other W: to John Wayne Birthplace

56 IA 92, Prole, to Indianola, Winterset
FStop W: Bussanmas Service/Shamrock, Kum & Go #56/Shell
Food W: Café, FastFood/K&G
TServ W: Bussanmas Service
Other W: Museum, Towing/Bussanmas

(53) Parking Area (NB)

52 CR G50, St Mary's, St Charles
Other W: to John Wayne Birthplace, Madison Co Museum, Covered Bridges of Madison Co

(51) Parking Area (SB)

47 CR G64, New Virginia, Truro

43 CR G76, IA 207, New Virginia
Gas E: Kum & Go◈
W: Total

36 IA 152, to US 69

34 Clay St, Osceola
Gas W: Kum & Go, Total
Other W: Terribles Lakeside **Casino Resort & Campground▲**

33 US 34, Osceola, Creston
FStop E: Osceola Travel Plaza/BP
Gas E: Casey's◈, Kum & Go
Food E: Family Table, Hardee's, McDonald's, Pizza Hut, Subway
W: KFC/Taco Bell
Lodg E: Best Western, Days Inn, Super 8
W: AmericInn, Blue Haven Motel
Med E: + Hospital
Other E: **IA State Hwy Patrol Post**, Auto Dealer, Auto Services, O'Reilly Auto Parts, Pamida Shopping, Grocery, Tires

(32) Osceola Rest Area (Both dir) (RR, Phones, Picnic, RVDump)

(31) Weigh Station (Both dir)

29 CR H45, Elk St, Osceola

22 CR J14, to US 69, Van Wert

18 CR J20, Van Wert, to Grand River, Garden Grove

12 IA 2, Decatur City, to Leon, Kellerton, Mount Ayr
TStop E: Country Corner/Shell
Gas E: Phillips 66◈
Food E: Rest/Country Corner, 50's Diner
Lodg E: to Little River Motel
Med E: + Hospital
Other E: LP/CC

(7) IA Welcome Center (NB) (RR, Phone, Picnic, Vend, RVDump)

4 US 69, Davis City, to Lamoni
Gas W: to Casey's, Kum&Go/BP

◈= Regular Gas Stations with Diesel ▲ = RV Friendly Locations ♥= Pet Friendly Locations
Red print shows large vehicle parking / access on site or nearby Brown Print = Campgrounds / RV PARKS

Food W: to Emu's Grill, Fastimes Rest, Outpost Café, Pizza Shack, Subway
Lodg W: Super 8, Chief Lamoni Motel
Other E: to Nine Eagles State Park▲
W: Auto Services, Banks,Cinema, Grocery

NOTE: WiFi Access Available at Rest Areas

CENTRAL TIME ZONE

IOWA
MISSOURI

CENTRAL TIME ZONE

NOTE: MM 214: Iowa State Line

114 to US 69, to Lamoni. IA
FStop W: Conoco State Line
Food W: FastFood/Conoco
Other W: RVDump/Walter Bros

(110) Weigh Station (Both dir)

106 MO N, East St N, Eagleville, Blythedale
TStop E: Eagleville Travel Express/66 (Scales)
W: Eagleville Texaco
Gas E: Conoco
Food E: Dinner Bell/Eagleville TE
W: Square Meal Café
Lodg E: Eagles Landing Motel/Eagleville TE
Tires W: Hutton Tire Center
TServ E: Eagleville TE/P66/Tires
Other E: Laundry/WiFi/Eagleville TE
W: I-35 RV Campground▲, to Eagle Ridge RV Park▲

99 CR A, Ridgeway
Other W: to Eagle Ridge RV Park▲

93 US 69 Spur, Bethany
Food W: Big Boys BBQ, Dos Chiquita's
Lodg W: Sunset Motel
Other E: Bethany Memorial Airport✈
W: Hillcrest Service Station, Bethany Tire & Auto

92 US 136, Miller St, Bethany, to Princeton
FStop E: Unlimited Convenience/Conoco
Gas W: Casey's, Kum & Go◈, Kwik Zone
Food W: Burger King, DQ, McDonald's, Pizza Hut, KFC/Taco Bell, Wendy's/K&G
Lodg W: Best Western♥, Family Budget Inn, Super 8
Med W: + Harrison Co Comm Hospital
Other W: Auto Dealer, Auto Repairs, ATMs, Banks, Grocery, Laundromat, Walmart sc

88 MO 13, to US 69, Bethany, to Gallatin (W 3mi Acc to Ex #92 Serv)

84 CR H, CR AA, to Gilman City
Other E: to appr 20 mi Crowder State Park▲

(81) Rest Area (Both dir)
(RR, Phones, Vend, Picnic)

80 SR B, SR N, Coffey

78 SR C, Coffey, to Pattonsburg

72 SR DD

68 US 69, Altamont, to Pattonsburg

64 MO 6, to US 69, Altamont, to Gallatin, Weatherby, Maysville
Other W: to appr 11mi Pony Express RV Park & Campground▲

61 US 69, to US 6, Winston, to Altamont, Jamesport
TStop E: Winston Truck Stop/Shell
Food E: Rest/Winston TS

54 US 36, Bus 35, to US 69, Cameron
FStop E: Country Corner AmPride/Cenex
TStop E: PTP/Jones Travel Mart/BP
Gas E: Shell◈
W: Phillips 66, Valero
Food E: Rest/Jones TM, Wendy's/Shell
W: Burger King, DQ, Domino's Pizza, Hardee's, KFC/Taco Bell, McDonald's, Ma & Pa's Kettle Diner, Sonic, Subway
Lodg E: Best Western♥, Crossroads Inn & RV Park▲, Comfort Inn♥
W: Days Inn, Econo Lodge♥, Holiday Inn Express, Super 8
TWash E: Jones TM
Other E: Laundry/RVDump/Jones TM
W: ATMs, Auto Services, Advance Auto Parts, Dollar General, Grocery, Kwik Lube & Car Wash, O'Reilly Auto Parts, Radio Shack, Walmart sc, MO Correction Facility, to appr 14mi Pony Express RV Park & Campground▲

52 CR BB, Lp 35, Cameron (NB)
(Gas & Food W to Bus 35, Acc to Ex #54)
Med E: + Cameron Regional Medical Center
Other W: to Cameron Memorial Airport✈

48 US 69, Cameron
Gas W: R&B Whistle Stop/Shamrock
Other E: to Wallace State Park▲
W: Down Under Camp Resort▲

40 MO 116, Lathrop, Polo, Plattsburg
FStop E: Trex Mart/66
Food E: Country Café/66
Tires E: Trex Mart/66

(35) Rest Area (NB)
(RR, Phones, Vend, Picnic)

(34) Rest Area (SB)
(RR, Phones, Vend, Picnic)

33 CR PP, Lathrop, to Lawson, Holt
FStop W: D&S Petroleum/Conoco, Phillips 66
Food W: Holt Cafe
Other E: JJ Campground▲

26 MO 92, 6th St Kearney, to Excelsior Springs
TStop W: Kearney Truck Plaza/Conoco (Scales), Pilot Travel Center #252 (Scales)
Gas E: Casey's, Conoco, P66◈, Shell◈
Food E: Pizza Hut, McDonald's, Sonic
W: Rest/Kearney TP, TacoBell/Pilot TC, Arby's, Burger King, Hardee's, Hunan Garden, Subway
Lodg E: Comfort Inn, Super 8
W: Country Hearth Inn♥, Econo Lodge
TServ W: Kearney TP/Tires
Other E: CVS, Grocery, Interstate Auto & Towing Service, Police Dept, Clay Co Reg'l Airport✈, to Watkins Mill State Park▲
W: Laundry/Kearney TP, Laundry/Love's TP, Family Dollar, Grocery

(23) Weigh Station (NB)

20 US 69, MO 33, Liberty, Excelsior Springs
Med E: + Liberty Hospital

17 MO 291, CR A, to I-435, Liberty
Gas W: Phillips 66◈
Food W: McDonald's, Subway
Med E: + Liberty Hospital
Other E: Access to Exit #16 Services
W: to Kansas City Int'l Airport✈

16 MO 152, W Kansas St, NE Barry Rd, Kansas City, Liberty
Gas E: BP, Conoco◈, Shell
W: Phillips 66
Food E: Arby's, Carlito's Mex Food, CiCi's Pizza, Fuji Japanese Steakhouse, KFC, Long John Silver, Pizza Hut, Perkins, Ponderosa, Starbucks, Subwy, Taco Bell, Texas Roadhouse, Village Inn, Wendy's
W: Applebee's, Bob Evans, Burger King, Back Yard Burgers, Chili's, Country Kitchen Cracker Barrel, Golden Corral, KFC, Longhorn Steakhouse, McDonald's, Panda Express, Smokestack BBQ, Steak n Shake, Subway, Taco Bell, Waffle House
Lodg E: Days Inn♥, Super 8♥
W: Comfort Suites, Fairfield Inn, Hampton Inn, Holiday Inn Express
Med E: + Liberty Clinic
Other E: ATMs, Banks, Auto Repairs, Auto Dealer, Enterprise RAC, Firestone, Grocery Lowe's, Sears Grand, Walgreen's, Museum Miller's Kampark▲, Liberty RV
W: ATM, Auto Services, Bank, Best Buy, Home Depot, NAPA, Office Depot, Radio Shack, Super Target, Walmart sc

14 US 69 (SB, Left exit), Pleasant Valley Rd, Liberty
TStop W: QT #179 (Scales) (NB Acc via Ex #13)
Gas E: Conoco◈, Sinclair
Food W: FastFood/QT, McDonald's
AServ E: Auto Services, Frank's Auto & Tow, Budget Auto Repair
Other E: I-35 RV Center, KC Ford Motor Plant
W: Civic Center, Police Dept

13 US 69, to Liberty Dr, Pleasant Valley Rd, Liberty (NB)
(Access to Ex #14 Services)

(12AB) Jct I-435, St. Louis, St Joseph

11 US 69N, Vivion Rd
Gas E: Shell
W: QT
Food E: McDonald's
W: Big Burger, Church's Chicken, Smoke Shack, Sonic, Stroud's Rest, Subway
Other W: to Antioch Shopping Center

10 N Brighton Ave, KC (NB)
(Access to Ex #11 Serv US 69N)

9 MO 269, Chouteau Trafficway
Gas E: Phillips 66, Sinclair
W: Amoco
Food E: IHOP, Outback Steakhouse, Subway
W: Wendy's
Other E: Festival Foods, Radio Shack, Target, to Harrah's Casino/Hotel/Restaurants
W: to Antioch Shopping Center

8C MO 1, NE Antioch Rd
Gas E: 7-11, Sinclair
W: Phillips 66
Food E: Domino's Pizza
W: Jumpin Catfish, Waffle House
Lodg E: Best Western, Inn Towne Lodge
Other W: Walgreen's, to Antioch Shopping Center

EXIT		MISSOURI
	NOTE:	**I-35 & I-29 below run together for next 6 exits, Exit #'s follow I-29SB.**
(8B)		**Jct I-29N, US 71N, to KCI Airport, St Joseph**
8A		**NE Parvin Rd, Ks City**
	Gas	**E:** Shell
	Lodg	**W:** Super Inn Motel
6AB		**MO 210, Armour Rd, N Ks City**
	Gas	**E:** Phillips 66◈ **W:** QT, Phillips 66, Shell
	Food	**E:** Arby's, Big Boy's, Burger King, Captain D's, Denny's, McDonald's **W:** Long John Silver, Pizza Hut, Taco Bell, Wendy's, Rest/American Inn
	Lodg	**E:** Baymont Inn, Days Inn♥ **W:** American 45 Inn, Country Hearth Inn, Quality Inn
	Med	**E:** + North KC Hospital
	Other	**E:** ATMs, Banks, **Harrah's Casino** **W:** Auto Services, ATMs, Banks, Conv Center, US Post Office, **Police Dept**
5B		**16th Ave (NB)**
5A		**Levee Rd, Bedford St**
4B		**Front St, Ks City (NB)**
	Other	**E:** Isle of Capri Casino & Rest
4A		**US 24, Independence Ave (SB)**
	Lodg	**E:** Capri Motel, Royale Inn Motel
	Other	**E:** Auto Services, Grocery
(3)		**Jct I-70W, to Topeka**
	NOTE:	**I-35 & I-29 above run together for next 6 exits, Exit #'s follow I-29NB.**
(2H)		**Jct I-70E**
2F		**Oak St, Independence Ave, W 5th St, Kansas City (WB)**
	Gas	**W:** Conoco
	Other	**W:** Restaurants, Auto Services
2D		**Delaware St, Downtown**
2C		**US 169N, Broadway Blvd, Downtown Kansas City**
2Y		**W 6th St, US 169N, Broadway (NB)**
2X		**US 24W, US 169S, I-70/40W (NB, LEFT Exit)**
2W		**W 12th St, Kemper Arena, Conv Center, Downtown KC**
2V		**14th St, Downtown (NB)**
(2U)		**Jct I-70E, to St Louis (SB, Left exit) Broadway, I-670, Topeka (NB)**
1D		**W 20th St (SB)**
1C		**W 27th St, SW Blvd, W Pennway (NB exit, SB reaccess)**
1B		**27th St, Penn Valley Dr, Broadway St (SB, LEFT exit)**
	Lodg	**E:** Best Western♥
	Med	**E:** + Trinity Lutheran Hospital
1A		**SW Trafficway (SB, LEFT exit)**

CENTRAL TIME ZONE

⬆ MISSOURI

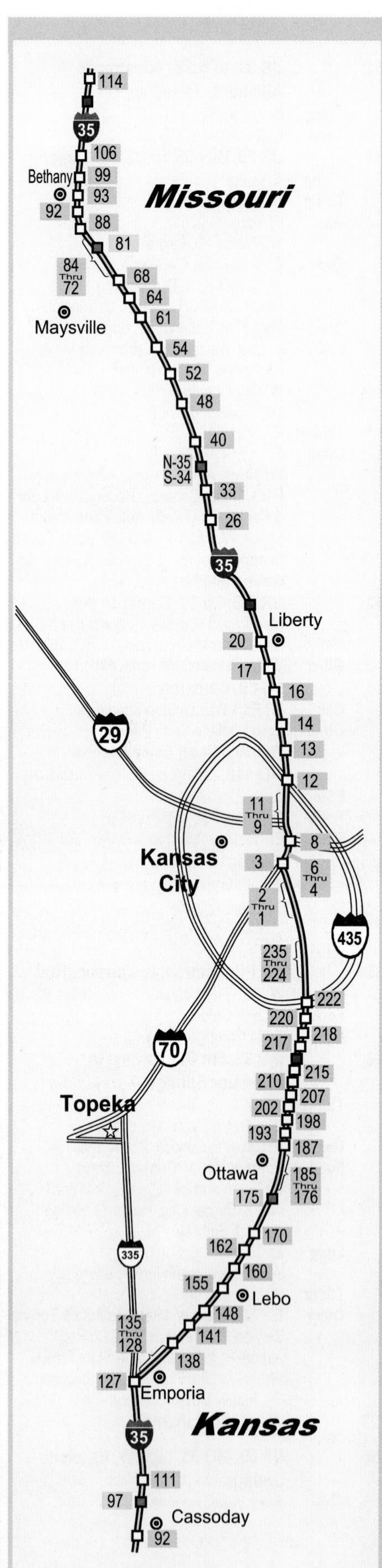

EXIT		KANSAS

⬇ KANSAS

	NOTE:	**MM 235: Missouri State Line**
235		**Eaton St, Cambridge Circle**
	Gas	**E:** QT
234		**US 169, 7th St Trafficway, Ks City, Rainbow Blvd (SB)**
	Gas	**E:** Phillips 66, QT, Shell
	Food	**E:** Applebee's, Arby's, Burger King, McDonald's, Rosedale BBQ, Sol Azteca Mexican Grill, Wendy's, Rest/BW
	Lodg	**E:** Best Western, Days Inn
	Med	**E:** + Univ of KS Medical Center
234A		**US 169S, Rainbow Blvd (NB)**
234B		**US 169N, 7th St Trafficway (NB)**
233A		**Mission Rd, SW Blvd**
	Food	**E:** Dagwood's Café, OK Joe's BBQ
	Lodg	**E:** Days Inn, Redwood Inn
	Other	**E:** Auto Repair, IGA
233B		**37th Ave, SW Blvd (SB)**
232B		**US 69N, 18th St Expy, Kansas City**
	Gas	**E:** QT, Phillips 66
	Food	**E:** McDonald's
	Lodg	**W:** Clark Motel
232A		**Lamar Ave, S 24th St**
	Gas	**E:** QT
(231A)		**Jct I-635N (fr NB, LEFT exit)**
231B		**US 69, Metcalf Ave (SB)**
230		**Antioch Rd, Mission**
	Gas	**W:** QT
	Food	**E:** Bob Evans, Chili's, Quiznos **W:** Sonic
	Other	**E:** Home Depot, Grocery, Cinemark 20
229		**Johnson Dr, Shawnee**
	Gas	**E:** Shell, Phillips 66 **W:** Phillips 66◈
	Food	**E:** Bob Evans, Chili's, Papa John's Pizza **W:** Café on Merriam
	Other	**E:** ATMs, Auto Services, Home Depot, PetSmart♥, Walgreen's **W:** Auto Services, **Walnut Grove Campground▲**
228B		**US 56E, US 69N, W 63rd St, Shawnee Mission Pkwy**
	Gas	**E:** QT, Shell
	Food	**E:** Checkers, Denny's, IHOP, Pizza Hut, Shoney's, Taco Bell, Winstead's **W:** Denny's, Long John Silver, Perkins. Steak 'N Shake
	Lodg	**E:** Comfort Inn, Drury Inn, Homestead Suites
	Other	**E:** Kmart, Pharmacy, **Police Dept**
228A		**67th St, Mission**
	Gas	**W:** Phillips 66
	Food	**E:** Burger King, Denny's
	Lodg	**E:** Comfort Inn, Fairfield Inn, Quality Inn
	Other	**E:** Kmart
227		**75th St, Overland Park**
	Gas	**E:** Circle K, Conoco, QT **W:** 7-11, QT◈, Shell
	Food	**E:** McDonald's, Mexican Rest, Perkins **W:** Backyard Burgers, Big Burger, KC BBQ, Ryan's Grill, Sonic, Subway, Sakura Japanese Rest, Taco Bell, Wendy's
	Lodg	**E:** Extended Stay America, Wellesley Inn **W:** Hampton Inn
	Med	**E:** + Shawnee Mission Medical Center

◈= Regular Gas Stations with Diesel ▲ = RV Friendly Locations ♥= Pet Friendly Loca-
Red print shows large vehicle parking / access on site or nearby **Brown Print = Campgrounds / RV PARKS**

EXIT	KANSAS
Other	**E:** Walmart **W:** Cinema III, Jiffy Lube
225B	**US 69, Overland Pkwy (SB)**
225A	**87th St, Overland Pkwy**
Gas	**E:** Amoco **W:** Phillips 66, BP, Shell
Food	**E:** Green Mill, Shoney's, Wendy's **W:** Arby's, DQ, El Caribe Mexican Rest, Holyland Café, Jalapenos Mex, KFC, Subway, Taco Bell, Zarda BBQ
Lodg	**E:** Holiday Inn, Microtel
Other	**E:** Grocery, Museum **W:** ATMs, Banks, Auto Services, Grocery, NTB, Museum, **Police Dept**
224	**95th St, Lenexa**
Gas	**E:** Phillips 66, Shell, Sam's **W:** Conoco, Costco
Food	**E:** Applebee's, Burger King, China Buffet, Chipolte Mexican Grill, Denny's, Einstein Bros, McDonald's, MiMi's Cafe, Nature's Table, On the Border, Outback Steakhouse, Rainforest Cafe, Ruby Tuesday, Santa Fe Café, Shogun, TGI Friday, Taco Bell, Winstead's **W:** KC Burgers, LC's BBQ, Taboulay Café
Lodg	**E:** Days Inn, Extended Stay, Holiday Inn, La Quinta Inn♥, Motel 6♥, Radisson, Super 8
Med	**E:** + Overland Park Reg'l Med Center
Other	**E:** ATMs, AMC 6, Banks, Advance Auto Parts, Best Buy, Enterprise, Firestone, Grocery, Oak Park Mall, Meineke, Jiffy Lube, Sam's Club **W:** Auto Services, Costco
(222B)	**Jct I-435W**
(222A)	**Jct I-435E**
220	**119th St, Olathe**
Gas	**E:** Conoco, Phillips 66, Shell
Food	**E:** Burger King, Carrabba's, China Café, Chipolte Mexican Grill, Cracker Barrel, IHOP, Joe's Crab Shack, Ks Machine Shed Rest, Long John Silver, McDonald's, Olive Garden, Rio Bravo, Ruby Tuesday, Steak n Shake, Souper Salad, Subway, Tres Hombres, Wendy's
Lodg	**E:** Comfort Suites, Fairfield Inn, Hampton Inn, Residence Inn, Value Place
TServ	**E:** Mid West Kenworth
Other	**E:** AMC 30, ATMs, Auto Dealers, Banks, Best Buy, Barnes & Noble, Goodyear, Home Depot, PetSmart♥, Radio Shack, Super Target, U-Haul, Vet♥ **W:** Bass Pro Shop
218	**135th St, Santa Fe St, to US 169, to KS 150, Olathe**
Gas	**E:** Amoco, Shell◈ **W:** BP, Phillips 66, QT
Food	**E:** Applebee's, Back Yard Burgers, Burger King, Guacamole Grill, Hardee's, Perkins, McDonald's, Shoney's, Taco Bell **W:** Denny's, Gate's BBQ, Good Fortune Chinese, Ponderosa, Taco Bell, Waffle House, Wendy's
Lodg	**W:** Days Inn, Villager Lodge
Other	**E:** ATMs, Auto Repairs, Banks, Big Lots, Dollar General, Enterprise RAC, Firestone, FedEx Office, Osco, Office Depot, Animal Hospital♥, Petland♥, **Walmart sc** **W:** Auto Dealers, Auto Services, Museum, Grocery, **Sheriff Dept**

EXIT	KANSAS
217	**Old Hwy 56 (SB exit only, NB reentry), (SB reaccess Ex #215) (Acc #215 Serv)**
215	**151st St, US 169, KS 7, Olathe, to Paola, Spring Hill**
TStop	**W:** Star Fuel Center #101/Shell (Scales)
Gas	**E:** Citgo, Phillips 66, QT, Shell **W:** Presto
Food	**E:** Culver's, DQ, Jumpin Catfish, Sonic, McDonald's, Outback Steaks, **W:** FastFood/Star FC, Applebee's, Java Jive, Burger King, Blimpie, Chili's, Red Lobster, Country Kitchen, McDonald's, Taco Bell, Waffle House, Wendy's
Lodg	**W:** Econo Lodge, Holiday Inn, Microtel, Sleep Inn
Med	**W:** + Olathe Medical Center
Other	**E:** Auto Repairs, Grocery, Home Depot, Target, Transmissions, Johnson Co Exec Airport✈, **Happy Camper RV** **W:** ATMs, Auto Services, Banks, Great Mall of the Great Plains, Jungle Jim's Playland of KS, **Police Dept**
(213)	**Weigh Station (Both dir)**
210	**US 56W, W 175th St, Gardner**
Gas	**W:** Phillips 66◈
Food	**W:** Arby's, kFC, McDonald's, Subway, Taco Bell, Waffle House
Lodg	**W:** Super 8
Other	**W: Walmart sc**, Towing, New Century Air Center and Business Park, Naval Air Museum
207	**Gardner Rd, Gardner**
Gas	**W:** Shell◈
Other	**E: Olathe Ford RV Center** **W:** to Gardner Muni Airport✈,
202	**Sunflower Rd, Edgerton**
Other	**W:** Holton Trailer Sales & Service
198	**KS 33, Poplar St, Wellsville**
Gas	**W:** Conoco
193	**Tennessee Rd, Ottawa, Wellsville**
Other	**W:** Antiques & More
187	**KS 68, E Logan, Ottawa, Peoria**
FStop	**W:** Zarco P66◈
Food	**W:** Sub Shop/P66
Other	**E:** Cottonwood Animal Hospital♥, **W:** Auto Dealer, Carwash/P66, Crist Auto & **RV** Sales, Franklin Co Visitor Center
185	**15th St, Marshall Rd, Ottawa (Gas/Food/Lodging 2mi W in Ottawa)**
183	**US 59, S Princeton St, Ottawa, to Lawrence, Garnett**
FStop	**W:** Jump Start #12/66
Gas	**W:** BP, Conoco◈, Murphy, Ottawa Mini Mart◈, Valero◈
Food	**W:** Applebee's, Burger King, China Palace, Country Kitchen, KFC, Long John Silver, McDonald's, Sirloin Stockade, Taco Bell, Wendy's
Lodg	**W:** Best Western♥, Comfort Inn, Days Inn♥, Econo Lodge♥, Knights Inn, Super 8, Travelodge♥,
Med	**W:** + Ransom Memorial Hospital
Other	**E:** to Ottawa Muni Airport✈, **W:** Advance Auto Parts, Auto Dealers, Auto Services, Auto Zone, Banks, Country Mart Grocery, Dollar General, Dollar Tree, Walgreen's, **Walmart sc**
182AB	**US 50, Eisenhower Rd, Ottawa**

EXIT	KANSAS
176	**Idaho Rd, Williamsburg, Homewood**
Other	**W: Homewood RV Park & Campground▲**
(175)	**Rest Area (Both dir) (RR, Ph, Vend, Pic, Pet, Wifi, RVDump)**
170	**KS 273, Dane Ave, John Brown Rd, Williamsburg, Pomona**
Gas	**W:** Sinclair◈
Food	**W:** Café/Sinclair
162	**KS 31S, Waverly**
160	**KS 31N, Melvern**
155	**US 75, Lebo, Beto Junction**
TStop	**E:** Travel Center of America #70 /Shell (Scales), BP/Amoco Travel Center
Food	**E:** CountryPride/Wendy's/TA TC, Subway/BPAmoco TC
Lodg	**E:** Wyatt Earp Inn
TServ	**E:** TA TC/Tires
Other	**E:** Laundry/WiFi/**RVDump**/TA TC, Laundry/WiFi/BPAmoco TC
148	**KS 131, Fauna Rd, Lebo**
FStop	**E:** S & S Lebo Plaza/Cenex
Gas	**E:** Casey's
Food	**E:** FastFood/S&S, Lebo Grill, Wendy's
Lodg	**E:** Universal Inn
Other	**W:** to Melvern Lake
141	**KS 130, Neosho Rapids, Hartford**
138	**CR U, Emporia**
135	**CR R1, Emporia, Thorndale**
Other	**W: Dieker Trailer Sales & Service/ Overnite Camping▲**
133	**US 50, 6th Ave, Emporia**
Gas	**E:** Casey's
Food	**E:** McDonald's, Pizza Hut
Lodg	**E:** Budget Host Inn
131	**Burlingame Rd, Emporia**
Gas	**E:** Conoco◈, Phillips 66
Food	**E:** DQ, Hardee's, Mr Good Cents Subs
Other	**E:** Auto & Tire Service, Grocery
130	**KS 99, Merchant St**
Gas	**E:** Phillips 66◈
Food	**E:** Bobby D's BBQ, Domino's Pizza, Subway
Med	**E:** + to Newman Regional Hospital
128	**Industrial Rd, Emporia**
TStop	**W:** Prairie Port Plaza/66 (Scales)
Gas	**E:** Conoco, Finish Line **W:** Shell
Food	**E:** Bruff's, Burger King, Coburn's Family Rest, Noah's, Pizza Hut, Subway **W:** Applebee's, Golden Corral, KFC, McDonald's, Montana Mike's, Pizza Hut, Starbucks, Taco Bell, Village Inn, Wendy's/P66
Lodg	**E:** Econo Lodge♥, GuestHouse Int'l, Motel 6♥, **W:** Candlewood Suites♥, Comfort Inn♥, Fairfield Inn, Holiday Inn Express♥
Med	**E:** + to Newman Regional Hospital
Other	**E:** ATMs, Aldi Grocery, Auto Services, Cinema 8, Family Dollar, Flinthills Mall, Goodyear, Walgreen's, **W:** Radio Shack, Staples, UPS Store, Verizon, **Walmart sc**
127C	**Jct I-35S, I-335, Ks Turnpike, to Topeka, Wichita (NB) US 50W, KS 57N, Newton (SB)**

◈= Regular Gas Stations with Diesel ▲ = RV Friendly Locations ♥= Pet Friendly Locations
Red print shows large vehicle parking / access on site or nearby **Brown Print = Campgrounds / RV PARKS**

EXIT — KANSAS

127B — US 50E, US 57S, Emporia
(NB exit, SB entr)

127A — US 50W, KS 57N, Newton
(SB, LEFT exit / LAST FREE Exit)
- **TStop** E: Flying J Travel Plaza #5083/Conoco (Scales), S & S #13/P66 (Scales)
- **Gas** E: Conoco◈, Shell◈
- **Food** E: Rest/FastFood/FJ TP, FastFood/SS, Arby's, Carlos O'Kelly's, Chester's Fried Chicken, China Buffet, Hardee's, Papa Johns Pizza, Wagon Wheel Grill,
- **Lodg** E: Americas Best Value Inn, Best Western, Days Inn♥, Rodeway Inn♥, Super 8♥
- **Other** E: Laundry/WiFi/RVDump/LP/FJ TP, Laundry/LP/S&S , Auto & Truck Services, Auto Dealers, Carwash/Shell, Grocery, NAPA, Tires4Less, Vet Hospital♥,
  W: Emporia RV Park & Campground▲ ,

NOTE: I -35 & Ks Tpk run together below. Exit #'s 19-92 follow KS Tpk.

(127) — TOLL Plaza, Ks Turnpike

(111) — Cattle Pens

(97) — Matfield Green Service Area
(LEFT Exit, Both dir)
- **FStop** Phillips 66 #6368
- **Food** McDonald's

92 — KS 177, Cassoday, Salina
- **TStop** E: Salina W TS, West Crawford 247
- **Gas** E: Cassoday Country Store

76 — US 77, El Dorado North
(Gas/Food/Lodg approx 4mi E)
- **Other** E: to El Dorado State Park▲

71 — KS 254, Central Ave, to KS 176
- **Gas** E: Conoco◈, Phillips 66◈
- **Food** E: Arby's, Braum's, Burger King, Chinese Chef, Golden Corral, KFC, Long John Silver, Pizza Hut, McDonald's, Prime Cut Steakhouse, Sonic, Subway, Taco Tico
- **Lodg** E: Best Western, El Dorado Motel, Holiday Inn Express, Sunset Inn, Super 8
- **Med** E: + Hospital
- **Other** E: ATMs, Banks, Auto & Tire Services, Cinema, Dollar General, Grocery, Museum, O'Reilly Auto Parts, Radio Shack, **Walmart SC, Deer Grove RV Park▲**

(65) — Towanda Service Area
(LEFT Exit, Both dir)
- **FStop** Phillips 66 #6369
- **Food** McDonald's

57 — 21st St, Andover Rd, Andover

53 — KS 96, Wichita
- **Gas** W: Conoco
- **Food** W: McDonald's, Two Bros BBQ, Subway, Wendy's/Conoco
- **Lodg** W: Courtyard, Cresthill Suites
- **Other** W: Raytheon/Beech Factory/Airport✈, Cinema, Lowe's, **Walmart sc**

50 — US 54, US 400, Kellogg Ave
- **Gas** E: Conoco◈
  W: Coastal
- **Food** E: Burger King, IHOP, McDonald's, Pizza Hut, Sonic, Subway
  W: Arby's, Denny's, Green Mill, Hooters, KFC, McDonald's, Red Lobster, Shoney's, Souper Salad, Steak & Ale, Spangles, Taco Bell
- **Lodg** E: Econo Lodge, Motel 6♥

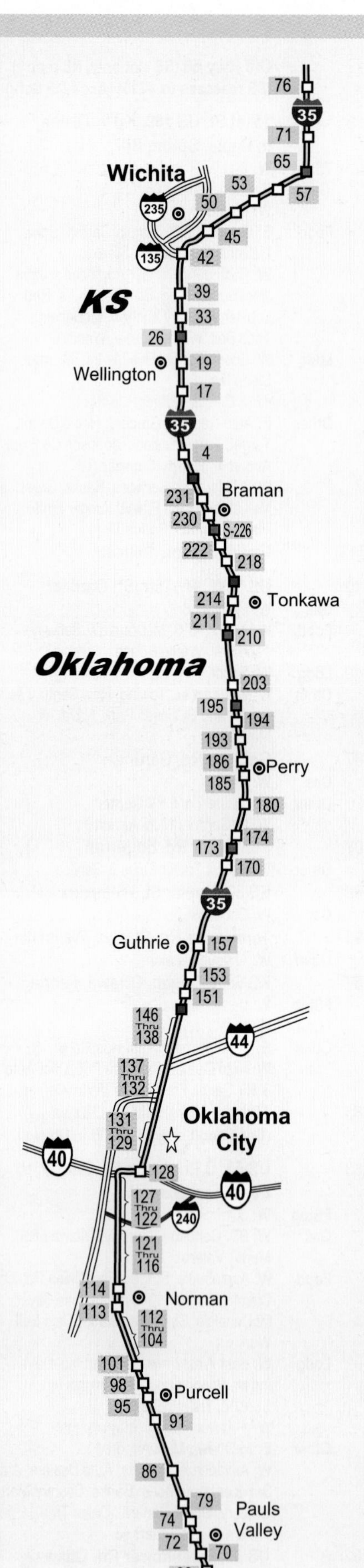

EXIT — KS / OK

- **Lodg** W: Best Western, Budget Inn, Comfort Inn, Days Inn, Fairfield Inn, Hampton Inn, Marriott, Residence Inn, Super 8, Wyndham Garden Hotel
- **Other** E: McConnell Air Force Base, Lowe's, Sears Grand, **Walmart sc**, Auto Dealers
  W: Advance Auto Parts, Auto Dealers, Barnes & Noble, Firestone, Pharmacy, Target, Towne East Square Mall

45 — KS 15, Wichita
- **Other** E: Boeing Factory, McConnell AFB
  W: K & R Travel RV Park▲ , Emery Park BMX Track

(42) — Jct I-135, I-235, US 81, to 47th St
(All Serv at 1st Exit)

39 — US 81, Haysville, Derby

33 — KS 53, Peck, Mulvane
- **Other** W: Winery

(26) — Belle Plain Service Area
(LEFT Exit, Both dir)
- **FStop** Phillips 66 #6370
- **Food** McDonald's

19 — US 160E, Wellington
(Serv 3 mi West)
- **TStop** W: Speedy Food N Fuel
- **Gas** W: Conoco
- **Food** W: KFC, DQ, Sonic
- **Lodg** W: Sunshine Inn
- **Other** **W: Wheatland RV Park▲**

(17) — TOLL Plaza

NOTE: I -35 & Ks Tpk run together above Exit #'s 19-92 follow KS Tpk

4 — US 166, E 160th St S, to US 81, South Haven, Arkansas City
- **TStop** E: Fleming Travel Plaza/66
- **Food** E: FastFood/Fleming TP, Junction Café, Rest/Economy Inn
- **Lodg** E: Economy Inn
- **Other** **W: Oasis RV Park▲** , Strickland Road Service, Ks Badlands Off Road Park

(1) — Weigh Station (Both dir)

⬆ KANSAS
⬇ OKLAHOMA

NOTE: MM 236: Kansas State Line

CENTRAL TIME ZONE

231 — US 177, Braman
- **TStop** E: Kanza Travel Plaza/Conoco (Scales)
- **Food** E: Grab & Dash/Kanza TP, Broadway Cafe
- **Lodg** E: Kanza Motel

230 — Braman Rd

(226) — OK Welcome Center (SB)
(RR, Phone, Picnic, Vend, RVDump)

222 — OK 11, Doolin Ave, Blackwell, to Medford, Alva, Newkirk
- **TStop** E: Jiffy Trip Truck Stop #24/Conoco
- **Gas** E: Shell◈, to Conoco
- **Food** E: Braum's, KFC/Taco Bell, McDonald's, Sam's Plainsman Rest, Subway, to Los Potros Mexican Rest, Pizza Hut, Sonic
- **Lodg** E: Americas Best Value Inn♥, Best Western♥, Comfort Inn♥, to Super 8

◈= Regular Gas Stations with Diesel ▲ = RV Friendly Locations ♥= Pet Friendly Loca-
Red print shows large vehicle parking / access on site or nearby Brown Print = Campgrounds / RV PARKS

EXIT		OKLAHOMA
	Med	E: + Blackwell Reg'l Hospital
	Other	E: to appr 2 mi: Banks, Blackwell City Golf Course, Dollar General, O'Reilly Auto Parts, NAPA, U-Haul, **Walmart**/Pharmacy,
218		**Hubbard Rd, Tonkawa**
	Other	W: Blackwell-Tonkawa Muni Airport✈
(217)		**Weigh Station** (Both dir)
214		**US 60, Thunderbird Rd, Tonkawa, to Lamont, Ponca City**
	Gas	W: Travel Center Cenex
	Food	W: Conestoga Restaurant
	Lodg	W: Western Motel
	Other	E: to appr 16 mi: Ponca City Reg'l Airport✈, Lodging, Services
		W: **Woodland RV Park▲**
211		**Fountain Rd, Tonkawa**
	TStop	W: Love's Travel Stop #213 (Scales)
	Food	W: Chesters/Subway/Love's TS
	Other	W: Laundry/WiFi/**RVDump**/Love's TS
(210)		**Parking Area** (Both dir)
203		**OK 15, Billings, to Marland**
	TStop	E: Cimarron Travel Plaza/Conoco (Scales)
	Food	E: DQ/FastFood/Cimarron TP
	Other	E: Laundry/Cimarron TP
(195)		**Parking Area** (Both dir)
194AB		**US 64, US 412, Cimarron Tpk, Stillwater, Tulsa**
193		**to US 412, US 64W** (NB)
186		**US 64E, Fir St, Perry**
	FStop	E: Sunmart #38/Mobil
		W: Exxon Travel Plaza
	Gas	E: Phillips 66◈,
	Food	E: Subway/Sunmart, Braums, McDonald's, Pizza Hut, Sonic, Taco Mayo
	Lodg	E: Super 8♥
		W: Comfort Inn♥, Holiday Inn Express, Regency Inn
	Med	E: + Perry Memorial Hospital
	Other	E: Auto Repairs, Banks, Homeland Grocery Museum, NAPA, **OK Hwy Patrol Post**, O'Reilly Auto Parts, Pharmacy, U-Haul, **Walmart**/Pharmacy,
185		**US 77, OK 164, Perry, Covington**
	TStop	W: Sooner's Corner/Conoco
	Food	W: FastFood/Rest/Sooner's Corner
	Lodg	E: American Inn
		W: Sooner's Corner **RV Park** & Motel
	TServ	W: Sooner's Corner/Tires
	Other	W: Laundry/**RVDump**/Sooner's Corner
180		**Orlando Rd, Perry**
174		**OK 51, W 6th Ave, Stillwater, to Hennessey** (Serv 12-14 mi E)
	Other	E: to Lake Carl Blackwell, OK State Univ, **to Cedar Crest RV Park & Campsite▲**, **Wildwood Acres RV Park▲**
180		**Orlando Rd, Perry**
(173)		**Parking Area** (Both dir)
170		**Mulhall Rd, 56th St, Stillwater**
157		**OK 33, Noble Ave, Guthrie, Cushing**
	FStop	W: Love's Travel Stop #218
	Gas	W: K&L Food Mart◈, Prime Food, Shell◈, Valero
	Food	W: Subway/Love's TS, Arby's, Braum's, DQ, El Rodeo Mexican, KFC, OK Most Famous BBQ, Pizza Hut

EXIT		OKLAHOMA
	Lodg	W: Best Western♥ & **RV Park▲**, Holiday Inn Express♥, Interstate Motel, Sleep Inn
	Med	W: + Hospital
	Other	W: WiFi/Love's TS, ATMs, Auto & Wrecker Service, Banks, Grocery, Museums, Pharmacy, **to Cedar Valley RV Park▲**, **Territorial Inn & RV Park▲**
153		**US 77, Guthrie** (NB, LEFT- Exit) (Gas/Food/B&Bs - 3mi W)
	TServ	W: Coker's Auto & Truck Repair
	Other	W: Auto Dealers, Enterprise RAC, Guthrie Muni Airport✈
151		**Seward Rd, Guthrie**
	FStop	E: Shell
	Other	E: **Pioneer RV Park▲**
		W: Mid America Cycle & ATV's
(149)		**Weigh Station** (Both dir)
146		**Waterloo Rd, Edmond**
	FStop	E: Edmond Travel Plaza/Shell
	Gas	W: Conoco
	Food	E: Steak & Catfish Barn
		W: Pizza/Conoco
	Other	W: Larry's Diesel Service, Auto repairs, Sooner Animal Hospital♥,
143		**Covell Rd, Edmond**
142		**Danforth Rd** (NB)
	Gas	W: to 7-11, Circle K/Shell
141		**US 77S, OK 66, 2nd St, Edmond**
	Gas	W: Conoco, Phillips 66◈
	Food	W: Braum's, CiCi's Pizza, Coyote Café, Country Kitchen, Denny's, DQ, KFC/ Taco Bell, IHOP, McDonald's, Marbo Chinese, Starbucks, Souper Salad, Western Sizzlin
	Lodg	W: Best Western♥, Comfort Suites, Fairfield Inn, Hampton Inn, Holiday Inn Express, Stafford Inn
	Med	W: + Columbia Edmond Med Center
	Other	W: ATMs, Auto & Tire Services, Animal Medical Center♥, Banks, FedEx Office, Firestone, Grocery, Laundromat, O'Reilly Auto Parts, PetCo♥, **Police Dept**, Radio Shack, Univ of Central OK, UPS Store, Walgreen's, **Walmart sc**,
140		**SE 15th St, Edmond**
139		**SE 33rd St, Frontage Rd**
138D		**Memorial Rd, Edmond**
	Other	W: to Mall, AMC 24, Lions Fun Park
138C		**Sooner Rd** (SB)
(138B)		**Jct Kilpatrick Turnpike**
	NOTE:	I-35 & I-44 run together below for 8 mi Exits #134-137, #'s follow I-35.
(138A)		**Jct I-44E Tpk, to Tulsa**
137		**NE 122nd St, Service Rd, North OKC, Edmond**
	TStop	E: Travel Stop #26/Shell
		W: Flying J Travel Plaza #5056 (DAND) (Scales), Love's Travel Stop #205 (Scales)
	Gas	E: Petro Plus 5, Valero◈
	Food	E: FastFood/Travel Stop, Charly's, IHOP, Kettle Rest
		W: CountryMkt/FastFood/FJ TP, Subway/TacoBell/Love's TS, Chuck's BBQ, **Cracker Barrel**, McDonald's, Sonic, Waffle House

EXIT		OKLAHOMA
	Lodg	E: Knights Inn♥, Sleep Inn,
		W: Comfort Inn, Days Inn♥, Economy Inn, Motel 6♥, Quality Inn♥, Red Carpet Inn, Super 8
	TWash	W: American Eagle TW
	Other	E: WiFi/TravelStop
		W: Laundry/WiFi/**RVDump/LP**/FJ TP, WiFi/**RVDump**/Love's TS, **Abe's RV Park▲**, Interstate Auto Repair, OKC Welcome/Visitor Center, Frontier City Theme Park
136		**Hefner Rd, OKC** (Access to Ex #137 Serv)
	Gas	W: Fuel at the Flag/Conoco◈
	Food	W: Rest/Conoco
	Other	W: Frontier City Theme Park
135		**Britton Rd, NE 93rd St, OKC**
134		**Wilshire Rd Blvd, NE 78th St**
	Lodg	W: Executive Inn
	Other	W: Blue Beacon TW, Tires
(133)		**Jct I-44W, Lawton, Amarillo**
	Other	W: State Capitol, Cowboy Hall of Fame
	NOTE:	I-35 & I-44 run together above for 8 mi. Exits #134-137, #'s follow I-35.
132B		**NE 63rd St** (NB)
	Gas	E: Conoco◈, Fuel at the Flag
	Food	E: Braum's
	Lodge	E: Remington Inn
	Other	W: Tinseltown 20, Museums, Zoo
132A		**NE 50th St, OKC**
	Lodg	E: Red Stone Inn
	Other	W: National Softball Hall of Fame, Oklahoma City Zoo, Omniplex, Air Space Museum, Firefighters Museum
131A		**NE 36th St, OKC**
	Gas	W: Phillips 66◈
	Other	W: Museum
130		**US 62E, NE 23rd St, OKC**
	Gas	E: Shell
	Food	E: Burger King, Beef & Bun
		W: KFC, Krispy King, TJ's Seafood
	Lodg	E: Deluxe Inn
		W: Relax Inn
	Other	E: Auto Services
		W: Auto, Towing & Wrecker Services, 45th Infantry Div Museum, State Capitol
129		**NE 10th St**
	FStop	E: Synergy Flash Mart #3/Conoco (Scales)
	Gas	E: Total
	Food	E: FastFood/FlashMart
		W: Tom's BBQ
	Med	W: + VA Medical Center, + University Hospital, + Childrens Hospital of OK, + Presbyterian Hospital
	Other	E: Wrecker Service
	NOTE:	I-35 runs with I-40 below for 2 exits. Exit #'s follow I-35.
(128)		**Jct I-40E, to Fort Smith** (SB, Left exit), **Reno Ave, Eastern Ave, MLK Ave** (SB)
127		**Eastern Ave, Reno Ave** (WB)
	TStop	W: JRS Travel Center (Scales), Stopping Center #16/Mobil (Scales)
	Gas	W: Shell
	Food	W: JRS Grill/Wendy's/JRS TC, IronSkillet/IronSkillet/Petro SC, Waffle House

◈ = Regular Gas Stations with Diesel ▲ = RV Friendly Locations ♥ = Pet Friendly Locations
Red print shows large vehicle parking / access on site or nearby Brown Print = Campgrounds / RV PARKS

EXIT — OKLAHOMA

Lodg — W: Bricktown Hotel, Econo Lodge, Quality Inn, Ramada Inn
TServ — W: Petro SC/Tires
TWash — W: Blue Beacon TW/Petro SC
Other — W: Laundry/JRS TC, Laundry/WiFi/ Petro SC, **Lewis RV Center**

(126) Jct I-40, W-Amarillo (NB, LEFT Exit) , E-Ft Smith, Jct I-235N, Edmond, Wichita, Jct I-35S, to Dallas (WB, LEFT exit)

NOTE: I-35 runs with I-40 above for 2 exits. Exit #'s follow I-35.

125D SE 15th St, Service Rd (SB)
Gas — E: Conoco◈, Save
W: 7-11
Food — E: El Sombrero Mexican, Skyline Rest.
Lodg — E: Green Carpet Inn
Other — W: Downtown Airpark✈

125B SE 15th St, Prospect Ave (NB)

125A SE 25th St, SE 29th St (SB)
Gas — W: Phillips 66
Food — E: Denny's, McDonald's, Sonic,Taco Bell, Waffle House
W: IHOP, Mama Lou's Rest
Lodg — E: Plaza Inn, Royal Inn, Super 8
TServ — E: R & R Diesel Service
Other — E: Auto & Tire Service
W: Auto Services

124B SE 29th St, SE 25th St (NB)
Food — E: Denny's, McDonald's, Waffle House
W: IHOP, Mama Lou's Rest
Lodg — E: Days Inn, Plaza Inn, Super 8
Other — E: Auto Services
W: Auto Services, **Access to Ex #125A**

124A Grand Blvd, OKC
Lodg — E: Bricktown Guest Suites
W: Drover's Inn, Executive Inn, Travelodge
TServ — E: Friday Truck Repair & Road Service

123B SE 44th St, OKC
Gas — E: Conoco◈
Food — E: Chelio's Mex Rest, Domino's, Sonic
W: DQ, Myrt's Diner, Pizza 44, Subway, Taco Mayo
Lodg — E: Best Value Inn, Courtesy Inn, Deluxe Inn
Med — W: **+ Integris SW Medical Center**
Other — E: Auto Services, **Roadrunner RV Park▲**
W: Auto Services, ATMs, Family Dollar, Grocery, US Post Office, **Boat City Motor & RV Sales**

123A SE 51st St, High Ave
Gas — E: Conoco◈
Food — W: Rest/Southgate Inn, Las Chalupas
Lodg — E: Best Value Inn
W: Southgate Inn
Other — E: **Roadrunner RV Park▲**

122B SE 59th St, Hillcrest St, OKC
FStop — W: City Mart #4/Valero
Gas — E: EZ Mart, Phillips 66◈
Food — E: Simple Simon's Pizza
W: FastFood/City Mart
Other — E: Auto Services, **Briscoes RV & Fun Park▲**
W: Repair Services

122A SE 66th St, Service Rd, OKC
Gas — W: 7-11
Food — E: Burger King, Luby's, McDonald's, Subway, Texas Roadhouse
W: Arby's

EXIT — OKLAHOMA

Lodg — E: Fairfield Inn, Ramada Inn, Residence Inn
Other — E: Best Buy, Firestone, Crossroads Mall, Cinema 8, Crossroads Mall 16, Tires Plus

(121B) Jct I-240, OK 3, US 62W, Lawton

121A SE 82nd St, Service Rd
Food — W: Denny's
Lodg — W: La Quinta Inn♥, Green Carpet Inn

120 SE 89th St, OKC
FStop — E: City Mart/Valero (Scales)
W: Love's Travel Stop #211
Food — E: FastFood/City Mart
W: Subway/Love's TS, Carl's Jr
Other — E: Laundry/City Mart
W: WiFi/Love's TS, Repair Services

119B N 27th St, OKC
Gas — E: Circle K/Shell◈
Food — E: Rest/Luxury Inn
Lodg — E: Best Western, Luxury Inn
Other — E: Repair Services
W: Repair Services, **Lee's RV City South**, Bryan Harley Davidson

119A Shields Blvd, Moore Ave (NB, L exit)
Lodg — W: Days Inn, Greentree Inn

118 N 12th St, Main St, Service Rd
Gas — E: Sinclair, Total
W: Phillips 66◈, Shell
Food — E: Pizza, Sonic
W: Arby's, Braums, DQ, Grandy's, KFC, Long John Silver, McDonald's, Pizza Hut, Subway, Western Sizzlin, Wendy's
Lodg — E: Super 8
W: Best Western♥, Candlewood Suites, Comfort Inn, Days Inn, Motel 6♥
Other — W: Auto Zone, **Walker RV Center**

117 OK 37, S 4th St, Main St, N 5th St
Gas — E: Shell
W: Valero
Food — W: Mr Burger, Maria's Mexican Rest
Lodg — W: Ramada Inn
Med — W: **+ Moore Medical Center**
Other — E: Auto Services
W: Bank, Pharmacy, **Walmart sc**

116 SW 19th St, Moore
Gas — E: Conoco, Shell
W: Murphy, Conoco
Food — E: BBQ House, Carl's Jr, McDonald's, Sonic, Taco Bell
W: Burger King, McDonald's, Subway
Lodg — W: La Quinta Inn♥
Other — E: Best Buy, Firestone, Goodyear, Office Depot, PetSmart♥, U-Haul
Other — W: ATMs, Aldi Grocery, CVS, Discount Tire, Dollar Tree, Harley Davidson, Home Depot, Lowe's, Radio Shack, Tires Plus, UPS Store, Walgreen's, **Walmart sc**,

114 Indian Hills Rd, 179th St, Norman
Food — E: Indian Hills Rest & Club
Lodg — E: Value Place
Other — E: **I-35 RV Sales**

113 US 77S, Franklin Rd (SB, LEFT exit)

112 Tecumseh Rd, Norman
Other — E: **RV General Store**, Max Westheimer Airport✈, Univ of OK

110A Interstate Dr, Robinson St (SB)

110B Interstate Dr, Robinson St (SB)

110 Robinson St, Norman (NB)
Gas — E: PetroStop
W: 7-11, Conoco, Phillips 66

EXIT — OKLAHOMA

Food — E: Carl's Jr, Cheddar's Cafe, Hardee's, Logan's Roadhouse, Sonic, Taco Bell, Western Sizzlin
W: Arby's, Braum's, BlackEyed Pea, **Cracker Barrel**, Danny's Steakhouse, House of Hunan, Joe's Crab Shack, Pizza Hut, Outback Steakhouse, Panda Garden, Rib Crib BBQ, Ryan's Grill, Santa Fe Cattle Co, Taste of China, Tulio's Mexican Rest, Waffle House
Lodg — E: Days Inn♥, Embassy Suites
W: Holiday Inn
Med — E: **+ Norman Regional Hospital, + Griffin Memorial Hospital**
Other — E: Albertson's, Auto Dealers, **Cruise America RV Rentals**, Griffin Park, Super Target, Tires Plus+, Univ of Ok Westheimer Airpark✈,
W: Cinemark 6, Carwash, Spotlight 14

109 W Main St, Norman
Gas — E: 7-11, Phillips 66, Shell, Murphy
W: Conoco◈
Food — E: CiCi's Pizza, Denny's, Golden Corral, Panera Bread, Prairie Kitchen, Subway, Taco Cabana, Waffle House
W: Applebee's, Burger King, Chili's, Don Pablo's, El Chico, Hooters, Olive Garden, McDonald's, On the Border, Pearls Oyster Bar, Pipers Coffee & Pastry, Piccadilly Cafeteria, Red Lobster, Souper Salad
Lodg — E: Days Inn, Econo Lodge, Guest Inn, Quality Inn, Super 8, Travelodge
W: Fairfield Inn, Hampton Inn, Hilton Garden Inn, La Quinta Inn♥
Other — E: Auto Zone, ATMs, Banks, Greyhound, Auto Dealers, Auto & Tire Services, Best Buy, Grocery, Lowe's, Target, Enterprise RAC, **Walmart sc**, Amtrak, Hertz RAC
W: ATMs, Banks, Barnes & Noble, Borders, IGA Grocery, Sam's Club, Sooner Fashion Mall,

108AB OK 74A, Lindsey St, OK 9, Tecumseh, University of Oklahoma
Gas — E: Citgo, Conoco, Shell
Food — E: Arby's, Braums, McDonald's, Panda Buffet, Subway, Taco Bell
W: IHOP, Johnny Carino's Italian, Red Robin, Souper Salad
Lodg — E: Villager Lodge, Residence Inn, Thunderbird Lodge
W: Country Inn, La Quinta Inn♥
Other — E: ATMs, Banks, Auto Services & Tires, Carwash, **to** Univ of Ok, OK Memorial Stadium, Owen Field✈
W: Home Depot, PetSmart♥

108A OK 9E, to Tecumseh

108B OK 74A, Lindsey St

106 OK 9W, Norman, to Chickasha, New Castle, Blanchard
FStop — W: Love's Travel Stop #260
Food — W: TacoBell/Love's TS
Other — E: **Floyd's Campers**
W: WiFi/Love's TS

104 OK 74S, Main St, Washington, to Goldsby
Gas — W: Shell, Sinclair◈
Other — E: Goldsby David J Perry Airport✈, **Floyd's Campers**
W: Andrew Service Center

EXIT		OKLAHOMA
101		**Ladd Rd, Washington**
98		**Johnson Rd, CR N4040, Purcell**
	Gas	E: Shamrock◈
95		**SR 74G, to US 77, Purcell, Lexington (SB LEFT exit)**
	Gas	E: Conoco◈, Love's, Shell
	Food	E: Carl's Jr, KFC, Pizza, Subway
	Lodg	E: Best Western
	Med	E: + Hospital
	Other	E: Grocery
91		**OK 74, to US 77, OK 39, Purcell, Maysville, Lexington**
	FStop	W: Star Travel Plaza/Shell
	Gas	E: Conoco◈, Love's◈, Phillips 66◈
	Food	E: Carl's Jr, McDonald's, Subway, Rest/Ruby's Inn W: FastFood/Star TP
	Lodg	E: Econo Lodge, Horse Country Inn, Ruby's Inn, Uptown Motel
	TServ	E: Diesel Dr, Precision Trailer Repair
	Med	E: + Hospital
	Other	E: Auto & Tire Services, Auto Dealers, Walmart sc
86		**OK 59, Wayne, Payne, Rosedale**
	Other	E: American RV Park▲
79		**OK 145E, Paoli**
	Gas	E: Phillips 66
74		**Kimberlin Rd, to OK 19, Pauls Valley**
72		**OK 19, Grant Ave, Pauls Valley, Lindsey, Maysville, Ada**
	FStop	E: Pauls Valley Travel Center/66 W: Love's Travel Stop #202
	TStop	E: Travel Plaza/Shamrock (Scales)
	Gas	E: Conoco◈, Murphy◈
	Food	E: Rest/FastFood/PV TC, Arby's, Braums, Ballard's D/I, Carl's Jr, Chicken Express, Denny's, KFC/Taco Bell, Pizza Hut, Sonic, Subway W: FastFood/Love's TS, Chaparral Steaks, McDonald's
	Lodg	E: Days Inn, Relax Inn, Sands Inn
	TWash	E: G&S TW
	TServ	E: Travel Plaza, Tire & Service, Truck Repair
	Other	E: Laundry/CB/Travel Plaza, Auto & Tire Services, ATMs, Banks, Auto Dealers, Grocery, Museum, Walmart sc, Royal Twin Theatre W: WiFi/Love's TS
70		**Airport Rd, Pauls Valley**
	Med	W: + Pauls Valley General Hospital
	Other	E: Animal Hospital♥, Pauls Valley Muni Airport✈
66		**OK 29, to US 77, Wynnewood, to Elmore City**
	FStop	E: Kent's
	Gas	W: Shell◈
	Food	E: Rest/Kent's
	Lodg	E: Motel/Kent's
64		**OK 17A, Wynnewood**
60		**Ruppe Rd, Wynnewood**
(58)		**Rest Area (Both dir) (RR, Phones, Pic, Pet, RVDump)**
55		**OK 7, Davis, to Duncan, Sulphur, Ada (All Serv 3-4 mi E in Davis)**
	FStop	E: Chickasaw Trading Post/Shamrock

EXIT		OKLAHOMA
	Gas	E: to Finish Line, Phillips 66 W: Conoco
	Lodg	E: Microtel
	Other	E: to Smokin Joe's BBQ & RV Park▲ W: Oak Hill RV Park▲
(53)		**Weigh Station (Both dir)**
51		**US 77, Davis, Turner Falls Area**
	Gas	W: Sinclair
	Food	W: Grill/Sinclair, Buffalo Gap BBQ
	Lodg	E: Canyon Breeze Motel & RV Park▲
	Other	E: to Chickasaw Nat'l Rec Area▲ W: Turner Falls▲ , Rose Grocery, RV Park & Canoe Rental▲
(49)		**Scenic View (SB)**
47		**US 77, Turner Falls Area**
	Other	W: Turner Falls▲
(46)		**Scenic View (NB)**
42		**OK 53W, Springer, Comanche**
	TStop	E: Sunmart #6/Exxon
	Food	E: FastFood/Sunmart
40		**US 77, OK 53E, Springer, Autrey, Ardmore, Airpark**
	TStop	E: Springer Shell
	Food	E: FastFood/Springer
	Other	E: Laundry/Springer, to appr 4 mi: Melody Ranch RV Park▲
33		**OK 142, Veterans Blvd, Ardmore**
	TStop	W: Flying J Travel Plaza/Conoco (Scales)
	Gas	E: Phillips 66◈
	Food	E: IHOP, Ryan's Grill W: CountryMarket/FastFood/FJ TP, McDonald's
	Lodg	E: Guest Inn, Holiday Inn, La Quinta Inn♥, Regency Inn, Super 8 W: Microtel♥
	TServ	W: Truck Lube Plus
	Other	E: ATMs, Banks, Acc Ex #132 E Serv E to US 77 W: Laundry/WiFi/RVDump/LP/FJ TP
32		**12th Ave NW, to US 77, Ardmore**
	FStop	W: Love's Travel Stop #266 (Scales)
	Gas	E: Phillips 66
	Food	E: Arby's, Burger King, Carl's Jr, Long John Silver, McDonald's, Ryan's Grill, Sirloin Stockade, Taco Bell W: Godfather's/Subway/Love's TS, McDonald's
	Lodg	W: Microtel
	Med	E: + Mercy Memorial Health Center
	TServ	E: Priest Auto & Truck Repair
	Other	E: ATMs, Banks, Grocery, Staples, Walgreen's, Walmart sc W: Laundry/WiFi/Love's TS
31B		**US 70W, W Broadway St, Ardmore, to Lone Grove, Waurika**
	FStop	W: Conoco
	Other	W: Ardmore RV Park▲ , Auto Dealers, Carwash, Westwood Animal Hospital♥
31A		**OK 199E, Ardmore, to US 77, to Dickson**
	Gas	E: Shell◈, Sinclair◈, Valero
	Food	E: Applebee's, Burger King, Broadway Café, BBQ Express, Cattle Rustler's Steakhouse, Denny's, El Chico, Golden China, Jack in the Box, KFC, Pizza Hut, McDonald's, Shoney's, Two Frogs Grill
	Lodg	E: Best Western♥, Comfort Inn♥, Days Inn♥, Hampton Inn, Holiday Inn, Motel 6♥

EXIT		OK / TX
	Other	E: Auto Zone, Budget Truck Rental, Carmike Cinema, Grocery, Museum, O'Reilly Auto Parts,
29		**US 70E, Ardmore**
	Other	E: Ardmore Downtown Executive Airport✈, Lake Murray State Park▲ W: Hidden Lake RV Resort▲
24		**OK 77S, Ardmore**
	Gas	E: Sinclair
	Other	E: to Lake Murray State Park▲
21		**Oswalt Rd, Marietta**
	Other	W: Ardmore/Marietta KOA▲
15		**OK 32, Memorial Dr, Marietta, Ryan**
	TStop	E: Valero #4430
	Gas	E: Phillips 66, Sinclair W: Phillips 66
	Food	E: FastFood/Valero, Carl's Jr, Denim's Rest, Hardee's, Pizza Hut, Sonic W: Hickory House BBQ , Subway
	Lodg	E: Lake Country Motel
	Med	E: + Hospital
	Other	E: Winn Dixie, Tires/Valero
5		**OK 153, Thackerville**
	Other	E: Red River Ranch RV Resort▲
(3)		**OK Welcome Center (NB) Rest Area (SB) (RR, Phone, Picnic, Vend)**
1		**US 77N, Thackerville**
	TStop	E: Thackerville Travel Plaza/Shamrock
	Food	E: FastFood/Thackerville TP
	Other	E: Laundry/Thackerville TP

CENTRAL TIME ZONE

⬆ OKLAHOMA
⬇ TEXAS

NOTE: MM 504: Oklahoma State Line

CENTRAL TIME ZONE

EXIT		TEXAS
504		**Frontage Rd, Gainesville**
(503)		**Parking Area (Both dir)**
(502)		**TX Welcome Center (SB) (RR, Phones, Picnic, Info)**
501		**FM 1202, Gainesville**
	Gas	W: Hilltop Conoco
	Food	W: Hilltop Café, Applebee's, Cracker Barrel, Harper's Grill
	Lodg	W: Hampton Inn
	Other	E: Auto Dealer W: Gainesville Prime Outlets, CAMPING▲
500		**FM 372, Service Rd, Gainesville**
	TStop	E: Hitchin Post AmBest Truck Stop/Shell (Scales), Gainesville Travel Stop/Citgo
	Food	E: Rest/Hitchin Post TS, Rest/ Gainesville/TS
	TWash	E: Gainesville TS
	TServ	E: Hitchin Post TS/Tires, Gainesville TS
	Other	E: Laundry/Hitchin Post TS, Laundry/ Gainesville TS
499		**Frontage Rd, Service Rd (NB)**
	Gas	E: Exxon, Gainesville Fuel Stop
	Food	E: Denny's
	Lodg	E: Budget Host Inn, Bed & Bath Inn, Super 8

◈ = Regular Gas Stations with Diesel ▲ = RV Friendly Locations ♥ = Pet Friendly Locations
Red print shows large vehicle parking / access on site or nearby Brown Print = Campgrounds / RV PARKS

EXIT		TEXAS
498A		**US 82E, Summit Ave, Sherman, Wichita Falls**
	FStop	E: E&M Mini Market/66
	TStop	E: (16mi) Whitesboro Truck Stop
	Gas	E: Exxon, Shell, Valero◈, Murphy
	Food	E: Catfish Louie's, Denny's, Golden Corral, KFC, Pizza Inn, Ranch House, Whataburger
	Lodg	E: Twelve Oaks Inn, Trails Inn Motel, Wagon Inn Motel
	Med	E: + Gainesville Memorial Hospital
	Other	E: ATMs, Banks, Auto & Tire Services, Big Lots, Dollar Tree, Enterprise RAC, Family Dollar, Grocery, **Walmart sc**, to appr 14mi: **Hwy 82 RV Park▲**
498B		**US 82W, W Summit Ave, Wichita Falls**
	Gas	W: Exxon◈
	Lodg	W: Best Western♥, Days Inn♥, Texas Motel
	Med	W: + N Texas Medical Center
	Other	W: Auto Repairs, Auto Dealer, ATMs, Gainesville Muni Airport✈, Gainesville Muni Golf Course, **David's RV & Trailer Park▲**, **1st Choice RV's**
497		**Frontage Rd, Gainesville (NB access Ex #498 serv, SB access #496 serv)**
496B		**TX 51, California St, to Decatur**
	Gas	E: Chevron, Conoco◈, Mobil W: Texaco
	Food	E: Burger King, Braum's, McDonald's, Starbucks, Taco Bell, Wendy's W: Chili's
	Lodg	E: Holiday Inn, Quality Inn, Ramada Ltd
	Other	E: ATMs, Banks, Auto Service, Grocery, Greyhound, Museum, **Police Dept**, City Park/**RVDump**/**Camping▲** W: Frank Buck Zoo, N Central Texas College
496A		**Weaver St (NB)**
495		**Frontage Rd, Service Rd (SB)**
494		**to FM 1306, CR 218, Gainesville**
(492)		**Parking Area (SB)**
491		**Spring Creek Rd**
(490)		**Parking Area (NB)**
489		**Hockley Creek Rd (SB)**
488		**Frontage Rd, Hockley Crk Rd (NB)**
487		**FM 922, Obuch St, Valley View**
	FStop	W: Lucky Lady #14/Chevron
	Food	W: FastFood/LuckyLady, DQ
	Other	W: Auto Repairs, Bank, US Post Office
486		**FM 1307, O'Brien St, Frontage Rd**
485		**Frontage Rd (SB exit, NB reacc)**
483		**FM 3002, Lone Oak Rd**
	Other	E: **Lone Oak RV Park▲**, to **Ray Roberts State Park▲**
482		**Chisam Rd, Sanger**
481		**View Rd, Sanger**
	Other	W: **Texas Sundown RV Resort▲**
480		**Lois Rd**
479		**Belz Rd, Sanger**
	Lodg	E: Sanger Inn

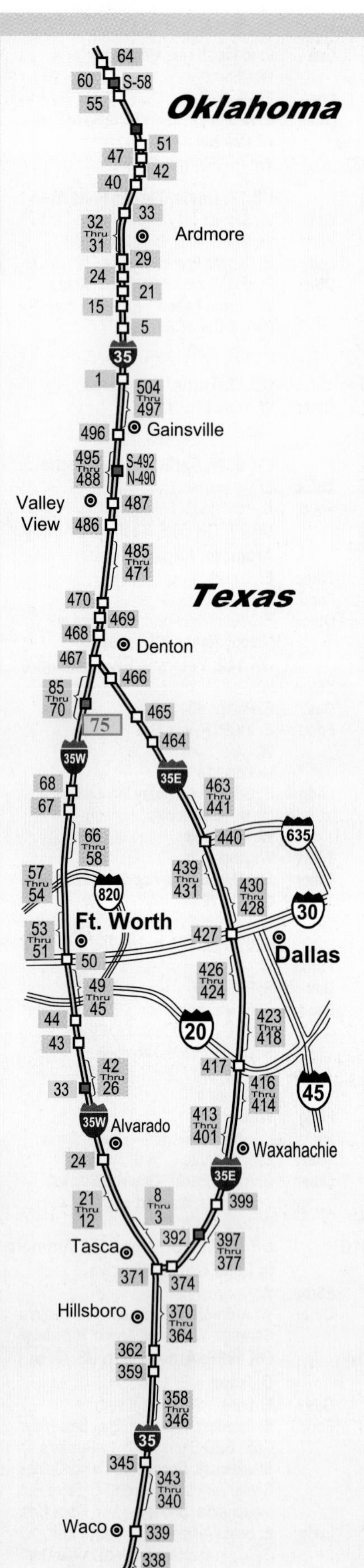

EXIT		TEXAS
	Other	E: **Indian Village Campground▲**
478		**FM 455, Chapman Dr, Sanger, to Pilot Point, Bolivar**
	Gas	E: Phillips 66, Shell W: Chevron
	Food	E: DQ, Mexican Rest, Sonic W: Chicken Express, Jack in the Box, Kirby's Rest, McDonald's, Subway
	Lodg	E: Sanger Inn
	Other	E: Grocery, Laundromat, Auto Repairs, **Police Dept** W: Family Dollar, IGA, **Wagon Master RV Park▲**
477		**Bus 35, 5th St, Keeton Rd, Sanger**
	Gas	E: Phillips 66 W: Shamrock◈
	Food	E: Mr Gatti's, No Frills Grill
	Other	W: **I-35 RV Center**, **Parkdale RV**
475B		**Rector Rd, Cowling Rd, Sanger**
475A		**FM 156, Denton, to Krum (SB)**
474		**Cowling TurnAround (NB)**
473		**FM 3163, Milam Rd, Denton**
	FStop	E: Love's Travel Stop #217
	Food	E: Subway/Love's TS
	Other	E: WiFi/Love's TS
472		**Ganzer Rd, Denton**
471		**US 77, N Elm St, to Loop 288, FM 1173, Denton, to Krum**
	FStop	W: FMB/Fina
	TStop	E: Travel Center of America #104/ Conoco (Scales) W: Sunpower Travel Plaza (Scales)
	Food	E: Rest/FastFood/TA TC, Good Eats Grill, Red River Coffee & Bagel W: Rest/Sunpower TP
	Tires	W: Sunpower TS
	TWash	W: Sunpower TS
	TServ	E: TA TC/Tires W: Denton Truck Clinic, Sunpower TS
	Med	W: + Denton Regional Med Ctr
	Other	E: Laundry/WiFi/TA TC, Factory Stores, TX Instruments W: Laundry/CB/Sunpower TP, **Funtime RV Sales/Camping World**
470		**Loop 288 (NB)**
469		**US 380, University Dr, Denton, to Decatur, McKinney**
	FStop	W: Golden Express/Conoco
	Gas	E: Phillips 66, RaceTrac W: Diamond Shamrock, Shell◈
	Food	E: Catfish King, Cracker Barrel, China Town Café, McDonald's, Texas Espresso W: DQ, Denny's, Waffle House
	Lodg	E: Best Western W: Excel Inn, Howard Johnson, Motel 6♥
	Med	E: + Denton Community Hospital W: + Columbia Medical Center
	Other	E: Albertson's/Pharmacy, Auto Services, Tires, Towing W: to Denton Muni Airport✈
468		**W Oak St, to FM 1515, Airport Rd Denton (SB)**
INTERSTATE 35E S		**I-35 continues below as I-35E to Dallas**
(467)		**Jct I-35W, S to Ft Worth, Jct I-35E to Dallas (SB), Jct I-35N to OKC (NB)**

◈= Regular Gas Stations with Diesel ▲ = RV Friendly Locations ♥ = Pet Friendly Loca-
Red print shows large vehicle parking / access on site or nearby Brown Print = Campgrounds / RV PARKS

466B **Ave D, Denton**
Gas E: Citgo, Exxon◈
Food E: Burger King, IHOP, McDonald's, Pancho's Mexican Buffet
Lodg E: Comfort Suites
W: Radisson
Other E: Dollar General, Univ of N TX

466A **McCormick St**
Gas E: Phillips 66, Shell◈
W: Citgo, Fina◈
Lodg E: Comfort Suites, Royal Hotel Suites
W: Radisson
Med E: + Denton Medical Clinic
Other W: Univ of N TX, Fouts Field

465B **US 377, Ft Worth Dr, Denton**
Gas E: Citgo, RaceTrac, Shamrock
W: Conoco, Phillips 66, Total
Food E: Kettle Rest, Taco Bueno, Whataburger
W: Frosty DriveN, Sonic, Taco Bell, Outback Steakhouse, Smokehouse Rest
Lodg E: La Quinta Inn♥
W: Days Inn
Other E: Auto Repair, Bank, Home Depot, U-Haul
W: Grocery, **RV Wurks**, **Post Oak Place RV Park▲**

465A **FM 2181, Teasley Lane**
Gas E: 7-11, Shell
W: Exxon, Fina, Shell
Food E: Applebee's, KFC, Olive Branch Pizza, Pizza Hut
W: Little Caesar's Pizza
Lodg E: Desert Sands Motor Inn, Hampton Inn
W: Best Value Inn, Super 8
Other E: Grocery, **N TX RV Repair**

464 **US 77, Dallas Dr, Denton**
Food E: Burger King, Island Crab, Wendy's
Lodg E: Quality Inn
Other E: ATMs, Banks, Kroger, Office Depot, **Walmart**, Golden Triangle Mall

463 **Lp 288, Lillian Miller Pkwy, to McKinney**
Gas E: Racetrac, Shell, Murphy
W: Chevron
Food E: Arby's, Burger King, Café China, CiCi's Pizza, Colters BBQ, Jason's Deli, Long John Silver, Wendy's
W: Black Eyed Pea, Chili's, Jack in the Box, Luby's Cafeteria, Red Lobster, Red Pepper's Chinese, Tia's TexMex
Other E: ATMs, Auto Services, Discount Tire, Enterprise RAC, Golden Triangle Mall, Goodyear, Kroger, Office Depot, PetCo♥, Target, **Walmart sc**, **River Lakes RV Park▲**
W: Albertson's, Fedex Office

462 **State School Rd, Mayhill Rd**
Gas E: Shell
W: Exxon
Food W: Café/Exxon
Med E: + Denton Regional Medical Center, + N Texas Hospital
Other E: **Explore USA RV Supercenter**, U-Haul
W: Auto Dealers, Grocery, **Funtime RV Sales**

461 **Post Oak Dr, Shady Shores Rd**
Other E: Auto Dealers
W: Auto Dealers

460 **Corinth St, Denton**
Gas E: Chevron◈
Other E: McClains RV Center

459 **Frontage Rd**
Food W: Mr Brisket BBQ
Other W: **Destiny Dallas RV Resort▲**, American Eagle Harley Davidson

458 **FM 2181, Swisher Rd, Teasley Ln, Frontage Rd, to Lake Dallas, Hickory Creek**
Gas E: Circle K, Phillips 66
W: Chevron, Exxon, Shell, Murphy
Food W: Burger King, ChikFilA, Jack in the Box, Mr Gatti's, McDonald's, Starbucks, Wendy's
Lodg E: Best Western
Other E: Grocery, O'Reilly Auto Parts, Rave Hickory Creek Cinemas 16, **McClain's RV Superstore, to** Lakeview Airport✈, Lakeview Marina
W: ATMs, Albertson's, Discount Tire, Radio Shack, **Walmart sc**

457B **Denton Dr, Hundley Dr, Lake Dallas (NB)**
Gas E: Chevron
W: Tetco
Food E: Chubby Burgers, Subway
W: Hickory Creek BBQ, McDonald's, Wendy's

457A **Frontage Rd, S Denton Dr, Hundley Dr, Lake Dallas (NB)**
Gas E: Allsup's
Food E: Papa's BBQ, Enrique's, Godfather's, Sonic, Salt & Peppers Smokehouse
Other E: Grocery, Police Dept

455 **Garden Ridge Blvd (SB)**

454B **Highland Village Rd (SB), Eagle Point Rd (NB), Garden Ridge Blvd, Lewisville**
Gas W: Citgo
Food W: Wendy's

454A **FM 407, Justin Rd (SB), Jones St, Lake Park Rd (NB)**
Gas E: Fina, Shamrock
W: Exxon, Murphy
Food E: Al's Chuck Wagon
W: McDonald's, Subway, Tx Hamburger Factory
Other E: Auto & Tire Service, Enterprise RAC, Lake Park Golf Course, **Lewisville Lake Park▲**
W: ATMs, Auto Services, Banks, Car Wash, Grocery, **Walmart**, Commercial Repair Service

453 **Service Rd, to Valley Ridge Blvd**
Gas W: Chevron
Food E: Subway
W: Burger King
Other E: Enterprise RAC, Auto Dealer, **May's RVs**, **Buddy Gregg Motorhomes**
W: Lowe's, Home Depot, Staples

452 **FM 1171, Main St, College Pkwy, Lewisville, to Flower Mound**
Gas E: Mobil, Shell
W: Chevron, Exxon◈, Shell
Food E: IHOP, McDonald's, Taco Bueno
W: ChikFilA, Golden Corral, Grandy's, McDonald's, Wendy's, Whataburger
Lodg E: Days Inn
W: Baymont Inn
Med E: + Columbia Medical Center
Other E: Auto Services, ATMs, Banks, Vet♥, Pharmacy
W: Grocery, Home Depot, Lowe's, Sam's Club, **Walmart sc**, Police Dept, Auto Services, ATMs, Banks

451 **Fox Ave, Lewisville**
Gas E: Shell◈
W: Chevron, Conoco◈, Shamrock
Food E: Braum's
W: Black Eyed Pea, Cracker Barrel, El Chico
Lodge W: Hampton Inn, Microtel
Other W: Auto Services, Midas

450 **Tx Bus 121, Lakeland Plaza, to Grapevine, McKinney**
FStop W: Whip n Stop/Fina
Gas E: 7-11, RaceTrac
W: Chevron, Citgo, QT, Texaco
Food E: BBQ, Mexican Rest
W: Asian Seafood Buffet, Bonanza, Buddy Ray's, Burger King, Chili's, KFC, Long John Silver, McDonald's, Pancho's, Subway, Taco Bell, Waffle House
Lodg E: Ramada Inn, Pine Motel
W: Best Value Inn, Crossroads Inn, J&J Motel, Super 8♥
Other E: Auto Services, Dollar General, Enterprise RAC, **Bob's RV Services**
W: ATMs, Banks, Auto Repairs, Hertz RAC, Firestone, Kroger/Pharmacy, Towing

449 **Corporate Dr, Lewisville**
Gas E: Phillips 66
W: Exxon
Food E: China Dragon, Dickeys BBQ, On the Border, Cajun Café, Hooter's
W: Chili's, Jack in the Box, Kettle Rest
Lodg E: Extended Stay, Motel 6♥
W: Best Western, InTown Suites, La Quinta Inn♥, Sun Suites
Other E: Auto & Diesel Repair, Cinema 10

448A **FM 3040, Round Grove Rd, Hebron Pkwy,Lewisville**
Gas E: 7-11
W: Exxon, RaceTrac, Murphy
Food E: ChikFilA, Chuck E Cheese's, Mimi's Café, Japanese Rest, Olive Garden, Saltgrass Steak House, Souper Salad, Subway
Food W: Carino's, Don Pablo, IHOP, Luby's, Famous Dave's BBQ, Good Eats Grill, McDonald's, Outback Steakhouse, Panda Express, Red Lobster, Spring Creek BBQ, Romano's Macaroni Grill, TGI Friday, Tony Roma, Wendy's
Lodg E: Homewood Suites
W: Comfort Suites, Fairfield Inn, Holiday Inn Express
Other E: ATMs, Banks, Auto & Tire Services, Best Buy, PetSmart♥, Target
W: ATMs, Banks, Budget, Carwash, Cinemark 12, Costco, Discount Tire, FedEx Office, Office Depot, Petland♥, Target, Vista Ridge Mall, **Walmart sc**, Raytheon

448B **Frontage Rd, to Spur 553, TX 121 (SB) (Access #448A Services)**

446 **Frankford Rd, Carrollton (SB)**
Gas E: RaceTrac, Texaco
Food E: Coltier's BBQ, Café, Ms Mary's Southern Cuisine
Other E: Auto Dealer, Auto Rental, Volvo, Indian Creek Golf Course

◈= Regular Gas Stations with Diesel ▲ = RV Friendly Locations ♥= Pet Friendly Locations
Red print shows large vehicle parking / access on site or nearby **Brown Print = Campgrounds / RV PARKS**

EXIT		TEXAS
445B		**Pres Geo Bush Frwy/Tpke (SB)**
445		**Pres Geo Bush Frwy/Tpke (NB)**
444		**Whitlock Lane, Sandy Lake Rd, Serv Rd, Luna Rd, Old Denton Rd**
	Gas	E: Texaco W: Chevron
	Food	E: Taco Bell, Tommy's BBQ W: McDonald's
	Lodg	W: Delux Inn
	Other	E: Repair Services, Tires, Towing W: Sandy Lake Amusement Park, Sandy Lake RV Park/RVDump▲
443C		**Frontage Rd, Old Denton Rd, Whitlock Lane (NB) (Acc #444 Serv)**
443B		**Belt Line Rd, Crosby Rd**
	Gas	E: Conoco, RaceTrac, Shell
	Food	E: Café on the Square, Chinese
	Other	E: ATMs, Banks, Albertson's, Firestone, Greyhound, NTB, Repair Services W: ATMs, Repair Services, to Dr Pepper Star Center
443A		**Service Rd, Crosby Rd (NB)**
442		**Valwood Pkwy, Dallas**
	Gas	E: Texaco W: Fina
	Food	E: DQ, Denny's, El Chico, Grandy's, Jack in the Box, Subway, Taco Bueno, Waffle House
	Lodg	E: Comfort Inn, Guest Inn, Red Roof Inn♥, Royal Inn W: Best Western, Days Inn
	Other	E: Auto Services, Kroger
441		**Valley View Ln, Serv Rd, Dallas**
	Gas	W: Exxon, Mobil
	Food	E: B& L Rest, Railroad China Rest W: Abuelo's, Michael's Cafe
	Lodg	W: Best Western, Days Inn, Econo Lodge, La Quinta Inn♥
(440B)		**Jct I-635E, to Garland**
(440C)		**Jct I-635W, to DFW Airport**
440A		**Forest Lane, to US 77 (NB)**
	Gas	E: Shell
	Food	E: Dickey's BBQ, Grandy's, IHOP
	Lodg	E: Courtyard, Motel 6♥
	Med	E: + RHD Memorial Medical Center
	Other	E: ATMs, Banks, Repair Services, Hertz RAC, to Northtown Mall
439		**Royal Lane**
	Gas	E: Shell, Shamrock W: Chevron, Star Mart
	Food	E: Exit Café, McDonald's, Whataburger, Wendy's W: Cheers Diner, Jack in the Box
	Other	E: Auto Services & Repairs, Greyhound W: Auto Services & Repairs
438		**Walnut Hill Lane, Dallas**
	Gas	E: Fina, Mobil, Shell W: Chevron, Texaco◊
	Food	E: Burger King, Denny's, Chili's, Hunan Café, Old San Francisco Steak House, Steak & Ale, Porterhouse Steaks & Seafood, Taco Bell, TGI Friday, Trail Dust Steak House, Wendy's
	Lodg	E: Comfort Inn, Country Inn, Drury Inn, Garden Inn, Hampton Inn, Walnut Inn
	Other	E: ATMs, Banks, Auto Repairs W: Speed Zone

Personal Notes

EXIT		TEXAS
437		**Manana Dr (NB)**
436		**Lp 12, Spur 348, W Northwest Hwy, to DFW, Irving (NB ex, SB reacc)**
	Gas	E: Chevron, Exxon◊ W: Exxon, RaceTrac
	Food	E: BlackEyed Pea, Bubba's 2, Chili's, Don Pablo, IHOP, Joe's Crab Shack, Olive Garden, Outback Steakhouse, Papas BBQ, Pappadeaux Seafood, Pappas Bros Steakhouse, Pappasito's Cantina, Tx Land & Cattle, Waffle House W: Jack in the Box, McDonald's, Neno Pizza & Pasta, Thai Rice, Waffle House
	Lodg	E: Baymont Inn♥, Best Western, Days Inn, Comfort Suites, Hearthside Extended Stay, Quality Inn, Radisson W: Best Value Inn, Century Inn, Delux Inn
	Other	E: to Dallas Love Field✈ W: ATMs, Auto Services, AMC 24, Grocery, Sam's Club, to TX Stadium
435		**Harry Hines Blvd, to W Northwest Hwy (NB ex, SB reaccess)**
	Gas	E: RaceTrac
	Food	E: Arby's
	Other	E: Repair Services, to Dallas Love Field✈
434B		**Regal Row, Dallas**
	Gas	E: Chevron, Fina
	Food	E: Denny's, Whataburger
	Lodg	E: Econo Lodge♥, La Quinta Inn♥ W: Fairfield Inn
	Other	W: TBC Indoor Racing
434A		**Empire Central**
	Gas	E: Chevron, Tetco W: Exxon

EXIT		TEXAS
	Food	E: McDonald's, Sonic, Tony's Mex Rest, Wendy's W: Burger King, Deli, Taco Bell
	Lodg	E: Budget Suites, Candlewood Suites, InTown Suites, Radisson♥, Red Roof Inn♥, Wingate Inn
	Other	E: Office Depot
433B		**Mocking Bird Lane, Dallas, Love Field Airport**
	Gas	E: Mobil, Tetco W: Chevron, Exxon, Shell
	Food	E: Jack in the Box W: Church's, McDonald's
	Lodg	E: Clarion Hotel, Crowne Plaza, Hawthorne Suites, Oak n Spruce Resort Club, Radisson, Residence Inn, Sheraton
	TServ	W: to Cummins Southern Plains
	Med	E: + Columbia Medical Arts Hospital, + St Paul Medical Center
	Other	E: to Dallas Love Field✈ W: Goodyear, Tires, U-Haul
432B		**TX 356, Commonwealth Dr**
	Gas	E: Texaco
	Lodg	E: Residence Inn W: Delux Inn
432A		**Inwood Rd, Dallas**
	Gas	E: Exxon W: Fina, Texaco
	Food	W: Whataburger
	Lodg	W: Hilton, Studio Plus
	Med	E: + SW Medical Center, St Paul Medical Center
431		**Motor St, Dallas**
	Gas	E: Shell W: Shell
	Food	E: Denny's W: Ninfa's Mexican Rest
	Lodg	E: Stouffer Hotel W: Embassy Suites, Homewood Suites, Marriott, Wilson World Hotel
	Med	E: + Children's Medical Ctr of Dallas
	Other	E: Int'l Apparel Mart W: Auto Repairs & Services
430C		**Wycliff Ave**
	Food	E: T-Bones Steakhouse
	Lodg	E: Stouffer Hotel W: Hilton, Renaissance Hotel
	Other	E: Dallas Market Hall, Dallas Trade Mart, World Trade Center
430B		**Market Center Bvd**
	Food	W: Denny's
	Lodg	W: Quality Inn, Sheraton Suites, Wyndham Hotel
	Other	E: Dallas Trade Mart, World Trade Center
430A		**Oak Lawn Ave**
	Gas	E: Texaco
	Food	E: Rudy's Country Store & BBQ
429D		**North Tollway (NB)**
429C		**Hi Line Dr, Victory Ave (NB)**
	Lodg	W: Best Western
	Other	E: American Airlines Center
429B		**Continental Ave**
	Gas	W: Exxon
	Food	W: McDonald's, Popeye's Chicken
429A		**Woodall Rogers Frwy, to I-45, to US 75, to Houston, Sherman**
428E		**Commerce St, Main St, Reunion Blvd, S Industrial Blvd (NB, LEFT exit)**
	Other	E: ATMs, Banks, Downtown,

◊ = Regular Gas Stations with Diesel ▲ = RV Friendly Locations ♥ = Pet Friendly Locations
Red print shows large vehicle parking / access on site or nearby Brown Print = Campgrounds / RV PARKS

EXIT		TEXAS
	Other	E: Museums, JFK Memorial, Greyhound, Restaurants, Hotels
		W: Dallas West MH & RV Park▲
(428D)		**Jct I-30W, Tom Landry Fwy, to Ft Worth (SB, LEFT exit)**
428B		**Industrial Blvd (SB), Jct I-30E (NB)**
(428A)		**Jct I-30E, to I-45S (SB, LEFT exit)**
427C		**Cadiz St, Industrial Blvd (NB)**
	Other	W: to Dallas Convention Center
(427B)		**Jct I-30E, Industrial Blvd**
427A		**Colorado Blvd, Dallas**
426C		**Jefferson Blvd**
	Gas	E: Texaco
		W: Shell
426B		**8th St, TX 180W**
	Gas	E: Texaco
		W: Shell
	Lodg	E: Classic Motel
		W: Lasanta Motel, Sun Valley Motel
	Other	W: Auto Services
426A		**Ewing Ave**
	Food	E: McDonald's
	Lodg	W: Circle Inn
425C		**Marsalis Ave, Ewing Ave**
	Gas	E: Chevron
		W: Mobil
	Food	E: McDonald's
	Lodg	E: Dallas Inn Motel
	Other	E: Dallas Zoo & Aquarium
425B		**Beckley Ave, 12th St**
	Gas	W: 7-11, Exxon
425A		**Zang Blvd, Beckley Ave**
	Gas	W: Exxon, Shamrock, Texaco
425		**W 12th St, Pembroke Ave (NB)**
424		**Illinois Ave, Dallas**
	Gas	E: 7-11, Chevron, Shamrock
		W: Exxon
	Food	E: DQ, BBQ, KFC
		W: IHOP, Jack in the Box, Taco Bell
	Lodg	W: Oak Tree Inn
	Med	W: + Hospital
	Other	W: Pharmacy, Kroger, Shopping Center
423B		**Saner Ave**
423A		**US 67, Cleburne (SB)**
422BA		**Kiest Blvd, RL Thornton Fwy, to US 67 (SB)**
	Gas	E: Shell
		W: Texaco
	Food	W: McDonald's
	Lodg	W: Dallas Inn
422B		**Kiest Blvd, to US 67 (NB)**
422A		**Beckley Blvd, to Kiest Blvd, to US 67 (NB)**
421B		**Lp 12, W Ledbetter Dr**
421A		**Lp 12, E Ledbetter Dr, to Ann Arbor Ave**
	Gas	E: RaceWay, Texaco
	Food	W: Luby's Cafeteria
	Lodg	E: Budget Inn, Howard Johnson, Motel 6♥
		W: Sunbelt Motel
420		**Laureland Rd, Dallas**
	Gas	W: Conoco, Mobil
	Lodg	E: Master Suite Hotel, Luxury Inn
		W: Embassy Inn, Linfield Inn

EXIT		TEXAS
419		**Camp Wisdom Rd**
	Gas	E: Exxon
		W: Chevron, Shell
	Food	W: McDonald's
	Lodg	E: Oak Cliff Inn
		W: Sun Crest Inn
	Other	E: Auto Repairs & Services
(418B)		**Jct I-20E, to Shreveport**
(418A)		**Jct I-20W, to Ft Worth**
417		**Wheatland Rd, Dallas (SB), Danieldale Rd, Lancaster (NB)**
	Other	E: Auto Services, Truck Service
416		**Wintergreen Rd, DeSoto**
	Gas	W: 7-11
	Food	W: Cracker Barrel, Waffle House
	Lodg	W: Holiday Inn, Red Roof Inn♥
	Other	E: Auto Care & Rental
		W: ATMs, Banks
415		**Pleasant Run Rd, Lancaster, DeSoto**
	Gas	E: Chevron, RaceTrac, Shell◈
		W: Chevron, Exxon
	Food	E: Subway, Waffle House
		W: Burger King, El Chico, KFC, Long John Silver's, Luby's, McDonald's, Pizza Inn, On the Border, Outback Steakhouse
	Lodg	E: Great Western Inn, Royal Inn, Spanish Trails Motel
		W: Best Western
	Med	E: + Columbia Medical Center
	Other	E: Cinemark 14, CarMax, Enterprise RAC
		W: ATMs, Banks, Enterprise RAC, Kmart, Kroger, Office Depot
414		**FM 1382, Belt Line Rd, Lancaster**
	Gas	W: One Stop
	Food	E: Chili's, Whataburger
		W: McDonald's, Joe's Pizza
	Other	E: Walmart sc
		W: Police Dept
413		**Parkerville Rd, Lancaster**
	Gas	W: Exxon, Total
	Food	W: Subway, Taco Bell
	Other	W: Auto Services, U-Haul
412		**Bear Creek Rd, Red Oak to Glen Heights, Lancaster**
	Gas	W: Shell◈
	Food	W: DQ, Jack in the Box
	Other	W: Police Dept, Dallas Hi Ho RV Park▲
411		**FM 664, Ovilla Rd, Red Oak**
	Gas	E: Exxon, RaceTrac
		W: Exxon, Texaco
	Food	E: Church's, McDonald's, Pizza Hut, Taco Bell, Whataburger
	Lodge	W: Howard Johnson
	Other	E: Grocery, Auto Service, Truck Service
410		**Red Oak Rd, Red Oak**
	TStop	E: NB Access Rd: Knox Super Stop/Shell (Scales)
	Food	E: FastFood/Knox SS, Denny's, Subway
	Lodg	E: Days Inn
	Other	W: Hilltop Travel Trailers/RVDump
408		**US 77, to TX 342**
406		**Sterrett Rd, Waxahachie**
405		**FM 387, Butcher Rd, to US 77**
	Gas	E: Chevron◈
404		**Lofland Rd**

EXIT		TEXAS
403		**US 287, to Corsicana, Ft Worth (Gas/Food/WalMart SC at 1st Exit E)**
	Other	E: Auto Dealer, Civic Center
401B		**US 287 Bus, FM 664, Ovilla Rd**
	Food	E: Chisolm Trail Steakhouse
	Lodg	E: Best Western, Comfort Inn, Super 8
	Med	E: + Baylor Medical Center
401A		**Brookside Rd, Waxahatchee**
	Lodg	E: Best Value Inn, Ramada
	Other	E: TX State Hwy Patrol Post
399B		**FM 1446 (SB)**
399A		**FM 66, Rogers St, to FM 876, FM FM 1446 (SB)**
399		**FM 66, Rogers St, to FM 876, FM 1446, Waxahachie (NB)**
	Gas	E: Shamrock
		W: Chevron, Fina, Star Mart
	Lodg	E: Texas Inn Motel
	Other	E: Auto Services, Tires, Towing
		W: to Screams Amusement Park
397		**US 77, Waxahachie**
(392)		**Ellis Co Rest Area (Both dir) (RR, Phones, Picnic, Vend, WiFi)**
391		**FM 329, Pecan Rd, to US 77, Forreston Rd**
386		**TX 34, Dale Evans Dr, Italy, Ennis**
	FStop	W: Tiger Mart/Exxon (Scales)
	Gas	E: Shell◈
	Food	E: FastFood/Shell, DQ
		W: FastFood/TigerMart
	Lodg	W: Italy Inn
	Other	W: Laundry/TigerMart
384		**Derrs Chapel Rd, Italy**
381		**FM 566, Water St, Crossmain St, Milford Rd, Milford**
377		**FM 934, Hillsboro**
374		**FM 2959, Carl's Corner**
	TStop	W: Carl's Corner Truck Stop (Scales)
	Food	W: Rest/Carl's
	Other	W: Laundry/Carl's
(371)		**Jct I-35W, to Ft Worth, Jct I-35S, to Austin, Jct I-35E, to Dallas**
(85A)		**Jct I-35E, to Dallas, Jct I-35N, to OKC**
INTERSTATE 35E N		**I-35E continues above thru Dallas**
INTERSTATE 35W S		**I-35W continues below thru Ft Worth**
84		**FM 1515, Bonnie Brae St**
	Med	E: + Denton Community Hospital
82		**FM 2449, to Ponder**
79		**Crawford Rd**
76		**FM 407, Argyle, to Justin**
	Gas	W: Phillips 66◈
	Other	W: Corral City RV Park▲, Paradise RV Park▲
(75)		**Parking Area (Both dir)**
74		**FM 1171, to Lewisville, Flower Mound**

◈= Regular Gas Stations with Diesel ▲ = RV Friendly Locations ♥= Pet Friendly Locations
Red print shows large vehicle parking / access on site or nearby Brown Print = Campgrounds / RV PARKS

72 **Dale Earnhardt Way, Justin (Access to Ex #70 Services)**

70 **TX 114, to Dallas, Bridgeport**
- Gas: E: Shell◊
- Food: E: Subway/Shell, **More Food 3 mi E**; W: Rest/Marriott
- Lodg: E: Corporate Suites Plus, Comfort Suites♥, Sleep Inn♥, **to** Best Western; W: Marriott,
- Other: E: **Northlake Village RV Park▲**, **to appr 3-3.5 mi:** Gas, Grocery, **Walmart sc**, **to** Dallas/Ft Worth Airport✈, W: Texas Motor Speedway, **to approx 11 mi: Skyview Ranch RV Park▲**

68 **Eagle Pkwy**
- Other: W: Ft Worth Alliance Airport✈

67 **Alliance Blvd**
- Other: W: Ft Worth Alliance Airport✈

66 **Keller-Haslet Rd, Westport Pkwy, Haslet**
- Gas: W: Mobil◊
- Food: W: Italian Bistro, Snooty Pig Cafe, Sonny Bryan's Smokehouse, Subway, Taco Bueno, Wendy's/Mobil
- Lodg: E: Hampton Inn, Residence Inn

65 **TX 170E, Ft Worth, Keller**
- TStop: E: Pilot Travel Center #434 (Scales)
- Food: E: Rest/McDonald's/Subway/Pilot TC
- Other: E: Laundry/WiFi/**RVDump**/Pilot TC, Cabela's/**RVDump**

64 **Golden Triangle Blvd, to Keller Hicks Rd, Keller**
- Other: E: Auto Dealer, Miles Automotive

63 **Park Glen Blvd, Heritage Trace**
- Gas: E: 7-11
- Food: E: Subway

61 **North Tarrant Pkwy**
- Other: E: **to appr 4 mi: Walmart sc**, Murphy, Addt'l Services

60 **US 287N, US 81N, to Decatur**

59 **Basswood Blvd (fr SB)**
- Gas: E: Chevron◊
- Food: E: Jack in the Box/Chevron, Sonic
- Other: E: Home Depot, Kaufmann Tire

58 **Western Center Blvd**
- Gas: E: 7-11, Shell
- Food: E: Black Eyed Pea, Braums, Chili's, Denny's, Genghis Grill, On the Border, Posados Cafe, Shady Oak BBQ, Saltgrass Steak House, Wendy's; W: Joe's Crab Shack, Rosa's Cafe, Starbucks, Waffle House, Whataburger
- Lodg: E: Baymont Inn, Best Western
- Other: E: ATMs, AT&T, FedEx Office; W: Budget Truck, Tires

(57B) **Jct I-820E**

(57A) **Jct I-820W, Melody Hills Dr**

(56B) **Jct I-820E (NB)**

56A **Meacham Blvd, Ft Worth**
- Gas: E: Shell◊; W: Texaco◊
- Food: W: Cracker Barrel, McDonald's, Subway
- Lodg: E: Hilton Garden Inn, Howard Johnson, La Quinta Inn♥
- Lodg: W: Baymont Inn, Holiday Inn, Radisson, Super 8
- Other: E: Carwash/Shell

55 **Pleasantdale Ave (NB)**

54C **33rd St, Long Ave (NB)**
- Gas: W: Conoco◊, Valero
- Lodg: W: Motel 6♥
- TServ: E: Kenworth Cummins Southern Plains, Tarrant Truck Repair; W: Ft Worth Gear & Axle, Vangard Trailers
- Med: E: **+ Medical Clinic**

54B **TX 183W, Papurt St**
- Gas: W: Gas, Quik Stop◊
- Lodg: E: Classic Inn Motel
- Other: W: Mr D's Tires

54A **TX 183E, NE 28th St, Ft Worth**
- FStop: W: Super Lady #2/Fina (Scales)
- Gas: E: 7-11, Gas, Texaco◊

54 **TX 183, Ft Worth**
- TStop: W: PTP/Drivers Travel Mart #412 (Scales)
- Food: W: FastFood/Drivers TM

53 **North Side Dr, Yucca Ave**
- Gas: E: Shell◊
- Lodg: W: Country Inn

52E **Carver St, Frontage Rd (NB)**

52D **Carver St, Pharr St**

52C **Pharr St**
- Gas: W: Texaco
- TServ: W: Freightliner, Southwest Int'l, CAT, Cummins

52B **US 377N, TX 347 Spur. Belknap St**
- Gas: W: Chevron
- Food: W: Sonic

52A **US 377N, TX 121, Belknap St**

(51A) **Jct I-30E to Abilene, (fr NB)**

51 **Spur 280, Downtown Ft Worth**

(50C A) **Jct I-30, US 287S, US 377S, to Dallas, Abilene**
- TServ: W: DARR Power Systems

50B **TX 180E (NB)**

49B **Rosedale St**
- Med: W: **+ Hospital**

49A **Allen St, Rosedale St (NB)**
- Gas: E: Chevron, Shell
- Med: W: **+ Hospital**

48B **Morning Side Dr (SB)**

48A **Berry St**
- Gas: E: Tetco/Chevron◊, Citgo, Quick Track; W: RaceTrac
- Food: E: McDonald's/Chevron, Texas Style Chicken & Seafood
- Other: E: Auto Zone, Grocery, Tire Universe; W: U-Haul

47 **Ripy St**
- Lodg: W: Metro Inn South

46B **Seminary Dr**
- Gas: E: Conoco, Raceway; W: Diamond Shamrock, Shell
- Food: E: Grandy's, Jack in the Box, Long John Silver's, Sonic, Taco Bell, Whataburger; W: Denny's, IHOP, Wendy's
- Lodg: E: Days Inn, Delux Inn, Super 7 Inn
- Med: W: **+ Seminary South Medical Clinic**
- Other: E: Laundromat, NAPA; W: Firestone, Grocery, Pharmacy, La Gran Plaza Mall

46A **Felix St (NB)**
- Gas: E: Mobil
- Food: E: Pulido's Mexican; W: Burger King, McDonald's
- Lodg: E: South Oaks Motel

(45B) **Jct I-20E, to Dallas**

(45A) **Jct I-20W, to Abilene**

44 **Altamesa Blvd, Ft Worth**
- Gas: W: Quick Way #2, Racetrac
- Food: W: Rig Steak House, Waffle House
- Lodg: E: Holiday Inn, Radisson Inn; W: Baymont Inn, Best Western, Motel 6♥, South Loop Inn Motel

43 **Sycamore School Rd**
- Gas: W: Exxon
- Food: W: Chicken Express, Jack in the Box, Sonic, Subway, Taco Bell, Whataburger
- Other: E: Miller Brewing Co; W: Home Depot, Radio Shack

42 **Everman Pky, Sycamore Schl Rd**
- FStop: E: QT #873 (Scales)
- Gas: E: Exxon
- Food: E: Deli/QT

41 **Risinger Rd, Ft Worth**
- Other: W: **McClains RV/Camping World**

40 **Garden Acres Dr, Ft Worth**
- TStop: E: Love's Travel Stop #281
- Food: E: Subway/Love's TS
- Lodg: E: Microtel
- Med: E: **+ Hospital**
- Other: E: WiFi/**RVDump**/Love's TS, **Happy Camper RV Center**; W: C&S Trailer World, **Fun Times RV Center**

39 **FM 1187, McAllister Rd, Rendon-Crowley Rd**
- Gas: W: Shell◊, Diamond Shamrock◊
- Food: W: Taco Bell, Waffle House
- Lodg: W: Howard Johnson
- Med: E: **+ Huguley Memorial Medical Center**

38 **Alsbury Blvd, Burleson**
- Gas: E: Chevron, Mobil◊; W: Citgo, RaceWay, Shell, Texaco
- Food: E: Chili's, Cracker Barrel, McDonald's, Old Country Steak House, On the Border; W: Arby's, Applebee's, Burger King, ChickFilA, Denny's, Donuts Plus, Logan's Roadhouse, Pancho's, Olive Garden, Red Lobster, Taco Cabana, TGI Friday
- Lodg: E: Holiday Inn Express, Super 8
- Med: W: **+ Medical Clinic**
- Other: E: ATMs, Discount Tire, Lowe's, Airport✈; W: ATMs, Albertson's, Banks, Best Buy, Borders, Carwash, Equine Hospital♥, PetSmart♥, Radio Shack, Staples, Verizon,

37 **TX 174, Wilshire Blvd, Cleburne (SB) (Access Ex #36 Serv)**
- Gas: W: Exxon, Shell
- Other: W: **to Walmart sc**

36 **Spur 50, FM 3391, TX 174S, Renfro St, Burleson**
- Gas: E: Citgo◊, Mobil; W: Chevron, Fina
- Food: E: Luby's, Sonic, Waffle House
- Lodg: E: Comfort Suites, Days Inn
- TServ: E: Prestige Trucks

34 **Briaroaks Rd, Hidden Creek Pkwy (SB)**
- Other: W: **Mockingbird Hill RV Park▲**

(33) **Johnson Co Rest Area (Both dir) (RR, Phones, Picnic, WiFi)**

◊ = Regular Gas Stations with Diesel ▲ = RV Friendly Locations ♥ = Pet Friendly Locations
Red print shows large vehicle parking / access on site or nearby Brown Print = Campgrounds / RV PARKS

EXIT		TEXAS
32		**Bethesda Rd, Burleson**
	Gas	E: Citgo, Valero
	Food	E: Rest/Five Star Inn
	Lodg	E: Five Star Inn
	Other	E: RV Ranch of S Ft Worth▲ W: Elk Horn RV Lodge▲ , Mockingbird Hill RV Park▲
30		**FM 917, Joshua, Burleson, Mansfield**
	FStop	W: KC Ranch House/Shell
	Gas	E: Shell◈
	Food	E: Sonic/Shell W: Rest/KC Ranch House
	TServ	E: AAA Truck Parts & Service, Quality Truck Service & Supplies
	Other	W: Elk Horn RV Lodge▲ , Lynn Smith RV Center
27		**FM 707, FM 604**
	Other	E: Ancira RV Center
26B		**Bus 35W, Alvarado (SB)**
26A		**US 67, Henderson St, Alvarado, Cleburne, Dallas**
	Gas	E: Chevron◈, Exxon, EZ Mart, Texaco
	Food	E: Chicken Express, DQ, McDonald's, KFC/Pizza Hut/Chevron, Sonic, Waffle House, Whataburger
	Lodg	E: Days Inn, La Quinta Inn♥, Super 8♥,
	Other	E: ATMs, Banks, Auto Services, Carwash, Dollar General, Family Dollar , Walmart sc, U-Haul W: RV Ranch of Cleburne
24		**FM 1706, FM 3136, Maple Ave, Alvarado**
	TStop	E: Alvarado Shell Travel Plaza
	Gas	E: Chevron, Conoco
	Food	E: Rest/Alvarado TP, Pizza, Subway
	Other	E: ATMs, Banks, Carwash, Family Dollar
21		**FM 2258 Barnesville Rd, to Greenfield**
17		**FM 2258**
16		**TX 81S, FM 201, Grandview**
15		**FM 916, Grandview, Maypearl**
	Gas	W: Chevron◈, Mobil, Shamrock
	Food	W: Ricks Tx BBQ/Chevron, Subway
12		**FM 67**
(8)		**FM 66, Itasca** W: Parking Area
	FStop	E: Stars & Stripes/Valero
	TStop	W: Exxon Smart Stop #33
	Food	E: Cafe/Stars & Stripes W: DQ
	Other	W: Auto Dealer
(7)		**FM 934** E: Parking Area
	Gas	W: Exxon
3		**FM 2959, Hillsboro Airport**
	Other	E: to Hillsboro Muni Airport✈
INTERSTATE 35W N		**I-35W above is thru Ft Worth.**
	NOTE:	**I-35SB continues below.**
(371)		**Jct I-35E, N to Dallas, Jct I-35S to Austin, Jct I-35W, to Fort Worth**

EXIT		TEXAS
370		**US 77N, Spur 579, Hillsboro**
	Other	W: to Hillsboro Muni Airport✈
368B		**FM 286, Old Brandon Rd, Service Service Rd, TX 22 (SB)**
	Gas	W: Exxon, Shamrock◈
	Food	E: Lone Star Steakhouse, Taco Bell, Wendy's W: DQ, McDonald's, Pizza Hut
	Lodg	W: Best Western, Comfort Inn
	Med	W: + Hospital
	Other	E: Prime Outlets Mall W: Repair Services& Wrecker
368A		**TX 22, TX 171, FM 286, Hillsboro, to Whitney, Corsicana**
	FStop	W: Quix'n/Shell
	TStop	E: Love's Travel Stop #231 (Scales)
	Gas	E: 7-11 W: Chevron, Exxon, Mobil, Murphy USA
	Food	E: ChestersGr/Subway/Love's TS, Arby's, Black Eyed Pea, Burger King, Chinese Buffet, Golden Corral, Grandy's, IHOP, McDonald's, Starbucks W: DQ, Jack in the Box, KFC, Whataburger
	Lodg	E: Holiday Inn Express, Motel 6♥ W: Best Western, Thunderbird Motel
	Other	E: Laundry/WiFi/Love's TS, Prime Outlets of Hillsboro W: Walmart sc, Auto Dealers
367		**FM 3267, Old Bynum Rd**
364B		**TX 81N, Hillsboro (fr NB, Left ex)**
364A		**FM 310, Hillsboro**
	FStop	W: Knox Fuel Stop (Scales)
	Gas	E: Conoco, Exxon◈
	Food	W: El Conquistador
362		**Chatt Rd, Hillsboro**
359		**FM 1304, Hillsboro**
	TStop	W: Sunmart #169/Mobil
	Food	W: FastFood/Sunmart
	TWash	W: Abbott Truck Wash
	Other	W: Laundry/Sunmart
358		**FM 1232, FM 1242E, CR 2341, Abbott**
	Gas	E: Exxon
	Food	E: Cafe
356		**CR 3102, Abest Rd**
355		**County Line Rd, Russels Dr, West**
	Other	E: Waco North KOA▲
354		**Marable St**
	Other	E: Waco North KOA▲
353		**FM 2114, Oak St, West**
	Gas	E: Citgo, Fina, Shell W: Citgo◈, Exxon
	Food	E: DQ, Jerry's Chicken Shack, Pizza House, Subway
351		**FM 1858, West**
349		**Wiggins Rd, West**
347		**FM 3149, Tours Rd**
346		**Ross Rd, Elm Mott, Ross**
	TStop	E: Ross Truck Stop/Shell W: Will's Petro Stop/Exxon
	Food	E: Rest/FastFood/Ross TS W: Rest/Will's PS
	Other	E: Laundry/Ross TS W: I-35 RV Park▲
(345)		**Parking Area (Both dir)**

EXIT		TEXAS
345		**Old Dallas Rd, Hilltop St**
	Other	W: I-35 RV Park▲ , Marek Truck Repair
343		**FM 308, Elm Mott Dr, Elm Mott**
	TStop	E: Ed's Truck Stop/Shell (Scales)
	Gas	E: Exxon, Fina◈ W: Chevron◈
	Food	E: Rest/FastFood/Ed's TS, DQ/Exxon, Junction Café, Eddie Ray's Smokehouse W: Dee's Donut Shop
	TWash	E: Ed's TS
	TServ	E: Ed's TS
	Other	E: Laundry/Ed's TS
342B		**US 77S Bus, Waco**
	Other	W: North Crest RV Park▲
342A		**FM 2417, Crest Dr, Waco**
	Gas	W: Exxon, Shamrock◈
	Food	W: DQ
341		**Craven Ave, to Lacy, Lakeview**
	Gas	E: Chevron W: BP◈, Shell
	Lodg	W: Interstate North Motel
	Other	W: North Crest RV Park▲
340		**Meyers Lane (NB)**
339		**Lp 340, Lake Shore Dr, Waco, to TX 6S, FM 3051, Lake Waco**
	Gas	E: Valero◈, HEB W: Chevron, Citgo, Shell
	Food	E: Domino's, Jack in the Box, Luby's, Pizza Hut, Sonic, Whataburger W: Burger King, Cracker Barrel, KFC, McDonald's, Papa John's, Starbucks
	Lodg	E: Country Inn Suites W: Hampton Inn, Kings Way, Knight's Inn
	Other	E: Auto Service, Advance Auto Parts, Dollar General, HEB, Home Depot, Radio Shack, Sam's Club, Walmart sc, to Concord RV Park▲
338		**Behren's Cr, Waco (SB)**
	FStop	E: K's Travel Center #3/Shell
338B		**Behrens Circle, Bell Mead (NB)**
	Gas	E: Shell W: Texaco◈
	Lodg	W: Days Inn, Hampton Inn, Hawthorn Suites, Knights Inn, Motel 6♥
338A		**US 84, to TX 31, Waco Dr, Bell Mead , Waco (NB)**
	Gas	E: Fina, HEB, Sam's W: Shell
	Lodg	E: Value Place
	Other	E: ATMs, Auto Zone, HEB, Sam's Club
337		**US 84, to TX 31, Waco Dr**
	Other	W: to Shady Rest RV Park▲
337B		**US 77N Bus (NB)**
337A		**US 77S Bus (NB)**
336		**Forrest St, Waco (NB)**
335C		**MLK Jr Blvd, Lake Brazos Dr**
	Gas	E: Texaco
	Food	E: River Café, Mickey's
	Lodg	E: River Place Inn, Holiday Inn W: Travel Inn
	Med	W: + Hospital
335B		**FM 434, University Parks Dr, Fort Fischer**
	Food	E: IHOP, Quiznos W: Arby's, Jack in the Box
	Lodg	E: Best Western W: Clarion, Lexington Inn, Residence Inn
	Other	E: Baylor Univ, Museums

◈= Regular Gas Stations with Diesel ▲ = RV Friendly Locations ♥= Pet Friendly Locations
Red print shows large vehicle parking / access on site or nearby Brown Print = Campgrounds / RV PARKS

EXIT		TEXAS
335A		**4th St, 5th St**
	Gas	E: Exxon◈, Texaco◈
		W: BP, Shamrock
	Food	E: Denny's, IHOP, Pizza Hut
		W: Fazoli's, McDonald's, Taco Bell
	Lodg	E: Best Western, La Quinta Inn♥
		W: Clarion Hotel
	Other	E: Baylor Univ
334B		**8th St (NB) US 77S, 17th St, 18th St**
	FStop	W: K's Travel Center/Shell
	Gas	E: Exxon
	Food	E: Denny's, Pizza Hut, Shoney's
		W: Long John Silver's, Pizza Inn, Sonic, Taco Bell, McDonald's
	Lodg	E: Best Western, La Quinta Inn♥
		W: Quality Inn
334		**US 77S, 18th St, 17th St**
	Gas	E: BP, Chevron, Mobil
		W: Phillips 66◈, Texaco
	Food	E: Burger King, Popeye's, Vitex
		W: DQ
	Lodg	E: Comfort Inn, Econo Lodge, Super 8
333A		**US 77, Loop 396, La Salle Ave, Valley Mills Rd Dr, Waco**
	Gas	E: Chevron
		W: RaceTrac, Valero
	Food	E: Denny's, El Chico, Waco Elite Café, Texas Roadhouse, Oasis Cafe
		W: Burrito King, Catfish King, DQ, Jack in the Box, Sonic, Taco Bueno
	Lodg	E: Lone Star Motel, Motel 6♥
		W: Comfort Inn, Mardi Gras Motel
	TServ	W: Volvo, Freightliner
	Other	E: Auto Services, Auto Dealer
		W: Auto Services, Auto Dealer
331		**New Rd, Waco**
	TStop	W: Flying J Travel Plaza #5089 (Scales)
	Gas	E: Chevron◈
		W: Valero
	Food	W: Rest/FastFood/FJ TP, Hooters, IHOP
	Lodg	E: New Road Inn, Rodeway Inn
		W: Quality Inn
	Other	W: Laundry/WiFi/RVDump/LP/FJ TS, Harley Davidson
330		**TX 6, TX 340, Meridian, Robinson**
	FStop	W: 1miW Tx 6: CEFCO #41/Shell
	Gas	E: Chevron
		W: Citgo
	Food	W: FastFood/CEFCO, McDonald's, Outback Steakhouse
	Lodg	E: New Road Inn
		W: Fairfield Inn, Extended Stay America
	TServ	W: DARR Power Systems
	Other	W: Best Buy, Lowe's, Walmart sc, to Quail Crossing RV Park▲
328		**FM 2063, Sun Valley Dr, FM 2113, Moody, Hewitt, Robinson**
	TStop	E: Pilot Travel Center #432 (Scales)
	Gas	W: Diamond Shamrock◈, Texaco◈
	Food	E: FastFood/Pilot TC, DQ, McDonald's, Pizza Hut
	Other	E: Laundry/WiFi/RVDump/Pilot TC
325		**FM 3148, Old Temple Rd, Robinson Rd, Hewitt**
	TStop	W: TJ's Truck Stop, Ceejay/Shell
	Food	W: Rest/Ceejay
	Other	W: Walkabout RV Center
323		**FM 2837W, Lorena (SB)**
	Gas	W: Conoco
	Food	W: Pizza House
	Other	W: One Way Auto & Diesel Service

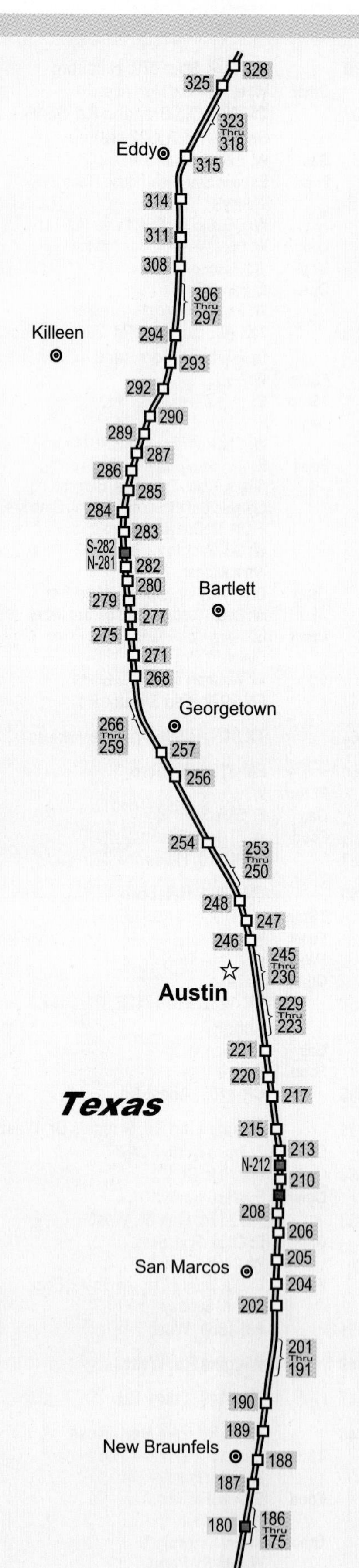

EXIT		TEXAS
322		**FM 2837E, Lorena**
	Gas	E: Phillips 66◈
		W: Chevron◈
319		**Woodlawn Rd, Bruceville**
(318)		**Parking Area (Both dir)**
318B		**Bruceville (SB)**
318A		**Frontage Rd, Bruceville**
315		**TX 7, FM 107, Eddy, to Moody, Chilton**
	TStop	W: CEFCO #47/Shell
	Food	W: FastFood/CEFCO
	Other	W: Bruceville Eddy RV Park▲, to Mother Neff State Park▲
314		**Blevins Rd, Chilton**
311		**Big Elm Rd, Troy**
	Other	W: All American RV Center
308		**FM 935, Troy**
	Gas	E: Shell
		W: Exxon
	Food	E: BBQ, Mexican Rest, Starbucks
	Other	W: All American RV Center
306		**FM 1237, Troy, to Pendleton**
	TStop	W: Love's Travel Stop #232
	Food	W: Subway/Love's TS
	TServ	W: All American Diesel & Tire
	Other	W: WiFi/RVDump/Love's TS, Temple RV Park & Sales▲
305		**Berger Rd, Temple**
	TStop	W: Truckers Heaven (Scales)
	Food	W: FastFood/Truckers Heaven
	Tires	W: Truckers Heaven
	TWash	W: Truckers Heaven
	Other	W: Laundry/Truckers Heaven, Temple RV Park & Sales▲
304		**Lp 363, Dodgen Loop, Temple**
	TStop	W: CEFCO #48/Shell (Scales)
	Gas	W: Diamond Shamrock◈
	Food	W: Wendy's/CEFCO
	Other	W: Laundry/CEFCO
303		**Spur 290, N 3rd St, Temple (SB)**
303B		**Spur 290, Bellair N, Mayborn Civic & Conv Center (NB)**
303A		**Spur 290, FM 1143, Industrial Blvd, N 3rd St (NB)**
	Gas	E: Diamond Shamrock
	Food	E: Fat Daddy's Rest, Jessie's Rest
	Lodg	E: Texas Inn
302		**Nugent Ave, Frontage Rd, to TX 53, Temple**
	Gas	E: EZ Way, Exxon◈, Texaco◈
		W: BP◈, Chevron
	Food	W: Denny's
	Lodg	E: Comfort Inn, Econo Lodge, Holiday Inn
		W: Days Inn, Motel 6♥, Stratford House
	Other	E: ATMs, Bank, Auto Services
		W: Auto Dealers
301		**TX 53, TX 36, FM 2305, Central Ave, Adams Ave, Temple**
	Gas	E: Diamond Shamrock, Texaco
		W: Valero
	Food	E: Arby's, ChickFilA, KFC, Long John Silver McDonald's, Starbucks, Subway, Taco Bell, Wendy's, Whataburger
		W: Catfish Shack

◈= Regular Gas Stations with Diesel ▲ = RV Friendly Locations ♥= Pet Friendly Locations
Red print shows large vehicle parking / access on site or nearby Brown Print = Campgrounds / RV PARKS

EXIT		TEXAS
	Lodg	E: La Quinta Inn♥ W: Best Western
	Other	E: ATMs, Auto Services, Firestone, HEB, Museum, Amtrak W: ATMs, Auto Services, Albertson's, Auto Dealers, Bell Co Harley Davidson to **Cedar Ridge Park▲** /Belton Lake, to Draughon-Miller Central Tx Regl Airport✈
300		**Ave H, 49th - 57th Streets, Temple**
	Gas	E: Shell W: Shell
	Food	E: Mexican Rest, TJ's Burgers
	Lodg	E: Oasis Motel, Temple Inn W: Westerner Motel
	Other	E: ATMs, Auto Services, Carwash, U-Haul, **Nick's Camper Sales**
299		**US 190E, TX 36, Loop 363, Gatesville, Cameron**
	Gas	E: Shell, Texaco◈ W: Exxon, Texaco
	Food	E: Doyle Phillips Steak House, Jack in the Box, Mexican Rest, Oldies Cafe W: Burger King, Chili's, IHOP, Luby's
	Lodg	E: Best Value Inn, Budget Inn
	Med	E: + Scott & White Memorial Hospital
	Other	W: Auto Dealers, **Ancira Motorhomes**, Best Buy, Home Depot, Target, U-Haul
298		**Frontage Rd (NB)**
297		**FM 817, Midway Dr, Temple**
	Gas	E: Citgo W: Shamrock
	Food	E: Mexican Grill
	Lodg	E: Classic Inn Motel, Super 8
	Other	E: **Family RV Sales**, Animal Clinic♥, W: Auto Dealer
294		**FM 93, 6th Ave, Belton**
294B		**FM 93, 6th Ave, Belton**
	Gas	E: Shell◈
	Food	E: McDonald's W: Old Time Pit BBQ, Pizza Hut, Sonic, Southwinds Rest, Taco Bell, Whataburger
	Lodg	W: Best Inns, River Forest Inn
	TServ	E: Santana's Truck Shop, McGuire Truck & Auto Repair
	Other	W: to DS Glory Summer Fun USA, Univ of Mary Hardin Baylor
294A		**Lp 253, Central Ave, Downtown**
	Gas	W: Shell◈
	Food	W: Burger King, Bobby's Burgers, Pizza Plus, Old Time Pit BBQ, Sonic
	Lodg	W: Ramada Inn
	Other	W: Auto Zone, Auto Services, Goodyear
293B		**TX 317, Main St, FM 436, US 190 (SB)**
293A		**US 190W, TX 317, FM 436, to Killeen, Fort Hood (NB)**
	TStop	E: CEFCO #54/Valero
	Gas	W: Mobil◈
	Food	E: FastFood/CEFCO W: Blimpie/Mobil
	Lodg	E: Budget Host, La Quinta Inn♥
	Other	W: **Belton/Temple/Killeen KOA▲**
292		**Loop 121, Belton (Access to Ex #293A Serv)**
	Other	W: **Belton/Temple/Killeen KOA▲**
290		**Shanklin Rd, Belton**
	Other	W: **Belton/Temple/Killeen KOA▲**, Picnic Area
289B		**Frontage Rd (NB)**

EXIT		TEXAS
289A		**Tahuaya Rd, Salado**
287		**Amity Rd, Salado**
286		**FM 2484, FM 1670, Salado**
	Other	W: to **Union Grove Park▲** /Stillhouse Hollow Lake
285		**FM 2268, Salado**
	Gas	E: Conoco W: Chevron
	Food	E: Subway W: Cowboys BBQ, Sonic
	Lodg	E: Holiday Inn Express
284		**Thomas Arnold Rd, Stagecoach Rd**
	Gas	E: Exxon W: Texaco◈
	Food	E: Burger King/Exxon, Arby's, Subway W: DQ
	Lodg	E: Stagecoach Inn W: Super 8
283		**FM 2268, to FM 2843, Salado**
282		**FM 2115, FM 2843, Salado**
	TStop	E: 2mi S: JD's Travel Center/Valero
	Food	E: Rest/JD's TC
	TServ	E: JD's TC/Tires,Lube&Oil
	Other	E: **Wagon Wheel RV Park▲**
(282)		**Bell Co Rest Area (SB) (RR, Phones, Picnic, Vend, WiFi)**
(281)		**Bell Co Rest Area (NB) (RR, Phones, Picnic, Vend, WiFi)**
280		**Frontage Rd, Prairie Dell**
279		**Frontage Rd, Hill Rd, Salado**
	Other	E: **Emerald Lake RV Park▲**
277		**Yankee Rd**
275		**FM 487, Jarrell, to Florence, Bartlett**
	TStop	E: PTP/Doc's One Stop/Shamrock (Scales), FJ TP/Sonterra Travel Center/Chevron (Scales)
	Gas	E: CEFCO #42/Exxon◈ W: Shell
	Food	E: Rest/Doc's One Stop, Burger King/ Denny's/FJ TP/Sonterra TC, McDonald's, Mexican Rest, Subway/Exxon
	Other	E: WiFi/Doc's OS, Laundry/WiFi/**RVDump/ LP**/FJ TP/S TC, Tire Shop/Exxon, Wiley's Wrecker Service
271		**Theon Rd, Jarrell**
	FStop	W: Texas Star Station #166/Shell
	Food	W: Subway/Texas Star
	Other	E: **ExploreUSA RV Supercenter**
268		**FM 972, Georgetown, Walburg**
	Other	E: **Crestview RV Center**
266		**TX 195, Georgetown, to Florence, Killeen**
	TStop	E: Sunmart #168/Mobil
	Gas	W: Exxon
	Food	E: FastFood/Sunmart
	Other	E: **Berry Springs RV Park▲**, **New Life RV Park▲**
264		**Bus 35, TX 418, Lakeway Dr, Georgetown**
	Other	E: Auto & Repair Services, **Berry Springs RV Park▲**, **New Life RV Park▲**, **San Gabriel River RV Camp Resort▲**, **East View RV Ranch▲** W: Georgetown Muni Airport✈

EXIT		TEXAS
262		**RM 2338, Andice Rd, Georgetown Lake Georgetown**
	Gas	E: Shamrock W: Exxon, Phillips 66, RaceTrac
	Food	E: KFC, Luby's, McDonald's, Pizza Hut, NY Burrito Wraps, Sonic W: Chuck Wagon, DQ, Georgetown BBQ, Hardee's, Riverview Steakhouse, Taco Bueno, Wendy's, Whataburger
	Lodg	E: Comfort Suites, Holiday Inn Express W: Days Inn, La Quinta Inn♥
	Other	E: Albertson's, ATMs, Auto Services, Enterprise RAC, Pharmacy, Radio Shack, Towing, UPS Store W: ATMs, Banks, Auto Services, Grocery, Wrecker Service
261A		**RM 2338, Williams Dr, Andice Rd, Lk Georgetown (Acc to #262 Serv)**
	Other	E: **Crestview RV**, **San Gabriel River RV Camp Resort▲**
261		**TX 29, W University Ave, Serv Rd Georgetown, to Taylor, Burnet**
	Gas	E: Chevron, Mobil, Shell◈ W: Chevron
	Food	E: Applebee's, Burger King, Chili's, Harry's BBQ, Rio Bravo
	Lodg	E: Red Poppy Inn, Holiday Inn Express
	Med	E: + Georgetown Hospital
	Other	E: ATMs, Banks, Auto Services, Family Dollar, Golf Course, Grocery, **Sheriff Dept**, Wrecker Service, Southwestern University, **Country Tyme RV Center**, **East View RV Ranch▲**, to **Shady River RV Resort▲** W: Best Buy, Home Depot, Office Depot, PetSmart♥, Target, **Walmart sc**
260		**RM 2243, Leander Rd, to Bus 35, Georgetown, to Leander**
	Gas	E: Jiffy Mart #2 W: Chevron/Tetco, Speedy Stop
	Food	W: Café, Jack in the Box, Pizza, Mexican
	Lodg	W: Holiday Inn, Quality Inn
	Med	E: + Georgetown Hospital
	Other	E: Auto Services, Georgetown Diesel & Auto Repair, Tires, Trailer Service W: to 8mi **Sunshine RV Park▲**
259		**Bus 35, Austin Ave, Georgetown**
	Other	E: **East View RV Ranch▲** W: **RV Outlet Mall**, to Inter space Caverns
257		**Westinghouse Rd, Frontage Rd**
	Other	E: Auto Dealers W: **Walkabout RV**
256		**FM 1431, CR 114, Chandler Rd, Round Rock**
	Other	E: Auto Dealers
254		**Lp 35, FM 3406, Old Settlers Blvd, Round Rock**
	Gas	E: 7-11, Chevron, Texaco W: Phillips 66, Shell
	Food	E: Arby's, Castaways Seafood, Lone Star Café, McDonald's, Sonic, Subway W: Cracker Barrel, Denny's, Golden Corral, Good Eats Café, Kona Ranch Steak Seafood, Rudy's Country Store, Saltgrass Steakhouse
	Lodg	E: Best Western W: Courtyard, Hilton Garden Inn, La Quinta Inn♥, Holiday Inn, Red Roof Inn♥, Springhill Suites

◈= Regular Gas Stations with Diesel ▲ = RV Friendly Locations ♥= Pet Friendly Locations
Red print shows large vehicle parking / access on site or nearby **Brown Print = Campgrounds / RV PARKS**

EXIT		TEXAS
	Med	E: + Round Rock Health Clinic
	Other	E: Auto Dealers, Cinemark 8, Firestone, Enterprise RAC, Fleetpride, Tires, Vet♥ W: Albertson's, ATMs, Auto Dealer, Auto Services & Repairs
253		**US 79, Palm Valley Blvd, Sam Bass Rd, to Old Settlers Blvd, Round Rock to Austin, Taylor**
	Gas	E: Phillips 66◈, Shell W: Exxon◈, Shell◈
	Food	E: Arby's, DQ, Damon's, KFC, Lone Star Café, Lonesome Dove W: K-Bob's Steakhouse, Mexican & Seafood Grill, Joe's Smokehouse, Popeye's, Roadhouse Grill
	Lodg	E: Best Western, Wingate Inn W: Country Inn, Super 8
	Other	E: ATMs, Auto Services, Banks, Rental Cars, **Police Dept, to Bullard's RV Park▲** W: Auto Services, US Post Office
252B		**RM 620, Frontage Rd**
	Gas	W: 7-11, BP
	Food	W: IHOP, Japanese Rest, McDonald's, Starbucks, Wendy's
	Other	W: Albertson's, Auto Services, Mall, Wholesale Tire
252A		**McNeil Rd, Frontage Rd**
	Gas	E: Shell◈ W: Fina, Phillips 66
	Food	E: Outback Steakhouse, Whataburger W: McDonald's, Wendy's
	Lodge	E: Days Inn, Candlewood Suites
	Other	E: ATMs, Banks, Auto Services, Tires W: Albertson's, **Adventure Time RV Rentals**
251		**Loop 35, Round Rock**
	Gas	W: Exxon, Shell
	Food	E: Chili's, CiCi's Pizza, McDonald's, Outback Steakhouse, Souper Salad, Whataburger W: Burger King, Jack in the Box, Luby's
	Lodg	E: Residence Inn W: Country Inn, Days Inn
	Other	E: Big Lots, Auto Services, Advance Auto Parts, Dollar General W: Albertson's, NTB, Walgreen's
250		**FM 1325, L Henna Blvd, Austin**
	Gas	E: Chevron, Mobil◈ W: Shell, Sam's
	Food	E: Applebee's, ChickFilA, Chili's, Jason's Deli, Joe's Crab Shack, McDonald's, Romano's Macaroni Grill, Subway W: Chuck E Cheese, Hardee's, Hooters, Olive Garden, Starbucks
	Lodg	E: Hampton Inn W: Baymont Inn, Hilton, Extended Stay America, Pinnacle Suites
	Other	E: ATMs, Best Buy, Discount Tire, FedEx Office, Goodyear, Home Depot, PetSmart♥, Target, **Walmart sc** W: ATMs, B&N, FedEx Office, Lowe's, Office Depot, PetCo♥, Sam's Club, Youngblood Tire & Auto, **Austin RV Park North▲**, **Blessing MH & RV Park▲**
248		**Grand Ave Pkwy, Pflugerville**
	FStop	E: **7701 N Gr Ave:** Tex Con Oil/Shell **FM 1825SE:** Speedy Stop #248
	Gas	E: RaceTrac, Shamrock W: Chevron
	Food	E: FastFood/Speedy Stop W: McDonald's/Chevron

Personal Notes

EXIT		TEXAS
	Lodg	W: Budget Suites
	Other	W: Auto Services, Fleet Service
247		**FM 1825, Pflugerville**
	FStop	E: **FM 1825SE:** Speedy Stop #248
	Gas	E: RaceTrac W: Exxon, Shell
	Food	E: Jack in the Box, Sonic, Wendy's W: KFC, Miller BBQ, Whataburger
	Lodg	W: Budget Suites, Quality Inn
	Other	E: Firestone, Cinema, HEB W: Diesel Tech, Goodyear
246		**Dessau Rd, Howard Lane, Austin**
	Gas	E: Citgo, Shell◈ W: Valero◈
	Food	W: IHOP, Whataburger
	Other	E: Home Depot, NTB, AAA Truck & Trailer W: Auto Services, **Smokey's RV Repair**
245		**FM 734, Parmer Lane, Yager Ln**
	Gas	W: 7-11, Exxon, Murphy USA
	Food	E: ChickFilA, Chili's, Johnny Carino's Italian Rest, Moe SW Grill, Panda Express, Subway W: Red Robin, Starbucks
	Lodg	W: Residence Inn, Springhill Suites
	Other	E: Best Buy, Hobby Lobby, Office Depot, NTB, Sports Authority, Target W: Lowe's, **Walmart sc**
244		**Frontage Rd, Austin (NB)**
243		**Braker Lane, Frontage Rd**
	Gas	E: Valero W: Shell◈
	Food	E: Jack in the Box, Subway, Whataburger W: Sweetie Pies, Taste of Brazil
	Lodg	W: Austin Motor Inn, Walnut Forest Motel

EXIT		TEXAS
	Other	E: Central TX Harley Davidson W: Albertson's, Auto Services, Dollar General, **to** IBM, Univ of TX/JJ Pickle Ctr
241		**Rundberg Lane**
	Gas	E: Exxon W: Chevron, Conoco, Shell
	Food	E: Golden Corral, Jack in the Box, Pizza, Mr Catfish, Mexican Rest
	Lodg	E: Extended Stay America, Ramada Inn, Wellesley Inn W: Austin Village Motor Inn, Budget Inn, Budget Lodge, Economy Inn, Motel 6♥, Red Roof Inn♥
	Other	E: Albertson's, Dollar General, Pharmacy, **Walmart sc**, U-Haul, TX Starter Service W: Auto Services, Grocery
240A		**US 183, Service Rd, Anderson Ln, to Lampasas, Lockhart**
	Gas	E: Exxon
	Gas	W: Chevron◈, Star Mart◈
	Food	E: Chili's, DQ, Jack in the Box, Old San Francisco Steak House W: Cancun Mexican Rest, McDonald's, Red Lobster
	Lodg	E: Days Inn, Hampton Inn, Wellesley Inn W: Best Western, Econo Lodge♥, Red Roof Inn♥, Sheraton, Super 8, Wingate Inn
	Other	E: Auto Services, Towing W: ATMs, Banks, Auto Services
240B		**US 183, Service Rd, Anderson Ln, to Lampasas, Lockhart (NB)**
	Gas	W: Star Mart
	Food	W: Burger Tex
	Lodg	W: Best Western, Sheraton
	Other	W: Daughters of the Republic of TX
239		**Service Rd, St Johns Ave, Anderson Ln, Austin**
	Gas	E: Shell W: Conoco◈, Exxon
	Food	E: Chili's, Fuddrucker's, Pappadeaux Seafood, Shoney's, Steak & Egg W: Applebee's, Denny's, Souper Salad, Sushi House
	Lodg	E: Best Value Inn, Days Inn, Doubletree Hotel, Drury Inn, Hampton Inn, Hawthorn Suites, Hearthside Suites, Studio 6 W: Amerisuites, American Inn, Comfort Inn, Country Inn, Holiday Inn Express, La Quinta Inn♥, Sheraton
	Med	E: + Cornerstone Hospital
	Other	E: Home Depot, **Walmart sc** W: ATMs, Auto Services, FedEx Office, Grocery, Greyhound, Highland Mall, Laser Quest, Office Depot
238BA		**US 290E, 51st St Frontage Rd (SB)**
238B		**Frontage Rd, US 290E, FM 2222, Koenig Ln, 51st St, to Houston**
	FStop	E: Conoco Fuel Mart
	Gas	E: Exxon, Chevron, Phillips 66, Shell W: Texaco
	Food	E: Burger King, Dixie's Roadhouse, El Torito, Fuddrucker's, Long John Silver, Pizza Hut, Tx Land & Cattle Steaks W: Bombay Bicycle Club, Captain's Seafood, Coco's, Carrabba's, IHOP
	Lodg	E: Doubletree Hotel, Embassy Suites, Econo Lodge, Holiday Inn, Red Lion Inn W: Country Inn, Courtyard, Drury Inn, Hilton, Quality Inn, Ramada

◈= Regular Gas Stations with Diesel ▲ = RV Friendly Locations ♥ = Pet Friendly Locations
Red print shows large vehicle parking / access on site or nearby Brown Print = Campgrounds / RV PARKS

EXIT		TEXAS
	Other	E: Capitol Plaza, Auto Services, ATMs, Banks, Dollar Tree, Grocery, Walgreen's W: Greyhound, Highland Mall, Office Depot to Univ of Tx/Austin
238A		**Frontage Rd, Reinli St, Clayton Ln, 51st St (Access same as #238B)**
	Food	E: CiCi's, Grandy's, McDonald's W: Captain's Seafood & Oyster Bar, Baby Acapulco, IHOP,
	Lodg	W: Courtyard, Drury Inn, Fairfield Inn, La Quinta Inn♥, Motel 6♥, Quality Inn, Ramada, Super 8♥
237B		**51st St, Cameron Rd (NB) (Access to Ex #238 Serv via Serv Rd)**
237A		**Airport Blvd, 51st St, 38 1/2 St**
	Food	E: Purple Sage BBQ W: Jack in the Box, Wendy's
	Lodg	E: Best Western
	Other	E: U-Haul
	Other	W: ATMs, Best Buy, HEB, Hancock Shopping Center, Univ of TX
	NOTE:	**Exits Below: Upper Level is Thru I-35, Lower Level is Downtown Access**
236B		**38 1/2 St, Austin**
	Gas	E: Chevron W: Texaco
	Other	E: ATMs, Auto Services, Planet Earth Adventures, U-Haul W: ATM, Bank, O'Reilly Auto Parts
236A		**26th—32nd Streets**
	Food	E: Sonic
	Lodg	E: Days Inn W: Rodeway Inn
	Med	W: + St David's Medical Center
	Other	W: LBJ Library & Museum, Museums, Tx Memorial Stadium, Galleries
235B		**Manor Rd, 26th St**
	Food	E: Denny's, Fuddruckers, Castaways W: Mexican Rest, Subway
	Lodg	E: DoubleTree Hotel, Super 8, Wingate W: Marriott, Ramada Inn
	Other	E: Disch Falk Stadium W: State Capitol, Univ of TX
235A		**15th St, MLK Blvd**
	Med	W: + Hospital
	NOTE:	**Exits Above: Upper Level is Thru I-35, Lower Level is Downtown Access**
234C		**6th St—12th St, State Capitol**
	Gas	E: Chevron, Exxon, Shell W: Exxon, Shell, Texaco
	Food	E: Denny's W: Wendy's
	Lodg	E: Doubletree Hotel, Super 8 W: Hilton Garden Inn, Radisson, Sheraton
	Med	W: + Breckenridge Hospital, + Children's Hospital of Austin
	Other	E: CVS, Museums W: Fall Creek Vineyards, Frank Erwin Center, Museums, State Capitol
234B		**Cesar Chavez St, 8th-3rd Sts (SB) Cesar Chavez St, 2nd-4th Sts (NB)**
	Gas	E: Chevron, Texaco W: Mobil
	Other	W: Courthouses, Museums
234A		**1st St, Lp 343, Cesar Chavez St, Holly St, Downtown**
	Food	E: Taco Bueno, Whataburger W: IHOP, Iron Works BBQ, Quiznos

EXIT		TEXAS
	Lodg	E: La Quinta Inn♥ W: Four Seasons Hotel
	Other	E: Auto Services W: ATMs, Banks, Austin Conv Center, Visitor Center
233A		**1st—4th Streets**
233BC		**Festival Beach Rd (NB)**
	Gas	E: Exxon, Shell W: Chevron
	Lodg	W: Holiday Inn
233		**Riverside Dr, Town Lake**
	Gas	E: Shell, Shamrock W: Chevron
	Lodg	E: Extended Stay America, Riverside Quarters, Wellesley Inn W: Holiday Inn
232B		**Woodland Ave**
	Gas	W: Shell
	Lodg	E: Guest Inn
232A		**Oltorf St, Live Oak**
	Gas	E: 7-11, Shell◈ W: Chevron, Exxon, Shell, Texaco
	Food	E: Carrow's, Luby's Cafeteria W: Denny's, Marco Polo
	Lodg	E: Exel Inn, La Quinta Inn♥, Motel 6♥, Park West Inn, Super 8 W: Clarion, Quality Inn
231		**Woodward St**
	Gas	E: Shell◈
	Food	E: Country Kitchen
	Lodg	E: Holiday Inn, Motel 6♥, Super 8
	Other	W: Home Depot
230A		**St Elmo Rd (SB)**
	Food	W: Chili's, KFC, Tx Land & Cattle Steakhouse, Wendy's, Whataburger, Umi Sushi Bar & Grill
	Lodg	W: Candlewood Suites, Days Inn, La Quinta Inn♥
	TServ	W: Hackney Auto & Truck Service
	Other	W: Auto Dealers, Auto Services, National Tire, Metropolitan 14
230B		**Ben White Blvd, US 290W, TX 71 Burleson Rd, Austin (SB)**
	FStop	E: Quick Mart #2/Conoco
	Gas	W: Chevron, Shell
	Food	W: Miller BBQ, Pizza Hut
	Lodg	E: Best Western W: Hawthorne Suites
	Other	W: Auto Services, Firestone
230		**US 290, TX 71, Ben White Blvd, St Elmo Rd, Austin (NB)**
	FStop	E: Speedy Stop #216/Conoco **9105 US290E**
	Gas	E: Shell, Sam's
	Food	E: Domino's Pizza, Jim's Rest, Subway, McDonald's, Western Steaks W: Furr's, IHOP
	Lodg	E: Comfort Suites, Fairfield Inn, Hampton Inn, Homewood Suites, Holiday Inn, Marriott, Omni Hotel, Red Roof Inn♥, Residence Inn, Springhill Suites W: Candlewood Suites, Hawthorn Suites, Days Inn, La Quinta Inn♥
	Med	W: + St David's South Hospital
	Other	E: Sam's Club, **Walmart** W: Auto Dealers, Auto Services
229		**Stassney Lane, Austin**
	Gas	E: Exxon W: Shell, Albertson's
	Food	E: Applebee's, McDonald's, Subway, Sonic, Taco Bell

EXIT		TEXAS
	Food	W: Burger King, Chili's, KFC, Long John Silver's, Whataburger
	ATServ	W: Hackney Auto & Truck Service
	Other	E: Cinemark Tinseltown, HEB, **Austin Lone Star RV Resort▲**, W: Albertson's, Auto Dealers, Lowe's, Firestone
228		**William Cannon Dr**
	Gas	E: Exxon, Shamrock W: Shell◈
	Food	E: Applebee's, McDonald's, Subway, Sonic, Taco Bell W: Burger King, Long John Silver, Whataburger, Wendy's
	Other	E: Discount Tire, Grocery, Radio Shack, Target, **Austin Lone Star RV Resort▲** W: Auto Dealers, Advance Auto Parts, Big Lots, CVS, Firestone, Pharmacy
227		**Lp 275, Slaughter Ln, S Congress**
	Gas	E: Shell◈ W: Tetco, Valero, Murphy
	Food	E: IHOP W: Chili's, Jack in the Box, Sonic, Starbucks, Steak n Shake, TGI Friday
	Other	E: Home Depot, Tires, Towing, Truck Service, U-Haul W: Albertson's, PetSmart♥, **Walmart sc**
226		**FM 1626, Slaughter Creek**
	Gas	E: Shell
225		**FM1626, Orion Creek Pkwy**
	Gas	E: Shell
	Other	E: Harley Davidson
223		**FM 1327, Buda**
221		**Loop 4, Buda**
	TStop	E: Dorsett's 221 Truck Stop (Scales)
	Gas	E: Chevron W: HEB
	Food	E: Rest/221 TS, McDonald's/Chevron W: **Cracker Barrel**, Jack in the Box, Subway
	Lodg	E: Best Value Inn
	TServ	E: 221 TS
	Other	E: Laundry/221 TS, **All Star RV Center, Camper Clinic II** W: HEB, Cabela's, Radio Shack, **Walmart sc**
220		**FM 2001, Buda, to Niederwald**
	Other	E: **Marshall's Traveland** W: **Crestview RV Park▲ & RV Center**
217		**Lp 4, CR 210, CR 131, Windy Hill Rd, Buda, Kyle**
	FStop	E: Tex Best #3/Conoco W: Diamond Shamrock
	Gas	W: Exxon◈
	Food	W: Pizza Hut/Shamrock, Burger King
	Lodg	W: Best Western
	Other	E: **Marshall's Traveland** W: **Evergreen RV Center, Beacon Lodge & RV Campground▲**
215		**Bunton Overpass**
	Gas	E: Exxon W: HEB
	Other	W: HEB
213		**FM 150, W Center St, Kyle**
	Gas	E: Diamond Shamrock◈, HEB W: Conoco
	Other	E: HEB, ATMs, Auto Services, Auto Zone, Tires W: Police Dept
(212)		**Parking Area (NB)**

◈= Regular Gas Stations with Diesel ▲ = RV Friendly Locations ♥= Pet Friendly Locations
Red print shows large vehicle parking / access on site or nearby **Brown Print = Campgrounds / RV PARKS**

EXIT		TEXAS
(211)		**Weigh Station (NB)**
210		**Yarrington Rd, Kyle**
	Other	W: Plum Creek RV Resort▲
(209)		**Weigh Station (SB)**
208		**Frontage Rd, San Marcos**
206		**US 81 Bus, Lp 82, Aquarena Springs Dr, San Marcos**
	Gas	E: Conoco◈, Shamrock W: Exxon◈, Mobil◈, Payless, Phillips 66, Shell◈, Texaco
	Food	W: Mamacita's, Popeye's Chicken, Sonic
	Lodg	W: Comfort Inn, La Quinta Inn♥, Motel 6♥, Ramada, Super 8, University Inn
	Other	E: Auto Services, Sheriff Dept W: Office Depot, Tourist Info, to Tx State Univ/SanMarcos
205		**TX 80, to TX 21, Hopkins St, TX 142, to Luling, Bastrop**
	Gas	E: Chevron, Conoco, Mobil, Shell◈ W: Circle K, Chevron, Shamrock
	Food	E: Arby's, DQ, Jason's Deli, Pit BBQ, McDonald's, Subway W: Applebee's, Burger King, CiCi's Pizza, Furr's, IHOP, Logan's, Long John Silver, McDonald's, Pizza Hut
	Lodg	W: Best Western, Days Inn, Microtel
	Other	E: ATMs, Auto Services, Banks, Dollar General, CVS, Grocery, Walmart sc, San Marcos Muni Airport✈, Pharmacy Pecan RV Park▲, Riverbend Park▲, Wolf Creek Ranch & Resort▲, Leisure Resort▲ W: ATMs, Auto Services, Best Buy, HEB, Office Depot, Target, Walgreen's, Tourist Info, Vet♥
204B		**Riverside Dr, CM Allen Pkwy (SB)**
	Gas	W: Chevron, Conoco◈, Shell◈
	Food	W: Chinese Buffet, KFC, Red Robin, Sonic
	Lodg	W: Best Western, Days Inn, Microtel, Parkside Inn, Red Roof Inn♥
	Other	W: Tourist Info, Auto Services
204A		**Lp 82W, TX 123E, San Marcos, to Seguin (SB)**
	FStop	W: San Marcos Truck Stop/Texaco
	Food	W: FastFood/San Marcos TS, DQ
	Lodg	W: Econo Lodge
	Tires	W: San Marcos TS
	Other	W: Laundry/LP/San Marcos TS, Amtrak, Auto Dealers, FedEx Office, Greyhound, Grocery
204		**Lp 82E, TX 123E (NB)**
	Gas	E: Conoco, Phillips 66, Shamrock
	Food	E: Golden Corral, Hardee's, Luby's Cafeteria, McDonald's, Whataburger
	Lodg	E: Best Western, Comfort Suites, Holiday Inn Express
	Med	E: + Hospital
	Other	E: Auto Dealers, Auto Service, Enterprise RAC
202		**FM 3407, Wonder World Dr**
	Gas	E: Shell, Sac n Pack W: Shamrock◈
	Food	E: Church's Chicken, Jack in the Box
	Med	E: + Central Tx Medical Center
	Other	E: Auto Service, Discount Tire, Lowe's, PetSmart♥, Sam's Club W: I-35 Tire & Service, Auto Services
201		**McCarty Lane, CR 233**
	Other	E: Auto Dealers W: Auto Dealers

EXIT		TEXAS
200		**Center Point Rd, San Marcos**
	Gas	W: Diamond Shamrock
	Food	E: Branding Iron, Cracker Barrel, Lone Star Cafe, Subway, Taco Bell, Wendy's W: Kip's Tx BBQ, Starbucks, Whataburger
	Lodg	W: AmeriHost Inn
	Other	E: Prime Outlets at San Marcos, Tanger Outlet Center
199		**Posey Rd, CR 235 (SB)**
	Other	W: Canyon Trail RV Resort▲
199A		**Posey Rd (NB)**
	Other	W: Canyon Trail RV Resort▲
196		**FM 1102, York Creek Rd, New Braunfels, San Marcos**
	Other	E: Southwest RV Center/Camping World, Roman Holiday Motorhomes
195		**Watson Ln, Old Bastrop Rd**
193		**Conrads Rd, Kohlenberg Rd**
	Gas	W: Travel Center of America #232/Shell (Scales)
	Food	W: CntryFare/Subway/Popeye's/TA TC
	TServ	W: TA TC
	Other	E: Camping World/Southwest RV Center, Roman Holiday Motorhomes W: Laundry/WiFi/RVDump/TA TC
191		**FM 306, FM 483, New Braunfels, Canyon Lake**
	FStop	W: Tex Best #5/Exxon
	Gas	E: Conoco◈, Texaco W: Chevron
	Food	E: Quizno's/Conoco W: FastFood/TexBest, Burger King
	Other	W: Guadalupe Valley Winery, Sundance Golf Course
190C		**Post Rd, Bus 35 (SB)**
190B		**Lp 35S, N Elliot Knox Blvd, New Braunfels, to TX 46 (SB)**
190A		**Frontage Rd, to TX 46 (SB)**
	Gas	E: Shell
	Food	W: McDonald's, Wendy's
	Lodg	W: Best Western, Comfort Suites, Quality Inn, Rodeway Inn
	Other	E: Discount Tire, Home Depot
190		**Frontage Rd, to Bus 35 (NB)**
	Lodg	E: Howard Johnson
	Other	E: Evergreen RV Center
189		**TX 46, TX 337, Seguin, Boerne**
	Gas	E: Conoco◈, Exxon, Texaco◈ W: Chevron, Diamond Shamrock
	Food	E: Luby's Cafeteria, Olive Garden, Oma's W: Applebee's, IHOP, McDonald's, Taco Bell, Wendy's, New Braunfels Smoke House, Taco Cabana
	Lodg	E: Fountain Motel, Oakwood Inn, Super 8 W: Days Inn, Hampton Inn, Holiday Inn, Motel 6♥, Rodeway Inn
	Med	W: + McKenna Memorial Hospital
	Other	E: Discount Tire, Home Depot, Office Depot, Lakeside RV Park▲, New Braunfels Muni Airport✈ W: Auto Services, New Braunfels Factory Stores,Museum, Peformace Auto & Truck Repair, Walgreen's, to Landa Park, Landa Falls, Waterpark
188		**Frontage Rd, New Braunfels**
187		**FM 725, Seguin Ave**
	Gas	E: Chevron

EXIT		TEXAS
	Gas	W: Exxon◈
	Food	E: Arby's, Burger King, CiCi's Pizza, Cow Pies, Long John Silver, Mamacita's, Subway, Whataburger W: Adobe Café, China Kitchen, Jack in the Box, Peking Rest
	Lodg	W: Budget Inn
	Med	W: + Hospital
	Other	E: Auto Dealers, Auto Services, Big Lots, Family Dollar, Grocery, Radio Shack, Police Dept W: CVS, Enterprise RAC, NAPA, Navarro's Truck & Auto Repair, Auto Services
186		**Walnut Ave, New Braunfels**
	Gas	E: Exxon, Valero, Murphy USA W: Shamrock, Shell, HEB
	Food	E: ChickFilA, Marina's Mexican Rest, McDonald's, Popeye's, Taco Bell W: KFC, Mr Gatti's, Papa John's, Starbucks
	Lodg	E: Executive Lodge, Red Roof Inn♥
	Other	E: Lowe's, Walmart sc W: Auto Zone, Auto Services, Cinema Walnut 6, Dollar Tree, HEB, Radio Shack, Target, Walgreen's, U-Haul
185		**Bus 35, Bus 81, Spur St, FM 1044**
184		**Lp 337, FM 482, Ruekle Rd, New Braunfels**
	TStop	E: Pilot Travel Center #330 (Scales)
	Gas	E: Shell◈
	Food	E: McDonald's/Pilot TC, Blimpie/Shell
	Other	E: Laundry/WiFi/Pilot TC, Auto Services, Auto Dealer, Hill Country RV Resort▲
183		**Solms Rd, New Braunfels**
	Gas	W: Exxon
182		**Engel Rd**
	Food	E: Pam's Country Kitchen W: Mesquite Pit BBQ
	Other	E: First RV of New Braunfels, Stahmann RV Sales W: Snake Farm, Noah RV Services
180		**Schwab Rd**
(180)		**Comal Co Rest Area (Both dir)** (RR, Phones, Picnic, WiFi, NB: RVDump)
178		**FM 1103, Cibolo, Hubertus Rd**
	Gas	E: Shell◈
177		**FM 482, FM 2252**
	Other	W: Stone Creek MH & RV Park▲
176		**Old Weiderstein Rd (Acc to Ex #175)**
175		**FM 3009, Roy Richard Dr, Natural Bridge Caverns Rd, Schertz, to Garden Ridge**
	Gas	E: Shamrock, HEB W: Shamrock◈, Shell◈, Murphy
	Food	E: Chili's, McDonald's, Miller BBQ, Mexican Rest, Sonic, Taco Cabana W: Arby's, Burger King, Denny's, Jack in the Box, KFC, Starbucks, Wendy's
	Lodg	W: Country Inn
	Other	E: HEB, Radio Shack, UPS Store W: Walmart sc
174A		**Frontage Rd, Schertz Pkwy**
	Food	E: Rudy's Country Store
	Other	W: S Texas RV Superstore, to Crestview RV Superstore
174B		**FM 1518, Selma, Schertz**
	Other	W: Enterprise RAC, Retama Park Racetrack, Crestview RV Superstore
	Food	E: Mama's Rest, Mexican Rest

◈= Regular Gas Stations with Diesel ▲ = RV Friendly Locations ♥= Pet Friendly Locations
Red print shows large vehicle parking / access on site or nearby Brown Print = Campgrounds / RV PARKS

EXIT **TEXAS**

173 **Olympia Pkwy, Old Austin Rd, Forum Blvd, Selma**
- Gas — E: Costco, Mobil, Shell, Valero
- Food — E: Chili's, ChickFilA, Hooters, IHOP, Outback Steakhouse, Peter Piper Pizza, Papouli's Greek Grill, Red Robin, Romano's Macaroni Grill, Starbucks, Subway, TGI Friday, Wendy's
- Other — E: ATMs, Best Buy, Borders, Costco, Home Depot, Office Max, PetSmart♥, Target/Pharmacy, UPS Store, to Randolph AFB
  W: Retama Park Racetrack

172 **Pat Booker Rd, Universal City, Randolph AFB, Toepperwein Rd, Live Oak (SB), Lp 1604, Anderson Loop, Forum Blvd (NB) TX 218**
- Lodg — E: Comfort Inn
- Other — E: ATM, Live Oak 18, **to** Randolph Air Force Base
  W: **to** Sea World

171 **TX 218, Pat Booker Rd, Universal City, Randolph AFB (NB)**

170 **Judson Rd, to Converse (SB)**
- Gas — W: Citgo, Exxon, Sam's
- Food — E: Denny's, Kettle Rest, Subway, Whataburger
- Lodg — E: Americas Best Value Inn, La Quinta Inn♥, Value Place
  W: Best Western, Hampton Inn
- Med — E: + NE Methodist Hospital, + Concentra Urgent Care
- Other — E: Auto Dealers, Enterprise RAC, Target
  W: Sam's Club

170B **Toepperwein Rd (NB)**

170A **Judson Rd, Converse (NB)**

169 **O'Connor Rd, Wurzbach Pkwy, San Antonio**
- FStop — W: Timewise #10/Shell
- Gas — E: Exxon◈, Phillips 66
  W: RaceTrac, Valero
- Food — E: McDonald's, Quiznos, Taco Cabana
  W: Jack in the Box, Jim's Coffee Shop, Little Caesar's, Mi Casa
- Lodg — W: Best Western, Days Inn, Econo Lodge
- Other — E: **El Monte RV Rentals, Iron Horse RV/LP/Rentals**
  W: **Greentree Village North Travel RV Park▲**, Auto Services, Tires

168 **Weidner Rd, Crosswinds Way**
- Gas — E: Exxon, Shamrock
  W: Mobil
- Lodg — E: American Motel, Days Inn
  W: Ramada Inn, Super 8
- Other — E: Auto Services
  W: Auto Services

167B **Starlight Terrace, Thousand Oaks Dr (SB)**
- Other — E: Auto & Truck Services
- Lodg — W: Best Western

167A **Randolph Blvd, Windcrest (SB)**
- Lodg — W: Best Western, Days Inn, Classic Inn, Motel 6♥, Ruby Inn
- Other — E: RV Center

167 **Starlight Terrace, Thousand Oaks Dr, San Antonio (NB)**

(166) **Jct I-410W, Loop 368S**
- Other — W: to Sea World

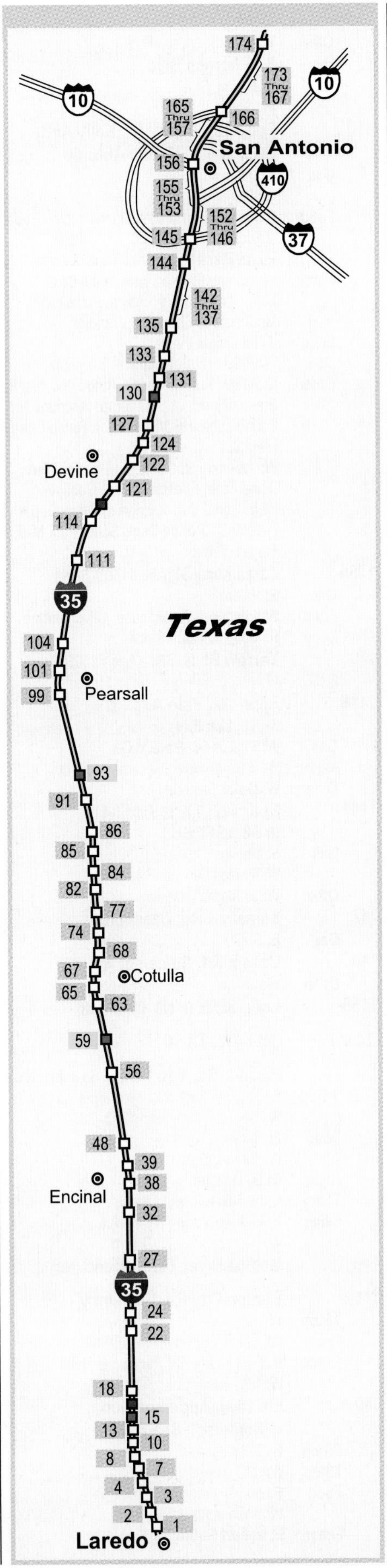

165 **FM 1976, Walzem Rd, Windcrest**
- Gas — E: Chevron, Shell, Valero◈
  W: Mobil
- Food — E: Applebee's, Burger King, CiCi's Pizza, Chuck E Cheese, Church's Chicken, Ghengis Khan, IHOP, Jack in the Box, Jim's Coffee Shop, Long John Silver, Luby's, Marie Callendar's, McDonald's, Olive Garden, Pizza Hut, Red Lobster, Shoney's, Starbucks, Subway, Taco Bell, Taco Cabana, Wendy's
  W: Mexican Rest, Sonic
- Lodg — E: Drury Inn, Hampton Inn
- Other — E: ATMs, Banks, Albertson's, Auto Zone, Big Lots, Discount Tire, Dollar General, Firestone, Home Depot, Office Depot, PetSmart♥, Radio Shack, Target, UPS Store, **Walmart sc**, Windsor Park Mall
  W: Auto Services, National Tire, **to TX RV Supply**

164B **Eisenhauer Rd**
- Gas — E: Exxon◈
- Lodg — E: Hawthorne Suites, Value Place

164A **Rittiman Rd, San Antonio**
- Gas — E: Exxon, Shell◈, Valero◈
  W: Chevron◈, Valero
- Food — E: Burger King, Cracker Barrel, Denny's, Church's Chicken, Jack in the Box, McDonald's, Taco Cabana, Whataburger
  W: Miller BBQ, Popeye's, Sonic, Wendy's
- Lodg — E: Best Value Inn, Best Western, Comfort Suites, Hallmark Inn, La Quinta Inn♥, Motel 6♥
- Other — E: Auto Services, Towing

163C **Holbrook Rd, Binz-Englemann Rd Ft Sam Houston (SB)**
- TServ — E: Cummins Southern Plains

163B **Petroleum Dr**

(163A) **Jct I-410S (SB, LEFT exit)**

(163) **Jct I-410S, George Beach Ave (NB)**
- Med — W: + Brooke Army Medical Center

(162) **Jct I-410S, FM 78, Kirby, Lp 13, WW White Rd (NB), to FM 78, George Beach Ave, Binz-Englemann Rd (SB)**
- Lodg — W: Holiday Inn, Microtel, Quality Inn
- Other — E: Auto & Towing Services

161 **Binz-Englemann Rd (NB) (Access #162 Serv)**

160 **Splashtown Dr (NB), AT&T Center Pkwy, Freeman Coliseum Rd (SB)**
- Gas — E: Exxon, Valero◈
  W: Conoco, Shamrock
- Food — W: Casey's BBQ, Mexican Rest, Rest/HI
- Lodg — E: Delux Inn
  W: Americas Best Value Inn, Days Inn, Howard Johnson, Holiday Inn, Microtel, Quality Inn, Super 8, Travelodge
- Other — E: Auto Services, Fleet Service, Freeman, Coliseum, Willow Springs Muni Golf Course, Splashtown, **San Antonio KOA▲**
  W: HEB, Ft Sam Houston

159B **Walters Ave , Ft Sam Houston (SB), AT&T Center Pkwy, Freeman Coliseum (NB)**
- Food — E: McDonald's
- Lodg — W: Econo Lodge

◈= Regular Gas Stations with Diesel ▲ = RV Friendly Locations ♥= Pet Friendly Locations
Red print shows large vehicle parking / access on site or nearby Brown Print = Campgrounds / RV PARKS

EXIT		TEXAS
	Other	E: San Antonio KOA▲
		W: to Fort Sam Houston
159A		**New Braunfels Ave**
	Gas	E: Exxon, Star Mart
		W: Chevron, Shamrock
	Food	W: Miller BBQ, Sonic
	Lodg	W: Antonian Inn
	Other	W: S Tx Diesel, to Fort Sam Houston
158C		**Alamo St, Austin St, Broadway (SB)**
(158B)		**Jct I-37S, US 281S, Corpus Christi (SB)**
158A		**US 281N, Johnson City (SB)**
(158)		**Jct I-37, US 281, Corpus Christi, Johnson City, Lp 368, Broadway (NB)**
157C		**St Mary's St, Quincy St, Lp 368, Broadway (NB)**
157B		**McCullough Ave, Brooklyn Ave**
	Med	W: + Metropolitan Methodist Hospital
157A		**San Pedro Ave, Main Ave, Lexington Ave**
	Lodg	E: Super 8
		W: Travelodge♥
	Med	E: + Baptist Medical Center
(156)		**Jct I-10W, US 87N, to El Paso**
155C		**W Commerce St, W Houston St, Market Square N Laredo St (SB)**
155B		**Durango Blvd, Downtown (NB), Frio St (SB)**
	Food	E: Miller's BBQ
		W: McDonald's
	Lodg	E: Best Western, Fairfield Inn, Courtyard, Holiday Inn, La Quinta Inn♥
		W: Motel 6♥, Radisson Inn
	Med	E: + Christus Santa Rosa Hospital
	Other	E: Univ of TX/San Antonio
		W: Court, Police Dept
155A		**Spur 536, S Alamo St, Frio St (SB), Spur 536, Guadalupe St (NB)**
	Gas	E: Exxon, Shell
		W: Conoco
	Food	E: Churchs Chicken, Denny's, McDonald's, Pizza Hut, Wendy's
	Lodg	E: Best Western, Comfort Inn, Mayfield Motel, Ramada Ltd
		W: Holiday Inn Express, Microtel, Riverside Lodging
	Other	E: Auto Services, Museums
154B		**S Laredo St, Cevallos St**
	Gas	E: Exxon, Texaco
	Food	E: McDonald's, Pizza Hut, Wendy's
	Lodg	E: Days Inn
154A		**San Marcos St, Nogalitos St, Loop 353S, Frontage Rd**
(153)		**Jct I-10E, US 90, US 87S, Del Rio, Houston, El Paso**
152B		**Malone Ave, Theo Ave**
	Gas	W: Phillips 66, Shamrock, Shell◈
	Food	E: Taco Cabana
152A		**Division Ave, San Antonio**
	Gas	E: Tetco/Chevron
		W: Gas
	Food	E: Miller BBQ, Whataburger
		W: Sonic
	Lodg	E: Quality Inn

EXIT		TEXAS
	Other	W: Auto Services, Tires
151		**Southcross Blvd**
	Gas	E: Exxon, Shell
		W: Shell◈
150B		**Loop 13, Military Dr, Kelly AFB, Lackland AFB, San Antonio**
	Gas	E: Valero
		W: Exxon
	Food	E: Applebee's, Arby's, Denny's, Don Pedro Mexican, El Pollo Loco, KFC, Peter Piper Pizza, Pizza Hut, Sonic, Taco Cabana
	Food	W: Hungry Farmer, Jack in the Box, Long John Silver's, Luby's, Pizza Hut, McDonald's, Shoney's, Wendy's
	Lodg	E: La Quinta Inn♥
	Med	W: + Southwest General Hospital
	Other	E: ATMs, Auto Services, Auto Zone, Banks, Brake Check, CVS, Cinema, Discount Tire, Econo Lube, HEB/Pharmacy, Radio Shack, U-Haul, Walgreen's,
		W: Albertson's, ATMs, Banks, Best Buy, Dollar Tree, Firestone Auto, Goodyear, HEB, Home Depot, Lowe's, Office Depot, Pharmacy, Police Dept, South Park Mall, Target, Verizon, Walgreen's,
150A		**Zarzamora St (Acc #150B Serv)**
	Gas	E: Valero
	Food	W: Longhorn Steakhouse, Olive Garden
	Lodg	E: Motel 6, Value Place
149		**Yarrow Blvd (SB) (Acc #150B Serv)**
	Med	W: + Southwest General Hospital
148B		**Spur 422, Palo Alto Rd (fr NB, Left Exit)**
	Gas	W: Phillips 66, Save 'n Go
	Med	W: + Southwest General Hospital
	Other	W: Dollar General
148A		**Spur 422, TX 16S, to I-410 (fr SB, LEFT Exit)**
	Gas	E: Chevron
		W: Phillips 66
	Other	W: to Alamo Dragway
147		**Somerset Rd, Cassin Rd**
	Gas	E: Shell◈
146		**Cassin Rd, Somerset Rd (NB)**
	Other	W: Leo's Truck & Trailer Repair
145B		**Loop 353N (fr NB, LEFT exit)**
(145A)		**Jct I-410, TX 16**
144		**Fischer Rd, Von Ormy, San Antonio**
	TStop	E: Tetco #308/Valero (Scales)
		W: Love's Travel Stop #242 (Scales)
	Food	E: Subway/Tetco
		W: Carl's Jr/Love's TS
	Lodg	E: D&D Motel
	TServ	E; to Sierra Diesel Truck Repair
	Other	E: Hidden Valley RV Park▲
		W: Laundry/WiFi/RVDump/Love's TS
142		**Medina River TurnAround (NB)**
141		**Benton City Rd, Von Ormy**
	TStop	W: Timewise Landmark/Shell
	Food	W: FastFood/Timewise, El Paradour Café
	Other	E: Fort Retire RV Park▲, U-Haul
		W: LP/Timewise
140		**FM 1604, Anderson Loop, to Somerset, Sea World**
	FStop	E: Tex-Best #4/Exxon
	TStop	W: AAA Travel Center/Valero (Scales)
	Food	E: Burger King/TexBest
		W: FastFood/AAA TC
	Other	E: to Fort Retire RV Park▲

EXIT		TEXAS
	Other	W: Laundry/AAA TC, Alamo River RV Resort▲, to Sea World
139		**Kinney Rd, Von Ormy**
137		**Shepherd Rd, Atascosa**
	Other	E: Diesel Service
		W: Diesel Service
135		**Luckey Rd, Lytle**
133		**US 81, TX 132, Lytle (SB)**
131		**FM 3175, Benton City Rd, Lytle**
	Gas	W: Conoco◈, HEB
	Food	W: DQ, McDonald's, Pig Stand, Sonic
	Lodg	W: Days Inn
	Other	W: AutoZone, Dollar General, HEB
(130)		**Medina Co Rest Area (Both dir) (RR, Phones, Pic, Pet, WiFi)**
127		**FM 471, Natalia**
124		**FM 463, Bigfoot Rd, Devine**
122		**TX 173, Hondo Ave, Devine, to Hondo, Jourdanton**
	Gas	E: Exxon◈
		W: Chevron
	Food	E: Church's Chicken/Exxon
		W: McDonald's/Subway/Chevron, Triple C Steak House
	Lodg	W: Devine Motel
	TServ	W: M&W Truck & Auto Service
	Other	E: Auto Dealer
		W: to Devine Muni Airport→
121		**TX 132N, Devine**
	Other	E: Gusville RV Park▲
(118)		**Weigh Station (Both dir)**
114		**FM 462, Moore, Big Foot, Yancey**
	Gas	E: Gas◈
	Other	E: US Post Office
111		**US 57, Pearsall, to Eagle Pass**
	FStop	W: Amigos Travel Center/Valero
104		**Bus 35, Pearsall (Acc #101 Serv-Approx 3 mi E)**
101		**FM 140, Pearsall, to Charlotte, Uvalde**
	FStop	E: Chevron
		W: Valley Mart #12/Exxon,
	TStop	W: AmBest/Pearsall Travel Center/Valero (Scales)
	Food	E: Cow Pokes BBQ
		W: FastFood/Exxon, Porterhouse Rest/Pearsall TC
	Lodg	E: Best Western, Rio Frio Motel, Royal Inn
		W: Budget Inn
	Med	W: + Frio Regional Hospital
	Other	E: appr 1.5 mi to N Oak St: HEB/Pharmacy, Walmart/Pharmacy, US Post Office, Addt'l food, lodging, services
		W: Laundry/BarbSh/WiFi/Pearsall TC
99		**US 35, FM 1581, Pearsall, Divot**
(93)		**Parking Area (Both dir)**
91		**FM 1583, Pearsall, Derby**
	Other	E: McKinley Field Airport→
86		**Loop 35, Dilley**
85		**FM 117, to Batesville, Garcia**
	Gas	W: Exxon◈
	Food	E: Pacho Garcia Café
		W: Rest/Relax Inn
	Lodg	E: Sona Inn♥
		W: Relax Inn♥

◈= Regular Gas Stations with Diesel ▲ = RV Friendly Locations ♥= Pet Friendly Locations
Red print shows large vehicle parking / access on site or nearby Brown Print = Campgrounds / RV PARKS

EXIT — TEXAS

- **Other** E: to Dilley RV Park▲
  W: Dilley Airpark✈

84 — TX 85, Leona St, Dilley, to Charlotte, Carrizo Springs
- **TStop** W: Frio Self Serve/Valero, Cleo's Travel Center #3/Shell
- **Gas** E: Super S Foods, to Valero
- **Food** W: FastFood/Frio SS, FastFood/Cleo's TC
- **Lodg** W: Executive Inn
- **Med** E: + Community General Hospital
- **Other** E: Super S Foods, Carwash/Super S, to Dilley Drug Store, US Post Office

82 — County Line Rd, CR 4700, Dilley

77 — FM 469, Cotulla, to Millett

74 — Gardendale

69 — Bus 35C, Frontage Rd, Cotulla (SB)
- **Gas** E: Super S Foods
- **Other** E: Family Dollar, Hardware Store, Super S Foods, **Access to #67**

67 — FM 468, Cotulla, to Big Wells
- **FStop** E: Cleo's Travel Center/Valero
  W: Tetco #70/Chevron (Scales)
- **Gas** E: Country Store/Conoco, Exxon◈
- **Food** E: FastFood/Cleo's TC, Wendy's/Exxon, DQ, Rest/Country Store
  W: McDonald's/Tetco
- **Lodg** E: Cotulla Executive Inn, Village Inn, to Cotulla Motel,
  W: Best Western♥
- **TWash** E: Cow Town Truck Wash
- **TServ** E: Valentine's Tires & Service
- **Other** E: to Cotulla-La Salle Co Airport✈

65 — Lp 35, TX 3408, Main St, Cotulla

63 — Elm Creek Interchange

(59) — Parking Area (Both dir)

56 — FM 133, Artesia Wells

48 — Caiman Creek Interchange

39 — TX 44, Ranch Rd 863, Encinal, to Laredo
- **FStop** E: Love's Travel Stop #298 (Scales)
- **Gas** W: Exxon◈
- **Food** E: Chesters/Subway/Love's TS
- **Other** E: Laundry/WiFi/Love's TS
  W: US Post Office

38 — TX 44, US 35, Encinal (NB)

32 — San Roman Interchange

27 — Callaghan Interchange

24 — Camino Columbia TOLL Rd

22 — Webb Interchange

(18) — US 83N, Laredo, to Carrizo Springs, Uvalde, Eagle Path, Del Rio
E: TX Info Center/Rest Area

(15) — Parking Area (Both dir)

(15) — Inspection Area (NB)

13 — Uniroyal Interchange, Laredo
- **TStop** E: Pilot Travel Center #377 (Scales),
  W: Flying J Travel Plaza # 730 (Scales), Travel Center of America #153 (Scales)

EXIT — TEXAS

- **Food** E: Subway/Pilot TC
  W: CountryMkt/FastFood/FJ TP, CountryPr/BKing/Subway/TacoBell/TA TC
- **TWash** E: Blue Beacon TW/Pilot TC
- **TServ** E: Southern Tire Center, Wingfoot Truck Care/Pilot TC
  W: TA TC
- **Other** E: Laundry/Pilot TC
  W: Laundry/WiFi/**RVDump/LP**/FJ TP, Laundry/WiFi/ChromeSh/TA TC

10 — Port Laredo, Carriers Dr (NB)

8B — Killam Ind Blvd, Lp 20, FM 3464, Bob Bullock Loop (SB)

8A — Lp 20, Bob Bullock Loop (NB)

8 — Lp 20, FM 3464, Bob Bullock Loop
- **Food** E: Carl's Jr, Quiznos, Wendy's
- **Lodg** E: Best Western
- **TServ** E: Rush Peterbilt Truck Center
- **Med** E: + Doctors Hospital of Laredo
- **Other** E: Advance Auto Parts, Best Buy, HEB/Pharmacy, Hobby Lobby,
  W: to Costco, **Deer Creek Village▲**

7 — Shiloh Dr, Las Cruces Dr (SB)
- **Lodg** E: Motel 9

4 — FM 1472, Del Mar Blvd, Santa Maria Ave, Laredo
- **FStop** W: **FM 1472& Killiam Blvd:** Laredo Fuel Center/Chevron, **8919 FM 1472:** Mart/Shell, **US 83S:** La Noria Truck Stop, **11801 FM 1472:** Speedy Stop#34/Exxon
- **TStop** W: **5301 Santa Maria:** Gateway Truck Terminal (Scales), **4mi N - Lp 20:** Discount Diesel (Scales)
- **Gas** E: Exxon◈, Chevron
- **Food** E: Applebee's, Burger King, CiCi's Pizza, DQ, IHOP, Jack in the Box, Johnny Carinos Italian Grill, Las Asadas Mexican, Lin's Grand Buffet, Posh Sushi, Quiznos, McDonald's, Shoney's, Whataburger
  W: Rest/Gateway TT, Golden Corral
- **Lodg** E: Comfort Suites, Extended Stay America♥, Hampton Inn, Residence Inn
  W: Motel/Gateway TT, Days Inn, Motel 6♥, Springhill Suites
- **TServ** W: Gateway TT/Tires
- **Other** E: ATMs, Albertson's, Best Buy, HEB, Lowe's, Northcreek 10 Cinema, Petland♥, Radio Shack, Target, UPS Store,
  W: CB/Gateway TT, Laredo Harley Davidson, to **Deer Creek Village▲**

3B — Mann Rd, Laredo
- **FStop** W: **5400 Santa Maria:** Leyendecker Oil/Exxon
- **Gas** E: Exxon
- **Food** E: Cattlemen's Café, Logan's Roadhouse, Luby's, Olive Garden
  W: Chili's, Golden Corral, Kettle Rest, Outback Steakhouse, Subway, Taco Cabana, Whataburger
- **Lodg** E: Embassy Suites, Fairfield Inn, Homewood Suites♥, Residence Inn
  W: Americana Inn, Family Garden Inn, Fiesta Inn,
- **Med** E: + Dr's Hospital Health Center
- **Other** E: ATMs, Auto Dealers, Budget RAC, Enterprise RAC, Lowe's, Mall de Norte, UPS Store, Auto & Truck Service

EXIT — TEXAS

- **Other** W: ATMs, Auto Services, Cinemark 12, Dollar General, Dollar Tree, Home Depot, Office Depot, **Walmart**

3A — San Bernardo Ave, Calton Rd
- **Gas** E: Texaco◈
  W: Chevron
- **Food** E: Chili's, ChickFilA, Dominos Pizza, Fuddrucker's, Jack in the Box, Long John Silver, Logan's Roadhouse, Luby's, Peter Piper Pizza, Sirloin Stockade
  W: Bill Miller's BBQ, Burger King, Coyote Creek Grill & Cantina, DQ, Dunkin Donuts, El Pollo Loco, Julep's, McDonald's, Pizza Hut, Popeye's Chicken, Taco Bell, Wendy's, Whataburger
- **Lodg** E: Fairfield Inn, Red Roof Inn♥
  W: Americas Best Value Inn, Best Western, Gateway Inn, La Hacienda Motor Hotel, Monterey Inn♥, Motel 6♥
- **Other** E: ATMs, Auto & Diesel Service, Advance Auto Parts, Banks, Carwash, Firestone, HEB/Pharmacy, Kmart, Kawasaki, Mall Del Norte, NAPA, O'Reilly Auto Parts, Pep Boys, Truck & Trailer Repair,
  W: Auto Services, Border Sporting Goods, Banks, Burlington Coat Factory, Grocery, Goodyear, Mexico Insurance, Office Max, PetCo♥, Radio Shack, Sam's Club, Towing

2 — US 59, Lafayette St, Intl Airport, to Corpus Christi, Houston
- **Gas** E: Conoco, Shell
  W: Chevron◈, Circle K, Exxon◈, Shell, Valero
- **Food** E: Jack in the Box
  W: Church's Chicken, Denny's, KFC, Little Mexico Rest, Pizza Hut, Raul's BBQ, Wendy's
- **Lodg** W: Courtyard, Holiday Inn, La Quinta Inn♥, Mayan Inn, Pan American Café & Motel
- **Med** E: + Laredo Medical Center
- **Other** E: ATMs, Auto Services, Auto Zone, to Laredo Int'l Airport✈, **Lake Casa Blanca State Park▲**
  W: ATMs, Advance Auto Parts, Auto Zone, Grocery, Mexican Insurance, Suzuki

1B — Park St, Frontage Rd
- **Gas** W: Conoco◈, Fina
- **Food** W: KFC, Pizza Hut, Popeye's Chicken
- **Lodg** W: Holiday Inn
- **Other** W: Auto Services, ATMs, Grocery

1A — Washington St, Frontage Rd
- **Gas** E: Exxon, Shell, Valero
  W: Exxon, Fina
- **Food** W: KFC, McDonald's, Wendy's
- **Other** E: Auto & Truck Repair
  W: Auto Services, Firestone, Goodyear

NOTE: I-35 begins/ends on US 83 in Laredo, TX

CENTRAL TIME ZONE

TEXAS

Begin Northbound I-35 from Laredo, TX to Duluth, MN.

◈= Regular Gas Stations with Diesel ▲ = RV Friendly Locations ♥= Pet Friendly Locations
Red print shows large vehicle parking / access on site or nearby Brown Print = Campgrounds / RV PARKS

S

EXIT	TEXAS

Begin Southbound I-37 from San Antonio, TX to Corpus Christi, TX.

TEXAS

CENTRAL TIME ZONE

NOTE: I-37 Begins/Ends on I-35, Exit # 158

(142B) **Jct I-35S, to Laredo (LEFT exit)**

(142A) **Jct I-35N, to Austin**

141C **Brooklyn Ave, McCullough Ave, Nolan St , Downtown (SB)**
- Gas W: Fina
- Food W: Denny's
- Lodg W: Days Inn, La Quinta Inn♥, Marriott

141B **McCullough Ave, Houston St (SB)**
- Food W: Denny's
- Lodg W: Days Inn, Hampton Inn, Hotel Indigo, Red Roof Inn♥, Residence Inn
- Med W: + Baptist Medical Center
- Other W: Auto Services, Greyhound, Municipal Auditorium, ATMs, Banks, Museums, Vietnam Vets Memorial, to Mall, the Alamo

141A **Commerce St, The Alamo,**
- Other W: Alamo Museum, IMAX, Visitor Center, Rivercenter Mall, US Post Office

141 **Commerce St, Downtown (NB)**
- Food E: Exit 141 Hamburgers & Seafood, Ruth's Chris Steak House
  W: Big Easy Cajun, Casa Rio, DQ, Denny's Fig Tree Rest, Hooters, Morton's Steak House, Planet Hollywood, Red Lobster, Starbucks, Steak Escape, Taco Bell, Tony Roma
- Lodg E: Holiday Inn
  W: AmeriSuites, Hilton, Homewood Suites, Hyatt, La Quinta Inn♥, Marriott, Riverwalk Vistas, Travelodge♥, Westin Hotel, Wyndham
- Other E: Amtrak, Grocery, SBC Center
  W: AMC 9, ATMs, Banks, Blum St Cellars Winery, Convention Center, Grocery, Hemisfair Arena, Hertz, IMAX, Museums, Rivercenter Mall, Tower of the Americas

140B **Market St, Durango Blvd, Frontage Rd, Alamodome (Acc to #141 Serv)**
- Food E: Bill Miller BBQ
- Other E: Auto Services, Grocery, to the Alamodome
  W: Courts, Police Dept

140A **Florida St, Carolina St**
- Gas E: Citgo◊
- Other W: Enterprise

(139) **Jct I-10W, US 87, US 90, to Houston, El Paso, Del Rio, Victoria**
- Other W: to Sea World

138C **Fair Ave (SB), Hackberry St (NB)**
- Gas W: Exxon, Petro Pantry, Shell
- Food E: DQ, Jack in the Box, KFC, Taco Bell
- Other E: Advance Auto Parts, Auto Zone, Brake Check, Dollar General, Dollar Tree, Family Dollar, Home Depot, Ken's Tires, Southeast Animal Hospital♥,

138B **New Braunfels Ave, W Southcross Blvd (SB)**
- Gas E: HEB
  W: Exxon

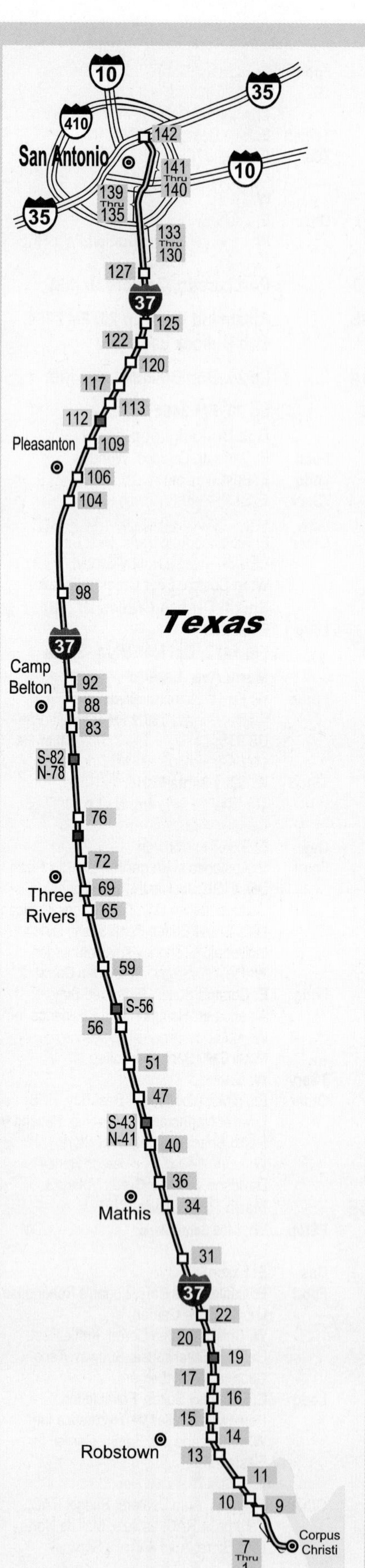

EXIT	TEXAS

- Food E: ChickFilA, Hong Kong Buffet, IHOP, Jim's, Little Caesars Pizza, McDonald's, Pizza Hut, Taco Cabana, Wendy's
  W: Burger King, Sonic
- Other E: ATMs, Banks, Cinemark 9, HEB, McCreless Shopping Center, **Acc to #138C**

138A **E Southcross Blvd (SB) (Acc to #138B Serv)**
- Med E: + Methodist Family Health Center

138AB **Gevers St, Southcross Blvd (NB) (Acc to #138B Serv)**

137 **Hot Wells Blvd, San Antonio**
- Food E: Popeye's Chicken
  W: IHOP
- Lodg W: Motel 6♥, Super 8
- Other W: Auto Service

136 **Pecan Valley Dr**
- Gas E: Citgo◊, Shell
- Food E: Church's Chicken, KFC/Taco Bell, Neptune's Seafood House, Pizza Hut, Rocky's Taco House
- Med W: + San Antonio State Hospital
- Other E: AMF Ponderosa Lanes, Auto Zone, Car Vel Skateland South, Family Dollar, La Fiesta Grocery

135 **Loop 13, Military Dr, Brooks AFB**
- Gas E: Shell, Valero
  W: Valero◊, HEB
- Food E: Jack in the Box
  W: Burger King, ChickFilA, Chili's, IHOP, Johnny Carino's Italian, Little Caesars Pizza, Longhorn Cafe, McDonald's, Panda Express, Peter Piper Pizza, Starbucks, Subway, Wingstop, Whataburger
- Lodg E: Best Western
  W: Brookside Inn, La Quinta Inn♥
- Other E: Auto Parts, Four Paws Animal Hospital♥, **Mission Trail RV Resort▲ / Sales & Service**,
  W: Advance Auto Parts, ATMs, AT&T, Auto Repairs, Auto Services, Avis RAC, Banks, Best Buy, Big Lots, Discount Tire, Dollar Tree, FedEx Office, HEB, Home Depot, Lowe's, Museum, Office Depot, PetCo♥, Radio Shack, Sprint, Target, **Travelers World RV Resort▲** , Walgreen's, **Walmart sc**, **to** Brooks AFB, Stinson Muni Airport✈

(133) **Jct I-410, US 281S, San Antonio**

132 **US 181S, to Floresville (SB), Presa St, Spur 122 (NB)**
- Gas E: Fina, Tetco/Shell, Valero
- Food E: Café, Mexican Rest
- Other E: Mission Gas/LP, Dollar General

130 **Southton Rd, Donop Rd, Elmedorf, Lake Braunig, San Antonio**
- FStop E: Tetco #303/Valero (Scales)
- Food E: FastFood/Tetco
- Lodg E: Comfort Inn
- Other E: RVDump/Tetco, **Braunig Lake RV Resort▲**

127 **San Antonio River TurnAround, Lake Braunig**

125 **Lp 1604, Anderson Loop, Elmendorf**
- FStop E: Tex Best #101/Conoco
  W: EZ Mart #601/Citgo
- Gas W: Exxon◊
- Food E: Burger King/TexBest, Mi Reina Mexican
  W: FastFood/EZ Mart, Miller BBQ
- Other E: **Riverside Ranch Nudist Resort▲**
  W: **Rustic Oaks Park▲**

◊= Regular Gas Stations with Diesel ▲ = RV Friendly Locations ♥= Pet Friendly Locations
Red print shows large vehicle parking / access on site or nearby Brown Print = Campgrounds / RV PARKS

EXIT		TEXAS
122		**Priest Rd, Mathis Rd**
120		**Hardy Rd, San Antonio**
117		**FM 536, Pleasanton**
113		**FM 3006, Pleasanton**
(112)		Parking Area (Both dir)
109		**TX 97, Pleasanton, Floresville**
	FStop	E: ZS Super Stop/Chevron
	Food	E: Rest/Super Stop
106		**FM 1334, Coughran Rd**
104		**Spur 199, Leal Rd, to US 281(SB), Jim Brite Rd, Pleasanton (NB)**
	TStop	E: Kuntry Korner/Shamrock
	Food	E: DQ, Rest/Kuntry Korner TS
	Lodg	E: Kuntry Inn Motel/KK TS
103		**US 281N, Leal Rd, Pleasanton (NB)**
98		**FM 541, to McCoy, Poth**
92		**US 281 Alt, Campbellton, Whitsett (SB)**
88		**FM 1099, to FM 791, Campbellton**
83		**FM 99, Campbellton, to Whitsett, Karnes City, Peggy**
	FStop	E: Shell
	Gas	W: Chevron◈
(82)		Rest Area (SB) (RR, Phones, Picnic)
(78)		Rest Area (NB) (RR, Phones, Picnic)
76		**US 281, FM 2049, Three Rivers, to Whitsett**
(75)		Weigh Station (SB)
(74)		Weigh Station (NB)
72		**US 281S, Three Rivers, Alice**
	Other	W: to Choke Canyon RV Park▲
69		**TX 72, King David Dr, to 281, Three Rivers, Kennedy**
	FStop	W: Handi Stop Shell
	TStop	W: Wolff's Travel Stop/Valero
	Food	W: Rest/Wolff's TS, BBQ/Deli/Shell
	Lodg	W: to 281: Econo Lodge, Regency Inn
	Tires	W: Wolff's TS
	Other	W: to Choke Canyon RV Park▲
65		**FM 1358, Oakville**
	Gas	W: Chevron
	Food	E: Van's BBQ
59		**FM 799, George West**
(56)		Parking Area (SB)
56		**US 59, to US 281, George West, to Beeville**
	FStop	E: Valero W: Tetco #80/Valero
	TStop	W: to Stripes #2157, George West Truck Stop/Shell
	Food	W: BurgerKing/Valero, FastFood/GW TS
	Other	W: LP/PetroPantry, to Smith Trailer & RV Park▲, Accurate Diesel Services
51		**Hailey Ranch Rd**
47		**FM 3024, FM 534, to Swinney**
	Other	W: Lake Corpus Christi/Mathis KOA▲

EXIT		TEXAS
(43)		Parking Area (SB)
(41)		Parking Area (NB)
40		**FM 888, Mathis**
	Other	W: Lake Corpus Christi/Mathis KOA▲
36		**TX 359E, to Skidmore**
	FStop	W: Texas Star Shell, Texaco Truck Stop
	Gas	W: Fuel Plus, Valero◈
	Food	W: McDonald's/Shell, Subway/Texaco, Pizza Hut, Rest/Ranch Motel
	Lodg	W: Mathis Motor Inn & RV Park▲, Ranch Motel
	Other	W: HEB, O'Reilly Auto Parts
34		**TX 359W, Mathis**
	Gas	W: Shamrock◈, Shell
	Food	W: Church's, DQ, Sonic, Van's BBQ
	Other	W: Mathis Motor Inn RV Park▲, to Sunrise Beach RV Park▲, Wilderness Lakes RV Resort▲, Riverlake RV Park▲ ATMs, Banks, Grocery, Auto Services, Towing
31		**TX 188, to Sinton, Rockport**
22		**TX 234, FM 796, to Edroy, Odem**
20B		**CR 54, Cooper Rd, Mathis**
(19)		Rest Area (Both dir) (RR, Phones, Vend, Picnic)
17		**US 77N, Mathis, to Odem, Sinton**
16		**Access Rd, Nueces River Park**
15		**Access Rd, Sharpsburg Rd, Red Bird Lane, Corpus Christi**
	Gas	W: Whistle Stop
	Food	E: Papa John's Pizza W: Burger King
14		**US 77, Red Bird Lane, Kingsville (Serv in Northwest Blvd area & US 77)**
	Gas	W: Circle K, RaceTrac, Shell, Shamrock◈
	Food	W: CiCi's, Denny's, K-Bob's Steakhouse, Pizza Hut, Popeye's, Quiznos, Sonic, TX A1 Steaks & Seafood, Whataburger
	Lodg	W: Comfort Inn
	Med	W: + Northwest Regional Hospital
	Other	W: ATMs, Banks, Auto Services, Firestone, Dollar Tree, Home Depot, Radio Shack, to US 77: Walmart sc
13B		**Sharpsburg Rd (NB)**
13A		**Leopard St, FM 1694, Callicoate Rd**
	Gas	W: Circle K
	Other	W: Evelyn's MH & RV Park▲
11B		**FM 24, Hart Rd, Violet Rd**
	Gas	E: Shell W: Circle K/Exxon◈, Valero◈
	Food	E: Chicken Shack W: DQ, KFC, McDonald's, Sonic, Subway, Pizza, Whataburger
	Lodg	E: Best Western, Hampton Inn W: La Quinta Inn♥
	Other	W: Auto Zone, Family Dollar, Grocery, O'Reilly Auto Parts, Walgreen's
11A		**FM 3386, McKinsey Rd**
	Gas	W: Circle K, Valero◈
	Lodg	W: La Quinta Inn♥
10		**Carbon Plant Rd**
9		**Rand Morgan Rd, Up River Rd**
	Gas	W: Citgo, Valero◈
	Food	W: Jim's Rest, Land & Sea Rest, Whataburger

EXIT		TEXAS
	Other	E: Koch Refinery W: Dollar General
7		**Suntide Rd, Tuloso Rd, Clarkwood Rd**
	Other	E: Koch Refinery W: Bank, ATM, Gulley's MH & RV Park▲
6		**Southern Minerals Rd**
5		**Corn Products Rd**
	Gas	E: Exxon W: PetroFleet
	Food	W: Restaurant
	Lodg	W: Eco Inn, Homegate Inn, Red Roof Inn♥, Super 8, Travelodge
	TServ	E: Ellison Truck Center/Kenworth W: Woody's Truck Center, Cummins Southern Plains
4B		**Lantana St, McBride Lane (SB)**
	Lodg	W: Motel 6♥
4A		**TX 358, to Padre Island (NB)**
	Gas	W: Shell◈
	Lodg	W: Drury Inn, Deluxe Inn, Holiday Inn, Quality Inn, Gulf Way Motel, TV Inn
	Other	W: Auto Services & Towing, Auto Rentals, Diesel Services, to Walmart sc, Corpus Christi Int'l Airport✈, Greyhound RV Park▲, Laguana Shores Village▲, to Marina Village Park▲, to Padre Palms RV Park▲, Pleasureland RV Center
4		**TX 44, TX 358, CC Intl Airport, Padre Island (NB)**
3B		**McBride Lane, Lantana St (NB)**
	Gas	E: Circle K W: Valero, USA Food Mart
	Lodg	W: Delux Inn, Rex Motel, Valley Motel
	Other	W: Greyhound Racetrack, Greyhound RV Park▲
3A		**Navigation Blvd, Corpus Christi**
	TStop	W: Corpus Christi Truck Stop (Scales)
	Gas	E: Shell W: Exxon
	Food	E: Rest/CC TS W: BBQ Man, Denny's, Miller BBQ, Las Milpas Mexican Rest
	Lodg	E: Clarion Inn W: Best Western, Days Inn, La Quinta Inn♥, Ramada Ltd, Rodeway Inn♥
	TServ	W: CC TS/Tires
	TWash	W: CC TS
	Other	W: Laundry/RVDump/CC TS, Diesel Services, Auto & Truck Services, Convention Center, Commercial Coach Works
2		**Up River Rd**
	Gas	E: Citgo W: Mobil
	Food	W: KFC, Pizza Hut, Sonic
	Lodg	W: Ramada Ltd
	Other	W: Hatch RV Park▲
1E		**Lawrence Dr, Nueces Bay Blvd**
	Gas	W: Circle K, Valero
	Other	W: Auto & Truck Service, Firestone, HEB, US Post Office
1D		**Port Ave, Brown Lee Blvd, Port of Corpus Christi (SB)**
	Gas	W: Citgo, Coastal
	Food	E: Pitmaster BBQ, Ray's BBQ
	Lodg	W: Howard Johnson

◈= Regular Gas Stations with Diesel ▲ = RV Friendly Locations ♥= Pet Friendly Locations
Red print shows large vehicle parking / access on site or nearby Brown Print = Campgrounds / RV PARKS

EXIT		TEXAS
	Other	E: Auto Service, Grocery W: Auto Services, Tire & Battery, Towing, Port of Corpus Christi
1C		**TX 286, Crosstown Expressway**
	Med	W: + Christus Spohn Memorial Hospital, to + Christus Spohn Hospital Shoreline, + Doctors Regional Medical Center
1B		**Brownlee Blvd, Port Ave (NB)**
	Gas	W: Chevron
1A		**Buffalo St, City Hall (SB)**
	Other	W: Auto Services, Courts, Blucher Convention Center, Memorial Coliseum, Greyhound, Car & Truck Shop, Sheriff Dept
1		**US 181, TX 35, to Portland**
	Other	E: Bayfront Plaza Conv Center, Museums, Tx State Aquarium, Visitor Info, to Puerto Del Sol RV Park▲ , to Sea Breeze RV Park▲
		W: Convention Center, Coliseum

NOTE: I-37 Begins/Ends at Shoreline Blvd in Corpus Christi, Tx

CENTRAL TIME ZONE

TEXAS

Begin Northbound I-37 from Corpus Christi to San Antonio, TX.

EXIT		WISCONSIN

Begin Southbound I-39 from Merrill, WI to Jct I-55 near Bloomington-Normal, IL.

WISCONSIN

CENTRAL TIME ZONE

NOTE: I-39 Begins/Ends on Bus 51 in Merrill

EXIT		WISCONSIN
211		**US 51 Bus, CR K, Merrill**
	Other	W: U-Haul, to Merrill Muni Airport✈
208		**WI 64, WI 70, Merrill**
	FStop	W: Pine Ridge Shell Travel Plaza
	Gas	W: BP◈, KwikTrip◈
	Food	W: Pine Ridge Rest/Shell, Burger King, China Inn, Diamond Dave's, Hardee's, McDonald's, Subway, Taco Bell, 3's Co
	Lodg	W: AmericInn, Pine Ridge Inn, Super 8
	Other	W: Auto Services, Auto Dealer, Piggly Wiggly, Museum, Radio Shack, U-Haul, Walmart, Jansen RV Sales & Service
205		**US 51 Bus, CR Q, River Ave, Merrill**
	TStop	E: Hwy 51 Truck Stop/Citgo
	Food	E: Rest/Hwy 51 TS
	Other	E: Laundry/WiFi/Hwy 51 TS
197		**CR WW, US 51, Brokaw, Wausau**
	FStop	W: Northside Citgo
194		**US 51Bus, CR K (SB), CR U, Wausau**
	Gas	E: KwikTrip, Mobil
	Food	E: McDonald's, Philly Subs
	Other	E: Auto Services, N Central Tech College
193		**Bridge St**
	Med	W: + Wausau Hospital
192		**WI 52E, WI 29W, Stewart Ave, to Abbotsford**
	Gas	E: Mobil, R-Store
	Food	E: Annie's American Café, Applebee's, Burger King, George's Rest, King Buffet, McDonald's, Noodles & Co, Pizza Chef, Starbucks, Subway W: 2510 Family Rest, Mandarin Chinese Rest
	Lodg	E: Baymont Inn, Exel Inn, Hampton Inn, La Quinta Inn♥, Plaza Hotel, Super 8
	Med	W: + Wausau Hospital
	Other	E: ATMs, Auto Services, Banks, Crossroads Cinema, ShopKO/Pharmacy, UPS Store, Animal Hospital♥, Marathon Co Park/RVDump
191		**Sherman St, Wausau (Access #192 Serv via S 24th Ave N)**
	FStop	E: 24th Ave to W Stewart: R-Store/BP
	Food	E: Applebee's, McDonald's, W: Burger King, Hardee's, Hereford & Hops
	Lodg	E: Hampton Inn, Super 8
	Med	W: + Wausau Hospital
	Other	E: Auto Services W: Auto Dealer, Home Depot
190		**CR NN, N Mountain Rd, to Rib Mtn Dr, Rib Mountain State Park**
	FStop	W: The Store #61/Citgo
	Gas	W: Mobil◈
	Food	E: Emma Krumbee's W: FastFood/The Store, Pizza, Subway
	Lodg	E: Howard Johnson W: Midway Hotel
	Other	E: to IGA W: Rib Mountain State Park▲ , WI State Hwy Patrol Post, Ski Area
188		**CR N, Rib Mountain Dr, US 51, Rib Mountain State Park**
	TStop	E: Rib Mountain Travel Center/BP (Scales)
	Gas	E: Phillips 66◈
	Food	E: Rest/RM TC, Country Kitchen, Fazoli's, Hong Kong Buffet, McDonald's, Pizza, Subway, Wendy's
	Lodg	E: Days Inn
	TServ	E: Peterbilt of WI
	Other	E: Laundry/WiFi/LP/RVDump/RM TC, Aldi, Auto Dealers, Best Buy, Dollar Tree, PetCo♥, PetSmart♥, Sam's Club, Tires Plus+, Walmart sc, King's Campers, Kenmark RV Rental
	NOTE:	**MM 187: I-39 Ends, US 51 continues NB (Exit #'s continue as I-39)**
187		**WI 29E, Wausau, to Green Bay (Gas/Food/Lodg Avail at 1st Ex #171)**
	FStop	E: to 4005 Westview: The Store #60/Citgo (Scales)
	Food	E: FastFood/The Store
185		**US 51 Bus, CR XX, Mosinee**
	FStop	E: R Store #11/Mobil
	Food	E: Cedar Creek Café, Culver's Family Rest, Green Mill Rest, Denny's, Subway
	Lodg	E: Comfort Inn, Holiday Inn, Lodge at Cedar Creek, Rodeway Inn, Stoney Creek Inn
	Other	E: ATM, Auto Service, Bank, Cedar Creek Factory Stores, Gander Mountain, Grocery, Harley Davidson, Visitor Center
(183)		**Rest Area (SB) (RR, Picnic)**
181		**Maple Ridge Rd, Mosinee**
	TServ	W: WI Kenworth
	Other	W: Brookside Village▲
179		**WI 153, East St, Mosinee**
	Gas	W: BP◈, KwikTrip, Shell◈
	Food	W: Hardee's, McDonald's, Subway/BP
	Lodg	W: Amerihost Inn
	Other	E: Central WI Airport✈
(178)		**Rest Area (NB) (RR, Picnic)**
175		**WI 34, Balsam Rd, Mosinee, Knowlton, to WI Rapids**
	Gas	W: Cyran's du Bay Pit Stop
171		**CR DB, Mosinee, to Knowlton**
	Other	W: to Lakeview Log Cabin Resort
165		**CR X, Saw Mill Rd, Stevens Point**
	Other	E: to Rivers Edge Campground & Marina▲
161		**US 51 Bus, Division St, Stevens Pt**
	Gas	W: BP, KwikTrip, R-Store
	Food	W: Country Kitchen, Cousin's Subs, Hardee's, KFC, McDonald's, Perkins, Papa John's Pizza, Pizza Hut, Subway,
	Lodg	W: Comfort Suites, Country Inn & Suites, Holiday Inn, Point Motel
	Other	W: Museum, Golf Course, Univ of WI/St Pt
159		**WI 66, Stanley St, Stevens Point**
	FStop	W: Kwik Trip #342
	Other	E: Stevens Pt Muni Airport✈, to 1903 Co Hwy Y: Jordan Co Park/RVDump ▲ W: Auto Dealer, Auto Services
158		**US 10, Stevens Point (SB)**
	Gas	E: Mobil◈ W: BP
	Food	E: Applebee's, Arby's, Culver's Family Rest, DQ, Fazoli's, Hong Kong Buffet, McDonald's, Shoney's, Subway, Taco Bell, Wendy's W: Hilltop Pub & Grill
	Lodg	E: Fairfield Inn, Holiday Inn Express♥, Holiday Inn W: La Quinta Inn♥
	Other	E: Grocery, Staples, Target, Tires Plus
158B		**US 10W, Stevens Point (NB)**
158A		**US 10E, Stevens Point (NB)**
156		**CR HH, McDill Ave, Stevens Point, to Whiting**
	Food	E: Cousin's Subs, Golden Corral, Subway
	Other	E: ATMs, Best Buy, Lowe's, PetCo♥, Walmart sc

◈ = Regular Gas Stations with Diesel ▲ = RV Friendly Locations ♥ = Pet Friendly Locations
Red print shows large vehicle parking / access on site or nearby Brown Print = Campgrounds / RV PARKS

153 CR B, Plover Rd, Plover
Gas W: BP, Mobil◈
Food W: Blake's Rest, Burger King/BP, Cousin Subs, IHOP, McDonald's, Subway
Lodg W: AmericInn, Hampton Inn, Sleep Inn
Other W: ATMs, Bank, Auto Services, Dollar Tree, Grocery, Truck Services

151 WI 54, US 51 Bus, Plover, to Waupaca
TStop E: Super 39 Shell (Scales)
Food E: Arby's/Super 39, 4 Star Family Rest
Lodg E: Elizabeth Inn
Other E: Laundry/CB/WiFi/Super 39, **Craft's Trading Center**

143 CR W, Main St, Bancroft, to WI Rapids
Gas E: Citgo◈
Food E: Cedarwood Family Rest
Other E: Auto Service, Grocery, **to Vista Royale Campground▲**

139 CR D, Plainfield, to Almond

136 WI 73, Plainfield, to WI Rapids
FStop E: Plainfield Amoco
TStop E: Plainfield Truck Stop/Mobil (Scales)
W: Plainfield 66 Travel Plaza
Food E: Rest/FastFood/Plainfield TS
W: FastFood/Plainfield TP
Lodg E: Motel/Plainfield TS
Other E: Laundry/Plainfield TS
W: Laundry/Plainfield TP

131 CR V, N Lake St, Hancock
Gas E: Hancock Mini Mart
Food E: Country Kettle Family Rest
Lodg E: Motel 51
Other E: **Hancock Village Park▲**, **Tomorrow Wood Campground▲**, Nordic Mountain Ski Resort

(126) Weigh Station (Both dir, Left Exit)

124 WI 21, E Follet Dr, Coloma
Gas E: Mobil◈
Food E: A&W, Lavore's on the Hill
Other E: Auto Dealers, **to Lake of the Woods▲**
W: **Coloma Camperland▲**

(120) Rest Area (SB)
(RR, Phone, Picnic, Vend)

(118) Rest Area (NB)
(RR, Phone, Picnic, Vend)

113 RD E, RD J, Westfield
FStop W: Pioneer Mini Store/Mobil
Gas W: BP, Marathon
Food W: Rest/FastFood/Pioneer MS, Burger King/BP, Point Pizza, McDonald's, Subway
Lodg W: Pioneer Motor Inn
Other W: Auto Services, Family Dollar, Grocery

106 WI 82W, WI 23E, Oxford
FStop W: Oxford Travel Center/Citgo
Food W: FastFood/Oxford TC
Lodg E: Crossroads Motel
Other E: Auto Service & Towing, **to Kilby Lake Campground▲**, **Buffalo Lake Camping Resort▲**
W: **to K&L Campground▲**, **Blue Lake Campground▲**

104 RD D, to WI 23, Montello, Oxford, to Packwaukee (NB, Diff reaccess)

100 WI 23W, CR P, Endeavor
Gas E: BP◈
Other W: **to Lake Mason Campground▲**

EXIT WISCONSIN

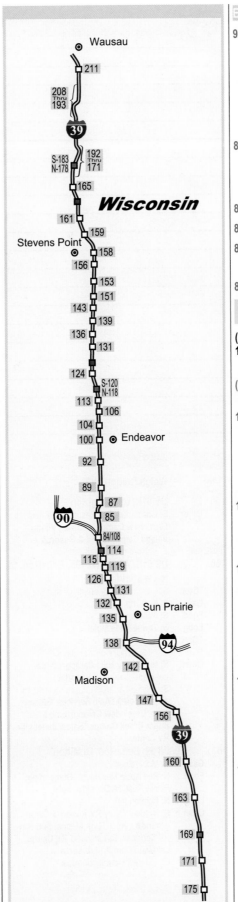

92 US 51S, Portage
FStop E: Kwik Trip #683
Gas E: Mobil
Food E: Big Mike's Super Subs, Culver's Family Rest, McDonald's, Subway, Taco Bell
Lodg E: Best Western, Ridge Motor Inn, Super 8
Other E: ATMs, Banks, Auto Zone, Dollar Tree, Radio Shack, Staples, Piggly Wiggly, Walgreen's, **Walmart sc**

89BA WI 16, to WI 127, Portage (SB)
Gas E: BP◈
Food E: Hitchin Post
Other E: Portage Muni Airport✈, Auto Dealer, Auto Services, Tires, Towing, Amtrak

89B WI 16, Wisconsin St (NB)

89A WI 16, Wisconsin St (NB)

87 WI 33, to I-90/94, Portage
(All Serv 3mi E to WI 16, Wisconsin St)
Other W: to Cascade Mountain Ski Area

85 Cascade Mountain Rd, Portage

NOTE: **I-39 runs with I-90 below. Exit #'s follow I-90.**

(84/108AB) Jct I-90, I-94
Jct I-39N, WI 78, to US 51N, Portage

(114) Rest Area (Both dir)
(RR, Phone, Picnic, Vend)

115 CR CS, CR J, Poynette, to Lake Wisconsin
FStop N: North Point Plaza/BP
Food N: FastFood/BP
TServ N: Graham's Auto & Truck Clinic
Other N: **to Little Bluff Campground▲**
S: **to Smokey Hollow Campground▲**

119 WI 60, Arlington, Lodi
Gas S: Mobil◈
Lodg S: Best Western
Other S: **Interstate RV Sales, Service & Rentals**

126 CR V, De Forest, to Dane
Gas N: BP, Phillips 66◈
S: Exxon◈
Food N: Culver's Family Rest, McDonald's, Subway
Lodg N: Holiday Inn
Other N: **KOA/Madison/RVDump▲**, WI State Hwy Patrol Post, Auto Services, Museum, Police Dept, Sheriff Dept

131 WI 19, Windsor, to Waunakee, Sun Prairie (Acc #132 Serv E to US 51S)
Gas N: Mobil, KwikTrip, Speedway
Food N: A&W, McDonald's
Lodg N: Days Inn, Windsor Lodging
TServ N: WI Kenworth
Other N: Auto Services

132 US 51, De Forest, Madison
TStop N: Citgo Travel Center (Scales), Truckers Inn/Shell (Scales)
S: Travel Center of America #50/Mobil (Scales)
Food N: Rest/Citgo TC, PineCone Rest/Truckers Inn
S: CountryPride/Subway/TacoBell/TA TC
TWash N: Truckers Inn
S: TA TC
TServ N: Truckers Inn/Tires
S: TA TC/Tires, Peterbilt, Freightliner

◈= Regular Gas Stations with Diesel ▲ = RV Friendly Locations ♥= Pet Friendly Locations
Red print shows large vehicle parking / access on site or nearby Brown Print = Campgrounds / RV PARKS

EXIT	WISCONSIN
Other	N: Laundry/Citgo TC, Laundry/BarbSh/CB/ RVServ/Truckers Inn, **Token Creek Co Park/RVDump▲**
	S: Laundry/WiFi/TA TC, **Wisconsin RV World, RV Custom Service & Rentals**, Dane Co Reg'l Airport✈, **to Camperland RV**
135BA	**US 151, Washington Ave, Madison, to Sun Prairie (EB)**
135ABC	**US 151, High Crossing Blvd, Madison, Washington Ave, to Sun Prairie (WB) (C=High Crossing Blvd, B=N, A=S)**
Gas	N: BP
	S: BP, Citgo, Shell, Sinclair
Food	N: KFC, Pizza, Subway
	S: Applebee's, Arby's, Country Kitchen, Cracker Barrel, Denny's, Hardee's, IHOP, KFC, Lotus Chinese, McDonald's, Mountain Jack's Steakhouse, Olive Garden, Pizza Hut, Pedro's Mex Rest, Red Lobster, TGI Friday, Steak n Shake, Tumbleweed Mex Rest, Wendy's
Lodg	N: Courtyard, Staybridge Suites, Woodfield Suites
	S: Best Western, Comfort Inn, Crowne Plaza, East Towne Suites, Econo Lodge, Exel Inn, Fairfield Inn, Hampton Inn, Holiday Inn, Heritage Inn, Microtel, Motel 6♥, Red Roof Inn♥, Select Inn
Med	S: + Meriter Hospital
Other	N: Auto Dealers, Auto Services, ATMs, Banks, Grocery, U-Haul
	S: ATMs, Auto & Truck Repairs, Banks, AniMart♥, Best Buy, Dane Co Reg'l Truax Field, East Towne Mall, Eastgate Cinema, FedEx Office, Firestone, Goodyear, Grocery, Home Depot, Midas, NTB, Office Depot, Penske, PetSmart♥, ShopKO, Target, **Walmart**,
NOTE:	**I-90W & I-94W run together Exits #138-48, approx 92 mi. Exit #'s follow I-90.**
(138A)	**Jct I-94, E to Milwaukee (fr EB, Left Exit)**
138B	**WI 30, Madison, to US 151 (fr WB, LEFT Exit)**
Other	S: Dane Co Airport✈, **Acc #135 Services**
142A	**US 12, US 18, Madison, to US 151 (WB, LEFT Exit)**
142B	**US 12, US 18, Madison, Cambridge**
142AB	**US 12, US 18, Madison, to US 151, to Cambridge (S Serv at 1st Exit/US 51)**
Gas	N: Mobil◈
	S: Cenex◈, Shell◈
Food	N: McDonald's, Subway
Lodg	N: Knights Inn, Wingate Inn
Other	N: Golf Course
	S: **to Dane Co Babcock Campground▲**
(146)	**Weigh Station (EB)**
147	**CR N, Cottage Grove, to Stoughton**
TStop	S: Road Ranger Travel Center/Citgo
Gas	S: BP
Food	S: FastFood/RR TC, Arby's/BP
Other	S: **to Lake Kegonsa State Park▲**

Personal Notes

EXIT	WISCONSIN
(148)	**Weigh Station (WB)**
156	**US 51N, to Stoughton**
Other	S: Coachman Golf Resort, Inn & Rest, **to Creekview Campground▲, Viking Village Campground & Resort▲**
Med	S: + Stoughton Hospital
160	**US 51S, WI 73, WI 106, Edgerton, to to Deerfield**
TStop	S: Edgerton AmBest Shell Oasis (Scales)
Gas	S: KwikTrip
Food	S: Rest/Edgerton Oasis
Lodg	S: Towne Edge Motel
TServ	S: Edgerton Oasis/Tires
Med	S: + Memorial Comm Hospital
Other	N: **to Hickory Hills Campground▲, Lakeland Camping Resort▲**
	S: Laundry/WiFi/**LP**/Edgerton Oasis, **to** Jana Airport✈, Auto Services, Grocery, Tires, **Creekview Campground▲, Sugar Creek Camper Sales, Janesville RV Center**
163	**WI 59, Edgerton, to Milton**
Gas	N: Mobil, Shell
Food	N: Red Apple Rest/Mobil, Burger King, Family Rest, McDonald's, Subs
Lodg	N: Comfort Inn
Other	N: **Hidden Valley RV Resort & Camp ground▲**, Rock River Marina, **Sun Ray RV Services, to Lakeland RV Center, Lakeland Camping Resort▲, Blackhawk Campgrounds▲**
(169)	**Rest Area (EB) (RR, Phone, Picnic, Vend)**
171AB	**WI 26, Milton Ave, Janesville (EB)**

EXIT	WISCONSIN
171A	**WI 26, Janesville (WB)**
FStop	N: Mulligan's Truck Stop/66
TStop	S: Road Ranger Travel Center #107/Citgo
Gas	S: BP, KwikTrip
Food	N: Cracker Barrel
	S: Rest/RR TC, Arby's, Applebee's, Country Kitchen, Culver's, Famous Dave's BBQ, Ground Round, Hardee's, Prime Quarter Steak House, Perkins, Milwaukee Grill
Lodg	N: Best Western, Hampton Inn, Motel 6
	S: Ramada Inn, Select Inn, Super 8
Med	S: + Mercy Hospital
Other	N: Auto Dealer, Auto Services
	S: ATMs, Banks, Auto Services, Grocery, Firestone, Target, **Walmart**, Janesville Mall
171B	**US 14, Humes Rd, Janesville (WB)**
171C	**US 14E, Janesville, Milton**
TStop	N: Travel Center of America #71/Mobil (Scales)
Food	N: Wendy's/TA TC, Damon's, Old Country Buffet, Steak n Shake
Lodg	N: Holiday Inn, Microtel
Med	S: + Mercy Hospital
Other	N: Laundry/WiFi/TA TC, Movies 10, Best Buy, Home Depot, Staples, Tires Plus
	S: Auto Dealers, ATMs, Banks, Kutter Harley Davidson
175A	**US 14 Bus, E Racine St**
Gas	S: BP
Food	S: DQ, Hardee's, Big Mike's Subs
Lodg	S: Lannon Stone Motel
Other	S: Black Hawk Golf Course, Auto Services
175B	**WI 11E, US 14 Bus, Janesville**
TStop	N: J & R Quick Mart/BP
Food	N: FastFood/J&R QM, Denny's, Subway
Lodg	N: Baymont Inn
177	**WI 11W, Avalon Rd, Janesville**
Other	S: Southern Wisconsin Reg'l Airport✈
183	**CR S, Shopiere Rd, Beloit**
TStop	S: Rollette Oil #4/Citgo
Food	S: FastFood/Rollette Oil
Med	S: + Beloit Memorial Hospital
Other	N: **Turtle Creek Campground▲**
185A	**WI 81, Milwaukee Rd, Beloit**
FStop	S: Speedway #4293
TStop	S: Pilot Travel Center #289 (Scales)
Gas	S: BP, Exxon, Shell
Food	S: TacoBell/Pilot TC, FastFood/Speedway, Applebee's, Arby's, Burger King, Country Kitchen, Culver's, Fazoli's, Hong Kong Buffet, McDonald's, Perkins, Wendy's
Lodg	S: Comfort Inn, Econo Lodge, Fairfield Inn, Holiday Inn Express, Super 8
Other	S: WiFi/Pilot TC, Auto Dealers, ATMs, Banks, Luxury 10 Cinemas, Tires Plus+, Staples, **Walmart sc**
(185B)	**Jct I-43N, to Milwaukee**
(187)	**WI Welcome Center (NB) (RR, Phone, Picnic, Vend, Info)**
NOTE:	**I-39 runs with I–90 above. Exit #'s follow I-90.**

CENTRAL TIME ZONE

↑WISCONSIN

◈= Regular Gas Stations with Diesel ▲ = RV Friendly Locations ♥= Pet Friendly Locations
Red print shows large vehicle parking / access on site or nearby Brown Print = Campgrounds / RV PARKS

EXIT ILLINOIS

ILLINOIS

CENTRAL TIME ZONE

NOTE: I-39 runs with I-90 below. Exit #'s follow I-90.

1 — US 51N, IL 75, S Beloit
- TStop — S: Flying J Travel Plaza #5097 (Scales), Road Ranger Travel Center #205 (Scales)
- Food — S: Rest/FastFood/FJ TP, Subway/RR TC
- Lodg — S: Knights Inn, Ramada Inn
- TServ — S: FJ TP
- Other — S: Laundry/WiFi/BarbSh/**RVDump/LP**/FJ TP, Auto Dealers, Auto Services, **Pearl Lake Campground▲**

(2) — IL Welcome Center (EB)
(RR, Phone, Pic, Vend, Info, **RVDump**)

3 — CR 9, Rockton Rd, Roscoe
- TStop — N: Love's Travel Stop #322 (Scales)
- Food — N: Hardee's/Love's TS
- Other — N: Laundry/WiFi/**RVDump**/Love's TS; S: Auto Museum

(75.5) — TOLL Plaza

(66) — CR 55, Riverside Blvd, Rockford
- TStop — S: Road Ranger Travel Center #211
- Gas — S: BP, Phillips 66
- Food — S: FastFood/RR TC, Arby's, Culver's, KFC, McDonald's, Subway, Wendy's
- Lodg — S: Days Inn
- Other — S: Auto Dealers, Auto Services, ATMs, Banks, Grocery

(63) — US 20 Bus, E State St, Rockford
- Gas — N: Phillips 66◈; S: BP, Mobil◈
- Food — N: **Cracker Barrel**, Subway/Phillips 66; S: Applebee's, Arby's, Burger King, Chili's, Country Kitchen, Denny's, Don Pablo, Hooters, IHOP, KFC, Lone Star Steak House, McDonald's, Machine Shed Rest, Olive Garden, Perkins, Ruby Tuesday, Steak n Shake, Tumbleweed Grill
- Lodg — N: Baymont Inn, Exel Inn; S: Alpine Inn, Best Western, Candlewood Suites, Comfort Inn, Courtyard, Fairfield Inn Hampton Inn, Holiday Inn Express, Quality Suites, Ramada Inn, Red Roof Inn♥, Residence Inn, Sleep Inn, Super 8
- Med — S: + St Anthony Medical Center
- Other — N: Greyhound, Museum; S: Amtrak, Auto Services, Best Buy, Home Depot, Lowe's, Office Depot, Sam's Club, Target, **Walmart**

(61) — Jct I-39S, US 20, US 51, Cherry Valley, to Rockford
- Other — S: Magic Waters Theme Park

(123) — Jct I-90E, TOLL, to Chicago

NOTE: I-39 runs with I–90 above (pg 175). Exit #'s follow I-90.

122AB — US 20E, Harrison Ave, Cherry Valley (NB: LAST FREE EXIT BEFORE TOLL)
- FStop — W: Oakview Diesel/Marathon
- Gas — W: Citgo
- Food — W: Rest/Oakview Diesel, Arby's, DQ, Burger King
- Other — W: Auto Dealer, B&N, Cherry Vale Mall, Cinema, **Collier RV Center**, Grocery, Kegel Harley Davidson,

EXIT ILLINOIS

119 — US 20W, to Freeport, Rockford
- Gas — W: BP, Phillips 66, Shell
- Food — W: BeefARoo, Burger King, Subway
- Other — W: Auto & Diesel Services, Tires, Quality Truck Repair, RC Truck & Auto Service

115 — CR 11, Baxter Rd, Rockford
- TStop — E: I-39 Express Lane/Shell (Scales)
- Food — E: FastFood/I-39 Expr Ln
- TWash — E: I-39 Expr Ln
- TServ — E: I-39 Expr Ln/Tires
- Other — E: Laundry/CB/I-39 Expr Ln; W: **Black Hawk Valley Campground▲**

111 — IL 72, Monroe Center
- Gas — W: BP◈

104 — IL 64, Lindenwood, Esmond, to Oregon, Sycamore
- Other — E: Cummins Northern IL

99 — IL 38, Rochelle, to De Kalb
- FStop — W: Super Pantry #14/BP
- TStop — W: Petro Stopping Center #59/Mobil (Scales), Road Ranger Travel Center #310/Citgo (Scales)
- Gas — W: Shell
- Food — W: IronSkillet/FastFood/Petro SC, Subway/RR TC, Arby's, DQ, Hardee's, McDonald's, Wendy's
- Lodg — W: Amerihost, Holiday Inn Express, Super 8
- TWash — W: BlueBeacon/Petro SC
- TServ — W: Petro SC/Tires
- Other — W: Laundry/BarbSh/Med/**RVDump/LP**/Petro SC, Auto Services, ATMs, Banks, Dollar General, Grocery, Radio Shack, Walgreen's

(97B) — IL 88W, TOLL, to Rock Falls

(97A) — IL 88E, TOLL, to Chicago

93 — CR 2, Perry Rd, Steward

87 — US 30, Lee, to Sterling, Rock Falls
- Other — **E: Shabbona Lake State Rec Area▲; W: to O'Connell's Jellystone RV Park▲, Mendota Hills Campground▲, Green River Oaks Camping Resort▲**

(85) — Willow Creek Rest Area (Both dir)
(RR, Phone, Pic, Vend, Pet, **RVDump**)

82 — CR 10, Chicago Rd, Paw Paw

72 — US 34, N 43rd Rd, Mendota, to Earlville
- FStop — W: Road Ranger Travel Center #140/Pilot
- TStop — W: Gromann I-39 Auto & Truck Plaza/BP (Scales)
- Food — W: Rest/Gromann ATP, McDonald's
- Lodg — W: Comfort Inn, Super 8
- Med — W: + Mendota Comm Hospital
- Other — W: Laundry/WiFi/Gromann ATP, Amtrak, Auto Services, Towing, Grocery, Grandpa's Farm, Mendota Airport✈

66 — US 52, N 37th Rd, Mendota
- Other — **E: to KOA LaSalle/Peru▲**

(59B) — Jct I-80W, to Des Moines
- Other — W: IL Valley Reg'l Airport✈

(59A) — Jct I-80E, to Chicago
- Other — **E: to KOA LaSalle/Peru▲**

57 — US 6, La Salle, to Peru
- Gas — W: to BP, Shell

54 — CR 23 Ext, Walnut St, Oglesby
- Gas — E: BP, Phillips 66, Shell

◈ = Regular Gas Stations with Diesel ▲ = RV Friendly Locations ♥ = Pet Friendly Locations
Red print shows large vehicle parking / access on site or nearby Brown Print = Campgrounds / RV PARKS

EXIT		ILLINOIS
	Food	E: Burger King, Hardee's, Subway
	Lodg	E: Holiday Inn Express
	Other	E: to Starved Rock State Park▲, Matthiessen State Park
52		**IL 251, Oglesby, to La Salle, Peru**
51		**IL 71, N 23rd Rd, Oglesby, to IL 251, to Hennepin**
48		**IL 54, N 20th Rd, Tonica**
	FStop	E: Tonica Truck Stop/BP
	Gas	E: Casey's
	Food	E: FastFood/Tonica TS
41		**IL 18, N 13th Rd, Lostant, to Streator, Henry**
35		**IL 17, Wenona, to IL 251, to Lacon**
	TStop	E: Wenona Travel Mart/BP, Shell
	Gas	E: Casey's
	Food	E: FastFood/Wenona TM, Burger King/ Subway/Shell, Pizza Hut
	Lodg	E: Super 8
	Other	E: RVDump/Shell
27		**CR 2, Minonk, to IL 251**
	TStop	E: Fast Break Travel Center/Shell (Scales)
	Gas	E: Casey's
	Food	E: Rest/FastFood/Fast Break TC
	Lodg	E: Motel 6♥
	Other	E: ATMs, Banks, Auto Services
22		**IL 116, Minonk, to IL 251, to Peoria, Benson, Pontiac**
14		**US 24, to IL 251, El Paso, to Peoria**
	FStop	E: Fast Break/Shell, Freedom Oil #47
	Gas	E: Casey's
	Food	E: FastFood/Fast Break, DQ, Hardee's, McDonald's, Subway, Woody's Family Rest
	Lodg	E: Days Inn W: Super 8
	Other	E: ATMs, **El Paso RV Center**, IGA, NAPA, Pharmacy, Radio Shack **W: Hickory Hills Campground▲**
8		**IL 251, CR 8, Hudson, Kappa**
	Other	E: Lake Bloomington W: **RV Camping▲**, Lake, Park
5		**CR 12, Hudson**
2		**US 51 Bus, Normal, Bloomington**
(1)		**Jct I-55,** **(Gas/Food/Lodg N to 1st Ex #165)** **(Travel Centers S to 1st Ex #160A)**

CENTRAL TIME ZONE

NOTE: **I-39 Begins/Ends on 1-55, Exit #164**

ILLINOIS

EXIT		CALIFORNIA

Begin Eastbound I-40 from Jct I-15 in Barstow, CA to US 17 in Wilmington, NC.

CALIFORNIA

PACIFIC TIME ZONE

NOTE: **I-40 begins/ends in Barstow on I-15**

EXIT		CALIFORNIA
1		**Montaro Rd, E Main St, Barstow**
	Gas	N: 76◈, Chevron x2, Mobil, Shell◈, Thrifty, Valero S: ArcoAmPm, Mirastar
	Food	N: Burger King, Carl's Jr, Carrow's, Chinese Food, CoCo's, Del Taco, Denny's, Donut Star, Frosty's Donuts, IHOP, Jack in the Box, Long John Silver's, McDonald's, Panda Express, Popeye's Chicken, Sizzler, Starbucks, Straw Hat Pizza S: McDonald's/Walmart
	Lodg	N: Astro Budget, Best Motel, Best Western, California Inn, Days Inn, Motel 6♥, Oak Tree Inn, Pennywise Inn, Quality Inn, Ramada Inn, Red Roof Inn, Super 8, Travelodge
	Other	N: Auto Zone, Auto Services, Amtrak, BJ's Natural Foods, Big Lots, Carwash/ Shell, Cinema, Radio Shack, U-Haul, Von's Grocery, **to Shady Lane RV Camp▲** S: Auto Service, **Walmart**
3		**Marine Corps Logistics Base**
5		**Nebo St, Daggett, to Rte 66 (EB)**
7		**A St, Daggett**
	FStop	N: DRS
	Food	N: Rest/Daggett TS
	Other	N: **Barstow/Calico KOA▲**, to Calico **Ghost Town Campground▲**
12		**Hidden Springs Rd, Barstow-Daggett Airport**
18		**National Trails Hwy, Newberry Springs**
	FStop	N: Calico Petroleum #2 S: Kelly's Market
	Other	N: **to appr 7mi: Twin Lakes RV Park▲** S: Auto Repair & Towing, LP
23		**Fort Cady Rd, Newberry Springs**
	FStop	N: Wesco Fuel & Food Texaco
	Food	N: Rest/Wesco TS S: Bagdad Café
	Lodg	S: Newberry Mountain **RV Park▲** & Motel
	Other	N: Laundry/Wesco TS
(28)		**Desert Oasis Rest Area (Both dir)**
	NOTE:	**EB: CLOSED, NO ETA ON OPEN** **(RR, Phones, Pic, Vend, Pet)**
33		**Hector Rd, to Rte 66**
50		**Ludlow Rd, Crucero Rd, Amboy, 29 Palms, Historic Rte 66, Ludlow**
	FStop	S: Ludlow Truck Stop
	Gas	N: to 76
	Food	S: Ludlow Café, Roy's Cafe
	Lodg	S: Ludlow Motel
	TServ	S: Ludlow TS
78		**Kelbaker Rd, to Amboy, Kelso**
100		**Essex Rd, Essex**
	Other	N: **to Providence Mountain State Park**, Mitchell Caverns
(106)		**Fenner Rest Area (Both dir)** **(RR, Phones, Pet)**
107		**Goffs Rd, Essex**
	FStop	N: Hi Sahara Oasis
	Other	S: **to 29 Palms Golf & RV Resort▲, Knott Sky RV Park▲, Joshua Tree RV Lake▲**
115		**Mountain Spring Rd, Essex Amboy, 29 Palms**
120		**Water Rd**
133		**US 95N, to Searchlight, Las Vegas**
139		**W Park Rd, River Rd Cutoff (EB)**
	Gas	N: Gas Mart, Texaco

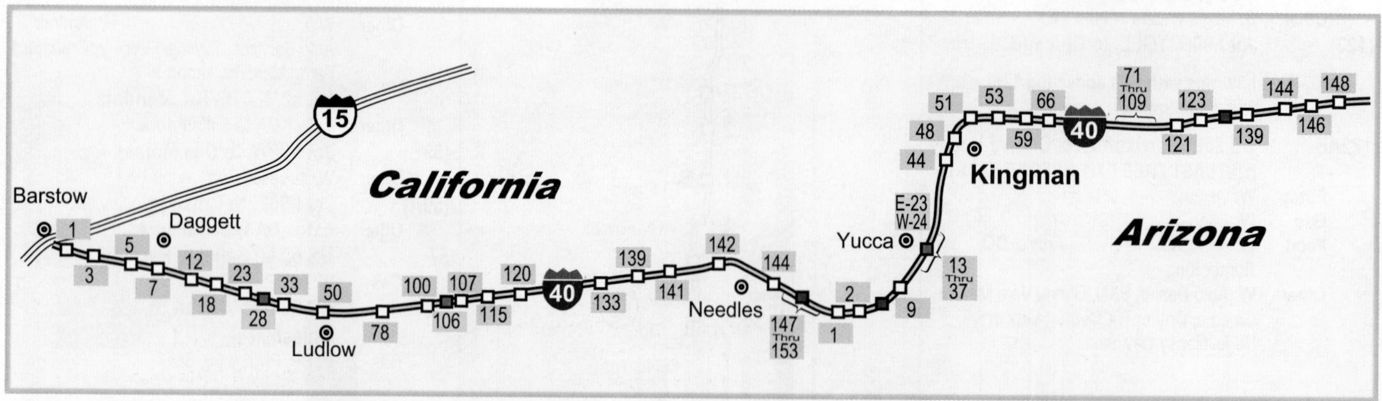

◈= Regular Gas Stations with Diesel ▲ = RV Friendly Locations ♥= Pet Friendly Locations
Red print shows large vehicle parking / access on site or nearby **Brown Print = Campgrounds / RV PARKS**

EXIT	CALIFORNIA
Food	N: Carl's Jr, China Garden, CA Pantry, Wagon Wheel Rest, Taco Bell
Lodg	N: Best Western Royal Inn♥ , Best Western Colorado River Inn♥, Sunset Inn
AServ	N: Texaco
Other	N: **Needles KOA▲** , **Fenders River Rd Resort** & **Motel▲** , **Rainbo Beach Resort▲** , **Desert View RV Resort▲** , to Avi Resort Casino & RV Resort▲
141	**W Broadway, Needles Hwy, River Rd, to AZ 95, Needles**
FStop	N: Westside Chevron
Gas	S: ArcoAmPm, Mobil◈, Shell
Food	N: Hungry Bear Rest, KFC S: Carl's Jr, Wagon Wheel, Taco Bell
Lodg	N: Best Hotel, Desert Mirage Inn,River Valley Motor Lodge, Robinson's Motel, Sage Motel S: Best Western Royal Inn♥, Best Western♥, Budget Inn, Needles Inn, Relax Inn
TServ	N: A&A Diesel Service, Great West Truck & Auto
Other	N: Fort Mohave Indian Reservation, **Needles Marina Park▲** , **to Spirit Mountain RV Park▲** , **Moon River RV Resort▲** , **Snowbird RV Resort▲** S: Auto Service, Auto Dealers, Grocery, **RV Service**, Tires, Transmissions
142	**J St, Needles**
Gas	N: 76, Valero
Food	N: Jack in the Box, McDonald's S: Denny's
Lodg	N: Traveler's Inn♥ S: Days Inn♥, Motel 6
Med	S: + CO River Medical Center
Other	N: Auto & Truck Repair, ATMs, Banks, Big O Tires, Museum, NAPA, Amtrak S: Courts, **CA State Hwy Patrol Post**
144	**US 95S, E Broadway, to Blythe**
FStop	N: Eastside Chevron
Gas	N: Mobil, Shell◈
Food	N: Burger King, Domino's Pizza, Roberto's Taco Shop
Lodg	N: Rte 66 Motel S: Best Value Inn♥
TServ	S: Big D Tire, Stout Comm'l Truck Tire Service
Med	S: + Family Care Clinic
Other	N: ATMs, Banks, Basha's, Laundromat, RiteAid, U-Haul S: Needles Airport✈, **to Calizona RV Park▲**
147	**Five Mile Rd US 95S, to Blythe**
Other	S: **Calizona RV Park▲** , Needles Airport✈
(148)	**Inspection Stop** (Produce Trucks) (EB)
(149)	**Inspection Stop** (All Vehicles) (WB)
153	**Park Moabi Rd, to Rte 66**
Other	N: **Moabi Reg'l Park▲**

PACIFIC / MOUNTAIN TIME ZONE

NOTE: **MM 155: Arizona State Line**

CALIFORNIA

EXIT	ARIZONA

ARIZONA

MOUNTAIN TIME ZONE

NOTE: **AZ = NO Daylight Savings Time**

EXIT		
1		**Topock Rd, CR 10, AZ 95, Topock, to Bullhead City, Laughlin, NV** (Gas & Serv approx 4 mi N)
2		**Needle Mountain Rd**
(3)		**Weigh Station** (Both dir)
9		**AZ 95S, Rice Dr, Lake Havasu City, London Bridge Rd, to Parker**
	TStop	S: Pilot Travel Center #211 (Scales)
	Food	S: Wendy's/Pilot TC
	Other	S: Laundry/WiFi/Pilot TC, **to Prospectors RV Resort▲** , **Lake Havasu Resort▲** , **Havasu Falls RV Resort▲** , **Havasu RV Resort▲** , Lake Havasu City Airport✈
13		**Franconia Rd**
20		**Gem Acres Rd, Bullhead City**
(23)		**Haviland Rest Area** (EB) (RR, Phones, Picnic)
(24)		**Haviland Rest Area** (WB) (RR, Phones, Picnic)
25		**Alamo Rd**
	Gas	N: Micromart◈
26		**Proving Ground Rd**
28		**Old Trails Rd**
37		**Griffith Rd**
44		**AZ 66, CR 10, Oatman Rd, Kingman**
	TStop	S: RoadysTS/Crazy Fred's Truck Stop
	Food	S: Café/Crazy Fred's, Burger Barn
	TWash	N: Truck Tub S: Crazy Fred's TS
	TServ	S: Crazy Fred's TS/Tires
	Other	S: Laundry/**LP**/WiFi/Crazy Fred's TS
48		**US 93N, to AZ 68, I-40 Bus, Beale St, Kingman, to Laughlin, Bullhead City, Las Vegas**
	FStop	N: Hallum Fuel Mart/Shell
	TStop	N: Travel Center of America #94/76 (Scales), USA AmBest Travel Center
	Gas	N: Express Stop◈, Mobil◈, Woody's S: Chevron◈, Circle K
	Food	N: Subway/USA TC, CountryPr/Popeye's/TA TC, House of Chan, Wendy's S: Quiznos/Chevron, Calico's, Carl Jr, Roadrunner Cafe
	Lodg	N: Budget Inn, Frontier Motel, Knights Inn S: Arizona Inn♥ , Motel 6♥, Beale Hotel, Hotel Brunswick, Quality Inn
	AServ	N: Auto & **RV** Service, Best Tire & Auto S: Chevron, One Stop Automotive
	TServ	N: TA TC/Tires, Great West Truck & Auto Service, Goodyear
	Other	N: Laundry/**LP**/WiFi/TA TC, **RVDump**/Mobil S: **Ft Beale RV Park▲** , **Canyon West RV Park▲** , ATM, Bank, Amtrak, Museum, **to Adobe RV Park▲** , **Sir Albert's RV Park▲** , **Golden Valley RV Park▲** , **Desert Sunset Park▲**
51		**Stockton Hill Rd, CR 20, Kingman**
	Gas	N: ArcoAmPm, Chevron, Circle K S: Circle K, USA Fuel, Safeway

EXIT	ARIZONA
Food	N: Chili's, Cracker Barrel, Domino's Pizza, Golden Corral, IHOP, In N Out Burgers, KFC, Panda Express, Papa John's Pizza, Sonic, Starbucks, Subway, Taco Bell, Whataburger S: DQ, Little Caesar's Pizza, Pizza Hut
Lodg	N: Hampton Inn, Travelodge
Med	N: + Kingman Regional Medical Center S: + Fastrax Urgent Care
Other	N: Albertson's, ATMs, Auto Dealers, Auto Zone, **AZ NW RV**, Banks, Big Lots, Brake Masters, Checkers Auto Parts, CVS, **Circle S Campground▲** , Dollar General, Holden's Auto & Truck Service, Home Depot, **Kingman KOA▲** , Mohave Comm College, Office Depot, PetCo♥, Safeway, Smith Food & Drug, Staples, **Trotter's RV**, True Value Hardware, **Walmart sc▲** , Walgreen's, Winston Tire, S: ATMs, Banks, CarQuest, Express Lube & Tires, Family Dollar, Kingman Muni Golf Course, Mohave Co Fairgrounds, Radio Shack, Safeway,
53	**AZ 66, I-40 Bus, Andy Devine Ave**
FStop	N: Shell
TStop	N: Flying J Travel Plaza #5050/Conoco (Scales)
Gas	N: Chevron, Mobil S: 76, Shell, Shell, Sinclair
Food	N: Cookery/FastFood/FJ TP, Arby's, Burger King, Denny's, Jack in the Box, McDonald's, Maddog's Doghouse Sports Bar & Grill, Pizza Hut, Taco Bell S: ABC Buffet, Dambar Steak House, JB's Rest, Lo's Chinese, Oyster's Mexican & Seafood, Sonic
Lodg	N: Days Inn, Econo Lodge, First Value Inn, Motel 6♥, Silver Queen Motel♥, Super 8, Travelodge S: Best Value Inn, Best Western♥, Best Western, Comfort Inn♥, Days Inn, Holiday Inn Express, High Desert Inn, Route 66 Motel, Rodeway Inn♥, Springhill Suites
TServ	N: Great West Commercial Tire, Goodyear
Other	N: Laundry/BarbSh/WiFi/**RVDump**/**LP**/FJ TP, ATMs, Banks, Basha's, Laundromat, Kmart, **Kingman KOA▲** , Mother Rd Harley Davidson, **Outdoorsman RV Center**, Pharmacy, Russell's Auto & **RV** Service, Tire World, **Trotter RV**, **Zuni Village RV Park▲** , to Kingman Airport✈, S: ATMs, Auto Service & Tires/Shell, Banks Economy Tire Service, NAPA, Penske, **Police Dept**, **Sunrise RV Park▲** ,
59	**CR 259, DW Ranch Rd, Kingman**
FStop	N: Love's Travel Stop #272
Food	N: Subway/Chesters/Love's TS
TWash	N: Freedom Truck Wash
Other	N: Laundry/WiFi/**RVDump**/Love's TS
66	**Blake Ranch Rd, Kingman**
TStop	N: Petro Stopping Center #315 /Mobil (Scales)
Food	N: IronSkllet/PizzaHut/Petro SC
TWash	N: Blue Beacon TW/Petro SC
TServ	N: Petro SC/Tires, Speedco
Other	N: Laundry/Petro SC, **Blake Ranch RV Park & Horse Motel**/**RVDump▲**
71	**Jct US 93S, to Wickenburg, Phoenix**
79	**Silver Springs Rd**
87	**Willows Ranch Rd**
91	**Fort Rock Rd, Kingman**

◈= Regular Gas Stations with Diesel ▲ = RV Friendly Locations ♥= Pet Friendly Locations
Red print shows large vehicle parking / access on site or nearby Brown Print = Campgrounds / RV PARKS

EXIT — ARIZONA

96 **Cross Mountain Rd, Seligman**

103 **Jolly Rd**

109 **Anvil Rock Rd**

121 **AZ 66, I-40 Bus, Chino St, Seligman (Access to Exit #123 Services)**
- Gas: **N:** Chevron, Exxon, Historic Rte 66 General Store/Mustang◈
- Food: **N:** Copper Cart Rest, Delgadillo's Snow Cap Rest, OK Saloon & Rte 66 Roadkill Cafe, Westside Lilo's Cafe, Rte 66 Gen'l Store
- Lodg: **N:** Deluxe Inn Motel, Rte 66 Mote,
- Other: **N:** Rte 66 Automotive Parts, Service & Towing, Seligman Sundries, US Post Office, Historic Rte 66 Genl Store/**LP**/ **Campground▲** , **to** Seligman Airport✈

123 **AZ 66, I-40 Bus, CR 5, Chino St, Seligman (Access to Ex #121 Serv)**
- FStop: **N:** Shell
  S: Johnsons Travel Center/Chevron
- Food: **N:** **to** Burgers, Copier Cafe, The Pizza Joint
  S: Subway/Johnsons TC
- Lodg: **N:** **to** Aztec Motel, Canyon Lodge, Romney Motel, Stage Coach 66 Motel♥, Supai Motel
- Other: **N:** **to** Asst'd Rte 66 Gift Shops, Grocery, **Seligman/Rte 66 KOA▲** ,

(132) **Weigh Station (Both dir)**

139 **Crookton Rd, to Rte 66, Ash Fork**

144 **I-40 Bus, Ash Fork (Acc to #146)**
- FStop: **S:** Hillside Texaco
- Gas: **S:** Chevron
- Other: **N:** Museum, **Ash Fork/Grand Canyon KOA▲**
  S: Laundry/Texaco/**Hillside RV Park▲** , Tourist Info

146 **AZ 89, Bus 40 Loop, Lewis Ave, Ash Fork, to Prescott (Acc to #144)**
- Gas: **N:** Mobil◈, Mustang
- Food: **N:** Cafe/Mustang, Ranch House Café, Route 66 Grill
- Lodg: **N:** Ash Fork Inn, Copperstate Motel

148 **County Line Rd, Williams**

149 **Monte Carlo Rd**

151 **Welch Rd (NO TRUCKS)**

(156) **Safety Pullout (WB)**

NOTE: MM 156: 6% Steep Grade next 5 mi

157 **Devil Dog Rd, Williams (NO TRUCKS)**

Personal Notes

EXIT — ARIZONA

161 **I-40 Bus, Bill Williams Ave, Williams, Golf Course Dr, Grand Canyon**
- Gas: **S:** Chevron◈, Mobil, Shell◈
- Food: **S:** Denny's, Parker House, Red's Steaks, Smokin Barrel
- Lodg: **S:** Best Western, Comfort Inn, Days Inn, Motel 6, Norris Motel, Westerner Motel
- Med: **S:** + Hospital
- Other: **N:** **Cataract Lake Co Park▲**
  S: ATMs, Family Dollar, Grocery, NAPA

163 **Grand Canyon Blvd, to AZ 73, Williams, Grand Canyon**
- Gas: **N:** Chevron◈
  S: Conoco, Mobil, Shell◈
- Food: **N:** Doc Holliday's Steakhouse, Subway/ Chevron
  S: Buckles, Jack in the Box, McDonald's, Pizza Hut, Rosa's Cantina

EXIT — ARIZONA

- Lodg: **N:** Fairfield Inn, Holiday Inn
  S: American Inn, Econo Lodge, Grand Canyon Hotel, Grand Motel, Knights Inn, Lodge on Rte 66, Rte 66 Inn, Rodeway Inn **x2**
- Other: **N:** **to Canyon Gateway RV Park▲** , **to** Williams Muni Airport✈
  S: Amtrak, Auto & Truck Repair, Perfection Automotive & Tires, **Railside RV Ranch▲** , **to** Bill Williams Ski Area

165 **AZ 64, I-40 Bus, Red Lake, Williams, Grand Canyon (Serv approx 4.5 mi N)**
- Gas: **N:** AJ's Mini Mart, Shell◈
- Lodg: **S:** Econo Lodge, El Rancho Motel, Motel 6♥, Mountain Side Inn, Rodeway Inn, Super 8, Travelodge
- Other: **N:** **Grand Canyon/Williams KOA▲ to Kaibab Natl Forest/Kaibab Lake Campground▲**
  S: **Railroad RV Park▲**

167 **Garland Prairie Rd, Circle Pines Rd**
- Other: **N:** **Williams/Circle Pines KOA▲**

171 **Pittman Valley Rd, Deer Farm Rd**
- Food: **S:** Rest/Quality Inn
- Lodg: **S:** Quality Inn

178 **Parks Rd, Williams**
- Gas: **N:** Mustang◈
- Other: **N:** **Ponderosa Forest RV Park▲**

(182) **Rest Area (EB)**
(RR, Phones, Vend, Pet, Weather)

(183) **Rest Area (WB)**
(RR, Phones, Vend, Pet, Weather)

185 **Transwestern Rd, Bellemont**
- TStop: **N:** Pilot Travel Center #180 (Scales)
- Food: **N:** McDonald's/Subway/Pilot TC
  S: 66 Roadhouse Grill
- Lodg: **N:** America's Best Value Inn
- TServ: **N:** Pilot TC
- Other: **N:** Laundry/WiFi/Pilot TC
  S: Navajo Army Depot, Nat'l Guard, Grand Canyon Harley Davidson, **Camping World Supercenter**

NOTE: MM 189: Elev 7335'

190 **A-1 Mountain Rd, Flagstaff**

191 **I-40 Bus, US 66, to Flagstaff, Grand Canyon (All Serv approx 5mi N)**
- Other: **N:** **Woody Mtn Campground & RV Park▲**

192 **Flagstaff Ranch Rd**
- Other: **N:** **Woody Mtn Campground & RV Park▲ , Kit Carson RV Park▲**

195 **AZ 89S, to US 180, Flagstaff (WB)**

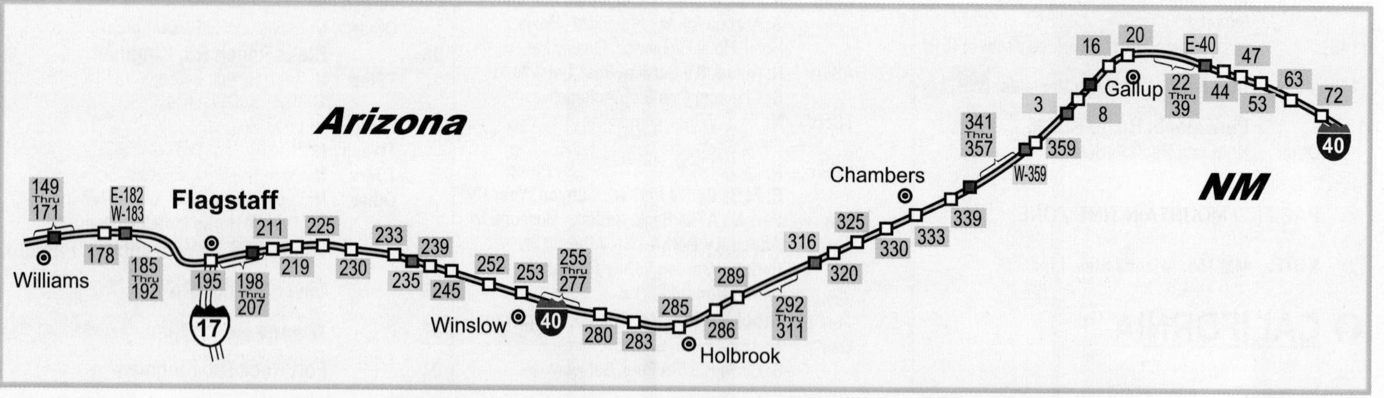

◈= Regular Gas Stations with Diesel ▲ = RV Friendly Locations ♥= Pet Friendly Locations
Red print shows large vehicle parking / access on site or nearby Brown Print = Campgrounds / RV PARKS

EXIT		ARIZONA
195B		**AZ 89N, to US 180, Flagstaff, to Grand Canyon**
	Gas	N: 76, Chevron◈, Circle K, Conoco◈, Exxon◈, Gasser, Mobil, Shell, Texaco◈
	Food	N: Arby's, Burger King, Carl's Jr, DQ, CoCo's, Denny's, Fazoli's, Fuddrucker's, IHOP, KFC, McDonald's, Olive Garden, Pizza Hut, Red Lobster, Sizzler, Village Inn
	Lodg	N: Amerisuites, Comfort Inn, Days Inn, Econo Lodge, Embassy Suites, Fairfield Inn, Hampton Inn, Hilton Garden Inn, La Quinta Inn♥, Quality Inn, Ramada Ltd, Rodeway Inn, Sleep Inn, Travelodge
	Med	N: + Flagstaff Comm Hospital
	Other	N: ATM's, Banks, B&N, Basha's Grocery, Cinema, Discount Tire, Kmart, Lowell Observatory, New Frontiers Natural Foods, Northern AZ Univ, Safeway, Staples, Target, Walgreen's, **Walmart**, **to US 66: Woody Mountain Campground & RV Park▲**, **Kit Carson RV Park▲** , Rt 66 RV & Auto Serv Center
(195A)		**Jct I-17S, AZ 89A, Sedona, Phoenix Northern Arizona University**
	Other	S: to Flagstaff Pulliam Airport✈
198		**Butler Ave, Flagstaff**
	TStop	S: AmBest/Little America Travel Center/ Sinclair (Scales)
	Gas	N: 76◈, Chevron, Conoco◈, Exxon◈, Giant◈, Shell, Fry's S: Mobil
	Food	N: Burger King, Country Host, Cracker Barrel, Denny's, McDonald's, Outback Steaks, Taco Bell, Rest/Econo Lodge S: Black Bart's Steakhouse
	Lodg	N: Best Western, Econo Lodge, Flagstaff Inn, Holiday Inn, Howard Johnson, Motel 6, Quality Inn, Ramada Inn, Relax Inn, Super 8, Travelodge S: Little America Hotel
	TServ	S: Little America/Tires
	Other	N: Auto Zone, Albertson's, Auto Dealers, Firestone, Fry's Grocery, NAPA, Sam's Club, RVDump/Conoco, U-Haul S: Laundry/WiFi/Little America TC, **Black Bart's RV Park▲**
201		**US 89N, I-40 Bus, US 180W, to Page, Grand Canyon**
	FStop	N: 7180 US 89N: Carter Travel Center/ Conoco
	Gas	N: 76, Chevron, Express Stop◈, Safeway S: Mobil◈
	Food	N: Arby's, Burger King, Del Taco, Jack in the Box, McDonald's, Pizza Hut, Ruby Tuesday, Sizzler Steak House, Wendy's
	Lodg	N: Best Western, Days Inn, Hampton Inn, Super 8 S: Fairfield Resort
	Med	N: + Hospital
	Other	N: LP/Carter TC, ATMs, Auto Services, Big O Tire, Banks, CVS, Cinemas, Checker Auto Parts, Discount Tire, Family Dollar, Flagstaff Mall, **Flagstaff Grand Canyon KOA▲** , **Flagstaff RV Sales & Service**/LP, Goodyear, Home Depot, **J&H RV Park▲** , PetCo♥, Safeway, AT Stadium, World Market
204		**Santa Fe Ave, to US 180, to US 89N, Walnut Canyon Rd**
	Other	S: Walnut Canyon Nat'l Monument
207		**Cosnino Rd**
(208)		**Weigh Station** (Both dir)
211		**CR 394, Flagstaff, Winona**
	Gas	N: Shell◈
	Other	N: Winona Trading Post
219		**NF 126, Twin Arrows**
225		**Buffalo Range Rd, Flagstaff**
230		**Old 66 Rd, Two Guns**
233		**Meteor Crater Rd, Flagstaff**
	Gas	S: Mobil
	Food	S: Subway/Mobil
	Other	S: **Meteor Crater RV Park▲**
(235)		**Meteor Crater Rest Area** (Both dir) **(RR, Phones, Picnic, Info, Pet)**
239		**Meteor City Rd, Red Gap Ranch Rd**
	Other	S: Meteor Crater Trading Post, to Meteor Crater
245		**AZ 99, Flagstaff, to Leupp**
252		**AZ 87S, I-40 Bus, Winslow, Payson**
	Gas	S: Shell◈
	Food	S: Burger King, Casa Blanca Café, Pizza Hut
	Lodg	S: Best Inn, Days Inn, Delta Motel, Rest Inn, Super 8, Travelodge
	Other	S: Auto Services, **Glenn's RV Repair**, Winslow Muni Airport✈
253		**N Park Dr, Winslow**
	TStop	N: Super American TS/USA Travel Center (Scales)
	Gas	N: Woody's S: Depot
	Food	N: Rest/Super Am TS, Arby's, Denny's, Captainn Tony's Pizza, Pizza Hut, Subway S: KFC, McDonald's, Subway, Taco Bell
	Lodg	S: Best Western, Comfort Inn, Econo Lodge♥, Motel 6♥
	Med	S: + Winslow Memorial Hospital
	TWash	N: Super Am TS
	Other	N: RVDump/WiFi/Super Am TS, Big O Tire, Dollar General, Laundromat, **Walmart SC**, Visitor Center, Santa Fe Station Golf Course S: Banks, Basha's Grocery, Family Dollar, Laundromat, NAPA, Safeway Grocery, Winslow Muni Airport✈
255		**Transcon Ln, to I-40 Bus, US 87S, Winslow, to Payson**
	TStop	S: Flying J Travel Plaza #5041 (Scales)
	Food	S: CountryMkt/FJ TP, China Inn, DQ, Sonic, Triple R's Home Cooking
	Lodg	N: Holiday Inn Express
	TServ	S: High Chaparrel Truck Repair, Winslow Truck Repair
	Other	N: **Freddy's RV Park▲** S: Laundry/BarbSh/WiFi/RVDump/LP/ FJ TP, Amtrak
257		**AZ 87N, AZ 66, to Second Mesa (Access to Ex #255 Serv S)**
	Other	N: **Homolovi Ruins State Park▲**
264		**Hibbard Rd, Winslow**
269		**Jackrabbit Rd**
	Gas	S: Jack Rabbit Trading Post◈
274		**I-40 Bus, to Joseph City**
	Gas	N: Speedy's
	Food	N: Mr G's Pizza
	Other	N: Laundry, U-Haul, **Dream Catcher RV Park▲** , **Norma's RV Park▲**
277		**I-40 Bus, Winslow, Joseph City**
	TStop	N: Love's Travel Stop #278 (Scales)
	Food	N: Subway/ChestersGr/Love's TS
	Other	N: WiFi/Love's TS
280		**Hunt Rd, Geronimo Rd**
	Other	N: Geronimo Trading Post
283		**Perkins Valley Rd, Golf Course Rd**
	FStop	S: Fuel Express/Shell
	Food	S: Rest/Fuel Express
	Other	S: Laundry/WiFi/Fuel Express
285		**I-40 Bus, US 180, Hopi Dr, to AZ 77, Holbrook**
	Gas	S: Giant◈, Mustang, Pacific Pride◈
	Food	S: Butterfield Stage Co, BBQ, Pizza Hut, Wayside Café
	Lodg	S: Best Inn♥, Budget Host Inn, Desert Inn, Holbrook Inn, Roseway Inn, Star Inn, Wigwam Motel
	Other	S: Auto Services, Family Dollar, Safeway
286		**AZ 77S, I-40 Bus, Navajo Blvd, US 180E, Holbrook, to Show Low**
	Gas	N: 76, Shamrock◈ S: Chevron◈, MiniMart, Woody"s◈
	Food	N: KFC, McDonald's, Pizza Hut, Roadrunner Café, Taco Bell S: DQ
	Lodg	N: 66 Motel, Best Inn, Comfort Inn, Holiday Inn Express, BW Sahara Inn, Super 8, Travelodge S: America's Best Value Inn, Budget Inn, Western Holiday Motel
	Med	S: + Petrified Forest Medical Center
	Other	N: Cinema, Dollar General, Vet♥, **OK RV Park▲** S: Auto Dealer, Auto Services, USPS
289		**I-40 Bus, Holbrook**
	Gas	N: Chevron◈, Hatch's, Mobil, Mustang◈
	Food	N: Denny's, Jerry's, McDonald's, KFC
	Lodg	N: Best Western,Comfort Inn, Days Inn, Econo Lodge, Motel 6♥, Ramada Inn
	Other	N: Holbrook Airport✈, **Holbrook/ Petrified Forest KOA▲**
292		**AZ 77N, to Keems Canyon**
	TStop	N: AmBest/Hopi Travel Plaza/Conoco (Scales)
	Food	N: Rest/FastFood/Hopi TP
	TWash	N: Hopi TP
	Other	N: Laundry/CB/Hopi TP
294		**Sun Valley Rd**
	Gas	S: Arizona Stage Stop
	Food	S: Arizona Stage Stop
300		**Goodwater Rd, Holbrook**
303		**Adamana Rd**
	Gas	S: Painted Desert Indian Center
311		**Petrified Forest National Park**
	Other	N: **Petrified Forest Nat'l Park**/Crystal Forest Gift Shop/**RVParking▲**
(316)		**Parking Area** (Both dir)
320		**Pinta Rd, Chambers**
325		**Pinta Rd, Navajo**
	FStop	S: Navajo Travel Center/Shell
	Food	S: Subway/Navajo TC
330		**McCarrell Rd, Chambers**
333		**US 191N, Chambers, Ganado**
	Gas	N: Chevron, GAS◈ S: Mobil◈
	Food	S: Rest/Best Western
	Lodg	S: Best Western

◈= Regular Gas Stations with Diesel ▲ = RV Friendly Locations ♥ = Pet Friendly Locations
Red print shows large vehicle parking / access on site or nearby Brown Print = Campgrounds / RV PARKS

EXIT		AZ / NM
339		**US 191S, Sanders, St Johns**
	Gas	S: Conoco◈
	Other	N: US Post Office
(340)		**Weigh Station / Inspection Station** (Both dir)
341		**Cedar Point Rd, Ganado**
	Gas	N: Amoco
343		**Querino Rd, Ganado**
346		**Pine Springs Rd**
	NOTE:	MM 347: Elevation 6000'
348		**St Anselm Rd, Ganado, Houck**
	Gas	N: Chevron
	Food	N: Pancake House Rest
351		**Allentown Rd, Ganado**
354		**Hawthorne Rd**
357		**Indian Hwy 12N, St Michael's, Lupton, Window Rock**
359		**Grants Rd, Ganado, Lupton**
	TStop	N: Speedy's Truck Stop
	Food	N: Rest/Speedy's
	TServ	N: Speedy's TS/Tires
	Other	N: Laundry/LP/Speedy's TS
(359)		AZ Welcome Center (WB) (RR, Phone, Picnic, Pet) Painted Cliffs Rest Area (EB)

MOUNTAIN TIME ZONE

NOTE: AZ = NO Daylight Savings Time

NOTE: MM 359: New Mexico State Line

ARIZONA

NEW MEXICO

MOUNTAIN TIME ZONE

(3)		Manuelito Welcome Center (EB) (RR, Phones, Picnic)
8		**NM 118, Rte 66, to Manuelito**
(12)		Weigh / Inspection Station (EB)
16		**I-40 Bus, NM 214, W Gallup**
	TStop	N: Love's Travel Stop #215, Navajo Travel Plaza/Armco, Travel Center of America #8 (Scales),
	Gas	S: Best Value, Chevron◈, Conoco, Rte 66 Mini Market, Shell
	Food	N: CntryPrideRest/Blimpie/TA TC, S: Subway/Chesters/Love's TS, Olympic Kitchen, NM Steak House, McDonald's, Mexican Rest, Taco Bell, Westend Donut & Deli
	Lodg	N: Howard Johnson/TA TC S: Americas Best Value Inn, Comfort Inn, Days Inn West♥, Econo Lodge♥, Hampton Inn, Microtel, Motel 6, Red Roof Inn♥, Travelodge♥
	TWash	N: Blue Beacon TW
	TServ	N: TA TC/Tires, Texaco TC/Tires S: Mike's Auto, Truck & RV Repair & Tires, RG Truck & RV Services
	Other	N: Laundry/WiFi/TA TC, Laundry/Tex TC, Kmart S: WiFi/Love's TS, Arrow Automotive, Carwash, USA RV Park/RVDump▲, UPS Store, Gallup Muni Airport✈,

Personal Notes

EXIT		NEW MEXICO
20		**US 491, NM 602S, Munoz Dr, to to Shiprock, Zuni**
	Gas	N: 7211, Giant◈, Texaco◈ S: Allsup's/Phillips 66◈, Shell◈
	Food	N: Applebee's Arby's, Burger King, Carl's Jr, Cracker Barrel, DQ, Denny's, Furr's, Golden Corral, KFC, McDonald's, Pizza Hut, Sizzler, Sonic, Taco Bell, Wendy's, S: Blake's Lotaburger, El Dorado Rest, El Sombrero Rest, Garcia's Sunset Grill, Plaza Cafe, Rte 66 Drive-In
	Lodg	N: Hampton Inn, Quality Inn♥, Ramada Ltd♥ S: America's Best Value Inn, Best Western, Days Inn East♥, Desert Skies Motel, Economy Inn♥, El Rancho Motel, Golden Desert Motel, Log Cabin Lodge, Rodeway Inn, Royal Holiday Motel♥, Sunset Motel, Super 8♥, Thunderbird Motel
	Med	S: + Gallup Indian Medical Center
	Other	N: Auto Zone, Auto Dealers, ATMs, Auto Services & Tires, Big Lots, Cedar Animal Medical Center♥, Checker Auto Parts, Cinema, Family Dollar, Firestone, Home Depot, Laundromat, Maloney Car Wash, NAPA, Pep Boys, Radio Shack, Rio West Mall, Safeway, UPS Store, Walmart sc, S: Amtrak, Auto Service & Tires/Shell, Auto Services, Aztec Twin Theatre, Banks, Big O Tires, Firestone, Goodyear, Premier Car Wash, US Post Office
22		**Ford Dr, Montoya Blvd**
	Gas	S: Armco, Chevron, Conoco, Giant◈, Macaya's, Texaco

EXIT		NEW MEXICO
	Food	S: Burger King, Carl's Jr, Church's Chicken, Earl's Rest, Hong Kong Buffet, Long John Silver, McDonald's, Papa John's, Pizza Hut, Subway, Taco Bell, Wendy's
	Lodg	S: Arrowhead Lodge, Blue Spruce Lodge, El Rancho Hotel, El Capitan Motel, Lariat Lodge, Redwood Lodge
	Other	S: Albertson's, Amtrak, Auto Services, RV & Truck Service, Carwash, Radio Shack, UPS Store, Walgreen's,
26		**I-40 Bus, NM 118, E Gallup**
	FStop	N: Chevron
	Gas	S: Conoco◈, Fina◈, Shell
	Food	N: Denny's S: Burger King, Blakes Lotaburger, KFC, McDonald's, Wendy's
	Lodg	N: Comfort Suites♥, La Quinta Inn♥, Sleep Inn♥ S: BW/Red Rock Inn, Road Runner Motel
	Med	S: + Gallup Hospital
	Other	N: Gallup KOA▲, to Red Rock State Park▲ S: NM State Hwy Patrol Post
33		**NM 400, McGaffey, Ft Wingate**
	Other	N: to Red Rock State Park▲
36		**Iyanbito**
39		**Refinery, Jamestown**
	TStop	N: Pilot Travel Center #305 (Scales)
	Food	N: Denny's/GrandmaMax's/Subway/Pilot
	TWash	N: Pilot TC
	TServ	N: Pilot TC/Boss Truck Shop/Tires
	Other	N: Laundry/BarbSh/WiFi/RVDump/Pilot TC
44		**Coolidge**
47		**Continental Divide** NOTE: Elev 7275'
	Gas	N: Chevron
	Other	N: US Post Office
53		**NM 371, NM 612, Gallup, to Chaco Canyon, Thoreau**
63		**NM 412, Prewitt, Bluewater St Park**
72		**Bluewater Village**
	Gas	N: Bowlins Bluewater Outpost/Exxon◈
	Food	N: DQ/Exxon
79		**NM 122, NM 605, Horizon Blvd, Milan, San Mateo**
	TStop	N: Love's Travel Stop #257, S: Petro Stopping Center #13/Mobil (Scales)
	Gas	N: Chaco Travel Center/Chevron
	Food	N: Subway/ChestersGr/Love's TS S: Iron Skillet/FastFood/Petro SC
	Lodg	N: Crossroads Motel
	TServ	S: Petro SC/Tires, Speedco
	Other	N: Wifi/Love's TS, Bar S RV Park▲ S: Laundry/Wifi/Petro SC, NM State Hwy Patrol Post, Grants-Milan Muni Airport✈
81A		**NM 53S, San Rafael (EB)**
	Other	S: Grants/Cibola Sands KOA▲, Blue Spuce RV Park▲
81B		**NM 53N, Grants (EB)**
	Gas	N: Phillips 66, Shell
	Food	N: Burger King, KFC, McDonald's
	Lodg	N: Sands Motel
	Med	N: + Cibola General Hospital
	Other	N: ATMs, Auto Dealers, Auto Services, Banks, Bert's Rte 66 Motorcycles, Flea Market, Museum, US Post Office
81		**NM 53, Grants, to San Rafael (WB)**

◈= Regular Gas Stations with Diesel ▲ = RV Friendly Locations ♥= Pet Friendly Locations
Red print shows large vehicle parking / access on site or nearby Brown Print = Campgrounds / RV PARKS

EXIT		NEW MEXICO
85		**I-40 Bus, NM 122, NM 547, Grants, Mt Taylor**
	Gas	**N:** Chevron, Conoco, Shell
	Food	**N:** 4 B's Rest, Chona's Cafe, Denny's, NM Steakhouse, Pizza Hut, Subway, Taco Bell, Rest/BW
	Lodg	**N:** Best Western♥, Comfort Inn, Days Inn♥, Economy Inn, Holiday Inn Express♥, Motel 6♥, Super 8, Travelodge♥
	Med	**N: + Cibola General Hospital**
	Other	**N:** Auto Zone, **Walmart sc**, Golf Course, **Lavaland RV Park▲**
89		**NM 117, Cubero, to Quernado**
	Gas	**N:** Citgo, Conoco
	Food	**N:** Stuckey's/Citgo
96		**NM 124, Cubero, McCartys**
100		**Acomita Rd, Cubero, to San Fidel**
(102)		**Sky City Rd, Casa Blanca, Acoma, Sky City**
		Acomita Rest Area (EB)
		S: (RR, Picnic)
	TStop	**N:** AmBest/Sky City Travel Center
	Food	**N:** Rest/McDonald's/Sky City TC
	Lodg	**N:** Sky City Hotel/Sky City TC
	Med	**N: + Hospital**
	Other	**N:** Laundry/BarbSh/ChromeSh/**Casino**/**RV Park▲** /Sky City TC
		S: Sky City Culteral Museum
104		**NM 124, to Cubero, Budville**
108		**NM 23, Paraje Dr, Casa Blanca**
	TStop	**N:** PTP/Dancing Eagle Travel Center/ Conoco
	Food	**N:** Rest/FastFood/DE TC
	Other	**N:** Laundry/**RVDump**/**RV Park▲** /Casino/ Grocery/DE TC
(113)		**Parking Area / Scenic View (Both dir)**
114		**NM 124, Rte 66, to Laguna**
	Gas	**N:** Conoco◈
117		**Mesita Rd, Casa Blanca**
126		**NM 6, Laguna, to Los Lunas**
131		**Canoncito School Rd, Laguna**
140		**Rio Puerco, Laguna**
	TStop	**S:** Route 66 Travel Center/Conoco
	Gas	**N:** Exxon◈
	Food	**S:** Rest/FastFood/Conoco
	Other	**S:** Laundry/Rte 66 TC, **Route 66 Casino**
149		**Paseo Del Vulcan Rd, Central Ave, Albuquerque, Paseo, Del Volcan**
	FStop	**S:** Nine Mile Hill Chevron, Hilltop Shamrock

EXIT		NEW MEXICO
	Food	**S:** Café, Hungry Cowboy Buffet, Tumbleweed Steakhouse
	Other	**N: Enchanted Trails RV Park & Trading Post▲ , American RV/Camping World**, Double Eagle II Airport✈
		S: American RV Park▲ , High Desert RV Park▲ , **Rte 66 RV** & Auto Repair
153		**98th St, Nolasco Rd**
	TStop	**S:** Flying J Travel Plaza #5032/Conoco (Scales)
	Food	**S:** Rest/FastFood/FJ TP, Hungry Cowboy Buffet, Tumbleweed Steakhouse
	Lodg	**S:** Microtel
	Other	**S:** Laundry/BarbSh/WiFi/**RVDump**/**LP**/ FJ TP, Auto Zone, Dollar Tree, **Palisades RV Park▲**
154		**Unser Blvd**
	Gas	**N:** Shamrock
		S: U Pump It
	Food	**S:** Hungry Cowboy Buffet
	Lodg	**S:** JB's Rte 66 Motel
	Other	**N:** Walgreen's, **to** Petroglyph Nat'l Monument
		S: Walgreen's
155		**NM 448, Coors Blvd, to Rio Rancho**
	Gas	**N:** Chevron, Duke City Fueling◈, Giant/Conoco◈, Shamrock◈
		S: Chevron, Circle K/Phillips 66◈, Shell
	Food	**N:** Applebee's, Arby's, Chili's, **Cracker Barrel**, Golden Corral, IHOP, McDonald's, Panda Express, Starbucks, Subway, Taco Cabana, Wendy's
		S: Del Taco, Denny's, Furr's, Marisco's Mexican Rest, Pizza Hut, Subway, Taco Bell, Village Inn
	Lodg	**N:** Westside Inn
		S: Comfort Inn, Days Inn, Hampton Inn, Holiday Inn Express, La Quinta Inn ♥, Motel 6 ♥, Motel 76, Quality Inn, Super 8
	Other	**N:** ATMs, Banks, Auto Zone, Brake Masters Brooks Grocery, Carwash, Dollar Tree, FedEx Office, Goodyear, Home Depot, Jiffy Lube, Midas, NAPA, Radio Shack, Staples, UPS Store, Walgreen's, **Walmart sc**, West Mesa Animal Hospital♥
		S: Albertson's, ATMs, Banks, Car Wash, Carwash/Shell, Discount Tire, U-Haul, **Dalon RV Sales & Service**
157A		**Rio Grande Blvd**
	Gas	**N:** Bubba's Conv Store, Valero
		S: Chevron, Shell
	Food	**N:** Burger King, Ned's
		S: Starbucks
	Lodg	**S:** Best Western, Econo Lodge, Hotel Albuquerque
	Other	**S:** Museums

EXIT		NEW MEXICO
157B		**12th St NW, Albuquerque (EB)**
	Gas	**N:** Fina
	Food	**N:** Arby's/Fina, Pueblo Harvest Cafe/Indian Cultural Center,
	Lodg	**N:** Holiday Inn Express, to Candlewood Suites♥
	Other	**N:** Indian Pueblo Cultural Center, Lowe's, Walgreen's
158		**8th St, 6th St, Albuquerque**
	FStop	**N:** Love's Travel Stop #210
	Gas	**S:** Chevron
	Food	**N:** Subway/Love's TS
	Lodg	**S:** Interstate Inn, Travelers Inn
	TServ	**N:** Big West Trucks
	Other	**N:** WiFi/**RVDump**/Love's TS, Big West Truck Sales & Service, U-Haul
159A		**6th St, 4th St, 2nd St, Broadway, University Blvd (EB)**
	FStop	**N: 6th St NW:** Love's Travel Stop #210
	TStop	**N: University Blvd NE:** Travel Center of America #81/Chevron (Scales)
	Gas	**N:** Chevron
		S: Diamond Shamrock
	Food	**N:** CountryPride/TA TC, Furr's, Whataburge
		S: Tony's Pizza, Village Inn
	Lodg	**N:** Comfort Inn, Fairfield Inn, La Quinta Inn♥, Rodeway Inn
		S: Interstate Inn, Hilton, Motel 6, Travelers Inn
	TServ	**N:** TA TC/Tires
		S: Great Basin Trucks
	Other	**N:** Laundry/WiFi/**RVDump**/TA TC, Dollar Tree, Family Dollar,
(159BC)		**Jct I-25, S-Las Cruces, N-Santa Fe**
159D		**University Blvd, to Menaul Blvd (WB)**
	TStop	**N:** Travel Center of America #81/Chevron (Scales)
	Gas	**N:** Circle K◈, Shell
		S: Valero◈
	Food	**N:** CountryPride/TA TC, Caso Chaco/ Ranchers Club/Hilton, Lindy's American Cafe, Range Cafe, Twisters, Village Inn
	Lodg	**N:** Candlewood Suites, Clubhouse Inn♥, Days Inn♥, Fairfield Inn, Hilton, Holiday Inn Express, La Quinta Inn♥, MCM Elegante, Ramada Inn, Red Roof Inn♥, Rodeway Inn, Super 8♥,
		S: Four Points Sheraton, Motel 6♥
	TServ	**N:** TA TC/Tires, Inland Kenworth
	Med	**S: + Carrie Tingley Hospital, + Univ Of NM Hospital**
	Other	**N:** Laundry/WiFi/**RVDump**/TA TC, Utility Trailer Interstate
		S: to Univ of NM

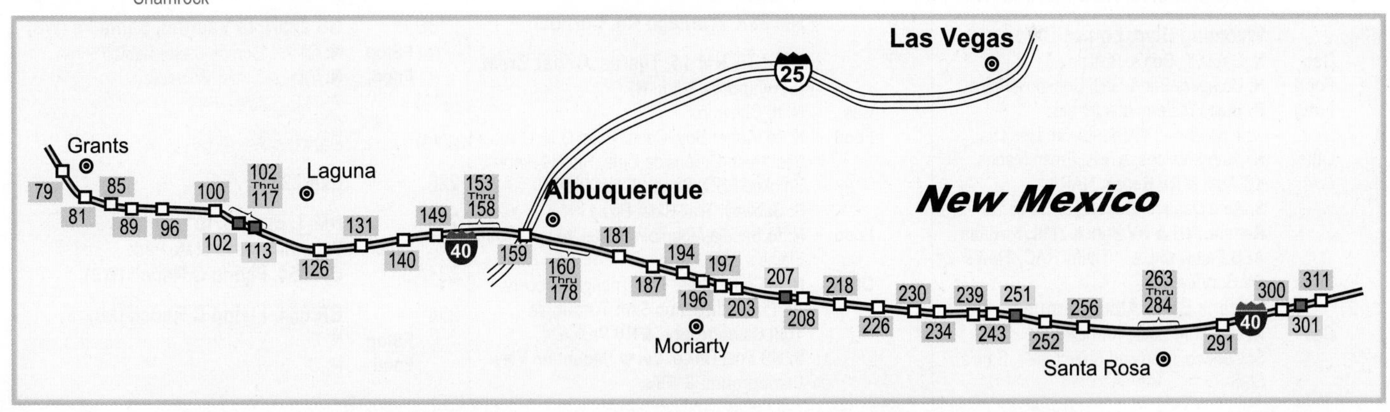

◈= **Regular Gas Stations with Diesel** ▲ = **RV Friendly Locations** ♥= **Pet Friendly Locations**

Red print shows large vehicle parking / access on site or nearby **Brown Print = Campgrounds / RV PARKS**

EXIT	NEW MEXICO

160 **Carlisle Blvd, Albuquerque**
- **Gas** N: 7-11/Fina, Circle K, Chevron, Shell
  S: Circle K, Economy GAS◈, Phillips 66◈, Shell
- **Food** N: Blake's Lotaburger, JB's, McDonald's, Pizza Hut, Richard's Mexican Rest, Rudy's Country Store & BBQ, Sonic, Village Inn, Whataburger
  S: Burger King, Subway, Taj Mahal Indian Cuisine, Whataburger
- **Lodg** N: Econo Lodge♥, Hampton Inn, Motel 6♥, Radisson Hotel & Waterpark, Residence Inn, Suburban Extended Stay♥
- **Med** S: + Univ of NM Hospital
- **Other** N: ATMs, Banks, Cost Plus World Market, Firestone Auto, Smith Food & Drug, Walgreen's, **Walmart sc**, **NM State Hwy Patrol Post**
  S: Auto Repair/Shell, Auto Service/**LP**/ Phillips 66, Blue Cross Animal Clinic♥, Laundromat, Penske Auto Center, Whole Foods Market

161B **San Mateo Blvd North (EB)**
- **Gas** N: Giant◈, Phillips 66◈, Shell
- **Food** N: Arby's, Burger King, Carl's Jr, Denny's, Dunkin Donuts, KFC, McDonald's, Peter Piper Pizza, Starbucks, Subway, Taco Bell, Wendy's
- **Lodg** N: La Quinta Inn♥
- **Other** N: ATMs, Auto Services, Big 5 Sporting Goods, Big Lots, Budget Truck Rental, FedEx Office, Good Shepherd Animal Clinic♥, Office Depot, Radio Shack, U-Haul

161A **San Mateo Blvd South (EB)**
(Many Serv S appr 1.5 mi to Central Ave)
- **Gas** S: Chevron◈
- **Food** S: Starbucks
- **Med** S: + Veteran's Medical Center
- **Other** S: appr 1.7mi: **Walmart sc**, **Asstd Serv**

161 **San Mateo Blvd (WB)**

162A **Louisiana Blvd South (EB)**

162B **Louisiana Blvd North (EB)**
- **Food** N: Fuddrucker's, Garduno's of Mexico, Hickory Pit BBQ, Le Peep, Romano's Macaroni Grill, Starbucks, Steak & Ale,
- **Lodg** N: AmeriSuites, Ambassador Inn, Hilton Garden Inn, Homewood Suites♥, Hyatt Pla Marriott, Sheraton
- **Other** N: ATMs, Apple, Banks, Barnes&Noble, Big O Tires, Borders, Coronado Mall, Discount Tire, FedEx Office, Firestone Auto, Regal Winrock Cinema 6, Sprint, St Francis Animal Clinic♥, Walgreen's, Winrock Mall,

162 **Louisiana Blvd, Albuquerque (WB)**

164 **Wyoming Blvd, Lomas Blvd**
- **Gas** N: Circle K, Don's, Phillips 66◈
- **Food** N: Bumpers Bar & Grill, Domino's Pizza
- **Lodg** N: Best Western, Luxury Inn
- **Med** N: + Kaseman Presbyterian Hospital
- **Other** N: Auto Services, ATMs, Fresh Market, KC Auto & **RV** Repair, NAPA
  S: Auto Dealers, **Desert RV Sales**, **El Rancho MH & RV Park▲**, **MIL/Kirtland AFB FamCamp▲**, Thrifty RAC, **Tom's RV Service**,

165 **Eubank Blvd, Albuquerque**
- **Gas** N: Chevron, Circle K/Phillips 66,
  S: Conoco, Diamond Shamrock◈, Sam's Club
- **Food** N: Applebee's, JB's, Owl Café, Panda Express, Sonic
  S: Bob's Burgers, Burger King, Boston Market, Chili's, Del Taco, Golden Corral, Golden Pride BBQ, Pizza Hut, Starbucks, Subway, Taco Bell, Twisters, Wendy's
- **Lodg** N: Days Inn♥, Econo Lodge, Freeway Inn, GuestHouse Inn♥, Holiday Inn Express, Howard Johnson, Quality Inn, Sandia Courtyard Hotel
- **Other** N: ATMs, Banks, Auto Services, Best Buy, Carquest, Office Max, Petco♥, Target, KC Auto & **RV** Repair
  S: ATMs, Auto Services, Auto Zone, Banks, Checkers Auto Parts, Costco, Home Depot, Office Depot, O'Reilly Auto Parts, Peerless Tires, PetSmart♥, Sam's Club, Towing, Walgreen's, **Walmart sc**, **MIL/Kirtland AFB FamCamp▲**

166 **Juan Tabo Blvd, Albuquerque**
- **Gas** N: Chevron, Phillips 66
- **Food** N: Burger King, Carrow's, McDonald's, Olive Garden, Pizza Hut, Twisters, Village Inn, Wendy's
  S: Chin's Chinese Food, Little Caesars Pizza, Sonic, Whataburger
- **Lodg** N: Americas Best Value Inn♥, Super 8,
- **Other** N: Albertson's, Banks, Big O Tires, Discount Tire, Dollar General, Family Dollar, Hobby Lobby, Outdoor Adventures, Pep Boys, Roller Skate City
  S: **Albuquerque Central KOA▲**, Auto Services, **Chisolm Trail RV**, Dollar General **El Monte RV Rental**, Grocery, **Holiday Travel Trailers Sales**, **United RV Sales**, Walgreen's,

167 **NM 556, Tramway Blvd, NM 333**
- **Gas** N: 7-11/Fina
  S: Chevron, Phillips 66, Shell, Smith's
- **Food** N: Papa John's Pizza
  S: Carl's Jr, Einstein Bagels, KFC, McDonald's, Pizza Hut, Starbucks, Subway, Taco Bell, Waffle House
- **Lodg** S: Americas Best Value Inn♥, Budget Host Inn♥, Comfort Inn, Deluxe Inn, Econo Lodge♥, Rodeway Inn, Sunset Inn, Travelodge♥, Value Place Hotel
- **Other** N: Carwash/7-11, Laundromat
  S: Albertson's, Auto Services, Banks, Dollar Tree, East Central Tire & Battery, Goodyear, PJ's Triumph Motorcycles, Smith's Food & Drug, Regal Four Hills 10 Cinema, Towing, U-Haul, UPS Store, **Chisolm Trail RV Repair & Service**, **Enchantment RV**, **Myers RV Center**, **Rocky Mountain RV & Marine Center**, **to** Kirtland AFB

170 **NM 333, Frontage Rd, Carnuel**

175 **NM 337, NM 14, Tijeras, Cedar Crest**
(Serv approx 2-3mi N)
- **Gas** N: to Chevron
- **Food** N: to Burger Boy, Cedar Point Grill, China's Best Rest, Greenside Cafe, Ribs Hickory Smoked BBQ, Sandia Crust Pizza
  S: Subway, Trail Rider Pizza
- **Lodg** N: **to** Sandia Mountain Hostel, **to** appr 4mi Elaine's B&B
- **Other** N: to Cedar Crest Tire, Triangle Grocery, US Post Office, **app 5mi: Turquoise Trail Campground & RV Park▲**
  S: US Post Office, Vet♥, **Mountain View Campground & RV▲**

178 **Zamora Rd, NM 333, Tijeras, Zuzax**
- **Gas** S: Chevron◈
- **Other** S: **Hidden Valley Camping Resort▲**

181 **NM 333, NM 217, Sedillo**
- **Gas** S: Phillips 66◈
- **Lodg** S: to Lazy K Ranch B&B
- **Other** S: Sandia Trailer

187 **NM 344, Edgewood**
- **Gas** N: Conoco◈, Jay's Service Center
  S: Phillips 66◈, Smith's
- **Food** N: DQ/Conoco, McDonald's/Walmart
  S: Home Run Pizza, McDonald's, Pizza Barn, Subway
- **Other** N: **Walmart sc**, **to** Sandia Airpark✈
  S: AutoZone, Dollar General, Ford, Grocery NAPA, **Red Arrow Edgewood Camp ground▲**, Smith's Food & Drug, US Post Office, Walgreen's, Zoo Animal Hospital♥

194 **NM 41, I-40 Bus, Moriarty, Escancia**
- **TStop** S: Travel Center of America #229/Shell (Scales)
- **Gas** S: Chevron, Conoco, Phillips 66◈
- **Food** S: CntryFare/BKing/PHut/TA TC, Arby's, El Comedor, KFC/Taco Belll, McDonald's, Mama Rosa's Rest, Shorty's BBQ
- **Lodg** S: Best Western♥, Motel 6♥
- **TServ** S: TA TC/Tires
- **Other** S: Laundry/BarbSh/WiFi/**RVDump**/**LP**/ TA TC, Alco, Auto Services, Auto Dealers, Banks, Dollar General, Grocery, **Kay's RV's**, Tires, **Acc to Exit #196 & #197**

196 **NM 41, Howard Cavasos Blvd, Estancia, Santa Fe**
- **Gas** S: Circle K, Phillips 66◈, Shell
- **Food** S: Lotaburger, Super China Buffet, Village Grill
- **Lodg** S: Comfort Inn♥, Lariat Motel, Super 8, Sunset Motel♥
- **Other** S: ATMs, Family Dollar, Grocery, Laundry, Pharmacy, Tires, Moriarty Airport✈

197 **Lp P, Abrahames Rd, Moriarty**
- **TStop** S: Lisa's Truck Center
- **Food** S: Rest/Lisa's TC
- **Lodg** S: Ponderosa Motel
- **TServ** S: Lisa's TC/Tires
- **Other** S: NAPA, **Access to #196/#194**

203 **Frontage Rd, Abrahames Rd**

(207) **Rattlesnake Draw Rest Area**
(Both dir)
(RR, Picnic, Horse Corrals)

208 **CR 60, Moriarty, Wagon Wheel**

218 **US 285, to Vaughn, Santa Fe (EB)**

218A **US 285S, to Vaughn, Santa Fe (WB)**

218B **US 285N, to Vaughn, Santa Fe (WB)**
- **FStop** N: Cline's Corner Travel Center/Shell
- **Food** N: Clines Corner Restaurant

(219) **Parking Area (WB)**

(220) **Parking Area (EB)**

226 **Exit 226**

230 **NM 3, Encino, to Villaneuva**
- **Other** S: **to Villaneuva State Park**

234AB **CR 054, Flying C Ranch (WB)**

234 **CR 054, Flying C Ranch (EB)**
- **FStop** N: Bowlin's Flying C Travel Center/Exxon
- **Food** N: DQ/Bowlin's

◈= Regular Gas Stations with Diesel ▲ = RV Friendly Locations ♥= Pet Friendly Locations
Red print shows large vehicle parking / access on site or nearby Brown Print = Campgrounds / RV PARKS

EXIT	NEW MEXICO
239	**Exit 239, CR 053, Encino**
243AB	**CR 4F, Milagro (WB)**
243	**CR 4F, Milagro (EB)**
FStop	N: D&R Chevron
Food	N: Café/Chevron
(251)	**Anton Chico Rest Area (Both dir) (RR, Picnic)**
252	**Exit 252**
256	**US 84N, NM 219, Anton Chico, to Santa Rosa, Las Vegas, Pastura**
263	**CR 4B, Santa Rosa, San Ignacio**
267	**NM 379, CR 4H, to Colonias**
FStop	N: Shell
Food	N: Stuckey's/Rest/Shell
273	**US 84, I-40E Bus, Coronado St, to US 54S, Santa Rosa, to Vaughn**
Gas	S: Chevron, Feed & Supply
Food	S: Mateo's Family Rest, KFC, Long John Silver, Joseph' s Cantina
Lodg	S: Rancho Motor Lodge, Best Western, Comfort Inn, Days Inn, La Quinta Inn♥, Motel 6♥, Ramada Ltd
Other	N: to **Santa Rosa Lake State Park▲** S: Banks, Carwash/Chevron, NAPA, **Santa Rosa Police Dept, Ramblin Rose RV Park▲**, **Access to Ex #275 Serv**
275	**I-40 Bus, US 54, Will Rogers Dr, Santa Rosa (Acc to Ex #277 Serv)**
Gas	N: to Phillips 66 S: Chevron, Fina, Shell◈
Food	N: Burger King, KFC/Long John Silver, McDonald's, Rte 66 Rest, TCBY, Taco Sol S: Comet II Drive-In,Joseph's Bar & Grill, Rte 66 Rest, Sun & Sand Rest
Lodg	N: Best Western Adobe Inn♥, Days Inn, La Quinta Inn♥, Travelodge S: American Inn, La Loma Lodge **& RV Park▲**, Sunset Motel, Sun n Sand Motel, Super 8, Tower Motel, Western Motel
Med	S: + **Guadalupe Co Hospital**
Other	N: Auto Services, Towing, **Santa Rosa Campground & RV Park/LP▲**, **to Santa Rosa Lake State Park▲** S: ATMs, Auto Services, CarQuest, Family Dollar, Laundromat, NAPA, **NM State Hwy Patrol Post**, T&D Food Mart, Tires, US Post Office
277	**US 84, US 54, I-40 Bus, Will Rogers Dr, Santa Rosa, to Fort Sumner (Access to Exit #275 Services)**
TStop	S: Travel Center of America #23/Shell (Scales), Love's Travel Stop #285
Gas	N: Chevron
Food	N: DQ, Denny's, Golden Dragon Rest, Lake City Diner, Silver Moon Rest S: CountryPride/Subway/TA TC, Carl's Jr/Love's TS
Lodg	N: Baymont Inn, Best Western Santa Rosa♥, Budget Inn, Comfort Inn♥, Hampton Inn, Holiday Inn Express♥, Motel 6♥, Quality Inn♥
TServ	S: TA TC/Tires, Big Rig Truck Service/Tires
Other	N: Silver Moon Auto, Truck & **RV** Service, **Santa Rosa Campground▲**, Rt 66 Auto Museum, **to appr 6mi: Santa Rosa Lake State Park▲** S: Laundry/CB/WiFi/TA TC, **RVDump**/WiFi/ Love's TS, Santa Rosa Muni Airport✈, **to Appr 41 mi: Lake Sumner State Park▲**, Ft Sumner, Billy the Kid Museum

Personal Notes

EXIT	NEW MEXICO
284	**Exit 284**
291	**Frontage Rd, Cuervo**
Gas	N: CUERVO GAS
Other	N: Wrecker Service
300	**NM 129, to NM 104, Newkirk**
Gas	N: Phillips 66◈
Other	N: **to Conchas Lake State Park**
(301)	**Newkirk Rest Area (Both dir) (WB CLOSED) (RR, Phones, Pic, Vend, RVDump)**
311	**Quay Rd, Tucumcari, Montoya**
321	**Frontage Rd, Tucumcari, Palomas**
FStop	S: Shell
Food	S: DQ/Stuckey's/Shell
329	**US 54, I-40Bus, to Rte 66, Tucumcari (Access to #331/#332 Serv)**
FStop	S: Tucumcari Travel Plaza
Food	N: Rest/Tristar Inn, Rest/PowWow Inn
Lodg	N: Redwood Lodge, to Tristar Inn Xpress♥ Motel Safari, PowWow Inn,
Other	N: Tucumcari Muni Golf Course, Mesa College, Convention Center
331	**Camino del Coronado**
332	**NM 104, NM 209, 1st St, Tucumcari**
TStop	N: MC Stop/Chevron
Gas	N: Allsup's/Phillips 66, Shell
Food	N: Subway/MC Stop, Blake's Lotaburger, Golden Dragon, K-Bob's, KFC, Long John Silver/A&W, McDonald's, Pizza Hut, Sonic,
Lodg	N: Americana Motel♥, Blue Swallow Motel

EXIT	NM / TX
Lodg	N: Best Western Discovery Inn♥, Buckaroo Motel, Days Inn♥, Friends Inn, Holiday Inn Express, La Quinta Inn♥, Microtel, Payless Inn, PowWow Inn, Travelers Motor Inn
TServ	N: John's Truck & **RV** Service
Med	N: + **Memorial Hospital**
Other	N: Laundry/MC Stop, Ace Hardware, Dollar General, Family Dollar, Greyhound, Lowe's Grocery, Mesalands Dinosaur Museum, **NM State Hwy Patrol Post**, Ostrich Ranch Tour, Pharmacies, Quay Co Fairgrounds, Tucumcari Mountain Cheese Factory, **Cactus RV Park▲**
333	**US 54, Mountain Rd, Tucumcari**
TStop	N: Love's Travel Stop #262 (Scales), Flying J Travel Plaza #5176◈ (Scales)
Gas	N: Circle K, Fina◈, Shell
Food	N: Arby's/Chester/Godfathers/Love's TS, CountryMarket/FastFood/FJ TP, McDonald's, Pizza Hut, Sonic
Lodg	N: Best Western, Comfort Inn, Holiday Inn, Historic Rte 66 Motel, Relax Inn, Super 8, Travelodge
TServ	N: Jack's Truck Repair
Other	N: WiFi/Love's TS, Laundry/WiFi/**RVDump/LP**/FJ TP, Auto Services, Museum, **to Mountain Rd RV Park▲**
335	**Lp 40, E Tucumcari Blvd, Tucumcari**
Gas	N: Conoco◈, Holiday Gas & Tire, Phillips 66
Food	N: Branding Iron Rest, Dean's Rest, Del's Rest, Denny's, Ken's Ice Cream, Kix on 66 Coffee Shop & Eatery,
Lodg	N: Econo Lodge♥, Gateway Inn, Hampton Holiday Inn, Motel 6♥, Palomino Motel, Quality Inn♥, Rodeway Inn♥, Super 8♥, Tucumcari Inn
Other	N: Auto Services, CarQuest, Kmart/ Pharmacy, NAPA, Tires, Towing, **Cactus RV Park▲**, **Empty Saddle RV Park▲**, **Kiva RV Park▲**, **Tucumcari Gas/LP**, **S: Tucumcari KOA▲**
339	**NM 286, NM 278, Tucumcari**
Other	N: Tucumcari Muni Airport✈
343	**Exit 343, Quay Rd AL**
356	**NM 469, 4th St, San Jon**
FStop	S: Fast Stop #24/P66
TStop	N: Drivers Travelmart #408/Citgo
Food	N: Taste of India Rest/Drivers TM
Lodg	S: San Jon Motel
TServ	N: Old Rte 66 Truck & Auto Service
Other	N: Laundry/WiFi/Drivers TM
(357)	**Weigh Station (EB)**
361	**Quay Rd M, San Jon, Bard**
369	**NM 93S, NM 392N, to Endee**
(373)	**NM Welcome Center (WB) (RR, Phone, Picnic, Vend, Pet)**

NOTE: MM 374: Texas State Line

MOUNTAIN / CENTRAL TIME ZONE

NEW MEXICO

TEXAS

MOUNTAIN / CENTRAL TIME ZONE

(0)	**I-40 Bus, to Glenrio**
(13)	**Picnic Area (Both dir)**

◈= Regular Gas Stations with Diesel ▲ = RV Friendly Locations ♥= Pet Friendly Locations
Red print shows large vehicle parking / access on site or nearby Brown Print = Campgrounds / RV PARKS

EXIT		TEXAS
15		**Ivy Rd, Adrian**
18		**FM 2858, CR 18, Gruhlkey Rd**
	Gas	S: Shell◈
	Food	S: Stuckey's/Rest/Shell
22		**TX 214, I-40 Bus, to Rte 66, Adrian**
	Gas	S: Phillips 66◈
	Food	N: Midpoint Cafe
		S: Cafe/P66
	TServ	N: Billy's Truck & Tire Service
	Other	N: Towing & Repair, US Post Office
23		**FM 290, TX 214, to Rte 66, Adrian**
28		**CR 29, Vega, to Landergin**
(31)		**Parking Area (EB)**
(32)		**Parking Area (WB)**
35		**I-40 Bus, Vega, Old Rte 66**
	Food	N: Sand's Café/Best Western
	Lodg	N: Best Western
	Other	N: Oversized Vehicle Permit Station, Walnut RV Park▲, Acc to #36
36		**US 385, S Main St, Vega, to Dalhart, Hereford**
	FStop	N: Allsup's #304/Conoco
	TStop	S: Kevin's Texas Quick Stop/Shell
	Gas	N: Shamrock, Fina◈
	Food	N: DQ, Boot Hill Saloon & Grill, Hickory Café,
		S: FastFood/TX QS,
	Lodg	N: Bonanza Motel♥, Days Inn♥, Vega Motel
	TServ	S: Tires/Tx QS
	Other	N: Repairs/Shamrock, US Post Office
		S: RVDump/Tx QS, Oversized Vehicle Permit Station,
37		**I-40W Bus, Vega (Acc to #36)**
	Other	N: Walnut RV Park▲
		S: Oldham Co Airport✈
42		**CR 42, Everett Rd, Vega**
49		**FM 809, N Locust St, Wildorado**
	FStop	S: Wildorado Fuel Club/Crist Fuel
	Other	S: LP/Crist Fuel
(53)		**Parking Area (EB)**
54		**Adkisson Rd, Amarillo**
(55)		**Parking Area (WB)**
57		**RM 2381, Amarillo, to Bushland**
	Gas	S: Shell◈
	Food	S: BBQ Barn
	Other	N: Bushland Mercantile, US Post Office
		S: Longhorn Trailer Inn & RV Park▲
60		**Arnot Rd, Amarillo, Bushland**
	FStop	S: Love's Travel Stop #250 (Scales)
	Food	S: Subway/Love's TS
	Other	N: Happy Tracks Horse Motel▲
		S: Laundry/WiFi/Love's TS, Oasis RV Resort/RVDump▲, Cadillac Ranch
62A		**Hope Rd, Helium Rd (EB)**
	Other	S: Amarillo West View RV Park▲, Sundown RV Resort▲,
62B		**I-40E Bus, Amarillo Blvd (EB)**
	Other	N: Fort Amarillo RV Park▲
62		**Old Rte 66, Hope Rd (WB)**
64		**Lp 335, Soncy Rd, Amarillo**
	Gas	S: Valero◈
	Food	N: Country Barn Steakhouse, Famous Dave's, Johnny Carino's, Joe's Crab Shack, Logan's Roadhouse, Red Robin
		S: Applebee's, DQ, Hooters, McDonald's On the Border, Ruby Tuesday, Subway
	Lodg	N: Comfort Inn, Country Inn♥, Drury Inn♥ Extended Stay America♥, Hilton Garden Inn
		S: Homewood Suites
	Other	N: ATMs, Cavenders Boot City, Discount Tire, Enterprise RAC, Gander Mountain
		S: ATMs, B&N, Best Buy, Carwash/Valero, Home Depot, Office Max, PetSmart♥, Target, ToysRUs, US Post Office, Westgate Mall, World Market
65		**Coulter Dr, Amarillo**
	Gas	N: BP, Phillips 66◈
		S: Chevron, Citgo, Shell
	Food	N: Arby's, Golden Corral, Luby's, Subway, Taco Bell, Waffle House
		S: Beef O'Brady's, Chuck E Cheese Pizza, CiCi's Pizza, Hoffbrau Steakhouse, Jason's Deli, McDonald's, Outback Steakhouse, Whataburger
	Lodg	N: Best Western, Courtyard, Days Inn, Executive Inn, Fairfield Inn, Interstate Motel, La Quinta Inn♥, Quality Inn, Residence Inn
		S: Fifth Season Inn, Hampton Inn, Ramada Inn, Sleep Inn, Super 8
	Med	N: + Baptist St Anthony Hospital, + NW Tx Hospital, + Amarillo Urgent Care
	Other	N: ATMs, Auto Dealers, Discount Tire, Firestone,
		S: ATMs, AT&T, Auto Services, Banks, Best Buy, Goodyear, Grocery, Jiffy Lube, Lowe's, Natural Grocer, UPS Store, Westgate Mall
66		**Bell St, Avondale St, Wolffin Ave**
	Gas	N: Citgo◈, Shell, Valero
		S: Chevron, Phillips 66◈, Shell
	Food	S: Arby's, Popeye's, Starbucks, Subway, Taco Bell, Waffle House
	Lodg	N: Fairfield Inn, Motel 6♥, Quality Inn♥
	Other	N: ATMs, Carwash/Valero, Carwash/Shell, Tripp's Harley Davidson
		S: Albertson's/Pharmacy, Firestone
67		**Western St, Avondale, Amarillo**
	Gas	N: Citgo, Shell
		S: Rudy's◈, Shamrock, Phillips 66
	Food	N: Beef Rigger Prime Rib, Black Eyed Pea, Burger King, Chili's, Frank's Bakery, McDonald's, Pancho's, Rosa's Cafe & Tortilla Factory, Sonic, Subway, Taco Bell
		S: Bangkok Tokyo, Blue Sky Texas, Catfish Shack, Cheddars Cafe, IHOP, Olive Garden, Rudy's Country Store & BBQ, Starbucks, Taco Cabana, Vince's Pizza, Waffle House
	Lodg	S: Baymont Inn♥, Holiday Inn Express
	Other	S: ATMs, Burlington Coat Factory, Discount Tire, FedEx Office, Firestone, NAPA, O'Reilly Auto Parts, PetCo♥, Radio Shack, Various Animal Services♥
68A		**Julian Blvd, Paramount Blvd**
	Gas	N: Chevron, Shell
		S: Valero
	Food	N: Arby's, Chili's, Pancho's, Wendy's
		S: Cajun Magic, Calico County Rest, Catfish Shack & Seafood Grill, El Chico, Fernando's Rest, Long John Silver, Malcolm's Ice Cream & Food, Pacific Rim Chinese, Pizza Hut, Pizza Planet, Red Lobster, Ruby Tequila's Mex Tex, Steak & Ale, Texas Roadhouse
	Lodg	S: Americas Best Value Inn♥, Baymont Inn♥, Comfort Suites, Travelodge♥
	Other	S: Auto Services, Enterprise RAC, Hertz RAC, Johnson Animal Hospital♥,
68B		**Georgia St, Amarillo**
	Gas	N: Shell
		S: Phillips 66, Valero
	Food	N: Dyers BBQ, Leal's Mexican, Macaroni Joe's, Sharky's Burrito, Subway/Shell, TGI Friday/Heritage Park/Ambassador
		S: Burger King, Carolina's Woodfired Italian Rest, David's Steaks & Seafood, Denny's, Dominos Pizza, Long John Silver, Moe's SW Grill, Roasters Coffee & Tea, Starbucks, Texas Roadhouse, Thai Arwan
	Lodg	N: Ambassador Hotel♥
		S: Holiday Inn Express,
	Med	S: + Hospital
	Other	S: Auto Dealers, Auto Services, Banks, Discount Tire, Home Depot, NAPA, Office Depot, Radio Shack, UPS Store, Walgreen's,

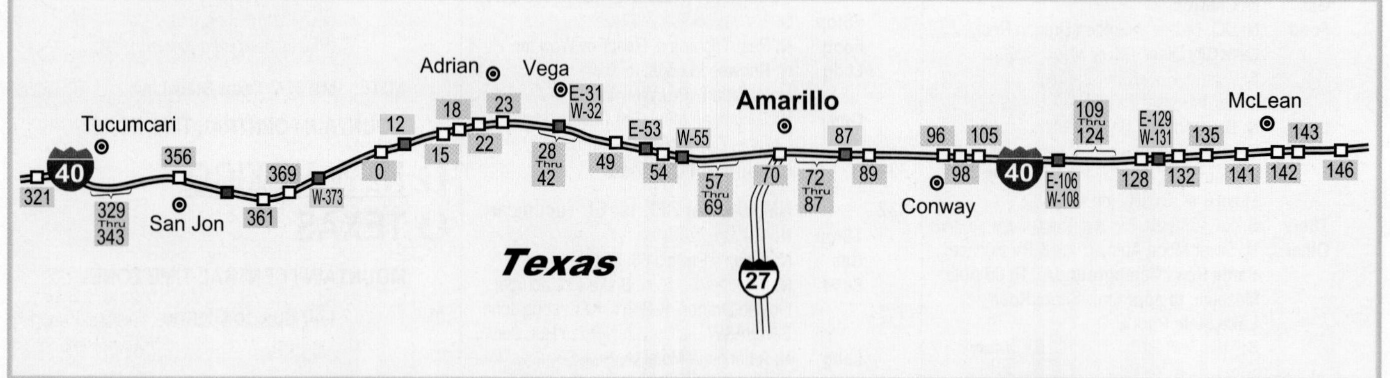

◈ = Regular Gas Stations with Diesel ▲ = RV Friendly Locations ♥ = Pet Friendly Locations
Red print shows large vehicle parking / access on site or nearby Brown Print = Campgrounds / RV PARKS

EXIT		TEXAS
69A		**Crockett St** (Acc to #68B)
69B		**Washington St, Amarillo College**
	Gas	S: Valero
	Food	N: Arnold Burgers S: DQ, Subway
	Lodg	N: La Casita del Sol, Parkview House B&B, Madison House B&B S: Martha's Midtown B&B
	Other	N: Albertson's S: Amarillo College, CVS, Museum, to I-27
(70/123A)		**Jct I-27S, US 60W, US 87, US 287**
71		**Ross St, Osage St, Arthur St**
	Gas	N: Conoco◈, Shamrock, Shell◈ S: Valero, Sam's
	Food	N: Burger King, Dominos Pizza, IHOP, Long John Silver, McDonald's, Popeye's Chicken, Subway, Tacos Garcia Cafe S: Arby's, Denny's, La Fiesta, Sonic, Taco Bell, Wendy's
	Lodg	N: Coach Light Inn, Comfort Inn, Days Inn, Holiday Inn, Microtel♥, Quality Inn♥, S: Hampton Inn, La Quinta Inn♥, Magnuson Hotel♥,
	Other	N: Auto Services, Jiffy Lube, Ryder, T-Anchor Flea Market S: Auto Dealers, Harbor Freight, Sam's Club, US Post Office, U-Haul
72A		**Lp 395, Nelson St, Quarter Horse Dr, Tee Anchor Blvd**
	Gas	S: Chevron, Shell◈
	Food	N: Cracker Barrel, KFC
	Lodg	N: Amarillo Value Inn, Ashmore Inn & Suites, La Kiva Hotel♥, Luxury Inn, Sleep Inn, Super 8♥, S: Camelot Suites
	Other	N: American Quarterhorse Museum S: LP/U-Haul/Chevron
72B		**Grand St, Bolton St, Amarillo**
	FStop	N: Pacific Pride
	Gas	N: Shell S: Exxon, Phillips 66, Murphy USA, Valero
	Food	N: Henk's BBQ, Jerry's Cafe, KFC S: Braums', Chicken Express, Coyote Bluff Cafe, El Bracero Mexican, Judy's Place, McDonald's, Pizza Hut, Pizza Palm, Sonic, Starbucks, Subway, Taco Villa, Whataburge
	Lodg	S: Motel 6♥
	Other	N: ATMs, D&H Generator Service, Family Dollar, O'Reilly Auto Parts, U-Haul S: ATMs, Advance Auto Parts, Auto Zone, Big Lots, Carwash, Carwash/P66, Dollar General, **Walmart** sc
73		**Eastern St, Bolton St, Amarillo**
	FStop	S: Taylor Chevron
	Gas	N: Shell◈ S: Discount Gas
	Food	N: Polly's, Stuckman's Rest
	Lodg	N: Dean Motel, Fiesta Motel, Motel 6♥, Value Place S: Best Western♥
	TServ	S: Amarillo Thermo King, Area Trailer Sales & Rentals, Cummins Southern Plains, High Plains Tire & Diesel Service
	Other	N: One Stop Auto & RV Service, **Amarillo RV Ranch▲**, Splash Waterpark S: Southern Tire Mart, Taylor Diesel
74		**Whitaker Rd, Amarillo**
	TStop	S: Love's Travel Stop #200 (Scales), Travel Center of America #55/Exxon (Scales)
	Food	N: Big Texan Rest S: Subway/Godfathers/A&W/Love's TS, Buckhorn/BurgerKing/PizzaHut/Popeye's/TA TC
	Lodg	N: Big Texan Motel, Best Value Inn S: Budget Inn
	TWash	S: Blue Beacon TW/TA TC, Red Baron, Eagle Truck Wash
	TServ	S: TA TC/Tires, Amarillo Truck Center, W Tx Peterbilt
	Other	N: **Amarillo Ranch RV Park▲**, Splash Waterpark S: WiFi/**RVDump**/Love's TS, Laundry/WiFi/**RVDump**/TA TC, UPS Store
75		**Lp 335, Lakeside Dr, Airport**
	TStop	N: Pilot Travel Center #436 (Scales) S: Petro Stopping Center #7/Mobil
	Gas	N: Phillips 66, Shell
	Food	N: McDonald's/Subway/Pilot TC, Country Barn, Waffle House S: Iron Skillet/FastFood/Petro SC
	Lodg	N: Americas Best Value Inn, Super 8♥
	TWash	S: Blue Beacon TW/Petro SC
	TServ	S: Petro SC/Tires, Peterbilt
	Other	N: Laundry/WiFi/**RVDump**/Pilot TC, **Overnite RV Park▲**, **to KOA/Amarillo▲** S: Laundry/WiFi/BarbSh/CB/Petro SC
76		**Spur 468, Int'l Airport, Amarillo** **Texas Travel Info Center** (Both dir) (RR, Ph, Pic, Vend, Weather, Playgr)
	TStop	N: Flying J Travel Plaza #5350/Conoco (Scales)
	Gas	N: Shell◈
	Food	N: Cookery/FastFood/FJ TP
	Lodg	N: Holiday Inn Express
	TWash	N: Buster's TW
	TServ	N: Bruckner's Trucks Sales & Service S: Speedco
	Other	N: Laundry/WiFi/BarbSh/**RVDump**/LP/FJ TP, Rick Husband Amarillo Int'l Airport✈ S: **Custom RV Center**
77		**FM 1258, Pullman Rd**
	TStop	N: Jesus Christ is Lord Travel Plaza (Scales) Cee Teez Truck Plaza
	Food	N: FastFood/Rest/JCIL TC, Rest/CTs TP
	Tires	N: CTs TP
	TWash	N: CTs TP
	TServ	N: Carrier Transporter Refrigeration, Stewart & Stevenson Truck Service S: Lakeside Trailer Repair, Utility Trailer
	Other	N: Laundry/WiFi/JCIL TC, Laundry/CT's TP
78		**US 287S** (EB), **FM 1258** (acc to #77)
80		**Spur 228, to US 287**
	Gas	N: Texaco
	Other	N: **A OK Camper Park▲**
81		**FM 1912, Amarillo**
	FStop	N: Fast Stop #25/P66
85		**Amarillo Blvd, Durrett Rd**
(87)		**Parking Area** (Both dir)
87		**FM 2373, Panhandle**
89		**FM 2161, to Old Rte 66**
96		**TX 207, Panhandle, Claude**
	Fstop	N: Love's Travel Stop #229
	Food	N: Subway/Love's TS, S: Café/Budget Host Inn, Cafe/Conway Inn,
	Lodg	S: Budget Host Inn, Conway Inn
	Other	N: WiFi/**RVDump**/Love's TS
98		**TX 207, Panhandle** (WB)
105		**FM 2880, Groom**
(106)		**Parking Area** (EB)
(108)		**Parking Area** (WB)
109		**FM 294, Groom**
	Other	N: G&J Truck Sales
110		**I-40E Bus, Groom, Old Rte 66**
	Gas	S: to Allsup's/Fina
112		**FM 295, Groom**
	Gas	S: to Allsup's/Fina, Gas
	Other	S: Bank, Grocery, Tires, US Post Office, Largest Cross in Western Hemisphere
113		**FM 2300, Groom**
	FStop	S: Stop n Shop/Texaco◈
	Food	S: DQ
	Lodg	S: Chalet Inn
114		**Lp 40 Bus, Groom**
121		**TX 70N, to Pampa**
124		**TX 70S, to Clarendon** (acc N to #128)
128		**FM 2477, to Lake McClellan, Panhandle Training Natl Guard**
	Other	N: **to McClellan Creek National Rec Area Grassland▲**, **Pampa City Park▲**,
(129)		**Donley Co Rest Area** (EB) (RR, Ph, Pic, Vend, WiFi, Shelter, Playgr)
(131)		**Gray Co Rest Area** (WB) (RR, Ph, Pic, Vend, WiFi, Shelter, Playgr)
132		**Johnson Ranch Rd**
135		**FM 291, Alanreed, Old Rte 66**
	FStop	S: Alanreed Travel Center/Conoco
	Food	S: Cafe/Alanreed TC
	Lodg	S: Motel/Alanreed TC
	Other	S: USPostOffice/**RVHookUps**/Alanreed TC
141		**I-40E Bus, McClean** (Acc to #142 Serv)
142		**TX 273, FM 3143, to McClean**
	FStop	N: Country Corner Shell
	Food	N: FastFood/Country Corner, Red River Steakhouse
	Lodg	N: Cactus Inn
	Other	N: Museums, **Country Corner RV Park**/**RVDump▲**
143		**McLean** (Access to Ex #142 Serv)
146		**County Line Rd**
	Other	N: McLean'Gray Co Airport✈
148		**FM 1443, Kellerville Rd, Kellerville**
152		**FM 453, Pakan Rd, Shamrock**
	FStop	S: T&M Truck Stop
	TServ	S: T&M TS/Tires
157		**FM 1547, FM 2474, FM 3075, Lela**
	Other	S: **to West 40 RV Park▲**
161		**I-40 Bus, Shamrock** (acc #163 Serv)
163		**US 83, Bus I-40, Shamrock, to Wheeler, Wellington** (Addtl Serv S to 66)
	FStop	S: Cantrell's Valero
	TStop	S: Midway Truck & Travel/Taylor Phillip66
	Gas	N: Chevron◈, Allsup's/Conoco◈, S: Quick Mart
	Food	N: Hasty's Burgers, Mitchell's Family Rest, Pizza Inn, Pizza Hut/Taco Bell S: Subway/Taylor's P66, Cicero's Green Frog Pizza, DQ, El Sombrero Mexican,Irish Inn Rest, McDonald's, Western Rest

◈= Regular Gas Stations with Diesel ▲ = RV Friendly Locations ♥= Pet Friendly Locations
Red print shows large vehicle parking / access on site or nearby **Brown Print = Campgrounds / RV PARKS**

EXIT		TX / OK
	Lodg	N: Best Western♥, Irish Inn Motel S: Blarney Inn, Budget Host Inn, Econo Lodge♥, Holiday Inn Express♥, Rte 66 Inn, Sleep Inn, Western Motel,
	TServ	S: PRS Road Service & Truck Repair/ Tires/Trailer Repair
	Med	S: + Shamrock General Hospital
	Other	N: Shamrock Muni Airport✈, S: LP/Cantrell's, Laundry/Taylor's, ATMs, Banks, Auto Services, C&H Supply, Dollar General, Goodyear, **K&K RV Park▲**, Pioneer West Museum, Shamrock CC Golf Course, US Post Office, **to West 40 RV Park▲**,
164		**Frontage Rd, I-40 Bus (acc #163 serv)**
(164)		**Weigh Station (EB)**
167		**FM 2168, Daberry Rd, Shamrock**
	FStop	N: Cantrell's Longhorn/Shamrock
	Other	N: Shamrock Muni Airport✈
169		**FM 1802, Carbon Black Rd**
(173)		**Picnic Area (EB)**
(176)		**Picnic Area (WB)**
(176)		**Livestock Inspection Area (WB)**
176		**Spur 30E, to Texola**

CENTRAL TIME ZONE

NOTE: MM 177: Oklahoma State Line

TEXAS
OKLAHOMA

CENTRAL TIME ZONE

EXIT		OKLAHOMA
1		**Grand Ave, N1675 Rd, Texola**
	TStop	S: Double D Fuel Stop
	Food	S: Rest/Double D FS, to Windmill Rest & Trading Post
	Other	S: Laundry/**RV Park**/**RVDump**/Dbl D FS
5		**I-40E Bus, Honeyfarm Rd, Erick, to Hollis**
7		**OK 30, Sheb Wooley Ave, Main St, Erick, to Sweetwater**
	TStop	S: Love's Travel Stop #253 (Scales)
	Food	N: Rafter T Rest S: Subway/Love's TS, Cowboys Rest & Trading Post, Main St Cafe & Bakery, Simple Simon's Pizza,
	Lodg	N: Premier Inn♥ S: Days Inn♥
	Other	S: Laundry/WiFi/Love's TS, **to** Grocery, Hardware Store, Honey Farm & Candle Shop, Museum, Pharmacy, Roger Miller Museum, US Post Office
(9)		**OK Welcome Center (EB) Rest Area (WB) (RR, Phones, Picnic, Pet, RVDump)**
11		**Bus I-40W, Erick (Acc to #7 Serv S)**
(13)		**Weigh Station (Both dir)**
14		**Hext Rd, Erick**
20		**US 283, I-40E Bus, 4th St, Sayre, to Magnum (Acc #23/#25 Serv N)**
	TStop	N: Flying J Travel Plaza #5093/Conoco (Scales)
	Food	N: CountryMarket/FastFood/FJ TP
	Lodg	N: AmericInn♥
	TWash	N: Industry TW
	Other	N: Laundry/WiFi/**RVDump**/**LP**/FJ TP, Hagerman Services, Sayre Muni Golf Course, Superior Lube Cars, Truck & **RV** Service
23		**OK 152, Madden Ave, to US 283, I-40 Bus, Sayre, to Cordell**
	FStop	N: AmPride Express S: Tosh Service Center/Shell,
	Gas	N: Jack's C-Store◈
	Food	N: Crazy Ladies Pastries & Bistro, Deb's Country Kitchen, River Bend Steakhouse S: Deli/Tosh SC
	TServ	S: Tosh SC/Tires
	Other	N: ATMs, Banks, Museum, Lumber Store
25		**I-40W Bus, N 4th St, US 66, to US 283, Sayre**
	Gas	N: Shell◈
	Food	N: Stardust Rest
	Lodg	N: Western Motel
	Med	N: + Sayre Memorial Hospital
	Other	N: Auto Dealer, Dollar General, OK SW Univ
26		**Cemetery Rd, Sayre**
	TStop	S: Travel Center of America #152 (Scales)
	Food	S: TacoBell/Subway/TA TC S: TA TC/Tires
	Other	N: Truck & Auto & Tire Repair, **to** Flying W Guest Ranch **(also acc via #32 or #34)** S: Laundry/WiFi/TA TC
32		**OK 34S, I-40E Bus, OK 6, Elk City, to Mangum, Carter (EB, LEFT Exit)**
34		**Merritt Rd, to Bus 40, OK 6, Elk City (All Serv 5-7 mi NE on OK 6)**
	TStop	**N: to 5100 W 3rd St:** Hutch's C-Store #103/Conoco
	Other	N: **to** Gas, Food, Lodging, Steve's Diesel & Truck Serv, Cinema, **Walmart**, Museum, **Elk City RV**, Elk City I-40 Speedway
38		**OK 6, S Main St, Elk City, to Altus**
	FStop	N: JC's Corner/Conoco,
	TStop	N: Hutch's #109/Phillips 66,
	Gas	N: Shell◈ S: Phillips 66◈
	Food	N: 20th St Diner, Arby's, Denny's/DI, Long John Silver, McDonald's, Quiznos, Western Sizzlin, Hog Trough S: Old Glory Cafe
	Lodg	N: Bedford Inn, Days Inn, to Rte 66: Best Western, Flamingo Inn, Super 8 S: Clarion Inn♥, Comfort Inn♥, Econo Inn♥, Holiday Inn, Ramada Inn♥
	Med	N: + Great Plains Reg'l Med Center
	Other	N: **Elk Creek RV Park▲**, L&R Tire & Car Center, Adams Garage, **Rolling Retreats RV Sales, Addtl Serv N to I-40 Bus** S: Hardware Store, Golf Course
40		**Eastern Ave, to Bus 40, Elk City (Access to #41 Serv)**
	Food	N: Portobello Grill
	Other	N: to Rte 66, **Ackley Park**
41		**OK 34N, I-40 Bus, to Rte 66, Elk City (EB LEFT Exit) (Most Serv on OK 66)**
	FStop	N: Love's Travel Stop #201
	Gas	N: Shell
	Food	N: Subway/Love's TS, Braum's, Denny's, El Charro, Home Cooking Café, Sonic, Subway
	Lodg	N: Ambassador Hotel, Economy Express Inn, Motel 6♥, **to** Standifer House B&B, Super 8, Travel Inn,
	TServ	N: Great Plains Tire Service
	Med	N: + Great Plains Reg'l Med Center
	Other	N: WiFi/Love's TS, ATMs, Auto Dealers, Auto Services, Elk City Reg'l Business Airport✈, **Elk Run RV Park▲**, Laundry, Pharmacy, Nat'l Rte 66 Museum, U-Haul, Walgreen's, **to Walmart**,
47		**CR 2080, Canute**
	Gas	S: Shell
	Food	S: Dominos Pizza
	Lodg	S: Sunset Inn
50		**Clinton Lake Rd, Canute**
	Other	N: **Elk City/Clinton KOA▲**, Clinton Lake
53		**OK 44, Foss, to Altus, Burns Flat**
	FStop	S: Pendleton's Truck Stop
	Food	S: FastFood/Pendleton's TS
	Tires	S: Pendleton's TS
	Other	**N: to appr 7mi: Foss State Park▲**
57		**Stafford Rd, Clinton**
61		**Haggard Rd, Clinton**

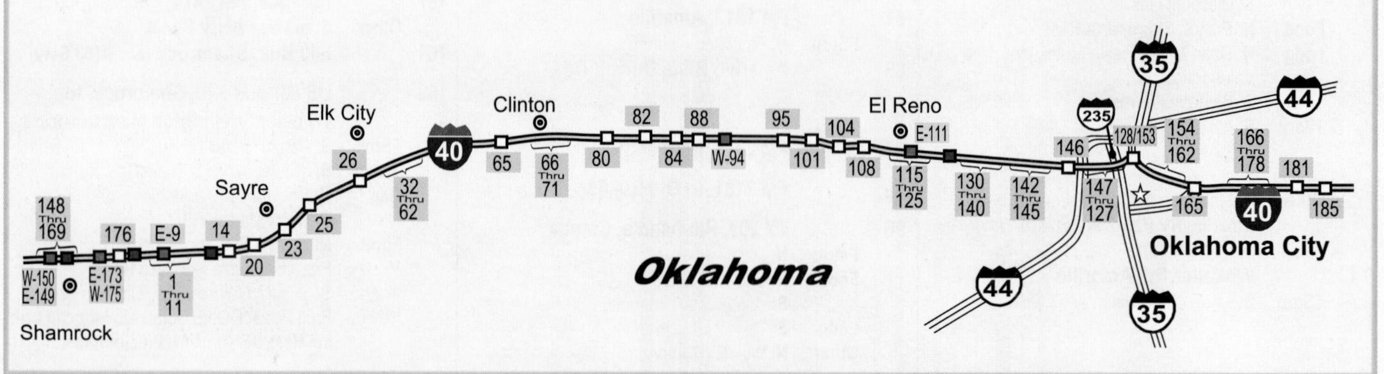

◈= Regular Gas Stations with Diesel ▲ = RV Friendly Locations ♥= Pet Friendly Locations
Red print shows large vehicle parking / access on site or nearby Brown Print = Campgrounds / RV PARKS

EXIT OKLAHOMA

62 Parkersburg Rd, Commerce Rd
Food N: Jigg's Smokehouse
Other S: Hargus RV Sales & Service/LP

65 I-40 Bus, Gary Blvd, Clinton (NO EB reaccess)
Gas N: Conoco◈, Shell◈
Food N: Adamo's Rte 66 Italian Villa, Adelina's Mexican, Country Kitchen/Ramada, Del Rancho, Long John Silver, McDonald's, Montana Mike's Steakhouse, Taco Mayo,
Lodg N: Budget Inn♥, Hampton Inn, to Midtown Travel Inn♥, Ramada Inn♥, Trade Winds Motel♥, Travelodge♥
Med N: + Clinton Reg'l Hospital
Other N: Dollar General, Family Dollar, Kmart/ Pharmacy, OK Rte 66 Museum, OK State Hwy Patrol Post

65A 10th St, Neptune Dr, Clinton
Gas S: Phillips 66◈
Food N: Braum's, Branding Iron, China King, KFC, Pizza Hut, Subway, Wong's Rest
Lodg N: Days Inn♥, Super 8
S: Econo Lodge♥,
Other N: Auto Services, Laundromat, Grocery, Winks RV Park▲
S: Challis Diesel Service, Parkers Truck Towing, Hargus RV Park▲

66 US 183, S 4th St, to I-40 Bus, Clinton, Cordell
FStop S: Fast Lane #300/66
TStop S: Domino Food & Fuel/Shell (Scales)
Food S: FastFood/Domino F&F,
Tires N: Great Plains Tire Service
TServ S: Freightliner
Other N: Auto Dealers, Auto Services, ATMs
S: Auto Dealers

69 Lp 40W, Gary Blvd, Clinton (WB) (Access to #66 & #65 Serv)
Other N: to Clinton Reg'l Airport✈

71 Custer City Rd, Clinton
FStop N: Love's Travel Stop #248
Food N: Subway/Love's TS
Other N: WiFi/Love's TS, to Clinton Reg'l Airport✈

80 OK 54, Weatherford, to Thomas
Gas N: Hutch's Conoco◈, Shell◈
Food N: Little Mexico
Lodg N: Economy Inn
Other N: Crowder Lake University Park

80A I-40E Bus, W Main St (EB, No reacc) (Access to #82 Serv)
Other N: Auto Services, Police Station

82 I-40W Bus, E Main St, Weatherford
Gas N: Conoco◈, Phillips 66, Shell, Shell◈, Valero◈,
Food N: Arby's, Braum's, Carl's Jr, Jerry's Rest, McDonalds, KFC/Taco Bell, Pizza Hut, Quiznos, Sonic, Subway/Shell, Taco Mayo, Vincio's Mexican Rest
Lodg N: Best Western, Comfort Inn, Fairfield Inn, Holiday Inn Express, Scottish Inn♥, Travel Inn
Med N: + Southwestern Memorial Hospital
Other N: Ace Hardware, ATMs, Auto Services, Auto Services/Conoco, Banks, Dollar General, Grocery, O'Reilly Auto Parts, Radio Shack, US Post Office, Walgreen's, Vet♥, to SW OK State Univ
S: Walmart SC,

84 Airport Rd, Weatherford
TStop N: Quick & Easy Travel Plaza/Phillips 66

Personal Notes

EXIT OKLAHOMA

TStop N: (Scales), Fast Lane Travel Plaza #101/ Texaco (Scales)
Food N: FastFood/Fast Lane TP, Lucille's Roadhouse
Lodg N: Holiday Inn Express, Travel Inn
Med N: + Weatherford Reg'l Hospital
Other N: Heartland Animal Hospital♥, Overnite Rte 66 RV Park▲, Thomas P Stafford Airport✈
S: Albert's Truck Service & Supply/Towing, Tin Star Shooting Range

88 OK 58, Hydro, Carnegie

(94) Parking Area (WB)

95 Bethel Rd, Hydro

101 US 281, OK 8, Hinton, to Anardarko
FStop S: Love's Travel Stop #385
TStop S: Hinton AmBest Travel Plaza/Shell
Gas N: to Hydro Quick Shop◈
Food S: FastFood/Hinton TP, Chesters/Godfathers/Love's TX
Lodg S: Microtel/Hinton TP
Other N: to Roman Nose State Park▲
S: Laundry/WiFi/Hinton TP, Red Rock Canyon State Park▲, Hinton Muni Airport✈

104 Methodist Rd, Hinton

108 Spur US 281N, Calumet, to Geary, Watonga
FStop N: Fast Lane Food Mart/P66
S: Love's Travel Stop #251
TStop N: Cherokee Travel Mart/Shell
Food N: FastFood/Fast Lane, Rest/FastFood/ Cherokee TM
S: Chesters/Godfathers/Love's TS

EXIT OKLAHOMA

TServ N: Cherokee TM/Tires
Other N: KOA Cherokee▲, to Roman Nose State Park▲
S: WiFi/Love's TS, Tires

(111) Parking Area (EB)

115 US 270, Calumet Rd, Calumet
Other N: to Good Life RV Resort▲
S: KOA Calumet▲

119 I-40 E Bus, OK 66, to El Reno

123 Country Club Rd, El Reno
FStop S: Phillips 66
Gas N: Conoco, Shell◈, Valero, Murphy◈
Food N: Arby's, Braum's, Carl's Jr, El Charro, KFC, Little Caesar's, McDonald's, Pizza Hut, Subway, Taco Bell
S: Denny's, Rest/BW
Lodg N: Comfort Inn, Motel 6♥
S: Best Western♥ & Hensley's RV Park▲ Days Inn, Regency Inn
Med N: + Parkview Hospital
Other N: ATMs, Banks, Dollar Tree, Grocery, Greyhound, Radio Shack, Walgreen's, Walmart sc, Lake El Reno
S: to El Reno Muni Airport✈

125 US 81, Bus 40, El Reno
Gas N: Conoco◈, Love's Country Store◈
Food N: China King Buffet, Serapio's Mex Rest, J & Kay Rest, Taco Mayo,Subway/Love's
Lodg N: Economy Express, Western Sands
Other N: Animal Hospital♥, Convention Center, Auto Dealers, Auto Services, Towing, Phil's Cycle & ATV's, Lucky Star Casino
S: United Auto & Truck Service

(130) Weigh Station (Both dir)

130 Banner Rd, El Reno, to Union City
FStop N: Shell Food Plaza
Food N: FastFood/Shell

132 Cimarron Rd, Yukon
Other S: Clarence Page Muni Airport✈

136 OK 92, 11th St, Garth Brooks Blvd, Yukon, Mustang
Gas N: Shell, Murphy◈
Food N: Braum's, Carl's Jr, Harry's Grill, KFC, Great Wall Chinese, McDonald's, Primo's Italian Rest, Santa Fe Cattle Co, Starbucks, Taco Mayo, Waffle House, Wendy's
S: Alfredo's Mexican Cafe, Chili's, Carino's, Pizza Hut, Quiznos, Rib Crib, Starbucks
Lodg N: Hampton Inn
S: Holiday Inn Express
Med S: + Canadian Valley Reg'l Hospital
Other N: Auto Zone, ATMs, Banks, Big O Tires, Big Lots, Blockbuster, Dollar General, Dollar Tree, Movies 5, Radio Shack, Walmart sc, Walgreen's
S: Auto Services, Lowe's, PetSmart♥, Staples, Target

137 Cornwell Dr, Czech Hall Rd
Other N: Albertson's/Pharmacy

138 OK 4, Mustang Rd, Yukon
Gas S: Conoco◈, Shell
Food N: Denny's
S: Arby's, Burger King, McDonald's, Sonic, Subway
Lodg N: Comfort Suites, Super 7 Motel
S: Best Western, Super 8, HOTEL
Other S: CVS, Grocery

139 John Kilpatrick Turnpike

◈ = Regular Gas Stations with Diesel ▲ = RV Friendly Locations ♥ = Pet Friendly Locations
Red print shows large vehicle parking / access on site or nearby Brown Print = Campgrounds / RV PARKS

EXIT		OKLAHOMA
140		**Morgan Rd, Okla City**
	TStop	N: Pilot Travel Center #460 (Scales), Travel Center of America #59/66 (Scales)
		S: Love's Travel Stop #203 (DAND), Flying J Travel Plaza #5027/Conoco (Scales) (DAND)
	Food	N: McDonald's/Pilot TC, CountryPride/Popeye's/TA TC
		S: Subway/Love's TS, Cookery/FastFood/FJ TP, Ricky's Cafe, Sonic
	TWash	S: Blue Beacon TW, G&S TW
	TServ	N: TA TC/Tires
		S: Fleet Service, Speedco
	Other	N: Laundry/WiFi/Pilot TC, Laundry/CB/WiFi/TA TC, Double L Tire Co
		S: WiFi/Love's TS, Laundry/BarbSh/WiFi/**RVDump/LP**/FJ TP
142		**Council Rd, OKC**
	TStop	S: Travel Center of America #36 (Scales)
	Gas	N: Shell, Sinclair
	Food	N: Applebee's, Braum's, McDonald's, Subway, Taco Bell, Waffle House
		S: CountryPride/BurgerKing/TA TC
	Lodg	N: Best Budget Inn
		S: Econo Lodge
	TWash	S: TA TC, TruckOMat
	TServ	N: Turbo Diesel of OK, Fleet Pride
		S: TA TC/Tires
	Other	N: Tires, **Lyons Repair**, **Motley RV Repair**
		S: Laundry/BarbSH/WiFi/**RVDump**/TA TC, **Council Rd RV Park▲**, **Griffith RV Services**
143		**Rockwell Ave, Okla City**
	Gas	N: 7-11, Shell◈
		S: Interstate Gas
	Food	N: Buffalo Wild Wings, Fire Mtn Grill, Pizza House Express
	Lodg	N: Rockwell Inn, Rodeway Inn
		S: Sands Motel
	TServ	N: Quality Diesel Service, Truck Pro
	Other	N: Best Buy, Harley Davidson World, Home Depot, PetCo♥, Tires +, **McClain's RV Superstore/Camping World**
		S: **A OK Campgrounds▲**, **Rockwell RV Park▲**, Price Auto & **RV** Repair
144		**MacArthur Blvd, OKC**
	Gas	N: Shell◈
		S: Conoco
	Food	N: Applebee's, Golden Corral, KFC, McDonald's, Sonic, Starbucks, Subway, Taco Cabana, Texas Roadhouse
		S: Ruby's, Signature Italian
	Lodg	N: Springhill Suites
		S: Econo Lodge, Green Carpet Inn, Microtel Inn, Quality Inn, Super 10 Motel, Travelodge
	TServ	N: Cummins Southern Plains
		S: Oklahoma Kenworth, Peterbilt
	Other	N: Auto Rental, Best Buy, Office Depot, PetSmart♥, Radio Shack, **Walmart sc▲**
		S: Garden Ridge, Sam's Club
145		**Meridian Ave, OKC**
	Gas	N: Conoco◈, Shell◈
		S: Phillips 66/Circle K◈, Shell
	Food	N: Denny's, McDonald's, On the Border, Outback Steakhouse
		S: Arby's, Burger King, Chili's, **Cracker Barrel**, IHOP, Kona Ranch Steaks, Panera Bread, Santa Fe Grill, Steak & Ale, Tony Roma, Wendy's, Waffle House
	Lodg	N: Best Western, Biltmore Hotel, Days Inn, Econo Lodge, Extended Stay America, Howard Johnson Express, Red Roof Inn♥, Residence Inn, Rodeway Inn, Super 8
		S: AmeriSuites, Best Value Inn, Comfort Suites, Clarion, Courtyard, Embassy Suites, Hampton Inn, Hilton Garden Inn, Holiday Inn Express, La Quinta Inn♥, Lexington Hotel, Motel 6♥, Regency Inn, Sleep Inn
	TServ	S: Sooner Great Dane Peterbilt
	Other	N: Auto Services, ATMs, Enterprise RAC
		S: Celebration Station, Shepler's
146		**Portland Ave (fr EB, no reaccess)**
	Gas	N: Shell◈
	Food	N: Subway
	Other	N: ATMs, Banks, White Water Bay Water Park
(147A)		**Jct I-44W, OK 3E, Dallas, Wichita (fr WB, LEFT exit)**
(147B)		**Jct I-44E, OK 3W (fr EB, LEFT exit)**
147C		**May Ave, Okla City (fr WB)**
	Other	N: Auto Services, **to** AllSports Stadium, **State Fair RV Park▲**
148A		**Agnew Ave, Villa Ave**
	FStop	N: Roadway Ventures/66
	Gas	S: Conoco◈
	Food	S: Braum's, Real BBQ, Taco Bell
	TWash	N: Signal Tank Wash
	TServ	N: International Service, Fleet Services
	Other	S: Harley Davidson World
148B		**Pennsylvania Ave (fr EB)**
	Gas	N: Shamrock◈
	TServ	S: HD Copland Int'l
	Other	S: to Downtown Airport✈
148C		**Virginia Ave (fr WB)**
149A		**Western Ave, Reno Ave**
	Gas	N: Total/Valero◈
		S: Conoco◈, Shell
	Food	N: McDonald's, Sonic, Subway/Valero, Taco Bell
		S: Burger King, Popeye's Chicken
	TServ	S: Jefferson Trailer Repair
	Other	N: Auto Services
		S: Auto Services, Downtown Airpark✈
149B		**Classen Blvd (fr WB)**
150A		**Walker Ave (fr EB)**
	Gas	S: Phillips 66
	Med	N: + St Anthony Hospital
	Other	N: Greyhound
150B		**Harvey Ave (No Reaccess)**
150C		**Robinson Ave, Downtown (WB)**
	Food	N: Zio's Italian
	Lodg	N: Courtyard, Renaissance Hotel, Sheraton Westin
	Other	N: Convention Center, AP Murrah Bldg Memorial, Museums, Hertz, Ford Center, Amtrak, Civic Center, Theatres, Bass Pro Shop
151A		**Byers Ave, Lincoln Blvd (EB)**
	Gas	N: Circle K/Conoco◈
	Food	N: Subway/Circle K, Earl's Rib Palace, Mickey Mantles Steakhouse, Toby Keith's I Love This Bar
	Lodg	N: Residence Inn
	Other	N: ATMs, Bass Pro Shop, Bricktown Stadium,
(151B)		**Jct I-35S, to Dallas (EB)**
(151C)		**Jct I-235N, State Capital, Edmond**
NOTE:		**I-40 below runs with I-35 Exit #'s follows I-35.**
127		**Eastern Ave, MLK Blvd (EB)**
	TStop	N: PTP/JRS Travel Center (Scales), Petro Stopping Center #16/Mobil (Scales)
	Gas	N: Shell
	Food	N: FastFood/JRS TC, IronSkillet/Petro SC, Cholita's Mexican Rest, Dale's BBQ, Waffle House
	Lodg	N: Best Western, Bricktown Hotel, Quality Inn, Econo Lodge, Ramada Inn
	TServ	N: Petro SC/Tires
	TWash	N: BlueBeacon TW/Petro SC
	Other	N: Laundry/JRS TC, Laundry/WiFi/Petro SC, **Lewis RV Center**
(128/153)		**Jct I-35N, to Edmond, Wichita**
NOTE:		**I-40 above runs with I-35 Exit #'s follows I-35.**
154		**Scott St, Reno Ave, OKC**
	Gas	N: Sinclair
		S: 7-11◈, Phillips 66◈
	Lodg	N: Value Place Hotel
155A		**Sunnylane Rd, to Del City**
	Gas	N: Conoco
		S: Shell
	Food	S: Braum's, Dunkin Donuts, Pizza Hut, Subway
	Lodg	S: Value Place Hotel
	Med	S: + Midwest Reg'l Medical Center
155B		**SE 15th St, Del City, Midwest City**
	Gas	N: ArcoAmPm, Express, Shell
		S: Conoco
	Food	S: Ashley's Country Kitchen
	Other	N: Grocery/Pharmacy
156A		**Sooner Rd**
	Gas	N: Conoco
	Food	N: Kettle, Ray's Steakhouse, Waffle House
	Lodg	N: Comfort Inn, Hampton Inn, Holiday Inn Express, La Quinta Inn♥, Sheraton
	Other	N: ATM, Auto Dealers, Home Depot, Radio Shack, Tires +, **Walmart sc**
		S: Auto Dealers
156B		**Hudibird Dr**
	Lodg	S: Motel 6♥
	Other	S: Auto Dealers
157A		**SE 29th St, to Midwest City**
	Gas	N: Conoco◈, Shell, Sam's
	Food	N: IHOP, Pizza Inn, Santa Fe Cattle Co
	Lodg	N: Best Western, Planet Inn Motel, Super 8
	Med	S: + Midwest Reg'l Medical Center
	Other	N: **Leisure Time RV**, Super 8
		S: Sam's Club
157B		**Air Depot Blvd**
	Gas	N: Conoco◈, Shell
	Food	N: Arby's, IHOP, Pizza Inn, Subway
	Lodg	N: Super 8
	Other	N: ATMs, Best Buy, Firestone, Lowe's, O'Reilly Auto Parts, Target, U-Haul, Walgreen's, OK Info Center
		S: Tinker AFB, Gate 1
157C		**Tinker Air Force Base, Eaker Gate**
159A		**Tinker AFB, Hruskocy Gate**
	Gas	N: Shell
	Food	N: China Grill
	Lodg	N: Executive Inn
	Other	N: Firestone, **Eastland Hills RV Park▲**
		S: Tinker AFB, Gate 7
159B		**Douglas Blvd, OKC**
	Gas	N: Phillips 66, Total

◈= Regular Gas Stations with Diesel ▲ = RV Friendly Locations ♥= Pet Friendly Locations

Red print shows large vehicle parking / access on site or nearby Brown Print = Campgrounds / RV PARKS

EXIT		OKLAHOMA
	Food	N: Denny's, McDonald's, Taco Bell
	Med	N: + Hospital
	Other	N: Eastland Hills RV Park▲ , Okie RV Park & Campground▲
		S: Tinker AFB
162		**Anderson Rd**
	Other	N: Lundy's Propane/LP
(165)		**Jct I-240W, to Dallas (WB)**
166		**Choctaw Rd, Choctaw**
	TStop	N: Love's Travel Stop #241 (Scales)
		S: Anderson Travel Plaza/66 (Scales)
	Food	N: Subway/Love's TS
		S: Rest/FastFood/Anderson TP
	TServ	S: Billy's 24Hr Road Service, Truck & Trailer Repair
	Other	N: Laundry/WiFi/Love's TS, OKC East KOA▲
		S: Laundry/BarbSh/WiFi/Anderson TP
169		**Peebly Rd, Newalla**
172		**Harrah Rd, Newalla**
	Gas	S: Shell
176		**OK 102N, McLoud Rd, McLoud**
	Gas	S: Love's Country Store #252
	Food	S: Subway/Love's, Curtis Watson's Rest
	Other	S: WiFi/Love's CS
178		**OK 102S, to Bethel Acres, Dale**
	Other	N: Firelake Grand Casino, Gas, Rest
181		**US 177, US 270, OK 3W, Shawnee to Stillwater, Tecumseh**
	FStop	S: Expo Stop/66
	Food	S: FastFood/Expo Stop
	Lodg	S: Budget Inn
	TWash	S: Expo Stop
	TServ	S: Days Diesel Service
	Other	S: Shawnee Expo Center, Shawnee Muni Airport✈, St Gregory's Univ, OK Baptist Univ
185		**OK 3E, Kickapoo St, Shawnee**
	Gas	N: Murphy
		S: Phillips 66◈
	Food	N: Braum's, Chili's, Garcia's, Red Lobster, Luby's Cafeteria, Taco Bueno
		S: Applebee's, CiCi's Pizza, Cracker Barrel, Garfield's, IHOP, McDonald's, Popeye's Chicken, Quiznos, Santa Fe Cattle Co, Shoney's, Starbucks, Taco Bell, Three Buddies BBQ & Burgers
	Lodg	N: Holiday Inn Express
		S: Hampton Inn♥, La Quinta Inn♥
	Med	S: + Shawnee Medical Center Clinic, + University Health Center
	Other	N: ATMs, Dollar Tree, Movie 6, Radio Shack, Shawnee Mall, Walgreen's, Walmart sc ▲ ,
		S: ATMs, CVS, Lowe's, Jones Theatres, Staples, Shawnee Muni Airport✈, St Gregory's Univ, OK Baptist Univ
186		**OK 18, Shawnee, to Meeker**
	Gas	N: Citgo◈, Shell
	Food	N: Denny's, Rest/Ramada
		S: Golden Corral, Sonic
	Lodg	N: Best Value Inn, Days Inn, Holiday Inn Express, La Quinta Inn♥, Motel 6♥, Ramada Inn, Super 8
		S: Colonial Inn, Super 8♥
	Other	S: Animal Hospital♥, Auto Dealers, Cinema 8, Vet♥,
192		**OK 9A, to Earlsboro**
	Gas	S: Shell◈
(197)		**Rest Area (Both dir) (RR, Phones, Picnic, Pet)**
200		**US 377, OK 99, Seminole, Prague**
	FStop	S: Love's Travel Stop #219, Seminole Food Mart
	TStop	S: to Seminole Nation Travel Plaza
	Food	S: Subway/Love's TS, Rest/Sem TP, Catfish Round-Up, Pit Stop Rest
	Other	S: Laundry/WiFi/Love's, Laundry/Sem TP, Round-Up RV Park▲, to Seminole State College, Mystic Winds Casino
212		**OK 56, Wewoka, to Cromwell**
	Gas	N: Conoco
		S: Shell◈
	Food	N: BBQ
		S: Café/Shell
	Other	S: Museum
217		**OK 48, Okemah, to Bristow, Holdenville**
	FStop	S: Total
	Food	S: Café/Total FS
	Other	N: to appr 12mi: Last Chance RV Park▲
221		**OK 27, US 62, Okemah, Wetumka**
	TStop	N: Okemah Travel Center/Shamrock
		S: Love's Travel Stop #274 (DAND)
	Gas	N: Conoco◈, Shell◈
	Food	N: FastFood/Okemah TC, Mazzio's Pizza, Sonic
		S: Chesters/A&W/Love's TS
	Lodg	N: Days Inn♥, OK Motel
	TServ	N: 24 Hr Truck Repair
	Med	N: + Creek Nation Comm Hospital
	Other	N: Laundry/Okemah TC, Auto & Tire Services, Okemah Flying Field✈
		S: WiFi/RVDump/Love's TS
227		**Clearview Rd, Okemah**
	Other	S: to Golden Pony Casino
231		**US 75S, Weleetka**
	FStop	S: Bernhardt's P66 Truck Stop
	Food	S: Cow Pokes Café, Rest/Bernhardt's TS
237		**US 62, to US 75, Henryetta**
	FStop	N: R&R Shell
	TStop	N: Mobile Services/Citgo
	Food	N: FastFood/Mobile Serv, Arby's, McDonald's, Pig Out Palace, Obee's Soup, Salad & Subs, KFC, Sheila's BBQ
		S: Hungry Traveler
	Lodg	N: Country Inn, Old Corral Motel
		S: Super 8
	TServ	N: Mobile Serv/Tires, Interstate Diesel
	Med	N: + Family Care Clinic
	Other	N: Henryetta RV Park▲ , Auto Services, ATMs, Carwash, Grocery, Museum, Towing
240A		**Indian Nation Turnpike (TOLL)**
240B		**US 62E, US 75N, to Okmulgee**
	Other	N: to Okmulgee/Dripping Springs State Park▲
247		**Tiger Mt Rd, Checotah**
(251)		**Parking Area (EB)**
(252)		**Parking Area (WB)**
255		**Pierce Rd, Service Rd**
	Other	N: Checotah/Lake Eufaula West KOA▲
259		**OK 150, Fountainhead Rd**
	Gas	S: Shell
	Lodg	S: Lake Eufaula Inn
	Other	S: to Fountainhead State Park▲
262		**Lotawatah Rd, to US 266**
	Gas	N: Phillips 66, Sinclair
264A		**US 69S, to Eufaula**
264B		**US 69N, to US 266, Muskogee**
	FStop	N: Checotah Truck Stop/P66
	TStop	N: Flying J Travel Plaza #5052/Conoco (Scales) (US69N to US 66W)
	Food	N: Rest/FastFood/FJ TP, Charlie's Chicken, McDonald's, Simple Simon's, Sooner Country Rest
	Lodg	N: Best Value Inn, Executive Inn
	Tires	N: M&J Tire, Checotah Tire & Lube
	TServ	N: Smith Diesel Repair
	Other	N: Laundry/WiFi/LP/FJ TP, ATMs, Bank, Auto Services, Dollar General, O'Reilly Auto Parts, Grocery, Walmart
265		**US 69 Bus, Checotah**
	TStop	N: Kwik N EZ Auto Truck Travel Plaza/ Shell
	Food	N: Kitchen Table Café, Pizza Hut, Sonic FastFood/KwiknEZ
	Lodg	S: Budget Inn
270		**Texanna Rd, Porum Landing**
	Gas	S: Sinclair

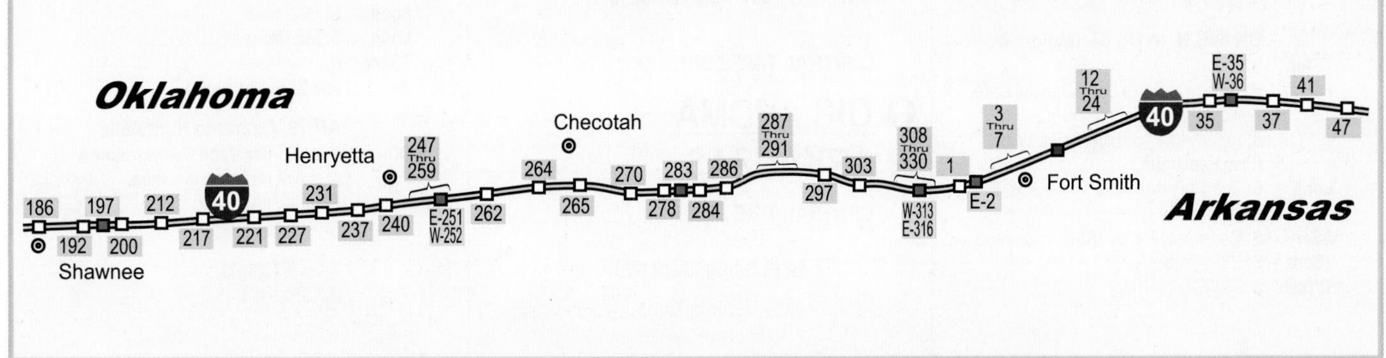

◈ = Regular Gas Stations with Diesel ▲ = RV Friendly Locations ♥ = Pet Friendly Locations
Red print shows large vehicle parking / access on site or nearby Brown Print = Campgrounds / RV PARKS

EXIT — OKLAHOMA

278 — **US 266, OK 2, Warner, Muskogee**
- FStop N: Jim Bob's Little Stores #21/66
- Food N: FastFood/JimBob's, Cowgirls D/I, McDonald's, Simple Simons, Subway
- Lodg N: Sleepy Travel Motel

(283) — **Scenic Turnout** (Both dir)

284 — **Ross Rd, Webbers Falls**

286 — **Muskogee Turnpike, to Muskogee, Tulsa**

287 — **OK 100N, Webbers Falls, Gore**
- TStop N: Love's Travel Stop #255
- Food N: Subway/Godfathers/Love's TS, Charlie's Chicken
- Lodg N: Sleepy Traveler
- TServ S: Tire Shop
- Other N: WiFi/Love's TS, **to MarVal Family Camping Resort▲**, **to Greenleaf State Park▲**

291 — **OK 10N, Carlile Rd, Gore**
- Other **N: to Webbers Falls Lock & Dam▲**

297 — **OK 82N, Vian, Talequah**
- Other **N: to 15mi: Tenkiller State Park▲**

303 — **Dwight Mission Rd, Sallisaw**
- Other N: Blue Ribbon Downs

308 — **US 59, I-40 Bus, Sallisaw, Poteau**
- FStop N: Greg's Mini Mart/66
- TStop S: Sallisaw Travel Center/Shell (Scales)
- Gas N: Citgo, Sinclair, Murphy
- Food N: Braum's, Dana's, McDonald's, Western Sizzlin, Wild Horse Mtn BBQ
  S: Rest/FastFood/Sallisaw TC
- Lodg N: Best Western, Days Inn, Golden Spur Inn, Microtel, Super 8
- TServ S: Sallisaw TC/Tires
- Med N: + Sequoyah Memorial Hospital
- Other N: Auto Services, Dollar General, Dollar Tree, Tires, Towing, **Walmart sc**, **to appr 10mi Brushy Lake State Park▲**
  S: Laundry/Sallisaw TC, Auto Dealer, **Sallisaw/Ft Smith W KOA▲**, Sallisaw Muni Airport✈, **to appr 6mi: Lakeside RV Campground▲**

311 — **US 64, Sallisaw, to Stillwell**
- TStop N: Ed's Truck Stop/66
- Food N: Rest/Ed's TS, Hardee's, Pizza Hut, Sonic, Subway, Taco Mayo
- Lodg N: Econo Lodge, Motel 6♥, Sallisaw Inn
- TServ N: Ed's TS/Tires
- Med N: + Sequoyah Memorial Hospital
- Other N: Laundry/Ed's TS, ATMs, Auto Zone, Dollar General, **Walmart sc**

(313) — **OK Welcome Center** (WB)
(RR, Ph, Pic, Vend, Pet, Info, RVDump)

(316) — **Rest Area** (EB)
(RR, Ph, Pic, Vend, Pet, Info, RVDump)

321 — **OK 64B N, to US 64, Muldrow**
- TStop S: Arena Truck Stop/Shell
- Food N: Broadway Joe's Café, Dandee Café, Sonic, Shadow Mountain BBQ
  S: Rest/Arena TS, Hickory Pit, Wild Rose Ranch BBQ
- Lodg S: Economy Inn/Arena Truck Stop, Best Value Inn
- AServ S: Carl's Auto Repair, K&K Automotive
- TServ S: B&W Truck Repair
- TWash S: B&W Truck Wash

Personal Notes

EXIT — OK / AR

325 — **US 64, Roland, Fort Smith**
- TStop N: Cherokee Nation Travel Plaza/Valero (Scales)
  S: Pilot Travel Center #196 (Scales), Roland Truck Stop/Shell (Scales)
- Gas S: Valero◈
- Food N: Subway/Bucks Grill/CN TP, 4 Star Diner
  S: Wendy's/Pilot TC, McDonald's/Roland's, El Celaya, Mazzio's Pizza, Smokey Joe's BBQ, Sonic, Subway
- Lodg N: Cherokee Inn/Cherokee Nation TP, Travelodge
  S: Interstate Inn
- Other N: Laundry/WiFi/**Casino**/Cherokee Nation TP, Tires, Towing
  S: Laundry/WiFi/Pilot TC, ATMs, Auto Services, AT&T, Banks, Dollar General, Grocery, Pharmacy, Tires

330 — **OK 64D S, Roland, to Dora, Fort Smith** (fr EB)

NOTE: **MM 331: Arkansas State Line**

CENTRAL TIME ZONE

↑ OKLAHOMA

↓ ARKANSAS

CENTRAL TIME ZONE

1 — **to Ft Smith, Dora** (WB)

(2) — **AR Welcome Center** (EB)
(RR, Phone, Picnic, Vend)

EXIT — ARKANSAS

3 — **Lee Creek Rd, Van Buren**
- Other **N: Park Ridge Campground▲**

5 — **AR 59, Fayetteville Rd, Van Buren, Siloam Springs**
(Addt'l serv 8mi S in Ft Smith)
- TStop S: Van Buren Travel Center (Scales)
- Gas N: Citgo, Phillips 66, Murphy
  S: Shell
- Food N: Arby's, Burger King, C&C Catfish, Chili's, Firehouse Subs, McDonald's, Popeye's Chicken, Santa Fe Café, Simple Simon's Pizza, Starbucks
  S: Braum's, Big Jake's Cattle Co, KFC, Mazzio's Pizza, Rick's Ribhouse, Sonic, Subway, Taco Bell, Waffle House, Wendy's
- Lodg N: Best Western, Hampton Inn
  S: Motel 6♥, Super 8♥
- Tires N: Cooley's Tires
- TWash S: TWA Truck Wash
- TServ N: Arkansas Kenworth
  S: Carco International
- Med S: + Crawford Memorial Hospital
- Other N: Auto Services, Advance Auto Parts, Dollar Tree, Dollar General, Lowe's, Radio Shack, Tires, **Walmart sc**, **to Park Ridge Campground▲**
  S: RVDump/Van Buren TC, ATMs, Banks, Auto Services, IGA, Walgreen's, **Outdoor Living RV Center/ Overland RV Park▲**

(7) — **Jct I-540S, US 71S, Fort Smith**
(All Serv at 1st Ex #2)

(9) — **Weigh Station** (Both dir)

(12) — **Jct I-540N, to Fayetteville**
- Other **N: to Lake Ft Smith State Park▲**
  S: Rick Yancey's RV

13 — **US 71, Alma, Fayetteville**
- FStop S: Alma Travel Mart/Citgo
- Gas N: Phillips 66◈, Shell
  S: Shamrock, Murphy◈
- Food N: Braum's Burger King, Cracker Barrel, DQ, KFC, Mazzio's, Subway, Taco Bell
  S: Braum's, McDonald's
- Lodg N: Comfort Inn, Meadors Motor Inn
  S: Days Inn
- TServ S: Long's Truck Service, Peterbilt
- Other N: O'Reilly Auto Parts, **to** Univ of AR, **Crabtree RV Center, Rentals & RV Park▲**, **Ft Smith/Alma KOA▲**, **to Lake Ft Smith State Park▲**
  S: Grocery, NAPA, Pharmacy, **Walmart sc**, **Rex Yancy's RV Superstore**

20 — **US 64, Mulberry, Dyer**
- TStop S: Kountry Xpress/Shell
- Gas N: Conoco◈
  S: Phillips 66
- Food S: Rest/Kountry Xpress
- Lodg S: Mill Creek Inn
- TServ N: Freightliner

24 — **AR 215, Mulberry**

35 — **AR 23, Ozark, to Huntsville**
- Other **S: to Turner Bend Campground▲**, **Aux Ark Park/Ozark Lake▲**

(35) — **Rest Area** (EB)
(RR, Phones, Picnic)

(36) — **Rest Area** (WB)
(RR, Phones, Picnic)

◈ = Regular Gas Stations with Diesel ▲ = RV Friendly Locations ♥ = Pet Friendly Locations
Red print shows large vehicle parking / access on site or nearby Brown Print = Campgrounds / RV PARKS

EXIT		ARKANSAS
37		**AR 219, Ozark**
	TStop	S: Love's Travel Stop #271
	Gas	S: Shell
	Food	S: Subway/Love's FS, McDonald's/Shell, KFC/Taco Bell
	Lodg	S: Days Inn♥
	Med	S: + Mercy Hospital/Turner Memorial
	Other	S: WiFi/Love's TS, Ozark Airport✈
41		**AR 186, Altus**
	Other	S: **Pine Ridge RV Park▲** , Mt Bethel Winery
47		**AR 164, Clarksville, to Coal Hill, Hartman**
55		**US 64, AR 109, Clarksville, Scranton**
	TStop	S: Hwy 109 Truck Plaza/Conoco (on AR 109—2mi S), Exxon Tigermart Auto Truck Center
	Gas	N: Citgo◈
	Food	N: Hardee's, Pizza Hut, Waffle Inn S: Rest/FastFood/Hwy 109 TP, FastFood/ Exxon TM, Catfish House, Kountry Kitchen Grill, Western Sizzlin'
	Lodg	N: Hampton Inn S: Days Inn
	TServ	S: Hwy 109 TP/Tires
	Other	N: AR State Hwy Patrol Post S: Laundry/**RVDump**/Hwy 109TP
57		**AR 109, Clarksville, Scranton**
	TStop	S: Exit 57 Auto Truck Express/Shell
	Gas	N: Citgo, Conoco◈
	Food	N: Subway, Tastee Taco S: FastFood/Ex 57 TE
	Other	N: to Univ of the Ozarks S: Laundry/**RVDump**/Ex 57 TE, Towing
58		**AR 103, AR 21, Clarksville**
	TStop	S: South Park Truck Stop/Shell
	Gas	N: Phillips 66, Shell◈ S: Murphy USA◈
	Food	N: KFC, McDonald's, Pizza Hut, Sonic, Waffle House, Wendy's, Woodward's S: Rest/S Park TS, Arby's
	Lodg	N: Best Western♥, Comfort Inn, Economy Inn, Super 8
	TWash	S: S Park TS
	TServ	S: S Park TS/Tires
	Med	N: + Johnson Reg'l Medical Center
	Other	N: ATMs, Banks, Auto Dealer, Dollar General, to Clarksville Muni Airport✈ S: Laundry/SP TS, Auto Dealers, **Walmart sc**
64		**US 64, Lamar, Clarksville**
	FStop	S: Valero
	Food	S: Rest/PizzaPro/Valero
	Other	S: **Dad's Dream RV Park▲**
67		**AR 315, Knoxville**
	Gas	S: GAS
(68)		**Rest Area (EB)** (RR, Phones, Picnic, Pet, Vend)
(70)		**Scenic Overlook (WB)**
(72)		**Rest Area (WB)** (RR, Phones, Picnic, Vend)
74		**AR 333, London, Russellville**
	Other	N: to Dardanelle Lake/**Piney Bay▲**
78		**US 64, Russellville**
	Gas	S: GAS
	Other	S: **Lake Dardanelle State Park▲** , **Shadow Mountain RV Park▲**
81		**AR 7, Russellville**
	Gas	N: SuperStop◈ S: Exxon◈, Fina, Phillips 66◈, Shell
	Food	N: Captain Blys Pies & More, Seven Forty Supper Club S: Arby's, Burger King, Cracker Barrel, Colton's Steak House & Grill, Dixie Cafe, Pizza Inn, Ruby Tuesday, Santa Fe Cafe, Subway, Waffle House
	Lodg	N: Days Inn, Motel 6♥, Lakeside Resort Motel & **RV Park▲** S: Best Western, Best Value Inn, Economy Inn, Fairfield Inn, Hampton Inn, Holiday Inn♥, Super 8
	Med	S: + Dardanelle Hospital
	Other	N: **Outdoor Living Center & RV Park/ RVDump▲** S: Goodyear, AR Tech Univ, **Shadow Mountain RV Park▲** , **RV Center**, to **Lake Dardanelle State Park▲**
83		**AR 326, Weir Rd**
84		**US 64, AR 331, to AR 7, Russellville**
	FStop	N: Hob Nob Shell (AR331N)
	TStop	N: Flying J Travel Plaza #5038/Conoco (Scales) S: Pilot Travel Center #430 (Scales)
	Gas	S: Phillips 66
	Food	N: Rest/FastFood/FJ TP S: Subway/Wendy's/Pilot TC, CiCi's Pizza, Country Joe's BBQ, Hardee's, Ryan's Grill, Shoney's, Waffle House
	Lodg	S: Comfort Inn
	TServ	N: Russellville Truck & Tire Repair S: Danny's Truck & Trailer Repair, Rick's Truck Repair International
	Other	N: Laundry/BarbSh/WiFi/**RVDump/LP**/ FJ TP, **Ivys Cove RV Retreat/RVDump▲** S: Laundry/WiFi/**RVDump**/Pilot TC, Auto Zone, ATMs, Auto Dealers, Banks, Grocery, Kmart, Lowe's, Staples, Tires,
	Other	S:Towing, **Walmart sc**, Valley Cinema, US Post Office, Russellville Muni Airport✈, To Lake Dardanelle/**Old Post Road Park▲**
88		**AR 363, Pottsville**
	TServ	S: Gala Creek Truck Service, Tires, Exit 88 Truck Wash
94		**AR 105, N Church St, Atkins**
	Gas	N: BP◈, Exxon◈, Shell◈
	Food	N: McDonald's/BP, Subway/Exxon, KFC/ Taco Bell, I-40 Grill, Jean's Country Kitchen, Sonic
101		**Fishlake Rd, Morrilton, Blackwell**
	FStop	N: Valero
	TStop	N: Blackwell Truck Stop (Scales)
	Food	N: Diner/Deli/Blackwell TS
	Other	N: Laundry/Blackwell TS
107		**AR 95, Oak Sts, Morrilton**
	TStop	S: Love's Travel Stop #267
	Gas	N: Shell◈ S: Shell
	Food	N: Morrilton Restaurant S: Subway/Love's TS, Wendy's
	Lodg	N: Days Inn, Scottish Inn
	Other	N: **Morrilton/Conway KOA/RVDump▲** S: WiFi/Love's TS
108		**AR 9, Bus 9, AR 287, Morrilton**
	Gas	S: Phillips 66, Shell◈, Murphy
	Food	S: Bonanza, KFC, McDonald's, Pizza Hut, Oretega's Mex Rest, Subway, Waffle House, Wendy's
	Lodg	N: Super 8 S: Days Inn, Super 8
	Med	S: + St Anthony's Healthcare Center
	Other	S: ATMs, Banks, Auto Dealers, Auto Services, Cinema, Dollar General, Goodyear, Kroger, Radio Shack, **Walmart sc**, to Morrilton Muni Airport✈, to **Lewisburg Bay MH & RV Park▲** , to **Petit Jean State Park▲**
112		**AR 92, to US 64, Plumerville**
117		**to US 64, Menifee**
124		**AR 25, US 64, Conway (EB)**
	Gas	S: Hess◈, Shell
125		**US 65N, US 65B, Conway, to Greenbrier, Harrison**
	FStop	S: Garrett's Truck Stop
	Gas	N: Conoco◈, Exxon◈, Phillips 66, Shell◈ S: Citgo, Exxon◈
	Food	N: Cracker Barrel, El Chico, Hardee's, McDonald's S: Burger King, CiCi's Pizza, IHOP, Outback Steakhouse, Ryan's Grill, Starbucks, Subway, Village Inn, Waffle House, Wendy's

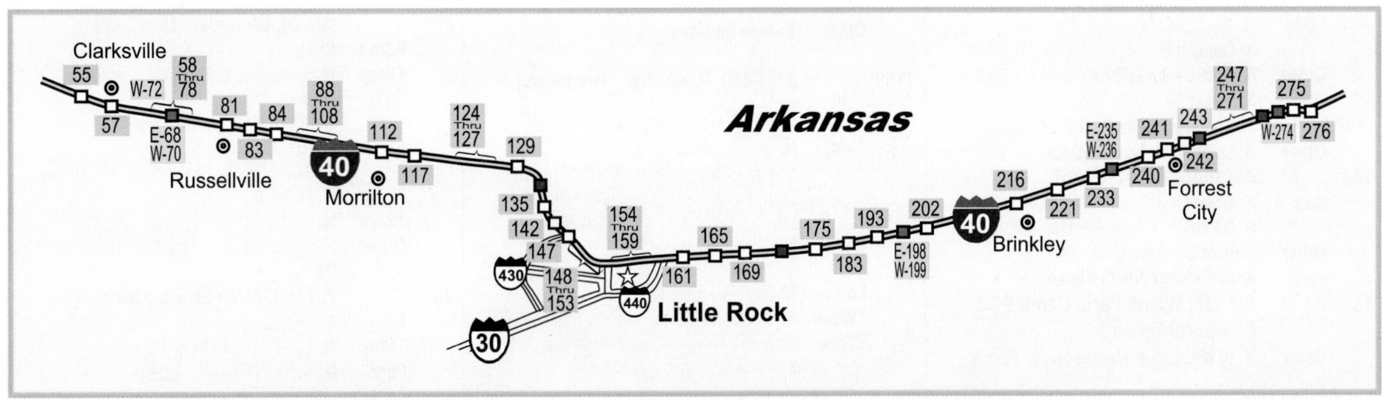

◈= Regular Gas Stations with Diesel ▲ = RV Friendly Locations ♥= Pet Friendly Locations
Red print shows large vehicle parking / access on site or nearby Brown Print = Campgrounds / RV PARKS

EXIT — ARKANSAS

Lodg **N:** Comfort Inn
S: Holiday Inn Express, Howard Johnson, Motel 6♥, Super 8
Med **S: + Conway Reg'l Medical Center**
Other **N:** Auto Services, Office Depot
S: ATMs, Banks, Dollar General, Dollar Tree, Kelly Tire, Lowe's, **Walmart sc**, Hendrix College

127 US 64, Conway, Vilonia, Beebe
Gas **N:** BP, Exxon
S: Raceway, Shell, Valero, Kroger
Food **N:** Arby's, Annie's Fam Rest, ChickFilA, Chili's, Denny's, Starbucks, Subway, Waffle House
S: Burger King, Dillon's Steakhouse, Gringo's TexMex, Hardee's, McDonald's, Panda Café, Taco Bell, Wendy's
Lodg **N:** Best Western, Comfort Inn, Days Inn, Hampton Inn
S: Best Value Inn, Conway Inn, Economy Inn, Kings Inn
Med **S: + Conway Reg'l Medical Center**
Other **N:** ATMs, Auto Dealers, Auto Services, Best Buy, Goodyear, Home Depot, NAPA, O'Reilly Auto Parts, PetSmart♥, Radio Shack, Target, **RV Center**
S: Auto Zone, Auto Services, ATMs, Big Lots, Banks, Carmike Cinema, Kroger, Natural Way Health Foods, Radio Shack, Walgreen's, Dennis F Cantrell Field✈, Central Baptist College, Univ of Central AR,

129AB US 65B, AR 286, Conway (WB)

129 US 65B, AR 286, Conway (EB)
FStop **S:** Mapco Express #3059
Gas **S:** Citgo, Exxon, Shell
Food **S:** Arby's, Rio Grande Mexican, Subway, Taco Place, Wendy's
Lodg **S:** Budget Inn, Continental Motel
Med **S: + Conway Reg'l Medical Center**
Other **N: RV Center**
S: ATMs, Auto Dealers, Midas, Wrecker & Repair services, **to COE/Toad Suck Ferry Park▲**, **AR State Hwy Patrol Post**

(133) Inspection Station (Both dir)

135 AR 89, AR 365, Mayflower
Gas **N:** Hess
S: Exxon◈, Valero
Food **S:** Sonic
Other **N: Mayflower RV Center, to** Camp Joseph T Robinson

142 AR 365, Morgan, Maumelle
FStop **N:** Morgan Valero **(MacArthur Dr)**
TStop **S:**AmBest/Morgan Truck Stop/Shell(Scales)
Gas **N:** Phillips 66
Food **S:** FastFood/Morgan TS, I-40 Rest, KFC/Taco Bell, McDonald's, Waffle House
Lodg **N:** Days Inn
S: Comfort Suites, Quality Inn, Super 8
Other **N:** Auto Services, **Trails End RV Park▲**
S: Diesel Service & Parts

(147) Jct I-430S, to Texarkana
Other **S: Little Rock North KOA▲**

148 AR 100, Crystal Hill Rd
Gas **N:** Shell
S: Citgo
Other **N:** Auto Services & Repairs
S: Little Rock North KOA▲

150 AR 176, Burns Park, Camp Pike, Camp Robinson
Other **N: to MIL/Camp Robinson RV Park▲**

EXIT — ARKANSAS

Other **S:** Burns Park Golf Course, **Burns City Park/RVDump▲**

152 AR 365, AR 176, 33rd St, to Levy
Gas **N:** Conoco, Shell
S: Exxon, Phillips 66, Shell
Food **N:** Burger King, McDonald's, Pizza Hut
S: Church's Chicken
Med **S: + Hospital**
Other **N:** Auto Zone, Fred's, Kroger, **Walmart**
S: Grocery, Radio Shack

153A AR 107, JFK Blvd, Main St
Gas **N:** Exxon, Mapco Express, Shell
S: Exxon
Food **N:** Deli
S: Bonanza, Waffle House
Lodg **N:** Travelodge
S: Country Inn, Hampton Inn, Holiday Inn, Howard Johnson, Motel 6♥
Med **S: + Hospital**
Other **N:** Animal Clinic♥

(153B) Jct I-30W, US 65S, to Little Rock

154 N Hills Blvd, to Lakewood (EB)

155 US 67, US 167, Jacksonville (fr EB, Left exit) (All Serv N on US 167)
Gas **N:** Phillips 66, Shell
Food **N:** Applebee's, Arby's, Chili's, Chuck E Cheese's, CiCi's Pizza, Denny's, Golden Corral, Hooters, IHOP, McDonald's, Outback Steakhouse, Pizza Hut, Red Lobster, Ryan's Grill, Sonic, Shorty's BBQ, Starbucks, Subway, TGI Friday, Wendy's
Lodg **N:** Best Western, Comfort Inn, Hampton Inn, Holiday Inn Express, La Quinta Inn♥, Super 8
Other **N:** ATMs, Auto Dealers, Auto Services, Barnes&Noble, Best Buy, Firestone, Gander Mountain, Harley Davidson, Home Depot, Lowe's, Office Depot, Pep Boys, PetSmart♥, Target, **Walmart sc**, Mall

156 Springhill Dr, N Little Rock
Gas **N:** Phillips 66
Food **N: Cracker Barrel**, Paradise Grill & Seafood
Lodg **N:** Fairfield Inn, Hampton Inn, Holiday Inn Express, La Quinta Inn♥, Residence Inn
Med **N: + Baptist Health Medical Center**

157 AR 161, to US 70, Prothro Rd, NLR
FStop **S:** Flash Market #123/Citgo
TStop **N:** Mid-State Truck Plaza (Scales)
Gas **N:** Exxon◈
S: Phillips 66◈, Shell◈
Food **S:** Burger King, McDonald's, Sonic, Subway, Taco Bell, Waffle House
Lodg **S:** Best Value Inn, Comfort Inn, Days Inn, Masters Inn, Rest Inn, Red Roof Inn♥, Super 8
Other **S:** Auto Services, Hills Mobile Truck & Trailer

(159) Jct I-440, River Port, Texarkana

161 AR 391, Galloway, NLR
TStop **N:** Love's Travel Stop #236
S: TruckOMat (Scales), Petro Stopping Center #26/Mobil (Scales) **(DAND)**, Pilot Travel Center #332 (Scales) **(DAND)**
Food **N:** Chesters/Love's TS
S: IronSkillet/Petro SC, Subway/Pilot TC
Lodg **S:** Days Inn, Galloway Inn
TWash **S:** TruckOMat, Blue Beacon TW/Pilot TC
TServ **N:** Trans America Tire, Freightliner
S: Petro SC/Tires, Speedco

EXIT — ARKANSAS

Other **N:** WiFi/Love's TS, **Camping World**
S: Laundry/BarbSh/WiFi/Petro SC, Laundry/WiFi/Pilot TC,

165 Kerr Rd, Lonoke

169 AR 15, Remington Rd, to Cabot

(170) Inspection Station (Both dir)

175 AR 31, Lonoke
TStop **N:** Crackerbox #35/Valero
Gas **N:** Phillips 66
S: Shell
Food **N:** McDonald's, Rest/Economy Inn
S: Pizza Hut, Sonic, Subway/Shell, Rest/Perry's Motel
Lodg **N:** Days Inn, Economy Inn, Holiday Inn Express, Super 8♥
S: Perry's Motel
Other **S:** ATMs, Banks, Grocery, **Walmart**

183 AR 13, Carlisle
FStop **S:** Conoco Truck Stop
Gas **S:** Exxon◈, Phillips 66◈
Food **S:** Nick's Catfish & BBQ, Subway, Sonic
Lodg **S:** Best Value Inn♥, Carlisle Motel

193 US 63, AR 11, Hazen, Des Arc, Stuttgart, Clarendon
FStop **S:** Hazen Super Stop #88/Shell
Gas **N:** Exxon
S: Citgo◈/T-Rick's
Food **S:** Outdoor Café, Subway
Lodg **S:** Super 8♥, Travel Inn
Other **S: T Rick's RV Park/RVDump▲**

(198) Rest Area (EB) (RR, Picnic, Vend)

(199) Rest Area (WB) (RR, Picnic, Vend)

202 AK 33, Biscoe

216 US 49, AR 17, Brinkley, Cotton Plant, Helena, Jonesboro
FStop **N:** Flash Market #49/Citgo
TStop **N:** Brinkley Travel Center/Shell
Gas **S:** Express◈, Exxon◈, Phillips 66, Valero
Food **N:** FastFood/Brinkley TC, Western Sizzlin, Rest/Super 8
S: Gene's BBQ, KFC, Laura's Diner, McDonald's, Pizza Hut, Sonic, Subway, Taco Bell, Waffle House
Lodg **N:** Baymont Inn, Best Inn, Days Inn & **RV Park▲**, Econo Lodge
S: Best Western, Budget Inn, Heritage Inn **& RV Park▲**
Med **S: + Brinkley Medical Clinic**
Other **S:** ATMs, Auto Services, Carwash, Family Dollar, Firestone, Kroger, NAPA, Laundromat, O'Reilly Auto Parts,

221 AR 78, Wheatley, Marianna
FStop **S:** Mapco Express #3154
TStop **N:** Sweet Pea's Exit 221Truck Stop #401/66,
S: Fuel Mart #640 Pit Stop/BP
Food **N:** Rest/Sweet Pea's TS
S: Subway/Mapco, PitStopDiner/FuelMart
Lodg **N:** Super 8
TServ **N:** Sweet Peas TS/Tires
Other **N:** Laundry/Sweet Pea TS, **Wheatley RV Park▲**

233 AR 261, Main St, Palestine
FStop **S:** Kwik Stop/BP
TStop **N:** Love's Travel Stop #275 (Scales)
Food **N:** Subway/Chesters/Love's TS

◈ = Regular Gas Stations with Diesel ▲ = RV Friendly Locations ♥ = Pet Friendly Locations
Red print shows large vehicle parking / access on site or nearby Brown Print = Campgrounds / RV PARKS

EXIT		ARKANSAS
	Food	S: FastFood/Kwik Stop
	Lodg	N: Rest Inn
	TServ	S: Tire Shop Truck Service
	Other	N: WiFi/RVDump/Love's TS S: B&E Tire Repair & Sales, White's Auto & Truck Repair
(235)		**Rest Area (EB)** **(RR, Phones, Picnic, Vend)**
239		**AR 1, Wynne, Marianne, Wheatley**
241B		**AR 1B N, Forrest City, Wynne**
	FStop	N: Forrest City AmocoBP
	Gas	N: Phillips 66◈
	Food	N: Denny's, HoHo Chinese, Popeye's/P66, Wendy's
	Lodg	N: Best Value Inn, Days Inn, Econo Lodge, Hampton Inn, Holiday Inn, Luxury Inn, Super 8
	Other	N: Auto Dealers, **AR State Hwy Patrol Post**
241A		**AR 1B S, Forrest City, Wynne**
	Gas	S: Citgo, Exxon, Shell, Murphy◈
	Food	S: Bonanza, Burger King, Hardee's, KFC, Granny's Country Diner, McDonald's, Pizza Hut, Ponderosa, Ole Sawmill Cafe, Subway, Taco Bell, Waffle House
	Lodg	S: Best Western
	Other	S: ATMs, Auto Service, Advance Auto Parts, Dollar General, Dollar Tree, Fred's, Grocery, O'Reilly Auto Parts, SavALot, Walgreen's, **Walmart sc**
242		**AR 284, Crowley's Ridge Rd, Forrest City**
	Med	S: + Forrest City Medical Center
	Other	N: to **Village Creek State Park▲**
(243)		**Rest Area (WB)** **(RR, Phones, Picnic, Pet, Vend)**
247		**AR 38E, Widener, to Hughes**
256		**AR 75, AR 275, Heth, Parkin**
	TStop	N: Mapco Express #3155
	Food	N: FastFood/Mapco Express
	Other	N: to appr 12 mi: **Parkin State Park**
260		**AR 149, Heth, to Earle**
	FStop	N: Valero
	TStop	N: Travel Center of America #33/BP (Scales) **(DAND)**
	Gas	N: Citgo S: Shell
	Food	N: CountryPride/BurgerKing/TacoBell/PizzaHut/TA TC, Subway/Citgo
	Lodg	N: Super 8
	TWash	N: TA TC
	TServ	N: TA TC/Tires
	Other	N: Laundry/WiFi/RVDump/TA TC, **Shell Lake Campground▲**

EXIT		ARKANSAS
	Other	S: Carwash, Diesel Services
265		**US 79, AR 218, Bings Store Rd, Crawfordsville, to Hughes**
271		**AR 147, Crawfordsville, Lehi**
	TStop	S: PJ's/66 **(W on US 70/79)**
	Gas	S: Exxon, Shell
	Food	S: FastFood/PJ's
	Other	S: Frank's Auto & Tractor Service
(273)		**Weigh Station (Both dir)**
(274)		**AR Welcome Center (WB)** **(RR, Phones, Pet, Info)**
275		**AR 118, Airport Rd, W Memphis**
	Other	S: Tilden Rodgers Sports Complex, W Memphis Muni Airport✈
276		**AR 76, Rich Rd (fr EB, diff reacc)**
	Gas	S: Exxon, Mapco, Phillips 66, Shell
	Food	S: Bonanza, Burger King, Krystal, McDonald's/Walmart, Mrs Winners, Pizza Inn, Popeye's Chicken, Shoney's
	Lodg	S: Ramada Ltd
	Other	S: ATMs, Banks, **Walmart sc**, Holiday Plaza Mall Shopping Center
	NOTE:	**I-40 runs with I-55 below, Exit #'s follow I-40.**
(277)		**Jct I-55N, Blytheville, St Louis**
278		**AR 77, 7th St, Missouri St, AR 191, W Memphis** **(Addt'l Serv S on Missouri St)**
	FStop	S: Flash Market #11/Shell **(S Serv Rd)**
	Gas	N: Citgo S: Love's◈, RaceTrac, Exxon, Mapco
	Food	S: Cracker Barrel, KFC, Krystal, Mrs Winners, TCBY, McDonald's, Pizza Hut, Shoney's, Subway, Wendy's
	Lodg	S: Quality Inn, Ramada Inn
	Med	S: + Crittenden Memorial Hospital
	Other	S: RVDump/Flash Market, Auto Services, ATMs, Goodyear, Kroger, Radio Shack, Walgreen's, **Walmart sc**, **Tom Sawyers Mississippi River RV Park/RVDump▲**
279A		**Ingram Blvd, W Memphis**
	Gas	S: Citgo◈, Exxon, Shell
	Food	S: Perkins, Shoney's, Waffle House
	Lodg	N: Comfort Inn, Ramada, Red Roof Inn♥, Rodeway Inn S: Best Value Inn, Days Inn, Econo Lodge♥, Hampton Inn, Holiday Inn, Howard Johnson, Motel 6♥, Relax Inn, Rodeway Inn
	Other	N: Southland Greyhound Park, U-Haul, S: Auto Dealers, Auto Services

EXIT		AR / TN
(279B)		**Jct I-55S, to Memphis, TN, Jackson, MS (EB)**
	NOTE:	**I-40 runs with I-55 above, Exit #'s follow I-40.**
(280/4)		**Club Rd, Southland Dr, Martin Luther King Jr Dr (I-55, Ex #4)**
	TStop	N: Pilot Travel Center #429 (Scales), Harris Travel Center/Shamrock S: Flying J Travel Plaza #5333/Conoco (Scales), Petro Stopping Center #11 (Scales), Love's Travel Stop #450 (Scales),
	Gas	N: BP◈
	Food	N: Subway/Wendy's/Pilot TC, FastFood/Harris TC S: Rest/FastFood/FJ TP, IronSkillet/FastFood/Petro SC, Subway/Love's TS, McDonald's, KFC/Taco Bell, Waffle House
	Lodg	N: Express Inn S: Best Western, Budget Inn, Sunset Inn, Super 8♥
	TWash	S: Blue Beacon TW, Crossroads TW
	TServ	N: CAT, Chrome Shop, Goodyear, Pinnacle Truck & Trailer S: Petro SC/Tires, Speedco, Southern Tire Mart
	Other	N: Laundry/WiFi/Pilot TC S: Laundry/BarbSh/WiFi/RVDump/LP/FJ TP, Laundry/CB/WiFi/Petro SC, WiFi/Love's TS, **Tom Sawyers Mississippi River RV Park/RVDump▲**, Southland Greyhound Park
281		**AR 131, Mound City Rd, Mound Mound City (WB)**
(282)		**Weigh Station (WB)**
	NOTE:	**MM 285: Tennessee State Line**

CENTRAL TIME ZONE

ARKANSAS
TENNESSEE

CENTRAL TIME ZONE

EXIT		AR / TN
(1)		**Riverside Dr, Front St (EB)** **TN WELCOME CENTER (NO TRUCKS)** **S: (RR, Phone, Picnic, Vend, Info)**
	Food	S: Felicia Suzanne's Rest, The Butcher Shop Steakhouse
	Lodg	S: Comfort Inn, Courtyard, Madison Hotel, Sleep Inn, Springhill Suites, Wyndham

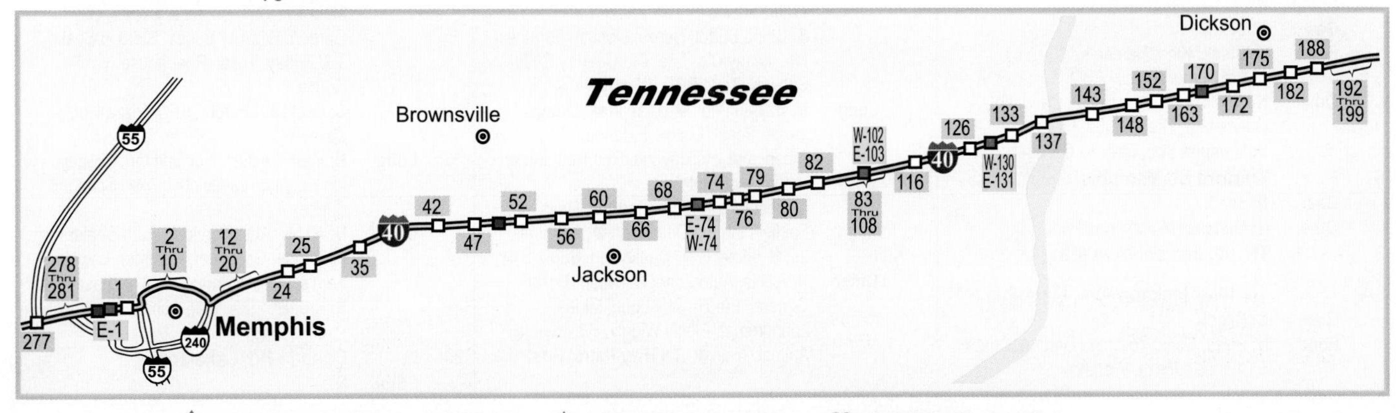

◈ = Regular Gas Stations with Diesel ▲ = RV Friendly Locations ♥ = Pet Friendly Locations
Red print shows large vehicle parking / access on site or nearby **Brown Print = Campgrounds / RV PARKS**

Other S: Convention Center, Museums, Pyramid Arena, Riverfront

1A Second St, Third St (WB ex, EB ent)
Food N: Starbucks
Lodg S: Crowne Plaza Hotel, Holiday Inn Select, Marriott, Wyndham Garden Hotel
Med N: + St Jude Research Center, + St Joseph Hospital
Other N: C&L Bus Repair Service, Downtown Animal Hospital♥,
S: Convention Center, Courts, Greyhound, Museums, **Police Dept**, Walgreen's

1B US 51, Danny Thomas Blvd (EB)

1C US 51S, Danny Thomas Blvd (WB)
Gas S: BP◈, Exxon
Food S: KFC, Subway/BP

1D US 51N, Danny Thomas Blvd (WB)
Med N: + St Jude Research Center, + St Joseph Hospital

(1E) Jct I-240S, to Jackson, MS (Acc Hosp Via 1st 2 Exits)
Med S: + Veteran's Medical Center, + Children's Medical Center, + Regional Medical Center, + Baptist Memorial Hospital, Univ of TN Hospital, + Methodist Hospital

1FG TN 14, Jackson Ave, Memphis (WB Exit, EB entr)
Gas S: Mapco
Food N: Church's Chicken
S: Tops BBQ
Lodg N: Rainbow Inn
Other N: Auto Services, **to** St Jude's Hospital
S: Auto Services, Laundromat, Memphis Zoo, to Rhodes College

2 Chelsea Ave (EB), Smith Ave (WB)
Gas N: Citgo
S: BP
Other N: Auto Services, Grocery

2A TN 300, to US 51, TN 3, Thomas St, to Millington (fr EB, LEFT Exit)
FStop N: Express Gas/BP
Gas N: BP
Food N: Church;s Chicken, Pit Bar-B-Q, Taco Bell, Tops BBQ,
Other N: Auto Services, Auto Zone, Dollar General, Family Dollar, Kroger, O'Reilly Auto Parts, Walgreen's

3 Watkins St, Memphis
FStop N: Texaco
Gas N: BP,
Other N: Auto Services, Family Dollar, Laundromat, Tire Shop, U-Haul
S: Mid South U-Pull-It Auto Parts

5 Hollywood St, Memphis
FStop N: Mapco Express
Gas N: BP
Food N: Burger King, Hardee's,
S: Fat Burger, Family BBQ
Other N: ATMs, Auto Service/BP, Carwash, Greyhound, Tires, Walgreen's
S: Memphis Zoo, Rhodes College

6 Warford St, Memphis
Gas N: Shell
Other N: Memphis Motorsports Park

8 TN 14, Jackson Ave (EB)

8A TN 14N, Jackson Ave, Memphis (WB)
Gas N: Citgo◈, Shell
Food N: Pizza, Sonic, **to** China Garden, Chuck E Cheese's Pizza, Wendy's
Lodg N: Days Inn, Sleep Inn♥
Med N: + Methodist Hospital
Other N: Auto Services, Carwash, Raleigh Tire, Stage Rd Animal Hospital♥, Big Lots, Goodyear, Jiffy Lube, Kmart, Raleigh Springs Mall, Theatre

8B TN 14S, Memphis (WB)
Gas S: Citgo◈
Food S: Central Park
Other S: Auto Zone, Auto Services, Family Dollar, Kelly Tire, Memphis Flea Market, O'Reilly Auto Parts

10 TN 204, Covington Pike, Memphis (South Serv appr 1mi to Summer Ave)
Gas N: BP
Food N: McDonald's, Wendy's
S: Backyard Burger Burger King, Central BBQ, Edo Japanese, Mortimer's Rest, Pizza Shack, Subway
Other N: Auto Dealers, Auto Services, Auto Rental, Dollar General, Grocery, NAPA, Sam's Club, Tires
S: Auto & Tire Services, Advance Auto Parts, Aldi Grocery, Animal Hospital♥, Banks, Kroger, Lowe's, O'Reilly Auto Parts, Walgreen's, **Access to #12A**

12A Summer Ave, US 64, US 70, US 79
FStop N: Mapco Express #3144
Gas N: Shell◈,
S: BP, Exxon, Star Mart
Food N: Pappy & Jimmy's, Waffle House
S: Arby's, Jack's BBQ Rib Shack Buffet, McDonald's, Pancho's, Rye Sushi, Wendy's
Lodg S: Best Value Inn, Comfort Inn, Days Inn
Other N: Auto Dealer, Auto Rental, Firestone, Garden Ridge, Golf & Games Family Park, Goodyear, Greyhound, Kmart, Malco Summer Drive-In Theatre, U-Haul, **Acc #12**
S: Auto Services, Cinema, Firestone, Piggly Wiggly Grocery, Penske Truck Rental, SavALot, Tires

12B Sam Cooper Blvd (fr WB, LEFT Exit)

(12C) Jct I-240, W to Jackson, I-40E to Nashville (fr EB, LEFT Exit)

10A Jct I-240W, Memphis ByPass,

(10B) Jct I-40E, to Nashville (WB)

12 Sycamore View Rd, to Bartlett
FStop S: Mapco Express #3144
Gas N: Citgo◈, Star Mart Texaco◈
S: Circle K◈/BP, Citgo, Exxon
Food N: Burger King, Cajun Catfish, Captain D's, Cracker Barrel, IHOP, KFC, McDonald's, Mrs Winner's, Perkins, Pizza Inn, Ruby Tuesday, Shoney's, Starbucks, Taco Bell, Waffle House
S: China Buffet, Dunkin Donuts, Fortune Inn, Jimmy C's Café, Old Country Buffet, Subway, Tops BBQ, Wendy's
Lodg N: Baymont Inn♥, Clarion♥, Drury Inn♥, Econo Lodge, Extended Stay America♥, Holiday Inn, Red Roof Inn♥, Value Place Hotel
S: Best Western, Comfort Inn, Days Inn, Fairfield Inn, La Quinta Inn♥, Memphis Inn♥, Motel 6♥, Quality Inn, Super 8♥,
Other N: ATMs, Auto Zone, Carwash, Dollar General, Fred's, Jiffy Lube, Midas, Laundromat, Piggly Wiggly, Walgreen's, Animal Clinic♥, **TN Hwy Patrol Post**
S: AT&T, Bass Pro Shop, Colonial Hardware, Super Suds Carwash, SW TN Comm College, **to Shelby Farms Park**

14 Whitten Rd
Gas N: Citgo, Mapco, Shell
S: Circle K/BP, Shell
Food N: Burger King/Shell, Quiznos, Sidecar Cafe
S: Backyard Burger/Shell
Lodg S: Travelers Inn, Bridgewater House B&B
Other N: Bumpis Harley Davidson, Penske Truck Rental, Polaris,
S: Dollar General, Walgreen's

15 Appling Rd, Cordova (WB)

15A Appling Rd S (EB)
Gas S: BP

15B Appling Rd N (EB)
Gas N: Circle K/BP

16 TN 177, Germantown Pkwy (EB)

16B TN 177N, Germantown Pkwy, Cordova (WB) (Acc to #18)
Gas N: 76, Shell
Food N: Abuelo's Mexican, Arby's, Bahama Breeze, Baskin Robbins, Burger King, ChickFilA, Chili's, Colton's Steakhouse, Danver's Rest, Eat Well Sushi & Grill, Guss's World Famous Fried Chicken, IHOP, J Alexander's, Joe's Crab Shack, Logan's Roadhouse, McDonald's, Melting Pot, On the Border, Romano's Macaroni Grill, Red Lobster, McDonald's, Starbucks, Taco Bell, Wendy's
Lodg N: Extended Stay Deluxe, Hampton Suites, Hyatt Place
Med N: + St Francis Hospital
Other N: ATMs, Auto Dealers, B&N, Best Buy, Dollar Tree, Hobby Lobby, Home Depot, Lowe's, Matco Cinema, Malco Stage Cinema 13, Office Depot, Sports Authority, Target, Walgreen's, Wolfchase Animal Hospital♥, Wolfchase Galleria Mall

16A TN 177S, Germantown (WB)
Gas S: Shell, Costco
Food S: Jim & Nick's BBQ, Shogun, Waffle House
Lodg S: Comfort Suites, Microtel♥, Quality Suites♥, Studio Plus, Wingate Inn
Other S: Auto Zone, Costco, Dick's Sporting Goods, Dollar General, Kroger, Verizon, Vet Pets Animal House♥, **to** Agricenter Int'l/RV Park▲

18 US 64, Somerville, Bolivar
Gas N: Shell
S: BP, Circle K, Citgo◈
Food N: Bob Evans, Burger King/Shell, Don Pablo, El Porto Mexican, Firebirds Rock Mountain Grill, Hooter's, Luby's, Olive Garden, Smokey Bones, Steak n Shake, TGI Friday, Texas Roadhouse, Waffle House
S: Backyard Burger, KFC, Pizza Hut, Zaxby's
Lodg N: Best Western, Fairfield Inn, Holiday Inn Express, La Quinta Inn♥, Springhill Suites
Other N: ATMs, Auto Services, Auto Dealers, Firestone, Goodyear, Hummer, Lowe's, Sam's Club, **Walmart sc**, Wolfchase Mall
S: Kroger, Pharmacy, Schnuck's Grocery/Pharmacy, UPS Store, Walgreen's

20 Canada Rd, Lakeland
FStop N: Shell

◈ = Regular Gas Stations with Diesel ▲ = RV Friendly Locations ♥ = Pet Friendly Locations
Red print shows large vehicle parking / access on site or nearby Brown Print = Campgrounds / RV PARKS

Gas N: BP
S: Exxon◈
Food N: FastFood/Lakeland Sh, **Cracker Barrel**, McDonald's, Waffle House,
S: Subway/Exxon, Cotton Cabin
Lodg N: Days Inn, Hotel Scottish, Relax Inn, Super 8♥
Other S: Factory Outlet Mall, Fireworks, Old Tyme Pottery, **Memphis East Campground▲**

24 TN 385, Millington, Collierville

24A TN 385W, Millington, Collierville

24B TN 385E, Millington, Collierville

25 TN 205, Airline Rd, Arlington
Gas N: Exxon◈, Shell◈
S: Horizon◈
Food N: Subway/Exxon, Chesters/Shell
S: Backyard Burger/Horizon
Other S: Tourist Info

35 TN 59, US 70, Somerville, Covington
FStop S: Longtown Travel Center/BP (Scales)
Food S: Rest/Longtown TC
Other S: CB/Longtown TC

42 TN 222, Stanton Rd, Somerville
TStop S: Pilot Travel Center #149 (Scales) **(DAND)**
Gas S: Exxon◈
Food N: Bozo's Hot Pit BBQ, Shirley's Grill
S: Chester's/Subway/Pilot TC, Café/Exxon,
Lodg N: Best Value Inn, Countryside Inn
S: Deerfield Inn
Other N: Earl's Wrecker Service & Tires
S: Laundry/WiFi/Pilot TC

47 TN 179, Darcyville Rd, Stanton
TStop S: Exit 47 Plaza (Scales)
Food S: Rest/Exit 47 Pl
Tires S: Exit 47 Pl

(49) Weigh Station (EB)

(50) Weigh Station (WB)

52 TN 76, TN 179, Koko Rd, to Whiteville
Gas S: Ko Ko Gas

56 TN 76, Anderson Ave, Brownsville, to Somerville
FStop N: Hopper Quik Stop #3/Exxon
S: Bell's Truck Stop/Exxon
Gas N: BP, Citgo◈, Shell
S: BP◈, Exxon◈
Food N: FastFood/Hooper QS, DQ, KFC, McDonald's, Pizza Hult, Subway/Citgo
S: Huddle House/Exxon
Lodg N: Best Western, Comfort Inn, Days Inn, Econo Lodge, O'Bannon Inn♥
Med N: **+ Hospital**
Other N: Tourist Info

60 TN 19, Mercer Rd, Brownsville

66 US 70, TN 1, Brownsville
FStop S: Gas Mart #628B (Scales)
Food S: FastFood/Gas Mart
Lodg S: Motel 6♥

68 TN 138, Providence Rd, Denmark
TStop S: Travel Center of America/Wilhites/Citgo (Scales)
Gas N: BP, Valero
Food S: Rest/Subway/TA TC
Lodg N: Ole South Inn, Scottish Inn
TServ S: TA TC/Tires
Other N: Wrecker Service, **Ft Pillow State Hist Park▲**
S: Laundry/WiFi/TA TC, **Joy-O RV Park▲**

EXIT TENNESSEE

(73) Madison Rest Area (Both dir) (RR, Phones, Picnic, Vend, Info)

74 Lower Brownsville Rd

76 TN 223S, Jackson
Other S: **Whispering Pines RV Park▲**, McKellar-Sipes Reg'l Airport✈

79 US 412, Jackson, Dyersburg
FStop S: Ash BP
Gas S: Exxon, Mapco
Food N: Red Robin
S: FastFood/Ash's, GG's Rest, Reggi's BBQ
Lodg S: Days Inn♥
Other N: Dick's Sporting Goods, Gander Mountain
S: **Jackson Mobile Village & RV Park▲**, Auto Services, Galloway's Truck & Auto Repair, Union Univ

80B US 45ByPass, to Milan
Gas N: BP◈, Exxon, Sam's Club, Murphy
Food N: Asahi Japanese Steakhouse, Backyard Burger, ChickFilA, Chili's, Corky's BBQ, IHOP, KFC, Lenny's Subs, Lone Star Steakhouse, Moe's SW Grill, Olive Garden, Perkins, Picasso Bistro Pizzeria, Red Robin, Ruby Tuesday, Steak n Shake, Starbucks, TGI Friday's, Wendy's
Lodg N: Baymont Inn, Comfort Inn, Country Inn, Jameson Inn
Med N: **+ Reg'l Hospital of Jackson**
Other N: AT&T, Best Buy, BooksAMillion,Cinema, Firestone Auto, Hobby Lobby, Home Depot, Lowe's, PetCo♥, PetSmart♥, Sam's Club, Stonehaven Veterinary♥, Union Univ, Verizon, **Walmart sc**

80A US 45 ByPass, to Jackson
Gas S: BP, Citgo, Coastal◈, Phillips 66◈
Food S: Applebee's, Arby's, Barnhill's Buffet, Burger King, Dunkin Donuts, El Chico Cafe, Logan's Roadhouse, McDonald's, Mrs Winner's, O'Charley's, Sonic, Subway, Taco Bell, Waffle House, Village Inn
Lodg S: Best Western, Comfort Inn, Days Inn, Doubletree Hotel, Econo Lodge♥, Fairfield Inn, Hampton Inn, Holiday Inn, Motel 6♥, Old Hickory Inn♥, Quality Inn, Supertel Inn
Med S: **+ Jackson Madison Co Hospital, + Minor Medical Clinic**
Other S: Auto Dealers, Auto Repairs, Bumpus Harley Davidson, Cinema 10, Dollar General, Kmart, Kroger, Penske Truck Rental, Victory Honda

82B US 45N, Highland Ave, Jackson
Gas N: Exxon, Texaco
Food N: **Cracker Barrel**,
Lodg N: Knight's Inn, Microtel
Other N: Auto Repairs, Batteries Plus, **TN State Hwy Patrol**, **to** University Pkwy Animal Hospital♥, **appr 4mi: Smallwoods RV**,

82A US 45S, Highland Ave, Jackson
Gas S: BP, Exxon, RaceTrac
Food S: Backyard BBQ, Burger King, Cajun Cookers BBQ, China Palace, Little Caesars Pizza, Los Portales Mexican Rest, Papa John's Pizza, Pizza Hut, Po Folks, Popeyes Chicken, Sakura Japanese, Shoney's, Sonic, Waffle House, Wendy's
Lodg S: Executive Inn♥, La Quinta Inn♥, Ramada Ltd, Super 8♥, Travelers Motel
Med S: **+ Jackson Madison Co Gen'l Hospital**

EXIT TENNESSEE

Other S: Advance Auto Parts, Auto Zone, Auto Repairs, Big Lots, Dollar General, Dollar Tree, Firestone, Fred's, Goodyear, Great Outdoor Store, Jackson Animal Clinic♥, Jackson Indoor Shooting Range, Kirkland's, Kroger, Laundromat, Office Depot, Old Hickory Mall, Parkway Animal Hospital♥, Radio Shack, Tractor Supply, UPS Store, **to** Lambuth Univ, **to appr 20 mi: Chickasaw State Park▲**, **app 42 mi: Big Hill Pond State Park**

83 Campbell St
Gas N: Exxon◈
Lodg S: Courtyard, Hampton Inn

85 Christmasville Rd, Jackson
FStop N: Express Food Mart & Deli/Exxon, Christmasville BP
TStop S: Pilot Travel Center #366 (Scales)
Gas S: Shell
Food N: Subs/BP
S: Denny's/Pilot TC, Lenny's Subs, Los Portales Mexican Rest, McDonald's, Reggi's BBQ, Sparky's Pizzeria & Grill,
Lodg N: Comfort Inn,
Other N: Dollar General
S: Laundry/WiFi/Pilot TC, Pringles Park, West TN Sportsplex

87 US 70, US 412, TN 1, Jackson, to Huntington, McKenzie
FStop S: BP Food Mart,
TStop S: Love's Travel Stop #244 (Scales)
Gas N: Coastal◈
Food S: Hardee's/Love's TS, Waffle House
Other N: Auto & Truck Service, U-Haul, Wildflower Farm
S: Laundry/WiFi/**RVDump**/Love's TS, Freightliner, Jackson Trailer Service, to Jackson State Comm College,

93 TN 152, Law Rd, to Lexington
Gas N: Phillips 66◈
S: BP, Global Fuels
Food N: Deli/P66
S: Global Cafe

101 TN 104, Wildersville
TStop N: 101 Travel Center/Conoco
Gas N: Exxon
Food N: Rest/101 TC
Other N: WiFi/CB/101 TC

(102) Parking Area (WB)

(103) Parking Area (EB)

108 TN 22, Huntington, Lexington, Parkers Crossroads
TStop N: I-Mart #108/66, Bull Market #19/Citgo
Gas N: BP◈
S: Exxon, Shell
Food N: BP/McDonald's, Bailey's Rest, DQ, Subway
S: The Cotton Patch Rest
Lodg N: Knight's Inn
S: Americas Best Value Inn♥,
Tires N: Bull Market
Med S: **+ Hospital**
Other N: **Parker's Crossroads RV Park & Campground▲**
S: Parkers Crossroads Visitor Center

116 TN 114, Westport
Other S: **to Natchez Trace State Park▲**

126 US 641, TN 69, Parsons, Camden
FStop N: Shell Food Mart
S: Holladay Shell

◈ = Regular Gas Stations with Diesel ▲ = RV Friendly Locations ♥ = Pet Friendly Locations
Red print shows large vehicle parking / access on site or nearby Brown Print = Campgrounds / RV PARKS

EXIT	TENNESSEE
TStop	N: North Forty Truck Stop/P66 (Scales), Sugar Tree Truck Stop
Gas	N: Exxon◊
	S: Dottie's Marine/BP◊,
Food	N: Rest/FastFood/N 40 TS, Rest/Sugar Tree TS, Interstate Cafe,
	S: Rest/Shell, Deli/Grill/BP
Lodg	S: Days Inn
TServ	N: Sugar Tree TS, B&W Truck Repair & Tires, Big John's Truck & Trailer Repair, Wilson's Repair,
Other	N: Laundry/BarbSh/**RVDump**/N 40 TS, **Northern Bedford Forrest State Park▲**
	S: Mousetail Landing State Park▲
(130)	**Benton Rest Area (EB)**
	(RR, Phones, Picnic, Pet, Vend)
(131)	**Benton Rest Area (WB)**
	(RR, Phones, Vend)
133	**TN 191, Birdsong Rd, Holladay**
Other	**N: to appr 9 mi: Birdsong Resort, Marina & RV Park▲**
	S: to Mousetail Landing State Park▲
137	**Cuba Landing, Waverly**
Gas	S: Citgo
Other	**N: TN River Mountain Getaways Lodging Cabins Resort & Campground▲**
143	**TN 13, Hurricane Mills, to Linden, Waverly**
FStop	N: Pilot Travel Center # 53 (Scales)
Gas	N: BP, Shell
	S: Exxon◊,
Food	N: Arby's/TJCinn/Pilot TC, Log Cabin, Loretta Lynn's Kitchen, McDonald's, Subway
	S: South-Side Rest
Lodg	N: Best Western, Days Inn♥, Holiday Inn Express, Knights Inn, Super 8
	S: Best Budget Motel
TServ	N: I-40 Auto & Truck Center
	S: Barnett's Wrecker Service, Tires
Other	N: Laundry/WiFi/Pilot TC, Greg's Tire & Repair, **Buffalo KOA▲**, **143 Off Road RV Park▲**, **to appr 7mi: Loretta Lynn's Ranch RV Park & Museum▲**
	S: appr 1 mi: Buffalo River Camping▲
148	**TN 229, TN 50, Barren Hollow Rd, to Centerville**
152	**TN 230, Only, to Bucksnort**
Gas	N: Citgo
Food	N: Rudy's Rest
Lodg	N: Travel Inn
163	**TN 48, Centerville, Dixon**
FStop	N: Phillips 66
Gas	S: Shell

EXIT	TENNESSEE
Other	N: Truck & Tire Repair 48 Tire
	S: CB Shop, **Tanbark Campground▲**
(170)	**Dickson Rest Area (Both dir)**
	(RR, Phones, Picnic, Vend)
172	**TN 46, Centerville, Dickson**
TStop	N: Pilot Travel Center #409 (Scales)
Gas	N: BP◊, Citgo, Exxon, Shell
	S: Phillips 66, Shell◊
Food	N: Wendy's/Pilot TC, Arby's, Burger King, Cracker Barrel, McDonald's, Ruby Tuesday, Subway/Citgo, Waffle House, to Bart's BBQ & Catfish Cooker
	S: O'Charley's, Sonic
Lodg	N: Best Western♥, Comfort Inn, Econo Lodge, Hampton Inn, Knights Inn, Motel 6♥, Quality Inn, South Ave Inn, Super 8♥ I-40 Motel
	S: Days Inn♥, Holiday Inn Express, Ramada Ltd♥
Med	N: + Hospital
Other	N: Laundry/WiFi/**RVDump**/Pilot TC, Renaissance Center, Roadside Services, **Dickson RV Park/LP▲**, NAPA, U-Haul, **to appr 4mi: Walmart sc**
176	**TN 840, Burns**
182	**TN 96, Dickson, Fairview, Franklin**
TStop	S: Flying J Travel Plaza #5051/Conoco (Scales), Horizon Family Travel Plaza **(NO TRUCKS)**
Gas	N: Express Fuel
Food	S: CountryMarket/FastFood/FJ TP, Backyard Burger/Horizon TP
Lodg	N: Fairview Inn
	S: Deerfield Inn,
Other	**N: to Montgomery Bell State Park▲**
	S: Laundry/WiFi/**RVDump/LP**/FJ TP
188	**TN 249, Kingston Springs Rd, Ashland City, Pegram, Kingston Springs**
TStop	S: Petro 2 #49/Mobil (Scales)
Gas	N: BP, Mapco Express◊, Shell
	S: Chevron
Food	N: Blimpie/Exprasess, Arby's/Shell, McDonald's, Pizza Pro, Sonic
	S: QuickSkillet/PizzaHut/Petro 2
Lodg	N: Best Western, Econo Lodge, Motown Inn, Relax Inn
TServ	S: Petro 2/Tires
Other	S: Laundry/BarbSh/WiFi/Petro 2, Sundown Trailers
192	**McCrory Lane, Pegram**
Other	**N: 1 mi GAS**
	S: Natchez Trace Parkway
196	**US 70S, Bellevue, Newsom Station**
Gas	N: Mapco Express

EXIT	TENNESSEE
Gas	S: BP, Mapco Express◊, Shell◊
Food	N: Shoney's
	S: Applebee's, Jack in the Box, Quiznos, O'Charley's, Pizza Hut, Subway, Sonic, Taco Bell, Waffle House
Lodg	S: Hampton Inn, Microtel
Med	S: + Baptist Bellevue Med Center
Other	N: Regal Cinema 12
	S: Bellevue Center Mall, Dollar Tree, Firestone, Grocery, Home Depot, Penske Truck Rental, PetCo♥, Publix, Staples, US Post Office, Walgreen's,
199	**TN 251, Old Hickory Blvd**
Gas	S: BP, Mapco Express, Sam's
Food	S: Sonic, Subway, Waffle House
Other	N: Wrecker Service
	S: Putt Putt Golf, Sam's Club, **Walmart**
201A	**US 70E, Charlotte Pike**
Gas	S: Citgo, BP, Mapco, Costco
Food	S: Arby's, Baskin Robbins, McDonald's, Pizza Hut, Red Robin, Taco Bell,
Other	S: Auto Service, Best Buy, Big Lots, Books AMillion, Costco, Firestone, Food Lion, PetSmart♥, Staples, Target, U-Haul, Verizon, World Market, West Meade Veterinary Clinic♥, **Acc to #204 S Serv**
201B	**US 70W, Nashville**
Gas	N: Exxon, Shell◊
Food	N: Cracker Barrel, Jim & Nick's BBQ, Krystal, Waffle House, Wendy's
Lodg	N: Super 8
Other	N: Dollar Tree, Lowe's, Radio Shack, **Walmart sc**
201	**US 70, TN 24, Charlotte Pike (WB)**
204B	**TN 155S, Briley Pkwy, Nashville Robertson Ave (WB)**
Gas	N: Exxon, Shell◊
Other	N: to John C Tune Airport✈
204A	**51st Ave N, Nashville (WB)**
Gas	S: Texaco
Food	S: Burger King, Church's, KFC, Krystal, Shoney's, Uncle Bud's Catfish, Waffle House, White Castle
Lodg	S: Baymont Inn, Best Western, Comfort Inn, Days Inn, Super 8
Other	S: Auto Zone, Auto Services, CVS, Enterprise RAC, Goodyear, Kroger, Walgreen's
204	**TN 155, Briley Pkwy, Nashville Robertson Ave, White Bridge Rd (EB) (Addtl Serv S to US 70/TN 24)**
205	**46th Ave, 51st Ave, W Nashville**
Gas	S: BP, Mapco Express, Shell
Food	S: McDonald's, Mrs Winner's

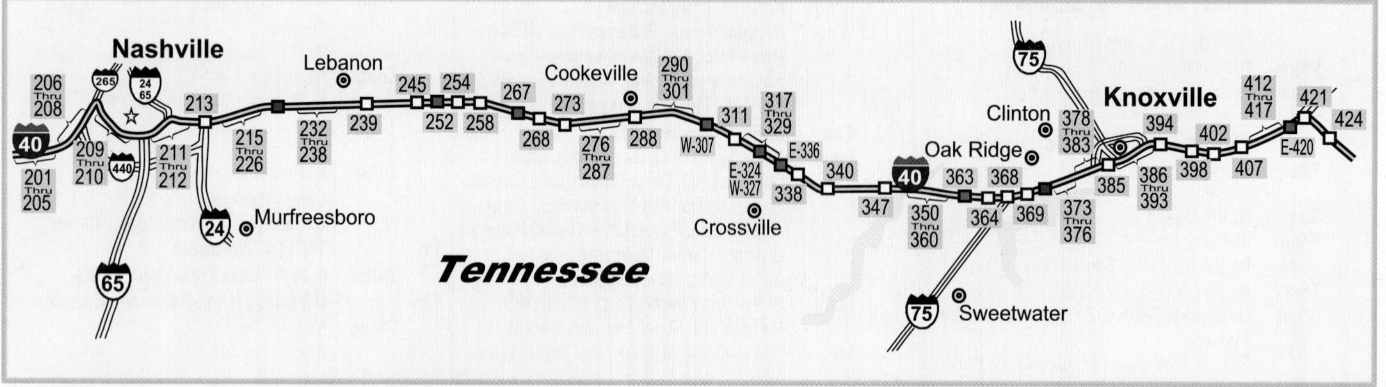

◊ = Regular Gas Stations with Diesel ▲ = RV Friendly Locations ♥ = Pet Friendly Locations
Red print shows large vehicle parking / access on site or nearby Brown Print = Campgrounds / RV PARKS

EXIT	TENNESSEE
Other	N: Harley Davidson S: Auto Services
(206)	**Jct I-440E, to Knoxville, Huntsville, Chattanooga (WB LEFT Exit)**
207	**28th Ave, Jefferson St**
Med	S: + Metro Nashville Gen'l Hospital, + Meharry Medical College
Other	N: Tn State Univ S: Fisk Univ
(208BA)	**Jct I-65N, to Louisville (EB LEFT Exit)**
(208)	**Jct I-65N, to Louisville**
209	**US 70, TN 24, US 70S, US 431, Church St, Charlotte Ave (EB exit, WB entr)**
Gas	N: Exxon S: BP, Exxon
Food	S: Burger King, Shoney's, White Castle
Lodg	N: Holiday Inn S: Best Western, Comfort Inn, Shoney's Inn
Med	S: + Baptist Hospital, + Columbia Centennial Medical Center
Other	N: Auto Services, Fleet Repair, Thrifty RAC Country Music Hall of Fame, Museums, State Capitol S: Auto & Tire Services, Auto Dealers, Budget RAC, Museums, Walgreen's
209A	**US 70S, US 431, Broadway**
209B	**US 70S, US 431 Demonbreun St**
Med	S: + Vanderbilt University Hospital
Other	N: Auto Services, Enterprise S: Music Row, Museums, Auto Services
(210)	**Jct I-65S, to Birmingham (WB Left ex)**
(210AB)	**Jct I-65S, to Birmingham**
210C	**US 31A, UA 41A, 2nd/4th Ave S**
Food	S: Brown's BBQ
TServ	S: Bestway Truck & Tire Service
Other	N: Auto Services S: Auto Services, Museums
(211B)	**Jct I-24W, Jct I-65N, Clarksville, Louisville (fr EB, LEFT exit)**
(211A)	**Jct I-65S, Birmingham, Jct I-40W, Memphis**
212	**Fesslers Lane**
TStop	S: Dailey's #604/Shell
Food	N: Nashville Smokehouse S: Burger King, Krystal, McDonald's
Lodg	S: Drake Inn, Music City Motor Inn
TServ	N: Goodyear Tire & Auto, Neely Coble Sunbelt Truck Center, Tn Truck Sales S: PM Truck Service, Total Truck & Trailer Service
Med	S: + Hospital
Other	S: Laundry/Dailey's, Auto Services, Auto Dealers, Auto Rentals
(213A)	**Jct I-24E, Jct I-40E, to Chattanooga**
(213AB)	**Jct I-24W, Jct I-440W**
213	**to US 41, Spence Lane**
Gas	N: Shell S: BP
Food	S: Hunan Chinese, Piccadilly Cafeteria, Pizza Hut, Red Lobster, Taco Bell, Waffle House
Lodg	S: Days Inn, Econo Lodge, Holiday Inn Express, Hawthorne Inn, Quality Inn, Ramada Inn, Scottish Inn

EXIT	TENNESSEE
TServ	N: Kenworth of TN S: Cummins Cumberland
215B	**TN 155N, Briley Pkwy (EB)**
Gas	N: Shell
Food	N: Denny's, Waffle House, Rest/Days Inn
Lodg	N: Days Inn, Embassy Suites, Holiday Inn, Hampton Inn, La Quinta Inn♥, Quality Inn, Residence Inn
215A	**TN 155S, Briley Pkwy (EB)**
Gas	S: Shell
Food	S: Steak Out
Lodg	S: Marriott, Radisson Inn, Ramada, Royal Inn
215	**TN 155, Briley Pkwy, Opryland**
Other	N: to N Nashville KOA▲
216A	**Nashville Int'l Airport (EB exit, WB entr) (NO TRUCKS)**
Other	N: Auto Rentals
216B	**Donelson Pike S, Airport (EB)**
216C	**TN 255, Donelson Pike N (EB)**
216	**TN 255, Donelson Pike, Nashville International Airport (WB)**
Gas	N: BP, Citgo, RaceTrac, Shell
Food	N: Arby's, Backyard Burgers, Burger King, Chili's, KFC, Little Caesar's Pizza, Papa John's Pizza, McDonald's, Outback Steakhouse, Ruby Tuesday, Shoney's, Subway, Taco Bell, Waffle House, Wendy's
Lodg	N: AmeriSuites, Country Inn Suites, Fairfield Inn, Hampton Inn, Holiday Inn Express, La Quinta Inn♥, Radisson Hotel, Red Roof Inn♥, Springhill Suites, Super 8, Wingate Inn, Wyndham Garden Hotel
Other	N: Cruise America, Laundromat, Kmart, Walgreen's S: Auto Rentals
219	**Stewarts Ferry Pike, Nashville**
Gas	N: Mapco Express S: Mapco Express, Shell
Food	S: Cracker Barrel, La Hacienda Mex Rest, Subway, Waffle House
Lodg	S: Best Value Inn, Best Western, Country Inn, Days Inn, Family Inn, Howard Johnson, Sleep Inn
Other	S: Cook Campground▲
221A	**TN 265, TN 45N, Central Pike, Old Hickory Blvd, Hermitage (EB)**
Med	N: + Summit Medical Center
221B	**TN 45S, Old Hickory Blvd (EB)**
221	**TN 45, Old Hickory Blvd**
Gas	N: BP, Exxon, Mapco Express, RaceWay S: Phillips 66, Shell
Food	N: Applebee's, Hardee's, IHOP, Jack in the Box, Music City Café, Waffle House S: McDonald's, Po Folks, Shooters Sports Bar
Lodg	N: Comfort Inn, Holiday Inn Express, Motel 6, Quality Inn, Ramada Inn, Super 8, Vista Motel
Med	N: + Summit Medical Center
Other	N: CVS, Kroger, Walgreen's S: to the Hermitage Public Use Area
(225)	**Weigh Station (EB)**
226A	**TN 171S, Mt Juliet Rd, Mt Juliet, Nashville (EB)**
226B	**TN 171N, Mt Juliet Rd, Mt Juliet, Nashville (EB)**

EXIT	TENNESSEE
226	**TN 171, Mt Juliet Rd, Mt Juliet, Nashville**
Gas	N: BP◈, Exxon, Mapco Express◈, Shell◈ S: Mapco Express◈
Food	N: Arby's, Captain D's, McDonald's/BP S: Cracker Barrel, Ruby Tuesday, Waffle House
Lodg	S: Microtel, Quality Inn
Med	S: + Walk In Clinic
Other	N: to COE/Cedar Creek Campground▲ S: Laundromat
(228)	**Weigh Station (WB)**
229A	**Beckwith Rd S (EB)**
229B	**Beckwith Rd N (EB)**
229	**Beckwith Rd (WB)**
232A	**TN 109S, Lebanon, to Gallatin (EB)**
232B	**TN 109N, Lebanon, to Gallatin (EB)**
232	**TN 109, Lebanon, to Gallatin (WB)**
Gas	N: Citgo, Mapco Express, Shell◈
Food	N: McDonald's, Subway, Waffle House S: Wendy's
Lodg	N: Best Western, Sleep Inn, HOTEL
Other	S: Countryside Resort RV Park▲
235	**TN 840, to Chattanooga, Murfreesbo**
236	**Hartmann Dr**
Gas	N: Mapco Mart, Shell
Food	N: Chili's, Outback Steakhouse
Med	N: + University Medical Center
Other	N: Home Depot, Lebanon Muni Airport✈
238	**US 231, Lebanon, Murfreesboro**
FStop	S: Scot Market #87/Citgo, Horizon Travel Plaza
TStop	S: Pilot Travel Center #411(Scales) (DAND)
Gas	N: BP, Exxon, Mapco Express, Shell◈
Food	N: Arby's, Cracker Barrel, Gondola Rest, Hardee's, Jack in the Box, McDonald's, Ponderosa, Waffle House, Wendy's S: FastFood/Scot Mkt, ChestersGr/ McDonald's/Subway/Pilot TC, O'Charley's, Santa Fe Cattle Co, Sonic
Lodg	N: Best Value Inn, Comfort Inn, Executive Inn, Hampton Inn, Holiday Inn Express S: Country Inn, Comfort Suites, Days Inn, Knights Inn, Super 8
Med	N: + Hospital
Other	N: Walmart sc, to Cumberland Univ S: Prime Outlets of Lebanon, Carwash, Laundry/WiFi/RVDump/Pilot TC, Cedars of Lebanon State Park▲, Shady Acres Campground▲, Timberline Campground▲, Family Campers▲, Bledsoe Creek State Park▲, RV Center
239A	**US 70E, Watertown (EB)**
TStop	S: Uncle Pete's Truck Stop/66 (Scales)
Food	S: Rest/FastFood/Uncle Pete's TS, Jalisco Mexican Rest
TServ	N: G&R Auto & Truck Repair S: Uncle Pete's TS/Tires
TWash	S: I-40 Repair & TW
Other	S: Laundry/WiFi/Uncle Pete's TS
239B	**US 70W, Lebanon, Smithville (EB)**
Gas	N: Citgo, RaceWay
Other	N: Auto Repairs
239	**US 70, Lebanon, Watertown**
245	**Linwood Rd**
Gas	N: BP◈

◈= Regular Gas Stations with Diesel ▲ = RV Friendly Locations ♥= Pet Friendly Locations
Red print shows large vehicle parking / access on site or nearby Brown Print = Campgrounds / RV PARKS

EXIT — TENNESSEE

287 TN 136, Cookeville, Sparta
- FStop S: Minit Mart #2293/Marathon
- TStop S: Pilot Travel Center #265 (Scales)
- Gas N: BP, Chevron◈, Exxon, Citgo, Shell◈
- Food N: Applebee's, Arby's, Burger King, Captain D's, ChickFilA, Chili's,
- Food N: Cracker Barrel, DQ, Golden Corral, IHOP, Jack In the Box, Long John Silver's, Logan's Roadhouse, McDonald's, Pizza Hut, Ponderosa, Outback Steakhouse, Red Lobster, Ruby Tuesday, Ryan's Grill, Shoney's, Steak 'n Shake, Starbucks, Subway, Waffle House, Wendy's
  S: FastFood/MinitMart, Blimpie/Pilot TC, Gondola Pizza, KFC
- Lodg N: Best Value Inn, Best Western♥, Clarion Inn, Comfort Inn, Days Inn, Garden Hotel, Hampton Inn, Ramada, Super 8
  S: Baymont Inn, Comfort Inn, Country Hearth, Country Inn, Econo Lodge
- TServ N: Walker Diesel Service
  S: Cumberland Tire & Truck
- Other N: Auto Services, CVS, Firestone, Harley Davidson, Kmart, Kroger, Lowe's, Mall, Sam's Club, Tires, **Walmart**, **TN Hwy Patrol Post**,
  S: WiFi/Pilot TC, Carmike 10 Cinema

(252) Parking Area (Both dir)

254 TN 141, to Alexandria

258 TN 53, Carthage, Gordonsville
- Gas N: BP, Exxon, Shell
  S: Citgo◈
- Food N: KFC/Taco Bell/Exxon, Connie's BBQ, McDonald's, Waffle House
- Lodg N: Comfort Inn

(267) Rest Area (Both dir)
(RR, Phones, Vend, Info)

268 TN 96, Buffalo Valley Rd, Center Hill Dam
- Other **S: to Edgar Evans State Park▲**

273 TN 56S, Smithville, McMinnville
- Gas S: BP◈, Phillips 66
- Food S: Rose Garden Restaurant
- Lodg S: Timber Ridge Inn

276 Old Baxter Rd
- Gas: N: Fuel Center
  S: Citgo◈
- Other N: Auto Service
  S: Jet Ski & Canoe Rental

280 TN 56N, Baxter, Gainesboro
- TStop N: Love's Travel Stop #330 (Scales)
- Gas N: Shell◈
- Food N: Subway/McDonald's/Love's TS
- Other N: WiFi/RVDump/Love's TS, **Twin Lakes RV Park & Catfish Farm▲**, TN Jaycee's Camp Discovery

286 TN 135, Burgess Falls Rd, S Willow Ave, Cookeville
- Gas N: BP, Exxon, RaceWay◈, Shell◈
  S: BP◈, Citgo◈
- Food N: Applebee's, Hardee's, Waffle House
  S: Rest/Star Motor Inn
- Lodg N: Key West Inn
  S: Star Motor Inn♥
- Med N: + Hospital
- Other N: Auto Dealer, Grocery, **Middle TN RV Center**

Personal Notes

EXIT — TENNESSEE

- Other S: Auto Repairs, American Car & **RV** Wash, **Burgess Falls State Park**

288 TN 111, Livingston, Sparta
- TStop S: Middle TN Auto/Truck Plaza/66 (Scales)
- Gas S: Citgo◈
- Food S: Subway/Mid TN ATP, Huddle House,
- Lodg S: Knights Inn
- Tires S: I-40 Truck Tire & Repair
- TWash S: Middle TN ATP
- TServ S: Middle TN ATP/Tires, Don's Truck Servic King's Truck Repair
- Other S: Laundry/RVDump/LP/Mid TN ATP

290 US 70N, Cookeville
- Gas N: BP
  S: Citgo
- Food S: Restaurant
- Lodg S: Alpine Lodge & Suites
- Other N: Outdoor Junction

300 US 70N, TN 84, Monterey, Livingston
- FStop N: The Convenience Mart/Citgo
- Food N: FastFood/Conv Mart, Cup N' Saucer Rest, Hardee's, Subway
- Lodg S: Garden Inn

EXIT — TENNESSEE

301 US 70N, TN 84, Monterey, Jamestown
- Gas N: Phillips 66, Shell
- Food N: Burger King, Subway
- Other N: Highland Manor Winery

(307) Parking Area (WB)

311 Plateau Rd
- Gas N: Citgo◈
  S: BP◈, Exxon
- Other N: Truck Sales & Parts

317 US 127, Crossville, Jamestown
- Gas N: BP◈, Chevron, Citgo, Exxon◈, Shell◈, Horizon Travel Plaza (NO TRUCKS)
  S: Citgo, Phillips 66, Murphy
- Food N: Huddle House, Rest/Ramada
  S: Cracker Barrel, Ponderosa, Ruby Tuesday, Ryan's Grill, Shoney's, Waffle House, Wendy's
- Lodg N: Best Value Inn, Best Western, La Quinta Inn♥, Ramada
  S: Days Inn, Heritage Inn, Scottish Inn
- Med S: + Hospital
- Other N: Auto Services, CAT, Flea Market, Wrecker Service
  S: Auto Dealers, Goodyear, Lowe's, Staples, Walgreen's, **Walmart sc**, **Cumberland Mountain Retreat Campground▲**,
- Other **S: to Ballyhoo Family Campground▲, Geronimo Campground▲, Lake Tansi RV Park▲, Cumberland Mountain State Park▲**

320 TN 298, Genesis Rd, Crossville
- TStop N: Pilot Travel Center #114 (Scales)
  S: Plateau Travel Plaza/BP (Scales)
- Gas S: Shell
- Food N: Wendy's/Pilot TC
  S: FastFood/Plateau TP, Catfish Cove, Krystal, Wendy's
- TServ S: Universal Tire
- Med S: + Hospital
- Other N: Laundry/WiFi/Pilot TC, Stonehaus Winery
  S: VT Outlet Mall

322 TN 101, Peavine Rd, Crossville
- Gas N: BP, Exxon, Phillips 66
  S: Texaco
- Food N: Bean Pot/BP, Hardee's, McDonald's
- Lodg N: Holiday Inn Express
  S: Comfort Suites, Fairfield Glade Resort, Super 8
- Med S: + Hospital
- Other **N: Bean Pot Campground▲, Ballyhoo RV Resort▲, to appr 4 mi: Spring Lake RV Resort▲, Deer Run RV Resort▲**
  S: Crossville/I-40 KOA▲, Lake's Rocky Top Retreat▲, TN Outdoors RV Center Sales & Service, Chestnut Hill Winery

(324) Cumberland Rest Area (EB)
(RR, Phones, Picnic, Vend)

(327) Cumberland Rest Area (WB)
(RR, Phones, Picnic, Vend)

329 US 70, Crab Orchard
- FStop N: Crab Orchard/BP
- Gas N: Exxon
- Other **N: to Crossville KOA▲**

(336) Parking Area (EB)

◈= Regular Gas Stations with Diesel ▲ = RV Friendly Locations ♥= Pet Friendly Locations
Red print shows large vehicle parking / access on site or nearby Brown Print = Campgrounds / RV PARKS

EXIT		TENNESSEE
338		**TN 299S, Westel Rd, Rockwood**
	FStop	S: Shell◈
	Gas	N: BP◈
	NOTE:	MM 340: Eastern / Central Time Zone
340		**TN 299N, Airport Rd**
	NOTE:	MM #341: EB: 4% Steep Grade 2mi
347		**US 27, Harriman, Rockwood**
	Gas	N: Phillips 66◈
		S: BP, Exxon, Shell◈
	Food:	N: Hardee's, KFC, Long John Silver, McDonalds, Pizza Hut, Taco Bell, Wendy's, Subway/Phillips 66
	Food	S: Captain D's, Cracker Barrel, Krystal/ Shell, Mexican Rest, Shoney's, Subway
	Lodg	N: Best Western♥
		S: Holiday Inn Express, Quality Inn, Super 8♥
	Med	N: + Hospital
	Other	N: Budget RAC, C & D Tire, Grocery, Hensley Tire, to Frozen Head State Park
		S: Advance Auto, Grocery, Kroger, to Appr 5mi: Walmart sc
	NOTE:	MM #350: EB: 7% Steep Grade
350		**US 70, TN 29, Pine Ridge Rd, Harriman, Midtown**
	Lodg	S: Midtown Motel
		S: Midtown Discount Tire, Lowe's, Kroger, to Caney Creek RV Resort & Marina▲
352		**TN 58S, Kingston**
	Gas	S: Exxon, RaceWay, Shell
	Food	N: Howard Johnson
		S: DQ, Hardee's, Jed's Family Steak House, McDonald's, Subway
	Lodg	N: Knights Inn
		S: Comfort Inn
	Other	N: Food Lion, NAPA
		S: to Watts Bar Lake, Four Seasons Campground▲, Watts Bar Lake Campground▲
355		**Lawnville Rd, Kingston**
	TStop	N: Pilot Travel Center #132
	Gas	N: Shell
	Food	N: FastFood/Pilot TC
	Other	N: WiFi/Pilot TC
		S: Heritage Propane/LP
356B		**TN 326, Gallaher Rd, Oak Ridge (WB)**
356A		**TN 58N, Gallaher Rd, Oak Ridge**
356		**TN 58, Gallaher Rd, to Oak Ridge**
	Gas	N: BP, Weigel's◈
		S: Citgo
	Food	N: Huddle House, Rest/Family Inns
	Lodg	N: DoubleTree Inn, Family Inn, Kings Inn
		S: Days Inn♥
	Other	N: Four Seasons Campground▲
360		**Buttermilk Rd, Lenoir City**
	Other	N: Southeast RV Center, Soaring Eagle Campground & RV Park▲
364		**Industrial Park Rd**
(363)		**Parking Area (Both dir)**
364		**US 321, TN 95, to Oak Ridge**
	Gas	N: Shell
	Food	N: Outback Steakhouse
	Lodg	N: Staybridge Suites
	Other	N: to TVA/Melton Hill Dam▲
		S: to Crosseyed Cricket Campground▲

EXIT		TENNESSEE
	NOTE:	I-40 & I-75 below run together for 18 mi, Exit #'s follow I-40.
(368)		**Jct I-75S, to Chattanooga**
369		**Watt Rd, W Knoxville**
	TStop	N: Flying J Travel Plaza #5034/Conoco
		S: Petro Stopping Center #12/Mobil (Scales), Travel Center of America #107/ BP (Scales)
	Food	N: Rest/FastFood/FJ TP
		S: IronSkillet/Petro SC, Perkins/BKing/ PizzaHut/TA TC
	TWash	S: Blue Beacon TW/Petro SC
		N: Fast Point Truck Wash
	TServ	N: Freightliner of Knoxville, Speedco
		S: Petro SC/Tires, TA TC /Tires, Knoxville Truck Sales
	Other	N: Laundry/WiFi/RVDump/LP/FJ TP, Shadrack Watersport & RV's
		S: Laundry/WiFi/RVDump/Petro SC, Laundry/CB/WiFi/TA TC
(372)		**Weigh Station (Both dir)**
373		**Campbell Station Rd, Farragut**
	FStop	S: Pilot Food Mart #221
	Gas	N: Amoco, Marathon, Shell
		S: BP, Conoco, Wiegel's
	Food	S: Cracker Barrel, Hardee's, Wendy's
	Lodg	N: Comfort Suites, Country Inn, Super 8
		S: Baymont Inn, Holiday Inn Express
	Other	N: Buddy Gregg Motorhomes
		S: Gander Mountain
374		**TN 131, Lovell Rd, Knoxville**
	TStop	N: Travel Center of America #13/BP (Scales)
		S: Pilot Travel Center #270 (Scales)
	Gas	N: Texaco
		S: Citgo, Pilot Food Mart, Speedway
	Food	N: CountryPride/FastFood/TA TC, McDonald's, Bojangles, Taco Bell, Waffle House
		S: Wendy's/Pilot TC, Arby's, Chili's, Krystal, Olive Garden, Shoney's, Tx Roadhouse, Wasabi Japanese, Rest/Days Inn
	Lodg	N: Best Western, Knights Inn, La Quinta Inn♥, Travelodge/TA TC, Vista Inn
		S: Comfort Inn, Days Inn, Homewood Suites, Motel 6♥, Red Roof Inn
	TServ	N: TA TC/Tires
	Other	N: Laundry/CB/BarbSh/WiFi/TA TC, Harley Davidson, Buddy Gregg MH
		S: WiFi/Pilot TC, Auto Dealers, ATMs, Banks, Best Buy, Lowes, Staples, Super Target, Walmart sc
376		**TN 162S, Maryville (EB)**
376A		**TN 162N, to Oakridge (WB)**
376B		**TN 162S, Maryville (EB)**
378AB		**Cedar Bluff Rd, Knoxville (WB)**
378		**Cedar Bluff Rd, Knoxville**
	Gas	N: Amoco, Pilot Travel Center, Texaco
		S: Exxon
	Food	N: Arby's, Burger King, Cracker Barrel, KFC, Long John Silver, McDonald's, Pizza Hut, Waffle House, Wendy's
		S: Applebee's, Bob Evans, Carraba's, Corky's Ribs & BBQ, Denny's, Fazoli's, Famous Dave's BBQ, Hops, IHOP, Outback Steakhouse
	Lodg	N: Econo Lodge, Hampton Inn, Holiday Inn, Ramada

EXIT		TENNESSEE
		S: Best Western, Courtyard, Comfort Inn, Extended Stay America, Jameson Inn, La Quinta Inn♥, Red Roof Inn♥, Sleep Inn
	Med	N: + Hospital
	Other	N: ATMs, Banks, Food Lion, Walgreen's
		S: ATMs, Banks, Auto Services, Best Buy, Carmike Cinema, Celebration Station, Lowe's, Staples, Walgreen's
379A		**Walker Springs Rd, Gallaher View,**
379		**Walker Springs Rd, Gallaher View, Bridgewater Rd (EB)**
	Gas	N: Exxon, Pilot Food Mart, Shell
		S: BP, Pilot, Texaco
	Food	N: McDonald's
		S: Bennett's Pit BBQ, Burger King, Chuck E Cheese's Pizza, Don Pablo, Logan's, Old Country Buffet, Ryan's Grill, Shoney's
	Lodg	N: Red Carpet Inn
		S: Holiday Inn, Scottish Inn
	Other	N: Sam's Club, Walmart sc
		S: Auto Zone, Auto Services, Goodyear, Pharmacy
380		**US 11, US 70, West Hills**
	Gas	S: BP, Citgo, Conoco, Pilot Food Mart, Shell, Weigel's
	Food	S: Arby's, Applebee's, BlackEyed Pea, Chili's, KFC, Krystal, Little Caesar's Pizza, Olive Garden, Texas Roadhouse
	Lodg	S: Howard Johnson, Quality Inn, Super 8
	Other	S: Food Lion, Kmart, Office Depot, U-Haul, Walgreen's, West Town Mall, TN State Hwy Patrol Post
383		**Papermill Dr, Knoxville**
	Gas	S: Amoco, BP, Citgo, Pilot Food Mart
	Food	S: Bombay Bicycle Club, Burger King, Captain D's, IHOP, McDonald's, Pizza Hut, Waffle House, Western Sizzlin'
	Lodg	N: Budget Inn, Holiday Inn
		S: Econo Lodge, Super 8
(385)		**Jct I-75N, Jct I-640E, to Lexington**
	NOTE:	I-40 & I-75 above run together for 18 mi. Exit #'s follow I-40.
386A		**University Ave, Middlebrook Pike, Henley St, Downtown, Conv Center**
386B		**US 129, Alcoa Hwy, Airport, Great Smoky Mountains, Univ of TN**
387		**TN 62, 17th St, 21st St, Western Ave**
	Med	S: + Children's Hospital
(387A)		**Jct I-275N, to Lexington**
388		**to US 441S, James White Pkwy, Univ of TN, Downtown (EB)**
388A		**James White Pkwy**
389		**Hall of Fame Dr**
389AB		**US 441N, Broadway, 5th Ave**
	Gas	N: BP, Conoco
	Food	N: Burger King, KFC, Krystal
	Other	N: CVS, Firestone, Kroger, Walgreen's
390		**Cherry St**
	FStop	N: Favorite Market #409/Shell
	Gas	N: Marathon, Pilot Food Mart, Weigel's
		S: Amoco, Exxon
	Food	N: Hardee's, Subway/Weigel's
		S: Arby's, KFC, Krystal, Wendy's
	Lodg	N: Red Carpet Inn
		S: Regency Inn

◈= Regular Gas Stations with Diesel ▲ = RV Friendly Locations ♥= Pet Friendly Locations
Red print shows large vehicle parking / access on site or nearby Brown Print = Campgrounds / RV PARKS

EXIT	TENNESSEE
TServ	N: Pemberton Truck Service, Truck Shop
Med	S: + Baptist Health System
Other	S: Advance Auto Parts, Auto Zone, Walgreen's
392AB	**US 11, Rutledge Pike**
392	**US 11W, Rutledge Pike**
Gas	S: Shell◈, BP
Food	S: Hardee's, Shoney's
Lodg	S: Family Inn
TServ	N: Cummins, International, Kenworth of Knoxville
Other	N: U-Haul S: Food City, Kroger, Laundromat,
(393)	**Jct I-640W, Knoxville ByPass, to I-75N, to Lexington**
394	**US 11E, US 25W, US 70, Asheville Hwy**
Gas	N: BP, Mobil◈, RaceWay S: Exxon, Shell◈
Food	N: Subway, Wendy's S: Waffle House
Lodg	N: Best Value Inn, Gateway Inn S: Days Inn
Other	N: Food Lion, Kmart S: CVS, Kroger, Walgreen's
398	**Strawberry Plains Pike**
FStop	N: Aztex BP S: Pilot Travel Center #219 (Scales)
TStop	N: Kwik Fuel Center/Exxon
Gas	N: Shell S: Citgo, Weigel's
Food	N: FastFood/Kwik FC, McDonald's, Outback Steakhouse, Ruby Tuesday, Waffle House, Wendy's S: Subway/Pilot TC, Arby's, Burger King, Cracker Barrel, Krystal, Puleo's Grill
Lodg	N: Baymont Inn, Country Inn, Courtyard, Comfort Suites, Econo Lodge, Hampton Inn, Quality Inn, Ramada Ltd, Super 8 S: Best Western, Fairfield Inn, La Quinta Inn♥, Motel 6, Quality Inn
Other	N: TN RV Sales & Service/Camping World S: WiFi/Pilot TC
402	**Midway Rd**
Other	N: River Island Golf Club
407	**TN 66, Kodak, to Sevierville, Pigeon Forge, Gatlinburg**
Gas	N: Citgo S: BP, Exxon, Shell
Food	N: Cracker Barrel, Huddle House/Citgo, McDonald's, Chop House, Rest/Bass Pro Shop S: Subway/Exxon, Wendy's
Lodg	N: Econo Lodge, Motel 6♥ S: Best Western♥, Comfort Suites, Days Inn, Holiday Inn Express, Quality Inn, Ramada Inn
Other	N: Bass Pro Shop, Smokie's Baseball Stadium S: Auto Dealers, Fireworks Supermarket, 407 Great Smokey Flea Market, **to** Sevierville/PigeonForge/Gatlinburg attractions, gas, food, lodging, **camping**, malls, restaurants, shopping, **Great Smoky Mountains National Park▲**
412	**Deep Springs Rd, Douglas Dam Dandridge**
TStop	N: Love's Travel Stop #306 (Scales) S: TR Truck/Auto Plaza/Chevron (Scales)
Food	N: Subway/Chesters/Love's TS, Apple Valley Cafe S: Rest/TR TAP
TServ	S: TR TAP/Tires
Other	N: WiFi/**RVDump**/Love's TS S: Laundry/**RVDump**/TR TAP
415	**US 25W, US 70, to Dandridge**
FStop	S: Shell
417	**TN 92, Dandridge, to Jefferson City**
TStop	N: Pilot Travel Center #226 (Scales)
Gas	N: BP S: Shell, Wiegel's
Food	N: Subway/Pilot TC, Captain's Galley, Hardee's, McDonald's, Perkins, Ruby Tuesday S: KFC, Shoney's, Waffle House
Lodg	N: Econo Lodge S: Hampton Inn, Holiday Inn Express♥, Jefferson Inn♥, Quality Inn♥, Super 8, **To appr 2 mi:** The Point Resort, Marina & **Dandridge Point RV Resort on the Lake▲**
TWash	N: Pilot TC
TServ	N: Pilot TC/Tires
Other	N: Laundry/WiFi/Pilot TC S: Advance Auto Parts, Food City, Vet♥,
(420)	**Jefferson Co Rest Area (EB)** **(RR, Phones, Picnic, Vend)**
(421)	**Jct I-81N, to Bristol (EB, LEFT Exit)**
424	**TN 113, Dandridge, White Pine**
FStop	N: FastTrax/BP
Food	N: Grill/BP
Other	S: **Jack Benny RV Resort & Campground▲**, **Lake Cove Resort▲**
(426)	**Jefferson Co Rest Area (WB)** **(RR, Phones, Picnic, Vend)**
432A	**US 411, to Sevierville**
Gas	S: BP, Shell, Texaco
Food	S: Rest/Family Inn
Lodg	S: Family Inn
432B	**US 25W, US 70, Newport, to Cosby (EB, LEFT Exit)**
TStop	N: PTP/Time Out Travel Center (Scales)
Gas	N: Exxon
Food	N: Huddle House/TimeOut TC, Lois's Family Rest, Grill/Exxon
Lodg	N: Relax Inn, Comfort Inn
TServ	N: Commercial Truck Center
Other	N: Laundry/TimeOut TC, Auto Dealers, Bowling, Laundromat/Carwash, Newport Tire, **TMC Campground▲**, **I-40/Newport /Smoky Mountain KOA▲**
435	**US 321, TN 32, Cosby Hwy, Newport to Gatlinburg, Cosby**
Gas	N: Exxon, Shell S: BP, Murphy
Food	N: Arby's, Burger King, Hardee's, KFC, La Carreta Mexi, McDonald's, Sagebrush, Shoney's, Subway, Taco Bell S: Bojangles, Buddy's BBQ, **Cracker Barrel**, Papa John's Pizza, Ryan's Grill, Ruby Tuesday, Waffle House, Wendy's,
Lodg	N: Motel 6♥ S: Best Western, Days Inn♥, Family Inn, Holiday InnExpress, Mountain Crest Inn♥, **Appr 4 mi:** Christopher Resort B&B
Med	N: + Hospital
Other	N: Advance Auto Parts, CVS, Cinema 4, Mustard Seed Health Store, O'Reilly Auto Parts, US Post Office S: Dollar Tree, Lowe's▲, SavALot, **Walmart sc▲**
440	**US 321S, TN 73, Wilton Springs Rd to Gatlinburg, Cosby**
TStop	N: Mtn View Truck Stop/Sunoco
Gas	S: BP
Food	N: Rest/MV TS
Lodg	N: Mountain View Motel
TServ	N: Mountain View Truck Service
Other	S: **to Adventure Bound Camping Resort/ Gatlinburg▲**, **Arrow Creek Campground▲**, **Jellystone Campground▲**
443	**Foothills Pkwy, Great Smoky Mtns Nat'l Park, Gatlinburg** **(NO COMMERCIAL VEHICLES)**
(446)	**TN Welcome Center (WB)** **(RR, Phones, Info) (NO Trucks)**
447	**Hartford Rd**
Gas	N: Downtown Hartford Citgo S: BP
Food	N: FastFood/DH Citgo, Pigeon River Smokehouse/BP,

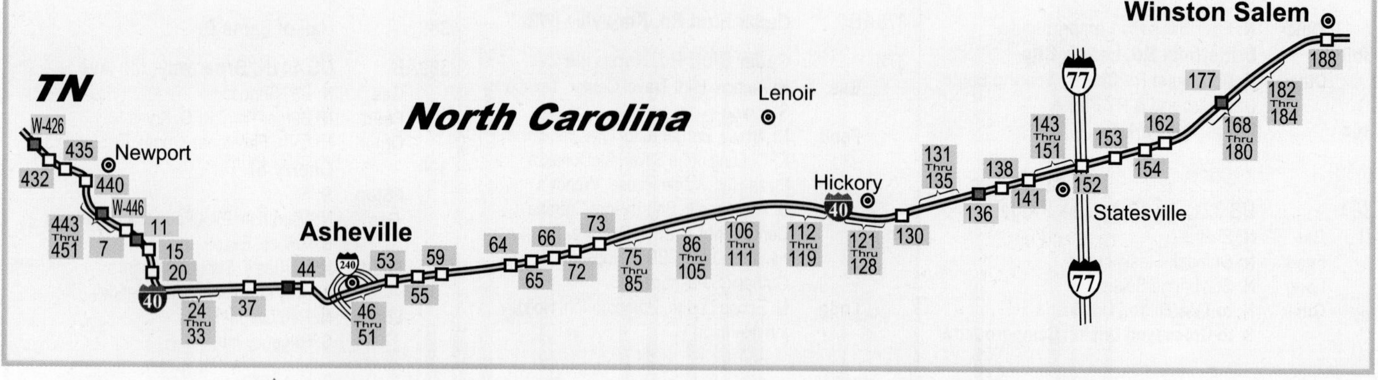

◈= Regular Gas Stations with Diesel ▲ = RV Friendly Locations ♥= Pet Friendly Locations
Red print shows large vehicle parking / access on site or nearby **Brown Print = Campgrounds / RV PARKS**

EXIT — TN / NC

Food — S: Shauan's Ice Cream & Coffee Shop, Beantree
Other — S: **Shauan's RV Park▲**, Whitewater Rafting Companies

451 — Waterville Rd

NOTE: MM 455: North Carolina State Line

EASTERN TIME ZONE

TENNESSEE
NORTH CAROLINA

EASTERN TIME ZONE

(4) — Tunnel (Both dir)

7 — Harmon Den Rd

(8) — Tunnel (Both dir)

(11) — NC Welcome Center (WB)
Rest Area (EB)
(RR, Phones, Picnic, Pet, Vend)

15 — Fines Creek

20 — US 276, Jonathan Creek Rd, Waynesville, to Maggie Valley
Gas — S: BP◊, Exxon◊
Food — S: J Creek Cafe
Lodg — S: Wynne's Creekside B&B
Other — S: to W Carolina Univ, Santa's Land, **Great Smoky Mtn Nat'l Park, Creekwood Farm RV Park▲, Pride RV Resort▲, Winngray Family Campground▲, Stone Bridge Campground▲**

24 — NC 209, Crabtree Rd, Waynesville, to Lake Junaluska, Hot Springs
TStop — N: Pilot Travel Center #393 (Scales)
S: Sam's Mart#45
Food — N: Subway/Pilot TC
S: Rest/Sam's, Haywood Café
Lodg — N: Midway Motel
TServ — N: Pilot TC/Tires
Other — N: WiFi/Pilot TC
S: Laundry/Sam's

27 — to US 19, US 23, US 74W, Clyde, Waynesville, (WB: Truck US 64W)
Gas — S: Shell
Food — S: Burger King/Shell, Shoney's, Subway, Taco Bell
Med — S: + Hospital
Other — S: Food Lion, Lowe's, to W NC State Univ

31 — NC 215, Champion Dr, Canton
FStop — S: Sandy's Auto/Truck Plaza/BP
Gas — S: Chevron, Exxon, Shell
Food — N: Sagebrush Steakhouse
S: Arby's/Shell, Burger King, McDonald's/Exxon, Subway, Taco Bell, Waffle House
Lodg — N: Econo Lodge
S: Comfort Inn
TServ — S: Cummins, Western Star
Other — S: Auto Dealer, Grocery

33 — Newfound Rd, to US 74
Other — N: **Mt Pisgah Campgrounds▲**

37 — East Canton (WB), Candler (EB)
TStop — N: Travel Center of America #221/Citgo (Scales)
Gas — N: AmocoBP
S: Exxon◊, Time Out

EXIT — NORTH CAROLINA

Food — N: Buckhorn/TA TC
Lodg — N: Quality Inn
S: Days Inn, Owl's Nest Inn
TServ — N: TA TC/Tires
S: Apollo Truck & Diesel Repair
Other — N: Laundry/WiFi/TA TC,
S: **Asheville West KOA▲, Laurel Bank Campground▲, Blue Ridge Motorcycle Campground▲, Riverside Camp ground▲, to appr 5 mi: Riverhouse Acres Campground▲**

(41) — Weigh Station (Both dir)

44 — US 74, W Asheville, US 19, US 23, Enka, Candler, W Ashville
FStop — N: Servco
Gas — N: BP, Chevron, Conoco, Exxon, Shell
S: Shell, Hess
Food — N: Burger King, Cracker Barrel, Pizza Hut, Hardee's, Krystal, Po Folks, Chinese, Waffle House, Wendy's
S: McDonald's, Shoney's, Subway
Lodg — N: Comfort Inn, Holiday Inn, Sleep Inn, Super 8
S: Ramada Inn
TServ — N: Freightliner
Med — N: + Reach Hospital
Other — N: Auto Services, CVS, Grocery, Lowe's
S: Food Lion, Home Depot, Pharmacy, Biltmore Square 6 Cinemas, **Mountain Retreat RV Park▲**

(46A) — Jct I-26E, US 74E, Truck US 64E, Hendersonville, Spartanburg (EB) **Asheville Airport** (EB: Truck US 64E)

(46B) — Jct I-26W, I-240, Asheville
(EB, Left Exit) (EB exit, WB entr)

47 — Brevard Rd, NC 191, W Asheville Farmers Market
Gas — S: Phillips 66◊
Food — S: Moose Café, Subway
Lodg — S: Comfort Inn, Hampton Inn, Super 8
TServ — S: Carolina Engine
Other — N: Asheville Speedway, Farmers Market, **Bear Creek RV Park▲**
S: to Biltmore Square

50B — US 25N, Asheville (WB)
Other — N: Biltmore Estate, Biltmore Village

50A — US 25S (WB)

50 — US 25, to NC 81, Hendersonville Rd, S Asheville (EB)
Gas — N: BP, Exxon◊, Shell◊
S: Hess, Phillips 66◊, Servco
Food — N: Arby's, Biltmore Dairy Bar & Grill, Hardee's, Long John Silver, McDonald's, Pizza Hut, Tx Roadhouse, TGI Friday
S: Apollo Flame Pizza, Atlanta Bread, Huddle House, Quincy's
Lodg — N: Baymont Inn, Doubletree Suites, Holiday Inn Express, Howard Johnson, Sleep Inn
S: Asheville Oaks Inn, Forest Manor Lodge, Holiday Inn Express
TServ — N: Baldwin Truck Service
Med — N: + Mission Memorial Hospital
Other — N: ATMs, Banks, Auto Services, Tires, Biltmore Estate, Biltmore Village
S: Auto Services, Towing

51 — US 25 Alt, Asheville
Other — N: to Biltmore Estate

EXIT — NORTH CAROLINA

53A — US 74E Alt , Blue Ridge Pkwy
Gas — S: BP, Phillips 66

(53B) — Jct I-240, US 74A, Asheville
(Addt'l services 2-3 miles North)
Gas — N: BP, Exxon
Food — N: Burger King, IHOP, Little Caesar's Pizza Olive Garden, Subway, Waffle House
Lodg — N: Comfort Inn, Days Inn, Econo Lodge
TServ — N: A Plus Truck Parts & Service
Other — N: Auto Services, Grocery

55 — to US 70, E Asheville, Black Mtn Hwy, Tunnel Rd
Gas — N: BP, Citgo, Conoco, Mobil
Food — N: Arby's, Hardee's, Waffle House
Lodg — N: Best Inn, Days Inn, Econo Lodge, Holiday Inn, Motel 6♥, Travelodge
Med — N: + VA Hospital
Other — N: **Mt Mitchell State Park▲, Topp's RV Park▲**, Grocery

59 — Swannanoa, to US 70
TStop — N: Lee's Exxon
Gas — N: BP, Servco, Shell◊
Food — N: Rest/Lee's Exxon, Burger King, Firehouse Grill, Subway/BP
Med — N: + St Joseph's Urgent Care
Other — N: Laundry/Lee's Exxon, **Asheville East KOA▲**, Warren Wilson College, **Miles RV Center & Campground▲**
S: **Mama Gertie's Hideaway Campground▲**

64 — NC 9, Black Mountain, Montreat Broadway St, Blue Ridge Rd
Gas — N: Exxon, Shell
S: BP◊, Phillips 66
Food — N: Pizza Hut, Subway/Shell
S: Arby's, Black Mountain BBQ, Camp Fire Steak & Buffet, Denny's, Huddle House, KFC, McDonald's, Taco Bell
Lodg — N: Super 8
S: Comfort Inn
Other — N: Grocery
S: Ingles Grocery, Pharmacy

65 — US 70W, Black Mountain
(WB exit, EB entr)

66 — Ridgecrest

(67.5) — TRUCK Info Center (EB)
(Trucks MUST Exit)

(70) — Truck RunAway Ramp (EB)

(70.5) — Truck RunAway Ramp (EB)

(70.8) — Truck RunAway Ramp (EB)

72 — US 70E, Old Fort (EB exit, WB entr)
Other — N: **to Tom Johnson Camping Center, to Mountain Stream RV Park▲, to Riverbreeze Campground▲**

73 — Old Fort
Gas — N: BP◊
S: Exxon◊
Food — N: Hardee's
S: McDonald's
Other — N: Auto & Tire Service
S: **to Catawba Falls Campground▲**

75 — Parker Padgett Rd, Old Fort
FStop — S: Stuckey's/Exxon
Food — S: DQ/Stuckey's/Exxon

81 — Sugar Hill Rd, Marion
TStop — S: Marion Travel Plaza/Exxon (Scales) (DAND)

◊= Regular Gas Stations with Diesel ▲ = RV Friendly Locations ♥= Pet Friendly Locations
Red print shows large vehicle parking / access on site or nearby Brown Print = Campgrounds / RV PARKS

EXIT — NORTH CAROLINA

Gas N: BP◈
Food N: Sugar Hill Rest
S: Rest/Marion TP
Med N: + McDowell Hospital

(82) **Rest Area (Both dir)**
(RR, Phones, Picnic, Pet, Vend)

83 **Ashworth Rd**

85 **US 221, N Main St, Marion, to Rutherfordton**
FStop S: Dollar Mart #10/Shell
Food S: Sagebrush Steakhouse
Lodg N: Hampton Inn
S: Days Inn
Other N: to Mountain Stream RV Park▲

86 **NC 226, Marion, Shelby**
TStop S: Love's Travel Stop #308 (Scales)
Gas N: Exxon◈
Food N: Godfather's Pizza, Hardee's, KFC
S: Chesters/Subway/Love's TC
Other N: to appr 6.5 mi: Riverbreeze Campground▲, Bear Den Campground▲, to Tom Johnson Camping Center
S: WiFi/Love's TS, NC Hwy Patrol Post, to Yogi Bears Jellystone Camp Resort▲

90 **Nebo, Lake James**
FStop S: Travel Store/AmocoBP
TStop N: Nebo Truck Stop/Exxon
Food N: Rest/Nebo TS
Other N: to Lake James State Park
S: Springs Creek RV Center

94 **Dysartsville Rd, Lake James**

96 **Kathy Rd**

98 **Causby Rd, Glen Alpine**

100 **Jamestown Rd, Morganton, Glen Alpine**
Gas N: BP◈
Food N: Waffle Shop
Lodg N: Eagle Motel
Other N: Auto Services, Auto Dealer

103 **US 64, Morganton, Rutherfordton**
Gas N: Exxon◈, Shell
S: Carswell, Marathon, RaceWay
Food N: Allison's Family Rest, Village Inn Pizza
S: Butch's BBQ, Checkers, Denny's, Hardee's, KFC, Mexican Rest, Subway, Taco Bell, Tokyo Diner Japanese Rest,
Lodg N: Super 8
S: Comfort Suites
TServ S: Dale's Truck Repair
Other N: ATMs, Auto Services, Enterprise RAC, Carwash/Exxon, Food Lion, Tires, Western Piedmont Comm College
S: ATMs, Dollar General, Food Lion, Grocery, Goodyear, Lowe's, Radio Shack, Tires, Walmart

104 **Enola Rd, Morganton**
Gas S: Citgo
Food S: ChickFilA
Med N: + to Broughton Hospital
Other S: ATMs, Big Lots, Food Lion, Grocery, Staples, NC State Hwy Patrol Post

105 **NC 18, Morganton, Shelby**
Gas N: BP, Chevron, Wilco◈
S: Shell◈, Texaco
Food N: Abele's Family Rest, Arby's, Captain D's Coffee House, Harbor Inn Seafood, McDonald's, Peking Express, Pizza Inn, Shoney's, Sonic, Wendy's, Zaxby's, Zeko's Village Rest

Personal Notes

EXIT — NORTH CAROLINA

Food S: El Paso Mexican Rest, Sagebrush Steak House, Waffle House
Lodg N: Hampton Inn, Red Carpet Inn
S: Plaza Inn, Quality Inn, Sleep Inn
Med N: + Grace Hospital, to + Broughton Hospital
Other N: ATMs, Auto Dealer, Joe's Tire Service, Pharmacy

106 **Bethel Rd, Morganton**
FStop S: Exxon
Lodg S: Economy Inn

107 **NC 114, Drexel Rd, Valdese**
Other S: Small Engine Repair

111 **Valdese, Millstone Ave, Abees Grove Church Rd (Serv N to US 70)**

112 **NC 1744, Mineral Springs Mtn Rd, Valdese (Serv N to US 70)**

113 **Malcolm Blvd, Rutherford College, Connelly Springs (Serv N to US 70)**
FStop N: Southern Convenience/66
Gas N: Citgo
Med N: + Hospital
Other N: Auto Dealer, CVS

116 **Rhodhiss, Icard**
FStop S: Jack B Quik #7/Marathon
Food N: Frosty's Drive-in
S: McDonald's/JBQ, Burger King, Granny's Country Kitchen, Rest/Icard Inn
Lodg S: Icard Inn

118 **Old NC 10**
Gas N: Shell◈

119A **Henry River (EB)**

119B **Hildebran, Longview (EB)**

EXIT — NORTH CAROLINA

119 **Hildebran, Henry River (WB)**
Gas N: Shell◈
Food N: Hardee's, KFC, Subway/Shell
Other N: ATMs, Banks

121 **Long View**

123A **Gastonia**

123B **Boone, Hickory Reg'l Airport**

123 **US 321, to US 70, to NC 127, Hickory, Lenoir, Lincolnton**
Other N: to Hickory Reg'l Airport✈

125 **NC 127, Hickory (WB), Lenoir-Rhyne College (EB)**
Gas N: Exxon◈, RaceTrac
S: Hess, Servco◈, Shell◈
Food N: Bojangles, Golden Corral, Peddler, Rock-Ola Café, Western Steer
S: Burger King, Carrabba's Rest, ChickFilA, CiCi's Pizza, Cracker Barrel, El Sombrero Mexican Rest, Fuddrucker's, Hardee's, Hooters, J&S Cafeteria, Kobe Japanese Rest, Longhorn Steakhouse, Outback Steakhouse, Red Lobster, Ruby Tuesday, Sagebrush Steak House, Steak & Ale, Waffle House, Wendy's, Zaxby's
Lodg N: Crowne Plaza,Red Roof Inn♥
S: Comfort Suites, Courtyard, Fairfield Inn, Hampton Inn, Holiday Inn, Jameson Inn, Sleep Inn
Med N: + Hospital
Other N: Auto Dealers
S: ATMs, Banks, Auto Services, Auto Dealers, Aldi Grocery, Food Lion, Hickory Metro Convention Center, Home Depot, Lowe's, Tire Kingdom, Valley Hills Mall, Blue Ridge Harley Davidson, Hickory Furniture Mart, Lenoir Rhyne College

126 **to US 70, Hickory, Newton**
FStop S: The Pantry #170
Gas S: Citgo, Phillips 66, Shell
Food S: Applebee's, Bob Evans, Chili's, IHOP, Libby Hill Seafood, McDonald's, O'Charley's
Lodg S: Holiday Inn Express
Other S: ATMs, Banks, Kmart, Lowe's, Office Depot, PetCo♥, Sam's Club, Walmart sc, UPS Store, to Hickory Furniture Outlets

128 **Fairgrove Church Rd, CR 1476**
FStop N: Speedy Mart/Solo
S: Citgo Gas Center
Gas N: BP, Shell
S: Phillips 66
Food N: McDonald's, Waffle House
S: Arby's, Bennett's Pit BBQ, Burger King, Harbor Inn Seafood, Mr Omelet, Shoney's, Wendy's, Rest/Days Inn
Lodg S: Affordable Suites, Best Western, Days Inn, Ramada Inn
TServ S: Carolina Engine, WhiteGMC Trucks, Newton Truck Service
Med N: + Catawba Valley Medical Center
Other S: NC Hwy Patrol Post, Catawba Valley College, to Hickory Motor Speedway

130 **Old US 70,**
Gas S: Citgo, Phillips 66
Food N: Dominos Pizza, Jack in the Box, Subway
Other N: Grocery, NAPA

132 **Mt Hope Church Rd, to NC 16, Conover, Taylorsville**
TStop N: WilcoHess Travel Plaza #308
Gas N: BP◈, Shell◈

◈= Regular Gas Stations with Diesel ▲ = RV Friendly Locations ♥= Pet Friendly Locations
Red print shows large vehicle parking / access on site or nearby Brown Print = Campgrounds / RV PARKS

EXIT		NORTH CAROLINA
	Food	N: Wendy's/Wilco TP S: Subway, Pizza
	Lodg	N: Hampton Inn, Holiday Inn Express
	Other	N: **Walmart sc**,
133		**US 70, to US 321, Rock Barn Rd**
	TStop	S: WilcoHess Travel Plaza #351 (Scales)
	Gas	N: Exxon
	Food	S: Subway/TacoBell/WilcoHess TP
	Other	S: Laundry/WilcoHess TP, Big Tire Service
135		**Oxford St, Claremont**
	Gas	S: Shell
	Food	S: Boxcar Grill, Burger King, Hardee's
	Lodg	S: Super 8
	Other	S: Dollar General, Grocery, **Carolina Coach & Camper**
(136)		Rest Area (Both dir) (RR, Phones, Picnic, Pet, Vend)
138		**NC 10, Oxford School Rd, Catawba**
	FStop	N: Bunker Hill Exxon
141		**Sharon School Rd, Statesville**
	Gas	N: Citgo
(143)		**Weigh Station (Both dir)**
144		**Old Mountain Rd, Statesville**
	FStop	N: Gran Prix
	Gas	N: BP◈ S: BP◈, Shell◈
	Food	N: Troy's 50's Rest
	Other	N: Repairs/BP S: Carwash/Shell
146		**Stamey Farm Rd, Statesville**
	TStop	S: Homer's Truck Stop/Citgo (Scales)
	Food	S: Rest/Homers TS
	TServ	S: Homers TS/Tires, Pro Tow Truck & Repair
	Other	S: Laundry/Homers TS, **to** Statesville Muni Airport✈
148		**US 64, NC 90, W Statesville, Taylorsville**
	Gas	N: Citgo◈, Exxon, Shell S: Travelers
	Food	N: Arby's, Burger King, KFC, Prime Steakhouse, McDonald's, Shiki Japanese Rest, Subway
	Lodg	N: Economy Inn
	Other	N: ATMs, Auto Services, CVS, Dollar General, Ingles Grocery, 84 Lumber, Repairs/Travelers S: Auto Services, Towing
150		**NC 115, Statesville, N Wilkesboro**
	Gas	N: BP◈, Citgo, Shell, Sheetz S: BP
	Food	N: Little Caesars Pizza
	Other	N: CVS, Food Lion, Fred's, **Family RV Center**
151		**US 21, Sullivan Rd, E Statesville, Harmony**
	Gas	N: Petro Express, Texaco, Wilco Hess◈ S: Exxon
	Food	N: Jersey Mikes Subs/Petro Express, Applebee's, Bojangles, Burger King, K&W, Chilis, Cracker Barrel, Golden Corral, KFC LJ Silver, McDonald's, Red Lobster, Sagebrush Steakhouse, Sokora Japanese Rest, Shoney's, Taco Bell, Wendy's, S: Hardee's, Huddle House, Lone Star Steakhouse, Waffle House, BBQ
	Lodg	N: Days Inn, Sleep Inn S: Econo Lodge, Holiday Inn Express♥, Masters Inn, Quality Inn, Travelodge

EXIT		NORTH CAROLINA
	Med	S: + Urgent Care, + Iredell Memorial Hospital
	Other	N: ATMs, Auto Dealers, Auto Services, CVS, Cinema, Home Depot, Lowe's, Radio Shack, Staples, Tire Kingdom, **Walmart sc**, S: ATMs, Banks, Dollar General, **NC State Hwy Patrol Post**, Laundromat
(152A)		**Jct I-77S, to Charlotte**
(152B)		**Jct I-77N, to Elkin**
153		**US 64, Mocksville Hwy (EB ex, WB ent) (Acc to #154 Serv)**
	Gas	N: Rickie's One Stop/BP
	Lodg	S: Hallmark Inn
154		**to US 64 (WB), Old Mocksville Rd (EB)**
	FStop	S: Fast Phil's #7/Citgo◈
	Food	S: Jay Bee's World Famous Hot Dogs
	Med	N: + Davis Community Hospital
162		**US 64, Statesville, Cool Springs**
	Gas	S: Shell
	Other	N: **to Lake Myers RV & Camp Resort▲** S: **Midway Campground Resort▲**
168		**US 64, to Mocksville**
	Gas	N: Exxon◈ S: BP◈
	Other	N: **to Lake Myers RV & Camp Resort▲**
170		**US 601, Mocksville, Yadkinville**
	FStop	S: BP
	TStop	N: AmBest/Horn's Auto Truck Plaza/Pure (Scales)
	Gas	N: Murphy◈ S: Exxon, Shell◈
	Food	N: Country Kitchen/Horn's ATP, La Carreta Mexican, Moe's Burger House, Subway S: Arby's, Burger King, KFC, Pizza Hut, McDonald's, Sagebrush Steakhouse, Taco Bell/Shell, Wendy's
	Lodg	S: Comfort Inn, Highway Inn, Quality Inn♥
	TWash	N: Horn's ATP
	TServ	N: Horn's ATP/Tires
	Med	S: + Davie Co Hospital
	Other	N: ATMs, Dollar Tree, Horn's Garage, TLC Auto Service, **Walmart sc**, **RV Superstore of Mocksville** S: ATMs, Advance Auto Parts, CVS, Carwash, Dollar General, Food Lion, Goodyear, Lowe's, Walgreen's, **Kamperz RV Service**
174		**Farmington Rd, Mocksville**
	FStop	N: Exxon
(177)		Rest Area (Both dir) (RR, Phones, Picnic, Vend)
180		**NC 801, Advance, Tanglewood, Bermuda**
	Gas	S: BP◈
	Food	N: Captain's Galley, Domino's Pizza S: McDonald's, Wendy's, Subway
	Other	N: Grocery, Pharmacy S: ATMs, Banks, CVS, Dollar General, Food Lion, Radio Shack, Walgreen's
182		**Harper Rd, Tanglewood, Bermuda (WB exit, EB entr)**
184		**CR 113, Clemmons Rd, Lewisville**
	Gas	N: Mobil, Shell S: BP◈, Wilco #120/Exxon◈, Kangaroo Express◈
	Food	N: Applebee's, IHOP, I Bambini, KFC S: Arby's, Burger King, Cracker Barrel, Dockside Seafood, Little Caesar's Pizza,

EXIT		NORTH CAROLINA
	Food	N: Mandarin Chinese, McDonald's, Mi Pueblo Mexican Rest, Pizza Hut, Sagebrush Steakhouse, Sonic, Taco Bell, Waffle House, Wendy's
	Lodg	N: Holiday Inn Express S: Super 8, Village Inn Golf & Conf Center
	Other	S: ATMs, Banks, Advance Auto Parts, CarQuest Auto Parts, CVS, Carwash, Dollar Tree, Grocery, Merchant Tire & Auto Center, Staples, US Post Office, Village Tires, Walgreen's,
188		**US 421, Bus 40, to Yadkinville (WB, difficult Reaccess)**
189		**US 158, Stratford Rd**
	Gas	N: BP, Exxon S: BP, Shell, Costco
	Food	N: Bojangles, Chili's, Golden Corral, McDonald's, Olive Garden, Red Lobster, Sagebrush, Texas Roadhouse S: Applebee's, Buffalo Wild Wings, Burger King, ChickFilA, Corky's BBQ, Dynasty Buffet, Five Guys Burgers, Hooters, Jason's Deli, Longhorn Steakhouse, Panera Bread, Romano's Macaroni Grill, Starbucks, Subway, Texas Land & Cattle
	Lodg	N: Best Western, Courtyard, Fairfield S: Extended Stay America, Hampton Inn, Hilton Garden Inn, La Quinta Inn♥, Sleep Inn, Springhill Suites
	Med	N: + Forsyth Memorial Hospital
	Other	N: Carmike 12, Dick's Sporting Goods, Walgreen's, Mall S: Barnes & Noble, Best Buy, Costco, CVS, Food Lion, Home Depot, Lowe's, PetSmart♥, Sam's Club, Target
190		**Hanes Mall Blvd, Silas Creek Pkwy (WB exit, EB entr)**
	Food	N: McDonald's, O'Charley's, Olive Garden, Ruby Tuesday, TGI Friday's S: Burger King, Little Caesar's Pizza, Lone Star Steakhouse, Outback Steakhouse, Oyster Bay Seafood, Souper Salad, Starbucks
	Lodg	S: Comfort Suites, Extended Stay America, Fairfield Inn, Microtel
	Med	N: + Forsyth Memorial Hospital
	Other	N: Auto Zone, Firestone, Kroger, Mall, Office Depot S: CVS, Food Lion, Goodyear
192		**NC 150, Peters Creek Pkwy , Downtown Winston Salem**
	FStop	N: WilcoHess #102
	Gas	N: Shell S: BP
	Food	N: Arby's, Bojangles, Burger King, Checkers, IHOP, Little Caesars, Monterey Mex, Old Country Buffet, Perkins, Pizza Hut, Red Lobster, Shoney's, Taco Bell S: McDonald's, Libby Hill Seafood
	Lodg	N: Innkeeper, Knights Inn S: Holiday Inn Express
	Med	N: + Crown Care Medical Center
	Other	N: Auto Zone, Big Lots, Kroger, Office Depot, NAPA, Radio Shack S: Auto Services, CVS, Food Lion
193C		**Silas Creek Pkwy, S Main St (WB)**
193A		**US 52S, NC 8S, Lexington**
193B		**US 52N, US 311N, NC 8N, Mt Airy**
	FStop	S: Wilco Hess
	Other	N: **to** Smith Reynolds Airport✈

◈= Regular Gas Stations with Diesel ▲ = RV Friendly Locations ♥= Pet Friendly Locations
Red print shows large vehicle parking / access on site or nearby Brown Print = Campgrounds / RV PARKS

EXIT	NORTH CAROLINA
193	**US 52, NC 8, US 311N, Lexington, Mount Airy**
195	**NC 109, Clemmonsville Rd, Thomasville**
FStop	**S:** WilcoHess #108
196	**US 311S, to High Point**
201	**Union Cross Rd**
Gas	**N:** Exxon◈, Quality Plus
Food	**N:** Burger King
Other	**N:** CVS, Food Lion
203	**NC 66, Kernersville, High Point**
Gas	**N:** BP, Citgo◈, Exxon **S:** Shell
Food	**N:** Clark's BBQ, Suzie's Diner, Waffle House, Wendy's **S:** Subway/Shell
Lodg	**N:** Quality Inn, Sleep Inn **S:** Holiday Inn Express
TServ	**N:** Bales & Truitt Truck Service
Other	**S: Camping World**
206	**Bus 40 N, US 421N, Kernersville, Downtown Winston-Salem (WB)**
208	**Sandy Ridge Rd, Colfax**
FStop	**N:** WilcoHess #295 **S:** Neighbor's Fuel Center #9
Other	**N: Holiday Kamper, Camping World/ Colfax RV Outlet/RVDump** **S:** Farmers Market
210	**NC 68, High Point, PTI Airport**
Gas	**N:** Phillips 66◈ **S:** Citgo, Exxon◈
Food	**N:** Arby's, Hardee's, Wendy's **S:** McDonald's/Citgo, Pizza Hut/Taco Bell, Shoney's, Subway
Lodg	**N:** Days Inn, Embassy Suites, Holiday Inn, Homewood Suites **S:** Ashford Suites, Best Western, Comfort Suites, Courtyard, Crestwood Suites, Fairfield Inn, Hampton Inn, Holiday Inn Express, Motel 6♥, Ramada Inn, Red Roof Inn♥, Residence Inn,
TServ	**N:** Whites' International, Volvo, Cummins, CAT, Carolina Kenworth, Freightliner, Piedmont Ford, Piedmont Truck Tires
Other	**N:** Piedmont Triad Int'l Airport✈
211	**Gallimore Dairy Rd, NC 1556**
212	**I-40E Bus, US 421S, to Bryan Blvd, Greensboro, PTI Airport**
212A	**to Bryan Blvd, PTI Airport (WB)**
212B	**I-40 Bus, US 421 (WB)**
212	**Chimney Rock Rd**
TServ	**S:** Carolina Engine, Carolina Diesel
213	**Guilford College Rd, Jamestown**
Gas	**N:** BP◈ **S:** Exxon, Sheetz
Food	**N:** Damon's Ribs
Lodg	**N:** Clarion, Radisson
Other	**S:** Auto Dealers, Carolina Veterinary♥, Dick's Sporting Goods, Gate City Lanes, **Access Ex #214 Serv**
214A	**Wendover Ave West (EB)**
Gas	**S:** Sam's
Food	**S:** Applebee's, Bojangles, ChickFilA, **Cracker Barrel**, Fuddruckers, Golden Corral, IHOP, Logan's Roadhouse, McDonald's, Red Lobster, Shoney's,

Personal Notes

EXIT	NORTH CAROLINA
Food	**S:** Steak 'n Shake, Subway, TGI Friday's, Wendy's
Lodg	**S:** AmeriSuites, Best Western, Courtyard, Hyatt Place, La Quinta Inn♥, Springhill Suites, Studio Plus, Wingate
Other	**S:** ATMs, Banks, Auto Services, Best Buy, Garden Ridge Goodyear, Grocery, Hobby Lobby, Home Depot, Lowe's, Sam's Club, Sports Authority, Target, **Walmart sc**
214B	**Wendover Ave East (EB)**
Gas	**N:** Exxon◈, Sheetz◈,Shell◈, Costco
Food	**N:** Bojangles, Burger King, K&W Cafeteria, Moe's SW Grill, Panera Bread, Ruby Tuesday, Shane's Rib Shack, Waffle House
Lodg	**N:** Extended Stay America, Fairfield Inn, Hilton Garden Inn, Holiday Inn Express♥, Microtel
Other	**N:** ATMs, Auto Dealers, Auto Services, Celebration Station, Costco, FedEx Office, Goodyear, PetCo♥, Staples
214	**Wendover Ave, Greensboro (WB)**
216	**NC 6W, Greensboro, Coliseum Area (fr EB, LEFT exit)**
217	**US 70A, US 29A, High Point Rd, Coliseum Area (EB) Koury Blvd (WB)**
Gas	**N:** Exxon◈, Shell◈ **S:** Crown, Exxon, Shell
Food	**N:** Arby's, Burger King, Chili's, Dunkin Donuts, Hooters, Lone Star Steakhouse, McDonald's, Olive Garden, Osaka, Perkins, Po Folks, Subway
Food	**S:** Bojangles, Carrabba's, Hardee's, Krispy

EXIT	NORTH CAROLINA
Food	**S:** Kreme, Kyoto, Nascar Café, Shoney's, Starbucks, Waffle House, Wendy's
Lodg	**N:** DoubleTree Hotel, Red Roof Inn♥, Super 8, Travelodge **S:** Comfort Inn, Days Inn, Drury Inn, Fairfield Inn, Hampton Inn, Residence Inn, Sheraton
Med	**S: + Prime Care Medical Center**
Other	**N:** ATMs, Carwash/Exxon, Burlington Coat Factory, Dollar General, Office Depot, **to** Greensboro Coliseum **S:** Auto Zone, Auto Services, Discount Tire, FedEx Office, Grocery, NAPA, Office Depot, Mall
(218)	**Jct I-85S, US 29, US 70W, High Point, Charlotte**
218A	**US 220S, to I-85S Bus, Asheboro (EB)**
218B	**Freeman Mill Rd (EB)**
219	**I-85S Bus, US 29S, US 70W, to US 220N, Greensboro (EB), to Charlotte (WB)**
220	**US 220S, Asheboro**
NOTE:	**I-40 below runs with I-85 Bus, Exit #'s 36-43. Exit numbers follow I-85 Bus.**
(219)	**Jct I-85S, to Charlotte, US 29S, US 70W, US 220 (WB)**
(36A)	**Jct I-85S, to Charlotte, US 29S, US 70W, US 220**
36B	**Randleman Rd, Greensboro**
Gas	**E:** BP, Kangaroo **W:** BP, Citgo, Shell, Solo
Food	**E:** CookOut, Mayflower Seafood, Waffle House, Wendy's **W:** Arby's, Burger King, Captain D's, Church's Chicken, DQ, Hardee's, KFC, McDonald's, Pizza Hut, Shoney's, Taco Bell
Lodg	**E:** Cavalier Inn **W:** Budget Motel
TServ	**E:** Cummins Diesel
Med	**E: + Piedmont Carolina Medical Clinic**
Other	**W:** Auto Services, Family Dollar, Food Lion, Harley Davidson of Greensboro, RiteAid
37	**S Elm St, Eugene St**
Gas	**E:** BP, Shell◈ **W:** Citgo◈, Crown
Food	**E:** Carolina Country Kitchen **W:** Bojangles, Sonic
Lodg	**E:** Days Inn, Econo Lodge♥, Knights Inn, Quality Inn, Super 8 **W:** Homestead Lodge, Ramada
Other	**E:** Home Depot **W:** Auto Repairs/Citgo, Auto Zone, Food Lion, NAPA, O'Reilly Auto Parts
38	**US 421S, to Sanford**
Gas	**E:** Exxon, Pit Stop
Food	**E:** Burger King, McDonald's, Old Hickory BBQ, Subway, Taco Bell, Wendy's
Med	**W: + Kindred Hospital**
Other	**E:** ATMs, Auto Services, CVS, Food Lion, Goodyear
39	**US 29N, US 70, US 220, US 421, Reidsville, Danville (NB, No reaccess)**
Other	**N:** KOA▲

◈= Regular Gas Stations with Diesel ▲ = RV Friendly Locations ♥= Pet Friendly Locations
Red print shows large vehicle parking / access on site or nearby Brown Print = Campgrounds / RV PARKS

EXIT		NORTH CAROLINA
41		**NC 6, E Lee St, Greensboro**
	Gas	E: Gastown
		W: BP◈, Shell◈
	Food	W: FastFood/BP
	Lodg	W: Holiday Inn Express, Quality Inn♥
	Other	E: to Greensboro Campground▲
		W: to Coliseum, KOA▲
43		**McConnell Rd**
	Gas	S: Shell
44		**to I-85S, US 70**
	NOTE:	I-40 above runs with I-85 Bus, Exit #'s 36-43. Exit #'s follow I-85 Bus.
	NOTE:	I-40 runs below with I-85N. Exit #'s follows I-85.
132		**Mt Hope Church Rd, McLeansville**
	TStop	W: WilcoHess Travel Plaza
	Gas	E: Citgo
	Food	W: Wendy's/WilcoHess TP, Café America
	Lodg	W: Hampton Inn
135		**Rock Creek Dairy Rd**
	Gas	W: Citgo, Exxon
	Food	W: Bojangles, Jersey Mike's, McDonald's
	TServ	W: Battleground Tire & Wrecker
	Other	W: CVS, Food Lion
138		**NC 61, to Gibsonville, Greensboro**
	TStop	W: Travel Center of America #2/BP (Scales)
	Gas	W: Shell◈
	Food	W: CountryPride/BKing/Popeye's/TA TC
	Lodg	W: Days Inn/TA TC
	TWash	W: TA TC
	TServ	W: TA TC/Tires
	Other	W: Laundry/WiFi/TA TC, Hawley's Camping Center
(139)		**Rest Area** (Both dir) (RR, Phones, Picnic, Vend)
140		**University Dr, Elon University**
	Other	W: Best Buy, Target
141		**Huffman Mill Rd, to Burlington**
	Gas	E: BP, Shell, Kangaroo
		W: Phillips 66◈, Shell
	Food	E: IHOP
		W: Applebee's, Arby's, Bojangles, Burger King, Cracker Barrel, Golden Corral, Hooters, KFC, McDonald's, Starbucks, Steak n Shake, Subway, Taco Bell
	Lodg	E: Hampton Inn Comfort Inn
		W: Best Western, Country Suites, Courtyard, Super 8
	Med	W: + Hospital
	Other	W: Auto Dealers, Food Lion, Walmart sc, Mall
143		**NC 62, Burlington**
	Gas	E: Citgo
		W: 76, Exxon
	Food	E: Wendy's/Citgo, Bob Evans, Hardee's Waffle House
		W: K&W, Libby Hill Seafood
	Lodg	W: Ramada Inn
	Other	W: Food Lion, Home Depot
145		**NC 49, Burlington, Liberty**
	FStop	E: Interstate Shell
	Gas	E: BP◈
		W: BP, Hess
	Food	E: FastFood/Interstate Sh, Captain D's, Shoney's
		W: Bojangles, Burger King, Hardee's, KFC, Subway, Waffle House
	Lodg	E: Microtel, Red Roof Inn♥

EXIT		NORTH CAROLINA
	Lodg	W: Econo Lodge, Holiday Inn, La Quinta Inn♥, Motel 6♥, Scottish Inn
	Other	E: Davis Harley Davidson, NC State Hwy Patrol Post
		W: Dollar General, Food Lion
147		**NC 87, to Pittsboro, Graham**
	Gas	E: BP, Servco
		W: Citgo, Exxon◈, Shell◈
	Food	E: Arby's, Bojangles, Burger King, Great Wall, Harbor House Seafood, Sagebrush, Subway, Wendy's
		W: Biscuitville, Hardee's, McDonald's, Taco Bell
	Med	W: + Hospital
	Other	E: Food Lion, Winn Dixie, Laundromat, Goodyear, NC State Hwy Patrol Post
		W: CVS, Grocery, Walgreen's
148		**NC 54, E Harden St, to Chapel Hill**
	FStop	S: Kangaroo Express #3791/Exxon
	Gas	S: BP◈, Quality
	Food	S: Waffle House, Grill/Kang Expr
	Lodg	S: Comfort Suites
		N: Econo Lodge, Travel Inn
	Other	S: Car Wash
150		**Haw River, to Roxboro, Graham**
	TStop	N: Flying J Travel Plaza #5332/Conoco (Scales), WilcoHess Travel Plaza #165 (Scales)
	Food	N: Rest/FJ TP, DQ/Wendy's/WH TP
	Lodg	N: Days Inn
	TWash	N: Blue Beacon TW
	TServ	N: Speedco
	Other	N: Laundry/BarbSh/WiFi/RVDump/LP/FJ TP, Laundry/WilcoHess TP
152		**Jimmie Kerr Rd, Trollingwood Rd**
	FStop	E: Pilot Travel Center #57 (Scales)
		W: Fuel City
	Food	E: McDonald's/Pilot TC
		W: Fuel City
	TWash	E: Pilot TC
	Other	E: Laundry/WiFi/Pilot TC
153		**NC 119, S 5th St, Mebane**
	Gas	E: BP, BP
		W: Exxon
	Food	E: Cracker Barrel, Ruby Tuesday, Taco Bell/KFC/PizzaHut/BP
		W: Burger King/Exxon, Sonic, Subway
	Lodg	E: Hampton Inn, Holiday Inn Express
	Med	W: + Hospital
	Other	E: ATMs, Banks, Lowe's, Golf Course
		W: CVS, Food Lion
154		**Oaks Rd, Mebane**
	FStop	W: Arrowhead Shell
	Gas	E: Sheetz
		W: BP, Citgo, Exxon◈, Shell
	Food	E: Blimpie/Shell
		W: Biscuitville, Bojangles, McDonald's, Waffle House, Rest/Budget Inn
	Lodg	W: Budget Inn
	Med	W: + Mebane Clinic
	Other	E: Walmart sc
		W: Winn Dixie, Hurdle Field
157		**Buckhorn Rd, Mebane**
	TStop	E: Petro Stopping Center #29/Mobil (Scales)
	Gas	E: BP
		W: Citgo
	Food	E: IronSkillet/FastFood/Petro SC
	TServ	E: Petro SC/Tires
		W: Diesel Service
	Other	E: Laundry/BarbSh/CB/WiFi/Petro SC
(158)		**Weigh Station** (Both dir)

EXIT		NORTH CAROLINA
160		**Efland**
	Gas	W: BP◈, Exxon◈
161		**to US 70E, NC 86N**
(163/259)		**Jct I-40E, to Raleigh**
		Jct I-85N, to Durham (WB)
	NOTE:	I-40 above runs with I-85. Exit #'s follow I-85.
261		**Hillsborough**
	Gas	N: BP, Citgo, Shell
	Food	N: Hardee's, McDonald's, Pizza Hut, Subway, Waffle House
	Lodg	N: Holiday Inn, Microtel
	Other	N: Visitor Info Center
263		**New Hope Church Rd**
266		**NC 86, to Chapel Hill**
	Gas	S: BP, Citgo, Exxon, Hess
	Food	S: Quiznos, Subway
	Other	N: Birchwood RV Park▲
		S: ATMs, Cinema, Food Lion
270		**US 15, US 501, Chapel Hill, Durham**
	Gas	S: BP, Exxon
	Food	N: Bob Evans, Hardee's, Outback Steak house, Wendy's
	Lodg	N: Comfort Inn
		S: Days Inn, Hampton Inn, Holiday Inn, Red Roof Inn♥, Sheraton
	Med	N: + Hospital
	Other	N: Best Buy, Home Depot, Walmart, to Duke Univ
		S: CVS, Lowe's
273B		**NC 54E, to Durham** (WB)
	Other	S: Univ of NC-Chapel Hill
273A		**NC 54W, to Chapel Hill** (WB)
273		**NC 54, Chapel Hill, Durham** (EB)
	Gas	N: Citgo, Shell◈
		S: BP◈
	Food	S: Hardee's
	Lodg	S: Hampton Inn, Holiday Inn Express
274		**NC 751, Hope Valley Rd, Durham, to Jordan Lake**
	Gas	S: BP, Kangaroo
	Food	N: Burger King, Waffle House
276		**Fayetteville Rd, Southpoint**
		Note: End Motorist Assistance
	Gas	N: Exxon◈, Phillips 66◈
	Food	N: McDonald's, Ruby Tuesday, Souper Salad, Waffle House, Wendy's
	Other	N: ATMs, Banks, Grocery, Mall, to NC Central Univ
278		**NC 55, to NC 54, Apex**
	Gas	N: Citgo
		S: Exxon◈, Mobil◈, Phillips 66
	Food	N: China One, Waffle House
		S: Arby's, Bojangles Chicken, Burger King, Golden Corral, KFC, McDonald's, Pizza Hut, Subway, Taco Bell, Wendy's
	Lodg	N: Fairfield Inn, Innkeeper, La Quinta Inn♥
		S: Candlewood Suites, Courtyard, Residence Inn
	Other	N: ATMs, Banks
		S: ATMs, Auto Services, Food Lion, Pharmacy
279A		**NC 147S, Durham Freeway, to Alexander Dr**
279B		**NC 147N, Durham Frwy (EB), Downtown Durham (WB)**

◈= Regular Gas Stations with Diesel ▲ = RV Friendly Locations ♥= Pet Friendly Locations

Red print shows large vehicle parking / access on site or nearby Brown Print = Campgrounds / RV PARKS

EXIT		NORTH CAROLINA
280		**Davis Dr, Durham**
	Lodg	S: Radisson
281		**Miami Blvd, Durham**
	Gas	N: BP, Shell
	Food	N: Wendy's
		S: Wok & Grille
	Lodg	N: Best Western, Marriott, Studio Plus
		S: Clarion, Homewood Suites, Wellesley
	Med	N: + Park Medical Center
282		**Page Rd, Durham**
	Food	S: McDonald's, Rest/Hilton, Rest/Sheraton
	Lodg	N: Holiday Inn
		S: Comfort Inn, Hilton, Sheraton, Wingate
(283)		**Jct I-540N, to US 70, Apex (EB)**
(283B)		**Jct I-540N, to US 70 (WB)**
(283A)		**Jct I-540W, to US 70 (WB)**
284A		**Airport Blvd W, RDU Airport (EB)**
284B		**Airport Blvd E, Int'l Airport (EB)**
284		**Airport Blvd, RDU Int'l Airport (WB)**
	Gas	S: BP◈, Citgo◈, Exxon, Shell◈
	Food	S: Cracker Barrel, Quiznos, Waffle House, Wendy's
	Lodg	S: Baymont Inn, Courtyard, Days Inn, Extended Stay America, Fairfield Inn, Hampton Inn, La Quinta Inn♥, Residence Inn
	Other	N: Auto Rentals
		S: Triangle Factory Shops
285		**Aviation Pkwy, Int'l Airport, Morrisville**
	Lodg	N: Hilton Garden Inn
	Other	S: Lake Crabtree Co Park
287		**Harrison Ave, Cary**
	Gas	S: BP, Shell
	Food	S: Arby's, McDonald's, Subway, Wendy's
	Lodg	S: Embassy Suites, Studio Plus
	Other	N: Wm B Umstead State Park▲
		S: Auto Services, Enterprise, Goodyear
289		**to I-440, US 1N, Wade Ave (WB) (diff reaccess)**
		to 440, to US 1N, Wade Ave (EB)
	Med	N: + Hospital
	Other	N: RBC Center, Carter Finley Stadium, Motorist Assistance Patrol
		S: Fairgrounds
290		**NC 54, Cary**
	Gas	N: Shell
		S: Citgo
	Food	N: Ole Time BBQ
		S: Carolina Chicken
	Lodg	N: Comfort Suites
		S: Hampton Inn

EXIT		NORTH CAROLINA
	Other	N: Amtrak
		S: Fairgrounds
291		**Cary Towne Blvd, Cary**
	Food	S: Burger King, McDonald's, Taco Bell
	Other	S: Cary Town Center Shopping
(293)		**Jct I-440E, US 1, US 64W, Sanford, Asheboro, Wake Forest, Raleigh**
293		**US 1, US 64W, Sanford, Asheboro**
293A		**US 1S, US 64W, Sanford, Asheboro**
	Gas	S: Citgo, Exxon, Shell
	Food	S: Hardee's, Ruth's Chris Steakhouse, Kabuki Japanese, Shoney's, Waffle House
	Lodg	S: Best Western, Fairfield Inn, Motel 6♥
	Other	S: ATMs, Auto Services, Grocery
293B		**Inner 440 Lp, US 1N, Raleigh, Wake Forest**
295		**Gorman St, Raleigh**
	Gas	N: Exxon, Kangaroo
	Food	N: Hardee's, McDonald's
	Other	N: NC State Univ, Coliseum
		S: Auto Services
297		**Lake Wheeler Rd**
	Gas	N: Exxon
		S: Citgo
	Food	N: Burger King
	Med	N: + Hospital
	Other	N: Farmers Market
298A		**US 70E, US 401S, NC 50S, Fayetteville, Garner, S Sanders St S**
	Gas	S: BP, Hess, RaceWay, Servco
	Food	S: Domino's Pizza, KFC, Shoney's
	Lodg	S: Claremont Inn, Days Inn, Innkeeper
	Other	S: Auto Services, Grocery, Sam's Club
298B		**US 401N, US 70W, NC 50N, Raleigh, S Sanders St North**
	Gas	N: Exxon, Shell
	Lodg	N: Red Roof Inn♥
	Other	N: Auto Services, Greyhound, Tires, Towing, Train Station
299		**Person St, Hammond Rd (EB diff reaccess)**
300		**Rock Quarry Rd (EB)**
300A		**Rock Quarry Rd South (WB)**
	Gas	S: BP, Exxon
	Food	S: Hardee's, Subway
	Other	N: Kroger
		S: Food Lion, Laundromat, Winn Dixie
300B		**Rock Quarry Rd North (WB)**
(301)		**Jct I-440W, US 64E, Rocky Mount (EB, LEFT Exit) (Exit Only)**

EXIT		NORTH CAROLINA
303		**Jones Sausage Rd**
	FStop	S: Country Cupboard #3/Shell
	Gas	N: BP◈, Shell◈
	Food	N: Burger King, Bojangles
		S: Smithfield BBQ
306		**US 70, Smithfield, Garner, Clayton, Goldsboro (EB)**
	Other	S: Hawley's Camping Center/RVDump
306A		**US 70W, Garner (WB)**
	Food	W: Chili's, McDonald's, Wendy's
	Other	W: BJ's, Best Buy, Target
306B		**US 70E, Smithfield, Clayton (WB)**
	Lodg	E: Suburban Lodge
	Other	E: Auto & Tire Service, 70 East Mobile Acres Park▲, Hawley's Camping Center/RVDump
312		**NC 42, Clayton, Fuquay-Varina, Garner**
	FStop	W: WilcoHess Travel Plaza #213
	Gas	W: BP◈, Citgo◈, Shell◈
	Food	E: DQ, Domino's, Huddle House, Ruby Tuesday, Waffle House
		W: Andy's, Burger King, Cracker Barrel, China King, Golden Corral, Smithfield Chicken & BBQ, McDonald's, Wendy's
	Lodg	E: Best Western, Holiday Inn, Quality Inn, Super 8
		W: Hampton Inn, Sleep Inn
	Other	W: Auto Repairs, CarQuest, Lowe's
		E: CVS, Food Lion
319		**NC 210, Benson, Smithfield, Angier**
	Gas	E: Citgo, Shell
		W: Mobil
	Food	E: FastFood/Citgo, McDonald's
		W: Café/Mobil, Subway, Waffle House, Wendy's
	Other	W: Food Lion
(324)		**Rest Area (Both dir) (RR, Phones, Picnic, Vend)**
325		**NC 242, to US 301, Benson**
	Gas	S: Citgo
(328A)		**Jct I-95S, Benson, Fayetteville**
(328B)		**Jct I-95N, Smithfield, Rocky Mount**
	Other	N: to Smithfield KOA▲
334		**NC 96, Benson, Meadow**
341		**NC 50, NC 55 (WB), to US 13 (EB), Newton Grove**
	Gas	N: Exxon◈
		S: BP, Shell
	Food	N: Hardee's
		S: McDonald's/BP, Subway

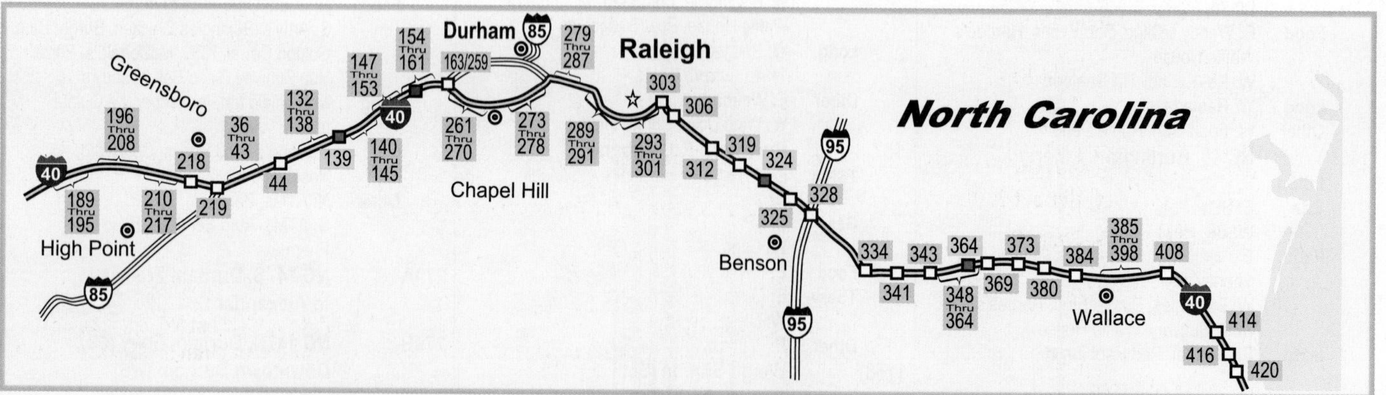

◈= Regular Gas Stations with Diesel ▲ = RV Friendly Locations ♥= Pet Friendly Locations
Red print shows large vehicle parking / access on site or nearby Brown Print = Campgrounds / RV PARKS

EXIT	NORTH CAROLINA
343	**US 701, Clinton (EB), to US 13, Newton Grove (WB)**
Gas	N: Exxon
348	**Suttontown Rd, Clinton**
355	**NC 403, to Faison, to US 117, to Goldsboro**
364	**NC 24W, Bus 24, to NC 50, Warsaw (EB), Clinton (WB)** Rest Area (Both dir) (RR, Phones, Picnic, Vend)
FStop	S: C Check #4/BP, Kangaroo Express #3130/Shell
TStop	N: WilcoHess Travel Plaza #225
Gas	S: Crown◈, Phillips 66◈
Food	N: Arby's/WilcoHess TP S: KFC, McDonald's, Smithfield's Chicken & BBQ, Subway, Waffle House, Wendy's, Bojangles/BP
Lodg	S: Days Inn, Holiday Inn Express
TServ	N: Joe's Truck Repair
Other	N: Auto Services S: Auto Services
369	**US 117, Warsaw, Magnolia**
373	**NC 24E, NC 903, Magnolia, Kenansville**
Gas	N: BP
Med	N: + Hospital
380	**Brices Store Rd, Rose Hill (EB), to Greenevers (WB)**
Gas	S: BP
384	**NC 11, Teachey, Wallace**
385	**NC 41, Wallace, Chinquapin**
Gas	N: Exxon
Lodg	N: Holiday Inn Express
Other	N: Hanchey's Auto & Truck Service
390	**US 117, Wallace**
398	**NC 53, Burgaw, Jacksonville** (All Serv Avail 3-4mi S in Burgaw)
Med	S: + Hospital
408	**NC 210, Hampstead, Rocky Point, Moores Creek Nat'l Battlefield, Topsail Island**
Gas	S: Exxon
Food	S: Café
TServ	S: Reeves Truck Repair
414	**Castle Hayne, Hampstead, Brunswick Co Beaches**
Gas	S: BP
Food	S: Hardee's
(416)	**Jct I-140W, US 17, to Shallotte, Myrtle Beach, Topsail Island (EB)**
(416A)	**Jct I-140W, US 17S, to Shallotte, Myrtle Beach (WB)**
Other	S: to USS NC Battleship Memorial
416B	**US 17N, to Topsail Island, Jacksonville (WB)**
420	**US 117N, NC 132N, Gordon Rd (EB)** (Addtl Serv Avail S on US 17)
Gas	N: Citgo◈ S: BP◈
Food	N: McDonald's, Perkins S: Subway
Other	S: Walmart sc, Howard RV Center, New Hanover Int'l Airport✈
420B	**US 117, NC 132N (WB)**
420A	**Gordon Rd (WB)**

EASTERN TIME ZONE

NORTH CAROLINA

Begin Eastbound I-40 from Wilmington, NC to I-5 in California.

EXIT	WISCONSIN

Begin Southbound I-43 from Green Bay, WI to Beloit, WI.

WISCONSIN

NOTE: I-43 begins/ends at Green Bay on US 41

CENTRAL TIME ZONE

EXIT	WISCONSIN
192B	**US 41S, US 141S, Deerfield Ave, Velp Ave, Appleton, Green Bay** (Serv South to Velp Ave)
Gas	W: BP◈, KwikTrip, Mobil, Shell◈
Food	W: Arby's, Burger King, McDonald's, Taco Bell
Lodg	W: AmericInn
Other	W: Auto Services, CVS, Family Dollar, Towing, RV Dealers, to Austin Straubel Int'l Airport✈
192A	**US 41N, US 141N, Appleton, Marinette, Iron Mountain**
TStop	E: 2mi N: Lineville Travel Mart/Mobil
Food	E: FastFood/Lineville TM, Barley's Deerfield Diner
Other	E: Laundry/Lineville TM W: Auto & Truck Services & Repairs
189	**Atkinson Dr, Velp Ave (SB)** **Port of Green Bay, Hurlbut St (NB)**
187	**Webster Ave, East Shore Dr**
Gas	W: Shell◈
Food	W: McDonald's, Wendy's
Lodg	W: Days Inn, Holiday Inn
Med	W: + Hospital
Other	E: RVDump/Bay Beach City Park W: Eagle Auto Repair
185	**WI 54, WI 57, University Ave, to Algoma, Sturgeon Bay**
Gas	W: Citgo, Mobil, Shell
Food	W: Cousin's Subs, Green Bay Pizza, Ponderosa, Subway, Taco Bell
Lodg	W: Tower Motel
Other	E: Univ of WI/GB W: Grocery, NAPA, Walgreen's
183	**CTH V, Mason St**
Gas	E: Shell◈ W: BP, Citgo, Mobil◈, Shell
Food	W: Applebee's, Burger King, Country Kitchen, Fazoli's, McDonald's, Perkins, Quiznos, Starbucks, Taco Bell
Lodg	E: Amerihost Inn, Country Inn W: Candlewood Suites
Med	E: + Aurora Baycare Medical Center
Other	W: ATMs, Banks, Auto Services, Grocery, Goodyear, Dollar Tree, Kmart, Osco, Office Max, PetCo♥, ShopKO, Tires Plus, Walmart, Walgreen's, East Town Mall
181	**CTH JJ, Eaton Rd, Manitowoc Rd**
Gas	E: Citgo◈ W: Express◈
Food	E: Blimpie/Citgo, Hardee's, McDonald's W: Subway/Express
Other	E: Home Depot, McCoy's Harley Davidson W: Grocery
180	**WI 172, to US 41, Straubel Airport**
TStop	W: Country Express AutoTruck Stop/ Citgo (Scales) (W to WI 172 & GV)
Gas	W: BP
Food	W: Rest/Country Express ATS, Burger King, McDonald's
Lodg	W: Best Western, Hampton Inn, Radisson
TWash	W: Country Express A/S
Med	W: + Hospital
Other	W: Laundry/WiFi/Country Express ATS
178	**US 141, to WI 29, CTH MM, Bellevue, Kewaunee**
TStop	E: I-43 Shell W: Circle T Truck Stop (Scales)
Food	E: FastFood/Shell, Rest/Redwood Inn
Lodg	E: Redwood Inn
TServ	E: Glenn's 24Hr Towing W: Circle T TS/Tires
Other	W: Laundry/Circle T TS
171	**WI 96, CTH KB, Greenleaf, Denmark**
FStop	E: Village Mart/Citgo
Food	E: FastFood/Village Mart, Lorrie's Café, McDonald's, Subway
Other	E: LP/Village Mart, Towing, Auto Service W: Shady Acres Campground▲
(169)	Maribel Rest Area (Both dir) (RR, Phone, Vend, Picnic)
164	**WI 147, CTH Z, Maribel, Mishicot** **WI 147, CTH Z, Maribel, Two Rivers**
FStop	W: Maribel Express/Citgo
TStop	W: Fun n Fast Travel Center/Citgo, OCS Hotstop Travel Plaza/Marathon (Scales)
Food	W: FastFood/OCS TP, Cedar Ridge
TServ	W: Citgo
Other	E: Maribel Caves State Park W: Laundry/RVDump/FunNFast TC, Laundry/ OCS TP, Devils River Campground▲
160	**CTH K, Kellnersville**
157	**CTH V, Hillcrest Rd, Manitowoc, to Mishicot, Francis Creek**
FStop	E: Citgo

◈= Regular Gas Stations with Diesel ▲ = RV Friendly Locations ♥= Pet Friendly Locations
Red print shows large vehicle parking / access on site or nearby Brown Print = Campgrounds / RV PARKS

EXIT **WISCONSIN**

Food E: Diner/Citgo

154 **US 10W, WI 310, to Two Rivers, Appleton**
Gas E: Mobil
W: Cenex
Med E: + Holy Family Memorial Med Center
Other E: Manitowoc Co Airport✈
W: to Rainbows End Campground▲

152 **US 10E, WI 42N, CTH JJ, Manitowoc**
Med E: + Holy Family Memorial Med Center

149 **US 151, WI 42S, Manitowoc, Chilton**
TStop E: Manitowoc Shell
Gas E: Mobil◈, Shell◈
W: BP
Food E: FastFood/Shell, Applebee's, Burger King, Country Kitchen, Culver's, Fazoli's, Perkins, Ponderosa, Starbucks, Wendy's
W: McDonald's/BP, Subway
Lodg E: Birch Creek Inn, Comfort Inn, Holiday Inn, Super 8♥
W: AmericInn
Med E: + Holy Family Memorial
Other E: LP/Shell, ATMs, Auto Dealers, Lowe's, PetCo♥, Tires Plus, Walmart sc

144 **CTH C, St. Nazianz, Newton**
Gas E: Mobil◈
Other E: Auto Repair

(142) **Weigh Station (SB)**

137 **CTH XX, North Ave, Cleveland, Kiel**
FStop E: Bonde's Quik Mart/Citgo
Food E: FastFood/Bonde's QM, Cleveland Family Rest
Other E: Wagner's RV Center

128 **WI 42, Sheboygan, Howards Grove**
FStop E: Interstate Plaza/BP (Scales)
TStop W: Citgo Oasis
Gas E: Mobil
Food E: Hardee's
W: Cousins Subs/Citgo
Lodg E: Comfort Inn
Other E: Laundry/Citgo, Gander Mountain

126 **WI 32, Sheboygan, Kohler, Fond du Lac, Plymouth**
Gas E: BP
Food E: Applebee's, Culver's, Hardee's, IHOP, McDonald's, Pizza Hut/Taco Bell
Lodg E: Baymont Inn, Ramada Inn, Super 8
Med E: + Hospital
Other E: Auto Dealers, Big Lots, Firestone, Tires, ShopKO, Walgreen's, Walmart, Mall

123 **WI 28, Sheboygan, Sheboygan Falls**
FStop E: Quality Q Mart/Citgo
Gas E: Mobil◈
Food E: McDonald's/Mobil, Perkins, Starbucks, Taco Bell, Wendy's
W: Arby's, Chili's
Lodg E: AmericInn, Holiday Inn Express
Other E: Auto Centers, Thunder Truck & Auto Repair, Harley Davidson
W: ATMs, Home Depot, Radio Shack, PetSmart♥, Target

120 **CTH V, CTH OK, Waldo, Sheboygan**
FStop E: Western Shores/66
Food E: Judie's
Lodg E: Sleep Inn
Other E: Kohler Andrae State Park▲
W: RV Center

116 **CTH AA, Foster Rd, Oostburg**

113 **WI 32N, CR H, LL, Cedar Grove**
TStop W: Hy-Way Service Center/Citgo

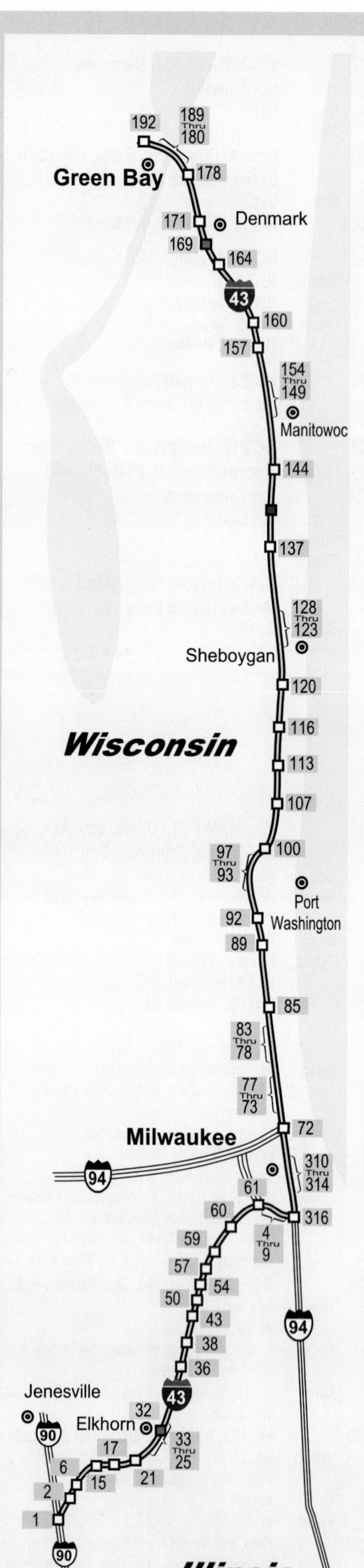

EXIT **WISCONSIN**

Food W: Country Grove Rest
Other W: Auto Repairs

107 **CTH D, Belgium, Lake Church**
TStop W: How-Dea Service Center/BP
Gas W: Mobil◈
Food W: Rest/FastFood/How-Dea SC, Hobos Korner Kitchen
Lodg W: AmericInn
TWash W: How-Dea SC
TServ W: How-Dea SC/Tires
Other W: Laundry/How-Dea SC, Harrington Beach State Park

100 **WI 32S, WI 84, CTH H, Fredonia, Port Washington**
Gas E: Citgo◈
Food E: Arby's, Burger King, McDonald's
Lodg E: Best Western

97 **WI 57N, Plymouth (NB exit, SB entr)**

96 **WI 33, Greeen Bay Dr, Saukville, Port Washington**
Gas E: Mobil◈
W: BP
Food E: Culver's Rest, Long John Silver/KFC
W: Subway
Lodg W: Super 8
Other E: Auto Dealers, Grocery, Walmart, Walgreen's

93 **WI 32N, WI 57, CTH V, Grafton, Port Washington**
Food E: Pied Piper Rest, Smith Bros Fish
Lodg E: Best Western

92 **WI 60, CTH Q, Grafton, Cedarburg**
Gas W: Citgo◈
Food E: Ghost Town Rest, Quiznos, Starbucks, Subway
Lodg W: Baymont Inn
Other W: Home Depot, Target

89 **CTH C, Cedarburg**
Gas W: Mobil◈
Lodg W: Stage Coach Inn
Med W: + St Mary Hospital

85 **WI 57S, WI 167, Mequon Rd, Thiensville**
Gas W: Citgo◈, Mobil
Food W: Café 1505, Cousins Subs, Culver's, McDonald's, Panera Bread, Starbucks, Subway, Wendy's
Lodg W: Best Western
Other W: ATMs, Banks, Cinema, Office Depot, Walgreen's

83 **CTH W, Port Washington Rd (NB ex, SB entr at County Line Rd)**

82BA **WI 32S, WI 100, Brown Deer Rd**
Gas E: BP
Food E: Cousins Subs, McDonald's, Pizza Hut, Outback Steakhouse, Qdoba Mex Rest
Lodg E: Courtyard
W: Sheraton
Other E: Best Buy, CVS, Cinema, Grocery, Walgreen's

82B **WI 100W, Brown Deer Rd**

82A **Brown Deer Rd E (NB)**
WI 32 S, Brown Deer Rd (SB)

80 **Good Hope Rd**
Gas E: BP, Mobil
Lodg E: Residence Inn
Other E: Grocery, Cardinal Stritch Univ

◈= Regular Gas Stations with Diesel ▲ = RV Friendly Locations ♥= Pet Friendly Locations
Red print shows large vehicle parking / access on site or nearby Brown Print = Campgrounds / RV PARKS

EXIT		WISCONSIN
78		**Silver Spring Dr, Milwaukee**
	Gas	E: BP, Mobil
	Food	E: Applebee's, BD Mongolian Rest, Boston Market, Burger King, Chinese, Denny's, Ground Round, Little Caesars Pizza, McDonald's, Perkins, Quiznos, Taco Bell, Tumbleweed Grill, Wendy's
	Lodg	E: Baymont Inn, Exel Inn, Woodfield Suites
	Med	W: + St Michael Hospital
	Other	E: ATMs, Banks, Barnes & Noble, Bayshore Mall, Firestone, Goodyear, Radio Shack, Walgreen's,
77B		**Hampton Ave W, Glendale (NB exit, SB entr)**
77A		**Hampton Ave E, Glendale (NB)**
	Lodg	E: Hilton
76B		**WI 57, WI 190W, Green Bay Ave, Capitol Dr (NB)**
76A		**WI 190E, Capitol Dr (NB)**
76AB		**WI 190, to WI 57, Green Bay Ave, Capitol Dr (SB)**
	Gas	W: Citgo
	Food	W: Burger King
	Other	E: Home Depot
75		**Atkinson Ave, Keefe Ave**
	Gas	E: Mobil W: BP, Citgo◊
74		**Locust St**
	Other	E: Police Dept
73C		**North Ave**
73B		**WI 145, Fond du Lac Ave**
73A		**4th St, Broadway**
72C		**Kilbourn Ave, Civic Ctr (NB) Highland Ave, Civic Ctr (SB)**
	Med	E: + St Mary's Hospital
	Other	E: Civic Center, Bradley Center Arena
	NOTE:	**I-43 below runs with I-94 thru Milwaukee, WI. Exit #'s follow I-94.**
(72B)		**Jct I-94W, US 41N, to Madison**
(72A)		**Jct I-794, Lakefront, Port of Milw**
310CAB		**Downtown Milwaukee (fr SB, LEFT Exit)**
311		**WI 59, National Ave, 6th St**
312AB		**Becher St, Mitchell St, Lapham Blvd, Greenfield Ave (WB)**
312B		**Becher St, Lincoln Ave**
312A		**Lapham Blvd, Mitchell St**
314A		**Holt Ave, Morgan Ave**
	Gas	E: Andy's◊
	Food	E: Applebee's, Jimmy John's, Starbucks, Subway
	Med	W: + St Francis Hospital
	Other	E: ATMs, Dollar General, Grocery, Home Depot, Pick 'n Save, Target
314B		**Howard Ave**
	Gas	E: Citgo, Mobil
	NOTE:	**I-43 above runs with I-94 thru Milwaukee. Exit #'s follow I-94.**
	NOTE:	**Below exits run with I-894 around Milwaukee, Exit #'s follow I-894.**

Personal Notes

EXIT		WISCONSIN
(316/ 10B)		**Jct I-43S, I-894W, to Beloit Jct I-94E, US 41S, to Chicago**
9AB		**WI 241, 27th St**
	Gas	E: BP, Clark, Citgo, Mobil
	Food	E: Arby's, Burger King, Cousins Subs, Dunkin Donuts, Famous Dave's BBQ, Pizza Hut, Rusty Skillet Rest W: Denny's, McDonald's, Taco Bell
	Lodg	W: Rodeway Inn E: Hospitality Inn, Suburban Motel
	Med	W: + Hospital
	Other	E: ATMs, Auto Zone, Auto Services, Auto Dealers, Big Lots, Dollar General, Pet World Warehouse Outlet♥, Target, Walgreen's, US Post Office, Carwash/Citgo W: ATMs, Banks, Advance Auto Parts, Auto Dealers, Auto Services
8AB		**WI 36, Loomis Rd**
	Gas	E: BP, Citgo
	Food	E: Los Mariachis Mexican Rest W: George Webb Rest
	Other	E: Carwash/BP, Carwash/Citgo, Walgreen's, W: Auto Services
7		**60th St**
	Gas	E: Speedway◊ W: Speedway
	Med	W: + Urgi Med Care Center
	Other	E: House of Harley Davidson, **Advance Camping Sales**
5AB		**S 76th St, S 84th St (NB)**
5B		**76th St, 84th St (SB, diff reaccess)**
	Food	E: Applebee's, Burger King, Ground Round, Hooters, KFC, Kopps, McDonald's,

EXIT		WISCONSIN
	Food	E: Olive Garden, Outback Steakhouse, Pizza Hut, Red Lobster, Wendy's
	Other	E: ATMs, B&N, Best Buy, Borders, Firestone, Goodyear, Office Depot, Grocery, Southridge Mall
5A		**WI 24, Forest Home Ave (SB)**
	Gas	E: Citgo
	Other	E: Carwash/Repairs/Citgo
(4/61)		**Jct I-43S, US 45S, to Beloit Jct I-894W, US 45N, to Fond du Lac**
	NOTE:	**I-43 runs above with I-894 around Milwaukee, Exit #'s follow I-894.**
60		**US 45S, WI 100, 108th St (fr SB, L ex)**
	Gas	E: BP, Citgo, Phillips 66 W: Phillips 66
	Food	E: Amore Italian Rest, Charcoal Grill W: McDonald's
	Other	W: ATMs, Aldi, Auto Services, Cinema, Grocery, Goodyear, Hertz RAC, Tires, Walgreen's, **Walmart**
59		**Layton Ave, Hales Corners (NB, LEFT Exit) (Acc to Exit #60 Serv)**
57		**Moorland Rd, Muskego, Berlin**
	Gas	W: Mobil◊
	Food	W: Applebee's, Atlanta Bread Co, McDonald's, Taco Bell, Tumbleweed, Texas Roadhouse
	Lodg	W: Baymont Inn, Best Western, Embassy Suites, Holiday Inn Express
	Other	W: Target
54		**CTH Y, Racine Ave, New Berlin**
	Gas	E: Citgo◊, KwikTrip
	Food	E: Cousins Subs, McDonald's
	Other	E: **Kastle Kampground▲**
50		**WI 164, Big Bend, Waukesha**
	Gas	W: Citgo◊
	Food	W: McDonald's
43		**WI 83, Mukwonago, Waterford**
	FStop	E: BJ's BP
	Gas	W: Citgo, Shell
	Food	W: Burger King, Cousins Subs, Culver's, McDonald's, Subway, Taco Bell
	Lodg	W: Sleep Inn
	Other	E: **to Country View Campground▲** W: Cinema, Home Depot, **Walmart sc**, Tire & Auto Services
38		**WI 20, East Troy, Waterford**
	TStop	W: Road Ranger #236
	Gas	W: BP, Clark, Shell
	Food	W: Subway/Road Ranger, Burger King, McDonald's/Shell
	Other	W: CarQuest, Auto Services, Towing
36		**WI 120, East Troy, Lake Geneva**
	TStop	W: Side View Travel Center/Citgo
	Lodg	E: Country Inn
33		**Bowers Rd, Elkhorn**
	Other	E: Apple Valley Resort & Golf Club
(32)		**Rest Area (Both dir) (RR, Phones, Picnic, Vend)**
29		**WI 11, Elkhorn, Burlington**
	Other	W: Fairgrounds
27AB		**US 12, Lake Geneva, Madison**
	Med	E: + Aurora Lakeland Medical Center
25		**WI 67, Elkhorn, Williams Bay**
	Gas	E: BP◊, Mobil W: Speedway◊
	Food	W: Burger King
	Lodg	E: AmericInn W: Lakeland Motel

◊= Regular Gas Stations with Diesel ▲ = RV Friendly Locations ♥= Pet Friendly Locations
Red print shows large vehicle parking / access on site or nearby Brown Print = Campgrounds / RV PARKS

EXIT		WISCONSIN
	Other	E: Auto Dealers W: DeHaan Auto & RV Center
21		**WI 50, E Geneva St, Delavan, to Lake Geneva**
	Gas	E: Shell◊ W: Mobil◊, Speedway◊
	Food	E: Chili's, Culver's, Domino's Pizza, Panera Bread, Quiznos, Starbucks, Subway W: Burger King, Hardee's, KFC, Pizza Hut, McDonald's, Subway, Taco Bell
	Lodg	W: Comfort Inn, Super 8
	Other	E: ATMs, Grocery, Lowe's, Radio Shack, Staples, **Walmart** sc, Greyhound Dog Track, Lake Lawn Resort
		W: ATMs, Auto Dealers, Auto Repairs, Grocery, ShopKO, Walgreen's
17		**CTH X, Delevan, Darien**
	Gas	W: BP
15		**US 14, CR C, Darien, to Janesville, Whitewater**
	Gas	E: Citgo◊
	Food	E: West Wind Diner
	Other	E: Auto Service, Tire Service, ATMs
6		**WI 140, Clinton, to Avalon**
	Gas	E: BP, Citgo
	Food	E: Subway
2		**CTH X, Hart Rd**
(1B)		**Jct I-90W, I-39N, to Madison**
(1A)		**Jct I-90E, I-39S, to Chicago** (Travel Ctrs & All Serv I-90, Ex #185A)
0		**WI 81, Beloit**

CENTRAL TIME ZONE

NOTE: **I-43 begins/ends I-90, Exit #183**

WISCONSIN

Begin Northbound I-43 at Jct I-90 from Beloit to Green Bay.

Begin Eastbound I-44 from Wichita Falls, TX to near I-55 in St. Louis, MO.

TEXAS

NOTE: **I-44 begins/ends in Wichita Falls**

CENTRAL TIME ZONE

EXIT		TEXAS
1A		**US 277S, 5th St, Central Freeway, Wichita Falls, to Abilene (SB)**
	FStop	E: on 287E Love's Travel Stop #269 (Scales)
	Gas	W: Conoco, Phillips 66
	Food	E: Subway/Love's TS W: Arby's, Burger King, IHOP, Papa John's Pizza, Popeye's, Subway, Whataburger
	Lodg	E: Holiday Inn, Howard Johnson, Knights Inn W: Econo Lodge
	Med	W: + Wichita Falls Gen'l Hospital
	Other	W: Wichita Falls RV Park▲
1B		**N 3rd St, Scotland Park (NB)**
	Food	E: Johnnie's Chicken
	Lodg	E: Scotland Park Motel W: Radisson
1C		**Vermont St, Tx Travel Info Center**
	Gas	E: Citgo
1D		**US 287 Bus, Iowa Park Rd**
	Gas	W: Conoco◊
	Food	W: El Chico, China Star, Whataburger
	Lodge	W: Days Inn, Eagle Inn, River Oaks Hotel, Travelers Inn
	Other	W: ATMs, Auto Services, Grocery
2		**Maurine St, Wichita Falls**
	Gas	E: 7-11◊, Shell◊ W: 7-11
	Food	W: DQ, Denny's, Long John Silver, Whataburger
	Lodg	E: Best Value Inn, Comfort Inn, Motel 6♥, Quality Inn W: Best Western♥, Candlewood Hotel, Hampton Inn, La Quinta Inn♥, Super 8
3A		**US 287, to Vernon, Amarillo**
	Gas	W: Shell
	Food	W: Carl's Jr
	Lodg	W: Ramada Ltd
3B		**Spur 325, to Sheppard AFB**
	Other	E: Sheppard AFB, Wichita Falls Muni Airport✈
3C		**FM 890, Municipal Airport**
	Gas	W: Shamrock, Murphy
	Food	W: Cracker Barrel
	Other	E: Wichita Falls Muni Airport✈ W: **Walmart** sc, Wichita Falls RV Center
4		**City Loop**
5		**Access Rd**
5A		**FM 3492, Missile Rd, Reilly Rd**
	Gas	W: Exxon◊
	Other	E: Sheppard AFB, Towing
6		**Bacon Switch Rd, Wichita Falls**
7		**East Rd**
(9)		**Picnic Area (Both dir)**
11		**FM 3429, Cropper Rd, Daniels Rd**

EXIT		TX / OK
12		**TX 240, Sheppard Rd, Burkburnett**
	Gas	E: Chevron, Phillips 66 W: 7-11, Fina, Shamrock
	Food	W: Braum's, Hardee's, KFC, McDonald's
	Lodg	W: Ranchouse Motel
	Other	W: Auto Services, Auto Dealer
13		**Glendale St, Burkburnett**
	Other	W: Family Dollar, SavALot, **Walmart**
14		**TX 240, Lp 267, 3rd St**
	Food	W: Circle H BBQ
	Other	W: Burkburnett RV Park▲

CENTRAL TIME ZONE

NOTE: **MM 15: Oklahoma State Line**

TEXAS

OKLAHOMA

CENTRAL TIME ZONE

EXIT		OKLAHOMA
1		**OK 36, Devol, to Grandfield**
5		**US 277N, US 281, Randlett** (NB: Last FREE Exit)
	Gas	E: Shamrock◊
(19)		**Begin TOLL, HE Bailey Turnpike**
20		**US 277N, US 281, OK 5, Walters**
(21)		**Service Plaza/OK Welcome Center**
	Gas	EZ Go Foods #44/66
	Food	McDonald's

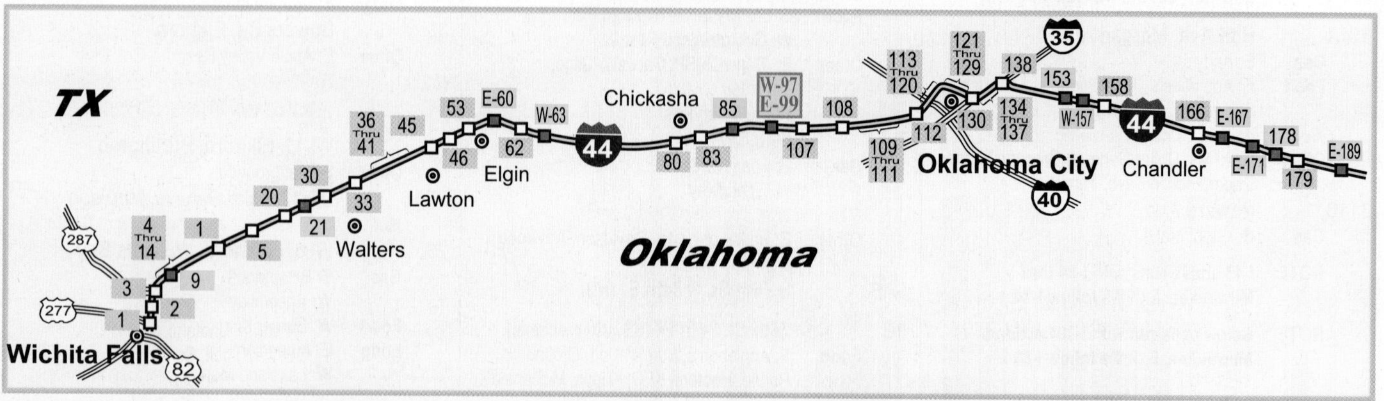

◊= Regular Gas Stations with Diesel ▲ = RV Friendly Locations ♥= Pet Friendly Locations

Red print shows large vehicle parking / access on site or nearby Brown Print = Campgrounds / RV PARKS

EXIT — OKLAHOMA

(30) **End TOLL**

30 **OK 36, Geronimo, Faxon, Frederick**

33 **US 281 Bus, 11th St, Lawton**
- Other: W: **Plaza RV & Trailer Park▲**, Lawton Muni Airport✈, Wrecker Service

36B **OK 7, Lee Blvd, to Duncan (SB)**

36A **OK 7, Lee Blvd, Lawton**
- FStop: W: Expressway Fina, Kids #3
- Gas: E: Phillips 66, Stripes/Valero◈
  W: Shamrock◈
- Food: W: Big Chef Rest, KFC/Taco Bell, Leo & Ken's Rest, Popeye's Chicken, Salas Mexican Rest, Sonic
- Lodg: W: LawtonInn, Motel 6♥
- Med: W: + SW Medical Center
- Other: W: Expressway Fina/Repairs/Tires, ATMs, Banks, Auto & Tire Services, Carwash, Towing, Fairgrounds, Animal Hospital♥,

37 **Gore Blvd, Lawton**
- Gas: E: Phillips 66
  W: Shamrock
- Food: E: Braum's, Los Tres Amigos, Sonic, Taco Mayo, Woody's BBQ, Rest/BW
- Med: E: + Kiowa Indian Hospital
  W: + Comanche Co Memorial Hospital
- Other: E: ATMs, Banks, Carwash, Penske Truck Rental
  W: ATMs, Banks, Office Depot, Harley Davidson, SavALot, Sheridan Mall, Central Mall, Cameron Univ

39A **US 62, Cache Rd (fr NB, LEFT exit)**
- Gas: W: Phillips 66, Smitty's Toot & Tote◈, Stripes/Valero, Total◈
- Food: W: Applebee's, Captain D's, Chili's, ChickFilA, Golden Corral, Long John Silver, KFC, Kimchi Garden Korean Rest, Ryan's Grill, Sam's BBQ, Sunrise & Shine Omelet Grill, Subway, Wendy's
- Lodg: W: Arrow Motel, Baymont Inn, Budget Inn, Deluxe Inn, Economy Inn, Holiday Inn, Ranch Motel, Red Lion Hotel, Relax Inn, Sheridan Inn, Super 9 Motel, Travel Inn
- Other: W: ATMs, Banks, Auto Services, Hibdon Tires Plus, Dollar General, U-Haul

39B **US 281 Bus, NW 2nd St, Lawton (SB)**
- Lodg: W: Americas Best Value Inn

40A **US 62, Rogers Lane, Lawton**
- Gas: E: Fina
- Lodg: W: Super 8
- Other: W: Fort Sill Military Res

40B **US 62W, to Cache, Altus (SB)**
- Lodg: W: Super 8
- Other: W: Fort Sill, Henry Post Army Air Field

40C **Post Rd, Gate Two, Fort Sill**

41 **Sheridan Rd, Fort Sill Key Gate**

45 **OK 49, Medicine Park, to Carnegie**
- Gas: W: Love's Country Store #263
- Food: W: Subway/Love's TS, Burger King
- Other: W: WiFi/Love's TS

46 **US 62E, US 277N, US 281, Elgin, Apache, Anadarko (NB: Last FREE Exit)**

53 **US 277, 8th St, OK 17, Elgin, to Lake Ellsworth, Fletcher, Sterling**
- Gas: E: Conoco, Shamrock
  W: Phillips 66

EXIT — OKLAHOMA

(60) **Parking Area (EB)**

62 **Whitfield Rd, Fletcher, to Elgin, Sterling (NB)**

(63) **Parking Area (WB)**

(79) **TOLL Plaza**

80 **US 81, US 277, to OK 92, Grand Ave, Chickasha, Duncan**
- FStop: E: Conoco◈
- Gas: E: Phillips 66◈, Shell◈
  W: Coastal, Conoco, Love's, Murphy
- Food: E: Burger King, Eduardo's Cafe, Western Sizzlin
  W: A&E Grill, Arby's, Braum's, Chicken Express, Denny's, El Rancho Mexican Rest Hardee's, KFC, Little Caesars Pizza, Long John Silver, Mazzio's, McDonald's, Napoli's Italian Rest, Pizza Hut, Sonic, Subway, Taco Bell, Taco Mayo
- Lodg: E: Americas Best Value Inn, Days Inn, Holiday Inn Express, Super 8
  W: Best Western, Budget Inn, Kings Inn, Ranch House Motel
- Other: E: ATMs, Auto Dealers, Auto Services, Carwash, Dollar Tree, Hibbett Sports, Hart Trailers
  W: Auto Zone, ATMs, Auto Services, CVS, Chickasha Lumber, Family Dollar, Firestone Grocery, Staples, Walgreen's, **Walmart sc**, **Chickasha RV Park▲**, **Western Center RV Park▲**, to OK College of Liberal Arts

83 **US 62, US 277, OK 9, Chickasha**
- FStop: N: 62 Truck Stop/Shamrock
- Gas: N: Conoco◈
- Food: N: Subway
- Other: N: **Time Out RV Park▲**

(85) **Service Plaza (Both dir, LEFT Exit)**
- FStop: EZ Go Foods #43/66
- Food: McDonald's

(97) **Picnic Area (WB)**

(98) **TOLL Plaza**

(99) **Parking Area (EB) Rest Area**

107 **US 62W, US 277S, Newcastle (No reacc NB, NB reacc via Serv Rd Past Ex #108)**
- TStop: N: Chickasaw Travel Plaza/Shamrock
- Food: N: KFC/Chickasaw TP, Pit Stop Grill, Sonic, Taco Mayo
- Lodg: N: Newcastle Motel
- Other: N: Laundry/Chickasaw TP, **Police Dept**

107A **Indian Hills Rd (SB)**

108 **OK 37W, NW 32nd to Tuttle, Minco**
- Gas: N: Phillips 66, Conoco◈
- Food: N: Braum's, Carl's Jr, Little Caesars Pizza, Mazzio's Pizza, McDonald's, Ribs n More
- Other: N: Dollar General, O'Reilly Auto Parts, **Walmart sc**
  S: to appr 8 mi: **A-AAA Adult RV Park▲**

108A **Frontage Rd (SB)**

109 **SW 149th St, Okla City**
- TServ: W: Southwest Diesel Service
- Other: W: Auto Service

110 **OK 37E, SW 134th St**
- Gas: S: Sinclair◈
- TServ: N: Southwest Diesel Service

111 **SW 119th St, OKC**
- Other: S: **Walker RV Center**

EXIT — OKLAHOMA

112 **SW 104th St**
- FStop: N: Hi-Way Grill & Service Station/Shell
- Gas: S: Valero
- Food: N: Grill/Shell

113 **SW 89th St, OKC**
- FStop: S: Love's Travel Stop #245
- Gas: S: Valero◈
- Food: S: Subway/Love's TS, McDonald's, Sonic, Taco Mayo
- Other: N: Will Rogers World Airport✈
  S: WiFi/Love's TS, CVS

114 **SW 74th St, OKC**
- Gas: S: Phillips 66, Sinclair
- Food: S: Braum's, Burger King, Taco Bell
- Lodg: N: Four Points Hotel
  S: Cambridge Inn
- Other: N: Will Rogers World Airport✈, Rental Cars, Women Pilots Museum
  S: Dollar General, **RV** & Truck Wash

(115) **Jct I-240E, US 62E, OK 3E, Ft Smith**

116A **SW 59th St**
- Gas: S: Conoco, Shell
- Other: N: Will Rogers World Airport✈

116B **Airport Rd (fr NB, LEFT Exit)**
- Other: N: Will Rogers World Airport✈

117AB **SW 44th St**
- Gas: E: Shell

118 **OK 152W, SW 29th St**
- Gas: N: Shell
  S: 7-11
- Food: S: Burger King, Captain D's, KFC, McDonald's, Taco Bell, Taco Bueno
- Lodg: N: Budget Inn, Bel-Aire Motel
- Other: S: Auto Zone, Walgreen's, Grocery, to Downtown Airpark✈

119 **SW 15th St**

(120A) **Jct I-40W, to Amarillo (NB, LEFT exit)**

(120B) **Jct I-40E, to Ft Smith (SB, LEFT exit)**

121B **NW 10th St W, Fair Park**
- Gas: N: Shell
- Other: N: Auto Services, Towing, **McClain's RV Superstore/Camping World**

121A **NW 10th St E, Fair Park**
- Gas: S: 7-11, Shell
- Other: S: All Sports Stadium, Fairgrounds, **State Fair Park▲**

122 **NW 23rd St, OKC**
- Gas: N: 7-11, Conoco
  S: Conoco
- Food: N: Church's Chicken, Long John Silver, Taco Mayo
  S: Arby's, Sonic
- Other: N: Tires Plus
  S: Big O Tire, Family Dollar

123A **NW 36th St, I-44, OK 66E**

123B **OK 66W, NW 39th St, to Warr Acres, to Bethany, Yukon**
- Food: N: Burger King, Carl's Jr, Meike's Rt 66, Quiznos, Taste of China
- Lodg: N: Carlyle Motel, Comfort Lodge, Hollywood Hotel, Nuhoma Motel
- Med: N: + First Med Urgent Care Clinic
- Other: N: to Wiley Post Airport✈

124 **North May Ave**
- Gas: N: Shell
- Food: S: Wendy's, Whataburger
  N: Subway/Shell, Sonic
- Lodg: N: Days Inn, Ramada, Super 8

◈ = Regular Gas Stations with Diesel ▲ = RV Friendly Locations ♥ = Pet Friendly Locations
Red print shows large vehicle parking / access on site or nearby Brown Print = Campgrounds / RV PARKS

EXIT		OKLAHOMA
	Other	N: O'Reilly Auto Parts
		S: Lowe's
125A		**Penn Ave, to NW Expy, NW 36th**
	Gas	N: Conoco◊
		S: Shell
	Food	N: Burger King/Conoco
		S: Braum's
	Lodg	N: Habana Inn
125B		**NW Expy, Classen Blvd, OKC (fr SB, LEFT exit)**
	Gas	N: Shell
	Food	N: Cajun Café, Garcia's, Moe's SW Grill, Olive Garden
		S: City Bites Subs, IHOP, McDonald's
	Lodg	S: AmeriSuites, Courtyard, Hawthorne Suites
	Other	N: Penn Square Mall, Radio Shack, Ross, **Walmart sc**
125C		**NW Expy (SB, LEFT Exit)**
126		**Western Ave, Grand Blvd**
	Lodg	S: Guest House Motel
(127)		**Jct I-235S, US 77, OKC, Edmond**
	Gas	N: Conoco, Shell
	Lodg	N: Best Western, Holiday Inn
128A		**Lincoln Blvd, State Capitol**
	Lodg	S: Holiday Inn, Oxford Inn, Whitten Inn♥
128B		**Kelly Ave**
	Gas	N: Conoco, Shamrock◊
	Food	N: Sonic, Subway/Shamrock
	Other	N: Cowboy Hall of Fame
129		**M L King Ave**
	Food	N: County Line BBQ
		S: McDonald's
	Lodg	N: Ramada
	Other	S: Family Dollar, Remington Park Race Track, Tinseltown 20, **Twin Fountains RV Park▲**
(130)		**Jct I-35S, to I-40, to Dallas**
	NOTE:	**I-44 runs below with I-35, Exit 134-137. Exit #'s follow I-35.**
133		**NE 63rd St (NB, Fr I-35)**
134		**Wilshire Blvd, NE 78th St**
	Lodg	W: Executive Inn
	Other	W: Blue Beacon TW
135		**Britton Rd, NE 93rd St**
136		**Hefner Rd, OKC**
	Gas	W: Conoco◊, Gas at the Flag
	Food	W: Rest/Conoco, DQ
	Other	W: Frontier City Theme Park
137		**NE 122nd St, to OKC**
	TStop	E: Travel Stop #26/Shell
		W: Flying J Travel Plaza #5036/Conoco (Scales), Love's Travel Stop #205 (Scales)
	Gas	E: Petro Plus 5, Shamrock◊
	Food	E: FastFood/Travel Stop, Charly's Rest
		W: CtryMarket/FastFood/FJ TP, Subway/Love's TS, **Cracker Barrel**, McDonald's, Sonic, Waffle House
	Lodg	E: Motel 6♥, Sleep Inn, Travelodge
		W: Comfort Inn, Days Inn, Economy Inn, Motel 6, Quality Inn, Red Carpet Inn, Super 8
	TWash	W: American Eagle TW
	Other	E: WiFi/Travel Stop
		W: Laundry/WiFi/**RVDump/LP**/FJ TP, WiFi/Love's TS, **Abe's RV Park▲**
(138)		**Jct I-35N, to Wichita**
(138A)		**Jct I-44E, Turner Turnpike (NB)**

Personal Notes

EXIT		OKLAHOMA
(138B)		**Jct Kilpatrick Turnpike (NB)**
	NOTE:	**I-44 runs above with I-35. Exit #'s follow I-35.**
(153)		**Parking Area (Both dir)**
(157)		**Service Area (WB)**
	FStop	Phillips 66
	Food	McDonald's
158		**OK 66, Rte 66, US 177, Wellston**
	Other	**N: to Country Homes Estates RV Park▲**
166		**OK 18, Price Ave, Chandler, to Cushing**
	FStop	S: EZ Go Foods #51/66
	Food	S: Little Caesars Pizza, Marsha's Rest
	Lodg	S: Econo Lodge♥, Lincoln Motel
	Other	**S: to Oak Glenn RV & MH Park▲**, Chandler Tire, Chandler Muni Airport✈, **to Sparks America Campground▲**
(167)		**Service Plaza (EB)**
	FStop	Phillips 66
(171)		**Parking Area (EB)**
(178)		**Service Plaza (Both dir, LEFT exit)**
	FStop	EZ Go Foods #53/66
	Food	McDonald's
179		**OK 99, Stroud, to Drumright**
	Gas	N: Citgo
		S: Phillips 66◊
	Food	N: Subway, Wendy's, Rest/BW
		S: Mazzio's Pizza, Sonic, Taco Mayo
	Lodg	N: Best Western
		S: Skyliner Motel, Sooner Motel
	Med	S: + Stroud Regional Medical Center
	Other	N: to Stroud Muni Airport✈

EXIT		OKLAHOMA
(183)		**TOLL Plaza**
(189)		**Parking Area (EB)**
(192)		**Parking Area (WB)**
196		**OK 48, OK 66, Bristow, Lake Keystone (Gas, Food, Lodg 2mi S in Bristow)**
(197)		**Service Plaza (EB)**
	FStop	Phillips 66
	Food	McDonald's
(204)		**Picnic Area (EB)**
(205)		**Picnic Area (WB)**
(207)		**Service Plaza (WB)**
	FStop	EZ Go Foods #52/66
211		**OK 33, OK 66, Kellyville, Sapulpa**
	FStop	S: Fastop #135/Shell
215		**OK 97, 9th St, Main St, Sapulpa, to Rte 66, Sand Springs**
	Gas	S: Kum & Go, Phillips 66◊
	Food	S: Arby's
	Lodg	N: Super 8
	Med	S: + Hospital
218		**Creek Turnpike, US 75A (NB)**
	Other	**S: Rte 66 RV Park▲, 66 MH & RV Park▲**
(221)		**Turner Tpk Begins WB, Ends EB**
221A		**57th West Ave, Tulsa**
221B		**OK 66, US 75A, to Creek Tpke (SB, LEFT exit)**
	Other	**S: Rte 66 RV Park▲, 66 MH & RV Park▲**
222A		**49th West Ave, Skelly Dr, Tulsa**
	TStop	S: QuikTrip #102 (Scales)
	Food	N: Carl's Jr, Kelly's Country Cooking Rest, Monterey Tex Mex Cafe
		S: Wendy's/QT, Arby's, Carl's Jr, McDonald's, Taco Bueno, Waffle House, Village Inn
	Lodg	N: Interstate Inn,
		S: Motel 6♥, Super 8, Economy Inn, Days Inn
	TServ	N: Mack
		S: Kenworth, Tulsa Freightliner, Volvo, Rush Truck Center, Les's Diesel Service
	Other	N: ATMs, 84 Lumber, Big Lots, Dollar General, Radio Shack
		S: ATMs
222B		**55th Pl S, Skelly Dr (NB)**
	Lodg	S: Days Inn, Economy Inn
222C		**56th St, Skelly Dr (SB)**
	Lodg	N: Gateway Motor Hotel, Interstate Inn, Super 9
(223A)		**Jct I-244E, MLK Expwy, Downtown Tulsa (SB)**
223B		**Gilcrease Expwy, 51st St (SB)**
223C		**33rd West Ave, Tulsa**
	Gas	S: Conoco
	Food	N: Braum's, Domino's Pizza
224		**US 75, Elmblood Ave, Union Ave, to Okmulgee, Bartlesville**
	Gas	N: QT◊
	Food	N: KFC, Mazzio's Pizza, Subway
	Lodg	S: Budget Inn, Royal Inn
	TServ	S: FWF Truck Sales
	Other	N: ATMs, Dollar General, Laundromat, Warehouse Market, **Tulsa Warrior RV Park▲**

◊= Regular Gas Stations with Diesel ▲ = RV Friendly Locations ♥= Pet Friendly Locations
Red print shows large vehicle parking / access on site or nearby **Brown Print = Campgrounds / RV PARKS**

EXIT — OKLAHOMA

225 — 51st St, Elwood Ave (SB)
- Other — N: to Cherry Hill MH & RV Park▲

226A — Riverside Dr
- Food — S: Village Inn
- Lodg — N: Stratford House Inn

226B — Peoria Ave, Tulsa
- Gas — N: QT, Shell
  S: Shell
- Food — N: China Wok, CiCi's Pizza, Egg Roll Express, Elmer's BBQ, Little Caesars, Pizza Hut, McDonald's, Taco Bell, Taco Bueno, Waffle House
  S: Braum's, Burger King, Kelly's Rest,
- Lodg — N: Super 8
- Other — N: ATMs, Banks, Hertz RAC, O'Reilly Auto Parts, Auto Services, Myers Duren Harley Davidson, Animal Hospital♥
  S: ATMs, Auto Zone, Dollar General, Grocery, Walgreen's, Carwash/Shell,

227 — Lewis Ave, Oral Roberts University
- Gas — S: Shell, Sinclair
- Food — S: El Chico, Steak Stuffers, Wendy's
- Other — S: Tires Plus, Walgreen's

228 — Harvard Ave, Tulsa
- Gas — N: Shell◈
  S: Citgo, Phillips 66
- Food — N: Shoney's, Subway
  S: Blimpie's, Bodean Seafood Rest, Chili's, Lone Star Steakhouse, Long John Silver, McDonald's, Osaka, Piccadilly's
- Lodg — N: Tradewinds East Inn, Towers Hotel, Trade Winds Central Inn
  S: Holiday Inn Express. Howard Johnson, Ramada Inn♥
- Other — S: Albertson's, Dollar Tree, Kelly Tire

229 — Yale Ave, St Francis Hospital
- Gas — N: Shell
  S: Phillips 66◈, QuikTrip
- Food — N: McDonald's
  S: Applebee's, Arby's, Braum's, Burger King, Carrabba's, Denny's, Don Pablo's, Outback Steakhouse, Red Lobster, Steak & Ale, Taco Bell, Village Inn
- Lodg — S: Baymont Inn♥, Comfort Inn, Days Inn, Holiday Inn Select, Red Roof Inn♥, Travelodge
- Med — S: + St. Francis Hospital, + Children's Medical Center
- Other — N: Tulsa Promenade Mall, Firestone, PetCo♥
  S: Celebration Station

230 — 41st St, Sheridan Rd
- Gas — N: Shell
- Food — N: Carl's Jr, On the Border, Subway, TGI Friday, Whataburger
  S: Ramsey's Steakhouse

EXIT — OKLAHOMA

- Lodg — N: La Quinta Inn♥
  S: Quality House
- Other — N: B&N, Goodyear, PetSmart♥
  S: Best Buy, Home Depot, to Sam's Club

231 — US 64, OK 51, Muskogee, E 31st St, Memorial Dr, Broken Arrow
- Gas — N: Phillips 66
  S: Shell
- Food — N: Whataburger
  S: Cracker Barrel, Cattleman's Steak House, IHOP, McDonald's, Village Inn
- Lodg — N: Best Value Inn, Days Inn, Ramada Inn, Travelodge
  S: Best Western, Comfort Inn, Courtyard, Econo Lodge, Extended Stay America, Fairfield Inn, Hampton Inn, Holiday Inn Express, Quality Inn, Sleep Inn, Studio Plus, Super 8
- Other — N: Police Dept
  S: Office Depot

232 — Memorial Dr, 31st St (SB) (Access #231 Services)

233B — East 21st St (SB)
- Gas — S: Citgo
- Food — S: El Chico
- Lodg — S: Comfort Suites
- Other — S: Dean's RV Superstore

234A — US 169, Mingo Valley Expy, S to Broken Arrow, N to Owasso

234B — Garnett Rd (NB)
- Gas — S: QT◈
- Food — N: Denny's, Mazzio's Pizza, Sonic
  S: Braum's
- Lodg — N: Econo Lodge, Motel 6♥

235 — East 11th St, Garnett Rd
- Gas — N: Phillips 66
- Food — N: Carl's Jr, Denny's, Lotta Burger, Sonic, Waffle House
  S: Taco Bueno
- Lodg — N: Executive Inn, Garnett Inn, Motel 6, Super 8
  S: Econo Lodge, National Inn
- Other — N: Dollar General, O'Reilly Auto Parts, Pharmacy

236A — 129th East Ave, E Admiral Pl (SB)
- TStop — N: Flying J Travel Plaza #5008/Conoco (Scales)
- Food — N: Rest/FastFood/FJ TP, McDonald's
- Other — N: Laundry/WiFi/RVDump/LP/FJ TP,

(236B) — I-244W, Downtown Tulsa, Airport
- Other — N: Tulsa Int'l Airport✈, to Mingo RV Park▲

238 — 161st East Ave, Tulsa, Catoosa
- TStop — N: Shell (Scales), QuikTrip #71 (Scales) Fiesta Mart #27 9187394240 161st

EXIT — OKLAHOMA

- Food — N: Rest/Shell, FastFood/QT, Country Kettle
  S: Arby's, Burger King
- Lodg — S: Microtel
- TServ — N: Bridgestone Tire & Auto
- Other — S: Walker RV Center, Tulsa RV Sales & Service

240A — OK 167N, 193rd East Ave, Catoosa
- FStop — N: Johnny's Quick Stop/Shell (4 mi N), Speedy's #1/66
- TStop — N: SunMart #46
- Gas — S: QT, Shell◈
- Food — N: Rest/Speedy's, Rest/SunMart, KFC, McDonald's, Pizza Hut, Taco Mayo, Waffle House, Wendy's
  S: Mazzio's Pizza, Sonic, Subway
- Lodg — N: Super 8
  S: Holiday Inn Express
- Other — N: KOA Tulsa▲, Ugly John's Custom Boats & RV
  S: Dollar General, Family Dollar, NAPA, Grocery, Auto & Tire Service

240B — US 412E, Choteau, Siloam Springs

241 — OK 66E, to Catoosa, Claremore

(241) — Will Rogers Tpk Begins EB, Ends WB

248 — OK 266, to OK 66, Claremore, to Catoosa

255 — OK 20, Claremore, to Pryor
- Gas — N: Citgo, Kum & Go
  S: Phillips 66
- Food — N: Arby's, Carl's Jr, McDonald's
- Lodg — N: Best Western, Days Inn, Super 8
- Med — N: + Claremore Reg'l Hospital
- Other — N: Walmart sc, to Willow Run MH & RV Park▲

(256) — Parking Area (SB)

(269) — Parking Area (NB)

269 — OK 28, Adair, to Chelsea (fr EB, No re-entry)

(271) — Picnic Area (SB)

283 — US 69, Big Cabin
- TStop — N: AmBest/Big Cabin Travel Plaza/Shell (Scales)
- Food — N: Cherokee Rest/FastFood/Big Cabin TP
- Lodg — N: Super 8/Big Cabin TP
- TWash — N: Big Cabin TP
- TServ — N: Big Cabin TP/Tires
- Other — N: Laundry/Big Cabin TP

(286) — TOLL Plaza

(288) — Service Plaza (Both dir)
- FStop — EZ Go Foods #47/66
- Food — McDonald's

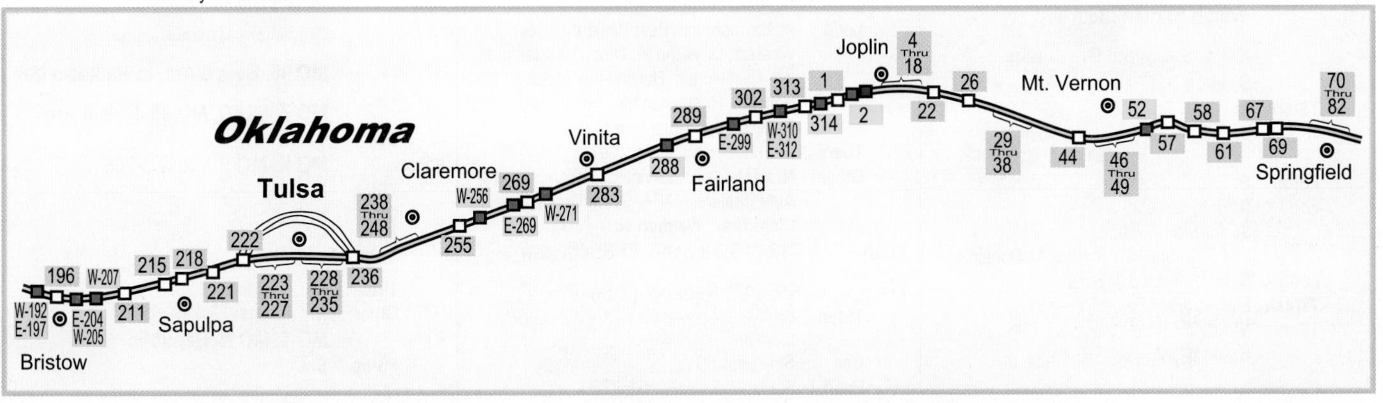

◈ = Regular Gas Stations with Diesel ▲ = RV Friendly Locations ♥ = Pet Friendly Locations
Red print shows large vehicle parking / access on site or nearby Brown Print = Campgrounds / RV PARKS

EXIT | OK / MO

289 **US 60, US 69, Vinita**
- FStop N: Phillips 66
- Gas N: Murphy
- Food N: Subway/66, Braum's, Carl's Jr, McDonald's, Pizza Hut
- Lodg N: Holiday Inn Express
- Med N: + Hospital
- Other N: Auto Dealers, Auto Services, Tires, Dollar General, Grocery, **Walmart sc**, **OK State Hwy Patrol Post**

(299) **Parking Area (NB)**

302 **US 59, US 69, US 60, Afton, to Fairland, Grove, Miami**
- FStop S: to Buffalo Ranch Travel Center/Citgo
- Food S: FastFood/Buffalo Ranch TC
- Lodg N: Shangri-La Inn
- Other N: **Bears Den Resort Campground▲**
  S: **Cedar Oaks RV Resort▲**

(310) **Parking Area (WB)**

(312) **Parking Area (EB)**

313 **OK 10, to US 69, OK 66, Miami**
- FStop N: Eastern Shawnee Travel Center/Citgo
- Gas N: Conoco◈, Love's Country Store◈,GAS
- Food N: Arby's, McDonald's, Okie Burger, Rest/BW
- Lodg N: Best Western, Deluxe Inn, Holiday Inn Express, Microtel, Super 8, Towneman Motel
- Med N: + Baptist Reg'l Hospital
- Other N: ATMs, Auto Services, Tires, Towing, **Miami RV & MH Park▲**, to Stables Casino, Buffalo Run Casino & Hotel
  S: Auto Dealers, High Winds Casino

(314) **Service Plaza/OK Welcome Ctr (WB)**
- FStop EZ Go Foods #48/66
- Food McDonald's

CENTRAL TIME ZONE

NOTE: MM 329: Oklahoma State Line

⇧ OKLAHOMA
⇩ MISSOURI

CENTRAL TIME ZONE

1 **US 400, US 166, Joplin, to Baxter Springs, KS**

(2) **MO Welcome Center (EB)**
Rest Area (WB)
(RR, Phone, Picnic)

(3) **Weigh Station (Both dir)**

4 **MO 43S, Coyote Dr, Joplin, Seneca**
- TStop N: Love's Travel Stop #282
  S: Petro Stopping Center #54/BP (Scales), Pilot Travel Center #317 (Scales)
- FStop S: Rapid Robert's #122/Conoco
- Food N: Hardee's/Love's TS
  S: IronSkillet/Blimpie/Petro, Wendy's/Pilot TC, Subway/Conono, McDonald's
- Lodg S: Motel/Petro SC, Sleep Inn
- TWash S: TruckOMat/Petro SC
- TServ N: Peterbilt
  S: Petro SC/Tires

Personal Notes

EXIT | MISSOURI

- Other N: WiFi/**RVDump**/Love's TS, **Zan's Creek Side Campground▲**
  S: Laundry/BarbSh/WiFi/**LP**/Petro SC, WiFi/Pilot TC, WiFi/ Rapid Robert's, **Joplin KOA▲**

6 **Bus 44, MO 43N, MO 86, Joplin, Hearns Blvd, to Racine**
- Gas N: BP
- Food N: Arby's, McDonald's, Pizza Hut
- Med N: + St Johns Regional Hospital

8BA **US 71 Bus, Range Line Rd, Joplin**
- Gas N: Citgo, Conoco, Kum & Go◈, Sam's
  S: Casey's, Citgo, Phillips 66
- Food N: Applebee's, Arby's, Bob Evans, CiCi's, Country Kitchen, Denny's, Gringo's Grill, IHOP, KFC, Kyoto, McDonald's,
- Food N: Olive Garden, Outback Steakhouse, Red Hot & Blue, Ruby Tuesday, Steak 'n Shake, Subway, Waffle House, Wendy's
  S: Cracker Barrel
- Lodg N: Baymont Inn, Best Value Inn, Best Western, Days Inn♥, Drury Inn, Hampton Inn, Fairfield Inn, Holiday Inn, Motel 6, Ramada, Residence Inn, Super 8♥
  S: Microtel, Towneplace Suites
- TServ N: Freightliner Trucks
- Other N: ATMs, Auto Services, Grocery, Lowe's, Auto Dealers, NAPA, Office Depot, Sam's Club, Tires, **Walmart sc**

11BA **US 71S, Neosho, Ft Smith (SB)**

11A **US 71S, Neosho, Ft Smith**
- TStop S: Flying J Travel Plaza #5080/Conoco (Scales)
- Gas S: Phillips 66
- Food S: CtryMkt/FastFood/FJ TP

EXIT | MISSOURI

- TWash S: Blue Beacon Truck Wash
- Other S: Laundry/BarbSh/WiFi/**RVDump/LP**/FJ TP

11B **MO 249N, to MO 66, Joplin**

15 **I-44 Bus, Rte 66, 7th St, Joplin (SB)**
- Lodg N: Tara Motel

18B **MO 59, US 71N, Carthage, Ks City**
- FStop N: to Flying W Conv Store
- Gas N: to Casey's, Murphy USA
- Food N: to Hardee's, Ranch House BBQ & Steaks, Taco Bell
- Lodg N: to Best Western, Budget Way Motel, Carthage Inn, Days Inn, Super 8
- Other N: to **Walmart sc**, Walgreen's, Auto Dealers, Auto Services, **Coachlight RV Center & Park▲**, **Big Red Barn RV Park▲**, **Precious Moments Cubby Bear's RV Park▲**

18A **MO 59, Carthage, to Diamond**
- Other S: **Ballard's Campground & Store▲**

22 **CR 100, 10th Rd, Carthage**
- FStop S: Express Truck Stop
- Food S: FastFood/Express TS
- Other N: **Colaw RV Parts & Salvage**

26 **MO 37, Bus 44, Sarcoxie, to Reeds**

29 **MO U, High St, Sarcoxie, La Russell**
- Gas S: Conoco, Kum & Go, Casey's Gen'l Store
- Food S: Subway/Kum&Go
- Other N: Antiques, Gift Shops, **WAC RV Park▲**
  S: ATM, Dollar General

33 **CR 1010, MO 97S, to Pierce City**
- FStop S: Zip Stop/Sinclair
- Food S: HungryHouseCafe/Sinclair

38 **MO 97, Stotts City, Pierce City**
- Gas N: Massie's Super Stop

44 **MO H, Bus 44, Mt. Vernon, Monett**
- Gas N: Citgo
- Lodg N: Walnuts Motel

46 **MO 39, MO 265, Bus 44, Mt Vernon to Aurora**
- TStop N: Travel Center of America #72/Conoco (Scales)
- Gas N: Phillips 66◈
  S: BP◈
- Food N: CountryPride/TA TC, Bamboo Garden, Country Kitchen, Hardee's, KFC/LJ Silver, McDonald's, Sonic, Subway, Taco Bell
- Lodg N: Super 8, USA Inn
  S: Comfort Inn
- TWash N: TA TC
- TServ N: TA TC/Tires
- Other N: Laundry/WiFi/TA TC, Dollar General, Family Dollar, O'Reilly Auto Parts

49 **MO 174, CR CC, to Chesapeake**

(52) **Rest Area (Both dir)**
(RR, Phones, Picnic, Vend)

57 **MO 96, Bois d'Arc, to Halltown (SB)**

58 **MO Z, MO O, MO 96, Bois d'Arc**
- Gas S: Shell◈

61 **MO K, MO PP, to MO 266**
- TStop N: Hood's Service Center/Cenex (Scales)
- Gas N: Phillips 66
- Food N: Rest/Hoods SC
- Lodg N: Motel/Hoods SC
- Tires N: Hoods SC
- Other N: Laundry/WiFi/**LP**/Hoods SC

67 **MO T, MO N, Republic**
- FStop S: Citgo

◈= Regular Gas Stations with Diesel ▲ = RV Friendly Locations ♥= Pet Friendly Locations
Red print shows large vehicle parking / access on site or nearby Brown Print = Campgrounds / RV PARKS

EXIT		MISSOURI
69		**MO 360, James River Expy, to US60**
70		**MO B, MO MM, Springfield**
	Gas	S: Phillips 66
	Other	S: **Springfield KOA▲**
72		**MO 266, Bus 44, Chestnut Expy**
	FStop	S: Coastal Super Stop
	Gas	S: Casey's
	Food	S: Casey's C/O Pizza, Hardee's, Subway, Taco Bell, Waffle House
	Lodg	S: Best Budget Inn, Ramada Ltd
	Other	N: **Travelers Park Campground▲**
75		**US 160, West ByPass, to Willard**
	Gas	S: Conoco, Phillips 66
	Lodg	S: Courtyard, La Quinta Inn♥
	Other	N: Springfield Reg'l Airport✈
77		**MO 13, Kansas Expy, to Bolivar**
	FStop	N: 4 mi N: Crossroads Convenience Store/Conoco
	Gas	S: Gas Plus, Phillips 66, QT
	Food	S: Arby's, Braum's, CiCi's, Golden Corral, IHOP, McDonald's, Papa John's, Subway, Taco Bell, Waffle House, Wendy's
	Lodg	N: Interstate Inn S: Econo Lodge
	Med	S: + Springfield Clinic
	Other	N: Lowe's, Central Bible College S: Mall, Big Lots, Dollar Tree, Grocery, Goodyear, O'Reilly Auto , Radio Shack, Staples, **Walmart sc**, Walgreen's
80A		**Bus 44, Glenstone Ave, Springfield**
	FStop	S: to 2mi S Johnson One Stop/Conoco
	Gas	S: Gas, Phillips 66◈, QT, Shell
	Food	S: Applebee's, Backyard Burgers, Bob Evans, Buckingham Smokehouse BBQ, Burger King, Captain D's, Costa Mesa Mexican Rest, Cracker Barrel, Denny's, Hardee's, KFC, Long John Silver, McDonald's, Pizza Hut, Rib Crib, Ruby Tuesday, Ryan's Grill, Shoney's, Steak 'n Shake, Subway, Taco Bell, Village Inn, Western Sizzlin
	Lodg	S: Americas Best Value Inn, Best Western, Best Western, Budget Inn, Candlewood Suites, Comfort Inn, Days Inn, Doubletree Hotel, Drury Inn, Economy Inn, Econo Lodge, Flag Ship Motell, Hampton Inn, Krystal Aire Inn, Lamplighter Inn, La Quinta Inn♥, Motel 6♥, Ozark Inn, Plaza Inn, Red Lion Hotel, Sheraton, Springfield Inn
	TWash	S: Kearney Street Truck Wash
	Med	S: + Doctors Hospital, + Ozarks Comm Hospital
	Other	S: LP/Johnson OS, ATMs, Auto Zone, Auto Services, Bass Pro Shop, Goodyear, O'Reilly Auto Parts, **Walmart**, Battlefield Mall, Fairgrounds, Zoo, S MO State Univ
80B		**Glenstone Ave, MO H**
	FStop	N: Rapid Robert's #123/Conoco (Scales)
	Gas	N: Phillips 66◈, Shell
	Food	N: Waffle House
	Lodg	N: Budget Lodge, Days Inn, Hotel 7, Microtel, Super 8
82A		**US 65S, to Branson, Sedalia**
	Gas	S: Phillips 66◈
	Food	S: McDonald's, Waffle House
	Lodg	S: American Inn, Days Inn, Microtel, Super 8
	TServ	S: Cummins Ozark Kenworth, White GMC Volvo, Peterbilt of Springfield
	Other	S: MO State Hwy Patrol Post
82B		**US 65N, to Branson, Sedalia**
84		**MO 744, Springfield**
	TServ	S: Peterbilt of Springfield
88		**MO 125, Strafford, to Fair Grove**
	FStop	N: Go Convenience #11/P66 (Scales)
	TStop	N: Travel Center of America #137/Amoco (Scales)
	Gas	S: Kum & Go◈, Conoco◈
	Food	N: CountryPride/Subway/TacoBell/ TA TC, Rest/Pizza/P66, McDonald's S: Dana's Cafe, Fox's Pizza Den, Grandaddy's BBQ
	Lodg	S: Super 8
	TWash	N: Quality Truck Wash, Kearney Truck Wash & Lube
	TServ	N: TA TC/Tires, P66, Cross Midwest Tire
	Other	N: Laundry/RVDump/P66, Laundry/ WiFi/TA TC, Red Rocket Fireworks, **Paradise in the Woods RV Park▲**, **Camping World** S: ATMs, Banks, Auto Service, Pharmacy, LP, **Strafford RV Park▲**
(89)		**Weigh Station (Both dir)**
96		**MO B, Marshfield, Northview**
	Other	N: **Paradise in the Woods RV Park▲**
100		**MO 38, Spur Dr, Marshfield**
	Gas	N: AmocoBP S: Conoco◈, Citgo◈, Kum & Go◈, Phillips 66◈, Shell
	Food	N: Tiny's Smokehouse BBQ S: Country Kitchen, El Charro, DQ, McDonald's, Pizza Hut, Sonic, Subway
	Lodg	N: Plaza Motel S: Holiday Inn Express
	Other	N: Goodyear, **Fountain Plaza MH & RV Park▲** S: Grocery, Pharmacy, **Walmart sc▲** , **RV Express RV Park▲**
107		**Sampson Rd, Marshfield**
113		**CR Y, CR J, MO M, Conway**
	Gas	N: Phillips 66 S: Conoco
	Food	N: Cafe
	Lodg	N: Budget Inn
118		**MO A, MO C, Phillipsburg**
	Gas	N: Conoco◈ S: Phillips 66
123		**Dove Rd, Phillipsburg**
	Gas	S: EZ Mart
	Other	S: **Happy Trails RV Center, Lebanon KOA▲**
127		**Bus Lp 44, Morgan Rd, Elm St, Lebanon**
	TStop	N: Clayton's Conoco (Scales)
	Gas	N: Phillips 66◈, Sinclair◈ S: Phillips 66◈
	Food	N: Rest/Clayton's TP, Ranch House, Waffle House
	Lodg	N: Days Inn, Econo Lodge, Hampton Inn, Holiday Inn Express, Rte 66 Inn Motel, Super 8, Travelers Inn
	TWash	N: Clayton's TP
	TServ	N: Clayton's TP/Tires
	Other	N: Laundry/LP/Clayton's TP, Auto Dealers, Kelly Tires S: Auto Dealers, to Floyd W Jones Lebanon Airport✈
129		**MO 5, MO 32, to Bus 44, MO 64, Lebanon, Hartville**
	Gas	N: Conoco, Kum & Go, Phillips 66◈ S: AmocoBP, Conoco◈
	Food	N: Applebee's, Bamboo Garden, Burger King, Country Kitchen, DQ, Jay's Family Rest, KFC, Long John Silver, Pizza Hut, Papa John's, McDonald's, Shoney's, Sonic, Subway, Taco Bell, Western Sizzlin S: Captain D's, Hardee's, Pizza Hut
	Lodg	N: Days Inn, Econo Lodge♥, Holiday Inn Express♥, Hampton Inn, Historic Rte 66 Inn, Super 8, Travelers Inn
	TServ	S: Johnson Service Center/Goodyear
	Med	N: + St John's Hospital
	Other	N: Auto Dealers, Advance Auto, Auto Zone, NAPA, O'Reilly Auto Parts, **to appr 9 mi: Oak Hill Campground▲** S: Auto Dealers, Dollar General, Lowe's, Ozark Harley Davidson, **Walmart sc**, **to** Floyd W Jones Lebanon Airport✈
130		**Bus 44, CR MM, Lebanon**
	Gas	N: Conoco, Phillips 66
	Food	N: Rest/BW
	Lodg	N: Best Western♥, Holiday Motel
	TServ	S: Johnson Service Center/Goodyear
	Med	N: + St John's Hospital
	Other	N: Forest Manor Motel & **RV Park▲**
135		**MO F, Lebanon, to Sleeper**
140		**MO T, MO N, to Stoutland**
	FStop	S: Phillips 66
	Food	S: Midway Chinese
145		**MO 133, Richland**
	TStop	N: Oasis Truck Plaza/Conoco/tires
	Food	N: Rest/Oasis TP
150		**MO 7, MO P, Richland, to Laquey**
153		**MO 17, Waynesville, to Buckhorn**
	FStop	N: Whitmore Farms/Cenex
	Gas	S: Shell◈
	Food	N: Rest/Whitmore Farms
	Lodg	N: Ft Wood Inn
	Other	S: **Glen Oaks RV Park▲**
156		**Hwy H, Bus Loop 44, Waynesville**
	Gas	N: Citgo◈, Smitty's
	Food	N: Smitty's, McDonald's, Subway
	Lodg	N: Star Motel
	Other	N: Dollar General, Grocery, Auto Dealers, **Covered Wagon RV Park▲** S: Fort Leonard Wood
159		**MO 17, Bus Lp 44, St Robert**
	Gas	N: Conoco S: BP◈, Phillips 66, Shell
	Food	N: DQ, Sonic S: Oakwood Café, Pine Steakhouse
	Lodg	N: Star Motel S: Microtel, Motel 6
	Med	S: + Mercy Medical Group
	Other	N: Goodyear, **Covered Wagon RV Park▲**
161A		**Bus 44S, Missouri Ave, St Robert, Ft Leonard Wood**
161B		**MO Y, Bus 44N, St Robert**
	FStop	S: St Robert Cenex
	Gas	N: Mobil◈ S: Conoco, Cenex◈
	Food	N: Cracker Barrel, Long John Silver, Pizza Hut, Popeye's, Ryan's Grill, Ruby Tuesday, Subway S: Arby's, Captain D's, Japanese Sushi, KFC, McDonald's, Subway, Taco Bell, Waffle House, Wendy's
	Lodg	N: Baymont Inn, Candlewood Suites, Comfort Inn, Fairfield Inn, Hampton Inn, Red Roof Inn

◈ = Regular Gas Stations with Diesel ▲ = RV Friendly Locations ♥ = Pet Friendly Locations

Red print shows large vehicle parking / access on site or nearby **Brown Print = Campgrounds / RV PARKS**

Lodg S: Budget Inn, Econo Lodge, Holiday Inn Express, Microtel, Motel 6, Ramada Inn
Other N: Dollar Tree, **Walmart sc**
S: Auto Zone, Firestone, Radio Shack

163 MO 28, St Robert, to Dixon
TStop N: Road Ranger #157/Pilot TC #547/ Citgo (Scales)
Gas S: Conoco
Food N: Chesters/Subway/Road Ranger/PTC
S: Country Cafe, Sweetwater BBQ
Lodg S: Best Western, Days Inn, Knights Inn, Super 8, Villager Lodge & **RV Park▲**
Other N: Laundry/WiFi/Road Ranger, **to appr 10 mi: Boiling Spring Campground▲**

169 MO J, Newburg
Other N: **Boiling Spring Campground▲**

172 MO D, CR 242, Jerome
Other N: **Arlington River Resort▲**

176 CR 8490, CR 7300, Sugar Tree Rd, Newburg

(178) Rest Area (Both dir)
(RR, Phone, Picnic, Vend)

179 MO T, Truman St, Newburg
Gas S: BP
Food S: Cookin from Scratch/BP

184 Bus Lp 44, to US 63S, Rolla
Gas S: Mobil, Phillips 66, Shell
Food S: Arby's, Burger King, Golden Corral KFC, Long John Silver's, McDonald's, Pizza Hut, Shoney's, Sirloin Stockade, Subway, Waffle House, Wendy's, Zeno's Steakhouse, Rest/BW
Lodg N: Comfort Suites
S: AmeriHost Inn, Best Western♥, Best Way Inn, Days Inn, Econo Lodge♥, Holiday Inn Express, Howard Johnson, Ramada Inn, Super 8, Travelodge, Western Inn, Zeno's Motel
Med S: + Hospital
Other S: Kroger, **Walmart sc**

185 MO E, Rolla
Gas S: Phillips 66
Food S: Applebee's, DQ, Hardee's, Subway, Taco Bell
Other S: **MO State Hwy Patrol Post**

186 US 63, Bus 44, N Bishop Ave, Rolla, Jefferson City
Gas N: Sinclair
S: AmocoBP, Mobil◈, Phillips 66
Food N: Steak 'n Shake
S: Denny's, Pizza Inn, Waffle House
Lodg N: Drury Inn, Hampton Inn, Sooter Inn
S: American Motor Inn
Med S: + Hospital
Other N: Lowe's

189 MO V, Rolla, Dillon
FStop N: Love's Travel Stop # 341 (Scales)
Food N: Subway/McDonald's/Love's TS
Other N: WiFi/Love's TS

195 US 68, MO 68, MO 8, St. James
Gas N: Conoco◈, Mobil◈, Phillips 66◈
S: Phillips 66◈, Circle S Gas
Food N: McDonald's, Pizza Hut, Subway
S: Burger King
Lodg N: Comfort Inn, Economy Inn, Ozark Motel
S: Finn's Motel
TServ N: Rays Tire & Service Center

203 MO F, MO ZZ, Cuba
Other N: **Blue Moon RV & Horse Park▲**

208 MO 19, Cuba, to Owensville
TStop N: Voss Truck Port (Scales)
Gas N: Phillips 66
S: Casey's, Delano◈, Mobil, Phillips 66
Food N: Rest/FastFood/Voss TP, Country Kitchen, Huddle House, Pizza Hut, Rest/ Best Western
S: Burger King, Hardee's, Jack in the Box, McDonald's, Sonic, Subway
Lodg N: Best Western♥, Super 8
S: Holiday Inn Express
TServ N: Voss TP/Tires
Other N: Laundry/BarbSh/WiFi/Voss TP
S: Auto Dealer, O'Reilly Auto Parts, **Walmart, RV Dealer, Onondaga Cave State Park▲ , Huzzah Valley Resort▲**

210 MO UU, Cuba
Other N: **Meramec Valley RV Campground▲**

214 CR H, CR 508, Leasburg
Gas N: Mobil◈

218 CR C, CR J, CR N, Bourbon
Gas N: Citgo◈
S: Mobil
Food S: Henhouse Rest
Lodg N: Budget Inn
Other S: **Blue Springs Ranch Campground▲ , Riverview Ranch Campground▲ , Bourbon RV Center**

225 MO 185, CR D, Sullivan
TStop S: Bobber Travel Center (Scales)
Gas N: Mobil, Phillips 66◈
S: Conoco
Food N: Domino's
S: Rest/Bobber TC, **Cracker Barrel**, Homer's BBQ, Jack in the Box, Pizza Hut, Sonic
Lodg N: Baymont Inn, Econo Lodge, Family Motor Inn, Super 8
S: Comfort Inn, Delta Motel
Med S: + **Missouri Baptist Hospital**
Other N: Vet♥, **to** Sullivan Reg'l Airport✈
S: Laundry/Bobber TC, Meramac Cinema I & II, Sullivan Memorial Airport✈

226 MO 185, Sullivan, to Oak Grove
TStop S: Flying J Travel Plaza #5047/Conoco
Gas S: Phillips 66
Food S: CtryMkt/FastFood/FJ TP, Denny's, Golden Corral, Hardee's, KFC, Pizza Hut, McDonald's, Steak 'n Shake, Subway
Other S: Laundry/BarbSh/WiFi/**RVDump/LP**/ FJ TP, Dollar General, O'Reilly Auto Parts,
Other S: **Walmart sc**, Cinema 6

230 MO JJ, MO W, Sullivan, to Stanton
Gas S: Phillips 66
Food S: Roosters Steak House
Lodg N: Stanton Motel
Other S: **Stanton/Meramec KOA▲**

(235) Rest Area (Both dir, LEFT exit)
(RR, Phones, Picnic, Vend)

(238) Weigh Station (Both dir)

239 MO 30, CR AB, CR WW, St Clair
Gas S: AmocoBP

240 MO 47, Main St, St Clair, Union
Gas N: Phillips 66◈, Sinclair
S: Mobil◈
Food N: Burger King, Taco Bell/P66
S: Hardee's, McDonald's, Subway
Lodg S: Budget Lodge, Super 8
Other N: **Frank Reed RV Center**
S: Dollar General, **3 R RV Service Center**

242 Old Hwy 66, St Clair

247 US 50, Union (SB), MO O, Villa Ridge (NB)

251 MO 100, Villa Ridge, to Washington
TStop N: Fuel Mart #634 (Scales), Mr. Fuel #1/ Conoco (Scales)
Food N: FastFood/Fuel Mart, FastFood/Mr Fuel

253 MO 100, Gray Summit, Eureka
Gas S: Phillips 66
Food S: Rest/Best Western
Lodg S: Best Western

257 Bus Lp 44, Viaduct St, Pacific
FStop S: Pilot Travel Center #208 (Scales)
Gas S: BP◈, Conoco, Mobil◈
Food S: Subway/Pilot TC, Hardee's, KFC, McDonald's, Taco Bell
Lodg N: Comfort Inn
S: Holiday Inn Express, Quality Inn
Other S: Laundry/WiFi/Pilot TC

261 Lp 44, Six Flags Rd, to Allenton
FStop S: Shell #28
Gas N: MotoMart◈
S: Phillips 66◈
Food N: Applebee's, Country Kitchen, KFC, Denny's, McDonald's, Lions Choice, Steak n Shake
Lodg N: Econo Lodge, Ramada Inn, Red Carpet Inn, Super 8
Other N: Auto Zone, **Walmart sc**, **to** Six Flags, **Yogi Bears Jellystone Park Resort▲**
S: **LP**/Shell, **St Louis West KOA▲**

264 MO 109, CR W, Eureka
Gas N: 7-11, Phillips 66
S: QT◈, Shell
Food N: Burger King, DQ, Domino's, KFC, McDonald's, Pizza Hut, Ponderosa, Smokers BBQ, Subway, Taco Bell, Wendy's, White Castle
Lodg N: Days Inn
Other N: Grocery, Firestone, NAPA, **Byerly RV Center**
S: Walgreen's

265 Williams Rd (NB)

266 Lewis Rd

269 Antire Rd, High Ridge, Beaumont

272 MO 141, Valley Park, Fenton
FStop S: MPC #23/66, Valley Park MotoMart
Gas N: MotoMart
S: 7-11, QT, Shell
Food S: Burger King, Culver's, McDonald's, Steak 'n Shake, Subway, Taco Bell
Lodg S: Drury Inn, Hampton Inn

274 Bowles Ave, Hwy Dr, Fenton
TStop N: Road Ranger #175/Pilot TC #533
Gas N: Shell◈
S: AmocoBP, Citgo◈, QT
Food S: **Cracker Barrel**, Denny's, McDonald's, Quiznos, Souper Salad, White Castle
Lodg S: Drury Inn, Econo Lodge, Fairfield Inn, Holiday Inn Express, Pear Tree Inn, Stratford Inn, Towneplace Suites
TServ S: Goodyear Truck Tire Center, Purcell Tire Co, Fabick Power Systems, Caterpillar
Other N: Daimler Chrysler Assembly Plant

275 Soccer Park Rd, Yarnell Rd (WB)
TStop N: Road Ranger #175/Pilot TC #533 (Scales)

◈ = Regular Gas Stations with Diesel ▲ = RV Friendly Locations ♥ = Pet Friendly Locations
Red print shows large vehicle parking / access on site or nearby **Brown Print = Campgrounds / RV PARKS**

EXIT		MISSOURI
	Food	N: Subway/RR/PTC, Burger King
	TServ	N: St Louis TP/Tires, Kenworth
	Other	N: Laundry/LP/RR/PTC
(276)		**Jct I-270, S - Memphis, N - Chicago**
277B		**US 61, US 67, US 50, Watson Rd, Lindbergh Blvd, St Louis**
	Gas	N: Shell
		S: Citgo, Phillips 66, Shell
	Food	N: Arby's, Chili's, Hardee's, Steak & Rice Chinese, Sunny China Int'l Buffet
		S: Bob Evans, Burger King, Denny's, House of Hunan, Longhorn Steakhouse, Steak n Shake
	Lodg	N: Best Western
		S: Comfort Inn, Days Inn, Econo Lodge, Hampton Inn, Holiday Inn
	Med	N: + St Joseph Hospital
		S: + Multi Medical Group
	Other	N: Lowe's, Office Depot, Target, **Walmart sc**, St Louis Comm College
		S: Home Depot, Sunset Hills Plaza Shopping Center, World Market
277A		**MO 366, Watson Rd (NB)**
	Med	S: + Hospital
278		**Big Bend Blvd, St Louis**
	Gas	N: Sam's
		S: Mobil◈, QT, Sinclair

EXIT		MISSOURI
	Food	N: Hardee's, Sonic
		S: Denny's
	Other	N: Sam's Club
279		**S Berry Rd, Big Bend Blvd (SB)**
280		**Elm Ave, St Louis**
	Gas	N: AmocoBP
		S: Shell
282		**Murdoch Ave, Laclede Stn Rd (NB)**
	Gas	N: Amoco, Mobil
	Food	N: McDonald's, Starbucks, Subway
283		**Shrewsbury Ave (SB)**
284A		**Jamieson Ave (NB)**
284B		**Arsenal St (SB)**
285		**Southwest Ave (fr SB, diff reacc)**
286		**Hampton Ave, St Louis**
	Gas	N: Mobil, Phillips 66, Shell
		S: Shell
	Food	N: Denny's, Jack in the Box, McDonald's, Steak 'n Shake, Subway, Taco Bell
		S: Burger King, Hardee's, Village Inn
	Lodg	S: Holiday Inn, Red Roof Inn♥
	Med	N: + Hospital
287A		**Kingshighway Blvd (NB)**

EXIT		MISSOURI
287B		**Vanderventer Ave**
288		**Grand Blvd, Downtown St. Louis**
	Gas	N: BP
	Food	S: Jack in the Box
	Med	N: + St Louis University Hospital, + Incarnate Word Hospital
		S: + Hospital
289		**Jefferson Ave**
	Gas	N: Citgo◈
		S: Conoco
	Food	N: Subway
		S: McDonald's
	Lodg	N: Holiday Inn Express
(290A)		**Jct I-55, S to Memphis (NB)**
290B		**18th St, Downtown St Louis (EB)**
290C/207		**S Tucker Blvd, Gravois Ave (SB)**

CENTRAL TIME ZONE

NOTE: **I-44 begins/ends on I-55, Exit #207BC**

MISSOURI

Begin Westbound I-44 from St. Louis, MO to Wichita Falls, TX.

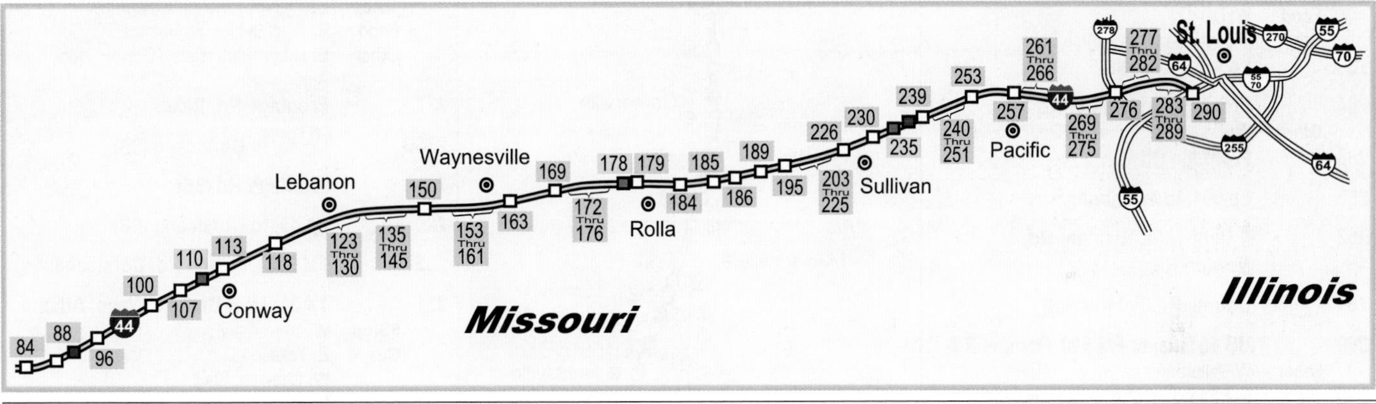

EXIT		TEXAS

Begin Southbound I-45 from Dallas to Galveston TX

TEXAS

CENTRAL TIME ZONE

NOTE: **I-45 begins/ends in Dallas**

EXIT		TEXAS
(286)		**to I-35E, to Denton**
285		**US 75N, Bryan St**
284C		**Bryan St, Ross Ave, N Central Expy**
	Other	W: Westin City Center, Plaza of the Americas, Arts District
(284AB)		**Jct I-30, W-Ft Worth, E-Texarkana**
	Med	E: + Baylor Univ Medical Center
283		**US 175E, Kaufman**
	Gas	E: Shell
		W: Kwik Stop, Shamrock

EXIT		TEXAS
	Food	E: Captain D's, Hardeman's BBQ
		W: KFC/Taco Bell
	Lodg	W: Colonial House Motel, Wayside Inn
	Other	E: Tire & Service Center
283A		**Lamar St**
283B		**Pennsylvania Ave, MLK Jr Blvd (SB)**
281		**Overton Rd, Dallas (SB)**
	Gas	E: Texaco
		W: Chevron
	Lodg	E: Lamar Motel
	Other	E: Auto Services
		W: Auto Services
280		**Linfield Rd, Illinois Ave**
	Gas	W: Texaco
	Lodg	E: Linfield Motel, Star Motel
		W: Luxury Inn Motel
	Other	E: Auto Services
		W: Auto Services
279		**Tx 12 Loop (SB)**

EXIT		TEXAS
279AB		**Tx 12 Loop (NB)**
	Med	W: + Veterans Medical Center
277		**Simpson Stuart Rd, Dallas**
	Gas	E: Conv Store
		W: Chevron
	Food	W: Whitehouse BBQ
	Lodg	E: ABC Motel
	Other	W: Paul Quinn College
(276B)		**Jct I-20E, to Shreveport**
(276A)		**Jct I-20W, to Ft Worth (Travel Center & All Serv 1st Exit W)**
275		**TX 310, S Central Expy, Dallas (NB, no reaccess)**
274		**Palestine St, Dowdy Ferry Rd, Hutchins**
	FStop	W: Tucker Oil (408 N Main)
	Gas	E: Exxon, Texaco

EXIT		TEXAS
	Food	W: BBQ Express, DQ, Jack in the Box, Smith's Rest
	Lodg	E: Gold Inn
	Other	W: Auto Services, Grocery, **Police Dept**
273		**Wintergreen Rd, Hutchins**
	Other	W: Hipps Bus Service
272		**Fulgham Rd, Hutchins**
	TStop	W: Love's Travel Stop #331 (Scales)
	Food	W: Carl's Jr/Love's TS
	Other	W: Laundry/WiFi/RVDump/Love's TS
(272)		**Weigh Station/Inspection Stn (SB)**
271		**Pleasant Run Rd, Wilmer**
270		**Belt Line Rd, Wilmer**
	TStop	W: Citgo Fuel Stop
	Gas	E: Shell◈, Texaco◈
		W: Exxon
	Food	W: DQ, Sonic, Subway, Taco Bell
	Other	W: **Police Dept**, Lancaster Airport✈
269		**Mars Rd, Wilmer**
268		**US 45 Bus, Malloy Bridge Rd, to Ferris**
267		**Frontage Rd**
266		**5th St, FM 660, Ferris**
	Gas	E: Fina
		W: Shamrock
	Food	W: DQ
	Other	W: Auto Services, **Police Dept**
265		**Lp 45, Ferris (NB)**
264		**Frontage Rd, Wester Rd**
	Other	W: Cortez Truck & Auto Repair
263A		**Frontage Rd**
263		**Lp 561, to Trumbull**
262		**S Central St, Risinger Rd, Newton Rd**
261		**County Rd, Palmer (NB)**
260		**US 45 Bus, to FM 818, Hampel Rd**
	Other	W: Auto Services
259		**FM 813, to FM 878, Palmer**
258		**Lp 45, US 75, Parker Hill Rd, Palmer**
	FStop	E: Exxon
	TStop	W: Sunmart #170/Mobil (Scales)
	Food	E: Subway/Exxon
		W: FastFood/Sunmart, Jenny's Café, Mexican Rest
	Lodg	W: Palmer House Motel
	TServ	W: Sunmart/Tires
	Other	W: Laundry/Sunmart
255		**FM 879, Ennis, to Garrett**
	Gas	E: Exxon◈
		W: Chevron◈
253		**Lp 45, Ennis**
	Gas	W: Shell
251B		**TX 34, Ennis Ave, to 35E, Ennis, to Kaufman, Italy**
	FStop	E: Tiger Mart #23/Exxon (2200 TX 34)
	Gas	E: Fina, Texaco◈
		W: Chevron◈, Exxon◈
	Food	E: Bubba's BBQ Steakhouse, McDonald's, Rest/Tiger Mart
		W: Arby's, AmeriMex Rest, Burger King, Braum's, Captain D's, Chili's, DQ, Golden Corral, Jack in the Box, McDonald's, KFC, Subway, Taco Bell, Waffle House, Wendy's, Whataburger

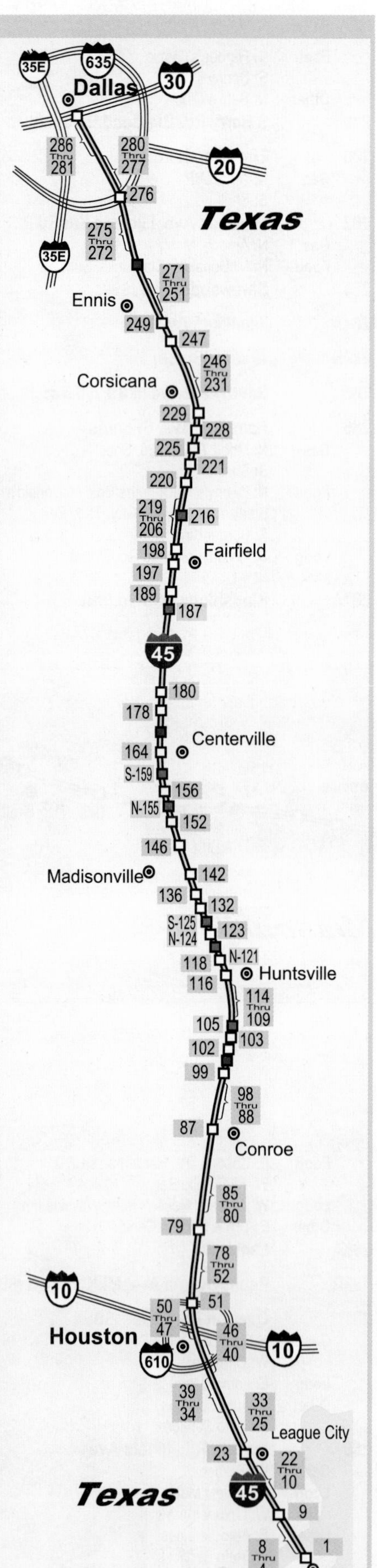

EXIT		TEXAS
	Lodg	E: Best Western, Holiday Inn Express
		W: Ennis Inn, Quality Inn
	Med	W: + Ennis Regional Medical Center
	Other	W: Auto Zone, Auto Dealers, Enterprise RAC, Grocery, **Police Dept**, Museum, Tires, Towing, **Walmart sc, to** Ennis Muni Airport✈, Tx Motorplex, **Jeff's RV Campground▲**
251A		**FM 1181, Creechville Rd, to Bus 45, Ennis (Serv W to Bus 45)**
	Other	W: **COE/Bardwell Lake/High View Park▲**
249		**Bus 45, FM 85, US 75, Ennis**
	FStop	W: Kwik Mart #6/Fina
	Food	W: Ennis Family Rest
	Lodg	E: Budget Inn
	TWash	W: Blue Beacon TW
247		**US 287N, to Waxahatchie**
246		**FM 1183, to Alma**
	Gas	W: Chevron, Phillips 66
244		**FM 1182, Ennis**
243		**Frontage Rd, Rice**
242		**Frontage Rd, Rice**
239		**FM 1126, Rice**
	Gas	W: Phillips 66
238		**FM 1603, Rice**
	TStop	E: Interstate Travel Center/Fina
	Food	E: Rest/FastFood/Interstate TC
	Other	E: Laundry/Interstate TC, H&H Truck & Auto Repair
237		**Frontage Rd, Rice**
235B		**Lp 45, to Corsicana (SB)**
235A		**Frontage Rd (SB)**
235		**Lp 45, to Corsicana (NB)**
232		**FM 3041, Roane Rd, Corsicana**
231		**TX 31, MLK Blvd, to Waco, Athens**
	FStop	W: Tiger Tote/Exxon
	Gas	E: Texaco◈
		W: Chevron, Shell◈
	Food	E: Jack in the Box
		W: Subway/Exxon, DQ, McDonald's
	Lodg	E: Colonial Inn
		W: Comfort Inn
	Other	W: Auto Dealers, Auto Services, ATMs, **to American RV Sales & Park▲**
229		**US 287S, Bus 287, to Palestine**
	Gas	E: Exxon◈, Shell◈
		W: Chevron
	Food	E: Wendy's/Exxon
		W: Catfish King, DQ, Waffle House
	Lodg	W: Days Inn, Royal Inn, Travelers Inn
	Other	W: Home Depot
228B		**Frontage Rd, Lp 45 (NB, LEFT exit)**
228A		**Frontage Rd, 15th St (NB)**
	Gas	E: Phillips 66
225		**FM 739, Corsicana, Angus, Mustang**
	TStop	E: Lucky 7 Quick Stop
	Gas	E: Chevron, Exxon
		W: Citgo◈, Shell
	Food	E: FastFood/Lucky 7 QS
	Other	E: Corsicana Muni Airport✈
221		**Frontage Rd, Corsicana**
220		**Frontage Rd, Richland**
219B		**Frontage Rd**

◈= Regular Gas Stations with Diesel ▲ = RV Friendly Locations ♥= Pet Friendly Locations
Red print shows large vehicle parking / access on site or nearby **Brown Print = Campgrounds / RV PARKS**

EXIT		TEXAS
219A		**TX 14, Richland, to Mexia (SB)**
	Gas	W: Richland Store
	Food	W: Dragon Palace
218		**FM 1394, Richland (NB)**
(216)		**Navarro Co Rest Area (Both dir) (RR, Phones, Picnic, WiFi)**
213		**FM 246, Richland, to Wortham, Streetman**
	Gas	E: Bonds Travel Shoppe
		W: Chevron, Texaco◈
	Food	W: Country Smoke House
211		**FM 80, Spur 114, Streetman, Kirvin**
206		**FM 833, Streetman, Fairfield**
198		**FM 27, Fairfield, Wortham**
	TStop	W: Love's Travel Stop #288
	Gas	E: Exxon, Shell
		W: Exxon
	Food	E: PJ's Café, BBQ/Shell
		W: FastFood/Love's TS, Gilberto's
	Lodg	W: Budget Inn, Super 8
	Med	E: + E Tx Medical Center
	Other	W: WiFi/RVDump/Love's TS, I-45 RV Park▲
197		**US 84, Teague St, Fairfield, Teague**
	FStop	W: Bond Texaco Truck Center
	TStop	W: I-45 Shell Truck Stop
	Gas	E: Chevron, Exxon, Fina
	Food	E: Jack in the Box/Exxon, Sam's BBQ/ Fina, DQ, McDonald's, Pizza Hut, Sonic, Subway, Texas Burger
		W: Rest/I-45 Shell TS
	Lodg	E: Regency Inn, Holiday Inn Express, Sam's Motel
		W: Best Value Inn, Super 8
	TServ	W: I-45 Shell TS/Tires
	Other	E: Pharmacy
		W: Auto Repairs
189		**TX 179, Teague, to Dew**
	TStop	E: Jet Travel Plaza/Exxon
	Food	E: FastFood/Jet TP, Dew Café
	Tires	E: Jet TP
	Other	E: Laundry/Jet TP
(187)		**Parking Area (Both dir)**
180		**TX 164, Buffalo, to Groesbeck**
178		**US 79, W Commerce, Buffalo**
	TStop	W: Buffalo Truck Stop/Shamrock, Tiger Mart Travel Plaza/Exxon (Scales), Sunmart #115/Mobil
	Gas	E: Shell
		W: Chevron
	Food	E: Café, Subway, Texas Burger, Weathervane Restaurant
		W: FastFood/Buffalo TS, FastFood/Tiger Mart TP, FastFood/SunMart, DQ, Pitt Grill, Sonic, Rainbow Rest
	Lodg	E: Wayside Inn
		W: Best Western, Economy Inn
	TServ	W: Triangle Tire
	Other	W: Laundry/Buffalo TS, Laundry/Tiger Mart
(166)		**Weigh Station (SB)**
164		**TX 7, Centerville**
	TStop	W: Woody's Diesel Express/Shell
	Gas	E: Woody's Smokehouse Shell
		W: Exxon
	Food	E: Country Cousins, Texas Burger
		W: FastFood/Woody's, DQ
	Lodg	E: Days Inn, Fiesta Motel

Personal Notes

EXIT		TEXAS
	Other	E: ATMs, Banks, Auto Services
		W: Laundry/Woody's
(159)		**Parking Area (SB)**
156		**FM 977, Leona**
	Gas	W: Exxon◈
(155)		**Parking Area (NB)**
152		**TX OSR, to Normangee**
	Gas	W: Chevron◈
	Other	W: Yellow Rose RV Park▲
146		**TX 75, Madisonville**
142		**US 190, TX 21, to Bryan, Crockett**
	Gas	E: Exxon◈, Texaco◈
		W: Citgo, Shamrock◈, Shell
	Food	E: Church's, Corral Café
		W: Lakeside Rest, McDonald's, Pizza Hut, Sonic, Subway, Texas Burger
	Lodg	E: Best Western, Madisonville Inn
		W: Budget Motel, Western Lodge
	Other	W: Auto Services, Towing
136		**Spur 67, Madisonville**
	Other	W: Home on the Range RV Park▲
132		**FM 2989, Huntsville**
(125)		**Walker Co Rest Area (SB) (RR, Phones, Picnic, Vend, WiFi)**
(124)		**Walker Co Rest Area (NB) (RR, Phones, Picnic, Vend, WiFi)**
123		**FM 1696, Huntsville**
(121)		**Parking Area (NB)**
118		**TX 75, Huntsville**
	TStop	E: Hitchin Post AmBest Truck Terminal/ Shell (Scales)

EXIT		TEXAS
	TStop	W: Pilot Travel Center #234 (Scales)
	Food	E: Rest/Hitchin Post TT
		W: Wendy's/Pilot TC
	Lodg	E: Econo Lodge, Motel 6♥, La Quinta Inn♥
	TWash	E: Hitchin Post TT/Tires
	TServ	E: Hitchin Post TT
		W: Pilot TC/Tires
	Other	E: Laundry/Hitchin Post TT, Huntsville Muni Airport→, Auto Dealers, Bowling Alley
		W: Laundry/WiFi/Pilot TC
116		**TX 30, US 190E, Huntsville**
	Gas	E: Citgo, Shamrock◈
		W: Chevron, Exxon, Shell
	Food	E: El Chico, Golden Corral, McDonald's
		W: Burger King, Chili's, CiCi's Pizza, IHOP, KFC, Pizza Hut, Subway, Taco Bell
	Lodg	E: Comfort Inn, Econo Lodge, Motel 6♥, La Quinta Inn♥
		W: Holiday Inn Express
	Other	E: Auto Dealers, to Sam Houston Teachers College
		W: Home Depot, Kroger, Office Depot, Walmart sc, Walgreen's, W Hill Mall
114		**FM 1374, Montgomery Rd, Huntsville**
	Gas	E: Exxon◈, Shell
		W: Chevron, Shamrock◈
	Food	E: DQ
	Lodg	E: Gateway Inn, Super 8
		W: Quality Suites
	Med	W: + Huntsville Memorial Hospital
	Other	W: Auto Services
113		**TX 19, Huntsville, Crockett (NB)**
112		**TX 75**
	Gas	E: Citgo
	Other	E: to Sam Houston State Univ
109		**TX P40, Huntsville**
	Other	W: to Huntsville State Park▲
(105)		**Picnic Area (Both dir)**
103		**TX 150, FM 1374, FM 1375, to New Waverly (SB)**
	Gas	W: Citgo
102		**TX 150, FM 1374, FM 1375, to New Waverly (NB)**
	Gas	E: Shell
(101)		**Weigh Station (NB)**
99		**Danville Rd, Shepard Hill Rd (SB)**
98		**Danville Rd, Shepard Hill Rd (NB)**
	Other	E: Convenience RV Park▲, The Catfish Pond▲
95		**Longstreet Rd, Willis**
	Other	W: to Castaways RV Park▲
94		**FM 1097, Willis**
	Gas	E: Kroger
		W: Chevron, Exxon, Shell
	Food	E: Jack in the Box, Sonic
		W: McDonald's, Subway
	Lodg	W: Best Western
	Other	E: Kroger, Lone Star/LP
		W: Auto & Diesel Service, Sunset Shores RV Park▲, to Omega Farms RV Retreat▲
92		**FM 830, Seven Coves Rd, Panorama Village, Willis**
	Lodg	W: to Seven Coves Resort

◈= Regular Gas Stations with Diesel ▲ = RV Friendly Locations ♥= Pet Friendly Locations
Red print shows large vehicle parking / access on site or nearby Brown Print = Campgrounds / RV PARKS

EXIT		TEXAS
	Other	W: Park on the Lake▲
91		**League Line Rd, Conroe**
	Gas	E: Chevron W: Shell
	Food	E: Subway, Wendy's W: Cracker Barrel
	Lodg	E: Comfort Inn
	Other	W: to Lake Conroe RV Resort & Marina▲
90		**FM 3083, Texas Nursery Rd**
	Other	E: to Montgomery Co Airport✈
88		**Lp 336, Wilson Rd, Conroe, to Cleveland, Navasota**
	FStop	E: 336 Shell
	Gas	E: Mobil, Shamrock W: Chevron
	Food	E: Arby's, McDonald's, Sonic, Subway W: KFC, Ryan's Grill
	Other	E: Cinema, Goodyear, Kroger, Walgreen's W: Lowe's, Sam's Club, Walmart sc to Lake Conroe RV & Camping Resort▲, to Havens Landing RV Resort▲
87		**TX 105, FM 2854, Conroe**
	Gas	E: Shamrock W: Exxon, Texaco◈
	Food	E: Burger King, CiCi's Pizza, Jack in the Box, Luther's BBQ, McDonald's, Outback Steakhouse, Village Inn W: Golden Corral, Luby's, Taco Bell
	Other	E: ATMs, Auto Services, Firestone, Kroger, Museum, Sunset Truck & Auto, to Country Place RV Park▲ W: ATMs, Bank, Grocery, Home Depot, Kroger, Target, to appr 13 mi: Houston North KOA▲
85		**Gladstell St, Conroe**
	Gas	E: Citgo◈ W: Shell◈
	Lodg	W: Days Inn, Motel 6♥
	Other	E: Auto Services
84		**TX 75N, Lp 336, Frazier St**
	Gas	E: Conoco, Texaco W: Shell
	Food	W: Pizza Hut, Taco Cabana
	Lodg	E: Holiday Inn, Ramada Inn
	Other	W: Albertson's, Kmart, Kroger, Tires
83		**Creighton Rd, Camp Starke Rd**
81		**FM 1488, Conroe, to Magnolia, Hempstead**
	FStop	W: Valero #591
	Gas	E: Citgo◈
	Other	W: Camperland
80		**Needham Rd (SB)**
79		**TX 242, College Park Dr, Needham**
	Gas	E: Texaco
	Food	E: McDonald's/Texaco W: Popeye's, Willie's Grill
	Lodg	W: Country Inn Suites
	Other	E: Outdoors & More RV Rentals, Woodland Lakes RV Resort▲ W: Firestone, Walmart sc
78		**Tamina Rd, Research Forest Dr (SB)**
	Gas	E: Conoco, Texaco W: Shamrock
77		**Woodland Pkwy, Robinson, Oak Ridge, Chateau Woods, Spring**
	Gas	E: Conoco◈, Texaco

EXIT		TEXAS
	Gas	W: Shamrock, Texaco
	Food	E: Babin's Steakhouse, Hooters, Pancho's, Pappadeaux Seafood, Saltgrass Steakhouse W: Benihana, Black Eyed Pea, ChickFilA, Luby's, Romano's, Outback Steakhouse
	Lodg	E: Budget Inn W: Comfort Inn, Days Inn, Hampton Inn, Homewood Suites, La Quinta Inn♥
	Med	E: + Urgent Care W: + Memorial Hospital
	Other	E: Home Depot, Office Depot, Sam's Club, Walgreen's, Police Dept W: Best Buy, Target, Woodlands Mall
76		**Research Forest Dr, Tamina Rd (SB)**
	Gas	E: Chevron◈, Conoco, Coastal, Shamrock, Texaco W: Exxon, Shell, Texaco
	Food	E: Long John Silver, Luther's BBQ, Pancho's Mexican Rest, Red Lobster W: Carrabba's, Chili's, El Chico, IHOP, Landry's Seafood, Kyoto, Olive Garden, Sweet Tomato, Starbucks, TGI Friday
	Lodg	W: Courtyard, Drury Inn, Hilton Garden Inn, Marriott, Residence Inn
	Med	W: + Memorial Hospital
	Other	W: ATMs, Banks, Auto Services, Cinema 17, Woodlands Mall
76B		**Woodlands Pkwy, Spring (NB)**
	Gas	E: Shamrock W: Shell
	Other	E: Auto Services, Police Dept W: FedEx Office, Goodyear, Woodlands Mall, Sunshare RV
76A		**Oakwood Dr (NB)**
73		**Rayford Rd, Sawdust Rd, Spring**
	TStop	W: Sunmart #116/Mobil
	Gas	E: Conoco, Shell W: Shell
	Food	E: Golden China, Jack in the Box, Mario's Mex Rest, McDonald's, Sonic W: FastFood/Sunmart, Cajun, Grandy's, Sam's Café, Sweet Bella, Subway
	Lodg	E: Hawthorn Suites, Holiday Inn Express W: Crossland Economy Studios, Red Roof Inn♥
	Other	E: ATMs, Auto Zone, Auto Services, Bank, Firestone, O'Reilly Auto Parts, UPS Store, Vet♥, to Rayford Crossing RV Resort▲ W: ATMs, Auto Services, Banks, FedEx Office, Goodyear, HEB, Goodyear, Kroger,
73A		**Frontage Rd, Hardy Toll Rd (SB)**
72		**Frontage Rd, Spring**
	Other	W: Spring Oaks RV & MH Park▲
70B		**Spring-Stuebner Rd, Spring**
	Other	W: Spring Oaks RV & MH Park▲
70A		**Louetta Rd, Spring Cyprus Rd, FM 2920, Spring, to Tomball**
	Gas	E: Exxon W: Chevron, Shell
	Food	E: McDonald's, Pizza Hut, Wendy's W: Burger King, Taco Bell, Whataburger
	Other	E: Old Town Spring Shopping, Walmart sc, Splashtown, Tourist Info, Walgreen's, Bates Motorhomes, Vaughn's RV

EXIT		TEXAS
		W: to David Wayne Hooks Memorial Airport✈, to Corral MH & RV Park of Tomball▲, to Burns RV Park▲
68		**Cypresswood Dr, Creekford Dr, Holzwarth Rd, Spring**
	Gas	E: Texaco◈ W: Chevron
	Food	E: Burger King, Pizza Hut/Taco Bell W: Denny's, Jack in the Box, Popeye's
	Lodg	W: Motel 6♥
	Other	E: Albertson's, Kroger, Walmart sc W: Home Depot, Lowe's, Office Depot, PetCo♥, Target, Walgreen's, Texan RV, Hornet Campers
66		**FM 1960, Houston, to Humble**
	Gas	E: Chevron, RaceTrac, Shell W: Chevron, Exxon, Shell, Star Mart
	Food	E: Jack in the Box, Potato Patch Rest, Pancho's, Popeye's W: Chili's, Grandy's, IHOP, Luby's, Luther's BBQ, McDonald's, Outback Steakhouse, Pizza Hut, Red Lobster, Steak & Ale, Subway
	Lodg	E: Days Inn W: Best Value Inn, Comfort Suites, Emerald Inn, La Quinta♥, Studio 6
	Med	W: + Houston Northwest Medical Center
	Other	E: Auto Dealers, Lonestar RV Sales, to George Bush Int'l Airport✈, PetSmart♥ W: Auto Dealers, ATMs, Banks, Kroger, Auto Services, NTB, Randall's, UPS Store
64		**Richey Rd, Houston**
	TStop	W: Flying J Travel Plaza #5094/Conoco (Scales)
	Gas	W: GasMart
	Food	E: Café, Pappasito's Cantina W: Rest/FastFood/FJ TP, Church's, Cracker Barrel, Jack in the Box, Joe's Crab Shack, Saltgrass Steakhouse, Whataburger
	Lodg	E: Holiday Inn, Lexington Hotel Suites W: Best Value Inn, La Quinta Inn♥
	Other	E: Sam's Club, Tires W: Laundry/WiFi/RVDump/LP/FJ TP, U-Haul, Cliff Jones RV
63		**Airtex Blvd, Rankin Rd, Houston**
	FStop	E: Sunmart #110/Mobil
	Gas	W: Chevron, RaceTrac
	Food	W: Cracker Barrel, Joe's Crab Shack, McDonald's, Saltgrass Steakhouse, Zio's Italian, Whataburger
	Lodg	W: Best Western, Guest House
	Other	E: Lone Star RV W: Celebration Station, De Montrond RV
62		**Rankin Rd, Kuykendahl Rd**
	FStop	E: Sunmart #190/Mobil
	Gas	W: Shell
	Food	W: Captain Seafood, Sonic
	Lodg	E: Executive Inn Express, Scottish Inn♥ W: Riata Inn, Sun Suites
	Other	W: Auto Dealers
61		**Greens Rd, Houston**
	Food	E: IHOP, Jack in the Box, McDonald's, Monterrey's W: Burger King, Luby's Cafeteria
	Lodg	E: Days Inn, Wyndham W: Comfort Inn
	Other	E: Greenspoint Mall
60D		**Beltway 8E, Houston (NB)**
	Lodg	E: Travelodge
60C		**Beltway 8E, Houston (SB)**

◈ = Regular Gas Stations with Diesel ▲ = RV Friendly Locations ♥ = Pet Friendly Locations
Red print shows large vehicle parking / access on site or nearby Brown Print = Campgrounds / RV PARKS

EXIT		TEXAS
60B		**Beltway 8, Sam Houston Toll W (SB) TX 525, Aldine Bender Rd (NB)**
	Other	E: Greenspoint Mall
60A		**W Dyna Dr, Aldine Bender Rd, N Belt Dr E, Beltway 8 (NB)**
	Other	E: Red Dot RV Park▲, Central Houston KOA/LP/RVDump▲
		W: Best Buy, Office Depot, **Walmart sc**
60		**Bell Tollway 8, Intercontinental Airport, Sam Houston Tollway**
59		**West Rd, Blue Bell Rd**
	Gas	E: Exxon, Shell
		W: Exxon
	Food	E: Burger King, Denny's, Long John Silver, McDonald's, Michoccan Mex Rest, Pappas Rest, Pizza Hut, Wendy's
		W: Chili's, Jalisco's, McDonald's, Starbucks Taco Bell, Whataburger
	Lodg	E: America's Best Value Inn
		W: Best Western
	Other	E: Carwash/Shell, Firestone, NTB
		W: Best Buy, Discount Tire, Kmart, Office Depot, Pep Boys, Penske, Radio Shack, Walgreen's, **Walmart sc**
57B		**TX 249, W Mt Houston Rd**
	Gas	E: Conoco◈, Exxon◈
		W: Shell
	Food	E: McDonald's
		W: Checker's, KFC, Pizza Inn, Sonic
	Lodg	W: Holiday Inn, La Quinta Inn, Ramada Inn
	Other	E: Auto Service, Enterprise RAC, Kroger, Tires
		W: Auto Dealer, Auto Services, CVS, Family Dollar
57A		**Gulf Bank Rd, Houston**
	FStop	E: Sunmart #133/Mobil
	Lodg	E: HiWay Inn
		W: Days Inn
	Other	E: Discount Tire,**Holiday World RV**,
		W: Auto Dealers, Enterprise RAC,
56C		**W Canino Rd (NB)**
56B		**Spur 261, Shepherd Dr, Little York Rd (SB)**
	Gas	W: Shell
	Food	W: Denny's, Luby's, McDonald's
	Lodg	W: Gulf Wind Motel, Houston Motor Inn, Passport Inn
	Other	W: Auto Dealers, **to** Post Office
56A		**Canino Rd, Houston (NB)**
	Other	E: **Holiday World RV**, PJ Trailers, Big Tex Trailers
		W: Auto Dealers, Auto Services
55B		**Rittenhouse St, W Little York Rd (NB)**
	Gas	E: Chevron
		W: Shell
	Food	E: China Border, Sam's BBQ, Whataburger
		W: Captain D's, Denny's, KFC, Popeye's
	Lodg	W: Best Value Inn, Econo Lodge
	Other	W: Harley Davidson, US Post Office
55A		**Rittenhouse St, Parker Rd, Yale St**
	TStop	E: Sunmart #119/Mobil
	Gas	E: Texaco
	Food	W: McDonald's
	Lodg	E: Olympic Motel
		W: Guest Motel, Town Inn
	Med	E: + **Columbia Medical Center**
	Other	E: Auto Services, Advance Auto Parts, Grocery, **Atlas Supply of TX**
		W: Auto Services, Walgreen's

EXIT		TEXAS
54		**Tidwell Rd, Houston**
	Gas	E: Exxon, Mobil, Shell
		W: Shell, Chevron
	Food	E: Aunt Bea's, Pancho's, Taco Cabana
		W: Starbucks
	Lodg	W: Scottish Inn, Southwind Motel, Sundown Inn
	Other	E: Big Lots, Family Dollar, **Propane/LP**
53		**Airline Dr, Victoria Dr**
	Gas	E: Chevron, Texaco
		W: Conoco
	Lodg	W: Villa Provencial Motor Inn
	Other	E: Northline Shopping Center
52B		**Crosstimbers St**
	Gas	E: Shell, Texaco◈
		W: Chevron, Exxon
	Food	E: Burger King, China Inn, Denny's, Hungry Farmer BBQ, Jack in the Box, KFC, Pizza Hut, McDonald's, Pappas BBQ, Sonic
		W: Monterey's, Wendy's, Whataburger
	Lodg	W: Econo Lodge, Luxury Inn, Palace Inn, Star Inn, Texan Inn
	TServ	W: Davenport Trucking & Wrecker
	Other	E: Northline Mall, Auto Services
		W: Auto Services, **Felton's RV Services**
52A		**Frontage Rd**
	Lodg	W: Road Runner, Northline Inn
(51)		**Jct I-610**
50		**Cavalcade St, Patton St (SB)**
	TStop	E: Love's Travel Stop #419 (Scales)
	Gas	E: Exxon, Shamrock, Star Mart
	Food	E: Wendy's/Love's TS
	Lodg	W: Astro Inn
	TServ	E: Alg Truck & Trailer Repair
	Other	E: Laundry/Love's TS, Auto Services
		W: Auto Services
50B		**Cavalcade St (NB)**
50A		**Patton St, Houston (NB)**
	TStop	E: Love's Travel Stop #419 (Scales)
	Gas	E: Citgo
	Food	E: Wendy's/Love's TS
	Other	E: Laundry/WiFi/Love's TS
49B		**N Main St, Houston Ave, Pecore St**
	Gas	W: Exxon◈, Texaco
	Food	W: KFC, McDonald's, Subway
49A		**Quitman St, Houston Ave**
(48AB)		**Jct I-10, W-SanAntonio, E-Beaumont**
(48B)		**Jct I-10W, to San Antonio (NB, LEFT exit)**
(48A)		**Jct I-10E, to Beaumont (SB, LEFT exit)**
47D		**Heiner St, Houston Ave, Dallas St, Allen Pkwy, Pierce Ave**
	Other	W: Police Dept
47C		**McKinney St, Bagby St, Smith St (SB)**
47B		**Houston Ave, Allen Pkwy E**
	Other	E: City Hall
47A		**Allen Pkwy W (Both dir, LEFT Exit)**
46AB		**US 59, W to Lake Jackson, E to Freeport**
46B		**US 59W, to US 288, to Lake Jackson (NB, LEFT exit)**
	Med	W: + to **Texas Medical Center**
	Other	W: **to** Rice Univ & Stadium, Houston Zoo

EXIT		TEXAS
46A		**US 59E, to Freeport (SB, LEFT exit)**
	Med	E: + St Joseph Hospital
	Other	E: **to** George Brown Convention Center
45A		**Scott St, Cullen Bvd, Spur 5 (SB)**
	Other	W: **to** TX Southern Univ
45		**Cullen Blvd, Scott St (NB)**
44C		**Cullen Blvd, Spur 5, Lockwood Dr, Elgin St (SB)**
	Other	W: Univ of Houston, Robertson Stadium, Hofheinz Pavilion
44B		**Calhoun St, Spur 5**
44A		**Lockwood Dr, Elgin St (NB)**
43A		**Telephone Rd, to US 90A**
43B		**Tellepsen St (NB)**
42		**US 90 Alt, Wayside Dr, Spanish Tr**
	Gas	E: Stop 'N Go
		W: Exxon
	Food	W: McDonald's
	Lodg	E: Days Inn, Gulf Freeway Inn
41B		**Griggs Rd, Broad St**
	Gas	W: Shamrock
	Lodg	E: Houtex Inn, Red Carpet Inn
	Other	W: Auto Services, Home Depot, Kmart, Lowe's, Mall, Office Depot,
41A		**Woodridge Dr**
	Gas	E: Shell
	Food	E: Denny's, McDonald's
		W: Brisket House, IHOP, Pappas BBQ
	Other	W: Auto Services, Home Depot, Mall
(40)		**Jct I-610**
(40C)		**Jct I-610W (NB, LEFT exit)**
(40B)		**Jct I-610E (fr SB, LEFT exit), TX 35 (SB)**
	Other	E: **to** Port of Houston Industrial Complex
40A		**Frontage Rd, Broadway St (NB)**
39		**Park Place Blvd, Broadway St**
	Gas	E: Valero
		W: Quick Mart
	Food	E: Jack in the Box, Taco House, Wendy's
38B		**Bellfort Ave, TX 3, Monroe Rd (Gas, food, Lodg W to Broadway St)**
38		**TX 3, Monroe Rd**
	Gas	E: Chevron◈, Shell
		W: Chevron, Shell, Texaco◈
	Food	E: Jack in the Box, Kip's, Lone Wolf Café, Luby's, Luther's BBQ, Wendy's
		W: Subway, Ninfa's Mexican
	Lodg	W: Best Western, Holiday Inn, Smile Inn, Super 8, Travel Inn
36		**College Ave, Airport Blvd**
	FStop	W: Airport Gas Mart
	Gas	E: Shell, Shamrock
		W: Exxon, Shell
	Food	E: Burger House, City Café, DQ, Smokey Joe's, Waffle House
		W: Damon's, Denny's, Taco Cabana
	Lodg	E: Best Value Inn, Roadway Inn
		W: Baymont Inn, Comfort Inn, Country Suites, Drury Inn, Hampton Inn, Holiday Inn, Marriott, Motel 6♥, Red Roof Inn♥, Regency Inn, Springhill Suites
	Other	E: ATMs, Auto Services, Banks, Firestone, Food City, Walgreen's, **RV Repair**, **to Just Passin Thru RV Park▲**
		W: Auto Repairs, Auto Rentals, **Lone Star RV Sales**, Wm P Hobby Airport✈

EXIT — TEXAS

35 Clearwood Dr, Edgebrook Dr
Gas E: Chevron, Exxon, RaceTrac
W: Shell
Food E: Burger King, China One, Grandy's, Jack in the Box, Subway, Waffle House
W: McDonald's, Pizza Hut
Lodg E: Airport Inn
W: La Quinta Inn♥

34 Almeda Genoa Rd, S Shaver Rd
Gas E: Conoco
W: Chevron, Murphy, Shamrock
Food W: Burger King, Wendy's
W: McDonald's, Taco Bell, Wendy's
Lodg W: Post Oak Inn, Scottish Inn
Other E: **Terry Vaughn RV's**
W: Almeda Mall, Best Buy, Dollar Tree, Kmart, NTB, Target, **Holiday World RV**

33 Fuqua St, Houston
Food E: Chili's, Luby's, Chili's, Mexico Lindo, Olive Garden, TGI Friday
W: Brown Sugar BBQ, Casa Ole', Black Eyed Pea, Golden Corral, Joe's Crab Shack, Outback Steakhouse, Steak & Ale
Other E: Auto Dealers, Comedy Club, Cinema
W: Auto Services, Almeda Mall, Sam's Club,

(32) Sam Houston TOLLway

31 FM 2553, Scarsdale Blvd
Gas W: Exxon, Shell
Food W: DQ, McDonald's
Med W: + Memorial Hospital
Other W: San Jacinto College

30 FM 1959, Dixie Farm Rd, Houston
Gas E: Conoco◈, Shell◈
W: RaceWay
Food E: Subway
Lodg E: Suburban Extended Stay
Other E: Ellington Field✈
W: **Lone Star RV Sales**

29 FM 2351, Choate Rd, Friendswood

27 El Dorado Blvd, Webster
Gas E: Texaco, Shamrock, Valero
Food E: DQ, Jack in the Box
W: Tx Roadhouse, Whataburger
Other E: Auto & Tire Services
W: Sam's Club, **Walmart sc**

26 Bay Area Blvd, Webster
Gas E: Exxon, Shell
W: Chevron, Shell
Food E: Angelo's Pizza & Pasta, Kettle, Lake Garden Chinese, Outback Steak House, Pappasito's, Red Lobster, Ryan's Grill, Romano's Macaroni Grill, Starbucks
W: Bennigan's, Burger King, Denny's, McDonald's, Olive Garden, On the Border Café, Rico's, Steak & Ale
Lodg E: Best Western, Comfort Suites, Hampton Inn, InTown Suites, La Quinta Inn♥,
Med E: + Columbia Medical Center, + Clear Lake Regional Medical Center
Other E: ATMs, Banks, Best Buy, FedEx Office, Cinema, Lowe's, Univ of Houston/CL
W: Baybrook Mall, ATMs, Banks, Office Depot, PetSmart♥, Target

25 FM 528, NASA Rd 1, Webster
Gas E: Express Mart, Texaco
Food E: Bayou Steak House, Chili's, CiCi's Pizza, Durango's Mexican Rest, Indian Rest, Saltgrass Steak House, Waffle House
W: Cajun Seafood, DQ, Hooters, Subway
Lodg E: Days Inn, Howard Johnson Express, Motel 6♥
Med E: + St John Hospital
Other E: ATMs, Big Lots, Cinemark 18, Dollar 8 Cinema, Home Depot, Kmart, Lyndon B Johnson Space Center, Office Depot
W: Challenger Seven Memorial Park, **Walmart**, **Bay RV Park▲**

23 FM 518, W Main St, League City
Gas E: RaceTrac, Shell◈, Star Mart
W: Exxon
Food E: Burger King, Jack in the Box, KFC, Grand Buffet, Kelley's Country Cookin, Pancho's Mex Buffet, Sonic, Subway
W: **Cracker Barrel**, McDonald's, Taco Bell, Village Pizza, Waffle House, Wendy's
Lodg W: Super 8
Other E: Auto Services, Kroger, Eckerd
W: Auto Services, ATMs, Banks, **Space Center RV Resort▲**

22 Calder Dr, Brittany Bay Blvd, TX 96 (Acc #23 Serv via Caulder Dr N)
Other E: Houston Gulf Airport✈
W: Visitors Center, **Safari MH Comm▲**

20 FM 646, to FM 517, Santa Fe, Bacliff
Gas W: Shamrock◈, Chevron
Other E: **to Green Caye RV Park▲**
W: PetCo♥, UPS Store, Vet♥

19 FM 517, Main St, Pine Dr, Hughes Rd, Dickinson
Gas E: Shell
W: Exxon, Star Mart
Food E: Pizza Inn, Mexican Rest, Village Pizza
W: KFC, Kettle, McDonald's, Pizza Hut, Subway, Taco Bell, Wendy's
Lodg W: Days Inn
Other E: Enterprise RAC, HEB, **Bay Colony RV Resort▲**, **Dues RV Center**, **Adventure Out RV Park▲**, **to Via Bayou RV Park▲**
W: Auto Rental, Kroger

17 Holland Rd, to FM 646, Dickinson

16 FM 1764, Texas City (SB)
Other E: Mall of the Mainland, **Access #15 Serv**

15 FM 1764, FM 2004, La Marque
Gas E: Shell
W: Mobil, Shell
Food E: China One, Gringo's, Jack in the Box, Olive Garden
W: Sonic, Subway, Waffle House, Whataburger, Wendy's
Lodg E: Fairfield Inn
Other E: Auto Dealers, Lowe's, Mall of the Mainland, **De Montrond Motorhomes**
W: Gulf Greyhound Park, **Walmart sc**

13 Delaney Rd, to FM 1764, FM 1765
Gas E: Chevron
Food E: Kelley's Rest, Village Pizza
Lodg W: Grand Suites, Super 8
Med E: + Mainland Medical Center
Other E: Mall of the Mainland
W: Gulf Greyhound Park, **Destination Luna RV Campground▲**

12 FM 1765, La Marque
Gas E: Circle T Quick Stop
W: Shell
Food E: Domino's Pizza, Jack in the Box, Sonic
Lodg W: Travel Inn
Other W: U-Haul, **Destination Luna RV Campground▲**

11 Vauthier St, La Marque

10 FM 519, Main St, Lake Rd
FStop W: Shoppers Mart #5/Shell
Gas E: Valero
Food E: McDonald's, Rocky's
Other E: MCH Wrecker Service, Auto & Truck Repair, **to** TX City Industrial Complex
W: **Oasis Resort & RV Park▲**, **to Gulf Holiday RV Park▲**, **Sunset RV Park▲**, **Highland Bayou RV Park▲**, **Lily's by the Bay RV Resort▲**, **Bob's Mobile RV Service**

9 Frontage Rd (SB)

8 Frontage Rd, Bayou Rd (NB)

7 TX 146, TX 6, TX 3, to Texas City, Hitchcock (SB)

7C TX 146, TX 6, TX 3, to Texas City, Hitchcock (NB)

7B TX 6, Hitchcock (NB, LEFT exit)

7A TX 146, TX 3, Texas City (NB)

6 Frontage Rd (SB)

5 Frontage Rd

4 Tiki Dr, Village Tiki Island, Galveston
Gas E: Tiki Island Store/Conoco◈

1C Ave J, Harborside Dr, Teichman Rd, 77th St, Port Industrial Rd, Galveston Island
FStop E: Island Food Mart/Shell
TStop E: Harborside Food Mart/Citgo
Gas E: Exxon
Food E: FastFood/**RVDump**/Harborside FM
W: American Grill, Clary's Seafood Rest
Lodg E: Howard Johnson, Motel 6♥,

1B Ave J, 71st St, 61st St

1A Spur 342, 61st St (Cont on TX 87 for serv)
Gas E: E-Z Mart
W: Exxon, Shell, Racetrac
Food E: Denny's
W: 61st St Diner, Leon's BBQ, Taco Bell
Lodg W: Days Inn
Other E: Enterprise, Home Depot, Target
W: ATMs, Banks, Auto Services, Office Depot, Walgreen's, Scholes Field✈, **to Bayou Haven RV Resort▲**

CENTRAL TIME ZONE

NOTE: I-45 begins/ends on TX 87 in Galveston

TEXAS

Begin Northbound I-45 from Galveston, TX to Dallas, TX.

◈ = Regular Gas Stations with Diesel ▲ = RV Friendly Locations ♥ = Pet Friendly Locations
Red print shows large vehicle parking / access on site or nearby Brown Print = Campgrounds / RV PARKS

EXIT		LOUISIANA
		Begin Southbound I-49 from Shreveport, LA to Lafayette, LA. (I-10, Exit #103 and I-20, Exit #17)

LOUISIANA

CENTRAL TIME ZONE

EXIT		LOUISIANA
(206)		**Jct I-20, E - Monroe, W - Dallas**
205		**Kings Hwy, Shreveport**
	Gas	W: Valero◈
	Food	E: McDonald's, Piccadilly's
		W: Burger King, Long John Silver, Subway, Taco Bell
	Med	W: + LSU Health Sciences Center
	Other	E: Mall St Vincent, ATMs, Banks
203		**Hollywood Ave, Pierremont Rd (Gas/Food/Lodg 2mi W)**
	Gas	W: Fina
	Other	W: to I-20, Shreveport Reg'l Airport✈
202		**LA 511E, 70th St**
	Gas	E: Raceway
		W: Circle K, Chevron
	Food	W: Sonic
	Other	W: Auto Services, Tires
201		**LA 3132, to Dallas, Texarkana**
199		**LA 526, Bert Kouns Industrial Loop**
	Gas	E: Chevron◈, Citgo, Exxon, RaceWay
		W: Express, Shell◈
	Food	E: Arby's/Chevron, Burger King, KFC, Taco Bell, Wendy's
		W: McDonald's
	Lodg	E: Comfort Inn
	Other	E: Home Depot
191		**LA 16, LA 3276, Stonewall, Frierson**
186		**LA 175, to Frierson, Kingston**
	TStop	E: Relay Station #3/Exxon (Scales)
	Food	E: Rest/Relay Stn
	Other	E: WiFi/Casino/Relay Stn
177		**LA 509, Mansfield, Carmel**
	TStop	E: Eagles Truck Stop/BP
	Food	E: Rest/Eagles TS
	Other	E: Laundry/Eagles TS
172		**US 84, to Mansfield, Grand Bayou**
169		**Asseff Rd**
162		**US 371, LA 177, Mansfield, Pleasant Hill, Coushatta, Evelyn**
155		**LA 174, Robeline, Ajax, Lake End**
	TStop	W: Spaulding Truck Stop
	Other	W: WiFi/Spauding TS, Ajax Country Livin at I-49 RV Park▲
148		**LA 485, to Allen, Powhatan**
142		**LA 547, Posey Rd**
138		**LA 6, Many, Natchitoches**
	TStop	W: Shop-A-Lott #10/Chevron
	Gas	E: BP, Exxon, RaceWay
		W: Casey's, Texaco◈
	Food	E: Shoney's, Wendy's
		W: FastFood/ShopALot, Burger King, Huddle House, McDonald's
	Lodg	E: Best Western, Holiday Inn Express, Super 8
		W: Comfort Inn, Econo Lodge, Hampton Inn
	Med	E: + Hospital
	Other	E: to Walmart sc, Albertson's, to NW State Univ, Natchitoches Reg'l Airport✈
	Other	W: Laundry/RVDump/ShopAlott TS,

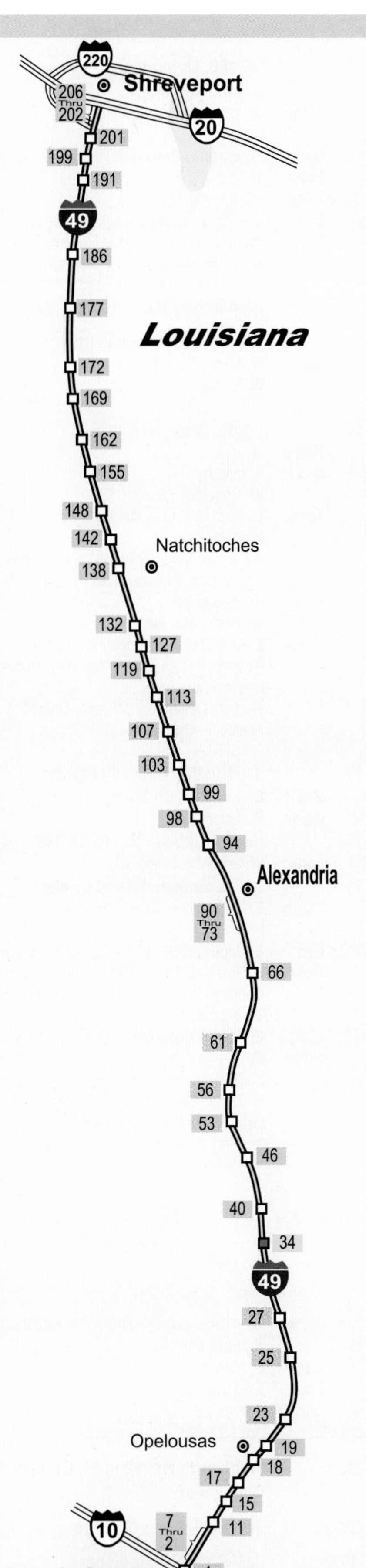

EXIT		LOUISIANA
	Other	W: Nakatosh RV Park▲, Dogwood Ridge Camper Park▲
132		**LA 478, CR 620, Natchitoches**
127		**LA 120, to Flora, Cypress**
	Gas	E: Citgo
119		**LA 119, Lena, to Derry, Gorum, Cloutierville**
113		**LA 490, Lena, to Chopin**
	Gas	E: Phillips 66◈
107		**to Lena, to US 1**
103		**LA 8W, Lena, to Flatwoods**
	Gas	E: Texaco
99		**LA 8E, LA 1200, to Boyce, Colfax**
98		**LA 1, Boyce, Colfax (NB)**
	Gas	E: Chevron
94		**PR 23, Rapides Station Rd, Boyce**
	FStop	E: Rapides Truck Stop
	Food	E: Café/Rapides TS
	Twash	E: Rapides TS
	Other	W: I-49 RV Center
90		**LA 498, Air Base Rd, Alexandria**
	TStop	W: Leebo's #9/Chevron
	Gas	W: Exxon◈, Mobil◈, Texaco◈
	Food	W: FastFood/Leebo's, Burger King, Chili's, Cracker Barrel, Eddie's BBQ, McDonald's
	Lodg	W: La Quinta Inn♥, Super 8, Travel Express Inn
	Other	W: Laundry/Leebo's, Alexandria Int'l Airport✈
86		**US 71, US 165, MacArthur Dr**
	FStop	W: (2161 LA 1 N of 165) A&M #5/Conoco
	Gas	W: Mobil, Shell, Texaco
	Food	W: Burger King, Cajun Landing, Pizza Hut, Ryan's Grill, Shoney's
	Lodg	W: Best Western, Comfort Inn, Clarion Inn, Crown Hotel, Hampton Inn, MacArthur Inn Motel 6♥, Quality Inn
	Other	W: Auto Repairs, Dollar General, Grocery, Towing, Cenla Camping Center, Freeman Parts, Specialty Hitches & RV Center, Superior RV
85B		**Monroe St, Medical Center Dr, Rapides Ave, Alexandria**
	Med	E: + Rapides Reg'l Medical Center
85A		**LA 1, MLK Dr, 10th St, Downtown**
	Other	W: Auto Repairs, Diesel Service, Towing
84		**US 167N, LA 28, LA 1, Pineville Expy, Casson St (NB, diff reacc)**
83		**Broadway Ave, to US 167,Bus 165, Alexandria (W Serv: 167N to Memorial Dr)**
	Gas	E: Fina, Express
		W: Texaco
	Food	W: Church's, Wendy's
	Other	W: Lowe's, Renegade Harley Davidson, Target, Walmart sc
81		**US 71N, LA 3250, Sugarhouse Rd, MacArthur Dr, to US 71, US 167 (Access to Ex #80 Services)**
80		**US 71, US 167, MacArthur Dr , Alexandria**
	TStop	W: I-49 Truck Plaza (Scales)
	Gas	W: Chevron◈, Exxon, Mobil, Shell, Albertson's
	Food	W: Rest/I-49 TP, Burger King, Carino's, Chili's, Hacienda Mex Rest, KFC, Logan's Roadhouse, McDonald's, Outback Steak house, Pizza Hut, Sonic,

◈= Regular Gas Stations with Diesel ▲ = RV Friendly Locations ♥= Pet Friendly Locations
Red print shows large vehicle parking / access on site or nearby Brown Print = Campgrounds / RV PARKS

EXIT — LOUISIANA

Food W: Subway, Taco Bell, Western Sizzlin
Lodg W: Best Western, Days Inn, Hampton Inn, Holiday Inn, Super 8
TServ W: to Timmons Int'l
Other W: Albertson's, ATMs, Banks, Cinema, Alexandria Mall, PetSmart♥, Sam's Club, U-Haul

73 LA 3265, PR 22, Lecompte, to US 165, Woodworth
FStop W: Tiger Fuel Stop/Exxon
Food W: FastFood/Tiger FS
Other W: to **Indian Creek Rec Area▲**, to Claiborne Range Military Res

66 LA 112, Forest Hill, Lecompte
Gas W: Leebo's/Chevron◈
Food W: Burger King/Leebo's

61 US 167, Cheneyville, to Turkey Creek, Meeker

56 LA 181, Cheneyville

53 LA 115, McArthur St, Bunkie (Gas/Food/Lodg/Casinos/Etc 4mi+ E)
TStop E: Sammy's Truck Auto Plaza/Chevron
Food E: Rest/Sammy's TAP
Other E: Laundry/**Casino**/WiFi/Sammy's TAP

46 LA 106, Bunkie, to St Landry
Other W: to **Chicot State Park▲**

40 LA 29, Ville Platte (Addtl Serv 8mi W)
TStop E: Tiger Trax #7/Exxon
Food E: Rest/FastFood/Tiger Trax
Other E: Laundry/**Casino**/Tiger Trax

(34) Grand Prairie Rest Area (Both dir) (RR, Phones, Picnic, RVDump)

27 LA 10, LA 182, Washington, Lebeau

25 LA 103, Washington, Port Barre
Gas W: Citgo, Mobil

23 US 167, LA 744, Opelousas, to Ville Platte
TStop E: I-49 Truck Stop/Texaco, Quarters Travel Plaza/Chevron
W: 167 Truck Stop/Exxon
Food E: Rest/I-49 TS, Subway/Quarters TP
W: Rest/FastFood/167 TS
Lodg W: Best Value Inn, Days Inn
Other E: Laundry/I-49 TS, **Casino**/Laundry/ Quarters TP
W: **Casino**/Laundry/167 TS

EXIT — LOUISIANA

19 US 190, Opelousas, Baton Rouge (SB)
TStop W: 12120 190W: Opelousas Truck Stop/ Conoco
Gas W: Exxon◈, Mobil
Food W: Rest/Op TS
Tires W: Tires/Op TS
Med W: + Opelousas General Hospital
Other W: Laundry/Op TS, Auto Repairs, Tires, ATMs, Banks, Lowe's, Museums, Tourist Info, St Landry Parrish Airport✈

19A US 190E, to Baton Rouge (NB)

19B US 190W, Opelousas (NB)
Gas W: Mobil, Tiger Trax Exxon◈
Food W: Blimpie
Med W: + Hospital

18 LA 31, Creswell Lane
FStop W: Valero
Gas E: Murphy◈
W: Chevron◈, Shell
Food E: Casa Ole, Little Caesar's Pizza, Subway, Rest/Hol Inn
W: Burger King, McDonald's, Pizza Hut, Ryan's Grill, Subway, Taco Bell, Wendy's
Lodg E: Holiday Inn
W: Best Value Inn, Days Inn
Other E: Auto Dealer, Evangeline Downs Racetrack & **Casino**, Dollar Tree, Home Depot, **Walmart sc**
W: Auto Dealer, CVS, Family Dollar, Firestone, **Opelousas City Park▲**, Walgreen's,

17 Judson Walsh Dr, Opelousas
Gas E: Texaco◈
Other W: Goodyear

15 Harry Guilbeau Rd, to LA 182
Lodg W: Best Value Inn

11 LA 93, Sunset, Grand Coteau
TStop E: Beau Chere Truck Stop/Chevron, USA Speedtrac
Gas E: Citgo◈, Exxon◈
Food E: Rest/FastFood/Beau Chere TS, Gram's Country Kitchen, Fast-Food/USA
W: Subway
Lodg E: Sunset Motor Inn
Other E: Laundry/Beau Chene TS, Laundry/USA, USA Raceway
W: Dollar General, Family Dollar, **Acadiana Wilderness Campground▲**

EXIT — LOUISIANA

7 LA 182
Lodg W: Acadian Motor Inn
Other W: **Premier RV**, **Primeaux RV**

4 LA 726, Carencro
Gas E: Depot
W: Chevron◈, Citgo, Texaco◈
Food W: Burger King, McDonald's, Popeye's
Lodg W: Economy Inn
TServ W: Mack/Kenworth
Other E: Auto & Engine Service
W: ATMs, Banks, Auto Services, U-Haul, **Foreman RV**

2 LA 98, Gloria Switch Rd
Gas E: Citgo, Chevron◈, Pit Stop
W: Shell
Food E: Blimpie/Citgo, Deli/Chevron, Chili's, IHOP, Wendy's
W: Church's Chicken, Domino's Pizza, Mexican Rest
Other E: Lowe's, **Stevens RV Center**, to appr mi: **Bayou Wilderness RV Resort▲**, to appr 9mi: **Poches Fish-n-Camp▲**
W: Prejeans Auto & Truck Repair

1B Point Des Mouton Rd, Lafayette
Gas E: Exxon◈, Star Mart Shell
Food E: Subway/Shell, Burger King
Lodg E: Motel 6♥, Plantation Motor Inn
Other E: Winn Dixie
W: Budget, Stelly's Auto & Truck Repair

(1A) Jct I-10, W to Lake Charles, E to Baton Rouge
Gas S: Chevron◈, RaceTrac, Shell, Albertson's, Murphy
Food S: Checker's, Kajun Kitchen, KFC, McDonald's, Pizza Hut, Shoney's, Taco Bell, Waffle House, Wendy's, Western Sizzlin'
Lodg S: Best Western, Comfort Suites, Fairfield Inn, Holiday Inn, Jameson Inn, La Quinta Inn♥, Quality Inn, Super 8
Med S: + Hospital
Other S: Albertson's, Dollar General, Firestone, Home Depot, RiteAid, **Walmart sc**

LOUISIANA

Begin Northbound I-49 from Lafayette, LA to Shreveport, LA. (I-10, Exit #103 and I-20, Exit #17

EXIT — ILLINOIS

Begin Southbound I-55 from Chicago, IL to New Orleans, LA.

ILLINOIS

NOTE: I-55 begins/ends on Lakeshore Dr/US 41

CENTRAL TIME ZONE

295 US 41, Lakeshore Dr, Chicago

293D Martin Luther King Dr (NB)
Gas E: BP
Food E: McDonald's
Med E: + Mercy Hospital
Other W: to Soldier Field, Museums, Aquarium

293C S State St (SB)
Gas E: Amoco
Food E: McDonald's
Med E: + Mercy Hospital

(293B) Jct I-90/94E, to Indiana

293A Wentworth Rd, 22nd St, Cermak Rd, Chinatown

(292B) Jct I-90/94W, to Chicago

(292A) Jct I-90/94E, to Indiana

292 Stewart Ave, Archer Ave, I-90/94N (SB)

290 Damen Ave, Ashland Ave, Western Ave
Gas E: Marathon
Food E: Burger King, Popeye's, Subway, White Castle
TServ E: Chicago Truck Center, Tony's Truck Service
Other E: Dollar Tree, Grocery, Target
W: Auto Services, Fleet Service, Truck & Auto Service

◈= Regular Gas Stations with Diesel ▲ = RV Friendly Locations ♥= Pet Friendly Locations
Red print shows large vehicle parking / access on site or nearby Brown Print = Campgrounds / RV PARKS

EXIT		ILLINOIS
289		**California Ave (NB)**
	FStop	E: Speedway #8315
	Food	E: Subway/Speedway
	Med	W: + St Anthony Hospital
288		**Kedzie Ave (SB, NB reacc)**
	Gas	E: Citgo, Speedway
	Food	E: Subway
287		**Pulaski Rd**
	Gas	E: Mobil◈, Shell
	Food	E: Burger King, Quiznos, Subway
	TServ	W: American Reefer Service, Mensik Fleet Service
	Other	E: ATMs, Auto Services, Auto Repairs, Advance Auto Parts, Aldi Grocery, Target, Towing, Walgreen's
286		**IL 50, Cicero Ave, Chicago, Cicero**
	FStop	E: 4759 IL 50: Mansoor Citgo W:2 blks N Cicero: Tuxedo Junction
	Gas	E: BP, Marathon, Phillips 66
	Food	E: McDonald's, Subway, Starbucks
	Lodg	E: Sportsman Inn Motel
	TServ	W: Fast Action Truck & Trailer, South Side Truck Service
	Other	E: Family Dollar, to Chicago Midway Airport✈ W: Hawthorne Race Course, Sportman's Park, Chicago Motor Speedway, Auto & Tire Services, ATMs, Grocery
285		**Central Ave, Chicago, Cicero**
	FStop	E: BP Connect #2705
	Gas	E: T&C Marathon W: Citgo
	Food	E: Burger King, Steak & Egger
	TServ	E: International Truck, BJ Truck & Trailer Repair, E&D Truck Repair
	Other	E: Auto Services
283		**IL 43, Harlem Ave, Lyons**
	Gas	E: Shell W: BP
	Food	E: Arby's, Burger King, Subway
	Other	W: Police Dept
282B		**IL 171W, Joliet Rd (NB)**
282A		**IL 171E, Archer Ave (NB)**
282		**IL 171, Archer Av, Joliet Rd (SB)**
	FStop	E: JJ Peppers Marathon
	Other	E: Amtrak W: General Motors ElectroMotive Plant, to Chicago Zoological Park
279B		**US 12N, US 20N, US 45N, LaGrange Rd, Joliet Rd**
	Gas	W: BP, Mobil, Shell, Sam's
	Food	W: Applebee's, Arby's, Boston Market, Burger King, KFC, Long John Silver, Lone Star Steakhouse, McDonald's, Pizza Hut, Popeye's, Subway, Taco Bell, Wendy's, White Castle
	Lodg	W: Holiday Inn, Hampton Inn
	Med	W: + to LaGrange Memorial Hospital
	Other	W: Auto Services, Auto Dealer, ATMs, Banks, Best Buy, Dollar Tree, Grocery, Discount Tire, Firestone, Home Depot, Pep Boys, NTB, Rental Cars, Sam's Club, Target/Pharmacy, Walmart
279A		**US 12S, US 20S, to Archer Ave, to I-294 TOLL, S to Indiana**
(277B)		**Jct I-294 (TOLL), S-Indiana (NB)**
(277A)		**Jct I-294 (TOLL), N-Wisconsin**

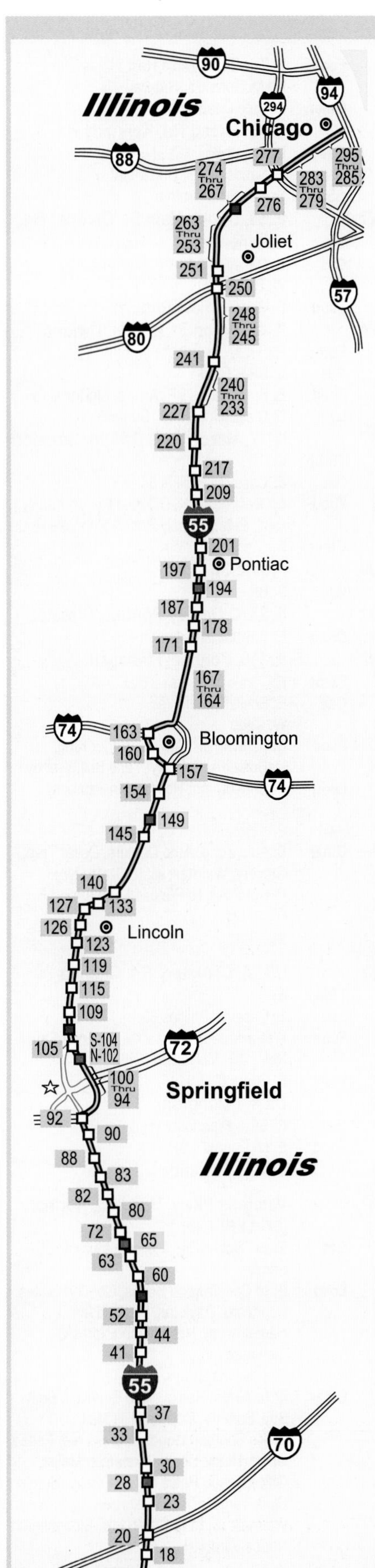

EXIT		ILLINOIS
276C		**Joliet Rd (NB, LEFT exit)**
276AB		**County Line Rd, Willowbrook**
	Food	E: Max & Erma's, Subway
	Lodg	E: Best Western, Extended Stay America, Marriott, Ramada Inn W: AmeriSuites, Springhill Suites
	TServ	E: Freightliner of Chicago
	Med	W: + Suburban Hospital
	Other	E: Police Dept
274		**IL 83, Kingery Hwy**
	Gas	E: Shell W: Mobil◈, Phillips 66, Shell
	Food	W: Bakers Square, Burger King, Dunkin Donuts, Denny's, Little Caesar's
	Lodg	E: Best Western W: Baymont Inn, Fairfield Inn, Holiday Inn, Red Roof Inn♥
	Other	W: ATMs, Staples, Target, Repairs, Towing, Tires, Police Dept
273AB		**Cass Ave, Darian**
	Gas	W: Shell
	Other	E: Argonne Nat'l Laboratory
271B		**Lemont Rd N, Downers Grove**
	Gas	W: Shell
271A		**S Lemont Rd**
	Lodg	E: Extended Stay America
(269)		**Jct I-355N (TOLL), Woodward Ave, West Suburbs**
(267)		**Weigh Station (NB)**
267		**IL 53, Bolingbrook, Romeoville**
	TStop	E: PTP/Greater Chicago I-55 Auto Truck Plaza/P66 (Scales)
	Gas	E: BP, W: Shell◈, Speedway◈
	Food	E: Rest/I-55 ATP, Bob Evans, Bono's Rest, Escapades Rest, McDonald's
	Food	W: Arby's, Bakers Square, Cheddar's, Denny's, Family Square Rest, Golden Corral, Hardee's, IHOP, KFC, Pizza Hut, Popeye's, Starbucks, Subway, Wendy's, White Castle
	Lodg	E: La Quinta Inn♥, Ramada Ltd, Super 8 W: AmericInn, Comfort Inn, Hampton Inn, Holiday Inn, Springhill Suites
	TWash	E: I-55 ATP
	TServ	E: NW Truck, I-55 ATP/Tires
	Med	W: + Hospital
	Other	E: Laundry/LP/I-55 ATP, **Air Stream of Chicago**, Home Depot, **US Adventure RV** W: Dollar General, Dollar Tree, Family Dollar, Goodyear, Grocery, Walgreen's, Walmart, U-Haul, **Camping World**
263		**Weber Rd, W Normantown Rd, W 127th St, Romeoville**
	Gas	E: BP◈, Gas City◈ W: Shell
	Food	E: Applebee's, Burger King, McDonald's, Popeye's, Quiznos, Subway, Starbucks, White Castle, Dunkin Donuts/Gas City W: Arby's, Cracker Barrel, Wendy's
	Lodg	E: Best Western W: Comfort Inn, Country Inn, Extended Stay America, Howard Johnson Express
	Other	E: Discount Tire, Grocery, Walgreen's W: CarWash/Shell, Home Depot, to Clow Int'l Airport✈
261		**IL 126W, E Main St, Plainfield (SB exit, NB reaccess)**

◈= Regular Gas Stations with Diesel ▲ = RV Friendly Locations ♥= Pet Friendly Locations
Red print shows large vehicle parking / access on site or nearby Brown Print = Campgrounds / RV PARKS

257 US 30, W Lincoln Hwy, Plainfield, Plainfield Rd, Joliet, Aurora
TStop W: Joliet I-55 Truck Stop/Clark (Scales)
Gas E: Shell
W: BP◈
Food E: Applebee's, Burger King, Chuck E Cheese's, Hardee's, Hooters, KFC, Lone Star Steakhouse, McDonald's, Pizza Hut, Red Lobster, Steak 'n Shake, Taco Bell, Texas Roadhouse, TGI Friday, Wendy's
W: Rest/Subway/I-55 TS
Lodg E: Comfort Inn, Fairfield Inn, Hampton Inn, Holiday Inn Express, Motel 6♥, Super 8
TWash W: I-55 TS
TServ W: I-55 TS/Tires
Other E: ATMs, Banks, Auto Services, Barnes & Noble, Best Buy, Cinemark 10 & 8, Discount Tire, Gander Mountain, Grocery, Home Depot, Office Depot, PetSmart♥, Pharmacy, Target, Westfield Louis Joliet Mall
W: Laundry/WiFi/I-55 TS, Auto Services

253 US 52, W Jefferson St, Joliet, to Shorewood
FStop W: BP Amoco Fuel Stop
Gas E: Citgo◈, Phillips 66, Shell
Food E: McDonald's, KFC/Pizza Hut, Wendy's
W: Ali Baba's Rest, Burger King, Subway
Lodg E: Best Western, Best Value Inn, Wingate Inn
Med E: + Provena St Joseph Medical Center
W: + Hospital
Other E: Harley Davidson, **Rick's RV Center▲**, Joliet Memorial Stadium, Joliet Jr College, Joliet Park District Airport✈,

251 IL 59, Cottage St, Shorewood, Plainfield (NB exit, SB reacc)

(250AB) Jct I-80, E-Toledo, W-Des Moines

248 US 6, W Eames St, Channahon Rd, Moriss, Joliet, Channahon
TStop E: Pilot Travel Center #473 (Scales)
Gas E: Citgo◈, Speedway
W: BP
Food E: Subway/Pilot TC, Daylight Donuts, Quiznos
W: McDonald's/BP
Lodg E: Manor House Motel
Other E: WiFi/Pilot TC, Radio Shack

247 CR 77, W Bluff Rd, Channahon

245 Arsenal Rd
Other E: Joliet Army Ammo Plant
W: Mobil Oil Refinery, Dow Chemical

241 N River Rd, Wilmington
Other W: **Des Plaines Fish & Wildlife Area▲ / RVDump**

240 CR 80, Lorenzo Rd, Wilmington
FStop E: Lorenzo Rd Fuel Stop/Valero
TStop W: RoadysTS/River Truck Plaza/Mobil (Scales)
Food W: Rest/FastFood/River TP
Lodg W: KnightsInn/River TP
Other W: Laundry/WiFi/CB/River TP

238 IL 129S, Strip Mine Rd, Braidwood (SB LEFT exit, NO SB reaccess)
Other E: **to Fossil Rock Rec Area▲**

236 IL 113, Coal City Rd, Coal City, Kankakee
Gas W: BP, Citgo, Mobil◈
Food E: The Good Table Rest
W: McDonald's, Subway
Other E: Auto Dealer

233 CR 37, Reed Rd, Kennedy Rd
Gas E: Marathon
Lodg E: Sands Motel, Sun Motel
AServ E: Repairs/Marathon

227 IL 53, CR 49, Main St, Gardner Rd, Gardner
Gas E: Casey's
W: BP◈
Food E: Gardner Haus Rest

220 IL 47, Union St, Morris, Dwight
FStop E: Circle K #1207/Marathon
Gas E: BP◈, Clark
Food E: Burger King/BP, Arby's, McDonald's
Lodg E: Classic Inn Hotel, Super 8

217 IL 17, Mazon Ave, Dwight, Streator
TStop E: Circle K #187/Shell
Gas E: Casey's, Phillips 66
Food E: Rest/Circle K, DQ, Old Rte 66 Family Rest, Pete's Family Rest & Pancake House
Other E: Laundry/Circle K

209 Prairie St, Odell
Gas E: BP

201 IL 23, O'Dell, to Pontiac, Streator
Other E: **Pontiac RV**, Airport✈

197 IL 116, Pontiac, Flanagan
FStop E: Pontiac BP Travel Mart
Gas E: Shell, Thornton's◈
W: Citgo
Food E: Subway/BP, Arby's, Burger King, McDonald's, Subway, Taco Bell, Wendy's
Lodg E: Comfort Inn, Holiday Inn Express, Super 8
Med E: + Hospital
Other E: Auto Zone, Auto Dealers, Dollar Tree, Grocery, **Walmart sc**, **IL State Hwy Patrol Post**, **to** Pontiac Muni Airport✈

(194) Rest Area (Both dir) (RR, Phones, Picnic, Vend)

187 US 24, Cemetery Rd, Chenoa
TStop E: Chenoa Thrifty Mart/Shell
Food E: Casey's, Phillips 66
Food W: FastFood/Chenoa TM, Chenoa Family Rest, DQ, McDonald's/P66
Lodg E: Super 8

178 CR 8, Lexington
Gas E: BP◈, Freedom◈
Food E: McDonald's/BP

171 CR 29, Towanda

167 Veterans Pkwy, Bus I-55, Normal (SB, LEFT Exit)
Gas E: **to** Circle K/BP, Meijer◈, Murphy USA, Sam's
Lodg E: **to** Candlewood Suites, Comfort Suites, Courtyard, Days Inn, Fairfield Inn, Hampton Inn, Holiday Inn Express, Signature Inn
Med E: + to Hospital
Other E: **to** ATMs, Banks, Auto Services, Best Buy, Borders, College Hills Mall, Dick's Sporting Goods, Dollar Tree, FedEx Office, Home Depot, Menard's, Meijer, Office Depot, Petco♥, Pharmacy, Sam's Club, Target, Tires, Walgreen's, **Walmart sc**, **to** IL State Univ, Bloomington Normal Airport✈

165AB US 51 Bus, Bloomington (NB)

165 US 51 Bus, N Main St, Bloomington, Normal (SB)
Gas E: Circle K/BP, Mobil◈, Qik n EZ, Shell
Food E: Arby's/Mobil, Burger King/Shell, China Star, Denny's, McDonald's/QuiknEZ Moe's SW Grill, Pizza Hut, Sly's BBQ, Steak 'n Shake, Subway, Uncle Tom's Pancake House
Lodg E: Best Western, Holiday Inn, Motel 6♥, Super 8
TServ W: McLean County Truck, Central Illinois Truck, Cummins, International Truck, White GMC Volvo/Kenworth
Med E: + to Hospital
Other E: ATMs, Dollar General, Dollar Tree, Grocery, NAPA, Walgreen's, **to** IL State Univ

(164) Jct I-39, US 51, Rockford, to Peru

NOTE: I-55 runs below with I-74. Exit #'s follow I-55.

(163) Jct I-74W, to Champaign, Peoria

160A US 150, IL 9, Market St, Bloomington
FStop E: Circle K #1251/Marathon, Speedway #8326, Freedom Oil #39
TStop E: Pilot Travel Center #299 (Scales), Travel Center of America #92/BP (Scales)
Gas E: BP, Shell
W: Citgo◈, WalMart
Food E: Wendy's/Pilot TC, CtryPride/Popeyes/ PizzaHut/TA TC, Arby's, Burger King, Carl's Jr, **Cracker Barrel**, Hardee's, KFC, McDonald's, Popeye's Chicken, Subway, Taco Bell
W: Bob Evans, Country Kitchen, Steak 'n Shake
Lodg E: Best Inn♥, Comfort Inn, Days Inn♥, Econo Lodge, Hawthorn Suites, Quality Inn
W: Country Inn, Hampton Inn, Holiday Inn Express, Wingate Inn
TWash E: Blue Beacon TW
TServ E: TA TC/Tires
Med E: + Hospital
Other E: Laundry/BarbSh/WiFi/Pilot TC, Laundry/WiFi/TA TC, ATMs, Dollar General, Grocery, NAPA, Radio Shack, **Walmart sc**, Factory Outlet Stores

160B US 150, IL 9, Market St
Gas W: Citgo◈, WalMart
Food W: Country Kitchen, Steak 'n Shake
Lodg W: Country Inn♥, Hampton Inn, Ramada Inn♥, Wingate Inn
Other W: Factory Outlet Mall, **Walmart sc**

NOTE: I-55 runs above with I-74. Exit #'s follow I-55.

157B Bus 55, US 51, Veterans Pkwy, Bloomington
Gas E: Shell
Food E: Rest/Parkway Inn, CJ's Rest
Lodg E: Parkway Inn, Sunset Inn

(157A) Jct I-74E to Indianapolis, I-55, US 51 to Decatur

154 CR 34, McLean, to Shirley

(149) Rest Area (Both dir) (RR, Phones, Picnic, Vend, Playgr)

◈ = Regular Gas Stations with Diesel ▲ = RV Friendly Locations ♥ = Pet Friendly Locations
Red print shows large vehicle parking / access on site or nearby Brown Print = Campgrounds / RV PARKS

EXIT — ILLINOIS

145 **US 136, McLean, Heyworth**
TStop W: RoadysTS/Dixie Travel Plaza/Citgo (Scales)
Gas W: Shell
Food W: Rest/Dixie TP, McDonald's
Lodg W: Super 8
TServ W: Dixie TP/Tires
Other W: Laundry/BarbSh/WiFi/Dixie TP

140 **CR 25, CR 6, Atlanta, Lawndale**
FStop W: Ray's Fast Stop
Food W: Country Aire Restaurant
Lodg W: I-55 Motel, Americas Best Value Inn

133 **I-55 Bus, Lincoln**
Gas E: Mini Mart Citgo
Lodg E: Budget Inn
Med E: + Hospital
Other E: McMillen's Camp-A-While▲, to Logan Co Airport✈, Amtrak, Lincoln College

(127) **Jct I-155N, to Peoria, Hartsburg**

126 **IL 10, IL 121, Lincoln, Mason City**
TStop E: Thorton's Travel Plaza/P66/ Pilot TC #514 (Scales)
Food E: Rest/FastFood/Thorton's TP, Burger King, Cracker Barrel, Hardee's, Long John Silver, McDonald's, Pizza Hut, Steak 'n Shake, Wendy's
Lodg E: Comfort Inn, Holiday Inn Express, Super 8
Med E: + Abraham Lincoln Memorial Hospital
TServ E: TNT Truck & Trailer Service
Other E: Laundry/Thornton's TP, Auto Zone, Auto Services, Dollar General, Grocery, Kroger, Radio Shack, Walmart sc,

123 **I-55 Bus Lp, to Lincoln**

119 **CR 12, Elkhart, to Broadwell**

115 **CR 10, Elkhart**
Gas W: Shell

109 **IL 123, CR 2, New Salem St, Williamsville, Petersburg**
TStop E: Love's Travel Stop #249 (Scales)
Food E: McDonald's/Love's TS
Other E: WiFi/RVDump/Love's TS

(107) **Weigh Station (SB)**

105 **IL 124, I-55 Bus Lp, Peoria Ave, Sherman Blvd, Sherman**
Gas W: BP, Casey's, Shell
Food W: DQ, Subway

(104) **Rest Area (SB)**
(RR, Phones, Picnic, Vend)

(102) **Rest Area (NB)**
(RR, Phone, Picnic, Vend)

100B **IL 54, Sangamon Ave, Clinton, Springfield**
Gas W: Circle K/BP, Shell◊, Speedway◊, Murphy USA
Food W: Arby's, Burger King, Culver's, Hickory River BBQ, McDonald's, Ryan's Gill, Sonic, Steak 'n Shake, Subway, Wendy's
Lodg W: Ramada Ltd
Other W: ATMs, Banks, Grocery, Lowe's, Menard's, Walmart sc, Harley Davidson, IL State Fairgrounds, to Capitol Airport✈

100A **IL 54, Springfield, Clinton**
TStop E: Road Ranger Travel Center #118/ Pilot TC #525 (Scales)
Food E: Rest/Road Ranger TC
Tires E: Road Ranger TC
TWash E: Powerline Truck Wash
TServ E: Kenworth/Volvo Trucks, American Truck Lube System

(98B) **Jct I-72, IL 97W, Clear Lake Ave**
Gas W: BP, Circle K, Shell◊
Food W: Hardee's, McDonald's, Starbucks, Subway, Taco Bell, Wendy's
Lodg W: Best Western, Best Rest Inn, Lincoln's Lodge, Parkview Motel, Shamrock Motel
TServ W: Ford Truck
Med W: + St John's Hospital
Other W: ATMs, Bergen Public Golf Course, Auto Services, Convention Center, Penske, Purcell Tire, Goodyear, Walgreen's

(98A) **Jct I-72, US 36E, to Decatur**

96A **IL 29S, Taylorville, Springfield**

96B **IL 29N, S Grand Ave**
Gas W: BP, Citgo◊, Road Ranger◊
Food W: Burger King, Godfather's Pizza, Popeye's Chicken
Lodg W: Quest Inn, Red Roof Inn♥, Super 8♥
Other W: ATMs, Auto Dealers, Auto Zone, Advance Auto Parts, Car Wash,Grocery, Greyhound, O'Reilly Auto Parts, Shop 'n Save

94 **Stevenson Dr, E Lake Shore Dr Springfield**
Gas W: Circle K/BP, Mobil◊
Food W: Applebee's, Arby's, Bob Evans, Carlos O'Kelley's, CiCi's Pizza, Denny's, Hooters, Hardee's, Little Caesars Pizza, Long John Silver, Maverick Steak House, McDonald's, Outback Steakhouse, Pizza Hut, Red Lobster, Smokey Bones BBQ, Steak 'n Shake, Taco Bell, Wendy's, Subway/Mobil, Quiznos/Circle K
Lodg W: Comfort Suites, Crowne Plaza Hotel, Days Inn, Drury Inn, Hampton Inn, Hilton Garden Inn, Holiday Inn Express, Pear Tree Inn, Signature Inn, Stevenson Inn
Other E: Springfield KOA▲
W: ATMs, Banks, Big Lots, Cinema, CVS, Dollar General, Radio Shack, ShopKO, Walgreen's, US Post Office, to Univ of IL/Springfield, Lincoln Land Comm College, A Mr Lincoln's Campground▲

92A **Bus Lp 55, 6th St, Springfield (SB)**

(92B) **Jct I-72W, US 36W, Jacksonville (SB)**

(92AB) **Jct I-72W, US 36W, Jacksonville (NB, LEFT exit)**
Gas W: Road Ranger, Thornton's
Food W: Arby's, Burger King, KFC, McDonald's, Subway, Taco Bell
Lodg W: Super 8, Travelodge
Other W: ATMs, Auto Dealers, Walgreen's, Walmart sc

90 **Toronto Rd, Springfield**
Gas E: Circle K/Shell, Qik-N-Ez◊,
Food E: Burger King, Cracker Barrel, Hardee's, Hen House, McDonald's, Subway, Taco Bell, Wendy's/QikNEz
Lodg E: Baymont Inn♥, Motel 6♥, Ramada Ltd
Med E: + Doctors Hospital
Other E: to Univ of IL/Springfield

88 **East Lake Shore Dr, to Chatham**
Other E: Springfield KOA▲, IL State Hwy Patrol Post
W: to Double J Campground & RV Park▲

83 **Old Rte 66, Glenarm**
Other W: to appr 4 mi: Double J Campground & RV Park▲

82 **IL 104, Divernon, Auburn, Pawnee**
FStop W: Auburn Travel Center (Scales)
Gas W: Marathon◊
Food W: FastFood/Auburn TC, Quiznos/Marathon
TServ W: Homestead Garage
Other W: Laundry/WiFi/RVDump/Auburn TC

80 **E Brown St, Divernon**
Gas W: Phillips 66◊
Food W: Bearden's Rest

72 **CR 17, Mine Ave, Farmersville**
FStop W: Jumpin Jimmy's
Gas W: Shell◊
Food W: FastFood/Jumpin Jimmy's, Subway, Rest/Art's Motel
Lodg W: Art's Motel

(65) **Rest Area (Both dir)**
(RR, Phones, Picnic, Vend, Playgr)

63 **IL 48, IL 127, Waggoner, Raymond**

60 **IL 108, to Carlinville**
FStop W: Shell
Food W: Café/Shell, Rest/Holiday Inn
Lodg W: Holiday Inn
Other E: Kamper Kampanion RV Park▲

(56) **Weigh Station (NB)**

52 **IL 16, to Rte 66, Litchfield**
TStop E: RoadysTS/Fast Stop Travel Center/P66 (Scales)
Gas E: BP, Conoco◊, Shell◊, Murphy USA Casey's General Store, Clark
Food E: BurgerKing/Fast Stop TC, Ariston Café, Arby's, DQ, Denny's, Hardee's, Jack in the Box/Conoco, Long John Silver/A&W, Maverick Steak House, McDonald's, Pizza Hut, Ruby Tuesday, Subway, Taco Bell, Wendy's
Lodg E: Americas Best Value Inn, Comfort Inn♥, Hampton Inn♥, Holiday Inn Express♥, Super 8♥
TServ E: Barney's Truck & Trailer, Den-Mar Truck Service
Med E: + St Francis Hospital
Other E: Laundry/Fast Stop TC, ATMs, Banks, Auto Dealers, Auto Services, Cinema, Dollar General, Dollar Tree, Goodyear, Grocery, IGA, Kroger, NAPA, Tires, Walgreen's, Walmart sc, to Litchfield Muni Airport✈
Other W: to Lankels Lazy Days Campground▲ IL State Hwy Patrol Post

44 **IL 138, Lakeview Dr, Mt Olive**
Gas E: Jumpin Jimmy's, Mobil◊
Food E: Crossroads Rest
Lodg E: Budget 10 Motel

41 **CR 12, Staunton Rd, to Staunton**
Gas W: Casey's Gen'l Store
Food W: DQ, Subway
Lodg W: Super 8♥
Med W: + Hospital

◊= Regular Gas Stations with Diesel ▲ = RV Friendly Locations ♥= Pet Friendly Locations
Red print shows large vehicle parking / access on site or nearby Brown Print = Campgrounds / RV PARKS

EXIT		ILLINOIS
37		**New Douglas Rd, Livingston**
	FStop	**W:** Meyer's BP Amoco
	Food	**W:** Country Inn Café
	Lodg	**W:** Country Inn
33		**IL 4, Worden, to Staunton, Lebanon**
	Gas	**W:** Schlechtes Service Station
	Food	**W:** Deli, Diggers Dugout
30		**IL 140, State St, Worden, Hamel**
	Gas	**W:** Shell
	Food	**E:** Rest/Inn Keeper
	Lodg	**E:** Inn Keeper
(28)		**IL Welcome Center (NB)** **Rest Area (SB)** (RR, Phones, Picnic, Vend)
23		**IL 143, Edwardsville, Highland, Marine**
	Gas	**E:** Phillips 66◈
	TServ	**E:** Joe's Car & Tractor Service
	Other	**W:** to Red Barn Rendezvous RV Park▲
(20B)		**Jct I-270W, to Kansas City**
(20A)		**Jct I-70E, to Indianapolis**
	NOTE:	**I-55 runs below with I-70E for 18 mi. Exit #'s follow I-55.**
18		**IL 162, Edwardsville Rd, Troy**
	TStop	**E:** Pilot Travel Center #249 (Scales), Travel Center of America #199/BP (Scales)
	Gas	**E:** ZX Gas Mart **W:** Phillips 66◈
	Food	**E:** Arby's/TJCinn/Pilot TC, CountryPride/TA TC, Burger King, DQ, Jack in the Box, KFC, Little Caesars Pizza, McDonald's, Perkins, Pizza Hut, Subway **W:** China Garden, Cracker Barrel, Taco Bell
	Lodg	**E:** Relax Inn **W:** Holiday Inn Express♥, Red Roof Inn♥, Scottish Inns, Super 8
	TWash	**E:** 18 Wheeler's Truck Wash
	TServ	**E:** TA TC/Tires, Carron's Auto & Truck Repair, Speedco
	Med	**E:** + Hospital **W:** to + Anderson Hospital
	Other	**E:** Laundry/WiFi/Pilot TC, Laundry/BarbSh/WiFi/TA TC, ATMs, Banks, Dollar General, Family Dollar, Grocery, Ace Hardware, U-Haul, Walgreen's
17		**US 40E, Troy**
	TServ	**E:** ADR Auto & Truck Repair, M&M Truck Repair
15AB		**IL 159, Center St, Collinsville, Maryville**
	Gas	**E:** Gas Mart/P66◈, Shell, ZX **W:** Conoco
	Lodg	**W:** Econo Lodge♥
	Other	**E:** ATMs, Auto Dealers, Auto Services, Car Wash, Dollar General, Grocery
(14)		**Weigh Station (SB)**
11		**IL 157, Bluff Rd, Collinsville, to Edwardsville**
	FStop	**W:** Moto Mart
	Gas	**E:** BP, Casey's, Shell
	Food	**E:** Denny's, Hardee's, Long John Silver, McDonald's, Pizza Hut, Waffle House Wendy's
	Food	**W:** Applebee's, Arby's, Bandanas BBQ, Bob Evans, Burger King, DQ, Ponderosa, Ruby Tuesday, Shoney's, Steak 'n Shake, White Castle

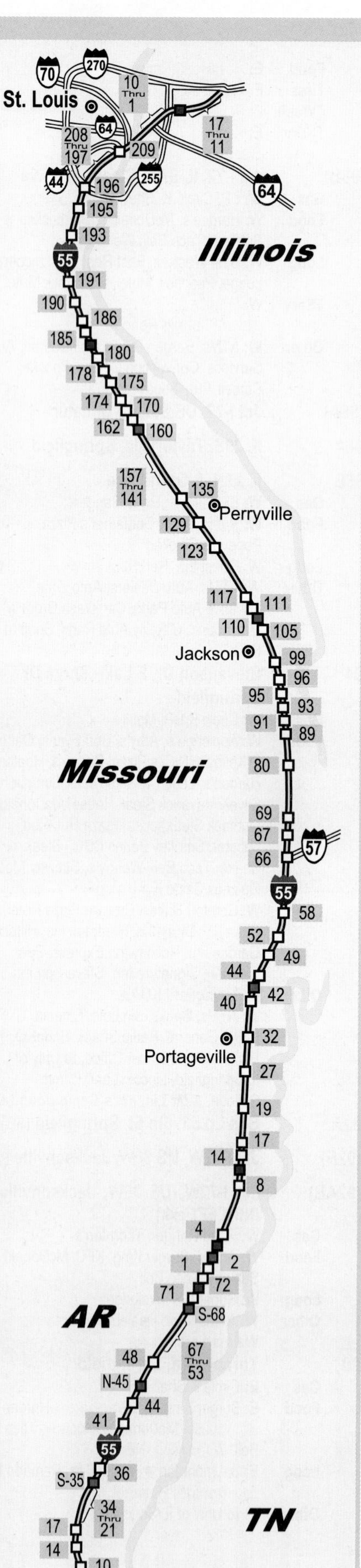

EXIT		IL / MO
	Lodg	**E:** America's Best Value Inn, Best Western, Comfort Inn, Days Inn, Howard Johnson, Motel 6♥, Pear Tree Inn **W:** Drury Inn♥, Fairfield Inn, Hampton Inn, Holiday Inn, Ramada, Super 8
	Other	**E:** ATMs, Home Depot, Radio Shack, Walgreen's, **Walmart sc**, Vet♥ **W:** ATMs, Auto Dealers, Splash City Family Water Park, Visitor Center, IL State Hwy Patrol Post
(10)		**Jct I-255, S to Memphis, N to I-270**
9		**Black Lane (NB, no reacc)**
	Other	**E:** to Fairmount Park Racetrack
6		**IL 111, Great River Rd, Wood River, Fairmont City, Washington Park**
	Gas	**E:** Phillips 66
	Lodg	**E:** Rainbow Court Motel
	Other	**E:** Grocery, Pharmacy
	NOTE:	**MM 5: NB: Begin Call Boxes**
4		**IL 203, Collinsville Rd, Granite City, E St Louis (NB)**
	TStop	**W:** Pilot Travel Center #313 (Scales) (SB: ACCESS VIA EXIT #4B)
	Gas	**E:** Phillips 66◈
	Food	**W:** Subway/TacoBell/Pilot TC
	Lodg	**E:** Western Inn
	TWash	**W:** Pilot TC
	TServ	**W:** Pilot TC/Tires
	Other	**W:** Laundry/WiFi/Pilot TC, Gateway Int'l Raceway
4B		**IL 203W, E St Louis (SB)**
4A		**IL 203E, Collinsville Rd (SB)**
3		**Exchange Ave, E St Louis**
(2)		**Jct I-64E, IL 3N, St Clair Ave**
2B		**3rd St (SB, LEFT exit)**
	Other	**W:** Casino Queen RV Park▲
2A		**MLK Bridge, to St Louis Downtown (SB, LEFT exit)**
1		**IL 3, to Sauget (SB)**
	NOTE:	**I-55 runs above with I-70E for 18 mi. Exit #'s follow I-55.**

CENTRAL TIME ZONE

⬆ ILLINOIS
⬇ MISSOURI

	NOTE:	**MM 209: Illinois State Line**

CENTRAL TIME ZONE

(209B)		**Jct I-70W, to Kansas City**
209A		**to St Louis Arch, Busch Stadium**
208		**7th St, Park Ave, Downtown**
	Gas	**W:** BP
	Food	**E:** Burger King, McDonald's **W:** Hardee's, Taco Bell
	Lodg	**W:** Drury Plaza, Marriott, Radisson. Park Ave B&B
	TServ	**E:** Broadway Ford Dealership
	Other	**E:** Haunted Theme Park
(207)		**Jct I-44W, to Tulsa (fr SB)**

◈ = Regular Gas Stations with Diesel ▲ = RV Friendly Locations ♥ = Pet Friendly Locations
Red print shows large vehicle parking / access on site or nearby Brown Print = Campgrounds / RV PARKS

EXIT		MISSOURI
(207B)		**Jct I-44W, to Tulsa (fr NB, LEFT Exit)**
207A		**MO 30, Russell Blvd, Gravois Ave**
	Gas	E: Citgo
	Food	E: Jack in the Box
206C		**Arsenal St, St Louis**
	Gas	W: Shell
	Other	E: Anheuser Busch Tour Center
206B		**S Broadway (NB, no reaccess)**
	Other	W: Auto & Truck Service
206A		**Potomac St (NB, no reaccess)**
205		**Gasconade St (SB ex, NB reaccess)**
	Med	W: + Alexian Bros Hospital
204		**Broadway, St Louis**
	Gas	E: Mobil
		W: Clark, Sinclair
	Food	W: Hardee's, McDonald's, Pizza Hut
	Med	W: + Alexian Bros Hospital
	Other	W: Radio Shack, Walgreen's
203		**Bates St, Virginia Ave**
	Gas	W: 7-11, BP
	Other	E: Auto Repair & Towing
202C		**Loughborough Ave, St Louis**
202B		**Germania Ave (SB exit, NB reacc)**
202A		**Carondelet Blvd (NB)**
201B		**Weber Rd (NB)**
201A		**Bayless Ave, St Louis**
	Gas	E: BP, QT, Shell
		W: 7-11, BP, Shell
	Food	E: McDonald's
		W: DQ, Jack in the Box, Subway, Taco Bell
	Other	W: Grocery, Goodyear, Pharmacy
200		**Union Rd (SB exit, NB reaccess)**
199		**Reavis Barracks Rd**
	Gas	E: BP, Shell
	Food	E: Steak n Shake
197		**US 61, US 50, Lindbergh Blvd**
	Gas	E: BP, Phillips 66
	Food	E: Applebee's, Arby's, Chuck E Cheese, Hooters, KFC, Long John Silver, McDonald's, Po Folks, Ruby Tuesday, Steak n Shake
		W: Bob Evans, Casa Gallerdo, Denny's Pasta House, Ponderosa, Shoney's
	Lodg	E: Holiday Inn, Super 8
		W: Motel 6♥, Oak Grove Inn
	Other	E: Advance Auto, ATMs, Banks, Best Buy, Auto Dealers, Goodyear, NTB, S County Center Mall, Auto Services
		W: Grocery, Auto Dealers, Costco, Office Depot, Target
(196B)		**Jct I-270W, to Kansas City (SB)**
(196A)		**Jct I-255E, to Chicago (SB)**
(196)		**Jct I-255E, to Chicago, I- 270W, to Kansas City (NB)**
195		**Butler Hill Rd, St Louis**
	Gas	E: Phillips 66
		W: Sinclair
	Food	W: Burger King, Hardee's, Subway, Taco Bell, Waffle House
	Lodg	E: Holiday Inn
		W: Econo Lodge
	Other	E: Walgreen's
193		**Meramec Bottom Rd**
	Gas	E: Mobil, QT
	Food	E: Cracker Barrel
	Lodg	E: Best Western♥
	Other	E: Howard RV Supercenter
191		**MO 141, Arnold**
	Gas	E: Citgo, PetroMart, QT, Shell
		W: Mobil, Phillips 66◈
	Food	E: Applebee's, Bandana's BBQ, CiCi's, China King, Denny's, Fazoli's, Hardee's, McDonald's, Steak n Shake
	Lodg	E: Drury Inn, Ramada Ltd
	Other	E: Mall, Grocery, **Walmart sc**, Bowling Center, Auto Services, Pharmacy
190		**Richardson Rd, Arnold**
	Gas	E: Express Mart, QT, Shell◈
		W: 7-11, Phillips 66◈, Shell◈
	Food	E: DQ, Domino's, Ponderosa, Pizza Hut, Subway, Taco Bell, White Castle
		W: Burger King, McDonalds, Ruby Tuesday, Waffle House
	Lodg	W: Comfort Inn
	Other	E: Arnold Cinema 14, Grocery, Firestone
		W: Grocery, Home Depot, Target, Walgreen's
186		**Imperial Main St, Imperial, Kimmswick**
	Gas	E: Conv Food Mart/Shell
185		**MO M, Barnhart, to Antonia**
	FStop	W: Express Mart/Citgo
	Food	W: Café
	Other	W: **LP**/ExpressMart, Walgreen's, **to St Louis South KOA▲**
(184)		**Weigh Station (Both dir)**
180		**CR Z, Pevely, to Hillsboro**
	TStop	W: Mr Fuel #3, I-55 Motor Plaza/66 (Scales)
	Gas	E: Mobil
	Food	E: Burger King, Country Kitchen, Domino's, KFC
		W: FastFood/Mr Gas, McDonald's/I-55MP
	Lodg	W: Super 8
	Other	E: IGA, Banks, ATMs, **to** I-55 Raceway
		W: Laundry/**LP**/I-55 MP
178		**Bus 55, McNutt St, Herculaneum**
	TStop	E: QuikTrip #611 (Scales)
	Gas	E: Shell
	Food	E: Wendy's/QT, **Cracker Barrel**, Jack in the Box, DQ, La Pachanga Mex Rest
	Other	E: **to** I-55 Raceway
		W: Auto Dealer
175		**Veterans Blvd, Festus, Crystal City**
	Gas	E: Phillips 66◈
		W: 7-11◈, Phillips 66◈
	Food	E: Arby's, Bob Evans, Captain D's, Fazoli's, McDonald's, Ryan's Grill, Steak n Shake, Subway, Taco Bell, Wendy's, White Castle
		W: Hardee's, Ruby Tuesday, Waffle House
	Lodg	E: Drury Inn, Holiday Inn Express
		W: Baymont Inn
	Other	E: Advance Auto, Grocery, Home Depot, Tires, **Walmart sc**, ATMs, Banks
		W: Cinema, Lowe's
174A		**US 67E, US 61, S Truman Blvd (Access #175 Services)**
	Gas	E: Phillips 66, WalMart
	Food	E: Arby's, McDonald's, Ryan's Grill
	Med	E: + Jefferson Memorial Hospital
	Other	E: **Walmart sc**, Festus Memorial Airport✈
174B		**US 67W, to Park Hills**
	FStop	W: One Stop
	Other	W: Tires, Towing, **RVDump**/One Stop, **Buff's RV**
170		**US 61, Festus**
	FStop	W: BP
	Other	W: **LP**/BP
162		**MO DD, MO OO, to US 61, Bloomsdale**
(160)		**Rest Area (Both dir) (RR, Phones, Picnic, Vend)**
157		**MO Y, to US 61, Bloomsdale**
	FStop	W: Bloomsdale Food Mart/Valero
	Gas	E: Phillips 66
154		**MO O, Ste Genevieve, Rocky Ridge**
150		**MO 32, MO B, MO A, Ste Genevieve**
	Gas	E: BP
		W: Phillips 66◈
	Food	E: DQ
	Med	E: + Hospital
	Lodg	W: Microtel
	Other	W: Auto Dealer
143		**MO M, MO N, MO J, St Mary, Ozora**
	TStop	W: AmBest/Ozora Truck & Travel Plaza/ Valero (Scales)
	Gas	W: Sinclair
	Food	W: Rest/FastFood/Ozora TP
	Lodg	W: Family Budget Inn
	TWash	W: Ozora TP
	TServ	W: Ozora TP/Tires
	Other	W: Laundry/WiFi/Ozora TP
141		**MO Z, St Mary**
135		**MO M, Perryville, Brewer**
129		**MO 51, Perryville Blvd, Perryville**
	FStop	E: Rhodes 101 Stop/P66
	Gas	E: MotoMart◈
		W: Rhodes 101 Stop Shell◈
	Food	E: Burger King, KFC, McDonald's, Skinny's Diner, Ponderosa, Sonic, Taco Bell
	Lodg	W: Best Western, Comfort Inn, Super 8
	Med	E: + Perry Co Memorial Hospital
	Other	W: **Walmart sc**, Auto Dealers, **Perryville/Cape Girardeau KOA▲**
123		**MO B, Perryville, to Biehle**
	FStop	W: Rhodes 101 Stop/66
	Food	W: Country Kettle Rest
117		**MO KK, Oak Ridge, to Appleton**
	Gas	E: Sewing's Travel Center
111		**MO E, Oak Ridge**
(110)		**Rest Area (Both dir) (RR, Phones, Picnic, Vend)**
105		**US 61, Jackson, Fruitland**
	Gas	E: BP◈, Casey's, Rhodes 101◈
		W: D-Mart
	Food	E: Casey's C/O Pizza, Pie Bird Cafe
		W: DQ, Pizza Inn
	Lodg	W: Drury Inn
	Other	W: McDowell South Truck, **RV** & Trailer Sales
99		**Bus 55, US 61, MO 34, Cape Girardeau, Jackson,**
	Gas	W: Murphy
	Food	W: DQ, Fazoli's, Subway
	Lodg	E: Super 8
	Other	E: **Cape Camping & RV Park▲** /**RVDump**, **Capetown RV Sales**
		W: **Walmart sc**
96		**MO K, William St, Cape Girardeau, Gordonville**
	Gas	E: BP, Citgo◈, D-Mart
		W: Shell

◈= Regular Gas Stations with Diesel ▲ = RV Friendly Locations ♥= Pet Friendly Locations
Red print shows large vehicle parking / access on site or nearby Brown Print = Campgrounds / RV PARKS

EXIT — MISSOURI

Food — E: Bob Evans, Blimpie, Burger King, Cracker Barrel, DQ, McDonald's, Logan's Roadhouse, Olive Garden, O'Charley's, Red Lobster, Ruby Tuesday, Ryan's Grill, Steak n Shake, Taco Bell, Sonic, Subway
W: Outback Steakhouse, White Castle
Lodg — E: Drury Lodge♥, Holiday Inn Express, Pear Tree Inn♥, Victorian Inn
W: Drury Inn, Hampton Inn
TServ — E: Purcell Tire
Med — E: + St Francis Medical Center
Other — E: ATMs, Banks, B&N, Best Buy, Big Lots, Grocery, Walgreen's, W Park Mall
W: ATMs, Cinema, Dollar Tree, Lowe's, Sam's Club, Staples, Target, **Walmart sc**

95 — **MO 74E, to US 61**

93B — **US 61, Cape Girardeau (NB)**

93A — **MO 74, Dutchtown (NB)**

93 — **MO 74W, Cape Girardeau (SB)**

91 — **CR AB, Nash Rd, Cape Girardeau, Scott City, Airport**
TStop — E: PTP/Rhodes Travel Center/66 (Scales)
Food — E: Rest/FastFood/Rhodes TC
TWash — E: Rhodes TC
Tires — E: Rhodes TC, Raben Tire
TServ — E: Sam's Service & Repair
Other — E: Laundry/WiFi/**RVDump**/Rhodes TC, Minor's Harley Davidson
W: Cape Girardeau Muni Airport✈, **Capetown RV Sales**

89 — **US 61, MO M, MO K, Main St, Scott City**
Gas — E: Rhodes 101, Shell
Food — E: Burger King, DQ, Sonic, Waffle Hut
Other — E: Dollar General, NAPA

80 — **MO 77, Benton**
Gas — W: BP◈, Express◈
Food — W: McDonald's/BP
Other — E: Auto Service

69 — **MO HH, Sikeston, Miner**
TStop — W: Keller Truck Service (Scales)

67 — **US 62, Malone St, Sikeston, Miner**
TStop — E: Break Time #3147/MFA
W: Keller Truck Service (Scales)
Gas — W: Citgo, Larry's Pit Stop
Food — E: Deli/Break Time, JD's Steakhouse
W: Rest/Keller TS, Burger King, Frankie's Country Cooking, McDonald's, Mex Rest, Pizza Hut, Ruby Tuesday, Shoney's, Sonic, Skinny's Diner, Taco Bell, Wendy's
Lodg — E: Best Western, Holiday Inn Express, Red Carpet Inn
W: Country Hearth Inn, Days Inn, Drury Inn, Pear Tree Inn, Ramada Inn, Super 8
TWash — W: Keller TS
TServ — E: Raben Tire, White GMC Volvo
W: Keller TS/Tires
Med — W: + Hospital
Other — E: **Hinton Park Campground▲**, **Town & Country RV Resort▲**, **RV America**
W: Laundry/Keller TS, Auto Zone, Auto Services, Family Dollar, Goodyear, Grocery, Walgreen's, **Walmart sc**, Sikeston Memorial Muni Airport✈

66B — **US 60W, to Poplar Bluff**

(66A) — **Jct I-57E, to Chicago, US 60W**

58 — **MO 80, Matthews, East Prairie**
TStop — E: Travel Center of America #51/Citgo
W: Flying J Travel Plaza #5074/Conoco (Scales), Love's Travel Stop #313 (Scales)
Food — E: CountryPride/TacoBell/TA TC
W: Rest/FastFood/FJ TP, Subway/Chesters/Love's TS
TWash — E: DJ's TW, Cranford's TW
TServ — E: TA TC/Tires
W: J & S Truck Repair
Other — E: Laundry/WiFi/TA TC
W: Laundry/BarbSh/WiFi/**RVDump**/FJ TP, WiFi/**RVDump**/Love's TS

52 — **MO P, New Madrid, Kewanee**
TStop — E: BJ's Travel Center/AmocoBP
Food — E: FastFood/BJ's TC

49 — **US 61, US 62, Lp 55, New Madrid (Access #44 Serv S to New Madrid)**

44 — **US 61, US 62, New Madrid**
Gas — E: Casey's, Express
Food — E: Casey's Pizza, Kinsey's Family Rest, Pro Pizza, Rosie's Grill
Lodg — E: Relax Inn & **Kampground▲**
Other — E: Auto Services, Tires, Towing

(42) — **MO Welcome Center (NB) Rest Area (SB) (RR, Phones, Picnic, Vend)**

40 — **MO EE, St Jude Rd, Marston**
TStop — E: Pilot Travel Center #301 (Scales)
W: Break Time #3149/MFA
Food — E: Arby's/TJCinn/Pilot TC
W: FastFood/BreakTime
Lodg — E: Super 8
W: Budget Inn
Other — E: Laundry/WiFi/Pilot TC

32 — **US 61, MO 162, Portageville**
FStop — W: Martin & Ivie Gas & Go/BP
Gas — W: Casey's
Food — W: FastFood/Martin&Ivie, McDonald's

27 — **MO K, MO A, MO BB, to Wardell**
Other — E: **to Hayti/Portageville KOA▲**

19 — **US 412, MO 84, Hayti**
FStop — E: Break Time #3153/MFA
TStop — E: Pilot Travel Center #442 (Scales) Hayti Travel Center (Scales)
Gas — W: BP, Conoco
Food — E: Arbys/TJCinn/Pilot TC, Rest/Hayti TC, Chubby's BBQ, KFC, McDonald's, Pizza Hut, Wendy's
W: BBQ, DQ, Pizza Inn
Lodg — E: Comfort Inn, Executive Inn
W: Budget Inn, Drury Inn
AServ — W: D&H Tire & Auto Repair
Tires — E: Raben Tire
TServ — W: Tatum Repair, Ace Wrecker & Repair
Med — W: + Medical Care
Other — E: Laundry/WiFi/**RVDump**/Pilot TC, MidContinent Airport✈, **to Hayti/ Portageville KOA▲**
W: ATMs, Bank, Auto Services, Goodyear

(17A) — **Jct I-155E, US 412, to Dyersburg, TN**

14 — **MO J, MOR H, MO U, Caruthersville, Braggadocio**

(10) — **Weigh Station (Both dir)**

8 — **MO 164, US 61, Steele**
TStop — W: AmBest/Deerfield Travel Plaza/BP (Scales)
Gas — E: Flash Market
Food — W: Subway/BP, Boss Hogg BBQ, Show Me Pizza

EXIT — MO / AR

Lodg — W: Deerfield Inn
TWash — W: Deerfield TP
Other — W: WiFi/Deerfield TP

4 — **MO E, Steele, to Cooter, Holland**

(3) — **Weigh Station (SB)**

(2) — **Rest Area (Both dir) (RR, Phones, Picnic, Vend)**

1 — **MO O, to US 61, Steele, to Holland**
Gas — E: RaceWay
W: Coastal, Shell◈

CENTRAL TIME ZONE

⬆ MISSOURI
⬇ ARKANSAS

NOTE: MM 72: Missouri State Line

CENTRAL TIME ZONE

72 — **State Line Rd (NB)**

(71) — **Weigh Station (SB)**

71 — **AR 150, Blytheville**
Gas — W: Citgo◈

(68) — **AR Welcome Center (SB) (RR, Phones, Picnic)**

67 — **AR 18, AR 151, Blytheville**
FStop — E: Hard Hat/Exxon
W: Flash Market #177/Citgo
TStop — E: Lone Wolf Truck Stop
Gas — W: BP◈
Food — E: Rest/Lone Wolf TS, Burger King, Chinese Buffet, Rest/Days Inn
W: Arby's, Grecian Steak House, Hardee's, KFC, Mazzio's Pizza, McDonald's, Perkins, Pizza Inn, Poor Boys Café, Shoney's, Sonic, Subway, Wendy's
Lodg — E: Days Inn
W: Comfort Inn♥, Hampton Inn, Travel Lodge Inn
Med — W: + Baptist Memorial Hospital
Other — E: Dollar Tree, Lowe's, **Walmart sc**, Blytheville Muni Airport✈
W: Animal Hospital♥, Auto Services, Family Dollar, Pharmacy, Blytheville AFB

63 — **US 61, Blytheville**
FStop — W: Shell
Gas — W: Dodge' Store◈, Citgo, Exxon
Food — W: McDonald's/Shell, Dodge's Chicken
Lodg — W: Best Western, Relax Inn
Tires — W: Raben Tire

57 — **AR 148, Burdette**

53 — **AR 158, Osceola, to Luxora, Victoria**

48 — **AR 140, Osceola (All Serv E in Osceola)**
TStop — E: Shell Truck Stop
Gas — E: Mobil◈
Food — E: Cotton Inn Rest, Huddle House
Lodg — E: Best Western, Days Inn, Deerfield Inn, Plum Point Inn
Med — E: + Baptist Memorial Hospital
Other — E: Osceola Muni Airport✈

(45) — **Rest Area (NB) (RR, Picnic, Phones)**

44 — **AR 181, to Wilson, Keiser**

◈ = Regular Gas Stations with Diesel ▲ = RV Friendly Locations ♥ = Pet Friendly Locations
Red print shows large vehicle parking / access on site or nearby Brown Print = Campgrounds / RV PARKS

EXIT		ARKANSAS
41		**AR 14, Dyess, to Marie, Leparto**
36		**AR 181, Bassett, to Evandale**
(35)		**Rest Area (SB) (RR, Picnic, Phones)**
34		**AR 118, Bassett, Joiner, Tyronza**
23AB		**US 63N, AR 77S, Gilmore, Marked Tree, Jonesboro, Turrell**
21		**AR 42, Turrell**
	TStop	W: Fuel Mart #798 (Scales)
	Food	W: FastFood/Fuel Mart
17		**AR 50, Clarkedale Rd, to Jericho**
14		**CR 4, James Mill Rd, Marion, Crawfordsville, Jericho**
	TStop	E: Fast Market #36/Citgo (Scales)
	Gas	W: Citgo◈
	Food	W: Stuckey's/Citgo
	Other	E: B&M Truck & Trailer Service W: **Memphis KOA▲**
10		**US 64, Marion, Sunset, Wynne**
	FStop	E: Mapco Express #3058
	Gas	E: BP, Citgo, Shell◈ W: BP, Shell
	Food	E: Sonic, Tops BBQ, McDonald's/Shell, Subway/Citgo W: Wendy's, Rest/Best Western
	Lodg	E: Inn of America W: Best Western
	Other	E: Grocery, Dollar General
(9)		**Weigh Station (Both dir)**
(8)		**Jct I-40W, to Little Rock**
7		**AR 77, Missouri St (SB ex, NB entr)**
	Gas	E: Texaco, Exxon, Mapco
	Food	E: Shoney's, Bonanza, Cracker Barrel, Krystal, Pizza Inn, Popeye's, Subway
	Lodg	E: Ramada Inn
	Other	E: ATMs, Banks
	NOTE:	**Next 4 Exits below run with I-40. Exit #'s follow I-40.**
(277)		**Jct I-55N, Blytheville, St Louis**
278		**AR 77, 7th St, Missouri St, AR 191, W Memphis (Addt'l Serv S on Missouri St)**
	FStop	S: Flash Market #11/Shell **(S Serv Rd)**
	Gas	N: Citgo S: Love's◈, RaceTrac, Exxon, Mapco
	Food	S: Cracker Barrel, KFC, KFC, Krystal, Mrs Winners, TCBY, McDonald's, Pizza Hut, Shoney's, Subway, Wendy's
	Lodg	S: Quality Inn, Ramada Inn
	Med	S: + Crittenden Memorial Hospital
	Other	S: RVDump/Flash Market, Auto Services, Goodyear, Kroger, Walgreen's, **Walmart sc, Tom Sawyers Mississippi River RV Park▲ /RVDump**
279A		**Ingram Blvd, W Memphis**
	Gas	S: Citgo◈, Exxon, Shell
	Food	S: Perkins, Shoney's, Waffle House
	Lodg	N: Comfort Inn, Ramada, Red Roof Inn♥, Rodeway Inn S: Days Inn, Econo Lodge♥, Hampton Inn, Holiday Inn, Howard Johnson, Motel 6♥, Relax Inn
	Other	N: U-Haul, Southland Greyhound Park S: Auto Dealers, Auto Services
(279B)		**Jct I-40E, to Memphis, Jackson**

EXIT		AR / TN
280/4		**Club Rd, Southland Dr, Martin Luther King Dr (I-55, Ex #4)**
	TStop	N: Pilot Travel Center #429 (Scales), Harris Travel Center/Shamrock S: Flying J Travel Plaza #5333/Conoco (Scales), Petro Stopping Center #11 (Scales), Love's Travel Stop #450 (Scales),
	Gas	N: BP◈
	Food	N: Subway/Wendy's/Pilot TC, FastFood/Harris TC S: Rest/FastFood/FJ TP, IronSkillet/FastFood/Petro SC, Subway/Love's TS, McDonald's, KFC/Taco Bell, Waffle House
	Lodg	N: Express Inn S: Budget Inn, Sunset Inn, Super 8♥
	TWash	S: Blue Beacon TW/Petro SC
	TServ	S: Petro SC/Tires, Speedco
	Other	N: Laundry/WiFi/Pilot TC S: Laundry/BarbSh/WiFi/RVDump/LP/FJ TP, Laundry/CB/WiFi/Petro SC, WiFi/RVDump/Pilot TC, **Tom Sawyers Mississippi River RV Park▲ /RVDump**, Southland Greyhound Park
	NOTE:	**Next 4 Exits above run with I-40. Exit #'s follow I-40.**
3B		**US 70, US 79, Club Rd, Broadway Blvd (NB, LEFT Exit)**
3A		**AR 131, Mound City Rd (NB exit, SB re-entry)**
(2)		**Weigh Station (NB)**
1		**Bridgeport Rd, W Memphis**

CENTRAL TIME ZONE

⬆ ARKANSAS
⬇ TENNESSEE

NOTE: MM 13: Arkansas State Line

CENTRAL TIME ZONE

EXIT		AR / TN
12C		**Delaware St, Metal Museum Dr**
12B		**Riverside Dr, Downtown**
12A		**East Crump Blvd, US 61, US 64 (NB)**
	TServ	E: G&W Diesel Service
11		**McLemore Ave, Presidents Island**
10		**South Parkway W, Memphis**
	Gas	E: BP◈, Conoco
	TServ	W: Haygood Truck & Trailer, TruckPro
9		**Mallory Ave, Memphis**
	TServ	E: Fruehauf, Great Dane Sales & Service
8		**Horn Lake Rd, Florida St (SB Exit, NB Ent)**
7		**US 61S, TN 14, 3rd St, to Vicksburg (difficult reaccess)**
	FStop	E: Mapco Express #3138 **(E on Mallory Ave)** W: Roadrunner Petro
	Gas	E: AmocoBP, Exxon W: Citgo
	Food	E: Interstate BBQ, Lotaburger, Taco Bell W: KFC, McDonald's, Subway
	Lodg	W: Rest Inn, Starlite Inn
	Other	E: Auto Services, Walgreen's W: Auto Services, Diesel Service, Towing,

EXIT		TN / MS
(6AB)		**Jct I-240, to I-40, to Nashville**
5B		**US 51, Elvis Presley Blvd, South Brooks Rd, Graceland, Memphis**
	Gas	W: BP, Citgo◈, Exxon, Phillips 66
	Food	W: Captain D's, KFC, Kettle, Taco Bell
	Lodg	W: American Inn, Graceland Inn, Super 7 Inn, Heartbreak Hotel
	Med	W: + Hospital
	TServ	W: Pinkston Diesel & Truck Repair, Stephens Truck Service, Roadway Diesel & Gas Repair
	Other	W: Advance Auto, Auto Services, Vet♥, Goodyear, Bell Brook Industrial Park, **D&N Camper Sales, Davis Motorhome Mart, Elvis Presley Blvd RV Park▲, Memphis Graceland RV Park & Campground▲**
5A		**South Brooks Rd, to US 51, Elvis Presley Blvd, Graceland (NB)**
	TStop	E: Mapco Express #3159
	Gas	E: AmocoBP, Exxon
	Food	E: Burger King, Crown Rest, Dad's Place, Mrs Winner's, Popeye's, Shoney's
	Lodg	E: Airport Inn, Clarion Hotel, Days Inn, Quality Inn, Travelodge
	TServ	E: Freightliner, Peterbilt of Memphis, Heavy Truck & Trailer Repair, Mid-America International, Cummins, Mid-South Diesel Service
	Other	E: ATMs, Bank, Memphis Int'l Airport✈
(3)		**TN Welcome Center (NB) (RR, Phones, Picnic, Vend)**
2AB		**TN 175, Shelby Dr, to White Haven**
	Gas	E: BP◈, Citgo, Conoco, Exxon W: BP, Citgo, Shell
	Food	E: Cheyenne Country, Pollards BBQ, Subway/Citgo W: Burger King, CK's Coffee Shop, Pizza Inn, IHOP, Mrs Winner's
	Lodg	E: Colonial Inn
	Other	E: Auto Services, Laundromat W: Family Dollar, Grocery, Goodyear, Southland Mall, U-Haul, Pharmacy

CENTRAL TIME ZONE

⬆ TENNESSEE
⬇ MISSISSIPPI

NOTE: MM 291.5: Tennessee State Line

CENTRAL TIME ZONE

EXIT		TN / MS
291		**State Line Rd, Main St, Southaven**
	Gas	E: Exxon, Horizon W: In n Out
	Food	E: Burger King, Interstate BBQ, Little Caesar's, McDonald's, Shoney's, Subway, Tops BBQ, Waffle House W: Capt D's, Checkers, Mrs Winner's, Sonic, Taco Bell, Wendy's
	Lodg	E: Best Value Inn, Comfort Inn, Holiday Inn Express♥, Quality Inn, Southern Inn W: Budget Inn, Travelers Inn
	Other	E: Firestone, Goodyear, Kroger, Penske, Walgreen's, **Southaven RV Park▲** W: ATMs, Banks, Auto Services, Cinema, Big Lots, Tires, RiteAid, Walgreen's, US Post Office, Pharmacy, **to Walmart sc**

EXIT		MISSISSIPPI
289		**MS 302, Goodman Rd, Horn Lake, Olive Branch, South Southaven**
	FStop	W: Goodman Rd Food Plaza/66
	Gas	E: 76, Shell, Sam's, Murphy W: BP, Phillips 66◈, Shell◈
	Food	E: Backyard Burgers, Burger King, Chick-Fil-A, Chili's, Fazoli's, IHOP, Krystal, McDonald's, Moe's SW Grill, Logan's Roadhouse, Lone Star Steakhouse, Outback Steakhouse, Smokey Bones BBQ, Steak n Shake, Starbucks, TGI Friday
	Food	W: Applebee's, Arby's, Bob Evans, Chuck E Cheese, Cracker Barrel, Hooters, KFC, Papa John's, Pizza Hut, Popeye's, Ryan's Grill, Texas Roadhouse, Waffle House, Wendy's, Zaxby's
	Lodg	E: Comfort Suites, Courtyard, Fairfield Inn, Hampton Inn, Residence Inn W: Days Inn, Drury Inn, Motel 6♥, Ramada Ltd, Sleep Inn
	TServ	E: E&W Auto/Truck Service W: Gateway Tire & Truck Service
	Med	E: + Baptist Memorial Hospital
	Other	E: Auto Dealers, Auto Services, ATMs, Dollar Tree, Grocery, Harley Davidson of DeSoto, Lowe's, NAPA, Office Depot, PetCo♥, Pharmacy, Sam's Club, **Walmart sc**, UPS Store W: Auto Services, Family Dollar, Home Depot, Kroger, Target, Walgreen's, Bruce Rossmeyer's Southern Thunder Harley Davidson, **Audubon Point RV Park▲**
(288)		**Future Exit, Nail Rd**
287		**Church Rd, Southaven**
	Gas	E: AmocoBP, Citgo◈ W: Shell◈
	Food	E: Chesters Fried Chicken/Texaco W: DQ/Shell, McDonald's, Quiznos, Subway, Waffle House
	Lodg	W: Country Hearth Inn, Magnolia Inn, Super 8
	Other	W: **Southaven RV Supercenter, EZ Daze RV Park▲ , Audubon Point RV Park▲**
(285)		**Weigh Station** (Both dir)
(285)		**Future Exit, Star Landing Rd**
284		**Nesbit Rd, to US 51, Pleasant Hill Rd, Nesbit**
	Gas	E: Wayne's Quick Stop/BP
	Food	E: Happy Daze
(283)		**Jct I-69S, MS 304S, to Tunica**
	NOTE:	**Begin NB I-55/I-69 concurrency, End SB**
280		**MS 304, US 51, Commerce St, Hernando**
	FStop	W: Chevron
	Gas	E: Exxon, Murphy W: BP, Citgo◈, Shell◈, Kroger
	Food	E: Captain D's, Guadalara Mex Grill, Huddle House, Sonic W: Subway/Chevron, Coleman's, BBQ, McDonald's, Papa John's, Pizza Hut, Quiznos, Wendy's
	Lodg	E: Budget Inn, Days Inn, Hernando Inn W: Super 8
	Other	E: Auto Services, NAPA, **Walmart sc** W: ATMs, Banks, Auto Services, Museum, Kroger, Piggly Wiggly, Tires, Visitor Center

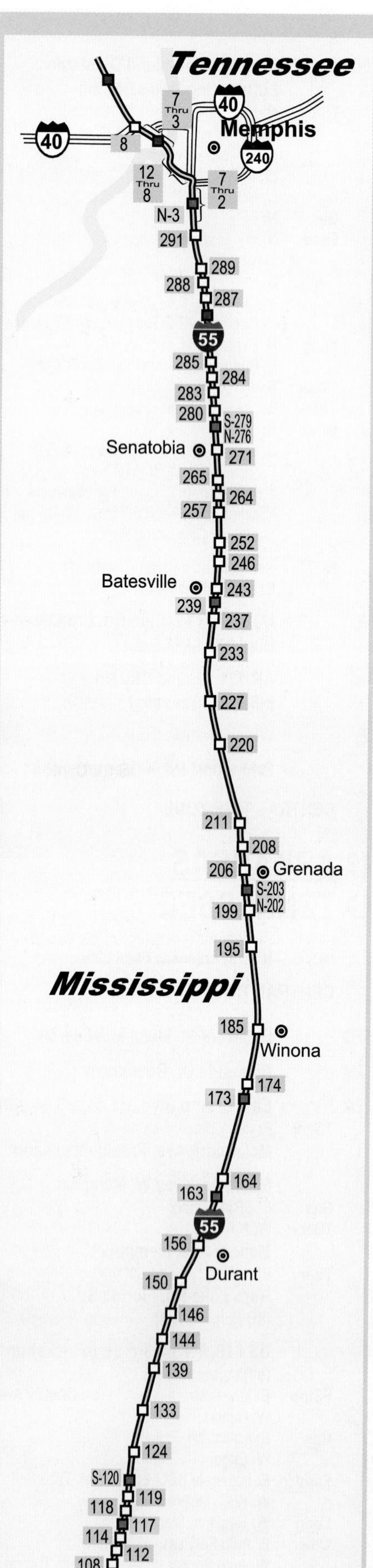

EXIT		MISSISSIPPI
(279)		**MS Welcome Center (SB)** (RR, Phones, Picnic, Sec24/7, **RVDump**)
(276)		**CLOSED - to reopen 8/11** **Hernando Rest Area (NB)** (RR, Phones, Picnic, Sec24/7, **RVDump**)
271		**MS 306, Cemetery Rd, to US 51, Coldwater, Independence**
	Gas	E: Coldwater Market & Deli W: AmocoBP, Citgo, Exxon
	Other	W: **Memphis South Campground & RV Park▲** , to COE/Hernando Point/ Arkabutla Lake
265		**MS 4, Main St, Senatobia, to Holly Springs, Tunica**
	TStop	W: Fuel Mart #622, Kangaroo Express
	Gas	W: Exxon
	Food	W: Huddle House/Kangaroo Exp, Coleman's BBQ, Domino's, Pizza Hut, Rio Lindo Mex Rest, Sonic, Subway, Taco Bell, Waffle House, Wendy's
	Lodg	W: Days Inn, Motel 6♥
	TServ	W: Kangaroo Exp/Tires
	Med	W: + N Oak Reg'l Medical Center
	Other	W: Laundry/Kangaroo Exp, ATMs, Bank, Auto Dealers, CarWash, Carquest, Grocery Pharmacy, **Walmart sc, Senatobia RV & Trailer Sales**, NW MS Comm College
263		**MS 740, to US 51, S Senatobia**
257		**MS 310, Oak Ave, Como**
	Gas	E: BP◈
	Other	E: to North Sardis Lake
252		**MS 315, Lee St, Sardis**
	FStop	W: Chevron
	Gas	E: Shell, Pure◈ W: BP, Shell◈
	Food	E: McDonald's, Nonnie & Pop's, BBQ, Sonic, Smokin Catfish
	Lodg	E: Lake Inn, Super 8 W: Knights Inn
	Med	E: + Hospital
	Other	E: **to John Kyle State Park▲** W: Grocery, Dollar General, Pharmacy
246		**MS 35, N Batesville**
	TStop	W: Maggie T's/Shell
	Gas	W: Gas Mart Mobil
	Food	W: Rest/Maggie T's
	Other	E: to Sardis Dam
243B		**MS 6W, Batesville, to Marks**
	Gas	W: Chevron◈, Exxon◈, Phillips 66◈, Shell◈
	Food	W: Captain D's, Cracker Barrel, DQ, Hardee's, Huddle House, McDonald's, KFC, Pizza Hut, Sonic, Subway, Taco Bell, Wendy's, Western Sizzlin
	Lodg	W: AmeriHost Inn, Comfort Inn, Days Inn, Hampton Inn, Holiday Inn, Ramada Inn
	Other	W: ATMs, Banks, Advance Auto, Auto Dealers, Auto Services, Dollar General, Diesel Services, Family Dollar, Grocery, Kroger, Lowe's, O'Reilly, Radio Shack, Tires, UPS Store, Outlet Stores
243A		**MS 6E, Batesville, to Oxford**
	FStop	E: Gas Mart Shell
	Gas	E: BP◈, Murphy USA◈
	Food	E: Backyard Burgers, Subway
	Med	E: + Tri Lakes Medical Center
	Other	E: **Walmart sc, to** S Sardis Lake
(239)		**Batesville Rest Area** (Both dir) (RR, Phones, Picnic, Sec24/7, **RVDump**)

◈= Regular Gas Stations with Diesel ▲ = RV Friendly Locations ♥= Pet Friendly Locations
Red print shows large vehicle parking / access on site or nearby Brown Print = Campgrounds / RV PARKS

EXIT		MISSISSIPPI
237		**Hentz Rd, to US 51, Courtland, Pope**
	FStop	W: Winters Travelstop/Pure
233		**CR 36, Oakland, Enid**
	Gas	W: Benson's
	Other	E: to COE/Wallace Creek/Enid Lake▲
227		**MS 32, Oakland, to Water Valley, Charleston**
	FStop	W: 55-32 Gas Mart/Exxon
	Gas	W: Shell◈
	Food	W: FastFood/55-32 GM
	Other	E: to George Payne Cossar St Park▲, COE/Water Valley Landing Campground/ Enid Lake▲
220		**MS 330, Tillatoba Rd, Tillatoba Oakland**
	TStop	E: Griffis Truck Stop
	Food	E: Rest/Griffis TS
	TServ	E: Griffis TS/Tires
	Other	E: Laundry/LP/WiFi/CB/Griffis TS
211		**MS 7, MS 333, Grenada, Coffeeville**
	FStop	W: 55-7 Gas Mart/Shell
	Gas	W: BP◈
	Food	W: FastFood/55-7 GasMart
	Other	E: Frog Hollow Campground▲
208		**Papermill Rd, Grenada**
	Other	E: Grenada Muni Airport✈
206		**MS 7, MS 8, Grenada, Greenwood**
	FStop	W: Shell
	Gas	E: Exxon◈, RaceWay W: Exxon
	Food	E: Burger King, Huddle House, La Cabana, McDonald's, Pizza Hut, Shoney's, Subway, Taco Bell, Western Sizzlin, Rest/BW
	Lodg	E: Best Value Inn, Best Western♥, Comfort Inn, Days Inn, Holiday Inn Express, Jameson Inn, Knights Inn, Quality Inn, Super 8 W: Country Inn, Econo Lodge
	Med	E: + Grenada Family Medical Clinic
	Other	E: Auto Dealers, Auto Services, Advance Auto Parts, Auto Zone, Dollar General,
	Other	E: Kroger, US Post Office, Walmart sc, to Hugh White State Park▲
(203)		**Parking Area (SB)**
(202)		**Parking Area (NB)**
199		**Trout Rd, Grenada, Elliott**
	Other	E: to Camp McCain Military Res
195		**MS 404, McCarley, to Duck Hill**
	Gas	W: Conoco◈
185		**US 82, Winona, to Greenwood**
	TStop	W: Pilot Travel Center #261 (Scales)
	Gas	E: Exxon, Shell◈
	Food	E: Huddle House, KFC, McDonald's, Pizza Hut, Subway W: TacoBell/Pilot TC
	Lodg	E: Magnolia Lodge, Relax Inn, Western Inn
	Med	E: + Tyler Holmes Memorial Hospital
	Other	E: MS State Univ, Ms Univ for Women W: Laundry/WiFi/Pilot TC, MS Valley State Univ
174		**MS 430, MS 35, Vaiden, Carrollton**
	FStop	E: Vaiden Shell
	TStop	E: 35-55 Travel Center/Chevron (Scales)
	Gas	W: Exxon◈
	Food	E: Rest/35-55 TC W: Stuckey's/Exxon
	Lodg	E: Motel/35-55 TC
	TServ	E: 35-55 TC
	Other	E: Laundry/WiFi/35-55 TC, Vaiden KOA/ RVDump▲
(173)		**Rest Area (SB)** (RR, Phones, Pic, Sec247, RVDump)
164		**MS 19, West**
	FStop	W: West Pit Stop/Pure
	TServ	W: West PS/Tires
	Other	W: WiFi/West PS
(163)		**Rest Area (NB)** (RR, Phones, Pic, Sec 247, RVDump)
156		**MS 12, Durant, Lexington**
	FStop	E: 55-12 Gas Mart/Shell
	Food	E: FastFood/55-12 GM
	Lodg	E: Super 8
	Med	W: + University Hospital
150		**State Park Rd, Georgeville Rd**
	Other	E: Holmes Co State Park▲
146		**MS 14, Goodman, Ebenezer**
	Other	W: to Little Red Schoolhouse
144		**MS 17, Pickens, Lexington**
	TStop	E: J's Truck Stop/Chevron W: Dickerson Petro #101/BP
	Food	E: Rest/J's TS W: Rest/Dickerson BP
	Other	E: WiFi/J's TS
139		**MS 432, Vaughan, Pickens, Benton**
133		**Vaughan Rd, Vaughan**
124		**MS 16, N Canton, Yazoo City**
(120)		**Parking Area (SB)**
119		**MS 22, MS 16, to US 51, Canton**
	FStop	E: Nancy's Restaurant & Fuel Center
	TStop	W: Love's Travel Stop #208 (Scales)
	Gas	E: AmocoBP◈, Exxon, Shell W: Chevron, Super Saver Citgo◈
	Food	E: Rest/Nancy's FC, McDonald's, Pizza Hut, Subway/BP, Sonic, Wendy's W: Arby's/Love's TS, Bumpers DriveIn, KFC, Two Rivers Rest, Western Sizzler
	Lodg	E: Days Inn W: Best Western, Comfort Inn, Econo Lodge, Hampton Inn, Holiday Inn Express
	Med	E: + Hospital
	Other	E: Discount Auto Repair, Ross Barnett Reservoir Upper Lake W: WiFi/RVDump/Love's TS
118AB		**Nissan Parkway, Canton**
	Other	E: Nissan North America Plant/Canton
(117)		**Parking Area (NB)**
114		**Sowell Rd**
112		**Gluckstadt Rd, Madison**
	FStop	E: Kangaroo #3424, C Store #635/Exxon
	Food	E: Subway/Kangaroo, Krystal/Exxon
	Lodg	E: Super 8
	Other	W: Camper Corral
108		**MS 463, Main St, Madison**
	Gas	E: Shell◈, Texaco◈ W: Exxon◈
	Food	E: Applebee's, Back Yard Burgers, ChickFilA, Chili's, Domino's/Texaco, Haute Pig Rest, Penn Station Subs W: KFC/Exxon, Bonefish Grill, Papito's Mex Grill, Pizza Inn, Wendy's
	Lodg	W: Hilton Garden Inn
	Other	E: Lowe's, Walmart sc W: CVS, Home Depot
105B		**Old Agency Rd, W Jackson St, Ridgeland**
	Gas	E: Chevron◈
105A		**Natchez Trace Pkwy, Ridgeland**
(104)		**Jct I-220W, West Jackson**
103		**County Line Rd, Jackson**
	Gas	E: BP, Circle K, Exxon◈, Shell W: Speedway
	Food	E: Applebee's, Burger King, ChickFilA, Cuco's Mex Rest, Fuddruckers, Hardee's, KFC, Mazzio's, McDonald's, Moe's SW Grill, On the Border, Roadhouse Grill, Ruby Tuesday, Romano's Macaroni Grill, Santa Fe Grill, Shoney's, Starbucks, Subway, Taco Bell, Wendy's
	Food	W: Logan Roadhouse, Olive Garden, Red Lobster
	Lodg	E: Cabot Lodge, Courtyard, Days Inn, Econo Lodge, Hilton, Homewood Suites, Staybridge Suites, Studio Plus W: Comfort Suites, Drury Inn, Motel 6
	Other	E: ATMs, Banks, B&N, Best Buy, Cinema 14, CompUSA, Goodyear, Northpark Mall, Office Depot, Sam's Club, Walmart, Auto Services, Auto Dealers W: Home Depot, PetSmart♥, Pharmacy, Target, Tougaloo College
102		**Beasley Rd, Briarwood Dr, Adkins Blvd, Jackson (SB)**
102B		**Beasley Rd, Adkins Blvd (NB)**
	Gas	E: BP, Chevron, Shell W: Exxon
	Food	E: Cracker Barrel, Fazoli's, Japanese Rest Mex Rest, Lone Star Steakhouse, Outback Steakhouse, Starbucks, Subway, Tony Roma W: McDonald's
	Lodg	E: Ramada Inn W: Best Western, Extended Stay Hotel, Fairfield Inn, Hampton Inn, InTown Suites, Jameson Inn
	Other	E: Auto Dealers, Enterprise RAC, Firestone, Office Depot, Kroger
102A		**Briarwood Dr, Frontage Rd (NB Exit, SB Entr)**
	Gas	E: BP, Phillips 66
	Food	W: Chili's, El Chico, Hops, McDonald's, Perkins, Red Lobster, Steak & Ale
	Lodg	E: La Quinta Inn♥ W: Best Value Inn, Comfort Inn, Fairfield Inn, Hampton Inn
	Other	W: Big Lots, Kmart, Office Depot
100		**Northside Dr, Downtown Jackson**
	Gas	E: BP, Chevron, Shell, Sprint W: AmocoBP, Exxon, Kangaroo
	Food	E: Burger King, Dunkin Donuts, Krystal, McDonald's, Papa John's, Piccadilly's, Shoney's, Subway, Wendy's, Western Sizzlin W: Hooters, IHOP, Pizza Hut, Shoney's, Waffle House
	Lodg	E: Holiday Inn W: Knights Inn, Super 8
	Other	E: ATMs, Auto Services, Auto Zone, Firestone, Goodyear, Pharmacy, Kroger, Office Depot, Winn Dixie
99		**Meadowbrook Rd (NB)**
98CB		**MS 25, Lakeland Dr, Carthage**
	Gas	E: Shell

◈= Regular Gas Stations with Diesel ▲ = RV Friendly Locations ♥= Pet Friendly Locations

Red print shows large vehicle parking / access on site or nearby Brown Print = Campgrounds / RV PARKS

EXIT MISSISSIPPI

Med E: + to River Oaks Hospital
W: + St. Dominic Memorial Hospital, Univ Ms Medical Center
Other E: Smith Wills Stadium, **LeFleur's Bluff State Park▲**, to Antonelli College, Jackson Int'l Airport✈
W: Veterans Memorial Stadium

98A Woodrow Wilson Dr, (NB LEFT exit) to State St (diff reaccess)
Med W: + University of Mississippi Medical Center, + VA Hospital
Other W: MS State Hwy Patrol Post

96C Fortification St, Jackson
Lodg E: Residence Inn
Med W: + Ms Univ Medical Center
Other E: Bellhaven College, Hawkins Field✈

96B High St, Downtown Jackson
Gas W: Shell◈, Kangaroo Exp/Texaco◈
Food W: Burger King, DQ, Domino's Pizza, Dunkin Donuts, Popeye's Chicken, Shoney's, Taco Bell, Waffle House, Wendy's
Lodg W: Best Western, Days Inn, Holiday Inn Express, Hampton Inn, Quality Inn, Regency Inn, Red Roof Inn♥
Other E: Auto Dealer
W: Convention Center, MS State Capitol, MS Coliseum, MS State Fairgrounds,

96A Pearl St, Downtown Jackson
Lodg W: Clarion,Holiday Inn, Regency
Other W: MS Museum of Art, Natural Science Museum, Coliseum, State Fairgrounds

NOTE: I-55 below runs with I-20. Exit #'s follow I-20.

(94/46) Jct I-20E, to Meridian, Jct I-55N, to Grenada, Memphis, US 49S

45 US 51, State St, Gallatin St (EB, LEFT exit)

45B US 51, State St (WB)
Gas N: Chevron
S: Speedway
Other N: Police

45A Gallatin St (WB)
TStop N: Petro Stopping Center #28/Mobil (Scales) **(Exit 45 EB)**
S: Pilot Travel Center #77 (Scales)
Gas N: Chevron
Food N: IronSkillet/Petro SC
S: McDonald's/Pilot TC
Lodg S: Knights Inn
TWash N: Blue Beacon TW/Petro SC
TServ N: Petro SC/Tires
Other N: Laundry/BarbSh/CB/**RVDump**/Petro SC, Amtrak, Auto Repairs, Tires
S: Laundry/WiFi/Pilot TC

(44/92C) Jct I-20W, to Vicksburg, US 49S, Jct I-55S, to New Orleans, McComb (WB, LEFT Exit)
Jct I-20W, US 49N, to Vicksburg, Yazoo City (NB, LEFT exit)

NOTE: I-55 above runs with I-20. Exit #'s follow I-20.

92B US 51N, State St, Gallatin St (NB)

92A McDowell Rd, Jackson
Gas W: BJ, BP, Dixie Gas, McFG, Shell,
Food W: Church's Chicken, McDonald's, Papa John's Pizza, Smiley's BBQ, Subway,Thai House, Waffle House, Wendy's

EXIT MISSISSIPPI

Lodg W: Super 8
Other E: U-Haul
W: Repair/Carwash/Shell, Brookshire's Grocery/Pharmacy, Fred's, Lawrence Veterinary Clinic♥, O'Reilly Auto Parts, RiteAid,

90B Daniel Lake Blvd, Cooper Rd (SB)
Gas W: BPx2, Kroger
Food W: Burger King
Other W: Auto Zone, Dollar General, Family Dollar, Harley Davidson of Central Ms, Kroger, Radio Shack, Tires, Walgreen's, **Acc to #92 W, N on Terry Rd**

90A Savanna St, Jackson
Gas W: BP
Food E: Charley's Steak & Seafood/Save Inn
W: Bo Don's Catfish & Seafood
Lodg E: Inn
Other E: Trikes & Bikes

88 Elton Rd, Jackson
Gas W: Chevron, Exxon◈
Food W: Subway/Chester/Exxon
Other W: Carwash/Chevron, Carwash, Penske Truck Rental

85 Siwell Rd, Byram
Gas E: Blue Sky BP
W: Byram Gas, Chevron◈, Exxon, Kangaroo Express/Texaco◈
Food E: El Sombrero Mexican Rest, Krystal, Penn's Rest, Relish Cafe, Swinging Bridge Fish House, Tin Shed BBQ
W: Backyard Burgers, Captain D's, Dragon Garden Chinese, KFC, McDonald's, Mazzio's, New China Buffet & Sushi, Pizza Hut, Popeye's Chicken, Sonic, Subway, Taco Bell, Waffle House, Wendy's
Lodg E: Comfort Inn, Value Place
W: Days Inn, Holiday Inn Express
Other E: Jackson Dragway Park, **Swinging Bridge RV Park▲**,
W: ATMs, Auto Services, Auto Zone, Banks, Carwash/Chevron, Carwash/Kang Exp, Dollar General, Grocery, NAPA, O'Reilly Auto Parts, **PawPaw's Camper City**, Pharmacy, Tires, Walgreen's,

81 Wynndale Rd, Terry
FStop W: Super Stop #44/Chevron

78 Cunningham St, Terry, to MS 473
FStop E: Red Apple/Texaco
Gas E: Pit Stop
W: Mac's #11
Food E: Subway/Texaco
Other E: Auto Service, Carwash, Grocery, **Police Dept**, US Post Office

72 MS 27, North Crystal Springs, to Vicksburg
FStop E: 27-55 Gas Plaza/66
Gas E: Exxon◈
Food E: Louise's BBQ, McDonald's, Popeye's Chicken, Subway/Exxon
Other E: Auto Service, Auto Dealer

68 Pat Harrison Dr, to US 51, S Crystal Springs
Other E: Auto Service

65 Byrd Town Rd, Hazlehurst, Gallman
Gas E: Stuckey's Gas
Food E: Stuckey's/Shell

61 MS 28, Hazlehurst, Fayette
Gas E: Exxon, Phillips 66◈, Murphy
Food E: Burger King, KFC, McDonald's, Pizza Hut, Wendy's, Western Sizzlin

EXIT MISSISSIPPI

Lodg E: Claridge Inn, Hilltop Motel, Western Inn Express
Med E: + Hardy Wilson Memorial Hospital
Other E: ATMs, Banks, Advance Auto Parts, Amtrak, Auto Services, CVS, Dollar General, Family Dollar, Fred's, Grocery, Pharmacy, **Walmart SC**

59 County Farm Rd, S Hazlehurst (Access #61 Serv via US 51N)

56 Tower Rd, Hazlehurst, Martinsville

(54) Hazlehurst Rest Area (Both dir) (RR, Ph, Pic, Pet, Vend, Sec, RVDump)

51 Sylvarena Rd, Wesson, Beauregard
TStop W: Country Junction Truck Stop/Chevron
Food W: Rest/Country Jct TS
TWash W: Country Jct TS
TServ W: Country Jct TS/Tires
Other E: **Timberlands Campground & Ranch▲**
W: Laundry/**RVDump**/Country Jct

48 Mt Zion Rd, Wesson

42 Dunn Ratcliff Rd, N Brookhaven
TStop E: Kasko Travel Center/Shell (Scales)
Gas E: Exxon,
Food E: Rest/Kasko TC
Lodg W: Super 8
Med E: + Hospital
Other E: Auto Dealers, Amtrak

40 Brookway Blvd, to MS 550, Downtown Brookhaven
Gas E: BP, Exxon, Shell◈, Murphy
Food E: Bob's Sandwich Shop, Bowie's BBQ, Burger King, CiCi's Pizza, Country Catfish & Steakhouse, Cracker Barrel, DQ, Domino's Pizza, El Sombrero Mexican, Golden China, Hal's BBQ, Inez Rest, KFC, Krystal, Little Caesars Pizza, McDonald's, Mitchell's Steak & Seafood, Oak Tree Rest, Pizza Hut, Shoney's, Taco Bell, Wendy's, Western Sizzlin Wood Grill,
Lodg E: America's Best Inn, Comfort Inn, Days Inn, Hampton Inn, Lincoln Inn♥, Spanish Inn Motel
Med E: + Kings Daughters Medical Center
Other E: ATMs, Auto Zone, Auto Dealers, Ace Hardware, Advance Auto Parts, Amtrak, Banks, Cinema 4, CarQuest, Dollar Tree, Grocery, Hibbett Sports, NAPA, O'Reilly Auto Parts, Radio Shack, RiteAid, US Post Office, Walgreen's, **Walmart sc, to appr 15 mi: Lake Lincoln State Park▲**,
W: Animal Medical Center♥, Home Depot

38 US 84, S Brookhaven, Natchez, Monticello, Meadville
FStop W: 84 Chevron
TServ W: 84 Chevron/Tires
Other W: **LP**/84 Chevron

30 Bogue Chitto, Norfield
TStop E: Bogue Chitto Auto/Truck Stop Shell
Food E: Rest/FastFood/Bogue Chitto ATS
Other E: Laundry/WiFi/Bogue Chitto ATS

(26) Parking Area (NB)

24 Freeman SW Rd, Summitt, Johnston Station, Lake Dixie Springs

(23) Parking Area (SB)

20A Lawrence St, Summit,
Stop E: BP,
Gas E: Stop n Shop◈

◈= Regular Gas Stations with Diesel ▲ = RV Friendly Locations ♥= Pet Friendly Locations
Red print shows large vehicle parking / access on site or nearby Brown Print = Campgrounds / RV PARKS

EXIT — MISSISSIPPI

- **Other** E: SW Mississippi Comm College

20B **US 98W, Summit, to Natchez**
- **FStop** W: Shawn Mart/P66, Exxon
- **Food** W: Subway/Exxon

18 **MS 570, Smithdale Rd, N McComb (Acc #17 W-Apache Dr & Marion Dr on E)**
- **FStop** W: Chevron
- **Gas** E: BP
- **Food** E: Burger King, McDonald's, Piccadilly's, Ruby Tuesday, Subway
  W: Arby's, Quiznos/Chevron, El Dorado Mexican Rest, Sante Fe Cattle Co
- **Med** E: + Hospital
- **Lodg** E: Holiday Inn Express
  W: Deerfield Inn, Hampton Inn, Hawthorne Suites, Ramada♥
- **Other** E: ATMs, AT&T, Banks, Auto Dealers, Auto Services, Edgewood Mall, Lowe's, Tires, Walgreen's, **Walmart sc**
  W: Auto Dealer, Carwash/Chevron

17 **Delaware Ave, Downtown McComb**
- **Gas** E: BP, Blue Sky, Chevron◈, Exxon, Pure, Raceway, Shell◈, Kroger
- **Food** E: Backyard BBQ, Burger King, China Palace, Church's Chicken/Exxon, DQ, Domino's Pizza, El Sombrero Mexican, Golden Corral, Huddle House, Krystal, McDonald's, New China Buffet, Pizza Hut, Pizza Inn, Popeye's Chicken, Subway/BP, TCBY/Chevron, Taco Bell, Tortilla Soup, Waffle House, Wendy's
- **Lodg** E: Best Western, Comfort Inn, Executive Inn, National Inn,
  W: Days Inn
- **Med** E: + SW Ms Reg'l Medical Hospital
- **Other** E: Auto Zone, ATMs, Banks, Amtrak, CVS, Dollar General, Family Dollar, Fred's, Grocery, Kroger, O'Reilly Auto Parts, RiteAid, UPS Store
  W: Auto Dealer

15B **MS 24W, MS 48, McComb, to Liberty**
- **FStop** W: Hwy 24 BP
- **Other** W: to Percy Quinn State Park▲

15A **US 98E, Presley Blvd, McComb, to Tylertown, Liberty (Most serv 1mi+/-)**
- **Gas** E: BP, Exxon, Pure, Shell
- **Food** E: Church's Chicken, Hardee's, KFC, Subway/Exxon, The Dinner Bell Rest
  W: to Mr Whiskers Family Catfish Rest
- **Lodg** E: Chameleon Motel
- **TServ** E: Peterbilt of McComb
- **Other** E: Advance Auto Parts, Auto Services, Carwash, Dollar General, Family Dollar, Grocery, Penske Truck Rental, Tires, **to appr 12 mi: Bogue Chitto Water Park▲**

13 **Fernwood Rd, McComb, Magnolia**
- **TStop** W: PTP/Fernwood Truck Stop/Conoco (Scales), Love's Travel Stop #393 (Scales)
- **Food** W: Fernwood Family Rest/Fernwood TS, Chesters/McDonald's/Love's TS
- **Lodg** W: Fernwood Motel/Fernwood TS
- **TWash** W: Fernwood TS
- **TServ** E: Interstate Trucking
  W: Fernwood TS/Tires
- **Other** E: McComb Pike Co Airport✈
  W: Laundry/LP/Fernwood TS, **Percy Quinn State Park▲**

10 **MS 48, to US 51, Magnolia (Addtl Serv 1-2 mi E in Magnolia)**
- **TStop** E: Magnolia Truck Stop

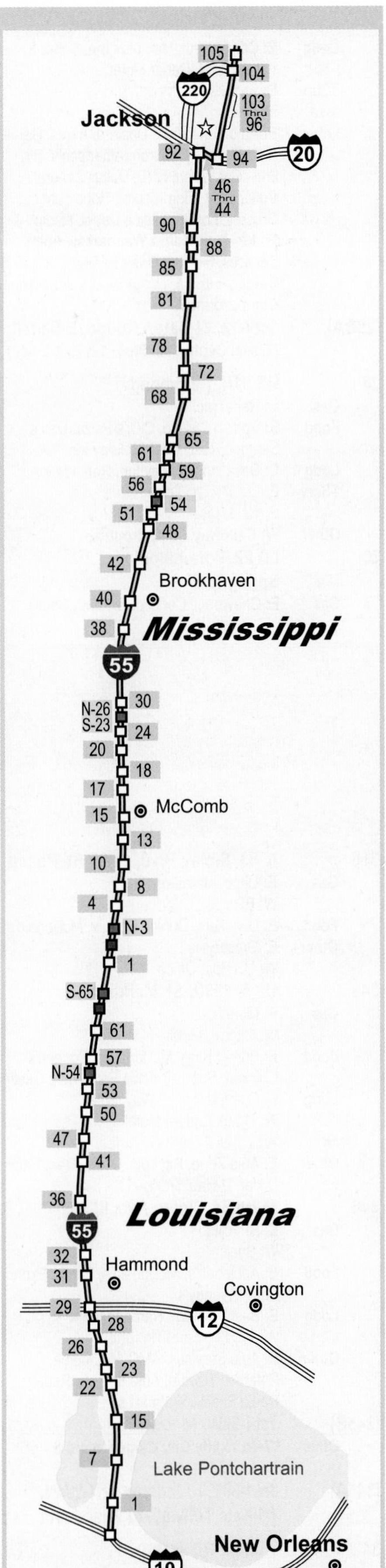

EXIT — MS / LA

8 **MS 568, Magnolia, to Gillsburg**
- **Other** E: Pike Co Speedway

4 **Chatawa Rd, to US 51, Osyka**

(3) **MS Welcome Center (NB)**
(RR, Phones, Picnic, Sec247, RVDump)

(2) **Weigh Station (NB)**

1 **MS 584, Osyka, to Gillsburg**
- **Other** E: Osyka Springs Campground▲

CENTRAL TIME ZONE

⬆ MISSISSIPPI
⬇ LOUISIANA

NOTE: MM 65: Mississippi State Line

CENTRAL TIME ZONE

(65) **LA Welcome Center (SB)**
(RR, Sec24, Vend, WiFi, Info, RVDump)

(64) **Weigh Station (NB)**

61 **LA 38, Ave G, Kentwood, Liverpool**
- **FStop** E: Chevron (DAND)
  W: Kangaroo Express #3988/Exxon, Kangaroo Express #3467
- **Gas** E: Raceway, Texaco
- **Food** E: Jam Fried Chicken & Seafood, Pizza Shack, Popeye's Chicken, Sonic
- **Other** E: ATMs, Auto Dealer, Auto Zone, Banks, Auto Dealer, Car Wash, Dollar General, Family Dollar, IGA, Laundromat, Pharmacy, **to appr 16.5mi: Silver Creek Campground▲**
  W: to appr mi: Great Discovery Inspiration Park▲

(59) **Weigh Station (SB)**

57 **LA 440, Kentwood, Tangipahoa**

(54) **Rest Area (NB) (CLOSED)**
(RR, Phones)

53 **LA 10, Fluker, Greensburg**

50 **LA 1048, Arcola, Roseland**
- **FStop** E: Chevron

46 **LA 16, Oak St, Amite, Montpelier**
- **FStop** W: to appr 2 mi: 30139 LA 16: St Helena's Express
- **TStop** W: to appr 2 mi: 30004 LA 16: Amite Plaza Truck Stop (Scales), 30096 LA 16: Forest Gold Truck Plaza & **Casino**
- **Gas** E: Exxon◈, Racetrac◈, Murphy USA◈
- **Food** E: Burger King, KFC, McDonald's, Mike's Catfish Inn, Popeye's, Sonic, Subway/Exxon, Subway, Wendy's
  W: Ardillo's, to Rest/Amita Plaza TS, Rest/ Forest Gold TP
- **Lodg** E: Comfort Inn
  W: Colonial Inn Motel
- **TServ** W: to Amite Plaza TS/Tires
- **Med** E: + Hood Memorial Hospital
- **Other** E: ATMs, Auto Services, Auto Zone, Carwash, Cinema, Fred's, Pharmacy, Tires, Towing, Winn Dixie, **Walmart sc**
  W: to Laundry/WiFi/**RVDump**/Amite Plaza TS, Laundry/Forest Gold TP, to **Sweetwater Campground▲**

◈= Regular Gas Stations with Diesel ▲ = RV Friendly Locations ♥ = Pet Friendly Locations
Red print shows large vehicle parking / access on site or nearby Brown Print = Campgrounds / RV PARKS

EXIT		LOUISIANA
40		**LA 40, Independence**
	Gas	E: Conoco
	Med	E: + Hospital
	Other	W: Indian Creek Campground & RV Park▲
36		**LA 442, Tickfaw**
	FStop	E: Tickfaw Pit Stop/Chevron
	Food	E: FastFood/Tickfaw PS
	Other	E: New Cherokee Beach Campground▲ Global Wildlife Center
32		**LA 3234, University Ave, Wardline Rd, Hammond**
	Gas	E: Chevron, Kangaroo◈ W: Chevron
	Food	E: Burger King, McDonald's, Sonic, Subway, Wendy's
	Lodg	E: Best Western
	Other	E: ATMs, Banks, to Southeastern LA Univ
31		**US 190, Albany, Hammond**
	FStop	E: Hammond Travel Plaza/Shell
	Gas	E: Chevron◈, Exxon◈
	Food	E: Applebee's, Burger King, Chili's, CiCi's Pizza, Cracker Barrel, Exxon/Subway, Krystal, McDonald's, Pizza Hut, Shoney's, Shorty's Ribs & Seafood, Waffle House, Wendy's

EXIT		LOUISIANA
	Lodg	E: Comfort Inn, Hampton Inn, Super 8, Value Place, Cedar Motel
	TServ	E: Bridgestone Tire & Auto
	Med	E: + Hospital
	Other	E: Auto Zone, Auto Dealers, ATMs, Banks, Auto Repairs/Chevron, Albertson's, Big Lots, Car Wash, CVS, Dollar General, Dollar Tree, Flea Market, Hobby Lobby, Grocery, Lowe's, Office Depot, Radio Shack, Walgreen's, **Walmart sc**, Auto Services, Hidden Oaks Family Campground▲ , Yogi Bear's Jellystone Campground▲
(29BA)		**Jct I-12, W-Baton Rouge, E-Slidell (Travel Center, All Serv, 1st Exit E #40)**
28		**US 51N, Hammond**
	Gas	E: RaceTrac
	Food	E: Catfish Charlie, CiCi's Pizza, Don's Seafood Rest, Rest /Holiday Inn
	Lodg	E: Days Inn, Holiday Inn, Ramada Inn
	TServ	E: Big Wheel Diesel Repair
	Med	E: + Hospital
	Other	W: Calloway Campground▲
26		**LA 22, Ponchatoula, Springfield**
	Gas	E: Chevron◈, Conoco, Exxon◈, Shell◈

EXIT		LOUISIANA
	Food	E: Burger King, KFC, McDonald's, Popeye, Sonic, Waffle House, Wendy's
	Lodg	E: Microtel
	Med	E: + Hospital
	Other	E: ATMs, Auto Zone, Dollar General, Pharmacy, Walgreen's, Winn Dixie
23		**US 51 Bus, Ponchatoula**
22		**Frontage Rd (SB exit, NB entr)**
15		**Manchac**
7		**Ruddock**
1		**US 51S, to I-10, LaPlace, to Baton Rouge (SB ex, NB entr) (Travel Center, All Serv, 1st Exit #209)**

EASTERN TIME ZONE

NOTE: I-55 begins/ends I-10, Exit #209

LOUISIANA

Begin Northbound I-55 from New Orleans, LA to Chicago, IL.

EXIT		ILLINOIS

Begin Southbound I-57 from Jct I-94 in Chicago, IL to Jct I-55 in St Louis, MO

ILLINOIS

NOTE: I-57 begins/ends on I-94, Exit #63

CENTRAL TIME ZONE

EXIT		ILLINOIS
(359)		**Jct I-94, E - Chicago, Indiana**
357		**IL 1, Halsted St, Chicago**
	Gas	E: BP, Mobil W: Marathon, Phillips 66, Shell
	Food	E: Ruby's Restaurant W: I-57 Rib House, McDonald's, Shark Fish
	Lodg	E: Grand Motel
	Other	E: Auto Repairs W: Walgreen's
355		**111th St, 112th St, Monterey Ave**
	Gas	W: BP, Frye's
354		**119th St**
	Gas	W: Citgo
	Food	W: Chili's, DQ, Panda Express
	Other	W: Dollar Tree, PetCo♥, Staples, Target
353		**127th St, Burr Oak Ave, Riverdale**
	Gas	E: Marathon, Shell W: BP, Gas City
	Food	E: Burger King, McDonald's, Subway, Wendy's
	Lodg	E: Best Western, Motel 6, Super 8
	Other	E: AZ Auto & Truck Service, Ace Hardware, Advance Auto Parts, Family Dollar, Grocery, Walgreen's

EXIT		ILLINOIS
350		**IL 83, Sibley Blvd, 147th St, Posen**
	Gas	E: Citgo, Marathon◈ W: BP
	Food	E: Checkers, Dunkin Donuts, McDonald's
	Other	E: Grocery W: US Post Office
348		**US 6, 159th St, Markham**
	Gas	E: Marathon◈ W: Citgo◈, Mobil◈
	Food	E: Burger King, McDonald's, Popeye's Chicken, Subway, Taco Bell, White Castle
	Lodg	E: Comfort Inn, Hi-Way Motel W: D-Lux Budget Motel
	Med	W: + Oak Forest Hospital
	Other	E: Auto Zone, Big Lots, Dollar Tree, Family Dollar, U-Haul, Walgreen's
346		**167th St, Cicero Ave, IL 50**
	Gas	E: BP, Citgo◈ W: Shell
	Food	E: Applebee's, McDonald's, Panda Express Sonic, Wendy's
	Lodg	E: Best Western, Ramada Inn♥
	Med	W: + Oak Forest Hospital
	Other	E: Auto Services, AMC 16 Cinema, Peterson Towing, Auto & Truck Repair, Radio Shack, **Walmart sc**,
(345B)		**Jct I-80W, to Iowa**
	Other	W: to Windy City Campground & Beach▲
(345A)		**Jct I-80E, to Indiana, to I-294N, TriState Tollway, to Wisconsin**
342B		**Vollmer Rd W (SB)**

EXIT		ILLINOIS
342A		**Vollmer Rd E (SB)**
	Gas	E: Shell
	Med	E: + St James Hospital
342		**Vollmer Rd, Matteson (NB)**
340B		**US 30W, 211th St, Lincoln Hwy**
	Other	W: Auto Dealers & Services, Lincolnway Animal Hospital♥, Walgreen's, to Terry's RV Center
340A		**US 30E, 211th St, Lincoln Hwy**
	Gas	E: BP, Citgo◈, Mobil, Shell, Sam's
	Food	E: Applebee's, Bob Evans, Chuck E Cheese's Pizza, Cracker Barrel, Denny's, Fuddrucker's, IHOP, JN Michael's Rest, McDonald's, Mr Benny's Steakhouse, Nino's Pizza, Olive Garden, Panda Express Panera Bread, Perros Bros Gyros, Pizza Hut, Quiznos Subs, Red Lobster, Starbucks Subway, Taco Bell, Wendy's
	Lodg	E: Americas Best Value Inn, Country Inn, Hampton Inn, Holiday Inn, La Quinta Inn♥, Matteson Motel
	Med	E: + to St James Hospital
	Other	E: ATMs, AT&T, Auto Services, Banks, Best Buy, Borders, CVS, Carwash, Discount Tire, Enterprise RAC, FedEx Office, Firestone Auto, Goodyear Auto, Grocery, Home Depot, Jiffy Lube, Lincoln Mall, Menard's, NTB, Office Max, Pep Boys PetSmart♥, Radio Shack, Sam's Club, Sports Authority, Target, ToysRUs, UPS Store, U-Haul, US Post Office, Verizon, Walgreen's, **Walmart**, W: Auto Dealers

◈= Regular Gas Stations with Diesel ▲ = RV Friendly Locations ♥= Pet Friendly Locations
Red print shows large vehicle parking / access on site or nearby Brown Print = Campgrounds / RV PARKS

EXIT ILLINOIS

339 **Sauk Trail, Richton Park**
Gas E: BP, Citgo◈
Food E: Domino's Pizza, Joe's Fish & Chicken, McDonald's, Uncle John's BBQ
Other E: Bowling, Grocery, Skate Center, Walgreen's, **Police Dept**

335 **CR 6, Monee Manhattan Rd, Monee**
TStop E: Petro Stopping Center #365/Mobil (Scales), Pilot Travel Center #39 (Scales)
Gas E: BP
Food E: IronSkillet/FastFood/Petro SC, McDonald's/Pilot TC, DunkinDonuts/ Subway/BP, Burger King, Lucky Burrito II, Max's Red Hots, Schoop's Hamburgers
Lodg E: Country Host Motel, Best Western, Holiday Inn Express, Super 8
TWash E: Petro SC, Blue Beacon TW
TServ E: Petro SC/Tires
Other E: Laundry/CB/WiFi/Petro SC, Laundry/ WiFi/Pilot TC, Carwash/LP/BP, **to appr 2 mi:** Governor's State Univ, Towing
W: Xtreme Plex

(332) **IL Welcome Center** (Both dir)
(RR, Ph, Pic, Pet, Vend, Info, RVDump)

(330) **Weigh Station** (Both dir)

327 **Wilmington Rd, Peotone, Wilmington**
Gas E: Casey's, Circle K/Shell
Food E: Pizza/Casey's McDonald's, Taco Bell
Other E: Will Co Fairgrounds

322 **CR 9, to US 45, US 52, Manteno, to Wilmington**
FStop W: Gas City #9
Gas E: BP, Phillips 66
Food E: Hardee's, Pizza Hut, McDonald's/BP, Subway/P66
W: FastFood/Gas City
Lodg E: Country Inn, Howard Johnson
Med E: + **Manteno State Hospital**
Other E: Land of Lincoln Harley Davidson
W: Penske Truck Rental

315 **IL 50, to US 45, US 52, Bourbonnais**
Gas E: Circle K/Shell
W: BP, Speedway
Food E: **Cracker Barrel**, Light House Pizza, McDonald's, Old Country Buffet, Pizza Hut, Red Lobster, Ruby Tuesday, Starbucks, TGI Friday, Tucci's
W: Applebee's, Arby's, Bakers Square, Checkers, Coyote Canyon, Denny's, Hardee's, IHOP, McDonald's, Lone Star Steakhouse, Old Country Buffet, Steak'n Shake, Starbucks, Subway, Taco Bell, Wendy's
Lodg E: America's Best Inn♥, Fairfield Inn, Hampton Inn, Holiday Inn Express♥
W: Motel 6♥, Northgate Motel, Quality Inn, Super 8
Other E: Aspen Ridge Golf Course, Antique Malls, Barnes& Noble, Best Buy, Cinemark 10, Hidden Cove Family Sportsplex, Midas, Radio Shack, Target, **Walmart sc**, **to Lake Alexander RV Park▲**
W: Auto Dealers, ATMs, Auto Services, Banks, Bradley Animal Hospital♥, **Brown & Brown RV Center**, Grocery, Kmart, Lowe's, Olivet Nazarene Univ, PetCo♥, **Quality MH & RV Service**, Strickler Planetarium, **Walmart sc**,

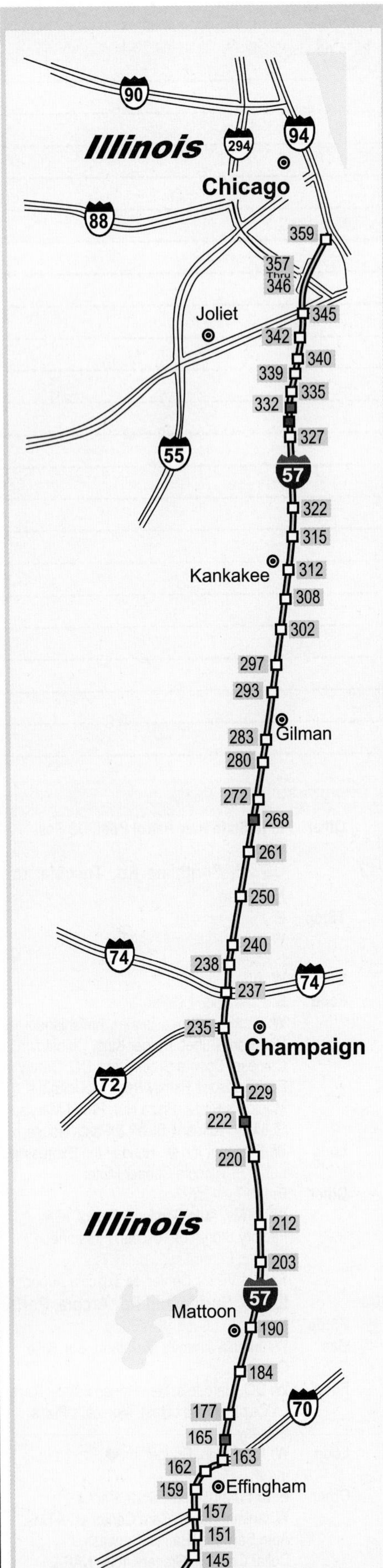

EXIT ILLINOIS

Other W: **to appr 2 mi:** Perry Farm Park/Exploration Station Childrens Museum, **to appr 8 mi: Kankakee River State Park▲**,

312 **IL 17, E Court St, Kankakee, Momence**
FStop W: BP
Gas W: Circle K/Shell, Marathon,
Food W: Captain Hook Fish & Chicken, McDonald's, Poor Boy Rest, Subway, Wendy's,
Lodg W: America's Best Value Inn♥, Magruder House B&B, Riverview Guest House B& B
TServ E: Chicago International Trucks
Med W: + **Provena St Mary's Hospital**
Other E: U-Haul, **to appr 6.5 mi: Twin Rivers Campground & Retreat▲**, **to appr Lake Alexander RV Park▲**
W: ATMs, Advance Auto Parts, Auto Services, Family Dollar, Laundromat, Railroad Museum, Walgreen's,

308 **US 45, US 52, Kankakee**
Gas W: Gas Depot
Food W: JJ Ruffles, KFC
Lodg W: Fairview Courts Motel, Hilton Garden Inn
Tserv E: I-57 Truck & Trailer Services, Midway Truck Parts
Other E: 123Jump Indoor Playground, Greater Kankakee Airport✈, Kankakee County Fairgrounds, **Kankakee South KOA▲**,
W: Dollar Tree, Grocery, Kankakee Comm College, **Walmart sc**, **to** Splash Valley Aquatic Park

302 **CR 37, CR 3400N, Chebanse**
Gas W: BP
TServ W: Ken's Truck Repair

297 **CR 4, Clifton**
Gas W: Phillips 66◈
Food W: DQ/P66
Other W: Auto Services, US Post Office

293 **IL 116, to US 45, Ashkum**
FStop E: BP
Food E: DQ, Subway/BP
W: The Loft
Other E: **IL State Hwy Patrol Post**, Meier Bros Tire Supply & Service/Auto/Truck/Farm, US Post Office

283 **US 24, CR 1700N, Gilman, Chatsworth**
TStop E: K&H Truck Plaza/BP(Scales),
W: Gilman TS Fast & Fresh
Food E: Rest/K&H TP, Burger King, DQ, McDonald's, Monical's Pizza
W: Subway/Gilman TS
Lodg E: Budget Host Inn♥, Motel 6♥, Super 8♥,
TServ E: K&H TP/Tires/Towing
Other E: Laundry/WiFi/K&H TP, Amtrak, Dollar General, NAPA, Pharmacy, U-Haul
W: **R&R RV Sales/RVDump**

280 **IL 54, CR 1450N, W Seminary Ave, to US 45, Onarga, Roberts**
Gas E: Casey's, Marathon, Phillips 66
Other E: Auto Repairs, Truck Service
W: **Lake Arrowhead RV Campground▲**

272 **CR 9, CR 800N, Buckley, Roberts**

(268) **Rest Area** (Both dir)
(RR, Phones, Picnic, Pet, Vend)

◈= Regular Gas Stations with Diesel ▲ = RV Friendly Locations ♥= Pet Friendly Locations
Red print shows large vehicle parking / access on site or nearby Brown Print = Campgrounds / RV PARKS

EXIT	ILLINOIS

261 **IL 9, W Ottawa Rd, Paxton, to Gibson City, Rankin**
- Gas: E: Casey's, Citgo; W: BP, Marathon
- Food: E: Hardee's, Pizza Hut, Subway; W: Country Gardens Rest
- Lodg: W: Paxton Inn♥, to appr 3 mi: TimberCreek B&B
- Other: E: Auto Dealer, Auto Services, Family Dollar, Laundromat, True Value Hardware, U-Haul, US Post Office; W: Paxton Airport✈

250 **US 136, Champaign Ave, Rantoul, Fisher**
- Gas: E: Circle K/BP, Phillips 66◈
- Food: E: Arby's, Burger King, Domino's Pizza, Hardee's, Long John Silver's, McDonalds, Monical's Pizza, Papa John's Pizza, Subway, Taco Bell/KFC,
- Lodg: E: Best Western♥, Days Inn, Super 8♥
- Other: E: ATMs, Amtrak, Auto Dealers, Auto Services, Banks, CVS, IGA, NAPA, SavALot, Walgreen's, **Walmart sc, to City Park/Prairie Pines Campground▲**, Rantoul Nat'l Aviation Center/Frank Elliott Field✈, Chanute Air Force Base,

240 **Market St, CR 20, Champaign**
- TStop: E: Road Ranger #132/Pilot TC #526/◈ Citgo(Scales)
- Food: E: Rest/McDonald's/Road Ranger
- TServ: E: Road Ranger/Tires, Road Ready Truck & Tire/Towing, Central IL Trucks Sales & Service/CIT Trucks,
- Other: E: WiFi/RR/Pilot TC; W: **D&W Lake Camping & RV Park▲**

238 **Olympian Dr St, Champaign**
- FStop: W: Super Pantry #48/Mobil
- Food: W: DQ/Mobil
- Lodg: W: Microtel♥,
- Other: E: to Prospect Ave appr 1.5mi: ATMs, Cinema, FOOD, LODGING, Target, **Walmart sc**,; W: ATMs, Banks, Tires

(237B) **Jct I-74W, to Peoria**

(237A) **Jct I-74E, to Indianapolis (All Serv, E to 1st Ex # 181)**
- Other: E: to Parkland College, Univ of IL

(235B) **Jct I-72W, to Decatur, Springfield**

(235A) **Jct I-72E, to Champaign, Urbana**
- Other: E: Serv Avail E to Mattis Ave, IL 10: Auto Services, Diesel Services, Food, to Univ of IL

232 **Curtis Rd, CR 13, Champaign**
- Lodg: E: to appr 2.5 mi to Dunlap Ave: Best Western, The Senators Inn B&B
- Other: E: Curtis Orchards & Pumpkin Patch

229 **CR 18, Monticello Rd, Champaign, to US 45, Monticello, Savoy, Tolono (Serv 2.5-4mi E, use US 45N)**
- FStop: E: Marathon◈
- Food: E: Rest/Marathon
- Other: E: Laundry/Marathon, to US 45N: Auto Services, Food, Radio Shack, South Side Veterinary Clinic, **Walmart sc**, Univ of IL - Willard Airport✈, Rental Cars

(222) **Rest Area (Both dir) (RR, Phones, Picnic, Pet, Vend)**

220 **US 45, Pesotum, Tolono**
- Gas: W: Citgo

Personal Notes

EXIT	ILLINOIS

- Other: E: IL State Hwy Patrol Post, US Post Office

212 **US 36, Southline Rd, Tuscola, to Newman**
- TStop: E: Fuel Mart #787; W: Road Ranger #139/Pilot TC #529 (Scales)
- Gas: W: BP
- Food: E: FastFood/FuelMart; W: FastFood/RoadRanger, Amishland Red Barn Buffet, Burger King, Chinatown Chinese, Coyote Creek Rest, DQ, Denny's, Four Seasons Family Rest, McDonald's, Monical's Pizza, Pizza Hut, Proud Mary's, Subway, Tuscany Steak & Pasta House,
- Lodg: W: Baymont Inn♥, Holiday Inn Express♥, Super 8, Tuscola Cooper Motel
- Other: E: LP/FuelMart; W: ATMs, Auto Services, Banks, IGA, Factory Stores of Tuscola, Firestone, Pamida Pharmacy, Quality Truck & Trailer Repair, Visitor Center, to Tuscola Airport✈

203 **IL 133, Springfield Rd, Arcola, Paris**
- FStop: E: Gasland Food Mart/Citgo
- Gas: W: Jumpin Jimmy's Marathon, Sun Rise Gas◈
- Food: W: DQ, Hardee's, Hen House Family Rest, La Cazuelas Mex Rest, Monical's Pizza, Subway
- Lodg: W: Arcola Inn, Budget Inn♥, Comfort Inn♥
- Other: E: to Walnut Point State Park▲; W: Animal Health Care Center♥, ATMs, Auto Services, Banks, Carwash, Dollar General, Grocery, IGA, NAPA,

EXIT	ILLINOIS

- Other: E: Towing, True Value Hardware, **Arcola Camper Stop▲**

192 **CR 1000N, Mattoon**

190B **IL 16W, Charleston Ave, Mattoon, to Windsor**
- Gas: W: Phillips 66, Murphy◈, Citgo, Huck's
- Food: W: Alamo Steakhouse, Arby's, Buffalo Wild Wings, Cracker Barrel, Domino's Pizza, KFC, McDonald's, Monical's Pizza, Pizza Hut, QQ Chinese Buffet, Steak 'n Shake, Taco Bell, Wendy's
- Lodg: W: Baymont Inn♥, Comfort Suites, Days Inn♥, Hampton Inn, Holiday Inn Express♥, Super 8
- Other: W: ATMs, Amtrak, Albin Animal Hospital♥, Banks, Big Lots, CVS, Cross Country Mall, **Cross Country RV Center**, Dollar General, Grocery, Hibbett Sports, Home Depot, Staples, Tidal Wave Carwash, Walgreen's, **Walmart sc, Wolf Creek State Park, Eagle Creek State Park, COE/ Campgrounds▲** /Lake Shelbyville

190A **IL 16E, Broadway Ave, Mattoon, to Charleston**
- Gas: E: BP◈
- TServ: E: Raben Tire Co
- Med: E: + Sarah Bush Lincoln Health Center
- Other: E: Coles Co Memorial Airport✈, to E IL Univ, **Happy Trails RV Rentals**

184 **US 45, IL 121, Mattoon (Addt'l Serv 3-4 mi W in Mattoon)**
- Gas: E: Marathon◈; W: Marathon◈,
- Food: W: McDonald's
- Lodg: W: Budget Inn
- Other: E: Lakeland College

177 **US 45, Neoga**
- TStop: E: Auto Truck FuelMart; W: ASW Truck Plaza/P66
- Gas: W: Casey's
- Food: E: Rest/Subway/AT FM; W: Rest/ASW TP, Casey's C/O Pizza, Villa Family Rest
- Other: E: WiFi/AT FM; W: Auto Repair

(165) **Rest Area (Both dir) (RR, Phones, Picnic, Vend)**

(163) **Jct I-70E, Indianapolis (SB, Left exit), Jct I-70W, to St Louis**

NOTE: I-57 below runs with I-70W for 6 mi. Exit #'s follow I-57.

162 **US 45, N 3rd St, Effingham**
- TStop: W: Pilot Travel Center #165 (Scales)
- Gas: E: Moto Mart; W: Citgo
- Food: W: McDonald's/Pilot TC, Subway/Citgo
- TWash: W: Pilot TC
- Med: E: + St Anthony's Memorial Hospital
- Other: E: Legacy Harley Davidson; W: Laundry/WiFi/LP/Pilot TC, **Crossroads RV Center, to appr 2 mi: Camp Lakewood RV Park▲**

160 **IL 32, IL 33, N Keller Dr, Effingham**
- TStop: W: Flying J Travel Plaza #5107/Pilot TC (Scales), Travel Center of America #35/ BP (Scales)
- Gas: W: BP, Marathon, Phillips 66, Murphy◈
- Food: E: KFC, Little Caesars Pizza, Lone Star Steakhouse, Papa John's Pizza, Pizza Hut

◈= Regular Gas Stations with Diesel ▲ = RV Friendly Locations ♥= Pet Friendly Locations
Red print shows large vehicle parking / access on site or nearby Brown Print = Campgrounds / RV PARKS

EXIT		ILLINOIS
		W: CountryMarket/FastFood/FJ TP, CountryPride/Popeye's/Sbarro/TA TC, Arby's, Burger King, Cracker Barrel, Denny's, Long John Silver, McDonald's, Ponderosa, Ryan's Grill, Ruby Tuesday, Steak n Shake, Starbucks, Subway, Taco Bell, TGI Friday, Wendy's
	Lodg	**E:** Comfort Inn, Fairfield Inn, Hampton Inn, **Addtl Lodging E to US 40/Fayette Ave** **W:** Hotel/FJ TP, Country Inn, Hilton Garden Inn, Holiday Inn Express♥, Motel 6, Rodeway Inn, Super 8♥,
	TWash	**W:** Blue Beacon TW/FJ TP, TA TC
	TServ	**W:** TA TC/Tires, Speedco, Peterbilt, Clarke Power Services
	Med	**E:** + St Anthony Memorial Hospital
	Other	**E:** ATMs, Auto Zone, Banks, Dollar General, Effingham Veterinary Clinic♥, Grocery, Kroger, O'Reilly Auto Parts, Walgreen's **W:** Laundry/WiFi/**RVDump/LP**/FJ TP, Laundry/BarbSh/WiFi/TA TC, ATMs, AT&T, Auto Dealer, Banks, **Camp Lakewood RV Park▲**, Dollar Tree, Menard's, Radio Shack, Towing, U-Haul, **Walmart sc**,
159		**Fayette Ave, Effingham**
	FStop	**E:** Jumpin Jimmy's Marathon
	TStop	**W:** Petro Stopping Center #21/Mobil (Scales), Truck-O-Mat (Scales)
	Gas	**E:** A-1, BP, Citgo◈, Phillips 66
	Food	**E:** China Buffet, Culver's, Hardee's, Neimerg's Steak House, Subway **W:** IronSkillet/Petro SC, Rest /BW
	Lodg	**E:** Abe Lincoln Motel, Comfort Suites♥, Econo Lodge, Howard Johnson Express♥, Lincoln Lodge♥, Paradise Inn, Rodeway Inn♥ **W:** Best Western♥
	TWash	**W:** Blue Beacon/Petro SC, TruckOMat
	TServ	**E:** Effingham Truck Sales **W:** Petro SC/Tires
	Med	**E:** + St Anthony's Memorial Hospital
	Other	**E:** ATMs, Auto Services, Amtrak, Auto Zone, Carwash, O'Reilly Auto Parts, Walgreen's, **to** Village Square Mall **W:** Laundry/BarbSh/CB/WiFi/Petro SC
(157)		**Jct I-70W, to St Louis (NB, LEFT exit)**
	NOTE:	**I-57 above runs with I-70W for 6 mi. Exit #'s follow I-57.**
151		**to IL 37, to IL 45, Mason, Watson**
	Other	**E:** to app 5 mi **Percival Springs Airport & Campground▲**, Effingham Co Memorial Airport✈, Scheid Diesel Service
145		**CR 29, Iowa St, Edgewood**
	Gas	**E:** Marathon
135		**IL 185, Washington St, Farina, Vandalia**
	FStop	**E:** RoadysTS/Jack Flash/BP
	Food	**E:** Subway/BP
	Other	**E:** Auto Dealer, Bank, U-Haul
127		**CR 8, CR 1050, Kinoka Rd, Alma, to Patoka, Kinmundy**
	Other	**E:** Kinmundy Truck & Auto Repair, **to 7 mi: Stephen A Forbes State Park▲**

EXIT		ILLINOIS
116		**US 50, W Main St, Salem, to Odin, Sandoval, Flora**
	Gas	**E:** Circle K/Shell, Huck's, **W:** Phillips 66, Murphy, Shell
	Food	**E:** Burger King, Domino's Pizza, KFC, Long John Silver, McDonalds, Pizza Hut, Pizza Man, Subway, Taco Bell, Wendy's **W:** Applebee's, Arby's, Denny's
	Lodg	**E:** Budget Inn **W:** Comfort Inn, Holiday Inn, Salem Inn, Super 8
	TServ	**E:** Fabick Cat **W:** Salem Tire Center, Salem Truck & Diesel
	Med	**E:** + to Township Hospital
	Other	**E:** Auto Zone, Auto Dealer, ATMs, Banks, CVS, Grocery, Landers Towing, NAPA, O'Reilly Auto Parts, Pharmacy, Salem-Leckrone Airport✈ **W:** Auto Dealers, Dollar Tree, **Walmart sc**
(114)		**Rest Area (Both dir) (RR, Phones, Pic, Vend, Pet, Playgr)**
109		**IL 161, E McCord St, Centralia**
	Gas	**W:** Gas◈
	Food	**W:** Biggies Café
	Other	**W:** Centralia Muni Airport✈
103		**CR 39, W South St, Dix**
	FStop	**E:** Illini Mart/P66
	Food	**E:** Deli/Illini Mart
	Lodg	**E:** Red Carpet Inn
(96)		**Jct I-64W, to St Louis**
95		**IL 15, Broadway St, Mt Vernon, Ashley**
	TStop	**W:** Travel Center of America #43/Citgo (Scales), Ambest/Huck's Travel Center (Scales), Pilot Travel Center #482 (Scales)
	Gas	**E:** BP◈, Marathon, Phillips 66, Kroger **W:** Shell
	Food	**E:** Bonanza, Burger King, Chili's, Cracker Barrel, Fazoli's, Hardee's, KFC, Little Caesars Pizza, Long John Silver, McDonald's, Pizza Hut, Steak n Shake, Subway, Taco Bell, Wendy's, Western Sizzlin
	Food	**W:** CountryPride/Popeyes/TA TC, Rest/FastFood/Huck's TC, Denny's/Pilot TC, Applebee's, Arby's, Burger King, Bob Evans, Chili's, Cracker Barrel, Lone Star Steakhouse, McDonald's, Ryan's Grill, Sonic, Subway
	Lodg	**E:** America's Best Value Inn, Comfort Suites, Drury Inn, Motel 6♥, Super 8 **W:** Comfort Inn, Days Inn, Fairfield Inn, Hampton Inn, Holiday Inn, Quality Inn
	TWash	**W:** TA TC, XVIII Wheelers Truck Wash
	TServ	**W:** TA TC/Tires, Freightliner
	Med	**E:** + Crossroads Comm Hospital
	Other	**E:** Auto Zone, ATMs, Animal Medical Center ♥, Banks, CVS, Dollar Tree, Kroger, O'Reilly Auto Parts, Radio Shack, Times Square Mall, Walgreen's, Animal Hospital♥, **to** Mt Vernon Airport✈, Jefferson Co Fairgrounds, **W:** Laundry/WiFi/TA TC, Laundry/Huck's TC, Laundry/WiFi/Pilot TC, Auto Dealer, Lowe's, NAPA, Outlet Mall, **Quality Times RV Park▲**, Staples, **Walmart sc**,
94		**Veterans Memorial Dr, Mt Vernon (Acc to #92 via E to S 42nd St)**

EXIT		ILLINOIS
(92)		**Jct I-64E, to Louisville (SB, LEFT exit)**
83		**North Ave, CR 42, Ina, Spring Garden**
	FStop	**E:** Lakeview General Truck Stop/Marathon
	TStop	**E:** Love's Travel Stop #318 (Scales)
	Food	**E:** Deli/LG TS, McDonald's/Love's TS
	Other	**E:** WiFi/**RVDump**/Love's TS, **to appr 2 mi: Sherwood Camping Resort▲** **W:** Rend Lake, **to** Rend Lake College
(79)		**Rest Area (SB) (RR, Phones, Pic, Vend, Pet, Playgr)**
77		**IL 154, Whittington, Sesser**
	Gas	**E:** Shell
	Food	**E:** Burton Café, Gibby's Lounge & Grill **W:** Seasons Rest (@ Golf Course)
	Lodg	**W:** to Rend Lake Resort & Rest, Season Lodge & Condos
	Other	**E:** Pheasant Hollow Winery, **Whittington Woods Campground▲**, **W: Wayne Fitzgerrell State Park▲**, **COE**/Rend Lake/**Gun Creek Rec Area▲**, Rend Lake Golf Course
(74)		**Rest Area (NB) (RR, Phones, Pic, Vend, Pet, Playgr)**
71		**IL 14, IL 34, Benton, Christopher**
	FStop	**W:** West City Shell
	Gas	**E:** Jumpin Jimmy's◈, Phillips 66 **W:** BP, Murphy
	Food	**E:** Arby's, Domino's Pizza, Hardee's, KFC/Taco Bell, Long John Silver, Pizza Hut, Wendy's **W:** FastFood/WC Shell, Applebee's, Burger King, McDonald's, Subway
	Lodg	**E:** Benton Gray Plaza Motel, Days Inn, Super 8
	Med	**E:** + Franklin Hospital
	Other	**E:** ATMs, Auto Dealers, Auto Dealers, Auto Zone, Banks, Carwash, CVS, Museum, O'Reilly Auto Parts, SavALot, Tires, U-Haul **W:** ATMs, Auto Services, Bank, **Benton KOA▲**, Benton Muni Airport✈, CVS, **Walmart sc, to COE**/Rend Lake/**S Marcum Rec Area▲**
65		**IL 149, W Main St, W Frankfort**
	Gas	**E:** BP, Shell **W:** Casey's
	Food	**E:** Hardee's, KFC, Long John Silver **W:** Burger King, Casey's Pizza, McDonald's, Triple E Plus
	Lodg	**E:** Gray Plaza Motel **W:** America's Best Value Inn
	Med	**E:** + Hospital
	Other	**E:** Grocery **W:** Auto Dealer, Auto Services, CVS, Dollar Tree, Factory Outlet Stores of America, Kmart, Kroger
59		**Herrin Rd, Broadway Blvd, Johnston City, Herrin**
	Gas	**E:** BP◈, Shell◈
	Food	**E:** DQ, Hardee's, McDonald's, Subway
	Med	**W:** + Herrin Hospital
	Other	**E:** ATMs, Bank, Auto Services, **to appr 2 mi: Arrowhead Lake Campground▲**
	Other	**W:** Golf Courses, **to appr 4 mi: Four Seasons Campground▲**

◈= Regular Gas Stations with Diesel ▲ = RV Friendly Locations ♥= Pet Friendly Locations
Red print shows large vehicle parking / access on site or nearby Brown Print = Campgrounds / RV PARKS

EXIT	ILLINOIS
54B	**IL 13W, W Deyoung St, Marion, to Carbondale, Murphysboro (Acc to Ex #53 via Halfway Rd on W)**
TStop	W: RoadysTS/Cheers Travel Center #220/BP (Scales)
Gas	W: Phillips 66, Sam's Club
Food	W: Rest/McDonald's/Marion TP, Applebee's, Burger King, Bob Evans, O'Charley's, Ryan's Grill, Red Lobster, Sonic, Steak n Shake, Taco Bell
Lodg	W: Best Inn, Country Inn, Drury Inn, Fairfield Inn, Hampton Inn, Motel 6♥, Super 8
TServ	W: Cheers TC/Tires
Med	W: + Heartland Regional Medical Center
Other	W: Laundry/CB/WiFi/Marion TP, ATM's, Animal Hospital♥, Auto Dealers, Black Diamond Harley Davidson, Enterprise RAC, Home Depot, IL Centre Mall, Sam's Club, Target, **Walmart sc**, Williamson Co Reg'l Airport✈
54A	**IL 13E, E Deyoung St, Marion**
Gas	E: Phillips 66, Kroger
Food	E: Arby's, Fazoli's, Hardee's, KFC, Long John Silver, Papa John's Pizza, Pizza Hut, Quiznos, Subway, Wendy's, Western Sizzlin
Lodg	E: Days Inn, Econo Lodge, Marion Gray Plaza Motel
Other	E: Auto Zone, ATMs, Auto Dealer, Auto Services, Advance Auto Parts, Aldi Grocery Banks, Dollar General, Kroger, Menard's, Radio Shack, US Post Office, UPS Store, Walgreen's,
53	**Main St, Marion (Acc to Ex #54 via Halfway Rd on W)**
Gas	E: to Marion Gas W: I-57 Moto Mart◈
Food	E: DQ, TCBY W: **Cracker Barrel**, 20s Hideout Steak House
Lodg	E: Motel Marion & **Campground▲** W: Comfort Suites, Holiday Inn Express, Quality Inn
TServ	E: Raben Tire Co
Med	E: + VA Medical Center, + First Priority Medical Center
Other	E: ATMs, Auto Services, Bowling Alley, NAPA, U-Haul, **Marion Campground & RV Park▲**
(46)	**Weigh Station (Both dir)**
45	**IL 148, N Refuge Rd, to IL 37, Marion, to Herrin, Pulleys Mill**
Gas	E: King Tut's◈
Food	E: Rameses
Other	E: to Lake of Egypt, Marina
(44)	**Jct I-24E, to Nashville**
(40)	**Turn Out / Scenic View (Both dir)**
40	**Goreville Rd, Jenkins Rd, Goreville**
Other	E: Hilltop Campground▲, to Ferne Clyffe State Park▲
36	**CR 4, Lick Creek Rd, Anna**
(32)	**Rest Area (Both dir) (RR, Phones, Pic, Vend, Info, Playgr)**

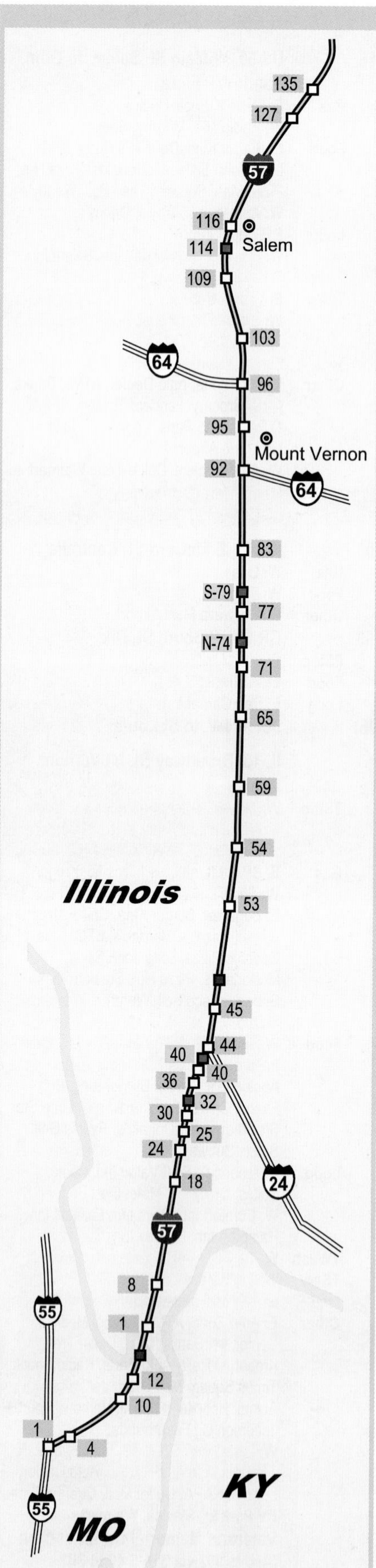

EXIT	IL / MO
30	**IL 146, Dongola, to Anna, Vienna Jonesboro, Mt Pleasant**
Gas	W: Shell◈
Food	W: Rest/Shell
TServ	W: Linson's Service Center
Med	W: + Union Co Hospital
25	**US 51N, Anna, to Carbondale (NB, LEFT exit)**
24	**CR 14, Cypress Rd, Dongola**
Gas	W: Cheers BP◈
Other	W: to Ulrich's Veterinary Clinic♥
18	**Ullin Rd, Ullin**
Gas	W: Fast Stop/Fill Up Mart◈
Food	W: Triple E BBQ
Lodg	W: Americas Best Value Inn
Other	W: Cache River Chevy & **RV**, **Addtl Services 1-2 mi W**
8	**Mounds Rd, to Mound City**
TStop	E: K & K Auto Truck Stop
Food	E: Rest/K & K TS
TServ	E: K & K TS/CBShop
1	**IL 3, to US 51S, Cairo**
Lodg	E: Days Inn
Other	E: Dollar General W: Cairo Reg'l Airport✈

CENTRAL TIME ZONE

⬆ ILLINOIS
⬇ MISSOURI

NOTE: MM 22 : Illinois State Line

CENTRAL TIME ZONE

EXIT	IL / MO
(18)	**Weigh Station (Both dir)**
12	**US 60, US 62, I-57 Bus, MO 77, Charleston, to Wyatt**
TStop	E: Cheers Travel Center (Scales) W: Sunshine Travel Center (Scales)
Gas	W: Casey's, Sinclair P66
Food	E: FastFood/Cheers TC W: Casey's C/O Pizza, KFC
Lodg	W: Econo Lodge
Other	W: ATMs, Banks, Auto Repairs, Grocery
10	**MO 105, Bus 57, Charleston, Prairie**
FStop	E: Pilot Travel Center #359 (Scales)
Gas	E: Charleston Boomland/AmocoBP W: Casey's
Food	E: Subway/Pilot TC, Rest/Boomland W: DQ, McDonald's, Pizza Hut
Lodg	W: Comfort Inn
Other	E: WiFi/Pilot TC, **Boomland RV Park & Campground▲**
4	**IL B, to US 62, Bertrand**
Other	W: Town & Country Camping▲
(1B)	**Jct I-55N, to St Louis (Gas/Food/Lodg/CG - 1st Ex #67)**
(1A)	**Jct I-55S, to Memphis**

CENTRAL TIME ZONE

NOTE: I-57 begins/ends I-55, Exit #66AB

⬆ MISSOURI

Begin I-57 Northbound from Jct I-55 in St Louis, MO to Jct I-94 in Chicago, IL

◈= Regular Gas Stations with Diesel ▲ = RV Friendly Locations ♥= Pet Friendly Locations
Red print shows large vehicle parking / access on site or nearby **Brown Print = Campgrounds / RV PARKS**

EXIT	GA / AL

Begin Southbound I-59 from Jct I-24 near Chattanooga, TN to Jct I-10 in LA.

GEORGIA

NOTE: **I-59 begins/ends on I-24, Exit #167**

CENTRAL TIME ZONE

(19) **Jct I-24W, to Nashville, Jct I-24E, to I-75, Chattanooga, TN**

17 **Slygo Rd, Trenton, to New England**
- Gas: **W:** Citgo◈
- Other: **W:** to Wilderness Outdoor Movie Theatre, to appr 2.5 mi: **Lookout Mountain KOA▲**

11 **GA 136, White Oak Gap Rd, Trenton**
- Gas: **E:** Chevron◈, Exxon◈, Kangaroo Express/ Citgo, **W:** BP, Kangaroo Express/Citgo, Mapco
- Food: **E:** Asian Garden, Burger King, Hardee's, McDonald's, Pizza Hut, Subway **W:** Huddle House, Krystal, Larry's Buffet, Randy's Rest, Taco Bell, Wendy's
- Lodg: **E:** Days Inn
- Other: **E:** Advance Auto Parts, CVS, Carwash/ Chevron, Family Dollar, Ingles Grocery, O'Reilly Auto Parts, US Post Office, **to Appr 4mi: Cloudland Canyon State Park▲**, **to appr 6 mi: The Landing Hang Gliding Resort & RV Park▲**, **W:** Auto Services, Bi-Lo, Carwash, Dollar General, Food Lion,

4 **Puddin Ridge Rd, Deer Head Cove Rd, to GA 58, US 11, Rising Fawn**
- TStop: **W:** Pilot Travel Center #415 (Scales)
- Gas: **E:** Citgo **W:** BP
- Food: **E:** Depot Diner, Rising Fawn Cafe **W:** Subway/Chesters/Pilot TC, Lazy Bones BBQ
- Tires: **W:** Pilot TC
- Other: **E:** US Post Office, **to appr 3 mi: R-Haven Overnight Family Park▲**, **W:** Laundry/WiFi/Pilot TC

EASTERN / CENTRAL TIME ZONE

GEORGIA
ALABAMA

NOTE: **MM 241: Georgia State Line**

CENTRAL / EASTERN TIME ZONE

(241) **AL Welcome Center (SB) (RR, Phone, Pic, Pet, Vend, RVDump)**

239 **CR 140, Valley Head, to US 11, Sulphur Springs Rd**
- Other: **E:** to appr 4 mi: Sequoyah Caverns & Ellis Homestead▲

231 **AL 40, AL 117, Valley Head, to US 11, Hammondville, Henagar**
- Gas: **W:** Victory
- Other: **E:** to Sequoyah Caverns▲, **Serenity Campground & Lake▲**, **DeSoto State Park▲**, **to appr 8.5 mi: Mentone Campground▲**, **W:** I-59 Flea Market

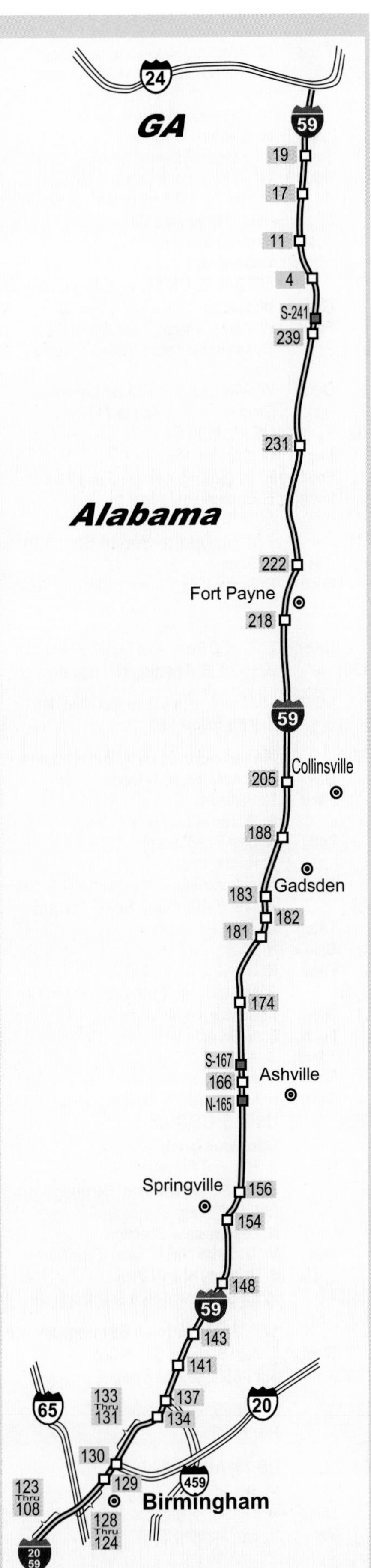

EXIT	ALABAMA

222 **US 11, AL 7, Fort Payne**
- Gas: **E:** Shell **W:** QuikStop, Citgo◈, Texaco
- Food: **E:** Arby's, Krystal, KFC, Jack's Rest, Pizza Hut, Subway, Western Sizzlin **W:** Waffle King
- Lodg: **E:** Ft Payne Inn, Rodeway Inn♥
- Other: **E:** Auto Dealer, ATMs, Banks, Cinema, Carwash, Foodland, SavALot, **to** Little River Canyon National Preserve **W:** Auto Repairs, Isbell Field✈, **Wills Creek RV Park▲**

218 **AL 35, Glenn Blvd, Fort Payne, Rainsville, Scottsboro**
- TStop: **W:** Kangaroo Express #3668
- Gas: **E:** Gas **W:** Chevron, Victory, Murphy◈
- Food: **E:** Asian Palace, Captain D's, China King, Fillin Station, Golden Rule BBQ, McDonald's, Papa John's Pizza, Pizza Hut, Quiznos, Taco Bell, Wendy's, Zaxby's **W:** Burger King, Cracker Barrel, Domino's Pizza, Hardee's, Huddle House, Ryan's Grill, Ruby Tuesday, Subway, Waffle House
- Lodg: **E:** Mountain View Motel **W:** Days Inn, Econo Lodge, Hampton Inn, Holiday Inn Express,
- Med: **W: + DeKalb Regional Medical Center**
- Other: **E:** Advance Auto Parts, Auto Zone, ATMs, Auto Dealer, Auto Services, Banks, Big Lots, Dollar General, Goodyear, O'Reilly Auto Parts, Tractor Supply, U-Haul, **to DeSoto State Park▲** **W:** ATMs, Auto Dealers, Dollar Tree, Hibbett Sports, Lowe's, Radio Shack, Verizo Walgreen's, **Walmart sc**

205 **AL 68, Collinsville, Crossville**
- FStop: **W:** BP
- Gas: **E:** Chevron **W:** Shell
- Food: **E:** Jack's, Patrick's Big Valley Rest, Smokin Joe's
- Lodg: **E:** Howard Johnson
- Other: **W:** Auto Repairs

188 **AL 211, to US 11, Noccalula Pkwy, Noccalula Falls, Gadsden**
- Gas: **E:** Jet Pep **W:** Jet Pep◈
- Other: **E:** Noccalula Falls & **Campground▲**

183 **US 278, US 431, Cleveland Ave, Forrest Ave, Attalla, Gadsden**
- Gas: **E:** Jet Pep◈, Shell **W:** Chevron, Exxon, Jet Pep, Texaco
- Food: **E:** Hardee's, Magic Burger, Waffle House, Wendy's **W:** McDonald's, Pizza Hut, Krystal, Subway, KFC/Taco Bell
- Lodg: **E:** Budget Inn, Days Inn♥, Econo Lodge, Rodeway Inn, Travelodge♥, **W:** Americas Best Inn
- Med: **E: + Riverview Regional Medical Center**
- Other: **E:** AL State Trooper Post, Banks, **W:** CVS,

(182) **Jct I-759E, Attalla, to Gadsden**

181 **AL 77, Gilbert Ferry Rd SE, Gadsden, Attalla, Rainbow City**
- TStop: **E:** Petro2 Stopping Center/BP (Scales)
- Gas: **W:** Citgo, Kangaroo◈, Pure◈
- Food: **E:** FastFood/Supermart TC, Austin's Steak&Seafood/Pizza/Café/Petro SC

EXIT — ALABAMA

Food W: Cracker Barrel, DQ, Domino's Pizza, Hardee's, Papa John's Pizza, Ruby Tuesday, Subway, Waffle House
Lodg E: Days Inn
W: Best Western, Comfort Suites, Holiday Inn Express
Other E: Laundry/BarbSh/Chiro/CB/WiFi/ RVDump/LP/ Petro SC, Gadsden Muni Airport/NE AL Reg'l Airport✈
W: Dollar Tree, O'Reilly Auto Parts, Radio Shack, Walmart sc

174 Steele Station Rd, Steele
FStop W: Chevron
TStop E: Love's Travel Stop #304 (Scales)
W: Steele City Truck Stop/Jet
Food E: Chester'sChicken/Subway/Love's TS
W: Rest/Steele City TS
TWash W: Steele City TS
TServ E: Tires/Love's TS
W: Steele City TS/Tires
Other E: RVDump/Love's TS , Alabama Int'l Dragway
W: Laundry/CB/Steele City TS

(167) Rest Area (SB)
(RR, Phones, Pic, Pet, Vend, RVDump)

166 US 231, Oneonta, Ashville
FStop E: Bama Chevron
W: Asheville Texaco
Food E: Jack's Family Rest
W: Huddle House, Subway, Taco Bell
Lodg E: American Inn

(165) Rest Area (NB)
(RR, Phones, Pic, Pet, Vend, RVDump)

156 AL 23, St Clair Springs, Springville
Other W: Walmart sc

154 AL 174, Marietta Rd, Springville, to Odenville
Gas W: Chevron, Shell◈, Texaco
Food W: Jack's Rest, McDonald's, Subway/ Texaco
Other W: Carwash/Chevron, Carwash/Shell,

148 Liles Ln, to US 11, Argo Pkwy, Argo
Gas E: BP

143 Deerfoot Pkwy, Trussville

141 Chalkville Rd, Trussville, Pinson
Gas E: BP◈, Shell◈, Texaco◈
W: Chevron, Citgo, Quick Shop #8/Exxon, Shell, Sam's
Food E: Applebee's, Arby's, Cracker Barrel, Lone Star Steakhouse, McDonald's, Papa John's Pizza, Pizza Hut, Subway, Taco Bell, Waffle House, Wendy's
W: Burger King, ChickFilA, Krystal, Little Caesars Pizza, Moe's SW Grill, Ruby Tuesday, Whataburger, Zaxby's
Lodg E: Comfort Inn, Holiday Inn Express, Jameson Inn♥
Other E: Harley Davidson
W: ATMs, Bank, Auto Services, CVS, Dollar Tree, PetSmart♥, Radio Shack, Sam's Club, Walgreen's, Walmart sc

(137) Jct I-459S, Tuscaloosa, Montgomery
(Serv at 1st Exit: US11, AL7)

134 AL 75, Roebuck Pkwy, Birmingham
Gas W: BP, Exxon, Shell, USA, Murphy
Food W: Burger King, ChickFilA, Chuck E Cheese's Pizza, McDonald's, Krystal,

EXIT — ALABAMA

Food W: Monterrey Mexican, Mrs Winner's Chicken, O'Charley's, Ruby Tuesday, Shoney's, Steak & Ale, Subway, Taco Bell, Waffle House, Wendy's
Lodg W: Best Inn
Med W: + Medical Center East
Other W: ATMs, Auto Services, Auto Rental, Banks, CVS, Enterprise RAC, Firestone, NTB, O'Reilly Auto Parts, Pharmacy, US Post Office, Walgreen's, Walmart sc,

133 4th Ave S, US 11, Birmingham (NB)
Gas W: Exxon
Food W: Arby's, Krystal, Papa John's Pizza, Shoney's, Starbucks, Subway, Waffle House
Other W: ATMs, Carwash, Dollar General, Grocery, RiteAid, Acc to #134

132 US 11, 80th St
Gas W: Chevron, Exxon
Food E: Burger King, Subway, Taco Bell
Lodg E: Delux Inn
Med E: + Hill Crest Hospital

131 77th St, Oporto-Madrid Blvd (NB)
Gas E: Exxon
Food E: Burger King, Church's Chicken, Subway, Taco Bell
Med E: + Hill Crest Hospital
Other E: CVS, O'Reilly Auto Parts, U-Haul

(130) Jct I-20, E-Atlanta, W-Tuscaloosa

NOTE: I-59S runs with I-20 to Meridian, MS Exit #'s follow I-20.

129 Messer Airport Hwy, Birmingham
Gas S: Conoco, Shell, Texaco
Food N: Hardee's
S: Huddle House, Holiday Inn
Lodg N: Best Inn, Sheraton
S: Holiday Inn
Other N: Auto Rentals, Birmingham Int'l Airport✈,

128 AL 79, Tallapoosa St, to Tarrant
TStop N: Kangaroo Express #3672
Gas N: Shell
Food N: FastFood/Kangaroo

126B 31st St, Sloss Furnaces, Civic Ctr
Gas N: Conoco, Shell
Food S: McDonald's
TServ S: K Diamond Truck Service
Med N: + Carraway Methodist Medical Center
Other S: Laundromat, W AL Tire Service

126A US 31S, US 280E, Carraway Blvd
Med S: + St Vincent Hospital

125 22nd St, Downtown Birmingham (SB, LEFT exit)
Lodg N: Best Western, Sheraton
Other N: AL Sports Hall of Fame, Civic Center
S: Museum, Sheriff Dept

125B 22nd St, Downtown Birmingham

125A 17th St, Downtown Birmingham (NB)
Other S: Auto Services, Greyhound

(124B) Jct I-65N, to Nashville

(124A) Jct I-65S, Montgomery, Huntsville

123 US 78, Arkadelphia Rd, to Jasper
TStop N: Pilot Travel Center #369 (Scales)
Gas N: BP, Chevron, Shell

EXIT — ALABAMA

Food N: Wendy's/Pilot TC, Charlie's Café, Popeye's
Lodg N: Days Inn♥
Med S: + Princeton Baptist Medical Center
Other N: Laundry/WiFi/Pilot TC, Auto Services
S: Bill Battle Coliseum, Birmingham Southern College

121 Bush Blvd, 19th St Ensley, Ave V (SB, no re-entry)
Gas N: BP, Exxon
Food N: Fat Burger

120 AL 269, 20th St Ensley, Ensley 5 Pts W Ave, Birmingham (diff reaccess)
Gas N: Crown
S: BP
Food N: KFC
Med S: + Hospital
Other N: Police Dept
S: Auto Dealer, AL State Fairgrounds, Fairgrounds Speedway, Birmingham Int'l Raceway

119B Ave I, Birmingham (SB, diff reacc)

119A Richard M Scrushy Pkwy, Gary Ave, Lloyd Nolan Pkwy, Fairfield
Gas N: BP, Chevron
S: Mobil
Food N: Burger King, Fairfield Seafood, Subway
S: Omelet Shop, Mama's Kitchen, Wings & Stuff
TServ S: Big Moe Spring & Alignment
Med S: + HealthSouth Metro West Hospital
Other S: Auto Services, U-Haul

118 Valley Rd, Fairfield
Lodg S: Fairfield Inn
Med S: + HealthSouth Metro West Hospital
Other S: Auto Services, U-Haul, to Western Hills Mall, Gas, Grocery, Restaurants

115 15th St, Jaybird Rd, Allison Bonnett Memorial Dr, to US 11, Birmingham
Gas N: Citgo, RaceTrac, Shell
Food N: Hardee's, Subway
Other S: to M&J RV Park▲

113 18th Ave, Jaybird Rd, Birmingham, Brighton, Lipscomb, Bessemer
FStop S: 20-59 Travel Center/Chevron
Food S: FastFood/20-59 TC

112 18th St, 19th St, to US 11, Bessemer
Gas N: Conoco, RaceTrac
S: Chevron
Food N: Jack's Hamburgers
S: Arby's, Burger King, Krystal
Other S: ATMs, Auto Services, Banks, Grocery, Greyhound, Tires, AL RV, General Auto & Truck Service

110 Visionland Pkwy

108 US 11, AL 5N, Academy Dr
Gas N: Exxon
S: BP, Citgo
Food N: Applebee's, Cracker Barrel, Santa Fe Steakhouse, Waffle House
S: Burger King, Cajun Landing Seafood, Milo's, McDonald's, Omelet Shop,
Lodg N: Best Western, Comfort Inn, Jameson Inn, Holiday Inn Express, Motel 6♥, Travelodge
S: Days Inn, Hampton Inn, Masters Economy Inn, Travelodge
Med S: + UAB West Medical Center

◈= Regular Gas Stations with Diesel ▲ = RV Friendly Locations ♥= Pet Friendly Locations
Red print shows large vehicle parking / access on site or nearby Brown Print = Campgrounds / RV PARKS

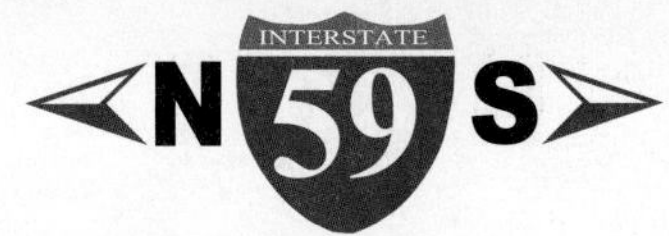

EXIT		ALABAMA
	Other	N: ATM, Bank, Civic Center, Visionland Theme Park, Watermark Place S: ATMs, Banks, Grocery, **Walmart sc**, Winn Dixie, Frank House Muni Golf Course, West Lake Mall , Outlet Mall
(106)		**Jct I-459N, Gadsden, Atlanta (South ByPass of Birmingham)**
104		**McAshen Dr, Rock Mountain Lakes, McCalla**
	TStop	S: Flying J Travel Plaza #5042/Conoco (Scales)
	Food	S: Rest/FastFood/FJ TP
	Other	S: Laundry/BarbSh/WiFi/LP/RVDump/FJ TP
100		**AL 216, McCalla, Abernant, Bucksville**
	TStop	S: Petro Stopping Center #19 (Scales)
	Gas	N: Citgo S: BP, Exxon
	Food	S: IronSkillet/Petro SC, Shenanigan's BBQ
	TServ	S: Petro SC/Tires
	Other	N: **McCalla RV Park▲** S: Laundry/WiFi/RVDump/Petro SC, Auto Repair, **Sheriff Dept**, Tannehill Nat'l Golf Course, Museum, **Tannehill Ironworks Historic State Park▲**
97		**US 11S, AL 5S, West Blocton**
	FStop	S: Caffee Jct BP, Rajpari Shell
	Gas	S: Exxon◈
	Food	S: Dots, KFC, Jack's Family Rest
89		**Mercedes Dr, Vance, Tuscaloosa**
	Lodg	N: Baymont Inn, Wellesley Inn
	Other	S: Mercedes Benz Auto Plant
86		**CR 59, Covered Bridge Rd, Cottondale, Brookwood, Vance**
	TStop	N: Brookwood Shell Truck Stop
	Food	N: Rest/Brookwood TS
(85)		**Rest Area** (Both dir) (RR, Phones, RV Dump)
79		**US 11, University Blvd, Coaling**
	Gas	S: Chevron◈
77		**CR 85, Buttermilk Rd, Cottondale**
	TStop	N: Travel Center of America #16/BP (Scales) S: WilcoHess Travel Plaza #5501 (Scales)
	Gas	N: Chevron
	Food	N: McDonald's/Chevron, CountryPride/Subway/Taco Bell/TA TC, Captain Jim's Seafood & Steak, Pizza Hut, Ruby Tuesday S: Wendy's/WilcoHess TP
	Lodg	N: Hampton Inn, Microtel Inn
	TServ	N: TA TC/Tires, Speedco
	TWash	N: Blue Beacon TW/TA TC
	Other	N: Laundry/WiFi/RVDump/TA TC S: Laundry/WilcoHess TP
76		**US 11, E Tuscaloosa, Cottondale**
	TStop	S: Pilot Travel Center #76 (Scales)
	Gas	N: Citgo◈, Exxon, Shell◈ S: Shell◈
	Food	N: Burger King, Cracker Barrel, Waffle House S: FastFood/Pilot TC
	Lodg	N: Comfort Inn, Scottish Inn, Super Inn S: Sleep Inn
	TServ	S: Southland Int'l Trucks
	Med	N: + US Vets Hospital
	Other	N: ATM, Bank, **Sunset II Travel Park▲** S: Laundry/WiFi/Pilot TC, Auto Service, Auto Dealers, **AL State Hwy Patrol Post**

EXIT		ALABAMA
73		**US 82, AL 6, McFarland Blvd, Tuscaloosa, Centreville**
	Gas	N: Chevron◈ x2, Exxon, RaceTrac, Shell◈ S: AmocoBP◈, Exxon, Shell, Sam's
	Food	N: Burger King, Captain D's, Krystal's, Long John Silver, Pizza Hut, Shoney's, Waffle House, S: Chili's, Hardee's, Huddle House, KFC, Lone Star Steakhouse, McDonalds, Piccadilly, Subway, Taco Bell, Taco Cabana, Waffle House, Wendy's, Western Sizzlin,
	Lodg	N: Best Value Inn, Best Western, Comfort Suites, Guest Lodge, Master's Inn, Shoney's Inn S: Country Inn, Econo Lodge, Days Inn, La Quinta Inn♥ , Motel 6♥, Quality Inn, Ramada Inn, Super 8
	Med	N: + DCH Reg'l Medical Center
	Other	N: ATMs, Banks, Big 10 Tire, CVS, Firestone, Goodyear, U-Haul, Mall, **Lake Lurleen State Park** S: ATMs, Banks, Enterprise RAC, FoodWorld, Fox 12 Cinema, Grocery, McFarland Mall, NAPA, Office Depot, RiteAid, Sam's Club, **Walmart sc**, **AL State Hwy Patrol Post**
(71B)		**Jct I-359, AL 69N, Tuscaloosa**
	Other	N: Univ of AL, Amtrak, Bryant-Denny Stadium, Coleman Coliseum, Stillman College
71A		**AL 69S, to US 11, LA 7, Moundville**
	Gas	N: Phillips 66 S: Chevron, Exxon◈, Shell
	Food	S: Arby's, Country Hic Café & BBQ, IHOP, Outback Steakhouse, Pizza Hut, Ryan's Grill, Waffle House, Wendy's
	Lodg	S: Courtyard, Fairfield Inn, Jameson Inn
	Other	S: ATMs, Advance Auto Parts, Auto Repairs, Firestone, L&H Truck Service, Lowe's, **Police Dept**
68		**Tuscaloosa Western ByPass (Gas 2 mi N in Tuscaloosa)**
62		**CR 10, CR 51, Holly Springs Lane, Fosters**
	Gas	N: BP
52		**US 11, US 43, Knoxville**
	FStop	N: Speedmart Fuel Center/Exxon, Kangaroo #3726
	Food	N: FastFood/Speedmart FC
45		**CR 208, AL 37, Union Rd, Eutaw**
	TStop	S: Trackside BP, Mott Oil #23
	Food	N: Cotton Patch Restaurant S: Hardee's, Southfork, Rest/Western Inn
	Lodg	S: Western Inn
	TServ	S: Trackside BP/Tires, Southfork Auto & Truck Center
	Other	S: Greene Co Greyhound Park
40		**AL 14, Eutaw, Aliceville**
	Med	S: + Hospital
	Other	N: **Tom Bevil Lock & Dam**
(39)		**Rest Area** (SB) (RR, Phones, RVDump)
(38)		**Rest Area** (NB) (RR, Phones, RVDump)
32		**CR 20, Boligee**
	TStop	N: Boligee Truck Stop/BP
	Gas	S: Chevron
	Food	N: Rest/FastFood/Boligee TS

EXIT		AL / MS
23		**CR 20, Gainesville, Epes**
17		**AL 28, Livingston, Boyd**
	TStop	S: 1st Stop Interstate Shell, Noble Truck Stop/Citgo (Scales)
	Gas	S: Chevron
	Food	S: Rest/FastFood/1st Stop, Rest/FastFood/Noble TS, Burger King, Pizza Hut
	Lodg	S: Comfort Inn
	TServ	S: Noble TS/Tires, Bullocks Truck Service
	Med	S: + Hospital
	Other	S: Laundry/Noble TS, Univ of W AL
8		**AL 17, York**
	TStop	S: PTP/York Truck Plaza/BP (Scales)
	Food	S: Deli/Rest/York TP
	Lodg	S: Days Inn/York TP
	TWash	S: York TP
	TServ	S: York TP/Tires
	Med	S: + Hospital
	Other	S: Laundry/CB/York TP, Bank, ATM
1		**AL 8, to US 80E, Cuba, Demopolis**
	TStop	S: Rocking Chair/P66
	Gas	S: Chevron, Dixie
	Food	S: Rest/Rocking Chair
(1)		**AL Welcome Center** (NB) (RR, Phones, RVDump)
	NOTE:	**I-20E & I-59N run together from Meridian, MS to Birminham, AL, Exit #'s follow I-20.**
		CENTRAL TIME ZONE

ALABAMA
MISSISSIPPI

EXIT		AL / MS
	NOTE:	**MM 172: Alabama State Line**
		CENTRAL TIME ZONE
	NOTE:	**I-20W & I-59S run together below to Meridian. Exit #'s follow I-20.**
(170)		**Weigh Station** (Both dir)
169		**US 11, US 80, Kewanee**
	FStop	S: Kewanee One Stop
	Food	S: Rest/Kewanee One Stop
165		**Garrett Rd, Toomsuba**
	TStop	S: Fuel Mart #631 (Scales)
	Gas	N: Shell, Texaco
	Food	N: Subway/Shell, Chesters/Texaco S: Arby's/FuelMart
	Other	S: **Meridian East/Toomsuba KOA▲**
(164)		**MS Welcome Center** (SB) (RR, Phones, Pic, Sec247, RVDump)
160		**Russell Mt Gilead Rd, Meridian**
	TStop	N: Travel Center of America #47P (Scales) S: Russell Shell #21
	Food	N: CountryPride/TA TC S: Rest/FastFood/Shell
	TServ	N: TA TC/Tires
	Other	N: Laundry/LP/TA TC, **Nanabe Creek Campground▲** S: Laundry/Shell

◈ = Regular Gas Stations with Diesel ▲ = RV Friendly Locations ♥ = Pet Friendly Locations
Red print shows large vehicle parking / access on site or nearby Brown Print = Campgrounds / RV PARKS

EXIT		MISSISSIPPI
157AB		**US 45, Macon, Quitman**
	Other	N: Benmark Coach & RV Park▲
154		**MS 19S, MS 39N, US 11N, US 80E, Butler, DeKalb (WB)**
	Gas	N: BP◈, Shell, Texaco S: Chevron, Conoco◈
	Food	N: Applebee's, Backyard Burgers, Cracker Barrel, Krystal, Waffle House
	Food	S: CiCi's Pizza, McDonald's, O'Charley's, Outback Steakhouse, Ryan's Grill, Taco Bell
	Lodg	N: Days Inn, Economy Inn, Hampton Inn, Holiday Inn, Howard Johnson, Relax Inn, Super 8 S: Comfort Inn, Jameson Inn, Scottish Inn, Microtel
	Other	N: Auto Dealers, U-Haul S: Mall, Harley Davidson, Sam's Club, RV Center, RVDump/Conoco
154AB		**MS 19S, MS 39N, US 11N, US 80E, Butler AL DeKalb, Naval Air Stn (EB)**
153		**MS 145S, 22nd Ave, Roebuck Dr, Downtown Meridian, Quitman**
	Gas	N: BP, Shell S: Chevron◈, Conoco◈, Exxon◈, Murphy
	Food	N: Arby's, Barnhill Buffet, Burger King, Captain D's, Chinese, Hardee's, KFC, McDonald's, Pizza Hut, Subway, Wendy's, Western Sizzlin S: Depot Rest, Waffle House
	Lodg	N: Relax Inn S: Astro Motel, Baymont Inn, Budget 8 Motel, Best Western, Econo Lodge, Holiday Inn Express♥, La Quinta Inn♥, Motel 6♥, Quality Inn, Sleep Inn
	Med	N: + Hospital
	Other	N: ATMs, Banks, Amtrak, Goodyear, Grocery, Museums, RiteAid S: Auto Dealers, ATMs, Best Buy, Budget Truck Rental, Lowe's, PetCo♥, Walmart sc
152		**29th Ave, MLK Jr Blvd, Meridian**
	Gas	N: Chevron◈
	Lodg	N: Ramada S: Royal Inn
151		**49th Ave, Valley Rd, Meridian**
	TStop	S: Pilot Travel Center #388 (Scales) (DAND)
	Food	S: Subway/Pilot TC
	Other	S: Laundry/WiFi/Pilot TC
150		**US 11S, MS 19N, Meridian, Philadelphia**
	FStop	S: Stuckey's Express #653/Chevron, Super Stop #10/Shell
	TStop	N: Queen City Truck Stop (Scales) (DAND)
	Food	N: Rest/Queen City TS S: FastFood/Stuckey's Exp
	TServ	N: Mack's Truck Service, QC TS/Tires
	Other	N: LP/Queen City TS, Okitibbee Lake S: Meridian Airport/Key Field✈
(149)		**Jct I-20W, to Jackson, Jct I-59S, to New Orleans**
	NOTE:	I-20W & I-59S run together above to Meridian. Exit #'s follow I-20.
142		**Meehan Savoy Rd, Meridian, to Savoy, Dunn's Falls**
137		**CR 370, N Enterprise, to Stonewall**

Personal Notes

EXIT		MISSISSIPPI
134		**MS 513, S Enterprise, Rose Hill**
126		**MS 18, Pachuta, Quitman, Rose Hill**
	FStop	E: Burns #6, BP Truck Plaza
	Food	E: FastFood/Burns #6, FastFood/BP TP
118		**CR 119, Vossburg, to Paulding, Stafford Springs, Waulkaway Springs**
113		**MS 528, N Pine Ave, Heidelberg, to Bay Springs**
	FStop	E: Stuckey's Express #619/Chevron
	TStop	E: JR's I-59 Truck Stop/BP
	Gas	E: Exxon, Shell
	Food	E: Rest/JR's TS, FastFood/Stuckey's, Subway/PizzaInn/Exxon
	Other	E: Laundry/RVDump/JR's TS, ATMs, Car Wash, U-Haul
(109)		**Parking Area (SB)**
(106)		**Parking Area (NB)**
104		**Main St, Sharon-Sandersville Rd, Laurel, to Sharon, Sandersville**
99		**US 11, N Laurel**
	Gas	E: T&B◈
	Food	E: Pizza Hut/Magnolia Motor Lodge
	Lodg	E: Magnolia Motor Lodge
	Other	E: Laurel KOA▲
97		**US 84E, Chantilly St, Meridian Ave, Waynesboro, Chantilly**
	TStop	E: 84E Truck Stop/Exxon (Scales), Kangaroo Express #3392

EXIT		MISSISSIPPI
	Gas	W: BP◈, Shell
	Food	E: HuddleHouse/FastFood/84E TS, Subway/Kangaroo, Hardee's, Ward's W: KFC, Vic's
	Lodg	E: Hotel/84E Truck Stop
	TServ	E: 84E TS
	Other	E: Laundry/CB/84 E TS W: Auto Services, B&W Towing, Carwash/ Shell, Keys Auto & Truck Repair , Tires, to Amtrak
96B		**MS 15S, Cooks Ave, to Richton**
96A		**4th Ave, Masonite Rd, Laurel**
	Other	E: Auto Service, Diesel Power Service
95C		**Beacon St, Downtown Laurel**
	Gas	E: Gas W: Pump n Save, Chevron
	Food	W: Burger King, Catfish One, Church's Chicken, McDonald's, Old Mexico Rest, Popeye's Chicken,Rest/Town House Motel
	Lodge	W: Town House Motel
	Med	W: + S Central Reg'l Medical Center
	Other	W: ATMs, Family Dollar, Museum, Pharmacy, Tires, Winn Dixie, US Post Office, to Shopping, Sawmill Square Mall, Laurel City Police Dept
95AB		**US 84W, MS 15N, 16th Ave, to Collins, Bay Springs**
	Gas	E: Pure W: Exxon◈, Texaco, Shell
	Food	W: DQ, KFC, McDonald's, Pizza Hut, Shoney's, Subway, Taco Bell, Waffle House, Wendy's
	Lodg	W: Comfort Suites, Econo Lodge, Hampton Inn, Holiday Inn Express, Super 8
	Med	W: + S Central Regional Med Center
	Other	W: Advance Auto, Auto Services, ATMs, Banks, Dollar General, Grocery, Lowe's, Office Depot, Walgreen's, Walmart sc, to Amtrak
93		**US 11, Ellisville Blvd, S Laurel, Fairgrounds, Industrial Park**
	Gas	W: Exxon◈, Shell
	Food	E: Hardee's W: Hardee's, Subway/Exxon
	Other	E: ATMs, Auto Services, Tires, Taylor Small Engine Service, to S Ms Fairgrounds Magnolia Center W: ATMs, Carwash/Shell, Hesler Noble Field✈
90		**US 11, Palmer Rd, Ellisville**
	FStop	E: Keith's Super Store #105/Texaco W: Dixie Oil #93 (DAD) (DAND)
	Other	E: Rogers Auto Parts
88		**MS 29, MS 588, Hill St, Ellisville**
	Gas	E: Chevron◈, Fast Tracs, BP W: Exxon◈
	Food	E: KFC, McDonald's, Pizza Hut, Subway, Domino's Pizza/Fast Tracs W: Ellisville Rest, Fisherman's Choice Seafood Rest, Glenda's Diner
	Lodg	W: Best Western
	Other	E: ATMs, Auto Services, Banks, Carwash, Dollar General, Family Dollar, Grocery, NAPA, Pharmacy, Carwash/BP, to Jones Co Comm College
85		**MS 590, Eubanks Rd, Ellisville**
80		**Moselle-Seminary Rd, Moselle**
	FStop	E: Keith's Super Store #115/BP
78		**Raymer Rd, Sanford Rd. Moselle**

◈= Regular Gas Stations with Diesel ▲ = RV Friendly Locations ♥= Pet Friendly Locations
Red print shows large vehicle parking / access on site or nearby Brown Print = Campgrounds / RV PARKS

EXIT		MISSISSIPPI
76		**Terminal Dr, Moselle**
	Other	W: Hattiesburg-Laurel Reg'l Airport✈
73		**Monroe Rd, Hattiesburg**
69		**Eatonville Rd, Glendale, Hattiesburg**
	Other	W: Auto Repairs
67B		**US 49N, Hattiesburg, to Jackson**
	FStop	W: Dandy Dan #523/BP, Maple Truck Stop (DAD)(DAND), Dandy Dan's #512/Pure,
	Gas	W: Chevron, Citgo, Shell
	Food	W: Subway/DandyDan's, Sonic, Waffle House, Wendy's
	Lodg	W: Best Western, Candlewood Suites, Hawthorne Suites, Holiday Inn
	Other	W: ATMs, Phillips Care Care Center, Carwash/Chevron, Carwash/Shell, JD Tire & Truck Service, **Shady Cove RV Park▲** , to appr 6 mi **Country Creek RV Super Center, Camper City, Okatoma Resort & RV Park▲** ,
67A		**US 49S, Hattiesburg, to Gulfport**
	TStop	E: Kangaroo Express #3845/Texaco
	Gas	E: Exxon, Shell
	Food	E: Krystal/Kangaroo Exp, Arby's, Burger King, Cracker Barrel, Conestoga Steak House, KFC, McDonald's, Pizza Hut, Sakura Japanese Rest, Starbucks, Taco Bell, Waffle House, Wingstreet
	Lodg	E: Budget Inn, Comfort Inn, Days Inn, Econo Lodge, Howard Johnson, Inn on the Hill, La Quinta Inn♥, Motel 6♥, Quality Inn, Ramada, Red Carpet Inn, Regency Inn, Scottish Inn, Sleep Inn, Super 8
	Other	E: Laundry/Kangaroo Exp, ATMs, Auto Services, Big 10 Tire, Dollar General, Hattiesburg Cycles, Hattiesburg Conv & Visitors Bureau/RVDump, Hattiesburg Lake Terrace Convention Center, Farmers Market, Car Wash, Greyhound, Avis RAC, Vet♥, to Univ of Southern MS
65		**US 98W, Hardy St, to Columbia (SB)**
	FStop	W: Kangaroo Express #3399/BP
	Gas	E: Dandy Dan's, Exxon, Shell◈, Texaco W: Dandy Dan's/BP, Shell, Sam's
	Food	E: Applebee's, Burger King, CiCi's Pizza, Cane's, Domino's Pizza, Front Porch BBQ, IHOP, Long John Silver, KFC, Krystal, McDonald's, Pizza Hut, Ponderosa, Quiznos, Starbucks, Subway, Taco Bell W: Subway/Kangaroo Exp, Arby's, Backyard Burger, Burger King, ChickFilA, Chili's, Hardee's, Lone Star Steakhouse, McDonald's, Olive Garden, Outback Steakhouse, Pizza Hut, Red Lobster, Ryan's Grill, Taco Bell, Waffle House, Wendy's, Zaxby's
	Lodg	E: Best Western Inn, Courtyard, Days Inn, Fairfield Inn, Western Motel W: Baymont Inn, Comfort Suites, Hampton Inn, Microtel, Sun Suites
	Med	E: + Immediate Care Medical Center, + Forrest Co Gen'l Hospital W: + Wesley Medical Center
	Other	E: Amtrak, ATMs, Auto Services, Banks, CVS, CarQuest, Deep South Cycles, Dollar General, Grocery, Goodyear, Home Depot, Walgreen's, University Tire, Vet♥, Univ of S MS,

EXIT		MISSISSIPPI
	Other	W: ATMs, Advance Auto Parts, Auto Zone, Best Buy, Auto Services, Banks, Cinema 9, Firestone, FedEx Office, Goodyear Auto, Grocery, Lowe's, Office Depot, PetSmart♥ Radio Shack, RiteAid, Sam's Club, Turtle Creek Mall, Target, UPS Store, Walgreen's, **Walmart sc**, **Ken Pickett RV Center**,
65AB		**US 98W, Hardy St, Hattiesburg (NB)**
60		**US 11, S Hattiesburg**
	TStop	W: Kangaroo Express #3395
	Gas	E: Shell◈ W: AmocoBP◈
	Food	W: Subway/Kangaroo Expr
	Other	E: Carwash/Shell, to Wm Carey College W: Peterbilt
59		**US 98E, Lucedale, Mobile, to US 49, to MS Gulf Coast**
	FStop	E: to US 49N: Dan's Truck Stop/BP
	Other	E: Thomas Tire Repair, to Hattiesburg Muni Airport✈, to appr 7 mi: **Cullen's RV Park▲** , **Paul B Johnson State Park▲** , **Mil/Camp Shelby Military Res/ Camp Shelby/Lake Walker Family Campground▲** ,
(56)		**Parking Area (SB)**
51		**MS 589, Purvis**
	FStop	W: Keith Super Stores/Chevron
	Other	W: Dunns Falls
41		**MS 13, Main Ave, Lumberton**
	Gas	W: Pure
	Other	W: to **Little Black Creek Water Park▲**
35		**Hillsdale Rd, Lumberton**
29		**MS 26, Poplarville, Wiggins**
	Gas	W: Kangaroo◈
	Food	W: Burger King
	Other	W: Pearl River Comm College
27		**MS 53, Poplarville, Necaise**
	FStop	W: to appr 2mi Kangaroo Express #3393
	Gas	W: Shell◈
	Other	E: Poplarville Pearl River Co Airport✈ W: Auto Dealer, Auto Services, Auto Zone, Addt'l Serv 2 mi W
19		**Savannah-Millard Rd, Poplarville**
15		**McNeill Steep Hollow Rd, Carriere**
	TStop	W: McNeill Travel Center
	Food	W: Rest/McNeill TC
	TServ	W: McNeill TC/Tires
	Other	W: WiFi/McNeill TP, to **Lacy RV Park Campground▲**
(14)		**Parking Area (SB)**
10		**W Union Rd, Carriere**
	TStop	E: Keith's Super Store/Chevron
	Food	E: HuddleHouse/FastFood/Keith's SS
	TServ	E: Keith's Super Store/Tires
	Other	E: Laundry/Keith's SS, to appr 6 mi: **Clearwater RV Park & Campground▲**
(8)		**Parking Area (NB)**
6		**MS 43N, Sycamore Rd, N Picayune**
	Gas	W: Chevron◈
	Lodg	W: Budget Host Inn
	Med	W: + Hospital
	Other	W: ATMs, CVS, Grocery, Winn Dixie
4		**MS 43S, Memorial Blvd, Picayune, Kiln**
	Gas	E: Murphy W: BP, Exxon◈, Shell◈, Spur

◈ = Regular Gas Stations with Diesel ▲ = RV Friendly Locations ♥ = Pet Friendly Locations

Red print shows large vehicle parking / access on site or nearby Brown Print = Campgrounds / RV PARKS

EXIT	MISSISSIPPI
Food	E: McDonald's, Ryan's Grill W: Burger King, Domino's, Golden China, Hardee's, KFC, McDonald's, Pizza Hut, Panda Palace, Popeye's, Shoney's, Taco Bell, Waffle House, Wendy's
Lodg	W: Comfort Inn, Days Inn, Heritage Inn
Med	W: + Crosby Memorial Hospital
Other	E: Auto Dealers, Home Depot, Picayune Vet Clinic♥, **Sun Roamers RV Resort▲**, Walgreen's, **Walmart sc**, W: Advance Auto, Animal Clinic♥, Amtrak, Auto Dealers, Firestone Auto, Fred's, Grocery, RiteAid, Radio Shack, Tires, **PawPaw's Camper City**, Picayune Pearl River Airport✈,
(2)	**MS Welcome Center (NB)** **(RR, Phones, Picnic, Vend, RVDump)**
(1)	**Weigh Station (Both dir)**

EXIT	MS / LA
1	**US 11N, MS 607, Nicholson, NASA Nat'l Space Tech Lab, Stennis Space Center, Naval Oceanographic Office**
Gas	W: Chevron◈, BP, Spur
Other	W: Auto & Truck Repairs, ATMs, Winn Dixie

CENTRAL TIME ZONE

MISSISSIPPI

LOUISIANA

CENTRAL TIME ZONE

EXIT	MS / LA
11	**Pearl River TurnAround**
NOTE:	**SB: Begin Motorist Call Boxes**
5B	**Honey Island Swamp**

EXIT	LOUISIANA
5A	**LA 41 Spur, Pearl River**
Gas	E: Chevron
Food	W: Café, Mama's Kitchen
3	**US 11S, LA 1090, Pearl River**
(1)	**Slidell Welcome Center (SB)** **(RR, Ph, Pic, Sec, Vend, Info, RVDump)**
(1CB)	**Jct I-10, E to Bay St Louis, W to New Orleans**
(1A)	**Jct I-12W, to Hammond**

CENTRAL TIME ZONE

NOTE: I-59 begins/ends I-12, Exit# 85AC
I-59 begins/ends I-10, Exit #267AB

LOUISIANA

Begin I-59 Northbound from Jct I-10 in LA to Jct I-24 in Chattanooga, TN

EXIT	MISSOURI

Begin Eastbound I-64 from Jct I-70 in Wentzville, MO to Chesapeake, VA

MISSOURI

CENTRAL TIME ZONE

EXIT	MISSOURI
(0)	**US 61N, Hannibal (WB exit, EB entr)**
(1)	**Jct I-70W, US 40W, to Kansas City, St Charles (WB exit, EB entr)**
(1A)	**Jct I-70W, US 40W, to Ks City**
(1B)	**Jct I-70E, St Charles (WB exit only)**
1C	**Prospect Rd, Wentzville**
2	**Lake St Louis Blvd**
4	**MO N**
6	**MO DD, Winghaven Blvd**
9	**MO K, O'Fallon, St Charles**
Gas	N: QT, Mobil
Food	N: Cracker Barrel, Culpeppers, Culvers, J Bucks, Joey's Seafood & Grill, Ruby Tuesday, Timber Creek Grill
Lodg	N: Country Inn, Staybridge Suites
10	**MO 94, St Charles (EB)** **(WB Access via Exit 9)**
Gas	N: QT
Food	N: Jack in the Box, McDonald's
Med	N: + Center Pointe Hospital
Other	N: ATMs, Bank, Auto Repairs, Tires, Walgreen's, Animal Hospital♥
11	**Research Park Circle** **(WB exit, EB ent)**
14	**Chesterfield Airport Rd, to MO 109, Long Rd, Chesterfield** **(EB exit, WB ent)**
Gas	S: Phillips 66
Lodg	S: Comfort Inn
Other	S: ATMs, Bank, Auto Repairs, Budget RAC, Tires, Aviation Museum, Spirit of St Louis Airport✈, **to appr 5 mi: Babler State Park▲**
14	**Spirit of St Louis Blvd** **(WB exit, EB entr)**
16	**Long Rd, Chesterfield** **(WB exit, EB ent)**
Gas	S: BP
Food	S: Central MO Pizza, Lisa's TX BBQ, McDonald's, Mr Goodcents
Other	S: Police Dept
17	**Boones Crossing St, Frontage Rd, Long Rd, Chesterfield Airport Rd**
Gas	S: BP, Mobil, Phillips 66
Food	S: Long Horn Steakhouse, NY Burrito Gourmet Wraps, O'Charley's, Old Country Buffet, Olive Garden, Quiznos, Red Lobster Sonic, Steak n Shake, Starbucks, Subway
Lodg	S: Hampton Inn, Hilton Garden Inn
Other	S: ATMs, Banks, Best Buy, Dollar Tree, Lowe's, Pharmacy, PetSmart♥, Sam's Club, Target, UPS Store, **Walmart**,
19A	**Chesterfield Pkwy N**
Gas	S: Shell
Food	N: Rest/DoubleTree S: Bahama Breeze, Keith's, Lettuce Leaf, Stoney River Rest
Lodg	N: Doubletree Hotel S: Homewood Suites
Other	N: Avis, ATM, Bank, Monsato Co, Pfizer Global R&D, **to** Arrowhead Airport✈, Creve Coeur Airport✈ S: ATMs, Auto Services, Bank, Chesterfield Mall, Tires

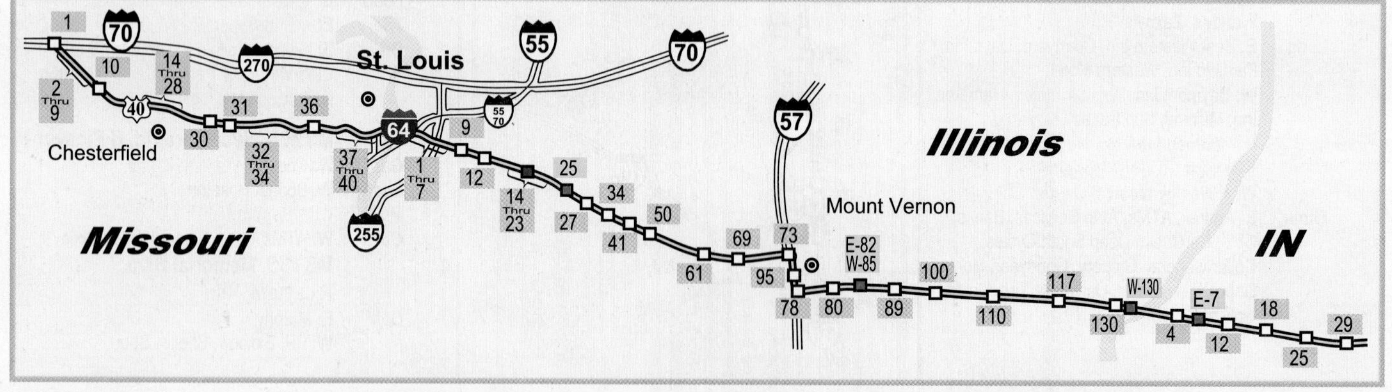

◈= Regular Gas Stations with Diesel ▲ = RV Friendly Locations ♥= Pet Friendly Locations
Red print shows large vehicle parking / access on site or nearby Brown Print = Campgrounds / RV PARKS

EXIT		MISSOURI
19B		**Clarkson Rd, Olive Blvd, MO 340**
	Gas	**N:** Amoco, Shell **S:** Mobil
	Food	**N:** Applebee's, Taco Bell, YiaYia's **S:** Aqua Vin, Crazy Bowls & Wraps, CA Pizza Kitchen, Chili's, Curry in a Hurry, Einstein Bros, Fuji Sushi, Hunan Express, KC Masterpiece, McDonald's, Panda Express, Pasta House, Quiznos Subs, Romano's Macaroni Grill, Starbucks
	Lodg	**N:** Hampton Inn, Residence Inn♥, Springhill Suites **S:** Drury Inn
	Other	**N:** ATMs, Banks, Goodyear, Grocery, Walgreen's **S:** ATMs, Banks, Clarkson 6 Cinema, FedEx Office, Grocery, PetCo♥, Trader Joe's, Wild Oats, UPS Store
20		**Chesterfield Pkwy, Frontage Rd (WB exit, EB entr) (Access to Ex #19B, #19A Serv)**
21		**Timberlake Manor Pkwy**
22		**MO 141, Woods Mill Rd, Chesterfield (Addt'l Serv 2-3 mi S to Clayton Rd)**
	Gas	**N:** 7-11, BP
	Food	**N:** Dock Café, McDonald', Wendy's **S:** Blimpie Subs, Dave's World Famous Bar & Rest, Hot Wok Café
	Lodg	**N:** Courtyard, Marriott
	Med	**N:** + St Luke's Hospital
	Other	**N:** Maryville Univ
23		**Maryville Centre Rd (WB exit, EB entr)**
24		**S Mason Rd, St Louis (WB) (Gas & Food S 1.5 mi to Clayton Rd)**
	Other	**N: MO State Hwy Patrol Post**
(25)		**Jct I-270, N to Chicago, S to Tulsa**
26		**New Ballas Rd, MO JJ, Clayton Rd**
	Gas	**S:** Shell, Shell
	Med	**N:** + St John's Mercy Heart Hospital **S:** + MO Baptist Medical Center
	Other	**S:** Auto Repairs/Shell, Auto Services, **Police Dept**
27		**Spoede Rd, St Louis**
28A		**US 61S, US 67, Lindbergh Blvd, Clayton Rd, Frontenac**
	Food	**S:** Brio Tuscan Grille, Canyon Cafe, Fleming's Prime Steak House, Italian Rest, Starbucks
	Lodg	**S:** Hilton
	Med	**S:** + Shriners Hospital for Children
	Other	**S:** ATMs, Bank, Grocery, **Police Dept**, Shopping Plaza, Mall
28B		**Clayton Rd (WB exit, EB entr)**
	Gas	**N:** BP, Texaco
	Food	**N:** Baskin Robbins, CoCo's, Grassi's Italian Rest, Starbucks
	Other	**N:** ATMs, Banks, Auto Services, Towing
30		**McKnight Rd, Ladue, St Louis**
31A		**I-170N, Clayton**
31B		**Brentwood Blvd, Hanley Rd**
	Gas	**N:** Shell **S:** BP, Mobil
	Food	**N:** Burger King, Cajun Café, Fazoli's, IHOP, KFC, Pasta House, Steak n Shake, St Louis Bread, Starbucks, TGI Friday **S:** Corwin's, Romano's Macaroni Grill, Subway
	Lodg	**N:** Residence Inn
	Other	**N:** AMC 6, Galleria Mall **S:** ATMs, Auto Services, Borders, Goodyear, Target, Whole Foods, Serra Mission Winery
32		**Hanley Rd, Brentwood Blvd**
	Gas	**S:** Shell, QT
	Food	**S:** McDonald's, Lion's Choice
	Other	**S:** ATMs, Auto Services, Best Buy, Home Depot, Sam's Club, Tires, **Walmart sc**, Whole Foods Market, **Police Dept**
33A		**Big Bend Blvd**
	Other	**S:** Auto Services, Tires, **Police Dept**
33B		**Bellevue Ave (EB exit, WB entr)**
	Gas	**N:** Texaco
	Med	**N:** + St Mary's Health Center
33C		**McCausland Ave**
	Gas	**N:** Amoco
	Food	**N:** Chinese Express, Del Taco
	Med	**N:** + St Mary's Health Center
34A		**Clayton Rd, Skinker Blvd (WB exit, EB entr)**
34B		**Hampton Ave, Forest Park**
	Gas	**S:** Mobil, Amoco
	Food	**S:** Courtesy Diner, Hardee's, Jack in the Box, Steak N Shake, Subway
	Med	**S:** + Forest Park Hospital
	Other	**N:** Golf Courses, Zoo
36A		**Kingshighway Blvd S, to I-44**
	Gas	**S:** Amoco
	Other	**S:** Auto Repairs
36B		**Boyle Ave (WB exit, EB entr) Vandeventer Ave (EB exit, WB entr)**
	Gas	**N:** BP **S:** Oil
	Lodg	**N:** Best Western, Chase Park Plaza, Marriott
	Med	**N:** + Barnes Jewish Hospital, + St Louis Children's Hospital
	Other	**S:** Auto Services
37A		**Market St, Bernard St (EB exit, WB ent)**
	Food	**S:** Shoney's
	Med	**S:** + St Louis University Hospital, + Cardinal Glennon Children's Hospital, + Bethesda General Hospital
37B		**Grand Blvd (EB exit, WB entr)**
	Gas	**N:** Oil, Shell
	Food	**N:** Asst'd
	Lodg	**N:** Courtyard, Drury Inn, Hampton Inn, Marriott
	Med	**N:** + John Cochrane VA Medical Center
	Other	**N:** Museums, Theatres
38A		**Forest Park Ave, Grand Blvd (WB exit, EB entr)**
	Other	**N:** Auto Services, Towing
38B		**Market St, 3000 West (WB exit, EB entr)**
38C		**Jefferson Ave, to I-44 (EB exit, WB ent)**
	Lodg	**N:** Courtyard
	Other	**N:** ATMs, Auto Services, Banks, Enterprise RAC, Firestone, **St Louis RV Park▲**
38D		**Chestnut St, 20th St (EB exit, WB ent)**
39A		**Market St, 21st St (WB exit, EB ent)**
	Lodg	**N:** Courtyard, Drury Inn, Hampton Inn, Hyatt Regency
39B		**14th St, St Louis (EB exit, WB entr)**
	Lodg	**N:** Marriott, Sheraton
39C		**11th St, Busch Stadium (EB exit, WB entr)**
	Lodg	**N:** Marriott, Sheraton
	Other	**N:** Courts, **Sheriff Dept**, Museums
40A		**9th St, Tucker Blvd, Busch Stadium (WB Exit Only)**
40B		**Broadway, 7th St, Stadium, Arch (EB exit, WB entr)**
	Gas	**S:** BP
	Food	Many Choices North & South
	Lodg	**N:** Drury Plaza, Marriott, Millennium Hotel, Westin Hotel
	Other	**N:** Busch Memorial Stadium, Cardinals Hall of Fame Museum, Gateway Arch, **to** Convention Centers, Courts, Museums **S:** Auto Services, Museum, **to** Darkness Haunted Theme Park
(40C)		**Jct I-55S to Memphis, Jct I-44W, to Tulsa (WB exit, EB entr) I-70W, Memorial Dr (WB exit, EB entr)**

CENTRAL TIME ZONE

NOTE: MM 41: Illinois State Line

⬆ MISSOURI
⬇ ILLINOIS

CENTRAL TIME ZONE

EXIT		ILLINOIS
1		**IL 3S, Cahokia, E St Louis**
	Other	**S: to** St Louis Downtown Airport✈, **Cahokia RV Parque▲**
2A		**MLK Memorial Bridge (WB, LEFT exit)**
2B		**3rd St, E St Louis (WB, LEFT exit)**
	Med	**S:** + St Mary's Hospital
	Other	**N: Casino Queen** Hotel & **RV Park▲** **S:** ATMs, Banks, **Police Dept**
2C		**MLK Memorial Bridge, Missouri Ave, Downtown (WB)**
3		**IL 3N, St Clair Ave, I-55N, I-70E, to Chicago, Indianapolis, to Gateway Int'l Raceway**
4		**Baugh Ave, N 15th St, St Clair Ave**
	Lodg	**N:** Blackmon's Motel
	Other	**S:** Auto Repair
5		**N 25th St, East St Louis**
6		**IL 111, N Kingshighway**
	Gas	**N:** BP, Mobil, Shell
	Food	**N:** Popeye's, China House **S:** Stoplight Restaurant
	Lodg	**N:** Econo Inn
	Other	**N:** ATMs

EXIT — ILLINOIS

(7) **Jct I-255, N to Chicago, S to Memphis, TN**

9 **IL 157, N 88th St, Caseyville, to Centerville, Belleville**
- **Gas** N: BP, Phillips 66
  S: BP◈
- **Food** N: Hardee's, Wendy's, Subway/P66
  S: Cracker Barrel, Domino's Pizza , DQ, Pizza Hut, McDonald's, Taco Bell
- **Lodg** N: First Western Inn
  S: Best Inn, Days Inn, Econo Lodge♥, Motel 6♥, Quality Inn
- **AServ** N: Phillips 66
  S: BP

12 **IL 159, N Illinois St, Fairview Heights, to Collinsville, Belleville**
- **Gas** N: Conv Food Mar/Shell◈
  S: BP, Mobil, Moto Mart◈
- **Food** N: Applebee's, Bob Evans, Carrabba's, Houlihan's, Joe's Crab Shack, Lotawata Creek, Olive Garden, Red Lobster, TGI Friday
  S: Boston Market, Burger King, Captain D's, Chili's, Denny's, Hardee's, IHOP, Longhorn Steakhouse, Little Caesars Pizza, Long John Silver's, McDonald's, Ponderosa Popeye's, Outback Steakhouse, Ruby Tuesday, Steak n Shake, Taco Bell
- **Lodg** N: Best Western, Drury Inn, Fairfield Inn, Hampton Inn, Ramada Inn, Sheraton, Super 8♥
- **Other** N: Michael's
  S: ATMs, Auto Services, Banks, B&N, Advance Auto Parts, Best Buy, Borders, Dobbs Tires, Firestone, FedEx Office, Goodyear Auto, Lowe's, NTB, PetCo♥, Natures Market, Craft Mall, St Clair Square Mall,Target, Walgreen's,

14 **W US 50, O'Fallon, to Shiloh**
- **Gas** N: QT, Shell
  S: Mobil, Conv Food Mart
- **Food** N: IHOP, Japanese Garden, Steak n Shake
  S: Chevys Fresh Mex, DQ, Hardee's, Jack in the Box, KFC, Lone Star Steakhouse, McDonald's, O'Charley's, Quiznos, Taco Bell, Western Sizzlin'
- **Lodg** N: Baymont Inn, Extended Stay America, Howard Johnson, Sleep Inn
  S: Candlewood Suites, Guest House Inn, Econo Lodge, Quality Inn
- **Other** N: ATMs, Auto Dealers, Banks, CVS
  S: ATMs, Banks, Cinema 15, Grocery, Home Depot, PetSmart♥, Sam's Club, Walmart sc,

16 **N Greenmount Rd, O'Fallon, Shiloh**
- **Food** N: Denny's, Sonic
  S: Applebee's, Cracker Barrel, Golden Corral, Quiznos Subs, St Louis Bread
- **Lodg** S: Holiday Inn Express
- **Other** S: ATMs, Grocery, Radio Shack, Target, UPS Store

(18) **Weigh Station (EB)**

19AB **US 50, IL 158, O'Fallon, Scott AFB, Air Mobility Dr, Scott Troy Rd**
- **Gas** N: Moto Mart
  S: Citgo◈
- **Food** N: Hero's Pizza/Subs
  S: Deli/Citgo, Ivory Chopsticks

EXIT — ILLINOIS

- **Lodg** N: Comfort Inn
- **Other** S: Mid-America Airport✈, Scott AFB

23 **IL 4, Mascoutah, Lebanon (Gas, Food, Lodg 4mi N in Lebanon)**
- **Other** S: Mid-America Airport✈, Scott AFB

(25) **Gateway Rest Area (Both dir) (RR, Phones, Picnic, Vend, Weather)**

27 **IL 161, New Baden**
- **Gas** N: Shell◈
- **Food** N: McDonald's, Outside Inn, Subway
- **Other** N: ATMs, Auto Services

34 **to Albers**

41 **IL 177, Okawville**
- **TStop** S: Road Ranger/Pilot TC #534
- **Gas** S: Gas Mart
- **Food** S: BurgerKingi/RR PTC, DQ, Hen House Rest, Subway
- **Lodg** S: Original Springs Hotel, Super 8
- **TServ** S: Ex 41 Service Center, Obermeier Truck Service, Gary's Tire Center

50 **IL 27, Nashville, to Carlyle**
- **FStop** S: Knapp Mart/Citgo
- **TStop** S: Little Nashville Truck Stop/Conoco (Scales)
- **Gas** S: BP, Shell◈
- **Food** S: Rest/Little Nashville TS, Deli/Citgo, Hardee's, McDonald's, Subway
- **Lodg** S: Best Western, Little Nashville Inn
- **TServ** S: Little Nashville TS/Tires
- **Med** S: + Hospital
- **Other** N: to Carlyle Lake

61 **US 51, Richview, Centralia**

69 **CR 9, Woodlawn Ln, Woodlawn**

NOTE: **I-64 below runs with I-57 for 5 mi. Exit #'s follow I-57.**

(73) **Jct I-57, N - Chicago, S - Memphis**

(78) **Jct I-57, S - Memphis, N - Chicago**

NOTE: **I-64 above runs with I-57 for 5 mi. Exit #'s follow I-57.**

80 **IL 37, Mt Vernon, Bakerville**
- **Gas** N: BP◈, Marathon◈
- **Food** N: Burger King/BP
- **Lodg** N: Royal Inn
- **Other** N: Auto Services, Towing, to Mt Vernon Outland Airport✈

(82) **Rest Area (EB) (RR, Phones, Picnic, Vend)**

(85) **Rest Area (WB) (RR, Phones, Picnic, Vend)**

89 **CR 17, Belle River, Bluford**

95 **IL 15, Broadway St, Mt Vernon**
- **TStop** W: Travel Center of America #43 (Scales), Huck's Travel Center (Scales), Pilot Travel Center #482 (Scales)
- **Gas** E: BP◈, Marathon, Phillips 66
  W: Shell
- **Food** E: Bonanza, Burger King, Fazoli's, Hardee's, KFC, McDonald's, Pizza Hut, Steak n Shake, Subway, Taco Bell, Wendy's, Western Sizzlin
  W: CountryPride/Popeyes/TA TC, Rest/ Huck's TC, Denny's/Pilot TC, Applebee's, Arby's, Burger King, Cracker Barrel, Lone Star Steakhouse, McDonald's, Ryan's Grill

EXIT — IL / IN

- **Lodg** E: Best Western, Comfort Suites, Drury Inn, Motel 6♥, South Gate Inn, Super 8
  W: Comfort Inn, Days Inn, Fairfield Inn, Hampton Inn, Holiday Inn, Quality Inn
- **TWash** W: XVIII Wheelers TW, TA TC
- **TServ** W: TA TC/Tires
- **Med** E: + Mt Vernon Hospital
- **Other** E: ATMs, Auto Zone, CVS, Kroger, Harley Davidson, Radio Shack, Walgreen's,
  W: Laundry/WiFi/TA TC, Laundry/Huck's TC, Laundry/WiFi/Pilot TC, Auto Dealers, ATMs, Lowe's, Outlet Mall, Staples, Walmart sc, Quality Times RV Park▲

100 **IL 242, Wayne City, McLeansboro**
- **Gas** N: Marathon◈

110 **US 45, Barnhill, Norris City, Fairfield**

117 **CR 20, Burnt Prairie**
- **FStop** S: Chuckwagon Charlie's/Marathon
- **Food** S: Cafe/Marathon

130 **IL 1, Grayville, Carmi**
- **FStop** N: Grayville Shell Plaza
- **Gas** S: Phillips 66◈
- **Food** N: Rest/BW, Subway
- **Lodg** N: Best Western, Super 8
- **Other** N: Auto Repairs

(130) **IL Welcome Center (WB) (RR, Phones, Pic, Vend, Info, Weather)**

NOTE: **MM 131.5: Indiana State Line**

⬆ ILLINOIS
⬇ INDIANA

EASTERN TIME ZONE

4 **IN 69S, Griffin, to New Harmony**
- **Gas** N: Depot
- **Food** N: Café/Depot
- **Other** S: to Harmony State Park

(7) **IN Welcome Center (EB) (RR, Phones, Picnic)**

12 **IN 165, Poseyville**

18 **IN 65, Cynthiana, Evansville**
- **FStop** S: I-64 Moto Mart

25B **US 41N, Terre Haute**
- **TStop** N: Flying J Travel Plaza #647 (Scales), Love's Travel Stop #414 (Scales), Pilot Travel Center #447 (Scales)
- **Food** N: Country Market/FJ TP, Wendy's/ Love's TS, Subway/TacoBell/Pilot TC
- **Lodg** N: Quality Inn♥
- **Tires** N: Pilot TC #395
- **TWash** N: Blue Beacon TW/Pilot TC
- **Other** N: Laundry/WiFi/RVDump/LP/FJ TP, Laundry/WiFi/Love's TS, Laundry/WiFi/ Pilot TC, Weather Rock Campground▲

25A **US 41S, Evansville, Haubstadt**
- **FStop** S: Busler #102/Citgo
- **TStop** S: Busler Truck Stop I-64 (Scales)
- **Gas** S: BP
- **Food** S: Rest/Busler TS, Arby's, Denny's, McDonald's
- **Lodg** S: Best Western♥, Comfort Inn, Holiday Inn Express, Super 8♥
- **TWash** S: Busler TS
- **TServ** S: Busler TS/Tires

◈ = Regular Gas Stations with Diesel ▲ = RV Friendly Locations ♥ = Pet Friendly Locations
Red print shows large vehicle parking / access on site or nearby Brown Print = Campgrounds / RV PARKS

EXIT		INDIANA
	Other	S: Laundry/Busler TS, IN State Hwy Patrol Post, Golf Course
(29A)		**Jct I-164, IN 57S, Evansville, to Henderson KY**
	TServ	S: Clarke Detroit Diesel
29B		**IN 57N, Petersburg**
	FStop	N: Circle A Food Mart #109/Sunoco (Scales)
	Food	N: Subway/Circle A FM
39		**IN 61, Lynnville, to Boonville**
	Gas	N: Shell
	Food	N: Pizza House, Rest/Old Fox Inn
	Lodg	N: Old Fox Inn
54		**IN 161, Tennyson, Holland**
57		**US 231, Dale, Jasper, Huntingburg**
	FStop	N: to 12 mi N to 1781 US 231: Sternberg's 24 N More/Citgo
	TStop	N: 231 AmBest Plaza (Scales),
	Gas	S: Shell◈
	Food	N: Rest/231 Plaza S: Denny's
	Lodg	N: Scottish Inns S: Baymont Inn, Motel 6♥
	TServ	N: 231 Plaza/Tires
	Med	N: + Hospital
	Other	N: Laundry/231 Plaza S: Abe Lincoln's Boyhood Home, to Lincoln State Park
(58)		**Rest Area (Both dir)** (RR, Phones, Picnic, Vend, Info)
63		**IN 162, Santa Claus, Ferdinand**
	Gas	N: Sunoco◈
	Food	N: Wendy's
	Lodg	N: Comfort Inn, Harvest Moon Motel
	Other	S: to appr 7 mi: Lake Rudolph RV Campground▲, Holiday World & Splashin Safari
72		**IN 145, Bristow, Birdseye**
79		**IN 37S, Tell City, St Croix**
(80)		**Parking Area (EB)**
(81)		**Parking Area (WB)**
86		**IN 37N, Sulphur, English**
92		**IN 66, Carefree, Leavenworth**
	TStop	S: Carefree Marathon, Country Style Plaza/ Shell (Scales), Days Inn Truck Stop/BP, Pilot Travel Center #478 (Scales)
	Food	S: Rest/Citgo, Rest/Country Style Plaza, Kathy'sKitchen/Days Inn TS, Subway/Pilot
	Lodg	S: Days Inn, The Leavenworth Inn
	Other	N: to Veringo Caves S: Laundry/WiFi/Shell, Laundry/WiFi/Pilot TC, to Wyandotte Caves

EXIT		INDIANA
(97)		**Parking Area (Both dir)**
105		**IN 135, Corydon, Palmyra**
	Gas	N: Citgo◈, Shell S: BP◈, Chevron
	Food	N: Big Boy, KFC S: Arby's, Burger King, Cracker Barrel, China Best Buffet, DQ, Hardee's, Lee's Famous Recipe Chicken, Long John Silver, McDonald's, O'Charley's, Papa John's Pizza, Ryan's Grill, Subway, Taco Bell, Waffle House, Wendy's, White Castle
	Lodg	N: Quality Inn, First Capitol Hotel♥ S: Baymont Inn, Hampton Inn, Holiday Inn Express, Super 8♥
	Med	S: + Hospital
	Other	S: ATMs, Auto Zone, Auto Dealers, CVS, Dollar General, Dollar Tree, Grocery, Radio Shack, Walgreen's, Walmart sc
113		**to Lanesville**
(115)		**IN Welcome Center (WB)** (RR, Phones, Picnic, Vend)
118		**IN 62, IN 64W, Georgetown**
	FStop	N: Gas 'n Stuff/Marathon
	Gas	N: Shell S: Marathon◈
	Food	N: Korner Kitchen, McDonald's
	Lodg	N: Days Inn, Motel 6♥
	Other	N: LP/GasnStuff, Grocery
119		**US 150W, to Greenville, Paoli**
	Gas	N: Citgo◈, Marathon
	Food	N: Domino's Pizza, Papa John's Pizza, Sam's Family Rest, Tumbleweed Grill
	Other	N: ATMs, RiteAid, Walgreen's
(121)		**Jct I-265E, to I-65** (EB, LEFT Exit)
123		**IN 62E, New Albany**
	Gas	N: BP, Bigfoot◈, Speedway S: BP, Marathon◈
	Food	S: DQ, Freedom Waffle,Minny's Café, Subway, Waffle & Steak
	Lodg	S: Hampton Inn, Hilton, Holiday Inn
	Med	S: + Hospital
	Other	N: ATMs, Firestone, Goodyear, Grocery

EASTERN TIME ZONE

NOTE: MM 124: Kentucky State Line

INDIANA

EXIT		KENTUCKY

KENTUCKY

EASTERN TIME ZONE

(1)		**Jct I-264, Louisville ByPass, Shively**
	TServ	S: Whayne Power Systems
3		**US 150E, 22nd St, Portland Ave**
	Gas	S: Chevron, Dairy Mart
	Food	S: DQ, McDonald's, Subway
	Other	S: Auto Repairs, to Simmons Bible College
4		**9th St, Roy Wilkins Ave, Downtown**
	Food	S: Various Rest S to US 60
	Other	S: Greyhound, Louisville Slugger Visitor Center, Museums, Science Center/IMAX, Courts, Police Dept
(5B)		**Jct I-65N, to Indianapolis (EB), 3rd St, River Rd, Downtown (WB)**
(5A)		**Jct I-65S, to Nashville**
	Med	E: + Univ of Louisville Hospital, + Kosair Childrens Hospital, + Jewish Hospital, Louisville Medical Center
(6)		**Jct I-71N, to Cincinnati (EB)**
	Med	E: + VA Medical Center (Ex #2)
7		**Story Ave, US 42, US 60, N Spring St, Mellwood Ave, Louisville**
	Gas	N: Speedway S: BP
	Food	S: Moby Dick Seafood Rest
	Other	S: Auto Repairs
8		**Grinstead Dr, Cherokee Pkwy** (Gas/Food/Lodg S to US 150)
	Gas	S: BP, Chevron, Swifty
	Food	N: Beef O'Brady's S: Chinese Bistro, KT's Rest & Bar
	Other	N: Southern Baptist Seminary S: to Expo Center, Presbyterian Seminary
10		**KY 2048, Cannons Lane**
	Other	S: Bowman Field Airport✈
(12A)		**Jct I-264W, Watterson Expwy (EB)**
	Med	N: + Baptist Hospital East S: + Norton Suburban Hospital
(12B)		**Jct I-264E, Watterson Expwy (EB)** (All Serv at 1st Ex #20AB/US 60) (Gas/Food/Lodg/Malls/Repairs)
(12)		**Jct I-264, Watterson Expwy, Airport, St Mathews, Churchill Downs (WB)**
	Other	W: to Freedom Hall, Fairgrounds
15		**KY 1747, Hurstbourne Pkwy, Jeffersontown, Middletown (WB)**
	Gas	N: BP◈, Chevron◈, Shell◈

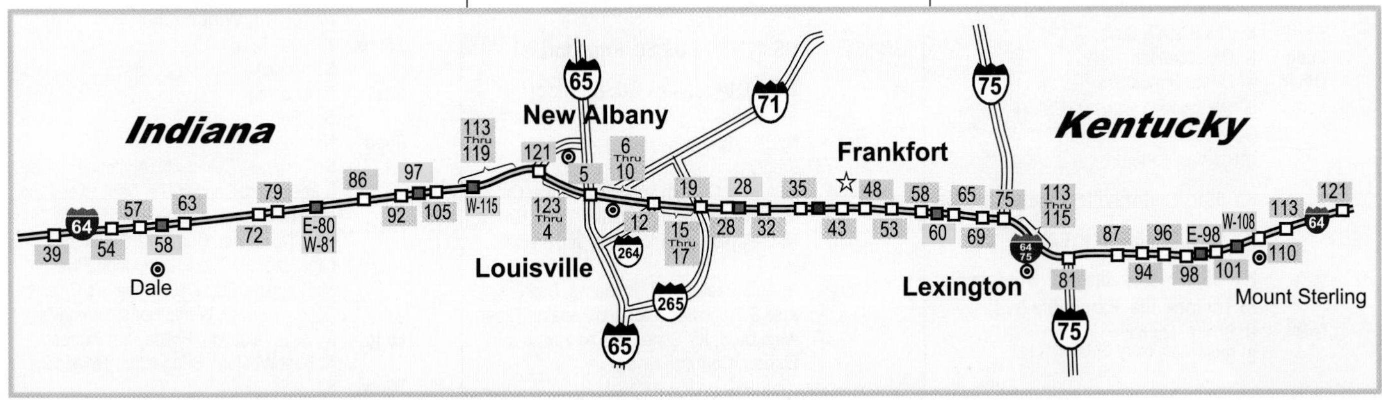

EXIT — KENTUCKY

Gas — S: BP◊, Shell, Thornton's, Meijer◊

Food — N: Arby's, Bob Evans, Burger King, Carrabba's, Chili's, Don Pablo, Lone Star Steakhouse, McDonald's, Olive Garden, Papa John's Pizza, Perkins, Romano's Macaroni Grill, TGI Friday, Waffle House
S: Applebee's, Chuck E Cheese's Pizza, Damon's, O'Charley's, Piccadilly's, Shoney's, Shogun Japanese, Starbucks, Wendy's

Lodg — N: AmeriSuites, Baymont Inn♥, Courtyard, Days Inn, Drury Inn, Holiday Inn, Red Roof Inn, Travelodge
S: Clarion Hotel, Days Inn, Extended Stay America, Hampton Inn, Marriott, Red Carpet Inn, Suburban Extended Stay

TServ — N: Cummins Cumberland
S: Clarke Detroit Diesel

Other — N: ATMs, Barnes & Noble, CompUSA, FedEx Office, Kroger, Lowe's, to Univ of Louisville/Shelby
S: ATMs, Auto Dealers, Auto Repairs, Auto Services, Banks, Cinema, CVS, Home Depot, Kroger, Office Depot, PetSmart♥, Radio Shack, Staples, Target, UPS Store, **Walmart sc**, Winn Dixie, Walgreen's

15A — KY 1747S, Hurstbourne Pkwy, Industrial Pkwy, Jeffersontown (EB)

15B — KY 1747S, Hurstbourne Pkwy (EB)

15C — KY 1747N, Hurstbourne Pkwy (EB)

17 — Blankenbaker Pky, Industrial Park, Jeffersontown

Gas — N: Marathon, Dairy Mart◊
S: BP, Citgo, Chevron, Shell, Thornton's◊

Food — S: Arby's, Backyard Burger, Burger King, Cracker Barrel, Kingfish, Rest, King Buffet, McDonald's, Ruby Tuesday, Subway, Taco Bell, Waffle House, Wendy's

Lodg — N: Staybridge Suites
S: Comfort Suites, Country Inn, Hampton Inn, Hilton Garden Inn, Holiday Inn Express Homestead Studio Suites♥, Jameson Inn, Microtel♥, Super 8, Wingate Inn

TServ — S: Clarke Detroit Diesel

Other — N: Bluegrass Harley Davidson
S: Sam's Club, Outlet Stores, McKendree College

(19A) — Jct I-265S, KY 841S

(19B) — Jct I-265N, KY 841N

Other — N: to **Tom Sawyer State Park**

28 — Veechdale Rd, Simpsonville

TStop — N: Pilot Travel Center #354 (Scales) **(DAND)**

Gas — S: BP◊

Food — N: Wendy's/Pilot TC, Rest/Old Stone Inn, Brandon's BBQ
S: JT's Pizza & Subs,

Lodg — N: Old Stone Inn

Other — N: Laundry/WiFi/Pilot TC

(28) — KY Welcome Center (EB)
Rest Area (WB)
(RR, Phone, Picnic, Vend, Info)

32A — KY 55S, Taylorsville, Finchville (EB)

32B — KY 55N, Shelbyville (EB)

32 — KY 55, Taylorsville Rd, Shelbyville, to Taylorsville, Finchville (WB)

Gas — N: Shell◊, Murphy
S: Shell

EXIT — KENTUCKY

Food — N: Arby's, Burger King, McDonald's, Waffle House
S: KFC, Subway, Wendy's

Lodg — N: Best Western, Country Hearth Inn, Days Inn, Ramada

Med — N: **+ Jewish Hospital**

Other — N: ATMs, Auto Dealer, Auto Service, Lee's Tire Center, **Walmart sc**, **Lake Shelby Campground▲**
S: ATMs, Bank, Auto Dealer, **to Taylorsville Lake State Park▲**

35 — KY 53, Mt Eden Rd, Shelbyville

Gas — N: BP◊, Chevron◊, Kroger
S: Shell◊

Food — N: BBQ, Cracker Barrel, McDonald's, Subway, Waffle House
S: FastFood/Shell

Lodg — S: Holiday Inn Express

Other — N: Kroger

(38) — Weigh Station (Both dir)

43 — KY 395, Waddy, Peytona, Shelbyville

TStop — N: Flying J Travel Plaza #5036/Conoco (Scales)
S: PTP/Waddy Travel Center/Citgo (Scales)

Food — N: Rest/FastFood/FJ TP
S: CountryMkt/FastFood/Waddy TC

TWash — S: Waddy TC

TServ — S: Tires/Waddy TC

Other — N: Laundry/WiFi/**RVDump**/**LP**/FJ TP
S: Laundry/**RVDump**/Waddy TC

48 — to KY 151, to US 60, Frankfort, to US 127S, Lawrenceburg

Gas — S: BP, Chevron, Shell◊

Food — S: Subway/Shell

Other — N: to Smith Diesel Service

53 — US 127, to Lawrenceburg, Frankfort

Gas — N: Chevron, Shell◊, Marathon, Speedway, Kroger, Murphy
S: BP, Marathon◊, Speedway

Food — N: Applebee's, Burger King, Chili's, Chuck E Cheese's Pizza, Hardee's, Longhorn Steakhouse, McDonald's, O'Charley's, Panera Bread, Pizza Hut, Quiznos, Steak 'n Shake, Shoney's, Subway, Taco Bell

Lodg — N: Best Value Inn, Days Inn, Hampton Inn, Holiday Inn Express, Marriott, Super 8

Med — N: **+ Frankfort Regional Medical Center**

Other — N: Advance Auto, Auto Services, ATMs, Carwash, Convention Center, Goodyear, Home Depot, Kmart, Kroger, Lowe's, Natures Way, Pharmacy, Office Depot **Walmart sc**, UPS Store, Capital City Airport✈, KY State Univ, State Capitol, **KY State Hwy Patrol Post**
S: Harrod's Diesel & Towing, Auto Service, Animal Hospital♥

53A — US 127S, to Lawrenceburg

53B — US 127N, to US 60, Frankfort

58 — US 60, Versailles Rd, Frankfort, Versailles

Gas — N: BP◊, Chevron◊, Marathon, Shell, Kroger

Food — N: Arby's, Captain D's, KFC, Market Café, McDonald's, Sandy's Steaks, White Castle

Lodg — N: Best Western, Bluegrass Inn, Fairfield Inn

Other — N: Auto Dealers, ATMs, Banks, Barker's Auto & Truck Service, Auto Repairs, Tires, Winn Dixie, KY State Univ, **to appr 5 mi: Elkhorn Campground▲**

EXIT — KENTUCKY

(60) — Rest Area (Both dir)
(RR, Phones, Vend)

65 — KY 341, to US 421, US 62W, Midway, Versailles

FStop — S: Midway Travel Center/Citgo

Other — S: Midway College

69 — US 62E, Paynes Depot Rd, Georgetown

Other — N: Georgetown College

NOTE: I-64 runs below with I-75 for 7mi. Exit #'s follows I-75.

(75) — Jct I-75N, to Cincinnati (EB)

Other — N: **to Kentucky Horse Park▲**

115 — KY 922, Newtown Pike, Lexington

Gas — E: Exxon◊, Shell
W: Chevron◊

Food — E: Cracker Barrel, McDonald's, Subway, Waffle House
W: Denny's, JWS Steakhouse, Post Rest

Lodg — E: Knights Inn, La Quinta Inn♥, Starwood Hotel & Resort
W: Embassy Suites, Holiday Inn, Marriott

TServ — S: Kentuckianna Truck & Trailer Repair, Whayne Power Systems, Volvo/GMC

Other — W: Auto Services
S: Truck & Auto Repairs, **Five Star RV Rental**

113 — US 27, US 68, Broadway, Paris Pike, Lexington, Paris

Gas — E: BP◊, Food Mart, Speedway, Thornton's
W: Chevron◊, Shell

Food — E: Waffle House, Rest/Ramada
W: Burger King, Fazoli's, Hardee's, Long John Silver, Penn Station E Coast Subs, Shoney's, Subway, Waffle House

Lodg — E: Ramada Inn
W: Catalina Motel, Congress Inn Motel, Days Inn, Red Roof Inn♥

Med — E: **+ VA Hospital**

Other — E: Auto Service, Bowling
W: ATMs, Auto Dealer, Auto Services, Carwash, Greyhound, Kroger, **Bluegrass RV/Cruise America**, **Northside RV**, to Univ of KY, Rupp Arena

(81/111) — Jct I-75S, to Knoxville (WB)
Jct I-64E, to Winchester, Ashland, Huntington, WV (LEFT Exit)

NOTE: I-64 runs above with I-75 for 7mi. Exit #'s follows I-75.

87 — KY 859, Bluegrass Station, Lexington Army Depot

94 — KY 1958, Truck KY 627S, Van Meter Rd, Winchester

TStop — N: Shell Food Mart #4 (Scales)
S: Speedway #8256/Marathon

Gas — N: Chevron◊
S: BP◊

Food — N: FastFood/Shell FM
S: FastFood/Speedway, Applebee's, Arby's Burger King, Captain D's, Cantuckee Diner, Domino's Pizza, El Rio Grande Rest, Fazoli's, Golden Corral, KFC, Hardee's, Little Caesars Pizza, Long John Silver, McDonald's, Pizza Hut, Popeye's Chicken, Sonic, Subway, Waffle House, Wendy's

Lodg — N: Best Value Inn, Holiday Inn Express
S: Best Western, Budget Inn, Travelodge

TServ — S: Bob Rayburn Truck Repair

◊= Regular Gas Stations with Diesel ▲ = RV Friendly Locations ♥= Pet Friendly Locations
Red print shows large vehicle parking / access on site or nearby Brown Print = Campgrounds / RV PARKS

EXIT — KENTUCKY

Med S: + Hospital
Other N: Codell Airport
S: Auto Zone, Auto Repairs, Auto Dealer, ATMs, Banks, Laundromat, Kroger, Lowe's, Office Depot, Radio Shack, Tires, **Walmart sc, to Fort Boonesborough State Park▲**

96 — KY 627, Truck KY 627N, to Winchester, Paris (EB)
TStop N: L to Ind Park: 96 Truck Stop/Citgo (Scales)
Gas N: BP◈
S: Marathon◈, Speedway
Food N: Rest/96 TS
Lodg S: Days Inn♥, Hampton Inn, Quality Inn
TWash N: 96 TS
TServ N: 96 TS/Tires, S&W Truck & Trailer Serv
Other S: Auto Dealer, Auto Services, ATMs, Banks, Grocery, Tires

96A — KY 627S, Maple St, Winchester (WB)

96B — KY 627N, Paris Rd, to Paris (WB)

98 — Bert T Combs Mountain Pkwy (EB)

(98) — Rest Area (EB)
(RR, Phones, Picnic, Vend)

101 — US 60, Winchester

(108) — Rest Area (WB)
(RR, Phones, Picnic, Vend)

110 — US 460, KY 11, Mt Sterling
Gas N: Chevron, Shell◈
S: BP◈, Exxon, Marathon, Speedway
Food N: **Cracker Barrel**, Krystal/Shell
S: Applebee's, Arby's, Burger King, Golden Corral, Hardee's, Huddle House, KFC, Long John Silver, McDonald's, Taco Bell
Lodg N: Fairfield Inn, Ramada Ltd
S: Budget Inn, Days Inn♥
Med S: **+ Mary Chiles Hospital**
Other S: Advance Auto, Auto Repairs, ATMs, Banks, Food Lion, **Walmart sc, to** Mt Sterling Montgomery Co Airport

113 — US 60, Midland Trail, Mt Sterling
FStop N: Super Express Stop #5/Chevron
TStop N: Pilot Travel Center #41 (Scales)
Food N: McDonald's/Subway/Pilot TC, Deli/Spr Exp Stop
Other N: Laundry/WiFi/Pilot TC

121 — KY 36, Owingsville, Frenchburg
TStop N: Appco/Marathon
Gas N: BP◈, Citgo◈
Food N: DQ, McDonald's, Subway
Lodg N: Best Western
Other N: Dollar General, Laundromat, Pharmacy

123 — US 60, Owingsville, to Salt Lick
Gas N: Chevron◈

EXIT — KENTUCKY

133 — KY 801, Morehead, to Sharkey, Farmers
TStop S: Eagle Travel Plaza (Scales)
Food S: Diner/Eagle TP
Lodg S: Comfort Inn
Other **S: to Outpost RV Park & Campground▲, Cave Run Lake RV Outlet, COE/Twin Knobs Rec Area▲, COE/Zilpo Rec Area▲**

137 — KY 32, Flemingsburg Rd, Morehead, to Flemingsburg
Gas N: BP
S: BP, Chevron◈, Exxon◈
Food N: Cutter's Road House, DQ
S: Burger King, China Star, Domino's Pizza, Hardee's, KFC, McDonald's, Papa John's Pizza, Jim Bo's Rest, Shoney's, Taco Bell
Lodg S: Days Inn, Holiday Inn Express, Knights Inn, Quality Inn, Mountain Lodge, Super 8
Other N: Big Lots, Kroger
Other S: Dollar General, Food Lion, Goodyear, Radio Shack, **Walmart**, **KY State Police Post**, Morehead St Univ

(141) — Rest Area (Both dir)
(RR, Phones, Picnic, Vend)

(147) — Weigh Station (Both dir)

156 — KY 2, KY 59, Olive Hill, Vanceburg
TStop S: Smokey Valley Truck Stop
Food S: Rest/Smokey Valley TS

161 — US 60, KY 182, to Olive Hill
TStop N: Appco #80 (Scales)
Gas S: Marathon◈
Other N: **Carter Caves State Resort Park▲**

172 — KY 1, KY 7, to AA Hwy, KY 9, Grayson, Maysville, Vanceburg
TStop N: First Class Travel Center/Citgo, Super Quik 8
S: Love's Travel Stop #418 (Scales)
Gas S: BP, Chevron, Exxon, Marathon, Speedway
Food N: FastFood/First Class TC, Domino's Pizza, Huddle House, KFC, Long John Silver, Shoney's, Subway, Western Steer
S: Wendy's/Love's TS, Arby's, Burger King, China House, DQ, Hardee's, KFC, McDonald's, Pizza Hut, Subway
Lodg N: American Inn, Country Squire Inn, Days Inn, Holiday Inn Express, Quality Inn
S: Super 8
TServ N: Clay's Tire, Grayson Tire & Svc Center, Grayson Truck Repair, CR Truck Sales, Interstate Truck Supply
S: Halls Bros

EXIT — KY / WV

TWash S: Miller's TW
Other N: **LP**/SuperQuik8, Dollar General, Dollar Tree, Grocery, ATMs, **Valley Breeze RV Campground▲, to Greenbo Lake State Park Resort**
S: WiFi/Love's TS, Auto Zone, Dollar General, Dollar Tree, Family Dollar, RiteAid, **to Grayson Lake State Park▲**

(173) — KY Welcome Center (WB)
Rest Area (EB)
(RR, Phones, Picnic, Vend)

179 — KY 67, Industrial Pkwy

181 — US 60, Grayson, Princess, Rush
TStop N: Exit 181 BP
Gas S: Marathon
Food N: Deli/Exit 181 TS

185 — KY 180, Catlettsburg, to Ashland
FStop N: Super Quik 24hr One Stop, Clark's Pump & Shop #21/BP
TStop S: Flying J Travel Plaza #5118 (Scales)
Gas N: Chevron
Food N: Subway/DQ/SQ, Arby's, Bob Evans, Burger King, Hardee's, Taco Bell, Wendy's
S: CountryMarket/FastFood/FJ TP
Lodg N: Budget Inn, Days Inn, Fairfield Inn, Hampton Inn, Holiday Inn Express, Knights Inn
TServ N: Whayne Power Systems
Other N: **LP**/SuperQuick9, Carwash/Super Quik, ATMs, **Walmart sc**, Animal Hospital♥, **KY State Police Post**,
S: Laundry/WiFi/**RVDump**/**LP**/FJ TP

191 — US 23, to Ashland, Louisa
Gas N: Exxon, Go Mart, Marathon◈, Speedway
Food N: Burger King, McDonald's, Subway, Waffle House
Lodg N: Holiday Inn Express, Quality Inn, Ramada Ltd
Med N: **+ Hospital**
Other N: RiteAid

EASTERN TIME ZONE

NOTE: MM 192: West Virginia State Line

⬆ KENTUCKY
⬇ WEST VIRGINIA

EASTERN TIME ZONE

1 — US 52S, WV 75, Kenova, Ceredo
Gas N: Exxon
Food N: Burger King, McDonald's, Pizza Hut
Lodg N: Hollywood Motel

Kentucky — Morehead — Huntington — Charleston — Beckley — *West Virginia*
123, 133, 137, 64, 141, 156, 161, 172, 173, 179, 181, 185, 191, 1, 6, 8, E-10, 11, 15, 18, 20, 28, 34, 37, 39, 40, 44 Thru 50, 53 Thru 58, 59, 77, 79, 101, 100, 99 Thru 96, 64, 95, 89 Thru 79, 74, 72, 69, 66 Thru 54, 48, 45, 44 Thru 42, 40, 121, 124, 125

◈ = Regular Gas Stations with Diesel ▲ = RV Friendly Locations ♥ = Pet Friendly Locations
Red print shows large vehicle parking / access on site or nearby Brown Print = Campgrounds / RV PARKS

EXIT — **WEST VIRGINIA**

Other N: Auto Repairs, Kenova RV & Auto Repair, ATM, Bank, SavALot, **Getaway RV Rentals**
S: Tri-State Airport✈, Rental Cars: Avis, Budget, Hertz, National

6 — US 52N, W Huntington, Ironton OH
Gas N: GoMart, Marathon, Shell, Speedway
Food N: DQ, Hardee's, Pizza Hut, Shoney's
Lodg N: Coach's Inn
Med N: + Hospital
Other N: Auto & Truck Services, Radio Museum, Tires, to Lawrence Co Airpark✈

8 — WV 152S, WV 527N, 5th St E
Gas S: Speedway
Food S: DQ, Laredo Steaks & Seafood
Med N: + Family Urgent Care Clinic
Other N: Huntington Museum of Art
S: Grocery

(10) — WV Welcome Center (EB)
(RR, Phones, Picnic, Vend)

(11) — Weigh Station (EB)

11 — WV 10, Hal Greer Blvd, Downtown
Gas N: BP, Chevron, Shell
Food N: Arby's, Bob Evans, Hugo's Pizza, McDonald's, Wendy's
Lodg N: Ramada Ltd, Super 8
Med N: + Cabell Huntington Hospital
Other N: to Marshall Univ, Civic Center
S: **Beech Fork State Park▲**

15 — US 60, 29th St E, Midland Trail, Huntington, Barboursville
FStop N: Go Mart #59
Gas N: Sunoco
S: Exxon
Food N: Arby's, Omelette Shoppe, Pizza Hut, Ponderosa, Wendy's, Rest/Econo Lodge
S: Golden Corral, KFC, McDonald's, Shoney's, Taco Bell
Lodg N: Colonial Inn Motel, Econo Lodge
S: Days Inn, Red Roof Inn♥, Stone Lodge
Med N: + Hospital
Other S: Auto Dealers, CVS, Grocery, Pharmacy, UPS Store, **Walmart**, **Hidden Trails Campground▲**, **Setzers RV World of Camping**

18 — US 60, to WV 2, Merrick Creek Rd, Barboursville
Gas S: Chevron
S: Hardee's
Other S: Home Depot, Kroger, Target

20 — US 60, Mall Rd, Barboursville (WB)
Gas N: Chevron, Exxon
S: BP, Exxon
Food N: Applebee's, Arby's, Bob Evans, Burger King, Chili's, CiCi's Pizza, China Max, Fiesta Bravo, Fuddrucker's, IHOP, Logan's Roadhouse, McDonald's, Olive Garden, Ruby Tuesday, Wendy's
S: Cracker Barrel, Gino's, Ponderosa, Subway, TCBY, Taco Bell
Lodg N: Comfort Inn, Holiday Inn, Ramada Inn
S: Best Western, Hampton Inn
Med N: + Emergi-Care Walk-In Med Ctr
Other N: Best Buy, Borders, Firestone, Lowe's, Huntington Mall, **Walmart sc**
S: Auto Dealer

20A — US 60W, West Mall Rd (EB)

20B — US 60E, East Mall Rd (EB)

28 — US 60, CR 13, Mason Rd, Milton
Gas S: Chevron, Exxon, Go Mart, Shell

Personal Notes

EXIT — **WEST VIRGINIA**

Food S: DQ, Granny K's Rest, McDonald's, Pizza Hut, Subway, Wendy's
Other S: Auto Services, Laundromat, Grocery, Pharmacy, **Huntington/Fox Fire KOA▲**

34 — CR 19, Hurricane Creek Rd, Teays Valley Rd, Hurricane
Gas N: Chevron
S: Chevron, Exxon, Shell, Sunoco
Food S: McDonald's, Pizza Hut, Subway
Lodg S: Days Inn, Super 8, Smiley's Motel
Med S: + Hospital
Other S: Auto Services, ATMs, Banks

(37) — Rest Area (Both dir)
(RR, Phones, Pic, Vend, **RVDump**)

(38) — Weigh Station (Both dir)

39 — WV 34, Hurricane, Scott Depot, Winfield, Teays Valley
FStop N: Go Mart #43
TStop S: Travel Center of America/76 (Scales)
Gas S: Exxon, Go Mart
Food N: Arby's/BP, Applebee's, Bob Evans, Hardee's, Rio Grande
S: CountryPride/TA TC, Burger King, Captain D's, Creek Side Café, Fazoli's, KFC, McDonald's, Kobe Japanese, Papa John's Pizza, Shoney's, Subway, Taco Bell, TCBY, Wendy's
Lodg N: Days Inn, Holiday Inn, Red Roof Inn♥
S: Hampton Inn
TServ S: TA TC/Tires
Med S: + Health Plus Walk-In Clinic
Other N: Advance Auto Parts, Grocery, Laundromat, US Post Office
S: Laundry/WiFi/TA TC, ATMs, Auto & Truck Services, Kroger, Pharmacy,

EXIT — **WEST VIRGINIA**

40 — US 35, Winfield, Pt Pleasant

44 — WV 817, St Albans
Gas S: Chevron◈

45 — WV 25, 1st Ave, Nitro
TStop N: Pilot Travel Center #243 (Scales)
Gas S: BP, Exxon
Food N: Arby's/TJCinn/Pilot TC, Hardee's
S: Biscuit World, Checkers, Gino's Pizza, McDonald's, Subway, Wendy's
Lodg S: Econo Lodge
Med S: + Modern Medicine Walk-In Clinic
Other N: Laundry/WiFi/Pilot TC

47 — WV 622, Goff Mountain Rd, Charleston (WB)
Gas N: Chevron, Exxon, Shell, Speedway
Food N: Biscuit World, Bob Evans, Captain D's, Domino's Pizza, Hardee's, McDonald's, Pizza Hut, Taco Bell, Wendy's
S: Arby's, Burger King, Cracker Barrel, CoCo's, DQ, Golden Corral, KFC, Shoney's, TGI Friday
Lodg N: Motel 6♥
S: Comfort Inn, Sleep Inn
TServ S: Mountain International
Med N: + Health Plus Walk-In Clinic
Other N: Auto & Tire Services/Repairs, Advance Auto Parts, CVS, Kroger,
S: Lowe's, **Walmart sc**, Dog Racetrack

47A — WV 622S, Goff Mountain Rd (EB)

47B — WV 622N, Cross Lanes (EB)

50 — WV 25, Fairlawn Ave, Institute
Gas S: Go Mart
Other S: WV State Univ

53 — WV 25, 10th St, Dunbar
Gas S: Go Mart
Food S: Captain D's, McDonald's, Shoney's, Subway, Wendy's
Lodg S: Super 8♥, Travelodge
Other S: Advance Auto Parts, CVS, Kroger, Police

54 — US 60, to WV 601, MacCorkle Ave, Jefferson Rd, Charleston
Gas S: Chevron, Citgo
Food N: Subway, TCBY
S: Bob Evans, KFC, Long John Silver, McDonald's, Taco Bell, Wendy's
Lodg N: Red Roof Inn♥
S: Days Inn
TServ S: Cummins Cumberland
Med N: + Health Plus Walk-In Clinic
S: + Thomas Memorial Hospital
Other N: Auto Dealers, Kroger
S: SavALot, Tires

55 — to WV 601, Kanawha Turnpike (WB)

56 — Montrose Dr, S Charleston
Gas N: Chevron, Exxon◈, SuperAmerica
Food N: Hardee's, Shoney's
Lodg N: Microtel, Ramada Plaza, Wingate Inn
S: Holiday Inn Express
Other N: Advance Auto Parts, Pharmacy

58A — US 119S, Oakwood Rd, Logan

58B — US 119N, Virginia St, Civic Ctr (EB)
Lodg S: Hampton Inn, Holiday Inn

58C — US 60, Lee St, Civic Center (EB) / US 60, Washington St (WB)
Gas N: BP, Exxon, GoMart
Med S: + Hospital

◈ = Regular Gas Stations with Diesel ▲ = RV Friendly Locations ♥ = Pet Friendly Locations
Red print shows large vehicle parking / access on site or nearby **Brown Print = Campgrounds / RV PARKS**

EXIT		WEST VIRGINIA
NOTE:		I-64 below follows I-77 between Charleston and Beckley. Exit #'s follow I-77.
(59/ 101)		**to Jct I-77N, Jct I-79N, Parkersburg, Clarksburg, Jct I-64W, to Huntington**
100		**Broad St, Capitol St**
	Gas	E: Chevron
	Food	E: Ponderosa
	Lodg	E: Fairfield Inn, Holiday Inn, Super 8
	Med	W: + St Francis Hospital
	Other	W: Auto Services, ATMs, CVS, Charles Town Center Mall, Kroger, Towing,
99		**WV 114, Greenbrier St, State Capitol**
	Gas	W: Citgo, Exxon
	Food	W: Domino's Pizza, Subway, Wendy's
	Other	W: Yeager Airport✈, Laidley Field, State Museum
98		**WV 61, 35th St Bridge (SB) (EB)**
	Gas	W: Sunoco
	Food	W: McDonald's, Shoney's, Subway, TacoBell/KFC, Wendy's
	Med	W: + Hospital
	Other	W: Univ of Charleston, WVU Charleston
97		**US 60W, Midland Trail, Kanawha Blvd, Charleston (NB) (WB)**
(96)		**WV Turnpike Begin/End**
96		**US 60E, Midland Trail, Belle**
	Food	E: Gino's Pizza
	Lodg	E: Budget Host Inn
	TServ	E: Walker Machinery
95		**WV 61, MacCorkle Ave**
	FStop	E: Go-Mart #31
	Gas	E: BP W: Ashland, Chevron, Exxon, GoMart
	Food	E: Bob Evans, Burger King, IHOP, Lone Star Steakhouse, McDonalds W: Applebee's, Captain D's, Cracker Barrel, Hooters, La Carreta Mexican Rest, Ponderosa, Shoney's, Southern Kitchen
	Lodg	E: Comfort Suites, Country Inn, Days Inn, Hawthorn Inn, Knights Inn, Motel 6♥, Red Roof Inn♥
	Other	E: Advance Auto Parts W: Kroger, Lowe's, NAPA, Mall, WVU Charleston, Univ of Charleston
89		**WV 61, WV 94, Marmet, Chesapeake**
	FStop	E: Market Express #7/Exxon
	Gas	E: Go-Mart, Shell, Sunoco
	Food	E: Subway/Exxon, Biscuit World, Gino's Pizza, Hardee's, KFC, Subway, Wendy's
	Other	E: Kroger, Pharmacy, Marmet Locks & Dam, Kanawha River
85		**US 60, WV 61, Chelyan, East Bank**
	Gas	E: GoMart◈
	Food	E: McDonald's, Shoney's
	Other	E: Kroger
(82)		**TOLL Plaza**
79		**CR 79/3, Cabin Creek Rd, Sharon**
74		**WV 83, Paint Creek Rd, Montgomery**
(72)		**Service Plaza (NB) (WB)**
	FStop	N: Exxon
	Food	N: Burger King, Starbucks, TCBY
	Other	N: RVDump

EXIT		WEST VIRGINIA
(69)		**Rest Area (SB) (EB)** (RR, Phones, Picnic)
66		**WV 15, Mahan**
	Gas	E: Sunoco
60		**WV 612, Mossy, Oak Hill**
	Gas	E: Exxon
(55)		**TOLL Plaza**
54		**CR 2, CR 23, Pax, Mt Hope**
	Gas	W: BP
48		**US 19N, N Beckley, Summersville** (Addt'l Serv E US 19/WV 16)
	Gas	E: BP◈
	Food	E: Subway/BP
	Lodg	E: Ramada Inn
(45)		**Service Plaza (Both dir)**
	TStop	S: Exxon
	Food	S: Biscuit World, Starbucks, TCBY
44		**WV 3, Harper Rd, Beckley**
	TStop	W: Go-Mart #50
	Gas	E: Chevron◈, Exxon, Marathon, Shell W: BP
	Food	E: Applebee's, Burger King, Hibachi Japanese Steakhouse, McDonald's, Omelet Shoppe, Outback Steakhouse, Pizza Hut, Western Steer W: Bob Evans, Cracker Barrel, Wendy's
	Lodg	E: Best Western, Comfort Inn, Courtyard, Fairfield Inn, Holiday Inn, Howard Johnson, Quality Inn, Super 8 W: Days Inn, Hampton Inn, Microtel, Park Inn
	Med	E: + Raleigh General Hospital
	Other	E: ATMs, Kroger, to Beckley Exhibition Coal Mine & Campground▲ W: Bob's Truck & Car Repairs, CVS, Kroger, College of WV
42		**WV 16, WV 97, Robert C Byrd Dr, Beckley, Mabscott**
	Gas	W: Amoco
	Food	W: Subway
	TServ	E: Walker Machinery
	Med	E: + VA Medical Center
	Other	W: to Twin Falls Resort State Park▲
(40/ 121)		**Jct I-64E, to Lewisburg Jct I-77S, Bluefield, Charleston (WB)**
NOTE:		I-64 above follows I-77 between Charleston and Beckley. Exit #'s follow I-77.
124		**US 19, Eisenhower Dr, Beckley** NOTE: Last FREE Exit WB
	Gas	N: Exxon, GoMart, Speedway
	Lodg	N: Honey Rock Motel, Pinecrest Motel
125		**WV 307, Airport Rd, Beaver (WB)**
	Gas	N: Shell S: Chevron, Exxon, GoMart
	Food	S: Hardee's, McDonald's, Pizza Hut
	Lodg	N: Sleep Inn S: Patriot Motel
	Other	N: Raleigh Co Memorial Airport✈
125A		**WV 307, Beaver (EB)**
125B		**Airport Rd (EB)**
129		**CR 9, Grandview Rd, Beaver (WB)**
	Gas	S: Exxon, Shell
	Other	N: Grandview State Park▲ S: Little Beaver State Park▲
129A		**CR 9S, Shady Spring (EB)**

EXIT		WEST VIRGINIA
129B		**CR 9N, Grandview Rd (EB)**
133		**CR 27, Pluto Rd, Bragg**
NOTE:		ALL TRUCKS MUST STOP (EB)
139		**CR 7, WV 20, Green Sulphur Springs, Sandstone, Hinton**
	Gas	S: Citgo◈
	Other	S: to Bass Lake Park▲, Bluestone State Park▲, Pipestem State Park▲, Rock Ridge Resort▲
143		**WV 20, Green Sulphur Springs, Meadow Bridge, Rainelle**
	Gas	N: Chevron
150		**CR 29, WV4, Dawson**
	Lodg	S: Dawson Inn & Campground▲
	Other	N: Summer Wind RV Park & Campground▲
156		**US 60, Midland Trail, Sam Black Church, Crawley, Rupert, Rainelle**
	Gas	N: Citgo◈, Exxon◈, Shell◈
161		**WV 12, Asbury, Alta**
	FStop	S: 161 Truck Stop/Chevron
	Food	S: Grandpa's Rest
	Other	S: to Greenbrier River Campground▲
169		**US 219, Lewisburg, Ronceverte**
	FStop	S: Exxon
	Gas	S: Shell
	Food	S: Applebee's, Arby's, Bob Evans, Hardee's, Shoney's, Western Sizzlin'
	Lodg	N: Days Inn S: Brier Inn, Econo Lodge, Hampton Inn, Rodeway Inn, Super 8
	Med	S: + Hospital
	Other	N: Greenbrier Valley Airport✈ S: ATMs, Auto Dealers, Cinema, Museums, Theatres, Lewisburg Fruit & Produce, Walmart sc, State Fairgrounds
175		**US 60, WV 92, White Sulphur Springs, Caldwell**
	FStop	N: Dixon's Auto Truck Stop/Shell
	Gas	N: Chevron, Exxon
	Food	N: Rest/Dixon's ATS, McDonald's, Taco Bell, Wendy's
	TServ	N: Dixon's ATS/Tires
	Other	S: to Greenbrier Mountainaire Campground▲, Greenbrier State Forest, Nat'l Radio Astronomy Observatory, Cass Scenic RR, Resort, Ski Areas
(179)		**WV Welcome Center (WB)** (RR, Phones, Picnic)
181		**US 60, WV 92, White Sulphur Springs, Caldwell (WB, diff reaccess)**
	Gas	N: Amoco, Shell
	Food	N: Hardee's, Pizza Hut, Taco Bell
	Lodg	N: Budget Inn, Old White Motel S: Allstate Motel
	Other	N: Food Lion, NAPA, Pharmacy, S: Twilight Overnite Campground▲, to Ski Areas, Nat'l Radio Astronomy Observatory
183		**VA 311, Crows (EB)**
	Other	S: to Moncove Lake State Park▲

EASTERN TIME ZONE

NOTE: MM 184: Virginia State Line

⋂ WEST VIRGINIA

◈ = Regular Gas Stations with Diesel ▲ = RV Friendly Locations ♥ = Pet Friendly Locations
Red print shows large vehicle parking / access on site or nearby Brown Print = Campgrounds / RV PARKS

VIRGINIA

EASTERN TIME ZONE

1 — **VA 198, Jerrys Runs Tr, Covington**

(2) — **VA Welcome Center (EB)**
(RR, Phones, Picnic)

7 — **VA 661, Midland Trail, Covington**

10 — **US 60E, VA 159S, to VA 311, Covington, to Callahan**
- Gas — S: Marathon◈
- Other — S: LP/Marathon

14 — **VA 154, Durant Rd, Covington, to Hot Springs**
- Gas — N: Exxon, Sunoco
- Food — N: Arby's/ Exxon, Hardee's, KFC, Little Caesars Pizza, Subway, Wendy's
- Lodg — N: Budget Motel, Town House Motel
- Other — N: Auto Zone, Auto Services, ATMs, CVS, Banks, Carwash, Family Dollar, Kroger
  S: Dollar Tree, **Walmart sc**

16 — **US 60W, US 220N, Covington, to Hot Springs**
- Gas — N: Amoco, Exxon, Shell
- Food — N: Burger King/Exxon, Western Sizzlin'
  S: Long John Silver, McDonald's
- Lodg — N: Best Value Inn, Best Western, Holiday Inn Express, Highland Motel, Pinehurst Motel
  S: Comfort Inn
- Other — S: Dollar General, Radio Shack

16B — **US 60W, US 220N, Covington (WB)**

21 — **VA 696, Covington, Lowmoor**
- Med — S: + Alleghany Regional Hospital

24 — **US 60E, US 220S, Clifton Forge**
- Gas — S: Shell◈
- Food — S: Hardee's, Taco Bell
- Other — N: Lancaster Comm College
  S: Amtrak, Auto Repairs, ATMs

27 — **US 60W Bus, US 220S, VA 629 Clifton Forge**
- Gas — S: Citgo◈, Exxon
- Other — N: to **Douthat State Park▲**

29 — **VA 269E, VA 42N, Clifton Forge**
- Gas — S: Exxon◈
- Food — S: Rest/Exxon
- Other — S: Repairs/Exxon

(33) — **Truck Parking Area (EB)**

35 — **VA 269, VA 850, Clifton Forge, Longdale Furnace**

43 — **VA 780, Goshen**

50 — **US 60, VA 623, Lexington**
(All Serv 3.5-5 mi S US 60 in Lexington)

55 — **US 11, to VA 39, Lexington, Goshen**
- Gas — N: Exxon◈
  S: Citgo◈, Texaco
- Food — N: Burger King, Ruby Tuesday, Waffle House
  S: Subway/Citgo, Applebee's, DQ, Redwood Family Rest, Shoney's
- Lodg — N: Best Western, Country Inn, Sleep Inn, Super 8♥, Wingate Inn
  S: Best Western, Comfort Inn, Country Inn, Econo Lodge, Holiday Inn Express
- Med — S: + Stonewall Jackson Hospital
- Other — N: ATMs, Auto Dealer, Banks, Blue Ridge Animal Clinic♥, Dollar Tree, Radio Shack, **Walmart sc**, **to Long's Campground▲**
  S: ATMs, Auto Service, Bank, **to** VA Military Institute, Washington & Lee Univ

NOTE: I-64 runs below with I-81. Exit #'s follow I-81.

(56/191) — **Jct I-81S, Roanoke**
Jct I-64W, Lewisburg WV, Beckley, to US 60, Charleston (NB, LEFT Exit)

195 — **US 11, Lee Hwy, Lexington**
- TStop — W: Lee Hi Travel Plaza/Shell (Scales)
- Gas — W: Citgo
- Food — E: Maple Hall Lodging & Dining
  W: Rest/Lee TP, Rest/Howard Johnson
- Lodg — E: Lexington Historic Inn, Maple Hall
  W: Days Inn, Howard Johnson, Ramada
- TServ — W: Lee Hi TP/Tires, VA Truck Center
- Other — W: Laundry/WiFi/**RVDump/RVPark**/Lee Hi TP

(199) — **Rest Area (WB) (SB)**
(RR, Phones, Picnic, Vend)

200 — **VA 710, Fairfield**
- FStop — W: Fairfield Exxon, Stop in Food Store #62/Shell
- Gas — E: BP
- Food — E: McDonald's/BP, Whistlestop Cafe
  W: Subway/Exxon
- TServ — W: Smith's Garage

205 — **VA 606, Raphine, Steeles Tavern**
- FStop — E: Orchard Creek Auto RV Plaza/Exxon
- TStop — E: Gas City, White's AmBest Truck Stop (Scales)
  W: WilcoHess Travel Plaza #735 (Scales)
- Gas — E: Sunoco
- Food — E: Rest/White's TS, Burger King/Orchard Creek
  W: Wendy's/WilcoHess TP, Rest/Days Inn
- Lodg — E: Motel/White's TS
  W: Days Inn, Howard Johnson
- TServ — E: White's TS/Tires/TWash
  W: Peterbilt
- Other — E: Laundry/White's TS, **Montebello Camping & Fish Resort▲**, **to Tye River Gap Campground▲**, **Crabtree Falls Campground▲**

213 — **US 11, to US 340N, Lee Jackson Memorial Hwy, Greenville, to Mint Spring, Waynesboro (NB)**
- TStop — E: Pilot Travel Center #396 (Scales)
- Gas — E: BP, Shell
- Food — E: Arby's/Pilot TC, Subway/BP, German Rest
- Lodg — E: Budget Host Inn
- Other — E: Laundry/WiFi/Pilot TC, **to Shenandoah Acres Resort▲**

213A — **US 11S, Greenville (SB)**

213B — **US 11N, Greenville (SB)**

217 — **VA 654, Mint Spring, Stuarts Draft**
- TStop — W: Kangaroo Express/Citgo
- Gas — E: BP, Exxon
- Food — E: Subway/BP
  W: AuntM's/Kangaroo
- Lodg — E: Days Inn
  W: Relax Inn
- Other — E: **to Walnut Hills Campground▲**, **Shenandoah Acres Resort▲**

220 — **VA 262, to US 11, Staunton**
- Gas — W: BP, Citgo, Exxon
- Food — W: Burger King, Hardee's, Hong Kong Buffet, McDonald's, Red Lobster
- Lodg — W: Budget Inn, Hampton Inn, Microtel
- Other — W: Advance Auto Parts, Shenandoah Harley Davidson

(221/87) — **Jct I-64E, Charlottesville, Richmond**
Jct I-81N, to Winchester

NOTE: I-64 above runs with I-81. Exit #'s follow I-81.

91 — **VA 608, Tinkling Spring Rd, Fisherville, Stuarts Draft**
- Gas — N: Shell
  S: Exxon, Sheetz
- Food — S: McDonald's/Exxon
- Lodg — N: Hampton Inn
- Med — N: + Augusta Medical Center

94 — **US 340, Waynesboro, Stuarts Draft**
- Gas — N: 7-11, Exxon
  S: Shell
- Food — N: Arby's, Burger King, Cracker Barrel, KFC, Japanese Steakhouse, McDonald's, Shoney's, Wendy's, Western Sizzlin

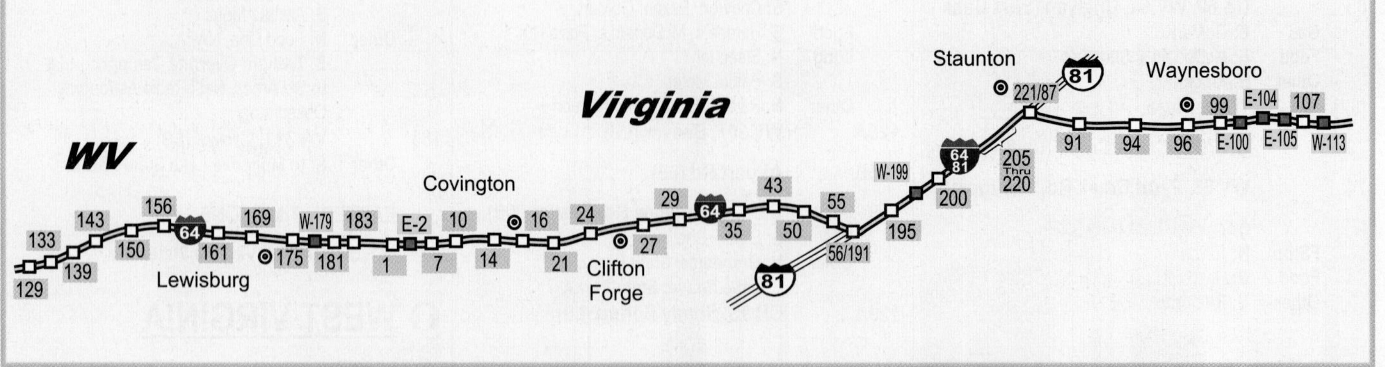

◈= Regular Gas Stations with Diesel ▲ = RV Friendly Locations ♥ = Pet Friendly Locations
Red print shows large vehicle parking / access on site or nearby Brown Print = Campgrounds / RV PARKS

EXIT		VIRGINIA
	Lodg	N: Days Inn, Holiday Inn Express, Super 8
	Med	N: + Hospital
	Other	N: Waynesboro Muni Airport✈, Vet♥, Brooks Auto & Truck Repair Center
		S: Ladd Auto & Truck Repair, Museum
96		**VA 624, Mt Torry Rd, Waynesboro, to Lyndhurst** (Trucks use lower gear on exit)
	Gas	N: Shell
	Food	N: Quality Inn
99		**US 250, Blue Ridge Pky, Skyline Dr, Waynesboro, Afton**
	Food	N: Colony House Motel
	Lodg	N: Colony House Motel
		S: Afton Inn
(100)		**Parking Area (EB) (NO Trucks/Bus)**
(104)		**Parking Area (EB) (NO Trucks/Bus)**
(105)		**Rest Area (EB)** (RR, Phones, Picnic, Vend)
107		**US 250, Rockfish Gap Tpk, Crozet**
	Gas	N: to Exxon
	Other	S: Misty Mountain Camp Resort▲
(113)		**Rest Area (WB)** (RR, Phones, Picnic, Vend)
114		**VA 637, Dick Woods Rd, Charlottesville, Ivy**
118AB		**US 29, Charlottesville, Lynchburg (Future 785)** (N Serv 2-4mi)
	Gas	N: AmocoBP, Citgo◈, Exxon, Shell
		S: Exxon◈
	Food	N: Blimpie, Hardee's, Shoney's, Subway
	Lodg	N: Best Western, Budget Inn, English Inn, Econo Lodge
	Med	N: + Univ of VA Medical Center
	Other	N: VA State Hwy Patrol Post, to Univ of VA
		S: Charlottesville KOA▲
120		**VA 631, 5th St, Charlottesville**
	Gas	N: Exxon◈, Shell
	Food	N: Amigos, Burger King, Domino's Pizza, Hardee's, Jade Garden, McDonald's, Taco Bell, Waffle House, Wendy's
	Lodg	N: Affordable Suites, Holiday Inn, Sleep Inn
	Other	N: Amtrak, CVS, Family Dollar, Food Lion, Greyhound, Laundromat, ATMs, Banks, Service Pro Auto & Truck Repair
121		**VA 20, Charlottesville (WB)**
	Gas	N: Amoco◈
		S: Exxon
	Med	N: + Martha Jefferson Hospital
	Other	N: Auto Repairs
		S: Visitor Center, Charlottesville KOA▲, to Monticello, Thomas Jefferson Home
121AB		**VA 20, Charlottesville, Scottsville**
124		**US 250, Richmond Rd, Charlottesvill Jefferson Hwy, Shadwell**
	Gas	N: Amoco, Shell, WilcoHess
	Food	N: Applebee's, Aunt Sarah's Pancake House, Burger King, McDonald's, Quiznos, Sticks Kebob Shop, Taco Bell, Tip Top Rest
	Lodg	N: Hilton Garden Inn
		S: Comfort Inn, Ramada Inn
	Med	N: + Hospital
129		**VA 616, Keswick, Boyd Tavern**
	Gas	S: BP
	Lodg	N: Keswick Hotel
	Other	S: Auto Repairs

EXIT		VIRGINIA
136		**US 15, James Madison Hwy, Zion Crossroad, Gordonsville, Palmyra**
	FStop	S: Crossing Point Citgo
	Gas	S: BP◈, Exxon◈, Shell◈
	Food	S: Burger King/Exxon, Blimpie/Citgo, McDonald's/BP, Rest/Crescent Inn
	Lodg	S: Crescent Inn, Zion Cross Roads Motel
	Other	S: WiFi/Crossing Point, Auto Repairs
143		**VA 208, Louisa, Ferncliff**
	Gas	S: Citgo◈, Exxon◈
	Other	N: to 7mi Small Country Campground▲
148		**VA 605, Shannon Hill Rd, Louisa**
152		**Old Fredericksburg Rd, to US 250, Goochland, Hadensville**
159		**US 522, Cross Country Rd, Gum Spring, Goochland, Jackson**
	Gas	N: Exxon◈
167		**VA 617, Oilville Rd, Oilville, Goochland**
	Gas	N: Exxon◈
		S: AmocoBP◈
(168)		**Rest Area (WB)** (RR, Phones, Picnic, Vend)
(169)		**Rest Area (EB)** (RR, Phones, Picnic, Vend)
173		**VA 623, Ashland Rd, Rockville**
	Gas	N: Citgo
		S: BP◈, Exxon◈, Shell◈
	Food	S: Bill's BBQ, Red Oak Café, Satterswhite Rest
	Other	N: Auto Repairs, Towing
		S: ATMs, Banks, Dollar General
175		**VA 288, Broad St, Manakin Sabot**
(177)		**Jct I-295, to I-95, to Washington, Norfolk, VA Beach, Williamsburg**
178A		**US 250S, Broad St, Richmond**
	Gas	S: 7-11, BP, Citgo
	Food	S: Baja Fresh Mex Grill, Burger King, Casa Grande, Captain D's, McDonald's, Taco Bell, TGI Friday, Wendy's
	Lodg	S: Candlewood Suites
	Other	S: ATMs, Auto Services, Banks, Best Buy, B&N, Dollar Tree, Goodyear, Home Depot, Lowe's, PetSmart♥, Regal Cinemas, Richmond Harley Davidson, Staples, Target, Tires, Walmart sc
178B		**US 250N, Broad St, Richmond**
	Gas	N: BP◈, Citgo, Exxon◈, Shell◈, Texaco
	Food	N: DQ, Great Taste Buffet, Starbucks, Thai Garden
	Lodg	N: AmeriSuites, Comfort Suites, Hilton Garden Inn, Hampton Inn
	Lodg	N: Homestead Suites♥, Marriott, Towneplace Suites
	Other	N: ATMs, Banks, Auto Services, Firestone, U-Haul
180		**Gaskins Rd, Richmond (EB)** (Addt'l Services N to Broad St)
	Gas	N: BP, Shell◈
	Food	N: DQ, Golden Corral, IHOP, O'Charley's, Ruby Tuesday
	Lodg	N: Courtyard, Fairfield Inn, Holiday Inn Express, Residence Inn, Studio Plus
	Med	N: + Universal Hospital
	Other	N: ATMs, Banks,Costco, FedEx Office, Goodyear, Lowe's, Office Depot, Sam's Club, UPS Store

EXIT		VIRGINIA
180AB		**Gaskins Rd (WB)**
181		**Parham Rd (EB) (Serv N to Broad St)**
	Med	N: + Henrico Doctors Hospital
181AB		**Parham Rd (WB)**
183		**US 250, Broad St, Glenside Dr (EB)** (Addt'l Services N to Broad St)
	Gas	N: Chevron
	Food	N: Bob Evans, McDonald's, Waffle House
	Lodg	N: Best Western, Comfort Inn, Embassy Suites, Super 8
	Med	S: + Henrico Doctors Hospital
	Other	N: CVS, Grocery, Mall,
183A		**US 250, Glenside Dr (WB)**
183B		**US 250, W Broad St (WB)**
183C		**Bethlehem Rd (WB)**
185		**US 33, Staples Mill Rd, Richmond** (Addt'l Serv S to Broad St)
	Gas	N: Exxon, Fast Fare, Texaco
		S: Shell
	Lodg	S: Holiday Inn
	Other	N: Auto & Truck Service, Amtrak, Towing
185A		**US 33, Dickens Rd (EB)**
185B		**US 33, Staples Mill Rd (EB)**
(186)		**Jct I-195S, to Powhite Pkwy, Richmond (SB/WB, LEFT exit)**
	NOTE:	I-64 below runs with I-95. Exit #'s follow I-95.
(187/79)		**Jct I-95N, to Washington (EB, LEFT exit) Jct I-64W, I-195S, Charlottesville**
78		**VA 161, N Boulevard, Hermitage Rd, Robin Hood Rd, Boulevard** (diff reaccess)
	Gas	E: Texaco
		W: BP, Citgo◈
	Food	E: Café, Zippy's
		W: Bill's Va BBQ
	Lodg	E: Holiday Inn
		W: Days Inn♥, Red Carpet Inn
	TServ	W: International, Lawrence Truck Service
	Med	E: + Richland Memorial Hospital
	Other	E: to Richmond Int'l Raceway
		W: Auto Services, U-Haul, Visitor Center, The Diamond, Parker Field
76B		**Gilmer St, W Leigh St, to US 1, US 301, Belvidere (SB)**
76A		**Chamberlayne Ave (NB)**
	Other	E: Dorsey RV
(75/190)		**Jct I-64E, VA Beach, Williamsburg, Norfolk, 7th St, N 5th St, Jct I-95S, to Rocky Hill, Miami**
	NOTE:	I-64 above runs with I-95. Exit #'s follow I-95.
192		**US 360, Mechanicsville Turnpike, Richmond, Mechanicsville**
	Gas	N: Chevron, Citgo◈
		S: BP, Citgo
	Food	N: McDonald's
		S: Church's, Hook Fish & Chips
	Other	N: Auto Services, to Richmond Int'l Raceway
		S: Auto Repairs, Sheriff Dept

◈= Regular Gas Stations with Diesel ▲ = RV Friendly Locations ♥= Pet Friendly Locations

Red print shows large vehicle parking / access on site or nearby Brown Print = Campgrounds / RV PARKS

EXIT	VIRGINIA
193AB	**VA 33, Nine Mile Rd, Richmond**
Gas	N: BP, Exxon
Food	N: Subway/Exxon, Burger King, Crab Lady, McDonald's S: Carolina BBQ
Med	S: + Richmond Community Hospital
Other	N: Auto Repairs S: Auto Repairs
195	**Laburnum Ave, to Williamsburg Rd, VA 33, US 60, VA 5, Richmond**
Gas	N: Chevron, Mobil, Shell S: BP, Exxon
Food	S: Applebee's, Burger King, China King, Hardee's, KFC, Little Caesar's Pizza, Popeye's Chicken, Shoney's, Subway, Taco Bell, Wendy's, Western Sizzlin'
Lodg	S: Airport Inn, Wyndham Garden Hotel
Other	N: Auto Repairs/Shell S: ATMs, Auto Services, Banks, CVS, Dollar General, Dollar Tree, Firestone, Grocery, Kroger, Radio Shack, RiteAid, Auto Rentals, Richmond Int'l Airport✈
197AB	**VA 156, S Airport Dr, E Nine Mile Rd, Williamsburg Rd, Sandston**
Gas	N: BP◈, Citgo, Shell◈ S: BP, Shell◈
Food	N: Bojangles Chicken, Domino's Pizza, Hardee's, Pizza Hut, Subway S: Arby's, Burger King, Ma & Pa's Diner, Waffle House
Lodg	S: Best Western, Comfort Inn, Days Inn, Econo Lodge, Hampton Inn, Homewood Suites, Microtel, Motel 6♥, Wingate Inn
Other	N: Advance Auto, CVS, Winn Dixie S: ATMs, Auto Services, Tires, Richmond Int'l Airport✈
(200)	**Jct I-295, N-Washington, DC, S to Rocky Mount, NC, US 60, VA 156**
(203)	**Weigh Station** (Both dir)
205	**New Kent Hwy, VA 33E, VA 249W, to US 60, Quinton, Bottoms Bridge**
Gas	N: BP◈, Exxon◈ S: Exxon, Shell◈
Food	N: Casa Pizza, Subway S: McDonald's
Other	N: Food Lion, US Post Office, Pharmacy
211	**VA 106, Emmaus Church Rd, Providence Forge, to Talleysville, Prince George, Hopewell**
TStop	N: Pilot Travel Center #159 (Scales)
Food	N: Subway/Pilot TC
Other	N: WiFi/Pilot TC S: Auto Service, Tires, New Kent Co Airport✈
(213)	**Rest Area** (Both dir) **(RR, Phones, Picnic, Vend)**
214	**VA 155, N Courthouse Rd, New Kent, to US 60, Providence Forge, Lanexa**
Gas	S: Exxon◈
Lodg	S: Jasmine Plantation B&B
Other	S: Colonial Downs Racetrack, **to Ed Allen's Campground▲, Rockahock Campground▲, Riverside Campground▲**
220	**VA 33E, Eltham Rd, Lanexa, to West Point**

EXIT	VIRGINIA
227	**VA 30, Old Stage Rd, Barhamsville Rd, to US 60, Toano, to West Point, Williamsburg**
FStop	S: Interstate Shell
Gas	S: Exxon◈
Food	S: McDonald's
231AB	**VA 607, to VA 30, Croaker Rd, Williamsburg, to Croaker, Norge**
Gas	N: 7-11 S: Shell◈
Food	S: Candle Factory, KFC, Trader Café, Wendy's
Other	S: **American Heritage RV Park▲, Outdoor World Williamsburg▲**
234AB	**VA 199, VA 646, Newman Rd, to Colonial Williamsburg**
Gas	S: 7-11, BP, Exxon◈, Mobil◈, Shell◈
Food	S: Blue Plate Diner, Burger King, ChickFilA, Hardee's, IHOP, KFC, Lightfoot Pancake & Steak House, McDonald's, Pierce's Pitt BBQ, Sonic, Starbucks, Subway, Top China
Lodg	S: Clarion Inn, Comfort Inn, Courtyard, Days Inn, Econo Lodge, Family Inn, Great Wolf Lodge Resort, Howard Johnson, Ramada Inn, Super 8, Travelodge
Other	N: **Williamsburg KOA▲** S: ATMs, Auto Services, Dollar General, Home Depot, Lowe's, PetCo♥, Radio Shack, Revolutionary Harley Davidson, **Walmart sc**, Williamsburg Outlet Mall, Williamsburg Pottery Mall, **Fair Oaks Family Campground▲, Scenic View RV Rentals, Williamsburg Pottery Campground▲**
238	**VA 143, Merrimac Trail, to US 60, Colonial Williamsburg, Camp Peary**
Gas	S: 7-11, Shell
Food	S: Ben & Jerry's, Captain George's Seafood, Cracker Barrel, Golden Corral, Hardee's, McDonald's, Outback Steakhouse, Olive Garden,
Lodg	S: Best Western, Comfort Inn, Country Inn, Days Inn, Econo Lodge, Hampton Inn, Holiday Inn, Howard Johnson, Marriott, Quality Inn, Ramada, Red Roof Inn♥, Sleep Inn, Travelodge
Other	N: Camp Peary Naval Reservation S: ATMs, Auto Services, Banks, Cinemas, Grocery, Rental Cars, Tires, **to appr 4 mi: Anvil Campground▲,**
242AB	**VA 199, Colonial Pkwy, Williamsburg**
Gas	N: BP S: 7-11, Crown, Shell
Food	N: Rest/Days Inn S: Burger King, McDonald's, Starbucks, Subway, Wendy's
Lodg	N: Days Inn S: Best Western, Clarion Hotel, Courtyard
Other	N: Cheatham Annex Naval Supply Center, US Naval Weapons Station, Water Country USA S: William & Mary College, Colonial Nat'l Historic Park, Busch Gardens
243A	**to US 60, VA 143W, Merrimac Trail, Pocahontas Trail, Busch Gardens, Williamsburg**
Other	S: **Carters Cove Campground▲**
243B	**VA 143W, Merrimac Trail, Williamsburg** (WB, LEFT exit)

EXIT	VIRGINIA
247	**VA 143, Merrimac Tr, Jefferson Ave (EB), VA 238, Yorktown Rd, Jefferson Ave** (WB, diff reacc)
Gas	N: 7-11, Citgo
250AB	**VA 105, Ft Eustis Blvd, Jefferson Ave, Warwick Blvd**
Gas	N: 7-11, Exxon◈, Sunoco, Dodge's
Lodg	S: Ft Eustis Inn, Holiday Inn Express
255	**VA 143, Jefferson Ave, Newport News, Williamsburg, Int'l Airport**
FStop	N: Shell◈
Gas	N: BP, Walmart, Sam's S: 7-11, Exxon◈, Raceway
Food	N: Castle Greek Italian, Chili's, Golden Corral, Hooters, Moe's SW Grill, Olive Garden, Panera Bread, Smokey Bones BBQ, Starbucks S: Applebee's, Beef O'Brady's, Bonefish Grill, Carrabba's, Cheddars Cafe, ChickFilA, **Cracker Barrel**, Don Pablo, Japan Samurai, KFC, McDonald's, Melting Pot Rest, Outback Steakhouse, Red Robin, Ruby Tuesday, Sakura Japanese Cafe, Starbucks, Subway, TGI Friday, Waffle House, Wendy's
Lodg	N: Comfort Suites, to Travelodge♥, S: Best Western, Comfort Inn, Hampton Inn, Microtel, Studio Plus,
Other	N: ATMs, Banks, Auto Dealers, Auto Services, Home Depot, Lowe's, Michael's, PetCo♥, Pharmacy, Sam's Club, **Walmart sc**, Newport News Williamsburg Int'l Airport✈, S: ATMs, Auto Services, B&N, Best Buy, Borders, CompUSA, Costco, Dick's Sporting Goods, NTB, Office Max, PetSmart♥, Pharmacy, Sears Auto Center Target, World Market, Patrick Henry Mall
255A	**VA 143S, Jefferson Ave**
255B	**VA 143N, Jefferson Ave, Airport**
256AB	**Oyster Pt Rd, Victory Blvd**
Gas	N: BP, Kangaroo Express/Citgo◈, Shell S: Citgo, Texaco
Food	N: 3 Amigos Mexican Rest, Burger King, Cavanaugh's Cafe & Bakery, ChickFilA, Fuddrucker's, Gus's NY Pizza, Ruby Tuesday, Starbucks, Texas Roadhouse S: Buffalo Wild Wings, Cold Stone Creamery, Kappo Nara Seafood & Sushi, KFC, McDonald's, Plaza Azteca Mexican Rest, Starbucks, Taco Bell, Villa Pizza
Lodg	N: Candlewood Suites, Courtyard, Hampton Inn, Hilton Garden Inn, Staybridge Suites♥, TownePlace Suites S: Crestwood Suites, Sleep Inn
Other	N: ATMs, Dollar Tree, Kmart,Kiln Creek Golf Course, Kroger, Pharmacy, Regal Cinema 14, UPS Store, Vet♥, **Walmart sc**, S: ATMs, Barnes & Noble, Bed Bath & Beyond, Carwash, Copy Max, FedEx Office, Office Depot, **Dixie RV Superstore**
258AB	**US 17, J Clyde Morris Blvd, Yorktown, Newport News**
Gas	N: BP, Shell◈, S: BP, Citgo◈,
Food	N: Chatfield's, Domino's Pizza, Strait Outta Philly, Waffle House S: Burger King, DQ, Hong Kong Rest, KFC/Taco Bell, Starbucks,

◈ = Regular Gas Stations with Diesel ▲ = RV Friendly Locations ♥ = Pet Friendly Locations
Red print shows large vehicle parking / access on site or nearby Brown Print = Campgrounds / RV PARKS

EXIT		VIRGINIA
	Lodg	N: Budget Lodge, Country Inn, Holiday Inn, Point Plaza, Super 8, S: Marriott, Motel 6♥,
	Med	S: + to Riverside Reg'l Medical Center
	Other	N: ATMs, Banks, 7-11, Advance Auto Parts, Family Dollar, Food Lion, S: ATMs, Dollar Tree, Radio Shack, Value City, to Christopher Newport Univ
261AB		**Hampton Roads Ctr Pky, Hampton**
	Gas	N: Exxon S: Citgo, Shell, Zooms
	Food	S: Anna's Italian Rest, Chuck E Cheese's Pizza, Fortune Garden, McDonald's, Peking Chinese, Plaza Azteca, Ruby Tuesday, Subway, Taco Bell/Pizza Hut, Topeka Steakhouse
	Lodg	N: Candlewood Suites, Suburban Lodge
	Med	N: + Hospital
	Other	N: ATMs, FedEx Office, Thomas Nelson Comm College S: ATMs, AMC Cinema, Banks, BooksA Million, Dollar Tree, Food Lion, RiteAid
262B		**Hampton Roads Center Pkwy (EB)**
	Med	N: + Hospital
262		**Magruder Blvd, Cunningam Dr (WB)**
	Gas	N: Exxon
	Lodg	N: Candlewood Suites, Country Inn, Suburban Lodge
	Other	N: Thomas Nelson Comm College
263AB		**US 258, VA 134, W Mercury Blvd, Cunningham Dr, James River Bridge, Hampton**
	Gas	N: Exxon, Shell S: 7-11, BP, Citgo, Exxon
	Food	N: Applebee's, Boston Market, Burger King, ChickFilA,Chili's, Denny's, Golden Corral, Hooters, IHOP, KFC, McDonald's, Olive Garden, Outback Steakhouse, Pizza Hut, Red Lobster, Tokyo Japanese Steakhouse, Waffle House, Wendy's S: Cracker Barrel, CiCi's Pizza, El Pollo Loco, Joe's Crab Shack, Lone Star Steakhouse, Old Country Buffet, Pizza Hut, Sonic, Waffle House
	Lodg	N: Comfort Inn, Courtyard, Days Inn♥, Embassy Suites, Extended Stay America, Fairfield Inn♥, Hampton Inn, Holiday Inn♥ Quality Inn♥, Red Roof Inn♥, Sheraton S: Best Western, Econo Lodge, Hampton Bay Plaza, Hilton Garden Inn, La Quinta Inn♥, Residence Inn, Savannah Suites, Springhill Suites
	Other	N: ATMs, Auto Services, Auto Dealers, Banks, Cinema, Coliseum Mall, Convention Center, Dollar Tree, Firestone, Goodyear,

EXIT		VIRGINIA
	Other	N: Grocery, Hampton Coliseum, NAPA, Office Depot, Target, U-Haul, Walgreen's, Walmart sc, S: Advance Auto Parts, ATMs, Auto Rental, Auto Services, Bass Pro Shop, Banks, BJ's Club, Big Lots, Dollar General, Enterprise RAC, Lowe's, Office Max, Pep Boys, Radio Shack, Walgreen's
(264)		**Jct I-664S, Dwntwn Newport News, Pembrook Pkwy, Suffolk**
265B		**VA 167, N Armistead Ave (WB)**
	Gas	N: 7-11,
	Other	S: Vet♥,
265A		**VA 134, N Armistead Ave, VA 167, LaSalle Ave, Hampton**
	Gas	N: Citgo, RaceWay S: BP
	Food	S: McDonald's, Taco Bell/KFC
	Lodg	N: Super 8
	Med	S: + Hospital
	Other	N: ATMs, Home Depot S: Advance Auto Parts, Family Dollar
265C		**Armistead Ave, Langley AFB, Rip Rap Rd (EB)**
	Other	S: Tops Auto & Truck Repair, Towing
267		**US 60, VA 143, W County St, Settlers Landing Rd, Woodland Rd**
	Food	S: Burger King
	Med	S: + Sentara Hampton General Hospital
	Other	N: Golf Course S: Darling Memorial Stadium, Hampton Univ
268		**VA 169, Mallory St, Franklin Blvd, Fort Monroe, Hampton**
	Gas	N: Citgo
	Food	N: Hardee's, McDonald's
	Med	S: + VA Medical Center
(269)		**Weigh / Inspection Station (EB)**
272		**W Ocean View Ave, Bayville St, Willoughby Beach, Norfolk**
	Food	S: Fisherman's Wharf Seafood Rest
	Lodg	S: Days Inn
273		**4th View St, W Ocean View Ave**
	Gas	N: BP◈
	Lodg	N: Econo Lodge, Super 8
274		**Bay Ave, Naval Air Station (WB)**
(276)		**Jct I-564, US 460E, Granby St (EB)**
276A		**US 460W, Granby St (EB)**
	Gas	S: AmocoBP, Exxon
	Food	S: Amigos, Pancake House, Mediterranean Café, Subway
	Other	S: ATMs, Banks, Kroger

EXIT		VIRGINIA
(276B)		**Jct I-564, US 460E, Granby St (WB)**
276C		**VA 165, E Little Creek Rd, to US 460, Norfolk (EB)**
	Gas	N: Shell S: BP, Exxon, Shell
	Food	S: McDonald's, KFC, Subway, Taco Bell, Wendy's
	Other	S: ATMs, Auto Zone, Banks, Dollar Tree, Grocery, Kroger, RiteAid, Walgreen's
277AB		**VA 168, Tidewater Dr, Thole St**
	Gas	N: 7-11 S: BP, Citgo
	Food	N: Bamboo Hut, Hardee's S: Hunan Express, Seafood Rest
	Med	S: + Hospital
	Other	N: Food Lion, Grocery S: Auto Repairs
278		**VA 194S, Chesapeake Blvd**
	Gas	S: Amoco, Exxon, Shell
	Food	S: Burger King, KFC, McDonald's
279		**VA 247, Norview Ave, Norfolk Int'l Airport, Chesapeake Blvd (EB)**
	Gas	N: Shell S: Shell
	Food	N: Golden Corral, Pizza Hut, Wendy's S: KFC, McDonald's
	Other	N: Auto Services, Dollar General, Food Lion, Kmart, Norfolk Int'l Airport✈,
279A		**Norview Ave S (WB)**
279B		**Norview Ave, Norfolk Int'l Airport**
	Other	N: Norfolk Int'l Airport✈
281		**VA 165, N. Military Hwy (WB) VA 165, N Robin Hood Rd (EB)**
	Gas	N: BP◈, Shell◈ S: Citgo, Exxon, Shell
	Food	N: Golden Corral, Pizza Hut, Wendy's
	Lodg	N: Econo Lodge S: Hampton Inn, Holiday Inn, Hilton
	Other	N: Auto Dealers, Kmart S: Firestone, Target
281A		**VA 165, Military Hwy, N Robin Hood Rd, Almeda Ave (EB)**
282		**US 13, VA 166, Northhampton Blvd, to Chesapeake Bay Bridge Tunnel**
	TStop	N: Big Charlie's Truck Plaza (Scales)
	Gas	N: Amoco, Exxon, Texaco
	Food	N: Rest/Big Charlie's TP, Burger King, McDonald's, Pizza Hut, Waffle House
	Lodg	N: Econo Lodge, Quality Inn, Sleep Inn, Wingate Inn,
	TServ	N: Big Charlie's TP/Tires
	Med	S: + Lake Taylor Hospital

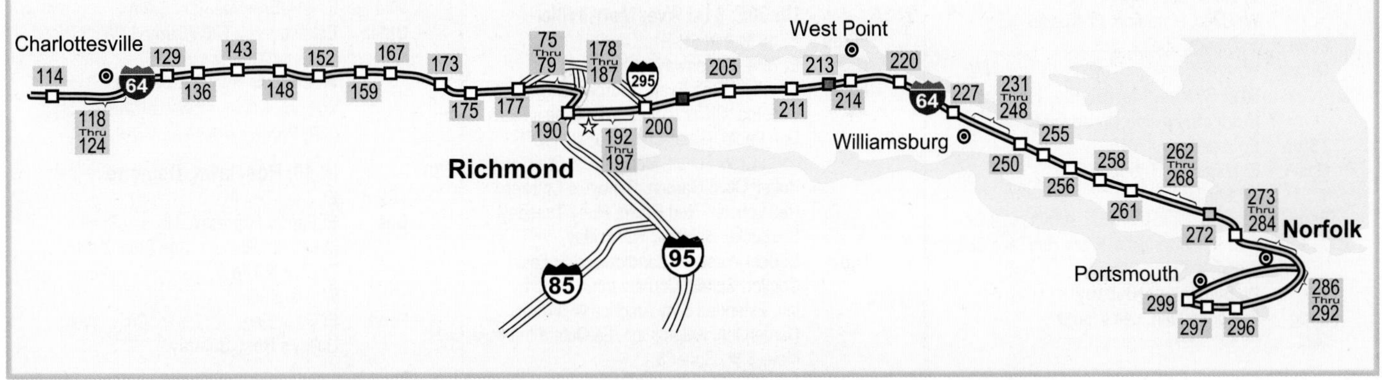

◈= Regular Gas Stations with Diesel ▲ = RV Friendly Locations ♥= Pet Friendly Locations
Red print shows large vehicle parking / access on site or nearby Brown Print = Campgrounds / RV PARKS

EXIT | VIRGINIA

Other N: Laundry/Big Charlie's TP, VA Wesleyan College, Auto Services, **to** Chesapeake Bay Bridge Tunnel
S: Auto Services, Tires

(284AB) Jct I-264 Norfolk, VA 44, VA Beach (N to Newtown Rd: Gas, Food, Lodg; S to Military Hwy: Gas, Food, Lodg, Mall)
Med N: + Sentara Leigh Hospital

286AB VA 407, Indian River Rd, Va Beach
Gas N: BP◊, Hess◊, Shell
S: Citgo, Exxon, Sunoco◊
Food N: Hardee's
S: Captain D's, Waffle House
Lodg S: Founders Inn & Conference Center

289AB Greenbrier Pkwy, Chesapeake
Gas N: Citgo, WaWa
Food N: Burger King, Subway, Taco Bell, Wendy's
S: Blimpie, Boston Market, Cheers Grill, Don Pablo, Flaming Wok, Fuddrucker's, Jason's Deli, Joe's Crab Shack, Kyoto Japanese, Lone Star Steakhouse, Landry's Rest, McDonald's, Old Country Buffet, Olive Garden, Panera Bread, Ruby Tuesday, Starbucks, Subway, Taco Bell
Lodg N: Hampton Inn♥ Holiday Inn♥, Motel 6♥, Red Roof Inn♥, Staybridge Suites, TownPlace Suites, Wellesley Inn
S: Comfort Suites, Courtyard, Extended Stay America, Fairfield Inn, Hilton Garden Inn, Homewood Suites, Residence Inn,
Other N: Auto Dealers, Food Lion, U-Haul
S: ATMs, Barnes & Noble, Best Buy, Cinema 13, Dollar General, Greenbrier Mall, Grocery, Michael's, NTB, Office Depot, Pharmacy, Target, TJ Maxx

290AB VA 168, Battlefield Blvd, Great Bridge
Gas S: BP◊, Shell
Food N: Applebee's, Burger King, Carrabba's, Chuck E Cheese's Pizza, Dunkin Donuts, Five Guys Burgers, Golden Corral, Grand China Buffet, Hardee's, Ryan's Grill, Starbucks, TGI Friday, Taco Bell, Waffle House, Wendy's
Lodg N: Days Inn, Hampton Inn, Super 8
TServ N: Tidewater Mack Trucks
Med N: + Chesapeake General Hospital
Other N: Dollar Tree, Home Depot, Lowe's, Sam's Club, US Post Office, Walgreen's, **Walmart sc**

(291AB) Jct I-464, US 17, VA 168, to Norfolk, Elizabeth City, Nags Head

292 VA 190, Great Bridge Blvd, VA 104, Dominion Blvd (WB)

296 US 17, Portsmouth, Elizabeth City, Chesapeake (WB)
Other S: to Chesapeake Campground▲

296A US 17N, Portsmouth (EB)
Lodg N: Colonial Motel, Days Inn

296B US 17S, Chesapeake (EB)

297 US 13, US 460, Military Hwy
Gas N: 7-11, Exxon
TServ N: Burton's Truck Repair, Carter Power Systems
Other N: Auto Repairs
S: Auto Repairs

(299AB) Jct I-264 Portsmouth, I-664 Suffolk, US 13, US 58, US 460, Norfolk

EASTERN TIME ZONE

NOTE: I-64 Begins/Ends on I-264

VIRGINIA

Begin Westbound I-64 from Chesapeake, VA to Jct I-70 in Wentzville, MO.

EXIT | INDIANA

Begin Southbound I-65 from Jct I-80/90 at Gary, IN to Jct I-10 near Mobile, AL.

INDIANA

NOTE: I-65 begins/ends on US12/US 20

EASTERN TIME ZONE

(262) Jct I-90 (TOLL), W-Chicago, E-Ohio, US 20, US 12, 16th Ave, Gary (NB)

261 E 15th Ave, to 16th Ave, US 12, US 20, Gary
Gas W: EZ Go Marathon
TServ E: Pozzo Mack Sales & Service
W: Cummins, Inland Detroit Diesel/ Allison, Lakeshore Truck Service

(259A) Jct I-80/94W, to Chicago

(259B) Jct I-80/94E, US 6, to Ohio

258 US 6 Bus, 37th Ave, Ridge Rd
Gas E: Mobil, Speedway◊
W: Citgo, Marathon, Phillips 66
Food E: Diner's Choice, Subway
Other W: Auto Services, Towing, IN Univ NW

255 61st St Ave, Merrillville, Hobart (Addt'l Serv W to Broadway)
TStop E: Speedway #7575
Gas E: Marathon, Thornton's
W: Shell
Food E: FastFood/Speedway, Arby's, Cracker Barrel, McDonald's, Pizza Hut/Taco Bell, Wendy's
W: Burger King, Subway
Lodg E: Comfort Inn, Lee's Inn♥
Med E: + St Mary Medical Center
Other E: Menard's, Midwest Auto & Tire Repair

253B US 30W, 81st Ave, Merrillville
Gas W: Gas City, Shell, Speedway◊, Meijer◊
Food W: Arby's, Applebee's, Blimpie, Celebration Station, Denny's, Dunkin Donuts, Golden Corral, Hooter's, House of Kobe, KFC, La Carreta, Lone Star Steakhouse, Max & Erma's, Old Chicago Pizza, Outback Steakhouse, Panda Express, Panera Bread Pizza Hut, Rio Bravo, Shoney's, Smoky Bones BBQ, Steak n Shake, Subway, Starbucks, Texas Corral, Wendy's, White Castle
Lodg W: Courtyard, Fairfield Inn, Hampton Inn, Holiday Inn Express, Radisson, Red Roof Inn♥, Residence Inn
Med W: + Prompt Medical Care, + Methodist Hospital of Merrillville
Other W: Auto Dealers, ATMs, Banks, CarQuest, Discount Tire, Dollar Tree, Firestone, FedEx Office, Grocery, Kmart, Meijer's, NTB, Staples, U-Haul, UPS Store, Walgreen's

253A US 30E, 81st Ave, Merrillville
FStop E: US 30 & IN 51: Gas City #51
Gas E: BP◊, Speedway◊, Costco
Food E: Arby's, Bob Evans, Burger King, Casa Gallardo, Chili's, Chuck E Cheese's Pizza, Don Pablo, Great China Buffet, IHOP, Joe's Crab Shack, McDonalds, Old Country Buffet, Olive Garden, Popeye's Chicken, Red Lobster, Red Robin, Ruby Tuesday, Starbucks, Subway, TGI Friday,
Lodg E: Best Western, Candlewood Suites, Comfort Suites, Country Inn, Economy Inn, Extended Stay America♥, Hilton Garden Inn, Knights Inn, La Quinta Inn♥, Motel 6♥, Super 8
Other E: **LP**/Gas City, AT&T, Auto Zone, Barnes & Noble, Best Buy, Borders, Cinemas, Costco, Firestone, Gander Mountain, Hobby Lobby, Home Depot, Lowe's, Michael's, Office Depot, Office Max, PetCo♥, Petland♥, Sam's Club, Southlake Mall, Target, TJ Maxx, Tire Barn, **Walmart sc**, **Rose RV Sales**

247 US 231, IN 8, Crown Point, Hebron
Gas W: Mobil
Med W: + Hospital

(241) Lake Co Weigh Station (Both dir)

240 IN 2, 181st Ave, Lowell, Hebron
TStop E: Flying J Travel Plaza #5119 (Scales) **(DAND)**, Pilot Travel Center #448 (Scales)
Gas W: Mobil, Speedway
Food E: Rest/FastFood/Flying J TP, McDonald's/Pilot TC
W: Burger King/Mobil
Lodg E: Super 8
TWash W: Anchor TW, Truck Wash
TServ E: Flying J TP/Tires
Med E: + Hebron Medical Center
Other E: Laundry/WiFi/**RVDump**/**LP**/FJ TP, Laundry/WiFi/Pilot TC
W: IN State Hwy Patrol Post

(231) Jasper Co Rest Area (Both dir) (RR, Phones, Pic, Pet, Vend, Info)

230 IN 10, Roselawn, Demotte
TStop E: Steel City Plaza 65
Gas E: Family Express◊, Holiday Shell, Marathon, Risner's Gas Stop, Zylstra's Service & Tire
W: Marathon
Food E: Rest/Steel City Plaza, China Wok, Holley's Rest, Subway

◊= Regular Gas Stations with Diesel ▲ = RV Friendly Locations ♥= Pet Friendly Locations
Red print shows large vehicle parking / access on site or nearby Brown Print = Campgrounds / RV PARKS

EXIT		INDIANA
	Food	W: Renfrow's, The Rodeo
	Med	W: + Lake Holiday Medical Clinic
	Other	E: Laundry/LP/Steel City Plaza W: CarQuest, CVS, Dollar General, IGA, Dr Bob's RV Repair, Lake Holiday Country Campground▲ , Pioneer Family Campground▲
215		**IN 114, Morocco, Rensselaer**
	FStop	E: Family Express #35◈
	TStop	W: Grandma's Travel Center (Scales), Trail Tree Truck Stop
	Gas	E: Kerr McGee, Phillips 66, Marathon
	Food	E: Arby's, DQ, KFC, McDonald's W: Rest/FastFood/Grandma's TC, Rest/FastFood/Trail Tree TS, Burger King
	Lodg	E: Holiday Inn Express, Knights Inn W: Economy Inn
	TServ	E: Anderson's Service W: Coopers Tire & Service
	Med	E: + Jasper Co Hospital
	Other	E: Auto Repair W: Laundry/Grandma's TC, Laundry/Trail Tree TS
205		**US 231, Remington, Rensselaer**
	TStop	E: Crazy D's (Scales)
	Gas	E: BP
	Food	E: Rest/Crazy D's
	Lodg	E: Carson Inn
	Med	E: + Hospital
	Other	E: Laundry/CB/Crazy D's
201		**US 24, US 231, Remington, Wolcott**
	FStop	W: Family Express◈, Remington Mobil
	TStop	W: Petro Stopping Center #75, Pilot Travel Center #34 (Scales)
	Food	W: IronSkillet/Petro SC, Subway/Pilot TC, Casey's C/O Pizza, KFC, McDonald's
	Lodg	W: Days Inn, Super 8
	TServ	W: Petro SC/Tires
	Other	W: Caboose Lake Campground▲
(196)		**White Co Rest Area (Both dir)** **(RR, Phones, Pic, Pet, Vend)**
193		**US 231, Wolcott, Chalmers**
	Gas	E: BP
	Food	E: DQ/BP
188		**IN 18, Brookston, Fowler**
178		**IN 43, W Lafayette, Delphi**
	Gas	E: Phillips 66, Shell
	Food	E: McDonald's, Subway, Wendy's
	Lodg	E: Days Inn, Econo Lodge
	Other	E: IN State Hwy Patrol Post W: to Purdue Univ
175		**IN 25, Lafayette, Delphi**
	Gas	E: Family Express◈,
	Med	E: + Hospital
	Other	E: Aretz Airport✈ W: Lafayette Travel Trailer Sales/ RVDump, to Purdue Univ
172		**IN 26, Lafayette, Rossville**
	Gas	E: Meijer◈◈ W: Circle K/BP◈, Shell, Speedway◈
	Food	E: Cracker Barrel, DQ, El Rodeo, Starbucks, Steak n Shake, Waffle House, White Castle W: Arby's, Bob Evans, Burger King, Chick-FilA, Chili's, Chuck E Cheese's Pizza, Cici's Pizza, Country Café, DQ, Damon's, Dennys Don Pablo, Golden Corral, Hunan House, IHOP, KFC, Logan's Roadhouse, McDonald's, Mountain Jack's, Olive Garden Outback Steakhouse, Pizza Hut, Steak 'n Shake, Subway, TGI Friday, Taco Bell

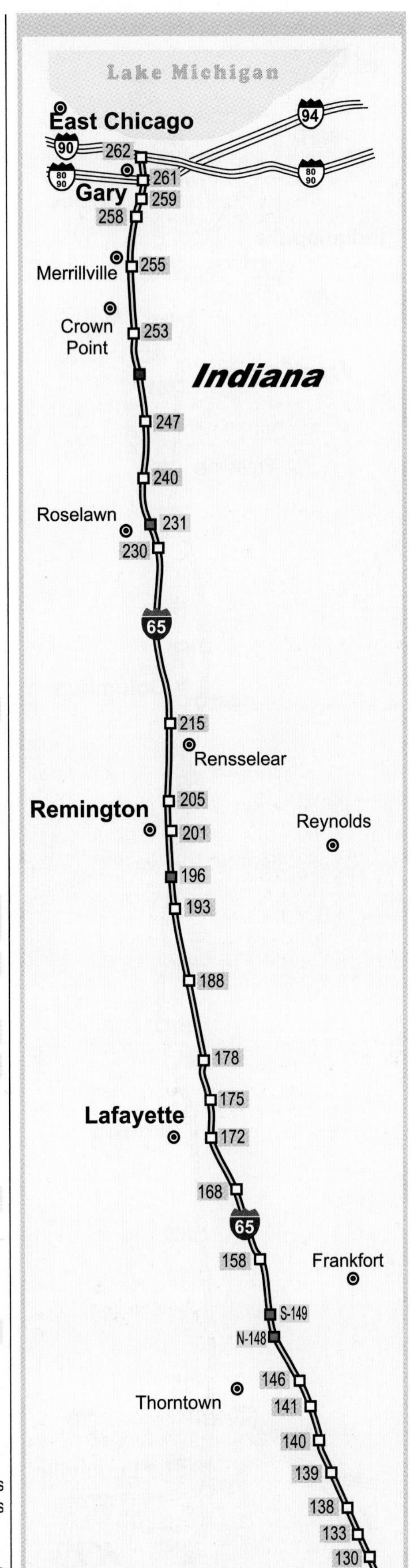

EXIT		INDIANA
	Lodg	E: Baymont Inn, Budget Inn, Candlewood Suites, Comfort Inn, Comfort Suites, Days Inn, Hawthorne Suites, Holiday Inn Express La Quinta Inn♥, Lee's Inn, Motel 6 W: Best Western, Dollar Inn, Fairfield Inn, Hampton Inn, Homewood Suites, Knight's Inn, Quality Inn, Radisson, Red Roof Inn, Signature Inn, Super 8
	TServ	W: Double D Truck Repair
	Med	W: + Hospital
	Other	E: Visitor Center W: Amtrak, Auto Dealers, Auto Services, CVS, Carwash, Discount Tire, Dollar Tree, Dollar General, Hobby Lobby, Home Depot, Lowe's, Museums, NAPA, Office Depot, Sam's Club, Target, TJ Maxx, Tippecanoe Mall, US Post Office, Verizon, Walgreen's, Walmart sc, to Purdue Univ
168		**IN 38, Lafayette, Dayton**
	FStop	E: Super Pantry Fuel Center #18/Mobil
	Food	E: FastFood/Super Pantry FC
158		**IN 28, Attica, Frankfort**
	FStop	E: to Good Oil/AmocoBP
	Med	E: + Hospital
	Other	E: Harley Davidson
(149)		**Boone Co Rest Area (SB)** **(RR, Phones, Picnic, Vend)**
(148)		**Boone Co Rest Area (NB)** **(RR, Phones, Picnic, Vend)**
146		**IN 47, Thorntown, Sheridan**
141		**US 52N, Lafayette Ave, Lebanon, Thorntown**
	Med	E: + Hospital
140		**IN 32, Lebanon, Crawfordsville**
	TStop	W: McClure Oil #52◈
	Gas	E: BP W: Shell
	Food	E: Denny's, McDonald's, White Castle W: FastFood/McClure, Arby's, Burger King, KFC, Ponderosa, Steak 'n Shake, Subway, Taco Bell
	Lodg	E: Comfort Inn, Econo Lodge W: Dollar Inn, Holiday Inn Express, Lee's Inn, Super 8
	Med	E: + Hospital
	Other	E: Auto Zone, Goodyear, Laundromat, NAPA, Tires
139		**IN 39, Lebanon St, Lebanon, Lizton**
	FStop	E: Gas America
	TStop	W: Flying J Travel Plaza #5069 (Scales)
	Gas	W: Phillips 66
	Food	E: Hardee's, Starbucks, Wendy's W: Rest/FastFood/FJ TP
	Lodg	W: Quality Inn, Ramada Inn
	TServ	W: to Jerry's Truck & Trailer Repair
	Other	W: Laundry/WiFi/RVDump/LP/FJ TP, David's Chocolates
138		**CR 100, N 156th St, Indianapolis Ave, Lebanon**
	Gas	E: BP◈
	Other	E: Auto Repairs W: Boone Co Airport✈
133		**IN 267, N 126th Rd, Lebanon, Brownsburg, Whitestown**
130		**IN 334, to Zionsville, Whitestown**
	TStop	E: Crystal Flash #34 W: Travel Center of America #173/BP (Scales)
	Gas	E: Shell

◈= Regular Gas Stations with Diesel ▲ = RV Friendly Locations ♥= Pet Friendly Locations
Red print shows large vehicle parking / access on site or nearby Brown Print = Campgrounds / RV PARKS

EXIT		INDIANA
	Food	**E:** FastFood/Crystal Flash, Burger King, Starbucks **W:** CountryPride/Popeye's/TA TC
	TServ	**W:** TA TC/Tires
	Other	**E:** CVS, Lowe's **W:** Laundry/WiFi/TA TC
(129)		**Jct I-865E, US 52E, to Ft Wayne, Columbus, OH (SB)**
124		**Delong Rd, 71st St, Indianapolis**
	Gas	**E:** BP
	Food	**E:** Hardee's, Max & Erma's Rest, Quiznos, Steak n Shake, Wendy's
	Lodg	**E:** Courtyard, Hampton Inn, Hilton Garden Inn, Residence Inn, Wingate Inn
	Other	**W:** Eagle Creek Park
(123)		**Jct I-465S, Peoria, St Louis (SB), Jct I-465N, Ft Wayne, Columbus Peoria (NB)**
	Other	**S:** to Eagle Creek Airpark✈, Indianapolis Motor Speedway
121		**Lafayette Rd, Indianapolis**
	Gas	**E:** Gas America, Speedway◈ **W:** BP, Circle K/Shell, Meijer
	Food	**W:** Applebee's, Arby's, Church's Chicken, Papa John's Pizza, Subway, Taco Bell, Wendy's
	Lodg	**E:** Lee's Inn, Quality Inn **W:** America's Best Value Inn, Travelodge
	Med	**W:** + Westview Hospital
	Other	**W:** ATMs, Auto Dealers, Auto Services, Banks, Borders, Batteries Plus, Cinema, Discount Tire, Family Dollar, FedEx Office, Firestone, Grocery, Lafayette Square, NAPA, PepBoys, Sears Auto Center, Tire Barn, Vet♥, **Acc to #119**
119		**38th St, N Kessler Blvd, Lafayette Rd, Fairgrounds (Acc to #121 Serv)**
	Gas	**W:** Meijer's◈, Speedway
	Food	**W:** Arby's, Chuck E Cheese's Pizza, CiCi's Pizza, KFC/Taco Bell, McDonald's, Lone Star Steakhouse, New China Buffet, Pizza Hut, Popeye's Chicken, Red Lobster, Starbucks, Taco Bell
	Lodg	**W:** Days Inn, Express Inn
	Med	**W:** + Westview Hospital
	Other	**E:** to IN State Fairgrounds **W:** ATMs, Auto Dealer, Auto Services, Best Buy, Cinema, Family Indoor Golf, Mall, NAPA, Office Depot, Staples, to Indianapolis Motor Speedway
117		**ML King Jr Dr, St Michigan Rd (SB)**
	Gas	**E** Marathon◈
116		**29th St, 30th St (NB)**
115		**21st St, Fall Creek Pkwy**
	Gas	**E:** Shell
	Med	**E:** + Methodist Hospital of IN
114		**W 11th St, ML King Jr St, to West St, to Downtown**
	Med	**W:** + University Hospital, + IN Univ Medical Center, + Riley Hospital for Children, + Wishard Memorial Hospital
113		**Illinois St, 11th St, Pennsylvania St, US 31, Meridian St, to Downtown**
(112A)		**Jct I-70E, to Columbus**
111		**Market St, Michigan St, Ohio St, Fletcher Ave, US 40, US 31**
	Other	**W:** to Indianapolis Zoo, RCA Dome, Victory Field, Convention Center
(110B)		**Jct I-70W, to St. Louis**

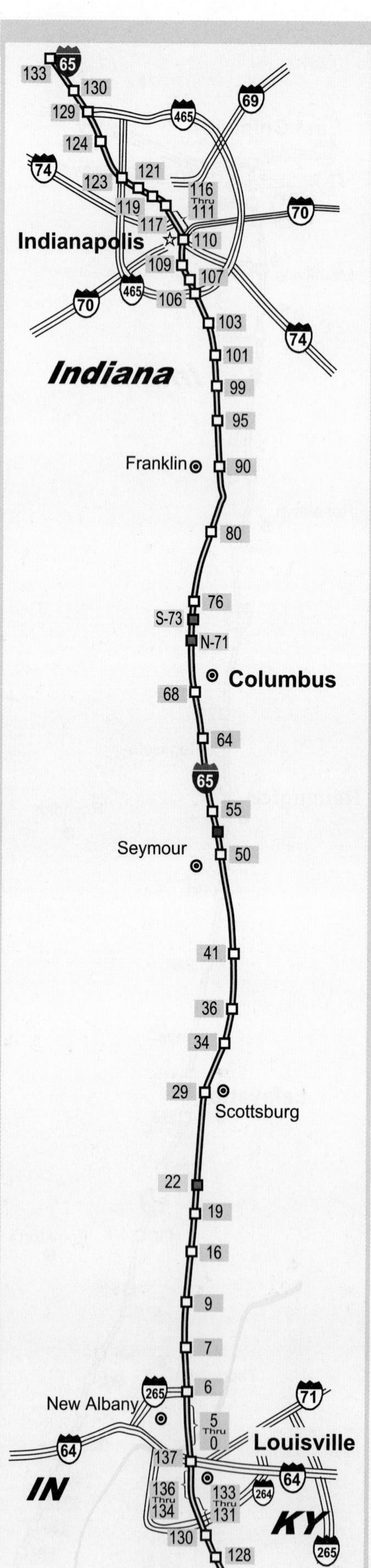

EXIT		INDIANA
110A		**Morris St, Prospect St**
109		**Raymond St**
	Gas	**W:** Speedway
	Med	**E:** + Hospital
	Other	**E:** CVS, Safeway
107		**Keystone Ave, Indianapolis**
	Gas	**E:** Mystik Food Mart **W:** Citgo, Phillips 66◈, Speedway◈, Valero
	Food	**W:** Burger King, Denny's, McDonald's, Starbucks, Subway, Wendy's
	Lodg	**E:** America's Best Value Inn **W:** Holiday Inn Express
	Med	**E:** + St Francis Hospital
	Other	**E:** Auto Repairs **W:** ATMs, Banks, Dollar General, Grocery, Univ of Indianapolis
(106)		**Jct I-465, I-74, Columbus, St Louis (All Serv E to 1st Ex, #52)**
103		**Southport Rd, Indianapolis**
	Gas	**E:** BP, Circle K/Shell, Meijer◈◈, **W:** Circle K, Speedway◈, Super 7
	Food	**E:** Arby's, ChickFilA, McDonald's/BP, Hardee's, Longhorn Steakhouse, Panda Express, Panera Bread, O'Charley's, Pizza Hut, Qdoba Mexican, Starbucks, Sonic, Taco Bell **W:** Bob Evans, Burger King, Carrabba's, **Cracker Barrel**, KFC, McDonald's, Starbucks, Steak 'n Shake, Texas Roadhouse, Waffle Steak, Wendy's
	Lodg	**W:** Best Western, Comfort Suites, Country Inn, Courtyard, Fairfield Inn, Hampton Inn, Jameson Inn, Quality Inn, Signature Inn, Super 8
	Med	**W:** + St Francis Hospital
	Other	**E:** ATMs, Auto Services, AT&T, Firestone, Home Depot, Indianapolis Southside Harley Davidson, Lowe's, Menard's, Pharmacy, Radio Shack, Staples, Target, **W:** ATMs, Auto & Tire Services, **IN State Fairgrounds Campground▲ , to Indy Lakes Campground▲**
101		**County Line Rd, Indianapolis**
	Gas	**W:** Murphy
	Food	**W:** BW3, Blimpie, Subway
	Lodg	**E:** Candlewood Suites **W:** HiltonGarden Inn, Holiday Inn Express, Value Place
	Med	**W:** + St Francis Hospital
	Other	**W:** ATMs, **Aaron RV Rental**, AT&T, Banks, Gander Mountain, Greenwood Park Mall, Greenwood Muni Airport✈, Kroger, Office Depot, Office Max, Pharmacy, **Walmart sc**,
99		**950N, Greenwood Rd, Greenwood**
	TStop	**E:** Road Ranger #226/Pilot TC #542/ Citgo (Scales)
	Gas	**W:** 7-11, Circle K/Shell
	Food	**E:** Subway/RR/Pilot TC **W:** Arby's, Bob Evans, Denny's, KFC, McDonald's, Subway, Starbucks, Taco Bell, Waffle & Steak, White Castle
	Lodg	**W:** Comfort Inn, InTown Suites, Red Carpet Inn, Red Roof Inn
	TServ	**W:** Road Ranger/Tires
	Med	**W:** + Hospital
	Other	**E:** Laundry/**RVDump**/Road Ranger/PTC **W:** Pharmacy, Sam's Club, Golf Course, **Stout's RV Sales/Camping World, All Good Mobile RV Services**

◈= Regular Gas Stations with Diesel ▲ = RV Friendly Locations ♥ = Pet Friendly Locations

Red print shows large vehicle parking / access on site or nearby Brown Print = Campgrounds / RV PARKS

EXIT INDIANA

95 CR 500N, Whiteland Rd, Whiteland

- **TStop** E: MT Travel Plaza #2774/Marathon Flying J Travel Plaza #656 (Scales) W: Love's Travel Stop #451 (Scales), Pilot Travel Center #37 (Scales)
- **Food** E: Rest/FastFood/MT TP, Country Market Rest/FastFood/FJ TP W: Arby's/Love's TS, McDonald's/Pilot TC
- **TWash** W: Pilot TC
- **TServ** E: MT Travel Plaza/Tires, Speedco W: Pilot TC/Tires, Scott Truck Systems, Whiteland Tire & Fleet
- **Other** E: Laundry/Marathon TP, Laundry/WiFi/ RVDump/LP/FJ TP W: Laundry/WiFi/Love's TS, Laundry/WiFi/ Pilot TC, Auto Repairs, to RV Center

90 IN 44, King St, Franklin, Shelbyville

- **Gas** W: Circle K/Shell
- **Food** W: Burger King, McDonald's, Subway, Waffle & Steak,
- **Lodg** W: Comfort Inn, Howard Johnson, Quality Inn, Super 7, Super 8
- **Med** W: + Johnson Memorial Hospital
- **Other** W: to Auto Services, ATMs, Banks, Museum, Franklin College, Golf Course

80 IN 252, Edinburgh, Flat Rock

- **Gas** W: Marathon◈, Shell◈
- **Other** E: Adventure RV Rentals W: Camp Atterbury Mil Res, Johnson Co Park & Rec Area▲ , Mobile RV Repair Service, Edmundson RV Sales

76A US 31S, Taylorsville, Columbus

- **FStop** E: Circle K 65/Shell
- **Gas** E: Speedway◈
- **Food** E: Burger King, KFC, Waffle & Steak
- **Lodg** E: Comfort Inn
- **Other** E: ATMs, Auto Dealers, to Columbus Bakalar Muni Airport✈

76B US 31N, Edinburgh

- **Gas** W: BP, Citgo◈, Thornton's◈
- **Food** W: Arby's, Cracker Barrel, Hardee's, Max & Erma's, McDonald's, Ruby Tuesday, Subway, Taco Bell
- **Lodg** W: Best Western, Hampton Inn, Holiday Inn Express, Red Roof Inn♥
- **TServ** W: White River Truck Repair, Greene's Truck Auto Service, Goodyear, Truck Wash
- **Other** W: Premium Outlets at Edinburgh, Mann's Harley Davidson, Blue's Canoe Livery, Driftwood Camp RV Park▲ , Camp Atterbury Military Res, Johnson Co Park & Rec Area▲ , Mark's Mobile RV Repair Service, Edmundson RV Sales

(73) Taylorsville Rest Area (SB) (RR, Phones, Picnic, Pet, Vend)

(71) Taylorsville Rest Area (NB) (RR, Phones, Picnic, Pet, Vend)

68 IN 46, Columbus, to Nashville, Bloomington

- **Gas** E: BP◈, Circle K/Shell, Circle K/Shell, Speedway◈, Sam's W: BP, Marathon, Swifty
- **Food** E: Burger King, Dimitri's, McDonald's, Starbucks, Subway, Waffle House, W: Arby's', Bob Evans, Denny's, Starbucks, Subway, Taco Bell, Wendy's
- **Lodg** E: Comfort Inn, Holiday Inn, Ramada Inn, Sleep Inn, Super 8 W: Courtyard, Days Inn, Knights Inn, Motel 6♥, Travelodge
- **Med** E: + Hospital
- **Other** E: ATMs, Cinema, Menard's, Museums, Sam's Club, Walgreen's, Walmart sc, W: ATMs, Banks, CVS, Dollar General, Grocery, U-Haul, Vet♥, to Westward Ho Campground▲ , The Last Resort Campground & RV Park▲ , Brown Co State Park▲

64 IN 58, to Ogilville, Walesboro

- **Gas** E: Marathon◈
- **Other** W: Woods n Waters Campground▲

55 IN 11, Seymour, to Jonesville

- **Gas** E: BP

(51) Weigh Station (Both dir)

50B US 50W, Seymour, N Vernon

- **Gas** W: BP, Shell◈, Speedway◈, Murphy USA
- **Food** W: Applebee's, Arby's, Bob Evans, Burger King, Captain D's, Chili's, Cracker Barrel, DQ, Denny's, Domino's Pizza, Hardee's, KFC, Long John Silver, Max & Erma's, McDonald's, Papa John's Pizza, Pizza Hut, Ryan's Grill, Santa Fe Mexican, Starbucks, Steak n Shake, Subway, Taco Bell, Tumbleweed Rest, Wendy's
- **Lodg** W: Hampton Inn, Holiday Inn Express, Knights Inn, Lee's Inn, Quality Inn
- **TServ** W: Cummins, Mack Trucks, Towing
- **Other** W: Auto Zone, Auto Dealers, Auto Repairs, ATMs, Aldi Grocery, Banks, Big Lots, CVS, Dollar General, Dollar Tree, Grocery, Home Depot, O'Reilly Auto Parts, Radio Shack, Staples, Tires, Walgreen's, Walmart sc

50A US 50E, Seymour, Brownstown

- **FStop** E: Seymour Marathon
- **TStop** E: Travel Center of America #65/BP (Scales)
- **Gas** E: Swifty
- **Food** E: CountryPride/TA TC, Tokyo Japanese Sushi Bar, McDonald's, Waffle House
- **Lodg** E: Allstate Inn, Days Inn, Econo Lodge, Motel 6♥, Super 8
- **TWash** E: TA TC
- **TServ** E: TA TC/Tires
- **Other** E: Laundry/WiFi/TA TC, Tanger Outlets, Visitor Center, Jiffy Lube, Great Escape

41 IN 250, Crothersville, Uniontown

- **FStop** W: Uniontown Fuel Stop
- **Food** W: Uniontown Rest/Uniontown FS
- **TServ** W: Uniontown Fuel Stop/Tires

36 US 31, Crothersville, Austin

- **Gas** E: Shell W: Marathon

34B IN 256W, W Main St, Austin (SB)

34A IN 256, W Main St, Austin (SB)

34 IN 256, W Main St, Austin (NB)

- **TStop** W: AmBest/Fuel Mart #783
- **Gas** E: BP
- **Food** E: Main St Family Rest, Tammy's Dairy Bar W: A&W
- **Other** E: Auto Services

29B IN 56W, W McClain Ave, Scottsburg

29A IN 56E, Scottsburg, Salem (SB)

29 IN 56, Scottsburg, to Salem (NB)

- **Gas** E: MotoMart, Speedway◈ W: Citgo◈, Circle K/Shell, Murphy USA◈
- **Food** E: Burger King, Cracker Barrel, KFC, Papa John's Pizza, Ponderosa, Sonic, Subway, Taco Bell, Rest/Mariann Motel W: Arby's, Domino's Pizza, McDonald's, Pizza Hut, Waffle & Steak, Wendy's
- **Lodg** E: Holiday Inn Express, Marianne Motel, Travel Inn W: Best Western, Hampton Inn, Quality Inn, Super 8
- **Med** E: + Hospital
- **Other** E: ATMs, Banks, Auto Services, Auto Dealers, Auto Zone, Advance Auto Parts, Ace Hardware, CVS, Family Dollar W: Big O Tire, Walmart sc, to appr 4mi: Yogi Bear Jellystone Raintree Campground▲

(22) IN Welcome Center (NB) Henryville Rest Area (SB) (RR, Phones, Picnic, Vend)

19 IN 160, Henryville, Charlestown

- **Gas** E: Circle K/Shell, Sprint◈
- **Food** E: Subway/Sprint

16 Memphis-Blue Lick Rd, Crone Rd, Memphis Rd, Memphis, Sellersburg

- **TStop** E: Love's Travel Stop #355 (Scales) W: Pilot Travel Center #152 (Scales)
- **Food** E: Subway/McDonald's/Love's TS W: Arby's/TJCinn/Pilot TC
- **Tires** W: Pilot TC
- **TWash** W: Pilot TC
- **Other** E: WiFi/Love's TS, Truck Sales, American Flea Market W: Laundry/WiFi/Pilot TC, Customers First RV Center

9 IN 311, Sellersburg, Speed

- **Gas** E: BP, Chevron, Circle K/Shell W: Dairy Mart
- **Food** E: Arby's, Cracker Barrel, DQ, Quiznos Subs, Waffle & Steak W: Burger King, McDonald's, Taco Bell
- **Lodg** E: Ramada Inn W: Comfort Inn
- **Other** E: ATMs, Auto Services, Banks, Grocery, Laundromat, O'Reilly Auto Parts, Pharmacy IN State Hwy Patrol Post

7 IN 60, Sellersburg, Clarksville

- **Gas** E: BP◈ W: Citgo
- **Food** W: KFC/Pizza Hut
- **Lodg** W: Days Inn
- **Other** E: Clark Co Airport✈

(6B) Jct I-265W, to I-64W, to New Albany, St Louis

- **Other** E: to IN Univ SE

(6A) Jct I-265E, IN 62, to Jeffersonville

- **Other** E: to US Military Res/IN Arsenal

5 Veterans Parkway, to US 31

- **Gas** W: Dairy Mart, Speedway, Murphy USA
- **Food** W: Asian Buffet, ChickFilA, Cheddar's Café Famous Dave's BBQ, IHOP, Longhorn Steakhouse, Olive Garden, Panera Bread, Pizza Hut, Ruben's Mexican Rest, Ruby Tuesday, Subway, Taco Bell
- **TServ** W: Wheatley Truck Services
- **Other** W: ATMs, AT&T, Bass Pro Shop, Best Buy, Lowe's, PetSmart♥, Sam's Club, Staples, Target, Verizon, Walmart sc, RV Center,

4 US 31N, IN 131S, McCullough Pike, Clarksville, Jeffersonville

- **Gas** E: Thornton's ◈ W: SavAStep, Speedway◈, Kroger

◈= Regular Gas Stations with Diesel ▲ = RV Friendly Locations ♥= Pet Friendly Locations
Red print shows large vehicle parking / access on site or nearby Brown Print = Campgrounds / RV PARKS

EXIT — IN / KY

Food — E: Dunkin Donuts/Subworks/Thornton's, White Castle
Food — W: Arby's, Applebee's, Bob Evans, Burger King, Captain D's, Chuck E Cheese's Pizza Denny's, Don Pablo, Fazoli's, Golden Corral, Hooters, Logan's Roadhouse, Long John Silver, Outback Steakhouse, Papa John's Pizza, Pizza Hut, Rally's, Red Lobster, Starbucks, Steak n Shake, Taco Bell, Wendy's
Lodg — E: Crest Motel, Value Place
W: Best Western♥, Candlewood Suites, Dollar Inn, Hampton Inn
TServ — E: KY Truck Sales, Freightliner, S & R Truck Tires, Dan's Truck & Diesel Repair
W: Goodyear
Other — W: ATMs, AT&T, Auto Zone, Auto Dealers, Bass Pro Shop, Big Lots, Dollar Tree, Firestone, Goodyear, Green Tree Mall, Hobby Lobby, Home Depot, Kroger, Office Depot, O'Reilly Auto Parts, Pep Boys, River Fair Family Fun Park, Sears/Auto, Target, US Post Office, Walgreen's,

2 — Eastern Blvd, to IN 131, Clarksville, Jeffersonville
Gas — E: Thornton's
W: Circle K/Shell, SavAStep, Swifty
Food — W: Denny's, Hungry Pelican, Ryan's Grill
Lodg — E: Best Inn, Comfort Suites, Motel 6♥, Super 8
W: Days Inn♥
Med — E: + Hospital
W: + Immediate Care Walk-In Clinic
Other — E: U-Haul
W: ATMs, Auto Services, Banks, Tires, Camping World

1A — W New Albany (NB)

1 — US 31S, 4th St, IN 62, Stansifer Ave, W 14th St, Jeffersonville, Clarksville
Food — W: Derby Dinner Playhouse
Lodg — W: Holiday Inn
Other — W: Cummins Cumberland, Louisville Metro KOA▲, Tom Stinnett RV Center/ Camping World

0 — US 31, Market St, 4th St, Court Ave, Jeffersonville
Gas — E: BP, Thornton's, Tobacco Rd
Food — E: Hardee's, McDonald's, Waffle & Steak
W: Buckhead Mtn Grill, Kingfish, Rocky's Italian Grill
Lodg — E: Alben Motel, River Falls Motel
W: Fairfield Inn, Ramada Inn, Sheraton
Med — E: + Hospital
Other — E: ATMs, Banks, Auto Services, Museums, Tires, Walgreen's

EASTERN TIME ZONE

⬆ INDIANA
⬇ KENTUCKY

NOTE: MM 138: Indiana State Line

EASTERN TIME ZONE

(137) — Jct I-71N, Jct I-64W, I-64E (NB)

136C — Jefferson St, Brook St (SB) Muhammad Ali Blvd (NB)
Gas — W: Chevron, Shell
Food — W: McDonald's, Papa John's

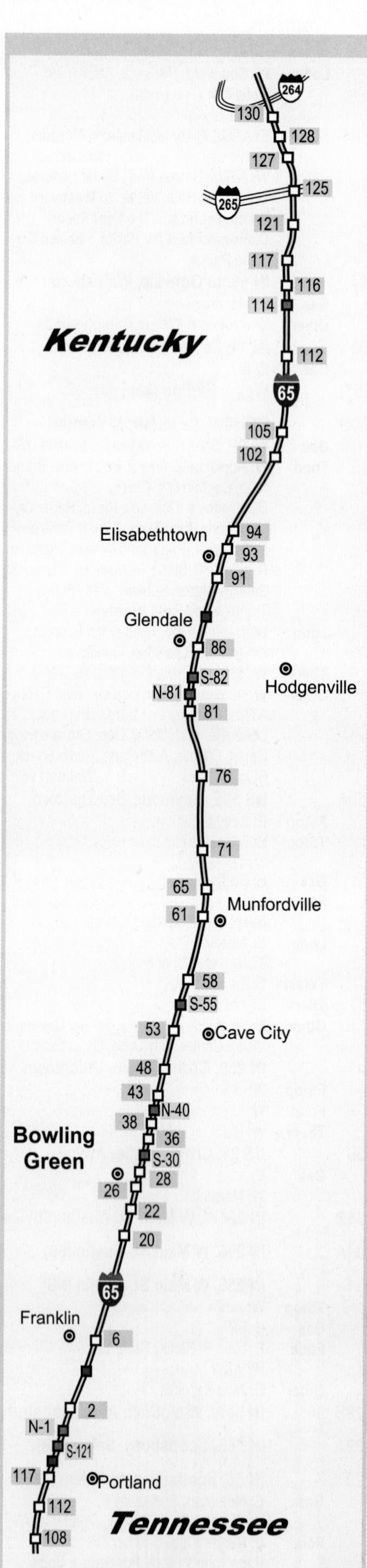

EXIT — KENTUCKY

Lodg — W: Comfort Inn, Courtyard, Days Inn, Hampton Inn, Hyatt, Marriott
Other — E: Walgreen's
W: Louisville Galleria, Museums, Tires

136B — E Gray St, S Brook St, Chestnut St Broadway St (NB)
Gas — W: Speedway, Thornton's
Lodg — W: Hilton, Holiday Inn
Med — E: + Jewish Hospital, + Norton Hospital, + Univ of Louisville Hospital, + Kosair Childrens Hospital

136A — College St, Jacob St, Brook St (NB)
Lodg — W: Holiday Inn
Other — E: Auto Services

135 — St Catherine St, Kentucky St
Gas — E: Big Foot, Circle K, Shell
Lodg — W: Alexander House, Dupont Mansion, Victorian Secret B&B

134B — Woodbine Ave
Gas — W: BP
Lodg — W: Days Inn, Quality Inn
Other — W: Harley Davidson

134A — S Preston St, Woodbine Ave

133 — Arthur St, Eastern Pkwy (SB)

133B — E Warnock St, Crittenden Dr (NB)
Food — E: Denny's, Papa John's Pizza, Subway
W: Cracker Barrel, McDonald's
Lodg — W: Country Hearth Inn

133A — Alt US 60, Eastern Pkwy (NB)
Gas — W: BP◈, Shell
Food — E: Denny's, Papa John's, Subway
W: McDonald's
Other — W: Univ of Louisville, to Churchill Downs

132 — Crittenden Dr, Louisville (SB)
FStop — W: Crittendon Drive BP
Food — E: Denny's
W: Arby's, Burger King, Cracker Barrel
Lodg — W: Country Inn, Hilton Garden Inn, Holiday Inn, Ramada Inn
TServ — E: Huber Tire
Other — E: Winn Dixie
W: KY Fair & Expo Center

(131BA) — Jct I-264, Watterson Expy, Freedom Way, Phillips Lane
Lodg — E: La Quinta Inn♥, Red Roof, Super 8
W: Airport Inn, Comfort Inn, Courtyard, Executive Inn, Hampton Inn
Other — W: KY Fair & Expo Center, Louisville Int'l Airport✈, Auto Rentals

130 — KY 61, Preston Hwy, Grade Ln
Gas — E: BP, Dairy Mart, Speedway, Thornton's
Food — E: Bob Evans, Burger King, Domino's, KFC, McDonald's, Ponderosa, Subway, Taco Bell, Waffle House, Wendy's
Lodg — E: Red Roof Inn♥, Super 8
Other — E: Auto Services, Auto Dealers, Big O Tire, Dollar General, Grocery, O'Reilly Auto Parts, Radio Shack, Staples, Tires Plus+, U-Haul, Right Stop RV Center
W: Louisville Int'l Airport✈, Warbirds Museum, Rental Cars

128 — KY 1631, Fern Valley Rd
Gas — E: BP, Chevron, Five Star, Thornton's, Sam's
Food — E: Arby's, Golden Wall Chinese, Hardee's, McDonald's, Outback Steakhouse, Shoney's, Subway, Subworks/Thornton's, Waffle House, White Castle
Lodg — E: Comfort Suites, Holiday Inn, InTown Suites, Jameson Inn
W: Holiday Inn

◈= Regular Gas Stations with Diesel ▲ = RV Friendly Locations ♥= Pet Friendly Locations
Red print shows large vehicle parking / access on site or nearby Brown Print = Campgrounds / RV PARKS

EXIT		KENTUCKY
	Other	E: Auto Services, ATMs, NAPA, Sam's Club, Walgreen's, Wrecker Service
		W: Ford Assembly Plant, Louisville Int'l Airport✈
127		**KY 1065, Outer Loop**
	Gas	W: Chevron, Marathon
	Food	E: Texas Roadhouse
		W: McDonald's
	Other	E: to Jefferson Mall, Kroger, Winn Dixie
		W: Louisville Motor Speedway, **Louisville RV Center**
(125)		**Jct I-265E, KY 841 (SB)**
125B		**Jct KY 841W**
(125A)		**Jct I-265E, KY 841E**
121		**KY 1526, Brooks Rd, Louisville, Brooks, Shepherdsville**
	TStop	W: Pilot Travel Center #356 (Scales)
	Gas	E: BP, Chevron, Marathon
		W: BP◈, Shell,
	Food	E: Arby's, Burger King, **Cracker Barrel**, McDonald's
		W: Subway/TacoBell/Pilot TC, Waffle House
	Lodg	E: Fairfield Inn, Hearthstone Inn♥, Holiday Inn Express
		W: Comfort Inn, Econo Lodge, Hampton Inn, Quality Inn
	Other	E: Scott's Auto & Truck Repair, **Tinker's Toy Interstate RV**
		W: WiFi/Pilot TC, Indoor Water Park/Comf Inn,Off Road Adventures, **Sunrise RV & Trailer Sales**,
117		**KY 44, Mt Washington Rd, 4th St, Shepherdsville**
	FStop	W: Five Star Food Mart
	Gas	E: BP, 44 Shell◈
		W: Chevron◈, Speedway◈, Kroger
	Food	E: Denny's, Hardee's, Rest/BW
		W: Arby's, Burger King, Fazoli's, KFC, Long John Silver, McDonald's, Papa John's, Sonic, Subway, Taco Bell, Waffle House, Wendy's, White Castle
	Lodg	E: Best Western, Days Inn♥
		W: Country Inn, Motel 6♥, Super 8
	Other	E: **Louisville South KOA▲**
		W: Ace Hardware, Advance Auto Parts, Big O Tires, Big Lots, Dollar General, Family Dollar, Kroger, Lowe's, NAPA, Pharmacy, RiteAid, SavALot
116		**KY 480, to KY 61, Cedar Grove Rd, Shepherdsville**
	TStop	E: Love's Travel Stop #238 (Scales)
	Gas	E: Shell◈
	Food	E: Chester's/Subway/Love's TS
	Other	E: Laundry/**RVDump**/WiFi/Love's TS
		W: **Grandma's RV Park ▲**, **Leisure Life RV Supercenter**
(114)		**Welcome Center Rest Area (Both dir)** (RR, Phone, Picnic, Pet, Vend)
112		**KY 245, to Clermont, Bardstown**
	Gas	E: Shell◈
	Other	E: to **My Old KY Home State Park**
105		**KY 61, Preston Hwy, Lebanon Jct**
	FStop	W: 105 Quik Stop
	TStop	W: Pilot Travel Center #399 (Scales)
	Gas	W: Citgo
	Food	W: Subway/McDonald's/Pilot TC, Back in Time Rest, Daddio's
	TServ	W: Pilot TC/Tires

EXIT		KENTUCKY
	Other	W: Laundry/WiFi/Pilot TC, Fort Knox Military Res
102		**KY 313, Joe Prather Highway, KY 434, Radcliff, Vine Grove**
94		**US 62, KY 61, Elizabethtown**
	Gas	E: Five Star Food Mart, Plaza 94 Food Mart, Marathon◈
		W: BP◈, Chevron◈, Speedway◈, Swifty, Kroger,
	Food	E: Denny's, Golden Corral, KFC/Taco Bell, Waffle House, White Castle
		W: Arby's, Burger King, Black Angus Grill, **Cracker Barrel**, KFC, McDonald's, Pizza Hut, Ryan's Grill, Ruby Tuesday, Shoney's, Subway, Texas Roadhouse, Wendy's
	Lodg	E: Days Inn♥, Quality Inn♥, Super 8
		W: Best Western, Country Hearth Inn, Fairfield Inn, Hampton Inn, Howard Johnson, La Quinta Inn♥, Motel 6♥, Ramada Inn
	Med	W: **+ Hardin Memorial Hospital**
	Other	E: Carwash/Plaza 94, **Elizabethtown Crossroads Campground▲**
		W: Advance Auto Parts, Auto Zone, CVS, Dollar General, Dollar Tree, Kroger, Skaggs **RV Country**, True Value Hardware, US Post Office, Walgreen's, **KY State Hwy Patrol Post**
93		**to Bardstown, Bluegrass Pkwy**
	Other	E: Makers Mark distillery, **to My Old KY Home State Park**
91		**US 31W, KY 61, Western KY Pkwy, Elizabethtown, Paducah**
	Gas	E: Chevron, Marathon◈, Shell
		W: Chevron◈
	Food	E: Back Yard Burgers, Long John Silver, McDonald's, Omelette House
		W: Jerry's Rest
	Lodg	E: Bluegrass Inn, Budget Holiday Motel, Common Wealth Lodge, Heritage Inn
		W: KY Cardinal Inn, E'Town Motel, Roadside Inn
	Med	W: **+ Hardin Memorial Hospital**
	Other	E: Auto Repairs, Orville's Diesel Service, Diesel Doc's, Budget, Ryder, U-Haul
		W: Towing, Wayne's Tire Center
(90)		**Weigh Station (Both dir)**
86		**KY 222, to US 31W, Glendale**
	TStop	E: Pilot Travel Center #48 (Scales)
		W: Petro Stopping Center #30/Mobil (Scales)
	Food	E: McDonald's/Pilot TC
		W: IronSkillet/FastFood/Petro SC, Depot Rest, Whistle Stop Rest
	Lodg	W: Glendale Economy Inn
	TWash	W: Blue Beacon/Petro SC
	TServ	W: Petro SC/Tires, Quality Diesel Service
	Other	E: Laundry/WiFi/Pilot TC, **Glendale Campground▲**
		W: Laundry/BarbSh/WiFi/Petro SC
(82)		**Rest Area (SB)** (RR, Phones, Picnic, Pet, Vend)
(81)		**Rest Area (NB)** (RR, Phones, Picnic, Pet, Vend)
81		**KY 84, Western Ave, Sonora**
	FStop	E: Sammy's Market/Marathon (DAD) (DAND)
	TStop	E: Pilot Travel Center #392 (Scales)
	Gas	E: Fast Way Food Mart BP
		W: Shell

EXIT		KENTUCKY
	Food	E: Rest/Sammy's, Subway/Pilot TC
	TWash	E: Blue Beacon/Pilot TC
	Other	E: Laundry/WiFi/**RVDump**/Pilot TC, to Abe Lincoln Birthplace
76		**KY 224, Upton-Talley Rd, Upton**
	Gas	E: Upton Mini Mart, Chevron◈
		W: Hawke's Service Station
NOTE:		**MM 75: Eastern / Central Time Zone**
71		**KY 728, Bonnieville**
65		**US 31W, Dixie Hwy, Munfordville**
	Gas	E: BP◈,
		W: Chevron◈, Shell
	Food	E: DQ, McDonald's, Pizza Hut
		W: Country Fixins, Sonic, Subway
	Lodg	E: Super 8
	Other	E: Advance Auto Parts, Dollar General, Family Dollar, Pamida
(61)		**Rest Area (Both dir)** (RR, Phones, Picnic, Pet, Vend)
58		**KY 218, to KY 335, Horse Cave**
	TStop	E: Love's Travel Stop #360 (Scales)
		W: Zack Bros Truck Stop /Chevron
	Gas	W: BP, Marathon◈
	Food	E: Chesters/McDonald's/Love's TS
		W: FastFood/ZB TS, Aunt B's Rest/ Budget Host Inn
	Lodg	W: Budget Host Inn, Country Hearth Inn, Hampton Inn
	Med	E: **+ Caverna Memorial Hospital**
	Other	E: WiFi/Love's TS, KY Down Under
		W: Auto & Truck Repairs/Marathon, **Horse Cave KOA/RVDump▲**
(55)		**Rest Area (SB)** (RR, Phones, Picnic, Pet, Vend)
53		**KY 70, KY 90, US 31W, Cave City**
	Gas	E: BP◈, Chevron◈, Marathon◈
		W: Shell, SuperAmerica
	Food	E: Burger King, **Cracker Barrel**, DQ, Jerry's Rest, KFC, Long John Silver, McDonald's, Pizza Hut, Subway, Sahara Steakhouse, Taco Bell, Wendy's
		W: Bel-Air, Joe's Diner, KFC, Subway
	Lodg	E: Best Western♥, Comfort Inn, Comfort Inn & Suites, Days Inn, Executive Inn, Knights Inn♥, Quality Inn, Super 8, WigWam Village
		W: Park View Motel, Oakes Motel &
	Other	E: Auto Services, ATM, Auto Dealer, Bank, Guntown Mtn, Museum, SavALot, Road & Field Diesel Service, Crystal Onyx Cave **& Campground▲**
		W: KY Action Park, Hillbilly Hound Fun Park, **Mammoth Cave Jellystone Park Camp Resort▲**, **Singin Hills Campground & RV Park▲**, **Mammoth Cave Nat'l Park▲**
48		**KY 255, to US 31W, Park City**
	FStop	E: Park City Shell
	Food	E: FastFood/Park City Shell
	Lodg	E: Parkland Motel
	Other	W: Diamond Caverns, **Diamond Caverns Campground▲**, **Mammoth Cave Nat'l Park▲**, **Singin Hills Campground & RV Park▲**
43		**Cumberland Pkwy (TOLL), Glasgow, Somerset**
	Other	E: to **Barren River Lake State Resort Park▲**, **COE/Barren River Lake/ The Narrows▲ /Tailwater Below Dam▲**

◈ = Regular Gas Stations with Diesel ▲ = RV Friendly Locations ♥ = Pet Friendly Locations

Red print shows large vehicle parking / access on site or nearby Brown Print = Campgrounds / RV PARKS

EXIT — KENTUCKY

(40) **Rest Area** (NB)
(RR, Phones, Picnic, Vend)

38 **KY 101, S Main St, Smiths Grove, US 68, KY 80, Scottsville**
- TStop W: Smith Grove BP Travel Center (Scales)
- Gas W: Chevron, Shell
- Food W: Rest/FastFood/Smith Grove TC, McDonald's, Wendy's
- Lodg W: Bryce Motel
- TServ W: Smith Grove TC/Tires/TWash
- Other E: COE/Barren River Lake/Tailwater Below Dam▲
  W: BarbSh/Smith Grove TC

36 **US 68, KY 80, Oakland**
(NB exit, SB reaccess only)

(30) **Rest Area** (SB)
(RR, Phones, Picnic, Pet, Vend)

28 **KY 446, to US 31W, US 68, Bowling Green, Plum Springs**
- Gas W: BP, Shell
- Food W: Hardee's, Jerry's Rest, Smokey Pig BBQ, Wendy's
- Lodg W: Best Western, Country Hearth Inn, Continental Inn, Value Lodge
- Other W: ATMs, Bank, Auto Services, National Corvette Museum, Tires, Towing, to Beech Bend Amusemart Park, Oval Track, Dragstrip, Splash Lagoon & Beech Bend Family Campground▲, Beech Bend State Park

26 **KY 234, Cemetary Rd**

22 **US 231, Scottsville Rd, Bowling Green, Scottsville**
- Gas E: Citgo◈, Marathon, Shell
  W: BP, Chevron◈, Marathon, RaceWay, Shell◈, Speedway◈
- Food E: Cracker Barrel, Culver's, DQ, Denny's, Domino's Pizza, Godfather's Pizza, Hardee's, Mancino Grinders & Pizza, Ryan's Grill, Sonic, Waffle House, Zaxby's
- Food W: Applebee's, Arby's, Bob Evans, Burger King, Captain D's, ChickFilA, Chuck E Cheese's Pizza, CiCi's Pizza, KFC, Krystal, Kyoto Steakhouse, Longhorn Steakhouse, Lone Star Steakhouse, McDonald's, Moe's SW Grill, O'Charley's, Olive Garden, OutBack Steakhouse, Panera Bread, Pizza Hut Santa Fe Steaks, Shoney's, Shogun of Japan, Smokey Bones BBQ, Starbucks, Taco Bell, TGI Friday, Waffle House, Wendy's, White Castle
- Lodg E: Best Western, Comfort Inn, Days Inn, Econo Lodge, Fairfield Inn, HomeTowne Suites, Holiday Inn, La Quinta Inn♥, Microtel, Quality Inn, Ramada Inn
  W: Baymont Inn, Candlewood Suites, Courtyard, Drury Inn♥, Hampton Inn, Motel 6♥, News Inn of BG, Red Roof Inn♥
- TServ W: Whayne Power Systems
- Med E: + Greenwood Urgent Clinic
  W: + Greenview Reg'l Hospital
- Other E: ATMs, Banks, Carwash/Shell, Car Wash Gander Mountain, Harley Davidson BG, IGA, Pharmacy, US Post Office, Vet♥, Camping World/RVDump
  W: Advance Auto Parts, Auto Dealers, ATMs, AMC Cinema, Banks, Barnes & Noble, Best Buy, Bowling Green KOA▲,

EXIT — KY / TN

- Other E: CVS, Carwash, Dollar General, FedEx Office, Goodyear, Greenwood Mall, Home Depot, Kroger, Lowe's, Office Depot, PetCo♥, Pharmacy, Sam's Club, Staples, Target, Trailer World, UPS Store, U-Haul, Walmart sc, Bowling Green Warren Co Reg'l Airport✈,

20 **William H Natcher Pky (TOLL), Bowling Green, Owensboro**
- Other W: to W Ky Univ, KY State Police

6 **KY 100, Franklin, Scottsville**
- TStop E: AmBest/Bluegrass Travel Plaza (Scales)
  W: Pilot Travel Center #46(Scales), Pilot Travel Center #438 (Scales)
- Gas E: BP◈
- Food E: FastFood/Bluegrass TP
  W: Subway/Pilot TC #46, Wendy's/Pilot TC #438
- Lodg W: Days Inn, Super 8
- TWash W: Pilot TW
- TServ W: Speedco, Bluegrass Truck & Tire Repair, Petro Lube Service & Tires
- Med W: + Hospital
- Other W: WiFi/Pilot TC #46, Laundry/WiFi/Pilot TC #438, Bluegrass Music RV Park▲

(4) **Weigh Station** (NB)

2 **US 31W, Nashville Rd, Franklin**
- TStop E: Flying J Travel Plaza #5053/Conoco (Scales), Keystop Truck Stop/Marathon
- Gas W: BP◈
- Food E: FastFood/Keystop TS, Rest/FastFood/FJ TP
- Food W: Cracker Barrel, Jim's BBQ, Shoney's, McDonald's, Waffle House, Subway/BP
- Lodg W: Best Value, Comfort Inn, Econo Lodge, Hampton Inn, Holiday Inn Express, Super 8
- Med W: + Hospital
- Other W: Laundry/BarbSh/WiFi/RVDump/LP/FJ TP

(1) **KY Welcome Center** (NB)
(RR, Phones, Picnic, Pet, Vend)

CENTRAL TIME ZONE

KENTUCKY
TENNESSEE

NOTE: MM 121.5: Kentucky State Line

CENTRAL TIME ZONE

(121) **TN Robertson Welcome Center** (SB)
(RR, Phones, Picnic, Vend)

(119) **Weigh Station** (Both dir)

117 **TN 52, Orlinda, Portland**
(Addtl Serv 4-5mi E in Portland)
- Gas E: Shell◈
  W: AmocoBP◈
- Lodg W: Budget Host Inn
- Med E: + Hospital

112 **TN 25, Cross Plains, Gallatin, Springfield**
- TStop W: Mapco Express #1028
- Gas E: BP
  W: Shell◈
- Food W: FastFood/Mapco Exp, Diddles Café, Trues BBQ
- TServ W: Mapco Exp

EXIT — TENNESSEE

108 **TN 76, Springfield Rd, White House, Springfield**
- Gas E: Keystop, Mapco Express
  W: AmocoBP
- Food E: Cracker Barrel, DQ, Hardee's, KFC, McDonald's, Taco Bell, Waffle House
  W: Rest/Days Inn, Red Lantern
- Lodg E: Holiday Inn Express
  W: Days Inn
- TServ W: American Coach & Truck
- Med W: + Hospital

104 **TN 257, Bethel Rd, Ridgetop, Goodlettsville**
- TStop E: Ridgetop Auto Truck Center/P66
- Gas W: Shell
- Food E: Rest/Ridgetop ATC
- Lodg E: Ridgetop Motel
- TWash E: Ridgetop ATC
- TServ E: Ridgetop ATC/Tires
- Other E: Laundry/Ridgetop ATC
  W: Owl's Roost Campground▲

98 **US 31W, US 41, TN 11, Goodlettsville Millersville, Springfield**
- Gas E: Citgo◈, RaceWay, Shell◈
  W: AmocoBP◈
- Food E: Subway, Waffle House
- Lodg E: Economy Inn
- Other E: Auto Services, Grocery, Blackwoods Truck Repair, Nashville Country RV Park▲
  W: Auto Services, Nashville I-65N Campground▲

97 **TN 174, Long Hollow Pike, Goodlettsville, Gallatin**
- FStop W: Dailey's Shell
- Gas E: BP◈, Exxon, Mapco Express
- Food E: Arby's, Captain D's, Cracker Barrel, China Express, KFC, McDonald's, Shoney's, Subway, Waffle House, Wendy's
  W: Bob Evans, Hardee's, Jack in the Box, Krystal, Little Caesar Pizza, Sonic
- Lodg E: Comfort Inn, Econo Lodge, Hampton Inn, Holiday Inn Express♥, Red Roof Inn♥, Shoney's Inn
  W: Baymont Inn, Motel 6♥
- Other E: ATMs, Banks, Kroger
  W: ATMs, Banks, Walgreen's, to Nashville I-65N Campground▲

96 **Rivergate Pkwy, Gallatin Pike, Two Mile Pkwy, Goodlettsville**
- Gas E: BP, Citgo◈, Phillips 66, Shell
  W: Chevron
- Food E: Arby's, Burger King, Cracker Barrel, Checkers, ChickFilA, Chili's, Chuck E Cheese, El Chico, Hooters, IHOP, Krystal, Lone Star Steakhouse, Mrs Winners, McDonald's, Olive Garden, Outback Steakhouse, Pizza Hut, Red Lobster, Starbucks, Subway, Steak n Shake, Waffle House, Wendy's
- Lodg E: Best Value Inn, Comfort Suites, Days Inn, Crestwood Suites, Quality Inn, Rodeway Inn, Red Roof Inn♥, Super 8
- Other E: ATMs, Auto Dealers, Auto Services, Banks, Best Buy, Boswell Harley Davidson, CVS, Cinemas, FedEx Office, Firestone, Goodyear, Home Depot, NTB, Office Depot, PepBoys, PetSmart♥, Rivergate Mall, Sam's Club, Sears Auto Center, Target, UPS Store, Walgreen's, Walmart,

◈= Regular Gas Stations with Diesel ▲ = RV Friendly Locations ♥= Pet Friendly Locations
Red print shows large vehicle parking / access on site or nearby Brown Print = Campgrounds / RV PARKS

EXIT — TENNESSEE

95 — **TN 386, Vietnam Vets Blvd, Hendersonville, Gallatin (NB)**

92 — **TN 45, Old Hickory Blvd, Madison (Serv E&W to US 31E or US 31W)**
- Med: E: + Nashville Memorial Hospital

90 — **US 31W, US 41, TN 155E, Briley Pky, Dickerson Pike, Nashville (NB)**
- Other: E: to Opryland

90B — **TN 155E, Briley Pkwy (SB)**
- Other: E: to Opryland, **Nashville KOA▲**

90A — **TN 155E, Briley Pkwy (SB)**

90A — **US 41, US 31W, Dickerson Pk (NB)**
- Gas: E: Citgo, Mapco Expr◊, Phillips 66, Shell◊
- Food: E: Arby's, Burger King, Captain D's, China King Buffet, Domino's Pizza, KFC, McDonald's, Mrs Winner's Chicken, Pizza Hut, Shoney's, Subway, Taco Bell, Waffle House, Wendy's
- Lodg: E: Days Inn, Econo Lodge, Sleep Inn, Super 8
- Med: W: + Skyline Medical Center
- Other: E: Advance Auto Parts, Banks, CVS, Kroger, Walgreen's, **Camping World**

(88B) — **Jct I-24W, to Clarksville**

(88A) — **Jct I-24E, to Nashville**

87AB — **US 431, TN 65, Trinity Ln, Nashville**
- TStop: E: Love's Travel Stop #429 (Scales)
- Gas: E: Circle K, Phillips 66
  W: BP, Chevron, Exxon
- Food: E: Subway/Love's TS, Krystal, White Castle
  W: Burger King, Captain D's, Denny's, Jack in the Box, McDonald's, Ponderosa, Subway, Taco Bell, Waffle House
- Lodg: E: Cumberland Inn, Delux Inn
  W: Best Value Inn♥, Comfort Inn♥, Days Inn♥, Quality Inn, Regency Inn, Super 8, Travelodge
- Med: W: + FHC Nashville
- Other: E: Auto Services, Grocery, Tires, **Holiday Mobile Village▲**
  W: Auto Services, **to** Jackson Truck & Trailer Repair, American Baptist College

(86) — **Jct I-24E, to I-40E, to Memphis**

85 — **US 41A, TN 12, Rosa L Parks Blvd**
- Gas: W: Exxon
- Food: W: Arby's, Krystal, McDonald's, Pizza Hut, Subway, Taco Bell
- Lodg: W: La Quinta Inn♥

NOTE: **I-65 below runs with I-40 for 2 exits. Exit #'s follow I-40.**

(84AB/208) — **Jct I-65N, I-40W, to Memphis**
Jct I-65N, I-40E, to Knoxville

209 — **US 70, TN 24, US 70S, US 431, Church St, Charlotte Ave**
- Gas: S: BP, Exxon
- Food: S: Burger King, Shoney's, White Castle
- Lodg: N: Holiday Inn
  S: Comfort Inn, Shoney's Inn
- Med: S: + Baptist Hospital, + Columbia Centennial Medical Center
- Other: N: Auto Services, Fleet Repair, Thrifty RAC, Museums, State Capitol
  S: Auto & Tire Services, Budget RAC, Museums

EXIT — TENNESSEE

209A — **US 70S, US 431, Broadway**
- Med: S: + Metro Nashville Gen'l Hospital

209B — **US 70S, US 431 Demonbreun St**
- Med: S: + Vanderbilt University Hospital, + Columbia Centennial Medical Center, + Baptist Hospital
- Other: N: Auto Services, ATMs, Banks, Courts, Enterprise RAC, Firestone, Goodyear, Country Music Hall of Fame & Museum, Gaylord Ent Center, Nashville Visitor Info, TN State Capitol, Ryman Auditorium, TN Convention Center, Nashville Muni Auditorium
- Other: S: Auto Services, ATMs, Banks, Budget RAC, Music Row, Museums

(210/211) — **Jct I-24E, I-40E, I-65S, Nashville, Chattanooga (SB) (WB, LEFT exit)**

(82/83) — **Jct I-65N, I-40W, to Memphis**

(82B) — **Jct I-40E, Knoxville (NB, LEFT Exit)**

NOTE: **I-65 above runs with I-40 for 2 exits. Exit #'s follow I-40.**

81 — **Wedgewood Ave, Nashville**
- Gas: W: BP, Exxon, Scot Market
- Food: W: Burger King, McDonald's, Mrs Winners Chicken
- Med: W: + Vanderbilt Univ Hospital, + Veterans Medical Center
- Other: E: to TN State Fairgrounds, Trevecca Nazarene Univ, Greer Stadium, Science Museum, Nashville Speedway USA
  W: CVS, Dollar General, Dollar Tree, Kroger, Walgreen's, U-Haul, **to** Museums, Belmont Univ, Vanderbilt Univ

(80) — **Jct I-440, W-Memphis, E-Knoxville (NB, LEFT Exit W) (SB, LEFT exit E)**

79 — **Armory Dr, Powell Ave, Nashville**
- Gas: E: Scot Market, Shell
- Food: E: Applebee's, Baja Border Café, Rice Bowl, Subway, Taco Bell, Wendy's
- Other: E: ATMs, Banks, Auto Services, Car Max, Cinema, Goodyear, PetSmart♥, UPS Store, One Hundred Oaks Mall, TN National Guard, **Police Dept**
  W: **to** CVS, Kroger, Walgreen's

78 — **TN 255, Harding Place (Addtl Serv E to US 31/Nolensville Pk)**
- Gas: E: Mapco Express, Marathon, Shell
- Food: E: **Cracker Barrel**, Santa Fe Cattle Co, Waffle House
- Lodg: E: La Quinta Inn♥, Red Roof Inn♥
- Med: E: to + Southern Hills Medical Center
- Other: E: **to** Museum, Nashville Zoo, Harding Mall

74AB — **TN 254, Old Hickory Blvd, Church St, Brentwood, Nashville**
- Gas: W: BP, Exxon, Mapco Exp, Shell, Texaco
- Food: E: Captain D's, Shoney's, Waffle House
  W: Mrs Winners Chicken, O'Charley's, Papa John's Pizza, Ruby Tuesday, Starbucks, Wendy's
- Lodg: E: AmeriSuites♥, Comfort Inn, Extended Stay America♥, Holiday Inn, Hilton, Steeple Chase Inn, Studio Plus
  W: Courtyard, Hampton Inn, Mainstay Suite
- Med: E: + Hospital
- Other: E: Target, Tires
  W: ATMs, Auto Services, Auto Dealers, Banks, CVS, Cinema, FedEx Office, Harris Teeter, Kroger, Office Depot, Tires, US Post Office, Walgreen's,

◊= Regular Gas Stations with Diesel ▲ = RV Friendly Locations ♥= Pet Friendly Locations
Red print shows large vehicle parking / access on site or nearby Brown Print = Campgrounds / RV PARKS

EXIT	TENNESSEE

71 **TN 253, Concord Rd, Brentwood**

69 **TN 441, Moores Lane, Franklin**
- Gas — **E:** Mapco Express◈, Shell; **W:** BP, Marathon, Shell◈
- Food — **E:** Applebee's, Cozymel's, Joe's Crab Shack, Japanese Rest, Krystal, Outback Steakhouse, Shogun, Sonic, Starbucks, Tony Roma's; **W:** McDonald's, Red Lobster, Romano's Macaroni Grill, Ruby Tuesdays, Subway, TCBY, Taco Bell
- Lodg — **E:** AmeriSuites, Homestead Studio, Red Roof Inn♥, Wingate Inn; **W:** Sleep Inn
- Other — **E:** Albertson's, ATMs, Banks, Home Depot, PetSmart♥, Publix; **W:** Best Buy, Barnes & Noble, Carmike Cinemas, Costco, CVS, Goodyear, Harley Davidson Cool Springs, Target, Walgreen's, Waldenbooks, Galleria Mall

68AB **Cool Springs Blvd, Franklin**
- Gas — **W:** Exxon, Shell
- Food — **W:** Carrabba's, Chili's, Jack in the Box, McDonald's, Ruby Tuesday, Starbucks, TGI Friday, Wendy's
- Lodg — **E:** Embassy Suites, Marriott; **W:** Country Inn, Hampton Inn
- Other — **W:** ATMs, Banks, Borders, Auto Services, Cinema, FedEx Office, Home Depot, Kroger, Lowe's, Office Depot, Staples, Sam's Club,UPS Store, Walgreen, **Walmart sc**,

65 **TN 96, Murfreesboro Rd, Franklin, Murfreesboro**
- Gas — **E:** Exxon, Mapco Expr, Shell◈; **W:** BP◈, Mapco Express◈, Shell◈
- Food — **E:** Cracker Barrel, Steak n Shake, Sonic; **W:** Arby's, Hardee's, Famous Chinese Buffet, KFC, McDonald's, Shoney's, Taco Bell, Waffle House, Wendy's
- Lodg — **E:** Best Value Inn, Comfort Inn, Days Inn♥ Holiday Inn Express, La Quinta Inn♥, Ramada; **W:** Best Western, Super 8
- Med — **E: + Williamson Medical Center**
- Other — **E:** Auto Dealer, Auto Services, Food Lion, Walgreen's; **W:** Animal Hospital♥, ATMs, Home Depot, Kroger, Publix, UPS Store, Walgreen's

61 **TN 248, Peytonsville Rd, Goose Creek ByPass, Franklin, Spring Hill**
- FStop — **E:** Kwik Sak #610
- TStop — **E:** Travel Center of America # 157/BP (Scales)
- Gas — **W:** Mapco Express, Scot Market
- Food — **E:** ForkintheRoad/TA TC; **W:** Rest/Goose Creek Inn
- Lodg — **W:** Goose Creek Inn
- TServ — **E:** TA TC/Tires; **W:** RLS Sales & Service
- Other — **E:** Laundry/WiFi/TA TC

59 **TN 840, E to Almaville, Murfreesboro, Lebanon**

53 **TN 396, Saturn Pkwy, Spring Hill (Gas, Food Lodg 3-4 mi W to US 31N)**

(49) **Parking Area (NB)**

EXIT	TENNESSEE

46 **US 412, TN 99, TN 273, Bear Creek Pike, Sylvester Chunn Hwy, Columbia, Chapel Hill**
- FStop — **W:** Stan's Rest & Country Store/Texaco, RP Williams Co
- TStop — **E:** Love's Travel Stop #346 (Scales)
- Gas — **E:** Chevron; **W:** BP
- Food — **E:** FastFood/Love's TS; **W:** Stan's Rest, Burger King, Cracker Barrel, Waffle House, Wendy's
- Lodg — **W:** Best Value Inn, Comfort Inn, Holiday Inn, Relax Inn
- TWash — **W:** RP Williams Co
- Med — **W: + Maury Regional Hospital, + Nashville Memorial Hospital**
- Other — **E:** WiFi/Love's TS, **Campers RV Family Campground▲, Travelers RV Park & Campground▲, to appr 13mi: Henry Horton State Park▲**

37 **TN 50, New Lewisburg Hwy, Columbia, Lewisburg**
- Med — **E: + Hospital**

32 **TN 373, Mooresville Hwy, Lewisburg, Columbia (Addt'l Serv 6-7 mi E in Lewisburg)**
- Gas — **E:** Williams Interstate Market/Exxon◈

27 **TN 129, Lynnville Rd, Cornersville (Addt'l Serv 4 mi E in Cornersville)**
- Other — **E: Texas T Campground▲**

(25) **Parking Area (SB)**

(24) **Parking Area (NB)**

22 **US 31A, Sam Davis Hwy, Lewisburg Hwy, TN 11, Cornersville, Pulaski, Lewisburg**
- TStop — **E:** The Tennessean Truck Stop/AmocoBP (Scales); **W:** Pilot Travel Center #406 (Scales)
- Gas — **W:** Serve & Go/Shell◈
- Food — **E:** Rest/FastFood/Tennessean TS, McDonald's, Subway
- Food — **W:** Deli/Pilot TC
- Lodg — **E:** Econo Lodge
- TServ — **E:** Tennessean TS/Tires
- Other — **E:** Laundry/WiFi/Tennessean TS; **W:** WiFi/Pilot TC

14 **US 64, TN 15, Fayetteville Hwy, Pulaski, Fayetteville**
- Gas — **E:** BP◈, Shell◈
- Other — **E: TN Valley RV Park▲**

6 **TN 273, Bryson Rd, Ardmore, Elkton**
- TStop — **E:** Shady Lawn Truck Stop/66 (Scales)
- Food — **E:** Rest/Shady Lawn TS
- Lodg — **E:** Best Value Inn
- TServ — **E:** Shady Lawn TS/Tires
- Other — **E:** Laundry/Shady Lawn TS

(3) **TN Giles Welcome Center (NB) (RR, Phones, Picnic, Vend, Info)**

1 **US 31, TN 7, Main St, Pleasant Hill Rd, Ardmore, to Pulaski, Lawrenceburg, Huntsville**
- Gas — **E:** Chevron◈, Exxon◈, Shell
- Food — **E:** Church's, DQ, Hardee's, Subway

CENTRAL TIME ZONE

⬆ TENNESSEE

EXIT	ALABAMA

⬇ ALABAMA

NOTE: MM 366: Tennessee State Line

CENTRAL TIME ZONE

365 **AL 53, Elkmont, to Ardmore, TN**
- Gas — **E:** Country Store
- Lodg — **E:** Budget Inn

(364) **AL Welcome Center (SB) (RR, Phones, Pic, Vend, Info, RVDump)**

361 **Sandlin Rd, Thach Rd, Elkmont**
- TStop — **W:** Pam's Truck Stop/Citgo
- Food — **W:** Rest/Pam's TS, Sonny G's BBQ
- TServ — **W:** Pam's TS/Tires
- Other — **W:** Morris Garage & Towing Service

354 **US 31S, AL 3, AL 99, Athens (Acc to #351 Serv via US 31S)**
- Gas — **W:** Chevron
- Food — **W:** Subway
- Med — **W: + Hospital**
- Other — **W:** ATMs, Banks, Auto Services & Repairs, **Northgate RV Travel Park▲**

351 **US 72, AL 2, Athens, Huntsville**
- Gas — **E:** BP, Exxon, RaceWay, Shell; **W:** Chevron, J Mart, Texaco◈, Murphy
- Food — **E:** BBQ, Burger King, Cracker Barrel, McDonald's, Subway/Shell, Waffle House, Wendy's; **W:** Applebee's, Arby's, Backyard Burger, Catfish Cabin, Hardee's, Krystal, Papa John's Pizza, McDonald's, Ruby Tuesday, Shoney's, Sonic, Starbucks, Subway
- Lodg — **E:** Comfort Inn, Country Hearth Inn, Hampton Inn; **W:** Best Western♥, Bomar Inn, Days Inn, Super 8♥, Sleep Inn♥
- Med — **W: + Hospital**
- Other — **E: to Bolton Service Center, Cagle's Motorhome Parts & Service**, Limestone Flea Market; **W:** ATMs, Auto Dealers, Auto Services, Banks, Big 10 Tire, Dollar General, Goodyear, Kroger, Lowe's, O'Reilly Auto Parts, Staples, **Walmart sc**, Athens State College, **to Joe Wheeler State Park▲**

(340) **Jct I-565, AL 20, Alt US 72, Huntsville, Decatur (NB)**
- Other — **E:** Huntsville Madison Co Int'l Airport✈, Redstone Arsenal

340A **Alt US 72, AL 20, Huntsville-Decatur Hwy, to Decatur (SB)**

(340B) **Jct I-565, Alt US 72, Huntsville (SB) (Services 7-10 mi W in Decatur)**
- Other — **E:** Huntsville-Madison Co Int'l Airport✈, NASA Space & Rocket Center

334 **AL 67, Point Mallard Pky, Decatur, Priceville, Somerville**
- FStop — **W:** J-Mart #567/BP
- TStop — **W:** Pilot Travel Center #441 (Scales)
- Gas — **E:** AmocoBP◈, RaceTrac◈; **W:** Chevron, Texaco
- Food — **W:** Subway/Wendy's/Pilot TC, Hardee's, BBQ Smokehouse, Krystal, McDonald's, Waffle House
- Lodg — **E:** Days Inn, Super 8, Southeastern Motel; **W:** Comfort Inn
- Med — **W: + North AL Reg'l Hospital**
- Other — **E:** Foodland

◈ = Regular Gas Stations with Diesel ▲ = RV Friendly Locations ♥ = Pet Friendly Locations
Red print shows large vehicle parking / access on site or nearby Brown Print = Campgrounds / RV PARKS

EXIT **ALABAMA**

W: Laundry/WiFi/**RVDump**/Pilot TC, Vet♥, American Truck Repair, **Hood Tractor & RV Center, Andy's RV Services, Wheeler Nat'l Wildlife Refuge**

328 AL 36, Main St, Hartselle
Gas W: AmocoBP, Chevron◊, Cowboys◊, Shell
Food W: Huddle House, Homestyle BBQ
Med W: + Hospital, + Hartselle Medical Center
Other W: ATMs, Banks, Auto Services, Kroger, Tires, Vet♥, N on US 31: **Walmart sc**

325 Thompson Rd, Hartselle

322 Hwy 55E, Pike Rd, Falkville, Eva
TStop E: J&J Oil/322 Truck Stop/BP
W: Love's Travel Stop #381 (Scales)
Gas W: Chevron
Food E: Rest/322 TS
W: Subway/McDonald's/Love's TS
Other W: ATMs, Trailers, **Falkville Police Dept**

318 US 31, AL 3, to Lacon, Vinemont
Gas E: BP
Food E: Stuckey's/DQ/BP

310 AL 157, Finis St John III Dr, Cullman, West Point, Fairview
FStop E: Dowd Hwy 157 Shell
Gas E: AmocoBP, Chevron, Conoco◊
W: BP, Exxon◊
Food E: Arby's, Backyard Burger, Burger King, **Cracker Barrel**, Denny's, McDonald's, Ruby Tuesday, Taco Bell, Waffle House
Lodg E: Best Western♥, Comfort Inn, Hampton Inn, Holiday Inn Express, Sleep Inn
W: Super 8
Med E: + Hospital
Other E: Cullman Towing, Auto Dealers, Auto Services, ATMs
W: **Cullman Campground▲**

308 US 278, AL 74, Cullman, Double Springs, Ave Maria Grotto
FStop E: US 31: Westside Shell
Gas W: Chevron
Food E: FastFood/Westside Shell, Rest/Days Inn, BBQ, Omelette Shop
W: Rest/Howard Johnson
Lodg E: Days Inn♥
W: Howard Johnson
Med E: + Hospital
Other E: Carmike Town Square 3, C&M Truck & Trailer Repair
W: Cullman Flea Market, Taylor Tire Service

304 AL 69N, CR 437, Cullman, Good Hope
TStop E: Jack's Truck Stop/Shell (Scales), Good Hope Exxon
Gas E: BP, Chevron, Texaco◊
W: JetPep◊
Food E: Rest/Jack's TS, Hardee's, Waffle House
Lodg E: Econo Lodge♥
TWash E: Jack's TS, Good Hope Exxon
TServ E: Jack's TS/Tires, Good Hope Exxon/ Tires, Mark's Truck Service, C& M Truck & Trailer Repair, Truck Express Lube
Med E: + Hospital
Other E: Laundry/Good Hope Exxon, ATMs, Auto Repairs, Laundromat, **Walmart**, **Good Hope Campground▲**
W: **Speegles Marina & Campground▲**, to Smith Lake

(302) Cullman Co Rest Area (Both dir) (RR, Phones, Picnic, Vend, RVDump)

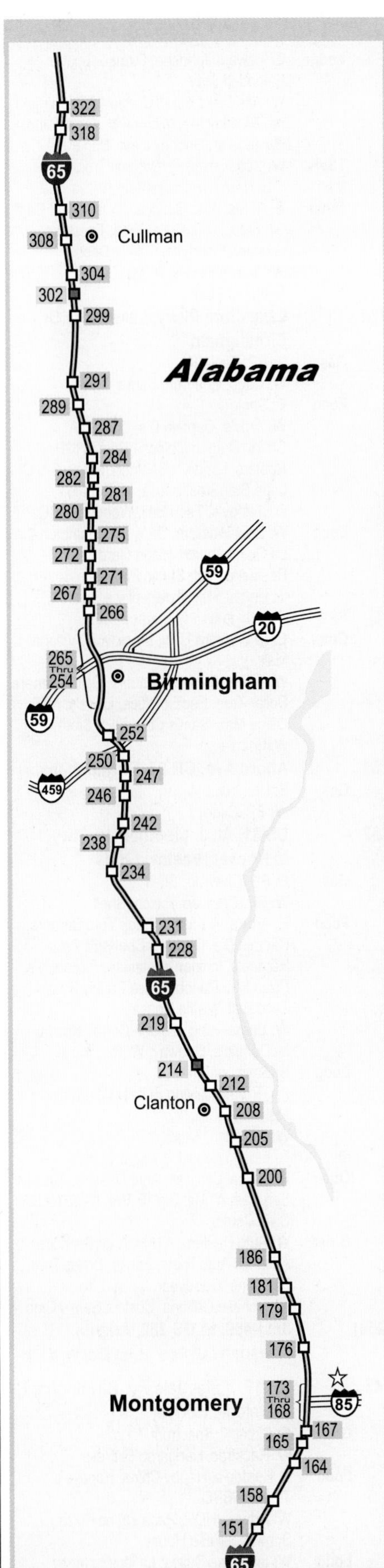

EXIT **ALABAMA**

299 AL 69S, CR 490, Cullman, Dodge City, Jasper
FStop W: 69 Chevron
TStop W: RoadysTS/Dodge City Travel Center/ Conoco (Scales)
Gas E: Citgo
W: BP◊, Shell◊, Texaco◊
Food W: Rest/Dodge City TC, Dodge City BBQ, Jack's Rest, Roadhouse BBQ & Grill, Subway
TServ E: Ray's Truck & Trailer Repair
W: Dodge City TC/Tires
Other E: **Millican RV**
W: Laundry/BarbSh/CB/WiFi/Dodge City TC, Dollar General, CarQuest, **Bremen Lake View Resort▲**

291 AL 91, Hanceville, Arkadelphia, Colony
TStop W: Parker's I-65 Truck Stop/Shell
Gas E: Conoco◊
Food E: AJ's BBQ
W: Rest/Parker's TS
Lodg W: Motel I-65/Parker's TS
TWash W: Parker's TS
Other E: **Country View RV Park▲**
W: WiFi/Tires/Parkers TS

289 CR 5, Hayden, Empire
Gas W: BP
Food W: Stuckey's/BP
Other W: **Rickwood Caverns State Park▲**

287 US 31N, AL 3, Bee Line Hwy, Hayden Garden City, Blount Springs
Gas E: Conoco◊, Citgo◊

284 US 31S, AL 160E, Warrior, Hayden
Gas E: Phillips 66, Shell◊
Food E: Bryant's Seafood, Perry's Catfish
Other W: **Rickwood Caverns State Park▲**, Scenic Drive

282 CR 140, Warrior Jasper Rd, Cane Creek Rd, Warrior, Robbins
Gas E: Chevron, Exxon, County Line Fuelz & Spirits◊
Food E: Hardee's, McDonald's/Exxon, Pizza Hut, Taco Bell
Other E: ATMs, Banks, Auto Services, Tires

281 Dana Rd, Warrior (Access to #282 Services)

280 to US 31, AL 3, Warrior, Kimberly
Other E: Auto Dealer, Enterprise RAC

275 to US 31, AL 3, Mary Buckelew Pky, Gardendale, Morris, Kimberly
Other E: Auto Service, Diesel Service

272 Mt Olive Rd, CR 112, Gardendale
Gas E: BP, Chevron
W: Chevron, Shell◊

271 Fieldstown Rd, CR 118, Gardendale
Gas E: Chevron, Circle K, RaceWay, Shell, Murphy
W: Shell
Food E: Arby's, ChickFilA, DQ, Fire Mountain Grill, Habanero's Mex Grill, Little Caesar's Pizza, McDonald's, Milo's Hamburgers, Pizza Hut, Ruby Tuesday, Shoney's, Subway, Taco Bell, Waffle House
W: **Cracker Barrel**
Lodg E: Microtel
W: Best Western
Other E: ATMs, Auto Services, Auto Zone, Banks, Civic Center, Dollar Tree, Firestone, Walgreen's, **Walmart sc**,

◊= Regular Gas Stations with Diesel ▲ = RV Friendly Locations ♥= Pet Friendly Locations
Red print shows large vehicle parking / access on site or nearby Brown Print = Campgrounds / RV PARKS

267 Walker Chapel Rd, Fultondale
Gas E: Chevron◈, Shell◈
W: BP, Chevron◈
Food E: Burger King, Domino's, Hardee's, O'Charley's, Outback Steakhouse, Waffle House
Lodg E: Comfort Suites, Fairfield Inn, Holiday Inn Express, Hampton Inn
Other E: ATMs, Banks, CVS, Dollar General, Grocery, Lowe's, RiteAid, Target, **Police Dept**

266 US 31, Fultondale, Birmingham
Gas E: Chevron, Raceway
Lodg E: Days Inn♥, Super 8

(265) Proposed Exit - US 78, Corridor X Freeway

264 41st Ave, Birmingham
TStop E: Flying J Travel Plaza #5091 (Scales),
Food E: CountryMarket/FastFood/FJ TP
Other E: Laundry/WiFi/**RVDump**/**LP**/FJ TP

263 33rd Ave (SB), 32nd Ave (NB)
Gas E: Chevron◈, Shell
W: Exxon
Food E: Hardee's, Little Caesars Pizza
Lodg E: Apex Motel, Oak Mountain Lodge
Other W: Auto Repair, **Colonial RV**

262B Finley Blvd, to US 78W, AL 4
TStop E: South Star Fuel Center (Scales)
W: Food N Gas/Conoco (Scales)
Gas E: AmocoBP, Bama Gas◈
W: Chevron, Citgo◈
Food E: FastFood/South Star FC
W: FastFood/Food N Gas, Captain D's, McDonald's, Popeye's Chicken, Shoney's
TServ E: South Star FC
Med E: + to Carraway Methodist Medical Ctr

262A 16th St N, 18th St N (NB)
Other E: to Civic Center

(261A) Jct I-20/59, E to Gadsden (SB, LEFT exit)

(261B) Jct I-20/59, W to Tuscaloosa (NB, LEFT exit)

260 US 11, 6th Ave N, Downtown (SB)
Gas E: BP, Shell
W: Chevron
Food E: Church's Chicken, Hardee's, Mrs Winners Chicken
Lodg W: Adam's Inn
Other W: Auto Services, Diesel Services

260B 2nd Ave N, US 78, US 11 (NB)

259B 4th Ave S, 11th St S (SB)

259A 6th Ave S (SB, diff reacc)
Gas E: BP
Food E: Waffle House
Lodg E: Best Western, Medical Center Inn
TServ E: Lynn Strickland Sales & Service
Med E: + Hospital

259 AL 149, 8th Ave S (NB, diff reacc)

258 Green Springs Ave
Gas E: BP, Chevron, Citgo
Food E: Irish Deli, Kebab & Curry

256AB Oxmoor Rd, Homewood (SB)

256 Oxmoor Rd, Homewood (NB)
Gas E: Exxon◈, Mobil◈, Shell
W: BP, Chevron
Food E: Arby's, Burger King, KFC, Subway
W: McDonald's, Shoney's, Waffle House
Lodge E: Howard Johnson, Oxmoor Lodge Extended Stay
W: Alta Vista Hotel, Comfort Inn, Fairfield Inn, Holiday Inn, Microtel♥, Quality Inn, Ramada♥, Shoney's Inn, Super 8
TServ W: Southland International Trucks
Med E: + Homewood Medical Clinic
Other E: ATMs, Auto Services, Auto Zone, Banks, Big Lots, CVS, Dollar Tree, Firestone, Grocery, Goodyear, Office Depot
W: Auto Services, ATMs, Banks, Batteries Plus

255 Lakeshore Pkwy, Lakeshore Dr, Birmingham
Gas E: BP, Circle K
W: Citgo, Chevron, Sam's Club
Food E: Sonic
W: Arby's, Captain D's, ChickFilA, Chili's, Dragon Chinese Rest, IHOP, Hooters, Landry's Seafood, Moe's SW Grill, Lone Star Steakhouse, McDonald's, O'Charley's, Taco Bell, Wendy's, BBQ
Lodg W: Best Western, Drury Inn, Hampton Inn, La Quinta Inn♥, Hilton Garden Inn, Residence Inn, Studio Plus, Sun Suites Extended Stay, Towneplace Suites
Med E: + Brookwood Medical Center
Other E: to Samford Univ, Brookwood Village Mall
W: ATMs, Banks, Cinemas, Dollar General, Dollar Tree, FedEx Office, Lowe's, NTB, Office Max, Sam's Club, UPS Store, **Walmart sc**,

254 Alford Ave, CR 97, Birmingham
Gas E: Chevron
W: BP, Citgo

252 US 31, AL 3, Montgomery Hwy, to Hoover, Vestavia Hills
Gas E: BP, Chevron, Shell
W: BP, Chevron, Exxon, Shell
Food E: Arby's, Aladdin's, Back Yard Burgers, Captain D's, Chuck E Cheese's Pizza, Hardee's, Ichiban Japanese, Piccadilly's, Pizza Hut, Ranch House Family Rest, Taco Bell, Waffle House
W: Burger King, Golden Corral, Krystal, McDonald's, Subway, Waffle House
Lodg E: Baymont Inn♥, Comfort Inn, Quality Inn, Premier Living Suites, Vestavia Motorlodge
W: Days Inn, Quality Inn
Med E: + Brookwood Medical Center
Other E: Animal Clinic♥, Auto Dealers, Auto Services, ATMs, Big 10 Tire, CVS, NAPA, Civic Center
Other W: Auto Dealers, ATMs, Auto Services, Advance Auto Parts, Banks, Dollar Tree, Firestone, Goodyear, RiteAid, **to** Riverchase Galleria, Costco, Sam's Club

(250) Jct I-459, to US 280, Atlanta, Gadsden (All Serv at 1st Exit W, #13)

247 CR 17, Valleydale Rd, Birmingham, to Helena, Hoover
Gas E: Circle K, Spectrum
W: Racetrac, Kangaroo Express
Food E: Hardee's, Happy China, Popeye's, Tin Roof BBQ
W: Arby's, IHOP, Papa Johns Pizza, Subway, Waffle House
Lodg W: In Towne Suites, La Quinta Inn♥, Oak Mountain Lodge
Med E: + Med Plex Care Center
Other E: ATMs, Banks, Grocery
W: Walgreen's

246 AL 119, Cahaba Valley Rd, Pelham
FStop W: The Store #4/BP
TStop W: Kangaroo Express #3682 (Scales)
Gas W: RaceTrac, Shell, Murphy
Food W: FastFood/Kangaroo Exp, Applebee's, Arby's, **Cracker Barrel**, ChickFilA, Golden Corral, Hooters, KFC, Krystal, McDonald's, O'Charley's, Pizza Hut, Ruby Tuesday, Shoney's, Sonic, Taco Bell, Texas Roadhouse, Waffle House, Wendy's
Lodg W: Best Western♥, Hampton Inn, Holiday Inn Express, Quality Inn, Ramada Ltd, Sleep Inn, Travelodge♥
Med W: + Hospital
Other E: Vet♥, **Country Sunshine RV Park▲**, **Oak Mountain State Park▲**
W: ATMs, AL Outdoors, Auto Services, Banks, CVS, Firestone, Grocery, Heart of Dixie Harley Davidson,

242 AL 52, Pelham, to Helena (Gas, Food, Serv W to US 31)
FStop E: Allen's Food Mart #74/Exxon
Gas E: Chevron◈, Shell
Food E: FastFood/Allen's FM
Lodg W: Shelby Motel
Tires E: Allen's FM
TServ E: 242 Tire & Truck Service
Other W: Staples, **Birmingham South CG▲**

238 US 31, AL 3, Alabaster
Gas E: Murphy◈
W: Chevron◈, Shell◈, Cannon KwikStop
Food E: ChickFilA, Habanero's, Moe's SW Grill, Ruby Tuesday, Subway, Taco Bell
W: Waffle House
Lodg W: Shelby Motor Lodge
Med W: + Baptist Shelby Medical Center
Other E: Best Buy, Lowe's, Target, **Walmart sc**, **Burton Campers**
W: Auto Services, CVS, Pharmacy, RiteAid, SavALot, Walgreen's

234 CR 87, Calera
Gas E: BP◈
W: Chevron◈, Shell◈
Food E: Subway/BP
Other E: **Cahaba RV**
W: Cain's Auto & Truck Service, Shelby Co Airport✈, Univ of Montevallo,

231 US 31, AL 3, Montgomery Hwy, to CR 22, AL 70, Calera, Saginaw
Gas E: BP◈, Shell
Food E: Captain D's, Cracker Barrel, Fish Market Rest, McDonald's, Mexican Rest, Subway
W: Donna's Café
Lodg E: Holiday Inn Express
Other E: Dollar Tree, **Walmart sc**, **Rolling Hills Campground▲**, **Burton Campers**
W: **Camper Repair Center**

228 AL 25, Calera, Montevallo
TStop E: Speed Track/Shell
Gas E: Citgo◈
W: Chevron◈
Food E: FastFood/SpeedTrack
W: to US 31
Lodg E: Best Value Inn♥, Days Inn
Other W: ATMs, Auto Repairs, Banks, Dollar General, Family Dollar, **to Brierfield Works State Park**

219 AL 42, Jemison, Thorsby
TStop E: PTP/Jemison Exxon

◈ = Regular Gas Stations with Diesel ▲ = RV Friendly Locations ♥ = Pet Friendly Locations
Red print shows large vehicle parking / access on site or nearby Brown Print = Campgrounds / RV PARKS

EXIT		ALABAMA
	Gas	E: Chevron◈ W: Shell
	Food	E: Subway/Exxon
	TServ	E: Exxon/Tires
	Other	E: Laundry/Exxon, **Peach Queen Campground▲** **W: Chilton Camper Sales/Central AL RV Sales & Service**
(214)		Clanton Rest Area (Both dir) (RR, Phones, Picnic, Vend, **RVDump**)
212		**AL 145, Lay Dam Rd, Clanton**
	TStop	W: Headco Truck Stop
	Gas	E: Chevron◈ W: BP
	Food	W: FastFood/Headco, Subway/BP
	Med	W: + Chilton Medical Center
	Other	E: Auto Repairs W: Gragg Field✈
208		**CR 28, Clanton, to Lake Mitchell**
	FStop	W: Allan's Food Mart #60/Exxon
	TStop	E: Love's Travel Stop #368 (Scales)
	Food	E: Arby's/Love's TS, Kountry Kitchen W: Shoney's
	Lodg	W: Guest House Inn
	Med	W: + Chilton Medical Center
	Other	E: WiFi/Love's TS **W: Dandy RV Sales**, Pecan Farm, Gragg Field✈
205		**US 31, AL 22, 7th St, Verbena, Clanton**
	FStop	E: Sunny Foods #6/Shell W: The Store #1/BP
	Gas	E: I-65 Kountry Mart W: Chevron◈, Murphy
	Food	E: McDonald's, Waffle House W: Burger King, Captain D's, Pizza Hut Hardee's, KFC, Subway, Taco Bell
	Lodg	E: Best Western♥, Days Inn♥, Holiday Inn Express, Scottish Inn W: Key West Inn
	Other	E: Peach Park W: Dollar General, Dollar Tree, Durbin Farm Market, **Walmart sc**,
200		**CR 59, Verbena**
	FStop	E: Shop N Fill #24/BP
	Gas	W: Shell◈
	Food	W: Stuckey's/DQ/Shell
186		**US 31, AL 3, Prattville**
	Gas	W: BP◈, Chevron, Citgo, Conoco◈
	Food	W: Country Diner, Vivian's Cafe
	Lodg	W: Pine Motel
	Med	W: + Prattville Baptist Hospital
	Other	E: Confederate Memorial Park
181		**AL 14, Fairview Ave, Millbrook, Prattville, Wetumpka, Coosada**
	Gas	E: Chevron◈, Entec◈ W: Exxon, Kangaroo, QV
	Food	W: Cracker Barrel, Ruby Tuesday, Subway, Waffle House, Wendy's
	Lodg	W: Best Western, Comfort Inn, Hometowne Suites, Super 8♥
	Med	W: + Prattville Baptist Hospital
179		**US 82, AL 6, Cobbs Ford Rd, Prattville, Millbrook**
	FStop	W: Petro Kwik Sak
	Gas	E: Chevron◈ W: JetPep, RaceWay, Shell, USA◈
	Food	E: Asian Grill, Catfish House, Fantail W: Hardee's, Longhorn Steakhouse, Subway, O'Charley's, McDonald's, Steak n Shake, Shoney's, Subway, Waffle House

EXIT		ALABAMA
	Lodg	E: Country Inn, Key West Inn♥ W: Days Inn, Econo Lodge, Holiday Inn, Hampton Inn, Jameson Inn♥, Marriott
	Other	E: Auto Services, **K&K Camping Center & Campground/LP▲**, **Clarks RV Center** W: ATMs, Auto Services, Banks, Bass Pro Shop, Food World, Office Depot, Prattville Auto & **RV** Service, Tires, UPS Store, **Walmart sc**, **to** Emerald Falls Adventure Park, **to Bakers RV Park▲**
176		**AL 143N, Montgomery, to Millbrook, Coosada (NB, NO reaccess)** **(Access #179 Serv, N to Cobbs Ford Rd)**
173		**AL 152, North Blvd, to US 231 (diff reaccess, Both dir)**
	Other	E: Montgomery Zoo
172AB		**Bell St, Clay St, Herron St, Downtown Montgomery**
	Gas	E: Amoco, KwikShop W: Chevron◈
	Lodg	E: Capitol Inn, Embassy Suites
	TServ	W: Southland International Trucks, AL Diesel Service
	Other	E: Auto Services, ATMs, Banks, Tires, Riverwalk Stadium, Troy Univ W: Auto Services, Maxwell AFB
(171)		**Jct I-85N, to Atlanta, Day St (SB, LEFT exit)**
	Food	W: Church's, Hardee's, McDonald's
	Other	E: **to** AL State Univ W: Auto Services, **to** Maxwell AFB
170		**Fairview Ave, Montgomery**
	Gas	E: Jack's Quick Mark, Citgo, Gas Depot W: Exxon
	Food	E: China King, Church's, Krystal, Pizza, McDonald's W: Hardee's, Seafood
	TServ	W: Cummins Alabama
	Other	E: Advance Auto Parts, Auto Zone, CVS, Huntington College, Tony's Tire Service, U-Haul, W: Family Dollar, Firestone, Grocery
169		**Edgemont Ave, Oak St (SB)**
	Gas	E: BP, Citgo, Exxon
	Food	E: McDonald's, Krystal
168		**US 80/82E, South Blvd, to US 31, US 231, US 331, Montgomery**
	FStop	W: Speedy #1, to US 31: Byrd's Pit Stop/66
	TStop	E: Travel Center of America #111/Citgo (Scales)
	Gas	E: Kangaroo, Spectrum, Entec◈ W: RaceTrac, Shell◈
	Food	E: CountryPride/TA TC, Arby's, Capt D's, Krystal, KFC, McDonald's, Shoney's, Taco Bell, Waffle House W: DQ, Hardee's, Quincy's, Wendy's, Subway/Shell
	Lodg	E: Best Inn, Best Western, Days Inn, Diplomat Inn, Economy Inn♥, Quality Inn W: Airport Inn, Econo Lodge, Holiday Inn, Inn South, Peddler's Motor Inn, Ramada Ltd, Super 8
	TWash	E: TA TC
	TServ	E: TA TC/Tires W: Curley's Tire & Auto, AL Spring & Brake
	Med	E: + Hospital
	Other	E: Laundry/CB/WiFi/TA TC, Auto Services, Grocery, U-Haul, **The Woods RV Park & Campground▲** W: Auto & Tire Services, U-Haul

EXIT		ALABAMA
167		**US 80W, Selma, to Meridian, MS**
	Gas	W: Citgo, PaceCar
	Food	W: Subway, Church's Chicken
	Lodg	W: Executive Inn
	Other	W: Dannelly Field/Montgomery Reg'l Airport✈, Winn Dixie, Hertz RAC, Auto Services
(165)		Proposed Exit - **Montgomery Outer Loop**
164		**US 31, AL 3, Mobile Hwy, Hope Hull, Montgomery**
	FStop	E: Petro Plus
	TStop	E: Saveway Travel Center (Scales)
	Gas	E: AmocoBP W: BP, Chevron, Exxon, Liberty
	Food	E: FastFood/Saveway TC, Momma's House W: Burger King/BP, Subway/Liberty, Waffle House
	Lodg	E: Lakeside Hotel W: Best Western, Hampton Inn, Motel 6♥
	Other	E: Laundry/Saveway TC, **Montgomery KOA▲**, Auto & Tire Services
158		**Tyson Rd, to US 31, Hope Hull, to Tyson, Hayneville**
	TStop	W: Flying J Travel Plaza (Scales)
	Gas	E: BP Stuckey's
	Food	E: Stuckey's/DQ/BP W: CountryMarket/FastFood/FJ TP
	Other	**E: Montgomery South RV Park▲** W: Laundry/WiFi/**RVDump**/**LP**/FJ TP
151		**AL 97, Hayneville, Letohatchee**
	Gas	W: BP, PaceCar
142		**AL 185, E Old Fort Rd, Fort Deposit, Logan**
	Gas	E: BP◈, Shell◈, USA W: Chevron
	Food	E: Subway W: Interstate Cafe
	Other	W: Priester's Pecans
(133)		Greenville Rest Area (Both dir) (RR, Ph, Pic, Vend, Weather, **RVDump**)
130		**AL Truck 10E, AL 185E, Greenville**
	Gas	E: BP◈, Chevron◈, Citgo, Shell W: Exxon, Glass 66, Texaco◈, Murphy
	Food	E: Arby's, Captain D's, Hardee's, KFC, McDonald's, Pizza Hut, Real Pit BBQ, Steak 'n Shake, Waffle House, Wendy's W: Burger King, Bates Turkey Rest, Cracker Barrel, Krystal, Ruby Tuesday, Shoney's, Subway, Taco Bell
	Lodg	E: Best Value Inn, Days Inn♥, Econo Lodge W: Best Western♥, Comfort Inn, Hampton Inn, Jameson Inn♥
	Other	E: Advance Auto Parts, CVS, Carwash/Chevron, Dollar General, Greenville Muni Airport✈ W: ATMs, Auto Dealer, Banks, Grocery, **Walmart sc**, **to appr 4mi: Sherling Lake Campground▲**
128		**AL 10, Pineapple Hwy, Greenville, Pine Apple**
	Gas	E: Shell◈ W: BP
	Food	E: The Smokehouse Rest
	Med	E: + Stabler Memorial Hospital
114		**AL 106, Georgiana, Starlington**
	Gas	E: BP, Chevron
	Med	E: + Georgiana Hospital

EXIT		ALABAMA
	Other	E: to Hank Williams Sr Museum
107		**CR 7, Hank Williams Rd, Georgiana, to Grace, Garland**
101		**AL 29, CR 29/22, Evergreen, Owassa**
	FStop	E: Owassa BP
		W: Owassa Food Store/Exxon
	Other	W: **Owassa Lakeside RV Park▲**
96		**AL 83, Liberty Hill Dr, Evergreen**
	TStop	W: PTP/McIntyre Travel Center/Citgo
	Gas	E: Chevron, Shell
		W: BP
	Food	E: Burger King, Hardee's, McDonald's, KFC/Taco Bell, Pizza Hut
		W: Subway/Chester/McIntyre TC, Waffle House
	Lodg	W: Comfort Inn, Days Inn
93		**US 84, AL 12, to Monroeville**
	FStop	E: Econ #12/Shell,USA Travel Center
		W: Diamond Gasoline #20/BP
	Food	W: FastFood/Diamond Gasoline
	Other	E: Greyhound, **Overnite Park▲**, **Pine Crest Park/Campground▲**
(89)		**AL Welcome Center (SB)**
		(RR, Ph, Pic, Vend, Weather, RVDump)
(85)		**Conecuh Rest Area (NB)**
		(RR, Ph, Pic, Vend, Weather, RVDump)
83		**CR 6, Castleberry, Lenox**
	Gas	E: Exxon◈, Texaco
	Food	E: Louise's Restaurant
	Other	E: **Country Sunshine RV Park▲**
77		**AL 41, Lenox, to Brewton, Repton**
	FStop	W: Range Shell #126, Econ #18/Citgo
	Food	W: Old Timer's Rest, Ranch House Rest
69		**AL 113, CR 17, Brewton, Flomaton, Wallace**
	TStop	E: Wallace Interstate Shell (Scales), Diamond Gasoline #5/Chevron
		W: Minute Stop #153
	Gas	E: BP
	Food	E: Subway/Chevron
		W: Huddle House
	TServ	E: Wallace Interstate/Tires
	Other	E: Laundry/**LP**/Wallace Interstate
57		**AL 21, Atmore, Uriah, Monroeville**
	FStop	E: RJ's Exxon
	Gas	E: Shell◈
		W: BP◈
	Food	E: RJ's BBQ/RJ's
		W: Creek Family Rest/BW
	Lodg	E: Royal Oaks B&B
		W: Best Western
	TServ	E: Atmore Tire & Retreading
	Other	E: Creek Bingo Palace & Ent Center
		W: to **Ponderosa RV Park▲**, to appr 12 mi: **Little River State Forest/Claude D Kelley State Park▲**
54		**CR 1, Atmore**
	FStop	E: Diamond Gasoline #21/BP
	Gas	E: Citgo◈
	Food	E: Subway/BP
45		**CR 47, Rabun, Perdido**
	FStop	W: Diamond Gasoline #18/BP
	Food	W: Subs&Pizza/Diamond Gas
37		**AL 287, Rabun Rd, Gulf Shores Pky Rabun, Bay Minette**
	Gas	E: BP
34		**AL 59, Bay Minette, Stockton**
	Med	E: + Hospital

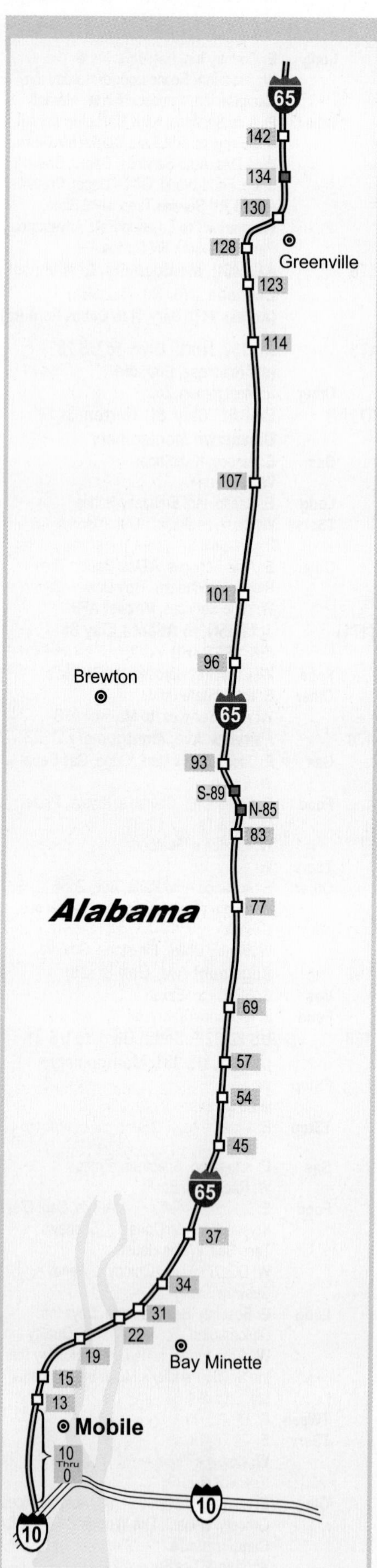

EXIT		ALABAMA
31		**AL 225, Bay Minette, Stockton, Spanish Fort**
	FStop	W: Minute Stop #159/Shell
	Food	W: FastFood/Minute Stop
	Other	E: **Historic Blakely State Park▲**
		W: **Live Oak Landing Campground▲**
22		**Sailor Rd, Creola**
	Other	W: to Mark Reynolds N Mobile Co Airport✈, **Dead Lake Marina & Campground▲**
19		**US 43, AL 13, Satsuma, Creola**
	FStop	E: Satsuma Chevron
		W: to appr 4 mi: Midway Truck Stop
	TStop	E: Pilot Travel Center #75 (Scales) (DAND)
	Gas	W: BP◈, Chevron, Shell
	Food	E: Arby's/TJCinn/Pilot TC, McDonald's, Waffle House
	Lodg	E: La Quinta Inn♥
	Other	E: Laundry/WiFi/**RVDump**/Pilot TC, Carwash/Chevron
		W: **I-65 RV Campground▲**
15		**CR 41, Celeste Rd, Saraland, Citronelle**
	Gas	E: Chevron
		W: Shell
	Food	W: Subway/Shell
13		**AL 158, AL 213, Industrial Pkwy, Saraland, Eight Mile, Citronelle**
	Gas	E: BP◈, Shell◈, Starvin Marvin, Murphy
		W: Exxon
	Food	E: McDonald's, Ruby Tuesday, Shoney's, Subway, Waffle House
		W: Pizza Inn, Subway
	Lodg	E: Days Inn, Comfort Suites, Holiday Inn Express, Quality Inn
		W: Hampton Inn
	TServ	E: On Site Truck & Trailer Repair
		W: Pitt & Son Truck Repair
	Other	E: **Walmart sc**, Auto & Diesel Services, **Saraland RV Sales, Stevens RV Repairs**
		W: **Co Park/Chickasabogue Park & Campground▲**, W AL Tire Service, to Univ of Mobile
10		**W Lee St, Chickasaw, Mobile**
	Gas	E: Conoco, Shell
	Food	E: Subway/Shell
	Lodg	E: America's Best Inn
(9)		**Jct I-165S, to I-10, Prichard, Downtown Mobile**
8AB		**US 45, AL 17, Prichard, Citronelle to Meridian, MS**
	TStop	W: Express Truck Wash & Fuel/Pride (Scales)
	Gas	E: Conoco, Glenn's Shell◈
		W: Conoco◈, Exxon, RaceWay, Diamond
	Food	E: Church's Chicken
		W: Burger King, McDonald's
	Lodg	E: Star Motel
	TWash	W: Express TW
	TServ	E: Cummins Alabama, Peterbilt of Mobile, Cummins/Onan
		W: Empire Truck Sales/Freightliner
	Other	E: Family Dollar
		W: Laundry/Express TW
5B		**US 98, AL 42, Moffett Rd, to Hattiesburg, MS**
	FStop	W: Minute Stop
	Gas	E: Exxon◈
	Food	E: Burger King, DQ, McDonald's
		W: Hardee's

◈ = Regular Gas Stations with Diesel ▲ = RV Friendly Locations ♥ = Pet Friendly Locations

Red print shows large vehicle parking / access on site or nearby **Brown Print = Campgrounds / RV PARKS**

EXIT — ALABAMA

	Lodg	W: Super 8
	TServ	E: Taylor Truck Service, Cummins Mid South W: Empire Truck Sales, Goodyear Truck Alignment & Retreading, Reliable Diesel Service
	Other	W: ATMs, Auto Services, **Moffett Rd RV, Aces RV Park▲ , Browns RV Park▲ , JR's RV Park▲**
5A		**Spring Hill Ave**
	Gas	E: Chevron, Shell◈ W: Chevron◈, Exxon, Shell◈
	Food	E: Burger King, DQ, McDonald's W: Waffle House
	Lodg	E: Crichton Lodging W: Extended Stay America, Wingate Inn
	Med	E: + USA Medical Center
	Other	E: Auto Zone, Auto Services, Big 10 Tire, Grocery, Pharmacy, Tires
4		**Dauphin St, Mobile**
	Gas	E: BP◈, Spectrum, Shell, Summit◈
	Food	E: Checker's, ChickFilA, Cracker Barrel, Krystal, McDonald's, Popeye's Chicken, Subway, Taco Bell, Waffle House, Wendy's
	Lodg	E: Comfort Inn, Red Roof Inn♥, Rodeway Inn W: Motel 6♥
	Med	W: + Spring Hill Medical Center

EXIT — ALABAMA

	Other	E: Auto Dealer, ATMs, Banks, Dollar General, Lowe's, RiteAid, **Walmart sc** W: Spring Hill College, Mobile Museum of Art, **to** Univ of S AL, ATMs, Banks
3AB		**CR 56, Airport Blvd, Mobile**
	FStop	W: Econ #21/Citgo
	Gas	E: BP W: Exxon, Shell **x2**, Spur◈
	Food	E: Burger King, ChickFilA, Golden China, Hooters, Deli, Mr Wok, Wendy's W: Arby's, Carrabba's, Chili's, Chuck E Cheese's Pizza, Denny's, El Monterey Mexican Rest, IHOP, Lone Star Steakhouse, O'Charley's, Olive Garden, Outback Steakhouse, Pizza Hut, Popeye's Chicken, Quiznos Subs, Red Lobster, Shoney's, Starbucks, Tony Roma, Waffle House
	Lodg	E: Marriott, Quality Inn W: Best Inn, Best Western, Courtyard, Days Inn, Drury Inn, Econo Lodge, Family Inn, Fairfield Inn, Hampton Inn, Holiday Inn, La Quinta Inn♥, Motel 6♥, Ramada Inn, Residence Inn, Towneplace Suites, Westmont Inn
	Med	W: + Spring Hill Medical Center, + Providence Hospital
	Other	E: ATMs, Banks, Best Buy, Barnes & Noble, Carwash, Colonial Mall, Firestone, Goodyear, Lowe's, Mobile Bay Harley Davidson, Sam's Club, Springdale Mall, Staples, Target,

EXIT — ALABAMA

	Other	W: ATMs, Banks, Dollar Tree, FedEx Office, Home Depot, Office Depot, Pep Boys, PetSmart♥, Radio Shack, Sam's Club, U-Haul, UPS Store, Walgreen's, Vet♥, **to** Univ of Southern AL, Mobile Reg'l Airport✈, **Crown Classic Coach**
1AB		**US 90, AL 16, Government Blvd**
	Gas	E: Chevron, BP W: Conoco, Shell◈
	Food	E: Burger King, Deli, McDonald's, Steak n Shake W: China Garden, Subway, Waffle House
	Lodg	E: Howard Johnson W: Bama Motel, Rest Inn
	Other	E: Hank Aaron Stadium, Auto Dealers, ATMs, Banks, Family Dollar, Theatres, Harley Davidson W: Auto Services, ATMs, Big 10 Tires
(0)		**Jct I-10, W to New Orleans, LA, Mississippi; E to Pensacola, FL (SB, LEFT Exit)**

CENTRAL TIME ZONE

NOTE: I-65 begins/ends on I-10, Exit #20

ALABAMA

Begin Northbound I-65 from Jct I-10 near Mobile, AL to Jct I-80/90 near Gary, IN.

INTERSTATE 66 E

EXIT — VIRGINIA

Begin Eastbound I-66 from Jct I-81 near Middletown, VA to Washington, DC

VIRGINIA

NOTE: I-66 begins/ends on I-81, Exit #300

EASTERN TIME ZONE

(1B)		**Jct I-81, N to Winchester**
(1A)		**Jct I-81, S to Roanoke (WB, LEFT exit)**
6		**US 340, US 522, Front Royal, Winchester, Linden**
	FStop	N: Quarles Food Store
	Gas	S: 7-11, Exxon, East Coast, Shell
	Food	N: FastFood/Quarles FS, Applebee's, **Cracker Barrel**, Panda Express, Starbucks, TGI Friday S: Arby's, Dunkin Donuts, Hardee's, Little Caesar's Pizza, McDonald's, Pizza Hut, Wendy's
	Lodg	S: Bluemont Inn, Blue Ridge Motel, Budget Inn, Cool Harbor Motel, Front Royal Motel, Hampton Inn, Quality Inn, Relax Inn, Shenandoah Motel, Super 8♥
	Med	S: + Warren Memorial Hospital
	Other	N: Auto Dealer, Lowe's, Staples, Target, **Walmart sc**

EXIT — VIRGINIA

	Other	S: Auto Repairs, ATMs, Banks, Big Lots, Cinema, Confederate Museum, Family Dollar, Tires, Towing, **to** Front Royal Airport✈, **Shenandoah National Park, Front Royal RV Campground▲ , Poe's Southfork Campground▲ , Gooney Creek Campground▲ , Low Water Bridge Campground▲ , Country Wave RV Resort▲** , Skyline Caverns
13		**VA 79, to VA 55, Linden, Front Royal (Access to #6 Serv via VA 55)**
	Gas	S: Exxon◈, Shell
	Food	S: The Apple House Rest
	Lodg	S: Super 8♥
	Other	S: Fox Meadow Winery, **to Shenandoah National Park,**
18		**VA 688, to VA 55, Markham**
23		**to VA 55, VA 729, US 17N (EB) US 17N, Delaplane, Winchester (WB)**
27		**Free State Rd, to VA 55, US 17, US 17 Bus, Marshall**
	Gas	N: Chevron◈, Citgo◈, Exxon◈
	Food	N: Marshall Diner, Old Salem Rest
	Other	N: ATMs, Bank, Auto & Truck Repair, IGA, Vet♥
28		**US 17, Winchester Rd, Marshall**
	Gas	N: 7-11, BP◈
	Food	N: McDonald's/BP, Fosters Grille, Subway
	Other	N: Animal Clinic♥, Food Lion, **Premier RV Repair**, Radio Shack, **Small Country Campground▲**

EXIT — VIRGINIA

31		**VA 245, Old Tavern Rd, The Plains, Great Meadow, Warrenton**
40		**US 15, Warrenton, Haymarket**
	FStop	S: to VA 55E: Q-Stop #616/Mobil
	Gas	S: Shell◈, Sheetz◈
	Food	N: Old Carolina Smokehouse S: McDonald's, Papa John's Pizza, Subway
	Other	N: **Greenville Farm Campground▲** S: ATM, Auto Repairs, Bank, Food Lion, Grocery, Home Depot, Police Dept
43A		**US 29S, Lee Hwy, Gainesville, to Warrenton, Charlottesville**
	Gas	S: 7-11, RaceWay, Shell◈, WaWa
	Food	S: Burger King, ChickFilA, Domino's Pizza, Five Guys Burgers, IHOP, McDonald's, MiMi's Cafe, Papa John's Pizza, Osaka Japanese, Ruby Tuesday, Subway, Taco Bell/KFC/Pizza Hut, Wendy's
	Lodg	S: Comfort Inn, Howard Johnson♥
	TServ	S: Patriot Truck
	Other	S: ATM, Auto & Tire Services, Bank, Best Buy, Golf Courses, Goodyear, Giant Grocery/Pharmacy, Lowe's, Nissan Pavilion PetSmart♥, Target, UPS Store, Walgreen's, World Market
43B		**US 29N, Lee Hwy, Gainesville**
	Gas	N: WaWa
	Other	N: **Manassas Nat'l Battlefield Park**
44		**VA 234S, Prince William Parkway, Manassas**
	TServ	S: Elliot Wilson Capitol Trucks

EXIT		VIRGINIA
	Other	S: Manassas Reg'l Airport✈
47		**VA 234 Bus, Sudley Rd, Manassas (EB)**
47A		**VA 234 Bus, Sudley Rd S (WB)**
	Gas	S: BP◈, Exxon, Raceway◈, Shell, Sunoco
	Food	S: Arby's, Bob Evans, Burger King, Chick-FilA, Chili's, Chipolte Mexican Grill, Damon's, Denny's, Domino's Pizza, Don Pablo, Hooters, Hunan Deli, KFC, Logan's Roadhouse, McDonald's, Olive Garden, Perfect Pita, Pizza Hut, Red Lobster, Red, White & Blue, Shoney's, Starbucks, TGI Friday, Taco Bell, Wendy's, Rest/BW
	Lodg	S: Best Western♥, Comfort Inn, Hampton Inn, Quality Inn, Red Roof Inn♥, Residence Inn, Super 8
	Med	S: + Prince William Hospital
	Other	S: ATMs, Auto Dealers, Auto Services, Best Buy, Budget RAC, Burlington Coat Factory, CVS, Cinemas, Costco, **Cruise America MH Rental**, Enterprise RAC, FedEx Office, Giant Grocery, Home Depot, Lowe's, Manassas Mall, NTB, Office Depot, Pep Boys, PetCo♥, PetSmart♥, Penske, Staples, **Reines RV Center/Camping World**, U-Haul, UPS Store, Walgreen's, **Walmart**, **to** Patriot Harley Davidson, Ben Lomond Reg'l Park/Splash Down Water Park, Amtrak, Museums, Subway Stations, **to** Quantico US Marine Corps Res, **Prince William Forest Park**
47B		**VA 234 Bus, Sudley Rd N (WB)**
	Gas	N: Shell◈
	Food	N: Cracker Barrel, Golden Corral, Pizza, Uno Chicago Grill, Wendy's
	Lodg	N: Country Inn, Courtyard, Fairfield Inn, Four Points Sheraton
	Other	N: **Manassas Nat'l Battlefield Park**, Nova Comm College, Regal Cinema
(49)		**Rest Area (Both dir) (RR, Phones, Picnic, Pet)**
52		**US 29, Lee Hwy, Centreville**
	Gas	N: Circle K S: 7-11, Exxon, Mobil◈
	Food	S: BBQ Country, Carrabba's, Domino's Pizza, Lone Star Steakhouse, McDonald's, Pizza Hut, Quiznos Subs, Ruby Tuesday, Starbucks, Wendy's
	Lodge	S: Springhill Suites
	Med	S: + Centreville Urgent Care
	Other	N: **Bull Run Park▲**, **Manassas Nat'l Battlefield Park**
	Other	S: ATMs, Banks, Auto Services, CVS, Centreville Multiplex Cinemas, Giant Foods, Nature Food Center, Radio Shack, Tires

EXIT		VIRGINIA
53		**VA 28, Sully Rd, to Lee Hwy, Centreville, Chantilly**
	Other	N: **to** Capitol Expo Center, Washington-Dulles Int'l Airport✈, Air & Space Museum **S: Access to Exit #52 Services**
55		**VA 7100, Fairfax Co Pky, Fairfax to US 50, to US 29**
	Gas	N: Exxon, Mobil, Sunoco S: Exxon
	Food	N: Applebee's, Burger King, Crab House, Logan's Roadhouse, Olive Garden, Red Robin, Pizza Hut, Red Robin, Starbucks, Wendy's
	Lodg	N: Hyatt, Residence Inn
	Med	N: + Fair Lakes Urgent Care Center, + Inova Fair Oaks Hospital
	Other	N: ATMs, Banks, Best Buy, BJ's Whls, Cost Plus World Market, Fair Lakes Shopping Center, Food Lion, PetSmart♥, Radio Shack, Target, **Walmart**, Whole Foods Market, S: Costco, Office Depot, **to** George Mason Univ, Patriot Center
55A		**VA 7100, Fairfax Co Pky, Fairfax, to US 29, Springfield (WB)**
55B		**VA 7100, Fairfax Co Pky, Fairfax, to US 50, Reston, Herndon (EB)**
(56)		**Weigh Station (Both dir)**
57A		**US 50S, Lee Jackson Hwy, Fairfax, Winchester**
	Gas	S: Amoco, Citgo, Shell
	Food	S: Chipolte Mexican Grill, CA Pizza, Italian Café, Subway
	Lodg	S: Candlewood Suites, Courtyard
	Other	S: ATMs, Banks, FedEx Office, Firearms Museum, Greyhound, Natural Foods, Office Depot, PetCo♥, UPS Store, Visitor Info, **to** George Mason Univ
57B		**US 50N, Lee Jackson Hwy, Fair Oaks, Winchester**
	Food	N: Arby's, Burger King, French Bakery, Grady's American Grill, Hunan Chinese, Chinese, Moby Dick House of Kabab, Popeye's Chicken, Romano's Macaroni Grill, Ruby Tuesday, Subway, Uno Chicago Grill
	Lodg	N: Extended Stay America, Extended Stay Deluxe, Hilton Garden Inn, Homestead Studio, Marriott
	Med	N: + Fair Oaks Urgent Care, + Inova Fair Oaks Hospital
	Other	N: ATMs, Banks, Cinema, FedEx Office, Fair Oaks Shopping Center, PetCo♥,

EXIT		VIRGINIA
	Other	N: Safeway, UPS Store, **Police Dept**, **to** Washington-Dulles Int'l Airport✈
60		**VA 123, Chain Bridge Rd, Fairfax, to Oakton, Vienna**
	Gas	N: Exxon, Mobil S: Exxon, Shell, Sunoco
	Food	N: McDonald's, Subway, Starbucks S: Bombay Bistro, Denny's, Fuddrucker's, Hooters, Minerva Indian Rest
	Lodg	S: Best Western, Econo Lodge, Hampton Inn, Holiday Inn Express
	Med	S: + Med First Urgent Care
	Other	N: ATMs, Banks, Auto Services S: ATMs, Auto Services, Banks, CVS, Patriot Harley Davidson, RiteAid
62		**VA 243, Nutley St, Vienna, Fairfax (GasFood N to MapleSt/ChainBridge Rd) (Addt'l Serv S to Arlington Blvd)**
	Gas	S: Exxon
	Food	S: Baja Fresh Mex Grill, McDonald's
	Lodg	S: **to** Vienna Wolf Trap Hotel
	Other	S: ATMs, Auto Services, Banks
(64)		**Jct I-495, N to Baltimore, S to Richmond**
(64A)		**Jct I-495, N to Baltimore (EB)**
(64B)		**Jct I-495, S to Richmond (EB, LEFT Exit)**
66		**VA 7, Leesburg Pike, Falls Church**
	Gas	N: Exxon S: 7-11, Xtra Mart, Sunoco
	Food	N: China King, Jerry's Subs, Starbucks S: Chicken Out, Indian Rest, Long John Silver, McDonald's, Pizza Hut
	Lodg	N: Westin Inn S: Inns of VA
	Other	N: **to** Tyson's Corner Shopping Center, ATMs, Banks, Gas, Food, Lodging S: ATMs, Banks, Auto Services, Subway
66B		**VA 7N, Leesburg Pike (WB)**
66A		**VA 7S, Leesburg Pike (WB)**
67		**VA 267N, Dulles Access Rd, I-495N, to Dulles Airport, Baltimore (WB)**
68AB		**Westmoreland St, Arlington (EB)**
69		**US 29, VA 237, Washington Blvd, Lee Hwy, Sycamore St, Arlington**
	Gas	N: Exxon
	Food	**S: Various - .5 mi S to Broad St**
	Lodg	S: Econo Lodge
	Other	N: ATMs, Banks, **Addt'l Serv North on Lee Hwy** S: ATMs, Auto Services, Banks

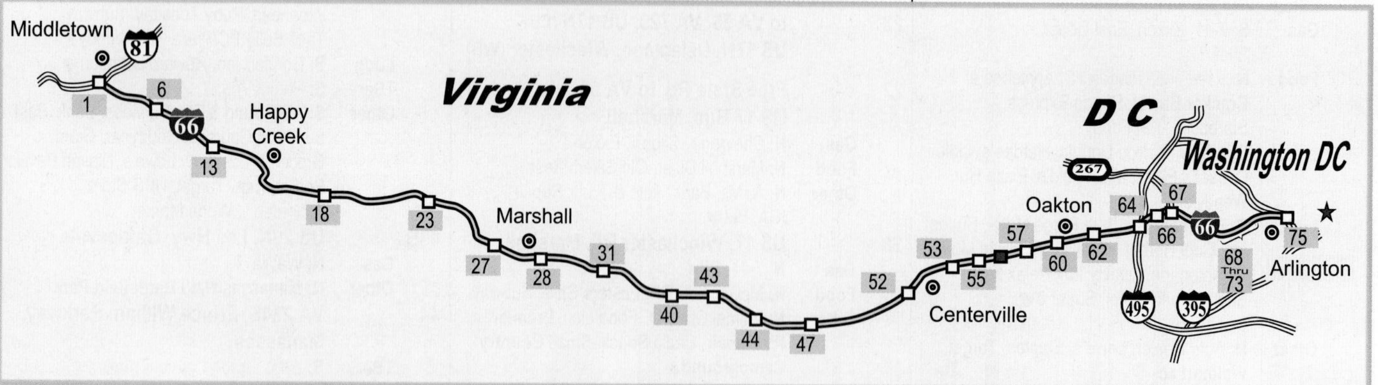

◈= Regular Gas Stations with Diesel ▲ = RV Friendly Locations ♥= Pet Friendly Locations
Red print shows large vehicle parking / access on site or nearby Brown Print = Campgrounds / RV PARKS

EXIT		VIRGINIA
71		**Glebe Rd, Fairfax Dr, VA 120, VA 337, Arlington** (WB, diff reaccess, ReAcc via Fairfax Dr)
	Gas	S: Exxon
	Food	S: Various Restaurants S on Glebe Rd
	Lodg	S: Comfort Inn, Holiday Inn
	Med	N: + Arlington Hospital
	Other	N: Gas, Food, Serv N to Lee Hwy S: ATMs, Auto Services, Banks, Cinema, Grocery, Pharmacy
72		**US 29, Lee Hwy, Spout Run Pkwy, Arlington** (EB, diff re-entry, Re-Enter via Lee Hwy/US 29)
	Gas	N: 7-11, Shell S: 7-11, Exxon
	Food	N: China Express, Pizza Hut S: Starbucks
	Lodg	N: Inns of VA
	Other	N: Auto Services, Grocery S: ATM, Bank, CVS, Courts, Grocery, Addtl Serv S to Wilson Blvd
73		**US 29, Lee Hwy, Fort Meyer Dr, N Lynn St, Arlington**
	Gas	S: Chevron
	Food	S: Burger King, McDonald's
	Lodg	N: Marriott S: Best Western, Holiday Inn, Hyatt
	Med	N: to + Georgetown Univ Hospital
	Other	N: to Georgetown Univ, Georgetown S: to Museums, Arlington Nat'l Cemetery, Marine Corps War Memorial, Shopping
75		**VA 110, Davis Hwy, to US 50, Arlington Blvd, Arlington, Ft Meyer**
	Other	S: to Arlington Nat'l Cemetery, Pentagon, Monuments, Shopping, Ronald Reagan Washington Nat'l Airport✈

EASTERN TIME ZONE

VIRGINIA

Begin Westbound I-66 from Jct US 50, Washington, DC to Jct I-81, Middletown, VA

EXIT		WEST VIRGINIA

Begin Eastbound I-68 from Jct I-79, Morgantown, WV to Hagerstown, MD.

WEST VIRGINIA

NOTE: I-68 begins/ends on I-79, Exit #148

EASTERN TIME ZONE

EXIT		WEST VIRGINIA / WV / MD
(0)		**Jct I-79, N-Washington, S-Fairmont**
1		**US 119, University Ave, Grafton Rd, Downtown Morgantown**
	Gas	N: Exxon◈ S: Chevron
	Food	N: Rest/Ramada Inn S: Subway
	Lodg	N: Comfort Inn, Ramada Inn, Almost Heaven B&B
	Other	S: Auto Repairs, Dollar Tree, Towing, Walmart sc,
4		**WV 7, Earl Core Rd, to Sabraton**
	Gas	N: BP◈, Exxon, Sheetz◈, Kroger S: Gas◈
	Food	N: Arby's, Blimpie/KFC/Exxon, Burger King, Hardee's, KFC, Long John Silver, McDonald's, Pizza Hut, Subway, Wendy's
	Lodg	N: Springhill Suites
	Other	N: ATMs, Advance Auto Parts, Auto Services, Banks, CVS, Dollar General, Family Dollar, Kroger, NAPA, SavALot, US Post Office
7		**CR 857, to US 119, Morgantown**
	Gas	N: BP, Exxon◈
	Food	N: Bob Evans, IHOP, Little Caesar's Pizza/ Subway/BP, Outback Steakhouse, Ruby Tuesday, Taco Bell/Exxon, Wendy's S: Tiberio's Pasta
	Lodg	N: Holiday Inn Express, Super 8
	Med	N: + Hospital
	Other	N: Auto Services, BooksAMillion, Family Dollar, Grocery, Lowe's, Tires, Triple S Harley Davidson, Morgantown Muni Airport✈, W Va Univ/Stadium
10		**CR 857, Fairchance Rd, to Cheat Lake, Morgantown**
	Gas	N: BP◈, Exxon◈
	Food	N: Little Caesars/BP, Ruby's & Ketchy's, Subway S: Burger King, Stone Crab Inn
	Lodg	S: Lakeview Resort & Conf Ctr
(12)		RunAway Truck Ramp (WB)
	NOTE:	WB: MM 15-10: Steep Grade
15		**CR 73/12, Bruceton Mills, Coopers Rock**
	Other	S: Coopers Rock State Forest▲
(16)		Weigh Station (WB)
(17)		RunAway Truck Ramp (EB)
23		**WV 26, Bruceton Mills**
	TStop	N: Little Sandy's Truck Stop/Mobil
	FStop	N: BFS Foods #10/BP
	Food	N: FastFood/BFS BP, Rest/Little Sandy's TS, Mill Place Rest, Pizza Pro, Twila's Family Rest
	Lodg	N: Maple Leaf Motel
	Other	N: LP/BFS BP, Family Dollar, US Post Office, to Glade Farms Campground▲
29		**CR 5, Hazelton Rd, Bruceton Mills**
	Gas	N: Mobil◈
	Other	S: to appr 4mi:Pine Hill Campground▲ , To appr 3 mi: Big Bear Lake Campland▲
(30)		WV Welcome Center (WB) (RR, Phones, Pic, Pet, Vend, Info)

EASTERN TIME ZONE

NOTE: MM 32: Maryland State Line

WEST VIRGINIA

MARYLAND

EASTERN TIME ZONE

EXIT		MARYLAND
4		**MD 42, Friendsville Rd, Maple St, to US 219, Friendsville**
	Gas	N: BP◈ S: Citgo◈
	Food	N: Jubilee Diner, Subs & Pizza
	Lodg	N: Riverside Hotel, Sunset Inn, Yough Valley Motel
	Other	N: ATM, Bank S: to Wisp Ski Resort
(8)		MD Welcome Center (EB) (RR, Phones, Picnic, Vend, Info)
14		**Garrett Hwy (EB)**

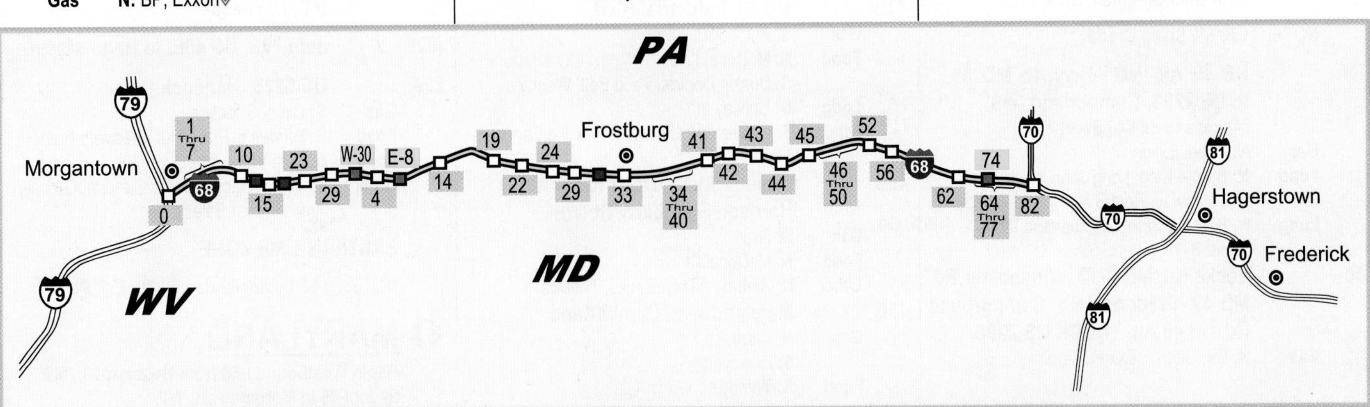

◈= Regular Gas Stations with Diesel ▲ = RV Friendly Locations ♥= Pet Friendly Locations
Red print shows large vehicle parking / access on site or nearby Brown Print = Campgrounds / RV PARKS

EXIT	MARYLAND
14A	**US 219S, Garrett Hwy S**
Other	S: to Wisp Ski Resort, Deep Creek Lake State Park▲, Garrett Co Airport✈
14B	**Garrett Hwy N, US 40, Nat'l Pike**
FStop	N: Keysers Ridge Auto Truck Stop/BP
Gas	N: Citgo◈
Food	N: Rest/Keysers Ridge TS, McDonald's
Other	N: Auto Repairs
19	**MD 495, to US 40 Alt, Grantsville, to MD 669, Swanton, Bittinger**
Gas	N: Exxon◈, Mobil
Food	N: Hey Pizza, Rest/Casselman Motel, Penn Alps Rest & Craft Shop
Lodg	N: Casselman Motel, Elliot House Victorian Inn
Other	N: ATMs, Banks, US Post Office, Casselman River State Park
22	**US 219N, to US 40 Alt, Chestnut Ridge Rd, to Meyersville, PA**
FStop	N: Fuel City/BP (Scales)
TStop	S: Pilot Travel Center #408 (Scales)
Gas	S: AmocoBP, Exxon
Food	N: Rest/Fuel City, Burger King, Subway S: Arby's/Pilot TC
Lodg	N: Little Meadows Motel S: Holiday Inn
TServ	S: Cummins
Other	N: Laundry/Fuel City, Pharmacy, Penn Alps Artesian Village S: Laundry/BarbSh/WiFi/Pilot TC, to New Germany State Park▲
24	**to US 40 Alt, Meyersdale Rd, Lower New Germany Rd**
NOTE:	MM 26: Eastern Continental Divide
NOTE:	EB: Area Prone to Low / No Visibility due to Fog
29	**MD 546, to US 40 Alt, Finzel Little Rd, Beall School Rd, Frostburg**
(31)	**Weigh Station (EB)**
NOTE:	WB: Area Prone to Low / No Visibility due to Fog
33	**Midlothian Rd, Braddock Rd**
Other	N: Frostburg State Univ
34	**MD 36, Frostburg, Westernport**
Gas	N: AmocoBP, Sheetz
Food	N: Burger King, McDonald's, Pizza Hut, Subway
Lodg	N: Days Inn, Hampton Inn
Med	N: + Hospital
Other	N: Auto Dealer, Auto Repairs, ATMs, Dollar General, Food Lion, RiteAid S: to Dans Mountain State Park
NOTE:	EB: 6% Steep Grade
39	**US 40 Alt, Nat'l Hwy, to MD 53, to US 220S, Cumberland (WB) (Access to Ex #40 Serv)**
Gas	N: Citgo, Exxon
Food	N: Burger King, Long John Silver, Pizza Hut, Subway, Rest/BW
Lodg	N: Best Western, Slumberland Motel, Super 8
40	**Vocke Rd, MD 53S, Winchester Rd, MD 49, Braddock Rd, Campground Rd, US 40 Alt, TRUCK US 220S**
Gas	N: BP, Citgo◈, Exxon, Mobil

Personal Notes

EXIT	MARYLAND
Food	N: Arby's, Bob Evans, Burger King, DQ, Denny's, KFC, Long John Silver, McDonald's, Pizza Hut, Ruby Tuesday, Wendy's, Rest/BW S: Applebee's, China Buffet, CiCi's Pizza
Lodg	N: Best Western, Comfort Inn, Slumber Land Motel, Super 8 S: Red Roof Inn
Med	N: + Hospital
Other	N: Advance Auto Parts, Budget RAC, CVS, Grocery, Highland Harley Davidson, Lowe's, Staples, U-Haul, MD State Hwy Patrol Post S: ATMs, Banks, Auto Services, Country Club Mall, Walmart sc
41	**to MD 49, Braddock Rd, Seton Rd (WB) (No Re-Entry to I-68)**
Med	N: + Sacred Heart Hospital
42	**US 220S, McMullen Hwy (EB), Fletcher Dr, Greene St, US220S (WB)**
Other	S: to Allegany Co Fairgrounds
NOTE:	EB: 6% Steep Grade
43A	**Johnson St (EB), Beall St (WB), to Alt MD 28, to W Va**
Gas	N: Sheetz
Other	N: ATMs, Banks, Court, Museums
43B	**MD 51, Industrial Blvd**
Gas	S: AmocoBP, Citgo◈
Food	N: McDonald's S: Dunkin Donuts, Taco Bell, Wendy's
Lodg	N: Holiday Inn
Other	S: Convention Center, to Mexico Farms Airport✈
43C	**Queen City Dr, Downtown (EB) Harrison St, Liberty St (WB)**
Gas	S: Shell
Food	N: McDonald's
Other	N: Amtrak, ATMs, Banks, Theatre
43D	**Maryland Ave, Cumberland**
Gas	N: Citgo S: Liberty◈
Food	N: Wendy's

EXIT	MARYLAND
Food	S: ChickFilA, Subway
Med	S: + Memorial Hospital of Cumberland
Other	N: Amtrak, ATMs, Banks, Downtown S: Grocery
44	**US 40 Alt, Baltimore Ave (WB) MD 639, Willow Brook Rd (EB)**
Other	S: Walmart sc, to Allegany College
45	**Hillcrest Dr, CR 952, Cumberland**
FStop	S: Fuel City/BP
46	**Baltimore Pike NE, to US 220N (EB) Naves Cross Rd, MD 144, Mason Rd NE, to US 220N (WB)**
Food	N: Lindy's Rest, Rest/Maryland Motel S: JB's Steak House
Lodg	N: Cumberland Motel, Maryland Motel
47	**MD 144, Baltimore Pike NE, US 220N, Cumberland (WB)**
50	**Pleasant Valley Rd, to MD 144**
Lodg	N: Rocky Gap Lodge & Golf Resort♥
Other	N: Rocky Gap State Park▲
52	**MD 144E, National Pike, Flintstone (EB, No Re-Entry)**
56	**MD 144, National Pike, Flintstone**
Gas	S: Sunoco
Other	S: Repairs/Sunoco, US Post Office,
62	**Fifteen Mile Creek Rd, US 40 Scenic**
64	**MV Smith Rd, Flintstone**
Other	S: Scenic Overlook: Green Ridge State Forest (Picnic, Phone)
68	**Orleans Rd, Little Orleans**
FStop	N: Belle Grove Auto Truck Stop/Exxon
Food	N: Rest/FastFood/Belle Grove ATS
72	**US 40 Scenic, High Germany Rd, Mann Rd, Little Orleans**
FStop	S: AmocoBP
(72)	**RunAway Truck Ramp (WB)**
74	**US 40E Scenic, Mountain Rd, Hancock (EB, No Re-Entry)**
(75)	**Rest Area / Sideling Hill Exhibit (NO Trucks) (Both dir) (RR, Phones, Picnic, Vend, Info)**
NOTE:	Both dir: 6% Steep Grade
(75)	**RunAway Truck Ramp (EB)**
77	**US 40W Scenic, MD 144E, Woodmont Rd, Hancock** NOTE: NO Thru Trucks Over 13T on MD 144 in Hancock.
Other	S: to Happy Hills Campground▲
(82C)	**Jct I-70W, US 522N, to Breezewood (EB, LEFT exit)**
(82B)	**Jct I-70E, US 40E, to Hagerstown**
82A	**US 522S, Hancock**
Gas	S: Citgo, Sheetz
Food	S: Hardee's, Pizza Hut, Weavers Rest
Lodg	S: Best Value Inn, Super 8
Other	S: ATMs, Banks, Dollar General, Grocery, Jimco Trailer Sales

EASTERN TIME ZONE

NOTE: I-68 begins/ends on I-70, Exit #1

MARYLAND

Begin Westbound I-68 from Hagerstown, MD to Jct I-79 in Morgantown, WV.

◈= Regular Gas Stations with Diesel ▲ = RV Friendly Locations ♥ = Pet Friendly Locations

Red print shows large vehicle parking / access on site or nearby Brown Print = Campgrounds / RV PARKS

EXIT	MICHIGAN

Begin Southbound I-69 from Port Huron, MI to Indianapolis, IN.

MICHIGAN

EASTERN TIME ZONE

NOTE: I-69 begins/ends on MI 25, PineGroveAve

NOTE: I-69 below runs with I-94. Exit #'s follow I-94.

275 — MI 25, Pine Grove Ave, Port Huron
- Gas — N: BP, Marathon, Shell, Speedway
- Food — N: McDonald's, Wendy's
- Lodg — N: Days Inn, Holiday Inn
- Med — S: + Port Huron Hospital
- Other — N: ATMs, Banks, Family Dollar, Can-Am Duty Free, **TOLL** Bridge to CANADA

(274) — Water St, to Lapeer Ave, Port Huron
MI Welcome Center Pt Huron #901
N: St Clair Co Rest Area (WB)
- FStop — S: By-Lo Speedy Q #6
- Gas — S: Speedway◈
- Food — N: Cracker Barrel
  S: Bob Evans
- Lodg — N: Best Western
  S: Comfort Inn, Fairfield Inn, Hampton Inn
- Other — N: Gilbert's Harley Davidson, **Pt Huron Twp Park Campground▲, to Lake Port State Park**

NOTE: I-69 above runs with I-94. Exit #'s follow I-94.

199 — I-69 Bus, Port Huron
- Gas — S: Mobil◈, Sam's
- Med — S: + Mercy Hospital
- Other — S: ATMs, Auto Services, Banks, Kmart SC, Kroger, Sam's Club, Truck Services

(198) — Jct I-94, S - Detroit, N - Canada

196 — Wadhams Rd, Lapeer Ave, Smiths Creek, Kimball
- FStop — N: By-Lo Speedy Q
- Gas — N: Shell◈
- Food — N: Burger King, Hungry Howie's Pizza McDonald's, Subway, Wendy's/Shell
- Other — N: Grocery, Pharmacy, At Your Service Auto & Truck Repair, **Pete's Camping Services, Port Huron KOA▲**

194 — Barth Rd, Taylor Dr, Smiths Creek
- Other — **N: Fort Trodd Family Campground RV Resort▲, to Ruby Campground▲**

189 — Wales Center Rd, Goodells

184 — MI 19, Kinney Rd, Memphis, Emmett
- FStop — S: Sunrise C-Store #29/Marathon
- TStop — N: Bisco's Truck Stop/Citgo (Scales)
- Food — N: Rest/FastFood/Bisco's TS
  S: FastFood/Sunrise
- TWash — N: Bisco's TS
- TServ — N: Bisco's TS/Tires
- Other — N: Laundry/**RVDump/LP**/Bisco's TS

180 — Riley Center Rd, Memphis
- Other — **N: Emmett KOA▲**

176 — Capac Rd, Capac
- FStop — N: Express Food Depot/BP (Scales)
- Food — N: McDonald's/Express BP
- Other — N: Auto & Truck Services

(174) — Rest Area St Clair Co #913 (WB)
(RR, Phones, Picnic, Vend, Info, Pet)

168 — MI 53, S Van Dyke Rd, Imlay City
- FStop — N: Speedway #8772, Spencer Oil/BP
- Food — N: Big Joe's Pizza & Chicken, Burger King, DQ, Little Caesars Pizza, Lucky's Steakhouse, McDonald's, New China Buffet, Taco Bell, Tim Horton's, Wendy's
- Lodg — N: Days Inn, M-53 Motel, Super 8
- Other — N: ATMs, Auto Zone, Auto Services, Grocery, Tires, Pharmacy, E&A Auto, Truck & **RV** Repair, Imlay City Service Center-**RV Repair**
  S: Woodland Waters Campground▲

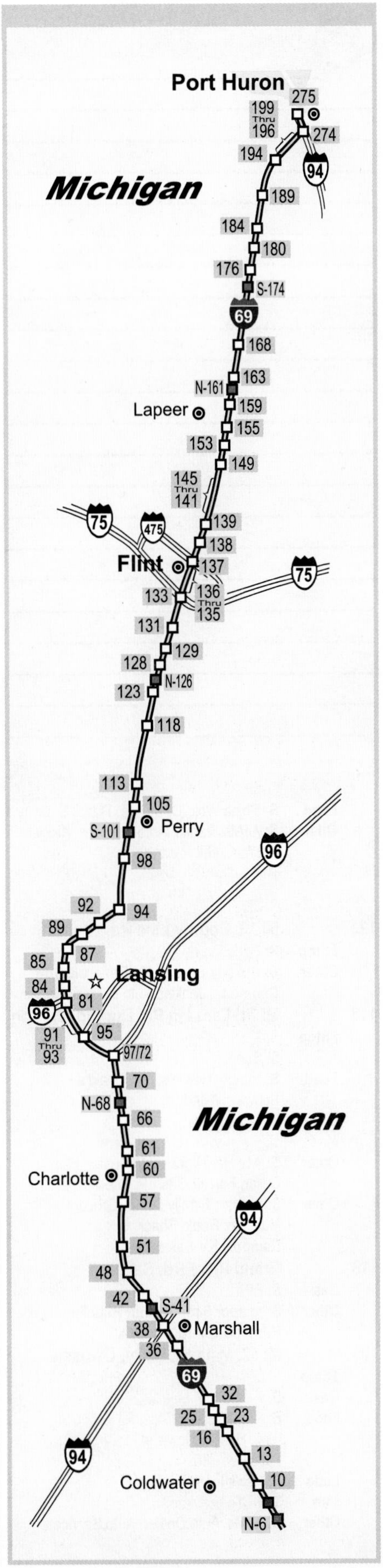

163 — Lake Pleasant Rd, Attica
- Other — N: Industrial Diesel Service, Greg's Truck & Auto Repair

(161) — Rest Area Five Lakes #629 (EB)
Lapeer Co (RR, Phones, Picnic, Vend)

159 — Wilder Rd, Lapeer

155 — MI 24, Lapeer Rd, Lapeer, Pontiac
- Gas — N: BP, Marathon◈, Meijer◈, Murphy
  S: Mobil◈
- Food — N: Arby's, Burger King, DQ, KFC, Little Caesars Pizza , McDonald's, Nick's Rest, Subway, Taco Bell, Tim Horton's, Wendy's, Greek & Amer Rest
- Lodg — N: Best Western, Fairfield Inn
- Med — N: + Lapeer Regional Hospital
- Other — N: ATMs, Auto Services, Auto Zone, Banks, Dollar Tree, Grocery, Kroger, Office Depot, Radio Shack, Tires, Vet♥, Amtrak, **MI State Hwy Patrol Post, to** Dupont Lapeer Airport✈, **RVDump**/City Park, **Walmart sc, Circle K RV's, Crystal Creek Campground▲**
  S: Auto Dealers, **to Metamora Hadley State Rec Area▲**

153 — Lake Nepessing Rd, Lapeer
- TStop — N: CMS Fueling Center/Marathon
- Other — N: CJ Auto & Truck Service
  S: Hilltop Campground▲

149 — Elba Rd, Lapeer
- Other — **S: Cummings RV & Trailer**

145 — MI 15, State Rd, Davison, Clarkston
- Gas — N: Shell◈, Speedway
  S: Mobil◈
- Food — N: Applebee's, Arby's, Big John Steak & Onion, Burger King, Country Sun Rest, Dunkin Donuts, Hungry Howie's, KFC, Little Caesars Pizza, McDonald's, Subway, Taco Bell, Tim Horton's
- Lodg — N: Comfort Inn
- Other — N: ATMs, Auto Services, Auto Dealer, Banks, Carwash, CVS, Kroger, RiteAid, Radio Shack, U-Haul

143 — Irish Rd, Davison
- Gas — N: Speedway◈
  S: Meijer◈, Shell◈
- Food — S: Dunkin Donuts, McDonald's/Shell
- Other — **N: to Outdoor Adventures/Lakeshore Resort▲, appr 5mi :Genesee Co Park/ Timber Wolf Campground▲**
  S: 7-11, Meijer

141 — Belsay Rd, Flint, Burton, Genesee
- FStop — S: Road Runner Express/Sunoco (DAND)
- Gas — N: Shell◈
- Food — N: Country Kitchen, McDonald's, Subway, Taco Bell, Wendy's/Shell
  S: Long John Silver/A&W/Road Runner, Little Caesars Pizza
- Other — N: ATMs, Grocery, Home Depot, **Walmart sc**, Carwash/Shell, Golf Course, **American RV**, to Athelone Williams Reg'l Airport✈

◈= Regular Gas Stations with Diesel ▲ = RV Friendly Locations ♥= Pet Friendly Locations
Red print shows large vehicle parking / access on site or nearby Brown Print = Campgrounds / RV PARKS

EXIT		MICHIGAN
	Other	S: ATMs, Bank, Car Wash, Family Dollar, RiteAid, **Bud's Trailer Center**
139		**Center Rd, Burton, Flint**
	Gas	N: Marathon, Speedway◈, Total S: Meijer◈
	Food	N: Applebee's, Boston Market, McDonald's, Old Country Buffet, Ponderosa, Quiznos, Starbucks, Subway, Tim Horton's, Wendy's S: Bob Evans, China 1, DQ, McDonald's, Walli's Rest
	Lodg	S: America's Best Inn♥, Super 8
	Other	N: ATMs, Auto Services, Banks, Bowling Center, Cinema, Discount Tire, Family Dollar, Grocery, Home Depot, Lowe's, Staples, Courtland Center Mall S: ATMs, Banks, Auto Services, Meijer, Office Depot, Target, Sports Arena, Vet♥
138		**MI 54, Dort Hwy, Flint**
	FStop	N: Speedway #8748
	Gas	N: BP S: Marathon, 7-11
	Food	N: Anna's Kitchen, Big John Steaks, Little Caesars Pizza, YaYa's Chicken S: Arby's, American Diner, Burger King, House of Hunan, KFC, McDonald's, Subway, Taco Bell
	Lodg	S: Travel Inn
	Med	N: + Genesys Regional Medical Center
	Other	N: ATMs, Auto Zone, RiteAid, Tires, Walgreen's, Golf Course, Amtrak S: ATMs, Auto Services, Campbells Auto & Truck Repair, Tri County Diesel, U-Haul
(137)		**Jct I-475, UAW Freeway, N to Saginaw, S to Detroit**
136		**Saginaw St, Downtown Flint**
	Med	N: to + Hurley Medical Center
	Other	N: ATMs, Banks, Courts, Greyhound, Convention Center, **Police Dept**, to Univ of MI/Flint S: Auto Services, Graff Truck Center
135		**Hammerberg Rd, Flint**
(133)		**Jct I-75, N - Saginaw, S - Detroit, US 23S to Ann Arbor (Gas/Food/Lodg N to 1st Exit, #117A)**
131		**MI 121, Bristol Rd, Miller Rd, American Veterans Hwy, Flint**
	Gas	N: Speedway, Sunoco S: Mobil
	Food	N: Arby's, Burger King, Chili's, Chuck E Cheese Pizza, Logan's, Long John Silver, Mongolian BBQ, Old Country Buffet, Outback Steakhouse, Ryan's Grill, Ruby Tuesday, Starbucks, Subway, Taco Bell
	Other	N: ATMs, Auto Rentals, Auto Services, Banks, Best Buy, Borders, Dale's Natural Foods, Discount Tire, FedEx Office, Firestone, Goodyear, Gander Mountain, NTB, Office Depot, Pep Boys, PetCo♥, PetSmart♥, Target, UPS Store, Mall S: Bishop Int'l Airport✈
129		**Miller Rd, Swartz Creek**
	Gas	S: Speedway, Kroger
	Food	S: Arby's, Burger King, DQ, McDonald's, Wendy's
	Other	N: Auto Service, GM Serv Parts Oper S: Kroger, Vet♥
128		**Morrish Rd, Swartz Creek**
	Gas	S: BP, Admiral

Personal Notes

EXIT		MICHIGAN
	Food	S: China Wok, CJ's Café, Pizza, Subway
	Other	S: ATMs, Banks, Auto Services, Kroger, Sports Creek Raceway
(126)		**Rest Area Genesee (EB) (RR, Phones, Picnic, Pet, Vend)**
123		**MI 13, County Line Rd, Lennon**
	FStop	N: Speedway #8797
	Other	S: **Holiday Shores RV Resort & Golf Course▲**, Jenkins Auto & Truck Repair
118		**MI 71, Lansing Rd, Durand, Vernon**
	FStop	S: Monroe Point Shell S: Sunoco
	Food	S: Hungry Howie's, McDonald's, Subway, Wendy's
	Lodg	S: Quality Inn
	Med	S: + Memorial Urgent Care
	Other	S: Ace Hardware, Auto Dealer, Family Dollar, **Ferrell Gas/LP**, RiteAid
	Other	S: Amtrak, Family Dollar, Grocery, Museum, Radio Shack, RiteAid, **Rainbow RV Sales**
113		**Grand River Rd, Bancroft**
	Gas	S: BP◈
	Other	S: to appr 6 mi **Walnut Hills Family RV Resort & Campground▲**
105		**MI 52, Main St, Perry, Owosso**
	TStop	S: Glitzy Ritz Auto Truck Plaza/Sunoco
	Gas	S: 7-11/Citgo, Mobil◈
	Food	S: Rest/Subway/Glitzy Ritz ATP, Burger King, Hungry Howie's, McDonald's, Taco Bell/P66
	Lodg	S: Heb's Inn♥
	Med	S: + Urgent Memorial Care
	Other	S: ATMs, Auto Dealer, Auto Services,

EXIT		MICHIGAN
	Other	S: Carwash/Mobil, Dollar General, Family Dollar, Harts Auto & **RV** Repair, IGA, **Police Dept**, RiteAid
(101)		**Rest Area Shiawassee Co (WB) (RR, Phones, Picnic, Vend, Pet)**
98		**Woodbury Rd, Haslett, to Laingsburg, Shaftsburg**
94		**Bus I-69, Saginaw Hwy, MI 78, Marsh Rd, Haslett, Lansing (Addtl Serv 4mi on Grand River Ave)**
	Gas	S: Speedway, Speedway
	Food	S: McDonald's/Speedway
	Other	S: Carwash/Speedway, Car Wash, Ferrell Gas/**LP**, **Gillette's Interstate RV**, Meijer, A& D Repair
92		**Webster Rd, Bath**
89B		**US 127N, Jackson (NB)**
89A		**US 127S, E Lansing (SB)**
87		**US 27, DeWitt, Lansing, to Clare**
	FStop	N: Speedway #8740
	Gas	N: BP◈ S: Speedway◈
	Food	N: FastFood/Speedway, Arby's, Burger King, Bob Evans, FlapJack's, Marco's, McDonald's, Little Caesars Pizza, Subway
	Lodg	N: Sleep Inn S: Amerihost Inn
	Med	N: + Delta Medical Center
	Other	N: ATMs, Auto Services, **Annie Rae RV** S: Auto Services, ATMs
85		**DeWitt Rd, Lansing, to DeWitt**
84		**Airport Rd, to I-96/69 Bus, Lansing**
	Other	S: to Capital City Airport✈, **Dennis Trailer Sales**
	NOTE:	**I-69 below runs with I-96. Exit #'s follow I-96.**
(81/ 90)		**Jct I-96W, Francis Rd,Grand Ledge (SB), Grand River Ave, Bus 69/96**
	TStop	W: Flying J Travel Plaza #5126 (Scales)
	Food	W: CountryMarket/FastFood/FJ TP
	Other	E: Capital City Airport✈ W: Laundry/WiFi/**RVDump**/**LP**/FJ TP
(91)		**Jct I-69N, US 27, to Flint, Clare**
93A		**I-69 Bus, MI 43W, W Saginaw Hwy to Grand Ledge**
	Gas	W: BP, Shell, Speedway◈
	Food	W: Arby's, Bob Evans, **Cracker Barrel**, McDonald's, Steak n Shake, Subway
	Lodg	W: Springhill Suites
	Other	W: Discount Tire, Lowe's, PetSmart♥, Staples, **Walmart**, FunTyme Park
93B		**I-69 Bus, MI 43E, W Saginaw Hwy**
	Gas	E: Shell, Speedway◈, Total, Meijer◈
	Food	E: Burger King, Carrabba's, Denny's, McDonald's, Mountain Jack's Steakhouse, Outback Steakhouse, Red Robin, TGI Friday
	Lodg	E: Best Western, Fairfield Inn, Hampton Inn, Holiday Inn, Motel 6♥, Quality Suites, Red Roof Inn♥, Residence Inn
	Med	E: + Delta Medical Center
	Other	E: AMC, Alamo RAC, ATMs, Auto Dealer, Auto Services, Banks, Better Health Market Big Lots, Carwash, Cinema, Enterprise RAC, FedEx Office, Firestone, Goodyear, Kroger, Midas, Office Max, Target,

◈= Regular Gas Stations with Diesel ▲= RV Friendly Locations ♥= Pet Friendly Locations
Red print shows large vehicle parking / access on site or nearby Brown Print = Campgrounds / RV PARKS

EXIT		MICHIGAN

Other — E: UPS Store, Lansing Mall, GM Lansing Assembly

(95) Jct I-496, Downtown Lansing
Med — E: to + Ingham Reg'l Medical Center
Other — E: to MI State Univ

(97/72) Jct I-69S, US 27, to Charlotte, Ft Wayne, I-96E, to Detroit, W to Grand Rapids

NOTE: I-69 above runs with I-96. Exit #'s follow I-96.

70 Lansing Rd, to I-96, Charlotte

(68) Potterville #829 Rest Area (NB)
Eaton Co (RR, Phones, Pic, Vend)

66 MI 100, Hartel Rd, Charlotte, Potterville, Grand Ledge
Gas — W: BP, Shell
Food — W: McDonald's, Subway

61 Lansing St/Rd, MI 79, Charlotte
FStop — E: Marathon
Gas — E: Mobil
W: Gas, Speedway
Food — E: Applebee's, Subway
W: Arby's, Big Boy, Biggby Coffee, Burger King, KFC, Little Caesars Pizza, McDonald's, Pizza Hut, Subway, Taco Bell, Top Chinese Buffet, Wendy's
Lodg — E: Comfort Inn, Crestview Motel
Med — W: + Hayes Green Beach Memorial Hospital
Other — E: ATMs, Auto Dealers, Auto Zone, Grocery, Tractor Supply, Walmart sc, Fitch H Beach Airport✈
W: ATMs, Advance Auto Parts, Auto Dealers, Auto Services, Banks, CarQuest, Carwash, Cinema, Family Dollar, Grocery, Radio Shack, Tires, Police Dept

60 MI 50, E Shepherd St, E Clinton Tr, Charlotte, Eaton Rapids
Gas — E: Meijer◈
Lodg — E: Holiday Inn Express
W: Super 8
Med — W: + Hospital
Other — E: Auto Services
W: Auto Services, Acc to Ex #61 Serv

57 Cochran Rd, Loop 69, Marshall Rd, Charlotte

51 Ainger Rd, Olivet

48 MI 78, Butterfield Hwy, Olivet, Bellevue, Lee Center
Gas — E: Citgo
Food — E: Subway, Taco Bell
Other — E: ATMs, Banks, Auto Service, Police

42 N Drive North, Marshall

(40) Rest Area Calhoun Co (SB)
(RR, Phones, Picnic, Vend, Pet, Info)

(38) Jct I-94, W to Chicago, E to Detroit

36 Michigan Ave, I-94 Bus, MI 96, Marshall, to I-94
Gas — E: Citgo◈, Mobil, Shell
Food — E: Applebee's, Arby's, Burger King, Little Caesars Pizza, McDonald's, Pizza Hut, Subway, Taco Bell, Wendy's
Lodg — E: Amerihost Inn, National House Inn
W: Arbor Inn, Howard's Motel, Imperial Motel

EXIT		MICHIGAN

Med — E: + Hospital
Other — E: ATMs, Auto Services, Auto Zone, Auto Dealers, Dollar Tree, Grocery, Radio Shack, RiteAid, Brooks Field Airport✈, MI State Hwy Patrol Post
W: Auto Services, Towing, Marshall RV

32 MI 227N, F Drive South, Marshall
Gas — E: Shell
Other — E: to Tri-Lake Trails Campground▲, Quality Camping▲

25 MI 60, Tekonsha, to Three Rivers, Jackson
FStop — E: Snappy Food Mart/BP, Tekonsha Sunoco
TStop — E: Te-Kon AmBest Travel Plaza/Citgo (Scales)
Food — E: FastFood/Snappy FM, Rest/Subway/Te-Kon TP, McDonald's
TWash — E: Te-Kon TP
TServ — E: Te-Kon TP/Tires, NAPA/Courtesy Car & Truck Parts & RV Repairs
Other — E: Laundry/Te-Kon TP, to Quality Camping▲
W: to Turtle Lake Nudist Resort▲

23 Marshall Rd, Tekonsha
Gas — E: Citgo
Other — W: to Potawatomie Rec Area▲

16 Jonesville Rd, Coldwater
Gas — W: AmocoBP
Other — W: Waffle Farm Campground▲, Love's Lazy Lagoon▲, Narrows Resort & Campground▲

13 US 12, I-69 Bus, E Chicago St, Coldwater, to Quincy, Batavia
Gas — E: Meijer◈, Speedway◈
W: BP, Citgo, Speedway◈, Sunoco
Food — E: Applebee's, Bob Evans, Super Grand Buffet
W: Arby's, Burger King, Chinese Rest, Cottage Inn Pizza, Coldwater Garden Rest, KFC, Little Caesars Pizza, McDonalds, Mr Gyros, Pizza Hut, Ponderosa, Subway, TCBY, Taco Bell, Wendy's
Lodg — E: Hampton Inn, Red Roof Inn♥
W: Cadet Motor Inn, Comfort Inn, Holiday Inn Express, Super 8, Chicago Pike Inn B&B
Med — W: + Hospital, + Family Medicine Clinic
Other: — E: Auto Zone, ATMs, Auto Services, Auto Dealer, Aldi's, Banks, Big Lots, Cinema, Dollar General, Dollar Tree, Grocery, Home Depot, Meijer,Radio Shack, SavALot, Walmart sc, Haylett's N Country Auto & RV Center, to Cottonwood Resort▲, to Historic Marble Springs Family Campground & Park▲, to appr 15 mi: Gateway Park Campground▲, Sugar Bush Park▲, Way-Back-In Campground▲
W: ATMs, Auto Services, Auto Dealers, Banks, RiteAid, Walgreen's, MI State Hwy Patrol Post, to Branch Co Mem'l Airport✈

10 Fenn Rd, to I-69 Bus, Coldwater

(8) Weigh Station (NB)

(6) MI Welcome Center (NB)
(RR, Phones, Picnic, Vend, Info)

3 Copeland Rd, Coldwater
Other — E: to Coldwater Lake Campground▲, Butler Resort▲

EXIT		MI / IN

Other — W: to Green Acres Campground▲, Coldwater River Campground▲

EASTERN TIME ZONE

⇑ MICHIGAN
⇓ INDIANA

NOTE: MM 158: Michigan State Line

EASTERN TIME ZONE

157 Baker Rd, Lk George Rd, to IN 120, Angola, Fremont, Jamestown
TStop — E: Petro2 Stopping Center #45/Mobil (Scales)
W: Pilot Travel Center #29 (Scales), Pioneer Auto Truck Stop/Shell
Food — E: Rest/FastFood/Petro SC
W: Wendy's/Pilot TC, Subway/Pioneer, McDonald's, Red Arrow Rest
Lodg — E: Lake George Inn/Petro SC
W: Holiday Inn Express, Redwood Motor Lodge
Other — E: Laundry/WiFi/Petro SC
W: Laundry/WiFi/Pilot TC, Prime Outlets at Fremont, to Barton Lake RV Sales & Service, Yogi Bear's Jellystone Camp▲, Manapogo Park▲

(156) Jct I-80/90 (TOLL), W to Chicago, E to Toledo, Ohio

154 IN 127, to IN 727, IN 120, W 400 N, Angola
Gas — W: Marathon◈
Food — E: Applebee's, Ruby Tuesday, Scoops
Lodg — E: Budgeteer Inn, Hampton Inn, Ramada Inn, Super 8, Travelers Inn
W: Pokagon Motel
Other — E: Oakhill Campground▲
W: Prime Outlets, Pokagon State Park▲, to Manapogo Park▲

150 CR 200W, Angola, Lake James
Gas — E: BP◈
W: Shell
Food — W: BB's Smokehouse, Caruso's Italian
Lodg — W: to Lake James Family Resort
Other — W: Fun Spot Amusement Park & Zoo

148 US 20, Angola, LaGrange (Addt'l Serv E to IN 127N)
FStop — E: Speedway #8336
Gas — E: Citgo◈, Gas America
Food — E: McDonald's, Subway, Hatchery, Rice Bowl, Timbers Rest, Wendy's
W: Best Western
Lodg — E: Redwood Motel
W: Best Western, Sycamore Hill B&B
TWash — E: Speedway
Med — E: + Hospital
Other — E: ATMs, Auto Services, Auto Dealers, Banks, Dollar General, Grocery, Towing, Golf Course, Happy Acres RV Park▲, Buck Lake Ranch▲, to Walmart sc, Panterra Coach & RV
W: Circle B Campground▲, to Gordon's Camping Resort▲, Tri State Steuben Co Airport✈

(144) Steuben Co Rest Area (SB)
(RR, Phones, Picnic, Vend, Info)

◈ = Regular Gas Stations with Diesel ▲ = RV Friendly Locations ♥ = Pet Friendly Locations
Red print shows large vehicle parking / access on site or nearby Brown Print = Campgrounds / RV PARKS

EXIT	INDIANA
140	**IN 4, State St, W 800S, Ashley, Hamilton, Hudson**
Gas	W: Ashley Deli, BP
Food	W: Deli, Cones & Coney, Pizza
Other	W: Auto Repairs, ATMs, Banks, Tires, to **Story Lake Resort▲**
134	**US 6, Grand Army of the Republic, Waterloo, Kendallville (Addt'l Serv E to IN 427)**
TStop	W: Kaghann's Korner/Marathon, Morning Star Truck & Auto Plaza/ BP
Food	W: Rest/Kaghann's Korner, Rest/Morning Star TAP
Lodg	E: Lighthouse Inn
Other	E: Amtrak
129	**IN 8, 7th St, Auburn, Garrett, Avilla**
Gas	E: BP◈, Clark, GasAmerica, Marathon◈, Shell, Speedway◈
Food	E: Applebee's, Arby's, Bob Evans, Burger King, DQ, McDonald's, Ponderosa, Pizza Hut, Subway, Taco Bell, Wendy's W: **Cracker Barrel**
Lodg	E: Best Western♥, Comfort Inn, Country Hearth Inn, Holiday Inn Express, La Quinta Inn♥
Med	E: **+ DeKalb Memorial Hospital**
Other	E: Auto Zone, ATMs, Auto Dealers, Auto Services, Banks, CVS , Cinema, Dollar General, Grocery, Kroger, Radio Shack, Staples, **Walmart sc**, Golf Course W: Home Depot, **to Indian Springs Resort Campground▲**
126	**CR 11A, Garrett, Auburn**
Other	E: Auburn Dekalk Airport✈ W: **Auburn/Ft Wayne North KOA▲ / RVDump**, **to Indian Springs Resort Campground▲**
(123)	**DeKalb Co Rest Area (Both dir) (RR, Phones) (Closed for renovation)**
116	**IN 1N, Dupont Rd, Ft Wayne, Cedarville-Leo, Huntertown**
Gas	E: Citgo W: BP◈, Speedway◈
Food	E: Burger King, Culver's W: Bob Evans, KFC, McDonald's, Mancino's Grinders & Pizza, Subway
Lodg	E: Comfort Suites W: AmericInn, Sleep Inn
Med	E: **+ Parkview North Hospital** W: **+ Dupont Hospital**
Other	W: ATMs, Banks, Auto Services, Golf Courses, Kroger, Walgreen's
(115)	**Jct I-469S, US 30E, to New Haven, Van Wert, Ohio**
112AB	**IN 327, Coldwater Rd, Ft Wayne (SB)**
Gas	E: BP◈, Marathon, Max Food Mart
Food	E: Arby's, AAJ India Rest, Burger King, Cork 'n Cleaver, Don Hall's Factory Rest, Lone Star Steakhouse, Old Country Buffet, Red River Steaks & BBQ, Steak n Shake, Taco Bell, Wendy's, Yokohama Japanese
Lodg	E: AmeriSuites, Marriott♥
Other	E: ATMs, Auto Services, Banks, Best Buy, Cinema 8, Dollar Tree, Grocery, Office Depot, NAPA, PetCo♥, Radio Shack, Walgreen's, **Walmart sc**, Glenbrook Square Mall, U-Haul, **to** Concordia Univ, IN Purdue Univ, Memorial Coliseum W: **to appr 13 mi: Indian Springs Resort Campground▲**

Personal Notes

EXIT	INDIANA
112A	**IN 327E, Coldwater Rd, Ft Wayne (NB)**
112B	**IN 327W, Coldwater Rd (NB)**
111B	**US 27S, IN 3N, Lima Rd, Ft Wayne, Kendalville**
Gas	W: BP◈, Marathon, Meijer◈, Sam's
Food	W: Applebee's, Burger King, **Cracker Barrel**, IHOP, KFC, Logan's Roadhouse, McDonald's, Mega Wraps, O'Charley's, Starbucks, Subway, Texas Roadhouse
Lodg	W: AmeriHost Inn, Baymont Inn, Best Value Inn, Candlewood Suites, Courtyard, Days Inn, Dollar Inn,Fairfield Inn, GuestHouse Inn, Hampton Inn, Lee's Inn, Studio Plus
Other	W: ATMs, Auto Services, Home Depot, Lowe's, Sam's Club, **Coleman Camper Center**
111A	**US 27S, IN 1S, Lima Rd, to IN 930, Ft Wayne**
Gas	E: Shell, Speedway
Food	E: Arby's, Chuck E Cheese Pizza, China Express, DQ, Don Pablo, Denny's, Fazoli's, Golden Corral, Hardee's, McDonald's, Starbucks, Subway, Wendy's
Lodg	E: Residence Inn
Other	E: ATMs, Auto Dealers, Auto Services, Banks, Discount Tire, FedEx Office, Grocery, Target, Glenbrook Square Mall
109B	**US 30W, US 33N, Ft Wayne, to Columbia City, Elkhart**
FStop	W: **to US 33N, 1mi:** Old Fort Travel Plaza/ Marathon

EXIT	INDIANA
TStop	W: **@ NA VanLines:** Speed-Ease, **to appr 8 mi - US 30W / CR N:** RoadysTS/County Line Travel Plaza (Scales)
Food	W: Chicken/Pizza/Subs/Co Line TP
TWash	W: County Line TP
TServ	W: Speed-Ease/Tires
Other	W: Laundry/Speed-Ease, Tires Plus, U-Haul, Laundry/County Line TP, **to Eel River Campground▲ , Blue Lake Campground & Resort▲**
109A	**IN 930E, Goshen Rd, Ft Wayne**
FStop	E: Ray's Truck Wash/Sunoco (Scales)
Tstop	E: Pilot Travel Center #881 (Scales)
Gas	E: BP
Food	E: PointRest/McDonald's/Subway/ Pilot TC, Liberty Diner
Lodg	E: Best Inn, Econo Lodge, Knights Inn, Motel 6♥, Quality Inn, Red Roof Inn♥
TWash	E: Blue Beacon Truck Wash/Pilot TC, Ray's TW,
TServ	E: Clarke Detroit Diesel/Allison, Cummins, Ft Wayne Truck Center/Kenworth, Wise International Trucks
Med	E: **+ Hospital**
Other	E: Laundry/BarbSh/CB/WiFi/Pilot TC, Goodyear, FW Childrens Zoo, U-Haul
105B	**IN 14W, Illinois Rd, Ft Wayne, South Whitley**
105A	**Illinois Rd, Ft Wayne**
Gas	E: BP, Meijer◈, Shell◈, Speedway
Food	E: Bob Evan's, O'Charley's, Steak 'n Shake, Smokey Bones BBQ, Subway
Lodg	E: Klopfenstein Inn
TServ	E: **to** Discover Volvo Trucks
Med	E: **+ St Joseph Hospital**
Other	E: ATMs, Auto Dealers, Auto Services, Animal Hospital♥, Banks, Barnes & Noble, Best Buy, Dollar Tree, FedEx Office, Grocery, Lowe's, PetSmart♥, Staples, UPS Store, **Walmart sc**, Jim Bailey's Harley Davidson, **to** Univ of St Francis
102	**US 24W, W Jefferson Blvd, Ft Wayne, Huntington**
Gas	W: BP, Marathon
Food	E: Casa D'Angelo, Subway, Taco Bell W: Applebee's, Arby's, Bob Evans, Carlos O'Kelly's, Captain D's, McDonald's, Outback Steakhouse, Pizza Hut, Starbucks, Sara's Family Rest, Wendy's
Lodg	E: Extended Stay America, Hampton Inn, Residence Inn W: Best Western, Comfort Suites, Holiday Inn Express, Hilton Garden Inn
Med	E: **+ Lutheran Hospital of IN**
Other	W: ATMs, Auto Services, Banks, Grocery, Kroger, UPS Store, Walgreen's, **IN State Hwy Patrol Post**
99	**Lower Huntington Rd, Ft Wayne**
Other	E: **to** Ft Wayne Int'l Airport✈, IN Nat'l Guard, General Mills W: GM Truck & Bus Group
96B	**Lafayette Center Rd, to US 24, Roanoke Station, Huntington**
Other	W: GM Truck & Bus Group
96A	**IN 469N, US 24E, to US 33S, US 27, New Haven, Decatur**
Other	E: **to** Ft Wayne Int'l Airport✈, IN Nat'l Guard, General Mills
(91)	**Wells Co Rest Area (SB) (RR, Phones, Picnic, Vend)**

◈= Regular Gas Stations with Diesel ▲ = RV Friendly Locations ♥= Pet Friendly Locations
Red print shows large vehicle parking / access on site or nearby Brown Print = Campgrounds / RV PARKS

EXIT		INDIANA
(89)		**Huntington Co Rest Area** (NB) (RR, Phones, Picnic, Vend)
86		**US 224, Markle Rd, Logan Rd, Huntington, Markle**
	Gas	E: Phillips 66, Sunoco
	Food	E: DQ, Pizza, Subway
	Lodg	E: Super 8
	Med	E: + Markle Medical Center
	Other	W: Markle State Rec Area, Little Turtle State Rec Area, Kil-So-Quah State Rec Area
(80)		**Weigh Station** (SB)
78		**IN 5, Warren Rd, Warren**
	TStop	W: AmBest/Steel City #472 (Scales)
	Gas	E: Sunoco◈
		W: Marathon◈
	Food	W: PopsCountryKitchen/FastFood/Steel City, McDonald's, Ugalde's Family Rest, Subway/Marathon
	Lodg	E: Huggy Bear Motel
		W: Comfort Inn, Motel 6
	Med	W: + Huntington Memorial Hospital
	Other	E: to appr 13 mi Blufton/Ft Wayne South KOA▲
		W: Laundry/WiFi/RVDump/Steel City, Boom City Fireworks
73		**IN 218, IN 5, Warren, La Fontaine**
64		**IN 18, Marion, Montpelier, Roll**
	TStop	E: Love's Travel Stop #323 (Scales)
	Gas	W: BP◈, Marathon◈
	Food	E: McDonald's/Love's TS
		W: Arby's, Subway
	Med	W: + Hospital
	Other	E: Laundry/WiFi/RVDump/Love's TS, Stone's Harley Davidson, to Ickes RV Surplus Supply, Wildwood Acres Campground
59		**US 35N, IN 22, Gas City, Upland** (Addtl Serv 3-4mi W-Gas City, E-Upland)
	TStop	W: McClure Oil #59
	Gas	E: Gas City, Valero
		W: Marathon◈, Shell◈
	Food	E: Burger King, Cracker Barrel, Subway/ Valero
		W: FastFood/McClure Oil, Arby's, McDonald's, KFC/Taco Bell, Starbucks
	Lodg	E: Best Western, Super 8, to This Old Barn B&B
		W: Holiday Inn Express
	TWash	W: Smitty's
	TServ	E: C&C Truck Service
	Other	E: Sports Lake Campground▲, to Mar-Brook Campground▲
55		**IN 26, Hartford City, Fairmount**
	Gas	W: Marathon
(51)		**Delaware Co Rest Area** (Both dir) (RR, Phones, Picnic, Vend)
45		**US 35S, IN 28, Alexandria, Muncie** (Addt'l Serv 4 mi W in Alexandria)
	TStop	E: Petro Stopping Center #374/Shell (Scales)
	Food	E: IronSkillet/TacoBell/Petro SC
	TServ	E: Petro SC/Tires
	Other	E: Laundry/WiFi/Petro SC, Big Oak Park▲
		W: to Hoosierland Park▲
41		**IN 332E, Muncie, Frankton** (Addt'l Serv 6-7mi E in Muncie)
	Gas	E: Citgo◈

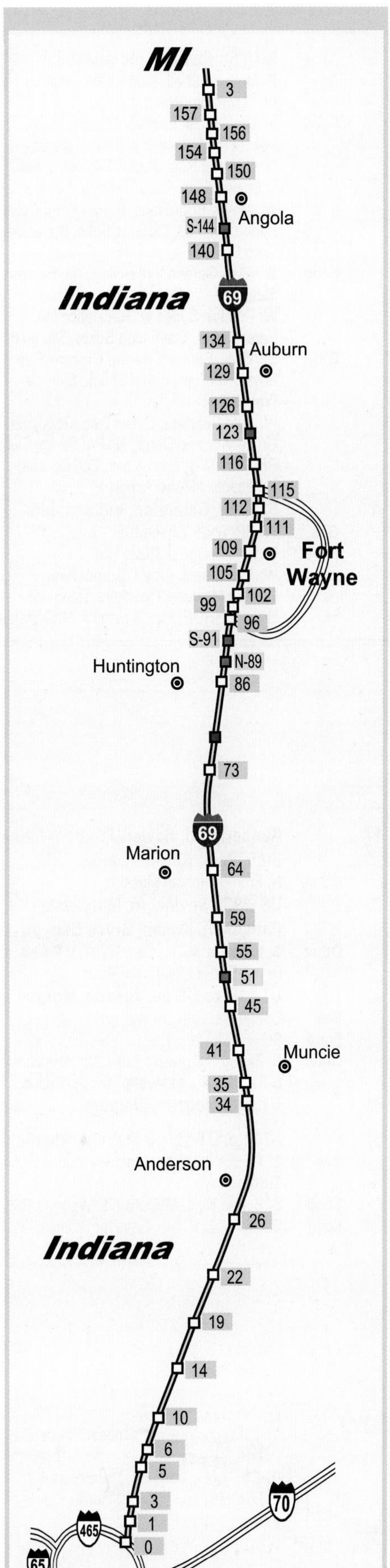

EXIT		INDIANA
	Med	E: + Ball Memorial Hospital
	Other	E: to Delaware Co Johnson Field✈, Ball State Univ
35		**IN 32, Main St, Daleville, Muncie Chesterfield, Anderson**
	Gas	E: AmocoBP
	Food	W: BBQ, Café, DQ, Pizza Hut
	Lodg	W: Hampton Inn
	TServ	W: Troy's Truck & Auto Service
	Other	E: Auto Repairs & Towing, Grocery
		W: to Timberline Campground▲, Mounds State Park▲, Anderson Muni Airport✈, Anderson Univ
34		**IN 67N, Commerce Rd, to IN 32, Main St, Daleville, Muncie, Chesterfield, Anderson**
	FStop	W: Gas America #41
	TStop	E: Pilot Travel Center #28 (Scales)
		W: Pilot Travel Center #446 (Scales)
	Gas	E: Shell
	Food	E: Subway/Pilot TC, FastFood/Shell, Arby's, Burger King, Taco Bell
		W: Rest/Pilot TC, McDonald's, Wendy's
	Lodg	E: Budget Inn
		W: Super 8
	TServ	E: Clarke Power Services/Allison, Bigelow Trailer Sales & Service
		W: Keep it Moving Truck & Trailer
	Other	E: WiFi/Pilot TC
		W: Laundry/WiFi/Pilot TC, ATMs, Banks, Central IN Auto & RV, Anderson Muni Airport✈, Great American Flea Market, Timberline Family Campground▲, Mounds State Park▲
26		**IN 9N, IN 109S, Scatterfield Rd, Anderson, Alliance**
	Gas	E: Meijer◈
		W: BP, Gas America, Marathon, Petro Mart◈, Speedway
	Food	E: Culver's, KFC, Ryan's Grill
		W: Applebee's, Arby's, Bob Evans, Burger King, Cracker Barrel, Culver's, IHOP, McDonald's, Little Caesars Pizza, Lone Star Steakhouse, Montana Mike's, Perkins, Pizza Hut, Red Lobster, Ruby Tuesday, Steak 'n Shake, Taco Bell, Waffle & Steak, Waffle House, Wendy's
	Lodg	E: Clarion Inn, Deluxe Inn, Hampton Inn, Quality Inn
		W: America's Best Inn♥, Baymont Inn, Comfort Inn, Days Inn, Econo Lodge, Fairfield Inn, Holiday Inn, Lee's Inn, Motel 6♥, Super 8
	TServ	W: Stoops Freightliner
	Med	W: + Community Hospital
	Other	E: Meijer
		W: ATMs, Auto Services, Auto Dealer, Aldi Grocery, Menard's O'Reilly Auto Parts, Radio Shack, Target, Tires, Tractor Supply, Visitor Center, Walmart SC, to Mounds State Park▲
22		**IN 67S, IN 9S, Pendleton Ave, Anderson, Pendleton**
	Gas	W: Gas America
	Food	W: Red Brick Inn Rest, Skyline Chili, Yesterday Drive-In
	Lodg	W: to Anderson Country Inn♥
	Other	W: Modern Trailer Sales

◈= Regular Gas Stations with Diesel ▲ = RV Friendly Locations ♥= Pet Friendly Locations
Red print shows large vehicle parking / access on site or nearby Brown Print = Campgrounds / RV PARKS

EXIT		INDIANA
19		**IN 38, Pendleton, Clarksville (Addtl Serv E to IN 67)**
	Gas	E: Marathon
	Food	E: DQ, McDonald's, Subway
	Other	W: to Pine Lake Camping & Fishing▲
14		**IN 13, Pendleton, Lapel, Fortville**
	TStop	W: Pilot Travel Center #362 (Scales)
	Food	W: Subway/Pilot TC
	Other	W: WiFi/Pilot TC, to Glo Wood Campground▲
10		**IN 238, Greenfield Ave, Olio Rd, Noblesville, Fortville**
	Med	E: + Hospital
6		**IN 37N, Noblesville (NB)**
	Gas	E: Shell
	Food	E: Blimpie, Chinese, Wendy's
5		**IN 37N, 116th St, Fishers**
	Gas	E: BP W: Shell, Speedway
	Food	W: BBQ, Hardee's, KFC, McDonald's, O'Charley's, Quiznos, Starbucks, Steak n Shake, Subway, Wendy's
	Lodg	W: Hampton Inn
	Other	W: ATMs, Auto Service, Target, Visitor Info, Police Dept, Cruise America RV Rental
3		**96th St, Fishers, Indianapolis**
	Gas	E: Meijer◈, Shell, Stop n Go◈, Murphy W: Marathon, Sam's
	Food	E: Applebee's, Blimpie, Cracker Barrel, Hardee's, McDonald's, Panera Bread, Qdoba Mex Rest, Ruby Tuesday, Steak 'n Shake, Starbucks, Wendy's W: Arby's, Bob Evans, Burger King, Culver, Panda Express, Quiznos Subs, Starbucks, Taco Bell
	Lodg	E: Hilton Garden Inn, Holiday Inn Express, Sleep Inn W: Comfort Suites♥, Residence Inn, Ramada Inn, Staybridge Suites, Studio 6
	Other	E: ATMs, Banks, Cinema, Grocery, Pep Boys, PetCo♥, Radio Shack, Staples, Walmart sc W: Auto Services, Dollar Tree, Goodyear, Grocery, Home Depot, NAPA, Sam's Club, PFM Car & & Truck Care, Golf Course, Indianapolis Metro Airport✈
1		**82nd St, Castleton, Indianapolis**
	Gas	W: BP, Shell, Speedway
	Food	E: Golden Corral, Pizza Hut W: Applebee's, Arby's, Burger King, Cancun Mexican, Checkers, Denny's, Hooters, IHOP, Max & Erma's, McDonald's, Olive Garden, Outback Steakhouse, Perkins, Pizza Hut, Red Lobster, Skyline Chili, Starbucks, Steak n Shake, Taco Bell, Tony Roma, Tuscany Italian Grill, Wendy's
	Lodg	E: Country Inn, Dollar Inn, Extended Stay America, Hilton, Super 8 W: Best Western♥, Candlewood Suites, Days Inn, Fairfield Inn, Hampton Inn, Red Roof Inn
	Med	E: + Community Hospital North, + Urgent Care Center
	Other	E: CVS, Lowe's, Walgreen's W: AMC Cinema, ATMs, Auto Services, Avis RAC, Banks, Best Buy, Costco, Discount Tire, Firestone, Goodyear, Kroger, National RAC, PetSmart♥, Tires, Target, Vet♥, Castleton Square Mall, Convention Center, Golf Course
(0)		**Jct I-465, Indianapolis ByPass, IN 37, Binford Dr, Lawrence**

NOTE: I-69 Begins/ends on I-465, Exits #37AB

EASTERN TIME ZONE

INDIANA

Begin Northbound I-69 from Indianapolis, IN Port Huron, MI.

EXIT		UTAH

Begin Eastbound I-70 at Jct I-15, near Cove Fort, UT to Baltimore, MD.

UTAH

NOTE: I-70 Begins/Ends on I-15, Exit #132

MOUNTAIN TIME ZONE

EXIT		UTAH
(0)		**Jct I-15, N to Salt Lake City, S to St George, to AZ, to NV**
1		**UT 161, Fillmore, Historic Cove Fort (Chain-Up Area)**
	Other	N: Paiute Indian Reservation
8		**Ranch Exit, Sevier**
(13)		**Brake Check Area (EB)**
(16)		**RunAway Truck Ramp (EB)**
17		**Kimberly Rd, Sevier, Fremont Indian State Park (Chain-Up Area)**
	Other	N: Fremont Indian Museum
23		**US 89S, Sevier, to Marysvale, Panguitch, Kanab, Bryce Canyon**
	Other	S: to Lizzie & Charlie's RV/ATV Park▲, Bryce Canyon National Park
25		**UT 118, to US 89, Joseph, Monroe**
	Gas	S: Flying U Country Store◈
	Food	S: Rest/Flying U CS
	Other	S: Flying U Country Store Campground & RV Park▲, to Mystic Hot Springs▲
31		**UT 258, Monroe, Elsinore**
37		**I-70 Lp, UT 120, S Main St, Richfield**
	Gas	S: Phillips 66◈, JR Munchie's/Conoco◈, Tesoro◈
	Food	S: Burger King, McDonald's, Wendy's/P66
	Lodg	S: Budget Host Inn, Days Inn, Quality Inn, Travelodge

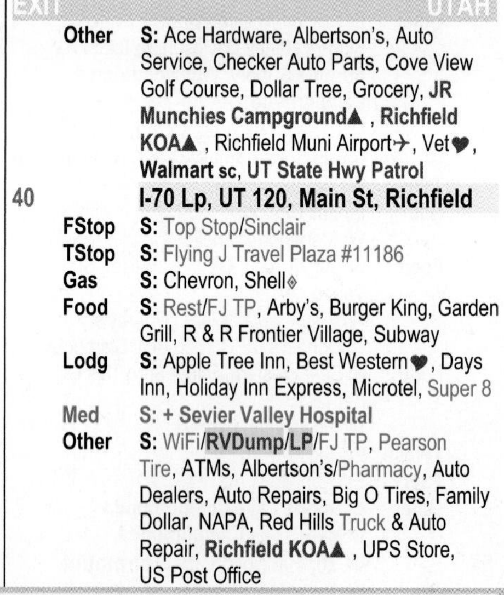

EXIT		UTAH
	Other	S: Ace Hardware, Albertson's, Auto Service, Checker Auto Parts, Cove View Golf Course, Dollar Tree, Grocery, JR Munchies Campground▲, Richfield KOA▲, Richfield Muni Airport✈, Vet♥, Walmart sc, UT State Hwy Patrol
40		**I-70 Lp, UT 120, Main St, Richfield**
	FStop	S: Top Stop/Sinclair
	TStop	S: Flying J Travel Plaza #11186
	Gas	S: Chevron, Shell◈
	Food	S: Rest/FJ TP, Arby's, Burger King, Garden Grill, R & R Frontier Village, Subway
	Lodg	S: Apple Tree Inn, Best Western♥, Days Inn, Holiday Inn Express, Microtel, Super 8
	Med	S: + Sevier Valley Hospital
	Other	S: WiFi/RVDump/LP/FJ TP, Pearson Tire, ATMs, Albertson's/Pharmacy, Auto Dealers, Auto Repairs, Big O Tires, Family Dollar, NAPA, Red Hills Truck & Auto Repair, Richfield KOA▲, UPS Store, US Post Office

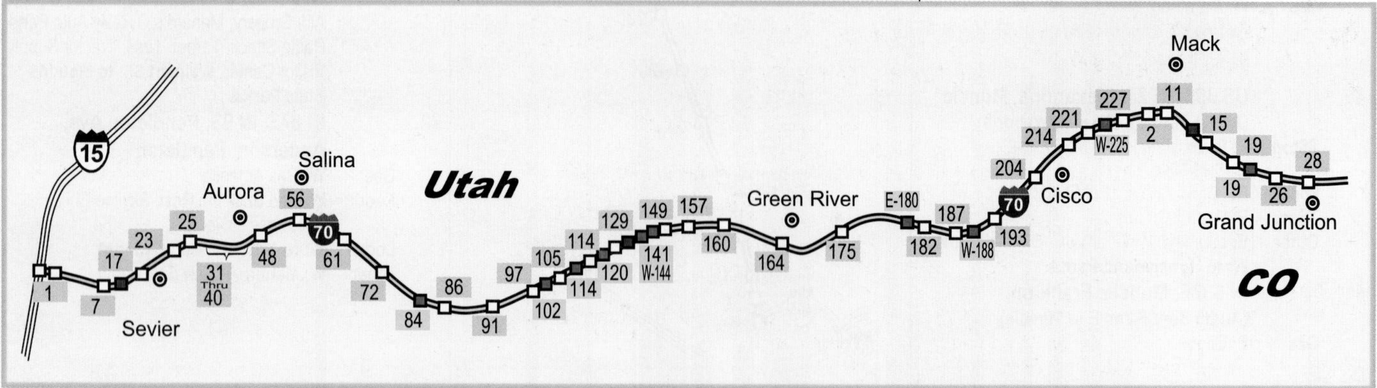

◈= Regular Gas Stations with Diesel ▲ = RV Friendly Locations ♥= Pet Friendly Locations
Red print shows large vehicle parking / access on site or nearby Brown Print = Campgrounds / RV PARKS

EXIT	UTAH
48	**UT 259, Old Hwy 89 to UT 24, to US 50, Richfield, Sigurd, Aurora**
NOTE:	EB: Gas Check! Next Fuel x #160
56	**State St, I-70 Bus, US 89N, to US 50, Salina, to Reno, Salt Lake City**
FStop	N: Salina Express/Sinclair
TStop	N: Scenic Quik Stop/P66
Gas	N: Conoco◈, Maverik
Food	N: Rest/Quik Stop, BurgerKing/Sinclair, Denny's, El Mexicano Rest, Subway,
Lodg	N: Best Western, Rodeway Inn, Ranch Motel, Super 8
TServ	N: Wheeler CAT,
Other	N: Laundry/QuikStop, Auto Repairs, **Butch Cassidy Campground▲**, CarQuest, Grocery, NAPA, **Salina Creek RV Campground▲**, U-Haul,
61	**Gooseberry Rd, Salina**
NOTE:	MM 69: Summit Elev 7076'
72	**Ranch Exit**
NOTE:	MM 83.5: Summit Elev 7923'
(84)	**Ivie Creek Rest Area (WB) (RR, Picnic, Info)**
86	**UT 72, Loa, Capital Reef Nat'l Park**
91	**UT 72, UT 10, Salina, to Emery, Huntington**
97	**Ranch Exit**
(102)	**Salt Wash View Area (Both dir) (RR, Info)**
108	**Ranch Exit**
(114)	**Devil's Canyon View Area (EB) (RR) Eagle Canyon View Area (WB) (RR, Info)**
116	**Moore Cutoff, Moore**
(120)	**Ghost Rocks View Area (Both dir) (RR, Info)**
131	**Ranch Exit**
(136)	**Brake Check Area (EB)**
(139)	**RunAway Truck Ramp (EB)**
(141)	**Black Dragon View Area (EB) San Rafael View Area (WB) (RR, Info)**
(141)	**RunAway Truck Ramp (EB)**
(144)	**Spotted Wolf View Area (WB) (RR)**
149	**UT 24, Hanksville, Lake Powell, to Capital Reef Nat'l Park, Bryce Canyon Nat'l Park**
157	**US 6W, US 191N, to Price, Salt Lake**
160	**I-70 Bus (EB), UT 19, W Main St, Green River (Access to #164 Serv)**
TStop	N: PTP/Gas n Go #13/Conoco
Gas	N: Chevron◈
Food	N: Arby's/Gas n Go, Burger King, Subway/ Chevron, Ben's Café, Ray's Rest,

EXIT	UT / CO
Lodg	N: Budget Inn, Robbers Roost Motel, Rodeway Inn, Sleepy Hollow Motel
Other	N: Laundry/Gas n Go, Amtrak, Museum, Auto Service, US Post Office, Green River Golf Course, AmeriGas Propane/LP, **Green River State Park, A OK RV Park▲ Shady Acres RV Park & Campground▲** /Silver Eagle Gas & Diesel/Blimpie
164	**UT 19, I-70 Bus (WB), E Main St, Green River (Access to #160 Serv)**
TStop	N: AmBest/West Winds Truck Stop/ Sinclair (Scales)
Gas	N: Short Stop◈
Food	N: West WindsRest/WW TS, Burger King, Rest/Book Cliff Lodge, Tamarisk Rest
Lodg	N: Motel/West Winds TS, Best Western, Book Cliff Lodge, Comfort Inn, Holiday Inn Express♥, Motel 6, Ramada Ltd♥, Super 8♥
TWash	N: West Winds TS
TServ	N: West Winds TS/Tires/**RV Repair**
Other	N: Laundry/**RVDump/LP**/West Winds TS, **Green River KOA▲**, **Shady Acres RV Park & Campground▲** /Silver Eagle Gas & Diesel/Blimpie, Museum, **Green River State Park**
NOTE:	WB: GAS Check! Next Fuel x #56
175	**Ranch Exit**
(180)	**Crescent Jct Rest Area (EB) (RR, Phone, Picnic)**
182	**US 191, Crescent Jct, to Moab**
Other	S: to appr 30mi: **Arches National Park, Canyonlands National Park, Dead Horse Point State Park, (Numerous Campgrounds & RV Parks)**
187	**Sego Canyon Rd, to UT 94, Thompson, to Thompson Springs**
FStop	N: Outwest Food n Food #34/Shell
(188)	**UT Thompson Welcome Center (WB) (RR, Phone, Picnic, Vending, Info)**
193	**Ranch Exit**
204	**UT 128, US 6 Bus, to Cisco**
214	**US 6 Bus, Thompson, to Cisco**
221	**Ranch Exit**
(226)	**Harley Dome View Area (WB) (RR)**
227	**Hay Canyon Rd, to US 6 Bus, Thompson, Westwater**

MOUNTAIN TIME ZONE

NOTE:	MM 232: Colorado State Line

↑ UTAH
↓ COLORADO

MOUNTAIN TIME ZONE

EXIT	COLORADO
2	**to Rabbit Valley Rd, Mack**
11	**US 6E, US 50, Loma, Mack (Serv 2-3 mi N)**
(14)	**Loma Weigh Station (Both dir)**
15	**CO 139N, 13 Rd, Loma, Rangely**
Other	N: to James Hutton Truck Repair, **Highline State Rec Area▲**
(19)	**CO 340, to US 6, US 50, Fruita** **S: CO Welcome Center (Both dir) (RR, Phones, Pic, Pet, Info, RVDump)**
TStop	S: Loco Travel Stop #17/Conoco
Gas	N: BP, Conoco◈ S: Shell◈
Food	N: Burger King, Munchies Pizza, Mex Rest S: Rest/SubwayLoco TS, Wendy's/Shell, Chinese Rest, McDonald's, Mexican Rest Pablo's Pizza, Rib City Grill, Taco Bell
Lodg	N: Balanced Rock Hotel S: Comfort Inn, La Quinta Inn♥, Super 8
Med	S: + St Mary's Hospital
TServ	S: Peterbilt
Other	N: ATMs, Auto Services, Banks, CarQuest, Grocery, NAPA, US Post Office, Walgreen's, S: Laundry/**LP**/Loco TS, ATMs, Adobe Creek Nat'l Golf Course, Desert Spring Vet♥, Dinosaur Journey Museum, **Monument RV Resort▲**, to CO Nat'l Monument, **CO River State Park**
26	**I-70 Bus, US 6, US 50E, 22 Road, Grand Junction, Delta, Montrose (Addt'l Serv 3- 5mi S in Grand Junction)**
TStop	N: 333 N 1st St: CRVS S: RoadysTS/Acorn Travel Plaza #2330/ Conoco
Food	S: FastFood/Acorn TP, Rest/Westgate Inn
Lodg	S: West Gate Inn
TServ	S: Transwest Trucks, Cummins Rocky Mountain, Mesa Truck & Trailer Repair
Other	N: 84 Lumber, **Junction West RV Park▲** S: Laundry/WiFi/Acorn TP, **Mobile City RV Park▲**, to Auto Dealers, ATMs, Auto Services, Amerigas/LP, Banks, **Big J RV Park▲**, **Bob Scott RV's**, City Market Food & Pharmacy, **Centennial RV**, **Gibson RV**, Mesa Mall, **to Grand Junction KOA▲**
28	**24 Rd, Redlands Pkwy, Grand Jct**
Gas	S: Stop N Save
Food	S: Black Bear Diner, IHOP, Olive Garden
Lodg	S: Holiday Inn Express
TServ	N: MHC Kenworth
Other	S: ATMs, Auto Services, Banks, Mesa Mall, Museums, Rental Cars
31	**Horizon Dr, Grand Junction**
Gas	N: Shamrock, Shell◈, Chevron, Marathon S: Loco/Conoco◈, Phillips 66◈
Food	N: CoCo's, Peppers, Shake, Rattle & Roll Diner, Village Inn, Wendy's S: Applebee's, Bin 707, Burger King, Denny's, Good Pastures Rest/Qual Inn, Pizza Hut, Shanghai Garden Rest, Starbucks, Subway/Loco, Taco Bell
Lodg	N: Americas Best Value Inn, Clarion, Comfort Inn, Courtyard, Grand Vista Hotel, Holiday Inn, La Quinta Inn♥, Motel 6♥, Ramada Inn, Residence Inn S: Affordable Inn, Best Western, Budget Host, Country Inn, DoubleTree Hotel, Mesa Inn, Quality Inn, Super 8
Med	S: to + St Mary's Hospital, + Community Hospital, + VA Med Ctr
Other	N: ATMs, Avis RAC, Budget RAC, Hertz RAC, Grand Jct Harley Davidson, NAPA, US Post Office, Walker Field✈, S: ATMs, Auto Services, Banks, Safeway/ Pharmacy, **to Mesa State College, Co River State Park, BLM/Nat'l Forest Info**

◈ = Regular Gas Stations with Diesel ▲ = RV Friendly Locations ♥ = Pet Friendly Locations
Red print shows large vehicle parking / access on site or nearby Brown Print = Campgrounds / RV PARKS

EXIT | COLORADO

37 — I-70W Bus, to CO 141, US 6, US 50E, Clifton, Grand Junction, Delta
- Gas — **S:** Conoco◈, Conoco, Sinclair
- Food — **S:** Burger King, Captain D's, KFC, McDonald's, Pizza Hut, Starbucks, Subway, Taco Bell, Texas Roadhouse, Village Inn
- Lodg — **S:** Best Western
- Other — **S:** ATMs, Albertson's, Auto Services, Auto Zone, Big Lots, Banks, Checker Auto Parts, Discount Tire, Family Dollar, Grocery, Walgreen's, **Walmart sc**, A1 Truck Repair, **RV Ranch @ Grand Junction▲**, **to Grand Junction KOA▲**, **Big J RV Park ▲**

42 — 37 3/10 Rd, to US 6, Palisade
(Gas, Food, Lodg S to US 6/8th St)
- Other — **S:** Grande River Vineyards

44 — I-70W Bus, US 6W, to Palisade
(Access to Ex #42 Serv 3-4 mi S)

46 — Cameo

47 — Island Acres, CO River State Park
- FStop — **S:** CRVS/Conoco
- Food — **S:** Rest/CRVS
- Other — **N: CO River State Park**
  S: Laundry/CRVS

49 — CO 65S, De Beque, to CO 330E, Grand Mesa, Collbran
- Other — **S: to Sundance RV Camp▲**, **to** Powderhorn Ski Area

(50) — Parking Area (EB)

62 — 45 1/2 Rd, De Beque
- FStop — **N:** CFN
- Food — **N:** Cafe/Trading Post
- Other — **N: to Canyon Lake Campground▲**

(75) — CR 300, CR 215, Parachute, Battlement Mesa
Parachute Rest Area (Both dir)
N: (RR, Phones, Picnic, Info)
- FStop — **N:** Shell Food Mart
- Gas — **N:** Sinclair◈
  S: Conoco◈
- Food — **N:** El Rio Café, Dragon Treasure Chinese, Hong's Garden, Mexican Cafe, Outlaws Rest, Subway, Sunrise Scramble
  S: Domino's Pizza, Wendy's/Conoco
- Lodg — **N:** America's Best Value Inn
  S: Candlewood Suites, Holiday Inn Express
- Other — **N:** Laundry/Shell FM, ATMs, Auto & Tire Services, NAPA, Radio Shack, US Post Office, Parachute Veterinary Clinic♥
  S: Valley Auto & Diesel, Golf Course, **to Battlement Mesa RV Park▲**

81 — CR 323, Rulison Rd, Rulison, Rifle

87 — to CO 13N, US 6E, US 24, Meeker, to West Rifle
(Acc #90 Serv/ Gas, Food, Lodg 2-3mi)

(90) — CO 13N, CR 346, Airport Rd, Rifle, Meeker
N: Rifle Rest Area (Both dir)
(RR, Ph, Vend, Pic, Info, RVDump)
- Gas — **N:** AmocoBP, Kum & Go, Phillips 66◈
  S: Conoco◈, Phillips 66◈
- Food — **N:** Base Camp Café, Pam's Country Cooking, Outlaws Rest, Texas Mesquite BBQ, The HideOut
  S: Burger King, Domino's Pizza, McDonald's, Sonic, Subway
- Lodg — **N:** Buckskin Inn♥, Winchester Motel
  S: Grand Timber Lodge, La Quinta Inn♥, Red River Inn, Rusty Cannon Motel
- Med — **S: + Grand River Medical Center**
- Other — **N:** ATMs, Banks, Advanced Auto & Truck Service, Auto Service/AmocoBP, Auto Services, Cinema, Grocery, Pharmacy, Towing, Towing/Conoco, **to Rifle Gap State Park▲**
  S: Auto Services, Silver Spur Outfitters, Auto Repairs, Thrifty RAC, Garfield Co Reg'l Airport✈, **Walmart sc**, Vet♥

94 — CR 315, Mamm Creek Rd, Garfield Co Airport Rd (Acc to #90 Serv)
- Other — **S:** Garfield Co Reg'l Airport✈

97 — 9th St, I-70 Bus, US 24, US 6, Silt
- Gas — **N:** Conoco◈, Kum & Go, Phillips 66
- Food — **N:** Miners Claim Rest, Silt Cafe
- Lodg — **N:** Red River Inn
- Other — **N: to Harvey Gap State Park**
  S: Heron's Nest/Viking RV Park▲

105 — CR 240, to US 6, US 24, Bruce Rd, New Castle
- Gas — **N:** Conoco◈, Kum & Go, Sinclair
  S: Phillips 66
- Food — **N:** Hong's Garden Chinese, New Castle Diner, Subway
- Lodg — **N:** Rodeway Inn
- Other — **N:** Grocery, Pharmacy, Bowling, Auto Service, **to Elk Creek Campground▲**

(107) — Parking Area (EB)

109 — US 6W, US 24, New Castle, Canyon Creek, Chacra

111 — CR 134, S Canyon Creek Rd, to US 6, US 24, Glenwood Springs

114 — Mel Ray Rd, US 6, US 24, W Glenwood, Glenwood Springs
- TStop — **N:** Tomahawk Auto Truck Plaza/Amoco
- Gas — **N:** 7-11, Shell
  S: Conoco◈, Kum & Go◈
- Food — **N:** Burger King, DQ, High Noon, Hombres Mexican, Fireside Family Steakhouse, Los Desperados, Marshall Dillons Steakhouse, Taco John's, Ocean Pearl Chinese
- Lodg — **N:** Affordable Inn, Best Value Inn, Budget Host Motel, First Choice Inn, Red Mountain Inn
  S: Quality Inn
- Other — **N:** Laundry/**LP**/Tomahawk ATP, ATMs, Auto Dealers, Auto Repairs, Banks, Big O Tire, Glenwood Springs Mall, Glenwood Springs Golf Course, Radio Shack, Staples, Taylors Auto & **RV** Center, Tires, Vet♥, **to Ami's Acres Campground▲**

(115) — W Glenwood Spgs Rest Area (EB)
(RR, Picnic)

116 — River Dr, 6th St, CO 82E, Grand Ave, Glenwood Springs, Aspen
NOTE: CO 82, Independence Pass, NO vehicles Over 35' / CLOSED during the winter
- Gas — **N:** Conoco◈, Shell◈
  S: 7-11, Conoco, Phillips 66◈, Sinclair
- Food — **N:** KFC, Pizza Hut, Smoking Willie's BBQ, Subway, Village Inn
  S: Arby's, Glenwood Canyon Brewing Co, Glenwood Café, Juicy Lucy's Steakhouse, McDonald's, Ron's Rib Shack, Sushi Bar, Starbucks, Taco Bell, Wendy's
- Lodg — **N:** Best Western, Glenwood Motor Inn, Hampton Inn, Holiday Inn Express, Hot Springs Lodge, Ramada Inn, Starlight Lodge Motel, Silver Spruce Motel♥
  S: Best Value Inn, Hotel Denver, Western Hotel
- Med — **S: + Valley View Hospital**
- Other — **N:** Auto Dealers, ATMs, Greyhound, Glenwood Caverns, Glenwood Hot Springs, Yampah Spa & Vapor Caves, Yampa Hot Springs
  S: ATMs, Auto Services, Amtrak, Banks, Cinema, Grocery, Goodyear, Good Health Store, NAPA, Museum, RiteAid, Tires, **Walmart**, Vet♥, Aspen Valley Harley Davidson, **CO State Hwy Patrol Post**, **Sheriff Dept**, Glenwood Springs Muni Airport✈, **to** Aspen, Snowmass, Buttermilk, Sunlight Mtn Ski Areas

(117) — No Name Tunnel

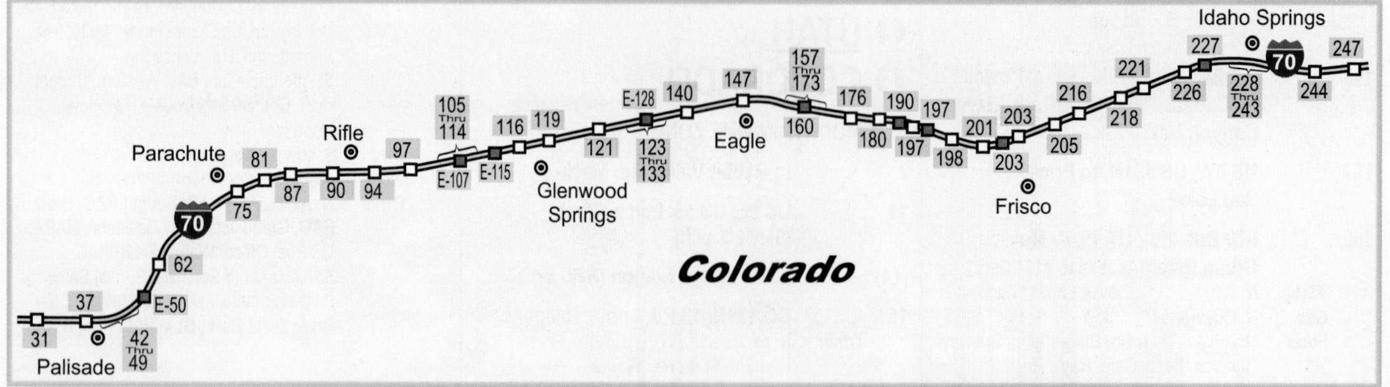

◈= Regular Gas Stations with Diesel ▲ = RV Friendly Locations ♥ = Pet Friendly Locations
Red print shows large vehicle parking / access on site or nearby Brown Print = Campgrounds / RV PARKS

EXIT		COLORADO
	NOTE:	MM 117-129: Vehicles Over 10,000 lbs GVW: NO PASSING, Use Right Lane next 12 miles.
(119)		**CR 129, No Name Exit, Glenwood Springs**
		Rest Area (Both dir) (RR, Phones, Picnic, RVCamping)
	Other	N: Glenwood Canyon Resort/Whitewater Rafting/Cabins/CO RV Park▲
(121)		**Grizzly Creek, to Hanging Lake**
	S:	Grizzly Creek Rest Area (Both dir) (RR, Picnic)
123		**Shoshone (EB, No EB reaccess)**
	Other	S: CO River Raft Access
(125)		**Hanging Lake (No EB reaccess)**
		Hanging Lk Rest Area (Both dir) (RR, Phones, Picnic)
(125)		**Hanging Lake Tunnel**
(127)		**Reverse Curve Tunnel (WB)**
(128)		Parking Area (EB)
(129)		**Bair Ranch**
	S:	Bair Ranch Rest Area (Both dir) (RR, Phones, Picnic) NO Vehicles Over 35'
	NOTE:	MM 117-129: Vehicles Over 10,000 lbs GVW: NO PASSING, Use Right Lane Next 12 miles
133		**CO River Rd, Dotsero, Gypsum**
	Other	N: to River Dance RV Resort▲, Deep Creek, BLM/Eagle River Rec Areas
140		**US 6E, Trail Gulch Rd, Gypsum**
	Gas	S: Phillips 66◈
	Food	S: Mexican Café, Pizza, Manuelito's
	TServ	S: Jerry's Auto & Truck Repair
	Other	S: Eagle Co Reg'l Airport✈, Rental Cars
(147)		**I-70 Bus, Eby Creek Rd, Eagle**
	S:	Rest Area (Both dir) (RR, Info)
	FStop	S: BP
	Gas	N: Shamrock◈ S: Conoco◈
	Food	N: Burger King, Domino's Pizza, McDonald's, Taco Bell/Shamrock S: Eagle Diner, Subway/BP, Wendy's
	Lodg	N: AmericInn, Comfort Inn, Holiday Inn Express S: Best Western, Suburban Lodge
	Other	S: ATMs, Auto Services, Banks, Grocery, Carwash, Museum, US Post Office, to Sylvan Lake State Park▲
157		**CO 131N, Eagle, to Wolcott, Steamboat Springs**
	Other	N: to Steamboat Springs Ski Area
(160)		Parking Area (Both dir)
(163)		**I-70 Bus, Edwards Access Rd, Edwards**
		Edwards Rest Area (Both dir) S: (RR, Phones, Picnic, RVDump)
	Gas	S: Conoco◈, Shell◈
	Food	S: Fiesta's, Gashouse, Main St Grill, Subway, Starbucks, Wendy's
	Lodg	S: Riverwalk Inn, Seven Lakes Lodge
	Other	S: ATMs, Banks, Auto Service, to Arrowhead Ski Area

Personal Notes

EXIT		COLORADO
167		**Avon Rd, Avon, Beaver Creek, Arrowhead, Nottingham Rd**
	Gas	N: Conoco, Phillips 66
	Food	N: Pizza Hut S: Burger King, Coyote Café, Denny's, Domino's Pizza, Outback Steakhouse, Quizno's Subs, Starbucks, Subway
	Lodg	S: Beaver Creek West Condos, Comfort Inn, Christie Lodge, Sheraton, Seasons at Avon, Vail Beaver Creek Resort
	Med	S: + Avon Medical Center
	Other	N: Auto & Tire Service S: ATMs, Banks, Beaver Creek Golf Course, Beaver Creek Ski Area, Grocery, Office Depot, Pharmacy, Radio Shack, Tourist Info,
168		**William J Post Blvd, Avon (Acc to #167 Serv via Beaver Crk Blvd)**
	Other	S: Home Depot, Walmart sc,
169		**US 6, Eagle, Vail (WB) (Access to #167 Serv)**
171		**US 24E, US 6W, Minturn, Leadville (Gas, Food & Lodging 3mi+ S)**
	Other	S: to Leadville Corral RV Park▲
173		**Frontage Rd, W Entrance, Vail**
	Gas	N: 7-11, Phillips 66, Shell◈ S: Conoco◈
	Food	N: McDonald's, Subway, Wendy's
	Lodg	N: Holiday Inn, Roost Lodge, West Vail Lodge, WildRidge Inn S: Marriott Streamside, Savory Inn, Vail Cascade Condos
	Other	N: ATMs, Grocery, Pharmacy, Safeway S: Repairs/Conoco, Vet♥

EXIT		COLORADO
176		**Frontage Rd, Spraddlecreek Rd, Vail Rd, Vail, Lions Head**
	Gas	S: Amoco◈, BP
	Food	S: La Cantina, Marble Slab Creamery, Mirabella Rest, Ore House Rest, Osaki Sushi Japanese Rest, Russell's Rest, Sweet Basil Rest, Terra Bistro
	Lodg	N: Wren Hotel S: Austria Haus Hotel, Evergreen Lodge, Holiday Inn, Lodge at Vail, Sitzmark Lodge, Vail Village Inn, Best Western
	Med	S: + Vail Valley Medical Center
	Other	S: ATMs, Grocery, Greyhound, Museums, Pharmacy, Tourist Info
180		**Bighorn Rd, Frontage Rd, East Entrance, Vail**
(183)		**RunAway Truck Ramp (WB)**
(186)		**RunAway Truck Ramp (WB)**
	NOTE:	WB: MM 189-181: 7% STEEP GRADE next 8 mi. Trucks Over 30,000#: Speed Limit 45mph
(189)		**Truck Brake Check Area (Both dir)** TRUCK Parking Area (Both dir)
	NOTE:	EB: MM 195-190: STEEP GRADE
(190)		Vail Pass Rest Area (Both dir) (RR, Phones, Picnic)
195		**CO 91S, Copper Rd, Wheeler Jct, Copper Mountain, Dillon, Frisco, to Leadville**
	Gas	S: Conoco◈
	Food	S: Alexanders on the Creek, Blue Moose Pizza, Columbine Café, Creekside Café, Imperial Palace Chinese Rest
	Lodg	S: Copper Mountain Resort, Copper Springs Lodge, Foxpine Inn
	Other	S: to Ski Cooper, Copper Mountain Ski Area
(197)		Parking Area (Both dir)
198		**Officers Gulch, Dillon**
201		**Main St, to Summit Blvd, Frisco to CO 9S, Breckenridge (EB only)**
	Gas	S: Conoco
	Food	S: Backcountry Brewery, Claim Jumper Rest, Country Kitchen, Farley's Chop House, KFC, Log Cabin Café, Pizza Hut, Subway, TCBY, Woody's
	Lodg	S: 1899 B&B, Blue Spruce Inn, Cedar Lodge, Cross Creek Resort, Frisco Lodge, Hotel Frisco CO♥, Sky-Vue Motel, Snowshoe Motel
	Other	S: Big O Tire, Grocery, NAPA, Walmart, Alpine Natural Foods, to Frisco Nordic Rec Area, Peninsula Rec Area, Tiger Run RV Resort▲
203		**CO 9S, Summit Blvd, Frisco, Breckenridge**
	Gas	S: 7-11, Conoco, Shamrock, Shell
	Food	S: Chili Parlor, Claim Jumper, KFC, Country Kitchen, Pizza Hut, Smoking Willie's BBQ, Starbucks, Subway, Taco Bell, Whiskey Creek, Rest/Hol Inn
	Lodg	S: Alpine Inn, Best Western, Holiday Inn♥, Ramada Ltd♥, Summit Inn
	Med	S: + Frisco Medical Center

EXIT — COLORADO

Other S: ATMs, Auto Services, Banks, Big O Tire, Discount Tire, Laundromat, NAPA, Pharmacy, Radio Shack, Safeway, **Walmart**, Towing/Shell, White Water Rafting, **to appr 6mi: Tiger Run RV Resort▲**

(203) Parking Area (Both dir)

205 **CO 9N, US 6E, Blue River Pkwy, Silverthorne, Dillon**

NOTE: **EB: Haz-Mat Mandatory Exit, NO Haz-Mat on EB I-70**

Gas N: 7-11, Conoco, Shell◈
S: Shamrock, Phillips 66, Tesoro

Food N: Burger King, Denny's, Old Chicago, Quiznos, Old Dillon Inn Mexican, Village Inn, Wendy's
S: Arby's, DQ, Dragon Chinese, BBQ, Pizza Hut, Ruby Tuesday, Starbucks, Subway

Lodg N: Days Inn♥, Hampton Inn, Howard Johnson, La Quinta Inn♥, Luxury Inn♥, Quality Inn, Sheraton, Alpine Hutte Lodge, Mountain Vista B&B, First Interstate Inn
S: Comfort Suites, Dillon Inn, Super 8, Days Inn, Best Western♥

Other N: Auto Dealers, Greyhound, **to White River Nat'l Forest▲**
S: ATMs, Laundromat, Grocery, Outlets at Silverthorne, **to** Keystone, Arapahoe Basin Ski Area

(209) **RunAway Truck Ramp (WB)**

(212) **RunAway Truck Ramp (WB)**

NOTE: **WB: MM 213-205: 7% Steep Grade next 8 mi, Trucks Over 30000# GVW, Speed Limit of 30mph.**

(213) Truck Brake Check Area (Both dir)
TRUCK Parking Area (Both dir)

NOTE: **MM 213-215: Eisenhower / Johnson Memorial Tunnel (Elev 11158'- highest point along the Interstate hwy system)**

NOTE: **Haz-Mat & Vehicles Over 13'11, MUST Use Loveland Pass**

NOTE: **MM 214: Pacific / Atlantic Continental Divide**

(215) Truck Brake Check Area (Both dir)
TRUCK Parking Area (Both dir)

216 **US 6W, Loveland Pass**

EXIT — COLORADO

NOTE: **WB: Haz-Mat-Mandatory Exit, NO Haz-Mat on EB I-70**

Other **S: to** Loveland Valley, Loveland Basin, Arapahoe Basin, Keystone Ski Areas

218 **Herman Gulch Rd, Idaho Springs**

221 **CR 321, CR 302, Stevens Gulch Rd, Bakerville, Idaho Springs**

NOTE: **EB: MM 226-229: 6% STEEP GRADE next 3 mi. Trucks Over 25,000# GVW: Speed Limit 45mph, Must Use Right Ln**

226 **Woodward Ave, Silver Plume**

Gas N: Buckley Bros

Lodg N: Brewery Inn

Other N: US Post Office

(227) Overlook Pull Out (Both dir)

228 **15th St, Georgetown**

Gas S: Conoco, Phillips 66, Shamrock◈

Food S: New Peking Garden, Mountainbuzz Café, Happy Cooker, Subway

Lodg S: All Aboard Inn, Georgetown Mountain Inn♥, Super 8

Other S: US Post Office

232 **US 40W, to Empire, Granby (WB: to Salt Lake City via I-70 or US 40)**

Other **N: to** Rocky Mtn Nat'l Park, Winter Park/ Mary Jane, SolVista Ski Areas

233 **Alvarado Rd, Lawson (EB)**

(234) **Stanley Rd, CR 308, Downieville, Dumont, Lawson**
Dumont Weigh Station (Both dir)

TStop N: Downieville Fuel Stop/Conoco/**LP**

Food N: FastFood/Downieville FS, Burger King, Starbucks

235 **CR 308, Stanley Rd, Dumont (WB)**

238 **Fall River Rd, CR 275, St Mary's Glacier, Alice**

239 **Stanley Rd, to I-70E Bus, Idaho Springs**

Gas N: BP, Phillips 66

Lodg N: Blair Motel

240 **CO 103, 13th Ave, Idaho Springs, Mount Evans, Golden**

Gas N: Shell, Sinclair

Food N: Two Bros Deli, McDonald's, Main St Rest, Picci's Pizzeria, Skipper's Ice Cream

Lodg N: Hanson Lodge, Miners Pick B&B
S: Baxter's on the Creek, Indian Springs Resort, Inn at Chicago Creek

Other N: ATMs, Laundromat
S: to Mt Evans, Nat'l Forest Info, Scenic Byway to CO 5, Mt Evans

EXIT — COLORADO

241AB **I-70W Bus, Colorado Blvd, Frontage Rd, CR 314, Idaho Springs**

Gas N: 7-11, BP, Phillips 66, Shell

Food N: A&W, AJ's Mex Rest, Cherry Blossom Asian Rest, Grampa's Shack, Hilldaddy's Wildfire Rest, King's, McDonald's, Marion's, Subway, Taco Bell

Lodg N: 6&40 National 9 Inn, Columbine Inn, H&H Motor Lodge, Heritage Inn, Idaho Springs Motel, JC Suites, Peoriana Motel

Other N: ATMs, Auto Services, Pharmacy, Safeway, US Post Office

(242) **Twin Tunnels**

243 **Frontage Rd, Central City Pkwy, Hidden Valley, Central City**

244 **US 6E, US 40, Evergreen, to CO 119, to Golden (EB, LEFT exit)**

NOTE: **WB: MM 246-244: 6% STEEP GRADE next 3 mi. Trucks Over 25,000# GVW: Speed Limit 45mph.**

247 **Beaver Brook, Floyd Hill (EB)**

248 **CR 65, Beaver Brook, Floyd Hill (WB)**

251 **El Rancho, to CO 74S, Evergreen Pkwy (EB)**

252 **CO 74S, Evergreen Pkwy, El Rancho Bergen Park, Evergreen (WB)**

Gas S: Conoco

Food S: Burger King, El Rancho Rest, McDonald's, Subway

Lodg S: Quality Suites

Other S: ATMs, Big O Tire, Home Depot, **Walmart**

253 **Genesee Dr, Chief Hosa, Golden**

Other **S: Chief Hosa Lodge & Campground▲**

NOTE: **EB: MM 254-259: 6% STEEP GRADE next 6 mi. Trucks Over 30,000# GVW: Speed Limit 35 mph, Must Use Low Gear & Right Lane**

(254) Overlook Pull Out (Both dir)

254 **Mt Vernon Country Club Rd, Genesee Park, Lookout Mountain**

Gas S: Conoco

Food S: Chart House Rest, Genesee Town Café & Pizza

Other S: **LP**/Conoco, US Post Office

256 **CO 45, US 40, Lookout Mountain, Mother Cabrini Shrine Rd**

Other **N: to** William Buffalo Bill Cody Grave & Museum, Mother Cabrini Shrine

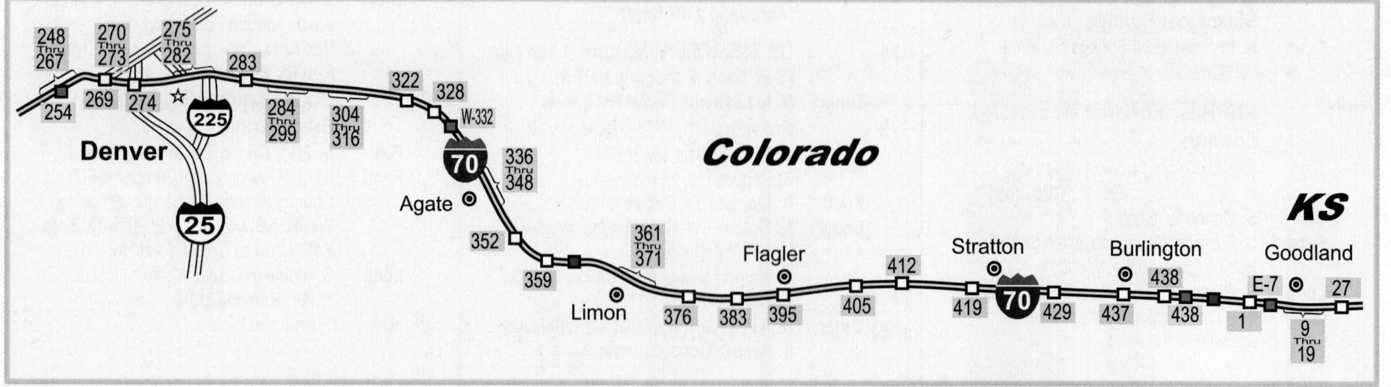

◈= Regular Gas Stations with Diesel ▲ = RV Friendly Locations ♥= Pet Friendly Locations
Red print shows large vehicle parking / access on site or nearby Brown Print = Campgrounds / RV PARKS

EXIT		COLORADO
(257)		**RunAway Truck Ramp (EB)**
259		**I-70E Bus, US 40, Colfax Ave, CO 26, CR 93, Golden, Morrison**
	Gas	N: Conoco
	Food	N: Arby's, Garden Grill, Quiznos
	Lodg	N: Hampton Inn
	Other	N: Heritage Square Funpark, **Dakota Ridge RV Park▲** , **to Golden Terrace South▲**
		S: to Red Rocks Amphitheater, Dinosaur Ridge
	NOTE:	**WB: MM 259-254: 6% STEEP UPHILL GRADE next 5 mi.**
260A		**CO 470E, Colorado Springs (EB)**
260B		**CO 470W, to US 6W, to CO 93, 6th Ave, Golden, Boulder (EB)**
261		**US 6E, 6th Ave (EB) (Addt'l Serv S to Union Blvd)**
	Lodg	S: Courtyard, Residence Inn, Sheraton
	Other	S: **Windish RV Center**
262		**I-70 Bus, US 40, Colfax Ave, to US 6, Golden, Lakewood**
	Gas	N: Sinclair
		S: Conoco, Shell
	Food	S: Outback Steakhouse, Romano's Macaroni Grill, Wendy's, Rest/Days Inn
	Lodg	S: Days Inn♥, Holiday Inn, Mountain View Motel, Ramada, Residence Inn
	Other	N: ATMs, PetCo♥, Five-R Trucks, **K&C RV/Camping World**, **Dakota Ridge RV Park▲**
		S: ATMs, Colorado Mills Mall, Office Max, Super Target, UPS Store, Jefferson Co Fairgrounds▲
263		**Denver West Blvd, Golden**
	Lodg	N: Marriott♥
	Other	N: Best Buy, Office Depot, Nat'l Renewable Energy Lab, Camp George West,
		S: Colorado Mills Mall
264		**CR 181, 32nd Ave, Youngfield St, Wheat Ridge, W Denver**
	Gas	N: Conoco
		S: 7-11, BP, Conoco, Shamrock
	Food	N: Country Café, Good Times
		S: Chili's, Chipolte MexGrill, McDonald's, Italian Rest, Noodles, Subway
	Lodg	S: La Quinta Inn♥
	Other	N: **RV America**
		S: ATMs, PetSmart♥, **Walmart**, Walgreen's, Vet♥, **Camping World**, **Steve Casey's RV**
265		**CO 58W, Golden, Central City (WB)**
	Other	N: to Coors Brewery, CO Schools of Mines
266		**CO 72W, Ward Rd, 44th Ave, Wheat Ridge, Arvada**
	TStop	S: Travel Center of America #174 (Scales)
	Gas	N: Shell
		S: Shamrock
	Food	S: Rest/TA TC
	Lodg	S: Quality Inn
	TWash	S: TA TC
	TServ	S: TA TC/Tires
	Other	S: Laundry/WiFi/TA TC, **Prospect RV Park**/RVDump▲
267		**CO 391, Kipling St, Wheat Ridge**
	Gas	N: 7-11, Amoco, Shell◈
		S: Conoco
	Food	N: Burger King, Carl's Jr, Denny's, Furrs

EXIT		COLORADO
	Food	N: Family Rest, Subway
		S: Taco Bell, Village Inn
	Lodg	N: American Inn, Holiday Inn Express, Motel 6♥
		S: Comfort Inn, Interstate Inn, Ramada Inn
	Med	S: + Lutheran Medical Center
	Other	N: Auto Dealer, Target
		S: **Ketelsen Campers of CO**
269A		**CO 121, Wadsworth Blvd (EB)**
	Gas	N: 7-11, Conoco◈, Phillips 66◈, Costco
	Food	N: Applebee's, Country Buffet, IHOP, Lone Star Steakhouse, McDonald's, Red Robin, Ruby Tuesday, Starbucks, Taco Bell
		S: China's Best, KFC, McDonald's, Red Lobster, Wendy's
	Med	S: + Hospital
	Other	N: ATMs, Advance Auto Parts, Auto Services, Costco, Home Depot, Lowe's, Office Depot, PetSmart♥, Sam's Club, Tires Plus, UPS Store
		S: ATMs, Discount Tire, **AAA Propane/LP**, to Freedom Harley Davidson, Walgreen's
(269B)		**Jct I-76E, to Ft Morgan, Ft Collins; Jct I-70E, to Denver (EB)**
269		**CO 121, Wadworth Blvd (WB)**
	Med	S: + Hospital
270		**Harlan St, to CO 95, Sheridan Blvd, Wheat Ridge, Commerce City (Lodging appr 3m S to US 70)**
	FStop	S: Valero
	Food	S: Arby's, El Paraiso, Cafe
	Other	N: U-Haul
		S: Lakeside Center Mall, Target, Lakeside Amusement Park
271A		**CO 95, Sheridan Blvd, Denver (WB)**
271B		**Lowell Blvd, Tennyson St (WB)**
272		**US 287, CO 88, Federal Blvd, to I-76, Denver**
	Gas	N: Amoco, Sinclair
	Gas	S: 7-11, Conoco
	Food	N: Burger King, Good Times, McCoy's, McDonald's, Pizza Hut, Subway, Taco Bell, Village Inn, Wendy's
		S: Rest/HJ, Popeye's Chicken
	Lodg	N: Motel 6♥
		S: Denver Inn, Howard Johnson♥
	Med	S: + to St Anthony's Hospital
	Other	N: Laundromat, Regis Univ
		S: to Invesco Field, Mile High Stadium
273		**Pecos St, W 48th St, Denver**
	Gas	S: Conoco, Phillips 66
	Food	N: Subs & Pizza
	Lodg	N: Best Western
	Other	N: Grocery, **Ryder Propane/LP**
(274)		**Jct I-25, N to Cheyenne, S to Colo Springs, Ft Collins**
	Other	N: to I-76, I-270
		S: to Amtrak, Greyhound, Coors Field, Invesco Field, Mile High Stadium, Denver Zoo, Six Flags
275A		**Washington St, Denver (WB)**
	FStop	S: Conoco @ Brighton, Denver Sinclair Fuel Stop
	Gas	N: Citgo
	Food	N: Pizza Hut
		S: McDonald's, Subway
275B		**CO 265N, Brighton Blvd, Denver**
	TServ	N: to Trans-West Freightliner

EXIT		COLORADO
	Other	N: Denver Coliseum, National Western Complex
275C		**York St, 45th Ave (EB)**
276A		**US 6E, US 85N, Steele St, Vasquez Blvd, Commerce City, Denver**
	TStop	N: Pilot Travel Center #316 (Scales)
	Gas	S: 7-11
	Food	N: Wendy's/DQ/Pilot TC
		S: Burger King
	Lodg	N: Colonial Manor, Western Motor Inn
	TWash	N: Blue Beacon/Pilot TC
	Other	N: Laundry/WiFi/Pilot TC, Mountain State Ford, to Mile High Greyhound Racing
276B		**CO 2, Colorado Blvd, (EB), to US 6E, to US 85N, Commerce City**
	Med	S: + Univ of CO Hospital
	Other	S: Denver Zoo, Denver Museum of Nature & Science
277		**Stapleton Dr, Frontage Rd, to Dahlia St, Holly St, Monaco St**
278		**CO 35, Quebec St, Commerce City, Denver**
	TStop	N: Sapp Bros.Truck Stop/Sinclair (Scales), Travel Center of America #148 (Scales)
	Gas	N: Shamrock
	Food	N: Rest/FastFood/Sapp Bros TS, CountryPride/PizzaHut/Popeyes/ Quiznos/TA TC, Denny's, Del Taco, Subway, TGI Friday,
		S: IHOP, McDonald's, Starbucks, Subway
	Lodg	N: Best Inn, Comfort Inn
		S: Courtyard, Guest House Hotel, Holiday Inn, Radisson, Ramada Inn, Red Lion Hotel
	TWash	N: Sapp Bros TS, Blue Beacon Truck Wash
	TServ	N: Sapp Bros TS/Tires, TA TC/Tires
	Med	S: + Next Care Urgent Care
	Other	N: Laundry/BarbSh/WiFi/Sapp Bros TS, Laundry/WiFi/HealthClinic/RVDump/TA TC, ATMs, Bass Pro Shop, Super Target, Mall, Rocky Mountain Arsenal,
	Other	N: Denver Coliseum, Mile High Greyhound Racing
		S: ATMs, Home Depot, Office Depot, PetSmart♥, Radio Shack, Sam's Club, UPS Store, **Walmart sc▲** , Walgreen's, Mall, **B & B RV Center**, Johnson & Wales Univ
(279)		**Jct I-270W, to I-25N, US 36W, to Boulder, Ft Collins (WB)**
280		**Havana St, Denver**
	Lodg	N: Embassy Suites
		S: Marriott
	Other	N: Rocky Mountain Arsenal
281		**Peoria St, Denver**
	FStop	N: Conoco
	Gas	N: 7-11, Phillips 66
		S: Conoco, Cenex, Shamrock◈
	Food	N: Big Bubba's BBQ, Burger King, McDonald's, Subway, Village Inn
		S: Denny's, IHOP, KFC, La Carreta Mex Rest, Pizza Hut, Subway, Taco Bell, Waffle House, Wendy's
	Lodg	N: Drury Hotel♥, Timbers Hotel
		S: Motel 6♥, Quality Inn, Star Motel
	Med	S: + Univ of CO Hospital
	Other	N: Big O Tires
		S: Auto Repairs, **Coast RV Center**
(282)		**Jct I-225S, Aurora, Peoria St, to I-25S, Colorado Springs**

◈ = Regular Gas Stations with Diesel ▲ = RV Friendly Locations ♥ = Pet Friendly Locations
Red print shows large vehicle parking / access on site or nearby Brown Print = Campgrounds / RV PARKS

EXIT		COLORADO
283		**Chambers Rd, Aurora**
	Gas	N: Conoco, Shell S: Shamrock, Phillips 66, Valero
	Food	N: Applebee's, Pizza Hut, Popeye's Chicken, Quiznos Subs, Sonic, Wendy's S: Burger King, Hardee's, Taco Bell
	Lodg	N: AmeriSuites, Country Inn, Hilton Garden Inn, Holiday Inn, Marriott, Residence Inn, Sleep Inn S: Extended Stay America
	Other	N: Safeway, Tires, U-Haul S: Greyhound, Kmart SC, **Mountain States RV Center**
284		**Pena Blvd, to E-470, CO 32 (EB)**
	Other	N: Denver Int'l Airport✈
285		**Airport Blvd, Pena Blvd, to CO 32, Tower Rd, Aurora, Denver**
	TStop	S: Flying J Travel Plaza #5061 (Scales)
	Gas	S: Shell◈
	Food	S: CountryMarket/FastFood/FJ TP, McDonald's/Shell
	Lodg	S: Comfort Inn, Crystal Inn/FJ TP
	Other	N: to Denver Int'l Airport✈ S: Laundry/WiFi/BarbSh/**RVDump/LP**/FJ TP, Mile High Harley Davidson, Grocery, to Buckley Air Nat'l Guard Base
286		**CO 32, Tower Rd, Aurora**
	Food	N: Chipolte Mex Grill, Del Taco
	Lodg	N: Comfort Suites, Country Inn, Hampton Inn, Microtel♥
	TServ	N: CAT
	Other	N: **Walmart sc ▲**, to Denver Int'l Airport✈ S: ATMs, Albertson's, Best Buy
288		**I-70 Bus, US 40W, US 287N, Colfax Ave (fr WB, 2 Ln LEFT exit) (Serv W on I-70 Bus/US 287)**
	Other	S: Buckley Air Nat'l Guard Base
(289)		**E-470 TOLL Way, Gun Club Rd, Colorado Springs, Ft Collins (NO Local Toll to Smith Rd, Colfax Ave, S Frontage, Gun Club Rd)**
(290.5)		**Aurora Weigh Station (Both dir)**
292		**CO 36E, Airpark Rd, Watkins**
	Other	S: Aurora Airpark✈
295		**CR 97, Lessig St, E Colfax Ave, I-70N Bus, to CO 36, Watkins**
	TStop	N: PTP/Tomahawk Auto Truck Plaza/Shell◈(Scales)
	Food	N: Rest/Tomahawk ATP
	Lodg	N: Country Manor Motel
	TServ	N: Tomahawk ATP/Tires
	Other	N: Laundry/**LP**/Tomahawk ATP, to Front Range Airport✈
299		**CR 113, Manila Rd, CR 28N, to CO 36, Bennett, Manila**
	FStop	N: Diamond Shamrock #2
	Food	N: FastFood/Diamond Shamrock
	Other	N: Front Range Airport✈
304		**1st St, CO 79N, CR 133, Bennett**
	Gas	N: Bennett Travel Shoppe/Conoco◈, King Soopers
	Food	N: Subway, to Bev's Kitchen, China Kitchen, High Plains Diner, Just Right Pizza, Country Rose Cafe
	Lodg	N: to Willow Tree Country Inn
	Other	N: King Soopers Food & Pharmacy
305		**CR 137, CR 34, Kiowa Bennett Rd, Kiowa (EB)**

Personal Notes

EXIT		COLORADO
(306)		**CO 36, Colfax Ave, Kiowa Bennett Rd, Kiowa, Bennett (WB) (NO EB Entry, Enter at Strasburg)** **Bennett Rest Area (Both dir)** **N: (RR, Phone, Picnic)**
310		**I-70 Bus, to CO 36, Wagner St, Frontage Rd, Strasburg**
	Gas	N: Conoco◈, Ray's Gas & Tire
	Food	N: B&K Pizza, Old Town Diner, The Pizza Shop, Slackers Rest.
	Lodg	N: Strasburg Inn
	Other	N: **Strasburg/Denver East KOA▲**, NAPA
316		**US 36E, CO 36W, Main St, Byers**
	Gas	N: Sinclair S: Gas
	Food	N: Rest/Budget Host Longhorn Motel S: Country Burger, The Golden Spike, Stagecoach Steakhouse
	Lodg	N: Budget Host Longhorn Motel S: Lazy 8 Motel
322		**CR 201, Peoria Rd, Peoria**
328		**I-70 Bus, Cedar St, Deer Trail**
	Gas	N: Phillips 66◈ S: Corner Gas
	Food	S: Brown Derby, Deer Trail Café
(332)		**Deer Trail Rest Area (WB) (RR, Phones, Picnic, Vend)**
336		**CR 178, to Lowland**
340		**I-70 Bus, CR 166, Agate**
348		**CR 134, to Cedar Point**

EXIT		COLORADO
352		**CO 86W, CR 142, to Kiowa**
354		**CR 118, Limon**
359		**I-70E Bus, to US 24, Limon (EB), US 24W, Colorado Springs (WB), US 40E, US 287S, Limon (Acc to #361 S to Main St/US24/40)**
	FStop	S: Gottschalk Oil/Valero
	TStop	S: Travel Center of America #228/Shell (Scales), Flying J Travel Plaza #5011(Scales)
	Gas	S: Phillips 66
	Food	S: CountryFare/Subway/TA TC, Arby's, CountryMkt/FastFood/FJ TP, Denny's, McDonald's, Oscar's Steak House
	Lodg	S: Best Western, Comfort Inn, Econo Lodge, Holiday Inn Express, Super 8, Tyme Square Inn,
	TServ	S: TA TC/Tires
	Other	S: Laundry/WiFi/TA TC, **RVDump/LP**/FJ TP, **CO State Hwy Patrol Post, to Limon MH & RV Park▲**
(360)		**Limon Weigh Station (Both dir)**
361		**to CO 71 (EB), I-70 Bus, US 24, US 40, US 287, Limon (Acc to #359 S to Main St/US24/40)**
	TStop	S: DJ Petroleum/Conoco (Scales)
	Gas	S: Phillips 66◈
	Food	S: DQ, Pizza Hut, Wendy's/P66
	Lodg	S: First Inn Gold, Midwest Country Inn, Silver Spur Motel, Travel Inn
	Other	N: Limon Muni Airport✈ S: ATMs, Family Dollar, Grocery, **Limon KOA▲**
363		**US 40E, US 287S, I-70 Bus, US 24, Hugo, Kit Carson (EB), I-70W Bus, US 24W, to CO 71, Limon (WB) (Gas Food Lodg S in Hugo)**
	Med	S: + Hospital (appr 12 mi)
	Other	N: Limon Muni Airport✈
371		**CR 31, CR 109, Genoa, Hugo**
	Med	S: in Hugo + Hospital
376		**CR 36, Genoa, Bovina**
(383)		**CR 63, Arriba** **Arriba Rest Area (Both dir)** **S: (RR, Phones, Picnic, RVCamping)**
	Gas	N: DJ Food Store/P66◈
	Food	N: Café/DJ Food Store
	Lodg	N: DJ Motel
395		**CR 5, Flagler**
	FStop	S: Country Store/Cenex
	Gas	N: Loaf N Jug◈
	Food	N: Dairy King, JC's Bar & Grill S: Café/Country Store
	Lodg	N: Little England Motel & **RV Park▲**
	TServ	S: Country Store/Tires
405		**CO 59, US 24, Seibert**
	FStop	S: Seibert Travel Plaza/Conoco
	Food	S: FastFood/Seibert TP
	Other	N: ATMs, Banks, Grocery, Post Office, **Shady Grove Wi-Fi Campground/RVDump/RVService▲**
412		**I-70 Bus, CR 23, Vona**
419		**CO 57N, CR 30, Colorado Ave, Stratton**
	FStop	N: AmPride/Cenex
	Gas	N: Conoco◈
	Food	N: Rest/BW, Dairy Treat

◈= Regular Gas Stations with Diesel ▲ = RV Friendly Locations ♥= Pet Friendly Locations
Red print shows large vehicle parking / access on site or nearby Brown Print = Campgrounds / RV PARKS

EXIT — CO / KS

Lodg N: Best Western, Claremont Inn
TServ N: Plains Diesel Service
Med N: + Stratton Medical Clinic
Other N: Marshall Ash Village RV Park▲, Trail's End Campground▲, Bernie's RV Service & Repair

429 CR 40, Bethune

437 US 385, I-70E Bus, Lincoln St, Burlington, Wray, Cheyenne Wells
FStop N: Amacks BPAmoco
TStop N: Travel Shoppe #4/Conoco
Gas N: Phillips 66◈
Food N: Interstate House/Conoco, FastFood/P66, Burger King, DQ, McDonald's, Sonic, Subway, The Route Steakhouse, Rest/Western Motor Inn, Rest/Burlington Inn
Lodg N: Burlington Inn, Chaparral Motor Inn, Comfort Inn, Sloan's Motel, Super 8, Western Motor Inn
TServ N: D & J Diesel
Med N: + Hospital
Other N: ATMs, Grocery, Goodyear
S: Kit Carson Airport✈

(438) CO Welcome Center (WB)
Rest Area (EB)
(RR, Phones, Picnic, Info, RVDump)

438 US 24, I-70W Bus, CR V, Rose Ave, Burlington
FStop N: PTP/Amacks BPAmoco
Gas N: Conoco, Sinclair
Food N: BJ's, Restaurant Panaderia
Lodg N: Comfort Inn, Hi-Lo Motel, Super 8
Med N: + Hospital
Other N: ATMs, Auto Dealers, CarQuest, Family Dollar, Goodyear, Grocery

MOUNTAIN TIME ZONE

NOTE: MM 451: Kansas State Line

↑ COLORADO
↓ KANSAS

MOUNTAIN / CENTRAL TIME ZONE

(0) Weigh Station (EB)

1 KS 267, CR 3, Kanorado

(7) KS Welcome Center (EB)
Rest Area (WB)
(RR, Ph, Pic, Vend, WiFi, Info, RVDump)

EXIT — KANSAS

9 CR 1, CR 64, Ruleton

12 CR 14, Caruso

17 Bus 24, KS 27, CR 19, Goodland, St Francis, Sharon Springs
FStop N: Frontier Equity Exchange/Conoco
S: Valero◈
TStop N: Presto #14/P66
Food N: Buffalo Inn, El Reynaldo's Mexican, KFC, Pizza Hut, McDonald's, Subway, Taco John's, Wendy's, Rest/BW
Lodg N: Best Western♥, Comfort Inn, Howard Johnson♥, Motel 6♥, Super 8
S: Holiday Inn Express, Welcome Inn
TWash N: Car/Truck/RV Wash
TServ N: Truck & Trailer Repair
Med N: + Goodland Regional Medical Center
Other N: ATMs, Pharmacy, Walmart sc, Tourist Info, Mid America Campground▲

19 Bus 24, KS 27 Spur, Goodland
Gas N: Sinclair◈
Food N: Pizza
Lodg N: Best Value Inn
Other N: Museum, Goodland KOA▲

27 KS 253, CR 29, Edson

NOTE: MM 35: Mountain/Central Time Zone

36 KS 184, CR 2, Brewster
Gas N: Fuel Depot◈

45 US 24, CR 11, CR 407, Levant

(48) Rest Area (Both dir)
(RR, Phone, Picnic, Vend, RVDump)

53 KS 25, CR 19, S Range Ave, Colby, Atwood, Leoti
FStop N: JJ Oil Co #8/Conoco
TStop N: Colby 24-7/BP
S: Petro 2/Oasis Travel Plaza/P66
Gas N: Amoco, Phillips 66, Total
Food N: DQ/Conoco, McDonald's/BP, Arby's, Burger King, City Limits Grill, KFC, Long John Silver, Pizza Hut, Subway, Taco John
S: Starbucks/Quiznos/Chesters/P66, McDonald's, Village Inn
Lodg N: Comfort Inn, Days Inn, Econo Lodge, Holiday Inn Express, Motel 6♥, Quality Inn, Super 8
S: Budget Inn, Crown Inn♥
TWash N: Truck Town Truck, Trailer & RV Wash
TServ N: JJ Oil/Conoco, Central Power/ONAN Truck & Bus Service, Detroit Diesel Allison, Cummins Diesel, CAT
Med N: + Citizens Medical Hospital

EXIT — KANSAS

Other N: ATMs, Auto Zone, Auto Dealers, Auto Services, Car Wash, Colby Comm College, Dollar General, Goodyear, Grocery, Radio Shack, Tourist Info, Walmart sc, Bourquins RV Park▲
S: Laundry/RVDump/Petro2 Oasis TP, Factory Outlet Stores, Auto Dealers

54 CR 20, Country Club Dr (Access to Ex #53 Serv)
TStop N: Bosselman Travel Center/Pilot TC #920
Other N: Bourquins RV Park▲

62 CR K, CR 24, Mingo
Gas N: AmPride◈

70 US 83, US 383, Rexford, Spica, Oakley
TStop S: RoadysTS/JJ Oil Co #6/P66
Gas S: Sinclair◈
Food S: Colonial Steakhouse
Lodg N: Free Breakfast Inn
TServ S: JJ Oil/P66
Med S: + Hospital
Other S: Prairie Dog Town, Museum, High Plains Camping▲

76 US 40W, Old Hwy 40, Oakley, Sharon Springs
TStop S: Travel Center of America/Shell (Scales)
Food S: Buckhorn/Subway/TA TC
Lodg S: Best Value Inn, First Interstate Inn, Econo Lodge, Ks Kountry Inn & RV Park▲
TWash S: Blue Beacon/TA TC
TServ S: TA TC/Tires
Med S: + Hospital
Other N: Auto Dealer, John Deere
S: Laundry/WiFi/TA TC

79 Campus Rd

85 KS 216, S Oak, Grinnell
Gas S: BP
Food S: Stuckey's/DQ/BP

93 KS 23, Grainfield, Gove
Gas N: Sinclair◈

95 KS 23, Hoxie, Grainfield
Other N: Betterbuilt Trailers

(97) Rest Area (Both dir)
(RR, Picnic, Vend, RVDump)

99 KS 211, Park
Gas N: Sinclair◈

107 KS 212, Castle Rock Rd, Quinter
FStop S: RC Petroleum/Shell
Gas N: Sinclair◈
Food N: Rest/Budget Host Inn
S: DQ
Lodg N: Budget Host Inn
Med N: + Hospital
Other N: Sunflower RV Campground▲

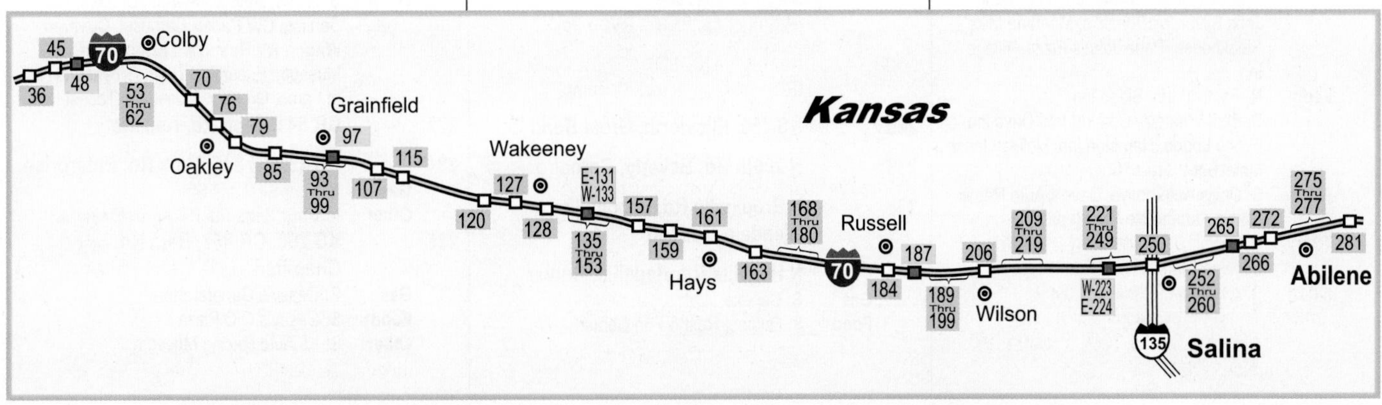

◈ = Regular Gas Stations with Diesel ▲ = RV Friendly Locations ♥ = Pet Friendly Locations
Red print shows large vehicle parking / access on site or nearby Brown Print = Campgrounds / RV PARKS

EXIT — KANSAS

115 KS 198N, Banner Rd, Collyer

120 Voda Rd

127 US 40 Bus, US 283, S 1st St, Wa Keeney, Ness City
FStop N: Town Pump/P66
TStop S: WaKeeney 24/7 Travel Plaza/BP
Gas S: Conoco◈
Food N: McDonald's/P66, Jade Garden, Pizza Hut
S: Real Country Café/BP, Subway/Conoco
Lodg N: Best Western, Ks Kountry Inn
S: Econo Lodge
TServ S: WaKeeney TP/Tires
Other S: Laundry/WaKeeney TP, **WaKeeney/ Hays KOA▲**

128 US 40 Bus, to US 283N, S 13th St, Wa Keeney, Hill City
FStop N: Sinclair
Lodg N: Ks Kountry Inn, Super 8
Med N: + Hospital
Other N: Always Christmas Shop

(131) Rest Area (EB)
RR, Picnic, RVDump)

(133) Rest Area (WB)
(RR, Picnic, RVDump)

135 KS 147, Ogallah

140 Riga Rd, Ogallah, Riga
Gas N: Schreiner Fuels◈
Other S: to Cedar Bluff State Park

145 KS 247, Ellis Ave, Washington St, Ellis
FStop S: AmBest/Ellis Travel Plaza/P66
Gas S: Casey's, Total
Food S: DQ/Pizza/Subway/Ellis TP, Alloway's, Bo's Landing, Casey's C/O Pizza, Matt's Rib Shack, Railroader Lanes & Dining Car,
Lodg S: Ellis House Inn
Other S: Laundry/PlayArea/Ellis TP, ATMs, Museums, **Lakeside Campground▲**

153 Yocemento Ave

157 US 183 South ByPass, 230th Ave, Hays, LaCrosse
Other S: Fort Hays Historic Site, Tourist Info

159 US 183, Vine St, Hays, Plainville
FStop S: Valero
TStop S: Golden Ox Truck Stop/Conoco
Gas N: Mirastar
S: BP, Holiday 66 Food Plaza
Food N: Applebee's, Carlos O'Kelly's, Golden Corral, IHOP, Quiznos
S: Arby's, China Garden, Country Kitchen, Hardee's, Imperial Garden, KFC, Long John Silver, McDonald's, Montana Mike's Steakhouse, Papa John's Pizza, Village Inn
Lodg N: Fairfield Inn, Sleep Inn
S: Best Western, Comfort Inn, Days Inn, Econo Lodge, Hampton Inn, Holiday Inn♥, Motel 6♥, Super 8
AServ S: Davis Automotive, Dave's Auto Repair Mike's Automotive Tire Repair
TServ N: Detroit Diesel, I-70 Truck Repair
S: Kansasland Tire, Hay's Mack
Med S: + Hayes Medical Center

EXIT — KANSAS

Other N: ATMs, Auto Dealer, Home Depot, Radio Shack, **Walmart sc**, **KS State Hwy Patrol Post**
S: Advance Auto Parts, Auto Dealers, Firestone, Grocery, Walgreen's, Mall

161 270th Ave, Commerce Pkwy

163 Toulon Ave

168 KS 255, Cathedral Ave, Victoria
Gas S: AmPride◈

172 Walker Ave

175 KS 257, Gorham Galatia Rd, 176th St, Gorham

180 181st St, Balta Rd, Balta

184 US 281, US 40 Bus, Russell, Hoisington
FStop N: 24-7 Store/BP
Gas N: AmPride, Phillips 66◈
Food N: McDonald's, Meridy's, Pizza Hut, Subway
Lodg N: AmericInn, Days Inn, Russell Inn, Super 8 Inn
TWash N: RV & Truck Wash
Med N: + Hospital
Other N: Oil Patch Museum, **Triple J RV Park▲**, **Fossil Creek RV Park▲**

(187) Rest Area (Both dir)
(RR, Phones, Picnic, RVDump)

189 US 40 Bus, 189th St, Pioneer Rd, Russell
Other N: Russell Muni Airport✈

193 193rd St, Bunker Hill Rd
TStop N: Sunmart #574/Conoco
Food N: Bear House Café/Conoco, Bunker Hill Café
Other N: Wilson Wildlife Area

199 KS 231, 200th Blvd, Dorrance
Gas S: Kerr-McGee

206 KS 232, Wilson, Lucas
Gas N: Conoco Travel Shoppe
Lodg N: Pioneer Village Motel & **Campground▲**
Other N: Smoky Hill Vineyards & Winery, to Lake Wilson▲

209 6th Rd, Wilson, Sylvan Grove

216 12th Rd, Vesper
Gas S: BP
Food S: DQ/Stuckey's/BP

219 KS 14S, Ellsworth
FStop S: Cliff's Service/Conoco
Tires S: Cliff's

221 KS 14N, to Lincoln

(223) Rest Area (WB)
(RR, Phones, Picnic, RVDump)

(224) Rest Area (EB)
(RR, Phones, Picnic, RVDump)

225 KS 156, Ellsworth, Great Bend

233 N 290th Rd, Beverly, Carneiro

238 N Brookville Rd, Brookville, Glendale, Tescott

244 N Hedville Rd, Hedville, Culver
Gas S: Cenex◈
Food S: Outpost Rest & Fun Center

EXIT — KANSAS

Other N: **Sundowner West RV Park▲**
S: Rolling Hills Wildlife Adventure, **Glasco RV Park▲**

249 N Halstead Rd, Trenton, Shipton

(250A) Jct I-135S, US 81S, to Wichita, Lindsborg

250B US 81N, to Concordia

252 KS 143, 9th St, Salina
TStop N: Petro 2 Truck Stop #81/Shell (Scales),
S: Bosselman Travel Center/Pilot #903/ Sinclair (Scales)◈, I-70 24-7/BP
Gas N: Valero◈
S: Pump Mart, Total
Food N: PizzaHut/Wendy's/Petro2, DQ, IHOP, Rest/Salina Inn, Rest/Super 8
S: Grandma Max's /Bosselman's TC, McDonald's, Ks Steak, Ponderosa
Lodg N: Best Inn, Days Inn, Holiday Inn Express, Motel 6♥, Salina Inn, Super 8
S: Best Western, Econo Lodge
TWash S: Blue Beacon TW/Petro2
TServ N: Palmer Truck & Trailer Repair
S: Bosselman TC/Tires, Inland Truck Parts, Central Detroit Diesel, Roberts Truck Center/Volvo
Other N: Laundry/Petro2, Smoky Hill Vineyards Winery, **Salina KOA▲**
S: Laundry/Bosselman TC, Laund/WiFi/BP, Salina Arts Center

253 Ohio St, Bicentennial Ctr, Salina
TStop S: Flying J Travel Plaza/Conoco (Scales)
Food S: CountryMarket/FastFood/FJ TP
TServ S: Kenworth
Med S: + Hospital
Other S: Laundry/WiFi/RVDump/LP/FJ TP, Harley Davidson

260 Niles Rd, New Cambria

(265) Rest Area (Both dir)
(RR, Phones, Picnic)

266 KS 221, Solomon Rd, Solomon
TStop S: Solomon Travel Center/Total (Scales)
Food S: Rest/Solomon TC

272 CR 829, Fair Rd, Solomon, to Abilene, Talmage

275 KS 15, Abilene, Clay Center
Gas S: Phillips 66, Shell, Alco Fuel Ctr
Food N: DQ
S: Burger King, La Fiesta, McDonald's, Pizza Hut, Subway
Lodg N: Brookville Hotel, Holiday Inn Express
S: Best Value Inn, Days Inn, Super 8
Med S: + Hospital
Other S: ATMs, Auto Zone, Auto Dealers, Auto Service, CW Parker Carousel, **Covered Wagon RV Resort▲**, Eisenhower Museum, Excursion Train, Greyhound Hall of Fame, Grocery, Museums, Tourist Info,

277 CR 841, Jeep Rd, Abilene

281 KS 43, CR 845, Mink Rd, Enterprise
Gas N: Four Seasons Shell
Other N: **Four Seasons RV Acres/Dealer▲**

286 KS 206, CR 857, Rain Rd, Chapman
Gas S: Casey's General Store
Food S: Casey's C/O Pizza
Other S: Ks Auto Racing Museum

◈= Regular Gas Stations with Diesel ▲ = RV Friendly Locations ♥= Pet Friendly Locations
Red print shows large vehicle parking / access on site or nearby Brown Print = Campgrounds / RV PARKS

EXIT	KANSAS

290 **Milford Lake Rd, Junction City**

(294) **Rest Area (WB)**
(RR, Picnic, Phone, RVDump)

295 **US 77, KS 18, Junction City, Marysville, Herrington**
- TStop N: Sapp Bros/P66 (Scales)
- Food N: Sapp Bros
- Lodg N: Motel 6♥
- TServ N: Sapp Bros/Tires
- TWash N: Sapp Bros
  S: Champion Car & Truck Wash
- Med N: + Hospital
- Other N: Laundry/WiFi/Sapp Bros, Harley Davidson, Flagstop Resort & RV Park▲, Milford State Park▲
  S: Owl's Nest Campground ▲, RV Center

296 **US 40 Bus, Washington St**
- FStop N: GS Conv Store/Cenex
- Gas N: BP, Phillips 66, Shell◈
- Food N: Country Kitchen, DQ, Hardee's, KFC, Long John Silver, McDonald's, Peking Rest, Sirloin Stockade, Sonic, Subway
- Lodg N: Budget Host & RV Park▲, Comfort Inn, Days Inn, Ramada Ltd
- Other N: Grocery

298 **East St, Chestnut St, Junction City**
- FStop N: Shell Travel Center (Scales)
- Food N: Burger King/Shell TC, Cracker Barrel, Arby's, Taco Bell
- Lodg N: Best Western, Courtyard, Holiday Inn
- Other N: Laundry/Shell TC, ATMs, Dollar Tree, Dollar General, Grocery, Walmart sc

299 **US 40 Bus, KS 57, J Hill Rd, Flint Hills Blvd, Junction City**
- Gas N: Handy's BP◈
- Food N: Stacy's Rest, Pizza/BP
- Lodg N: Econo Lodge, Dream Land Motel, Great Western Inn, Red Carpet Inn, Super 8
- Other N: Laundromat

300 **US 40 Bus, KS 57, Council Grove**
- Lodg N: Dream Land Motel

301 **Henry Rd, Fort Riley, Marshall Field**
- Lodg N: Dream Land Motel, Sunset Motel & RV Park▲
- Other N: Ft Riley Military Reservation, Custer's House, Calvary Museum

303 **KS 18, Clarks Creek Rd, Ft Riley, Ogden, Manhattan**

304 **Humboldt Creek Rd, Jct City**
- NOTE: Low Clearance 13'9"

307 **CR 901, McDowell Creek Rd**

EXIT	KANSAS

(309) **Rest Area (Both dir)**
(RR, Phones, Picnic, RVDump)

311 **Moritz Rd**

313 **KS 177, Pillsbury Dr, Manhattan, Council Grove (Serv N in Manhattan)**

316 **CR 911, Deep Creek Rd**

318 **Frontage Rd, Manhattan**

323 **Frontage Rd, Tallgrass Rd, Alma**

324 **Wabaunsee Rd, Alma**
- Other N: Grandma Huerney Natural Foods

328 **KS 99, Alma, Wamego**
- Other N: Oz Museum
  S: Museum

333 **KS 138, Paxico**
- Other N: Auto Repairing & Towing, Wyldewood Cellars

335 **Snokomo Rd, Skyline Scenic Dr, Paxico**
- Other N: Paxico Shops, Mill Creek RV Park▲

(336) **Rest Area (Both dir, Left exit)**
(RR, Phones, Picnic, WiFi, RVDump)

338 **Vera Rd, McFarland, Vera**

341 **KS 30, Windy Hill Rd, Maple Hill, St Marys**
- FStop S: 24-7 Maple Hill Truck Stop/BP
- Food S: Café/Maple Hill TS
- Other S: RVDump/Maple Hill TS

342 **Eskridge Rd, Keene Blacktop Rd**

343 **Frontage Rd, Ranch Rd, Maple Hill**

346 **Carlson Rd, Willard, Rossville, Dover**

347 **W Union Rd, Topeka**

350 **Valencia Rd, Topeka**

351 **Frontage Rd, Patton Rd (EB)**

353 **KS 4, Auburn Rd, to Eskridge**

(355) **Jct I-470S, US 75S**
- Med S: + Veteran's Medical Center
- TServ S: Martin Truck Service

356 **Wanamaker Rd, Topeka**
- TStop S: Topeka Travel Plaza (Scales)
- Gas S: BP, Phillips 66◈
- Food N: Sirloin Stockade
  S: Rest/Topeka TP, Applebee's, Boston Market, Burger King, Chili's, Chuck E Cheese's Pizza, Cracker Barrel, Coyote Canyon, Denny's, Golden Corral, Hooters, IHOP, KFC, McDonald's, Old Country Buffet, Olive Garden, Panera Bread, Perkins, Pizza Hut, Red Lobster, Shoney's, Steak 'n Shake, Taco Bell, Timberline Steaks, Wendy's
- Lodg N: AmeriSuites
  S: Candlewood Suites, Clubhouse Inn, Comfort Inn, Country Inn, Days Inn, Econo Lodge, Fairfield Inn, Hampton Inn, Motel 6♥, Quality Inn, Sleep Inn, Super 8
- TServ S: Topeka TP/Tires
- Med N: + Tallgrass Immediate Care Center
- Other S: Laundry/Topeka TP, ATMs, Best Buy, Banks, Grocery, FedEx Office, Home Depot, Lowe's, Office Depot, Sam's Club, Walmart sc, West Ridge Mall

EXIT	KANSAS

357A **Fairlawn Rd, SW 6th Ave, Topeka**
- Gas S: Phillips 66
- Food S: Rest/Holiday Inn
- Lodg S: Holiday Inn, Motel 6♥

357B **Danbury Lane, Topeka (WB)**

358 **US 75, KS 4, Gage Blvd (EB)**
- Other N: Topeka KOA▲

358A **US 75N (WB)**
- Other N: Topeka KOA▲

358B **Gage Blvd (WB)**
- Gas S: Conoco
- Food S: McDonald's, Subway, Wendy's
- Aserv S: Huntington Park Auto Center
- Med S: + Hospital
- Other S: Zoo, Rain Forest

359 **MacVicar Ave, Topeka**
- Other S: Hummer Sports Park

361A **1st Ave, Alt US 75, Topeka Blvd (EB, NO reaccess)**
- Other S: Ryder

361B **3rd St, Monroe St (EB)**

362A **4th St, Madison St (WB)**
- Lodg S: Ramada Inn

362B **8th Ave, Downtown Topeka**
- Lodg S: Days Inn

362C **10th Ave, Madison St**
- Gas N: BP
- Lodg N: Ramada
- Other N: KS State Capitol Bldg

363 **Adams St, Branner Trafficway**

364A **California Ave, Topeka**
- Gas S: BP◈, Conoco
- Food S: Burger King, McDonald's, Pizza Hut, Rosa's Mexican, Subway
- Other S: Auto Zone, Walgreen's

364B **US 40, KS 4, Carnahan Ave, Deer Creek Trafficway**

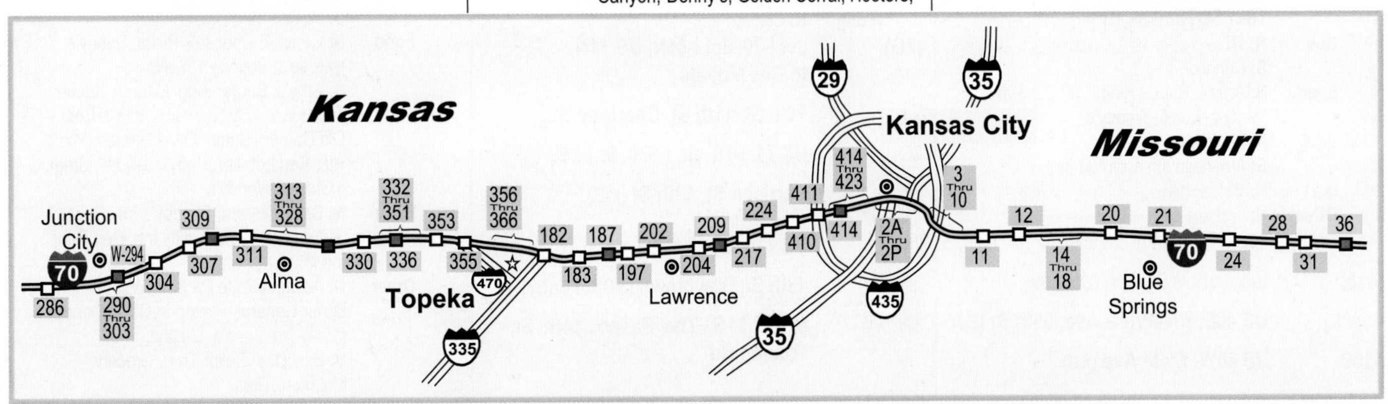

◈= Regular Gas Stations with Diesel ▲ = RV Friendly Locations ♥= Pet Friendly Locations
Red print shows large vehicle parking / access on site or nearby Brown Print = Campgrounds / RV PARKS

EXIT	KANSAS
365	**21st St, Rice Rd, Topeka**
NOTE:	I-70 below runs with KS Tpk. Exit #'s follow KS Tpk.
(366)	**Jct I-470W, to Wichita**
(367)	**TOLL Plaza**
(183)	**Jct I-70W, US 40, KS 4, Topeka, Salina**
(182)	**Jct I-335, I-470, KS Tpk, Emporia, Wichita** (LEFT exit)
(187)	**Topeka Service Plaza** (Both dir)
FStop	Conoco
Food	Hardee's
197	**KS 10, Lawrence, Lecompton**
202	**US 59, West Lawrence**
Gas	S: BP, Phillips 66
Food	S: Mr Goodcents Subs & Pasta
Lodg	S: Hampton Inn, Holiday Inn, Quality Inn, Ramada Inn, Super 8
Med	S: + Hospital
Other	S: Firestone, to Univ of KS
204	**US 24, US 59, E Lawrence**
Gas	S: Citgo
Food	S: Burger King
Lodg	S: Bismark Inn, Jayhawk Motel
Med	S: + Hospital
(209)	**Lawrence Service Plaza** (Both dir, LEFT exit)
FStop	EZ Go #70/Conoco
Food	McDonald's
(217)	**TOLL Plaza**
224	**KS 7, S 130th St, to US 73, Bonner Springs, Leavenworth**
NOTE:	Last FREE Exit
Gas	N: Shell S: Citgo
Food	N: KFC, Waffle House S: McDonald's, Mr Goodcents Subs & Pasta, Ross's Steakhouse
Lodg	N: Holiday Inn Express, Super 8
Other	N: Verizon Amphitheater S: Walmart sc
NOTE:	I-70 above runs with KS Tpk. Exit #'s follow KS Tpk.
410	**110th St**
Other	N: Ks Speedway
(411A)	**Jct I-435S, Overland Park**
(411B)	**Jct I-435N, St Joseph**
Other	N: to Woodlands Race Track, KCI Int'l Airport✈
414	**78th St, Kansas City**
Gas	N: QT S: Conoco
Food	N: Arby's, Burger King, Cracker Barrel, Hardy's, Sonic, Wendy's
Lodg	N: Microtel S: American Inn, Comfort Inn
Med	N: + Hospital
Other	N: Walgreen's
(414)	**Parking Area** (Both dir)
(415)	**Inspection Station** (Both dir)
415A	**US 40E, Riverview Ave, 65th St** (EB)
415B	**US 40W, State Ave** (EB)

EXIT	KS / MO
415	**Riverview Ave, 65th St, US 40, State Ave** (WB)
417	**57th St, Kansas City**
(418A)	**Jct I-635S, to Overland Park**
TStop	S: I-635 SB, Exit 3: QT, Shamrock
(418B)	**Jct I-635N, to Missouri**
419	**Park Dr, 38th St, State Ave** (Serv 3-5 mi N on State Ave)
420A	**Jct US 69S, 18th St Expy**
420B	**18th St, Kansas City**
Gas	N: Conoco
Lodg	N: Eagle Inn Motel
Med	N: + Hospital
421A	**Service Rd, to Railroad Yard** (WB)
(421B)	**Jct I-670W**
422A	**US 69N, US 169S, 7th St TrWy** (EB)
422B	**US 69, US 169, 7th St TrWy** (WB)
422C	**Service Road**
422D	**Central Ave** (EB) **6th St, Reynolds Ave** (WB)
423A	**5th St** (EB)
423B	**James St, 3rd St** (EB)
423C	**US 24, US 169, Minnesota Ave, Washington Blvd**
423D	**Fairfax District**

CENTRAL TIME ZONE

NOTE: MM 424: Missouri State Line

⬆ KANSAS
⬇ MISSOURI

CENTRAL TIME ZONE

EXIT	MISSOURI
(2A)	**Jct I-35S, to Wichita**
2B	**Beardsley Rd**
2C	**US 169N, Broadway, 5th St, Airport**
2D	**Main St, Delaware St, Downtown**
2E	**MO 9, 6th St, Oak St**
2F	**Oak St, Independence Ave** (WB)
2H	**US 24E, Independence Ave**
Lodg	N: Comfort Inn
(2G)	**Jct I-29, Jct I-35N, US 71N, to Des Moines**
2J	**10th St, 11th St, Charlotte St**
2L	**US 71, I-70 Alt, I-670, to I-35S**
2K	**Harrison St, 12th St** (WB)
Med	N: + Hospital
2M	**US 71S, Downtown**
2P	**13th St, Downtown** (NO Re-Entry)
3A	**to US 71S, The Paseo, 14th St, Truman Rd**
3B	**Brooklyn Ave** (EB)
3C	**Prospect Ave, 14th St**
4A	**Benton Blvd, E Truman Rd** (EB)
4B	**18th St, Askew Ave**
Other	N: Pioneer College, American Jazz Museum. Negro League Baseball Museum
4C	**23rd St**
5A	**27th St, Mersington Ave** (EB)
5B	**31st St, Myrtle Ave** (EB)
5C	**29th St, Jackson Ave** (WB)
6	**Van Brunt Blvd**
Gas	N: 7-11 S: BP
Food	S: McDonald's, Subway, Taco Bell
Med	S: + VA Hospital
Other	S: Carwash, Family Dollar, NAPA
7A	**31st S, US 40E**
7B	**Manchester Trafficway**
TServ	N: Arrow Truck Sales
(8A)	**Jct I-435S, to Wichita**
(8B)	**Jct I-435N, to Des Moines**
9	**Blue Ridge Cut-Off, Kansas City**
Gas	N: Conoco S: BP, Sinclair
Food	N: Denny's, Wendy's S: Taco Bell
Lodg	N: Clarion Hotel, Drury Inn♥ S: Holiday Inn
Med	N: + Hospital
Other	S: Arrowhead Stadium, KC Museum, Royals, Water Park, Welcome Center/ RVDump
10	**Sterling Ave** (EB)
11	**US40, Blue Ridge Blvd, Sterling Ave**
Gas	N: QT, Conoco, Shell S: 7-11, BP, GasMart, Sinclair
Food	N: Burger King, Bob Evans, Gates & Son BBQ, McDonald's, Long John Silver, Rosie's Café, Sonic, Subway, V's Italian Rest S: Applebee's, Hong Kong Buffet, Old Country Buffet, Papa John's, Taco Bell
Lodg	N: Budget Inn, Delux Inn, Sports Stadium Motel
Other	N: Stadium RV Park▲ S: Blue Ridge Mall, Family Dollar, O'Reilly Auto Parts, Walmart sc
12	**Noland Rd, Independence, Ks City**
Gas	N: QT, Shell◊ S: Phillips 66
Food	N: Chuck E Cheese's Pizza, Denny's, Hardee's, Shoney's, Sonic S: Arby's, Burger King, Country Kitchen, Fuddruckers, McDonald's, KFC/TBell, Old Country Buffet, Olive Garden, Pizza Hut, Red Lobster, Ruby Tuesday, Steak n Shake, Wendy's
Lodg	N: Best Western, Shoney's Inn, Super 8 S: American Inn, Quality Inn, Red Roof Inn♥
Other	N: Advance Auto Parts, ATMs, CVS, Dollar General, Firestone,Office Depot, Osco, Walgreen's, U-Haul S: Best Buy, Dollar Tree, Grocery, Museum, Tires,

◊= Regular Gas Stations with Diesel ▲ = RV Friendly Locations ♥= Pet Friendly Locations
Red print shows large vehicle parking / access on site or nearby Brown Print = Campgrounds / RV PARKS

14 Lee's Summit Rd, Independence
Food S: Cracker Barrel, Olive Garden, Steak n Shake
Other S: Home Depot

(15AB) Jct I-470, MO 291, Independence, Liberty, Lees Summit

(15A) Jct I-470S, MO 291S, Lees Summit

15B MO 291N, Independence
Gas N: 7-11, QT, Phillips 66
Food N: Applebee's, Arby's, Bob Evans, Burger King, Chili's, Denny's, Hops, Lone Star Steakhouse, McDonald's, Starbucks, TGI Friday
Lodg N: Fairfield Inn, Residence Inn
Other N: ATMs, Albertson's, Barnes & Noble, Best Buy, Sam's Club, Target, Walmart sc, Mall

17 Little Blue Pkwy, 39th St, US 40, Memorial Pkwy, Blue Springs
Gas S: QT, Costco
Food N: Applebee's, Joe's Crab Shack, Romano's Macaroni Grill, O'Charley's, On the Border, Starbucks
S: Carrabba's, Hooters, IHOP, Kobe Japanese Rest, Outback Steakhouse, Wendy's
Lodg N: Comfort Suites, Hilton Garden Inn
S: Holiday Inn Express
Med N: + Hospital
Other N: Mall
S: ATMs, Costco, CompUSA, Lowe's

18 Woods Chapel Rd, NW Duncan Rd, Blue Springs, Independence, Lake Tapawingo, Fleming Park (Access to Ex #20 Services)
Gas N: Quik Stop/BP
S: Conoco, QT, Phillips 66◈
Food N: King Dragon
S: China Kitchen, KFC/Taco Bell, McDonald's, Pizza Hut, Waffle House
Lodg N: American Inn, Best Value Inn, Interstate Inn, Microtel
Other N: Blue Springs Harley Davidson, Carwash, Jefferson Service Center
S: Dave's Service Center, Laundromat

20 MO 7, Lake Lotawana, Blue Springs
Gas N: Phillips 66◈, Sinclair, Valero
S: BP◈, QT, Shamrock, Shell
Food N: Backyard Burger, Bob Evans, Pizza Hut, Quiznos, Sonic
S: Applebee's, Arby's, Burger King, China Buffet, Captain D's, Denny's, Einstein Bros, Golden Corral, KFC, Long John Silver, McDonald's, Starbucks, Subway, Wendy's, Village Inn
Lodg N: Econo Lodge, Motel 6♥, Ramada, Sleep Inn, Super 8
S: Hampton Inn, Holiday Inn Express, Quality Inn
Other N: ATMs, Ace Hardware, Auto Service, Dollar General, Grocery, Home Depot, O'Reilly Auto Parts, Walgreen's
S: ATMs, Advance Auto Parts, Auto Services, Firestone, Goodyear, Grocery, NAPA, Office Depot, Radio Shack

21 Adams Dairy Pkwy
Gas S: Phillips 66◈, Murphy
Food S: Burger King/P66, Bob Evans
Lodg S: Courtyard, Rodeway Inn, Sleep Inn
Other S: ATMs, Grocery, Home Depot, Walmart sc

24 US 40, MO AA, MO BB, Main St, Grain Valley, Buckner
FStop N: McLeroy Oil Co
TStop N: Apple Trail Travel Center/P66 (Scales)
S: Conoco Travel Center (Scales)
Food N: Rest/Apple Trail TC
S: Subway/Conoco TC
Lodg N: Comfort Inn, Travelodge
S: Kozy Inn Motel
Other N: Laundry/WiFi/RVDump/Apple Trail TC, Country Campers & RV Center▲, Nationwide RV, Show Me Campers & Boats
Other S: Trailside RV Center, Trailside RV Park▲

28 MO F, MO H, Broadway St, Oak Grove, Levasy
TStop N: Travel Center of America #52/Conoco (Scales)
S: Petro Stopping Center #70/BP (Scales), Quik Trip #150 (Scales)
Food N: Rest/Popeye's/PizzaHut/TA TC
S: Rest/Blimpie/DQ/Wendy's/Petro SC, Deli/QT, Hardee's, KFC, McDonald's, Subway, Waffle House
Lodg N: Days Inn
S: Econo Lodge
TWash N: Blue Beacon TW/TA TC, Quality TW
S: TruckOMat/Iowa80/Petro SC
TServ N: TA TC/Tires
S: Petro SC/Tires, Speedco
Other N: Laundry/CB/WiFi/RVDump/TA TC, KC East/Oak Grove KOA▲
S: Laundry/WiFi/RVDump/Petro SC, Laundry/QT, Walmart sc

31 MO Z, 2nd St, MO D, Bates City
Gas S: BP◈
Food S: Bates City BBQ, Sonic, Taco John's
Lodg S: Bates City Motel & Campground▲
TServ S: Mid America Truck Center
Other S: Flea Market, Fireworks, Pyro City Fireworks

(36) TRUCK Parking (Both dir)

37A MO 131, Odessa, Wellington

37 MO 131, Odessa, Wellington
FStop S: Odessa BP
Gas S: BP, Shell
Food N: Countryside Family Dining
S: McDonald's, Pizza Hut, Taco John's
Lodg S: Odessa Inn, Parkside Inn
Other N: Country Gardens RV Park▲, New Oak Winery
S: ATMs, Auto Dealer, Auto Services, Grocery, O'Reilly Auto Parts, Prime Outlets of Odessa, Grand Junction KOA▲

38 MO 131S, Johnson Dr, Odessa (WB)
FStop S: Odessa BP
Gas S: Shell
Food S: McDonald's, Sonic, Subway, Wendy's

41 MO M, MO O, Lexington
Other N: I-70 Speedway

(43) Weigh Station (Both dir)

45 MO H, to Mayview

49 MO 13, Higginsville, Warrensburg
TStop N: Pilot Travel Center #443 (Scales)
Gas N: BP
Food N: McDonald's/Subway/Pilot TC
S: Rest/Super 8
Lodg N: Best Western, Best Value Inn
S: Camelot Inn, Super 8
Other N: Laundry/RVDump/Pilot TC, U-Haul, R&S Towing
S: Interstate RV Campground▲

52 MO T, Blue Jay Rd, Aullville

(57) Rest Area (Both dir) (RR, Phones, Picnic, Vend)
NOTE: WB: LAST Rest Area in MO

58 MO 23, Main St, Concordia
FStop S: Fat Boyz/Conoco
TStop N: Travel Center of America #18 (Scales)
Gas N: Casey's
S: Breaktime, Shell
Food N: CountryPride/PizzaHut/Subway/TA TC
S: Biffles Smokehouse BBQ, Hardee's, KFC, McDonald's, Topsy's Rest
Lodg S: Budget Inn, Days Inn, Fannie Lee B&B, Travelodge
TServ N: TA TC/Tires
Other N: Laundry/WiFi/TA TC, ATMs, Dollar General
S: NAPA, St Paul's College, RV Center

62 MO Y, MO W, Elm St, Concordia, Emma

66 MO 127, Locust St, Sweet Springs, Mt Leonard, Knob Noster
Gas S: Conoco, Phillips 66, Break Time, MFA
Food S: Aunt Bea's Bakery, Brownsville Station Rest, Sweet Water Rest, Sonic
Lodg S: Motel 6♥, Peoples Choice Motel, Super 8

71 MO K, MO EE, Marshall, Houstonia

74 MO YY, CR 329, Sweet Springs
TStop N: Betty's Truck Stop/Shell
Food N: Rest/Betty's TS
Lodg N: Betty's Motel
TServ N: Betty's TS/Tires

78A US 65S, to Sedalia
FStop S: Break Time #3068/MFA
Other S: Lazy Days Camping▲, MO Valley College, Fairgrounds, Historic Sites

78B US 65N, to Marshall
FStop N: Conoco
Other N: Fireworks, Whitman Air Force Base✈

84 MO J
Gas N: BP
Food N: Stuckey's/DQ/BP

89 MO K, MO Z, Bryant Bottom Rd, Blackwater, to Arrow Rock

98 MO 135, CR 41, Arrow Rock, Boonville, Lamine, Pilot Grove
TStop S: Dogwood Truck Stop/Conoco
Gas S: Shell◈
Food S: DogwoodRest/Dogwood TS
TServ S: Dogwood TS/Tires, Tony's Diesel Service

101 I-70 Bus, US 40, MO 5, Ashley, Boonville, Tipton
TStop N: Pilot Travel Center #44 (Scales)
S: Love's Travel Stop #347
Food N: Arby'sWendy's/Pilot TC, Burger King
S: Hardee's/Love's TS
Lodg N: Comfort Inn♥, Holiday Inn Express
TWash N: Pilot TC
TServ N: Pilot TC
Other N: Laundry/WiFi/Pilot TC, Auto Dealers

◈ = Regular Gas Stations with Diesel ▲ = RV Friendly Locations ♥ = Pet Friendly Locations
Red print shows large vehicle parking / access on site or nearby Brown Print = Campgrounds / RV PARKS

EXIT		MISSOURI
	Other	S: RVDump/Love's TS, Auto Dealers
103		**MO B, Main St, Boonville**
	TStop	S: Boonville Truck Stop/Conoco (Scales)
	Gas	N: Break Time, Phillips 66◈, Speedy's Gas S: BP Cenex◈
	Food	N: Cowboy Toad, Domino's, La Hacienda Mex Rest, Pizza Hut, McDonald's, Sonic, Subway, Taco Bell, KFC/Long John Silver S: Bobber Cafe/Boonville TS, Arby's, DQ, Mr Goodcents Subs
	Lodg	N: Days Inn, Super 8
	Med	S: + Cooper Co Memorial Hospital
	Other	N: ATMs, Dollar General, Radio Shack, **Walmart**, **RV Express Park▲** S: Laundry/RVDump/Boonville TS, **Windmill Campground▲**, **Bobber Lake Campground▲**, **to** Isle of Capri Casino & Hotel
(104)		**Rest Area (Both dir)** **(RR, Phones, Picnic, Vend)**
106		**Bus 70, MO 87, Boonville, Bingham Rd, Prairie Home**
	Gas	N: Cenex, Conoco◈, Phillips 66◈
	Food	N: Diner 87, Rest/Atlasta Motel
	Lodg	N: Atlasta Motel
111		**MO 179, MO 98, Overton, Wooldridge**
	Gas	S: Phillips 66◈
	Other	S: Tires/Repair/P66
115		**MO BB, Roby Farm Rd, Rocheport**
	Other	N: Les Bourgouis Winery, **to State Park**
117		**MO J, MO O, Harrisburg, Huntdale**
121		**US 40W, MO 240, MO UU, Columbia, Fayette**
	TStop	N: PTP/Midway Truck Plaza/Conoco (Scales)
	Gas	N: Phillips 66
	Food	N: Rest/Midway TP
	Lodg	N: Budget Inn
	TServ	N: Midway TP, Goodyear, Truck & Tire Service
	Other	N: Laundry/RVDump/Midway TP, Central Methodist Univ, UMC Dairy Farm
124		**MO 740, MO E, Stadium Blvd**
	Gas	N: Break Time S: Phillips 66, Shell
	Food	S: Applebee's, Alexander's Steakhouse, Burger King, G&D Steak House, Great Wall Chinese Buffet, Hardee's, KFC, Pasta House, Red Lobster, Subway, Taco Bell, Rest/Holiday Inn
	Lodg	N: Extended Stay America, Motel 6♥ S: Baymont Inn, Days Inn, Drury Inn, Holiday Inn
	Other	S: Columbia Mall, ATMs, Auto Services, Best Buy, Radio Shack, Target, UPS Store, **Walmart**, **to** Univ of MO
125		**West Blvd, N Creasy Springs Rd, Lp 70, I-70 Bus, Columbia**
	Gas	S: Break Time◈, Conoco◈, Phillips 66◈, Shell
	Food	S: Denny's, El Maguey, Hong Kong, Long John Silver, Olive Garden, Outback Steakhouse, Pizza Hut, Perkins, Red Lobster, Ryan's Grill, Wendy's
	Lodg	S: Delux Inn, Econo Lodge, Howard Johnson, Scottish Inn
	Other	S: Advance Auto Parts, Auto Dealers, ATMs,Firestone, Grocery, U-Haul
126		**MO 163, Providence Rd, Columbia**
	Gas	N: BP S: BP, Break Time◈
	Food	N: Bandana's BBQ, Country Kitchen S: Burger King, McDonald's, Pizza Hut, Sonic, Subway, Taco Bell
	Lodg	N: Best Value Inn, Quality Inn, Red Roof Inn
	Med	S: + Hospital
	Other	N: Auto Dealers S: ATMs, Auto Zone, Dollar General, Enterprise RAC, Grocery, O'Reilly
127		**MO 763, Rangeline St, Columbia**
	Gas	N: Break Time◈ S: Phillips 66◈
	Food	N: McDonald's, Waffle House S: Burger King, DQ, Sonic, Taco Bell
	Lodg	N: Budget Host, Ramada, Travelodge S: Super 7
	Other	N: Auto Dealers, Dollar General, Harley Davidson S: Bass Pro Shop
128		**I-70 Bus, Columbia (WB, LEFT exit)**
	Gas	S: Conoco◈
	Med	S: + Hospital
	Other	S: Stephens College
128A		**to US 63N, Jefferson City, Moberly**
	Gas	N: BP, Casey's, QT S: Conoco◈
	Food	N: Bob Evans, Burger King, **Cracker Barrel**, Golden Corral, Hooters, KFC, Lone Star Steakhouse, McDonald's, Ruby Tuesday, Steak n Shake, Taco Bell S: Applebee's, Chili's, CiCi's Pizza, IHOP, Longhorn Steakhouse, Quiznos Subs, Subway
	Lodg	N: Fairfield Inn, Hampton Inn, Hilton Garden Inn, Residence Inn, Super 8 S: Best Western, Candlewood Suites, Holiday Inn Express, La Quinta Inn♥, Motel 6♥, Wingate Inn
	Other	N: Bass Pro Shop, Home Depot, **Cottonwoods RV Park▲** S: ATMs, Bank, Grocery, Lowe's, Sam's Club, Staples, **Walmart sc**, **Finger Lakes State Park▲**, Pine Grove Village
131		**St Charles Rd, Lake of the Wood Rd**
	Gas	N: BP, Phillips 66◈ S: Conoco◈
	Food	S: Sonic, Subway/P66
	Lodg	N: Super 8
	Other	N: Mid-America Harley Davidson, Lakeview Mall, Tourist Info S: **RV Park▲**
133		**MO Z, Rangeline Rd, to Centralia**
	TServ	N: Fabick Cat, Bobcat S: Kenworth
	Other	N: **Loveall's RV**
137		**MO DD, MO J, Millersburg**
	TServ	S: Freightliner
144		**MO M, MO HH, Cort 223, to Hatton**
	Other	S: **Shoemaker RV Center, Crooked Creek Campground▲**
148		**US 54, CR 201, Gold Ave, CR 211, Kingdom City**
	TStop	S: FastLane/P66, Gasper's Travel Center/ Shell (Scales), Petro Stopping Center #18 / Mobil (Scales), Westland Travel Center/ Conoco (Scales)
	Gas	N: BP, Phillips 66◈
	Food	N: Taco Bell S: McDonald's/FastLane, Arby's/Gasper's TC, Iron Skillet/FastFood/Petro SC, Subway/Westland TC
	Lodg	N: Holiday Inn S: Comfort Inn, Days Inn, Red Carpet Inn, Super 8
	TServ	S: Gasper's TC/Tires, Petro SC/Tires
	Other	N: Nostalgia Village USA, Tourist Info, MO Military Academy, **to** Mark Twain Lake S: Laundry/Gasper's TC, Laundry/BarbSh/ RVDump/Petro SC, Lake of the Ozarks
155		**MO A, MO Z, Fulton, Auxvasse**
161		**MO YY, MO D, Williamsburg, Old US 40, CR 177, Bachelor, Calwood**
	TStop	S: Jump Stop Travel Center/Conoco
	Gas	S: Ray's Garage
	Food	S: Rest/Jump Stop TC
(166)		**Rest Area (EB)** **(RR, Phones, Picnic, Vend)**
(169)		**Rest Area (WB)** **(RR, Phones, Picnic, Vend)**
170		**MO 161, MO J, Danville, Montgomery City**
	Gas	N: Citgo, Phillips 66

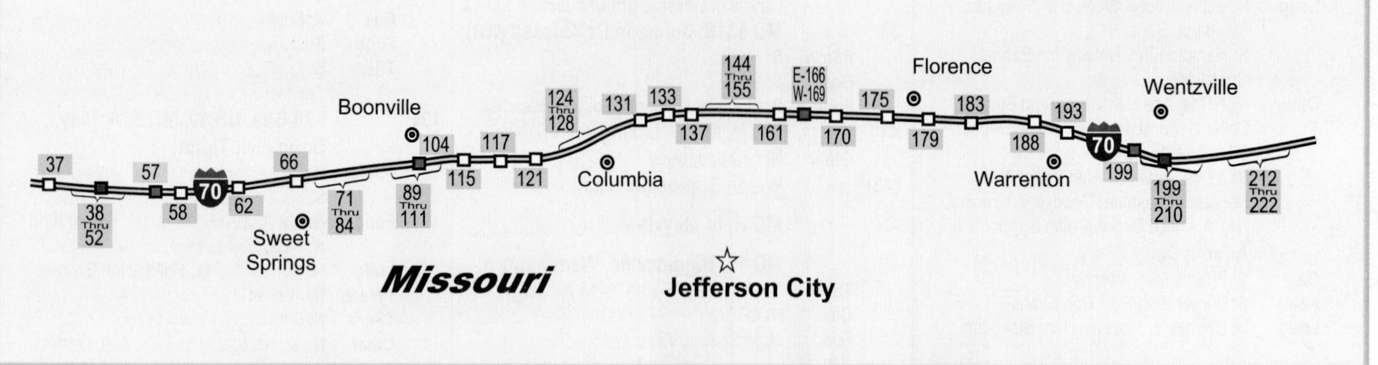

◈ = Regular Gas Stations with Diesel ▲ = RV Friendly Locations ♥ = Pet Friendly Locations
Red print shows large vehicle parking / access on site or nearby Brown Print = Campgrounds / RV PARKS

EXIT | MISSOURI

Other N: Graham Cave State Park▲, Kan-Do Kampground▲
S: Lazy Day Campground▲

175 MO 19, Boonslick Rd, New Florence, Hermann, Montgomery City
FStop N: Abel's Fuel Center #17/Shell, Junction Fuel & Grocery/BP
Gas N: Phillips 66
Food N: McDonald's/Shell, Hardee's, Maggie's Café, Pizza Cabin,
Lodg N: Best Inn, Super 8, Harbour Haus Inn
Other N: Cuno RV, Stone Hill Winery, to Mark Twain Lake, Cannon Dam (appr 51 mi)
S: Hermann Winery, Adam Punate Winery

179 MO F, High Hill
Lodg S: I-70 Budget Motel, Colonial Inn

183 MO Y, MO NN, MO E, N 1st St, CR 250, Jonesburg
Gas S: Fastlane/66, Shell
Other N: Jonesburg Gardens Campground▲

188 MO A, MO B, Warrenton
TStop S: Flying J Travel Plaza #5016/Conoco (Scales)
Food S: Cookery/FastFood/FJ TP
Lodg S: Budget Inn
Other S: Laundry/WiFi/RVDump/LP/FJ TP

193 MO 47, Warrenton, to Hawk Point, Marthasville
Gas N: 7-11, Phillips 66◈, ZX
S: BP, Casey's, Phillips 66◈, Shell
Food N: Burger King, DQ, Jack in the Box, Pizza Hut, McDonald's, Subway, Waffle House
S: Denny's, Hardee's, KFC, Taco Bell
Lodg N: Days Inn, Holiday Inn Express, Super 8
S: AmeriHost, Budget Host Inn
Other N: ATMs, Banks, Family Dollar, Grocery, Walmart sc
S: ATMs, Auto Dealers, Auto Zone, Auto Services, Kelly Tires, NAPA, Outlet Mall

(199) Rest Area (Both dir) (RR, Phones, Picnic)

199 Wildcat Dr, MO H, to MO M to MO J, Wright City (WB)
Gas N: Shell
Food N: McDonald's
TServ S: Porter Truck Sales, Volvo

200 MO J, MO F, Elm Ave, Wright City
Gas N: Citgo◈, Shell◈, MidWest Petro
S: Phillips 66
Food N: Abilene's Rest, Mexican Rest
S: Big Boy
Lodg S: Super 7 Inn
TServ N: Freightliner
Other N: Chiropractor

203 MO T, MO W, Foristell
TStop N: Travel Center of America #175/BP (Scales), Mr Fuel #4 (Scales)
S: Foristell Truck Stop/P66
Food N: Rest/Popeye's/PizzaHut/TacoBell/TA TC FastFood/Mr Fuel
S: Rest/Foristell TS
Lodg N: Best Western
TServ N: TA TC/Tires, Fabick CAT
Other N: Laundry/WiFi/TA TC
S: Marlen Gas Co/LP

(205) Weigh Station (Both dir)

208 Pearce Blvd, Wentzville Pkwy, Wentzville
Gas N: Citgo, QT◈
S: BP, Shell, Phillips 66

EXIT | MISSOURI

Food N: McDonald's, Pizza Hut, Steak n Shake, Taco Bell, Wendy's, Waffle House
S: Captain D's, Hardee's, Pizza
Lodg S: Super 8
Med N: + Hospital
Other N: ATMs, Banks, Best Buy, Grocery, Home Depot, Walgreen's, Bill Thomas Camper
S: Walmart, Pinewood RV Park▲

209 MO Z, Church St, to New Melle (WB)
Gas S: Phillips 66
Food N: DQ

210AB US 40S, US 61, to I-64, Wentzville
TStop S: Wentzville P66
Gas S: Conoco, Shell
Food S: Rest/Wentzville P66
Lodg N: Budget Inn, Econo Lodge, Knights Inn

212 MO A, Freymuth Rd, Lake St Louis
Gas S: Citgo◈, Mobil
Food S: Arby's, Burger King, Willie's Steaks
Lodg N: Ramada Econo Lodge, Knights Inn
S: Holiday Inn
Other N: General Motors Assembly Plant, Freedom RV

214 Lake St Louis Blvd, Lake St Louis
Gas S: Phillips 66◈, Shell
Food S: Denny's, Hardee's, Subway
Lodg S: Days Inn
Med S: + St Joseph Hospital West
Other N: Ryder, Marina
S: Grocery

216 Bryan Rd, W Terra Ln, O'Fallon
Gas S: Casey's, Conoco, Phillips 66
Lodg N: Super 8
TServ N: Peterbilt

217 MO K, Veterans Memorial Pkwy, MO M, S Main St, O'Fallon
Gas N: BP, QT
S: Citgo◈, Dirt Cheap, Fina, Shell, Phillips 66, ZX
Food N: Burger King, Hardee's, Jack in the Box, Ponderosa, Taco Bell, Waffle House
S: Arby's, Bob Evans, IHOP, Lion's Choice, Longhorn Steakhouse, McDonald's, Papa John's Pizza, Pizza Hut, Steak 'n Shake, Stefanina's Pizza,
Lodg S: O'Fallon Motel
Other N: Firestone, Radio Shack, Cherokee Camping▲
S: ATMs, Auto Zone, Grocery, Lowe's, Midas, Walgreen's, RV Center

219 Belleau Creek Rd, TR Hughes Blvd, Cool Springs Rd, O'Fallon
Gas S: QT
Lodg S: Comfort Inn

220 MO 79, Salt Lick Rd, St Peters, to Elsberry
Gas S: 7-11, BP
Food S: Hardee's, McDonald's, Quiznos, Smokehouse Rest, Sonic, Subway
Other N: Cherokee Camping & Fishing▲

222 MO C, Mid Rivers Mall Dr, St Peters
FStop S: QuikTrip #608 (Scales)
Gas S: Citgo, Mobil
Food N: Burger King
S: Arby's, Bob Evans, Chili's, Hardee's, Jack in the Box, Joe's Crab Shack, Olive Garden, McDonald's, Pizza Hut, Red Robin, Ruby Tuesday, Steak 'n Shake, Subway, Steak Escape, Taco Bell, Wendy's

EXIT | MISSOURI

Lodg S: Drury Inn, Extended Stay America
Other N: Auto Dealers, Daniel Boone Monument
S: ATMs, Auto Zone, Auto Services, Barnes & Noble, Best Buy, Big Lots, Costco, Discount Tire, Grocery, U-Haul, Walgreen's, Westfield Mall

224 MO 370E
TServ N: Kenworth
Other S: Auto Dealer

225 Cave Springs Rd, Harry Truman Rd, St Peters, St Charles
Gas N: BP, Citgo, Shell
S: Conoco, Mobil, QT, ZX
Food N: Patty's Café, Taco Bell, Wendy's
S: Burger King, Denny's, Ground Round, IHOP, Jack in the Box, Long John Silver, McDonald's, Pasta House, Pizza Hut, Ponderosa, Red Lobster, Steak n Shake, Subway
Lodg N: Hampton Inn, Knights Inn, Motel 6♥
S: Holiday Inn Express, Budget Motel
Med S: + Hospital
Other N: Auto Dealers, U-Haul
S: ATMs, Budget RAC, Firestone, Grocery, Home Depot, Office Depot, Target

227 Zumbehl Rd, St Charles
Gas N: Shell, ZX
S: BP, Mobil
Food N: Burger King, Culpepper's
S: Applebee's, Black Eyed Pea, Boston Market, Bob Evans, Chevy's Mexican, CiCi's Pizza, Fratelli's, Golden Corral, Hardee's, Little Caesars Pizza, Lone Star Steakhouse, Old Country Buffet, Popeye's Chicken, Quiznos Subs, Subway, Taco Bell
Lodg N: Econo Lodge, Super 8
S: Best Western, Comfort Inn, Red Roof Inn♥, TownPlace Suites, Travelodge
Other N: Cinema, Grocery, Lowe's
S: ATMs, Auto Services, Big Lots, Dollar Tree, Grocery, Sam's Club, Walmart, Glendale Christian Family Resort, Access to Ex #228

228 MO 94, First Capitol Dr, St Charles, to Weldon Springs
Gas N: Citgo, Phillips 66, Shell
S: Mobil, Shell, QT
Food N: Arby's, DQ, Hardee's, Long John Silver, Papa John's Pizza, Pizza Hut, Steak 'n Shake, Wendy's
S: Chuck E Cheese's Pizza, Fazoli's
Lodg S: Best Western, Days Inn, InTowne Suites
Other N: ATMs, Advance Auto Parts, Auto Zone, Auto Services, Firestone, Grocery, Radio Shack, Walgreen's
S: Lynnwood Univ

229 5th St, River Rd, St Charles (EB)
Gas N: BP, Mobil◈
S: Phillips 66, QT
Food N: Burger King, Denny's, Jack in the Box, McDonald's, Subway, Waffle House
S: Cracker Barrel
Lodg N: Baymont Inn, Best Western, Comfort Suites, Quality Inn, St Charles Hotel
S: Comfort Inn, Days Inn, Fairfield Inn, Ramada Inn, Suburban Lodge
Other N: Bass Pro Shop, Casino, Walgreen's,
S: Convention Center, Mall, RV Park▲

◈ = Regular Gas Stations with Diesel ▲ = RV Friendly Locations ♥ = Pet Friendly Locations
Red print shows large vehicle parking / access on site or nearby Brown Print = Campgrounds / RV PARKS

EXIT		MISSOURI
229A		**S 5th St, S River Rd (WB)**
229B		**Bus 70N, 5th St (WB)**
231AB		**Earth City Expy, Maryland Hts Expy**
	FStop	N: MPC #62/P66
	Gas	S: Mobil
	Food	N: Jack in the Box/P66, McDonald's S: Burger King, Town Square Café
	Lodg	N: Candlewood Suites, Courtyard, Fairfield Inn, Residence Inn, Sheraton, Studio Plus S: Holiday Inn Express, Wingate Inn
	Other	S: Harrah's Riverport Casino, Riverport Amphitheatre, RV Park▲
(232)		**Jct I-270, N-Chicago, S-Memphis**
234		**MO 180, St. Charles Rock Rd, Bridgeton**
	Gas	N: Phillips 66, Shell
	Food	N: Applebee's, Casa Gallardo's, Hatfield/McCoy Rest, Lone Star Steakhouse, Long John Silver, McDonald's, Old Country Buffet, Ponderosa, Red Lobster, Shoney's, Steak n Shake, Taco Bell
	Lodg	N: Knights Inn
	Med	N: + Hospital
	Other	N: ATMs, Best Buy, Office Depot, Sam's Club, Target, Walgreen's
235AB		**US 67, Lindberg Blvd (WB)**
235A		**US 67S, Lindberg Blvd**
	Gas	S: Shell
	Food	S: Steak 'n Shake, TGI Friday
	Lodg	S: Crown Plaza, Embassy Suites, Homestead Inn, Radisson
	Other	S: ATMs, Auto Services, Firestone, Mall
235B		**US 67N, Lindberg Blvd**
	Gas	N: Shell
	Food	N: Rest/Holiday Inn
	Lodg	N: Econo Lodge, Holiday Inn, Howard Johnson
	Other	N: St Louis Int'l Airport✈
235C		**MO B, Cypress Rd, Nat'l Bridge Rd**
	Other	N: St Louis Int'l Airport✈
236		**Lambert St Louis Int'l Airport**
	Gas	S: BP
	Food	S: CoCo's, Hardee's, Rafferty's
	Lodg	S: Best Western, Days Inn, Drury Inn, Hampton Inn, Holiday Inn, Hilton Garden Inn, Marriott, Motel 6♥
237		**MO 115, Natural Bridge Rd (EB)**
	Gas	S: Phillips 66, Shell
	Food	S: Arby's, Burger King, Denny's, Jack in the Box, Pizza Hut, Steak 'n Shake, Waffle House, Wendy's
	Lodg	S: Best Western, Days Inn, DoubleTree Hotel, Travelodge

EXIT		MISSOURI
238A		**Lambert St. Louis Airport (WB)**
(238B)		**Jct I-170S**
(238C)		**Jct I-170N**
239		**Hanley Rd**
	Gas	S: Mobil
	Food	S: McDonald's
240		**MO N, Florissant Rd**
	Gas	N: BP
	Food	N: McDonald's, Taco Bell
241A		**Stanwood Dr, Bermuda Ave**
	Gas	S: Shell, Sinclair
241B		**MO U, Lucas-Hunt Rd**
	Gas	N: Shell
	Gas	S: Citgo
242		**Jennings Station Rd**
	Gas	N: Shell
243		**Goodfellow Blvd**
243A		**Riverview Blvd**
243B		**Bircher Blvd, Riverview Blvd (WB)**
243C		**Bircher Blvd (EB)**
244A		**Riverview Blvd, Bircher Blvd (EB) Union Blvd (WB)**
244B		**N Kingshighway Blvd**
245A		**Shreve Ave, Bircher Ave**
	Gas	S: BP
245B		**W Florissant Ave, Bircher Blvd**
246A		**Broadway (WB), E Carrie Ave (EB)**
	Gas	N: Mobil◊
	Other	N: Freightliner
246B		**Adelaide Ave**
247		**Grand Blvd, St Louis**
	FStop	N: MPC #42/P66
	Lodg	N: First Western Inn
248A		**N 9th St, Salisbury St (WB) N 11th St, Salisbury St (EB)**
	Gas	S: BP, Mobil◊
248B		**Branch St, N 9th St (WB) N 11th St, St Louis Ave (EB)**
249A		**Madison St (WB), Howard St (EB)**
	Gas	N: Phillips 66◊
	Other	N: Busch Stadium, Riverboat Gambling
249C		**Cass Ave, N Broadway, 6th St (EB)**
250A		**Cole St, N Broadway**
	Lodg	N: Econo Lodge, Embassy Suites S: Drury Inn, Hampton Inn, Holiday Inn
	Other	N: Convention Center

EXIT		MO / IL
250B		**Memorial Dr, Downtown**
	Gas	S: Shell
	Food	S: McDonald's
	Lodg	S: Adams Mark, Days Inn, Radisson
(251A)		**Jct I-55S, to Memphis, to I-44, Downtown**
251B		**Memorial Dr (WB)**

CENTRAL TIME ZONE

NOTE: MM 252: Illinois State Line

⬆ MISSOURI
⬇ ILLINOIS

CENTRAL TIME ZONE

NOTE: I-70 runs below with I-55 Exit #'s follow I-55.

EXIT		MO / IL
1		**IL 3, to Sauget (SB)**
2A		**MLK Bridge, to St Louis Downtown (SB, LEFT exit)**
2B		**3rd St (SB, LEFT exit)**
	Other	W: Casino Queen RV Park▲
2C		**MLK Memorial Bridge (SB)**
(2)		**Jct I-64E, IL 3N, St Clair Ave**
3		**Exchange Ave, St Clair Ave, E St East St Louis**
4A		**IL 203E, Collinsville Rd (SB)**
4B		**IL 203W, E St Louis (SB)**
4		**IL 203, Collinsville Rd, Granite City, E St Louis (NB)**
	TStop	W: Pilot Travel Center #313 (Scales) SB: Access via Exit #4B
	Gas	E: Phillips 66◊
	Food	W: Subway/TacoBell/Pilot TC
	Lodg	E: First Western Inn
	TWash	W: Pilot TC
	TServ	W: Pilot TC/Tires
	Other	W: Laundry/WiFi/Pilot TC, Gateway Int'l Raceway

NOTE: MM 5: EB: Begin Motorist Call Boxes

EXIT		MO / IL
6		**IL 111, Great River Rd, Wood River, Fairmont City, Washington Park**
	Gas	E: Phillips 66◊
	Lodg	E: Royal Relax Inn, Royal Budget Inn, Indian Mound Motel

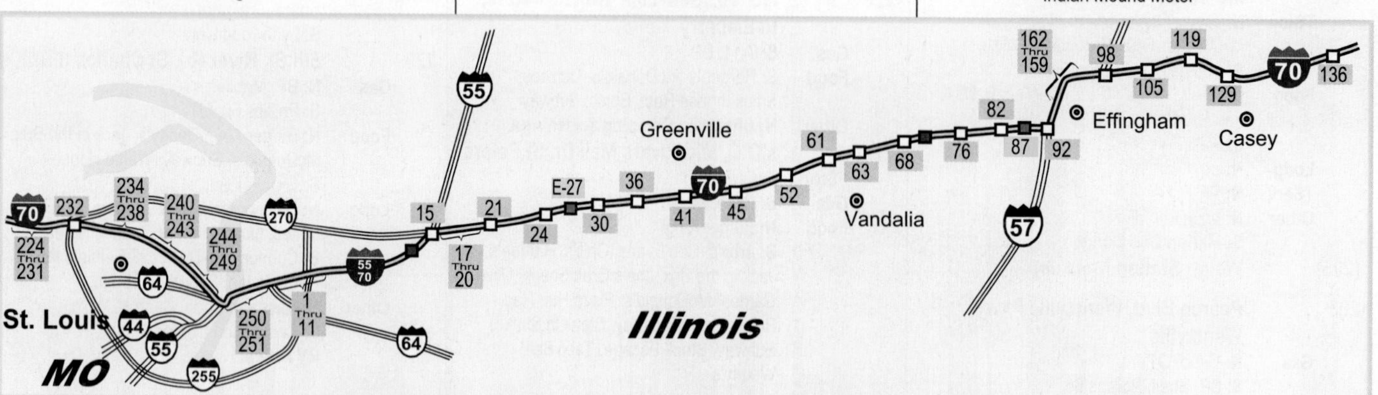

◊= Regular Gas Stations with Diesel ▲ = RV Friendly Locations ♥= Pet Friendly Locations
Red print shows large vehicle parking / access on site or nearby Brown Print = Campgrounds / RV PARKS

EXIT ILLINOIS

Other E: Grocery, Pharmacy, **Safari RV Park▲**, Indian Mounds Golf Course, **to Cahokia Mounds State Park**
W: **to Horseshoe Lakes State Park**, Lakeside Airport✈

9 Fairmont Ave, Black Lane (NB exit, SB reaccess)
Other E: **to** Fairmount Park, **Cahokia Mounds State Park**

(10) Jct I-255, S-Memphis, N to I-270

11 IL 157, Bluff Rd, Collinsville, to Edwardsville
FStop W: Moto Mart
Gas E: BP, Casey's, Shell
Food E: Denny's, Hardee's, Long John Silver, McDonald's, Waffle House, Wendy's
Food W: Arby's, Applebee's, Bandanas BBQ, Bob Evans, Burger King, DQ, Pizza Hut, Ruby Tuesday, Steak 'n Shake, White Castle, Rest/Hol Inn
Lodg E: Best Western, Howard Johnson, Motel 6♥
W: Comfort Inn, Days Inn, Drury Inn♥, Fairfield Inn, Holiday Inn, Super 8
Other E: **Randy's Trailer Town**
W: Auto & Tire Service, Auto Dealers, Convention Center, Visitor Center, **IL State Hwy Patrol Post**

(14) Weigh Station (SB)

15AB IL 159, Vandalia St, Maryville Rd, Collinsville, Maryville
Gas E: Citgo, Phillips 66◊, Shell
W: Conoco
Lodg W: Econo Lodge

17 US 40E, to Troy, St Jacob
TServ E: ADR Auto & Truck Repair, M&M Truck Repair

18 IL 162, Edwardsville Rd, Troy
TStop E: Pilot Travel Center #249 (Scales), Travel Center of America #199/BP (Scales)
Gas W: Phillips 66◊
Food E: Arby's/TJCinn/Pilot TC, Rest/TA TC, Burger King, DQ, Jack in the Box, KFC, Little Caesar's Pizza, McDonald's, Perkins, Pizza Hut, Subway
W: China Garden, **Cracker Barrel**, Taco Bell
Lodg E: Relax Inn
W: Holiday Inn Express♥, Red Roof Inn♥, Scottish Inns, Super 8
TWash E: 18 Wheeler's Truck Wash
TServ E: TA TC/Tires, Carron's Auto & Truck Repair
Med W: **+ Anderson Hospital**
Other E: Laundry/WiFi/Pilot TC, Laundry/BarbSh/TA TC, Family Dollar, Grocery

(20A) Jct I-70E, to Indianapolis

(20B) Jct I-270W, to Kansas City

(15AB) Jct I-55, N-Chicago, S-St Louis, I-270W, to Kansas City

NOTE: **I-70 runs above with I-55 for 18 mi. Exit #'s follow I-55.**

21 IL 4, Marine, to Lebanon, Staunton

NOTE: **MM 23: WB: Begin Motorist Call Boxes**

24 IL 143, Marine, Highland
Med S: + Hospital

EXIT ILLINOIS

(27) IL Welcome Center (EB) Silver Lake Rest Area (WB) (RR, Phones, Picnic, Vend, Weather)

30 US 40, to IL 143, Steiner Rd, Highland
Gas S: Shell◊
Food S: Blue Springs Restaurant
Med S: **+ Hospital**
Other S: **to Tomahawk Campground▲**

36 US 40, CR 21, 475E, Pocahontas
Gas S: AmocoBP◊, Phillips 66◊
Food S: Rest/Powhatan Motel
Lodg S: Powhatan Motel, Tahoe Motel, Wikiup Motel

41 US 40E, to Greenville, 970E

45 IL 127, to US 40, Greenville, to Carlyle Lake, Carlyle
Gas N: Citgo◊, Phillips 66◊, Shell◊
Food N: KFC, McDonald's, Rest/BW
S: Circle B Western Steakhouse
Lodg N: Best Western, Budget Host Inn, Super 8
Med N: **+ Greenville Regional Hospital**
Other N: Auto Services, Towing
S: **to** Greenville Airport✈

52 CR 10, Maple St, Mulberry Grove
Gas N: Citgo◊
Other S: **Cedarbrook RV Park & Campground▲**

61 US 40, Vandalia, Mulberry Grove
FStop S: Roadys TS/Fastop Travel Center (Scales)
Gas S: Phillips 66, Murphy◊
Food S: KFC/Taco Bell, Ponderosa
Lodg S: Ramada
Other N: Vandalia Muni Airport✈
S: Auto Services, NAPA, **Walmart sc**,

63 US 51, US 40, Vandalia, Pana
Gas S: BP, Marathon, Shell◊
Food N: Long John Silver
S: DQ, Hardee's, KFC, McDonald's, Pizza Hut, Subway, Wendy's
Lodg N: Days Inn
S: Jay's Inn♥, Travelodge
Med S: **+ Fayette Co Hospital**
Other S: Grocery, Pharmacy

68 US 40, Brownstown, Bluff City

(71) Weigh Station (EB)

76 US 40, CR 7, 2125E, St Elmo

82 IL 128, CR 25, 300th St, Altamont
Gas N: Casey's, Stuckey's/Citgo◊, Marathon, Speedway◊
Gas S: Phillips 66
Food N: McDonald's, Subway
Lodg N: Altamont Motel, Knights Inn
S: Super 8

(87) Rest Area (Both dir) (RR, Phones, Picnic, Vend)

(92) Jct I-57, N - Chicago, S - Memphis

NOTE: **I-70 below runs with I-57 for 6 mi. Exit #'s follow I-57.**

159 Fayette Ave, Effingham
FStop E: Econo Fuel Express/Citgo
TStop W: Petro Stopping Center #21/Mobil (Scales), Truck-O-Mat (Scales)
Gas E: BP, Phillips 66
Food E: China Buffet, Culver's, Hardee's, Neimerg's Steak House, Subway
W: IronSkillet/Petro SC, Rest/BW

EXIT ILLINOIS

Lodg E: Abe Lincoln Motel, Comfort Suites♥, Econo Lodge, Howard Johnson Express♥, Lincoln Lodge♥, Paradise Inn, Rodeway Inn♥
W: Best Western♥
TWash W: Blue Beacon/Petro SC, TruckOMat
TServ E: Effingham Truck Sales/International
W: Petro SC/Tires
Other E: ATMs, Amtrak, Auto Services, Carwash, **to** Village Square Mall, Effingham Co Memorial Airport✈
W: Laundry/BarbSh/CB/WiFi/Petro SC

160 IL 32, IL 33, N Keller Dr, Effingham
TStop W: Flying J Travel Plaza #5107 (Scales), Travel Center of America #35/BP (Scales)
Gas E: BP, Shell
W: Phillips 66, Murphy◊
Food E: KFC, Lone Star Steakhouse
W: Rest/FastFood/FJ TP, CountryPride/Popeye's/Sbarro/TA TC, Arby's, Burger King, **Cracker Barrel**, Denny's, Long John Silver, McDonald's, Ponderosa, Ryan's Grill, Ruby Tuesday, Steak n Shake, Starbucks, Subway, Taco Bell, TGI Friday, Wendy's
Lodg E: Comfort Inn, Hampton Inn
W: Hotel/FJ TP, Country Inn, Hilton Garden Inn, Holiday Inn Express♥, Motel 6, Ramada Ltd, Super 8♥, Travelodge
TWash W: Blue Beacon TW/FJ TP, TA TC
TServ W: TA TC/Tires, Speedco, Peterbilt, Clarke Power Services
Med E: **+ St Anthony's Memorial Hospital**
Other E: ATMs, Banks, Dollar General, Grocery, Kroger, Walgreen's
W: Laundry/WiFi/**RVDump/LP**/FJ TP, Laundry/BarbSh/WiFi/TA TC, ATMs, Towing, U-Haul, **Walmart sc**, **Camp Lakewood RV Park▲**

162 US 45, N 3rd St, Effingham
TStop W: Pilot Travel Center #165 (Scales)
Gas E: Moto Mart
W: Citgo
Food W: McDonald's/Pilot TC
TWash W: Pilot TC
Med E: **+ St Anthony's Memorial Hospital**
Other E: Legacy Harley Davidson
W: Laundry/WiFi/**LP**/Pilot TC, **Crossroads RV Center, Camp Lakewood RV Park▲**

NOTE: **I-70 above runs with I-57 for 6 mi. Exit #'s follow I-57.**

(98) Jct I-57N, to Chicago

105 Montrose
Gas S: BP◊, Citgo◊, Shell
Food S: Rest/Montarosa Motel
Lodg S: Montarosa Motel

119 IL 130, Greenup, Charleston
Gas S: BP◊, Citgo◊, Phillips 66, Shell
Food S: DQ, Dutch Pan Restaurant
Lodg S: Budget Host Inn

129 IL 49, Casey, Kansas
Gas S: BP◊, Casey's, Citgo◊, Speedway
Food S: DQ, Hardee's, KFC, McDonald's, Pizza Hut
Lodg S: Comfort Inn
Other S: Casey Muni Airport✈

136 to Martinsville
Gas S: BP◊

EXIT		IL / IN
147		**IL 1, Marshall, Paris**
	FStop	S: Marshall Junction 66
	Gas	S: Jiffy◊, Casey's
	Food	N: Hardee's, Jerry's Rest
		S: Burger King, McDonald's, Pizza Hut
	Lodg	S: Peak's Motor Inn, Super 8
(149)		**IL Welcome Center (WB)** **(RR, Phones, Picnic, Vend, Weather)**
(151)		**Weigh Station (WB)**
154		**US 40W**

CENTRAL TIME ZONE

NOTE: MM 157: Indiana State Line

⬆ ILLINOIS
⬇ INDIANA

CENTRAL TIME ZONE

EXIT		INDIANA
1		**US 40E, W National Rd, W Terre Haute, to Terre Haute**
(2)		**IN Welcome Center (EB)** **(RR, Phones, Picnic, Vend, Info)**
3		**Darwin Rd, W Terre Haute**
7		**US 41, US 150, Terre Haute**
	Gas	N: BP, Marathon◊, Thornton's◊
		S: Jiffy, Shell, Speedway◊, Sunoco, Sam's
	Food	N: Arby's, Bob Evans, Cracker Barrel, Fazoli's, Hardee's, IHOP, Little Caesars Pizza, Pizz Hut, Shoney's, Steak n Shake, Texas Roadhouse, Starbucks
		S: DQ, Damon's Ribs, Hardee's, Denny's, Long John Silver, McDonald's, Olive Garden, Outback Steakhouse, Red Lobster, Subway, Taco Bell, Wendy's
	Lodg	N: Comfort Suites, Days Inn, Dollar Inn, Drury Inn, Econo Lodge, Fairfield Inn, Signature Inn, Super 8
		S: Hampton Inn, Holiday Inn, Motel 6♥
	TServ	N: GMC/Volvo
		S: McCord Tire & Auto Service
	Med	S: + Hospital
	Other	N: Auto Zone, **IN State Hwy Patrol Post**
		S: ATMs, Auto Dealers, Big Lots, Gander Mountain, Harley Davidson, Kroger, Sam's Club, **Walmart sc**, Walgreen's
11		**IN 46, Hulman Rd, Terre Haute**
	TStop	N: Pilot Travel Center #297 (Scales)
	Gas	N: Thornton's◊
	Food	N: Arby's/TJCinn/Pilot TC, Burger King, McDonald's
	TServ	N: Russ Fisher Truck Parts
	Other	N: WiFi/Pilot TC, Hulman Reg'l Airport✈
		S: **Terre Haute KOA▲**
23		**IN 59, Brazil, Linton**
	TStop	N: Pilot Travel Center #444 (Scales)
		S: Brazil 70 AmBest Truck Stop/Shell (Scales), Road Ranger #141/Citgo (Scales)
	Gas	S: Sunoco◊
	Food	N: McDonald's/Subway/Pilot TC
		S: Rest/Brazil 70 TS, Subway/RoadRanger, Burger King, Ike's Great American Rest, Rally/Sunoco
	Lodg	S: Howard Johnson
	TServ	S: Brazil 70 TS
	Med	N: + Hospital
	Other	N: Laundry/WiFi/Pilot TC, **to appr 20 mi Willow Rose RV Park ▲**, **to appr 17 mi Fallen Rock Park Campground▲**
		S: Laundry/Brazil70 TS, Ex 23 70 CB Shop
37		**IN 243, Cloverdale, Putnamville**
	FStop	S: Marathon #211
	Other	N: **Dogwood Springs Campground▲**
41		**US 231, IN 43, Cloverdale, to Greencastle, Spencer**
	TStop	S: PTP/Cloverdale Travel Plaza (Scales)
	Gas	S: BP◊, Shell
	Food	N: Long Branch Steakhouse
		S: Rest/FastFood/Cloverdale TP, Burger King, Arby's, KFC, McDonald's, Wendy's
	Lodg	N: Midway Motel
		S: Best Western, Budget Inn, Days Inn, Dollar Inn, Holiday Inn Express, Super 8
	TWash	S: Cloverdale TP
	TServ	S: Cloverdale TP/Tires
	Med	N: + Hospital
	Other	N: **Cloverdale RV Park▲**
		S: Laundry/Cloverdale TP, **to appr 11 mi Hickory Hills Campground▲**
51		**Little Point Rd, CR 1100W, IN 42, Stilesville**
	Gas	S: Koger's Country Mart
	TServ	S: Curtin Garage & Wrecker Service, Koger's Garage
59		**IN 39, Clayton, Belleville, Monrovia**
	TStop	S: Travel Center of America #102/Citgo (Scales)
	Gas	N: Marathon
	Food	S: CountryPride/NobleRomans/TA TC
	TServ	S: TA TC/Tires
	Other	S: Laundry/WiFi/**LP**/TA TC
(64)		**Rest Area (Both dir)** **(RR, Phones, Picnic, Vend, Info)**
66		**IN 267, Quaker Blvd, Plainfield, to Mooresville**
	Gas	N: BP, Shell, Speedway◊, Thornton's◊
	Food	N: Arby's, Bob Evans, Cracker Barrel, Hog Heaven BBQ, McDonald's, Perkins, Quiznos, Subway, Wendy's
	Lodg	N: Amerihost Inn, Comfort Inn, Days Inn, Dollar Inn, Hampton Inn, Holiday Inn Express, Lee's Inn, Super 8
	Other	N: Harley Davidson, Winery
(73A)		**Jct I-465S, I-74E**
(73B)		**Jct I-465N, I-74W**
75		**Airport Expwy, to Raymond St, to I-465, I-74 (WB)**
	Gas	N: Marathon, Speedway
	Food	N: Denny's, Waffle & Steak
	Lodg	N: Adams Mark, AmeriSuites, Baymont Inn, Fairfield Inn, La Quinta Inn♥, Motel 6♥, Residence Inn, Wellesley Inn
	Other	N: Indianapolis Int'l Airport✈
77		**Holt Rd, Indianapolis**
	Gas	S: Shell
	Food	S: McDonald's
	TServ	S: Cummins, Discover Volvo Trucks, Ford, Fruehauf, Kenworth of Indianapolis
78		**Harding St, to Downtown**
79A		**West St, S Capitol Ave (EB)** **Capitol Ave, S Missouri St (WB)**
79B		**Illinois St, W McCarty St**
(80)		**Jct I-65S, to Louisville**
83A		**Michigan St, Ohio St, Fletcher Ave, Indianapolis**
(83B)		**Jct I-65N, to Chicago**
85AB		**Rural St, Keystone Ave (WB)**
	Gas	N: Amoco
		S: Marathon
85A		**Rural St (EB)**
85B		**Rural St, Keystone Way (EB)**
87		**Emerson Ave**
	Gas	N: BP, Speedway
	Food	N: McDonald's/BP
89		**Shadeland Ave, 21st St, Jct I-465, (fr EB)**
	Gas	S: Circle K, Shell, Speedway
	Food	N: Bob Evans, Waffle House
		S: Black Angus, Burger King, Damon's, Red Lobster, Subway, Wendy's
	Lodg	N: Comfort Inn, Hampton Inn, Motel 6

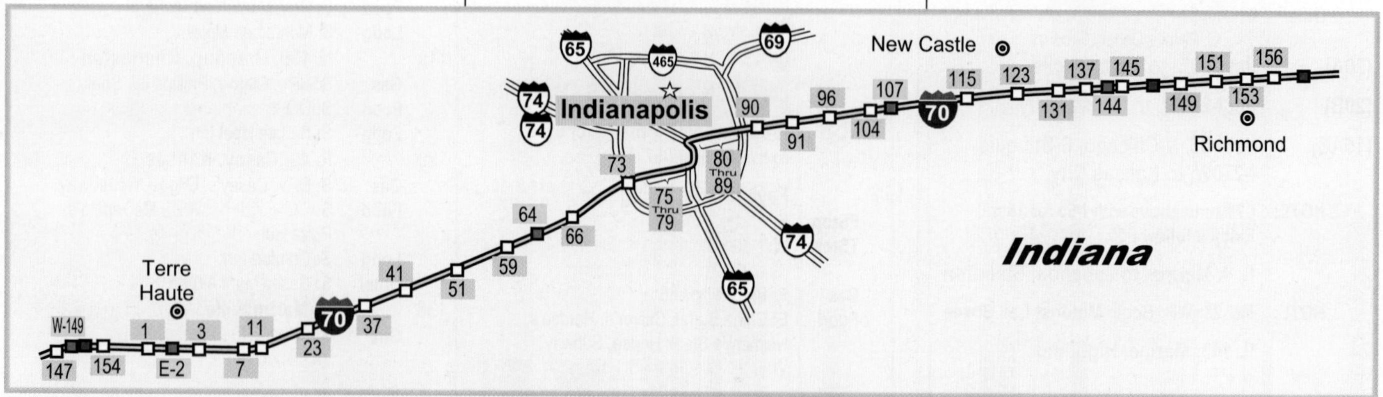

◊ = Regular Gas Stations with Diesel ▲ = RV Friendly Locations ♥ = Pet Friendly Locations
Red print shows large vehicle parking / access on site or nearby Brown Print = Campgrounds / RV PARKS

EXIT		INDIANA
	Lodg	S: Budget Inn, Fairfield Inn, Holiday Inn, Knights Inn, La Quinta Inn♥, Ramada Ltd
	Other	S: CVS
(90)		**Jct I-465, Louisville, Ft Wayne (WB)**
91		**Post Rd, E 21st, E 25th St**
	Gas	N: 7-11/Marathon S: BP, Shell
	Food	N: Cracker Barrel, Denny's, Joe's Crab Shack, McDonald's, Outback, Wendy's S: Hardee's, Taco Bell, Waffle & Steak
	Lodg	N: Baymont Inn, La Quinta Inn♥, Suburban Lodge S: Best Western, Days Inn, Dollar Inn, Quality Inn, Super 8
	Other	N: IN State Hwy Patrol Post S: ATMs, CVS, Grocery, Home Depot
96		**600W, Greenfield, Mt Comfort**
	TStop	N: Pilot Travel Center #30 (Scales)
	Gas	N: Gas America S: Shell
	Food	N: PizzaHut/Pilot TC, Burger King, Wendy's S: McDonald's
	Other	N: WiFi/Pilot TC, Heartland Resort▲ S: Indianapolis KOA▲, RV Center, RV Park▲
104		**IN 9, State St, Greenfield, Maxwell**
	Gas	N: Gas America S: Shell, Sunoco, Murphy
	Food	S: Applebee's, Arby's, Bob Evans, Burger King, Cracker Barrel, Hardee's, KFC, McDonald's, Starbucks, Steak n Shake, Taco Bell, Waffle House, Wendy's
	Lodg	S: Comfort Inn, Dollar Inn, Holiday Inn Express, Lee's Inn, Super 8
	Other	S: ATMs, Advance Auto Parts, Big Lots, Big O Tire, CVS, Home Depot, Walmart sc
(107)		**Rest Area (Both dir)** (RR, Phones, Pic, Vend, RVDump)
115		**IN 109, Knightstown, Wilkinson**
	TStop	N: Gas America #43 (Scales)
	Food	N: Rest/GA, Burger King
	Other	N: CB/Laundry/RVDump/GA
123		**IN 3, Spiceland, New Castle**
	FStop	S: BP
	TStop	S: Flying J Travel Plaza #5111 (Scales)
	Gas	N: Shell, Speedway, Murphy S: Marathon, Phillips 66
	Food	N: Denny's, McDonald's S: Rest/FastFood/FJ TP
	Lodg	N: All American Inn, Days Inn, Holiday Inn Express
	TServ	N: Hartley Truck Parts S: Hopkins Towing
	Med	N: + Hospital
	Other	N: ATMs, CarQuest, Walmart, RV Park▲ S: Laundry/WiFi/RVDump/LP/FJ TP
131		**Wilbur Wright Rd, New Lisbon**
	TStop	S: Hoosier Heartland Travel Plaza/ Marathon (Scales)
	Food	S: KFC/TacoBell/Hoosier TP
	TServ	S: Hoosier TP/Tires
	Other	S: New Lisbon Family Campground▲
137		**IN 1, Cambridge City, Connersville, Hagerstown**
	FStop	S: Crazy D's/Clark (Scales)
	Gas	S: Gas America, Shell
	Food	S: Rest/Crazy D's, Burger King, McDonald's

Personal Notes

EXIT		INDIANA
	TServ	S: Crazy D's/Tires
	Other	S: Laundry/Crazy D's, to appr 16mi: Whitewater River Campground▲
(144)		**Rest Area (Both dir)** (RR, Phones, Picnic, Vend)
145		**Centerville Rd, Centerville**
	Gas	N: BP
	Food	N: DQ/Stuckey's/BP
	Lodg	N: Super 8
	TServ	N: Goodyear
(148)		**Weigh Station (Both dir)**
149A		**IN 38S, Williamsburg Pike**
	Other	S: Tom Raper RV Center
149B		**US 35N, IN 38N, Richmond**
	TStop	N: Love's Travel Stop #222 (Scales)
	Food	N: Hardee's/Love's TS
	Other	N: Laundry/WiFi/RVDump/Love's TS S: RV Center
151		**US 27, Chester Blvd, Richmond, to Fountain City, Chester (WB)**
	Other	N: Richmond KOA▲, RV Center
151AB		**US 27, Chester Blvd, Richmond, to Fountain City, Chester (EB)**
	Gas	S: Meijer◊, Speedway, Shell, Sunoco
	Food	N: Maverick Rest S: Bob Evans, Burger King, McDonald's, Pizza Hut, Subway, Wendy's
	Lodg	S: Comfort Inn, Super 8
	Other	N: Richmond KOA▲, RV Center
153		**IN 227, Richmond, Whitewater**
	Other	N: Deer Ridge Camping Resort▲, Grandpa's Farm Campground RV Park▲

EXIT		IN / OH
156A		**US 40, National Rd, Richmond, Lewisburg, OH**
	Gas	S: Shell, Speedway, Murphy
	Food	S: Applebee's, Bob Evans, Burger King, Cracker Barrel, Golden Corral, McDonald's, O'Charley's, Red Lobster, Ryan's Grill, Steak n Shake, Texas Roadhouse, White Castle
	Lodg	S: Days Inn, Holiday Inn, Hampton Inn, Lee's Inn, Knights Inn
	Other	S: ATMs, Firestone, Goodyear, Kroger, Lowe's, Pharmacy, Target, U-Haul, Walmart sc
156B		**US 40, National Rd, Richmond, Lewisburg, OH, New Paris, OH**
	FStop	N: Fuel Mart #604
	TStop	N: Petro Stopping Center (Scales)
	Gas	N: Highway Oil, Swifty N: Iron Skillet/PizzaHut/Petro SC
	TWash	N: Blue Beacon TW/Petro SC
	TServ	N: Petro SC/Tires
	Other	N: Laundry/BarbSh/CB/WiFi/Petro SC
(156)		**Weigh Station (WB)**

EASTERN TIME ZONE

NOTE: **MM 157: Ohio State Line**

INDIANA

OHIO

EASTERN TIME ZONE

(1)		**Weigh Station (EB)**
1		**OH 35E, Eaton (EB exit, WB reaccess)**
(3)		**OH Welcome Center (EB)** **Rest Area (WB)** (RR, Phones, Pic, Pet, Vend, Info-EB)
10		**US 127, Eaton, Greenville**
	TStop	N: Travel Center of America #11/BP (Scales) S: Pilot Travel Center #286 (Scales)
	Gas	N: Marathon
	Food	N: CountryPride/BKing/Subway/TA TC S: Subway/Pilot TC
	Lodg	S: Budget Inn, Econo Lodge
	TWash	N: TA TC
	Other	N: Laundry/CB/WiFi/TA TC S: Laundry/WiFi/Pilot TC
14		**OH 503, Lewisburg, W Alexandria**
	Gas	N: Sunoco◊ S: Lewisburg Food Mart/Citgo◊
	Food	N: Subway/Sunoco
	Lodg	N: Super Inn Motel
	Other	N: ATM, Golf Course, Grocery, RiteAid
21		**CR 533, Arlington Rd, Brookville**
	FStop	S: Speedway #1219
	Gas	N: Gas America S: BP◊
	Food	N: Subway/GA S: Arby's, DQ, KFC/Taco Bell, McDonald's, Subway, Waffle House, Wendy's
	Lodg	S: Days Inn, Holiday Inn Express
	Other	S: Dollar General, Family Dollar, IGA, RiteAid
24		**OH 49N, Brookville-Salem Pike, Brookville, Clayton, Greenville (EB, no EB reaccess)**
	Gas	S: Sunoco◊
	Other	N: Dayton KOA▲

◊= Regular Gas Stations with Diesel ▲ = RV Friendly Locations ♥= Pet Friendly Locations
Red print shows large vehicle parking / access on site or nearby Brown Print = Campgrounds / RV PARKS

EXIT		OHIO
26		**OH 49S, Salem Ave (EB), Hoke Rd, Clayton, Trotwood (WB)**
	Gas	N: Shell, Murphy◈
	Food	N: Bob Evans, Subway, Wendy's
	Other	N: ATMs, Radio Shack, **Walmart sc**, OH State Hwy Patrol Post, S: to Hara Arena
29		**OH 48, Main St, Dayton, Englewood**
	Gas	N: BP, Speedway, Sunoco◈, Valero S: Meijer◈
	Food	N: Arby's, Bob Evans, Perkins, Pizza Hut, Skyline Chilil, Taco Bell, Tim Horton's, Wendy's S: McDonald's, Steak n Shake, Subway, Tumbleweed SW Grill, Waffle House
	Lodg	N: Best Western, Hampton Inn, Holiday Inn, Motel 6♥, Super 8♥ S: Comfort Inn, Motel 6♥, Red Roof Inn♥
	TServ	N: Cummins Diesel Service
	Other	N: ATMs, Advance Auto Parts, Big Lots, Englewood Truck Towing, Family Dollar, Grocery, **McNulty RV Center**, O'Reilly Auto Parts, Pharmacy, Thunderbowl Lanes, S: Hara Arena, Meijer
32		**Dayton Int'l Airport, Vandalia**
	Other	N: Dayton Int'l Airport✈
(33A)		**Jct I-75S, to Dayton (All Serv at 1st Exit S, #60)**
(33B)		**Jct I-75N, to Toledo**
36		**OH 202, Old Troy Pike, Huber Hts**
	Gas	N: Shell, Speedway◈ S: BP◈, Sunoco◈, Kroger
	Food	N: Applebee's, El Toro, Pizza Hut, Ruby Tuesday, Steak n Shake, Subway, Taco Bell, Waffle House, Wendy's S: Arby's, Bob Evans, Burger King, CiCi's Pizza, Long John Silver, McDonald's, White Castle
	Lodg	N: Baymont Inn S: Days Inn, Hampton Inn, Holiday Inn Express
	TServ	N: Ed's Truck & Trailer, CAT, Western Ohio Freightliner
	Other	N: Auto Services, ATM, Cinema, Dick's Sporting Goods, Grocery, Hobby Lobby, Gander Mountain, Lowe's, PetSmart♥, Radio Shack, Staples, Target, Vet♥, S: ATMs, CVS, Cinemas, Kroger, OH State Hwy Patrol
38		**OH 201, Brandt Pike, Dayton**
	Gas	N: Marathon, Meijer S: Shell
	Food	S: Bob Evans, Denny's, McDonald's, Sonic, Tim Horton's, Waffle House, Wendy's
	Lodg	S: America's Best Value Inn, Comfort Inn,
	Other	N: Meijer S: ATM, **Walmart sc**
41		**OH 4, OH 235, Dayton Lakeview Rd, Dayton, New Carlisle**
	Gas	N: BP◈, Sunoco◈
	Food	N: McDonald's, Subway, Wendy's
(44A)		**Jct I–675S, to Cincinnati (EB)**
44B		**Medway (EB)**
(44)		**Jct I-675, to Cincinnati (WB)**
47		**OH 4N, to Springfield (EB exit, WB reaccess)**
	Gas	N: Speedway
	Other	N: **Enon Beach Campground▲**
48		**Enon-Xenia Rd, to OH 4, Enon, Donnelsville (WB exit, EB reaccess) (Access to Ex #47 Serv)**
52A		**OH 68S, Xenia**
	Other	S: to Springfield Beckley Muni Airport✈, Antioch College, **John Bryan State Park**
52B		**OH 68N, Urbana**
54		**OH 72, Limestone St, Springfield, Cedarville**
	Gas	N: BP◈, Shell, Speedway◈, Sunoco◈ S: Swifty
	Food	N: Arby's, Bob Evans, China Gate, Cracker Barrel, Denny's, Domino's Pizza, Hardee's, KFC, Little Caesar's Pizza, Long John Silver, McDonald's, Perkins, Rally's, Subway, Taco Bell/Pizza Hut, Wendy's
	Lodg	N: Comfort Inn, Days Inn, Hampton Inn, Holiday Inn, Quality Inn, Ramada Ltd, Red Roof Inn, Super 8
	Other	N: ATM, Advance Auto Parts, Auto Service, Big Lots, CVS, Clark State Comm College, Family Dollar, Kroger, Rite Aid, Walgreen's, Wittenburg Univ
59		**OH 41, S Charleston Pike**
	TStop	S: Prime Fuel Center
	Gas	S: BP◈, Clark◈
	Med	N: + Hospital
	Other	N: Mid OH Harley Davidson, Clark Co Fairgrounds/RVDump, OH Nat'l Guard, **OH State Hwy Patrol Post** S: Antique Mall
62		**US 40, E National Rd, Springfield**
	Gas	N: Rich
	Food	S: Pizza
	Lodg	N: Harmony Motel
	Other	N: Auto Services, Melody Cruise Drive-In Theatre, **to appr 2.5mi: Buck Creek State Park**, S: **Tomorrow's Stars RV Resort▲**, **Beaver Valley Resort▲**, **Crawfords Market & Campground▲**
66		**OH 54, N Urbana St, to US 40, S Vienna, Catawba, S Charleston**
	FStop	N: Fuel Mart #764
	Gas	S: Speedway◈
	Other	S: **Crawford RV Park▲**, **Beaver Valley Campground▲**, Golf Course, US Post Office
(71)		**Rest Area (Both dir) (RR, Phones, Pic, Pet, Vend)**
72		**OH 56, London, Mechanicsburg**
	Gas	N: Marathon
	Med	S: + Hospital
	Other	S: Auto Repair, Madison Co Airport✈, Madison Co Fairgrounds
79		**US 42, W Jefferson, London**
	FStop	S: Speedway #5360
	TStop	N: Pilot Travel Center #454 (Scales) S: Travel Center of America /BP (Scales)
	Gas	S: Sunoco◈
	Food	N: Arby's/TJCinn/Pilot TC, Waffle House, S: McDonald's, Taco Bell, Wendy's, Country Pride/Pizza Hut/Popeye's/TA TC, Subway/Speedway
	Lodg	S: Holiday Inn Express, Knights Inn, Motel 6
	TWash	S: Red Baron TW/TA TC
	TServ	S: TA TC/Tires
	Med	S: + Hospital
	Other	N: Laundry/WiFi/Pilot TC, Trailers S: Laundry/WiFi/TA TC, **OH State Hwy Patrol Post**
80		**OH 29, Mechanicsburg, Urbana**
	TServ	S: Truck Repair
	Other	S: **OH State Hwy Patrol Post**,
85		**OH 142, CR 7, Georgesville Rd, W Jefferson, to Plain City**
	Other	S: **to appr 6.5 mi: Alton RV Park▲**
91		**CR 3, Hilliard Rome Rd (EB)**
91A		**CR 3S, Hilliard Rome Rd, Columbus, Hilliard, New Rome**
	Gas	S: BP◈, Marathon◈
	Food	S: Bob Evans, Steak 'n Shake
	Lodg	S: Best Western, Country Inn, Microtel
	Other	S: **to appr 4 mi: Alton RV Park▲**
91B		**CR 3N, Hilliard Rome Rd, Columbus, Hilliard, New Rome**
	Gas	N: Shell, Speedway◈, Meijer◈, Murphy, Sam's

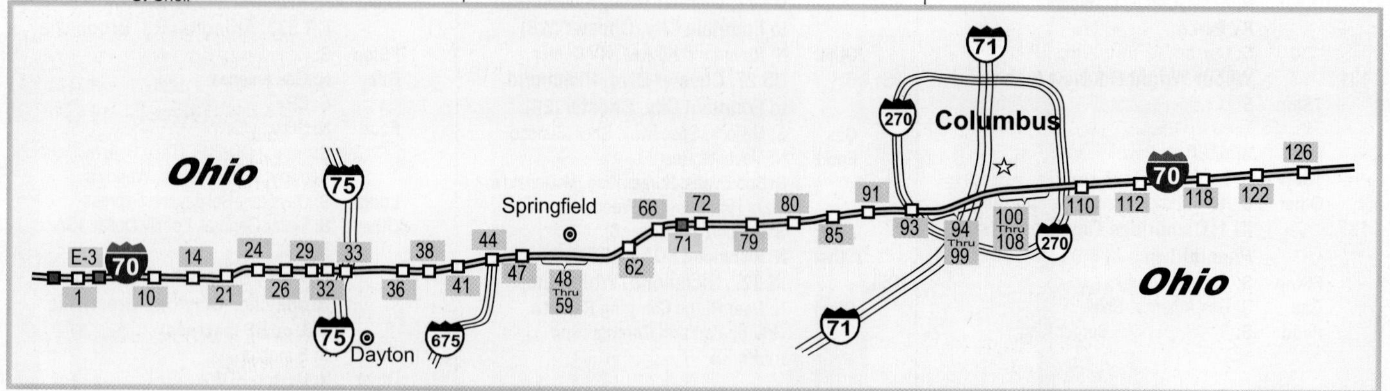

◈= Regular Gas Stations with Diesel ▲ = RV Friendly Locations ♥ = Pet Friendly Locations
Red print shows large vehicle parking / access on site or nearby Brown Print = Campgrounds / RV PARKS

EXIT		OHIO
	Food	N: Applebee's, Arby's, Big Boy, Buffalo Wild Wings, Burger King, ChickFilA, Chipolte Mexican Grill, CICi's Pizza, Cracker Barrel, Culver's, Fazoli's, Golden Chopsticks, Hooters, KFC, McDonald's, Outback Steakhouse, Perkins, Red Robin, Ruby Tuesday, Taco Bell/Pizza Hut, Texas Roadhouse, Wendy's, White Castle
	Lodg	N: America's Best Value Inn, Comfort Suites, Hampton Inn, Hawthorn Inn, Holiday Inn Express, La Quinta Inn♥, Motel 6♥, Red Roof Inn♥, Super 8
	Other	N: ATMs, Advance Auto Parts, Auto Services, Banks, Big Lots, Carwash, Cinema, Dick's Sporting Goods, Discount Tire, Firestone, Gander Mountain, Giant Eagle Grocery/Pharmacy, Kroger, Meijer, Midas, Petland♥, Radio Shack, Sam's Club, Starplex 10 Cinema, Target, US Post Office, **Walmart sc**
	NOTE:	**Through trucks carrying Haz-mat MUST use I-270 around Columbus.**
(93A)	**Jct I-270S, Col ByP, Cincinnati (EB)**	
(93B)	**Jct I-270N, Col ByP, Cleveland (EB)**	
(93)	**Jct I-270, Columbus ByPass, S - Cincinnati, N - Cleveland (WB)**	
94	**Wilson Rd, Columbus**	
	TStop	S: Pilot Travel Center #213 (Scales)
	Gas	N: Circle K/Marathon◈, UDF/Mobil S: BP, Shell, Speedway,
	Food	N: Subway/Circle K S: Wendy's/Pilot TC, Waffle House, McDonald's, Subway, Taco Bell, White Castle
	Lodg	S: Econo Lodge
	Other	S: Laundry/WiFi/Pilot TC, Auto Services, Carwash, Carwash/BP, Carwash/Shell,
95	**Hague Ave (WB)**	
	Gas	S: Sunoco
(96)	**Jct I-670 (EB, LEFT exit)**	
97	**US 40, W Broad St**	
	Gas	N: Valero◈
	Food	N: Arby's, Burger King, KFC, McDonald's, Pizza Hut/Taco Bell, Subway, Tim Horton's, Wendy's, White Castle
	Lodg	N: Knights Inn
	Med	N: + Mt Carmel Hospital
	Other	N: ATM's, Auto Services, CVS, Convention Center, Cooper Stadium, Nationwide Arena US Post Office, U-Haul, S: Auto Zone, Walgreen's, US Post Office
98A	**US 62, OH 3, Central Ave, Sullivant Ave (WB) (Acc to #98B)**	
98B	**Mound St (WB, diff reaccess)**	
	Gas	S: Marathon
	Food	S: Long John Silver, McDonald's
	Med	N: to + Mt Carmel West Hospital
	Other	S: Auto Repair, Buckeye Tire, Cooper Stadium
(99A)	**Jct I-71S, to Cincinnati**	
99B	**OH 315N, Dwntwn, Worthington (EB)**	
99C	**Rich St, Town St (WB)**	
100A	**US 23S, Front St, High St**	
	Gas	S: Shell
	Food	S: BW3's, Ludlow's, Plank's Rest, Tommy's Tony's Italian Rest, Victory Bar & Grill

EXIT		OHIO
	Lodg	S: Best Western, Clarmont Inn
	Med	S: + Grant Hospital
	Other	S: ATMs, Brewery District, Convention Center, German Village, OH Statehouse
100B	**US 23N, 4th St, Livingston Ave (EB) E Fulton St, US 23, US 33 (WB)**	
	Food	N: Brown Bag Deli, Cup O'Joe, Michael's Bistro, Max & Erma's, Roosters, Starbucks
(101A)	**Jct I-71N, to Cleveland**	
101B	**18th St (EB, No reaccess)**	
	Med	S: + Children's Hospital
	Other	S: Auto Zone, E Columbus Veterinary Hospital♥
102	**Miller Ave, Kelton Ave**	
	Med	S: + Children's Hospital
103A	**Main St, Bexley, US 40E (EB)**	
	Food	N: KFC, Starbucks,
	Other	N: Auto Services, CVS, Kroger
103B	**Alum Creek Dr, Livingstone Dr (fr EB, diff reaccess)**	
	Gas	N: BP, Speedway◈, Thornton's, Kroger S: Shell
	Food	N: Domino's, Subway, Taco Bell S: McDonald's, White Castle, Wendy's
	Med	S: + Hospital
	Other	N: Family Dollar, Kroger
105A	**US 33, College Ave, Lancaster (EB)**	
	Gas	S: 7-11/Citgo
105B	**James Rd, Bexley (WB)**	
	Food	N: Great Wall Chinese, McDonald's
	Other	N: Port Columbus, Int'l Airport✈
107	**OH 317, Hamilton Rd (WB)**	
107A	**OH 317S, Hamilton Rd S (EB)**	
	Gas	S: BP, Citgo◈, Sunoco◈
	Food	S: Arby's, Bob Evans, Burger King, McDonald's, Olive Garden, Papa John's Pizza, Pizza Hut, Red Lobster, Steak 'n Shake, Subway, Taco Bell, White Castle
	Lodg	S: Columbus Gatehouse Inn, Fort Rapids Resort Indoor Waterpark, Hampton Inn, Hawthorn Suites, Holiday Inn, Knights Inn, Residence Inn
	Other	S: ATM, Auto Repair, AT&T, Cinema, Dollar General, Eastland Mall, Fort Rapids Resort & Waterpark, Pep Boys, Petland♥, Pharmacy, Sprint, Staples, T-Mobile,
107B	**OH 317N, Hamilton Rd, Columbus, Whitehall (EB)**	
	Gas	N: Mobil, Sunoco
	Food	N: Arby's, Burger King, Church's Chicken, Golden Corral, KFC, Long John Silver's, Massey's Pizza, Pizza Hut, Wendy's, White Castle,
	Other	N: Advance Auto Parts, Auto Repair, Auto Services, CVS, **Cruise America Motorhome Rental**, Kroger/Pharmacy, NAPA, U-Haul, Walgreen's, Whitehall Animal Hospital♥
(108)	**Jct I-270, N to Cleveland, S to Cincinnati (EB)**	
(108A)	**Jct I-270S, to Cincinnati (WB)**	
(108B)	**Jct I-270N, to Cleveland (WB)**	
	NOTE:	**Through trucks carrying haz-mat MUST use I-270 around Columbus.**
110	**CR 117, Brice Rd, Reynoldsburg**	

EXIT		OHIO
110A	**CR 117, Brice Rd S (EB)**	
	Gas	S: BP, Meijer◈, Shell, Sunoco, Speedway, Kroger
	Food	S: Applebee's, Arby's, Boston Market, Burger King, Chipolte Mexican Grill, El Chico Mexican Rest, Genji Japanese, KFC, McDonald's, Perkins, Ruby Tuesday, Skyline Chili, Starbucks, Subway, Taco Bell Tim Horton's, Waffle House, Wendy's, White Castle
	Lodg	S: America's Best Value Inn, Comfort Suites, Econo Lodge, Motel 6♥
	Other	S: Advance Auto Parts, Aldi, AT&T, Auto Dealers, Best Buy, Burlington Coat Factory, Brush Animal Hospital♥, CVS, Cinema City, Discount Tire, Dollar Tree, Enterprise RAC, **Farber RV's**, FedEx Office, Hertz RAC, Hobby Lobby, Kroger, Lowe's, Magic Mountain Fun Center, Meijer, Michael's, NTB, PetSmart♥, Penske Truck Rental, Sam's Club, Sprint, Sports Authority, Target, U-Haul, US Post Office, Walgreen's,
110B	**CR 117, Brice Rd N, Reynoldsburg (EB)**	
	Gas	N: Speedway, Sunoco, Thornton's
	Food	N: Arby's, Bob Evans, Burger King, Genji Japanese Steak House, Pizza Hut, Popeye's Chicken, Roadhouse Grill, Ryan's Grill, Waffle House
	Lodg	N: Best Western, Days Inn, Extended Stay America, La Quinta Inn♥, Red Roof Inn♥, Super 8
	Other	N: Antique Mall, Auto Services, Family Dollar, Grocery, Home Depot, O'Reilly Auto Parts
112A	**OH 256E, Reynoldsburg Baltimore Rd, Pickerington**	
	Gas	S: Exxon, Speedway
	Food	S: Arby's, Bob Evans, Cafe Meditterranea, CiCi's Pizza, Cracker Barrel, KFC, Mexican Grill, Longhorn Steakhouse, McDonald's, Long John Silver, Steak n Shake, Wendy's
	Lodg	S: Best Western, Hampton Inn, Hawthorne Suites, Holiday Inn Express
	Med	S: + America's Urgent Care
	Other	S: Advance Auto Parts, Barnes & Noble, CVS, Cross Creeks Animal Hospital♥, Firestone, Giant Eagle Foods/Pharmacy, Golf Course, Kroger, Motorcycle Museum & Hall of Fame, NAPA,
112B	**OH 256W, Reynoldsburg Baltimore Rd, Reynoldsburg**	
	Gas	N: BP, Shell, Sunoco◈, Kroger, Murphy, Sam's
	Food	N: Chipolte Mexican Grill, KFC, Logan's Roadhouse, McDonald's, Noodles & Co, O'Charley's, Olive Garden, Panera Bread, Smokey Bones BBQ, TGI Friday
	Lodg	N: Country Inn, Fairfield Inn, Lenox Inn
	Other	N: ATMs, Best Buy, Gander Mountain, Golf Course, NTB, Radio Shack, Sam's Club, Sprint, Staples, T-Mobile, Target, Tire Kingdom, Walgreen's, **Walmart sc**,
112C	**Blacklick-Eastern Rd**	
	Gas	N: BP, Exxon, Speedway, Kroger
118	**OH 310, Hazelton Etna Rd**	
	Gas	N: BP, Speedway◈, Sunoco S: Duke◈
	Food	N: Etna Pizza, McDonald's/BP S: Subway/Duke

◈= Regular Gas Stations with Diesel ▲ = RV Friendly Locations ♥= Pet Friendly Locations
Red print shows large vehicle parking / access on site or nearby Brown Print = Campgrounds / RV PARKS

EXIT		OHIO
	Other	N: Etna Towing, Candle Shop, US Post Office
		S: RCD Rv's
122		**OH 158, Baltimore Rd, 5th St, CR 40, Pataskala, Kirkersville, to Baltimore**
	TStop	S: Flying J Travel Plaza #5030 (Scales)
	Food	S: CountryMarket/FastFood/FJ TP
	Lodg	N: Regal Inn
	Other	S: Laundry/BarbSh/WiFi/RVDump/LP/ FJ TP
126		**OH 37, Lancaster Rd, Hebron, Granville, Lancaster, Millersport**
	FStop	N: Certified #423/Citgo
	TStop	N: Pilot Travel Center #285 (Scales)
		S: Travel Center of America #39/BP (Scales) Truck-O-Mat (Scales)
	Gas	N: Starfire Express◈
		S: Sunoco◈
	Food	N: ChestersChicken/Subway/Pilot TC
		S: CountryPride/Popeye's/Sbarro/TA TC
	Lodg	S: Delux Inn, Red Roof Inn♥
	TWash	S: Truck-O-Mat
	TServ	S: TA TC/Tires, Eastern OH Truck & Trailer
	Other	N: WiFi/Pilot TC, LP/Certified
		S: Laundry/WiFi/CB/TA TC
129A		**OH 79S, to Buckeye Lake**
	TStop	S: Duke's Travel Plaza/BP (Scales)
	Gas	S: Citgo, Shell
	Food	S: Rest/Duke's TP, Burger King, Subway, McDonald's, Wendy's
	Lodg	S: Duke's Inn, Super 8
	AServ	S: Joe's Auto Service, A-1 Auto Parts
	TWash	S: Beechridge Truck Wash
	TServ	S: Duke's TP/Tires
	Other	S: Laundry/Duke's TP, Grocery, U-Haul, Tourist Info, State Park, Buckeye Lake/ Columbus East KOA▲
129B		**OH 79N, Hebron Rd, Buckeye Lake, Hebron, Heath**
	FStop	N: Speedway #9385
	Gas	N: Kroger
	Other	N: Kroger, Buckeye Outdoors
(131)		**Rest Area (Both dir) (RR, Phones, Pic, Pet, Vend)**
132		**OH 13, Jacksontown Rd, Newark, Thornville, Somerset**
	Gas	S: BP, Shell
141		**OH 668, Brownsville Rd, Brownsville to Gratiot (EB exit, WB reacc)**
142		**US 40, Mt Perry Rd, Gratiot (WB exit, EB reaccess difficult)**
	Other	N: Camping▲
152		**US 40, National Rd, Zanesville**
	Gas	N: BP, Exxon, Starfire◈

EXIT		OHIO
	Food	N: McDonald's, A&W
	Lodg	N: Super 8
	TServ	N: White GMC/Volvo/Cummins
	Other	N: to appr 6 mi: Campers Grover RV Park▲
153A		**OH 146W, State St**
	Gas	N: Speedway◈
		S: Marathon
153B		**Maple Ave, to OH 60N (WB, NO re-entry)**
	Gas	N: BP, Moto Mart
	Food	N: DQ, KFC, Papa John's Pizza, Wendy's
	Med	N: + Hospital
	Other	N: Colony Square Mall
154		**5th St, to US 40 (EB, NO re-entry)**
155		**OH 60, OH 146, Underwood St (WB), 7th St (EB)**
	Gas	S: Exxon◈
	Food	N: Bob Evans, Olive Garden, Red Lobster, Shoney's, Steak 'n Shake, Tumbleweed
		S: Cracker Barrel, Subway, Wendy's
	Lodg	N: Comfort Inn, Fairfield Inn, Hampton Inn
		S: AmeriHost Inn, Baymont Inn, Best Western, Econo Lodge, Travelodge
	Med	N: + Hospital
	Other	N: Wolfie's Family Camping▲, to Muskingun River Parkway State Park▲
		S: Fink's Harley Davidson, RiteAid,
157		**OH 93, to US 22, US 40, Zanesville**
	Gas	N: BP, Duke
		S: Marathon, Shell◈
	Food	S: Blimpie's, Subs Express
	Other	S: OH State Hwy Patrol Post, Zanesville KOA▲
160		**OH 797, CR 52, US 40, Zanesville, Airport, East Pike, Sonora**
	TStop	N: Love's Travel Stop #221 (Scales)
	Gas	S: BP, Exxon◈, Starfire Express
	Food	N: Arby's/Love's TS
		S: Denny's, McDonald's, Wendy's
	Lodg	S: Best Value Inn, Best Western, Days Inn, Holiday Inn, Red Roof Inn♥, Super 8
	Other	N: Laundry/WiFi/RVDump/Love's TS
		S: Flea Market, Zanesville Muni Airport✈, OH State Hwy Patrol Post
(163)		**Rest Area (WB) (RR, Phones, Picnic, Pet, Vend)**
164		**US 22, US 40, National Rd, Norwich**
	Gas	N: BP
	Lodg	N: Baker's Motel
	Other	N: Museum, Pottery Outlets, Shopping
169		**OH 83, Friendship Dr, West Rd, New Concord, Cumberland**
	FStop	N: 1mi N to US 40: Fuel Mart #706
	Gas	N: BP

EXIT		OHIO
	Food	N: Dairy Duchess, Domino's Pizza, Subway
(173)		**Weigh Station (Both dir)**
176		**OH 723, US 22, US 40, to Cambridge**
	Gas	N: Sunoco◈
	Lodg	N: Budget Inn
	Other	N: Civic Center, OH State Hwy Patrol
178		**OH 209, Southgate Rd, Cambridge**
	TStop	S: Pilot Travel Center #6 (Scales)
	Gas	N: BP◈, Shell, Kmart Express, Sheetz◈
		S: Speedway, Murphy USA◈
	Food	N: Bob Evans, Cracker Barrel, Denny's, DQ, KFC, McDonald's, Ruby Tuesday, Taco Bell, USA Steak Buffet, Waffle House
		S: Subway/Pilot TC, Burger King
	Lodg	N: Best Western, Budget Host, Cambridge Inn, Comfort Inn♥, Days Inn, Super 8♥
		S: AmeriHost Inn
	Med	N: + Hospital
	Other	N: 84 Lumber, Advance Auto Parts, Auto Zone, Auto Dealer, Big Lots, CVS, Dollar General, Kroger, Tractor Supply, U-Haul,
		S: WiFi/Pilot TC, Cinema, Cambridge Airport✈, King Pin Lanes, Museum, Spring Valley Campground▲, Walmart sc, Winery,
(180A)		**Jct I-77S, to Marietta, Charleston**
(180B)		**Jct I-77N, to Cleveland**
186		**US 40, OH 285, Wintergreen Rd, Old Washington, to Senecaville**
	FStop	S: Go Mart #57
	Gas	N: BP
		S: BP, Fuel Mart
	Other	N: to appr 4 mi: Barnyard Campground▲
		S: Fairgrounds, Camping▲, Seneca Lake
(189)		**Rest Area (EB) (RR, Phones, Picnic, Pet, Vend)**
193		**OH 513, Batesville Rd, Quaker City**
	TStop	N: Fuel Mart #727 (Scales)
	Gas	N: BP, Shell
	Food	N: Pizza/BP
	Other	N: R&R Auto & Truck Repair
198		**CR 114, Barnesville, Fairview**
	Other	N: Penny Royal Opera House, US Post Office
202		**OH 800, Barnesville, Woodfield**
	FStop	S: U-Save Fuel Mart
	Med	S: + Hospital
204		**US 40E, National Rd, CR 100, Bethesda (EB exit, WB reaccess)**
208		**OH 149, Belmont Morristown Rd, Belmont, Morristown, Bethesda**
	FStop	N: Two-O-Eight Fuel Plaza/BP

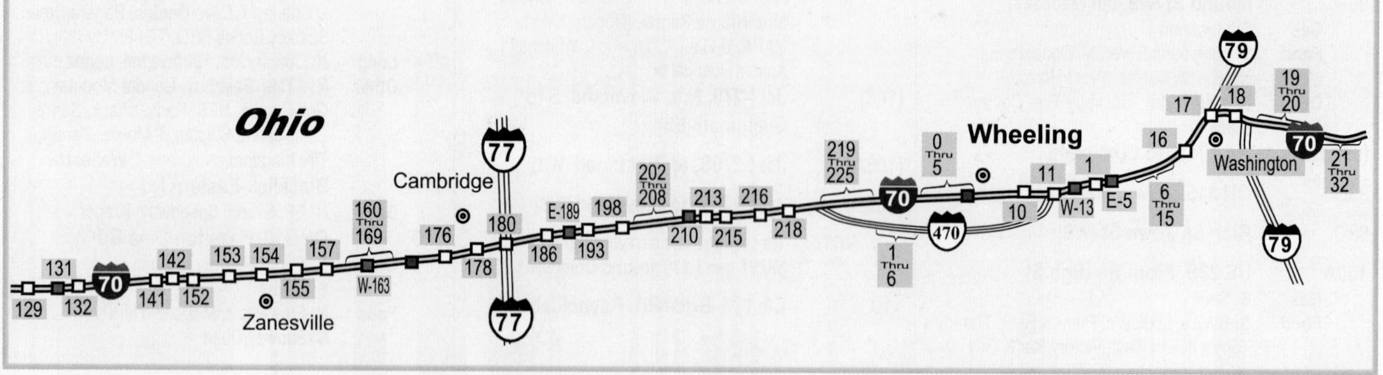

◈= Regular Gas Stations with Diesel ▲ = RV Friendly Locations ♥= Pet Friendly Locations
Red print shows large vehicle parking / access on site or nearby Brown Print = Campgrounds / RV PARKS

EXIT — OHIO

Gas — **S:** Chevron◈, Marathon
Food — **N:** Deli/McDonald's/208 FP, Quiznos, Schlepp's Family Rest
Lodg — **N:** Arrowhead Motel, Sunset Motel
TServ — **S:** Terex Truck Service
Med — **N:** + Morristown Clinic
Other — **N:** LP/208 FP, Cannonball Motor Speedway,
S: Golf Course, Valley Harley Davidson,

(210) **Rest Area (Both dir)**
(RR, Phones, Pic, Pet, Vend, Info-WB)

213 **OH 331, Airport Rd (WB), Flushing, US 40 (EB), St Clairsville**
Gas — **S:** BP, Marathon◈, Sunoco◈
Food — **S:** Mi Ranchito, Subway
Lodg — **S:** Twin Pines Motel
TWash — **S:** Valley 1 Auto/Semi Coin Wash
Other — **S:** Sheriff Dept, Alderman Airport✈

215 **US 40, National Rd, St Clairsville**
Gas — **N:** Citgo, Chevron
Food — **N:** Burger King, Domino's Pizza, Subway

216 **OH 9, St Clairsville**
Gas — **N:** BP
S: Marathon
Other — **S:** Fairgrounds

218 **CR 28A, Mall Rd, Banfield Rd, to US 40, St Clairsville, to Blaine**
Gas — **N:** BP◈, Citgo, Exxon
S: USA◈
Food — **N:** Applebee's, Arby's, Burger King, Denny's, Eat 'n Park, Outback Steakhouse, Pizza Hut,Red Lobster, Steak n Shake, Taco Bell, W Texas Steaks, Wendy's
S: Bob Evans, Bonanza, Cracker Barrel, Long John Silver, Longhorn Steakhouse, McDonald's, Starbucks, Undos Pizza
Lodg — **N:** Best Value Inn, Econo Lodge, Hampton Inn, Holiday Inn Express♥, Knight's Inn, Red Roof Inn♥, Super 8
S: Fairfield Inn
Med — **N:** + Urgent Care
Other — **N:** Auto Zone, Auto Dealers, ATMs, Dollar General, Dollar Tree, Grocery, Kroger, Lowe's, Sam's Club, Staples, **Walmart sc**, **RV Center**, **OH State Hwy Patrol Post**
S: CVS, Cinema, Kroger, OH Valley Mall

(219) **Jct I-470, to Washington, PA, Wheeling, WV**

220 **CR 214, National Rd, US 40, Bellaire-High Ridge Rd, Bridgeport**
Gas — **N:** Citgo, Exxon, Sunoco◈
S: Chevron◈, Marathon,
Lodg — **N:** Holiday Inn Express
S: Days Inn, Plaza Motel

225 **Marion St, to US 40, to US 250W, OH 7, Bridgeport, Martins Ferry**
Gas — **N:** Marathon, Starfire Express, Sunoco
S: Exxon, Gulf
Food — **N:** KFC, Papa John's Pizza, Pizza Hut, Wendy's
S: Domino's Pizza
Med — **N:** + Hospital
Other — **N:** Auto Zone, ATMs, Family Dollar, NAPA, Wheeling Downs, **to Austin Lake Park & Campground▲**

EASTERN TIME ZONE

NOTE: **MM 226: West Virginia State Line**

OHIO

EXIT — WEST VIRGINIA

WEST VIRGINIA

EASTERN TIME ZONE

0 **US 250, US 40, Zane St, Wheeling**
Gas — **N:** Exxon◈

(1) **Tunnel**

1A **US 40, WV 2, Main St, Wheeling**
Lodg — **S:** Best Western

1B **US 250S, WV 2, S Wheeling**

2A **US 40, National Rd, to WV 88**
Gas — **N:** Exxon, Sheetz, Kroger
Food — **N:** Bob Evans, Hardee's, Long John Silver, Papa John's Pizza, Perkins, Subway, TJ's
Lodg — **N:** Hampton Inn, Springhill Suites
Other — **N:** Advance Auto Parts, CVS, Kroger, NTB, Radio Shack

2B **Armory Dr, Washington Ave**
Gas — **N:** Exxon, Kroger
Food — **N:** Subway
Other — **N:** Kroger

(3) **Weigh Station (WB)**

4 **US 40, WV 88N (EB)**
Gas — **S:** BP, Exxon

(5A) **Jct I-470W, to Columbus (WB)**

5 **US 40, WV 88S, Wheeling, Elm Grove, Triadelphia**
Gas — **N:** Marathon
S: Exxon◈, Mobil
Food — **N:** Christopher's Cafe, Hoss's Steak & Seafood, Pizza Hut, Subway, Wendy's
S: Arby's, DQ, McDonald's
Lodg — **N:** Super 8
Other — **N:** Family Dollar, Grocery, Pharmacy,
S: Advance Auto Parts, Auto Dealers, ATMs, Laundromat, NAPA, RiteAid

10 **CR 65, Cabela Dr**
Food — **N:** Applebee's, Bob Evans, Cheddars Cafe, Cracker Barrel, Eat 'n Park, McDonald's, Olive Garden, Panera Bread, Wendy's
Other — **N:** Best Buy, BooksAMillion, Cabela's, PetCo♥, Target, **Walmart sc**

11 **CR 41, Dallas Pike Rd, Triadelphia, Wheeling**
TStop — **N:** Travel Center of America (Scales)
S: AmBest/Dallas Pike Fuel Center/Citgo (Scales)
Gas — **S:** Exxon, Mobil◈
Food — **N:** Rest/TA TC
S: Rest/FastFood/Dallas Pike FC, DQ/ Mobil
Lodg — **N:** Comfort Inn, Days Inn
S: Holiday Inn Express
TServ — **N:** TA TC/Tires
Other — **N:** Laundry/BarbSh/WiFi/TA TC
S: Laundry/**RVDump**/Dallas Pike FC

(13) **WV Welcome Center (WB)**
(RR, Phones, Pic, Pet, Vend, RVDump)
Note: RVDump Closed in Winter Months

EASTERN TIME ZONE

NOTE: **MM 14.5: Pennsylvania State Line**

WEST VIRGINIA

EXIT — PENNSYLVANIA

PENNSYLVANIA

EASTERN TIME ZONE

1 **Maple Ave, West Alexander**

(5) **PA Welcome Center (EB)**
(RR, Phones, Picnic, Vend)

6 **Old National Pike, US 40, PA 231, Claysvillle, West Alexander**
TStop — **S:** Petro 2 #83 (Scales)
Gas — **N:** Exxon
Food — **S:** Rest/Sbarro/Subway/Petro2
TServ — **S:** Petro2/Tires
Other — **S:** Laundry/WiFi/**RVDump**/Petro2

11 **Jolly School Rd (EB), Buffalo Church Rd (WB), to PA 221, S Bridge Rd, Washington, Taylorstown**
Other — **S: to** Washington Co Airport✈

15 **US 40, Chestnut St, Washington**
Gas — **S:** BP, Starfire, Sunoco◈, Valero
Food — **N:** USA Steak Buffet
S: Bob Evans, Denny's, Hardee's, Long John Silver, McDonald's, Pizza Hut, Wendy'
Lodg — **S:** Comfort Suites, Days Inn, Econo Lodge, Interstate Motel, Ramada Inn♥, Red Roof Inn♥
TServ — **S:** International
Other — **N:** Laundry, Grocery
S: Auto Repairs, ATMs, Banks, Dollar General, Franklin Mall, Gander Mountain, Pharmacy, Tires,Vet♥, Washington & Jefferson College, Washington Co Airport✈

16 **Sheffield St, Jessop Pl, Wilmington St**
Other — **S:** Pat's Auto & Truck Repair

17 **PA 18, Jefferson Ave, Washington**
Gas — **N:** Crossroads Food Mart, Get n Go
S: Nick's Service Station, Sunoco
Food — **N:** DQ, McDonald's
S: Barry's, Burger King, Domino's Pizza, Little Caesar's Pizza, Subway
Other — **N:** Carwash, Family Dollar, RiteAid
S: ATMs, Advance Auto Parts, Grocery

NOTE: **I-70 & I-79 run together below, Exits 19-21, Exit #'s follow I-70.**

(18) **Jct I-79N, to Pittsburgh**

19AB **US 19, Murtland Ave, Washington Rd**
Gas — **N:** BP, Sam's
S: AmocoBP◈, Exxon, Sunoco, Valero
Food — **N:** Applebee's, Arby's, Cracker Barrel, McDonald's, Outback Steakhouse, Panera Bread, Ponderosa, Red Lobster, Red Robin, Starbucks, Subway, TGI Friday, Texas Roadhouse
S: Bob Evans, Burger King, Chinese Rest, CiCi's Pizza, KFC, Long John Silver, McDonald's, Pizza Hut, Shoney's, Taco Bell
Lodg — **N:** Springhill Suites
S: Hampton Inn, Motel 6♥
Med — **S:** + Washington Hospital
Other — **N:** ATMs, Auto Dealers, Grocery, Lowe's, PetSmart♥, Sam's Club, Target, **Walmart sc**,
S: Big Lots, Firestone, Home Depot, Staples Washington Mall, **PA State Hwy Patrol**

20 **PA 136, Beau St, Washington**
Other — **S: Washington/Pittsburg SW KOA▲**

EXIT	PENNSYLVANIA
(21)	**Jct I-79S, to Morgantown, Waynesburg**
NOTE:	I-70 & I-79 run together above Exit #'s follow I-70.
25	**PA 519, Eighty Four, Glyde**
FStop	S: 7-11 #185/BP
Gas	N: GetGo S: Sunoco
Food	S: 7-11/Diner/BP
Other:	S: CB Shop/BP
27	**Brownlee Rd, Somerset Dr, Eighty Four, Dunningsville**
Lodg	S: Avalon Motor Inn
31	**McIlvaine Rd, to PA 917, Sprowls Rd, Bentleyville, Kammerer**
Food	N: Carlton Kitchen
Lodg	N: Carlton Motel
32A	**PA 917, Pittsburgh Rd, Bentleyville (Trucks Use Exit #32B)**
32B	**Wilson Rd, to PA 917, Bentleyville**
TStop	S: Pilot Travel Center #348 (Scales)
Gas	S: AmocoBP◈, Sheetz
Food	S: DQ/Subway/Pilot TC, Burger King, McDonald's
Lodg	S: Best Western, Holiday Inn Express
TWash	S: Blue Beacon TW/Pilot TC
Med	S: + Hospital
Other	S: Laundry/WiFi/Pilot TC, Advance Auto Parts, Grocery, RiteAid
35	**PA 481, Charleroi, to Centerville**
36	**Twin Bridges Rd, Charleroi, Lover (WB exit, NO re-entry)**
37AB	**PA 43, Mon Fayette Expwy**
39	**Maple Dr, Charleroi, Speers**
Gas	S: Exxon
Food	N: Lorraine's Family Rest
40	**PA 88, Pennsylvania Ave, Belle Vernon, Charleroi, Dunlevy**
Gas	N: Amoco, Sunoco
41	**PA 906, Main St, Belle Vernon**
42	**Fayette Ave, N Belle Vernon**
Gas	S: BP, Exxon, Pantry, Sunoco◈
Food	S: DQ, McDonald's/BP
42A	**Tyrol Blvd, to PA 906, Monessen**
43	**PA 201, Rostraver Rd (EB)**
43AB	**PA 201, Rostraver Rd, Belle Vernon, to Donora, Pricedale (WB)**
Gas	S: Exxon
Food	S: Burger King, Denny's, Hoss's Steak & Seafood, KFC, Little Caesars Pizza,

EXIT	PENNSYLVANIA
Food	N: Long John Silver, McDonald's, Pizza Hut Ponderosa, Starbucks, Subway, Wendy's
Lodg	N: Hampton Inn
Med	N: + Hospital
Other	S: ATMs, Advance Auto Parts, Big Lots, CVS, Grocery, Kelly Auto Parts, Lowe's, Radio Shack, Staples, **Walmart sc**
44	**Indian Hill Rd, to PA 201, Arnold City**
46AB	**PA 51, to Pittsburgh, Uniontown**
Gas	N: Exxon, BP◈ S: GetGo
Food	N: Burger King
Lodg	N: Sleeper Inn S: Holiday Inn, Relax Inn
Other	N: Auto Dealers, Cerini Harley Davidson,
49	**Dutch Hollow Rd, Turkeytown Rd, to PA 981, Smithton**
TStop	N: Flying J Travel Plaza (Scales), Smithton Truck Stop/Citgo (Scales)
Food	N: CountryMkt/FJ TP, Rest/Smithton TS
Lodg	N: Motel/Penn Stn TP, Motel/Smithton TS
TWash	N: Smithton, Southwestern Star Trucks, Trucks of W Pa
TServ	N:FJ TP
Other	N: Laundry/WiFi/RVDump/LP/FJ TP, Laundry/WiFi/Smithton TS
51AB	**PA 31, Mt Pleasant Rd, Ruffs Dale, West Newton, Mt Pleasant**
53	**PA 3010, Huntingdon St, Ruffs Dale, West Newton, to Yukon**
54	**Waltz Mill Rd, Ruffs Dale, Madison**
Gas	S: Rhodes Service Station
Other	N: Madison/Pittsburgh SE KOA▲
57	**Center Ave, New Stanton**
Gas	N: Exxon, Sheetz S: BP
Food	N: Bob Evans, KFC, McDonald's, Pizza Hut, Quiznos, Subway, Wendy's S: Cracker Barrel
Lodg	N: Budget Inn, Comfort Inn, Days Inn, Fairfield Inn, Quality Inn, Super 8 S: New Stanton Motel
TServ	N: Fox & James Freightliner
57A	**New Stanton, Hunker (WB)**
NOTE:	I-70 below runs with I-76/PA Turnpike, (TOLL), for 86 mi. Exit #'s follow I-76. EB: Begin Call Box Area.
(58)	**Jct I-76/PA Turnpike (TOLL)**
(75)	**Jct I-70W, US 119, to PA 66**
(78)	**New Stanton Service Plaza (WB)**
FStop	W: Sunoco

EXIT	PENNSYLVANIA
Food	W: McDonald's, King's Family Rest
91	**PA 711, Donegal**
Gas	S: BP, Exxon◈, Sunoco◈
Food	S: DQ, Hardee's/Pizza Hut/BP
Lodg	S: Days Inn, Donegal Motel
TServ	N: Freightliner
Other	N: Hidden Valley Ski Resort, Laurel Mtn Ski Resort, Seven Springs Ski Resort, **Laurel Hill State Park**
(94)	**Parking Area (WB)**
110	**PA 601, to US 219, Somerset**
Gas	N: Sheetz S: Exxon, Shell◈
Food	N: Hoss's Steak & Seafood, Pizza Hut
Food	S: Arby's, China Garden, Dunkin Donuts KFC, Long John Silver, McDonald's
Lodg	N: Dollar Inn, Economy Inn S: Best Western, Budget Host Inn, Days Inn, Holiday Inn, Hampton Inn, Knights Inn, Ramada Inn, Super 8
Other	N: Auto Dealers, Advance Auto Parts, Flight 93 Memorial, Somerset Historical Center, S: Harley Davidson
(112)	**Somerset Service Plaza (Both dir)**
FStop	Sunoco #7077/#7076
Food	S: Big Boy, Cinnabon, Hot Dog City, Roy Rogers, Starbucks N: Burger King, Cinnabon, Hot Dog City, Hershey's Ice Cream
(123)	**Allegheny Mountain Tunnel (Headlights on / Check Hazmat Restr)**
(142)	**Parking Area (WB)**
146	**US 220, to I-99, Bedford**
FStop	N: RG's Travel Plaza/BP, SAC Shop/BP
Gas	N: Sheetz
Food	N: China Inn, Denny's, Ed's, Hoss's Steak & Seafood, Pizza Hut, Wendy's
Lodg	N: Best Western, Econo Lodge, Quality Inn, Super 8, Travelodge S: Hampton Inn
TServ	N: Shaw Mack
Other	N: Bedford Airport✈, **to Shawnee State Park, Blue Knob State Park**
(147)	**Midway Service Plaza (Both dir)**
FStop	Sunoco #7078/#7079
Food	S: Cinnabon, Hot Dog City, Sbarro N: Cinnabon, Hot Dog City, KFC, TCBY, Sbarro, Starbucks
147/161	**US 30, Lincoln Hwy, to I-70E, Breezewood, Everett**
FStop	S: Breezewood BP
TStop	S: Travel Center of America /Mobil (Scales), Petro 2 (Scales)

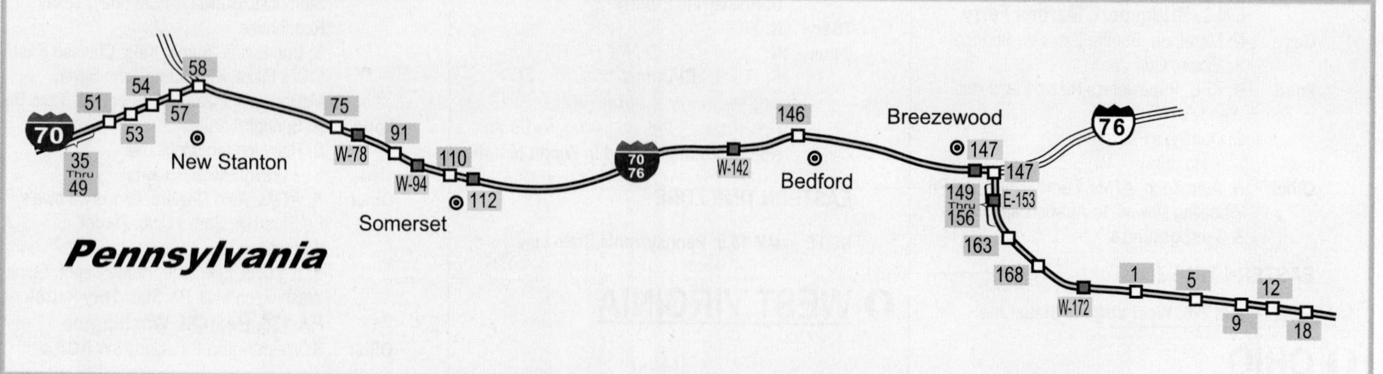

◈= Regular Gas Stations with Diesel ▲ = RV Friendly Locations ♥= Pet Friendly Locations
Red print shows large vehicle parking / access on site or nearby **Brown Print = Campgrounds / RV PARKS**

EXIT PA / MD

Gas S: BP◈, Exxon◈, Sheetz, Shell, Sunoco◈
Food S: Rest/DQ/Dominos/Subway/TA TC, Perkins/FastFood/Petro 2, Arby's, Big John's Steak & Buffet, Bob Evans, Bonanza, Burger King, DQ, Denny's, Hardee's, KFC, McDonald's, Pizza Hut, Taco Bell, Wendy's
Lodg N: Best Western, Econo Lodge
S: Comfort Inn, Holiday Inn Express, Quality Inn, Ramada Inn
TWash S: Blue Beacon TW/Petro 2
TServ S: TA TC/Tires, Petro 2/Tires
Other S: Laundry/BarbSh/WiFi/TA TC, Laundry/CB/WiFi/Petro 2

NOTE: **I-70 above runs with I-76/PA Turnpike, (TOLL) for 86 mi. Exit #'s follow I -76.**

149 **Breezewood Rd (EB), Lighthouse Rd (WB), to US 30W, Everett, Breezewood (difficult reaccess WB)**
Food S: Blimpie, Denny's, McDonald's
Lodg S: Redwood Motel, Wildwood Inn
Other S: **Brush Creek Campground▲**

151 **PA 915, Valley Rd, Crystal Spring**
Food N: Cornerstone Cafe
Other N: Fischer's Garage
S: **Brush Creek Campground▲**

(153) **Rest Area (EB)**
(RR, Phones, Picnic, Pet, Vend)

156 **PA 643, Flickerville Rd, Old Rte 126, Crystal Spring, Town Hill**
FStop N: Town Hill Travel Plaza/Sunoco
Food N: Rest/Town Hill TP
Lodg N: Days Inn/Town Hill TP

163 **PA 731S, Old Rte 126, Mill Hill Rd, Warfordsburg, Amaranth**

168 **US 522N, Great Cove Rd, PA 484, Buck Valley Rd, Warfordsburg**
Gas N: Exxon◈

(172) **PA Welcome Center (WB)**
(RR, Phones, Picnic, Pet, Vend, Info)

EASTERN TIME ZONE

NOTE: **MM 172: Maryland State Line**

PENNSYLVANIA
MARYLAND

EASTERN TIME ZONE

(1A) **Jct I-68W, US 40W, to Cumberland (WB, Left exit)**

EXIT MARYLAND

1B **US 522S, Hancock, Winchester, VA (WB, Left exit)**
Gas S: Citgo◈, Pit Stop Gas, Sheetz◈
Food S: Hardee's, Pizza Hut, Subway, Weaver's Rest
Lodg S: Best Value Inn, Super 8
Other S: Auto Service, Auto Dealer, Dollar General, Grocery, Laundromat, Pharmacy, Visitor Info, **Fleetwood Travel Trailers of MD**

3 **MD 144W, E Main St, Hancock (WB Left exit, diff reaccess WB)**
TStop S: Hancock Truck Stop/BP
Gas S: AC&T◈
Food S: Rest/Hancock TS, Hardee's, Pizza Hut
Lodg S: Motel/Hancock TS
Tires S: Hancock TS
Other S: WiFi/Hancock TS, Auto Repair

5 **MD 615, Millstone Rd (EB Left exit, NO immed EB reaccess)**

9 **US 40, National Pike, Big Pool, Indian Springs (EB, Left exit)**

12 **MD 56, Big Pool Rd, Indian Springs**
FStop S: Big Pool AC&T/Exxon
Other S: **Ft Frederick State Park**

18 **MD 68, Clear Spring Rd, Clear Spg**
Gas N: BP, Chevron
S: Exxon◈
Food N: McDonald's
S: Windy Hill Family Rest
Other N: Ski Area

24 **MD 63, Greencastle Pike, Hagerstown Williamsport, Huyett**
TStop N: Pilot Travel Center #150 (Scales)
Food N: Subway/Pilot TC
Other N: WiFi/Pilot TC
S: **Hagerstown/Antietam Battlefield KOA▲**

(26AB) **Jct I-81, N - Harrisburg, S - Roanoke**
Other N: Hagerstown Reg'l Airport✈

28 **MD 632, Downsville, Hagerstown**
Gas N: Shell
Food N: Bob Evans, Burger King, ChickFilA, Domino's Pizza, Pizza Hut, Shoney's, Western Sizzlin
Lodg N: Country Inn
Other N: Advance Auto Parts, Auto Zone, Auto Services, Grocery, **Yogi Bear's Jellystone Campground▲**

29 **MD 65, Sharpsburg Pike (WB)**

29AB **MD 65, Sharpsburg, Hagerstown**
FStop N: Sharpsburg Pike AC&T/Exxon

EXIT MARYLAND

Gas N: Sheetz, Sunoco◈
S: Shell◈
Food N: Longhorn Steakhouse, Pizza Hut, Starbucks, Subway
S: Blimpie/Shell, Burger King, Cracker Barrel, McDonald's, Waffle House, Wendy's
Lodg S: Sleep Inn♥
Med N: + Hospital
Other N: Auto Repair, Prime Outlets, **MD State Hwy Patrol Post**
S: Greyhound, **to** Antieam Battlefield

32AB **US 40, Hagerstown**
Gas N: 7-11, BP, Exxon, Sunoco
Food N: Bob Evans, Burger King, DQ, Denny's, McDonald's, Pizza Hut, Popeye's Chicken, Red Horse Steaks, Subway,Taco Bell, Texas Roadhouse
Lodg N: Comfort Suites, Days Inn, Hampton Inn, Holiday Inn, Quality Inn, Sheraton, Super 8
Med N: + Hospital
Other N: Auto Dealers, CVS, Dollar Tree, Goodyear, Grocery, Outlet Mall
S: Auto Dealers

35 **MD 66, Mapleville Rd, Hagerstown, Beaver Creek, Boonsboro**
Other S: **to appr 4 mi: Greenbrier State Park, To appr 6mi: Washington Monument State Park**

(39) **Rest Area (Both dir)**
(RR, Phones, Pic, Pet, Vend, Info)

42 **MD 17, Myersville Rd, Myersville**
Gas N: Exxon, Sunoco◈
S: BP◈
Food N: Burger King, McDonald's
Other N: **Greenbrier State Park, Gambrill State Park**

48 **US 40E, Frederick (EB, no reaccess) (Serv avail to WB via Exit #49, then N)**
Gas N: Chevron, Citgo◈, Exxon◈, Shell, Sunoco
Food N: Arby's, Bob Evans, Burger King, Denny's, McDonald's, Outback Steakhouse Pizza Hut, Red Lobster, Ruby Tuesday, Starbucks, Subway, Taco Bell, Wendy's
Lodg N: Comfort Inn, Holiday Inn
Other N: 7-11, Auto Services, CVS, Grocery, Home Depot, Tires, **to** Ft Detrick Mil Res

49 **US 40W Alt, Braddock Hts, Middletown (WB, no reaccess)**
Other S: **Washington Monument State Park**, Ski Area

52 **US 340W, US 15S (WB)**

52A **US 340W, US 15S, Charlestown WV**

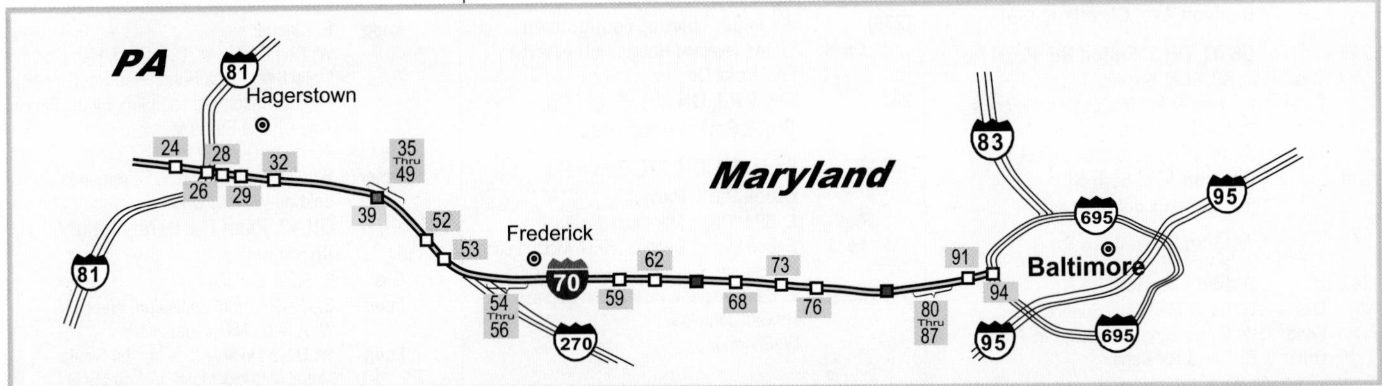

◈= Regular Gas Stations with Diesel ▲ = RV Friendly Locations ♥= Pet Friendly Locations
Red print shows large vehicle parking / access on site or nearby **Brown Print = Campgrounds / RV PARKS**

EXIT		MARYLAND
52B		**US 15N, US 40W, Gettysberg (EB)**
(53)		**US 15N, US 40W, Gettysberg (WB) Jct I-270S, to Washington (EB)**
54		**MD 355, Urbana Pike, to MD 85, Buckeystown Pike (EB), MD 355, to MD 85, to I-270 (WB), Frederick**
	Gas	**N:** Amoco, Costco **S:** Chevron, Exxon◈, Sheetz, Shell
	Food	**S:** Arby's, Bob Evans, Burger King, **Cracker Barrel**, El Paso, KFC, Longhorn Steakhouse, McDonald's, Papa John's Pizza, Popeye's Chicken, Ruby Tuesday, Subway, Waffle House, Wendy's
	Lodg	**N:** Travelodge **S:** Days Inn, Econo Lodge, Fairfield Inn, Hampton Inn, Holiday Inn Express, Sleep Inn
	Other	**S:** ATMs, Auto Dealers, Best Buy, CVS, Home Depot, Lowe's, Mall, Sam's Club, Staples, **Walmart**,
55		**Reich's Ford Rd, Smiths St, South St, MD144, Frederick**
	Gas	**N:** Citgo, Sheetz
	Other	**N:** Frederick Muni Airport✈
56		**MD 144, Baltimore Nat'l Pike (EB), Patrick St (WB), Frederick (WB reaccess difficult)**
	Gas	**N:** Citgo, Sheetz
	Food	**N:** Burger King, McDonald's, Taco Bell, Waffle House, Wendy's
	Other	**N:** Dollar General, **Triangle RV Center**

EXIT		MARYLAND
59		**MD 144W, Old National Pike, Meadow Rd, Frederick (WB)**
62		**MD 75, Green Valley Rd, New Market, Libertytown, Hyattsville**
	Gas	**N:** Mobil◈, Shell
	Food	**N:** Domino's Pizza, Dunkin Donuts, McDonald's
(64)		**Weigh / Inspection Station (EB)**
(66)		**Truck Parking (EB)**
68		**MD 27, Ridge Rd, Mt Airy, Damascus**
	Gas	**N:** 7-11, AmocoBP◈, Shell **S:** Exxon◈
	Food	**N:** Arby's, Burger King, KFC, McDonald's, Papa John's Pizza, Pizza Hut, Roy Rogers, TCBY
	Other	**N:** ATMs, Auto Dealers, Grocery Stores, RiteAid, Radio Shack, Safeway, US Post Office, **Walmart**, **S: Patuxent River State Park**
73		**MD 94, Woodbine Rd, Woodbine**
	Gas	**N:** Shell **S:** BP◈, Citgo
	Food	**N:** Dunkin Donuts, McDonald's, Pizza Hut, Subway
	Other	**N:** to appr 6mi: **Ramblin Pines RV Park▲** **S: Patuxent River State Park**
76		**MD 97, Roxbury Mills Rd, Hoods Mills Rd, Cooksville, Westminster**
(79)		**Weigh / Inspection Station (WB)**

EXIT		MARYLAND
80		**MD 32, Sykesville Rd, W Friendship, Sykesville, Columbia**
	Gas	**S:** Citgo
	Food	**S:** Subway
82		**US 40E, Baltimore National Pike, Marriottsville, Ellicott City (EB)**
83		**Marriottsville Rd, to US 40E (WB exit, NO reaccess)**
87AB		**US 29, to MD 99, Columbia, Ellicott City, Columbia Pike (WB, Left Exit) (All Serv South to US 40)**
	Gas	**N:** BP◈, Shell, Sunoco
	Food	**N:** Burger King, BBQ, Domino's Pizza, McDonald's, Papa John's Pizza, Subway, Wendy's
	Other	**N:** ATMs, Auto Dealers, Advance Auto Parts, Goodyear, Grocery, Home Depot, NAPA, RiteAid, **Walmart**, Tires, **Patapsco Valley State Park**
(91AB)		**Jct I-695, Baltimore Beltway, Towson, Glen Burnie**
	Other	**N:** Gas/Food/Lodg, Best Buy, Firestone, Grocery, Mall, Staples **S:** to Baltimore-Washington Intl Airport✈
94		**MD 122, Security Blvd, Woodlawn**

EASTERN TIME ZONE

NOTE: **I-70 begins/ends on Security Blvd**

MARYLAND

Begin Westbound I-70 from Baltimore, MD to Jct I-15, near Cove Fort, UT.

EXIT		OHIO

Begin Southbound I-71 in Cleveland, OH to Jct I-65 in Louisville, KY

OHIO

NOTE: **I-71 starts/ends in OH: I-90, Exit #170B & on I-490, Exit #1A**

EASTERN TIME ZONE

EXIT		OHIO
(247B)		**Jct I-90W, Jct I-490E**
247A		**14th St, Clark Ave, Cleveland**
246		**OH 176, Jennings Fwy, Jennings Rd Denison Ave, Cleveland (SB)**
245		**US 42, OH 3, Fulton Rd, Pearl Rd**
	Gas	**E:** BP, Shell, Sunoco
	Food	**E:** China Town, McDonald's, Wendy's
	Med	**E:** + Metro Health Medical Center
	Other	**E:** CVS, Cleveland Zoo, U-Haul
244		**Denison Ave, 65th St (NB, Left exit, diff reaccess)**
242		**W 130th St, Bellaire Rd**
242AB		**W 130th St, Bellaire Rd**
	Gas	**W:** Citgo, Marathon, Sunoco
	Food	**W:** Burger King, Little Caesars Pizza
	Other	**E:** Auto & RV Repair **W:** Auto Services, Discount Tire
240		**W 150th St, Cleveland**
	Gas	**E:** Marathon, Speedway◈ **W:** BP◈
	Food	**E:** Denny's, Deli, Rest/Marriott **W:** Burger King, Subway/BP, Taco Bell, Rest/Hol Inn
	Lodg	**E:** Marriott♥ **W:** Baymont Inn, Holiday Inn, La Quinta Inn♥
	Other	**E:** ATMs, Banks, Tires **W:** Auto Services, ATM, Bank
239		**OH 237, Airport (SB)**
	Other	**W:** Office Max, **to** Airport✈
(238)		**Jct I-480, Toledo, Youngstown**
	Other	**W:** to Cleveland Hopkins Int'l Airport✈, Ford Motor Co
237		**Snow Rd, OH 291, Engle Rd, Brook Park, Parma (NB)**
237AB		**Snow Rd, OH 291, Engle Rd, Brook Park, Parma**
	Gas	**E:** BP◈, Citgo, Marathon, Shell
	Food	**E:** Bob Evans, Denny's, KFC, McDonald's, Ponderosa, Subway
	Lodg	**E:** Best Western, Holiday Inn Express, Howard Johnson **W:** Sheraton
	Med	**E:** + Parma Medical Center
	Other	**E:** Auto Services, Carwash/Shell **W:** Ford Motor Co, Cleveland Hopkins Int'l Airport✈
235		**Bagley Rd, to US 42, Pearl Rd, US 291, Engle Rd, Berea, Middleburg Heights**
	Gas	**E:** Speedway **W:** BP◈, Speedway, Shell
	Food	**E:** Bob Evans **W:** Arby's, Back Home Buffet, Burger King, Damon's, Denny's, Friendly's, McDonald's, Max & Erma's, Olive Garden, Perkins, Pizza Hut, Panera Bread, Taco Bell
	Lodg	**E:** Clarion **W:** Comfort Inn♥, Courtyard, Hampton Inn Motel 6♥, Plaza Hotel, Red Roof Inn♥, Residence Inn, Ramada Inn, Studio Plus, Towneplace Suites♥
	Med	**W:** + SW General Health Center
	Other	**W:** Grocery, Pharmacy, Fairgrounds, Baldwin-Wallace Univ
234		**OH 42, Pearl Rd, Parma Heights Strongsville**
	Gas	**E:** Shell, Sunoco◈
	Food	**E:** House of Hunan, Italian, Wendy's **W:** A Slice Above, Jennifer's
	Lodg	**W:** Days Inn♥, Kings Inn, La Siesta Motel, Metricks Motel, Village Motel

◈= Regular Gas Stations with Diesel ▲ = RV Friendly Locations ♥= Pet Friendly Locations
Red print shows large vehicle parking / access on site or nearby **Brown Print = Campgrounds / RV PARKS**

EXIT **OHIO**

Other — **E:** Auto Dealer, Laundromat, Lowe's
W: Home Depot, **Walmart**

(233) — **Jct I-80, OH Turnpike (TOLL), to Toledo, Youngstown**

231B — **OH 82, N Royalton, Strongsville**
Gas — **W:** BP◈, Marathon◈, Sunoco◈
Food — **W:** Applebee's, County Kitchen, Panera Bread, Longhorn Steakhouse, Romano's Macaroni Grill, Red Lobster, Subway/BP
Other — **W:** Borders, Grocery, Iceland USA, Pharmacy, South Park Center, Target, Mall

231A — **OH 82, Royalton Rd, Strongsville**
Gas — **E:** Shell
Food — **E:** Rest/Holiday Inn
Lodg — **E:** Holiday Inn Select, Motel 6♥, Red Roof Inn

231 — **OH 82, Strongsville (NB)**

226 — **OH 303, Center Rd, Brunswick**
Gas — **E:** Shell◈
W: BP, Marathon◈, Sunoco◈, GetGo
Food — **E:** Pizza Hut
W: Arby's, Applebee's, Bob Evans, Burger King, CiCi's Pizza, Little Caesar's Pizza, McDonald's, Pizza Hut, Starbucks, Subway, Steak 'n Shake, Taco Bell, Tony Roma's, Wendy's
Lodg — **W:** Howard Johnson Express, Sleep Inn♥
Other — **E: Sirpilla RV Center/Camping World**
W: ATM, Dollar General, Grocery

(225) — **Rest Area (NB)**
(RR, Phones, Picnic, Pet)

(224) — **Rest Area (SB)**
(RR, Phones, Picnic, Pet)

222 — **OH 3, Weymouth Rd, Medina**
Other — **W:** Medina Co Fairgrounds,

(220) — **Jct I-271N, to Erie, PA (NB)**

218 — **OH 18, Medina Rd, Medina, Akron**
Gas — **E:** BP◈, Citgo◈, Shell◈, Sunoco◈
W: Speedway, SuperAmerica◈
Food — **E:** Blimpie's, Burger King, DQ, **Cracker Barrel**, McDonald's, Perkins
W: Arby's, Bob Evans, Denny's, McDonald's Pizza Hut, Wendy's, Waffle House
Lodg — **E:** Best Value Inn, Holiday Inn Express, Super 8♥, Travelers Choice
W: Hampton Inn, Motel 6♥, Red Roof Inn♥
Med — **W: + Immediate Care Center**
Other — **E:** Medina Muni Airport✈, **Avalon RV** & Marine, Bank, ATM
W: ATM, Banks, Century Harley Davidson, Grocery, Medina Co Fairgrounds, Pharmacy, Walsh Univ

(209) — **Jct I-76, to Akron, US 224, Lodi, Seville**
TStop — **W:** Pilot Travel Center #13 (Scales), Travel Center of America #15/BP (Scales)
Food — **W:** CountryKitchen/Subway/Pilot TC, CountryPr/BKing/Popeye/Starbucks/TA TC
Lodg — **W:** Super 8♥
TWash — **W:** Blue Beacon TW/TA TC
TServ — **W:** TA TC/Tires, Speedco
Other — **E: Maple Lakes Campground▲**
W: Laundry/WiFi/Pilot TC, Laundry/WiFi/ RVDump/TA TC

204 — **OH 83, Avon Lake Rd, Burbank, Lodi, Wooster**
TStop — **E:** Love's Travel Stop #332 (Scales)

EXIT **OHIO**

W: Pilot Travel Center #287 (Scales)
Gas — **E:** BP◈, Duke◈
Food — **E:** Hardee's/Love's TS
W: Wendy's/Pilot TC, Burger King, Bob Evans, McDonald's, Taco Bell
Lodg — **E:** Plaza Motel
Med — **W: + Lodi Comm Hospital**
Other — **E:** WiFi/Love's TS
W: Laundry/WiFi/Pilot TC, Prime Outlets of Lodi, Auto Dealers

198 — **OH 539, Congress Rd, W Salem**

(197) — **Rest Area (Both dir)**
(RR, Phones, Picnic, Pet, Vend)

196 — **OH 301, Elyria Rd, W Salem**
(NB exit, NO NB re-entry)

(190) — **Weigh Station (SB)**

186 — **US 250, Main St, Ashland, Wooster**
FStop — **W:** GoAsis Travel Plaza **(NO SEMIS)**
Gas — **E:** Marathon
Food — **E:** Perkins
W: PHut/Starbucks/Taco Bell/GoAsis TP, Bob Evans, Denny's, Jake's,Java Hut Cafe, McDonald's, Starbucks, Wendy's
Lodg — **W:** AmeriHost Inn, Days Inn♥, Holiday Inn Express, Super 8♥
Med — **W: + Samaritan Hospital**
Other — **E: to 7mi Hickory Lakes Campground▲**
W: ATMs, Dollar General, Grandpa's Village, Home Depot, UPS Store, **Walmart sc**, **OH State Hwy Patrol**, **to** Ashland Univ, Ashland Co Airport✈

176 — **US 30, Mansfield, Wooster**
(Addtl'l Serv 3.5 mi W on US 30)
Lodg — **E:** Econo Lodge, Ohio Hilltop
W: Best Value Inn/Mansfield Inn♥
Med — **W: + Hospital**
Other — **E: COE/Charles Mill Lake Park▲**, **to** Wooster College
W: RV Centers, to Mansfield Muni Airport✈

173 — **OH 39, Lucas Rd, to Mansfield**

169 — **OH 13, Mansfield, Bellville, Mt Vernon**
Gas — **E:** Marathon◈, Murphy
W: Marathon
Food — **E:** Applebee's, **Cracker Barrel**, Steak 'n Shake, Wendy's, Subway/WalMart
W: Arby's, Bob Evans, Burger King, McDonald's, Taco Bell
Lodg — **E:** AmeriHost Inn, Best Western, La Quinta Inn♥
W: Hampton Inn, Super 8, Travelodge♥
Med — **W: + Hospital**
Other — **E: Walmart sc, to Mohican State Park, Malabar Farm State Park**
W: OH State Hwy Patrol Post

165 — **OH 97, Bellville, Lexington**
Gas — **E:** BP, Shell◈, Speedway◈
Food — **E:** Burger King, Dutch Heritage Amish Rest, KC's Steak & Ribs, McDonald's, Subway
W: Wendy's
Lodg — **E:** Days Inn, Comfort Inn, Economy Inn, Knights Inn, Quality Inn
W: Mid Ohio Motel, Ramada
Other — **E: to Mohican State Park**, Ski Area, **to app 12mi: KOA▲**
W: to Mid Ohio Race Track

151 — **OH 95, Mt Gilead, Fredericktown**
TStop — **E:** Mt Gilead Truck Plaza/Duke

◈= **Regular Gas Stations with Diesel** ▲ = **RV Friendly Locations** ♥= **Pet Friendly Locations**
Red print shows large vehicle parking / access on site or nearby **Brown Print = Campgrounds / RV PARKS**

EXIT — OHIO

Gas E: Marathon
W: Sunoco◊, Shell◊
Food E: Gathering Inn Rest, McDonald's, Wendy's
Lodg E: Best Western
W: Knights Inn♥
Med W: + Hospital
Tires E: Mt Gilead TP
Other E: Laundry/Mt Gilead TP, **OH State Hwy Patrol Post**, ODOT Facility
W: **to appr 6mi: Mt Gilead State Park**, Mid-OH Race Track

140 — OH 61, Marengo, to Mt Gilead, Cardington
TStop E: Pilot Travel Center #455 (Scales)
Gas W: BP, Duke, Sunoco
Food E: Arby's/TJCinn/Pilot TC
W: Farmstead Rest, Subway/Sunoco, Taco Bell/BP
Other E: Laundry/WiFi/Pilot TC, **OH Country Music & RV Park▲**
W: 61 & 71 CB Shop, **Cardinal Center Campground▲**

131 — US 36, OH 37, Sunbury, Delaware
TStop E: Flying J Travel Plaza #5028/Conoco (Scales), Pilot Travel Center #14 (Scales)
Gas W: BP◊, Shell
Food E: Rest/FastFood/Flying J TP, Subway/Pilot TC, Burger King, McDonald's, Starbucks
W: Arby's, Bob Evans, **Cracker Barrel**, KFC, Long John Silver, McDonald's, Wendy's, Waffle House, White Castle
Lodg W: Days Inn, Hampton Inn, Holiday Inn Express
Med W: + Hospital
Other E: Laundry/WiFi/**RVDump/LP**/Flying J TP, WiFi/Pilot TC, Golf Course, Harley Davidson, **to appr 7mi: Autumn Lakes Family Campground▲**
W: Flea Market, **Alum Creek State Park, Alum Creek RV & Marina Campground▲**

(129) — Weigh Station (NB)

(128) — Rest Area (Both dir)
(RR, Phones, Picnic, Pet, Vend)

121 — OH 750, Polaris Pkwy, Gemini Pl, Columbus
Gas E: BP, Mobil, Shell
W: BP, Circle K/Shell, Marathon, Costco, Kroger
Food E: Bonefish Grill Buffalo Wild Wings, Dynasty Express, McDonald's, Polaris Grill, Quiznos Subs, Skyline Chili, Starbucks, Steak n Shake
W: Subway/Marathon, Applebee's, Arby's, Bob Evans, Carrabba's, ChickFilA, Chipolte Mexican Grill, Hooters, Max & Erma's, O'Charley's, MiMi's Café, Olive Garden, Qdoba, Quaker Steak & Lube, Red Robin, Red Lobster, Smokey Bones BBQ, Starbucks, TGI Friday, Texas Roadhouse, Tim Horton's, Waffle House, Wendy's
Lodg E: Best Western, Hampton Inn, Wingate Inn
W: Candlewood Suites, Comfort Inn, Extended Stay, Hilton Garden Inn
Med E: + St Ann's Hospital
Other E: Amphitheater
W: ATMs, Banks, Best Buy, Barnes & Noble, Costco, Kroger, Lowe's, Office Max,

EXIT — OHIO

Other E: PetSmart♥, Pharmacy, Polaris Fashion Mall, Target, **Walmart sc**,

NOTE: Haz-Mat Trucks MUST use I-270 around Columbus.

(119B) — Jct I-270W, Col ByP, to Indianapolis

(119A) — Jct I-270E, Col ByP, to Wheeling

(119) — Jct I-270, Columbus ByPass, E to Wheeling, W to Indianapolis (NB)

NOTE: Haz-Mat Trucks MUST use I-270 around Columbus.

117 — OH 161, Dublin Granville Rd, Columbus, to Worthington
Gas E: BP◊, Shell, Speedway◊, Sunoco
W: Shell, Speedway, Giant Eagle/GetGo
Food E: Burger King, China Wok, Golden Corral, KFC, Lone Star Steakhouse, Max & Erma's, McDonald's, Pastabilities, Outback Steakhouse, Red Lobster, Shell's Seafood, Subway, Super Seafood Buffet, White Castle
W: Bob Evans, Casa Fiesta, Don Pablo's, Domino's Pizza, Pizza Hut, McDonald's, Olive Garden, Otani Japanese, Waffle House, Wendy's
Lodg E: Comfort Inn, Days Inn, Holiday Inn Express, Knight's Inn, Motel 6♥
W: AmeriHost, Best Western, Clarion, Country Inn, Crowne Plaza, Econo Lodge, Extended Stay America, Hampton Inn, Rodeway Inn, Super 8
Other E: Advance Auto Parts, CVS, Firestone, Grocery, Staples, Walgreen's
Other W: ATM, Best Way Auto Care, Bowling, Cinema, Continent Mall, Family Dollar, Grocery, Laundromat, Walgreen's, **to** OSU Airport✈

116 — US 23, Morse Rd, Sinclair Rd
Gas E: BP, Shell, Speedway
W: Sunoco
Food E: Grandad's Pizza, Max & Erma's, McDonald's, Subway, Yogi's Hoagies
W: La Hacienda Mexican Rest
Lodg E: Howard Johnson
W: Best Value Inn, Motel 6♥
Med E: + Urgent Care
Other E: ATM, Auto Dealer, Auto Repair, CVS, Kroger, Pep Boys
W: Ohio School for the Deaf, **to** Anheuser Busch Sports Park

115 — Cooke Rd, to US 23, Columbus
Gas W: Sunoco
Other W: Auto Repair & Towing

114 — North Broadway St, Columbus
Gas W: Sunoco
Food W: Subway
Med W: + Riverside Methodist Hospital

113 — Weber Rd, Columbus
Gas E: Weber Rd Market/Auto Service
W: Speedway◊
Other W: Auto Services, NAPA

112 — Hudson St, Columbus
Gas E: Shell, Marathon
Food E: Wendy's
Lodg E: Holiday Inn Express
Other E: Auto Repair, Crew Stadium, Tires
W: Grocery, Lowe's, NTB

EXIT — OHIO

111 — 17th Ave, to US 23, Summit St
(Gas & Food approx 1mi W to Summit St)
Food W: McDonald's
Lodg W: Comfort Suites, Days Inn
Other W: Ohio Expo Center & State Fairgrounds, Crew Stadium

110B — 11th Ave, Columbus
Med W: + OSU Hospitals & Clinics
Other W: Ohio Expo Center & State Fairgrounds

110A — 5th Ave (SB)
Gas E: Sunoco
W: Citgo, Valero
Food E: KFC, McDonald's, White Castle
W: Wendy's
Other N: Auto Zone

(109A) — Jct I-670W (SB)

(109B) — Jct I-670E, Leonard Ave, Cleveland Ave (NB) (difficult reaccess)
Med W: + Veteran's Medical Center
Other E: **to** Port Columbus Int'l Airport✈
W: Fort Hays Army Res, Columbus St Comm College

109C — Spring St, Downtown
(SB, Left exit)
Other W: Columbus St Comm College

108B — US 40, US 62, Broad St, Oak St
Gas E: BP, Marathon
Other E: Franklin Park Observatory
W: Pro Care Automotive Service, ATM, **to** State Capitol, Supreme Court

108A — Main St, Main-Rich St Connector, Columbus (SB)
Food W: JP's BBQ, McDonald's
Other W: ATM, Pharmacy, Downtown

NOTE: I-71 below runs with I-70 . Exit #'s follow I-70.

(107/ 101A) — Jct I-70E, to US 23N, Wheeling (SB)
Jct I-71N, to Cleveland

100B — US 33, US 23, Fulton St (SB)
US 33, US 23, Livingston Ave (NB)

100A — Fulton St, High St (NB)

99C/99B — OH 315N, Columbus, Downtown
OH 315N, to Worthington

(99A/ 106A) — Jct I-70W, to Dayton, Indianapolis
Jct I-71S, to Cincinnati
(I-71 NB, Left exit)

NOTE: I-71 above runs with I-70 . Exit #'s follow I-70.

105 — Greenlawn Ave, Columbus
Gas E: BP, SuperAmerica
W: Marathon
Food W: White Castle
Med W: + Hospital
Other W: ATM, Cooper Stadium, German Village

104 — OH 104, Frank Rd, Columbus
Gas W: Certified, Mobil

NOTE: Haz-Mat Trucks MUST use I-270 around Columbus.

(101B) — Jct I-270W, to Indianapolis

(101A) — Jct I-270E, to Wheeling

◊ = Regular Gas Stations with Diesel ▲ = RV Friendly Locations ♥ = Pet Friendly Locations
Red print shows large vehicle parking / access on site or nearby **Brown Print = Campgrounds / RV PARKS**

EXIT		OHIO
	NOTE:	Haz-Mat Trucks MUST use I-270 around Columbus.
100		**CR 135, Stringtown Rd, Grove City**
	FStop	W: Speedway #1231
	Gas	E: BP
		W: BP, GetGo, Sunoco
	Food	E: Bob Evans, ChickFilA, Chipolte Mexican Grill, DQ, Longhorn Steakhouse, O'Charley's, Olive Garden, Panda Express, Red Robin, Roosters, Smokey Bones BBQ, Starbucks, Steak 'n Shake, Subway, White Castle
		W: Applebee's, Arby's, Burger King, Capt D's, CiCi's Pizza, Cracker Barrel, Damon's, KFC, McDonald's, Papa John's Pizza, Perkins, Ruby Tuesday, Starbucks, Taco Bell, Tim Horton's, Waffle House, Wendy's
	Lodg	E: Best Western, Drury Inn, Hampton Inn, Hilton Garden Inn, Holiday Inn, La Quinta Inn♥, Motel 6, Red Roof Inn♥, Super 8
	Lodg	W: Comfort Inn, Microtel, Saver Motel, Value Inn
	Med	W: + Urgent Medical Care, Urgent Dental Care
	Other	E: Best Buy, Discount Tire, Home Depot, PetSmart♥, Staples, TJ Maxx, Target, **Walmart sc**
		W: ATM, Auto Zone, Beulah Park Racetrack, Big Lots, CVS, Goodyear, Grocery, Kroger, Radio Shack, UPS Store, Walgreen's,
97		**OH 665, London-Groveport Rd, Groveport**
	Gas	E: Marathon, Sunoco, Kroger, Meijer
	Food	E: Arby's, McDonald's, Quiznos, Subway, Tim Hortons, Wendy's
	TServ	E: Peterbilt, ELW Co, RW Diesel Svc
	Med	E: + Urgent Care
	Other	E: Scioto Downs Racetrack
		W: ATM, Pharmacy, Eddie's Repair Service,
94		**US 62, OH 3, Harrisburg Rd, Grove City, Orient, Harrisburg**
	Gas	E: BP
		W: Sunoco◈
	Other	W: Beulah Park Track
84		**OH 56, Mt Sterling, London**
	Gas	E: BP, Circle K, Sunoco, Kroger
		W: Eddie's Super Service
	Food	E: Subway/BP
	Lodg	E: Royal Inn
	Other	E: Flea Market, Kroger, **to COE/Deer Creek State Park, Deer Creek Camping Resort▲**
75		**OH 38, Bloomingburg, Midway**
	Gas	W: Sunoco◈
69		**OH 41, OH 734, Jeffersonville, Solon**
	TStop	E: Flying J Travel Plaza #5046/Conoco (Scales)
	Gas	W: BP, Marathon, Shell◈
	Food	E: CountryMkt/FastFood/FJ TP
		W: Subway/Shell, Arby's, Wendy's
	Lodg	W: AmeriHost Inn, Quality Inn
	Med	E: + Fayette Co Memorial Hospital
	Other	E: Laundry/WiFi/RVDump/LP/FJ TP, **Walnut Lake Campground▲**, Barker's Towing, Flea Market, Home Works Outlet Mall
		W: Family Dollar

EXIT		OHIO
(67)		**Rest Area (Both dir) (RR, Phones, Picnic, Pet, Vend)**
65		**Old US 35 NW, to US 35, Jeffersonville, Washington CH**
	FStop	E: True North #757/Shell
	TStop	E: Travel Center of America #139/BP (Scales)
		W: Fuel Mart #643 (Scales), Love's Travel Stop #352 (Scales)
	Food	E: CountryPride/PizzaHut/Popeye/TA TC, Bob Evans, Burger King, Long John Silver/ Taco Bell, McDonald's, Waffle House, Wendy's, Werner's BBQ
		W: Hardee's/Love's TS
	Lodg	E: AmeriHost Inn, Hampton Inn, Super 8
		W: Budget Motel, Econo Lodge
	TServ	E: TA TC/Tires
		W: Fuel Mart
	Med	E: + Fayette Co Memorial Hospital
	Other	E: Laundry/WiFi/TA TC, Prime Outlets
		W: WiFi/RVDump/Love's TS
58		**OH 72, Sabina, Jamestown**
(54)		**Weigh Station (SB)**
50		**US 68, Wilmington, Xenia**
	FStop	W: Mt Pleasant Shell
	TStop	W: Pilot Travel Center #16 (Scales)
	Gas	W: BP◈
	Food	W: Subway/Pilot TC, DQ/BP, Max & Erma's, McDonald's, Wendy's
	Lodg	W: Budget Inn, Holiday Inn
	TServ	W: Goodyear
	Other	E: Clinton Field✈
		W: WiFi/Pilot TC, Convention Center, Wilmington College, Auto & Truck Repair
(48)		**Weigh Station (NB)**
45		**OH 73, Wilmington, Waynesville**
	Gas	E: BP, Marathon◈
	Med	E: + Clinton Memorial Hospital
	Other	E: **to Thousand Trails RV Park▲**, Wilmington College, Airborne Airpark✈
		W: Flea Market, **to Caesar Creek State Park▲**
36		**CR 7, Wilmington Rd, Oregonia**
	Other	E: **to Olive Branch Campground▲**, Fort Ancient State Memorial
(34)		**Rest Area (Both dir) (RR, Phones, Pic, Pet, Vend, Info)**
32		**OH 123, Lebanon, Morrow**
	Gas	E: BP, Citgo, Marathon, Valero
	Food	E: Country Kitchen
		W: Bob Evans, Skyline Chili
	Other	E: **Morgan's Riverside Campground▲**, Warren Co Fairgrounds, Ft Ancient
		W: **to Cedarbrook Campground▲**, Lebanon Raceway
28		**OH 48, Lebanon, S Lebanon**
	Other	W: **to** Lebanon Raceway, **OH State Hwy Patrol Post, to Cedarbrook Campground▲**
25AB		**OH 741, Kings Mill Rd, Mason**
	Gas	E: Shell, Speedway◈
		W: BP, Exxon
	Food	E: El Toro, McDonald's, Popeye's Chicken/ Shell, Ruby Tuesday, Taco Bell
		W: Arby's, Big Boy, Bob Evans, Burger King, GoldStar Chili, Outback Steakhouse, Perkins, Skyline Chili, Subway/Exxon, Waffle House, Wendy's

EXIT		OHIO
	Lodg	E: Comfort Suites, Great Wolf Lodge, Kings Island Resort
		W: Best Western, Hampton Inn, Microtel, Super 8
	Other	E: Cinema, Kings Island Amusement Park, **Kings Island Campground▲**
		W: CVS, Kroger, Kings Golf Center, The Beach Water Park
24		**Western Row Rd, Kings Island Dr (NB, Exit only)**
	Gas	E: Sunoco
	Lodg	E: Kings Island Resort, Great Wolf Lodge
	Other	E: Kings Island Amusement Park, Laser Kraze, **Kings Island Campground▲**
19		**Mason Montgomery Rd, Fields Ertel Rd, US 22, OH 3, Cincinnati**
	Gas	E: BP, Shell, Sunoco, Meijer◈, Speedway, Sam's Club
		W: Ameristop, BP◈, Marathon◈, Shell
	Food	E: Arby's, Bob Evans, Cracker Barrel, Golden Corral, KFC, Little Caesars Pizza, McDonald's, Olive Garden, Pizza Hut, Taco Bell, TGI Friday, Wendy's, White Castle
		W: Amon Steak House, Applebee's, Burger King, Carrabba's, Chipolte Mexican Grill, Fuddrucker's, GoldStar Chili, Lone Star Steakhouse, Mimi's Cafe, O'Charley's, Qdoba Mexican Rest, Red Robin, Romano's Macaroni Grill, Steak n Shake, Skyline Chili, Subway, Waffle House, Wendy's
	Lodg	E: Comfort Inn, Quality Inn, Signature Inn
		W: AmeriSuites, Best Western, Days Inn, Kings Luxury Inn, La Quinta Inn♥, Marriott, Quality Inn, Ramada Ltd, Red Roof Inn♥
	Med	W: + Children's Medical Center, +Jewish Medical Center
	Other	E: Auto Zone, Auto Dealers, Auto Repairs, Best Buy, Barnes & Noble, Costco, Firestone, Goodyear, Kroger, Office Max, PetSmart♥, Radio Shack, Sam's Club, Target, Tires, Vet♥, Walgreen's,
		W: ATM, Animal Hospital♥, Auto Repair, Borders, Grocery, Home Depot, Lowe's, NAPA, Staples, UPS Store, **Walmart sc**, Wild Oats Market
(17B)		**Jct I-275W, to I-75**
(17A)		**Jct I-275E, to OH 52**
	NOTE:	Through trucks MUST take I-275 around Columbus, OH.
15		**Pfeiffer Rd, Blue Ash, Montgomery**
	Gas	W: BP, Shell◈, Sunoco◈
	Food	W: Ambo Japanese, Applebee's, Bob Evans, Brown Dog Café, Buffalo Wild Wings & Rings, Subway
	Lodg	W: Clarion Inn, Courtyard, Crowne Plaza, Embassy Suites, Hampton Inn, Holiday Inn Express, Red Roof Inn♥
	Med	E: + Bethesda North Hospital
	Other	W: ATMs, Auto Services, Banks, Office Depot, Cincinnati Blue Ash Airport✈
14		**OH 126, Ronald Reagan Hwy, Cross County Hwy, to I-75**
12		**US 22, OH 3, Kenwood Rd, Montgomery Rd, Cincinnati, Madeira, Silverton**
	Gas	E: BP◈, Shell, Sunoco
		W: Chevron

◈ = Regular Gas Stations with Diesel ▲ = RV Friendly Locations ♥ = Pet Friendly Locations

Red print shows large vehicle parking / access on site or nearby Brown Print = Campgrounds / RV PARKS

EXIT — OHIO

Food E: Arby's, Bob Evans, Burger King, Chipolte Mex Rest, KFC/Long John Silver, LoneStar Steakhouse, Outback Steakhouse Panera Bread, Red Lobster, Ruby Tuesday Subway, TGI Friday, Wendy's
W: Burger King, IHOP, McDonald's, Max & Erma's, Potbelly's, Starbucks, Taco Bell
Lodg E: Best Western
W: Hannerford Suites
Med W: + Jewish Hospital
Other E: Auto Dealers, Firestone, Goodyear, Pep Boys
W: ATM, Auto Repair, Barnes & Noble, Firestone, Kenwood Town Center, Mall & Cinema, Staples,

11 Kenwood Rd (NB, diff reaccess) (Access Services at Exit #12)
Gas W: Chevron
Med W: + Hospital

10 Stewart Ave, Silverton (NB)
Gas W: Marathon◈

9 Red Bank Expwy, Fairfax
Gas W: Mobil, Speedway

8 Highland Ave, Ridge Ave (SB)

8C Ridge Ave (NB)
Gas E: BP, Meijer, Sam's
W: Marathon◈, Shell, Speedway
Food E: IHOP
W: Denny's, Golden Corral, McDonald's, Pizza Hut, Subway, Taco Bell, Wendy's
Lodg E: Motel 6
W: Howard Johnson
Other E: Auto Zone, Sam's Club, Target
W: Auto Services, Big Lots, Goodyear, Grocery, Home Depot, Lowe's, Office Depot, **Walmart**

8B OH 562, Norwood Lateral Expy (NB)

8A Ridge Ave S (NB)

7 OH 562, Norwood Lateral (SB)

6 OH 561, Williams Ave, Edwards Rd (SB), Edmondson Rd, to OH 561, Smith Rd (NB)
Gas E: BP, Shell, Speedway
W: Shell
Food E: Bonefish Grill, Boston Market, BW3, China Bistro, Don Pablo, Fuddrucker's, Gold Star Chili, J Alexander's, La Rose, Longhorn Steakhouse, Max & Erma's, PF Chang's, Starbucks
Other E: ATM, Auto Repair, Rockwood Commons and Pavilion
W: Midas

5 Dana Ave, Montgomery Rd
Other W: Cincinnati Zoo, Xavier Univ

3 William Howard Taft Rd, to US 42, Reading Rd (SB)
Other W: Cincinnati Zoo, Univ of Cincinnati

2 US 42, Reading Rd, Gilbert Ave, Dorchester Ave, Eden Park Dr (NB, Left Exit)

(1J) Jct I-471S, Newport, Ky (SB) Downtown, Riverfront, Third St (SB) Dwntwn, Riverfront, Second St (NB)
Other Cintas Center, Freedom Center, Paul Brown Stadium, Great American Ball Park

(1A) US 50W, River Rd Jct I-75N, to Dayton (SB)

EXIT — KY / OH

⬆ OHIO
⬇ KENTUCKY

NOTE: MM 193: Ohio State Line

EASTERN TIME ZONE

NOTE: SB I-71 below runs with I-75 to Ex#173. Exit #'s follows I-75.

192 5th St, Crescent Ave, Covington (SB) US 25, US 127, 9th St, 5th St (NB)
Gas E: BP, Speedway, Shell
Food E: Burger King, Goldstar Chili, Hardee's, KFC, McDonald's, Subway, Taco Bell, Waffle House, White Castle
Lodg E: Courtyard, Extended Stay America, Holiday Inn, Radisson
W: Hampton Inn
Other E: Riverboat Casino

191 9th St, Pike St (SB), 12th St (NB)
Med E: + Hospital

189 KY 1072, Kyles Lane, Ft Wright
Gas W: BP◈, Marathon◈, Shell◈, Speedway
Food W: Hardee's, Pizza Hut, Skyline Chili, Sub Station
Lodg W: Days Inn, Lookout Motel, Ramada
Other W: Grocery, Vet♥, Walgreen's

188 US 25, US 127, Dixie Hwy, Fort Mitchell, Covington
Gas E: Sunoco
Gas W: Marathon◈, Speedway, Shell
Food E: Little Caesars Pizza
W: Indigo Cafe
Lodg W: Days Inn, Holiday Inn, Rodeway Inn, USA Hotel
Other W: Museum

186 KY 371, Buttermilk Pike, Crescent Springs, Ft Mitchell, Covington
Gas E: BP◈, Citgo◈
W: BP, Shell, Sunoco◈
Food E: DQ, Oriental Wok, Papa John's Pizza, Subway
W: Arby's, Bob Evans, Bonefish Grill, Burger King, Chipolte Mexican Grill, Dominos Pizza, Goldstar Chili, Long John Silver, McDonald's, Miyajo Sushi & Steakhouse, Outback Steakhouse, Pizza Hut, Rima's Diner, Subway
Lodg E: Cross Country Inn, Drawbridge Inn♥, Super 8
W: Best Western
Other E: Banks, KY Speedway, US Post Office
W: Crescent Springs Animal Hospital♥, Dollar Tree, FedEx Office, Grocery, Hardware Store, Home Depot, Walgreen's

(185) Jct I-275, W to Cincinnati Airport, I-275E, to I-471

184 KY 236, Donaldson Rd, to Erlanger (NB)

184B KY 236W, Commonwealth Ave, Donaldson Hwy, Erlanger
Gas W: Ron's Svc Ctr, Speedway, Sunoco
Food W: Waffle House
Lodg W: Comfort Inn, Days Inn, Econo Lodge, Howard Johnson, Motel 6, Wingate
Med W: + Doctors Urgent Care
Other W: Home Depot, Lazer Craze, Lowe's, Penske Truck Rental, Staples, Walgreen's,

EXIT — KENTUCKY

Other W: Cincinnati-N Ky Int'l Airport✈

184A KY 236E, Commonwealth Ave, Donaldson Hwy, Erlanger
Gas E: BP, Marathon
Food E: Double Dragon, Rally's
Other E: US Post Office, **Police Dept**

182 KY 1017, Turfway Rd, Florence
Gas E: BP, Shell
W: Meijer◈
Food E: Big Boy, Lee's Chicken, McDonald's, New Wok, Ryan's Grill
W: Applebee's, Burger King, Cici's Pizza, Cracker Barrel, Famous Dave's BBQ, Fuddrucker's, Golden Corral, Longhorn Steakhouse, O'Charley's, Rafferty's, Shell's Seafood, Steak 'n Shake, Subway, Tumbleweed SW Grill, Wendy's
Lodg E: Clarion Inn, Courtyard, Days Inn, Fairfield Inn, Howard Johnson, Rodeway Inn, Signature Inn
W: Extended Stay America, Hampton Inn, Hilton, Hyatt, La Quinta Inn♥, Red Roof Inn, Springhill Suites, Studio Plus
Med W: + St Luke Hospital West
Other E: Big Lots, CVS, FedEx Office, Grocery, Office Depot, US Post Office
W: Beckfield College, Best Buy, Dick's Sporting Goods, Grocery, Home Depot, Laser Adventure, Lowe's, Meijer, PetSmart♥, Sam's Club, Target, Turfway Park Racing

181 KY 18, Burlington Pike, Florence, Burlington
TStop E: Travel Center of America/Sunoco (Scales)
Gas E: Speedway, Swifty
W: BP◈, Chevron, Shell
Food E: Arby's/PizzaHut/Popeye/Subway/TA TC, Waffle House
W: Applebee's, Chili's, Chipolte Mexican Grill, **Cracker Barrel**, Hooters, IHOP, Lone Star Steakhouse, O'Charley's, Red Robin, Taco Bell, Wendy's
Lodg E: America's Best Value Inn, Best Western
W: Microtel, Suburban Extended Stay
TServ E: Tires/TA TC
Med W: + Hospital
Other E: Laundry/WiFi/TA TC, Auto Services, Enterprise RAC, Vet♥
W: ATMs, Auto Services, Auto Dealers, City of Florence Golf Course, Florence Mall, Harbor Freight Tools, Kroger, ProCare Automotive Service, Staples, Verizon, Vet♥, **Walmart sc**,

180A Steinberg Dr, Mall Rd (SB)
Food W: Cathay Kitchen, China Max, Hardee's, Pizza Hut, Olive Garden, Old Country Buffet Skyline Chili, Subway
Other W: ATMs, Florence Mall, Kroger, Pep Boys, Staples, Walgreen's

180 US 42, US 127, Dixie Hwy, Mall Rd, Florence, Union
Gas E: BP◈, Speedway, Thornton's
W: BP, Chevron◈, Shell◈, Speedway
Food E: Bob Evans, Burger King, Captain D's, Dunkin Donuts, Frisch's Big Boy, Long John Silver, McDonald's, Pizza Hut, Red Lobster, Smokey Bones BBQ, Starbucks, Subway, Wendy's
Food W: Arby's, Burger King, McDonald's, KFC, Perkins, Ponderosa, Taco Bell, Waffle House, White Castle

◈ = Regular Gas Stations with Diesel ▲ = RV Friendly Locations ♥ = Pet Friendly Locations
Red print shows large vehicle parking / access on site or nearby Brown Print = Campgrounds / RV PARKS

EXIT		KENTUCKY
	Lodg	E: Holiday Inn, Knights Inn, Motel 6♥, Quality Inn, Super 8
		W: Ramada, Travelodge
	Other	W: Ace Hardware, Auto Services, Auto Zone, Barnes & Noble, CVS, Kroger, Midas, NTB, Pep Boys, **RV Center**, Tires Plus, U-Haul, Walgreen's
178		**KY 536, Mt Zion Rd, Florence**
	Gas	E: BP◈, Mobil, Shell, Sunoco◈
	Food	E: Goldstar Chili, Jersey Mike's Subs, McDonald's, Rally's/BP, Sonic, Steak n Shake, Subway
	Other	E: Bank, George's Car & Truck Repair, Goodyear, Harley Davidson, Kroger, Middendorf Animal Hospital♥, Pharmacy
(177)		**KY Welcome Center (SB)**
		Rest Area (NB)
		(RR, Phones, Pic, Pet, Vend, RVDump)
175		**KY 338, Richwood Dr, Walton**
	TStop	E: Travel Center of America/BP (Scales), Pilot Travel Center #278 (Scales)
		W: Pilot Travel Center #321 (Scales)
	Gas	W: BP, Shell◈
	Food	E: Rest/TacoBell/TA TC, Subway/Pilot, Arby's, Burger King, White Castle
	Food	W: Subway/Pilot TC, McDonald's, Skyline Chili, Waffle House, Wendy's/BP
	Lodg	E: Comfort Inn, Holiday Inn Express
		W: Econo Lodge
	TServ	E: TA TC/Tires
	Other	E: Laundry/WiFi/TA TC, WiFi/Pilot TC, **RV Park▲**, to Richwood Flea Market
		W: WiFi/Pilot TC, **to Big Bone Lick State Park▲**
(173/ 77)		**Jct I-71S, to Louisville**
		Jct I-75S, to Lexington
	NOTE:	**I-71 above runs with I-75 to OH. Exit #'s follow I-75.**
(75)		**Weigh Station (SB)**
72		**KY 14, Verona Mudlick Rd, Verona**
	Gas	E: BP◈, Chevron◈
	Other	E: U-Haul, **to appr 6mi: Oak Creek Campground▲**
62		**US 127, Warsaw, to Glencoe**
	FStop	W: Marathon
	TStop	E: Exit 62 Fuel Stop & Restaurant
	Food	E: Rest/Exit 62 FS
		W: Rest/Marathon
	Lodg	W: 127 Motel
	TServ	E: Exit 62 FS/Tires
57		**KY 35, Sparta, Warsaw**
	Gas	E: Marathon◈
		W: BP◈
	Lodg	W: Ramada Inn♥
	Other	E: **Sparta Campground▲**
		W: KY Speedway
55		**KY 1130, Sparta**
	TStop	W: Love's Travel Stop (Scales)
	Food	W: McDonald's/Subway/Love's TS
	Other	E: **Sparta Campground▲**
		W: KY Speedway
44		**KY 227, Carrollton, Indian Hills**
	Gas	W: BP◈, Chevron◈, Marathon, Shell, USA◈, Kroger, Murphy USA
	Food	W: Arby's, Burger King, KFC, Long John Silver, McDonald's, Sonic, Subway, Taco Bell, Waffle House
	Lodg	W: Best Western, Comfort Inn, Econo Lodge, Hampton Inn, Holiday Inn Express, Super 8

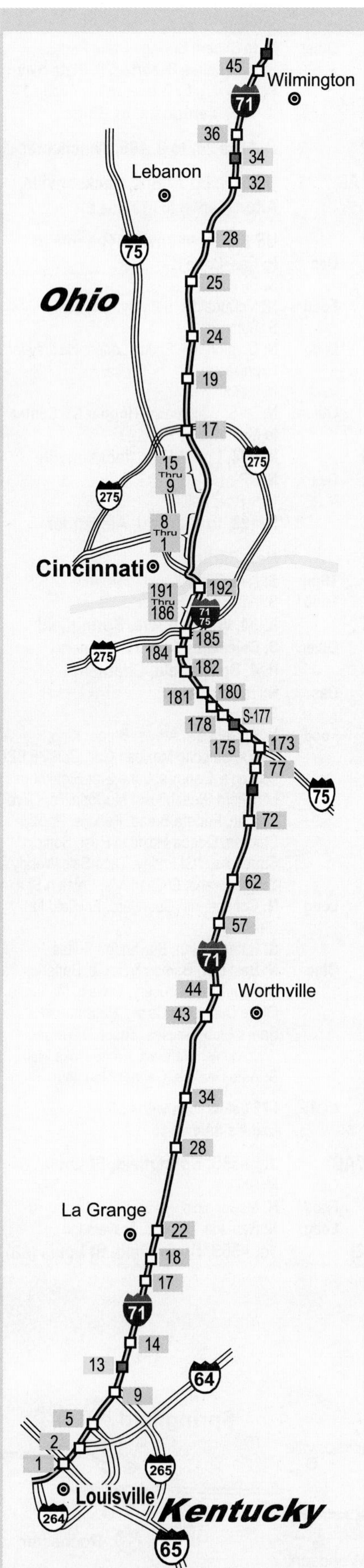

EXIT		KENTUCKY
	Med	W: + to Carroll Co Memorial Hospital
	Other	W: Auto Zone, Carroll Co Animal Clinic♥, Dollar General, Flea Market, Kroger, Radio Shack, RiteAid, SavALot, Wallace Veterinary Clinic♥, **Walmart sc**,
43		**KY 389, Carrollton, to KY 55**
34		**US 421, Campbellsburg, Bedford**
	Gas	W: Citgo◈, Marathon◈
28		**KY 153, Pendleton, KY 146, to US 42, Newcastle, Sulphur**
	TStop	E: Pilot Travel Center #50 (Scales)
		W: Pilot Travel Center #440 (Scales)
	Gas	E: Marathon◈
	Food	E/W Subway/McDonald's/Pilot TC
	TServ	E: Dan's Truck & Diesel
		W: Pilot TC/Tires, SpeedCo
	Other	E: Laundry/WiFi/Pilot TC, **to Lake Jericho Rec Area▲**
		W: Laundry/WiFi/Pilot TC
22		**KY 53, S 1st St, La Grange**
	Gas	E: Marathon, Super America, Kroger
		W: Chevron◈, Shell, Swifty
	Food	E: Applebee's, Burger King, Papa John's Pizza, Rally's, Sonic, Subway, Waffle House, Wendy's
		W: Arby's, **Cracker Barrel**, DQ, Domino's Pizza, Hometown Pizza, KFC, Long John Silver, McDonald's, Subway, Taco Bell
	Lodg	E: Best Western, Days Inn, Holiday Inn Ex
		W: Comfort Suites, Super 8
	Med	**E: + First Stop Urgent Care, + Baptist Hospital Northeast**
	Other	E: AT&T, Big O Tire, Car Wash, Dollar General, Eagle Creek Golf Course, Kroger, Radio Shack, Walgreen's, **Walmart sc**,
		W: Advance Auto Parts, Auto Services, Flea Market, Grocery, NAPA, RiteAid, SavALot, Tires, US Post Office, Vet♥
18		**KY 393, La Grange, Buckner**
	Gas	W: Marathon
17		**KY 146, Buckner, Crestwood, Pewee Valley**
	Gas	W: Shell◈, Thornton's◈
14		**KY 329 Crestwood, Pewee Valley**
	Gas	E: Chevron, Shell
	Food	E: Starbucks
(13)		**Rest Area (Both dir)**
		(RR, Phones, Picnic, Pet, Vend)
(9B)		**Jct I-265W, KY 841, to I-65**
(9A)		**Jct I-265E, KY 841, to I-65**
	Gas	E: Speedway
	Lodg	E: Hilton Garden Inn
	Other	E: **to Sawyer State Park**
(5)		**Jct I-264, Watterson Expy (SB Left exit)**
2		**Zorn Ave, Louisville**
	Gas	W: BP, Chevron
	Food	W: Kingfish Rest, Rest/Ramada Inn
	Lodg	W: Ramada Inn
	Med	E: + VA Hospital
(1B)		**Jct I-65, N to Indianapolis, S to Nashville (Left Exit)**
(1A)		**Jct I-64W, to St Louis**

KENTUCKY

Begin Northbound I-71 from Louisville, KY to Cleveland, OH.

◈ = Regular Gas Stations with Diesel ▲ = RV Friendly Locations ♥ = Pet Friendly Locations
Red print shows large vehicle parking / access on site or nearby Brown Print = Campgrounds / RV PARKS

EXIT	MO / IL
	Begin Eastbound I-72 from Hannibal, MO to near Jct I-57 in Champaign, IL.

MISSOURI

NOTE: I-72 begins/ends near I-57, Ex #235B in IL

CENTRAL TIME ZONE

156 US 61, US 36 Bus, Hannibal, to New London, Palmyra
- Gas N: BP, Conoco◈, Murphy
  S: Shell◈, Ayerco Conv Store
- Food N: Burger King, Country Kitchen, Golden Corral, Hardee's, McDonald's, Papa John's Pizza, Pizza Hut, Sonic, Subway, Taco Bell
  S: DQ, Domino's Pizza, Gran Rio Mex, KFC, Wendy's
- Lodg S: Comfort Inn, Days Inn, Econo Lodge, Holiday Inn Express, Howard Johnson, Super 8♥
- Other N: ATMs, Banks, Big Lots, Dollar General, Dollar Tree, Kroger, **Walmart sc**, **to Bay View Campers Park▲**
  S: Auto Zone, ATMs, Banks, Family Dollar, Grocery, O'Reilly Auto Parts, Pharmacy, Walgreen's, **Injun Joe Campground▲**

157 US 61 Bus, US 36 Bus, MO N, MO 79, Hannibal, Palmyra
- Gas N: BP, Conoco, Shell, Ayerco P66
- Lodg N: Super 7, Travelodge
- Other S: Pharmacy, **to American RV Center**

CENTRAL TIME ZONE

MISSOURI

ILLINOIS

CENTRAL TIME ZONE

1 IL 106, to Hull

(4AB) Jct I-172N, to Quincy

10 IL 96, to IL 106, Kinderhook, to Hull, Payson

20 CR 4, to IL 106, Barry
- FStop S: Barry Travel Plaza/P66
- Gas S: Shell◈
- Food S: Wendy's
- Other S: Laundry/Barry TP, Golf Course

31 CR 2, CR 3, New Salem, Pittsfield (Serv appr 5 mi S in Pittsfield)
- Med S: + Hospital

35 US 54, IL 107, Pittsfield, Griggsville (Serv appr 4 mi N in Griggsville)
- Med S: + Hospital
- Other N: to Siloam Springs State Park▲
  S: Pine Lakes Resort▲, IL State Hwy Patrol Post, to Pittsfield Muni Airport→

46 IL 100, Meredosia, to Bluffs

52 Old Rte 36, to IL 106, Winchester

60AB US 67N, Lp 72 Bus, Jacksonville, Alton (Serv N to I-72 Bus E)

64 US 67, Jacksonville, Greenfield
- Gas N: Gas, Circle K◈
  S: BP◈
- Food N: McDonald's, Subway, Chinese
  S: Subway
- Lodg N: Comfort Inn, Econo Lodge, Holiday Inn Express
- Med N: + Hospital
- Other N: CVS, Walgreen's, **Hopper RV Center**, to Muni Airport→

68 IL 104, Lp 72 Bus, Jacksonville
- Gas N: BP
- Med N: + Hospital

76 IL 123, to Ashland, Alexander

82 New Berlin
- TStop S: New Berlin Travel Plaza/P66
- Food S: FastFood/New Berlin TP

91 IL 54, Wabash Ave, Springfield
- Other S: **Coleman's Country Campers**

93 IL 4, Springfield, Chatham
- Gas N: Thornton's◈
  S: Meijer◈
- Food N: Applebee's, Arby's, Burger King, Chili's, Chipolte Mexican Grill, Corky's BBQ, Damon's, Denny's, Lone Star Steakhouse, Longhorn Steakhouse, McDonald's, Olive Garden, Panera Bread, Perkins, Popeye's Chicken, Qdoba Mexican Rest, Sonic, Starbucks, TGI Friday, Taco Bell, Wendy's
  S: Bob Evans, O'Charley's, Steak n Shake
- Lodg N: Comfort Inn, Courtyard, Fairfield Inn, Sleep Inn
  S: Hampton Inn, Staybridge Suites
- Other N: Best Buy, Barnes & Noble, Batteries Plus, Discount Tire, Grocery, Lowe's, Menard's, Office Depot, PetCo♥, PetSmart♥, Sam's Club, Staples, ShopKO, Target, Walgreen's, **Walmart**, White Oaks Mall
  S: Auto Dealers, Gander Mountain

NOTE: I-72 below runs with I-55. Exit #'s follow I-55.

(97AB) Jct I-55S, Springfield, St Louis
- Gas N: Shell
- Food N: McDonald's
- Lodg N: Ramada, Super 8, Travelodge

(92) Jct I-55S, Springfield, St Louis (SB)

94 Stevenson Dr, East Lake Dr
- Gas W: Circle K, BP, Mobil◈
- Food W: Arby's, Bob Evans, Denny's, Hardee's, Hooters, Long John Silver, Maverick Steakhouse, McDonald's,
- Food W: Outback Steakhouse, Quiznos, Pizza Hut, Red Lobster, Smokey Bones BBQ, Steak n Shake, Subway, Taco Bell, Wendy's
- Lodg W: Comfort Suites, Days Inn, Drury Inn, Hampton Inn, Hilton Garden Inn, Holiday Inn Express, Microtel, Signature Inn
- Other E: **to app 7mi: KOA▲**
  W: Auto Dealers, CVS, Dollar General, Radio Shack, Walgreen's, US Post Office, **RV Center & Campground▲**

96AB IL 29N, Grand Ave, Springfield, Taylorville
- TStop W: RoadRanger/Citgo
- Gas W: BP
- Food W: Burger King
- Lodg W: Red Roof Inn, Super 8
- Other W: Auto Zone, Auto Dealers, Grocery

(98AB/ 103AB) Jct I-72, US 36E, to Decatur Jct I-55, N to Chicago, S to St Louis, IL 97W, to Springfield

NOTE: I-72 above runs with I-55. Exit #'s follow I-55.

104 Mechanicsburg Rd
- Food N: Hardee's, McDonald's, Starbucks, Wendy's
- Lodg N: Best Western, Best Rest Inn

108 Riverton

114 Mechanicsburg, Buffalo

122 to Mt Auburn, Illiopolis
- Gas N: Citgo

128 Niantic

133AB US 51S, US 36E, Pana, Decatur
- Gas S: Citgo◈, Phillips 66◈
- Food S: Subway/P66
- Lodg S: Days Inn, Holiday Inn Select

138 IL 121, Decatur, Lincoln
- Med S: + Hospital

141AB US 51N, Decatur, Bloomington
- Gas N: Circle K/Shell
- Food N: Applebee's, **Cracker Barrel**, Country Kitchen, McDonald's, O'Charley's, Pizza Hut, Red Lobster, Steak n Shake, Subway, Taco Bell, Texas Roadhouse
  S: Arby's, Burger King, Quiznos
- Lodg N: Baymont Inn♥, Comfort Inn, Country Inn, Fairfield Inn, Hampton Inn, Ramada♥, Wingate Inn

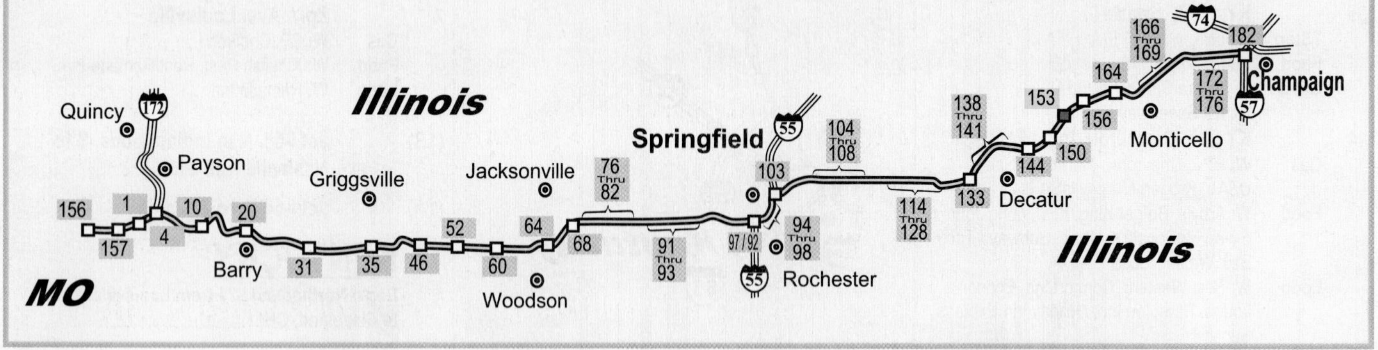

◈= Regular Gas Stations with Diesel ▲ = RV Friendly Locations ♥ = Pet Friendly Locations
Red print shows large vehicle parking / access on site or nearby Brown Print = Campgrounds / RV PARKS

EXIT		ILLINOIS
	Med	S: + Hospital
	Other	N: Auto Dealers, Advance Auto, Best Buy, Dollar Tree, Golf Course, Harley Davidson, Hickory Pt Mall, Lowe's, Menard's, PetSmart♥, Staples, S: ATMs, PetCo♥, Radio Shack, Sam's Club, Target, Walgreen's, **Walmart** sc,
144		**IL 48, Decatur, Oreana**
	FStop	S: RoadRanger #134
	TStop	N: Oasis Truck Stop/Marathon, S: Pilot Travel Center #368 (Scales)
	Food	S: McDonald's/Subway/Pilot TC
	Lodg	S: Sleep Inn
	Med	S: + Hospital
	Other	S: Laundry/Pilot TC,
150		**Argenta Rd, IL 25, to IL 48**
(153)		**Rest Area** (Both dir) (RR, Phone, Picnic, Pet, Vend)
156		**IL 48, Cisco, Weldon**
	Other	N: to appr 3mi: Friends Creek Co Park▲
164		**IL 5, Bridge St, DeLand, Monticello**
	Food	S: Hardee's, McDonald's, Pizza Hut
	Med	S: + John & Mary Kirby Hospital
	Other	S: Platt Co Airport✈
166		**IL 105, Monticello**
	Gas	S: Mobil◈
	Food	S: Rest/BW
	Lodg	S: Best Western♥
	Med	S: + John & Mary Kirby Hospital
	Other	S: Auto Dealers, Platt Co Airport✈
169		**Garfield Ave, White Heath**
172		**IL 10, Seymour, Lodge, Clinton**
176		**IL 47, to Mahomet**
(182AB)		**Jct I-57, N - Chicago, S - Memphis, to I-74**

CENTRAL TIME ZONE

ILLINOIS

Begin Westbound I-72 from Champaign, IL to Jct US-61 in Hannibal, MO.

EXIT		NORTH CAROLINA

Begin Southbound I-73 from Virginia Border to to South Carolina Border.

NORTH CAROLINA

I-73 in NC is being constructed in segments. We have listed what is currently signed as I-73 or Future I-73. Other roads, mainly US Highways that are part of the Future I-73 Corridor will be noted without exit details This will change as new partsof I-73 are open to traffic. We have tried to be as accurate as possible and List Exit #'s and Mile Markers where available.

EXIT		NORTH CAROLINA
(Segment 1)		US 220/Future I-73 Corridor, (Va Border/ US 220 to NC 68), (Current plans show construction to begin after 2015)
(Segment 2)		US 220, NC 68 to US 220/NC 68 Connector (Construction 2010-2013)
(Segment 3)		US 220/NC 68 Connector from Summerfield to NC 68, N of Greensboro (Construction to start 2013)
(Segment 4)		NC 68/Bryan Blvd (from US 220- NC 68 Conn to Greensboro Urban Loop (Future I-73/I-840)
109		**NC 68S, High Point**
(107)		**FUTURE Exit - Piedmont-Triad Int'l Airport**
3/105		**Bryan Blvd, PTI Airport**
2/104		**W Friendly Ave**
(Segment 5)		Greensboro Urban Lp Freeway (Bryan Blvd to US 220) Future I-73/I-840, I-73, US 421)
103B/80		**US 421N , Winston-Salem**
103A/80		**US 421S, Greensboro**
102/78		**Wendover Ave**
121A/		**Groometown Rd** (fr I-85S Exit #120) (SB for I-85, Bus 85 are 97A & 97B)
(98)		**FUTURE EXIT - High Point Rd**
(97A)		**Jct I-85, US 29S, US 70W, to High Point, Charlotte**
97B		**Bus Lp 85, US 29N, US 70E, to Greensboro**
(97)		**Jct I-85, Bus 85, US 29, US 70 (SB)**
	NOTE:	NB: joins US 421N on Greensboro Loop SB: leaves US 421S onto US 220S
95		**US 220, Asheboro, Rockingham**
(79)		**Jct I-85, US 29, US 70, Burlington, Charlotte** (SB)
79B		**Bus 85S, US 29S**
79A		**Bus 85N, US 29N**
(78)		**Jct I-85N, US 421S, to Durham, Raleigh** (SB)
(78B)		**Jct I-73N, US 421N, Winston-Salem, to Groometown Rd** (NB) (Use Ex #79B to access I-85S)
	NOTE:	SB End Future I-73/74. Begin I-73/74
51		**US 220 Bus N, NC 134S, Ulah, Troy**
49		**New Hope Church Rd, Asheboro**
45		**NC 705, Little River Rd, Seagrove, Robbins**
	Gas	E: Quik Chek
	Other	E: Wheatley Truck Repair
41		**Black Ankle Rd, Seagrove**
39		**Alt US 220, Star, Ether, Steeds**
36		**Spies Rd, Star, Robbins** (Serv W to Alt US 220)
	Other	W: to Montgomery Co Airport ✈
77		**Old Randleman Rd, Greensboro**
	Gas	W: Summer Food Mart, BP
74		**NC 62, Climax, High Point**
71		**US 220 Bus S, Level Cross**
67		**High Point St, Randleman**
	Gas	E: Tank and Tummy
	Food	E: Bojangles, Hardee's, McDonald's, Soprano's Rest, Wendy's
	Other	E: Express Care
65 (Seg 7/8)		**US 311, High Point, Randleman** (US 220, Future I-73, Future I-74: 2013+) (Future I-74 starts SB, Ends NB) (Addt'l Serv E to Bus US 220N)
	Gas	Quik N Easy, Exxon
63		**Pineview St**
62		**Spero Rd**
60		**to US 220 Bus N, Fayetteville St, Vision Dr**
59		**NC 1462, Presnell St** (Serv E to US 220 Bus)
59A		**Presnell Dr**
59B		**to Bus US 220**
58		**NC 42, Salisbury St, Lexington Rd, Asheboro** (Both dir, LEFT Exit) (Addt'l Services E to US 220 Bus)
	Gas	E: Amoco, Servco
56		**US 64, NC 49, to Raleigh, Lexington, Charlotte**
	Gas	E: BP, Gulf, Wilco W: Exxon
	Food	E: Arby's, Bamboo Garden, Burger King, Dixie Express, Huddle House, McDonald's W: Heritage Diner
	Lodg	E: Asheboro Inn, Days Inn W: Super 8
	Other	E: Grocery
55		**McDowell Rd**
	Gas	E: Tank and Tummy, Oil
	Food	W: K&W Cafeteria
	NOTE:	NB End I-73/74, Begin Future I-73/74
33		**NC 24, NC 27, Biscoe**
	Gas	W: Quik Chek
	Food	W: Chinese Rest
	Lodg	W: Days Inn
	Other	W: Food Lion
28		**NC 211, Candor, Pinehurst**
	FStop	E: WilcoHess Travel Center
	Gas	W: Quik Chek
	Food	E: Wendy's W: Chinese Rest, Hardee's
24		**Alt US 220N, Candor**
22		**Tabernacle Church Rd**
18		**Norman**
16		**NC 73**
13		**J Barwell Rd, Haywood Parker Rd**
11		**Millstone Rd, to NC 73W, Ellerbe**
8		**Bus US 220N, Ellerbe**

NORTH CAROLINA

◈= Regular Gas Stations with Diesel ▲ = RV Friendly Locations ♥= Pet Friendly Locations
Red print shows large vehicle parking / access on site or nearby Brown Print = Campgrounds / RV PARKS

EXIT		IOWA

Begin Eastbound I-74 from Jct I-80 in Davenport, IA to Jct I-75 in Cincinnati, OH.

IOWA

NOTE: **I-74 begins/ends on I-80, Exit #298**

CENTRAL TIME ZONE

(0) **Jct I-80, W to Des Moines, E to Chicago (WB, Left exit)**

1 **E 53rd St, Davenport**
- Gas **E:** Phillips 66
  W: AmocoBP, Murphy
- Food **E:** Arby's, Bamboo Garden, Chili's, Golden Corral, IHOP, Texas Roadhouse, Wendy's
  W: Red Robin, Ruby Tuesday, Steak 'n Shake, Subway, Taco Bell
- Lodg **E:** Country Inn, Hampton Inn, Residence Inn, Staybridge Suites
  W: Sleep Inn
- Other **E:** Golf Course
  W: Best Buy, PetSmart♥, Staples, Target, **Walmart sc**, Walgreen's, Hamilton Tech College, **US Adventure RV Center**

2 **US 6W, Spruce Hill Dr, Kimberly Rd, Bettendorf, Davenport**
- Gas **E:** Gary's Quik Service, Phillips 66
  W: AmocoBP◈, Citgo, Sam's
- Food **E:** Domino's, Mother Hubbard Cupboard, Old Chicago Pizza, Shoney's
  W: Applebee's, Bob Evans, Burger King, Panera, Red Lobster
- Lodg **E:** Courtyard, Heartland Inn♥, The Lodge Hotel♥, Ramada, Super 8
  W: Days Inn, Econo Lodge, Fairfield Inn, La Quinta Inn♥
- Other **E:** Auto Dealers, Auto Service, Golf Course, Lowe's, U-Haul
  W: Auto Services, ATM, Banks, PetCo♥, Sam's Club, Staples, Northpark Mall, Kaplan Univ, **IA State Hwy Patrol Post**

3 **Middle Rd, Locust St, Kimberly Rd, Bettendorf, Davenport**
- Gas **W:** One Stop Mart
- Food **W:** China Taste, McDonald's, Pizza Hut, Quiznos, Starbucks, Subway
- Lodg **W:** Holiday Inn
- Med **W: + Genesis Medical Center**
- Other **W:** Goodyear, Home Depot, Walgreen's, ShopKO, Golf Course, **to** Putnam Museum & IMAX

4 **US 67, Grant St, State St, Riverfront**
- Gas **E:** BP, Phillips 66◈, Shell
- Food **E:** Ross Restaurant

EXIT		IA / IL

- Food **W:** Village Inn
- Lodg **E:** Abbey Hotel, Traveler Motel, Isle of Capri Casino & Hotel
  W: City Center Motel
- Other **E:** Auto Services, CarQuest
  W: Dollar General, NAPA

CENTRAL TIME ZONE

IOWA

ILLINOIS

CENTRAL TIME ZONE

1 **River Dr, Moline (EB)**
- Other **E:** Visitor Info

2 **7th Ave, to IL 92, Moline**

3 **23rd Ave, Ave of the Cities, Moline**

4AB **IL 5, John Deere Rd, Moline**
- Gas **N:** BP, Citgo
  S: Citgo, Mobil
- Food **N:** Applebee's, Burger King, Old Country Buffet, Ryan's Grill, Starbucks, Steak 'n Shake, Wendy's
  S: Arby's, Burger King, Denny's, IHOP, Long John Silver, Pizza Hut, Subway, Taco Bell, Wendy's
- Lodg **S:** Best Western, Comfort Inn♥, Fairfield Inn, La Quinta Inn♥, Super 8
- Med **S: + Trinity Medical Center**
- Other **N:** Lowe's, Staples, **Walmart sc**, Tires, Blackhawk College, John Deere Co World Hdqtrs
  S: Auto Dealers, Best Buy, Firestone, Grocery, FedEx Office, Office Max, Pharmacy, PetCo♥, Southpark Mall, **to Blackhawk State Park**

NOTE: **I-74 runs with I-280 to MM14, Jct I-80**

(5A) **Jct I-280W, US 6W, to Des Moines**

5B **US 6E, Quad City Airport, Moline**
- Food **S:** Denny's, McDonald's, Montana Jack's
- Lodg **S:** Country Inn, First Choice Inn♥, Hampton Inn, Holiday Inn Express, La Quinta Inn♥,Quality Inn, The Fifth Season Hotel♥
- Other **S:** Quad City Int'lAirport✈, **to** Niabi Zoo

(6) **Weigh Station (EB)**

(8) **Weigh Station (WB)**

(14) **Jct I-80, E-Chicago, I-80/280W, to Des Moines**

EXIT		ILLINOIS

NOTE: **I-74 runs with I-280 to MM 14, Jct I-80**

24 **IL 81, Lynn Center, Andover**
- Other **S: to appr 15mi: Gibson's RV Park & Campground▲**

(28) **Rest Area (EB)**
(RR, Phones, Picnic, Vend, RVDump)

(30) **Rest Area (WB)**
(RR, Phones, Picnic, Vend, RVDump)

32 **IL 17, Woodhull, Alpha**
- TStop **S:** Woodhull Truck Plaza/Mobil (Scales)
- Gas **N:** BP◈, Shell
- Food **S:** Rest/Woodhull TP, Homestead Rest, Subway
- Other **N: to Shady Lakes Campground▲**
  S: Laundry/Woodhull TP

46AB **US 34, Galesburg, Monmouth, Kewanee (Serv 3.5mi S in Galesburg)**
- FStop **S:** Mobil **(1.75 mi E of US 34)**
- Other **S: Lake Storey Campground▲**

48 **Main St, E Galesburg (EB)**

48AB **Main St, Galesburg (WB)**
- Gas **S:** Clark, Hy-Vee, Mobil, Phillips 66
- Food **S:** Hardee's, KFC, McDonald's, Jalisco's Mex Rest, Pizza Hut, Taco Bell
- Lodg **N:** Best Western♥
  S: Days Inn, Holiday Inn Express, Relax Inn, Super 8
- Other **S:** Galesburg Muni Airport✈

51 **CR 9, Henderson St, CR 10, US 150, Galesburg, Knoxville**
- FStop **S:** Knoxville Travel Mart/BP **(CR 9S)**
- TStop **S:** The Junction/66 **(US 150)**
- Gas **S:** Casey's General Store
- Food **S:** Hardee's, McDonald's, Subway
- Other **S:** Laundry/Junction, Fairgrounds

54 **US 150, to IL 97, Knoxville, Gilson, Dahinda, Lewistown**
- Other **N:** Golf Course, **Dean's RV Service, Best Holiday Trav-L Park▲, Galesburg East Campground▲**
  S: Whispering Oaks Campground▲

(62) **Rest Area (Both dir)**
(RR, Phones, Picnic, Vend, Weather)

71 **CR R18, to IL 78, US 150, Brimfield, Canton, Kewanee, Elmwood**

75 **CR R25, N Maher Rd, Brimfield, Oak Hill**

82 **CR 18, CR R40, Edwards, Kickapoo**
- FStop **S:** Freedom Oil/Shell
- Gas **N:** Mobil◈
- Food **S:** SubExpress/Freedom Oil

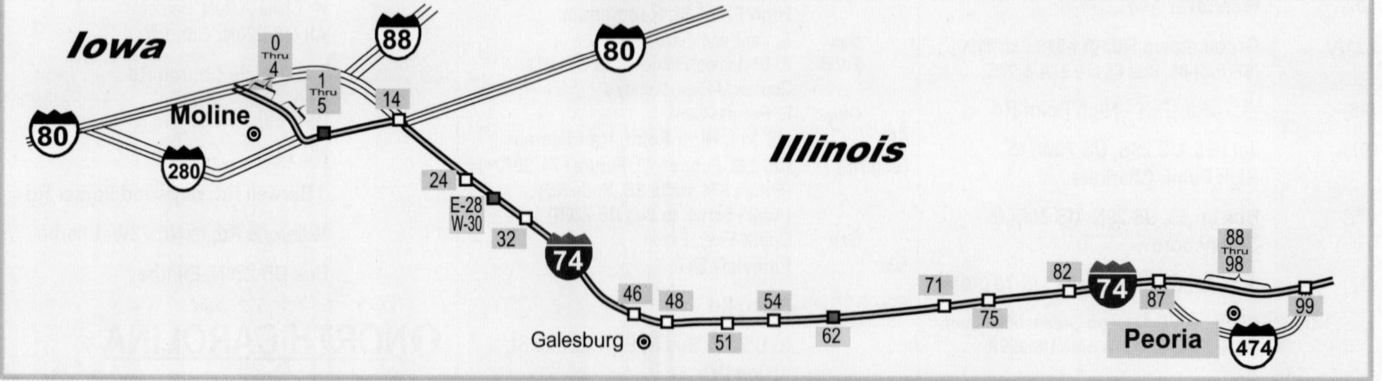

◈= Regular Gas Stations with Diesel ▲ = RV Friendly Locations ♥= Pet Friendly Locations
Red print shows large vehicle parking / access on site or nearby Brown Print = Campgrounds / RV PARKS

EXIT — ILLINOIS

Other — N: Jubilee College State Park, Wildlife Prairie State Park

(87A) Jct I-474E, to Indianapolis
Other — S: to Greater Peoria Reg'l Airport✈

87B Jct IL 6N, to Chillicothe

88 Sterling Ave, to US 150W, War Memorial Dr, Peoria
Lodg — N: Springhill Suites

89 US 150E, War Memorial Dr
Gas — N: BP, Clark
Food — N: Bob Evans, Burger King, Denny's, IHOP, Ned Kelly's Steakhouse, Outback Steakhouse, Perkins, Pizza Hut, Red Lobster, Subway, Wendy's
Lodg — N: Baymont Inn, Best Western♥, Comfort Suites♥, Extended Stay America, Red Roof Inn♥, Residence Inn, Sleep Inn, Super 8
Med — N: + to Proctor Hospital
Other — N: Lowe's, Northwoods Mall, Target, Tires, Walgreen's, Walmart sc, to IL Central College

90 Gale Ave, Peoria
Gas — N: Circle K
S: Speedway
Other — S: Kmart

91 University St, Peoria (EB)

91AB University St, Peoria
Gas — N: BP, Phillips 66
Other — S: Auto Zone, Walgreen's, Walmart, to Bradley Univ, Shea Stadium, Museum, Expo Gardens, Fairgrounds

92A IL 40N, IL 88, Knoxville Ave

92B to IL 40S, Glen Oak Ave, Downtown
Med — N: + St Francis Med Center, VA Hospital
S: + Methodist Med Center
Other — S: Peoria Civic Center, O'Brien Field

93 to US 24, IL 29, Washington St (EB), Adams St, Jefferson Ave (WB)
Lodg — S: Mark Twain Hotel♥
Other — S: Riverplex, Tourist Info, Greater Peoria Reg'l Airport✈, Riverfront, Downtown

94 IL 40N, Riverfront Dr, Downtown
Gas — S: Citgo
Food — S: Burger King/Citgo, Papa John's Pizza, Steak 'n Shake
Other — S: Lowe's, Office Max, Radio Shack, Walmart sc

95 US 150W, IL 116, N Main St (WB)

95A US 150, IL 116, N Main St (EB)
Gas — S: BP

EXIT — ILLINOIS

Food — S: Applebee's, Bob Evans, Hardee's, Long John Silver, Subway
Lodg — S: Baymont Inn♥, Motel 6♥
Other — S: Advance Auto Parts, CVS, Dollar General, Kroger, ShopKO, Walgreen's

95B US 150, IL 8E, Camp St (EB)
Other — N: Par-A-Dice Riverboat Casino, IL Central College

96 to IL 8, Washington St (EB), to US 15
Food — N: Subway, Wendy's
Lodg — N: Super 8
Other — N: Eastside Sports Complex

98 Pinecrest Dr, Peoria

(99) Jct I-474 W, to Moline Rock Island, Pekin, Peoria Reg'l Airport

(101) Jct I-155 S, IL 121, to Lincoln

102AB IL 121, N Morton Ave, Morton (EB)

102 IL 121, N Morton Ave, to US 150, Jackson St, Morton (WB)
TStop — N: Morton Travel Center/Mobil (Scales)
Gas — N: BP, Casey's, Citgo◈
S: Clark, Shell◈
Food — N: Arby's/Morton TC, Blimpie/Citgo, Burger King, Cracker Barrel, Country Kitchen, Morton Family Rest, Taco Bell, Wendy's
S: Judy's Rest, KFC, McDonald's, Subway
Lodg — N: Best Western, Comfort Inn, Days Inn, Holiday Inn Express, Townhouse Inn
Other — N: Laundry/WiFi/Morton TC
S: CVS, Kroger

112 IL 117, Deer Creek, Goodfield
FStop — N: Freedom Oil #77/Shell
Food — N: Subway/Freedom Oil

(114) Rest Area (Both dir)
(RR, Ph, Pic, Vend, Weather, RVDump)

120 CR 153, W Washington St, Carlock

(122) Weigh Station (Both dir)

125 US 150, Mitsubishi Motorway, Normal, to Bloomington

NOTE: I-74 runs below with I-55 for 6 mi. Exit #'s follow I-55.

(163/127) Jct I-74W, to Champaign, Peoria Jct I-55N, US 51, to Chicago S to St Louis, I-74W, to Peoria

160A US 150, IL 9, Market St, Bloomington, Pekin
FStop — E: Circle K/Citgo, Speedway #8326, Freedom Oil #39
TStop — E: Pilot Travel Center #299 (Scales), Travel Center of America #92/BP (Scales)

EXIT — ILLINOIS

Gas — E: BP, Clark, Shell
Food — E: Wendy's/Pilot TC, CountryPride/Popeyes PizzaHut/TA TC, Arby's, Burger King, Carl's Jr, Cracker Barrel, Hardee's, KFC, McDonald's, Subway, Taco Bell
Lodg — E: Best Inn♥, Comfort Inn, Days Inn♥, Econo Lodge, Hawthorn Suites, Quality Inn
TWash — E: Blue Beacon TW
TServ — E: TA TC/Tires
Med — E: + Hospital
Other — E: Laundry/BarbSh/WiFi/Pilot TC, Laundry/WiFi/TA TC, Grocery, NAPA, Pharmacy, Walmart

160B US 150, IL 9, Market St
Gas — W: Citgo◈
Food — W: Country Kitchen, Steak 'n Shake
Lodg — W: Country Inn♥, Hampton Inn, Ramada Inn♥, Wingate Inn
Other — W: Factory Outlet, Walmart

(157A/134A) Jct I-74E, to Indianapolis, I-55, US 51, to Decatur Jct I-55, S to Memphis, N to Chicago

157B/134B Bus 55, US 51, Veteran's Pkwy, Bloomington
Gas — E: Shell◈
Food — E: Rest/Parkway Inn, CJ's
Lodg — E: Parkway Inn, Sunset Inn

NOTE: I-74 runs above with I-55 for 6 mi. Exit #'s follow I-55.

135 US 51S, US 51N Bus, Bloomington
Gas — N: Mobil◈
S: Shell◈
Food — N: McDonald's
Other — S: Budget Truck Rental

142 CR 27, CR 36, Downs
Gas — N: BP◈

149 CR 21, Le Roy, Clinton Lake
TStop — N: Love's Travel Stop #367 (Scales)
S: Le Roy Truck Plaza/Shell (Scales)
Gas — N: BP◈, Freedom Oil
Food — N: Arby's/Love's TS, KFC, McDonald's, Subway
S: Rest/LeRoy TP
Lodg — S: Super 8
Other — N: Grocery, Pharmacy, Moraine View State Park, Wildwood Campground▲

152 US 136, Le Roy, to Heyworth

(156) Rest Area (Both dir)
(RR, Phones, Picnic, Vend, Weather)

159 IL 54, Farmer City, Gibson City
Gas — S: Casey's General Store
Food — S: Farmer City Café, Peoples Cafe
Lodg — S: Budget Motel, Days Inn

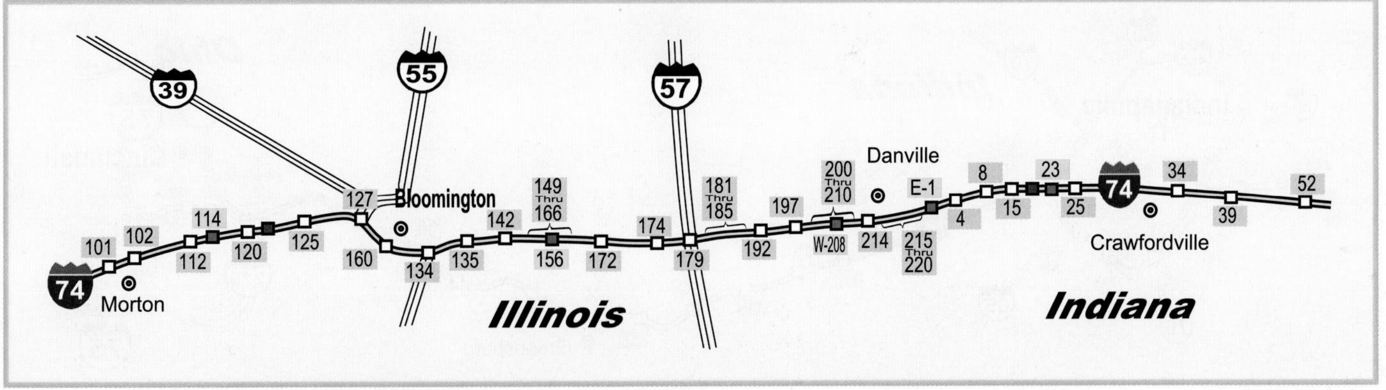

◈ = Regular Gas Stations with Diesel ▲ = RV Friendly Locations ♥ = Pet Friendly Locations
Red print shows large vehicle parking / access on site or nearby Brown Print = Campgrounds / RV PARKS

EXIT		ILLINOIS
166		**CR 2, Mansfield**
	Gas	S: BP
172		**IL 47, Mahomet, Gibson City**
	Gas	S: Mobil, Shell◈
	Food	S: Arby's, Hardee's, Subway
	Lodg	S: Heritage Inn
	Other	S: CVS, Grocery, Laundromat, NAPA
174		**Prairie View Rd, to CR 50, Lake of the Woods Rd, Mahomet**
	FStop	N: Super Pantry #42/Mobil
	Gas	N: Casey's, BP◈
	Food	N: Pickle Tree Farm Rest, Subway
	Other	N: **Tincup RV Park▲ , RV Center**
(179AB)		**Jct I-57, S - Memphis, N - Chicago**
181		**Prospect Ave, Champaign, Urbana**
	Gas	N: Meijer◈, Murphy, Sam's S: Clark, Freedom Oil◈, Mobil
	Food	N: Applebee's, Burger King, Chili's, Culver's, Damon's, Hardee's, Lone Star Steakhouse, O'Charley's, Old Country Buffet, Outback Steakhouse, Red Lobster, Ryan's Grill, Steak 'n Shake, Subway, Wendy's S: Arby's, KFC, Long John Silver
	Lodg	N: Courtyard, Drury Inn, Extended Stay America, Fairfield Inn S: Days Inn, Econo Lodge
	Other	N: ATMs, Bank, Advance Auto Parts, Auto Dealers, Auto Services, Best Buy, Dollar Tree, Lowe's, Market Place Mall, Office Depot, Sam's Club, Staples, Target, Tires, **Walmart sc**, S: Dollar General, Home Depot, Walgreen's
182		**Neil St, Champaign**
	Gas	S: Mobil
	Food	N: Bob Evans, Chevy's Mexican Rest, Denny's, McDonald's, Olive Garden, Smokey Bones BBQ, Subway, Taco Bell
	Lodg	N: Baymont Inn, Comfort Inn, La Quinta Inn♥, Red Roof Inn♥ S: Howard Johnson
183		**Lincoln Ave, Urbana**
	Gas	S: Mobil◈, Speedway
	Food	S: Urbana's Garden Rest, Rest/Hol Inn
	Lodg	S: Holiday Inn, Holiday Inn Express, Ramada Ltd♥, Sleep Inn, Super 8
	Other	S: to Univ of IL/Urbana-Champaign
184		**US 45, Cunningham Ave, Urbana**
	Gas	S: Circle K, Freedom Oil◈, Super America
	Food	S: Cracker Barrel, Domino's Pizza, Hickory River Smokehouse, Longhorn Steakhouse, Ned Kelly's Steakhouse, Steak 'n Shake
	Lodg	N: Park Inn S: Best Value Inn, Best Western, Eastland Suites, Motel 6♥

EXIT		ILLINOIS
	TServ	S: Ron's Truck & Auto Repair
	Other	N: Auto Dealers S: Firestone, Grocery, Laundromat,
185		**US 150, IL 130, University Ave**
192		**CR 12, N Main St, St Joseph**
197		**IL 49S, 2700E, Ogden, Royal**
200		**IL 49N, Rankin, Fithian**
	Other	N: **Five Bridges RV Park▲**
206		**CR 10, Oakwood Rd, Oakwood, Potomac**
	TStop	N: I-74 Auto Truck Plaza/Marathon (Scales) Colonial Pantry Travel Plaza/66 (Scales) S: Oakwood Truck Plaza/Marathon (Scales)
	Gas	S: Casey's
	Food	N: Rest/I-74 ATP, FastFood/Colonial TP S: Oaks Grill/Oakwood TP, McDonald's
	TServ	N: I-74 ATP/Tires, Truck & Trailer Repair
	Other	N: Laundry/**LP**/Colonial Pantry TP S: Laundry/Oakwood TP
(208)		**IL Welcome Center (WB)** **Rest Area (EB)** **(RR, Ph, Pic, Vend, Pet, Info, Weather)**
210		**US 150, W Main St, MLK Dr**
	Med	N: + Hospital
214		**G St, Tilton**
215		**US 150, IL 1, Gilbert St, Danville**
	Gas	N: Speedway S: Casey's, Clark, Speedway◈
	Food	N: Arby's, Burger King, Hardee's, Long John Silver, McDonald's, Pizza Hut, Steak n Shake, Subway, Taco Bell S: Burger King, Family Restaurant
	Lodg	N: Best Western, Days Inn S: Budget Motel
	Med	N: + Hospital
	Other	N: Grocery, Pharmacy S: Auto Dealers, Auto Zone, Family Dollar, Grocery,
216		**CR 6, Perrysville Rd, Bowman Ave**
	Gas	N: Freedom Oil, Mobil◈
220		**Lynch Rd, to US 136, Danville**
	TStop	N: Lynch Creek Plaza/Marathon (Scales)
	Gas	N: BP◈
	Food	N: Big Boy, What's Cooking Rest
	Lodg	N: Best Western♥, Comfort Inn, Fairfield Inn, Holiday Inn Express, Redwood Motor Inn, Super 8
	Other	N: Laundry/Tires/Lynch CP
	NOTE:	**MM 221: Indiana State Line**

ILLINOIS

EXIT		INDIANA

INDIANA

EASTERN TIME ZONE

(1)		**IN Welcome Center (EB)** **(RR, Ph, Picnic, Vend, Info, RVDump)**
4		**IN 63, Covington, Perrysville, W Lebanon, Newport**
	TStop	N: Pilot Travel Center #339 (Scales)
	Gas	N: BP
	Food	N: Arby's/TJCinn/Pilot TC, Beef House Rest, Wendy's
	Other	N: Laundry/WiFi/Pilot TC
8		**S Stringtown Rd, Covington**
	Gas	N: Shell
15		**US 41, US 136, Veedersburg**
	Gas	S: Marathon◈, Phillips 66
(19)		**Weigh Station (EB)**
(23)		**Rest Area (Both dir)** **(RR, Phones, Vend)**
25		**IN 25, Waynetown, Wingate**
	Other	S: **Charlarose Lake & Campground▲**
34		**US 231, IN 43, Crawfordsville**
	TStop	S: Crawfordsville Travel Plaza/Marathon (Scales)
	Gas	S: BP, Gas America, Shell
	Food	S: Burger King, KFC, McDonald's
	Lodg	S: Candlewood Suites, Comfort Inn, Days Inn, Holiday Inn Express, Ramada, Super 8
	TWash	S: Truck Wash of America
	TServ	S: D & B Truck Service
	Med	S: + Hospital
	Other	S: Laundry/Crawfordsville TP, **Crawfordsville KOA▲ , Sugar Creek Campground▲**
39		**IN 32, Crawfordsville, to Lebanon**
	TStop	S: Pilot Travel Center #247 (Scales)
	Food	S: Subway/Pilot TC
	Other	S: Laundry/WiFi/Pilot TC
52		**IN 75, Jamestown**
(57)		**Rest Area (Both dir)** **(RR, Phones, Picnic, Vend)**
58		**IN 39, N State St, Lizton, Lebanon**
61		**CR 275E, Jeff Gordon Blvd, Pittsboro**
	TStop	S: Love's Travel Stop #319 (Scales)
	Food	S: Godfathers/Subway/Love's TS
	Other	S: WiFi/**RVDump**/Love's TS

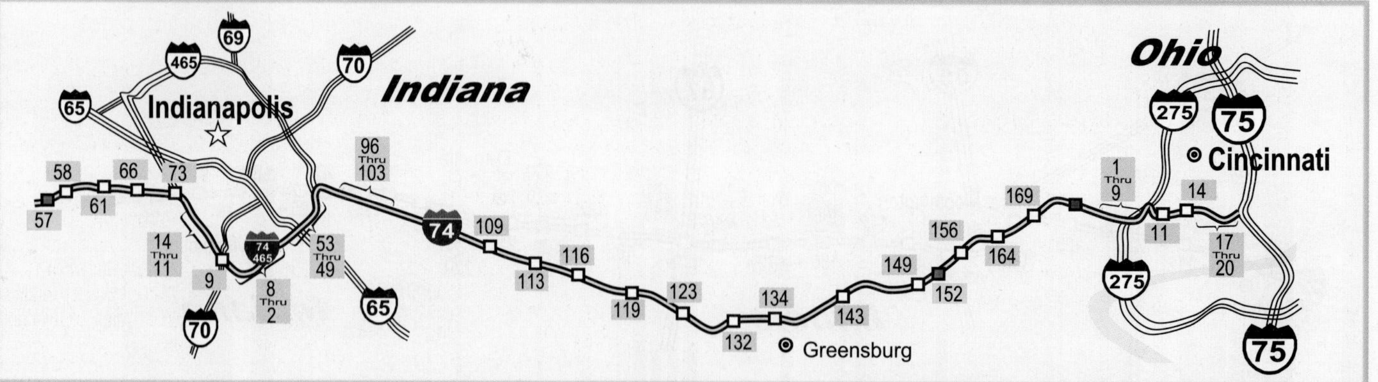

◈ = Regular Gas Stations with Diesel ▲ = RV Friendly Locations ♥ = Pet Friendly Locations
Red print shows large vehicle parking / access on site or nearby Brown Print = Campgrounds / RV PARKS

EXIT		INDIANA
66		**IN 267, N Green St, Brownsburg**
	Gas	**N:** Circle K/Shell, Circle S Mart/Citgo
		S: BP◈, Speedway◈, Kroger
	Food	**N:** Applebee's, Hardee's, Steak'n Shake, Subway
		S: Arby's, Bob Evans, Burger King, KFC, McDonald's, Mediterranean Pizza, Starbucks, Taco Bell, Wendy's, White Castle
	Lodg	**N:** Hampton Inn, Holiday Inn Express
		S: Comfort Suites, Super 8
	Med	**S: + Family Medicine Immed Care**
	Other	**N:** Big O Tires, Cinema, Jiffy Lube, Midas, Westwood Animal Hospital♥,
		S: Dollar Tree, CVS, Kroger/Pharmacy, Lowe's, O'Reillly Auto Parts, Radio Shack, **Walmart sc**
68		**Ronald Regan Pkwy,**
	Other	**S:** Brownsburg Animal Clinic♥, Clermon Golf Course, to O'Reillly Raceway Park, Sunset Bowling
	NOTE:	**I-74 runs below with I-465 for 21 mi. Exit #'s follow I-465.**
(73A/ 16B)		**Jct I-465S, Indianapolis ByPass, Crawfordsville Rd, Jct I-74 (Acc Services via Crawfordsville Rd)**
	Gas	**N:** Circle K, Circle K/Shell
	Food	**N:** Applebee's, El Rodeo, Hardee's, Mazatlan Mexican Rest, White Castle
		S: Denny's, Long John Silver, McDonald's, Quiznos Subs, Taco Bell,
	Lodg	**N:** Budget Inn,
		S: Clarion Inn, Dollar Inn, Motel 6, Red Roof Inn
	Other	**N:** Advance Auto Parts, Banks, Firestone, Goodyear, Kroger, PetCo♥, Radio Shack, US Post Office,
		S: Bank, CVS, Grocery, Noah's Westside Animal Hospital♥, Sprint,
(73B/ 16A)		**Jct I-465N, to I-65, to I-865, Crawfordsville Rd, to Chicago, Ft Wayne, Jct I-74**
14AB		**W 10th St, Indianapolis**
	Gas	**N:** Marathon, Shell
		S: BP, Gas America, Speedway
	Food	**N:** Pizza Hut, Wendy's
		S: Arby's, Hardee's, McDonald's, Noble Roman's Pizza, Taco Bell
	Med	**N: + Hospital**
	Other	**N:** Grocery, Lowe's
		S: CVS
13AB		**US 36E, Rockville Rd, Danville**
	Gas	**N:** Citgo
		S: Speedway
	Food	**N:** Burger King
		S: Bob Evans
	Lodg	**N:** Comfort Inn, Sleep Inn, Wingate Inn
		S: Best Western
	Other	**N:** Sam's Club
12AB		**US 40E, Washington St, Plainfield**
	Gas	**N:** BP
		S: Phillips 66, Shell, Thornton's
	Food	**N:** Burger King, Fazoli's, McDonald's, Taco Bell, White Castle
		S: Arby's, Burger King, Hardee's, KFC, Long John Silver, Omelet Shop, Pizza Hut, Steak 'n Shake, Subway, Wendy's
	Lodg	**S:** Dollar Inn
	Med	**+ Hospital**

EXIT		INDIANA
	Other	**N:** Auto Zone, Dollar General, Kroger, Laundromat, Walgreen's, U-Haul
		S: Goodyear, Laundromat, Target
11AB		**Airport Expy, Indianapolis Int'l Airport**
	Gas	**S:** BP
	Food	**S:** Burger King
	Lodg	**N:** Adams Mark, Baymont Inn, Days Inn, Courtyard, Extended Stay America
		S: Holiday Inn, Hilton, La Quinta Inn♥, Ramada, Residence Inn, Wellesley Inn
(9AB)		**Jct I-70, E to Indianapolis, W to Terra Haute**
8		**IN 67S, Kentucky Ave**
	Gas	**S:** BP◈, Speedway, Shell
	Food	**S:** Denny's, Hardee's, KFC
	Med	**S: + Hospital**
7		**Mann Rd (WB)**
4		**IN 37S, Harding St, Indianapolis, Martinsville, Bloomington**
	TStop	**N:** Mr Fuel #6 (Scales), Pilot Travel Center #318 (Scales)
		S: Flying J Travel Plaza #5440/Conoco
	Gas	**S:** Marathon
	Food	**N:** FastFood/Pilot TC, FastFood/MrFuel, Omelet Shoppe
		S: Cookery/FastFood/FJ TP, Hardee's, McDonald's, Waffle & Steak, White Castle
	Lodg	**N:** Best Value Inn, Super 8
		S: Knights Inn
	TWash	**S:** Blue Beacon TW/FJ TP
	TServ	**S:** FJ TP/Tires, Stoop's Freightliner, Paul's Trailer Sales & Service
	Other	**N:** Laundry/WiFi/MrFuel, WiFi/Pilot TC
		S: Laundry/BarbSh/CB/WiFi/**RVDump/LP**/FJ TP
2AB		**US 31S, IN 37, East St, Indianapolis**
	Gas	**N:** BP, Speedway
		S: Shell, Sunoco
	Food	**N:** Arby's, Burger King, DQ, Golden Wok, Hardee's, KFC, Long John Silver, Papa John's, McDonald's, Old Country Buffet, Pizza Hut, Ponderosa, Steak & Ale, Steak 'N Shake, Wendy's,White Castle
		S: Applebee's, Bob Evans, Denny's, Red Lobster
	Lodg	**S:** Best Inn, Comfort Inn, Days Inn, Four Winds Resort & Marina, Holiday Inn Express, Ramada Inn, Ramada Ltd
	Other	**N:** Auto Zone, Auto Dealers, CVS, Dollar General, Family Dollar, Firestone, Kroger, Goodyear, Office Depot, Radio Shack, Target, U-Haul
(53AB)		**Jct I-65, N to Indianapolis, S to Louisville**
52		**Emerson Ave, Beech Grove, Indianapolis**
	Gas	**N:** Shell, Speedway
	Gas	**S:** Shell, Speedway◈
	Food	**N:** Burger King, Domino's Pizza, KFC, Subway, Taco Bell, Wendy's
		S: Arby's, DQ, Fazoli's, Hardee's, Pizza Hut, McDonald's, Steak 'n Shake, Subway, White Castle
	Lodg	**N:** Motel 6♥
		S: Holiday Inn, Red Roof Inn♥, Super 8
	Med	**N: + Hospital**
	Other	**N:** CVS
		S: Auto Zone, Kmart, Walgreen's

EXIT		INDIANA
(49AB/ 94)		**Jct I-74E, US 421S Jct I-465/I-74W, I-465N, I-421N Southwestern Ave, Columbus, OH; Ft Wayne**
	NOTE:	**I-74 runs above with I-465 for 21 mi. Exit #'s follow I-465.**
96		**Post Rd, Indianapolis**
	Gas	**N:** Marathon◈
		S: Shell◈
	Food	**N:** McDonald's, Subway/Marathon
		S: Wendy's
99		**Acton Rd, Southeastern Ave**
	Other	**N:** Buck Creek Winery
101		**Pleasant View Rd, Fairland**
	Gas	**N:** Marathon
103		**N700W, London Rd, to Boggstown**
109		**W400N, Fairland Rd, Fairland**
	TStop	**N:** Pilot Travel Center #242 (Scales)
	Food	**N:** McDonald's/Pilot TC
	Other	**N:** WiFi/Pilot TC, Indiana Downs, Shelbyville Muni Airport✈
		S: RV Park▲
113		**IN 9, Shelbyville, Greenfield**
	FStop	**S:** Crystal Flash #10
	Gas	**N:** Gas America◈
		S: BP, Shell
	Food	**N:** **Cracker Barrel**, Santa Fe Cattle Co, Wendy's
		S: McDonald's, Subway/Crystal Flash, Waffle & Steak
	Lodg	**S:** America's Best Value Inn, Best Western, Comfort Inn, Days Inn, Hampton Inn, Holiday Inn, Knights Inn♥, Super 8
	Med	**S: + Hospital**
116		**IN 44, to IN 9, Shelbyville, Manilla**
	FStop	**N:** Big Foot #28/Shell
	Gas	**S:** BP, Marathon, Shell, Swifty, Kroger, Murphy
	Food	**S:** Applebee's, Arby's, Burger King, Bob Evans, China Inn, DQ. Denny's, Domino's Pizza, Golden Corral, McDonald's, Pizza Hut, Starbucks, Subway, Taco Bell, Wendy's
	Lodg	**S:** Lee's Inn
	Med	**S: + Hospital**
	Other	**S:** Ace Hardware, Advance Auto Parts, ATMs, Auto Dealers, Big Lots, CVS, Dollar General, Dollar Tree, Grocery, Kroger, NAPA, Radio Shack, Walgreen's, **Walmart sc**
119		**IN 244E, Waldron, Milroy, Andersonville**
123		**N CR 8W, St Paul, Middletown**
	Other	**S: Hidden Paradise Campground▲, Thorntree Lake Campground▲**
132		**US 421S, Greensburg (EB)**
	Gas	**S:** BP
	Lodg	**S:** Hampton Inn
134AB		**IN 3, to US 421, Greensburg, Rushville, Columbus**
	Gas	**S:** Big Foot, BP◈, Shell, Speedway◈
	Food	**S:** Arby's, Big Boy, Burger King, Chili's, Hardee's, Little Caesar's Pizza, KFC, McDonald's, Papa John's, Ponderosa, Subway, Taco Bell, Waffle House, Wendy's
	Lodg	**S:** Best Western, Fairfield Inn, Holiday Inn, Lee's Inn

◈ = Regular Gas Stations with Diesel ▲ = RV Friendly Locations ♥ = Pet Friendly Locations

Red print shows large vehicle parking / access on site or nearby **Brown Print = Campgrounds / RV PARKS**

EXIT		IN / OH
	Other	S: Advance Auto, Auto Zone, Big O Tire, CVS, Dollar General, Dollar Tree, Grocery, NTB, Radio Shack, Staples, Walgreen's, **Walmart sc**
143		**CR 850E, Greensburg, to New Point, St Maurice**
	TStop	N: Petro Stopping Center #73 (Scales)
	Gas	S: Marathon
	Food	N: IronSkillet/FastFood/Petro SC
	TServ	N: Petro SC/Tires
	Other	N: Laundry/WiFi/Petro SC
149		**IN 229, Walnut St, Batesville, to Oldenburg**
	Gas	N: Shell◊, Sunoco S: BP
	Food	N: McDonald's, Subway, Wendy's S: Arby's, Skyline Chili, Waffle House
	Lodg	N: Hampton Inn S: Comfort Inn, Sherman House
	Med	S: + Hospital
	Other	N: Dollar General, Kroger S: Pharmacy
(152)		**Rest Area (Both dir)** **(RR, Phones, Picnic, Pet, Vend)**
156		**IN 101, CR 875E, Sunman, Milan**
	Gas	S: Exxon◊
164		**IN 1, Woodbridge Ln, W Harrison, Lawrenceburg, St Leon**
	Gas	N: Exxon, Shell◊ S: BP◊
	Food	N: Christina's Family Rest

EXIT		OHIO
169		**US 52W, West Harrison, Brookville**
(171)		**Weigh Station (WB)**

EASTERN TIME ZONE

NOTE: MM 171.5: Ohio State Line

INDIANA
OHIO

EASTERN TIME ZONE

EXIT		OHIO
1		**New Haven Rd, Harrison**
	Gas	N: BP◊ S: Marathon, Shell, Speedway◊, Sunoco
	Food	N: Cracker Barrel, Gold Star Chili S: Arby's, Burger King, Hardee's, Pizza Hut, McDonald's, Shoney's, Waffle House, Wendy's, White Castle
	Lodg	N: Comfort Inn S: Holiday Inn, Quality Inn
	Other	N: Home Depot, Tires S: Auto Zone, Big Lots, CVS, Firestone, Kroger, Goodyear, Walgreen's
(2)		**Weigh Station (EB)**
3		**Dry Fork Rd, Harrison**
	FStop	S: 74 Fuel Stop/Shell
	Gas	N: Citgo
	Food	S: Burger King, McDonald's
	Other	N: Cincinnati West Airport✈
(5)		**Jct I-275S, to Kentucky**
7		**OH 128, Cleves, to Hamilton**
	Gas	N: BP◊, Marathon◊
	Food	N: Wendy's
(9)		**Jct I-275N, to I-75, to Dayton (WB)**
11		**Rybolt Rd, Harrison Ave, Cincinnati**
	Gas	S: BP
	Food	S: Rest/Imperial House
	Lodg	S: Imperial House
14		**N Bend Rd, to Cheviot**
	Gas	N: Citgo, Speeedway◊, Shell, Sam's S: BP
	Food	N: McDonald's, Pizza Hut, Perkins, Subway, Wendy's S: Bob Evans
	Lodg	S: Tri-Star Motel
	Med	N: + Hospital
	Other	N: Grocery, Sam's Club, Tires, Walgreen's
17		**Montana Ave, W Fork Rd (WB)**
18		**US 27N, Colerain Ave, Beekman St**
19		**Elmore St, Colerain Ave, to Spring Grove Ave, William Dooley Byp (WB)**
(20)		**Jct I-75, N to Dayton, S to Cincinnati (EB)**

EASTERN TIME ZONE

NOTE: I-74 begins/ends on I-75, Exit #4

OHIO

Begin Westbound I-74 at Jct I-75 in Cincinnati, OH to Davenport, IA.

Begin Eastbound I-74 from Virginia Border to to South Carolina Border.

NORTH CAROLINA

EASTERN TIME ZONE

I-74 in NC is being constructed in segments. We have listed what is currently signed as I-74 or Future I-74. Other roads, mainly US Highways that are part of the Future I-74 Corridor will be noted without exit details. This will change as new parts of I-74 are open to traffic.
We have tried to be as accurate as possible and List Exit #'s and Mile Markers where available.

NOTE: I-74 below runs with I-77 from VA Border to Exit #101/Jct I-74.

EXIT		NORTH CAROLINA
(105)		**NC Welcome Center (SB)** **(RR, Phones, Picnic, Vend, Info)**
(103)		**Weigh Station (Both dir)**
(101)		**Jct I-74E, Mount Airy, to Winston-Salem (fr SB, Left Exit)**

NOTE: I-74 above runs with I-77 to VA Border. I-74 begins below to Mt Airy.

EXIT		NORTH CAROLINA
(5)		**Jct I -77, N to Wytheville, VA; S to Statesville**
6		**NC 89, to I-77, W Pine St, Mt Airy**
	TStop	S: Brintle Travel Plaza/Citgo (Scales)
	Gas	N: Citgo, BP, Exxon S: Marathon◊
	Food	N: Subway S: Rest/Brintle TP, Subway, Wagon Wheel Rest
	Lodg	S: Best Western
	TServ	S: Brintle TP/Tires, Pooles 89 Truck Service & Car Repair
8		**Red Brush Rd, Mount Airy**
	Gas	N: Exxon
	Other	S: Pine Ridge Golf Course
11		**US 601, Rockford Rd, Mt Airy, White Plains, Dobson** **(Serv 2 mi+ E on US 601)**
	Gas	N: Citgo, Texaco
	Food	N: Arby's, Biscuitville, Burger King, Chinese Rest, Golden Corral, Hardee's, Little Caesars, Japanese Rest, Long John Silver, Mex Rest, Ruby Tuesday, Subway, Taco Bell, Waffle House, Wendy's
	Lodg	N: Best Western, Hampton Inn, Quality Inn
	Med	N: + Northern Hospital of Surry Co
	Other	N: ATMs, Auto Services, Banks, Carolina Tire, Grocery, Pharmacy, **Walmart sc**
13		**Park Dr**
(17/140)		**US 52N, Mount Airy (EB)** **Jct I-74W, to I-77, to Wytheville, VA**
	Other	N on US 52: to Downtown Mt Airy, Mt Airy/Surry Co Airport✈

NOTE: EB: End I-74, Begin US 52/Future I-74 Corridor. Exit #'s below follow US 52.

EXIT		NORTH CAROLINA
136		**Cook School Rd, Pilot Mtn**
135		**Pilot Mountain (EB, Left Exit)**
134		**NC 268, Pilot Mtn, Elkin**
	Gas	N: Citgo, Exxon, Wilco
	Food	N: Cousin Gary's Family Rest, McDonald's, Mountain View Rest, Wendy's
	Lodg	N: Best Western
	Other	N: ATMs, Auto Services, Golf Course, Grocery
131		**Pilot Mountain State Park**
	Other	W: Pilot Mountain State Park
129		**Perch Rd, Pinnacle**
	Gas	N: BP
	Food	N: EJ's Rest, Trails End Grill
	Other	N: Auto Services
(129)		**Scenic Overlook (NO TRUCKS)**
123		**S Main St, King, Tobaccoville**
	Gas	S: BP, Chevron, Shell
	Food	N: Domino's Pizza, McDonald's/BP, Stratford BBQ, Waffle House, Wendy's S: Burger King, KFC,
	Lodg	N: Econo Lodge
	Other	N: Banks, Grocery, O'Reilly Auto Parts, RiteAid,
122		**Moore/RJR Dr**
120		**Westinghouse Rd**
118		**NC 65, Rural Hall, Bethania**

◊= Regular Gas Stations with Diesel ▲ = RV Friendly Locations ♥= Pet Friendly Locations
Red print shows large vehicle parking / access on site or nearby Brown Print = Campgrounds / RV PARKS

EXIT	NORTH CAROLINA
NOTE:	(Construction to begin 2012) EB: Future I-74 to be routed onto Winston-Salem Northern Beltway. WB: to be routed onto US 52/Future I-74 from Winston-Salem Beltway.
NOTE:	Begin US 311/Future I-74 Corridor (Construction to begin by 2011)
(55)	I-40, US 311N, Winston-Salem
56	Ridgewood Rd
59/31	Union Cross Rd, Winston-Salem
Gas	N: Marathon
Other	N: Tire & Auto Services, to I-40 S: Golf Courses
60/30	High Point Rd, Kernersville
Gas	S: Little Cedar Groceries
63/27	NC 66, Kernersville
Other	S: Auto Services
65/25	Bus US 311S, N Main St, High Point (Serv available S on N Main)
66/24	Johnson St, High Point
Other	N: Golf Course, City Park/Oak Hollow Family Campground ▲
67/23	NC 68, Eastchester Dr, to I-40 PTI Airport
Gas	S: 76, Kelly C-Store, Marathon
Food	S: ChickFilA, Chu's Express, Garfield's, Juice n Java, La Hacienda Mex Rest, Sbarro, Wendy's
Lodg	S: Courtyard
Other	S: ATMs, Auto & Tire Services
69/21	Greensboro Rd
Gas	N: Amoco, BP S: Citgo, Oil
Food	N: Henry James BBQ S: Fortune Cookie Express, McDonald's
70/20	Kivett Dr, High Point
Other	N/S: Auto, Tire, Towing Services
71A/19B	E Green Dr
71B/ 19A	US 311S, Bus 85, US 29, US 70, Thomasville, Greensboro
71	US 311S, Bus 85, US 29, US 70, Thomasville, Greensboro
NOTE:	EB I-74 to continue under construction On US 311 Bypass to US 220. WB to be routed to under construction US 311 Bypass to current US 311.
(75AB)	Jct I -85, N to Greensboro, S to Charlotte
79	Cedar Square Rd
NOTE:	US 311/Future I-74 to be under Construction Thru 2012. US 311 Bypass from E of I-85, Archdale, to US 220, Sophia.
NOTE:	I-74 will join I-73 about 1mi S of Current Jct US 311/US 220. Road Is signed US 220/Future I-73/Future I-74. Expect construction. Future I-74 runs with Future I-73 below. Exit #'s follow Future I-73.
65 (Seg 7/8)	US 311, High Point, Randleman (US 220, Future I-73, Future I-74: 2013+) (Future I-74 starts SB, Ends NB) (Addt'l Serv E to Bus US 220N)
Gas	E: Quik N Easy

EXIT	NORTH CAROLINA
Gas	W: Exxon
(Future)	Future - Jct I-74W, High Point, to Winston-Salem
63	Pineview St, Randleman
62	Spero Rd, Asheboro (Services E to US 220 Bus)
60	to US 220 Bus N, Fayetteville St, Vision Dr
59	NC 1462, Presnell St (Services E to US 220 Bus)
59B	to Bus US 220, Fayetteville St
59A	Presnell Dr
58	NC 42, Salisbury St, Lexington Rd, Asheboro (Both dir, LEFT Exit) (Addt'l Services E to US 220 Bus)
Gas	E: Amoco, Servco
56	US 64, NC 49, to Raleigh, Lexington, Charlotte
Gas	E: BP, Gulf, Wilco W: Exxon
Food	E: Arby's, Bamboo Garden, Burger King, Dixie Express, Huddle House, McDonald's W: Heritage Diner
Lodg	E: Asheboro Inn, Days Inn W: Super 8
Other	E: Grocery
56B	US 64W, NC 49S, to Lexington, Charlotte
56A	US 64E, NC 49N, to Siler City, Raleigh
55	McDowell Rd
Gas	E: Tank and Tummy, Oil
Food	W: K&W Cafeteria
NOTE:	NB End I-73/74, Begin Future I-73/74 SB End Future I-73/74. Begin I-73/74
51	US 220 Bus N, NC 134S, Ulah, Troy
49	New Hope Church Rd, Asheboro
45	NC 705, Little River Rd, Seagrove, Robbins
Gas	E: Quik Chek
Other	E: Wheatley Truck Repair
(44)	Rest Area (Both dir) (RR, Ph, Pic, Vend)
41	Black Ankle Rd, Seagrove
39	Alt US 220, Star, Ether, Steeds
36	Spies Rd, Star, Robbins (Serv W to Alt US 220)
Other	W: to Montgomery Co Airport ✈
33	NC 24, NC 27, Biscoe
Gas	W: Quik Chek
Food	W: Chinese Rest
Lodg	W: Days Inn
Other	W: Food Lion
28	NC 211, Candor, Pinehurst
FStop	E: WilcoHess Travel Center
Gas	W: Quik Chek
Food	E: Wendy's W: Chinese Rest, Hardee's
NOTE:	NB: Begin I-73/I-74, SB End, Begin US 220, Future I-73/I-74.
24	Alt US 220N, Candor

EXIT	NORTH CAROLINA
22	Tabernacle Church Rd
18	Norman
16	NC 73
13	J Barwell Rd, Haywood Parker Rd
11	Millstone Rd, to NC 73W, Ellerbe
8	Bus US 220N, Ellerbe
NOTE:	NB Begin Frwy, SB End
(22)	Future - Bus Lp I-73, Bus Lp I-74, Rockingham
NOTE:	(Construction to begin after 2015) NB I-73/74 to be routed onto Planned US 220 Bypass Fwy to current US 220 SB to be routed onto Planned US 220 Bypass to US 74 Bypass.
(15)	Future - US 74W, Monroe, Charlotte
NOTE:	Begin US 74, Future I-73, Future I-74, NB End, SB Begin. Exit #'s are US 74.
(12/ 311)	US 1, Rockingham, Southern Pines, Cheraw, to US 220, Ellerbe, Asheboro, Greensboro
(7/316)	NC 177, Hamlet
NOTE:	NB joins US 74 Rockingham Bypass from NC 38 Corridor from SC Border. SB leaves US 74 Rockingham Bypass along NC 38 Corridor to SC Border.
(168/319)	NC 38, Hamlet, Bennettsville
NOTE:	I-73 proposed to leave I-74/US 74 on future fwy at or near NC 38. Begin EB Future I-74 / US 74 .
(320)	NC 381. Hamlet, Gibson
(321)	Bus US 74, Hamlet (WB)
NOTE:	Begin US 74, I-74
207	Bus US 74, Lauringburg (EB)
208	NC 79, Gibson (WB)
209	US 15, US 401N, US 501, N to Fayetteville, S to Bennettsville
210	Bus US 15, US 401, Laurinburg
211	US 501S, Rowland, Myrtle Beach
212	to Bus 74, Laurinburg
213	Bus US 74, Maxton, E Laurinburg
216	Maxton-Laurinburg Airport Rd
217	NC 71, Maxton, Red Springs
220A	Bus US 74W, Maxton (EB)
220	Alt US 74, Bus US 74, Maxton (WB)
220B	Alt US 74E (EB)
223	Cabinet Shop Rd
226	NC 710, Pembroke, Red Springs
203	Dew Rd, Pembroke
207	Back Swamp Rd
(209)	Jct I-95, US 301, N to Fayetteville, S to Florence

◈= Regular Gas Stations with Diesel ▲ = RV Friendly Locations ♥= Pet Friendly Locations
Red print shows large vehicle parking / access on site or nearby Brown Print = Campgrounds / RV PARKS

EXIT	NORTH CAROLINA
(209B)	Jct I-95N, US 301N, to Lumberton, Fayetteville
(209A)	Jct I-95S, US 301S, to Florence
( )	Future - Rest Area (tbo in 2009)
210	Alt US 74
212	NC 41, Lumberton, Fairmont
NOTE:	EB End Fwy, WB Begin
(228)	NC 242, Evergreen
(234)	NC 410, Bus US 74, NC 130E, Chadbourn, Bladenboro
NOTE:	MM 236: EB: I-74 routed onto existing US 74/76 fwy around Whiteville, WB routed from existing fwy around.
NOTE:	EB Begin Fwy, EB End
(236)	US 76, I-20W, Chadbourn, FairBluff
(238)	Union Valley Rd
(239)	US 701 Bypass, Whiteville, Clarkton
(242)	Bus US 74/76, Whiteville
NOTE:	EB End Fwy, WB Begin
(260)	US 74, US 76, I-20E, Wilmington
(285)	US 17N, Supply, Wilmington
(294)	NC 904, Grissettown, Ocean Isle Beach
(298)	US 17S, to Myrtle Beach
	EASTERN TIME ZONE
NOTE:	MM 301: South Carolina State Line

NORTH CAROLINA

Begin Northbound I-74 from South Carolina Border to Virginia Border.

EXIT		MICHIGAN
		Begin Southbound I-75 from the Canada / Michigan border to Miami, FL.

MICHIGAN

EXIT		MICHIGAN
NOTE:		I-75 begins/ends at Int'l Toll Bridge
		EASTERN TIME ZONE
(0)		Canadian Customs (NB), US Customs (SB) (All Vehicles MUST Stop)
(394)		I-75 Bus, MI 129, Easterday Ave, W Portage Ave, Sault Ste Marie, to Toledo, OH
NOTE:		NB: LAST USA exit before TOLL
		W: MI Welcome Center (NB) (RR, Phone, Picnic, Info, Weather) (Addt'l serv on W Portage Ave/NE)
	FStop	W: Holiday Station #262
	Gas	E: Citgo◈
	Food	E: Applebee's, Arby's, McDonald's W: Freighters Rest, Lakeside Pub, Subway
	Lodg	E: Holiday Inn Express♥
	Other	E: Sault Ste Marie Muni Airport✈, River of History Museum, Tower of History, Lake Superior State Univ
392		I-75 Bus, 3 Mile Rd, Sault Ste Marie
	FStop	E: I-75 BP
	TStop	E: Admiral Ship Store/Marathon
	Gas	E: Mobil◈, Shell, USA◈
	Food	E: FastFood/Admiral, Applebee's, Arby's, Burger King, Country Kitchen, Great Wall Chinese, Jeff's Fifties Cafe, La Senorita, McDonald's, Subway, Wendy's
	Lodg	E: Best Value Inn, Best Western, Budget Host, Comfort Inn, Days Inn, Hampton Inn, Motel 6♥, Plaza Motor Motel, Super 8
	Med	E: + Hospital
	Other	E: LP/Admiral, ATM, Auto, Grocery, NAPA, RiteAid, Walmart, MI State Hwy Patrol Post, Sault Ste Marie Muni Airport✈ W: Varsity Cinemas
(389)		Sault Ste Marie Rest Area (NB) (RR, Phones, Picnic, Vend, Info)
386		MI 28, 9 Mile Rd, Dafter, Newberry
	Food	E: Sharolyn Rest/Motel
	Lodg	E: Sharolyn Motel, Sunset Motel
	Other	W: to Brimley State Park, Minnow Lake Campground▲, Bay Mills Resort & Casino
379		Gaines Hwy, Kincheloe
	Other	E: to Barbeau Area, Clear Creek Campground▲
378		MI 80, Tone Rd, Kincheloe, Kinross
	Other	E: Chippewa Co Int'l Airport✈
373		MI 48, W 19 Mile Rd, Rudyard
	Gas	W: AmocoBP◈
359		MI 134, St Ignace, DeTour Village, Drummond Island
	Other	E: to Loons Pt Campground▲, Cedarville RV Park & Campground▲
352		MI 123, Newberry, to Moran
348		I-75 Bus Loop, St Ignace, Evergreen Shores, Castle Rock Rd, to Allentow
	Gas	E: Shell
	Food	E: Shore's Rest
	Lodg	E: Comfort Inn, Days Inn, Great Lakes Motel, Harbor Pointe, Holiday Inn Express, Pines Motel, Quality Inn, Sands Motel
	Other	E: Castle Rock Campark▲, Tiki Travel Park▲, MI State Hwy Patrol Post, Mackinac Co Airport✈
(346)		St Ignace Rest Area (SB) (RR, Phone, Picnic) (Closed Winter)
345		Portage St, to US 2, St Ignace (SB)
	Gas	E: Marathon
	Other	W: Lakeshore Park Campground▲
344A		I-75 Bus Loop, St Ignace (NB)
	Gas	E: Shell
	Food	E: Northern Lights Rest, Subway
	Lodg	E: Comfort Inn, Quality Inn
	Med	E: + Hospital
	Other	E: US Post Office, MI State Hwy Patrol, Straits State Park
344B		US 2W, Manistique (NB)
	TStop	W: St Ignace Truck Stop/BP
	Gas	W: Holiday◈, Shell◈
	Food	W: Big Boy, Burger King, Hardee's, McDonald's, Miller's Camp Rest, Seafood Palace, UpNorth Rest
	Lodg	W: Quality Inn♥, Super 8
	Other	W: LP/St Ignace TS, St Ignace/Makinac Island KOA▲
344		I-75 Bus, US 2W, St Ignace (SB)
(344)		St Ignace Welcome Center (NB) (RR, Phones, Picnic, Info, Weather)
(343)		TOLL Booth, to TOLL Bridge
(341)		TOLL, Mackinac Bridge W-Lake Michigan, E-Lake Huron
339		Jamet St, Mackinaw City
	Gas	E: AmocoBP W: Phillips 66, Shell
	Food	E: Audie's Family Rest, Big Boy, DQ, KFC, McDonald's, Subway W: Darrow's Rest
	Lodg	E: Budget Host Inn, Days Inn, Econo Lodge, Lighthouse View Motel, Super 8 W: Holiday Inn Express
(338)		US 23, Mackinaw Hwy (SB) MI 108, Mackinaw Hwy (NB) Mackinaw City Welcome Center E: (Both dir) (RR, Phones, Picnic, Info, Weather)
	FStop	E: Next Door Store #17/Marathon
	Gas	E: BP
	Food	E: Anna's Country Buffet, Burger King, DQ, Mackinaw Pizza, Subway
	Lodg	E: Baymont Inn, Courtyard
	Other	E: Mackinaw City/Mackinac Island KOA▲
337		MI 108, Mackinaw Hwy, Cheboygan to US 23, Huron Ave (NB, diff reacc)
	Gas	E: Citgo◈
	Food	E: Rest/Embers Motel, Dockside Deli, Lighthouse Rest, Mario's
	Lodg	E: Best Western♥, Embers Motel, Kings Inn, Starlite Budget Inn, Sundown Motel
	Other	E: Mackinaw City/Mackinac Island KOA▲, Tee Pee Campground▲, Old Mill Creek State Park, Mackinaw Mill Creek Camping▲, W: Wilderness State Park

◈= Regular Gas Stations with Diesel ▲ = RV Friendly Locations ♥= Pet Friendly Locations
Red print shows large vehicle parking / access on site or nearby Brown Print = Campgrounds / RV PARKS

EXIT		MICHIGAN
336		**US 31S, Petoskey, Charlevoix (SB)**
(328)		**Hebron Rest Area #408 (SB)** (RR, Phones, Picnic, Info) (NO Truck/RV) (Closed Winter)
326		**CR C66, Levering Rd, to Cheboygan**
	Gas	E: Marathon
	Med	E: + Hospital
322		**CR C64, Riggsville Rd, Cheboygan (Serv 8mi E in Cheboygan)**
(317)		**Topinabee Rest Area (NB) (Closed Winter)** (RR, Phones, Picnic, Info, View)
313		**MI 27N, Straits Hwy, Indian River, to Topinabee**
	Lodg	W: Navajo Motel, Topinabee Motel
	Other	E: Indian River RV Resort & Camp▲, Indian River Country Cabins ▲
310		**MI 68, Indian River, Burt Lake, Afton**
	Gas	W: AmocoBP◈, Shell
	Food	W: Burger King, Café, DQ, Indian River Steak House
	Lodg	E: Holiday Inn Express W: Coach House Motel, Indian River Motel & Cottages
	Other	E: Pigeon Bay Campground▲, Yogi Bear Jellystone Campground▲ W: Burt Lake State Park, Indian River Trading Post▲, Crooked River RV Park▲
301		**CR C58, Afton Rd, Wolverine**
	Gas	E: Marathon◈
	Other	E: Elkwood Campground▲ W: Sturgin River Campground▲
290		**CR C48, N Old 27, Vanderbilt**
	Gas	E: BP W: Andy's Mobil
	Food	E: Gateway Rest
	Other	E: LP/BP W: RVDump/Mobil
(287)		**Vanderbilt Rest Area #406 (SB)** (RR, Phones, Picnic, Vend, Info, View)
282		**I-75 Bus, MI 32, Main St, Gaylord**
	FStop	E: Forward Shell Food Mart W: Chalet Marathon, Gaylord Fuel Stop
	Gas	E: 7-11, BP◈, Clark, Holiday, Speedway◈ W: BP◈, Shell◈
	Food	E: Arby's, Burger King, DQ, La Senorita, KFC, McDonald's, N MI Seafood, Quiznos, Red Rose Rest, Subway, Wendy's W: Applebee's, Big Boy, Bob Evans, China 1, Culver's, Mancino's Grinders & Pizza, Hut, Ponderosa, Ruby Tuesday, Red Rose Rest, Sweet Basil, Spicy Bob's Ital Express, Starbucks, Subway, Taco Bell
	Lodg	E: Baymont Inn♥, Best Western♥, Best Value Inn, Downtown Motel, Quality Inn, Royal Crest Motel♥ W: Hampton Inn, Holiday Inn Express
	Med	E: + Hospital
	Other	E: Auto Dealer, Family Dollar, Grocery, RiteAid, Golf Courses, Otsego Co Fairgrounds, MI Sheriff Office, MI State Hwy Patrol Post W: LP/Marathon, ATMs, Auto Dealer, Big Lots, Dollar Tree, Home Depot, Grocery, Lowe's, Walmart sc, Golf Course, Otsego Co Airport✈, Gaylord Alpine RV Park & Campground▲, Burnside RV Center

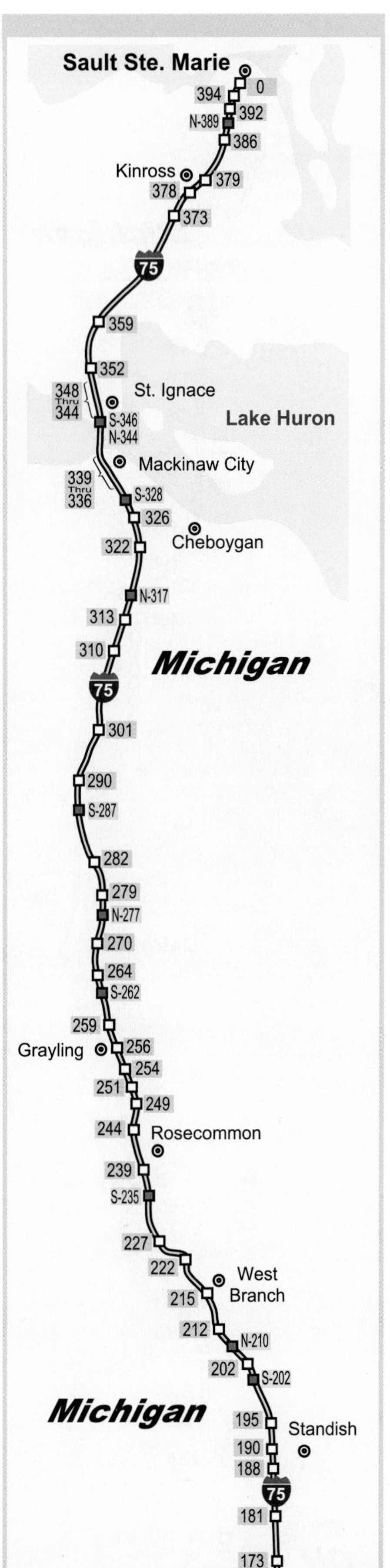

EXIT		MICHIGAN
NOTE:		**MM 279: 45th Parallel—Halfway Point between the Equator & North Pole**
279		**I-75 Bus, Old US 27, Gaylord**
	FStop	E: South End Marathon
	Gas	E: Mobil◈, Shell
	Food	E: Burger King, Mama Leones Italian, Subway/Marathon
	Lodg	E: Econo Lodge, Timberly Motel
	Other	E: Auto Dealers, Gaylord KOA▲, MI Sheriff, MI State Hwy Patrol Post W: to Otsego Lake State Park, Beaver Creek Resort & RV Park▲, Golf Courses
(277)		**Gaylord Rest Area #405 (NB)** (RR, Phones, Picnic, Vend, Info)
270		**Marlette Rd, Gaylord, Waters**
	TStop	E: Hilltop BP Truck Stop
	Food	E: Rest/Hilltop TS
	Other	W: Grocery, to Otsego Lake State Park
264		**CR 612, Frederic, Grayling**
	Other	E: Hartwick Pines St Park North Ent, Camp Grayling MI Nat'l Guard Military Res
(262)		**Hartwick Pines Rest Area #404 (SB)** (RR, Phones, Picnic, Vend, Info)
259		**I-75 Bus, MI 93, Hartwick Pines Rd, Downtown Grayling, Traverse City**
	Other	E: Hartwick Pines St Park South Ent, Camp Grayling MI Nat'l Guard Mil Res W: Grayling Army Air Field✈, Camp Grayling MI Nat'l Guard Miilitary Res
256		**N Down River (SB), to I-75 Bus, IN 93, IN 72, Grayling**
254		**I-75 Bus, MI 72, Grayling (NB, L exit)**
	Gas	W: Admiral, BP, Citgo, Phillips 66, Shell, Speedway
	Food	W: A&W, Burger King, DQ, Hardee's, KFC, Little Caesars, McDonald's, Pizza Hut, Subway, Taco Bell, Wendy's
	Lodg	W: Days Inn, Holiday Inn, Super 7 Inn
	TWash	W: Wagon Wheel Cleaning Center
	TServ	W: MI CAT
	Med	W: + Hospital
	Other	W: CarQuest, Grocery, RiteAid
(252)		**Grayling Rest Area #403 (NB)** (RR, Phones, Pic, Pet, Vend, Info)
251		**4 Mile Rd, Grayling**
	TStop	W: Charlie's Country Corner/Marathon
	Food	W: FastFood/Charlie's CC
	Lodg	W: Super 8
	Other	E: Yogi Bear Jellystone RV Camp▲ W: Laundry/RVDump/LP/Charlie's CC, Camp Grayling MI Nat'l Guard Mil Res
249		**US 127S, CR 301, Claire, Roscommon (SB, no reaccess)**
	Other	W: to N Higgins Lake State Park
244		**I-75 Bus, CR200, W Federal Hwy, Old MI 76, Roscommon**
	FStop	W: Knight Enterprises/Sunoco
	Food	E: Tee Pee Rest
	Lodg	E: Tee Pee Motel
	Other	W: Higgins Hills RV Park▲, to North Higgins Lake State Park, Higgins Lake
239		**MI 18, Roscommon Rd, I-75 Bus, Lake St, Houghton Lake, Gladwin**
	Other	W: Higgins Lake State Park
(235)		**Nine Mile Hill Rest Area (SB)** (RR, Phones, Picnic, Vend)

◈= Regular Gas Stations with Diesel ▲ = RV Friendly Locations ♥= Pet Friendly Locations
Red print shows large vehicle parking / access on site or nearby Brown Print = Campgrounds / RV PARKS

EXIT		MICHIGAN
227		**MI 55W, W Branch Rd, St Helen**
		(Serv 5mi W in Prudenville)
	Other	**W:** to Houghton Lake
222		**MI 76, St Helen Rd, St Helen**
215		**I-75 Bus MI 55E, Old MI 76, West Branch, Tawas City**
	Gas	**E:** Citgo◈
	Lodg	**E:** La Hacienda Motel
	Med	**E:** + Hospital
	TServ	**E:** West Branch Diesel Repair
	Other	**E:** Schmitt Tire, **MI Sheriff, MI State Hwy Patrol Post**, W Branch Comm Airport✈
212		**I-75 Bus, Cook Rd, West Branch, to MI 76, Alger Rd, to MI 55**
	FStop	**E:** 7-11/Marathon
		W: Jaxx Snaxx W Branch/BP
	Gas	**E:** Shell
	Food	**E:** Arby's, Burger King, McDonald's, Taco Bell, Wendy's, Subway/Shell
	Lodg	**E:** Quality Inn, Super 8
	Med	**E:** + Hospital
	Other	**E:** ATM, Home Depot, **Walmart sc**, Tanger Outlet Mall, West Branch Comm Airport✈, **MI State Hwy Patrol, to Outdoor Adventures/Lake of the North Resort▲**
(210)		**W Branch Rest Area (NB)**
		(RR, Phone, Picnic, Vend)
202		**MI 33, Brock Rd, Alger Rd, Alger**
	FStop	**E:** Mobil
	Gas	**E:** BP, Shell
	Food	**E:** Subway/Pizza/Shell
	Other	**E: Greenwood Campground▲**
(202)		**Alger Rest Area (SB)**
		(RR, Phones, Picnic, Vend)
195		**W Sterling Rd, Sterling, Omer**
	Gas	**E:** Forward, Sunrise Side Towing
	Food	**E:** Dave & Kathie's, Iva's
	Other	**E: River View Campground & Canoe▲ , Crystal Creek Campground▲ , Outdoor Adventures/Rifle River Resort▲**
190		**MI 61, Standish, to MI 76, US 23**
	Gas	**W:** Mobil, Shell
	Food	**E:** A&W, Little Caesars Pizza, Moon Gate Chinese, N Forest Café, Subway, Taco Bell, Wheeler's Rest
	Lodg	**E:** Forward Lodging, In Town Motel
	Other	**E: Big Bend Campground▲ , Riverbend Campground▲**
188		**US 23, S Huron Rd, Standish**
	Other	**E:** Standish Industrial Airport✈, **to Big Bend Campground▲ , Riverbend Camp ground▲ , Outdoor Adventures/ Saginaw Bay Resort▲ , Outdoor Adventures/Wilderness Resort ▲**
181		**Pinconning Rd, Pinconning**
	TStop	**W:** Pinconning Express Stop/Sunoco
	Gas	**E:** Mobil, Shell◈, Speedway
	Food	**E:** McDonald's/Shell, Pizza, Subway
		W: FastFood/Pinconning ES
	Lodg	**E:** Pinconning Trail House Motel
(175)		**Linwood Rest Area (NB)**
		(RR, Phone, Picnic, Vend)
173		**Linwood Rd, Linwood**
	Gas	**E:** BP◈, Mobil◈
	Other	**E: Hoyle's Marina & Campground▲**
168		**Beaver Rd, Kawkawlin, to Willard**
	Other	**E:** Bay City State Park

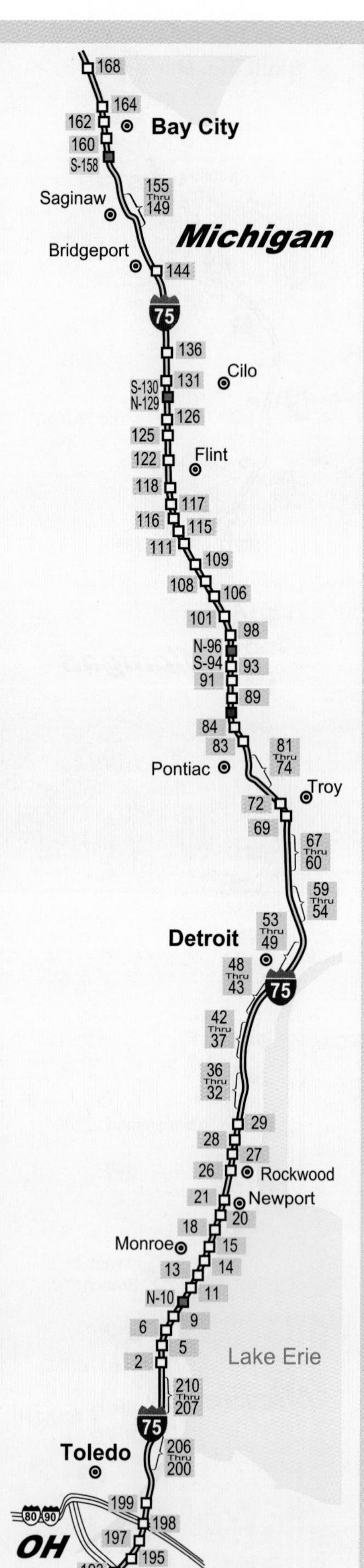

EXIT		MICHIGAN
164		**Wilder Rd, MI 13 Conn, Bay City**
	Gas	**E:** Meijer◈
	Food	**E:** Cracker Barrel, McDonald's, Pizza
	Lodg	**E:** AmericInn
162		**US 10W, MI 25, Midland, Bay City**
162B		**US 10W, Midland (NB)**
	Other	**W: to appr 12mi Valley Plaza Resort▲**
162A		**MI 25, Bay City (NB)**
160		**MI 84, Westside Saginaw Rd**
	Gas	**E:** Mobil◈, Shell
		W: 7-11, Speedway
	Food	**E:** Dunkin Donuts/Shell, Subway/Mobil
		W: Berger Family Rest, Burger King, McDonald's
	Lodg	**W:** Bay Valley Hotel & Resort, Econo Lodge
	Other	**E: to Finn Rd Campground▲**
		W: International RV World
(158)		**Bay City Rest Area (SB)**
		(RR, Phone, Picnic, Vend)
(155)		**Jct I-675, Downtown Saginaw**
154		**Adam St, Saginaw, Zilwaukee**
153		**MI 13, Bay City Rd, Saginaw**
151		**MI 81, Washington Rd, Saginaw, Caro, Reese**
	TStop	**E:** M-81 Express/Sunoco
		W: Flying J Travel Plaza (Scales)
	Food	**E:** BurgerKing/M-81 Express
		W: Wendy's/FJ TP
	TWash	**W:** Coty's Hi-Pressure Wash
	TServ	**E:** Upper Lakes Tire
		W: Fruehauf Parts & Service, MI CAT
	Other	**E:** Laundry/M-81 Express
		W: Laundry/WiFi/**RVDump/LP**/FJ TP
(150)		**Jct I-675N, Saginaw**
149AB		**MI 46, Holland Ave, Saginaw**
	Gas	**W:** Amoco, Circle K, Sunoco, Speedway◈
	Food	**W:** Arby's, Burger King, Big John Steak & Onion, McDonald's, Taco Bell, Wendy's
	Lodg	**W:** Best Western, Motel 6♥, Welcome Inn
	TServ	**W:** Scott Tire Sales
	Med	**W:** + Hospital
	Other	**W:** Grocery
144		**Dixie Hwy, Bridgeport, Frankenmuth**
144A		**Dixie Hwy, Bridgeport (NB)**
	FStop	**E:** Speedway (Scales)
	TStop	**E:** North Star Travel Plaza/Marathon (Scales
	Gas	**E:** Shell
	Food	**E:** Subway/Marathon, Blimpie/Shell
	Lodg	**E:** Heidelberg Inn Motel
	Other	**E: to Yogi Bear's Jellystone RV Park Campground▲**
144B		**Dixie Hwy, Bridgeport, Frankenmuth**
	TStop	**W:** Travel Center of America #198/Citgo (Scales)
	Gas	**W:** Mobil
	Food	**W:** CountryPride/TA TC, Arby's, Burger King, **Cracker Barrel**, McDonald's, Peking City, Subway, Taco Bell, Wendy's
	Lodg	**W:** Baymont Inn, Days Inn, Villager Lodge
	TServ	**W:** TA TC/Tires
	Other	**W:** Laundry/WiFi/**RVDump**/TA TC, IGA, Pharmacy, **MI State Hwy Patrol Post**

◈ = Regular Gas Stations with Diesel ▲ = RV Friendly Locations ♥ = Pet Friendly Locations

Red print shows large vehicle parking / access on site or nearby **Brown Print = Campgrounds / RV PARKS**

EXIT		MICHIGAN
136		**MI 54, MI 83, Birch Run Rd, Birch Run**
	FStop	**E:** Conlee Travel Center #2/Mobil **W:** Birch Run Express Stop/Sunoco, Fast Pax/Marathon
	Gas	**E:** Shell **W:** 7-11, BP
	Food	**E:** Exit Rest, Little Caesars, KFC, Subway **W:** Arby's, Bob Evans, McDonald's, Quiznos, Starbucks, Taco Bell, Tony's Birch Run, Wendy's
	Lodg	**E:** Best Western, Comfort Inn, Holiday Inn Express♥, Super 8 **W:** Country Inn
	Other	**E:** CarQuest, Laundry, **Pine Ridge RV Campground▲**, **RV Center**, **Frankenmuth Jellystone Park▲** **W:** Pharmacy, Prime Outlets, Auto Dealers
131		**MI 57, Vienna Rd, Clio, to Montrose, Thetford Center**
	Gas	**E:** Shell, Sunoco **W:** AmocoBP◈, Mobil◈
	Food	**E:** Arby's, Big John Steak & Onion, Burger King, KFC, McDonald's, Taco Bell, Subway **W:** Big Boy, Wendy's
	Other	**E:** Auto Zone
(130)		**Clio Rest Area (SB)** **(RR, Phones, Picnic, Vend)**
(129)		**Dodge Rd Rest Area (NB)** **(RR, Phones, Picnic, Vend, Info)**
126		**Mt Morris Rd, Mount Morris**
	FStop	**E:** Amir's Mini Mart **W:** I-75 BP #8
	TStop	**E:** Quick-Sav #7/BP (Scales)
	Food	**E:** FastFood/BP
	Other	**W:** I-75 Malls, ATMs, Carwash
(125)		**Jct I-475, UAW Freeway, Flint**
122		**Pierson Rd, Flint, Flushing**
	Gas	**E:** AmocoBP, Clark, Marathon **W:** Citgo, Shell, Meijer◈
	Food	**E:** KFC, McDonald's, Ponderosa, Subway **W:** Arby's, Bob Evans, Burger King, Cracker Barrel, Denny's, Long John Silver, Pizza Hut, Red Lobster, Taco Bell, Wendy's, YaYa's Chicken
	Lodg	**E:** Super 8 **W:** Baymont Inn, Great Western Inn, Ramada Inn, Sheraton Inn
	Other	**W:** ATMs, Discount Tire, Home Depot
118		**MI 21, Corunna Rd, Flint, Owasso**
	Gas	**E:** Sunoco, Kroger **W:** AmocoBP, Citgo, Mobil, Shell
	Food	**E:** Badawest Lebanese Rest, Big John Steak & Onion, Burger King, Hardee's, Little Caesar's, Taco Bell **W:** Burger King, Domino's, Happy Valley Oriental
	Lodg	**W:** Economy Motel
	Med	**E:** + McLaren Reg'l Med Center
	Other	**E:** Advance Auto, Dollar General, Kroger, Pharmacy, RiteAid **W:** Auto Zone, CarQuest. Home Depot, Lowe's, Pharmacy, Sam's Club, **Walmart**, **MI State Hwy Patrol Post**
117		**Miller Rd, to I-69 (SB)**
117B		**Miller Rd, Flint (NB)**
	Gas	**E:** Speedway◈, Sunoco◈ **W:** Amoco, Speedway

Personal Notes

EXIT		MICHIGAN
	Food	**E:** Applebee's, Arby's, Don Pablo, Fuddrucker's, KFC, McDonald's, Lone Star Steakhouse, Subway **W:** Bob Evans, Burger King, Chuck E Cheese Pizza, Hooters, Old Country Buffet, Olive Garden, Outback Steakhouse, Pizza Hut, Starbucks, Taco Bell, Wendy's
	Lodg	**E:** Comfort Inn, Motel 6♥, Sleep Inn **W:** Howard Johnson, Red Roof Inn♥, Super 8
	Other	**E:** Grocery **W:** Best Buy, Goodyear, Office Depot, Target, U-Haul, Genesee Valley Center Mall
(117A)		**Jct I-69, E-Lansing, W-Pt Huron (NB)**
116B		**MI 121, Bristol Rd, Am Vets Hy (SB)**
116A		**MI 121, Amer Veterans Hwy (SB)**
116		**MI 121, American Veterans Hwy**
	FStop	**W:** Bristol Mobil **(SB 116B)**
	Gas	**E:** Amoco, Citgo, Speedway◈
	Food	**E:** KFC, McDonald's
	Lodg	**E:** Days Inn **W:** Econo Lodge
	TServ	**E:** Scott Tire Sales
	Other	**E:** Auto Zone, GM Truck & Bus Assembly Plant, **to I-475** **W:** Bishop Int'l Airport✈
115		**US 23S, to Ann Arbor, MI (SB)** **(Serv at Ex #90 on US 23, W Hill Rd)**
(111)		**Jct I-475N, UAW Frwy (NB)**

EXIT		MICHIGAN
109		**MI 54, Dort Hwy, Grand Blanc Rd (Difficult reaccess SB)**
	Gas	**E:** Marathon
	Food	**E:** Big Boy, Damon's, Wendy's
108		**Holly Rd, Grand Blanc**
	Gas	**E:** Marathon **W:** BP
	Food	**E:** Quiznos **W:** McDonald's
	Lodg	**E:** AmeriHost Inn
	Med	**W:** + Genesys Reg'l Medical Center
106		**MI 54, Dixie Hwy, S Saginaw Rd Holly (SB, Left Exit, NO NB return)**
101		**Grange Hall Rd, to Ortonville, Holly**
	Gas	**E:** Sunoco
	Other	**E:** Holly State Rec Area, Yogi Bear's Jellystone RV Campground/RVDump▲, Clear Water Campground▲ **W:** Groveland Oaks County Park, Seven Lakes State Park
98		**E Holly Rd, Holly, Springfield**
	FStop	**E:** E Holly Truck Stop/Sunoco
(96)		**Davisburg Rest Area (NB)** **(RR, Phones, Picnic, Vend, Info)**
(94)		**Clarkston Rest Area (SB)** **(RR, Phones, Picnic, Vend, WiFi)** **NOTE: SB: Last Rest Area in MI**
93		**US 24, Dixie Hwy, Clarkston, Springfield**
	Gas	**E:** BP◈, Kroger **W:** Speedway
	Food	**W:** McDonald's, Subway, Wendy's
	Other	**W:** Pontiac Lake State Rec Area
91		**MI 15, N Main St, Ortonville Rd, Clarkston, Ortonville, Waterford**
	Gas	**E:** Marathon **W:** Shell◈
	Food	**W:** Clarkston Café, Mesquite Rest
	Lodg	**W:** Mill Pond Inn
89		**Sashabaw Rd, Clarkston**
	Gas	**E:** Shell◈ **W:** AmocoBP
	Food	**E:** Ruby Tuesday **W:** McDonald's, Subway, Wendy's
(86)		**Weigh Station (SB)**
84		**Baldwin Rd, Auburn Hills (SB)**
	Gas	**E:** Shell, Sunoco◈ **W:** Mobil
	Food	**E:** Arby', Big Boy, Joe's Crab Shack, Longhorn Steakhouse, Wendy's **W:** Chili's, McDonald's, Sbarro, Starbucks, Steak n Shake
	Lodg	**W:** Towne Suites
	Other	**E:** Best Buy, Costco, Discount Tire, Office Max, PetCo♥, Staples, Target, UPS Store Great Lakes Crossing Outlet Mall **W:** Circuit City, FedEx Office
84AB		**Baldwin Rd, Auburn Hills (NB)**
83		**Joslyn Rd, Auburn Hills**
	Gas	**E:** Meijer◈, Sam's
	Food	**E:** Applebee's, McDonald's, Olive Garden
	Other	**E:** Foodtown, Sam's Club, Tires
83AB		**Joslyn Rd**
81		**I-75 Bus, Lapeer Rd, MI 24, Pontiac (difficult reaccess)**
	Gas	**E:** AmocoBP
	Other	**E:** The Palace Arena

◈= Regular Gas Stations with Diesel ▲ = RV Friendly Locations ♥= Pet Friendly Locations
Red print shows large vehicle parking / access on site or nearby **Brown Print = Campgrounds / RV PARKS**

EXIT — MICHIGAN

79 — University Dr, Auburn Hills, Pontiac Rochester Hills, Rochester
- Gas: E: Amoco; W: Speedway◈
- Food: E: Domino's Pizza, Dunkin Donuts, Subway; W: Big Buck Brewery & Steakhouse, McDonald's, Mountain Jack's Steakhouse, Taco Bell, Tim Horton's, Wendy's
- Lodg: W: AmeriSuites, Comfort Inn, Courtyard Inn, Candlewood Suites, Fairfield Inn, Holiday Inn, Hampton Inn, Motel 6♥
- Med: W: + Hospital
- Other: W: A&S RV Center/RVDump

78 — Chrysler Dr, Auburn Hills
- Other: E: Daimler Chrysler Tech Center

77AB — MI 59, Veterans Memorial Frwy, E to Utica, W to Pontiac
- Other: W: Pontiac Silverdome Stadium

75 — Square Lake Rd (NB, Left Exit)

74 — Adams Rd, Troy

72 — Crooks Rd, Troy
- Food: W: Quiznos, Red Robin, Starbucks
- Lodg: W: Embassy Suites, Hilton Inn, Marriott

69 — W Big Beaver Rd, Troy
- Gas: W: AmocoBP, Shell
- Food: W: Denny's, Ruth Chris Steakhouse
- Lodg: E: Drury Inn, Marriott; W: Candlewood Hotel

67 — Rochester Rd, E Big Beaver Rd
- Gas: E: Marathon, Mobil, Shell
- Food: E: Arby's, Burger King, Dunkin Donuts, KFC, Mr Pita, Popeye's Chicken
- Food: W: Mountain Jack Steakhouse
- Lodg: W: Embassy Suites, Holiday Inn, Red Roof Inn♥
- Other: E: Discount Tire, Office Depot, Radio Shack; W: Tires

65AB — 14 Mile Rd, Troy, Madison Heights
- Gas: E: Mobil, Shell; W: Mobil
- Food: E: Bob Evans, Burger King, Chili's, Denny's, Logan's Roadhouse, McDonald's, Panera Bread Co, Steak & Ale, Taco Bell, Wendy's; W: Applebee's, Big Fish Seafood Rest, McDonald's, Outback Steakhouse, White Castle
- Lodg: E: Motel 6♥, Red Roof Inn♥; W: Best Western, Econo Lodge, Extended Stay America, Fairfield Inn, Hampton Inn, Residence Inn
- Med: E: + Walk-In Clinic
- Other: E: ATMs, Banks, CompUSA, Firestone, Goodyear, FedEx Office, Office Depot, Pharmacy, Sam's Club, Target, UPS Store, Oakland Mall; W: ATMs, Banks, CVS, Discount Tire, Grocery

63 — 12 Mile Rd, Madison Heights
- Gas: E: Marathon, Speedway; W: Mobil, Marathon, Costco
- Food: E: Blimpie's, McDonald's, Red Lobster; W: Denny's, Dunkin Donuts/Marathon
- Med: W: + Hospital
- Other: E: Kmart, Home Depot; W: Pharmacy, Costco

62 — 11 Mile Rd, 10 Mile Rd W
- Gas: E: Mobil; W: BP, Mobil

Personal Notes

EXIT — MICHIGAN

- Food: E: Domino's Pizza; W: Hardee's, KFC, Taco Bell

(61) — Jct I-696, E-Port Huron, W-Lansing
- Other: W: to Hazel Park Raceway

60 — 9 Mile Rd, Hazel Park
- Gas: E: Mobil◈; W: Mobil, Shell
- Food: E: China One, DQ, McDonald's, Subway; W: Big Boy, Wendy's
- Lodg: E: Guesthouse Inn

59 — MI 102, 8 Mile Rd, Highland Park
- Gas: E: Amoco; W: 76, Shell
- Food: E: Arby's, Burger King, Subway, Wendy's
- Lodg: E: Bali Motel
- Other: E: Family Dollar, Grocery, Pharmacy; W: MI State Fairgrounds

58 — 7 Mile Rd, Highland Park, Detroit
- Gas: W: AmocoBP◈

57 — McNichols Rd, Highland Park
- Gas: E: BP

56AB — MI 8, Davison Freeway

55 — Caniff Ave, Holbrook St, Detroit
- Gas: E: Mobil
- Food: W: KFC, Taco Bell
- Other: W: Daimler Chrysler Gen'l Offices

54 — Grand Blvd, Clay St, Detroit
- Gas: W: BP, Shell
- Food: W: Super Coney Island

(53B) — Jct I-94, Ford Fwy, to Port Huron, Chicago

EXIT — MICHIGAN

53A — Warren Ave, Detroit
- Gas: E: Shell; W: AmocoBP
- Food: E: Little Caesars Pizza, McDonald's
- Med: E: + Hospital
- Other: W: Detroit Institute of Arts

52 — Mack Ave, Detroit
- Gas: E: Shell
- Food: E: McDonald's
- Med: W: + Children's Hospital of Michigan, Harper Hospital, + Detroit Receiving Hospital

(51C) — Jct I-375, Chrysler Freeway, Flint
- Other: E: Comerica Park, Ford Field, Civic Ctr, Tunnel to Canada, Greektown, Greektown Casino, Joe Louis Arena, Cobo Hall, MGM Grand Casino

51B — MI 3, Gratiot Ave (NB, Left exit)

51A — MI 1, Woodward Ave

50 — Grand River Ave, Downtown
- Gas: W: AmocoBP

49B — MI 10, Lodge Freeway (SB)

49A — Rosa Parks Blvd
- Gas: W: Mobil
- Med: E: + Hospital
- Other: E: Tiger Stadium

49 — Rosa Parks Blvd

(48) — Jct I-96, Jeffries Freeway, Lansing (I-96 begins/ends I-75 Ex# 48)

47B — Porter St, to Windsor Canada
- FStop: E: Ammex
- Other: E: Bridge to Canada, DutyFree 24/7

47A — MI 3, Clark St, Fort St, Detroit
- FStop: E: USA Fuel Mart/BP

46 — Livernois Ave, Downtown Detroit
- TStop: E: Detroit Truck Stop/Marathon
- Food: E: KFC

45 — Fort St, Springwells Ave
- Gas: E: BP◈; W: Mobil
- Food: W: McDonald's, Wendy's

44 — Dearborn St (NB exit, NO NB re-entry)
- FStop: E: Dearborn Food Mart/Citgo

43 — MI 85, Fort St, Schaefer Hwy (NB)
- TStop: W: Motor City Truck Plaza/Marathon, Fuel Mart of America/BP (SB 43B)
- Gas: E: AmocoBP, Sunoco
- TServ: W: Marathon Motor City TP/Tires
- Other: W: Ford Plant

43B — MI 85, Fort St, Schaefer Hwy (SB)

43A — MI 85, Fort St, Schaefer Hwy (SB)

42 — Outer Dr, Detroit
- Gas: W: BP◈, Mobil◈
- Food: E: Coney Island
- Med: E: + Oakwood Medical Center

41 — MI 39, Southfield Rd, Lincoln Park
- FStop: W: Marathon
- Food: E: A&W, Tim Hortons; W: Dunkin Donuts
- Lodg: E: Budget Inn; W: Sleep Inn
- TServ: W: Speedy Muffler King
- Other: W: Pharmacy

40 — Dix Hwy, to IN 85, Lincoln Park
- Gas: E: Citgo, Marathon, Speedway; W: Mobil, Shell

◈ = Regular Gas Stations with Diesel ▲ = RV Friendly Locations ♥ = Pet Friendly Locations
Red print shows large vehicle parking / access on site or nearby Brown Print = Campgrounds / RV PARKS

EXIT		MICHIGAN
	Food	E: Pizza, Ponderosa W: Burger King, DQ, Dunkin Donuts, Long John Silver, McDonald's, Pizza Hut, Taco Bell
	Lodg	W: Holiday Motel
	TServ	E: Downriver
	Other	E: Pharmacy W: CVS, Foodland, Firestone
37		**Northline Rd, Allen Rd, Southgate**
	FStop	W: Allen Rd Mini Mart/Citgo
	Gas	E: AmocoBP, Mobil, Speedway
	Food	E: Pizza W: Arby's, Burger King, McDonald's
	Lodg	E: Holiday Inn W: Best Value, Comfort Suites, La Quinta Inn♥
	Other	E: Auto Repair Service, Sam's Club W: Wayne Co Comm College
36		**Eureka Rd, Southgate, Taylor**
	Gas	E: BP, Shell, Speedway W: Meijer◈
	Food	E: Bob Evans, Denny's, Fire Mountain Grill W: Baker's Square, Famous Dave's BBQ, Hooters, Mountain Jack's Steakhouse, Rio Bravo, Subway, Wendy's
	Lodg	E: Ramada Inn, Super 8 W: Red Roof Inn♥
	Other	W: ATMs, Banks, Best Buy, CVS, Discount Tire, FedEx Office, Home Depot, PetCo♥, Staples, Southland Center Mall
35		**US 24, Telegraph Rd (NB, Left exit)**
34B		**Sibley Rd, Wyandotte (SB)**
34A		**Dix Toledo Hwy, Trenton (SB)**
34		**Dix Toledo Hwy, Sibley Rd (NB)**
	FStop	W: Sunoco Plaza **(SB: Access via 34B)**
	Gas	W: AmocoBP
	Food	W: McDonald's, Subway
32		**West Rd, Woodhaven, Trenton**
	TStop	E: AmBest/Detroiter Travel Center/Citgo (Scales)
	Gas	E: Meijer◈, Speedway◈ W: AmocoBP, Shell
	Food	E: Cafe/Deli/Detroiter TC, Applebee's, Bob Evans, Burger King, Dunkin Donuts, Long John Silver, Panera Bread, Pizza Hut, Taco Bell, White Castle W: Country Skillet, McDonald's
	Lodg	E: Motel/Detroiter TC W: Best Western, Knight's Inn, Holiday Inn Express♥
	TWash	E: Detroiter TC
	TServ	E: Detroiter TC
	Other	E: Laundry/BarbSh/**RVDump**/Detroiter TC, ATMs, Discount Tire, Firestone, Home Depot, Kroger, Office Depot, Target, **Walmart**, Ford Woodhaven Stamping Plant W: Pharmacy
29		**Gibraltar Rd, Flat Rock (NB)**
	Gas	W: Marathon
	Lodg	W: Sleep Inn
29AB		**Gibraltar Rd, Flat Rock**
28		**MI 85, Fort St (NB)**
27		**N Huron River Dr, Rockwood**
	Gas	E: Marathon◈ W: Speedway◈
	Food	E: Benito's Pizza, Huron River Rest, Ocean Chinese
	Lodg	E: Huron River Inn

EXIT		MI / OH
26		**S Huron River Dr, Rockwood**
	Gas	E: Sunoco◈
	Food	E: Dixie Café
21		**Newport Rd, Swan Creek Rd, Newport**
	TStop	W: Newport Travel Center/Marathon
	Gas	E: AmocoBP
	Food	E: TacoBell/Amoco W: FastFood/Newport TC
	Other	E: Newport Auto Repair, Jerry's Towing, US Post Office W: Laundry/**LP**/Newport TC
(20)		**Jct I-275N, to Flint**
18		**Nadeau Rd, Monroe**
	TStop	W: Pilot Travel Center #284 (Scales)
	Food	W: Arby/TJCinn/Pilot TC
	Other	W: WiFi/Pilot TC, **Shady Creek RV Park & Campground▲**
15		**MI 50, N Dixie Hwy, Monroe**
	TStop	W: Pilot Travel Center #24 (Scales), TravelCenter of America #69/BP (Scales)
	Gas	E: Shell
	Food	E: Bob Evans, Burger King, Red Lobster W: Subway/Pilot TC, CountryPride/PizzaHut/Popeye/Quiznos/TA TC, Denny's, **Cracker Barrel**, McDonald's, Wendy's
	Lodg	E: Best Value Inn, Best Western, Hampton W: Holiday Inn Express, Knights Inn
	TWash	W: TA TC
	TServ	W: TA TC/Tires
	Other	W: WiFi/Pilot TC, Laundry/WiFi/TA TC
14		**Elm Ave, to Monroe**
13		**Front St, Monroe**
11		**Laplaisance Rd, Monroe**
	Gas	W: Amoco, Marathon, Speedway
	Food	W: Burger King, McDonald's, Wendy's
	Lodg	W: AmeriHost Inn, Comfort Inn
	Other	W: **Harbortown RV Resort▲**, Outlet Mall, **MI State Hwy Patrol Post**
(10)		**MI Welcome Center (NB) (RR, Phones, Pic, Vend, Info, Playgr)**
9		**S Otter Creek Rd, to La Salle**
(8)		**Weigh Station (Both dir)**
6		**Luna Pier Rd, Erie, Luna Pier**
	TStop	W: Luna Pier Fuel Center/Sunoco
	Food	E: Gander's
	Lodg	E: Super 8
	Other	W: Laundry/Luna Pier FC
5		**Erie Rd, Erie, to Temperance**
2		**Summit St, Erie, Temperance**

EASTERN TIME ZONE

↑ MICHIGAN

↓ OHIO

NOTE: MM 211: Michigan State Line

EASTERN TIME ZONE

EXIT		OHIO
210		**OH 184, E Alexis Rd, Toledo**
	FStop	W: **to 5715 Enterprise Blvd:** Quick Fuel #2304
	TStop	W: Pilot Travel Center #15 (Scales)
	Gas	W: BP◈, Meijer◈
	Food	W: Subway/Pilot TC, Arby's, Bob Evans, Burger King, McDonald's, Taco Bell, Wendy's
	Lodg	W: Comfort Inn, Fairfield Inn, Hampton Inn,Raceway Motel, Sunset Motel
	TServ	W: Alexis Diesel & Truck Service, Ron's Diesel Service, John's Standard Diesel Service, Bi-State Ford Truck
	Other	W: WiFi/Pilot TC, Raceway Park, North Towne Square Mall, Meijer,Tires Plus, Toledo Speedway
209		**Ottawa River Rd (NB)**
	Gas	E: BP, Sunoco
	Food	E: Little Caesar's Pizza
	Other	E: Foodtown, RiteAid
(208)		**Jct I-280S, to I-80/90, to Cleveland**
207		**La Grange St, (SB) Stickney Ave (NB)**
	FStop	W: **to 812 Matzinger Rd:** Convenience Express
	Gas	E: BP, Citgo, Sunoco
	Food	E: McDonald's, Wendy's
	Other	E: Family Dollar, Kroger, RiteAid
206		**Phillips Ave, to US 24**
205B		**Berdan Ave, to US24 (NB, No reacc)**
	Other	E: Daimler Chrysler Toledo Assembly Plant
205A		**Willy's Pkwy, to Jeep Pkwy**
(204)		**Jct I-475W, to US 23, Maumee, Sylvania, Ann Arbor (NB Left Exit)**
203B		**US 24, OH 51, N Detroit Ave**
	Gas	W: BP, Shell
	Food	W: KFC, McDonald's, Wendy's
	Other	W: Pharmacy, Grocery, U-Haul, Museum
203A		**Bancroft St, to OH 51, Dwntwn (NB)**
202B		**Collingwood Blvd, to Dorr St (SB)**
202A		**Dorr St, Indiana Ave, to Washington St, Downtown Toledo (SB)**
	Gas	E: BP
	Food	W: McDonald's
	Lodg	E: Radisson, Wyndham
	Med	E: + Hospital
	Other	E: Convention Center, Zoo
201A		**OH 25S, Anthony Wayne Trail, Maumee, Toledo Zoo**
201B		**OH 25N, Downtown Toledo (NB)**
	Food	E: Bronze Boar, Dirty Bird, Fricker's, Grumpy's, Spaghetti Warehouse
	Lodg	E: Radisoon, Riverfront Hotel, Seagate Hotel
	Other	E: Fifth Third Field, COSI, Conv Center
200		**South Ave, Kuhlman Ave**
199		**OH 65, N-Miami St, S-Rossford**
199AB		**OH 65, N-Miami St, S-Rossford**
	Gas	E: 76, Sunoco
	Lodg	E: Days Inn
198		**Wales Rd, Oregon Rd, Rossford, Northwood**
	FStop	E: Wales Rd Shell
	Food	E: Subway/Shell, Arby's, China Wok, Pizza Hut
	Lodg	E: AmeriHost Inn, Baymont Inn, Comfort Inn
197		**Buck Rd, Perrysburg, to Rossford**
	Gas	E: Shell◈ W: BP, Sunoco◈

◈ = Regular Gas Stations with Diesel ▲ = RV Friendly Locations ♥ = Pet Friendly Locations
Red print shows large vehicle parking / access on site or nearby Brown Print = Campgrounds / RV PARKS

EXIT **OHIO**

Food E: Tim Horton's, Wendy's
W: Denny's, McDonald's
Lodg W: American Inn, Knights Inn♥

(195) Jct I-80/90, OH Turnpike (TOLL) (SB) OH 795, Indiana Rd (NB)
FStop E: Barney's #15
Gas E: BP◈,
Food E: Subway/Barney's
Lodg E: Courtyard

193 US 20, US 23S, Perrysburg, Fremont
Gas E: BP◈, Meijer, Sunoco, Kroger
W: Speedway◈
Food E: Arby's, Big Boy, Bob Evans, Burger King Chili's, China City, Cracker Barrel, IHOP, McDonald's, Subway, Taco Bell, Wendy's
Lodg E: Best Western, Comfort Suites, Days Inn, Holiday Inn Express
W: La Quinta Inn♥
Other E: ATMs, Banks, Kroger, Lowe's, PetSmart♥, Target, Walgreen's, to appr 7 mi: Toledo East/Stony Ridge KOA▲
W: Auto Zone, Signature Harley Davidson

(192) Jct I-475N, US 23N (NB, Left exit) to Maumee, Ann Arbor, MI

187 OH 582, Middleton Pike, Bowling Green, to Haskins, Luckey

181 OH 64, E Wooster St, OH 105, Bowling Green Rd, Bowling Green
Gas E: Meijer◈
W: BP, Citgo◈, Speedway, Sunoco◈
Food W: Bob Evans, Big Boy, Burger King, Chipolte Mex Grill, Fricker;'s, Little Caesars, McDonald's, Ranch Steak & Seafood, Starbucks, Subway, Tim Horton's, Waffle House, Wendy's
Lodg E: Holiday Inn Express
W: Best Western, Buckeye Inn, Days Inn, Hampton Inn, Quality Inn
Med W: + Wood Co Hospital
Other W: Wood Co Airport✈, Golf Course, to Bowling Green State Univ

179 US 6, Bowling Green, to Fremont
Other E: Cactus Flats Campground▲
W: Fire Lake Camper Park▲

(178) Wood Co Rest Area (Both dir)
(RR, Phones, Picnic, Vend)

(175) Weigh Station (NB)

171 OH 25, Cygnet Rd, Cygnet

168 Eagleville Rd (SB), Quarry Rd (NB) North Baltimore
FStop E: Fuel Mart #714

167 OH 18, Deshler Rd, N Baltimore, to Fostoria
TStop E: Petro Stopping Center #25/Mobil (Scales)
W: Love's Travel Stop #356 (Scales)
Gas W: Sunoco◈
Food E: IronSkillet/FastFood/Petro SC, McDonald's, Pizza Hut
W: Arby's/Love's TS
Lodg W: Crown Inn
TWash E: Blue Beacon TW/Petro SC
TServ E: Petro SC/Tires, Buckeye Truck Repair, D & R Towing & Repair Service
Other E: Laundry/BarbSh/WiFi/Petro SC
W: WiFi/Love's TS, Dollar General

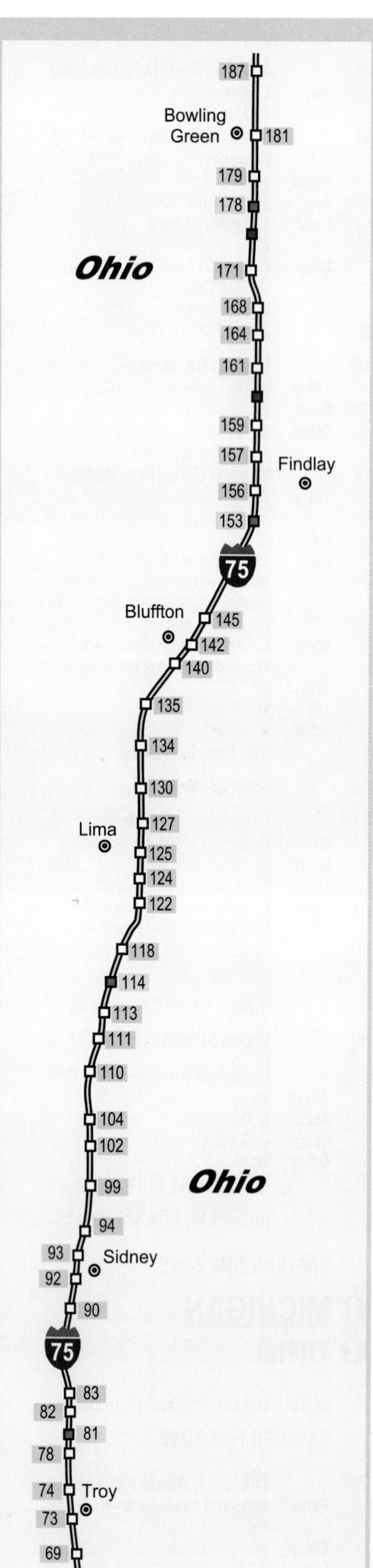

EXIT **OHIO**

164 OH 613, Market St, Van Buren, Fostoria, McComb
TStop W: Pilot Travel Center # 360 (Scales)
Food W: Subway/TacoBell/Pilot TC
Other E: Shady Lake Campground▲, Van Buren Lake State Park
W: WiFi/Pilot TC

(162) Weigh Station (SB)

161 CR 99, Findlay
FStop E: Speedway #8502
Gas E: Shell
Food E: Subway
Lodg E: Comfort Suites
Med E: + Physicians Plus Urgent Care
Other E: Quick Lane Repair & Tire, Shadylake Campground▲, OH State Hwy Patrol Post

159 US 224, OH 15, W Trenton Ave, Findlay, to Ottawa, Tiffin
Gas E: BP◈, Speedway◈, Swifty
W: Shell◈, Murphy
Food E: Burger King, Dakota Grill, Domino's, McDonald's, Ponderosa, Subway, Taco Bell, Wendy's
W: Bob Evans, Cracker Barrel, Denny's, Max & Erma's, Outback Steakhouse, Steak n Shake, Subway, Waffle House
Lodg E: Drury Inn, Red Roof Inn♥, Rodeway Inn♥, Super 8♥
W: Country Inn, Hampton Inn, Holiday Inn Express, Quality Inn♥
TServ W: Easter Tire & ReTreading
W: Peterbilt of NW Ohio
Med E: + Hospital
Other E: Cinema, Golf Course, Pharmacy, Univ Of Findlay
W: ATMs, Auto Dealers, Walmart sc

157 OH 12, W Main Cross St, Findlay Columbus Grove
TStop W: Highway Travel Center
Gas E: GasAmerica◈, Marathon◈
Food E: Blimpie, Noble Roman's
W: CountryGriddleRest/Highway TC, Big Boy, Fricker's, Pilgrim Family Rest
Lodg E: Days Inn
W: Best Value Inn, Econo Lodge
Tires W: Cooper Tire
TServ E: Sparks Comm'l Tire, Phillips Garage
W: Miami Industrial Trucks, Helton Ent,
Other W: Laundry/WiFi/Highway TC

156 US 23/68, OH 15E, Findlay, to Carey
TServ E: Findlay Int'l
Med E: + Hospital
Other E: Findlay Airport✈

(153) Rest Area (Both dir)
(RR, Phones, Picnic, Vend)

145 OH 235, Bluffton, Mt Cory, Ada
Gas W: Gastown
Other E: Twin Lakes Park
W: Kirtland's Auto Repair Center

142 OH 103, Bluffton, Arlington
FStop E: BP
Gas E: Sterling◈, Sunoco◈
W: Marathon, Shell
Food E: Denny's, Eagles Nest Rest.
W: Arby's, Burger King, KFC, McDonald's, Subway, Taco Bell
Lodg E: Knights Inn
W: Comfort Inn
ATS W: Ken's Auto & Truck Service

◈ = Regular Gas Stations with Diesel ▲ = RV Friendly Locations ♥ = Pet Friendly Locations
Red print shows large vehicle parking / access on site or nearby Brown Print = Campgrounds / RV PARKS

EXIT		OHIO
	Med	W: + Blanchard Valley Reg'l Hospital
	Other	E: Car Wash, Bluffton College, Bluffton Airport✈
140		**Bentley Rd, OH 103, Bluffton**
135		**Lincoln Hwy, Main St, to OH 696, US 30, Beaverdam, Lima,Delphos**
	TStop	W: Pilot Travel Center #457 (Scales), Flying J Travel Plaza #5039 (Scales)
	Gas	E: Speedway #3547
	Food	W: McDonald's/Subway/Pilot TC, Cookery/FastFood/FJ TP
	TWash	E: Blue Beacon Truck Wash
	TServ	W: Pilot TC/Bridgestone Tire & Auto, Beaverdam Fleet Services
	Other	W: Laundry/WiFi/Pilot TC, Laundry/ BarbSh/WiFi/**RVDump/LP**/FJ TP
134		**OH 696, Napoleon Rd, Beaverdam Upper Sandusky (NB, NO NB re-entry)**
130		**Blue Lick Rd, Lima**
	Gas	E: Citgo, Marathon◈
	Food	E: Northside Pizza
	Lodg	E: Americas Best Value Inn
127		**OH 81, Findlay Rd, Lima, to Ada (SB)**
	Gas	W: BP, Clark, Marathon◈, Speedway
	Food	W: Waffle House, Rest/Days Inn
	Lodg	W: Comfort Inn, Days Inn, Econo Lodge
	TServ	E: E&R Trailer W: Easter Tire Truck Auto & RV, Whiteford Kenworth
	Med	W: to + St Rita Medical Center
	Other	E: Northland Auto Service W: Gilroy's Auto Service
127AB		**OH 81, Findlay Rd, Lima, to Ada**
125AB		**OH 309E, OH 117E, Lima**
125B		**OH 309W, OH 117W, Lima**
125		**OH 309, OH 117, Lima (NB)**
	FStop	W: Shell
	Gas	E: BP◈, Speedway, Sam's
	Food	E: Arby's, Bob Evans, Big Boy, Burger King, Captain D's, **Cracker Barrel**, McDonald's, Olive Garden
	Food	E: Pizza Hut, Red Lobster, Ryan's Grill, Skyline Chili, TCBY, Taco Bell, Texas Roadhouse, Wendy's W: Damon's, Papa John's
	Lodg	E: Courtyard, Holiday Inn, Hampton Inn, Motel 6♥ W: Country Inn, Travelodge
	Med	W: + Lima Memorial Hospital
	Other	E: ATMs, Banks, Carwash/BP, Grocery, Harbor Freight Tools, Sam's Club, Walgreen's, **Walmart sc**, **RV Center**, Co Fairgrounds W: ATMs, Advance Auto Parts, Auto Services, Dollar General, Laundromat, Grocery, RiteAid
124		**E 4th St, Lima**
	Other	E: **OH State Hwy Patrol Post**, to Lima Allen Co Airport✈
122		**OH 65, St Johns Ave, Lima, Ottawa**
	FStop	E: Speedway #5236 W: Four Star Food Mart/Shell (DAND)
	TServ	W: Buckeye Truck Center/International, S&S Volvo/GMC Truck Center, King Bros Truck Center, Stoops Freightliner
120		**W Breese Rd, Lima, Ft Shawnee**
	FStop	W: Fuel Stop
	Other	W: Lima Harley Davidson

EXIT		OHIO
118		**E Main St, National Rd, Lima, Wapakoneta, to Cridersville**
	FStop	W: Fuel Mart
	Gas	W: Speedway #782◈
	Food	W: Subway/FuelMart, Bears Den, Bella Mama, Village Café, Westside Pizza
	Other	W: ATMs, Banks, Car Wash, Baker Animal Hospital♥
(114)		**Rest Area (Both dir) (RR, Phones, Picnic, Vend)**
113		**OH 67, Wapakoneta, Uniopolis (Acc to #111 via W to OH 67)**
111		**Bellefontaine St, Wapakoneta**
	TStop	E: Travel Center of America #82/Marathon (Scales)
	Gas	W: BP◈, Shell, Murphy USA
	Food	E: CountryFare/TA TC W: Arby's, Bob Evans, Burger King, DQ, Captain D's, Comfort Zone Diner, El Azteca Mexican Rest, Lucky Stars Rest, McDonald's, Pizza Hut, Taco Bell, Waffle House, Wendy's
	Lodg	E: Knights Inn W: Comfort Inn, Holiday Inn Express, Super 8, Travelodge
	TServ	E: TA TC/Tires, Sterling/Western Star
	Other	E: Laundry/WiFi/TA TC, **OH State Hwy Patrol Post**, **Wapakoneta KOA▲**, **Lakewood Village Resort ▲**, **to appr 4 mi: Glacier Hills Lake RV Sales & Parts & Campground▲** W: ATMs, Advance Auto Parts, Auto Services, Astro Lanes, CVS, Carwash/ Shell, Car Wash, Family Dollar, Grocery, Pharmacy, Lowe's, O'Reilly Auto Parts, Radio Shack, Safeway Auto Lube, **Walmart sc**, Neil Armstrong Air & Space Museum
110		**US 33, to St Mary's, Bellefontaine**
	Other	E: **OH State Hwy Patrol Post**, **to Wapakoneta/Lima South KOA▲**, **to appr 4 mi: Glacier Hills Lake RV Sales & Parts & Campground▲** **W: to Easy Campground ▲**
104		**OH 219, CR 22, Botkins Rd, Botkins**
	FStop	W: Botkins Marathon
	Gas	W: Shell
	Food	W: Subway/Shell
	Lodg	W: Budget Host Inn
	Other	W: ATMs, Auto & Tires Services, US Post Office
102		**OH 274, Botkins, to New Bremen, Jackson Center**
	Other	E: **to Thor Industries**
99		**OH 119, Main St, Anna, to Minster**
	TStop	E: Joe Stop 99 Diesel (Scales)
	Gas	W: Gas America, Marathon
	Food	W: Subway/Marathon, Wendy's
	TWash	W: Five Star Truck Wash
	TServ	E: L&O Tire Service/Joe Stop 99 W: Truck Repair & Towing
	Other	E: Auto Repair Unlimited W: Movin On CB Sales, **to Lake Loramie State Park▲**
94		**CR 25A, Sidney**
93		**OH 29, St Mary's Ave, Sidney (Gas, Food E to Russell Rd)**

EXIT		OHIO
92		**OH 47, W Michigan St, Sidney**
	Gas	E: Shell, Speedway◈ W: BP, Citgo◈, Sunoco◈, Valero◈, Murphy USA◈
	Food	E: Applebee's, Arby's, Subway, Taco Bell, Wendy's W: BW3, Bob Evans, Burger King, China Garden Buffet, Culver's, KFC, Long John Silver/A&W, McDonald's, Perkins, Pizza Hut, Waffle House
	Lodg	E: GreatStone Castle B&B, Lodge & Spa W: Comfort Inn, Country Hearth Inn, Days Inn♥, Holiday Inn, Quality Inn, Travel Inn
	Med	E: + Wilson Memorial Hospital
	Other	E: ATMs, Auto Zone, Auto Services, Auto Lube, Banks, Aldi's, CVS, Dollar General, Grocery, NAPA, Walgreen's W: Auto Dealers, ATMs, Big Lots, Lowe's, Enterprise RAC, Kroger, Precision Auto Wash, Radio Shack, Staples, U-Haul, Vet♥, **Walmart sc**, **to Hickory Hills Lakes RV Sales & Campground▲**
90		**Fair Rd, Sidney**
	Gas	E: Sunoco W: Marathon◈
	Food	W: DQ/Marathon
	Lodg	W: Hampton Inn
83		**CR 25A, Piqua**
	Gas	W: Super Station/Marathon
	Food	W: NobleRoman's/Café/SuperStation
	Lodg	W: Red Carpet Inn
	Other	E: Dollar General W: ATMs, Auto Dealers, Bowling Lanes, Enterprise RAC, **Paul Sherry RV Center**, to Picqua Airport✈
82		**OH 36, E Ash St, Piqua, to Urbana**
	Gas	E: Valero, Murphy W: Citgo, Speedway,
	Food	E: Arby's, China East Chinese, China Garden Buffet, DQ, El Sombrero Mexican Rest, KFC, Long John Silver, Pizza Hut, Sonic, Taco Bell, Waffle House, Wendy's W: Bob Evans, Burger King, **Cracker Barrel**, El Tapatio Mexican Rest, McDonald's, Quiznos, Red Lobster
	Lodg	W: Comfort Inn♥, Knights Inn, La Quinta Inn♥
	Other	E: ATMs, Banks, Big Lots, Car Wash, Cinema, Cingular, Dollar Tree, Goodyear, Gover Harley Davidson, Home Depot, Petland♥, **Walmart sc**, **OH State Hwy Patrol Post** W: ATMs, Aldi's, Radio Shack, Miami Valley Center Mall, U-Haul
(81)		**Rest Area (Both dir) (RR, Phones, Picnic, Vend)**
78		**CR 25A, Troy**
	Med	E: + Upper Valley Medical Center
	Other	E: Miami Co Fairgrounds
74AB		**OH 41, Main St, Troy, Covington**
74		**OH 41, W Main St, Troy, Covington**
	Gas	E: BP◈ W: Shell, Speedway◈, Meijer◈
	Food	E: China Garden, Little Caesar's, Long John Silver, McDonald's, Perkins, Pizza Hut, Subway W: Applebee's, BW3, Big Boy, Bob Evans, Burger King, DQ, El Rancho Mex Rest, Ruby Tuesday, Outback Steakhouse, Panera Bread, Steak n Shake

◈= Regular Gas Stations with Diesel ▲ = RV Friendly Locations ♥= Pet Friendly Locations
Red print shows large vehicle parking / access on site or nearby Brown Print = Campgrounds / RV PARKS

EXIT		OHIO
	Lodg	W: Best Value Inn♥, Fairfield Inn, Hampton Inn, Holiday Inn Express, Knights Inn, Residence Inn
	Med	E: + Upper Valley Medical Center
	Other	E: Goodyear, Pharmacy, Miami Co Fairgrounds W: Auto Zone, CVS, Hobart Arena, Lowe's, Meijer, Staples, Tire Discounters, Tractor Supply, **Walmart sc**
73		**OH 55, Troy, to Ludlow Falls**
	Gas	E: BP, Shell, Kroger
	Food	E: Jersey Mike's Subs, Papa John's, Waffle House, Wendy's
	Lodg	E: Best Western, Econo Lodge, Super 8
	Med	E: + Hospital
	Other	E: ATMs, Dollar General, Kroger
69		**CR 25A, Tipp City**
	Gas	E: BP, Citgo, Starfire◈
	Food	E: Subway
	Other	E: Auto Dealers, **RV Center**
68		**OH 571, Main St, Tipp City, W Milton**
	Gas	E: BP◈, Shell, Speedway W: Citgo◈, Speedway◈
	Food	E: Burger King, McDonald's, Subway W: Arby's, Big Boy, Bob Evans, Hickory Rivers Smokehouse, Wendy's
	Lodg	W: Holiday Inn Express, Travelodge
	Other	E: CVS, Family Dollar, Grocery, Goodyear
64		**Northwoods Blvd, Vandalia**
	Gas	E: Kroger
	Food	E: El Toro Mex Rest, Family Garden Rest, Quzinos
	Other	E: Kroger, Dollar Tree
63		**US 40, National Rd, Vandalia**
	Gas	E: Speedway◈ W: BP◈, Shell, Speedway
	Food	W: Arby's, KFC, McDonald's, Pizza Hut, Subway, Taco Bell, Waffle House, Wendy's
	Lodg	E: Crossroads Motel W: Super 8, Travelodge
	Other	W: Grocery, Kroger, Pharmacy, Dayton Int'l Airport✈
	NOTE:	**SB: Ongoing construction thru 2011**
(61B)		**Jct I-70W, to Indianapolis, to Dayton Int'l Airport✈**
(61A)		**Jct I-70E, to Columbus**
59		**Wyse Rd, Benchwood Rd, Dayton**
	Gas	W: Speedway, Murphy, Sam's Club
	Food	E: Azteca Grande Mexican Rest W: Arby's, Bob Evans, **Cracker Barrel**, Don Pablo, El Rancho Grande, Golden Corral, Hooters, Joe's Crab Shack, Lone Star Steakhouse, Max & Erma's, Olive Garden, O'Charley's, Outback Steakhouse, Ryan's Grill, Ruby Tuesday, Smokey Bones BBQ, Skyline Chili, Steak 'N Shake, Tim Horton's, Wendy's
	Lodg	E: Hawthorn Suites, Howard Johnson, Residence Inn W: Comfort Inn, Country Inn, Courtyard, Drury Inn, Extended Stay America, Fairfield Inn, Hampton Inn, Knights Inn, Motel 6♥, Ramada, Red Roof Inn♥
	TServ	E: Miami Valley International
	Other	E: ATM, Auto Service, Discount Tire, FedEx Office, **RV Center** W: ATMs, Banks, Office Depot, Petland♥, Radio Shack, Sam's Club, **Walmart sc**, Walgreen's, **RV Center**, **Brookville KOA▲**

EXIT		OHIO
58		**Needmore Rd, Wright Bros Pkwy**
	Gas	E: BP◈, Shell, Thornton's W: Marathon◈, Speedway◈, Sunoco◈, Swifty, Kroger
	Food	E: Big Boy, Hardee's, McDonald's/Shell W: Arby's, Burger King, Captain D's, Domino's Pizza, Long John Silver, McDonald's, Roosters, Waffle House, Wendy's
	Lodg	E: Dayton Executive Hotel
	Other	E: ATMs, Budget Truck Rental, Goodyear, Suburban Tire, Tire Express,
	Other	W: ATM, Advance Auto Parts, Auto Repairs, Kroger, O'Reilly Auto Parts, Walgreen's, US Post Office
57B		**Wagner Ford Rd, Dixie Dr**
	Gas	E: Sunoco W: Mobil, Speedway, UDF
	Food	W: Little Caesars Pizza, Subway
	Lodg	E: Holiday Inn W: Days Inn
	TServ	W: Dayton-Evans Motor Truck
	Other	W: Pharmacy, Kelly Tire, TDC Road & Truck Service
57A		**Neva Dr, Dayton (NB exit, SB reacc)**
56B		**Stanley Ave W, Dayton (SB)**
56A		**Stanley Ave E, Dayton (SB)**
56		**Stanley Ave, Dayton**
	FStop	E: True North #704/Shell
	Gas	W: Clark
	Food	W: Dominos, Gold Star Chili, Great Steak Co, McDonald's, Taco Bell, Wendy's
	Lodg	W: Dayton Motor Hotel, Plaza Motel, Royal Motel
	Other	E: N Dayton Truck Services, Owen's Road Services
55		**Keowee St, Dayton (SB)**
55B		**Keowee St N, Leo St (NB)**
	Gas	W: BP
	Other	E: Chrysler Corp Dayton Thermal Prod
55A		**Keowee St (NB)**
54C		**OH 4, Webster St, to Springfield**
	Med	E: + Children's Medical Center
	Other	E: to Wright Patterson AFB
54B		**OH 48, Main St, Dayton**
	Gas	W: BP
	Food	W: Benjamin's Burgers, Chicken Louie's
	Med	W: + Grandview Medical Center
54A		**Grand Ave (SB Left exit, NB entr)**
	Med	W: + Grandview Medical Center
53B		**OH 49, W 1st St, Salem Ave, Downtown Dayton**
	Lodg	E: Days Inn
53A		**OH 49, 3rd St, 2nd St, Dayton**
	Gas	E: Sunoco
	Lodg	E: Crowne Plaza, DoubleTree Hotel
	Med	W: + Grandview Medical Center
	Other	E: Convention Center, Courthouse, City Hall
52B		**OH 35, W to Eaton, E to Dayton**
52A		**Albany St, Stewart St (SB)**
51		**Nicholas Rd, Edwin C Moses Blvd**
	Gas	W: BP◈
	Food	W: McDonald's, Wendy's
	Lodg	W: Courtyard, Econo Lodge
	Med	E: + Dayton Heart Hospital, + Miami Valley Hospital

EXIT		OHIO
	Other	E: Montgomery Co Fairgrounds, Univ of Dayton, Arena, Stadium
50B		**OH 741S, Springboro Rd (SB exit, NB entr)**
50A		**Dryden Rd, Dayton**
	Gas	E: Citgo W: Sunoco
	Food	W: Subway, TJ's Rest
	Lodg	W: Holiday Inn, Super 8
	Other	E: Auto Service, Dayton Emergency Vet♥
47		**Central Ave, Dixie Hwy, Dayton Moraine, Kettering, W Carrollton**
	Gas	E: Marathon, Sunoco W: BP, Speedway
	Food	E: Big Boy, Waffle House W: McDonald's, Pizza Hut, Taco Bell, Wendy's
	Med	E: + Kettering Memorial Hospital
	Other	E: Auto Services W: US Post Office, Moraine Air Park✈
44		**OH 725, Miamisburg-Centerville Rd**
	Gas	E: BP◈, Shell, Speedway W: BP, Marathon, Shell
	Food	E: Applebee's, Blimpie's, Burger King, Captain D's, Chuck E Cheese Pizza, Denny's, Dunkin Donuts, Fuddrucker's, Friendly's, Golden Corral, Hardee's, KFC, McDonald's, Max & Erma's, O'Charley's, Olive Garden, Pizza Hut, Red Lobster, Roosters, Steak 'n Shake, Subway, Taco Bell, TGI Friday, Wendy's W: Bob Evans, Jersey Mike Subs, Perkins
	Lodg	E: Comfort Suites, Courtyard, DoubleTree Hotel, Extended Stay America, Hawthorne Suites, Hilton, Holiday Inn, Homewood Suites, Motel 6♥, Residence Inn, Springhill Suites, Studio 6, Suburban Lodge W: Knights Inn, Quality Inn, Ramada, Red Roof Inn♥, Signature Inn, Super 8, Yankee Mill Inn
	Med	E: + Southview Hospital, Budget Care Medical Walk-In Center W: + Sycamore Hospital Kettering, Medical Center
	TServ	E: Clarke Detroit Diesel
	Other	E: ATMs, Auto Services, Dayton Mall, Best Buy, Barnes & Noble, Borders, CompUSA, Cinema, Cub Foods/Pharmacy, Discount Tire, Dick's Sporting Goods, Firestone, Goodyear, Home Depot, Lowe's, NTB, Office Depot, Pep Boys, PetSmart♥, Sam's Club, Target/Pharmacy, Tire Discounters, **Walmart sc**, W: Dollar General, NAPA
(43)		**Jct I-675N, Dayton, to Columbus**
	NOTE:	**NB: Ongoing construction thru 2011**
38		**OH 73, E 2nd St, W Central St, Springboro, to Franklin**
	Gas	E: BP, Shell, Speedway, Sunoco W: Circle K, RoadRanger/Exxon◈, Shell, Swifty, Murphy USA
	Food	E: Applebee's, Arby's, Bob Evans, Long John Silver, Hardee's, Lacomedia Dinner Theater, McDonald's, Perkins, Pizza Hut, Skyline Chili, Subway, Taco Bell, Tim Horton's, Wendy's W: Big Boy, Cazadores Mexican, McDonald's

◈ = Regular Gas Stations with Diesel ▲ = RV Friendly Locations ♥ = Pet Friendly Locations

Red print shows large vehicle parking / access on site or nearby Brown Print = Campgrounds / RV PARKS

EXIT **OHIO**

Lodg E: Hampton Inn, Holiday Inn Express
W: Econo Lodge, Knights Inn

Other E: ATMs, Kroger, Radio Shack, Tire Discounters, UPS Store, Animal Medical Center♥, to Dayton Wright Bros Airport✈
W: ATMs, Auto Zone, Dollar General, Dollar Tree, Grocery, NAPA, Walgreen's, **Walmart sc**,

36 **OH 123, Franklin, to Lebanon**

TStop E: Pilot Travel Center #9 (Scales) **(DAND)**

Gas E: BP, Exxon◈
W: Marathon, Sunoco

Food E: PizzaHut/Subway/Pilot TC, Wendy's/Exxon, McDonald's, Waffle House
W: White Castle

Lodg E: Quality Inn

TWash E: Truck Wash Express

TServ E: Truck Lube USA, Steve's Towing, Truck & Trailer Repair

Med W: to **+ Atrium Medical Center**

Other E: Laundry/WiFi/Pilot TC, U-Haul

32 **OH 122, Franklin, to Middletown**

Gas E: BP, Duke
W: Marathon, Meijer◈, Speedway, Murphy USA

Food E: McDonald's, Waffle House
W: Applebee's, Bob Evans, **Cracker Barrel**, Frisch's Big Boy, Gold Star Chili, Golden Corral, Hardee's, KFC, Lone Star Steakhouse, McDonald's, Olive Garden, Old Country Buffet, O'Charley's, Sonic, Steak 'n Shake, Wendy's

Lodg E: Americas Best Value Inn, Ramada Inn, Red Carpet Inn, Super 8♥
W: Best Western, Country Hearth Inn♥, Drury Inn, Fairfield Inn, Hawthorne Suites, Holiday Inn Express♥

Med W: **+ Doctor's Urgent Care Clinic, + Middletown Regional Hospital**

Other E: Auto Dealers, CVS, Walgreen's
W: ATMs, Auto Services, Big Lots, Cinema, CVS, Dollar General, Jiffy Lube, Kohl's, Kroger/Pharmacy, Lowe's, Meijer/Pharmacy, Sears Auto Center, Staples, Target/Pharmacy, Tires, Tire Discounters, Vet ♥, **Walmart sc**, Towne Mall, to Hook Field Muni Airport✈

29 **OH 63, Hamilton Lebanon Rd, Lebanon, to Monroe, Hamilton**

FStop E: Marathon

TStop E: Stony Ridge Travel Center (Scales)

Gas E: Shell◈
W: Speedway◈,

Food E: S R Diner/Stoney Ridge TC, WhiteCastle/Marathon, Popeye's/Shell, Burger King, Gold Star Chili, McDonald's, Waffle House, Wendy's
W: McDonald's, Subway

Lodg E: Motel/Stony Ridge TC, Comfort Inn,
W: Hampton Inn, Howard Johnson

TWash E: Interstate Truck Care

TServ E: Bishop Truck Care, S&C Towing & Recovery, CB Shoppe

Other E: Laundry/Stony Ridge TC, Coyote Ridge Saloon & Dance Hall, to Lebanon Warren Co Airport✈
W: Auto Technics, Flea Market, Cincinnati Premium Outlet Mall,

EXIT **OHIO**

(28) **Rest Area** (Both dir) (RR, Phones, Picnic, Vend, Info)

24 **OH 129W, Michael A Fox Hwy, Middletown, to Hamilton**

22 **Tylersville Rd, West Chester, to Hamilton, Mason**

Gas E: BP, Marathon, Sunoco
W: Shell, Speedway◈, Thornton's, Meijer◈

Food E: Arby's, Bob Evans, Bonefish Grill, Burger King, Fazoli's, GoldStar Chili, KFC, Johnny Carino's, IHOP, Long John Silver, McDonald's, Perkins, Pizza Hut, Subway, Ruby Tuesday, Taco Bell, TGI Friday, Waffle House
W: O'Charley's, Steak 'n Shake, Starbucks

Lodg E: Econo Lodge, Howard Johnson
W: Wingate Inn

Med E: **+ Urgent Care**

Other E: ATMs, Big Lots, Firestone, Home Depot, Kroger, Radio Shack, Target, Tires Plus, Walgreen's
W: Car-X Auto Service,Tire Discounters, **Walmart**

21 **Cincinnati-Dayton Rd**

Gas W: Mobil◈, Shell, Speedway◈

Food E: Arby's, Big Boy
W: Papa John's, Subway, Waffle House

Lodg E: Holiday Inn Express
W: Knights Inn

Other W: **Walmart sc**, Vet♥, **Camperland RV Center**

19 **Union Centre Blvd, West Chester, to Fairfield, Hamilton**

Gas W: BP, Marathon, Shell

Food W: Applebee's, Bob Evans, Burger King, Chipolte Mexican Grill, Dickey's BBQ, Don Pablo, Max & Erma's, Red Robin, Roadhouse Grill, Starbucks

Lodg W: Comfort Inn, Courtyard, Marriott, Sleep Inn, Staybridge Suites

NOTE: **Through trucks MUST take I-275 around Cincinnati.**

(16) **Jct I-275, to I-71, I-74, to Columbus, Indianapolis**

Lodg E: Red Roof Inn♥
W: Econo Lodge, Extended Stay America, Residence Inn

TServ E: Peterbilt of NW Ohio

NOTE: **Through trucks MUST take I-275 around Cincinnati.**

15 **Sharon Rd, Chester Rd, Cincinnati, to Glendale, Sharonville (Many Servi W to OH747, then N)**

Gas E: BP, Chevron, Marathon◈, Shell, Sunoco, Thornton's #551
W: Speedway, Costco

Food E: Big Boy Bob Evans, **Cracker Barrel**, Jim Dandy's Family BBQ, Pizza Hut, Ruby Tuesday, Skyline Chili, Subworks/Thornton's, Waffle House,
W: Arby's, Burger King, Captain D's, Chuck E Cheese Pizza, Jim Dandy's BBQ, Long John Silver, McDonald's, Pizza Hut, Ruby Tuesday, Starbucks, Subway, Texas Roadhouse, Taco Bell, Wendy's

◈= Regular Gas Stations with Diesel ▲ = RV Friendly Locations ♥= Pet Friendly Locations
Red print shows large vehicle parking / access on site or nearby Brown Print = Campgrounds / RV PARKS

EXIT — OHIO

Lodg — E: Baymont Inn, Country Inn, Drury Inn, Fairfield Inn, Hampton Inn, Holiday Inn Express, Hilton Garden Inn, La Quinta Inn♥, Motel 6♥, Ramada Inn, Red Roof Inn♥
W: Comfort Inn, Extended Stay America, Econo Lodge, Residence Inn, Signature Inn Super 8, Sheraton, Travelodge
TServ — E: Clarke Detroit Diesel, Kenworth of Cincinnati
Other — E: Ford Plant, Golf course
W: ATMs, Auto Repair, Convention Center, to Tri County Mall, Costco, Dick's Sporting Goods, Target

14 — Glendale Milford Rd, Cincinnati
Gas — W: Swifty
Lodg — W: Americas Best Value Inn, Quality Inn, Travelodge & **RV Park▲**, Wingate
Med — E: + **Evendale Medical Center**
Other — E: ATMs, Auto Services, Walgreen's
W: to Brown Mackie College

13 — Shepherd Lane, Shepherd Ave

12 — Cooper Ave (SB) to Wyoming Ave, Davis St to Jefferson Ave (NB)

10 — Galbraith Rd, Arlington Hts (SB)
Gas — E: Shell, Speedway, Sunoco
Other — E: Budget RAC, Pharmacy

10B — Galbraith Rd, Arlington Hts (NB, Left Exit)

10A — Ronald Reagan Cross County Hwy

9 — OH 4, Paddock Rd, Vine St, OH 561, Seymour Ave
Gas — E: Speedway
Food — E: White Castle
Other — E: Hamilton Co Fairgrounds

8 — Towne St, to Paddock Rd (NB)

7 — OH 562, to I-71

6 — Mitchell Ave, St Bernard
Gas — E: Marathon, Shell, Speedway
W: BP◊
Food — E: KFC, Wendy's, White Castle
W: McDonald's, Subway
Lodg — E: Holiday Inn Express
Med — E: + **VA Hospital**
Other — E: Kroger, Tires, Car Wash
W: Walgreen's, to Cincinnati Zoo

(4) — Jct I-74W, US 52W, US 27N, to Indianapolis

3 — Hopple St, to US 27S, US 127S (NB, Left Exit)
Gas — E: Marathon
W: BP, Shell
Food — E: Big Boy, Subway, White Castle, Wendy's
Lodg — E: Budget Host Inn, Days Inn, Interstate Motel, Rest Inn
Med — W: + **Hospital**

2B — Western Hills Viaduct, to US 27, US 127, Cincinnati, Harrison Ave
Gas — W: BP
Food — W: McDonald's, Subway

2A — Western Ave, Liberty St (SB)

2 — Harrison Ave, Cincinnati

1H — Western Ave, Ezzard Charles Dr (SB) (ReAccess from 8th St)

Personal Notes

EXIT — OH / KY

1G — Freeman Ave, Gest St, 8th St W, (SB) to US 50W, OH 264 (NB)
FStop — W: Marathon

1F — 7th St, Downtown Cincinnati (SB)
Lodg — W: Holiday Inn

1E — 5th St, US 127, I-71N, US 50

(1) — Jct I-71N, to I-471, to Cincinnati

EASTERN TIME ZONE

↑ OHIO
↓ KENTUCKY

NOTE: MM 193: Ohio State Line

EASTERN TIME ZONE

NOTE: I-75 below runs with I-71 to Ex #173. Exit #'s follows I-75.

192 — 5th St, Crescent Ave, Covington (SB) US 25, US 127, W 9th, W 5th (NB)
Gas — E: BP, Speedway
Food — E: Burger King, Hardee's, KFC, McDonald's Riverview Revolving Rest, Skyline Chili, Subway, Waffle House
Lodg — E: Courtyard, Extended Stay America, Holiday Inn, Radisson
W: Hampton Inn

191 — W 9th St, Pike St, W 12th St
Med — E: + **Hospital**

EXIT — KENTUCKY

189 — KY 1072, Kyles Lane, Ft Wright
Gas — W: Marathon, Speedway
Lodg — W: Days Inn, Lookout Motel, Ramada

188 — US 25, Dixie Hwy, Fort Mitchell
Gas — E: Sunoco
W: Marathon, Speedway
Food — E: Little Caesar's Pizza
W: Indigo Cafe
Lodg — W: Holiday Inn

186 — KY 371, Buttermilk Pike, Ft Mitchell
Gas — E: BP◊, Citgo◊
W: BP, Shell, Sunoco◊
Food — E: Oriental Wok, Rest/Drawbridge Inn
W: Bob Evans, Burger King, Long John Silver, McDonald's, Outback, Subway
Lodg — E: Cross Country Inn, Drawbridge Inn
Other — W: Grocery, Home Depot, Walgreen's

(185) — Jct I-275, W to Cincinnati Airport

184 — KY 236, Erlanger

184AB — KY 236, Commonwealth Ave, Donaldson Hwy, Erlanger
Gas — E: BP, Marathon
W: Ron's Svc Ctr, Speedway, Sunoco
Food — E: Double Dragon Chinese
W: Southern Kitchen, Waffle House
Lodg — E: Days Inn, Chandler Inn
W: Comfort Inn, Days Inn, Econo Lodge
Med — W: + **Doctors Urgent Care**
Other — E: US Post Office, **Police Dept**
W: Cincinnati N Ky Int'l Airport✈

182 — KY 1017, Turfway Rd, Florence
Gas — E: BP, Shell
W: Meijer◊
Food — E: Big Boy, Lee's Chicken, Ryan's Grill
W: Applebee's, **Cracker Barrel**, Famous Dave's BBQ, Longhorn Steakhouse, Ming Garden, Rafferty's, Shell's Seafood, Steak 'n Shake, Subway
Lodg — E: Courtyard, Fairfield Inn, Signature Inn
W: Extended Stay America, Hampton Inn, Hilton, La Quinta Inn♥
Med — W: + **St Luke Hospital West**
Other — E: ATM, Big Lots, Office Depot
W: Best Buy, Home Depot, Lowe's, Sam's Club, Target

181 — KY 18, Burlington Pike, Florence, Burlington
TStop — E: Travel Center of America/Sunoco (Scales)
Gas — E: Speedway, Swifty
W: ProCare Auto Service/BP, Chevron
Food — E: Arby/PizzaHut/Popeye/Subway/TA TC, Waffle House
W: Applebee's, Cheddars Cafe, Chili's, **Cracker Barrel**, Hooters, IHOP, Lone Star Steakhouse, O'Charley's, Wendy's
Lodg — E: Best Value Inn
W: Microtel, Suburban Lodge
TServ — E: TA TC/Tires
Med — W: + **Hospital**
Other — E: Laundry/WiFi/TA TC, ProCare Auto Service
W: ATMs, Auto Dealers, Dollar Tree, Staples, Tire Discounters, **Walmart sc**

180A — Steinberg Dr, Mall Rd (SB)
Food — W: Cathay Kitchen, China Max, Olive Garden, Hardee's, Old Country Buffet, Subway, Taco Bell
Other — W: Florence Mall, Kroger, Walgreen's

◊ = Regular Gas Stations with Diesel ▲ = RV Friendly Locations ♥ = Pet Friendly Locations
Red print shows large vehicle parking / access on site or nearby Brown Print = Campgrounds / RV PARKS

180 **US 42, US 127, Florence, Union**
Gas E: BP◈, Speedway, Thornton's
W: BP, Chevron, Shell◈, Speedway
Food E: Bob Evans, Burger King, Captain D's, Dunkin Donuts, Long John Silver, McDonald's, Pizza Hut, Red Lobster, Subway, Wendy's
W: Arby's, KFC, Perkins, Ponderosa, Waffle House, White Castle
Lodg E: Holiday Inn, Travelodge
W: Knight's Inn, Motel 6♥, Ramada, Super 8, Wildwood Inn
Other W: Auto Zone, CVS, NTB, Walgreen's

178 **KY 536, Mt Zion Rd**
Gas E: BP◈, Mobil, Shell◈, Sunoco◈
Food E: Gold Star Chili, Jersey Mike's Subs, Steak 'n Shake, Subway
Other E: Grocery, Goodyear

(177) **KY Welcome Center (SB)**
Rest Area (NB)
(RR, Phones, Picnic, Vend, RVDump)

175 **KY 338, Richwood Dr, Walton**
TStop E: Travel Center of America/BP (Scales), Pilot Travel Center #278 (Scales)
W: Pilot Travel Center #321 (Scales)
Gas W: BP, Shell◈
Food E: CountryPride/TacoBell/TA TC, Subway/Pilot, Arby's, Burger King, White Castle
W: Subway/Pilot TC, Wendy's/BP, McDonald's, Skyline Chili, Waffle House
Lodg E: Holiday Inn Express
W: Econo Lodge
TServ E: TA TC/Tires
Other E: Laundry/WiFi/TA TC, WiFi/Pilot TC, **Florence RV Park▲**
W: WiFi/Pilot TC

(173) **Jct I-71S, to Louisville**

NOTE: **I-75 above runs with I-71 to OH. Exit #'s follow I-75.**

171 **KY 14, KY 16, Walton**
TStop W: Flying J Travel Plaza #5400 (Scales) **(DAD)**
Gas E: BP, Citgo
Food E: Waffle House
W: Cookery/FastFood/FJ TP
TWash W: Blue Beacon TW/FJ TP
TServ W: Quick Lube Truck Center
Other W: Laundry/WiFi/**RVDump/LP**/FJ TP, **Oak Creek Campground▲**, **Delightful Days RV Center**

(168) **Weigh Station (SB)**

166 **KY 491, Violet Rd, Crittenden**
Gas E: BP, Marathon◈, Sunoco
W: Chevron, Shell◈
Food E: McDonald's
W: Subway, Wendy's
Other E: U-Haul, **to Cincinnati South Good Sam Campground▲**

159 **KY 22, KY 467, Broadway St, Taft Hwy, Dry Ridge**
Gas E: BP, Shell◈
W: Marathon, Speedway◈, Sunoco◈
Food E: Arby's, Burger King, KFC, McDonald's, Lil Shrimp, Waffle House, Wendy's
W: **Cracker Barrel**, Shoney's
Lodg E: Country Inn, Dry Ridge Motor Inn, Microtel, Super 8
W: Hampton Inn, Holiday Inn Express

Med E: **+ Hospital**
Other E: ATMs, Dollar General, Radio Shack, **Walmart sc**, **I-75 Camper Village▲**
W: ATMs, Banks, Auto Dealer, Grocery, Tires, Dry Ridge Outlet Mall

156 **Barnes Rd**

154 **KY 36, US 25, Williamstown**
Gas E: Chevron◈, Texaco◈
W: BP◈, Marathon◈
Food E: Chester's Fr Chicken, Red Carpet Rest
W: Williamstown Pizza, El Jalisco Mexican
Lodg E: Fountain Inn, Knights Inn
W: Americas Best Value Inn♥, Days Inn
Med E: **+ Hospital**

144 **KY 330, Corinth, to Owenton**
TStop E: Noble's Fuel/Marathon
Gas E: Marathon,
W: BP
Food E: Rest/Noble's
TServ E: Noble's Fuel/Tires
Other E: CBShop/Noble's, **to appr 1.5 mi: Three Springs Campground▲**

136 **KY 32, Porter Rd, to Sadieville**
Gas W: Marathon

(131) **Weigh Station (NB)**

129 **KY 620, Delaplain Rd, to US 25, Cherry Blossom Way, Georgetown**
TStop E: Pilot Travel Center #353 (Scales)
W: Pilot Travel Center #047 (Scales)
Gas W: Shell
Food E: Wendy's/Pilot TC, Waffle House
W: McDonald's/Pilot TC
Lodg E: Days Inn, Motel 6♥
TWash E: First American Truck Wash
TServ E: Clarke Power Services/L&G Truck Repair, I-75 Truck Repair, Bluegrass International Trucks & Busses, Fleet Service Inc, Pilot Truck Care Center, East Side Wrecker Service,
Other E: Laundry/WiFi/Pilot TC, Georgetown Toyota Plant,
W: Laundry/WiFi/Pilot TC

(127) **Rest Area (Both dir)**
(RR, Phones, Picnic, Vend)

126 **US 62, to US 460, Cherry Blossom Way, Georgetown**
(Acc betw #126&129 via Cherry Blssm)
Gas E: BP, Chevron, Marathon, Murphy USA◈
W: BP, Shell, Marathon, Speedway◈
Food E: Applebee's, Big Boy, CiCi's Pizza, Golden Corral, McDonald's, O'Charley's, Papa John's, Starbucks, Steak 'n Shake
W: **Cracker Barrel**, KFC, Waffle House
Lodg E: Econo Lodge
W: Best Western, Comfort Suites, Country Inn, Fairfield Inn, Hampton Inn, Holiday Inn Express, Hilton Garden Inn, Microtel, Quality Inn, Super 8
Med W: **+ Hospital**
Other E: ATMs, Banks, 84 Lumber, Lowe's, Radio Shack, **Walmart sc**, Tender Care Animal Clinic♥
W: ATMs, Auto Dealers, Carwash/Shell, Clark's Tire & Auto Service, Outlet Mall,

125 **US 460, Paris Pike/Rd, Connector Rd, Georgetown (NB)**
(Acc Ex #126 via E to Connector Rd or W via Cherry Blossom Way)
Gas E: BP◈, Shell
W: Chevron, Swifty

Food E: Rest/Flag Inn,
W: Arby's, DQ, Little Caesars Pizza, Long John Silver, Wendy's
Lodg E: Econo Lodge, Flag Inn, Super 8
W: Winner's Circle Motel
Med W: **+ Georgetown Community Hospital**
Other E: U-Haul
W: Advance Auto Parts, Big Lots, Hibbett Sporting Goods, Kmart, Radio Shack, Central KY Vet Center♥

120 **KY 1973, Iron Works Pk, Lexington**
TStop W: AmBest/PTP/Donerail Travel Plaza/ Citgo (Scales)
Gas W: Circle K/BP
Food W: FF/Donerail TP, Sam's Rest, **to** Rest/Sunset Motel
Lodg W: **to** Sunset Motel
Med W: **+ Hospital**
Other E: **Ky State Horse Park/Museums & Campground/RVDump▲**
W: ATMs, Penske Truck Rental, Golf Course

NOTE: **I-75 below runs with I-64 for 7 mi. Exit #'s follow I-75.**

(118/75) **Jct I-64W, Frankfort, Louisville (SB)**

115 **KY 922, Newtown Pike, Bluegrass Pkwy, Lexington**
Gas E: Exxon, Shell
W: Chevron◈
Food E: **Cracker Barrel**, McDonald's, Waffle House
W: Denny's
Lodg E: Fairfield Inn, Knight's Inn, La Quinta Inn♥, Sheraton
W: Embassy Suites, Holiday Inn, Marriott
Med W: **to + Eastern State Hospital**

113 **US 27, US 68, Broadway Rd, Paris Pike, Paris, Lexington**
Gas E: BP◈, Speedway
W: Chevron◈, Shell
Food E: Waffle House
W: Fazoli's, Subs
Lodg E: Ramada Inn
W: Days Inn, Red Roof Inn
Med W: **to + Ventral Baptist Hospital, + VA Hospital**
Other E: Joyland Bowl & Park, KY Horse Center
W: ATMs, Car Wash, Kroger, **NorthsideRV Center**, **Bluegrass RV**, **to** Lexington Convention Center, Univ of KY, Stadiums, Rupp Arena

(111/81) **Jct I-64E, to Winchester, Ashland, Huntington, WV**

NOTE: **I-75 above runs with I-64 for 7 mi. Exit #'s follow I-75.**

110 **US 60, Winchester Rd, Lexington**
(Acc to #108 W to Sir Barton Way)
FStop W: Speedway #9393
Gas W: Shell, Thornton's◈, Murphy USA
Food W: Arby's, Bob Evans, Bonefish Grill, **Cracker Barrel**, International Buffet, McDonald's, Shoney's, Waffle House
Lodg W: Baymont Inn, Best Western, Country Inn, Hampton Inn, Howard Johnson, Holiday Inn Express, Microtel, Motel 6♥, Ramada, Super 8
TServ W: International Trucks, Mack
Med W: **+ Appalachian Reg'l Hospital**

◈= **Regular Gas Stations with Diesel** ▲ = **RV Friendly Locations** ♥= **Pet Friendly Locations**
Red print shows large vehicle parking / access on site or nearby **Brown Print = Campgrounds / RV PARKS**

EXIT		KENTUCKY
	Other	W: ATMs, Banks, Lowe's, Sportmans Warehouse, **Walmart sc**,
108		**KY 1425, Man O'War Blvd (Acc to #110 W to Sir Barton Way)**
	Gas	W: BP◈, Citgo◈, Shell, Speedway, Meijer, Chevron
	Food	W: Applebee's, Arby's Backyard Burgers, Burger King, Carrabba's, ChickFilA, Chipolte Mex Rest, Damon's, Don Pablo, Fire Mtn Grill, Gold Star Chili, Logan's Roadhouse, Max & Erma's, Outback Steakhouse, Starbucks, Steak 'n Shake, Taco Bell, Ted's Montana Grill, Waffle House, Wendy's
	Lodg	W: Courtyard, Hilton, Homestead Suites, Sleep Inn
	Med	W: + to Hospital
	Other	W: ATMs, Banks, B&N, Best Buy, Car Wash, Garden Ridge, Harley Davidson, Meijer, Office Max, Radio Shack, Regal Cinemas, Target/Pharmacy, Walgreen's,
104		**KY 418, Athens Boonesboro Rd, Lexington**
	Gas	E: Exxon◈, Shell W: BP◈, Speedway
	Food	E: Wendy's/Exxon, Arby's, Hooters, Subway, Waffle House W: Arby's, Jerry's
	Lodg	E: Holiday Inn, Red Roof Inn♥ W: Comfort Inn, Days Inn, Econo Lodge
	TServ	W: Whayne Power Systems
	Med	W: + Hospital
99		**US 25N, US 421N, Lexington**
97		**US 25S, US 421S, Richmond, Clay's Ferry Landing**
	TStop	E: Clays Ferry Travel Center/Marathon (Scales)
	Food	E: HuddleHouse/Clays Ferry TC, Blimpie's, McDonald's
	Other	E: Laundry/Clays Ferry TC, GI Joe's CB Radio, **to Ft Boonesborough State Park**
95		**KY 627, KY 3055, Richmond, to Winchester, Boonesborough**
	FStop	W: Dishman's Shell Food Mart
	TStop	E: Love's Travel Stop #291 (Scales)
	Food	E: Arby's/TJCinn/Love's TS W: Burger King/Dishman's
	Other	E: Laundry/WiFi/Love's TS, **Fort Boonesborough State Park**
90		**US 25, US 421, Richmond, Irvine**
	Gas	E: BP◈, Shell W: Citgo, Exxon, Shell
	Food	E: **Cracker Barrel**, Outback Steakhouse W: Arby's, Big Boy, Hardee's, Pizza Hut, Subway, Waffle House, Wendy's
	Lodg	E: Best Western, Knights Inn, La Quinta Inn♥, Red Roof Inn♥ W: Days Inn, Motel 6, Super 8
	Other	E: Richmond Flea Market
87		**KY 876, Barnes Hill Rd, Richmond, Lancaster, Richwood**
	Gas	E: BP◈, Chevron, Citgo, Shell◈, Speedway W: BP◈
	Food	E: Arby's, Burger King, Denny's, Dunkin Donuts, Fazoli's, Hardee's, Hooters, KFC, Krystal, Little Caesar's Pizza, Long John Silver, McDonald's, Papa John's Pizza, Pizza Hut, Taco Bell, Waffle House W: Bob Evan's, Ryan's Grill, Steak 'n Shake, Sonny's BBQ, Starbucks

EXIT		KENTUCKY
	Lodg	E: Best Western, Econo Lodge, Holiday Inn W: Comfort Suites, Hampton Inn, Holiday Inn Express, Jameson Inn
	Med	E: + Hospital
	Other	E: ATM, AT&T, Big Lots, Eastern Ky Univ, Enterprise RAC, Goodyear, Hobby Lobby, Kroger, Office Depot, RiteAid, **Walmart sc**, Winn Dixie, **KY State Police Post** W: Barnes Mill Animal Hospital♥, Mall
83		**Duncannon Lane,**
	Other	W: Eastern KY Univ
77		**KY 595, Walnut Meadow Rd, Berea**
	Gas	W: BP, Shell
	Food	W: Subway/BP, Columbia Steak House, Huddle House
	Lodg	W: Country Inn, Days Inn, Holiday Inn Express♥
	Med	E: + Hospital
	Other	E: Berea College W: Vet♥
76		**KY 21, Chestnut St, Lancaster Rd, Berea**
	TStop	W: 76 Fuel Center
	Gas	E: BP, Citgo, Shell, Speedway◈ W: BP, Chevron, Marathon◈
	Food	E: Arby's, Burger King, **Cracker Barrel**, DQ, KFC, Long John Silver, Little Caesars, McDonald's, Subway, Taco Bell, Wendy's W: Lee's Chicken, Pantry Family Rest
	Lodg	E: Budget Inn, Holiday Motel, Howard Johnson, Knights Inn, Super 8 W: Comfort Inn, Econo Lodge, Fairfield Inn
	TServ	W: 76 TC/Tires
	Med	E: + Hospital
	Other	E: ATMs, Banks, Auto Service, Dollar General, Radio Shack, **Walmart sc**, Berea College W: ATMs, U-Haul, **Walnut Meadows RV Park & Campground▲**, **OH! KY Campground & RV Park▲**
62		**US 25, to KY 461, Renfro Valley, Mt Vernon**
	TStop	E: Derby City South Travel Plaza
	Gas	E: Shell W: BP, Chevron, Shell, Marathon
	Food	E: Hardee's, KFC, Waffle House W: DQ, Denny's, McDonald's, Wendy's
	Lodg	E: Country Hearth Inn, Heritage Inn, Renfro Valley Inn W: Days Inn, Econo Lodge
	Med	W: + Hospital
	Other	E: Renfro Valley Entertainment Center, KY Music Hall of Fame, **Renfro Valley KOA▲**
59		**US 25, US 150, Mt Vernon, Livingston**
	TStop	E: Mount Vernon Fuel Center
	Gas	E: BP, Marathon◈, Shell◈ W: BP
	Food	E: Pizza Hut, Rest/Kastle Inn
	Lodg	E: Kastle Inn
	TServ	E: Mt Vernon FC/Tires
49		**KY 909, to US 25, Livingston**
	TStop	W: 49er Diesel Center/Shell
	Food	W: 49er Diner/49er DC
	Other	W: Laundry/49er DC
41		**KY 80, London, Somerset**
	TStop	W: Petrol Auto Truck Center/Clark, London Auto Truck Center/BP (Scales) Clark's Shell
	Gas	E: Chevron, Marathon, Speedway

EXIT		KENTUCKY
	Gas	W: Chevron, Marathon
	Food	E: Arby's, Burger King, DQ, McDonald's, KFC, Pizza Hut W: **Cracker Barrel**, Long John Silver, McDonald's/Chevron, Shiloh Rest, Subway, Taco Bell, Waffle House, Wendy's
	Lodg	E: Best Western, Econo Lodge, Days Inn, Holiday Inn Express, Quality Inn, Red Roof Inn♥, Sleep Inn, Super 8 W: Hampton Inn, Budget Host Inn & **RV Park▲**, Westgate Inn Motel & **RV Park▲**
	TWash	W: London ATC
	Med	E: + St Joseph London Hospital W: + Urgent Care
	Other	E: ATMs, Auto Services, CVS, Dollar General, Kroger, Pharmacy, **KY State Police**, Tires, Tourist Info Center/**RVDump** W: Laundry/Petrol ATC, Laundry/WiFi/London ATC, Tourist Info, to Daniel Boone National Forest
38		**KY 192, Somerset Rd, London, Daniel Boone Pkwy**
	FStop	E: Exit 38 Truck Plaza Shell
	Gas	E: BP◈, Citgo◈, Speedway◈
	Food	E: Burger King, Captain D's, Domino's Pizza, Huddle House, Krystal, Perkins, McDonald's, Ponderosa, Starbucks, Taco Bell
	Lodg	E: Comfort Suites, Country Inn, Days Inn, Hampton Inn, Holiday Inn Express, Ramada Ltd
	TServ	E: CAT Truck Service, Western Star
	Med	E: + Hospital
	Other	E: Laundry/Shell, ATMs, Advance Auto Parts, Car Wash, Office Depot, Pharmacy, **Walmart sc**, US Post Office, **to Levi Jackson State Park▲**, to London Corbin Airport Magee Field✈
(34)		**Weigh Station (Both dir)**
29		**US 25, US 25E, Hwy 770, Corbin**
	TStop	E: Pilot Travel Center #231 (Scales) **(DAND)**, Corbin Travel Plaza/Marathon (Scales) W: Love's Travel Stop #321 (Scales)
	Gas	E: BP, Murphy USA W: BP◈, Chevron◈, Shell◈
	Food	E: Subway/McDonalds/Pilot TC, Rest/FastFood/Corbin TP, Burger King, Huddle House, Shoney's, Taco Bell W: Hardee's/Love's TS, **Cracker Barrel**, Krystal/BP, Sonny's BBQ, Taco Bell
	Lodg	E: Quality Inn, Super 8 W: Baymont Inn, Comfort Inn, Fairfield Inn, Hampton Inn, Knights Inn
	TWash	E: Blue Beacon Truck Wash
	TServ	E: Corbin TP/Tires W: Q-Fix
	Other	E: Laundry/WiFi/Pilot TC, Laundry/WiFi/Corbin TP, Lowe's, **Walmart sc**, **to Cumberland National Park, Pine Mountain State Park** W: **RVDump**/WiFi/Love's TS, **Corbin KOA▲**, **to Laurel River Lake Rec Area**
25		**US 25W, Cumberland Falls Hwy, Corbin**
	FStop	W: Fast Track Truck Stop #2/BP
	Gas	E: Speedway◈ W: Shell
	Food	E: Applebee's, Burger King, Jerry's Rest, McDonald's W: Arby's, China Garden Buffet, Subway, Waffle House

◈= Regular Gas Stations with Diesel ▲ = RV Friendly Locations ♥= Pet Friendly Locations

Red print shows large vehicle parking / access on site or nearby Brown Print = Campgrounds / RV PARKS

EXIT — KY / TN

	Lodg	E: Country Inn, Days Inn, Holiday Inn Express W: Best Western, Mountain View Lodge, Regency Inn
	Med	E: + Hospital
	Other	E: Auto & Truck Service, Repair & Towing W: ATMs, Vet♥, to **Cumberland Falls State Park**
15		**US 25W, Williamsburg**
	Gas	E: to Exxon W: Chevron◈, Shell
	Food	E: to Domino's Pizza/Exxon
	Other	E: to ATMs, Bank, Dollar General, US Post Office W: to Williamsburg Whitley Co Airport✈
11		**KY 92, Williamsburg**
	TStop	W: Pilot Travel Center #437 (Scales)
	Gas	E: BP◈, Exxon◈, Shell W: Shell◈
	Food	E: Arby's, DQ, Hardee's, KFC, McDonald's, Pizza Hut, Subway, Taco Bell/BP W: Wendy's/Pilot TC, Burger King, Huddle House, Krystal, Long John Silver
	Lodg	E: Cumberland Inn, Super 8 W: Days Inn, Williamsburg Motel & **RV Park▲**
	Other	E: ATMs, Auto Services, Dollar General, Firestone, Grocery, NAPA, U-Haul, Ky Splash Waterpark, to Univ of the Cumberlands W: Laundry/WiFi/**RVDump**/Pilot TC, ATMs, **Walmart sc**
(1)		**KY Welcome Center (NB)** **(RR, Phones, Picnic, Vend)**

EASTERN TIME ZONE

⬆ KENTUCKY
⬇ TENNESSEE

NOTE: MM 161.5: Kentucky State Line

EASTERN TIME ZONE

(161)		**TN Welcome Center (SB)** **(RR, Phones, Picnic, Vend)**
160		**US 25W, TN 9, Jellico**
	FStop	W: Shell
	Gas	E: BP, Citgo, Exxon◈, Marathon W: BP
	Food	E: KFC, Rest/Jellico Motel, Subway/Exxon W: Arby's/Shell, Hardee's, Wendy's
	Lodg	E: Jellico Motel, Best Value Inn W: Days Inn
	Med	W: + Hospital
	Other	W: to **Indian Mountain State Park▲**

NOTE: MM 156: Steep Grade Next 4 mi

156		**Rarity Mountain Rd**
144		**Stinking Creek Rd, Jacksboro**
141		**TN 63, H Baker Hwy, Jacksboro, La Follette, Huntsville, Oneida**
	FStop	W: Pilot Travel Center #224 (Scales)
	Gas	E: Shell
	Food	E: Stuckey's/Shell, Perkins W: Subway/Pilot TC, Stuckey's/Shell
	Lodg	W: Comfort Inn
	Other	W: WiFi/Laundry/Pilot TC

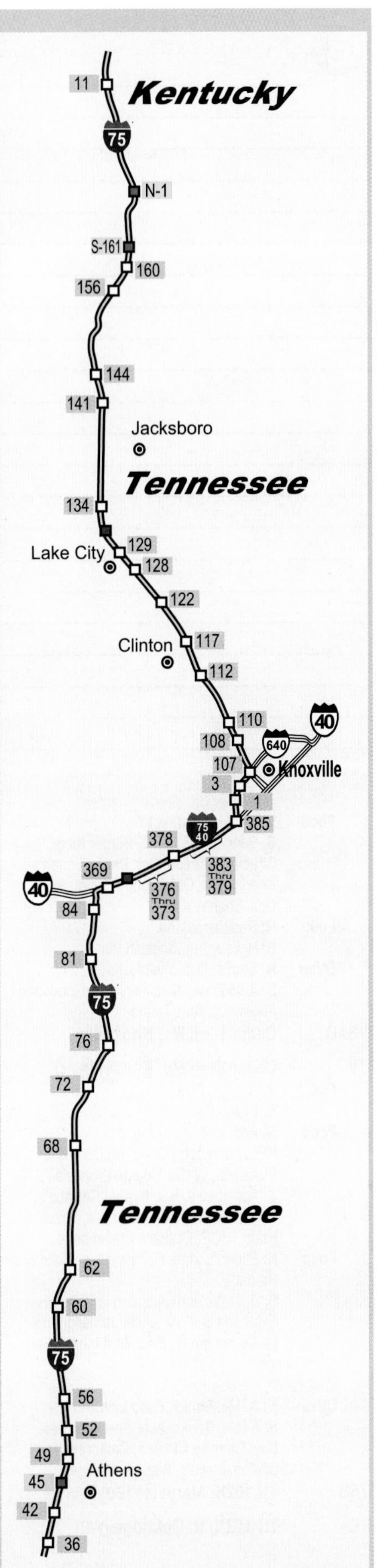

EXIT — TENNESSEE

134		**US 25W, TN 63, Caryville, La Follette, Jacksboro**
	Gas	E: Shell W: BP
	Food	E: Waffle House W: Shoney's
	Lodg	E: Econo Lodge, Family Inn, Hampton Inn, Super 8 W: Budget Host Inn
	Med	E: + Hospital
	Other	E: to **Cove Lake State Park▲**
(130)		**Weigh Station (Both dir)**
129		**US 25W S, TN 116, Lake City**
	Gas	E: BP, Mystik, Sunoco W: Citgo, Exxon, Shell
	Food	W: Burger King, Cracker Barrel, KFC, McDonald's
	Lodg	W: Days Inn, Lambs Inn Motel
128		**US 441, TN 71, to Lake City**
	Gas	E: BP, Sunoco W: Exxon◈, Shell
	Lodg	W: Blue Haven Motel, Days Inn, Lake City Motel
	TServ	E: Precision Truck & Trailer Repair W: Hicks Truck Service
	Other	E: U-Haul, to Mtn Lake Marina & **Campground▲**
122		**TN 61, Andersonville Hwy, Norris, Andersonville, Clinton**
	TStop	W: Kwik Fuel Center #122/P66 (Scales)
	Gas	E: Shell W: Exxon, Marathon◈
	Food	E: Shoney's W: Burger King, Hardee's, Krystal, McDonald's, Shoney's, Waffle House, Wendy's
	Lodg	W: Best Western, Comfort Inn, Super 8
	Other	E: **Fox Inn Campground▲**, IGA, Museum of Appalachia W: Laundry/Kwik FC, Food Lion, ATMs
117		**TN 170, W Raccoon Valley Rd, Heiskell, to Powell**
	TStop	E: Pilot Travel Center #403 (Scales)
	Gas	E: BP◈
	Food	E: BurgerKing/Subway/Pilot TC
	Lodg	W: Valley Inn Motel
	Other	E: WiFi/Pilot TC W: **Volunteer RV Park▲**, **Escapees Raccoon Valley RV Park▲**
112		**TN 131, Emory Rd, Powell**
	Gas	E: BP◈, Chevron W: Exxon, Shell◈
	Food	E: Buddy's BBQ, Krystal, McDonald's, Starbucks, Wendy's W: Hardee's, Shoney's, Waffle House
	Lodg	E: Country Inn, Holiday Inn Express W: Comfort Inn
	Other	E: CVS, Ingles
110		**Callahan Dr, Knoxville**
	Gas	E: Coastal, Weigels W: BP
	Food	E: Rest/Quality Inn W: Burger King, Chili's, McDonald's
	Lodg	E: Knights Inn, Quality Inn, Rodeway Inn W: Scottish Inn
108		**Merchant Dr, to 25W, Knoxville**
	Gas	E: BP◈, Citgo◈, Pilot◈, Texaco, Weigels W: Pilot/Conoco, Shell

EXIT	TENNESSEE
Food	**E:** Applebee's, Cracker Barrel, Denny's, Hooters, Logan's Roadhouse, O'Charley's, Olive Garden, Ryan's Grill, Pizza Hut, Sagebrush, Starbucks, Waffle House **W:** Arby's, Bob Evans, Burger King, Great American Steak & Buffet, IHOP, McDonald's, Outback Steakhouse, Red Lobster, Subway, Waffle House
Lodg	**E:** Best Western, Comfort Inn, Days Inn, Hampton Inn, Howard Johnson, Ramada, Sleep Inn **W:** Comfort Suites, Econo Lodge, Clarion Inn, Family Inn, La Quinta Inn♥, Red Roof Inn♥, Super 8
Other	**E:** CVS, Ingles **W:** ATMs, Advance Auto Parts, Kroger, Walgreen's
NOTE:	**I-640 Knoxville ByPass runs with I-75 below. Exit #'s follow I-640.**
(107)	**Jct I-640E, Knoxville ByPass**
3	**TN 25W, Clinton Hwy, Clinton**
Gas	**N:** BP, Texaco
Food	**N:** Hardee's, KFC, Krystal, Long John Silver, Pizza Hut, Taco Bell, Wendy's
Other	**N:** CVS, Kroger
3B	**Gap Rd NW, Knoxville (NB)**
(3A)	**Jct I-75N, to Lexington, I-275S, to Knoxville**
1	**TN 62, Western Ave**
Gas	**N:** Exxon◊, Marathon, RaceTrac, Shell **S:** BP, Texaco
Food	**N:** Golden Corral, Hardee's, Krystal, Ruby Tuesday, Shoney's, Taco Bell, Wendy's **S:** Hardee's, Krystal, Subway
TServ	**E:** Cummins Cumberland
Other	**N:** CVS, Kroger, Walgreen's **S:** Auto Services, US Post Office
NOTE:	**I-640 Knoxville ByPass runs with I-75 above. Exit #'s follow I-640.**
NOTE:	**I-40 & I-75 below run together for 18 mi. Exit #'s follow I-40.**
(385)	**Jct I-75N, Jct I-640E, to Lexington**
383	**Papermill Rd, TN 372, Knoxville**
Gas	**S:** Amoco, BP, Citgo, Pilot
Food	**S:** Bombay Bicycle Club, Burger King, Captain D's, IHOP, McDonald's, Pizza Hut, Waffle House, Western Sizzlin'
Lodg	**N:** Budget Inn, Holiday Inn **S:** Econo Lodge, Super 8
380	**US 11, US 70, West Hills**
Gas	**S:** BP, Citgo, Conoco, Pilot, Shell, Weigel's
Food	**S:** Arby's, Applebee's, BlackEyed Pea, Chili's, KFC, Krystal, Little Caesar's, Olive Garden, Texas Roadhouse
Lodg	**S:** Howard Johnson, Quality Inn, Super 8
Other	**S:** ATMs, West Town Mall, Food Lion, Office Depot, PetSmart♥, U-Haul, Walgreen's, **TN State Hwy Patrol Post**
379A	**Walker Springs Rd, Gallaher View**
379	**Walker Springs Rd, Gallaher View, Bridgewater Rd**
Gas	**N:** Exxon, Pilot, Shell **S:** BP, Pilot, Texaco

Personal Notes

EXIT	TENNESSEE
Food	**N:** McDonald's/Pilot **S:** Bennett's Pit BBQ, Burger King, Chuck E Cheese, Don Pablo, Logan's Roadhouse, Old Country Buffet, Ryan's Grill, Shoney's
Lodg	**N:** Red Carpet Inn **S:** Holiday Inn, Scottish Inn
Other	**N:** Sam's Club, **Walmart sc** **S:** Auto Zone, Auto Services, Goodyear, Pharmacy, Auto Dealer
378AB	**Cedar Bluff Rd, Knoxville**
378	**Cedar Bluff Rd, Knoxville**
Gas	**N:** Amoco, Pilot, Texaco **S:** Exxon
Food	**N:** Arby's, Burger King, Cracker Barrel, KFC, Long John Silver, McDonald's, Pizza Hut, Waffle House, Wendy's **S:** Applebee's, Bob Evans, Carraba's, Corky's Ribs & BBQ, Denny's, Fazoli's, Hops, IHOP, Outback Steakhouse
Lodg	**N:** Econo Lodge, Hampton Inn, Holiday Inn, Ramada **S:** Best Western, Comfort Inn, Courtyard, Extended Stay America, Jameson Inn, La Quinta Inn♥, Red Roof Inn♥, Sleep Inn
Med	**N: + Hospital**
Other	**N:** ATMs, Banks, Food Lion, Walgreen's **S:** ATMs, Banks, Auto Services, Best Buy, Carmike Cinema, Celebration Station, Lowe's, Staples, Walgreen's
376B	**TN 162S, Maryville (EB)**
376A	**TN 162N, to Oakridge (WB)**

EXIT	TENNESSEE
376	**TN 162S, Maryville (EB)**
374	**TN 131, Lovell Rd, Knoxville**
TStop	**N:** Travel Center of America #13/BP (Scales) **S:** Pilot Travel Center #270 (Scales)
Gas	**N:** Texaco **S:** Citgo, Pilot Food Mart, Speedway
Food	**N:** CountryPride/FastFood/TA TC, McDonald's, Taco Bell, Waffle House **S:** Wendy's/Pilot TC, Arby's, Chili's, Krystal, IHOP, Olive Garden, Shoney's, Texas Roadhouse, Wasabi Japanese,
Lodg	**N:** Best Western, Knights Inn, La Quinta Inn♥, Travelodge/TA TC, Vista Inn **S:** Days Inn, Homewood Suites, Motel 6♥, Springhill Suites
TServ	**N:** TA TC/Tires
Other	**N:** Laundry/CB/BarbSh/WiFi/TA TC, **Buddy Gregg Motorhomes** **S:** WiFi/Pilot TC, Auto Dealers, ATMs, Banks, Target, **Walmart sc**
373	**Campbell Station Rd, Farragut**
FStop	**S:** Pilot Food Mart #221
Gas	**N:** Shell◊, Marathon **S:** BP
Food	**S:** Cracker Barrel, Hardee's, Wendy's/Pilot
Lodg	**N:** Comfort Suites, Country Inn, Super 8 **S:** Baymont Inn, Holiday Inn Express
Other	**N: Buddy Gregg Motorhomes▲** **S:** Gander Mountain
(372)	**Weigh Station (Both dir)**
369	**Watt Rd, W Knoxville**
TStop	**N:** Flying J Travel Plaza #5034/Conoco (Scales) **S:** Petro Stopping Center (Scales), Travel Center of America #107/BP (Scales)
Food	**N:** Cookery/FastFood/Flying J TP **S:** IronSkillet/Petro SC, Perkins/B King/PizzaHut/TA TC
TWash	**N:** Fast Point Truck Wash **S:** Blue Beacon TW/Petro SC
TServ	**N:** Freightliner of Knoxville, Speedco **S:** Petro SC/Tires, TA TC/Tires
Other	**N:** Laundry/WiFi/**RVDump/LP**/FJ TP, **Shadrack Watersport & RV's** **S:** Laundry/WiFi/**RVDump**/Petro SC, Laundry/CB/WiFi/TA TC, Fireworks
(368/84A)	**Jct I-75S, to Chattanooga** **Jct I-40E, I-75N, to Knoxville**
(84B)	**Jct I-40W, to Nashville (Left exit)**
NOTE:	**I-40 & I-75 above run together for 18 mi. Exit #'s follow I-40.**
81	**US 321, TN 73, Lenoir City, Oak Ridge, Great Smoky Mtns Nat'l Park**
Gas	**E:** BP◊, Exxon◊, Mobil, Shell◊, Murphy **W:** Citgo◊, Shell◊, Mobil
Food	**E:** Burger King, Buddy's BBQ, Chili's, Cracker Barrel, KFC, McDonald's, Shoney's, Waffle House, Wendy's, Zaxby's, Rest/KI, Subway/Exxon **W:** Ruby Tuesday
Lodg	**E:** Days Inn, Hampton Inn, Holiday Inn Express, Inn of Lenoir, Kings Inn, Super 8 **W:** Comfort Inn, Econo Lodge, Ramada Ltd
Other	**E:** Home Depot, **Walmart sc**, Radio Shack, **to** Ft Loudon Dam, **Smoky Mtns Nat'l Park, to app 18 mi** Smoky Mountain Harley Davidson

◊= Regular Gas Stations with Diesel ▲ = RV Friendly Locations ♥= Pet Friendly Locations
Red print shows large vehicle parking / access on site or nearby Brown Print = Campgrounds / RV PARKS

EXIT **TENNESSEE**

76 **TN 324, Hotchkiss Valley Rd E, Sugar Limb Rd, Lenoir City**
- Other E: to Watts Bar Lake
- W: to TN Valley Winery

72 **TN 72, Loudon**
- Gas E: BP, Shell◈
- W: Citgo
- Food E: McDonald/BP, Wendy/Shell, Hardee's
- Lodg E: Country Inn, Super 8♥
- W: Best Value Inn♥
- Other W: **Express RV Park▲**

68 **TN 323, Pond Creek Rd, Loudon, to Philadelphia**
- Gas E: BP◈, Sunoco
- Other E: Sweetwater Valley Cheese Farm

62 **TN 322, Oakland Rd, Sweetwater**
- Gas E: Phillips 66
- W: 48's Fireworks
- Food E: Dave's Rest, Dinner Bell Rest
- Other W: **Sweetwater KOA▲** , Trailer Center

60 **TN 68, Lost Sea Pike, Sweetwater, to Spring City, Lost Sea**
- FStop W: Kangaroo Express #3599/Citgo
- Gas E: BP, Marathon, RaceWay, Shell◈
- W: BP◈, Conoco
- Food E: Burger King, Huddle House, KFC, McDonald's, Bradley's Pit BBQ, Wendy's
- W: Aunt M's Fr Chicken/Kangaroo, **Cracker Barrel**, Hardee's
- Lodg E: Best Value Inn, Comfort Inn, Days Inn, Knights Inn, Super 8
- W: Best Western, Magnuson Hotel, Quality Inn
- Other E: to Lost Sea Underground Lake
- W: Flea Market, Tourist Info, **Tellico Plains KOA▲**

56 **TN 309, Union Grove Rd, Niota**
- TStop E: PTP/Crazy Ed's/BP (Scales)
- Food E: Rest/Crazy Ed's, Front Porch Rest
- TServ E: Crazy Ed's/Tires
- Other E: **TN Country Campground▲**

52 **Hwy 305, Mt Verd Rd, Athens**
- Gas E: BP, Citgo
- W: BP, Exxon
- Food E: Subway
- Lodg E: Heritage Motel
- W: Ramada Inn♥, Travelodge
- Other E: **Overniter RV Park▲** , Mayfield Dairy Tour

49 **TN 30, Athens, to Decatur**
- Gas E: BP, Conoco, Kangaroo, RaceWay, Shell◈
- W: Shell
- Food E: Applebee's, Burger King, Hardee's, KFC, McDonald's, Krystal, Ruby Tuesday, Shoney's, Steak n Shake, Subway, Waffle House, Wendy's, Western Sizzlin
- W: **Cracker Barrel**
- Lodg E: Days Inn, Econo Lodge, Hampton Inn, Holiday Inn Express, Homestead Inn, Knights Inn, Motel 6♥, Super 8
- W: Homestead Inn
- Med E: + Hospital
- Other E: **Athens I-75 Campground & Park▲**

(45) **McMinn Rest Area (Both dir) (RR, Phone, Picnic, Vend, Info) (CLOSED)**

42 **TN 39, Riceville Rd, Calhoun**
- Gas E: Citgo
- Lodg E: Relax Inn, Rice Inn

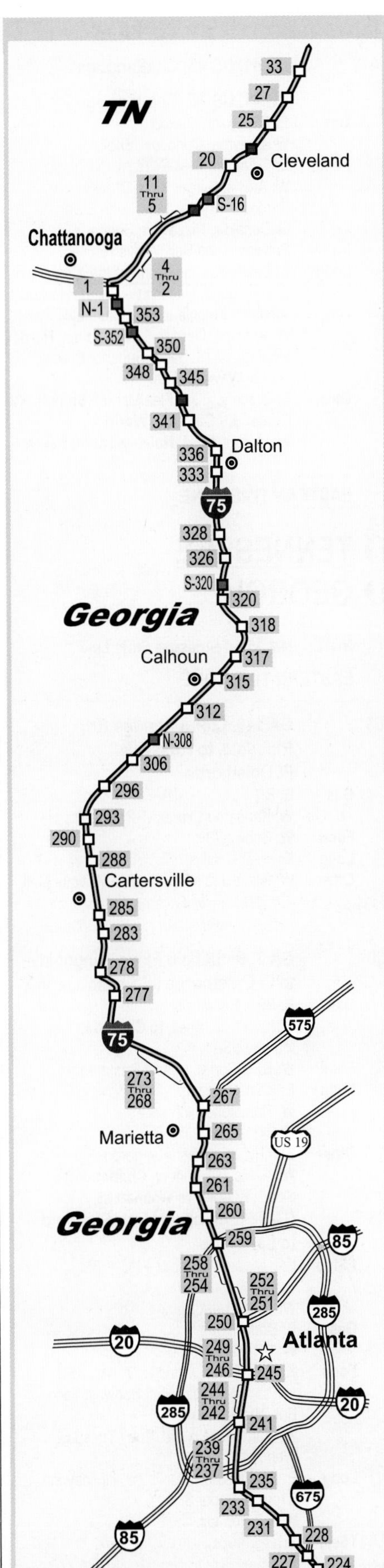

EXIT **TENNESSEE**

- Other E: **Mouse Creek Campgound▲**

36 **TN 163, Big Spring Calhoun Rd, Lamontville Rd, to Calhoun**

33 **TN 308, Lauderdale Memorial Hwy, Charleston**
- TStop W: Ponderosa Truck Plaza/Shell (Scales), Love's Travel Stop #364 (Scales)
- Gas E: Citgo
- Food W: Rest/Ponderosa TP, McDonald's/Arby's/McDonald's/Love's TP
- TServ W: Ponderosa TP/Tires
- Other E: **Exit 33 Campground▲**
- W: Laundry/Ponderosa TP, Laundry/WiFi/**RVDump**/Love's TS

27 **Sgt Paul Huff Pkwy, Cleveland**
- FStop W: BP
- Gas E: Phillips 66, Murphy
- W: Exxon, Texaco
- Food E: Applebee's, Chili's, CiCi's, Golden Corral, IHOP, McDonald's, O'Charley's, Outback Steakhouse, Panera Bread, Ryan's Grill, Steak 'n Shake, Taco Bell
- W: Denny's, Hardee's, Waffle House
- Lodg E: Jameson Inn
- W: Comfort Inn, Hampton Inn, Quality Inn, Ramada, Royal Inn, Super 8
- TServ E: Cleveland Tire Center
- Other E: AutoZone, CVS, Dollar Tree, Food Lion, Goodyear, Home Depot, Lowe's, PetCo♥, Staples, **Walmart sc**, Grocery, Bradley Square Mall
- W: Target

25 **TN 60, 25th St NW, Georgetown Rd, Cleveland, to Dayton**
- FStop E: Orbit Chevron
- Gas E: BP, Citgo, RaceWay, Texaco◈
- W: Shell
- Food W: Bojangles, Burger King, **Cracker Barrel**, Hardee's, McDonald's, Waffle House, Wendy's, Zaxby's
- W: Perkins, Uncle Bud's Catfish
- Lodg E: Colonial Inn, Days Inn, Econo Lodge, Economy Inn, Fairfield Inn, Howard Johnson, Knights Inn, Quality Inn, Red Carpet Inn, Travel Inn
- W: Baymont Inn, Economy Inn♥, Holiday Inn, Wingate Inn
- Med E: + Hospital
- Other E: Tourist Info, Golf Course, CarWash, Lee Univ, Comm College

(23) **Weigh Station (NB)**

20 **US 74, TN 311 to US 64 ByPass E, to Cleveland**
- Gas E: Exxon, Shell
- W: Exxon◈, Horizon◈
- Food E: Golden Corral, Hardee's, McDonald's, Subway, Taco Bell
- Other W: **Chattanooga N/Cleveland KOA▲**

(16) **Scenic View (SB)**

(13) **Weigh Station (SB)**

11 **US 11E N, US 64E, Ooltewah**
- Gas E: BP, Chevron, Citgo, RaceWay, Shell, Murphy
- W: BP◈, Kangaroo
- Food E: Arby's, Burger King, **Cracker Barrel**, Hardee's, McDonald's, Subway, Taco Bell, Quiznos, Wendy's, Zaxby's
- W: Krystal, Waffle House
- Lodg E: Hotel

◈= **Regular Gas Stations with Diesel** ▲ = **RV Friendly Locations** ♥= **Pet Friendly Locations**

Red print shows large vehicle parking / access on site or nearby **Brown Print = Campgrounds / RV PARKS**

EXIT		TENNESSEE
	Lodg	W: Super 8♥
	Med	E: + Family Walk-In Medical Center
	Other	E: Grocery, Publix, **Wal-Mart sc**
		W: to **Harrison Bay State Park▲**
9		**Volunteer Ordinance Rd**
7		**Lee Hwy, to US 64W, US 11S, TN 317, to Chattanooga (SB)**
	Gas	E: Exxon
		W: Chevron, Shell
	Food	W: Taco Bell, Waffle House
	Lodg	W: AmeriSuites, Best Inn, Best Western, Comfort Inn, Days Inn, Econo Lodge, Motel 6♥
	Other	W: Harley Davidson
7A		**Lee Hwy, TN 317E, to Summit, Collegedale (NB)**
7B		**Bonny Oaks Dr, US 64, US 11, TN 317W, Chattanooga (NB)**
5		**Shallowford Rd, Hamilton Place Blvd, to US 11, US 64, Chattanooga**
	Gas	W: BP, Citgo, Exxon, Shell
	Food	E: Arby's, CiCi's, Famous Dave's BBQ, Hops Grill, Krystal, Logan's Roadhouse, McDonald's, Old Country Buffet, Romano's Macaroni Grill, Red Lobster, Steak 'n Shake, Starbucks, Taco Bell
		W: Applebee's, Cracker Barrel, Golden Corral, KFC, Domino's, McDonald's, O'Charley's, Pizza Hut, Rio Bravo, Sonic, Shoney's, Subway, Waffle House, Wendy's
	Lodg	E: Comfort Suites, Courtyard, Quality Inn, Wingate Inn
		W: Country Inn, Days Inn, Fairfield Inn, Guesthouse Inn, Hampton Inn, Hilton Garden Inn, Homewood Suites, Holiday Inn Knights Inn, La Quinta Inn♥, Ramada Ltd, Red Roof Inn, Sleep Inn
	Med	W: + Hospital
	Other	E: ATMs, Auto Service, B&N, Best Buy, Firestone, Home Depot, Lowe's, Office Depot, PetSmart♥, Staples, Walgreen's, **Walmart sc**, Grocery
		W: ATMs, CVS, Grocery, Goodyear, Univ of TN/Chattanooga
4A		**Hamilton Place Blvd (NB, diff reacc)**
	Food	E: Bonefish Grill, Carrabba's, DQ, Grady's, Hardee's, Outback Steakhouse, Olive Garden, Red Lobster, Ruby Tuesday, TGI Friday
	Lodg	E: Courtyard
	Med	E: + Physicians Walk-In Clinic
	Other	E: ATMs, Firestone, Staples, World Market, Hamilton Place Mall, Tourist Info
4		**TN 153N, to US 64, US 11**
	Other	W: to Lovell Field Airport✈
3B		**TN 320W, E Brainerd Rd**
3A		**TN 320W, E Brainerd Rd**
3		**TN 320W, E Brainerd Rd (SB)**
	Gas	E: AmocoBP
	Food	E: Baskin Robbins
	Other	E: Concord Public Golf Course
		W: to Lovell Field Airport✈
(2)		**Jct I-24W, to I-59, Lookout Mtn, Chattanooga, Nashville (NB, Left Ex)**
(1)		**TN Welcome Center (NB)** (RR, Phones, Picnic, Vend)
1B		**US 41W, US 46, Chattanooga**

EXIT		TN / GA
1A		**US 41, US 46, Chattanooga**
1		**US 41, US 46, Chattanooga**
	Gas	E: BP, Exxon, Texaco
		W: Chevron, Conoco◈, Shell◈
	Food	E: Country Vittles Buffet, Trip's Seafood
		W: Arby's, Burger King, Cracker Barrel, Hardee's, Krystal, Long John Silver, McDonald's, Pizza Hut, Shoney's, Subway, Taco Bell, Waffle House
	Lodg	E: Best Value Inn, Comfort Inn, Crown Inn, Econo Lodge, Hawthorne Suites, Howard Johnson, Knights Inn, Ramada Ltd
		W: Best Inn, Days Inn, Fairfield Inn, Holiday Inn Express, Super 8, Superior Creek Lodge, Waverly Hotel
	Other	E: Grocery, CVS, Flea Market, **Shipp's RV Center ▲ / Camping World**
		W: U-Haul, **Best Holiday Trav-L Park▲**

EASTERN TIME ZONE

⬆ TENNESSEE
⬇ GEORGIA

NOTE:		MM 355: Tennessee State Line

EASTERN TIME ZONE

EXIT		
353		**GA 146, Cloud Springs Rd, Ringgold, to Rossville, Ft Oglethorpe**
	Gas	E: BP
		W: Kangaroo Express/BP◈, Shell
	Food	W: Subway/BP
	Lodg	E: Knights Inn
	Other	W: Island Joe's Food & Fun, Antique Mall
(352)		**GA Welcome Center (SB)** (RR, Phones, Picnic, Vend, RVDump)
350		**GA 2, Battlefield Pkwy, Ringgold, to Ft Oglethorpe (W Serv to app 3mi)**
	Gas	E: BP◈, Kangaroo
		W: RaceTrac, Shell, to Conoco◈, Murphy USA
	Food	W: BBQ Corral, to Asst Restaurants
	Lodg	E: Hometown Inn
		W: Hamptonon Inn
	Med	E: + Hospital
	Other	E: ATMs, Carwash/Kangaroo, Freightliner
		W: ATMs, GA Winery, **Chattanooga South KOA▲**, to **Walmart sc**,
348		**GA 151, Alabama Hwy, Ringgold, to LaFayette**
	FStop	E: Kangaroo Express #3553/BP, Sunset Market #9/Shell
		W: Shell Fuel Center #1027
	Gas	E: Conoco
		W: BP, Kangaroo
	Food	E: Aunt Effie's, Cracker Barrel, KFC, McDonald's, Pizza Hut, Subway, Taco Bell, Waffle House
		W: Hardee's, Krystal, Ruby Tuesday, Wendy's
	Lodg	E: Best Western, Days Inn, Holiday Inn Express, Super 8
		W: Comfort Inn
	TServ	E: JTS Truck Sales
		W: Peterbilt of Lookout Mountain, Yates, Freightliner

EXIT		GEORGIA
	Other	E: Advance Auto, CVS, Family Dollar, Grocery, **N GA RV Country, All Aboard RV & Trailer Depot**
		W: ATMs, Auto Dealers, Ace Hardware, Playtime Amusement Park/Holcomb Rd, **Northgate RV Center**
345		**US 41, US 76, GA 3, Ringgold, Tunnel Hill**
	TStop	W: AmBest/Choo Choo Truck Wash Plaza (Scales), PTP/Cochran's Travel Center/ MidniteOil (Scales), Kangaroo Express #3622 (Scales)
	Gas	E: BP
		W: Chevron
	Food	E:
		W: Rest/ChooChoo TWP, Rest/Cochran's TC, Subway/Kangaroo, Waffle House
	Lodg	W: Friendship Inn
	TWash	W: Choo Choo TW
	TServ	W: Cochran's TC/Tires
	Other	E: U-Haul
		W: Laundry/Cochran's TC, Bell's Towing, Bell's Wrecker Service
(343)		**Weigh Station (Both dir)**
341		**GA 201, N Varnell Rd, Tunnel Hill-Varnell Rd, Tunnel Hill**
	Gas	W: Chevron, Shell
	Other	W: Assorted Carpet Outlets
336		**US 41, US 76, GA 3, Chattanooga Rd, Dalton, Rocky Face**
	FStop	E: Fast Food & Fuel/Conoco (GA 71N & US 76 N ByPass)
	Gas	E: Chevron, RaceTrac, Shell, Murphy USA
		W: BP◈, Exxon
	Food	E: Blimpie/Chevron, Mr Biscuit, Waffle House, Wendy's
		W: Denny's, Los Pablos Mexican Rest, Wendy's,
	Lodg	E: Econo Lodge, Howard Johnson
		W: Best Western, Guest Inn, Motel 6♥, Royal Inn, Super 8
	Med	E: + Hamilton Hospital
	Other	E: ATMs, Banks, Checker Auto Parts, Higdon Animal Hospital♥, Home Depot, **Walmart sc**, Whitfield Animal Hospital♥, **Whitfield Co Sheriff Dept**
		W: GA State Hwy Patrol Post
333		**GA 52, GA 71, Walnut Ave, Dalton**
	Gas	E: BP◈, Exxon, RaceTrac◈, Kangaroo/ Citgo, Kroger
		W: Shell
	Food	E: Applebee's, Burger King, ChickFilA, Captain D's, CiCi's Pizza, Cracker Barrel, DQ, Fuddruckers, IHOP, KFC, Long John Silver, Longhorn Steakhouse, McDonald's, Outback Steakhouse, O'Charley's, Sonic, Shoney's, Starbucks, Steak 'n Shake, Taco Bell, Waffle House, Wendy's
		W: Chili's, Red Lobster
	Lodg	E: America's Best Inn, Days Inn, Hampton Inn, Travelodge
		W: Comfort Inn, Country Inn, Courtyard, Jameson Inn, La Quinta Inn, Quality Inn, Ramada Inn, Wellesley Inn, Wingate Inn
	Other	E: ATMs, Banks, Auto Dealers, Auto Service/Exxon, Kroger/Pharmacy, Mountain Creek Harley Davidson, Petland♥, Pharmacy, Walgreen's, Tanger Outlet Mall
		W: NW Georgia Trade Center

◈= Regular Gas Stations with Diesel ▲ = RV Friendly Locations ♥= Pet Friendly Locations
Red print shows large vehicle parking / access on site or nearby **Brown Print = Campgrounds / RV PARKS**

EXIT		GEORGIA
328		**SR 3 Conn, to US 41, S Dalton ByPass, Dalton**
	TStop	E: Pilot Travel Center #319 (Scales)
	Gas	E: Food Mart/BP◈, Exxon
	Food	E: Arby's/TJCinn/Pilot TC, Blimpie/BP, Country Kitchen, Waffle House, Wendy's
	Lodg	E: Super 8♥
	Other	E: WiFi/Pilot TC, Comm'l Driver License Facility W: Various Carpet Outlets
326		**Carbondale Rd, CR 665, to US 41N, GA 3, Carbondale, Dalton**
	FStop	W: Mapco #3511/Exxon
	TStop	E: Pilot Travel Center #421 (Scales)
	Gas	E: Chevron◈ W: BP
	Food	E: McDonald's/Subway/Pilot TC, BBQ, Pizza
	Lodg	E: Country Boy Inn
	TWash	E: Pilot TC
	TServ	E: Pilot TC/Tires W: Cummins South
	Other	E: Laundry/WiFi/**RVDump**/Pilot TC, ATMs, Greyhound/Pilot TC,
320		**GA 136, Hill City Rd, Resaca, to LaFayette**
	TStop	E: Flying J Travel Plaza #5470/Conoco (Scales)
	Food	E: Rest/FastFood/FJ TP
	TWash	E: Dependable TW
	TServ	E: Reece Truck Service/Tires
	Other	E: Laundry/BarbSh/WiFi/**RVDump/LP**/FJ TP, C& C Electronics/CB
(320)		**Rest Area (SB)** **(RR, Phones, Picnic, Vend, RVDump)**
318		**US 41, GA 3, Dixie Hwy, Calhoun**
	TStop	E: WilcoHess Travel Plaza #3005 (Scales)
	Gas	W: Shell◈
	Food	E: DQ/Wendy's/WilcoHess TP, Hardee's, Huddle House W: Chuckwagon Rest, Rest/Duffy's Motel
	Lodg	E: Best Western, Knights Inn W: Best Inn, Budget Inn, Duffy's Motel, Smith Motel, Super 8
	Other	E: Laundry/WilcoHess TP
317		**GA 225, Chatsworth Hwy NE, Calhoun, Chatsworth**
	Gas	W: BP
	Lodg	W: Express Inn
315		**GA 156, Red Bud Rd, Calhoun**
	Gas	E: BP, Citgo◈, Kangaroo W: BP◈, Liberty, Shell
	Food	E: Shoney's, Subway, Waffle House W: Arby's
	Lodg	E: Ramada Inn, Scottish Inn W: Days Inn, Oglethorpe Inn
	Med	W: + Gordon Hospital
	Other	E: ATM, Auto Service, Food Lion, **Calhoun KOA▲**
312		**GA 53, Fairmont Hwy, Calhoun to Fairmont, Rome**
	Gas	E: BP, Shell◈ W: Chevron◈, Kangaroo, RaceWay, Murphy, Kroger
	Food	E: **Cracker Barrel**, Denny's, Rest/Budget Host Inn W: Arby's, Bojangle's, Burger King, Captain D's, Checkers, DQ, Golden Corral, Hickory House BBQ, Huddle House, IHOP, KFC, Krystal, Long John Silver, McDonald's Pizza Hut, Ruby Tuesday, Starbucks,

EXIT		GEORGIA
	Food	W: Subway, Taco Bell, Waffle House, Wendy's
	Lodg	E: Budget Host Inn, Country Inn, Quality Inn W: Comfort Inn, Days Inn, Hampton Inn, Holiday Inn Express, Jameson Inn, Royal Inn
	Other	E: Prime Outlets, **GA State Hwy Patrol** W: ATMs, Auto Zone, Auto Dealers, CVS, Dollar General, Goodyear, Home Depot, Kroger, Office Depot, **Walmart sc**
(308)		**Rest Area (NB)** **(RR, Phone, Picnic, Vend, RVDump)**
306		**GA 140, Folsom Rd, Adairsville, to Summerville, Rome**
	TStop	E: Patty's Truck Stop/Citgo (Scales), QT #757 (Scales) W: All American Truck Stop (Scales)
	Gas	E: Cowboys◈, Shell W: BP◈, Chevron, Exxon
	Food	E: Rest/Patty's TS, **Cracker Barrel**, Wendy's W: Rest/All Amer TS, Bamboo Garden, Burger King, Hardee's, McDonald's, Owens BBQ, Subway, Taco Bell, Waffle House, Wendy's, Zaxby's
	Lodg	W: Best Western, Comfort Inn, Ramada Ltd, Relax Inn
	TWash	E: Patty's TS W: All Amer TS
	TServ	E: Patty's TS/Tires
	Other	E: Laundry/Patty's TS, Adairsville Towing & Auto W: ATMs, Food Lion, **Harvest Moon RV Park▲**
296		**CR 630, Cassville-White Rd, Cartersville, White**
	TStop	E: Travel Center of America/Exxon (Scales), Pilot Travel Center #67 (Scales) **(DAND)**
	Gas	E: Food & Fuel, Pure, Texaco W: Chevron, Citgo, Shell
	Food	E: CountryPride/BurgerKing/Popeye/Pizza Hut/Taco Bell/TA TC, McDonald's/Subway/Pilot TC, Country BBQ & Grill W: Waffle House
	Lodg	E: Sleep Inn W: Americas Best Inn, Budget Host Inn, Howard Johnson Express Inn♥
	TWash	E: Pilot TC
	TServ	E: TA TC/Tires
	Other	E: Laundry/BarbSh/WiFi/Med/**RVDump**/TA TC, Laundry/WiFi/Pilot TC, CB Shop W: **Cartersville/Cassville-White KOA▲**
293		**US 411, GA 61, Chatsworth Hwy, Cartersville, to White**
	FStop	W: Gas N Go/Citgo
	Gas	E: BP◈, Texaco W: Chevron◈
	Food	W: Cafe, BBQ, Waffle House
	Lodg	E: Quality Inn W: Holiday Inn
	Other	W: ATMs, Harley Davidson of Cartersville, Museum, **GA State Hwy Patrol Post**
290		**GA 20, Canton Hwy, Cartersville, to Rome, Canton**
	FStop	E: Kangaroo Express #3675
	Gas	E: Chevron◈, Exxon◈ W: BP, Shell, Murphy USA
	Food	E: Arby's, McDonald's, Wendy's, Subway/Exxon, W: **Cracker Barrel**, BBQ, Shoney's, Subway, Waffle House

EXIT		GEORGIA
	Lodg	E: Best Western, Comfort Inn, Econo Lodge, Motel 6♥ W: Days Inn, Hampton Inn,
	Med	W: + Cartersville Hospital
	Other	E: ATMs, Car Wash, P&J Tires, W: ATMs, to Auto Services, Dollar Tree, Firestone, Lowe's, Tires, U-Haul, **Walmart sc**,
288		**GA 113, Main St, Cartersville**
	FStop	W: KangarooExpress #3653/BP
	Gas	W: Exxon◈
	Food	W: Applebee's, Blimpie, Burger King, ChickFilA, McDonald's, Mrs Winner's, Krystal, Pizza Hut, Subway, Waffle House
	Lodg	W: Fairfield Inn, to Knights Inn, Quality Inn
	Other	W: ATMs, to Auto Dealers, Auto Services, Banks, Kroger, Pharmacy, Staples, Target, US Post Office
285		**CR 633, Red Top Mountain Rd, Cartersville, Emerson**
	Gas	E: Texaco
	Lodge	E: Red Top Mountain Lodge
	Other	E: **to appr 1.5 mi Red Top Mountain State Park▲**
283		**CR 397, Emerson-Allatoona Rd**
	Other	E: **to appr 2 mi Allatoona Landing Campground▲**
278		**CR 633, Glade Rd, Acworth**
	Gas	E: BP◈, Shell W: Chevron, Citgo
	Food	E: Subway/BP W: Burger King, Country Club Café, KFC, Krystal, Pizza Hut, Subway, Taco Bell, Waffle House, Western Sizzlin
	Lodg	E: Americas Best Value Inn, Guest House Inn W: Red Roof Inn♥
	Other	E: **Old 41 Campground▲ , COE/Clark Creek North Campground▲ , COE/McKinney Campground▲ , to appr 3mi** Holiday Harbor Marina & Resort▲ , W: ATMs, Auto Zone, Big Lots, CVS, Carwash/Chevron, Grocery, Ingles, NAPA, Radio Shack
277		**GA 92, Alabama Rd, Acworth**
	Gas	E: BP, RaceTrac, W: Shell◈
	Food	E: Hardee's, Shoney's, Waffle House W: McDonald's, Subway, Waffle House, Wendy's, Zaxby's
	Lodg	E: Comfort Suites, Holiday Inn Express, La Quinta Inn♥, Ramada W: Best Western, Days Inn, Econo Lodge, Quality Inn, Super 8
	Other	E: **COE/Payne Campground▲** W: ATMs, CVS, Dollar General, Goodyear, Publix, Walgreen's
273		**Wade Green Rd, to GA 92, Kennesaw**
	Gas	E: BP, Citgo◈, RaceTrac W: Conoco, Texaco, Kroger
	Food	E: Arby's, Burger King, China King, Mrs Winner, McDonald's, Papa John's, Subway, Taco Bell, Waffle House W: Blimpie/Texaco, Starbucks, Wendy's
	Lodg	E: Rodeway Inn, Sleep Inn, Travelodge
	Other	E: ATMs, Publix, Pharmacy, Tires W: ATMs, Home Depot, Jiffy Lube, Kroger, Walgreen's, Shiloh Veterinary Hospital♥

◈= Regular Gas Stations with Diesel ▲ = RV Friendly Locations ♥= Pet Friendly Locations
Red print shows large vehicle parking / access on site or nearby Brown Print = Campgrounds / RV PARKS

EXIT		GEORGIA
271		**Chastain Rd, to I-575N**
	Gas	**E:** Pacer Fuel/Chevron
		W: Citgo, Save, Shell◈
	Food	**E:** California Dreaming, ChickFilA, Cracker Barrel, Dunkin Donuts, O'Charley's, Panda Express
		W: Arby's, Waffle House, Wendy's
	Lodg	**E:** Best Western, Comfort Inn, Embassy Suites, Extended Stay America, Fairfield Inn, Residence Inn
		W: Country Inn, La Quinta Inn, Spring Hill Suites, Sun Suites
	Med	**E:** + Physician's Immed Med Clinic
	Other	**E:** ATMs, Goodyear, **Walmart**, Outlet Mall
		W: ATMs, Discount Tire, Penske Truck Rental, Kennesaw State Univ, Cobb Co Airport McCollum Field✈
269		**GA 5, to US 41, Barrett Pkwy, Kennesaw, to Marietta, to I-575**
	FStop	**E:** Shell Food Mart
	Gas	**E:** Chevron
		W: ArcoAmPm/BP, Exxon, Costco
	Food	**E:** Applebee's, Atlanta Bread, Burger King, Fuddrucker's, McDonald's, Longhorn Steakhouse, Olive Garden, Piccadilly's, Red Lobster, Shoney's, Starbucks, Smokey Bones BBQ, Waffle House
		W: ChickFilA, Chili's, Chuck E Cheese's, Golden Corral, Joe's Crab Shack, On the Border, Outback Steakhouse, Rafferty's, Roadhouse Grill, Sweet Tomato, Starbucks, Steak 'n Shake, TGI Friday
	Lodg	**E:** Econo Lodge, Holiday Inn Express, Red Roof Inn♥, Super 8
		W: Comfort Inn, Days Inn, Hampton Inn, Hilton Garden Inn, Sleep Inn, Town Place Suites, Quality Inn, Wingate Inn
	Med	**W:** + Hospital
	Other	**E:** ATMs, Big 10 Tire, B&N, Firestone, Home Depot, Publix, Sears Auto Center, Town Center at Cobb Mall
	Other	**W:** ATMs, Auto Dealers, Best Buy, Borders, Costco, Dick's Sporting Goods, Office Depot, PetSmart♥, Target, Tires, Cobb Place Shopping Center
(268)		**Jct I-575N, GA 5N, to Canton**
267A		**GA 5N, Canton Rd**
267B		**to US 41S, GA 5S, Marietta**
	Med	**W:** + Hospital
265		**GA 120 Lp, N Marietta Pkwy, Marietta, Roswell**
	Gas	**W:** Chevron, Shell◈
	Food	**W:** Arby's, Bojangles, Sonny's BBQ
	Lodg	**W:** Budget Inn, Crown Inn, Days Inn, Spinnaker Resort, Sun Inn, Travel Motel
	Med	**W:** + Hospital, + Medical Care Center
	Other	**E:** Nat'l Bus Sales
		W: White Water Park, Six Flags, American Adventure Amusement Park
263		**120W, Marietta, S Marietta Pkwy, 120E, Roswell, Southern Poly**
	Gas	**E:** Chevron◈, QT, Texaco
		W: QT, Exxon◈, RaceTrac
	Food	**W:** Applebee's, Captain D's, China Kitchen, Chili's, DQ, Hardee's, Piccadilly's, Subway
	Lodg	**W:** Baymont Inn, Best Western, Crowne Plaza, Fairfield Inn, Hampton Inn, Ramada Ltd, Regency Inn, Super 8, Wyndham
	Other	**W:** ATMs, Bowling Center, Pharmacy, U-Haul, **Brookwood RV Park▲**,

EXIT		GEORGIA
261		**GA 280, Delk Rd, Lockheed, to Dobbins AFB**
	Gas	**E:** Exxon◈, RaceTrac, Shell
		W: BP, Chevron, Shell
	Food	**E:** Denny's, Hardee's, McDonald's, KFC, Ruby Tuesday, Spaghetti Warehouse, Texas BBQ, Waffle House
		W: Cracker Barrel, China Chef, Mexican Rest, Waffle House
	Lodg	**E:** Budget Inn, Courtyard, Drury Inn, Motel 6♥, Scottish Inn, Sleep Inn, Super 8, Travelers Inn
		W: Best Inn, Comfort Inn, Days Inn, Fairfield Inn, Holiday Inn, La Quinta Inn♥, Wingate Inn
	Other	**E:** ATM, Publix Grocery
		W: ATMs, **RVs n Such**, to Dobbins AFB
260		**CR 1720, Windy Hill Rd, Smyrna**
	Gas	**E:** BP, Shell
		W: Citgo, Shell, Texaco
	Food	**E:** Deli, Famous Dave's BBQ, Fuddrucker's, Los Bravos, Mrs Winner's, Pappasito Cantina, Pappadeaux Seafood, Starbucks, Subway, TGI Friday
		W: Arby's, ChickFilA, McDonald's, Popeye, Waffle House, Wendy's, $3 Cafe
	Lodg	**E:** Crown Plaza, Econo Lodge, Extended Stay, Hilton Garden Inn, Hyatt Regency♥, Marriott, Travelodge
		W: Best Western, Country Inn, Days Inn, Courtyard, DoubleTree Hotel, Masters Inn, Radisson, Red Roof Inn♥
	Med	**W:** + Hospital
	Other	**E:** CVS, FedEx Office
		W: ATMs, Auto Dealers, Best Buy, FedEx Office, Target
(259)		**Jct I-285, E-Augusta, W-Birmingham**
(259A)		**Jct I-285E, Atlanta ByPass, to Augusta, Greenville (SB)**
(259B)		**Jct I-285W, Atlanta ByPass, to Birmingham, Montgomery (SB)**
	NOTE:	**All through trucks MUST take I-285 around Atlanta. West ByPass is shorter.**
258		**Akers Mill Rd, Cumberland Blvd**
	Food	**W:** Hooter's, Longhorn Steakhouse, Subway
	Lodg	**W:** Homewood Suites, Embassy Suites, Residence Hotel, Sheraton
	Other	**W:** Galleria Specialty Mall, AMC 15, Cumberland Mall, Cobb Co Conv & Visitor Center, Costco, Office Max, PetSmart♥, UPS Store
256		**to US 41, Mt Paran Rd, CR 624, GA 3, US 41, Northside Pkwy**
	Med	**W:** + Hospital
255		**to US 41, West Paces Ferry Rd, Northside Pkwy**
	Gas	**E:** Chevron, Shell◈, BP
		W: Exxon
	Food	**E:** ChickFilA, China Moon, DQ, Flying Biscuit Cafe, Goldberg's Bagels & Deli, Houston's, McDonald's, Steak 'n Shake, Starbucks, Willy's Mexican Grill
	Med	**W:** + Hospital
	Other	**E:** ATMs, Banks, CVS, Publix, Paces Ferry Vet Clinic♥
254		**Moores Mill Rd**

EXIT		GEORGIA
252		**Howell Mill Rd, to US 41, GA 3**
252B		**Howell Mill Rd, to US 41, GA 3**
	Gas	**E:** Exxon, Shell◈
		W: Shell◈
	Food	**E:** ChickFilA, Domino's, Hardee's, McDonald's, Willy's Mexican Grill
		W: Arby's, Einstein Bros, KFC, Long John Silver, Piccadilly, Subway, Taco Bell, Waffle House, Wendy's, US BBQ
	Lodg	**E:** Budget Inn
		W: Castlegate Hotel, Holiday Inn
	Med	**E:** + Hospital
	Other	**E:** Grocery, Goodyear, Office Depot, Pharmacy, PetSmart♥, US Post Office
		W: ATMs, Ace Hardware, Jiffy Lube, Kroger, Firestone, **Walmart sc**, Northside Drive Pet Hospital♥
252A		**US 41, GA 3, Northside Dr, Ga Dome**
	Gas	**W:** BP, Shell
	Food	**W:** Hickory BBQ, Krystal, McDonald's, Waffle House
	Lodg	**W:** Days Inn
(251)		**Jct I-85N, Greeneville, to I-75N, to Chattanooga, TN (SB Left Exit)**
250		**Williams St, 10th St NW (NB) 17th St NW, Techwood Dr (SB)**
	Lodg	**E:** Hampton Inn, Residence Inn, Regency Suites
		W: Courtyard, Sleep Inn, Travelodge
	Other	**E:** B&N, Office Depot, Publix, Pharmacy
		W: Ga Inst of Technology
249D		**US 29, US 278, Linden Ave, Spring St, 10th St, to US 19, 228**
	Gas	**E:** BP, Chevron
	Food	**E:** Checker's, Pizza Hut
		W: McDonald's
	Lodg	**E:** Fairfield Inn, Regency Suites, Residence Inn
		W: Comfort Inn, Courtyard, Holiday Inn Express
	Med	**E:** + Crawford Long Hospital
	Other	**E:** to Civic Center, Museums, Walgreen's, US Post Office
249C		**Downtown Atlanta, Williams St, Ga Dome, Aquarium (SB)**
249B		**Pine St, Peachtree St NE, Atlanta Civic Center (NB)**
249A		**Courtland St, Baker St (SB)**
	Lodg	**W:** Marriott, Red Roof Inn
	Other	**W:** GA State Univ
248D		**Ellis St, Jesse Hill Dr, JW Dobbs Ave (SB)**
	Lodg	**W:** Baymont Inn, Sheraton, Wyndham
	Other	**W:** UPS Store
248C		**Freedom Pkwy, Carter Center, International Blvd (NB)**
	Med	**E:** + Atlanta Medical Center
248B		**Edgewood Ave, Auburn Ave, Butler St, JW Dobbs Ave (NB)**
	Med	**E:** + Grady Memorial Hospital
248A		**Martin Luther King Jr Dr, State Capitol, Stadium (SB)**
(247)		**Jct I-20, E-Augusta, W-Birmingham (SB-E Left Lane, NB-W-Left Lane)**
246		**Central Ave, Georgia Ave, Fulton St Abernathy Blvd, Turner Field**
	Gas	**E:** BP

◈= Regular Gas Stations with Diesel ▲ = RV Friendly Locations ♥= Pet Friendly Locations
Red print shows large vehicle parking / access on site or nearby **Brown Print = Campgrounds / RV PARKS**

EXIT		GEORGIA
	Lodg	E: Hampton Inn, Holiday Inn
	Other	E: to Stadium, Turner Field, Enterprise RAC, Atlanta Drivers License Dept, Ryder, U-Haul W: to Coliseum, GA State Univ
245		**Washington St, Ormond St (NB)**
	Lodg	E: Comfort Inn, Country Inn, Holiday Inn, Hampton Inn
	Other	E: Tires, U-Haul W: State Capitol
244		**University Ave, Pryor St**
	Gas	E: Chevron, Exxon
	TServ	E: Cummins South, Southern Freight W: Brown Transport, Ford Trucks, Freight Direct, Great Dane Trailers
	Other	E: NAPA, Pharmacy, Tires
243		**GA 166, Langford Pkwy**
	Other	E: Lakewood Park, Amphitheatre, Raceway
(242)		**Jct I-85S, Atl Airport, Montgomery**
241		**Cleveland Ave**
	Gas	E: BP, Chevron W: Shell, Citgo, Marathon
	Food	E: Checkers, Church's Chicken, McDonald's, Subway W: Burger King, Krystal, Pizza Hut
	Lodg	E: Palace Inn W: American Inn, Days Inn, Travelodge
	Med	W: + Hospital
	Other	E: ATM, Advance Auto Parts, KMart W: CVS, Kroger, U-Haul
239		**US 19, US 41, Henry Ford II Ave, Central Ave, CW Grant Pkwy**
	Gas	E: Chevron◈ W: BP, Citgo
	Food	E: Checkers, Waffle House W: ChickFilA, Krystal, McDonald's
	Lodg	W: Best Western
(238A)		**Jct I-285E, 407E, to Augusta, Greenville**
(238B)		**Jct I-285W, 407W, Atlanta Airport, to Chattanooga**
237A		**to GA 85S, Riverdale (SB)**
237		**to GA 85, GA 331, Forest Pkwy, Fort Gillem**
	TStop	E: Happy Store (Scales), PTP/Patriot Travel Center (Scales)
	Gas	E: Chevron, Exxon W: BP
	Food	E: FastFood/HS, Fast Food/Patriot, Burger King, McDonald's, Waffle House W: Subway
	Lodg	E: Econo Lodge, Motel 6♥ W: Comfort Suites, Days Inn, Ramada Ltd
	TWash	E: Happy Store, Patriot
	TServ	E: Happy Store/Tires, Patriot/Tires W: FStop Sales & Service
	Other	E: Laundry/Happy Store, Laundry/CB/WiFi/LP/Patriot, Grocery, Farmers Market, GA DOT, Aviation Museum W: GA State Hwy Patrol
235		**US 19, US 41, Jonesboro, to Griffin (NB reacc on Westside of Hwy)**
	FStop	W: Fuel Mart #638
	Gas	E: Chevron, Exxon◈, Phillips 66, Hess W: Racetrac, Shell
	Food	E: Waffle House, Hardee's W: Shoney's, Waffle House, Burger King, KFC, Krystal, Red Lobster

Georgia
227
224
222
221
218
McDonough
216
212
75
Jackson
205
Griffin
201
198
193
75
188
187
Forsyth
186
185
181
S-179
177
175 Thru 167
15
475
9
N-8
75
5
3
Macon
165 Thru 160
156
155
152
149
146
Fort Valley
144
142
138
136
135
134
Georgia
75
127
122
Hawkinsville
121
S-118
117
112
Vienna
109
104
Cordele
102
101
99
97
92
N-85
84
Ashburn
82
80
78
S-76
75
71

EXIT		GEORGIA
	Lodg	E: Travelodge, Super 8, Howard Johnson W: Best Value Inn, Comfort Inn, Days Inn, Econo Lodge, Holiday Inn Express, Super 8
	TServ	E: Atlanta Freightliner, Stith Equipment
	Med	W: + Southern Reg'l Medical Center
	Other	E: Atlanta RV Center W: ATM, Dollar General, Office Depot
233		**GA 54, Jonesboro Rd, Morrow, Jonesboro, Lake City**
	Gas	E: BP, Chevron, Citgo◈, Gulf, Murphy USA◈ W: Circle K, Exxon, Food Mart
	Food	E: RJ BBQ, Cracker Barrel, Krystal, Taco Bell, Mrs Winners, Waffle House, Wendy's W: KFC, Pizza Hut, Long John Silver, McDonald's, Outback Steakhouse, Shoney's,
	Lodg	E: Best Western, Days Inn, Drury Inn W: Hampton Inn, Quality Inn, Red Roof Inn♥
	Med	W: + Immediate Medical Care
	Other	E: ATMs, Banks, Walmart sc, Morrow Animal Hospital♥, Morrow Police Dept Clayton State Univ W: ATMs, Auto Services, Banks, Best Buy, Clayton Co Harley Davidson, Costco, Firestone, Goodyear, Southlake Mall, Sam's Club
231		**CR 28, Mt Zion Blvd, Morrow**
	Gas	E: QT, Citgo, Conoco, Exxon W: Chevron, Gas Xpress
	Food	W: Arby's, Blimpie, Chili's, McDonald's, Longhorn Steakhouse, Steak 'n Shake, Waffle House, Wendy's
	Lodg	W: Country Inn, Extended Stay America, Sun Suites, Sleep Inn
	Other	W: ATMs, AMC 24, Best Buy, Barnes & Noble, Costco, HH Gregg, Home Depot, Kaufman Tire, NTB, Publix, Pharmacy, Sports Authority, Target, UPS Store
228		**GA 138, GA 54, Stockbridge Hwy, Stockbridge**
	Gas	E: Exxon, RaceWay W: BP, Chevron, Sunoco
	Food	E: Arby's, Burger King, CiCi's Pizza, Golden Corral, IHOP, Krystal, McDonald's, Long John Silver, Shoney's , Subway, Taco Bell, Waffle House, Wendy's W: Waffle House
	Lodg	E: Best Western, Comfort Inn, Days Inn, Holiday Inn, La Quinta Inn♥, Motel 6, Red Roof Inn♥, Shoney's Inn
	Other	E: ATMs, Goodyear, Lowe's, Kroger, Office Depot, Tires W: Auto Dealer, CVS, U-Haul
(227)		**Jct I-675N, Atlanta ByPass, to I-285E, Augusta, Greenville (NB)**
224		**Hudson Bridge Rd, Eagle's Landing Parkway, Stockbridge**
	Gas	E: BP, Citgo, Phillips 66, Texaco◈ W: QT, Murphy
	Food	E: ChickFilA, Outback Steakhouse, KFC, McDonald's, Subway, Waffle House W: Arby's, Blimpie, China Café
	Lodg	E: AmeriHost Inn♥, Microtel W: Baymont Inn, Super 8
	Med	E: + Henry General Hospital

◈= Regular Gas Stations with Diesel ▲ = RV Friendly Locations ♥= Pet Friendly Locations
Red print shows large vehicle parking / access on site or nearby Brown Print = Campgrounds / RV PARKS

EXIT		GEORGIA
	Other	E: ATMs, Banks, Publix, Walgreen's W: ATMs, Batteries Plus, Kroger, Walgreen's, **Walmart sc**, Hudson Bridge Animal Clinic♥,
222		**GA 351, Jodeco Rd, McDonough**
	Gas	E: Pantry, Citgo, Texaco W: BP, Chevron◊
	Food	E: Waffle House, Hardee's
	Other	W: **Atlanta South RV Resort▲, Access to Ex #221 via Mt Olive Rd**
221		**Jonesboro Rd, McDonough, Lovejoy**
	TStop	E: Travel Center
	Gas	E: BP, Williams
	Food	E: FastFood/TC W: Burger King, Chili's, CiCi's Pizza, Golden Corral, Hooters, Hong Kong Café, Logan Roadhouse, McDonald's, O'Charley's, Wendy's, Yuki Japanese
	Lodg	E: Days Inn
	TServ	E: Stirling
	Other	W: ATMs, Best Buy, BJ's Club, Books A Million, Dick's Sporting Goods, Home Depot, Radio Shack, Sam's Club, Staples, Target, Flea Market, to **Atlanta South RV Park ▲**
218		**GA 20, GA 81, Hampton McDonough**
	FStop	W: Fuel Stop #359
	Gas	E: QT, RaceTrac Texaco, Murphy W: Speedway
	Food	E: Applebee's, Arby's. Cracker Barrel, McDonald's, Mrs Winner, Subway, Wendy's W: Pizza, Subway, Waffle House
	Lodg	E: Best Western, Hampton Inn, Super 8 W: Comfort Inn, Econo Lodge, Masters Inn♥
	Other	E: ATMs, Lowe's, **Walmart sc**, **McDonough RV Center, RV Sales** **W: RV Repairs**
216		**GA 155, McDonough**
	FStop	E: Liberty Center Texaco W: Kangaroo #3333
	Gas	E: Chevron◊, Shell◊ W: BP, Citgo, RaceTrac
	Food	E: Waffle House, BBQ W: Krystal, Shoney's, Waffle House
	Lodg	E: Beset Value Inn, Days Inn, Microtel Inn W: Country Inn, Quality Inn, Sleep Inn
	TServ	W: Kenworth
212		**Bill Gardner Pkwy, Locust Grove Rd, to US 23, Locust Grove, Hampton, Jackson**
	Gas	E: BP◊, Chevron, Exxon◊, Liberty, Shell W: Chevron, Citgo◊, Exxon
	Food	E: BurgerKing/Chevron, McDonald's/BP, Denny's, DQ, Hardee's, Huddle House, Taco Bell, Waffle House, Wendy's, Zaxby's
	Lodg	E: Econo Lodge, Executive Inn, Ramada Ltd, Red Roof Inn W: Country Inn, Super 8, Scottish Inn
	Other	E: Tanger Factory Outlet Mall, Atlanta Motor Speedway
205		**GA 16, Griffin, Jackson**
	FStop	E: Jackson Super Mart/BP
	Gas	E: Citgo◊ W: BP, Chevron◊
	Food	E: Simmons Smokehouse BBQ
	Other	W: **Forest Glen RV Park▲**
201		**GA 36, Barnesville-Jackson Rd, Jackson, Barnesville**
	FStop	W: Interstate BP
	TStop	E: WilcoHess Travel Plaza #3030 (Scales), Travel Center of America/Citgo (Scales) (DAND), Love's Travel Stop #307(Scales) (DAND) W: Flying J Travel Plaza #5280/Conoco (Scales)
	Food	E: DQ/Wendy's/WilcoHess TP, Rest/Subw/TBell/TA TC, McDonald's/Love's TS W: Rest/Hardee's/FJ TP, Fast Food/Interstate BP, O'Rudy's Rib Shack, Buckner's Family Rest
	TWash	E: Blue Beacon TW/TA TC, Jason's TW W: Eagle TW/FJ TP
	TServ	E: TA TC/Tires, GA Motor Truck , Hinkle Interstate Truck Tires, Jackson Tire Center W: Speedco, 201 Truck Service
	Other	E: Laundry/WilcoHess TP, Laundry/WiFi/TA TC, WiFi/Love's TS W: Laundry/WiFi/**RVDump/LP**/FJ TP, **RV Connection, Sagon RV Supercenter**
198		**CR 277, Highfalls Rd, Jackson**
	Food	W: High Falls BBQ
	Other	E: **Buck Creek Campground▲, High Falls State Park** W: **High Falls Campground▲**
193		**CR 275, Johnstonville Rd**
	Gas	E: BP
(189)		**Weigh Station** (Both dir)
188		**GA 42, N Lee St, Forsyth**
	Gas	E: Liberty◊, Shell
	Food	E: Captain D's, Pizza Hut/TacoBell/KFC, Subway
	Lodg	E: Best Value Inn, Best Western, Budget Inn W: Sundown Lodge
	Other	E: Ingles, Pharmacy, **Indian Springs State Park▲**
187		**GA 83, Cabaniss Rd, Lee St, Forsyth**
	Gas	W: BP, Citgo◊, Marathon, Texaco, Murphy USA
	Food	W: Burger King, Captain D's, Hardee's, McDonald's, Pizza Hut, Subway, Taco Bell, Waffle House, Wendy's
	Lodg	E: Econo Lodge, Regency Inn W: Days Inn
	Other	W: ATMs, Advance Auto Part, CVS, Dollar General, Family Dollar, **Walmart**
186		**Juliette Rd, Tift College Dr, CR 271**
	Gas	W: BP◊, Minit Mart, Shell
	Food	W: Waffle House, Hong Kong Café, DQ
	Lodg	W: Hampton Inn, Holiday Inn Express, Super 8
	Other	W: **Forsyth KOA▲**
185		**GA 18, Harold Clark Pkwy, Forsyth**
	Gas	E: Shell W: BP, Shell◊
	Food	E: Pippin's BBQ W: Shoney's
	Lodg	E: Comfort Inn, Comfort Suites
	Other	E: **L&D Campground▲, GA State Hwy Patrol Post**
181		**CR 34, Rumble Rd, Forsyth, to Smarr**
	FStop	E: Rumble Road BP
	Gas	E: Shell◊
	Food	E: Stuckey's/BP
	Other	E: Roy's Auto & 24hr Repair, Tires
(179)		**Monroe Co Rest Area #22** (SB) (RR, Phones, Picnic, Vend, **RVDump**)
(177)		**Jct I-475S, GA 408, Macon ByPass, to Valdosta** (SB)
175		**Pate Rd, to GA 19, to US 41** (NB, No Re-entry)
172		**to US 23, Dames Ferry, Bass Rd**
	Gas	W: Citgo◊
	Food	E: BBQ, McDonald's, Starbucks,
	Other	E: Bass Pro Shop
171		**Riverside Dr, US 23, Dames Ferry** (Access to Exit #169)
	Gas	E: BP, Marathon◊
	Food	E: Backyard Burger, **Cracker Barrel**, Hooters, Huddle House
169		**to GA 19, to US 41, US 23, Arkwright Rd**
	Gas	E: Shell, BP◊ W: Chevron, Conoco◊
	Food	E: Carrabba's, China Gourmet, Outback Steakhouse, Waffle House W: Applebee's, Arby's, Backyard Burger, Burger King, ChickFilA, Chili's, Chinese Rest, **Cracker Barrel**, Dunkin Donuts, El Azteca Mex, Hooters, KFC, Krystal, Longhorn Steakhouse, McDonald's, Papa John's, Popeye's, Ryan's Grill, Rio Bravo, Steak n Shake, Subway, Waffle House
	Lodg	E: Comfort Inn, Courtyard, Fairfield Inn, La Quinta Inn♥, Residence Inn, Red Roof Inn♥, Red Roof Inn, Super 8 W: Hampton Inn, Holiday Inn, Quality Inn, Ramada Inn, Wingate Inn
	Med	W: + Hospital
	Other	W: ATMs, Auto Dealers, Banks, Barnes & Noble, FedEx Office, Kroger, Pharmacy, Publix, Radio Shack, RiteAid
167		**GA 247, N Pierce Ave, Macon**
	Gas	W: BP◊, Chevron, Exxon, Marathon◊, Shell◊
	Food	W: Applebee's, Arby's, Pizza Hut, Red Lobster, Texas Cattle Co, Waffle House, Wendy's
	Lodg	W: Best Western, Budget Inn, Comfort Inn, Days Inn, Econo Lodge, Holiday Inn Express, Howard Johnson, Motel 6
	Other	W: Goodyear, Pharmacy
(165)		**Jct I-16E, to Savannah** (SB, Left Ex)
164		**US 41, GA 19, Georgia Ave, Macon**
	Med	E: + Medical Center of Central GA
163		**GA 74, Mercer University Dr**
	Gas	W: Marathon◊
	Lodg	W: Red Carpet Inn
	Other	E: Mercer Univ
162		**US 80, GA 22, Eisenhower Pkwy**
	Gas	W: Chevron, Flash
	Food	W: Captain D's, IHOP, McDonald's, Mrs. Winners, Subway, Taco Bell, Wendy's
	Other	W: ATMs, Goodyear, Home Depot, Office Depot, PetSmart♥, Walgreen's, Colonial Mall
160		**US 41, GA 247, to GA 74 Spur, to Rocky Creek Rd, Houston Ave** (NB)
	Gas	E: RaceWay, Marathon, Mini Food Store W: BP, Chevron, Enmark◊

◊= Regular Gas Stations with Diesel ▲ = RV Friendly Locations ♥= Pet Friendly Locations
Red print shows large vehicle parking / access on site or nearby Brown Print = Campgrounds / RV PARKS

EXIT GEORGIA

Food E: Johnny V's, Waffle House
W: Arby's, KFC, McDonald's, Subway, Waffle House
Lodg E: Masters Inn, Magnolia Court Motel
Other W: Auto Services, Dollar General, Grocery

160A US 41, GA 247, to Houston Ave (SB)

160B Rocky Creek Rd, to US 41 (SB)

NOTE: Follow I-475 below to bypass Macon. Exit #'s follow I-475 for next 15 mi.

15 US 41, Bolingbroke
Gas W: Exxon◈, Marathon◈

9 Zebulon Rd, Wesleyan College
Gas E: Shell, Murphy◈
W: Citgo, Exxon, Marathon
Food E: ChickFilA, Fuddruckers, Japanese Rest, Krystal, Margarita's Mex Grill, McDonald's, Pizza Hut, Popeye's Chicken, Sonic, Taco Bell, Waffle House, Wendy's
Lodg E: Baymont Inn, Fairfield Inn, Sleep Inn
Med W: + Hospital
Other E: ATMs, Banks, Tires, **Walmart sc**

(8) Bibb Co Rest Area #19 (NB)
(Next RA on I-75 138mi)
(RR, Phone, Picnic)

5 GA 74, Macon, Thomaston, Mercer University Dr
Food E: Waffle House
W: Grill Works, Church's Chicken
Lodg W: Howard Johnson

3 US 80, GA 22, Macon, Roberta, Macon College
Gas E: Oil, RaceTrac, Spectrum
W: Shell
Food E: **Cracker Barrel**, Chesterfield Cafe, Indian Rest, JL's Open Pit BBQ, McDonald's, Subway,Waffle House
W: Burger King
Lodg E: Days Inn, Hampton Inn, Knights Inn, Motel 6, Ramada, Rodeway Inn, Super 8, Travelodge
W: Scottish Inn, Econo Lodge, Knights Inn
Other E: to Colonial Mall, Best Buy, Staples, Central GA Tech College
W: Macon State College

(156) Jct I-475N, GA 408, Macon ByPass, to Atlanta (NB, LEFT exit)

NOTE: Follow I-475 above to bypass Macon. Exit #'s follow I-475 for next 15 mi.

155 CR 740, Hartley Bridge Rd, Macon
Gas E: BP◈, Shell, Kroger
W: Citgo◈, Exxon
Food E: Hong Kong Garden, KFC, Wendy's
W: McDonald's, Subway, Waffle House
Lodg W: Amer Best Value Inn
Other E: Kroger
W: Advance Auto Parts, CVS,

(152) NEW EXIT: Sardis Ch Rd

149 GA 49, Byron, to Fort Valley
FStop W: Marathon Fuel Stop #2, Byron Citgo, Flash Foods #264/BP
Gas E: Enmark, Shell
W: RaceWay
Food E: Burger King, Denny's, McDonald's, Krystal, Shoney's, Subway, Waffle House, Wendy's, Zaxby's
W: Country Cupboard, Huddle House, Mex Rest, Popeye's, Subway, Waffle House
Lodg E: Best Western, Holiday Inn Express
W: Comfort Inn, Days Inn, Econo Lodge, Passport Inn, Super 8
TServ W: Tires/Citgo, Sterling Western, CAT
Other E: Peach Outlet Shops, Various Outlet Stores, **Mid State RV Center**
W: CarQuest, NAPA, Auto Dealers, **Interstate RV Center**, **Camping World**
Sun Coast RV Center

146 GA 247, Centerville Rd, Byron, to Centerville
FStop W: Raceway Food Mart #2502
TStop W: Pilot Travel Center #267 (Scales)
Gas E: Flash Foods, Exxon◈, Shell, Enmark◈
Food E: Outback Steakhouse, Subway, Waffle House, River Bend Fish Camp & Grill
W: Arby's/TJCinn/Pilot TC
Lodg E: Budget Inn, Comfort Suites, Economy Inn, Hampton Inn
W: Red Carpet Inn
Other E: Robbins AFB
W: Laundry/WiFi/Pilot TC, **Mid Ga RV Service**

144 Russell Pkwy, Fort Valley

142 GA 96, Housers Mill Rd, Ft Valley
Gas E: Chevron◈, Shell
Other E: **Perry Ponderosa Park Campground▲**

138 GA 11 Conn, N Perry Pkwy, Thompson Rd, Perry
FStop E: Super Food Mart/Texaco
Food E: FastFood/Super Food Mart
Other W: Perry Ft Valley Airport✈

136 US 341, GA 7, Sam Nunn Blvd, Perry
FStop E: Flash Foods #267
W: Mini Foods #65/Conoco
Gas E: Amoco, Chevron, Speedway
W: Chevron, RaceWay, Texaco
Food E: Arby's, Burger King, Captain D's, ChickFilA, Jalisco Mex Grill, KFC, Krystal, Longhorn Steakhouse, McDonald's, Red Lobster, Sonny's BBQ, Subway, Waffle House, Wendy's, Zaxby's
W: Applebee's, Angelina's Italian Garden Cafe
Lodg E: Great Inn, Hampton Inn, Howard Johnson, Jameson Inn♥, Super 8♥
W: Comfort Inn, Econo Lodge, Holiday Inn♥, Knights Inn, Quality Inn♥
Med E: + Hospital
Other E: Advance Auto Parts, Dollar Tree, Kroger, NAPA, Pharmacy, Radio Shack, **Walmart sc**, **Bolands RV Park▲**
W: **Crossroads of GA Campground▲**

135 US 41, GA 127, Marshallville Rd, Perry, Fort Valley
Gas E: BP◈, Exxon, Shell, Flash Foods
Food E: **Cracker Barrel**, DQ, Huddle House, Subway, Waffle House
Lodg E: Best Western♥, Crossroads Motel, Howard Johnson, Passport Inn, Red Carpet Inn, Relax Inn, Rodeway Inn♥, Travelodge
Med E: + Hospital
Other E: Kmart, Kroger, GA Fairgrounds, Welcome Center
W: **Fair Harbor RV Park & CG▲** , GA State Hwy Patrol Post

134 to US 41, GA 7, S Perry Pkwy, Perry, Marshallville
Gas E: Texaco◈
Lodg E: HOTEL
Other E: Ga Fairgrounds

127 GA 26, Montezuma, Hawkinsville
Gas W: Chevron
Other E: **Twin Oaks RV Park▲**

122 GA 230, 2nd St, Unadilla
Gas E: Dixie◈
Lodg W: Red Carpet Inn

121 US 41, GA 7, Pine Ave, Unadilla, to Pinehurst
FStop W: All State Truck Stop (Scales)
Gas E: BP, Flash Foods Shell/Stuckey's◈
Food E: DQ/Stuckey's, Cotton Patch Rest, Don Ponchos
W: Rest/All State TS
Lodg E: Days Inn, Economy Inn, Scottish Inn
W: Regency Inn
TServ W: All State TS/Tires
Other E: Grocery, Tires, **Southern Trails RV Resort▲**
W: Laundry/WiFi/**LP**/All State TS

(118) Dooly Co Rest Area #14 (SB)
(RR, Phones, Picnic, **RVDump**)

117 to US 41, Pinehurst-Hawkinsville Rd, Pinehurst
TStop W: Pinehurst Travel Center/BP (Scales)
Food W: Rest/Pinehurst TC
Other W: Laundry/Pinehurst TC

112 GA 27, Vienna, Hawkinsville
FStop W: Rachel's BP
Gas E: Pure
W: Marathon
Other E: **to Hillside Bluegrass RV Park▲**

109 GA 215, Union St, Vienna, Pitts
TStop E: Pilot Travel Center #398 (Scales)
Gas W: BP◈, Citgo◈, Shell
Food E: FastFood/Pilot TC
W: Hardee's, Huddle House, Popeye's, Subway, Vienna Cafe
Lodg W: Executive Inn
Med E: + Hospital
W: + Dooly Medical Center
Other E: Laundry/WiFi/Pilot TC
W: to Middle GA Tech College

(107) Dooly Co Rest Area #13 (NB)
(RR, Phones, Picnic, Vend, **RVDump**)

104 Farmers Market Rd, Cordele
Gas W: Conoco/P66
Lodg W: Cordele Inn

102 GA 257, Cordele, Hawkinsville
Gas E: Shell
Food W: Smokies BBQ
Med W: + Hospital

101 US 280, GA 90, GA 30, Cordele, Abbeville, Presidential Route
TStop E: Pilot Travel Center #416 (Scales)
Gas E: Exxon◈, Shell
W: BP◈, Chevron, Liberty, RaceWay
Food E: Arby's/TJCinn/Pilot TC, Denny's, Golden Corral, Marise's Country Cooking, Waffle House
W: Burger King, Captain D's, DQ, **Cracker Barrel**, Farm House Rest, Hardee's, KFC, Krystal, McDonald's, Pizza Place, Shoney's, Wendy's, Zaxby's
Lodg E: Days Inn, Fairfield Inn, Ramada
W: Ashburn Inn, Best Western, Comfort Inn Delux Inn, Econo Lodge, Hampton Inn, Holiday Inn, Super 8, Travelodge

◈= Regular Gas Stations with Diesel ▲ = RV Friendly Locations ♥= Pet Friendly Locations
Red print shows large vehicle parking / access on site or nearby Brown Print = Campgrounds / RV PARKS

EXIT		GEORGIA
	Other	E: GA State Hwy Patrol Post
		W: Laundry/WiFi/Pilot TC, CVS, Dollar General, CarWash, Family Dollar, Grocery, Radio Shack, Winn Dixie, **Walmart sc**, to appr 9mi **GA Veterans State Park▲**
99		**GA 300, GA-FL Pkwy, Albany, Sylvester**
	Gas	W: BP
	Lodg	W: Country Inn
97		**GA 33, Rock House Rd, Cordele Wenona, Sylvester**
	TStop	W: Travel Center of America/BP (Scales)
	Food	W: CountryPride/PizzaHut/Popeyes/TA TC
	Lodg	E: Royal Inn
	TWash	W: TW
	TServ	W: TA TC/Tires, Carter Thermo King, Perlis
	Other	E: **Cordele RV Campground▲**
		W: Laundry/CB/WiFi/TA TC, **Cordele KOA▲**
92		**CR 357, Arabi Rd, Arabi**
	Gas	E: Chevron/Plantation House
		W: BP◊
	Other	W: **Southern Gates RV Park▲**
(85)		**Turner Co Rest Area #10** (NB) (RR, Phones, Picnic, Vend, RVDump)
84		**GA 159, North St, Ashburn, Amboy**
	TStop	W: A-1 Truck Stop/Chevron
	Gas	E: Shell◊
	Food	W: DQ/Subway/A-1 TS
	Lodg	W: Ashburn Inn & **RV Park▲**
	Other	W: Laundry/A-1 TS
82		**GA 107, GA 112, Washington Ave, Sylvester, Ashburn, Fitzgerald**
	Gas	W: BP, Chevron, TC Gas
	Food	W: Huddle House, Krystal, McDonald's, Shoney's, Waffle House
	Lodg	W: Best Western, Days Inn, Super 8
	Other	W: Ashburn Tire Service, O'Reilly Auto Parts, RiteAid
80		**Bussey Rd, Sycamore**
	FStop	W: Shorty's 26 Chevron
	TStop	E: Exxon Truck Plaza
	Gas	E: Qwik Stop
	Food	E: Deli/Exxon TS
	Lodg	E: Budget Lakeview Inn
	TServ	E: Exxon TS
		W: S GA Diesel Services, Clark's Diesel Services, Allen's Tire & Auto Truck **RV** Service
	Other	E: Laundry/Exxon TP
78		**GA 32, Jefferson Davis Hwy, Sycamore, Ocilla**
(76)		**Turner Co Rest Area #9** (SB) (RR, Phones, Picnic, Vend, RVDump)
75		**CR 252, Inaha Rd, Sycamore**
	Gas	E: Chevron
		W: BP/Stuckey's
	Food	W: DQ/Stuckey's/BP
71		**CR 11, Willis Still Rd, Sunsweet**
69		**CR 421, Chula-Brookfield Rd**
	Gas	E: Phillips 66◊
	Food	E: Rest/Red Carpet Inn
	Lodg	E: Red Carpet Inn
		W: to Shalom House B&B
66		**CR 410, Brighton Rd**

EXIT		GEORGIA
64		**I-75 Bus Loop, US 41, Tifton**
	Gas	E: BP◊
		W: Petro
	Med	E: + Hospital
63B		**Whiddon Mill Rd, 8th St, Tifton**
	Gas	E: AmocoBP, Exxon, Shell
	Food	E: Hardee's, KFC, Krystal, Subway
	Lodg	E: Budget Inn, Davis Bros Motor Lodge
	Med	E: + Hospital
	Other	E: Pharmacy, Winn Dixie
63A		**King Rd, 2nd St, Tifton**
	Gas	E: Chevron
		W: Citgo, Shell◊
	Food	E: Arby's, Burger King, McDonald's, Krystal, Taco Bell
		W: Waffle House
	Lodg	E: Econo Lodge, Super 8♥
		W: Quality Inn♥, Travelodge
62		**to US 82, GA 520, to US 319, GA 35, Tifton, Sylvester, Moultrie**
	Gas	E: BP, Citgo, Exxon◊
		W: BP, RaceWay, Shell◊
	Food	E: Applebee's, **Cracker Barrel**, Golden Corral, Waffle House, Western Sizzlin'
		W: Burger King, Captain D's, Longhorn Steakhouse, Shoney's, Starbucks, Waffle House, Wendy's/Shell
	Lodg	E: Comfort Inn, Courtyard, Hampton Inn, Microtel
		W: Days Inn, Holiday Inn, Ramada Ltd
	Med	E: + Walk-In Medical Center
	Other	E: Advance Auto Parts, Tires
		W: Auto Dealers, Carwash/Shell, Lowe's, **Walmart sc**
61		**CR 299, Omega Rd, Tifton**
	TStop	W: Citgo Travel Plaza
	Food	W: Stuckey's/WaffleKing/Citgo TP
	Lodg	E: Days Inn, Motel 6
	TWash	W: Citgo TP
	TServ	W: Prince Truck Ctr/WhiteGMC Volvo
	Other	W: Laundry/Citgo TP, Little River Harley Davidson, **The Pines Campground▲**, **RV Overnite▲**
60		**CR 418, Central Ave, Tifton**
	TStop	W: Pilot Travel Center #192 (Scales)
	Gas	E: Circle K, Chevron
	Food	W: Rest/Subway/Pilot TC
	TWash	W: Blue Beacon TW/Pilot TC
	TServ	W: Pilot TC/Tires, Ten Speed Truck Service
	Other	W: Laundry/WiFi/**RVDump**/Pilot TC, **Amy's S GA RV Park & RV Center▲**
59		**CR 204, Southwell Blvd, Widdon Rd, to US 41, GA 7, Tifton**
	TStop	E: Love's Travel Stop #325 (Scales)
	Food	E: Hardee's/Love's TS
	Other	E: WiFi/**RVDump**/Love's TP, Lairsey's Auto Service Center, U-Haul, Henry Tift Myers Airport✈
55		**CR 418, Omega Eldorado Rd, Tifton**
49		**GA 547, Kinard Bridge Rd, Lenox**
	FStop	W: Lenox BP
	Gas	E: Chevron, Dixie◊
		W: Phillips 66◊
	Food	W: Stella's Diner
	Lodg	W: Knights Inn
(48)		**Cook Co Rest Area #6** (SB) (RR, Phones, Picnic, RVDump)
(46)		**Cook Co Rest Area #5** (NB) (RR, Phones, Picnic, RVDump)

EXIT		GEORGIA
45		**CR 253, Barneyville Rd**
41		**Roundtree Bridge Rd, Moultrie Rd, Sparks, to GA 37, US 41**
39		**GA 37, W 4th St, Adel, Moultrie, to Nashville, Lakeland**
	TStop	W: Adel Truck Plaza/Citgo (Scales)
	Gas	E: Shell◊, Dixie, Chevron
		W: BP
	Food	E: McDonald's/Shell, Hardee's, Subway, Waffle House, Wendy's
		W: HuddleHouse/Stuckeys/Adel TP, Burger King, Captain D's, China Buffet, Popeye's, Taco Bell, Western Sizzlin, IHOP/DaysInn
	Lodg	E: Budget Lodge, Scottish Inn♥, Super 8♥
		W: Days Inn♥, Hampton Inn
	TServ	W: Adel TP/Tires
	Med	E: + Memorial Hospital
	Other	E: RiteAid, Winn Dixie, ATMs, Auto Service
		W: Laundry/Adel TP, Cook Co Airport✈, **Reed Bingham State Park**
37		**CR 216, Old Quitman Rd, Adel**
32		**CR 240, Old Coffee Rd, Adel, Cecil**
	Gas	W: Chevron
	Other	W: **Cecil Bay RV Park▲**
29		**US 41, GA 122, GA 7, Sheriff's Boys Ranch, Hahira, to Lakeland**
	TStop	W: Big Foot Travel Center BP
	Gas	E: Jimmy's 66, Pure
	Food	E: City Café, Joyce's Fried Chicken
		W: Apple Valley Rest/BF TC, Blimpie/BP
	Lodg	W: Knights Inn, Super 8
(24)		**Weigh Station** (Both dir)
22		**I-75 Bus, US 41S, N Valdosta Rd, Moody AFB, Valdosta**
	Gas	E: BP, Shell◊
		W: Citgo◊
	Food	W: Burger King/DQ/Stuckeys/Citgo
	Lodg	W: Days Inn♥/Citgo
	Med	E: + Smith Northview Hospital
18		**GA 133, St Augustine Rd, Valdosta, Moultrie, Valdosta St University**
	Gas	E: BP, Citgo, Exxon, Shell◊
		W: BP, RaceWay, Shell◊
	Food	E: Applebee's, Arby's, Burger King, China Garden, ChickFilA, **Cracker Barrel**, Denny's, Hooters, KFC, McDonald's, Longhorn Steakhouse, Red Lobster, Outback Steakhouse, Sonic, Subway, Taco Bell, Waffle House, Wendy's
	Lodg	E: Best Western◊, Country Inn, Comfort Suites, Courtyard, Days Inn, Fairfield Inn, Hampton Inn, Holiday Inn, Howard Johnson, La Quinta Inn♥, Quality Inn, Rodeway Inn, Scottish Inn
		W: Econo Lodge, Sleep Inn
	Other	E: ATMs, Best Buy, Home Depot, Publix, Target, Walgreen's, **Walmart**, Valdosta Mall
		W: **River Park RV Park▲**
16		**US 84, US 221, GA 38, Valdosta**
	FStop	E: Big Foot Travel Stop Citgo, Jack Rabbit #4/BP
	TStop	W: Buzz's Auto Truck Plaza/Shell (Scales)
	Gas	E: Phillips 66, Fina, Sam's
	Food	E: Blimpie/Citgo, Burger King, IHOP, Japanese Steak House, McDonald's, Pizza Hut, Sonic, Shoney's, Waffle House, Wendy's

◊= Regular Gas Stations with Diesel ▲ = RV Friendly Locations ♥= Pet Friendly Locations
Red print shows large vehicle parking / access on site or nearby Brown Print = Campgrounds / RV PARKS

EXIT		GEORGIA
		W: HuddleHouse/Buzz's ATP, Austin Cattle Co
	Lodg	E: Days Inn♥/Citgo, Guest House Inn♥, Hampton Inn, Holiday Inn, Motel 6, Quality Inn♥, Ramada Ltd♥, Super 8♥
		W: Comfort Inn♥, Knights Inn
	TServ	W: Buzz's ATP/Tires
	Med	E: + Hospital
	Other	E: Sam's Club, **Walmart sc**, Convention Center
		W: Laundry/Buzz's ATP
13		**CR 785, Old Clyattville Rd, Valdosta**
	Other	E: Valdosta Reg'l Airport✈
		W: **to appr 4mi:** Wild Adventures Theme Park
11		**GA 31, Colin P Kelly Jr Hwy, Valdosta, to Madison FL**
	TStop	E: Pilot Travel Center #73 (Scales), Wilco Hess Travel Plaza #3050 (Scales)
	Gas	W: BP
	Food	E: Subway/Pilot TC, Stuckey's/WilcoHess TP, Waffle House
	Lodg	E: Travelers Inn
	TWash	E: Blue Bird Truck Wash, TW/Pilot TC
	TServ	E: Pilot TC/Tires, Hwy 31 Truck & Tire Repair
		W: All Star International, S&S Truck Repair
	Other	E: WiFi/Pilot TC, Laundry/WiFi/**RVDump**/WilcoHess TP, Valdosta Reg'l Airport✈
5		**GA 376, Clyattville-Lake Park Rd, Lake Park, Madison**
	TStop	W: GA-FL Fuel Center/Shell, Citgo TP
	Gas	E: Chevron, Phillips 66, RaceWay, Shell
	Food	E: ChickFilA, China Garden, Farm House Rest, Hardee's, Krystal, Shoney's, Sonny BBQ, Subway, Waffle House
		W: FastFood/Citgo TP, **Cracker Barrel**, McDonald's, Pizza Hut, Taco Bell
	Lodg	E: Holiday Inn, Guest House Inn, Quality Inn
		W: Days Inn, Hampton Inn, Super 8, Travelodge
	Other	E: Preferred Outlets of Lake Park, Flea Market, NAPA, Winn Dixie, **Valdosta/Lake Park KOA▲**, **Eagles Roost RV Resort▲**, **Travel Country RV Center**
		W: **Suncoast RV Center & CG▲**
(3)		**GA Welcome Center** (NB) (RR, Phone, Picnic, Vend, **RVDump**)
2		**Lake Park Rd, Lake Park, Bellville**
	TStop	E: Travel Center of America/BP #128 (Scales)
	W:	Flying J Travel Plaza #5044/Conoco (Scales)
	Gas	E: Shell◈
	Food	E: Rest/Arby's/TA TC, Lakeside Rest
		W: Rest/FastFood/FJ TP
	Lodg	E: Best Western
		W: Lake Park Inn
	TWash	W: Lake Park Truck & **RV** Wash
	TServ	E: TA TC/Tires, Speedco, Great American Chrome Shop
		W: CB Shop
	Other	E: Laundry/WiFi/TA TC
		W: Laundry/BarbSh/WiFi/**RVDump/LP**/FJ TP

EASTERN TIME ZONE

ⓘ GEORGIA

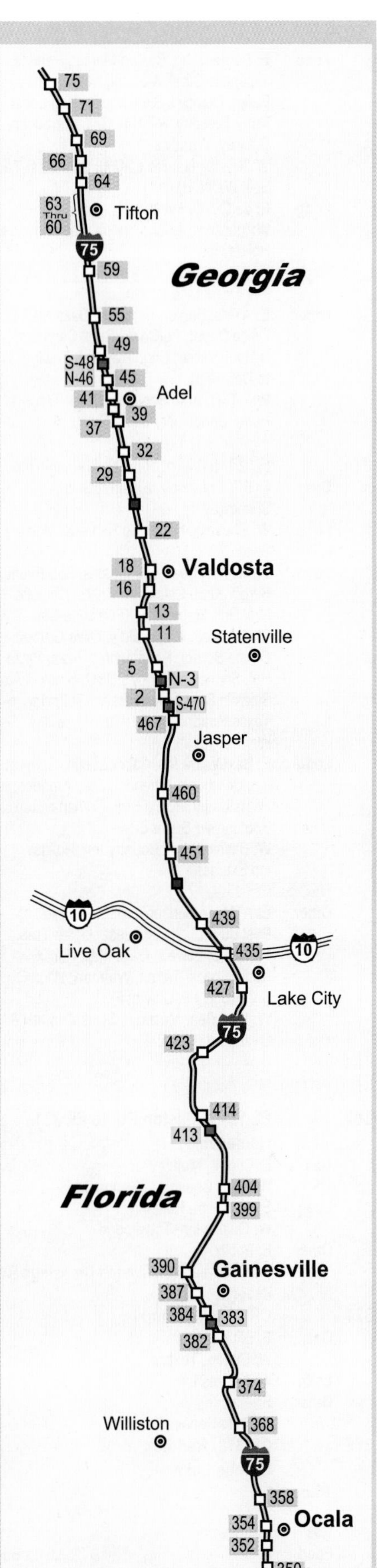

ⓘ FLORIDA

EXIT		FLORIDA
	NOTE:	**MM 471: Georgia State Line**
		EASTERN TIME ZONE
	NOTE:	**MM 471: SB: Begin Motorist Call Boxes**
(470)		**FL Welcome Center** (SB) (RR, Phone, Picnic, Vend, Info)
467		**FL 143, Jennings**
	FStop	W: Johnson & Johnson #9/Exxon
	Gas	E: Chevron, Texaco
		W: Amoco
	Food	W: Burger King, Jennings House Rest.
	Lodg	W: Budget Lodge, Econo Lodge, N Florida Inn
	Other	W: Fireworks Super Center, **Jennings Outdoor Resort & Campground▲**
460		**FL 6, Jennings, to Jasper, Madison**
	TStop	E: Johnson & Johnson #14/Exxon
	Gas	E: RaceWay, Texaco
		W: BP, Shell◈, Texaco
	Food	E: HuddleHouse/J&J, Sheffield's Country Kitchen
	Lodg	E: Days Inn♥, Scottish Inns
	ATServ	W: Dennis Garage
	Med	E: + Hospital
	Other	E: Laundry/BarbSh/J&J, Walker's Pecan House
451		**US 129, FL 51, Jasper, Live Oak (Gas, Food, Lodging E to Jasper)**
	Med	E: + Madison Co Memorial Hospital
	Other	W: **Spirit of the Suwanee Music Park▲**
(450)		**Weigh Station / Agricultural Inspection** (Both dir)
439		**FL 136, White Springs, Live Oak**
	Gas	E: BP◈, Gate◈
	Food	E: McDonald's, BB Ann's Country Cafe
	Lodg	E: Scottish Inn
		W: Best Value Inn
	Other	E: **Suwannee Valley Campground▲**, **Lee's Country Campground▲**, **Stephen Foster State Folk Center▲**, **to Kelly's RV Park▲**
		W: Powell's Auto Service, U-Haul
(435)		**Jct I-10, E-Jacksonville, W to Tallahassee**
427		**US 90, Lake City, Live Oak**
	NOTE:	Low Clearance 14' 4"
	Gas	E: BP, Chevron◈, Gas N Go, Exxon, Shell, Murphy USA
		W: BP, Shell
	Food	E: Applebee's, Arby's, Burger King, Cedar River Seafood, Cracker Barrel, DQ, Hardee's, IHOP, KFC, Krystal, Pizza Hut, McDonald's, Ryan's Grill, Red Lobster, Ruby Tuesday, Sonny's BBQ, Steak 'n Shake, Taco Bell, Texas Roadhouse, Waffle House, Wendy's
		W: Bob Evans, Shoney's, Waffle House
	Lodg	E: Best Inn, Days Inn, Driftwood Inn, Howard Johnson, Holiday Inn, Jameson Inn♥, Knights Inn, Ramada Ltd, Rodeway Inn, Scottish Inns
		W: Best Western, Comfort Inn, Country Inn, Courtyard, Econo Lodge, Hampton Inn, Motel 6♥, Quality Inn, Red Roof Inn
	Med	E: + Lake City Medical Center

◈ = Regular Gas Stations with Diesel ▲ = RV Friendly Locations ♥ = Pet Friendly Locations
Red print shows large vehicle parking / access on site or nearby Brown Print = Campgrounds / RV PARKS

Other E: ATMs, Auto Services, Auto Zone, Advance Auto Parts, CVS, CarWash, Kmart Lake City Mall, Lowe's, NAPA, Office Max, Radio Shack, Tires, Tire Kingdom, True Value Hardware, UPS Store, **Walmart** sc, **In & Out RV Park▲**, **to Oak N Pines RV Campground▲**, **Lake City KOA▲**
W: Auto Dealers, **Wayne's RV Resort▲**, **Travel Country RV Center**

423 FL 47, Lake City, to Fort White
Gas E: Mobil, Shell◈
W: BP◈, Chevron
Food W: Little Caesar's, Subway
Lodg E: Super 8
TServ E: Ring Power/CAT
W: Tom Nehl Truck Co/Freightliner, Mike's Truck & Auto
Other E: to Lake City Muni Airport✈
W: **Casey Jones Campground▲**, **Neverdunn's Slow & Easy Living RV Park▲**

414 US 41, US 441, Lake City, Ellisville
FStop W: S&S Food Store #38/Shell, B&B Food Store #32/BP
TStop W: Country Station Truck Plaza (Scales)
Gas E: Chevron, Texaco
Food W: Huddle House, Subway
Lodg E: Travelers Inn
W: Travelodge, Motel/Country Station TP
TServ W: Country Station TP/Tires
Other E: **October Bend RV Park▲**
W: Laundry/LP/Country Station TP, **E-Z Stop RV Park▲**, **Turning Wheels RV Center**, **O'Leno State Park▲**

(413) Rest Area (Both dir)
(RR, Phone, Picnic, Vend)

404 CR 236, High Springs, Alachua, Lake Butler
Gas E: Citgo, Shell◈
Lodg E: HOTEL
Other W: **High Springs Campground▲**

399 US 441, ML King Blvd, Alachua, High Springs
Gas E: BP◈, Exxon
W: Chevron, Citgo◈, Exxon
Food E: McDonald's, Pizza Hut, Taco Bell, Sonny's BBQ, Subway, Waffle House
W: KFC, Wendy's
Lodg E: Econo Lodge, Quality Inn
W: Days Inn, Ramada Ltd
Other E: CarWash, **Travelers Campground▲**, **JD Sanders RV Center**
W: Greyhound, **to River Rise Resort▲**

390 FL 222, NW 39th Ave, Gainesville
Gas E: Exxon◈, Kangaroo◈
W: BP◈, Chevron◈
Food E: Burger King, McDonald's, Sonny's BBQ, Wendy's
W: Cross Creek Café
Lodg W: Best Western
Other E: UPS Store, Publix, Walgreen's, Santa Fe Comm College
W: Gainesville Harley Davidson, Auto Repair/BP

387 FL 26, NW 8th Ave, Gainesville
Gas E: BP, Citgo, Shell◈, Speedway, Texaco
W: BP, Citgo, Chevron◈, Exxon◈, Gator

EXIT FLORIDA

Food E: Burger King, Boston Market, Perkins, Japanese Steak & Sushi, New Century Buffet, Quincy's Steakhouse, Red Lobster, Ruby Tuesday, Rib City Grill, Starbucks, Subway, Wendy's
W: Krystal, Hardee's, KFC, Shoney's, Taco Bell, Waffle House
Lodg E: La Quinta Inn♥
W: Days Inn, Econo Lodge, Fairfield Inn♥, Holiday Inn
Med E: + Immediate Care Walk-In Clinic, + N Florida Reg'l Medical Center
Other E: ATMs, Bank, Pharmacy, Oaks Mall, Office Depot, PetCo♥, Shell/Carwash, U-Haul, Vet♥, Citgo Repair & Towing, to Univ of FL
W: ATMs, Auto Services, Dollar Tree, Home Depot, Jiffy Lube, Publix, Walgreen's, Tires

384 FL 24, SW Archer Rd, Gainesville
Gas E: BP, Chevron◈, Exxon◈, Shell, Speedway
W: Chevron, Kangaroo Express, Mobil◈, Shell
Food E: Atlanta Bread, Bennigan's, Bob Evans, Burger King, ChickFilA, Chili's, Chipolte Mex Grill, Hops Grill, KFC, Lone Star Steakhouse, McDonald's, Olive Garden, On the Border, Papa John's Pizza, Pizza Hut, Shoney's, Sonny's BBQ, Steak & Ale, Steak 'n Shake, Taco Bell, TGI Friday, Texas Roadhouse, Waffle House
W: Cracker Barrel
Lodg E: Best Value Inn, Cabot Lodge, Comfort Inn, Courtyard, Extended Stay America, Hampton Inn, Motel 6♥, Ramada, Red Roof Inn♥, Super 8
W: Baymont Inn, Country Inn, Holiday Inn Express
Med E: + N FL Reg'l Medical Center
Other E: ATMs, Albertson's, Barnes & Noble, Best Buy, CVS, CarQuest, Dollar Tree, Firestone, Lowe's, Oaks Mall, Publix, Radio Shack, Target, **Walmart**, Winn Dixie, **Suburban LP**, Univ of FL
W: Fred Bear Museum, **Sunshine MH & Over Nite Park▲**

(383) Rest Area (Both dir)
(RR, Phones, Picnic, Vend, Sec24/7)

382 FL 121, Williston Rd, to FL 331 Gainesville
Gas E: Citgo◈, Mobil◈
W: BP◈, Chevron◈, Kangaroo◈
Lodg E: Gator Inn, Rest Inn
W: Quality Inn, Travelodge
Other E: Publix
W: Goodyear, **to Williston Crossings RV Resort▲**

374 CR 234, Micanopy
Gas E: BP, Chevron
W: Citgo◈, Texaco
Lodg W: Knights Inn
Other E: Antique Mall
W: Auto Repairs/Texaco

368 CR 318, Reddick, Orange Lake
TStop E: Petro Stopping Center #23/Mobil (Scales)
Gas E: Chevron
Food E: IronSkillet/Wendy's/Petro SC, Jim's BBQ
TServ E: Petro SC/Tires

EXIT FLORIDA

Other E: Laundry/BarbShop/**RVDump/LP**/Petro SC, Dave's Towing, Pro Automotive, U-Haul, Midway Transmissions, **Water's Edge Oaks RV Park▲**, **Sportman's Cove▲**, **South Shore Fish Camp▲**
W: **Grand Lake RV Resort▲**, **Ocala North RV Park▲**

358 CR 326, Ocala
TStop E: Pilot Travel Center # 424 (Scales)
W: Pilot Travel Center #92 (Scales)
Gas E: BP◈, Mobil◈
W: Chevron◈
Food E: Arby's/TJCinn/Pilot TC, Chuck & Von's BBQ To Go, McDonald's/Mobil
W: Wendy's/Pilot TC, DQ, McDonald's
TServ E: Ocala Freightliner
W: American Auto & Truck Repair, 326 Chrome Shop, 10-4 CB Store, Trucker Svc Ctr Oil & Lube, I-75 Truck Sales
Other E: Laundry/WiFi/Pilot TC, Harley Davidson, **Liberty RV & Marine Center**
W: Laundry/WiFi/Pilot TC

354 US 27, FL 500, Ocala, Williston
Gas E: BP, RaceTrac
W: BP◈, Chevron, Circle K, Shell, Texaco◈
Food E: Burger King, Krystal, Rascal's BBQ
W: Huckle Berry Finn's Rest, Waffle House
Lodg E: Payless Inn
W: Budget Host Inn, Comfort Suites, Days Inn, Howard Johnson, Ramada, Travelodge
TServ W: American Diesel Service, Martin Truck & Tire
Other E: **Wild Frontier Campground▲**
W: ATM, Dollar General, Publix, Winn Dixie Walgreen's, Super Flea Market, **Oak Tree Village Campground▲**, **Arrowhead Campsites▲**, **Williston Crossings RV Resort▲**, **Turning Wheel RV Center**

352 FL 40, W Silver Springs Blvd, Ocala, to Silver Springs
Gas E: BP◈, Citgo, RaceTrac
W: Shell◈, Texaco
Food E: McDonald's, PizzaHut/Taco Bell, Wendy's, Whataburger
W: Denny's, Dunkin Donuts, Waffle House
Lodg E: Days Inn, Economy Inn, Quality Inn, Motor Inns Motel & **RV Park▲**
W: Comfort Inn, Hornes Motor Lodge, Red Roof Inn♥, Super 8, Travelodge
Other E: **to Wilderness RV Park Estates▲**, **Silver River State Park**, **to Wild Frontier RV Park▲**
W: **Holiday Trav-L RV Park▲**, to Ocala Int'l Airport✈, **Turning Wheel RV Center**

350 FL 200, College Rd, Ocala, Silver Springs, to Hernando, Dunnellon
Gas E: Chevron, Citgo, RaceTrac, Shell◈, Texaco◈
W: BP, Chevron, Sam's
Food E: Applebee's, Arby's, Bob Evans, Burger King, Chili's, ChickFilA, Chuck E Cheese's Pizza, Hooters, Hops, Krystal, McDonald's, Lone Star Steakhouse, Olive Garden, Outback Steakhouse, Papa John's, Perkins, Ruby Tuesday, Shoney's, Sonny's BBQ, Subway, Taco Bell, TGI Friday, Wendy's
W: Burger King, Cracker Barrel, KFC, Steak 'n Shake, Waffle House

◈= Regular Gas Stations with Diesel ▲ = RV Friendly Locations ♥= Pet Friendly Locations
Red print shows large vehicle parking / access on site or nearby Brown Print = Campgrounds / RV PARKS

EXIT FLORIDA

Lodg E: La Quinta Inn♥, Hampton Inn, Hilton
W: Best Western, Courtyard, Country Inn, Fairfield Inn, Holiday Inn Express, Residence Inn
Med E: + Hospital
Other E: ATMs, Advance Auto Parts, Auto Dealers, Best Buy, Barnes & Noble, CVS, Dollar General, Goodyear, Home Depot, Lowe's, PetSmart♥, Publix, Pep Boys, Target, Tires, Walgreen's, **Walmart sc**, UPS Store, Paddock Mall
W: Sam's Club, Tires, **Ocala KOA▲**, **Ocala RV Camp Resort▲**, **Camperville Of America**, **River Creek RV Resort▲**

(346) **Rest Area Marion Co (SB)** (RR, Phones, Picnic, Vend, Sec24/7)

(345) **Rest Area Marion Co (NB)** (RR, Phones, Picnic, Vend, Sec24/7)

341 **FL 484, Ocala, Belleview, Dunellon**
TStop W: Pilot Travel Center #293 (Scales)
Gas E: Chevron, Citgo, Exxon◈, Shell
W: BP
Food W: Arby's/DQ/TJCinn/Pilot TC, Cracker Barrel, Dunkin Donuts, McDonald's, Sonny's BBQ, Waffle House
Lodg E: Microtel, Sleep Inn
W: Hampton Inn
Other W: WiFi/Pilot TC, BP/Auto & **RV** Repair, **Ocala Ranch RV Park▲**

(338) **Weigh Station (Both dir)**

329 **FL 44, Wildwood, Inverness**
TStop E: Pilot Travel Center #95 (Scales), PTP/Gate #1142 (Scales)
W: Travel Center of America/BP (Scales)
Gas E: Mobil◈
Food E: Steak n Shake/Gate, Burger King, Denny's, IHOP, McDonald's, Waffle House, Wendy's
W: CountryPride/PizzaHut/Popeye/Subway/TA TC
Lodg E: Budget Suites, Days Inn, Economy Inn, Microtel, Super 8, Wildwood Inn
Tires E: Tommy's Tire Shop
TWash E: Wildwood TW
W: TA TC
TServ E: 75 Truck Service Center, All Fleet Refrigeration, Wildwood CB Shop
W: TA TC/Tires, 75 Chrome Shop
Other E: WiFi/Pilot TC, Laundry/Gate, Auto Svc, **Wildwood KOA▲**
W: Laundry/WiFi/TA TC

(328) **FL Tpk (TOLL), to Orlando, to Miami (fr SB, Left Exit)**

321 **CR 470, Lake Panasoffkee, Bushnell, Sumterville**
FStop W: Lake Panasoffkee BP
TStop E: Spirit Travel Center (Scales)
Food E: Rest/Spirit TC
W: Hardee's/Subway/BP
Lodg W: Motel USA
TServ W: BP/Tires
Other W: **Countryside RV Park▲**, **Turtleback RV Resort▲**

314 **FL 48, Bushnell**
Gas E: BP◈, Citgo, Murphy
W: Hess, Shell◈, Sunoco◈
Food E: DQ/Citgo, Chinese, Dunkin Donuts, McDonald's, KFC, Pizza, Subway, Taco Bell, Wendy's

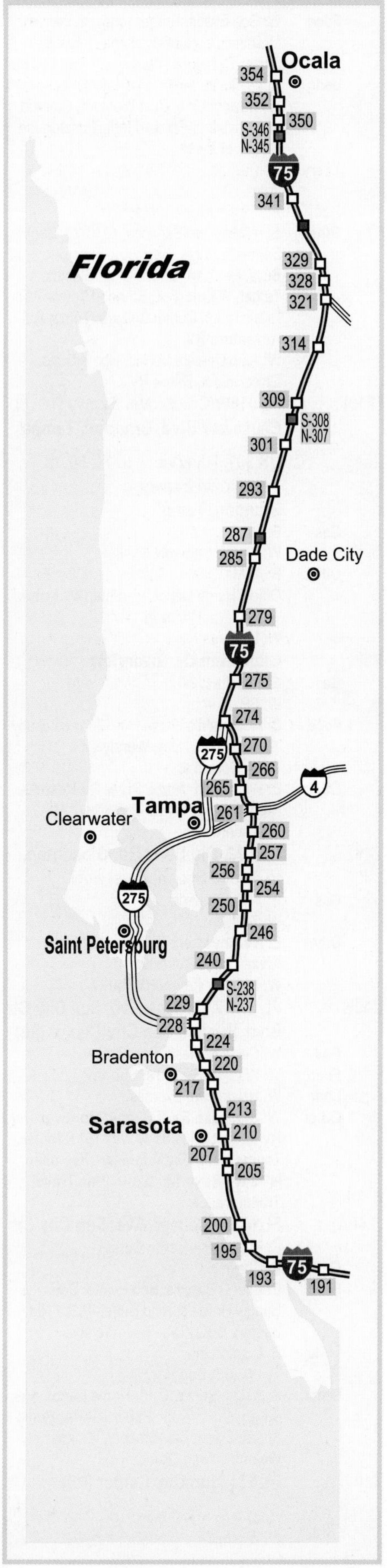

Florida

Ocala, Dade City, Tampa, Clearwater, Saint Petersburg, Bradenton, Sarasota

EXIT FLORIDA

Food W: Beef O'Brady's, McDonald's, Sonny's BBQ, Waffle House
Lodg E: Best Western, GuestHouse Inn, Rodeway Inn
W: Microtel
Other E: **Walmart sc**, Webster Flea Market, Farmers Market, ATMs, Auto Services, Banks, Winn Dixie, **Red Barn RV Resort & MH Park▲**, **Oaks RV Resort▲**, **Blueberry Hill RV Resort▲**, **Florilow Oaks Camp▲**, **Dade Battlefield State Park**, to **Sunshine Village MH Comm & RV Resort▲**
W: **Flagship RV Sales & Service**

309 **CR 476B, Bushnell, Webster**
Other E: **Breezy Oaks RV Park▲**, **Sumter Oaks RV Park▲**

(308) **Rest Area (SB)** (RR, Phones, Picnic, Pet, Vend)

(307) **Rest Area (NB)** (RR, Phones, Picnic, Pet, Vend)

301 **US 98, FL 50, Orlando, Brooksville**
Gas E: BP, RaceTrac, Speedway, Murphy
W: Hess◈, Chevron◈, Sunrise
Food E: Arby's, Cracker Barrel, Denny's, McDonald's, Waffle House, Wendy's
W: Burger King, Subway
Lodg E: Days Inn
W: Best Western, Hampton Inn
Med W: + Hospital
Other E: ATMs, Dollar General, Pharmacy, Winn Dixie, to **Webster Travel Park▲**, **Sunshine Village MH & RV Resort▲**

293 **CR 41, Blanton Rd, Dade City**
Other W: **Travelers Rest Resort▲**

285 **FL 52, San Antonio, to Dade City, New Port Richey**
TStop E: Flying J Travel Plaza #5037/Conoco (Scales)
W: Four Star Fuel Mart/Citgo (Scales)
Food E: CountryMarket/FastFood/FJ TP
W: Rest/Four Star FM, Waffle House
Med E: + Pasco Reg'l Medical Center
Other E: Laundry/BarbSh/WiFi/**RVDump/LP**/FJ TP, Costco, **Marathon Coach**

279 **FL 54, Zephyrhills, Land O' Lakes, Wesley Chapel**
Gas E: Hess◈, RaceTrac, Shell
W: 7-11, BP, Circle K◈, Marathon
Food E: Applebee's, Burger King, Carino's, Sonny's BBQ, Subway, Waffle House, Wendy's
W: Cracker Barrel, Denny's, KFC, McDonald's, Outback Steakhouse
Lodg W: Best Western, Comfort Inn, Holiday Inn Express, Sleep Inn
Other E: Ace Hardware, Advance Auto Parts, Publix, Walgreen's, Winn Dixie, **Leisure Days RV Resort▲**, **Ralph's Travel Park▲** **Happy Days RV Park▲**, to **Jim's RV Park▲**
W: Best Buy, Goodyear, PetSmart♥, Sweet Bay Grocery, **Quail Run RV Park▲**

(278) **Rest Area Pasco Co (Both dir)** (RR, Phones, Pic, Pet, Vend, Sec247)

275 **FL 56, to Zephyrhills**
Gas E: Shell
Lodg E: Hampton Inn

(274) **Jct I-275S, to Tampa, St Petersburg (SB)**

◈ = Regular Gas Stations with Diesel ▲ = RV Friendly Locations ♥ = Pet Friendly Locations
Red print shows large vehicle parking / access on site or nearby Brown Print = Campgrounds / RV PARKS

EXIT	FLORIDA

270 **CR 581, Bruce B Downs Bvd, Tampa**
- Gas E: 7-11, Hess◈, Mobil, Shell◈
  W: 7-11
- Food E: Boston Market, Burger King, ChickFilA, Golden China, Lee Roy Selmon's, Moe's SW Grill, Panera Bread, Papa John's Pizza, Ruby Tuesday, Starbucks, Steak 'N Shake, Subway, Taco Bell
  W: McDonald's, Olive Garden, Red Lobster
- Lodg E: Comfort Inn, Holiday Inn Express, Wingate Inn
- Other E: Home Depot, Publix, Tires, Walgreen's
  W: BJ's Club, Lowe's

266 **CR 582A, CR 579, E Fletcher Ave, Morris Bridge Rd, Tampa**
- Gas E: Circle K
  W: 7-11, Mobil, Shell◈
- Food W: Bob Evans, Great American Grill, Hooters, Starbucks, Wendy's
- Lodg W: Courtyard, Days Inn, Hampton Inn, Hilton Garden Inn, Residence Inn, Sleep Inn
- Med E: + Hospital, + Moffitt Cancer Center

265 **FL 582, Fowler Ave, Temple Terrace**
- Gas W: BP, Shell
- Food W: Burger King, Denny's, McDonald's, Perkins, Ryan's Grill
- Lodg W: Holiday Inn, La Quinta Inn♥, Ramada Inn, Wingate Inn
- Other E: **Happy Traveler RV Park▲**
  W: to Busch Gardens, Universal Studios

(261) **Jct I-4, E-Orlando, W-Tampa, US 92, FL 600, to Brandon (NB)**
- Gas E: BP, Citgo, Chevron
- Food E: Bob Evans, **Cracker Barrel**, Danny's All American Diner, Subway, Wendy's
- Lodg E: Camp Knox Motel, Hampton Inn, Masters Inn, Suites Motel
- TServ W: Cummins SE (W to exit 6C)
- Other E: **Lazydays RV Supercenter/Rally Park▲**
  W: **RV Mobile Service**, Vandenburg Airport✈

260 **FL 574, ML King Blvd, Mango (SB)**

260B **FL 574W, ML King Blvd, Mango**
- Gas W: BP, Hess
- Food W: McDonald's, Subway
- Lodg W: AmeriSuites, Hilton Garden Inn, Radisson, Residence Inn
- TServ W: Kenworth of Central FL
- Other E: Grocery, Walgreen's
  W: Grocery, US Post Office, CitiBank Center, FL State Fairgrounds

260A **FL 574E, ML King Blvd, Mango**
- Gas E: Chevron, Citgo, RaceTrac, Shell
- Food E: McDonald's, Quiznos, Waffle House

257 **FL 60, Adamo Dr, Brandon Blvd, Causeway Blvd, Tampa, to Brandon**
- Gas E: Circle K, Mobil, Shell
  W: Citgo, Circle K, Shell
- Food E: Chili's, Chuck E Cheese's Pizza, Denny's, Don Pablo, Olive Garden, Moe's SW Grill, Outback Steakhouse, Panda Express, Papa John's Pizza, Red Lobster, Romano's Macaroni Grill, Sam Seltzer's Steakhouse, Smokey Bones BBQ, Steak 'N Shake, TGI Friday, Wings Gone Wild
  W: Bob Evans, Burger King, Hooters, McDonald's, Subway, Sonny's BBQ, Sweet Tomatoes, Wendy's
- Lodg E: La Quinta Inn♥, Holiday Inn
  W: Baymont Inn, Best Western, Comfort Inn, Days Inn, Fairfield Inn, Hampton Inn, Red Roof Inn♥
- TServ W: Freightliner of Tampa, Tampa Mack Sales
- Med E: + Brandon Reg'l Hospital
- Other E: ATMs, Auto Services, AMC 20, Banks, Barnes & Noble, Best Buy, Firestone, Pep Boys, Petco♥, Sam's Club, Staples, Target, **Walmart sc**, Brandon Towne Mall, Hillsborough Comm College, **Tom's RV, Adventure RV**
  W: Auto Dealers, ATMs, Home Depot, Office Depot, **Bates RV**

(256) **FL 618W/Crosstown Expwy (TOLL), Causeway Blvd, Brandon, Tampa**

254 **US 301, Riverview, to FL 60, to Crosstown Expwy, Brandon, Tampa**
- Gas E: Mobil
  W: 7-11◈, Chevron, Shell
- Other E: ATMs, Banks, Costco, CVS, FedEx Office, Home Depot, PetSmart♥, Publix, Walgreen's, **Walmart**
  W: **La Mesa RV**, Freightliner

250 **Gibsonton Dr, Riverview**
- Gas E: Racetrac, 7-11
  W: BP, Murphy
- Food E: McDonald's, Pizza Hut, Quiznos, Ruby Tuesday, Taco Bell, Wendy's
  W: McDonald's
- Other E: Winn Dixie, **Alafia River RV Resort▲**, **Hidden River Travel Resort▲**
  W: **Walmart sc**

246 **CR 672, Big Bend Rd, Gibsonton, to Apollo Beach, Riverview**
- Gas E: 7-11, Chevron
  W: 7-11
- Other E: **RV Anywhere Service**, **to Hidden River Travel Resort▲**
  W: **Holiday Palms RV Park▲**

240B **FL 674W, College Ave, Sun City Ctr Blvd, Ruskin, Sun City Center (SB)**
- Gas W: Circle K, Hess, RaceTrac
- Food W: KFC, McDonald's, Subway
- Lodg W: Holiday Inn Express
- Other W: **Sun Lake RV Resort▲**, **to River Oaks RV Resort▲**, **Hide-A-Way RV Resort▲**, **Tampa South RV Resort▲**, **Hawaiian Isles RV Resort▲**, **Lone Pine Travel Trailer Park▲**

(240A) **FL 674E, College Ave, Sun City Ctr**
E: Ruskin Welcome Center
- Gas E: Chevron
- Food E: Beef O'Brady's, Bob Evans, Denny's, Hungry Howie's, King Buffet, Pizza Hut, Sonny's BBQ, Taco Bell, Wendy's
- Lodg E: Comfort Inn
- Med E: + South Bay Hospital
- Other E: ATMs, Banks, CVS, Home Depot, Kash & Karry, Pharmacy, Publix, NAPA, Radio Shack, Sweet Bay Grocery, Walgreen's, **Walmart**, Winn Dixie

240 **FL 674, Sun City Center (NB)**

(238) **Rest Area Hillsborough Co (Both dir) (RR/Fam, Ph, Pic, Vend, Pet, Sec24/7)**

229 **CR 6, Moccasin Wallow Rd, to Parrish, Palmetto**
- Other W: **Winterset Travel Trailer Park▲**, **Terra Ceia RV Resort▲**, **Fiesta Grove RV Resort▲**, **Frog Creek RV Campground▲**, **Fisherman's Cove RV Resort▲**

(228) **Jct I-275N, to St Petersburg**

224 **US 301, Ellenton, to Palmetto**
- TStop W: Pilot Travel Center #89 (DAND)
- Gas E: BP, Chevron, RaceTrac, Shell◈
- Food E: Applebee's, Checkers, Little Caesars Pizza, McDonald's, Ruby Tuesday, Wendy's
  W: Subway/Pilot TC, Denny's, Oyster Bar, Shoney's, Waffle House
- Lodg E: Hampton Inn, Sleep Inn
  W: GuestHouse Inn, Ramada Ltd
- Other E: Kmart, Publix, Walgreen's, US Post Office, Ellenton Outlet Mall/Prime Outlets, Ellenton Ice & Sports Complex, Darlene's Shell, Tourist Info, **Ellenton Gardens CG▲**

220B **FL 64W, Bradenton (NB)**
- FStop W: Circle K Truxtop #1686/76
- Gas W: BP◈, Hess, RaceTrac, Shell
- Food W: Burger King, **Cracker Barrel**, Wendy's McDonald's, Sonny's BBQ, Waffle House
- Lodg W: Comfort Inn, Days Inn, Econo Lodge, Holiday Inn Express, Motel 6♥
- Med W: + Hospital
- Other W: ATMs, Banks, Manatee River Harley Davidson, Publix, Winn Dixie, **Walmart sc**, Vet♥, **Dream RV Center**, **Encore RV Resort▲**

220A **FL 64E, Zolfo Springs (NB)**
- Other E: **Lake Manatee State Rec Area▲**

220 **FL 64, Bradenton, Zolfo Springs (SB)**
- Other E: **Lake Manatee State Park▲**

217B **FL 70W, Bradenton, Myakka City**
- Gas W: BP◈, Circle K, Exxon◈, Shell
- Food W: Arby's, Applebee's, Bob Evans, ChickFilA, McDonald's, Starbucks, Subway
- Other W: CVS, Publix, Lowe's, Tires, **Pleasant Lake RV Resort▲**, **Horseshoe Cove RV Resort▲**, **to Arbor Terrace RV Resort▲**, **Tropical Gardens Travel Park▲**, **Linger Lodge RV Resort▲**

217A **FL 70, Bradenton, Myakka City**
- Gas E: Hess◈
- Food E: Wing Factory, Subs/Pizza/Hess
- Other E: ATMs, Banks, Carwash, Grocery

217 **FL 70, Bradenton, Arcadia, Myakka City, Lakewood Ranch (SB)**

213 **University Pkwy, to Sarasota, to International Airport**
- Gas E: Chevron◈
  W: Chevron
- Food E: Alamo Steakhouse Grill, Chili's, China Coast, Quiznos, Subway/Chevron
  W: Atlanta Bread, Bonefish Grill, Carrabbas Ruby Tuesday, Wendy's
- Lodg E: Fairfield Inn, Holiday Inn
  W: Comfort Suites, Courtyard, Residence Inn, Springhill Suites
- Other E: Publix, Walgreen's
  W: BJ's, CVS, Staples, Target, Sarasota/ Bradenton Int'l Airport✈, Sarasota Outlet Center, Ringling Museum, Sarasota Jungle Gardens, Sarasota Classic Car Museum, **Sarasota Lakes RV Resort▲**

◈ = Regular Gas Stations with Diesel ▲ = RV Friendly Locations ♥ = Pet Friendly Locations
Red print shows large vehicle parking / access on site or nearby Brown Print = Campgrounds / RV PARKS

EXIT FLORIDA

210 **FL 780, Fruitville Rd, Sarasota**
Gas W: BP◈, Chevron, Mobil◈
Food W: Applebee's, Bob Evans, Burger King, ChickFilA, Don Pablo, KFC, Longhorn Steakhouse, McDonald's, Perkins, Subway, Taco Bell
Lodg W: AmericInn
Med W: + Hospital
Other E: **Sun N Fun RV Resort/RVDump▲**
W: ATMs, Advance Auto Parts, Dollar Tree, Pharmacy, Publix, Radio Shack, Sam's Club, Target, Winn Dixie, Shopping at St Armand Circle, **Campbell RV**, **Adventure RV**

207 **Bee Ridge Rd, Sarasota**
Gas W: BP, Mobil◈, Shell
Food W: Arby's, Chili's, Checker's, McDonald's, Pizza Hut, Steak 'n Shake, Taco Bell, Woody's BBQ
Lodg W: Hampton Inn
Med W: + Dr's Hospital of Sarasota
Other W: ATMs, Dollar Tree, Goodyear, Home Depot, Publix, Radio Shack, Sweet Bay Foods, Walgreen's, **Walmart**

205 **FL 72, Clark Rd, Sarasota, Arcadia**
Gas W: BP◈, Exxon◈, Mobil
Food W: Applebee's, Arby's, Burger King, ChickFilA, McDonald's, Quiznos, Starbucks, Waffle House, Wendy's
Lodg W: Comfort Inn, Country Inn, Ramada
Other W: ATMs, CVS, Publix, Walgreen's, **Beach Club RV Resort▲**, **Windward Isle RV Park▲**, **Sarasota RV Center**

200 **FL 681S, Venice, Osprey (SB)**
Med W: + Hospital

195 **Laurel Rd, Nokomis, Laurel (Serv 3.5mi W in Nokomis & Laurel)**

193 **Jacaranda Blvd, Venice**
Gas W: Chevron, Citgo◈, Hess◈, RaceTrac
Food W: Cracker Barrel, McDonald's, Waffle House
Lodg W: Best Western, Holiday Inn Express
Med W: + Hospital
Other W: **Caribbean Bay Club**, **Palm & Pines Mobile & RV Park▲**

191 **River Rd, Venice, to North Port, Warm Mineral Springs, Englewood (Serv 3mi W in Venice)**
Other W: Venice Airport✈, Buchanan Airport✈, **Venice Campground▲**, **Ramblers Rest▲**

182 **Sumter Blvd, North Port**
Other W: **Myakka River RV Park▲**

179 **Toledo Blade Blvd, North Port**

170 **CR 769, Kings Hwy, Port Charlotte**
FStop W: Kings Chevron
Gas E: 7-11◈, RaceTrac
W: BP, Hess◈, Mobil
Food W: Denny's, McDonald's, Cracker Barrel, Pizza Hut, Waffle House, Wendy's
Lodg E: Holiday Inn, Hampton Inn
Other E: **Walmart sc**
W: Advance Auto Parts, CVS, Dollar General, Grocery, Publix, Walgreen's, US Post Office

167 **CR 776, Harborview Rd**

164 **US 17, FL 35, Punta Gorda, Arcadia**
TStop E: Duncan Rd Shell

Personal Notes

EXIT FLORIDA

Gas E: Chevron◈, RaceWay
W: Circle K
Food W: McDonald's
Med W: + Hospital
Other E: **Waters Edge RV Resort▲**, **Charlotte Harbor RV Park▲**, Charlotte Co Airport✈, **Lettuce Lake Travel Resort▲**

(161) **CR 768, Jones Lp Rd, Punta Gorda**
E: Rest Area Charlotte Co (Both dir) (RR, Phones, Picnic, Vend, Sec24/7)
TStop W: Pilot Travel Center #94 (Scales)
Gas W: BP◈
Food W: Arby's/TJCinn/Pilot TC, Burger King, Pizza Hut, Taco Bell, Waffle House, Wendy's
Lodg W: Motel 6♥, Days Inn, Super 8
Other E: Charlotte Co Airport✈
W: WiFi/Pilot TC, Golf Course, **Punta Gorda RV Resort▲**, **Encore RV Park▲**,

(160) **Weigh Station (Both dir)**

158 **CR 762, Tuckers Grade**
Gas W: Circle K
Other E: Babcock-Webb Wildlife Area
W: **Pelican Perch RV Park▲**, **Our Family RV Center**

143 **FL 78, Bay Shore Rd, N Ft Myers**
Gas E: Citgo◈
W: RaceTrac◈
Other E: **Seminole Campground▲**, **Up River Campground▲**
W: **Pioneer Village Mobil & RV Park▲**

141 **FL 80, Palm Beach Blvd, Ft Myers**
Gas E: BP◈, Chevron, Exxon
W: 7-11, RaceTrac, Hess◈

EXIT FLORIDA

Food E: Cracker Barrel, Waffle House
W: Hardee's, Little Caesar's Pizza, Perkins, Pizza Hut, Sonny's BBQ, Subway, Taco Bell
Lodg E: Comfort Inn
Other E: Pharmacy, Publix, **Orange Harbor RV Park▲**
W: Big Lots, CVS, Dollar General, Publix, Radio Shack, **North Trail RV Center**

139 **Luckett Rd, Ft Myers**
TStop W: Pilot Travel Center #352 (Scales)
Food W: Subway/Pilot TC, Grandma's Kitchen
TServ W: Pilot TC/Tires
Other E: **Cypress Woods RV Park▲**, **RV Center**
W: Laundry/WiFi/Pilot TC, **Camping World**, **RV Park▲**

138 **FL 82, MLK Blvd, Ft Myers**
Gas E: Hess◈
W: Citgo◈, Speedway
TServ W: Cummins SE, Wallace Int'l

136 **FL 884, Colonial Blvd, Ft Myers**
Gas W: 7-11, BP, Shell◈, Murphy
Food W: Bob Evans, Steak 'n Shake
Lodg W: Baymont Inn, Courtyard, Howard Johnson, La Quinta Inn♥, Super 8
Med W: + Hospital
Other E: Home Depot
W: ATMs, Lowe's, **Walmart sc**

(131) **Daniels Pkwy, International Airport, Fort Myers, Cape Coral**
E: Cape Coral Rest Areas Lee Co (Both dir) (RR/Fam, Ph, Pic, Pet, Vend, Sec24/7)
Gas E: BP◈
W: Hess◈, RaceTrac, Shell
Food E: Subway/BP
W: Arby's, Bob Evans, Burger King, Cracker Barrel, Denny's, McDonald's, Waffle House, Wendy's
Lodg W: Best Western, Country Inn, Hampton Inn, Sleep Inn, Springhill Suites
Med W: + Hospital
Other E: Southwest Florida Int'l Airport✈, to **Golden Palms Motorcoach Estates▲**
W: Tires. Publix

128 **Alico Rd, San Carlos Park**
Gas E: Costco
W: Hess◈
Food W: Subway, Wendy's
Lodg E: Hilton Garden Inn, Homewood Suites
Other E: ATMs, Bass Pro Shop, Best Buy, Costco, Petco♥, Staples, Super Target
W: to **Woodsmoke Camping Resort/RVDump▲**

123 **CR 850, Corkscrew Rd, Estero**
Gas E: BP◈
W: 7-11, Chevron, Hess◈
Food E: McDonald's, Perkins, Starbucks, Subway
Other E: CVS, Grocery, Publix
W: Lowe's, Tires

116 **Bonita Beach Rd, Bonita Springs**
Gas E: Chevron◈
W: BP, Shell, Albertson's
Food W: Bob Evans, McDonald's, Waffle House
Lodg W: Baymont Inn, Hampton Inn, Holiday Inn Express
Other E: Publix
W: Albertson's, CVS, **Imperial RV Park▲**

◈ = Regular Gas Stations with Diesel ▲ = RV Friendly Locations ♥ = Pet Friendly Locations
Red print shows large vehicle parking / access on site or nearby Brown Print = Campgrounds / RV PARKS

EXIT		FLORIDA
111		**CR 846, Immokalee Rd, Naples Park**
	Gas	E: 7-11, Mobil W: Shell◈
	Food	E: Bob Evans, Pizza Hut W: McDonald's
	Lodg	E: Hampton Inn
	Med	W: + Hospital
	Other	W: ATMs, Albertson's, CVS, Publix, Super Target, **Walmart sc**
107		**CR 896, Pinebridge Rd, Naples**
	Gas	E: BP◈ W: Chevron◈, RaceTrac, Shell◈
	Food	E: McDonald's/BP W: Applebee's, Burger King, IHOP, Perkins, Waffle House
	Lodg	W: Best Western, Hilton Garden Inn
	Other	E: Publix, Walgreen's W: Tires, Harley Davidson
105		**CR 886, Golden Gate Pkwy**
101		**FL 84, CR 951, Naples**
	NOTE:	**SB: LAST Free Exit before TOLL**
	Gas	W: Mobil◈, Shell◈
	Food	W: Burger King, Checkers, Cracker Barrel, McDonald's, Subway, Waffle House
	Lodg	W: Baymont Inn, Comfort Inn, La Quinta Inn♥, Red Roof Inn♥, Super 8
	Other	W: **RV Center, RV Park▲ , Naples/Marco Island KOA▲**
(100)		**TOLL Plaza** (Both dir)
80		**FL 29, to Everglades City**
(71)		**Big Cypress Nat'l Preserve**
(63)		**Rest Area Collier Co** (Both dir) (RR, Phones, Pic, Pet, Vend, Sec247)
49		**FL 833, Government Rd** (NB)
	TStop	E: Miccosukee Service Plaza/Mobil
	Other	E: Laundry/M SP
(41)		**Picnic Area** (SB)
(38)		**Picnic Area** (NB)
(34)		**Rest Area Broward Co** (Both dir) (RR, Phones, Pic, Pet, Vend, Sec247)
(32)		**Picnic Area** (Both dir)
(26)		**TOLL Plaza** (WB)
	NOTE:	**Begin NB/End SB Callboxes**
23		**US 27, FL 25, Miami, South Bay**
	NOTE:	**Begin I-75N TOLL Road**
22		**Glades Pkwy, Arvida Pkwy, Ft Lauderdale**
21		**FL 84W, Indian Trace** (NB)
	Gas	W: Citgo◈
19		**I-595E, FL 869** (TOLL), **Sawgrass Expwy, Ft Lauderdale**
15		**Royal Palm Blvd, Weston**
	Gas	W: Exxon
	Food	E: Pastability W: Subway, Wendy's
	Lodg	E: AmeriSuites, Courtyard W: Marriott, Residence Inn

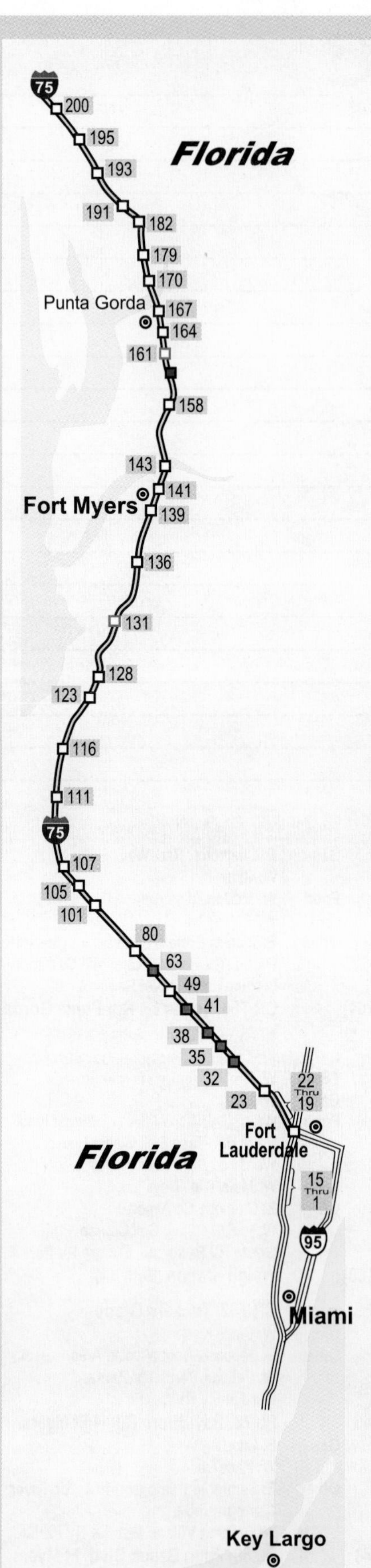

EXIT		FLORIDA
	Other	W: Best Buy
13B		**FL 818, Griffin Rd W**
	Gas	W: 7-11
	Food	W: Chili's, McDonald's
	Other	W: Home Depot, Publix, Auto Dealers
13A		**FL 818, Griffin Rd E, SW 46th St**
	Gas	E: Shell◈
	Food	E: Burger King, Outback Steakhouse, Waffle House
	Med	E: + Hospital
	Other	E: Publix
11B		**Sheridan St W, SW 72nd St, Pembroke Pines**
	Gas	W: Shell
	Food	W: Cracker Barrel, McDonald's, Starbucks Subway, TGI Friday
	Other	W: Publix, Lowe's
11A		**SW 72nd St, Sheridan St E**
	Gas	E: Chevron
	Lodg	E: Hampton Inn, Holiday Inn
9B		**FL 820W, Pines Blvd**
	Gas	W: Mobil, 76, Shell
	Food	W: KFC/TacoBell, McDonald's, Sweet Tomatoes
	Lodg	W: Grand Palms Hotel Resort
	Other	W: ATMs, Advance Auto Parts, Costco, Publix, Tires
9A		**FL 820E, Pines Blvd**
	Gas	E: Shell
	Food	E: Arby's,Chili's, Romano's Macaroni Grill, Shell's Seafood, Starbucks, Subway, Wendy's
	Other	E: Best Buy, B&N, BJ's, Home Depot, Target, Walgreen's, **CB Smith Co Park▲ / RVDump**
7B		**Miramar Pkwy West**
	Gas	W: Shell
	Food	W: Starbucks
7A		**Miramar Pkwy East**
	Gas	E: Chevron
	Food	E: McDonald's, Subway, Wendy's
	Lodg	E: Hilton Garden Inn, Wingate Inn
	Other	E: Home Depot, Publix, Walgreen's
5		**to FL 821S, FL Tpk (TOLL) (SB)**
4		**NW 186th St, Miami Gardens Dr**
	Gas	E: BP, Chevron
	Food	E: IHOP, McDonald's, Subway
	Other	E: CVS, Publix
2		**NW 138th St, Graham Dairy Rd**
	Gas	W: Mobil, Shell
	Food	W: McDonald's, Subway, Wendy's
	Other	W: Publix, Walgreen's
1B		**FL 826S, Palmetto Expwy**
1A		**FL 826N, Palmetto Expwy**
	NOTE:	**I-75 begins/ends on FL 826**

EASTERN TIME ZONE

FLORIDA

Begin Northbound I-75 from Miami, FL to the MICHIGAN / CANADA border.

◈ = Regular Gas Stations with Diesel ▲ = RV Friendly Locations ♥ = Pet Friendly Locations
Red print shows large vehicle parking / access on site or nearby Brown Print = Campgrounds / RV PARKS

EXIT **COLORADO**

Begin Eastbound I-76 from near Julesburg, CO To near Jct I-80 in Big Springs, NE.

COLORADO

NOTE: I-76 begins/ends on I-70, Ex #269B

MOUNTAIN TIME ZONE

1A **CO 121, Wadsworth Blvd, Arvada (WB)**
- **Gas** N: 7-11, Conoco, Phillips 66, Costco
- **Food** N: Applebee's, Burger King, to Cheesecake Therapy, Chipolte Mexican Grill, Country Buffet, Fazoli's, IHOP, Kokora Japanese Rest, Lone Star Steakhouse, McDonald's, Namiko's Japanese Rest, Red Robin, Ruby Tuesday, Starbucks, Subway, Taco Bell, Texas Roadhouse, S: Amici's Pizzeria, Burger King, Boston Market, China's Best, El Jaliciense Mexican Rest, In 'N Out Burger, KFC, Mi Cabana/ Salsa's Mexican Rest, New Canton Rest, Raliberto's Mexican Food, Red Lobster, Wendy's,
- **Med** N: + Hospital, + Next Care Urgent Care
- **Other** N: AMC Old Town 14 Cinema, Advance Auto Parts, Auto Services, Costco, Discount Tire, Dollar Tree, FedEx Office, Goodyear, Home Depot, Lowe's, Office Depot, Office Max, PetSmart♥, Radio Shack, Sam's Club, Sports Authority, T-Mobile, Tires Plus, S: AAA Propane/LP, Auto Services, Big Lots, Discount Tire, O'Reilly Auto Parts, Midas, Pep Boys, Pharmacy, Safeway, US Post Office, Walgreen's,

1B **CO 95, Sheridan Blvd, Arvada**

3 **US 287, Federal Blvd, S to I-70, N to US 36/Denver Boulder Turnpike**
- **Gas** N: Shamrock◈ S: Sinclair
- **Food** S: McDonald's, Pizza Hut, Taco House
- **Lodg** N: Valley Motel S: Joy Motor Hotel, Primrose Motel, White Rock Motel
- **Other** N: Carwash, Nolan's RV & Marine S: Advance Auto Parts, **Delux RV Park▲**, Fireworks, Hermosa Veterinary Clinic♥, Regis Univ

4 **Pecos St, Denver**

(5) **Jct I-25, N to Ft Collins, Boulder, S to Denver, Colo Springs (EB)**

(5AB) **Jct I-25, S-Denver, N to Ft Collins, Boulder (WB)**

EXIT **COLORADO**

(6) **Jct I-270E, to I-70E, Limon, DIA (EB)**

(6A) **I-270E, to I-70E, Limon, DIA (WB)**
- **Other** E: Many Serv S to 1st Exit: x2b-Grocery, Tire & Diesel Services, **Walmart sc**,

(6B) **I-270W, to I-25N Ft Collins, US 36W Boulder (WB)**

8 **CO 224, 74th Ave, to US 85, Commerce City, to Welby (EB) (Diff Reacc - via S to US 85/ 6 / Vasquez Blvd) (Access to Exit #10 Services)**
- **FStop** S: Shoco Oil◈◈
- **Gas** S: Shamrock◈
- **Food** S: Butcher Block Cafe
- **Lodg** S: Crestline Motor Motel
- **TWash** S: Shoco Oil
- **TServ** S: All Maintenance Towing & Repair, Beall Trailers Sales & Service, IMCO Trailer Sales & Service, Interstate Turbo Supply
- **Other** S: Buckeye Welding, O'Reilly Auto Parts, **Roadbear RV Rentals & Sales**, Transwest Auto, Truck, **RV**, & Trailer Sales& Service, **to S on US 85 appr 2mi:** Grocery, Tires, Diesel Services, **Walmart sc**

9 **US 85S, US 6W, to CO 2S, Brighton Blvd, Commerce City (WB)**
- **Gas** S: Shell◈
- **TServ** S: Freightliner
- **Other** S: CO State Hwy Patrol Post

10 **88th Ave, Henderson**
- **Gas** N: Phillips 66◈
- **Food** N: Blimpie/P66
- **Lodg** N: Holiday Inn Express♥, Super 8
- **Other** S: Mile High Flea Market, 88 Drive-In Theatre, Acc via Service Rd: Tire Center, Western Truck Parts,

11 **96th Ave, Henderson**
- **Other** S: Diesel Repair Services, Leadbetter Small Animal Hospital♥,

12 **US 85N, Greeley, Brighton (fr EB, Left Exit)**
- **Other** N: Diversified Truck & **RV** Repair

16 **CO 2W, Sable Blvd, 120th Ave, Brighton, Commerce City**
- **TStop** N: PTP/Tomahawk Auto Truck Plaza/Shell (Scales)
- **Food** N: Rest/FastFood/Tomahawk ATP
- **TWash** N: Tomahawk ATP
- **TServ** N: Tomahawk ATP/Tires
- **Other** N: Laundry/Chiro/Tomahawk ATP

(18) **Jct I-470E (TOLL), to DIA, Limon, Aurora, Colorado Springs (WB)**

EXIT **COLORADO**

20 **136th Ave, Barr Lake, Brighton (Access to Ex #21/22 via Buckley Rd N)**
- **Other** **N: Barr Lake RV Park▲**, N to acc # **S: Barr Lake State Park▲**

21 **144th Ave, Brighton (Access to Ex #22 Serv-N to US 85)**
- **Food** N: Buffalo Wild Wings, ChickFilA, Chili's, KFC/Long John Silver's, McDonald's, Quiznos Subs, Subway, Taco Bell
- **Lodg** N: Holiday Inn Express
- **Other** N: Dick's Sporting Goods, Discount Tire, Dollar Tree, Home Depot, Kohl's, Lowe's, Michael's, Office Depot, PetSmart♥, Sprint, Super Target, Verizon,

22 **152nd Ave, Bromley Lane, to US 85, Brighton (most serv nw to US 85)**
- **Gas** N: Shamrock◈, Amer Pride, GasAMat, King Sooper
- **Food** N: Applebee's, Arby's, KFC, Starbucks, Wendy's
- **Lodg** N: Best Western, Comfort Inn, Hampton Inn, Sleep Inn, Super 8
- **Med** N: + Platte Valley Medical Center
- **Other** N: ATMs, Ace Hardware, Albertson's, Brighton Animal Clinic♥, Kmart, King Soopers, Lowe's, Peerless Tire, Penske Truck Rental, Pharmacy, Radio Shack, UPS Store, **Walmart sc**,

25 **Frontage Rd, 160th Ave, CO 7W, Brighton, Lochbuie**
- **Gas** N: Shell◈
- **Other** N: Big O Tires, Safeway, Walgreen's, Auto & Truck Services S: Staples

31 **CO 52, Hudson, Prospect Valley**
- **TStop** N: Love's Travel Stop #377 (Scales)
- **Gas** S: Conoco◈, Phillips 66◈
- **Food** N: Carl'sJr/Subway/Love's TS S: El Faro, Pepper Pod Rest, Mex Rest
- **Other** N: WiFi/Love's TS **S: Denver NE Pepper Pod Campground▲**, US Post Office

34 **CR 49, Kersey Rd, Hudson, Greeley, Kersey**

39 **I-76 Bus, Market St, Keenesburg**
- **Gas** S: Phillips 66◈
- **Food** S: Corner Kitchen, Coffee Bistro
- **Lodg** S: Keene Motel
- **Other** S: Auto Supply, Antique Store

48 **CR 73, Roggen, to CO 79, Bennett**
- **Gas** N: Shell◈

49 **Painter Rd, CR 386 (WB)**

57 **CO 51, CR 91, Orchard**

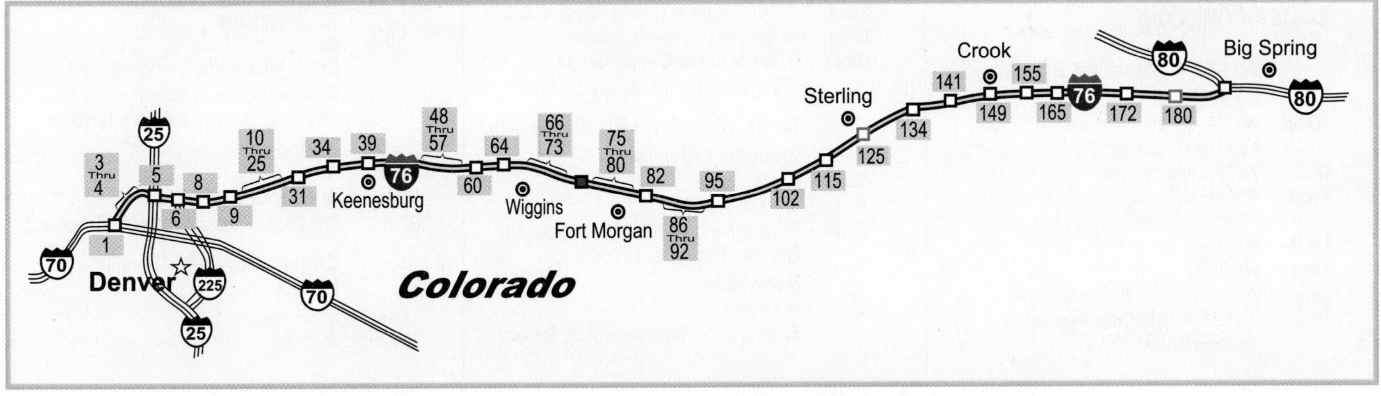

◈= Regular Gas Stations with Diesel ▲ = RV Friendly Locations ♥= Pet Friendly Locations

Red print shows large vehicle parking / access on site or nearby Brown Print = Campgrounds / RV PARKS

COLORADO

60 — **to CO 144, to Orchard**

64 — **US 6E, Central Ave, Wiggins (EB) (Access to #66 Services)**
- Other — S: Hardware Store, Wiggins Auto Supply, US Post Office

(66A) — **CO 39, CO 52, Wiggins, Goodrich**
Rest Area (Both dir)
S: (RR, Phone, Picnic, Vend)
- FStop — N: Wiggins Junction Truck Stop/P66; S: Stub's Gas & Oil/Sinclair
- Food — N: Rest/Wiggins Jct TS
- TServ — N: Wiggins Jct/Tires/Towing
- Other — S: LP/Stub's

66B — **US 34W, CR R, Greeley (WB)**

73 — **Long Bridge Rd, CR 12, Ft Morgan**

(75) — **Weigh Station (Both dir)**

75 — **I-76 Bus, US 34, Ft Morgan**
- Gas — S: Loaf 'n Jug◊
- Food — S: Rest/Clarion Inn
- Lodg — S: Clarion Inn♥, **to appr 2 mi:** Country Comfort Motel♥ & **RV Park▲**,
- Other — N: Great West Trailer & Truck; S: I-76 Speedway

79 — **CO 144, Weldona, Log Lane Village (fr WB, no re-entry)**

80 — **CO 52, Main St, Ft Morgan, Raymer**
- Gas — S: Conoco◊x2, Sav-O-Mat, Shell◊, Valero◊
- Food — S: Arby's, DQ, KFC, Little Bamboo Chinese Rest, McDonald's, Memories Rest/BW, Mexican Rest, Taco John's, Sonic, Subway
- Lodg — S: Best Western♥, Central Motel♥, Days Inn, Sands Motel, Super 8,
- Med — S: + Co Plains Hospital
- Other — N: Golf Course, **to** Ft Morgan Muni Airport✈, Riverside Park; S: Amtrak, Auto Services, Auto Zone, Big O Tire, Ft Morgan Museum, Laundromat, NAPA, RiteAid, Safeway, Valley Drive-In Theatre, Walgreen's

82 — **CR 20, Barlow Rd, Ft Morgan**
- FStop — N: Conoco Outpost; S: Phillips 66
- Food — N: Maverick's Country Grill; S: Burger King,Subway/Walmart, to Country Steak Out Rest
- Lodg — N: Comfort Inn, Rodeway Inn♥
- Other — S: Dollar Tree, Morgan Comm College, Morse Cycle Sales & Service, **Walmart sc**,

86 — **CR 24, Dodd Bridge Rd, Ft Morgan**

89 — **CR 27, Hospital Rd, Brush**
- Gas — S: Grocery Kart, Sinclair
- Food — S: Subway
- Lodg — S: Empire Motel
- Med — S: + E Morgan Co Hospital
- Other — S: Beaver Creek Veterinary Clinic♥, Dollar General, Family Dollar, Ft Morgan Muni Golf Course, Grocery Kmart/ Pharmacy, NAPA,

90A — **CO 71S, to US 34, Colorado Ave, Brush, Limon, Akron**
- FStop — S: Acorn Food Store #2380/Conoco
- Food — S: McDonald's, Subway
- Lodg — S: Microtel♥,

90B — **CO 71N, Snyder**
- TStop — N: PTP/Tomahawk Truck Plaza/Shell (Scales)
- Food — N: Rest/Tomahawk TP, Pizza Hut, Peking China Buffet, Wendy's
- Lodg — N: Econo Lodge♥
- TServ — N: Tomahawk ATP/Tires

92AB — **to US 6E, I-76 Bus, to US 34, CO 71, Brush, Limon**
- Other — S: Brush Muni Airport✈

95 — **CR 33, Hillrose**

102 — **CO Q, Akron, to Merino**

115 — **CO 63, Merino, to Atwood, Akron**
- FStop — N: Atwood Sinclair
- Food — N: Café/Sinclair FS; S: Atwood Steakhouse

(125) — **I-76 Bus, US 6W, to CO 138, CO 14, CO 62S, Sterling, Otis, Atwood**
Rest Area (Both dir)
N: (RR, Phone, Pic, Vend, RVDump)
- FStop — S: Phillips 66
- TStop — N: AmPride #2/Cenex
- Gas — N: Conoco, Sinclair, SavOMat
- Food — N: Arby's, Burger King, McDonald's, Sonic, Taco John's, Wendy's; S: FastFood/P66, McDonald's, Quiznos, Rest/Ramada
- Lodg — N: Best Western♥, First Interstate Inn, **to appr 2 mi:** Crest Motel, Fountain Lodge, Oakwood Inn, Sterling Motor Lodge; S: Comfort Inn, Ramada Inn♥, Super 8♥, Travelodge♥
- TServ — N: Sterling Diesel Service
- Med — N: + Sterling Reg'l Hospital
- Other — N: Laundry/AmPride, Auto Dealers, Big O Tires, Bowling, Cinema, Golf Course, Grocery, North Eastern Jr College, Overland Trail Park & Museum, Pharmacy, Radio Shack, US Post Office, Veterinary Medical Clinic♥, Walgreen's, **Walmart sc**, **Sterling RV**, **Sterling State Park**; **S: Buffalo Hills Campground & RV Park▲**

134 — **CR 55, Iliff**

141 — **CR 67, CR 65, Crook, Proctor**

149 — **CO 55, Crook, to Fleming**
- TStop — S: Kuskie Interstate Svc & Café/Sinclair

155 — **CR 93, Red Lion Rd, Fleming**

165 — **CO 59, CR 15, Sedgwick, Haxtun**
- Gas — N: Lucy's Place

172 — **CR 27, CR 29, Ovid**

(180) — **US 385, CR 45, Julesburg, Holyoke**
N: CO Welcome Center (Both dir) (RR, Phone, Vend, Pet, Info, RVDump)
- FStop — N: Flying JTravel Plaza #5014/Conoco
- Gas — N: Texaco; S: Conoco◊
- Food — N: Rest/FJ TP, Subway
- Lodg — N: Budget Host Inn, Grand Motel
- Med — N: + Sedgwick Co Memorial Hospital
- Other — N: WiFi/LP/FJ TP, Julesburg Muni Airport✈

MOUNTAIN TIME ZONE

NOTE: I-76 begins/ends on I-70, Ex #269B

NOTE: MM 184: Nebraska State Line

⇑ COLORADO

⇓ OHIO

NOTE: Begin/End I-76 on I-71, Exit #209

EASTERN TIME ZONE

(1) — **Jct I-71, N-Cleveland, S-Columbus, US 224W, to Lodi**
- TStop — W: Travel Center of America/BP, Pilot Travel Center #13
- Gas — W: 76, Citgo, Sunoco
- Food — W: CountryPride/B King/Popeye/Starbucks/ TA TC, Subway/Pilot TC, McDonald's
- Lodg — W: Super 8♥
- Tires — W: TA TC
- Other — W: Laundry/WiFi/RVDump/TA TC, WiFi/Pilot TC, to **Chippewa Valley Campground▲**

2 — **OH 3, Wooster Pike Rd, Seville, Medina**
- Gas — N: Circle K; S: Citgo◊
- Food — N: DQ, Hardee's, Huddle House, Subway
- Lodg — N: Comfort Inn, Hawthorne Inn
- Other — N: **Maple Lakes Campground▲**

(6) — **Weigh Station (Both dir)**

7 — **OH 57, Wadsworth Rd, Wadsworth, to Rittman, Medina**
- Gas — N: Marathon◊
- Med — S: + Hospital
- Other — S: Wadsworth Muni Airport✈, Akron Univ

9 — **OH 94, High St, Wadsworth, N Royalton**
- Gas — N: Circle K; S: BP◊, Citgo, Marathon, Shell, Sunoco
- Food — N: Arby's, Bob Evans, Burger King, DQ, McDonald's, Pizza Hut, Ponderosa, Subway, Taco Bell, Wendy's; S: Casa Del Rio, Country Café, Denny's
- Lodg — N: Holiday Inn Express, Ramada; S: Legacy Inn♥
- Other — N: Pharmacy, Goodyear, Grocery, Home Depot, NTB, Radio Shack, **Walmart sc**; S: Auto Zone, Auto Service, RiteAid

11 — **OH 261, Akron Rd, Wadsworth, Norton**
- Gas — N: Speedway
- Other — S: Lowe's, PetCo♥, Target

13AB — **OH 21, S - Massillon, N - Cleveland**

14 — **CR 17, Cleveland-Massillion Rd, Norton**
- Gas — S: BP, Marathon
- Food — S: Charlie's Rest

◊= Regular Gas Stations with Diesel ▲ = RV Friendly Locations ♥= Pet Friendly Locations
Red print shows large vehicle parking / access on site or nearby **Brown Print = Campgrounds / RV PARKS**

EXIT		OHIO
16		**Barber Rd, Norton Ave, Barberton**
	Gas	S: Gas, Sunoco
	Med	S: + Hospital
17		**Wooster Rd, East Ave (WB)**
	Gas	N: Duke
	Other	N: Auto Services
17A		**State St (EB, No EB re-entry)**
	Food	N: Arby's, Iguana's, Long John Silver, McDonald's, Subway, Wendy's
	Other	N: Rolling Acres Mall, Goodyear, NTB, Firestone
17B		**OH 619, Wooster Rd, to Barberton, Wooster (EB)**
	Gas	N: Marathon
	Food	N: Family Restaurant
	Med	S: + Hospital
	Other	S: Tires
(18)		**Jct I-277, US 224E, to I-77, Canton, Mogadore, Barberton**
19		**Kenmore Blvd (EB), Battles Ave (WB)**
(20)		**Jct I-77, N-Cleveland, S-Akron (EB)**
21A		**East Ave (WB, no WB re-entry)**
	Gas	N: 76
21B		**Bowery St , Lakeshore Ave, Downtown (EB)**
21C		**OH 59E, MLK Frwy (EB), Dart Ave, (WB), Downtown Akron**
	Med	N: + Akron General Med Center
	Other	N: to Akron Zoo
22A		**Main St, Broadway, Downtown**
	Other	N: ATM, Amtrak, Convention Center
22B		**Grant St, Wolf Ledges Blvd**
	Gas	S: BP
	Food	S: McDonald's
	Lodg	N: Quaker Crown Plaza
	Other	N: ATM, Akron Univ, Quaker Square, Inventors Hall of Fame
(23A)		**Jct I-77S, to Canton**
23B		**OH 8N, Buchtel Ave, to Cuyahoga Falls, Univ of Akron (fr EB Left Exit)**
24A		**Johnston St, Inman St (WB)**
24		**Arlington St, Kelly Ave (EB)**
	Other	S: to Akron Fulton Int'l Airport✈
24B		**Arlington St, Kelly Ave (WB)**
25A		**Martha Ave, Seiberling St (EB)**
25B		**Englewood Ave, Seiberling St (EB)**
25		**Martha Ave, Market St (WB)**
	Other	N: Goodyear Rubber Co

EXIT		OHIO
26		**OH 18, E Market St, Brittain Rd, Mogadore, N Springfield**
	FStop	N: Knacks Morgan's Truck Plaza/Marathon (EB: Access Via Exit #25B)
	Gas	N: Circle K◈, Shell S: Gas
	Food	S: Arby's, McDonald's, Subway, Wendy's
	Other	S: ATM, Auto Service, Akron Rubber Bowl
27		**Gilchrist Rd, to OH 91, Akron**
	Gas	S: Marathon◈, Sunoco
	Food	N: Bob Evans, S: Hardee's, Wendy's, Subway/Marathon
	Lodg	S: Best Western
	Other	N: Goodyear Metroparks S: Truck & Trailer Repair
29		**OH 532, Southeast Ave, Tallmadge, Mogadore**
	Gas	N: Duke S: Citgo
	Other	N: Summit Racing Parts Store
31		**CR 18, Tallmadge Rd, to Kent**
	Food	N: Applebee's, Beef O'Brady's, Quiznos
	Other	N: Dollar Tree, Lowe's, Walmart sc, to Summit Co Fairgrounds
33		**OH 43, Kent, Hartville**
	Gas	N: BP◈ S: Speedway◈
	Food	N: Bob Evans, Burger King, Pizza Hut S: McDonald's, Subway, Wendy's
	Lodg	N: Alden Inn, Comfort Inn, Days Inn, Hampton Inn, Holiday Inn Express, Quality Inn, Relax Inn, Super 8
	Other	N: to Kent State Univ S: Cherokee Park Family Campground▲ Akron Mogadore Reservoir▲
38A		**OH 44S, Ravenna Louisville Rd, Rootstown, Ravenna (EB)**
38B		**OH 44N, OH 5, Ravenna Louisville Rd, Rootstown, Rd (EB)**
38		**OH 44, to OH 5, Ravenna Louisville Rd, Ravenna, Rootstown (WB)**
	Gas	N: BP, Speedway◈ S: Dairy Mart, Marathon
	Food	N: McDonald's, Taco Bell, Wendy's S: Burger King, Cracker Barrel, David's
	Med	N: + Regency Hospital
	Other	S: Auto Repair, Grocery, Randolph Fairgrounds, NEO College of Medicine, Friendship Acres RV Park▲
43		**OH 14, Rootstown, Ravenna, Alliance**
	FStop	S: Certified Oil #410
	Other	N: West Branch State Park▲ S: Truck Repair

EXIT		OHIO
(46)		**Rest Area (Both dir) (RR, Phones, Picnic, Pet)**
48		**OH 225, Alliance, Diamond, Palmyra**
	Other	N: Country Acres Campground▲ , Leisure Lake Park S: to Berlin Lake
54		**OH 534, Lake Milton, Newton Falls**
	Gas	S: BP
	Other	N: Green Acres Lake Park▲ , Lake Milton State Park
57		**CR 65, Bailey Rd, to OH 45, Warren**
	Other	N: to GM Lordstown Assembly Plant S: Leonard Truck & Trailer
	NOTE:	**I-76 runs with I-80/OH Tpk Below. Exit #'s follow I-80**
(61/ 218)		**Jct I-80/76, OH Tpk (TOLL) (EB joins, WB Ends)**
232		**OH 7, Market St, North Lima, to Boardman, Youngstown**
	TStop	S: Pilot Travel Center #011 (Scales)
	Gas	N: Shell, Sheetz S: Shell◈, Speedway◈
	Food	N: DQ S: FastFood/Pilot TC
	Lodg	N: Budget Inn, Economy Inn, Holiday Inn Express, Microtel, Quality Inn♥, Ramada S: Davis Motel, Rodeway Inn
	Med	N: + Hospital
	TWash	S: Pilot TC
	Other	S: WiFi/Pilot TC, to appr 10 mi Beaver Creek State Park , Ponderosa Park, Chaparral Family Campground▲
(234)		**I-680N, Youngstown, Poland (WB)**
		S: FastFood/Pilot TC
	Lodg	N: Budget Inn, Economy Inn, Holiday Inn Express, Quality Inn♥, Ramada S: Davis Motel, Rodeway Inn
	Med	N: + Hospital
	TWash	S: Pilot TC
	Other	S: WiFi/Pilot TC, to appr 10 mi Beaver Creek State Park , Ponderosa Park, Chaparral Family Campground▲
(234)		**I-680N, Youngstown, Poland (WB)**
(237)		**Glacier Hills Service Plaza (EB) Mahoning Valley Service Plaza (WB)**
	TStop	Valero
	Food	McDonald's
	Other	Picnic

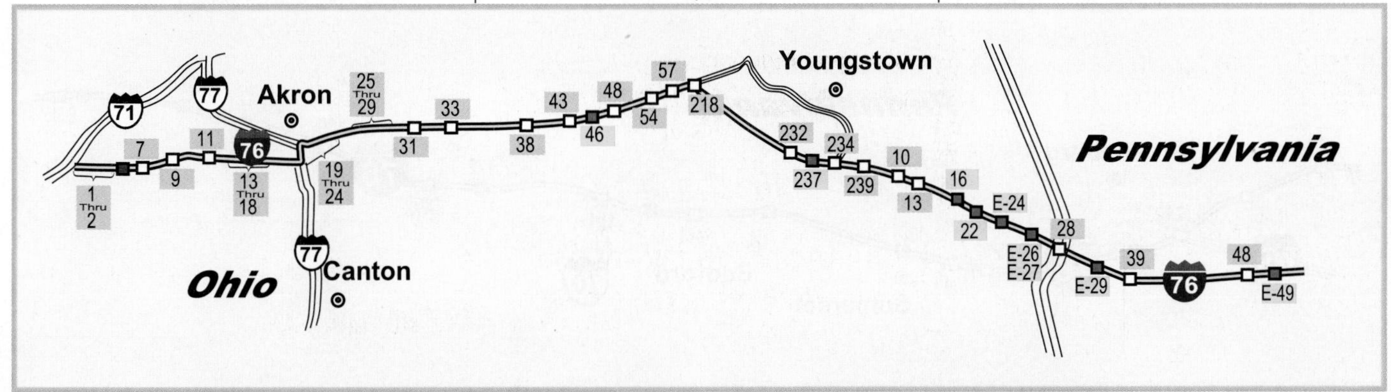

◈= Regular Gas Stations with Diesel ▲ = RV Friendly Locations ♥= Pet Friendly Locations
Red print shows large vehicle parking / access on site or nearby Brown Print = Campgrounds / RV PARKS

EXIT		OH / PA
(239)		TOLL Booth (EB End, WB Begin)
	NOTE:	I-76 runs with I-80/OH Tpk above. Exit #'s follow I-80.
	EASTERN TIME ZONE	
	NOTE:	MM 241: Pennsylvania State Line

OHIO
PENNSYLVANIA

EXIT		PENNSYLVANIA
	EASTERN TIME ZONE	
(1.5)		TOLL Booth
	NOTE:	Begin EB/End WB Call Box Area EB for next 326 mi.
(2)		Parking Area (EB)
(6)		Parking Area (EB)
10		PA 60 (TOLL), James E Ross Hwy, to Pittsburgh, Newcastle
	Other	S: to Pittsburgh Int'l Airport
13		PA 18, Big Beaver Blvd, Beaver Falls, Ellwood City
	Food	N: Rest/Holiday Inn S: Rest/Conley Inn, Giuseppe's Italian Rest
	Lodg	N: Alpine Inn, Beaver Valley Motel, Hilltop Motel, Holiday Inn ♥ S: Conley Inn
(16)		Parking Area (Both dir)
(22)		Zelienople Travel Plaza (EB) E: PA WELCOME CENTER
	FStop	Sunoco
	Food	Roy Rogers, Mrs Fields Cookies, Hershey's Ice Cream
(24)		Parking Area (EB)
(26)		Parking Area (EB)
(27)		Parking Area (EB)
28		US 19, Perry Hwy, to I-79, Cranberry, to Pittsburgh, Erie
	Gas	N: Amoco/BP◈, Exxon◈, Sheetz, Sunoco, Costco, GetGo S: BP◈
	Food	N: Arby's, Bob Evans, Burger King, CiCi's Pizza, Dennys, Dunkin Donuts, Eat n Park, Hardee's, Long John Silver, Lone Star Steakhouse, Max & Erma's, McDonald's, Panera Bread, Papa John's Pizza, Perkins, Pizza Hut, Primanti Bros, Subway, Wendy's S: China Garden, Quaker Steak & Lube
	Lodg	N: Comfort Inn, Fairfield Inn, Hampton Inn, Holiday Inn Express, Hyatt Place, Marriott, Motel 6 ♥, Red Roof Inn ♥, Super 8, Sheraton S: Residence Inn
	Med	N: + UPMC Hospital
	Other	N: ATMs, Auto Services, Banks, Barnes & Noble, Best Buy, CarQuest, Cinema, Costco, Cranberry Mall, FedEx Office, Goodyear, Grocery, Home Depot, Office Max, Pep Boys, PetCo ♥, Pharmacy, Radio Shack, RiteAid, Staples, Target, UPS Store, US Post Office, Walgreen's, **Walmart sc**,
(29)		Parking Area (EB)
(30)		TOLL Plaza
39		PA 8, William Flynn Hwy, Gibsonia, to Pittsburgh, Butler, Butler Valley
	Gas	N: Exxon◈, GetnGo, Sheetz S: BP, Sunoco◈
	Food	N: Applebee's, Eat 'n Park, Max & Erma's, McDonald's, Starbucks S: Arby's, Burger King, DQ, Dunkin Donuts, Panera Bread, Quiznos, Subway, Taco Bell, Wendy's
	Lodg	N: Comfort Inn, Richland Hotel S: Econo Lodge
	Other	N: Advance Auto Parts, Auto Dealers, Dollar Tree, Grocery, Lowe's, Pharmacy, Ross Park Mall, Target, Vet ♥, **Walmart**, S: Auto Zone, CVS, Firestone, Goodyear, Home Depot, Radio Shack, Tire & Auto Services
48		to PA 28, Pittsburgh, New Kensington
	Gas	N: 76, Shell, S: Exxon◈, GetGo
	Food	S: Bob Evans, Burger King, Denny's, Eat 'n Park, KFC, Fuddrucker's, McDonald's, Ponderosa, Primani Bros, Subway, Taco Bell, Wendy's
	Lodg	S: Comfort Inn, Days Inn, Holiday Inn, Holiday Inn Express, Super 8, Valley Motel
	TServ	S: Cummins Interstate Power
	Other	N: RiteAid S: ATM, Grocery, Target
(49)		Oakmont Service Plaza (EB)
	FStop	Sunoco
	Food	Burgers Etc, Hershey's Ice Cream, Nathan's Hot Dogs, Pizza
(57)		Jct I-376, US 22, Penn-Lincoln Pkwy, Monroeville, to Pittsburgh
	FStop	S: Stop #22/Citgo
	Gas	S: BP, Sheetz
	Food	S: Arby's, Bob Evan's, Burger King, CiCi's Pizza, ChickFilA, Chinese, Chuck E Cheese's Pizza, Damon's, Denny's, DunkinvDonuts, Eat 'n Park, Golden Corral, Lone Star Steakhouse, Max & Erma's, McDonald's, Olive Garden, Outback Steakhouse, Primanti Bros, Quiznos, Red Lobster, Starbucks, Taco Bell, Wendy's
	Lodg	N: East Exit Motel S: Comfort Suites, Courtyard, Days Inn ♥, Extended Stay America, ExecuStay, Hampton Inn, Holiday Inn ♥, Radisson, Red Roof Inn ♥, Springhill Suites, Sunrise
	Med	S: + Forbes Regional Hospital
	Other	N: CCAC Boyce Campus S: ATM, Auto Services, Auto Dealers, Banks, Big Lots, Borders, Expo Mart, FedEx Office, Firestone, Lowe's, Monroeville Mall, NTB, Office Depot, Office Max, Petco ♥, PetSmart ♥, Pharmacy, Radio Shack, Target, UPS Store, to Three Rivers Stadium,
67		US 30, Lincoln Hwy, Irwin, to Greensburg, McKeesport
	FStop	S: W on US 30: Marathon
	Gas	N: BP◈, Sheetz S: Gulf, Sunoco, Sunoco
	Food	N: Blimpie/BP, Pizza S: Arby's, Bob Evans, Burger King, CiCi's Pizza, DQ, Denny's, Dunkin Donuts, Eat 'n Park, Long John Silver, McDonald's, Panera Bread, Pizza Hut, Quiznos Subs, Taco Bell
	Lodg	N: Motel 3 S: Holiday Inn Express, Penn Irwin Motel
	TServ	N: Fox & James
	Med	S: + Walk-In Medical Clinic, + Westmoreland Hospital
	Other	N: Auto Service, ATM, Bank, Laundromat, **RV Center**, to St Vincent College, Seton Hill Univ S: Advance Auto Parts, Auto Service, ATMs Banks, CarQuest, Grocery, Dollar Tree, Radio Shack, RiteAid, Target, **RV Center**
	NOTE:	I-76/PA Tpk runs with I-70 below. Exit #'s follow I-76.
(74.5)		Hemphill Service Plaza (EB)
	FStop	Sunoco
	Food	Breyer's, McDonald's
(75)		Jct I-70W, to US 119, PA 66 (TOLL), New Stanton, Greensburg, Wheeling
	Gas	N: Sunoco S: BP◈, Exxon, Sheetz, Sunoco
	Food	N: Cedar Steakhouse/Motel S: Bob Evans, Eat 'n Park, McDonald's X2, Chinese, **Cracker Barrel**, KFC, Pizza Hut, Quzinos, Subway, Wendy's

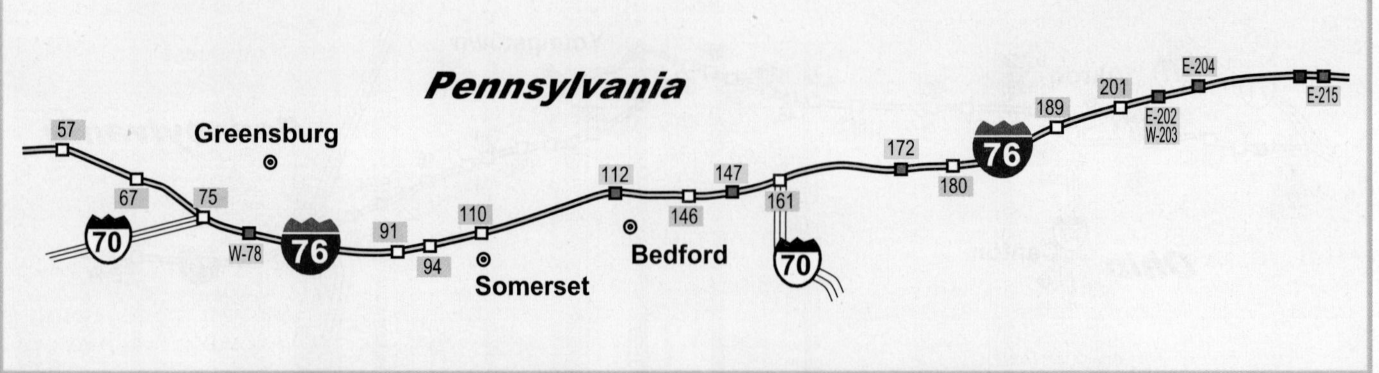

◈= Regular Gas Stations with Diesel ▲ = RV Friendly Locations ♥= Pet Friendly Locations
Red print shows large vehicle parking / access on site or nearby Brown Print = Campgrounds / RV PARKS

EXIT		PENNSYLVANIA
	Lodg	N: Cedar Motel S: Budget Inn, Comfort Inn, Days Inn, Fairfield Inn, Howard Johnson, Quality Inn, Super 8
	Other	N: to Univ of Pittsburgh/Greensburg S: to Madison KOA▲, Camping▲
(78)		**New Stanton Service Plaza (WB)**
	FStop	Sunoco #7089
	Food	Kings Family Rest, McDonald's
91		**PA 31, to PA 711, Donegal, to Ligonier, Uniontown (NO Trucks PA 31W)**
	Gas	S: BP, Exxon◈, Sunoco◈
	Food	S: DQ, Hardees/Pizza/BP, Subway/Exxon
	Lodg	S: Days Inn
	Other	N: to St Vincent College S: Donegal Campground▲, Laurel Highlands Campland▲, Mountain Pines RV Resort▲, to Rivers Edge Campground▲, Kooser State Park, Laurel Hill State Park, Ohiopyle State Park, Seven Springs Ski Resort, Hidden Valley Ski Resort, Laurel Mtn Ski Resort
(94)		**Parking Area (WB)**
110		**PA 601, Center Ave, to US 219, to PA 31, Somerset, Johnstown** NOTE: Tunnel Restrictions for HazMat
	TStop	S: Jim's Auto Truck Stop
	Gas	N: KwikFill, Sheetz S: Exxon, Shell◈
	Food	N: Hoss's Steak & Sea House, Pizza Hut S: Arby's, Burger King, KFC, Long John Silver, McDonald's, Starbucks, Subway, Wendy's
	Lodg	N: A1 Economy Inn, Inn at Georgian Place S: Best Western, Days Inn, Hampton Inn, Holiday Inn, Knights Inn, Quality Inn♥, Ramada Inn, Super 8♥
	TServ	N: Truck Service S: Beckwith Machinery, Jim's Auto & Truck Service
	Med	S: + Hospital
	Other	N: Auto Services, Auto Dealers, Ryder, U-Haul, Factory Shops at Georgian Place, to Somerset Co Airport✈, to Woodland Campsites▲, Flight 93 Memorial S: ATMs, Banks, Glades Court Mall, Greyhound, Penske, Pharmacy, Harley Davidson, to Hidden Valley Resort, Pioneer Park Campground▲, Scotty Camping Resort & RV Sales▲
(112)		**Somerset Service Plaza (Both dir)**
	FStop	Sunoco
	Food	E: Big Boy, Cinnabon, Hershey's Ice Cream Roy Rogers, Starbucks W: Burger King, Cinnabon, Hot Dog City, Hershey's Ice Cream
(123)		**Allegheny Mtn Tunnel (Headlights on)**
146		**US 220 Bus, to I-99, to US 220, Bedford, to Altoona, Johnstown** NOTE: Tunnel Restrictions for HazMat
	FStop	N: RG's Travel Plaza/BP
	TStop	N: SAC Shop/BP (US 220)
	Gas	N: Sheetz
	Food	N: Arena Rest, Burger King, China Inn, Denny's, Ed's Steak House, Hoss's Steak & Sea House, Long John Silver, Pizza Hut, McDonald's, Wendy's
	Lodg	N: Best Western♥, Econo Lodge, Quality Inn♥, Super 8, Travelodge S: Hampton Inn, Janey Lynn Motel

EXIT		PENNSYLVANIA
	TServ	N: Truck Service & Parts S: Rte 220 Truck Repair
	Other	N: Laundry/WiFi/SAC BP, Bedford Airport✈, Bedford Co Airport✈, to Shawnee State Park, Blue Knob State Park S: Friendship Village Campground & RV Park▲
(147)		**Midway Service Plaza (Both dir)**
	FStop	Sunoco #7078/#7079
	Food	E: Cinnabon, Hershey's Ice Cream, Hot Dog City, Sbarro W: Cinnabon, Hershey's Ice Cream, KFC, Sbarro, Starbucks
(161)		**Jct I-70E, to US 30, Lincoln Hwy, Breezewood, Everett (Serv N to US 30)**
	FStop	N: Breezewood BP
	TStop	N: Gateway Travel Plaza/Valero Travel Center of America #75 (Scales), Petro 2 #84/Shell (Scales)
	Gas	N: Exxon◈, Mobil◈, Sunoco◈
	Food	N: GatewayRest/DQ/Dominos/Subway/ TA TC, Perkins/Blimpie/HersheyIC/Petro 2, Café/Sunoco, Arby's, Big John's Steak & Buffet, Bob Evans, Bonanza Steakhouse, Burger King, Denny's, Domino's Pizza, Hardee's, KFC, Pizza Hut, Starbucks, Subway, Taco Bell, Wendy's
	Lodg	N: Gateway Travel Lodge/Holiday Inn Express/Gateway TC, Best Western, Comfort Inn, Econo Lodge, Heritage Inn, Howard Johnson, Penn Aire Motel, Quality Inn, Ramada Inn
	TWash	N: Blue Beacon TW/Petro 2
	TServ	N: TA TC/Tires, Petro 2/Tires
	Other	N: Laundry/BarbSh/RadioShack/WiFi/ TA TC, Laundry/BarbSh/CB/WiFi/Petro 2, Breezewood Campground▲
	NOTE:	I-76/PA Tpk runs with I-70 above. Exit #'s follow I-76.
(172)		**Sideling Hill Service Plaza (Both dir)**
	FStop	Sunoco
	Food	Big Boy, Burger King, Hershey's Ice Cream, Popeye's Chicken, Starbucks
180		**US 522, Fort Littleton, Mount Union, McConnellsburg, Mercersburg** Note: Tunnel Restrictions-HazMat
	Gas	N: BP◈, GAS◈
	Food	N: Fort Family Rest
	Lodg	N: Downes Dixie Motel #2
	Med	N: + Hospital
	Other	N: PA State Hwy Patrol Post S: to Cowans Gap State Park▲
(187)		**Tuscarora Mtn Tunnel (Headlights on)**
189		**PA 75, Ft Loudon, Willow Hill**
	Food	S: Rest/Willow Hill Motel
	Lodg	S: Willow Hill Motel
(197)		**Kittatinny Mtn Tunnel (Headlights on)**
(199)		**Blue Mtn Tunnel (Headlights on)**
201		**PA 997, Blue Mountain, Chambersburg, Shippensburg** Note: Tunnel Restrictions-HazMat
	Food	S: Rest/Johnnie's Motel
	Lodg	S: Johnnie's Motel, Kenmar Motel
	Other	S: to Letterkenny Ord Depot Area
(202)		**Parking Area (EB)**

EXIT		PENNSYLVANIA
(203)		**Blue Mountain Service Plaza (WB)**
	FStop	Sunoco
	Food	Hershey's Ice Cream, Nathan's, Roy Rogers
(204)		**Parking Area (EB)**
(214)		**PA State Hwy Patrol Post (WB)**
(215)		**Parking Area (EB)**
(219)		**Plainfield Service Plaza (EB)**
	FStop	Sunoco
	Food	Hershey's Ice Cream, Hot Dog City, Roy Rogers
(224)		**Parking Area (EB)**
226		**US 11, Harrisburg Pike, to I-81, Carlisle, Harrisburg**
	FStop	N: I-81 Carlisle Fuel Stop/Citgo
	TStop	N: Gables of Carlisle All American Plaza/ Shell(Scales), Petro Stopping Center (Scales), Flying J Travel Plaza #5200 (Scales), Pilot Travel Center #342 (Scales)
	Gas	N: BP S: Exxon, Sheetz
	Food	N: FastFood/GablesofCarlisle, IronSkillet/ NobleRoman/Petro SC, Rest/FastFood/ Flying J TP, Wendy's/Pilot TC, Arby's, Bob Evans, Eat 'n Park, McDonald's, Middlesex Diner, Subway, Waffle House S: Hoss's Steakhouse & Sea House
	Lodg	N: Best Western, Hampton Inn, Howard Johnson, Quality Inn♥, Ramada, Rodeway Inn, Super 8 S: Best Western, Motel 6♥, Pike Motel
	TWash	N: Blue Beacon TW/Petro SC, Gables
	TServ	N: Petro SC/Tires, Gables/Tires
	Med	S: + Carlisle Regional Medical Ctr
	Other	N: Laundry/Gables, Laundry/BarbSh/CB/ WiFi/Petro SC, Laundry/WiFi/RVDump/LP/ Flying J TP, Laundry/WiFi/Pilot TC, ATM, Grocery, Greyhound, Dickerson College, Carlisle Campground▲ S: Auto Service, Budget, U-Haul, Animal Clinic♥, to US Army War Coll Carlisle Barracks, to Carlisle Airport✈
236		**US 15, Gettysburg Pike, Mechanicsburg, to Gettysburg, Harrisburg**
	Gas	N: BP, Mobil, Shell S: Sheetz
	Food	N: Brothers Pizza, Issac's Rest & Deli, Mary's Family Rest, Papa John's Pizza, Subway S: Arby's, Burger King, Cracker Barrel, Hong Kong Chef, Hoss's Steak & Sea House, McDonald's, Quiznos, Wendy's
	Lodg	N: Comfort Inn, Country Inn, Courtyard, Econo Lodge, Hampton Inn♥, Holiday Inn, Homewood Suites S: Best Western, Wingate Inn
	Med	N: + Hospital
	Other	N: Auto Service, Tires, U-Haul, to BJ's, Capital City Mall, State Capitol S: ATMs, Auto Services, Banks, Dollar General, Grocery, RiteAid, to Messiah College, Gettysburg National Military Park
(237)		**Parking Area (EB)**
(242)		**Jct I-83, Memorial Hwy, Harrisburg**
	Gas	N: BP, Hess, Mobil
	Food	N: Bob Evans, Doc Holliday's Steakhouse, Eat 'n Park, McDonald's, Pizza Hut

◈= Regular Gas Stations with Diesel ▲ = RV Friendly Locations ♥= Pet Friendly Locations
Red print shows large vehicle parking / access on site or nearby Brown Print = Campgrounds / RV PARKS

EXIT		PENNSYLVANIA
	Lodg	N: Best Western, Comfort Inn, Holiday Inn♥, Motel 6♥, Rodeway Inn, Travel Inn S: Days Inn, Highland Motel
	Other	N: Animal Hospital♥, Capital City Airport✈, to State Capitol Complex
(247)		**Jct I-283, to PA 283, Lancaster, Hershey, Harrisburg**
	Gas	N: Exxon, Sunoco
	Food	N: Taco Bell, Wendy's
	Lodg	N: Best Western, Days Inn, Rodeway Inn
	TServ	N: to Cummins Power Systems
	Other	N: Harrisburg East Campground▲, to State Capitol S: Etnoyer's RV World & Mobile RV Repair, Penn State Univ, Harrisburg Int'l Airport✈
(250)		**Highspire Service Plaza (EB)**
	FStop	Sunoco
	Food	Nathan's, Cinnabon, Hershey's Ice Cream, Sbarro
(253)		**Parking Area (EB)**
(254)		**Parking Area (WB)**
(255)		**Parking Area (WB)**
(258)		**Lawn Service Plaza (WB)**
	FStop	Sunoco
	Food	Burger King, Cinnabon, Hot Dog City, Hershey's Ice Cream, Starbucks
	Other	RV Dump
(263)		**Parking Area (EB)**
(264)		**Parking Area (EB)**
266		**PA 72, Lebanon Rd, Manheim, Lebanon, Lancaster**
	FStop	N: Hess Express #38429
	Gas	N: Mobil
	Food	N: Blimpie/Hess, Café
	Lodg	N: Red Carpet Inn, Rodeway Inn, Farmers Hope Inn♥ & Restaurant S: Hampton Inn
	Med	N: + Hospital (in Lebanon)
	Other	N: Auto Service, Harley Davidson, Pinch Pond Family Campground▲, to Starlite Camping Resort▲, Refreshing Mountain Camp▲ S: Auto Service, Mt Hope Winery, Gretna Oaks Campground▲
(268)		**Parking Area (EB)**
(269)		**Parking Area (EB)**
(270)		**Parking Area (EB)**
(280)		**Truck Inspection Station (WB)**
286		**US 222, to PA 272, Denver, Reading, Lancaster**
	FStop	N: Al's Exxon
	Gas	N: Citgo◈, Shell◈ S: Sunoco
	Food	N: Park Place Diner & Rest, Zia Maria Ital Rest, Rest/Black Horse Lodge
	Food	S: Casual's Neighborhood Café, Baskin Robbins/Dunkin Donuts
	Lodg	N: Black Horse Lodge, PA Dutch Motel, Penn Amish Motel S: Comfort Inn♥, Econo Lodge, Holiday Inn, Red Carpet Inn

EXIT		PENNSYLVANIA
	Other	N: Dutch Cousins Camping▲, Shady Grove Campground▲, to Hickory Run Family Campground▲, Lake in Wood Resort▲, Oak Creek Campground▲, Starlite Camping Resort▲, to Cocalico Creek Campground▲, Refreshing Mountain Camp▲, to Sun Valley Campground▲, Reading Outlet Center S: Red Run Campground▲, to Dutch Wonderland, Lancaster Outlet Center, Tanger Outlet Center, Rockvale Outlets
(289)		**PA State Hwy Patrol Post (EB)**
(290)		**Bowmansville Service Plaza (EB)**
	FStop	Sunoco
	Food	Chicken Express, Hershey's Ice Cream, Pizza Hut Express, Snack Bar, Starbucks
(291)		**Parking Area (EB)**
(294)		**Parking Area (WB)**
(295)		**Parking Area (EB)**
(297)		**Parking Area (EB)**
(298)		**Jct I-176, PA 10, Morgantown Expy, Reading, Morgantown**
	Gas	S: Exxon, Sheetz
	Food	N: Rest/Heritage Motel S: McDonald's, Rest/Holiday Inn
	Lodg	N: Heritage Motel S: Holiday Inn♥, Red Carpet Inn
	Med	N: + St Joseph Medical Center S: + Reading Hospital
	Other	N:Walmart, to Lake in Wood Resort▲, Sun Valley Campground▲, to VF Outlet Village, Maple Grove Raceway, to French Creek State Park S: ATMs, Banks, Animal Hospital♥, RiteAid, to Berry Patch Campground▲
(300)		**Parking Area (WB)**
(305)		**Peter J Camiel Service Plaza (WB)**
	FStop	Sunoco
	Food	Cinnabon, Hershey's Ice Cream, Nathan's, Roy Rogers, Sbarro, Starbucks
312		**PA 100, Exton, Chester Springs, Pottstown, W Chester, Downington**
	Gas	N: Valero S: Sunoco◈, WaWa
	Food	S: Hoss's Steak & Sea House, Quiznos, Red Robin, Starbucks
	Lodg	S: Best Western, Comfort Inn, Extended Stay America, Fairfield Inn, Hampton Inn, Holiday Inn Express, Residence Inn
	Med	S: + Hospital
	Other	N: Smaltz Harley Davidson S: ATMs, Banks, QVC Studio Park, to Mall, Target, Shady Acres Campground▲, Brandywine Creek Campground▲, Marsh Creek State Park
(325)		**Valley Forge Service Plaza (EB)**
	FStop	Sunoco
	Food	Burger King, Nathan's, Pizza Uno, Starbucks

NOTE: I-76 WB above runs with PA Tpk. EB continues as I-276.

NOTE: Begin WB TOLL, End EB on I-76

NOTE: Begin WB, End EB Call Box Area WB for next 326 mi

EXIT		PENNSYLVANIA
(326)		**Jct I-76, I-276E/PA Tpk, to US 202, Valley Forge, Bristol, New Jersey (fr EB, Left exit)**
327		**PA 363, Gulph Rd, Mall Blvd, King of Prussia, to Valley Forge**
	Gas	N: Exxon◈
	Food	N: Ruth's Chris Steak House
	Lodg	S: Holiday Inn Express, Homestead Suites, MainStay Suites, McIntosh Inn, Radisson, Sheraton, Sleep Inn, Scanticon Valley Forge Motel
	Other	N: King of Prussia Mall S: Valley Forge Convention Center, AmeriGas/LP
328A		**US 202S, DeKalb Pike, to US 422, West Chester, Norristown**
	Other	S: PetSmart♥, Staples, Trader Joe's, UPS Store
328B		**US 202N, DeKalb Pike, King of Prussia**
	Gas	N: Exxon◈, Lukoil, Mobil, Sunoco, WaWa
	Food	N: Arby's, Burger King, CA Café, Chili's, ChickFilA, Friendly's, Lone Star Steakhouse, KFC, McDonald's, Morton's Steakhouse, Ruby King of Prussia Diner, Starbucks, Subway, Sullivan's Steakhouse, TGI Friday
	Lodg	N: Best Western, Comfort Inn, Crowne Plaza, Econo Lodge, Fairfield Inn, Holiday Inn, Motel 6♥
	Other	N: ATMs, Auto Services, Banks, Best Buy, Borders, Costco, Cinemas, IMAX, King of Prussia Mall, PetCo♥, Pharmacy, Staples, Tires, UPS Store
330		**PA 320, Gulph Rd, Gulph Mills**
	Other	S: to Villanova Univ, Valley Forge Military Academy
(331A)		**Jct I-476S, Veterans Memorial Hwy, Chester (fr WB, Left exit)**
(331B)		**Jct I-476N, Veterans Memorial Hwy, Plymouth Meeting, PA 23, Conshohocken (EB)**
332		**PA 23, Conshohocken (WB)**
337		**Hollow Rd, River Rd, Gladwyne (WB)**
338		**Belmont Ave, Green Lane, Philadelphia**
	Gas	S: Sunoco, WaWa
	Med	N: + Roxborough Memorial Hospital
	Other	N: Pharmacy
339		**US 1S, City Line Ave (fr WB, Left exit)**
	Lodg	S: Holiday Inn, Homewood Suites, NA Motor Inn
	Other	N: to Philadelphia Univ S: to St Joseph's Univ
340A		**Kelly Dr, Lincoln Dr, to Germantown (fr EB, Left Exit)**
	Med	N: + Roxborough Memorial Hospital
	Other	N: CVS
340B		**US 1N, Roosevelt Blvd, Philadelphia (fr EB, Left Exit)**
341		**Montgomery Dr, W River Dr (NO Trucks Permitted)**
342		**US 13, US 30W, Girard Ave, Philadelphia**
	Gas	S: Sunoco

◈ = Regular Gas Stations with Diesel ▲ = RV Friendly Locations ♥ = Pet Friendly Locations
Red print shows large vehicle parking / access on site or nearby Brown Print = Campgrounds / RV PARKS

EXIT		PENNSYLVANIA
	Other	**N:** Girard College **S:** Philadelphia Zoo
343		**Spring Garden St, Haverford Ave (EB)**
(344)		**Jct I-676E, US 30, Vine St, Central Philadelphia (fr EB, Left Exit, NO EB re-entry)**
345		**30th St, Market St (exit only)**
	Other	**S:** Amtrak, Drexel Univ
346A		**South St, Philadelphia (Left exit)**
	Med	**S:** + Childrens Hospital, + Univ of PA Hospital
	Other	**S:** Univ of PA
346B		**Grays Ferry Ave, University Ave (fr WB, Exit only)**
	Other	**S:** Civic Center
346C		**28th St (EB), Vare Ave (WB)**
347		**Passyunk Ave (WB)**
	Med	**N:** + Methodist Hospital
347A		**Penrose Ave, to PA 291, to I-95S (EB, Left exit)**
	Other	**S:** to Philadelphia Int'l Airport✈, Sun Oil, Gulf Oil, Commanders Naval Base
347B		**Passyunk Ave, Oregon Ave (fr EB, Left Exit)**

EXIT		PENNSYLVANIA
348		**PA 291W, Penrose Ave, to Chester (WB, Left Exit)**
	Lodg	**S:** America's Best Inn
	Other	**S:** Philadelphia Int'l Airport✈
349		**PA 611, Broad St, Sports Complex**
	Gas	**N:** Sunoco
	Med	**N:** + Methodist Hospital
	Other	**S:** Lincoln Financial Field, Citizens Bank Park, Wachovia Center, PA Naval Business Center
350		**Packer Ave, 7th St, to I-95 (EB, Exit Only)**
	TStop	**S:** to 3540 S Lawrence: Walt Whitman Truck Stop (Scales)
	Food	**S:** Rest/WW TS
	Lodg	**S:** Holiday Inn
	TServ	**S:** WW TS/Tires
	Other	**S:** Laundry/**RVDump**/WW TS, Ports
351		**Vietnam Veterans Memorial Hwy, Front St, to I-95, N to Trenton, S to Chester (WB)**
(352)		**Neshaminy Service Plaza (WB)**
	FStop	Sunoco
	Food	Burger King, Nathan's, Starbucks Breyers, McDonald's, Nathan's
358		**US 13, Delaware**
	Gas	**N:** WaWa **S:** Getty, Mobil, Sunoco

EXIT		PA / NJ
	Lodg	**S:** Comfort Inn

EASTERN TIME ZONE

NOTE: **MM 359: New Jersey State Line**

PENNSYLVANIA

NEW JERSEY

EASTERN TIME ZONE

(2)		**Jct I-676N, I-76WB**
1D		**US 130N, PA 168, to NJ Tpk, Camden Waterfront, Blackhorse Pike (WB)**
1C		**US 130S, Market St, Brooklawn, Westville**
(1B)		**Jct I-295N, to NJ Tpk, Trenton**
(1A)		**Jct I-295S, DE Memorial Bridge**
(0)		**NJ 42S, Atlantic City**

NEW JERSEY

Begin Westbound I-76 from Jct I-295 in NJ to Jct I-71 near Cleveland, OH.

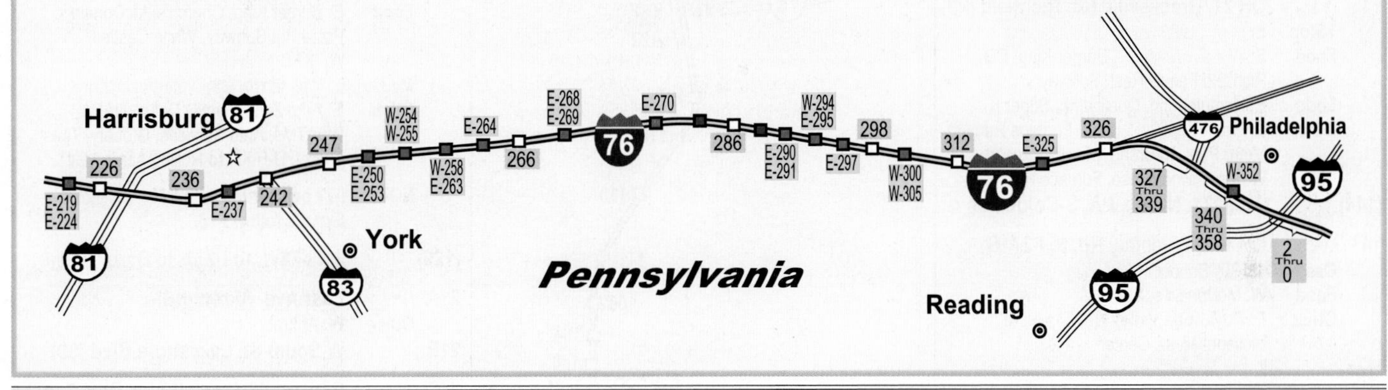

EXIT		OHIO

Begin Southboundl - 77 from Jct I-90 in Cleveland, OH to Jct I-26 in Columbia, SC.

OHIO

NOTE: **I-77 Starts/Ends on I-26, Exit #116 in SC**

EASTERN TIME ZONE

163C		**E 9th St, Carnegie Ave, Cleveland**
	Other	**W:** ATMs, Jacobs Field, Gund Arena, to Cleveland Conv Center, Cleveland Browns Stadium, Rock & Roll Hall of Fame
(163AB)		**Jct I-90, W-Toledo, E- Erie, PA (NB)**
162B		**E 22nd, E 14th (NB)**
	Med	**E:** + St Vincent Charity Hospital

EXIT		OHIO
162A		**E 30th St, Woodland Ave, to US 422, OH 8, OH 43**
(161B)		**Jct I-490W, to I-71, E 55th St, Toledo to I-90W**
161A		**OH 14, Broadway Ave (NB)**
160		**Pershing Ave (NB)**
	Med	**E:** + St Michael Hospital
159B		**Fleet Ave, Cleveland**
	Gas	**E:** BP◈
	Food	**E:** Subway/BP
159A		**Harvard Ave, Newburgh Heights**
	FStop	**W:** Speedway #3328
	Gas	**W:** BP◈, Marathon
	Food	**W:** Subway/BP
	Other	**W:** WiFi/Speedway

EXIT		OHIO
158		**Grant Ave, Cuyahoga Heights**
157		**OH 21, OH 17, E 71st St, Brecksville Rd, Granger Rd (SB)**
	Other	**E:** Tires **W:** Vet♥
(156)		**Jct I-480, to Toledo, Youngstown**
	Other	**W:** to Cleveland Hopkins Int'l Airport✈, Cleveland Metroparks Zoo
155		**Rockside Rd, Seven Hills, Independence**
	Gas	**E:** Shell, Sunoco **W:** BP◈
	Food	**E:** Bob Evans, Bonefish Grill, Delmonico's, Denny's, McDonald's, Outback Steakhouse, Shula Steak House, Wendy's, Rest/Hol Inn **W:** Applebee's, Damon's, Red Lobster, Longhorn Steakhouse, Rest/Clarion

EXIT		OHIO
	Lodg	E: Baymont Inn, Comfort Inn, DoubleTree Hotel, Embassy Suites, Holiday Inn, Red Roof Inn♥
		W: Clarion, Courtyard, Hampton Inn, Hyatt Place, Residence Inn, Sheraton
	Med	W: + Urgent Care
	Other	E: ATMs, Banks, Auto Repair, NTB, Carwash/Shell, Walgreen's, to Garfield Mall **Cuyahoga Valley Nat'l Park**
		W: ATMs, Banks, **to** Shopping Center, Grocery, Office Max, Pharmacy
153		**Pleasant Valley Rd, Seven Hills, Independence**
151		**Wallings Rd, Broadview Hts**
149		**OH 82, Broadview Hts (NB)**
149AB		**OH 82, E Royalton Rd, Brecksville, Broadview Heights (SB)**
	Gas	E: BP
	Food	W: Boneyard Grill, CoCo's, Domino's Pizza
	Lodg	W: Tally Ho
	Other	E: Golf Course, Museum, **Cuyahoga Valley National Park, Brecksville Reservation**
147		**Miller Rd, to OH 21 (SB)**
	Other	E: BF Goodrich Headquarters
(146)		**I-80/OH Tpk (TOLL), to Toledo, Youngstown, OH 21, Brecksville Rd (Access #145 Serv before Toll)**
145		**OH 21, Brecksville Rd, Richfield (NB)**
	TStop	E: Pilot Travel Center #130 (Scales)
	Food	E: Wendy's/Pilot TC, Burger King, DQ, Richfield Family Rest, Subway
	Lodg	E: Hampton Inn, Quality Inn, Super 8
	Other	E: Laundry/WiFi/Pilot TC, Furnace Run Metro Park, **to** Brandywine Ski Resort
		W: Brushwood Lake, Furnace Run Park
(144)		**Jct I-271, N-Erie, PA, S-Columbus**
143		**OH 176, Wheatley Rd, to I-271S**
	Gas	W: BP, Sunoco
	Food	W: McDonald's, Subway
	Other	E: **Cuyahoga Valley Nat'l Park, to** Blossom Music Center
(141)		**Rest Area (Both dir) (RR, Phones, Picnic, Vend)**
138		**Ghent Rd, Akron**
	Gas	W: Circle K◈
	Food	W: Vaccaro's Italian Rest
	Other	E: **to Sand Run Metro Park**
		W: **to Bath Nature Preserve**
137AB		**OH 18, Medina Rd, Akron, Fairlawn, Medina**
	Gas	E: BP, Circle K, Marathon, Shell, Speedway
		W: Citgo
	Food	E: Applebee's, Baja Fresh Mex Grill, Bob Evans, Chili's, Chipolte Mex Grill, Cracker Barrel, Friendly's, Golden Corral, Max & Erma's, Lonestar Steakhouse, McDonald's,
	Food	E: Olive Garden, Red Lobster, Panera Bread, Romano's Macaroni Grill, Ruby Tuesday, Steak 'n Shake, Starbucks, Taco Bell, Wendy's
		W: Burger King, Damon's, Don Pablo, Fuddrucker's, Mario's, Outback Steakhouse TGI Friday
	Lodg	E: Courtyard, Holiday Inn, Hampton Inn, Motel 6, Quality Inn, Super 8, Hilton, Sheraton

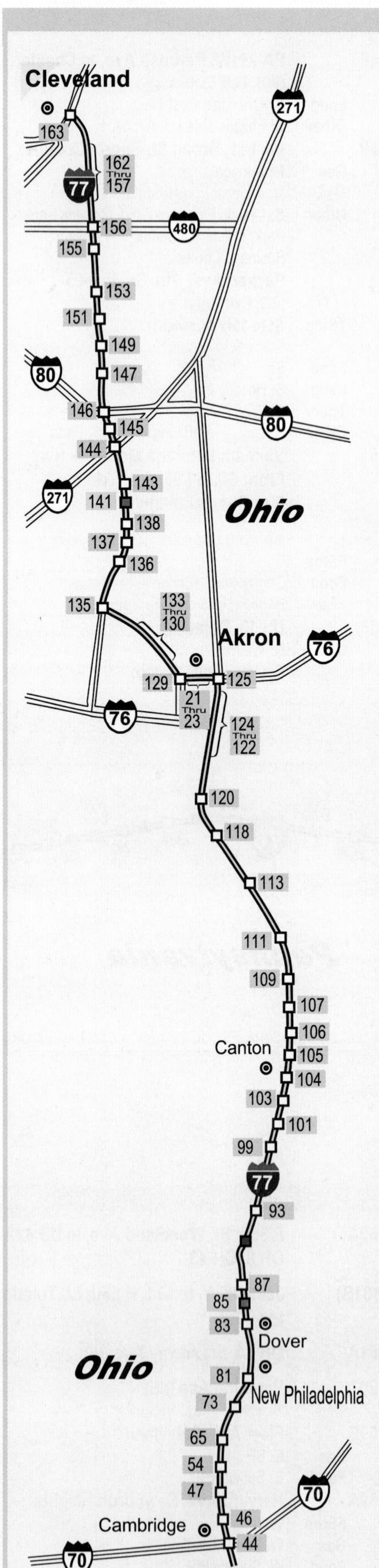

EXIT		OHIO
	Lodg	W: Best Western, Comfort Inn, Extended Stay America, Radisson, Residence Inn, Studio Plus
	Med	E: + Medical Clinic
	Other	E: ATMs, Auto Services, Bank, Best Buy, FedEx Office, Firestone, Goodyear, NTB, Grocery, Home Depot, Lowe's, Office Max, PetSmart♥, Pharmacy, RiteAid, Sam's Club, Staples, Target, **Walmart**, UPS Store, Summit Mall, to Univ of Akron, to Hale Farm & Village, **to** Blossom Music Center
		W: ATM, Bank, Medina Muni Airport✈, **Avalon RV & Marine**
136		**OH 21S, to Massillon (fr NB, Left exit)**
135		**CR 17, Cleveland-Massillon Rd (NB)**
133		**Ridgewood Rd, Miller Rd, Akron**
	Gas	E: Citgo◈
	Food	E: Wendy's
132		**White Pond Rd Dr, Mull Ave**
131		**OH 162, Copley Rd, Akron**
	Gas	E: Citgo
		W: BP◈, Marathon◈
	Food	E: China Star, Church's, Pizza
		W: McDonald's, Pizza Hut
	Other	E: Grocery, US Post Office, **to** Akron Zoo
130		**OH 261, Wooster Ave, Vernon Odom Blvd, Akron**
	Gas	E: BP, Circle K
	Food	E: Burger King, Church's, McDonald's, Pizza Hut Subway, White Castle
		W: KFC
	Med	E: + to Akron Gen'l Medical Center
	Other	E: Auto Zone, Family Dollar, NAPA
		W: ATMs, Auto Services, Grocery, Tires, Target, U-Haul, **to** Rolling Acres Mall
	NOTE:	**I-77 below runs with I-76. Exit #'s follow I-76.**
(129)		**Jct I-76W, to I-277, to Barberton**
21A		**East Ave, Akron (NB)**
	Other	W: Amtrak
21B		**W South St, Lakeshore Blvd (SB)**
21C		**Bowery St, Russell Ave, Dart Ave, to OH 59, Akron**
22A		**Main St, Broadway St**
	Other	W: Zeigler Tire
22B		**Wolf Ledges Pkwy, Grant St**
	Other	E: Center Auto Machine Gas & Diesel Shop
		W: Greyhound Bus Lines
(23A/ 125B)		**Jct I-76E, to Youngstown I-77S, to Canton**
	NOTE:	**I-77 above runs with I-76. Exit #'s follow I-76.**
125A		**OH 8N, to Cuyahoga**
124B		**Lovers Lane, Cole Ave, Akron**
124A		**Archwood Ave, Firestone Blvd**
123B		**OH 764, Wilbeth Rd, Waterloo Rd**
	Other	E: Akron Fulton Int'l Airport✈
123A		**Waterloo Rd**
(122AB)		**Jct I-277, US 224E, to I-76, Akron, Barberton, Mogadore**
	Other	E: Akron Fulton Int'l Airport✈

◈= Regular Gas Stations with Diesel ▲ = RV Friendly Locations ♥= Pet Friendly Locations
Red print shows large vehicle parking / access on site or nearby Brown Print = Campgrounds / RV PARKS

EXIT | OHIO

120 **CR 15, Arlington Rd, Akron, Green**
- Gas: E: Speedway◊; W: BP, Speedway
- Food: E: Applebee's, Denny's, Friendly's, IHOP, Pizza Hut, Ryan's Grill, Waffle House, White Castle; W: Bob Evans, Burger King, Blimpie, IHOP, McDonald's, Starbucks, Subway, Taco Bell, Wendy's, White Castle
- Lodg: E: Comfort Inn, Quality Inn, Red Roof Inn♥; W: Fairfield Inn, Hampton Inn
- Other: E: ATMs, Banks, Dollar General, Home Depot, Pharmacy, **Walmart**; W: ATMs, Auto Service, Auto Dealers, Goodyear, Grocery, Regal Cinema 18, **Camping World**, **Sirpilla RV**, **to Portage Lakes State Park▲**

118 **OH 241, Massillon Rd, to OH 619, Green, Uniontown**
- Gas: E: Speedway◊; W: Circle K, GetGo
- Food: E: Pizza, Subway; W: Arby's, Lucky Star Chinese, Lunch Box Deli, McDonald's, Menches Bros Rest, Quiznos
- Lodg: W: Cambria Suites, Super 8
- Other: W: ATMs, Banks, Grocery, **to Portage Lakes State Park▲**

113 **Akron-Canton Reg'l Airport, Canton**
- Lodg: W: Hilton Garden Inn
- Other: W: Akron Canton Reg'l Airport✈, Tourist Info, **Clay's RV Center**

111 **Portage St, North Canton**
- TStop: E: Travel Center of America #95/Marathon (Scales)
- Gas: E: Circle K, Sunoco◊; W: BP◊, Speedway, Sam's Club
- Food: E: CountryPride/TA TC, Burger King, KFC, Geisen Haus, Subway; W: Carrabba's, **Cracker Barrel**, Don Pablo, Einstein Bros Bagels, IHOP, Longhorn Steakhouse, McDonald's, Panera, Pizza Hut, Quiznos, Red Robin, Starbucks, Taco Bell, Wendy's
- Lodg: W: Best Western, Microtel, Motel 6♥
- TWash: E: TA TC
- TServ: E: TA TC/Tires
- Other: E: Laundry/WiFi/TA TC, Auto Services, Car Wash, Cinemark 10; W: ATMs, Banks, BJ's, Best Buy, Borders, Freedom Harley Davidson, Gander Mountain, Grocery, Home Depot, Lowe's, Office Max, Sam's Club, **Walmart**, Tinseltown, **to** Kent State Univ/Stark

109 **Everhard Rd, Whipple Ave (SB)**
- Food: W: Bob Evans, Boston Market, CiCi's Pizza, Chili's, ChickFilA, DQ, Friendly's, Hometown Buffet, Max & Erma's, Panera Bread, Quiznos, Ruby Tuesday, Starbucks, Steak Escape, Taco Bell
- Lodg: W: Courtyard, Days Inn, Holiday Inn, Knights Inn♥, Parke Resident Suites, Red Roof Inn♥
- Other: W: ATMs, Auto Services, Banks, Belden Village Mall, NTB, PetSmart♥, Pharmacy, Tires, Target

109B **Everhard Ave (NB)**
- Gas: E: Citgo, Speedway◊
- Food: E: Burger King, Denny's, Fazoli's, McDonald's, Subway, Taco Bell, Waffle House

Personal Notes

EXIT | OHIO

- Lodg: E: Comfort Inn, Fairfield Inn, Hampton Inn♥, Residence Inn♥
- Other: E: **Little Guy Teardrop Camper Sales**

109A **Whipple Ave, Everhard Rd (NB)**
- Gas: W: Marathon
- Food: W: Applebee's, Arby's, Bob Evans, Damon's, Eat 'n Park, Fuddrucker's, Lone Star Steakhouse, Mulligan's Pub, Outback Steakhouse, Olive Garden, Pizza Hut, Ponderosa, Red Lobster, Romano's Macaroni Grill, Subway, TGI Friday, Wendy's
- Lodg: W: Days Inn, Knights Inn, Sheraton
- Other: W: ATMs, Auto Service, Belden Village Mall, Best Buy, Firestone, FedEx Office, Office Max, PetCo♥, Radio Shack, Target, UPS Store, **to** Kent State Univ/Stark

107B **US 62, Canton, to Alliance**
- Other: E: Malone College, **to** Mt Union College

107A **OH 687, Fulton Rd, Fulton Dr**
- Gas: E: Marathon; W: Circle K
- Food: E: Subway, Woody's Rootbeer Stand
- Other: W: Pro Football Hall of Fame

106 **13th St NW, 12th St NW, Canton**
- Med: E: + Mercy Medical Center
- Other: E: Pharmacy, Civic Center, McKinley Presidential Museum, Discovery World

105B **OH 172, Tuscarawas St (SB)**

105A **6th St SW (SB, diff reaccess)**

105 **OH 172, W Tuscarawas St (NB)**
- Gas: E: Stop n Go, Sunoco; W: Citgo
- Food: E: McDonald's, Subway; W: Hungry Howie's Pizza, KFC

EXIT | OHIO

- Med: W: + Aultman Hospital
- Other: E: Water Works Park, Discover World, McKinley Museum, National First Ladies Museum; W: Laundromat, Pharmacy, **to** Shopping Center, Perry Diesel Services, Stark Co Fairgrounds

104B **US 30, US 62W, East Liverpool, Massillon (NB)**

104A **OH 30E, East Liverpool (NB)**

104 **US 30, US 62, East Liverpool, Downtown Canton, Massillon (SB)**

103 **OH 800S, Cleveland Ave, Canton**
- Gas: E: Citgo, Speedway
- Food: E: Arby's, Burger King, McDonald's, Subway, Taco Bell, Waffle House

101 **OH 627, Faircrest St, Canton**
- TStop: E: Gulliver's 77 Travel Plaza/Citgo (Scales)
- Gas: E: Speedway, Shell
- Food: E: Rest/Gulliver's TP, Wendy's, McDonald's/Speedway
- Other: E: Laundry/CB/Gulliver's TP

99 **Fohl St SW, to Navarre**
- Gas: W: Shell
- Other: E: **to appr 4.5 mi: Bear Creek Resort Ranch/KOA▲**

93 **OH 212, Bolivar, to Zoar**
- Gas: E: Speedway; W: Citgo
- Food: E: McDonald's, Pizza Hut, Subway, Wendy's; W: DQ/Citgo
- Lodg: E: Sleep Inn
- Other: E: Golf Course, Grocery, NAPA, Pharmacy, **to Bear Creek Resort Ranch/KOA▲**

(92) **Weigh Station (Both dir)**

87 **US 250, CR 74, Wooster Ave, to OH 21, Dover, Strasburg, Massillon, Wooster**
- FStop: W: Sibley Fuel Mart
- Gas: W: Citgo◊
- Food: W: Lugnut Café, McDonald's, Quiznos, Rosalie's Rest, Subway
- Lodg: W: Ramada Ltd, Twins Motel

(85) **Rest Area (Both dir) (RR, Phones, Picnic)**

83 **OH 39, OH 211, Dover, Amish Country, to Sugarcreek, Dover**
- Gas: E: BP, Speedway◊; W: Marathon
- Food: E: Bob Evans, KFC, McDonald's, Shoney's, Subway, Wendy's; W: DQ/Marathon
- Lodg: E: Hospitality Inn; W: Comfort Inn
- Med: E: + Hospital
- Other: E: Auto Dealers, Vet♥, Ziegler Tire

81 **US 250W, US 250 Bus, OH 39, W High Ave, CR 21, CR 52, Dover, New Philadelphia**
- TStop: W: Eagle Auto Truck Plaza/BP
- Gas: E: Kwik Fill, Sheetz, Speedway
- Food: E: Rest/Eagle ATP, Burger King, Denny's, Hog Heaven BBQ, Hong Kong Chinese, Long John Silver, McDonald's, Pizza Hut, Taco Bell, Texas Roadhouse

◊= Regular Gas Stations with Diesel ▲ = RV Friendly Locations ♥= Pet Friendly Locations
Red print shows large vehicle parking / access on site or nearby Brown Print = Campgrounds / RV PARKS

EXIT — OHIO

Lodg — E: Hampton Inn, Holiday Inn, Knights Inn♥ Motel 6♥, Schoenbrunn Inn, Super 8
TServ — W: Peterbilt
Med — E: + Hospital
Other — E: ATMs, Advance Auto Parts, ,Grocery, **Walmart sc**, U-Haul, Tourist Info, Schoenbrunn Village
W: Adventure Harley Davidson, **RV Park▲**

73 — OH 751, CR 21, Stone Creek
Gas — W: Marathon

65 — US 36, Newcomerstown, Coshocton, Port Washington
TStop — W: Newcomerstown Truck Stop/Duke (Scales)
Gas — W: BP, Marathon
Food — W: Duke's Fam Rest, McDonald's, Wendy's
Lodg — W: Hampton Inn, Super 8
TServ — W: Duke TS/Tires
Other — W: Laundry/Duke TS, **to** Tri City Airport✈, **To appr 16 mi: Roscoe Colonial RV Resort▲**

54 — OH 541, CR 831, Plainfield Rd, Kimbolton
Gas — W: BP
Food — W: Jackie's Family Rest
Other — E: **to appr 6 mi: Big Sky Campground▲ , Appr 10 mi: Salt Fork State Park▲**

47 — US 22, Cadiz Rd, Cambridge, Cadiz
Gas — W: BP
Med — W: + Hospital
Other — E: **to appr 4.5mi: Hillview Acres Campground▲ , to Salt Fork State Park, to appr 9.5 mi: Winterset Lakes Campground▲ ,**
W: to Austin Lake Park & Campground▲

46 — US 40, Wheeling Ave, Cambridge, Old Washington (SB)

46B — US 40, Cambridge, Old Washington
FStop — W: FuelMart #708/Ashland
Gas — W: BP, Exxon◊, Speedway◊
Food — W: Burger King, J&K Rest, McDonald's, Long John Silver, Exxon/Wendy's
Lodg — W: Longs Motel
Other — W: ATMs, Auto Repairs, Grocery

46A — US 40E, Old Washington (NB)

(44B) — Jct I-70W, Cambridge, to Columbus (fr NB, Left exit) (TStop, Gas, Food, Lodg avail @ 1st exit W, # 178 on I-70)
Med — W: + Hospital
Other — W: ATMs, Tourist Info, Winery, Shopping, Museum , **Spring Valley Campground▲ ,** Cambridge Muni Airport✈

(44A) — Jct I-70E, to Wheeling, WV

41 — OH 209, OH 821, CR 35, Main St, Byesville
Gas — W: BP◊, KwikFill, Starfire Express
Food — W: McDonald's
Other — W: Family Dollar, Grocery, Cambridge Muni Airport✈

(40) — Rest Area (NB) (RR, Phones, Picnic, Vend)

37 — OH 313, Clay Pike Rd, Pleasant City, Senecaville, Buffalo City
Gas — E: BP, Duke
Food — E: Buffalo Grill, BBQ, Subway
TServ — E: Truck Service
Other — E: US Post Office, **to approx 7mi Buffalo Hills Camping Resort▲** , Senecaville

EXIT — OH / WV

Other — E: Lake, **to appr 8 mi: Seneca Lakes Park & Marina▲**

(36) — Rest Area (SB) (RR, Phones, Picnic, Vend)

28 — OH 821, Main St, Public Rd, Caldwell, Belle Valley
Gas — E: Sunoco◊
Food — E: Marianne's Rest
Other — E: Grocery, US Post Office, **Wolf Run State Park▲** , Noble Co Airport✈

25 — OH 78, Caldwell, Woodsfield
TStop — E: Pilot Travel Center #309 (Scales)
Gas — E: BP, Sunoco◊
Food — E: Arby's/TJCinn/Pilot TC, Lori's Family Rest, McDonald's, Subway/Sunoco
Lodg — E: Best Western
Other — E: Laundry/WiFi/Pilot TC, ATM, Auto Repair, Tourist Info, US Post Office

16 — OH 821, Macksburg, Dexter City

6 — OH 821, Marietta, Lower Salem
FStop — W: Miller's AmPm/BP
Gas — E: Exxon
Lodg — W: Best Western
Med — W: + Hospital

(4) — OH Welcome Center (NB) (RR, Phones, Picnic, Vend, Info)

1 — OH 7, Newport Pike, Marietta
TStop — E: Go Mart #58
Gas — W: BP◊, Duke◊, Speedway◊
Food — E: China Gate, CiCi's Pizza, DQ, Ryan's Grill
W: Applebee's, Arby's, Bob Evans, Burger King, Captain D's, KFC, McDonald's, Pizza Hut, Shoney's, Subway, Taco Bell, Wendy's
Lodg — E: Comfort Inn♥, Economy Lodge, Holiday Inn, Lafayette Hotel
W: Best Value Inn, Hampton Inn, Super 8
Med — W: + Marietta Memorial Hospital
Other — E: ATMs, Auto Dealers, Grocery, Lowe's, Harley Davidson, **Walmart sc**, **Landing's Family Campground▲ , Marietta RV & Outdoor World**
W: ATMs, Auto Zone, Big Lots, Carwash, CVS, Kroger, Marietta College, **OH State Hwy Patrol**

EASTERN TIME ZONE

⬆ OHIO
⬇ WEST VIRGINIA

NOTE: MM 186: Ohio State Line

EASTERN TIME ZONE

185 — WV 14, WV 31, Highland Ave, Williamstown, Vienna WV Welcome Center/Rest Area
Gas — W: 7-11, Gas n Goods
Food — W: Family Rest, Subway
Lodg — W: Days Inn
Other — W: **to** Fenton Art Glass Factory Tour

179 — WV 2N, WV 68, Emerson Ave, North Parkersburg, Vienna
Gas — E: Exxon
W: BP

EXIT — WEST VIRGINIA

Lodg — W: Red Carpet Inn
Med — W: + Camden Clark Memorial Hospital
Other — E: Wood Co Airport/Mid OH Valley Reg'l Airport✈
W: **to** OH Valley College

176 — US 50, 7th St, Dowtown Parkersburg Clarksburg
Gas — W: 7-11, GoMart, Speedway, Kroger
Food — W: Bob Evans, Burger King, Long John Silver, McDonald's, Mountaineer Family Rest, Omelet Shoppe, Shoney's, Wendy's
Lodg — W: Knights Inn, Motel 6♥, Parkersburg Inn, Red Roof Inn♥
Other — E: **to N Bend State Park**

174 — WV 47, Staunton Ave, Davisville
Gas — E: Exxon◊
W: Citgo
Other — E: WVU/Parkersburg
W: **to** Oil & Gas Museum

173 — WV 95, Camden Ave, Downtown Parkersburg
Gas — E: Marathon◊
W: BP
Food — W: Hardee's
Med — W: + Hospital

170 — WV 14, Mineral Wells
FStop — E: Pifer's Service Center/BP
TStop — E: PTP/Liberty Truck Stop (Scales), New Parkersburg Truck Stop (Scales)
Gas — E: Chevron
Food — E: Rest/Liberty TS, FastFood/NP TS, McDonald's, Subway, Taco Bell, Wendy's
W: Cracker Barrel
Lodg — E: Comfort Suites, Hampton
W: AmeriHost, Microtel
TWash — E: Liberty TS
TServ — E: Liberty TS/Tires, NP TS/Tires
Other — E: Laundry/CB/WiFi/Liberty TS, Laundry/WiFi/NP TS, US Post Office, WV Motor Speedway

(169) — Weigh Station (Both dir)

(167) — WV Welcome Center (SB) Rest Area (NB) (RR, Phones, Picnic, Vend, RVDump)

161 — CR 21, CR 17, Rockport

154 — CR 1, Medina Rd

146 — WV 2S, US 33W, Ravenswood, to WV 68, Silverton
Gas — W: BP◊, Exxon, Marathon◊
Lodg — W: Scottish Inns
Other — W: **Camping▲**

138 — US 33E, WV 62S, Ripley
TStop — E: Love's Travel Stop #378
Gas — E: BP◊, Exxon, Marathon
W: Exxon◊
Food — E: Chesters/McDonald's/Love's TS KFC, Long John Silver, McDonald's, Pizza Hut, Taco Bell, Wendy's, Rest/BW
W: Ponderosa, Shoney's, Subway
Lodg — E: Best Western, Super 8
W: Holiday Inn Express
Med — W: + Jackson General Hospital
Other — E: ATMs, Cinema, Kroger, NAPA, RiteAid, Tractor Supply, **Walmart**, **Ruby Lake Campground▲**

132 — WV 21, Ripley, Fairplain
FStop — E: Fairplain 7-11/BP #5521, Go Mart #33

◊ = Regular Gas Stations with Diesel ▲ = RV Friendly Locations ♥ = Pet Friendly Locations
Red print shows large vehicle parking / access on site or nearby Brown Print = Campgrounds / RV PARKS

EXIT		WEST VIRGINIA
	Food	E: Burger King/BP
	Lodg	W: 77 Motor Inn
	TServ	E: International
	Other	E: RV Park▲
124		**WV 34, CR 19, Kentuck Rd, Kenna**
	Gas	E: Exxon
	Food	E: Family Rest
119		**WV 21, Kenna, Goldtown**
116		**CR 21, Haines Branch, Sissonville, Charleston**
	Other	E: Ripplin Waters Campground▲
114		**WV 622, Sissonville Dr, Charleston, Pocatalico, Sissonville**
	Gas	E: Mountain Mart Gas & Grocery
111		**CR 29, Tuppers Creek Rd**
	Gas	W: BP◈
	Food	W: Subway/BP
106		**CR 27, Edens Fork Rd**
	Gas	W: Chevron◈
(104)		**Jct I-79N, to Clarksburg**
102		**US 119, Westmoreland Rd, O'Dell Ave, Crescent Rd, Charleston**
	Gas	E: 7-11, BP, Go Mart
	Food	E: China Garden, Hardee's
	Lodg	E: Paisley Motor Inn
	Other	E: Pharmacy, Grocery, Yeager Airport✈
	NOTE:	**I-77 below follows I-64 between Charleston and Beckley. Exit #'s follow I-77.**
(101/59)		**Jct I-64, W to Huntington, E to Beckley**
100		**Broad St, Capitol St, Charleston**
	Gas	W: Chevron
	Lodg	W: Fairfield Inn, Holiday Inn, Super 8, Embassy Suites, Marriott
	Med	W: + St Francis Hospital
	Other	W: CVS, Kroger, Charlestown Town Center Mall
99		**WV 114, Greenbrier St, State Capitol**
	Gas	W: Citgo, Exxon
	Food	W: Domino's Pizza, McDonald's, Wendy's
	Other	E: Yeager Airport✈ W: to State Capitol, Museum
98		**WV 61, 35th St Bridge (SB)**
	Gas	W: Sunoco
	Food	W: McDonald's, Shoney's, Subway, TacoBell/KFC, Wendy's
	Med	W: + Hospital
	Other	W: Univ of Charleston, WVU
97		**US 60W, Midland Trail, Kanawha Blvd Charleston (NB)**
96		**US 60E, Midland Trail, Belle**
	Food	E: Gino's Pizza
	Lodg	E: Budget Host Inn
	TServ	E: Walker Machinery
(96)		**WV Turnpike Begins/Ends**
95		**WV 61, MacCorkle Ave, Charleston**
	FStop	E: Go Mart #31
	Gas	E: BP◈ W: Ashland, Chevron, Exxon, Marathon
	Food	E: Bob Evans, IHOP, McDonald's, Wendy's W: Applebee's, Arby's, Captain D's, Cracker Barrel, Hooters, La Carreta Mex, Pizza Hut, Shoney's

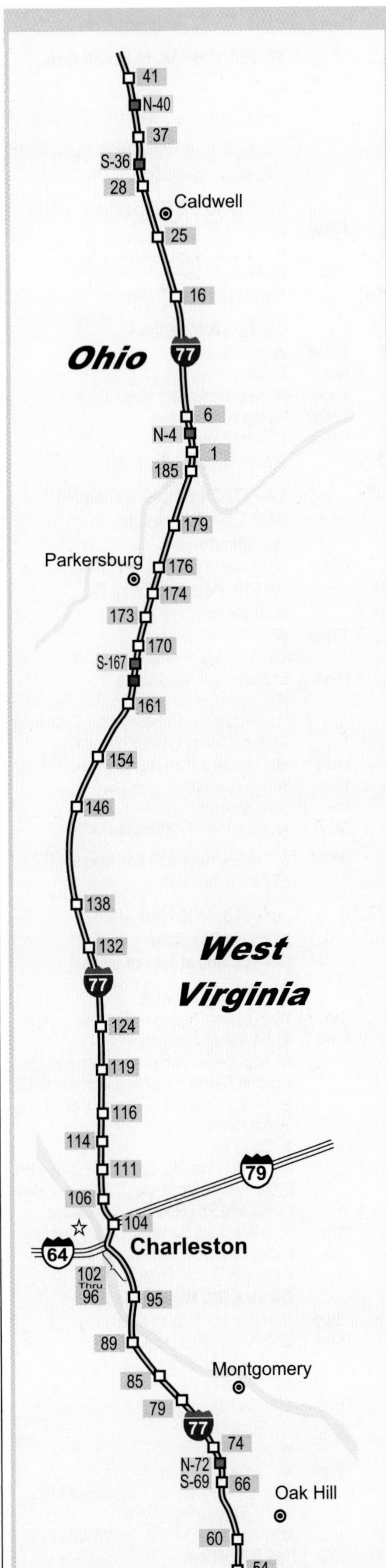

EXIT		WEST VIRGINIA
	Lodg	E: Comfort Suites, Country Inn, Dyas Inn,
	Other	E: Advance Auto Parts, Kmart W: Grocery, Lowe's, Mall, Vet♥, WVU, Univ of Charleston
89		**WV 61, WV 94, Marmet, Chesapeake**
	FStop	E: Market Express #7/Exxon
	Gas	E: Go-Mart, Shell, Sunoco
	Food	E: Subway/Exxon, Biscuit World, Gino's Pizza, Hardee's, KFC, Subway, Wendy's
	Other	E: Kroger, Pharmacy
85		**US 60, WV 61, Chelyan, East Bank**
	Gas	E: Go Mart◈
	Food	E: McDonald's, Shoney's
	Other	E: Kroger, Tires, WVU Inst of Tech
(82)		**TOLL Plaza**
79		**CR 79/3, Cabin Creek Rd, Sharon**
74		**CR 83, Paint Creek Rd**
	Other	E: WVU Inst of Tech
(72)		**Morton Service Plaza (NB)**
	FStop	Exxon
	Food	Burger King, Starbucks, TCBY
	Other	RVDump
(69)		**Rest Area (SB)** **(RR, Phones, Picnic, Vend)**
66		**CR 15, to Mahan**
	Gas	E: Sunoco◈
60		**WV 612, Oak Hill, Mossy**
	Gas	E: Exxon◈
(55)		**TOLL Plaza**
54		**CR 2, CR 23, Pax, Mt Hope**
	Gas	W: BP
48		**US 19N, N Beckley, Summersville** **(E on US 19 for addt'l food, WalM, etc)**
	Gas	E: BP◈
	Food	E: Subway/BP
	Lodg	E: Ramada Inn
	Other	E: Appalachian Bible College
(45)		**Tamarack Travel Plaza (Both dir)**
	TStop	Exxon
	Food	BiscuitWorld, Burger King, Sbarro's, Starbucks, TCBY
	Other	RVDump
44		**WV 3, Harper Rd, Beckley**
	TStop	W: Go-Mart #50
	Gas	E: Chevron◈, Exxon, Marathon, Shell W: BP
	Food	E: Applebee's, Burger King, Hibachi Japanese Steakhouse, McDonald's, Omelet Shoppe, Outback Steakhouse, Pizza Hut, Western Steer W: Bob Evans, Cracker Barrel, Wendy's
	Lodg	E: Best Western, Comfort Inn, Courtyard, Fairfield Inn, Holiday Inn, Howard Johnson, Quality Inn, Super 8 W: Days Inn, Hampton Inn, Microtel
	Med	W: + Raleigh General Hospitall
	Other	W: CVS, Kroger, Mountain State Univ, College of WV, Exhibition Coal Mine/ RV Camping▲
42		**WV 16, WV 97, Robert C Byrd Dr, to Mabscott**
	Gas	W: AmocoBP◈
	Food	W: Subway
	TServ	E: Walker Machinery
	Med	E: + Hospital, VA Med Center
	Other	W: Walmart sc, to Twin Falls Resort Park▲

◈= Regular Gas Stations with Diesel ▲ = RV Friendly Locations ♥= Pet Friendly Locations

Red print shows large vehicle parking / access on site or nearby Brown Print = Campgrounds / RV PARKS

EXIT — WV / VA

(40) **Jct I-64E, to Lewisburg**

NOTE: **I-77 above follows I-64 between Charleston and Beckley. Exit #'s follow I-77.**

(35) **Rest Area** (Both dir) (RR, Phones, Picnic, RVDump)

(30) **TOLL Plaza**

28 **CR 48, Odd Rd, Ghent, Flat Top**
- Gas — **E:** BP, Marathon◈
- Lodg — **E:** Glade Springs Resort, **to** Appalachian Resort Inn; **W:** Econo Lodge
- Other — **E:** US Post Office, **to** Ski Area

20 **US 119, to Camp Creek**
- FStop — **E:** Exxon◈
- Other — **W: Camp Creek State Park▲**

(17) **Bluestone Travel Plaza** (NB)

(17) **Weigh Station** (NB), **Parking** (SB)
- FStop — Exxon
- Food — Roy Rogers, Starbucks, TCBY
- Other — RVDump

14 **WV 20, CR 7, Athens Rd, Princeton**
- Gas — **E:** Citgo
- Other — **E: to Princeton/Pipestem KOA▲ , Pipestem Resort Park▲ , Lake Ridge RV Resort Family Campground▲ ,** Concord College

(9) **WV Turnpike Begins/Ends**

(9) **US 460, Veterans Memorial Hwy, Princeton; Pearisburg, VA**
WV WELCOME CENTER
E: (RR, Phone, Picnic, Vend)
- FStop — **E:** Blue Flash FoodMart #460
- TStop — **E:** I-77 Truck Stop
- Gas — **W:** BP◈, Chevron◈, Exxon, Marathon◈
- Food — **W:** Applebee's, Bob Evans, DQ, **Cracker Barrel**, Hardee's, McDonald's, Omelette Shoppe, Shoney's, Wendy's
- Lodg — **W:** Comfort Inn, Days Inn, Hampton Inn, Ramada, Sleep Inn, Super 8
- Med — **W:** + Hospital
- Other — **E: Walmart sc**; **W: WV State Hwy Patrol Post**

7 **CR 27, Twelve Mile Rd, Ingleside** (NB, Exit only, NO re-entry)

5 **WV 112** (SB, Exit only, NO re-entry)

1 **US 52N, US 460, CR 290, Bluefield** (Serv 5mi W in Bluefield)
- Med — **W:** + Hospital
- Other — **W: Ashland KOA▲ ,** Bluefield State College

EASTERN TIME ZONE

WEST VIRGINIA
VIRGINIA

NOTE: **MM 67: West Virginia State Line**

EASTERN TIME ZONE

66 **US 52, VA 598, to East River Mtn**

64 **US 52, VA 61, to Rocky Gap**

EXIT — VIRGINIA

62 **VA 606, Bastian, to South Gap**

(61) **VA Welcome Center** (SB) (RR, Ph, Pic, Pet, Vend, Info, Playgr)

(59) **Rocky Gap Rest Area Bland Co** (NB) (RR, Phones, Picnic, Pet, Vend)

58 **VA 666, to US 52, Bastian**
- FStop — **E:** BP; **W:** Kangaroo Express
- Gas — **W:** Exxon◈

(56) **RunAWay Ramp** (NB)

52 **US 52, VA 42, Bland**
- FStop — **W:** Sentry Food Mart #28/Shell
- Gas — **E:** Citgo
- Food — **W:** Rest/Big Walker Motel
- Lodg — **W:** Big Walker Motel
- Other — **E:** Conv Store

(52) **Weigh Station** (Both dir)

47 **VA 717, CR 601, Krenning Rd, Deer Trail, Wytheville, Max Meadows**
- Other — **W: to Deer Trail Park & Campground▲**

41 **VA 610, Peppers Ferry Rd, Wytheville**
- TStop — **W:** Kangaroo Express, Travel Center of America #143/BP (Scales)
- Food — **E:** Sagebrush Steakhouse; **W:** FastFood/Kangaroo Express, Rest/ Popeye/Subway/TacoBell/TA TC, Country Kitchen, Wendy's, Rest/Ramada
- Lodg — **W:** Comfort Suites, Hampton Inn, Ramada
- TServ — **W:** TA TC/Tires
- Med — **W:** + Hospital
- Other — **W:** Laundry/WiFi/RVDump/TA TC

NOTE: **I-77 below runs with I-81 next 9 mi. Exit #'s follow I-81.**

(40/72) **Jct I-81S, to Bristol, US 52 I-77N, to Bluefield** (Serv located at 1st exit on I-81)

73 **US 11S, Wytheville**
- Gas — **W:** BP, Citgo, Kangaroo Express
- Food — **E:** Sagebrush Steakhouse; **W:** Applebee's, Bob Evans, Burger King, **Cracker Barrel**, Chinese, Hardee's, KFC, Pizza Hut, Ocean Bay Seafood, Shoney's, Waffle House
- Lodg — **E:** Sleep Inn; **W:** Budget Host Inn, Days Inn, Holiday Inn, Econo Lodge, Motel 6♥, Quality Inn, Red Carpet Inn, Red Roof Inn, Travelodge
- Other — **W:** ATMs, Auto Services, CVS, Food Lion, Harley Davidson, Pharmacy, Tires, Wytheville Comm College

77 **Service Rd, Wytheville**
- FStop — **E:** WilcoHess C Store #605
- TStop — **E:** Kangaroo Express/Citgo, Flying J Travel Plaza #5420 (Scales); **W:** WilcoHess Travel Plaza #606 (Scales)
- Food — **E:** Subway/Kangaroo Express, Rest/FJ TP, Burger King; **W:** Arby's/WilcoHess TP
- TWash — **W:** TruckOMat/WilcoHess TP
- Other — **E:** Laundry/BarbSh/WiFi/RVDump/LP/ FJ TP, **Wytheville KOA▲**; **W:** Laundry/WilcoHess TP, **VA State Hwy Patrol Post**

EXIT — VIRGINIA

80 **US 52S, VA 121N, Max Meadows, Fort Chiswell**
- FStop — **W:** Sentry Food Mart #21
- TStop — **E:** Flying J Travel Plaza #1123 (Scales)
- Gas — **E:** BP◈; **W:** AmocoBP
- Food — **E:** Cooker/Wendy's/FJ TP, BurgerKing/BP; **W:** Family Rest, McDonald's
- Lodg — **E:** Hampton Inn, Super 8; **W:** Comfort Inn♥
- TWash — **E:** Blue Beacon TW/FJ TP
- TServ — **E:** FJ TP/Tires; **W:** Speedco
- Other — **E:** Laundry/WiFi/**LP**/FJ TP, Ft Chiswell Outlet Mall, **Ft Chiswell RV Park▲**

(81/32) **Jct I-81N, US 11, Roanoke I-77S, to Charlotte**

NOTE: **I-77 above runs with I-81 next 9 mi. Exit #'s follow I-81.**

24 **VA 69, Lead Mine Rd, Austinville, to Poplar Camp**
- FStop — **W:** Citgo
- Gas — **E:** Pure
- TServ — **E:** Poplar Camp Truck Repair

19 **VA 620, Coulson Church Rd, Hillsville**
- Other — **W:** Twin Co Airport✈

14 **US 58, US 221, Hillsville, Galax**
- FStop — **W:** Cockerham Fuel Center #4/Chevron
- Gas — **E:** Race In; **W:** EZ Stop, On the Way
- Food — **E:** Burger King, Pizza Hut; **W:** DQ, McDonald's, Shoney's, Wendy's
- Lodg — **E:** Comfort Inn, Red Carpet Inn; **W:** Best Western, Comfort Inn, Hampton Inn, Holiday Inn Express, Quality Inn, Super 8
- Med — **E:** + Hospital
- Other — **E: to Lake Ridge RV Resort Family Campground▲**; **W: Carrollwood Campground▲ , to appr 19 mi: Deer Creek RV Resort▲**

8 **VA 148, VA 755, Chances Creek Rd, to US 52, Fancy Gap**
- FStop — **W:** Kangaroo Express #3367/Citgo
- Gas — **W:** BP, Exxon
- Lodg — **W:** Days Inn, Country View Inn
- Other — **E: Fancy Gap/Blue Ride KOA▲ , Fancy Gap Cabins & Campgrounds▲ , UTT's Campground▲**

(6) **RunAWay Ramp** (SB)

(4) **RunAWay Ramp** (SB)

(3) **RunAWay Ramp** (SB)

1 **VA 620, Lambsburg Rd, Old Pipers, Gap Rd, Lambsburg**

(1) **VA Welcome Center** (NB) (RR, Phones, Picnic, Info)

EASTERN TIME ZONE

VIRGINIA

◈ = Regular Gas Stations with Diesel ▲ = RV Friendly Locations ♥ = Pet Friendly Locations
Red print shows large vehicle parking / access on site or nearby Brown Print = Campgrounds / RV PARKS

EXIT	N CAROLINA

NORTH CAROLINA

NOTE: MM 105: Virginia State Line

EASTERN TIME ZONE

(105) NC Welcome Center (SB)
(RR, Phones, Picnic, Vend, Info)

(103) Weigh Station (Both dir)

(101) **Jct I-74E, Mt Airy, to Winston-Salem** (fr SB, Left exit)

100 **NC 89, Mount Airy, to Galax, Va**
- TStop — E: PTP/Brintle Travel Plaza/Citgo (Scales)
- Gas — E: Exxon◈, Marathon◈, Shell
- Food — E: Rest/Brintle TP, Subway/Marathon, Wagon Wheel Rest
- Lodg — E: Best Western, Comfort Inn
- TServ — E: Brintle TP/Tires
- Other — E: Laundry/Brintle TP; W: to appr 17mi Deer Creek RV Resort▲

93 **Zephyr Rd, Dobson, Surry**
- FStop — E: Fast Track Shell #119
- Gas — E: Citgo◈; W: On the Way Food Store
- Food — E: FastFood/FT Shell, Diner
- Lodg — E: Surry Inn
- Other — E: Camping▲

85 **CC Camp Rd, Elkin, to US 21 ByP**
- Gas — W: Exxon◈, Shell◈
- Other — E: to Elkin Muni Airport→

83 **US 21 ByP, to Sparta** (NB, Left exit)

82 **NC 67, Jonesville, Elkin, Boonville**
- FStop — E: Four Bros Food Store #300/BP; W: G&B Food Mart #290/Exxon
- Gas — E: Chevron◈, Citgo
- Food — E: Arby's; W: Bojangles, Cracker Barrel, Glenn's BBQ, Jordan's Country Rest, McDonald's, Waffle House, Wendy's
- Lodg — E: Holiday Inn Express; W: Comfort Inn, Days Inn, Hampton Inn
- Other — E: Holly Ridge Family Campground▲; W: Grocery, Pharmacy, Vet♥

79 **US 21 Bus, US 21S, Jonesville, to Arlington**
- Gas — E: Shell; W: Shell◈
- Food — W: Sally Jo's Kitchen
- Lodg — E: Super 8; W: Country Inn

73AB **US 421, Hamptonville, to Winston-Salem, Wilkesboro**
- FStop — E: Fast Track Shell #143
- Food — E: FastFood/FT Shell
- Lodg — E: Welborn Motel, Yadkin Inn

(72) Rest Area (NB)
(RR, Phones, Picnic, Vend)

65 **NC 901, Union Grove, Harmony**
- FStop — W: Union Grove Quick Stop/BP, Fast Track Shell #137, Knight's BP
- Food — W: FastFood/FT Shell, Burger Barn
- Other — E: Van Hoy Farms Family Campground▲; W: Fiddlers Grove Campground▲, New Hope Stables & Campgrounds▲

(62) Rest Area (SB)
(RR, Phones, Picnic, Vend)

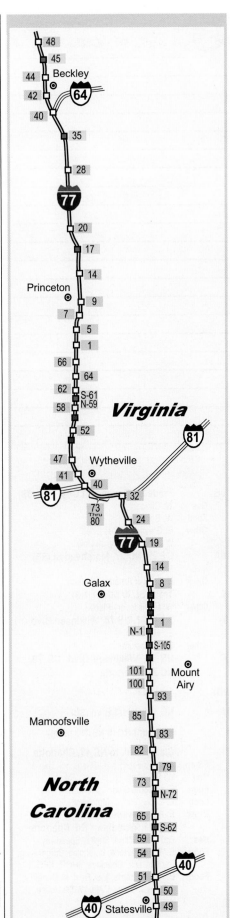

EXIT	N CAROLINA

59 **NC 1890, Tomlin Mill Rd, Statesville**

54 **US 21, Statesville, to Turnersburg**
- FStop — W: Fast Track Shell #130
- Gas — E: Citgo
- Other — W: Staples

(51B) **Jct I-40W, to Hickory**

(51A) **Jct I-40E, to Winston Salem**

50 **E Broad St, Statesville**
- Gas — E: BP, Citgo◈, Kangaroo◈, Shell
- Food — E: Arby's, Bojangles, Burger King, Domino's, Hardee's, IHOP, Long John Silver, McDonald's, Pizza Hut, Starbucks, Subway, Wendy's
- Lodg — E: Fairfield Inn, Red Roof Inn♥
- Med — W: + Iredell Memorial Hospital
- Other — E: ATMs, Banks, Dollar General, Dollar Tree, Grocery, Pharmacy, Signal Hill Mall, UPS Store, US Post Office; W: to Carolina Mountain Sports

49B **Salisbury Rd, to I-70, to Downtown**
- Gas — E: USA Mart Chevron; W: Amoco, Citgo, Exxon
- Food — E: KFC, Waffle House
- Lodg — W: Best Value Inn
- Other — W: Auto Services

49A **US 70E, Statesville**
- FStop — E: Kangaroo Express #3195
- Gas — E: BP, Circle K, Shell
- Food — E: Waffle House
- Lodg — E: Comfort Inn, Holiday Inn, Motel 6♥, Super 8
- Other — E: Lane's Tire & Auto, Tilley Harley Davidson, Camping World/RVDump

45 **Amity Hill Rd, Statesville, to Troutman, Barium Springs**
- FStop — W: Chevron
- Other — E: Statesville KOA▲, Rent Me RV America

42 **US 21, NC 115, Troutman**
- TStop — E: WilcoHess Travel Plaza #357 (Scales)
- Food — E: Subway/TacoBell/WilcoHess TP
- Other — W: to Lake Norman State Park▲

(39) Rest Area (Both dir)
(RR, Phones, Picnic, Vend)

(38) Weigh Station (Both dir)

36 **NC 150, W Plaza Dr, Mooresville**
- Gas — E: Exxon, Shell; W: BP◈, Citgo, Shell◈, Servco, BJ's
- Food — E: Applebee's, Bob Evans, Burger King, Denny's, McDonald's, Pizza Hut, Taco Bell, Waffle House, Wendy's; W: Arby's, Cracker Barrel, Golden Corral, Hardee's, Hooters, Kyoto's, Subway
- Lodg — E: Days Inn, Fairfield Inn, Holiday Inn; W: Hampton Inn, Sleep Inn, Super 8
- Other — E: Grocery, Staples, Walmart sc; W: Food Lion, Lowe's, Walgreen's

33 **US 21N, Mooresville**
- Gas — E: Phillips 66; W: BP, Citgo◈
- Food — E: McDonald's, Subway
- Lodg — E: Springhill Suites
- Med — E: + Hospital

31 **Langtree Rd**

30 **Griffith St, Davidson**
- Gas — E: Exxon◈

◈= Regular Gas Stations with Diesel ▲ = RV Friendly Locations ♥= Pet Friendly Locations
Red print shows large vehicle parking / access on site or nearby Brown Print = Campgrounds / RV PARKS

EXIT		N CAROLINA
28		**Catawba Ave, to US 21, NC 73, to Lake Norman, Cornelius**
	Gas	E: AmocoBP, Citgo
	Food	E: Bojangles, Subway, Rest/Hol Inn W: Burger King, Domino's Pizza, Jersey Mike's, KFC, Kobe, Little Caesars Pizza, Lone Star Steakhouse, McDonald's, Pizza Hut, Taco Bell, Wendy's
	Lodg	E: Hampton Inn, Holiday Inn W: Best Western, Comfort Inn, Econo Lodge, Microtel, Quality Inn,
25		**NC 73, Sam Furr Rd, Huntersville, to Concord, Lake Norman**
	Gas	E: Shell◊ W: Circle K◊
	Food	E: Burger King, Chili's, Fuddruckers, McDonald's, O'Charley's, Wendy's W: Arby's, Bob Evans, Bojangles, Carrabba's, DQ, Outback Steakhouse, Subv
	Lodg	E: Country Suites, Hawthorn Inn, Quality Inn W: Candlewood Suites, Courtyard, Residence Inn, Sleep Inn
	Other	E: ATMs, Banks, Home Depot, Lowe's, Target, Winn Dixie W: ATM, Food Lion
23		**Gilead Rd, Huntersville**
	Gas	E: BP, Citgo, Shell W: Sam's Mart
	Food	E: Captain's Galley, Hardee's, Subway, Waffle House, Wendy's
	Lodg	E: Holiday Inn Express, Red Roof Inn♥
	Med	W: + Presbyterian Hospital
	Other	E: ATM, Pharmacy, Food Lion, US Post Office W: ATM, CVS, Grocery
18		**NC 24, to US 21, Charlotte Harris Blvd, Reames Rd**
	Gas	E: BP, Phillips 66◊, Shell◊, Sam's Mart
	Food	E: Arby's, Bob Evans, Corner Deli & Grill, Jack in the Box, Quiznos, Waffle House W: ChikFilA, The Grape, Food Court
	Lodg	E: Comfort Suites, Fairfield Inn, Hilton Garden Inn, Suburban Extended Stay
	TServ	E: Carolina Engine
	Med	E: + Hospital
	Other	W: Northlake Mall, FedEx Office
16AB		**US 21, Sunset Rd, Charlotte**
	TStop	W: AmBest/Charlotte Travel Plaza/Shell (Scales)
	Gas	E: Circle K W: Citgo, Circle K
	Food	E: Captain D's, Hardee's, KFC, McDonald's, Taco Bell, Wendy's W: FastFood/Charlotte TP, Bubba's BBQ, Bojangles, Denny's, Domino's, Jack in the Box, Waffle House
	Lodg	E: Days Inn, Super 8 W: Microtel, Sleep Inn
	Other	E: ATMs, Auto Zone, CVS, Auto & Truck Services, Tires W: Laundry/Charlotte TP, CVS, Food Lion, Family Dollar, **Charlotte Bus & RV Sales**
(13AB)		**Jct I-85, N to Greensboro, S to Spartanburg**
12		**LaSalle St, Charlotte**
	Gas	W: Citgo◊, Shell◊
(11AB)		**Jct I-277, NC 16, Brookshire Fwy**
10C		**Trade St, 5th St, Downtown (SB)**

Personal Notes

EXIT		N CAROLINA
10B		**Trade St, Downtown Charlotte (SB)**
	Gas	W: Citgo
	Food	W: Bojangles
	Other	E: Greyhound Bus Lines W: Johnson C Smith Univ
10A		**US 29, NC 27, Morehead St (SB)**
	Med	E: + Hospital
	Other	E: Bank of America Stadium
10		**Trade St, W 5th St (NB)**
	Other	W: to Discovery Place
(9)		**Jct I-277, US 74, Wilkinson Blvd**
	Med	E: + Hospital
	Other	E: to Stadium
9C		**US 74, Wilkinson Blvd, US 29, NC 27, Charlotte**
(9B)		**Jct I-277**
9A		**NC 160, West Blvd (SB)**
8		**Remount Rd (fr NB, NO reacc)**
7		**Clanton Rd, to NC 49, Charlotte**
	FStop	E: Petro Express #10/Citgo
	Gas	W: BP, Shell
	Food	E: to South Blvd
	Lodg	E: Econo Lodge, Motel 6♥, Super 8
	Other	E: Auto Services, Tires
6A		**US 521, Woodlawn Rd, Charlotte**
	Gas	E: 76, BP, Citgo, Shell◊, Speedway◊
	Food	E: Arby's, Azteca, Bojangles, Burger King, Captain D's, Checkers, IHOP, KFC,
	Food	E: Krispy Kreme, Mex Rest, McDonald's, Shoney's, Steak & Ale, Waffle House, Wendy's

EXIT		NC / SC
	Lodg	E: Best Western, Days Inn, Four Points Sheraton, Howard Johnson, Ramada
	Other	E: CVS
6B		**NC 49, Tryon St, US 521, Woodlawn Rd, Billy Graham Pkwy**
	Gas	W: Phillips 66, Petro Express
	Food	W: McDonald's, Omaha Steak House, Wendy's
	Lodg	W: Embassy Suites, Extended Stay Hotel, Holiday Inn, Homestead Studio, La Quinta Inn♥, InTown Suites, Summerfield Suites
	Other	W: Charlotte Coliseum, to Charlotte Douglas Int'l Airport✈
5		**Tyvola Rd, to US 49, US 521, Charlotte**
	Gas	E: Citgo◊, Petro Express, Texaco
	Food	E: Black Eyed Pea, Chili's, China King, Carolina Country BBQ, Hooters, Lone Star Steakhouse, McDonald's, Sonny's BBQ, Subway
	Lodg	E: Candlewood Suites, Comfort Inn, Hampton Inn, Marriott, Quality Inn, Residence Inn W: Extended Stay, Wingate Inn
	Other	E: Grocery, Target W: to Charlotte Coliseum
4		**Nations Ford Rd, Charlotte**
	Gas	E: AmocoBP, Circle K, Citgo W: Shell
	Food	E: Caravel Seafood, Shoney's W: Burger King
	Lodg	E: Best Inn, Knights Inn, Motel 6, Ramada
	Other	E: Grocery
3		**Arrowood Rd, to I-485 (SB)**
	Gas	E: Shell
	Food	E: Bob Evans, Jack in the Box, Long John Silver, McDonald's, Sonic, Wendy's W: Bojangles, Café, Ruby Tuesday
	Lodg	E: AmeriSuites, Courtyard, Fairfield Inn, Holiday Inn Express, Mainstay Suites, Staybridge Suites, TownePlace Suites W: Hampton Inn
	Other	E: CVS, Family Dollar, Food Lion W: to Walmart, Tires
2		**Arrowood Rd (NB), to I-485 (SB) (Access to Ex #3 Serv)**
(1)		**NC Welcome Center (NB) (RR, Phones, Picnic, Vend)**
1		**Westinghouse Blvd, to I-485**
	Gas	E: BP◊, Shell◊ W: BP, Exxon, Shell◊, Petro Express
	Food	E: Jack in the Box, Subway, Waffle House W: Burger King
	Lodg	E: Super 8

EASTERN TIME ZONE

⬆ NORTH CAROLINA
⬇ SOUTH CAROLINA

NOTE: MM 91: North Carolina State Line

EASTERN TIME ZONE

90		**US 21, Carowinds Blvd, Ft Mill**
	Gas	E: Petro Express, Shell W: 76, Circle K, Exxon, Petro, Shell

◊= Regular Gas Stations with Diesel ▲ = RV Friendly Locations ♥= Pet Friendly Locations
Red print shows large vehicle parking / access on site or nearby Brown Print = Campgrounds / RV PARKS

EXIT		S CAROLINA
	Food	**E:** Burger King, Denny's **W:** Cracker Barrel, KFC, Shoney's, Wendy's
	Lodg	**E:** Days Inn, Super 8 **W:** Best Western, Comfort Inn, Holiday Inn Express, Motel 6♥, Plaza Hotel, Sleep Inn
	Other	**E:** CAMP▲, **National RV Rentals** **W:** Carowinds Amusement Park, Outlet Mall, Carolina Pottery, **Carowinds Camp Wilderness Resort▲**
(89)		**SC Welcome Center (SB)** **(RR, Phones, Picnic, Vend, Info)**
(88)		**Weigh Station (NB)**
88		**SC 98, Gold Hill Rd, to Pineville**
	Gas	**W:** Exxon◈, Gate◈, Shell◈
	Food	**W:** Bojangles, John's Place, Logan Farms & Market Cafe
	Other	**W:** Auto Dealers, **Charlotte/Ft Mill KOA▲**, **Tracy's RV**
85		**SC 160, Fort Mill**
	Gas	**E:** Exxon **W:** BP◈, Circle K
	Food	**E:** Subway **W:** Backyard Burger, Bojangles, Wendy's
(84)		**Weigh Station (SB)**
83		**SC 49, Sutton Rd, Fort Mill**
	TStop	**W:** Love's Travel Stop #333 (Scales)
	Food	**W:** Godfathers/ChesterFr/Love's TS
	Other	**W:** WiFi/**RVDump**/Love's TS
82C		**SC 161, Celanese Rd, York**
	Gas	**W:** Allsup's, Petro Express
	Food	**W:** Chinese Bistro, Hooters, Outback Steakhouse, Sonic, Starbucks
	Lodg	**W:** Courtyard
	Med	**W:** + **Piedmont Medical Center**
	Other	**W:** ATMs, CVS, Grocery, **to** Bryant Field✈
82B		**US 21, Cherry Rd, Rock Hill (SB)**
	Gas	**W:** Exxon, Petro Express, RaceTrac◈
	Food	**W:** Arby's, Burger King, Bojangles, Captain's Galley, ChickFilA, Denny's, Firebonz BBQ, McDonald's, Pizza Hut, Sake Express, Sakura Japanese, Subway, Taco Bell, Waffle House
	Lodg	**W:** Best Western, Country Inn, Days Inn, Howard Johnson, Microtel, Regency Inn, Super 8♥
	Other	**W:** ATMs, Advance Auto Parts, Auto Dealers, Auto Services, Dollar General, Family Dollar, Firestone, Grocery, Office Depot, Pep Boys, Pharmacy, Towing, U-Haul, Winthrop Univ, Winthrop Coliseum
82A		**US 21, Cherry Rd (NB)**
	Gas	**E:** Food Mart
	Food	**E:** IHOP, Sonny's BBQ, Steak 'n Shake, Zaxby's
	Lodg	**E:** Quality Inn, Ramada Inn
	Other	**E:** ATM, Greyhound, Home Depot, PetSmart♥
79		**SC 122, Dave Lyle Blvd, Downtown**
	Gas	**E:** BP **W:** Petro Express
	Food	**E:** Applebee's, Charanda's Mex Rest, ChickFilA, Cracker Barrel, Hardee's, Longhorn Steakhouse, O'Charley's, Ryan's Grill, Ruby Tuesday

EXIT		S CAROLINA
		W: Bob Evans, Chili's, McDonald's, Olive Garden, Moe's SW Grill, Panera, Quiznos, Sagebrush, Subway, Taco Bell, Wendy's
	Lodg	**E:** Hampton Inn, Wingate Inn **W:** Hilton Garden Inn
	Med	**W:** + **Piedmont East Urgent Care Center**
	Other	**E:** ATMs, Banks, Food Lion, Cox Harley Davidson, Lowe's, Radio Shack, Staples, Discount Tire, Tire Kingdom, Rock Hill Galleria Mall, Rock Hill Truck Services, **Walmart sc▲** **W:** ATMs, Best Buy, Target, UPS Store, **to** York Tech College
77		**US 21, SC 5, Anderson Rd**
	FStop	**W:** Pride Truck Stop (Scales) **W:** Cone Oil #220
	Gas	**E:** BP◈, Citgo◈, Exxon◈ **W:** Exxon
	Food	**E:** Subway **W:** Bojangles, KFC, McDonald's, Papa John's, Subway, Waffle House
	Other	**E:** Cox Harley Davidson **W:** Laundry/Pride TS, Auto Service
75		**Porter Rd, Rock Hill**
	Gas	**E:** Texaco◈
	Other	**E:** Fireworks
73		**SC 901, Mt Holly Rd, Rock Hill**
	FStop	**E:** Crenco Auto Truck Plaza #8/Exxon **W:** Citgo
	TStop	**E:** Flying J Travel Plaza (Scales)
	Food	**E:** CountryMarket/FastFood/FJ TP
	Other	**E:** Laundry/WiFi/**RVDump/LP**/FJ TP
(66)		**Rest Area (Both dir)** **(RR, Phones, Picnic, Vend)**
65		**SC 9, SC 901, Lancaster Hwy, Richburg, to Lancaster, Chester**
	FStop	**E:** Shell **W:** Crenco Auto Truck Plaza #2/Exxon
	Gas	**E:** BP
	Food	**E:** Subway, Waffle House **W:** Burger King, Country Omelet, KFC, McDonald's
	Lodg	**E:** Days Inn, Econo Lodge, Relax Inn **W:** Comfort Inn, Rodeway Inn, Super 8
	Other	**W:** Laundry/Crenco ATP
62		**SC 56, Old Richburg Rd, Richburg, to SC 9, SC 901, Fort Lawn**
55		**SC 97, Great Falls Rd, to Chester**
	Gas	**E:** Exxon◈
48		**SC 200, Winnsboro, to Great Falls**
	TStop	**E:** Grand Central Station/Shell (Scales) **W:** WilcoHess Travel Plaza #932 (Scales)
	Food	**E:** Rest/Grand Central Station **W:** DQ/Wendy's/WH TP
	TWash	**E:** Grand Central
	TServ	**E:** Grand Central/Tires
	Other	**E:** Laundry/Grand Central **W:** Laundry/**RVDump**/WH TP
46		**SC 20-42, Camp Welfare Rd, White Oak, Winnsboro**
41		**SC 20-41, Old River Rd, Winnsboro**
34		**SC 34, Ridgeway, Camden**
	FStop	**W:** Sharp Shoppe #5/Exxon
	TStop	**E:** AmPm Food Mart
	Food	**W:** Blimpie/Exxon, Lois's, Waffle House
	Lodg	**E:** Ridgeway Motel **W:** Ramada Ltd
	Med	**W:** + **Hospital**

◈= Regular Gas Stations with Diesel **▲ = RV Friendly Locations** **♥= Pet Friendly Locations**
Red print shows large vehicle parking / access on site or nearby **Brown Print = Campgrounds / RV PARKS**

EXIT		S CAROLINA
	Other	E: Ridgeway Campground/RVDump▲
32		**Peach Rd, Ridgeway**
27		**Blythewood Rd, to US 21, Blythewood**
	Gas	E: BP◈, Exxon◈
	Food	E: Bojangles/Exxon, KFC/Pizza Hut, McDonald's, Subway, Waffle House, Wendy's,
	Lodg	E: Comfort Inn, Days Inn, Holiday Inn Express
	Other	E: Carwash/BP, Grocery, Pharmacy, Tires W: Food Lion
24		**US 21, Wilson Blvd, Blythewood, to Columbia**
	FStop	E: Pitt Stop #3/Shell, BP
	Food	E: Subway/Shell, Myers BBQ
22		**Killian Rd, to US 21, Columbia**
	Gas	E: Murphy
	Food	E: McDonald's, Monterrey Mexican Rest,
	Other	E: Auto Dealers, **Walmart sc, to** CVS, Budget Truck Rental, Lowe's, Walgreen's,
19		**SC 555, Farrow Rd, LeGrand Rd**
	Gas	E: BP◈, Exxon, Shell◈ W: Shell◈
	Food	E: **Cracker Barrel**, Wendy's W: Waffle House
	Lodg	E: Courtyard, Residence Inn
	Med	E: + Providence Hospital NE
	Other	E: Carquest, Pharmacy,
18		**US 277, to I-20W, Columbia (SB)**
17		**US 1, Two Notch Rd, to I-20**
	Gas	E: BP, Circle K/76, Kangaroo
	Food	E: Arby's, Burger King, Harbor Inn Seafood, Texas Roadhouse, Tiffany's Bakery & Eatery, Waffle House W: Bojangles, Chili's, Hooters, IHOP, Outback Steakhouse, Waffle House
	Lodg	E: Fairfield Inn, Holiday Inn, InTown Suites, Columbia Plaza Hotel,Quality Inn, Wingate W: AmeriSuites, Baymont Inn♥, Comfort Suites, Econo Lodge, Hampton Inn, Holiday Inn, Microtel, Motel 6♥, Red Roof Inn♥, Travelodge
	Med	E: + Doctors Care Urgent Care
	Other	E: ATMs, Banks, Bi-Lo, Gregg Animal Hospital♥, Grocery, RiteAid, Royal Z Bowling, Spring Valley Animal Hospital♥, Target, U-Haul, US Post Office, **Walmart▲ Center, Sesquicentennial State Park** W: ATMs, Auto Services, Banks, Columbia Mall, Home Depot, Tires, **to I-20**

EXIT		S CAROLINA
(16B)		**Jct I-20W, to Augusta**
(16A)		**Jct I-20E, to Florence**
(16AB)		**Jct I-20, W-Atlanta, E-Florence (fr NB, Left exit to WB)**
15		**SC 12, Percival Rd, Ft Jackson (SB)**
	Gas	W: Exxon, Shell
15B		**SC 12W, Percival Rd, Ft Jackson (NB)**
15A		**SC 12E, Percival Rd, Ft Jackson (NB)**
	Other	E: Ft Jackson Miil Res
13		**Decker Blvd, to SC 12 (NB)**
	Gas	W: El Cheapo, Spinx
	Other	W: Budget Truck Rental, Penske Truck Rental, Staples
12		**Imboden St, to SC 12, Forest Dr, Strom Thurmond Blvd**
	Gas	W: BP◈, Kangaroo Express, Shell◈, Sam's
	Food	E: Burger King, W: Bojangles, ChickFilA, Fatz Cafe, Golden Corral, Hardee's, McDonald's, Starbucks, Steak & Ale, Subway
	Lodg	W: Extended Stay America, Marlboro Inn, Super 8
	Med	E: + Hospital
	Other	E: Fort Jackson Museum, Ft Jackson Military Res W: AT&T, Hobby Lobby, Sam's Club, U-Haul, **Walmart SC▲**
10		**SC 760, Fort Jackson Blvd, to US 76 US 378, SC 16**
	Gas	W: BP
	Food	W: Applebee's, Bojangles, Ruby Tuesday, Subway
	Lodg	W: Econo Lodge, Liberty Inn
	Other	E: Ft Jackson Museum, Ft Jackson, **MIL/ Weston Lake Rec Area▲**
9B		**SC 262, Leesburg Rd, Columbia, to US 76, US 378, Sumter (SB)**
9A		**US 76/378, Columbia, Sumter (SB)**
9		**US 76, US 378, to SC 262, Leesburg Rd, Columbia, to Sumter (NB)**
	Gas	E: BP, Citgo, Hess◈, Kangaroo◈, Murphy W: Circle K/76, Corner Pantry,

EXIT		S CAROLINA
	Food	E: Arby's, Captain D's, ChickFilA, Domino's Pizza, KFC, McDonald's, Pizza Hut, Ruby Tuesday, Shoney's, Subway, Waffle House, Zaxby's W: CiCi's Pizza, Hardee's, Jimmy John's, Panera Bread, Sonic, Starbucks, Wendy's
	Lodg	E: Best Western, Candlewood Suites, Comfort Inn, Country Inn, Days Inn, Holiday Inn Express, La Quinta Inn♥, Plaza Inn, Quality Inn, Sleep Inn, Towneplace Suites, W: America's Best Value Inn, Econo Lodge, Howard Johnson, Rodeway Inn
	Med	E: + Doctors Care Urgent Care W: + Hospital, VA Medical Center
	Other	E: Advance Auto Parts, Aldi, Auto Zone, CVS, Carquest, Dollar Tree, Enterprise RAC, Firestone, Grocery, Lowe's, NAPA, Piggly Wiggly, Radio Shack, RiteAid, Tire Kingdom, U-Haul, US Post Office, Walgreen's, **Walmart sc▲**, W: ATMs, Grocery, Pharmacy, RiteAid, Staples, Target, U-Haul, USC School of Med, Woodhill Mall,
6		**SC 768, Shop Rd, Columbia (SB)**
	Other	W: to State Fairgrounds, Coliseum
6B		**SC 768W, Shop Rd, Columbia (NB)**
6A		**SC 768E, Shop Rd, Columbia (NB)**
5		**SC 48, Bluff Rd, Gadsen**
	Gas	E: 76 W: Shell
	Food	W: Burger King/Shell
	Other	W: to Columbia Owens Downtown Airport✈
2		**12th St Ext, to Cayce**
1		**US 21, US 176, SC 73, US 321 (Serv on US 176/US 21)**
	Other	W: to Cayce Speedway
(0)		**Jct I-26, W - Spartanburg, E - Charleston (to EB, Left exit)**

EASTERN TIME ZONE

NOTE: I-77 begins/ends on I-90, Ex #172A

SOUTH CAROLINA

Begin Northbound I-77 from Jct I-26 in Columbia, SC to Jct I-90 in Cleveland, OH.

EXIT		PENNSYLVANIA

Begin Eastbound I-78 from Jct I-81 near Fredericksburg, PA to Jct I-95 in Newark, NJ.

PENNSYLVANIA

NOTE: Begin/End I-78 on I-81, Ex #89

EASTERN TIME ZONE

EXIT		PENNSYLVANIA
(1A)		**Jct I-81S, to Harrisburg (Left exit)**
(1B)		**Jct I-81N, to Hazelton**
6		**PA 343, Legionaire Dr, to US 22, Fredricksburg, Lebanon (EB)**
	FStop	S: Pacific Pride
	Other	S: Farmers Pride Airport✈, to appr 5mi: **Jonestown KOA▲**
8		**US 22W, to PA 343, Fredericksburg, Lebanon (WB)**
10		**PA 645, Camp Swatara Rd, Myerstown, Frystown**
	TStop	N: Gables of Frystown/Shell (Scales) S: Frystown All American Plaza/Pilot TC #518 (Scales)
	Food	N: Deli/Gables S: Rest/All Amer Pl
	Lodg	S: All American Motel/All Amer Pl
	TServ	S: All American Plaza/Tires/TWash
	Other	S: Laundry/CB/WiFi/LP/All Amer Pl
13		**PA 501, Lancaster Ave, Bethel**
	FStop	N: Shell
	TStop	S: I-78 Truck Stop/Exxon
	Food	S: Rest/I-78 TS
	TServ	S: Midway Truck Service, Towing

◈= Regular Gas Stations with Diesel ▲ = RV Friendly Locations ♥= Pet Friendly Locations
Red print shows large vehicle parking / access on site or nearby Brown Print = Campgrounds / RV PARKS

EXIT		PENNSYLVANIA
15		**Court St, Frantz Rd Midway, Grimes** (NO Trucks)
16		**Midway Rd, Bethel, Midway**
	FStop	**N:** Midway Exxon Travel Center, Midway Fuel & Truck Wash/Citgo
	Food	**N:** Midway Diner
	Lodg	**N:** Comfort Inn
	TWash	**N:** Midway Exxon TC
	Other	**N:** Auto & Truck Repair
17		**PA 419, Four Point Rd, Bethel, to Rehrersburg**
	Gas	**N:** Best◈
	Lodg	**N:** Lamplighter Motel
	Other	**N:** Truck Repair, Tires
19		**PA 183, Bethel, to Strausstown**
	Gas	**S:** Shell◈
	Other	**S: to** Bashore & Stoudt Country Winery, Calvaresi Winery, Clover Hill Winery
23		**Mountain Rd, Shartlesville**
	FStop	**N:** Sunoco
	Food	**N:** Stuckeys/DQ/Sunoco
		S: Blue Mountain Family Rest, Haag's PA Dutch Rest/Haags Motel, Riverboat Saloon
	Lodg	**N:** Dutch Motel
	Lodg	**S:** Scottish Inn, Haag's Motel
	Other	**N: PA Dutch Campsites▲ , Martin's RV Center, Appalachian Campsites▲ , Mountain Springs Camping Resort▲**
		S: to Blue Marsh Lake
29A		**PA 61S, Hamburg, to Reading**
	Food	**S:** Hamburg Diner
	Other	**S:** Grocery
29B		**PA 61N, to Pottsville**
	FStop	**N:** Square One Market/Shell
	Food	**N:** Burger King, Cracker Barrel, Italian Rest, Subway, Taco Bell, Wendy's
	Lodg	**N:** Microtel
	Other	**N: Boat n RV Superstore, RV Center, Cabela's/RVDump, to** Hawk Mountain, Blue Mtn Airport✈, **to app 9mi Christmas Pines Campground▲**
30		**N 4th St, Hamburg**
	Gas	**S:** Getty, Mobil
	Food	**S:** Subway, Rest/Amer Hse Htl
	Lodg	**S:** American House Hotel
	Other	**S:** ATMs, Banks, Hamburg Truck Service, **Tom Schaeffer RV Superstore**
35		**PA 143, Lenhartsville**
	Other	**N: Blue Rocks Family Campground▲ , Robin Hill Camping Resort▲**
		S: PA Dutch Folk Culture Center
40		**PA 737, Krumsville, Kutztown**
	Gas	**S:** Shell◈
	Food	**S:** Skyview Country Rest

Personal Notes

EXIT		PENNSYLVANIA
	Lodg	**N:** Top Motel
	Other	**N: Pine Hill RV Park▲ , Robin Hill Camping Resort▲**
45		**PA 863, Kutztown, to Lynnport, New Smithville**
	FStop	**N:** Bandit Truck Stop #1/Sunoco
	Gas	**N:** Exxon
	Food	**N:** FastFood/Bandit TS, DeMarco's Italian Rest, Subway/Exxon
	Lodg	**S:** Super 8
	Other	**N:** WiFi/Bandit TS
49AB		**PA 100, Fogelsville, Trexlertown**
49A		**PA 100S, to Trexlertown**
	Gas	**S:** Shell, Sunoco, WaWa
	Food	**S:** Burger King, Damons, Starlite Diner, Taco Bell, Yocco's Hot Dogs
	Lodg	**S:** Hampton Inn, Hilton Garden Inn, Holiday Inn, Sleep Inn, Staybridge Suites
	Other	**S:** ATMs, Grocery Store, Grover Hill Winery, **PA State Hwy Patrol Post**

EXIT		PENNSYLVANIA
49B		**PA 100N, to Fogelsville**
	Food	**N:** Arby's, Cracker Barrel, Long John Silver, Pizza Hut
	Lodg	**N:** Comfort Inn, Hawthorne Suites
	Other	**N:** ATM, Auto Services, Bank, Pharmacy,
	Other	**N:** Purcell Tire, Tires, **to Allentown KOA▲**
51		**US 22E, to I-476, Pa Tpk, to PA 309N PA 33N, Whitehall** (EB, exit only)
	Other	**to** Lehigh Valley Int'l Airport✈
53		**PA 309N, to I-476N, Pa Tpk** (WB)
54		**US 222, Hamilton Blvd** (EB, Exit only)
	Gas	**N:** Hess
		S: Sunoco, WaWa
	Food	**N:** Boston Market, Burger King, Carrabba's, Dunkin Donuts, McDonald's, Mangos, Perkins, Subway, TGI Friday, Wendy's
		S: Hunan Chinese, Pizza Hut
	Lodg	**N:** Comfort Suites, Holiday Inn Express, Howard Johnson
		S: Days Inn, Wingate Inn
	Other	**N:** ATMs, FedEx Office, Grocery, Cedar Crest College, Muhlenberg College, Wild Water King Park, Dorney Park,
		S: U-Haul, Tires
54A		**US 222S, Hamilton Blvd** (WB)
54B		**US 222, Hamilton Blvd** (WB)
55		**PA 29s, Cedar Crest Blvd**
	Gas	**S:** Post & Shell
	Food	**S:** Cafe
	Med	**S: + Lehigh Valley Hospital**
	Other	**S:** Indian Museum
57		**Lehigh St, Allentown**
	Gas	**N:** Hess◈
		S: Turkey Hill, Getty
	Food	**N:** Arby's, IHOP
		S: Bennigan's, Burger King, Bob Evans, Dunkin Donuts, Friendly's, McDonald's, Perkins, Subway, Taco Bell, Wendy's
	Lodg	**N:** Days Inn
	Other	**N:** ATM, Big Lots, CVS, Family Dollar, Grocery, Home Depot, Queen City Muni Airport✈, Mack Truck WHQ
		S: ATMs, Banks, Auto Dealers, Grocery, PetCo♥, Staples, Tires, UPS Store, South Mall
58		**Emmaus Ave, Allentown** (WB)
	Gas	**S:** Gulf, Turkey Hill
	Other	**N:** Pharmacy
		S: ATMs, Banks, Grocery, Pharmacy
59		**Rock Rd, to PA 145, Summit Lawn** (EB)
60		**PA 309S, Quakertown** (EB)
	Other	**N:** DeSales Univ

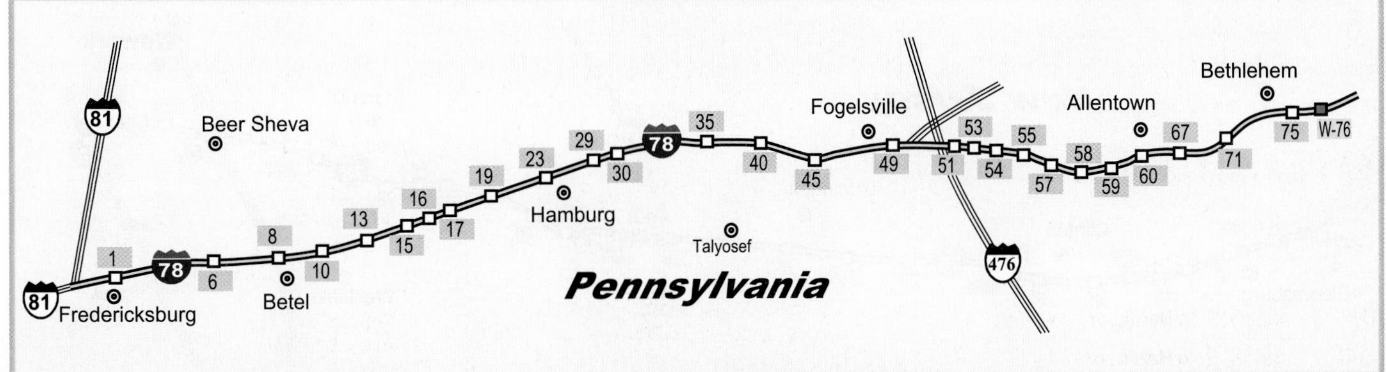

◈= Regular Gas Stations with Diesel ▲ = RV Friendly Locations ♥ = Pet Friendly Locations
Red print shows large vehicle parking / access on site or nearby Brown Print = Campgrounds / RV PARKS

EXIT		PA / NJ
60A		**PA 309S, Quakertown (WB)**
	Other	N: DeSales Univ
60B		**PA 145N, S 4th St, Quakertown, Coopersburg (WB)**
67		**PA 412, Hellertown Rd, Hellertown, to Bethlehem**
	Gas	N: Turkey Hill
		S: Citgo, Mobil◈, Sunoco
	Food	N: Wendy's
		S: Burger King, McDonald's, Waffle House
	Lodg	N: to Comfort Suites
		S: to Holiday Inn Express
	Med	N: + to St Luke's Hospital
	Other	N: to Lehigh Univ, Historic Bethlehem
71		**PA 33N, to US 22, Bethlehem, to Easton, Stroudsburg, Pocono Mtns**
	Other	N: Lowe's, Staples, to Lehigh Valley Int'l Airport✈
75		**Morgan Hill Rd, to PA 611, Easton, to Philiadelphia**
	Gas	N: Turkey Hill
	Food	N: McDonald's, Perkins
	Lodg	N: Best Western
	Other	N: to Lafayette College, Crayola Attractions
(75)		**TOLL Plaza (WB)**
(76)		**PA Welcome Center (WB) (RR, Phones, Picnic, Vend, Info)**

EASTERN TIME ZONE

NOTE: MM 77: New Jersey State Line

PENNSYLVANIA
NEW JERSEY

EASTERN TIME ZONE

EXIT		NEW JERSEY
3		**US 22, NJ 173, Phillipsburg**
	FStop	N: PTP/US Gas, Michael Petroleum
	TStop	N: Penn-Jersey Truck Stop (US 22N)
	Gas	N: Citgo◈, Getty
	Food	N: Rest/PennJersey TS, Applebee's, Burger King, China Grill Buffet, McDonald's, Panera Bread, Ruby Tuesday
	Lodg	N: Clarion Hotel, Phillipsburg Inn
	Med	N: + Hospital
	Other	N: ATMs, Banks, Grocery, Home Depot, Lowe's, Pharmacy, Staples, Target, Walmart sc
4		**CR 637, Main St, Stewartsville (WB, Exit only)**
	Lodg	N: Stewart Inn

Personal Notes

EXIT		NEW JERSEY
(6)		**Weigh Station (Both dir)**
6		**CR 632, Bloomsbury Rd, Asbury (EB, Exit Only)**
7		**NJ 173, Clinton St, Bloomsbury**
	TStop	S: Travel Center of America #48/Mobil
	TStop	S: Pilot Travel Center #280 (Scales)
	Gas	S: Citgo◈
	Food	S: CountryPride/Burger King/TA TC, Subway/Pilot TC, Rest/KrispyKreme/Citgo
	TServ	S: TA TC/Tires/TWash
	Other	N: Jugtown RV Park▲
		S: Laundry/WiFi/TA TC, WiFi/Pilot TC
(8)		**Picnic Area (Both dir)**
11		**NJ 173, West Portal, Pattenburg**
	Gas	N: Coastal, Shell◈
	Other	N: Jugtown RV Park▲ , NJ State Hwy Patrol Post

EXIT		NEW JERSEY
12		**CR 625, Perryville Rd, CR 635, Charlestown Rd, NJ 173, Hampton, Clinton, to Jutland, Norton**
	TStop	N: Johnny's Truck Stop/Citgo (Scales) Pilot Travel Center #190 (Scales)
	Gas	N: Exxon◈
		S: Shell◈
	Food	N: Rest/Johnny's TS, Rest/Pilot TC
	TServ	N: Johnny's TS/Tires
	Other	N: Laundry/BarbSh/Johnny's TS, Spruce Run State Park
13		**Rupell Rd, to NJ 173W, Clinton**
	TStop	N: Clinton Truck Stop
	Food	N: Clinton Diner
15		**CR 513, NJ 173E, Clinton, Pittstown**
	Gas	N: Citgo, Exxon, Shell◈
	Food	N: Subway
		S: Cracker Barrel, Hunan Wok
	Lodg	N: Holiday Inn Select
		S: Hampton Inn
	Other	N: Red Mill Museum Village
		S: Dollar Tree, Grocery, Walmart
16		**NJ 31, Center St, Clinton, to CR 513, to Washington (EB) (Acc to Ex #17)**
17		**NJ 31, Annandale, to CR 513, to Clinton, Flemington**
	FStop	N: Hampton Mobil
	Gas	N: Exxon, Hess
	Food	N: King Buffet, McDonald's
18		**CR 626, Beaver Ave, US 22, Annandale, to Lebanon**
20		**CR 639, Cokesbury, Lebanon (WB)**
	Gas	S: Exxon, Shell
	Food	S: Deli, Dunkin Donuts, Diner
	Lodg	S: Courtyard, Fountain Motel
	Other	S: Lebanon Train Station, Round Valley State Park
24		**CR 523, Oldwick Rd, to CR 517, to Oldwick, to US 22, Whitehouse**
26		**NJ 523 Spur, North Branch, CR 665**
(29)		**Jct I-287, to US 202, US 206, to I-80, to I-95, to Morristown, Somerset**
(32)		**Scenic Overlook (WB) (NO Trailers, Trucks)**
33		**CR 525, Liberty Corner Rd, Basking Ridge, Bernardsville, Martinsville**
	Gas	S: Exxon, Sunoco
	Food	N: Rest/Somerset Hills Hotel
	Lodg	N: Courtyard, Somerset Hills Hotel

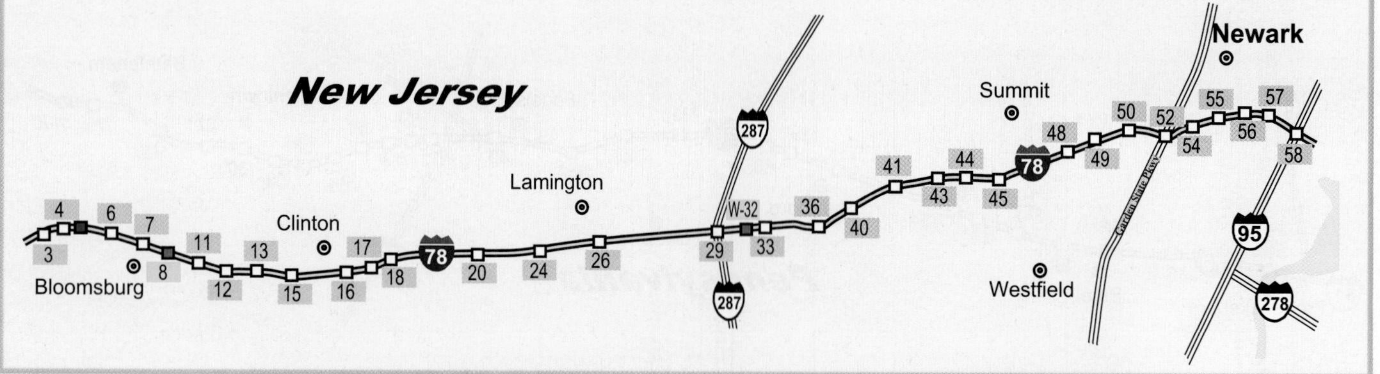

◈ = Regular Gas Stations with Diesel ▲ = RV Friendly Locations ♥ = Pet Friendly Locations
Red print shows large vehicle parking / access on site or nearby Brown Print = Campgrounds / RV PARKS

EXIT		NEW JERSEY
36		CR 651, King George Rd, Basking Ridge, Warrenville
	Gas	N: Exxon
40		CR 531, Hillcrest Rd, The Plainfields
	Gas	S: BP
	Med	S: + Hospital
41		Dale Rd, to CR 663, CR 44, Watchung, to Berkeley Heights, Scotch Plains
43		Oak Way, CR 39, CR 642, Diamond Hill Rd, Watchung, New Providence
	Other	N: Lucent Technologies S: Watchung Reservation
44		CR 527, Glenside Ave, Berkeley Hts (EB)
45		CR 36, CR 527, Glenside Ave (EB)
48		to NJ 24, NJ 124W, to I-287N, Springfield, to Morristown
	NOTE:	MM 48: I-78 divides to I-78 Expr & I-78
49AB		NJ 124, Springfield Ave, to NJ 82, to Vauxhall, Maplewood, Union (EB
50AB		CR 30, CR 630, Union, Millburn (WB)
	Gas	N: Exxon, Mobil
	Other	N: Home Depot, US Post Office
52		NJ Garden State Pkwy (NO Trucks)
54		Winans Ave, Fabyan Place, to CR 601, Newark, Irvington, Hillside (EB)
55		Leslie St, Fabyan Pl, Newark, to Hillside, Irvington (WB)
	Gas	N: BP, Getty, Hess
	Food	N: Wendy's
	Med	S: + Newark Beth Israel Med Ctr
56		Hillside Ave, Peddie St, Newark Clinton Ave (Fr EB, Left exit)
57		US 1S, US 9S, US 22, Newark International Airport
	Lodg	S: Best Western, Courtyard, Days Inn, Hilton, Hampton Inn,Holiday Inn, Marriott, Sheraton
58AB		US 1N, US 9N, NJ Tpk, Newark

EASTERN TIME ZONE

↑ NEW JERSEY

Begin Westbound I-78 from Jct I-95 in Newark, NJ to Jct I-81 near Fredericksburg, PA

Begin Southbound I-79 from Erie, PA to Jct I-77 in Charleston, WV.

PENNSYLVANIA

NOTE: I-79 begins/ends on PA 5, Ex #183A

EASTERN TIME ZONE

EXIT		PENNSYLVANIA
183B		PA 5W, 12th St, Erie (NB)
	Gas	W: Citgo, Sunoco
	Food	W: Applebee's, Bob Evans, Chinese, KFC, Italian Rest, McDonald's, Taco Bell
	Lodg	W: Comfort Inn, Thunderbird Motel
	Med	W: + Priority Care
	Other	W: ATMs, Advance Auto, Big Lots, CVS, Dollar General, Grocery, Pharmacy, Tires, U-Haul, Vet♥, Waldameer Amusement and Water Park, Golf Course, to Erie Int'l Airport✈, Presque Isle State Park, Sara's Campground▲
183A		PA 5E, PA 290, 12th St (NB, Exit only)
	FStop	E: Greengarden Shell
	Other	E: to Gannon Univ, Lampe Marina Campground▲
182		US 20, 26th St, Erie (fr SB, Exit only)
	Gas	E: Citgo, KwikFill W: BP, Country Fair
	Food	E: Subway W: Arby's, Burger King, Hoss's Steak & Sea House, Little Caesars, McDonald's, Pizza Hut, Subway, Super China Buffet, Tim Hortons
	Lodg	W: Village Motel
	Med	E: + St Vincent Health Center W: + Hamot Medical Center
	Other	E: Auto Service, Family Dollar, Grocery, Commercial Truck Repair, to Erie Zoo W: ATMs, Auto Services, CVS, Grocery, Dollar General, U-Haul, to Erie Int'l Airport✈
180		Interchange Rd, to US 19, Erie, to Waterford
	Gas	W: Citgo◊
	Food	E: Arby's, Eat 'n Park, KFC, Lone Star Steakhouse, Max & Erma's, McDonald's, Outback Steakhouse, Olive Garden, Panda Express, Ponderosa, Red Lobster, Roadhouse Grill, Smokey Bones BBQ, Starbucks, Subway, Wendy's
	Lodg	E: Fairfield Inn, Homewood Suites♥ (Addt'l lodg S on US 19)
	Med	E: + Millcreek Community Hospital
	Other	E: ATMs, Auto Dealers, Banks, Best Buy, B&N, Borders, FedEx Office, Gander Mountain, Firestone, Goodyear, Office Depot, Office Max, PetCo♥, Mill Creek Mall, Home Depot, Lowe's, Pharmacy, Target, UPS Store , Walmart, Sam's Club, Tinseltown, Family First Sports Park
(178B)		Jct I-90W, to Cleveland, OH
(178A)		Jct I-90E, to Buffalo, NY
74		West Rd, McKean
	Other	W: Erie KOA▲
166		US 6N, Edinboro, Albion, Washington
	Gas	E: Country Fare, Sheetz
	Food	E: Burger King, McDonald's, Perkins, Ital Rest, Subway, Taco Bell, Wendy's
	Lodg	E: Edinboro Inn
	Other	E: Walmart sc, Golf Course, Campbell Pottery, Edinboro Univ, Wooden Nickel Buffalo Farm, Gift Shop & Rest
(163)		PA Welcome Center (SB) Rest Area (NB) (RR, Phones, Picnic, Vend, Info)
154		PA 198, Saergertown, Conneautville
147B		US 6W, US 322W, US 19S, Conneaut Lake
	Gas	W: BP, Sheetz, Kwik Fill
	Food	W: Burger King, King's Rest, McDonald's, Ponderosa, Red Lobster
	Lodg	W: Quality Inn, Super 8
	Other	W: ATMs, Auto Zone, Auto Dealers, Dollar General, Grocery, Goodyear, Staples, Walmart sc▲ , Port Meadville Airport✈, PA State Hwy Patrol Post, to Conneaut Lake Park, Pymatuning Deer Park, Pymatuning State Park/Lake, to Pineview Camplands▲ , Playland Camping Park▲
147A		US 6E, US 322, US 19N, Meadville
	Gas	E: Country Fair
	Food	E: Applebee's, Cracker Barrel, Chovy's Italian, Hoss's Steak & Sea House, Perkins, Super China Buffet
	Lodg	E: Days Inn♥, Holiday Inn Express, Motel 6♥
	Med	E: + Meadville Medical Center
	Other	E: Advance Auto, Grocery, Home Depot, Allegheny College, to appr 7mi Brookdale Family Campground▲
141		PA 285, Meadville, to US 19, Custards, to Geneva, Cochranton
	TStop	W: Exit 141 Auto Truck Stop
	Food	W: Rest/Ex 141 ATS
	Other	E: to appr 6.5mi French Creek Campground▲ W: LP/Ex 141 ATS
(135)		Rest Area (Both dir) (RR, Phones, Picnic, Vend)
130		PA 358, Sandy Lake Greenville Rd, to Sandy Lake, Greenville
	Med	W: + Greenville Regional Hospital
	Other	E: Maurice Goddard State Park, to Goddard Park Vacationland▲ W: to Thiel College, appr 7mi Farma Family Campground▲
121		US 62, Franklin Rd, Jackson Center, to Mercer, Franklin
	FStop	W: Jiffy Mart/Sunoco
	Other	W: to RV Village Camping Resort▲ , PA State Hwy Patrol Post
(116B)		Jct I-80W, to Sharon, Mercer
(116A)		Jct I-80E, to Clarion

◊= Regular Gas Stations with Diesel ▲ = RV Friendly Locations ♥= Pet Friendly Locations
Red print shows large vehicle parking / access on site or nearby Brown Print = Campgrounds / RV PARKS

EXIT		PENNSYLVANIA
113		**PA 208, Leesburg Grove City Rd, to PA 258, to Grove City, Leesburg**
	Gas	E: BP, Citgo◈ W: KwikFill, Sheetz
	Food	W: Eat 'n Park, Hoss's Steak & Sea House, McDonald's, Wendy's, Subway, Elephant & Castle Pub & Rest
	Lodg	W: Americana Inn, Comfort Inn, Hampton Inn, Holiday Inn Express, Super 8, E&C
	Med	E: + Hospital
	Other	E: to Grove City College W: Grove City Airport✈, Prime Outlets at Grove City, **Mercer/Grove City KOA▲**, to Westminster College
(110)		**Rest Area (SB)** **(RR, Phones, Picnic)**
(108)		**Rest Area (NB)** **(RR, Phones, Picnic)**
105		**PA 108, New Castle Rd, to Slippery Rock, New Castle** **(Addt'l Serv 3-5 mi E in Slippery Rock)**
	Food	E: Rest/Evening Star Motel
	Lodg	E: Evening Star Motel
	Other	E: **Slippery Rock Campground▲**, to Slippery Rock Univ
99		**US 422, Benjamin Franklin Hwy, New Castle Rd, Portersville, to Prospect, New Castle, Butler**
	TStop	W: Pilot Travel Center #81 (Scales)
	Food	W: McDonald's/Subway/Pilot TC
	Other	E: Big Butler Fairgrounds, **Moraine State Park, to Lake Arthur Family Campground▲** W: Laundry/Pilot TC, New Castle Harley Davidson, Living Treasures Animal Park, **Cooper's Lake Campground▲**, **Rose Point Park Campground▲**
96		**PA 488, Portersville Rd, to US 422, to US 19, to Prospect, Portersville**
	Other	E: **Bear Run Campground▲**, to **Moraine State Park** W: **to McConnell Mill State Park**
88		**Little Creek Rd, Harmony, to US 19, PA 68, to Zelienople** **(SB Ex, NB reacc) (Access #87 Serv)**
	Other	W: **Indian Brave Campground▲**
87		**PA 68, Evans City Rd, Harmony, to US 19, Zelienople (NB Ex, SB reacc)**
	Gas	W: Exxon
	Food	W: Burger King, Pizza Hut, Subway
	Lodg	W: Zelienople Motel
	Other	W: Greyhound, **Indian Brave Campground▲**
85		**US 19, PA 528, Evans City** **(NO Trucks) (SB Ex, diff NB reacc)**
83		**PA 528, Lindsay Rd, to US 19, Evans City, Zelienople (NB Exit, SB reaccess) (NO Trucks)**
	NOTE:	**Trucks over 10,000# to Evans City, Use Exit #87**
	Med	W: + Butler Memorial Hospital
(81)		**Picnic Area (Both dir) (Phones)**
(80)		**Truck Scales (SB)**
78		**PA 228, Cranberry Twp, to US 19, Mars, Cranberry (fr NB, exit only)**
	Gas	E: 7-11, Texaco W: Exxon◈, Sheetz, Sunoco, GetGo

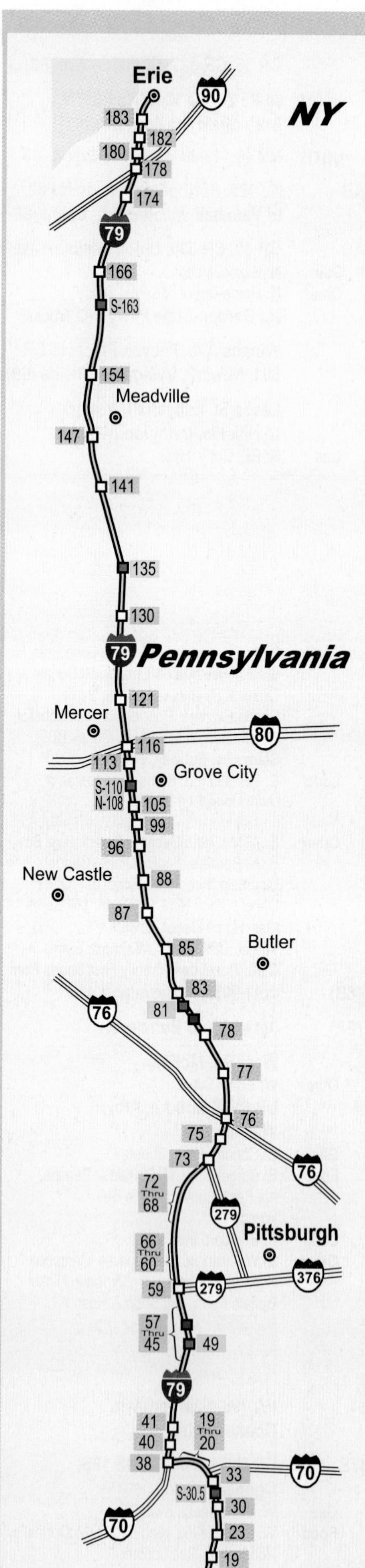

EXIT		PENNSYLVANIA
	Food	E: Applebee's, Dunkin Donuts, Hereford & Hops Steakhouse, McDonald's, Moe's SW Grill, Olive Garden, On the Border, Quiznos, Red Robin, Smokey Bones BBQ, Starbucks, Subway W: Burger King, CiCi's, Denny's, Fatburger, Jersey Mike's, Long John Silver, Panera Bread, Papa John's Pizza, Primanti Bros, Quaker Steak & Lube, Subway, Wendy's
	Lodg	E: Marriott W: Fairfield Inn, Hampton Inn, Residence Inn
	Med	W: + UPMC Hospital
	Other	E: ATMs, Lowe's, PetSmart♥, Pharmacy, Staples, Target, Vet♥
	Other	W: ATMs, Auto Services, Banks, Barnes & Noble, Best Buy, Cinema 8, Costco, Firestone, Goodyear Comm'l, Goodyear, Grocery, Home Depot, Office Max, PetCo♥, Pharmacy, Radio Shack, **Walmart sc▲**, UPS Store, US Post Office, Vet♥, Cranberry Mall
77		**US 19, to I-76, PA Tpk (TOLL), to Harrisburg, Youngstown, OH (fr SB, exit only) (Acc to #78/76 Serv)**
	NOTE:	**NO Trucks over 13'6" on I-76 / PA Tpk**
76		**to US 19N, Perry Hwy, Cranberry (NB, Left Exit only) (Acc Ex #78 Serv)**
	Gas	W: BP◈, Exxon
	Food	W: Arby's, Bob Evans, Burger King, Eat 'n Park, Lone Star Steakhouse, Max & Erma's Perkins
	Lodg	W: Comfort Inn, Four Points Sheraton, Holiday Inn Express♥, Hyatt Place♥, Motel 6♥, Red Roof Inn♥, Super 8
	Med	W: + UPMC Hospital
	Other	W: ATMs, Auto Services, FedEx Office
75		**Warrandale Bayne Rd, to US 19S, Warrendale, Rte 8, OH River Blvd, Red Belt (NB, Exit only)** **(Acc to Ex # 76-78 Serv via US 19)**
73		**PA 910E, Wexford Bayne Rd, Orange Belt, Wexford**
	Gas	E: BP, UniMart, Gas/T-Bones Groc W: Exxon◈
	Food	E: Eat 'n Park, King's Family Rest, Oriental Express, Pizza, Starbucks W: Carmody's Rest, Stone Mansion Rest
	Lodg	E: America's Best Inn♥
	Med	E: + Hospital
	Other	E: FedEx Office, T-Bones Marketplace
(72)		**I-279S, to Pittsburgh (SB, Left exit)**
68		**Blackburn Rd, Mount Nebo Rd North Park, Yellow Belt**
66		**PA 65, Ohio River Blvd, (NB) Glenfield Rd, to PA 65, (SB) to Emsworth, Sewickley**
	Med	W: + Hospital
	Other	W: to North Shore Areas: PA 65S
65		**Grand Ave, Neville Island (NB), to PA 51, Corapolis, Yellow Belt (fr SB, Exit Only)**
64		**PA 51, Coraopolis, McKees Rocks (NB)**
	NOTE:	**NB: TRUCK ALERT—WINDING ROAD ROLL OVER AREA NEXT 2 1/4 mi**

◈= Regular Gas Stations with Diesel ▲ = RV Friendly Locations ♥= Pet Friendly Locations
Red print shows large vehicle parking / access on site or nearby Brown Print = Campgrounds / RV PARKS

EXIT	PENNSYLVANIA
60B	**PA 60N, to US 22W, US 30W, Pittsburgh Intl Airport, Robinson (SB)**
Food	W: McDonald's
Lodg	W: AmeriSuites♥, Holiday Inn Express, Red Roof Inn
60A	**PA 60S, Crafton (SB)**
Gas	E: Exxon
Food	E: King's Family Rest, Primanti Bros
Lodg	E: Comfort Inn, Econo Lodge, Motel 6♥, Travel Inn
Med	E: + Hospital
59B	**US 22W, US 30W (NB)**
Other	W: to Allegheny Co Settlers Cabin Park▲, Greater Pittsburgh Int'l Airport✈, PA Air National Guard
(59A)	**Jct I-279N, US 22E, US 30E, to Pittsburgh**
Other	E: to Heinz Field, Univ of Pittsburgh, Carnegie Mellon Univ
57	**Noblestown Rd, to I-279, Carnegie**
55	**PA 50, Washington Pike, Bridgeville, Heidelberg, Kirwan Heights**
Gas	E: Sunoco
Food	E: Arby's, Bob Evans, CiCi's Pizza, DQ, Damons, Eat 'n Park, KFC, McDonald's, Pizza Hut, Starbucks, Subway, Taco Bell, Wendy's
Med	E: + Kane Memorial Hospital
Other	E: ATMs, Auto Services, Big Lot, Firestone, Goodyear, Home Depot, Laundromat, Mall, Pharmacy, UPS Store, Walmart▲,
54	**PA 50, Millers Run Rd, Bridgeville (fr SB, Exit only)**
Gas	E: BP◈, Exxon◈ W: Sunoco
Food	E: Burger King, McDonald's, Wendy's
Lodg	E: Holiday Inn Express W: Knights Inn
TServ	W: Firestone Tire & Auto
Med	E: + Hospital
Other	E: Grocery, Laundromat, Pharmacy
(50.5)	**Weigh Station (Both dir)**
(49)	**Rest Area (Both dir) (RR, Phone, Picnic)**
48	**PA 1032, Southpointe Blvd, Canonsburg, to Southpointe, Hendersonville**
Food	E: Big Jim's Roadhouse W: Jackson's Rest, Subway
Lodg	W: Hilton Garden Inn
45	**McClelland Rd, to PA 980 (SB, NB reacc), Weavertown Rd, to PA 980, to US 19, Canonsburg (NB exit, SB entrance),**
Gas	E: Sheetz W: BP, Citgo
Food	W: Hoss's Steak & Sea House, KFC, Long John Silver, McDonald's, Pizza Hut, Quiznos, Starbucks, Subway, Taco Bell, Wendy's
Lodg	W: Super 8
Other	W: ATM, Auto Services
43	**PA 519, Hill Church Houston Rd, to US 19, Canonsburg, Houston, Eighty Four**
Gas	E: Amoco◈, Sunoco

EXIT	PENNSYLVANIA
Gas	W: Sunoco
Med	E: + Canonsburg General Hospital
Other	W: Auto Services, to Jones RV
41	**Racetrack Rd, to US 19, Washington Meadow Lands**
Gas	E: Exxon W: BP◈
Food	E: McDonald's, Waffle House, Wendy's
Lodg	E: Comfort Inn, Holiday Inn
Other	E: The Meadows Race Track & Casino W: Washington Co Fairgrounds
40	**Locust Ave, Pike St, Meadow Lands (NB, NO re-entry)**
Other	W: Washington Co Fairgrounds, Museum
NOTE:	**I-79 below runs with I-70. Exit #'s follow I-70.**
(38/18)	**Jct I-70W, to Wheeling, WV (fr NB, Left exit) Jct I-79N, to Pittsburgh**
19AB	**US 19, Murtland Ave, Washington Rd**
Gas	N: BP S: AmocoBP◈, Exxon, Sunoco
Food	N: Applebee's, Arby's, Cracker Barrel, McDonald's, Ponderosa, Red Robin, Red Lobster, Starbucks, Subway, TGI Friday S: Bob Evans, Burger King, Chinese Rest, CiCi's Pizza, KFC, Long John Silver, McDonald's, Pizza Hut, Shoney's, Taco Bell
Lodg	N: Springhill Suites S: Hampton Inn, Motel 6♥
Med	S: + Washington Hospital
Other	N: ATMs, Auto Dealers, Grocery, Lowe's, PetSmart♥, Sam's Club, Target S: Washington Mall, Firestone, Home Depot, Staples, Walmart sc▲, PA State Hwy Patrol Post
20	**PA 136, Beau St, Washington**
Other	S: Washington/Pittsburg SW KOA▲
(21)	**Jct I-79S, to Morgantown, Waynesburg**
(34)	**Jct I-70E, to New Stanton (fr SB, Left exit)**
NOTE:	**I-79 above runs with I-70. Exit #'s follow I-70.**
33	**US 40, Maiden St, Washington, to Laboratory**
Gas	W: Amoco
Other	W: Washington/PittsburghSW KOA▲
(30.5)	**Parking / Weigh Area (SB)**
30	**US 19, Waynesburg Rd, Amity Ridge Rd, Washington, Amity, Lone Pine**
23	**Ten Mile Rd, Amity, to Marianna, Prosperity**
19	**PA 221, to US 19, Ruff Creek, Jefferson**
14	**PA 21, Roy E Furman Hwy, Waynesburg, Masontown**
FStop	E: Deputy Dawg Amoco
Gas	W: 7-11, Exxon, Sheetz, GetGo
Food	W: Deputy Dawg Sub Shop, Burger King, DQ, Golden Wok, KFC, Long John Silver, McDonald's, Subway, Wendy's

EXIT	PA / WV
Lodg	E: Comfort Inn W: Econo Lodge, Holiday Motel, Super 8
Med	W: + Hospital
Other	E: Greene Co Airport✈ W: ATMs, Auto Dealers, Auto Service, Big Lots, CVS, Grocery, PA State Hwy Patrol,
7	**Kirby-Garards Fort Rd, Waynesburg, to Kirby, Garards Fort**
(6)	**PA Welcome Center (NB) (RR, Phone, Picnic, Vend, Info)**
1	**Bald Hill Rd, Mount Morris**
TStop	E: BFS Truck Auto Plaza/Citgo (Scales)
Gas	W: BP◈, Marathon
Food	E: Rest/BFS TAP
Other	E: Laundry/BFS TAP W: Mt Morris Campground▲
	EASTERN TIME ZONE

⬆ PENNSYLVANIA
⬇ WEST VIRGINIA

NOTE:	**MM 160: Pennsylvania State Line**
	EASTERN TIME ZONE
(159)	**WV Welcome Center (SB) (RR, Phones, Picnic, Vend, RVDump)**
155	**US 19, Osage Rd, to WV 7, Osage Granville, Morganton**
Gas	E: Sheetz, GetGo
Food	E: Arby's, Burger King, ChickFilA, CiCi's Pizza, Golden Corral, Long John Silver, Longhorn Steakhouse, McDonald's, Olive Garden, Shoney's, Starbucks, Texas Roadhouse
Lodg	E: Best Western, Econo Lodge, Euro Suites, Hampton Inn, Holiday Inn, Quality Inn, Residence Inn
Med	E: + Ruby Hospital
Other	E: ATMs, Auto Service, Banks, Barnes & Noble, Best Buy, CVS, PetCo♥, Sam's Club, Target, Tires, UPS Store, Walmart sc▲, WV Univ
152	**US 19, CR 49, Downtown Morgantown, Westover**
Gas	E: BP◈, Exxon
Food	E: McDonald's, Pizza Hut, Subway, Taco Bell, Western Sizzlin' W: Bob Evans, Burger King
Lodg	E: Econo Lodge
Other	E: ATMs, Auto Services, Tires W: ATMs, Auto Services, Lowe's, Office Max, Mall, Tires
(148)	**Jct I-68E, Morgantown, to US 119, Grafton, to Cumberland, MD**
Gas	E: Exxon◈
Food	E: Rest/Ramada Inn
Lodg	E: Almost Heaven B&B, Comfort Inn, Ramada Inn
Other	E: WVU Football Stadium, Tygart Lake State Park
146	**CR 77, Goshen Rd, to US 119**
Other	W: Sport Rider Outdoors
(141)	**Weigh Station (Both dir)**
139	**CR 33, Prickets Creek, E Fairmont**
TStop	W: K & T Truck Stop/BP (Scales)

◈ = Regular Gas Stations with Diesel ▲ = RV Friendly Locations ♥ = Pet Friendly Locations
Red print shows large vehicle parking / access on site or nearby Brown Print = Campgrounds / RV PARKS

EXIT		WEST VIRGINIA
	Gas	E: Chevron
		W: Exxon
	Food	W: Rest/K&T TS
	TServ	W: K & T TS/Tires
	Other	W: Laundry/K&T TS
137		**WV 310, Downtown Fairmont**
	Gas	E: BP, Exxon◈
	Food	E: Subway
		W: KFC, McDonald's, Wendy's
	Lodg	E: Holiday Inn
	Med	W: + Hospital
	Other	E: Grocery
		W: UPS Store, Fairmont State Univ
135		**CR 64, Millersville Rd, to Pleasant Valley Rd, Fairmont**
133		**CR 64/1, Kingmont Rd, Fairmont**
	FStop	E: BFS Foods #39/BP
	Gas	W: Chevron◈
	Food	E: Subway/BP, Cracker Barrel
	Lodg	E: Super 8
		W: Comfort Inn, Days Inn, Red Roof Inn♥
	Other	E: Mountain Man RV Center
		W: Fairmount Muni Airport✈
132		**US 250, Adams St, S Fairmont**
	Gas	W: Exxon, Sunoco
	Food	E: Arby's, Bob Evans, Hardee's, McDonald's, Subway, Taco Bell
	Lodg	E: Days Inn, Red Roof Inn♥
	TServ	E: Cummins Cumberland
	Med	W: + Hospital
	Other	E: ATMs, Advance Auto Parts, Grocery, Harley Davidson, Middletown Mall, Sam's Club, Walmart sc▲,
		W: Auto Dealers, Trailer City RV Center, Fairmont State Univ
125		**WV 131, Grande Meadow Rd, Saltwell Rd, Bridgeport**
	Gas	W: Exxon◈
	Lodg	W: Super 8
124		**WV 279, to US 50E, Bridgeport**
	Other	E: to Benedum Airport✈
(123)		**Rest Area (Both dir)** (RR, Phones, Picnic, Vend, RVDump)
121		**CR 24, Meadowbrook Rd**
	Gas	E: GoMart, Sheetz
		W: Exxon◈
	Food	E: Bob Evans, Blimpie/GoMart
		W: Arby's, Burger King, Ponderosa
	Lodg	E: Hampton Inn
		W: Econo Lodge, Super 8
	Other	E: to Benedum Airport✈
		W: Pharmacy, Target, Mall
119		**US 50, W Main St, Clarksburg, Bridgeport**
	Gas	E: Chevron◈, Exxon◈, GoMart, Speedway
	Food	E: Denny's, Hardee's, KFC, Little Caesars Pizza, Long John Silver, McDonald's, Shoney's, Subway, TCBY, Taco Bell
	Lodg	E: Comfort Inn, Days Inn, Holiday Inn, Knights Inn, Sleep Inn, Towne House Motor Lodge East
	Med	E: + Hospital
	Other	E: ATMs, Big Lots, Grocery, Home Depot, Kroger, Lowe's, Sam's Club, Walmart sc▲, Salem Int'l Univ, to Harrison Marion Regional Airport✈
117		**WV 58, Smithfield Ave, Anmoore**
	FStop	W: 7-11 #5602/BP
	Food	E: Arby's, Applebee's, Burger King, Ruby Tuesday, Ryan's Grill, Subway

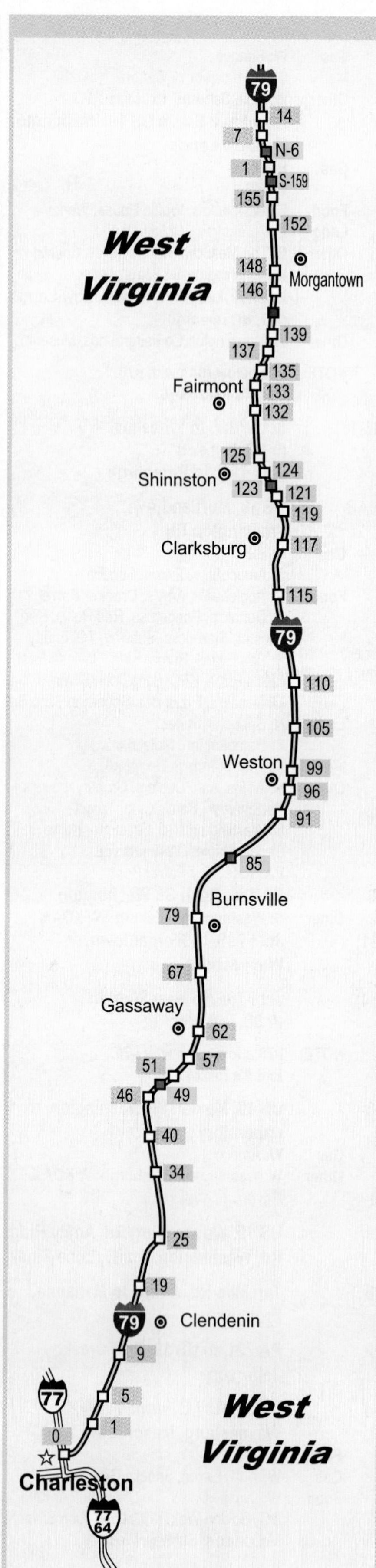

EXIT		WEST VIRGINIA
	Other	E: ATMs, Bank, Grocery, Staples, Walmart sc▲
115		**WV 20, Mt Clare, to Stonewood**
	Gas	E: BP, Chevron, Exxon
110		**WV 270, Milford Rd, Lost Creek Rd, Lost Creek**
105		**CR 7, to US 19, Jane Lew**
	TStop	E: Jane Lew Truck Stop/Chevron (Scales)
	Gas	W: Exxon
	Food	E: Rest/Jane Lew TS
	TServ	E: Jane Lew TS/TWash/Tires
	Other	E: Laundry/Jane Lew TS
99		**US 33, US 119, Weston, Horner**
	Gas	E: Exxon, Sheetz
		W: BP
	Food	E: McDonald's, Subway
		W: Hardee's, Pizza Hut, Wendy's
	Lodg	E: Comfort Inn, Days Inn, Super 8
	Med	W: + Hospital
	Other	E: Kroger, Walmart, Pharmacy
		W: NAPA
96		**CR 30, CR 19/39, Weston**
	Other	E: Stonewall Jackson State Park
91		**US 19, Weston, to Roanoke**
	Other	E: Stonewall Jackson Lake State Park
(85)		**Rest Area (Both dir)** (RR, Phones, Picnic, Vend, RVDump)
79		**WV 5, 5th Ave, 5th St, Burnsville, Glenville**
	Gas	E: Exxon
		W: Go Mart, Shell
	Food	E: Rest/Motel 79
	Lodg	E: Motel 79
	Other	E: Glenville State College, Burnsville Dam
67		**WV 15, US 19, Flatwoods**
	FStop	E: Go Mart #44, Lloyd's Food Store/ Chevron
	TStop	E: John Skidmore Truck Stop/Ashland
	Gas	E: Exxon◈
	Food	E: Rest/John Skidmore TS, DQ, KFC, McDonald's, Waffle Hut
		W: Shoney's, Wendy's
	Lodg	E: Days Inn
		W: John Skidmore Motel/Pennzoil
	Tires	W: John Skidmore TS
	Other	E: to Sutton Lake Rec Area
62		**WV 4, State St, Sutton, Gassaway**
	Gas	W: Go Mart
	Food	W: Long John Silver, Pizza Hut
	Med	W: + Hospital
	Other	W: CVS, Kroger
57		**US 19S, Mountaineer Expwy, Beckle Summersville**
51		**WV 4, to Frametown, Strangetown**
(49)		**Rest Area (Both dir)** (RR, Phone, Pic, Vend, RVDump)
46		**CR 11, Servia Rd, Duck**
40		**WV 16, Big Otter, Nebo, Wallback**
	FStop	E: Go Mart #86
		W: Big Otter Food Mart/Exxon
34		**WV 36, Wallback, Clay, Newton**
25		**CR 29, Big Sandy Creek, Amma**
	Gas	E: Exxon◈
19		**US 119, Bufflick Rd, Spencer Rd, to WV 4, to Clendenin**
	Gas	E: BP◈
	Food	E: BiscuitWorld

◈= Regular Gas Stations with Diesel ▲ = RV Friendly Locations ♥= Pet Friendly Locations
Red print shows large vehicle parking / access on site or nearby Brown Print = Campgrounds / RV PARKS

EXIT		WEST VIRGINIA
9		**CR 43, Frame Rd, Elkview**
	Gas	E: Go Mart◈ W: Exxon◈, Speedway◈
	Food	W: Bob Evans, McDonald's, Ponderosa, Subway, Arby's/Exxon
	Other	W: ATMs, Advance Auto Parts, CVS, Kroger
5		**WV 114, CR 41, Copper Creek Rd, Charleston, to Big Chimney**
	Gas	E: Exxon
	Food	E: Hardee's
1		**US 119, Pennsylvania Ave, Mink Shoals, to Charleston**
	Food	E: Family Rest
	Lodg	W: Sleep Inn
	Other	E: Yeager Airport✈, Coonskin Park
(0)		**Jct I-77, S to Charleston, N to Parkersburg**
	NOTE:	I-79 starts/ends on I-77, Ex #104

WEST VIRGINIA

Begin Northbound I-79 from Jct I-77 in Charleston, WV to Erie, PA.

Begin Eastbound I-80 from San Francisco, CA to Jct I-95 in Englewood, NJ.

CALIFORNIA

PACIFIC TIME ZONE

NOTE: 1-80 begins/ends on 7th St, San Fran

EXIT		CALIFORNIA
1		**7th St, 8th St, Harrison St, Bryant St, Downtown San Francisco (EB)**
1C		**9th St, Civic Center (WB)**
1B		**US 101N, Golden Gate Bridge (WB)**
1A		**US 101S (WB, Left exit)**
2		**4th St, Embarcadero (EB)**
2C		**Fremont St (WB)**
2B		**Harrison St (WB, Left exit)**
2A		**5th St (WB, Left exit)**
4A		**Treasure Island (EB, Left exit)**
4B		**Yerba Buena Island (EB)**
4		**Treasure Island Rd (WB, Left exit)**
	TServ	S: Cummins West
	Other	S: US Coast Guard SF
(7)		**TOLL Plaza (WB)**
8A		**Maritime St, W Grand Ave, to I-880, Harbor Terminals, Oakland**
	Other	S: Oakland Army Base
(8B)		**I-580E, Oakland, Hayward Stockton; I-880S (WB, Left exit) (end shared I-580)**
9		**Powell St, Emeryville (EB begins shared with I-580)**
	Gas	N: Shell S: Beacon
	Food	N: Chevy's Mexican Rest S: Burger King, Denny's, Starbucks
	Lodg	N: Holiday Inn S: Courtyard, Sheraton, Wyndham
	Other	S: ATMs, Borders, Grocery, Trader Joe's
10		**CA 13, Ashby Ave, Shellmound St, Berkeley**
11		**University Ave, Berkeley**
	Gas	S: 76, Beacon
	Lodg	N: Doubletree Inn S: Holiday Inn Express, Marina Lodge Motel, University Inn
	Other	S: to Univ of CA/Berkeley, Amtrak, Berkeley Aquatic Park
12		**Gilman St**
	Other	N: Golden Gate Fields Racetrack
13		**to I-580, Albany (WB) (Begin share I-580)**
13A		**Buchanan St, Albany (EB)**
	Lodg	S: Meyer Motel
(13B)		**Jct I-580W, Point Richmond**
14A		**Central Ave, Richmond, El Cerrito**
	Gas	S: 76, Shell, Valero
	Food	S: Burger King, KFC
	Other	S: ATMs, Costco, Mall
	Other	N: Golden Gate Fields Racetrack
14B		**Carlson Blvd, Richmond**
	Gas	N: 76
	Lodg	N: Forty Flags Motel S: Super 8
15		**Potrero Ave, Cutting Blvd, El Cerrito**
	Gas	N: ArcoAmPm S: Chevron
	Lodg	S: Best Inn
16A		**Mac Donald Ave (EB)**
16B		**San Pablo Ave (EB)**
	Gas	N: 76 S: Chevron
16		**San Pablo Ave, Richmond (WB)**
17		**Solano Ave (EB), McBryde Ave**
	Gas	N: 7-11, ArcoAmPm S: Chevron
	Food	N: Burger King, KFC, Taco Bell S: Wendy's
	Med	N: + Dr's Medical Center
	Other	S: Albertson's, Safeway, B & L RV
18		**San Pablo Dam Rd**
	Gas	N: 76, 7-11, Shell S: Shell
	Food	N: Burger King, Denny's, McDonald's
	Lodg	N: Holiday Inn
	Med	N: + Hospital
	Other	N: Albertson's, Pharmacy, UPS Store
19A		**El Portal Dr, San Pablo, El Sobrante**
	Gas	N: Shell
	Food	S: McDonald's
19B		**Hilltop Dr, Richmond**
	Gas	N: Chevron, Shell S: Hilltop Fuel◈
	Food	N: Olive Garden, Red Lobster, Subway S: BBQ
	Lodg	N: Courtyard, Extended Stay America
	Other	N: Albertson's, Firestone, Hilltop Mall Walmart sc▲
20		**Richmond Pkwy, to I-580, Fitzgerald Dr, Pinole, San Pablo**
	Gas	N: Chevron S: Chevron, Shell

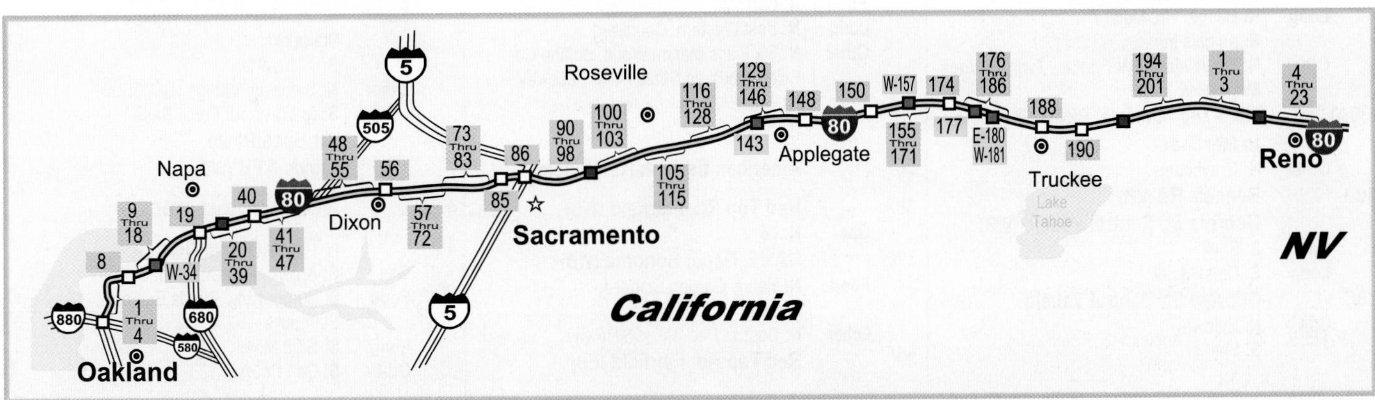

◈= Regular Gas Stations with Diesel ▲ = RV Friendly Locations ♥ = Pet Friendly Locations
Red print shows large vehicle parking / access on site or nearby Brown Print = Campgrounds / RV PARKS

EXIT		CALIFORNIA
	Food	N: McDonald's, Red Lobster, Subway S: Applebee's, Outback Steakhouse, Starbucks
	Lodg	S: Motel 6♥
	Other	N: ATMs, Auto Dealers, Barnes & Noble, B Dalton, Hilltop Mall, PetSmart♥, Greyhound S: FedEx Office, Grocery, Staples, Target
21		**Appian Way, Pinole**
	Gas	N: Beacon S: Valero◈
	Food	N: McDonald's S: Burger King, Hometown Buffet, KFC, Panda Express, Sizzler, Subway, Starbucks, Taco Bell, Wendy's
	Lodg	S: Days Inn, Motel 6♥
	Other	N: Grocery, Pharmacy, Safeway S: Albertson's, Auto Zone, Best Buy, Goodyear, UPS Store
22		**Pinole Valley Rd, Pinole**
	Gas	S: 76, 7-11, Chevron◈, Shell
	Food	S: China House, Jack in the Box, Pizza, Subway, Waffle Shop
	Other	S: Albertson's
23		**CA 4, John Muir Pkwy, Willow Ave, San Pablo Ave, Hercules, Stockton**
	Gas	N: Shell
	Food	N: Starbucks
	Other	S: Albertson's, Pharmacy
24		**Willow Ave, to CA 4, Rodeo, Hercules**
	Gas	N: 76◈ S: Circle K◈
	Food	N: Pizza S: Burger King
	Other	N: Grocery, NAPA
26		**Cummings Skyway, to CA 4, to San Pablo Ave, Martinez, Concord**
27		**Crockett Port Costa, Crockett**
(28)		**TOLL Plaza (EB)**
29A		**CA 29, Sonoma Blvd (EB), Maritime Academy Dr (WB)**
	Gas	N: Chevron
	Food	N: Subway
	Lodg	N: Motel 6♥, Rodeway Inn
	Other	N: Car Wash
29B		**Sequoia Ave (EB), Magazine St (WB)**
	Lodg	N: Budget Inn, El Rancho Inn
29C		**Magazine St, Vallejo (EB)**
	Gas	N: Shell S: 7-11
	Food	N: Hickory Pit S: McDonald's
	Lodg	N: Budget Inn, Motel 7 S: Knights Inn
	Other	N: **Tradewinds RV Park▲, Twin Bridges MH Park▲**
(30A)		**Jct I-780, Curtola Pkwy, Benecia, to Martinez**
	Other	N: Greyhound
30B		**Benecia Rd (EB) Georgia St, Central Vallejo (WB)**
	Gas	S: Shell
	Lodg	S: Crest Motel
30C		**Georgia St, Central Vallejo**
	Gas	N: Safeway S: Shell◈

EXIT		CALIFORNIA
	Food	S: Mandarin Chinese, Starbucks/Shell
	Lodg	S: California Motel
31A		**Solano Ave, Springs Rd, Vallejo**
	Gas	N: Chevron◈ S: Beacon, Chevron, QuikStop
	Food	N: Burger King, Church's S: DQ, McDonald's, Pizza Hut, Subway
	Lodg	N: Best Value Inn, Travelodge S: Islander Motel, Relax Inn
	Other	N: Albertson's, RiteAid, U-Haul S: Walgreen's
31B		**Tennessee St, Vallejo, Mare Island**
	Gas	S: 76, Valero
	Food	S: Jack in the Box
	Lodg	S: Great Western Inn, Quality Inn
	Other	N: CarQuest S: **Sunset Trailer Park▲**
32A		**Redwood Pkwy (EB)**
	Other	S: FedEx Office
32B		**Redwood St (EB)**
32		**Redwood St, Vallejo (WB)**
	Gas	N: 76, Shell, Stop & Save S: Shell
	Food	N: Denny's, Annie's Panda Garden S: Indian Rest, Little Caesar's Pizza
	Lodg	N: Days Inn, Motel 6♥
	Med	N: + Hospital
	Other	N: Albertson's, Auto Services, Tires, **Crane's RV Refrig Service** S: Auto Dealers, Auto Zone, Safeway, Target
33		**CA 37, Auto Mall Columbus Pkwy, Marine World Pkwy, Vallejo (EB)**
	Gas	N: Chevron
	Food	N: Carl's Jr S: Applebee's, Black Angus Steakhouse, IHOP, McDonald's, Mountain Mike's Pizza, Panda Express, Red Lobster , Subway, Taco Bell, Wendy's
	Lodg	N: Best Western, Courtyard S: Comfort Inn, Ramada Inn♥
	Other	N: ATMs, Grocery, Six Flags Marine World, Co Fairgrounds S: ATMs, Banks, Best Buy, Costco, Dollar Tree, Home Depot, Office Max, Pep Boys, PetCo♥
33A		**Auto Mall Columbus Pkwy (WB)**
	Gas	N: Chevron
	Food	N: Carl's Jr,
	Lodg	N: Best Western, Courtyard
	Other	N: Six Flags Marine World, Solano Co Fairgrounds
33B		**CA 37, Marine World Pkwy, San Rafael (WB)**
	Gas	N: Chevron
	Food	N: Carl's Jr,
	Lodg	N: Best Western, Courtyard
	Other	N: Six Flags Marine World, Solano Co Fairgrounds, **to** Sears Point Raceway
(34)		**Hunter Hill Rest Area (WB)** **(RR, Phones, Picnic, Info)**
36		**American Canyon Rd, Vallejo**
39A		**Red Top Rd, Fairfield (WB)**
	Gas	N: 76
39B		**CA 12, Napa, Sonoma (WB)**
	Food	N: Happy Garden Chinese, Subway
	Other	N: Costco, Pharmacy, Safeway
39		**Red Top Rd, Fairfield (EB)**

EXIT		CALIFORNIA
(40)		**Jct I-680, Benecia, San Jose (WB) I-680, Green Valley Rd, Benecia (EB)**
41		**Suisun Valley Rd, Green Valley Rd, Fairfield**
	Gas	S: 76◈, ArcoAmPm, Chevron, Flyers◈, Shell◈
	Food	S: Arby's, Burger King, Carl's Jr, Denny's, Jack in the Box, McDonald's, Starbucks, Subway, Taco Bell, Wendy's
	Lodg	S: Best Western, Comfort Inn, Days Inn, Econo Lodge, Fairfield Inn, Hampton Inn, Holiday Inn Express, Overniter Lodge
	Other	N: Solano Comm College S: **Ray's RV, Camping World/RVDump**
(42)		**Weigh Station (Both dir)**
43		**CA 12, Rio Vista, Chadbourne Rd (EB), Abernathy Rd, Suisun City (WB)**
	Other	S: Pharmacy, **Walmart**, Anheuser-Busch Brewery, Jelly Belly Factory Tour
44A		**Abernathy Rd (EB)**
44B		**W Texas St, Fairfield (EB)**
44		**W Texas St, Rockville Rd (WB)**
	Gas	N: Shell S: 76, Exxon, Valero
	Food	N: Chuck E Cheese's Pizza, Denny's, In 'N Out Burger S: DQ, Jack in the Box, McDonald's
	Lodg	N: Extended Stay America, Holiday Inn Select S: Economy Inn, Sleepy Hollow Motel
	Other	N: ATMs, FedEx Office S: ATMs, Home Depot, Target, Walgreen's
45		**Travis Blvd, Fairfield**
	Gas	N: ArcoAmPm, Chevron, Shell S: Shell
	Food	N: Burger King, Chuck E Cheese's Pizza, Denny's, McDonald's, Starbucks, Subway, Taco Bell S: Applebee's, Carino's, China Express, Mimi's Café, Panda Express, Red Lobster, Starbucks, Subway
	Lodg	N: Extended Stay America, Holiday Inn, Motel 6♥ S: Hilton Garden Inn
	Med	S: + Northbay Medical Center
	Other	N: ATMs, Banks, Grocery, PetCo♥, Fairfield Harley Davidson, **CA State Hwy Patrol Post** S: ATMs, Best Buy, Firestone, Office Max, Trader Joe's, Westfield Mall
47		**Waterman Blvd, Air Base Pkwy (EB)**
	Gas	S: 7-11
	Food	N: Dynasty Chinese, Hungry Hunter, Starbucks
	Med	S: + Hospital
	Other	N: Safeway, **Village RV Center** S: **to** Travis Air Force Base
47A		**Air Base Pkwy, Travis AFB (WB)**
47B		**Waterman Blvd (WB)**
48		**N Texas St, Fairfield**
	Gas	S: ArcoAmPm, Chevron, Shell
	Food	S: Burger King, Panda Express, Starbucks
	Lodg	S: EZ 8 Motel
	Other	S: Golf Course

◈ = Regular Gas Stations with Diesel ▲ = RV Friendly Locations ♥ = Pet Friendly Locations
Red print shows large vehicle parking / access on site or nearby **Brown Print = Campgrounds / RV PARKS**

EXIT		CALIFORNIA
51A		**Lagoon Valley Rd, Cherry Glen Rd, Fairfield, Vacaville**
51B		**Pena-Adobe Rd**
	Other	S: Lagoon Valley Regional Park
52		**Cherry Glen Rd (WB)**
53		**Alamo Dr, Merchant St**
	Gas	N: Chevron, Shell◈ S: 76
	Food	N: Bakers Square, Lyon's S: Jack in the Box, KFC, McDonald's, Pizza Hut, Starbucks, Stir Fry Chinese
	Lodg	N: Alamo Inn
54A		**Davis St, Vacaville**
	Gas	N: Chevron S: QuikStop
	Food	N: McDonald's/Chevron, Outback Steakhouse
	Lodg	N: Hampton Inn
	Other	S: Grocery
54B		**Peabody Rd Elmira (EB), Mason St (WB)**
	Gas	N: Chevron S: 7-11, ArcoAmPm
	Food	S: Carl's Jr
	Lodg	N: Hampton Inn, Royal Motel, Super 8
	Other	N: Albertson's, ATMs, Auto Zone, Big O Tire, Firestone, Goodyear, NAPA, Pharmacy S: Auto Repair/Shell, Costco, Goodyear, Greyhound
55		**Monte Vista Ave, Allison Dr, Nut Tree Parkway**
	Gas	N: 76, Citgo, Shell S: ArcoAmPm, Chevron
	Food	N: Arby's, Burger King, Denny's, IHOP, McDonald's, Taco Bell, Wendy's S: Applebee's, Baja Fresh Mexican, Carl's Jr, Chili's, HomeTown Buffet, Jack in the Box, McDonald's, KFC, Starbucks
	Lodg	N: Best Western, Super 8 S: Courtyard, Fairfield Inn, Holiday Inn Express, Motel 6, Residence Inn
	Med	S: + Vaca Valley Hospital
	Other	N: America's Tire, Firestone, Goodyear, U-Haul, Lee's MH & RV Park▲ S: ATMs, CompUSA, Pharmacy, Safeway, Sam's Club, Staples, Target, Tires, Walmart▲, Vacaville Premium Outlets
(56)		**I-505, Winters, Redding, Orange Dr (EB), I-505N, Redding (WB)**
	Lodg	S: Courtyard, Fairfield Inn, Holiday Inn, Motel 6♥, Residence Inn
	Other	N: Weslo's RV Center, Vacaville Nut Tree Airport✈, Vineyard RV Park▲ S: ATMs, FedEx Office, Home Depot, Staples, UPS Store, Vacaville Harley Davidson
57		**Leisure Town Rd, Vaca Valley Pky**
	Food	S: Jack in the Box, Kings Buffet
	Lodg	S: Extended Stay America
	Other	N: Nelson's RV Parts & Service S: Auto Dealers
59		**Meridian Rd, Weber Rd**
60		**Midway Rd, Lewis Rd, Elmira**
	Other	N: to appr 7mi: Vineyard RV Park▲
63		**CR 238, Dixon Ave, Grant Rd, Dixon**
	Gas	N: Chevron S: ArcoAmPm, Shell

Personal Notes

EXIT		CALIFORNIA
	Food	S: Carl's Jr, KFC/A&W
	Lodg	S: Super 8
	Other	N: RVDump/LP/Chevron
64		**CR 124, Pitt School Rd**
	Gas	S: Chevron, Valero, Safeway◈
	Food	S: Arby's, Burger King, Denny's, IHOP, McDonald's, Pizza Hut, Starbucks, Subway
	Lodg	S: Best Western, Microtel
66		**CA 113S, Curry Rd, First St (EB) (EB Begin Shared CA 113, WB End)**
66A		**CA 113S, Rio Vista, Dixon**
	FStop	S: CFN/Ramos Oil/Shell
	Gas	S: 76◈, ArcoAmPm, Valero
	Food	S: Cattleman's Steakhouse, Jack in the Box, Popeye's/Valero
	Lodg	S: Comfort Suites
	Other	S: Walmart▲
66B		**Milk Farm Rd, Dixon (WB)**
	FStop	S: CFN/Ramos Oil
67		**CR 104, Pedrick Rd**
69		**Kidwell Rd**
70		**CA 113N, Davis, to Woodland (WB Begin Shared CA 113, EB End)**
	Other	N: Univ of CA/Davis Airport✈
71		**Old Davis Rd, UC Davis Off Ramp**
72		**Richards Blvd, Davis (EB)**
	Gas	N: Shell S: Chevron
	Food	N: Café Italia, In 'N Out Burger S: Applebee's, IHOP, KFC, Wendy's
	Lodg	N: Aggie Inn, Best Western, Econo Lodge, Hallmark Inn, University Park Inn S: Comfort Suites, Holiday Inn Express

EXIT		CALIFORNIA
	Other	N: ATMs, Auto Services, NAPA, Amtrak, Greyhound, Univ of CA/Davis S: Jiffy Lube
72A		**Richards Blvd South, Davis**
72B		**Richards Blvd, Davis (WB)**
73		**Olive Dr (WB)**
75		**Mace Blvd, Chiles Rd, Davis**
	Gas	N: Arco S: Chevron, Shell, Valero◈
	Food	S: Burger King, Denny's, McDonald's, Mountain Mikes, Subway, Taco Bell, Wendy's
	Lodg	S: Howard Johnson, Motel 6♥
	Other	S: Auto Dealers, La Mesa RV
78		**East Chiles Rd, CR 32A, CR 32B, Frontage Rd**
81		**Enterprise Blvd, W Capital Ave, Industrial Blvd, W Sacramento**
	FStop	N: W Sacramento Truck Stop/Chevron S: CFN / Ramos Oil #1580
	Gas	S: 76◈
	Food	N: Eppie's Rest S: Denny's, Quiznos, Starbucks, Subway
	Lodg	N: Granada Inn
	Other	S: Sacramento West/Old Town KOA▲
82		**I-80 Bus Lp, US 50, S Lake Tahoe (EB, Left exit) US 50E, Bus Loop 80, Sacramento (WB)**
83		**Reed Ave, W Sacramento**
	Gas	N: 76◈ S: Shell◈
	Food	N: Jack in the Box, Panda Express, Quiznos, Starbucks, Subway S: In 'N Out Burger, McDonald's/Shell
	Lodg	N: Extended Stay America, Hampton Inn
	TServ	S: Cummins West
	Other	S: Home Depot, Walmart SC
85		**W El Camino Ave, El Centro Rd**
	TStop	N: AmBest/Sacramenta 49er Travel Plaza/ Shell (Scales)
	Gas	N: Chevron◈
	Food	N: SilverSkilletRest/49er TP, Burger King, Subway/Chevron
	Lodg	N: Motel/49er TP, Fairfield Inn, Super 8
	TWash	N: 49er TP
	TServ	N: 49er TP/Tires
	Other	N: Laundry/CB/Chiro/Med/WiFi/RVDump/ LP/49er TP
(86)		**Jct I-5, N-Redding, S-Sacramento, Los Angeles, S to CA 99**
88		**Truxel Rd, Sacramento**
	Gas	N: Chevron, Shell◈, Sam's
	Food	N: Applebee's, Chili's, Chipolte Mex Rest, Del Taco, Hooters, MiMi's Cafe, On the Border, Panera Bread, Qdoba Mexican, Quiznos, Starbucks, TGI Friday
	Other	N: ATMs, Barnes & Noble, Best Buy, Home Depot, Michael's, PetSmart♥, Sam's Club, Staples, Target, Walmart▲, Mall, to Arco Arena
89		**Northgate Blvd, Sacramento**
	Fstop	N: CFN / Ramos Oil #3962
	Gas	S: Circle K, Shell◈, Valero◈
	Food	S: Burger King, Carl's Jr, IHOP, KFC, Long John Silver, McDonald's, Taco Bell
	Lodg	S: Extended Stay America, Red Roof Inn♥ Quality Inn

◈ = Regular Gas Stations with Diesel ▲ = RV Friendly Locations ♥ = Pet Friendly Locations
Red print shows large vehicle parking / access on site or nearby Brown Print = Campgrounds / RV PARKS

EXIT — CALIFORNIA

Other N: Arco Arena
S: Big Lots, Dollar Tree, Goodyear, Grocery, Pep Boys, Tires

90 Norwood Ave
Gas N: ArcoAmPm, Valero
Food N: Jack in the Box/Arco, McDonald's, Starbucks, Subway
Other N: Grocery, RiteAid,

91 Raley Blvd, Marysville Blvd
Gas N: ArcoAmPm, Chevron◈

92 Winters St
Other N: McClellan AF Base

93 Longview Dr, Light Rail Station

94A Watt Ave (EB)
Gas N: 7-11, 76, ArcoAmPm, Shell
Food N: Carl's Jr, Carrow's, DQ, Jack in the Box, KFC, Pizza Hut, Taco Bell, The Golden Egg Café
S: Burger King, Denny's, Starbucks
Lodg N: Days Inn, Motel 6♥
Other N: McClellan AFB

94B Auburn Blvd (EB)
Med S: + Heritage Oaks Hospital

94 Light Rail Stations (WB, Left exit)

95 to I-80 Bus, Capital City Frwy, Sacramento, to CA 99S

96 Madison Ave
Gas N: Beacon, Chevron, Valero
S: 76, ArcoAmPm, Shell
Food N: Brookfield's, Denny's, Java Coffee, Jack In the Box, Starbucks
S: Boston Market, Burger King, El Pollo Loco, IHOP, Jack in the Box, McDonald's, Panda Express, Starbucks, Subway, Taco Bell
Lodg N: Motel 6♥, Super 8, Vagabond Inn
S: Holiday Inn, La Quinta Inn♥
Other N: McClellan AFB
S: Auto Service, Goodyear, Office Depot, Target, U-Haul, Walgreen's

98 Greenback Lane, Elkhorn Blvd
Gas N: 76, Circle K
Food N: Carl's Jr, McDonald's, Pizza Hut C/O, Subway, Taco Bell
Med N: + Intermediate Care Medical Clinic
Other N: Pharmacy, Radio Shack, Safeway

(100) Weigh Station (Both dir)

100 Antelope Rd, Citrus Heights
Gas N: 76
Food N: Burger King, Carl's Jr, Giant Pizza, KFC, Little Caesar's Pizza, Long John Silver, McDonald's, Subway, Taco Bell
Other N: Albertsons, Dollar Tree, Pharmacy, US Post Office

102 Riverside Ave, Auburn Blvd, Citrus Heights, Roseville
Gas N: Arco, Valero◈
S: Flyers◈, Shell
Food N: Starbucks, Subway
S: Jack in the Box
Other S: Auto Zone, NAPA, **RV Center**, Tires

103AB Douglas Blvd (WB)
Gas N: 76, ArcoAmPm, Chevron, Exxon
S: Shell
Food N: Burger King, Claim Jumper, DQ, Jack in the Box, KFC, McDonald's, Taco Bell
S: Carl's Jr, Carrow's, Del Taco, Denny's
Lodg N: Best Western, Extended Stay America, Heritage Inn
S: Hampton Inn, Oxford Suites
Med S: + Roseville Hospital
Other N: Ace Hardware, Big Lots, Big O Tires, Dollar Tree, Firestone, Goodyear, Grocery, Pharmacy, Radio Shack, Trader Joe's
S: Albertson's, Laundromat, Pharmacy, Office Depot, PetCo♥, RiteAid, Target

103 Douglas Blvd, Sunrise Ave (WB)

105A Atlantic St, Eureka Rd (EB) Eureka Rd, Taylor Rd (WB)
Gas S: 76, Chevron, Pacific Pride, Shell
Food S: Brookfields, Black Angus, Carvers Steaks & Chops, In 'N Out, Panda Express, Taco Bell, Wendy's
Lodg S: Marriott
Other S: America's Tire, Auto Dealers, Home Depot, Mall, PetSmart♥, Sam's Club, **RVDump**/Chevron

105B Taylor Rd Rocklin (EB), Atlantic St (WB), Roseville
Gas S: 76
Food N: Cattlemen's Rest
Lodg S: Courtyard, Fairfield Inn, Hilton Garden Inn, Holiday Inn Express, Residence Inn
Other N: **RV Center**, Grocery

106 CA 65, to Lincoln, Marysville
Gas N: Shell
Food N: Applebee's, Carl's Jr, IHOP, Jack in the Box, McDonald's, On the Border, Red Robin, Subway
Lodg N: Comfort Suites
Other N: ATMs, Auto Zone, Barnes & Noble, Costco, Grocery, **Walmart**

108 Rocklin Rd
Gas N: Exxon, Flyers
S: ArcoAmPm
Food N: Arby's, Burger King, Carl's Jr, China Gourmet, Denny's, Jack in the Box, KFC, Starbucks, Subway, Taco Bell
Lodg N: Days Inn, Howard Johnson, Microtel
S: Marriott, Rocklin Park Hotel
Med N: + Medical Clinic
Other N: **Camping World**, **Gamel RV Center**, Pharmacy, CarQuest, Radio Shack, Safeway

109 Sierra College Blvd
Gas N: 76, Chevron◈
Food N: Carl's Jr, McDonald's/Chevron
Lodg N: Days Inn
Other N: **Loomis RV Park**/**RVDump**▲

110 Horseshoe Bar Rd, Loomis

112 Penryn Rd, Loomis
Gas N: 76, Gasco
Food S: Cattle Baron

115 Indian Hill Rd, Newcastle Rd, Hidden Trail Rd, Newcastle
Gas S: ArcoAmPm, Flyer's
Food S: Denny's
Other S: **CA State Hwy Patrol Post**

116 CA 193, Taylor Rd, Lincoln
Other S: Wagner's Truck Repair, **RV Center**

118 Ophir Rd (WB)

119A Maple St (EB), Nevada St (WB), Auburn
Gas S: Shell
Food S: Shanghai Rest, Tio Pepe

119B CA 49, CA 193, to Grass Valley, Placerville
Gas N: Shell
Food N: Granny's Café, Java Junction
Lodg N: Holiday Inn
Med N: + Hospital
Other N: Laundromat, Grocery, Pharmacy, Staples

119C Elm Ave, Auburn
Gas N: 76, Shell
Food N: Blimpie, Taco Bell
Lodg N: Holiday Inn
Other N: Amtrak, Albertson's, Pharmacy, U-Haul

120 Lincoln Way (EB), Russell Rd (WB) (Access Ex #121 Serv)
Gas S: BP, Shell

121 Auburn Ravine Rd, Foresthill
Gas N: Flyers◈, Thrifty, Valero
S: 76◈, ArcoAmPm◈, Chevron◈, Shell◈
Food N: Arby's, Denny's, Taco Bell
S: Bakers Square, Burger King, Carl Jr, Country Waffles, DQ, Jack in the Box, KFC, McDonald's, Sizzler, Starbucks, Subway
Lodg N: Best Inn, Foothills Motel, Motel 6♥, Sleep Inn, Super 8
S: Best Western, Country Squire Inn, Quality Inn, Travelodge
Other S: Grocery, **Auburn State Rec Area**

122 Bowman Rd, Lincoln Way, Auburn (Access Ex #121 Serv)

123 Bell Rd, Auburn
Med N: + Hospital
Other N: **Auburn RV Park**▲

124 Dry Creek Rd

125 Clipper Gap Rd, Placier Hills Rd, Auburn, Meadow Vista

128 Orchard Rd, Applegate
Gas N: Applegate Gas◈
Food N: Cruise In
Lodg N: The Original Firehouse Motel
S: Applegate Motel
Other N: LP/ Applegate Gas

129 Applegate Rd, Heather Glen

130 Paoli Lane, Applegate, Colfax
Gas S: Weimar Country Store◈

131 Weimar Crossroad, Canyon Way

133 S Auburn St, to Placer Hills Rd, Canyon Way, Colfax

135 CA 174, S Auburn Ave, Canyon Way, Colfax, Grass Valley
Gas N: 76◈, Chevron
S: Chevron◈, Valero◈
Food N: McDonald's, Pizza Factory, Rosy's Café, Starbucks, Taco Bell
S: Subway
Lodg N: Colfax Motor Inn
Other N: Best Hardware, Grocery, Laundromat, NAPA
S: **Sierra RV**

139 Rollins Lake Rd, Magra Rd (WB)

140 Magra Rd, to Rollins Lake Rd, Secret Town Rd, Colfax

143 Magra Rd, Gold Run Rd, Dutch Flat

◈ = Regular Gas Stations with Diesel ▲ = RV Friendly Locations ♥ = Pet Friendly Locations
Red print shows large vehicle parking / access on site or nearby Brown Print = Campgrounds / RV PARKS

EXIT	CALIFORNIA
(143)	Gold Run Rest Area (Both dir) (RR, Phones, Picnic, Pet)
144	**Gold Run Rd, Sawmill (WB)**
145	**Ridge Rd, Dutch Flat**
Gas	S: Tesoro◈
Food	N: Monte Vista
Other	N: CAMP▲ S: CA State Hwy Patrol Post
146	**Alta Bonnynook Rd, Alta, Dutch Flat**
148A	**Crystal Springs Rd, Alta**
148B	**Baxter Rd, Alta**
150	**Drum Forebay Rd, Alta**
155	**Blue Canyon Rd, Putt Rd, Alta**
Other	S: Blue Canyon-Nyack Airport✈
156	**Nyack Rd, Alta**
FStop	S: Shell
Food	S: Burger King/Shell FS, Nyack Cafe
(157)	Vista Point (WB)
158A	**Emigrant Gap (EB)**
Gas	S: Shell◈
Food	S: Café/Rancho Sierra Inn
Lodg	S: Rancho Sierra Inn
158B	**Laing Rd (EB)**
158	**Emigrant Gap, Laing Rd (WB)**
160	**Yuba Gap Rd, Crystal Lake Rd**
161	**CA 20, Soda Springs, Nevada City**
164	**Eagle Lakes Rd, Crystal Lake Rd**
Other	N: CAMP▲
165	**Cisco Rd, Cisco Grove, Norden**
Gas	S: Mobil, Valero◈
Other	N: RV CAMP/RVDump▲
166	**Donner Pass Rd, Hampshire Rocks Rd, Norden, to Big Bend (EB)**
168	**Rainbow Rd, Big Bend**
Food	S: Rest/Rainbow Lodge
Lodg	S: Rainbow Inn
171	**Donner Pass Rd, Troy, Kingvale**
Gas	S: Shell
174	**Donner Pass Rd, Soda Springs**
FStop	S: 76
Food	S: Rest/Donner Summit Lodge
Lodg	S: Donner Summit Lodge
176	**Boreal Ridge Rd, Soda Springs, Castle Peak**
Food	S: Rest/Boreal Inn
Lodg	S: Boreal Inn
(177)	Donner Summit Rest Area (Both dir) (RR, Phones, Picnic) (CLOSED thru 4/11)
(180)	Vista Point (EB)
180	**Donner Lake Rd, Truckee**
Lodg	S: Donner Lake Village Resort, Richards Motel
(181)	Vista Point (WB)
184	**Donner Pass Rd, Truckee**
FStop	N: Shell S: Chevron
Gas	S: 76
Food	N: Mountain Grill S: Donner House Rest, Donner Lake Pizza
Lodg	N: Sunset Inn S: Alpine Village Motel, Holiday Inn Express

Personal Notes

EXIT	CALIFORNIA
Other	S: Donner Memorial State Park, CAMP/RVDump▲
185	**CA 89S, Truckee, to Lake Tahoe (EB Begin shared CA 89, WB end)**
Gas	N: Sierra Super Stop S: Shell
Food	N: Burger King, DQ, La Bamba, Little Caesars Pizza, Panda Express, Pizza, Sizzler, Starbucks S: Burger King, China Garden, KFC, McDonald's, Subway
Lodg	N: Sunset Inn S: Inn at Truckee, Super 8
Med	N: + Tahoe Forest Hospital
Other	N: CA Hwy Patrol Post, Ace Hardware, CarQuest, NAPA, Radio Shack, RiteAid, Safeway S: Albertson's, Long's Pharmacy, RV CAMP▲
186	**Donner Pass Rd, Central Truckee (reaccess WB only)**
Gas	S: 76
Food	S: Dragonfly, Ponderosa, Truckee Diner, Wagontrain Cafe
Lodg	S: Alta Hotel, Cottage Hotel, Truckee Hotel
Med	N: + Hospital
Other	S: Amtrak
188A	**Donner Pass Rd, to CA 89N, CA 267S, Truckee (EB)**
188B	**CA 89N, Sierraville, CA 267S, Kings Beach (EB) (EB End shared CA 89)**
Other	S: Truckee Tahoe Airport✈

EXIT	CALIFORNIA
188	**CA 89N, Sierraville, CA 267S, Kings Beach, Truckee ByPass (WB) (WB begin Shared CA 89)**
Other	N: Coachland RV Park/RVDump▲
190	**Prosser Village Rd, Truckee**
(191)	Weigh Station (WB)
194	**Hirschdale Rd**
Gas	S: United Trails Gen'l Store
Other	S: RV CAMP▲
199	**Floriston Way, Floriston**
201	**Farad**

PACIFIC TIME ZONE

NOTE: MM 208: Nevada State Line

⇑ CALIFORNIA
⇓ NEVADA

PACIFIC / MOUNTAIN TIME ZONE

EXIT	NEVADA
1	**Gold Ranch Rd, Verdi (WB)**
2	**Gold Ranch Rd, I-80 Bus, 3rd St**
Gas	N: ArcoAmPm◈/Gold Ranch, Terrible's Chevron◈
Food	N: Jack in the Box/Sierra Café/Gold Ranch
Lodg	N: Gold Ranch Hotel, Casino & RV Resort▲
3	**Verdi Rd, Verdi (WB)**
(4)	Weigh Station (EB)
4	**Boomtown-Garson Rd, Verdi**
TStop	N: AmBest/Boomtown Casino Truck Stop (Scales) (***CLOSED INDEFINITELY***)
Food	N: Cassidy's Steakhouse/Sundance Cantina SilverScreenBuffet/Starbucks/FastFood/ Boomtown TS
Lodg	N: Boomtown Hotel
Other	N: Laundry/RVDump/Boomtown TS & Reno KOA/Boomtown RV Park▲
(4.5)	Scenic View (EB)
5	**I-80 Bus, NV 425, to E Verdi (WB)**
(6)	Parking Area (Both dir)
7	**W 4th St, Reno, Mogul**
8	**W 4th St, US 40, NV 647 (EB)**
9	**Robb Dr, Reno**
Gas	N: 76◈ Jackson's/Chevron◈,
Food	N: Domino's Pizza, Jimmy John's, Port of Subs, Starbucks, Tahoe Burger
Other	N: Grocery, Longs Drugs
10	**McCarran Blvd, Reno**
Gas	N: 7-11, ArcoAmPm, Safeway◈ S: 7-11
Food	N: Arby's, Burger King, Carl's Jr, Chili's El Pollo Loco, IHOP, Jack in the Box, McDonald's, Starbucks, Taco Bell S: Little Caesars/Kmart
Lodg	S: Inn at Summit Ridge
Med	S: + Urgent Care
Other	N: Albertson's, Big O Tire, Dollar Tree, Grocery, Kragen Auto Parts, PetSmart♥, Safeway, ShopKO, Tires Plus+, Walgreen's, Walmart sc, to Bonanza Terrace RV Park▲ S: Home Depot

◈= Regular Gas Stations with Diesel ▲ = RV Friendly Locations ♥ = Pet Friendly Locations
Red print shows large vehicle parking / access on site or nearby Brown Print = Campgrounds / RV PARKS

EXIT		NEVADA
12		**Keystone Ave, Reno**
	Gas	**N:** 7-11, ArcoAmPm
		S: 76◈, Chevron, Exxon
	Food	**N:** Pizza Hut, Starbucks
		S: Coffee Grinder Inn, Jack in the Box, KFC, McDonald's, Port of Subs, Ritz Café, Taco Bell, Wendy's
	Lodg	**N:** Gateway Inn, Motel 6♥
		S: Carriage Inn, Courtyard, Crest Inn, Donner Inn, El Tavern Motel, Gold Dust West Casino & Motel, Travelodge
	Med	**S:** + Family & Urgent Medical Care, + Medina Medical Center
	Other	**N:** CVS, Grocery, Laundromat, Pharmacy
		S: Albertson's, Greyhound, Olsen Tire, Pharmacy, Radio Shack, Shopping, **Keystone RV Park▲**, **Chism Trailer Park▲**, to Casinos
13		**Sierra St, Center St, US 395 Bus, Virginia St, Reno**
	Gas	**N:** Shell
		S: Chevron, Shell◈
	Food	**N:** Breakaway, Carl's Jr, Giant Burger, Jimmy John's Gourmet Sandwiches, Jimboy's Tacos
		S: DQ, McDonald's, Sterling's Seafood Steakhouse
	Lodg	**N:** Capri Motel, Silver Dollar Motor Lodge, Sundance Motel
		S: Aspen Motel, Chalet Motel, Flamingo Hilton, Golden West Motor Lodge, Monte Carlo Motel, Silver Legacy Resort Casino, Sands Hotel & Casino, Savoy Motor Lodge, Showboat Inn
	Med	**S:** + St. Mary's Hospital
	Other	**N:** Fleischmann Planetarium, to Univ of NV, **Bonanza Terrace RV Park▲**, **Shamrock RV Park▲**
		S: NAPA, Walgreen's, to Univ of NV/Reno, The Gambler Casino, Circus Circus Hotel & Casino, Eldorado Hotel & Casino Harrah's, Silver Legacy Resort Casino, The Nugget, Various Casinos, **Silver Sage RV Park▲**, **Reno RV Park▲**
14		**Wells Ave**
	Gas	**S:** Chevron, Shell
	Food	**S:** Carrow's, Denny's
	Lodg	**N:** Motel 6♥
		S: Days Inn, Econo Lodge, Holiday Inn Diamonds Casino, Motel 6, Reno Hotel & Casino
	Other	**N:** Washoe Co Fairgrounds
15		**US 395, to Carson City, Susanville**
	Gas	**N:** Chevron, Shell◈

Personal Notes

EXIT		NEVADA
	Food	**N:** Arby's, Burger King, Chinese, Del Taco, Sonic, Subway, Taco Bell
	Lodg	**S:** Alejos Inn, Everybody's Inn Motel, Gold Coin Motel, HiWay 40 Motel
	Other	**N:** Home Depot, **Walmart**, **Bonanza Terrace RV Park▲**, Bonanza Casino, **Shamrock RV Park▲**, to appr 15mi: **Bordertown Casino & RV Resort**/Fuel/LP
		S: **Reno Hilton KOA▲**, to Reno Tahoe Int'l Airport✈
16		**Prater Way, E 4th St, Sparks**
	FStop	**S:** PacPride/Nite N Day
	Gas	**N:** ArcoAmPm
		S: ArcoAmPm◈, Chevron
	Food	**N:** Jack's Coffee Shop, Plantation Station
		S: Gallett's Coney Island Bar

EXIT		NEVADA
	Lodg	**N:** Motel 6♥, Pony Express Lodge
		S: Gold Coin Motel, Hilton
	Other	**N:** Rail City Casino
17		**Rock Blvd, Nugget Ave, Sparks**
	FStop	**S:** to Glendale & Intl Way CFN / Western Energetix
	Gas	**N:** ArcoAmPm, Exxon
	Food	**N:** Jack's Coffee Shop
	Lodg	**N:** Craig Motel, Grand Sierra Resort, Casino, & **RV Park▲**, Nugget Hotel & Casino, Safari Motel, Victorian Inn, Wagon Train Motel
	Other	**N:** Laundromat, Rail City Casino
		S: Baldini's Sports Casino
18		**NV 445, Pyramid Way, Nugget Ave, Victorian Ave, Sparks**
	Food	**N:** Steak Buffet, Victoria's Steak House
		S: John's Oyster Bar, Steakhouse Grill
	Lodg	**N:** DeSoto Hotel, Lariat Motel, Nugget Courtyard, Sunrise Motel, Silver Club Hotel & Casino
		S: Nugget Hotel & Casino
	TServ	**S:** Cummins Intermountain
	Med	**N:** + Occu-Family Care
	Other	**N:** Victorian Mall, Casinos
19		**McCarran Blvd, Nugget Ave, Sparks**
	TStop	**N:** Travel Center of America #172 (Scales)
	Gas	**N:** Chevron◈
	Food	**N:** Truckers Grill/TA TC, Applebee's, Arby's, Black Bear Diner, Burger King, El Pollo Loco, IHOP, Jack in the Box, KFC, McDonald's, Sizzler, Subway, Wendy's
		S: Denny's, BJ's BBQ, Super Burrito
	Lodg	**N:** Aloha Inn, Western Village Inn & Casino
		S: Quality Inn, Motel 6
	TWash	**N:** TA TC
	TServ	**N:** TA TC/Tires
	Other	**N:** Laundry/WiFi/RVDump/LP/TA TC, Big Lots, CVS, Dollar Tree, Kragen Auto Parts, Long Drugs, Mall, Pep Boys, Radio Shack, Safeway, Pharmacy, **Victorian RV Park▲**, **Sparks Marina RV Park▲**
20		**Sparks Blvd, E Greg St, Sparks**
	Gas	**N:** Shell◈
	Food	**N:** Carl's Jr, Outback Steakhouse
	Lodg	**S:** Super 8
	Other	**N:** Best Buy, Factory Outlets of NV, Target
21		**Vista Blvd, E Greg St, Sparks**
	TStop	**S:** Alamo Travel Center/Petro Stopping Center #338 (Scales) **EB: Acc via Exit #20**
	Gas	**N:** Chevron, KwikStop
	Food	**N:** Del Taco, McDonald's
		S: IronSkillet/FastFood/Petro SC
	Lodg	**N:** Fairfield Inn
		S: Super 8♥/Petro SC

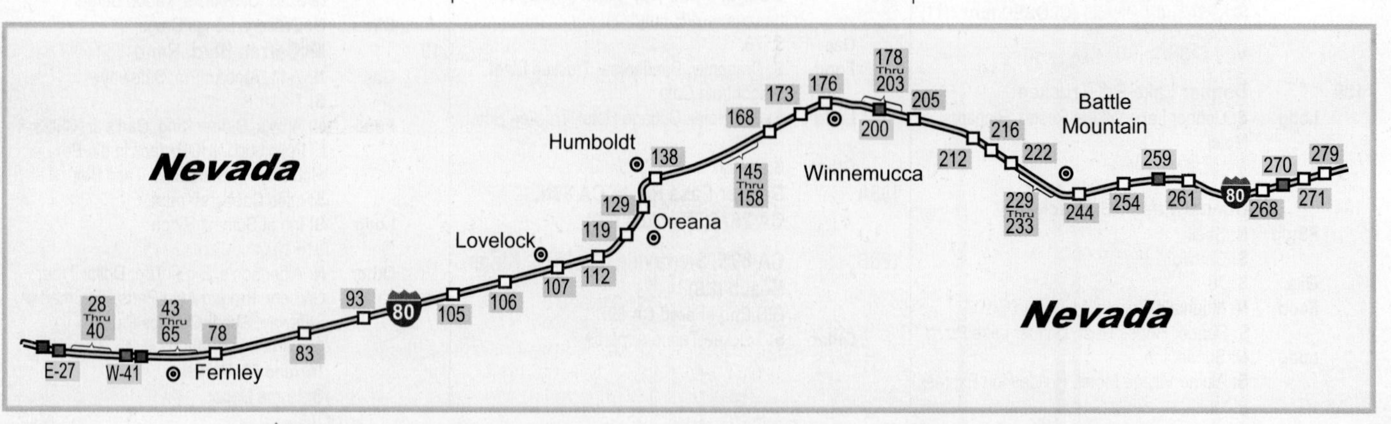

◈= Regular Gas Stations with Diesel ▲ = RV Friendly Locations ♥= Pet Friendly Locations
Red print shows large vehicle parking / access on site or nearby **Brown Print = Campgrounds / RV PARKS**

EXIT		NEVADA
	TWash	S: Petro SC
	TServ	S: Petro SC/Tires, Allison, International, Kenworth, Freightliner
	Med	N: + Hospital
	Other	N: Joe Gandolio Arena S: Laundry/BarbSh/CB/Chiro/**Casino**/Petro SC
22		**Canyon Rd, Lockwood Dr**
23		**Mustang Ranch Rd, Sparks**
	Gas	S: Chevron◈
	Food	N: Mustang Station Café
(25)		**Weigh Station (WB)**
(27)		**Scenic View (EB)**
28		**NV 655, to Waltham Way, Patrick**
32		**Clark Station Rd, Virginia City**
	TStop	S: Golden Gate Auto Truck Plaza (Scales)
	Food	S: FastFood/Golden Gate ATP
36		**Derby Dam**
38		**Orchard**
40		**NV 421, Painted Rock, Reno**
(41)		**Rest Area (WB)** **(RR, Phones, Picnic, RVDump)**
(42)		**Weigh Station (EB)**
43		**NV 427, Wadsworth, Pyramid Lake**
	Other	N: Pyramid Lake Indian Res/Gas◈/**Camping▲**
46		**NV 427, US 95 Alt, W Main St, W. Fernley, Silver Springs, Wadsworth** **(Addtl Serv S to US 50, Acc to #48)**
	TStop	N: Love's Travel Stop #246 (Scales) S: Pilot Travel Center #340 (Scales)
	Gas	S: to Chevron, Exxon
	Food	N: Arby's/Love's TS S: DQ/Wendy's/Pilot TC, to China Chef, La Fiesta Mex Rest
	Lodg	S: Lazy Inn,
	TWash	S: Blue Beacon Truck Wash/Pilot TC, Speedco
	Other	N: Laundry/WiFi/Love's TS S: Laundry/**Casino**/WiFi/Pilot TC, to **Fernley RV Park▲** , **Chukars Sports Casino**, US Post Office
48		**NV 343, US 50 Alt, E Fernley** **(Addtl Serv S to US 50, Acc to #46)**
	TStop	N: Big Wheel Truck Stop (Scales) S: to US 50: CFN/Winners Corner #50/76
	Gas	S: Jakes's Gas, Shell◈, to US 50: 7-11, Chevron, Exxon
	Food	N: Rest/FastFood/Big Wheel TS S: Domino's Pizza, Jack in the Box, KFC, McDonald's, Pizza Factory, Starbucks, Rest/Silverado Casino to Black Bear Diner, Subway
	Lodg	S: Best Western♥ & **RV Park▲** , Super 8♥
	Other	N: **Casino**/Big Wheel TS S: ATMs, Banks, Auto Zone, **Casinos**, D&D Tire, Goodyear, Grocery, Kragen Auto Parts, Lowe's, Radio Shack, **Silverado Casino**, True Value Hardware, U-Haul, **Walmart sc**, **to appr 4mi Desert Rose RV Park▲**
65		**Nightingale Rd, to Hot Springs**
78		**to Jessup**

EXIT		NEVADA
(83)		**US 95S, to Fallon, Las Vegas** **Rest Area (Both dir)** **S: (RR, Phone, Picnic)**
93		**Ragged Top Rd, Lovelock**
105		**80 Bus Lp, Lovelock, to Toulon**
	Gas	N: Shell◈
	Food	N: La Casita Rest
	Lodg	N: Brookwood Motel & **MH RV Park▲**
106		**Main St, Downtown Lovelock** **(Access from Exit #105 or #107)**
	FStop	N: Chevron
	Gas	N: 76, Shell◈
	Food	N: Longhorn Saloon, McDonald's, Pizza Factory, Ranch House Rest
	Lodg	N: Cadillac Motel, Covered Wagon Motel, Sage Motel
	Med	N: + Pershing General Hospital
	Other	N: Sturgeon's Restaurant/**Casino**/Inn, Laundromat, NAPA, Pharmacy
107		**Airport Rd, E Lovelock (WB)**
	Gas	N: Exxon
	Food	N: Rest/Lovelock Inn
	Lodg	N: Lovelock Inn
112		**Coal Canyon Rd, to US 395, NV 396**
119		**Etna Rd, Lovelock-Unionville Rd, to Rochester, to Oreana**
129		**NV 401, Rye Patch Reservoir Rd**
	FStop	S: Rye Patch Truck Stop
	Food	S: Café/Rye Patch TS
	Other	S: Rye Patch Reservoir, **Rye Patch State Recreation Area▲**
138		**Humboldt House Interchange Rd**
145		**NV 416, Imlay**
	Other	N: Village Store & **Campground▲**
149		**NV 400, Imlay, Mill City, to Unionville**
	TStop	N: Travel Center of America #181/Arco (Scales) **(WB Access Via Ex #151)**
	Food	N: ForkinRoad/Subway/TacoBell/TA TC
	Lodg	N: Knights Inn♥/TA TC
	TServ	N: TA TC/Tires
	Other	N: Laundry/WiFi/TA TC, ATM, **I-80 CG▲** S: General Store & **Camping▲**
151		**NV 415, Mill City, Dun Glen** **(WB Access to Ex #149)**
(158)		**Cosgrave Rd, to Cosgrave** **Rest Area (SB)** **S: (RR, Phone, Picnic, RVDump)**
168		**to Rose Creek**
173		**I-80 Bus, NV 289, Winnemucca**
	Other	S: to Winnemucca Muni Airport✈
176		**US 95N, I-80 Bus, NV 289, Winnemucca Blvd, Downtown**
	FStop	N: Pacific Pride S: CFN/Western Energetix **3245 W Potato Rd**
	TStop	S: Flying J Travel Plaza #5025 (Scales), Pilot Travel Center #485 (Scales)
	Gas	S: Chevron◈, Shell◈
	Food	S: CrossRoadDeli/FJ TP, Subway/Pilot TC, Arby's, Burger King, Denny's, KFC, Pizza Hut, Round Table Pizza, Taco Time, Taco Bell
	Lodg	S: Best Western, Days Inn, Holiday Inn Express, Motel 6♥, Quality Inn, Ramada, Santa Fe Inn, Super 8, Winner's Hotel & **Casino**, Red Lion Inn & **Casino**

EXIT		NEVADA
	TServ	S: Freightliner
	Med	S: + Humbolt General Hospital
	Other	S: Laundry/WiFi/**RVDump/LP**/FJ TP, Laundry/**Casino**/**RVDump**/Pilot TC, Auto Dealer, Auto Service, Grocery, Goodyear, Schwab Tire, **Walmart sc▲** , **Model T Casino & RV Park▲** , Winnemucca Indian Colony
178		**I-80 Bus, E 2nd St, to US 40, NV289, US 95, Winnemucca Blvd**
	Gas	S: Chevron, Exxon, Maverick, Shell
	Food	S: Burger King, China Gate, El Mirador Mexican, Pizza Hut, Subway
	Lodg	S: Best Western, Park Motel, Overland Hotel, Scottish Inn, Super 8, Thunderbird Hotel
	Med	S: + Humbolt General Hospital
	Other	S: Grocery, Pharmacy, Amtrak, Golf Course, **Winnemucca KOA▲** , **Casinos**
180		**I-80 Bus, US 40, Winnemucca Blvd**
	Other	S: **High Desert RV Park▲**
(187)		**to Button Point** **Rest Area (Both dir)** **S: (RR, Phones, Picnic, RVDump)**
194		**NV 790, Golconda, Midas**
	Gas	N: Water Hole Gas & Store
	Food	N: Bar Z & Grill
	Lodg	N: Water Hole Motel
	Other	N: Grocery, US Post Office
(200)		**Parking Area (Both dir)**
203		**to Iron Point**
205		**to Pumpernickel Valley**
212		**Stonehouse Hwy, Stonehouse**
(216)		**Valmy** **Rest Area (Both dir)** **(RR, Phones, Picnic, RVDump)**
	FStop	N: CFN/76
	Food	N: Rest/Golden Motel
	Lodg	N: Golden Motel
222		**to Mote**
229		**I-80 Bus, NV 304, to NV 305, Downtown Battle Mountain** **(Acc to #231/#233 Serv)**
	Gas	N: Shell◈
	Lodg	N: Battle Mountain Inn, Big Chief Motel, Nevada Hotel
	Med	N: + to Hospital
	Other	N: Grocery, Te-Moak Indian Res S: Te-Moak Indian Res, **Mill Creek Rec Area▲**
231		**NV 305, S Broad St, Battle Mtn** **(Acc to #233/#229 Serv)**
	FStop	N: **to 345 N 1st St:** CFN/Western Energetix
	TStop	N: Broadway Flying J Travel Plaza #511307/76 (Scales) **(EB Acc via Ex #229)**
	Gas	N: Chevron◈
	Food	N: BroadwayDiner/Blimpie/FJ TP, Donna's Diner, Mama's Pizza
	Lodg	N: BattleMountainInn/FJ TP, Comfort Inn, Nevada Hotel, Owl Motel, Super 8
	TServ	N: North Nevada Tire, Smith Detroit Diesel, Allison, Ed's Tire Service
	Med	N: + to Battle Mountain Gen'l Hospital
	Other	N: Laundry/WiFi/**RVDump/LP/RVPark**/FJ TP, ATMs, Grocery, NAPA, Radio Shack, Auto & Truck Service S: **Mill Creek Rec Area▲**

◈ = Regular Gas Stations with Diesel **▲ = RV Friendly Locations** **♥ = Pet Friendly Locations**
Red print shows large vehicle parking / access on site or nearby **Brown Print = Campgrounds / RV PARKS**

EXIT		NEVADA
233		**NV 304, Hill Top Rd, Battle Mountain to NV 305 (Acc to #231/#229 Serv)**
	Other	S: Battle Mountain Airport✈
244		**to Argenta**
254		**to Dunphy**
(259)		**Rest Area (Both dir) (RR, Picnic, RVDump)**
261		**NV 306, Crescent Valley, Beowawe**
268		**to Emigrant**
(270)		**Parking Area (Both dir)**
271		**Frenchie Rd, to Palisade**
279		**NV 278, NV 221, I-80 Bus, Carlin, Eureka (EB)**
280		**NV 766, Central Carlin, Eureka**
	FStop	S: to 424 Chestnut St CFN/Western Energtix
	TStop	S: Pilot Travel Center #387 (Scales)
	Gas	S: Shell, Sinclair
	Food	S: Subway/Pilot TC, BurgerKing/Shell, Chin's Café, Pizza Factory, Whistle Stop Cafe, State Café
	Lodg	S: Best Inn, Cavalier Motel
	TServ	N: Anderson Diesel Repair
	Other	N: WiFi/Casino/RVDump/Pilot TC, Grocery
282		**to I-80 Bus, NV 221, Carlin, Eureka**
292		**Maggie Creek Ranch Rd, Hunter**
298		**80 Bus Loop, NV 535, West Elko**
	Other	S: Te-Moak Indian Reservation
301		**NV 225, Mountain City Hwy, Elko, I-80 Bus, NV 535 (Acc to #302 via S to Idaho St)**
	FStop	S: 920 Mtn City Hwy CFN/Western Energtix
	Gas	N: Maverick S: Conoco◈, Phillips 66◈, Texaco◈, Smith's
	Food	N: Arby's, McDonald's, Papa Murphy's, Round Table Pizza, 9 Beans & a Burrito S: KFC, New China Café, Starbucks, Sierra Java, Taco Bell
	Lodg	N: Oak Tree Inn♥, Shilo Inn S: American Inn, Key Motel, Manor Motor Lodge, Ruby Hill Motel, Stampede Motel
	TServ	S: Cummins Intermountain, Western Tire Center, Elko Truck Services
	Med	S: + Hospital
	Other	N: ATM, Big 5 Sporting Goods, Grocery, Home Depot, Laundromat, **Walmart sc**, Ruby View Golf Course S: ATMs, Avis RAC, Car Quest, Checker Auto Parts, Family Dollar, Grocery, IGA, Les Schwab Tires, Office Max, Pharmacy, Smith Food & Drug, U-Haul, Casinos, Elko Reg'l Muni Airport✈, RVDump/P66, RVDump/Shell, Cimarron West/Store/Texaco◈ Car Wash/Rest/ /LP/RV Park▲, RV Dealer
303		**NV 535, I-80 Bus, East Elko (Acc to #302 via S to Idaho St)**
	FStop	N: CFN/Chevron S: Bonus Star Mart #53/Sinclair
	Gas	S: Chevron, Conoco◈, Shell, Tesoro◈
	Food	S: Burger King, Coffee Mug, Cowboy Joe, Golden Corral, McDonald's, Pizza Hut, Subway, Taco Time, Wendy's
	Lodg	S: Best Western♥/RVPark▲ /Casino, Days Inn, Elko Motel, Hi Desert Inn, Hilton Garden Inn, Holiday Inn, Motel 6♥, Microtel, Park View Inn, Red Lion Inn & Casino, Super 8
	TServ	S: CAT, Allison, Cummins
	Med	S: + NE Nevada Reg'l Hospital
	Other	N: Golf Course S: ATMs, Albertson's, Amtrak, Auto Dealers, Elko Convention Center, Pharmacy, Iron Horse RV Resort▲, Double Dice RV Park▲, Valley View RV Park▲, to Ryndon Campground RV Park▲
310		**NF 421, E Idaho St, to Osino**
(312)		**Weigh Station (Both dir)**
314		**CR 721A, CR 742, Elko, to Ryndon, Devils Gate**
	Other	S: to Ryndon Campground RV Park▲
317		**NF-423, CR 71, to Elburz**
321		**NV 229, Halleck, Ruby Valley**
328		**River Ranch**
333		**NV 230, Deeth, Starr Valley**
343		**NV 230, Deeth, to Welcome**
	Other	N: Welcome Station RV Park▲
348		**6th St, Wells, Crested Acres**
351		**I-80 Bus, NV 223, Humboldt Ave**
	Gas	N: Tesoro◈
	Lodg	N: Chinatown Motel
	Other	N: Grocery, US Post Office, Mountain Shadows RV Park▲, to PL/Angel Lake Campground▲, Crossroads RV Park▲
352AB		**US 93, Great Basin Hwy, 6th St, I-80 Bus, NV 223, Wells**
	FStop	N: CFN/Western Energetix 881 6th St
	TStop	N: Flying J Travel Plaza #5102 S: Flying J Travel Plaza #5068/Conoco (Scales), Love's Travel Stop #365 (Scales)
	Gas	N: Chevron, Shell
	Food	N: FastFood/FJ TP, Burger King, Dee's, Old West Inn Casino & Café, Ranch House S: Cookery/FastFood/FJ TP, McDonald's/Love's TS
	Lodg	N: Best Western, Motel 6♥, Rest Inn, Super 8, Wagon Wheel Motel
	TWash	N: Roadway Diesel
	TServ	N: Intermountain Car & Truck Repair, Roadway Diesel, Goodyear
	Other	S: Laundry/Casino/WiFi/RVDump/LP/ FJ TP
(354)		**Parking Area (EB)**
360		**Moor**
365		**Independence Valley**
(373)		**Rest Area (Both dir) (RR, Picnic)**
376		**Pequop**
378		**NV 233, to Oasis, Montello**
	FStop	N: Country Store & Gas
387		**Shafter**
398		**Pilot Peak**
407		**Wendover Blvd, Wendover**
(410)		**US 80 Bus Loop, US 93 Alt, Wendover Blvd, Wendover NV Welcome Center (WB) S: (RR, Phone, Info)**
	TStop	S: Pilot Travel Center #147 (Scales)
	Gas	S: Chevron◈, Shell◈, Sinclair
	Food	S: Arby's/TJCinn/Pilot TC, Burger King, McDonald's, Pizza Hut, Subway
	Lodg	S: Best Western, Days Inn, Motel 6♥, Nevada Crossing Hotel, Peppermill Inn & Casino/RVPark▲, Red Garter Hotel & Casino, Rainbow Hotel & Casino, Super 8, Stateline Hotel & Casino
	Other	S: Laundry/Casino/WiFi/Pilot TC, Grocery, Goodyear, Stateline RV Park▲, Silver Sage RV Park▲, Wendover KOA▲, Wendover Air Force Aux Field✈
	NOTE:	MM 411: Utah State Line

NEVADA

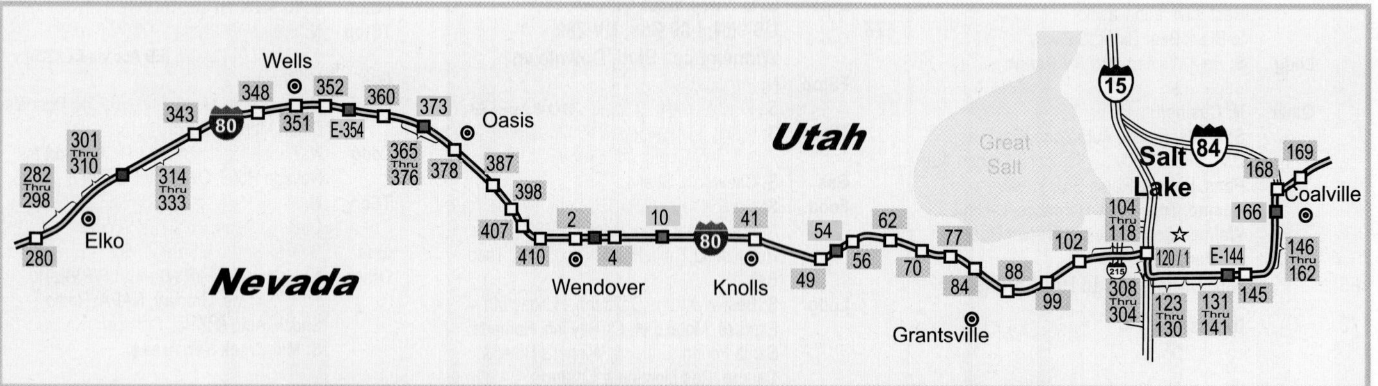

◈ = Regular Gas Stations with Diesel ▲ = RV Friendly Locations ♥ = Pet Friendly Locations
Red print shows large vehicle parking / access on site or nearby Brown Print = Campgrounds / RV PARKS

EXIT UTAH

UTAH

MOUNTAIN / PACIFIC TIME ZONE

2 UT 58, Wendover Blvd, Wendover (WB diff reaccess)
- Gas S: R Place #4/Shell◈
- Food S: Subway, Taco Poblano Mexican Rest
- Lodg S: Best Western, Bonneville Inn, Days Inn♥, Knights Inn, Motel 6♥, Quality Inn, Western Ridge Motel
- Other N: Danger Cave State Park, S: ATM, Auto Services, CarQuest, Family Dollar, Grocery, Museum, Tires, US Post Office, U-Haul, Vet♥, Wendover Airport/AFB✈, to NV Casinos, RV Parking & Camping▲

(3) Port of Entry / Weigh Station (Both dir)

NOTE: EB: CHECK YOUR FUEL Next Ex #99

4 Salt Flats Rd, Bonneville Speedway
- FStop N: Bonus Star Mart/66 (Scales) Hardy Ent/Wendover TS/Sinclair
- Food N: Café
- Other N: Bonneville Salt Flats State Park

(10) Salt Flats Rest Area (Both dir) (RR, Phones, Pic, Vend, Pet, Info)

41 Knolls

49 to Clive

(54) Grassy Mtn Rest Area (Both dir) (RR, Phones, Picnic, Vend)

56 to Aragonite

62 Military Area, Lakeside

70 Delle
- FStop S: Delle Auto & Truck Plaza/Sinclair
- Food S: Café/Delle ATP
- Lodg S: Motel/Delle ATP

77 UT 196, Rowley, Dugway

84 UT 138, Grantsville, Tooele

88 to Grantsville

99 UT 36, Tooele, Stansbury
- TStop S: Flying J Travel Plaza #5015/Conoco (Scales), Travel Center of America #60/ Tesoro (Scales)
- Gas S: Chevron, Shell◈
- Food S: Rest/FastFood/FJ TP, CountryPride/ BurgerKing/TacoBell/TA TC, Subway/ Chevron, McDonald's
- Lodg S: Oquirrh Motor Inn & RV Park▲
- TWash S: Blue Beacon TW/TA TC
- TServ S: TA TC/Tires
- Other S: Laundry/WiFi/RVDump/LP/FJ TP, Laundry/WiFi/RVDump/TA TC, Tooele Army Depot

NOTE: WB: CHECK YOUR FUEL Next Ex #4

102 UT 201, to Magna (EB)
- Med S: + Hospital

104 UT 202, Saltair Dr, Magna
- Other N: Great Salt Lake State Park

111 S7200W, Salt Lake City

113 S5600W, UT 172, Salt Lake City
- Gas N: Phillips 66
- Food N: Perkins, Pizza Hut, Pizza Palace, Subwa
- Lodg N: Best Western, Comfort Inn, Fairfield Inn, Hampton Inn, Hilton, Holiday Inn, Holiday Inn Express, Quality Inn, Super 8

114 Wright Bros Dr (WB) (Access to Ex #113 Serv)
- Lodg N: Courtyard, Holiday Inn, La Quinta Inn♥, Microtel, Residence Inn

115 UT 154, Bangerter Hwy, Salt Lake City Airport
- Other N: Salt Lake City KOA▲

(117) Jct I-215, N-Ogden, S-Provo

118 UT 68, Redwood Rd, to Temple
- TStop N: Love's Travel Stop #436 (Scales)
- Gas N: 7-11, Chevron◈, Maverik, Tesoro S: 7-11
- Food N: Arby's/ Love's TS, Burger King, Carl's Jr, Denny's, KFC, Subway, Taco Bell,
- Lodg N: Airport Inn, Baymont Inn, Candlewood Suites, Comfort Suites, Days Inn, Dream Inn, Holiday Inn Express, Motel 6, Quality Inn, Radisson, Sheraton
- Med N: + Hospital
- Other N: Laundry/Love's TS, Salt Lake City KOA▲

(120) Jct I-15N, to Ogden

121 W 600S, UT 269, Salt Lake City

NOTE: I-80 below runs with I-15. Exit #'s follow I-15.

(308) Jct I-80W, Airport, Reno

307 400 South , UT 186 (SB), 400 South HOV Exit (NB)
- Gas E: Chevron, Food Mart
- Food E: Various
- Lodg E: Courtyard, Hampton Inn, Rio Grande Hotel, Renaissance Suites, Residence Inn
- Other E: Amtrak, Enterprise RAC, Aquarium, Museum, Auto Repair, Grocery, Banks W: Grocery

306 600 South, UT 269 (NB)
- Gas E: Chevron, Maverick, Sinclair
- Food E: Denny's, McDonald's, Rest/Hilton, Salty Dogs, Rest/Quality Inn, Rest/ Ramada, Rest/Travelodge
- Lodg E: Ameritel Inn, Best Western, Embassy Suites, Hilton, Motel 6♥, Quality Inn, Ramada, Red Lion Hotel, Super 8, Travelodge♥
- Other E: Amtrak, Enterprise RAC, Aquarium, Museum, Auto Repair, Grocery, Banks

(305C-A) Exit to SB Collector (SB)

305D 900 South (NB)
- Gas E: Chevron, Sinclair
- Food E: Artic Circle, Chinese, Mexican
- Lodg E: Best Inns, Holiday Inn
- Other E: Auto Repairs, Tires

305C 1300S, Salt Lake City
- Gas E: Maverik
- Food E: Various
- Other E: Auto Repairs, Tires, Banks

305B 2100S, UT 201, Salt Lake City (Addt'l Serv W to UT 68)
- FStop E: Premium Oil/Chevron
- Gas E: 7-11, Petro Mart, Costco
- Food E: FastFood/Prem Oil, Burger King, Carl Jr's, IHOP, McDonald's, Subway
- Lodg E: Marriott
- Other E: LP/Prem Oil, Costco, Home Depot,

305A UT 201W, 900W, Salt Lake City (Addt'l Serv W to UT 68)
- TStop W: Flying J Travel Plaza #50007
- Food W: Rest/FJ TP, Wendy's
- TWash W: Blue Beacon/FJ TP
- TServ W: Diesel Repair
- Other W: Laundry/WiFi/RVDump/LP/FJ TP, Goodyear, NAPA, Banks, Repair

(305A-D) Exit to NB Collector (NB)

(304) Jct I-80E, to Cheyenne, Denver (Gas & Lodging at 1st Exit on I-80E)
- TServ E: Cummins Intermountain

NOTE: I-80 above runs with I-15. Exit #'s follow I-15.

(123AB) I-15, N to Ogden, S to Provo

122 2100S, UT 201, Salt Lake City

124 US 89, State St
- Gas N: 7-11, Chevron S: Sinclair
- Food N: Burger King, Central Park, Subway, Taco Bell, Wendy's S: KFC, Pizza Hut
- Lodg S: Ramada Ltd
- Other N: ATM, Auto Dealers, Discount Tire

125 UT 71, 7th East

126 UT 181, 13th East, Sugar House
- Gas N: Chevron, Shell
- Food N: KFC, Olive Garden, Pizza Hut, Red Lobster, Sizzler, Taco Bell, Wendy's

127 UT 195, S2300E, to Holladay

(128) Jct I-215S (EB)

129 UT 186W, Foothill Dr, Parleys Way
- Med N: + Hospital

(130) Jct I-215S (WB)

131 Quarry

132 Ranch Exit

133 Utility Exit (EB)

134 UT 65, Park City, Emigration & East Canyons

137 Lambs Canyon Rd, Lambs Canyon

140 Parleys Summit
- Gas S: Sinclair◈
- Food S: Cafe

141 Homestead Rd, Jeremy Ranch
- Gas N: Phillips 66
- Food N: Blimpie/P66, Pizza Hut

(144) Scenic View (EB)

145 UT 224, Kimball Junction, Park City
- Gas S: 7-11, Chevron, Shell
- Food S: Arby's, Denny's, JB's, Little Caesars, McDonalds, Panda Express, Quiznos, Ruby Tuesday, Subway, Taco Bell, Wendy's
- Lodg S: Best Western, Hampton Inn, Holiday Inn Express
- Other N: Park City RV Resort▲ S: Grocery, Tanger Outlet Center at Park City, US Post Office, Walmart, Powderwood Resort▲ , Ski Area

146 US 40, Silver Creek Rd, Park City, to Heber, Provo
- FStop N: Bell's Silver Creek Junction/Sinclair

◈= Regular Gas Stations with Diesel ▲ = RV Friendly Locations ♥= Pet Friendly Locations
Red print shows large vehicle parking / access on site or nearby Brown Print = Campgrounds / RV PARKS

EXIT		UT / WI
	Food	N: Blimpie's/Sinclair
150		**Ranch Exit**
155		**UT 32, Main St, Wanship Rd, Peoa, Wanship, Kamas**
	Gas	S: Sinclair◈
	Food	N: Café/Spring Chicken Inn
	Lodg	N: Spring Chicken Inn
	Other	S: Rockport State Park
162		**W 100 St, UT 280, Coalville**
	TStop	N: Holiday Hills/66
	Gas	S: Chevron◈, Sinclair, Shell
	Food	S: Denise's Home Plate Rest,
	Lodg	N: Best Western♥
		S: Moore Motel
	Other	N: LP/Holiday Hills, Holiday Hills Campground/RVDump▲
		S: Auto Service/Chevron, Grocery, Laundromat, NAPA, Pharmacy, Towing, US Post Office, Echo Res Rec Area
(166)		**Scenic Area** (Both dir)
(168)		**Jct I-84, W to Ogden, E to Cheyenne**
169		**Echo Dam Rd, Echo**
(170)		**Welcome Center** (WB) Rest Area (EB) (RR, Phones, Pic, Vend, Info, RVDump)
178		**Emory** (WB)
(180)		**Port of Entry / Weigh Station** (WB)
185		**Castle Rock**
187		**Ranch Exit**
191		**Wahsatch Rd, Coalville**

MOUNTAIN TIME ZONE

NOTE: MM 197: Wyoming State Line

⬆ UTAH
⬇ WYOMING

MOUNTAIN TIME ZONE

EXIT		WYOMING
(1)		**Old Utah Port of Entry** (EB), **Weigh Station** (WB)
3		**US 189, 30, Harrison Dr, Evanston**
	TStop	N: Flying J Travel Plaza #5180 (Scales)
	Gas	N: Chevron◈, Phillips 66, Sinclair, Tesoro
	Food	N: Cookery/FJ TP, Burger King, JB's, KFC, Lottie's, Rest/BW
		S: KFC/Taco Bell, McDonald's
	Lodg	N: Best Western, Comfort Inn, Country Inn, Days Inn, Economy Inn♥, Hampton Inn, Holiday Inn Express, Howard Johnson
	Med	S: to + Evanston Reg'l Hospital
	Other	N: Laundry/WiFi/FJ TP, Golf Course
		S: Fireworks, Penske Truck Rental, Tires
5		**WY 89N, WY 150S, Front St, Downtown Evanston**
	Gas	N: Chevron◈, Maverik, Sinclair
	Food	N: Arby's, Dragon Wall Chinese, McDonald's, Sonic, Subway
	Lodg	N: Super 8
	Med	N: + Hospital
		S: + WY State Mental Hospital
	Other	N: Auto Zone, Car Wash, Family Dollar, NAPA, Walmart sc▲
(6)		**I-80 Bus, US 189, WY 89, Bear River Dr, Evanston** S: WY Welcome Center (SB) (RR, Phones, Picnic, Info, RVDump)
	TStop	N: Pilot Travel Center #141 (Scales), Four Stars Sinclair Truck Stop
	Food	N: Subway/Pilot TC, Kelly's Roadhouse Grill, Mexican Rest
	Lodg	N: Best Value Inn, Evanston Inn, Holiday Inn Express, Prairie Inn, Motel 6♥
	Other	N: Laundry/WiFi/Pilot TC, Laundry/Sinclair, CarQuest, Goodyear, Grocery, Racetrack, Bear River State Park, Bear River RV Park▲ , Philips RV Park▲
10		**Painter Rd, CR 180**
13		**Divide Rd**
(14)		**Parking Area** (Both dir)
15		**Guild Rd** (EB)
18		**US 189, CR 181, Kemmerer**
21		**Coal Rd**
23		**Bar Hat Rd**
24		**CR 141, CR 173, Leroy Rd**
(28)		**Parking Area** (Both dir)
28		**French Rd**
30		**Bigelow Rd, Fort Bridger**
	TStop	N: Travel Center of America #188/ Tesoro (Scales)
	Food	N: ForkinRoad/BurgerKing/TacoBell/TA TC
	TServ	N: TA TC/Tires
	Other	N: Laundry/WiFi/TA TC
33		**Union Rd**
34		**I-80 Bus Loop, to Fort Bridger**
	Gas	S: Phillips 66
	Lodg	S: Wagon Wheel Café & Motel
	Other	S: Fort Bridger RV Campground▲
39		**WY 412N WY 414S, Lyman, to Carter Mountain View**
(41)		**WY 413, Lyman** Rest Area (Both dir) S: (RR, Phones, Picnic)
	TStop	N: Gas N Go #15
	Food	N: Rest/FastFood/GasnGo, Cowboy Café, Taco Time
	Lodg	N: Gateway Inn
	TServ	N: GasNGo/Tires
	Other	S: Lyman KOA▲
48		**I-80 Bus, Lyman, Fort Bridger**
53		**Church Butte Rd**
(60)		**Parking Area** (Both dir)
61		**WY 374, Cedar Mountain Rd, to Granger**
66		**US 30, Kemmerer, Pocatello**
68		**WY 374E, Little America**
	FStop	N: AmBest/Little America Fuel Center/ Sinclair (Scales)
	Food	N: Rest/Little America TC
	Lodg	N: Hotel/LA TC
	TServ	N: LA TC/Tires
	Other	N: Laundry/RVDump/LP/LA TC, Camp▲
(71)		**Parking Area** (Both dir)
72		**Westvaco Rd, to WY 374, McKinnon**
83		**WY 372, LaBarge Rd**
85		**Covered Wagon Rd, Green River**
	Other	S: Adams RV Sales & Service, Tex's Travel Camp▲
89		**US 30 Bus, WY 374, Flaming Gorge Way, Green River**
	FStop	S: Sinclair◈
	Gas	S: Exxon,
	Food	S: Domino's Pizza, Krazy Moose Rest, McDonald's, Penny's Diner, Pizza Hut, Ponderosa
	Lodg	S: Desmond Motel, Oak Tree Inn♥, Sweet Dreams Inn, Super 8, Walker Motel, Western Motel♥
	Other	S: RV Service
91		**I-80 Bus, US 30, to WY 530** (Services same as Exit #89)
	Gas	S: Loaf 'n Jug
	Food	S: Artic Circle, McDonald's, Pizza Hut

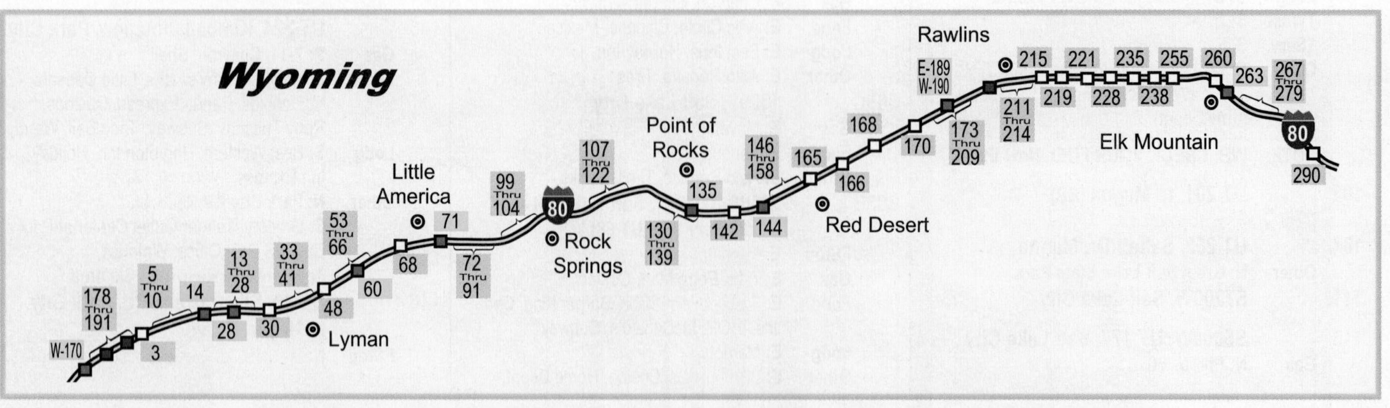

◈= Regular Gas Stations with Diesel ▲ = RV Friendly Locations ♥= Pet Friendly Locations
Red print shows large vehicle parking / access on site or nearby Brown Print = Campgrounds / RV PARKS

EXIT		WYOMING
	Lodg	S: Coachman Inn, Flaming Gorge Motel♥, Mustang Motel,
	Other	S: Auto Services, Budget Truck Rental, To **Flaming Gorge Nat'l Rec Area▲**
99		**US 191, WY 373, East Flaming Gorge Rd, Rock Springs**
	FStop	S: Cruel Jack's Travel Plaza/Sinclair
	Food	S: Rest/Cruel Jack's TP, Rodeo Grill, Ted's Supper Club
	Other	**N: to appr 1 mi: Rock Springs/Green River KOA▲**
		S: Laundry/Cruel Jack's TP
102		**I-80 Bus, US 30 Bus, Dewar Dr, to WY 376, WY 430, Rock Springs**
	Gas	N: Exxon, Sinclair◈
		S: Kum & Go, Loaf 'n Jug, Mobil◈
	Food	N: Applebee's, Denny's, KFC/Long John Silver, Pam's BBQ, Sizzler, Taco Time,
		S: Arby's, Burger King, IHOP, JB's, Pizza Hut, Quiznos, Sizzler, Starbucks, Subway, Village Inn, Wendy's
	Lodg	N: Americas Best Value Inn, Comfort Inn, Motel 6♥, La Quinta Inn♥, Ramada Ltd, The Inn at Rock Springs
		S: Budget Host Inn, Comfort Inn, Hampton Inn, Holiday Inn Express, Homewood Suites, Motel 8, Quality Inn, Super 8, Wingate Inn,
	Med	**S: + Memorial Hospital of Sweetwater Co**
	Other	N: Auto Dealers, Cummins Rocky Mountain **Don's RV & Repair**, Dollar Tree, Flaming Gorge Harley Davidson, Home Depot, Kmart, Smith's Food & Drug, US Post Office,
		S: Albertson's, Auto Zone, Big O Tires, Checker Auto Parts, NAPA, Radio Shack, Sports Authority, Staples, UPS Store, Walgreen's, **Walmart sc**,
103		**College Dr, Rock Springs**
	Gas	S: Loaf 'n JugConoco
	Food	S: Domino's Pizza
	Med	**S: + Memorial Hospital**
	Other	S: Western WY Comm College
104		**US 191N, Elk St, Rock Springs**
	TStop	N: Flying J Travel Plaza #5017(Scales), Outlaw Sinclair
	Gas	N: Exxon, Shell
		S: Exxon◈
	Food	N: Thad's/FastFood/FJ TP, McDonald's, BurgerKing/Sinclair, TacoTime
	Lodg	N: Best Western, Econo Lodge
		S: Days Inn
	TServ	N: Cummins Intermountain
	Other	N: Laundry/WiFi/**RVDump/LP**/FJ TP, Laundry/Sinclair, Auto Dealers, Grocery
107		**I-80 Bus, US 30, WY 376, WY 430, Rock Springs, Pilot Butte Ave**
	Gas	N: Mobil◈, Phillips 66◈
	Lodg	S: Springs Motel
111		**Baxter Rd**
	Other	S: Rock Springs Sweetwater Co Airport✈
122		**WY 371, to Superior**
130		**Point of Rocks**
	Gas	N: Conoco◈
	Food	N: Rest/Conoco
(135)		**Parking Area (Both dir)**
136		**Black Butte Rd**
139		**Red Hill Rd**
142		**Bitter Creek Rd**
(144)		**Rest Area (Both dir) (RR, Phones, Picnic) (Next RA 102 mi)**
146		**Patrick Draw Rd**
150		**Table Rock Rd, Wamsutter**
	Gas	S: Major/Sinclair◈
152		**Bar X Rd**
154		**B L M Rd**
156		**G L Rd**
158		**Tipton Rd**
165		**Red Desert**
	Gas	S: Saveway Gen'l Store
166		**Booster Rd**
168		**Frewen Rd, Wamsutter**
170		**Rasmussen Rd**
173		**Wamsutter Crooks Gap Rd, CR 23, Wamsutter**
	FStop	S: Wamsutter Conoco
	TStop	N: Love's Travel Stop #310 (Scales), Sinclair Fuel Stop
		S: Phillips 66 Travel Center
	Food	N: Chester/Subway/Love's TS, FastFood/Sinclair TS
		S: Rest/FastFood/P66 TC
	Lodg	S: Sagebrush Motel
	TServ	N: Sinclair TS/Tires
		S: Wamsutter Conoco/Tires
	Other	N: WiFi/**RVDump**/Love's TS
		S: Laundry/P66 TC
184		**Continental Divide Rd**
187		**WY 789S, Baggs Rd, Wamsutter**
(189)		**Parking Area (EB)**
(190)		**Parking Area (WB)**
196		**Riner Rd**
201		**Daley Rd**
204		**Knobs Rd, Rawlins**
206		**Hadsell Rd**
209		**Johnson Rd, Rawlins**
	TStop	N: Flying J Travel Plaza #5040/ (Scales)
	Food	N: Cookery/FastFood/FJ TP
	Other	N: Laundry/WiFi/**RVDump/LP**/FJ TP
(211)		**Weigh Station (WB)**
211		**I-80 Bus, US 30 Bus, to WY 789N, Spruce St, Rawlins**
	FStop	N: West End Sinclair
	Gas	N: Conoco◈, Exxon◈, Phillips 66
	Food	N: JB's, Rest/BW
	Lodg	N: Best Western, Econo Lodge, Express Inn♥, Ferris Mansion B&B, Golden West Motel, Knights Inn♥, La Bella Motel, Motel 7, Rawlins Motel, Super 8, Sunset Motel, Travelodge♥
	Med	**N: + Memorial Hospital of Carbon Co, + Rawlins Urgent Care**
	Other	**N: American Presidents Campground▲**, Auto Dealer, Auto Services, Family Dollar, Frontier Prison Museum, Laundromat, Memory Lanes Bowling Alley, **RV World Campground▲**, **Westen Hills Campground & Miniature Golf▲**, V-1 Propane/**LP**,
214		**WY 78, Higley Blvd, Rawlins**
	TStop	S: Travel Center of America #234/Shell (Scales)
	Food	S: CountryFare/Subway/TA TC
	Lodg	N: Microtel
		S: America's Best Value Inn♥,
	TServ	S: TA TC/Tires
	Other	**N: Rawlins KOA▲**,
		S: Laundry/**RVDump**/TA TC,
215		**I-80 Bus, US 30 Bus, US 287 BypP, Cedar St, Rawlins**
	Gas	N: Conoco◈, Phillips 66, Shell, Sinclair
	Food	N: China House, McDonald's, Pizza Hut, Subway, Taco John, Wendy's, Rest/Days In
	Lodg	N: 1st Choice Inn♥, Days Inn♥, Hampton Inn♥, Holiday Inn Express♥, Key Motel♥, Quality Inn
	TServ	N: Truck & Radiator Repair, Western Truck Repair
	Other	N: Auto Dealers, Auto Services, CarQuest, Grocery/Pharmacy, O'Reilly Auto Parts, Pamida Pharmacy, Radio Shack, Tires, Rawlins Muni Airport✈
219		**Lincoln Ave, W Sinclair**
221		**WY 76, E Sinclair**
	FStop	N: I-80 Travel Plaza/66
	Food	N: Rest/I-80 TP
(228)		**Fort Steele Rd** **Rest Area (Both dir)** **N: (RR, Phones, Picnic, Pet)**
235		**US 30E, US 287S, WY 130E, Hanna, Walcott, Saratoga**
	FStop	N: Shell
	Food	N: Café/Shell
238		**Peterson Rd**
255		**WY 72, Hanna, Elk Mountain**
	Gas	N: Conoco◈
260		**CR 402, Elk Mtn Medicine Bow Rd**
(262)		**Parking Area (Both dir)**
(267)		**Wagonhound Rd** **Rest Area (Both dir)** **S: (RR, Phones, Picnic)**
272		**WY 13N, to Arlington**
	Gas	N: Exxon
279		**Cooper Cove Rd, Dutton Creek Rd**
290		**CR 59, Quealy Dome Rd, Laramie**
	TStop	S: Sinclair
	Food	S: FastFood/Sinclair
	TServ	S: Sinclair
	Other	S: Laundry/Sinclair
297		**WY 12, Herrick Lane**
310		**CR 322, Curtis St, N Laramie**
	TStop	N: Pilot Travel Center #308 (Scales), Diamond Shamrock/Valero #4552
		S: Petro Stopping Center #303 (Scales)
	Food	N: Wendy's/Pilot SC, Café/Valero,
		S: IronSkillet/Petro SC
	Lodg	N: Days Inn, Econo Lodge, Holiday Inn Express, Motel 8, Quality Inn, Super 8
		S: AmeriHost Inn, Fairfield Inn,
	TWash	N: Pilot TC
		S: Blue Beacon TW/Petro SC
	TServ	S: Petro SC/Tires
	Med	**N: + Hospital**
	Other	N: Laundry/WiFi/Pilot TC, Grocery
		S: Laundry/WiFi/Petro SC, **Laramie KOA▲**

◈= Regular Gas Stations with Diesel ▲ = RV Friendly Locations ♥= Pet Friendly Locations
Red print shows large vehicle parking / access on site or nearby Brown Print = Campgrounds / RV PARKS

EXIT		WYOMING
311		**WY 130, WY 230, Snowy Range Rd, Laramie, Snowy Range**
	FStop	S: High Country Sportsman/Sinclair
	Gas	S: Conoco◈, Phillips 66◈
	Food	S: McDonald's, Subway
	Lodg	S: Best Value Inn, Howard Johnson, Travel Inn
	Other	S: Laundry/LP/RVDump/High Country Sportsman, **RV Center**, Ski Area, Univ of WY
313		**US 287, 3rd St, Laramie** **N: Port of Entry**
	Gas	N: Conoco◈, Exxon, Phillips 66, Shell◈
	Food	N: Burger King, Denny's, Great Wall Chinese, McDonald's, Village Inn
	Lodg	N: First Inn Gold, Sunset Inn, Motel 8 S: Holiday Inn, Motel 6♥, Ramada
	Med	N: + Ivinson Memorial Hospital
316		**I-80 Bus, US 30, Grand Ave, Laramie**
	Gas	N: Conoco◈, Albertson's
	Food	N: Applebee's, Arby's, Burger King, Hong Kong Buffet, JB's, McDonald's, Taco Bell, Taco John's, Wendy's
	Lodg	N: Comfort Inn, Sleep Inn
	Med	N: + Ivinson Memorial Hospital
	Other	N: Albertson's, **Walmart sc**, Univ of WY
	NOTE:	**MM 317: EB: 5% Steep Grade for 6 mi**
(322)		**Chain-Up Area** (Both dir)
(323)		**WY 210, Happy Jack Rd, Laramie**
	NOTE:	**Highest Elev point on I-80**
		Rest Area (Both dir) N: (RR, Phones, Picnic)
329		**Vedauwoo Rd**
(333)		**Parking Area** (Both dir)
335		**Buford Rd, Laramie**
	FStop	S: 24 Hr Gas & Diesel
	Food	S: Rest/24Hr G&D
339		**Remount Rd**
(341)		**Parking Area** (Both dir)
342		**Harriman Rd**
(344)		**Parking Area** (Both dir)
345		**Warren Rd, Cheyenne**
348		**Otto Rd**

EXIT		WYOMING
358		**I-80 Bus, US 30, WY 225, Otto Rd, W Lincolnway, Cheyenne**
	TStop	N: AmBest/Little America Travel Center/ Sinclair, Big D Truck Stop/Exxon **(WB: Access via Ex #359)**
	Food	N: Rest/Little America TC, Rest/FastFood/ Big D TS, Denny's, Outback Steakhouse, Pizza Inn, Village Inn
	Lodg	N: Motel/Little America TC, Days Inn, Econo Lodge, Hampton Inn, La Quinta Inn♥, Luxury Inn, Motel 6♥, Super 8, Wyoming Motel
	Med	N: + Hospital
	Other	N: Laundry/WiFi/LP/Big D TS, Home Depot
(359A)		**Jct I-25S, US 87S, to Denver**
(359C)		**Jct I-25N, US 87N, to Casper**
(362)		**Jct I-180, US 85, Central Ave, Cheyenne, to Greeley, CO**
	FStop	S: Diamond Shamrock #4550
	Gas	S: Conoco◈, Safeway
	Food	N: Arby's, Applebee's, Golden Corral, Hardee's S: Subway/Conoco, Burger King, Sonic, Taco John
	Lodg	N: Lariat Motel S: Holiday Inn, Round Up Motel
	TServ	N: Cheyenne Truck Center
	Med	S: + Hospital
	Other	N: Greyhound S: Safeway
364		**I-80 Bus, WY 212, S College Dr, E Lincolnway, Cheyenne**
	Gas	N: Shell
	Food	N: Burger King, Chili's, IHOP, McDonald's, Papa John's Pizza, Pizza Hut, Taco Bell
	Lodg	N: Cheyenne Motel, Fleetwood Motel
	Med	N: + Hospital
	Other	N: Auto Zone, Grocery
367		**Campstool Rd, Cheyenne**
	TStop	N: Cheyenne Travel Plaza/Sinclair, Pilot Travel Center #402 (Scales)
	Food	N: Arby's/Sinclair, Subway/Pilot TC
	Other	N: Laundry/RVDump/Cheyenne TP, Laundry/Pilot TC, **Cheyenne KOA▲**
370		**US 30, Field Station Rd, to Archer**
	TStop	N: Sapp Bros/Spirit (Scales)
	Food	N: Rest/Sapp Bros TS
	Lodg	N: Big G Motel/Sapp Bros TS
	TServ	N: Sapp Bros TS/Tires
(371)		**Port of Entry / Check Station** (WB)

EXIT		WY / NE
377		**WY 217, Hillsdale Rd, Cheyenne, Hillsdale**
	TStop	N: Travel Center of America #187/Amoco
	Food	N: Buckhorn/BurgerKing/TacoBell/TA TC
	Lodg	N: Motel/TA TC
	TServ	N: TA TC/Tires
	Other	N: Laundry/WiFi/TA TC, **WY RV Park & Campground▲**
386		**US 30, WY 213, WY 214, Burns, Carpenter**
	TStop	N: Antelope Truck Stop
	Food	N: Rest/Antelope TS
	Other	N: Laundry/Antelope TS
391		**Egbert South Rd, Burns**
(401)		**I-80 Bus, US 30 Bus, WY 215, Pine Bluffs** **WY Welcome Center** (Both dir) S: (RR, Phones, Picnic, Info)
	TStop	N: AmPride/Cenex, RaceTrac
	Gas	N: Sinclair
	Food	N: FastFood/AmPride, Rest/FastFood/ RaceTrac
	Lodg	N: Gater's Travel & Motel
	TServ	N: AmPride TS
	Other	N: Auto Repair/Sinclair, US Post Office, **Pine Bluff RV Park▲**
	NOTE:	**MM 402: Nebraska State Line**

⬆ WYYOMING

⬇ NEBRASKA

MOUNTAIN TIME ZONE

EXIT		NEBRASKA
1		**NE 53B, State Line Rd, Bushnell**
8		**NE 53C, CR 17, to Bushnell**
(10)		**Kimball Rest Area** (EB) (RR, Phones, Picnic, Info)
(18)		**Weigh Station** (EB)
20		**NE 71, S Chestnut St, Kimball**
	FStop	N: Travel Shop/Sinclair
	Food	N: Pizza Hut, Subway S: Burger King
	Lodg	N: Best Value Inn, Days Inn, First Interstate Inn, Super 8
	Med	S: + Hospital
	Other	S: **Twin Pines RV Park▲**, Kimball Muni Airport✈

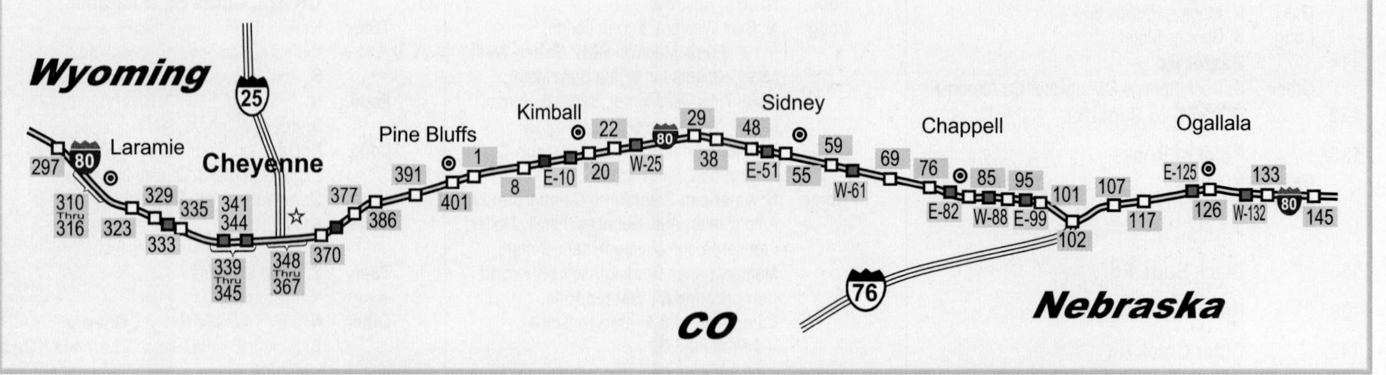

◈= Regular Gas Stations with Diesel ▲ = RV Friendly Locations ♥= Pet Friendly Locations
Red print shows large vehicle parking / access on site or nearby Brown Print = Campgrounds / RV PARKS

EXIT — NEBRASKA

22 — **NE 53E, Kimball, East Entrance**
Other — N: Kimball KOA▲

(25) — **Kimball Rest Area (WB)**
(RR, Phones, Picnic)

29 — **NE 53A, Dix**

38 — **NE 17B, Potter**
Gas — N: Cenex◈, Shell

48 — **NE 17C, Sidney, to Brownson**

(51) — **Sidney Rest Area (EB)**
(RR, Phones, Picnic, Observation Area)

55 — **I-80 Bus, NE 19, Sidney**
(Serv 3mi N in Sidney)

59 — **I-80 Bus, NE 17J, to US 30, US 385, Sidney, Bridgeport**
TStop — N: Sapp Bros Travel Center/Shell **US 385**
Gas — N: Conoco◈
S: BP◈, Phillips 66
Food — N: FastFood/Sapp Bros, KFC/TacoBell/Conoco, Arby's, McDonald's, Perkins, Quiznos, Runza Rest, Taco John
Lodg — N: AmericInn, Comfort Inn, Days Inn, Motel 6♥, Super 8
S: Holiday Inn
Other — N: WiFi/Sapp Bros, ATMs, **Walmart sc**, **Bear Family RV Park▲**, **RV Center**, Cabela's/**RVDump**
S: Sidney Muni Airport✈

(61) — **Sidney Rest Area (WB)**
(RR, Phones, Picnic)

69 — **NE 17E, to Sunol**

76 — **NE 17F, to Lodgepole**

(82) — **Chappell Rest Area (EB)**
(RR, Phones, Picnic)

85 — **NE 25A, Chappell**
Gas — N: AmPride
Other — N: US Post Office, Billy G Ray Field✈, **Creekside RV Park▲**

(88) — **Chappell Rest Area (WB)**
(RR, Phones, Picnic)

95 — **NE 27, Julesburg, Oshkosh**

(99) — **Scenic View (EB)**

101 — **US 138, Big Springs, Julesburg**

(102) — **Jct I-76S, to Denver**

107 — **NE 25B, Big Springs**
TStop — N: Bosselman Travel Center/Pilot #904/Sinclair (Scales), Total #4419
Food — N: GrandmaMax/LittleCaesars/Subway/Bosselman TC
Lodg — N: Best Value Inn
TWash — N: Bosselman TC
TServ — N: Bosselman TC/Tires
Other — N: Laundry/WiFi/Bosselman TC, Laundry/Total, **to appr 25mi:** Lake McConaughy, **Eagle Canyon Hideaway▲**

117 — **NE 51A, Brule**
TStop — N: Happy Jack/Sinclair
Food — N: FastFood/Happy Jack
Other — N: Laundry/**RVDump**/**RVPark▲** / HappyJack

Personal Notes

EXIT — NEBRASKA

(125) — **Ogallah Rest Area (EB)**
(RR, Phones, Picnic, Info)

126 — **US 26, NE 61, Ogallala, Grant**
TStop — N: Sapp Bros Travel Center/Shell
S: Travel Center of America #90/76 (Scales)
Gas — N: BP, Phillips 66◈, Sinclair, Texaco
S: Conoco◈, Phillips 66◈
Food — N: Deli/Sapp Bros TC, Arby's, Burger King, Country Kitchen, McDonald's, Pizza Hut, Taco John, Valentino's
S: CountryPride/TA TC, KFC, Panda Chinese, Wendy's
Lodg — N: Best Western, Days Inn, Holiday Inn Express, Plaza Inn
S: Comfort Inn, Econo Lodge♥, Super 8
TServ — S: TA TC/Tires
Med — N: + Hospital
Other — N: WiFi/Sapp Bros TC, ATM, Dollar General, Grehound, NAPA, Safeway, **Scottsbluff/Chimney Rock KOA▲**, **to appr 25mi** Lake McConaughy, **Eagle Canyon Hideaway▲**
S: Laundry/WiFi/**RVDump**/TA TC, **Open Corral Campground▲**, **Country View Campground▲**

(132) — **Ogallala Rest Area (WB)**
(RR, Phones, Picnic, Info)

133 — **NE 51B, Ogallala, to Roscoe**

145 — **NE 51C, Paxton Elsie Rd S, Paxton**
Gas — N: Texaco◈/Ole's
Food — N: Ole's Big Game Steakhouse & Lounge
Lodg — N: Ole's Lodge/Paxton Days Inn/**Ole's RV Park & Campground▲**

EXIT — NEBRASKA

NOTE: **MM 149: Central / Mountain Time Zone**

158 — **NE 25, Sutherland, Wallace**
Gas — N: Ozzie's General Store
S: Sinclair◈

(160) — **Sutherland Rest Area (Both dir)**
(RR, Phones, Picnic)
(WB: Historical Site Oregon Trail)

164 — **NE 56C, Dickens Rd, Hershey**
TStop — N: Western Convenience Truck Stop (Scales)
Gas — N: KwikStop
Food — N: Rest/Western Conv TS
Other — N: Laundry/**RVDump**/Western Conv TS

177 — **US 83, North Platte, McCook**
Gas — N: BP, Conoco◈, Shell◈, Sinclair◈
S: Phillips 66, Shell◈
Food — N: Applebee's, Arby's, Burger King, DQ, McDonald's, Quiznos, Rogers Diner, Subway, Village Inn, Wendy's, Whiskey Creek Steakhouse
S: Taco Bell/Conoco, Rest/Shell, Bud's Steakhouse, Country Kitchen, Mi Ranchito, Perkins
Lodg — N: Best Western, Hampton Inn, Hospitality Inn, Motel 6♥, Oak Tree Inn, Quality Inn
S: Comfort Inn, Days Inn, Holiday Inn Express, Ramada, Super 8
TServ — N: High Plains Power Systems
S: Mid America Diesel, Herbst Towing & Repair, Truck & Trailer Repair
Med — N: + Great Plains Regional Medical
Other — N: ATMs, Advance Auto Parts, Auto Services, Banks, Budkes Harley Davidson, Carmike Mall Cinemas, Ft Cody Trading Post, Go-Karts Rides & Games, Goodyear, Grocery, **Holiday Trav-L/Holiday RV Park & Campground▲**, Laundromat, Mall, Mid Plains Tech College, Staples, Towing, UPS Store, **Walmart sc▲**, **NE State Hwy Patrol Post**, **to** Buffalo Bill's Ranch, **Buffalo Bill State Rec Area**, **RV Repair**
S: Auto Dealers, Kmart, **to Lake Maloney State Rec Area**

179 — **NE 56G, to US 30, to N Platte**
TStop — S: Flying J Travel Plaza #5059/Conoco (Scales)
Gas — N: Casey's, Sinclair
Food — S: CountryMarket/FastFood/FJ TP
Lodg — N: La Quinta Inn♥
TWash — S: Red Arrow Truck & **RV** Wash
TServ — S: Boss Truck Shop
Other — N: Golf Course, **to** N Platte Reg'l Airport✈
S: Laundry/WiFi/**RVDump/LP**/FJ TP

(182) — **Weigh Station (Both dir)**

190 — **NE 56A, Maxwell, Ft McPherson**
FStop — N: Ranchland C-Store/Sinclair
Other — S: **Ft McPherson Campground**/**RVDump▲**

(194) — **Brady Rest Area (Both dir)**
(RR, Phones, Picnic, Info)

199 — **NE 56D, Brady**
Gas — N: Brady One Stop
Food — N: DQ/Brady OS

211 — **NE 47, S Lake Ave, Gothenburg**
FStop — N: Plaza Shell
TStop — N: I-80 Pit Stop/Sinclair
Gas — S: Sinclair/KOA
Food — N: Rest/FastFood/I-80 Pit Stop, McDonald's, Pizza Hut, Runza Rest

◈ = Regular Gas Stations with Diesel ▲ = RV Friendly Locations ♥ = Pet Friendly Locations
Red print shows large vehicle parking / access on site or nearby Brown Print = Campgrounds / RV PARKS

EXIT NEBRASKA

Lodg N: Pony Express Inn, Super 8♥, Travel Inn
Med N: + Gothenburg Memorial Hospital
Other N: Auto Services, Auto Dealers, Museum, to Quinn Field✈
S: Gothenburg KOA▲

222 NE 21, NE 22, S Meridian Ave, Cozad
FStop N: Gas N Shop/66
Gas N: BP, Sinclair
Food N: Burger King, DQ, Pizza Hut, Subway
Lodg N: Budget Host Circle S Motel
S: Motel 6♥
Other N: Cozad Muni Airport✈

(226) Cozad Rest Area (EB)
(RR, Phones, Picnic)

(227) Cozad Rest Area (WB)
(RR, Phones, Picnic)

231 NE 24A, Rd 428, Lexington
Other S: Exit 231 Truck Wash

237 US 283, Plum Creek Pkwy, Lexington, Arapahoe, Elwood
FStop N: AmPride
TStop S: NebraskaLand Tire Truck Center/Sinclair
Gas N: Conoco, Phillips 66◈
Food N: Amigo's, Arby's, Burger King, KFC, McDonald's, Pizza Hut, Wendy's
S: Rest/Nebraskaland
Lodg N: Comfort Inn, Days Inn, First Interstate Inn, Holiday Inn Express, Minuteman Motel
S: Super 8
TServ S: NebraskaLand/Tires
Other N: ATMs, Advance Auto Parts, Dollar General, Goodyear, Grocery, Walmart sc▲, to Jim Kelly Field✈
S: Laundry/NebraskaLand

248 NE 24B, Rd 444, Overton
TStop N: Mian Bros Travel Center/BPAmoco
Food N: Rest/MB TC
Other N: Laundry/MB TC

257 US 183, Elm Creek, Holdrege
TStop N: Bosselman Travel Center/Pilot #901/Sinclair (Scales)
Food N: LittleCaesars/Subway/TacoExpress/Bosselman TC
Lodg N: First Interstate Inn
Other N: Laundry/WiFi/Bosselman TC, Sunny Meadows Campground▲

263 NE 10B, Odessa Rd, Odessa
TStop N: Sapp Bros Travel Center/Shell
Food N: Rest/Deli/Sapp Bros TC
Lodg S: to Lakeside Motel & RV Park▲
TServ N: Sapp Bros TC/Tires

EXIT NEBRASKA

Other N: Laundry/WiFi/LP/Sapp Bros TC
S: Union Pacific State Rec Area

(269) Kearney Rest Area (EB)
(RR, Phones, Picnic, Info, Fishing)

(271) Kearney Rest Area (WB)
(RR, Phones, Picnic, Info, Fishing)

272 NE 44, 2nd Ave, Kearney, Axtell
Gas N: Phillips 66◈, Shamrock, Shell◈
S: BP, Shamrock◈
Food N: Amigo's, Arby's, Burger King, DQ, Country Kitchen, McDonald's, Perkins, Pizza Hut, Red Lobster, Runza Rest, Taco Bell, Valentino's, Wendy's, USA Steak Buffet, Whiskey Creek Wood Fire Grill, Rest/Hol Inn, Rest/Ramada
S: Grandpa's Steakhouse, Skeeter's BBQ
Lodg N: AmericInn, Best Western, Comfort Inn, Country Inn, Days Inn, Fairfield Inn, Hampton Inn, Holiday Inn, Ramada, Super 8, Western Inn, Wingate, Cranewood Country Inn & RV Park ▲
S: Fort Kearney Inn, Holiday Inn Express
Med N: + Good Samaritan Hospital
TServ N: Cummins Great Plains
Other N: ATM, Auto Dealers, Banks, Goodyear, Grocery, Office Max, UPS Store, Vet♥, to Hilltop Mall, Walmart sc▲, Fairgrounds, Univ of NE/Kearney, Clyde & Vi's Campground▲
S: Fort Kearney Historical Park▲

279 NE 10, Gibbon, Minden
FStop S: Ft Kearney Trading Post/Shell
Other N: to Kearney Muni Airport✈
S: to appr 12mi S: Pioneer Village Rest/Motel/Campground▲

285 NE 10C, Lowell Rd, Gibbon
Gas N: Petro Oasis
Lodg S: Country Inn
Other N: Windmill State Park▲

291 NE 10D, Shelton
Other N: War Axe State Park

300 NE 11, 40D Spur, Wood River
TStop S: Bosselman Travel Center/Pilot #912/Sinclair (Scales)
Food S: GrandmaMax/Subway/Bosselman FS
Lodg S: Laundry/WiFi/Bosselman FS, Wood River Motel & Campground▲

305 NE 40C, 80th Rd, CR 26, Alda Rd, Wood River, Alda, Junita
Rest Area (WB)
(RR, Phones, Picnic)
FStop N: Gas N Shop #33/Sinclair
TStop N: Travel Center of America #193 (Scales)
Food N: CountryPride/TA TC

EXIT NEBRASKA

TServ N: TA TC/Tires
Other N: Laundry/WiFi/RVDump/TA TC, RVDump/GasNShop

312 US 34, US 281, Alda, to Grand Island, Hastings, Doniphan
(N Serv are appr 5mi N)
TStop N: Bosselman Travel Center/Pilot #902/Sinclair (Scales)
Gas N: Phillips 66
S: BP
Food N: GrandmaMax/Subway/TacoExpress/Bosselman TC,
S: Rest/USA Inn, 9 Bridges Family Rest
Lodg N: Holiday Inn Express, Holiday Inn
S: USA Inn
TWash N: Diamond TW
TServ N: Graham Tire, Boss Truck Shop
S: High Plains Power Systems, NE Truck Center, Peterbilt
Med N: + Hospital
Other N: Laundry/WiFi/RVDump/Bosselman TC, Morman Island State Rec Area, to Rich & Son's Camper Sales/RVDump, to Sam's Club, Central Reg'l NE Airport✈, to US 34E/Walmart sc▲
S: to appr 15mi Hastings Campground▲

314 Locust St, Grand Island

(315) Grand Island Rest Area (EB)
(RR, Phones, Picnic, Vend, Info, Fishing)

(317) Grand Island Rest Area (WB)
(RR, Phones, Picnic, Vend, Info)

318 NE 2, to US 34, Grand Island
Other S: Grand Island KOA▲

324 NE 41B, Giltner Spur, to Giltner

332 NE 14, Aurora
TStop S: Love's Travel Stop #309 (Scales), Fast Fuel #2/Sinclair
Gas N: Casey's, Shell◈
Food N: McDonald's, Pappy Jack's, Subway, Rest/Hamilton Motor Inn
S: Arby's/Love's TS
Lodg N: Hamilton Motor Inn
Other N: City Park/Streeter Park/RVDump
S: WiFi/RVDump/Love's TS, Laundry/FastFuel

338 NE 41D, Aurora, Hampton

342 NE 93A, Rd B, Henderson, Sulton
TStop S: Fuel Mart #791
Food S: FastFood/Fuel Mart
Lodg S: First Interstate Inn
Other N: Prairie Oasis RV Park & Campground▲

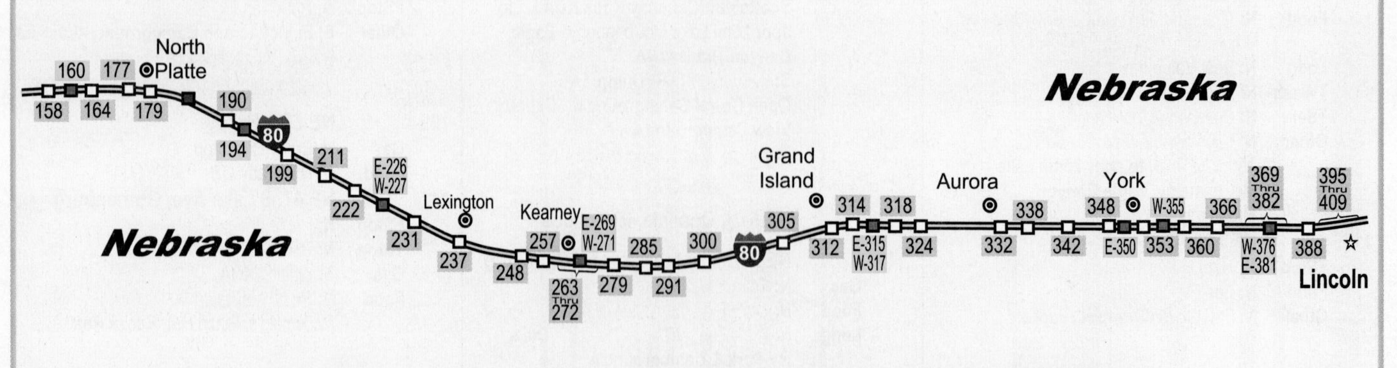

◈= Regular Gas Stations with Diesel ▲ = RV Friendly Locations ♥= Pet Friendly Locations
Red print shows large vehicle parking / access on site or nearby Brown Print = Campgrounds / RV PARKS

EXIT	NEBRASKA
348	**NE 93E, York, to Bradshaw**
(350)	**York Rest Area (EB)** (RR, Phones, Picnic, Vend, Info)
353	**US 81, York, Geneva**
TStop	**N:** Sapp Bros/Sinclair (Scales) **S:** Crossroads Fuel Stop/Shell, Petro Stopping Center #62/66 (Scales)
Gas	**N:** BP◈, Shell◈
Food	**N:** Subway/Sapp Bros, Amigo's, Arby's, Burger King, Country Kitchen, KFC, McDonald's, Wendy's **S:** Rest/FastFood/Crossroads FS, IronSkillet/PizzaHut/Petro SC, Applebee's, Chris's Steak House/ USA Inns
Lodg	**N:** Best Western, Comfort Inn, Days Inn, Quality Inn, Super 8, Y Motel & **RV Park▲** **S:** Holiday Inn Int'l, USA Inn
TWash	**S:** Blue Beacon TW/Petro SC
TServ	**S:** Petro SC/Tires
Other	**N:** Laundry/WiFi/Sapp Bros, Auto Dealers, ATMs, **Walmart sc▲** , **to** York Muni Airport✈ **S:** WiFi/Crossroads FS, Laundry/WiFi/ **RVDump/LP**/Petro SC
(355)	**York Rest Area (WB)** (RR, Picnic, Phone, Vend, Info)
360	**NE 93B, York, to Waco, Exeter**
TStop	**N:** Fuel Mart #642
Food	**N:** Rest/Fuel Mart
Other	**S: Double Nickel Campground▲**
366	**NE 80F, CR 462, Beaver Crossing, to Utica**
369	**NE 80E, CR 420, Beaver Crossing**
373	**NE 80G, CR 364, Goehner**
Gas	**N:** Sinclair
(376)	**Goehner Rest Area (WB)** (RR, Phones, Picnic, Vend)
379	**NE 15, Seward, Fairbury**
Gas	**N:** Phillips 66 **S:** Shell◈
Food	**N:** McDonald's
Lodg	**N:** Super 8
Med	**N:** + Hospital
Other	**N: Walmart sc▲**
(381)	**Blue River Rest Area (EB)** (RR, Phones, Picnic, Vend)
382	**Matzke Hwy, to US 34, Seward, to US 6, Milford**
Other	**N: to Branched Oak Lake State Rec Area▲**
388	**NE 103, CR 154, Crete**
Other	**N: Pawnee Lake State Rec Area▲**
395	**US 6, NW 48th St, Lincoln**
TStop	**S:** AmBest/Original Shoemaker's Truck Stop/Shell (Scales), PTP/Don&Randy Shoemakers Truck Stop/P66
Gas	**N:** Sinclair
Food	**N:** Runza Rest **S:** Rest/Shoemaker's TS
Lodg	**S:** Cobbler Inn/DR Shoemakers, Shoney's Inn, Super 8, Travelodge
TWash	**S:** DR Shoemaker's TS
TServ	**S:** DR Shoemaker's TS/Tires, Freightliner
Other	**N: NE State Hwy Patrol Post** **S:** Laundry/DR Shoemaker's TS

EXIT	NEBRASKA
396	**US 6, W O St, Lincoln (EB)**
Gas	**S:** GasNShop◈
Food	**S:** Blimpie, Mexican Rest,
Lodg	**S:** Super 8, Travelodge
TServ	**S:** High Plains Power Systems
397	**US 77S, Lincoln, to Beatrice**
Gas	**S:** Conoco
Lodg	**S:** Congress Inn Motel, Red Carpet Inn, Super 8, Travelodge
399	**W Adams St, NW 12th St, Cornhusker Hwy, to I-180, Lincoln**
Gas	**N:** BP◈, Phillips 66 **S:** Cenex
Food	**N:** Denny's, McDonald's, Perkins, Quiznos
Lodg	**N:** Best Western, Best Value Inn♥, Comfort Inn, Days Inn, Hampton Inn, Holiday Inn Express, Motel 6♥, Sleep Inn **S:** Econo Lodge, Inn 4 Less Motel
TServ	**S:** Cornhusker International
Other	**N:** Lincoln Muni Airport✈ **S:** to Lincoln State Fairgrounds▲
(401)	**I-180, US 34, to 9th St, Lincoln (EB)**
Other	**S: Campaway RV Resort & Campground▲**
(401A)	**I-180, US 34E, to 9th St, Lincoln**
401B	**US 34W**
403	**27th St, Lincoln**
Gas	**S:** Conoco◈, Mobil, Phillips 66◈, Shell
Food	**S:** Wendy's/Conoco, Subway/P66, Applebee's, Arby's, Burger King, CiCi's, **Cracker Barrel**, DQ, Golden Corral, IHOP, McDonald's, Popeye's, Ruby Tuesday, Valentino's, Village Inn
Lodg	**S:** AmericInn, Best Western♥, Baymont Inn, Comfort Suites, Country Inn, Fairfield Inn, Lincoln SettleInn♥, Microtel♥, Ramada Ltd, Red Roof Inn♥, Super 8
Other	**S:** ATMs, Auto Dealers, Grocery, Home Depot, Sam's Club, **Walmart sc**, **to** State Fairgrounds▲ , Univ of NE East, **Leach Camper Sales/RVDump**
405	**US 77, 56th St, Lincoln**
Gas	**S:** Conoco, Phillips 66
Food	**S:** Misty's
Lodg	**S:** Howard Johnson, Motel 6♥
409	**US 6, Waverly, East Lincoln**
(416)	**Weigh Station (Both dir)**
420	**NE 63, 238th St, Greenwood, Ashland**
FStop	**N:** Speedy Mart/Shell
TStop	**N:** Cubby's Greenwood Travel Plaza/ Conoco (Scales)
Food	**N:** Rest/Greenwood TP **S:** Corner Rest
Lodg	**S:** Big Inn
Other	**N:** Laundry/Greenwood TP, **Pine Grove Campgrounds▲**
(425)	**Platte River Rest Area (EB)** (RR, Phones, Picnic, Vend, Info)
426	**Ashland, Mahoney State Park**
Other	**N: to Eugene T Mahoney State Park**/ Lodge/Rest/**Campground▲** /Family Aquatic Center/Other Activities
(432)	**Melia Hill Rest Area (WB)** (RR, Phones, Picnic, Info)
432	**US 6, NE 31, Gretna, Ashland**
TStop	**S:** Flying J Travel Plaza #5012/Conoco (Scales)

EXIT	NEBRASKA
Gas	**N:** Sinclair
Food	**N:** McDonald's **S:** Cookery/FastFood/FJ TP
Lodg	**N:** Super 8
Other	**N:** Laundry/BarbSh/WiFi/**RVDump/LP**/ FJ TP, NE Crossing Factory Outlet Stores, **to appr 12 mi: W Omaha KOA▲**
439	**NE 370, Omaha, to Gretna, Bellevue**
Gas	**N:** Phillips 66◈
Food	**N:** Blimpie, The Happy Chef
Lodg	**N:** Days Inn, Suburban Inn
Med	**S:** + Hospital
440	**NE 50, S 144th St, Omaha, to Springfield, Louisville**
FStop	**N:** Wally's Place/Conoco
TStop	**N:** Sapp Bros Travel Center/Shell (Scales
Gas	**S:** BP◈
Food	**N:** Rest/Subway/Deli/Sapp Bros TC, **Cracker Barrel**, Hardee's, McDonald's, Subway
Lodg	**N:** Ben Franklin Motel, Budget Inn, Comfort Inn♥, Days Inn, Quality Inn
TWash	**N:** Classic TW
TServ	**N:** Sapp Bros TC/Tires
Med	**N:** + Hospital
Other	**N:** Laundry/BarbSh/Massg/WiFi/ Sapp Bros TC
442	**126th St, Harrison St, Omaha**
Lodg	**S:** Hampton Inn
Other	**N:** Millard Airport✈
444	**Q St, L St, Omaha** (Access to Ex #445 Serv)
445	**US 275, NE 92, I/L/Q St, Center Rd**
Gas	**N:** Cenex◈ **S:** Conoco◈, QT◈, Sinclair
Food	**N:** Austin's Steakhouse, NE Steak & Grill, Perkins, Village Inn **S:** Arby's, Burger King, Hardee's, Hong Kong Café, McDonald's, Long John Silver, Valentino's, Wendy's
Lodg	**N:** Clarion, Residence Inn, Sheraton **S:** Comfort Inn, Days Inn, Econo Lodge♥, Hampton Inn, Holiday Inn Express, Hawthorne Suites, Motel 6♥, La Quinta Inn♥, Super 8
Med	**N:** + Hospital
Other	**N:** Sam's Club, **Walmart sc**, Lucent Tech, **AC Nelsen RV World** **S:** Albertson's, Goodyear
(446)	**Jct I-680N, Downtown, to Boystown, Irvington**
448	**84th St, Papillion**
Gas	**N:** BP, Shell **S:** Phillips 66◈, QT, Shell
Food	**N:** Arby's, Denny's, McDonald's, Subway, Taco Bell **S:** Wendy's
Lodg	**N:** Econo Lodge
Other	**N:** Goodyear, Grocery, NAPA **S:** Auto Dealers, CarQuest, Grocery, Tires, U-Haul
449	**72nd St, La Vista, Ralston**
Gas	**N:** BP **S:** Phillips 66◈
Food	**N:** Burger King, Perkins, Rest/Hol Inn
Lodg	**N:** Baymont Inn, Comfort Inn, DoubleTree, Hampton Inn, Holiday Inn, Homewood Suites, Howard Johnson, Quality Inn, Super 8, Travelodge

◈= Regular Gas Stations with Diesel ▲ = RV Friendly Locations ♥= Pet Friendly Locations
Red print shows large vehicle parking / access on site or nearby Brown Print = Campgrounds / RV PARKS

EXIT		NE / IA
	Med	N: + Hospital
	TServ	S: Kenworth of Omaha
	Other	N: College of St Mary, Golf Course
450		**60th St, Omaha**
	Gas	N: Conoco, Phillips 66◊, Shell S: Phillips 66◊
	Food	S: Country Kitchen
	Lodg	S: Microtel, Relax Inn
	TServ	N: Cummins Allison
	Other	N: Univ of NE/Omaha
451		**42nd St, Omaha**
	Gas	N: 76, Phillips 66, Texaco S: Phillips 66
	Food	S: Burger King, McDonald's, Taco Bell
	Med	N: + Douglas Co Hospital
(452)		**Jct I-480N, US 75N, US 75S**
453		**24th St (EB)**
454		**13th St, Omaha**
	Gas	N: BP◊, Shamrock S: Phillips 66◊
	Food	N: Burger King, KFC, McDonald's
	Lodg	N: Comfort Inn
	Med	N: + St Joseph's Hospital
	Other	N: to Omaha Botanical Gardens S: to IMAX, Rosenblatt Stadium, Zoo
	NOTE:	MM 455: Iowa State Line

CENTRAL TIME ZONE

⇑ NEBRASKA
⇓ IOWA

CENTRAL TIME ZONE

EXIT		IOWA
(1A)		**Jct I-29N, to Sioux City (EB, Left exit)**
	NOTE:	I-80 below runs with I-29. Exit #'s follow I-80.
1B		**24th St, Council Bluffs**
	TStop	N: Pilot Travel Center #329 (Scales), Sapp Bros Travel Center/Shell (Scales)
	Gas	N: Conoco, Sinclair
	Food	N: Arby's/TJCinn/Pilot TC, Rest/BurgerKing/Sapp Bros TC
	Lodg	N: American Inn, Best Western, Super 8
	TWash	N: Blue Beacon TW/Sapp Bros TC
	TServ	N: Sapp Bros/Tires, Peterbilt, Speedco
	Other	N: Laundry/WiFi/Pilot TC, Laundry/WiFi/LP/Sapp Bros TC, Dog Track, Bluffs Run Casino, Mid America Center
3		**IA 192N, S 4th St, S Expressway St, Council Bluffs, Lake Manawa**
	TStop	S: Travel Center of America #66 (Scales), Phillips 66
	Gas	N: Casey's
	Food	S: CountryPride/PizzaHut/TA TC, Applebee's, Burger King, Cracker Barrel, DQ, Golden Corral, Long John Silver, McDonald's, Perkins, Red Lobster, Subway, Taco Bell
	Lodg	S: Days Inn, Fairfield Inn, Motel 6♥, Settle Inn
	TWash	S: TruckOMat
	TServ	S: TA TC/Tires
	Other	S: Laundry/WiFi/TA TC, Advance Auto Parts, Auto Dealers, Sam's Club, U-Haul, Walmart▲, Lake Manawa State Park
(4)		**Jct I-29S, to Kansas City (WB, Left ex)**
	NOTE:	I-80 above runs with I-29. Exit #'s follow I-80.
5		**Madison Ave, Council Bluffs**
	Gas	N: AmocoBP S: Conoco, Shell
	Food	N: Burger King, KFC, McDonald's, Pizza Hut, Subway S: DQ, Valentino's, Village Inn
	Lodg	N: Heartland Inn S: Western Inn Motor Lodge♥
	Other	N: ATMs, Grocery, Target, Walgreen's, Mall of the Bluffs
8		**US 6, Kanesville Blvd, Council Bluffs, Oakland**
	Gas	N: Coastal, Fill & Food, Phillips 66
	Other	N: IA Western Comm College S: IA State Hwy Patrol Post, to Council Bluffs Muni Airport✈
17		**G30, Magnolia Rd, Underwood**
	TStop	N: Underwood Truck Stop/66
	Food	N: Rest/Underwood TS, Rest/I-80 Inn
	Lodg	N: I-80 Inn, Underwood Motel
	TServ	N: A 1 Truck Repair
(19)		**IA Welcome Center (EB) Rest Area (WB)** (RR, Phone, Pic, Vend, RVDump, WiFi, Weather)
23		**IA 244, L55, 298th St, Neola**
	FStop	S: Kum & Go #23
	Other	S: Arrowhead Park▲
(27)		**Jct I-680W, to N Omaha, Sioux City (fr EB, Left exit)**
29		**L66, 335th St, Minden**
	Gas	S: Phillips 66◊
(32)		**Parking Area (Both dir)**
34		**M16, 385th St, Avoca, Shelby**
	FStop	N: Taylor Quick-Pik/Shell
	Food	N: Country Pizza, DQ/Shell
	Lodg	N: Shelby Country Inn & RV Park▲
40		**US 59, Avoca Ln, Avoca, Harlan**
	TStop	N: Wings America Travel Center/Conoco (Scales)
	Gas	S: Shell◊
	Food	N: Rest/FastFood/Wings Amer TC S: Embers, Parkway Café & Campground▲
	Lodg	N: Motel 6♥ S: Avoca Motel
	TWash	N: Wings Amer TC
	Med	N: + Hospital
	Other	N: Laundry/BarbSh/RVDump/LP/Wings Amer TC S: Parkway Café & Campground▲, Pottawattamie Co Fairgrounds▲
(44)		**Weigh Station (Both dir)**
46		**M47, 505th St, Walnut Antique City Dr, Walnut**
	FStop	S: Kum & Go #46
	Gas	S: BP
	Food	S: The Villager Rest, McDonald's
	Lodg	S: Red Carpet Inn & RV Park▲, Super 8, Antique City Inn B&B
	Other	N: to Prairie Rose State Park▲
51		**M56, Marne**
54		**IA 173, Mame, Atlantic, Elk Horn, Kimballton (Serv appr 6mi N)**
	Other	N: to Danish Windmill, Danish Museum
57		**N16, Atlantic**
	Med	S: + to Hospital
60		**US 6W, US 71W, Atlantic, Villisca, Audubon**
	TStop	S: Valley Oil Co/66
	Gas	S: Shamrock
	Food	S: Rest/P66
	Lodg	S: Days Inn
	TServ	S: Valley Oil/Tires
64		**N28, Anita, to Wiota**
70		**IA 148, Anita, to Exira**
	Other	S: to Lake Anita State Park▲
75		**G30, Anita Adair Rd, Adair**
76		**N54, 5th St, Adair**
	FStop	N: Kum & Go #76
	Gas	N: AmocoBP, Casey's◊

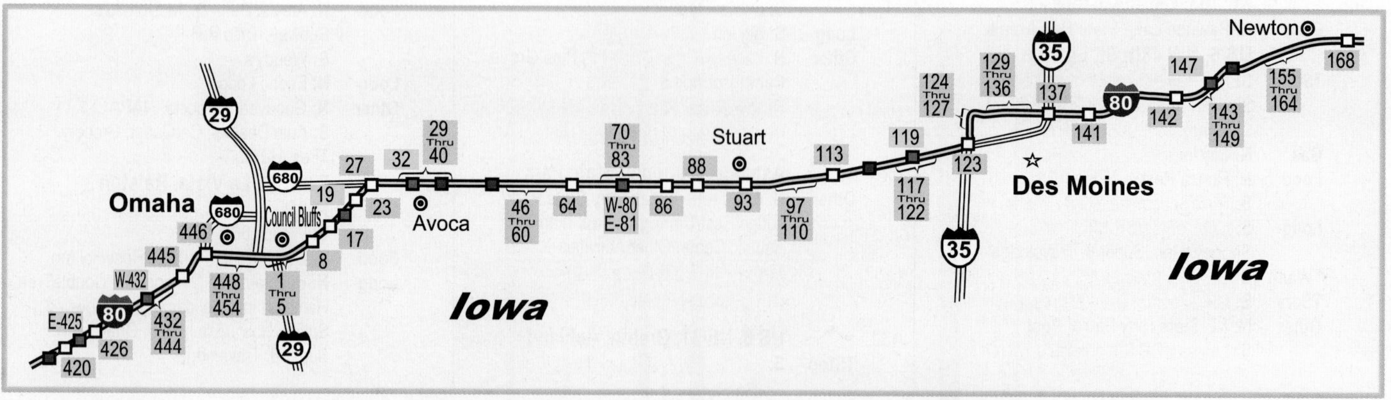

◊ = Regular Gas Stations with Diesel ▲ = RV Friendly Locations ♥ = Pet Friendly Locations
Red print shows large vehicle parking / access on site or nearby Brown Print = Campgrounds / RV PARKS

EXIT		IOWA
	Food	N: Happy Chef, Subway/Kum & Go
	Lodg	N: Budget Inn, Super 8
	Other	N: Auto Repair
(80)		Rest Area (WB) (RR, Phone, Pic, Vend, RVDump, WiFi)
(81)		Rest Area (EB) (RR, Phone, Picnic, Vend, RVDump, WiFi)
83		**N77, Antique County Dr, Casey**
86		**IA 25, to Guthrie Center, Greenfield**
	Other	S: to Springbrook State Park▲
88		**P20, Redwood Ave, Pinewood Ave, Casey, to Menlo**
93		**P28, Division St, to Stuart, Panora**
	TStop	N: Prairie Dog Truck Travel Center/ Conoco (Scales) S: Stuart 66 Truck Stop
	Gas	N: BP◈
	Food	N: FastFood/Prairie Dog TTC, Burger King, McDonald's, Subway S: Rest/Stuart TS, Country Kitchen
	Lodg	N: AmericInn♥, Super 8 S: New Edgetowner Motel
97		**P48, Casey, to Dexter**
100		**F 60, P53, El Paso Ave, Eldorado Ave, Dexter, Redfield**
104		**P57, I Ave, De Soto, Earlham**
106		**F90, P58, 360th St, L Ave**
	Other	N: to Des Moines West KOA▲
110		**US 169, US 6, Desoto, Adel, Winterset**
	Gas	S: Casey's, Kum & Go
	Lodg	S: De Soto Motor Inn, Edgetowner Motel
	Other	S: John Wayne Birthplace, Tourist Info, Covered Bridges of Madison Co
113		**R16, Van Meter**
(114)		Weigh Station (EB)
117		**R2, Waukee, Booneville**
	Gas	S: Kum & Go
	Food	S: Rube's Steakhouse
	Other	N: Timberline Campground▲
(119)		Rest Area (Both dir) (RR, Phone, Picnic, Vend, WiFi, RVDump)
121		**74th St, Jordan Creek Pkwy, Waukee, W Des Moines**
	Gas	N: BP, Hy-Vee S: Kum & Go
	Food	N: West Diner S: Arby's, Burger King, McDonald's, Perkins, Taco John
	Lodg	N: Hampton Inn, Hawthorne Suites S: Fairfield Inn, Quality Inn, Motel 6♥
	Other	N: Grocery, Home Depot, Target
122		**60th St, W Des Moines (EB)**
	Gas	S: Kum & Go
(123A)		**I-235E, W Des Moines, Des Moines St Fairgrounds (EB, Left Exit)**
(123B)		**I-35S, to Kansas City**
(123)		**I-35/I-80N, I-35 S-Kansas City, I-235E to Des Moines**

Personal Notes

EXIT		IOWA
NOTE:		I-80 below runs with I-35 for 14mi. Exit #'s follow I-80.
124/72C		**University Ave, Clive**
	Gas	N: BP, Kum & Go, QT S: Phillips 66
	Food	N: Cracker Barrel S: Applebee's, Bakers Square, Chili's, Colton's Steakhouse, Don Pablo, KFC, McDonald's, Outback Steakhouse, Romano's Macaroni Grill
	Lodg	N: Baymont Inn, Best Western, Country Inn, La Quinta Inn♥, Ramada S: Chase Suites, Courtyard, Fairfield Inn, Heartland Inn, Holiday Inn, Marriott, Residence Inn, Wildwood Lodge
	Med	N: + Hospital S: + Mercy West Health Center
	Other	S: ATMs, Banks, Barnes & Noble, Best Buy, CompUSA, Lowe's, World Market
125		**US 6, Hickman Rd, W Des Moines, Clive, Adel**
	TStop	N: Love's Travel Stop #411 (Scales)
	Food	N: Denny's/FastFood/Love's TS
	Lodg	S: Clarion, Comfort Suites, Sleep Inn
	Other	N: Laundry/WiFi/LP/Love's TS S: Goodyear, to Living History Farms
126		**Douglas Ave, Urbandale, Des Moines**
	TStop	N: Pilot Travel Center #373 (Scales)
	Gas	S: Kum & Go◈
	Food	N: GrandmaMax/Pilot TC S: Dragon House
	Lodg	S: Days Inn, Econo Lodge

EXIT		IOWA
	TWash	N: Pilot TC
	TServ	N: Pilot TC/Tires
	Other	N: Laundry/WiFi/RVDump/Pilot TC
127		**IA 141, Urbandale, Grimes, Perry**
	FStop	N: Swift Stop/66
	Food	N: Subway/66 S: Quiznos
	Other	S: Target
129		**NW 86th St, Urbandale, Camp Dodge**
	Gas	N: Kum & Go S: BP, Phillips 66
	Food	N: Burger King, McDonald's S: Arby's, Culver's, Ember's
	Lodg	N: Hilton Garden Inn, Stoney Creek Inn S: Microtel
131		**IA 28S, NW 58th St, Merle Hay Rd, Urbandale, Des Moines**
	Gas	N: Casey's, QT S: BP◈, QT, Sinclair◈
	Food	N: North End Diner, Quiznos, Shoney's, Rest/BW S: Arby's, Burger King, Country Kitchen, Denny's, Famous Dave's BBQ, Hostetler's BBQ, KFC, McDonald's, Perkins, Pizza Hut, Village Inn, Wendy's
	Lodg	N: Best Inn♥, Best Western♥, Ramada♥ S: Comfort Inn♥, Days Inn, Holiday Inn, Quality Inn, Sheraton, Super 8
	Med	S: + VA Hospital
	Other	N: Grocery, Goodyear S: ATMs, Auto Dealers, Best Buy, Firestone, Office Depot, Walgreen's, Mall
135		**IA 415, 2nd Ave, Polk City**
	Gas	S: Coastal, QT
	TServ	N: Interstate Detroit Diesel S: Freightliner
	Med	S: + Hospital
	Other	N: IA State Hwy Patrol Post, Easter Seals Camp
136		**US 69, E 14th St, Ankeny**
	FStop	S: QT #562 (Scales)
	Gas	N: BP◈, Phillips 66, Sinclair S: Casey's, Citgo◈
	Food	N: Bonanza Steak House, Country Kitchen, Rest/BW S: Burger King/QT FS, KFC, Kin Folks BBQ, Long John Silver, McDonald's, Pizza Hut, Village Inn, Wendy's
	Lodg	N: Best Western, Motel 6♥ S: 14th Street Inn, Ramada, Red Roof Inn
	TServ	N: Cummins Great Plains, White Volvo/ GMC of Des Moines S: Mack Trucks, Midstates Ford Truck
	Other	S: Advance Auto Parts, Goodyear, RV Center, Easter Seals Camp
(137A/87)		**Jct I-235W, to Des Moines**
(137B/87)		**Jct I-35N, to Minneapolis** (fr NB, Left Exit)
NOTE:		I-80 above runs with I-35 for 14mi. Exit #'s follow I-80.
141		**US 65S, Altoona, Des Moines (EB) Pleasant Hill, Des Moines (WB)**
	Other	WB: IA State Fairgrounds
142A		**US 6W, Altoona (EB)**
142B		**US 65N, Bondurant, Marshalltown** (EB, Left exit)

◈= Regular Gas Stations with Diesel ▲ = RV Friendly Locations ♥= Pet Friendly Locations
Red print shows large vehicle parking / access on site or nearby Brown Print = Campgrounds / RV PARKS

EXIT		IOWA
142		**US 6W, US 65N, Altoona, Bondurant**
	TStop	S: Bosselman Travel Center/Pilot #913/ Sinclair (Scales)
	Food	S: GrandmaMax/FastFood/Bosselman TC, Big Steer Rest, Burger King, McDonald's, Pizza Hut, Subway, Taco John
	Lodg	S: Adventureland Inn, Country Inn, Holiday Inn, Howard Johnson, Motel 6♥ Settle Inn & Suites♥
	TWash	S: Blue Beacon TW/Bosselman TC
	TServ	S: Bosselman TC/Tires, International
	Other	N: to Plaza RV Center, Griff's Valley View RV Park▲ S: Laundry/WiFi/Bosselman TC, Walmart sc, Williamsburg Outlet Mall, Prairie Meadows Horse Racing & Casino, Adventureland Resort, Adventureland RV Park▲
143		**1st Ave N, CR S14, Altoona, Bondurant**
	Gas	S: Casey's
	Food	S: Settle Inn
(147)		**Rest Area (Both dir) (RR, Phone, Picnic, Vend, WiFi)**
149		**S27, NE 112th St, Mitchellville (DO *NOT* PICK UP HITCHIKERS)**
(151)		**Weigh Station (WB)**
155		**IA 117, Colfax, Mingo, Prairie City**
	FStop	S: Kum & Go #32
	TStop	N: PTP/Colfax Valley Travel Center/BP (Scales)
	Gas	S: Casey's
	Food	N: McDonald's/Colfax Valley TC
	Lodg	S: Comfort Inn
	TServ	N: Colfax Valley TC/Tires
	Other	N: Laundry/Colfax Valley TC
159		**F48, to S52, Newton, Baxter**
164		**US 6, IA 14, Newton, Monroe**
	Gas	N: BP, Kum & Go, Phillips 66◈
	Food	N: Country Kitchen, KFC, Perkins S: Rest/Best Western, Newton Inn
	Lodg	N: Days Inn♥, Ramada♥, Super 8 S: Best Western
	Med	N: + Hospital
	Other	S: to Lake Red Rock, Central College Casinos, Horse Racing
168		**IA Speedway Dr, Newton**
	TStop	S: Love's Travel Stop #361 (Scales)
	Gas	N: Casey's◈
	Food	N: Arby's, Taco John S: McDonald's/Chesters/Love's TS
	Other	N: Walmart sc, Best Holiday Trav-L-Park/Rolling Acres RV Park▲, IOWA Speedway S: Newton Muni Airport✈
173		**IA 224N, T22S, Kellogg, Sully**
	Gas	N: Phillips 66◈
	Food	N: IA Best Burger Café/P66 & Kellogg RV Park▲
	Other	N: to Rock Creek State Park▲ S: Chk for open dates: Camp Lake Pla-Mor Campground▲
179		**T38, Grinnell, to Lynnville, Oakland Acres**
(180)		**Rest Area (Both dir) (RR, Phone, Picnic, Vend, WiFi, RVDump/EB)**
182		**IA 146, Grinnell, New Sharon**
	Gas	N: Casey's
	Food	N: AJ's Steakhouse, Country Kitchen, KFC, Taco Bell
	Lodg	N: Budget Inn, Country Inn, Days Inn, Econo Lodge, Super 8
	Other	N: Grocery, Walmart, Grinnell College, Grinnell Reg'l Airport✈ S: Fun Valley Ski Area
191		**US 63, Montezuma St, Malcolm, Tama, Montezuma**
	TStop	S: Fuel Mart #794
	Food	S: Rest/Fuel Mart
	Other	S: Fun Valley Ski Area
197		**V18, Brooklyn**
	FStop	N: Randhawa's Travel Center/BP
	Food	N: Rest/Randhawa's TC
	Other	N: LP/Randhawa's TC
201		**IA 21, Brooklyn, to Belle Plaine, Deep River**
	TStop	N: AmBest/Shortstop Travel Plaza/66 S: KwikStar #303 (Scales)
	Food	N: QtrPostCare/Subs/Shortstop TP, S: Rest/FastFood/KwikStar
	Lodg	N: Motel/Shortstop TP
	TServ	S: KwikStar/Tires
	Other	N: Laundry/Shortstop TP S: Laundry/WiFi/KwikStar
205		**V38, B Ave, Victor**
(208)		**Rest Area (Both dir) (RR, Phone, Picnic, WiFi, RVDump/EB)**
211		**V52, H Ave, Ladora, Millersburg**
	Other	N: Lake Iowa Park
216		**V66, M Ave, Williamsburg, to Marengo, North English**
	FStop	N: Kum & Go #443/Shell
220		**IA 149S, V77N, Highland St, to US 6, Williamsburg, Parnell (NEXT 2 EXITS—Amana Colonies)**
	FStop	N: Landmark Handymart/66
	Gas	N: BP, Casey's
	Food	N: McDonald's, Pizza Hut, Subway
	Lodg	N: Crest Motel, Super 8 S: Days Inn, Ramada
	Other	N: Outlet Mall
225		**US 151N, W21S, U Ave, Homestead, Cedar Rapids, Amana Colonies**
	Gas	S: BP, Phillips 66
	Food	S: Colony Haus, Colony Village, Little Amana Rest, Maid-Rite, Rest/DI
	Lodg	N: Comfort Inn S: Days Inn, Holiday Inn, My Little Inn, Econo Lodge, Super 8
	Other	N: to Amana Colonies, Amana Colonies RV Park▲
230		**W38, Black Hawk Ave, Oxford**
	Other	N: Sleepy Hollow Campground▲, FW Kent Park, Kalona Village Museum
(237)		**Rest Area (Both dir) (RR, Phone, Picnic, Vend, WiFi, RVDump)**
237		**Ireland Ave, Tiffin**
	Other	N: FW Kent Park
239A		**US 218S, IA 27, Mount Pleasant, Keokuk**
(239B)		**I-380, US 218N, Cedar Rapids, Waterloo**
240		**Coral Ridge Ave, 27th Ave, to US 6, Coralville, North Liberty**
	Gas	N: Phillips 66 S: BP, Conoco, Phillips 66
	Food	N: McDonald's, Steak n Shake, Village Inn, Wendy's S: Applebee's, Chili's, Olive Garden, Outback Steakhouse, Red Lobster
	Lodg	N: AmericInn, Country Inn, Ramada Inn S: Days Inn♥, Holiday Inn Express
	Other	N: Walmart sc, Harley Davidson, Colony Country Campground▲ S: ATMs, Barnes & Noble, Best Buy, Grocery, Lowe's, Target, Tires, U-Haul, Coral Ridge Mall, Univ of IA/Oakdale, to IA City Muni Airport✈
242		**1st Ave, Coralville, Iowa City**
	FStop	S: Kum & Go #201
	Gas	S: BP, Conoco
	Food	S: Arby's, Burger King, Country Kitchen, McDonald's, KFC, Lone Star Steakhouse, Perkins, Pizza Hut, Subway, Taco Bell

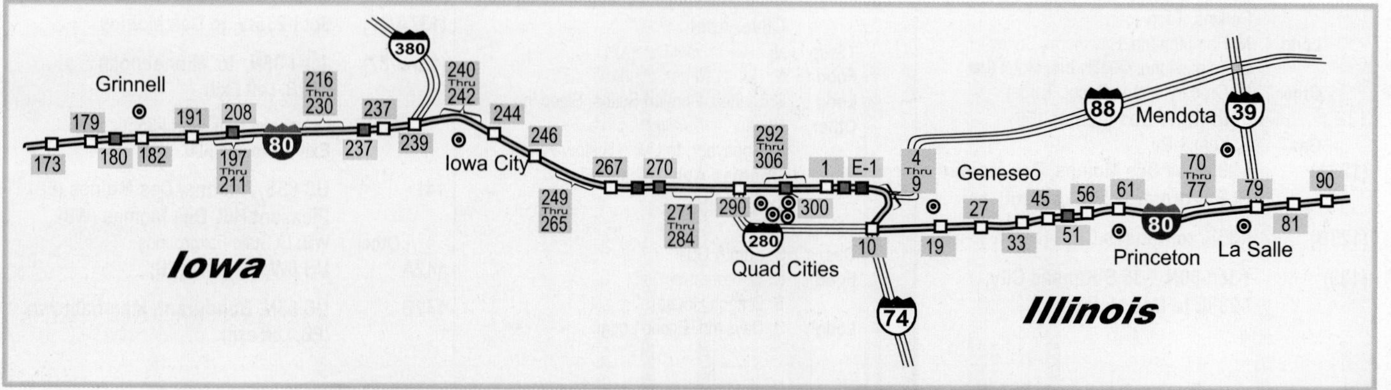

◈= Regular Gas Stations with Diesel ▲ = RV Friendly Locations ♥= Pet Friendly Locations
Red print shows large vehicle parking / access on site or nearby Brown Print = Campgrounds / RV PARKS

EXIT		IOWA
	Lodg	N: Hampton Inn, Holiday Inn S: Baymont Inn, Best Western, Comfort Inn, Days Inn, Fairfield Inn, Motel 6♥, Red Roof Inn♥,Super 8♥
	Med	S: + VA Hospital, + Univ of IA Hospital
	Other	S: Walgreen's, Visitor Info, Firefighters Memorial, Univ of IA
244		**W66, Dubuque St, Downtown, Iowa City**
	Med	S: + Hospital
	Other	N: Coralville Lake
246		**IA 1, Dodge St, Iowa City, to Mt Vernon**
	Gas	N: BP◊, Phillips 66 S: Sinclair
	Lodg	N: Highlander Inn, Quality Inn S: Country Suites, Travelodge♥
249		**F44, Herbert Hoover Hwy, Iowa City**
254		**X30, Baker Ave, Downey St, West Branch, to Buchanan, West Liberty**
	Gas	N: BP◊, Casey's S: Kum & Go, Phillips 66
	Food	S: McDonald's
	Lodg	S: Best Value Inn, Presidential Inn
	Other	N: Herbert Hoover Historical Site & Presidential Museum
259		**X40, Garfield Ave, West Liberty**
	FStop	S: J&M Oil/BP
	Food	S: FastFood/J&M Oil
	Lodg	S: Econo Lodge
	Other	N: Herbert Hoover National Library & Museum S: RVDump/J&M Oil, West Liberty KOA▲
265		**X46, Atalissa Rd, Atalissa**
	TStop	S: AmBest/Diesel Depot/66 (Scales)
	Food	S: Birdie's/Chesters/AustinBluesBBQ/ Diesel Depot
267		**IA 38N, X54S, Moscow Rd, Tipton, Moscow**
	Food	S: The Cove Café
	Other	N: Cedar River Campground▲
(268)		**Weigh Station (WB)**
(270)		**IA Welcome Center (WB) Rest Area (EB) (RR, Phone, Pic, Vend, WiFi, RVDump)**
271		**US 6W, IA 38S, Wilton, Muscatine**
277		**Y26, Yankee Ave, Durant, Bennett**
280		**Y30, 20th Ave, Durant, Stockton, New Liberty**
	Other	S: IA State Hwy Patrol Post
284		**Y40, 60th Ave, Walcott, Plain View**
	TStop	N: IA 80 Travel Center of America #77/BP (Scales), Pilot Travel Center #43 (Scales) S: Pilot Travel Center #268 (Scales)
	Gas	N: Phillips 66
	Food	N: IA 80Kitchen/Blimpie/DQ/Wendys/ IA 80 TA TC, Arby's/TJCinn/Pilot TC, Gramma's Kitchen S: Subway/Pilot TC, McDonald's
	Lodg	N: Comfort Inn, Super 8 S: Days Inn
	TWash	N: Blue Beacon TW/IA 80 TA TC
	TServ	N: IA 80 TA TC/Tires, Speedco
	Other	N: Laundry/BarbSh/CB/WiFi/IA 80 TA TC, Laundry/WiFi/Pilot TC S: WiFi/Pilot TC, Cheyenne Camping Center

EXIT		IA / IL
(290)		**Jct I-280E, US 6E, to Rock Island, Moline (fr WB, LEFT Exit)**
	TServ	S: Cummins Great Plains, Peterbilt
	Other	S: Quad City Airport✈
292		**IA 130W, Northwest Blvd, Davenport, Maysville**
	TStop	N: Flying J Travel Plaza #5071/Conoco (Scales)
	Gas	S: BP, Sinclair
	Food	N: Cookery/FastFood/FJ TP S: Machine Shed Rest
	Lodg	N: Hotel/FJ TP S: Comfort Inn
	Other	N: Laundry/BarbSh/WiFi/RVDump/LP/ FJ TP, Interstate RV Park & Campground▲, Water Park, IMAX, Putnam Museum S: Hidden Lake Campground▲
295A		**US 61S, Brady St, Davenport, Downtown, Riverfront**
295B		**US 61N, Eldridge, De Witt**
295		**US 61, Brady St, Davenport**
	Gas	N: BP S: BP◊, Shell
	Food	S: Burger King, Country Kitchen, Cracker Barrel, Hardee's, Hooters, McDonald's, Steak 'n Shake, Village Inn
	Lodg	S: Baymont Inn, Best Western, Days Inn, Heartland Inn, Motel 6, Residence Inn
	Other	N: Davenport Muni Airport✈, Scott Co Park, Terry Frazer RV Center S: ATMs, Auto Zone, Auto Dealers, Northpark Mall, US Adventure RV
(298)		**Jct I-74E, to Bettendorf, Davenport, to Peoria**
(300)		**Rest Area (Both dir) (RR, Phone, Picnic, Vend, WiFi)**
301		**Middle Rd, Bettendorf**
(306)		**US 67, Cody Rd, Le Claire, Bettendorf, Clinton N: IA Welcome Center (WB) (RR, Phone, Picnic) (NO Trucks)**
	Gas	N: BP, Phillips 66◊ S: BP◊
	Food	N: Subway, Cowboy Steaks
	Lodg	N: Comfort Inn, Super 8
	Other	N: Buffalo Bill Museum

CENTRAL TIME ZONE

NOTE: MM 307: Illinois State Line

⬆ IOWA
⬇ ILLINOIS

CENTRAL TIME ZONE

EXIT		IA / IL
1		**IL 84, 20th St, Great River Rd, E Moline, Savanna**
	Gas	N: BP S: Citgo
(1)		**IL Welcome Center (EB) (RR, Phone, Picnic, Info)**

EXIT		ILLINOIS
(2)		**Weigh Station (Both dir)**
4A		**IL 92S, IL 5S, Silvis**
	Other	S: to Quad City Downs, Lundeen Campground▲
(4B)		**Jct I-88, IL 92E, Sterling, Rock Falls**
7		**Cleveland Rd, Colona, Green Rock**
	Gas	N: Shell◊
9		**US 6, Colona, to Geneseo**
	Other	N: Niabi Zoo, Winery
(10)		**From EB:**
	AHEAD	**Jct I-74E, to Peoria (EB) to Galesburg, Western IL Univ**
	1st Rt	**Jct I-280W, I-74W, to Moline, Rock Island (EB) to Quad City Airport✈**
	2nd Rt	**Jct I-80E, to Chicago (EB)**
		From WB:
	AHEAD	**Jct I-280W, I-74, Moline, Rock Island**
	1st Rt	**Jct I-80W, to Davenport**
	2nd Rt	**Jct I-74E, to Peoria**
19		**IL 82, Geneseo, Cambridge**
	FStop	N: Beck Oil/P66
	Gas	N: BP, Shell
	Food	N: Hardee's, McDonald's, Subway S: KFC
	Lodg	N: Deck Plaza, Oakwood Motel
	Med	N: + Hospital
	Other	N: Walmart, Geneseo Campground▲, RV Center
27		**CR 5, Atkinson, to Galva**
	TStop	N: Atkinson Plaza #93/Mobil
	Gas	N: Casey's
	Food	N: Rest/Atkinson Plz
	TWash	N: Atkinson Plz
	Other	N: LP/Atkinson Plz
33		**IL 78, Annawan, Kewanee, to Prophetstown**
	Gas	S: Mobil◊, Phillips 66◊
	Food	S: The Loft, Olympic Flame
	Lodg	S: Holiday Inn Express
	Other	S: Johnson Sauk Trail State Park
45		**IL 40, 900 St E, Peoria, Sterling**
	Gas	N: Marathon◊
	Food	N: Rest/Marathon, Rest/Days Inn
	Lodg	N: Days Inn
	Other	N: to President Ronald Reagan birthplace S: Hennepin Canal State Park▲
(51)		**Great Sauk Trail Rest Area (Both dir) (RR, Ph, Pic, Vend, RVDump, Weather)**
56		**IL 26, N Main St, Princeton, Dixon**
	TStop	N: Road Ranger #225/Pilot TC/ Citgo (Scales)
	Gas	S: BP, Phillips 66, Shell
	Food	N: Rest/FastFood/Road Ranger S: Burger King, Country Kitchen, KFC, McDonald's, Taco Bell, Wendy's
	Lodg	N: Super 8 S: Comfort Inn, Days Inn, Princeton Motel
	TWash	N: Road Ranger
	TServ	N: Road Ranger/Tires
	Other	N: Laundry/Road Ranger S: ATMs, Auto Services, Auto Dealers, Amtrak Station, Dollar General, Grocery, Walmart sc,
(61)		**Jct I-180S, to Hennepin**
70		**IL 89, S Main Ave, Ladd, to Spring Valley**

◊= Regular Gas Stations with Diesel ▲ = RV Friendly Locations ♥= Pet Friendly Locations
Red print shows large vehicle parking / access on site or nearby Brown Print = Campgrounds / RV PARKS

EXIT		ILLINOIS
73		**CR 76, Plank Rd, Peru**
	TStop	N: Sapp Bros Travel Center◈◈ (Scales)
	Food	N: Rest/FastFood/Sapp Bros TC
	TServ	N: Sapp Bros TC/Tires
	Other	N: Laundry/WiFi/LP/Sapp Bros TC,
		S: IL Valley Reg'l Airport✈
75		**IL 251, Peru, Mendota**
	FStop	N: Clocktower Shell
	TStop	N: Crazy D's (Scales)
	Gas	N: BP
		S: BP
	Food	N: Arby's, McDonald's, Taco Bell, Rest/Tiki Inn
		S: Applebee's, Bob Evans, Culver's, Red Lobster, Steak 'n Shake, Subway, Wendy's
	Lodg	N: Baymont Inn, Econo Lodge, Kings Inn, Motel 6♥, Super 8♥, Tiki Inn & RV Park▲
		S: Fairfield Inn, La Quinta Inn♥
	Med	S: + Hospital
	Other	N: Laundry/Crazy D's
		S: Auto Dealers, Auto Zone, Grocery, Goodyear, Home Depot, Midas, Staples, Target, Walgreen's, Walmart, Peru Mall, IL Valley Comm College
77		**IL 351, St Vincent Ave, La Salle**
	TStop	S: Flying J Travel Plaza #5076 (Scales)
	Food	S: CountryMarket/FastFood/FJ TP
	Lodg	S: Daniels Motel
	TWash	S: FJ TP
	Other	S: Laundry/BarbSh/WiFi/RVDump/LP/FJ TP, IL State Hwy Patrol Post
(79)		**Jct I-39N, US 51, N to Rockford, S to Bloomington**
(79A)		**I-39S, US 51, Bloomington, Normal**
(79B)		**I-39N, US 51, to Rockford**
81		**IL 178, CR 43, E 8th Rd, Utica**
	TStop	N: Love's Travel Stop #351 (Scales)
	Gas	S: BP, Shell◈
	Food	N: McDonald's/Subway/Love's TS
	Other	N: WiFi/RVDump/Love's TS, La Salle/Peru KOA▲
		S: Hickory Hollow Campground▲, Starved Rock State Park▲
90		**IL 23, Ottawa, De Kalb**
	Gas	N: BP
		S: BP◈, Shell
	Food	N: Cracker Barrel, Taco Bell, Subway/BP
		S: China Inn, Country Kitchen, Dunkin Donuts, McDonald's, KFC, Ponderosa
	Lodg	N: Hampton Inn, Holiday Inn Express
		S: Comfort Inn, Super 8, Travelodge
	Med	N: + Hospital

EXIT		ILLINOIS
	Other	N: Auto Dealers
		S: ATMs, Kroger, Harley Davidson, Pharmacy, Walmart, US Post Office, Ace RV Center
93		**IL 71, Ottawa, Oswego**
	FStop	N: JMP Oil #76/Mobil
	TStop	N: Oasis Clocktower Shell
	Food	N: Rest/Oasis CS
	TServ	N: Oasis CS/Tires
	Other	N: Skydive Chicago RV Park▲
97		**CR 15, E 24th Rd, Marseilles**
	Other	S: Glenwood RV Resort▲, Troll Hollow Campground▲, Illini State Park▲
105		**Seneca Rd, Morris, Seneca**
	Other	S: Whispering Pines RV Sales
112		**IL 47, US 6, Division St, Morris, to Yorkville**
	FStop	N: Northside Fuel/Citgo
	TStop	N: Travel Center of America #236/BP (Scales)
	Gas	S: BP, Mobil, Shell
	Food	N: Rest/Quiznos/Romines, Chili's
		S: Burger King, KFC, McDonald's, Maria's, Morris Diner, Pizza Hut, Subway, Taco Bell, Wendy's
	Lodg	N: Comfort Inn, Days Inn♥, Holiday Inn Express
		S: Morris Motel, Park Motel, Super 8♥
	TServ	N: TA TC/Tires
	Med	S: + Morris Hospital
	Other	N: Laundry/WiFi/Romines TC, Grundy Co Fairgrounds
	Other	S: ATMs, Auto Services, Grocery, Radio Shack, Walgreen's, Walmart sc, Pro Source Motorsports
(117)		**Rest Area (EB)** (RR, Phone, Picnic, Weather)
(118)		**Rest Area (WB)** (RR, Phone, Picnic, Weather)
122		**CR 11, Ridge Rd, Minooka**
	FStop	N: McCoy's Citgo
	TStop	S: Pilot Travel Center #236 (Scales)
	Gas	S: BP
	Food	S: Arby's/TJCinn/Pilot TC, DQ, McDonald's, Subway, Wendy's,
	Other	S: Laundry/WiFi/Pilot TC, Grocery
(126AB)		**Jct I-55, N-Chicago, S-St Louis**
127		**Houbolt Rd, Empress Rd, Joliet**
	Gas	N: 7-11, BP
	Food	N: Burger King, Cracker Barrel, McDonald's
	Lodg	N: Fairfield Inn, Hampton Inn, Ramada
	Other	N: Harley Davidson, Joliet Park Airport✈
		S: Empress River Casino

EXIT		ILLINOIS
130AB		**IL 7, Larkin Ave, Joliet**
	Gas	N: Citgo, Clark, Marathon, Speedway, Shell, Thornton◈
	Food	N: Bob Evans, Burger King, Dunkin Donuts, KFC, Pizza Hut, Steak 'n Shake, Subway, Taco Bell, Wendy's, White Castle
	Lodg	N: Comfort Inn, Holiday Inn Express, Microtel, Motel 6♥, Red Roof Inn♥, Super 8
	TServ	N: International
	Med	N: + Hospital
	Other	N: Grocery, Goodyear, Kmart, Sam's Club, Walmart
131		**Center St, US 6, Railroad St, S Raynor Ave**
	Other	N: to Riverboat Casino
132AB		**US 52E, IL 53, Chicago St**
	Other	N: Harrah's Joliet Casino, Amtrak
133		**Richards St, Joliet**
134		**CR 54, Briggs Rd**
	Gas	N: Speedway
		S: 7-11◈
	Other	N: Martin Campground▲
		S: Starting Line Campground▲, Chicago Land Speedway, Rte 66 Speedway
137		**US 30, Maple St, Lincoln Hwy, New Lenox**
	Gas	S: Speedway◈
	Food	N: Rest
	Food	S: Burger King, KFC, McDonald's, Pizza Hut, Taco Bell
	Other	N: ATMs
		S: Grocery, Walgreen's
(143)		**Weigh Station (EB)**
145AB		**US 45, 96th Ave, Mokena**
	FStop	S: Shell Food Mart
	Gas	N: Gas City
		S: BP, Gas City
	Food	N: Subway/Gas City
		S: Burger King, DQ, Denny's, Subway, Wendy's, White Castle
	Lodg	S: Super 8
(147)		**Weigh Station (WB)**
148AB		**IL 43, Harlem Ave, Tinley Park**
	FStop	N: Speedway
	Food	N: Subway/Speedway, Burger King, Chicago Café, Cracker Barrel, Wendy's
	Lodg	N: Baymont Inn, Comfort Suites, Fairfield Inn, Holiday Inn Select, Sleep Inn
	Other	S: Windy City Campground & Beach▲
(151AB)		**Jct I-57, S-Memphis, N-Chicago** (Left Exits)

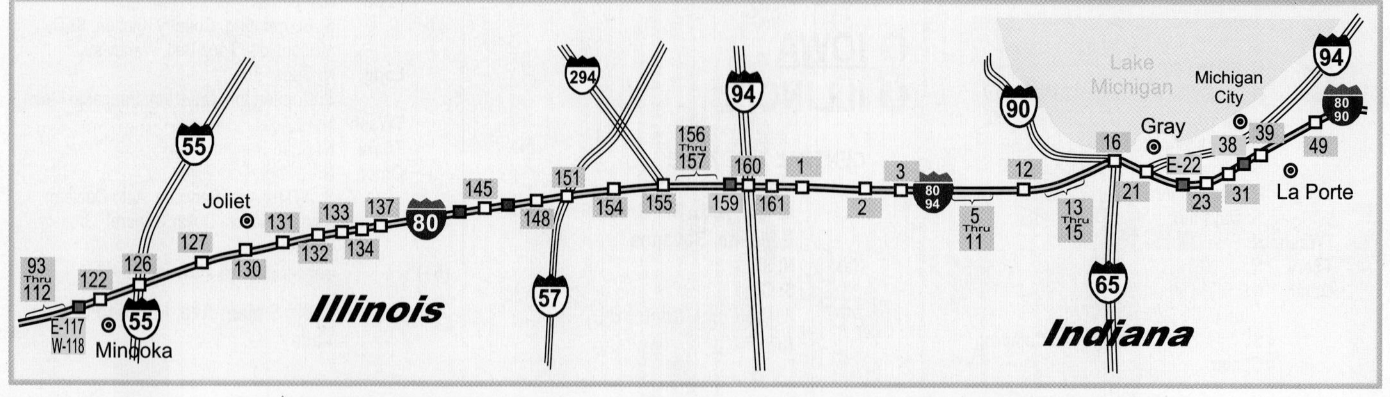

◈= Regular Gas Stations with Diesel ▲ = RV Friendly Locations ♥= Pet Friendly Locations

Red print shows large vehicle parking / access on site or nearby Brown Print = Campgrounds / RV PARKS

EXIT — **IL / IN**

154 — **Kedzie Ave, Hazel Crest (EB)**

(155) — **Jct I-294N (TOLL), Tri State Tollway, to Wisconsin**

NOTE: I-80 below runs with I-294.
Exit #'s follow I-80.

156 — **Dixie Hwy (EB)**

157 — **IL 1, Halsted St, Hazel Crest**
- Gas — N: Citgo◊, Marathon◊
  S: Shell, Speedway
- Food — N: Burger King
  S: Applebee's, Arby's, Dunkin Donuts, KFC, Popeye's, McDonald's, Subway, Taco Bell, Wendy's
- Lodg — N: Best Western, Comfort Inn, Hilton Garden Inn, Hampton Inn, Holiday Inn, Motel 6♥, Sleep Inn
  S: Days Inn, Rodeway Inn, Super 8
- TServ — N: K&J Truck Tire Repair
- Other — S: ATMs, Auto Services, Firestone, Goodyear, Home Depot, Pharmacy, Target

(159) — **Lincoln Oasis (Both dir)**
- FStop — Mobil
- Food — Burger King, TCBY

160A — **IL 394S, to Danville**

(160B) — **Jct I-94W, to Chicago**

NOTE: EB End TOLL, WB Begin TOLL Road
I-80 above runs with I-294.
Exit #'s follow I-80.

161 — **US 6, IL 83, Torrence Ave, Lansing**
- FStop — S: Park Service/Mobil
- Gas — N: BP
  S: Gas City, Marathon
- Food — N: Arby's, Bob Evans, Checkers, Chili's, Hooters, IHOP, Olive Garden, On the Border, Wendy's
  S: Burger King, DQ, Dunkin Donuts, McDonald's, Pappy's Gyros
- Lodg — N: Comfort Suites, Days Inn, Extended Stay America, Fairfield Inn, Red Roof Inn♥, Ramada Inn, Sleep Inn, Super 8
- Med — N: + Ingalls Urgent Aid Walk-In Clinic
- Other — N: ATMs, Auto Services, Auto Dealers, Best Buy, Grocery, Home Depot
  S: ATMs, Grocery, Sam's Club, Walgreen's

CENTRAL TIME ZONE

NOTE: MM 163: Indiana State Line

ILLINOIS
INDIANA

CENTRAL TIME ZONE

NOTE: I-80 runs with I-94 below.
Exit #'s follow I-94.

1 — **US 41N, Calumet Ave, Hamilton**
- Gas — N: BP◊, Gas City◊
  S: BP, Gas City, Marathon, Shell
- Food — N: Dunkin Donuts, Subway/BP
  S: Arby's, Burger King, Starbucks, Taco Bell, Wendy's
- Other — N: ATM, Firestone, Laundromat, Walgreen's
  S: CVS, Grocery

Personal Notes

EXIT — **INDIANA**

2AB — **US 41S, IN 152N, Indianapolis Blvd, Hamilton, Hammond**
- TStop — S: Pilot Travel Center #31 (Scales)
- Gas — N: SavAStop, Shell
  S: Thorntons
- Food — N: Arby's, Domino's, Dunkin Donuts
  S: Subway/Pilot TC, Burger King, Little Caesar's, Taco Bell
- Lodg — S: Ameri Host Inn
- Med — N: + Hospital
  S: + Hospital
- Other — N: to Purdue Univ/Calumet
  S: WiFi/Pilot TC, Grocery

3AB — **Kennedy Ave, Hammond**
- Gas — N: Clark, Speedway
  S: Citgo, Speedway
- Food — N: Burger King, Dominos, McDonald's
  S: Cracker Barrel, Subway, Wendy's
- Lodg — S: Courtyard, Fairfield Inn, Residence Inn
- Other — N: Walgreen's, NAPA

5AB — **IN 912, Cline Ave, Gary, Hammond**
- Gas — S: BP, Clark, Shell, Speedway
- Food — S: Arby's, Bob Evans, Burger King, DQ, McDonald's, Pizza Hut, White Castle
- Lodg — S: Best Western, Motel 6♥

6 — **Burr St, Gary**
- TStop — N: Travel Center of America #10/BP (Scales), Pilot Travel Center #271 (Scales)
- Gas — N: BP
  S: Shell◊
- Food — N: CountryPride/Chester/PizzaHut/TacoBell TA TC, Subway/Pilot TC
- TWash — N: Pilot TC
- TServ — N: TA TC/Tires

EXIT — **INDIANA**

- Other — N: Laundry/CB/WiFi/TA TC, WiFi/Pilot TC

9AB — **Grant St, Gary**
- TStop — S: Love's Travel Stop #417 (Scales), Steel City AmBest Truck Plaza (Scales)
- Food — N: Chicago Hot Dogs
  S: Denny's/FastFood/Love's TS, Rest/Fast Food/Steel City TP, Burger King, DQ, KFC, McDonald's, Subway
- Other — N: Laundromat, Walgreen's
  S: Laundry/WiFi/RVDump/LP/Love's TS, ATMs, Auto Zone, Grocery, Firestone, Outlet Mall

10AB — **IL 53, Broadway, Gary**
- Gas — N: Citgo, Marathon
  S: BP, Citgo
- Food — N: Broadway BBQ
  S: DQ, Rally's

(11) — **Jct I-65S, Indianapolis (EB)**

(12A) — **Jct I-65S, to Indianapolis (WB)**

(12B) — **Jct I-65N, to Gary, IN**

13 — **Central Ave (EB, No re-entry)**

15A — **US 6E, IN 51S, to US 20, Lake Station**
- TStop — S: Road Ranger Travel Center #240/ Citgo (Scales)
- Gas — S: Mobil◊, Shell
- Food — S: Subway/RoadRanger, Burger King, DQ, Papa John's, Long John Silver, Wendy's
- Other — S: Walgreen's

15B — **US 6W, IN 51N, Ripley St, Melton Rd, Central Ave, Gary, Lake Station**
- TStop — N: Road Ranger Travel Center #239/Citgo (Scales), Flying J Travel Plaza #5085 (Scales), Travel Center of America #219/BP (Scales), Dunes Center Truck Stop (Scales)
- Food — N: Subway/Road Ranger TC, Rest/ FastFood/FJ TP, Buckhorn/Popeyes/ Subway/TA TC, McDonald's, Ponderosa
- TWash — N: Road Ranger, FJ TP, TA TC
- TServ — N: FJ TP/Tires, TA TC/Tires, Dunes Center TS/Tires
- Other — N: Laundry/BarbSh/CB/WiFi/FJ TP, Laundry/WiFi/TA TC

NOTE: I-80 runs with I-94 above.
Exit #'s follow I-94.

NOTE: I-80 below runs with I-90 to Elyria OH.
Exit #'s follow I-90.
I-94 continues East to Detroit.

(16/21) — **Jct I-90W, Jct I-94E, IN TOLL Road**

(22) — **George Ade Service Area (EB)**
John McCutcheon Service Area (WB)
- FStop — BP #70512/#70511 (Scales)
- Food — Hardee's, Hershey's Ice Cream

23 — **600W, Portage, Port of Indiana**
- Gas — N: Marathon, Shell
  S: AmocoBP, Marathon
- Food — S: Burger King, Dunkin Donuts, KFC, Jimmy John Subs, First Wok, McDonald's, Starbucks, Subway, Wendy's
- Lodg — N: Comfort Inn, Holiday Inn Express
- Other — N: Yogi Bear's Jellystone Park▲
  S: Grocery, Walgreen's, US Post Office

(24) — **TOLL Plaza**

EXIT		INDIANA
31		**IN 49, Chesterton, Valparaiso**
	Lodg	**N:** Hilton Garden Inn
	Other	**N: Sand Creek RV Park▲**
(38)		**Truck Rest Area** (Both dir)
39		**US 421, Westville, Michigan City (Serv Appr 5mi N)**
	Other	**N: Michigan City Campground▲**
49		**IN 39, La Porte (Gas, Food, Lodg appr 4 mi S)**
	Lodg	**S:** Cassidy Motel & **RV Park▲**
	Other	**N: to Sand Creek Campground▲**
(56)		**Knute Rockne Service Area** (EB) **Wilbur Shaw Service Area** (WB)
	FStop	BP #70510/#70509
	Food	McDonald's, DQ
	Other	**RVDump**
	NOTE:	**MM 62: Central / Eastern Time Zone**
72		**US 31, St Joseph Valley Pky, South Bend, to Plymouth, Niles**
	FStop	**N:** Speedway #6674 (Scales)
	TStop	**N:** Pilot Travel Center #35 (Scales)
	Food	**N:** Subway/Pilot TC **S:** McDonald's, Ponderosa, Taco Bell
	Lodg	**N:** Super 8 **S:** Days Inn, Quality Inn
	TServ	**S:** Whiteford Kenworth
	Other	**N:** WiFi/Speedway, WiFi/Pilot TC **S:** Amtrak, Michiana Reg'l Transportation Center Airport✈, South Bend Reg'l Airport✈, **IN State Hwy Patrol Post**
77		**IN 933, US 31 Bus, South Bend, to Notre Dame University**
	Gas	**N:** Meijer◈, Mobil, Phillips 66 **S:** Marathon, Phillips 66◈
	Food	**N:** Arby's, Burger King, DQ, Damon's, Fazoli's, McDonald's, Papa John's, Pizza Hut, Ponderosa, Steak & Ale, Subway **S:** Bob Evans, Denny's, Perkins, Taco Bell, Wendy's
	Lodg	**N:** Comfort Suites, Days Inn, Hampton Inn, Motel 6♥, Ramada Inn, Super 8 **S:** Best Inn, Howard Johnson, Holiday Inn, Knights Inn, Inn at St. Mary's, Signature Inn, Wingate Inn
	Other	**N:** Walgreen's **S:** to Notre Dame Univ
83		**IN 331, Capital Ave, Granger, to Mishawaka**
	Gas	**N:** BP◈, Citgo, Phillips 66◈ **S:** Meijer
	Food	**N:** Applebee's, Arby's, Olive Garden, Panda Express, Pizza Hut, Taco Bell, Wendy's **S:** Arby's, Burger King, Carrabba's, Chili's, Lone Star Steakhouse, McDonald's, Outback Steakhouse, Ryan's Grill, Steak 'n Shake, Subway, TGI Friday
	Lodg	**N:** Carlton Lodge, Fairfield Inn, Hampton Inn, Holiday Inn, Super 8 **S:** Best Western, Courtyard, Extended Stay America, Studio Plus
	Other	**N:** Best Buy, CVS, Kroger, Office Depot, Target, Walgreen's, Mall, **South Bend East KOA▲** **S:** Auto Dealers, Discount Tire, Lowe's, Sam's Club, **Walmart sc**
(90)		**George Craig Service Area** (EB) **Henry Schricker Service Area** (WB)
	TStop	BP #70508/#70507
	Food	Burger King, Pizza Hut, Starbucks
	Other	**RVDump**
92		**IN 19, Cassopolis St, Elkhart**
	Gas	**N:** 7-11, Phillips 66◈ **S:** Marathon◈, Shell, Speedway
	Food	**N:** Applebee's, **Cracker Barrel**, Perkins, Steak 'n Shake, Starbucks **S:** Arby's, Bob Evans, Burger King, KFC, Long John Silver, McDonald's, Olive Garden, Red Lobster, Ryan's Grill, Taco Bell, Texas Roadhouse, Wendy's
	Lodg	**N:** Best Western, Comfort Suites, Country Inn, Econo Lodge, Hampton Inn, Holiday Inn Express, Knights Inn, Quality Inn, Sleep Inn **S:** Budget Inn, Days Inn, Jameson Inn, Ramada, Red Roof Inn♥, Super 8
	Med	**S:** + Hospital
	Other	**N:** Grocery, CVS, **RV Repair, Tiara RV Center, Elkhart Campground▲** **S:** ATMs, AutoZone, Walgreen's, **Walmart sc**, Elkhart City Airport✈, **Holiday World RV Center, Michiana RV, Cruise America, to Camping World/ RVDump**
96		**CR 17, Elkhart**
101		**IN 15, Bristol, to Goshen**
	Gas	**S:** 7-11, Speedway◈
107		**US 131, IN 13, Middlebury, Constantine (Addt'l Serv 5 mi S in Middlebury)**
	FStop	**N:** Marathon **S:** Snappy Food Mart/BP
	Lodg	**N:** Plaza Motel
	Other	**S: Elkhart Co/Middlebury KOA▲, Eby's Pines Campground▲**
(108)		**Truck Rest Area** (Both dir)

EXIT		IN /OH
121		**IN 9, Howe, Sturgis, LaGrange**
	Food	**N:** Applebee's, Golden Corral, Wendy's
	Lodg	**N:** Hampton Inn, Travel Inn Motel, Comfort Inn, Knights Inn **S:** Holiday Inn, Super 8
	Med	**N:** + Hospital **S:** + Hospital
	Other	**N: Walmart** **S: to Grand View Bend RV Park/RVDump**
(126)		**Gene Porter Service Area** (EB) **Ernie Pyle Service Area** (WB)
	FStop	Mobil #70572
	Food	Hardee's
	Other	**RVDump**
(144)		**Jct I-69, US 27, Fremon, Angola, Fort Wayne, Lansing**
	TStop	**N:** Petro 2 #45/Mobil (Scales), Pilot Travel Center #29 (Scales), Pioneer Auto Truck Stop/Shell **(At Exit #157 on I-69)**
	Gas	**S:** Marathon◈
	Food	**N:** Rest/FastFood/Petro2, Wendy's/Pilot TC
	Lodg	**N:** Redwood Lodge **S:** Hampton Inn, Holiday Inn Express, Super 8, Travelers Inn
	TServ	**S:** Cummins, Discover Volvo Trucks
	Other	**N:** Laundry/WiFi/**LP**/Petro2, Laundry/WiFi/ Pilot TC **S:** Outlet Mall, U-Haul
(146)		**JR Riley Service Area** (EB) **Booth Tarkenton Service Area** (WB)
	FStop	Mobil #70580/#70580
	Food	McDonald's
(153)		**IN TOLL Plaza**

EASTERN TIME ZONE

NOTE: MM 157: Ohio State Line

⬆ INDIANA
⬇ OHIO I-80/OH TPK

EASTERN TIME ZONE

NOTE: I-80 / OH TPK runs below with I-90. Exit #'s follow I-80.

Begin TOLL EB, End WB

EXIT		OHIO
(2.7)		**TOLL Plaza Westgate**
2		**OH 49, Edon, Edgerton, to US 20, Allen MI**
	Gas	**N:** Mobil
	Food	**N:** Burger King, Subway

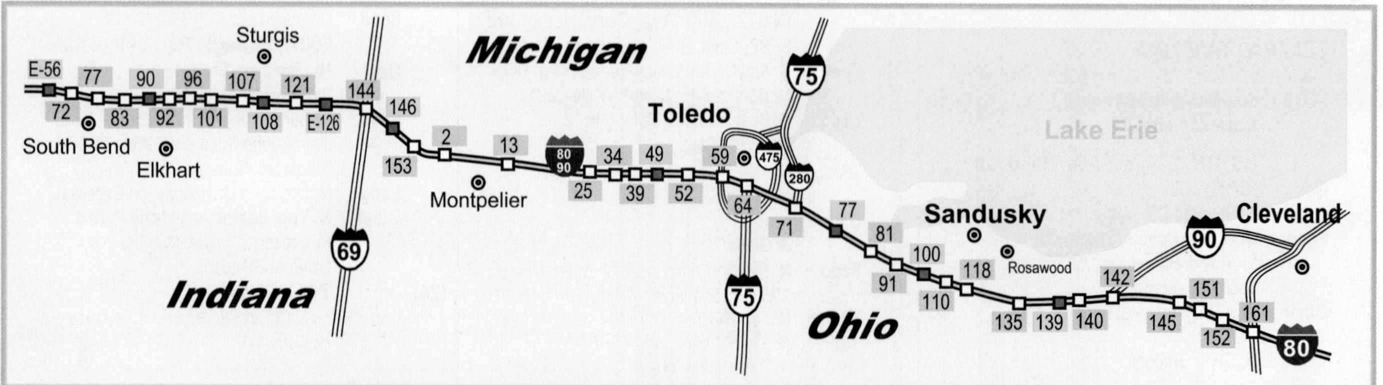

◈= Regular Gas Stations with Diesel ▲ = RV Friendly Locations ♥= Pet Friendly Locations
Red print shows large vehicle parking / access on site or nearby **Brown Print = Campgrounds / RV PARKS**

EXIT		OHIO
13		**OH 15, US 20 Alt, Holiday City, Montpelier, Bryan**
	FStop	S: Holiday City Stop N Go/Sunoco, Hutch's Karry Out/Marathon
	Food	S: Subway/Marathon, Country Fair Rest
	Lodg	S: Econo Lodge♥, Holiday Inn Express, Ramada Inn
	TServ	S: Hutch's Marathon/Tires
	Other	N: **Lazy River Resort Campground▲**, **to appr 7 mi: Loveberry's Funny Farm Campground▲**
25		**OH 66, Archbold-Fayette, Burlington**
	Lodg	S: to Sauder Heritage Inn
	Other	N: **to to appr 4.5 mi: Harrison Lake State Park▲** S: **to Hidden Valley Campground▲**
34		**OH 108, Wauseon, Napoleon**
	TStop	S: Turnpike Shell
	Gas	S: Circle K, DM, Mobil
	Food	S: Subway/Shell, Burger King, Pizza Hut, McDonald's, Smith's Rest, Taco Bell, Wendy's
	Lodg	S: Arrowhead Motel♥, Best Western, Holiday Inn Express, Super 8
	TServ	S: Turnpike Shell, Wood Truck Service
	Med	S: + Hospital
	Other	N: Fulton Co Fairgrounds/**RVDump▲**, **appr 5mi Sunny's Shady Rec Area▲**, **to appr 18mi Lake Hudson Rec Area▲** S: ATMs, Auto Service, Family Dollar, **Walmart**
39		**OH 109, Delta, Lyons**
	TStop	S: Country Corral/Citgo
	Food	S: Rest/Country Corral,
	Other	S: Delta Wings Airport✈, Maumee State Forest
(49)		**Fallen Timbers Service Plaza (EB) Oak Openings Service Plaza (WB)**
	TStop	Valero
	Food	Nathan's, Cinnabon, Pizza Uno, Great American Bagel
	Other	Picnic
52		**OH 2, Swanton, Toledo Airport**
	Lodg	S: Days Inn, Quality Inn
	Other	N: CFS Truck & Fleet Repair S: Grocery, Budget, U-Haul, Express Auto & Truck Service, Toledo Express Airport✈, **RV Center, to Big Sandy Campground▲**, **Twin Acres Campground▲**, **Bluegrass Campground▲**, **Hidden Lake Campground▲**, **Betty's Country Campground▲**
59		**US 20, Reynolds Rd, to I-475, to US 23, Maumee, Toledo**
	Gas	N: BP◈, Shell, Speedway◈ S: Meijer◈, Speedway
	Food	N: Arby's, Bob Evans, Damon's, Dragon Buffet, Little Caesars, McDonald's, Olive Garden, Pizza Hut, Steak n Shake, Waffle House S: Fazoli's, Outback Steakhouse, Red Lobster, Taco Bell
	Lodg	N: Clarion, Econo Lodge, Holiday Inn, Motel 6♥, Quality Inn S: Baymont Inn, Courtyard, Country Inn, Comfort Inn, Days Inn, Econo Lodge, Fairfield Inn, Hampton Inn, Homewood Suites, Red Roof Inn♥, Super 8
	Med	N: + to Medical Univ of OH/Toledo S: + St Luke's Hospital

EXIT		OHIO
	Other	N: ATMs, Advance Auto, Banks, FedEx Kinko's, Grocery, Goodyear, Kmart, RiteAid, Walgreen's, Southwyck Mall, Auto & **RV** Repair, **to** Toledo Stadium S: Auto Dealers, UPS Store
(64)		**Jct I-75N, Perrysburg, Toledo**
	Other	to Bowling Green State Univ, Toledo Zoo, Fifth Third Field
71		**I-280, OH 420, Perrysburg, Stony Ridge, Toledo, to I-75N, Detroit**
	TStop	N: I-280/1B: Petro Stopping Center #17/ Mobil (Scales), Flying J Travel Plaza #5450/Conoco (Scales) S: Travel Center of America #87/BP (Scales), Fuel Mart #641 (Scales), Pilot Travel Center #12 (Scales)
	Food	N: IronSkillet/PizzaHut/Petro SC, Cookery/ FastFood/Flying J TP S: CountryPride/BurgerKing/TacoBell/ TA TC, Rest/Fuel Mart, McDonald's/Pilot TC, Wendy's
	Lodg	N: Motel/Petro SC, Howard Johnson, Crown Inn, Ramada Ltd, Stony Ridge Inn, Vista Inn Express, to Super 8,
	TWash	N: Blue Beacon TW/Petro SC S: Fuel Mart
	TServ	N: Petro SC/Tires S: TA TC/Tires, Fuel Mart/Tires, 795 Tire Service, Williams Detroit Diesel
	Other	N: Laundry/BarbSh/WiFi/Petro SC, Laundry BarbSh/WiFi/**RVDump/LP**/FJ TP, to Metcalf Field✈ S: Laundry/WiFi/TA TC, Laundry/Fuel Mart, WiFi/Pilot TC, **to appr 4.5 mi: Toledo East/Stony Ridge KOA▲**
(77)		**Wyandot Service Plaza (EB) Blue Heron Service Plaza (WB)**
	TStop	Valero
	Food	Hardee's, Gloria Jeans Coffees, Mancino's Italian Eatery
	Other	WiFi, Picnic Area, **RVDump/OverNite▲**
81		**OH 51, Elmore, Gibsonburg, Woodville**
	Other	S: **Wooded Acres Campground▲**, **to Eagle Lake Camping Resort▲**
91		**OH 53, Fremont, Port Clinton, to US 6, US 20, US 2, Sandusky**
	FStop	S: BP #137
	Lodg	N: Days Inn S: Comfort Inn, Fremont Turnpike Motel, Hampton Inn, Holiday Inn
	Med	S: + Hospital
	Other	N: to Lake Erie Islands, Rutherford B Hayes Presidential Center, **to RV Dealer**, **Shade Acres Campground▲**, Erie Islands Resort & Marina▲ S: **Wooded Acres Campground▲**, **RV Dealer**, Fremont Airport✈, **to Cactus Flats Campground▲**
(100)		**Comm Perry Service Plaza (EB) Erie Islands Service Plaza (WB)**
	TStop	Valero
	Food	Burger King, Carvel, Cinnabon, Einstein Bros, Starbucks, Sbarro
	Other	WiFi, Picnic Area
110		**OH 4, Bellevue, Sandusky, Attica**
	Other	N: to Cedar Point, **Lazy J RV Resort▲**
118		**US 250, Sandusky, Norwalk, Milan**
	Gas	N: Marathon, Speedway
	Food	N: McDonald's, Subway S: Homestead Rest

EXIT		OHIO
	Lodg	N: Best Western, Comfort Inn, Colonial Inn South & **Milan Travel Park▲**, Days Inn, Fairfield Inn, Great Wolf Lodge, Hampton Inn, Holiday Inn Express, Kalahari Resort, Motel 6♥, Super 8
	Other	N: **Walmart sc**, **to** Cedar Point, Lake Erie S: **OH State Hwy Patrol Post**, **to** Milan Thomas Edison Museum, **Wilcart RV**, **Pin Oak RV**, Norwalk Raceway Park
135		**Baumhart Rd, to OH 2, Amherst, Vermilion, Huron, Sandusky**
	Other	N: **to Swift Hollow RV Resort▲**, **Neff Bros RV/RVDump**
(139)		**Vermilion Valley Service Plaza (EB) Middle Ridge Service Plaza (WB)**
	TStop	Valero
	Food	Burger King, Great Steak, Manchu Wok, Panera, Popeye's, Starbucks, TCBY
	Other	Picnic, WiFi, **RVDump/OverNite▲**
140		**OH 58, Leavitt Rd, Amherst, Oberlin**
	Gas	N: Sunoco◈
	Food	N: Subway/Sunoco
	Other	S: to Lorain Co Reg'l Airport ✈
(142)		**I-90E, to OH 2, W Cleveland (EB)**
	Other	to Cleveland, Erie PA, Buffalo NY
	NOTE:	**I-80/OH TPK runs above with I-90. Exit #'s follow I-80.**
	NOTE:	**I-80/OH TPK below continues EB. To Exit #218. Exit #'s follow I-80.**
145		**OH 57, Lorain Blvd, to I-90, Elyria, Lorain**
	Gas	N: BP◈, Shell, Speedway S: Shell, Speedway
	Food	N: McDonalds/BP, Applebee's, Arby's, Bob Evans, Burger King, Country Kitchen, Denny's, Fazoli's, Lone Star Steakhouse, Pizza Hut, Red Lobster, Smokey Bones BBQ, Subway, Wendy's
	Lodg	N: Best Western, Comfort Inn, Country Inn, Days Inn♥, Econo Lodge, Holiday Inn, Red Carpet Inn, Red Roof Inn♥ S: Howard Johnson Express♥, Super 8
	Med	S: + to Elyria Memorial Hospital
	Other	N: ATMs, Auto Services, Best Buy, Family Dollar, Firestone, Grocery, Goodyear, Home Depot, Lowe's, NTB, Pharmacy, PetSmart♥, Staples, Sam's Club, Target, **Walmart**, Elyria Midway Mall S: Laundromat, **OH State Hwy Patrol Post**, **to Cascade Park**
(151)		**I-480E, to N Ridgeville, Cleveland, Cleveland Hopkins Int'l Airport (EB)**
152		**OH 10, Lorain Rd, North Olmstead, Cleveland**
	Gas	N: BP, Marathon, Sheetz, Speedway◈ S: BP
	Food	N: McDonald's
	Lodg	N: Motel 6, Super 8
	Other	N: Grocery, U-Haul, **Crystal Springs Campground▲**, **Moore's RV Sales & Service**
(161)		**I-71, to US 42, Pearl Rd, to I-480, Cleveland, to US 82, Strongsville (Gas, Food, Lodg on US 42)**
	Gas	N: Circle K
	Food	N: Mad Cactus, Pizza Hut, Subway
	Lodg	N: Days Inn
	Med	N: + Hospital

◈ = Regular Gas Stations with Diesel ▲ = RV Friendly Locations ♥ = Pet Friendly Locations
Red print shows large vehicle parking / access on site or nearby Brown Print = Campgrounds / RV PARKS

EXIT — **OHIO**

Other N: Home Depot, to Cleveland Hopkins Int'l Airport✈, Browns Stadium, Rock & Roll Hall of Fame & Museum, Jacobs Field

(170) **Towpath Service Plaza (EB)**
Great Lakes Service Plaza (WB)

TStop Valero
Food Burger King, Panera Bread, Pizza Hut/KFC, Starbucks
Other Picnic Area, WiFi

173 **OH 21, Brecksville Rd, Richfield, to I-77, to I-271, Cleveland, Akron**

TStop N: I-77 X146: Pilot Travel Center #130 (Scales)
Gas S: BP
Food N: Wendy's/Pilot TC
S: DQ, Subway
Lodg N: Holiday Inn Express, Howard Johnson, Lake Motel
S: Hampton Inn, Quality Inn, Super 8
Tires N: Pilot TC
TServ S: Richfield Radiator Repair
Other N: Laundry/WiFi/Pilot TC, BF Goodrich Hdqtrs, to Jacobs Field/Gund Arena, Cleveland Browns Stadium, Rock & Roll Hall of Fame/Museum, Great Lakes Science Center, Brandywine Ski Area

180 **OH 8, to 271N, to I-90E, Akron**

Gas N: Marathon
S: BP◈, Starfire Express
Lodg N: Clarion, Comfort Inn, Country Inn, Days Inn, Hampton Inn, Holiday Inn, Hudson Inn, Knights Inn, La Quinta Inn♥, Motel 6♥
Other S: Kamper City/RVDump, Cuyahoga Valley National Park

(187) **Jct I-480, OH 14, Streetsboro**

Gas S: BP, DM, Shell, Sheetz
Food S: Arby's, Bob Evans, Burger King, DQ, Denny's, KFC, Long John Silver, Perkins, Ruby Tuesday, Subway, Taco Bell
Lodg S: Comfort Inn, Econo Lodge, Fairfield Inn, Hampton Inn, Holiday Inn Express, Microtel, Super 8, Towneplace Suites♥, Wingate Inn
Other N: Woodside Lake Park▲, to Tinker's Creek State Park, to Geauga Lake & Wildwater KingdomCG▲
S: ATMs, Auto Services, CVS, Firestone, Grocery, Home Depot, Staples, Walmart, Mall, to Kent State Univ, Mar-Lyn Lake Park/Streetsboro KOA▲, Hudson Springs Park, Valley View Lake Park▲

193 **OH 44, Ravenna**

Other S: Mills Airport✈, Portage Co Airport✈

(197) **Brady's Leap Service Plaza (EB)**
Portage Service Plaza (WB)

TStop Valero

EXIT — **OHIO**

Food McDonald's, Krispy Kreme, Popeye's, Sbarro, Starbucks
Other OH Marketplace, Picnic, WiFi, RVDump/OverNite▲

209 **OH 5, Newton Falls, Warren**

TStop N: PTP/Short Stop Travel Plaza/Marathon (Scales)
Food N: KountryKubboardRest/Short Stop TP
Lodg N: Budget Lodge
S: Econo Lodge, Holiday Inn Express
TServ N: Short Stop TP/Tires, Youngstown Warren Reg'l Airport✈
Other N: Laundry/Short Stop TP
S: to appr 5mi Country Acres Campground▲, Ravenna Ordinance Plant

215 **Ellsworth Bailey Rd, Lordstown (EB)**

Other N: GM Plant

216 **Hallock Young Rd, to OH 45, Lordstown (WB)**

NOTE: **I-80/OH TPK continues above Exit #'s follow I-80.**

NOTE: **OH TPK continues below to PA. (OH TPK below runs with I-76 EB to exit #237)**

218 **CR 18, Mahoning Ave, I-76W to Akron, I-80E, to I-680, to OH 11, Youngstown, Pittsburgh, NY City**

232 **OH 7, Market St, N Lima, to Youngstown**

TStop S: Pilot Travel Center #011 (Scales)
Gas N: Shell, Sheetz
S: Shell◈, Speedway◈
Food N: DQ
S: FastFood/Pilot TC
Lodg N: Budget Inn, Economy Inn, Holiday Inn Express, Quality Inn♥, Ramada
S: Americas Best Value Inn, Davis Motel, Rodeway Inn
Med N: + Hospital
TWash S: Pilot TC
Other S: WiFi/Pilot TC, to appr 10 mi Beaver Creek State Park, Ponderosa Park, Chaparral Family Campground▲

(234) **I-680N, Youngstown, Poland (WB)**

(237) **Glacier Hills Service Plaza (EB)**
Mahoning Valley Service Plaza (WB)

TStop Valero
Food McDonald's

(239) **TOLL Plaza Eastgate**

NOTE: **End TOLL EB, Begin WB**

EXIT — **OH / PA**

OH / PA Border

NOTE: **OH I-80 continues EB End TOLL, WB Begin TOLL**

223B **OH 46N, Niles, Warren (WB)**

223A **OH 46S, Austintown, Canfield (WB)**

223 **OH 46, Austintown, Canfield, Youngstown, Niles (EB)**

TStop N: Pilot Travel Center #3 (Scales)
S: AmBest Fuel Mart #730 (Scales), Travel Center of America #58 (Scales)
Gas N: Citgo◈
S: BP◈, Sunoco
Food N: McDonald's/Pilot TC, Bob Evans, Burger King
S: CountryPride/TA TC, Arby's, Cracker Barrel, McDonald's, Perkins, Starbucks, Taco Bell, Wendy's
Lodg N: Best Value Inn, Comfort Inn
S: Super 8/TA TC, Best Western♥, Country Inn, Econo Lodge, Hampton Inn, Knights Inn, Sleep Inn, Super 8
TWash S: Blue Beacon TW/TA TC
TServ S: TA TC/Tires
Freightliner Trucks, White/GMC Volvo
Other N: Laundry/WiFi/Pilot TC
S: Laundry/CB/WiFi/RVDump/TA TC

224 **OH 11S, to Canfield (WB)**

224A **OH 11S, to Canfield (EB)**

(224B) **I-680S, Youngstown (EB)**

226 **Salt Springs Rd, to I-680S, Girard, to McDonald, Youngstown**

TStop S: Mr Fuel #5 (Scales), Petro Stopping Center #20/Mobil (Scales), Pilot Travel Center #281 (Scales)
Gas N: BP◈, Sheetz
Food N: Subway/BP, McDonald's, Waffle House
S: Rest/Mr Fuel, Iron Skillet/Petro SC, Arby's/TJCinn/Pilot TC
TWash S: Blue Beacon TW/Petro SC, Eagle Truck Wash, Frank's Truck Wash
TServ S: Petro SC/Tires, Speedco, OH Cat
Other S: Laundry/CB/BarbSh/Med/Massg/WiFi/Petro SC, WiFi/Pilot TC

227 **US 422, State St, Girard, Niles, Youngstown**

Gas N: Shell◈
Food N: Burger King, Subway

228 **OH 11N, Ashtabula (fr EB, Left exit)**

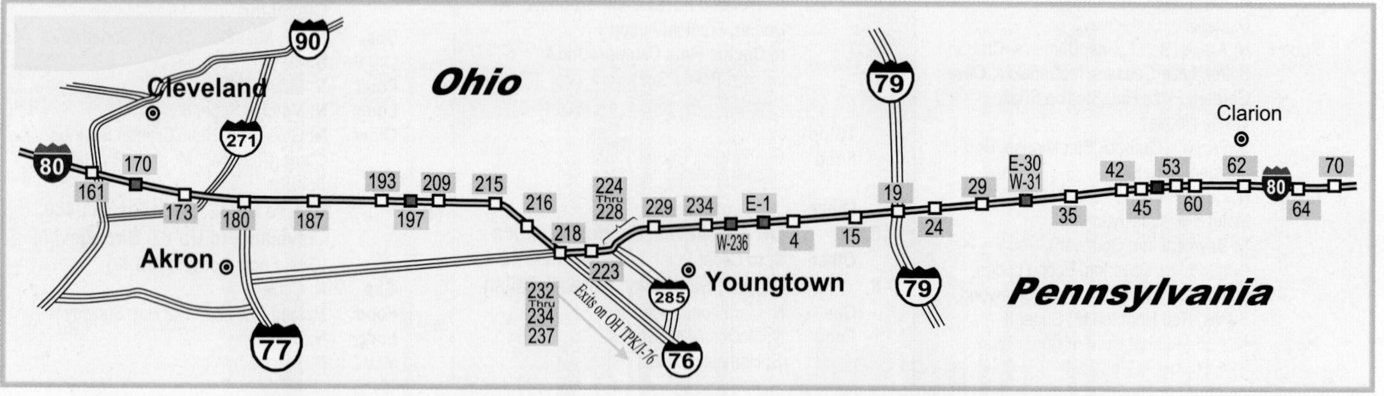

◈= Regular Gas Stations with Diesel ▲ = RV Friendly Locations ♥= Pet Friendly Locations
Red print shows large vehicle parking / access on site or nearby Brown Print = Campgrounds / RV PARKS

EXIT — OH / PA

229 — OH 193, Belmont Ave, Youngstown
- Gas: N: Speedway◊; S: Shell
- Food: S: Arby's, Bob Evans, Burger King, KFC, Denny's, Long John Silver, McDonald's, Perkins, Pizza Hut, Subway, Taco Bell, Wendy's, Western Sizzlin'
- Lodg: N: American Inn, Days Inn, Hampton Inn, Holiday Inn, Super 8; S: Days Inn, Econo Lodge, Quality Inn
- Med: N: + Hospital
- Other: S: ATMs, Advance Auto, AutoZone, Big Lots, Firestone, Grocery, Goodyear

234AB — US 62, OH 7, Main St, Hubbard (EB)

234 — US 62, OH 7, Main St, Hubbard, Youngstown, to Sharon, PA (WB)
- TStop: N: EB Access via Ex #234B: PTP/Truck World/Shell (Scales), Flying J Travel Plaza #5112 (Scales), Love's Travel Stop #370 (Scales)
- Food: N: GlobeRest/Truck World, CountryMarket/FastFood/FJ TP, Chesters/Subway/Love's TS, Arby's, Burger King, McDonald's, Waffle House
- Lodg: N: Motel/Truck World, Motel/FJ TP, Best Western
- TWash: N: Blue Beacon TW/Truck World
- TServ: N: Truck World/Tires; S: Youngstown Kenworth
- Other: N: Laundry/CB/BarbSh/Truck World, Laundry/WiFi/RVDump/LP/FJ TP, Homestead RV Center, Hubbard's Heaven Family Campground▲, Chestnut Ridge Park & Campground▲

(236) — OH Welcome Center (WB)
(RR, Phones, Picnic, Vend, Info)

EASTERN TIME ZONE

NOTE: MM 237: Pennsylvania State Line

⮉ OHIO I-80/OH TPK
⮋ PENNSYLVANIA

EASTERN TIME ZONE

(1) — PA Welcome Center (EB)
(RR, Phone, Picnic, Vend, Info)

4A — PA 60S, New Castle
- Gas: N: Sunoco; S: DM
- Food: S: DQ, Diner
- Other: S: PA Motor Sports Museum

4B — PA 60N, to PA 18, Sharon, Hermitage, W Middlesex, Farrell
- Gas: N: BP, Sunoco
- Food: N: Subway
- Lodg: N: Comfort Inn, Holiday Inn, Radisson
- Other: N: Rocky Springs Campground▲, to appr 14mi Shenango Valley RV Park▲

15 — US 19, Perry Hwy, Mercer
- Gas: N: BP
- Food: N: Burger King, McDonald's, Rest/HJ
- Lodg: N: Howard Johnson
- Other: N: PA State Hwy Patrol Post, to RV Village Camping Resort▲, Rocky Springs Campground▲; S: Jct 19-80 Campground▲

EXIT — PENNSYLVANIA

(19A) — Jct I-79S, to Pittsburgh
- Other: S: to Grove City Airport✈, Mercer/Grove City KOA▲

(19B) — Jct I-79N, to Erie

24 — PA 173, Sandy Lake Rd, Grove City, Sandy Lake
- Med: S: + Hospital
- Other: N: to Goddard Park Vacationland Campground▲

29 — PA 8, Pittsburgh Rd, Harrisville, Barkeyville, Franklin
- TStop: S: Kwik Fill Auto Truck Plaza #229 (Scales), Exit 29 Fuel Stop/Citgo, Travel Center of America #67/BP (Scales)
- Food: N: Arby's, Burger King; S: Rest/KwikFill ATP, FastFood/Exit 29, CountryPr/Subway/TA TC
- Lodg: N: Comfort Inn, Days Inn, Super 8
- TServ: S: TA TC/Tires
- Other: S: Laundry/WiFi/TA TC, to Slippery Rock Univ, Venango Regional Airport✈

(30) — Rest Area (EB)
(RR, Phone, Picnic, Vend)

(31) — Rest Area (WB)
(RR, Phone, Picnic, Vend)

35 — PA 308, Butler St, Clintonville
- FStop: N: Phoenix Quik Stop

42 — PA 38, Emlenton
- TStop: N: Emlenton Travel Center/Citgo (Scales)
- Gas: N: Exxon◊
- Food: N: Rest/Emlenton TC, Subway/Exxon
- Lodg: N: Motel/Emlenton TC
- TServ: N: Emlenton TC/Tires
- Other: N: Laundry/WiFi/Emlenton TC, Gaslight Campground▲

45 — PA 478, Emlenton, St Petersburg

53 — Canoe Ripple Rd, to PA 338, Knox
- Gas: N: Exit 7 Gulf
- Food: N: BJ's Eatery, Wolf's Den Rest
- TServ: S: Good Tire Service
- Other: N: Wolf's Camping Resort▲, to Colwell's Campground▲

(57) — Weigh Station (Both dir)

60 — PA 66N, to Shippenville
- Gas: N: QuikStop
- Other: N: PA State Hwy Patrol Post, to appr 3mi Clarion Co Airport✈, Rustic Acres Campground▲

62 — PA 68, Clarion
- Gas: N: 7-11, BP; S: KwikFill◊
- Food: N: Arby's, Burger King, Cozumel, Eat 'n Park, Long John Silver, McDonald's, Perkins, Pizza Hut, Subway, Taco Bell
- Lodg: N: Comfort Inn, Hampton Inn, Holiday Inn, Microtel, Quality Inn, Super 8
- Med: N: + Clarion Hospital
- Other: N: Advance Auto Parts, ATMs, Bank, Grocery, Staples, Walmart sc, Mall, Clarion Univ, to appr 11mi Kalyumet Campground▲, Cook Forest State Park▲

64 — PA 66S, Clarion, New Bethlehem
- Other: N: to Clarion Univ; S: to Piney Meadows Park▲, Penn Wood Campground▲

EXIT — PENNSYLVANIA

70 — US 322, Strattanville
- TStop: N: Keystone All American Plaza/Shell (Scales)
- Food: N: Rest/Keystone Plz
- TServ: N: Keystone Plz/Tires
- Other: N: Laundry/Keystone Plz

73 — PA 949, Corsica
- Other: N: to Clear Creek State Park, Cook Forest State Park▲, Campers Paradise Campground▲

78 — PA 36, Brookville, Sigel
- TStop: N: Travel Center of America #3/BP (Scales), Flying J Travel Plaza #5092 (Scales)
- Gas: S: Citgo, Sheetz, Sunoco
- Food: N: Country Pr/TacoBell/TA TC, Country Market/FastFood/FJ TP, McDonald's, Pizza Hut; S: Arby's, Burger King, Plyer's Pizza & Family Rest, Subway
- Lodg: N: Howard Johnson/TA TC, Super 8♥; S: Days Inn♥, Gold Eagle Inn, Holiday Inn Express
- TServ: N: TA TC/Tires, FJ TP/Tires
- Other: N: Laundry/WiFi/RVDump/TA TC, Laundry/WiFi/RVDump/LP/FJ TP, RV Dealer, to Clear Creek State Park, Cook Forest State Park▲, Campers Paradise Campground▲

81 — PA 28, Brookville, to Hazen
- Med: S: + Hospital

86 — PA 830, PA 810, Reynoldsville

(88) — Rest Area (Both dir)
(RR, Phones, Picnic)

90 — PA 830E, DuBois Reg'l Airport

97 — US 219, Buffalo-Pittsburgh Hwy, Falls Creek, Du Bois, Brockway
- TStop: S: Sheetz Travel Center #194 (Scales), Pilot Travel Center #336 (Scales)
- Food: S: FastFood/Sheetz TC, Arby's/TJCinn/Pilot TC, Dutch Pantry Rest
- Lodg: S: Best Western, Holiday Inn Express
- Med: S: + DuBois Reg'l Medical Hospital
- Other: N: PA State Hwy Patrol Post; S: Laundry/Sheetz TC, Laundry/WiFi/Pilot TC, DuBois Harley Davidson, Penn State/DuBois

101 — PA 255, Du Bois, Penfield
- Gas: N: BP; S: Citgo, Sheetz
- Food: S: Arby's, Burger King, Domino's, Eat 'n Park, Hoss's Steak & Sea House, Italian Oven, McDonald's, Perkins, Ponderosa, Red Lobster, Ruby Tuesday, Subway, Taco Bell, Wendy's
- Lodg: N: Best Western, Hampton Inn; S: Clarion, Ramada Inn
- Med: S: + DuBois Reg'l Medical Hospital
- Other: N: to appr 10mi Parker Dam State Park▲; S: ATMs, Banks, Auto Services, Grocery, Lowe's, Staples, Walmart, DuBois Mall, PA State Hwy Patrol Post

111 — PA 153, Penfield, Clearfield
- NOTE: Trucks over 5 Tons, Use Ex #120. Highest Pt on I-80 E of the Mississippi
- Med: S: + Hospital
- Other: N: SB Elliott State Park, to Parker Dam State Park▲; S: Curwensville Lake Rec Area▲

◊= Regular Gas Stations with Diesel ▲ = RV Friendly Locations ♥ = Pet Friendly Locations
Red print shows large vehicle parking / access on site or nearby Brown Print = Campgrounds / RV PARKS

EXIT		PENNSYLVANIA
120		**PA 879, Clearfield, Shawville**
	TStop	**N:** Sapp Bros Travel Center/Shell (Scales)
	Gas	**S:** BP, Sheetz, Snappy's
	Food	**N:** Cafe/Deli/FastFood/Sapp Bros TC **S:** Arby's, Burger King, Dutch Pantry, McDonald's, KFC/PizzaHut/TacoBell, Tacamba's Mex Rest
	Lodg	**S:** Days Inn, Comfort Inn, Econo Lodge, Holiday Inn Express, Super 8
	TServ	**N:** Sapp Bros/Tires, Cumberland Truck Parts **S:** Cummins, Purcell Tire
	Med	**S:** + Clearfield Hospital
	Other	**N:** Laundry/BarbSh/WiFi/Sapp Bros TC **S:** ATM, Lowe's, **Walmart sc** Pharmacy, Clearfield Co Fairgrounds, **to Curwensville Lake Rec Area▲**
123		**PA 970, Woodland, Shawville**
	FStop	**S:** Pacific Pride
	Other	**N: Woodland Campground▲** **S: PA State Hwy Patrol Post**
133		**PA 53, Winburne, Grassflat, to Kylertown, Phillipsburg**
	TStop	**N:** Kwik Fill Auto Truck Plaza #226 (Scales)
	Gas	**N:** Sunoco
	Food	**N:** Rest/Kwik Fill ATP
	Lodg	**N:** Motel/Kwik Fill ATP
	TServ	**N:** Kwik Fill ATP/Tires
	Med	**S:** + Hospital
	Other	**S: to** Mid State Reg'l Airport✈, **Black Moshannon State Park**
(146)		**Rest Area** (Both dir) **(RR, Phone, Picnic)**
147		**Beech Creek Rd, PA 144, Snow Shoe**
	TStop	**N:** Snow Shoe Auto Truck Plaza/Citgo, Reese Truck Stop/Exxon
	Food	**N:** Rest/Snow Shoe ATP, Rest/Reese TS
	TServ	**N:** Reese TS/Tires
	Other	**N:** Laundry/Reese TS, Grocery
158		**US 220S Alt, to I-99, PA 150, Bellafonte, Altoona, Milesburg**
	NOTE:	**Steep grade on exit, Use low gear**
	TStop	**N:** Bestway Travel Center/Shell (Scales), Travel Center of America #214/Amoco
	Gas	**N:** Citgo
	Food	**N:** Rest/FastFood/Bestway TC, Buckhorn/TA TC
	Lodg	**N:** Motel/Bestway TC, Holiday Inn
	TServ	**N:** Best Way TC/Tires, TA TC/Tires
	Other	**N:** Laundry/CB/WiFi/Bestway TC, Laundry/WiFi/TA TC, **to Bald Eagle State Park** **S: PA State Hwy Patrol Post, to** Beaver Stadium

EXIT		PENNSYLVANIA
161		**US 220S, PA 26, Bellefonte, Howard (Future I-99S)**
	Gas	**S:** Kwik Fill, Shell
	Other	**N: Fort Bellafonte Campground▲, Bellefonte/State College KOA▲, to Bald Eagle State Park** **S: Centre RV Dealer, to** Penn State Univ, **to Woodward Cave▲, Lake Raystown Resort & Lodge▲**
(171)		**Parking Area** (Both dir)
173		**PA 64, Nittany Valley Dr, Hall, Lamar, to Mill Hall**
	TStop	**N:** Pilot Travel Center #1 (Scales) **S:** Travel Center of America #68/Mobil (Scales), Flying J Travel Plaza #5113 (Scales)
	Gas	**S:** Citgo
	Food	**N:** Subway/Pilot TC, McDonald's, Perkins, Rest/Comfort Inn **S:** CountryPride/Subway/TA TC, Country Market/FastFood/FJ TP
	Lodg	**N:** Comfort Inn
	TServ	**S:** TA TC/Tires
	Other	**N:** Laundry/WiFi/Pilot TC, **PA State Hwy Patrol Post** **S:** Laundry/WiFi/TA TC, Laundry/WiFi/**RVDump/LP**/FJ TP
178		**US 220, Frank O'Reilly Hwy, Mill Hall, to Lock Haven** **(Addt'l Serv 5mi N in Mill Hall)**
	Gas	**S:** Citgo◈
	Food	**N:** Belle Springs Family Rest
	Other	**N:** Clinton Co Fairgrounds/Speedway, **to Bald Eagle State Park**, Lock Haven Univ
185		**PA 477, Long Run Rd, Loganton**
	Gas	**N:** Mobil **S:** Valley Service
	Other	**N: Holiday Pines Campground▲** **S: to Raymond B Winter State Park**
192		**Valley Rd, PA 880, Ranchtown Rd, Carroll, Loganton, Jersey Shore**
	TStop	**N:** Pit Stop Travel Center/Citgo
	Food	**N:** Pit Stop Rest/Pit Stop TC
	Med	**S:** + Hospital
	Other	**N:** Laundry/Pit Stop TC, **to Ravensburg State Park, McCall Dam State Park**
(194)		**Rest Area** (Both dir) **(RR, Phone, Picnic)**
(194)		**Weigh Station** (Both dir)
199		**Mile Run Rd, Lewisburg**
210A		**US 15S, to Lewisburg (Exit only)**
	Gas	**S:** Citgo
	Food	**S:** Bonanza/Comfort Inn

EXIT		PENNSYLVANIA
	Lodg	**S:** Comfort Inn, Holiday Inn Express
	Other	**S:** Sunbury Bucknell Univ, Lewisburg Federal Penitentiary, **to appr 6 mi Williamsport South/Nittany Mtn KOA▲, to appr 13mi River Edge RV Camp & Marina▲, Little Mexico Campground▲, Penn's Creek Campground▲, Hidden Valley Camping Resort▲**
210B		**US 15N, to Williamsport (Exit only)**
	Other	**N:** to Reptiland Zoo, Little League Hall of Fame/Museum, Int'l HQ
212A		**PA 147S, to Milton**
(212B)		**I-180W, to Williamsport**
215		**PA 254, Milton, Limestoneville**
	TStop	**N:** Bressler's Truck Plaza (Scales) **S:** Petro Stopping Center/Shell (Scales)
	Food	**N:** Rest/Bressler's TP **S:** Iron Skillet/Subway/Petro SC
	TWash	**S:** Eagle Truck Wash/Petro SC
	TServ	**N:** Bressler's TP/Tires **S:** Petro SC/Tires
	Other	**N:** Laundry/Bressler's TP **S:** Laundry/CB/WiFi/**RVDump**/Petro SC
(219)		**Rest Area** (EB) **(RR, Phones, Picnic)**
(220)		**Rest Area** (WB) **(RR, Phones, Picnic)**
224		**PA 54, Continental Blvd, to Danville**
	Gas	**N:** BP, Mobil◈ **S:** Shell◈
	Food	**N:** Country Kitchen, Subway **S:** Dutch Kitchen, McDonald's
	Lodg	**N:** Quality Inn **S:** Days Inn, Hampton Inn, Red Roof Inn♥, Travelodge
	Med	**S:** + Hospital
	Other	**S: to appr 8mi Splash Magic Campground & RV Resort▲**
232		**PA 42, Mall Blvd, Bloomsburg, Buckhorn**
	TStop	**N:** Travel Center of America #212/BP (Scales)
	Gas	**N:** Shell◈
	Food	**N:** Buckhorn/Subway/TA TC, **Cracker Barrel**, KFC, Perkins, Ruby Tuesday, Wendy's
	Lodg	**N:** Econo Lodge, Holiday Inn Express
	TServ	**N:** TA TC/Tire
	Other	**N:** Laundry/WiFi/TA TC, Home Depot, Columbia Mall, **Turner's High View Campground▲**

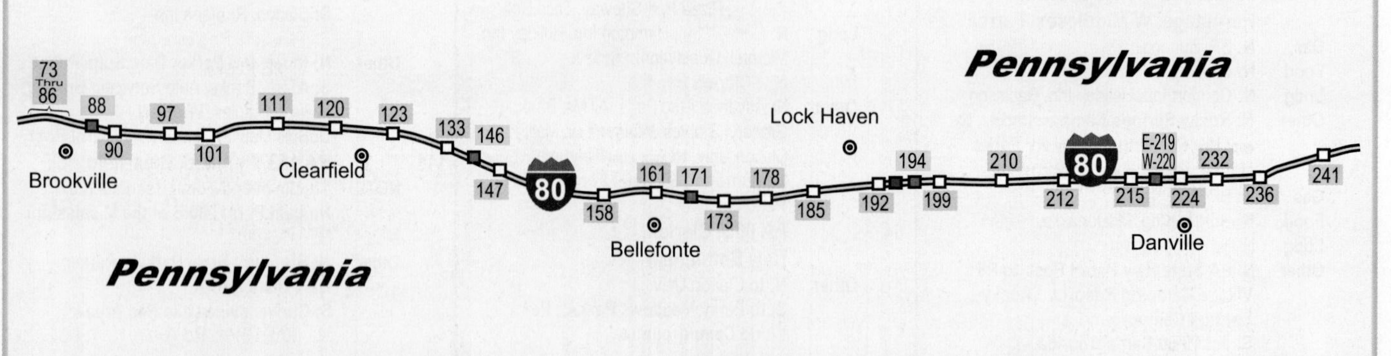

◈= Regular Gas Stations with Diesel ▲ = RV Friendly Locations ♥= Pet Friendly Locations
Red print shows large vehicle parking / access on site or nearby Brown Print = Campgrounds / RV PARKS

EXIT		PENNSYLVANIA
	Other	S: Lowe's, Walmart sc, Knoebel's Amusement Park, to appr 4-6mi: Indian Head Campground▲, Shady Rest Campground▲, Mt Zion Family Campground▲
236A		PA 487S, to Bloomsburg (WB)
236B		PA 487N, Light St (WB)
236		PA 487, Light St, Bloomsburg
	Gas	S: Sunoco, UniMart
	Food	S: Denny's
	Lodg	S: Hampton Inn, Inn at Turkey Hill
	Med	S: + Bloomsburg Hospital
	Other	N: to appr 4mi: Deihl's Camping Resort▲ S: Cinema Center, Bloomsburg Univ, Bloomsburg Muni Airport ✈
241A		US 11S, to Lime Ridge
	Gas	S: Coastal, Shell, Sheetz◊
	Food	S: Applebee's, Arby's, Burger King, China Queen, Long John Silver, McDonald's, Pizza Hut, Subway, Wendy's
	Lodg	S: Budget Host Inn, Tennytown Motel
	Other	S: ATMs, Auto Dealers, Advance Auto, Big Lots, CVS, Grocery, Staples, U-Haul, Walmart sc, Bloomsburg Muni Airport✈, PA State Hwy Patrol Post
241B		US 11N, to Berwick
	Lodg	N: Red Maple Inn, Super 8
	Med	N: + Hospital
242		PA 339, Nescopeck to Mifflinville, Mainville
	TStop	N: Brennan's Auto Truck Plaza/Shell (Scales), Love's Travel Stop #324 (Scales) S: Kreiser Truck Stop/Citgo
	Food	N: Rest/Brennan's ATP, Arby's/Love's TS, McDonald's S: FastFood/Kreiser TS
	Lodg	N: Super 8
	TServ	N: Brennan's ATP/Tires
	Other	N: Laundry/CB/Brennan's ATP, WiFi/ RVDump/Love's TS
(246)		Rest Area (Both dir) (RR, Phones, Picnic)
(246)		Weigh Station (Both dir)
256		PA 93, Berwick Hazelton Hwy, Drums, Conyngham, Nescopeck
	TStop	N: Pilot Travel Center #298 (Scales)
	Gas	N: Sunoco S: Shell◊
	Food	N: Subway/Pilot TC S: Brass Buckle, Tom's Kitchen, Stewarts
	Lodg	N: Lookout Motor Lodge S: Best Value Inn, Days Inn, Hampton Inn
	Med	S: + Hospital
	Other	N: WiFi/Pilot TC, Penn State Univ/Hazelton, to appr 7mi Moyers Grover Campground & Country RV▲, to Jim Thorpe Camping Resort▲
(260A)		Jct I-81S, to Harrisburg
(260B)		Jct I-81N, to Wilkes-Barre (Fr EB, LEFT Exit)
262		PA 309, N Hunter Hwy, Drums, to Mountain Top, Hazleton
	Gas	N: BP, Shell
	Food	N: Mountain View Rest, Wendy's

EXIT		PENNSYLVANIA
	Lodg	N: Econo Lodge, Holiday Inn Express, Mountain View Motel
	Other	S: PA State Hwy Patrol Post
(270)		Rest Area (EB) (RR, Phones, Picnic, Vend)
273		PA 940, to PA 437, Church St, Whitehaven, Freeland
	NOTE:	NO Trucks with Underclearance less than 15' on PA 940E
	Gas	N: BP, Mobil
274		PA 534, Hickory Run State Park
	TStop	N: Bandit Truck Stop/Sunoco #2, AmBest/ Hickory Run Travel Plaza/Exxon (Scales)
	Food	N: FastFood/Bandit TS, Rest/Hickory Run TP
	TServ	N: Hickory Run TP/Tires
	Other	N: WiFi/Hickory Run TP, to Hickory Run State Park, Lehigh Gorge Campground & RV Center/LP▲
277		PA 940, Lake Harmony, to I-476, PA Tpk (TOLL), Wilkes-Barre, Allentown
	Gas	N: BP, Shell, WaWa
	Food	N: Arby's, Burger King, Denny's, Gino's, McDonald's, Rest/Howard Johnson
	Lodg	N: Comfort Inn, Days Inn, Econo Lodge, Howard Johnson, Mountain Laurel Resort
284		PA 115, Blakeslee, to Ski Areas
	Gas	N: WaWa S: Exxon◊
	Food	N: Rest/Blakeslee Inn
	Lodg	N: Best Western, Blakeslee Inn S: Tudor Inn
	Other	N: PA State Hwy Patrol Post S: to appr 5mi: WT Family Campground RV Sales & Service▲, to Pocono Int'l Raceway, Wilkes Barre Ski Area, Jack Frost Ski Area, Big Boulder Ski Area
(293)		I-380N, to Scranton (fr EB, LEFT Exit)
	NOTE:	Trucks to WilkesBarre: Use I-380N
(295)		Rest Area (EB) (RR, Phones, Picnic, Vend)
298		PA 611, to Scotrun, Mt Pocono
	Gas	N: Shell, Sunoco◊
	Food	N: Plaza Deli, Anthony's Steakhouse, Scotrun Diner
	Lodg	N: Scotrun Motel
	Other	N: Four Seasons Campground▲, PA State Hwy Patrol Post, to Mt Pocono, Camel Back Ski Area
299		PA 715, Singer Ave, Tannersville
	Gas	N: BP, Mobil S: Sunoco
	Food	N: Deli, Friendly's, Rest/Chateau Inn S: Tannersville Diner
	Lodg	N: Ramada, Chateau Inn, Great Wolf Lodge S: Days Inn, Summit Resort
	Other	N: Four Seasons Campground▲, The Crossings Factory Outlet Mall S: to Big Pocono State Park, Camelback Ski Area
302A		PA 33S, to US 209S, Snydersville
302B		PA 611N, Bartonsville
	TStop	N: AmBest/Crossroads Travel Center (Scales), Bartonsville Travel Center
	Food	N: Rest/Subway/TBell/PHut/Crossroads TC
	Lodg	N: Comfort Inn, Howard Johnson, Knights Inn
	TWash	N: Bartonsville TC

EXIT		PA / NJ
	TServ	N: Crossroads TC/Tires
	Other	N: Laundry/CB/Crossroads TC, Lowe's S: Pocono Vacation Park▲
302		PA 611, Bartonsville
	Other	S: to appr 6mi Silver Valley Campsites▲
303		9th St, Stroudsburg (EB)
	Gas	N: BP
	Food	N: Arby's, Boston Market, Pizza Hut
	Other	N: Stroud Mall, ATMs, Cinemas, CVS
304		US 209S, to PA 33S, Stroudsburg to Snydersville (WB)
	Other	S: to appr 6mi Silver Valley Campsites▲
305		US 209 Bus, Main St, Stroudsburg
	Gas	N: Mobil S: Exxon
	Food	N: Perkins S: Damon's
	Lodge	N: Quality Inn S: Alpine Motel
	Other	N: to Stroud Mall
306		Dreher Ave (WB)
307		PA 611, Park Ave, to PA 191 (EB), PA 191, Broad St (WB)
	Gas	N: Gulf
	Food	N: Chinese, KFC, McDonald's, Mex Rest
	Lodg	N: Best Western, Hampton Inn, Hillside Inn S: Days Inn
308		Prospect St, E Stroudsburg
	Gas	N: Shell, WaWa
	Food	N: Arby's, Burger King, McDonald's
	Lodg	S: Budget Motel, Super 8
	Med	N: + Pocono Medical Center
	Other	N: ATMs, Auto Service, Grocery, Goodyear Kmart, NAPA, Tires, Walmart sc, Univ
309		US 209, PA 447, Seven Bridge Rd, Stroudsburg, Marshalls Creek
	Gas	N: Exxon◊
	Food	N: Rest/Pocono Grand Hotel
	Lodg	N: Shannon Inn, Pocono Grand Hotel S: Super 8
	Med	N: + Pocono Medical Center
	Other	N: Grocery, RiteAid, Pocono Flea Market, The Christmas Factory, to appr 7mi Otter Lake Camp Resort▲, Delaware Water Gap KOA▲, Cranberry Run CG▲, Mountain Vista Campground▲
(310)		Foxtown Hill Rd, Broad St, to PA 611, DE Water Gap S: PA Welcome Center (WB) (RR, Phone, Picnic, Vend, Info)
	Gas	S: BP, Gulf
	Food	S: Water Gap Diner
	Lodg	S: Deer Head Inn, Pocono Inn
	Other	N: to appr 6mi Delaware Water Gap KOA▲ Foxwood Family Campground▲ S: to Driftstone on the Delaware Campground▲

EASTERN TIME ZONE

NOTE: MM 311: New Jersey State Line

⬆ PENNSYLVANIA
⬇ NEW JERSEY

EASTERN TIME ZONE

1		NJ 606, River Rd (WB)

◊= Regular Gas Stations with Diesel ▲ = RV Friendly Locations ♥= Pet Friendly Locations
Red print shows large vehicle parking / access on site or nearby Brown Print = Campgrounds / RV PARKS

EXIT		NEW JERSEY
(2)		**Weigh Station (EB)**
3		**Hainesburg River Rd, Columbia**
4A		**Decatur St, to US 611 Alt, US 46E, NJ 94, Portland, Columbia (EB)**
4B		**NJ 94, US 46E, US 611 Alt (EB)**
	FStop	**S:** Columbia Fuel Stop/Shell
4C		**NJ 94N, Columbia (EB)**
4		**NJ 94, US 46, Columbia, Portland (WB)**
	FStop	**S:** Columbia Fuel Stop/Shell
	TStop	**N:** Travel Center of America #6/Mobil (Scales)
	Food	**N:** McDonald's, CountryPride/Pizza Hut/ TacoBell/TA TC
	Lodg	**N:** Days Inn
	TServ	**N:** TA TC/Tires
	Other	**N:** Laundry/WiFi/TA TC, **Worthington State Forest, to** appr 7mi **Camp Taylor Campground▲** **S: Delaware River Family Campground▲**
(6)		**Scenic Overlook (WB) (Autos only)**
(7)		**NJ Welcome Center (EB) (RR, Phone, Picnic, Vend)**
12		**CR 521, Hope Blairstown Rd, Hope, Blairstown, Great Meadows**
	Gas	**S:** Shell
	Other	**N: to** appr 5mi **TripleBrook Family Camping Resort▲**
19		**CR 517, Hackettstown, Andover**
	Gas	**S:** Shell
	Food	**S:** Rest/Panther Valley Inn
	Lodg	**S:** Panther Valley Inn
	Med	**S: + Hospital**
	Other	**N: Panther Lake Camping Resort▲**
(21)		**Scenic Overlook (Both dir)**
25		**US 206, Newton, Stanhope**
	Gas	**N:** Exxon **S:** Shell
	Food	**N:** McDonald's, Subway
	Lodg	**N:** Extended Stay American, Residence Inn, Wyndham Garden
	Other	**N: to Green Valley Beach Family Campground▲ , appr 4mi Columbia Valley Campground▲ , Panther Lake Camping Resort▲ , Windy Acres Campground▲** **S:** Sam's Club
26		**US 46, Main St, Netcong, to Budd Lake, Hackettstown (WB)**
	Gas	**N:** Exxon, Mobil **S:** Shell
	Food	**N:** Cattleman's Steakhouse **S:** Golden Bowl
	Lodg	**N:** Days Inn **S:** Best Western, Comfort Suites, Kennedy's Bud Lake Motel
	Other	**N: to Goodland Nudist Country Club▲** **S:** ATMs, CVS, Lowe's, Staples, Sam's Club, **Walmart**, **Delaware River Family Campground▲ , Fla-Net Park▲**
27		**US 206S, NJ 183, Netcong, Flanders, Sommerville**
	Gas	**N:** Mobil◈ **S:** B&S Auto Repair, Exxon, Shell
	Food	**N:** Circle Grill, El Coyote, Perkins **S:** Chili's, Longhorn Steakhouse, Wendy's Mandarin House, McDonald's, Romano's Macaroni Grill
	Other	**N:** Auto services **S:** ATMs, Auto service, **Walmart Fla-Net Park▲**
28		**CR 631, US 46, to NJ 10, Landing, Ledgewood, Lake Hopatcong**
	Gas	**S:** GasNGo, Gulf, Hess, Shell
	Food	**S:** Burger King, Deli, Diner, Domino's, KFC, McDonald's, Pizza Hut, Outback Steakhouse, Red Lobster, Ruby Tuesday, Subway, TGI Friday, Tom's Diner, Wendy's
	Lodg	**S:** Days Inn, Kingstown Motel, Roxbury Circle Motel
	Other	**S:** ATMs, Auto Services, BJ's, CVS, Roxbury Mall, Grocery, Tires, **Walmart**, Walgreen's
30		**CR 615, Howard Blvd, Ledgewood, to Mount Arlington**
	Gas	**N:** CF, Exxon◈
	Food	**N:** China City, **Cracker Barrel**, IHOP
	Lodg	**N:** Courtyard, Holiday Inn Express
(32)		**TRUCK Rest Area (WB)**
34		**CR 634, Main St, to NJ 15, Wharton, to Sparta, Randolph**
	Gas	**N:** Exxon, Gulf
	Food	**N:** Deli, Ming Court Buffet, Subway **S:** Hot Rod's BBQ, Maria's Pizzeria, Ming's Kitchen, Pancho Villa
	Med	**S: + St Clares Hospital**
	Other	**N:** Grocery, Laundromat, RiteAid, **to Valley Beach Family Campground▲**
34A		**NJ 15S, Wharton, to Dover (WB)**
34B		**NJ 15N, Wharton, to Sparta (WB)**
	Other	**N: to** Picatinny Arsenal, appr 14mi **Beaver Hill Campground▲ , to Cedar Ridge Campground▲ , Kymer's Camping Resort▲**
35AB		**CR 661, Mt Hope Ave, Dover**
35		**CR 661, Mt Hope Ave, Dover**
	Gas	**S:** Exxon
	Food	**S:** Olive Garden, Steak Escape, Subway, Starbucks, Wendy's
	Lodg	**S:** Hilton Garden Inn
	Med	**S: + Urgent Medical Care**
	Other	**S:** ATMs, Best Buy, PetSmart♥, **Walmart**, Rockaway Townsquare Mall
37		**CR 513, Hibernia Ave, Rockaway**
	Gas	**N:** Exxon, Shell
	Food	**N:** Damon's, Hibernia Diner **S:** Sherwood's Deli
	Lodg	**N:** Best Western, Hampton Inn
	Med	**S: + Hospital**
38		**US 46E, to NJ 53, Denville (EB)**
	Gas	**N:** Exxon, Sunoco **S:** Shell
	Food	**N:** Burger King, Wendy's
	Med	**N: + Hospital**
39		**US 46, to NJ 53, Denville (WB)**
	Gas	**N:** Exxon, Getty, Shell, Sunoco
	Food	**N:** Banzai Steak House, Denville Diner, Ichiban's, King's Palace, Starbucks, Sushi
	Med	**N: + St Clare's Hospital**
42		**NJ 46, NJ 202, Parsippany, Morris Plains**
42ABC		**US 202, Cherry Hill Rd, to US 46, Parsippany, US 202, to NJ 10, Morris Plains (Serv N to US 46)**
(43)		**Jct I-287, to US 46, Morristown, Boonton, Mahwah**
(43A)		**Jct I-287, to US 46, Morristown, Boonton, Mahwah**
45		**CR 637, Beverwyck Rd, to US 46, to Lake Hiawatha, Whippany (EB)**
	Gas	**N:** BP, Gulf
	Food	**N:** Burger King, Chili's, IHOP, Outback Steakhouse, Taco Bell, Wendy's, Stockyard Steakhouse/Hol Inn
	Lodg	**N:** Holiday Inn, Howard Johnson, Ramada Inn, Red Roof Inn♥
	Other	**N:** ATMs, Best Buy, Grocery, Pharmacy, Staples
(47A)		**Jct I-280E, Newark (EB)**
47B		**US 46, Parsippany (EB)**
47		**US 46W, Parsippany (WB)**

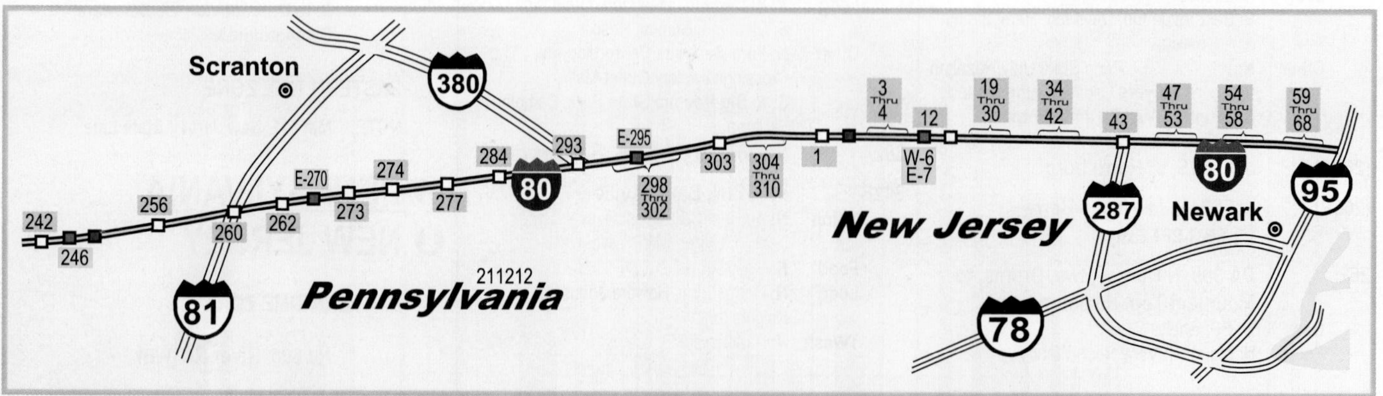

◈= Regular Gas Stations with Diesel ▲ = RV Friendly Locations ♥= Pet Friendly Locations
Red print shows large vehicle parking / access on site or nearby Brown Print = Campgrounds / RV PARKS

EXIT		NEW JERSEY
48		**Hook Mtn Rd, to US 46, Pine Brook, The Caldwells, Lincoln Park, Montville, Pinebrook (WB)**
	Gas	S: Coastal, Getty
	Food	S: Don Pepe II Rest, Wendy's
	Lodg	S: Holiday Inn, Sunset Motel
52		**Two Bridges Rd, to US 46, Fairfield, Lincoln Park, Caldwells**
	Other	S: to Essex Co Airport✈
53		**US 46E, NJ 23, Wayne, Butler, Verona**
	Gas	S: Exxon, Mobil, Sunoco
	Food	S: Applebee's, Burger King, McDonald's, Hooters, Red Lobster, Ruby Tuesday, Steak & Ale, TGI Friday, Wendy's
	Lodg	S: Holiday Inn, Ramada Inn
	Other	S: ATMs, Auto Services, Costco, Firestone, Home Depot, Staples, Target, Willowbrook Mall
54		**CR 642, Minnisink Rd, Totowa, Little Falls**
	Gas	S: BP
	Other	S: Best Buy, Office Depot, Staples
55AB		**CR 646, Union Blvd, Totowa, Little Falls**
56		**CR 636, McBridge Ave (WB)**
56AB		**CR 636, Squirrelwood Rd, Little Falls, W Paterson, Paterson**
	Gas	S: Mobil
57AB		**NJ 19, Main St, Downtown Paterson, Clifton**
57C		**Main St, Paterson (WB)**
58AB		**Madison Ave, Patterson, Clifton**
	Gas	N: Exxon
	Med	S: + St Joseph's Reg'l Medical Center
59		**Market St (WB)**
60		**NJ 20, to US 46, Hawthorne**
61		**NJ 507. Garfield, Elmwood Park**
	Gas	S: Sunoco
62		**Garden State Pkwy (WB)**
62A		**to Garden State Pkwy , Saddlebrook**
	Gas	N: Shell
	Lodg	N: Howard Johnson, Marriott S: Holiday Inn
62B		**Saddle River Rd (EB)**
63		**to NJ 4, NJ 17N, Rochelle Park, Paramus, Lodi, Fairlawn**
	Gas	N: BP, Citgo, Hessd
64AB		**to NJ 4, NJ 17, to US 46E, Newark, Rochelle Park, Paramus**
	Gas	S: BP, Exxon
	Lodg	S: Hilton
	Med	N: + Hackensack Univ Med Center
65		**Green St, Teterboro, S Hackensack**
	Gas	S: Exxon
	Lodg	S: Airport Motel, Marriott
	Other	S: to Walmart, Teterboro Airport✈
66		**Hudson St, Hackensack, Little Ferry**
	Other	N: Costco
67		**Bogota, Ridgefield Park (EB)**
(68A)		**Jct I-95S, NJ 46, NJ Tpk (TOLL)**
(68B)		**Jct I-95N, George Washington Bridge, New York**

EASTERN TIME ZONE

NOTE: NJ TPK / I-95 continues into NY

NEW JERSEY

Begin Westbound I-80 from Jct I-95 in Englewood, NJ to San Francisco, CA

Begin Southbound I-81 from Canada/New York border to Jct I-40 near Knoxville, TN.

NEW YORK

NOTE: I-81 begins/ends at NY/CANADA border

EASTERN TIME ZONE

NOTE: NYS is NOT mileage based exits. Listed is Mile Marker/Exit #.

EXIT		NEW YORK
(183)		**US/CANADA Border, Customs, AmEx Duty Free** Be Prepared to STOP
182/52		**CR 191, Island Rd, De Wolf Point**
	NOTE:	**NB: LAST US EXIT**
179/51		**Island Rd, Island State Parks**
	Gas	E: Citgo W: Sunoco
	Food	E: South of the Border Café
	Lodg	E: Torchlite Lodge & Motel
(178)		**1000 Islands Bridge (NB: TOLL)**
177/50		**NY 12, Alexandria Bay, Clayton**
	NOTE:	**NB: Last FREE Exit Before TOLL**
		NY Welcome Center (SB) **(RR, Phone, Pic, Info)** **Rest Area (NB)** **(RR, Phone, Pic, NY State Police)**
	Gas	W: Citgo, Mobil
	Food	E: Beefers Diner & Steakhouse, Kountry Kottage, Subway
	Lodg	E: Bridgeview Motel, Rock Ledge Motel
	Med	E: + Hospital
	Other	E: Keewaydin State Park▲ , Pine Tree Point Resort▲ W: Captain Clayton CG▲ , Thousand Island CG▲
(174)		**Rest Area (NB)** **(RR, Phone, Pic, Vend, Info, NY St Police)**
167/49		**NY 411, Plank Rd, Theresa**
(166)		**Parking Area (SB)**
(162)		**Parking Area (NB)**
160/48		**NY 342, Fort Drum, Black River (SB) to US 11, to NY 37 (NB), Watertown**
	FStop	E: Nice n Easy Grocery #36/Citgo
	TStop	E: Longways Truck Stop/Mobil, Sugar Creek Store #590/Sunoco
	Food	E: FastFood/Nice n Easy, Rest/Longways TS, FastFood/Sugar Creek,
	Lodg	E: Allen's Budget Motel, Microtel, Royal Inn
	Other	E: Laundry/WiFi/LP/Sugar Creek, Fort Drum Military Res
(159)		**Parking Area (Both dir)**
157/47		**NY 12, Bradley St, Watertown, Clayton**
	FStop	E: Nice n Easy Grocery/Mobil
	Other	E: PetCo♥, RV Center
156/46		**NY 12F, Coffeen St, Watertown**
	Gas	E: Mobil W: Citgo
	Food	E: Cracker Barrel, Diner
	Med	E: + Urgent Care
	Other	E: ATM, Home Depot W: FedEx Office, Jefferson Comm College, Watertown Muni Airport✈, to appr 6mi Black River Bay Campground▲
155/45		**NY 3, Arsenal St, Watertown**
	Gas	E: Citgo, Mobil, Sunoco W: Fastrac
	Food	E: Applebee's, Arby's, Buffalo Wild Wings, Burger King, China Café, Denny's, Dunkin Donuts, KFC, McDonald's, Panda Buffet, Pizza Hut, Ponderosa, Ruby Tuesday, Starbucks, Taco Bell, Wendy's W: Bob Evans, Panera Bread, Pizza Hut, Red Lobster, Texas Roadhouse
	Lodg	E: Days Inn, Econo Lodge, Hampton Inn, Holiday Inn Express W: Ramada Inn
	Med	E: + Hospital
	Other	E: ATMs, Advance Auto Parts, Aldi Foods, Auto Dealers, Auto Zone, Big Lots, Dollar General, Dollar Tree, Grocery, Laundromat, Michael's, Pharmacy, Radio Shack, RiteAid, Staples, TJ Maxx, UPS Store, US Post Office, Walgreen's W: ATMs, Best Buy, Borders, Cinemas, Gander Mountain, Grocery, Kmart, Lowe's, PetCo♥, Salmon Run Mall, Sam's Club, Target, Walmart sc, to Bedford Creek Marina & Campground▲ , Westcott State Park▲
(151)		**Parking Area (NB)**
150/44		**NY 232, Watertown Center (Serv 4 mi E in Watertown)**
	Med	E: + Hospital
(150)		**Rest Area (SB)** **(RR, Phone, Picnic, NY St Police)**
148/43		**to US 11, Kellogg Hill**

EXIT	NEW YORK
146/42	**NY 177, Smithville, Adams Center**
Gas	E: Mobil, Sunoco
141/41	**NY 178, Church St, Adams, Henderson**
Gas	E: Citgo◈
Food	E: McDonald's
135/40	**NY 193, Ellisburg, Pierrepont Manor**
Other	W: **Southwick Beach State Park**
(134)	Parking Area (Both dir)
133/39	**CR 90/94, Lilac Park Dr, Mannsville**
131/38	**US 11, Mannsville**
128/37	**CR 15 (NB), CR 22A (SB), Sandy Creek, Lacona, Boylston**
Gas	W: Gas Mart, Sunoco◈
Food	E: J&R Diner W: Subway
Lodg	E: Harris Lodge
Other	W: Laundromat, Oswego Co Fairgrounds, **Sandy Island Beach State Park**
121/36	**CR 2, Richland Rd, Pulaski (SB, No reaccess)** **NY 13, Rome St, to US 11, Pulaski (NB, No reaccess)**
Gas	E: Citgo W: KwikFill, Mobil
Food	E: Ponderosa W: Arby's, Burger King, McDonald's, Stefano's Pizza, Waffleworks
Lodg	E: Redwood Motel W: Super 8
Other	E: **Stoney's Pineville Campground▲**, **Fox Hollow Salmon River Lodge▲** W: ATMs, Auto Dealer, Grocery, Pharmacy, NAPA, Fish Hatchery, **Selkirk Shores State Park, NY State Police**
119/35	**to US 11, Tinker Cavern Rd**
115/34	**NY 104, to Mexico, Oswego**
TStop	E: Sun-Up Auto Truck Plaza/Sunoco Ezze Auto Truck Stop (Scales)
Food	E: Rest/SunUp ATP, Rest/Ezze ATS
Lodg	W: La Siesta Motel
Other	E: WiFi/BarbSh/**LP**/SunUp ATP, Laundry/ Ezze ATS, **Steamside Campground▲** W: **to J & J Campground▲**, **Salmon Country Marina & Campground▲**, **Yogi Bear Jellystone Campground▲**
111/33	**NY 69, E Main St, Parish**
FStop	E: Sunoco/Grist Mill Rest
Gas	W: Kwik Fill, Mobil◈
Food	E: Grist Mill Rest
Lodg	E: Parish Motel
Other	E: **to appr 4mi Bass Lake Resort▲**, **appr 8mi Up Country Family Campground▲**
104/32	**NY 49, Central Square**
TStop	E: Penn Can Truck Stop/Mobil
Gas	W: Fastrac
Food	E: FastFood/Penn Can TS W: Burger King, Hardee's, McDonald's
TWash	E: Penn Can TS
Other	E: WiFi/**LP**/Penn Can TS W: Grocery
(101)	**Inspection Station (SB)**
(101)	Rest Area (SB) (RR, Phones, Picnic) **(Next RA 73 mi)**
100/31	**Bartel Rd, to US 11, Brewerton**
Gas	W: Mobil, Sunoco

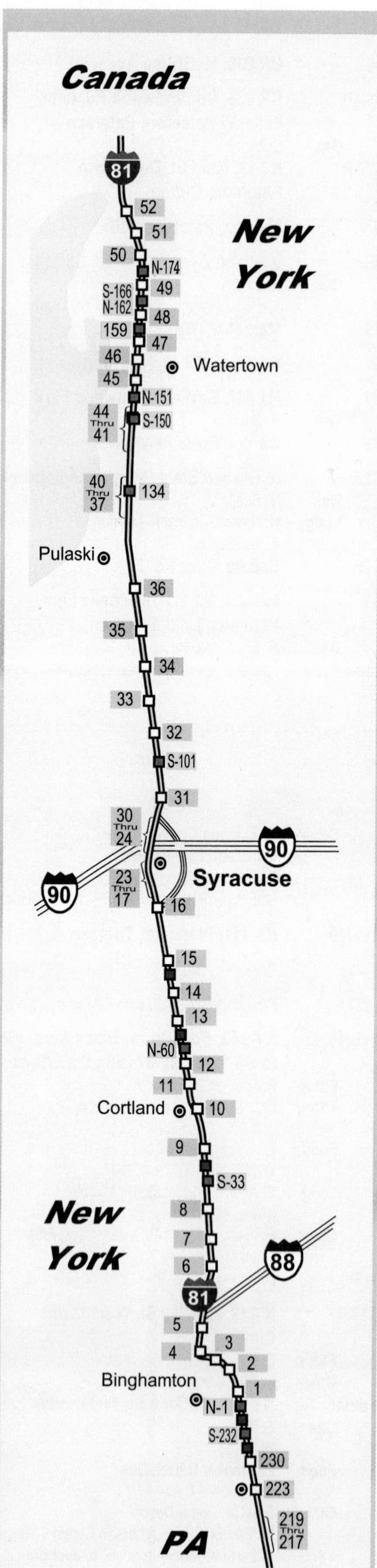

EXIT	NEW YORK
Food	E: Good Golly Rest W: Burger King, Dunkin Donuts, McDonald's, Subway
Lodg	W: Holiday Inn Express
Other	E: **Oneida Shores Co Park▲** W: Laundromat, Pharmacy, **Walmart**
95/30	**NY 31, Cicero, Bridgeport**
Gas	E: Hess, Mobil, Sunoco W: Kwik Fuel
(93/29)	**Jct I-481, NY 481, S to Syracuse, DeWitt, N to DeWitt, Oswego (SB: Use I-481 to ByPass) (Serv @ 1st Ex, Ex #10)**
92/28	**Taft Rd, N Syracuse (SB)**
91/27/28	**Syracuse Airport, Taft Rd, N Syracuse (NB)**
Gas	E: Mobil W: KwikFill
Food	W: Burger King, Ponderosa, Taco Bell, Wendy's
Lodg	E: Ledge Inn W: Traveler's Motel
Other	E: Pharmacy, USMC Reserve Training Center, NY Army Natl Guard, Hancock Field USAF Base, **NY State Police**
92/27/26	**US 11, Syracuse Airport, Mattydale, Syracuse (SB)**
Gas	E: Mobil, Sunoco W: Hess◈, Kwik Fill, Mobil
Lodg	W: Econo Lodge, Rest Inn
Other	E: ATMs, Big Lots, Staples W: Auto Dealers, Auto Services, US Post Office, **NY State Police**
90/26	**US 11, Brewerton Rd, Mattydale (NB)**
Gas	E: Citgo, Mobil W: Hess, KwikFill
Food	E: Asian 98 Buffet, China Road, Café, Friendly's, Pizza Hut W: Beneventos Italian, Burger King, McDonald's, Ponderosa, Sal's Seafood, Taco Bell, Wendy's
Lodg	E: Red Carpet Inn W: Candlewood Suites, Rest Inn
Other	E: Pharmacy, USMC Reserve Training Center, NY Army Natl Guard, Hancock Field USAF Base
(89/25A)	**Jct I-90, NY ThruWay, Rochester, Buffalo, Albany**
88/25	**7th North St, Liverpool**
TStop	E: Pilot Travel Center #380 (Scales)
Gas	W: Mobil
Food	E: McDonald's/Pilot TC W: Bob Evans, Colorado Mine Co Steak house, Denny's, Friendly's, Tully's Good Times, Rest/Ramada Inn
Lodg	W: Days Inn, Econo Lodge, Quality Inn, Ramada Inn, Super 8
TWash	E: Express Wash/Pilot TC
TServ	E: Valerino Auto & Truck Repair, Syracuse Crank & Machine
Other	E: Laundry/WiFi/Pilot TC, Auto Services
87/23AB/ 22	**NY 298, to I-690W, Hiawatha Blvd, Bear St, Carousel Center Dr (SB)**
Gas	W: Hess
Food	E: Market Diner, Wendy's
Other	E: Alliance Bank Stadium, Amtrak, Greyhound, Carousel Center

◈= Regular Gas Stations with Diesel ▲ = RV Friendly Locations ♥= Pet Friendly Locations
Red print shows large vehicle parking / access on site or nearby **Brown Print = Campgrounds / RV PARKS**

EXIT NEW YORK

87/24AB/23 **NY 370, Hiawatha Blvd, Park St, Old Liverpool Rd, Onandaga Lake Pkwy, Liverpool (NB)**
NOTE: Trucks / Vehicles 9'+ MUST use Old Liverpool Rd to Liverpool
Gas W: Hess
Food E: Market Diner, Wendy's
Other E: Alliance Bank Stadium, Amtrak, Greyhound, Carousel Center
W: Mall

86/22 **NY 298, Sunset Ave, Court St (NB)**

85/21 **Spencer St, Catawba St (SB)**

84/20 **Franklin St, West St, Downtown Syracuse (SB)**

84/19 **Clinton St, Salina St (SB)**

(84) **I-690, E Syracuse, Baldwinsville, Fairgrounds (NB), I-690E, (SB)**

83/18 **Adams St, Harrison St**
Lodg E: Genesee Inn, Marriott, Marx Hotel, Sheraton
W: Hotel Syracuse, Harbor Inn
Med E: + Hospital
Other E: CVS, to Syracuse Univ

82/17 **S Salina St, Brighton Ave, State St**

(81/16A) **I-481N, to De Witt (fr SB, Left exit) (NB: Use 481N to ByPass)**

77/16 **US 11, Nedrow, Onondaga Nation Territory**
Gas W: Hess, Daniels Car Care/Mobil
Food W: McDonald's, Nedrow Diner, Pizza Hut
Other W: Onandaga Indian Res

73/15 **US 20 (SB), to US 11 (NB), La Fayette**
FStop E: Nice n Easy Grocery #7/Sunoco
Food E: Deli, Pizza
W: McDonald's
Other E: Grocery, NAPA, US Post Office, NY State Police

(70) **Inspection Station (Both dir)**

66/14 **NY 80, US 11, Tully**
FStop E: Nice n Easy Grocery #12/Sunoco
Food E: Deli/Nice n Easy
Food W: Burger King
Lodg E: Best Western
Other E: Highland Forest Co Park

62/13 **NY 281, Tully, to Preble**

(60) **Inspection Station (NB)**

(60) **Rest Area (NB) (RR, Phones, Picnic, Info, NY St Police)**

54/12 **US 11, NY 41, NY 281, Cortland, Homer, Ithaca**
FStop W: Express Mart #323/Mobil
Gas W: KwikFill
Food W: Applebee's, Burger King, Fabio's Italian, Pizzeria
Lodg W: Budget Inn, Country Inn
Other W: to Fillmore Glen State Park

52/11 **NY 13, Clinton Rd, Cortland, Ithaca**
Gas W: Mobil
Food E: Denny's
W: Arby's, Bob Evans, Friendly's, Little Caesars Pizza, McDonald's, Subway, Taco Bell, Wendy's, Rest/Holiday Inn

Personal Notes

EXIT NEW YORK

Lodg E: Comfort Inn, Super 8
W: Holiday Inn
TServ W: Cortland Tire Service
Other E: Yellow Lantern Kampground▲
W: Pharmacy, Grocery, Advance Auto, Courtland Co Chase Field✈, Fillmore Glen State Park

49/10 **US 11, NY 41, Cortland, McGraw**
FStop W: Express Mart #308/Mobil
TStop W: Pit Stop Travel Center/Citgo
Gas W: Sunoco
Food W: Subway/Expr Mart, BurgerKing/PizzaHu Pit Stop TC, Diner, Pizza Express
Lodg W: Cortland Motel, Days Inn♥
Other W: LP/Express Mart, Laundry/WiFi/LP/ Pit Stop TC

38/9 **NY 221, Main St, Marathon**
Gas W: Citgo, XtraMart
Food W: Kathy's Diner, NY Pizzeria, Reilly's Café, Rest/3 Bear Inn
Lodg W: Three Bear Inn
Other W: Grocery, Yogi's Campground▲, Country Hills Campground▲, Bowman Lake State Park

(33) **Inspection Station (SB)**

(33) **Rest Area (SB) (RR, Phones, Picnic, NY St Police)**

30/8 **NY 79, to US 11, to NY 26, to NY 206, Whitney Point (SB)**
Gas E: Hess, Mobil
Food E: McDonald's, Subway
Lodg E: Point Motel

EXIT NEW YORK

28/8 **NY 26, to US 11, to NY 79, to NY 206, Whitney Point (NB)**

21/7 **US 11, Castle Creek**

16/6 **US 11, NY 12, to I-88E (SB), US 11, NY 12, Chenango Bridge (NB)**
Gas E: Exxon, Hess◈, Mobil
W: Kwik Fill, Mobil
Food E: Burger King, Denny's, Pizza Hut, McDonald's, Ponderosa, TCBY, Wendy's
Lodg W: Days Inn, Comfort Inn, Motel 6♥
Other E: CVS, Grocery, Lowe's, Staples, Northgate Speedway, Broome Co Comm College Norwich Binghamton Reg'l Airport✈

(15) **Jct I-88E, to Albany (NB)**

14/5 **US 11, Front St NB), to I-88 (SB)**
Gas E: Mobil, Valero
Food E: Great Wall Chinese
W: Applebee's, Cracker Barrel, Quiznos, Starbucks
Lodg E: Howard Johnson, Riverfront B&B, Super 8
W: Days Inn, Fairfield Inn, Motel 6♥, Super 8
Other E: Broome Co Comm College

13 **NY 17W, Owego, Elmira (fr NB, Left exit)**

12/4 **NY 7, Binghamton, Hillcrest**
Gas W: Express Mart, Mobil
Food W: Subway
Lodg W: Howard Johnson, Super 8
Other W: ATM, CVS, Grocery

12/3 **Broad Ave, Downtown (NB)**
Gas W: Exxon

9/3 **Colesville Rd, Industrial Park, Binghamton (SB)**
TStop W: NB: Acc Via Ex #2 Travel Center of America #207 (Scales), Love's Travel Stop #403 (Scales)
Gas W: Exxon
Food W: Buckhorn/TA TC, Wendy's/Love's TS, KFC, McDonald's
Lodg W: Del Motel, Holiday Inn, Super 8, Wright Motel
Other W: Laundry/WiFi/TA TC, Laundry/WiFi/ Love's TS, CVS, Grocery

(7) **NY 17, New York, I-86E (SB, Left Exit)**

7/2 **US 11, Five Mile Pt (SB) I-86E, NY 17, US 11, New York, Industrial Park (NB)**

4/1 **Cedarhurst St, to US 11, NY 7, Kirkwood, Conklin**
Gas W: Mobil
Lodg W: Kirkwood Motel, Larrabee B&B

(1) **NY Welcome Center (NB) (RR, Phone, Picnic, Vend, NY St Police)**

(1) **Inspection Station (NB)**

NOTE: **NYS is NOT mileage based exits. Listed is Mile Marker/Exit #.**

NEW YORK

◈= Regular Gas Stations with Diesel ▲ = RV Friendly Locations ♥ = Pet Friendly Locations
Red print shows large vehicle parking / access on site or nearby Brown Print = Campgrounds / RV PARKS

EXIT PENNSYLVANIA

PENNSYLVANIA

NOTE: MM 233: New York State Line

EASTERN TIME ZONE

(232) **PA Welcome Center (SB)**
(RR, Phone, Pic, Pet, Info)

(232) **Truck Scales (SB)**

230 **PA 171, to US 11, Great Bend, Susquehanna**
Gas E: Mobil, Valero
W: Exxon◈, Sunoco◈
Food W: Burger King, Country Kitchen, McDonald's, Subway, Rest/Colonial Motel
Lodg W: Colonial Brick Inn

223 **PA 492, New Milford, Lakeside**
Gas W: Gulf◈, Mobil
Other W: **Montrose Campsites▲**, **East Lake Campground▲**

219 **PA 848, Harford Rd, PA 2081, New Milford, to Gibson**
TStop W: Flying J Travel Plaza #5062/Shell (Scales), Gibson Travel Plaza/Exxon
Food W: CountryMarket/FastFood/FJ TP, McDonald's/Gibson TP
Lodg W: Holiday Inn Express
TServ W: Gibson Truck & Tire Service
Other E: **April Valley Campsites▲**, PA State Hwy Patrol Post
W: Laundry/WiFi/**RVDump/LP**/FJ TP

217 **PA 547, Harford**
TStop E: PTP/Liberty Travel Plaza/Exxon, Penn Can Travel Plaza/Getty
Food E: Subway/Liberty TP, Rest/Penn Can TP
TServ E: Penn Can TS/Tires
Other E: CB/Liberty TP

211 **PA 92 (SB), PA 106 (NB), Lenox**
Gas W: Mobil◈, Shell◈
Food W: Lenox Rest
Other W: to appr 6mi: **Shore Forest CG▲**

(208) **PA Welcome Center (SB)**
(RR, Phones, Picnic, Info)

206 **PA 374, Lenoxville, to Glenwood**
Other E: to ELK Mountain Ski Resort

(203) **Rest Area (NB)**
(RR, Phones, Picnic)

202 **PA 107, Fleetville, Tompkinsville**

201 **PA 438, East Benton**
Gas W: Mobil◈

199 **PA 524, Scott**
TStop E: Scott 60 Truck & Travel Plaza/Gulf, BP 60
Gas W: Exxon
Food E: Rest/FastFood/Scott 60 TTP
W: Subway/Exxon
Lodg W: Motel 81
TWash E: Scott 60 TTP
Tires E: Scott 60 TTP

197 **PA 632, Clarks Summit, Waverly**
Gas W: Sunoco
Food W: Deli
Other E: Food Mart, RiteAid

194 **US 6W, US 11, to I-476S, PA Tpk, Clarks Summit**
Gas W: Shell◈, Sheetz, Sunoco◈
Food W: Burger King, Damon's, Domino's Pizza, Dunkin Donuts, Friendly's, Garlic Jim's, Kyoto, McDonald's, Pizza Hut, Quiznos,

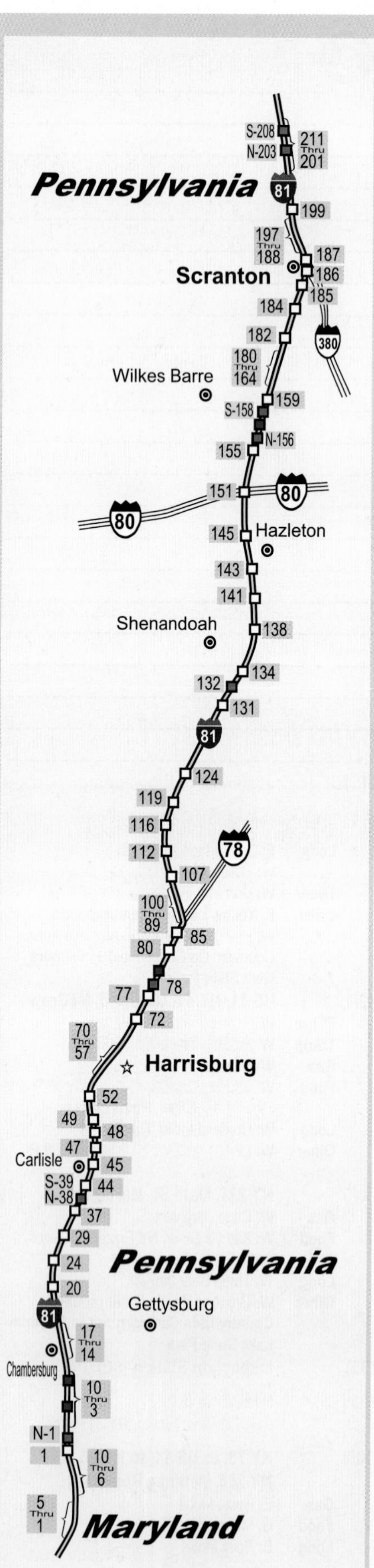

EXIT PENNSYLVANIA

Food W: Subway, Starbucks, Taco Bell, Waffle House, Wendy's
Lodg W: Comfort Inn, Econo Lodge, Hampton Inn, Nichols Village Inn, Ramada
Other W: ATMs, Advance Auto Parts, Grocery, Pharmacy, Radiio Shack, RiteAid, Tires, UPS Store, to appr 8 mi **Highland CG▲**, appr 14 mi **Yogi Bear Jellystone Park Camp Resort▲**

191B **to US 11, Scranton Expwy, Scranton**
NOTE: Trucks Over 10.5 Tons, Use Ex #185
Other W: to Lackawanna Coal Mine Tour, Anthracite Museum

191A **US 6E Bus, Dickson City, Carbondale**
Gas E: Shell◈, Sheetz◈
Food E: Applebee's, Arby's, Burger King, China Buffet, Chuck E Cheese's Pizza, Denny's, Don Pablo, Five Guys Cafe, Lone Star Steakhouse, McDonald's, Old Country Buffet, Olive Garden, Perkins, Pizza Hut, Red Lobster, Red Robin, Ruby Tuesday, Smokey Bones BBQ, Subway, Texas Roadhouse, TGI Friday, Wendy's
Lodg E: Days Inn, Fairfield Inn, Residence Inn
Other E: ATMs, Borders, Electric City Harley Davidson, Firestone, Grocery, Home Depot, Michael's, Pep Boys, PetSmart♥, Radio Shack, Target, TJ Maxx, Tires, Viewmont Mall, **Walmart sc**,

190 **Main Ave, Dickson City**
Gas E: Sam's
Food E: Arby's, Charlie Brown's Steakhouse, Golden Corral, Old Country Buffet, Pizza Hut, Uno Chicago Grill, Wendy's
Lodg E: Fairfield Inn, Residence Inn
Other E: ATMs, Viewmont Mall, Best Buy, Gander Mountain, Lowe's, Sam's Club, Staples, Endless Mountain Theater
W: Auto & Truck Repairs, **Royal RV Center**

188 **PA 347, Blakely St, Scranton, to Throop, Dunmore**
Gas E: Sunoco◈, Sheetz
W: Mobil
Food E: China World Buffet, McDonald's, Quiznos, Wendy's
W: Burger King, Pizza, Subway
Lodg E: Days Inn, Dunmore Inn, Sleep Inn, Super 8♥
TServ E: Motor Truck Equipment Co, Freightliner
Other E: CVS, Grocery, PA State Hwy Patrol Post, Penn State Scranton Campus
W: to Marywood Univ

(187) **Jct I-84E, I-380S, US 6E, to Milford, Mt Pocono, Carbondale**
Other E: to appr 20mi: **Keen Lake Camping & Cottage Resort▲**

186 **Drinker St, Dunmore (NB)**
Gas E: Mobil, Valero
W: Citgo, Exxon
Lodg E: Holiday Inn

185 **Central Scranton Expressway (NB Left Exit, SB Exit Only)**
Other W: UPS Store, to Scranton Memorial Stadium, Univ of Scranton

184 **PA 307, Moosic St (SB), River St, to PA 307 (NB), Scranton**
Gas W: Citgo, Exxon, USA
Food W: Dunkin Donuts, Pizza
Lodg W: Clarion
Med W: + Hospital
Other W: ATMs, CVS, Dollar Tree, Grocery

◈= Regular Gas Stations with Diesel ▲ = RV Friendly Locations ♥= Pet Friendly Locations
Red print shows large vehicle parking / access on site or nearby Brown Print = Campgrounds / RV PARKS

EXIT		PENNSYLVANIA
182		**Montage Mountain Rd, Davis St (NB)**
	Gas	E: Exxon W: Mobil
	Food	E: Ruby Tuesday W: McDonald's, Waffle House, Wendy's
	Lodg	E: Comfort Inn, Courtyard, Hampton Inn W: Econo Lodge
	Other	W: CVS, US Post Office
182B		**Davis St (SB)**
182A		**Montage Mountain Rd (SB)**
180		**US 11, Birney Ave, to PA 502 Moosic (fr NB, Left Exit)**
	Gas	W: BP◈
	Food	W: Subway/BP
178B		**PA 315S, to Avoca**
	TStop	W: Petro Stopping Center #63 (Scales)
	Food	W: IronSkillet/PizzaHut/Petro SC
	TServ	W: Petro SC/Tires
	Other	W: Laundry/BarbSh/Massg/WiFi/**RVDump**/Petro SC
178A		**PA 315N, to Wilkes Barre, Scranton Int'l Airport**
	Food	E: Damon's
	Lodg	E: Holiday Inn Express
	Other	E: Wilkes-Barre Scranton Intl Airport✈
175B		**PA 315N, to Dupont (SB)**
175A		**PA 315S, to I-476/PA TPK to Pittston (SB)**
175		**PA 315N, to I-476/PA TPK, Dupont, Pittston (NB)**
	FStop	W: Hi-Way Auto & Truck Plaza/Getty
	TStop	W: Pilot Travel Center #370 (Scales) **(SB Access via Ex# 175B)**
	Gas	E: Mobil◈, Sunoco
	Food	E: Arby's, BBQ Express, Dunkin Donuts, McDonald's, Perkins W: Wendy's/Pilot TC
	Lodg	E: Knights Inn♥, Quality Inn, Super 8
	TServ	W: Hi-Way ATP/Tires, Pilot TC/Tires
	Other	W: Laundry/WiFi/Pilot TC, **Walmart**
170B		**PA 309N, Wilkes-Barre**
	Gas	W: Exxon◈, Sunoco◈ W: Sunoco◈
	Food	W: McDonald's, Perkins, Pizza Hut, Lone Star Steakhouse, TGI Friday
	Lodg	E: Best Western W: Days Inn, Hampton Inn, Holiday Inn, Red Roof Inn♥, Woodlands Inn
	Med	W: **+ US Veterans Hospital**, **+ Mercy Family Health Center**
	Other	W: Wyoming Valley Mall, Kings College, Wilkes Univ
170A		**PA 115S, Bear Creek**
	Gas	E: Exxon◈, Sunoco◈
	Lodg	E: Best Western, East Mountain Inn
	Med	E: **+ Wyoming Valley Medical Center**
	Other	E: to Pocono Downs Racetrack
168		**Highland Park Blvd, Wilkes-Barre**
	Gas	W: Sheetz
	Food	W: Applebee's, Bob Evans, Burger King, Chili's, **Cracker Barrel**, Ground Round, McDonald's, Olive Garden, Panera, Outback Steakhouse, Red Robin, Smokey Bones BBQ, Starbucks, Wendy's
	Lodg	W: Best Western, Hilton Garden Inn, Ramada Inn, Travelodge
	Other	W: ATMs, Arena Hub Plaza, Best Buy, Barnes & Noble, FedEx Office, Lowe's, Office Depot, PetCo♥, Sam's Club, Target, **Walmart sc**, Wachovia Arena, Wyoming Valley Mall,
165B		**PA 309 Bus, Wilkes-Barre (NB, Left ex)**
	Gas	W: BP◈
	Food	W: McDonald's, Perkins, Taco Bell
	Lodg	W: Comfort Inn, Econo Lodge
	Other	W: ATM, Auto Services
165A		**PA 309S, Mountain Top (NB)**
165		**PA 309S, PA 309 Bus, Mountain Top, Wilkes-Barre (SB)**
164		**PA 29N, Ashley, Nanticoke**
159		**Church St, Mountain Top, Nuangola**
	Gas	W: BP
	NOTE:	**MM 158: Begin Call Box SB, End NB**
(158)		**Rest Area (SB)** **(RR, Phones, Picnic)**
(157)		**Truck Scales (SB)**
(156)		**Rest Area (NB)** **(RR, Phones, Picnic)**
(155)		**Truck Scales (NB)**
155		**Blue Ridge Trail, Mountain Top, to Dorrance, Drums**
	TStop	E: Blue Ridge Plaza
	Gas	E: Sunoco
(151B)		**Jct I-80W, to Bloomsburg**
(151)		**Jct I-80E, to Stroudsburg**
145		**PA 93, Berwick Hazelton Hwy, Susquehanna Blvd, W Hazelton**
	Gas	E: Shell, Sunoco◈, Shell, Turkey Hill
	Food	E: Friendly's, Ground Round, Long John Silver, McDonald's, Perkins, Pizza Hut, Taco Bell, Wendy's
	Lodg	E: Comfort Inn, Fairfield Inn, Ramada Inn W: Candlewood Suites, Hampton Inn
	Med	E: + Hospital
	Other	E: Auto Dealers, Aldi Grocery, Dollar Tree, Hazelton Muni Airport✈, Penn St Univ/Hazelton W: **PA State Hwy Patrol Post**
143		**PA 924, Hazelton**
	FStop	W: Uni-Mart/Exxon
	Lodg	W: Residence Inn
	Other	W: to appr 8mi **Red Ridge Lake Campground▲**
141		**PA 424E, to PA 309, Hazelton**
138		**PA 309, McAdoo, Tamaqua**
134		**Grier Ave, Delano**
(132)		**Parking Area (Both dir)**
131B		**PA 54W, to Mahanoy City**
	Gas	W: Exxon, Shell
131A		**PA 54E, to Hometown**
	Other	E: to Bendinsky Airport✈, **Locust Lake State Park▲**, **Tuscarora State Park**
124B		**PA 61N, to Frackville**
	FStop	W: Central Hwy Oil Co/Gulf
	Gas	W: Hess, Mobil
	Food	W: Dutch Kitchen Rest, Pizza, Subway, Taco Bell
	Lodg	W: Econo Lodge, Inn 81, Rodeway Inn
	Med	W: **+ Good Samaritan Reg Med Center**
	Other	W: RiteAid, **PA State Hwy Patrol Post**
124A		**PA 61S, to St Clair**
	Food	E: **Cracker Barrel**, Granny's, McDonald's
	Lodg	E: Holiday Inn Express, Granny's Motel
	TServ	E: Cleveland Bros CAT
	Other	E: ATMs, Laundromat, Schuylkill Mall, Pioneer Coal Mine Tunnel, Anthracite Coal Museum, 3 mi **Walmart sc**
119		**Highridge Park Rd, Gordon Mtn Rd Pottsville, Ashland, Gordon**
	Lodg	E: Country Inn
	Med	E: + Hospital
116		**PA 901, Sunbury Rd, Pottsville, to Minersville, Hegins**
	Other	W: Schuylkill Co Airport✈
112		**PA 25, E Main St, Tremont, Hegins**
	Other	W: **Camp-A-While Campground▲**
	NOTE:	**MM 108: Begin Call Box NB, End SB**
107		**US 209, Tremont, Tower City**
	Food	E: Carter Mtn Girls Cafe, Family Rest, Pizza
104		**TR 634, to Tremount Rd, PA 125, Tremont, Ravine**
	TStop	W: PTP/Raceway Truck Stop/Exxon
	Food	W: Rest/Raceway TS, Rachel's Country Kitchen
	TServ	W: Raceway TS/Tires
	Other	E: **Echo Valley Campground▲** W: Laundry/Raceway TS
100		**PA 443, Pine Grove**
	FStop	W: Empire Fuel Stop/Sunoco
	TStop	W: Gooseberry Farms Travel Plaza (Scales)
	Gas	E: Exxon◈
	Food	E: McDonald's W: Rest/Gooseberry Farm, Arby's, Subway
	Lodg	E: Comfort Inn W: Econo Lodge, Hampton Inn
	TServ	W: Gooseberry Farms TC/Tires
	Other	W: to appr 5mi **Twin Grove Park & Campground▲**, **Swatara State Park▲**
90		**PA 7, Old Forge Rd, to US 22, Jonestown, Annville, Lebanon**
	TStop	E: Love's Travel Stop #366 (Scales)
	Gas	E: Hess, Shell W: Exxon
	Food	E: Chesters/McDonald's/Love's TS, Subway/Exxon, Wendy's
	Lodg	E: Days Inn W: Best Western, Quality Inn
	Other	E: WiFi/Love's TS, **PA State Hwy Patrol Post**, **Lickdale Campground▲**, to appr 5 mi **Jonestown/I-81/I-78 KOA▲** W: Fort Indiantown Gap Military Res
(89)		**Jct I-78E, to Allentown (fr SB, Left exit)**
85B		**Fort Indiantown Gap (NB)**
	Gas	W: Mobil
	Food	W: Family Rest
	Other	W: PA National Guard Res, **Memorial Lake State Park**
85A		**PA 934S, Fisher Ave, Annville (NB)**
	TStop	E: Ono Truck Center/Shell
	Other	E: Laundry/Ono TC, Auto Services, Tires, Lebanon Valley College
85		**PA 934S, to US 22, Annville, Ono Ft Indiantown Gap (SB)**

◈ = Regular Gas Stations with Diesel ▲ = RV Friendly Locations ♥ = Pet Friendly Locations

Red print shows large vehicle parking / access on site or nearby **Brown Print = Campgrounds / RV PARKS**

EXIT	PENNSYLVANIA
80	**to PA 743, Grantville, Hershey (fr NB, Exit only)**
Gas	E: Mobil◈ W: Exxon◈, Shell
Lodg	E: Econo Lodge, Hampton Inn W: Comfort Inn, Holiday Inn
Med	E: + Greater Hanover Medical Center
Other	E: to appr 16mi: Hershey Attractions, Hershey Highmeadow Campground▲ W: Penn National Racetrack
(79)	**Weigh Station (Both dir)**
(78)	**Rest Area (Both dir) (RR, Phones, Picnic)**
77	**PA 39, Linglestown Rd, Harrisburg, to Hershey, Manada Hill**
FStop	W: Gables of Harrisburg/Shell (Scales)
TStop	E: Pilot Travel Center #245 (Scales) W: Travel Center of America #12 (Scales), WilcoHess Travel Plaza #7001 (Scales)
Gas	E: Exxon◈, Mobil◈
Food	E: PizzaHut/Pilot TC, Café/Mobil W: CountryPride/TA TC, Perkins/WH TP, Subway/Gables
Lodg	E: Country Hearth, Country Inn, Howard Johnson, Scottish Inn W: Daystop Inn/TA TC, Comfort Inn
TServ	W: TA TC/Tires, WH TP/Tires, Diesel Injection & Turbo Service
Other	E: WiFi/Pilot TC, PA State Hwy Patrol, West Hanover Winery, to Hershey Attr W: Laundry/CB/WiFi/TA TC, Laundry/WiFi/WH TP
72B	**Linglestown (NB)**
72A	**to US 22, Paxtonia (NB)**
72	**Mountain Rd, Harrisburg, Paxtonia, Linglestown (SB)**
Gas	E: Citgo◈, Hess◈, Shell, Sunoco◈
Food	E: Applebee's, Burger King, Great Wall, McDonald's, Red Robin, Wendy's
Lodg	E: Holiday Inn Express, Quality Inn W: Baymont Inn, Best Western
Med	E: + Penn State Hershey Medical Center
Other	E: Advance Auto Parts, CVS, Grocery, Harley Davidson, U-Haul
(70)	**Jct I-83S, US 322E, PA Tpk, to Hershey, York (fr SB, Left exit)**
Other	E: to Harrisburg Int'l Airport✈
69	**Progress Ave, Harrisburg**
Gas	E: 7-11, Gulf
Food	E: Cracker Barrel, Moe's SW Grill, Romano's Macaroni Grill, Starbucks W: Arby's, China Chef, Damon's, Nature's Table, Middle Eastern Rest, Western Sizzlin
Lodg	W: Best Western♥, Red Roof Inn♥
Other	E: National Civil War Museum, PA State Hwy Patrol Post W: Widener Univ
67B	**US 22W, US 322, Lewistown**
67A	**US 22E, to PA 230, Cameron St**
66	**Front St, Downtown Harrisburg (fr SB, Exit Only)**
Gas	W: Exxon
Food	W: McDonald's, Pizza Hut, Wendy's
Lodg	W: Days Inn, Super 8
Med	E: + Hospital
Other	E: US Navy Marine Reserve, Amtrak, Bus Terminal

EXIT	PENNSYLVANIA
65B	**US 11N, US 15, Marysville (SB)**
65A	**US 11S, US 15, Enola (SB)**
Gas	E: Mobil, Sunoco◈
Food	E: DQ, Eat 'n Park, KFC, McDonald's, Subway, Wendy's
Lodg	E: Quality Inn
Other	E: ATMs, Advance Auto Parts, Dollar Tree, Kmart, Radio Shack, RiteAid, to Central PA College
65	**US 11, US 15, Enola, Marysville (NB**
61	**PA 944, Wertzville Rd, Enola**
Med	E: + Hospital
59	**PA 581E, US 11 (SB), to I-83 (NB), Camp Hill (fr SB, Left exit) (Trucks to Gettysburg, Use PA 581E)**
Other	E: appr 3 mi: Food & Lodging
57	**PA 114, New Willow Mill Rd, to PA 944, US 11, Mechanicsburg**
Other	W: to Paradise Stream Family Campground▲
52B	**US 11S, Middlesex, to I-76, Pa Tpk, Pittsburgh, Philadelphia (NB)**
FStop	W: Gables of Carlisle/Shell (Scales)
TStop	W: Petro Stopping Center #36 (Scales), Love's Travel Stop #407 (Scales)
Food	W: IronSkillet/FastFood/Petro SC, Wendy's/Love's TS, Arby's, Dunkin Donuts, Hoss's Steak & Sea House, McDonald's, Subway, Waffle House, Rest/HJ,
Lodg	W: Hampton Inn, Howard Johnson, Quality Inn♥, Ramada Inn
TWash	W: Blue Beacon TW/Petro SC, Gables of Carlisle TW
TServ	W: Petro SC/Tires
Other	W: Laundry/BarbSh/CB/WiFi/Petro SC, Laundry/WiFi/Love's TS, Eddie's Tire & Auto Service, Greyhound, Carlisle Fairgrounds, Carlisle Campground▲
52A	**US 11N, New Kingstown (NB)**
FStop	E: I-81 Carlisle Fuel Stop/Citgo
TStop	E: Flying J Travel Plaza #5200 (Scales)
Food	E: Country Market/FastFood/FJ TP , Bob Evans, Duffy's, Middlesex Diner
Lodg	E: America's Best Inn, Econo Lodge, Holiday Inn, Hotel Carlisle, Motel 6, Super 8
TServ	E: FJ TP/Tires
Other	E: Laundry/WiFi/RVDump/LP/FJ TP, Auto Dealer, U-Haul
52	**US 11, Harrisburg Pike, to I-76, PA Tpk, Carlisle, to New Kingstown,**
49	**PA 641, High St (SB, diff reaccess)**
Gas	W: Hess
Food	E: Red Robin, Starbucks W: Burger King, McDonald's, Pizza Hut
Other	E: PetSmart♥, Target, Carlisle Airport✈ W: Carlisle Plaza Mall, Office Max, Target, Dickinson College
48	**PA 74, York Rd (NB, diff reaccess)**
Gas	W: Gulf, Hess, Kwik-Fill
Food	W: Blue Mountain Krinkles, Burger King, Farmer's Market Rest, McDonald's, Red Robin, Rillo's, Starbucks
Other	E: Aldi, Dollar Tree, PetSmart♥, RiteAid, Target, Carlisle Airport✈ W: CVS, Grocery, Lowes, Radio Shack, Carlisle Plaza Mall
47B	**PA 34N, Hanover St (SB)**
Gas	W: Gulf, Mobil

EXIT	PENNSYLVANIA
Food	W: Applebee's, Chili's, Panera Bread, Papa John's Pizza, Subway
Other	W: ATMs, Carlisle Fairgrounds, Carlisle Mall, CVS, Greyhound, Grocery, Home Depot, Pharmacy, RiteAid, TJ Maxx, Walmart sc, US Army War College,
47A	**PA 34S, Hanover St (SB)**
Food	E: Cracker Barrel
Lodg	E: Sleep Inn
Other	E: Carlisle Airport✈
47	**PA 34, Hanover St, Carlisle (NB)**
45	**College St, Walnut Bottom Rd**
Gas	E: BP◈, Mobil, Shell
Food	E: Bonanza Steakhouse, Dunkin Donuts, Great Wall Buffet, McDonald's, Shoney's
Lodg	E: Days Inn, Holiday Inn, Super 8
Med	W: + Hospital
Other	E: Grocery, Staples, Target, UPS Store, Western Village RV Park▲
44	**PA 465, Allen Rd, to Plainfield**
Gas	W: Sheetz
Food	W: Subway
Lodg	E: Fairfield Inn
Other	E: PA State Hwy Patrol Post W: Carlisle Fairgrounds
(39)	**Rest Area (SB) (RR, Phones, Picnic)**
(38)	**Rest Area (NB) (RR, Phones, Picnic)**
37	**PA 233, Centerville Rd, Newville**
Other	E: Pine Grove Furnace State Park W: to Col Denning State Park
29	**PA 174, King St, Walnut Bottom Rd, Shippensburg, Walnut Bottom**
TStop	E: Pharo's Truck Stop (Scales)
Gas	E: Sunoco
Food	E: Rest/Pharo's TS W: Chinatown, Subway, Wendy's
Lodg	E: Budget Host Inn W: AmeriHost Inn, Best Western
TServ	E: Pharo's TS/Tires
Med	W: + Seavers Medical Center
Other	E: Laundry/CB/Pharo's TS W: Shippensburg Univ, Shippensburg Airport✈, Walmart sc,
24	**PA 696, Fayette St, Old Scotland Rd**
20	**PA 997, Black Gap Rd, to PA 696, Chambersburg, Scotland**
FStop	W: RGS Food Shop #9/BP
Gas	E: Exxon◈ W: Sunoco
Food	E: Flamers Burger, McDonald's, Subway
Lodg	E: Comfort Inn, Super 8 W: Sleep Inn
Other	E: ATMs, Chambersburg Mall, Gander Mountain, to Caledonia State Park, Mont Alto State Park W: to Chambersburg Muni Airport✈, Letterkenny Army Depot
17	**Walker Rd (fr NB, Exit only)**
Gas	W: Sheetz
Food	W: Bruster's, Fuddrucker's, Moe's SW Grill, Panera Bread. Quiznos, Red Robin, TGI Friday
Lodg	W: Country Inn
Other	W: Auto Dealer, Grocery, PetSmart♥, Staples, Target
16	**US 30, Lincoln Hwy, Chambersburg, Gettysburg (fr SB, Exit only)**
Gas	E: Exxon, Sheetz W: Hess◈

◈ = Regular Gas Stations with Diesel ▲ = RV Friendly Locations ♥ = Pet Friendly Locations
Red print shows large vehicle parking / access on site or nearby Brown Print = Campgrounds / RV PARKS

EXIT		PA / MD
	Food	E: Arby's, KFC, Hong Kong Rest, Perkins, Popeye's, Shoney's, Waffle House W: Burger King, Dunkin Donuts, Long John Silver's, McDonald's, Pizza Hut, Starbucks, Taco Bell
	Lodg	E: Days Inn, Four Points Hotel W: Best Western, Travelodge
	Med	W: + Hospital
	Other	E: ATMs, Dollar Tree, Food Lion, Grocery, Lowe's, Radio Shack, **Walmart sc**, **PA State Hwy Patrol Post** W: ATMs, Advance Auto Parts, Grocery, Walgreen's, **to** Wilson College
14		**PA 316, Wayne Ave, Chambersburg**
	Gas	W: Exxon, KwikFill, Sheetz, Shell
	Food	E: Bob Evans, Cracker Barrel W: Applebee's, Arby's, China Buffet, Denny's, Dunkin Donuts, Little Caesar's Pizza, Red Lobster,Subway, Wendy's
	Lodg	E: Hampton Inn W: Fairfield Inn, Econo Lodge, Holiday Inn Express, Quality Inn
	Other	W: CVS, Dollar Tree, Grocery, Staples
(11)		**Truck Scales (SB)**
10		**PA 914, Marion**
(7)		**Truck Scales (NB)**
5		**PA 16, Buchanan Tr, Greencastle, Waynesboro**
	FStop	E: Greencastle Food Mart/Sunoco
	TStop	E: Travel Center of America #213/BP
	Gas	W: Exxon◈
	Food	E: Buckhorn/TA TC, Arby's, McDonald's, Subway W: Hardee's, Rest/Greencastle Motel
	Lodg	E: RodewayInn/TA TC, Econo Lodge♥ W: Castle Green Motel
	TServ	E: TA TC/Tires
	Med	W: + John L Grove Medical Center
	Other	E: Laundry/CB/WiFi/TA TC, **to** White Tail Ski Resort
3		**US 11, Molly Pitcher Hwy**
	Gas	E: Molly Pitcher Mini Mart/Exxon
	Food	E: Rest/Pizza
	Lodg	E: Comfort Inn
(1)		**PA Welcome Center (NB) (RR, Phones, Picnic, Vend, Info)**
1		**PA 163, Mason-Dixon Rd**
	Food	W: Mason-Dixon Rest
	Lodg	W: Best Value Inn, Knights Inn♥, State Line Motel
	Other	E: Washington Co Reg'l Airport✈ **W: Keystone RV Center**

⬆ PENNSYLVANIA
⬇ MARYLAND

NOTE: MM 12: Pennsylvania State Line

EASTERN TIME ZONE

EXIT		
10AB		**Showalter Rd, to US 11, Hagerstown, Maugansville**
9		**Maugans Ave, Maugansville, Hagerstown (NB)**
	Gas	E: Sheetz, Shell
	Food	E: McDonald's, Taco Bell, Waffle House W: Burger King
	Lodg	E: Hampton Inn W: Microtel

West Virginia
S-25
23
20
16
14
13
12
8
5
N-2
323
321
S-320
Winchester
317
315
313 Thru 302
300
66
298
296
291
283
Woodstock
81
279 Thru 277
273
269 Thru 264
N-262
257
251
247
245
Virginia
243
240
235
227
225
64
Stauton
222
221
220
81 64
217
213
205
200
195
S-195
191
Lexington
188
64
180
175
168
81
167
162
156
150
Virginia
146
143
Roanoke

EXIT		MD / WV
	TServ	W: Martin WhiteGMC, Mack Trucks
	Other	E: Washington Co Reg'l Airport✈
8		**Maugansville Rd (SB exit, NB reacc)**
7AB		**PA 58, Cearfoss Pike, to US 11, to US 40, Hagerstown**
6AB		**US 40, E to Hagerstown, W to Huyett**
	Gas	E: Exxon◈, Shell
	Food	E: Golden Crown Chinese, Perkins, Steak-Out, Wendy's W: Arby's, IHOP, KFC, McDonald's, Ryan's Grill, Subway, TGI Friday
	Lodg	E: Comfort Suites, Days Inn, Holiday Motel, Quality Inn, Super 8
	Med	E: + Hospital
	Other	W: ATMs, Grocery, Home Depot, **Walmart sc**
5B		**Halfway Blvd N, tHagerstown (NB)**
5A		**Halfway Blvd S, Hagerstown (SB)**
5		**Halfway Blvd, to US 11, Hagerstown**
	TStop	E: Pilot Travel Center #179 (Scales) W: AC&T Fuel Center (Scales)
	Gas	E: Sheetz, Shell W: Exxon
	Food	E: McDonald's/Subway/Pilot TC, Burger King, CiCi's Pizza, Chinatown, Crazy Horse Steakhouse, Golden Corral, McDonald's, Olive Garden, Outback Steakhouse, Pizza Hut, Red Lobster, Shoney's, Western Sizzlin W: Rest/AC&T FC
	Lodg	E: Country Inn, Holiday Inn Express, Motel 6♥, Plaza Hotel W: AC&T FC, Super 8
	TServ	E: Massey Ford Trucks W: AC&T FC/Tires, C Earl Brown Freightliner
	Other	E: Laundry/WiFi/Pilot TC, ATMs, Auto Services, Auto Dealers, CVS, Firestone, Grocery, Lowe's, Office Depot, PetCo♥, Sam's Club, Staples, Target, Valley Mall W: Laundry/WiFi/**RVDump**/AC&T FC
(4)		**I-70E, to Frederick, Washington, Baltimore, I-70W, to Hancock, to I-68, Cumberland**
2		**US 11, Williamsport**
	FStop	W: Williamsport Sunoco
	Gas	E: Chevron W: Exxon, Shell
	Food	W: McDonald's, Waffle House
	Lodg	W: Red Roof Inn♥
	Other	**E: Woodman of the World Campground▲** **W: Hagerstown / Antietam Battlefield KOA▲**
1		**MD 63, MD 68, Williamsport**
	Gas	W: Citgo
	Lodg	W: State Line Motel
	Other	**E: Yogi Bear's Jellystone Park CG▲**

⬆ MARYLAND
⬇ WEST VIRGINIA

NOTE: MM 26: Maryland State Line

EASTERN TIME ZONE

(25)		**WV Welcome Center (SB) (RR, Phone, Picnic, Info)**

◈ = Regular Gas Stations with Diesel ▲ = RV Friendly Locations ♥ = Pet Friendly Locations

Red print shows large vehicle parking / access on site or nearby Brown Print = Campgrounds / RV PARKS

EXIT	WV / VA
23	**US 11, Marlowe, Falling Waters**
Gas	W: 7-11, Shell
Other	E: Falling Waters Campground▲ W: RV Center
20	**WV 901, Spring Mills Rd, Martinsburg**
Gas	W: Shell◈
Lodg	E: Econo Lodge W: Holiday Inn Express
(19)	**Turn Out (SB)**
16	**WV 9E, N Queen St, Shepherdstown, WV 9W, Berkeley Springs**
Gas	E: Citgo, Exxon◈, Sheetz W: Shell◈
Food	E: China King, Denny's, Hoss's Steak & Sea House, KFC, Long John Silver, McDonald's, Waffle House
Lodg	E: Comfort Inn, Knight's Inn, Super 8, Travelodge
Med	W: + Hospital
14	**CR 13, Dry Run Rd, Tennessee Ave, Martinsburg**
13	**CR 15, King St, Downtown**
Gas	E: BP◈, Sheetz
Food	E: Applebee's, Burger King, Cracker Barrel, Kobe Japanese, Outback Steak house, Pizza Hut, Shoney's, Wendy's
Lodg	E: Hampton Inn, Holiday Inn, Relax Inn, Scottish Inn
Med	E: + Hospital
Other	E: Amtrak, Tanger Outlet Mall, Walmart sc,
12	**WV 45, Winchester Ave**
Gas	E: Citgo◈, Sheetz, Shell◈
Food	E: Arby's, Bob Evans, ChickFilA, Hardee's, McDonald's, Papa John's, Ryan's Grill, Ruby Tuesday, Taco Bell, Waffle House, Wendy's
Lodg	E: Comfort Suites, Economy Inn, Relax Inn, Scottish Inn
Med	E: + VA Medical Center
Other	E: ATMs, Auto Zone, Auto Services, Grocery, Lowe's, Mall
8	**CR 32, Tablers Station Rd, Inwood**
Other	E: to Eastern WV Reg'l Airport✈
5	**WV 51, Inwood, Charlestown**
Gas	E: 7-11, Exxon, Sheetz, Shell◈
Food	E: Burger King, McDonald's, Pizza Hut, Subway, Waffle House
Lodg	E: Hampton Inn
Other	E: ATMs, Food Lion W: to Lazy A Campground▲
(2)	**WV Welcome Center (NB)** (RR, Phone, Picnic, Vend, Info)

EASTERN TIME ZONE

⬆ WEST VIRGINIA
⬇ VIRGINIA

NOTE: MM 324: West Virginia State Line

EASTERN TIME ZONE

EXIT	VIRGINIA
323	**VA 669, US 11, Clear Brook, Whitehall, Winchester**
TStop	W: Flying J Travel Plaza #5073(Scales)
Gas	E: Exxon
Food	W: CountryMarket/FastFood/FJ TP
Other	W: Laundry/BarbSh/WiFi/RVDump/LP/ FJ TP
321	**VA 672, to US 11, Hopewell Rd, Brucetown Rd, Clearbrook**
FStop	E: Old Stone Truck Stop/Citgo
Food	E: Old Stone Rest
(320)	**VA Welcome Center (SB)** (RR, Phones, Picnic, Vend, Info)
317	**US 11, VA 37, Martinsburg Pike, Winchester, Stephenson**
Gas	W: Citgo, Exxon◈, Liberty◈, Sheetz◈
Food	W: Burger King, Denny's, McDonald's
Lodg	W: Comfort Inn♥, Courtyard, Econo Lodge♥, Holiday Inn Express
Med	W: + Hospital
Other	E: Mountain Lake Campground▲ W: Various Museums, to appr 3mi Candy Hill Campground▲, appr 12mi The Cove Campground▲
315	**VA 7, Berryville Pike, Winchester, to Berryville**
Gas	E: Exxon, Sheetz W: Chevron◈, Exxon, Liberty◈, Shell◈
Food	E: 220 Seafood Rest, Quiznos, Starbucks W: Arby's, Burrough's Steak & Seafood, Captain D's, Hardee's, Little Caesar's, McDonald's, Shoney's, Subway, Wendy's
Lodg	W: Hampton Inn, Shoney's Inn
Med	W: + Winchester Hospital
Other	E: Veramar Vineyard, to appr 9.5mi Watermelon Park▲ W: ATMs, Auto Zone, Food Lion, CVS, Greyhound
313AB	**US 17, US 50, US 522, Winchester**
313	**US 17, US 50, US 522, Winchester**
Gas	E: BP◈, Exxon, Shell◈ W: Sheetz
Food	E: Cracker Barrel, Golden Corral, Hoss's Steak & Sea House, Hardee's, IHOP, Texas Roadhouse, Waffle House W: Bob Evans, Buffalo Wild Wings, Chili's, CiCi's Pizza, KFC, McDonald's, Olive Garden, Perkins, Ruby Tuesday, Subway, Wendy's, Rest/Qual Inn
Lodg	E: Comfort Inn, Fairfield Inn, Holiday Inn♥, Red Roof Inn♥, Sleep Inn, Super 8, Travelodge♥ W: Best Western, Hampton Inn, Holiday Inn Express, Quality Inn, Wingate Inn
Med	W: + Winchester Medical Center
Other	E: ATMs, Big Lots, Food Lion, Costco, Apple Blossom Mall, Winchester Harley Davidson, to Winchester Reg'l Airport✈ W: ATM, Apple Blossom Mall, Borders, Grocery, Home Depot, Kroger, Lowe's, Office Max, Pharmacy, Staples, Target, UPS Store, Walmart sc, Shenandoah Univ, The Log Cabin Campground▲
310	**VA 37, to US 11, to US 50W, to US 522, Winchester**
Food	W: Dragon Garden, McDonald's, Outback Steakhouse
Lodg	W: to Best Value Inn, to Country Inn, Echo Village Budget Motel, Days Inn, Relax Inn, Royal Inn
Med	W: + Hospital
Other	W: ATM, Auto Services, CarQuest, to appr 6 mi Candy Hill Campground▲
307	**VA 277, Fairfax St, Fairfax Pike, Stephens City, Greenway Court**
TStop	W: to 5116 Main St: High Point Truck Stop
Gas	E: 7-11, Chevron, Shell W: Exxon, Sheetz
Food	E: Arby's, Burger King, KFC/Taco Bell, McDonald's, Roma's Italian Rest, Subway, Waffle House, Wendy's, Western Steer W: Dunkin Donuts, High Point Rest
Lodg	E: Comfort Inn♥, Holiday Inn Express
Other	E: ATMs, Banks, Advance Auto Parts, Dollar General, Food Lion, Miller Hardware, RiteAid, Walgreen's, Stephens City Animal Hospital♥ W: ATMs, Laundromat
(304)	**Weigh Station (Both dir)**
302	**Reliance Rd, VA 627, Middletown**
Gas	E: Exxon◈ W: 7-11, Liberty◈
Food	W: Rest/Wayside Inn
Lodg	W: Super 8♥, Wayside Inn
Other	W: Rte 11 Potato Chip Factory, Battle of Cedar Creek CG▲, Camping World
(300)	**Jct I-66E, to Washington, DC, Skyline Dr, Shenandoah Natl Park (SB, Left Exit)**
298	**US 11, Strasburg**
Gas	E: BP◈, Exxon◈, Shell
Food	E: Arby's, Burger King, Denny's, McDonald's
Lodg	E: Fairfield Inn, Hotel Strausburg, Ramada Inn
Other	E: ATM, Family Dollar, Grocery, RiteAid, Battle of Cedar Creek Campground▲
296	**VA 55, US 48, John Marshall Hwy, Strasburg**
291	**VA 651, Mt Olive Rd, Toms Brook**
TStop	W: Love's Travel Stop #305 (Scales), WilcoHess Travel Plaza #705 (Scales)
Food	W: Arby's/TJCinn/Love's TP, Milestone Rest/DQ/WH TP
Lodg	E: Budget Inn
TWash	W: WilcoHess TP
TServ	W: Love's TP/Tires
Other	W: WiFi/Love's TP
283	**VA 42, Reservoir Rd, Woodstock**
Gas	E: BP, Chevron, Liberty, Shell W: Exxon◈, Sunoco
Food	E: Arby's, Dunkin Donuts, Hardee's, KFC, Joe's Steakhouse, McDonald's, Pizza Hut, Ponderosa, Taco Bell, Wendy's W: Cracker Barrel, Subway
Lodg	E: Budget Host Inn♥, Comfort Inn♥, Hampton Inn, Holiday Inn Express
Med	E: + Hospital
Other	E: RiteAid, Massanutten Military Academy W: ATMs, Dollar Tree, Lowe's, Walmart sc
279	**VA 185, Stoney Creek Blvd, to US 11, Edinburg**
Gas	E: BP◈, Exxon◈, Shell◈
Food	E: Edinburg Mill Rest, Subway
Other	E: Creekside Campground▲, to appr 11mi Luray Country Waye RV Resort▲, Fort Valley Horse & Mule Campgr▲
277	**VA 614, Bowmans Crossing**
273	**VA 292, VA 703, Mt Jackson**
TStop	E: Shenandoah Truck Center/Liberty (Scales), Sheetz Travel Center #701 (Scales)
Gas	E: 7-11, Exxon◈

◈= Regular Gas Stations with Diesel ▲ = RV Friendly Locations ♥ = Pet Friendly Locations
Red print shows large vehicle parking / access on site or nearby Brown Print = Campgrounds / RV PARKS

EXIT		VIRGINIA
	Food	E: Blimpie's/Liberty TC, Wendy's/Sheetz TC Burger King, China King, Denny's
	Lodg	E: Best Western, Shenandoah Valley Inn
	Other	E: Laundry/WiFi/LP/Shenandoah TC, Laundry/Sheetz TC, Food Lion, US Post Office, to Ski Area
269		**VA 730, Caverns Rd, to US 11, Mt Jackson, Shenandoah Caverns**
	Gas	E: Chevron◈
264		**US 211, New Market, Timberville, Luray**
	Gas	E: BP◈, Chevron◈, Exxon◈, Shell◈ W: 7-11
	Food	E: Burger King, McDonald's, Pizza Hut, Southern Kitchen, Taco Bell
	Lodg	E: Budget Inn♥, Quality Inn W: Days Inn♥
	Other	E: to Shenandoah Nat'l Park
(262)		**New Market Rest Area (Both dir) (RR, Phones, Picnic, Vend, Info)**
257		**US 11, Lee Jackson Memorial Hwy, to VA 259, N Valley Pike, Broadway**
	Gas	E: Liberty
	Food	E: BK/Godfathers/Liberty
	Other	E: Harrisonburg/New Market KOA▲, Endless Caverns & RV Resort▲
251		**US 11, N Valley Pike, Harrisonburg**
	Gas	W: Exxon◈
	Lodg	W: Economy Inn
247B		**US 33W, to US 11, Harrisonburg**
247A		**US 33E, Harrisonburg**
247		**US 33, E Market St, Harrisonburg**
	Gas	E: BP◈, Royal, Shell W: Exxon◈, Sheetz, Texaco
	Food	E: Applebee's, Bob Evans, Captain D's, Chili's, CiCi's, Golden Corral, IHOP, Long John Silver, O'Charley's, Outback Steak house, Ponderosa, Red Lobster, Ruby Tuesday, Shoney's, Starbucks, Taco Bell, Texas Steakhouse, Waffle House, Wendy's W: Arby's, Golden China, Hardee's, KFC, Kyoto, McDonald's, Pizza Hut, Subway
	Lodg	E: Best Western, Candlewood Suites, Comfort Inn, Courtyard, Econo Lodge, Hampton Inn, Holiday Inn, Jameson Inn♥, Motel 6♥, Shoney's Inn, Sleep Inn
	Med	W: + Hospital
	Other	E: ATMs, Auto Services, B&N, Banks, Costco, Firestone, Food Lion, Home Depot, Kroger, Lowe's, Office Depot, PetSmart♥, PetCo♥, Staples, Target, UPS Store, Walmart sc, Valley Mall W: ATMs, Advance Auto Parts, CVS, Food Lion, James Madison Univ, Memorial Stadium
245		**VA 659, Port Republic Rd, to US 11, Harrisonburg**
	Gas	E: Exxon◈, Liberty◈, Texaco
	Food	E: Blimpie/Liberty, Subway/Exxon, China Express, Little Caesar's, McDonald's W: Starbucks
	Lodg	E: Days Inn♥, Howard Johnson
	Med	W: + Hospital
	Other	W: FedEx Office, James Madison Univ
243		**US 11, S Main St, Harrisonburg**
	TStop	W: Harrisonburg Travel Center (Scales)
	Gas	W: 7-11, Exxon◈, Liberty
	Food	W: Rest/Harrisonburg TC, Burger King, Cracker Barrel, McDonald's, Pizza Hut,

EXIT		VIRGINIA
	Food	W: Taco Bell, Waffle House
	Lodg	E: Country Inn, W: Holiday Inn Express♥, Ramada Inn♥, Red Carpet Inn♥, Super 8♥
	TWash	W: Harrisonburg TC
	TServ	W: Mack, Kenworth, ThermoKing, Trailers, Southside Auto Truck & RV Service
	Other	W: Laundry/WiFi/Harrisonburg TC,
240		**VA 257, VA 682, Mt Crawford**
	Gas	W: Exxon◈
	Food	W: Burger King, Country Buffet, Village Inn
	Other	W: Bridgewater Air Park✈, Vet♥, to appr 10 mi Natural Chimneys Campground▲
235		**VA 256, US 11, Weyers Cave Rd, Weyers Cave, Grottoes**
	FStop	W: Deno's Food Mart #10/BP
	Gas	E: Shell◈ W: Exxon
	Food	E: Subway
	TServ	W: Freightliner
	Other	E: Grand Caverns, Shenandoah Valley Reg'l Airport✈
(232)		**Mt Sydney Rest Area (NB) (RR, Phones, Picnic, Vend, Info)**
227		**VA 612, Laurel Hill Rd, Verona**
	FStop	E: BP
	Gas	W: Citgo◈, Exxon, Shell◈
	Food	E: Waffle Inn W: Arby's, Burger King, Chili's, Hardee's, McDonald's, Wendy's
	Lodg	W: Knights Inn
	TServ	E: Interstate Auto & Truck Repair
	Other	E: Food Lion, to Waynesboro North 340 Campground▲ W: CVS, RiteAid, Carwash/Shell, Food Lion, to Staunton/Verona KOA▲
225		**VA 275, Woodrow Wilson Pkwy, VA 262, Staunton, Waynesboro**
	Food	E: Rest/Q I W: Rest/H I
	Lodg	E: Quality Inn W: Days Inn, Holiday Inn♥
222		**US 250, Jefferson Hwy, Staunton, Fisherville**
	Gas	E: Citgo, Exxon, Texaco W: Sheetz, Wilco #741◈
	Food	E: Cracker Barrel, McDonald's, Shoney's, Texas Steakhouse, Wendy's W: Burger King, Chili's, Ryan's Grill, Waffle House
	Lodg	E: Best Western♥, Guesthouse Inn, Sleep Inn♥, Shoney's Inn W: Comfort Inn, Econo Lodge, Microtel, Super 8♥
	Other	W: ATMS, Auto Zone, Amtrak, Lowe's, Walmart sc, VA State Hwy Patrol Post,
	NOTE:	**I-81 below runs with I-64. Exit #'s follow I-81.**
(221/ 87)		**Jct I-64E, Skyline Dr, Shenandoah Nat'l Park, to Charlottesville, Richmond, Blue Ridge Pkwy**
220		**VA 262, to US 11, Staunton**
	Gas	W: BP, Citgo, Exxon, Shell
	Food	W: Arby's, Burger King, Hardee's, KFC, McDonald's, Red Lobster
	Lodg	W: Budget Inn, Hampton Inn, Microtel
	Other	W: Shenandoah Harley Davidson, RV Center

EXIT		VIRGINIA
217		**VA 654, White Hill Rd, Staunton, Stuarts Draft, Mint Spring**
	FStop	W: Kangaroo Express/Citgo
	Gas	E: BP◈, Exxon◈ W: Liberty
	Food	E: Subway/BP W: Aunt M's/Kangaroo
	Lodg	E: Days Inn♥ W: Relax Inn♥
	Other	E: to appr 8mi Shenandoah Acres Resort W: appr 4mi Walnut Hills Campground & RV Park▲
213B		**US 11W, VA 340, Greenville (SB)**
213A		**US 11E, VA 340, Greenville (SB)**
213		**US 11, Staunton, Greenville**
	TStop	E: Pilot Travel Center #396 (Scales)
	Gas	E: BP, Shell
	Food	E: Arby's/TJCinn/Pilot TC, Subway/BP, German Rest
	Lodg	E: Budget Host Inn♥
	Other	E: Laundry/WiFi/Pilot TC, to Walnut Hills Campground & RV Park▲
205		**VA 606, Raphine Rd, Raphine, Steeles Tavern, Vesuvius**
	TStop	E: AmBest/RoadysTS/White's Truck Stop (Scales), Orchard Creek Auto & RV Plaza/Exxon, Smiley's Fuel City W: WilcoHess Travel Plaza #735 (Scales)
	Food	E: Rest/Subway/Starbucks/White's TS, BurgerKing/Orchard Plaza W: Wendy's/WH TP, Rest/D I
	Lodg	E: Whites Motel♥/White's TS W: Days Inn
	TWash	E: White's TS
	TServ	E: White's TS/Tires W: Peterbilt
	Other	E: Laundry/CB/WiFi/White's TS, to Crabtree Falls Campground▲, Tye River Gap Campground▲ W: RV Center
200		**VA 710, Sterrett Rd, Fairfield**
	FStop	W: Stop In Food Store #62/Shell, Fairfield Exxon
	Gas	E: BP◈, Texaco
	Food	E: Fairfield Diner, McDonald's/BP W: Subway/Exxon, Whistlestop Cafe
	TServ	W: Smith's Garage
198		**New Exit**
(195)		**Fairfield Rest Area (SB) (RR, Phones, Picnic, Vend, Info)**
195		**US 11, Lee Hwy, Lexington**
	TStop	W: PTP/Lee-Hi Travel Plaza/Shell (Scales)
	Gas	W: Citgo◈
	Food	E: Rest/Maple Hall Country Inn W: Berky's Rest/Lee Hi TP, Aunt Sarah's Pancake House
	Lodg	E: Maple Hall Country Inn, Lexington Historic Inn W: Days Inn, Howard Johnson♥, Ramada Inn
	TServ	W: Lee-Hi TP/Tires/VA Truck Center
	Other	W: Laundry/BarbSh/WiFi/LP/Lee Hi TP/ Campground▲, Auto Repair
(191/ 56)		**Jct I-64W, to Charleston (fr NB, Left Exit)**
	NOTE:	**I-81 above runs with I-64. Exit #'s follow I-81.**
188B		**US 60W, to Lexington**

◈ = Regular Gas Stations with Diesel ▲ = RV Friendly Locations ♥ = Pet Friendly Locations
Red print shows large vehicle parking / access on site or nearby Brown Print = Campgrounds / RV PARKS

EXIT — VIRGINIA

188A **US 60E, to Buena Vista**

188 **US 60, E-Buena Vista, W-Lexington (Serv 3-5mi E)**
Gas E: Exxon
W: Exxon
Food E: Hardee's, KFC, Long John Silver, Taco Bell, McDonald's, Pizza Hut, Wendy's
Lodg E: Budget Inn, Comfort Inn, Days Inn
W: Days Inn, Hampton Inn, Holiday Inn
Other E: to Stonewall Jackson Home, Museum
W: Auto Dealers, to VA Military Institute, Washington & Lee Univ

180 **US 11, S Lee Hwy, Natural Bridge Glasglow (fr SB, Left Exit)**
Gas E: Shell◊
W: Shell◊
Food E: Fancy Hill Rest
W: Pink Cadillac Diner
Lodg E: Relax Inn, Red Carpet Inn
W: Budget Inn
Other W: to **Natural Bridge/Lexington KOA▲**

175 **US 11, Natural Bridge, Glasgow**
Gas E: Exxon
Other E: to Natural Bridge Hotel, Attractions
W: **Yogi Bear's Jellystone Park Resort▲**, Speedway, Zoo, Museum

168 **VA 614, Arcadia Rd, Buchanan**
Gas E: Shell
Food E: Burger King, Rest/Wattstull Motel
Lodg E: Wattstull Motel
Other E: to appr 6mi **Middle Creek CG▲**

167 **US 11, Buchanan (SB)**

162 **US 11, Lee Hwy N, Buchanan**
FStop W: Texaco
Gas E: Exxon◊
Food W: Subway/Texaco

(158) **Troutville Rest Area (SB)**
(RR, Phones, Picnic, Vend, Info)

156 **Brughs Mill Rd, VA640, to US 11, to US 220, Fincastle, Troutville**
Gas E: Exxon◊

150B **US 220N, Daleville**

150A **US 220S, to 460E, Cloverdale**

150 **US 220, Roanoke Rd, Lee Hwy, Troutville, Roanoke, Cloverdale**
FStop E: Kangaroo Express/Citgo
TStop E: Travel Center of America #21/BP(Scales), Pilot Travel Center #258 (Scales)
Gas W: BP◊, Exxon◊
Food E: CountryPride/TA TC, Subway/Pilot TC, Burger King, Cracker Barrel, Hardee's, McDonald's, Shoney's, Taco Bell, Waffle House, Wendy's
W: Bojangles, Pizza Hut
Lodg E: Days Inn/TA TC, Comfort Inn♥, Holiday Inn Express, Quality Inn, Red Roof Inn♥, Travelodge
W: Econo Lodge, Howard Johnson♥, Super 8
TWash E: Truckwash
TServ E: TA TC/Tires, Carter Power Systems, Montvale Truck Service VA Truck Center/GMC
Other E: Laundry/WiFi/TA TC, WiFi/Pilot TC, CVS, 84 Lumber, Winn Dixie, **Berglund RV Center**, **McFarland RV Park▲**

(149) **Weigh Station (Both dir)**

EXIT — VIRGINIA

146 **VA 115, Plantation Rd, Roanoke, to Hollins, Cloverdale**
Gas E: Exxon, Shell◊
Food E: Burger King, Hardee's, Harbor Inn Seafood, McDonald's, Subway
Lodg E: Country Inn, Fairfield Inn, Hampton Inn, Knights Inn
W: Days Inn
Other E: Hollins Univ

(143) **Jct I-581, US 220, Roanoke (fr SB, Left Exit) (Serv at 1st 2 exits) (Addt'l Services on Hershberger Rd)**
Gas E: BP, Exxon, Shell
Food E: Chinese, Mex Rest, Pizza, Waffle House
Lodg E: Hampton Inn, Holiday Inn, Knights Inn, Quality Inn, Ramada Inn, Super 8
TServ E: Highway Motors, Wood's Fleet & Truck Service
Other E: ATMs, Staples, Target, **Walmart sc**, Mall, Harley Davidson, Roanoke Reg'l Airport✈

141 **VA 419, N Electric Rd, to VA 31, Roanoke, to Salem**
Gas E: BP, Liberty, Texaco
W: BP◊, Citgo
Food E: Burger King, Hardee's, McDonald's
W: Fuddrucker's
Lodg E: Baymont Inn, Holiday Inn Express, La Quinta Inn, Quality Inn
Med E: + Hospital

140 **VA 311, Thompson Memorial Dr, Salem, Newcastle**
Other S: to Roanoke College

137 **VA 112, Wildwood Rd, Salem**
Gas E: BP, Exxon, GoMart, Sheetz, Shell◊
Food E: Applebee's, Arby's, Burger King, Denny's, Hardee's, KFC, Long John Silver, McDonald's, Omelette Shoppe, Shoney's, Starbucks, Taco Bell, Wendy's
Lodg E: Comfort Inn, Econo Lodge♥, Knights Inn, Super 8
W: Best Value Inn, Holiday Inn, Howard Johnson Express♥
Other E: ATMs, Auto Zone, Big Lots, Dollar Tree, Food Lion, Goodyear, Kroger, Lowe's, O'Reilly Auto Parts, **Snyder's RV**, Verizon, Walgreen's, **Walmart sc**,
W: Havens State Game Refuge

132 **VA 647, Dow Hollow Rd, to US 11, US 460, Salem, Dixie Cavern**
Gas E: Citgo, Shell
Lodg E: Budget Host Inn
Other E: Dixie Caverns & Pottery Shop/ **CG▲**, VA State Hwy Patrol Post

(129) **Ironto Rest Area (NB)**
(RR, Phones, Picnic, Vend, Info)

128 **US 11, VA 603, N Fork Rd, Elliston**
TStop W: Stop In Food Store #144/Exxon
Gas E: Shell
Food W: Subway/Stop In FS

118ABC **US 11, US 460, Christiansburg, Blacksburg**
FStop E: RoadysTS/Stop In Food Store #40/Shell (118C)
W: Charlie's Market/Crown
Gas W: BP, Exxon, RaceWay, Shell
Food E: Denny's, Cracker Barrel
W: McDonald's, Hardee's, Pizza Hut, Ruby Tuesday, Shoney's, Waffle House, Wendy's, Western Sizzlin

EXIT — VIRGINIA

Lodg E: Days Inn♥, Fairfield Inn, Holiday Inn, Quality Inn♥, Super 8♥ (118C)
W: Econo Lodge♥, Howard Johnson, Rodeway Inn♥ (118C)
Med W: + Hospital
Other E: **Interstate Overnight Park▲** (118C)
W: Auto Dealers, ATMs, Banks, Advance Auto, U-Haul, 84 Lumber, to VA Tech, to **New River Junction Campground▲**

114 **VA 8, W Main St, Christiansburg**
Gas W: Citgo
Food W: Burger King, Hardee's
Lodg W: Budget Inn

109 **VA 177, Tyler Rd, VA 600, Radford**
TStop W: Radford Travel Center/BP
Lodg W: appr 4 mi Best Western♥, Comfort Inn La Quinta Inn♥, Super 8♥
Med W: + Hospital

(108) **Radford Rest Area (Both dir)**
(RR, Phones, Picnic, Vend, Info)

105 **VA 232, VA 605, 1st St, Quarry Rd, Little River Rd, Radford**
Gas E: Marathon
Other E: **Sportsman Campground▲**

101 **VA 660, State Park Rd, Dublin**
TStop W: RoadysTS/Stop In Truck Stop/ Shell #142 (Scales)
Gas W: Kangaroo/Marathon◊
Food W: Omelette Shop/Taco Bell/StopIn, DQ
Lodg E: Claytor Lake Inn, Sleep Inn
TServ W: StopIn TP/Tires
Other E: to **Claytor Lake State Park**
W: Laundry/Stopin TS, Radford Army Ammunition Plant

98 **VA 100N, Cleburne Blvd, Dublin**
TStop W: Liberty #120 Truck Stop
Gas E: Exxon◊
W: Marathon
Food E: Subway/Exxon, Shoney's
W: Arby's, Burger King, Fatz Cafe, McDonald's, Waffle House, Wendy's
Lodg E: Comfort Inn♥, Hampton Inn, Holiday Inn Express
W: Super 8, Travel Inn
Med W: + Pulaski Comm Hospital
Other W: Dollar General, Museum, Visitor Info, Vet♥, **Walmart sc**, Hwy Patrol, to New River Valley Airport✈, County Fairgrounds

94AB **VA 99N, Pulaski (NB)**

94 **VA 99, Old Rte 100, Pulaski**
Gas E: BP
W: Exxon, Hess
Food W: Hardee's, Kimono, KFC, McDonald's
Lodg E: Days Inn♥
Med W: + Pulaski Comm Hospital

92 **Service Rd, VA 658, Draper**

89AB **VA 100, Wysor Rd, to Hillsville, US 11, Lee Hwy, to Pulaski**
Other E: to appr 14mi **Lake Ridge RV Resort Family CG▲**, **Camp Jellystone▲**

86 **VA 618, Service Rd, Max Meadows**
TStop W: PTP/I-81 Travel Plaza
Food W: AppletreeRest/I-81 TP
Lodg W: Motel/I-81 TP
TServ W: I-81 TP/Tires
Other W: Laundry/I-81 TP

84 **VA 619, VA 618, Major Grahams Rd, to Grahams Forge, Wytheville**
TStop W: Love's Travel Stop # 239 (Scales), Kangaroo Express

◊= Regular Gas Stations with Diesel ▲ = RV Friendly Locations ♥= Pet Friendly Locations
Red print shows large vehicle parking / access on site or nearby **Brown Print = Campgrounds / RV PARKS**

EXIT — VIRGINIA

Food — W: Chesters/Subway/Love's TS
Lodg — W: Fox Mountain Inn & Rest, Gateway Motel
Other — W: WiFi/**RVDump**/Love's TS

NOTE: I-81 below runs with I-77. Exit #'s follow I-81.

(81/32) **Jct I-77S, to Charlotte**
Jct I-81N, US 11, to Roanoke

80 **US 52S, VA 121N, Ft Chiswell Rd, Fort Chiswell, Max Meadows**
FStop — W: Kangaroo Express/Citgo
TStop — E: Flying J Travel Plaza #1123 (Scales)
Gas — E: BP◈
W: BP
Food — E: Cookery/Wendy's/FlJ TP, Burger King/BP, Pappy's Ital Amer Rest, Wendy's
W: McDonald's
Lodg — E: Hampton Inn, Super 8
W: Comfort Inn
TWash — E: Blue Beacon TW/FJ TP
TServ — E: FJ TP/Tires
W: Speedco, K&C Chrome Shop
Other — E: Laundry/WiFi/**LP**/FJ TP, Ft Chiswell Outlet Mall, **Fort Chiswell RV Park▲**
W: Little Valley RV Center

77 **Service Rd, Chapman Rd, Lee Hwy, Wytheville**
FStop — E: WilcoHess C Store #605
TStop — E: Kangaroo Express/Citgo, Flying J Travel Plaza #5420 (Scales)
W: WilcoHess Travel Plaza #606 (Scales)
Food — E: Subway/Kangaroo Express, Cookery/FastFood/FJ TP, Burger King
W: Arby's/WH TP
TWash — W: TruckOMat, WilcoHess TP
Other — E: Laundry/BarbSh/WiFi/**RVDump**/**LP**/FJ
W: Laundry/WH TP, **VA State Hwy Patrol Post**, **Wytheville KOA▲**

73 **US 11S, Wytheville**
Gas — E: BP, Citgo, Kangaroo, Mobil, Shell
Food — E: Applebee's, Bob Evans, Burger King, **Cracker Barrel**, DQ, Great Wall Chinese, Hardee's, KFC, Pizza Hut, Ocean Bay Seafood, Shoney's, Waffle House
Lodg — E: Budget Host Inn, Days Inn, Econo Lodge, Holiday Inn, La Quinta Inn♥, Motel 6♥, Quality Inn, Red Carpet Inn, Red Roof Inn, Super 8, Travelodge
Other — E: ATMs, CVS, Grocery, K-Mart, Harley Davidson Wytheville

(72/40) **Jct I-77N, to Bluefield**
Jct I-81S, to Bristol, US 52
(Serv at 1st exit on I-77N, #41)

NOTE: I-81 above runs with I-77. Exit #'s follow I-81.

70 **US 21, US 52, Wytheville**
Gas — E: BP◈, Exxon
W: Citgo, Exxon, Kangaroo
Food — E: Arby's, McDonald's, Subway, Wendy's
W: Long John Silver, Pizza Hut, Ruby Tuesday, Scrooge's
Lodg — W: Comfort Inn, Econo Lodge
Med — E: + Hospital
Other — E: CVS, Food Lion, Lowe's, **Walmart sc**

67 **US 11, W Lee Hwy, Wytheville**
(NB exit, SB Reaccess)

(61) **Rural Retreat Rest Area (NB)**
(NO Trucks) (RR, Phone, Picnic, Vend)

EXIT — VIRGINIA

60 **VA 90, Rural Retreat**
Gas — E: Chevron◈, Sunoco
Food — E: McDonald's, Subway, Pizza Plus, Tuscan Italian Grill
Other — E: to appr 3.5mi **Rural Retreat Lake Park▲**, **Mount Rogers Nat'l Rec Area▲**

54 **VA 683, to US 11, Rural Retreat, Atkins, Groseclose, Marion**
TStop — E: Village Truck Stop/Shell
Gas — E: Exxon
Food — E: DQ/Exxon
Lodg — E: Relax Inn
Other — E: Mountain Empire Airport✈

(53) **Smyth Rest Area (SB)**
(RR, Phones, Picnic, Vend, Info)

50 **VA 622, US 11, Nicks Creek Rd, Atkins, Marion**
Gas — W: Citgo◈, Exxon
Food — W: Atkins Diner, Subway
Lodg — W: Comfort Inn

47 **US 11, N Main St, Marion**
Gas — W: BP, Chevron, Exxon◈
Food — W: Arby's, Burger King, McDonald's, Family Rest, Little Caesar's, Sonic
Lodg — W: Best Western, Comfort Inn, Econo Lodge, Rodeway Inn
Med — W: + Hospital
Other — W: ATMs, Auto Services, Auto Zone, Auto Dealers, Kmart, RiteAid, **Walmart**, to **Hungry Mother State Park▲**

45 **VA 16, S Commerce St, Marion**
Gas — E: BP, Exxon, Valero
Food — E: Appletree Rest, Hardee's, KFC
Other — E: **Mount Rogers National Rec Area**, **Houndshell Campground▲**, **Grayson Highlands State Park**

44 **Washington Ave, US 11, Marion Service Rd (SB exit, NB reaccess)**
Service Rd, US 11, Lee Hwy, Marion (NB, SB reaccess)
Gas — W: Marathon

39 **US 11, VA 645, Ridgefield Rd**
Food — E: Rest/Budget Inn
Lodg — E: Budget Inn
Other — W: **Interstate Campground▲**

35 **VA 107, White Top Ave, Chilhowie**
Gas — E: Citgo, Shell
W: Chevron, Exxon◈, Food City
Food — W: McDonald's, Subway
Lodg — E: Knights Inn
Other — E: to **Mount Rogers National Rec Area▲**, **Grindstone Campground▲**
W: Food City, Pharmacy

32 **US 11, Lee Hwy, Chilhowie**

29 **VA 91, Maple St, Glade Spring**
TStop — E: Petro Stopping Center #72 (Scales)
Gas — E: Shell◈, Valero
W: Chevron◈, Coastal, Exxon
Food — E: IronSkillet/KrispyKreme/Petro SC, Rest/Glade Economy Inn
Lodg — E: Glade Economy Inn, Swiss Inn, Travelodge
TServ — E: Petro SC/Tires
Other — E: Laundry/WiFi/Petro SC

26 **VA 737, College Dr, Meadowview, to Emory**
Other — W: to Emory & Henry College

24 **VA 80, VA 50, Meadowview**

EXIT — VIRGINIA

22 **VA 704, Enterprise Rd, to US 11, Abingdon**

19 **US 11, US 58 Alt, Abingdon**
TStop — E: Roadrunner #134/Shell
Gas — W: Chevron◈, Citgo, Exxon◈
Food — E: Subway/Roadrunner
W: Burger King, **Cracker Barrel**, Harbor House Seafood, Huddle House, Wendy's
Lodg — E: Holiday Lodge
W: Alpine Motel, Days Inn, Empire Motor Lodge, Holiday Inn Express, Quality Inn
Other — E: Lowe's, to appr 10mi: **Callebs Cove CG▲**, to **Mt Rogers Nat'l Rec Area▲**

17 **US 58 Alt, VA 75, Abingdon**
Gas — E: Valero
W: Chevron, Citgo, Exxon
Food — E: Domino's Pizza, Long John Silver
W: Arby's, Hardee's, KFC, Pizza Hut, McDonald's, Shoney's, Taco Bell
Lodg — E: Hampton Inn
W: Martha Washington Inn, Super 8
Med — W: + Hospital
Other — E: to appr 8.5 mi **Wolf Lair Village CG▲**, **Lake Front Family CG▲**, **Lake Shore CG▲**
W: Advance Auto Parts, CVS, Dollar General, Food City, Kmart, Kroger

14 **US 19N, VA 140, Jonesboro Rd**
Gas — W: Chevron◈, Exxon, Shell◈
Food — W: McDonald's, DQ, Subway
Lodg — E: Maxwell Manor B&B
W: Comfort Inn, Comfort Suites
Other — W: to appr 7mi **Riverside Campground▲**

(13) **Abingdon TRUCK Rest Area (NB)**
(RR, Phone, Picnic, Vend, Info)

13 **Spring Creek Rd, US 611, to US 11, US 19, Abingdon**
Gas — W: Shell◈
TServ — W: Blue Ridge Kenworth, Peterbilt
Other — W: VA Highlands Airport✈

10 **US 11, US 19, Lee Hwy, Bristol**
FStop — W: Exit 10 Quick Stop/BP
Gas — W: Chevron, Marathon
Lodg — W: Beacon Motel, Evergreen Motel, Red Carpet Inn, Skyland Inn

7 **Old Airport Rd, Bristol**
Gas — E: Citgo, Shell◈
W: BP◈, Conoco◈
Food — E: **Cracker Barrel**
W: Chili's, Damon's, Golden Corral, IHOP, Kobe Japanese, Logan's Roadhouse, McDonald's, Osaka Japanese Rest Outback Steakhouse, Perkins, Prime Sirloin Buffet, Ruby Tuesday, Starbucks, Sagebrush Steakhouse, Subway,
Lodg — E: La Quinta Inn♥, Quality Inn
W: Courtyard, Holiday Inn, Microtel, Motel 6♥
Med — W: + Lee Urgent Medical Care
TServ — W: Goodpasture White/GMC
Other — W: ATMs, Advance Auto, Auto Services, Banks, Bowling, Cinemas, Dollar General, Food City, Grocery, Home Depot, Lowe's, Office Depot, PetSmart♥, Pharmacy, Target, UPS Store, **Walmart sc**

5 **US 11, US 19, Lee Hwy, Bristol**
Gas — E: Chevron, Citgo, Shell
W: Exxon◈
Food — E: Arby's, Burger King, Hardee's, KFC, Long John Silver, McDonald's, Shoney's

◈ = Regular Gas Stations with Diesel ▲ = RV Friendly Locations ♥ = Pet Friendly Locations
Red print shows large vehicle parking / access on site or nearby **Brown Print = Campgrounds / RV PARKS**

EXIT **VA / TN**

Lodg E: Budget Inn, Crest Motel, Super 8
W: Comfort Inn

Other E: ATMs, CVS, Food Lion, Walgreen's, US Post Office, Black Wolf Harley Davidson
W: ATMs, Atlas Yamaha, Blevins Tire, Crabtree Towing, Kelly Tire, **Lee Hwy Campground▲**

(3) **Jct I-381S, to Bristol**

Gas E: Chevron, Citgo◈, Conoco, Exxon◈

Food E: Applebee's, Pizza Hut, Ryan's Grill

Lodg E: Enchanted Lodge, Days Inn, Econo Lodge

1 **US 58, US 421, Bristol, Gate City**

Gas E: Chevron, Appco/Citgo, Zoomerz

Food E: Burger King, ChickFilA, KFC, Krispy Kreme, Long John Silver, McDonald's, Wendy's

Lodg E: Budget Host Inn, Howard Johnson, Knights Inn

Med E: + Hospital

Other E: ATMs, Auto Dealers, Auto Services, CVS, Food Lion, Kroger, Sears Auto Center, Walgreen's, **Walmart**, Bristol Mall, Animal Medical Clinic♥

(0) **VA Welcome Center (NB) (NO Trucks) (RR, Phone, Picnic, Vend, Info)**

EASTERN TIME ZONE

⬆ VIRGINIA
⬇ TENNESSEE

NOTE: MM 75: Virginia State Line

EASTERN TIME ZONE

(75) **TN Welcome Center (SB) (RR, Phones, Picnic, Vend, Info)**

74B **US 11W, Lee Hwy, Bristol, Kingsport**

Gas W: Exxon, Valero

Food W: Rest/Bristol Lodge

Lodg W: Bristol Lodge

TServ W: WE Truck & Diesel Repair

Other W: Towing

74A **TN 1, State St, to US 11E, US 421, Bristol, Kingsport (Addtl Serv 2-3 mi E in VA)**

Gas E: appr 2 mi E Shell, Roadrunner/BP

Food E: appr 2 mi E in VA Usual Brand Fast Food

Lodg E: Days Inn♥, Hampton Inn

Med E: + Wellmont Reg'l Medical Center

Other E: ATMs, Allstate Trailers, appr 2 mi ATMs, Auto Services, CVS, Kroger, Walgreen's, **Walmart**, U-Haul, Bristol Mall

69 **TN 394, TN 37, to US 11E, Blountville**

Gas E: Roadrunner/BP◈

Food E: Subway/BP, Arby's, Burger King, Domino's, McDonald's

Other E: Advance Auto Parts, **to appr 4-5mi** Appalachian Caverns, Bristol Motor Speedway, **All American Campground▲**, **Blue Ox Campground/BMS▲**, **Earhart Campground▲**, **Farmer Bob's Camp ground▲**, **Lakeview RV Park▲**, **Race-way Cove Campground▲**, **Red Barn Campground▲**, **Thunder Valley Camp ground▲**,

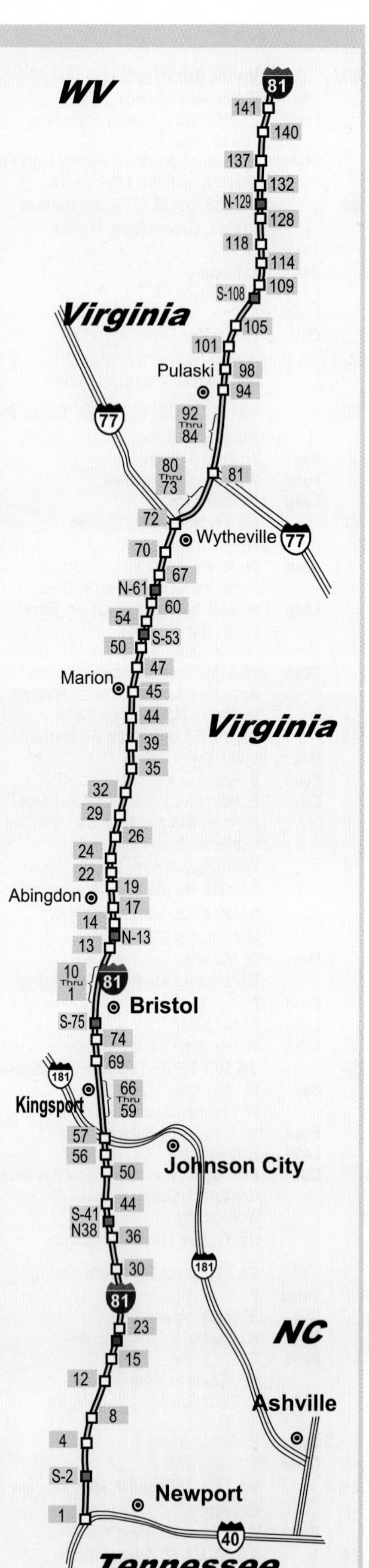

EXIT **TENNESSEE**

Other E: **Twin City Drive-In Campground▲**, **Camp at the Lake Campground▲**, **to Cherokee Trails Campground & Stables▲**

66 **TN 126, Memorial Blvd, Blountville, to Kingsport**

Gas W: Chevron◈

Food W: McDonald's

Other W: Factory Stores, Carolina Pottery

63 **TN 357, to TN 75, Airport Pkwy, Kingsport**

TStop W: Appco #23/P66

Gas E: Roadrunner/BP◈, Exxon, Shell◈
W: Roadrunner/BP

Food E: Cracker Barrel, Wendy's, TacoBell/ Krystal/Exxon, Subway/Shell

Lodg E: La Quinta Inn♥, Sleep Inn♥
W: America's Best Value Inn, Red Carpet Inn♥

TServ W: Stowers Machinery CAT

Other E: Tri City Reg'l Airport✈
W: Dollar General, Sam's Club, Marsh/**LP**, **Rocky Top Campground & RV Park▲**, **Bristol/Kingsport KOA/RVDump▲**, Countryside Winery

59 **TN 36, Ft Henry Dr, Kingsport, to Johnson City**

Gas E: BP, Speedy Mart/Citgo◈
W: Roadrunner/BP, Citgo, Shell, Sunoco

Food W: Arby's, Burger King, Edo Japanese Grill, Hardee's, Huddle House, La Carretta Mex, Little Caesars Pizza, McDonald's, Pal's, Perkins, Piccadilly, Subway, Wendy's

Lodg E: Super 8
W: Best Western♥, Comfort Inn

Other E: Companion Animal Hospital♥
W: ATMs, Banks, Advance Auto Parts, CVS, Carwash, Dollar General, Dollar Tree, Firestone, Food City, Ingles, Mail Box Etc, US Post Office, Vet♥, Walgreen's, **to appr 2 mi: Walmart SC**, Ft Henry Mall, **to Warrior's Path State Park▲**

(57AB) **Jct I-26, US 23 S-Johnson City, I-181, US 23N to Kingsport**

56 **Fordtown Rd, Kingsport**

TServ E: Smokey Mountain Truck Center

50 **TN 93, to TN 81, Fall Branch, Jonesborough**

Other W: TN State Hwy Patrol Post

44 **Jearoldstown Rd, Chuckey**

Gas E: Exit 44 Market

Other E: I-81 Motorsports Park/**Camp▲**

(41) **Greene Co Rest Area (SB) (RR, Phones, Picnic, Vend)**

(38) **Greene Co Rest Area (NB) (RR, Phones, Picnic, Vend)**

36 **TN 172, Baileyton Rd, Baileyton, Greeneville**

TStop E: Pilot Travel Center #51 (Scales)**(DAND)**
W: Travel Center of America #36 (Scales), Roadrunner #119/Shell

Gas W: BP◈

Food E: Subway/Pilot TC
W: Rest/TA TC, Subway/Shell, Pizza Plus

Lodg W: 36 Motel

TServ W: TA TC/Tires, Looney's Truck & Trailer

Med W: + Medical Center

◈ = Regular Gas Stations with Diesel ▲ = RV Friendly Locations ♥ = Pet Friendly Locations
Red print shows large vehicle parking / access on site or nearby **Brown Print = Campgrounds / RV PARKS**

EXIT		TENNESSEE
	TWash	E: McAmis Truck Wash
	Other	E: WiFi/Pilot TC
		W: Laundry/TA TC, ATMs, Family Dollar, **Around Pond RV & Campground▲**, **Baileyton RV Park▲**
30		**TN 70, to TN 66, Lonesome Pine Trail, Bulls Gap, to Greeneville, Rogersville**
	Gas	E: Exxon◈
	Food	E: DQ/Stuckey's/Exxon
23		**US 11E, TN 24, Bulls Gap, Greenville**
	TStop	W: Kwik Fuel #23/P66 (Scales)
	Gas	E: BP, Mobil, Quick Stop
		W: Quick Shop/Exxon
	Food	E: Subway, Wendy's
		W: McDonald's, TacoBell
	Lodg	W: Best Western, Super 8
	Other	E: to **Davy Crockett State Park▲**
		W: Bulls Gap Racetrack, Tony's Wrecker Service & Repair
(21)		**Weigh Station (SB)**
15		**TN 340, Fish Hatchery Rd**
12		**TN 160, Morristown, Lowland**
	Gas	E: Phillips 66
		W: Shell◈
8		**US 25E, TN 32, Morristown, to White Pine, Dandridge (Addt'l Serv 5mi N on US 25E)**
	NOTE:	**25E: NO Trucks in Cumberland Gap Tunnel**
	Gas	W: Shell◈, BP◈
	Food	W: Cracker Barrel, Hardee's, Rest/HI
	Lodg	W: Holiday Inn, Parkway Inn, Super 8
	Other	W: to **Walmart sc**, Dollar Tree, Auto & Truck Services, Food, Gas, Lodging, Colboch Harley Davidson
4		**TN 341, Roy J Messer Hwy, White Pine Rd, White Pine**
	TStop	E: Pilot Travel Center #412 (Scales)(DAND)
		W: WilcoHess Travel Plaza #4001 (Scales)
	Food	E: McDonald's/Pilot TC
		W: Huddle House, Wendy's/WilcoHess TP
	Lodg	W: Days Inn
	Other	E: Laundry/WiFi/RVDump/Pilot TC
		W: Laundry/WilcoHess TP
(2)		**Jefferson Co Rest Area (SB) (RR, Phones, Picnic, Vend)**
(1B)		**Jct I-40E, to Asheville, NC (fr SB, Left Exit)**
(1A)		**Jct I-40W, to Knoxville, to I-75**

EASTERN TIME ZONE

NOTE: **I-81 starts/ends on I-40, Exit #421**

TENNESSEE

Begin Northbound I-81 from Jct I-40 near Dandridge TN to NY/Canada border.

Begin Eastbound I-82 at Jct I-90 near Ellensburg, WA to Jct I-84 near Hermiston, OR.

WASHINGTON

NOTE: **I-82 begins/ends Exit #110, I-90**

PACIFIC TIME ZONE

EXIT		WASHINGTON
3		**WA 821S, Thrall Rd**
	Other	S: **Yakima River RV Park▲**
(8)		**Manastash Ridge Viewpoint (Both dir)**
11		**Military Rd, Ellensburg**
	Other	N: US Military Res Yakima Training Ctr
(22)		**Selah Creek Rest Area (WB) (RR, Phones, Picnic, RVDump)**
(24)		**Selah Creek Rest Area (EB) (RR, Phones, Picnic, Info, RVDump)**
26		**Firing Center Rd, WA 821S, WA 823S, Harrison Rd, Selah**
	Gas	S: 7-11, Shell
	Other	S: to appr 16mi **Stagecoach RV Park▲**
29		**E Selah Rd**
30A		**WA 823S (WB)**
30B		**Rest Haven Rd, Selah (WB)**
30		**WA 823, Rest Haven Rd, Selah (EB)**
31B		**US 12, Yakima, Naches (EB)**
31		**US 12, Yakima, Naches, to Chinook Pass, White Pass (fr WB, Left exit)**
	FStop	S: to 1408 N 1st PacPride/Roadrunner
	Gas	S: ArcoAmPm◈, Exxon, Shell
	Food	S: Amer Mex Rest, Artic Circle, Black Angus, Gasperetti's, Golden Moon Chinese, Jack in the Box, Ital Rest, Olive Garden, Red Lobster, Waffles Cafe, Wendy's
	Lodg	S: All Star Motel, Best Western, Clarion♥, Days Inn♥, Motel 6♥, Ramada Ltd♥, Yakima Inn
	Med	S: + Yakima Reg'l Medical Center
	Other	S: ATMs, Albertson's, **Woodland Park▲**, **Trailer Inns RV Park▲**, **North Acres MH Park▲**, **Trailer Village MH & RV Park▲**, to Sun Tides Golf Course & **RV Park▲**
33A		**Fair Ave, Terrace Hts Dr (EB)**
33B		**Terrace Hts Dr, Yakima (EB)**
33		**Yakima Ave, Terrace Hts Dr, Fair Ave, Yakima (WB)**
	Gas	N: Chevron, Shell◈
		S: 7-11, ArcoAmPm
	Food	N: Chesters/Shell, Burger King, DQ, McDonald's
		S: DQ, Domino's, Libby's Rest, Sub Shop, Taco Bell
	Lodg	N: Oxford Inn, Oxford Suites
		S: Cedar Suites♥, Fairfield Inn, Hilton Garden Inn, Holiday Inn Express♥, Red Lion Hotel♥
	Med	S: + Yakima Reg'l Medical Center
	Other	N: Auto Dealer, **Walmart sc**, Auto & RV Service
		S: ATMs, Auto Services, Cinema, Firestone, Les Schwab Tires, Office Max, PetCo♥, Safeway, Target, Tires, UPS Store, Yakima Convention Center, Yakima Sundome
34		**WA 24E, Nob Hill Blvd, Yakima, to Moxee City**
	Gas	S: 7-11, ArcoAmPm, Chevron◈
	Food	S: Arby's, McDonald's, Mexican Rest
	TServ	S: Cummins NW, Kenworth NW, Mobil Fleet Service
	Other	N: Auto Dealer, **Yakima KOA▲**, **Yakima Sportman State Park▲**
		S: ATMs, Auto Services, UPS Store, Valley Mall, State Fair Park, Yakima Speedway, **Casino Caribbean**, **Circle H RV Ranch▲**, **Aubrey's RV Center**, to **Nob Hill Casino**
36		**US 82, Valley Mall Blvd, Old Town Rd, Union Gap, Yakima**
	FStop	S: PacPr/Rainier Place/ArcoAmPm
	TStop	S: AmBest/GearJammer Travel Plaza/Shell (Scales)
	Gas	S: BJ's Get N Go
	Food	S: Rest/GearJammer TP, Applebee's, Burger King, Denny's, Jack in the Box, IHOP, Miner's D/I Rest, McDonald's, Old Country Buffet, Outback Steakhouse, Shari's, Skippers Seafood, Starbucks, Subway
	Lodg	S: Motel/GearJammer TP, Best Western, Pioneer Motel, Quality Inn, Super 8
	TWash	S: GearJammer TP
	TServ	S: GearJammer TP/Tires, Western Peterbilt
	Med	S: + Valley Medi-Center
	Other	S: Laundry/WiFi/RVDump/LP/Gear Jammer TP, ATMs, Best Buy, Borders, Costco, Cinemas, FedEx Office, Tires, Goodyear, Home Depot, Lowe's, Office Depot, PetCo♥, PetSmart♥, RiteAid, Safeway, ShopKO, Valley Mall, Yakima Air Terminal✈, **Canopy Country RV Center**
37		**US 97S, Main St, Union Gap, Yakima, Wapato (EB)**
38		**Main St, US 97, Yakima (WB, Left exit) (Acc to x36 Serv)**
40		**Thorp Rd, Parker Rd, Yakima Valley Highway, Wapato**
44		**Wapato Rd, Yakima Valley Hwy**
	Gas	N: Shell◈

EXIT | WASHINGTON

50 **WA 22E, Buena Rd, to US 97S, Zillah, to Toppenish (Serv appr 3mi S)**
- Food S: Dad's Rest, KFC, McDonald's, Pizza, Subway, Taco Bell,
- Lodg S: Best Western, El Corral Motel
- Med S: + Hospital
- Other S: ATMs, Safeway, to Yakama Nation RV Resort▲, Yakima Nation Legends Casino

52 **Zillah Rd, Meyers Rd, Zillah**
- Gas N: Chevron, Cherry Patch Mini Mart, Shell
- Food N: El Porton, McDonald's, Subway
- Lodg N: Comfort Inn
- Other S: to Yakama Indian Res

54 **Yakima Valley Hwy, Division Rd, Zillah, (National Historic Site)**
- Other S: Grocery, RVDump, Teapot Dome Service Station

58 **WA 223S, Van Belle Rd, Granger**
- FStop S: Granger Place/Conoco
- TStop S: RoadysTS/Granger Travel Plaza/ Chevron (Scales)
- Food S: Deli/Pizza/Subs/DinoJava/Granger TP
- Other S: Laundry/MoneyMart/LP/Granger TP, U-Haul/Granger TP(TW/Tires& Oil Future), to Yakama Indian Reservation

63 **Sunnyside Rd, Yakima Valley Hwy, Outlook, Sunnyside, Granger (Acc to Ex #67 Serv 3mi N)**
- Lodg N: Country Inn♥, Travel Inn
- Other N: Sunnyside RV Park▲

67 **Midvale Rd, 1st St, Sunnyside**
- Gas N: CFN/Chevron◈
- Food N: Jack in the Box
- Med N: + Hospital
- Other N: Bi-Mart, Pharmacy, Safeway

69 **WA 241, Waneta Rd, to WA 24, Sunnyside, to Mabton**
- FStop N: PacPride/The Outpost/Shell
- Gas N: ArcoAmPm◈, Texaco◈
- Food N: Arby's, Burger King, China Grove, DQ, KFC, McDonald's, Pizza Hut, Subway, Taco Bell
- Lodg N: Best Western♥, Rodeway Inn♥, Country Inn♥, Travel Inn
- Med N: + Sunnyside Comm Hospital
- Other N: LP/The Outpost, ATMs, Auto Repairs, Banks, Dollar Tree, Grocery, Les Schwab Tires, RiteAid, Radio Shack, Staples, Tires, Walmart sc, Vet♥, Mid Valley Mall, Sunnyside Muni Airport✈

Personal Notes

EXIT | WASHINGTON

73 **W Wine Country Rd, Yakima Valley Hwy, Grandview**
- Gas S: Grandview Market/Exxon, Smitty's Conoco◈ & Car Wash
- Food S: Eli & Kathy's Family Rest, New Hong Kong Rest, Subway
- Lodg S: Apple Valley Motel
- Other S: ATMs, Auto Repairs, Les Schwab Tires, Laundromat, Pharmacy, Safeway, Smitty's RV Overniter▲

75 **E Wine Country Rd, Grandview (Access to Ex #73 Serv)**
- FStop S: Pacific Pride 501 E Wine Country Rd

(76) **Weigh Station (EB)**

(80) **Gap Rd, Wine Country Rd, Prosser**
S: Prosser Rest Area (Both dir) (RR, Phone, Picnic, Info, RVDump)

EXIT | WASHINGTON

- TStop S: Horse Heaven Hills Travel Plaza/Shell
- Food S: Blue Goose Rest, KFC, McDonald's, Speedway Café, Subway
- Lodg S: Best Western♥, Barn Motor Inn/Rest/ RV▲
- Med S: + Prosser Memorial Hospital
- Other S: WiFi/RVDump/LP/Horse Heaven Hills TP, Wine Country RV Park▲, Auto Dealers, Hinzerling Winery, Prosser Airport✈

82 **Wine Country Rd, E Meade Ave, Prosser, to WA 22, to Mabton, to WA 221, to Paterson (Access to Ex #80 Serv)**

88 **Gibbon Rd**

93 **Yakitat Rd, to Benton City 1st St, WA 225, to WA 240, Benton City, to Richland, Kennewick, Pasco, to WA 224E, W Richland**
- Other N: Beach RV Park▲, Elm Grove RV Park▲, to appr 6mi RV Village Resort▲

(102) **Jct I-182, US 12E, to US 395, Richland, to Pasco**
- Other N: to Richland Airport✈, to App 6mi Horn Rapids RV Resort▲, Sandy Heights RV Resort▲

104 **Dallas Rd, Goose Gap Rd, Richland, Kennewick**
- Gas N: Conoco◈

109 **Badger Rd, Clearwater Ave**
- Gas N: SunMart, Shell
- Other N: to appr 3 mi+ Food, Lodging, Columbia Center Mall, Tri-Cities RV Park▲, Wrights Desert Gold Motel & RV Park▲, Vista Field Airport✈

113 **Jct US 395, to I-182, to Kennewick, Pasco (Serv 3-5mi N)**
- FStop N: Tesoro Truck Stop (S Ely & W 4th)
- Gas N: Exxon, Murphy
- Food N: Rest/Tesoro TS, Burger King, Café, Carl Jr's, Fiesta Mexican, Jack in the Box, McDonald's, Starbucks, Subway
- Lodg N: Best Western, Econo Lodge, Holiday Inn Express, La Quinta Inn♥
- TServ N: Eagle Freightliner, Freedom Truck Center
- Med N: + Greater Columbia Regional
- Other N: RVDump/Tesoro TS, ATMs, Grocery, Home Depot, Radio Shack, Walgreen's, Walmart sc, to Tri-Cities Airport✈, to Franklin Co RV Park at TRAC▲

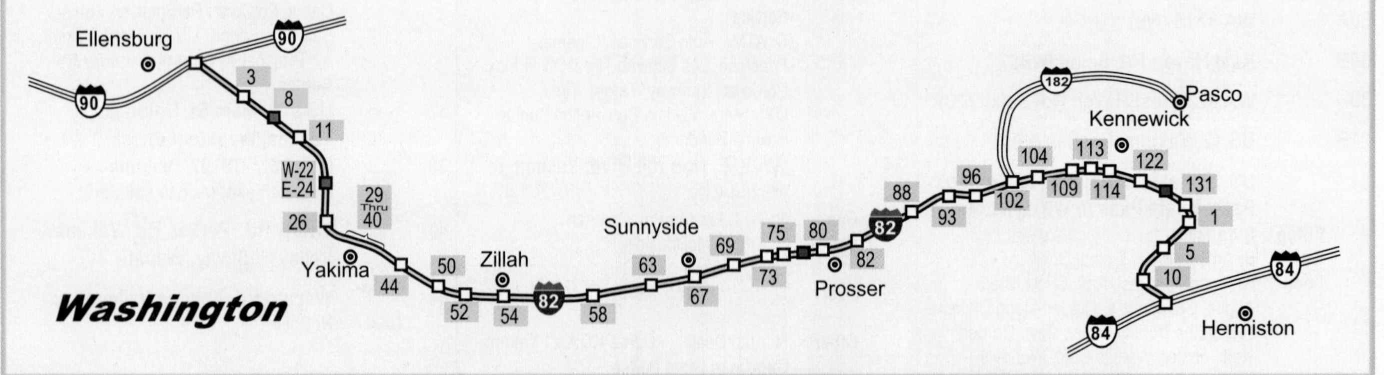

◈= Regular Gas Stations with Diesel ▲ = RV Friendly Locations ♥= Pet Friendly Locations
Red print shows large vehicle parking / access on site or nearby Brown Print = Campgrounds / RV PARKS

EXIT	WASHINGTON
114	**WA 397, Locust Grove Rd**
122	**Coffin Rd**
(130)	**Port of Entry / Weigh Station (WB)**
131	**WA 14W, McNary Rd, Plymouth Rd, Kennewick, Plymouth, Vancouver**

PACIFIC TIME ZONE

NOTE: MM 132: Oregon State Line

WASHINGTON

EXIT	OREGON

OREGON

PACIFIC TIME ZONE

EXIT		OREGON
1		**US 395S, US 730, Columbia River Hwy, Umatilla, Hermiston**
		OR Welcome Center (SB)
		WEIGH STATION (SB)
	FStop	W: Tesoro #62180
	TStop	W: CFN/Crossroads Truck Stop/Shell
	Food	W: Rest/Crossroads TS, Subway/Tesoro,
	Lodge:	E: Desert River Inn W: Lamplighter Motel, Umatilla Inn
	Med	W: + Umatilla Urgent Care
	TServ	W: Krome Diesel Repair/Tires/Crsrds TS
	Other	E: Comm'l Tire Center, Wildood RV Park▲, RV Repair, RV Center, to appr 5mi Wal-Mart sc W: NAPA, Pharmacy, OR State Hwy Patrol Post, Shady Rest MH & RV, to Oasis RV Park▲,
5		**Power Line Rd**
10		**CR 1232, Walker Rd, Westland**
	Med	E: + Good Shepherd Comm Hospital
	Other	E: to Pioneer RV Park▲, to Hermiston Muni Airport✈ W: Umatilla Ordinance Depot

NOTE: I-82 begins/ends at Exit #179, on I-84

OREGON

Begin Westbound I-82 at Jct I-84 near Hermiston, OR to Jct I-90 Ellensburg, WA.

EXIT		PENNSYLVANIA

Begin Southbound I-83 in Harrisburg, PA to Fayette St, Exit #1 in MD.

PENNSYLVANIA

EASTERN TIME ZONE

EXIT		PENNSYLVANIA
(51B)		**Jct -81N, to Hazelton**
(51A)		**Jct I-81S, US 322W, Carlisle, Chambersburg (Left Exit Only)**
50B		**US 22W, Harrisburg, Progress**
50A		**US 22E, Jonestown Rd, Colonial Park, Harrisburg,**
	Gas	E: Shell, Sunoco
	Food	E: Applebee's, Arby's, Colonial Park Diner, McDonald's, Long John Silver, Olive Garden, Red Lobster, Red Robin, Subway, Taco Bell W: Friendly's, KFC, Roberto's Pizza
	Other	E: ATMs, Colonial Park Mall, Best Buy, CVS, Costco, Goodyear, Home Depot, NTB, Target, Tires
48		**Union Deposit Rd, Harrisburg**
	Gas	E: Sunoco W: BP
	Food	E: Arby's, Burger King, Denny's, Hong Kong Chef, Lone Star Steakhouse, Panera Bread, Wendy's W: Hardee's, McDonald's, Outback Steakhouse, Starbucks, Subway, Waffle House
	Lodg	E: Sheraton W: Comfort Inn, Fairfield Inn
	Med	E: + Comm General Hospital
	Other	E: ATMs, Grocery, Pharmacy, Staples W: ATMs, Lowe's, Office Depot, Office Max, UPS Store, State Farm Complex
47		**US 322E, Derry St, Paxton St, Eisenhower Blvd, Hershey (SB, Exit Only)**
	Other	E: Home Depot, to Hershey Park & Attractions, Milton Hershey Medical Center, Hershey Highmeadow CG▲
46B		**US 322E, to Hershey (NB)**
	FStop	E: Hess Express
	Other	E: Home Depot, PetSmart♥, Cummins
(46A)		**Jct-283S, to I-76, PA Tpk (SB) (Services Accessible I-283)**
	Other	S: to Harrisburg Int'l Airport✈, to Harrisburg East Campground▲
45		**Paxton St, Harrisburg**
	Gas	E: Sheetz
	Food	E: Applebee's, Burger King, ChickFilA, Fuddrucker's, Pizza Hut, Wendy's
	Other	E: ATMs, Auto Dealers, Auto Services, Bass Pro Shop, Harrisburg Mall, Radio Shack,
44B		**17th St (SB), 19th St (NB)**
	Gas	E: Pacific Pride, Hess, Sunoco
	Food	E: Benihana, Hardee's
	Other	E: ATMs, Auto Dealers, Auto Services, Advance Auto Parts, CarQuest, Firestone
44A		**13th St, to PA 441, Harrisburg**
	Gas	W: Chevron
	Other	W: DMV
43		**2nd St, to State Capitol**
	Lodg	W: Crowne Plaza
	Med	W: + Hospital
	Other	W: Amtrak, Greyhound, State Capitol
42		**3rd St, Lemoyne**
41B		**Louther St, Highland Park (NB)**
	Gas	W: Mobil
	Food	W: KFC, Subs
41A		**PA 581W, Camp Hill (Both, Left Exit)**
40B		**Simpson Ferry Rd, New Cumberland**
	Gas	W: BP◈, Shell
	Food	W: McDonald's, Subway
40A		**Limekiln Rd, New Cumberland**
	Gas	E: BP, Mobil W: Hess
	Food	E: Bob Evans, McDonald's, Pizza Hut
	Lodg	E: Comfort Inn, Fairfield Inn, Holiday Inn, Rodeway Inn, Travelodge W: Best Western, Motel 6♥, Travel Inn
(39B)		**Jct I-76, PA TPK (TOLL), to Philadelphia, Pittsburgh**
	Other	E: to Harrisburg Int'l Airport✈
39A		**PA 114, Lewisberry Rd**
	Lodg	E: Days Inn
	Other	E: Capitol City Airport✈
38		**Evergeen Rd, Pleasant View Rd, Reesers Summit, New Cumberland**
36		**PA 262, Fishing Creek**
	Gas	E: Hess W: Citgo, Shell
35		**PA 177, Lewisberry**
	Gas	W: Mobil
	Food	E: Hillside Cafe
	Lodg	W: Alpine Inn
	Other	W: Gifford Pinchot State Park, Ski Roundtop
(35)		**Parking Area (SB)**
(35)		**Weigh Station (SB)**
34		**Valley Green (NB)**
	FStop	E: Hess Express #38422
	Food	E: Blimpie/Hess
	Lodg	E: Super 8
	Other	E: UPS Store, Parks Away Parks Campground▲
(33)		**Weigh Station (NB)**
33		**PA 392, Old Trail Rd, Yocumtown**
	FStop	E: Hess Express
	Food	E: Burger King, McDonald's, Two Brothers Italian Grill
	Lodg	E: Super 8
	Other	E: ATMs, Family Dollar, Radio Shack W: Valley Green Veterinary Hospital♥
32		**PA 382, Newberrytown**
	FStop	E: Rutter's Farm Stores #53
	Gas	W: Exxon◈
	Food	E: Pizza Hut/Rutters FS
	Other	W: Gifford Pinchot State Park, Ski Roundtop

◈ = Regular Gas Stations with Diesel ▲ = RV Friendly Locations ♥ = Pet Friendly Locations
Red print shows large vehicle parking / access on site or nearby Brown Print = Campgrounds / RV PARKS

EXIT — PENNSYLVANIA

28 — PA 295, Susquehanna Tr, York, to Strinestown, Zions View
- FStop — W: Rutters Farm Store #54
- Food — W: Wendy's, Interstate 83 Diner
- Other — W: ATMs, York Auto Auction

24 — PA 238, Church Rd, to PA 181, York, Emigsville
- Gas — E: to Hess Exress
  W: Rutters Farm Store
  W: 4 Brothers Restaurant
- Other — W: US Weightlifting Hall of Fame

22 — US 83S, PA 181, to US 30W (SB), PA 181N, N George St (NB)
(Access to Ex #21B Serv via PA 181)
- Gas — E: Rutter's Farm Store #53
  W: Rutter's Farm Store
- Lodg — E: Comfort Inn, Homewood Suites
- Other — E: ATMs, Car Wash, Sportsmans Liquidation
  W: Vet♥

21 — US 30, to Gettysburg (SB)

21B — US 30W, to PA 181, York, to Gettysburg (NB)
- Gas — W: BP, Exxon, Mobil
- Food — W: Burger King, China Kitchen, Denny's, Dunkin Donuts, Damon's, El Rodeo Mexican Rest, Hardee's, Hooters, Hoss's Steak & Seafood House, KFC, Lone Star Steakhouse, McDonald's, Memphis Blues BBQ, Olive Garden, Pizza Hut, Ruby Tuesday, Smokey Bones BBQ, Subway, Taco Bell, TGI Friday, Wendy's
- Lodg — W: Best Western, Holiday Inn, Red Roof Inn, Super 8
- Other — W: West Manchester Mall, York Expo Center, ATMs, AT&T Store, Auto Dealers, Auto Services, CVS, Dick's Sporting Goods, Gander Mountain, Grocery, Jiffy Lube, Laugermans's Harley Davidson, Pep Boys, PetCo♥, PetSmart♥, Staples, Target, **Walmart sc**, **Ben Franklin Campground RV Park▲**, **to Conewago Isle Campground▲**

21A — US 30E, Arsenal Rd, York (NB)
- Gas — E: Rutter's Farm Store
- Food — E: Bob Evans, Round the Clock Diner, San Carlos
- Lodg — E: Days Inn, Holiday Inn, Motel 6♥, Sheraton
- Med — E: + Hospital
- Other — E: ATMs, Enterprise RAC, Harley Davidson Plant & Museum

19B — PA 462W, Market St (SB)

19A — PA 462E, Market St (SB)
- Gas — E: Hess, Mobil
- Food — E: Applebee's, Arby's, Perkins, Outback Steakhouse, Red Lobster, Starbucks, Taco Bell, Wendy's
- Lodg — E: Quality Inn
- Med — E: + Hospital
- Other — E: York Mall, ATMs, Advance Auto Parts, Dollar General, Grocery, NTB, Sam's Club, Walgreen's, **Walmart sc**

19 — PA 462, Market St (NB)

18 — PA 124, Mt Rose Ave
- Gas — E: Mobil, Rutters Farm Store
- Food — E: Burger King, Denny's
- Lodg — E: Budget Host Inn
- Other — E: CVS, Penn State Univ/York Campus

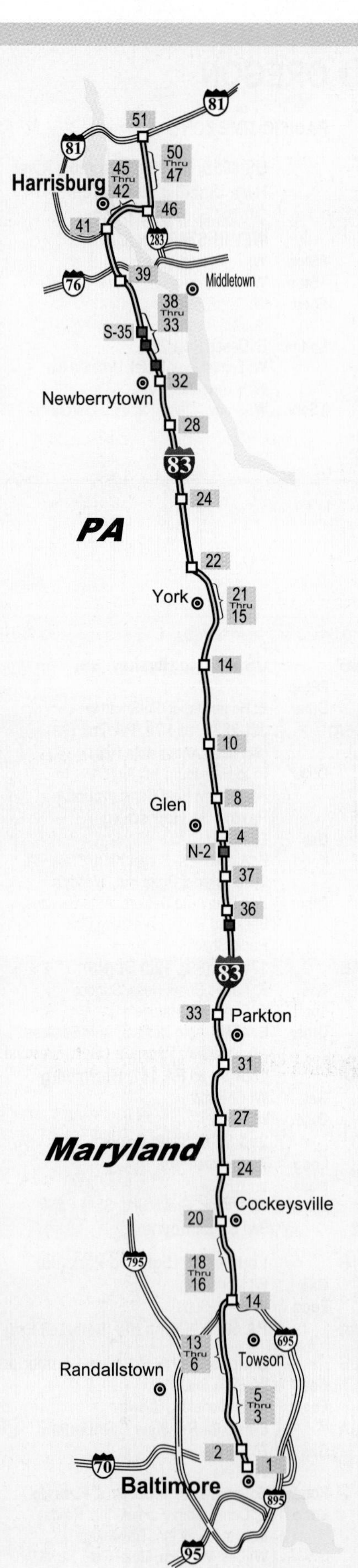

EXIT — PA / MD

16B — PA 74N, Queen St
- Gas — W: Exxon
- Food — W: McDonald's, Subway, Taco Bell
- Other — W: York College, CVS, Dollar General, Dollar Tree, Walgreen's

16A — PA 74S, Queen St, York
- Gas — E: Mobil
- Food — E: **Cracker Barrel**, Pizza Hut, Ruby Tuesday
- Lodg — E: Country Inn

15 — US 83 N, S George St
- Med — W: + Hospital
- Other — W: York College of PA

14 — PA 182, Leader Heights
- Gas — W: Exxon, Rutters, Sunoco
- Food — W: McDonald's, PizzaHut/Rutters
- Lodg — W: Comfort Inn, Holiday Inn Express
- Other — W: **Indian Rock Campground▲**, Ryan Auto & **RV** Parts

10 — PA 214, Loganville
- Food — W: Lee's Rest, Pizza
- Lodg — W: Midway Motel
- Other — W: **PA State Hwy Patrol Post**

8 — PA 216, Glen Rock
- Lodg — W: Rocky Ridge Motel
- Other — E: Amish & Farmers Market

4 — PA 851, Shrewsbury
- FStop — E: Tom's Mobil, Tom's Cigarette Cellar #22/Crown
- Gas — W: Exxon◈
- Food — E: **Cracker Barrel**, Ruby Tuesday
  W: Arby's, ChickFilA, McDonald's, Subway
- Lodg — E: Hampton Inn
- Other — E: Home Depot
  W: ATMs, Advance Auto Parts, CVS, Dollar Tree, Grocery, Radio Shack, **Walmart sc**, Naylor Winery

NOTE: NB: NO Trucks Over 13' 6" Beyond Exit #4

(2) — PA Welcome Center (NB)
(RR, Phone, Picnic, Info)

EASTERN TIME ZONE

⬆ PENNSYLVANIA
⬇ MARYLAND

NOTE: MM 38: Pennsylvania State Line

EASTERN TIME ZONE

NOTE: I-83 begins/ends in MD on Fayette St

37 — Freeland Rd, Parkton (SB)

36 — MD 439, Old York Rd, Parkton, Maryland Line, Bel Air
- Other — W: to appr 5mi **Morris Meadows Campground▲**

(35) — Weigh Station (SB)

33 — MD 45, York Rd, Parkton
- Gas — E: Exxon◈

31 — Middletown Rd, Parkton, Wiseburg, Rayville

27 — MD 137, Mt Carmel Rd, Parkton
- Gas — E: Exxon◈
- Other — E: Grocery, US Post Office, Pharmacy, **Gunpowder Falls State Park**

◈= Regular Gas Stations with Diesel ▲ = RV Friendly Locations ♥= Pet Friendly Locations
Red print shows large vehicle parking / access on site or nearby **Brown Print = Campgrounds / RV PARKS**

EXIT		MARYLAND
10A		**Northern Pkwy E, Baltimore (NB)**
24		**Belfast Rd, Sparks Glencoe, to Butler, Sparks**
20AB		**Shawan Rd, Cockeysville, to Hunt Valley, Shawan**
	Gas	E: BP, Exxon◈
	Food	E: Burger King, Carrabba's, Caribou Coffee, Chipolte Mexican Grill, Damon's, McDonald's, Outback Steakhouse, Panera Bread, Quiznos, Wendy's
	Lodg	E: Courtyard, Econo Lodge, Embassy Suites, Hampton Inn, Marriott
	Other	E: ATMs, Grocery, Sears Auto Center, Walmart, Mall, Baltimore Convention Center W: Oregon Ridge Park/Nature Center
18		**Cockeysville Rd, Warren Rd (NB, Exit only)**
	FStop	E: Southern States
	Gas	E: Exxon
	Lodg	E: Residence Inn
17		**Padonia Rd, Lutherville Timonium**
	Gas	E: BP◈, Hess
	Food	E: Applebee's, Bob Evans, Chili's, Romano's Macaroni Grill
	Lodg	E: Days Inn, Extended Stay America
	Other	E: ATMs, Auto Dealers, Grocery, RiteAid
16		**Timonium Rd (SB)**
	Gas	E: Sunoco◈
	Food	E: Steak & Ale
	Lodg	E: Extended Stay America, Holiday Inn
	Other	W: MD State Fairgrounds
16B		**Timonium Rd West (NB)**
16A		**Timonium Rd East (NB)**
(14)		**Jct I-695N,**
(13)		**Jct I-695S, Glen Burnie, Towson**
	Med	+ Hospital
	Other	MD State Hwy Patrol Post

Personal Notes

EXIT		MARYLAND
12		**Ruxton Rd, Towson (NB, Exit Only)**
	Other	E: to Robert E Lee Park
10		**Northern Pky, Baltimore (SB)**
	Med	E: + Hospital
10B		**Northern Pkwy W, Baltimore (NB)**

EXIT		MARYLAND
9AB		**Cold Spring Lane, Baltimore (SB)**
9B		**Cold Spring Lane W (NB)**
9A		**Cold Spring Lane E (NB)**
8		**MD 25, Falls Rd (NB)**
7B		**28th St (fr SB, Left Exit)**
	Med	E: + Hospital
7A		**Druid Park Lake Dr (SB)**
	Other	W: Druid Lake Park, to Baltimore Conservatory, Zoo
6A		**US 1, North Ave, Mt Royal Ave (SB)**
6B		**US 1, North Ave, to W 28th St, to Druid Park Lake Dr (NB)**
5		**MD 2, St Paul St, Calvert St, Maryland Ave, Downtown (SB)**
4		**Guilford Ave (SB), Eager St (NB), MD 2, St Paul St, Mt Royal Ave, Downtown, Baltimore (SB)**
3		**Fallsway, Chase St, (NB) Guilford Ave, Madison St (SB)**
2		**N Holiday St, E Pleasant St (fr SB, Left Exit)**
1		**E Fayette St, Downtown**
	Other	W: to National Aquarium, M&T Bank Stadium, to US 395

EASTERN TIME ZONE

NOTE: I-83 begins/ends at Exit #70 on I-81

MARYLAND

Begin Northbound I-83 in Baltimore to Jct I-81 near Harrisburg, PA.

EXIT		OREGON

Begin Eastbound I-84 from Portland, OR to Jct I-90 near Sturbridge, MA.

OREGON

NOTE: I-84 Begins/Ends on I-90, Ex #9 in MA
I-84 Begins/Ends on I-5, Ex #301

PACIFIC TIME ZONE

EXIT		OREGON
1A		**OR 99E, 12th Ave, Lloyd Blvd (WB)**
	Food	N: Quiznos, Asst'd Café's & Restaurants
	Lodg	N: Courtyard, DoubleTree Hotel, La Quinta Inn♥, Inn at Conv Center, Residence Inn, Shilo Inn S: Dunes Motel, Executive Lodge
	Med	N: + Legacy Emanuel Hospital
	Other	N: Convention Center, Lloyd Center, Rose Garden Arena S: Office Depot
1B		**33rd Ave, Lloyd Blvd (EB)**
	Gas	N: 76, Pacific Pride, Shell◈
	Food	S: Pizza Hut, Wendy's
	Other	N: Grocery, RiteAid S: Auto Dealers
2		**39th Ave (EB), Halsey St (WB)**
	Gas	N: Chevron, Shell
	Food	N: Blackwell's Steak Grill, Burger King, McDonald's, Pagoda, Poor Richard's, Quiznos, Subway
	Lodg	N: Banfield Value Inn, Econo Lodge
	Med	S: + Providence Portland Hospital
3		**Glisan St, 60th Ave (EB)**
	Gas	S: KC's MiniMart
	Med	S: + Providence Portland Hospital
4		**68th Ave, Halsey St (EB)**
5		**OR 213, 82nd Ave (EB ex, diff reacc)**
	Gas	N: 7-11, Shell S: Chevron, Shell
	Food	N: DQ, Chinese S: Burgerville USA, Chinese Village, Elmer's, McDonald's, Pizza Hut, Subway, Taco Bell, Wendy's
	Lodg	N: Days Inn, Cabana Motel S: Comfort Inn, Microtel
(6)		**Jct I-205S, Salem, Oregon City (EB)**
7		**Hasley St, Gateway District (EB)**
	Gas	S: ArcoAmPm Chevron
	Food	S: Carl's Jr, Carrow's, Subway
(8)		**I-205N, Seattle, Portland, Airport (EB, Exit only)**
	Other	N: to Portland Int'l Airport✈
(9)		**102nd Ave, Portland (EB) I-205, S to Oregon City, Salem, N to Seattle (WB, Left exit)**
10		**122nd Ave (EB)**

◈= Regular Gas Stations with Diesel ▲ = RV Friendly Locations ♥= Pet Friendly Locations
Red print shows large vehicle parking / access on site or nearby Brown Print = Campgrounds / RV PARKS

EXIT	OREGON
13	**181st Ave, Gresham, Fairview**
Gas	**N:** Chevron **S:** 7-11, Circle K
Food	**S:** Burger King, Francis Xavier's, IHOP, Jungs Dynasty, Little Caesars Pizza, McDonald's, Shari's, Wendy's
Lodg	**N:** Hampton Inn **S:** Comfort Suites, Extended Stay America, Econo Lodge, Quality Inn, Sleep Inn, Sheraton, Super 8♥
Other	**S:** ATMs, Auto Services, Safeway, Vet♥
14	**207th Ave, Fairview**
Gas	**N:** Shell◈
Food	**N:** CJ's Café, Gin Sun Rest & Lounge
Other	**N: Portland Fairview RV Park▲ , Rolling Hills RV Park▲ , American Dream RV Center**, Blue Lake Auto & **RV Repair**
16	**238th Dr, Wood Village, Gresham**
Gas	**N:** ArcoAmPm◈ **S:** Chevron
Food	**N:** Jack in the Box, Chinese, Quiznos
Lodg	**N:** Travelodge♥ **S:** Best Western, McMenamins Edgefield
Med	**S: + Legacy Mt Hood Medical Center**
Other	**N: Walmart sc▲ , Olinger Travel Homes/Camping World** **S: RV Center**
17	**Marine Dr, 257th Ave, Graham Rd, Frontage Rd, Troutdale, Portland**
TStop	**S:** Travel Center of America #183/Arco (Scales), Love's Travel Stop #449(Scales)
Gas	**S:** Chevron
Food	**N:** Wendy's **S:** Buckhorn/Subway/Popeyes/TA TC, Hot & Cold Deli/Love's TS, Arby's, McDonald's, Shari's, Taco Bell
Lodg	**N:** Holiday Inn Express♥ **S:** Best Value Inn/TA TC, Comfort Inn♥, Motel 6♥
TServ	**S:** TA TC/Tires
Other	**N:** Portland Troutdale Airport✈, **Blue Lake RV** **S:** Laundry/WiFi/TA TC, Laundry/WiFi/ RVDump/LP/Love's TS, ATMs, Columbia Gorge Premium Outlets, **to** Mount Hood Comm College, **Sandy Riverfront RV Resort▲**
18	**Lewis & Clark State Park**
Other	**S:** RR, Picnic, Trails, Beach, Boat Ramp, **to appr 6mi Crown Point RV Park▲**
22	**Corbett Hill Rd, Corbett**
Food	**S:** Rest/Chinook Inn
Lodg	**S:** Royal Chinook Inn
Other	**S: to Steep Grade: Crown Point RV Park▲**

EXIT	OREGON
(23)	**Corbett Scenic View (WB)**
25	**Rooster Rock State Park (NO Trucks)**
28	**to Bridal Veil State Park (EB)**
30	**Benson State Park (EB)**
31	**Multnomah Falls (Left Exit, Both dir)**
35	**Columbia River Scenic Hwy Ainsworth State Park**
Other	**S: RV/Camp▲** , **RVDump**, Elec, Showers, RR, Playground, Walking/Hiking Trail, Picnic, Waterfall, Amphitheater
37	**Warrendale Rd, Tumalt Rd, Cascade Locks, Warrandale (WB)**
40	**Bonneville Dam**
Other	**N:** Bonneville Dam, Bonneville Fish Hatchery, Bonneville Lock & Dam
41	**Eagle Creek Rec Area**
44A	**US 30E, Cascade Locks (EB) Bridge of the Gods to WA**
Gas	**N:** Chevron, Shell◈
Lodg	**N:** Best Western, Bridge of the Gods Motel, Econo Lodge
Other	**N:** Sternwheeler Columbia Gorge, Port of Cascade Locks & Marine Park, **Sternwheeler RV Park▲**
44B	**US 30, Cascade Locks (WB)**
Other	**N: Cascade Locks/Portland East KOA▲**
(44.9)	**Weigh Station (EB)**
47	**Herman Creek Rd, Forest Ln (WB)**
(49)	**Pull Off Area (EB)**
51	**Wyeth Rd, Herman Creek Rd, Cascade Locks, Wyeth**
(54)	**Weigh Station (WB)**
(55)	**Starvation Peak Trail Head (EB) (RR, Phones)**
55	**Starvation Creek State Park**
56	**Viento State Park**
Other	**N: RV/Camp▲** , Elec, Showers, Picnic, Beach Access, Hiking, Playground
(58)	**Mitchell Pt Overlook (EB)**
60	**Service Rd, Morton Rd (WB exit, No re-entry)**
(61)	**Hood River Pull Out Area (WB)**

EXIT	OREGON
62	**US 30E, OR 35, Cascade Ave, Westcliff Dr, Hood River**
Gas	**S:** Chevron◈, Shell◈
Food	**N:** Charburger Country, Red Panda **S:** McDonald's, Quiznos, Shari's, Subway, Starbucks, Taco Bell
Lodg	**N:** Columbia Gorge Hotel, Vagabond Lodge♥ **S:** Comfort Suites, Lone Pine Motel, Red Carpet Inn, Stonehenge Inn
Med	**S: + Hospital**
Other	**S:** ATMs, Laundromat, Grocery, **Walmart**, Auto Dealers, **to** Hood River Airport✈
63	**2nd St, Hood River**
Gas	**N:** 76d, Shell
Food	**S:** Burger King, Chinese, Hood River Rest, Horse Feathers
Lodg	**S:** Hood River Hotel, Riverview Lodge
Med	**S: + Hospital**
Other	**S: to** Hood River Airport✈, **818 Riverside Dr** Hood River Waste Treatment Plant/ **RVDump**
64	**OR 35, Button Bridge Rd, US 30W, Hood River, to White Salmon, WA**
Gas	**N:** Chevron, Shell **S:** Exxon
Food	**N:** McDonald's, Starbucks, Taco Time
Lodg	**S:** Oak Street Hotel
Other	**N: OR State Hwy Patrol Post**
(66)	**Hood River Rest Area (WB) (RR, Picnic)**
69	**US 30E, Mosier**
73	**Memaloose State Park**
Other	**N: Camp/RV▲** , Elec, Showers, RR, **RVDump**
(73)	**Mosier Rest Area (Both dir) (RR, Phone, Picnic, RVDump/EB)**
76	**Rowena River Rd, The Dalles, Rowena, Mayer State Park**
82	**Chenoweth Rd, to US 30, W 6th St Columbia River Discovery Center**
Gas	**S:** Shell◈, Astro◈, Exxon
Food	**S:** Arby's, Burger King, Cousins, Pietro's Pizza, Subway, Wendy's
Lodg	**S:** Country Cousins Inn, Motel 6♥, Oregon Trail Motel
Other	**S:** Columbia River Discovery Center
83	**US 30E, The Dalles (EB)**
Gas	**S:** Chevron, Exxon, Shell◈
Food	**S:** Arby's, Burger King, DQ, Skipper's Seafood, McDonald's, Subway, Taco Bell

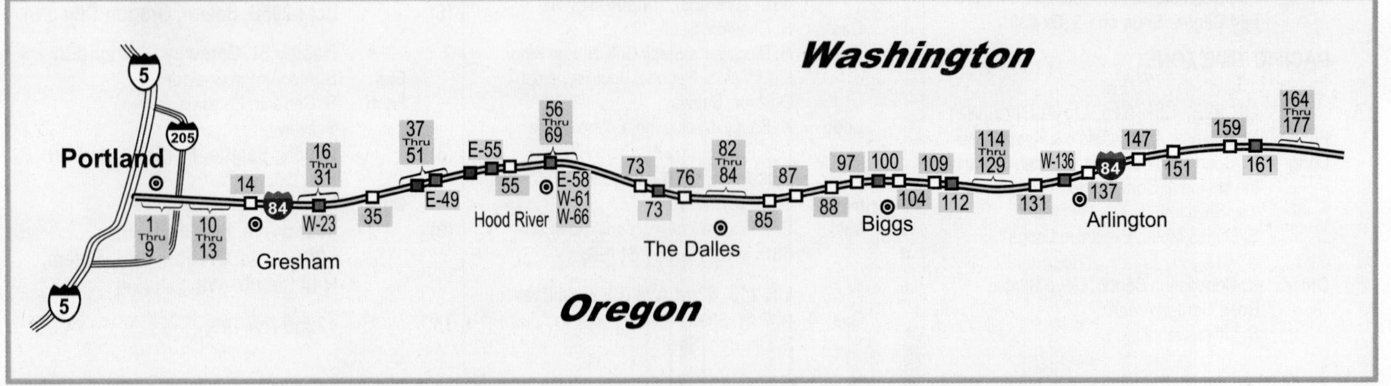

◈= Regular Gas Stations with Diesel ▲ = RV Friendly Locations ♥= Pet Friendly Locations
Red print shows large vehicle parking / access on site or nearby Brown Print = Campgrounds / RV PARKS

EXIT		OREGON
	Lodg	S: Best Western, Days Inn, Quality Inn, Shilo Inn, Super 8
	Other	N: NAPA S: Albertson's, RiteAid, Staples
84		**2nd St, to US 30W, The Dalles (WB) (Access to Ex #83 Serv)**
(85)		**Riverfront Park Rd, The Dalles** **N: Riverfront Park Rd (RR, Phone, Pic, Playgr, Marina)**
	Gas	S: 76◈, Chevron
	Food	S: Burgerville USA, Casa El Miridor, The Wagon Seafood & Steaks
	Lodg	S: Best Western
	Med	S: + Hospital
	Other	S: Auto Services & Repairs
87		**US 197, US 30W, The Dalles, Maupin, Dufur, Bend**
	Gas	N: 76, Chevron, Shell
	Food	S: Big Jim's, McDonald's
	Lodg	N: Comfort Inn, Shilo Inn♥
	Other	N: OR State Hwy Patrol Post, Lone Pine RV Park▲, to Columbia Hills RV Village▲, to Wishbone Campground▲, to The Dalles Muni Airport✈ S: to Dufur RV Park, appr 20 mi Wasco Co Fairgrounds▲, to Pine Hollow Lakeside Resort & RV Park▲
88		**to The Dalles Dam**
	Other	N: to Dalles Dam
97		**OR 206, Celilo Park, The Dalles, Celilo, Wasco**
	Other	N: Celilo Park S: Celilo Village▲, Deschutes River Rec Area▲
(100)		**Scenic Area: Columbia River Gorge, Deschutes River**
104		**US 97, Wasco, Biggs Junction, to Yakima, Bend**
	TStop	S: Pilot Travel Center #195 (Scales), Grand Central Travel Stop
	Gas	S: Circle K/76◈, hevron
	Food	S: McDonald's/Pilot TC, Linda's Rest/ Subway/TS, Noble Romans/Circle K, Dinty's Café, Jack's Fine Food,
	Lodg	S: Biggs Motel, Dinty Motor Inn, Travelodge
	Other	N: to Peach Beach RV Park▲, Maryhill State Park▲ S: WiFi/Pilot TC, Auto Repair, to Wasco State Airport✈
109		**US 30, John Day Dam Ln, Rufus**
	FStop	S: Pacific Pride
	Gas	S: BP, Shell◈
	Food	S: Bob's Texas T-Bone

EXIT		OREGON
	Lodg	S: Rufus Rocks Motel♥, Tyee Motel
	Other	N: John Day Visitor Center S: Bob's Budget RV & Trailer Park▲, Rufus RV Park▲, Deschutes State Park▲, to appr 18mi Sherman Co Fairgrounds, Sherman Co RV Park▲
(112)		**Rufus Parking Area (Both dir)**
114		**John Day Dam, LePage Park Rd**
	Other	S: COE/LePage Park/RVDump
123		**Quinton Canyon Rd, Phillippi Canyon, Lewis & Clark Trail**
129		**Blalock Canyon Rd, Arlington, Blalock, Lewis & Clark Trail**
131		**Woelpern Rd (EB, No re-entry)**
(136)		**Arlington Scenic View (WB)**
137		**OR 13, Arlington, Condon**
	Gas	S: 76, Shell◈
	Food	S: Happy Canyon, Village Inn
	Lodg	S: Arlington Motel
	Other	S: Grocery, Columbia River RV Park▲, Arlington RV & MH Park▲, Arlington Muni Airport✈
147		**OR 74, Heppner Hwy, Arlington, to Ione, Heppner, Blue Mountain Scenic Byway**
151		**Three Mile Canyon**
159		**Tower Rd, Boardman Rd, Boardman**
	Other	S: Boardman Airstrip✈, Boardman Bombing Range
(161)		**Boardman Rest Area (Both dir) (RR, Phone, Picnic, Vend, Info/EB)**
164		**N Main St, Boardman**
	FStop	N: Main St Shell
	TStop	N: Devon Oil/Shell 76
	Gas	N: Chevron◈ S: Shell◈
	Food	N: C&D Drive In S: Nomad Rest
	Lodg	N: Dodge City Inn, Riverview Motel S: Econo Lodge
	Other	N: Boardman RV Park & Marina▲ S: ATMs, Auto Services, Grocery
165		**Messner Rd, Port of Morrow**
	FStop	S: Pacific Pride
168		**US 730, Columbia River Hwy, to Irrigon, Umatilla**
	Other	N: to appr 8 mi: Oasis RV Park▲
171		**CR 930, Patterson Ferry Rd, Frontage Rd, Irrigon**

EXIT		OREGON
177		**Umatilla Army Depot, Hermiston**
(179)		**Jct I-82W, Umatilla, to Yakima, Kennewick**
180		**Westland Rd, Westland, Hermiston, to McNary Dam**
	FStop	S: Western Express/Shell
	Food	S: FastFood/Western Express
	TServ	N: Truck Body Trailer & Repair, Freightliner
	Other	N: LP/Western Express
182		**OR 207, Hermiston Hwy, Hermiston, Lexington**
	TStop	N: RoadysTS/Space Age Fuel Travel Center (Scales)
	Food	N: FastFood/Space Age TC
	Lodg	N: Comfort Inn
	Med	N: + Hospital
	Other	N: Laundry/RVDump/LP/Space Age FC, appr 3mi Pioneer RV Park▲
(187)		**Stanfield Rest Area (Both dir) (RR, Phone, Pic, Vend, Horse)**
188		**US 395N, OR 32, Stanfield, Hermiston, Old Pendleton River Rd, Echo**
	TStop	N: Pilot Travel Center #390 (Scales)
	Gas	N: Chevron◈
	Food	N: Subway/McDonald's/Pilot TC, Denny's
	Lodg	N: appr 4-5 mi Best Western, Oak Tree Inn, Oxford Suites, Economy In
	Med	N: + Hospital
	Other	N: Laundry/WiFi/RVPark▲/Pilot TC, to appr 6mi Hat Rock Campground▲, Stage Gulch RV Park▲, Pilot RV Park▲, Greyhound, Hermiston Muni Airport✈ S: Fort Henrietta RV Park▲
193		**Whitmore Rd, Stage Gulch Rd, OR 320, Echo, Lexington**
198		**McClintock-Lorenzen Rd**
199		**Yoakum Rd, Pendleton**
202		**Barnhart Rd, Pendleton**
207		**US 30E, Pendleton Hwy, Pendleton**
	Gas	N: Chevron◈, Shell◈
	Food	N: DQ, Taco Bell
	Lodg	N: Longhorn Motel, Travelodge♥, Vagabond Inn
	Other	N: Lookout RV Park▲, Brooke RV Park▲, Eastern OR Reg'l Airport✈
209		**US 395S, to US 30, OR 37, Pendleton, to Burns**
	Gas	N: ArcoAmPm, Safeway S: 76◈, Exxon, Shell

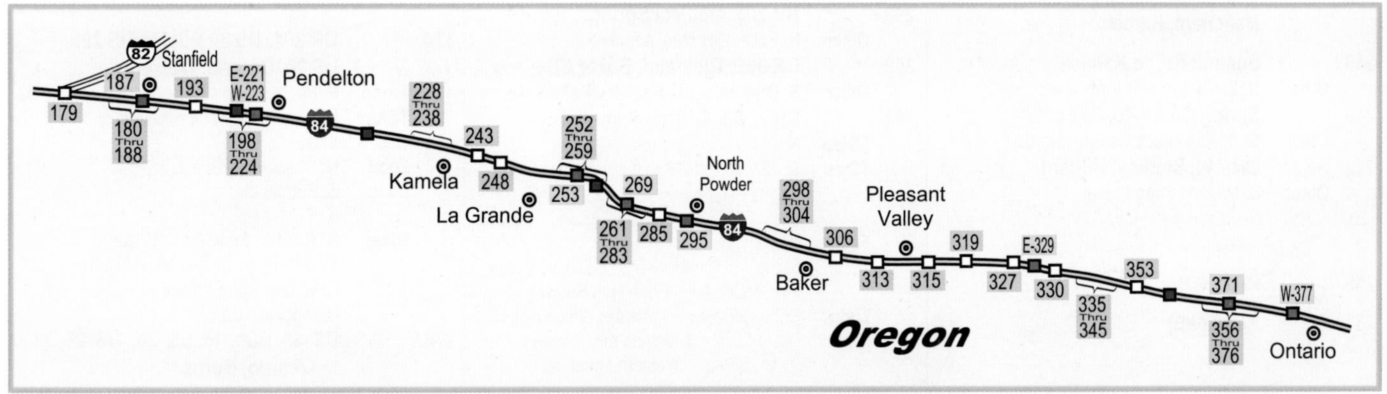

◈= Regular Gas Stations with Diesel ▲ = RV Friendly Locations ♥= Pet Friendly Locations

Red print shows large vehicle parking / access on site or nearby Brown Print = Campgrounds / RV PARKS

Food — N: Jack in the Box, KFC, Taco Bell
S: Arby's, Burger King, Denny's, Pizza, McDonald's, Rooster's, Subway, Wendy's
Lodg — N: Oxford Suites, Travelodge♥
S: Econo Lodge
TServ — N: Cummins
Med — N: + Hospital
Other — N: ATMs, Grocery, RiteAid, Safeway, **Walmart sc**, **Camp Da-Kon-Ya▲**
S: ATMs, Auto Dealers, Grocery, Les Schwab Tire, **Thompson RV Center**, Heritage Station Museum/RVDump

210 — OR 11, Oregon-Washington Hwy, Pendleton, Walla Walla
FStop — S: Pacific Pride
Gas — N: 76, Exxon
S: 76◈, Shell◈
Food — S: Kopper Kitchen, Shari's
Lodg — S: Best Western, Holiday Inn Express♥, Motel 6♥, Red Lion Hotel
Med — N: + Hospital
Other — N: **Catalpa Tree RV Park▲**, **Wild Rose RV Park▲**
S: Grocery, **Mountain View RV Park▲**, OR State Hwy Patrol Post

213 — US 30, Pendleton Hwy (WB) (Addtl Serv 3-5 mi N)
Other — N: **Oregon Trail RV Park▲**

216 — OR 331, to OR 11, Milton-Freewater, Walla Walla, Mission, Umatilla Indian Reservation
TStop — N: PacPride/Arrowhead Travel Plaza (Scales)
Food — N: Rest/Arrowhead TP
Lodg — N: Wildhorse Casino Resort & **RVPark▲**
Other — N: WiFi/LP/Arrowhead TP, Wildhorse Golf Course

(220) — RunAway Truck Ramp (WB)

(221) — Scenic View (EB)

(223) — Scenic View (WB)

224 — Poverty Hill Rd, Old Emigrant Rd, Umatilla Indian Reservation

(227) — Weigh Station (WB) Brake Inspection Area

(228) — Deadman Pass, Evergreen Ln
Pendleton Rest Area (Both dir) (RR, Phone, Picnic, Vend)

234 — Old Emigrant Hill Scenic Frontage Rd, Pendleton, Meacham
Other — N: **Emigrant Spring State Park▲**

235 — Emigrant Spring State Park (WB)

238 — Beaver Creek Rd, Pendleton, Meacham, Kamela

243 — Summit Rd, to Kamela
Other — N: Emily Summit State Park

248 — Spring Creek Rd, to Kamela
Other — S: **Spring Creek Campground▲**

252 — OR 244, Starkey, Hilgard
Other — S: **Hilgard State Park▲**

(253) — Rest Area (Both dir) (RR, Picnic)

256 — Perry (EB)

257 — Perry (WB)

(258) — Weigh Station (EB)

259 — US 30E, LaGrande (EB)
Gas — S: Chevron, Exxon, Shell
Food — S: Smokehouse Rest, BurgerKing/Exxon
Lodg — S: Royal Motor Inn♥

261 — OR 82, LaGrande, Elgin
FStop — S: PacPride/Buy Rite/Exxon
TStop — N: Gem Stop/Chevron
Gas — N: Shell◈
S: 76◈, Chevron◈, Exxon◈
Food — N: Denny's, Pizza Hut, Subway
S: DQ, Little Caesars, McDonald's, Taco Time, Skipper's, Wendy's
Lodg — N: Howard Johnson, LeGrande Inn
S: Best Value Inn, Best Western, Super 8
TServ — N: Eagle Truck & Machine Co
S: Trail West Truck Service Center
Med — S: + Grande Ronde Hospital
Other — N: OR State Hwy Patrol Post, Auto Dealers, **Walmart**, **Thunder RV**, **Island City Trailer Sales**, **La Grande Rendezvous RV Park▲**
S: Albertson's, RiteAid, Safeway, E OR Univ, **Curt's RV Service & Repair**

265 — US 30, OR 203, LaGrande, Union
TStop — S: Flying J Travel Plaza #10120/Exxon (Scales)
Food — S: Blue Mtn Rest/FastFood/FJ TP
Lodg — S: Royal Motor Inn♥
TServ — S: Freightliner
Other — N: **to appr 8mi: Eagles Hot Lake RV Resort▲**
S: Laundry/WiFi/FJ TP, East OR Univ

268 — Foothill Rd, Union
Other — N: **to appr 8mi: Eagles Hot Lake RV Resort▲**

(269) — La Grande Rest Area (Both dir) (RR, Phone, Picnic, Vend, RVDump)

270 — Ladd Canyon Rd (EB)

273 — Brush Creek Rd, Ladd Creek

278 — Clover Creek

283 — Wolf Creek Rd

285 — US 30E, Haines, OR 237, N Powder
FStop — N: North Powder Co-Op/Cenex
Food — N: Rest/Cenex
Lodg — N: Powder River Motel
Other — S: to Ski Area, Anthony Lakes

NOTE: MM 287.5: 45th Parallel halfway between the North Pole & the Equator

(295) — Baker City Rest Area (Both dir) (RR, Phone, Picnic, Vend)

298 — OR 203, Medical Springs, Haines
Other — N: Baker City Muni Airport✈

302 — OR 86E, Richland, Baker City
Other — S: **Oregon Trails West RV Park/Gas▲**

304 — OR 7, Baker City, Sumpter
FStop — N: Baker City Chevron
TStop — S: CFN/AmBest/Roadys/Baker Truck Corral/Sinclair (Scales), Jacksons Food Mart #83/Shell
Food — N: Burger King/Chevron
S: Country Cafe/Baker TC, Blimpie/Jackson FM, McDonald's, Pizza Hut, Subway
Lodg — S: Motel/Baker TC, Always Welcome Inn, Best Western, Eldorado Inn, Rodeway Inn ♥, Super 8, Western Motel
TServ — S: Baker TC/Tires
Med — S: + St Elizabeth's Hospital
Other — S: Laundry/**RVDump/LP**/Baker TC, Carwash/**RVDump/LP**/Jackson FM, Albertson's, RiteAid, Safeway, **Mountain View Holiday Trav-L-RV Park▲**

306 — US 30W, Baker City
Gas — S: Gilly's Service Center/Chevron◈
Food — S: Burger Bob's Drive-In, Inland Café, Janet's Cook Shack
Lodg — S: Budget Inn, **Baker City Motel & RV Park▲**, OR Trail Motel, Western Motel
Other — S: OR State Hwy Patrol Post

313 — Pleasant Valley (EB)

315 — Pleasant Valley (WB)

317 — Old Hwy 30, Pleasant Valley (WB)

319 — Pleasant Valley

327 — Durkee
FStop — N: Oregon Trail Travel Center/Cenex
Food — N: Café/Cenex TS
Other — N: RVDump/Cenex TS

330 — Plano Rd, Cement Plant Rd, Nelson
Other — S: Cement Plant

(335) — to Weatherby
N: Rest Area (Both dir) (RR, Phone, Picnic, Vend)

338 — Lookout Mountain
Other — N: **OR Trail RV Park▲**

340 — Rye Valley

342 — Lime (EB)

345 — US 30 Bus, Huntington Hwy, Huntington, Lime

NOTE: MM 351: PACIFIC/MOUNTAIN Time Zone

353 — US 30, to Huntington, Farewell Bend
TStop — N: Farewell Bend Travel Plaza
Food — N: Deli/Farewell Bend TP

(354) — Weigh Station (EB)

356 — OR 201N, to Weiser, ID
Other — N: **Oasis RV Park & Campground▲**, **Catfish Junction RV Park▲**, **Snake River RV Park▲**

362 — Moores Hollow Rd

(371) — Rest Area (Both dir) (RR, Picnic)

371 — Stanton Blvd

374 — OR 201, US 30 Bus, to US 20, US 26, Ontario, Weiser
FStop — S: Pacific Pride
TStop — N: Love's Travel Stop #372 (Scales)
Gas — S: Shell◈
Food — N: Chesters/Subway/Love's TS
Lodg — S: Budget Inn
Med — S: + Hospital
Other — N: **Ontario State Park**/RVDump
S: U-Haul, to Ontario Muni Airport✈, **Lake Owl State Park▲**, **Country Campground▲**

376A — US 30 Bus, to US 20, US 26, to Ontario, Burns

EXIT		OR / ID
376B		**to US 95, Payette**
376		**US 30, US 95, Idaho Ave, Ontario, Payette**
	TStop	**S:** Pilot Travel Center #232 (Scales)
	Gas	**N:** Chevron
		S: Shell◈
	Food	**N:** Burger King, Country Kitchen, DQ, Denny's, McDonald's, China Buffet
		S: Arby's/TJCinn/Pilot TC, BBQ, Chinese, DJ's Rest, Sizzler, Skippers Seafood, Taco Bell, Wendy's, Winger's Diner
	Lodg	**N:** Best Western, Colonial Motor Inn, Motel 6♥, Sleep Inn, Super 8
		S: Economy Inn, Holiday Motor Inn, Oregon Trail Motel, Rodeway Inn
	Med	**S:** + Hospital
	Other	**N:** ATMs, Auto Dealers, Home Depot, Staples, **Walmart sc▲**, **OR State Hwy Patrol Post**
		S: Laundry/WiFi/**RVDump**/Pilot TC, Ontario Muni Airport✈, Auto Dealers, NAPA, Tires, Radio Shack, U-Haul, Museum
(377)		**OR Welcome Center (WB) (RR, Phone, Picnic, Vend, Info, WiFi)**

MOUNTAIN TIME ZONE

NOTE: MM 378: Idaho State Line

⬆ OREGON
⬇ IDAHO

MOUNTAIN TIME ZONE

EXIT		IDAHO
(1)		**ID Welcome Center (EB) (RR, Phone, Picnic, Vend, Info, WiFi)**
3		**US 95, Fruitland, Payette**
	Gas	**N:** Shell◈
	Food	**N:** A&W **Addtl food 3.5mi**
	Other	**N: Exit 3 RV Park▲ , Hells Canyon Rec Area, Hollis RV Repair**
		S: Neat Retreat RV Park▲
9		**US 30 Bus, New Plymouth**
13		**Black Canyon Rd, Caldwell, Bliss**
	TStop	**S:** Stinker Station #45/Sinclair (Scales)
	Food	**S:** Rest/FastFood/Stinker
	Lodg	**S:** Motel/Stinker
	Other	**S:** Laundry/Stinker
17		**Oasis Rd, Caldwell, Sand Hollow**
	Gas	**N:** Sinclair
	Food	**N:** Sandhollow Country Café
	Lodg	**S:** Wild Rose Manor B&B
	Other	**N: Country Corners Campground & RV Park/RVDump▲**
25		**ID 44E, Caldwell, Middleton**
	Gas	**N:** 44 Quick Stop/Shell◈
26		**US 20, US 26, Nyssa, Burns, Caldwell, Notus**
	Gas	**S:** Stinker/Sinclair
	Other	**N: Caldwell Campground & RV Park▲**
27		**I-84 Bus, ID 19, Centennial Way, to US 95, Caldwell, Wilder**
	FStop	**S: 122 Simplot Blvd:** Pacific Pride
	TStop	**S: approx 11mi 128 5th St/Wilder:** Jackson Food Store #3/Shell (Scales)
	Other	**S:** Laundry/**RVDump**/Jackson FS
28		**10th Ave, Caldwell**
	Gas	**N:** Maverik Country Store
		S: Chevron, Jackson FS/Shell◈
	Food	**S:** Carl's Jr, DQ, Jack in the Box, Mr. V's, Pizza Hut, Wendy's
	Lodg	**N:** I-84 Motor Inn
		S: Holiday Motel♥, Sundowner Motel♥
	Med	**S: + West Valley Medical Center**
	Other	**N:** Birds of Prey Harley Davidson
		S: ATMs, Auto Zone, Banks, Bruneel Tire Factory, Paul's Market/Pharmacy, Walgreen's, Canyon Co Court House, Golf Course
29		**US 20E, US 26E, Franklin Rd, Caldwell, Boise, Garden City**
	TStop	**N:** Flying J Travel Plaza #5002/Conoco (Scales)
		S: Sage Travel Plaza/Sinclair
	Food	**N:** CountryMarket/FastFood/FJ TP
		S: Rest/FastFood/Sage TP, Cattleman's Café, McDonald's, Perkins
	Lodg	**S:** Best Western, La Quinta Inn♥
	Med	**S: + W Valley Hospital**
	Other	**N:** Laundry/WiFi/**RVDump/LP**/FJ TP, **Ambassador RV Resort/RVDump▲** Caldwell Industrial Airport✈
	Other	**S:** Laundry/**RVDump/LP**/Sage TP, ATMs, Banks, Auto Dealers, Auto Services, Albertson's/Pharmacy, Auto Zone,Best Buy, Conger Small Animal Hospital♥, Les Schwab Tires, NAPA, RiteAid, Tires, True Value, **Walmart sc**, Albertson College, College of ID, Fairgrounds/**RVDump, Nelson's Out West RV's**
33AB		**ID 55S, Karcher Rd, Nampa (WB)**
33		**ID 55S, Karcher Rd, Midland Blvd, Nampa (EB) (Acc #29 via W to Nampa Caldwell Blvd)**
	Gas	**S:** Jackson FS, Maverik
	Food	**N:** Olive Garden, Qdoba Mexican Grill, Starbucks, TGI Friday, Wingers
		S: Acapulco Grill, Applebee's, Arby's, Carl's Jr, IHOP, Jack in the Box, Jade Garden, Jalapeno Rest, Outback Steakhouse, Red Robin, Shari's, Taco Bell
	Other	**N:** Best Buy, Costco, Cost Plus World Market, PetCo♥, Target, Caldwell Industrial Airport✈
		S: ATMs, Auto Repairs & Services, Big O Tires, Big Lots, Dollar Tree, Edwards 21 Cinemas, Home Depot, Office Depot, Pharmacy, ShopKO, Staples, Sports Authority, Triangle Truck Center, UPS Store, Karcher Mall, **Freedom Boat & RV, Bob'sRV Center, Happy Trails RV, appr 7mi Decoy RV Park▲**
35		**ID 55S, Nampa Blvd, Nampa**
	TStop	**S:** CFN/Gem Stop Truck Stop/Jackson Food Store #85/Shell
	Food	**S:** FastFood/Jackson FS, Burger King, Blazen Burgers, Denny's, KFC, McDonald's, Pizza Hut
	Lodg	**S:** Rodeway Inn, Shilo Inn, Super 8
	Med	**S: + Hospital**
	TWash	**S:** Jackson FS
	Other	**S:** Laundry/WiFi/Jackson FS, ATM, Auto Service, Tires, Fred Meyer, Pharmacy, Walgreen's
36		**Franklin Blvd, Nampa**
	FStop	**S:** Chevron
	TStop	**S:** PacPr/Jackson Food Store #5/Shell (Scales)
	Gas	**N:** Maverik
	Food	**N:** Elmer's, Jack in the Box
		S: FastFood/Jackson FS
	Lodg	**N:** Shilo Inn
		S: Sleep Inn
	TWash	**S:** Action **RV** & Truck Wash, Jackson FS
	TServ	**S:** Western ID Freightliner
	Med	**S: + Hospital**
	Other	**N: Nelson Freeway RV's**
		S: Laundry/**RVDump**/Jackson FS, **Mason Creek RV Park/RVDump▲ , ID RV Service & Repair, Seventh Heaven RV & Marine Superstore,** Western Marine
38		**I-84 Bus, ID 45S, Garrity Blvd,**
	Gas	**N:** Chevron◈
		S: Phillips 66◈, Shell
	Food	**N:** Port of Subs, Subway
		S: McDonald's/66
	Lodg	**N:** Hampton Inn
		S: Holiday Inn Express

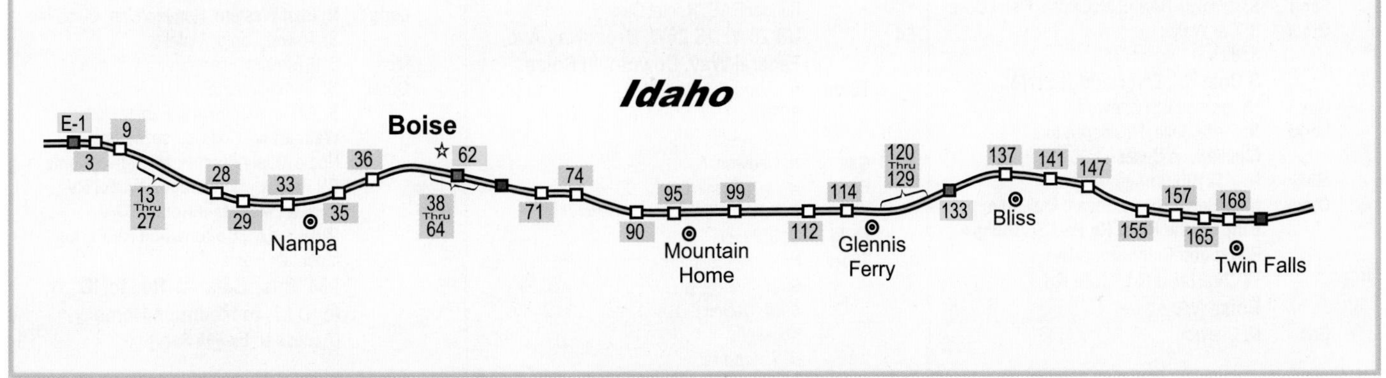

◈= Regular Gas Stations with Diesel ▲ = RV Friendly Locations ♥= Pet Friendly Locations
Red print shows large vehicle parking / access on site or nearby Brown Print = Campgrounds / RV PARKS

EXIT — IDAHO

Med S: + Mercy Health Center
Other N: Auto Dealers, Sam's Club, **WalMart sc**
S: **Garrity Blvd RV Park**/RVDump▲, **Earl's RV, RV Furniture Center**, Nampa Muni Airport✈

44 — 1st St, Meridian Rd, ID 69S, Meridian, Kuna
FStop N: **234 W Franklin:** Pacific Pride
Gas N: Chevron◈, Sinclair
S: Shell◈
Food N: Bolo's Pub, DQ, KFC, McDonald's, Pizza Hut, Quiznos, Shari's, Starbucks, Subway, Taco Bell, Tony Roma's, Wendy's
S: JB's Family Rest, Pizza Hut
Lodg N: Best Western, Motel 6♥, Wyndham
S: Mr. Sandman Motel
TServ N: Idaho Fleet Service
S: Western States Truck Shop/CAT
Other N: ATMs, Auto Repairs, Banks, CarQuest, Grocery, Home Depot, Les Schwab Tires, Pharmacy, Sierra Trading Post, Meridian Speedway, **Boise-Meridian RV Resort**/RVDump▲
S: U-Haul, Vet♥, **Playground RV Park**▲, **Bodily RV Center**/RVDump, Roaring Springs Waterpark, Boondocks Fun Center

46 — ID 55N, Eagle Rd, McCall
FStop N: **to 549 Partridge Pl appr 3mi** Pacific Pride◈◈
S: **to 3291 E Pine** CFN/Jackson Food Store #105
Gas N: Chevron◈◈, Shell◈
Food N: IHOP, McDonald's, Subway
S: Durango's Mexican, NY Deli, Quiznos, Subway, TCBY
Lodg N: Holiday Inn Express
Med N: + St Luke's Meridian Medical Center
Other N: FedEx Office, PetSmart♥, Office Depot, Pharmacy, **Fiesta RV Park**▲, **to appr 7mi: Hi-Valley RV Park**▲
S: High Desert Harley Davidson, Carwash/ Jackson FS, UPS Store, US Post Office

(49) — Jct I-184, W Boise (fr EB, Left Exit)
Other N: **to 1st Ex** Boise Town Square Mall, **to** Bogus Basin Mountain Resort, Ski Area

50A — W Overland Rd, Boise (EB)
Gas S: Phillips 66, Jackson FS
Food S: Black Angus, Burger King, CK Hawaiian BBQ, ChuckARama Buffet, Goodwood BBQ, Johnny Carino's Italian, McDonald's, Pollo Rey Mex Rest, On the Border, Starbucks
Lodg S: Ameritel Inn, Budget Host Inn, Hilton Garden Inn, Homewood Suites, Oxford Suites
Other S: Car Wash, Lowe's, **Walmart sc**

50B — S Cole Rd, Overland Rd (EB)
Gas S: Stinker/Shell, Maverik
Food S: Cracker Barrel, McGrath's Fish House
Other S: Car Wash, Commercial Tire, Costco

50A — S Cole Rd, Overland Rd (WB)
Gas N: Jackson FS, Chevron
Lodg N: Plaza Suite, Residence Inn, Candlewood Suites
Med N: + St Alphonsus Hospital
Other N: **to** Boise Towne Square Mall, **to appr 6 mi: On the River RV Park**/RVDump▲, **Riverpond Campground**▲

50B — W Overland Rd, Cole Rd, Boise (WB)
Gas N: Chevron

Personal Notes

EXIT — IDAHO

Food N: Cobby's Sandwich Shop, Eddie's, McDonald's, Outback Steakhouse, Pizza Hut, Subway, Taco Bell

52 — Orchard St, Boise (Access to Ex #50AB Serv N)
FStop N: **to 3712 Chinden Blvd 3.5mi** Pacific Pride◈◈
Gas N: Shell
Food N: Jack in the Box

53 — Vista Ave, Boise Airport
Gas N: Shell, Sinclair
S: Chevron
Food N: McDonald's, Pizza Hut
S: Denny's, McDonald's, Kopper Kitchen, Pizza Hut
Lodg N: Cambria Suites, Extended Stay America, Fairfield Inn, Hampton Inn, Holiday Inn Express♥, Super 8
S: Best Western, Comfort Inn, Holiday Inn, Inn America, Motel 6♥, Sleep Inn
Other N: **ID State Hwy Patrol Post**
S: Boise Air Terminal/Gowen Field✈, Budget RAC, Rental Cars

54 — US 20W, US 26W, Broadway Ave, Federal Way, Downtown Boise
TStop N: Flying J Travel Plaza #10380 (Scales)
S: Travel Center of America #167/ Tesoro (Scales)
Gas N: Chevron◈
Food N: Rest/FastFood/FJ TP
S: Buckhorn/Subway/TacoBell/TA TC
Lodg S: Shilo Inn
TServ N: Cummins Intermountain, NW Equipment
S: TA TC/Tires, Lake City International, Smith Detroit Diesel-Allison, Trebar Kenworth
Med N: + Hospital

EXIT — IDAHO

Other N: Laundry/WiFi/**RVDump/LP**/FJ TP, NAPA, **to** Boise State Univ, Boise Zoo
S: Laundry/WiFi/TA TC, Boise Air Terminal/ Gowen Field✈, **Mountain View RV Park**/RVDump▲

57 — ID 21 Gowen Rd, Boise, Idaho City
Gas N: Albertson's
S: Chevron, Shell
Food N: Jack in the Box, Perkins, Subway
S: Burger King/Chevron, McDonald's
Lodg N: Best Western
TServ N: Boise Peterbilt, Cummins Rocky Mtn
Other N: Albertson's, Micron Technology, Simplot Sports Complex, **to Lucky Peak State Park**
S: Boise VF Factory Outlet Mall, Jack's Tires & Oil, ID Ice World

59A — Eisenman Rd (EB)

59B — Federal Way (EB)

59 — Memory Rd, Eisenman Rd, S Federal Way, Boise (WB) (Access to Ex #57 Serv)

(62) — Rest Area (Both dir) (RR, Phone, Picnic, Vend)

64 — Kuna More Rd, Boise

(67) — Weigh Station (Both dir)

71 — Orchard Access Rd, Boise, Mayfield, Orchard
TStop S: PacPride/Boise Stage Stop/Sinclair (Scales)
Food S: Rest/Boise SS
Lodg S: Motel/Boise SS
TWash S: Boise SS
TServ S: Boise SS/Tires
Other S: Laundry/CB/WiFi/**RVDump**/Boise SS, Ada Co Nat'l Guard Maneuver Area

74 — Simco Rd

90 — I-84 Bus, Frontage Rd, to ID 51, ID 67, Mountain Home (Access to Ex #95 Serv-3mi)

95 — US 20E, Idaho Falls (EB), ID 51S, American Legion Blvd, Mountain Home, Elko
FStop S: Sunset C-Store/Sinclair
TStop N: Pilot Travel Center #350 (Scales)
Gas N: Chevron
S: Mirastar
Food N: Arby's/TJCinn/PilotTC KFC, Jack in the Box, Subway
S: Golden Crown Rest, Jade Palace Rest, McDonald's, Subway, Wendy's
Lodg N: Best Western, Hampton Inn, Sleep Inn
S: Towne Center Motel♥
Med S: + Elmore Hospital
Other N: Laundry/WiFi/Pilot TC
S: ATMs, Albertson's, Family Dollar, **Walmart sc**, Golf Course, Mountain Home Muni Airport✈, **Mountain Home RV Park**▲, **The Wagon Wheel RV Park**▲, **Mountain Home KOA**/RVDump▲, **Cottonwood RV Park**▲, Mountain Home AFB

99 — I-84 Bus, Bennett Rd, to ID 51, to ID 67, to Mountain Home (Access to Ex #95 Serv)

◈= Regular Gas Stations with Diesel ▲ = RV Friendly Locations ♥= Pet Friendly Locations
Red print shows large vehicle parking / access on site or nearby Brown Print = Campgrounds / RV PARKS

EXIT	IDAHO

112 — I-84 Bus, Hammett Hill Rd, to ID 78W, Glenns Ferry, Murphy
Other S: Cold Springs Winery, to Bruneau Dunes State Park

114 — I-84 Bus, ID 30, to ID 78, Cold Springs Rd (WB)

120 — I-84 Bus, N Bannock Ave, Glenns Ferry (EB) (Access to Ex #121 Serv)
Other S: Trail Break RV Park▲ ,

121 — I-84 Bus, King Hill Loop, E 1st Ave, Glenns Ferry
Gas S: Sinclair
Food S: Oregon Trail Café, Café/Hanson's Motel, Pizza, Rest/Carmela Winery
Lodg S: Hanson's Motel, Harvester Inn, Redford Motel
Other S: Power Pop RV Stop▲ , Carmela Winery, Glenns Ferry Muni Airport✈, Carmela RV Park▲ , Three Island State Park▲

125 — Paradise Valley, Grave Rd, King Hill

129 — Parks Loop Rd, Gopher Knoll Rd, King Hill

(133) — Rest Area (Both dir)
(RR, Phone, Picnic, Vend)

137 — I-84 Bus, US 26, to US 30, Pioneer Rd, Bliss
(Access to Ex #141 Serv-1.5mi)

141 — US 26E, Gooding, Snoshone (EB), US 30E, Buhl, Bliss (WB)
TStop S: Stinker Station #74/Sinclair, Roadrunner, Ziggy's Express/66, (EB: Access via Ex #137)
Gas S: Hagerman Shell
Food S: Rest/Ziggy's, Larry & Mary's Café, Ox Bow Café, Riley Creek Rest, Skinny Pig, Snake River Grill
Lodg S: Amber Inn Motel, Y-Inn Motel, to appr 8mi: Hagermann Valley Inn, Billingsley Creek Lodge
Med N: + Hospital
Other S: Laundry/Stinker, WiFi/Roadrunner, Hagerman RV Village▲

147 — 2300 S, Hagerman, to Tuttle
Other S: High Adventure River Tours, Malad Gorge State Park

155 — ID 46 Spur, Wendell, Hagermann
(Access to Ex #157 Sev)
Other N: Intermountain Motor Homes & RV Park/RVDump▲ , Bert Harbaugh Motors
S: Thousand Springs Resort▲ , to Mineral Hot Springs & Campground▲

EXIT	IDAHO

157 — ID 46N, Idaho St, Wendell, Gooding
FStop S: Wendell Gas & Oil/Sinclair
Food N: Family Rest, Pizza, Subway
S: Farmhouse Rest
Lodg N: Hub City Inn
Other N: Intermountain Motor Homes & RV Park/RVDump▲ , to 210 S Shohone St: City RVDump
S: RVDump/Wendell G&O

165 — ID 25E, Main St, Appleton Rd, to US 93, Jerome
(Access to Ex #168 Serv)
Gas N: Valley Co-Op, Sinclair◈
Food N: China Village, Café, Family Dinner
Lodg N: Holiday Motel, Towles Motel
TServ N: Centennial Truck Service, Fleet Tire Service
Med N: + St Benedicts Hospital
Other N: Auto Services, ATMs

168 — ID 79N, Jerome
FStop N: Honker's Mini Mart/Sinclair (Scales)
Gas N: Chevron, Mirastar, Shell
Food N: FastFood/Honkers, Jerome Café, McDonald's, Sonic, Wendy's/Shell
Lodg N: Best Western, Crest Motel
TServ N: Kenworth
Other N: Laundry/RVDump/LP/Honkers, Tires, Walmart sc, Brockman's RV Sales
S: ID RV & Marine

(171) — Rest Area (EB)
(RR, Phone, Picnic, Vend)

(171) — Weigh Station (EB)

173 — US 93, Jerome, Twin Falls, Sun Valley Wells, Missoula
(S Serv are appr 5mi S in Twin Falls)
TStop N: Flying J Travel Plaza #5116 (Scales)
Food N: Rest/FastFood/FJ TP
Lodg N: Days Inn/FJ TP
TWash N: Blue Beacon TW/FJ TP
S: Wiley's Truck Wash
TServ N: FJ TP/Tires
Med S: + Magic Valley Memorial Hospital
Other N: Laundry/WiFi/LP/FJ TP, Twin Falls/ Jerome KOA/RVDump▲
S: appr 8.5mi: South 93 RV Park▲ , Bish's RV, College of Southern ID, Twin Fa Sun Valley Reg'l Airport✈, Shoshone Falls Park

182 — ID 50, Eden, to Hansen, Twin Falls, Eden
TStop S: PacPride/AmBest/Travelers Oasis Travel Plaza/Shell (Scales)
Gas N: Sinclair/Anderson Campground▲
Food S: Rest/Blimpie/TacoBell/Travelers TP
Lodg S: Amber Inn

EXIT	IDAHO

TServ S: Travelers TP/Tires/Towing
Other N: Anderson Campground/RVDump▲ , Gary's Freeway RV, Xtreme Motorsports& RV
Other S: Laundry/Travelers TP, Oregon Trail Campground▲ & Family Fun Center

188 — Valley Rd, to Eden, Hazelton

194 — ID 25W, Ridgeway Rd, Hazelton, Eden
TStop S: R&E Greenwood Travel Plaza/Sinclair
Food S: Café/Sinclair
Other S: Laundry/RVDump/Sinclair

201 — ID 25E, Kasota Rd, to Paul, Rupert

208 — I-84 Bus, ID 27, Burley, Paul
FStop S: Chevron, Sinclair
(Both Chevron & Sinclair DAD/DAND)
TStop N: Hub Plaza/P66 (Scales)
Gas S: Shell◈, Mirastar◈
Food N: FastFood/Hub Plz
S: Arby's, Burger King, Jack in the Box, McDonald's, JB's Family Rest, Perkins, Wendy's
Lodg N: Super 8
S: Best Western, Budget Motel, Fairfield Inn, Starlite Motel
Med S: + Hospital
Other N: Cassia Co Fairgrounds/RVDump
S: ATMs, Auto Dealers, Auto Services, Kelly Tire, Walmart sc, Golf Course, to Snake River Rec Area

211 — I-84 Bus, US 30W, Burley (EB), ID 24, Rupert, Heyburn (WB)
FStop N: Stinker Station #66/Sinclair
TStop S: Love's Travel Stop #334 (Scales)
Gas N: Chevron
Food N: A&W, Café
S: Carl'sJr/Love's TS, Jill's
Lodg N: Tops Motel
TWash N: Truck Wash
Med N: + Hospital
Other N: Country RV Village▲
S: Laundry/WiFi/RVDump/Love's TS, to Burley Muni Airport✈, Heyburn Riverside RV Park/RVDump▲

216 — ID 25W, to Rupert (EB), ID 77S, to Declo (WB)
FStop N: Conoco 66/Village of Trees
Gas S: Pit Stop/Shell◈
Other N: Village of Trees RV Resort/RVDump▲ , to Lake Walcott State Park▲

(222) — Jct I-86, US 30E, to Pocatello

228 — ID 81, Yale Rd, to Declo, Malta

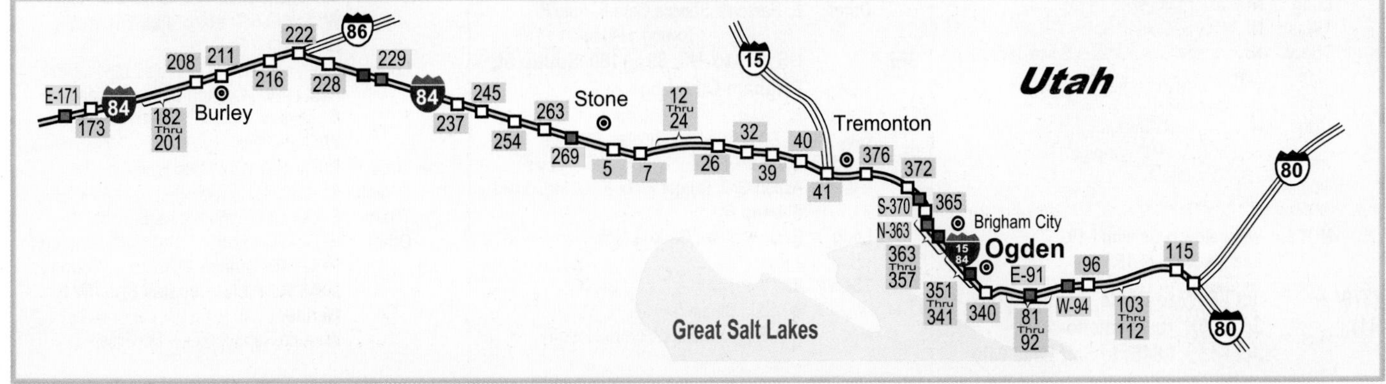

◈= Regular Gas Stations with Diesel ▲ = RV Friendly Locations ♥= Pet Friendly Locations
Red print shows large vehicle parking / access on site or nearby Brown Print = Campgrounds / RV PARKS

EXIT		ID / UT
(229)		Rest Area (Both dir) (Next RA 97mi) (RR, Phone, Picnic, Vend)
(229)		Weigh Stations (Both dir)
237		**Idahome Rd**
245		**Sublett Rd, Malta, Sublett**
	TStop	N: Mountain View Truck Stop/Sinclair
	Food	N: Rest/Mtn View TS
254		**Sweetzer Rd**
263		**Juniper Rd, Juniper**
(269)		Rest Area (Both dir) (RR, Picnic)

MOUNTAIN TIME ZONE

NOTE: MM 275: Utah State Line

IDAHO
UTAH

MOUNTAIN TIME ZONE

EXIT		
5		**UT 30, Snowville, to Park Valley, to Elko, NV**
7		**Snowville**
	TStop	N: Flying J Travel Plaza #1139 (Scales)
	Food	N: FastFood/Flying J TP, Mollie's Café, Ranch House Diner, Subway
	Lodg	N: Outsiders Motel
	Other	N: WiFi/RVDump/LP/FJ TP, Lottie Dell Campground & RV Park▲
12		**Ranch Exit**
16		**Ranch Exit, Hansel Valley**
17		**Ranch Exit**
20		**Blue Creek**
24		**Valley**
26		**UT 83S, Howell, Thiokol**
32		**Ranch Exit**
39		**to I-15, Garland, Bothwell**
	Med	N: + Hospital
40		**I-84 Bus, UT 102, Tremonton, Bothwell**
	FStop	N: Jim & Dave's Sinclair
	TStop	N: RJ's Fuel Stop/Sinclair (Scales), CFN/Golden Spike Travel Plaza/Chevron
	Food	N: BurgerKing/Quiznos/RJ's FS, Rest/Golden Spike TP, Denny's, McDonald's, Wendy's
	Lodg	N: Western Inn♥
	TWash	N: RJ's FS, Golden Spike TP
	TServ	N: RJ's FS/Tires, Golden Spike TP/Tires, Transport Diesel Service
	Med	N: + Hospital
	Other	N: Laundry/RVDump/RJ's FS, Laundry/BarbSh/WiFi/RVDump/LP/Golden Spike TP, Interstate Auto & Truck Center, Jack's RV Sales

NOTE: I-84 below runs with I-15. Exit #'s follow I-15.

EXIT		
(379/41)		**Jct I-84W to Boise, Tremonton** **Jct I-15N, to Pocatello** **Jct I-15S, I-84E, to Salt Lake City**

Personal Notes

EXIT		UTAH
376		**UT 13, N 5200 St W, Tremonton, to UT 102, Garland, Bear River (lodging N to UT 102W)**
	FStop	E: Exxon Travel Center
	Gas	E: Conoco◊
	Food	E: Arby's/Exxon TC, Crossroads Family Rest, JC's Country Diner, Subway
	Lodg	E: Marble Motel, Sandman Motel W: Western Inn♥
	Other	E: Co Fairgrounds
372		**UT 240, Honeyville, to UT 13, UT 38, Bear River**
	Other	E: Crystal Hot Springs Campground▲
(370)		Rest Area (SB) (RR, Phone, Picnic, Vend)
365		**900 North St, Brigham City (EB), UT 13, Corinne (WB)**
	Other	E: Brigham City Airport✈
363		**Forest St, Brigham City**
	Other	E: Parson's Service Center, Auto & Truck Repair, Towing, U-Haul
362		**US 91, to US 89, 1100 South St, Brigham City, Logan**
	FStop	E: Flying J Travel Plaza #1188 (Scales)
	Gas	E: 7-11, Chevron, Sinclair, Mirastar
	Food	E: Rest/FastFood/Flying J TP, Arby's, Aspen Grill, Burger King, KFC, McDonald's, Subway
	Lodg	E: Crystal Inn, Galaxie Motel, Howard Johnson
	TServ	E: Willard Auto & Diesel Service W: S&M Diesel Service
	Med	E: + Brigham City Comm Hospital

EXIT		UTAH
	Other	E: WiFi/LP/RVDump/FJ TP, Golden Spike RV Park▲, Walker Cinemas, Auto Dealers, Auto Zone, Checkers Auto Parts, Walmart sc, Eagle Mtn Golf Course, Logan State Univ
(363)		Perry Rest Area (NB) (RR, Phones, Picnic)
(361)		Port of Entry / Weigh Station (Both dir)
357		**750N, UT 360, UT315, N Willard, Perry, Willard Bay**
	TStop	E: Flying J Travel Plaza #1125 (Scales)
	Food	E: CountryMarket/FastFood/FJ TP
	Other	E: Laundry/WiFi/RVDump/LP/FJ TP, Brigham City/Perry South KOA▲, Police Dept W: Willard Bay State Park▲
351		**UT 126, to US 89, S Willard, Pleasant View, Willard Bay**
	Other	W: Willard Bay State Park▲
(349)		Emergency Pull Out (NB)
349		**2700 N, UT 134, Ogden, Farr West, Pleasant View**
	Gas	E: 7-11, Chevron, Maverik, Phillips 66 W: Conoco◊
	Food	E: Arby's, McDonald's, Melinas Mex Rest, Subway, Wendy's
	Other	E: Auto Repair, Fort Carson Army Res Center W: Tips RV
346		**Pioneer Rd, Ogden, Harrisville, Defense Depot**
	Gas	W: Excel Conv Store
	TServ	W: Diesel Service
	Other	E: Mulligan's Golf Course, Fort Carson Army Res Center
344		**UT 39, 1200S, 12th St, Ogden**
	TStop	W: Pilot Travel Center #294 (Scales)
	Gas	E: Chevron, Phillips 66, Shell◊
	Food	E: Rest/BW, Jeremiah's, Hogi Yogi W: DQ/Subway/TacoBell/Pilot TC, CJ's Rest & Bakery
	Lodg	E: Best Western W: Holiday Inn Express, Sleep Inn
	TServ	W: General Diesel Services
	Other	E: Steve's Car Care W: WiFi/Pilot TC
343		**UT 104, 21st St, Wilson Lane**
	FStop	W: Super Stop Shell
	TStop	E: Flying J Travel Plaza #5001/Conoco (Scales), Wilson Lane Chevron
	Gas	W: Phillips 66
	Food	E: Rest/FastFood/FJ TP, Arby's/Wilson Lane, Cactus Red's, McDonald's, Mi Rancho Rest, Rest/Comf Sts, Rest/HI W: FastFood/Texaco, Café/Super 8, Blimpie
	Lodg	E: Flying J Inn/FJ TP, Big Z Motel, Best Rest Inn♥, Comfort Suites, Holiday Inn Express♥ W: Super 8♥
	Tires	E: Flying J TP, Wilson Lane
	TWash	E: Wilson Lane Service
	TServ	E: Ogden Diesel Sales & Service
	Other	E: Laundry/BarbSh/CB/WiFi/RV Dump/LP/FJ TP, RV Dump/Wilson Lane, Century MH & RV Park▲, Justus Bros RV & Marine W: Auto Repair, Diesel Services

◊ = Regular Gas Stations with Diesel ▲ = RV Friendly Locations ♥ = Pet Friendly Locations
Red print shows large vehicle parking / access on site or nearby Brown Print = Campgrounds / RV PARKS

EXIT	UTAH
342	**UT 53, Pennsylvania Ave, 24th St, Ogden** (NB)
FStop	E: Sinclair
Food	W: Sunrise Cafe
Other	E: ATM, Animal Hospital♥ Auto Repair, Fort Buenaventura State Park
341B	**UT 79, 31st St, Ogden**
Other	W: Ogden Hinckley Airport✈, U-Haul
341A	**UT 79, 31st St, Hinckley, to UT 204, US 89, Ogden** (Serv E to Wall St/UT204/US89)
Gas	E: 7-11
Food	E: Arby's, Golden Corral, Skippers
Lodg	E: Days Inn♥
Med	E: + Hospital
Other	E: Newgate Mall, to Weber St Univ
(340)	**Jct I-84E, to Cheyenne** (SB, Left exit)

NOTE: I-84 above runs with I-15. Exit #'s follow I-15.

EXIT	UTAH
81	**UT 26, to I-15S, Riverdale**
Gas	N: Conoco◈, Sinclair
Food	N: Applebee's, Carl's Jr, Chili's, La Salsa Mex Rest, IHOP, McDonald's S: McDonald's
Lodg	S: Motel 6♥
Other	N: ATMs, Auto Dealers, Home Depot, Harley Davidson, Lowe's,
Other	N: PetSmart♥, Sam's Club, Target, Walmart sc, Wilderness RV
85	**Adams Ave Pkwy, Uintah, S Weber**
Med	N: + Ogden Reg'l Medical Center
87A	**US 89N, to I-15, UT 203, Ogden**
87B	**US 89S, to I-15, UT 193, Salt Lake City**
87	**US 89, Ogden, Salt Lake City** (EB)
Gas	S: Shell, Chevron
Food	N: Wendy's, Village Inn
(91)	Rest Area (EB) (RR, Picnic)
92	**UT 167, Mountain Green, to Huntsville** (EB)
(94)	Rest Area (WB) (RR, Picnic)
96	**to UT 167, Peterson, Mountain Green, Enterprise, Stoddard**
Gas	S: Sinclair
Other	N: to Powder Mountain, Snow Basin, Nordic Valley Ski Areas
103	**UT 66, Morgan**
Gas	S: 7-11, Chevron
Food	S: Subway, Chicken Hut, Steph's Drive In, Spring Chicken Cafe
Other	S: Fairgrounds, East Canyon
106	**Ranch Exit**
108	**Devils Slide, Taggert**
111	**Croydon**
112	**Henefer**
115	**Henefer, Echo**
(120)	**Jct I-80, W to Ogden, E to Cheyenne**

MOUNTAIN TIME ZONE

NOTE: I-84 Begins/Ends on I-80, Exit #168

UTAH

Resume WB I-84 at Jct I-80, near Echo, UT to near I-5 in Portland, OR.

EXIT	PENNSYLVANIA

Resume I-84EB from Jct I-81 near Dunsmore, PA to Jct I-90 near Sturbridge, MA.

PENNSYLVANIA

NOTE: I-84 Begins/Ends on I-81, Exit #186/187

EASTERN TIME ZONE

EXIT	PENNSYLVANIA
(0)	**Jct I-81, US 6W, to Wilkes-Barre, Binghamton, NY** (WB) **US 6E, Expressway, to Carbondale** (WB, Exit only) **Begin I-84 / I-380 EB, End WB**
1	**Tigue St, Dunmore**
Gas	N: Shell S: Mobil
Food	S: Anna Marie's Rest
Lodg	S: Holiday Inn♥
2	**PA 435S, Scranton, to Elmhurst** (EB, Left Exit only)
(4)	**Jct I-380S, to Mt Pocono** (fr WB, Left exit)
8	**PA 247N, Line Rd, to PA 348, Lake Ariel, to Mount Cobb, Hamlin** NOTE: NO Trucks over 10.5 Tons on PA 247
FStop	S: Joe's Kwik Mart/Mobil
Gas	N: Gulf◈
17	**PA 191, Twin Rocks Rd, Sterling, to Newfoundland, Hamlin**
TStop	N: Howe's 84 AmBest Auto Truck Plaza/ Exxon (Scales)
Food	N: Rest/Howe's ATP
Lodg	N: Comfort Inn
TServ	N: Howe's ATP/Tires
Other	N: Laundry/Howe's ATP S: Spring Hill Airpark✈, PA State Hwy Patrol Post
20	**PA 507, Greentown, Lake Wallenpaupack**
TStop	N: Lakewood 84/Exxon
Food	N: Rest/Lakewood 84
Other	N: WiFi/Lakewood 84
(26)	Rest Area (Both dir) (RR, Phone, Picnic, Info)
(26)	Weigh Station (Both dir)
26	**PA 390, Greentown, Tafton**
TStop	N: Promised Land Fuel Stop/Exxon
Food	N: FastFood/Promised Land FS
Other	S: to Promised Land State Park
30	**PA 402, Tafton to Porters Lake, Blooming Grove** NOTE: PA 402S: 10 Ton Weight Limit
Other	N: PA State Hwy Patrol Post
34	**PA 739, Dingman Tpk, Tafton, to Dingmans Ferry, Lords Valley**
Gas	S: Sunoco◈
Food	S: McDonald's
46	**US 6, to Milford** (Addt'l Serv 3mi S in Milford)
Gas	S: Citgo◈, Hilltop Xtra Mart◈, Turkey Hill
Food	S: Big Willie's BBQ, Apple Valley Family Rest, Waterwheel Cafe

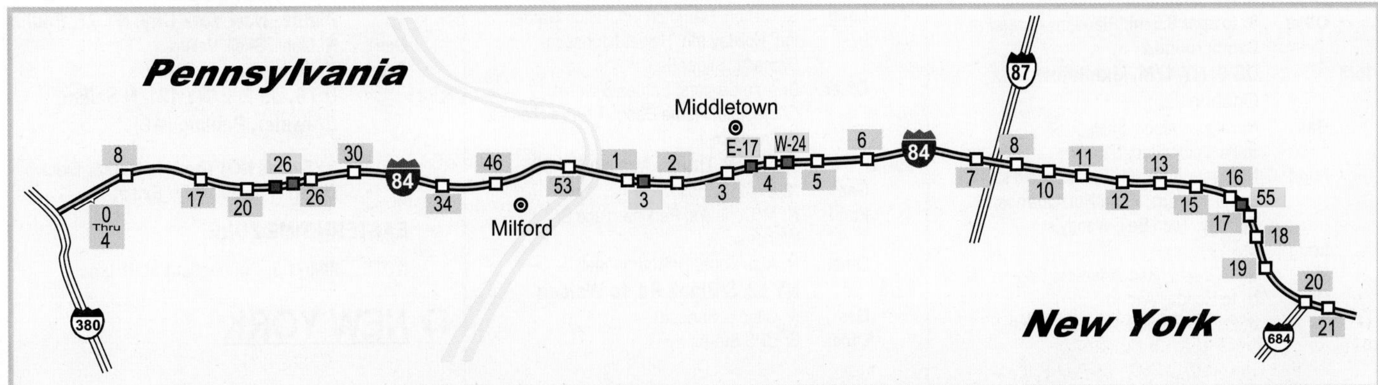

◈= Regular Gas Stations with Diesel ▲ = RV Friendly Locations ♥= Pet Friendly Locations
Red print shows large vehicle parking / access on site or nearby Brown Print = Campgrounds / RV PARKS

EXIT — PA / NY

Lodg — **S:** Red Carpet Inn, to Milford Motel, Myer Motel, Cliff Park Inn, Mt Haven Resort **to appr 11 mi: Harmony Ridge Farm & Campground▲**

(53) US 6, US 209, Matamoras
NOTE: **US 209S: NO Trucks**
N: PA Welcome Center (WB)
Rest Area (EB) (NO TRUCKS 7am-7pm)
(RR, Phone, Picnic, Info)
Gas — **N:** Shell, Turkey Hill, Exxon
S: Mobil◈
Food — **N:** Applegrill, Little Caesars Pizza, Stewarts Family Rest, Taco Palace
S: McDonald's, Little Caesars, Perkins, Subway, Wendy's, Westfall Family Rest
Lodg — **S:** Best Western, Riverview Inn, Scottish Inn
Other — **N:** Auto Zone, **TriState Campground▲**
S: ATMs, Grocery, Home Depot, Lowe's, Pharmacy, Staples, **Walmart sc**, **River Beach Campsites▲**

EASTERN TIME ZONE

NOTE: **MM 54: New York State Line**

PENNSYLVANIA
NEW YORK

EASTERN TIME ZONE

NOTE: **NYS does NOT use Mile Marker Exits. Listed is Mile Marker / Exit #.**

.66/1 US 6, NJ 23, CR 15, to NY 97, Port Jervis, Sussex NJ
Gas — **N:** Sunoco◈
S: Citgo◈, CF, Mobil◈
Food — **N:** Arlene & Tom's, Baskin Robbins, Dunkin Donuts, Ponderosa
S: DQ, McDonald's, Village Pizza
Lodg — **N:** Painted Aprons Motel, Shady Brook Motel
S: Comfort Inn
Med — **N: + Bon Secours Comm Hospital**
Other — **N: 84 Rayewood RV Center**, Tri State Golf Carts, **to Butler Home & RV**
S: Mall, **to High Point State Park▲ /NJ, Rockview Valley Campground▲ /NJ, Cedar Ridge Campground▲ /NJ, to appr 8.5 mi: Pleasant Acres Farm Campground▲**

(3) Parking Area (Both dir)

5/2 CR 35, Mountain Rd, to US 6, Port Jervis, Smith Corners
Food — **S:** Greenville's Firehouse Deli
Other — **S: to appr 8.5 mi: Pleasant Acres Farm Campground▲**

15/3 US 6, NY 17M, Middletown, Goshen
Gas — **N:** Citgo◈, Mobil, Shell
S: 84 Quick Stop, Sunoco◈
Food — **N:** Burger King, IHOP, McDonald's, NY Buffet, Perkins, Pizza Hut, Quiznos, Subway, Taco Bell, Wendy's
Lodg — **S:** Days Inn
Med — **N: + Orange Reg'l Medical Center**
Other — **N:** to Randall Airport✈
S: Rudy's Towing, US Post Office

EXIT — NEW YORK

(17) Rest Area (EB)
(RR, Phone, Picnic, NY St Police)
Random DOT Inspections

19/4 NY 17 (FUTURE I-86), W-Binghamton, E-New York (Serv at 1st Ex on NY 17)
Gas — **N:** Getty, Mobil, Sunoco
S: Citgo◈, Mobil
Food — **N:** Applebee's, Chuck E Cheese's Pizza, Denny's, Friendly's, KFC, McDonald's, Olive Garden, Perkins, Red Lobster, Ruby Tuesday, Subway, Taco Bell, Wendy's
S: Chili's, Outback Steakhouse, Red Robin, TGI Friday
Lodg — **N:** Howard Johnson, Super 8
S: Courtyard, Hampton Inn, Holiday Inn
Med — **N: + Orange Reg'l Medical Center**
Other — **N:** ATMS, Auto Services, Best Buy, CVS, Borders, Firestone, Gander Mountain, Home Depot, Lowe's, PetCo♥, PetSmart♥, RiteAid, Sam's Club, Staples, **Walmart sc**, Crystal Run Mall, U-Haul, Randall Airport✈

(24) Rest Area (WB)
(RR, Phone, Picnic, NY St Police)
Random DOT Inspections

28/5 NY 208, Montgomery, to Walden, Maybrook
TStop — **S:** Travel Center of America #210 (Scales)
Gas — **N:** Exxon, Mobil
S: Hess◈
Food — **N:** Burger King, Cascarino's, McDonald's
S: Buckhorn/PizzaHut/TA TC, Subway
Lodg — **S:** Motel/TA TC, Super 8
TServ — **S:** TA TC
Other — **N:** Grocery, Pharmacy, **to** Orange Co Airport✈, **to Winding Hills Golf Club/ Campground▲**
S: Laundry/WiFi/TA TC

33/5A NY 747, International Blvd, Stewart Int'l Airport

34/6 NY 17K, Montgomery, Newburgh
TStop — **N:** Pilot Travel Center #394 (Scales)
Gas — **N:** Mobil
S: Exxon◈
Food — **N:** Arby's/TJCinn/Pilot TC, Airport Diner, Deli, KFC
Lodg — **N:** Comfort Inn
S: Courtyard
Other — **N:** Laundry/WiFi/Pilot TC
S: Stewart Int'l Airport✈

36/7A NY 300S, to I-87, Albany, New York
Gas — **S:** Citgo, Sunoco
Food — **S:** Applebee's, Burger King, Denny's, Café Int'l, China City, TGI Friday
Lodg — **S:** Clarion, Hampton Inn, Hilton Garden Inn, Holiday Inn, Howard Johnson, Ramada, Super 8
Other — **S:** Auto Dealers, Barnes & Noble, Greyhound, Home Depot, Lowe's, Target, **Walmart sc**,

36/7B NY 300N, Union Ave, to NY 32
Gas — **N:** Exxon, Mobil
Food — **N:** McDonald's, Perkins, Taco Bell, Wendy's
Other — **N:** Auto Zone, Newburgh Mall

37/8 NY 52, S Plank Rd, to Walden
Gas — **N:** Citgo◈, Sunoco
Other — **S:** UPS Store

EXIT — NEW YORK

39/10 US 9W, NY 32, Newburgh
NOTE: **EB: Last FREE Exit Before TOLL**
Gas — **N:** Citgo, Mobil, Shell
S: Exxon◈, Sunoco◈
Food — **N:** Bagel World, Bruno Pizza, Burger King, McDonald's, Perkins, Pizza Hut
S: Alexis Diner, Family Deli
Lodg — **N:** Budget Inn, Economy Inn
Med — **S: + Hospital**

(41) TOLL Booth (EB)

41/11 NY 9D, NY 52 Bus, Beacon, Wappingers Falls
Gas — **N:** Mobil◈
Med — **N: + Castlepoint VA Hospital**
Other — **N:** Dutchess Stadium

44/12 NY 52E, Main St, Fishkill
Gas — **N:** Coastal, Valero
S: Mobil, Sunoco, Sam's Club,
Food — **S:** I-84 Diner
Other — **N:** UPS Store

46/13 US 9, S-Peekskill, N-Poughkeepsie
Gas — **N:** Citgo, Gulf, Mobil◈
S: Hess◈
Food — **N:** Burger King, Charlie Brown Steakhouse, Cracker Barrel, Denny's, Pizza Hut, Ruby Tuesday, Starbucks, Taco Bell, Wendy's
S: McDonald's, Pizza Hut, Subway
Lodg — **N:** Courtyard, Extended Stay America, Hampton Inn, Hilton Garden, Holiday Inn, Homestead Suites, Ramada Inn, Residence Inn, Sierra Suites
TServ — **N:** HO Penn Machinery
Other — **N:** ATMs, Grocery, Pharmacy, Sam's Club, **Walmart sc**, **to** Duchuss Co Airport✈
S: Home Depot

50/15 CR 27, Lime Kiln Rd, to NY 52, E Fishkill, Hopewell Junction

52/16 Taconic State Pkwy, N to Albany, S to NY (NO Trucks)

(55) Rest Area (Both dir)
(RR, Phones)
Random DOT Inspections

59/17 CR 40, Ludingtonville Rd, to NY 52
Gas — **S:** Hess◈, Sunoco
Food — **S:** Blimpie/Hess, Rest, Deli

62/18 NY 311, Lake Carmel, Patterson
Gas — **S:** BP

65/19 NY 312, to NY 22, Brewster, Carmel
Food — **S:** Applebee's, McDonald's, Wendy's
Med — **S: + Hospital**
Other — **N: NY State Police**
S: Home Depot

(68/20) I-684, US 6, US 202, NY 22, White Plains, New York City, NY 22, Paulin
Gas — **N:** Mobil, Shell, Valero
Food — **N:** Burger King, McDonald's

69/21 US 6, US 202, NY 121, N Salem, Brewster, Pauling (WB)

NOTE: **NYS does NOT use Mile Marker Exits. Listed is MileMarker / Exit #.**

EASTERN TIME ZONE

NOTE: **MM 71.5: Connecticut State Line**

NEW YORK

◈= Regular Gas Stations with Diesel ▲ = RV Friendly Locations ♥= Pet Friendly Locations
Red print shows large vehicle parking / access on site or nearby Brown Print = Campgrounds / RV PARKS

EXIT	CONNECTICUT

CONNECTICUT

EASTERN TIME ZONE

NOTE: CT does NOT use Mile Marker Exits. Listed is MileMarker / Exit #.

.36/1 — **Saw Mill Rd, Danbury (WB, Exit only)**

(.78/2) — **US 6, US 202, Mill Plain Rd, Old Ridgeberry Rd, Danbury (EB)**
S: CT Welcome Center (EB)
(RR, Phone, Picnic, Info, RVDump)
S: Weigh Station (EB)
- Gas — **N:** Exxon◈
- Food — **N:** Bambino Pizza, Desert Moon Mex Grill, Rosy Tomorrows, Starbucks
- Lodg — **N:** Comfort Suites, Hilton Garden Inn; **S:** Sheraton♥, Springhill Suites
- Other — **N:** Pharmacy, Staples

1/2A — **US 6, US 202, Mill Plain Rd (WB)**

1/2B — **Old Ridgeberry Rd (WB)**

3/3 — **US 7S, Park Ave, Airport, Norwalk (fr EB, Exit Only / fr WB, LEFT Exit)**
- Food — **S:** Charley's Grilled Subs, Cosmos Brick Oven, Great Wraps, Kitchen Café, Uno Chicago Grill
- Other — **S:** CVS, Danbury Fair Mall, Danbury Muni Airport✈, to **Wooster Mtn State Park**

4/4 — **US 6W, US 202W, Lake Ave**
- Gas — **N:** Shell◈, Xtra
- Food — **N:** Abe's Steak & Seafood House, Chuck's Steakhouse, Soup 2 Nutz; **S:** Dunkin Donuts, McDonald's
- Lodg — **N:** Residence Inn♥; **S:** Ethan Allen Hotel♥, Maron Hotel♥, Super 8
- Other — **N:** CVS, Laundromat, Pharmacy; **S:** Staples, UPS Store

5/5 — **CT 37, CT 39, CT 53, Main St, Downtown Danbury, Bethel**
- Gas — **N:** Shell, Sunny Mart; **S:** Mobil, Citgo
- Food — **S:** Taco Bell
- Lodg — **N:** Best Value Inn
- Med — **S:** + Danbury Hospital
- Other — **N:** to **Squantz Pond State Park**; **S:** W CT State Univ, Costco, to **Putnam Memorial State Park**

6/6 — **CT 37, North St, New Fairfield (WB)**
- Gas — **N:** Gulf, Texaco, Mobil; **S:** BP
- Food — **N:** Burger King, McDonald's, Moon Star Chinese, Pizza; **S:** KFC
- Med — **N:** + Hospital
- Other — **N:** CVS, Grocery, Pharmacy

7/7 — **US 7N, US 202E, New Milford, Brookfield (Both dir, Exit only) (fr EB, LEFT Exit) (Serv on Federal Rd)**
- Lodg — **S:** Quality Inn
- Other — **N:** Home Depot, Staples, UPS Store, to appr 24mi **Hemlock Hill Camp Resort▲**; **S:** Auto Services, Tires

8/8 — **US 6E (EB), Newtown Rd, Bethel**
- Gas — **N:** Gulf, Mobil◈; **S:** BP, Shell, Sunoco
- Food — **S:** Bertucci's Brick Oven Rest, Burger King, Chili's, Denny's, Friendly's, McDonald's, Outback Steakhouse, Taco Bell
- Lodg — **S:** Best Western, Courtyard, Hampton Inn, Holiday Inn, Howard Johnson, Microtel, Stony Hill Inn, Travel Inn, Wellesley Inn
- Other — **S:** ATMs, Auto Dealers, Auto Services, Banks, CVS, PetCo♥, Target, Tires, Walmart, Dave's RV Center

11/9 — **CT 25, to US 6, Brookfield, Bridgeport, New Milford, Hawleyville Newtown (Acc Ex #8 Serv via US 6)**

15/10 — **US 6W, Church Hill Rd, Newtown, Sandy Hook (WB, Exit Only)**
US 6W, Newton Business Dist (EB)

NOTE: Low Bridge on US 6-12'7", Alt Use Ex# 9
- Gas — **S:** Mobil◈, Shell
- Food — **N:** Katherine's Kitchen, Subway; **S:** Newtown Pizza Palace, Sandy Hook Family Diner
- Other — **S:** CVS, Grocery, Pharmacy, US Post Office, UPS Store

16/11 — **CT 34, Derby, New Haven**
- Other — **S:** Vet♥

19/13 — **River Rd (EB)**

20/14 — **CT 172, Main St, South Britain**
- Gas — **N:** Mobil
- Food — **N:** Starbucks
- Other — **N:** CT State Hwy Patrol Post; **S:** to **Kettletown State Park▲**

22/15 — **US 6E, CT 67, Southbury, Seymour, Ski Area, Oxford, Woodbury**
- FStop — **N:** Hine Bros/Mobil
- Gas — **N:** Shell
- Food — **N:** Dunkin Donuts, McDonald's
- TServ — **N:** Hine Bros/Tires
- Other — **N:** Kmart, Grocery, Golf Courses

25/16 — **CT 188, Middlebury, Southford**
- Gas — **N:** Mobil
- Lodg — **N:** Crowne Plaza
- Other — **N:** to Quassy Amusement Park; **S:** Waterbury Oxford Airport✈

30/17 — **CT 63, CT 64, Middlebury, to Watertown, Naugatuck**
- Gas — **N:** Mobil; **S:** Mobil◈
- Food — **N:** Maggie McFly's Rest; **S:** Maples Rest, Subway

31.5/18 — **Chase Pkwy (EB),W Main St, Highland Ave (WB)**
- Gas — **N:** Exxon
- Med — **N:** + Waterbury Hospital
- Other — **N:** CVS, Naugatuck Valley Comm College

32/19 — **CT 8S, Naugatuck, Bridgeport (fr EB, Exit Only / fr WB, LEFT Exit)**

32/20 — **CT 8N, Torrington (fr EB, LEFT Exit / fr WB, Exit Only)**
- Gas — **N:** Shell
- Food — **N:** McDonald's
- Other — **N:** to **Black Rock State Park▲**, **White Pines Campsites▲**

33/21 — **Meadow St, Bank St (fr EB, Exit only)**
- Gas — **N:** 7-11, Gulf, Hess; **S:** Exxon
- Food — **N:** Diorio Rest, Subway
- Lodg — **N:** Courtyard
- Other — **S:** Home Depot, PetSmart♥, Pharmacy

33/22 — **Baldwin St (EB), Union St (WB), Downtown Waterbury**
- Food — **N:** Arby's, Burger King, Chili's, McDonald's, Olive Garden, Ruby Tuesday, TGI Friday
- Lodg — **N:** Holiday Inn Express
- Med — **N:** + St Mary's Hospital
- Other — **N:** Auto Services, B&N, Sears, Tires, Walgreen's, Brass Mill Center Mall, **to Walmart (1mi-Wolcott St)**

34/23 — **CT 69, Wolcott, Prospect (EB, Exit Only), Hamilton Ave (WB), Waterbury (Access to Ex #22 Serv)**

35/24 — **Harpers Ferry Rd, Waterbury (WB)**
- Gas — **S:** Texaco, DM, Getty

36/25 — **Harpers Ferry Rd (EB), E Main St, Scott Rd, Reidville Dr (WB)**
- Gas — **N:** Exxon, Gulf◈; **S:** Mobil
- Food — **N:** China Buffet, Dunkin Donuts, Grinders, Subway, Taylors Family Rest; **S:** Burger King, Friendly's, McDonald's, Nino's Rest
- Lodg — **S:** Super 8
- Other — **S:** CVS, BJ's, Grocery

36/25A — **Austin Rd, Waterbury (EB)**
- Lodg — **N:** CT Grand Hotel
- Other — **N:** Costco

38/26 — **CT 70, Waterbury Rd, Chesire, Waterbury, Prospect**

(40/27) — **I-691E, to Meriden, Middletown (EB)**

41/28 — **CT 322, Meridien Waterbury Rd, Marion, Southington, Milldale**
- TStop — **S:** Travel Center of America #154 (Scales)
- Gas — **N:** Sam's Food Store; **S:** Mobil
- Food — **S:** CountryPride/TA TC, Applebee's, Burger King, Blimpie, China Gourmet, DQ, Dunkin Donuts, Grace's Rest, Milldale Diner
- Lodg — **S:** Days Inn
- TServ — **S:** TA TC/Tires
- Other — **N:** **Hemlock Hill RV**; **S:** Laundry/BarbSh/WiFi/TA TC

(41/27) — **Jct I-691E, to Meriden (WB)**

(42) — **Rest Area (EB)**
(RR, Phone, Picnic, RVDump)

42/29 — **CT 10, Milldale (WB, LEFT Exit) (Access to Exits #27 & 30 Serv)**

43/30 — **W Main St, Marion Ave, Downtown Southington, Plantsville**
- Gas — **S:** Getty, Mobil, Main St Food Mart
- Food — **S:** Gene's Corner House Rest, Italian Rest, Pig Out BBQ, Pizza, Steve's Rest
- Med — **S:** + Hospital
- Other — **N:** Mt Southington Ski Area

44/31 — **CT 229, West St, Bristol**
- Gas — **N:** Mobil, Sunoco; **S:** Citgo
- Food — **N:** Dunkin Donuts/Mobil
- Lodg — **S:** Residence Inn

46/32 — **CT 10, Queen St, Southington**
- Gas — **N:** Exxon, Shell; **S:** Hess, Mobil, Sunoco
- Food — **N:** Bertucci's Brick Oven, Burger King, Chili's, Denny's, McDonald's, KFC, Pizza Hut, Outback Steakhouse, Starbucks, Subway, Taco Bell; **S:** El Sombrero, Friendly's, Little Caesars, Ponderosa, Subway, Wendy's
- Lodg — **N:** Motel 6♥; **S:** Howard Johnson Express, Holiday Inn Express, Traveler Inn

EXIT	CONNECTICUT
Med	N: + Hospital
Other	N: CVS, Grocery, PetCo♥, Staples, Custom Camper
49/33	**CT 72W, to Bristol (fr EB, Left Exit / fr WB, Exit Only)**
Other	N: Redman's Trailer Sales, Crowley RV
49/34	**CT 372, Crooked St, Plainville**
Gas	N: Sunoco
Food	N: Applebee's, Friendly's, Long John Silver, McDonald's, Pizza, Starbucks, Wendy's
Lodg	N: Advance Motel, Hotel Plainville
Other	N: Lowe's, Grocery, PetSmart♥, CT Dept of Motor Vehicles, Robertson Airport✈
50/35	**CT 72E, to CT 9, New Britain, Middletown (fr WB, Left Exit)**
51/36	**Slater Rd (fr EB, Left Exit)**
53/37	**to US 6W (EB), Fienemann Rd**
Gas	N: Shell
Lodg	N: Marriott S: Extended Stay America
Other	N: Hertz RAC
54/38	**US 6W, Bristol (WB)**
54/39	**CT 4, Farmington (fr EB, Left Exit / fr WB, Exit Only)**
Med	N: + Univ of CT Health Center
55/39A	**CT 9S, Newington, New Britain (Both dir, Exit only)**
56/40	**CT 71, New Britain Ave, Corbins Corner**
Gas	S: Shell, Sunoco
Food	S: Joe's Grill, Olive Garden, Red Robin, Starbucks, Wendy's
Lodg	S: Courtyard
Other	S: Westfarms Mall, B&N, Borders, Best Buy, Office Depot, Target
57/41	**S Main St, Elmwood**
58/42	**Trout Brook Dr, Elmwood (WB, Left Exit)**
58/43	**Park Rd, W Hartford (fr EB, Left exit)**
Other	N: St Joseph College, U Conn Campus
59/44	**Prospect Ave (EB), Oakwood Ave**
Gas	N: Exxon, Shell
Food	N: Burger King, McDonald's
TServ	N: Toce Bros Tire
Other	N: Pharmacy

EXIT	CONNECTICUT
60/45	**Flatbush Ave (WB, Left Exit)**
60/46	**Sisson Ave, Downtown (fr EB, Left Exit / fr WB, Exit only)**
Other	N: U Conn Law School, Hartford College for Women, Hartford Seminary, Mark Twain House, Harriet B Stowe House
61/47	**Sigourney St (WB, Exit Only)**
Med	N: + St Francis Hospital
61/48A	**Asylum St, Downtown (EB)**
Other	S: Civic Center, Bus & Train Stations
61/48B	**Capital Ave (EB, Exit Only)**
61/48	**Asylum St, Downtown (WB, Exit Only)**
Med	S: + Hartford Hospital
Other	S: Bus & Train Stations, Trinity College
61/49	**Ann St, High St (EB)**
Other	S: Civic Center, Trumbull St
62/50	**Main St (EB), US 44W, to I-91S (WB) (fr WB, Exit Only)**
Other	S: Civic Center
Lodg	S: Marriott
(62/51)	**Jct I-91N, Springfield, Bradley Int'l Airport**
(62/52)	**Jct I-91S, New Haven (EB, Exit Only)**
62/53	**US 44E, Connecticut Blvd, E River Dr, East Hartford (EB)**
63/54	**CT 2W, Downtown Hartford (fr WB, Left exit)**
63/55	**CT 2E, Norwich, New London (fr EB, Exit Only / fr WB, Left Exit)**
63/56	**Governor St, E Hartford, Downtown E Hartford (fr EB, Left exit)**
64/57	**CT 15S, to I-91S, Charter Oak Br, NY City (WB, Left Exit)**
65/58	**Roberts St, Burnside Ave, Silver Lane, E Hartford**
Food	S: Hong Kong Buffet, Mr Steak
Lodg	N: Holiday Inn, Nantucket Island Resort, Wellesley Inn
Other	S: Goodwin College, Pratt & Whitney, Rentschler Field, Hartford Brainard Airport✈

EXIT	CONNECTICUT
(66/59)	**Jct I-384E, to Providence (EB, Exit only), Spencer St, Silver Lane (WB)**
Other	S: to appr 4.5 mi Nickerson Park Family Campground▲
NOTE:	MM 67.42: Begin EB / End WB, Left Lane Truck Prohibition
67/60	**US 6, US 44, Middle Tpk West, Manchester, Burnside Ave (EB)**
Gas	S: Mobil
Med	S: + Hospital
(68/61)	**Jct I-291W, to Windsor, to Bradley Int'l Airport**
69/62	**Buckland St (EB), Middle Tpk, Buckland St (WB)**
Gas	N: Exxon◈ S: Mobil, Xtra
Food	N: Boston Market, Chili's, Friendly's, Hooters, Hops, KFC, Olive Garden, Taco Bell, Vinny T's S: Burger King, Carrabba's, Dunkin Donuts, Ground Round, McDonald's, Subway, Texas Roadhouse, Wendy's
Lodg	N: Fairfield Inn
Other	N: ATMs, Banks, Borders, Firestone, Home Depot, PetCo♥, PetSmart♥, Sam's Club, Buckland Hills Mall S: ATMs, Banks, Auto Services
71/63	**CT 30, CT 83, Deming St, Manchester, South Windsor**
Gas	N: Shell S: Getty, Xtra Mart, Shell, Sunoco
Food	N: Applebee's, McDonald's, Hometown Buffet, Outback Steakhouse, Panera Bread, Romano's Macaroni Grill, TGI Friday, Uno Chicago Grill S: Roy Rogers Rest, Shea's Amer Grill
Lodg	N: Courtyard, Residence Inn S: Best Value Inn, Super 8, Extended Stay America
Med	S: + Hospital
Other	N: Best Buy, Barnes & Noble, Office Depot, Walgreen's, **Walmart** S: Auto Dealers, Grocery, Pharmacy, **Certified On Site RV Service**
73/64	**CT 30, CT 83, Vernon, Bus Distr, Rockville**
Gas	N: Mobil, Sunoco
Food	N: Denny's, Damon's, McDonald's, Taco Bell S: Chuckwagon, Elmo's Sea Catch, George's Seafood & Prime Rib

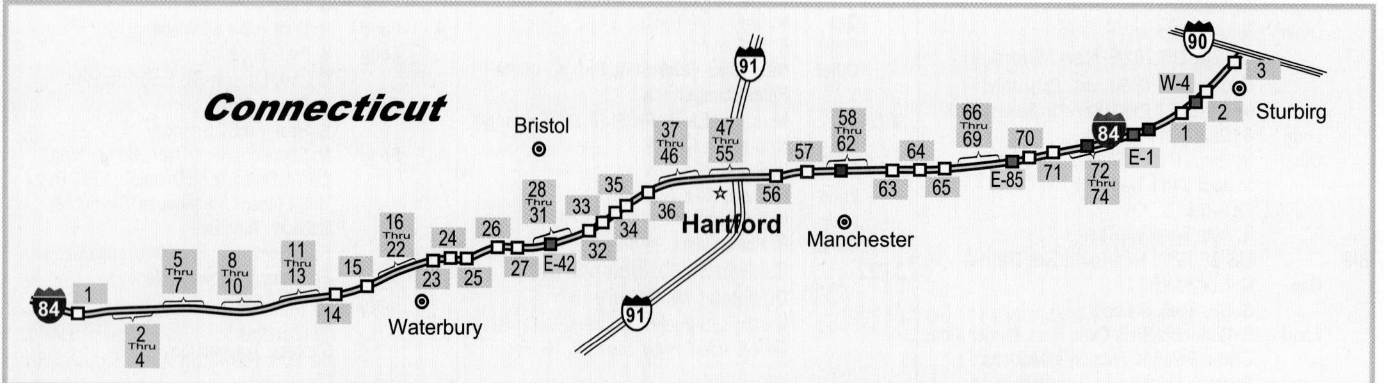

EXIT	CONNECTICUT
Lodg	N: Holiday Inn Express S: Quality Inn
Other	N: ATMs, Advance Auto Parts, CVS, Firestone, Goodyear, Grocery, Staples
75/65	**CT 30, CT 83, Vernon Center**
Gas	N: Mobil, Shell
Food	N: Burger King, Denny's, KFC, Pizza Hut
Lodg	N: Comfort Inn, Howard Johnson♥
Med	N: + Rockville Gen'l Hospital
Other	N: ATMs, CarQuest, Pharmacy, Grocery
76/66	**CT 85, Tunnel Rd, Vernon, Bolton**
77/67	**CT 31, Mile Hill Rd, Vernon, Rockville, Coventry**
Gas	N: Mobil, Shell
Food	N: Burger King, China Taste, McDonald's Outback Steakhouse
Med	N: + Hospital
Other	N: Grocery, Vernon Police Dept, to appr 7mi Del-Aire Camping Resort▲ , to Stafford Speedway
81/68	**CT 195, Merrow Rd, Tolland, Mansfield**
FStop	N: Tolland Getty
Gas	N: Mobil S: Citgo
Food	N: Subway S: Capt Matt's Lobster House, Lee's Garden, Villa Italiana
Lodg	N: Tolland Inn
84/69	**CT 74, to US 44, Willington, Putnam (fr WB, Exit only)**
Other	N: to Del-Aire Campground▲ S: CT State Hwy Patrol Post, Brialee RV & Tent Park▲ , to Charlie Brown Campground▲ , appr 4.5 mi Nickerson Park Family Campground▲ , Peppertree Camping▲ , Moosemeadow Camping Resort▲
(85/69)	CT Welcome Center (EB) Rest Area (Both dir) (RR, Phones, Vend, RVDump)
85/70	**CT 32, Stafford Springs (EB, Exit only), Willington, Willimantic**
Gas	S: Mobil, Sunoco
Med	N: + Hospital
Other	N: Wilderness Lake Campground & Resort▲ , to appr 6.5 mi Mineral Springs Family Campground▲ , appr 11mi Oak Haven Family Campground▲ ,

EXIT	CT / MA
Other	N: appr 17mi Sunsetview Farm Camping Area▲ , to Stafford Motor Speedway S: appr 17mi Waters Edge Campground▲
88/71	**CT 320, Ruby Rd, Willington**
TStop	S: Travel Center of America #22/Shell (Scales)
Food	S: CountryPride/BurgerKing/TA TC
Lodg	S: Econo Lodge♥, Rodeway Inn♥
TWash	S: TA TC
TServ	S: TA TC/Tires
Other	S: Laundry/WiFi/RVDump/TA TC
92/72	**CT 89, Hillside Rd, Fish Pt Rd, Stafford Spgs, Ashford, Westford**
Lodg	N: Ashford Motel
Other	N: Roaring Brook Co-Op Campground▲ S: to appr 7mi Brialee RV & Tent Park▲
93/73	**CT 190, Buckley Hwy, Union, Stafford Springs**
Other	N: CT State Hwy Patrol Post, Roaring Brook Co-Op Campground▲ , to Mineral Springs Family Campground▲ , to Stafford Motor Speedway S: Bigelow Hollow State Park to appr 8mi Beaver Pines Campground▲ ,
Other	S: to Chamberlain Lake Campground▲
(95.5)	Weigh Station (WB)
97/74	**CT 171, Holland Rd, Stafford Springs, Union, to Holland, MA**
FStop	S: Citgo
Food	S: Traveler's Rest

NOTE: CT does NOT use Mile Marker Exits. Listed is Mile Marker / Exit #.

NOTE: MM 98: Massachusetts State Line

CONNECTICUT
MASSACHUSETTS

EASTERN TIME ZONE

NOTE: MA does NOT use Mile Marker Exits. Listed is Mile Marker / Exit # .

(1)	Picnic Area (EB)

EXIT	MASSACHUSETTS
(3)	Weigh Station (WB)
1/2.5	**MA 15, Mashapaug Rd, Haynes St, Sturbridge, Southbridge**
FStop	S: Mobil Mart
TStop	S: Pilot Travel Center #222 (Scales)
Gas	S: Shell◊
Food	N: CountryKitchen/Pilot TC, Sbarro/ RoyRogers/Mobil
Lodg	S: Quality Inn/Pilot TC
Med	S: + Hospital
Other	S: Laundry/WiFi/Pilot TC, Outdoor World-Sturbridge Resort▲ , Westville Lake Rec Area
(4)	Picnic Area (WB)
2/5	**MA 131, Sturbridge**
Lodg	S: Days Inn, Historic Inn
Other	S: Yogi Bear's Jellystone Park Camp Resort▲ , to Southbridge Muni Airport✈
3AB/9	**US 20, Main St, Charlton Rd, Sturbridge, Worchester**
TStop	S: PTP/New England Truck Stop
Gas	N: Citgo, Mobil◊ S: Citgo
Food	N: Burger King, McDonald's S: Rest/NE TS, Applebee's, Colonial House Family Rest, Charlie's, Cracker Barrel, Gracie's Roadside Café, Subway, Wendy's
Lodg	N: Best Western, Carriage House Inn, Hampton Inn, Old Sturbridge Village Lodge, Super 8, Travelodge S: Comfort Inn, Public House Historic Inn & Resort, Rodeway Inn
Other	S: ATMs, Grocery, Staples, Walmart N: US Post Office

NOTE: MA does NOT use Mile Marker Exits. Listed is Mile Marker / Exit # .

EASTERN TIME ZONE

NOTE: I-84 Begins/Ends on I-81, Ex #186 in PA

MASSACHUSETTS

Begin Westbound I-84 from Jct I-90 near Sturbridge, MA to Jct I-81 in Dunmore, PA.

EXIT	VIRGINIA

Begin Southbound I-85 from Jct I-95 near Richmond to Jct I-65 in Montgomery, AL.

VIRGINIA

NOTE: I-85 begins/ends on I-95, Exit #51

EASTERN TIME ZONE

EXIT	VIRGINIA
69	**Washington St, Wythe St, Petersburg**
(68)	**Jct I-95, Crater Rd, Petersburg**
65	**Squirrel Level Rd, Petersburg**
Gas	W: BP◊
63AB	**US 1, US 460 Bus, Petersburg**
TStop	W: Thrift Mart Truck Plaza/Exxon
Gas	E: Chevron◊, Shell W: AmocoBP
Food	E: Burger King, Waffle House W: Blimpie, Hardee's, McDonald's
Lodg	E: Holiday Inn Express
Med	W: + Central State Hospital
Other	W: Laundry/Exxon, Auto Repairs
61	**US 460 Bus, Airport St, Petersburg, to Blackstone**
FStop	E: East Coast Oil/Mapco Express #4064
Gas	W: Shell◊, Valero
Food	E: Subway/Mapco, Huddle House
Other	E: LP/Mapco, to appr 4mi Camptown Campground▲ W: Picture Lake Campground▲ , Dinwiddie Co Airport✈
(55)	Dinwiddie Rest Area (Both dir) (RR, Phone, Picnic, Vend, Info)
53	**VA 703, Carson Rd, Dinwiddie**
Gas	W: Exxon◊
Food	W: Rumorz Cafe
Other	E: appr 5mi Camptown Campground▲
48	**VA 650, Hamilton Arms Rd, DeWitt**

◊= Regular Gas Stations with Diesel ▲ = RV Friendly Locations ♥= Pet Friendly Locations
Red print shows large vehicle parking / access on site or nearby Brown Print = Campgrounds / RV PARKS

EXIT		VIRGINIA
42		**VA 40, McKenney Hwy, McKenney**
	FStop	**W:** Citgo
	Gas	**W:** Exxon
	Lodg	**W:** Economy Inn
39		**VA 712, Old Stage Rd, Warfield, to Rawlings**
	TStop	**W:** AmBest/Davis Travel Center #108/ Exxon (Scales)
	Gas	**W:** Citgo◈
	Food	**W:** Subway/Davis TCNottoway Rest/Motel
	Lodg	**W:** Nottoway Motel
	Other	**W:** WiFi/**RVDump**/Davis TC
34		**VA 630, Sturgeon Rd, Warfield**
	Gas	**W:** Exxon◈
(32)		**Alberta Rest Area (Both dir) (RR, Phone, Picnic, Pet, Vend)**
28		**US 1, VA 46, Alberta, Lawrenceville**
	Gas	**W:** Exxon
	Lodg	**W:** Alberta B&B
	Other	**W:** Kenbridge Tire & Auto Service, US Post Office
27		**VA 46, Alberta, to Blackstone, Lawrenceville (SB)**
	Other	**E:** Southside VA Comm College
24		**VA 644, Meredithville**
	Other	**E:** US Post Office
(22)		**Weigh station (Both dir)**
15		**US 1, South Hill, to Kenbridge (Acc to Ex #12 Serv via US 1W)**
	Gas	**E:** Citgo **W:** Shell, Valero
	Food	**W:** Kahills Rest, Rumorz Cafe
	Other	**E:** Auto Repair
12B		**US 58, VA 47, Atlantic St, South Hill, Norfolk**
	Gas	**W:** Amoco, Citgo◈, Exxon◈, Kangaroo◈, Petrol
	Food	**W:** Brian's Steakhouse, Burger King, **Cracker Barrel**, Denny's, Down Home Buffet, Hardee's, KFC/Taco Bell, McDonald's, New China Rest, Pizza Hut, Subway, Wendy's
	Lodg	**W:** Americas Best Value Inn, Days Inn
	Med	**W: + Hospital**
	Other	**W:** Auto Dealers, Auto Repairs, Advance Auto Parts, CVS, Carwash/Amoco, Dollar General, Family Dollar, Food Lion, Goodyear, Grocery, Home Depot, Laundromat, Tires, Towing
12A		**US 58, VA 47, Atlantic St, South Hill, Norfolk**
	FStop	**E:** Slip In Shell, **appr 5mi S:** Red Barn
	Gas	**E:** BP◈, RaceWay
	Food	**E:** Applebee's, Arby's, Arnold's Diner, Domino's Pizza, Nest Egg Café, Quiznos, Sonic, Subway
	Lodg	**E:** Best Western, Comfort Inn♥, Fairfield Inn♥, Hampton Inn, Holiday Inn Express, Super 8
	Other	**E:** ATMs, Dollar Tree, **Walmart SC**, Towing, Mecklenburg Brunswick Reg'l Airport✈
4		**VA 903, Bracey, Lake Gaston**
	FStop	**W:** Slip In Shell
	TStop	**E:** Simmons Travel Center/Exxon (Scales)
	Gas	**E:** BP◈,
	Food	**E:** JctRest/FastFood/Simmons TC, DQ/ Subway/BP **W:** Countryside Rest, Memphis Grill, Pizza Hut/Quiznos/KrispyKreme/Shell
	Lodg	**W:** Lake Gaston Inn

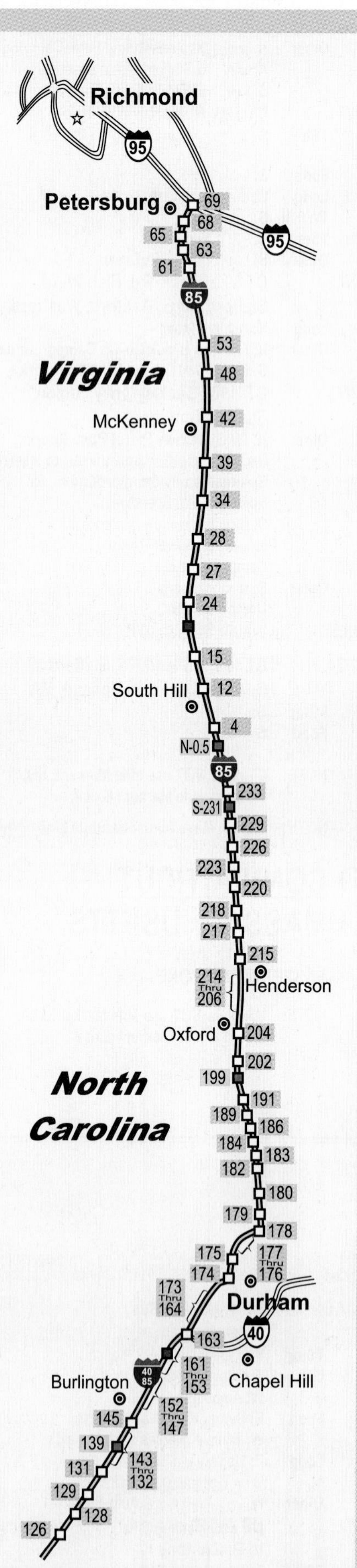

EXIT		VA / NC
	TServ	**E:** Simmons TC/Tires
	Other	**E:** Laundry/WiFi/Simmons TC, U-Haul
(.5)		**VA Welcome Center (NB) (RR, Phones, Picnic, Vend)**
		EASTERN TIME ZONE

⬆VIRGINIA
⬇NORTH CAROLINA

	NOTE:	**MM 234: Virginia State Line**
		EASTERN TIME ZONE
233		**US 1, Norlina, Wise**
	TStop	**E:** Wise Truck Stop/Citgo
	Food	**E:** Rest/Wise TS
	Lodg	**E:** Budget Inn
(231)		**NC Welcome Center (SB) (RR, Phone, Picnic)**
229		**Oine Rd, to Norlina**
226		**Ridgeway Rd**
223		**Manson Rd**
	Gas	**E:** BP◈
220		**US 1, US 158, Fleming Town Rd, Henderson, Norlina, Middleburg**
	TStop	**W:** Chex Truck Stop/Exxon (Scales)
	Gas	**E:** BP◈
	Food	**W:** Rest/Chex TS
	Lodg	**W:** Motel/Chex TS
	TWash	**W:** Chex TS
	TServ	**W:** Chex TS/Tires
	Other	**W:** Laundry/CB/WiFi/Chex TS, **to Kerr Lake State Rec Area**
218		**US 1 ByPass, to Raleigh (SB ex, NB entr)**
217		**NC 1319, Henderson**
215		**US 1, US 158E ByPass, Parham Rd, Garnett St, Henderson (fr NB diff reacc, Re-enter Next Exit N)**
	FStop	**E: to 2101 Garnett** Pacific Pride
	Gas	**E:** Citgo◈, Hess, Shell
	Food	**E:** 220 Seafood, Burger King, Subway
	Lodg	**E:** Ambassador Inn, Best Value Inn, Budget Host Inn, Comfort Inn, Econo Lodge Howard Johnson, Scottish Inn
	Other	**E:**Budget Truck Rental, Goodyear, Grocery
214		**NC 39, Andrews Ave, Henderson**
	Gas	**E:** BP, Shell
213		**US 158, Dabney Dr, Henderson**
	Gas	**E:** BP, Shell **W:** Exxon, Shell
	Food	**E:** Bamboo Garden, Bojangles, Denny's, KFC, McDonald's, Papa John's Pizza, Ruby Tuesday, Subway, Wendy's **W:** ChickFilA, Golden Corral, McDonald's, Pizza Hut, Taco Bell
	Lodg	**W:** Holiday Inn Express
	Other	**E:** Auto Zone, Banks, CVS, Family Dollar, Food Lion/Pharmacy, Goodyear, Radio Shack, Staples, Winn Dixie **W:** Auto Dealers, Auto Services, Dollar Tree, Lowe's, RiteAid, Staples, Tires, Tractor Supply, **Walmart SC**
212		**NC 1128, Ruin Creek Rd, Henderson (Access to Ex #213 Serv)**
	Gas	**E:** Shell◈ **W:** BP
	Food	**E:** Cracker Barrel, Mexican Rest

◈= Regular Gas Stations with Diesel ▲ = RV Friendly Locations ♥= Pet Friendly Locations
Red print shows large vehicle parking / access on site or nearby Brown Print = Campgrounds / RV PARKS

EXIT — NORTH CAROLINA

Food W: Gary's BBQ, Golden Corral
Lodg E: Days Inn, Hampton Inn
W: Holiday Inn Express, Jameson Inn, Sleep Inn
Med W: + Maria Parham Hospital

209 NC 1126, Poplar Creek Rd

206 US 158, Oxford, Roxboro
Gas W: Exxon◈
Other W: U-Haul/Exxon

204 NC 96, Linden Ave, Oxford
Gas E: BP◈
W: Exxon, Shell, Trade/Hess◈
Food W: Burger King, KFC, McDonald's, Pizza Hut, Subway, Taco Bell, Wendy's
Lodg E: Comfort Inn, Kings Inn
W: Best Western, Econo Lodge
Med W: + Hospital
Other E: Auto Dealers, U-Haul
W: ATMs, Dollar General, Family Dollar, Grocery, Pharmacy, Radio Shack, **Walmart SC**

202 US 15, Oxford, Clarksville
Gas W: Citgo
Lodg W: Crown Motel

(199) Rest Area (Both dir)
(RR, Phone, Picnic, Pet)

191 NC 56, Butner, Creedmoor
FStop E: Trade Mart #27/WilcoHess
W: Rose Mart #2/Shell
Gas E: BP◈
W: Exxon◈
Food E: Bob's BBQ, Bojangles, Burger King, KFC, McDonald's, Pizza Hut, Sonic, Taco Bell, Wendy's
W: Domino's Pizza, Hardee's
Lodg E: Comfort Inn, Econo Lodge♥
W: Best Western, Holiday Inn Express, Ramada Ltd
Other E: Food Lion, Pharmacy

189 NC 1103, Butner

186 US 15N, Creedmoor (SB)

186AB US 15, Creedmoor (NB)
Other E: **Falls Lake State Rec Area▲**

183 Redwood Rd, Durham
Gas E: Days Inn
Food E: Redwood Cafe
Lodg E: Days Inn
Other E: Durham Skypark Airport✈

182 Red Mill Rd, Durham
Gas E: Redmill Quick Stop/Exxon
Food E: Perky's Pizza

180 Glenn School Rd
Gas W: William Bros Country Store/Heritage

179 East Club Blvd
Gas E: C-Mart/Exxon

178 US 70E, ByP, to Airport (NB)

177B NC 55, Avondale Dr, Durham
FStop E: WilcoHess C-Store #191
Gas W: Amoco, BP, Shell
Food W: Arby's, Dunkin Donuts, Hong Kong Buffet, Hardee's, KFC, McDonald's, Pizza Hut

177C NC 55N, Avondale Dr (NB)

177A US 501 Bus, US 15 Bus, Roxboro St, Downtown Durham
Gas W: BP
Lodg W: Chesterfield Motel

176B US 501N, Duke St , Roxboro

EXIT — NORTH CAROLINA

176A Gregson St
Gas E: Shell, Texaco
Food E: BBQ n Stuff, Biscuitville, Burger King, Cajun Café, ChickFilA, Ruby Tuesday, Subway, Yamato Japanese
Med E: + Duke Univ Medical Center
W: + Durham Reg'l Hospital
Other E: Amtrak, Northgate Mall, **to** Duke Univ
W: Staples, Durham Co Stadium

175 NC 157, Guess Rd, Durham
Gas E: Shell◈
W: AmocoBP◈, Kangaroo Express
Food E: Hog Heaven BBQ, Pizza Hut
W: Bojangles, Honey's Rest, IHOP, Rudino's Pizza & Grinders, Texas Roadhouse
Lodg E: Best Value Inn♥, Holiday Inn Express♥, Super 8
W: Red Roof Inn♥
Other W: CVS, Home Depot, Kroger, PetSmart♥

174A Hillandale Rd
Gas W: BP◈
Food W: China King, Papa's Grill, Shoney's
Lodg W: Courtyard, Hampton Inn, Howard Johnson
Other W: Pharmacy, Winn Dixie, UPS Store

174B US 15S ByPass, US 501S, Chapel Hill (SB exit, NB entr)

173 US 15, US 501S, Cole Mill Rd, Durham (diff reaccess)
Gas E: BP, Exxon◈, Shell
Food E: Arby's, Bojangles, Burger King, Checkers, ChickFilA, **Cracker Barrel**, Dominos Pizza, Dunkin Donuts, Galley Seafood, McDonald's, Starbucks, Subway, Taco Bell/KFC, Waffle House, Wendy's
Lodge E: Days Inn, Fairfield Inn, Hilton, Innkeeper, Quality Inn
Med E: + Hospital
Other E: Advance Auto Parts, Auto Zone, CVS, Kroger, Laundromat, Pharmacy, RiteAid

172 NC 147S, to US 15S, US 501S (NB exit, SB entr)

170 US 70, to NC 751, Duke University
Food E: Harbor Bay Seafood
Lodg E: Best Western
Other E: Auto Services, **Cruise America Motor Home Rental**
W: **Eno River State Park**

165 NC 86, Hillsborough, to Chapel Hill
TStop E: Express America Truck Stop (Scales)
Gas W: BP◈
Food E: Rest/Expr Amer TS, McDonald's, Papa John's Pizza, Subway
W: Heartland Steakhouse, Wendy's
Other E: Home Depot, **Walmart sc**

164 S Churton St, Hillsborough
Gas E: Kangaroo/BP, Citgo◈
W: Exxon◈, Shell
Food E: McDonald's
W: Burger King, Hardee's, KFC/Taco Bell, Pizza Hut, Occoneechee Steakhouse, Waffl House, Wendy's
Lodg E: Holiday Inn Express
W: Microtel, Southern Country Inn
Other W: Auto Dealers, All Pro Auto Parts, Auto Zone, Firestone, Food Lion, Goodyear, Sanchez Auto Care, Wagner Tire & Auto

EXIT — NORTH CAROLINA

NOTE: I-85 below runs with I-40. Exit #'s follow I-85.

(163) Jct I-40E, to Raleigh

161 to US 70E Conn, NC 86, Efland

160 Mt Willing Rd, US 70E Conn, Efland
Gas W: BP◈, Exxon◈

(159) Weigh Station (Both dir)

157 Buckhorn Rd, Mebane
TStop E: Petro Stopping Center #29/Mobil (Scales)
Gas E: BP◈
W: Exxon, Mobil
Food E: IronSkillet/FastFood/Petro SC
TServ E: Petro SC/Tires
Other E: Laundry/BarbSh/CB/WiFi/Petro SC

154 Mebane Oaks Rd, Mebane
FStop W: Arrowhead Shell
Gas E: Sheetz◈, Shell◈, Murphy USA
W: BP, Exxon◈
Food E: Quiznos
W: Bojangles, China Garden, La Fiesta, McDonald's, Roma's Pizza, Waffle House
Lodg W: Budget Inn
Other E: Dollar Tree, Tires, **Walmart sc**,
W: Advance Auto Parts, Auto Zone

153 NC 119, S 5th St, Mebane
Gas E: BP Pepsi Jct◈, Citgo
W: Tommy's Mini Mart/P66
Food E: **Cracker Barrel**, Hibachi Rest, KFC, Jersey Mike's Subs, Pizza Hut, Smithfield's Chicken & BBQ, Taco Bell
W: Burger King, Mex Rest, Subway
Lodg E: Hampton Inn, Holiday Inn Express
Other E: Lowe's
W: CVS, Food Lion, Vet♥

152 NC 1981, Trollingwood Rd, Mebane
FStop E: Speedway
TStop E: Pilot Travel Center # 57 (Scales)
W: Fuel City/Circle K Truck Stop #5364
Food E: McDonald's/Pilot TC
W: FastFood/Circle K TS
TWash E: Pilot TC
Other E: Laundry/WiFi/Pilot TC, Greyhound/Pilot

150 Jimmie Kerr Rd, Haw River, Graham
TStop W: Flying J Travel Plaza #5332 (Scales), WilcoHess Travel Plaza #165 (Scales)
Food W: Cookery/FastFood/FJ TP, DQ/Wendy's/WilcoHess TP
Lodg W: Days Inn
TWash W: Blue Beacon TW/FJ TP
TServ W: Speedco
Other W: Laundry/BarbSh/WiFi/**RVDump**/**LP**/FJ TP, Laundry/WilcoHess TP

148 NC 54, E Harden St, Graham to Chapel Hill, Carrboro
FStop E: Kangaroo Express #3791
Gas E: BP◈, Quality Plus
Food E: Waffle House
Lodg E: Comfort Suites
W: Embers Motor Lodge, Econo Lodge

147 NC 87, Main St, Graham, Pittsboro
Gas E: BP
W: Exxon◈, Shell◈
Food E: Arbys, Burger King, Bojangles, Harbor House Seafood, Sagebrush Steakhouse, Sonic, Starbucks, Subway, Wendy's
W: Biscuitville, McDonald's, Taco Bell
Lodg E: Affordable Suites of America

◈= Regular Gas Stations with Diesel ▲ = RV Friendly Locations ♥= Pet Friendly Locations
Red print shows large vehicle parking / access on site or nearby Brown Print = Campgrounds / RV PARKS

Med W: + Hospital

Other E: ATMs, Auto Dealers, Advance Auto Parts, Food Lion, Goodyear, Laundromat, RiteAid, Ve♥t, Winn Dixie
W: ATMs, CVS, Lowe's, Walgreen's, **Graham Police Dept**

145 NC 49, Maple Ave, Downtown Burlington, Liberty

FStop E: Interstate Shell

Gas E: BP◈
W: BP, Hess

Food E: Captain D's
W: Biscuitville, Bojangles, Burger King, China Inn, Hardee's, KFC, Waffle House

Lodg E: Econo Lodge, Microtel, Motel 6♥
W: Best Value Inn, Days Inn, Holiday Inn, La Quinta Inn♥, Quality Inn, Scottish Inn

Other E: Davis Harley Davidson, **NC State Hwy Patrol Post**
W: ATMs, Food Lion, Outlet Mall, Radio Shack, RiteAid,

143 NC 62, Alamance Rd, Downtown Burlington, Alamance

Gas E: Citgo
W: Circle K, Exxon, Kangaroo Express

Food E: Bob Evans, Hardee's, Waffle House
W: K&W Cafeteria, Libby Hill Seafood

Lodg W: Ramada Inn

Other E: JR Outlet, Burlington Muni Airport✈
W: Auto Dealers, Food Lion, Home Depot, Greyhound, Train Station

141 Huffman Mill Rd, Burlington

Gas E: BP, Kangaroo,
W: Crown, Phillips 66◈, Texaco

Food E: IHOP, Mayflower Seafood, Outback Steakhouse
W: Applebee's, Arby's, Bojangles, Biscuitville, Burger King, ChickFilA, China Gate, **Cracker Barrel**, Golden Corral, Hooters, Indian Rest, KFC, Krystal, McDonald's, O'Charley's, Panera Bread, Rock-Ola Café, Ruby Tuesday, Starbucks, Steak 'n Shake, Subway, Taco Bell

Lodg E: Comfort Inn, Hampton Inn
W: Best Western, Country Inn, Courtyard, Super 8

Med E: + Alamance Hospital

Other W: Auto Dealers, Food Lion, Kmart SC, Office Max, **Walmart sc**, UPS Store, Burlington Square Mall, **to** Elon College

140 University Dr, Burlington, Elon

Other W: Best Buy, PetSmart♥, Target, **to** Elon Univ

(139) Rest Area (Both dir) (RR, Phone, Picnic, Vend)

138 NC 61, Whitsett, Gibsonville, Greensboro

TStop W: Travel Center of America #2/BP (Scales)

Gas W: Shell◈

Food W: CountryPr/Burger King/Popeye/TA TC

Lodg W: DaysInn/TA TC

TWash W: TA TC

TServ W: TA TC/Tires

Other W: Laundry/WiFi/TA TC, **Hawley's Camping Center**

135 Rock Creek Dairy Rd, Whitsett

Gas W: Citgo, Exxon

Food W: Bojangles, Jersey Mike's, McDonald's

Other W: CVS, Food Lion

132 Mt Hope Church Rd, McLeansville

TStop W: WilcoHess Travel Plaza #308

EXIT NORTH CAROLINA

Gas E: Stop & Save/Citgo
W: Shell◈

Food E: Subway, Pizza Corner
W: Wendy's/WilcoHess TP

Lodg W: Hampton Inn

Other W: ATMs

(131A) Jct I-840, to US 70, Greensboro

(131) Jct I-85N/I-40E (Left exit)

NOTE: I-85 above runs with I-40. Exit #'s follow I-85.

129 Youngs Mill Rd, Greensboro

128 Alamance Church Rd

126B US 421, Greensboro, Sanford

126A US 421S, Sanford

126 US 421, Sanford, Greensboro

FStop S: The Pantry/Kangaroo Express #170

124 S Elm Eugene St, Greensboro

Food E: Cracker Barrel

122 US 220, Greensboro, Asheboro (Future I-73 South)

122B US 220S, Asheboro, Greensboro

122C US 220N, Asheboro, Greensboro

122A Groometown Rd, to Grandover Parkway (SB)

(121) Jct I-73N, US 421W to I-40W, Winston-Salem (SB)

(120B) Jct I-73N, US 421W to I-40W, Winston-Salem (NB)

120A I-85 Bus N, US 29N, US 79E, Greensboro (NB exit, SB entr)

119 Groometown Rd (NB)

Gas W: Phillips 66◈

118 I-85 Bus S, US 29S, US 70W, to High Point, Jamestown

Lodg W: Grandover Resort

113 NC 62, Liberty Rd, High Point, Archdale

FStop E: Moose Tracks/Citgo

Gas W: BP◈

Lodg W: Best Western

111 US 311, N Main St, Downtown High Point, to Archdale

Gas W: BP◈, Citgo, Exxon, Shell◈

Food E: Biscuitville, Bojangles, Hardee's, Little Caesar's Pizza, Subway, Wendy's
W: Waffle House

Lodg E: Innkeeper
W: Comfort Inn, Fairfield Inn, Hampton Inn, Holiday Inn Express

Med W: + Hospital

Other E: CVS, Dollar General, Food Lion
W: Advance Auto Parts, Firestone

108 Hopewell Church Rd, Trinity

106 Finch Farm Rd, Trinity, Thomasville

FStop E: Quik Shop-Gas Stop/Exxon

103 NC 109, Randolph St, Thomasville

Gas E: Citgo, Shell
W: BP◈, Coastal, Crown, Hess

Food E: Arby's, Taco Bell
W: Burger King, China Garden, Golden Corral, Hardee's, KFC, McDonald's,

EXIT NORTH CAROLINA

Food E: Pizza Hut, Subway, Waffle House

Lodg W: Country Hearth Inn, Howard Johnson, Quality Inn

Other E: CVS, Grocery, **Walmart sc**
W: ATMs, Auto Zone, Advance Auto Parts, Food Lion, Family Dollar, Tires, Walgreen's

102 Lake Rd, Thomasville

Gas W: Phillips 66, Shell◈

Lodg W: Days Inn, Microtel

Med W: + Hospital

(99) Rest Area (Both dir) (RR, Phone, Picnic, Vend)

96 US 64, Lexington, Asheboro,

Gas E: Exxon
W: Chevron◈

94 Old US 64, Raleigh Rd, Lexington

Gas E: Shell

91 NC 8, Cotton Grove Rd, Lexington

Gas E: BP◈, Citgo, Phillips 66, Shell◈
W: Exxon◈, QM

Food E: McDonald's, Sonic, Subway, Wendy's
W: Applebee's, Arby's, Burger King, Cracker Barrel, Hardee's, Taco Bell

Lodg E: Comfort Suites, Super 8
W: Country Hearth Inn, Holiday Inn Express

Med W: + Lexington Memorial Hospital

Other E: Food Lion, **to appr 8mi High Rock Lake Marina & Campground▲**
W: Grocery, **Walmart**

88 NC 47E, Hargrave Rd, Linwood, High Rock Lake

Gas W: BP◈

87 I-85N Bus, US 52N, US 29N, US 70E, Lexington, Winston-Salem (NB Exit, SB entr)

86 NC 47, Belmont Rd, Linwood

TStop E: Bill's Truck Stop/66 (Scales)

Food E: Rest/Bill's TS

TServ E: Bill's TS/Tires

Other E: Laundry/Bills TS

85 Clark Rd, Linwood

Other W: **Crosswinds Family Campground▲**

83 NC 150E, to Spencer (NB ex, SB entr) US 29S, US 70W, NC 150W, Spencer Linwood (SB Left Exit, NB entr)

81 Long Ferry Rd, Salisbury, Spencer

Gas E: Exxon◈

79 Andrew St, Salisbury, Spencer

76B US 52N, E Innes St, Salisbury

76A US 52S, E Innes St, Salisbury

76 US 52, E Innes St, Salisbury

Gas E: BP, RaceTrac, Speedway
W: Circle K◈, Exxon◈, Shell

Food E: Applebee's, IHOP, Little Caesar's, Lone Star Steakhouse, Shoney's
W: Blue Bay Seafood, Bojangles, Burger King, Captain D's, ChickFilA, Hardee's, KFC, O'Charley's, Outback Steakhouse, Pizza Hut, Starbucks, Waffle House, Wendy

Lodg E: Days Inn, Happy Traveler Inn, Sleep Inn, Studio Suites, Super 8
W: Budget Inn, Comfort Suites, Howard Johnson Express

Med E: + Hospital

Other E: ATMs, CVS, Food Lion, Lowe's, Staples, Tilly's Harley Davidson
W: Auto Zone, Family Dollar, Firestone,

EXIT — NORTH CAROLINA

Other W: Goodyear, Office Depot, **Walmart**

75 — US 601N, Jake Alexander Blvd, Salisbury, Rowan
- FStop W: WilcoHess C-Store #363
- Gas W: BP, Exxon◈, Rushco, Shell◈
- Food E: Arby's, Farmhouse Rest
  W: Burger King, Fire Mountain Grill, Ichiban, Jasmine's, McDonald's, Pizza Hut, Sagebrush Steakhouse, Subway, Waffle House, Wendy's
- Lodg E: Ramada
  W: Best Western, Days Inn, Hampton Inn, Holiday Inn
- Other W: Auto Dealers, **Walmart**

74 — Julian Rd, Salisbury
- Lodg E: Affordable Suites of America

72 — Peach Orchard Rd

71 — Peeler Rd, Salisbury
- TStop E: PTP/Derrick Travel Plaza/Shell (Scales)
  W: WilcoHess Travel Plaza #364 (Scales)
- Food E: CW's Rest/Derrick TP
  W: Bojangles/Subway/TB/WilcoHess TP
- TWash E: Derrick TP
- TServ E: Derrick TP/Tires
- Other E: Laundry/BarbSh/CB/WiFi/LP/Derrick TP

70 — Webb Rd, Salisbury
- Other E: Flea Market
  W: NC State Hwy Patrol Post

68 — US 29, US 601S, NC 152, Rockwell Hwy, China Grove, Rockwell

63 — Lane St, Kannapolis
- TStop E: Pilot Travel Center #56 (Scales)
- Gas W: Exxon◈
- Food E: Subway/Pilot TC, Waffle House
  W: Hardee's, KFC
- Other E: Laundry/WiFi/Pilot TC

60 — Dale Earnhardt Blvd, Copperfield Blvd, Kannapolis, Concord
- Gas E: BP, Exxon◈, Kangaroo Express
  W: BP◈
- Food E: Bojangles, Bob Evans, **Cracker Barrel**, Wendy's
  W: Johnny Carino's, Logan's Roadhouse, McDonald's, Ruby Tuesday, Subway
- Lodg E: Hampton Inn, Sleep Inn
  W: Holiday Inn Express
- Med E: + Hospital
- Other W: Sam's Club, **Walmart sc**

(59) — Rest Area (Both dir) (RR, Phone, Picnic, Vend)

58 — US 29, US 601, Concord Pkwy, Cannon Blvd, Ridge Ave, US 29A, Kannapolis Hwy, Concord
- Gas E: BP, Crown, Exxon, Shell◈, Wilco◈
  W: Phillips 66, Wilco Food Mart
- Food E: Applebee's, Burger King, Captain D's, ChickFilA, Golden Corral, KFC, Little Caesars, McDonald's, Mexican Rest, O'Charley's, Pizza Hut, Subway, Shoney's, Starbucks, Taco Bell, Waffle House, Wendy's
  W: CiCi's Pizza, IHOP, Ryan's Grill
- Lodg E: Best Value Inn, Colonial Inn, Holiday Inn Express, Rodeway Inn
  W: Comfort Inn, Econo Lodge, Fairfield Inn, Microtel, Mainstay Suites, Park Inn
- Med E: + NE Medical Center
- Other E: Auto Dealers, Auto Services, Food Lion, FedEx Office, UPS Store, U-Haul,

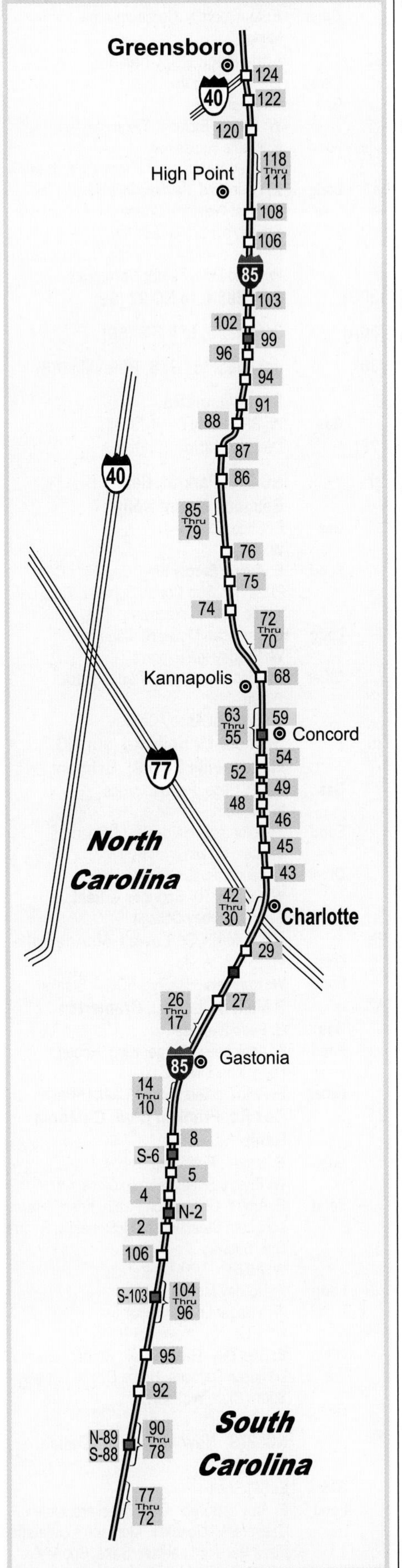

Greensboro
High Point
Kannapolis
Concord
Charlotte
Gastonia
North Carolina
South Carolina

EXIT — NORTH CAROLINA

Other E: tCarolina Mall, Mall 8, **NC State Hwy Patrol Post, to** Lowe's Motor Speedway
W: Grocery, Home Depot, Pharmacy, Target, Vet♥, Greyhound, Family Adventures Fun Park

55 — NC 73, Davidson Hwy, Concord, Huntersville
- Gas E: Exxon◈, Shell
  W: 76◈, Phillips 66◈, Shell
- Food E: McDonald's, Waffle House
  W: Huddle House
- Lodg W: Days Inn
- Other E: to Lowe's Motor Speedway

54 — Kannapolis Pkwy, Geo Liles Pkwy

52 — Poplar Tent Rd
- Gas E: Shell◈
  W: Exxon
- Other E: to Lowe's Motor Speedway, Race Driving Schools, **Fleetwood RV Race Campground▲**
  W: Concord Reg'l Airport✈

49 — Concord Mills Blvd, Speedway Blvd
- Gas E: BP, Shell◈
  W: Citgo, Petro Express
- Food E: Arby's, Bob Evans, Bojangles, BBQ, Carrabba's, Chuck E Cheese, Cracker Barrel, Hooters, KFC, McDonald's, Quaker Steak & Lube, Quiznos, Subway
  W: Alabama Grill, Applebee's, Panera Bread, Olive Garden, Red Lobster, Steak 'n Shake, Texas Roadhouse, TGI Friday
- Lodg E: Comfort Suites, Hampton Inn, Holiday Inn Express, Sleep Inn, Springhill Suites, Suburban Extended Stay♥, Wingate Inn
  W: Days Inn
- Other E: Lowe's Motor Speedway, Driving Schools, **Fleetwood RV Race Campground/RVDump▲, Tom Johnson Camping Center**
  W: AMC Cinemas, Bass Pro Shop, Concord Mills Mall, Discount Tire, PetCo♥, Radio Shack, Concord Reg'l Airport✈

(48) — Jct I-485, to US 29, Charlotte

46 — Mallard Creek Church Rd (SB)
- Gas E: Exxon, Wilco◈
  W: Exxon, Petro Express

46B — Mallard Creek Church Rd (NB)

46A — Mallard Creek Church Rd, to US 29

45B — NC 24, WT Harris Blvd, Charlotte

45A — NC 24, WT Harris Blvd, Charlotte

45 — NC 24, WT Harris Blvd, Charlotte
- Gas E: Phillips 66◈, Sonic Mart
- Food E: Applebee's, Bojangles, Burger King, Chili's, Hops, McDonald's, Max & Erma's, Shoney's, TGI Friday, Waffle House
  W: McDonald's, Romano's Macaroni Grill, Subway, Wendy's
- Lodg E: Courtyard, Drury Inn, Extended Stay America, Hilton, Hampton Inn, Holiday Inn, Homewood Suites, Microtel, Residence Inn, Sleep Inn
  W: Springhill Suites, Towneplace Suites
- Med E: + Hospital
- Other E: Best Buy, Food Lion, Lowe's, Office Depot, Radio Shack, Sam's Club, Walgreen's, **Walmart**, Mall, Univ of NC/Charlotte
  W: Food Lion, Pharmacy

◈= Regular Gas Stations with Diesel ▲ = RV Friendly Locations ♥= Pet Friendly Locations
Red print shows large vehicle parking / access on site or nearby Brown Print = Campgrounds / RV PARKS

EXIT		NORTH CAROLINA
43		**City Blvd, to NC 24, US 29 (NB)**
42		**to US 29, NC 49 (NB exit, SB entr)**
41		**Sugar Creek Rd, Charlotte**
	Gas	E: RaceTrac, Shell◈
		W: 76, BP◈, Exxon◈
	Food	E: Bojangles, McDonald's, Taco Bell, Wendy's
		W: Shoney's, Waffle House
	Lodg	E: Best Value Inn, Brookwood Inn, Continental Inn, Econo Lodge, Economy Inn, Microtel, Motel 6♥, Red Roof Inn
		W: Comfort Inn, Country Hearth Inn, Days Inn, Ramada Inn, Rodeway Inn, Super 8
40		**Graham St, Charlotte**
	Gas	E: Exxon◈
		W: Citgo
	Food	E: Hardee's, Hereford Barn Steakhouse
	Lodg	E: Howard Johnson
	TServ	E: Adams Int'l Trucks, Peterbilt Carolina, Tar-Heel Ford Trucks, Volvo/GMC,
		W: Freightliner, Mack Truck
39		**Statesville Ave, Charlotte**
	TStop	E: Pilot Travel Center #275 (Scales)
	Gas	W: Shell◈
	Food	E: Subway/Pilot TC
	Lodg	W: Knights Inn
	TServ	W: Bradley's Truck Service
	Other	E: WiFi/Pilot TC, CarQuest, Carwash
(38)		**Jct I-77, US 21, N to Statesville, S to Columbia**
	TServ	W: Carolina Engine
37		**Beatties Ford Rd**
	Gas	E: Phillips 66◈, Shell◈
		W: BP
	Food	E: Burger King, KFC, McDonald's, Subway, Taco Bell
		W: McDonalds Cafeteria
	Lodg	W: Travelodge
	Other	E: ATMs, CVS, Food Lion, Johnson C Smith Univ
36		**NC 16, Brookshire Blvd, to US 74E, Downtown Charlotte**
	Gas	E: BP◈
		W: Exxon, RaceTrac, Speedway
	Food	W: Burger King, Jack in the Box
	Med	E: + Hospital
35		**Glenwood Dr**
	Gas	E: Circle K, Shell◈
	Lodg	E: Knights Inn
34		**NC 27, Freedom Dr, Tuckaseegee Rd, Charlotte, Lincolnton**
	Gas	E: BP◈, Circle K
	Food	E: Bojangles, Burger King, IHOP, Mayflower Seafood, McDonald's, Pizza Hut, Taco Bell, Wendy's
	Lodg	W: Howard Johnson, Ramada Inn
	Med	E: + Pro-Med Minor Emergency Center
33		**US 521, Billy Graham Pkwy, to Charlotte Douglas Int'l Airport**
	Gas	E: 76◈, Crown
		W: Exxon◈
	Food	E: Krystal, KFC/Taco Bell, Wendy's
		W: Cracker Barrel, Waffle House
	Lodg	E: Comfort Suites, Days Inn, Hawthorne Suites, Royal Inn, Sheraton, Springhill Suites
	Lodg	W: Best Value Inn, Fairfield Inn, La Quinta Inn♥, Hampton Inn, Microtel, Red Roof Inn♥, Sheraton

EXIT		NORTH CAROLINA
	Other	E: to Airport✈, Coliseum Area, Farmers Market
32		**Little Rock Rd, Charlotte**
	FStop	W: Sam's Mart/Shell
	Gas	E: Exxon
		W: Crown, Exxon◈, Texaco
	Food	E: Waffle House
		W: Arby's, Hardee's, Shoney's, Subway
	Lodg	E: Courtyard, Fairfield Inn, Holiday Inn
		W: Best Western, Country Inn, Motel 6♥, Shoney's Inn, Wingate Inn
	Other	E: Tires, **Fieldridge Acres Campground▲**
		W: Food Lion, Family Dollar, Pharmacy
(30B)		**Jct I-485N, to NC 27 (SB)**
(30A)		**Jct I-485S, to I-77S (SB)**
(30)		**Jct I-485, to I-77S, Pineville (NB)**
29		**Sam Wilson Rd**
	Gas	W: BP, Handy Dandy/Shell◈
(28)		**Weigh Station (Both dir)**
27		**NC 273, Park St, Beatty Dr, Belmont, Mount Holly**
	Gas	E: Citgo, Exxon◈
		W: BP◈
	Food	E: Arby's, Burger King, Captain's Cap, Pizza Hut, Sub Corral, Subway, Taco Bell, Waffle House, Wendy's
	Lodg	E: American Motel, Heritage Inn
		W: Holiday Inn Express
	Other	E: Food Lion, NAPA, Radio Shack, Walgreen's
		W: Belmont Abbey College
26		**Belmont-Mt Holly Rd (SB), NC 7, McAdenville Rd (NB), Belmont**
	Gas	E: BP, Citgo, Petro Express
		W: Circle K
	Food	E: Bojangles, Hardee's, McDonald's, Western Sizzlin
	Other	E: Laundromat, Grocery, Pharmacy
		W: **Quality RV Services & Rentals**, Belmont Abbey College
23		**NC 7, Main St, Lowell, McAdenville**
	Gas	W: Exxon, World
	Food	W: Hardee's, Hillbilly's BBQ & Steaks
22		**S Main St, Lowell, Cramerton**
	Gas	E: Petro Express
	Food	E: Applebee's, Burger King, Hooters, Long John Silver, Zaxby's
	Other	E: Auto Dealers, Sam's Club, U-Haul
21		**Cox Rd, Franklin Blvd, Gastonia Ranlo**
	Gas	E: Citgo◈, Petro Express
		W: Exxon, Shell, Petro Express
	Food	E: Arby's, Chili's, Don Pablo, Krispy Kreme, Longhorn Steakhouse, McDonald's, Ryan's Grill, Subway
		W: IHOP
	Lodg	E: Holiday Motel
		W: Villager Lodge, Super 8
	Med	W: + Gaston Memorial Hospital
	Other	E: Best Buy, Gaston Mall, Grocery, Harley Davidson Carolina, Home Depot, Lowe's, Sam's Club, **Walmart**,
		W: Pharmacy
20		**NC 279, New Hope Rd, Dallas, Gastonia**
	Gas	E: BP, Shell
	Food	E: Arby's, Burger King, Checkers, Little Caesars, McDonald's, Morrison's Cafeteria, Pizza Hut, Red Lobster, Sake, Shoney's,

EXIT		NORTH CAROLINA
	Food	E: Taco Bell
	Food	W: Bojangles, Captain D's, **Cracker Barrel**, KFC, Outback Steakhouse, Texas Roadhouse, Waffle House
	Lodg	E: Best Western, Hampton Inn, Holiday Inn Express, Ramada
		W: Comfort Suites, Courtyard, Fairfield Inn, Hampton Inn
	Med	W: + Gaston Memorial Hospital
	Other	E: Advance Auto Parts, Eastridge Mall Firestone, Grocery, Laundromat, Office Depot, Target, UPS Store,
19		**NC 7, Ozark Ave, Long Ave, Gastonia**
	Gas	E: Shell, World
	Other	E: Amtrak, Greyhound
17		**US 321, N Chester St, Gastonia, to Lincolnton**
	Gas	E: Exxon◈
		W: Citgo◈, Petro Express◈ x2, Texaco
	Food	W: McDonald's, Pancake House, Waffle House, Wendy's, Western Sizzlin
	Lodg	E: Days Inn, Villager Lodge
		W: America's Best Value Inn, Holiday Inn Express, Microtel, Motel 6♥
	TServ	W: Freightliner
	Other	W: Shooting Range, to Gaston College
14		**NC 274, Bessemer City Rd, East Bessemer City, W Gastonia**
	FStop	W: Grab & Go/Citgo
	Gas	E: Phillips 66
	Food	E: Burger King, McDonald's, Subway
		W: Waffle House
	Lodg	W: Affordable Suites of America, Express Inn
13		**Edgewood Rd, Bessemer City**
	Gas	W: BP, Exxon◈
	Lodg	W: Economy Inn
	Other	W: **Young RV**
10B		**US 74W, Kings Mountain (NB)**
10A		**US 29, US 74E, Shelby (NB)**
10		**US 29N, US 74, Kings Mountain, Shelby (SB)**
8		**NC 161, York Rd, Kings Mountain**
	Gas	E: Exxon
		W: BP
	Food	W: Burger King, Hardee's, McDonald's, KFC, Taco Bell, Waffle House
	Lodg	E: Holiday Inn Express
		W: Comfort Inn, Quality Inn
	TServ	W: Sterling Equipment Co.
	Med	W: + Hospital
(6)		**Rest Area (SB)** (RR, Phones, Picnic, Vend)
5		**Dixon School Rd, Kings Mountain**
	TStop	E: AmBest/Kings Mountain Travel Center/ Shell (Scales)
	Gas	E: Citgo
	Food	E: Rest/FastFood/Kings Mtn TC, 50's Diner
	TServ	E: Kings Mtn TC/Tires
	Other	E: Laundry/RVDump/Kings Mtn TC, Tobacco Outlet
4		**US 29S, NC 216 (SB Exit, NB entr)**
(2)		**NC Welcome Center (NB)** (RR, Phone, Pic, Vend, Info, Weather)

◈= Regular Gas Stations with Diesel ▲ = RV Friendly Locations ♥= Pet Friendly Locations
Red print shows large vehicle parking / access on site or nearby Brown Print = Campgrounds / RV PARKS

EXIT — NC / SC

2 — NC 216, Battleground Rd, Kings Mountain
- Gas — W: Chevron
- Other — E: **to Kings Mountain Nat'l Military Park**

EASTERN TIME ZONE

⬆ NORTH CAROLINA
⬇ SOUTH CAROLINA

NOTE: MM 106.5: North Carolina State Line

EASTERN TIME ZONE

106 — US 29, E Blacksburg, Grover
- TStop — W: WilcoHess Travel Plaza #905 (Scales)
- Gas — E: BP; W: Exxon
- Food — W: DQ/Wendy's/WilcoHess TP
- Other — E: **to Kings Mountain State Park▲**; W: Laundry/WilcoHess TP, ATMs, Budget RAC, Fireworks

104 — Rd 99, Blacksburg
- TStop — E: Love's Travel Stop #397
- Food — E: McDonald's/Subway/Love's TS
- Other — W: Fireworks

(103) — SC Welcome Center (SB) (RR, Phone, Picnic, Vend, Info)

102 — SC 198, Mtn St, Blacksburg, Earl
- FStop — E: Gasland #8/BP
- TStop — W: Flying J Travel Plaza #5510 (Scales)
- Gas — E: Shell; W: Citgo
- Food — E: Hardee's; W: Cookery/FastFood/FJ TP, McDonald's, Waffle House
- Other — E: ATMs, Fireworks; W: Laundry/BarbSh/WiFi/LP/FJ TP (RV Dump Closed)

100 — SC 5, Blacksburg Hwy, Blacksburg, to Rock Hill, Shelby
- TStop — W: Sharma Petroleum/Sunoco (Scales)
- Food — W: Subway/Sharma
- Other — E: **to Kings Mountain State Park▲**

98 — Frontage Rd, Blacksburg (NB) (Exit Only / Re-access at Ex #100)
- TStop — E: Broad River Truck Stop
- Food — E: Rest/Broad River TS
- Tserv — E: Broad River TS/Tires

96 — SC 18, Shelby Hwy, Shelby
- TStop — E: Kangaroo #3438
- Gas — W: Sunoco
- Food — E: Krystal/Kangaroo
- Other — E: Laundry/Kangaroo, ATMs, Cherokee Speedway

95 — Hampshire Dr, to SC 18, Limestone St (NB), Rd 82, Pleasant School Rd, Gaffney, Shelby (SB)
- FStop — E: Mini Mart Food Store #3406
- TStop — E: Kangaroo Express, Mr Waffle Auto & Truck Plaza; W: Norma's Truck Stop
- Food — E: Mr Waffle, Auntie M's Cafe/Kang Exp, Dog House Café; W: Rest/Norma's Truck Stop
- Lodg — E: Gaffney Inn, Shamrock Motel
- Med — E: **+ Upstate Carolina Medical Center**

EXIT — SOUTH CAROLINA

92 — SC 11, Floyd Baker Blvd, to SC 150, Gaffney, Boiling Springs, NC
- Gas — E: Citgo, Murphy, Petro Express; W: Exxon, Texaco◈
- Food — E: Applebee's, Blue Bay Seafood, Burger King, Bojangles, KFC, McDonald's, Pizza Hut, Ruby Tuesday, Ryan's Grill, Sagebrush Steakhouse, Sonic, Subway, Taco Bell, Wendy's, Western Sizzler; W: Fatz Cafe, Waffle House
- Lodg — E: Jameson Inn, Super 8; W: Homestead Lodge♥, Quality Inn♥
- Other — E: Grocery, Pharmacy, **Walmart sc**

90 — SC 105, SC 81, Hyatt St, Gaffney
- TStop — E: Pilot Travel Center #453 (Scales)
- Gas — E: BP◈, Kangaroo Express; W: Citgo, Gasland, Petro Express
- Food — E: Arby's/TJCinn/Pilot TC, Bronco Mex Rest, Subway, Waffle House; W: BurgerKing/Citgo, Cracker Barrel, La Fogata Mex Rest, Outback Steakhouse
- Lodg — E: Red Roof Inn, Sleep Inn; W: Hampton Inn
- Other — E: Laundry/WiFi/RVDump/Pilot TC, **Pinecone Campground▲**; W: Prime Outlets at Gaffney

(89) — Rest Area (NB) (RR, Phones, Picnic, Vend)

(88) — Rest Area (SB) (RR, Phones, Picnic, Vend)

87 — Rd 39, Green River Rd, Macedonia Rd, Gaffney
- Other — E: **Pinecone Campground▲**

83 — SC 110, Horry Rd, Battleground Rd, Cowpens, Cowpens Battlefield
- TStop — W: Roadys/Mr Waffle Auto Truck Plaza/ Citgo (Scales)
- Gas — E: HotSpot
- Food — E: Red Rooster , Subway; W: Rest/Mr Waffle ATP
- TWash — W: Mr Waffle ATP
- TServ — E: Horton's Truck Repair; W: Mr Waffle ATP/Tires
- Other — W: Laundry/Mr Waffle ATP, Cowpens Battlefield, Abbott Farms, Fireworks

82 — Frontage Rd (NB)

80 — Rd 57, Gossett Rd (NB)

78 — US 221, Chesnee Hwy, Chesnee, Spartanburg
- Gas — E: Shell◈; W: Exxon◈, RaceTrac◈
- Food — E: Blimpie/Shell, Hardee's; W: Arby's, Bojangles, Burger King/Exxon, Hardee's, McDonald's, Southern BBQ, Subway, Wendy's, Waffle House
- Lodg — E: Motel 6♥, Sun 'n Sand Motel; W: Hampton Inn
- Other — W: Advance Auto, Dollar General, Grocery, Spartanburg Harley Davidson

77 — I-85 Bus S, Spartanburg

75 — SC 9, Spartanburg, Boiling Springs
- Gas — E: Exxon; W: BP◈, Citgo, RaceTrac
- Food — E: Denny's; W: Burger King, Long John Silver, McDonald's, Pizza Hut, Steak & Ale, Waffle House, Zaxby's

EXIT — SOUTH CAROLINA

- Lodg — E: Best Western, Red Roof Inn; W: Comfort Inn, Days Inn
- Med — E: **+ Spartanburg Hospital**
- Other — E: Dollar General; W: CVS, Grocery, Auto Service, US Post Office, **Masters RV Center**

72 — US 176, to I-585, Spartanburg, Inman, Downtown
- Gas — W: BP, RaceTrac
- Other — E: to Univ of SC/Spartanburg

(70B) — Jct I-26W, to Asheville
- Other — W: **Cunningham RV Park▲**

(70A) — Jct I-26E, to Columbia

(70) — Jct I-26, W to Asheville, NC, E to Columbia

69 — I-85 Bus N, to Spartanburg (NB Exit, SB entr)

68 — SC 129, to Wellford, Greer (SB)

66 — US 29, Greenville Hwy, Spartanburg, to Wellford, Lyman
- Other — W: **to Flowermill RV Park▲ , Creekside RV Park▲**

63 — SC 290, E Main St, Duncan, Moore, Spartanburg
- FStop — E: Kangaroo Express #3414/Citgo
- TStop — W: Pilot Travel Center #310 (Scales), Travel Center of America #25/BP (Scales)
- Gas — E: Circle K, Exxon; W: Shell
- Food — E: Burger King, Denny's, Jack in the Box, Pizza Inn, Taco Bell, Waffle House; W: Wendy's/Pilot TC, CountryPride/TA TC, Arby's, Bojangles, Hardee's, McDonald's, Waffle House, Wendy's
- Lodg — E: Hampton Inn, Jameson Inn, Microtel; W: Days Inn/TA TC, Days Inn, Holiday Inn Express, Quality Inn
- TServ — W: TA TC/Tires
- Other — W: Laundry/WiFi/Pilot TC, Laundry/CB/ WiFi/TA TC, **Sonny's Campground▲**

60 — SC 101, Greer, Woodruff
- FStop — E: Grand Foodstuff #2
- Gas — E: BP, Citgo◈; W: Exxon
- Food — E: Subway; W: Burger King
- Other — W: BMW Assembly Plant

58 — Brockman McClimon Rd, to SC 101
- Other — W: BMW Assembly Plant

57 — Aviation Dr, Airport
- Other — W: Greenville Spartanburg Int'l Airport✈

56 — SC 14, Greer, Pelham
- FStop — W: Sphinx #121
- Gas — E: Shell◈; W: BP◈
- Other — W: LP/Spinx, **Outdoor RV & Marine World**

54 — Pelham Rd, Greenville
- Gas — E: BP◈, Citgo◈; W: BP◈, Sphinx
- Food — E: Burger King, Waffle House; W: Applebee's, Ca Dreamin, ChickFilA, Hardee's, Jack in the Box, Joe's Crab Shack, Logan's Roadhouse, Mayflower Seafood, Max & Erma's, McDonald's, On the Border, Ruby Tuesday, Romano's Macaroni Grill, Starbucks, Tony Roma, Wendy's

◈= Regular Gas Stations with Diesel ▲ = RV Friendly Locations ♥= Pet Friendly Locations
Red print shows large vehicle parking / access on site or nearby **Brown Print = Campgrounds / RV PARKS**

EXIT	SOUTH CAROLINA
Lodg	**E:** Best Western **W:** Comfort Suites, Courtyard, Extended Stay America, Fairfield Inn, Hampton Inn, Holiday Inn Express, MainStay Suites, Microtel, Residence Inn, Wingate Inn
Other	**E:** Harley Davidson **W:** CVS, FedEx Office, Goodyear, Grocery, Radio Shack
(52)	**Weigh Station (NB)**
(51C)	**Jct I-385N, Greenville, Downtown**
(51B)	**Jct I-385S, to Columbia**
(51)	**Jct I-385, SC 146, Woodruff Rd, Columbia, Greenville (Acc #48 Serv)**
Gas	**E:** Hess, Spinx **W:** BP, Kangaroo Express, RaceWay, Shell
Food	**E:** Bob Evans, Burger King, Chili's, Fatz Café, Fuddrucker's, IHOP, MiMi's Café, Monterey Mexican, Waffle House **W:** Carrabba's, Capri's Italian Rest, Cracker Barrel, Flat Rock Grille, Jack in the Box, K&W, McDonald's, MiMi's Café, Ruby Tuesday, Salsarita's, Subway, Sushi, TGI Friday, Waffle House
Lodg	**E:** Drury Inn♥, Hampton Inn, Staybridge Suites **W:** Crowne Plaza♥, Days Inn, Fairfield Inn, Holiday Inn Express, La Quinta Inn♥, Microtel, Towneplace Suites
Other	**E:** ATMs, Auto Services, Best Buy, Barnes & Noble, Discount Tire, Frankie's Funpark, Goodyear, Lowe's, Sam's Club, Staples, **Walmart sc**, **W:** ATMs, BJ's, Best Buy, Firestone, Haywood Mall, Home Depot, Lowe's, Office Max, PetSmart♥, Target,
50	**Woodruff Rd**
48AB	**US 276, Laurens Rd, Greenville, Mauldin, Laurens**
48	**US 276, Mauldin, Greeenville**
Gas	**W:** BP, Exxon◈, Murphy
Food	**E:** Waffle House **W:** Arby's, Bojangles, Burger King, Happy China, Hooters, Jack in the Box, KFC, Melting Pot, Ryan's Grill, Roadhouse Grill, Subway, Taco Bell, Zaxby's
Lodg	**E:** Red Roof Inn **W:** Best Inn, Days Inn, Embassy Suites, Phoenix Inn, Sleep Inn
Other	**E:** Car Max **W:** Auto Dealers, Auto Zone, Advance Auto, Auto Repairs, Best Buy, CVS, Office Depot, PetSmart♥, UPS Store, Haywood Mall, Convention Center, Greenville Downtown Airport✈
47	**Mauldin Rd**
46	**Mauldin Rd, SC 291, Pleasantburg Dr, US 25, Augusta Rd**
46C	**Mauldin Rd, to US 25, SC 291**
Gas	**W:** Citgo, Shell, Spinx
Food	**W:** Jack in the Box, Subway
Lodg	**W:** Comfort Inn, InTowne Suites, Quality Inn

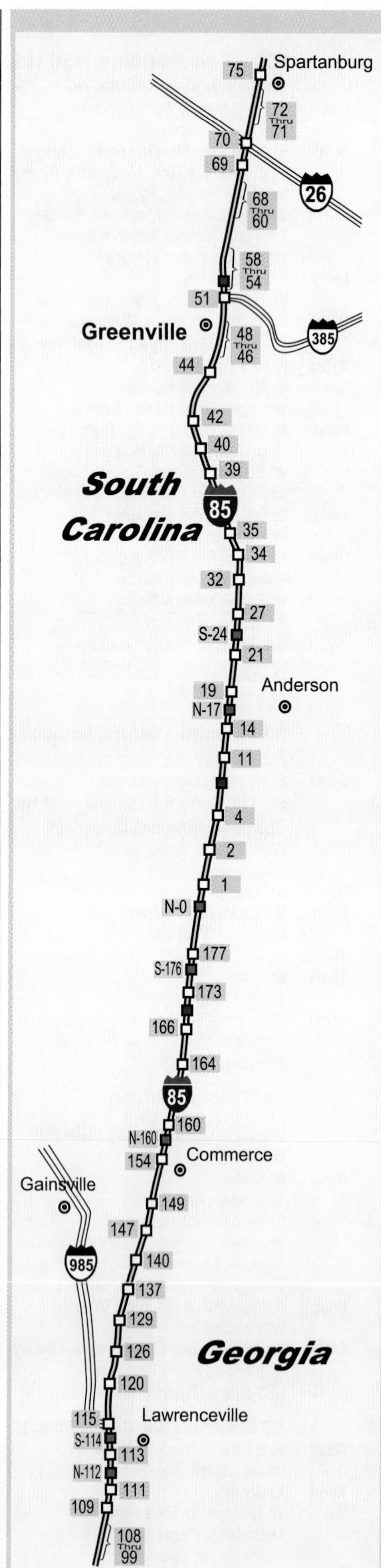

EXIT	SOUTH CAROLINA
Other	**E:** to Greenville Muni Stadium **W:** Grocery **W:** Advance Auto, CVS, Grocery, Home Depot, Tires, **to** Greenville Tech
46B	**SC 291, Pleasantburg Dr, to US 25**
Food	**E:** Waffle House **W:** Burger King, Jack in the Box, Logan's
Lodg	**W:** Economy Inn, Travelers Inn
46A	**Mauldin Rd, SC 291S, Augusta Rd, to Greenwood**
Gas	**E:** Chevron, Spinx
Lodg	**E:** Holiday Inn, Motel 6♥, Southern Suites
Other	**E:** to Springwood RV Park▲, Donaldson Center Airport✈
44B	**White Horse Rd, US 25**
FStop	**E:** Spinx Travel Plaza #138
Gas	**W:** RaceTrac
Food	**E:** Subway/Spinx **W:** McDonald's, Waffle House
TServ	**W:** Cherokee Kenworth
Med	**W:** + Greenville Hospital, + Childrens Hospital
Other	**E:** to Springwood RV Park▲ **W:** Sun Coast RV, Wrecker
44A	**Piedmont Hwy, SC 20 (SB Exit, NB entr)**
Other	**E:** Auto Service, LC Diesel Service
44	**US 25, White Horse Rd, SC 20, Piedmont Hwy, Greenville (NB)**
(42)	**Jct I-185 (TOLL), US 29N, Downtown Greenville, Columbia**
40	**SC 153, SC 190, Piedmont, Easley**
Gas	**E:** Exxon **W:** Pantry, RaceTrac, Shell
Food	**E:** Waffle House **W:** Arby's, Burger King, Cracker Barrel, Hardee's, Huddle House, KFC, McDonald's Pizza Hut, Subway
Lodg	**W:** Executive Inn, Super 8
Other	**W:** Grocery, Pharmacy
39	**SC 143, River Rd, to SC 153 (Access to Ex #40 Serv)**
Gas	**W:** Shell◈
Other	**E:** to Ivy Acres RV Park▲
35	**SC 86, Anderson Hwy, Piedmont**
TStop	**E:** Pilot Travel Center #63 (Scales)
Gas	**W:** BP◈
Food	**E:** McDonald's/Pilot TC
Other	**E:** WiFi/Pilot TC
34	**US 29, Anderson, Williamston (SB Left Exit, NB entr)**
32	**SC 8, Easley Hwy, Pelzer, Easley, Williamston, Belton**
Gas	**E:** Shell◈
27	**SC 81, Williamsburg Rd, Anderson**
TStop	**W:** Anderson Travel Center (Scales)
Gas	**E:** BP◈, Exxon
Food	**E:** Arby's, McDonald's, Waffle House **W:** Rest/Anderson TC
Lodg	**E:** Holiday Inn Express
Tires	**E:** Anderson TC
Other	**E:** Laundry/WiFi/Anderson TC
(24)	**Rest Area (SB) (RR, Phones, Picnic, Vend)**
21	**US 178, Liberty Hwy, Anderson, Liberty (Access to Ex #19 Serv)**
FStop	**E:** Liberty Crossroads/Shell

◈ = Regular Gas Stations with Diesel ▲ = RV Friendly Locations ♥ = Pet Friendly Locations
Red print shows large vehicle parking / access on site or nearby Brown Print = Campgrounds / RV PARKS

EXIT		SC / GA
	Food	E: Applebee's, O'Charley's, Ruby Tuesday
	Lodg	E: La Quinta Inn♥, Quality Inn, Super 8
19A		**US 76W**
19B		**US 76E**
19		**US 76, Clemson Hwy, to SC 28, Pendleton, Anderson, Clemson, to Abbeville, Greenwood**
	Gas	E: BP, Exxon◊ W: RaceWay Trac
	Food	E: Chili's, Fuddrucker's, Hardee's, Jack in The Box, O'Charley's, Olive Garden, Texas Roadhouse W: Cracker Barrel, Hooters, McDonald's, Outback Steakhouse, Waffle House, Wendy's
	Lodg	E: Best Value Inn, Days Inn, La Quinta Inn♥, Mainstay Suites, Quality Inn W: Comfort Suites, Country Inn, Fairfield Inn, Hampton Inn, Holiday Inn Express, Jameson Inn
	Other	E: Best Buy, Harley Davidson, Sam's Club, Target, **Walmart sc**, Auto Dealers W: to Clemson Univ, to appr 20 mi Crooked Creek RV Park▲
(17)		**Rest Area (NB)** (RR, Phone, Picnic, Vend)
14		**SC 187, Williams Rd, Townville, Anderson, Pendleton, Clemson**
	FStop	E: Fuel Club
	Gas	W: AmocoBP◊
	Food	E: Huddle House
	Lodg	W: Budget Inn
	Other	E: Anderson/Lake Hartwell KOA▲
11		**SC 24, SC 243, Townville, Anderson, to Westminster**
	FStop	E: Sunoco #2687
	Gas	E: Exxon◊ W: Shell◊
	Food	E: Subway W: Circles Café
	Other	W: to appr 15mi Crooked Creek RV Park▲
(9)		**Weigh Station (NB)**
4		**SC 243, Old Dobbins Bridge Rd, to SC 24, Fair Play**
	FStop	E: A & V Quick Stop (Scales)
	Gas	E: Exxon W: Russell's Gen'l Store/Marathon
2		**SC 59, Fair Play Blvd, Fair Play**
	Other	E: Fireworks
1		**SC 11, Walhalla, Westminster** (NB Exit and Entrance)
	Other	W: Lake Hartwell State Park
(0)		**SC Welcome Center (NB)** (RR, Phones, Picnic, Vend, Info)

⬆ SOUTH CAROLINA
⬇ GEORGIA

NOTE: MM 179: South Carolina State Line

EASTERN TIME ZONE

EXIT		GEORGIA
177		**GA 77S, Whitworth Rd, Lavonia, to Elberton, Hartwell**
	Gas	E: BP◊
	Other	E: to Hart State Park▲

Personal Notes

EXIT		GEORGIA
(176)		**GA Welcome Center (SB)** (RR, Phone, Picnic, Vend, RVDump)
173		**GA 17, Jones St, Lavonia, Toccoa**
	Gas	E: RaceTrac W: Exxon◊, Shell
	Food	E: Hardee's, La Cabana, McDonald's, Subway, Taco Bell, Wendy's W: Arby's, Burger King, Pizza Hut, Shoney's, Waffle House, Zaxby's
	Lodg	E: Best Western, Sleep Inn W: GuestHouse Inn, Super 8
	Other	E: Dollar General, RiteAid W: Sunset Campground▲, to Tugaloo State Park▲
(171)		**Weigh Station (NB)**
(169)		**Weigh Station (SB)**
166		**GA 106, GA 145, Carnesville, Toccoa**
	TStop	E: WilcoHess Travel Plaza #3001 (Scales) W: Echo Auto Truck Plaza/Chevron (Scales)
	Food	E: Wendy's/WilcoHess TP W: Rest/Echo ATP
	TServ	W: Echo ATP/Tires
	Other	E: Laundry/WilcoHess TP
164		**GA 320, Church Rd, Carnesville** (Serv E to Commerce Rd / GA 59)
	TStop	W: Carnesville Truck Stop
	Gas	E: BP
	Other	E: Auto Service, Dollar General, U-Haul

EXIT		GEORGIA
160		**GA 51, Sandy Cross Rd, Carnesville, Homer, Royston, Elberton**
	TStop	E: Shell Travel Plaza (Scales) W: Flying J Travel Plaza #5096 (Scales), Petro Stopping Center #60 (Scales)
	Food	E: Chesters/Subway/Shell TP W: CountryMarket/FastFood/FJ TP, IronSkillet/PizzaHut/Petro SC
	TWash	W: Blue Beacon TW/Petro SC
	TServ	W: Petro SC/Tires
	Other	E: Laundry/Shell TP, to Victoria Bryant State Park▲ W: Laundry/WiFi/RVDump/LP/FJ TP, Laundry/BarbSh/CB/RVDump/Petro SC
154		**GA 63, Martin Bridge Rd, Commerce**
149		**US 441, GA 15, Commerce, Homer**
	TStop	E: Travel Center of America #156 (Scales)
	Gas	E: Shell, Murphy USA W: BP, Citgo, RaceTrac◊
	Food	E: Buckhorn/TA TC, Captain D's, El Azteca, Grand Buffet, Longhorn Steakhouse, Sonny's BBQ, Shoney's, Taco Bell/Pizza Hut, Waffle House, Zaxby's W: Applebee's, Arby's, Burger King, Checkers, ChickFilA, Cracker Barrel, Denny's, KFC, La Fiesta Grill, McDonald's, Pizza Hut, Ruby Tuesday, Ryan's Grill, Starbucks, Subway, Waffle House, Wendy's
	Lodg	E: Days Inn, Dandelion Inn♥, Hampton Inn, Red Roof Inn♥, Scottish Inn W: Americas Best Inn, Best Western, Holiday Inn Express, Howard Johnson♥, Jameson Inn♥, Quality Inn♥, Super 8
	TServ	E: TA TC/Tires
	Med	E: + Commerce Hospital
	Other	E: Laundry/WiFi/TA TC, ATMs, Auto Dealer, Dollar General, Dollar Tree, Pharmacy, Radio Shack, **Walmart sc**, Tanger Outlet Mall 1, County Boys RV Park▲
	Other	W: Auto Dealers, Home Depot, Tanger Outlet Mall 2, Tires, Lightnin RV, The Pottery Campground▲, Atlanta Dragway
147		**GA 98, Maysville Rd, Commerce, Maysville**
	FStop	E: Fuel Mart #636
	TStop	E: Flying J Travel Plaza #5169 (Scales)
	Gas	W: Cody's Fuel
	Food	E: Rest/FastFood/FJ TP
	Med	E: + Commerce Hospital
	Other	E: Laundry/WiFi/RVDump/LP/FJ TP
140		**GA 82, Dry Pond Rd, Pendergrass**
	Other	E: to Jackson Co Airport✈
137		**US 129, GA 11, Pendergrass, Gainesville, Jefferson**
	TStop	W: QT #737 (Scales)
	Gas	E: RaceTrac◊, Shell
	Food	E: Arby's, McDonald's, Waffle House, Zaxby's W: Deli/QT, Burger King, Waffle House, Wendy's
	Lodg	E: Comfort Inn
	Other	W: ATMs, Pendergrass Flea Market
129		**GA 53, Winder Hwy, Braselton, Hoschton, Lanier Raceway**
	TStop	W: Pilot Travel Center #66 (Scales)

◊= Regular Gas Stations with Diesel ▲ = RV Friendly Locations ♥= Pet Friendly Locations
Red print shows large vehicle parking / access on site or nearby Brown Print = Campgrounds / RV PARKS

Gas E: BP, Chevron, Shell◊
Food E: Subway/BP, Waffle House
W: McDonald's/Pilot TC, **Cracker Barrel**, Domino's Pizza, Stonewall's BBQ
Other W: Laundry/WiFi/Pilot TC

126 GA 211, Winder Hwy, Hoschton, Braselton, Winder
Gas E: Shell◊
W: BP◊
Food E: Subway, Waffle House
W: Chateau Elan, Papa John's
Lodg W: Chateau Elan Resort, Holiday Inn Express
Other W: Chateau Elan Winery & Resort, Golf Course, Chateau Animal Hospital♥

120 CR 134, Hamilton Mill Pkwy, Hamilton Mill Rd, Buford
Gas E: BP, QT◊
W: Chevron, Shell◊, Murphy USA
Food E: Arby's, McDonald's, Ninja's Japanese Steakhouse, Shane's Rib Shack, Starbucks, Subway, The Fieldhouse, Wendy's, Zaxby's
W: ChickFilA, Chili's, Front Porch Country Cooking, Hardee's, Huddle House/Shell, Subway
Other E: ATMs, Banks, Auto Services, Home Depot, Kohl's, Publix, **RV World of GA**
W: ATMs, CVS, Car Wash, O'Reilly Auto Parts, Tires Plus, **Walmart sc**

115AB GA 20, Buford Dr NE, Buford

115 GA 20, Buford Dr NE, Buford, Lawrenceville, to I-985
Gas E: QT, to Racetrac, Citgo
W: BP, Chevron, QT◊
Food W: Arby's, Burger King, Chili's, ChickFilA, Chuck E Cheese, Longhorn Steakhouse, McDonald's, MiMi's Cafe, Moe's SW Grill, O'Charley's, Olive Garden, On the Border, Red Lobster, Romano's Macaroni Grill, Starbucks, Subway, TGI Friday, Waffle House
Lodg W: Country Inn, Courtyard, Hampton Inn, Springhill Suites, Wingate Inn
Med E: + Hospital
Other E: to Walgreen's
W: ATMs, Banks, Apple Store, Best Buy, Borders, Cingular, Costco, Dick's Sporting Goods, FedEx Office, Firestone, HH Gregg, Lowe's, Office Max, PetCo♥, PetSmart♥, Sam's Club, Staples, Target, UPS Store, **Walmart sc**, Mall of GA , **to Southland Motorhome**

(114) Rest Area (SB)
(RR, Phone, Picnic, Vend)

(113) Jct I-985N, Gainesville, GA 365, Lanier Pkwy, Lake Lanier Islands, Buford Dam (NB)

(112) Rest Area (NB)
(RR, Phones, Picnic, Vend)

111 GA 317, Lawrenceville - Suwanee Rd, Suwanee, Lawrenceville
FStop E: FA Simms Oil #104/66
Gas E: BP
W: Chevron◊, RaceTrac, Shell, Murphy USA

Food E: Applebee's, Arby's, Blimpie, Burger King, ChickFilA, **Cracker Barrel**, Pizza Hut, Outback Steakhouse, Subway, Taco Bell, Waffle House, Wendy's
W: CiCi's Pizza, Denny's, McDonald's, Moe's SW Grill, Waffle House
Lodg E: Best Western♥, Comfort Inn♥, Comfort Suites, Fairfield Inn, Sun Suites♥
W: Days Inn, Motel 6♥, Super 8
Other E: ATMs, Banks, CVS, Kaufmann Tire, Publix, UPS Store
W: ATMs, Banks, Dollar Tree, Lowe's, Mail Depot, Office Depot,Radio Shack, Tires Plus, **Walmart sc**, Auto Repair/Shell, Carwash/Chevron

109 Old Peachtree Rd, Lawrenceville
Gas E: QT◊
Food E: Jim & Nick's BBQ, McDonald's, Quiznos
W: Waffle House
Other E: ATMs, Banks,
W: ATMs, Home Depot, Mercy Animal Hospital♥, **Access to Ex #111**

108 Sugarloaf Pkwy
Food W: Carrabba's, ChickFilA, Roadhouse Grill
Lodg E: Hampton Inn, Homewood Suites
W: Hilton Garden Inn, Holiday Inn
Other E: ATMs, Banks, CVS, Suburban Tires, Discover Mills,
W: ATMs, Banks, Gwinnett Convention Center,

107 GA 120, Duluth Hwy, to GA 316, Duluth, Lawrenceville
Gas E: Shell
W: BP, Chevron, QT
Food E: Burger King, Carino's, Zaxby's
W: McDonald's, Subway, China Gate
Lodg W: La Quinta Inn♥, Suburban Extended Stay
Med E: + Gwinett Medical Center
Other E: ATMs, Banks, CVS, Discount Tire, Discover Mills, Suburban Tire, **to Appalachee RV Center**

106 GA 316E, Lawrenceville ByPass (NB, Exit only)
Other E: **to Lightnin RV**, Gwinnett Co Airport/ Briscoe Field✈

104 Pleasant Hill Rd, Duluth, Norcross
Gas E: Chevron, Circle K, Exxon, RaceTrac
W: BP◊, Phillips 66, QT, Shell, Murphy
Food E: Burger King, ChickFilA, Carrabba's, Joe's Crab Shack, Romano's Macaroni Grill, Smoky Bones BBQ, Starbucks, Subway, TGI Friday, Waffle House, Wendy's
W: Applebee's, Arby's, Burger King, Checkers, Chili's, Hooters, IHOP, KFC, Olive Garden, McDonald's, On the Border, Panda Express, Pizza Hut, Red Lobster, Ryan's Grill, Shoney's, Starbucks, Steak 'n Shake, Taco Bell, Waffle House, Wendy's
Lodg E: Candlewood Suites, Comfort Suites, Country Inn, Hampton Inn, Holiday Inn Express, Marriott, Residence Inn, Studio 6
W: Courtyard, Days Inn, Hyatt, Quality Inn, Wellesley Inn, Wingate Inn
TServ E: International Trucks
Other E: ATMs, Best Buy, CVS, FedEx Office, Goodyear, Home Depot, Office Depot, Publix, Walgreen's

Other W: Art City Art World, Auto Dealers, Auto Repairs, Banks, Barnes & Noble, Batteries Plus, Firestone, Goodyear, Gwinnett Place Mall, Kroger, PetCo♥, PetSmart♥, Staples, Target, UPS Store, Venture Cinemas, **Sagon RV**, **Walmart sc**,

103 CR 557, Steve Reynolds Blvd (NB) (Access to Ex #104 Serv)
Gas W: QT
Food W: Starbucks, Waffle House
Lodg E: Sun Suites
W: InTown Suites
Other W: Costco, Sam's Club, Target

102 GA 378, Beaver Ruin Rd, Norcross
Gas E: Shell◊
W: BP, QT
Other W: **Casey's Mobile RV Repair**

101 Indian Trail Rd, CR 560, Lilburn Rd, Norcross
Gas E: QT◊, Shell◊
W: BP◊, Chevron, Speed Mart
Food E: Blimpie, Krystal, KFC, McDonald's, Taco Bell, Shoney's, Starbucks, Waffle House
W: Arby's, DQ, Little Caesars, Waffle House, Wendy's
Lodg E: GuestHouse Inn, Shoney's Inn, Suburban Lodge, Super 8
W: Red Roof Inn♥
Other E: **Jones RV Park▲**
W: CVS, Grocery, Lowe's, Outlet Mall

99 GA 140W, Jimmy Carter Blvd, Norcross, Doraville
Gas E: BP, Exxon, Phillips 66◊, Shell
W: Chevron, Citgo, QT◊
Food E: Burger King, ChickFilA, Chili's, **Cracker Barrel**, Denny's, McDonald's, Long John Silver, Pizza Hut, Steak & Taco Bell, Wendy's
W: Arby's, Hooters, Pappadeaux Seafood, Shoney's, Waffle House
Lodg E: Best Western, Comfort Inn, Courtyard, Motel 6♥, La Quinta Inn♥, Travelodge
W: Country Inn, Drury Inn, Microtel
TServ W: Peachstate Ford
Med E: + GA Family Medicine Center
Other E: Budget RAC, CVS, Firestone, Hertz RAC, Office Depot, U-Haul, UPS Store, Walgreen's,
W: Auto Zone, Big 10 Tire, NTB, Tires

96 Pleasantdale Rd, Northcrest Rd Northcrest Rd (NB)
FStop W: QT #707 (Scales)
Gas W: Exxon
Food E: Burger King
W: Deli/QT, Waffle House
Lodg W: Howard Johnson, US Economy Lodge

(95B) Jct I-285W, to Chattanooga, Birminham (SB)

(95A) Jct I-285E, to Macon, Augusta (SB)

(95) Jct I-285, Atl ByP, E to Augusta, W to Chattanooga (NB)

94 Chamblee Tucker Rd, Atlanta, Chamblee, Tucker
Gas E: BP, Shell
W: QT◊, Shell
Food E: Chinese
W: DQ, Waffle House
Lodg E: Masters Inn
W: Motel 6♥, Red Roof Inn♥
Other W: to Mercer Univ

◊= Regular Gas Stations with Diesel ▲ = RV Friendly Locations ♥= Pet Friendly Locations
Red print shows large vehicle parking / access on site or nearby **Brown Print = Campgrounds / RV PARKS**

EXIT		GEORGIA
93		**Shallowford Rd, to Briarcliffe Rd, Doraville**
	Gas	E: Shell
		W: Circle K, Shell◈
	Food	E: Waffle House, Blimpie/Shell
		W: Quality Inn, Chicken Plaza
	Lodg	E: Super 8
		W: Quality Inn
	Other	E: Laundromat, Publix, U-Haul
91		**US 23, GA 155, Clairmont Rd, Decatur, to Airport**
	Gas	E: Express, Chevron, Speedway
		W: Amoco, BP
	Food	E: IHOP, McDonald's, Popeye's
		W: Waffle House, Roadhouse Grill, Starbucks, Pizza
	Lodg	W: Clairmont Lodge, Days Inn, Marriott, Wingate Inn
	Other	E: CVS, IGA
		W: Laundromat, Grocery, Pharmacy, Sam's Club, DeKalb-Peachtree Airport✈, Emory Univ
89		**GA 42, N Druid Hills Rd**
	Gas	E: Amoco, Crown, QT◈
		W: BP, Chevron◈, Exxon, Hess
	Food	E: Arby's, Burger King, McDonald's, Piccadilly, Taco Bell
		W: Pizza Hut, Waffle House
	Lodg	E: Courtyard, Homestead Suites
		W: Hampton Inn, Microtel, Radisson, Red Roof Inn♥
	Med	E: + Hospital
	Other	E: CVS, Target, to Oglethorpe Univ
88		**to GA 400N, Cheshire Bridge Rd, Lenox Rd (SB)**
	Gas	E: BP, Exxon, Shell, Spur
	Food	E: Waffle House, Sonny's BBQ
	Lodg	E: Baymont Inn
87		**GA 400N, Harvey Mathis Pkwy, Cumming (NB)**
86		**GA 13S, Peachtree St (SB), GA 13N, Buford Hwy (NB)**
	Gas	E: BP, Chevron
	Food	E: Denny's, Wendy's
	Lodg	E: Intown Suites, Piedmont Inn
		W: Ramada
	NOTE:	**I-85 below runs with I-75. Exit #'s follow I-75.**
(85/251)		**Jct I-85N, to Greeneville, SC Jct I-75N to Marietta, Chattanooga, TN**
84/ 250		**17th St, 14th St, 10th St, to GA Tech (SB, Exit only)**
250		**10th St, 14th St, GA Tech (NB)**
249D		**US 78, US 278, North Ave (SB)**
	Gas	E: BP
	Food	E: Checker's, Pizza Hut
		W: McDonald's
	Lodg	W: Comfort Inn, Holiday Inn Express
249D		**US 29, US 19, Spring St, W Peachtre St, to US 78, US 278 (NB)**
249C		**Downtown Atlanta, Williams St, Georgia Dome (SB, Exit Only)**

EXIT		GEORGIA
249B		**Pine St, Peachtree St, Civic Center, (NB, Exit Only)**
	Med	E: + Crawford Long Hospital
249A		**Courtland St, GA St Univ (SB, Exit only)**
	Other	W: GA State Univ
248D		**J W Dobbs Ave,Edgewood Ave (SB)**
248C		**GA 10E, Freedom Pkwy, Carter Center, Andrew Young Int'l Blvd**
248B		**Edgewood Ave, Auburn Ave, Butler St, J W Dobbs Ave**
248A		**MLK Jr Dr, State Capitol (SB)**
(247)		**Jct I-20, E to Augusta, W to Birmingham**
246		**Fulton St, Central Ave, Downtown**
	Gas	E: BP
	Lodg	E: Hampton Inn, Holiday Inn
	Other	E: Torner Field, Atlanta Zoo
		W: to Coliseum, GA State Univ
245		**Abernathy Blvd, Capitol Ave (NB exit, SB ent)**
	Lodg	E: Holiday Inn, Hampton Inn
	Other	E: Turner Field
		W: State Capitol
244		**University Ave, Pryor St**
	Gas	E: Chevron, Exxon
	TServ	E: Cummins South, Southern Freight
		W: Brown Transport, Ford Trucks, Freight Direct, Great Dane Trailers
243/ (242/ 77)		**GA 166, Lankford Pkwy, East Point Jct I-85S, to Atlanta Airport, Montgomery**
	NOTE:	**I-85 above runs with I-75. Exit #'s follow I-75.**
77		**GA 166, Langford Pky, Lakewood Fwy (NB exit, SB entr) US 19, US 41, Metropolitan Pkwy, GA 3 (SB exit, NB entr)**
76		**Cleveland Ave, Atlanta**
	Gas	E: BP, Citgo◈, Hess, Phillips 66
		W: Amoco, Texaco
	Food	E: Arby's, Burger King, Mrs Winners
		W: KFC, Church's
	Lodg	E: Days Inn, New American Inn
	Med	W: + Hospital
	Other	E: CVS, Kroger, to Atlanta Tech
75		**Sylvan Rd, Central Ave, Hapeville**
	Gas	E: Fina, Shell◈
	Food	E: ChickFilA, McDonald's, Waffle House
	Lodg	E: InTown Suites
		W: Mark Inn
74		**Loop Rd (SB exit, NB entr) (Access to Ex #73 Serv)**
	Lodg	E: Residence Inn
73		**Virginia Ave (SB)**
73B		**Virginia Ave West (NB)**
	Gas	W: Chevron, Shell
	Food	W: Arby's, BBQ Kitchen, KFC, Sandwich Factory, Steak & Ale, Waffle House
	Lodg	W: AmeriSuites, Crowne Plaza, DoubleTree, Econo Lodge, Fairfield Inn, Hampton Inn, Holiday Inn

EXIT		GEORGIA
73A		**Virginia Ave East (NB)**
	Gas	E: Citgo◈
	Food	E: Hardee's, IHOP, McDonald's, Pizza Hut, Ruby Tuesday, Waffle House, Wendy's
	Lodg	E: Courtyard, Hilton, Marriott, Red Roof Inn♥, Residence Inn, Sheraton
72		**GA 6, Camp Creek Pkwy, Atlanta Airport, Air Cargo**
	Gas	W: Amoco, Chevron, Shell
	Med	E: + Grady Medical Center
	Other	E: Hartsfield Jackson Atl Intl Airport✈
		W: Goodyear
71		**GA 139, Riverdale Rd, Airport, Camp Creek Pkwy, Air Cargo**
	Gas	E: QT
	Food	E: Ruby Tuesday, Rest/Hol Inn
		W: Rest/Westin
	Lodg	E: Courtyard, Fairfield Inn, Hampton Inn, Holiday Inn, Hyatt, La Quinta Inn♥, Microtel, Sheraton, Sleep Inn, Super 8, Wingate Inn
		W: Embassy Suites, Hilton Garden Inn, Marriott, Westin
(70)		**Jct I-285, E to Macon, Augusta, W to Birmingham, Chattanooga (SB ex, NB entr)**
69B		**GA 279, Old National Hwy (NB)**
	Gas	E: BP, Chevronx2, Citgo, Texaco
		W: Chevron, Conoco◈, Shell, Texaco
	Food	E: Burger King, Checkers, El Ranchero, Indian Rest, McDonald's, Taco Bell, Waffle House, Wendy's
		W: City Café Diner, Subway, Waffle House
	Lodg	E: Clarion, Comfort Inn, Days Inn, Howard Johnson, Motel 6♥, Quality Inn
		W: Econo Lodge, Hilton Garden Inn
	Other	E: Auto Repairs, Firestone, Grocery , Pharmacy, U-Haul
		W: Advance Auto, Auto Zone, Family Dollar, Kroger, Radio Shack, Target
69A		**GA 14 Spur, S Fulton Pkwy (NB, Left Exit)**
69		**GA 279, GA 14 Spur (SB)**
(68)		**Jct I-285, E to Macon, Tampa, FL N to Birmingham, Chattanooga, TN**
66		**Flat Shoals Rd, CR 1384,Union City (Access to Ex #64 Serv)**
	FStop	W: Chevron Food Mart #122
	Food	W: Waffle House
	Lodg	W: Motel 6♥
64		**GA 138, Jonesboro Rd, Union City, Jonesboro**
	Gas	E: BP◈
		W: Chevron, QT, Shell◈
	Food	E: Waffle House
		W: Arby's, Burger King, ChickFilA, **Cracker Barrel**, IHOP, Krystal, McDonald's Pizza Hut, Subway, Taco Bell, Waffle House, Wendy's
	Lodg	E: Econo Lodge, Ramada, Super 8
		W: Baymont Inn, Best Western, Comfort Inn, Days Inn, Holiday Inn Express, Microtel, Red Roof Inn♥
	Other	E: Auto Dealers
		W: Auto Repairs, Big Lots, Carwash, Dollar Tree, Firestone, Goodyear, Kroger, NTB, PepBoys, Shannon Mall, Walgreen's, **Walmart sc**,

◈= Regular Gas Stations with Diesel ▲ = RV Friendly Locations ♥= Pet Friendly Locations
Red print shows large vehicle parking / access on site or nearby Brown Print = Campgrounds / RV PARKS

EXIT		GEORGIA
61		**GA 74, Senoia Rd, Fairburn**
	TStop	E: Greenway Fairburn Family Travel Center/BP (Scales) (DAND)
	Gas	E: Chevron◈, RaceTrac, Shell W: Citgo◈, Marathon, Pit Stop, Phillips 66◈
	Food	E: Rest/Fairburn TC, Chili's, Dunkin Donuts, McDonald's Subway, Wendy's, Waffle House, Zaxby's
	Lodg	E: Hampton Inn, Sleep Inn, Wingate Inn W: Efficiency Motel
	Other	E: Laundry/Fairburn TC, Carwash
56		**Collinsworth Rd, CR 548, Palmetto, Tyrone**
	Gas	E: BP, Marathon
	Food	E: Frank's Family Rest
	Other	W: South Oaks RV & MH Park▲ , Pine Acres MH & RV Park▲
51		**GA 154, McCollum-Sharpsburg Rd**
	Gas	E: BP, Phillips 66 W: Shell
	Food	E: Blimpie, Hardee's W: Krystal, Waffle House
47		**GA 34, Newnan, Peachtree City**
	FStop	W: Lakeside Shell
	Gas	E: Chevron◈, HotSpot◈ , QT, Shell◈ W: Exxon, Phillips 66, RaceTrac
	Food	E: Arby's, Applebee's, CiCi's Pizza, Cracker Barrel, Longhorn Steakhouse, McDonald's, Mama Lucia's, Moe's SW Grill, Panda Express, Pizza Inn, Ryan's Grill, Starbucks, Subway, Waffle House, Wendy's W: Burger King, Golden Corral, IHOP, Krystal, Waffle House, Zaxby's
	Lodg	E: Best Western, Country Inn, Hampton Inn, Jameson Inn, Springhill Suites W: Comfort Inn, Holiday Inn Express, La Quinta Inn♥, Motel 6♥
	Med	W: + Hospital
	Other	E: ATMs, Best Buy, Goodyear, Home Depot, Kaufmann Tires, Lowe's, Office Max, PetSmart♥, Target, Walmart sc, Outlet Mall, Tourist Info W: Auto Dealers, BJ's, Office Depot, Publix, Target, Tires Plus, UPS Store, Univ of W GA/Newnan
(Future)		**FUTURE 2010: Poplar Rd, to GA 26, GA 34, 154**
	Med	W: (FUTURE)+ Piedmont Newnan Hosp
41		**US 27A, US 29, GA 14, to GA 16, Newnan, Moreland**
	TStop	E: Pilot Travel Center # 422 (Scales) W: Greenway Stores #612/BP (Scales)
	Gas	W: Phillips 66
	Food	E: Subway/Wendy's/Pilot TC W: McDonald's, Waffle House
	Lodg	W: Days Inn, Ramada, Rodeway Inn, Super 8
	TWash	E: Pilot TC
	Other	E: Laundry/WiFi/RVDump/Pilot TC, Newnan-Coweta Co Airport✈
35		**US 29, GA 14, Grantville, Moreland**
	Gas	W: Phillips 66◈
28		**GA 54, GA 100, Hogansville**
	FStop	W: Money Back #14/AmocoBP
	TStop	W: Hogansville 66 Truck Plaza (Scales), Love's Travel Stop #376 (Scales)
	Gas	E: Shell◈

EXIT		GA / AL
	Food	E: Janie's Country Kitchen W: Rest/66 TP, Arby's/Love's TS, McDonald's, Rogers BBQ, Subway, Waffle House, Wendy's
	Lodg	W: Days Inn, Econo Lodge
	TWash	W: Baileys TW/66 TP
	Tires	W: 66 TP
	Other	W: Flat Creek Campground▲
(22)		**Weigh Station (Both dir)**
(21)		**Jct I-185S, to Columbus, Ft Benning**
18		**GA 109, Greenville Rd, LaGrange, Greenville, Warm Springs**
	Gas	E: Chevron◈ W: RaceTrac, Shell◈, BP◈, Spectrum◈
	Food	W: Applebee's, Burger King, Church's Chicken, Cracker Barrel, Hoofer's Rest, IHOP, Ryan's Grill, Subway, Waffle House, Wendy's, Zaxby's
	Lodg	W: AmeriHost Inn♥, Best Western, Holiday Inn Express, Jameson Inn, Quality Inn, Super 8
	Med	W: + Hospital
	Other	W: ATMs, Auto Dealers, Auto Repairs, Banks, Home Depot, Hoofers RV Park▲ , LaGrange Mall, Walmart,
14		**US 27, GA 1, LaGrange**
	Gas	W: BP, Pure Food Mart
	Food	W: Church's Chicken
	Lodg	W: Hampton Inn
	Other	W: GA State Hwy Patrol Post
13		**GA 219, Whitesville Rd, LaGrange**
	FStop	W: Money Back #5/AmocoBP
	TStop	E: Roadys/LaGrange Travel Center/ Shell (Scales) W: Pilot Travel Center #69 (Scales)
	Food	E: Rest/LaGrange TC, Waffle House W: Subway/Pilot TC, McDonald's
	Lodg	E: Days Inn
	TServ	E: LaGrange TC/Tires
	Med	W: + West GA Medical Center
	Other	E: Laundry/WiFi/LaGrange TC W: WiFi/Pilot TC, GA Tech, Callaway Airport✈
6		**Kia Blvd, Kia Pky, West Point**
	Other	W: Kia Motor Plant & Training Facility
2		**GA 18, West Point, Pine Mountain, Callaway Gardens**
	Gas	E: Shell◈
	Food	E: Church's Chicken, KFC, Subway
	Lodg	E: Travelodge
(1)		**GA Welcome Center (NB)** **(RR, Phone, Picnic, Vend, Info)**

EASTERN TIME ZONE

↑ GEORGIA
↓ ALABAMA

EASTERN / CENTRAL TIME ZONE

79		**US 29, AL 15, Valley, Lanett**
	Gas	E: BP◈ , Murphy USA W: Jet Pep, QV, Phillips 66◈
	Food	E: Arby's, Burger King, Captain D's,

EXIT		ALABAMA
	Food	E: Hardee's, KFC, Krystal, McDonald's, Taco Bell, Waffle House, Wendy's
	Lodg	W: Days Inn, Econo Lodge
	Med	E: + Hospital
	Other	E: Dollar General, Dollar Tree, Pharmacy, Walmart sc, to Valley View Airport✈ W: ATMs, Auto Zone, CVS, Kroger, O'Reilly Auto Parts
(78)		**AL Welcome Center (SB)** **(RR, Phone, Picnic, Vend, RVDump)**
77		**CR 208, Valley, Huguley**
	TStop	E: Spectrum #40
	Food	E: Waffle King
	Lodg	E: Holiday Inn Express
	Med	E: + Hospital
	NOTE:	**MM 76: Eastern / Central Time Zone**
70		**CR 388, to Cusseta**
	TStop	E: AmBest/Bridges Travel Plaza/Shell (Scales)
	Gas	E: BP
	Food	E: CountryPride/Subway/Bridges TP
	TWash	E: Bridges TP
	TServ	E: Bridges TP/Tires
	Other	E: Laundry/Bridges TP W: Fireworks
66		**Andrews Rd, to US 29, AL 15**
64		**US 29, AL 15N, Opelika**
	Gas	E: BP W: Tiger Fuel◈
	Lodg	E: GuestHouse Inn
62		**US 280E, US 431, Opelika, Phenix City**
	FStop	E: Spectrum #22/BP
	Gas	E: Chevron, Liberty W: Jet Pep, Shell
	Food	E: Burger King, Denny's, McDonald's, Shoney's, Subway W: Cracker Barrel, Waffle House, Western Sizzlin'
	Lodg	E: Holiday Inn, Knights Inn, Red Carpet Inn, Travelodge W: Comfort Inn, Days Inn, Econo Lodge, Motel 6, Travelodge
	Other	E: Lakeside RV Park▲ , Opelika RV Outlet W: Auto Dealers, Grocery, Outlet Mall, Flea Market, Harley Davidson
60		**AL 51, AL 169, Opelika, Hurtsboro**
	Gas	E: BP◈, RaceTrac W: Shell◈
	Food	E: Hardee's W: Krystal, Wendy's
58		**US 280W, AL 38W, Gateway Dr, Opelika**
	Gas	W: BP, Chevron, Liberty
	Food	W: Arby's, ChickFilA, Golden Corral, Outback Steakhouse, Starbucks, Subway, Taco Bell
	Lodg	W: Best Western, Homestead Suites, Tiger Inn
	Med	W: + East AL Medical Center
	Other	W: ATMs, Best Buy, BooksAMillion, Home Depot, Kroger, Lowe's, Office Depot, Pharmacy, Target
57		**Glenn Ave, Auburn**
	Gas	W: Exxon, QV
	Food	W: Waffle House
	Lodg	W: Hilton Garden Inn
	Other	W: Auburn Opelika Airport✈

◈= Regular Gas Stations with Diesel ▲ = RV Friendly Locations ♥= Pet Friendly Locations
Red print shows large vehicle parking / access on site or nearby Brown Print = Campgrounds / RV PARKS

EXIT		ALABAMA
51		**US 29, AL 147, College St, Auburn**
	Gas	E: BP◈ W: RaceWay, Exxon
	Food	W: Arby's, Krystal, McDonald's, Ruby Tuesday, Sonic, Waffle House, Zaxby's
	Lodg	E: Best Western, Hampton Inn, Sleep Inn W: Comfort Inn, Econo Lodge, Microtel♥, Sleep Inn
	Med	W: + Auburn Urgent Care
	Other	E: Pet Vet♥, Surfside Water Park, Golf Course, **Leisure Time Campground▲**, **Bar W RV Park▲**, **Chewacle State Park▲** W: ATMs, Banks, AL Outdoors, Advance Auto Parts, Auto Dealers, Auto Services, Tires, Vet ♥, Winn Dixie, **Walmart sc**, to Auburn Univ
(51)		FUTURE: **Beehive Rd, Auburn construction 2010-2012**
(44)		Rest Area (Both dir) (RR, Ph, Pic, Vend, Sec247, RVDump)
42		**AL 186E, to US 80, Wire Rd, Tuskegee, to Phenix City, Columbus**
	TStop	W: PacPr/Torch 85 Truck Stop/AmocoBP
	Food	W: Rest/Torch 85 TS
	TWash	W: Torch 85 TS
	Tires	W: Torch 85 TS
38		**AL 81, Tuskegee, Notasulga**
	Other	E: to airport
32		**AL 49N, Tuskegee, Franklin**
	Gas	E: BP◈
	Med	E: + Hospital
	Other	E: to Tuskegee Univ
26		**AL 229N, Franklin Rd, Tallassee**
	Gas	E: Shell◈
22		**to US 80, AL 138 to AL 8, Shorter**
	TStop	E: Petro 2/Chevron (Scales) **(DAND)**
	Gas	E: Exxon◈
	Food	E: QuickSkillet/Petro2
	Lodg	E: Days Inn
	Other	E: Laundry/WiFi/Petro2, **Wind Drift Travel Park▲**, Macon Co Greyhound Park
16		**AL 126, Cecil, Waugh, Mt Meigs**
	FStop	E: Entec BP
	Food	E: Subway/BP
(13)		**Future Exit-Montgomery Outer Lp**
11		**US 80, AL 110, Mitylene, Mt Meigs**
	Gas	E: Exxon◈, Liberty◈ W: Chevron◈
	Food	E: Cracker Barrel, Waffle House
	Lodg	E: Best Western, Holiday Inn Express, Sleep Inn
	Other	E: Home Depot, **Walmart sc**
9		**AL 271, to US 231, to Taylor Rd, Auburn Univ at Montgomery**
	Gas	W: Citgo◈

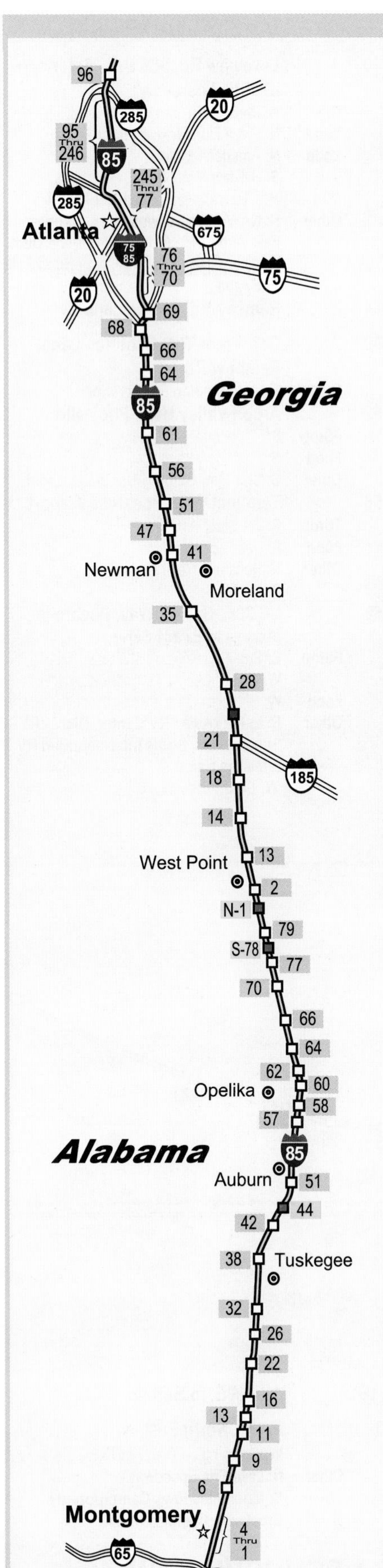

EXIT		ALABAMA
	Food	E: Applebee's, Arby's, Bonefish Grill, ChickFilA, Chili's, McDonald's, Moe's SW Grill, Ruby Tuesday, Starbucks, Subway, Wendy's, Whataburger
	Lodg	E: Hampton Inn
	Med	W: + Hospital
	Other	E: ATMs, BooksAMillion, Costco, Target, The Shoppes at Eastchase W: Southern Christian Univ, Auburn Univ/ Montgomery, Golf Course
6		**US 80, US 231, AL 21, Eastern Blvd, Wetumpka, Troy, Maxwell AFB**
	Gas	E: Chevron, Exxon◈, Liberty, RaceWay, Texaco W: BP, Citgo, Liberty◈, Shell
	Food	E: Arby's, Carrabba's, ChickFilA, Cracker Barrel, Don Pablo, Golden Corral, KFC, McDonald's, O'Charley's, Olive Garden, Popeye's, Shogun, Smokey Bones BBQ, Starbucks, Taco Bell, Texas Roadhouse, Waffle House, Wendy's, Whataburger, Zaxby's W: Burger King, Lone Star Steakhouse, McDonald's, Outback Steakhouse, Waffle House
	Lodg	E: Best Inn, Comfort Inn, Country Inn, Courtyard, Extended Stay America, Fairfield Inn, Hampton Inn, Quality Inn, Residence Inn, Springhill Suites, Super 8 W: Best Western, Comfort Suites, Drury Inn Econo Lodge♥, Motel 6
	Other	E: Barnes & Noble, Home Depot, Lowe's, PetSmart♥, Radio Shack, Target, **Walmart sc** W: Auto Dealers, Sam's Club, **to** Eastdale Mall, Faulkner Univ, Gunter AFB
4		**Perry Hill Rd**
	Gas	W: Chevron
	Food	W: Hardee's
	Lodg	W: Hilton Garden Inn, Homewood Suites
	Other	E: Grocery, Pharmacy
3		**Ann St**
	Gas	E: BP◈, Chevron W: Exxon, PaceCar, Murphy USA
	Food	E: Arby's, Captain D's, Dominos Pizza, Hardee's, KFC, Krystals, McDonald's, Taco Bell, Waffle House, Wendy's
	Lodg	E: Days Inn
	Other	E: Big 10 Tire W: ATMs, Dollar Tree, Office Depot, Radio Shack, **Walmart sc**
2		**Mulberry St (SB), Forest Ave (NB)**
	Med	W: + Jackson Hospital
	Other	W: Huntingdon College
1		**Union St (SB), Court St (NB), Downtown**
	Gas	E: BP◈, Exxon
	Med	W: + Hospital
	Other	E: to AL State Univ W: Bank, **to** Troy State Univ, Crawford Stadium

CENTRAL TIME ZONE

NOTE: I-85 Begins/Ends on I-65, Exit #171

⬆ ALABAMA

Begin NB I-85 from Jct I-65 in Montgomery, AL, to Jct I-95 near Richmond, VA.

◈ = Regular Gas Stations with Diesel ▲ = RV Friendly Locations ♥ = Pet Friendly Locations
Red print shows large vehicle parking / access on site or nearby Brown Print = Campgrounds / RV PARKS

EXIT IDAHO

Begin Eastbound I-86 from Jct I-84 near Burley, ID to Jct I-15, Pocatello, ID.

IDAHO

NOTE: I-86 Begins/Ends on I-15, Ex #72
I-86 Begins/Ends on I-84, Ex #222

(1) **Jct I-84E, to Ogden (WB)**

15 **Raft River Rd, Yale Rd N, Albion, Raft River Area**

(19) Rest Area (EB)
(RR, Phone, Picnic, Vend)

21 **Barkdull Rd, Coldwater Rd, Osborn Lp, Coldwater Area, American Falls**

28 **Register Rd, Park Lane, Massacre Rocks State Park**
- Other N: to Massacre Rocks State Park/ RVCamp/RVDump▲

(31) Rest Area (WB)
(RR, Phone, Picnic, Vend, Trails)

33 **Rock Creek Rd, Neeley**

36 **I-86 Bus, American Falls, ID 37S, Rockland Hwy, Rockland**
- Gas N: Jackson Food Store/Shell◊
- Lodg N: Falls Motel
- Med N: + Harms Memorial Hospital
- Other W: Indian Springs Swimming & RV Park▲

EXIT IDAHO

40 **Lakeview Rd, I-86 Bus, American ID 39N, Aberdeen**
- Gas N: Phillips 66◊
- Food N: Pizza Hut, Mexican Rest
- Lodg N: American Motel
  S: Hillview Motel♥
- Med N: + Harms Memorial Hospital
- Other N: NAPA, Les Schwab Tires, American Falls Airport✈, Amer Falls Police Dept, to Willow Bay Rec Area, American Falls Rec Area

44 **Ramsey Rd, Boone Lane**

49 **Gas Plant Rd, Schaffer Lane, Rainbow Rd**
- Other Fort Hall Indian Reservation

52 **Arbon Valley Hwy, Pocatello**
- FStop S: Bannock Peak Truck Stop/Sinclair
- Food S: FastFood/Bannock TS
- Other S: Sho-Ban Gaming Casino Outpost

56 **Terminal Way, Pocatello Airport**
- TStop S: Jet Stop/Sinclair (Scales)
- Food S: FastFood/JetStop
- Other N: Pocatello Reg'l Airport✈
  S: LP/Jet Stop

58 **US 30E, Garrett Way, Pocatello (Access to Ex #61 Serv)**
- FStop E: Smoking Hot Deals/Sinclair
  W: Cowboy West Truck Stop
- Food W: Shifters Café/Cowboy West TS
- Other E: to ParkAway RV Center, Bish's RV Supercenter, Bob's Intermountain RV & Marina Sales
  W: LP/Cowboy W TS

EXIT IDAHO

61 **US 91, Yellowstone Ave, Chubbuck, Pocatello**
- FStop N: Jackson Food Stop #30/Shell
  S: Flying J C Store
- Gas N: Exxon
  S: Phillips 66◊
- Food N: FastFood/Jackson FS, Artic Circle, Burger King, Johnny B Goode, Pizza Hut, Subway, Wendy's
  S: Del Taco, Denny's, IHOP, McDonald's, Red Lobster, Subway
- Lodg N: Motel 6♥, Ramada♥
- TServ S: Western States Equipment/CAT, Kenworth
- Other N: ATMs, Banks, Family Dollar, Grocery, U-Haul, Budget RV Park▲, Crossroads RV Center▲,
  S: RVDump/Jackson FS, ATMs, Banks, Home Depot, Lowe's, PetCo♥, ShopKO, Staples, Starbucks, UPS Store, Walmart sc, Walgreen's, Eagle Rock Harley Davidson, Pine Ridge Mall, Westwood Mall, Bish's RV Supercenter

(63AB/71) **Jct I-15, N to Idaho Falls, Butte. S to Salt Lake City (Serv at 1st Ex I-15S)**

MOUNTAIN TIME ZONE

NOTE: I-86 Begins/Ends on I-84, Ex #222
I-86 Begins/Ends on I-15, Ex #72

IDAHO

Begin Westbound I-86 from Jct I-15 near Pocatello, ID to Jct I-84 near Burley, ID.

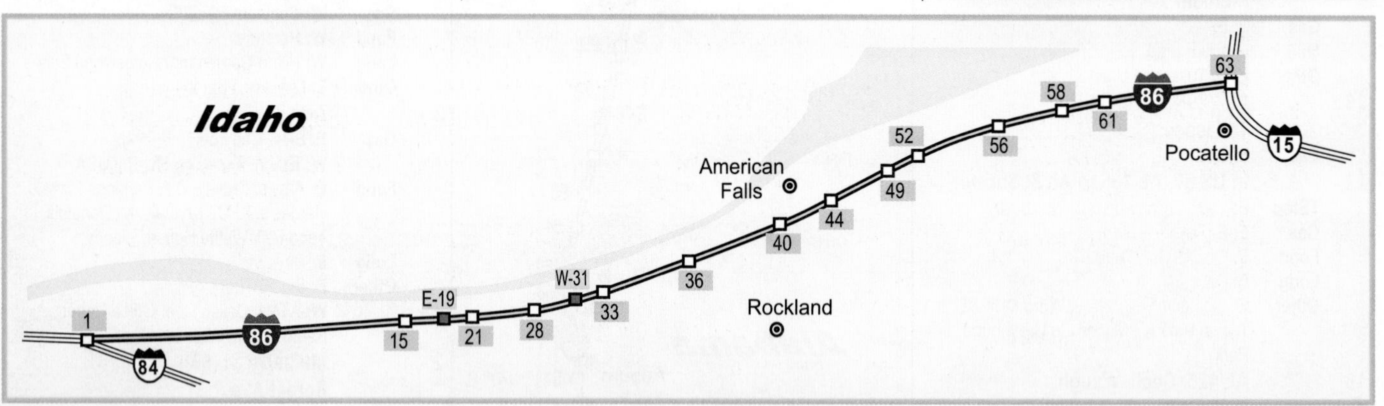

EXIT PENNSYLVANIA

Begin Eastbound I-86 from North East, PA to Jct I-87 near Highland Falls, NY.

PENNSYLVANIA

NOTE: I-86 Begins/Ends on I-90, Exit #37
I-86 Begins/Ends on I-87, Exit #16

EASTERN TIME ZONE

(1A) **Jct I-90W, to Erie**

EXIT PA / NY

(1B) **Jct I-90E, to Buffalo**

3 **PA 89, North East, Wattsburg**
- Other N: Lake Erie Speedway
  S: Moon Meadows Campground▲, Creekside Campground▲

PENNSYLVANIA

EXIT NEW YORK

NEW YORK

EASTERN TIME ZONE

NOTE: NYS does NOT use Mile Marker Exits. Listed is Mile Marker / Exit #.

1/4 **NY 426, N East Rd, to NY 430, Sherman, Findley Lake**
- Food N: I-86 Express Rest
  S: Curly Maple Rest, Country Kitchen

◊= Regular Gas Stations with Diesel ▲ = RV Friendly Locations ♥= Pet Friendly Locations
Red print shows large vehicle parking / access on site or nearby Brown Print = Campgrounds / RV PARKS

EXIT		NEW YORK
	Lodg	N: Holiday Inn Express S: Blue Heron Inn, Findley Lake Inn
	Other	N: Family Affair Campground▲ S: Peek 'n Peak Resort & Conf Center▲, Peek 'n Peak Ski Resort▲, to French Creek R&R Campground▲, Paradise Bay Park Campground▲
10/6		**NY 76, Osborne St, Sherman**
	Gas	N: Sherman Service Center, Sherman Country General
	Food	N: Village Pizzeria
	Lodg	N: Sherman Hotel, Millers Angel Inn
16/7		**CR 33, Panama-Stedman Rd, Panama**
18/8		**NY 394, W Lake Rd, Ashville, to Mayville, Lakewood**
	Gas	N: Hogan's Hut/Mobil◈
	Other	S: James Lakefront Camping▲
20/9		**NY 430E, E Lake Rd, Main St, Bemus Point (EB ex, WB entr)**
	Gas	N: Bridgeview One Stop/Mobil
	Food	N: Gracie's on Main, Main St Pizzeria, Italian Fisherman
	Lodg	N: Lenhart Hotel, Redwood Ranch Motel
20/10		**to NY 430W (EB, LEFT Exit)**
	Other	N: Wildwood Acres Campground▲
21/10		**NY 430, Bemus Point (WB)**
(24)		**NY Welcome Center (EB)** (RR, Phone, Picnic, Info)
(24)		**Weigh Station (EB)**
26/11		**Strunk Rd, Jamestown**
	Lodg	S: Apple Inn
28/12		**NY 60, N Main St, Jamestown**
	TStop	S: Main Express Travel Plaza/Mobil
	Gas	N: KwikFill◈
	Food	S: McDonald's/Main Express, Bob Evans
	Lodg	S: Comfort Inn, Hampton Inn
	Other	N: Harley Davidson, Chautauqua Co Jamestown Airport✈ S: Airport✈, Jamestown Comm College, NY State Hwy Patrol Post
31/13		**NY 394, E Main St, Falconer**
	Gas	S: Mobil
	Food	S: Burger King
	Lodg	S: Budget Inn, Red Roof Inn♥
36/14		**US 62, Frewsburg Rd, Kennedy, Warren, PA**
	Other	S: to Forest Haven Campground▲, Homestead Park Campground▲, Kinzua Lake Campground▲

Personal Notes

EXIT		NEW YORK
(38)		**Picnic Area (Phone) (WB)**
38/15		**School House Rd, Randolph**
	Other	S: Randolph Airport✈
(39)		**Picnic Area (Phone) (EB)**
40/16		**W Main St, Randolph, Gowanda**
	TStop	N: Wilson Farms #166/Mobil
	Food	N: Rest/FastFood/Wilson Farms, R&M Rest
	Other	N: WiFi/LP/Wilson Farms, Pope Haven Campground▲
(45)		**Seneca Nation Allegany Res (EB)**
46/17		**NY 394, W Perimeter Rd, Randolph, Steamburg, Onoville**
	TStop	S: M&M Diesel Mart
	Food	N: HideAWay Rest
	Other	N: Highbank Campground▲ S: LP/M&M Diesel Mart
48/18		**NY 280, Salamanca, Allegany State Park, Quaker Run Area**
52/19		**Allegany State Park Rd 2, Red House Area, Salamanca**
57/20		**NY 353, NY 417, Broad St, Salamanca**
	FStop	N: Seneca One Stop

EXIT		NEW YORK
	Food	N: McDonald's, Burger King
	Other	N: LP/Seneca OneStop, Seneca-Iroquis Museum, Rail Museum, Casino
60/21		**US 219N, Parkway Dr, Salamanca**
(22)		**PROPOSED NEW EXIT** **US 219N, Springville, Buffalo**
69/23		**US 219S, Limestone, Carrollton, Bradford, PA**
	TStop	N: M&M Allegany Jct Truck Stop
	Food	N: Subway/Allegany TS
(71)		**Seneca Nation Allegany Res (WB)**
(73)		**Rest Area (WB)** (RR, Phone, Picnic, Info)
(73)		**Weigh Station (WB)**
75/24		**NY 417, W Five Mile Rd, Allegany**
	Lodg	S: Country Inn & Suites, Allegany Motel, Lantern Motel
	Other	S: St Bonaventure Univ
78/25		**Buffalo St, Olean** **(Serv 2-3 mi S on Constitution Ave)**
	Gas	S: Citgo, KwikFill
	Food	S: Applebee's, Burger King, Pizza Hut, Quiznos, Tim Horton's
	Lodg	S: Comfort Inn, Country Inn, Microtel
	Other	S: Convention Center, BJ's, Home Depot, Walart
79/26		**NY 16, N Union St Ext, Olean**
	Gas	S: Wilson Farms/Mobil
	Food	S: Burger King
	Lodg	S: Hampton Inn
	Med	S: + Olean General Hospital
87/27		**NY 16, NY 446, Hinsdale**
	Gas	S: Crosby Dairyland
	Food	N: Burger King, Denny's Hut Family
	Other	N: Triple R Camping Resort & Trailer Sales▲, to Cattaraugus Co Olean Airport✈, Olean Munil Airport✈, to Emerald Acres Campground▲, Whispering Pine Campground▲
92/28		**NY 305, Genesee St, Cuba**
	Gas	S: Exxon, Sunoco
	Food	N: Cruisers Cafe S: Fox's Pizza Den, McDonald's
	Lodg	N: Cuba Coachlight Motel S: St James Hotel
	Other	N: Maple Lane Campground & RV Park▲
99/29		**NY 275, Friendship, Bolivar**
	Gas	S: Mobil
	Food	S: Subway
(101)		**Rest Area (EB)** (RR, Phone, Picnic)

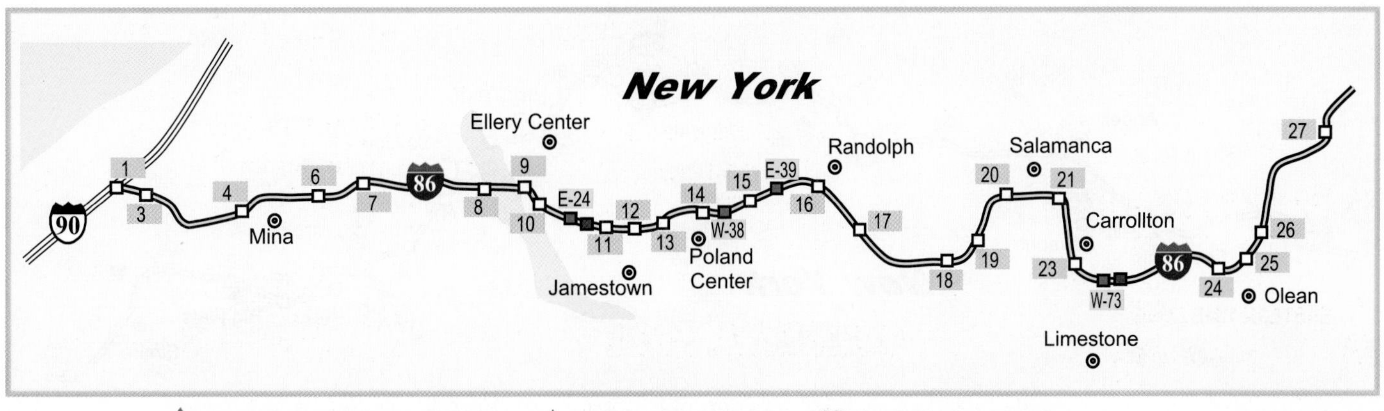

◈= Regular Gas Stations with Diesel ▲ = RV Friendly Locations ♥= Pet Friendly Locations
Red print shows large vehicle parking / access on site or nearby Brown Print = Campgrounds / RV PARKS

EXIT — NEW YORK

(101) **Weigh Station (EB)**

105/30 **NY 19, Belmont, Wellsville**
- **TStop** S: All American Plaza
- **Food** S: Rest/All Amer Pl
- **TWash** S: All Amer Pl
- **Other** N: to appr 9mi Evergreen Trails Campground▲
  S: WiFi/LP/All Amer Pl, Riverside Park Campground▲

109/31 **Clossek Ave, Angelica**
- **Gas** N: Citgo
- **Food** N: Rest/American Hotel
- **Lodg** N: Park Circle B&B, American Hotel
- **Other** N: to McCarthy Ranch▲ , Allegany Co Fairgrounds

117/32 **CR 2, Karrdale Ave, West Almond**

NOTE: MM 117.2: WB: Highest Elev on I-86
MM 117.3: EB: 2080'

124/33 **CR 2, Karr Valley Rd, to NY 21, Almond, Andover**
- **Gas** S: Tops Market/Mobil
- **Other** S: Lake Lodge Campground▲ , Kanakadea Park Campgrounds▲

(125) **Scenic View (EB)**

129/34 **NY 36, Genesee St, Arkport, Hornell**
- **Food** N: Dunkin Donuts, McDonald's
  S: Angel's, Ruperts
- **Lodg** S: Econo Lodge
- **Other** N: Walmart , to appr 7 mi Sun Valley Campsites▲ , to Sugar Creek Glen Campground▲
  S: Kanakadea Park Campground▲

138/35 **CR 70, Avoca, Howard**
- **Other** S: to Lake Demmon Rec Area

(146/36) **Jct I-390N, NY 15N, Rochester (fr WB, Left Exit)**
- **Other** N: to Tumble Hill Campground▲

146.5/37 **NY 53, Bath, Kanona, Prattsburg**
- **TStop** S: Wilson Farms AmBest #167/Sunoco (Scales), Pilot Travel Center #322 (Scales)
- **Food** S: Rest/Wilson Farms, Subway/Pilot TC
- **TWash** S: Wilson Farms
- **Other** N: to Wagon Wheel Campground▲
  S: Laundry/WiFi/LP/Wilson Farms, Laundry/WiFi/Pilot TC

(147) **Rest Area (WB)**
(RR, Phone, Picnic)

150/38 **NY 54, W Washington St, Bath, Hammondsport**
- **Gas** N: KwikFill, Mobil
- **Food** N: Arby's, Burger King, Chinese Buffet, Dunkin Donuts, McDonald's, Pizza Hut

EXIT — NEW YORK

- **Lodg** N: Budget Inn, Days Inn
- **Med** S: + US Veterans Medical Center
- **Other** N: Advance Auto, Auto Repair, Grocery, Kmart, Hickory Hill Family Camping Resort▲ , Campers Haven▲ , NY State Police
  S: Wilkens RV Center

153/39 **CR 11, Babcock Hollow Rd, to NY 415, Bath**
- **Other** N: to Sanford Lake
  S: Babcock Hollow Campground▲

157/40 **NY 226, CR 12, Lamoka Ave, Savona**
- **Gas** N: Savona Arrow Mart/Mobil◈
- **Food** N: Mom's Savona Diner, Subway/Mobil

(160) **Rest Area (EB)**
(RR, Phone, Picnic)

(101) **Weigh Station (EB)**

161/41 **CR 333, Campbell**
- **Gas** S: Sunoco
- **Other** N: Campbell Camping▲
  S: to Cardinal Campground▲

165/42 **CR 26, Meads Creek Rd, to NY 415, Painted Post, Coopers Plains**
- **Other** N: NY State Police

(167) **Picnic Area (Phone) (WB)**

168/43 **NY 415, Coopers-Bath Rd, Painted Post**
- **Gas** N: Pump n Pantry, Wilson Farms
  S: Sunoco
- **Food** N: Burger King, Denny's, McDonald's, Pizza Hut
- **Lodg** S: Hampton Inn
- **Other** N: CarQuest, Pharmacy

169/44 **US 15S, NY 417W, Painted Post, Future 99, Gang Mills, Williamsport**
- **Lodg** S: Best Western, Holiday Inn

170/45 **NY 415, Coopers-Bath Rd, Riverside (WB ex, EB entr), NY 352, Denison Pkwy, Downtown Corning (EB ex, WB entr)**
- **Food** S: Bob Evans, Burger King, Ponderosa, Subway, Wendy's
- **Lodg** S: Fairfield Inn

172/46 **NY 414, Corning, Watkins Glen**
- **Gas** S: Citgo◈
- **Food** S: Garcia's Mexican, Pizza Hut
- **Lodg** S: Comfort Inn, Days Inn, Staybridge Suites♥, Radisson Hotel♥
- **Other** N: Corning KOA▲ , to appr 5mi Ferenbaugh Campsites▲
  S: Corning Museum of Glass, to Sunflower Acres Family Campground▲

EXIT — NEW YORK

175/47 **NY 352, Gibson, Downtown**

176.8/48 **NY 352, East Corning**
- **Gas** S: Citgo

178/49 **Olcott Rd, Canal St, Big Flats**
- **Other** N: Elmira/Corning Reg'l Airport✈

180/50 **CR 63, Kahler Rd, Elmira**
- **Other** N: Elmira/Corning Reg'l Airport✈, Soaring Museum

181/51A **CR 35, Chambers Rd, Elmira**
- **Gas** N: Mobil◈, Sunoco◈
- **Food** N: Chili's, McDonald's, Olive Garden, Outback Steakhouse, Red Lobster, Ruby Tuesday
  S: Applebee's, China Inn, Panera Bread, TGI Friday
- **Lodg** N: Country Inn, Hilton Garden Inn
  S: Econo Lodge, Relax Inn
- **Other** N: Firestone, Mall
  S: B&N, Best Buy, Grocery, Petco♥, Lowe's, Sam's Club, Staples, Walmart

181/51B **Colonial Dr (WB, exit only) (Access to Ex #51 Serv)**

182/52 A **Commerce Center Dr (EB) (Access to Ex #51 Serv)**

52B **NY 14, CR 64, Elmira, Watkins Glen (EB)**

52AB **NY 14, CR 64, Watkins Glen, Elmira (WB)**
- **Lodg** N: Holiday Inn, Howard Johnson

183.5/53 **Horseheads**

185/54 **NY 13, to Ithaca, Horseheads, to Cayuga Lake**

189/56 **NY 352, Church St (EB), CR1, Water St (WB), Elmira, Jerusalem Hill**
- **Gas** S: Citgo, KwikFill
- **Food** S: Hoss's Steak & Sea House, Pizza Hut McDonald's
- **Lodg** S: Holiday Inn

195/58 **CR 2/8/60, Lowman, Wellsburg**
- **Other** S: Gardner Hill Campground▲

(199) **Rest Area (WB)**
(RR, Phone, Picnic)

200/59 **NY 427, CR 3, CR 60, Wyncoop Creek Rd, Chemung, Wellsburg**
- **FStop** N: Dandy Mini Mart #10

203/59A **CR 56, White Wagon Rd, Waverly, Wilawana, PA**

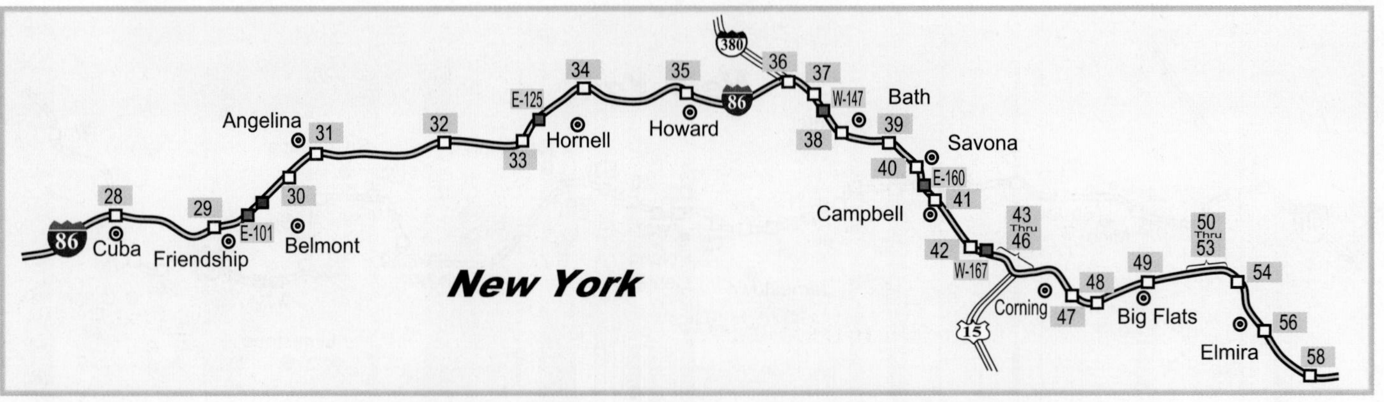

◈= Regular Gas Stations with Diesel ▲ = RV Friendly Locations ♥= Pet Friendly Locations
Red print shows large vehicle parking / access on site or nearby Brown Print = Campgrounds / RV PARKS

EXIT	NEW YORK
NOTE:	MM 204.2: State Border
205/60	**US 220, to Waverly NY, Sayre, PA**
Gas	S: Citgo, Mobil
Lodg	N: O'Brien's Inn
Other	S: Kmart, Grocery, RiteAid
NOTE:	MM 205.8: State Border
206/61	**NY 34, PA 199, to Waverly NY, Sayre, PA**
Gas	S: KwikFill, Citgo
Food	S: McDonald's
Lodg	S: Best Western
Other	S: Joe's RV Center
(212)	**Rest Area (EB)** (RR, Phone, Picnic)
(212)	**Weigh Station (EB)**
215/62	**NY 282, River Rd, Nichols**
FStop	S: Dandy Mini Mart #14/Citgo
Other	S: RV Center
219/63	**CR 509, Stanton Hill Rd, CR 502, River Rd, Nichols, Lounsberry**
TStop	S: Lounsberry Truck Stop/Exxon
Food	S: Lounsberry TS
Other	S: WiFi/LP/Lounsberry TS
(221)	**Rest Area (WB)** (RR, Phone, Picnic)
(221)	**Weigh Station (WB)**
224/64	**CR 503, Southside Dr (EB), NY 434, (WB), to NY 96, Owego, Ithaca**
224/65	**NY 17C, NY 434, Owego**
Gas	N: Mobil◈
Food	N: Burger King, KFC, Subway, Wendy's
Lodg	N: Hampton Inn, Holiday Inn Express
Other	N: Grocery, Pharmacy
231/66	**NY 434, Valley View Dr, NY 17C, Apalachin, Endicott, Campville**
FStop	S: Express Mart #357/Mobil
Gas	S: KwikFill
Food	S: Blue Dolphin Diner, McDonald's
Lodg	S: Dolphin Inn, Quality Inn
TWash	S: Express Mart
Other	S: LP/Express Mart
237/67	**NY 26, to NY 434, Endicott, Vestal** (Serv S on NY 26 to NY 434)
Gas	S: Valero
Food	S: Burger King, McDonald's, Olive Garden, Red Lobster, Starbucks, Subway, Taco Bell, TGI Friday, Uno Pizza
Other	N: Tri-Cities Airport✈ S: Advance Auto, Grocery, Lowe's, Sam's Club, Tires, WalMart

EXIT	NEW YORK
238/68	**CR 44, Old Vestal Rd** (EB ex, WB entr) (NO Re-entry to NY 17)
240/69	**NY 17C, E to Westover** (EB ex, WB entr), **W to Endwell** (WB ex, EB entr)
241/70	**NY 201S, Johnson City**
Gas	N: Exxon, Hess, Valero
Food	N: Blimpie, Friendly's, Great China Buffet, Buffet, McDonald's, Pizza Hut, Ponderosa, Quiznos, Ruby Tuesday, Taco Bell
Lodg	N: Best Western, Hampton Inn
Other	N: Grocery, Gander Mountain, Mall S: Home Depot
243/71	**CR 69, Airport Rd, Binghamton (EB) Airport Rd, Johnson City (WB)**
Other	N: Binghamton Reg'l/Edwin Link Field✈
244/72	**Mygatt St, Clinton St (WB, exit only), US 11, Front St (EB, exit only)**
NOTE:	MM 244.5: EB: Kamikaze Curve ALERT
(245)	**Jct I-81N, to I-88, Syracuse, Albany** (EB, Left Exit) **NY 17W, Owego, Elmira** (WB, Left Exit)
NOTE:	I-81 below runs with NY 17. Exit #'s are I-81, Mile Marker / Exit #.
12/4	**NY 7, Binghamton, Hillcrest**
Gas	W: Express Mart, Mobil
Food	W: Subway
Lodg	W: Howard Johnson, Super 8
Other	W: ATM, CVS, Grocery
12/3	**Broad Ave, Downtown** (WB ex, EB entr)
Gas	W: Exxon
9/3	**Colesville Rd, Industrial Park Binghamton** (EB exit, WB entr)
TStop	W: NB: Access Via Ex #2: Travel Center of America #207 (Scales), Pilot Travel Center #170 (Scales)
Gas	W: Exxon
Food	W: Buckhorn/TA TC, Wendy's/Pilot TC, KFC, McDonald's
Lodg	W: Del Motel, Holiday Inn, Super 8, Wright Motel
Other	W: Laundry/WiFi/TA TC, Laundry/WiFi/ Pilot TC, CVS, Grocery
(7/75)	**NY 17, New York, I-86E** (SB, Left Exit) **Jct I-81, US 11, Binghamton, Scranton, PA** (WB)
NOTE:	I-81 above runs with NY 17. Exit #'s are I-81, Mile Marker / Exit #.
251/76	**Haskins Rd, Johnson Rd, Foley Rd, Windsor**

EXIT	NEW YORK
254/77	**CR 47, Place Rd, North Rd, West Windsor**
Gas	N: Mobil◈
256/78	**CR 28, Dunbar Rd, Windsor, Occanum**
258/79	**NY 79, Main St (EB), CR 28, Old NY 17, Chapel St, (WB), Windsor**
Gas	N: Xtra Mart, Sunoco◈
Food	N: Pizza Wings & Things, Subway S: Yesteryear's Diner
Other	N: Lakeside Campground▲
261/80	**CR 225, State Line Rd (EB), CR 28, Old NY 17 (WB), Damascus**
Gas	N: Mighty Mart 7/Exxon◈
Food	N: J&K Family Diner
Other	N: Forest Lake Campground▲
263/81	**E Bosket Rd, CR 28, Windsor**
269/82	**NY 41, McClure, Sanford**
Other	N: Kellystone Park S: Oquaga Lake State Park, Guestward Ho Family Campground▲
273/83	**CR 28, Old NY 17, Deposit, Oquaga Lake**
Other	S: to Oquaga Lake
275/84	**NY 8, NY 10, Deposit, Walton**
Gas	N: Citgo◈, Deposit Country Store
Food	N: Wendy's, Timbers
Lodg	N: Deposit Motel, Laurel Bank Motel
Other	N: NY State Hwy Patrol Post
85	**Hale Eddy**
86	**Silver Lake Rd, Roods Creek Rd**
87	**NY 97, to PA 191, NY 268, Cadosia, Hancock, Calicoun**
Gas	S: Getty, Mobil, Sunoco
Food	S: Circle E Diner, McDonald's, Subway
Lodg	S: Colonial Motel
87A	**NY 268, Old State Rd, Cadosia, Hancock** (WB ex, EB entr)
292/89	**CR 17, Old State Rd, Hancock, Fishs Eddy**
(294)	**Rest Area (WB)** (RR, Phone, Picnic) **Weigh Station (WB)**
296/90	**NY 30, Old State Rd, Harvard Rd, East Branch, Downsville**
Gas	N: Sunoco
Other	N: Oxbow Campsites▲, Beaver Del Hotel & Campsites▲, Del Valley Campground▲, to appr 9mi Peaceful Valley Campsite▲

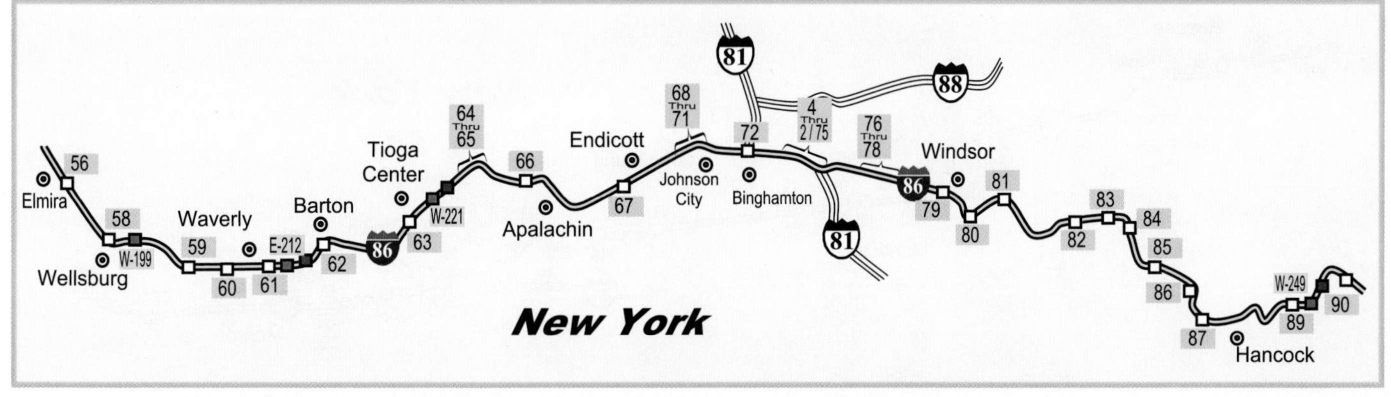

◈= Regular Gas Stations with Diesel ▲ = RV Friendly Locations ♥= Pet Friendly Locations
Red print shows large vehicle parking / access on site or nearby Brown Print = Campgrounds / RV PARKS

EXIT	NEW YORK
302/92	**CR 17, Roscoe, Cooks Falls, Horton**
Gas	S: Sunoco◈
Other	N: Russell Brooks Campsites▲
305/93	**CR 17, Roscoe, Cooks Falls** (WB exit, EB entr)
310/94	**NY 206, Roscoe, Tennanah Lk (EB) Walton (WB), Oneonta, Lew Beach**
Gas	N: Exxon◈, Sunoco◈ S: Mobil◈
Food	N: Roscoe Diner, 1910 Coffees Shop
Lodg	N: Rockland House, Roscoe Motel, Tennanah Lake Motel
Other	N: Roscoe Campsites▲, Butternut Grove Campsites▲, Miller Hollow Campground▲, Beaverkill State Campgrounds ▲ S: Twin Islands Campsites▲
(313)	Rest Area (EB) (last rest area on I-86) (RR, Phone, Picnic, Vend)
(313)	**Weigh Station (EB)**
316/96	**CR 178, White Roe Lake Rd, Livingston Manor, Lew Beach**
318/97	**CR 178, Livingston Manor, Morrston**
321/98	**CR 176, Parksville, Cooley**
Other	N: Hunter Lake Campground▲
324/99	**Main St, to NY 52, to NY 55, Liberty**
Gas	S: Exxon, Sunoco
325/100A	**NY 52, to NY 55, Liberty** (WB ex, EB entr)
326/100	**NY 52, Liberty, Loch Sheldrake**
Gas	N: Sunoco S: Citgo, Exxon◈, Mobil
Food	N: Burger King, McDonald's, Taco Bell S: Dunkin Donuts
Lodg	N: Best Inn, Days Inn S: Budget Inn, Lincoln Motel, Liberty Motel
Other	N: Neversink River Campground▲, to appr 10 mi Yogi Bear's Jellystone Park▲ S: Auto Dealers, Grocery
327/101	**Ferndale, Swan Lake**
Gas	S: Exxon◈
Food	N: Manny's Steakhouse & Seafood S: Burger King, McDonald's, Wendy's
Lodg	S: Days Inn
331/102	**CR 174, to Harris-Bushville Rd, Monticello, Harris, Bushville**
Other	S: to Swan Lake Campground▲
333/103	**Rapp Rd, Monticello** (WB ex, EB entr)
335/104	**NY 17B, Jefferson St, Monticello, Raceway**
Gas	S: Citgo, Exxon◈
Food	S: Tilly's Diner
Lodg	S: Best Western, Raceway Motel
Other	S: to Happy Days Campground▲, Swinging Bridge Lake Campground▲, Raceway, Sullivan Co Int'l Airport✈
337/105AB	**NY 42, Pleasant St, Monticello, to Kiamesha, Forestburg**
Gas	S: Citgo, Mobil, Stewarts, Valero
Food	S: Burger King, Chinatown, Crown Fried Chicken, Pizza Hut, Wendy's
Lodg	N: Rosemond Motel & Campsites▲ S: Econo Lodge, Ramada, Travel Inn
Other	N: Walmart sc, Lazy G Campground▲
339/106	**Cimarron Rd, East Monticello (WB)**
340/107	**CR 173, CR 161, Heiden Rd, South Fallsburg, Monticello, Bridgeville**
Food	S: Mana Rest, Old Homestead Rest
341/108	**CR 173, Holiday Mountain Trail, Monticello, Bridgeville (EB)** (Access Services at Ex #109)
342/109	**Katrina Falls Rd, Rock Hill Dr, to CR57/58, Rock Hill, Woodridge**
Gas	N: Exxon◈ S: Mobil
Food	N: Rock Hill Diner, Land & Sea Rest
Lodg	N: Rock Hill Lodge
Other	N: Hilltop Farm Campsites▲, Yogi Bear's Jellystone Camp▲, Mountaindale Campground▲
343/110	**Lake Louise Marie, Wanaksink Lake (EB), Fall Brook Rd, CR 172, Rock Hill, Lake Louise Marie, Wanaksink Lake, Wolf Lake (WB)**
344/111	**Wolf Lake Rd, Rock Hill (EB)**
347/112	**Masten Lake, Yankee Lake, Wurtsboro, Mountaindale**
Other	N: to Catskill Mountain Ranch & Camping Club▲
349/113	**US 209, Wurtsboro, Ellenville**
Gas	N: Mobil◈, Stewarts
Food	N: A&B Diner, Benny's Café, Danny's Village Inn, Subway S: Giovanni's Café
Lodg	N: Days Inn♥
Other	N: Berentsens Campground▲ S: to appr 8mi Oakland Valley Campground▲, to American Family Campground▲
352/114	**CR 171, Bloomingburg, Highview, Wurtsboro** (WB, exit only) (Reacc next exits, No re-entry to NY17)
354/115	**Burlingham Rd** (WB ex, EB entr)
Other	N: Berentsens Campground▲, Rainbow Valley Campground▲
354/116	**NY 17K, Bloomingburg, Newburgh**
Gas	S: Citgo, Mobil
Other	S: to Korn's Campground▲, Rainbow Valley Campground▲
357/118	**CR 76, Bloomingburg Rd, Brown Rd, Middletown, Fair Oaks**
Gas	S: Exxon◈, Mobil
Food	S: Fair Oaks Deli
Lodg	N: Heritage Motel
359/119	**NY 302, Middletown, Pine Bush**
361/120	**NY 211, Middletown, Montgomery**
Gas	N: Mobil, Sunoco S: Mobil
Food	N: Olive Garden S: Arby's, Burger King, China Buffet, Denny's, KFC, Red Lobster, Taco Bell
Lodg	N: Middletown Motel, Howard Johnson, Super 8
Other	N: Best Buy, Grocery, Sam's Club, Walmart S: AutoZone, Grocery, Home Depot, Kmart, Pharmacy, Staples, U-Haul
(362/121)	**Jct I-84, E to Newburgh, W to Port Jervix**
363/122	**CR 67, Crystal Run Rd, E Main St**
Gas	N: Mobil S: Getty
Food	N: TGI Friday, Outback Steakhouse
Lodg	N: Hampton Inn, Holiday Inn, Marriott
Other	S: Randall Airport✈, Fantasy Balloon Flights
365/122A	**Fletcher St, Goshen**
366/123	**US 6W, NY 17M W, Middletown, Port Jervis, FUTURE I-86**
369/124	**NY 17A, to NY 207, Goshen, Florida**
Gas	N: Exxon, Mobil
Food	N: Burger King, Goshen Diner, Pizza Hut
Lodg	N: Comfort Inn, Goshen Inn
Other	N: CVS S: Black Bear Campground▲
367/125	**NY 17M E, South St, Future I-86**
370/126	**NY 94, Chester, Florida**
Gas	N: Shell, Sunoco
Food	N: McDonald's, Wendy's
Lodg	N: Holiday Inn Express

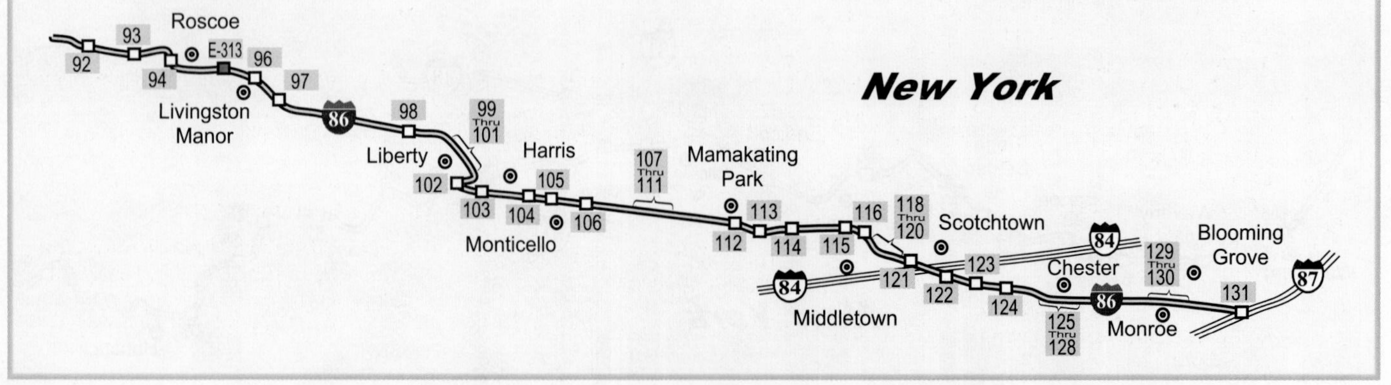

◈= Regular Gas Stations with Diesel ▲ = RV Friendly Locations ♥= Pet Friendly Locations
Red print shows large vehicle parking / access on site or nearby Brown Print = Campgrounds / RV PARKS

EXIT	NEW YORK
Other	N: Grocery, Pharmacy S: Black Bear Campground▲
372/127	**Lehigh Ave, Chester, Greycourt Rd, Sugar Loaf, Warwick (WB ex, EB entr)**
374/128	**CR 51, Craigville Rd, Oxford Depot (WB Exit Only, NO Re-entry to NY 17)**
375/129	**Museum Village Rd, to Monroe (NO re-entry to NY 17)**
376/130	**NY 208, Monroe, Washingtonville**
Gas	N: Sunoco◈
	S: Mobil◈
Food	S: Burger King, Pizza Hut
379/130A	**US 6E, Bear Mountain, Future I-86, (EB exit, WB entr) (WB)**
Gas	S: Exxon, Mobil
Food	S: Chili's, McDonald's, TGI Friday
Other	N: Outlet Mall S: BJ's, Home Depot, Staples, Wal-Mart sc
379.6/131	**NY 17S, NY 32, Newburgh, Suffern (EB), US 6E, NY 17S, NY 32, Harriman (WB)**
(380)	**Jct I-87, NY THRUWAY (TOLL), to Albany, New York (EB ex, WB entr), NY 17, Future I-86 (WB)**
NOTE:	**NYS does NOT use Mile Marker Exits. Listed is Mile Marker / Exit #.**

(I-86 Begins/Ends on I-87, Exit #16)
(EASTERN TIME ZONE)

NEW YORK

Begin I-86 at Jct I-87 to Jct I-90 near North East, PA.

Begin Southbound I-87 from Champlain to NYC.

NEW YORK

EASTERN TIME ZONE

EXIT	NEW YORK
NOTE:	**I-87 Begins/Ends at the Canada Border**
NOTE:	**NYS does NOT use Mile Marker Exits. Listed is MileMarker / Exit #.**
(333)	**US/Canada Border, NY St Line US Customs/New York (SB), Canadian Customs/Quebec (NB)**
333/43	**US 9, Champlain**
TStop	W: Champlain Peterbilt (Scales)
Food	W: FastFood/Peterbilt TS
TWash	W: Peterbilt TS
TServ	W: Peterbilt TS/Tires
Other	E: World Duty Free W: Laundry/BarbSh/WiFi/LP/Peterbilt TS
331/42	**US 11, Mooers, Rouses Point, Champlain**
FStop	W: Garceau Exxon
TStop	W: Rte 11 Mobil, 11-87 Truck Plaza (Scales)
Gas	E: Mobil
Food	E: Peppercorn Family Rest, Chinese, Three Forks Pizza & Deli W: Rest/FastFood/11-87 TP, McDonald's, Subway
TWash	W: 11-87 TP
TServ	W: 11-87 TP/Tires
Other	E: Grocery, Laundromat, Pharmacy W: WiFi/Garceau Exxon, Laundry/WiFi/ 11-87 TP
325/41	**NY 191, CR 23, Chazy, Sciota**
(319)	**NY Welcome Center (SB)** Rest Area (NB) (RR, Phone, Pic, SB: Info, NY St Police)
318/40	**NY 456, Plattsburgh, Beekmantown, Point au Roche**
Gas	E: Mobil◈
Food	E: Café/Stonehelm Motel
Lodg	E: Stonehelm Motel
Other	E: Monty's Bay Campsites▲ W: Plattsburgh RV Park▲
314/39	**NY 314, Moffitt Rd, Plattsburgh, Cumberland Head, Plattsburgh Bay**
Gas	E: Stewarts
Food	E: Gus' Red Hots, McDonald's
Lodg	E: Chateau Motel, Rip Van Winkle Motel, Super 8♥
Other	E: Plattsburgh RV Park▲ , Cumberland Bay State Park W: Shady Oaks RV Park▲
312/38	**NY 22N, NY 374, Plattsburgh, to Tupper Lake, Sarnac Lake**
Gas	E: Mobil, Sunoco
TServ	W: Plattsburgh Diesel Service
Med	E: + Hospital
310/37	**NY 3, Plattsburgh, Morrisonville, Saranac Lake**
Gas	E: Short Stop◈, Sunoco, Stewarts W: BP, Exxon, Mobil, Sunoco◈
Food	E: Burger King, Domino's, IHOP, KFC, McDonald's, Papa John's Pizza, Pizza Hut, Quiznos, Subway, Wendy's W: Applebee's, Ponderosa, Red Lobster
Lodg	E: Comfort Inn, Holiday Inn W: Baymont Inn, Best Western♥, Days Inn, Econo Lodge, Microtel, Quality Inn, Super 8
Med	E: + Champlain Valley Hospital
Other	E: Auto Dealers, Big Lots, Firestone, Grocery, Sam's Club, Walmart sc, State Univ of NY, CarWash W: Auto Repair, Kmart, Grocery, Miidas, Walmart sc, Lowe's, Clinton Co Airport✈, Twin Ells Campsites▲
308/36	**NY 22, Plattsburgh Air Force Base, Lake Champlain Shore, Plattsburgh**
TStop	E: Exit 36 Truck Stop/Mobil (Scales)
Gas	E: Citgo
Tires	E: Exit 36 TS
TServ	E: MA Jerry Co/International, Charlebois Truck Parts W: Phil's Auto & Truck Service
Other	E: BarbSh/WiFi/LP/Exit 36 TS, Plattsburgh AFB W: NY State Police, to Northway Airport✈
(304)	**NY Welcome Center (SB)** Rest Area (NB) (RR, Phones, Picnic)
302/35	**NY 442, Bear Swamp Rd, Peru, Valcour, Port Kent**
TStop	E: Chase's Mobil #2
Gas	W: Wilson Farms, Mobil
Food	E: Dunkin Donuts/Subway/Mobil W: Crickets, McDonald's
TWash	E: Chase's
Other	E: Amtrak, AuSable Point Campground▲ Iroquis RV Park & Campground▲ , to appr 12mi AuSable Pines Campground & RV Sales▲
NOTE:	**MM 143: Begin SB Call Boxes, End NB**
296/34	**NY 9N, Keeseville, AuSable Chasm, AuSable Forks**
Gas	W: Sunoco◈
Food	E: Mac's Diner, Pleasant Corner Rest
Lodg	W: Shamrock Motel
Other	E: Holiday Travel Park▲ W: Lake Placid KOA, AuSable River Campsites▲ , to appr 12mi AuSable Chasm Campground▲
292/33	**US 9, NY 22, Keeseville, Willsboro, Essex-Ferry**
Gas	E: Mobil
Lodg	E: Chesterfield Motel
281/32	**CR 12, Stowersville Rd, Lewis, to Willsboro**
FStop	W: Pierce's Service Station
(280)	**Picnic Area (NB, NO Trucks)** Rest Area (SB) (RR, Phone, Picnic)
275/31	**NY 9N, Westport, Elizabethtown**
Gas	E: Mobil
Lodg	E: Hilltop Motel
Med	W: + Hospital
Other	E: NY State Police, to appr 7mi Barber Homestead Park▲
(270)	**Rest Area (NB)** (RR, Phone, Picnic)
262/30	**US 9, NY 73, North Hudson, Keene, Keene Valley**
Other	W: Lake Placid KOA▲
(257)	**Rest Area (Both dir)** (RR, Phones, Picnic) NOTE: SB: Border Patrol
252/29	**CR 2, Boreas Rd, North Hudson, Newcomb**
Other	E: Yogi Bear's Jellystone Park▲ W: Blue Ridge Falls Campground▲

◈ = Regular Gas Stations with Diesel ▲ = RV Friendly Locations ♥ = Pet Friendly Locations
Red print shows large vehicle parking / access on site or nearby Brown Print = Campgrounds / RV PARKS

EXIT	NEW YORK
240/28	**NY 74E, Crown Point, Schroon Lake, Ticonderoga Ferry**
Gas	E: Sunoco◈, Stewarts
Lodg	E: Starry Nite Cabins
Other	E: On the River Campground▲, NY State Hwy Patrol Post, Medcalf Acres Riverfront Campground▲, Schroon Lake Airport✈
(239)	**Rest Area (NB) (RR, Phones, Picnic)**
239/27	**US 9, Schroon Lake (NB, diff reacc)**
Gas	E: Stewarts
Lodg	E: Elm Tree Cabins & Motel
237/26	**US 9, Valley Farm Rd, Pottersville**
235/26	**US 9, Pottersville (NB)**
FStop	W: Pottersville Nice N Easy/Mobil
Food	E: Café Andirondack, Hometown Deli W: Black Bear Diner
Lodg	E: Lee's Corner Motel
Other	E: Ideal Campground▲, Eagle Point Campsite▲ W: WiFi/Nice N Easy
231/25	**NY 8, Chestertown, Hague, Brant Lake**
FStop	W: Riverside Nice N Easy #1501/Mobil, Buckman's Family Fuel
Other	E: Rancho Pines Campground▲, Country Haven Campground▲, Riverside Pines Campground▲, Hidden Pond Campsite▲ W: WiFi/Nice N Easy
225/24	**CR 11, Bolton Landing-Riverbank Rd, Bolton Landing, Warrensburg**
Other	E: Bakersfield East Campground▲, to Scenic View Campground▲, Ridin Hy Ranch Resort▲ W: Lake George Schroon Valley Resort▲, to Schroon River Campsites▲
(223)	**Picnic Area (Phone) (SB)**
(222)	**Picnic Area (Phone) (NB)**
217/23	**CR 35, Diamond Point Rd, to US 9, to NY 28, Lake George, Warrensburg, Diamond Point**
FStop	W: Exit 23 Truck Stop/Citgo
Gas	W: Mobil
Food	W: McDonald's
Lodg	W: Super 8, Seasons B&B, White House Lodge
Other	E: to appr 6mi Schroon River Resort▲, W: WiFi/LP/Ex 23 TS, Warrensburg Travel Park▲, Queen Village Campground▲, Crazy Creek Campground▲, Schroon River Campsite▲, to appr 14mi Daggett Lake Campsites▲, Glen-Hudson Campsite▲
213/22	**US 9, NY 9N, Lake Shore Dr, Lake George Village, Diamond Point**
Gas	E: Citgo, Mobil
Food	E: China Wok, Guiseppe's, Jasper's Steak & More, McDonald's, Pizza Hut, Luigi's, Subway, Taco Bell
Lodg	E: Adirondack Oasis, Blue Moon Motel, Econo Lodge, Lake Motel, Quality Inn, Sundowner Motel, Travelodge
Other	E: Mohawk Campground▲, Shoreline Cruises of Lake George, Ft William Henry Museum

87
Champlain
43
42
41
S-319
40
39
38
Plattsburg
37
New York
36
S-304
35
34
33
87
32
N-280
Elizabethtown
31
N-270
30
257
29
28
Schroon Lake
239
27
26
25
24
S-223
N-222
87
Warrensburg
23
22
21
20
19
Glens Falls
18
201

EXIT	NEW YORK
211/21	**NY 9N, to US 9, Lake George, Lake Luzerne**
Gas	E: Mobil, Stewarts W: Mobil◈
Food	E: Barnsider BBQ, George's, Jasper's, Lake George Pancake House
Lodg	E: Best Western, Comfort Inn, Harbor Motel, Holiday Inn, Howard Johnson, Lyn-Aire Motel, Ramada, Super 8, Studio Motel, Village Motor Inn W: King John's Manor Cabins, Lake George Luzerne Gardens Motel
Other	E: Whippoorwill Campsites▲ W: to Alpine Lake RV Resort▲, to Juniper Woods Campground
207/20	**US 9, NY 149, W Mountain Rd, Lake George, to Fort Ann, Whitehall, Queensbury**
Gas	E: Mobil, Shell, Sunoco◈
Food	E: Log Jam Rest, Montcalm Rest
Lodg	E: Days Inn, French Mtn Motel, Capri Village, Kay's Motel
Other	E: Lake George Campsites▲, NY State Police, Great Escape Fun Park, Factory Outlet Stores W: Saugerties/Woodstock KOA▲, Brookside Campground/RVDump▲
205/19	**US 9, NY 254, Aviation Rd, to US 209, Glens Falls, Hudson Falls, Queensbury**
Gas	E: Citgo, Hess W: Mobil, Stewarts
Food	E: Burger King, China Buffet, Friendly's, KFC, McDonald's, Olive Garden, Pizza Hut, Ponderosa, Red Lobster, Taco Bell W: 7 Steers Western Grill
Lodg	E: Econo Lodge, Sleep Inn W: Ramada Inn
Other	E: Advance Auto Parts, CVS, Firestone, Goodyear, Home Depot, Staples, Mall, Walmart, Floyd Bennett Memorial Airport✈ W: NY State Police, to Rondout Valley Resort▲
203/18	**CR 28, Main St, to NY 32, NY 299, NY 213, Corinth Rd, New Paltz, Glens Falls, Queensbury**
Gas	E: Hess◈, Mobil, Citgo W: Stewarts
Food	E: Carl R's Café, Pizza Hut, Subway W: Lone Bull Pancake House, Nicky's Pizzeria, McDonald's
Lodg	W: Best Inn, Super 8
Med	E: + Hospital
Other	E: CVS, U-Haul W: to appr 20mi So-Hi Campground▲, Sacandaga Campground▲
(201)	**Rest Area (Both dir) (RR, Phones, Picnic)**
199/17	**US 9, Saratoga Rd, Gansvoort, South Glens Falls, Moreau St Park**
FStop	E: Moreau Xtra Mini Mart/Sunoco
TStop	E: Nice N Easy/Mobil, KC Truck Stop/Getty
Gas	E: Citgo
Food	E: FastFood/Nice N Easy, Blimpie, Dunkin Donuts, Winslow's Diner
Lodg	E: Landmark Motor Inn, Swiss American Motel, Town & Country Motel
TServ	E: Nice N Easy

◈= Regular Gas Stations with Diesel ▲ = RV Friendly Locations ♥= Pet Friendly Locations
Red print shows large vehicle parking / access on site or nearby Brown Print = Campgrounds / RV PARKS

EXIT	NEW YORK
Other	E: BarbSh/WiFi/LP/Nice N Easy, Laundry/BarbSh/WiFi/LP/KC TS, **American RV Campground▲**
	W: Moreau Lake State Park
193.2/16	**CR 33, Ballard Rd, Wilton, Gurn Springs**
TStop	W: Wilton Travel Plaza/Sunoco
Gas	W: Mobil, Stewarts
Food	W: Rest/Wilton TP
TServ	W: Wilton TP/Tires
Other	**E: Cold Brook Campsites▲ , NY State Police**
	W: Laundry/WiFi/LP/Wilton TP, **Alpine Haus RV Center, to appr 7mi Saratoga Springs Resort▲ , Fort Bink Campground▲**
188.6/15	**NY 50, NY 29, Saratoga Springs, Gansvoort, Schuylerville**
Gas	E: Hess◈, Mobil
Food	E: Applebee's, Burger King, Denny's, Golden Corral, KFC, McDonald's, Ruby Tuesday, TGI Friday
Lodg	E: Super 8
	W: Residence Inn, Saratoga Motel
Other	E: Best Buy, BJ's, Kmart, Grocery, Home Depot, Lowe's, Staples, Target, **Walmart sc**, Wilton Mall
	W: to Alpine Lake RV Resort▲ , to appr 8mi Saratoga RV Park▲
187.1/14	**NY 9P, Y 29, Saratoga Springs, Saratoga Lake, Schuylerville**
Gas	E: Stewarts, Mobil
	W: Citgo
Lodg	E: Longfellow Inn, Saratoga Springs Motel
	W: Holiday Inn, Malta Motor Court
Other	**E: Lee's RV Park▲**
183/13	**US 9, Ballston Spa, Saratoga Lake, Saratoga Springs**
Gas	W: Mobil, Stewarts
Lodg	E: Post Road Lodge
	W: Coronet Motel, Hilton Garden Inn
Other	**E: Northway RV, Ballston Spa State Park**
175/12	**NY 67, Dunning St, Malta, Ballston Spa**
Gas	E: Mobil◈, Sunoco
Food	E: Malta Diner, McDonald's, Subway
Lodg	E: Fairfield Inn
Other	E: CVS, Grocery
175/11	**CR 80, Round Lake Rd, Curry Ave, Burnt Hill, Round Lake**
TStop	W: Exit 11 Truck Stop/Citgo
Gas	W: Sunoco
Food	W: FastFood/Ex 11 TS, Gran-Prix Grill
Lodg	W: Gran-Prix Inn
Other	W: WiFi/LP/Exit 11 TS
174.3/10	**Ushers Rd, Ballston Lake, Jonesville**
Gas	E: Hess◈, Sunoco◈
	W: Stewarts
(172.1)	**Rest Area (NB)**
	(RR, Phones, Picnic, Info, NY St Police)
(172.1)	**Truck Inspection Station (NB)**
171.4/9	**NY 146 E/W, Clifton Park, Rexford, Halfmoon, Waterford**
Gas	E: Hess◈, USA
	W: Mobil, Sunoco◈

Personal Notes

EXIT	NEW YORK
Food	E: Burger King, Chili's, Cracker Barrel, Hardee's, Pizza Hut, Red Robin
	W: Applebee's, Denny's, Dunkin Donuts, Friendly's, McDonald's, Outback Steakhouse, TGI Friday, Wendy's
Lodg	E: Comfort Inn
	W: Best Western, Hampton Inn
Med	**W: + Medi-Call**
Other	E: Grocery, Home Depot, Laundromat, Lowe's, Pharmacy
	W: AutoZone, CVS, Kmart, Mall, NY **State Police, Freedom RV**
169.9/8A	**CR 91, Groom's Rd, Clifton Park, Waterford**
Other	E: Wal-Mart sc
168.4/8	**Vischer Ferry Rd, Crescent Rd**
Gas	E: Hess◈
	W: Coastal◈
Food	E: McDonald's, Blimpie/Hess
	W: MrSub/Coastal
164/6+7	**NY 2/7W, Troy, Schenectady (SB)**
164.5/7	**NY 7E, Troy (NB)**
	(All Services E on US 9)
Gas	E: Hess◈, Mobil
Food	E: McDonald's, Subway
Lodg	E: Hampton Inn, Holiday Inn Express
Med	**E: + Hospital**
Other	E: Auto Dealers, Auto Services, Grocery, Outlet Mall
163.9/6	**NY 7W, NY 2, to US 9, Troy, Schenectady, Watervilet (NB)**
Gas	E: Mobil

EXIT	NEW YORK
Gas	W: Mobil
Food	E: Applebee's, Dakota's, Golden Wok, Ground Round, McDonald's, Panera
	W: Chuck E Cheese Pizza, Carrabba's, Friendly's
Lodg	W: Clarion, Microtel, Super 8
Other	E: Latham Circle Mall, CVS, Lowe's, Sam's Club, Staples, **Walmart**
	W: Target, Albany Co Airport✈
162/4+5	**NY 155, Albany Airport, Latham (SB)**
161/5	**NY 155, CR 153, Latham (NB)**
Lodg	E: Econo Lodge
161/4	**Albany-Shaker Rd, Albany, Airport (E Serv on Wolf Rd)**
Gas	E: Hess◈, Mobil, Sunoco
Food	E: Arby's, Denny's, Long John Silver, McDonald's, Olive Garden, Pizza Hut, Outback Steakhouse, Real Seafood, Romano's Macaroni Grill, Red Lobster
Lodg	E: Best Western, Courtyard, Hampton Inn, Holiday Inn, Red Roof Inn
Other	E: Auto Dealers, CVS, Firestone, Albany Airport✈
(160/3)	**Future EXIT Albany Int'l Airport**
159.3/2	**NY 5, Central Ave, to Wolf Rd, Schenectady, Albany**
	(Addt'l E Serv on Wolf Rd)
Gas	E: Mobil, Sunoco
	W: Mobil, Exxon
Food	E: Applebee's, Chili's, IHOP, Lone Star Steakhouse, Panchos Mexican, Starbucks, Wendy's
	W: Domino's, Delmonico's Italian Steak House, Garcia's, Red Lobster, Truman's
Lodg	E: Days Inn, Econo Lodge, Park Inn
	W: Ambassador Motor Inn, Comfort Inn, Howard Johnson, Northway Inn, Super 8
Other	E: BJ's, B&N, Firestone, Goodyear, Laundromat, Staples, Target, Mall
NOTE:	**I-87 below runs with NY St Thruway (TOLL). Exit #'s are MM / Thruway.**
(158/1)	**Jct I-87S, Jct I-90, W to Buffalo, E to Albany, Boston, NY State Thruway (TOLL) (SB)**
(158.1)	**Washington Ave TOLL Plaza**
NOTE:	**SB Begin TOLL, NB End**
(157/24)	**Jct I-90E, to Albany, Jct I-87N, to Plattsburgh, Montreal (NB), I-87S to NYC (Thruway cont with I-90W)**
(150/23)	**Jct I-787, US 9W, Albany, Troy, Glenmont, Rensselaer**
FStop	W: Petro 9W
TStop	E: (I-787, Ex 2NB/3SB) Riverside Travel Plaza (Scales), Big Main Truck Stop
Gas	E: Mobil
Food	E: Rest/FastFood/Riverside TP, Rest/Big Main TS,
	W: Applebee's, Dunkin Donuts, Johnny B's Diner, Wendy's
Lodg	E: Comfort Inn, Days Inn
	W: Econo Lodge, Quality Inn, Stone Ends Motel
TWash	E: Riverside TP
TServ	E: Riverside TP/Tires
Med	**E: + Hospital**

EXIT		NEW YORK
	Other	E: Laundry/BarbSh/WiFi/LP/Riverside TP, Laundry/BarbSh/WiFi/LP/Big Main TS, to Knickerbocker Arena, Times Union Center, Albany Airport✈
(148)		Picnic Area (Phone) (SB)
143.7/22		**NY 144, NY 396, Selkirk**
(143/ 21A)		**to Jct I-90E, to Mass Tpk, Boston (to I-90W, Thruway- Cont on I-87N)**
(136)		New Baltimore Service Area
	FStop	Mobil
	Food	Roy Rogers, TCBY, Mrs Fields, Starbucks
	Other	LP
133.3/21B		**US 9W, NY 81, Coxsackie, Ravena, New Baltimore, Athens**
	TStop	W: 21B Travel Plaza (Scales)
	Gas	W: Sunoco
	Food	W: Rest/21B TP
	Lodg	W: Best Western
	TWash	W: 21B TP
	Other	W: Laundry/BarbSh/WiFi/LP/21B TP, Boat & RV Center
122.6/21		**NY 23, Catskill, Cairo**
	Gas	E: Mobil, Sunoco◈
	Food	E: Rest/Catskill Motor Lodge
	Lodg	E: Catskill Motor Lodge
	Other	E: Home Depot
(112)		Malden Service Area (NB) Picnic Area (Phone) (SB)
	FStop	Mobil
	Food	McDonald's, Carvel
110/20		**NY 32, NY 212, Saugerties, Woodstock, Hunter, Tannersville**
	Gas	E: Mobil◈, Stewarts W: Hess◈, Sunoco◈
	Food	E: McDonald's, Subway W: Blimpie/Hess, McDonald's, Land & Sea Grill & Steakhouse, Subway
	Lodg	W: Comfort Inn, Howard Johnson
(108)		Picnic Area (NB)
(108)		Inspection Station (NB)
(107)		Ulster Service Area (SB)
	FStop	Mobil
	Food	Nathan's, TCBY, Roy Rogers, Mrs Field, Cinnabon
100.1/19		**NY 28, Onteora Trail, to I-587, US 209, Kingston, Rhinecliff Bridge**
	Gas	E: Citgo◈, Mobil
	Food	E: Gateway Diner W: Rest/Ramada Inn
	Lodg	E: Holiday Inn, Super 8 W: Ramada Inn, Super Lodge
	Other	E: Grocery, Walgreen's, Zoo, Bus Station
	NOTE:	**MM 19-21: Catskill Ski Region**
84.8/18		**NY 299, Main St, New Paltz, Poughkeepsie, Hyde Park**
	Gas	E: Citgo◈, Mobil W: Sunoco
	Food	E: China Buffet, College Diner W: Burger King, McDonald's, Subway

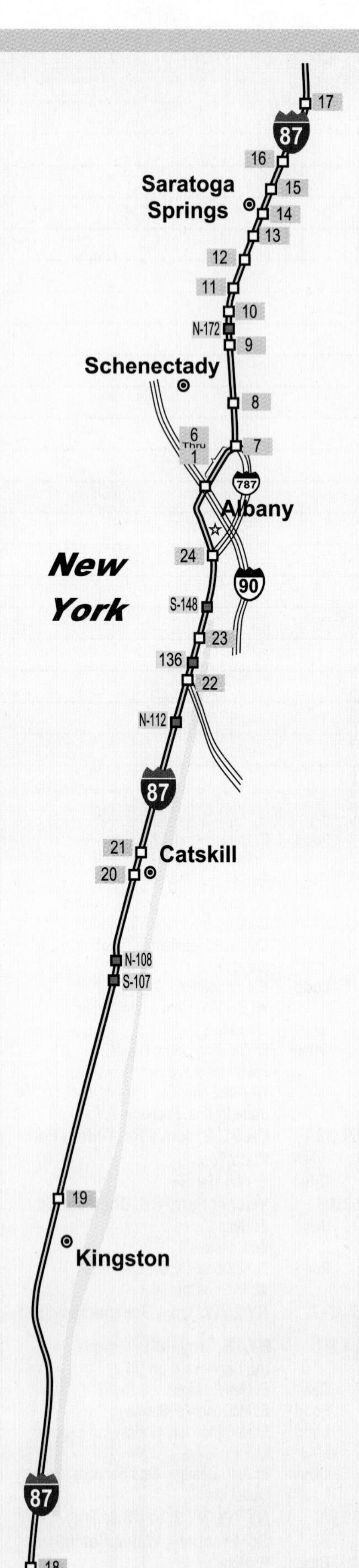

EXIT		NEW YORK
	Lodg	E: 87 Motel, Econo Lodge, Days Inn W: Super 8
	Other	W: Grocery, Laundromat, Pharmacy
(75)		Plattekill Service Area (NB)
	FStop	Mobil
	Food	Nathan's, Big Boy, Cinnabon
(74.8)		Modena Service Area (SB)
	FStop	Mobil
	Food	Arby's, McDonald's, Carvel
68.9/17		**NY 300, Union Ave, to I-84, NY 17K, Newburgh, Int'l Airport, Bear Mtn**
	Gas	E: Exxon, Mobil, Sunoco◈ W: Citgo◈
	Food	E: Applebee's, Burger King, Denny's, Cafe Int'l, China City, McDonald's, Subway, Taco Bell
	Lodg	E: Clarion, Holiday Inn, Hampton Inn, Ramada Inn, Super 8
	Other	E: Auto Dealers, Auto Services, Greyhound Grocery, Harley Davidson, Home Depot, Mall, Pharmacy, **Walmart**, W: Stewart Int'l Airport✈
(53.8)		**Woodbury TOLL Plaza (NB)**
	NOTE:	**NB Begin TOLL, SB End**
54/16		**US 6, NY 17, West Point, Harriman (Future I-86) Bear Mtn, Middletown, Monticello, Liberty, Monroe, Woodbury Outlets Blvd**
	Gas	W: Exxon◈
	Other	W: **Walmart sc**, Woodbury Outlet Mall, NY State Police
(41.8)		Sloatsburg Service Area (NB) Ramapo Service Area (SB)
	FStop	Sunoco
	Food	NB: Burger King, Sbarro, Dunkin Donuts SB: McDonald's, Carvel
40.1/15A		**NY 17N, NY 59, (NB), NY 17 (SB) Sloatsburg, Hillburn, Suffern**
(38.9/15)		**Jct I-287S, to NJ 17S, New Jersey**
	NOTE:	**I-87S & I-287 run together**
35.4/14B		**Airmont Rd, Suffern, Montebello**
	Gas	W: Exxon◈
	Food	W: Airmont Diner, Applebee's, Friendly's, J & R Lobster & Seafood, Outback Steakhouse, Starbucks
	Lodg	E: Holiday Inn, Inn at Gulfshores W: Wellesley Inn
	Med	W: + Hospital
	Other	W: Grocery, Walgreen's, Walmart
(33.1)		**Spring Valley TOLL Plaza (NB) (Truck TOLL Only)**
32.3/14A		**Garden State Pkwy, Spring Valley, to New Jersey (Passenger Cars Only)**
31.6/14		**NY 59, Grandview Ave (NB), NY 59, Pascack Rd (SB), Spring Valley, Nyack, Nanuet**
	Gas	E: Shell◈ W: Citgo

◈= Regular Gas Stations with Diesel ▲ = RV Friendly Locations ♥= Pet Friendly Locations
Red print shows large vehicle parking / access on site or nearby Brown Print = Campgrounds / RV PARKS

EXIT	NEW YORK
Food	**E:** Denny's, McDonald's, Subway **W:** Dunkin Donuts, Great China, IHOP, Red Lobster, Taco Bell
Lodg	**E:** Fairfield Inn **W:** Days Inn, Nanuet Inn
Other	**E:** Grocery, Mall, Target **W:** Grocery, Home Depot, Staples
29.7/13	**Palisades Interstate Pkwy N/S, to Ft Lee, Pekskill, Bear Mtn, NJ (Passenger Cars Only)**
27.5/12	**NY 303, Vriesendael Rd, West Nyack, Palisades Center Dr**
Gas	**W:** Mobil
Food	**W:** Grill 303, Outback Steakhouse, Panda Express, Romano's Macaroni Grill
Lodg	**W:** Nyack Motor Lodge
Other	**W:** Best Buy, Barnes & Noble, BJ's, Home Depot, Staples, Target, Mall, Grocery, Pharmacy
26.2/11	**Main St, High Ave, to US 9W, Highland Ave, NY 59, Nyack**
Gas	**E:** Mobil **W:** Shell◈
Lodg	**E:** Best Western, Super 8
Med	**W:** + Hospital
25.5/10	**US 9W, Hillside Ave, Ft Lee, Nyack, S Nyack (NB)**
(21.8)	**Tappan Zee Bridge TOLL Plaza (SB)**
21.6/9	**US 9, Broadway, NY 119, Tarrytown White Plains Rd, Sleepy Hollow**
Gas	**E:** Hess, Shell **W:** Mobil
Lodg	**E:** Marriott **W:** Hilton
20.1/8A	**NY 119, Saw Mill Pkwy North, Elmsford (SB)**
(20.1/8)	**Jct I-287E, Cross Westchester Expy, to Saw Mill Pkwy, Rye, White Plains**
Other	to Saw Mill State Park, Taconic State Park
19.1/7A	**Saw Mill River Pkwy, Yonkers, Bronx, Katonah (NO SB entry)**
Other	to Saw Mill State Park, Taconic State Park
16.6/7	**NY 9A, Ardsley, Saw Mill River Rd, Dobbs Ferry, Ardsley (NB)**
Med	**W:** + Hospital
(15.8)	Ardsley Service Area (NB)
FStop	Sunoco
Food	Burger King, Popeye's, TCBY
(14.2)	**Yonkers TOLL Plaza**
13.6/6A	**Corporate Dr, to Ridge Hill**
Other	**W:** Costco, Home Depot
12.7/6	**Tuckahoe Rd E/W, Yonkers, Bronxville**
Gas	**W:** Gulf, Mobil
Lodg	**E:** Tuckahoe Motor Inn **W:** Holiday Inn

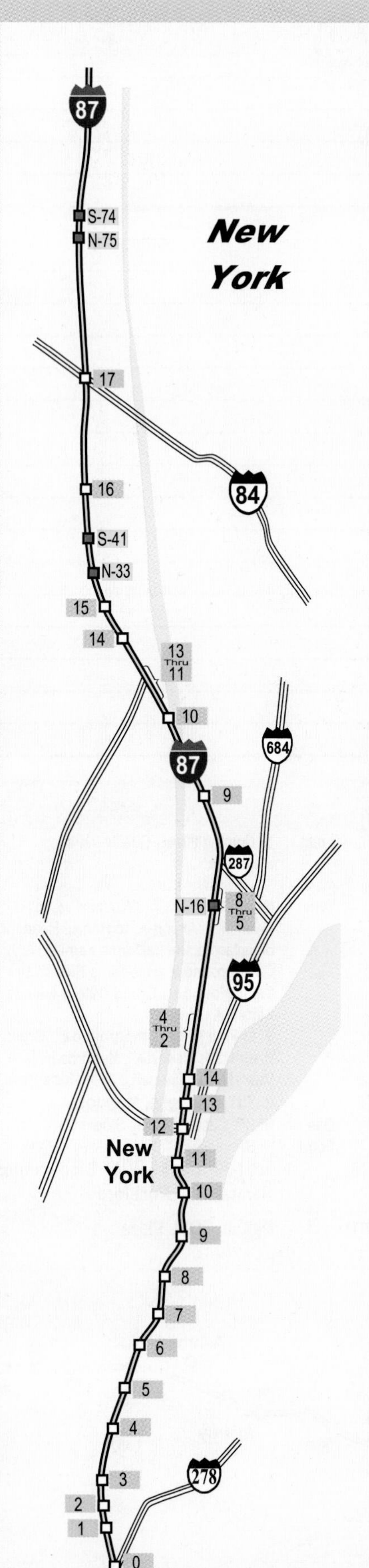

EXIT	NEW YORK
11.5/5	**NY 100N Central Park Ave, Yonkers**
Gas	**E:** Shell, Sunoco
10.9/4	**Cross Country Pkwy (W/E NB), Mile Square Rd, Yonkers Ave (SB), Yonkers, Bronxville**
Gas	**E:** Getty **W:** Shell
Other	**E:** Cross Country Mall **W:** to Yonkers Speedway
9.5/3	**Mile Square Rd, Yonkers (NB)**
9.2/2	**Central Park Ave, to Yonkers Ave, Yonkers, Mt Vernon (NB)**
Other	**E:** Yonkers Raceway
8.8/1	**Hall Place, McLean Ave**
NOTE:	**I-87 runs above with NY State Thruway (TOLL). Exit #'s are MM / Thruway.**
8.8/14	**McLean Ave (NB)**
Gas	**E:** Shell
8/13	**West 233rd St**
8/12	**Mosholu Pkwy (NB)**
7/11	**Van Cortlandt Pk S**
6/10	**West 230th St**
5/9	**Fordham Rd, Bronx**
Med	**E:** + Hospital
Other	**E:** Fordham Univ
5/8	**West 179th St, Cedar Ave (NB)**
(4/7)	**Jct I-95, Cross Bronx Expy, Throgs Neck Bridge to New Haven CT, Geo Washington Bridge to Newark, NJ**
3/6	**E 161st St (SB)**
Other	**E:** to Yankee Stadium
2/5	**W 155th St, E 153rd St, Macombs Dam Bridge**
2/4	**E 149th St (NB)**
Other	**E:** to Yankee Stadium
1/3	**E 138th St, Grand Concourse, Madison Ave Bridge**
1/2	**Willis Ave, 3rd Ave Bridge**
1/1	**E 134th St, Brook Ave (SB)**
Gas	**E:** Hess
(0)	**Jct I-278, Bruckner Expy, Triborough Bridge**

NOTE: NYS does NOT use Mile Marker Exits. Listed is MileMarker/Exit #.

NOTE: I-87 begins/ends on I-278, Exit #47

EASTERN TIME ZONE

NEW YORK

Begin Northbound I-87 from New York City to Champlain, NY.

◈= Regular Gas Stations with Diesel ▲ = RV Friendly Locations ♥= Pet Friendly Locations
Red print shows large vehicle parking / access on site or nearby Brown Print = Campgrounds / RV PARKS

Begin Eastbound I-88 from Jct I-80 near Rock Island, IL to Jct I-290, near Hillside, IL.

ILLINOIS

CENTRAL TIME ZONE

NOTE: I-88 Begins/Ends at Jct I-290

(0) **IL 5, IL 92, W to Moline, Rock Island, Sterling, Rock Falls (WB)**
Other S: to Lundeen's Landing Campground▲

(1A) **Jct I-80E, to I-74, Peoria**

(1B) **Jct I-80W, to Des Moines**

2 **Former IL 2**

6 **IL 92E, 38th Ave, Hillsdale, Joslin**
Other S: 3mi Spirit in the Oaks Campground▲, Sunset Lake Campground▲, to Geneseo Campground▲

10 **IL 2, Moline Rd, Hillsdale, Pt Byron**
TStop S: Hillsdale Fast Break (Scales)
Food S: Mama J's/Hillsdale
Other N: to Camp Hauberg Campground▲

18 **CR 13, Albany Rd, Erie, Albany**

26 **IL 78, Crosby Rd, Lyndon, to Morrison, Prophetstown**
Other N: to Morrison Rockwood State Park▲
S: to Prophetstown State Park▲

36 **Como Rd, to Moline Rd, US 30, Rock Falls Rd, Sterling, Clinton**
Other S: Crow Valley Campground▲

41 **IL 40, IL 88, Hoover Rd, Rock Falls, Sterling (Use N Serv as Last Free Exit)**
Gas N: Casey's, Marathon, Mobil, Shell◊
Food N: Arby's, Culver's, Hardee's, KFC, McDonald's, Red Apple Family Rest, Subway
Lodg N: All Seasons Motel, Country Inn, Holiday Inn♥, Super 8
Med N: + Hospital
Other N: Grocery, Goodyear, Walgreen's, Walmart, Leisure Lake Campground▲
S: Whiteside Co Airport✈

44 **US 30, E Rock Falls Rd, Rock Falls**
NOTE: LAST FREE EXIT

(53) **Dixon TOLL Plaza, Ronald Reagan Memorial Tollway**

54 **IL 26, Dixon**
TStop N: DND Travel Plaza/BP (Scales)
Food N: Rest/FastFood/DND TP, Hardee's, Pizza Hut

Personal Notes

Lodg N: Comfort Inn♥, Quality Inn♥, Super 8♥
Med N: + KSB Hospital
Other N: Laundry/DND TP, Walmart sc, to Dixon Muni Airport✈, to Ronald Reagan Birthplace, Lake LaDonna Family Campground▲, Hanson's Hideaway Campground▲, Grand Detour Islands Retreat▲
S: to Pine View Campground▲, Green River Oaks Resort▲, Mendota Hills Resort▲, O'Connell's Jellystone Park

76 **IL 251, Rochelle, Mendota**
Gas N: BP, Casey's, Shell, Stop n Go
Food N: Blimpie/BP, TJ Cinn, Casey's Pizza

(78) **Jct I-39, US 51, S to Bloomington, Normal, N to Rockford**

(91) **DeKalb TOLL Plaza**

92 **Fairview Dr, to IL 23, IL 38, Annie Glidden Rd, DeKalb, Sycamore IL 251 (All Serv 3 mi N to IL 38/W Lincoln Hwy)**
Fstop Stop n Go #527/BP
Other N: DeKalb Taylor Muni Airport✈, to Sycamore RV Resort▲

(93) **DeKalb Oasis (Both dir)**
FStop S: Mobil
Food S: McDonald's, Panda Express, Starbucks, Subway
Other S: WiFi

94 **Peace Rd, to IL 23, IL 38, DeKalb, Taylor**
Other N: DeKalb Taylor Muni Airport✈, N IL Univ, to Sycamore RV Resort▲

109 **IL 47, Sugar Grove (EB ex, WB reacc)**

114 **IL 56W, to IL 30, to IL 47, Aurora, Sugar Grove (WB ex, EB reacc)**

115 **Orchard Rd, Aurora (Serv S to Galena Blvd)**
Gas S: 7-11
Food S: Blackberry Café, Chili's, IHOP, KFC, McDonald's, Pizza Hut, Starbucks, Subway, Taco Bell
Lodg S: Hampton Inn
Med S: + Dreyer Medical Clinic
Other N: Auto Dealers
S: CVS, Home Depot, Walmart, Auto Repair, to Hide-A-Way-Lakes Camping & RV Park▲, to Blackberry Historical Farm Village

117 **IL 31, IL 56, to IL 25, Aurora, Batavia**
Gas N: Citgo◊, Marathon
S: Mobil, Thorntons
Food S: Denny's, McDonald's, Popeye's
Lodg S: Baymont Inn, La Quinta Inn♥
Med S: + Indian Trail Medical Center
Other S: Auto Zone, Walgreen's, U-Haul

(118) **Aurora TOLL Plaza**

119 **CR 77, Farnsworth Ave, to Kirk Rd**
Gas S: Mobil◊, Phillips 66, Shell, Speedway
Food N: New Ser Family Rest, Papa Bear Family Rest
S: McDonald's, Little Caesar, Subway, Taco Bell, Wok In
Lodg N: Fox Valley Inn, Motel 6♥
Other N: Outlet Stores

123 **IL 59, Naperville, Warrenville**
Gas S: Mobil◊
Food S: Cracker Barrel, Steak 'n Shake, Subway, Wendy's

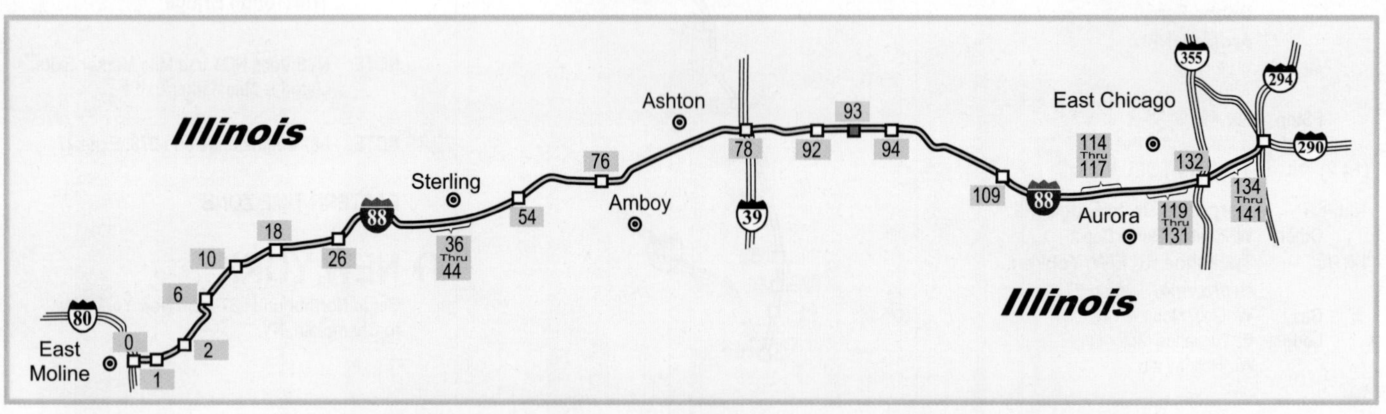

◊= Regular Gas Stations with Diesel ▲ = RV Friendly Locations ♥= Pet Friendly Locations
Red print shows large vehicle parking / access on site or nearby Brown Print = Campgrounds / RV PARKS

EXIT		ILLINOIS
	Lodg	**N:** Marriott
		S: Country Inn, Hawthorn Suites, Red Roof Inn♥, Sleep Inn, Townplace Suites
	Other	**N:** Odyssey Fun World
125		**Winfield Rd, Warrenville**
	Gas	**N:** BP
		S: BP, Phillips 66
	Food	**N:** Arby's, McDonald's
		S: Chipolte Mexican Grill, McDonald's, Max & Erma's, Red Robin
	Lodg	**N:** Residence Inn♥
		S: Springhill Suites
	Other	**N:** Walgreen's
		S: Target
128		**CR 23, Naperville Rd, Naper Blvd, Naperville, Lisle, Wheaton**
	Gas	**S:** Mobil, Shell
	Food	**S:** Bob Evans, Chevy's, Fresh Mex, McDonald's, TGI Friday
	Lodg	**N:** Hilton, Marriott, Wyndham
		S: Best Western, Courtyard, Days Inn♥, Fairfield Inn, Holiday Inn Select, Hampton Inn
	Other	**S: Mendota Hills Camping Resort▲**
130		**IL 53, Lincoln Ave, Lisle (Exit Both Dir, EB reaccess)**
	Gas	**N:** BP
	Food	**N:** McDonald's
	Other	**N: Walmart**
(131)		**I-355S, to US 34, Joliet (EB)**
(132)		**I-355S, to IL 56, NW Suburbs (WB)**
134		**CR 9, Highland Ave, Downers Grove (Exit Both Dir, EB reaccess)**
	Food	**N:** CiCi's Pizza, Fuddrucker's, Hooters, Joe's Crab Shack, Kyoto, Olive Garden, Potbelly Sandwiches, Red Lobster, Ruby Tuesday, Starbucks, TGI Friday
		S: Elliot's Deli, Parker's Ocean Grill
	Lodg	**N:** Comfort Inn, Embassy Suites, Extended Stay America, Hampton Inn, Homestead Suites, Hyatt Place, Red Roof Inn♥, Residence Inn, Townplace Suites
	Med	**S: + Good Samaritan Hospital**
	Other	**N:** ATMs, Auto Services, Best Buy, FedEx Office, Firestone, Office Max, PetSmart♥, Pharmacy, Target, Walgreen's, Yorktown Center Mall
		S: Pharmacy, UPS Store
(135.5)		**Meyers Rd TOLL Plaza (EB)**
136		**IL 15, Midwest Rd, Oakbrook (EB)**
	Gas	**N:** Shell, Costco
	Food	**N:** Denny's, McDonald's, Starbucks
	Lodg	**N:** Holiday Inn, La Quinta Inn♥
	Other	**N:** Costco, Home Depot, Walgreen's
137		**IL 83S, Kingery Hwy (WB)**
	Lodg	**N:** Hilton Garden Inn, Hyatt, InTown Suites, La Quinta Inn♥, Marriott
		S: Residence Inn
	Other	**N:** FedEx Kinko's, Office Max, Oak Brook Center Mall
137		**Spring Rd, W 22nd St, to Cermak Rd to I-83N (WB)**
138		**IL 8N, Cermak Rd, to to IL 83N**
(138)		**York Rd TOLL Plaza**
(139)		**I-294S, Tri-State Tollway, Indiana**
(140.5)		**I-294, Tri-State Tollway (TOLL), S to Indiana, N to O'Hare, Milwaukee I-290, W to Rockford, IL 38W**
(141)		**I-290, E to Chicago, Mannheim Rd, to US 12, US 20, US 45**

CENTRAL TIME ZONE

NOTE: I-88 Begins/Ends at Jct I-80 near Hampton

ILLINOIS

Begin Eastbound I-88 from Jct I-290 near Rock Island, IL to Jct I-80, near Hampton, IL

Begin I-88 from Jct I-81 in Binghamton to Jct I-90 in Schenectady.

NEW YORK

NOTE: I-88 Begins/Ends I-90, Exit# 25A

EASTERN TIME ZONE

NOTE: NYS does NOT use Mile Marker Exits. Listed is MileMarker/Exit #.

EXIT		NEW YORK
(0)		**Jct I-81, to NY 17, N to Syracuse, S to Binghamton (WB), Jct I-88E, NY 7E (EB)**
	Other	**S: Hillcrest RV**
1/1		**NY 7W, to Binghamton (WB, no reacc)**
2/2		**NY 12A W, to Chenango Bridge**
4/3		**NY 369, Port Crane**
	Gas	**S:** FasTrac◈, KwikFill
	Other	**N: Chenango Valley State Park**
8/4		**NY 7E, to NY 7B, Sanitaria Springs**
	FStop	**S:** Hess Express #32379
12/5		**Martin Hill Rd, to Belden**
	Gas	**N:** Exxon◈
	Other	**N: Belden Hill Campground▲**
15/6		**NY 79, to NY 7, Harpursville, Ninevah**
	TStop	**S:** Quickway Food Store #74/Citgo
	Food	**S:** FastFood/QW FS
	Other	**S:** WiFi/LP/QW FS, **to Forest Lake Campground▲**, to appr 15 mi **Lakeside Campground▲**
23/7		**NY 41, to Afton**
	Gas	**N:** Mobil, Xtra
	Other	**N: Echo Lake Resort Campground▲**
		S: to appr 6mi **Kellystone Park Campground▲**
29/8		**NY 206, Bainbridge, Masonville**
	FStop	**N:** Xtra Mart/Sunoco
	Gas	**N:** Mobil
	Food	**N:** TacoBell/XtraMart, Bob's Family Diner
	Other	**N:** Kmart, **Riverside RV Park▲**
		S: to appr 5mi Oquaga Creek State Park▲
32/9		**NY 8, to NY 7, Sidney, Utica**
	Gas	**N:** Citgo◈, Hess◈, Mobil◈
	Food	**N:** Burger King, Gavin's Pizzeria & Steak House, Little Caesars, McDonald's, Pizza Hut, Subway
	Lodg	**N:** Super 8
	Med	**N: + Hospital**
	Other	**N:** ATMs, Bank, Auto Services, Grocery US Post Office, Sidney Muni Airport✈, **to appr 3mi Tall Pines Riverfront Campground▲**
37/10		**NY 7, to Unadilla**
	Gas	**N:** Kwikfill
	Other	**N: NY State Police**
(39)		**Rest Area (EB) (RR, Phone, Picnic)**

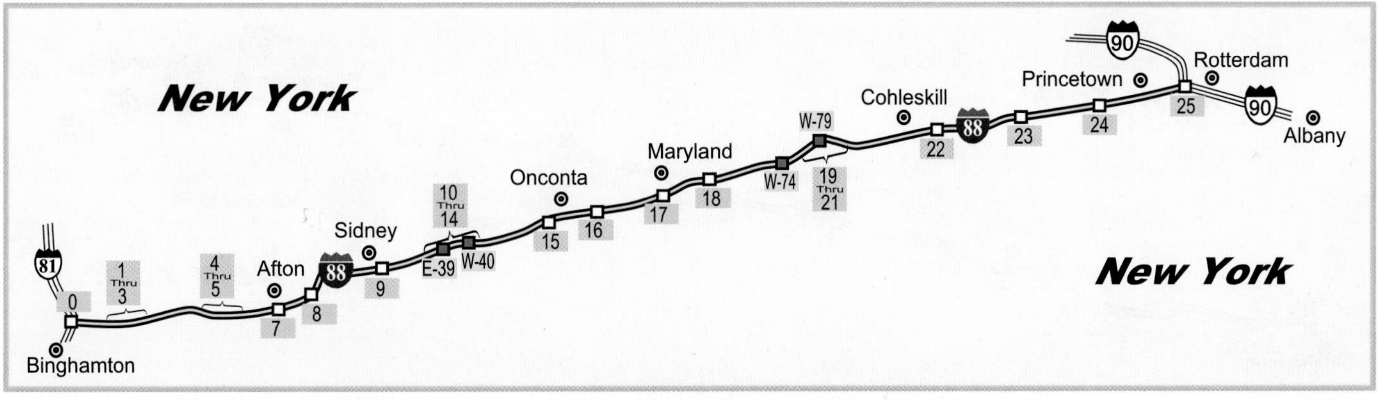

EXIT — NEW YORK

40/11 — **NY 357, Franklin, Unadilla, Delhi**
- Other: S: appr 4mi Unadilla/I-88/Oneonta KOA▲

(40) — Rest Area (WB)
(RR, Phone, Picnic)

46/12 — **NY 7, Otego**
- TStop: S: Quickway Food Store #73/Citgo
- Food: S: FastFood/QW FS
- Other: S: WiFi/LP/QW FS

53/13 — **NY 7, NY 205, Oneonta**
- Gas: N: Citgo, Hess, Mobil
- Food: N: Burger King, McDonald's, Ponderosa
- Lodg: N: Hampton Inn, Maple Terrace Motel, Oasis Motor Inn
- Other: N: Auto Dealers, Auto Services, Grocery, Pharmacy, to appr 16mi Meadow-Vale Campsites▲

55/14 — **NY 28E, Main St, Oneonta, Delhi (Access to Ex #15 Serv)**
- Gas: N: Kwikfill, Stewarts, Sunoco
- Food: N: Deli
  S: Denny's, McDonald's, Taco Bell
- Lodge: N: Clarion, Oneonta Motel, Town House Motor Inn
- Other: N: ATMs, Banks, CVS, Dollar General, Grocery, Pharmacy, Harwick College, State Univ

56/15 — **NY 28, NY 23, Oneonta, Davenport**
- FStop: S: Quickway Food Store #69
- Gas: S: Hess, KwikFill, Mobil, BJ's
- Food: S: TacoBell/QW FS, Applebee's, Brookes BBQ, Denny's, McDonald's, Italian Rest, Neptune Diner, Quiznos, Subway, Wendy's
- Lodg: S: Budget Inn, Holiday Inn, Super 8
- TWash: S: QW FS
- Med: N: + Hospital
- Other: N: Pharmacy, to Soccer Hall of Fame
  S: WiFi/LP/QW FS, ATMs, Auto Services, Banks, BJ's, Borders, Grocery, Home Depot, Office Max, Walmart sc, Southside Mall, Leatherstocking RV

58/16 — **NY 7, to Emmons**
- Food: N: Arby's, Burger King, Farmhouse Rest, Pizza Hut
- Lodg: N: Rainbow Inn

61/17 — **NY 28N, to NY 7, Colliersville, Cooperstown**
- Gas: N: Mobil◈
- Food: N: Homestead Rest
- Lodg: N: Best Western, Redwood Motel
- Other: N: to appr 14mi Hartwick Highlands Campground▲ , to Baseball Hall of Fame

Personal Notes

EXIT — NEW YORK

71/18 — **to Schenevus**
- Gas: N: Citgo

(74) — Rest Area (EB)
(RR, Phone, Picnic)

77/19 — **to NY 7, Worcester**
- Gas: N: Stewarts, Sunoco◈

(79) — Rest Area (WB)
(RR, Phone, Picnic)

88/20 — **NY 7S, NY 10, to Richmondville**
- Gas: S: Sunoco, Mobil◈
- Lodg: S: Econo Lodge
- Other: S: Hi View Campground▲

90/21 — **NY 7, NY 10, to Cobleskill, Warnerville**
- Gas: N: Mobil◈, Hess

EXIT — NEW YORK

- Food: N: Burger King, Pizza Hut
- Other: N: Walmart sc, to State Univ of NY

95/22 — **NY 7, NY 145, Cobleskill, Middleburgh**
- FStop: N: Hess Express
- Gas: N: Mobil
- Food: N: Arby's, Burger King, McDonald's, Subway, Taco Bell, Rest/Howe Caverns Motel
- Lodg: N: Best Western, Holiday Motel, Howe Caverns Motel
- Med: N: + Hospital
- Other: N: Twin Oaks Campground▲ , Howe Caverns
  S: Happy Trails RV Parts & Service, NY State Police

100/23 — **NY 7, NY 30, NY 30A, to Schoharie, Central Bridge**
- Gas: N: Mobil
  S: Mobil◈
- Food: S: Dunkin Donuts, McDonald's
- Lodg: S: Holiday Inn Express
- Other: N: Locust Park Campground▲ , Hideaway Campground▲

112/24 — **US 20, NY 7, to Duanesburg**
- Gas: N: Mobil
  S: Mobil, Stewarts
- Food: S: Duanesburg Diner
- Other: N: NY State Police

117/25 — **NY 7, to Rotterdam, Schenectady, to US 20, NY 70/107/52/103**
NOTE: EB: Last FREE Exit
- TStop: S: Pilot Travel Center #494 (Scales)
- Food: S: DunkinDonut/Subway/Pilot TC, Burger King, McDonald's, Midway Café, Topps Diner
- Other: N: WiFi/LP/Pilot TC, 3 mi Frosty Acres Campground▲
  S: White RV Specialists

(117.5) — **Jct I-90, NY Thruway (TOLL), to Albany, Buffalo**

NOTE: NYS does NOT use Mile Marker Exits. Listed is Mile Marker /Exit #.

EASTERN TIME ZONE

NOTE: I-88 Begins/Ends I-90, Exit# 25A

NEW YORK

Begin I-88 from Jct I-90 in Schenectady to Jct I-81 in Binghamton.

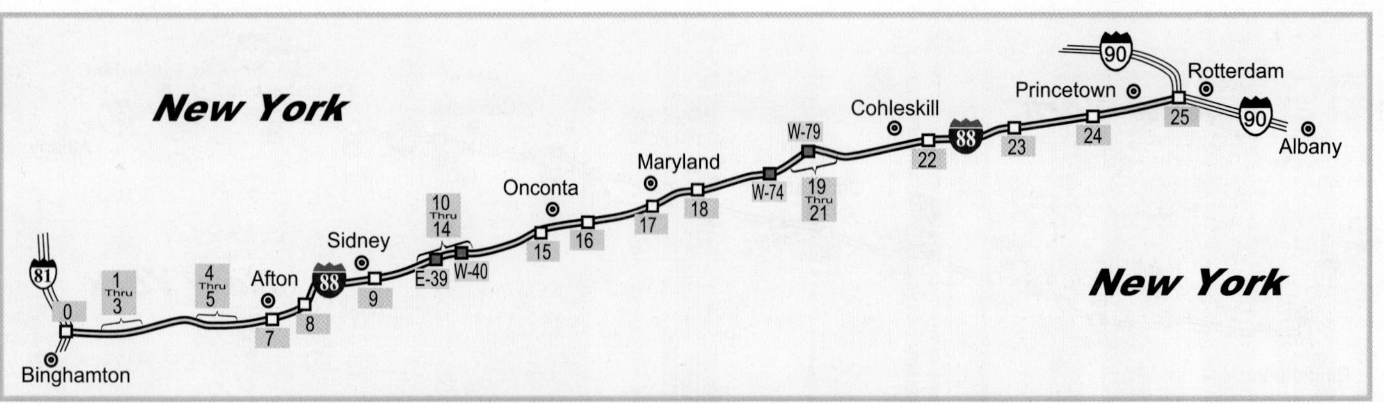

◈= Regular Gas Stations with Diesel ▲ = RV Friendly Locations ♥= Pet Friendly Locations
Red print shows large vehicle parking / access on site or nearby Brown Print = Campgrounds / RV PARKS

EXIT	VERMONT

Begin Southbound I-89 from Canada/VT border to Jct I-93 near Concord, NH.

VERMONT

EASTERN TIME ZONE

(130) **VT State Line, US / Canada Border**

(129.5) **Rest Area (SB)**
(RR, Phone, Picnic, Vend)

129/22 **US 7S, Swanton, Highgate Springs**
- Gas: E: Mobil◈
- Other: E: AmEx Duty Free

NOTE: MM 129: 45 degrees N Latitude: Mid Point between N Pole & Equator

123/21 **VT 78, 1st St, to US 7, Swanton**
- TStop: E: Champlain Farms/Exxon; W: Hometown Sunoco, Swanton Mobil Mart
- Gas: W: Shell
- Food: W: Big Wok, Dunkin Donuts, McDonald's

117/20 **VT 207, to US 7, St Albans**
- Gas: W: Mobil, Shell◈
- Food: W: Burger King, McDonald's, Pizza Hut
- Other: W: Auto Dealers, Grocery, Laundromat, Staples

113/19 **VT 104, to US 7, VT 36, St Albans**
- TStop: W: The Jolly Short Stop/Exxon (Scales)
- Gas: W: Mobil, Shell◈
- Food: W: FastFood/Jolley SS
- Lodg: W: Econo Lodge
- TWash: W: Jolley SS
- TServ: W: Jolley SS/Tires
- Med: W: + Hospital
- Other: W: Laundry/WiFi/**RVDump**/Jolly SS, Amtrak, Auto Dealers, **VT State Hwy Patrol Post**

(111) **Rest Area (Both dir)**
(RR, Phones, Picnic, Vend, Info)

106/18 **US 7, VT 104A, Georgia, Fairfax**
- FStop: E: Maplefields/Mobil
- Gas: E: Shell
- Other: E: **Homestead Campground▲**

97/17 **US 2, US 7, Colchester, Lake Champlain Islands**
- Gas: E: Mobil, Shell◈
- Other: W: **to appr 4mi Lone Pine Campsites▲**

(96) **Weigh Station (Both dir)**

91/16 **US 2, US 7, to VT 15, Roosevelt Hwy Colchester, Essex Jct, Winooski**
- FStop: W: Champlain Farms/Shell
- Gas: E: Mobil; W: Citgo
- Food: E: Friendly's; W: Burger King, McDonald's, Diner
- Lodg: E: Hampton Inn; W: Fairfield Inn, Motel 6
- Other: W: **to appr 4mi Lone Pine Campsites▲**

90/15 **VT 15, Winooski, Burlington**
(NB Exit, SB reaccess)
- Gas: W: Mobil
- Lodg: E: Days Inn

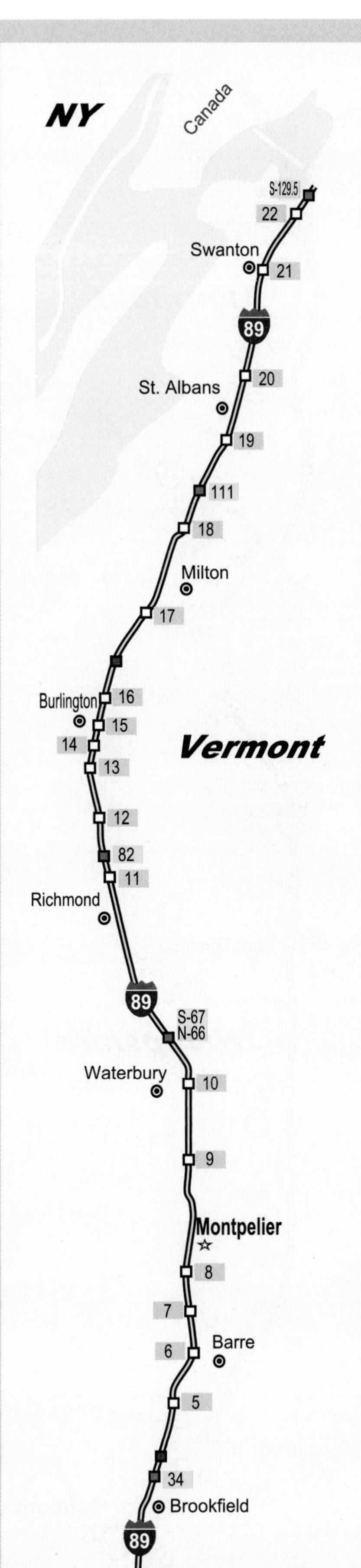

EXIT	VERMONT

- Other: E: Burlington Int'l Airport✈, Ft Ethan Allen

88/14 **US 2, Burlington**
- Gas: E: Exxon, Mobil, Shell◈; W: Exxon, Mobil
- Food: E: Applebee's, Burger King, Dunkin Donuts, Friendly's, KFC, McDonald's, Outback Steakhouse, Quiznos
- Lodg: E: Best Western, Clarion, Comfort Inn, Days Inn, Holiday Inn, University Inn; W: Sheraton
- Med: W: + Hospital
- Other: E: B&N, Grocery, Pharmacy, Mall, Natural Foods Market, Burlington Int'l Airport✈; W: Advance Auto, Greyhound, Staples

(87/13) **Jct I-189, to US 7, Shelburn**
(All Services W to US 7N/S)
- Other: W: **Shelburne Camping Area▲**

84/12 **VT 2A, St George Rd, to US 2, Williston**
- Gas: E: Mobil, Sunoco◈
- Food: W: Chili's, Friendly's, Ponderosa, Longhorn Steakhouse
- Lodg: E: Fairfield Inn; W: Marriott, Residence Inn
- Other: E: ATMs, Bank, Best Buy, Grocery, Home Depot, Staples, **Walmart**, **VT State Hwy Patrol Post**

(82) **Rest Area (Both dir)**
(RR, Phone, Picnic, Vend)

78/11 **US 2, to VT 117, Richmond**
- Gas: W: Mobil◈
- Food: E: Checkered Rest
- Lodg: E: Checkered House Motel

(67) **Parking Area (SB)**

(66) **Parking Area (NB)**

63/10 **VT 100, to US 2, Waterbury**
- Gas: E: Mobil◈, Exxon◈; W: Citgo
- Lodg: E: Best Western

58/9 **US 2, to VT 100B, Middlesex**
- Gas: W: Getty
- Food: W: Rest/Camp Meade Motor Inn
- Lodg: W: Camp Meade Motor Inn
- Other: W: **VT State Hwy Patrol Post**

53/8 **US 2, VT 12, Montpelier**
- Gas: E: CF, Exxon◈, Mobil, Sunoco
- Food: E: Subway
- Other: E: Grocery

50/7 **to US 302, VT 62, Berlin Corners**
- FStop: E: Maplewood Ltd/Mobil
- Food: E: Applebee's
- Lodg: E: Comfort Inn
- Med: E: + Hospital
- Other: E: Auto Dealers, Grocery, Staples

46/6 **VT 63, to VT 14, S Barre**
(Serv 4-5 mi in Barre)
- Other: E: **Limehurst Lake Campground▲**

43/5 **VT 64, to VT 12, VT 14, Northfield**

(34) **Rest Area (Both dir)**
(RR, Phone)

(33) **Weigh Station (Both dir)**

30/4 **VT 66, Randolph**
NOTE: STEEP Grade on hill
- Gas: W: Mobil
- Food: W: McDonald's
- Med: W: + Hospital
- Other: E: **Lake Champagne Campground▲**

◈= Regular Gas Stations with Diesel ▲ = RV Friendly Locations ♥= Pet Friendly Locations
Red print shows large vehicle parking / access on site or nearby Brown Print = Campgrounds / RV PARKS

EXIT	VT / NH
22/3	**VT 107, Main St, S Royalton, to Bethel, Rutland**
Gas	E: Shell◈
	W: Citgo◈
Other	W: VT State Hwy Patrol Post, to approx 8mi White River Valley Campground▲
13/2	**VT 132, to VT 14, Sharon**
Gas	W: Citgo◈, Mobil
Food	W: Dixie's Kitchen
(9)	**VT Welcome Center (NB)** (RR, Phone, Vend) **Weigh Station (Both dir)**
3/1	**US 4, Woodstock, Quechee**
Gas	E: Shell◈
	W: Mobil
Food	W: Dunkin Donuts
Lodg	E: Hampton Inn, Super 8
Other	W: Quechee Pine Valley KOA▲
(1)	**Jct I-91, N to St Johnsbury, S to Brattleboro (Serv E to 1st x11)**

EASTERN TIME ZONE

VERMONT
NEW HAMPSHIRE

NOTE: MM 61: Vermont State Line

60/20	**NH 12A, Main St, W Lebanon, Claremont**
Gas	E: Mobil, Sunoco
	W: Citgo◈
Food	E: KFC, Chili's, 99 Rest, Mex Rest, Subway, Weathervane Seafood Rest
	W: Applebee's, Burger King, Denny's, Friendly's, Japanese Rest, McDonald's, Pizza Hut, Weathervane Seafood, Wendy's
Lodg	W: Fireside Inn
Other	E: Grocery, Pharmacy
	W: ATMs, Auto Services, Auto Zone, BJ's, Best Buy Borders, CVS, Grocery, Home Depot, Radio Shack, Staples, Walmart, Lebanon Muni Airport✈
58/19	**US 4, NH 10, Mechanic St, Lebanon, Hanover**
Gas	E: Exxon◈, Shell
Food	E: Little Caesars, Blimpie/Shell
Other	E: Family Dollar, Laundry, Grocery, Radio Shack, Harley Davidson
	W: Lebanon Muni Airport✈
(57)	**NH Welcome Center (SB)** (RR, Phones, Picnic, Vend) **Weigh Station (Both dir)**
56/18	**NH 120, Lebanon, Hanover**
TStop	E: Exit 18 Truck Stop/Getty (Scales)
Gas	W: Citgo◈, Shell
Food	E: Rest/Exit 18 TS
Lodg	E: Days Inn, Residence Inn
TServ	E: Exit 18 TS/Tires/TWash
Med	W: + Hospital
Other	E: Laundry/WiFi/LP/Exit 18 TS
54/17	**US 4, NH 4A, Enfield, Canaan**
Other	E: Mascoma Lake Campground▲
52/16	**Eastman Hill Rd, Enfield**
FStop	W: Exit 16 Mobil
TStop	E: Evans Exit 16 Truck Stop/Exxon
Food	E: Subway/Ex 16 TS
	W: Burger King/Ex 16 Mobil
Other	W: Whaleback Ski Area

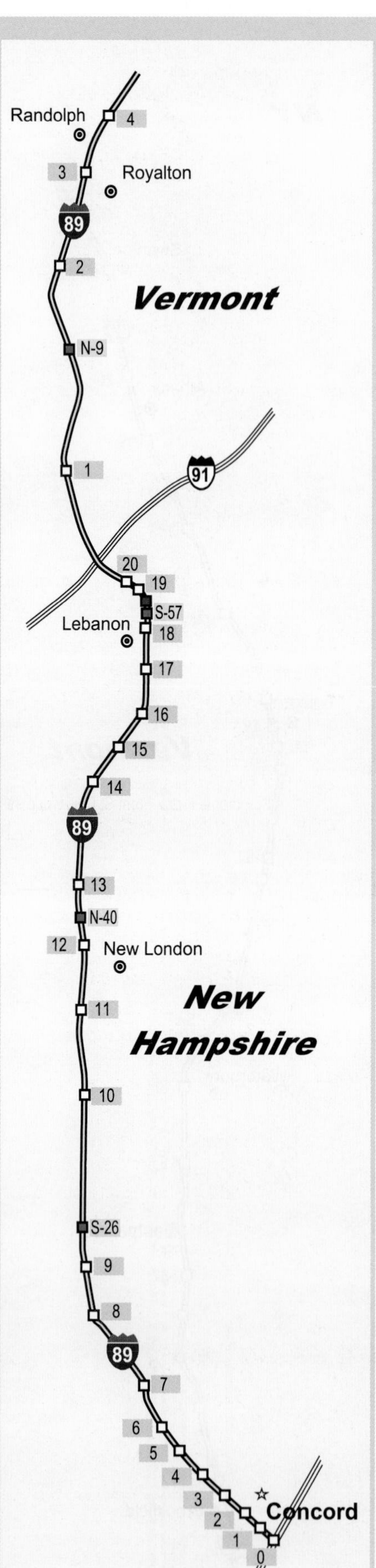

EXIT	NEW HAMPSHIRE
50/15	**Smith Pond Rd, Enfield, Montcalm**
48/14	**N Grantham** (SB exit, NB reaccess)
43/13	**NH 10, Grantham, Croydon, Newport**
Gas	E: General Store/Gulf
	W: Mobil
Other	W: to North Star Campground▲, Appr 13mi Crow's Nest Campground▲
(40)	**Rest Area (NB)** (RR, Phones, Picnic, Vend)
37/12A	**Georges Mills Rd, Springfield Rd, Sunapee, Georges Mills**
Other	W: Crow's Nest Campground▲
35/12	**NH 11W, NH 114, Newport Rd, New London, Sunapee**
Lodg	E: Maple Hill Farm Inn
Med	E: + Hospital
31/11	**NH 11E, King Hill Rd, New London**
27/10	**Gile Pond Rd, to NH 114, Sutton**
(26)	**Rest Area (SB)** (RR, Phones, Picnic, Vend)
20/9	**NH 103, Main St, Warner, Bradford**
Gas	E: Citgo, Exxon, Mobil◈
Food	E: Dunkin Donuts, McDonald's
Other	W: to appr 6mi Northstar Campground▲
17/8	**NH 103, Warner (NB ex, SB reacc)**
15/7	**NH 103, Davisville, Contoocook**
11/6	**NH 127, Maple St, Contoocook**
Other	E: Sandy Beach RV Resort▲
	W: appr 3mi Keyser Pond Campground▲, appr 6mi Mile Away Campground▲
9/5	**US 202, NH 9, Hopkinton, Henniker (NB, Left Exit)**
Other	W: appr 3mi Keyser Pond Campground▲ Appr 6mi Mile Away Campground▲, Appr 10mi Cold Springs Camp Resort▲, Appr 30mi Idle Times Campground▲
7/4	**US 202, NH 9, to NH 103, Contoocook, Hopkinton** (NB Ex, SB reacc)
4/3	**Stickney Hill Rd, Concord** (NB ex, SB reacc)
2/2	**NH 13, Clinton St, Concord**
Med	E: + Hospital
Other	W: Friendly Beaver Campground▲, to appr 6miCold Springs Camp Resort & RV Sales/Service/Rentals▲
1/1	**Logging Hill Rd, South St, Bow**
Gas	E: Mobil
Lodg	E: Hampton Inn
(0)	**Jct I-93, N to Concord, S to Manchester**

EASTERN TIME ZONE

NOTE: I-89 Begins/Ends I-93, MM 36

NEW HAMPSHIRE

Begin Northbound I-89 near Concord, NH to Vermont / Canada border.

◈ = Regular Gas Stations with Diesel ▲ = RV Friendly Locations ♥ = Pet Friendly Locations
Red print shows large vehicle parking / access on site or nearby Brown Print = Campgrounds / RV PARKS

EXIT — WASHINGTON

Begin Eastbound I-90 from near Jct I-5 in Seattle, WA to near Jct I-93 in Boston MA.

WASHINGTON

NOTE: **I-90 Begins/Ends on I-93, Ex #20**
I-90 Begins/Ends on I-5, Ex #164

2A — **4th Ave S (WB)**
Other — W: Qwest Field, Safeco Field, Amtrak

(2CB) — **Jct I-5, S to Tacoma, Portland, OR; N to Everett, Vancouver, BC**

3 — **Rainier Ave South, Seattle (EB)**
Gas — N: Shell◈
Food — S: Burger King, McDonald's, Wendy's

NOTE: **Tunnel, Mercer Island Floating Bridge, Tunnel**

3A — **Rainier Ave South (WB)**

3B — **Rainier Ave North (WB)**

6 — **W Mercer Way (EB)**

7 — **Island Crest Way (WB)**

7A — **77th Ave (EB)**

7B — **Island Crest Way (EB)**

7AB — **76th Ave, 80th Ave, Island Crest Way (EB)**
Gas — S: 76, Shell◈
Food — S: McDonald's, Starbucks, Subway
S: Islander Steakhouse
Lodg — S: Travelodge
Other — S: Auto Repair/Shell, Walgreen's

7C — **80th Ave SE (fr WB, LEFT Exit)**

8 — **East Mercer Way, Mercer Island**

9 — **Bellevue Way**

(10A) — **Jct I-405, N to Everett, Vancouver, S to Renton, Tacoma (EB)**

10B — **SE 36th St, 128th Ave (EB)**

(10) — **Jct I-405, N to Everett, Vancouver, S to Renton, Tacoma (WB)**

10C — **Richards Rd, Factoria Blvd (EB)**

11 — **Eastgate Way, 156th Ave, 150th Ave (WB)**
Gas — N: Shell
S: 76, Shell◈
Food — N: DQ, Lil John's, McDonald's, Starbucks
S: Denny's, Pizza Hut, Outback Steakhouse
Lodg — N: Days Inn, Eastgate Motel, Embassy Suites, Silver Cloud Inn
S: Candlewood Suites, Homestead Suites
Other — N: Safeway, Animal Hospital♥
S: Albertson's, RiteAid

11A — **150th Ave SE, SE 36th/35th St, Eastgate Way (EB)**

11B — **148th Ave SE (EB)**

13 — **Lakemont Blvd, West Lake Sammamish Parkway, Bellevue, Issaquah, to Redmond**
Food — S: Starbucks
Other — S: Grocery, UPS Store, Vet♥

15 — **WA 900S, 17th Ave, Renton Rd, Issaquah Rd, Issaquah, to Renton**
Gas — N: ArcoAmPm, Costco
S: Shell
Food — N: IHOP, Red Robin
S: Burger King, Cascade Garden, Jack in the Box, Denny's, McDonald's, Subway, Starbucks, Taco del Mar
Lodg — N: Holiday Inn, Motel 6♥
Other — N: ATMs, B&N, Costco, Lowe's, Grocery, Office Depot, PetSmart♥, Trader Joe's, **to Lake Sammamish State Park/RVDump**
S: PetCo♥, RiteAid, Safeway, Target, Harley Davidson, **Issaquah Highlands Camping▲**

17 — **E Lake Sammamish Pkwy, Front St, Issaquah**
Gas — N: 76
S: ArcoAmPm, Chevron, Shell
Food — N: McDonald's, Qdoba Mex, Starbucks
S: Extreme Pizza, Front St Deli, Skippers
Other — N: Albertson's, Home Depot, Walgreen's, **Issaquah Village RV Park/RVDump▲**
S: Auto Repair, Big O Tire, Staples, U-Haul

18 — **Sunset Way, Highlands Dr**
Gas — S: Shell
Food — S: Domino's, Shanghai Garden
Lodg — S: Issaquah B&B

20 — **High Point Way, Issaquah**

22 — **82nd St, High Pt Way, to WA 203, Preston Fall City Rd, Preston**
Gas — N: Chevron, Shell◈
Food — N: Savannah's, Espresso Cafe, Subway
Other — N: **to Snoqualmie River RV Park & Campground▲**
S: **Blue Sky RV Park▲**

25 — **Snoqualmie Pkwy, Snoqualmie WA 18W, Auburn, Federal Way**

27 — **N Bend Way, Snoqualmie, to North Bend (EB)**

31 — **WA 202E, Bendigo Blvd, North Bend, Snoqualmie**
Gas — N: 76◈, Chevron, Shell◈
Food — N: Arby's, DQ, McDonald's, Taco Time
Lodg — N: North Bend Motel, Sunset Motel
Other — N: Safeway, Factory Stores at North Bend, **PL/Tinkham Campground▲**, **PL/Denny Creek Campground▲**, **WA State Hwy Patrol Post**

32 — **436th Ave SE, North Bend, Tanner**
Food — S: Gordy's Steak & BBQ Smokehouse

34 — **468th Ave SE, North Bend**
FStop — N: Edgewick Shell & Deli
TStop — N: Travel Center of America #176 (Scales)
Food — N: Ken's/TA TC, Subway/Edgewick Shell
Lodg — N: Edgewick Inn, Nor'west Motel & **RV Park▲**
TServ — N: TA/Tires, Cascade Diesel Truck & **RV**
Other — N: WiFi/CB/TA TC, LP/Edgewick Shell

38A — **Homestead Valley Rd, Olallie State Park (EB)**

38B — **Homestead Valley Rd, Fire Training Center (WB)**
Other — S: **Olallie State Park**

42 — **Tinkham Rd**

45 — **Bandera Rd**

47 — **Asahel Curtis Rd, North Bend, Asahel Curtis, Denny Creek**

52 — **WA 906 W, Summit Rd, Snoqualmie Summit Rec Area (EB)**

NOTE: **MM 53: Snoqualmie Summit Elev 3022'**

53 — **E Summit Rd, to WA 906, Snoqualmie Summit Rec Area**
Gas — S: Chevron
Food — S: Family Pancake House
Lodg — S: Best Western

54 — **WA 906, Hyak, Cle Elum**

(56) — **Parking Area (EB)**

62 — **Kachess Lake Rd, Cle Elum, Stampede Pass, Kachess Lake**
Other — N: to Lake Kachess
S: to Stampede Pass

63 — **Cabin Creek Rd**

70 — **Railroad St, Lake Easton State Park, Easton**
Gas — N: Shell◈
Food — N: Mtn High Hamburgers, Parkside Cafe
Other — N: **Silver Ridge Ranch Campground▲**

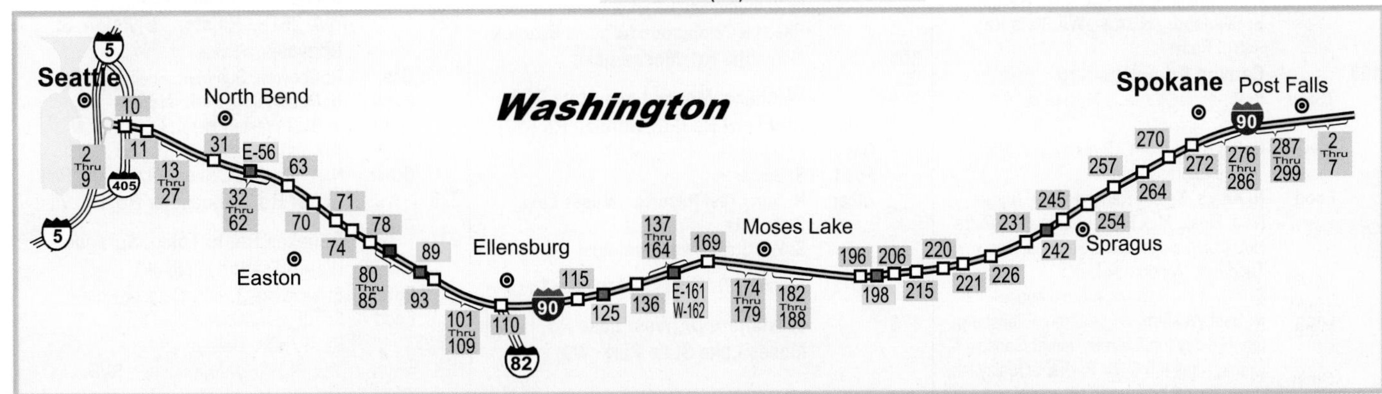

◈= **Regular Gas Stations with Diesel** ▲ = **RV Friendly Locations** ♥= **Pet Friendly Locations**
Red print shows large vehicle parking / access on site or nearby **Brown Print = Campgrounds / RV PARKS**

EXIT		WASHINGTON
	Other	S: Lake Easton Resort▲ , Lake Easton State Park/RVDump▲
71		**Railroad St, Easton**
	Gas	S: CB's Café & Grocery◈
74		**Nelson Siding Rd**
	Other	S: Sun Country Golf Resort & RV Park▲
78		**Golf Course Rd, Nelson**
(80)		**Weigh Station (Both dir)**
80		**Bullfrog Rd, to Roslyn**
84		**WA 903, 1st St W (EB), Cle Elum, Oakes Ave (WB)**
	Gas	N: 76, Chevron◈, Conoco, Shell◈
	Food	N: Burger King, Caboose Bar & Grill, DQ, El Caporal, Los Cabos, Mama Vallone's Steakhouse, Yum Yang Chinese
	Lodg	N: Best Western, Hummingbird Inn, Stewart Lodge, Timber Lodge Motel
	Med	N: + Cle Elum Urgent Care Center
	Other	N: ATMs, Auto Services, Safeway, Beverly Campground▲ , PL/Kachess Campground▲ S: Whispering Pines RV Center, Mountain River Trails Camping▲
85		**WA 970, to US 97N, Wenatchee, WA 903, I-90 Bus, Cle Elum**
	FStop	N: Willette's Shell Service, Storey Service
	Gas	N: Conoco
	Food	N: Rest/Willette's Shell, Cottage Café
	Lodg	N: Cascade Mountain Inn, Cle Elum Travelers Inn, Wind Blew Inn Motel
	Tires	N: Willette's Shell
	Other	N: LP/RVDump/Willette's Shell, Cle Elum Muni Airport✈, Trailer Corral RV Park▲ S: Eagle Valley Campground▲
(89)		**Cle Elum Rest Area (Both dir)** (RR, Ph, Pic, Vend, WiFi, RVDump)
93		**Elk Heights Rd**
101		**Thorp Hwy, Thorp**
106		**Cascade Way, I-90 Bus, Ellensburg, US 97N to Wenatchee**
	TStop	N: Love's Travel Stop #413 (Scales)
	Gas	N: 76, Chevron, Conoco◈, Texaco
	Food	N: Subway/Love's TS, Jack in the Box, DQ, Perkins S: Wild West Ranch
	Lodg	N: I-90 Inn Motel, Hampton Inn
	TWash	N: Cascade Truck & RV Wash Gibson Truck Wash
	Other	N: Laundry/WiFi/Love's TS, Bowers Field Airport✈, Central WA Univ, Canopy Country RV Center, Wild Goose Casino, US Post Office, to Icicle River RV Park▲ S: Ellensburg KOA▲ , WA State Hwy Patrol Post
109		**Canyon Rd, Ellensburg**
	TStop	S: Broadway/Flying J Travel Plaza/ Exxon (Scales)
	Gas	N: Big B Mini Mart, Chevron, Sun Mart, Toad's Express Mart◈
	Food	N: Arby's, Bar 14 Ranch House, Burger King, Fiesta Mex Rest. McDonald's, Pizza Hut, Quiznos, Skippers Seafood, Subway, Taco Bell, Windbreak Deli S: Saks/FJ TP, Buzz in Steakhouse
	Lodg	N: Best Western, Comfort Inn, Ellensburg Inn, Holiday Inn Express, Inn at Goose Creek, Nites Inn & RV Park▲ , Quality Inn, N: Super 8, Thunderbird Motel S: Best Inn, Days Inn,
	Med	N: + to Kittitas Valley Comm Hospital
	Other	N: ATMs, Bank, Auto Services, Cinema Grocery, Les Schwab Tire, Pharmacy, Radio Shack, RiteAid, Vet♥ S: Laundry/WiFi/LP/FJ TP, R & R RV Park▲ , to Riverview Campground▲
(110)		**I-82E, US 97S, to Yakima, Tri Cities**
115		**Badger Pocket Rd, Kittitas**
	FStop	N: Exit 115 Auto Truck Stop/Shell
	Food	N: FastFood/Ex 115 ATS
	Other	N: LP/Exit 115 ATS
(125)		**Ellensburg Rest Area (Both dir)** (RR, Phone, Picnic, WiFi)
136		**Huntzinger Rd, Vantage, Gingko State Park**
	Gas	N: Texaco◈
	Food	N: Golden Harvest, Ft Wanapum Inn
	Lodg	N: Vantage Riverstone Resort & RV Park ▲
	Other	N: Ginkgo State Park▲ S: Vantage Airport✈,
137		**WA 26E, to Othello, Pullman, WA State Univ, to WA 243, to Tri Cities** (Vista Viewpoints Ex #137E-Both dir)
	NOTE:	Frontage Rd Access Ex #143-174
143		**Silica Rd, Quincy**
	Other	N: to the Gorge Amphitheatre, Wild Horse Campground▲
149		**WA 281N, Quincy, Wenatchee, Royal Anne Ave, George**
	FStop	S: 300 Washington Way PacPride/George Scales(Scales)
	Gas	S: Exxon◈
	Food	S: Martha's Inn Café, Rest/George Scales
	Other	N: to Crescent Bar Resort, Marina & Campground▲ , Gorge Amphitheatre, U-Haul, Wild Horse Campground▲
151		**WA 281N, Ephrata, WA 283N, George, Quincy, Wenatchee**
	FStop	N: Midway Mini Mart/Shell
	Lodg	N: to Best Western, Travelodge
	Other	N: Shady Tree RV, to Stars & Stripes RV Park▲ , Oasis RV Park▲ & Golf, Ephrata Muni Airport✈
154		**Adams Rd, Quincy**
(161)		**Moses Lake Rest Area (Both dir)** (RR, Phone, Pic, WiFi, RVDump)
164		**Dodson Rd, Road C, Ephrata**
	Other	S: Sun Basin RV Park & Campground▲ to Potholes State Park▲ , 16mi Mar Don Resort & Campground▲ , Last Resort▲
169		**Hiawatha Rd, Moses Lake**
174		**Westlake, Moses Lake State Park Pritchard Rd (EB), Hansen Rd (WB)**
	Gas	S: Conoco◈
	Food	S: Burger Inn
	Other	N: Sun Crest Resort▲ , Moses Lake State Park S: WA State Hwy Patrol Post
	NOTE:	Frontage Rd Access Ex #174-143
175		**Westshore Dr, West Lake Rd, Moses Lake State Park (WB)**
176		**I-90 Bus, Lakeshore Dr, Moses Lake**
	Gas	N: Cenex, Exxon◈, Shell◈
	Food	N: Mex Rest, Perkins
	Lodg	N: Best Western♥, Heritage Suites♥, Interstate Inn, Microtel, Motel 6, Super 8♥ S: Lakeshore Resort Motel
	Other	N: Golf Course, Big Sun Resort▲ , Lakefront RV Park▲ , Desert Oasis RV Park▲
	NOTE:	Frontage Rd Access Ex #179-184
179		**WA 17N, Moses Lakes, WA 17S, to US 395S, Othello, Kennewick**
	TStop	N: Ernie's Truck Stop #9/Chevron (Scales)
	Gas	N: Conoco◈, Exxon, Shell◈
	Food	N: FastFood/Ernie's TS, Arby's, Burger King, Denny's, Shari's, Starbucks
	Lodg	N: Best Value Inn♥, Holiday Inn Express, Inn at Moses Lake, Shilo Inn, Travelodge
	Med	N: + Hospital
	Other	N: Laundry/Ernie's TS, Safeway, US Post Office, Pharmacy, TLC Mobile RV Repair, Sun Country RV, to Grant Co Fairgrounds, Grant Co Int'l Airport✈, Moses Lake Muni Airport✈, Cascade Campground▲ , to Sun Lake State Park, R&R RV Park▲ S: I-90 RV, Willows Trailer Village▲ , to 15mi: Sage Hills Golf Club & RV Resort▲ , 15mi Potholes State Park▲ , 14 mi Mar Don Resort & Campground▲ , Last Resort▲
182		**Road O, Moses Lake, to Wheeler**
184		**Road Q, Raugust Rd, to Wheeler**
	NOTE:	Frontage Rd Access Ex #184-179
188		**Rd U, Warden Rd, to Ruff, Warden**
196		**Deal Rd, Lind, Schrag**
	Other	N: to Lincoln Recreation & RV Park▲
(198)		**Rest Area (Both dir)** (RR, Phone, Picnic, WiFi, WB: RVDump, Weather)
206		**WA 21, to Odessa, Lind**
215		**Paha Packard Rd, Ritzville**
220		**W 1st Ave, Ritzville, US 395S, Kennewick, Pasco**
	FStop	N: Vista 24hr Fuel Stop, Jake's Exxon
	Food	N: Jake's Café, Blue Bike Café, Whispering Palms Rest
	Lodg	N: Best Value Inn♥, Top Hat Motel, West Side Motel
	Other	N: Laundry/Vista Astro QM, Auto Repair, Les Schwab Tires, Ritzville Muni Airport✈, WA State Hwy Patrol Post
221		**WA 261S, Ralston, Division St, Ritzville**
	Gas	N: Chevron, Sun Mart, Shell◈
	Food	N: McDonald's, Perkins, Zip's
	Lodg	N: Best Western♥, La Quinta Inn♥
	Med	N: + E Adams Rural Hospital
	Other	N: ATMs, Golf Course, Ritzville City Park
226		**Coker Rd, Schoessler Rd, Ritzville**
231		**Danekas Rd, to Tokio, Sprague Weigh Station (Both dir)**
	FStop	S: Templins Country Corner/Exxon◈
	Food	S: Templin's Corner Café
(242)		**Rest Area (Both dir)** (RR, Ph, Pic, Info, Weather, RVDump)

◈ = Regular Gas Stations with Diesel ▲ = RV Friendly Locations ♥ = Pet Friendly Locations

Red print shows large vehicle parking / access on site or nearby Brown Print = Campgrounds / RV PARKS

EXIT	WASHINGTON
245	**WA 23, to WA 231, Sprague, to Harrington, Edwall, St John**
Gas	**S:** Chevron◈
Food	**S:** Viking Drive In
Lodg	**S:** Purple Sage Motel♥, Sprague Motel & **RV Park▲**
Other	**S:** Grocery, US Post Office, **to Klink's Williams Lake Resort▲**, **appr 7mi: Four Seasons Campground▲**, **Sprague Lake Resort▲**
254	**Old State Hwy, Fishtrap Rd**
257	**WA 904E, to Tyler, Cheney, to East WA University**
264	**WA 902, Salnave Rd, Cheney, Medical Lake**
Other	**N:** to **Dan's Landing▲**, **Ruby's Resort on Silver Lake▲**, **Silver Lake Camp▲**, **West Medical Lake Resort▲**, **Mallard Bay Resort▲** **S:** to Eastern WA Univ, **10mi :Peaceful Pines Campground▲**
270	**WA 904W, Four Lakes, Cheney**
Gas	**S:** Exxon
Other	**N:** to 7mi: **Peaceful Pines RV Park▲** **S:** to appr 15mi: **Klinks Williams Lake Resort▲**
272	**WA 902W, Hayford Rd, Aero Rd, Spokane, to Medical Lake**
TStop	**S:** Petro Stopping Center #339 (Scales)
Gas	**N:** Shell◈
Food	**S:** IronSkillet/Subway/Starbucks/Petro SC
Lodg	**S:** Super 8
TServ	**S:** Petro SC/Tires, Freightliner
Other	**N:** to Fairchild AFB, **Overland Station RV Park▲** **S:** Laundry/BarbSh/WiFi/Petro SC, **Ponderosa Falls RV Resort▲**, **Yogi Bear's Jellystone Park▲**
276	**Grove Rd, Geiger Blvd, I-90 Bus**
TStop	**N:** Flying J Travel Plaza #106/Exxon (Scales)
Gas	**S:** Shell◈
Food	**N:** Saks/Subway/FJ TP, Denny's
Lodg	**N:** Airway Express Inn, Best Western
Other	**N:** WiFi/**LP**/FJ TP, Spokane Int'l Airport✈, **WA State Hwy Patrol Post**
277	**US 2W, Garden Springs Rd, to I-90 Bus, Spokane Int'l Airport (WB)**
Lodg	**N:** Cedar Village Motel, Days Inn, Hampton Inn, Holiday Inn, Motel 6♥, Ranch Motel, Travelodge
277A	**Abbott Rd, Garden Springs Rd, to US 90 Bus, Spokane Int'l Airport, US 2W (EB)**
277B	**US 2W, Wenatchee, Spokane Int'l Airport, to Fairchild AFB, Grand Coulee Dam (EB)**
279	**US 195S, to Pullman, Colfax, WA State University**
280	**Maple St, Walnut St, Downtown Spokane (EB)**
Food	**S:** Burger King, IHOP, Taco Bell
280A	**Maple St, Walnut St, Downtown (WB)**
Gas	**N:** Cenex, Conoco◈, Shell◈
Food	**N:** Perkins, Subway
Lodg	**N:** Tiki Lodge
Med	**S:** + Deaconess Medical Center

EXIT	WASHINGTON
Other	**N:** Grocery, NAPA
280B	**Howard St, Wall St, Lincoln St, 3rd Ave, Downtown (WB)**
Gas	**N:** Chevron, Conoco◈, Shell
Food	**N:** Burger King, Carl's Jr, Deli, IHOP, Molly's Family Rest, Jack in the Box, Spaghetti Factory, Taco Bell
Lodg	**N:** Trade Winds Motel, Davenport Hotel, Hotel Lusso, Montvale Hotel, Ramada, Rodeway Inn
Other	**N:** ATMs, CarWash, Grocery
281	**US 2E, US 395N, Division St, Downtown, Newport, Colville**
Gas	**N:** Citgo, Shell, Tesoro◈
Food	**N:** Arby's, Dick's Hamburgers, McDonald's, Jack in the Box, Perkins, Pizza Hut, Starbucks, Subway, Taco Time, Waffles Café
Lodg	**N:** Best Value Inn, Econo Lodge, Howard Johnson **S:** Quality Inn, Madison Inn
Med	**S:** + Sacred Heart Medical Center
Other	**N:** Amtrak, Divine's Auto Center & Towing, Firestone, Les Schwab Tire, U-Haul
282	**2nd Ave, Hamilton St (EB)**
Gas	**N:** Shell◈
Food	**N:** Something Else Deli, Shogun
Lodg	**N:** Budget Saver Motel, Shilo Inn
282A	**Hamilton St (WB)**
Other	**N:** to Wa State Univ/Spokane, Gonzaga Univ
282B	**2nd Ave, Trent Ave (WB)**
Other	**N:** Office Depot, Ray's Truck & **MH** Service
283A	**Altamont St**
Gas	**N:** Circle K/76
283B	**Thor St, Freya St**
Gas	**N:** Chevron, Conoco◈, Tesoro◈ **S:** Citgo, Shell
Food	**N:** Burger Basket, CJ's Pizza, Peking Garden, McDonald's, Calgary Steak House, Little Caesars Pizza
Lodg	**N:** Park Lane Motel & **RV Park▲**
285	**Sprague Ave, Spokane**
Gas	**N:** Shell, Costco **S:** Exxon
Food	**N:** Denny's, IHOP, Wendy's **S:** Mandarin House, Puerto Vallarta, Starbucks, Subway, Taco Bell, Zip's
Lodg	**N:** Maple Tree Motel & **RV Park▲**
Other	**N:** Costco, Home Depot, Lowe's, Radio Shack **S:** Auto Dealers, Auto Services, Tires
286	**Broadway Ave, Spokane**
TStop	**N:** Broadway/Flying J Travel Plaza #511308/Conoco (Scales)
Gas	**S:** 7-11, Tesoro
Food	**N:** Saks/FJ TP, Zip's
Lodg	**N:** Best Inn, Comfort Inn
TServ	**N:** FJ TP/Tires, International Trucks, Inland Truck Center, Les Schwab Tires, Northland Peterbilt, Western States CAT, Spokane Diesel, White/Volvo/GMC, Titan Truck, Goodyear
Other	**N:** WiFi/**RVDump/LP**/FJ TP **S: Airstream of Spokane, Johnson RV Repair**
287	**Argonne Rd, Mullan Rd, Spokane Valley, to Millwood**
Gas	**N:** Exxon, Holiday◈, Albertson's **S:** Chevron, Exxon, 76◈
Food	**N:** Burger King, Denny's, Dominos Pizza, Jack in the Box, Longhorn BBQ, McDonald,

EXIT	WASHINGTON
Food	**N:** Panda Express, Starbucks, Subway, Wendy's **S:** Casa De Oro, Godfather's Pizza, Little Caesar's, Perkins, Starbucks, Sub Shop
Lodg	**N:** Motel 6♥, Super 8 **S:** Holiday Inn Express, Quality Inn, Maple Tree Motel & **RV Park▲**, Park Lane Motel & **RV Park▲**
Other	**N:** Albertson's, Auto Services, Hardware Store, Walgreen's, **RV Rentals** **S:** RiteAid, Safeway/Pharmacy, **Trailers Inn RV Park▲**
289	**WA 27, Pines Rd, Opportunity**
FStop	**S:** Divine's Shell
Gas	**N:** 7-11
Food	**N:** Matthew's Rest **S:** Applebee's, Brown Bag, Denny's, Jack in the Box, Jimmy Chang's, Quiznos
Lodg	**S:** Best Western
Med	**S:** + Valley Hospital & Medical Center
Other	**S: RVDump**/Divine's Shell, Walgreen's
291A	**Evergreen Rd**
Gas	**S:** Shell
Food	**N:** Arby's, Azteca, Black Angus, Boston's Gourmet Pizza, Flaming Wok, Ivar's Seafood's Bar, IHOP, McDonald's, Outback Steakhouse, TGI Friday, Wendy's
Lodge	**N:** Oxford Suites
Other	**N:** ATMs, Best Buy, Tires, Spokane Valley Mall, Sportsman's Warehouse
291B	**Sullivan Rd (EB), Indiana Ave (WB), Veradale**
Gas	**N:** Chevron, Shell **S:** 76, Shell◈, Tesoro
Food	**N:** Arby's, McDonald's, Tony Roma, Red Robin **S:** DQ, Jack in the Box, KFC, McDonald's, Mongolian BBQ, Panda Express, Pizza Hut, Quiznos, Shari's Rest, Starbucks, Subway, Taco Bell, Wendy's
Lodg	**N:** La Quinta Inn♥, Residence Inn **S:** Comfort Inn
Other	**N:** Auto Services, Barnes & Noble, Best Buy, Staples, Tires, **Mobil RV Repair** **S:** ATMs, Auto Services, Dollar Tree, Fred Meyer, Grocery, PetSmart♥, Target, Walgreen's, **Walmart sc**
293	**Barker Rd, Green Acres, Spokane**
Gas	**N:** Conoco◈ **S:** Exxon◈, Shell◈
Food	**N:** Wendy's **S:** Subway/Exxon
Lodg	**N:** Alpine Motel & **RV Park▲**
Other	**N: Spokane KOA▲** **S: N Country RV & Boat**
294	**Appleway Ave, I-90 Bus, Opportunity (WB)**
296	**Appleway Ave Liberty Lake Rd, Liberty Lakes, Otis Orchards**
Gas	**N:** Shell◈ **S:** Conoco, Chevron, Safeway
Food	**S:** Burger King, McDonald's, Pizza Hut, Starbucks, Subway, Taco Bell
Lodg	**N:** Best Western **S:** Comfort Inn
Other	**N:** Auto Dealers **S:** Albertson's, Home Depot, Safeway, Tires, **RNR RV Center**
299	**Spokane Bridge Rd** **N: Port of Entry/Weigh Station (WB)**

◈= Regular Gas Stations with Diesel ▲ = RV Friendly Locations ♥= Pet Friendly Locations
Red print shows large vehicle parking / access on site or nearby **Brown Print = Campgrounds / RV PARKS**

EXIT		WA / ID
		WA Welcome Center (WB) **N: (RR, Phones, Picnic, Info)**
	Gas	**N:** Shell, Gas n Go

PACIFIC TIME ZONE

NOTE: MM 300: Idaho State Line

WASHINGTON

IDAHO

2 Pleasant View Rd, Post Falls, McGuire
- TStop — **N:** Flying J Travel Plaza #5005/Conoco (Scales)
- Gas — **N:** Shell; **S:** Exxon◊
- Food — **N:** Thad's/FJ TP, Burger King, McDonald's, Toro Veijo III; **S:** Cabin Rest, Jack in the Box, Zip's
- Lodg — **N:** Howard Johnson Express; **S:** Riverbend Inn, Sleep Inn
- TWash — **N:** Splash N Dash Truck & **RV** Wash
- TServ — **N:** Post Falls Performance
- Other — **N:** Laundry/WiFi/**RVDump/LP**/FJ TP, Cabela's, U-Haul, **Suntree RV Park/ RVDump▲**; **S:** Post Falls Outlet Mall, Prime Outlet Mall, Greyhound Racetrack

5 I-90 Bus, Spokane St, Post Falls
- Gas — **N:** Shell◊, GasMart, 76◊; **S:** Pacific Pride◊, Handy Mart
- Food — **N:** Golden Dragon, Hunters Steakhouse, Rob's Seafood & Burgers, Whitehouse Grill; **S:** Milltown Grill Rest
- Lodg — **S:** Red Lion Hotel♥
- Other — **N:** Perfection Tire & Auto Repair/Les Schwab Tires, **Seltice RV**; **S: Pop's RV Service & Repair**

6 I-90 Bus, Seltice Way (WB ex, EB entr)
- Gas — **N:** 7-11, HiCo Country Store
- Food — **N:** Caruso's Deli, Del Taco, La Cabana Mexican, Paul Bunyan Rest, Pizza Hut; **S:** Arby's, Little Caesar's Pizza
- Med — **N: + North ID Medical Care Center, + After Hours Urgent Care Clinic, + NW Specialty Hospital**
- Other — **N:** ATMs, Auto Zone, Banks, Grocery, Vet♥, Walgreen's; **S:** Grocery, Tires, Vet♥, **McCall RV Resort▲**

7 ID 41N, Rathdrum, Spirit Lake
- Gas — **N:** Exxon◊, Murphy; **S:** Chevron
- Food — **N:** La Cocina, Pizza Factory, Starbucks, Subway, Wendy's; **S:** Capone's Pub & Grill, Denny's, Hot Rod Café, KFC, McDonald's, Rancho Veijo, Subway, Taco Bell
- Lodg — **S:** Comfort Inn
- TServ — **S:** Northern Diesel, Ross Point Truck Repair, **Boat & RV Werkes**
- Other — **N:** Dollar Tree, Radio Shack, **Walmart sc, Coeur d'Alene RV Resort/RVDump▲**; **S:** Auto Services, U-Haul, **McCall RV Resort▲**

(8) ID Welcome Center (EB)
Rest Area (WB)
(RR, Phone, Picnic, Vend, Info)

(9) Weigh Station (EB)

11 Northwest Blvd, Coeur d'Alene
- Gas — **N:** Texaco◊; **S:** Exxon, Quik Stop◊
- Food — **N:** Top of China Buffet II; **S:** Deli, Joey's Smokin BBQ, Outback Steakhouse, Subway, Sunshine Trader
- Lodg — **S:** Days Inn♥, Garden Motel, Holiday Inn Express, Blvd Motel **& RV Park/RVDump▲**
- Other — **N:** Public Golf Course, Lowe's; **S: River Walk RV Park▲, to Blackwell Island RV Park▲**, North ID College, **to appr 25mi** Coeur d'Alene Casino & Hotel

12 US 95, N Lincoln Way, Lewiston, Sandpoint, Moscow
- Gas — **N:** Chevron, Exxon◊, Holiday◊, Shell◊, Costco, Safeway
- Food — **N:** Applebee's, Arby's, Burger King, Chili's, Domino's Pizza, Dragon House Rest, Elmer's Rest, JB's Rest, McDonald's, Perkins, Pizza Hut, Red Lobster, Taco Bell; **S:** Jack in the Box, Qdoba Mex Grill, Quiznos, Sub Shop, Shari's
- Lodg — **N:** Best Western, Guest House Inn, La Quinta Inn♥, Motel 6♥, Shilo Inn, Super 8♥
- Med — **N + Idaho Immediate Care Center**; **S: + Kootenai Medical Center, + After Hours Urgent Care**
- Other — **N: RVDump**/Holiday, ATMs, Banks, Auto Services, Costco, Dollar Tree, Enterprise RAC, Fred Meyer, Grocery, Office Depot, Home Depot, Les Schwab Tires, Safeway, U-Haul, Walgreen's, Kootenai Co Fairgrounds, Coeur d'Alene Airport✈, **to 15mi** Silverwood Theme Park/**RVPark▲**, **Bambi RV Park/RVDump▲, Magic Carpet RV Center, Tamarack RV Park▲, To Alpine Country Store & RV Park▲**; **S:** Albertson's, RiteAid, ShopKO, Staples, **Blackwell Island RV Park▲**, Wild Waters Water Park

13 4th St, 3rd St, to Government Way, Coeur d'Alene
- Gas — **N:** Conoco◊; **S:** Exxon◊
- Food — **N:** Carl's Jr, DQ, Denny's, IHOP, KFC, Little Caesar's Pizza, Taco John's, Wendy's; **S:** Subway
- Lodg — **N:** Comfort Inn, Fairfield Inn
- Other — **N:** NAPA, Radio Shack, Tire, Auto Services **Ericksons RV Sales/Service/Rentals**; **S:** Wild Waters Water Park

14 15th St, Coeur d'Alene
- Other — **N: Coeur d'Alene Pkwy State Park**

15 I-90 Bus, 23rd St, Sherman Ave
- TStop — **S:** Tesoro to Go
- Gas — **S:** Cenex◊
- Food — **S:** FastFood/Teroso, Down the Street, Moon Rest, Café, Zip's
- Lodg — **S:** Cedar Motel **& RV Park/RVDump▲**, Budget Saver Motel, El Rancho Motel♥, Flamingo Motel, Holiday Motel, Japan House Suites, La Quinta Inn♥, Resort City Inn, Sandman Motel, State Motel
- Other — **S:** Laundry/**RVDump/LP**/Tesoro, NAPA

17 Mullan Trail Rd

22 ID 97S, Harrison, to St Maries
- Food — **N:** Wolf Lodge Steakhouse
- Lodg — **N:** Wolf Lodge Inn
- Other — **S: Wolf Lodge RV Campground▲, Coeur d'Alene KOA/RVDump▲, appr 3mi PL/Beauty Creek Campground▲ appr 7mi Squaw Bay Resort & Marina/ RVDump▲, to Lake Coeur d'Alene Rec Area**

(24) ChainUp (EB) / Removal Area (WB)

28 Cedar Creek Rd, 4th of July Pass Rec Area (Turn off Lanes, Both dir)
NOTE: Elev 3069'
- Other — Ski & Snowmobile Area

(32) Weigh Station / ChainUp Area (WB)

34 ID 3S, Cataldo, Rose Lake, St Maries
- FStop — **S:** Junction Quick Stop/Conoco
- Gas — **S:** Rose Lake General Store◊
- Food — **S:** Rose Lake Rest, Country Chef Café

39 Old Mission State Park
- Other — **S: Visitor Center / RR / Picnic**

40 Latour Creek Rd, Cataldo
- Other — **S: Kahnderosa RV Campground/ RVDump▲**

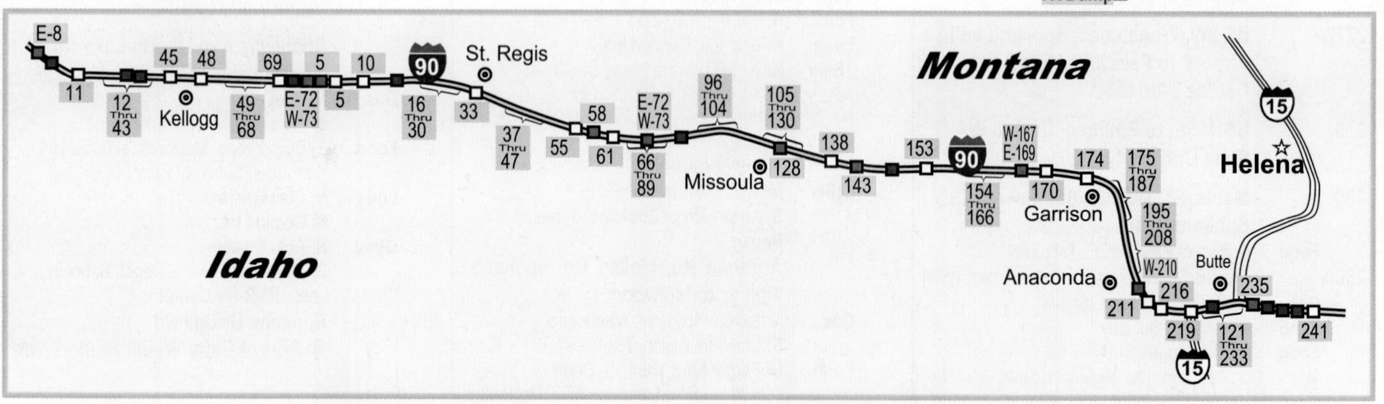

◊= Regular Gas Stations with Diesel ▲ = RV Friendly Locations ♥= Pet Friendly Locations
Red print shows large vehicle parking / access on site or nearby Brown Print = Campgrounds / RV PARKS

EXIT		IDAHO
43		**Coeur d'Alene River Rd, Kingston**
	Gas	**S:** Kingston Kwik Stop/Exxon
	Other	**N: Country Lane RV Resort▲**
		S: RVDump/Exxon, **to appr 12mi: BLM/ Bumblebee Campground▲**
45		**Division St, Pinehurst**
	FStop	**S:** Carousel Gas & Tire
	Gas	**S:** Chevron◈, Conoco◈
	Other	**S: By the Way RV Park▲ , Pinehurst RV**
48		**Airport Rd, Murray, Smelterville**
	TStop	**N:** Silver Valley Car & Truck Stop
	Food	**N:** Rest/Silver Valley CTS
	Lodg	**N:** Motel/Silver Valley CTS
	Other	**N:** RVDump/LP/Silver Valley CTS, Shoshone Co Airport✈
49		**I-90 Bus, Bunker Ave, Kellogg**
	Gas	**N:** Conoco◈
	Food	**N:** McDonald's, Subway, Sam's D/I
		S: Gondola Café/Silver Mountain
	Lodg	**N:** Silverhorn Motor Inn, Silver Ridge Mountain Lodge
		S: Baymont Inn
	Med	**N: + Shoshone Medical Center**
	Other	**N:** Silver Mountain Resort
		S: to New St City/RVDump
50		**Hill St, Kellogg (EB)**
	Gas	**S:** Conoco
	Lodg	**N:** Trail Motel
	Other	**S: Silver Mountain Resort/Rec Area▲**
51		**Division St, Kellogg, Wardner**
	Gas	**N:** Conoco◈
	Med	**N: + Hospital**
	Other	**N:** Auto Dealers
		S: Kellogg RV Center
54		**Big Creek Rd, Elk Creek, Murray**
	Other	**N:** Miners Memorial, Crystal Gold Mine
57		**I-90 Bus, 3rd St, Wallace, Osburn**
	Gas	**S:** Shell◈
	Other	**S: Blue Anchor RV Park▲**
60		**Markwell Ave, Wallace, Silverton**
	Lodg	**S:** Molly B'Damm Motel
61		**I-90 Bus, Front St, Wallace**
	Gas	**S:** Conoco◈, Exxon
	Food	**S:** Albi's Steakhouse, Brooks Rest, Deb's Café, Pizza Factory, Wallace Café, Silver Lantern D/I
	Lodg	**S:** Wallace Inn, Brooks Hotel, Stardust Hotel, Ryan Hotel
62		**I-90 Bus, ID 4, Wallace, Burke**
	Gas	**S:** Exxon
	Food	**S:** Jameson Rest/Saloon/Inn
	Med	**S: + Hospital**
64		**Golconda**
65		**Grouse Creek Rd**
66		**Gold Creek**
67		**Lower Mill St**
68		**I-90 Bus, River St, Mullan (EB)**
	Gas	**N:** Exxon◈
	Food	**N:** Mullan Cafe
69		**I-90 Bus, Atlas Rd, Mullan**
(70)		**RunAWay Truck Ramp (WB)**
(71)		**RunAWay Truck Ramp (WB)**
(72)		**Scenic Area (EB)**

Personal Notes

EXIT		ID / MT
(73)		**Scenic Area (WB)**
	NOTE:	**EB: TRUCK INFO**
		Lookout Pass: Elev 4680'

PACIFIC / MOUNTAIN TIME ZONE

NOTE: **MM 73.88: Montana State Line**

⬆ IDAHO
⬇ MONTANA

MOUNTAIN TIME ZONE

(0)		**Lookout Pass** NOTE: **Elev 4680**
	Other	Lookout Pass Ski & Recreation Area Rest/**RVPark▲** , Tourist Info, Ski Area
(5)		**Lookout Pass Rest Area (Both dir) (RR, Picnic, ChainUp / Remove)**
5		**Taft Area, Saltese**
10		**Saltese Rd, Saltese, St Regis**
	Lodg	**N:** Mangold Gen'l Store & Motel
(15)		**Weigh Station (Both dir, Left Exit)**
16		**Haugan Rd, Haugan, St Regis**
	FStop	**N:** Lincoln's Silver Dollar/Exxon
	Food	**N:** Rest/Silver Dollar Bar
	Lodg	**N:** Motel/Silver Dollar & **RV Park▲**
	Other	**N:** Casino/Silver Dollar
18		**Thompson De Borgia Rd, De Borgia, Henderson**
	Lodg	**N:** Pinecrest Motel, Black Diamond Guest Camp Ranch♥ & **Resort▲**

EXIT		MONTANA
22		**Henderson Rd, St Regis**
	Other	**S: to appr 5mi: BLM/Cabin City Campground▲**
25		**Drexel Rd, St Regis**
26		**Ward Creek Rd (EB only)**
29		**Fishing Access (WB ex & reacc)**
30		**Two Mile Rd, St Regis**
33		**MT 135, Old US 10, St Regis**
	FStop	**N:** St Regis Travel Center/Conoco
	Gas	**N:** Exxon, SInclair
	Food	**N:** Rest/St Regis TC, Frosty Drive In, OK Café & Casino
	Lodg	**N:** Little River Motel, Super 8♥
	Other	**N: Campground St Regis/RVDump▲ , St Regis Riding Stables Campground▲ Nugget RV Resort▲**
37		**Sloway Rd, Sloway Area**
43		**Southside Rd, Dry Creek Rd, Superior**
47		**River St, 4th Ave, to Diamond Rd, MT 257, Superior**
	TStop	**S:** Town Pump #3800/Pilot #911/Exxon
	Gas	**N:** Conoco◈
	Food	**N:** Café, Rock 'n Rodeo Bar & Grill
		S: FastFood/Town Pump
	Lodg	**N:** Big Sky Motel, Hilltop Motel
	Med	**N: + Mineral Community Hospital**
	Other	**N:** Grocery, Pharmacy
		S: Casino/Laundry/TownPump
55		**Lozeau Rd, Lozeau, Superior**
(58)		**Quartz Flats Rest Area (Both dir) (RR, Phone, Picnic)**
61		**Tarkio Rd, Alberton**
66		**Fish Creek Rd, Albertson**
70		**Old Hwy 10, Alberton, Cyr (WB exit, EB reaccess)**
(72)		**Parking Area (EB)**
(73)		**Parking Area (WB)**
75		**MT 507, Railroad St, Alberton**
	Lodg	**S:** Ghost Rail Inn B&B, Rivers Edge Resort/ Motel/Rest/Casino/**RV Park & Campground**/RVDump▲
77		**CR 507, Petty Creek Rd, Alberton (Acc Ex #75 W on Fred Thompson Rd)**
82		**Nine Mile Rd, Huson**
85		**Frontage Rd, Huson Rd, Huson**
	Other	**S:** Larry's Six Mile Casino & Cafe
89		**MT 263, Frenchtown, Huson**
	Gas	**S:** Conoco◈
	Food	**S:** Alcan Bar & Café, Coffee Cup Rest, Eugene's Pizza, King Ranch Rest
	Other	**S:** Axmen Propane
(93)		**Inspection Station (Both dir)**
96		**US 93N, I-90 Bus, MT 200W, Missoula, Kalispell**
	TStop	**N:** PacPride/Muralt's AmBest Travel Plaza/ Conoco (Scales)
		S: Crossroads Travel Center/Sinclair
	Food	**N:** Muralts Cafe/Muralt's TP
		S: Rest/Crossroads TC

EXIT		MONTANA
	Lodg	N: DaysInn♥/Muralt's TP
		S: Redwood Lodge
	TWash	N: Muralt's TP
	TServ	N: Muralt's TP/Tires, Freightliner, Ford, GMC, Kenworth, Peterbilt, Volvo, Wabash, Utility & Thermo King, NW Truck & Trailer
		S: Transport Equipment, Missoula Truck & Auto Body
	Other	N: Laundry/BarbSh/WiFi/RVSvc/RVDump/LP/Muralts TP, Wye West Casino/Muralt's TP, Yogi Bear's Jellystone Park Camp Resort/RVDump▲, Jim & Mary's RV Park/RVDump▲, Outpost Campground /RVDump▲, to approx 98 miles EdgeWater RV Resort and Motel ▲
		S: Laundry/WiFi/RVDump/LP/Crossroads TC, Missoula RV Repair, U-Haul, to Missoula Int'l Airport✈
99		**Airway Blvd, Broadway St, Missoula (Access to Ex #101 Serv)**
	Gas	S: Mobil◈
	Lodg	S: Wingate Inn
	TServ	S: Interstate Power Systems
	Other	S: Montana Harley Davidson, Missoula Int'l Airport✈
101		**US 93, Grant Creek Rd, Reserve St, Missoula**
	FStop	S: Harvest States Cenex
	TStop	S: Deano's Travel Plaza/Exxon
	Gas	N: Conoco◈
		S: Conoco
	Food	N: Cracker Barrel, Mac Kenzie River Pizza, Starbucks
		S: Rest/Deano's TP, 4 B's, Arby's, Fiesta En Jalisco, IHOP, Kadena's, McDonald's, Montana Club, Johnny Carino's, Java Junction, Quiznos, Taco Time
	Lodg	N: Best Western♥, C'Mon Inn
		S: America's Best Inn, Comfort Inn, Courtyard, Hampton Inn, Hilton Garden Inn, Microtel, Ruby's Inn, Super 8
	TServ	S: CAT, Cummins NW, Western Truck
	Med	S: + Community Medical Center
	Other	S: RVDump/Harvest St Cenex, RVDump/Casino/Deano's TP, Albertson's, Auto Dealers, Auto Services, ATM's, Banks, Barnes & Noble, Best Buy, Costco, Firestone, Home Depot, Les Schwab Tires, PetSmart♥, REI, Staples, Target, Tire-Rama, Walgreen's, Walmart sc, to Southgate Mall, Bob Wards, Golf Courses, Missoula KOA/RVDump▲, Bretz RV & Marine/RVDump, Gull Boats & RV, Rangitsch Bros RV, Silver Creek Casino, Jokers Wild Casino, Lucky Lil's Casino, Casinos, to appr 12mi Lolo Hot Springs RV Park▲
104		**US 93S, Orange St, to Hamilton**
	Gas	S: Conoco◈, Sinclair
	Food	S: Depot, Double Front Café, Pagoda Chinese, Starbucks, Subway, Taco John's
	Lodg	S: Days Inn, Holiday Inn, Inn on Broadway♥, Mountain Valley Inn, Orange St Inn, Red Lion Inn
	Med	S: + St Patrick Hospital
	Other	S: FedEx Office, Greyhound, Pharmacy, Safeway, Tire-Rama, UPS Store, Whitefish KOA▲
105		**I-90 Bus, US 12, Van Buren St, Greenough Dr, Missoula**
	Gas	S: Conoco◈, Exxon, Pacific Pride◈, Sinclair◈

Personal Notes

EXIT		MONTANA
	Food	S: Burger King, Finnegan's Family Rest, Little Caesars Pizza, McDonald's, Pizza Hut, Subway, Taco Bell
	Lodg	S: Campus Inn, Creekside Inn♥, DoubleTree Hotel, Family Inn, Holiday Inn Express, Ponderosa Lodge♥, Thunderbird Motel
	Other	S: ATMs, Albertson's, Auto Services, PetSmart♥, Pharmacy, Univ of MT
107		**MT 200, Broadway St, E Missoula (Access to Ex #105 via S)**
	TStop	N: Ole's Truck Stop/Conoco
	Gas	N: Sinclair
	Food	N: Rest/Ole's TS
	Lodg	N: Aspen Motel
109		**MT 200E, Milltown, to Bonner, Great Falls**
	TStop	N: Town Pump #8500/Pilot #905/Exxon (Scales)
	Food	N: Arby's/Subway/TownPump
	TServ	N: Boss Truck Shop
	Other	N: Laundry/BarbSh/Casino/WiFi/LP/TownPump
113		**Turah Rd, Turah**
	Other	S: Turah RV Park/RVDump▲
120		**MT 210, Mullan Rd, Clinton**
126		**Rock Creek Rd, Clinton, Rock Creek Rec Area**
	Gas	S: Rock Creek Lodge
	Food	S: Rock Creek Lodge, Pioneer Rest/Ekstroms Stage Station

EXIT		MONTANA
	Lodg	S: Rock Creek Lodge, to 4mi Elkhorn Guest Ranch
	Other	S: Ekstroms Stage Station Campground/RVDump▲, Rock Creek Lodge RV/RVDump, to 12 mi PL/Grizzly Campground▲, appr 18 mi PL/Harry's Flat Campground▲, 15 mi PL/Dalles Campground▲
(128)		Parking Area (Both dir)
130		**Beavertail Rd, Clinton**
	Other	S: Beavertail Hill State Park▲
138		**Drummond Frontage Rd, Clinton, Bearmouth Area**
	Other	N: Chalet Bearmouth Motel/Restaurant/RV Park & Campground/RVDump▲
(143)		Bearmouth Rest Area (Both dir) (RR, Phone, Picnic)
(151)		Weigh Station (Both dir)
153		**MT 1, US 10A, Frontage Rd, Drummond, to Philipsburg (EB exit, WB reaccess) (Acc to Ex #154)**
	Other	N: to appr 6 mi Good Time Camping & RV Park▲
		S: to appr 25mi The Inn at Philipsburg/Motel/RV Park & Campground▲
154		**MT 271, Front St, Drummond, Philipsburg (WB ex, EB reaccess)**
	Gas	S: Conoco◈, Sinclair
	Food	S: Wagon Wheel Cafe
	Lodg	S: Sky Motel, Wagon Wheel Motel
162		**Jens Rd, Gold Creek**
166		**Gold Creek Rd, Gold Creek**
	Other	S: to Camp Mak-A-Dream
(167)		Gold Creek Rest Area (WB) (RR, Phone, Picnic)
(169)		Gold Creek Rest Area (EB) (RR, Phone, Picnic)
170		**Phosphate Rd, Gold Creek**
174		**US 12E, Garrison, Helena (EB)**
175		**US 12E, Garrison, Helena (WB)**
	Other	N: to Riverfront RV Park/RVDump▲
179		**Beck Hill Rd, Garrison**
184		**I-90 Bus, Boulder Rd, Deer Lodge**
	FStop	S: Town Pump #9150/Exxon
	TStop	S: I-90 Auto Truck Plaza/Conoco
	Gas	S: Cenex◈
	Food	S: Rest/I-90 ATP, 4 B's Rest, Broken Arrow Casino & Steakhouse, Coffee House, McDonald's, Outlaw Café, Scharf's Family Rest
	Lodg	S: Super 8♥, Scharf's Motor Inn, Western Big Sky Inn
	Other	N: Deer Lodge KOA▲
		S: Casino/TownPump, Casino/RVDump/I-90 ATP, Indian Creek Campground/RVDump▲, Auto Repairs, Les Scwab Tires, IGA, Safeway
187		**I-80 Bus, Main St, Deer Lodge (Access to Ex #184 Serv)**
	Other	N: Deer Lodge KOA/RVDump▲
		S: to Deer Lodge City & Co Airport✈
195		**Racetrack Rd, Deer Lodge**
197		**MT 273, Galen Rd, Anaconda**

◈= Regular Gas Stations with Diesel ▲ = RV Friendly Locations ♥= Pet Friendly Locations
Red print shows large vehicle parking / access on site or nearby Brown Print = Campgrounds / RV PARKS

EXIT	MONTANA
201	**MT 48, Anaconda, Warm Springs**
Other	S: to Anaconda Airport✈, Big Sky RV Park & Campground▲, Willow Springs RV Park & Campground▲
208	**MT 1, Anaconda** (All Serv 3-5 mi S in Anaconda)
Med	S: + Hospital
(210)	Parking Area (WB)
211	**Fairmont Rd, to MT 441, Butte, Gregson, Fairmont, Hot Springs**
Other	S: to appr 2.5 mi Fairmont RV Park▲, Fairmont Hot Springs Resort & Golf Course
216	**Ramsey Rd, Nissler Rd, Butte**
NOTE:	I-90 below runs with I-15 for appr 8 mi. Exit #'s follow I-15.
(219/ 121)	**Jct I-15S, to Dillon, Idaho Falls Jct I-90W to Missoula, I-15S to Idaho Falls, I-15N/I-90E to Butte**
122	**MT 276, Butte, Rocker** N: Weigh Station (Both dir)
TStop	E: Flying J Travel Plaza #5130 (Scales) W: Town Pump Travel Plaza #5600/ Pilot #908/Conoco
Food	E: Cookery/Arby's/FJ TP W: Arby's/Subway/McDonald's/Town Pump TP
Lodg	E: Rocker Inn W: Motel 6♥
TServ	E: Rocker Repair
Other	E: Casino/Laundry/WiFi/RVDump/LP/ FJ TP W: Laundry/Casino/TownPump TP
(124)	**Jct I-115, Butte City Center, Harrison Ave, Montana St (NB)**
126	**Montana St, Butte**
Gas	E: Thriftway, Town Pump◈ W: Cenex, Kum & Go
Food	W: Jokers Wild Casino & Rest
Lodg	W: Budget Motel, Eddy's Motel
Med	W: + St James Healthcare
Other	W: Butte KOA/RVDump▲, Grocery
127B	**I-15 Bus N, Harrison Ave, Butte (NB)**
127A	**I-15 Bus S, Harrison Ave, Butte (NB)**
127	**I-15 Bus, Harrison Ave, Butte (SB)**
Gas	E: Conoco, Exxon, Sinclair, Town Pump W: Conoco, Town Pump
Food	E: 4 B's Rest, Arbys, Burger King, DQ, Godfather's, KFC, McDonald's, Perkins, Taco Bell, Wendy's W: Rest/Red Lion Hotel, Denny's, Hanging Five Family Rest, Papa John's Pizza, Papa Murphy's, Quiznos
Lodg	E: Best Western, Hampton Inn, Super 8 W: Comfort Inn, Days Inn, Holiday Inn Express, Red Lion Hotel
Other	E: Casinos, Auto Dealers, Grocery, Kmart, Walmart sc, Our Lady of the Rockies, Butte Plaza Mall, Bert Mooney Airport✈, Rocky Mtn RV Sales & Srv, Al's RV Center W: RVDump/Town Pump, Casino, Grocery, Hospital♥, NAPA, Animal
(129/ 227)	**Jct I-90E to Billings, Jct I-15S/I-90W to Butte, N-Helena**
NOTE:	I-90 above runs with I-15 for appr 8 mi. Exit #'s follow I-15.

Personal Notes

EXIT	MONTANA
(230)	ChainUp / Removal Area (Both dir)
233	**Homestake, Continental Divide**
(235)	Parking Area (Both dir)
(237)	Pull-Off (EB)
(238.5)	RunAWay Truck Ramp (EB)
(240.5)	ChainUp / Removal Area (Both dir)
241	**Pipestone Rd, Whitehall**
Other	S: Pipestone RV Park/RVDump▲
249	**MT 55, MT 69, Whitehall**
TStop	S: Town Pump Travel Plaza #8945/Exxon
Food	S: CountrySkillet/Subway/Lucky Lil's Casino/TownPump TP
Lodg	S: Super 8
Other	S: Laundry/LP/TownPump TP, Whitetail Creek RV Park▲
256	**MT 69, MT 2, MT 359, Whitehall, Cardwell, Boulder**
Gas	S: Corner Store/Conoco
Other	S: RVDump/Conoco, to Lewis & Clark Caverns State Park/RVDump▲, to Yellowstone Nat'l Park
267	**Milligan Canyon Rd, Cardwell**
274	**US 287, Three Forks, Helena, Ennis**
TStop	S: Town Pump Travel Plaza #350/Pilot #910/Exxon (Scales)
Gas	N: Conoco
Food	N: Cattlemen's Cafe S: Subway/TownPump TP
Lodg	N: Fort Three Forks Motel♥ & RV Park/ HorseCorrals▲

EXIT	MONTANA
Other	S: Laundry/Casino/LP/WiFi/Town Pump, Three Forks KOA/RVDump▲
278	**US 10, MT 2, Three Forks, Trident**
Gas	S: 3 Forks Sinclair
Food	S: 3 Forks Café, D&L Country Diner, Stageline Pizza
Lodg	S: Broken Spur Motel
Other	N: to Missouri River Headwaters State Park S: 3 Forks Sinclair/RVDump, Marble's Laundry/RVDump, Golf, 3 Forks Airport✈
283	**Buffalo Jump Rd, Three Forks, Logan**
Other	S: to Madison Buffalo Jump State Park
288	**MT 288, Manhattan, Amsterdam**
Gas	N: Thriftway/Conoco◈
Food	N: Café on Broadway, Garden Cafe, Sir Scott's Oasis Steakhouse
Other	N: Manhattan RV Park/RVDump▲
298	**MT 347, Amsterdam Rd, (EB) MT 291, MT 85, Jackrabbit Ln (WB) Belgrade, W Yellowstone**
TStop	S: Flying J Travel Plaza/Conoco (Scales)
Gas	N: Cenex◈,Conoco, Exxon◈
Food	N: Burger King, McDonald's, Pizza Hut, Subway S: Rest/FJ TP
Lodg	S: Motel/FJ TP, Best Inn, Holiday Inn♥, La Quinta Inn♥, Super 8
Other	N: Albetson's, IGA, NAPA, Whalen Tire, Gallatin Field Airport✈ S: Laundry/WiFi/LP/FJ TP, to appr 8mi Bozeman KOA▲
305	**MT 412, N 19th Ave, Bozeman**
Gas	N: Exxon
Food	S: Arby's, Burger King, Denny's, Johnny Carino's, Perkins, Pizza Hut
Lodg	N: AmericInn S: C'Mon Inn, Wingate Inn
Other	S: Rest Area, Bozeman Ford Lincoln Mercury RV, ATMs, Bank, Costco, Home Depot, Lowe's, Target
306	**I-90 Bus, US 10, US 191N, N 7th, Bozeman**
Gas	N: Conoco, Sinclair S: Conoco◈, Exxon, Sinclair◈
Food	N: McDonald's S: Applebee's, Hardee's, Subway, Taco Bell, Wendy's
Lodg	N: Best Value Inn, Fairfield Inn, Microtel, Ramada S: Best Western♥, Comfort Inn♥, Days Inn♥, Hampton Inn, Hilton Garden Inn, Holiday Inn♥, Sunset Motel & Trailer Park▲
Other	N: C&T Mobile Home Repair, Whalen Tire S: RVDump/Conoco, ATMs, Banks, Big O Tires, Firestone, Grocery, IGA, Kmart, Pharmacy, Walmart sc, U-Haul, to MT State Univ
309	**US 191S, Main St, Bozeman**
FStop	S: Town Pump #9110/Exxon Town Pump #8927/Exxon
Gas	S: Exxon, Sinclair
Food	S: 4 B's, Black Angus Steakhouse, Eastside Diner, Montana Ale Works
Lodg	S: Continental Motor Inn, Ranch House Motel, Western Heritage Inn
Med	S: + Hospital
Other	N: Sunrise Campground/RVDump▲

◈= Regular Gas Stations with Diesel ▲ = RV Friendly Locations ♥ = Pet Friendly Locations
Red print shows large vehicle parking / access on site or nearby Brown Print = Campgrounds / RV PARKS

EXIT		MONTANA
	Other	S: Jackpot Casino East, Lucky Dog Saloon
313		**Bozeman Trail Rd, Bear Canyon Rd**
	Other	S: Bear Canyon Campground/RVDump▲
316		**Trail Creek Rd, Bozeman**
(319)		**ChainUp / Removal Area (Both dir)**
319		**Jackson Creek Rd**
324		**Ranch Access**
330		**I-90 Bus Loop, US 10, Livingston**
	TStop	N: Yellowstone Truck Stop
	Food	N: Rest/Yellowstone TS
	TServ	N: Yellowstone TS/Tires
	Other	N: Laundry/RVDump/Yellowstone TS
333		**US 89S, Park St, Livingston, to Yellowstone Park**
	TStop	S: Town Pump #610/Conoco
	Gas	N: Conoco, Exxon, Sinclair S: Cenex, Exxon
	Food	N: Pizza Hut S: FastFood/TownPump, Hardee's, McDonald's, Subway
	Lodg	N: Best Western♥, Budget Host Motel, Econo Lodge♥, Travelodge♥ S: Comfort Inn, Super 8
	Med	N: + Hospital
	Other	N: Grocery, Pharmacy, Oasis RV Park▲ S: Laundry/CarWash/Casino/Town Pump, Albertson's, Pharmacy, Osen's RV Park & Campground/RVDump▲, Livingston/Paradise Valley KOA/ RVDump▲, to Yellowstone
337		**I-90 Bus, Livingston, Local Access**
340		**US 89N, White Sulphur Springs**
343		**MT 295, Mission Creek Rd**
350		**East End Access**
352		**Ranch Access**
354		**MT 563, Big Timber, Springdale**
362		**Frontage Rd, Big Timber, DeHart**
367		**I-90 Bus Lp, US 191, US 10, Big Timber, Harlowton**
	TStop	N: WB: Acc Ex #370: Town Pump #922/ Exxon
	Gas	N: Conoco
	Food	N: Country Skillet/FastFood/Town Pump
	Lodg	N: Super 8
	Other	N: Laundry/Town Pump S: Spring Creek Campground & Trout Ranch/RVDump▲
384		**Bridger Creek Rd, Greycliff**
392		**Division St, Reed Point**
	Gas	N: Sinclair
	Other	N: US Post Office
396		**Ranch Access**
400		**Springtime Rd, Columbus**
408		**MT 78, N 9th St, Columbus**
	TStop	S: Town Pump #8924/Pilot #906/Exxon (Scales)
	Gas	S: Conoco
	Food	S: CountrySkillet/McDonald's/T Pump, Apple Village Café
	Lodg	S: Super 8/T Pump
	Med	S: + Hospital
	Other	S: Laundry/Casino/WiFi/RVDump/T Pump
(418)		**Columbus Rest Area (Both dir) (RR, Phone, Picnic)**
426		**Old US 10, Park City**
	TStop	S: Kum&Go #829/Cenex
	Food	S: Rest/FastFood/Kum&Go
	Other	S: Laundry/WiFi/LP/Kum&Go
433		**I-90 Bus Lp, W Laurel (EB ex, Wb entr)**
434		**US 212, US 310, Laurel, Red Lodge**
	FStop	N: Town Pump/Exxon
	Gas	N: Cenex◈, Conoco◈
	Food	N: Deli/T Pump, Burger King, Hardee's, Pizza Hut
	Lodg	N: Best Western, Howard Johnson, Russell Motel
	Other	N: Casino/CarWash/T Pump, RVDump/ Cenex, IGA, Pharmacy, to Laurel Airport→
437		**Frontage Rd, US 212, MT 2, Laurel**
	TStop	S: Pelican Truck Plaza/Sinclair (Scales)
	Food	S: Rest/FastFood/Pelican TP
	Lodg	S: Motel/Pelican TS & RV Park▲
	Tires	S: Pelican TP
	Other	S: Laundry/Casino/RVDump/LP/Pelican TP
(439)		**Weigh Station (Both dir)**
443		**Zoo Dr, to Shiloh Rd, Billings**
	Gas	S: Cenex
	Other	N: Zoo S: I-90 Motors & RV, Beartooth Harley Davidson, Billings RV
446		**I-90 Bus, Laurel Rd, Mullowney Ln, King Ave, Billings**
	TStop	N: Sinclair West Parkway
	Gas	N: Conoco, Holiday◈ S: Conoco, Exxon
	Food	N: Rest/Sinclair, Burger King, Denny's, Fuddrucker's, Olive Garden, Outback Steakhouse, Perkins, Red Lobster S: Cracker Barrel
	Lodg	N: C'Mon Inn, Comfort Inn♥, Days Inn♥, Fairfield Inn, Quality Inn♥, Super 8 S: Best Western♥, Holiday Inn♥, Motel 6♥, Kelly Inn♥, Ramada Inn♥, Red Roof Inn♥
	TServ	N: Sinclair/Tires, Interstate Tire Rama, Tractor & Equipment Co, Kenworth
	Other	N: Laundry/Sinclair, RVDump/Holiday, Casino's, Costco, Best Buy, Albertson's, Home Depot, Lowe's, Mall, PetSmart♥, Office Depot, Target, Wal-Mart sc, Big Sky Campground/RVDump▲
447		**Billings Blvd, Billings**
	Gas	N: Conoco◈
	Food	N: McDonald's, 4 B's
	Lodg	N: Hampton Inn, Sleep Inn, Super 8♥
	Other	S: Billings KOA▲
450		**MT 3, 27th St, Billings**
	Gas	N: Conoco◈, Sinclair, Exxon
	Food	N: Pizza Hut, Denny's, Perkins
	Lodg	N: War Bonnet Inn, Howard Johnson♥
	Med	N: + Hospital
	Other	N: to Billings Logan Int'l Airport→ S: Billings KOA/RVDump▲, Yellowstone River Campground/ RVDump▲
452		**US 87N, Billings, to Lockwood, Roundup**
	FStop	N: Town Pump/Conoco
	TStop	S: Kum&Go #824/Cenex
	Gas	N: Exxon◈, Cenex, Holiday◈
	Food	N: Arby's/TownPump, Elmer's, Peking Express, Subway, Taco Bell, Wendy's S: FastFood/Cenex
	Other	N: Casino/T Pump, Albertson's, CarQuest, Office Depot, Target, Walmart sc, U-Haul, Fairgrounds, Metra RV Center S: Laundry/Kum&Go
455		**Johnson Lane, Billings**
	TStop	S: Flying J Travel Plaza #5490/Conoco
	Gas	S: Exxon
	Food	S: Cookery/FastFood/FJ TP, Burger King, Subway
	TWash	S: Fly In Wash
	Other	S: Laundry/WiFi/RVDump/LP/FJ TP
(456A)		**Jct I-94, Hardin, Sheridan**
(456B)		**Jct I-94E, Miles City, Bismarck (WB)**
462		**Pryor Creek Rd, Indian Creek Rd, Huntley**
	Other	S: Crow Indian Reservation
469		**Arrow Creek Rd**
(476)		**Hardin Rest Area (Both dir) (RR, Phone, Picnic)**

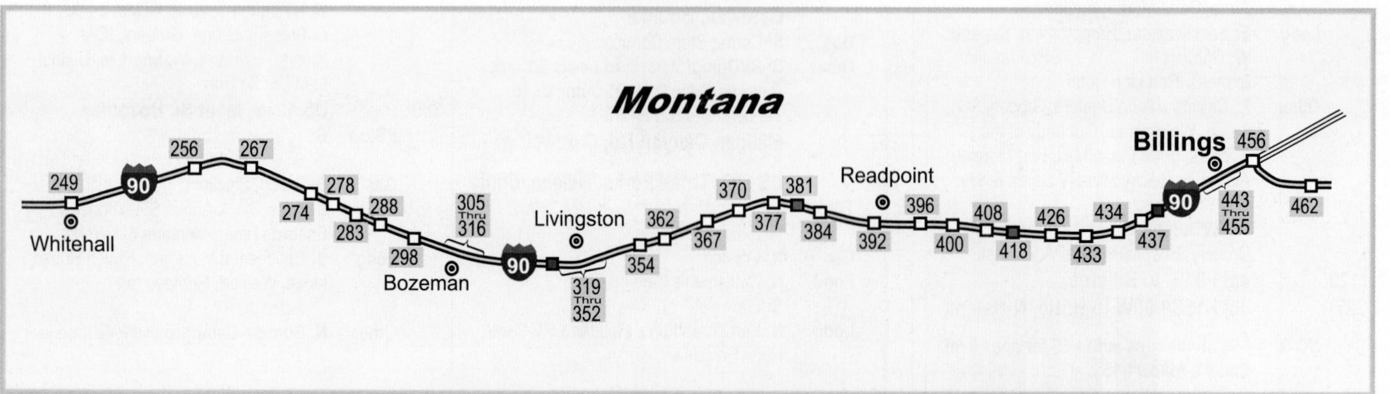

◈= Regular Gas Stations with Diesel ▲ = RV Friendly Locations ♥= Pet Friendly Locations
Red print shows large vehicle parking / access on site or nearby Brown Print = Campgrounds / RV PARKS

EXIT		MT / WY
478		**CR 30, Fly Creek Rd, Hardin**
484		**Frontage Rd, Hardin, Toluca**
495		**I-90 Bus Lp, MT 47, MT 313, Hardin**
	FStop	**N:** Interstate Texaco **S:** Town Pump #1710/Exxon, Red Eagle Shell
	TStop	**S:** Broadway/Flying J Fuel Stop/Conoco
	Gas	**S:** Sinclair◈
	Food	**N:** Purple Cow **S:** FastFood/Flying J FS, FastFood/TownPump, McDonald's
	Lodg	**S:** American Inn, Super 8, Lariat Motel
	Med	**S:** + Hospital
	Other	**N: Hardin KOA/RVDump▲ , Grand View Campground/RVDump▲ , Sunset Village RV/RVDump** **S:** WiFi/**RVDump/LP**/FJ FS, **Casino**/TP
497		**I-90 Bus, MT 47, 3rd St, Hardin**
	Med	**S:** + Hospital
	Other	**S:** Crow Indian Res
503		**Frontage Rd, Dunmore**
509		**Crow Agency**
	Gas	**N:** Conoco
	Food	**N:** Chester Fried Chicken
(509)		**Weigh Station** (Both dir)
510		**US 212E, Garryowen**
	Gas	**N:** Exxon◈ **S:** Little Big Horn
	Food	**N:** Crow's Nest Cafe
	Lodg	**S:** Little Big Horn **Casino** & Motel **& Campground▲**
	Med	**N:** + Hospital
	Other	**S:** Little Big Horn Battlefield Nat'l Mon
514		**MT 451, Garryowen**
	Gas	**N:** Conoco
	Other	**S: 7th Ranch RV Camp/RVDump▲**
530		**US 87, MT 463, Lodge Grass**
	Gas	**S:** Cenex◈
544		**MT 457, Wyola**
549		**CR 382, MY 451, to Aberdeen**
	MOUNTAIN TIME ZONE	
	NOTE:	**MM 558: Wyoming State Line**

⇑ MONTANA
⇓ WYOMING

EXIT		WYOMING
1		**CR 65, Barker Rd, Parkman**
9		**US 14W, Ranchester, Dayton**
	Gas	**S:** Big Country Oil
	Lodg	**S:** Foothills Motel & **Campground▲**
	Other	**S: Lazy R Campground▲ , to Bear Lodge Resort & Campground▲**
14		**WY 345, Acme Rd, Ranchester**
(15)		**Parking Area** (WB)
16		**WY 339, Sheridan, to Decker**
20		**I-90 Bus, US 87S, Main St, Sheridan** **S: WY Port of Entry** (WB)
	FStop	**S:** Red Eagle #17/Shell
	TStop	**S:** Common Cents Travel Plaza #210/Exxon
	Gas	**S:** Conoco, Cenex, Kum&Go
	Food	**S:** Country Kitchen/CommonCents TP, Little Caesar's, McDonald's, Pizza Hut, Pablo's Rest, Subway, WY Rib & Chop House
	Lodg	**S:** Super 8♥, Stage Stop Motel, Trails End Motel
	TServ	**S:** Steve's Truck Service
	Other	**N: Sheridan/Big Horn Mtns/KOA▲** **S:** Laundry/CommonCents TP, Safeway, Kmart
23		**WY 336, 5th St, Sheridan** **Rest Area** (Both dir) **N:** (RR, Phone, Picnic, **RVDump**)
	Gas	**N:** Rock Stop◈ S: Cenex, Holiday, Maverik, Shell
	Food	**N:** Subway/Rock Stop **S:** Artic Circle, Bubba's BBQ, KFC, WY Rib & Chop House
	Lodg	**S:** Alamo Motel, Best Western, Bramble Motel **& RV Park▲** , Motel 6♥, Sheridan Inn, Sundown Motel
	Med	**S: + Sheridan Memorial Hospital**
	Other	**S:** ATMs, Kmart, Pharmacy, Tires, Auto Services, **Peter D's RV Park/RVDump▲ , Summertime RV Service**
370		**US 191, I-90 Bus, Big Timber**
	Gas	**N:** Conoco, Exxon, Sinclair
	Other	**S: Spring Creek Campground & Trout Ranch/RVDump▲**
377		**Frontage Rd, Greycliff**
	Other	**S: Big Timber KOA/RVDump▲**
(381)		**Greycliff Rest Area** (Both dir) (RR, Phone, Picnic)
25		**I-90 Bus, Brundage Ln, US 14E, Sheridan, Big Horn**
	Gas	**S:** Conoco◈, Exxon◈, Holiday, Maverik
	Food	**S:** Arby's, Burger King, Golden China, JB's Family Rest, Perkins, Prime Dining, Subway, Taco Bell, Wendy's
	Lodg	**N:** Comfort Inn **S:** Days Inn♥, Holiday Inn♥, Mill Inn

EXIT		WYOMING
	Other	**N: Dalton's RV Center** **S:** Firestone, Grocery, Pharmacy, Walgreen's, **Walmart sc**, Auto Service, Mall, Sheridan Jr College, Sheridan Co Airport✈, **Sheridan RV Park▲ , RVDump**/Washington Park
(31)		**Parking Area** (EB)
33		**Meade Creek Rd, Big Horn, Story**
37		**Prairie Dog Creek Rd, Story**
(39)		**Parking Area** (WB)
44		**US 87N, Piney Creek Rd, Buffalo, to Story, Banner**
	Other	**N:** Fort Phil Kearney
47		**Shell Creek Rd, Buffalo**
51		**CR 39, Lake Ridge Rd, Buffalo, Monument Rd, to Lake Desmet**
	Other	**N:** Lake Stop Resort/Motel/**RVPark▲**
53		**Rock Creek Rd**
56A		**I-90 Bus, I-25 Bus, Main St, to Buffalo** (EB ex, WB entr) **(All Serv at 1st Exit, I-25S, x299)**
	Other	**S:** Johnson Co Airport✈, **Buffalo KOA▲ , to appr 3.5mi Big Horn Mountain Campground▲**
(56B)		**I-25S, Buffalo, Casper, Cheyenne** **(All Serv at 1st Exit S x299)**
	Other	**S: Buffalo KOA▲ , to Mountain View Motel & Campground▲ , to Indian Campground▲**
	NOTE:	**EB: CHECK YOUR FUEL! No Services Between Exits #58 & #124.**
58		**I-90 Bus, US 16, US 87, Buffalo, Ucross, I-25**
	TStop	**S:** Big Horn Travel Plaza, Kum&Go/Cenex
	Gas	**S:** Shell◈, Sinclair
	Food	**S:** Rest/Big Horn TP, McDonald's, Pizza Hut, Subway
	Lodg	**S:** Best Value Inn♥, Best Western♥, Comfort Inn♥, Econo Lodge♥, Super 8♥, Wyoming/WYO Motel
	Med	**S: + Family Medical Center**
	Other	**S: RVDump**/Cenex, **Buffalo KOA▲ , Big Horn Mountains Campground▲ , Deer Park RV Park & Campground▲ /RVDump▲ , Indian Campground▲ ,** Carousel Park
(59)		**Parking Area** (Both dir)
65		**Red Hills Rd, Tipperary Rd**
(68)		**Parking Area** (Both dir)

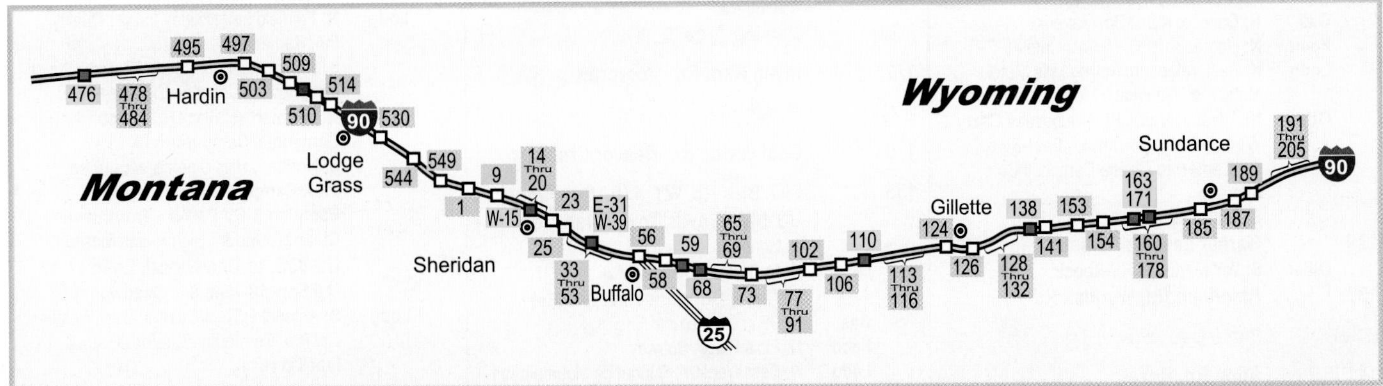

◈= Regular Gas Stations with Diesel ▲ = RV Friendly Locations ♥= Pet Friendly Locations
Red print shows large vehicle parking / access on site or nearby Brown Print = Campgrounds / RV PARKS

EXIT	WYOMING
69	**Dry Creek Rd, Buffalo**
73	**Crazy Woman Creek Rd**
77	**Schoonover Rd, Buffalo**
82	**Indian Creek Rd, Buffalo**
88	**Powder River Rd, Buffalo** Rest Area (Both dir) N: (RR, Phone, Picnic)
91	**Dead Horse Creek Rd**
102	**Barber Creek Rd, Gillette**
106	**Barlow Rd, Kingsbury Rd**
(110)	Parking Area (Both dir)
113	**Wild Horse Creek Rd**
116	**Force Rd**
124	**I-90 Bus, Skyline Dr, to US 14, US 16W, WY 50, Gillette**
FStop	N: Shell Food Mart
Gas	N: Conoco◈ S: Cenex◈, Kum&Go◈
Food	N: Long John Silver, Pizza Hut, Subway
Lodg	N: Best Western♥, Budget Inn, Comfort Inn, Hampton Inn, Motel 6♥, Super 8♥
Med	N: + Campbell Co Memorial Hospital
Other	N: to PL/Green Tree's Crazy Woman Campground▲
NOTE:	**WB: CHECK YOUR FUEL! No Services Between Exits #124 & #58.**
126	**WY 59, Douglas Hwy, Gillette**
TStop	S: Flying J Travel Plaza
Gas	N: Cenex◈, Conoco S: Exxon, Shell
Food	N: McDonald's, Subway, Prime Rib Rest, Starbucks S: Cookery/FJ TP, Applebee's, Arby's, Bootlegger's Rest, Burger King, DQ, China Buffet, Golden Corral, KFC, Perkins, Pizza Hut, Quiznos, Starbucks, Taco Bell, Wendy's
Lodg	N: Best Value Inn♥, Mustang Motel, Smart Choice Inn, S: Clarion♥, Days Inn, Fairfield Inn, Holiday Inn Express ♥, Wingate Inn
Other	N: Discount Tire, Grocery, Pharmacy, Radio Shack, Tires S: Laundry/WiFi/RVDump/LP/FJ TP, Albertson's, Advance Auto, Auto Dealers, Big O Tire, Goodyear, Home Depot, Pharmacy, Walmart sc
128	**I-90 Bus, Gillette, US 14W, US 16W** Port Of Entry
Gas	N: Conoco, Kum&Go, Maverik◈
Food	N: Hardee's, KFC, Mona's Café
Lodg	N: Best Value Inn, Rolling Hills Motel, Motel 6♥, National 9 Motel, Quality Inn
Other	N: AdvancedAuto, PL/Greentrees Crazy Woman Campground▲, East Side RV Center, to Gillette Campbell Co Airport✈ S: High Plains Campground▲
129	**Garner Lake Rd, Gillette**
Other	S: WY Marine & RV Repair
132	**American Rd, Wyodak Rd**
(138)	Parking Area (Both dir)
141	**Adon Rd, Rozet**

Personal Notes

EXIT	WYOMING
153	**I-90 Bus, to US 14E, to US 16E, Moorcraft, Newcastle, Aglett** Rest Area (Both dir) N: (RR, Phone, Picnic, RVDump)
Other	N: Devils Tower KOA▲
154	**I-90 Bus, E Moorcroft, US 14E, Devils Tower, US 16E, Newcastle**
TStop	S: PTP/Coffee Cup Fuel Stop #5/Conoco
Food	S: FastFood/CoffeeCup FS, Donna's Diner, Hub Café, Subway
Lodg	S: Cozy Motel, Moorcourt Motel, WY Motel, Rangeland Court Motel & RV Park▲
160	**Wind Creek Rd, Moorcroft**
(163)	Parking Area (Both dir)
165	**Pine Ridge Rd, Wagner Rd, to Pine Haven**
Other	N: to appr 9mi Keyhole State Park/ RVDump▲
(171)	Parking Area (Both dir)
172	**Inyan Kara Rd, Moorcroft**
(177)	Parking Area (Both dir)
178	**Coal Divide Rd, Beaver Creek Rd**
185	**I-90 Bus, to WY 116, Sundance, US 14W, Devils Tower Natl Mon**
Gas	S: Conoco◈
Other	N: to Devils Tower KOA▲
187	**WY 585, Sundance, Newcastle**
Gas	N: BP◈, Conoco◈
Food	N: Flo's Place, Subway
Lodg	N: Best Western, Sundance Mountain Inn

EXIT	WY / SD
(189)	**I-90 Bus, US 14W, Sundance, Newcastle** S: WY Port of Entry / Weigh Station Rest Area (Both dir) S: (RR, Phones, Info, Picnic, RVDump)
TStop	N: Sundance BP Travel Center
Food	N: Subway
Lodg	N: Best Western♥
Med	N: + Hospital
Other	N: Laundry/Sundance TC S: Mountain View Campground▲
191	**Moskee Rd, Sundance**
199	**WY 111, to Aladdin**
205	**CR 129, Sand Creek Rd, Beulah**
Gas	N: Stateline Station
Food	N: Buffalo Jump Saloon & Steakhouse
NOTE:	**MM 207: South Dakota State Line**

⬆ WYOMING
⬇ SOUTH DAKOTA

MOUNTAIN TIME ZONE

EXIT	SOUTH DAKOTA
(1)	SD Welcome Center (EB) (RR, Phone, Picnic, Info, RVDump)
2	**Shenk Ln, Spearfish**
Other	N: McNenny State Fish Hatchery
8	**McGuigan Rd, W Spearfish**
Other	S: Spearfish KOA▲
10	**I-90 Bus, US 85N, Spearfish, to Belle Fourche**
Gas	S: Valley Corner Gas/Casino
Food	S: Burger King, Guadalajara Mexican, Golden Dragon, Subway, Wendy's
Lodg	S: Days Inn♥
Other	S: Auto Dealers, Grocery, Jos Field Dreams CG▲, Spearfish KOA ▲
12	**E Jackson Blvd, Spearfish**
Gas	S: Mini Mart, Sinclair
Food	S: Bay Leaf Café, Bell's Steakhouse, China Town, Country Kitchen, Domino's, Millstone Fam Rest, Pizza Ranch
Lodg	S: Best Western♥, Travelodge♥
Med	S: + Lookout Memorial Hospital
Other	S: Black Hills State College, Spearfish Campground▲, Spearfish KOA▲
14	**27th St, I-90 Bus, US 14A, Spearfish**
Gas	S: AmocoBP Speedy Mart
Food	N: Applebee's S: PizzaRanch/HJE, Applebee's, KFC, Long John Silver, Perkins
Lodg	N: Fairfield Inn, Holiday Inn♥, Quality Inn, Ramada S: All American Inn, Best Western, Super 8♥, Howard Johnson Express♥
Other	N: Walmart sc, Black Hills Airport✈, Centennial Campground▲ S: Northern Hills Cinema, Mountain View Campground▲, Chris's Camping & RV Park▲, Trout Haven Campground▲, High Plains Museum
17	**US 85S, to Deadwood, Lead** **(All Serv 10-15mi S in Deadwood)**
Lodg	S: AmericInn/Rest/Casino, Best Western/ Casino, ComfortInn/Casino, Historic Franklin Hotel,

◈= Regular Gas Stations with Diesel ▲ = RV Friendly Locations ♥= Pet Friendly Locations
Red print shows large vehicle parking / access on site or nearby Brown Print = Campgrounds / RV PARKS

EXIT		SOUTH DAKOTA
	Lodg	S: Hampton Inn/FourAcesCasino/Rest, Holiday Inn Express/Gold Dust Casino/ Rest, Super 8
	Other	S: Deadwood KOA▲ , Elkhorn Ridge RV Resort & Cabins▲ , Hidden Valley CG▲ , Fish N Fry CG▲ , Deadwood Gulch Resort & Gaming▲ , Whistler Gulch CG▲
23		**SD 34W, Laurel St, Whitewood**
	Gas	S: April's Place◈, BP
	Food	S: Shea's Family Rest
	Lodg	S: Tony's Motel
	Other	N: RV Center
30		**I-90 Bus, SD 34, Boulder Canyon Rd, US 14A, Sturgis, Deadwood**
	Gas	N: BP, Cenex◈
		S: BJ's Country Store, Conoco◈
	Food	N: China Buffet, McDonald's, Pizza Hut, Subway
		S: Burger King, McDonald's, Subway
	Lodg	N: Days Inn♥, Canyon Inn, Holiday Inn Express, Motel 6♥
		S: Super 8♥
	Other	N: CarQuest, Laundromat, Grocery, Tires, Radio Shack, Iron Horse Campground▲ , Glencoe Campground▲ , Free Spirit Campground▲
		S: Deadwood KOA▲ , Hidden Valley Campground▲ , Fish N Fry Campground▲ , Wild Bill's Campground▲ , Fort Meade, to Recreational Springs Resort▲
32		**I-90 Bus, SD 79N, Junction Ave, Sturgis, Fort Meade**
	Gas	N: Conoco, BP, CommonCents
	Food	N: Subway/Conoco, Taco John's
	Lodg	N: Best Western♥, Lantern Motel, Star Lite Motel, South Pine Motel
	Med	N: + Fort Mead VA Medical Center
	Other	N: Casino/BW, Fort Meade, Big Rig RV Park▲ , Glencoe Campground▲ , Mt Rodney Luxury Coach Park/Mt Rodney's Downtown RV & Camping Park▲ , Bob & Lea's Campground▲ , Vanocker Campground▲
34		**Old Stone Rd, Pleasant Valley Dr**
	Other	S: Katmandu RV Park & Campground▲ , No Name City RV Park & Cabins▲ , Black Hills National Cemetary
37		**Pleasant Valley Dr, Sturgis**
	Other	N: Elkview Campground & Resort▲
		S: Bulldog Campground▲ , Rush-No-More RV Park & Campground▲
(38)		**Port of Entry / Weigh Station (EB)**
40		**214th St, Sturgis, Tilford**
(42)		**Rest Area (Both dir)** (RR, Phone, Picnic, Info, RVDump/Wtr)
44		**218th St, Bethlehem Rd, Piedmont**
	Other	S: Bethlehem RV Park▲ , Jack's RV
46		**Piedmont Rd, Elk Creek Rd**
	Gas	S: Conoco◈
	Food	N: Elk Creek Steakhouse
	Other	N: Covered Wagon Resort▲ , Lazy JD RV Park▲ , Elk Creek Resort & Lodge & Campground▲
48		**Stagestop Rd, Blackhawk**
	Gas	S: Sinclair
	Food	S: Classics Bar & Grill, Mike's Pizza
	Lodg	S: Ramada Inn♥, Super 8
	TServ	N: Northwest Peterbilt
	Med	S: + Piedmont Medical Center
	Other	S: Casino/Ramada Inn, Bethlehem Road RV Park▲
51		**Foothills Blvd, I-90 Bus, SD 79, Black Hawk Rd, Blackhawk**
	Other	N: Three Flags RV Park▲
55		**Deadwood Ave, Rapid City**
	TStop	S: Bosselman Travel Center/Pilot #918 Sinclair (Scales)
	Food	S: Rest/Pilot TC
	TWash	S: Superior TW/Pilot TC
	TServ	N: Butler CAT
		S: Pilot TC/Boss Truck Shop/Tires, West River International
	Other	N: Rushmore Mall, Harley Davidson, Lazy JD RV Park▲
		S: Laundry/BarbSh/RVDump/LP/ Pilot TC, Golf Course
(57)		**Jct I-190, US 16W, Rapid City, to Mt Rushmore**
	Gas	S: Conoco
	Food	S: Hardee's, Little Caesars, McDonald
	Lodg	S: Alex Johnson♥, Days Inn, Holiday Inn♥, Howard Johnson Express, Radisson
	Other	S: Happy Holiday Resort & Campground▲ , Hart Ranch Resort▲ , Lazy JD RV Park▲ , Lake Park CG & Cottages▲ , Lazy J RV Park & CG▲ , Mystery Mountain Resort ▲
58		**Haines Ave, Rapid City**
	Gas	N: Conoco, Shell
		S: Mini Mart◈, Conoco
	Food	N: Applebee's, Chili's, Hardee's, IHOP, Red Lobster, Mall Food Court
		S: Taco John's, Wendy's
	Lodg	N: Best Value Inn♥
	Med	S: + Hospital
	Other	N: Rushmore Mall, Best Buy, Lowe's, Target, Tires Plus+
		S: ShopKO
59		**N La Crosse St, Rapid City**
	Gas	N: BP, Phillips 66, Shell
		S: Cenex◈, Exxon, Murphy USA
	Food	N: Burger King, Denny's, Fuddruckers, Olive Garden, Outback Steakhouse, TGI Friday
		S: Chuck E Cheese, Golden Corral, McDonald's, Millstone Rest, Perkins, Red Lobster, Subway
	Lodg	N: Best Western♥, Country Inn, Econo Lodge♥, GrandStay Residential Suites, Holiday Inn Express♥, Quality Inn, Super 8♥
		S: AmericInn, Comfort Inn, Days Inn, Fair Value Inn, Foothills Inn♥, Grand Gateway Hotel, Hampton Inn, Microtel♥, Motel 6♥, Quality Inn♥, Ramada Inn♥
	Other	N: SD State Hwy Patrol Post, Mall, Tires
		S: Sam's Club, Target, Tires, Walgreen's, Walmart sc
60		**I-90 Bus, SD 79, North St, Rapid City, Mt Rushmore (fr WB, Left Exit)**
	Food	S: Bonanza, Hong Kong Café, Great Wall, KFC, Long John Silver
	Lodg	S: Budget Inn, Comfort Inn, Four Seasons Motel, Gold Star Motel
	Med	S: + Hospital
	Other	S: Berry Patch CG▲ , Hart Ranch Resort▲ , Menard's, Michael's, PetCo♥, TJ Maxx
61		**Elk Vale Rd, St Patrick St, Rapid City**
	TStop	N: Flying J Travel Plaza/Conoco (Scales)
	Food	N: CountryMarket/FastFood/FJ TP
		S: Arby's, McDonald's
	Lodg	S: Comfort Suites, Fairfield Inn, La Quinta Inn, Sleep Inn
	TWash	N: FJ TP
	TServ	S: Hills Brake & Equipment Black Hills Truck & Trailer
	Other	N: Laundry/BarbSh/WiFi/RVDump/ LP/FJ TP, RV Center, Cabela's,
		S: Rapid Towing, Watiki Indoor Waterpark, I-90 RV & Auto, Lazy J RV Park & Campground▲ , Rapid City KOA▲
63		**Ellsworth AFB Comm'l Entrance, Box Elder, (EB exit, WB reacc)**
67		**Liberty Blvd, Ellsworth AFB,Main Main Entrance (WB)**
67AB		**Liberty Blvd (EB)**
(69)		**Parking Area (Both dir)**
78		**161st Ave, New Underwood**
	Gas	S: Steve's General Store

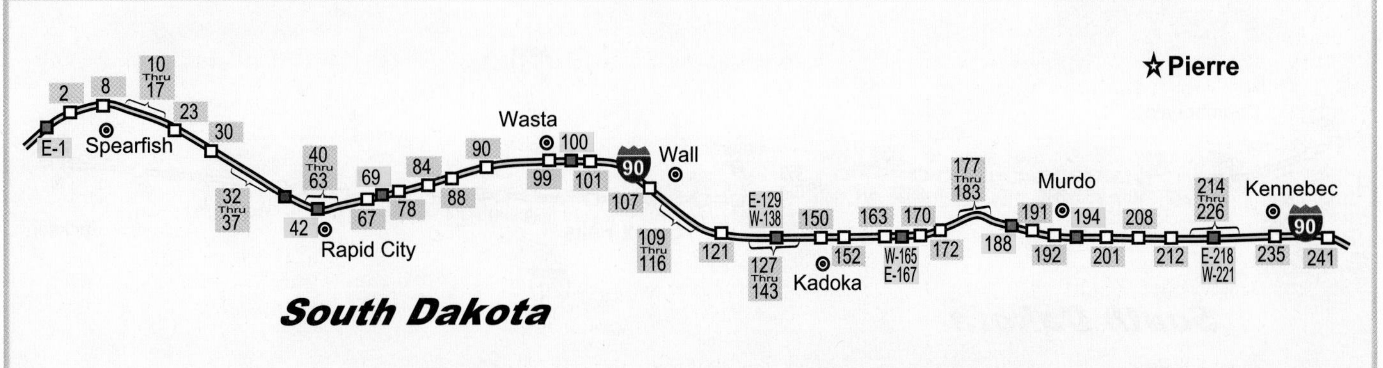

◈= Regular Gas Stations with Diesel ▲ = RV Friendly Locations ♥= Pet Friendly Locations
Red print shows large vehicle parking / access on site or nearby Brown Print = Campgrounds / RV PARKS

EXIT — SOUTH DAKOTA

Food S: Diamond Café
Lodg S: Jake's Motel
Other S: Boondocks Campground▲

84 CR 497, 167th Ave, Duncan Rd

88 171st Ave (EB exit, WB reaccess)

90 173rd Ave, CR C492, Owanka

99 Base Line Rd, Wasta
Gas N: BP◈
Food N: Packard Café
Lodg N: Redwood Motel
Other N: US Post Office, Sunrise RV Park & Campground▲

(100) Rest Area (Both dir)
(RR, Phone, Picnic, Info, RVDump/Wtr)

101 CR T504, Jensen Rd

107 168th Ave, Cedar Butte Rd

109 W 4th Ave, Wall

110 I-90 Bus, SD 240, Glenn St, Wall, Badlands Loop
Gas N: BP◈, Exxon, Phillips 66
Food N: Cactus Café, DQ, Elkton House Rest, Subway
Lodg N: Best Western♥, Best Value Inn, Days Inn, Econo Lodge♥, Elk Motel, Homestead Motel, Kings Inn, Knights Inn, Motel 6♥, Sunshine Inn, Super 8, Wall Motel
Other N: NAPA, US Post Office, Pharmacy, Sleepy Hollow Campground▲, Arrow Cg▲, to Badlands Nat' Park

112 US 14E, to Phillip

116 239th St, Wall

121 Big Foot Pass, CR C511, to US 14

127 CS 23A, Big Foote Rd, Kadoka

(129.5) Scenic View (EB)

131 SD 240, Badlands Loop, CR 8, Badlands Interior, Kadoka
Gas S: BP, Conoco
Other S: Badland Circle 10/Motel/Rest/ Campground▲, to appr 9 mi Badlands Nat'l Park, to appr 15 mi Badlands/ White River KOA▲

(138) Scenic View (WB)

143 SD 73N, Kadoka, to Phillip
Med N: to + Hospital

150 SD 73S, I-90 Bus, Kadoka
FStop S: Discount Fuel/Conoco
Gas S: BP
Food N: Rest/Dakota Inn
S: Happy Chef
Lodg N: Dakota Inn
S: Best Western, Budget Host, Downtowner Motor Inn, Super 8, Ponderosa Motel & RV Park▲
Other S: Laundromat, to Pine Ridge Indian Res

152 I-90 Bus, Kadoka, S Creek Rd
TStop N: Badlands Travel Stop/66
Food N: Rest/Badlands TS
Lodg S: Best Western
Other N: Laundry/Tires/Badlands TS
S: Kadoka Campground▲

163 SD 63S, Belvidere
Gas S: BP◈, Sinclair◈

(165) Rest Area (EB)
(RR, Phone, Picnic, RVDump)

(167) Rest Area (WB)
(RR, Phone, Picnic, RVDump)

170 SD 63N, to Midland
Gas N: Shell
Other N: Belvidere East KOA▲

172 to Cedar Butte

177 NO Access

183 Okaton

(188) Parking Area (Both dir)

NOTE: MM 190: Central / Mountain Time Zone

191 Old US 16, Murdo

192 US 83, I-90 Bus, Murdo, White River
TStop N: Triple H Truck Stop/Shell
Gas N: BP◈, Phillips 66, Sinclair
Food N: Rest/Triple H TS, KFC/P66, Murdo Drive In, Tee Pee
Lodg N: AmericInn, Best Western♥, Days Inn♥, Lee Motel, Super 8, Tee Pee Motel & RV Park▲
S: Country Inn
TServ N: Triple H TS/Tires
Other N: Laundry/LP/Triple H TS, Grocery

(194) Parking Area (Both dir)

201 CR N13, Draper

208 CR S10, Draper

212 US 83N, SD 53, Ft Pierre, Pierre
TStop N: PTP/Coffee Cup Fuel Stop #8/66
Food N: Vivian Jct Rest

214 US 83, SD 53, Vivian

(218) Rest Area (EB)
(RR, Phones, Picnic, RVDump)

220 NO Access

(221) Rest Area (WB)
(RR, Phones, Picnic, Info, RVDump)

225 I-90 Bus, SD 16, Presho
FStop N: New Frontier Station/Conoco
Gas N: Sinclair◈
Food N: Café/Frank's Hutch's Motel, Pizza
Lodg N: Coachlight Inn, Hutch's Motel
Other N: New Frontier RV Park▲

226 I-90 Bus, US 183S, Presho, Winner (Access Serv at Ex #225)

235 SD 273, I-90 Bus, Kennebec
Gas N: Conoco◈
Lodg N: Budget Host Inn
Other N: Kennebec KOA▲

241 to Lyman

248 SD 47N, Reliance
Gas N: BP◈, Cenex

251 SD 47N, Reliance, Gregory, Winner
Other N: to Golden Buffalo Casino

260 SD 50, Dougan Ave, Oacoma
FStop S: Oasis Pump & Pack/Conoco
Gas N: BP◈, Shell◈
Food N: Taco John's
Lodg N: Days Inn♥, Comfort Inn♥, Holiday Inn Express, Oasis Kelly Inn♥
Other N: Al's Oasis/Rest/Motel/River Ranch Resort/Campground▲, Familyland Camping▲, Hi & Dri Camping▲, Cedar Shore Resort▲

263 Main St, Chamberlain, Crow Creek Sioux Tribal Headquarters
Gas N: Sinclair◈
Food N: Casey's Café, McDonald's, Pizza Hut, Subway, Taco John's
Lodg N: Best Western♥, Riverview Inn, Super 8♥
Other N: IGA

(264) Rest Area (Both dir)
(RR, Phone, Info, Picnic, View, RVDump)

265 I-90 Bus, SD 50, 344th Ave, Chamberlain
FStop S: Vet's Whoa & Go/Conoco
Gas N: BP
Other S: Keiner's Kampground▲, Happy Camper Park▲

272 SD 50, Pukwana

284 SD 45N, Main St, Kimball
FStop N: CBS Miller Oil/Corner Bottle Stop
Tstop N: Corner Pantry Café/66
Gas N: BP

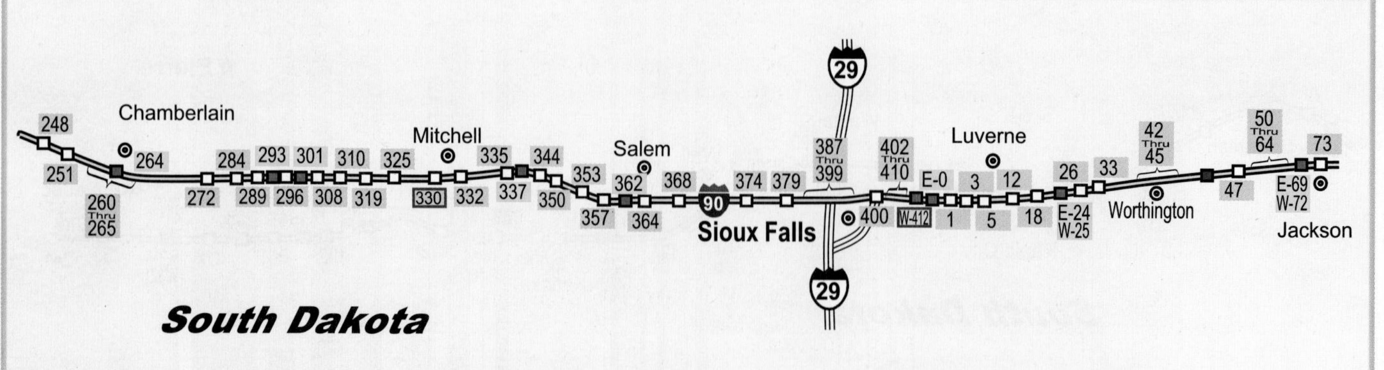

◈= Regular Gas Stations with Diesel ▲ = RV Friendly Locations ♥= Pet Friendly Locations
Red print shows large vehicle parking / access on site or nearby Brown Print = Campgrounds / RV PARKS

EXIT		SOUTH DAKOTA
	Food	N: Diner/Corner Panty
	Lodg	N: Super 8, Dakota Winds
	Other	N: Parkway Campground▲
289		**SD 45S, Kimball, to Platte**
	Other	S: to Snake Creek/Platte Creek Rec Area
(293)		Parking Area (Both dir)
296		**CR 11, White Lake**
	Gas	S: Cenex, Shell
	Lodg	N: White Lake Motel
(301)		Rest Area (Both dir) (RR, Phone, Picnic, RVDump)
308		**I-90 Bus, SD 258, to Plankinton**
	Gas	N: Phillips 66◊
	Food	N: Al's I-90 Café
	Lodg	N: Super 8
310		**US SD 281, Plankinton, to Stickney, Aberdeen**
	TStop	S: PTP/Coffee Cup Fuel Stop #4/Conoco
	Food	S: FastFood/Coffee Cup FS
319		**Mt Vernon**
	Gas	N: Cenex
325		**Betts Rd, 403rd Ave**
	Other	S: Famil-E-Fun Campground▲
330		**SD 37N, Mitchell, Corn Palace** N: Weigh Station (Both dir)
	TStop	N: West Haven Cenex
	Gas	N: Shell◊
	Food	N: AJ's, Country Kitchen, DQ, Happy Chef
	Lodg	N: Holiday Inn, Motel 6♥
	Med	N: + Hospital
	Other	N: RV Center, RonDee's Campground▲, Mitchell KOA▲, to Mitchell Muni Airport✈ Lake Mitchell Campground▲ S: Dakota Campground▲, Jack's RV
332		**I-90 Bus, SD 37S, Mitchell**
	TStop	N: Cenex, I-90 Fuel Services/Pilot Travel Center #919 (Scales)
	Gas	N: BP, Phillips 66 S: Highland Travel Plaza/Shell◊, Murphy
	Food	N: Rest/Subway/Pilot TC/I-90 TC, Arby's, Bonanza Steak House, Burger King, Country Kitchen, Embers Rest, Hardee's, Kinders Rest, McDonald's, Perkins, Pizza Hut S: TacoBell/Godfathers/Highland TP, Quiznos
	Lodg	N: AmericInn, Best Western, Comfort Inn, Days Inn, Super 8, Thunderbird Lodge S: Corn Palace Motel, Hampton Inn, Kelly Inn
	TServ	N: Pilot TC/ I-90 TC/Tires
	Med	N: + Hospital
	Other	N: Laundry/Pilot/I-90 TC, Auto Services, ATMs, Advance Auto Parts, Corn Palace, Pharmacy, R & R Campground▲, Rondees Campground▲, to Mitchell Muni Airport✈, Dakota Wesleyan Univ S: Cabela's/RVDump, Dollar Tree, Menard's, Radio Shack, Highland Mall, Walmart sc
335		**Riverside Rd**
	Other	N: Mitchell KOA▲
(337)		Parking Area (Both dir)
344		**SD 262E, Fulton, Alexandria**
	Gas	S: Shell◊
350		**SD 25, Emery, Farmer**
	Other	N: to home of Laura Ingalls Wilder

EXIT		SOUTH DAKOTA
353		**431st Ave, Spencer, Emery**
	FStop	N: AmBest/Fuel Mart #645
	TStop	S: Travel Center of America/Amoco (Scales)
	Food	S: FastFood/TA TC
	Other	S: Laundry/WiFi/TA TC
357		**Bridgewater, Canova**
(362)		Rest Area (Both dir) (RR, Ph, Pic, RVDump, SD Hwy Patrol)
364		**US 81, Canistota, Salem, Yankton**
368		**445th Ave, Canistota**
	Other	S: RVFishing.com RV Park▲
374		**451st Ave, to SD 38, Montrose** (Serv 3-4 mi N in Montrose)
	Other	S: Lake Vermillion Rec Area▲
379		**SD 19, 456th Ave, Humboldt, to Madison**
	Gas	N: Mobil◊
	Food	N: Cafe
387		**SD 151, 463rd Ave, Hartford**
	FStop	N: Tammen Oil/66
	Tires	N: 66
390		**SD 38, Sioux Falls, Buffalo Ridge, Hartford**
	Gas	S: Buffalo Ridge, Phillips 66
	Food	S: Buffalo Ridge, Pizza Ranch
(396AB)		**Jct I-29, S-Sioux City, N-Fargo**
399		**I-90 Bus, SD 115, Cliff Ave, Sioux Falls**
	FStop	S: Kum&Go #613/Cenex
	TStop	N: Frontier Village Truck Stop/Sinclair (Scales) S: Pilot Travel Center #349 (Scales)
	Gas	N: Phillips 66◊ S: Holiday◊
	Food	N: Rest/Frontier Village TS S: Grandma's/Subway/Pilot TC, Burger King, McDonald's, Perkins, Taco John's
	Lodg	S: Comfort Inn, Country Inn, Days Inn, Econo Lodge, Super 8
	TWash	S: Blue Beacon TW/Pilot TC
	TServ	S: Pilot TC/Tires, American Rim & Brake, Crossroads Trailer, Cummins Great Plains Diesel, Dakota White/GMC Volvo, Diesel Machinery, Graham Tire, International Dealer, Peterbilt Dealer, Sheehan Mack, Sioux Falls Kenworth, T&W Tires, Boss Truck Shop
	Med	S: + Hospital
	Other	N: Laundry/CB/Frontier Village TS, Sioux Falls KOA▲, Spaders RV S: Laundry/BarbSh/WiFi/Pilot TC
(400)		**Jct I-229S, Sioux Falls, Sioux City**
402		**CR 121, S 478th Ave, EROS Data Center**
	Other	N: Yogi Bear's Jellystone Resort▲
406		**SD 11, 482nd Ave, Brandon, Corson**
	FStop	S: PTP/Coffee Cup Fuel Stop #7/BP (Scales
	Gas	S: Sinclair◊
	Food	S: Brandon Steakhouse, DQ, Domino's, McDonald's, Subway
	Lodg	S: Holiday Inn Express
	Other	S: Golf Courses, to Big Sioux State Rec Area
410		**CR 105, 486th Ave, Valley Springs, Garretson**
	Other	N: Palisades State Park▲

EXIT		SD / MN
(412)		SD Welcome Center (WB) Port of Entry / Weigh Station (WB) Rest Area (EB) (RR, Phone, Picnic, RVDump/WB)
	NOTE:	MM 412: Minnesota State Line

SOUTH DAKOTA
MINNESOTA

CENTRAL TIME ZONE

EXIT		MINNESOTA
(0)		MN Welcome Center (EB) (RR, Phone, Picnic, Info, Vend)
1		**MN 23, CR 17, Beaver Creek, Manley, Jasper, Pipestone**
	Other	N: Split Rock Creek State Park
3		**CR 4, Beaver Creek (EB)**
5		**CR 6, Beaver Creek**
	Gas	N: Shell◊
12		**US 75, S Kniss Ave, Luverne, to Pipestone, Rock Rapids**
	Gas	N: Casey's Gen'l Store, Cenex◊, FuelTime◊, Phillips 66◊, Shell◊
	Food	N: Chit Chat Rest, China Inn, Pizza Hut, McDonald's, Subway, Taco John's S: Magnolia Lounge & Steakhouse
	Lodg	N: Comfort Inn S: Super 8♥
	Med	N: + Luverne Community Hospital
	Other	N: Blue Mounds State Park▲, Auto Dealers, Split Rock Creek State Park S: Luverne Muni Airport✈
18		**CR 3, Magnolia, Kanaranzi**
(24)		Adrian Rest Area (EB) (RR, Phone, Picnic, Vend)
(25)		Adrian Rest Area (WB) (RR, Phone, Picnic, Vend)
26		**MN 91, Adrian, to Lake Wilson, Ellsworth**
	Gas	S: Cenex◊
33		**CR 13, Jones Ave, Rushmore**
42		**MN 266N, CR 25, Worthington, Reading, Wilmont**
	Lodg	S: Days Inn♥, Super 8♥
43		**US 59, Humiston Ave, Worthington**
	FStop	S: Cenex AmPride Fuel Stop, Plaza 66/66
	Gas	N: Conoco◊ S: BP, Casey's, Shell, Murphy
	Food	S: Arby's, Country Kitchen, DQ, KFC, Ground Round, Perkins, McDonald's, Pizza Hut, Subway
	Lodg	N: Travelodge♥ S: AmericInn, Budget Inn, Holiday Inn Express
	Med	S: + Hospital
	Other	N: Worthington Muni Airport✈ S: ATMs, Dollar Tree, Family Dollar, Grocery, ShopKO, Walmart sc, Auto Dealers, Visitor Center, Pioneer Village, Northland Mall, Campbell Soup
45		**MN 60, Worthington, Windom** S: MN Welcome Center Rest Area
	TStop	N: Blue Line Travel Center/BP (Scales) S: AmBest/Worthington Travel Plaza/Shell

◊= Regular Gas Stations with Diesel ▲ = RV Friendly Locations ♥= Pet Friendly Locations
Red print shows large vehicle parking / access on site or nearby Brown Print = Campgrounds / RV PARKS

EXIT		MINNESOTA
	Food	N: Rest/Blue Line TC
		S: McDonald's, King Wok Buffet
	Lodg	S: Sunset Inn
	Other	N: Laundry/RVDump/Blue Line TC
		S: Wheel Camping & Marine Center▲
(46)		**Weigh Station (EB)**
47		**CR 53 (EB)**
50		**MN 264S, CR 1, Round Lake**
57		**CR 9, Round Lake, Oakabena**
64		**MN 86, Lakefield**
	Gas	N: Standard Station, Mitch's Corner
	Food	N: Hilltop Café
	Lodg	N: Windmill Motel
(69)		**Clear Lake Rest Area (EB)** (RR, Phones, Picnic, Vend)
(72)		**Des Moines Rest Area (WB)** (RR, Phones, Picnic, Vend, PlayArea)
73		**US 71, Jackson, Windom**
	TStop	N: Vets Whoa & Go Fuel Stop #2/Conoco
	Gas	S: BP, Casey's General Store
	Food	N: Burger King, Santee Crossing Family Rest
		S: China Buffet, DQ, Casey's C/O Pizza, Pizza Ranch, Subway
	Lodg	N: Best Western♥, Econo Lodge, Super 8♥
		S: Budget Host Inn, Earth Inn
	Med	S: + Jackson Medical Center, + Jackson Clinic
	Other	N: Jackson KOA▲, Jackson Muni Airport✈, Auto Dealers, RVDump/ Burger King
		S: Kilen Woods State Park
80		**CR 29, Alpha**
87		**MN 4, Main St, Sherburn**
	Gas	S: Cenex
93		**MN 263S, CR 27, Welcome**
	Gas	S: Cenex
	Food	S: Welcome Cafe
	Other	S: Checkers Welcome Campground▲
99		**CR 39, 190th Ave, Fairmont**
102		**I-90 Bus W, MN 15, State St, Fairmont** (EB: Use MN 15 to MN 60E, Mankato)
	TStop	S: Whoa & Go/SuperAmerica, NuMart/ Cenex
	Gas	S: Conoco◈, Phillips 66◈
	Food	S: Happy Chef, McDonald's, Perkins, Pizza Hut, Subway
	Lodg	S: Budget Inn, Comfort Inn♥, Holiday Inn♥, Super 8♥

EXIT		MINNESOTA
	Med	S: + Hospital
	Other	S: CarQuest, Goodyear, Fairmont Muni Airport✈
107		**MN 262N, CR 53, Granada, Imogene**
	Other	S: Flying Goose Campground▲
113		**CR 1, Blue Earth, Huntley, Gukeen**
(119)		**Rest Area (Both dir)** (RR, Phone, Picnic, Vend, PlayArea)
119		**US 169, Blue Earth, Mankato**
	FStop	S: Blue Earth Auto & Truck Stop/ Sinclair
	Gas	S: Shell◈
	Food	S: Country Kitchen, McDonald's, Pizza Hut, Subway
	Lodg	S: AmericInn, Budget Inn, Super 8
	TServ	S: Blue Earth ATS/Tires
	Med	S: + Hospital
	Other	S: Walmart, Fairbault Co Fairgrounds/ RVDump
128		**MN 254S, CR 17, Easton, Frost**
134		**MN 253S, CR 21, Bricelyn**
138		**MN 22, Wells**
146		**MN 109W, CR 6, Alden, Wells**
	TStop	S: Petrol Pumper AmBest #73/BP
	Gas	S: Cenex
	Food	N: Café
154		**MN 13, to US 65, US 69, Albert Lea, Manchester**
	FStop	N: Vets Whoa & Go/SuperAmerica
	Other	S: Spam Museum, Visitor Center
157		**CR 22, Bridge Ave, Albert Lea, Bancroft**
	FStop	S: Budget Mart #5119/Mobil
	Gas	S: Conoco
	Food	S: Applebee's, Arby's, McDonald's
	Lodg	S: AmericInn, Holiday Inn Express
	Med	S: + Hospital
	Other	S: Grocery, Harley Davidson, Pharmacy, Mall, Albert Lea Muni Airport✈
(159AB)		**Jct I-35, N-Twin Cities, Albert Lea, S to Des Moines**
(162)		**Hayward Rest Area (EB)** (RR, Phone, Picnic, Vend, PlayArea)
163		**CR 26, Hayward** (Serv 4-5mi S in Hayward)
	Other	S: Myre Big Island State Park▲
166		**CR 46, Oakland Rd, Hayward**
	Other	N: to Albert Lea/Austin KOA▲
(171)		**Oakland Woods Rest Area (WB)** (RR, Phone, Picnic, Vend, PlayArea)

EXIT		MINNESOTA
175		**MN 105S, I-90 Bus E, CR 46, Oakland Ave, Austin**
	FStop	S: Apollo #3/Conoco
	Gas	S: BP
	Food	S: McDonald's
	Lodg	N: Countryside Inn
	Other	S: River Side Campground▲
177		**US 218N, 14th St NW, Blooming Prairie, Austin** (WB: Use 218N for Owatonna)
	Gas	N: Holiday
		S: Sinclair◈
	Food	N: Applebee's, Arby's, KFC, Quiznos
		S: Hardee's, Burger King, Subway
	Lodg	S: Super 8♥
	Other	N: Grocery, Staples,Target, Mall
178A		**Broadway St, Mapleview, CR 45, 4th St NW, Downtown**
	Gas	S: BP, Conoco◈, Sinclair
	Food	N: Perkins
		S: Burger King
	Lodg	N: AmericInn, Days Inn♥, Holiday Inn♥
	Med	S: + Hospital
	Other	S: Spam Museum, Visitor Center
178B		**6th St NE, Downtown Austin**
179		**11th Dr NE, 10th Pl, Austin**
	TStop	N: Austin Auto Truck Plaza/Citgo (Scales)
	Food	N: Rest/Austin ATP
	TWash	N: Austin ATP
	Other	N: Laundry/Austin ATP
180A		**I-90 Bus W, Oakland Place NE (WB)**
180B		**US 218S, 21st St NE, Lyle**
	Gas	S: Shell
	Lodg	S: Austin Motel
	Other	N: Jay C Hormel Nature Center
		S: Austin Muni Airport✈
181		**28th St NE**
	Other	S: Austin Muni Airport✈
183		**MN 56, 590th Ave, Brownsdale, Rose Creek**
	Gas	S: Cenex
187		**CR 20, 630th Ave, Elkton**
	Other	S: Beaver Trails Campground & RV Park▲
189		**CR 13, 650th Ave, Elkton**
193		**MN 16E, CR 7, Dexter, Preston, Grand Meadow**
	TStop	S: Windmill Travel Center/66
	Food	S: Rest/Windmill TC
	Lodg	S: Budget Inn

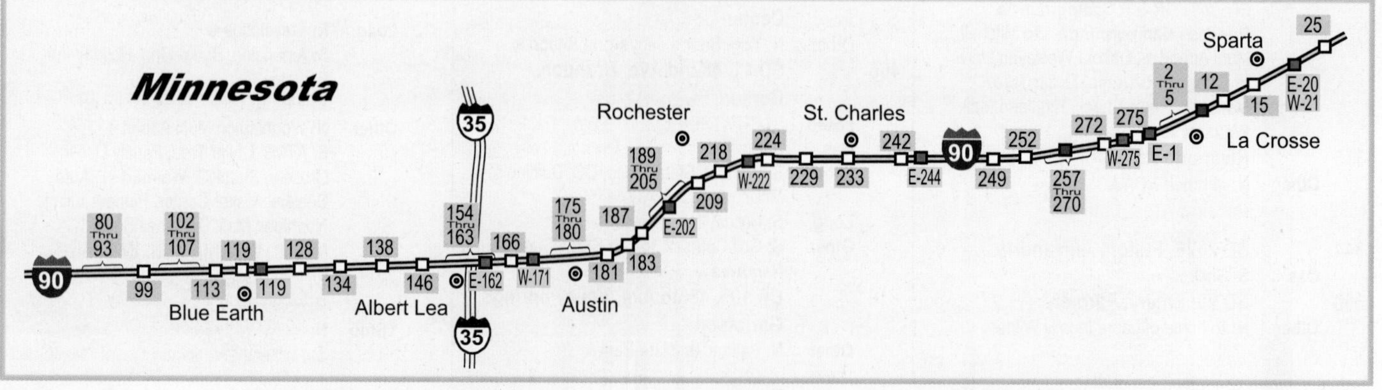

◈= Regular Gas Stations with Diesel ▲ = RV Friendly Locations ♥= Pet Friendly Locations
Red print shows large vehicle parking / access on site or nearby Brown Print = Campgrounds / RV PARKS

EXIT		MINNESOTA
(202)		High Forest Rest Area (EB) (RR, Phones, Picnic, Vend, PlayArea)
205		CR 6/8, Stewartville, High Forest
209A		US 63S, MN 30E, Stewartville (EB)
	Gas	S: KwikTrip
	Food	S: DQ
	Lodg	S: AmericInn ♥
209B		US 63N, MN 30W, Rochester, (EB) US 63, MN 30, Stewartville (WB)
	Med	N: + Hospital (10mi N)
	Other	N: Autumn Woods RV Park ▲, Rochester Int'l Airport ✈, Willow Creek RV Park & Campground ▲
209		US 63N, MN 30W, Rochester (EB), US 63, MN 30, Stewartville (WB)
218		US 52, Chatfield (EB), Rochester (WB)
	Gas	S: BP ◈
	Med	N: + Hospital (9mi N)
	Other	N: Autumn Woods RV Park ▲, Brookside RV Park ▲ S: Rochester/Marion KOA ▲
(222)		Marion Rest Area (WB) (RR, Phones, Picnic, Vend, PlayArea)
224		MN 42N, CR 7, Eyota, Elgin, Plainview
229		CR 10, Chatfield St, Dover
233		MN 74, Chatfield, St Charles
	TStop	S: Amish Market Square Auto Truck Plaza/Texaco
	Gas	N: KwikTrip
	Food	N: Del's Café, Hometown Café, Pizza Factory, Subway S: Rest/Amish Market
	Tires	S: Amish Mkt Sq ATP/Tires
	Other	N: Whitewater State Park S: RVDump/LP/Amish Market
242		CR 29, Utica, Lewiston
(244)		Enterprise Rest Area (EB) (RR, Phone, Picnic, Vend, PlayArea)
249		MN 43S, Rushford
	TServ	N: Peterbilt
252		MN 43N, Winona (All Serv 7 mi N in Winona)
	Med	N: + Hospital (7mi N)
	Other	N: to Pla-Moor Campground & Marina ▲, to Great River Bluffs State Park, Winona Muni Airport ✈
257		MN 76S, Houston, Ridgeway, Witoka
	Other	S: Money Creek Haven Campground ▲
(260)		Weigh Station (Both dir)
266		CR 12, CR 3, Dakota, Nodine
	TStop	S: PTP/Truckers Inn/BP (Scales)
	Food	S: Rest/FastFood/Truckers Inn
	Lodg	S: Motel/Truckers Inn
	TWash	S: Truckers Inn
	TServ	S: Truckers Inn/Tires
	Other	N: Great River Bluff State Park S: Laundry/Truckers Inn
	NOTE:	EB: MM 268 thru MM 269 STEEP GRADE

Personal Notes

EXIT		MN / WI
269		to US 61N, US 14W, CR 12, Cr 101, Dakota (EB), I-90W Albert Lea, US 61N, US 14W, Winona (WB)
	Other	N: Pla-Mor Campground & Marina ▲
270		CR 12, Center St (EB), CR 101, River St (WB), to US 14/61, Dakota
272A		CR 12, Dresbach (EB)
272B		CR 12, Dresbach (EB)
272		CR 12, Dresbach (WB)
275		US 61S, US 14E, to MN 16, La Crescent, La Crosse (All Serv 4-5 mi S in La Crescent)
(275)		MN Welcome Center (WB) (RR, Phone, Picnic, Vend, Info)
	NOTE:	MM 275: Wisconsin State Line

↑ MINNESOTA
↓ WISCONSIN

CENTRAL TIME ZONE

EXIT		
(1)		WI Welcome Center (EB) (RR, Phone, Picnic, Vend, Info)
2		CR B, French Island
	Gas	N: Mobil ◈ S: Citgo ◈
	Food	S: Adams Ribs & Steak House
	Lodg	S: Days Inn
	TServ	N: International
	Other	N: La Crosse Muni Airport ✈

EXIT		WISCONSIN
3		WI 35N, Onalaska (EB), US 53S, WI 35, La Crosse, Onalaska (WB)
	FStop	S: KwikTrip #767
	Gas	S: Speedway ◈
	Food	S: Burger King, Country Kitchen, Embers KFC, McDonald's, North Country Steak Buffet, Pizza Hut, Subway
	Lodg	N: Onalaska Inn S: Best Western, Exel Inn, Hampton Inn, Night Saver Inn, Roadstar Inn, Super 8
	Med	S: + Hospital
	Other	S: Univ of WI/La Crosse, Viterbo College
3A		US 53S, WI 35S, La Crosse (EB)
	Other	S: Univ of WI/La Crosse, Viterbo College
3B		WI 35N, Onalaska (EB)
4		US 53N, WI 157, to WI 16, La Crosse, Onalaska, Midway, Holmen
	Gas	S: Citgo, KwikTrip
	Food	S: Applebee's, Bakers Square, Burger King, Famous Dave's BBQ, Hardee's, Hong Kong Buffet, McDonald's, Panera, Red Lobster, Subway, Taco Bell, Wendy's
	Lodg	S: Comfort Inn, Days Inn
	Med	S: + Hospital
	Other	N: Harley Davidson S: Grocery, Goodyear, Kmart, Office Depot, Sam's Club, ShopKO, Valley View Mall
5		WI 16, Onalaska, W Salem (EB), WI 16, Onalaska, La Crosse (WB)
	Gas	S: Holiday ◈, KwikTrip ◈
	Food	N: Outback Steakhouse, Quiznos S: Applebee's, Carlos O'Kelly, Chuck E Cheese, Hong Kong Buffet, McDonald's, Olive Garden, Perkins, Subway, TGI Friday
	Lodg	N: Baymont Inn, Hampton Inn, Microtel S: Holiday Inn Express
	Med	S: + Hospital
	Other	N: ATMs, Bank, Grocery, Home Depot, Walmart sc, S: Best Buy, ShopKO, Mall
(10.6)		Weigh Station (EB)
12		CR C, Neshonoc Rd, West Salem
	TStop	N: I-90 Cenex
	Food	N: Rest/I-90 Cenex
	Lodg	S: AmericInn
	Tires	N: I-90 Cenex
	Other	N: RV Center, Lakeside Camp Resort ▲, Neshonoc Campground ▲
15		WI 162, Bangor, Rockland
	Gas	N: Spur
	Other	N: Grocery
(20)		Rest Area (EB) (RR, Phone, Picnic, Vend)
(21)		Rest Area (WB) (RR, Phone, Picnic, Vend)
25		WI 27, to WI 71N, WI 21, Sparta, Rockland, Melvina
	FStop	S: Cenex #27, Kwik Trip #318, Amish Cheese House Shell
	Gas	N: Citgo S: Phillips 66
	Food	N: Burger King, Country Kitchen, Happy Chef, Hardee's, McDonald's, Pizza Hut S: Burger King, KFC, Subway
	Lodg	N: Country Inn, Super 8
	Other	S: Walmart sc

◈ = Regular Gas Stations with Diesel ▲ = RV Friendly Locations ♥ = Pet Friendly Locations
Red print shows large vehicle parking / access on site or nearby Brown Print = Campgrounds / RV PARKS

EXIT		WISCONSIN
28		**WI 16, to WI 71S, Sparta**
	FStop	N: Kwik Trip #317
	Gas	N: BP
	Other	N: Sparta Ft McCoy Airport✈
		N/S: Fort McCoy Military Res
41		**WI 131, Superior Ave, Tomah**
	Gas	N: Mobil◈, KwikTrip◈
	Food	N: Chinese, Cafe
	Lodg	N: Days Inn, Park Motel
	Med	N: + Hospital
	Other	N: Bloyer Field✈, Amtrak, **WI State Hwy Patrol Post**
43		**US 12, WI 16, Tomah**
	Gas	N: KwikTrip◈
	Med	N: + Hospital
	Other	N: Bloyer Field✈
	NOTE:	I-90 below runs with I-94 for 93 mi. Exit #'s follow I-90.
(45A)		**Jct I-94W, Twin Cities (EB) (L exit)**
(45B)		**Jct I-90/94E, Wisconsin Dells, Madison (EB), I-90W La Crosse, I-94W St Paul (WB)**
(47.5)		**Weigh Station (WB)**
48		**CR PP, Tomah, Oakdale**
	TStop	N: Road Ranger #209/Citgo (Scales)
		S: Love's Travel Stop # 345 (Scales)
	Food	N: Rest/Road Ranger
		S: Hardee's/Love's TS
	Other	N: Laundry/RoadRanger, **Oakdale KOA▲**
		S: WiFi/Love's TS
(51)		**Weigh Station (EB)**
55		**CR C, CR H, US 12, WI 16, Camp Douglas, Volk Field**
	TStop	S: Camp Douglas BP
	Gas	S: Mobil◈
	Food	S: Subway/Mobil
	Lodg	S: Walsh's K&K Motel, Travelers Rest
	TServ	S: CL Chase Truck Service
	Other	N: **Mill Bluff State Park**, Camp Williams Military Res
		S: Laundry/Camp Douglas BP
61		**WI 80, CR A, New Lisbon, Necedah**
	TStop	N: New Lisbon Travel Center/Citgo, The Bunk House/Mobil
	Food	N: Rest/Bunk House
	Lodg	N: Motel/Bunk House
	Other	N: Laundry/**RVDump**/New Lisbon TC, Laundry/**RVDump**/Bunk House, **to Buckhorn State Park, Ken's Marina & Campground▲**
		S: Mauston New Lisbon Union Airport✈

EXIT		WISCONSIN
69		**WI 82, Mauston, Necedah**
	TStop	N: Pilot Travel Center #164 (Scales) Citgo Travel Plaza
		S: Kwik Trip #775/BP (Scales)
	Gas	N: Shell
		S: Citgo◈
	Food	N: Wendy's/Pilot TC, FastFood/Citgo TP, Country Kitchen
		S: Rest/KwikTrip, McDonald's, Pizza Hut, Roman Castle Rest
	Lodg	N: Best Western, Country Inn, Super 8
		S: The Alaskan Motel
	Med	S: + Hospital
	Other	N: Laundry/WiFi/Pilot TC
		S: Laundry/**RVDump**/KT, Mauston New Lisbon Union Airport✈, Auto Dealers , Walgreen's, **Walmart**
(74)		**Rest Area (EB)** (RR, Phone, Picnic, Vend)
(75)		**Rest Area (WB)** (RR, Phone, Picnic, Vend)
79		**WI HH, Rock St, Lyndon Station**
	TStop	S: Lyndon Station BP
	Food	S: FastFood/Lyndon Station
85		**US 12, WI 16, Wisconsin Dells**
	Lodg	S: Days End Motel
	TServ	S: Rocky Arbor Truck & Trailer Repair
	Other	N: **Rocky Arbor State Park, Sherwood Forest Camping & RV Park▲**
		S: **Bass Lake Campground▲** , **Crockett Resort Camping & RV▲** , **Arrowhead Resort Campground▲** , **Dells Timberland Camping Resort▲** , **Wisconsin Dells KOA▲** , **Edge O'Dells Camping & RV Resort▲**
87		**WI 13N, Wisconsin Dells, to WI 23E, Briggsville**
	FStop	N: Interstate BP
	Gas	N: Citgo◈, Mobil◈, Shell
	Food	N: Burger King, Country Kitchen, Pedros, Denny's, Perkins, Rococo's Pizza, Taco Bell, Wendy's
	Lodg	N: Best Western, Comfort Inn, Days Inn, Holiday Inn, Howard Johnson, Super 8
	Other	N: **RVDump**/Interstate BP, Amtrak, Christmas Mountain Village & Ski Area, **American World Resort & RV Park▲** , **Sherwood Forest Camping & RV Park▲** , **Erickson's Tepee Park Campground▲** , **Wisconsin Dells KOA▲**
89		**WI 23, Lake Delton, Reedsburg**
	Gas	N: Mobil◈
	Food	N: Howie's, Internet Cafe

EXIT		WISCONSIN
	Lodg	N: Country Squire Inn, Grand Marquis Inn, Hilton Garden Inn, Sandman Inn
	Other	S: Home Depot, **Walmart sc**, **Mirror Lake State Park, Country Roads RV Park▲**
92		**US 12, Baraboo, Lake Delton**
	Gas	N: BP◈, Cenex◈, Citgo◈, Mobil◈, Sinclair
	Food	N: Cracker Barrel, Damon's, Denny's, McDonald's, Subway/Sinclair
	Lodg	N: AmericInn, Camelot Inn, Del Rancho, Grand Marquis Inn, Ramada Ltd
		S: Travelodge
	Med	S: + **to Hospital 7mi S**
	Other	N: WI Cheese Museum
		S: Wisconsin Opry, Baraboo Wisconsin Dells Airport✈, **Fox Hill RV Park & Campground▲** , **Yogi Bear's Jellystone Park, Dell Boo Campground▲** , **Mirror Lake State Park**
106		**WI 33, Portage, Baraboo**
	FStop	N: Lake Morgaune Mobil
	Gas	S: BP
	Lodg	S: Cascade Mountain Motel
	Med	N: + Hospital
	Other	N: Portage Muni Airport✈
		S: Cascade Mountain Ski Area, **Sky High Camping Resort▲** , **Devil's Lake State Park**
	NOTE:	I-90 continues EB with I-94 & I-39. Exit #'s follow I-90.
108A		**WI 78S, to US 51N, Wausau, Merrimac**
	TStop	S: Petro Stopping Center #53 (Scales)
	Gas	S: Phillips 66
	Food	S: Subway/Petro SC, Little Caesars
	Lodg	S: Comfort Suites, Days Inn
	TServ	S: Petro SC/Tires
	TWash	S: Blue Beacon TW/Petro SC
	Other	S: Laundry/WiFi/Petro SC, **Devil's Lake State Park**
(108B)		**I-39N, Wausau, Merrimac, Portage**
	Med	N: + Hospital
	Other	N: to WI Dells, Portage Muni Airport✈
(113)		**Rest Area (Both dir)** (RR, Phone, Pic, Vend, **RVDump**)
115		**CR CS/J, Poynette, Lake Wisconsin**
	FStop	N: North Point Plaza/BP
	Food	N: McDonald's, Subway
119		**WI 60, Arlington, Lodi**
	Gas	S: Mobil◈
	Food	S: Rococo's Pizza
	Lodg	S: Best Western
	Other	S: **Interstate RV Center**

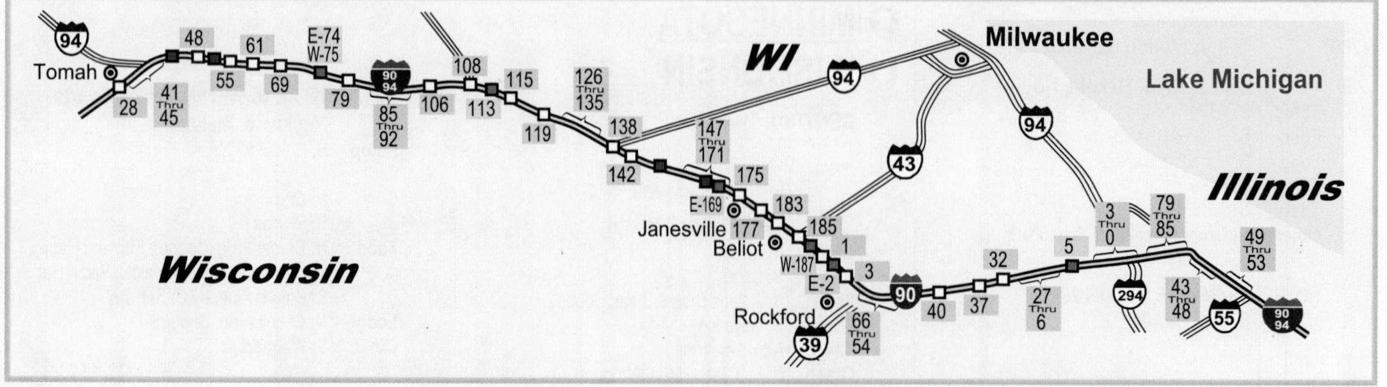

◈= Regular Gas Stations with Diesel ▲ = RV Friendly Locations ♥= Pet Friendly Locations
Red print shows large vehicle parking / access on site or nearby Brown Print = Campgrounds / RV PARKS

EXIT — WISCONSIN

126 — CR V, De Forest, Dane
- Gas: N: BP, Phillips 66◈
  S: Citgo, Exxon◈
- Food: N: Arby's, McDonald's, Subway
- Lodg: N: Holiday Inn Express

131 — WI 19, Waunakee, Sun Prairie
- Gas: N: Mobil, KwikTrip, Speedway
- Food: N: McDonald's, Taco Bell/Speedway
- Lodg: N: Days Inn, Super 8
  S: Country Inn Suites
- TServ: N: Kenworth
- TWash: N: Windsor Truck Wash
- Other: N: Walgreen's

132 — US 51, Madison, De Forest
- TStop: N: Hwy 51 Citgo, AmBest/Truckers Inn #1/Shell (Scales)
  S: Travel Center of America #50/Mobil (Scales)
- Food: N: Rest/Hwy 51, Rest/Truckers Inn
  S: CountryPride/Subway/TacoBell/TA TC
- TWash: N: Truckers Inn
- TServ: N: Truckers Inn/Tires, Peterbilt of WI, Volvo/White/GMC/Freightliner
  S:TA TC/Tires, Brad Ragan Truck, Auto & **RV** Tire Service
- Other: N: Laundry/Hwy 51, Laundry/BarbSh/CB/Truckers Inn
  S: Laundry/WiFi/TA TC, **WI RV World, Camperland RV**

135A — US 151S, Washington Ave, Madison
- Gas: S: BP, Shell, Sinclair
- Food: S: Applebee's, Chili's, Country Kitchen, Cracker Barrel, Denny's, Dunkin Donuts, Hardee's, IHOP, KFC, McDonald's, Mtn Jack's Steakhouse, Olive Garden, Perkins, Ponderosa, Red Lobster, Tumbleweed Grill, Steak 'n Shake, Wendy's
- Lodg: S: Best Western, Comfort Inn, Fairfield Inn, Econo Lodge, Hampton Inn, Holiday Inn, Madison Suites, Microtel, Motel 6♥, Residence Inn, Select Inn
- Other: S: Best Buy, Mall, WI State Hwy Patrol Post, Dane Co Reg'l Airport✈

135B — US 151N, Washington Ave

135C — High Crossing Blvd (WB)
- Lodg: N: Courtyard, Staybridge Suites
  S: East Town Suites, Microtel

(138A) — I-94E, Milwaukee (EB, Left exit)

138B — WI 30W, Madison (WB, Left exit)

NOTE: I-90 runs with I-94 above for 93 mi. Exit #'s follow I-90.

NOTE: I-90 runs below with I-39 to IL State Line. Exit #'s follow I-90.

142A — US 12W, US 18W
- Gas: S: Cenex, Shell
- Food: S: Arby's, Denny's, Wendy's
- Lodg: S: AmericInn, Days Inn, Holiday Inn Express, Quality Inn
- Med: S: + Hospital
- Other: S: to Univ of WI

142B — US 12E, US 18E
- FStop: N: Wagner's Mobil
- Food: N: McDonald's, Subway
- Lodg: N: Knights Inn, Motel 6♥, Ramada Inn, Wingate Inn

(145.5) — Weigh Station (EB)

EXIT — WISCONSIN

147 — CR N, Cottage Grove, Stoughton
- TStop: S: Road Ranger #136/Citgo
- Gas: S: BP
- Food: S: FastFood/Road Ranger, BurgerKing/BP
- Other: N: Grocery

(147.8) — Weigh Station (WB)

156 — US 51N, Stoughton
- Lodg: S: Coachmen's Inn

160 — US 51S, WI 73, to WI 106, Edgerton, Deerfield
- TStop: S: Edgerton AmBest Oasis (Scales)
- Food: S: Rest/Oasis
- TServ: S: Edgerton Oasis/Tires
- Lodg: S: Towne Edge Motel
- Other: N: **Hickory Hills Campground▲**
  S: Laundry/WiFi/**LP**/BP, Jana Airport✈

163 — WI 59, Edgerton, Milton, Newville
- Gas: N: Mobil, Shell
  S: BP
- Food: N: Burger King/Shell, McDonald's, Red Apple/Mobil
- Lodg: N: Comfort Inn
- Other: N: **Blackhawk Campground/Sales/Svc▲, Hidden Valley RV Resort & Campground▲, Lakeland Camping Resort▲, Lakeview Lodge & Campground▲**

(169) — Rest Area (EB)
(RR, Phone, Picnic, Vend)

171A — WI 26, Milton Ave, Janesville (EB)
- FStop: N: Mulligan's Truckstop/66
- TStop: S: Road Ranger #107/Citgo
- Food: N: Cracker Barrel
  S: Rest/Road Ranger
- Lodg: N: Best Western, Hampton Inn, Motel 6♥
- Other: N: Auto Dealers, **Blackhawk Campground▲**

171A — WI 26N, Milton Ave, Janesville (WB)
- FStop: N: Mulligan's Truckstop/P66
- Food: N: Cracker Barrel
- Lodg: N: Best Western, Hampton Inn, Motel 6♥
- Other: N: to **Yogi Bear's Jellystone Park▲, Pilgrim's Campground▲**

171B — US 14W, Janesville (EB)
US 14W, WI 26S (WB)
- Lodg: S: Oasis Motel, Ramada Inn, Super 8

171C — US 14, Humes Rd, Janesville
- TStop: N: Travel Center of America #71/Mobil (Scales)
- Food: N: Wendy's/TA TC
  S: Asia Buffet, Milwaukee Grill
- Lodg: N: Holiday Inn Express, Microtel
  S: Ramada Inn, Super 8
- Other: N: Laundry/TA TC, Auto Dealers

175C — WI 14E

175A — US 14 Bus, Racine St
- Gas: S: BP
- Food: S: Hardee's
- Lodg: S: Lannon Stone Motel

175B — WI 11E, Janesville
- TStop: N: J&R Quick Mart/BP
- Food: N: Subway/QuickMart, Denny's
- Lodg: N: Baymont Inn

177 — WI 11W, WI 351, Avalon Rd, Avalon, Janesville
- Gas: S: BP, KwikTrip
- Other: S: S WI Reg'l Airport✈

EXIT — WI / IL

183 — CR S, Shopiere Rd, Beloit
- TStop: N: Rollette Oil #4/Citgo
- Med: N: + Hospital
- Other: N: **Turtle Creek Campground▲**

185A — WI 81W, Milwaukee Rd, Beloit
- FStop: S: Speedway #4293
- TStop: S: Pilot Travel Center #289 (Scales)
- Gas: S: BP, Exxon◈, Shell
- Food: S: TacoBell/Pilot TC, Applebee's, Arby's, Country Kitchen, Hong Kong Buffet, McDonald's, Perkins, Wendy's
- Lodg: S: Comfort Inn, Econo Lodge, Fairfield Inn, Holiday Inn Express, Super 8
- Other: S: Auto Dealers, Staples, Tires +, **Walmart sc**

(185B) — Jct I-43N, to Milwaukee

(187) — WI Welcome Center (WB)
(RR, Phones, Picnic, Vend, Info)

NOTE: I-90 runs above with I-39 WB to Ex #138. Exit #'s follow I-90.

CENTRAL TIME ZONE

NOTE: MM 188: Illinois State Line

⬆ WISCONSIN
⬇ ILLINOIS

CENTRAL TIME ZONE

NOTE: I-90 below runs with I–39. Exit #'s follow I-90.

1 — US 51N, IL 75W, S Beloit
- TStop: S: Flying J Travel Plaza #5097 (Scales), Road Ranger Travel Center #205 (Scales)
- Food: S: Rest/FastFood/FL TP, Rest/Subway/RR TC
- Lodg: S: Knights Inn, Ramada Inn
- TServ: S: FJ TP
- Other: S: Laundry/WiFi/BarbSh/**RVDump/LP**/FJ TP, Auto Dealers, Auto Services, **Pearl Lake RV Park & Campground Sales & Service▲**, to **Finnegan's RV Center**

(2) — IL Welcome Center (EB)
(RR, Phone, Picnic, Vend, Info, **RVDump**)

76/3 — CR 9, Rockton Rd, Roscoe
- TStop: N: Love's Travel Stop #322 (Scales)
- Food: N: Hardee's/Love's TS
- Other: N: Laundry/WiFi/**RVDump**/Love's TS
  S: Auto Museum

NOTE: I-90 runs below with Tollway. Exit #'s follow Tollway.

(75.5) — S Beloit TOLL Plaza

69 — IL 173

66 — CR 55, Riverside Blvd, Rockford
- FStop: S: Road Ranger Travel Center #211
- Gas: S: BP, Phillips 66◈
- Food: S: FastFood/RR TC, Arby's, Culver's, KFC, McDonald's, Subway, Wendy's
- Lodg: S: Days Inn
- Other: S: Auto Dealers, Auto Services, ATMs, Banks, Grocery

63 — US 20 Bus, E State St, Rockford
- Gas: N: Phillips 66◈
  S: BP, Mobil◈
- Food: N: Cracker Barrel, Subway/Phillips 66

EXIT		ILLINOIS
	Food	S: Applebee's, Arby's, Burger King, Chili's, Country Kitchen, Denny's, Don Pablo,KFC, Hooters, IHOP, Lone Star Steakhouse, McDonald's, Machine Shed Rest, Olive Garden, Perkins, Ruby Tuesday, Steak n Shake, Tumbleweed Grill
	Lodg	N: Baymont Inn, Exel Inn S: Alpine Inn, Best Western, Candlewood Suites, Comfort Inn, Courtyard, Fairfield Inn Hampton Inn, Holiday Inn Express, Quality Suites, Ramada Inn, Red Roof Inn, Residence Inn, Sleep Inn, Super 8
	Med	S: + St Anthony Medical Center
	Other	N: Greyhound, Museum S: Amtrak, Auto Services, Advance Auto Parts, B&N, Best Buy, Borders, CompUSA, Discount Tire, Dollar Tree, Home Depot, Lowe's, Office Depot, Pharmacy, ShopKO, Sam's Club, Target, Wal-Mart
(61/123)		**Jct I-39S, US 51S, to US 20, Cherry Valley, to Rockford Jct I-90E, TOLL, to Chicago**
	Other	S: Magic Waters Theme Park, to **Blackhawk Valley Campground▲**
	NOTE:	**I-90 above runs with I–39 and Tollway. Exit #'s follow Tollway.**
	NOTE:	**I-90 below continues with Tollway. Exit #'s follow Tollway.**
(55)		**Belvidere TOLL Plaza (WB)**
(54.5)		**Belvidere Oasis (Both dir)**
54		**Belvidere-Genoa Rd, Belvidere, Sycamore**
	Other	N: to Boone Co Fairgrounds, to appr 5 mi **Holiday Acres Camping Resort▲** S: to **Sycamore RV Resort▲**
(40)		**TOLL Plaza (EB)**
37		**US 20, Grant Hwy, Hampshire, Elgin, Marengo**
	TStop	N: Travel Center of America #44/BP (Scales), AmBest/Arrowhead Oasis (Scales), Road Ranger #235/Citgo (Scales)
	Food	N: CountryPride/BurgerKing/Popeye's/ TA TC, Rest/Arrowhead, Subway/RR, Wendy's
	Lodg	N: Super 8
	TWash	N: Arrowhead TW
	TServ	N: TA TC/Tires, Arrowhead/Tires
	Other	N: Laundry/WiFi/**RVDump**/TA TC, Laundry/CB/WiFi/Arrowhead, to appr 4mi **Lehman's Lakeside RV Resort▲**, **Chicago Northwest KOA▲**
32		**IL 47, Woodstock (WB)**
	Food	N: Culver's, Great Steak & Potato, Starbucks, Subway, Taco Bell
	Other	N: Prime Outlet Stores, Botts Welding & Truck Service, to appr 14 mi **Will Oaks Campground▲**
27		**CR 34, Randall Rd, Elgin**
	Food	N: Jimmy's Charhouse, Starbucks
	Lodg	N: Country Inn, Comfort Suites
	Med	S: + to Provena St Joseph Hospital
	Other	S: Train Station, **Walmart**
(25)		**TOLL Plaza**
24		**IL 31N, State St, Elgin**
	Gas	N: Thornton's◈ BP

Personal Notes

EXIT		ILLINOIS
	Food	N: Alexander's, Cracker Barrel, McDonald's, Quiznos, Wendy's
	Lodg	N: Hampton Inn, Marriott, Quality Inn, Super 8, Towneplace Suites
	Other	N: ATMs, Auto Services, Firestone, NTB, Spring Hill Mall, UPS Store S: Judson College
23		**IL 25, Dundee Ave, Elgin**
	Gas	S: Shell, Speedway◈
	Food	S: Arby's, Subway
	Lodg	N: Days Inn
	Med	S: + Hospital
21		**Beverly Rd, Elgin (WB)**
	Other	N: Sears Arena
19		**IL 59, Sutton Rd, Barrington**
	Lodg	N: Marriott
	Med	S: + Hospital
	Other	N: Cabela's
17		**Barrington Rd, Schaumburg (WB)**
	Gas	S: 7-11, BP, Shell
	Food	S: Chili's, IHOP, Lone Star Steakhouse, Max & Erma's, Romano's Macaroni Grill, Steak 'n Shake, TGI Friday
	Lodg	S: Baymont Inn, Candlewood Suites, Hampton Inn, Hilton Garden Inn, Hyatt Place, La Quinta Inn♥, Red Roof Inn♥
	Med	S: + St Alexius Medical Center
	Other	N: to Cabela's S: ATMs, Auto Services, Pharmacy, Sam's Club, Target, Tires
13		**Roselle Rd, Schaumburg (WB)**
	Food	N: Medieval Times Dinner Theatre S: Ho Luck Rest, Outback Steakhouse, Red Lobster, Super China Buffet

EXIT		ILLINOIS
	Lodg	N: Extended Stay America S: Country Inn, Holiday Inn, Homestead Suites, Wingate Inn
	Other	N: Harper College S: Auto Dealers
(11)		**Jct I-290, IL 53, IL 58, Golf Rd, Rolling Meadows, Elk Grove**
	Food	N: Ming's Chinese, Hong Kong Cafe S: Joe's Crab Shack, Olive Garden, Stir Crazy Café, Morton's
	Lodg	N: Holiday Inn, Radisson S: AmeriSuites, Hyatt, Residence Inn, Springhill Suites
	Other	S: Woodfield Mall, Costco, Sam's Club
9		**Arlington Heights Rd, Golf Rd**
	Gas	N: BP S: Shell
	Food	N: Applebee's, Arby's, Baja Fresh, Chili's, Denny's, Magnum's Steakhouse, Panda Express, Starbucks, Sushi Rest, Yanni's Greek Rest
	Lodg	N: AmeriSuites, Courtyard, DoubleTree, Extended Stay America, Holiday Inn Express, Motel 6♥, Red Roof Inn, Wingate Inn S: Sheraton Suites♥
	Med	N: + NW Medical Center
	Other	N: ATMs, Auto Services, Banks, Golf Courses, Firestone, NTB, Sam's Club, **Walmart**, US Army Reserve Center S: Golf Courses, Tires
6		**Elmhurst Rd, Des Plaines, Elk Grove Village, Mt Pleasant (WB)**
	Gas	N: 7-11, Citgo, Mobil S: Amoco, BP, Marathon
	Food	S: Burger King, Dunkin Donuts, Lou's Pizzeria, McDonald's, Subway
	Lodg	N: Country Inn S: Comfort Inn, Days Inn, Excel Inn, Holiday Inn, Howard Johnson, InTowne Suites
	Other	N: Sam's Club
(5)		**Des Plaines Oasis (Both dir)**
	FStop	Mobil
	Food	McDonald's, Panda Express, Starbucks
	Other	CarWash
3		**IL 72, Lee St, Higgins Rd (WB)**
	Food	N:Cafe La Cave, Chili's, Chipolte Mex Grill, IHOP, Potbelly Sandwiches, Starbucks, Steak 'n Shake, Subway S: Elliots Deli, Harry Carey's Ital Steakhouse, Nick's Fish Market
	Lodg	N: Extended Stay America, Quality Inn, Radisson, Residence Inn, Wyndham S: Best Western, Holiday Inn Select, Holiday Inn Express, Travelodge
	Other	N: Allstate Arena S: Train Station, O'Hare Airport✈
(2)		**TOLL Plaza**
(1)		**Jct I-294N, Tri State Tollway, to Wisconsin (WB) Jct I-294, I-190, Wisconsin, Indiana, O'Hare Airport (EB)**
(.5)		**TOLL Plaza Begin/End IL NW Tollway**

◈= Regular Gas Stations with Diesel ▲ = RV Friendly Locations ♥= Pet Friendly Locations
Red print shows large vehicle parking / access on site or nearby Brown Print = Campgrounds / RV PARKS

EXIT		ILLINOIS
(0)		US 190W, Chicago O'Hare, to I-294S, Tri State Tollway (WB) I-90E, Kennedy Expy, Chicago Lp (EB)
	NOTE:	I-90 above runs with Tollway. Exit #'s follow Tollway.
	NOTE:	I-90 below continues as Kennedy Expy. Exit #s follow Kennedy Expy
79A		IL 171, Cumberland Ave S
	Food	S: Deli, Subway, Triangle Cafe
	Lodg	S: Clarion, Marriott
	Other	S: Train Station, Greyhound Terminal
79B		IL 72, Higgins Rd, Cumberland Ave
	Gas	N: Citgo, Mobil
	Food	N: Chicago Hot Dog Factory, Denny's, Hooters, McDonald's, Porters Steak House, Outback Steakhouse, Starbucks
	Lodg	N: AmeriSuites, Holiday Inn, Marriott
	Other	N: Grocery, Walgreen's
80		Canfield Rd (WB)
81A		IL 43, Harlem Ave
	Gas	S: BP, Shell
	Food	S: Hansen's Fish Pier, Mr K's, Sally's Pancakes, Wendy's
	Med	N: + Resurrecton Medical Center
	Other	S: Train Station
81B		Sayre Ave
82A		Nagle Ave
82B		Bryn Mawr Ave (WB)
82C		Avondale Ave, Austin Ave (EB)
83AB		Foster Ave, Central Ave (WB)
	Gas	N: BP
	Food	N: Checkers, Dunkin Donuts
	Other	N: Walgreen's
84		Lawrence Ave
	Gas	N: BP
	Food	S: Dunkin Donuts, McDonald's, Subway
(85)		I-94W, Skokie, Chicago
	NOTE:	I-90 below runs with I-94 . Exit #'s follow I-94.
43A		Wilson Ave (WB)
(43B)		Jct I-90W
43C		Montrose Ave
43D		Kostner Ave
44A		IL 19, Keeler Ave
	Gas	N: BP, Shell
	Other	N: Wrigley Field
44B		Pulaski Rd, Irving Park Rd
	Gas	N: BP, Mobil
45A		Addison St
45B		Kimball Ave
	Gas	N: Marathon◈
		S: Marathon, Mobil
	Food	S: Dunkin Donuts, Subway, Wendy's
45C		Kedzie Ave, Belmont Ave
46A		California Ave
	Gas	S: Mobil
	Food	S: IHOP, Popeye's Chicken
	Other	N: Laundromat
46B		Diversey Ave

EXIT		ILLINOIS
47A		Western Ave, Fullerton Ave
	Gas	N: Citgo, Phillips 66
		S: Marathon
	Food	N: Dunkin Donuts, Popeye's, Subway
	Other	N: Home Depot
47B		Damen Ave
48A		Armitage Ave
	Gas	N: Mobil
		S: BP
48B		IL 64, North Ave, Ashland Ave
	Gas	N: BP
		S: BP, Shell
	Food	S: Huddle House
49A		Division St
	Gas	S: BP, Shell
49B		Augusta Blvd, Milwaukee Ave
50A		Ogden Ave
50B		Ohio St
51A		Randolph St, Lake St (WB)
51B		Lake St, Randolph St (EB), Washington Blvd, Ohio St (WB)
51C		Madison, Washington Blvd (WB) Randolph, Washington (EB)
51D		Washington, Madison St (EB) Monroe St, Madison St (WB)
51E		Madison St, Monroe St (EB) Adams St, Monroe St (WB)
51F		Monroe St, Adams St (EB)
51G		Adams St, Jackson Blvd (EB)
51HI		Van Buren St, I-290, Congress Pkwy, West Suburbs
52A		Taylor St, Roosevelt Rd (EB)
	Gas	N: Shell
		S: Citgo
52B		Roosevelt Rd, Taylor St (WB)
52C		18th St (EB)
	Gas	N: Shell
53		Cermak Rd, Archer Ave, I-55 (EB)
53A		Archer Ave, I-55 (EB), Cermak Rd, S Canalport Ave (WB)
(53B)		Jct I-55, Stevenson Expy
(53C)		Jct I-55, St Louis, Lake Shore Dr
54		31st St
	Med	N: + Hospital
55A		35th St
55B		Pershing Rd
56A		43rd St
56B		47th St (EB)
57A		51st St
	Food	N: McDonald's
	Other	N: Chicago District Police Hdqtrs
57B		Garfield Blvd
	Gas	S: Mobil, Shell
	Food	N: Checkers
		S: Wendy's
58A		59th St

EXIT		IL / ID
58B		63rd St (EB)
	Gas	N: Shell
		S: BP
	Med	S: + Hospital
(59A)		Jct I-94E (EB)
	NOTE:	I-90 above runs with I-94 . Exit #'s follow I-94.
		Begin/End Chicago Skyway Toll Rd
6		State St, to I-94E (WB)
Exit		St Lawrence Ave (WB)
5.5		E 79th St (WB)
5		Stony Island Ave, to IL 41
3		E 87th St (WB)
Exit		TOLL Plaza
Exit		92nd St (EB)
(2)		Chicago Skyway Plaza
	Gas	AmocoBP
	Food	McDonald's
1		US 12, US 20, US 41, Indianapolis Blvd, 106th St, State Line Rd (EB)
	Gas	S: BP◈, Shell◈
	Food	S: Burger King, McDonald's
(0)		Begin/End Chicago Skyway Toll Rd

CENTRAL TIME ZONE

NOTE: MM 103: Indiana State Line

⬆ ILLINOIS

⬇ INDIANA

EXIT		
(0)		Begin IN TOLL EB, End WB
1		US 12, US 20, US 41, 106th St, 108th St, Indianapolis Blvd
	Gas	N: BP◈, Mobil, Shell◈
	Food	S: Burger King, KFC, McDonald's
	Other	S: Amtrak
(1)		TOLL Plaza
3		IN 912E, Cline Ave, Hammond, Gary
5		US 41, Calumet Ave, Hammond
	FStop	N: IMK Truck Stop GasARoo
		S: Speedway #8305
	Gas	N: Gas City
		S: Marathon
	Food	S: Arby's, Dunkin Donuts, KFC, McDonald's, Taco Bell, White Castle
	Lodg	S: AmericInn, Ramada Inn, Super 8
	Other	S: AutoZone, Walgreen's, Car/Truck Wash
10		IN 912, Cline Ave, Gary
	Other	N: Gary Reg'l Airport✈, Trump IN Casino
14A		Grant St, Buchanan St, Gary
	Med	S: + Methodist Hospital
	Other	N: US Steel
14B		IN 53, Broadway
	Other	N: US Steel
		S: Greyhound Terminal, Train Station
(17)		Jct I-65, US 12, US 20, Dunes Hwy, to Indianapolis

◈= Regular Gas Stations with Diesel ▲ = RV Friendly Locations ♥= Pet Friendly Locations
Red print shows large vehicle parking / access on site or nearby Brown Print = Campgrounds / RV PARKS

EXIT | INDIANA

NOTE: I-90 below runs with I-80EB. Runs separately WB. I-80 & I-94 run together WB.

(21) Jct I-80W (IL TOLL), Jct I-94E, to Detroit, US 6W, IN 51, to Des Moines
(Serv on IN 51)
- **TStop** N: Road Ranger Travel Center #239/Citgo (Scales), Flying J Travel Plaza #5085 (Scales), Travel Center of America #219/BP (Scales), Dunes Center Truck Stop (Scales)
- **Food** N: Subway/Road Ranger TC, Rest/FastFood/FJ TP, Buckhorn/Popeyes/Subway/TA TC, McDonald's, Ponderosa
- **TWash** N: Road Ranger, FJ TP, TA TC
- **TServ** N: FJ TP/Tires, TA TC/Tires, Dunes Center TS/Tires
- **Other** N: Laundry/BarbSh/CB/WiFi/FJ TP, Laundry/WiFi/TA TC

(22) George Ade Service Area (EB) John T McCutcheon Service Area (WB)
- **FStop** BP #70512/#70511
- **Food** Hardee's

23 600W, Portage, Port of Indiana
- **Gas** N: Marathon, Shell
  S: AmocoBP, Marathon
- **Food** S: Burger King, Dunkin Donuts, KFC, Jimmy John Subs, First Wok, McDonald's, Starbucks, Subway, Wendy's
- **Lodg** N: Comfort Inn, Holiday Inn Express
- **Other** N: Yogi Bear's Jellystone Park▲
  S: Grocery, Walgreen's, US Post Office

(24) Indiana TOLL Plaza

31 IN 49, Chesterton, Valparaiso
- **Med** S: + Hospital
- **Other** N: to appr 4mi Sand Creek RV Park▲

(38) TRUCK Rest Area (Both dir)

39 US 421, Westville, Michigan City

49 IN 39, La Porte, Rolling Prairie
(Addt'l services 4 mi S in La Porte)
- **Lodg** N: Hampton Inn
  S: Best Value Inn, Cassidy Motel & RV Park▲

(56) Knute Rockne Service Area (EB) Wilbur Shaw Service Area (WB)
- **FStop** BP #70510/#70509
- **Food** McDonald's, DQ
- **Other** Phone, RVDump

NOTE: MM 62: Central / Eastern Time Zone

72 US 31, St Joseph Valley Pkwy, South Bend, to Plymouth, Niles
- **FStop** N: Speedway #6674 (Scales)
- **TStop** N: Pilot Travel Center #35 (Scales)
- **Food** N: Subway/Pilot TC
  S: McDonald's, Ponderosa, Taco Bell
- **Lodg** N: Super 8
  S: Days Inn, Quality Inn
- **TServ** S: Whiteford Kenworth
- **Other** N: WiFi/Speedway, WiFi/Pilot TC
  S: Amtrak, Michiana Reg'l Transportation Center Airport ✈, South Bend Reg'l Airport✈, IN State Hwy Patrol Post

77 IN 933, US 31 Bus, South Bend, to Notre Dame University
- **Gas** N: Meijer◇, Mobil, Phillips 66
  S: Marathon, Phillips 66◇
- **Food** N: Arby's, Burger King, DQ, Damon's, Fazoli's, McDonald's, Papa John's, Pizza Hut, Ponderosa, Steak & Ale, Subway
  S: Bob Evans, Denny's, Perkins, Taco Bell, Wendy's
- **Lodg** N: Comfort Suites, Days Inn, Hampton Inn, Motel 6♥, Ramada Inn, Super 8
  S: Best Inn, Howard Johnson, Holiday Inn, Knights Inn, Inn at St. Mary's, Signature Inn, Wingate Inn
- **Other** N: Auto Zone, NAPA, Radio Shack, Walgreen's
  S: to Notre Dame Univ

83 IN 331, Capital Ave, Granger, to Mishawaka
- **Gas** N: BP◇, Citgo, Phillips 66◇
  S: Meijer◇
- **Food** N: Applebee's, Arby's, Olive Garden, Panda Express, Pizza Hut, Taco Bell, Wendy's
  S: Arby's, Burger King, Carrabba's, Chili's, Lone Star Steakhouse, McDonald's, Outback Steakhouse, Ryan's Grill, Steak 'n Shake, Subway, TGI Friday
- **Lodg** N: Carlton Lodge, Fairfield Inn, Hampton Inn, Holiday Inn, Super 8
  S: Best Western, Courtyard, Extended Stay America, Studio Plus
- **Other** N: Best Buy, CVS, Kroger, Office Depot, Target, Walgreen's, Mall, South Bend KOA▲
  S: Auto Dealers, B&N, Discount Tire, Lowe's, Sam's Club, Walmart sc

(90) George N Craig Service Area (EB) Henry F Schricker Service Area (WB)
- **TStop** BP #70508/#70507
- **Food** Arby's, Burger King, Pizza Hut, Starbucks
- **Other** RVDump

92 IN 19, Cassopolis St, Elkhart
- **Gas** N: 7-11, Phillips 66◇
  S: Marathon◇, Shell, Speedway
- **Food** N: Applebee's, Cracker Barrel, Perkins, Steak 'n Shake, Starbucks
  S: Arby's, Bob Evans, Burger King, KFC, Long John Silver, McDonald's, Olive Garden, Red Lobster, Ryan's Grill, Taco Bell, Texas Roadhouse, Wendy's
- **Lodg** N: Best Western, Comfort Suites, Country Inn, Econo Lodge, Hampton Inn, Holiday Inn Express, Knights Inn, Quality Inn, Sleep Inn
  S: Budget Inn, Days Inn, Jameson Inn, Ramada, Red Roof Inn♥, Super 8
- **Med** S: + Hospital
- **Other** N: ATMs, Grocery, CVS, RV Repair, Tiara RV Center, Elkhart Campground▲
  S: ATMs, AutoZone, CarQuest, Dollar Tree, Walgreen's, Walmart sc, Elkhart City Airport✈, Holiday World RV Center, Michiana RV, Cruise America, to Camping World/RVDump

96 Elkhart East
- **Gas** S: 7-11, BP◇
- **Food** S: McDonald's, Subway

101 IN 15, Bristol, to Goshen
- **Gas** S: Speedway◇

107 US 131, IN 13, Constatine, Middlebury
(Addt'l Serv 5 mi S in Middlebury)
- **FStop** N: Marathon
  S: Snappy Food Mart/BP
- **Lodg** N: Plaza Motel
- **Other** S: Eby's Pines RV Park▲, Elkhart Co/Middlebury KOA▲, to Coachman RV Factory

(108) TRUCK Rest Area

121 IN 9, Howe, Sturgis, LaGrange
- **Food** N: Applebee's, Golden Corral, Wendy's
- **Lodg** N: Hampton Inn, Travel Inn Motel, Comfort Inn, Knights Inn
  S: Holiday Inn, Super 8
- **Med** N: + Hospital
  S: + Hospital
- **Other** S: to Grand View Bend RV Park/RVDump

(126) Gene Porter Service Area (EB) Ernie Pyle Service Area (EB)
- **FStop** Mobil #70572
- **Food** Hardee's
- **Other** RVDump

(144) Jct I-69, US 27, Fremont, Angola, Fort Wayne, Lansing
- **TStop** N: Petro 2 #45/Mobil (Scales), Pilot Travel Center #29 (Scales), Pioneer Auto Truck Stop/Shell (At Exit #157 on I-69)

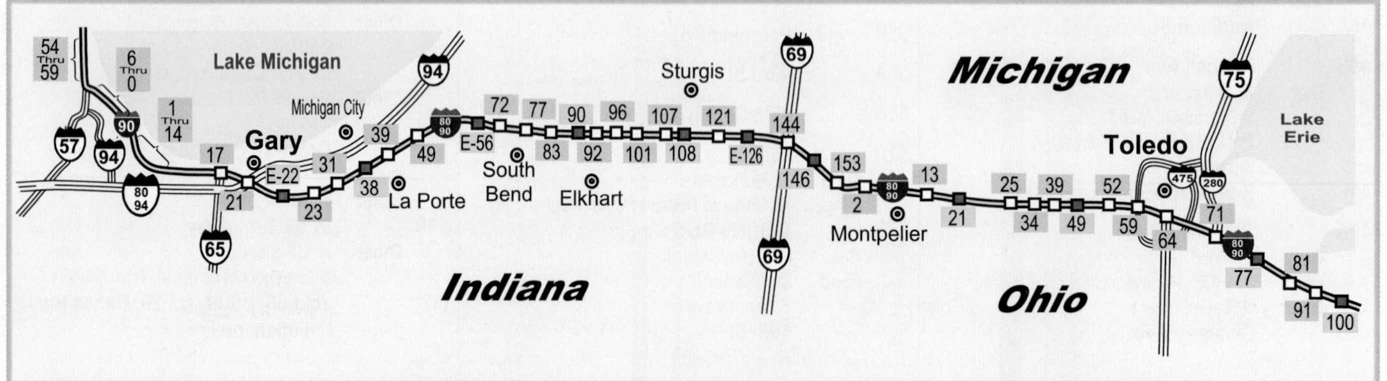

◇= Regular Gas Stations with Diesel ▲ = RV Friendly Locations ♥ = Pet Friendly Locations
Red print shows large vehicle parking / access on site or nearby Brown Print = Campgrounds / RV PARKS

EXIT **IN / OH**

Gas S: Marathon◊
Food N: Rest/FastFood/Petro2, Wendy's/Pilot TC
Lodg N: Redwood Lodge
S: Hampton Inn, Holiday Inn Express, Super 8, Travelers Inn
TServ S: Cummins, Discover Volvo Trucks
Other N: Laundry/WiFi/LP/Petro2, Laundry/WiFi/Pilot TC
S: Outlet Mall, U-Haul

(146) J R Riley Service Area (EB)
Booth Tarkington Service Area (EB)
FStop Mobil /#70580
Food McDonald's

(153) Indiana TOLL Plaza

EASTERN TIME ZONE

NOTE: MM 157: Ohio State Line

INDIANA
OHIO

NOTE: I-90 runs below with I-80. Exit #'s follow I-80.

NOTE: EB: Begin TOLL, WB End

(2.7) TOLL Plaza Westgate

2 OH 49, Edon, Edgerton, to US 20, Allen MI
Gas N: Mobil
Food N: Burger King, Subway

13 OH 15, US 20 Alt, Holiday City, Montpelier, Bryan
FStop S: Holiday City Stop N Go/Sunoco, Hutch's Karry Out/Marathon
Food S: Subway/Marathon, Country Fair Rest
Lodg S: Econo Lodge♥, Holiday Inn Express, Ramada Inn
TServ S: Hutch's Marathon/Tires
Other N: Lazy River Resort Campground▲, to appr 7 mi Loveberry's Funny Farm Campground▲

(21) Tiffin River Service Plaza (EB)
Indian Meadow Service Plaza (WB)
TStop Sunoco #7106/#7105
Food Hardee's
Other Picnic, RVDump/Overnite▲

25 OH 66, Archbold-Fayette, Burlington
Lodg S: to Sauder Heritage Inn
Other N: to Harrison Lake State Park▲
S: to Hidden Valley Campground▲

34 OH 108, Wauseon, Napoleon
TStop S: Turnpike Shell
Gas S: Circle K, DM, Mobil
Food S: Subway/Shell, Burger King, Pizza Hut, McDonald's, Smith's Rest, Taco Bell, Wendy's
Lodg S: Arrowhead Motel♥, Best Western, Holiday Inn Express, Super 8
TServ S: Turnpike Shell, Wood Truck Service
Med S: + Hospital
Other N: Fulton Co Fairgrounds/RVDump▲, appr 5mi Sunny's Shady Rec Area▲, to appr 18mi Lake Hudson Rec Area▲
S: ATMs, Auto Service, Family Dollar, Walmart

39 OH 109, Delta, Lyons
TStop S: Country Corral/Citgo
Food S: Rest/Country Corral,

Personal Notes

EXIT **OHIO**

Other S: Delta Wings Airport✈, Maumee State Forest

(49) Fallen Timbers Service Plaza (EB)
Oak Openings Service Plaza (WB)
TStop Valero
Food Nathan's, Cinnabon, Pizza Uno, Great American Bagel
Other Picnic

52 OH 2, Swanton, Toledo Airport
Lodg S: Days Inn, Quality Inn
Other N: CFS Truck & Fleet Repair
S: Grocery, Budget, U-Haul, Express Auto & Truck Service, Toledo Express Airport✈, RV Center, to Big Sandy Campground▲, Twin Acres Campground▲, Bluegrass Campground▲, Hidden Lake Campground▲, Betty's Country Campground▲

59 US 20, Reynolds Rd, to I-475, to US 23, Maumee, Toledo
Gas N: BP◊, Shell, Speedway◊
S: Meijer◊, Speedway
Food N: Arby's, Bob Evans, Damon's, Dragon Buffet, Little Caesars, McDonald's, Olive Garden, Pizza Hut, Steak n Shake, Waffle House
S: Fazoli's, Outback Steakhouse, Red Lobster, Taco Bell
Lodg N: Clarion, Econo Lodge, Holiday Inn, Motel 6♥, Quality Inn
S: Baymont Inn, Courtyard, Country Inn, Comfort Inn, Days Inn, Econo Lodge, Fairfield Inn, Hampton Inn, Homewood Suites, Red Roof Inn♥,

EXIT **OHIO**

Med N: + to Medical Univ of OH/Toledo
S: + St Luke's Hospital
Other N: ATMs, Advance Auto, Banks, FedEx Kinko's, Grocery, Goodyear, Kmart, RiteAid, Walgreen's, Southwyck Mall, Auto & RV Repair, to Toledo Stadium
S: Auto Dealers, UPS Store

(64) Jct I-75N, Perrysburg, Toledo
Other to Bowling Green State Univ, Toledo Zoo, Fifth Third Field

(71) I-280, OH 420, Perrysburg, Stony Ridge, Toledo, to I-75N, Detroit
TStop N: I-280/1B: Petro Stopping Center #17/Mobil (Scales), Flying J Travel Plaza #5450/Conoco (Scales)
S: Travel Center of America #87/BP (Scales), Fuel Mart #641 (Scales), Pilot Travel Center #12 (Scales)
Food N: IronSkillet/PizzaHut/Petro SC, Cookery/FastFood/FJ TP
S: CountryPride/BurgerKing/TacoBell/TA TC, Rest/Fuel Mart, McDonald's/Pilot TC, Wendy's
Lodg N: Motel/Petro SC, Howard Johnson, Crown Inn, Ramada Ltd, Stony Ridge Inn, Super 8, Vista Inn Express
TWash N: Blue Beacon TW/Petro SC
S: Fuel Mart
TServ N: Petro SC/Tires
S: TA TC/Tires, Fuel Mart/Tires, 795 Tire Service, Williams Detroit Diesel
Other N: Laundry/BarbSh/WiFi/Petro SC, Laundry/BarbSh/WiFi/RVDump/LP/FJ TP, to Metcalf Field✈
S: Laundry/WiFi/TA TC, Laundry/Fuel Mart, WiFi/Pilot TC, Toledo East/Stony Ridge KOA▲

(77) Wyandot Service Plaza (EB)
Blue Heron Service Plaza (WB)
TStop Valero
Food Hardee's, Gloria Jeans Coffees, Mancino's Italian Eatery
Other WiFi, Picnic Area, RVDump/OverNite▲

81 OH 51, Elmore, Gibsonburg, Woodville
Other S: Wooded Acres Campground▲, to Eagle Lake Camping Resort▲

91 OH 53, Fremont, Port Clinton, to US 6, US 20, US 2, Sandusky
FStop S: BP #137
Lodg N: Days Inn
S: Comfort Inn, Fremont Turnpike Motel, Hampton Inn, Holiday Inn
Med S: + Hospital
Other N: to Lake Erie Islands, Rutherford B Hayes Presidential Center, to RV Dealer, Shade Acres Campground▲, Erie Islands Resort & Marina▲
S: Wooded Acres Campground▲, RV Dealer, Fremont Airport✈, to Cactus Flats Campground▲

(100) Comm Perry Service Plaza (EB)
Erie Islands Service Plaza (WB)
TStop Valero
Food Burger King, Carvel, Cinnabon, Einstein Bros, Starbucks, Sbarro
Other WiFi, Picnic Area

110 OH 4, Bellevue, Sandusky, Attica
Other N: to Cedar Point, Lazy J RV Resort▲

◊ = Regular Gas Stations with Diesel ▲ = RV Friendly Locations ♥ = Pet Friendly Locations
Red print shows large vehicle parking / access on site or nearby Brown Print = Campgrounds / RV PARKS

EXIT	OHIO
118	**US 250, Sandusky, Norwalk, Milan**
Gas	N: Marathon, Speedway
Food	N: McDonald's, Subway S: Homestead Rest
Lodg	N: Comfort Inn, Colonial Inn South & **Milan Travel Park▲**, Days Inn, Fairfield Inn, Great Wolf Lodge, Hampton Inn, Holiday Inn Express, Motel 6♥, Super 8
Other	N: **Walmart sc**, to Cedar Point, Lake Erie S: **OH State Hwy Patrol Post**, to Milan Thomas Edison Museum, **Wilcart RV**, **Pin Oak RV**, Norwalk Raceway Park, S: to appr 10 mi **Berlin Heights Holiday Park▲**
135	**Baumhart Rd, to OH 2, Amherst, Vermilion, Huron, Sandusky**
Other	N: to **Swift Hollow RV Resort▲**, **Neff Bros RV/RVDump** S: to appr 8mi **Berlin Heights Holiday Park▲**
(139)	**Vermilion Valley Service Plaza (EB) Middle Ridge Service Plaza (WB)**
TStop	Valero
Food	Burger King, Great Steak, Manchu Wok, Panera, Popeye's, Starbucks, TCBY
Other	Picnic, WiFi, **RVDump/OverNite▲**
140	**OH 58, Leavitt Rd, Amherst, Oberlin**
Gas	N: Sunoco◊
Food	N: Subway/Sunoco
Other	S: to Lorain Co Reg'l Airport ✈
(142)	**Jct I-90E, to OH 2, W Cleveland (EB)**
Other	to Cleveland, Erie PA, Buffalo NY
NOTE:	**I-90WB runs above with I-80/OH TPK. Exit #'s follow I-80.**
145AB	**OH 57, Lorain, Elyria, to I-80E, OH Tpk**
145	**OH 57, Lorain Blvd, Lorain, Elyria, to I-80E, OH Tpk**
Gas	N: BP◊, Speedway, Shell S: Shell, Speedway
Food	N: Applebee's, Bob Evans, Country Kitchen, Denny's, Lone Star Steakhouse, Red Lobster, Smokey Bones BBQ, Subway, Wendy's
Lodg	N: Best Western, Comfort Inn, Country Suites, Econo Lodge, Holiday Inn S: Journey Inn, Super 8
Med	N: + Hospital
Other	N: Mall, Best Buy, Firestone, Goodyear, Lowe's, PetSmart♥, Staples, **Walmart** S: Home Depot, **OH State Hwy Patrol**

EXIT	OHIO
148	**OH 351, OH 254, Avon**
Gas	S: BP, Speedway
Food	S: Arby's, Cracker Barrel, Burger King, McDonald's, Ruby Tuesday, Subway
Other	S: CVS, Dollar General, Dollar Tree, Gander Mountain, Grocery, Sam's Club, Tires, Lorain Co Comm College
151	**OH 611, Colorado Ave, Avon, Sheffield**
TStop	N: Pilot Travel Center #4 (Scales)
Gas	N: BP◊ S: BJ's
Food	N: Subway/Pilot TC, Dianna's Deli, McDonald's
Lodg	N: Fairfield Inn
Other	N: Lake Erie Harley Davidson, **Avon RV Superstore** S: BJ's
153	**OH 83, Avon Belden Rd, Avon**
Gas	N: BP, Circle K, Murphy's, Shell S: Speedway, Costco
Food	N: Burger King, McDonald's, Perkins S: Bob Evans, IHOP, Panera, Wendy's
Other	N: Best Buy, **Walmart** S: CVS, Costco, Home Depot, Target
156	**OH 113, Crocker Rd, Bassett Rd, Westlake, Bay Village**
Gas	N: BP, Shell S: Marathon◊
Food	S: Applebee's, Bob Evans, Max & Erma's, McDonald's, Subway, Wendy's
Lodg	N: Extended Stay America, Holiday Inn, Marriott, Red Roof Inn♥, Residence Inn S: Hampton Inn
Med	S: + Hospital
Other	S: Mall, Cinema, CVS, Grocery, Kmart, UPS Store
159	**OH 252, Columbia Rd, Westlake**
Gas	N: Speedway S: BP
Food	N: Carrabba's, Dave & Buster's, Joe's Crab Shack, Outback Steakhouse, Tony Roma S: Houlihan's, McDonald's
Lodg	N: Courtyard, Super 8
Med	N: + Lakewood Medical Center
Other	S: CVS, Grocery, NTB, UPS Store
160	**Clague Rd, Westlake, Rocky River (WB) (Access to Ex #159 Serv)**
161	**OH 2E, OH 254, Detroit Rd, Rocky River, Lakewood (EB)**
162	**Hilliard Blvd, Rocky River (WB)**
Other	S: to Westgate Mall

EXIT	OHIO
164	**McKinley Ave, Lakewood**
165	**Warren Rd, W 140th St, Bunts Rd, Lakewood (EB)**
165A	**Warren Rd, Cleveland (WB)**
Med	N: + Hospital
165B	**W 140th St, Bunts Rd (WB)**
Gas	N: Marathon
166	**W 117th St, Cleveland**
Gas	N: BP, Shell
Other	N: Carwash, Home Depot
167	**OH 10, Lorain Ave, West Blvd, Cleveland (EB)**
167A	**98th St, West Blvd (WB)**
167B	**OH 10, Lorain Ave (WB)**
169	**W 44th St, W 41st St**
Med	N: + Hospital
170A	**Wade Ave, US 42, W 25th St, OH 3, Scranton Rd, Cleveland (EB)**
(170B)	**Jct I-71S, I-176, Columbus (EB)**
(170C)	**I-490E, to I-77, South Akron (EB)**
(170B)	**Jct I-71S, to Columbus, to I-176, Parma, Zoo (WB)**
171C	**W 14th St, Abbey Ave (WB)**
171	**Abbey Ave, Fairfield Ave, W 14th (WB)**
171A	**US 422S, OH 14, Ontario Ave (EB)**
171B	**US 422N, OH 14, OH 8, OH 10 (EB)**
Other	to Cleveland Browns Stadium, Convention Center, Jacobs Field
(172)	**Jct I-77S, to Akron (WB)**
(172A)	**Jct I-77S, to Akron (EB)**
172B	**E 9th St, Central Ave (EB)**
Med	S: + St Vincent Hospital
Other	N: Jacobs Field, Gund Arena
172C	**E 22nd St, Central Ave, to Carnegie Ave West (EB)**
Other	to Cuyahoga Comm College, to Cleveland State Univ
172D	**Carnegie Ave E, to Euclid Ave, OH 20, Cleveland (EB)**
173A	**Prospect Ave E, to Euclid Ave, US 20, Jacobs Field, Gund Arena (WB)**

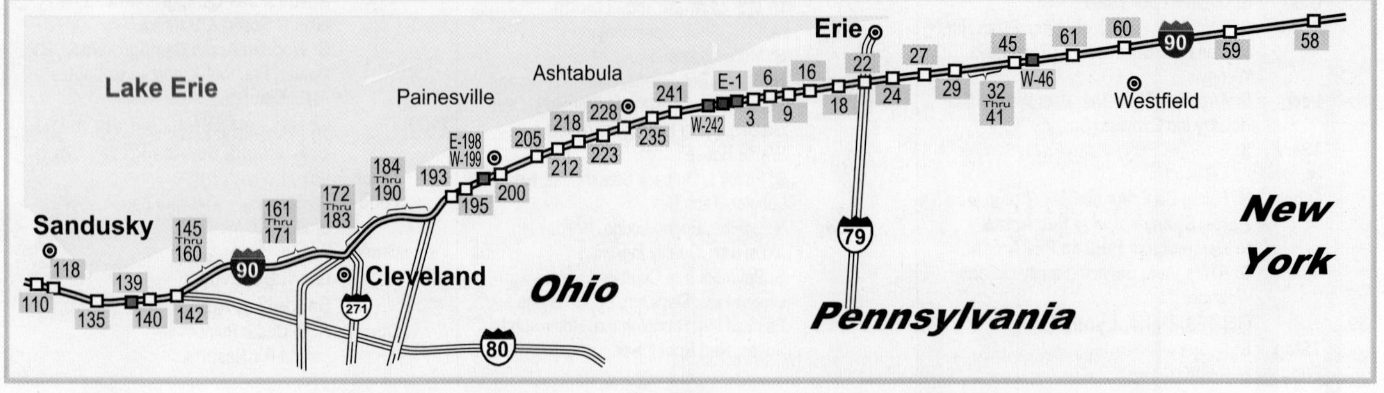

◊= Regular Gas Stations with Diesel ▲ = RV Friendly Locations ♥= Pet Friendly Locations
Red print shows large vehicle parking / access on site or nearby Brown Print = Campgrounds / RV PARKS

EXIT — OHIO

173B **US 322, Chester Ave East (EB)**
E 24th St, Chester Ave (WB)
- Other — **N:** Cleveland St Univ, Playhouse Square

173C **Superior Ave, E 30th St (EB),**
E 26th St, US 6, St Clair Ave (WB)

174A **Lakeside Ave (EB)**

174B **OH 2W, Lakewood (EB, SHARP Curve)**
OH 2W, Downtown Cleveland (WB)
- Other — **N:** Burke Lakefront Airport✈, **to** The Flats, Rock & Roll Hall of Fame, Amtrak Station, Cleveland Browns Stadium, Convention Center, Port of Cleveland

175 **E 55th St, Marginal Rd**

176 **E 72nd St**

177 **University Circle, Martin Luther King Dr (NO Trucks)**
- Med — **S:** + Hospital

178 **Eddy Rd, to Bratenahl**

179 **OH 283E, Lake Shore Blvd (EB)**

180 **E 140th St, E 152nd St (WB)**

180A **E 140th St, Cleveland (EB)**

180B **E 152nd St (EB)**

181 **E 156th St (WB) (NO Trucks)**

182A **E 185th St, Cleveland (EB)**
Villaview Rd, Neff Rd (WB)
- FStop — **S:** Marathon Mart
- Gas — **N:** BP
  S: BP, Shell, Speedway
- Other — **N:** Home Depot

182B **E 200th St, Waterloo Rd (EB)**
Lakeland Blvd, E 200th St (WB)
- Gas — **N:** BP
  S: BP
- Med — **N:** + Hospital
- Other — **N:** Laundromat

183 **Lakeland Blvd, E 222nd St**
- Gas — **N:** Sunoco◈

184 **OH 175, E 260th St, Babbitt Rd (WB)**

184A **Babbitt Rd (EB)**

184B **OH 175, E 260th St (EB)**
- Gas — **N:** BP
- Other — **S:** Euclid Square Mall, Cuyahoga Co Airport✈

185 **OH 2E, Painesville (fr EB, Left exit)**

186 **US 20, Euclid Ave, Euclid, Wickliffe**
- Gas — **N:** Sunoco
  S: Shell
- Food — **N:** Denny's, Joe's Crab Shack, McDonald's
  S: KFC, Pizza Hut, Sidewalk Café
- Lodg — **N:** Hampton Inn, Sheraton
- Other — **S:** CVS, Firestone, Kmart, Laundromat

187 **OH 84, Bishop Rd, Wickliffe, to Willoughby Hills, Richmond Hts**
- Gas — **S:** BP, Shell
- Food — **S:** Burger King, McDonald's, Subway
- Lodg — **S:** Holiday Inn
- Med — **S:** + Hospital
- Other — **S:** CVS, Grocery, Laundromat, Sam's Club, Cuyahoga Co Airport✈, Bryant & Stratton College

(188) **Jct I-271S, to Akron, Columbus**

EXIT — OHIO

189 **OH 91, Sam Center Rd, Willoughby, Willoughby Hills**
- Gas — **N:** BP◈, Shell
- Food — **N:** Bob Evans, Burger King, **Cracker Barrel**, Damon's, Eat 'n Park, Subway
- Lodg — **N:** Courtyard, Fairfield Inn, Travelodge
- Med — **N:** + Hospital
- Other — **N:** CVS, Walgreen's, **to** Classic Field

(190) **Jct I-271S, Akron, Columbus**

193 **OH 306, Broadmoor Rd, Mentor, Kirtland, Willoughby**
- Gas — **N:** BP, Shell, Speedway
  S: Marathon
- Food — **N:** McDonald's, Ponderosa, Red Lobster
  S: Burger King, Roadhouse Grill
- Lodg — **N:** Comfort Inn, Motel 6♥, Super 8
  S: Days Inn, Red Roof Inn♥, Travelodge
- Other — **N:** Lakeland Comm College, Holden Arboretum, Lake Farmpark

195 **OH 615, Center St, Mentor, Kirtland Hills**

(198) **Rest Area (EB)**
(RR, Phone, Picnic)

(199) **Rest Area (WB)**
(RR, Phone, Picnic)

200 **OH 44, Painesville, Chardon**
- Gas — **S:** BP◈, Sunoco◈
- Food — **S:** CK's Steakhouse, McDonald's, Waffle House
- Lodg — **S:** AmeriHost Inn, Quail Hollow Resort
- Med — **N:** + Hospital
- Other — **S: OH State Hwy Patrol Post**, Lake Erie College, **Headlands Beach State Park**

205 **CR 227, Vrooman Rd, to OH 86**
(NB: NO Trucks)
- Gas — **S:** BP◈

212 **OH 528, River St, Madison Rd, Madison, Thompson**
- Gas — **N:** Marathon◈
- Food — **N:** McDonald's, Potbelly Sandwiches

218 **OH 534, Geneva, Geneva on the Lake**
- TStop — **N:** Geneva Auto Truck Plaza #227/ Kwik Fill (Scales)
- Gas — **N:** BP, Sunoco
- Food — **N:** Best Friends Rest, KFC, McDonald's, Lighthouse Grill, Pizza Hut, Wendy's
- Lodg — **N:** Howard Johnson
- TWash — **N:** Geneva Truck Wash
- Med — **N:** + Hospital
- Other — **N: to** appr 7mi **Indian Creek Resort▲**, **Willow Lake Campground▲**, **Geneva State Park▲**

223 **OH 45, Austinburg, W to Warren, E to Ashtabula**
- TStop — **N:** Flying J Travel Plaza /Shell (Scales)
  S: Pilot Travel Center #2 (Scales)
- Gas — **S:** BP
- Food — **N:** Rest/FastFood/Flying J TP
  S: FastFood/Pilot TC, Burger King, McDonald's
- Lodg — **N:** Best Value Inn, Comfort Inn, Holiday Inn Express, Sleep Inn, Travelodge
  S: Hampton Inn

EXIT — OH / PA

- TWash — **S:** Pilot TC
- Other — **N:** Laundry/BarbSh/WiFi/**RVDump**/**LP**/FJ TP, **to Hide-A-Way Lakes Campground▲**, **to** 10mi **Indian Creek Resort▲**
  S: Laundry/Pilot TC, Grand River Academy, Kent State Univ

228 **OH 11, Ashtabula, Youngstown, to OH 46, Jefferson**
- Med — **N:** + Hospital

235 **OH 84, OH 193, Kingsville**
- FStop — **N:** Circle K #5564
  S: Fuel Mart/Speedway
- TStop — **S:** Travel Center of America/BP (Scales)
- Gas — **N:** Grab & Go
- Food — **S:** Rest/FastFood/TA TC, Kay's Place
- Lodg — **N:** Dav-Ed Motel
  S: Kingsville Motel
- TServ — **S:** TA TC/Tires, Kingsville Towing/ Recovery
- Other — **N: Locust Lane Campground▲**, **Village Green Campground▲**
  S: Laundry/WiFi/TA TC

241 **OH 7, Conneaut, Andover**
- Food — **N:** Burger King, McDonald's
  S: Beef & Beer Rest
- Lodg — **N:** Days Inn
- Other — **N:** CVS, Grocery, Kmart, **Evergreen Lake Park Campground▲**
  S: to Bayshore Family Camping▲

(242) **OH Welcome Center (WB)**
(RR, Phone, Picnic, Info)
Weigh Station (WB)

EASTERN TIME ZONE

NOTE: MM 244: Pennsylvania State Line

⬆ OHIO
⬇ PENNSYLVANIA

(1) **PA Welcome Center (EB)**
(RR, Phone, Picnic, Vend, Info)
Weigh Station (EB)

3 **US 6N, Cherry Hill, W Springfield**
- TStop — **S:** Stateline BP (Scales)
- Food — **N:** Blue Plate Rest
  S: Rest/Stateline BP
- Lodg — **N:** EJ's Motel, Sunset Motel
- TServ — **S:** Stateline BP/Tires
- Other — **S:** Laundry/Stateline BP, **to Whispering Trails Campground▲**

6 **PA 215, Girard, Albion, E Springfield**
- Gas — **S:** Sunoco
- Lodg — **S:** Miracle Motel
- Other — **N: Pine Lane Campground▲**, **Erie Bluffs State Park, Virginia's Beach Lakefront Cottages & Camping▲**

9 **PA 18, Platea, Girard**
- Gas — **N:** Gulf
- Lodg — **S:** Green Roof Inn
- TServ — **N:** Penn Detroit Diesel
- Other — **N: PA State Hwy Patrol Post**

16 **PA 98, Avonia Rd, Fairview, Franklin Center**
- Other — **N: to** Erie Int'l Airport✈, **Follys End Campground▲**, **Pine Lane Campground▲**, **Erie Bluffs State Park**

EXIT	PENNSYLVANIA
18	**PA 832, Sterrettania Rd, McKean, Presque Isle State Park**
Gas	N: Citgo, Shell◈
Food	N: Burger King
Lodg	S: Best Western
Other	N: **Hills Family Campground▲**, **Sara's Campground on the Beach▲**, Waldameer Amusement Park & Water World, **Presque Isle State Park** S: **Erie KOA▲**
(22A)	**Jct I-79S, to Pittsburgh**
(22B)	**Jct I-79N, to Erie**
24	**US 19, Peach St, Waterford (Exit only)**
Gas	N: Citgo◈, Kwik Fill S: Citgo, Exxon, Sunoco
Food	N: Applebee's, Burger King, Chuck E Cheese, Cracker Barrel, Damon's, Eat 'n Park, Golden Corral, Longhorn Steakhouse, McDonald's, Panera Bread, Ponderosa, Quaker Steak & Lube, Taco Bell, TGI Friday, Wendy's S: Bob Evans
Lodg	N: Courtyard, Motel 6♥ S: Comfort Inn, Country Inn, Econo Lodge, Hampton Inn, Holiday Inn, Microtel
Med	N: + St Vincent Health Center
Other	N: ATMs, Best Buy, Grocery, Home Depot, Lowe's, PetSmart♥, Sam's Club, Staples, Target, **Walmart** Greyhound, Mill Creek Mall, Tinseltown S: Family First Sports Park, **Sparrow Pond Family Campground & Rec Center▲**, **Boyer RV Center**, **Shorehaven Campground▲**
27	**PA 97, Perry Hwy, State St, Erie, Waterford**
FStop	S: Holiday Shell Truck Stop
TStop	S: Pilot Travel Center #311 (Scales)
Gas	N: Citgo◈, Kwik Fill
Food	N: Arby's, Barbato's Italian, McDonald's S: FastFood/Shell, FastFood/Pilot TC
Lodg	N: Best Western, Days Inn♥, Red Roof Inn♥ S: Blue Spruce Motel, Quality Inn♥
Med	N: + Hamot Medical Center, + US Veterans Medical Center
Other	N: Amtrak, Erie Zoo, WW II Monument, U-Haul, Erie Veterans Memorial Stadium
29	**PA 8, Wattsburg Rd, Parade St, Erie, to Hammett**
Gas	N: Country Fair/Citgo S: Kwik Fill
Food	N: Wendy's S: Rest/Travelodge

EXIT	PA / NY
Lodg	S: Travelodge
TServ	S: Lake Erie Ford Trucks, Peterbilt, Tri-Star Truck Service, Cummins, Five Star International
Other	S: Mercyhurst College
32	**PA 430, PA 290W, Station Rd, Erie, Wesleyville, Colt Station**
Gas	N: Citgo
TServ	S: Beckwith CAT, Freightliner
Other	S: **PA State Hwy Patrol Post**, **to Moon Meadows Campground▲**, **Creekside Campground▲**
35	**PA 531, Depot Rd, Erie, Harborcreek**
TStop	N: Travel Center of America/BP (Scales)
Food	N: Rest/FastFood/TA TC
Lodg	N: Rodeway Inn♥/TA TC
TWash	N: Blue Beacon TW/TA TC
TServ	N: TA TC/Tires
Other	N: Laundry/WiFi/RVDump/TA TC S: **to Moon Meadows Campground▲**
(37)	**Jct I-86 E, to Jamestown, NY**
Other	S: **to Creekside Campground▲**
41	**PA 89, North East**
Gas	N: Shell
Food	N: New Harvest Rest & Pub
Lodg	N: Super 8, Vineyard B&B
Other	S: **to Creekside Campground▲**, **Family Affair Campground▲**, **Campers Hill Campground▲**
45	**US 20, Buffalo Rd, State Line, North East**
TStop	N: Kwik-Fill Auto Truck Plaza (Scales) S: Stateline BP, North East Truck Plaza (Scales)
Food	N: McDonald's, Jammin Vine S: Rest/NE TP, Subway/Stateline BP
Lodg	S: Red Carpet Inn
TServ	S: NE TP
Other	N: Heritage Wine Cellar
(46)	**Weigh Station (WB)**
(46)	**PA Welcome Center (WB)** (RR, Phone, Picnic, Vend, Info)

EASTERN TIME ZONE

NOTE: MM 47: New York State Line

PENNSYLVANIA
NEW YORK

NOTE: NY does not use Mile Marker Exits. We have listed Mile Marker / Exit #.

EXIT	NEW YORK
495/61	**NY 815, Shortman Rd, Ripley**
TStop	N: Ripley State Line Truck Stop/Shell (Scales)
Food	N: Rest/Ripley SL TS
Lodg	N: Pines Motel
TServ	N: Ripley SL TS/Tires
Other	N: Laundry/LP/Ripley SL TS, **Lakeshore RV Park▲**
(494)	**TOLL Plaza**
485/60	**NY 394, N Portage St, Westfield, to Mayville**
Gas	N: Keystone◈
Lodg	S: Thruway Holiday Motel
Med	S: + Hospital
Other	N: **Westfield/Lake Erie KOA▲**, **Blue Water Beach Campground▲**, **Lake Erie State Park** S: **to Camp Chautauqua▲**, Webb's Lake Resort
468/59	**NY 60, Bennett, Rd, Dunkirk, Fredonia**
FStop	S: Wilson Farms Mobil
Gas	S: Kwik Fill◈, Citgo, Murphy
Food	S: Arby's, Bob Evans, China King, KFC, McDonald's, Perkins, Wendy's
Lodg	S: Best Western♥, Comfort Inn♥, Clarion♥, Days Inn♥
Med	S: + Hospital
Other	S: LP/Wilson Farms, ATMs, Grocery, Home Depot, NAPA, RiteAid, **Walmart sc**, **NY State Hwy Patrol Post**,
455/58	**US 20, NY 5, Irving, Silver Creek**
TStop	N: Seneca Hawk, Seneca One Stop, Native Pride Travel Center
Gas	S: Atlantic, Kwik Fill
Food	N: Rest/Seneca Hawk, Rest/Native Pride TC S: Burger King, Subway, Sunset Grill, Tim Horton's, Tom's Family Rest
TWash	N: Native Pride TC
Med	N: + Lake Shore Health Care Center
Other	N: WiFi/BarbSh/LP/Seneca Hawk, Seneca OS, WiFi/LP/Native Pride TC, Golf Course
(447)	**Angola Service Plaza (Both dir)**
FStop	Mobil
Food	Denny's, McDonald's
445/57A	**Eden, Angola**
(443)	**Parking Area (Both dir)**
436/57	**NY 75, Camp Rd, Hamburg, Aurora**
TStop	N: Exit 57 Truck Plaza (Scales)
Gas	S: Kwik-Fill◈, Mobil◈
Food	N: Rest/FastFood/Ex 57 TP, Bob Evans, Denny's, McDonald's, Tim Horton's, Wendy's S: Arby's, Burger King, Camp Rd Diner, Pizza Hut, Subway

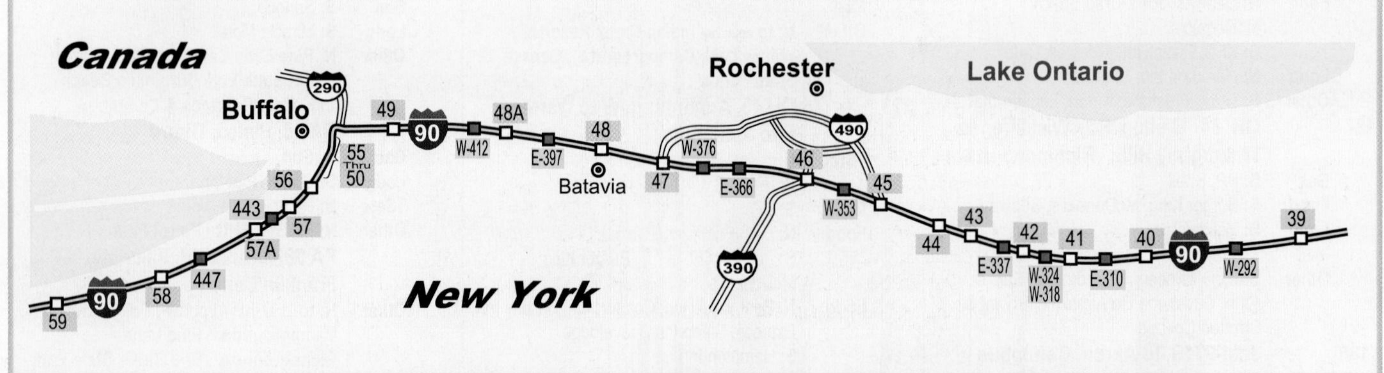

◈ = Regular Gas Stations with Diesel ▲ = RV Friendly Locations ♥ = Pet Friendly Locations
Red print shows large vehicle parking / access on site or nearby Brown Print = Campgrounds / RV PARKS

EXIT	NEW YORK
Lodg	N: Motel/Exit 57 TP, Days Inn♥, Comfort Inn♥, Red Roof Inn♥, Tallyho Motel S: Holiday Inn
TWash	N: Exit 57 TP
TServ	N: Exit 57 TP/Tires
Other	N: WiFi/**LP**/Ex 57 TP, Auto Dealers, to Mall, Buffalo Speedway, Erie Co Fairgrounds, **Ballard's Camping Center Sales/Service/Campground▲** S: Goodyear, **Camping World RV Sales**, To Hilbert College
432/56	**NY 179, Mile Strip Rd, Blasdell, Orchard Park**
Gas	N: Sunoco
Food	N: Family Rest, Burger King S: Applebee's, Chuck E Cheese, Outback Steaks, McDonald's, Olive Garden, Pizza Hut, Ruby Tuesday, TGI Friday, Wendy's
Lodg	N: Econo Lodge♥
Other	S: Grocery, Home Depot, McKinley Mall, to **Buffalo RV**, Erie Comm College, Ralph Wilson Stadium
(430)	**TOLL Plaza**
429/55	**Ridge Rd, Orchard Park, Lackawanna (EB), US 219, Ridge Rd (WB)**
Food	S: Arby's, Denny's, Wendy's
TServ	N: Kenworth Truck of Upstate NY
Other	S: FedEx Kinko's, Grocery, Home Depot,
427/54	**NY16, NY400, W Seneca, E Aurora**
(426/53)	**Jct I-190, Downtown Buffalo, Niagra Falls (TOLL)**
425/52A	**William St**
423/52	**Walden Ave, Buffalo, Cheektowaga**
TStop	S: AmBest/Jim's Truck Plaza/Sunoco (Scales)
Food	N: Applebee's, Arby's, Bob Evan's, Famous Dave's BBQ, IHOP, McDonald's, Ruby Tuesday, Starbucks, Subway, TGI Friday, Tim Horton's, Wendy's S: Rest/Jim's TP, Alton's, Fuddrucker's, McDonald's, Olive Garden, Pizza Hut, Smokey Bones BBQ, Starbucks
Lodg	N: Hampton Inn, Residence Inn♥ S: Sheraton, Millenium Airport Hotel
Med	N: + St Joseph Hospital
Other	N: Grocery, Goodyear, Office Depot, PetSmart♥, Target, **Walmart** S: Laundry/**LP**/Jim's TP, ATMs, Best Buy, Sam's Club, Walden Galleria Mall
422/51	**NY 33, Buffalo Niagara Int'l Airport**
Lodg	S: Best Western, Comfort Suites♥, Days Inn, Holiday Inn♥, Homewood Suites♥, Quality Inn
Other	S: NY State Hwy Patrol Post
421/50A	**Cleveland Dr (EB)**
(420/50)	**Jct I-290, to Niagara Falls (EB-Last Free Exit)**
Other	N: to appr 9 mi **Leisurewood Rec Comm & Campground▲**
(420)	**TOLL Plaza**
417/49	**NY 78, Transit Rd, Buffalo, Depew, Lockport**
Gas	N: Mobil S: Kwik Fill, Mobil

EXIT	NEW YORK
Food	N: Arby's, Chili's, **Cracker Barrel**, Don Pablo, Dunkin Donuts, McDonald's, Old Country Buffet, Perkins, Ponderosa, Pizza Hut, Red Lobster, Ruby Tuesday, Shogun, Starbucks, Subway, TGI Friday, Wendy's S: Bob Evans, Salvatores Ital Gardens
Lodg	N: Clarion, Econo Lodge, Fairfield Inn, Microtel, Ramada Inn♥ S: Howard Johnson, Garden Place Hotel, Red Roof Inn♥, Residence Inn♥
Med	N: + Hospital
Other	N: ATMs, Auto Services, Auto Dealers, Banks, B&N, BJ's, Cinema, Dollar General, Fedex Office, Firestone, Grocery, Home Depot, Lowe's, Office Depot, Pharmacy, Radio Shack, Target, Tires, UPS Store, **Walmart sc**, Eastern Hills Mall, to Erie Comm College, Epic Sports Center S: Greater Buffalo Int'l Airport✈, **All Seasons RV, to Samcoe RV**
(412)	**Clarence Service Plaza (WB)**
FStop	Sunoco
Food	Burger King, Pizza Hut, Mrs Fields
402/48A	**NY 77, Allegheny Rd, Pembroke, Corfu, Medina, Akron, Six Flags Darien Lake, to NY 5, NY 33**
TStop	S: Flying J Travel Plaza #5049 (Scales), Travel Center of America (Scales)
Food	S: CountryMarket/FastFood/FJ TP, Rest/TA TC, Exit 48A Diner
TWash	S: TA TC
TServ	S: TA TC/Tires
Other	N: to appr 6mi **Leisurewood Rec Comm & Campground▲** S: Laundry/BarbSh/WiFi/**RVDump/LP**/FJ TP, Laundry/WiFi/**RVDump**/TA TC, **Darien Lake Theme Park & Camping Resort▲**, to **Skyline Camping Resort & RV Sales▲**, to appr 4.5mi **Sleepy Hollow Lake Resort Campground▲**, to appr 6mi **Darien Lake State Park▲**
(397)	**Pembroke Service Plaza (EB)**
FStop	Sunoco
Food	Burger King, Popeye's, TCBY
390/48	**NY 98, Oak St, Batavia, Albion, Attica**
Gas	S: Citgo
Food	S: Aby's, Bob Evans, Denny's, Perkins
Lodg	N: Hampton Inn S: Best Western, Days Inn, Holiday Inn, Quality Inn, Ramada♥, Super 8
Med	S: + Hospital
Other	N: Genesee Co Airport✈, **NY State Police** S: Auto Zone, Auto Dealers, Auto Repairs, CVS, Home Depot, Tires, **Wal-Mart sc**, Dwyer Stadium, to **Lei-Ti Campground▲**
(379/47)	**Jct I-490, to NY 19, Leroy, Rochester**
TStop	N: 490 Truck Stop/Coastal
Other	N: **LP**/490 TS S: to **Lei-Ti Too Campground▲**
(376)	**Ontario Service Plaza (WB)**
FStop	Mobil
Food	McDonald's, Ben & Jerry's
TServ	AJ Ulgiati Enterprises
(366)	**Scottsville Service Plaza (EB)**
FStop	Mobil
Food	Burger King, Dunkin Donuts, TCBY

EXIT	NEW YORK
(362/46)	**Jct I-390 , Rochester, Corning Henrietta (Serv N on NY 253)**
TStop	N: Western Truck Stop/Citgo
Gas	N: Hess
Food	N: McDonald's, Wendy's
Lodg	N: Country Inn, Days Inn♥, Fairfield Inn, Microtel, Red Roof Inn♥, Super 8♥
TServ	N: Regional International
Other	N: WiFi/**LP**/Western TS
(353)	**Parking Area (EB)**
(351/45)	**Jct I-490, NY 96, Victor Rd, Victor, Fairport, Rochester**
Gas	S: Kwik Fill
Food	N: TGI Friday S: Burger King, Chili's, Denny's, Wendy's
Lodg	N: Hampton Inn S: Holiday Inn Express, Microtel, Royal Inn
Other	N: Eastview Mall S: **Ballatyne RV & Marine**, Bristol Woodlands
(350)	**Seneca Service Plaza (WB)**
FStop	Mobil
Food	Burger King, Sbarro, Mrs Fields
347/44	**NY 332, Rochester Rd, Victor, Canandaigua**
FStop	S: Wilson Farms #142/Mobil
Food	S: KFC, McDonald's, Subway
Lodg	S: Best Value Inn, Econo Lodge
Other	S: **Canandaigua/Rochester KOA▲** , **NY State Police**
340/43	**NY 21, Main St, Manchester, Palmyra**
Gas	S: Mobil◊
Food	S: Steak-Out Rest, McDonald's
Lodg	S: Roadside Inn
(337)	**Clifton Spring Service Plaza (EB)**
FStop	Sunoco
Food	Roy Rogers, Sbarro, TCBY
327/42	**NY 14, to NY 318, Geneva, Lyons**
TStop	S: Wilson Farms AmBest #184/Mobil (Scales)
Food	S: Rest/Wilson Farms
Lodg	S: Relax Inn
Other	N: to appr 20mi **Cherry Grove Campground▲** S: Laundry/**LP**/Wilson Farms
(324)	**Junius Ponds Service Plaza (WB)**
FStop	Sunoco
Food	Dunkin Donuts, Roy Rogers
(318)	**Parking Area (WB)**
317/41	**NY 414, Ridge Rd, Mound Rd, NY 318, Waterloo, Clyde**
FStop	S: Nice N Easy #21/Mobil
TStop	S: Petro Stopping Center #71 (Scales)
Food	S: IronSkillet/Subway/Petro SC, Country Diner
TWash	S: Petro SC
TServ	S: Petro SC/Tires
Other	S: Laundry/BarbSh/CB/WiFi/Petro SC, Waterloo Outlet Mall, to **Hejamada Campground & RV Park▲**
(310)	**Port Byron Service Plaza (EB)**
FStop	Mobil
Food	McDonald's, Ben & Jerry's
304/40	**NY 34, Weedsport, Auburn, Oswego**
FStop	S: Fast Track Market #210
TStop	S: The Pit Stop Auto Truck Plaza/Sunoco
Gas	S: Qwik Fill

EXIT	NEW YORK
Food	S: Arby's, Arnold's Family Rest, Ashby's Fish & Grill, Old Erie Diner, Village Diner
Lodg	S: Best Western, Days Inn, Microtel
Other	N: Riverforest RV Park▲ , Whitford Airport✈ S: WiFi/LP/Pit Stop ATP, to Hejamada Campground & RV Park▲
(292)	**Warners Service Plaza (WB)**
FStop	Mobil
Food	McDonald's, Ben & Jerry's
(290/39)	**Jct I-690, NY 690, Syracuse, Fulton, to Solvay, Baldwinsville, Onondaga Lake, State Fairgrounds**
Other	N: Camping World RV Center
286/38	**NY 57, Liverpool, Syracuse, Fulton, Oswego**
Gas	N: Hess, KwikFill S: Mobil, Sunoco
Food	N: Pier 57 Rest, Pizza Hut S: Burger King
Lodg	N: Super 8
283/37	**Electronics Pkwy, 7th St, Syracuse**
Gas	S: Hess, Mobil
Food	S: Bob Evans, Denny's, Ground Round, McDonald's, Colorado Steaks
Lodg	S: Days Inn, Hampton Inn, Quality Inn, Ramada Inn, Super 8
(283/36)	**Jct I-81, N to Watertown, S to Binghamton Courtland, Syracuse, 1000 Islands, Syracuse Airport**
TStop	S: I-81, #25 Pilot Travel Center #380 (Scales)
Food	S: FastFood/Pilot TC
Other	N: Syracuse Hancock Int'l Airport✈, USMC Reserve Training Center S: WiFi/Pilot TC
(280)	**DeWitt Service Plaza (EB)**
FStop	Sunoco
Food	McDonald's, Ben & Jerry's
279/35	**NY 298, Syracuse, East Syracuse**
Gas	S: Mobil, Kwik Fill
Food	S: Denny's, McDonald's
Lodg	S: Comfort Inn, Days Inn, Fairfield Inn, Embassy, Hampton Inn, Holiday Inn, Howard Johnson, Marriott, Microtel, Motel 6♥, Red Roof Inn♥, Super 8
(277/34A)	**Jct I-481, Syracuse, Chittenango (EB) Syracuse, Oswego (WB)**
(266)	**Chittenango Service Plaza (WB)**
FStop	Sunoco
Food	Dunkin Donuts, Sbarro, TCBY
262/34	**NY 13, Canastota, Oneida (EB), Canastota, Chittenango (WB)**
FStop	S: Nice N Easy Sunoco
Gas	S: Mobil◇

EXIT	NEW YORK
Food	S: Arby's, McDonald's
Lodg	S: Days Inn♥
Other	N: The Landing Campground▲ , Verona Beach State Park▲ , Boxing Hall of Fame
(256)	**Parking Area (WB)**
253/33	**NY 365, Verona, Rome (EB), Verona, Oneida (WB)**
FStop	S: SavOn Diesel
Gas	N: Citgo, Sunoco
Lodg	N: Verona Motor Inn S: Super 8
Med	S: + Hospital
Other	N: Turning Stone Resort & Casino/RV Park▲ , The Landing Campground▲
(250)	**Parking Area (EB)**
(244)	**Oneida Service Plaza (EB)**
FStop	Sunoco
Food	Burger King, Sbarro, TCBY
243/32	**NY 233, Westmoreland, Rome**
Food	S: Carriage Motor Inn
Lodg	S: Carriage Motor Inn
Other	N: Oneida Co Airport✈, Griffiss AFB
(233/31)	**Jct I-790, NY 8 NY 12, Utica, Rome, St Lawrence Seaway, 1000 Islands, Watertown, Norwich**
FStop	N: North Utica Citgo
Gas	N: Fastrac, BJ's S: Hess◇
Food	N: Burger King, Subway S: Denny's, Dunkin Donuts, Friendly's, McDonald's, Pizza Hut, Taco Bell, Wendy's
Lodg	S: Best Western♥, Hampton Inn, Radissor Red Roof Inn♥, Super 8♥
Other	N: ATMs, BJ's, Big Lots, Grocery, Lowe's, Laundromat, Pharmacy, Walmart sc, West Canada Creek Campsites▲ , Trail's End Campground▲
(227)	**Schuyler Service Plaza (WB)**
FStop	Sunoco
Food	McDonald's, Breyer's
Other	NY State Police
220/30	**NY 28, Herkimer, Mohawk**
Gas	N: Mobil◇, Fastrac34A)
Food	N: Applebee's, Burger King, Denny's, Friendly's, McDonald's, Subway/Mobil, Tony's Pizzeria
Lodg	N: Budget Motel, Herkimer Inn
TServ	S: Eggers, Cary & Corrigan Tires
Med	S: + Hospital
Other	N: Auto Dealer, Auto Services, ATMs, Goodyear, RiteAid, Walmart sc, West Canada Creek Campsites▲ , to appr 7 mi Herkimer KOA▲ S: Grocery, to Baseball Hall of Fame

EXIT	NEW YORK
211/29A	**NY 169, Front St, Little Falls, Dolgeville**
Lodg	N: Best Western♥
Other	N: Crystal Grove Diamond Mine & Campground▲
(210)	**Indian Castle Service Plaza (EB) Iroquois Service Plaza (WB)**
FStop	Sunoco
Food	Roy Rogers, Bob's Big Boy, Mrs Fields Burger King, Dunkin Donuts, TCBY
194/29	**NY 10, Canajoharie, Sharon Springs**
FStop	S: Betty Beaver Fuel Stop/Getty
Gas	N: Stewarts S: Sunoco
Food	S: McDonald's, Pizza Hut
Lodg	S: Rodeway Inn♥
(184)	**Parking Area (Both dir)**
182/28	**NY 30A, Fultonville, Fonda**
TStop	N: Betty Beaver Fuel Stop/Getty, Travel Center of America (Scales), AmBest/FultonvilleSuper Stop/Citgo (Scales)
Food	N: Buckhorn/TA TC, Rest/Fultonville SS
Lodg	N: Motel/TA TC, Motel/Fultonville SS
TWash	N: Betty Beaver FS, Fultonville SS
TServ	N: TA TC/Tires
Med	N: + Hospital
Other	N: Laundry/LP/Betty Beaver FS, Laundry/WiFi/CB/TA TC, Laundry/CB/WiFi/LP/Fultonville SS
174/27	**NY 30, Minaville Rd, Amsterdam**
Gas	N: Mobil34A)
Food	N: Diner/Super 8 Motel
Lodg	N: Super 8, Valley View Motor Inn
Med	N: + Hospital
(172)	**Mohawk Service Plaza (EB)**
FStop	Sunoco
Food	McDonald's, Breyer's
(168)	**Pattersonville Service Plaza (WB)**
FStop	Sunoco
Food	Bob's Big Boy, Starbucks, TCBY
(162/) 26	**Jct I-890, NY 5, NY 5S, Scotia, Schenectady, Rotterdam**
(159/ 25A)	**Jct I-88S, Schenectady, Binghamton Cooperstown, Oneonta**
(154/25)	**Jct I-890, NY 7, 146, Schenectady**
(153)	**Guilderland Service Plaza (EB)**
FStop	Sunoco
Food	McDonald's, Mr Sub, Ben & Jerry's
(148/24)	**Jct I-87N, I-90E, Albany, Montreal (EB, Left Exit), I-90W, I-87S, New York, Buffalo, to US 20 (WB)**

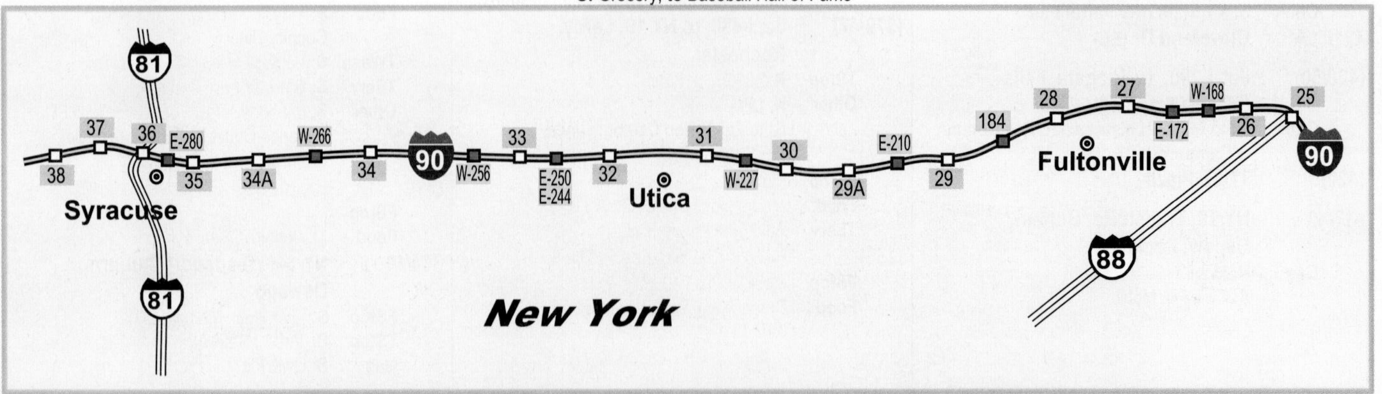

◇= Regular Gas Stations with Diesel ▲ = RV Friendly Locations ♥= Pet Friendly Locations
Red print shows large vehicle parking / access on site or nearby Brown Print = Campgrounds / RV PARKS

EXIT — NEW YORK

(148) **TOLL Plaza**

02/1S **Western Ave, to US 20**
NOTE: **WB: Last FREE Exit Before TOLL**
Other **S:** ATMs, Restaurants, Best Buy, Home Depot, Sam's Club, **Walmart**, Cross Gates Mall

(04/1N) **Jct I-87N, to Saratoga, Montreal, Albany Int'l Airport**

1/2 **Fuller Rd, to NY 5, US 20, Western Ave, Univ of Albany**

2/3 **State Offices, NYS Police Academy**

2/4 **NY 85, Albany, to Slingerlands, Voorheesville**

3/5 **Everett Rd, to NY 5, College of St Rose**
Gas **S:** Hess
Food **S:** Denny's, Friendly's, McDonald's, Pizza Hut, Subway, Taco Bell
Lodg **S:** Clarion, Quality Inn
Other **S:** Advance Auto, Auto Dealers, Auto Services, CVS, Auto Zone, Home Depot

3/5A **Corporate Woods Blvd**

5/6 **US 9, New Loudon Rd, Loudonville, Arbor Hill, Henry Johnson Blvd**
Gas **N:** Stewarts
Med **N:** + Hospital

(6/6A) **Jct I-787, Albany, Troy, Watervliet, to NY 7, South Mall Expy**
Other **S:** to Downtown Albany, Empire State Plaza

7/7 **Washington Ave, Rensselaer (EB)**

7/8 **NY 43, Sand Lake Rd, US 4, Broadway, Defreestville, Sand Lake**
Other **N:** to Joseph L Bruno Stadium, Hudson Valley Comm College

10/9 **US 4, E Greenbush Rd, Troy Rd, Troy, Greenbush, Glens Falls**
Gas **N:** Mobil
S: Citgo, Stewarts
Food **N:** Applebee's, McDonald's, Panera Bread, Starbucks, Subway
S: Cracker Barrel, Denny's, Wendy's
Lodg **N:** Holiday Inn Express
S: Econo Lodge, Fairfield Inn
Other **N:** ATMs, Grocery, Home Depot, Staples, PetSmart♥, Bank, Target, **Walmart sc**

13/10 **Miller Rd, E Greenbush**
Gas **S:** Mobil◈, Stewarts
Food **S:** Dunkin Donuts, Pizza Hut, Weather Vane Rest

EXIT — NY / MA

14/11 **US 9, US 20, E Greenbush, Nassau**
Gas **N:** Citgo◈, Hess◈
S: Mobil
Food **S:** Burger King
Lodg **S:** Econo Lodge, Rodeway Inn
Other **N: NY State Police**

(18) **Rest Area (WB)**
(RR, Phone, Picnic, Vend)

20/12 **US 9, Hudson**
Gas **S:** Mobil◈, Xtra, Sunoco◈
TStop **S:** Pilot Travel Center #146 (Scales)
Food **S:** Subway/McDonald's/Pilot TC
Other **S:** WiFi/Pilot TC

(B1) **TOLL Plaza**

(B6/B1) **Jct I-90W, US 9, Albany, Hudson (WB)**

B15/B2 **NY 295, Taconic State Pkwy**
Other **S: Woodland Hills Campground▲**

(B18) **TOLL Plaza**

B23/B3 **NY 22, NY 10, Austerlitz, New Lebanon, W Stockbridge, Mass**
FStop **N:** Canaan Super Stop/Citgo (Scales)
Gas **S:** Sunoco◈
Food **N:** Rest/Canaan SS
Other **N:** Laundry/Canaan Super Stop
S: Camp Waubeeka Family Campground▲, Woodland Hills CG▲

EASTERN TIME ZONE

NOTE: **MM 391: Massachusetts State Line**

⬆ NEW YORK
⬇ MASSACHUSETTS

NOTE: **MA does not use Mile Marker Exits. We have listed Mile Marker / Exit #.**

3/1 **MA 41, Great Barrington Rd, West Stockbridge**
Food **N:** Orient Express Rest
Lodg **N:** Marble Inn, Pleasant Valley Motel

TOLL Plaza (EB Begin Toll, WB End)

(8) **Lee Travel Plaza (Both dir)**
FStop **E/W:** Gulf
Food **E:** McDonald's, D'Angelo's, Edy's Ice Cream, Pretzels, Fresh City
W: McDonald's
Other **E:** Visitor Info

11/2 **US 20, Housatonic St, to MA 102, Lee, to Pittsfield, Adams**
FStop **N:** Lee Shell

EXIT — MASSACHUSETTS

TStop **S:** Lee Travel Plaza
Gas **N:** Citgo, Sunoco
S: Shell
Food **N:** Burger King, McDonald's, Pizza Hut
Lodg **N:** Best Western, Pilgrim Inn, Super 8, Sunset Motel
S: Inn at Lee Plaza, Best Value Inn♥
Other **N: Walker Island Family Campground▲**
S: Outlet Stores, **Camp Overflow▲, Prospect Mountain Campground & RV Park▲, Bonny Rigg Campground▲,**

(12) **Parking Area (Both dir)**

(29) **Blandford Travel Plaza (Both dir)**
FStop **E/W:** Gulf
Food **E:** McDonald's
W: McDonald's, Honey Dew, Pizza

NOTE: **MM: 29: Steep Grade, Trucks use Right Lane, LOW Gear**

(35.5) **RunAWay Truck Ramp (EB)**

40/3 **US 202, MA 10, Westfield, Southampton, Northampton**
Gas **N:** Mobil
S: Shell
Food **N:** New England Pizza
S: Dunkin Donuts, Friendly's, Napoli II Italian Rest, Subway, Wendy's
Lodg **S:** Econo Lodge
Med **S:** + Noble Hospital
Other **N:** Barnes Muni Airport✈, **MA State Police Barracks, Walker Island Family Campground▲, Windy Acres Family Campground▲**
S: Camp Overflow▲, Sodom Mountain Campground▲, Southwick Acres Campground▲, Bonny Rigg Campground▲

(41) **MA State Hwy Patrol Barracks (WB)**

(45/4) **Jct I-91, US 5, Hartford, Springfield, Holyoke (Serv on US 5)**
Gas **S:** Mobil
Food **N:** Dunkin Donuts
S: Piccadilly, Outback Steakhouse
Lodg **N:** Welcome Inn
S: Best Western, Hampton Inn♥, Knights Inn♥, Quality Inn, Red Roof Inn♥, Springfield Inn, Super 8
Med **N:** + Providence Hospital
Other **N:** Holyoke Mall, Univ of MA, Amherst, Holyoke Soldiers Home
S: Basketball Hall of Fame, Six Flags

49/5 **MA 33, Memorial Dr, MA 141, Chicopee, Westover Field**
Gas **N:** Sunoco, Stop & Shop

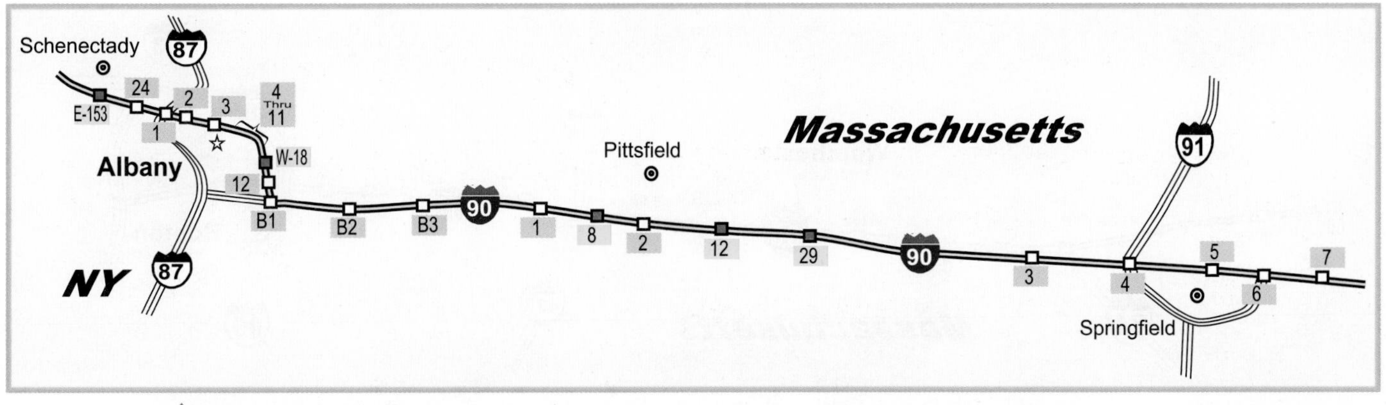

◈ = Regular Gas Stations with Diesel ▲ = RV Friendly Locations ♥ = Pet Friendly Locations
Red print shows large vehicle parking / access on site or nearby Brown Print = Campgrounds / RV PARKS

EXIT		MASSACHUSETTS
	Food	N: Applebee's, Arby's, Burger King, Dunkin Donuts, Denny's, Pizza Hut, Starbucks, Subway, Wendy's
	Lodg	N: Days Inn♥, Hampton Inn, Super 8♥
	Other	N: BJ's, Grocery, Home Depot, Staples, Tires, **Walmart**, Mall, U-Haul, Westover Air Force Base, Westover Metro Airport✈
(51/6)		**Jct I-291, Springfield, Hartford CT**
	TStop	S: AmBest/Pride Travel Center
	Food	S: McDonald's/Subway/Pride TC
	Lodg	N: Motel 6♥, Ramada Inn
54/7		**MA 21, Center St, Ludlow, Belchertown**
	Gas	N: Sunoco, Mobil
	Food	N: Burger King, Friendly's, McDonald's, Joy's Country Kitchen, Subway
	Lodg	S: Comfort Inn
	Med	N: + Hospital
	Other	N: CVS, Grocery
(56)		**Ludlow Travel Plaza (Both dir)**
	FStop	E/W: Gulf
	Food	E: McDonald's, Honey Dew W: Boston Market, Honey Dew
63/8		**MA 32, Thorndike St, to US 20, Palmer, Amherst, Ware (Addt'l Serv on US 20S)**
	Gas	S: Citgo, Shell◇
	Food	S: Dunkin Donuts, McDonald's, Subway
	Med	N: + Hospital
	Other	N: **Pine Acres Family Camp Resort▲** S: Grocery, CVS, **Oak Haven CG▲**
(78/9)		**Jct I-84, to US 20, EB - Hartford, Sturbridge, WB-Hartford, NY City (Serv on I-84S, Ex #3AB)**
	TStop	S: #3A New England Truck Stop (Scales) I-84, Ex #1: Pilot Travel Center #222 (Scales)
	Food	S: Rest/NE TS, **Cracker Barrel**, Subway, Wendy's, Gracie's Roadside Cafe
	Lodg	S: Motel/NE TS, Best Western♥, Comfort Inn, Hampton Inn, Super 8♥
	TServ	S: NE TS/Tires
	Other	S: Laundry/NE TS, Southbridge Muni Airport✈, **MA State Police Barracks**, **Oak Haven Campground▲**, **Yogi Bear's Jellystone Park Resort▲**, **Sunset View Farm Camping Area▲**, **Quinebaug Cove Campground▲**
(79)		**MA State Police Barracks (EB)**
(79)		**TOLL Plaza**
(80)		**Charlton Travel Plaza (EB)**
	FStop	E: Gulf
	Food	E: McDonald's, Auntie Anne's, Ben & Jerry's, Papa Gino's
	Other	E: **MA State Hwy Patrol**, Visitor Info

EXIT		MASSACHUSETTS
(84)		**Charlton Travel Plaza (WB)**
	FStop	W: Gulf
	Food	W: McDonald's, Auntie Anne's, Ben & Jerry's, Papa Gino's
	Other	W: Visitor Info
(87)		**Weigh Station (EB)**
(90/10)		**Jct I-395S, I-290E, MA 12, Auburn, Worcester, New London**
	Gas	N/S: Shell
	Food	N: Piccadilly's, Papa Gino's S: Applebee's, Friendly's, Golden Lion, Chuck's Steakhouse, Wendy's
	Lodg	N: Comfort Inn, La Quinta Inn♥, S: Ramada Inn
	Med	S: + Hospital
	Other	N: Auburn Reg'l Mall, **Pine Acres Family Camping Resort▲** S: CVS, **MA State Police Barracks**, **Indian Ranch Resort▲**, **Lake Manchaug Camping▲**
93/10A		**US 20, to MA 146, MA 122A, Worcester, Providence**
96/11		**MA 122, Millbury, Worcester, to Providence, RI**
	TServ	N: Southworth Milton S: Dario Diesel Volvo Trucks
	Med	N: + Hospital
(104)		**Westborough Travel Plaza (WB)**
	FStop	W: Gulf
	Food	W: Auntie Anne's, Ben & Jerry's, Boston Market, Dunkin Donuts
(106/ 11A)		**Jct I-495, N to New Hampshire, S to Cape Cod, Maine**
111/12		**MA 9, Framingham, Marlborough**
	Gas	N: Circle K, Getty, Hess
	Food	N: Subway, Ground Round
	Lodg	N: Residence Inn♥, Sheraton♥ S: Econo Lodge, Framingham Inn, Motel 6♥
	Med	N: + Hospital
(115)		**Framingham Travel Plaza (WB)**
	FStop	W: Gulf
	Food	W: McDonald's, Boston Market, Auntie Anne's, Edy's Ice Cream, Honey Dew
117/13		**MA 30, Framingham, Natick**
	Gas	S: Exxon, Mobil◇
	Food	S: Burger King, Naked Fish, McDonald's
	Lodg	S: Courtyard, Hampton Inn, Peabody Hotel, Red Roof Inn♥, Travelodge
	Med	S: + Hospital
	Other	S: BJ's, Home Depot, Lowe's, Mall, Target, **Walmart sc**

EXIT		MASSACHUSETTS
(118)		**Natick Travel Plaza (EB)** **NOTE: Last Travel Plaza on Mass Pike**
	FStop	E: Gulf
	Food	E: McDonald's, Dunkin Donuts, Papa Gino's
(123/14)		**Jct I-95, MA 128, MA 30, Portsmouth, Providence (WB)**
(124)		**TOLL Plaza (EB End TOLL, WB Begin)**
(124/15)		**Jct I-95, MA 128, MA 30, Weston Portsmouth, Providence (EB)**
125/16		**Washington St, West Newton (EB)** **NOTE: Last FREE Exit Before TOLL**
	Gas	S: Mobil
	Other	S: Auto Services
126/17		**Washington St, Newton, Watertown**
131/18		**Allston, Cambridge, Brighton (EB, Left exit) Cambridge St, Soldiers Field Rd, River St Bridge**
131/19		**Cambridge TOLL Plaza, Beacon Park**
131/20		**Allston, Brighton, Cambridge (EB)**
(131)		**TOLL Plaza**
132/21		**Massachusetts Ave (WB)**
133/22		**Dartmouth St, Prudential Center, Copley Square (WB)**
133/22A		**Clarendon St (WB)**
133/23		**Arlington St (WB)**
133/23		**Downtown Boston, South Station**
(134/24)		**Jct I-93N, Central Artery (Left exit)**
(134/ 24C)		**Jct I-93S, Quincy (Left exit) Haul Rd, Dorchester (WB)**
25		**South Boston Northern Ave, World Trade Center (WB), TOLL Plaza-Ted Williams Tunnel**
138/26		**Logan Int'l Airport, Merge to 1A N, McClellan Hwy, East Boston**
	NOTE:	**I-90 Begins/Ends on I-5, Exit #164 in Seattle, WA**

EASTERN TIME ZONE

NOTE: MM 160: Massachusetts State Line

MASSACHUSETTS

Begin WB I-90 from Jct I-93 in Boston, MA to I-5 in Seattle, WA.

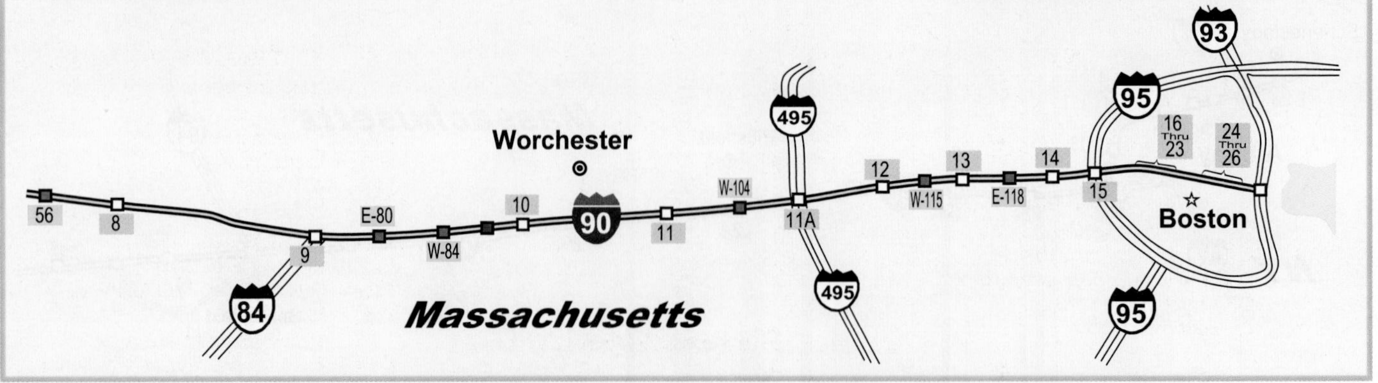

◇= Regular Gas Stations with Diesel ▲ = RV Friendly Locations ♥ = Pet Friendly Locations
Red print shows large vehicle parking / access on site or nearby Brown Print = Campgrounds / RV PARKS

EXIT — VERMONT

Begin Southbound I-91 from Canada/VT border to Jct I-95 in New Haven, CT.

VERMONT

EASTERN TIME ZONE

NOTE: VT does not use Mile Marker Exits. We have listed Mile Marker / Exit #.

NOTE: Rest Area Hours 7am-11pm

(178) **US/Canada Border, US Customs, VT State Line**

177/29 **to US 5, Caswell Ave, Derby Line**
- Gas — W: Derby Irving Mainway◈
- Lodg — W: Derby Village Inn
- Other — E: AmEx Duty Free

NOTE: MM 176: Latitude 45 degrees North, MidPoint between Equator & North Pole

(175) **VT Welcome Center (SB)** (RR, Phone, Picnic, Vend, Info)

172/28 **US 5, VT 105, Derby, Newport**
- FStop — E: Champlain Farms/Exxon, Short Stop #113/Mobil
- Gas — E: Citgo, Gulf; W: Gulf◈, Shell◈
- Food — W: Craving Rest, McDonald's, Village Pizza, Roasters Café & Deli
- Lodg — E: Border Motel; W: Pepins Motel, Super 8, Top of the Hills Hotel
- Med — W: + Hospital
- Other — E: VT State Hwy Patrol Post; W: RiteAid, Border Patrol, Elk Newport State Airport✈

170/27 **VT 191, to US 5, VT 105, Newport**
- Gas — W: Exxon/Carwash
- Med — W: + Hospital

(166.5) **Parking Area (NB)**

162/26 **to US 5, VT 58, Orleans, Irasburg**
- Gas — E: Irving◈, Lanoues Serv Stn, Sunoco; W: Royers Service Station
- Food — E: Loon's Landing, Orleans Pizza Place, Just Good Food, Subway; W: Martha's Diner
- Other — E: to Will-O-Wood Campground▲

156/25 **VT 16, Glover Rd, to US 5, Barton, Hardwick**
- Gas — E: Barton Irving Mainway◈, Barton One Stop Mini Mart/Mobil◈
- Food — E: Village Coffee House
- Lodg — E: Pinecrest Motor Court
- Other — E: Belview Campground▲

(154) **Parking Area (NB)**

(150.5) **Highest Elev on I-91 (1856')**

(143) **Scenic View (NB)**

(141) **Rest Area (SB)** (RR, Phone, Picnic, Vend, Info)

140/24 **VT 122, Gilman Rd, Lydonville, Wheelock, Sheffield (NB)**
VT 122, to VT 114, Burke, Lyndon Center, Lydonville (SB)
- Gas — E: Nick's Mini Mart, Irving Mainway
- Food — E: Asia Rest, Sweet Basil Café, Subway
- Lodg — E: Lynburke Motel
- Other — E: Lyndon State College

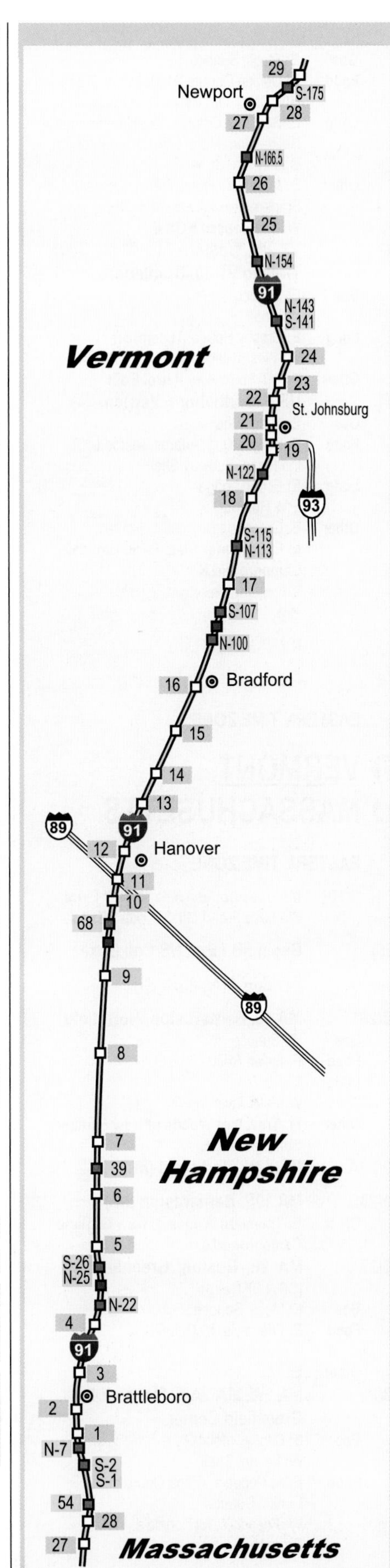

EXIT — VERMONT

137/23 **US 5, Memorial Dr, to VT 114, Lyndonville, Lydon, Burke**
- Gas — E: Mobil
- Food — E: Dunkin Donuts/Mobil, McDonald's
- Lodg — E: Colonnade Inn; W: Lyndon Motor Lodge
- Other — N: White Caps Campground▲, Burke Mountain Ski Area, Lake Willoughby, Lyndon State College

133/22 **Hospital Dr, to US 5, St Johnsbury**
NOTE: STEEP Grade-Trucks Low Gear
- Gas — E: Citgo◈
- Food — E: Pizza Hut, TacoBell/KFC
- Med — E: + Hospital

131/21 **to US 2, to US 5, St Johnsbury, Montpelier**
- Gas — E: Western Ave Station
- Lodg — E: Fairbanks Inn
- Other — E: to Moose River Campground▲, Rustic Haven Campground▲, Breezy Meadows Campground▲; W: Sugar Ridge RV Village & Camp ground▲

129/20 **US 5, to US 2, St. Johnsbury, Passumpsic** (Serv 2-3mi E in St Johnsbury)
- Gas — E: Irving Mainway◈, Shell◈
- Lodg — W: Comfort Inn
- Other — E: VT State Hwy Patrol Post

(128/19) **Jct I-93S, to Littleton, New Hampshire, (Truck Route) to US 2**

(122) **Scenic View (NB)**

121/18 **US 5, Barnet, Peecham**
NOTE: Steep Grade on exit ramp
- Other — E: to Warner's Campground▲; W: to appr 5mi Harvey's Lake Cabins & Campground▲, Stillwater Campground▲

(115) **Parking Area (SB)**

(113) **Parking Area (NB)**

110/17 **US 302, to US 5, Wells River, Barre, Woodsville, NH**
- TStop — W: P&H Truck Stop (Scales)
- Food — E: Warners Gallery Rest; W: Rest/P&H TS
- Med — E: + Hospital
- Other — E: to appr 10mi Crazy Horse Campground▲; W: Laundry/P&H TS, to Pleasant Valley Campground▲, Ricker Pond Campground▲

(107) **Parking Area (SB), Weigh Station (SB)**

(100) **Rest Area (NB)** (RR, Phone, Picnic, Vend, Info)

98/16 **VT 25, Waits River Rd, to US 5, Bradford, Barre**
- Gas — E: Mobil◈
- Food — E: Hungry Bear Rest
- Lodg — E: Bradford Motel
- Other — W: VT State Hwy Patrol Post

92/15 **Lake Morey Rd, to US 5, Fairlee, to Oxford, NH**
- Gas — E: Citgo◈, Mobil, Shell◈
- Food — E: Fairlee Diner, Pizza, Your Place
- Lodg — E: Fairlee Motel; W: Lake Morey Inn
- Other — E: Jacobs Brook Campground▲

◈ = Regular Gas Stations with Diesel ▲ = RV Friendly Locations ♥ = Pet Friendly Locations
Red print shows large vehicle parking / access on site or nearby Brown Print = Campgrounds / RV PARKS

EXIT — VERMONT

84/14 **VT 113, Main St, to US 5, Fairlee to Thetford**
Other E: Rest 'N Nest Campground▲
75/13 **VT 10A, Main St, to US 5, Norwich, to Hanover, NH**
Med E: + Hospital
Other E: to Dartmouth College
72/12 **Bugbee St, to US 5, to US 4, White River Junction, Wilder**
Gas E: Gulf◈, Mobil
70/11 **US 5, White River Junction**
Gas E: Exxon◈, Mobil, Sunoco
W: Citgo, Shell
Food E: Crossroads Café, John's Place, McDonald's, Mustard Seed Deli
Lodg E: Comfort Inn, Pines Motel
W: Best Western, Hampton Inn, Holiday Inn Express, Super 8
TServ E: Gateway Ford Trucks
Other E: US Post Office, Amtrak, Auto Dealers
69/10 **Jct I-89, N to Barre, Montpelier, S to Airport, New Hampshire**
(68) **Rest Area** (Both dir) (RR, Phone, Picnic, Vend, Info)
(67) **US Customs Check Point / Weigh Station (SB)**
61/9 **US 5, VT 12, Hartland, Windsor**
Med E: + Hospital
51/8 **VT 131, to US 5, VT 12, Ascutney, Windsor**
Gas E: Citgo◈, Mobil, Sunoco◈
Food E: Red Barn Rest, Roadside Cafe
Med E: + Hospital
Other E: Running Bear Camping Area▲
42/7 **US 5, VT 11, VT 106, Springfield**
TStop W: On the Run Mobil
Food W: FastFood/Mobil, Paddock Seafood
Lodg W: Holiday Inn Express
Med W: + Hospital
Other W: Laundry/Mobil, Tree Farm Campground▲
(39) **Parking Area** (Both dir)
35/6 **US 5, VT 103, Bellows Falls, Rockingham, Rutland**
Gas E: Shell
W: Sunoco◈
Other W: VT State Hwy Patrol Post
29/5 **Westminster St Hwy, to US 5, to VT 12, Westminster, Walpole NH**
(26) **Parking Area** (SB)
(25) **Parking Area** (NB)
(23) **Weigh Station** (SB)
(22) **Parking Area** (NB)
18/4 **US 5, VT 4, Putney**
Gas W: Sunoco◈
Food E: Rest/Putney Inn
W: Curtis BBQ
Lodg E: Putney Inn
Other W: Brattleboro KOA▲
12/3 **VT 9E, to US 5, Brattleboro, Keene, Chesterfield, NH**
NOTE: SB: Clearance 13'9", Ex #2 alt
FStop E: Citgo

EXIT — VT / MA

Gas E: Mobil, Sunoco
Food E: Dunkin Donuts, McDonald's, Pizza Hut, Steak Out Rest
Lodg E: Best Inn, Colonial Inn, Hampton Inn, Holiday Inn, Motel 6♥ Lamplighter Inn, Quality Inn, Super 8
Other E: Auto Mall, Home Depot, Grocery, Staples, U-Haul, US Post Office
W: Brattleboro KOA▲
9/2 **VT 9W, Western Ave, Molly Stark Trail, to VT 30, Brattleboro**
Gas E: Sunoco
W: Shell
Lodg E: Crosby House, Tudor B&B
W: West Village Motel
Other W: VT State Hwy Patrol Post
8/1 **US 5, Brattleboro, Vernon**
Gas E: Mobil, Shell◈
Food E: Burger King, Adams Seafood, VT Inn Pizza, Subway/Shell
Lodg E: Econo Lodge
Med E: + Hospital
Other E: Grocery, Walgreen's, Amtrak, to Ft Drummer State Park, Hinsdale Campground▲
(7) **VT Welcome Center** (NB) (RR, Phone, Picnic, Vend, Info)
(2) **Parking Area** (SB)
(1) **Parking Area** (NB)

EASTERN TIME ZONE

↑ VERMONT
↓ MASSACHUSETTS

EASTERN TIME ZONE

NOTE: MA does not use Mile Marker Exits. We have listed Mile Marker / Exit #.

(55) **Begin SB / End NB Call Boxes**
(54) **Parking Area** (Both dir)
50/28 **MA 10, Bernardston, Northfield**
Gas W: Sunoco
Food E: Italian Rest
Lodg E: Fox Inn
W: Falls River Inn
Other W: Travelers Woods of New England Campground▲
50/28A **MA 10N, Northfield (NB)**
50/28B **MA 10S, Bernardston (NB)**
Other E: Travelers Woods of New England Campground▲
46/27 **MA 2E, Boston, Greenfield (SB, LEFT exit)**
Gas E: Mobil, Sunoco
Food E: Friendly's, McDonald's
Med E: + Hospital
Other E: CVS
43/26 **MA 2W, MA 2A E, Mohawk Trail, Greenfield Center**
Gas E: Citgo◈, Mobil
W: Exxon, Shell
Food E: Applebee's, China Gourmet, Dunkin Donuts
W: Friendly's, McDonald's, Pizza Hut

EXIT — MASSACHUSETTS

Lodg E: Howard Johnson
W: Candlelight Resort Inn, Marriott, Super 8
Med E: + Hospital
Other E: Auto Dealers, Mtn View Auto Repair
W: BJ's, Home Depot, Grocery, Pharmacy, Staples, Auto Services, Peppermint Park Camping Resort▲, Country Aire Campground▲
(37) **Weigh Station** (Both dir)
35/25 **MA 116, Conway Rd, Deerfield, Conway (SB) (Difficult reaccess)**
Gas E: Mobil
Lodg E: Red Roof Inn♥
Other E: Yankee Candle Co
34/24 **US 5, MA 10, Deerfield, Whately**
FStop W: Whately Truck Stop/Exxon
Gas E: Mobil
Food E: Sara's Café & Deli
W: Rest/Whately TS
Lodg E: Motel 6♥
Other E: Yankee Candle Co
(34) **Parking Area** (Both dir)
31/23 **US 5, MA 10, Whately (SB)**
30/22 **US 5, MA 10, Whately (NB)**
27/21 **US 5, MA 10, Allen Rd, N King St, Northampton, Hatfield, Whately**
Gas W: Sunoco
Lodg W: Country View Motel
Other W: MA State Hwy Patrol Post
26/20 **US 5, MA 9, MA 10, Hadley, Northampton (SB)**
Gas W: Citgo
Food W: Burger King, Friendly's, McDonald's
Med W: + Hospital
Other W: ATMs, Auto Dealers, CVS, Grocery, Laundromat
25/19 **MA 9, Bridge St, Damon Rd, Northampton, Amherst**
Gas W: Citgo
Food E: Websters Fish Hook Rest.
Lodg W: Hampshire Inn
Med W: + Hospital
23/18 **US 5, Mt Tom Rd, Northampton, Easthampton**
Gas E: Mobil
W: Shell
Food W: Friendly's, McDonald's, Spaghetti Freddy's, Roberto's
Lodg E: Clarion Hotel
W: Best Western, Northampton Lodging
(18) **Scenic Area** (Both dir)
16/17 **MA 141, Easthampton, Holyoke Ctr**
Gas E: Citgo◈, Mobil◈
Food E: Real China, Deli, Subway
Lodg E: Super 8
Other E: Walgreen's
16/17A **MA 141E, Holyoke Ctr (NB)**
16/17B **MA 141W, Easthampton (NB)**
14/16 **US 202, Cherry St, Holyoke, S Hadley, Westfield**
Food E: Burger King, Denny's, McDonald's

◈= Regular Gas Stations with Diesel ▲ = RV Friendly Locations ♥= Pet Friendly Locations
Red print shows large vehicle parking / access on site or nearby Brown Print = Campgrounds / RV PARKS

EXIT		MASSACHUSETTS
	Lodg	E: Yankee Peddler Inn & Rest
12/15		**Lower Westfield Rd, to US 5, Holyoke, Ingleside**
	Gas	E: Shell
	Food	E: Cracker Barrel, Friendly's, JP's Rest, Ruby Tuesday, Surf n Turf, Wendy's
	Lodg	E: Holiday Inn
	Other	E: Holyoke Mall, Best Buy, Target
(11/14)		**Jct I-90, MA Turnpike (TOLL), E to Boston, W to Albany, NY**
9/13		**US 5, S-Springfield, N-Riverdale St**
	Gas	W: Mobil, Sunoco◈
	Food	E: Bickford's Family Rest, Chili's, Donut Dip, Empire Buffet, Longhorn Steakhouse, On the Border, Outback Steakhouse W: Burger King, Calamari's Seafood Grill, Friendly's, McDonald's, KFC, Old Country Buffet, Pizza Hut, Wendy's
	Lodg	E: Comfort Inn, Quality Inn♥, Red Roof Inn♥, Residence Inn W: Best Western, Econo Lodge, Elsie's Motel, Hampton Inn
	Other	E: Mall, Home Depot W: Auto Dealers, Costco, Grocery, Pharmacy
(9/12)		**I-391N, Chicopee, Holyoke Center (fr NB, Right Two Lanes)**
8/11		**US 20W, W Springfield (SB)**
	Gas	E: Mobil
	Med	E: + Hospital
8/10		**Main St, Chicopee, Springfield (NB)**
	Gas	E: Mobil
	Med	W: + Hospital
7/9		**US 20W, MA 20A, W Springfield (NB)**
	NOTE:	Trucks Use US 20W to Springfield
(7/8)		**Jct I-291E, US 20E, Boston (SB) I-291E, US 20E, to I-90 (NB) (Both dir: Use Right Two Lanes)**
7/7		**Columbus Ave, Springfield Ctr (SB)**
6/6		**Springfield Ctr (NB), Union St (SB)**
	FStop	W: Pride◈
	Food	E: Various Rest
	Lodg	E: Marriott, Sheraton
	Med	E: + Hospital
	Other	E: Greyhound Station W: to Basketball Hall of Fame
5/5		**Broad St (NB)**
5/4		**MA 83, Main St, Springfield E Longmeadow (SB)**
	TStop	W: Broad St Truck Stop/Sunoco
	Gas	E: Mobil◈, Sunoco, Texaco
	Food	E: McDonald's, Wendy's
4/3		**US 5N, to MA 57, Agawam (SB) Columbus Ave, W Springfield**
	Gas	E: Pride, Sunoco
	Other	W: Southwick Acres Campground▲, Sodom Mountain Campground▲
4/2		**MA 83, Forest Park, to E Longmeadow (NB)**
4/1		**US 5S, Longmeadow (SB)**

EXIT		MA / CT
(0)		**End SB / Begin NB Call Boxes**

EASTERN TIME ZONE

⬆ MASSACHUSETTS
⬇ CONNECTICUT

EASTERN TIME ZONE

NOTE: **CT does not use Mile Marker Exits. We have listed MM / Exit #.**

EXIT		MA / CT
58/49		**US 5, Enfield St, Enfield, to Longmeadow MA**
	Gas	E: Citgo, Mobil, Valero W: Gas & Service
	Food	E: Friendly's, McDonald's, Steve's Boston Seafood W: DQ, Cloverleaf Cafe
	Lodg	E: Crown Plaza Hotel, Marriott W: Cloverleaf Motel
56/48		**CT 220, Elm St, Enfield, to Thompsonville (Acc to Ex #47 Serv)**
	Gas	E: Mobil
	Food	E: Arby's, Burger King, Denny's, Dunkin Donuts, McDonald's, TGI Friday, Wendy
	Other	E: CVS, Grocery, Home Depot, Target, Asnuntuck Comm College, U-Haul
55/47		**CT 190, Hazard Ave, Enfield, W to Suffield, E to Hazardville**
	Gas	E: Citgo
	Food	E: Dunkin Donuts, Ground Round, KFC, McDonald's, Olive Garden, Pizza Hut, Red Lobster, Taco Bell
	Lodg	E: Motel 6♥, Red Roof Inn♥
	Other	E: ATMs, Auto Zone, B&N, CVS, Goodyear, Staples, Walgreen's, Mall, Stafford Speedway
53/46		**US 5, King St, Enfield**
	Gas	E: Mobil
	Lodg	W: Super 8
51/45		**CT 140, Bridge St, Warehouse Pt, E Windsor, Ellington**
	Gas	E: Shell W: Sunoco
	Food	E: Burger King, Cracker Barrel, Great Wall, Kowloon Rest, Sophia's W: Maine Fish Market & Rest
	Lodg	E: Comfort Inn W: Best Western, Ramada
	Other	E: Laundromat, **Walmart** W: AmTrak
50/44		**US 5S, Prospect Hill Rd, E Windsor**
	Gas	E: Citgo, Mobil
	Food	E: Dunkin Donuts, Wendy's
	Lodg	E: Holiday Inn Express
	Other	E: Longview RV
49/42		**CT 159, S Main St, Windsor Locks**
	Gas	W: Citgo, Gulf
49/41		**Center St (SB) (Exits with #39)**
	Gas	W: Shell
	Lodg	W: Howard Johnson
48/40		**Bradley Field Connector, to Bradley Int'l Airport**
	Lodg	W: Sheraton, Baymont Inn, Days Inn, DoubleTree Inn, Fairfield Inn, Homewood Suites, Motel 6♥

EXIT		CONNECTICUT
	Other	W: Conn Air Nat'l Guard
47/39		**Kennedy Rd, Center St (NB) (Exits with #41)**
	Gas	E: Shell◈
46/38		**CT 75, Poquonock Ave, Windsor**
	Gas	E: Mobil◈
	Food	E: China Sea, Dunkin Donuts, McDonald's, Pizza Rama, Subway W: Rivercity Grille Rest.
	Lodg	W: Courtyard, Hilton Garden Inn
45/37		**CT 305, Bloomfield Ave, Windsor**
	Gas	E: Mobil◈
	Lodg	W: Residence Inn
	Other	E: Amtrak
44/36		**CT 178, Park Ave, Bloomfield**
43/35B		**CR 218, Windsor, Bloomfield**
	Gas	W: Shell
(43/35A)		**I-291E, to Manchester**
(43/35)		**I-291, Windsor, CT 218, Bloomfield**
41/34		**CT 159, Windsor Ave (NB), North Main St (SB), Hartford**
	Gas	E: Shell◈ W: Citgo◈
	Food	W: Ranch House, Lunch Box Cafe
	Lodg	W: Flamingo Inn
	Med	W: + Hospital
40/33		**Jennings Rd, Hartford**
	Gas	W: Exxon◈
	Food	W: Burger King, McDonald's, Quiznos, Subway
	Lodg	W: Marriott, Motel 6♥, Super 8
	Other	E: CT State Hwy Patrol Post
(39/32B)		**Jct I-84W, Trumbull St, Waterbury (fr NB, LEFT exit)**
(39/32A)		**Jct I-84W, Trumbull St, Waterbury**
38/31		**State St (SB)**
	Other	W: Various Dining & Lodging, Constitution Plaza, Greyhound Station State Capitol
(38/30)		**Jct I-84E, CT 2, East Hartford (SB) New London (fr SB, LEFT exit)**
37/29A		**Whitehead Hwy, Capitol Area (fr NB, LEFT exit)**
	Other	W: State Capitol, CT Conv Center, Civic Center, Old State House
37/29		**US 5, CT 15, to CT 2, I-84E, to E Hartford, Boston (NB)**
37/27		**Airport Rd (NB), Brainard Rd (SB)**
	Gas	E: Shell◈ W: Mobil
	Food	E: Chowder Pot IV, McDonald's W: Airport Rd Café, Burger King, Dunkin Donuts, Wendy's
	Lodg	E: Days Inn
	TServ	E: Interstate Ford, Nutmeg International
	Other	E: Hartford-Brainard Airport✈ W: Oasis Truck Tire Center
36/28		**CT 15S, Newington, Wethersfield, (NB), US 5S, CT 15, Berlin Tpk (SB)**
35/27		**Brainard Rd, Airport Rd (NB)**
	Gas	E: Shell◈
	Food	E: Chowder Pot IV, McDonald's
	Lodg	E: Days Inn
	TServ	E: Interstate Ford, Nutmeg International
	Other	E: Hartford-Brainard Airport✈

◈ = Regular Gas Stations with Diesel ▲ = RV Friendly Locations ♥ = Pet Friendly Locations
Red print shows large vehicle parking / access on site or nearby **Brown Print = Campgrounds / RV PARKS**

EXIT		CONNECTICUT
34/26		**Mart St, Old Wethersfield (SB)**
	Other	E: Motor Vehicle Dept
34/25		**CT 3N, Glastonbury, Wethersfield (NB)**
34/25		**CT 3N, Glastonbury CT 3S, Wethersfield**
32/24		**CT 99, Silas Deane Hwy, Rocky Hill, Wethersfield**
	Gas	E: Mobil W: Mobil, Shell
	Food	E: Bickford's Family Rest, Dakota Rest, On the Border Rest W: Denny's, D'Angelo's, Ground Round, KFC, Hometown Buffet, McDonald's, Panda King, Red Lobster, Wendy's
	Lodg	E: Great Meadow Inn, Howard Johnson W: Best Western, Hampton Inn, Motel 6♥
	Other	W: Auto Zone, CVS, Lowe's, Tru Value Hardware, Walgreen's, **Walmart**,
30/23		**CT 3, West St, Rocky Hill**
	Gas	E: Citgo, Mobil
	Food	E: Marriott W: D'Angelo's, Elizabeth's Rest.
	Lodg	E: Marriott
	Other	E: **Dinosaur State Park**
28/22		**CT 9, N to New Britain, S to Middletown, Old Saybrook**
	Other	S: **Nelson's Family Campground▲**
27/21		**CT 372, Berlin Rd, Cromwell, Berlin**
	Gas	E: Sunoco W: Citgo, Mobil, Shell
	Food	E: Franco's Pizzeria, Diamond Trio, Friendly's, Wooster St Pizza Shop W: Blimpie's, Burger King, McDonald's, Subway
	Lodg	E: Comfort Inn, Crowne Plaza W: Courtyard, Holiday Inn, Super 8
	Other	W: Grocery, **Walmart**, **Longview RV**
24/20		**Country Club Rd, Middle St**
(22)		**Rest Area (NB)** **(RR, Phone, Picnic, Vend, RVDump)**
(22)		**Weigh Station (NB)**
21/19		**Baldwin Ave, Preston Ave (SB)**
(20/18)		**I-691W, to Meriden, Waterbury (SB) CT 66E, Middlefield, Middletown (NB)**
19/17		**CT 15S, W Cross Pkwy, E Main St, (NO Comm'l Vehicles) (SB), CT 15N, Berlin Tpk, to I –691, CT 66 (NB)**
	Gas	W: BP
	Food	W: Great Wall Chinese
	Lodg	W: East End Hotel, Extended Stay America, Hampton Inn, Residence Inn
	Other	W: Powder Ridge Ski Area
18/16		**E Main St, Shelton (NB)**
	Gas	E: Mobil, Valero W: BP, Gulf, Sunoco
	Food	E: American Steakhouse, Little Caesar's Pizza, NY Pizza, Subway W: Burger King, KFC, McDonald's, Pizza Hut, Royal Guard Fish & Chips,cTaco Bell

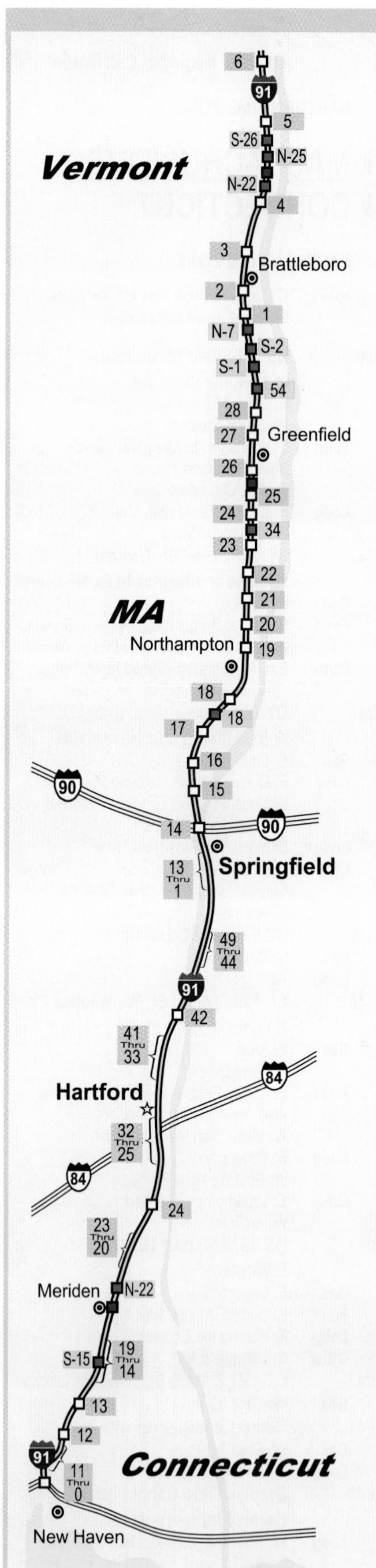

EXIT		CONNECTICUT
	Lodg	E: Candlewood Suites, Hampton Inn W: Days Inn, Howard Johnson
	Med	E: + Hospital
	Other	E: CVS, Grocery
16/15		**CT 68, Barnes Rd, Wallingford, Yalesville, Durham**
	Lodg	E: Marriott
(15)		**Rest Area (SB)** **(RR, Phone, Picnic, Vend, RVDump)**
14/14		**CT 150, E Center St, Wallingford Woodhouse Ave**
11/13		**to US 5, Wallingford, North Haven (fr NB, Left Exit)**
	Other	W: **Wharton Brook State Park**
9/12		**US 5, Washington Ave**
	Gas	E: Citgo, Shell, Valero W: Exxon
	Food	E: Boston Market, Burger King, China Buffet, Dunkin Donuts, Rustic Oak Steak, McDonald's, Subway, Wendy's W: Athena Diner, Roy Rogers
	Lodg	W: Holiday Inn
	Other	E: CVS, Walgreen's W: Grocery, Pharmacy
8/11		**CT 22, New Haven (NB) (Access to Ex #12 Serv)**
	Gas	E: Citgo
	Food	E: Hunan Rest
7/10		**CT 40, Mt Carmel, Hamden (SB), Hamden, Cheshire (NB)**
5/9		**Montowese Ave, North Haven**
	Gas	W: Sunoco
	Food	W: Sbarro, Subway
	Other	W: BJ's, Home Depot, Target
3/8		**CT 17, CT 80, Middletown Ave**
	Gas	E: 7-11, BP◈, Exxon, Shell W: Mobil
	Food	E: Burger King, Dunkin Donuts, KFC, McDonald's, Pizza Hut, Taco Bell
	Lodg	E: Days Inn
	Other	E: Lowe's, **Walmart**
3/7		**Ferry St, Fair Haven (SB)**
2/6		**US 5, Willow St, Blatchley Ave (fr NB, Left exit)**
2/5		**US 5, State St, Fair Haven (NB)**
2/4		**State St, Downtown (SB)**
1/3		**Trumbull St**
1/2		**Hamilton St (NB access fr I-95 only)**
(0)		**Jct I-95N, CT Tpk, New London (SB, Left exit)**
0/1		**CT 34W, Downtown, New Haven (SB)**

NOTE: CT does not use Mile Marker Exits. We have listed Mile Marker / Exit #.

EASTERN TIME ZONE

NOTE: I-91 Begins/Ends at Exit # 48, I-95

CONNECTICUT

Begin Northbound I-91 from Jct I-95 in New Haven, CT to Vermont/Canada border

◈ = Regular Gas Stations with Diesel ▲ = RV Friendly Locations ♥ = Pet Friendly Locations
Red print shows large vehicle parking / access on site or nearby Brown Print = Campgrounds / RV PARKS

EXIT	VT / NH

Begin Southbound I-93 from Jct I-91 near St Johnsbury, VT to Jct I-95 in Boston, MA.

VERMONT

NOTE: **I-93 begins/ends Exit #19, I-91 VT and/or I-95 Ex #12, Dedham, MA**

EASTERN TIME ZONE

NOTE: **VT does not use Mile Marker Exits. We have listed Mile Marker / Exit #.**

(11/2/1) **Jct I-91, N to St Johnsbury, S to White River Junction VT 18, to US 2, St. Johnsbury**
- **Lodg** N: Aime's Motel
- **Other** N: **Moose River Campground▲**

(1) **VT Welcome Center (NB)** (RR, Phone, Picnic, Vend)

EASTERN TIME ZONE

VERMONT

NEW HAMPSHIRE

EASTERN TIME ZONE

NOTE: **NH does not use Mile Marker Exits. We have listed Mile Marker / Exit #.**

130.5/44 **NH 18, NH 135, Littleton, Monroe, to Waterford, VT**
Rest Area (SB) (8a-8p)
W: (RR, Phone, Pic, Vend, Info, View)

126.2/43 **NH 135, to NH 18, Dalton Rd, Littleto**
- **Med** S: + Little Regional Hospital
- **Other** E: **Crazy Horse Campground▲**

124.6/42 **US 302, NH 10, Dartmouth College Hwy, Littleton, Woodsville**
- **Gas** E: Citgo, Cumberland, Sunoco
  W: Mobil
- **Food** E: Burger King, Cantina Di Gerardo, Clam Shell, Dunkin Donuts, McDonald's, Pizza Hut, Italian Oasis Rest, Subway
  W: 99 Rest & Pub, Applebee's, Asian Garden Rest
- **Lodg** E: Country Squire Motel, Littleton Motel, Maple Leaf Motel, Thayers Inn
  W: Econo Lodge♥, Hampton Inn
- **Other** E: Grocery, Laundromat, Pharmacy
  W: Auto Dealers, Grocery, Staple, Tires, **Walmart**, **Littleton/Lisbon KOA▲**, **Mink Brook Family Campground▲**

122.6/41 **to US 302, NH 18, NH 116, Gilmantor Hill Rd, Littleton, Whitefield**
- **Gas** E: Irving◈
- **Food** E: Rest/Eastgate Motor Inn
- **Lodg** E: Eastgate Motor Inn

121/40 **US 302, NH 10E, NH 18, NH 116, Bethlehem, Twin Mountain**
- **Gas** E: Exxon
- **Lodg** E: Pinewood Motel
- **Other** E: **Snowy Mountain Campground▲**, **Apple Hill Campground/RVDump▲**, **Tarry Ho Campground & Cottages▲**, Twin Mountain Airport✈

119.4/39 **NH 18, NH 116, Bethlehem (SB) N Franconia, Sugar Hill**

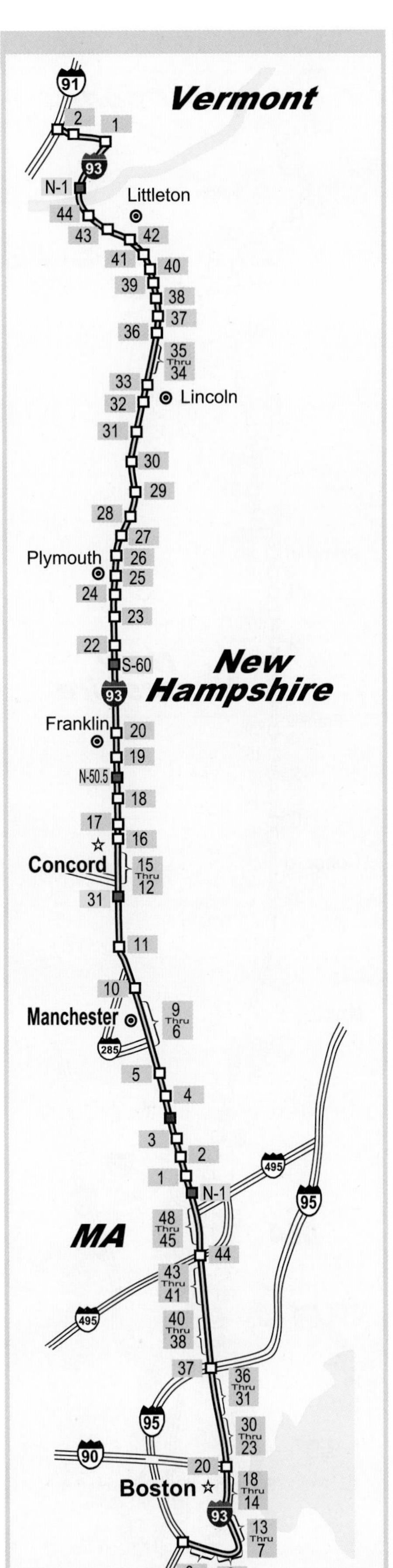

EXIT	NEW HAMPSHIRE

116.8/38 **Wallace Hill Rd, Easton Rd, to NH 18, NH 116, NH 117, NH 142, Franconia, Sugar Hill, Lisbon**
- **Gas** W: Mobil
- **Food** W: Franconia Café, Franconia Seafood & Dairy Bar, Subway
- **Lodg** E: Red Coach Inn
  W: Cannon Mtn Motor Lodge, Gale River Motel, Hillwinds Motel,
- **Other** W: Grocery, US Post Office, **Fransted Family Campground▲**, Cannon Mtn Ski Area, Franconia Airport✈

115.6/37 **NH 142, Forest Hill Rd, to NH 18, Franconia, Bethlehem (NB)**
- **Gas** W: Mobil
- **Food** W: Above the Notch, Franconia Village House Rest
- **Lodg** W: Cannon Mtn View Lodge
- **Other** W: **Fransted Family Campground▲**, to **Franconia Notch State Park**

113.2/36 **NH 141, Butterhill Rd, to US 3N, to S Franconia, Twin Mtn (SB), NH 141(NB)**

112.6/35 **US 3N,Twin Mtn, Lancaster (NB)**
- **Other** E: to **Rogers Campground & Motel▲**, **Beaver Trails Campground▲**, **Twin Mtn KOA▲**, **Twin Mtn Motor Court & RV Park▲**, **Tarry Ho Campground & Cottages▲**, **Beech Hill Campground▲**

NOTE: **MM 103-112: I-93 interrupted below for Franconia Notch Parkway. Two Lanes NB, Single Lane SB.**

111/34C **NH 18, Echo Lake Beach, Peabody Slopes, Cannon Mountain**

110/34B **Cannon Mountain Tramway**
Cannon Mtn Ski Area, Old Man of the Mountains Museum, NE Ski Museum, **Cannon RV Park▲**

109 **Trailhead Pkg (SB), Boise Rock, Old Man Historic Site (NB)** NO Trucks
Picnic Area, Scenic Overlook

108 **Lafayette Place Campground (SB) Trailhead Parking (NB/SB)**
(Single Lane NB, Two Lanes SB)

107 **The Basin**
Scenic View, Picnic

106/34A **US 3, The Flume Gorge, Park Info Center**

NOTE: **MM 103-112: I-93 interrupted above for Franconia Notch Parkway.**

102.4/33 **US 3, Daniel Webster Hwy, N Woodstock, N Lincoln**
- **Gas** E: Irving◈
- **Food** E: Notch View Country Kitchen, Longhorn Palace
  W: Eagle Cliff
- **Lodg** E: Drummer Boy Motor Inn, Mount Coolidge Motel, Red Doors Motel
  W: Cozy Cabins, Mount Liberty Motel
- **Other** W: Smitty's Auto Repair, **Country Bumpkins Campground▲**, Clarks Trading Post
  N: Whales Tale Water Park, Indian Head Viewing

◈= Regular Gas Stations with Diesel ▲ = RV Friendly Locations ♥= Pet Friendly Locations
Red print shows large vehicle parking / access on site or nearby Brown Print = Campgrounds / RV PARKS

EXIT **NEW HAMPSHIRE**

100.6/32 **NH 112, Kancamagus Hwy, N Woodstock , Lincoln**
Gas E: Citgo, Mobil
W: Mobil
Food E: Dunkin Donuts, Emperor Chinese, Earl of Sandwich, Flapjack's, Seven Seas Rest, McDonald's, White Mtn Bagel Co
Lodg E: Comfort Suites, Mill House Inn
W: Carriage Motel, Woodstock Inn
Other E: Loon Mtn Ski Resort
W: Grocery, **Maple Haven Resort▲** , **Lost River Valley Campground▲** , White Mountains Motorsports Park

97.3/31 **to NH 175, Tripoli Rd, N Woodstock**
Other W: **Woodstock KOA▲**

94.8/30 **US 3, Daniel Webster Hwy, Woodstock, Thornton**

88.6/29 **US 3, Daniel Webster Hwy, Campton, Thornton**
Lodg W: Gilcrest Motel
Other E: **Pemi River Campground▲** , **Clear Stream Natural Campground▲**

86.8/28 **NH 49, to NH 175, Campton Village Rd, Waterville Valley, Campton**
Gas E: Citgo, Mobil
W: Citgo
Food E: Campton Pizza
W: Sunset Grill
Lodg W: Inn
Other W: Convention Center, Tourist Info, **Branch Brook Campground▲**

83.6/27 **Blair Rd, to US3, W Campton**
Lodg E: Super 8

81/26 **US 3, NH 25, NH 3A, Plymouth, Rumney**
Gas W: to Mobil, Kwik Stop
Food W: McDonald's
Lodg W: Best Inn, Pilgrim Motel
Med W: + Hospital
Other W: to **Jacobs Brook Campground▲** , **Newfound RV Park▲** , Plymouth State Univ, Tenney Mountain Ski Area, Plymouth Muni Airport

80.2/25 **NH 175A, Bridge St, Holderness Rd, Plymouth**
Gas W: Irving◈
Food W: Ashland Mtn View Deli, Fosters Steakhouse, Main St Station, Plymouth Bagels, Tom Bros Pizza
Lodg W: Comman Man Inn & Spa
Med W: + Hospital
Other W: Plymouth State Univ

NOTE: MM 76:CAUTION Dangerous Crosswinds

75.3/24 **US 3, NH 25, Ashland, Holderness, Squam Lake Region, Science Ctr**
Gas E: Irving Mainway, Mobil◈
Food E: Burger King, Subway
Lodg E: Comfort Inn
Other E: Museum, **Ames Brook Campground▲** **Mountain View Family Campground▲** , **The Inn at Bethel Woods Campground▲**

69.2/23 **NH 104, NH 132, New Hampton, Meredith, Bristol**
Gas E: Kwik Stop, Irving◈
Food E: Dunkin Donuts, Rossi's, Subway
Other E: **Twin Tamarack Family Camping▲** , **Clearwater Campground▲** , **Bear's Pine Woods Campground▲** to US 3, Lake Winnipisaukee Region

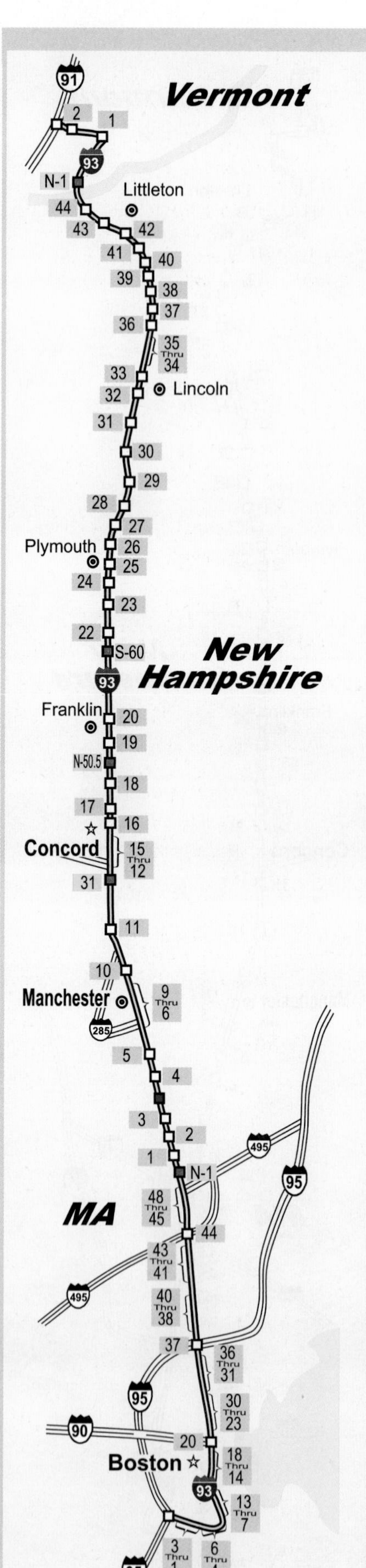

EXIT **NEW HAMPSHIRE**

Other W: Ragged Mtn Ski Area, Ruggles Mine **Yogi Bear's Jellystone Campground▲** , **Davidson's Country Campground▲** , **Newfound RV Park▲**

61/22 **NH 127, New Hampton Rd, Sanbornton, W Franklin**
Med W: + Franklin Reg'l Hospital

(60) **Rest Area (SB)**
(RR, Phone, Picnic, Vend, Info)

57/20 **US 3, NH 11, NH 132, NH 140, Franklin, Laconia, Tilton**
Gas E: Exxon◈, Irving◈, Mobil
Food E: Applebee's, Burger King, Dunkin Donuts, KFC, Kalliopes Rest, McDonald's, Tilt'n Diner, Wendy's
Lodg E: Super 8
Other E: BJ's, Home Depot, Staples, Outlet Mall
W: Auto Dealers, **Walmart**, **to Thousand Acres Family Campground▲**

54.8/19 **NH 132, Park St, Tilton, Northfield, Franklin (NB)**
Gas W: Exxon
Med W: + Hospital
Other W: NH Veterans Home

(50.5) **Rest Area (NB)**
(RR, Phone, Picnic, Vend, Info)

48/18 **West Rd, to NH 132, Centerbury, Boscawen**
Gas E: Mobil
Other E: Shaker Village Historic Site

44.5/17 **US 4W, Holt Rd, to US 3, NH 132, Penacook, Boscawen (NB)**

17E **to NH 132 (SB)**

17W **US 4W, to US 3, Penacook, Boscawen (SB)**
Other W: Veterans Cemetery

40/16 **NH 132, Mountain Rd, Portsmouth St, East Concord**
Gas E: Mobil◈, Complete Car Care

39/15B **US 202W, to US 3, N Main St**
Gas W: Citgo, Hess
Food E: Family Buffet
W: Friendly's
Lodg W: Courtyard
Med W: + Hospital
Other W: Convention Center

(39/15A) **I-393E, US 4E, US 202E, Main St, Concord, to Loudon, Portsmouth**
Other to NH Tech Inst, Planetarium, Speedway

39/14 **NH 9, Loudon Rd, State Offices**
FStop E: Loudon Rd Shell
Gas E: Mobil, Sunoco
W: Citgo, Exxon◈, Hess
Food E: Boston Market, Pizzeria Uno, Family Buffet, Olive Garden, Panera Bread, Outback Steakhouse, Ruby Tuesday
Lodg W: Holiday Inn
Med W: + Hospital
Other E: ATMs, Advance Auto Parts, Auto Zone, Grocery, Pharmacy, US Post Office, U-Haul, **Walmart sc**, Everett Area, NH Air Nat'l Guard
W: Cinema 93 Video, State Library, Capitol, Museum of NH History

38/13 **US 3, Manchester St, Downtown**
FStop E: Fred's Kwik Stop & Deli/Sunoco

◈= Regular Gas Stations with Diesel ▲ = RV Friendly Locations ♥= Pet Friendly Locations
Red print shows large vehicle parking / access on site or nearby Brown Print = Campgrounds / RV PARKS

EXIT		NEW HAMPSHIRE
	Gas	E: Mobil◈ W: Hess
	Food	E: Cityside Grill, Dunkin Donuts W: D'Angelo's, Hawaiian Isle II, KFC, McDonald's
	Lodg	W: Best Western, Comfort Inn, Fairfield Inn
	TServ	W: Yankee GMC Trucks, Kenworth, Concord Tire & Auto Service
	Other	E: RV Center W: NAPA, Firestone,
37/12N		**NH 3A N, S Main St, Concord**
	Gas	E: Exxon, Irving W: Mobil
	Food	E: Subway W: Pizza
	Lodg	E: Days Inn W: Hampton Inn
	Med	W: + Hospital
	Other	E: Auto Dealers
37/12S		**NH 3A S, to I-89, to Bow Junction**
	TStop	E: Bow Jct Irving Mainway
	Gas	E: Citgo◈
	Food	E: Subway/Irving
	Other	E: Laundry/WiFi/Irving
(36)		**TOLL Begins/Ends**
(36)		**Jct I-89N, to Lebanon, White River Junction, VT, to US 202, NH 9W, Bow, Keene, Claremont**
(31)		**Rest Area (Both dir) (RR, Phone, Picnic, Vend, Info) (NH Liquor Store)**
29/11		**TOLL Plaza, Hackett Hill Rd, to NH 3A, Bow, Hooksett**
	TStop	E: Mr Mike's Travel Plaza/Citgo
	Food	E: Rest/Mr Mike's TP
	Other	E: Laundry/Mr Mike's TP
(29)		**TOLL Begins/Ends**
(26)		**Jct I-293S, Everett Tpk, Manchester, Nashua, Airport (fr SB, Left 2 Lanes, Left exit), Jct I-93S, Salem, Boston (fr SB, Right 2 Lanes)**
26/10		**NH 3A, W River Rd, Hooksett** NOTE: **NB: Last FREE Exit before TOLL**
	FStop	E: Irving Mainway #1511
	Gas	W: Exxon, Mobil
	Food	E: Wendy's
	Other	E: UNH Manchester, NH Tech College W: BJ's, Home Depot, Staples, Target
24/9		**US 3, NH 28, N to Hooksett, S to Manchester**
	Gas	E: Exxon, Mobil W: Manchester Market & Gas, Sunoco
	Food	E: Chantilly's Rest, Pizza Hut W: D'Angelo Grilled Sandwiches, KFC, La Carreta, Luisa's Italian Pizzeria, Shogun, Shorty's Mexican Road House
	Other	E: Twin Oaks Campground▲, Big Bear State Park & Campground▲, Southern NH Univ
22/8		**Bridge Rd, Wellington Rd, to NH 28A, Manchester**
	Med	W: + US Veterans Medical Center
	Other	W: Civic Arena
21/7		**NH 101E, Seacost, Portsmouth (fr SB, Left Exit/ fr NB, Exit Only)**

EXIT		NEW HAMPSHIRE
21/6		**Candia Rd (NB), Hanover St (SB), Candia, Manchester**
	FStop	W: Kwik Stop Mobil
	Gas	W: Citgo◈, Shell
	Food	E: Wendy's
	Med	W: + Hospital
19		**Jct I-293N, NH 101W, to Manchester, Bedford, Airport (fr NB, Left exit / fr SB, Exit only)**
	Other	W: Gas, Food, Lodge, Airport, Malls
15/5		**NH 28, N Londonderry**
	FStop	E: RMZ Truckstop/Sunoco
	Gas	E: 7-11 W: Exxon◈
	Food	E: Poor Boys Family Dining, Burger King, Applebee's, Dunkin Donuts W: Honey Dew, TD's Deli
	Lodg	W: Sleep Inn
	Other	E: **Walmart**, Grocery, LBP Towing & Auto Repair W: Manchester Airport✈, Stonyfield Farm
12/4		**NH 102, Nashua Rd, Derry, to Londonderry**
	FStop	E: Freedom Fuel & Food/Citgo
	Gas	E: Mobil, Sunoco◈, Shell W: Exxon◈, Getty, Hess, Shell◈
	Food	E: **Cracker Barrel**, Derry Pizza, Dunkin Donuts W: Ginger Garden Chinese, McDonald's, Jerome's Deli, Papa Gino's, Wendy's
	Med	E: + Hospital
	Other	W: Cinema 8, Grocery, K-Mart, Home Depot, Walgreen's, Hudson Speedway
(7)		**Weigh Station (Both dir)**
6/3		**NH 111, Indian Rock Rd, Windham, N Salem, Canobie Lake, Hudson**
	Gas	E: Mobil, Oasis Gas & MiniMart W: Sunoco
	Food	E: Windham House of Pizza, McDonald's W: Dunkin Donuts, Subway
	Other	E: Canobie Lake Park, Searles Castle
3/2		**Pelham Rd, to NH 38, NH 97, Salem**
	Gas	W: Mobil
	Food	E: Pudgy's Pizza W: A&A Rest, Margarita's, Loafer's
	Lodg	E: Red Roof Inn♥ W: Holiday Inn, Fairfield Inn
	Other	E: Canobie Lake Park
2/1		**Rockingham Park Blvd, to NH 28, NH 38, Salem**
	FStop	E: Rockingham Fuel/Citgo
	Gas	E: 7-11, Exxon, Getty
	Food	E: Bickford's Family Rest, Burger King, Chili's, Denny's, Friendly's, McDonald's, Papa Gino's, 99 Rest & Pub
	Lodg	E: Park View Inn
	Other	E: AMC 20,B&N, Best Buy, Home Depot, Grocery, Staples, Target, Walgreen's, Rockingham Park Racetrack, Mall
(1)		**NH Welcome Center (NB) (RR, Phone, Picnic, Vend, Info)**

NOTE: **NH does not use Mile Marker Exits. We have listed Mile Marker / Exit #.**

EASTERN TIME ZONE

⬆ NEW HAMPSHIRE

EXIT		MASSACHUSETTS

⬇ MASSACHUSETTS

NOTE: **MM 47: New Hampshire State Line**

EASTERN TIME ZONE

NOTE: **MA does not use Mile Marker Exits. We have listed Mile Marker / Exit #.**

NOTE: **MM 47: Begin / End Call Boxes**

EXIT		MASSACHUSETTS
45.8/48		**MA 213E, Methuen, Haverhill**
45.2/47		**MA 213, Pelham St, Pelham, Methuen**
	Gas	E: Sunoco W: Getty
	Food	E: McDonald's, Outback Steakhouse W: Fireside Rest, Julie's II Roast Beef & Seafood
	Lodg	W: Days Inn, Guest Towers Inn
43.9/46		**MA 110, MA 113, Lawrence, Dracut**
	Gas	E: Getty W: Citgo
	Food	E: Burger King, McDonald's, Pizza Hut W: Dunkin Donuts, Pizza
	Lodg	W: Motel 110
	Med	E: + Hospital
42.7/45		**River Rd, Andover, S Lawrence**
	Gas	W: Mobil
	Lodg	E: Courtyard, Hawthorne Suites, Wyndham W: Residence Inn, Springhill Suites
(41/44BA)		**Jct I-495, S to Lawrence, N to Lowell**
39.6/43		**MA 133, Lowell St, Andover**
	Gas	E: Mobil
	Food	E: Dunkin Donuts/Mobil
	Lodg	E: Ramada
38/42		**Dascomb Rd, Andover, Tewksbury**
35/41		**MA 125, Ballardvale St, Wilmington, Andover, N Andover**
	Other	E: to Camp Forty Acres Campground▲
34.1/40		**MA 62, Wilmington, N Reading**
33/39		**Concord St, Wilmington**
31.4/38		**MA 129, Lowell St, Wilmington**
	Gas	W: Mobil
29.7/37C		**Commerce Way, Atlantic Ave**
(29/37BA)		**Jct I-95, S-Waltham, N-Peabody (Serv at 1st Exit S on I-95)**
27.5/36		**Montvale Ave, Woburn, Stoneham**
	FStop	W: Bob's Fuel Stop/Mobil
	Gas	E: Mobil W: 7-11, Exxon, Mobil, Shell
	Food	E: Kyoto Japanese Rest W: Bickford's Family Rest, Dunkin Donuts, Friendly's , McDonald's, Wendy's
	Lodg	E: Courtyard W: Best Western, Comfort Inn

EXIT	MASSACHUSETTS
26.4/35	**Winchester Highlands, Melrose (SB)**
Gas	E: Sunoco
25.8/34	**MA 28N, Main St, Stoneham (NB)**
Gas	W: Mobil
Food	W: Friendly's
Med	W: + Hospital
23.5/33	**MA 28, Fellsway West, Winchester**
Med	W: + Lawrence Memorial Hospital
22.8/32	**MA 60, Salem St, Riverside Ave, Medford, Medford Square, Malden**
Gas	E: 93 Services, Mobil W: Getty, Mobil
Food	E: Ronny's Place W: Alamo Roast Beef & Seafood, Chili Garden, Mystic Deli, Papa Geno's
Lodg	W: AmeriSuites
Other	W: ATMs, Auto Services, CVS, UPS Store, Walgreen's
22/31	**MA 16E, Revere (SB), MA 16, Mystic Valley Pkwy, Arlington (NB)**
Other	E: to Meadow Glen Mall, Gateway Center W: Auto Services
22/30	**MA 38, Mystic Ave, Medford (SB)**
FStop	W: Mr C's Truck Stop/Sunoco
Gas	W: Fred's Auto Center
Other	W: ATMs, Auto Zone, to Tufts Univ
20.6/29	**MA 28, MA 38, Somerville (NB)**
20.2/28	**Sullivan Square, Charlestown (SB), to MA99, Charlestown (NB)**
Gas	W: Gulf, Hess
Food	E: 99 Rest, Dunkin Donuts
Lodg	E: La Quinta Inn ♥
Other	E: ATMs, Home Depot, Staples, Assembly Square Mall W: Auto Dealers, Auto Services, Grocery
18.9/27	**US 1N, Tobin Bridge (NB, Left 2 lanes)**
19/26	**MA 28, MA 3N, Storrow Dr, North Station, Cambridge, Beacon Hill (SB, Exit only)**
Lodg	W: Holiday Inn
Med	W: + MA General Hospital
Other	W: to Museum of Science, Cambridgeside Galleria Mall, MA Inst of Tech
18.5/26	**Storrow Dr, North Station (NB)**
18/24B	**Logan Airport, MA 1A (SB)**
18/24A	**Gov't Center, North End (SB)**
17.5/23	**Purchase St, S Boston Waterfront (SB), Gov't Center, North End (NB)**
Other	E: NE Aquarium, UPS Store W: City Hall, Quincy Market, Faneull Hall Marketplace, FedEx Kinko's
(16.4/20)	**Jct I-90, E to Logan Airport, Worcester, to I-90W, S Boston, South Station, Chinatown (NB)**
Other	E: Boston Tea Party Ship & Museum
20A	**South Station (SB)**
20B	**to I-90W, Mass Pike, Albany St, South Boston, South End (SB)**
15.9/18	**Mass Ave, Roxbury, Andrew Sq (SB) Boston, to NB Frontage Rd, Mass Ave, Roxbury (NB)**
FStop	W: Mass Ave Sunoco Station
Med	W: + Boston Medical Center

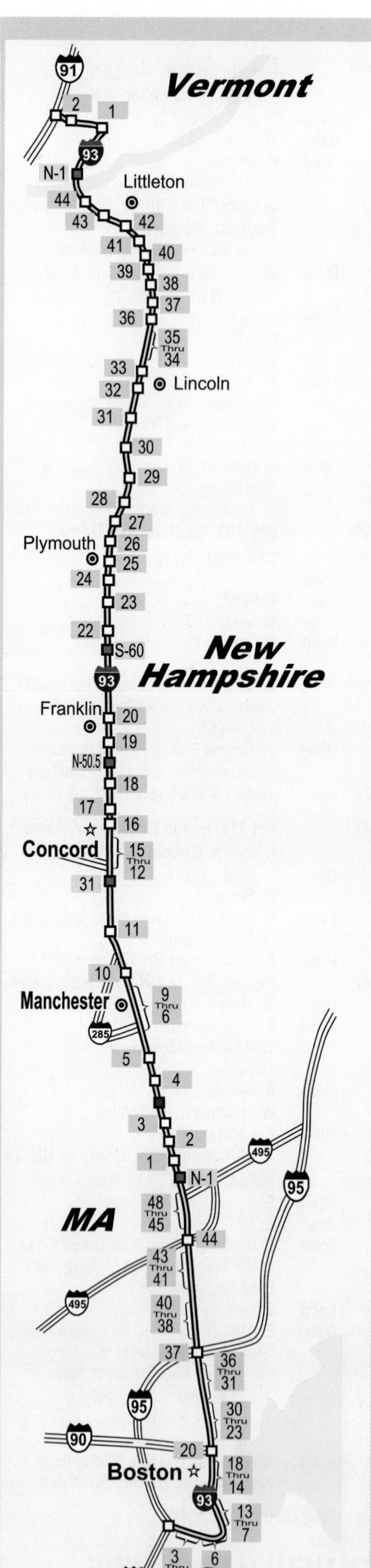

EXIT	MASSACHUSETTS
15.5/16	**Southampton St, Andrew Square (NB)**
Gas	W: Shell
Lodg	W: Holiday Inn Express
Other	W: Home Depot
14.7/15	**Columbia Rd, JFK Library, Edward Everett Square**
Gas	W: Shell
13.2/14	**Morrissey Blvd, JFK Library (NB)**
13/13	**Freeport St, Dorchester (NB)**
Gas	W: 7-11
Other	W: CVS
12.1/12	**MA 3A S, Neponset, Quincy (SB)**
Gas	E: Shell W: 7-11, Exxon, Shell
Food	W: Arby's, Boston Market, Ground Round
Lodg	E: Best Western
Other	W: Auto Zone, Auto Dealers, Auto Service, CVS, Staples, Walgreen's
11.3/11B	**to MA 203, Granite Ave, Ashmont (SB)**
11.3/11A	**Granite Ave, E Milton (SB)**
11.3/11	**to MA 203, Granite Ave, Ashmont (NB)**
10.4/10	**Squantum St, Milton (SB)**
9.7/9	**Bryant Ave, W Quincy (SB) Adam St, Milton, N Quincy (NB)**
Gas	W: Mobil, Shell
8.4/8	**Furnace Brook Pkwy, Quincy**
Med	E: + Hospital
7.4/7	**MA 3S, Braintree, Cape Cod (SB) I-93S, US 1S, to I-95, Dedham, Providence (SB) (Rt 2 lanes)**
7.2/7	**MA 3S, Cape Cod, I-93N, US 1, Boston (NB) (Rt 2 lanes)**
6.7/6	**MA 37, W Quincy, Braintree**
Gas	E: Mobil W: Sunoco
Food	E: D'Angelo's, Pizza, TGI Friday
Lodg	E: Sheraton W: Extended Stay, Hampton Inn, Holiday Inn Express
Other	W: Auto Services, Mall
4.5/5BA	**MA 28, N - Milton, S - Randolph**
Gas	W: Shell, Sunoco, Texaco
Food	W: D'Angelo's, Dunkin Donuts, IHOP
Lodg	W: Holiday Inn
3.8/4	**MA 24S, Brocktown, New Bedford (fr SB, Left exit)**
3/3	**Houghtons Pond, Ponkapoag Trail**
2/2BA	**MA 138, N-Milton, S-Stoughton**
Gas	E: Mobil, Sunoco, Shell
(0/1)	**Jct I-95N, US 1S, Portsmouth, NH I-95S, Providence RI**

NOTE: MA does not use Mile Marker Exits. We have listed Mile Marker / Exit #.

EASTERN TIME ZONE

MASSACHUSETTS

Begin Northbound I-93 from Jct I-95 south of Dedham, MA to Jct I-91 near St Johnsbury,VT.

◇= Regular Gas Stations with Diesel ▲ = RV Friendly Locations ♥= Pet Friendly Locations
Red print shows large vehicle parking / access on site or nearby Brown Print = Campgrounds / RV PARKS

EXIT	MONTANA

Begin Eastbound I-94 from Jct I-90 in Billings, MT to I-69 in Pt Huron, MI.

MONTANA

NOTE: I-94 Begins/Ends on I-90, Ex #456

MOUNTAIN TIME ZONE

(0) **Jct I-90, W-Billings, E-Sheridan**

6 **MT 522, Pryor Creek Rd, Huntley**
- Gas N: Express Way
- Food N: Ernie's Bakery & Deli, Pryor Creek Café & Grill, Sam's Cafe
- Lodg N: Yellowstone Inn & Cabins

14 **S 16th Rd, Ballantine, Worden**
- Gas N: Tiger Town
- Food S: Longbranch Cafe Casino

23 **S 31st St, US 312, Pompeys Pillar**

36 **Reed Creek Rd, Waco, Custer**

(38.2) **Rest Area (EB)** (RR, Phone, Picnic) (Open 4/15-11/15)

(41.3) **Rest Area (WB)** (RR, Phone, Picnic) (Open 4/15-11/15)

47 **MT 310, 5th St, Custer**
- Gas S: Custer Station◈
- Food S: D&L Café, Junction City Saloon
- Lodg S: D&L Motel
- Other S: Conv Store

49 **MT 47, Custer, Hardin**
- Other S: to Ft Custer Rest & Bar, Grandview Campground▲, Little BigHorn Battlefield

53 **Tullock Rd, Bighorn, Hysham**

63 **Ranch Access, Bighorn**

(65) **Rest Area (Both dir)** (RR, Phone, Picnic)

67 **US 10, US 312, MT 311, Bighorn, Hysham (All Serv appr 2mi N)**

72 **MT 384, Sarpy Creek Rd, Bighorn**

82 **Reservation Creek Rd, Forsyth**

87 **MT 39, Forsyth, to Colstrip**

93 **US 12W, Forsyth, Roundup**
- FStop N: Town Pump #8932/Exxon
- Gas N: Kum&Go/Cenex
- Food N: Big Sky Café, DQ, Fitzgerald's, Pizza, Top That Eatery
- Lodg N: Best Western, Howdy Motel, Montana Inn, Rails Inn Motel, Restwell Motel
- Med N: + Rosebud Health Care Center
- Other N: Lucky Lil's Casino, Buff's Bar & Casino, Tom's Casino, Vet♥

95 **18th Ave, Forsyth**
- Food N: Hong Kong Rest
- Med N: + Hospital
- Other N: Art's Tires & Service, Forsyth Auto Repair, Gamble Repair, Grocery, Pharmacy
- S: Wagon Wheel Campground▲

(99) **Weigh Station (Both dir)**

103 **MT 447, MT 446, Rosebud Creek Rd, Rosebud**

106 **Butte Creek Rd, Rosebud**

(113) **Rest Area (WB) (Open 4/15-11/15)** (RR, Phone, Picnic, RVDump)

(114) **Rest Area (EB) (Open 4/15-11/15)** (RR, Phone, Picnic, RVDump)

117 **Graveyard Creek Rd, Rosebud, Hathaway**

126 **Moon Creek Rd, Miles City**

128 **Local Access**

135 **I-94 Bus, Miles City, Jordan**
- Other N: to Miles City KOA/RVDump▲

138 **MT 59, S Haynes Ave, Miles City, US 312, to Broadus**
- TStop N: Kum&Go #820/Cenex, Town Pump #8300/Pilot #907/Exxon
- Gas N: Conoco◈
- Food N: Rest/Deli/DQ/McDonald's/Town Pump/Pilot TC, 4 B's Family Rest, Blimpie, Gallaghers Family Rest, Hardee's, KFC, Pizza Hut, Subway, Taco John's, Wendy's
  - S: Hunan Chinese
- Lodg N: Best Western, Budget Inn, Econo Lodge♥, Motel 6♥
  - S: Comfort Inn, GuestHouse Inn, Holiday Inn Express, Super 8
- Other N: Laundry/RVDump/Kum&Go, Laundry/CarWash/WiFi/Casino/TP Pilot, Auto Dealers, ATMs, Ace Hardware, Albertson's, Grocery, O'Reilly Auto Parts, Pharmacy, Radio Shack, Walmart sc, Meadows RV Park▲

141 **I-94 Bus, US 12E, Miles City, Baker**
- Other N: Use #135: Miles City KOA/RVDump▲, Big Sky Camp & RV Park/RVDump▲

148 **Valley Dr E, Ismay**

159 **Frontage Rd, Diamond Ring, Ismay**

169 **Powder River Rd, Terry**

176 **MT 253, Airport Rd, Terry**
- Gas N: Cenex, Conoco◈
- Food N: Diner, Roy Rogers Saloon, Terry's Landing
- Lodg N: Diamond Motel & Campground▲, Kempton Hotel
- Med N: + Hospital
- Other N: Small Town RV Campground▲
  - S: Terry Airport✈

185 **MT 340, Terry, Fallon**

192 **Bad Route Rd, Glendive**
- S: Rest Area (Both dir) (RR, Phone, Picnic, Info)
- S: Weigh Station (Both dir)

198 **CR 260, Cracker Box Rd, Glendive**

204 **Whoopup Creek Rd, Glendive**

206 **Pleasant View Rd, Glendive**

210 **I-94 Bus, MT 200S, Glendive, Circle**
- Gas S: Cenex◈
- Food S: McDonald's
- Other S: Auto Dealers, Auto Services, Bowling

211 **MT 200S, Circle (WB, diff WB reacc)**

213 **MT 16, Glendive, Sidney**
- TStop S: Trail Star Truck Stop/Sinclair
- Gas N: Exxon◈
  - S: Cenex◈, Conoco◈
- Food S: Rest/Trail Star TS, McDonald's, Pizza Hut, Subway
- Lodg S: Parkwood Motel, Riverside Inn♥
- Other N: MT State Hwy Patrol Post
  - S: Laundry/Trail Star TS, ATMs, Grocery, Albertson's/Pharmacy, Auto Dealer, Green Valley Campground/RVDump▲

215 **I-94 Bus, N Merrill Ave, Glendive**
- Gas N: Conoco
  - S: Exxon◈, Holiday, Sinclair◈
- Food N: CC's Family Café, Rustic Inn, Rest/Yellowstone River Inn
  - S: Hardee's, Subway, Taco John's
- Lodg N: Comfort Inn, Days Inn, Super 8, Yellowstone River Inn
  - S: Best Western,
- Med S: + Hospital
- Other N: Glendive Campground/RVDump▲, ATMs, Glendive Dinosaur Fossil Museum, Museums, Casino/Yellowstone River Inn to Makoshika State Park▲
  - S: Riverview RV Park▲

224 **Griffith Creek, Frontage Rd**

231 **Hodges Rd**

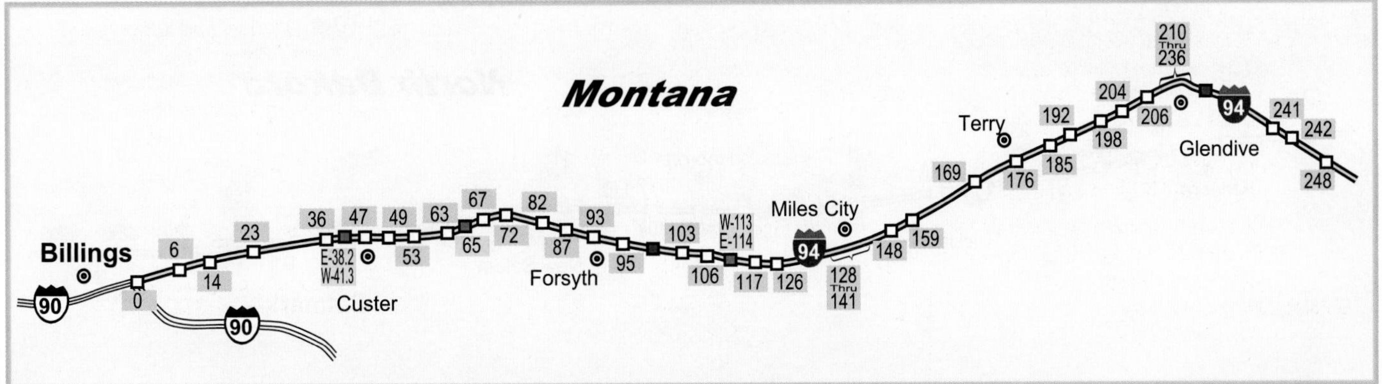

◈= Regular Gas Stations with Diesel ▲ = RV Friendly Locations ♥= Pet Friendly Locations
Red print shows large vehicle parking / access on site or nearby Brown Print = Campgrounds / RV PARKS

EXIT — MT / ND

236 Ranch Access

(240) Weigh Station (Both dir)

241 I-94 Bus, MT 261, Wibaux, Baker (EB, NO EB reaccess) (Acc to #242)
- Gas: S: Amsler Conv Store◊
- Lodg: S: Beaver Creek Inn, Super 8

242 I-94 Bus, MT 7, to MT 261, Wibaux, Baker (WB)
Rest Area (Both dir)
S: (RR, Phone, Picnic)

248 Carlyle Rd, Wibaux

MOUNTAIN TIME ZONE

NOTE: MM 250: North Dakota State Line

MONTANA
NORTH DAKOTA

MOUNTAIN TIME ZONE

(1) Weigh Station (Both dir)

1 ND 16, 1st Ave NW, Beach
- FStop: S: Interstate Cenex
- TStop: S: Flying J Travel Plaza #5004 (Scales)
- Food: S: Rest/FastFood/FJ TP, Backyard Rest, Crazy Charlie's, DQ, La Playa
- Lodg: S: Buckboard Inn
- TServ: S: Walz Truck Repair Service, W Dakota Truck Repair/Auto/Towing/Tires/RV
- Other: S: Laundry/WiFi//RVDump/LP/FJ TP, LP/Cenex, Beach Field✈

7 Home on the Range

10 Sentinel Butte, Camp Hump Lake

18 Buffalo Gap, Sentinel Butte

(21) Scenic View (EB)

23 W River Rd, Medora (WB)

24 Historic Medora, T Roosevelt National Park / South Unit

27 Historic Medora (EB)
- Other: S: Medora Campground▲

32 T Roosevelt Nat'l Park, Painted Canyon Visitor Area
Rest Area (Both dir)
N: (RR, Phone, Picnic)

36 Fryburg

EXIT — NORTH DAKOTA

42 US 85, Belfield, Grassy Butte, Williston
- TStop: S: Super Pumper #22/Tesoro
- Gas: S: Interstate Conoco◊
- Food: S: Trapper's Kettle Rest & Pizzeria
- Lodg: S: Trapper's Inn♥ & RV Park▲
- Other: S: Laundry/Tesoro, NAPA, US Post Office

51 CMC 4511, Belfield, South Heart

59 I-94 Bus, 30th Ave W, City Center, Dickinson (Access to Ex #61 Serv)
- Gas: S: Conoco◊
- Lodg: S: Oasis Motel, Queen City Motel
- Other: S: Camp on the Heart Campground▲

61 ND 22, 3rd Ave W, Dickinson, Kill Deer
- FStop: N: The General Store/Cenex
- Gas: N: Simonson's Station Store◊
  S: Cenex◊, Conoco, Holiday◊, Tesoro
- Food: N: Applebee's, Arby's, Bonanza Steak House, Burger King, El Sombrero Mex Rest, Happy Joe's Pizza, Skipper's Seafood, Taco Bell, Wendy's
  S: China Doll Chinese, Country Kitchen, Domino's, KFC, Pizza Hut, McDonald's, Perkins, Subway/Walmart
- Lodg: N: AmericInn, Comfort Inn, Days Inn, Holiday Inn Express
  S: Best Western, Budget Inn, Quality Inn, Super 8, Travel Host Motel
- Med: S: + St Joseph's Hospital
- Other: N: RVDump/LP/Gen'l Store, Albertson's, Auto Services, Goodyear, Laundromat, NAPA, North Park Campground▲, O'Reillly Auto Parts, Pharmacy, Prairie Hills Mall, Radio Shack, Tires, True Value Hard ware, UPS Store,Vet♥ , Walmart sc,
  S: Auto Repair/Conoco, Auto Dealers, Dakota Dino Museum, Dickinson State Univ ND State Hwy Patrol Post

64 I-94 Bus, Dickinson (Acc to #61 Serv)
- TStop: S: Tiger Discount Truck Stop/Tesoro
- Food: S: FastFood/Tiger Disc TS, Dakota Diner
- TServ: S: George's Tire Shop, NW Tire, Schmidt Repair
- Other: S: Laundry/Tiger TS

72 CMC 4531, Gladstone, Lefor

78 94 R Ave SW, Gladstone, Taylor

84 ND 8, Richardton, Mott
- FStop: N: Cenex C-Store
- Food: N: Wrangler Cafe
- Med: N: + Richardton Memorial Hospital

90 CMC 4510, Richardton, Antelope

EXIT — NORTH DAKOTA

97 CR 90, Hebron
- Gas: N: Farmers/Cenex◊,
- Food: N: Pizza, Wagon Wheel Cafe
- Lodg: N: Brick City Motel

102 CR 139, Hebron, Glen Ullin, Lake Tschida (Serv S 3-4 mi in Glen Ullin)
- Gas: S: Crossroads Express
- Food: S: Rondes Family Cafe
- Lodg: S: M&M Motel, Red Roof Inn
- Other: S: Glen Ullin Muni Airport✈, Glen Ullin Memorial Park Campground▲

108 CR 88, 65th Ave, Glen Ullin (Serv 3-4 mi S in Glen Ullin)

110 ND 49, Glen Ullin, Beulah

113 Glen Ullin, Geck Township

117 CR 87, New Salem, Dengate

(119) Rest Area (Both dir)
(RR, Phone, Picnic)

120 New Salem, Blue Grass, Ullin

123 CR 86, New Salem, Almont

127 ND 31, New Salem, Hannover
- FStop: S: U-Serve/Cenex
- Food: S: Sunset Inn Café
- Lodg: S: Sunset Inn, Sunset Motel
- Other: S: Grocery, Laundromat, Pharmacy

134 CR 84, New Salem, to Judson, Sweet Briar Lake

(135) Scenic View (WB)

140 33rd Ave, Mandan, Crown Butte, Crown Butte Dam

NOTE: MM 143: Mountain / Central Time Zone

147 I-94 Bus, ND 25, to ND 6, Mandan
- TStop: S: PTP/Freeway 147 Truck Stop/ Sinclair (Scales)
- Food: S: Rest/Freeway 147 TS
- Other: S: Laundry/RVDump/LP/Frwy 147 TS

(151) Scenic View (EB)

152 ND 6, Sunset Dr, Mandan
- Gas: N: Conoco
  S: Tesoro
- Food: S: Fried's Family Rest, Los Amigos
- Lodg: N: Best Western, Ridge Motel♥
- Med: S: + Hospital
- Other: N: Casino/Ridge Motel
  S: RVDump/Tesoro

153 Mandan Ave, Mandan
- Gas: S: Cenex, StaMart◊, Tesoro

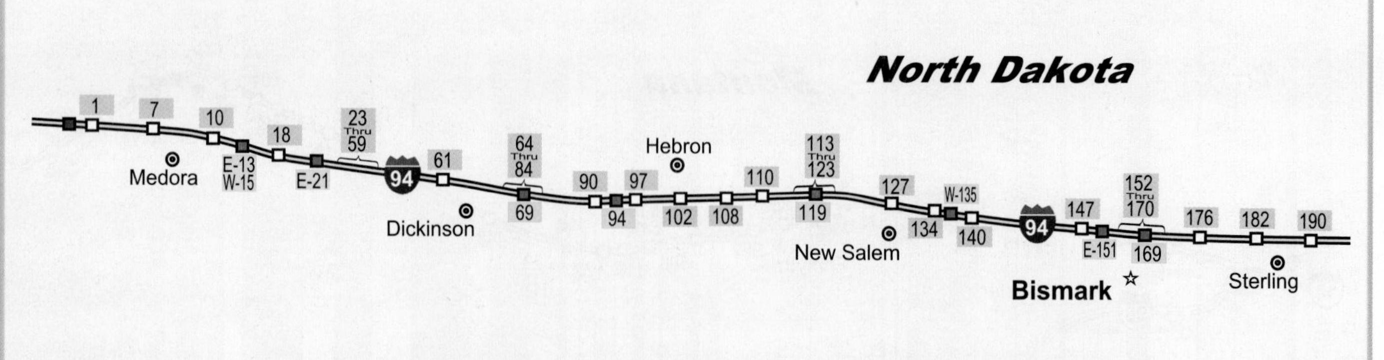

◊= Regular Gas Stations with Diesel ▲ = RV Friendly Locations ♥= Pet Friendly Locations
Red print shows large vehicle parking / access on site or nearby Brown Print = Campgrounds / RV PARKS

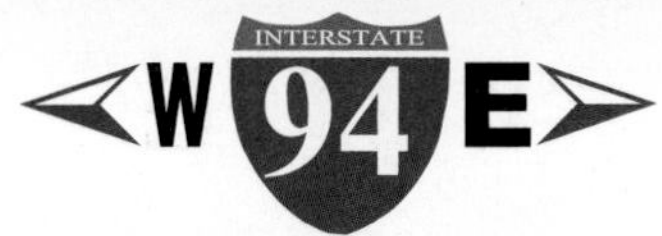

EXIT NORTH DAKOTA

Exit	Type	Services
	Food	S: Burger King, Dakota Farms Family Rest, Hardee's, McDonald's, Pizza Hut, Subway, Taco Johns', Wendy's
	Lodg	S: N Country Inn, TP Motel
	Other	S: ATMs, Auto Dealers, Auto Services, Goodyear, Grocery, Golf Course, Tires, Old Town Tavern 72 Casino
155		**I-94 Bus, to ND 6 (WB, Left exit) (Access to Serv at Ex #153)**
	Other	S: Corral Sales RV Superstore, to Ft Lincoln State Park▲ , Rough Rider Harley Davidson
(156)		**I-194, ND 810, W Bismarck Expy, NC 1804, W Bismarck, E Mandan**
	Other	S: to Dakota Zoo, Kirkwood Mall, Bismarck Muni Airport✈, Raging Waters Waterpark
157		**Divide Ave, Tyler Pkwy, Bismarck**
	Gas	N: Conoco◈
		S: Cenex◈
	Food	N: Cracker Barrel, Johnny Carino's Italian, McDonald's, Quiznos, Starbucks, Taco John's, Texas Roadhouse, Wendy's
	Other	N: RVDump/LP/Conoco, Best Buy, Dollar Tree, Lowe's, PetSmart♥,
		S: RVDump/Cenex, Banks, Bismarck State College, Grocery, Pharmacy,
159		**US 83N, ND 1804, State St, Bismarck, Minot, Willton**
	Gas	N: Gas Plus, Best Stop◈, Sinclair◈
		S: Conoco◈, StaMart, Tesoro◈
	Food	N: Applebee's, Arby's, Burger King, China Star, Hooters, KFC, McDonald's, Mex Rest, Perkins, Red Lobster, Royal Fork Buffet, Ruby Tuesday, Subway, Taco Bell
		S: East 40 Chophouse, DQ, Hardee's, Pizza Hut, Starbucks, Subway, Taco Bell, Taco del Mar, Wendy's, Wood House
	Lodg	N: AmericInn, Candlewood Suites, Comfort Inn♥, Comfort Suites, Country Inn, Fairfield Inn, Hampton Inn, Holiday Inn Express, Motel 6♥
		S: Best Western, Days Inn, Kelly Inn♥, Select Inn♥, Super 8
	Med	S: + Hospital
	Other	N: ATMs, Bismarck Animal Clinic♥, CVS, Gateway Mall, Grand Theatres, Grocery, Hobby Lobby, Home Depot, Kmart, Menard's, Pharmacy, Tires, U-Haul, Walmart sc,
		S: O'Reilly Auto Parts, to Kirkwood Mall
161		**N Bismarck Expy, Centennial Rd**
	FStop	N: Cenex C-Store
	TStop	S: StaMart Travel Center #15/Tesoro (Scales)
	Food	S: Rest/StaMart TC, McDonald's
	Lodg	S: Ramada Ltd♥
	TServ	S: Butler CAT Engine Service, Johnson Trailer Sales, Trucks of Bismarck
	Other	N: LP/RVDump/Cenex, Bismarck KOA/ RVDump▲
	Other	S: Laundry/RVDump/StaMart TC, Capital RV Center, River City Boats, Tires, Vet♥, appr 3mi: Hillcrest Acres Campground▲
(169)		**Rest Area (Both dir) (RR, Phones, Pic, Pet, Vend)**
170		**158th St NE, Menoken**
	Other	S: A Prairie Breeze RV Park▲
176		**236th St NE, Sterling, McKenzie**
182		**US 83S, ND 14, Sterling, Wing**
	TStop	S: Tops Truck Stop/Cenex
	Food	S: Rest/Tops TS, Darnell's Cafe
	Lodg	S: Tops Motel
	Other	S: Laundry/Tops TS
190		**405th St NE, Driscoll**
195		**20th Ave SE, Steele, Long Lake**
200		**ND 3, Mitchell Ave N, Steele, to Dawson, Tuttle**
	TStop	S: PTP/Coffee Cup Fuel Stop #2/Conoco
	Gas	S: Cenex
	Food	S: FastFood/Coffee Cup, Lone Steer Rest
	Lodg	S: Lone Steer Motel, Casino & RV Park▲ , OK Motel & Campground▲
205		**30th Ave SE, Steele, Robinson**
208		**ND 3S, Lake Ave, Dawson, Napolean**
	Food	S: Dawson Cafe
214		**39th Ave SE, Tappen**
	Gas	S: Marlin's Standard
217		**42nd Ave SE, Tappen, Pettibone**
(221)		**Rest Area (EB) (RR, Phone, Picnic, Vend, RVDump)**
221		**CR 39, CR 70, Medina, Crystal Springs**
(224)		**Rest Area (WB) (RR, Phone, Picnic, Vend, RVDump)**
228		**ND 30S, CR 39, Medina, Streeter**
230		**1st Ave S, 55th Ave SE, Medina**
	Gas	N: Cenex◈
	Food	N: Coffee Cup Café, Medina Cafe
	Lodg	N: Medina's Cozy Corners Motel, North Country Lodge/Motel
233		**CR 68, 58th Ave SE, Medina, to Halfway Lake**
238		**CR 67, 5th Ave, Euclid Ave, Cleveland, to Windsor, Gackle**
242		**67 1/2 Ave SE, Cleveland, Windsor**
245		**70th Ave SE, Cleveland, Oswego**
248		**CR 65, 74th Ave SE, Jamestown, Lippert Township**
251		**CMC 4728, Jamestown, Eldridge**
(254)		**Rest Area (Both dir) (RR, Phone, Picnic, Vend)**
256		**US 52, US 281, Truck, 81st Ave SE, Jamestown, Woodbury**
	Other	S: Jamestown Campground▲
257		**I-94 Bus, 17th St SW, to US 52, US 281, Jamestown (EB, Left Exit)**
258		**US 281, US 52, Jamestown, Edgly**
	FStop	N: Interstate Sinclair
	TStop	S: Super Pumper #26/Conoco
	Gas	N: BP
	Food	N: Arby's, DQ, Depot, Hardee's, McDonald's, Pizza Ranch, Taco Bell
		S: Subway/SuperPumper, Applebee's, Burger King, Embers Rest. Little Caesar's, Perkins, Paradiso Mex Rest, Super Buffet
	Lodg	N: Buffalo Motel, Comfort Inn, Days Inn, Gladstone Inn & Suites♥, Holiday Inn Express, Jamestown Motel, Ranch House Motel
		S: Best Western, Quality Inn♥, Super 8
	TServ	N: James River Diesel Service
	Med	N: + Jamestown Hospital
	Other	N: Auto Repair, Auto Dealers, Firestone, Jamestown Mall, Civic Center, ND Sports Hall of Fame, Museum, Jamestown College Jamestown Reg'l Airport✈, Jamestown Speedway, Stutsman Co Fairgrounds, Frontier Fort Campground▲ , to appr 7mi Lakeside Marina & Campground▲
		S: ATMs, Buffalo Mall, Cinemas, Countryside RV, Dale's Motorsports, Harley Davidson, Uncle Bob's Trailers, Walmart SC,
260		**I-94 Bus, 14th St, to US 52, US 281, Jamestown**
	TStop	N: Jamestown Truck Plaza/BP (Scales)
	Gas	N: Stop 'n Go
	Food	N: Rest/Jamestown TP
	Lodg	N: Budget Lodge, Star Lite Motel♥
	TWash	N: Jamestown TP
	TServ	N: Jamestown TP/Tires
	Med	S: + ND State Hospital

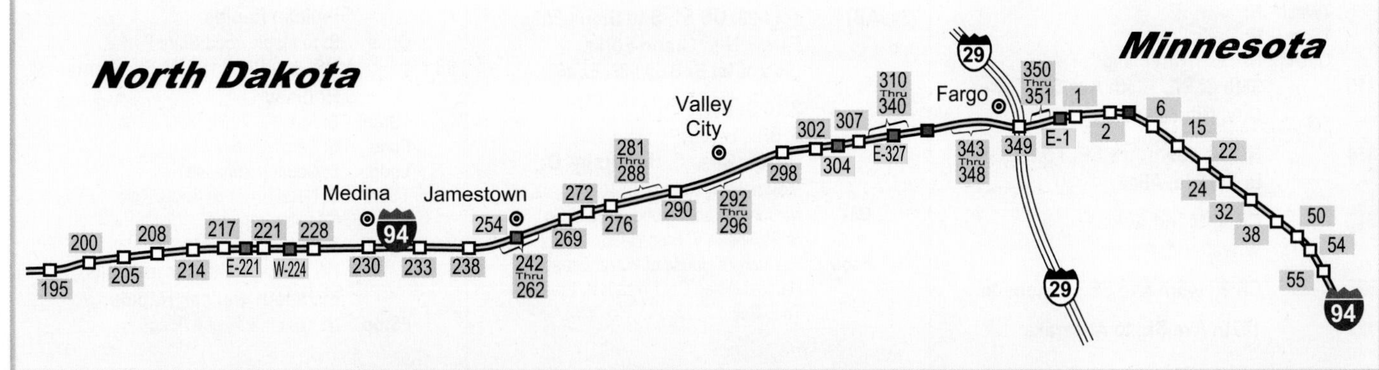

◈= Regular Gas Stations with Diesel ▲ = RV Friendly Locations ♥= Pet Friendly Locations
Red print shows large vehicle parking / access on site or nearby Brown Print = Campgrounds / RV PARKS

EXIT — NORTH DAKOTA

Other — N: Laundry/Jamestown TP, Buffalo Museum, Golf Course , Stutsman Harley Davidson

262 — Frey Rd, Jamestown, Bloom
Other — N: to Jamestown College, Jamestown Reg'l Airport✈

269 — CR 62, Jamestown, Spiritwood

272 — 97th Ave SE, Sanborn, to Urbana

276 — CR 7, 101st Ave SE, Eckelson
Other — S: Prairie Haven Campground▲ /Gas

281 — CR 11, 106th Ave SE, Sanborn, to Litchville

283 — ND 1N, Valley City, Rogers

288 — ND 1S, 113th Ave SE, CR 22N, Valley City, to Oakes

290 — I-94 Bus, US 52, Main St, CR 19, Valley City (Access to Ex #292 Serv)
Gas — N: Cenex, Tesoro◈
Food — N: Burger King, Kenny's Rest, Pizza Hut, Subway
Lodg — N: Bel-Air Motel, Valley City Motel
S: Flickertail Inn
Med — N: + Hospital
Other — N: LP/Dakota Plains Co-Op, Auto Dealers, Family Dollar, NAPA

292 — CR 21, 8th Ave SW, Valley City, to Kathryn
TStop — N: John's I-94 Tesoro
Food — N: Sabir's Dining & Lounge
Lodg — N: AmericInn, Super 8, Wagon Wheel Inn & RV Park▲
TServ — N: Berger Auto & Diesel Repair
Med — N: + Mercy Hospital
Other — N: to Barnes Co Muni Airport✈, Auto Dealers, to appr 14mi: COE/Lake Ashtabula▲
S: Public Golf Course

294 — I-94 Bus, US 52 Bus, Valley City (Access to Ex #292 Serv)
Med — N: + Hospital
Other — N: Wagon Wheel Inn & RV Park▲

296 — CR 27, 121st St SE, Valley City, Peak

298 — Cuba

302 — ND 32, Oriska, Fingal

(304) — Rest Area (Both dir, Left exit) (RR, Phone, Pic, Pet, Vend, Info)

307 — CR 1, 132nd Ave SE, Tower City
TStop — N: Tower Fuel Stop/Mobil
Food — N: Rest/Tower FS, Tower View Café
Lodg — N: Tower Motel & Campground▲
TWash — N: Tower FS
TServ — N: Tower FS/Tires
Other — N: Laundry/RVDump/Tower FS

310 — 36th St SE, 135th Ave SE, Tower City, Hill Township

314 — ND 38, 139th Ave SE, Tower City, to Buffalo, Alice

317 — CR 3, 142nd Ave SE, Wheatland, Ayr

320 — CR 7, 145th Ave SE, to Embden

322 — 147th Ave SE, to Absaraka

EXIT — NORTH DAKOTA

324 — CR 5, 149th Ave SE, Wheatland, to Chaffee

(327) — TRUCK Parking Area (EB)

328 — 153rd Ave SE, Casselton, to Lynchburg, Everest

331 — ND 18, Casselton, Leonard
Gas — N: Gordy's Travel Plaza◈, Cenex
Food — N: Gordy's Café, Subway
Lodg — N: Governors Inn & Conf Center/Rest/RV Park▲
Other — N: NAPA
S: Casselton Reg'l Airport✈

(337) — TRUCK Parking Area (WB)

338 — CR 11, Meridian Rd, Mapleton

340 — CR 15, 165th Ave SE, Mapleton, to Kindred, Davenport

(342) — Weigh Station (Both dir)

342 — 38th St NW, Mapleton, to Raymond

343 — I-94 Bus, US 10, W Fargo
TStop — N: West Fargo Truck Stop
Food — N: FastFood/W Fargo TS, Speedway Rest
Lodg — N: Hi-10 Motel, Sunset Motel, Days Inn, Super 8
Other — N: LP/W Fargo TS, Adventure RV Sales, Fargo Harley Davidson

346AB — Sheyenne St, West Fargo (WB)

346 — CR 17, Sheyenne St, West Fargo to Horace (EB)
Gas — N: Sooper Stop, Stop N Go
S: RJ's Conoco◈

348 — 45th St SW, Fargo
TStop — N: Petro Stopping Center #61/Mobil (Scales)
Gas — N: BP, Cenex
Food — N: IronSkillet/FastFood/Petro SC, Johnny Carino's, Culver's, Denny's, IHOP, McDonald's, Mongolian Grill, Mexican Grill, Qdoba Mexican Rest, Olive Garden, Pizza Hut, Quiznos, Space Aliens Bar & Grill, Subway, Wendy's
S: Applebee's, Culver's Rest, DQ, Famous Dave's, Golden Corral, KFC, Pizza Hut
Lodg — N: C'Mon Inn, Hilton Garden Inn, Mainstay Suites, Sleep Inn, Staybridge Suites, Wingate Inn
S: La Quinta Inn♥, Settle Inn
TWash — N: Blue Beacon/Petro SC
TServ — N: Petro SC/Tires
Other — N: Laundry/RVDump/LP/Petro SC, Home Depot, NAPA, Office Depot, Sam's Club, Target, Walmart sc
S: Red River Zoo

(349AB) — Jct I-29, US 81, S to Sioux Falls, Fargo, N to Grand Forks (Serv at 1st Ex S on I-29, Ex #62)

350 — 25th St SW, Fargo
Gas — S: BP◈, Holiday

351 — US 81 Bus, S University Dr, Downtown Fargo
Gas — N: Conoco, Loaf n Jug, Stop N Go
S: Phillips 66◈, Stop-N-Go
Food — N: Duane's House of Pizza, Great Harvest Bread Co, Pizza Hut, Starbucks, Taco Bell

EXIT — ND / MN

Food — S: Burger King, Denny's, Domino's, KFC, McDonald's, N American Steak Buffet, Randy's Diner, Subway, Taco Bell
Lodg — N: Dakota Day Inn
S: Expressway Inn, Rodeway Inn
Med — N: + Dakota Medical Center
Other — N: Greyhound, AutoZone, Pharmacy
S: Blue Wolf Casino

NOTE: MM 352: Minnesota State Line

NORTH DAKOTA
MINNESOTA

CENTRAL TIME ZONE

1A — US 75, S 8th St, Moorhead
Gas — N: Phillips 66, Brady's Service Ctr
S: Bud's Amoco & Service Center, Casey's Gen'l Store
Food — N: Burger King, Little Caesar's, Qdoba Mexican Grill, Starbucks, Village Inn
S: Hardee's, Snap Dragon, Speak Easy Rest & Lounge, Subway
Lodg — N: Courtyard
S: AmericInn, Grand Inn♥, Super 8
Other — N: CarWash/Repairs/Towing/Brady's, MN State Univ/Moorhead, MSU Planetarium, Moorhead Center Mall

1B — 20th St (EB exit, WB reaccess)
Gas — S: Stop N Go
Other — N: MN State & Tech College

(1) — MN Welcome Center (EB) (RR, Phones, Picnic, Vend, Info)

2 — I-94 Bus, US 52, Main Ave, to US 10, Moorhead
Gas — N: Holiday Station Store◈
Food — N: China Buffet, Perkins
Lodg — N: Guest House Motel
Other — N: Larry's RV, Moorhead/Fargo KOA▲ , to US 10: ATMs, Target, Walmart

(5) — Weigh Station (EB)

6 — MN 336, CR 11, to US 10, Glyndon, to Sabin, Dilworth
Other — N: to Buffalo River State Park▲

15 — MN 10, Barnesville, Downer, Sabin

22 — MN 9, CR 55, Barnesville
Gas — S: Barnesville Gen'l Store, Barnesville AmocoBP, Cenex◈

24 — MN 34, Barnesville, Detroit Lakes
Gas — S: Cenex◈
Other — N: Golf Course
S: Wagner City Park Campground/RVDump▲

32 — MN 108E, CR 30, Lawndale, Pelican Rapids
Other — S: to Maplewood State Park▲

38 — US 52, CR 11, MN 88, Center St, Rothsay
TStop — S: Rothsay Truck Stop/Tesoro
Food — S: Rest/Rothsay TS
Lodg — S: Comfort Zone Inn
TServ — S: Neuleib Repair Shop, Rothsay Truck & Trailer Repair
Other — S: LP/Rothsay TS

50 — US 59N, CR 88, Fergus Falls, Elizabeth, Pelican Rapids
FStop — N: Interstate Fuel & Food

◈= Regular Gas Stations with Diesel ▲ = RV Friendly Locations ♥= Pet Friendly Locations
Red print shows large vehicle parking / access on site or nearby Brown Print = Campgrounds / RV PARKS

EXIT		MINNESOTA
	Food	N: Rest/Interstate F&F
	Other	N: RVDump/LP/Interstate F&F
54		**MN 210W, W Lincoln Ave, Fergus Falls, Breckenridge**
	TStop	N: Kum & Go #107
	Gas	N: Amoco, Casey's, Holiday Station
	Food	N: Applebee's, Burger King, Hardee's, KFC,McDonald's, Mabel Murphy's, Pizza Hut, Perkins, Pizza Ranch, Subway
	Lodg	N: AmericInn♥, Best Western, Comfort Inn♥, Days Inn♥, Motel 7, Super 8
	Med	N: + Fergus Falls State Hospital
	Other	N: RVDump/Holiday, ATMs, Auto Services, Auto Dealers, Grocery, Home Depot, NAPA, Radio Shack, Target, Tires Plus, Westridge Mall, **Walmart**, MN State & Tech College S: Fergus Falls Muni Airport✈
55		**CR 1, Wendell Rd, Fergus Falls**
57		**MN 210E, CR 25, Fergus Falls**
	Other	N: to Swan Lake Resort Campground▲
(60)		Rest Area (EB) (RR, Phone, Picnic, Vend)
61		**US 59S, CR 82, Fergus Falls, to Elbow Lake**
	TStop	N: Big Chief Truck Stop/Citgo
	Food	N: Rest/Big Chief TS
	Other	N: WiFi/Big Chief TS, to Swan Lake Resort & Campground▲ S: River N Woods Campground▲
67		**CR 35, Dalton**
	Other	N: Big Island Campsite▲
(69)		Rest Area (WB) (RR, Phone, Picnic, Vend)
77		**MN 78N, CR 10, Barrett, Ashby**
	Other	N: Ashby Resort & Campground▲, Prairie Cove Campground & RV Park▲
82		**MN 79W, CR 41, Evansville, Elbow Lake**
	Other	S: Tipsinah Mounds Campground▲
90		**CR 7, Brandon**
97		**MN 114, CR 40, Alexandria, Garfield, Lowry**
	Other	N: Alexandria Oak Park▲
(100)		Rest Area (EB) (RR, Phones, Picnic, Vend)
100		**MN 27, Alexandria**
	TStop	N: PTP/Pipeline Travel Plaza◊
	Food	N: Subway/Pipeline TP
	Other	N: Steinbring Motorcoach & Service

EXIT		MINNESOTA
103		**MN 29, MN 27, Alexandria, Glenwood**
	FStop	N: B&H Self Serve
	Gas	N: Citgo, Holiday Station Store
	Food	N: Burger King, Country Kitchen, Culver's, Hardee's, KFC, McDonald's, Perkins, Taco Bell, Wendy's S: Rudy's Red Eye Grill
	Lodg	N: AmericInn, Days Inn♥, Ramada Ltd♥, Super 8♥ S: Country Inn♥, Holiday Inn♥
	TServ	S: Steussy's Diesel Service
	Med	N: + Douglas Co Hospital, + Midway Medical Clinic, + VA Hospital
	Other	N: RVDump/Holiday, ATMs, Pharmacy, Target, **Walmart sc**, Chandler Field, Jiffy Lube, Midas, Sun Valley Resort & Campground▲, Steinbring Motorcoach & Service, to appr 6mi: Scenic View RV Campground▲ S: Alexandria RV
(105)		Rest Area (WB) (RR, Phones, Picnic, Vend)
114		**MN 127, CR 3, Osakis, Westport**
	Other	N: to Sportmens Motel & RV Park▲, Midway Beach Resort & Campground▲, Head of the Lakes Resort▲
119		**CR 46, CR 91, 137th Ave, West Union, Sauk Centre**
124		**CR 72, Beltline Rd, Sinclair Lewis Ave, Sauk Centre (EB exit, no reacc)**
127		**US 71, MN 28, Sauk Centre, Glenwood, Willmar**
	TStop	N: Holiday Super Stop S: PTP/Truckers Inn #6/BP (Scales)
	Gas	N: Casey's Gen'l Store, Super America
	Food	N: DQ, Hardee's, Pizza Hut, McDonald's S: Rest/Truckers Inn
	Lodg	N: AmericInn♥, Best Value♥, Super 8♥
	TWash	S: Truckers Inn
	TServ	S: Truckers Inn/Tires, St Cloud Truck Sales
	Med	N: + St Michael's Hospital
	Other	N: Auto Repairs, Tires, Head of the Lakes Resort▲ S: Laundry/Truckers Inn, Sauk Centre Muni Airport✈, Midwest RV Service
131		**MN 4S, Meire Grove, Paynesville**
135		**MN 13, S 2nd Ave E, Melrose**
	Gas	N: Mobil◊, Tesoro◊
	Gas	S: Conoco◊
	Food	N: Burger King, Subway S: DQ
	Lodg	S: Super 8♥

EXIT		MINNESOTA
	Med	N: + Melrose Hospital
	Other	N: ATMs, Grocery, NAPA, Auto Repairs & Towing/Mobil, Sauk River City Park/ RVDump S: Grocery
137		**MN 237, CR 65, New Munich**
140		**MN 11, 1st Ave S, Freeport**
	Gas	N: Conoco◊
	Food	N: Pioneer Supper Club, Charlie's Café
	Lodg	N: Pioneer Inn
	Other	N: US Post Office
147		**MN 238N, MN 10, 8th St S, Albany**
	Gas	N: Holiday Station◊, QuikMart, Shell
	Food	N: DQ, Hillcrest Family Rest S: KFC, Subway
	Lodg	N: Country Inn
	Med	N: + Albany Medical Center
	Other	N: RVDump/Holiday, ATMs, Car Wash, IGA, Laundromat
(152)		Rest Area (Both dir) (RR, Phone, Picnic, Vend)
153		**CR 9, Avon Ave S, Avon**
	Gas	N: Avon QuikMart◊, Avon Shell◊
	Food	N: Neighbors BBQ & Smokehouse
	Lodg	N: AmericInn♥
	Other	N: Grocery, US Post Office S: to El Rancho Manana Campground▲
156		**CR 159, 135th Ave N, Avon, St John's University**
158		**CR 75, St Joseph, St. Cloud, Waite Park (EB, Left Exit, No reacc)**
	Other	N: to St Cloud Campground & RV Park▲
160		**CR 2, St. Joseph, Cold Springs**
164		**MN 23, Waite Park, St Cloud, Rockville (Serv 3-4 mi N in Waite Park)**
167AB		**MN 15, St. Cloud, Kimball (EB), MN 15, to US 10W, to MN 371N, St Cloud, Kimball, Brainerd (WB) (Serv 4 mi N in St Cloud)**
	Med	N: + Hospital
	Other	N: to St Cloud Campground & RV Park/RVDump▲
171		**CR 75, CR 7, St Cloud, St Augusta**
	TStop	N: Pilot Travel Center #134 (Scales)
	Gas	N: Cenex S: Holiday Station
	Food	N: FastFood/Pilot TC, FastFood/Cenex
	Lodg	N: AmericInn, Holiday Inn Express
	TServ	N: Casey's Truck Repair, Joe's Auto & Truck Repair, Heartland Tire & Service

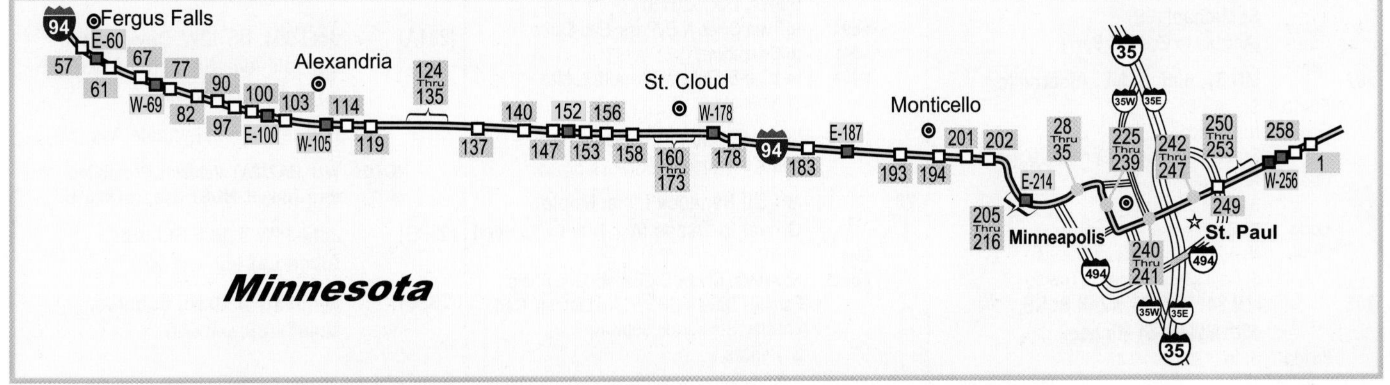

◊= Regular Gas Stations with Diesel ▲ = RV Friendly Locations ♥= Pet Friendly Locations
Red print shows large vehicle parking / access on site or nearby Brown Print = Campgrounds / RV PARKS

EXIT		MINNESOTA
	Other	N: WiFi/RVDump/Pilot TC
		S: RVDump/Holiday, **Pleasureland RV Center/RVDump**
173		**CR 75, Opportunity Dr**
(178)		**Fuller Lake Rest Area (WB) (RR, Phone, Picnic, Vend)**
178		**MN 24, Clearwater, Annandale**
	TStop	N: Petro 2/Clearwater Travel Plaza/ Citgo (Scales)
	Gas	N: Holiday Station◈
	Food	N: Rest/FastFood/Petro2/Clw TP, Burger King, DQ, Subway
	Lodg	N: Best Western, Budget Inn
	TServ	N: Petro2/Clw TP
	Other	N: Laundry/**RVDump/LP**/Petro2/Clw TP, Grocery, **St Cloud/Clearwater/I-94 KOA▲**, **to St Cloud Campground & RV Park▲**, Leaders Clear Lake Airport✈
		S: Clearwater Auto Parts, **A-J Acres Campground/RVDump▲**
183		**CR 8, Elder Ave NW, Hasty, Clearwater, Silver Creek**
	TStop	S: AmBest/Olsen's Truck Stop (Scales)
	Food	S: Pump House Rest&Deli/Olson's TS
	TServ	S: Petrol Pumper/Tires
	Other	N: **Miesner RV Services, Northern RV & Boat**
		S: Laundry/WiFi/Petrol Pumper, **Olson's Campground▲**, **Lake Maria State Park**
(187)		**Enfield Rest Area (EB) (RR, Phone, Picnic, Vend)**
193		**MN 25, Pine St, Monticello, Buffalo**
	FStop	S: Tom Thumb/BP
	Gas	N: Holiday Station Store◈, Marathon, Kwik Stop, Conoco◈
		S: Super America◈
	Food	N: Burger King, DQ, KFC, Mex Rest, Perkins, Quiznos, Taco Bell
		S: Applebee's, Arby's, Culver's, McDonald's, Pizza Factory, Subway
	Lodg	N: AmericInn, Rand House B&B
		S: Best Western, Days Inn, Select Inn
	TServ	S: Hoglund Bus Co Sales & Service
	Med	N: + Big Lake Hospital
	Other	N: ATMS, Auto Value Parts Store, Grocery Home Depot, Pharmacy, Radio Shack, Target, **River Terrace Park▲**, **Monticello Center, to Big Lake RV**
		S: LP/TomThumb, Checker Auto Parts, Auto Dealers, **Walmart sc**, Pilots Cove Airport✈, **Lake Maria State Park**
194		**Fenning Ave NE, Monticello (Access to Ex #193 Serv)**
201		**MN 19, La Beaux Ave, Albertville, St Michael (EB) (Access to Ex #202 Serv)**
202		**MN 37, 60th St NE, Albertville**
	FStop	S: Pat's Shell
	Gas	N: Conoco◈
		S: Amoco, Casey's Gen'l Store, Mobil
	Food	N: Burger King, Subway
		S: Hot Stuff Pizza/Pat's
	Lodg	N: Country Inn
	Other	N: Albertville Premium Outlets
		S: Dale's Auto Repair & Towing
205		**MN 241, CR 36, 42nd St SE, 45th St NE, St Michael**
	FStop	S: to Super America #4554

EXIT		MINNESOTA
207		**MN 101, CR 81, Main St, Rogers, Elk River, to US 169N**
	TStop	N: Travel Center of America #190/Citgo (Scales)
	Gas	N: Super America◈
		S: BP, Holiday Station Store
	Food	N: Fulton'sRest/TA TC, Arby's, Applebee's, Burger King, Culver's, Rest, Denny's, Dominos Pizza, McDonald's, Subway, Taco Bell, Wendy's
		S: Black Bear Lodge & Saloon, Country Kitchen, DQ, Embers Rest, Guadalajara Mexican Rest, Subway
	Lodg	N: Hampton Inn, Super 8
		S: AmericInn
	TServ	N: TA TC/Tires, Goodyear, MN Trailer Sales
		S: Campbell Diesel Service, Glen's Truck Center, Boyer Trucks
	Other	N: Laundry/WiFi/**RVDump**/TA TC, ATMs, Best Buy, Cabela's/**RVDump**, **Camping World**, Discount Tire, Goodyear, Grocery, Lowe's, Lube & CarWash, Target, Tires Plus, UPS Store, Vet♥, Walgreen's,
		S: CVS, Grocery
(212)		**FUTURE Exit, MN 610E**
213		**CR 30, 97th Ave N, 93rd Ave N, Osseo, Maple Grove**
	Gas	N: Maple Square Fuel & Wash, Phillips 66, Super America◈
		S: Holiday◈
	Food	S: Culver's Rest, McDonald's, Quiznos
	Other	S: Goodyear, Sam's Club, Target, Tires, Walgreen's, **Walmart sc**, **Minneapolis NW KOA▲**
(214)		**Elm Creek Rest Area (EB) (RR, Phones, Picnic, Vend)**
215		**CR 109, Weaver Lake Rd, Maple Grove, Osseo**
	Gas	N: Super America◈, Citgo
	Food	N: Bakers Square, Burger King, DQ, Cattle Co Steakhouse, Chuck E Cheese's Pizza, Don Pablo, Famous Dave's, HOPS Grill, Joe's Crab Shack, KFC, McDonald's, Little Caesars Pizza, Papa John's Pizza, Pizza Hut, Starbucks, Subway, Taco Bell, Wendy's
		S: Applebee's, Fuddrucker's
	Lodg	N: Hampton Inn, Staybridge Suites
	Other	N: ATMs, Banks, Barnes & Noble, Best Buy, Borders, FedEx Office, Gander Mountain, Goodyear, Grocery, Mall, **Modern RV**, PetCo♥, Tires Plus, US Post Office, Walgreen's,
(216)		**Jct I-94E, I-694E, I-494S (EB), I-94W, US 52 (WB)**
	I-694:	to Twin Cities N ByPass, Eau Claire
	I-94:	to Downtown
	I-494:	to Minn-St Paul Int'l Airport✈, Mall of America
	NOTE:	**I-94 runs below with I-694. Exit #'s follow I-694.**
28		**MN 61, Hemlock Lane, Maple Grove, to Osseo (Acc N to Ex 15 Serv)**
	Gas	S: BP
	Food	N: Arby's, Chuck E Cheese, Don Pablo, Famous Dave's BBQ, Olive Garden, Red Lobster, Starbucks, Subway
		S: Perkins

EXIT		MINNESOTA
	Lodg	N: Holiday Inn, Hampton Inn
		S: Select Inn, Travelodge
	Other	N: ATMs, Best Buy, Grocery, Tires
29AB		**US 169, to Osseo, Hopkins**
30		**Boone Ave, Minneapolis**
	Food	N: Rest/Northland Inn
	Lodg	N: Northland Inn Hotel, Sleep Inn
	Other	S: Discount Tire, Home Depot
31		**MN 81, MN 8, Lakeland Ave, Downtown Minneapolis**
	Gas	N: Shell, SuperAmerica◈
	Food	N: DQ, Wendy's
	Lodg	N: Ramada Inn
		S: Best Value Inn, Budget Host Inn, Super 8
	Other	S: Crystal Airport✈
33		**CR 152, Brooklyn Blvd**
	Gas	N: Mobil, Shell
		S: BP
	Other	S: Family Dollar, Grocery, Walgreen's
34		**Shingle Creek Pkwy, to MN 100**
	Gas	N: Mobil
	Food	N: Cracker Barrel, Denny's, Olive Garden, TGI Friday
		S: Boston Market, Indian Rest, Panera Bread, Pizza Hut
	Lodg	N: AmericInn, Baymont Inn, Comfort Inn, Super 8
		S: Inn on the Farm
	Other	S: ATMs, Best Buy, Target, Tires
35A		**Dupont Ave, MN 100, Robbinsdale**
(35B)		**Jct I-94E, Downtown Minneapolis**
(225 /35C)		**Jct I-694E, MN 252N, to MN 610 (WB)**
	NOTE:	**I-94 runs above with I-694. Exit #'s follow I-694.**
226		**53rd Ave N, 49th Ave N**
	Food	S: DQ, Pizza
	Lodg	S: Camden Motel
	Other	S: Grocery
228		**Dowling Ave N, Minneapolis**
229		**26th Ave N, CR 81, CR 66, Broadway Ave, Plymouth Ave (EB), CR 152, N Washington Ave (WB)**
	Gas	N: Holiday
	Food	S: Subway, Taco Bell, Wendy's
	Other	S: Grocery, Target, Walgreen's
230		**W Broadway, N Plymouth, 4th St N, US 52, MN 55W, W Suburbs (EB) CR 40, Glenwood Ave, MN 55 (WB)**
	NOTE:	**EB: HAZMAT Vehicles Prohibited thru Tunnel. MUST Use Exit #231A.**
(231A)		**Jct I-394, US 12W, Downtown Lyndale Ave, Hennepin Ave (EB), I-394, US 12W (WB)**
231B		**Hennepin Ave, Lyndale Ave (WB)**
	NOTE:	**WB: HAZMAT Vehicles Prohibited thru Tunnel. MUST Use Exit #231B.**
(233B)		**Jct I-35W S, to S Suburbs, Albert Lea (EB, Left exit)**
(233C)		**Jct I-35W N, to NE Suburbs, Duluth (EB, Left exit)**

◈= Regular Gas Stations with Diesel ▲ = RV Friendly Locations ♥= Pet Friendly Locations
Red print shows large vehicle parking / access on site or nearby **Brown Print = Campgrounds / RV PARKS**

EXIT	MINNESOTA

233A **11th St, Downtown (WB)**

234A **MN 55E, Hiawatha Ave**
Other S: to Minn St Paul Int'l Airport✈

(233C) **Jct I-35W S, Albert Lea (WB, Left exit)**

234B **5th St, Downtown (WB, diff reaccess)**

234C **CR 152, Cedar Ave (WB)**

235A **25th Ave, Riverside Ave**

235B **Huron Blvd, University of MN**
Med N: + Hospital
Other N: Univ of MN

236 **MN 280, to I-35W N, University Ave**
Med N: + St Paul Veterans Center

237 **Vandalia St, Cretin Ave N**
FStop N: N to Cleveland Ave: Pro Stop Fuel
TServ N: Kenworth
Other N: AmTrak

238 **MN 51, Snelling Ave, St Paul**
Gas S: Citgo
Food N: Applebee's, Best Steak House, McDonald's, Perkins
Other N: to Zoo, State Fairgrounds

239A **Hamline Ave (WB, No reaccess)**
Food N: Hardee's
Lodg N: Sheraton
Med N: + Hospital
Other N: ATMs, Grocery, Target

239B **CR 51, Lexington Pkwy, St Paul**
Gas N: BP, Super America
Food N: Best Steak House, DQ, Hardee's, KFC, Pizza Hut, White Castle
Med N: + Hospital

240 **CR 53, Dale St**
Other S: St Paul College

241A **CR 56, 12th St, Marion St, Kellogg Blvd, to (EB) I-35E, State Capitol**
Other N: State Capitol, Vietnam Memorial

241B **5th St, 10th St W, St Paul (EB)**

(241C) **Jct I-35E S, to Albert Lea (WB)**
NOTE: NO Trucks over 9000# GVW

(242B) **Jct I-35E N, US 10W (EB, Left exit)**

242A **12th St, State Capitol (WB)**
Med N: + Regions Hospital
S: + St Joseph's Hospital

(242B) **Jct I-35E N, US 10W (WB)**

242C **7th Ave, MN 5 (EB, Exit only)**

242D **US 52S, MN 3, 6th St, Downtown St Paul (fr WB, Left exit)**

243 **US 61, Mounds Blvd, Kellogg Blvd (fr EB, Left Exit, diff reacc)**
Other N: Metropolitan State Univ
S: St Paul Downtown Holman Field

244 **US 10E, US 61S, Hastings, Prescott**

245 **R 65, White Bear Ave, St Paul**
Gas N: Super America
S: BP
Food N: Embers, Hardee's, Pizza Hut, Subway
S: Arby's, Bakers Square, Burger King, Davanni's Pizza, Ground Round, KFC, McDonald's, Perkins, Taco Bell
Lodg N: Excel Inn, Travelodge
Other S: ATMs, Auto Dealer, Firestone, Target, Pharmacy

246A **Ruth St (EB, No reacc)**

Personal Notes

EXIT	MINNESOTA

246BC **CR 68, McKnight Rd**
Lodg S: Holiday Inn
Other N: 3M, Petland♥

247 **MN 120, Century Ave, St Paul**
Gas S: Super America
Food N: Denny's, Toby's Rest
S: McDonald's
Lodg N: Super 8
S: Country Inn

(249AB) **Jct I-694, Jct I-494**
I-494S: to Mall of America, Minn St Paul Intl Airport✈
I-694N: to Twin Cities North ByPass, St Cloud

250 **CR 13, Radio Dr, Inwood Ave, Lake Elmo, Woodbury**
Gas S: Holiday Station Store
Food S: Blimpie, Don Pablo, India Palace, Machine Shed, Quiznos, Starbucks, Sushi Tango, Taco Bell, TGI Friday, Wendy's
Lodg N: Hilton Garden Inn, Wildwood Lodge
Med S: + Health Partners Clinic
Other N: Auto Repairs, Best Buy, Lake Elmo Reg'l Park▲
S: ATMs, Animal Hospital♥, Auto Service, Borders, Circuit City, CompUSA, Home Depot, Grocery, Office Max, PetSmart♥, Tires Plus

251 **CR 19, Woodbury Dr, Keats Ave**
Gas S: Kwik Trip, Super America◈
Food S: Applebee's, Arby's, Burger King, Chili's, Chipolte Mex Grill, Outback Steakhouse, Food Court/Horizon Outlet Ctr
Lodg S: Extended Stay America, Holiday Inn Express
Other N: Lake Elmo Reg'l Park▲

EXIT	MN / WI

Other S: ATMs, Auto Repairs, Gander Mountain, Horizon Outlet Center, Sam's Club, Tires, Walmart, to St Paul East RV Park▲

253 **MN 95S, CR 15, Manning Ave, Lake Elmo, St Paul, Hastings**
Other N: Lake Elmo Airport✈
S: to Afton State Park▲, St Croix Bluff's Reg'l Park▲

(254) **Weigh Station (WB)**

(256) **MN Welcome Center (WB)**
(RR, Phones, Vend, Picnic, Info)

258 **MN 95N, CR 18, St Croix Trail, Lakeland, Afton, Stillwater**
Other S: Afton State Park, Afton Alps Ski Area

NOTE: MM 259: Wisconsin State Line

MINNESOTA
WISCONSIN

CENTRAL TIME ZONE

1 **WI 35N, 2nd St S, Hudson**
Gas N: Auto Stop Gas, Freedom Valu Ctr◈, Holiday Station Store, Mike's Standard
Food N: Corby's, DQ, Dragon Pearl, Subway
Lodg N: Dibbo Hotel, Grapevine Inn B&B, Phipps Inn
S: Best Western, Comfort Inn♥, Super 8
Med N: + Hudson Hospital
Other N: Rick's Auto Service, to Willow River State Park▲
S: Hudson Cinema 9

2 **CR F, Carmichael Rd, Hudson**
S: WI Welcome Center (EB)
Hudson Rest Area (WB)
(RR, Phone, Picnic, Vend, Info)
Gas N: BP, Holiday
S: Kwik Trip◈, Freedom Valu◈
Food N: Applebee's, Cousins Subs, KFC
S: Arby's, Burger King, Country Kitchen, Denny's, Kingdom Buffet, McDonald's, Taco Bell, Wendy's
Lodg N: Best Value Inn♥, Royal Inn
S: Best Western, Comfort Inn♥, Fairfield Inn, Holiday Inn Express
Med S: + Hudson Memorial Hospital
Other N: ATMs, Auto Dealers, Grocery, Pharmacy, Target
S: ATMs, Auto Dealers, Checker Auto Parts, Grocery, Home Depot, Pharmacy, Tires Plus, Walmart

3 **WI 35S, Hudson, River Falls**
Lodg S: Stageline Inn
Other S: to Univ of WI/River Falls

4 **US 12, CR U, 60th St, Hudson, Burkhardt, Somerset**
TStop N: Travel Center of America #192/Mobil (Scales)
Gas N: Mr Convenience/Citgo◈
Food N: Rest/TA TC, Jr Ranch Bar & Grill
Lodg N: Best Value Inn
TServ N: TA TC/Tires
Other N: Laundry/WiFi/TA TC, to Willow River State Park▲, Float Rite Park

(8) **Weigh Station (EB)**

10 **WI 65, Roberts, River Falls, New Richmond,**
Other N: to Rivers Edge Tubing, Camping, Rest
S: to Univ of WI/River Falls

◈= Regular Gas Stations with Diesel ▲ = RV Friendly Locations ♥= Pet Friendly Locations
Red print shows large vehicle parking / access on site or nearby Brown Print = Campgrounds / RV PARKS

EXIT WISCONSIN

16 **CR T, Baldwin, Hammonds**
Gas N: AmocoBP
Lodg N: Hammond Hotel

19 **US 63, Baldwin, Ellsworth**
TStop S: Ray's Super Truck Stop/Citgo
Gas N: Freedom Valu◊, Kwik Trip #747/BP◊
Food N: A&W, DQ, Hardee's, McDonald's, Subway/KT
S: Rest/Ray's SS, Coachman Supper Club
Lodg N: AmericInn
S: Super 8
Med N: + Baldwin Area Medical Center
Other S: LP/Ray's Super TS

24 **CR B, Woodville, Spring Valley**
Gas N: Stop-A-Sec/Mobil
Food N: Woodville Cafe
Lodg N: Woodville Motel

28 **WI 128, Wilson, Glenwood City, Spring Valley, Elmwood**
TStop S: Kwik Trip #603/BP
Food S: Rest/KT

32 **CR Q, to Knapp**

41 **WI 25, N Broadway St, to US 12, Menomonie, Barron, Wheeler (WB)**
Gas N: Cenex
S: Holiday Station Store, SA/Speedway◊
Food N: Applebee's, China Buffet, Old 400 Depot Café, Quiznos
S: Arby's, Country Kitchen, Green Mill Rest, KFC, Kernel Rest, McDonald's, Perkins, Pizza Hut, Taco Bell, Wendy's
Lodg S: AmericInn, Country Inn♥, Motel 6♥, Super 8♥
Other N: Auto Repair Dollar Tree, Grocery, Radio Shack, **Walmart sc**, **to** Skyport Airport✈, **Twin Springs Resort Campround▲**
S: Auto Repair, Advance Auto, Auto Dealers, ATMs, Grocery, O'Reilly Auto Parts, Walgreen's

(43) **Menomonie Rest Area (Both dir)**
(RR, Phone, Picnic, Vend, Info, Weather)

45 **CR B, Menomonie**
TStop N: Exit 45 Auto Truck Plaza/Cenex (Scales)
S: Kwik Trip #674/BP (Scales)
Food N: Rest/Ex 45 ATP
S: Subway/KT, Country Kitchen
Lodg S: Comfort Inn
TServ S: Kenworth, International
Other N: LP/Ex 45 ATP
S: Laundry/KT, **Aok RV Sales & Service**, Menomonie Muni Airport/Score Field✈, Univ of WI

EXIT WISCONSIN

(48.3) **Weigh Station (WB)**

52 **US 12, WI 29, WI 40, Elk Mound, Chippewa Falls, Colfax, Green Bay**

59 **Partridge Rd, CR EE, to US 12, WI 312E, Eau Claire, Elk Mound**
TStop N: Mega Express #1/BP, Holiday Station Store #16 (Scales)
Food N: Burger King/Mega Expr, Subway/Holiday Anderson's Grill & Bar, Embers Rest, McDonald's, Peppermill Rest
Lodg N: AmericInn♥, Days Inn, Super 8
TServ N: Peterbilt, Eau Claire Diesel Service, Badger Truck Refrigeration, River States Truck & Trailer
S: Eau Claire Truck & Trailer, Fabco Engine Systems
Med N: + Hospital
Other N: LP/Mega Express, Interstate Auto & Towing, Golf Course, U-Haul, Chippewa Valley Reg'l Airport✈

65 **WI 37, WI 85, to US 12, Eau Claire, Mondovi**
(Addt'l serv N to US 12)
Gas N: Exxon
Food N: Arby's, A&W, China Buffet, Green Mill Rest/Hol Inn, Godfather's Pizza, Hardee's, McDonald's, Red Lobster, Taco Bell, Wendy's
Lodg N: Best Western♥, Comfort Inn♥, Days Inn♥, Hampton Inn, Highlander Inn, Holiday Inn, Super 8
Med N: + Sacred Heart Hospital
Other N: Univ of WI/Eau Claire, **to Ferry St:** Eau Claire Wasterwater Plant/RVDump
S: Tires

68 **WI 93, to US 53, US 12, Eau Claire, to Eleva, Altoona**
Gas N: BP, Holiday Station, KwikTrip
Food N: Burger King, DQ, Quiznos, Red Robin
Lodg N: Econo Lodge♥
Other N: Auto Dealers, Goodyear, to Oakwood Mall/Cinema
S: Auto Dealers, **US RV Supercenter**

70AB **US 53, S Hastings Way, Eau Claire, Chippewa Falls, Altoona**
Gas N: Conoco◊, Handy Mart, Holiday, KwikTrip
Food N: Applebee's, Buffalo Wild Wings, Fazoli's, McDonald's, Olive Garden, Panera Bread, Starbucks, TGI Friday, Timber Lodge Steakhouse
Lodg N: Country Inn♥, Grand Stay Residential Suites, Heartland Inn♥

EXIT WISCONSIN

Other N: ATMs, Banks, Auto Services, Best Buy, Borders, Gander Mountain, Grocery, Office Depot, PetCo♥, Pharmacy, Sam's Club, Target, Tires, **Walmart sc**, Oakwood Mall, Cinema, 50/50 Factory Outlet

81 **CR HH, to US 53, to CR KK, Strum, Foster, Fall Creek, Augusta**

88 **US 10, 10th St, to US 53, to CR R, Osseo, Fairchild, Strum, Augusta**
FStop N: Direct Travel Center/Mobil
S: SA/Speedway #4523
TStop N: AmBest/Golden Express Travel Plaza (Scales)
Gas S: Kwik Trip
Food N: ElderberryRest/Golden Express TP, DQ, Hardee's
S: Hardee's, McDonald's, Moe's Diner, Subway, Taco John's
Lodg N: Ten Seven Inn, Super 8
S: Red Carpet Inn♥
TServ N: Golden Express TP/Tires
Med S: + Osseo Area Medical Center
Other N: Laundry/Golden Express TP, **Stoney Creek RV Resort & Campground▲**

98 **WI 121, CR FF, Hixton, Northfield, Alma Center, Pigeon Falls**
Gas S: Farmers Co-Op/Cenex◊
Food N: York's Last Resort
S: Jackie's Inn Bar & Grill

105 **WI 95, CR FF, Hixton, Alma Center, Taylor**
TStop S: Hixton Travel Plaza
Gas S: Cenex◊, Citgo
Food S: Rest/Hixton TP, Hixton Café
Lodg N: Motel 95 & **Campground▲**
Other N: **Hixton/Alma Center KOA▲**
S: Laundry/LP/Hixton TP, ATMs,

115 **US 12, WI 27, Black River Falls, Merrillan, Melrose**
Gas S: I-94 Mobil Express, Holiday◊
Food S: Hardee's, KFC, Sunrise Inn Family Rest, Subway
Lodg N: River Crest Resort
S: E&F Motel
Med S: + Black River Memorial Hospital
Other S: Goods Times **RV**, Auto & Trailer

116 **WI 54, Main St, to WI 27, Black River Falls, Wisconsin Rapids**
FStop N: Black River Crossing Oasis/BP
TStop S: Kwik Trip #648, Flying J Travel Plaza #5010 (Scales)
Food N: Perkins, Subway, Taco John's
S: Rest/FJ TP, Burger King, McDonald's, Oriental Kitchen

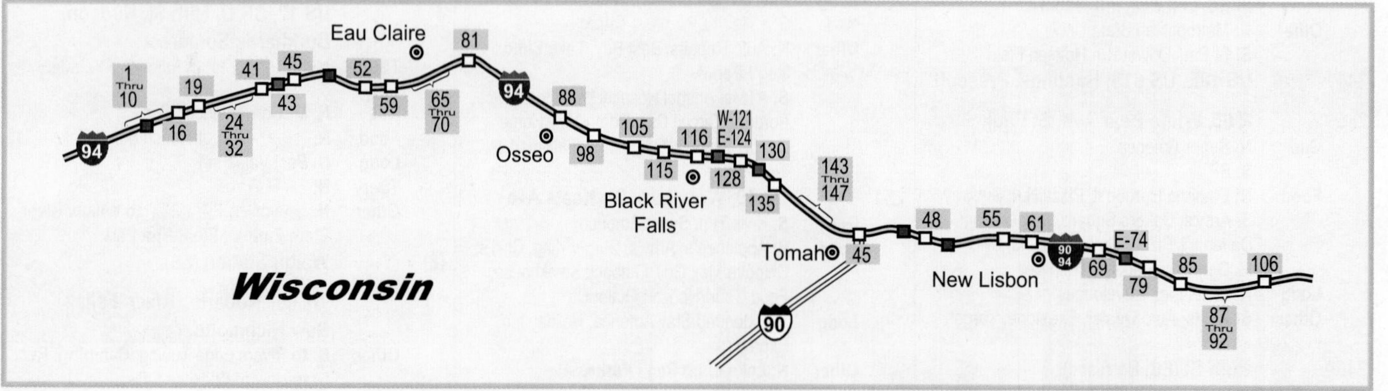

◊ = Regular Gas Stations with Diesel ▲ = RV Friendly Locations ♥ = Pet Friendly Locations
Red print shows large vehicle parking / access on site or nearby Brown Print = Campgrounds / RV PARKS

EXIT		WISCONSIN
	Lodg	N: Best Western♥, Holiday Inn, Majestic Pines Hotel & Casino, Super 8 S: Days Inn
	TWash	S: FJ TP
	TServ	S: FJ TP/Tires
	Med	S: + Black River Falls Hospital
	Other	N: RVDump/LP/Blk River Oasis Crossing, Parkland Village Campground▲ S: Laundry/KT, Laundry/WiFi/RVDump/LP/FJ TP, Walmart sc, Hwy 54 Towing & Repair, Black River Falls Area Airport✈
(121)		Black River Falls Rest Area (WB) (RR, Phone, Picnic, Vend, Info, Weather)
(124)		Millston Rest Area (EB) (RR, Phone, Picnic, Vend, Info, Weather)
128		CR O, Mill St, Black River Falls, Millston, Warrens
(130)		Rest Area (Both dir) (RR, Phones, Picnic, Vend)
135		CR EW, Warrens
	Gas	N: Citgo
	Other	N: Jellystone Park Camp Resort▲
143		US 12, N Superior Ave, Tomah (EB) WI 21, Eaton Ave, Necedah (WB)
	TStop	S: Kwik Trip #796/BP (Scales)
	Gas	N: Mobil◊ S: Mobil, Shell◊, Murphy's◊
	Food	N: Long John Silver, Perkins, Rest/Spr8 S: Rest/KT, Culver's, Ground Round, KFC, McDonald's, Subway, Taco Bell
	Lodg	N: AmericInn, Holiday Inn♥, Microtel, Super 8♥ S: Motel/KT, Cranberry Country Lodge♥, Comfort Inn, Econo Lodge♥
	Med	S: + Tomah Memorial Hospital, + VA Hospital
	Other	N: Humbird Cheese Mart, Whispering Pines Campground▲ S: Laundry/WiFi/RVDump/KwikTrip, Advance Auto, Dollar Tree, U-Haul, Walmart sc, to Ft McCoy Military Res
145		Industrial Ave
	NOTE:	I-94 runs with I-90 below for 93 mi. Exit #'s follow I-90.
(147)		Jct I-90W, to La Crosse I-90/94E, Wisconsin Dells, Madison
(45A)		Jct I-94W, Twin Cities (EB LEFT exit)
(45B)		Jct I-90/94E, Wisconsin Dells, Madison (EB), I-90W La Crosse, I-94W St Paul (WB)
(47.5)		Weigh Station (WB)
48		CR PP, Tomah, Oakdale
	TStop	N: Road Ranger #209/Citgo (Scales)
	Food	N: Rest/Road Ranger
	Other	N: Laundry/RoadRanger, Oakdale KOA▲
(51)		Weigh Station (EB)
55		CR C, CR H, US 12, WI 16, Camp Douglas, Volk Field
	TStop	S: Camp Douglas BP
	Gas	S: Mobil◊
	Food	S: Subway/Mobil
	Lodg	S: Walsh's K&K Motel, Travelers Rest
	TServ	S: CL Chase Truck Service

Personal Notes

EXIT		WISCONSIN
	Other	N: Mill Bluff State Park, Camp Williams Military Res S: Laundry/Camp Douglas BP
61		WI 80, CR A, New Lisbon, Necedah
	TStop	N: New Lisbon Travel Center/Citgo, The Bunk House/Mobil
	Food	N: Rest/Bunk House
	Lodg	N: Motel/Bunk House
	Other	N: Laundry/RVDump/New Lisbon TC, Laundry/RVDump/Bunk House, to Buckhorn State Park, Ken's Marina & Campground▲ S: Mauston New Lisbon Union Airport✈
69		WI 82, Mauston, Necedah
	TStop	N: Pilot Travel Center #164 (Scales) Citgo Travel Plaza S: Kwik Trip #775/BP (Scales)
	Gas	N: Shell S: Citgo◊
	Food	N: Wendy's/Pilot TC, FastFood/Citgo TP, Country Kitchen S: Rest/KwikTrip, McDonald's, Pizza Hut, Roman Castle Rest
	Lodg	N: Best Western, Country Inn, Super 8 S: The Alaskan Motel
	Med	S: + Hospital
	Other	N: Laundry/WiFi/Pilot TC S: Laundry/RVDump/KT, Mauston New Lisbon Union Airport✈, Auto Dealers , Walgreen's, Walmart
(74)		Rest Area (EB) (RR, Phone, Picnic, Vend)
(75)		Rest Area (WB) (RR, Phone, Picnic, Vend)

EXIT		WISCONSIN
79		WI HH, Rock St, Lyndon Station
	TStop	S: Lyndon Station BP
	Food	S: FastFood/Lyndon Station
85		US 12, WI 16, Wisconsin Dells
	Lodg	S: Days End Motel
	TServ	S: Rocky Arbor Truck & Trailer Repair
	Other	N: Rocky Arbor State Park, Sherwood Forest Camping & RV Park▲ S: Bass Lake Campground▲ , Crockett Resort Camping & RV▲ , Arrowhead Resort Campground▲ , Dells Timberland Camping Resort▲ , Wisconsin Dells KOA▲ , Edge O'Dells Camping & RV Resort▲
87		WI 13N, Wisconsin Dells, to WI 23E, Briggsville
	FStop	N: Interstate BP
	Gas	N: Citgo◊, Mobil◊, Shell
	Food	N: Burger King, Country Kitchen, Pedros, Denny's, Perkins, Rococo's Pizza, Taco Bell, Wendy's
	Lodg	N: Best Western, Comfort Inn, Days Inn, Holiday Inn, Howard Johnson, Super 8
	Other	N: RVDump/Interstate BP, Amtrak, Christmas Mountain Village & Ski Area, American World Resort & RV Park▲ , Sherwood Forest Camping & RV Park▲ , Erickson's Tepee Park Campground▲ , Wisconsin Dells KOA▲
89		WI 23, Lake Delton, Reedsburg
	Gas	N: Mobil◊
	Food	N: Howie's, Internet Cafe
	Lodg	N: Country Squire Inn, Grand Marquis Inn, Hilton Garden Inn, Sandman Inn
	Other	S: Home Depot, Walmart sc, Mirror Lake State Park, Country Roads RV Park▲
92		US 12, Baraboo, Lake Delton
	Gas	N: BP◊, Cenex◊, Citgo◊, Mobil◊, Sinclair
	Food	N: Cracker Barrel, Damon's, Denny's, McDonald's, Subway/Sinclair
	Lodg	N: AmericInn, Camelot Inn, Del Rancho, Grand Marquis Inn, Ramada Ltd S: Travelodge
	Med	S: + Hospital (7mi S)
	Other	N: WI Cheese Museum S: Wisconsin Opry, Baraboo Wisconsin Dells Airport✈, Fox Hill RV Park & Campground▲ , Yogi Bear's Jellystone Park, Dell Boo Campground▲ , Mirror Lake State Park
106		WI 33, Portage, Baraboo
	FStop	N: Lake Morgaune Mobil
	Gas	S: BP
	Lodg	S: Cascade Mountain Motel
	Med	N: + Hospital
	Other	M: Portage Muni Airport✈ S: Cascade Mountain Ski Area,Sky High Camping Resort▲ , Devil's Lake State Park
	NOTE:	I-94 continues EB with I-90 & I-39. Exit #'s follow I-90.
108A		WI 78S, to US 51N, Wausau, Merrimac
	TStop	S: Petro Stopping Center #53 (Scales)
	Gas	S: Phillips 66
	Food	S: Subway/Petro SC, Little Caesars
	Lodg	S: Comfort Suites, Days Inn
	TWash	S: Blue Beacon TW/Petro SC

◊= Regular Gas Stations with Diesel ▲ = RV Friendly Locations ♥= Pet Friendly Locations
Red print shows large vehicle parking / access on site or nearby Brown Print = Campgrounds / RV PARKS

EXIT	WISCONSIN
TServ	S: Petro SC/Tires
Other	S: Laundry/WiFi/Petro SC, Devil's Lake State Park
(108B)	**Jct I-39N, to Wausau, Merrimac, Portage**
Med	N: + Hospital
Other	N: to WI Dells, Portage Muni Airport✈
(113)	**Rest Area (Both dir)** (RR, Phone, Picnic, Vend, RVDump)
115	**CR CS/J, Poynette, Lake Wisconsin**
FStop	N: North Point Plaza/BP
Food	N: McDonald's, Subway
119	**WI 60, Arlington, Lodi**
Gas	S: Mobil◈
Food	S: Rococo's Pizza
Lodg	S: Best Western
Other	S: Interstate RV Center
126	**CR V, De Forest, Dane**
Gas	N: BP, Phillips 66◈ S: Citgo, Exxon◈
Food	N: Arby's, Burger King, Culver's Rest, McDonald's, Subway
Lodg	N: Holiday Inn Express
131	**WI 19, Waunakee, Sun Prairie**
Gas	N: Mobil, KwikTrip, Speedway◈
Food	N: McDonald's, Taco Bell/Speedway
Lodg	N: Days Inn, Super 8 S: Country Inn Suites
TWash	N: Windsor Truck Wash
TServ	N: Kenworth
Other	N: Walgreen's
132	**US 51, Madison, De Forest**
TStop	N: Hwy 51 Citgo, PTP/Truckers Inn #1/ Shell (Scales) S: Travel Center of America #50/Mobil (Scales)
Food	N: Rest/Hwy 51, Rest/Truckers Inn S: CountryPride/Subway/TacoBell/TA TC
TWash	N: Truckers Inn
TServ	N: Truckers Inn/Tires, Peterbilt of WI, Volvo/White/GMC/Freightliner S:TA TC/Tires, Brad Ragan Truck, Auto & RV Tire Service
Other	N: Laundry/Hwy 51, Laundry/BarbSh/ CB/Truckers Inn S: Laundry/WiFi/TA TC, WI RV World, Camperland RV
135A	**US 151S, Washington Ave, Madison**
Gas	S: BP, Shell, Sinclair
Food	S: Applebee's, Chili's, Country Kitchen, Cracker Barrel, Denny's, Dunkin Donuts, Hardee's, IHOP, KFC, McDonald's, Mtn Jack's Steakhouse, Olive Garden, Perkins, Ponderosa, Red Lobster, Tumbleweed Grill, Steak 'n Shake, Wendy's

EXIT	WISCONSIN
Lodg	S: Best Western, Comfort Inn, Fairfield Inn, Econo Lodge, Hampton Inn, Holiday Inn, Madison Suites, Microtel, Motel 6♥, Residence Inn, Select Inn
Other	S: ATMs, Best Buy, Mall, WI State Hwy Patrol Post, Dane Co Reg'l Airport✈
135B	**US 151N, Washington Ave**
135C	**High Crossing Blvd (WB)**
Lodg	N: Courtyard, Staybridge Suites S: East Town Suites, Microtel
(138A)	**Jct I-94E, Milwaukee (EB, Left exit)**
138B/240	**WI 30W, to Madison (WB, Left exit)**
NOTE:	I-94 runs with I-90 above for 93 mi. Exit #'s follow I-90.
244	**CR N, Sun Prairie, Cottage Grove, Sun Prairie**
Gas	S: Stop 'n Go
Food	S: Blimpie, Black Bear Inn, McDonald's, Papa Jimmy's Pizzeria, Village Inn
Lodg	S: Shortstop Inn
Other	N: Madison KOA▲
250	**WI 73, Deerfield, Marshall**
259	**WI 89, CR V, CR G, Lake Mills, Marshall, Waterloo**
FStop	S: Kwip Trip #306
TStop	N: Lake Oasis Travel Plaza/Citgo (Scales)
Gas	S: BP◈, Roman's Quick Stop/Mobil
Food	N: Rest/Lake Oasis TP S: McDonald's, Pizza Pit, Subway
Lodg	N: Rodeway Inn S: Bade's Resort, Fargo Mansion Inn B&B, Pyramid Motel
TWash	N: Lake Oasis TP
TServ	N: Lake Oasis TP/Tires
Other	N: Laundry/Lake Oasis TP S: to Pilgrims Campground▲
(261)	**Lake Mills Rest Area (EB)** (next RA 86 mi) (RR, Phone, Picnic, Vend, Info, Weather)
(263)	**Johnson Creek Rest Area (WB)** (RR, Phone, Picnic, Vend, Info, Weather)
267	**N Watertown St, WI 26, Frontage St, Johnson Creek, Watertown**
TStop	N: Pine Cone Travel Plaza/Shell (Scales)
Gas	N: BP◈ S: Citgo
Food	N: Rest/Pine Cone TP, Arby's, 2 Loons Café, McDonald's/BP, S: A&W, Culver's, KFC/Citgo, Subway

EXIT	WISCONSIN
Lodg	N: Comfort Inn, Days Inn♥
TServ	N: J & L Tire
Med	N: + Watertown Memorial Hospital
Other	N: Laundry/Pine Cone TP, Goodyear, Watertown Muni Airport✈ S: to Fort Atkinson, Ft Atkinson Muni Airport✈
275	**CR F, CR B, Oconomowoc, Concord Sullivan, Ixonia**
Gas	N: Concord Gen'l Store/BP◈
AServ	S: Gesell's Auto Service
277	**Willow Glen Rd, to CR B, to CR Dr (EB exit, WB reaccess)**
282	**WI 67, Summit Ave, to CR B, CR Dr, Oconomowoc, Dousman**
Gas	N: Mobil. SA/Speedway
Lodg	N: Hilton Garden Inn, Olympia Resort & Spa
Med	N: + Hospital
Other	N: ATMs, Pharmacy, Target
283	**CR P, N Sawyer Rd (WB, Exit only)**
285	**CR C, Genesee St, Delafield**
Gas	N: Mobil
Food	N: Andrews Rest, Loaf & Jug Rest
Lodg	N: Delafield Hotel♥
287	**WI 83, Delafield, Hartland, Wales**
Gas	S: BP
Food	N: Applebee's, Hardee's, McDonald's, Perkins, Starbucks S: Burger King, DQ, Subway
Lodg	N: Country Pride Inn, Holiday Inn Express S: La Quinta Inn♥
Other	N: Golf Course, Golf Course, Best Buy, Walgreen's S: Grocery, Home Depot, Pharmacy, PetCo♥, Target, Tires Plus, Walmart
290	**CR SS, Prospect Ave, Pewaukee**
291	**CR G, Meadowbrook Rd, Pewaukee**
Gas	S: BP
Food	N: Rest/Country Inn
Lodg	N: Country Inn
293AB	**CR T, Waukesha, Pewakee (EB)**
Gas	S: Mobil
Food	S: Denny's, Hardee's, McDonald's, Mr Wok, Peking House, Rocky Rococo, Taco Amigo, Wendy's
Lodg	N: Country Inn S: Best Western
TServ	S: Peterbilt of WI
Other	N: GE Medical Systems S: ATM's, Firestone, Grocery, Office Depot, Radio Shack, Walgreen's,

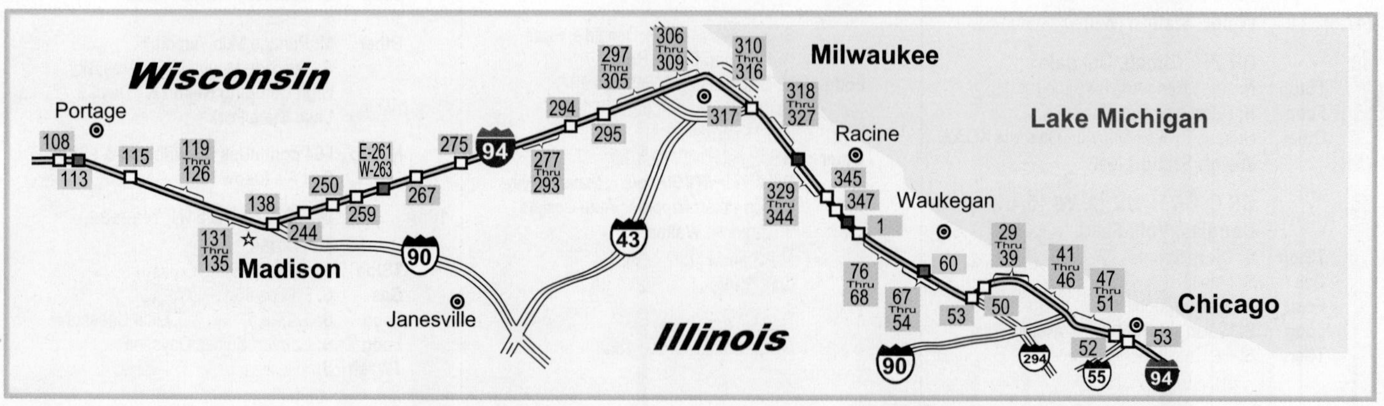

◈= Regular Gas Stations with Diesel ▲ = RV Friendly Locations ♥= Pet Friendly Locations
Red print shows large vehicle parking / access on site or nearby Brown Print = Campgrounds / RV PARKS

EXIT		WISCONSIN
	Other	S: Waukesha Co Fairgrounds, Waukesha Co Airport
293		**CR T, Grandview Blvd, Waukesha Pewaukee (WB)**
293C		**WI 16, Waukesha, Pewaukee, Oconomowoc (WB)**
	Other	N: GE Medical Systems, to UPS Store
294		**CR J S, WI 164N, Pewaukee Rd, Pewaukee, Waukesha**
	Gas	N: Mobil
	Food	N: WI Machine Shed Rest S: Taste of Italy
	Lodg	N: Comfort Suites
	TServ	S: Peterbilt of WI
295		**WI F, WI 164, CR F, Waukesha, Sussex**
	FStop	N: Kwik Trip #396 S: Hopson Oil/66
	Med	N: + Aurora Health Center S: + Hospital
297		**US 18, WI 164S, CR JJ, Barker Rd, Waukesha, Blue Mound Rd, Barker**
	Gas	N: BP, Mobil
	Food	N: Applebee's, Burger King, Chuck E Cheese's Pizza, KFC, McDonald's, Melting Pot, Olive Garden, Perkins, Starbucks, Subway, Tony Roma's, Zorba's Greek, Wendy's S: Arby's, Cousin's, Dunkin Donuts, Famous Dave's BBQ, McDonald's, Taco Bell,
	Lodg	N: Baymont Inn, Comfort Inn, Fairfield Inn, Motel 6♥ S: Holiday Inn, Select Inn, Super 8
	Other	N: ATMs, Advance Auto Parts, Best Buy, CompUSA, Grocery, S: WI State Hwy Patrol, Auto Dealers, Firestone, Home Depot, Sam's Club, Target, Tires Plus, Walgreen's
301AB		**Moorland Rd, Brookfield (EB)**
	Gas	N: BP, Mobil S: Mobil
	Food	N: Fuddrucker's, McDonald's, Pizza Uno, Rocky Rococo, Wong's Wok S: Outback Steakhouse
	Lodg	N: Courtyard, Marriott, Sheraton S: Country Inn, Embassy Suites, Midway Hotel, Residence Inn
	Other	N: Barnes & Noble, Firestone, Goodyear, Office Depot, PetCo♥, Walgreen's, Mall S: Walgreen's
301A		**Moorland Rd S, New Berlin (WB)**
301B		**Moorland Rd N, Brookfield (WB)**
304AB		**WI 100, S 108th St, Milwaukee (EB)**
	Gas	N: Citgo, Shell◊ S: Phillips 66, Speedway◊
	Food	N: McDonald's, Pizza Hut, Qdoba Mex Rest, Starbucks, Taco Bell S: Dunkin Donuts, Steakhouse 100, Wendy's
	Lodg	N: Best Western, Exel Inn, Westwood Inn
	TServ	S: Central WhiteGMC
	Other	N: to Milwaukee Co Zoo, Oceans of Fun S: Auto Dealers, Auto Services, U-Haul
304B		**WI 100N, Milwaukee (WB)**
304A		**WI 100S, Milwaukee (WB)**

EXIT		WISCONSIN
305B		**US 45N, Fond du Lac, Appleton**
(305A)		**Jct I-894E, US 45S, to Chicago**
306		**WI 181, 84th St, Milwaukee**
	Med	N: + Hospital
	Other	S: Pettit National Ice Center, WI State Fairgrounds▲ /RVDump
307A		**68th St, 70th St**
307B		**Hawley Rd, Milwaukee**
308A		**VA Center, Milwaukee County Stadium, Mitchell Blvd (Left exit)**
308B		**Miller Park Way**
	Other	Milwaukee Co Stadium, Miller Park
308C		**US 41N, Lisbon Ave, Milwaukee**
	Other	N: to Washington Park Zoo
309A		**35th St, Milwaukee**
	Gas	N: SA/Speedway
309B		**26th St, St. Paul Ave (EB) 25th St, 2nd St, Clybourn St (WB)**
	Other	N: Pabst Mansion, Marquette Univ
	Med	N: + Aurora Sinai Medical Center, + Milwaukee Hospital
	Other	N: Marquette Univ
	NOTE:	I-94 below runs with I-43. Exit numbers follow I-94.
310A		**13th St, N Ember Lane (EB)**
(310B)		**Jct I-43N, to Green Bay**
(310C)		**Jct I-794E, Downtown Milwaukee**
311		**WI 59, National Ave, 6th St**
312A		**Lapham Blvd, Mitchell St (EB)**
312B		**Becher St, Lincoln Ave (EB)**
312AB		**Becher St, Mitchell St, Lapham Blvd, Greenfield Ave (WB)**
314A		**Holt Ave (EB)**
314B		**Howard Ave (EB)**
314AB		**Howard Ave, Holt Ave (WB)**
(316)		**Jct I-43, I-894 (EB) I-894W, I-43S, I-894 ByPass, Beloit (WB, Left exit)**
	NOTE:	I-94 above runs below with I-43. Exit numbers follow I-94.
317		**Layton Ave, Milwaukee**
	Gas	E: Clark
	Food	E: Prime Quarter Steakhouse W: Big City Pizza, Howard Johnson
	Lodg	E: Holiday Inn W: Howard Johnson
318		**WI 119, Airport, Mitchell Field**
	Other	E: Amtrak, Gen'l Mitchell Int'l Airport
319		**College Ave, CR ZZ, Milwaukee**
	Gas	E: SA Speedway, Shell W: BP, Citgo

EXIT		WISCONSIN
	Food	E: McDonald's, Perkins W: Boy Blue French Cuisine
	Lodg	E: Country Inn, Econo Lodge, Exel Inn, Hampton Inn, Ramada Inn, Red Roof Inn♥
	Other	E: Penske W: Grocery, Laundromat
320		**CR BB, Rawson Ave, Oak Creek, Milwaukee**
	Gas	E: BP, Mobil
	Food	E: Burger King
	Lodg	E: La Quinta Inn♥ W: Park Motel
	Other	E: Cinema
322		**WI 100, Ryan Rd, Oak Creek**
	TStop	W: Flying J Travel Plaza #5124 (Scales), Pilot Travel Center #40 (Scales)
	Gas	W: Shell◊
	Food	E: McDonald's, Perkins, Wendy's W: CountryMarket/FastFood/FJ TP, Subway/Pilot TC, Arby's, Country Kitchen, Starbucks
	Lodg	W: Travelers Motel, Sunrise Motel, Value Inn
	TWash	W: Blue Beacon TW/Pilot TC
	TServ	E: Cummins Truck Service W: Freightliner, Kenworth
	Other	W: Laundry/WiFi/RVDump/LP/FJ TP, WiFi/Pilot TC
325		**US 41N, 27th St, Oak Creek, Franklin, Racine (WB ex, EB entr)**
326		**Seven Mile Rd, Caledonia**
	Gas	E: BP W: Mobil
	Lodg	E: Hi View Motel, Seven Mile Motel
	Other	E: Yogi Bear's Jellystone Park▲
327		**CR G, Caledonia**
	Other	W: U-Haul
(327.3)		**Weigh Station (EB)**
329		**CR K, Northwestern Ave, Racine, Thompsonville, Franksville**
	TStop	E: Love's Travel Stop #432 (Scales)
	Gas	N: Mobil, Phillips 66
	Food	E: Denny's/HotColdDeli/Love's TS
	Lodg	E: Days Inn
	TServ	W: D&D Truck Repair, Racine Truck Sales & Equipment
	Other	E: Laundry/WiFi/RVDump/Love's TS, Greyhound Racetrack W: to Happy Acres Kampground▲
333		**WI 20, Washington Ave, Sturtevant, Racine, Waterford**
	FStop	E: I-94/20 Shell Plaza, Kwik Trip #686
	TStop	W: Citgo Auto Truck Plaza, Petro Stopping Center #68/Mobil (Scales)
	Food	E: Cousins Subs/I-94/20 Shell, Burger King, McDonald's W: Wendy's/Citgo ATP, IronSkillet/Petro SC, Black Bear Bar & Grill, Culver's
	Lodg	E: Paul's Motel, Holiday Inn Express, Ramada Ltd W: Best Western, Comfort Inn,
	TServ	W: Petro SC/Tires, Pomp's Tire Service, Lakeside International
	Other	W: Laundry/WiFi/Citgo ATP, Laundry/WiFi/RVDump/Petro SC, RV Center
335		**WI 11, Durand Ave, Sturtevant, to Racine, Burlington**
	Gas	N: Kwik Trip

◊ = Regular Gas Stations with Diesel ▲ = RV Friendly Locations ♥ = Pet Friendly Locations
Red print shows large vehicle parking / access on site or nearby Brown Print = Campgrounds / RV PARKS

EXIT		WI / IL
	Lodg	S: Travelers Inn Motel & Campground▲
	Other	N: Amtrak Stations
		S: Sylvania Airport✈
337		**CR KR, 1st St, County Line Rd**
	Other	E: to Sanders Park, Great Lakes Dragway
339		**CR E, 12th St, Somers, Sturtevant**
	FStop	N: Toor Petro/Marathon
340		**WI 142, CR S, Burlington Rd, Kenosha, Burlington**
	Gas	N: Mobil◈
	Food	N: Wispride Cheese
		S: Mars Cheese Castle, Star Bar
	Lodg	S: Easter Day Motel
342		**WI 158, Kenosha**
	TServ	S: Kenosha Truck & Equipment
	Other	N: Kenosha Reg'l Airport✈
344		**WI 50, 75th St, Kenosha, Bristol, Salem, Lake Geneva**
	Gas	N: Shell◈, Citgo◈
		S: BP, Speedway
	Food	N: Noodles & Co, Quiznos, Pizza Hut, Starbucks, Wendy's
		S: Arby's, Brat Stop, Chef's Table, Cracker Barrel, Denny's, KFC, Long John Silver, McDonald's, Perkins, Taco Bell, Wendy's
	Lodg	N: Baymont Inn, Country Inn, La Quinta Inn♥, Super 8
		S: Best Western, Comfort Suites, Days Inn, Value Inn♥
	Other	N: ATMs, Best Buy, Gander Mountain, Walgreen's
		S: Outlet Mall, Shopping
345		**CR C, Wilmot Rd, Pleasant Prairie**
	FStop	S: Kenosha Truck Stop/P66
		E: WI Welcome Center (WB) Kenosha Rest Area (EB) (RR, Ph, Pic, Vend, Weather, WiFi)
347		**WI 165, CR Q, 104th St, Lakeview Pkwy, Pleasant Prairie**
	Gas	N: BP◈
	Food	N: McDonald's
	Lodg	N: Radisson
	Other	N: Factory Outlet Center
(349.8)		**Weigh Station (WB)**

CENTRAL TIME ZONE

NOTE: **MM 350: Illinois State Line**

WISCONSIN
ILLINOIS

CENTRAL TIME ZONE

EXIT		
1A		**CR 19, CR A1, Russell Rd, Zion**
	TStop	W: Travel Center of America #30 (Scales), Toor's Car & Truck Plaza/Citgo (Scales)
	Food	W: CountryPride/PizzaHut/TA TC, Rest/Toor's CTP
	TWash	W: TA TC
	TServ	W: TA TC/Tires, Peterbilt
	Other	W: Laundry/WiFi/RVDump/TA TC
1B		**US 41S, to Waukegan**
	Other	E: Sky Harbor RV Center

NOTE: **Begin EB / End WB TriState Tollway, Edens Expy Spur**

EXIT		ILLINOIS
76		**IL 173, Rosecrans Rd, Wadsworth**
(73.5)		**TOLL Plaza**
70		**IL 132, Grand Ave, Gurnee, Waukegan**
	Gas	E: Speedway◈
		W: Mobil, Shell
	Food	E: Burger King, Chuck E Cheese's Pizza, Cracker Barrel, Dunkin Donuts/Baskin Robbins, IHOP, Joe's Crab Shack, McDonald's, Olive Garden, Outback Steakhouse, Subway
		W: Applebee's, Boston Market, Chili's, Denny's, Lone Star Steakhouse, Max & Erma's, McDonald's, Panda Express, Pizza Hut, Ruby Tuesday, Starbucks, Steak 'n Shake, TGI Friday, Taco Bell, Wendy's, White Castle
	Lodg	E: Baymont Inn, Comfort Suites, Country Inn, Hampton Inn, La Quinta Inn♥
		W: Fairfield Inn, Holiday Inn
	Other	E: to Six Flags
		W: Auto Zone, Bass Pro Shop, Borders, Firestone, Grocery, Home Depot, Menard's, PetSmart♥, Pharmacy, Radio Shack, Sam's Club, Target, Walmart, Outlet Mall
68		**IL 21, Milwaukee Ave, Gurnee, Libertyville, Graysflack (EB)**
	Med	S: + Hospital
	Other	S: to Six Flags
67		**IL 120, Belvidere Rd, Gurnee (WB)**
64		**IL 137, Buckley Rd, Lake Bluff**
	Med	E: + VA Medical Center
62		**IL 176, Rockland Rd, Park Ave, Libertyville, Lake Bluff (WB)**
(60)		**Lake Forest Oasis (Both dir)**
	FStop	Mobil
	Food	KFC, McDonald's, Panda Express, Starbucks, Subway, Taco Bell
59		**IL 60, Townline Rd, Lake Forest**
57		**IL 22, Half Day Rd, Deerfield**
54		**Deerfield Rd, Deerfield (WB)**
(53.5)		**TOLL Plaza**
(53)		**Jct I-294S, to O'Hare Int'l Airport**
50		**IL 43, Waukegan Rd, Northbrook (EB)**
	Gas	S: Amoco, Shell
	Food	N: Baha Fresh, Boston Market, China Palace, Hunan Garden, Kegon Japanese
		S: KFC
	Lodg	N: Embassy Suites, Red Roof Inn♥
	TServ	S: CVS Truck & Auto Repair
	Other	N: Best Buy, Borders, Home Depot

NOTE: **Begin WB / End EB TriState Tollway, Edens Expy Spur**

EXIT		
29		**US 41, to Waukegan, Tri State Tollway (WB)**
30AB		**IL 68, Dundee Rd, Northbrook (WB, difficult reaccess)**
31		**Tower Rd, Frontage Rd, Winnetka (EB)**
	Other	S: Auto Dealers
33AB		**Willow Rd, Winnetka**
	Gas	S: Shell
	Food	S: Starbucks

EXIT		ILLINOIS
34A		**US 41S, Skokie Rd, Wilmette (EB)**
34BC		**E Lake Ave, Wilmette (WB)**
	Gas	N: BP
		S: BP, Shell
	Food	N: Panda Express, Starbucks
35		**Old Orchard Rd, Skokie**
	Gas	N: BP, Shell
	Lodg	S: Hampton Inn
	Med	N: + Hospital
37AB		**IL 58, Dempster St, Skokie**
39AB		**Touhy Ave, Skokie**
	Gas	N: BP◈, Shell
		S: Citgo, Mobil, Shell
	Food	S: Chili's, Chuck E Cheese's Pizza, Dunkin Donuts, McDonald's, Starbucks, Subway
	Lodg	N: Radisson
		S: Holiday Inn
	Other	S: Auto Services
41C		**IL 50, Cicero Ave, to US 41, to I-90, Lincolnwood (WB)**
41AB		**US 14, Caldwell Ave, Peterson Ave, Chicago**
41C		**IL 50S, to I-90W (EB)**
42		**W Foster Ave (WB)**
43A		**Wilson Ave (WB)**
(43B)		**Jct I-90W (WB)**
43C		**Montrose Ave**
43D		**Kostner Ave**
44A		**IL 19, Keeler Ave**
	Gas	N: BP, Shell
	Other	N: Wrigley Field
44B		**Pulaski Rd, Irving Park Rd**
	Gas	N: BP, Mobil
45A		**Addison St (EB)**
45B		**Kimball Ave**
	Gas	N: Marathon◈
		S: Gas Depot, Marathon, Mobil
	Food	S: Dunkin Donuts, Pizza Hut, Subway, Wendy's
	Other	S: ATMs, Grocery, Radio Shack, Walgreen's
45C		**Kedzie Ave, Belmont Ave**
46A		**California Ave**
	Gas	S: Mobil
	Food	S: IHOP, Popeye's Chicken
	Other	N: Laundromat
46B		**Diversey Ave**
47A		**Western Ave, Fullerton Ave**
	Gas	N: Citgo, Phillips 66, Costco
		S: Marathon
	Food	N: Burger King, Dunkin Donuts, Popeye's Chicken, Starbucks, Subway
	Other	N: ATMs, Costco, Home Depot, Staples, Target
47B		**Damen Ave (WB)**
48A		**Armitage Ave**
	Gas	N: Mobil
		S: BP
	Other	S: Best Buy

◈= Regular Gas Stations with Diesel ▲ = RV Friendly Locations ♥= Pet Friendly Locations
Red print shows large vehicle parking / access on site or nearby Brown Print = Campgrounds / RV PARKS

EXIT		ILLINOIS
48B		**IL 64, North Ave**
	Gas	N: BP
		S: Gas Depot, Shell
	Food	S: Huddle House
	Other	N: Home Depot
49A		**Division St**
	Gas	S: BP, Shell
49B		**Augusta Blvd, Milwaukee Ave**
50A		**Ogden Ave**
50B		**Ohio St**
	Gas	S: Marathon
51A		**Randolph St, Lake St (WB)**
51B		**Lake St, Randolph St (EB), Washington Blvd, Randolph St (WB)**
51C		**Madison, Washington Blvd (WB) Randolph, Washington (EB)**
51D		**Washington, Madison St (EB)**
51E		**Madison St, Monroe St (EB) Adams St, Monroe St (WB)**
	Other	S: Walgreen's
51F		**Monroe St, Adams St (EB)**
51G		**Adams St, Jackson Blvd (EB)**
51HI		**Van Buren St, I-290, Congress Pkwy, West Suburbs**
52A		**Taylor St, Roosevelt Rd (EB)**
	Gas	N: Shell
		S: Citgo
52B		**Roosevelt Rd, Taylor St (WB)**
52C		**18th St (EB)**
	Gas	N: Shell
53		**W Cermak Rd, S Archer Ave (EB)**
53A		**Archer Ave, I-55 (EB), Cermak Rd, S Canalport Ave (WB)**
(53B)		**Jct I-55 S, Stevenson Pkwy**
(53C)		**Jct I-55, Lake Shore Dr, Downtown**
54		**31st St**
	Med	N: + Hospital
55A		**35th St**
55B		**Pershing Rd**
56A		**43rd St**
	Gas	S: Citgo◈

EXIT		ILLINOIS
56B		**47th St (EB)**
57A		**51st St**
	Food	N: McDonald's
	Other	N: Chicago District Police Hdqtrs
57B		**Garfield Blvd**
	Gas	S: Mobil, Shell
	Food	N: Checkers
		S: Wendy's
58A		**59th St**
58B		**63rd St (EB)**
	Gas	N: Shell
		S: BP
	Med	S: + Hospital
(59A)		**Jct I-94E, I-90E, to Indiana (EB)**
	NOTE:	**I-94 runs with I-90 above. Exit #'s follow I-94.**
59B		**69th St**
59C		**71st St**
	Gas	N: BP
	Food	S: McDonald's
60A		**75th St (EB)**
	Gas	N: Mobil, Shell
	Food	S: KFC, Popeye's
60B		**76th St**
	Gas	N: BP, Mobil, Shell
	Other	N: Walgreen's
60C		**79th St**
	Gas	N: Shell
		S: Citgo◈
61A		**83rd St (EB)**
	Gas	N: Shell
	Other	N: IL State Hwy Patrol Post
61B		**87th St**
	Gas	N: BP, Shell
	Food	N: Burger King, McDonald's
	Other	S: Grocery, Pharmacy, Home Depot
62		**US 12, US 20, 95th St**
	Gas	N: Shell
		S: BP
(63)		**Jct I-57S, to Memphis**
65		**95th St, 103rd St, Stony Island Ave**
66A		**111th St**
	Gas	S: Shell
	Other	S: Wentworth Tire Center, Firestone
66B		**115th St**
68AB		**130th St**
69		**Beaubien Woods**
70AB		**Dolton Ave, Dolton**

EXIT		ILLINOIS
71AB		**Sibley Blvd, IL 83**
	Gas	N: Mobil◈
		S: BP, Shell
	Food	N: McDonald's, Popeye's, Subway
		S: Arby's, Dunkin Donuts, Long John Silver's, KFC, Ponderosa, Red Lobster, Wendy's, White Castle
	Lodg	N: Baymont Inn
	Other	N: Grocery, Pharmacy
		S: Grocery
73AB		**US 6, 159th St, S Holland**
	TStop	N: AmBest Truck-O-Mat (Scales)
	Gas	S: Marathon
	Food	N: Fuddruckers, Outback Steakhouse
		S: Little Caesars Pizza, McDonald's, Subway
	Lodg	S: Cherry Lane Motel, Dutch Motel
	TWash	N: TruckOMat
	NOTE:	**I-94 runs below with I-80 for 3 mi. Exit #'s follow I-80.**
74A/160A		**IL 394S, to Danville**
(74B/ 160B)		**Jct I-80W, Jct I-294 (TOLL) Jct I-94, W to Chicago**
161		**US 6, IL 83, Torrence Ave**
	FStop	S: Park Service/Mobil
	Gas	N: BP
		S: Gas City
	Food	N: Arby's, Bob Evans, Chili's, Hooters, IHOP, Olive Garden, On the Border, Wendy's
		S: Al's Hamburgers, Café Borgia, DQ, Dunkin Donuts, Golden Crown, Pappy's Gyros, McDonald's
	Lodg	N: Best Western, Comfort Suites, Days Inn, Extended Stay America, Fairfield Inn, Holiday Inn, Red Roof Inn♥, Sleep Inn, Super 8
		S: Pioneer Motel
	Med	N: + Ingalls Urgent Aid Walk-In Clinic
	Other	N: Auto Dealers, Auto Services, ATMs, Best Buy, Firestone, Grocery, Home Depot, Radio Shack
		S: Walgreen's, Sam's Club
	NOTE:	**I-94 runs above with I-80 for 3 mi. Exit #'s follow I-80**

CENTRAL TIME ZONE

NOTE: MM 77: Indiana State Line

⬆ ILLINOIS

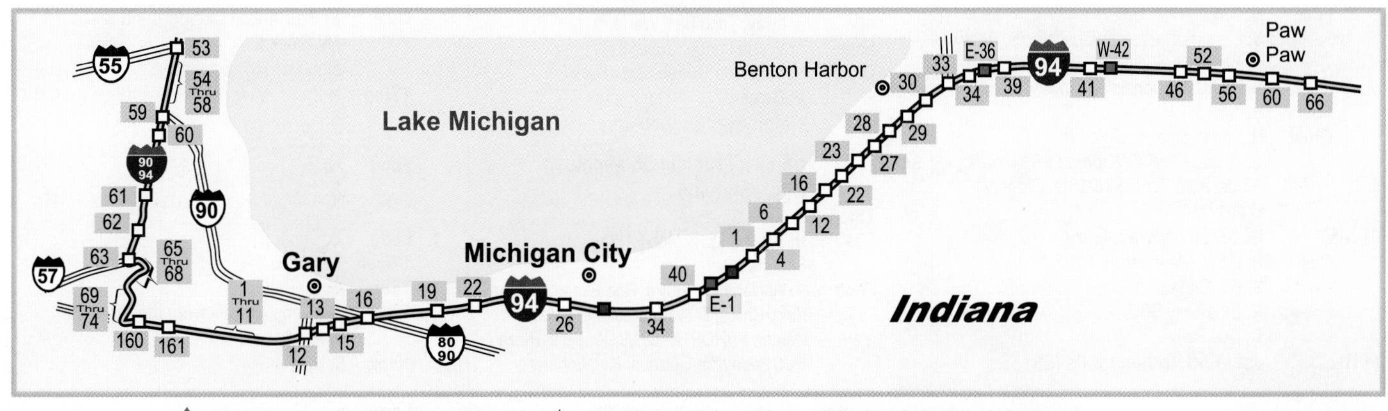

◈= Regular Gas Stations with Diesel ▲ = RV Friendly Locations ♥= Pet Friendly Locations

Red print shows large vehicle parking / access on site or nearby Brown Print = Campgrounds / RV PARKS

EXIT | INDIANA

INDIANA

CENTRAL TIME ZONE

NOTE: I-94 runs with I-80 below. Exit #'s follow I-94.

1 **US 41N, Calumet Ave, Hamilton**
- Gas N: BP◈, Gas City◈
  S: BP, Marathon, Mobil◈, Shell
- Food N: Baskin Robbins/Dunkin Donuts, Subway/BP
  S: Arby's, Burger King, Starbucks, Subway, Taco Bell, Wendy's
- Other N: Firestone, Laundromat, Walgreen's
  S: CVS, Grocery, Radio Shack, Staples, Target, Vet♥,

2AB **US 41S, IN 152N, Indianapolis Blvd, Hamilton, Hammond**
- TStop S: Pilot Travel Center #31 (Scales)
- Gas N: SavAStop, Shell
  S: Thorntons
- Food N: Arby's, Domino's, Dunkin Donuts
  S: Subway/Pilot TC, Burger King, Little Caesar's, Taco Bell
- Lodg S: Ameri Host Inn
- Med N: + Hospital
  S: + Hospital
- Other N: to Purdue Univ/Calumet
  S: WiFi/Pilot TC, ATMs, Cabela's, Dollar General, Grocery

3AB **Kennedy Ave, Hammond**
- Gas N: Clark, Mobil◈, Speedway
  S: Citgo, Speedway
- Food N: Burger King, Dominos, McDonald's
  S: Cracker Barrel, Subway, Wendy's
- Lodg S: Courtyard, Fairfield Inn, Residence Inn
- Other N: NAPA, Walgreen's,

5AB **IN 912, Cline Ave, Gary, Hammond**
- Gas S: BP, Clark, Shell, Speedway
- Food S: Arby's, Bob Evans, Burger King, DQ, McDonald's, Pizza Hut, White Castle
- Lodg S: Best Western, Motel 6♥

6 **Burr St, Gary**
- TStop N: Travel Center of America #10/BP(Scales) Pilot Travel Center #271 (Scales)
- Gas N: BP
  S: Shell◈
- Food N: CountryPride/Chester/PizzaHut/Taco Bell/TA TC, Subway/Pilot TC
- TWash N: Pilot TC
- TServ N: TA TC/Tires
- Other N: Laundry/CB/WiFi/TA TC, WiFi/Pilot TC

9AB **Grant St, Gary, to Chicago, IL**
- TStop S: 9A: Love's Travel Stop #417 (Scales), AmBest/Steel City Truck Plaza (Scales)
- Food N: Chicago Hot Dogs
  S: Denny's/HotColdDeli/Love's TS, Rest/FastFood/Steel City TP, Burger King, DQ, KFC, McDonald's, Subway
- TServ S: Tires, Truck Wash
- Other N: Laundromat, Walgreen's
  S: Laundry/WiFi/RVDump/LP/Love's TS, ATMs, Auto Zone, Firestone, Grocery, Outlet Mall

10AB **IN 53, Broadway, Gary**
- Gas N: Citgo, Marathon
  S: BP, Citgo
- Food N: Broadway BBQ
  S: DQ, Rally's

(11) **Jct I-65S, Indianapolis (EB)**

EXIT | INDIANA

(12A) **Jct I-65S, to Indianapolis (WB)**

(12B) **Jct I-65N, to Gary, IN**

13 **Central Ave (EB, No re-entry)**

15A **US 6E, IN 51S, to US 20, Lake Station**
- TStop S: Road Ranger Travel Center #240/Citgo
- Gas S: Mobil◈, Shell
- Food S: Subway/RoadRanger, Burger King, DQ, Papa John's, Long John Silver, Wendy's
- Other S: Walgreen's

15B **US 6W, IN 51N, Ripley St, Melton Rd, Central Ave, Gary, Lake Station**
- TStop N: Road Ranger Travel Center #239/Citgo (Scales), Flying J Travel Plaza #5085 (Scales), Travel Center of America #219/BP (Scales), Dunes Center Truck Stop (Scales)
- Food N: Subway/Road Ranger TC, Cookery/FastFood/FJ TP, Buckhorn/Popeyes/Subway/TA TC, McDonald's, Ponderosa
- TWash N: Road Ranger, FJ TP, TA TC
- TServ N: FJ TP/Tires, TA TC/Tires, Dunes Center TS/Tires
- Other N: Laundry/BarbSh/CB/WiFi/FJ TP, Laundry/WiFi/TA TC

(16/21) **Jct I-90, Jct I-80, US 6, IN 51**

NOTE: I-94 runs with I-80 above. Exit #'s follow I-94.

19 **IN 249, Crisman Rd, Portage, Port of Indiana**
- Gas S: Shell, Citgo
- Food S: Andy's, Burger King, Denny's, Cactus Carlos, KFC. Subway
- Lodg S: Days Inn, Dollar Inn, Hampton Inn, Inn, Ramada Inn, Super 8, Travel Inn
- TServ N: Great Lakes Peterbilt GMC
- Other N: Bass Pro Shop

22AB **US 20, Melton Rd, Chesterton, Porter, Burns Harbor**
- FStop S: Steel City Express (Scales)
- TStop N: Travel Center of America /Mobil (Scales)
  S: Pilot Travel Center #445 (Scales)
- Food N: FastFood/Steel City, Rest/Subway/TA
  S: McDonald's/Subway/Pilot TC
- TWash N: Blue Beacon TW/TA TC
- TServ N: TA TC/Tires
- Other N: Laundry/CB/WiFi/TA TC
  S: Laundry/RVDump/Pilot TC, Auto Dealers, Camp-Land RV Center

26AB **IN 49, Chesterton, Porter**
- Gas S: BP, Speedway◈
- Food S: Applebee's, Burger King, Dunkin Donuts, KFC, Little Caesars, Long John Silver, McDonald's, Pizza Hut, Quiznos, Subway, Taco Bell, Wendy's
- Lodg S: Econo Lodge, Super 8
- Other N: to Indian Dunes State Park
  S: Grocery, Walgreen's

(29) **Weigh Station (Both dir)**

34AB **US 421, Franklin St, Michigan City, Westville**
- TStop S: Steel City (Scales)
- Gas N: BP◈, Citgo◈, Mobil◈, Shell, Speedway◈
- Food N: Applebee's, Arby's, Bob Evans, Burger King, Chili's, Culver's Rest, Denny's, Damon's, IHOP, KFC, McDonald's, Pizza Hut, Popeye's, Quiznos, Red Lobster,

EXIT | IN / MI

- Food N: Ryan's Grill, Starbucks, Steak 'n Shake, Subway, Taco Bell, Wendy's
  S: FF/Steel City
- Lodg N: Comfort Inn, Days Inn, Holiday Inn, Knights Inn, Red Roof Inn, Super 8
- Med N: + Hospital
- Other N: ATMs, Auto Dealers, Auto Zone, Auto Service, Dollar Tree, Grocery, Lowe's, Radio Shack, **Walmart**
  S: Laundry/Steel City, Auto Dealers, Harley Davidson

40AB **US 20, US 35, Michigan City, South Bend, La Porte**
- FStop S: Speedway #6661
- Med N: + Hospital
- Other N: Michigan City Muni Airport✈

(42) **IN Welcome Center (WB) (RR, Phone, Picnic, Vend)**

CENTRAL TIME ZONE

NOTE: MM 46: Michigan State Line

INDIANA

MICHIGAN

EASTERN TIME ZONE

(1) **MI Welcome Center (EB) (RR, Phone, Picnic, Vend, Info, WiFi)**

1 **MI 239, La Porte Rd, New Buffalo**
- TStop S: Plaza One Truck Stop (Scales)
- Gas N: Shell
  S: Speedway
- Food N: Dominics Ital Rest, McDonald's, Quiznos, Wheel Inn Rest
  S: Arby's, Wendy's, Zeke's
- Lodg N: Best Western, Holiday Inn Express
  S: Obrien Inn
- Other N: CarWash/Shell, AmTrak, Rogers Wrecker Service, Tire & Auto Services, Golf Course
  S: Four Winds Casino Resort

(2) **Weigh Station (Both dir)**

4AB **US 12, E-Niles, W-New Buffalo Pulaski Hwy, S Red Arrow Hwy**
- TStop N: J &J 12&60 Truck Stop
- Food N: Rest/J&J TS, Pizza Hut, Redamak's Tavern
- Lodg N: Harbor Grand Hotel, New Buffalo All Suites Inn, White Rabbit Inn B&B
- Other N: MI State Hwy Patrol Post
  S: Dale's Auto Service, M&N Towing Service, U-Haul

6 **Union Pier Rd, Union Pier**
- Other E: Bob-A-Ron Campground & RV Sales▲

12 **Sawyer Rd, Sawyer**
- TStop N: Dunes Auto Truck Plaza/Citgo (Scales)
  S: Travel Center of America #116/Amoco (Scales)
- Food N: FastFood/Dunes ATP
  S: Country Pride/Burger King/Pizza Hut/Popeyes/Taco Bell/TA TC
- Lodg S: Super 8
- TWash N: Dunes TW
- TServ S: TA TC/Tires
- Other N: Kamp Across from the Dunes▲
  S: Laundry/WiFi/TA TC

◈= Regular Gas Stations with Diesel ▲ = RV Friendly Locations ♥= Pet Friendly Locations
Red print shows large vehicle parking / access on site or nearby Brown Print = Campgrounds / RV PARKS

EXIT		MICHIGAN
16		**MI 12N, Red Arrow Hwy, Bridgman**
	TStop	N: USA Travel Center/Marathon (Scales)
	TStop	S: Bridgman Travel Center (Scales)
	Gas	N: Bridgman Amoco◈
		S: Speedway
	Food	N: A&W/Amoco
		S: McDonald's, Pizza Pizza Hut, Subway
	Lodg	S: Bridgman Inn
	Other	N: Kamp Across from the Dunes RV Park▲, Warren Dunes State Park, Weko Beach Campground▲
22		**Grand Mere Rd, John Beers Rd, Stevensville**
	Gas	S: P&R Shell, H&S Gas & Food Mart
	Other	N: Grand Mere State Park
23		**I-94 Bus E, Red Arrow Hwy, Stevensville, St Joseph, Benton Harbor**
	Gas	N: Admiral Station, Central Station Food Mart, Lakeshore Shell Food Mart◈, Marathon◈
	Food	N: Bob's Big Boy, Burger King, Cracker Barrel, Culver's, DQ, Long John Silver, McDonald's, Papa John's Pizza, Popeye's Chicken, Subway, Tony's Family Rest
		S: Cajun Deli, Schuler's Rest
	Lodg	N: Baymont Inn♥, Candlewood Suites♥, Comfort Suites, Park Inn♥, Ray's Motel
		S: Hampton Inn♥
	Other	N: Walgreen's
27		**US 33, MI 63, St Joseph, Niles**
	Gas	N: I-94 AmocoBP
	Food	N: Dino's Family Rest, Qdoba Mex Grill, McDonald's, Taco Bell, Wendy's
	Lodg	N: Econo Lodge♥
	Other	S: Goodyear, Wingfoot Comm'l Tire
28		**US 31S, MI 139, Fair Ave, Nickerson Ave, Scottsdale Rd, Benton Harbor**
	TStop	N: Speedway #8718
	Gas	N: Citgo◈, Quik Shop, Marathon
	Food	N: Burger King, Country Kitchen, DQ, KFC, Little Caesar's Pizza, Pizza Hut, Subway, Taco Bell, Wendy's
	Lodg	N: Howard Johnson♥, Rodeway Inn♥
		S: Lake Breeze Hotel
	Med	N: + Lakeland Hospital
	Other	S: ATMs, Auto Zone, Big Lots, Dollar Tree, Office Depot, RiteAid, Target, Tires, MI State Hwy Patrol Post
29		**Pipestone Rd, Benton Harbor**
	FStop	S: Pri Mar Fuel Center #10/Mobil
	Gas	N: Meijer◈, Total
	Food	N: Applebee's, Burger King, China Buffet, Denny's, El Rodeo Mex Rest, Great Steak & Potato, Hacienda Mex Rest, IHOP,

EXIT		MICHIGAN
	Food	N: McDonald's, Jimmy's Family Buffet, Pizza Hut, Red Lobster, Sophia's House of Pancakes, Steak 'n Shake, Subway, Texas Corral
		S: Bob Evans
	Lodg	N: Best Western♥, Courtyard, Motel 6♥, Red Roof Inn♥
		S: Comfort Suites, Holiday Inn Express
	Med	N: + Urgent Care Medical Walk-In
	Other	N: ATMs, Best Buy, Dollar Tree, Grocery, Home Depot, Goodyear, Lowe's, Radio Shack, Meijer, PetSmart♥, Staples, Tires, Walgreen's, Mall, Walmart sc
30		**US 31, Napier Ave, Benton Harbor**
	TStop	N: Flying J Travel Plaza #5121 (Scales)
	Gas	N: Shell
	Food	N: FastFood/FJ TP
	Lodg	N: Super 8
	TWash	N: Blue Beacon TW/FJ TP
	TServ	N: FJ TP/Tires
	Other	N: Laundry/WiFi/LP/FJ TP, Discount Tire, Tires, Orchard Mall, Animal Care Center♥
		S: Lake Michigan College
33		**I-94 Bus, E Main St, Downtown St Joseph, Bar Harbor (WB)**
	Other	N: Benton Harbor Airport✈
(34)		**I-196N, US 31N, South Haven, Holland, Grand Rapids**
	Other	N: to Coloma/St Joseph KOA▲, Dune Lake Campground▲
(36)		**Rest Area (EB)** (RR, Phone, Picnic, Vend, Info)
39		**Friday Rd, Church St, Columa, Millburg, Deer Forest**
	Gas	N: Speedway, Randy's Svc Ctr/Towing
		S: BP◈
	Food	N: McDonald's, Pizza Hut, Subway
	Other	N: ATMs, Ace Hardware, Family Dollar, Krenek RV Super Center
41		**MI 140, Watervliet Rd, Watervliet**
	Gas	N: Dave's AmocoBP
		S: Pri Mart Quik Shop
	Food	N: Subway, Taco Bell
		S: Burger King, Waffle House
	Other	N: to Covert/South Haven KOA▲, Paw Paw River Campground▲
(42)		**Rest Area (WB)** (RR, Phones, Picnic, Vend, Info)
46		**CR 687, 64th St, Hartford**
	Gas	N: Hartford Shell◈
	Food	N: McDonald's
		S: Patio Donut Shop
	Other	S: Thousand Adventures Travel Inn Resort▲

EXIT		MICHIGAN
52		**CR 365, 52nd St, Lawrence**
	Gas	N: Lawrence Self Serve, Village Marathon
	Food	N: Waffle House
	Other	S: to Oak Shores Campground▲, Timber Trails RV Park▲
56		**MI 51, CR 671, Paw Paw, to Decatur, Dowagiac**
	FStop	S: Citgo
	TStop	S: Road Hawk Travel Center/Marathon (Scales)
60		**MI 40, Paw Paw, Lawton**
	Gas	N: AmocoBP, Speedway◈
	Food	N: Arby's, Big Boy, Burger King, Chicken Coop, McDonald's, Pizza Hut, Taco Bell, Wendy's
	Lodg	N: Comfort Inn♥, Econo Lodge, Super 8♥
	Med	N: + Lakeview Community Hospital
	Other	N: Pharmacy, UPS Store, US Post Office, St Julian Winery, Warner Winery
66		**CR 652, 24th St, Main St, Mattawan**
	FStop	N: Speedway #6604 (Scales)
	Gas	S: Shell
	Food	N: Subway/Speedway, Mancino's Italian
	Other	N: Family Dollar
72		**9th St, Kalamazoo, Oshtemo**
	FStop	N: Short Stop Citgo
	Gas	N: Speedway◈
	Food	N: Arby's, Burger King, Culver's, McDonald's, Taco Bell, Wendy's
		S: Burger King, Cracker Barrel
	Lodg	N: Hampton Inn
		S: Fairfield Inn
(73)		**Rest Area (EB)** (RR, Phone)
74AB		**US 131N, I-94 Bus, to Kalamazoo, Grand Rapids, Three Rivers (EB)**
	Other	N: to W MI Univ
74B		**US 131N, Grand Rapids(WB, Exit only)**
74A		**US 131S, Three Rivers**
75		**Oakland Dr, Portage, Kalamazoo**
76A		**Westnedge Ave S, Portage**
	Gas	S: Shell
	Food	S: Applebee's, Bob Evans, Burger King, Carrabba's, Chili's, Chuck E Cheese Pizza, Chinese Buffet, Culvers,Fazoli's, KFC, Logan's Roadhouse, Mountain Jack's, McDonald's, Noodles & Co, Olive Garden, Panera Bread, Peking Palace, Pizza Hut, Qdoba Mexican Rest, Red Lobster, Red Robin, Subway, Taco Bell, Wendy's
	Lodg	S: Holiday Motel

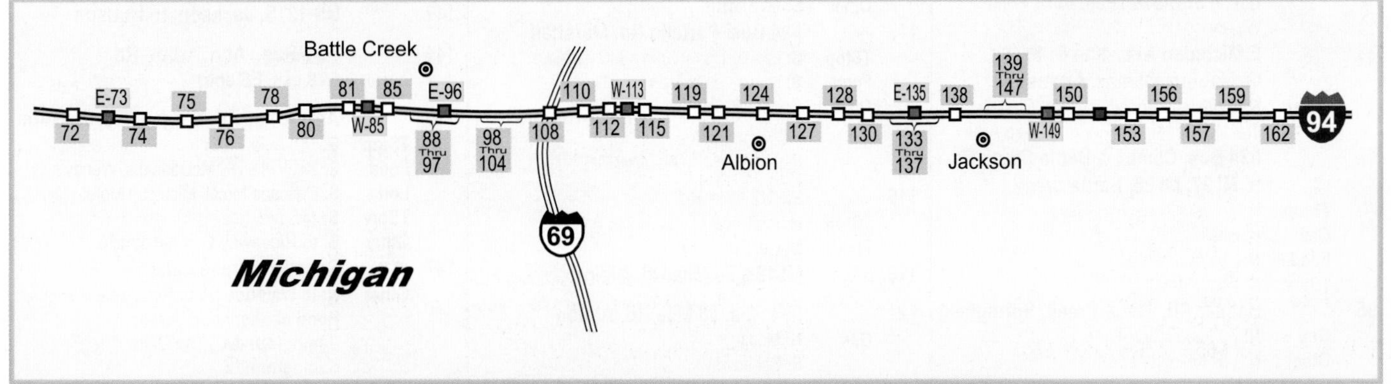

◈= Regular Gas Stations with Diesel ▲ = RV Friendly Locations ♥= Pet Friendly Locations
Red print shows large vehicle parking / access on site or nearby Brown Print = Campgrounds / RV PARKS

Other S: ATMs, Auto Services, Banks, Southland Mall, Crossroads Mall, Auto Dealers, Auto Zone, B&N, Best Buy, Dollar Tree, Firestone, Grocery, Home Depot, Pep Boys Radio Shack, Sam's Club, Target, Tires, World Market, Walgreen's

76B Westnedge Ave N, Kalamazoo
FStop N: Speedway #3561
Gas N: Admiral, Meijer◊
Food N: Arby's, Hooters, IHOP, Papa John's, Pappy's Mexican, Outback Steakhouse, Mancino's Italian, Steak 'n Shake, Subway, Taco Bell
Lodg N: Quality Inn
Other N: ATMs, Big Lots, Discount Tire, Gander Mountain, Goodyear, Lowe's, Meijer, Office Depot, RiteAid

78 Portage Rd, Kilgore Rd, Portage
Gas N: Circle K
S: Mobil, Shell, Marathon
Food N: Cottage Inn Pizza, Hungry Howie's Pizza, Subway, Taco Bob's, Uncle Ernie's Pancake House
S: McDonald's, Pizza King, Gum Ho Chinese, Taco Bell
Lodg N: Hampton Inn, Residence Inn♥
S: Airport Inn, Country Inn, Lee's Inn♥
Other S: Sam's Club, Kalamazoo/Battle Creek Int'l Airport✈, Aviation History Museum

80 Sprinkle Rd, Cork St, Kalamazoo
FStop N: Double O Express/Marathon
Gas N: Citgo◊, Speedway◊
S: BP◊, Speedway◊l
Food N: Arby's, Burger King, Chicken Coop, Denny's, Perkins, Taco Bell
S: McDonald's, Subway, Wendy's
Lodg N: Best Western♥, Clarion Hotel♥, Fairfield Inn, Holiday Inn Express, Red Roof Inn♥
S: Comfort Inn, Days Inn, Econo Lodge, Motel 6♥, Quality Inn
TServ N: GMC/Volvo Trucks
S: Mi CAT
Other N: ATMs, Auto Services, Car Wash, Spring Rd Veterinary Clinic♥

81 I-94 Bus Loop (WB)
(Serv 1st Ex & Acc to Ex #80 N Serv)
Other N: Kalamazoo Co Fairgrounds▲

(85) Rest Area (WB)
(RR, Phone, Picnic, Vend)

85 35th St S, Augusta, Galesburg
Gas N: Shell◊
Food N: FastFood/Shell, McDonald's
Other N: Galesburg Speedway, **to Shady Bend Campground▲**
S: **to Timber Lake Campground & Riding Stables▲**, Peterson & Sons Winery

88 E Michigan Ave, 40th St S, Galesburg, Climax, Augusta
Other N: Galesburg Speedway, Fort Custer Training Center, **Ft Custer St Rec Area**

92 I-94 Bus, Climax & Battle Creek Rd to MI 37, MI 96, Battle Creek
TStop N: Arlene's Truck Stop/Citgo
Gas: N: Shell
Food N: Rest/Arlene's TS
TServ N: Glen's Tire Center

95 Helmer Rd, Battle Creek, Springfield
Gas N: Ps Food Mart/Citgo◊
Other N: WK Kellogg Airport✈

EXIT MICHIGAN

(96) Rest Area (EB)
(RR, Phone, Picnic, Vend)

97 Capital Ave, 5 Mile Rd, B Dr N, Beckley Rd, Battle Creek
Gas N: BP, Clark
S: Citgo, Shell
Food N: Arby's, Lakeview Family Rest, Lone Star Steakhouse, McDonald's, Red Lobster
Food S: Applebee's, Bob Evans, Burger King, Cracker Barrel, Denny's, Don Pablo, Old Country Buffet, Pancake House, Subway, Taco Bell, Wendy's
Lodg N: Comfort Inn, Knights Inn♥, Ramada Inn♥
S: Battle Creek Inn, Baymont Inn♥, Best Western, Days Inn♥, Fairfield Inn, Hampton Inn, Motel 6♥, Ramada, Super 8♥
Other S: Lakeview Square Mall, ATMs, Firestone, Goodyear, Lowe's, Target, UPS Store, Mahrle's Harley Davidson

98A MI 66S, to Sturgis
Gas S: Citgo◊, Meijer◊
Food S: Chili's, McDonald's, Steak 'n Shake, Ruby Tuesday, Taco Bell
Lodg S: Super 8
Other S: ATMs, Best Buy, Discount Tire, Grocery, Lowe's, Sam's Club, Staples, Walgreen's, **Walmart sc, to Camper Village▲**

(98B) Jct I-194N, MI 66, to Battle Creek

100 Beadle Lake Rd, Battle Creek
FStop S: Jim Hazel's Fuel Stop
Food N: Moonraker Rest

103 Jct I-94 Bus, MI 96, Battle Creek
(WB exit, EB entr)

104 to MI 96, 11 Mile Rd, Michigan Ave
FStop S: Pilot Travel Center #17, Interstate Truck & Car Stop
TStop S: Te-Khi AmBest Travel Plaza/Sunoco
Food S: Rest/Te-Khi TP
Lodg S: Quality Inn
TWash S: Te-Khi TS
TServ S: Te-Khi TS
Other S: Laundry/WiFi/Te-Khi TP, WiFi/Pilot TC

(108) Jct I-69, I-94 Bus, N to Lansing, S to Ft Wayne
Other S: **Tri Lake Trails Campground▲**

110 17 Mile Rd, Old 27, Marshall
FStop S: Brewer Park Ps Food Mart
TStop N: Pioneer Auto Truck Stop/Shell
Food N: Rest/Subway/Pioneer ATS, Country Kitchen
Lodg S: Hampton Inn, Holiday Inn Express
Med S: + Hospital
Other S: **MI Sheriff**

112 I-94 Bus, Partello Rd, Marshall
TStop S: Love's Travel Stop #336 (Scales)
Food S: Hardee's/Love's TS
Other S: WiFi/**RVDump**/Love's TS

(113) Rest Area (WB)
(RR, Phone, Picnic, Vend, Info)

115 22 1/2 Mile Rd
TStop N: PTP/One Fifteen Truck Stop
Food N: Rest/115 TS

119 MI 199, 26 Mile Rd, Albion

121 I-94 Bus, 28 Mile Rd, Albion
Gas N: Mobil
S: Speedway◊

EXIT MICHIGAN

Food N: Arby's
S: Burger King, McDonald's, Pete's Place, Pizza Hut
Lodg N: Best Western♥
S: Super 9 Inn♥
Med S: + Trillium Hospital
Other S: ATMs, Auto Dealers, Auto Zone, Dollar General, Family Dollar, Pharmacy, Radio Shack

124 MI 99, I-94 Bus, Eaton Rapids, Albion, Parma, Springport

127 N Concord Rd, Parma, Concord

128 Michigan Ave, Parma
TStop N: Parma Travel Center/BP (Scales)
Gas N: Petro Shop◊
Food N: Burger King
Lodg S: Hilltop Farm
Other N: Laundry/Parma TC

130 N Parma Rd, Parma
TStop S: Parma Citgo Truck Stop/Citgo
Rest S: Rest/Parma TS

133 Dearing Rd, Parma, Spring Arbor

(135) Rest Area (EB)
(RR, Phone, Picnic, Vend, Info)

136 I-94 Bus, MI 60, Jackson, Spring Arbor

137 Airport Rd, Jackson
Gas N: 7-11, Shell, Meijer◊
S: BP, Sam's
Food N: Denny's, McDonald's, Subway
S: Cracker Barrel, Olive Garden
Other N: Laundromat
S: Kmart, Sam's Club, Jackson Co Airport✈

138 US 127N, MI 50, Lansing, Jackson
Gas S: Marathon, Shell, Total
Food N: Red Lobster
S: Bob Evans, Ground Round, KFC, Long John Silver, McDonald's, Pizza Hut, Old Country Buffet, Outback Steakhouse, Pizza Hut
Lodg N: Comfort Inn, Fairfield Inn, Holiday Inn, Super 8
S: Best Motel, Motel 6♥
Other S: Best Buy, Home Depot, Lowe's, Pharmacy, Target, Walgreen's

139 MI 106, Cooper St, Jackson
Gas S: Citgo, Marathon
Food S: Jackson Café, Subway
Med S: + Hospital
Other N: **MI State Hwy Patrol Post**
S: Amtrak Station

141 Elm Rd, Jackson

142 US 127S, Jackson, to Hudson

144 I-94 Bus, Ann Arbor Rd
(WB exit, EB entr)

145 Ann Arbor Rd, Sargent Rd, Jackson
TStop S: 145 Auto Truck Plaza/Mobil (Scales)
Food S: Rest/145 TP, McDonald's, Wendy's
Lodg S: Cascade Motel, Michigan Motel
TServ S: 145 TP/Tires
Other S: **to Hideaway Campground▲**

147 Race Rd, Grass Lake
Other N: **to Waterloo State Rec Area, Robin Hood of Sherwood Forest Campground▲, The Oaks Campground▲**

◊= Regular Gas Stations with Diesel ▲ = RV Friendly Locations ♥= Pet Friendly Locations
Red print shows large vehicle parking / access on site or nearby Brown Print = Campgrounds / RV PARKS

EXIT		MICHIGAN
	Other	S: Grass Lake Resort▲, Greenwood Acres Family Campground▲, to MI Int'l Speedway
(149)		**Rest Area (WB)** (RR, Phone, Picnic, Vend, Info)
150		**Mt Hope Rd, Grass Lake**
	Gas	S: Grass Lake Mini Mart, Mobil
	Food	S: Subway
	Other	N: Waterloo State Rec Area, to Robin Hood of Sherwood Forest, Portage Lake Family Campground▲ S: Apple Creek Resorts-Grass Lake
(151)		**Weigh Station (Both dir)**
153		**Clear Lake Rd, Grass Lake, Waterloo**
	Gas	N: Clear Lake Oil/Marathon◈
156		**Kalmbach Rd, Grass Lake**
	Other	N: Waterloo State Rec Area
157		**Old 12, Pierce Rd, Chelsea**
159		**MI 52, Main St, Chelsea, Manchester**
	Gas	N: Chelsea AmocoBP◈, Mobil◈
	Food	N: Big Boy, McDonald's, Schumm's, Taco Bell, Wendy's
	Lodg	N: Comfort Inn, Holiday Inn Express
	Med	N: + Chelsea Community Hospital
	Other	N: RVDump/Mobil, Auto Service/Amoco, CVS, Lloyd Bridges Traveland RV▲
162		**Old 12, Fletcher Rd, Jackson Rd, Chelsea, Dexter**
	FStop	S: Chelsea Plaza/Clark
	Food	S: Subway/Chelsea Plaza
167		**Baker Rd, Dexter**
	FStop	S: Wolverine Truck Stop
	TStop	N: Pilot Travel Center #21 (Scales) S: Pilot Travel Center #296 (Scales), Travel Center of America #89/BP (Scales)
	Food	N: Subway/Pilot TC S: Arby's/TJCinn/Pilot TC, CountryPride/TC
	TWash	S: Blue Beacon TW/TA TC
	TServ	S: TA TC/Tires
	Other	N: WiFi/Pilot TC, Hell Creek Ranch Campground▲ S: Laundry/WiFi/TA TC
(168)		**Rest Area (EB) (Next RA 87 mi)** (RR, Phone, Picnic, Vend, Info)
169		**Zeeb Rd, Ann Arbor**
	Gas	N: AmocoBP◈ S: Citgo◈, Mobil
	Food	N: Baxter's Deli, German Rest, McDonald's S: Arby's, Pizza Hut, Subway, Taco Bell, Wendy's
	Other	S: Lowe's, Harley Davidson

EXIT		MICHIGAN
171		**MI 14, Plymouth, to Ann Arbor, Flint (EB, Left Exit)**
172		**I-94 Bus, Jackson Rd (EB), Jackson Ave (WB), to Ann Arbor**
	Gas	N: AmocoBP, Marathon, Shell S: Sunoco
	Food	N: DQ, KFC, Panda House, Knight's Steakhouse
	Food	S: Michigan Inn, Webers
	Lodg	S: Best Western, Garden Point Inn, Weber's Inn
	Med	S: + Hospital
	Other	N: Kroger, Staples, Tires, Mall
175		**Ann Arbor Saline Rd, Ann Arbor**
	Gas	N: BP, Marathon, Shell
	Food	N: Applebee's, Lone Star Steakhouse, Old Country Buffet, Panera, Subway S: McDonald's, Joe's Crab Shack, Outback Steakhouse
	Lodg	N: Candlewood Hotel
	Other	N: Mall, ATMs, Office Depot S: ATMs, Best Buy, Grocery, Target
177		**State St, Ann Arbor**
	Gas	N: BP, Mobil, Shell S: Citgo, Total
	Food	N: Max & Erma's, Olive Garden, Romano's Macaroni Grill S: McDonald's, Taco Bell
	Lodg	N: Courtyard, Fairfield Inn, Hampton Inn, Holiday Inn, Holiday Inn Express, Red Roof Inn♥, Residence Inn, Sheraton S: Motel 6♥
	Other	N: to Univ of MI, Grocery, Mall S: Ann Arbor Municipal Airport✈
180AB		**US 23, I-94 Bus, S to Toledo, N to Flint (EB)**
180B		**US 23N, to Flint (WB)**
	Other	N: to Univ of MI
180A		**US 23S, S to Toledo (WB)**
	Gas	N: Meijer◈, Speedway S: Shell
	Food	N: Burger King, Taco Bell S: McDonald's, Subway
	Other	N: ATMs, Grocery, Walmart
181		**US 12W, Michigan Ave (EB)**
181B		**Michigan Ave East (WB)**
181A		**US 12W, Michigan Ave, Saline (WB)**
183		**US 12 Bus, Huron St, Ypsilanti**
	Gas	N: Marathon◈
	Food	S: McDonald's
	Lodg	S: Marriott
	Med	N: + Hospital

EXIT		MICHIGAN
	Other	N: Ford Motor Co, Eastern MI Univ S: MI State Hwy Patrol Post
185		**US 12E, Michigan Ave, Ypsilanti (EB Exit, WB entr)**
	Other	Willow Run Airport✈, GM Plant
186		**Williard Rd, Willow Run Airport (WB Exit, EB Entr)**
	Other	Willow Run Airport✈, GM Plant
187		**Rawsonville Rd, Belleville**
	Gas	S: Mobil◈, Speedway◈
	Food	S: Burger King, Denny's, Hardee's, KFC, Little Caesars Pizza, Lone Star Steakhouse, Pizza Hut, Wendy's
	Other	S: RiteAid, Detroit/Greenfield KOA▲
190		**Belleville Rd, Belleville**
	Gas	N: Amoco, Marathon, Meijer◈ S: Shell
	Food	N: Applebee's, Cracker Barrel, McDonald's, Taco Bell, Wendy's S: Burger King, China City, China King, Domino's, Subway
	Lodg	N: Hampton Inn, Holiday Inn, Red Roof Inn♥ S: Super 8
	Other	N: CVS, U-Haul, Camping World, Walt Michaels RV Center/RVDump, Walmart, Wayne Co Fairgrounds S: Laundromat, US Post Office
192		**Haggerty Rd, Belleville**
	Gas	N: Mobil
(194A)		**Jct I-275S, to Toledo (EB)**
(194B)		**Jct I-275N, to Livonia, Novi (EB)**
(194)		**Jct I-275, N-Livonia, S-Toledo (WB)**
196		**Wayne Rd, Wayne, Romulus**
	Gas	N: Citgo, Shell S: Mobil, Total
	Food	N: McDonald's S: Burger King
197		**Vining Rd, Romulus**
198		**Merriman Rd, Middle Belt Rd, Detroit Metro Wayne Co Airport**
	FStop	N: M& J Petro
	Gas	N: Speedway S: Metro Gas
	Food	N: American Grill, Bob's Big Boy, Bob Evans, Beirut Rest, Fortune Chinese, Leonardo's Pizzeria & Rest, McDonald's, Merriman St Grill, Subway S: Denny's, McDonald's, Wendy's
	Lodg	N: Baymont Inn, Best Western, Comfort Inn, Clarion, Courtyard, Crown Plaza, Doubletree Hotel, Extended Stay America, Hampton Inn, Hilton Suites, Motel 6♥, Quality Inn, Relax Inn

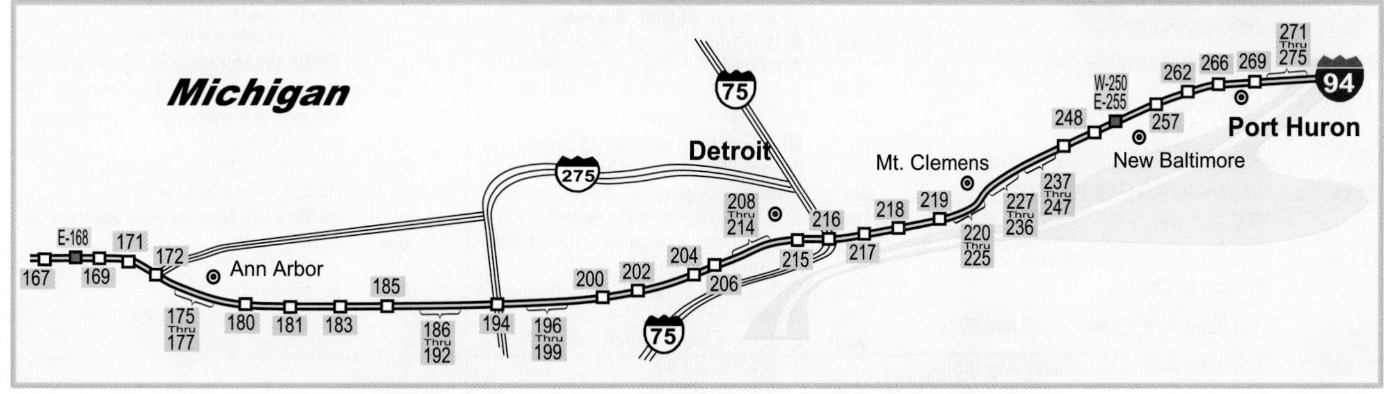

◈ = Regular Gas Stations with Diesel ▲ = RV Friendly Locations ♥ = Pet Friendly Locations
Red print shows large vehicle parking / access on site or nearby Brown Print = Campgrounds / RV PARKS

EXIT		MICHIGAN
	Lodg	S: Days Inn, Howard Johnson, Super 8
199		**Middle Belt Rd, Romulus (Acc to Serv at Ex #198)**
200		**Ecorse Rd, Taylor**
	TStop	N: Madco Truck Plaza/Marathon (Scales) (EB: Access via Exit #198)
	Food	N: Rest/Madco TP
	TWash	N: Madco TP
	TServ	N: Madco TP/Tires
	Other	N: Laundry/Madco TP
202A		**US 24N, Telegraph Rd, Dearborn Hts**
	Gas	N: Shell
	Food	N: Pizza Hut, Taco Bell, Wendy's
	Lodg	N: Casa Bianca Motel
	Other	N: Grocery, Walgreen's, to Henry Ford Museum & Greenfield Village
202B		**US 24S, Telegraph Rd, Taylor**
	FStop	S: Metro Truck Plaza/BP
	Gas	S: Citgo, Marathon◈, Mobil, Shell
	Food	S: Burger King, Pizza Hut, Red Lobster
	Lodg	S: Quality Inn
	TServ	S: Metro TP/Tires
	Med	S: + Oakwood Heritage Hospital
	Other	S: Laundry/Metro TP, CVS, Walmart
204		**MI 39, Southfield Freeway, Pelham Rd, Allen Park, Dearborn**
206A		**Oakwood Blvd S, Allen Park (WB)**
206B		**Oakwood Blvd N, Allen Park (WB)**
206		**Oakwood Blvd, Allen Park (EB)**
	Gas	N: Marathon S: BP, Mobil
	Food	S: Burger King, Pizza Hut, Subway
	Lodg	S: Best Western, Holiday Inn Express
	TServ	S: Belle Tire
	Med	N: + Oakwood Hospital
208		**Greenfield Rd, Schaefer Rd**
	FStop	S: to Fuel Mart of America
209		**Rotunda Dr, Dearborn (WB ex, EB entr)**
210A		**US 12, Michigan Ave, Wyoming Ave, Dearborn**
	FStop	S: MAH Fuel & Auto Service, MI & WY Food Shop/BP
	TStop	S: Wyoming Fuel Plaza/Truck City
	Food	S: Drake's Iron Skillet, WY Lunch
	TWash	S: MAH
	TServ	S: MAH
210B		**MI 153, Ford, Rd, Addison St (WB Exit, EB entr)**
	Gas	N: Mobil
211A		**Lonyo St (WB exit, EB entr)**
211B		**Central Ave, Cecil Ave (WB exit, EB entr)**
212		**Livernois Ave (WB)**
212A		**Livernois Ave, Detroit (EB)**
	FStop	S: I-94 & Livernois Marathon
212B		**Warren Ave (EB)**
213A		**W Grand Blvd, Warren Ave (EB, Left exit)**
(213B)		**Jct I-96, Lansing, Ambassador Bridge to Canada**
214		**Linwood Ave, Grand River Ave (WB)**
214A		**Linwood Ave, Grand River Ave (EB)**

EXIT		MICHIGAN
214B		**Trumbull Ave (EB exit, WB entr)**
215		**MI 10, Downtown Detroit (EB)**
215A		**MI 10S, Downtown, Tunnel to Canada**
215B		**MI 10N, Lodge Freeway**
215C		**MI 1, Woodward Ave, John R St**
(216A)		**Jct I-75, N to Flint, S to Toledo, Chrysler Frwy, Tunnel to Canada**
216B		**Russell St (EB, Exit only)**
217		**Chene St, E Grand Blvd, Mount Elliot Ave (WB)**
217A		**Chene St, E Grand Blvd (EB)**
217B		**Mount Elliott Ave (EB)**
218		**MI 53, Van Dyke Ave**
	Gas	N: AmocoBP, Mobil
219		**MI 3, Gratiot Ave**
	Gas	N: Marathon S: BP
	Food	N: McDonald's, KFC
220A		**French Rd (EB)**
220B		**Conner Ave, City Airport**
	Gas	N: BP, Kwik Fill
	Lodg	N: Travel Inn
222A		**Outer Dr, Chalmers Ave**
	Gas	N: AmocoBP◈, Marathon
	Food	N: Little Caesar's, White Castle
222B		**Harper Ave (EB exit, WB entr)**
223		**Cadieux Ave**
	Gas	S: Amoco, Shell, Sunoco
	Food	S: McDonald's, Taco Bell, Wendy's
224A		**Moross Rd**
	Gas	S: Shell
224B		**Allard Ave, Eastwood Ave**
225		**MI 102, 8 Mile Rd, Vernier Rd**
227		**9 Mile Rd, St Clair Shores**
	Gas	N: Mobil, Speedway, Sunoco S: Mobil
	Food	N: Mama Rosa's, McDonald's, Taco Bell, Wendy's
	Lodg	S: Shore Point Motor Lodge
	Other	N: CVS, Grocery, US Post Office
228		**10 Mile Rd**
	Gas	N: Amoco, Shell
	Food	N: Eastwind , Jet's Pizza
(229)		**Jct I-696W, to 11 Mile Rd**
	Gas	N: BP S: BP, DM, Speedway
230		**12 Mile Rd, St Clair Shores**
	Gas	N: Marathon, Citgo S: Marathon
	Food	N: Burger King, Buffet World, Outback
	Other	N: CVS, Mall, Walmart
231		**MI 3, Gratiot Ave (EB, Left exit) (EB exit, WB entr)**
	Gas	N: Shell, Speedway
	Food	N: Applebee's, Arby's, Big Boy, Chuck E Cheese, Denny's, Mountain Jack's, Pizza Hut, Texas Roadhouse
	Lodg	N: Best Western, Days Inn, Knights Inn, Super 8
	Other	N: Discount Tire, Firestone, Sam's Club, Target, Mall, U-Haul

EXIT		MICHIGAN
232		**Little Mack Ave, Roseville**
	Gas	N: Sunoco S: AmocoBP, Meijer◈, Speedway◈
	Food	N: Bob Evans, Famous Dave's BBQ S: Dunkin Donuts, **Cracker Barrel**, IHOP
	Lodg	N: Comfort Inn, Microtel, Holiday Inn Microtel, Red Roof Inn♥, Super 8 S: Baymont Inn
	Other	N: Sam's Club S: Home Depot
234A		**Harper Ave S, Clinton Twp**
234B		**Harper Ave N, Clinton Twp**
234		**Harper Ave, Clinton Twp**
	Gas	N: Amoco, Citgo, Sunoco◈ S: Mobil
	Food	N: Pizza, Subway S: Little Caesar's Pizza, Subway
235		**Shook Rd (WB exit, EB entr)**
236		**16 Mile Rd, Metropolitan Pkwy**
	Food	S: McDonald's, Subway
	Med	S: + Hospital
237		**N River Rd, Mt Clemens**
	FStop	N: North River AmocoBP
	Gas	N: Mobil◈
	Food	N: McDonald's
	Lodg	N: Comfort Inn
	Other	N: RV Center
240A		**Rosso Hwy E, to MI 59, Utica (EB)**
240B		**Rosso Hwy W, to MI 59, Utica (EB)**
240		**Rosso Hwy, to MI 59, Utica**
	Gas	N: 7-11, BP, Marathon, Speedway
	Food	N: Arby's, Bob Evan's, McDonald's, O'Charley's, Tim Horton
	Lodg	N: Best Western
	Other	N: **Walmart**
241		**21 Mile Rd, Selfridge (Access to Ex #240 Serv)**
	FStop	N: M&M Gas & Grocery/Citgo
	Gas	N: Marathon
	Food	N: Quiznos, Subway
	Other	N: CVS
243		**23 Mile Rd, MI 29, to MI 3, MI 59, New Baltimore, Utica**
	FStop	S: Speedway #2314
	Gas	N: Marathon, Meijer◈, Shell◈, Sunoco S: Marathon◈
	Food	N: Applebee's, Arby's, McDonald's, Outback Steakhouse, Starbucks, Steak 'n Shake, Texas Roadhouse, White Castle, Wendy's S: Big Boy, Taco Bell
	Lodg	N: Chesterfield Motel
	Other	N: ATMs, Discount Tire, Home Depot, Lowe's, Staples, Walgreen's, Target, MI CAT, **Roseville RV Center**
247		**MI 19, Washington St, New Haven Rd, New Baltimore, New Haven (EB exit, WB entr)**
	FStop	N: New Haven Citgo
	Food	N: NobleRomansPizza/NH Citgo, New Haven Coney Island, AM Donut
248		**26 Mile Rd, New Haven, Marine City**
	Gas	N: BP S: 7-11, Mobil
	Food	N: McDonald's
(250)		**Rest Area (WB) (Next RA 62 mi) (RR, Phone, Picnic, Vend)**

◈= Regular Gas Stations with Diesel ▲ = RV Friendly Locations ♥= Pet Friendly Locations
Red print shows large vehicle parking / access on site or nearby Brown Print = Campgrounds / RV PARKS

EXIT		MICHIGAN
(255)		**Rest Area (EB)** (RR, Phone, Picnic, Vend)
257		**Division Rd, Adair, Casco, St Clair**
	FStop	S: 257 BP
	Other	S: MI State Hwy Patrol Post
262		**Wadhams Rd, St Clair**
	FStop	S: Road Hawk Travel Center/Marathon (Scales)
	Other	N: St Clair Thousand Trails▲ , to Port Huron KOA▲
		S: Laundry/Road Hawk TC
266		**I-94 Bus, MI 25, Gratiot Rd, Smiths Creek, Marysville**
	FStop	S: Sunrise/Marathon
	Gas	S: Shell, Plum's Conv Store
	Food	S: Burger King, Big Boy, KFC, Little Caesar's Pizza, McDonald's, Taco Bell
	Lodg	S: Days Inn, Microtel, Super 8
	Med	S: + Hospital
	Other	N: St Clair Co Int'l Airport✈
		S: Auto Zone, CVS
269		**Range Rd, Dove St, Port Huron**
	Gas	N: Speedway◈
	Food	N: Burger King
	Lodg	N: AmeriHost
	NOTE:	I-94 runs with I-69 below. Exit #'s follow I-94.
(271)		**Jct I-69W, to Flint** **Jct I-69E, to Pt Huron**
274		**Water St, Lapeer Ave, Pt Huron** MI Welcome Center (WB) N: (RR, Phone, Picnic, Vend, Info)
	FStop	S: ByLo Speedy Q #6
	Gas	S: Speedway◈
	Food	N: Cracker Barrel
		S: Bob Evans
	Lodg	N: Best Western, Ramada Inn
		S: Comfort Inn, Fairfield Inn, Hampton Inn, Knights Inn
	Other	N: Lake Port State Park
275		**I-69 Bus, MI 25, Pine Grove Ave, Port Huron, Toll Bridge to Canada (EB, LEFT exit)**
	Gas	S: BP, Clark, Shell, Speedway
	Food	S: McDonald's, Wendy's, White Castle
	Lodg	S: Best Western, Days Inn, Holiday Inn
	Other	S: CanAm Duty Free, Pharmacy
	NOTE:	I-94 begins/ends on MI 25

MICHIGAN

EXIT		MAINE
		Begin Southbound I-95 from Canada / Maine border to Miami, FL.

MAINE

EASTERN TIME ZONE

EXIT		MAINE
(306)		**US/Canada Border, US Customs, ME State Line**
305		**Airport Rd, to US 2, Military St, Houlton (Last US Exit)**
	Other	E: Houlton Int'l Airport✈, AmEx Duty Free
302		**US 1, North St, Houlton, Downtown, Presque Isle** W:ME Welcome Center (SB) Rest Area (NB, RR, Phone, Picnic, Info)
	FStop	W: Doc's Place/Citgo
	TStop	W: Travelers Irving Big Stop/FJ TP (Scales)
	Gas	E: Irving Mainway◈
	Food	E: Burger King, KFC, McDonald's, Pizza Hut, Tangs Chinese
		W: BigStopRest/Irving Big Stop, Governor Rest & Bakery, Tim Horton's, Subway
	Lodg	E: Scottish Inns
		W: Ivey's Motor Lodge, Stardust Motel
	TServ	W: Irving Big Stop/Tires, Hogan Tire
	Med	E: + Houlton Reg'l Hospital
	Other	E: Houlton Tire, Grocery, Pharmacy, VIP Auto Center, to Houlton Int'l Airport✈, to Greenland Cove Campground▲
		W: LP/Irving, Auto Dealers, Walmart, ME State Hwy Patrol Post, My Brothers Place Campground▲
291		**US 2, Silver Ridge Rd, Oakfield, Smyrna Mills, New Limerick**
286		**Oakfield Rd, to US 2, ME 212, ME 11, Oakfield, Smyrna Mills**
	Gas	W: Irving Mainway◈, Valero◈
	Food	W: Crossroads Café, A Place to Eat
	Other	W: to appr 4mi Birch Point Campground & Cottages▲
276		**ME 159, to US 2, Island Falls, Patten**
	Gas	E: Citgo
	Other	E: to appr 4mi Birch Point Campground & Cottages▲
	Other	W: to Baxter State Park, Matagamon Wilderness
264		**Main St, ME 158, ME 11, Sherman**
	FStop	E: Shell
	TStop	W: Irving Big Stop/Circle K
	Gas	E: Mobil
	Food	E: Rest.Shell
		W: Rest/Irving BS
	Lodg	W: Katahdin Valley Motel
	Other	E: to Barnett's Cabins & Camping▲
		W: LP/Irving
259		**Casey Rd, Pond Rd, to US 2, ME 11 Benedicta, Sherman (NB ex, SB reacc)**
(252)		**Scenic View Mt Katahdin (NB) (May-Oct) (RR, Phone, Picnic)**
244		**ME 157, Medway Rd, Medway, Millinocket, Mattawamkeag**
	TStop	W: Irving Big Stop/Circle K
	Food	W: Rest/Irivng BS, Gram's Place
	Lodg	W: Gateway Inn
	Other	W: to Baxter State Park, Pine Grove Campground & Cottages▲ , Katahdin Shadows Campground▲ , Hidden Springs Campground▲ , Big Moose Inn Cabins & Campground▲
(243)		**Rest Area (Both dir)** (RR, Phone, Picnic, Vend)
227		**to ME 16, US 2, Penobscot Valley Ave, Lincoln (All Serv in Lincoln)**
	Gas	E: Doc's Place, Irving Conv
	Food	E: McDonald's, China Light, Taco Bell, Subway, Mill St Diner, Steak & Stuff
	Lodg	E: Briarwood Motor Inn, Thomas Motel
	Med	E: + Penobscot Valley Hospital
	Other	E: Lincoln Reg'l Airport✈, to Sleeping Bear Camping▲
217		**ME 155, ME 6, Howland, LaGrange Enfield, Milo**
	Gas	E: Citgo, Irving◈
	Food	E: Little Peter's Seafood
	Other	E: Lakeside Campground & Cabins▲
199		**ME 6, Old Town, to Alton, LaGrange, Milo (NB ex, SB reacc)**
(198)		**Weigh Station (Both dir)**
197		**ME 43, Old Town, Hudson, Milford**
	Gas	E: Exxon, Mike's Car Service
	Food	E: Wendy's
	Other	E: DeWitt Field Airport✈, Grocery, to Greenwood Acres Campground▲
193		**Stillwater Ave, Old Town, Orono**
	Gas	E: Citgo◈, Irving◈, Mobil◈
	Food	E: Burger King, China Garden, Governor Rest, KFC, McDonald's, Subway
	Lodg	E: Best Western
	Other	E: Dollar Tree, Grocery, Univ of ME/Orono
		W: Pushaw Lake Campground▲
191		**Kelly Rd, Orono, Veazie**
187		**Hogan Rd, Bangor, Veazie**
	Gas	E: Exxon, Mobil, Sam's Club
		W: Exxon◈, Irving, Doc's Place
	Food	E: Denny's
		W: Applebee's, Arby's, Bugaboo Creek Steakhouse, Burger King, Chili's, KFC, McDonald's, Olive Garden, Pizza Hut, Quiznos, Red Lobster, Smokey Bones BBQ, Starbucks, Wendy's, 99 Rest
	Lodg	E: Courtyard, Hilton Garden Inn,
		W: Bangor Motor Inn, Comfort Inn♥, Country Inn, Days Inn, Hampton Inn
	TServ	E: Bangor Peterbilt
	Med	E: + Hospital
	Other	E: Auto Dealers, Sam's Club
		W: Advance Auto Parts, Bangor Mall, Best Buy, Burlington Coat Factory, Carwash/ Exxon, Cinema 1-8, Goodyear, Home Depot, Office Depot, Staples, Target, UPS Store, Walmart
186		**Stillwater Ave, Bangor (Access to Ex #187)**
185		**ME 15, Broadway, Bangor, Brewer**
	Gas	E: Irving
		W: Mobil, Exxon
	Food	E: Tri-City Pizza
		W: China Light, Friendly's, Governor's, KFC, McDonald's, Pizza Hut
	Med	E: + Hospital
	Other	W: ATMs, Firestone, Grocery, RiteAid

◈= Regular Gas Stations with Diesel ▲ = RV Friendly Locations ♥= Pet Friendly Locations

Red print shows large vehicle parking / access on site or nearby Brown Print = Campgrounds / RV PARKS

EXIT | MAINE

184 ME 222, Union St, Ohio St, Airport
Gas E: Citgo, Exxon
W: Exxon, Mobil◈
Food W: Burger King, Captain Nick's, McDonald's, Subway, Wendy's
Lodg W: Four Points Sheraton
Other E: Auto Service/Citgo, RiteAid, **Holden Family Campground▲**
W: Budget Truck Rental, Dollar Tree, Grocery/Pharmacy, Staples, University College, Bangor Int'l Airport✈, **Paul Bunyan Campground▲ , to appr 5mi Pleasant Hill RV Park & Campground▲**

183 US 2, US 2A, ME 100, Hammond St
Gas E: Exxon, Gulf
Food E: Subway, Papa Gambino's Pizza & Subs
Other W: Bangor Int'l Airport✈

182B to US 2W, ME 100W, Hermon
Gas W: Irving◈, Mobil◈
Food W: Barnaby's, Dunkin Donuts, Ground Round, Jason's NY Style Pizza
Lodg W: Days Inn♥, Econo Lodge♥, Fairfield Inn, Holiday Inn, Howard Johnson♥, Motel 6♥, Ramada♥, Super 8, Travelodge
Other W: Cinema, Family Fun Bowling Center, Generator Sales, **Gopher Ridge RV Park▲** , Tire Warehouse, **Webb's RV Center**, Bangor Int'l Airport✈

(182A) Jct I-395S, ME 15, to US 1A, ME 9, Bangor, Brewer
TServ E: Freightliner
Other E: Bangor Muni Golf Course, Beal College, Brewer Airport✈, Downtown, Museum, USS ME Monument, WW II Memorial, **to Red Barn Campground▲**

180 Coldbrook Rd, Hampden, Hermon
TStop W: Dysart's Service/Citgo (Scales)
Gas E: Dysart Conv Store
Food W: Rest/Dysart's
Lodg W: Best Western♥
TWash W: Dysart's
TServ W: Dysart's
Other W: Laundry/**RVDump**/Dysart's, **Pumpkin Patch RV Resort▲ , to Wheeler Stream Camping Area▲**

(178) Rest Area (SB)
(RR, Phone, Picnic, Vend, Info)

(176) Rest Area (NB)
(RR, Phone, Picnic, Vend, Info)

174 ME 69, Hampden Rd, Carmel Rd N, Carmel, Winterport
Gas E: Citgo◈
Other W: **Shady Acres RV & Campground▲**

167 to ME 69, ME 143, Lakins Rd, Etna, Dixmont
Other W: Ring Hill Airport✈, **Stetson Shores Campground▲**

161 ME 7, Moosehead Trail, to US 2, ME 100, E Newport, Plymouth

159 Ridge Rd, to US 2, ME 100, Newport, Dexter, Plymouth (SB)
Other W: **Sebasticook Lake Campground▲ , Christie's Campground▲**

157 ME 11, ME 100, Ox Bow Rd, to US 2, ME 7, Newport, Dexter
TStop W: Irving Big Stop/FJ TP/Circle K
Gas W: Citgo, Mobil◈

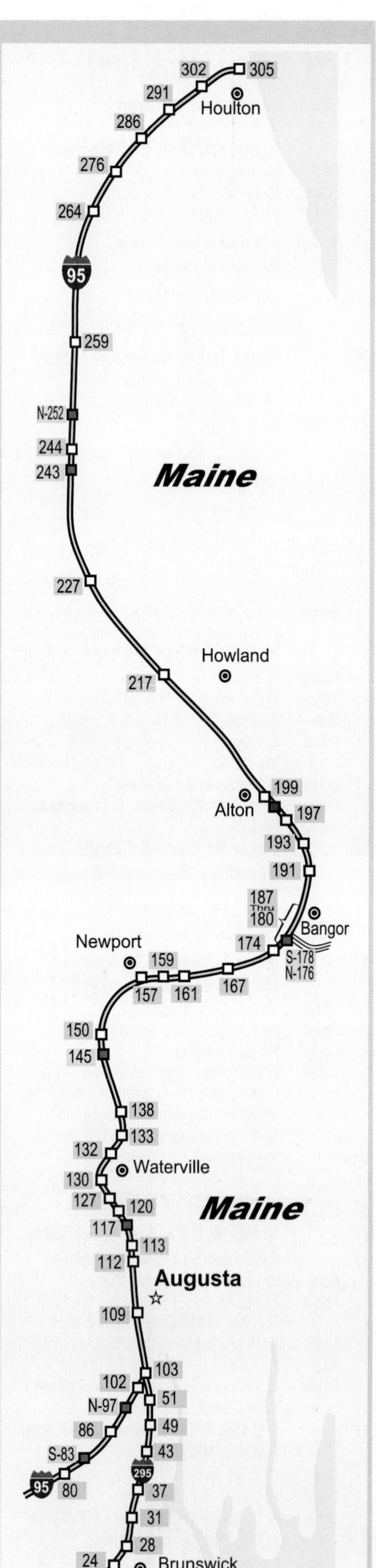

EXIT | MAINE

Food E: Burger King, Dunkin Donuts
W: BigStopRest/Irving BS, House of Pizza, Pat's Pizza, Front Porch Rest BBQ & Grill, Sail In Cafe, Sawyers Dairy Bar, Subway
Lodg W: Lovely's Motel, Pray's Motel
Med E: + Hospital
Other W: **LP**/Irving, ATMs, Auto Dealers, Budget Truck Rental, CarQuest, Grocery, Newport Ent Center, Pharmacy, Radio Shack, US Post Office, **Walmart sc, to** Moose Mtn, Sugarloaf Ski Area, **Skowhegan/Canaan KOA▲ , Palmyra RV Resort/Palmyra Golf▲**

150 Weeks Rd, Somerset Ave, to ME 11/100/152, Pittsfield, Palmyra, Hartland, Burnham
Gas E: Mobil
Food E: Subway
Lodg E: Pittsfield Motor Inn
Med E: + Hospital
Other E: Auto Services, Family Dollar, Grocery, RiteAid, to Pittsfield Muni Airport✈

(145) Rest Area (Both dir)
(RR, Phone, Picnic, Vend)

138 Hinckley Rd, Baker St, Clinton
Gas W: Citgo◈

133 US 201, Main St, Fairfield, Skowhegan, Quebec City
TStop W: Irving Big Stop
Food W: Rest/Deli/Irving
Other W: Laundry/Irving, **to appr 7mi: Skowhegan/Canaan KOA▲**

132 ME 139, Western Ave, Fairfield
TStop W: Pilot Travel Center #958 (Scales)
Gas E: Gene's Market/Gas
Food W: Rest/Subway/Pilot TC
TServ W: Pilot TC/Tires
Other E: Pharmacy
W: Laundry/**LP**/Pilot TC

130 ME 104, Main St, Waterville
Gas E: Mobil
Food E: Arby's, McDonald's, Ruby Tuesday, Starbucks, Subway, Wendy's
Lodg E: Best Western, Comfort Inn, Fireside Inn, Holiday Inn
Med E: + to ME Gen'l Medical Center
Other E: Auto Dealers, ATMs, Square Cinema, Grocery, Home Depot, KMart, Pharmacy, Radio Shack, Staples, **Walmart sc, to** Colby College

127 ME 11, ME 137, Kennedy Memorial Dr, Waterville
Gas E: Citgo, Irving◈, Mobil
W: Exxon◈, Valero
Food E: Applebee's, Angelo's, Burger King, McDonald's, Papa John's Pizza, Pizza Hut, Quiznos, Subway, Weathervane Seafood
W: China Express
Lodg E:Budget Host, Econo Lodge, Hampton Inn
Med E: + Inland Hospital
Other E: Auto Dealers, Auto Zone, Cinema, Grocery, RiteAid, Tire Warehouse, **Walmart, Countryside Camping▲ , to appr 10mi Green Valley Campground▲** Waterville Robert Lefleur Airport✈
W: CVS, Carwash, **Mid-ME Marine & RV,**

120 Lyons Rd, Sidney, Augusta

(117) Rest Area (Both dir)
(RR, Phone, Picnic, Vend)

113 ME 3, to ME 104, Augusta

◈= Regular Gas Stations with Diesel ▲ = RV Friendly Locations ♥= Pet Friendly Locations
Red print shows large vehicle parking / access on site or nearby **Brown Print = Campgrounds / RV PARKS**

EXIT		MAINE
112		**ME 8, ME 11, ME 27, N to Belgrade, S to Augusta (SB)**
	Gas	E: Citgo, Getty W: Irving◈
	Food	E: Denny's, Ground Round, Longhorn Steakhouse, Olive Garden, Panera Bread, Red Robin, Ruby Tuesday W: Taco Bell, Wendy's, 99 Rest
	Lodg	E: Holiday Inn W: Comfort Inn, Fairfield Inn
	Other	E: ATMs, Augusta Civic Center, Banks, Barnes & Noble, Grocery, Home Depot, Radio Shack, Sam's Club, Staples, **Walmart sc**, Univ of ME/Augusta W: Advance Auto Parts
112A		**ME 11, ME 27, S-Augusta (NB)**
112B		**ME 11, ME 27, N-Belgrade (NB)**
109		**US 202, ME 11/17/100, E to Augusta, W to Winthrop (NB)**
109B		**US 202, ME 11/17/100, W to Winthrop (SB)**
	Gas	W: Exxon, Getty, Valero
	Food	W: Ponderosa, Tea House Chinese
	Lodg	W: Econo Lodge♥, Motel 6♥, Quality Inn, Super 8
	Other	W: Auto Dealers, Auto Services, ATMs, Enterprise RAC, Grocery/Pharmacy, ME Comm'l Tire, PetCo♥, **Scott's Recreation**
109A		**US 202, ME 11/17/100, E to Augusta (SB)**
	Gas	E: Irving◈, Shell
	Food	E: Applebee's, Arby's, Burger King, DQ, KFC, McDonald's, Oyster Bar & Grill, Subway, Tim Horton's, Wendy's
	Lodg	E: Best Western, Senator Inn
	Other	E: Auto Services, Big Lots, Children's Discovery Museum, Dollar Tree, Grocery, Mailing Center, Target, Tires, Augusta State Airport✈
	NOTE:	**I-95 below runs with ME Tpk**
(103)		**Jct I-495S, Maine Tpk, to Litchfield, Gardiner**
102		**ME 9, ME 126, Lewiston Rd, Gardiner, to Sabbatus**
(100)		**Gardiner TOLL Plaza**
(97)		**Litchfield Service Plaza (NB)**
	FStop	Mobil
	Food	Burger King
86		**ME 9, Middle Rd, Sabattus, to Richmond, Lisbon**
(83)		**Lewiston Service Plaza (SB)**
	FStop	Mobil
	Food	Burger King
80		**ME 196, Lisbon St, Lisbon, Lewiston**
	FStop	W: Gendron's U-Save
	Gas	W: Getty, Mobil, Shell
	Food	W: Burger King, Carribou Café, Dunkin Donuts, Governor's Rest, KFC, Little Caesar's Pizza, McDonald's, Tim Horton's,
	Lodg	W: Motel 6♥, Ramada Inn, Super 8, Travelodge
	Med	W: **+ St Mary's Regional Med Center, + Central ME Medical Center, + Concentra Urgent Care**

EXIT		MAINE
	Other	W: Advance Auto Parts, CVS, Cinema, Dollar Tree, Family Dollar, NAPA, RiteAid, Staples, Tire Warehouse, UPS Store
75		**to US 202, ME 4, ME 100, Kittyhawk Ave, Auburn**
	FStop	E: FJ TP/Irving Mainway #1475/Circle K, **3.5 mi to 249 US 202:** Ness Oil
	Food	E: Rest/Auburn Inn
	Lodg	E: Auburn Inn, Sleepytime Motel
	TServ	W: Freightliner
	Other	W: Auburn Lewiston Muni Airport✈
(67)		**New Gloucester TOLL Plaza**
63		**US 202, ME 115, ME 26, ME 100, Gray, New Gloucester**
	Gas	E: Mobil, Oil W: Gary's
	Food	E: Dunkin Donuts, McDonald's, Subway
	Other	E: Ace Hardware, RiteAid, W: **to 26N:** Sunday River Ski Resort, Mt Abram Ski Area
(58)		**Cumberland Service Plaza (Hours 6a-10p)**
	FStop	Mobil
	Food	Burger King, TCBY
53		**ME 26, ME 100, Falmouth, Portland**
	Gas	E: Irving◈
52		**Falmouth Spur, to I-295, US 1 Falmouth, Freeport**
48		**Larrabee Rd, Riverside St, to ME 25, US 302, Westbrook, Portland**
	FStop	W: Mobil
	Gas	E: Citgo, BJ's W: Exxon, Shell
	Food	E: Applebee's, Burger King, Subway W: Denny's, KFC, McDonald's, Panda Garden, Ruby Tuesday, Tim Horton's, Valle's Steakhouse, Wendy's
	Lodg	E: Ramada Inn, Rodeway Inn W: Holiday Inn, Howard Johnson, Motel 6♥, Super 8, Travelodge
	TServ	W: Freightliner
	Other	E: Auto Dealers, ATMs, BJ's, Grocery, Lowe's, **Walmart** W: Auto Dealers, Auto Service, Grocery, Home Depot, Pharmacy, Tires
47		**Rand Rd, Westbrook Arterial, to MI 25, Portland**
46		**Jetport Rd, to ME 9, ME 22, Congress St, Portland (Acc #45 Serv)**
	Other	E: Portland Int'l Jetport✈ W: Auto & Truck Service
45		**to ME Mall Rd, Payne Rd, to US 1, ME 9, I-295, S Portland**
	Gas	E: Gulf, Mobil, Shell
	Food	E: Bugaboo Creek Steakhouse, Chili's, Friendly's, IHOP, Old Country Buffet, Olive Garden, Outback Steakhouse, Panda Express, Panera Bread, Romano Macaroni Grill, Ruby Tuesday, Starbucks, TGI Friday, Tim Horton, Weathervane Seafood W: Applebee's, Starbucks
	Lodg	E: Comfort Inn, Courtyard, Days Inn, Econo Lodge, Fairfield Inn, Hampton Inn, Hilton Garden Inn, Residence Inn, Sheraton Towneplace Suites W: Holiday Inn Express, Marriott
	Other	E: ATMs, AAA, Banks, Best Buy, Borders, Grocery, Office Depot, PetCo♥, Staples,

EXIT		MAINE
	Other	E: Sam's Club, Tires, **Walmart**, ME Mall, Portland Int'l Jetport✈, **to** Kenworth
44		**to ME 114, Jct I-295N, S Portland, Downtown (NB) (Acc to Ex #45 Serv)**
42		**Haigais Pkwy, to US 1, Scarborough**
	Lodg	E: Millbrook Motel, Oak Leaf Motel, Moosehead Motel, Shady Pine Motel
	Other	E: NE Truck Tires, Scarborough Downs Racetrack W: Beech Ridge Motor Speedway
(36)		**Jct I-195E, Saco, Old Orchard Beach**
	Lodg	E: Hampton Inn
	Other	E: **to Saco/Old Orchard Beach KOA▲**
32		**ME 111, Biddiford**
	FStop	E: Irving/Circle K
	Food	E: Dunkin Donuts, Ruby Tuesday, Subway, Wendy's W: Applebee's, Olive Garden, Panera Bread, Starbucks
	Lodg	E: America's Best Value Inn, Biddiford Motel, Comfort Suites
	Med	E: **+ Hospital**
	Other	E: Advance Auto Parts, Auto Zone, Cinema Grocery, Pharmacy, **Walmart sc**, Biddiford Ice Arena, Biddiford Muni Airport✈ W: ATMs, Best Buy, Home Depot, Lowe's, PetSmart♥, Staples, Target
25		**ME 35, Kennebunk, to US 1**
	Lodg	E: Turnpike Motel W: Lodge at Kennebunk
	TServ	E: Freightliner
(24)		**Kennebunk Service Area (Both dir)**
	FStop	Mobil
	Food	Burger King, Popeye's, TCBY Burger King, Sbarro, TCBY
19		**ME 109, ME 9, Wells, Sanford**
	Other	W: Amtrak, **to appr 5 mi: Pinderosa Camping Area▲**
(7)		**York TOLL Plaza**
	NOTE:	**Begin NB/End SB TOLL**
	NOTE:	**I-95 above runs with ME Tpk**
7		**to US 1, ME 91, Yorks, Ogunquit (Last Free Exit NB)**
	Gas	E: Irving◈, Mobil◈, Shell
	Food	E: Greenleaves Chinese, Mandarin Inn, Ruby's Grill, Safina's Italian Rest.
	Lodg	E: York Commons Inn, Mic Macmotel
	Med	E: **+ York Hospital**
	Other	E: Auto Dealers, ATMs, Grocery W: **to appr 10 mi: Pinderosa Camping Area▲**
(6)		**Weigh Station (NB)**
(3)		**Weigh Station (SB)**
(3)		**ME Welcome Center (NB) (RR, Phone, Picnic, Vend, Info)**
3		**to US 1N, ME 236, Coastal Route, Kittery (NB)**
2		**ME 236, Dow Hwy, Kittery (NB)**
	TStop	E: Kittery Travel Stop/Irving (Scales)
	Food	E: Rest/Irving TS, Bagel Caboose, DQ, Sunrise Grill, Tasty Thai
	Lodg	E: Ramada
	Other	E: Kittery Animal Hospital♥,

◈= Regular Gas Stations with Diesel ▲ = RV Friendly Locations ♥= Pet Friendly Locations

Red print shows large vehicle parking / access on site or nearby **Brown Print = Campgrounds / RV PARKS**

EXIT		ME / NH
1		**Dennot Rd, to ME 103** **(NB ex, SB reacc)**
	Gas	E: Citgo, Sunoco
	Food	E: Sue's Seafood, Warren's Lobster House
	Lodg	E: Days Inn, Blue Roof Motel, NorEaster Motel, Inn at Portsmouth Harbor
	Other	E: to Portsmouth Naval Base

EASTERN TIME ZONE

MAINE
NEW HAMPSHIRE

NOTE: Listings show Mile Marker / Exit #

17/7		**Market St, Woodbury Ave, Portsmouth Bus Distr, Waterfront Historic Sites**
	Food	W: Applebee's, Bickford's Family Rest, Chuck E Cheese's Pizza, Panera Bread, Ruby Tuesday, Texas Roadhouse, Wendy's
	Lodg	E: Sheraton W: Courtyard, Hampton Inn, Homewood Suites
	Other	W: BJ's, Grocery, Pep Boys, Home Depot, **Walmart sc**,
15/6		**Woodbury Ave, Portsmouth (NB)**
	Gas	E: Shell
	Lodg	E: Anchorage Inn, Best Inn, Holiday Inn
14/5		**Spaulding Tpk, US 4, NH 16, Newington, Dover (SB)** **NH Tpk, US 1 ByP, (NB, Exit only)** **I-95N, to Maine (NB, Left 3 lanes)**
	FStop	E: O'Brien's #2/Citgo **(US 1 ByP)**
	TStop	E: Hanscom's Truck Stop **(US 1 ByP)**
	Lodg	E: Best Inn, Best Western, Fairfield Inn, Holiday Inn
	Med	E: + Portsmouth Reg'l Hospital
	Other	E: CVS, RiteAid,
(14)		**Begin/End TOLL Road**
13/4		**Spaulding Tpk, US 4, NH 16, NH Lakes, Newington, Dover** **(NB, Left exit)**
12/3A		**Grafton Rd, Pease Int'l Tradeport Airport, Trailways (SB)**
12/3B		**NH 33, Greenland Rd, Portsmouth**

NOTE: SB: Last Exit Before TOLL

12/3		**NH 33, Greenland Rd, Portsmouth**
	FStop	W: Exit 3 Truck Stop/Sunoco
	TStop	W: Travel Center of America (Scales) **(SB: Access via Exit #3B)**
	Food	W: Buckhorn/TA TC
	Other	**E: Shel-Al Campground▲** W: Laundry/WiFi/TA TC, Golf Course, Target
(6)		**Hampton TOLL Plaza**
6/2		**NH 101, Hampton, Exeter**
	Other	E: to US 1/1A, Hampton Beach W: to Manchester, Epping
(1)		**Begin/End TOLL Road**
1/1		**NH 107, to US 1, Seabrook**
	FStop	E: Seabrook One Stop/Sunoco
	Gas	E: Getty W: Citgo

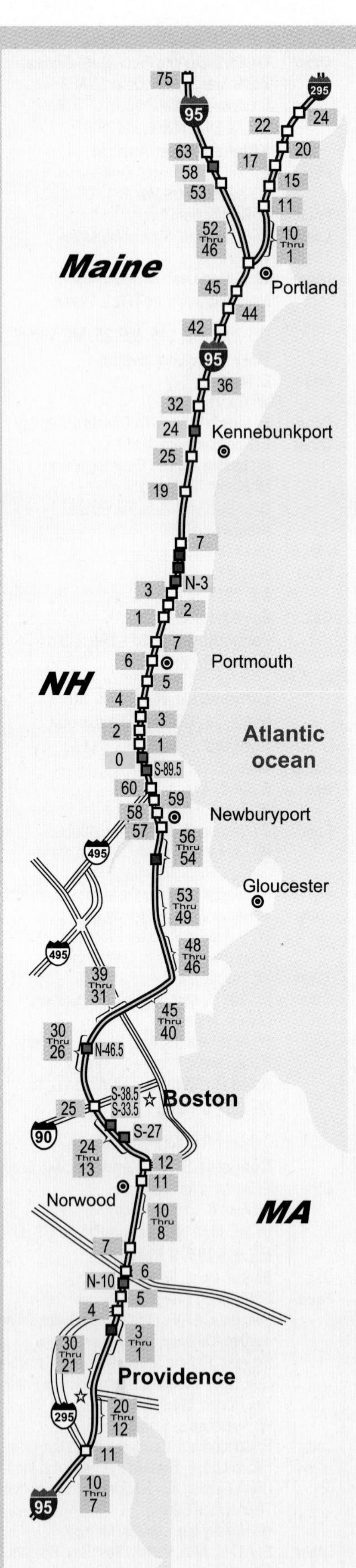

EXIT		NH / MA
	Food	E: Applebee's, Burger King, Dunkin Donuts, McDonald's, Rock in Lobster, Starbucks, Steak & Seafood, Subway, Wendy's W: Capt K's Seafood, Master MacGrath's
	Lodg	E: Hampshire Inn, Holiday Inn Express W: Best Western
	Other	E: ATMs, Auto Zone, CVS, Grocery, Home Depot, Lowe's, Laundromat, Staples, Tires, **Walmart** W: Sam's Club, Greyhound Park, **Green Gate Campground▲ , Exeter Elms Family Campground▲**
(0)		**NH Welcome Center (NB)** **(RR, Phone, Picnic, Info)**

EASTERN TIME ZONE

NEW HAMPSHIRE
MASSACHUSETTS

EASTERN TIME ZONE

NOTE: Listings show Mile Marker / Exit #

(89.5)		**MA Welcome Center (SB)** **(RR, Phone, Picnic, Vend, Info)**
89.5/60		**Main St, MA 286, US 1, Beaches, Salisbury**
	Gas	W: Pump & Pantry
	Food	E: Lena's Seafood
	Lodg	W: Johnson's Motel
	Other	**E: Black Bear Family Campground▲ , Rusnik Campground▲**
(88.8/59)		**Jct I-495S, Worcester (SB, rt 2 ln)**
87.2/58		**MA 110, to I-495S, W - Amesbury, E - Salisbury (SB)**
	Gas	E: Sunoco◈ W: Irving, Mobil
	Food	E: China Buffet, Crossroads Pizza, Dunkin Donuts, Frankie's Roast Beef, Sylvan St Grill, Winners Circle W: Burger King, McDonald's, Papa Gino's
	Lodg	W: Fairfield Inn
	Other	**E: Pines Camping Area▲ , Beach Rose RV Park▲** , Auto Dealers, U-Haul, Penske W: Auto Dealers, Pharmacy,
58A		**MA 110E, to Salisbury (NB)**
87.4/58B		**MA 110W, to I-495 (NB)**
85.7/57		**MA 113, Storey Ave, Newburyport, W Newbury**
	Gas	E: Mobil, Shell, Sunoco
	Food	E: Dunkin Donuts, Friendly's, McDonalds, Jade Chinese, Papa Gino's
	Med	E: + Hospital
	Other	E: ATMs, Walgreen's, Grocery
82.6/56		**Scotland Rd, South St, Byfield, Newbury, W Newbury**
	Other	E: MA State Hwy Patrol
80.9/55		**Central St, Byfield, Newbury**
	Gas	E: Prime Energy
	Food	E: Village Diner
(79)		**Weigh Station (Both dir)**
77/54		**MA 133, Main St, W - Georgetown, E - Rowley (SB)**
77.1/54A		**MA 133, Main St, E - Rowley (NB)**
77.3/54B		**MA 133W, to Georgetown (NB)**

◈= Regular Gas Stations with Diesel ▲ = RV Friendly Locations ♥ = Pet Friendly Locations
Red print shows large vehicle parking / access on site or nearby Brown Print = Campgrounds / RV PARKS

EXIT	MASSACHUSETTS
75.4/53	**MA 97, Boxford, Topsfield**
72.9/52	**Topsfield Rd, Boxford, Topsfield**
71.2/51	**Endicott Rd, Topsham, Middleton**
68.6/50	**US 1, Topsfield, to MA 62, Danvers**
Gas	E: Exxon, Mobil
Food	W: Quiznos, Subway, Supino's Italian
Lodg	W: Sheraton
Other	E: Beverly Muni Airport✈ W: ATMs, CVS, Staples
67.9/49	**MA 62, Danvers, Middletown (NB)**
66.5/48	**Centre St, Danvers (SB)**
Food	W: Italian Rest
Lodg	W: Comfort Inn, Extended Stay America, Village Green
66.3/47AB	**MA 114, S - Peabody, N - Middleton (NB)**
Gas	E: Exxon◈, Shell, Sunoco
Food	E: Friendly's, Papa Gino's W: Chili's, McDonald's
Lodg	W: Motel 6♥, Residence Inn
Other	E: ATMs, Lowe's, **Walmart** W: Auto Dealers, Home Depot
65.1/46	**US 1S, Boston**
Gas	W: Gulf, Shell, Sunoco
Food	W: Burger King, Seawitch Seafood
Lodg	W: Mario's Motor Inn, Sir John Motel
65/45	**MA 128N, Gloucester, Peabody**
65/44AB	**US 1, MA 129, Peabody, Boston, Everett**
FStop	W: Best Auto Truck Stop
Gas	E: Shell W: Shell
Food	W: Rest/Best ATS, Bickford's Family Rest, Carrabba's, Wendy's
Lodg	W: Holiday Inn
Med	E: + Hospital
Other	E: MA State Hwy Patrol Post
63/43	**Walnut St, Lynnfield, Saugus**
62/42	**Salem St, Audubon Rd, Wakefield**
Gas	E: Mobil, Sunoco
Lodg	W: Sheraton
60/41	**Main St, Vernon St, Lynnfield, Wakefield**
59/40	**MA 129, Wakefield, N Reading**
Gas	E: Exxon
Other	W: Camp Curtis Guild Natl Guard Res
58/39	**North Ave, Wakefield, Reading**
Gas	E: Exxon W: Shell
Lodg	E: Best Western
Med	E: + Hospital
57/38AB	**MA 28, Main St, Reading**
Gas	E: Gulf, Shell, Hess◈ W: Exxon, Mobil, Shell
Food	E: Baja Fresh, Bickford's Family Rest, Dunkin Donuts, Ground Round, 99 Rest, Subway W: McDonald's
Med	E: + Hospital
Other	E: CVS, Grocery
(56/37AB)	**Jct I-93, S - Boston, N - Manchester**
55/36	**Washington St, Woburn, Winchester**
Gas	E: Getty W: Mobil, Shell
Food	E: Dunkin Donuts, Far East, Nick's Oasis W: D'Angelo's, McDonald's, 99 Rest
Lodg	E: Crowne Plaza W: Comfort Inn, Fairfield Inn, Hampton Inn, Red Roof Inn♥
Other	E: Auto Dealers, BJ's, Staples, W: ATMs, CVS, Lowe's, Hogan Tire, Mall, Office Depot, US Post Office
54/35	**MA 38, Main St, Wilmington, Woburn**
FStop	W: Jimmy's Garage/Mobil
Food	W: Baldwin's, Applebee's
Lodg	E: Ramada W: Sierra Suites
Other	W: ATMs, Grocery
53/34	**Winn St, Burlington, Woburn**
52/33AB	**US 3S, MA 3A N, Cambridge St, Winchester, Burlington**
Gas	W: Citgo, Hess
Food	E: Chuck E Cheese Pizza, Papa Razzi's, Outback Steakhouse, Bickford's Family Rest
Lodg	W: Marriott
Med	W: + Hospital
Other	E: CVS
51/32BA	**Middlesex Tpk, to US 3, Burlington, Arlington**
Gas	E: Mobil, Shell
Food	E: Burger King, Charlie's, McDonald's W: Boston Market, Chili's, Romano Macaroni Grill
Lodg	E: Sheraton, Staybridge Suites W: Howard Johnson, Homestead Village
Med	W: + Hospital
Other	W: Mall, ATMs, Staples
32A	**US 3N, Lowell, Nashua, NH (SB)**
32B	**Middlesex Tunrpike (NB)**
48/31AB	**MA 4, MA 225, Hanscom AFB, Lexington, Carlisle, Bedford**
Gas	E: Mobil, Shell W: Shell, Exxon
Food	E: Starbucks W: McDonald's
Lodg	W: Holiday Inn Express, Quality Inn
Other	W: Hanscom Field, Hanscom AFB
47/30AB	**MA 2A, Concord, E Lexington**
Gas	E: Shell
Lodg	W: Sheraton
Other	W: Minute Man Nat'l Historic Park, Hanscom AFB
(46.5)	**Service Area (NB)**
FStop	Mobil
Food	McDonald's
46/29AB	**MA 2E, Cambridge Tpk, Lexington**
45/28AB	**Trapelo Rd, Belmont, Lincoln**
Gas	E: Exxon◈, Mobil◈, Shell
Food	E: Burger King, Friendly's, McDonald's
44/27AB	**Totten Pond Rd, Winter St, Waltham**
Gas	E: Shell
Food	E: Best Western, Home Suites Hotel, Hilton Garden Inn
Lodg	E: Best Western, Courtyard, Hometree Suites, Homestead Studio, Sheraton W: Doubletree, Marriott
Other	W: Costco, Home Depot
43/26	**US 20, Weston St, Boston Post Rd, to MA 117, Waltham, Weston**
Gas	E: Sunoco W: Mobil
Med	E: + Hospital
(42/25)	**Jct I-90, MA Tpk/TOLL**
41/24	**MA 30, South Ave, Weston, Newton, Wayland, Waltham**
Gas	E: Mobil
Lodg	E: Marriott
Med	E: + Hospital
40/23	**to Recreation Rd, to MA Tpk, to MA 30 (NB)**
39/22AB	**Grove St**
Lodg	E: Holiday Inn Express
Other	E: Greyhound
(38.5)	**Service Area (SB)**
FStop	Mobil
Food	McDonald's
38/21AB	**MA 16, Washington St, Newton, Lower Falls, Wellesley**
Med	E: + Hospital
36/20AB	**MA 9, Worcester St, Wellesley Hills Boston, Brookline**
35/19AB	**Highland Ave, Newton, Highlands**
Gas	E: Gulf, Hess W: Shell
Food	E: Ground Round, McDonald's, Mighty Subs W: IHOP, Bickford's Family Rest
Lodg	E: Sheraton
Other	E: PetCo♥, Staples
34/18	**Great Plain Ave, W Roxbury**
(33.5)	**Parking Area (SB)**
33/17	**MA 135, Needham, Wellesley**
31/16AB	**MA 109, High St, Dedham, Westwood**
29/15AB	**US 1, to MA 128, MA 1A, Dedham**
Gas	W: Shell◈
Food	E: Bickford's Family Rest, Chili's, Joe's Grill, Panera Bread, TGI Friday W: Dunkin Donuts, Burger King
Lodg	E: Comfort Inn, Holiday Inn, Residence Inn W: Budget Inn
Med	E: + Walk-In Medical Center
Other	E: ATMs, BJ's, Best Buy, Costco, Grocery
28/14	**East St, Canton St, Westwood**
Lodg	E: Hilton
TServ	E: Cummins, Kenworth
(27)	**Rest Area (SB)** **(RR, Phone, Picnic)**
26.5/13	**Railway Station, University Ave**
Other	W: Amtrak
(26/12)	**Jct I-93N, Braintree, Boston**
NOTE:	**Begin SB/End NB Motorist Call Boxes**
23/11AB	**Neponset St, Norwood, Canton**
Gas	E: Citgo, Sunoco W: Gulf
Med	W: + Hospital
Other	W: Norwood Memorial Airport✈
20/10	**Coney St, to US 1, to MA 27, Sharon, Walpole** **(fr SB, diff reaccess/Serv W on US 1)**
Gas	W: Shell

◈ = Regular Gas Stations with Diesel ▲ = RV Friendly Locations ♥ = Pet Friendly Locations
Red print shows large vehicle parking / access on site or nearby Brown Print = Campgrounds / RV PARKS

EXIT MA / RI

Food W: IHOP, McDonald's, Pizza Hut, Taco Bell, 99 Rest
Lodg W: Best Western
Other W: Mall, ATMs, Auto Services, CVS, Home Depot, Staples, Walgreen's

19/9 US 1, to MA 27, Walpole (SB to Gillette Stadium)
Gas W: Exxon, Mobil, Shell
Food W: Bickford's Family Rest
Lodg W: Holiday Inn Express
Other W: ATMs, Grocery, Walmart

16.6/8 S Main S, Sharon, Mechanic St, Foxboro

13/7AB MA 140, S-Mansfield, N-Foxboro
Gas W: Mobil
Food E: 99 Rest, Piccadilly
Lodg E: Comfort Inn, Courtyard, Holiday Inn, Red Roof Inn♥, Residence Inn
Other E: Foxborough Business Center

(11/6AB) Jct I-495, N to Worcester, S to Cape Cod
Other N: to Gillette Stadium, to US 1 Normandy Farms Family Camping Resort▲, to Circle CG Farm Campground▲

(10) MA Welcome Center (NB)
(RR, Phone, Picnic, Vend, Info)
(Parking Area) (SB)

6.9/5 to MA 152, Attleboro
Gas W: Gulf◈
Food W: Wendy's
Med E: + Hospital
Other W: Laundromat, Grocery, Pharmacy

(5.9/4) Jct I-295, to Woonsocket, Warwick

4.2/3AB MA 123, Norton, Attleboro
Gas E: Shell◈
Med E: + Hospital

(3) Weigh Station (Both dir)
Picnic Area (NB)

1.5/2B US 1A N, to US 1, Attleboro

1/2A US 1A S, Pawtucket RI (NB), Newport Ave (SB), Attleboro
Gas E: Mobil, Shell, Sunoco
Food E: McDonald's, Olive Garden
Other E: ATMs, Grocery, Home Depot

.2/1 US 1 S, Broadway, Pawtucket (SB)
Gas W: Gulf, Sunoco
Food W: Burger King, Taco Bell
Lodg E: Days Inn

EASTERN TIME ZONE

⬆ MASSACHUSETTS
⬇ RHODE ISLAND

NOTE: MM 43: Massachusetts State Line

EASTERN TIME ZONE

NOTE: Exits list Mile Marker / Exit #.

43/30 East St, Central Falls, Roosevelt Ave, Pawtucket
Food E: Dunkin Donuts, Subway
Other E: Greyhound

43/29 US 1, Broadway, Cottage St (NB), US 1, to RI 114, Pawtucket (SB)

Personal Notes

EXIT RHODE ISLAND

42/28 RI 114, Water St, School St (NB)
Gas E: Sunoco

42/27 Pearl St, Garden St, to US 1, Downtown Pawtucket (NB), US 1, George St, to RI 15, Providence, Pawtucket (SB)
Gas W: Shell, Sunoco◈
Food W: Burger King, Dunkin Donuts
Lodg W: Comfort Inn
Med W: + Hospital

41/26 RI 122, Main St, Pawtucket, Downtown (NB)

40/25AB RI 126, Foch St, to US 1,N Main St, Smithfield Ave (NB)

40/25 RI 126, Foch St, to US 1,N Main St, Smithfield Ave, Providence (SB)
Gas E: Hess, Shell
W: Gulf◈ Valero
Med E: + Hospital
Other E: ATMs, CVS, Grocery

39/24 Branch Ave, Providence
Gas W: Mobil

39/23 RI 146, US 44, Woonsocket, Downtown, State Offices (NB), Charles St, to RI 146N (SB)

38/22ABC US 6W, RI 10, Downtown Providence to Hartford, CT
22A: **US 6W, ME 10, Hartford Ct**
Univ of RI-Providence, Amtrak
22C: Providence Place Civic Center, Mall

37/21 Washington St, Franklin St, Broadway (NB), Atwells Ave (SB)

EXIT RHODE ISLAND

Lodg E: Holiday Inn
Other E: Civic/Convention Center
W: Auto & Tire Services

(37/20) Jct I-195, US 6E, East Providence, Cape Cod

36/19 Eddy St, to RI 1A, Allens Ave (SB)
Med W: + Hospital

35/18 US 1A, Thurbers Ave, Providence
Gas W: Shell
Food W: Burger King
Med W: + Hospital

34/17 US 1, Elmwood Ave (NB)
Other E: Roger Williams Park & Zoo

34/16 RI 10, to US 1, to RI 2/12, Cranston
Other E: Roger Williams Park & Zoo

32/15 Jefferson Blvd, Warwick, Cranston
Gas E: Getty◈, Mobil
Food E: Bickford's Family Rest, Bugaboo Creek Steakhouse, Dunkin Donuts, Shogun Steak & Seafood
Lodg E: Courtyard, La Quinta Inn♥, Motel 6♥
Other E: U-Haul
W: Coastal International Trucks, Colony RV Dealer, Budget RAC

31/14AB RI 37, to RI 2, Cranston, to US 1, Jefferson Blvd, Warwick
Gas W: Shell, Sunoco
Food W: Burger King
Other E: Lincoln Ave Auto & Truck Service

30/13 Airport Connector Rd, to US 1, to TF Green State Airport, Warwick
Gas E: Exxon, Mobil
Food E: Capelli's Italian Rest, Dave's Bar & Grill, Great House Chinese, Legal Seafood
Lodg E: Best Western, Comfort Inn, Hampton Inn, Hilton Garden Inn, Holiday Inn Express Homewood Suites♥, Homestead Hotel♥, Radisson, Residence Inn♥, Sheraton
Other E: TF Green Int'l Airport✈

(28/12B) Jct I-295N, RI 113, to RI 2 (SB)

28/12A RI 113E, East Ave, Warwick (SB)

28/12 RI 113E, East Ave, to RI 5, Warwick (NB)
Gas E: Sunoco, Shell◈
Food E: Ocean Express Seafood, Remington's
Lodg E: Crowne Plaza
Other E: ATMs, Lowe's
W: ATMs, Walmart, Warwick Mall

28/11 I-295N, Woonsocket (NB, Left exit)

10AB Rte 117, E to Warwick, W to West Warwick (SB)

27/10 RI 117, Centerville Rd, Warwick (NB)
Med W: + Hospital
Other E: Park & Ride

25/9 RI 4S, E Greenwich, N Kingstown (SB, Left exit)

8AB RI 2, Quaker Lane, S to RI 4, E Greenwich, N to West Warwick (NB)

8 RI 2, Quaker Ln, W Warwick (SB)
Gas E: Shell◈
W: Sunoco◈
Food E: Dunkin Donuts, McDonald's, Outback Steakhouse, Ruby Tuesday
W: 99 Rest, Applebee's, Denny's, Papa Gino's, TGI Friday, Wendy's

◈= Regular Gas Stations with Diesel ▲ = RV Friendly Locations ♥= Pet Friendly Locations
Red print shows large vehicle parking / access on site or nearby Brown Print = Campgrounds / RV PARKS

EXIT — RHODE ISLAND

Lodg E: Extended Stay America
W: Comfort Suites, Marriott, Open Gate Motel, Springhill Suites

Med W: + Hospital

Other E: Walgreen's
W: Auto Dealers, ATMs, Best Buy, Mall, Grocery, Lowe's, Sam's Club, **Arlington RV SuperCenter/RVDump**, **Camping▲**

21/7 **New London Tpike, W Greenwich, Coventry, West Warwick**

Gas E: Ray's Service/Mobil◈

Food W: Applebee's, Cracker Barrel, Denny's, Quiznos, Wendy's

Lodg W: Hampton Inn, Wingate Inn

Other E: Auto repairs/Mobil, ATMs, BJ's Club, Home Depot, **Walmart sc**

20/6A **Hopkins Hill Rd**

Other W: Park & Ride, Technology Park

18/6 **RI 3, Nooseneck Hill Rd, Division Rd W Greenwich, to Coventry**

Gas E: Shell◈, Sunoco◈

Food W: Dunkin Donuts, Mark's Grill, Pizza, Tim Horton's

Lodg E: Best Western, Super 8

15/5AB **RI 102, Victory Hwy, W Greenwich, S to N Kingstown, Exeter, N-Foster, West Greenwich**

TStop W: PTP/RI's Only 24 Hr A/T Plaza (Scales)

Food W: FastFood/RI's ATP

Lodg W: Classic Motor Lodge

TServ W: RI's ATP

Other E: **Wawaloam Campground▲**
W: Laundry/CB/WiFi/RI ATP, **to appr 7mi Oak Embers Campground▲**

(10) **Weigh Station**
Picnic Area (SB)

9/4 **RI 3, to RI 165, Wyoming, Arcadia, Exeter (NB)**

Other W: **Arcadia State Park, to appr 8mi Oak Embers Campground▲**

7/3AB **RI 138, E-Kingstown Rd, to US 1, Kingston, Newport, W-to RI 3, Wyoming, Hope Valley**

Gas W: Exxon, Hess, Mobil, Valero

Food E: McDonald's, Tim Horton's, Wendy's
W: Bickford's, Pizza

Lodg E: Cookie Jar B&B
W: Stagecoach House, Sun Valley Inn

Other E: ATMs, Grocery, Pharmacy, Richmond Airport✈, Univ of RI
W: ATMs, CVS, **RI State Hwy Patrol, Whispering Pines Campground▲**

(6) **RI Welcome Center (NB)**
(RR, Phone, Picnic, Vend, Info)
(Closed daily 2a-5a)

4/2 **Woodville Alton Rd, Hope Valley, Hopkinton, Alton**

Other W: **Whispering Pines Campground▲**

1/1 **RI 3, Main St, Ashaway, Hopkinton, Westerly**

Med E: + Hospital

Other E: **Holly Tree Camper Park▲ , Frontier Family Camper Park▲ , to Misquamicut State Park, Burlingame State Park, to Timber Creek RV Resort▲**

NOTE: MM 0: Begin NB / End SB Call Boxes Listings show Mile Marker/ Exit #.

ⓘ RHODE ISLAND

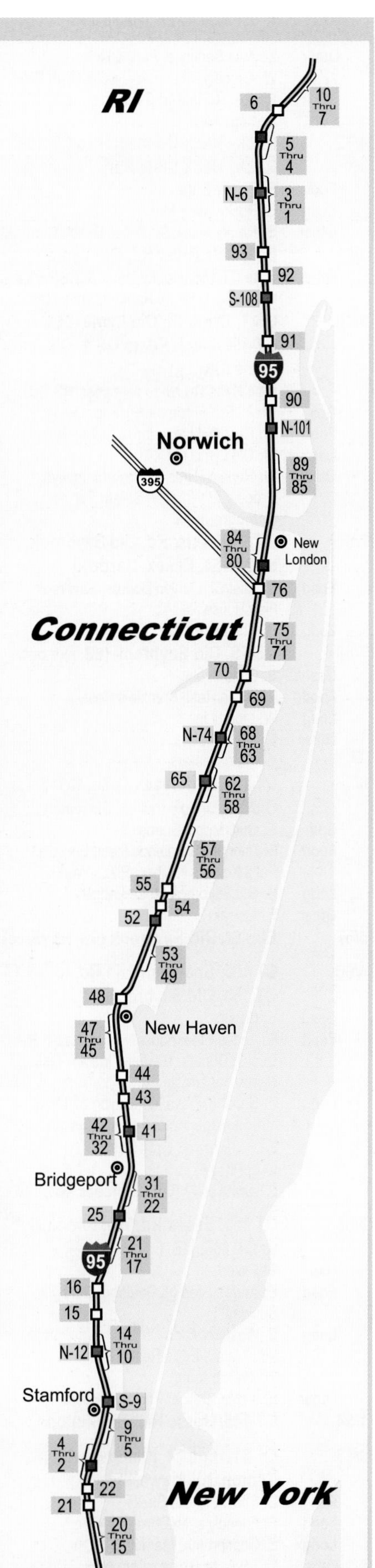

EXIT — CONNECTICUT

ⓘ CONNECTICUT

NOTE: MM 112: Rhode Island State line

EASTERN TIME ZONE

NOTE: Exits show Mile Marker / Exit #

111/93 **CT 216, Clark Falls Rd, Clark Falls, N Stonington, to CT 184, Ashaway, RI**

FStop W: Spicer Plus Food & Fuel/Mobil

TStop W: R&R Truck Stop/Republic Auto & Truck Plaza (Scales)

Gas E: Shell

Food W: Rest/R&R TS, McDonald's, Tim Horton's

Lodg W: Budget Inn, Stardust Motel

TServ W: Republic ATP

Other E: **to Frontier Family Camper Park▲**

109/92 **CT 49, Pendleton Hill Rd, to CT 2, N Stonington, Pawcatuck (SB)**

Other E: **to Worden Pond Family Campground▲**
W: **Highland Orchards Resort Park/ RV Dealer▲**

(108) **CT Welcome Center (SB)**
(RR, Phone, Picnic, Vend, Info, RVDump)

108/92 **CT 49, Pendleton Hill Rd, to CT 2, Pawcatuck, N Stonington (NB)**

Food W: Rest/Cedar Park, Rest/Randall's

Lodg W: Cedar Park Inn, Randall's

104/91 **Taugwonk Rd, CT 234, Pequot Tr, Stonington, Borough**

Med E: + Hospital

102/90 **CT 27, Whitehall Ave, Mystic**

Gas E: Mobil
W: Mobil, Shell◈

Food E: Bickford's Family Rest, Friendly's, McDonald's, Quiznos, Starbucks
W: Ashby's, Ground Round, Pizza Grille, Subway/DunkinDonuts/Shell

Lodg E: AmeriSuites, Econo Lodge, Howard Johnson, Hilton, Holiday Inn
W: Best Western, Comfort Inn, Days Inn, Residence Inn

Other E: Factory Outlet Mall, Mystic Seaport, Mystic Aquarium, Cinema, Amtrak
W: Auto Dealers, **Seaport Campground▲**

(101) **Scenic Overlook (NB, NO Trucks)**

100/89 **Allyn St, Mystic St, Mystic, to US 1**

98/88 **CT 117, North Rd, Groton, Noank, Groton Point, Downtown Groton**

Lodg W: Hampton Inn, Marriott

Med S: + Emergency Medical Center

Other E: to Groton New London Airport✈, **Bluff Point State Park, Haley Farm State Park**

97/87 **CT 349, Clarence B Sharp Hwy, to US 1, Industrial Area (SB, Left exit)**

Lodg E: Econo Lodge, Quality Inn

Other E: Groton New London Airport✈

96/86 **US 1,CT 12, CT 184, Groton (NB, Left exit)**

Gas W: Hess, Shell◈

Food E: Applebee's, 99 Rest
W: Flanagan's, Dunkin Donuts, IHOP, KFC, Marcie's Pancake House/Rest, NY Family Pizza, Russell's Ribs, Rosie's Diner, Taco Bell

◈= Regular Gas Stations with Diesel ▲ = RV Friendly Locations ♥= Pet Friendly Locations
Red print shows large vehicle parking / access on site or nearby Brown Print = Campgrounds / RV PARKS

EXIT — CONNECTICUT

Lodg E: Hampton Inn, Knights Inn, Quality Inn
W: Best Way Inn, Best Western, Clarion, Groton Inn, Super 8
Other W: ATMs, Grocery, **Walmart**, New London Naval Sub Base, USS Nautilus, WW II Sub Museum

95/85 Bridge St, to US 1N, Thames St, Downtown Groton (NB exit, NO NB reaccess)
Gas E: Quick Stop Deli
Food E: Boomer's Café, Norm's Diner
Lodg E: Quality Inn

94/84 CT 32, Downtown New London (SB)

94/83 US 1, CT 32, New London (SB), Briggs St, Huntington St, CT 32 (NB)
Other E: Ferries to Block Island, Fishers Island
W: Malls, US Coast Guard Academy

92/82A Frontage Rd, Coleman St, Briggs St, to US 1, CT 32, CT 85
Gas E: Mobil
W: Sunoco
Food E: Dunkin Donuts, Pizza Hut
W: American Steakhouse, Chili's, Golden Wok, Panda Buffet, Outback Steakhouse
Lodg W: Red Roof Inn♥
Other E: Auto Services, ATMs, Staples, Tires

92/82 CT 85, Broad St, to I-395, Waterford
Gas W: Mobil
Food E: Real Italian Pizzeria
W: Burger King, Charley's, D'Angelo's, Olive Garden, Panda Express, Ruby Tuesday, Subway, Wendy's
Lodg W: Fairfield Suites, Holiday Inn
Med E: + Hospital
Other W: ATMs, Best Buy, Crystal Mall, PetCo♥, Home Depot, Target, **Salem Farms Campground▲** ,

(90) Weigh Station (Both dir)

90/81 Cross Rd, Waterford
Gas W: BJ's
Food W: McDonald's, Rock & Roll Pizza House
Lodg W: Rodeway Inn♥
Other W: ATMs, BJ's Club, Grocery, Lowe's, **Walmart sc**

88/80 Parkway N, Oil Mill Rd (SB) (Access to Ex #81 Services)

(86/76) Jct I-395N, CT Tpk, to Norwich, Plainfield (SB, LEFT exit) I-95N, New London, Providence (SB, Right 2 lanes)
395N: Foxwood Resort & Casino, Mohegun Sun Casino

88/75 US 1, Boston Post Rd, E Lyme, Waterford, Flanders
Lodg E: Blue Anchor Motel
Med E: + Hospital

87/74 CT 161, Flanders Rd, East Lyme, Flanders, Niantic
Gas E: Citgo, Mobil, Sunoco◈, Texaco
W: Shell
Food E: Burger King, Bickford's Family Rest, Dunkin Donuts
W: Flanders Pizza, King Garden Chinese, Flanders Fish Market & Rest, Flanders House Café, McDonald's, Wendy's
Lodg E: Best Value Inn, Best Western, Days Inn, Motel 6♥, Sleep Inn

Other E: Auto Services, Park & Ride
W: Grocery, Pharmacy, **Aces High RV Park▲ , to Island Campground & Cottages▲**

84/72 Rocky Neck Connector to CT 156, Rocky Neck State Park
Food E: Pier IV Café
Lodg E: Rocky Neck Motor Inn
Other E: **Rocky Neck SP**/Public Beach/**Camp▲**

84/71 Four Mile River Rd, Old Lyme
Other E: to CT 156, **Rocky Neck State Park▲**
W: to US 1, Stone Ranch Military Res.

79/70 US 1, Lyme St, Old Lyme (SB), CT 156, Neck Rd, to US 1, Old Lyme (NB) (use Halls Rd (W) to reaccess NB/SB)
Gas W: All Pro Automotive/Irving, Shell◈
Food W: Rest/Old Lyme Inn, Chinese Rest
Lodg W: Old Lyme Inn
Other W: Repairs/Tires All Pro Automotive, Grocery, Pharmacy, **Salem Farms Campground▲**

78/69 CT 9N, Essex Rd, Old Saybrook, to CT 154, Essex, Hartford
Food E: Rest/Cl, Dunkin Donuts, Saybrook Fish House
Lodg E: Comfort Inn♥

77/68 US 1S, Old Saybrook (SB, exit only)
Gas E: Citgo, Mobil
Food E: Italian Rest, Frankie's Rest
Lodg W: Liberty Inn
Other E: Auto Dealers
W: Auto Dealers

76/67 CT 154, Middlesex Tpke, to US 1, Old Saybrook (NB ex, SB reacc)
Gas E: Gulf, Mobil, Sunoco
Food E: Andriana's Seafood Rest, Emilio's, Pat's Kountry Kitchen, Pizza Works
Lodg E: Old Saybrook Motor Lodge
Other E: Amtrak

76/67 Elm St, Old Saybrook (SB, NB reacc)

74/66 CT 166, Spencer Plain Rd, to US 1, CT 153, Old Saybrook
Gas E: Citgo◈
Food E: Angus Steakhouse, Aleia's Italian Rest, Dunkin Donuts, Gateway Indian Rest, Nishiki Japanese
Lodg E: Super 8, Days Inn, Saybrook Motor Inn, Heritage Motor Inn, Knights Inn

(74) CT Welcome Center (NB) (RR, Phone, Picnic, Vend, Info)
CT State Hwy Patrol, Phones (SB)

73/65 CT 153, Essex Rd, Westbrook, to CT 166, US 1
Gas E: Exxon
Food E: Andy's Steak & Seafood, Denny's, Subway
Lodg E: Westbrook Inn B&B, Angels Watch Inn, Waters Edge Resort & Spa
W: Welcome Inn
Other E: ATMs, Tanger Factory Outlets

71/64 CT 145, Horse Hill Rd, Clinton

69/63 CT 81, High St, Killingworth Tpk, Clinton, Killingworth
Gas E: Shell, Citgo◈, Shell◈
Food E: Friendly's, McDonald's, Wendy's
Lodg E: Comfort Inn, Marriott
Other E: CVS, to Griswold Airport✈
W: ATMs, Clinton Crossing Outlet Mall

66/62 Hammonaset Conn, Duck Hole Rd, Hammonaset State Park, Madison
Other E: **State Park**/Public Beach/**Camping▲** , Griswold Airport✈
W: **Riverdale Farm Campground▲ , Keith's RV & Trailer Repair**

(65) Madison Service Area (Both dir)
FStop Mobil
Food McDonald's

65/61 CT 79, Durham Rd, Madison (Gas/Food/Lodg E to US 1)

64/60 Mungertown Rd, Madison (SB, No reacc) (Food & Lodg E to US 1)

61/59 Goose Lane, to US 1, Guilford
Gas E: Mobil, Shell◈
Food E: Dunkin Donuts, Ichiban Japanese Steakhouse, McDonald's, Rio Grande Steakhouse, Wendy's
Lodg E: Comfort Inn, Tower Inn

60/58 CT 77, Church St, Guilford
Gas E: Getty, Mobil
Food E: Friendly's, Subway

59/57 US 1, Boston Post Rd ,Guilford
Food E: Quattro's Italian
W: Anthony's, Roadhouse Grille
Lodg E: Frenchmans Reef Beach
W: Guilford Suites Hotel

56/56 Leetes Island Rd, Branford, to US 1, CT 139, Stony Creek, New Haven
FStop W: Leetes Island Fuel/Berkshire Farms
TStop W: Travel Center of America #171 (Scales)
Gas W: Mobil
Food W: PizzaHut/Popeyes/Subway/TA TC, Dunkin Donuts, Friendly's, USS Chowder Pot, Starbucks,
Lodg E: Advanced Motel
W: Ramada Inn
TServ W: Freightliner of Southern CT
Med W: **+ Coastline Medical Emer Center**
Other E: ATMs, Grocery, Pharmacy
W: Laundry/WiFi/TA TC, ATMs

55/55 US 1, E Main St, Branford
Gas E: Mobil, Sunoco, Thornton's
W: Citgo, Exxon◈, Mobil◈
Food E: Dunkin Donuts, Lynn's Deli, Marco Pizzeria, Shoreline Buffet, McDonald's
W: Gourmet Wok, Parthenon Diner, Margarita's Mexican, Salerno Pizza
Lodg E: Economy Inn, Holiday Inn Express, Motel 6♥
W: Days Inn♥
Other E: Walgreen's

53/54 Cedar St, CT 740, Branford
Gas E: A&M Service Stn, Mobil
Food E: Branford Townhouse Diner & Rest, Fortune Village Chinese, La Luna
W: Lion City Chinese
Lodg E: By the Sea Inn & Spa
Other E: Auto Dealers, Staples

(52) Branford Service Area (Both dir)
FStop Mobil
Food McDonald's
Other ATM, Gift Shop

52/53 Branford Connector to US 1, CT 142, CT 146, Short Beach (NB, NO reaccess

50/52 CT 100, N High St, East Haven (SB)
Gas E: Citgo
Food E: Subway
Other E: to Tweed New Haven Airport✈

◈= Regular Gas Stations with Diesel ▲ = RV Friendly Locations ♥= Pet Friendly Locations
Red print shows large vehicle parking / access on site or nearby Brown Print = Campgrounds / RV PARKS

EXIT		CONNECTICUT
50/51		**US 1, Frontage Rd, East Haven**
	Gas	**E:** Hess, Sunoco **W:** Gulf, Mobil, Shell
	Food	**E:** Boston Market, Chili's, Friendly's, McDonald's **W:** Dunkin Donuts, Wendy's
	Lodg	**E:** Quality Inn♥
	Other	**E:** Auto Services, **to** Tweed New Haven Airport✈ **W:** ATMs, Radio Shack
49/50		**Woodward Ave, Lighthouse Pt (NB)**
	Other	**E: to** Tweed New Haven Airport✈, US Naval/Marine Reserve, Ft Nathan Hale
49/49		**Stiles St, to US 1, New Haven (NB)**
(47/48)		**Jct I-91N, to Hartford, Yale Univ (SB exit only, NB left exit)**
47/47		**CT 34, Downtown New Haven (fr NB, Left exit)**
47/46		**Long Wharf Dr, Sargent Dr**
	Gas	**E:** Shell **W:** Mobil◈
	Food	**E:** Rusty Scrupper Rest **W:** Brazi's Rest
	Lodg	**W:** Fairfield Inn, Residence Inn
	Med	**E:** + Hospital
	Other	**W:** Amtrak, Greyhound Station
46/45		**CT 10, Grasso Blvd (SB)**
46/44		**CT 122, Kimberley Ave, to CT 10**
45/43		**Campbell Ave, Downtown (NB, NO Trucks)** **CT 122, First Ave (SB)**
	Med	**W:** + Veterans Hospital
	Other	**W:** Univ of New Haven
44/42		**CT 162, Saw Mill Rd, West Haven**
	Gas	**E:** Mobil **W:** Shell, 7-11
	Food	**E:** Billy's Café, Pizza Hut, Great Wall **W:** American Steakhouse, El Gallo, D'Angelo's, Dunkin Donuts, Friendly
	Lodge	**E:** Econo Lodge **W:** Best Western
	Other	**W:** ATMs, Staples
42/41		**Marsh Hill Rd, Orange**
	Food	**W:** Outback Steakhouse
	Lodg	**W:** Courtyard
(41)		**Milford Service Area (Both dir)**
	FStop	Exxon #13987/#13986
	Food	McDonald's
	Other	ATM, Gift Shop
41/40		**Old Gate Lane (NB), Woodmont Rd (SB), to US 1, Milford**
	TStop	**E:** Secondi Truck Stop/Citgo (Scales), Pilot Travel Center #255 (Scales)
	Gas	**E:** Shell **W:** Mobil
	Food	**E:** Wendy's/Pilot TC, **Cracker Barrel**, Dunkin Donuts, D'Angelo's, Duchess Family Rest **W: to US 1:** Chili's, Boston Market, Taco Bell
	Lodg	**E:** Best Value Inn, Comfort Inn, Milford Inn, Mayflower Motel
	TWash	**E:** Blue Beacon TW/Pilot TC
	TServ	**E:** Mayflower Kenworth
	Other	**E:** Laundry/WiFi/Pilot TC, Laundry/ Secondi TS, ATMs,

Personal Notes

EXIT		CONNECTICUT
39AB		**US 1, Boston Post Rd, Milford**
	Gas	**E:** Gulf◈ **W:** Mobil
	Food	**E:** Athenian Diner, Friendly's, Hooters, Pizzeria Uno **W:** Burger King, Chili's, Dunkin Donuts, KFC, Little Caesars, Miami Subs, Panda Express, McDonald's, Steak & Sword Rest, Subway, Taco Bell, Wendy's
	Lodg	**E:** CT Tpk Motel, Howard Johnson, Super 8
	Med	**E:** + Milford Hospital
	Other	**E:** Tires, Walgreen's **W:** Auto Dealers, ATMs, Grocery, Mall, Pharmacy, US Post Office
39/38		**Milford Pkwy, to Merritt Pkwy, CT 15, Wilbur Cross Pkwy (NO Comm'l Vehicles/Trucks)**
38/37		**High St, Milford (NB, no NB reacc)**
37/36		**Plains Rd, Milford, Stratford**
	Gas	**E:** Exxon
	Lodg	**E:** Hampton Inn
	Med	**E:** + Hospital
36/35		**School House Rd, Bic Dr, Milford to US 1**
	Gas	**E:** Citgo
	Food	**E:** Subway, Wendy's
	Lodg	**E:** Fairfield Inn **W:** Marriott, Red Roof Inn♥, Springhill Suites
	Other	**E:** Auto Dealers
35/34		**US 1, Bridgeport Ave, Milford**
	Gas	**E:** Gulf, Shell

EXIT		CONNECTICUT
	Food	**E:** Belair Seafood, Denny's, Gourmet Buffet, Dunkin Donuts, McDonald's. Taco Bell
	Lodg	**E:** Devon Motel, Liberty Rock Motel
34/33		**Ferry Blvd, to US 1, CT 110, Devon Stratford (NB, no NB reaccess)**
	Gas	**E:** Shell, Sunoco
	Food	**W:** Ponderosa, Villa Pizza
	Other	**E:** Laundromat, Staples, Walgreen's **W:** ATMs, Home Depot, **Walmart sc**
33/32		**W Broad St, Stratford**
	Gas	**E:** BP **W:** Gulf
	Food	**W:** Dunkin Donuts, Italian Rest
32/31		**Honeyspot Rd (NB), South Ave (SB)**
	Gas	**E:** Gulf◈ **W:** Citgo◈
	Food	**E:** New Honeyspot Diner
	Lodg	**E:** Camelot Motel, Honeyspot Motor Lodge
31/30		**CT 113, Lordship Blvd (NB), Surf Ave (SB), Stratford**
	Gas	**E:** Shell **W:** Sunoco
	Lodg	**E:** Ramada Inn
	Other	**E: to** Sikorsky Memorial Airport✈
30/29		**CT 130, CT Ave, Stratford Ave, Seaview Ave, Bridgeport**
	Med	**W:** + Hospital
30/28		**Ann St, Pembroke St, Main St, Waterview Ave, Bridgeport**
	Gas	**E:** BP
	Food	**E:** La Familia Rest
29/27		**Lafayette Blvd, Downtown (SB)**
	Other	**W:** Greyhound Station, Amtrak
29/27A		**CT 25, CT 8, Trumbull, Waterbury**
27		**Frontage Rd, Lafayette St (NB)**
	Other	**E:** Port Jefferson Ferry **W:** Amtrak, Greyhound
28/26		**Wordin Ave, Bridgeport**
28/25		**CT 130, Fairfield Ave (SB), State St, Commerce Dr (NB)**
	Gas	**E:** Getty **W:** Gulf
27/24		**Chambers St, to US 1, (SB), Kings Hwy (NB), Black Rock Turnpike**
	Food	**E:** Black Rock Oyster Bar & Grill, Antonio's Rest, D'Angelo Deli
	Lodg	**E:** Bridgeport Motor Inn
26/23		**US 1, Kings Hwy, Fairfield**
	Gas	**E:** Sunoco◈
	Other	**E:** Home Depot
25/22		**CT 135, N Benson Rd (SB)**
(25)		**Fairfield Service Area (Both dir)**
	FStop	**NB/SB:** Mobil
	Food	**NB:** McDonald's **SB:** McDonald's, Hebrew Nat'l Hot Dogs, Hot Subs
	Other	ATM, Gift Shop
24/21		**Mill Plain Rd, Fairfield**
	Gas	**E:** Mobil
24/20		**Bronson Rd, Southport (SB, NB reacc)**
23/19		**US 1, Post Rd, Southport (SB) Center St, Old Post Rd (NB)**
	Gas	**W:** Shell

◈= Regular Gas Stations with Diesel ▲ = RV Friendly Locations ♥= Pet Friendly Locations
Red print shows large vehicle parking / access on site or nearby **Brown Print = Campgrounds / RV PARKS**

EXIT	CONNECTICUT
21/18	**Sherwood Island State Park**
Gas	W: Mobil
Other	E: Sherwood Island State Park, Beach
	W: CT State Hwy Patrol Post
18/17	**CT 33, CT 136, Saugatuck Ave, Westport**
17/16	**East Ave, Norwalk**
Gas	E: Mobil, Shell◈
Food	E: East Side Cafe, Penny's Diner
16/15	**US 7, Norwalk, Danbury**
Gas	E: Shell, Sunoco
	W: Getty
Med	W: + Norwalk Hospital
Other	W: Norwalk Police Dept
15/14	**Fairfield Ave, Norwalk (NB)**
	US 1, Connecticut Ave, Norwalk (SB)
Gas	W: BP◈, Coastal
Food	W: China King, Pizza Hut, Silver Star Diner
Med	W: + Norwalk Hospital
Other	E: CT State Hwy Patrol
	W: ATMs, Barnes & Noble, Best Buy, Firestone, Grocery, Laundromat, PetSmart♥, Sports Authority
13/13	**US 1, Boston Post Rd, Darien**
Gas	W: Mobil, Shell
Food	W: Burger King, Dunkin Donuts, Driftwood Diner, IHOP, McDonald's, Pasta Fare, Wendy's
Lodg	W: Doubletree Hotel, Marriott
Other	W: ATMs, Costco, Grocery, Home Depot, Pharmacy, Staples, Tires, Trader Joe's, **Walmart**, Norwalk Comm College
(12)	**Darien Service Area (NB)**
FStop	Mobil
Food	McDonald's, Hebrew Nat'l, Hot Subs
Other	ATM, Gift Shop
	CT Welcome Center
12/12	**CT 136, Tokeneke Rd, Rowayton (NB)**
11/11	**US 1, Boston Post Rd, Darien**
Gas	E: BP
	W: Exxon
Food	W: Rest/Howard Johnson
Lodg	W: Howard Johnson
10/10	**Noroton Ave, Darien**
Gas	W: Getty, Mobil, Shell
(9)	**Darien Service Area (SB)**
FStop	Mobil
Food	McDonald's
Other	ATM, Gift Shop
9/9	**US 1, CT 106, Seaside Ave, Stamford, Glenbrook**
Gas	W: Gulf
Food	W: McDonald's, Stamford Pizza
Lodg	E: Stamford Motor Inn
Other	W: Vet
8/8	**Elm St (SB), Atlantic St (NB)**
Gas	W: Exxon, Sunoco
Food	E: Mandarin Rest, Sam's Place
Lodg	W: Budget Inn, Holiday Inn
Other	E: Greyhound, Amtrak, U-Haul
7/7	**CT 137N, Greenwich Ave (NB), Atlantic St (SB), Stamford**
Lodg	E: Westin Hotel
7/6	**Harvard Ave (NB), West Ave (SB)**
Gas	E: Exxon
	W: Shell
Food	E: Vincent's Steakhouse
	W: Boston Market, Subway, Taco Bell

EXIT	CT / NY
Med	W: + Hospital
Other	W: Firestone
6/5	**US 1, E Putnam Ave, Riverside**
Gas	W: Shell
Food	W: Hunan Café, McDonald's, Taco Bell
Lodg	W: Howard Johnson, Hyatt
Other	W: Grocery, Staples, Pharmacy, US Post Office
4/4	**Indian Field Rd, Greenwich**
3/3	**Steamboat Rd, Arch St, Greenwich**
Gas	W: Mobil, Shell
Food	E: Atlantis, Manero's
Lodg	E: Greenwich Harbor Inn
Med	W: + Hospital
Other	E: Bruce Museum
(2)	**Weigh Station (NB)**
1/2	**Delavan Ave, Byram Shore Rd, Greenwich**

NOTE: Listings show Mile Marker / Exit #.

EASTERN TIME ZONE

⬆ CONNECTICUT
⬇ NEW YORK

EASTERN TIME ZONE

EXIT	CT / NY
22	**Midland Ave, Port Chester, Rye**
Gas	W: BP, Shell
Med	W: + Hospital
Other	W: ATMs, Grocery, Home Depot, Staples
(21)	**Jct I-287W, US 1N, Tappan Zee, Port Chester, White Plains**
20	**US 1S, Rye, Port Chester (NB)**
19	**Playland Pkwy, Rye, Harrison**
18B	**Mamaroneck Ave, White Plains**
18A	**Fenimore Rd, Mamaroneck**
17	**Chatsworth Ave, Larchmont (NB)**
(7)	**New Rochelle TOLL Plaza (NB)**
16	**North Ave, Cedar St, New Rochelle (LAST exit before NB TOLL)**
Food	E: McDonald's, Taco Bell
Lodg	E: Ramada
Med	E: + Hospital
15	**US 1, New Rochelle, The Pelhams**
Gas	E: Getty, PitStop
	W: Scot
Food	E: Thruway Diner
Other	E: ATMs, CVS, Costco, Home Depot
14	**Hutchinson River Pkwy S, Whitestone Br (fr SB, NO Trucks) (SB exit, NB entr)**
13	**Conner St, Baychester Ave**
Gas	E: Gulf◈
	W: BP
Food	W: McDonald's
Lodg	E: Econo Lodge
	W: Holiday Motel
TServ	E: Frank's Truck & Auto, Mack
Other	E: Car Wash
12	**Baychester Ave (fr NB, Left exit) (NB exit, SB entr)**

EXIT	NY / NJ
11	**Bartow Ave, Co-op City Blvd**
Gas	E: Mobil, Shell
	W: BP, Shell, Sunoco
Food	E: Applebee's, Burger King, Checker's, McDonald's, Red Lobster
Other	E: ATMs, Staples
	W: ATMs, Grocery, Home Depot
10	**Gun Hill Rd (NB, Left exit, SB entr)**
9	**Hutchinson River Pkwy N**
8C	**Pelham Pkwy West**
8B	**Orchard Beach, City Island**
8A	**Westchester Ave (SB ex, NB entr)**
7C	**Country Club Rd, Pelham Bay Park (NB exit, NB entr)**
7B	**E Tremont Ave (SB ex, NB entr)**
(7A)	**Jct I-695 (SB), to I-295S, Throgs Neck Bridge (SB exit, NB entr)**
(12)	**Jct I-295S, Throgs Neck Bridge (NB exit, SB entr)**
(11)	**Jct I-278W, Bruckner Expressway, Triboro Bridge (SB exit, NB entr)**
(10)	**Jct I-678S, Bruckner Blvd, Whitestone Bridge**
5B	**Castle Hill Ave (NB exit, SB entr)**
5A/8	**White Plains Rd, Westchester Ave**
4B	**Rosedale Ave, Bronx River Pkwy**
(4A)	**Jct I-895S, Sheridan Expwy (NB exit, SB entr)**
3	**Third Ave (SB ex, NB entr)**
2B	**US 1N, Webster Ave (NB)**
2A	**Jerome Ave, to I-87**
(1C)	**Jct I-87, Deegan Expwy, Amsterdam Ave, Albany, Queens (SB)**
(3NS)	**Jct I-87, Deegan Expwy, Amsterdam Ave, Albany, Queens (NB)**
2	**Harlem River Dr, Amsterdam Ave, to FDR Dr, Manhattan (NB exit, SB entr)**
1	**US 9, NY 9A, W 178th St, W 181st St, Henry Hudson Pkwy, George Washington Bridge (TOLL)**

EASTERN TIME ZONE

⬆ NEW YORK
⬇ NEW JERSEY

EASTERN TIME ZONE

NOTE: Listings show Mile Marker / Exit #.

EXIT	NY / NJ
123/74	**Palisades Pkwy (SB)**
73AB	**NJ 67, Center Ave, Lemoine Ave**
122/72	**US 9 W, to Palisades Int'l Pkwy (SB) US 1S, US 9S, US 46, Ft Lee (NB)**
121/71	**Broad Ave, Leonia, Englewood**

◈ = Regular Gas Stations with Diesel ▲ = RV Friendly Locations ♥ = Pet Friendly Locations
Red print shows large vehicle parking / access on site or nearby Brown Print = Campgrounds / RV PARKS

EXIT	NEW JERSEY
120/70	CR 12, Degraw Ave, Teaneck
(119/69)	Jct I-80W, to Paterson (SB)
118/68	US 46, Challenger Blvd
NOTE:	I-95 runs with NJ Tpk below.
117/18	US 46E, Ft Lee, Hackensack
(115)	Vince Lombardi Service Area (NB)
FStop	Shell
Food	Bob's Big Boy, Roy Rogers
116/16E,17	NY 3, Lincoln Tunnel, Secaucus
(114)	TOLL Plaza
113/16W	NY 3, Secaucus, Rutherford
Gas	E: Hess, Shell
(112)	Alexander Hamilton Service Area (SB)
FStop	Sunoco
Food	Roy Rogers
(109/15W)	Jct I-280, Newark, Harrison
107/15E	US 1, US 9, Newark, Jersey City
(105/14)	I-78W, US 1, US 9, Holland Tunnel, Newark Airport
102/13A	Newark Airport, Elizabeth Seaport
(100/13)	Jct I-278, Elizabeth, Staten Island
96/12	Carteret, Rahway
(93)	Grover Cleveland Serv Area (NB) Thomas Edison Serv Area (SB)
FStop	Sunoco
Food	Bob's Big Boy, Roy Rogers, Starbucks, TCBY
91/11	US 9, Garden State Pkwy, Woodbury Shore Points
(88/10)	I-287, NJ 440, Metchuen, Percy Amboy, Outerbridge Crossing
83/9	US 11, US 1, NJ 18, New Brunswick, East Brunswick
Gas	E: Hess◈
Food	E: Grand Buffet, On the Border W: Denny's, Fuddruckers
Lodg	E: Days Inn, Motel 6 W: Holiday Inn Express, Sheraton
(79)	Joyce Kilmer Service Area (NB)
FStop	Sunoco
Food	Burger King, Starbucks
74/8A	Cranbury, Jamesburg
(72)	Molly Pritcher Service Area (SB)
FStop	Sunoco
Food	Bob's Big Boy, Nathan's, Roy Rogers, Starbucks, TCBY
67/8	NJ 33, Hightstown, Freehold
Gas	E: Exxon◈
Food	E: Diners
Lodg	E: Hampton Inn, Holiday Inn, Quality Inn
Other	E: Grocery Store
(60/7A)	Jct I-95/195, W-Trenton, E-Neptune
NOTE:	I-95 runs with NJ Tpk above.
NOTE:	I-95 below runs with I-195. Exit #'s follow I-195.
6	Edgebrook Rd
5AB	US 130

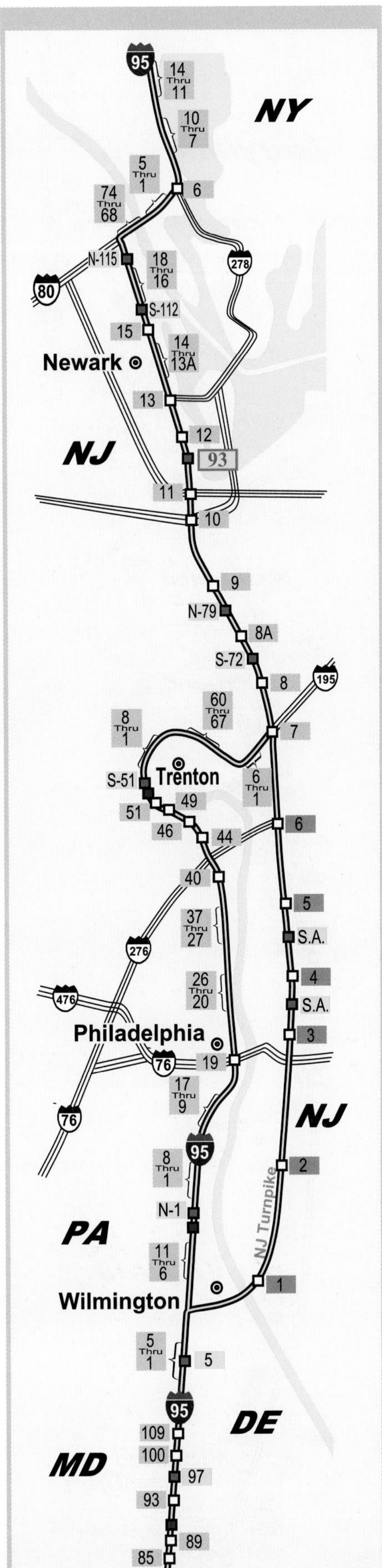

EXIT	NJ / PA
3AB	Yardville Hamilton Square Rd
2	Lakeside Blvd, Arena Dr, Broad St
1AB	US 206
NOTE:	I-95 above runs with I-195. Exit #'s follow I-195.
NOTE:	I-95 below runs with I-295. Exit #'s follow I-295.
(60B)	Jct I-95N/I-295N
61AB	Arena Dr, NJ 620
62	Old Olden Ave (SB, reacc NB only)
63AB	Nottingham Way, NJ 33
64	E State St
65AB	Sloan Ave
67AB	US 1, to Trenton, New Brunswick
Gas	E: Shell W: BP◈, Mobil◈
Food	W: Applebee's, Charlie Brown's Steakhouse, Chili's, Denny's, Hooters, Joe's Crab Shack, Olive Garden, Pizza Hut, Red Lobster, TGI Friday, Wendy's
Lodg	E: Howard Johnson W: AmeriSuites, Extended Stay, Red Roof Inn♥
Other	E: Auto Dealers W: ATMs, Best Buy, Firestone, Grocery, Home Depot, Lowe's, NTB, Staples, Walmart, Mall
NOTE:	I-95 above runs with I-295. Exit #'s follow I-295. I-95 runs for next 10 exits around Trenton.
NOTE:	I-95S continues below, Exit #'s follow I-95.
8B	Princeton, Trenton
8A	CR 546, Franklin Corner Rd, Trenton
7AB	US 206, Lawrenceville Rd, Trenton
5AB	Federal City Rd (SB)
4	NJ 31, Pennington Rd, Pennington
Gas	E: Exxon W: Mobil
3AB	CR 611, Scotch Rd, Trenton
Other	E: Mercer Co Airport✈
2	CR 579, Bear Tavern Rd, Trenton
Gas	E: Exxon, Mobil W: BP
1	NJ 29, River Rd, Trenton
Other	W: NJ State Hwy Patrol Post

EASTERN TIME ZONE

⬆ NEW JERSEY
⬇ PENNSYLVANIA

NOTE: MM 51: New Jersey State Line

EASTERN TIME ZONE

(51)	PA Welcome Center (SB) (RR, Phone, Picnic, Vend)

◈= Regular Gas Stations with Diesel ▲ = RV Friendly Locations ♥= Pet Friendly Locations
Red print shows large vehicle parking / access on site or nearby Brown Print = Campgrounds / RV PARKS

EXIT		PENNSYLVANIA
(51)		**Weigh Station (SB)**
51BA		**Taylorsville Rd, Morrisville W - New Hope, E - Yardley (SB)**
51		**Taylorsville Rd, Morrisville**
	Other	W: Washington Crossing Hist Park
49		**PA 332, Newtown Yardley Rd**
	Lodg	W: Hampton Inn
	Med	W: + Hospital
	Other	W: to Tyler State Park
46AB		**US 1, N - Morrisville, S - Langhorne**
	Other	W: to I-276, PA Tpk
44		**US 1 Bus, PA 413, Langhorne, Penndel, Levittown**
	Gas	E: Shell◈
		W: Mobil◈
	Food	E: Chuck E Cheese, Classic Steaks & Hoagies, Dunkin Donuts, Friendly's, Panera Bread, Ruby Tuesday, Wendy's
		W: Denny's, McDonald's
	Med	E: + Hospital
	Other	E: ATMs, Auto Dealers, Grocery, Lowe's, Mall, Sam's Club, Pharmacy, Harley Davidson
		W: U-Haul
40		**to PA 413, to PA Tpk, to US 13**
37		**PA 132, Bensalem, to PA Turnpike, to US 1**
	TStop	E: to State Rd S: PacPride/Bensalem Travel Plaza
	FStop	W: Jai Sunoco
	Gas	W: BP, Shell
	Food	W: Burger King, Denny's, IHOP, KFC
	Other	E: Neshaminy State Park
		W: Firestone, Radio Shack, Philadelphia Park Race Track
35		**PA 63W, Woodhaven Rd, to US 13, to US 1, to NE Philadelphia Airport**
	Gas	W: Mobil, Exxon, Sunoco
	Food	W: Arby's, KFC, McDonald's, Perkins, Pizza Hut, Taco Bell, Wendy's
	Lodg	W: Hampton Inn
	Med	W: + Hospital
	Other	E: Park & Ride, Amtrak
		W: ATMs, CompUSA, Grocery, Home Depot, NTB, Walmart, Mall
32		**Academy Rd, Linden Ave**
	Med	W: + Hospital
30		**PA 73, Cottman Ave, Rhawn St**
27		**Bridge St, Harbison Ave (SB), Lefevre St, Aramingo Ave (NB)**
	Gas	W: Getty
	Med	W: + Hospital
	Other	W: Pharmacy
26		**Aramingo Ave, Betsy Ross Bridge, to NJ 90**
25		**Allegheny Ave, Castor Ave**
	Gas	W: Getty, WaWa
	Med	W: + Hospital
23		**Girard Ave, Lehigh Ave.**
	Gas	W: Exxon, Shell
	Food	W: Pizza Hut, Dunkin Donuts, Ruby Tuesday
	Med	W: + Hospital
(22)		**to I-676, US 30, Central Philadelphia**
20		**Columbus Blvd, Washington Ave**
	Gas	E: BP, Mobil, Sunoco

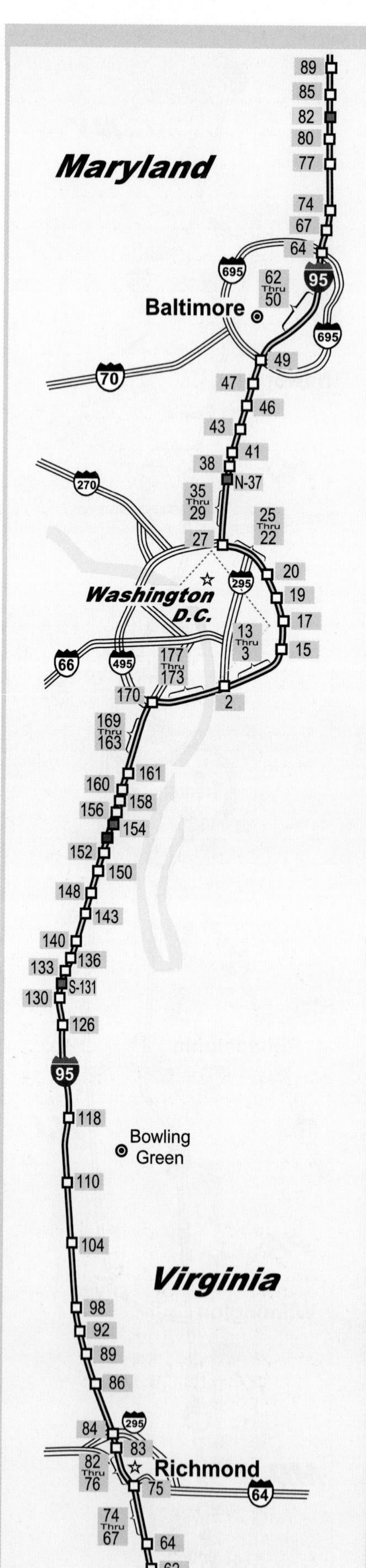

EXIT		PENNSYLVANIA
	Food	E: Burger King, Boston Market, Chuck E Cheese, Hooters, McDonald's
	Other	E: ATMs, Auto Services, Grocery, Home Depot, Staples, Target, Walmart
(19)		**Jct I-76E, Walt Whitman Bridge (All services W to Oregon Ave)**
17		**PA 611N, Broad St, Pattison Ave**
	Med	W: + Hospital
	Other	W: to Naval Shipyard, to Stadium
15		**Enterprise Ave, Island Ave (SB)**
14		**Bartram Ave, Essington Ave (SB)**
13		**PA 291W, to I-76W, Valley Forge (fr NB, Exit Only)**
	Gas	E: Exxon◈
	Lodg	E: Hilton, Residence Inn, Westin Hotel
12B		**Cargo City (SB)**
12A		**to PA 291, Phila Int'l Airport (SB)**
	Lodg	W: Courtyard, Embassy, Fairfield Inn
12		**Philadelphia Int'l Airport (NB)**
	Lodg	W: Courtyard, Embassy Suites
10		**PA 291E, Bartram Ave, Cargo City (NB)**
	Food	E: Hunan Garden
	Lodg	E: Econo Lodge, Renaissance Hotel
		W: Courtyard, Extended Stay America, Fairfield Inn, Hampton Inn, Microtel
9AB		**PA 420, Wanamaker Ave, Essington, S-Essington, N-Prospect Park**
	Gas	E: Coastal, Sunoco◈, Valero◈
	Food	E: Denny's, Shoney's
	Lodg	E: Comfort Inn, Econo Lodge, Evergreen Hotel, Holiday Inn, Motel 6♥, Red Roof Inn♥
	Other	E: John Heinz Nat'l Wildlife Refuge, Westinghouse
8		**Ridley Park, Chester Waterfront**
(7)		**Jct I-476N, to Plymouth Meeting**
6		**to PA 320, to PA 352, Edgemont Ave, Providence Ave, Chester**
	Lodg	W: Days Inn, Howard Johnson
	Med	W: + Hospital
	Other	W: ATMs, Radio Shack, Walmart, Widener Univ,
5		**Kerlin St (NB)**
4		**US 322E, to NJ, Bridgeport**
3B		**Highland Ave (SB)**
3A		**US 322W, West Chester (SB)**
	TServ	W: Watkins Motor Trucks
3		**Highland Ave (NB)**
2		**PA 452, Market St, to US 322W**
	Gas	W: Exxon, Getty
	Food	W: McDonald's
1		**Chichester Ave, Marcus Hook**
(1)		**Weigh Station (NB)**
(1)		**PA Welcome Center (NB) (RR, Phone, Picnic, Info)**

EASTERN TIME ZONE

PENNSYLVANIA

◈= Regular Gas Stations with Diesel ▲ = RV Friendly Locations ♥= Pet Friendly Locations
Red print shows large vehicle parking / access on site or nearby Brown Print = Campgrounds / RV PARKS

DELAWARE

NOTE: MM 23: Pennsylvania State Line

EASTERN TIME ZONE

NOTE: Exits show Mile Marker / Exit #.

NOTE: MM 23: Begin SB/End NB Call Boxes

(22/11) **Jct I-495S, DE 92, Naamans Rd, Claymont, Port of Wilmington**
- Gas: E: WaWa; W: Gulf◊
- Food: E: China Star, Wendy's
- Lodg: W: Holiday Inn
- Other: E: ATMs, Goodyear, Grocery; W: ATMs, Home Depot, Pharmacy, Radio Shack

21/10 **Harvey Rd, Claymont (No NB reacc)**

19/9 **DE 3, Marsh Rd, Wilmington**
- Other: E: Bellevue State Park, DE State Hwy Patrol Post

17/8AB **US 202, DE 202, Concord Pike, Wilmington, West Chester**

16/7B **DE 52, Delaware Ave, N Jackson St, W 10th St (SB)**

16/7A **DE 52, Delaware Ave, N Adams St, W 11th St (SB)**

15/7 **DE 52, Delaware Ave (NB)**
- Lodg: E: Courtyard, Sheraton

14/6 **N Jackson St, to DE 48, to DE 4 (SB), DE 4, Maryland Ave, to DE 48, MLK Blvd, Lancaster Ave (NB) Downtown Wilmington**
- Food: E: Joe's Crab Shack, Lee's Chinese
- Other: E: Greyhound, Amtrak

(12/5D) **Jct I-495, Port of Wilmington, Philadelphia**

(10.6/5C) **Jct I-295, NJ Turnpike, DE Memorial Bridge**

11/5B **DE 141N, Newport**

10/5A **DE 141, US 202S, to US 13, New Castle, Newport**
- Lodg: E: Radisson
- Other: E: New Castle Co Airport✈

8/4B **DE 58, DE 7N, Churchmans Rd, Newark, Stanton, Wilmington**
- Food: W: Applebee's, Chili's, Longhorn Steak House, Ruby Tuesday
- Lodg: W: Courtyard, Country Suites, Days Inn, Fairfield Inn, Hilton, Red Roof Inn♥
- Med: W: + Christiana Hospital
- Other: E: ATMs, Costco, Mall; W: DE Park Racetrack

7.6/4A **DE 1, DE 7S, Newark, New Castle**
- Food: E: Food Court/Mall, Ruby Tuesday
- Med: W: + Christiana Hospital
- Other: E: Christiana Mall; W: DE Park Racetrack

7/3 **DE 273, Christiana Rd, Newark, W to Newark, E to Dover (SB)**

Personal Notes

6.6/3B **DE 273, Christiana Rd, Newark, W to Newark (NB)**
- Gas: E: Exxon◊
- Food: E: Bob Evans, Chinese Rest, Wendy's; W: Denny's
- Lodg: W: Best Western, Hawthorne Suites, Residence Inn

6.3/3A **DE 273, Christiana Rd, Newark, E to Dover (NB)**
- Gas: W: Shell, Getty
- Food: W: Denny's, Pizza Hut, Rest/Hol Inn
- Lodg: W: Comfort Inn, Hampton Inn, Holiday Inn

(5) **Service Area (Both dir, Left exit)**
- FStop: Exxon, Sunoco
- Food: Big Boy, Roy Rogers, Sbarro, Taco Bell, TCBY

2/1AB **DE 896, S College Ave, N-Newark, S-Middletown, to US 301**
- Gas: W: Exxon, Mobil, Shell◊
- Food: W: Boston Market, Diner, Dunkin Donuts, Friendly's, McDonald's
- Lodg: W: Howard Johnson, Quality Inn
- Other: W: Univ of DE-Campus & Stadium

(0/1) **DE Turnpike TOLL Plaza**
DE State Hwy Patrol

NOTE: MM 1: Begin NB/End SB Call Boxes

NOTE: Exits show Mile Marker / Exit #.

EASTERN TIME ZONE

DELAWARE

MARYLAND

NOTE: MM 110: Delaware State Line

EASTERN TIME ZONE

109AB **MD 279, Elkton Rd, to MD 213, Elkton, Newark, DE**
- TStop: E: Petro Stopping Center #51 (Scales); W: Travel Center of America #19/Mobil (Scales)
- Gas: E: Shell◊
- Food: E: IronSkillet/Petro SC, Cracker Barrel, KFC, McDonald's, Waffle House; W: CountryPride/Subway/TA TC
- Lodg: E: Days Inn, Elkton Lodge, Hampton Inn, Hawthorn Suites, Knights Inn♥, Motel 6♥
- Tires: E: Petro SC
- TWash: E: Blue Beacon TW
- TServ: W: TA TC
- Med: E: + Union Hospital of Cecil Co
- Other: E: Laundry/Petro SC; W: Laundry/WiFi/CB/Med/RVDump/TA TC, to Univ of DE

100 **MD 272, North East Rd, North East**
- TStop: E: Flying J Travel Plaza (Scales)
- Gas: W: Mobil
- Food: E: Rest/FastFood/FJ TP, McDonald's
- Lodg: E: Crystal Inn/FJ TP
- Other: E: Laundry/WiFi/RVDump/LP/FJ TP, ATMs, MD State Hwy Patrol; W: Cecil Comm College, Zoo

(97) **Chesapeake House Service Area (Both dir, Left exit)**
- FStop: Exxon, Sunoco
- Food: Burger King, Popeye's, Pizza Hut, Starbucks

93 **MD 222, MD 275, Perrylawn Dr, Perryville, Port Deposit**
- TStop: E: Pilot Travel Center #290 (Scales)
- Gas: E: Exxon◊
- Food: E: Subway/Pilot TC, DQ, Denny's, KFC
- Lodg: E: Comfort Inn
- Other: E: WiFi/Pilot TC, ATMs, Prime Outlets Mall; W: MD State Hwy Patrol Post

(93) **Weigh Station (SB)**

(93) **TOLL Booth (NB)**

89 **MD 155, Level Rd, Havre de Grace**
NOTE: NB: Last exit BEFORE TOLL
- Med: E: + Hospital
- Other: W: to Susquehanna State Park

85 **MD 22, Aberdeen Throughway, Churchville Rd, Aberdeen**
- Gas: E: 7-11, Amoco, Crown◊, Shell◊
- Food: E: Applebee's, Appleby's, Bob Evans, Burger King, Fast Eddie's Pit Beef, Golden Corral, KFC, Little Caesar's, McDonald's, Olive Tree Rest, Pizza Hut, Subway, Taco Bell, Wendy's
- Lodg: E: Clarion Hotel♥, Days Inn♥, Holiday Inn, La Quinta Inn♥, Red Roof Inn♥, Super 8♥, Travelodge♥; W: Courtyard, Residence Inn
- Other: E: ATMs, Dollar Tree, Dollar General, Grocery, Pharmacy, Radiio Shack, Target; W: Ripken Stadium

◊ = Regular Gas Stations with Diesel ▲ = RV Friendly Locations ♥ = Pet Friendly Locations
Red print shows large vehicle parking / access on site or nearby Brown Print = Campgrounds / RV PARKS

EXIT — MARYLAND

(82) MD House Service Area
(Both dir, Left exit)
- FStop: Exxon, Sunoco
- Food: Big Boy, Roy Rogers, Sbarro, TCBY

80 MD 543, Creswell Rd, Bel Air, Riverside, Churchville
- Gas: E: 7-11, BP, Crown◈, Mobil◈
- Food: E: Bliss Coffee & Wine Bar, Burger King, China Moon Chinese Rest, Cracker Barrel, Riverside Pizza, Ruby Tuesday, Waffle House
- Lodg: E: Country Inn, Extended Stay America, Springhill Suites, Wingate Inn
- Other: E: to appr 4mi Bar Harbor RV Park▲

77AB MD 24, Emmorton Rd, Abingdon, Edgewood, Bel Air
- Gas: E: Exxon◈, Shell; W: Exxon◈, WaWa
- Food: E: Burger King, Country Kitchen, Denny's, Vitale's Rest, Waffle House, Rest/BW; W: KFC, McDonald's
- Lodg: E: Best Western♥, Comfort Inn, Days Inn, Hampton Inn, Holiday Inn Express, La Quinta Inn♥, Ramada Inn, Sleep Inn
- Med: W: + Hospital
- Other: W: BJ's, Grocery, Pharmacy, Petco♥, Target, Walmart

74 MD 152, Mountain Rd, Joppa, Joppatowne, Fallston
- Gas: E: Citgo◈, Exxon◈
- Food: E: IHOP, McDonald's, Wendy's, Addt'l Food S to US 40
- Lodg: E: Super 8♥
- Med: E: + Hospital
- Other: E: Days RV Center

67AB MD 43, White Marsh Blvd, to US 40, MD 7, to US 1, I-695, White Marsh
- FStop: E: S&E Truck Stop, White Marsh Truck Stop (MD 43E to US 40N)
- Gas: E: BP◈, Crown, Shell, Sunoco; W: 7-11, Exxon◈
- Food: E: Burger King; W: Chili's, China Wok, ChickFilA, Don Pablo, Fuddruckers, Lin's China Buffet, McDonald's, Olive Garden, Philip's Seafood Grill, Red Lobster, Ruby Tuesday, Starbucks, Taco Bell, TGI Friday
- Lodg: W: Fairfield Inn, Hilton Garden Inn, Hampton Inn, Residence Inn
- Other: E: Best Buy, Target, to Gunpowder Falls State Park; W: ATMs, Auto Services, B&N, Grocery, FedEx Kinkos, Staples, Tires, White Marsh Mall

(64AB) Jct I-695 Beltway, W to Towson, E to Essex
(NB, B-WB-Left exit, SB-EB-Left exit)

(62) Jct I-895S, Harbor Tunnel (SB)

61 US 40, Pulaski Hwy, Rosedale (NB)
- Other: E: Park & Ridge, Industrial Park; W: MD Truck Tire Serv

60 Moravia Rd, to US 40, I-8895 (NB)
- Gas: E: Citgo◈

59 MD 150, Eastern Ave, Baltimore
- Gas: E: Sunoco; W: AmocoBP◈, Exxon, Hess
- Food: E: Glass Grill, Ice Cream Factory; W: Broadway Diner, China East, Dunkin Donuts, Subway, Wendy's
- Med: W: + John Hopkins Bayview Med Ctr

EXIT — MARYLAND

- Other: E: to Eastpoint Mall; W: Home Depot, Kimmel Tire & Auto Center, US Post Office

58 Dundalk Ave (NB)
- Gas: E: Citgo, Mobil

57 O'Donnell St (SB), Interstate Ave (NB)
- FStop: E: Midway Truck Stop
- TStop: E: Travel Center of America #216 (Scales)
- Food: E: Buckhorn/Subway/TA TC, KFC, McDonald's, Sbarro
- Lodg: E: Best Western
- TWash: E: Baltimore Truck Wash
- TServ: E: TA TC/Tires
- Other: E: Laundry/WiFi/CB/TA TC

(56) Ft McHenry Tunnel TOLL Plaza

56 Keith Ave, Baltimore

55 McComas St, Key Hwy
NOTE: NB: Last Exit Before TOLL - NO Services
- Other: W: Ft McHenry Nat'l Monument

54 MD 2, Hanover St

(53) Jct I-395N, Downtown, Oriole Pk

52 MD 295, Baltimore-Washington Pkwy, Russell St, BWI Int'l Airport

51 Washington Blvd

50 Caton Ave (NB), Desoto Rd (SB), to Wilkens Ave, US 1, US 1A
- Gas: E: Hess◈, Shell
- Food: E: Caton House, McDonald's
- Lodg: E: Holiday Inn Express
- Med: E: + Hospital

(49AB) I-695, W-Towson, E-Glen Burnie
(W to I-70, I-83, E to I-97)

(47AB) I-195, o tMD 166, Catonsville
(I-195 to BWI Airport)

(46) I-895N, Harbor Tunnel Thrwy (NB)

43 MD 100, Elkridge, Glen Burnie
- Gas: E: Citgo◈, Exxon
- Food: E: Wendy's
- Lodg: E: Best Western, Red Roof Inn

41AB MD 175, Waterloo Rd, to US 1, Elkridge, Columbia, Jessup
- TStop: E: Travel Center of America #151 (Scales)
- Gas: E: Exxon◈, Shell; W: Crown
- Food: E: CountryPride/Subway/TA TC, Burger King, McDonald's; W: Bob Evans, Olive Garden, TGI Friday
- Lodg: E: Knights Inn/TA TC, Holiday Inn, Fairfield Inn, Red Roof Inn♥, Super 8; W: Homewood Suites
- TServ: E: TA TC/Tires
- Med: W: + Hospital
- Other: E: Laundry/WiFi/CB/TA TC, MD State Hwy Patrol Post; W: to John Hopkins Univ

38AB MD 32, Patuxent Fwy, to US 1, Jessup, Ft Meade, Columbia
(All Serv at 1st Exit E to US 1)

(37) MD Welcome Center (NB)
Rest Area (SB)
(RR, Phone, Picnic, Vend, Info, RVDump)

35AB MD 216, Scaggsville Rd, Laurel
(All Serv at 1st Exit E to US 1)

EXIT — MARYLAND

33AB MD 198, Sandy Spring Rd, Laurel
(Addt'l Serv E to US 1)
- Gas: E: Exxon; W: Exxon, Shell
- Food: E: Domino's; W: Blimpie, Outback Steakhouse
- Lodg: W: Holiday Inn
- Med: E: + Laurel Regional Hospital

29AB MD 212, Powder Mill Rd, Beltsville, Calverton
- Gas: E: 7-11 appr 1mi; W: Exxon◈
- Food: W: Baskin Robbins, Danny's, Flagship Deli, KFC, McDonald's, Sunrise Cafe, Sun Spot Café, T & J's Rest, Wendy's, Rest/Sheraton
- Lodg: W: Fairfield Inn, Sheraton♥
- Other: E: Cherry Hill Park/RVDump▲, El Monte RV Rentals & Sales; W: CVS, Grocery

(27) Jct I-495, Washington ByPass, to Silver Spring

NOTE: I-95 runs with I-495E below around Washington, DC. Exit #'s follow I-495.

25AB Cherry Hill Rd, US 1, Baltimore Blvd, Laurel, College Park
- Gas: E: 7-11, Amoco, Exxon◈, Shell; W: Shell
- Food: E: Arby's, Austin Steak House, Burger King, Danny's, McDonald's, Starbucks, Wendy's; W: College Park Diner, Dunkin Donuts, Hard Times Cafe, IHOP, Kebab Rest, Pizza, Starbucks
- Lodg: E: Holiday Inn; W: Econo Lodge, Hampton Inn, Days Inn, Ramada Inn, Super 8
- Other: E: Cherry Hill Park▲, RiteAid, Tires, Queenstown RV & Marine Service; W: Grocery, Home Depot, Pharmacy, Auto Services & Tires, Queenstown RV & Marine Sales, College Park Airport✈, to Univ of MD/College Pk

24 Greenbelt Station Rd (SB)
- Other: W: Auto Dealers

23 MD 201, Kenilworth Ave, Greenbelt
- Gas: W: Shell
- Food: E: Rest/Marriott, Starbucks; W: Boston Market, Checker's, Popeye's, Starbucks, TGI Friday
- Lodg: E: Marriott; W: Courtyard, Residence Inn
- Other: W: CVS, Grocery, Pharmacy, Staples, Target, Tires, Beltway Plaza Mall

22 MD 295, Baltimore Washington Pkwy, Greenbelt

22AB MD 295, Baltimore Washington Pkwy, Greenbelt
- Food: E: Starbucks
- Lodg: E: Holiday Inn, Days Inn, Howard Johnson
- Other: E: to Nasa Goddard Space Flight Ctr

20AB MD 450, Annapolis Rd, Lanham
- Gas: E: Mobil; W: 7-11, Chevron, Shell, Sunoco
- Food: E: McDonald's, Jerry's, Pizza Hut, Red Lobster, Rest/DI, Rest/BW; W: Chesapeake Bay Seafood House, KFC, Popeye's, Wendy's

◈ = Regular Gas Stations with Diesel ▲ = RV Friendly Locations ♥ = Pet Friendly Locations
Red print shows large vehicle parking / access on site or nearby Brown Print = Campgrounds / RV PARKS

EXIT	MARYLAND
Lodg	**E:** Best Western, Days Inn, Red Roof Inn♥ **W:** Ramada Inn
Med	**W:** + Hospital
Other	**W:** CVS, Grocery, Office Depot, Radio Shack, Safeway, Staples, Tires, Auto Dealers, Auto Services
19AB	**US 50, Annapolis, Washington**
17AB	**MD 202, Landover Rd, Hyattsville, Bladensburg, Upper Marlboro**
Food	**E:** Outback Steakhouse, Ruby Tuesday **W:** China Restaurant, IHOP
Lodg	**E:** Holiday Inn
Other	**W:** Sam's Club
15AB	**MD 214, Central Ave, Upper Marlboro**
FStop	**W:** Crown, Exxon
Gas	**W:** Shell
Food	**E:** Rest/Hampton Inn **W:** Jerry's, McDonald's, Pizza Hut, Wendy's
Lodg	**E:** Hampton Inn, Extended Stay America **W:** Days Inn, Motel 6♥
Other	**E:** FedEx Center, to Six Flags **W:** U-Haul, Goodyear, Home Depot, Staples
13	**Ritchie Marlboro Rd, Upper Marlboro**
11AB	**MD 4, Pennsylvania Ave, Upper Marlboro, Washington**
Gas	**W:** Exxon, Sunoco
Food	**W:** Applebee's, Arby's, IHOP, Pizza Hut, Starbucks, Taco Bell, Wendy's
Other	**W:** CVS, MD Hwy Patrol Post
9	**Forestville Rd, Suitland Pkwy, to PA Ave (SB), MD 337, Allentown Rd, Andrews Air Force Base (NB)**
Gas	**E:** Crown, Shell
Food	**E:** Checker's, McDonald's, Popeye's
Lodg	**E:** Holiday Inn Express, Ramada Inn, Super 8
Med	**E:** + Hospital
Other	**E:** U-Haul, Andrews AFB
7AB	**MD 5, Branch Ave, Temple Hills, Waldorf, Silver Hill**
Gas	**E:** Exxon, Sunoco **W:** Shell◈
Lodg	**W:** Days Inn, Econo Lodge
Med	**W:** + Hospital
4AB	**MD 414, St Barnabas Rd, Oxon Hill, Marlow Heights**
Gas	**E:** Citgo, Exxon **W:** Exxon◈, Shell
Food	**E:** Bojangles, Burger King, McDonald's, KFC, Outback Steakhouse, Wendy's **W:** McDonald's
Lodg	**E:** Red Roof Inn♥
Other	**E:** Grocery, Home Depot, Staples
3AB	**MD 210, Indian Head Hwy, Oxon Hill, Forest Heights**
Gas	**E:** Mobil, Shell **W:** 7-11, BP◈, Crown, Shell
Food	**E:** Danny's, Pizza Hut, Taco Bell **W:** CiCi's, McDonald's, Wendy's
Lodg	**E:** Best Western, Park Inn
Other	**E:** Advance Auto Parts **W:** Safeway

EXIT	MD / VA
(2AB)	**Jct I-295N, to Washington**
NOTE:	**I-95 runs with I-495E above around Washington, DC. Exit #'s follow I-495.**
	EASTERN TIME ZONE

⬆ MARYLAND
⬇ VIRGINIA

EXIT	MD / VA
NOTE:	**MM 178: Maryland State Line**
	EASTERN TIME ZONE
177CBA	**US 1, Richmond Hwy, GW Mem'l Hwy, Fort Belvoir, to Alexandria**
Gas	**W:** Exxon, Hess, Shell
Food	**E:** Diner, Domino's, Great American Steak Buffet, Western Sizzlin', Rest/RRI
Lodg	**E:** Hampton Inn, Red Roof Inn♥, Travelers Inn, Statesman Motel
Other	**E:** Auto Dealers **W:** Amtrak
NOTE:	**SB: Expect construction near X176, Telegraph Rd, thru 2012.**
176AB	**VA 241, Telegraph Rd, Alexandria**
Gas	**E:** Exxon, Hess◈
Lodg	**W:** Courtyard, Holiday Inn
NOTE:	**NB: Expect construction near X176, Telegraph Rd, thru 2012.**
174	**Eisenhower Ave, Alexandria**
173	**VA 613, Van Dorn St, Alexandria, to Franconia**
Gas	**W:** Exxon, Shell
Food	**W:** Dunkin Donuts, Jerry's, McDonald's, Papa John's Pizza, Red Lobster
Lodg	**E:** Comfort Inn
Other	**W:** ATMs, Grocery, NTB, Radio Shack
(170B)	**Jct I-395N, to Washington**
(170A)	**Jct I-495N, to Rockville**
NOTE:	**I-95 runs above with I-495 around Washington, DC. Exit #'s follow I-95.**
169	**VA 644, Old Keene Mill Rd, Franconia Rd, Springfield (SB) Franconia-Springfield Pky (NB)**
Gas	**E:** Mobil **W:** Mobil, Shell
Food	**E:** Bertucci's, Sbarro **W:** Bob Evans, Chesapeake Bay Seafood, Chili's, KFC, Long John Silver, McDonald's, Outback Steakhouse, Pizza Hut, Popeye's, Subway
Lodg	**E:** Best Western, Courtyard, Days Inn, Hampton Inn, Hilton **W:** Holiday Inn Express, Red Roof Inn♥, Townplace Suites
Med	**E:** + Hospital
Other	**E:** Barnes & Noble, Firestone, Springfield Mall **W:** ATMs, Auto Dealers, Auto Services, CVS, Grocery, Radio Shack,
169A	**VA 644, Franconia Rd (SB)**
169B	**VA 644, Old Keene Mill Rd, Loisdale Rd, Spring Mall Rd (SB)**

EXIT	VIRGINIA
167	**VA 617, Backlick Rd, Fullerton Rd (SB, diff reacc)**
166AB	**VA 7100, VA 617, Fairfax Co Pky, Springfield, Ft. Belvoir, Newington**
Gas	**E:** Exxon◈ **W:** Exxon
Lodg	**E:** Hunter Motel
Other	**E:** Davison Airfield✈, Fort Belvoir Mil Res **W:** Costco, Fort Belvoir Military Res
163	**VA 643, Lorton Rd, Lorton**
Gas	**E:** Shell **W:** Shell
Food	**W:** Burger King, Gunston Wok
Lodg	**W:** Best Western, Comfort Inn
Other	**E:** Amtrak, Davison Airfield✈, Fort Belvoir Military Res
161	**US 1, Richmond Hwy, Loran, Woodbridge (SB Left ex, No NB reacc)**
Gas	**E:** Crown, Exxon, Shell
Food	**E:** Denny's, McDonald's, Taco Bell
Lodg	**E:** Econo Lodge, Hampton Inn, Inn of VA, Quality Inn
Other	**E:** Amtrak
160AB	**VA 123N, Gordon Blvd, Woodbridge, Occoquan, Lake Ridge**
Gas	**E:** Mobil **W:** Exxon◈, Mobil, Shell
Food	**E:** Subway **W:** KFC, McDonald's
Lodg	**E:** Econo Lodge, Hampton Inn, Quality Inn
Other	**E:** Grocery, Amtrak, Diamond Labs
158AB	**VA 3000, VA 639, Prince William Pky, Horner Rd, Woodbridge**
Gas	**W:** 7-11, Exxon, Shell, Sunoco, WaWa
Food	**W:** ChickFilA, IHOP, Red Lobster, Romano Macaroni Grill, Starbucks, Subway, Taco Bell, Wendy's
Lodg	**W:** Courtyard, Country Inn, Fairfield Inn, Holiday Inn Express, Residence Inn, Sleep Inn, WyteStone Suites
Other	**W:** ATMs, FedEx Office, PetSmart♥, Sam's Club, **Walmart**, to BJ's
156	**Optiz Blvd, to VA 784 (SB), VA 784, Dale Blvd, Woodbridge (NB)**
Gas	**E:** Exxon, WaWa **W:** Chevron, Exxon, Mobil, Shell
Food	**E:** McDonald's, Taco Bell **W:** Burger King, Bob Evans, Chesapeake Bay Seafood House, Chli's, Dunkin Donuts, Jerry's Subs & Pizza, Lone Star Steak House, McDonald's, Olive Garden, Pizza Hut, Outback Steakhouse, Ruby Tuesday, Sakura Japanese Steak & Seafood, Starbucks
Lodg	**W:** Best Western, Days Inn
Med	**E:** + Potomac Hospital
Other	**E:** Auto Dealers, Grocery, N Va Comm College **W:** ATMs, CVS, Costco, Firestone, Staples, U-Haul, Potomac Mills Outlet Mall, Dale City Animal Hospital♥
(154)	**Dale City TRUCK Rest Area (Both dir) NOTE: Trucks ONLY Rest Area (RR, Phone, Picnic, Vend)**
(154)	**Weigh Station (Both dir)**
152AB	**VA 234, Dumfries Rd, Dumfries**
Gas	**E:** BP◈, Shell◈

EXIT	VIRGINIA
Gas	W:7-11, Exxon, Shell
Food	E: Golden Corral, KFC, McDonald's, Subway, Taco Bell W: Cracker Barrel, Starbucks, Waffle House
Lodg	E: Super 8, Sleep Inn W: Days Inn, Econo Lodge, Hampton Inn, Holiday Inn Express
Other	E: Walmart W: to appr 2.5mi: Prince William Trailer Village/RVDump▲
150AB	**VA 619, Joplin Rd, Triangle**
Gas	E: Exxon, Shell◈
Food	E: Burger King, Dent's Seafood, McDonald's, Wendy's
Lodg	E: Best Value Inn, Ramada Inn, US Inn
Other	E: Quantico US Marine Corps Res W: Quantico Nat'l Cemetery, Prince William Forest Park
148	**Russell Rd, US Marine Corps Base, Quantico**
Lodg	E: Crossroads Inn, Spring Lake Motel
143AB	**VA 610, Garrisonville Rd, US 1, Jefferson Davis Hwy, Stafford**
Gas	E: BP, Exxon, Shell◈ W: Amoco◈, Citgo◈, WaWa
Food	E: Carlos O'Kelly's, DQ, Imperial Gardens, Little Caesars, KFC, King St Blues, McDonald's, Pizza Hut, Ruby Tuesday, Shoney's, Subway, Taco Bell, VA BBQ W: Applebee's, Burger King, Bob Evans, ChickFilA, Dunkin Donuts, Golden Corral, Hardee's, McDonald's, Kobe Japanese, Popeye's, Starbucks, Taco Bell, Wendy's
Lodg	E: Days Inn, Hampton Inn, Towneplace Suites W: Comfort Inn, Country Inn, Holiday Inn Express, Super 8, Wingate Inn
Other	E: ATMs, Big Lots, Grocery, Laundromat, Pharmacy, Radio Shack, Tires, Aquia Pines Camp Resort▲ W: ATMs, Auto Zone, Best Buy, CVS, Grocery, Home Depot, Lowe's, Staples, Target, Walmart
140	**VA 630, Courthouse Rd, Stafford**
Gas	E: Texaco◈ W: BP◈, Shell◈
Food	E: McDonald's
136	**VA 627, to US 1**
Gas	E: Chevron
Other	E: Centreport RV Sales & Service W: Stafford Reg'l Airport✈
133B	**US 17W, Warrenton Rd (SB)**
133A	**US 17E, Warrenton Rd (SB)**
133	**US 17, US 17 Bus, Warrenton Rd, Fredericksburg, Falmouth (NB)**
FStop	W: East Coast Oil/Mapco Express #4050
TStop	W: Servicetown Truck Plaza (Scales)
Gas	E: Exxon◈, Mobil◈, RaceWay W: Chevron, Shell◈
Food	E: Arby's, Burger & Kabob Place, Tex-Mex Grill, Paradise Diner, Taco Mexico & More, Rest/H J W: Servicetown Diner/TP, Hardee's, McDonald's, Outback Steakhouse, Perkins, Pizza Hut, Ponderosa, Popeye's, Sam's Pizza, Subway, Taco Bell, Waffle House, Wendy's, Rest/Qual Inn

EXIT	VIRGINIA
Lodg	E: Motel 6♥, Howard Johnson W: Best Inn, Comfort Suites, Days Inn♥, Holiday Inn♥, Quality Inn♥, Sleep Inn, Super 8, Wingate Hotel, Travelodge
TWash	W: Blue Beacon TW
TServ	W: Road Runners Truck & Tire Services, ABC Truck & Tire Repair
Other	E: Auto & Tire Service W: ATMs, CVS, Auto Service, Bowling Grocery,
(131)	**Fredericksburg Welcome Ctr (SB) (RR, Phone, Picnic, Vend)**
130AB	**VA 3, Plank Rd, Fredericksburg, Culpepper**
Gas	E: BP◈, WaWa W: 7-11, Crown, Exxon◈, Shell, Sheetz, WaWa
Food	E: Arby's, Bob Evans, Carlos O'Kelly's, CiCi"s Pizza, Friendly's, Hardee's, Hunan Inn, Lone Star Steakhouse, KFC, Popeye's Chicken, Shoney's, Tops China Buffet, Wendy's W: Applebee's, Boston Market, Burger King, Carrabba's, Cracker Barrel, Chili's, Denny's, Fuddrucker's, IHOP, Joe's Crab Shack, McDonald's, O'Charley's, Outback Steakhouse, Olive Garden, Panera, Pizza Hut, Popeye's, Red, Hot & Blue, Red Lobster, Ruby Tuesday, Santa Fe Grill, Starbucks, Taco Bell, TGI Friday, Waffle House, Wendy's
Lodg	E: Best Western♥, Hampton Inn♥, Quality Inn W: Best Western♥, Holiday Inn Select, Hilton Garden Inn, Ramada Inn, Super 8
Med	E: + Hospital
Other	E: Home Depot, Pep Boys, Radio Shack, Staples, to Univ of Mary/WA W: Spotslyvania Mall, ATMs, BJ's, Best Buy, FedEx Office, Grocery, Lowe's, NTB, Office Depot, Target, Walmart sc, US Post Office
126AB	**US 1, US 17S, Fredericksburg (NB)**
126	**US 1, US 17S, Fredericksburg (SB)**
FStop	W: RaceWay Fuel Stop
Gas	E: BP, Citgo, Exxon, Mobil, Shell◈ W: Exxon, WalMart
Food	E: Arby's, Denny's, Friendly's, Garden Terrace Rest, Golden Corral, Hooters, McDonald's, Pancho Villa Mex Rest, Pizza Hut, Ruby Tuesday, Subway, Waffle House, Vital Felice Italian Rest, Wendy's W: Applebee's, Bob Evans, Burger King, ChickFilA, Cracker Barrel, Chili's, KFC, Golden Corral, Longhorn Steakhouse, McDonald's, Wendy's
Lodg	E: Days Inn♥, Econo Lodge♥, Fairfield Inn, Hampton Inn, Ramada Inn, TownePlace Suites♥ W: Comfort Inn, Sleep Inn, Wytestone Suites
Other	E: Auto Dealers, Auto Services, ATMs, CVS, Goodyear, Radio Shack, Tires, UPS Store, Vet/Animal Hospital♥, Safford RV, Fredericksburg/WA DC S KOA▲ W: ATMs, FedEx Office, Walmart sc, Massaponax Factory Outlet Center, Vet/Animal Hospital♥

EXIT	VIRGINIA
118	**VA 606, Mudd Tavern Rd, Woodford, Thornburg**
Gas	E: BP, Shell◈ W: Citgo◈, Exxon, Shell, Valero
Food	W: Burger King, McDonald's
Lodg	E: Quality Inn W: Holiday Inn Express
Other	E: Fredericksburg KOA▲
110	**VA 639, Ladysmith Rd, Ruther Glen**
Gas	E: Shell◈ W: Citgo◈, Exxon◈
104	**VA 207, Rogers Clark Blvd, Ruther Glen, to Carmel Church, Bowling Green**
TStop	E: Mr Fuel #2 (Scales), Petro Stopping Center #56/Shell (Scales), Love's Travel Stop #435 (Scales) W: Flying J Travel Plaza #5033 (Scales)
Gas	E: BP◈, Exxon◈ W: Exxon◈
Food	E: Rest/Petro SC, Subway/DQ/Love's TS, McDonald's W: Rest/FastFood/FJ TP, Waffle House
Lodg	E: Howard Johnson♥, Super 8 W: Comfort Inn, Days Inn, Red Roof Inn♥, Quality Inn, Travelodge♥
TWash	E: Blue Beacon TW/Petro SC
TServ	E: Petro SC/Tires, Speedco
Other	E: Laundry/WiFi/Petro SC, Laundry/Love's TS W: Laundry/BarbSh/WiFi/RVDump/LP/FJ TP, ATMs, US Post Office
98	**VA 30, Kings Dominion Blvd, Doswell**
TStop	E: Doswell All American Travel Plaza/Texaco (Scales)
Gas	E: 7-11, Exxon
Food	E: Rest/All Amer TP, Burger King, Denny's, Subway
Lodg	E: Best Western, Econo Lodge/Doswell AA TP
TWash	E: All American TP
TServ	E: All American TP/Tires
Other	E: Laundry/RVDump/All Amer TP, Paramount's Kings Dominion Fun Park/Campground▲, All American CG▲ W: #1 Towing/Repair
92AB	**VA 54, Courthouse Rd, Ashland (NB)**
92	**VA 54, Courthouse Rd, Ashland (SB)**
FStop	W: Mapco Express #4068
TStop	W: Travel Center of America (Scales)
Gas	E: Mobil W: Citgo, Exxon, Shell◈
Food	W: Rest/TA TC, Arby's, Burger King, Cracker Barrel, KFC, McDonald's, Pizza Hut, Perkins, Ponderosa, Ruby Tuesday, Taco Bell, Wendy's
Lodg	W: Budget Inn, Comfort Inn, Days Inn♥, Econo Lodge♥, Hampton Inn, Howard Johnson♥, Microtel, Quality Inn, Sleep Inn, Super 8♥
TServ	W: TA TC/Tires
Other	W: Laundry/WiFi/CB/TA TC, ATMs, CVS, Food Lion, Amtrak, U-Haul
89	**VA 802, Lewistown Rd, Ashland**
TStop	E: Travel Center of America #142 (Scales)
Gas	E: Shell
Food	E: CountryPride/PizzaHut/TA TC
Lodg	W: Cadillac Motel
TServ	E: TA TC/Tires

◈= Regular Gas Stations with Diesel ▲ = RV Friendly Locations ♥= Pet Friendly Locations
Red print shows large vehicle parking / access on site or nearby Brown Print = Campgrounds / RV PARKS

EXIT		VIRGINIA
	Other	E: Laundry/WiFi/CB/TA TC, Hanover Co Muni Airport✈, **Americamps Richmond North▲** W: **Kosmo Village Campground▲**, Auto Dealers, **RV Center**
86		**VA 656, Sliding Hill Rd, Ashland, Atlee, Elmont**
	Gas	E: BP, Sheetz W: 7-11, Mobil, Shell◈
	Food	W: Applebee's, Burger King, Chili's, ChickFilA, McDonald's, O'Charley's, Panera Bread, Red Robin, Ruby Tuesday, Shoney's, Sbarro, Subway, Wendy's
	Lodg	W: Best Western, Springhill Suites
	Other	W: Mall, ATMs, Firestone, Goodyear, Target, Walgreen's
(84AB)		**I-295, to I-64, Glen Allen, Norfolk, Williamsburg, Charlottesville**
83AB		**VA 73, Parham Rd, Richmond**
	Gas	W: 7-11, Exxon, Shell◈
	Food	W: Denny's, Hardee's, KFC, Little Caesar's, McDonald's, Subway, Taco Bell, Waffle House, Wendy's
	Lodg	W: Econo Lodge, GuestHouse Inn, Holiday Inn, Quality Inn, Sleep Inn
	Med	W: + Hospital
	Other	W: ATMs, CVS, Food Lion, Kroger, Lowe's, **Walmart sc**
82		**US 301, VA 2, Chamberlayne Ave**
	Gas	E: Mobil◈
	Food	E: McDonald's, Rest/RRI
	Lodg	E: Red Roof Inn♥, Super 8, Travelodge♥
81		**US 1N, Brook Rd, Wilmer Ave (NB)**
80		**Westbrook Ave, VA 161, Hermitage Rd (NB, no NB reaccess)**
(79)		**Jct I-64W, I-195S, Charlottesville**
78		**N Blvd (SB), Hermitage Rd (NB)**
	Gas	W: Citgo◈
	Food	E: Double T's Café W: Bill's VA BBQ, Rest/Days Inn
	Lodg	E: Holiday Inn W: Comfort Inn, Days Inn, Prestige Inn
	TServ	W: Dolan International
	Med	W: + Hospital
76B		**Lehigh St, Gilmer St, to US 1, US 301, Belvidere St (SB)**
	Lodg	E: Quality Inn
76A		**Chamberlayne Ave, Richmond (NB)**
(75)		**Jct I-64E, Williamsburg, Norfolk N 3rd St (SB), N 7th St (NB)**
74C		**US 33, US 250, Broad St (SB) US 360, N 17th St (NB)**
74B		**Franklin St, to US 60 (SB)**
(74A)		**Jct I-195N, Downtown Exprwy**
73		**Maury St, Commerce Rd**
69		**VA 161, Commerce Rd, Richmond**
	Gas	W: Exxon◈, Shell◈
	Food	W: Hardee's, McDonald's
	Lodg	W: Holiday Inn, Red Roof Inn♥
	TServ	W: VA Truck Center
	Other	E: Port of Richmond
67AB		**VA 895E (TOLL), to I-295, VA 150, to US 60, to US 360**

EXIT		VIRGINIA
64		**VA 613, Willis Rd, Richmond**
	Gas	E: Exxon, Shell W: 7-11, Mobil◈, Shell◈
	Food	E: Arby's, Waffle House W: Burger King, McDonald's
	Lodg	E: Best Value Inn, Econo Lodge, Ramada W: Country Inn, Sleep Inn, Super 8, VIP Inn
	TServ	E: Kenworth
	Other	E: **Hayden's RV Center** W: Flea Market
62		**VA 288, to Powhite Pkwy**
61AB		**VA 10, W Hundred Rd, Chester, Chesterfield, Hopewell**
	Gas	E: RaceTrac W: 7-11◈, Crown, Exxon◈, Shell
	Food	E: Imperial Seafood House W: Applebee's, Burger King, Captain D's, **Cracker Barrel**, Denny's, Hardee's, Hooters, McDonald's, Pizza Hut, O'Charley's, Starbucks, Taco Bell, Waffle House, Western Sizzlin'
	Lodg	E: Comfort Inn, Courtyard, Hampton Inn, Holiday Inn Express, Homewood Suites, Quality Inn W: Clarion, Country Inn, Days Inn, Fairfield Inn, Super 8
	TServ	E: VA Truck Center
	Med	E: + Hospital
	Other	W: ATMs, CVS, Lowe's, RiteAid, Winn Dixie, Targe, John Tyler Comm College, **Pocahontas State Park▲**
58		**VA 746, Ruffin Mill Rd (NB), VA 620, Woods Edge Rd, Colonial Heights, Walthall, Richmond**
	TStop	E: Pilot Travel Center #384 (Scales)
	Gas	E: Shell, WaWa W: Chevron◈
	Food	E: Wendy's/Pilot TC W: Subway, Rest/Interstate Inn
	Lodg	E: Chester Inn W: Interstate Inn, Days Inn
	TWash	E: Pilot TC
	Other	E: Laundry/Pilot TC
54		**VA 144, Conduit Ave, Temple Ave, Colonial Heights, Hopewell**
	Gas	E: BP, Citgo, Crown, Exxon, Shell W: Shell
	Food	E: Arby's, Great Steak & Fry, Golden Corral, La Carreta, Old Country Buffet, Outback Steakhouse, Red Lobster, Taco Bell, Sagebrush Steakhouse, Wendy's W: Hardee's, McDonald's, Subway
	Lodg	E: Comfort Inn, Hampton Inn, Hilton Garden Inn
	Other	E: Mall, ATMs, Home Depot, Sam's Club, Staples, Target, **Walmart** W: U-Haul, **to** VA State Univ
53		**Southpark Blvd, Colonial Heights (Access to Ex #54 Serv)**
52AB		**US 301, E Bank St, Washington St, Wythe St (SB), US 301, Bank St, Petersburg (NB)**
	Gas	E: Citgo, Crown, Shell◈ W: Shell
	Lodg	E: Best Value Inn, Econo Lodge, Holiday Inn, Howard Johnson, Star Motel W: Quality Inn, Ramada Inn

EXIT		VIRGINIA
(51)		**Jct I-85S, Durham, Atlanta**
50ABCD		**US 460, County Dr, Petersburg (NB)**
	Lodg	E: American Inn, CA Inn, Rodeway Inn Knights Inn, Flagship Inn Super 8, Travelodge, Howard Johnson, Star Motel, Royal Inn W: Quality Inn, Ramada Inn
	Other	E: Petersburg Nat'l Battlefield W: Greyhound
50		**US 301, US 460, S Crater Rd (SB) to US 460, County Dr, Petersburg US 301, Wythe, Washington (NB)**
	Gas	E: 7-11, BP
	Lodg	E: Flagship Inn, Knights Inn
	Med	W: + Hospital
48AB		**Wagner Rd, Petersburg**
	Gas	E: Exxon W: Chevron◈, Exxon, Shell
	Food	E: McDonald's W: Hardee's, KFC, McDonald's, Pizza Hut, Ponderosa, Subway, Taco Bell
	Other	W: Auto Dealers, Auto Services, US Post Office
47		**VA 629, Rives Rd, Petersburg**
	Gas	W: Citgo, Shell
	Lodg	W: Heritage Motor Lodge
(46)		**Jct I-295N, to Washington (fr SB, Left exit)**
45		**US 301, S Crater Rd, Petersburg**
	Gas	E: Shell◈ W: Exxon
	Food	W: Rest/BW, Rest/Days Inn, Rest/Qual Inn
	Lodg	E: Hampton Inn W: Best Western♥, Comfort Inn, Days Inn♥, Holiday Inn Express, Quality Inn
41		**US 301, VA 35, VA 156, Courtland**
	FStop	E: US Gas/Chevron
	Food	E: Nino's Rest W: Rest/Rose Garden Inn
	Lodg	E: Econo Lodge W: Rose Garden Inn, Travelodge
	Other	E: **Petersburg KOA▲**
(40)		**Weigh Station (Both dir)**
37		**VA 623, Carson**
	Gas	W: BP◈, Shell
(37)		**Carson Rest Area (NB) (RR, Phone, Picnic, Vend, Playground)**
33		**VA 602, St John Church Rd, Cabin Point Rd, S 301, Stony Creek**
	TStop	W: AmBest/Davis Travel Center/Exxon (Scales)
	Gas	W: Chevron◈
	Food	W: Denny's/Starbucks/Subway/Davis TC, Burger King
	Lodg	W: Hampton Inn♥, Sleep Inn♥
	TServ	W: Davis TC/Tires
	Other	W: Laundry/Davis TC
31		**VA 40, US 301, Stony Creek, Waverly**
	FStop	W: Carter's One Stop/Shell
	Food	W: Carter's Rest, Stony Creek BBQ
	Other	W: Carters Car & Truck Repair, Tires
24		**VA 645, Owen Rd, Jarratt**
20		**VA 631, Jarratt Rd, Jarratt**
	Gas	W: Exxon◈, Shell◈
17		**US 301, Jarratt**
	Food	E: China Star/Reste Motel

◈= Regular Gas Stations with Diesel ▲ = RV Friendly Locations ♥= Pet Friendly Locations
Red print shows large vehicle parking / access on site or nearby Brown Print = Campgrounds / RV PARKS

EXIT — VA / NC

Lodg — E: Knights Inn, Reste Motel
Other — E: **Yogi Bear's Jellystone Camp Resort▲**

13 — VA 614, Otterdam Rd, Emporia
TStop — E: Emporia Travel Plaza/Shell
Lodg — E: Dixie Motel
Other — E: **RVDump**/Shell

12 — US 301 (NB)

11AB — US 58, Emporia, S Hill, Norfolk
TStop — W: Sadler Travel Plaza/Shell (Scales)
Gas — E: BP◈, Exxon, Shell
W: Citgo, Exxon, Petrol
Food — E: Burger King, Cracker Barrel, Hardee's, KFC, Long John Silver, McDonald's, Pizza Hut
W: RestBuffet/Sadler TP, Bojangles/Exxon
Lodg — E: Best Value Inn♥, Holiday Inn Express, Fairfield Inn, Marriott, US Inn
W: Best Western♥, Days Inn♥, Hampton Inn♥, Holiday Inn Express, Quality Inn, Sleep Inn
TServ — W: Sadler TP/Tires
Med — E: + Hospital
Other — E: Auto Services, CVS, Food Lion, Radio Shack, **Walmart sc**
W: Laundry/**RVDump**/Sadler TP

8 — US 301, Skippers Rd, Emporia
TStop — E: Simmons Travel Center #2/AmocoBP (Scales)
Gas — E: Citgo
Food — E: Rest/Red Carpet Inn, Rest/Simmons TC, Denny's
Lodg — E: Comfort Inn♥, Red Carpet Inn♥
TServ — E: Simmons TC/Tires
Other — E: Laundry/Simmons TC

4 — VA 629, Moores Ferry Rd, Skippers
TStop — E: Love's Travel Stop #317 (Scales)
Food — E: McDonald's/Love's TS
Lodg — W: Econo Inn
Other — E: WiFi/**RVDump**/Love's TS
W: **Cattail Creek RV Park▲**

(1) — VA Welcome Center (NB) (NO TRUCKS)
(RR, Phone, Pic, Vend, Info, Playgr)

EASTERN TIME ZONE

⬆ VIRGINIA
⬇ NORTH CAROLINA

NOTE: MM 181: Virginia State Line

EASTERN TIME ZONE

(181) — NC Welcome Center (SB)
(RR, Phone, Picnic, Vend)

180 — NC 48, Pleasant Hill Rd, Pleasant Hill, Gaston, Lake Gaston
TStop — W: Pilot Travel Center #58 (Scales)
Food — W: Subway/Pilot TC
Other — W: WiFi/Pilot TC

176 — NC 46, Garysburg, Gaston
Gas — E: Texaco
W: Shell
Food — E: Stuckey's/Texaco
W: Rest/Comfort Inn
Lodg — W: Comfort Inn

173 — US 158, Weldon, Roanoke Rapids
Gas — E: Shell, BP◈, Texaco◈
W: BP◈, Exxon, RaceTrac, WalMart

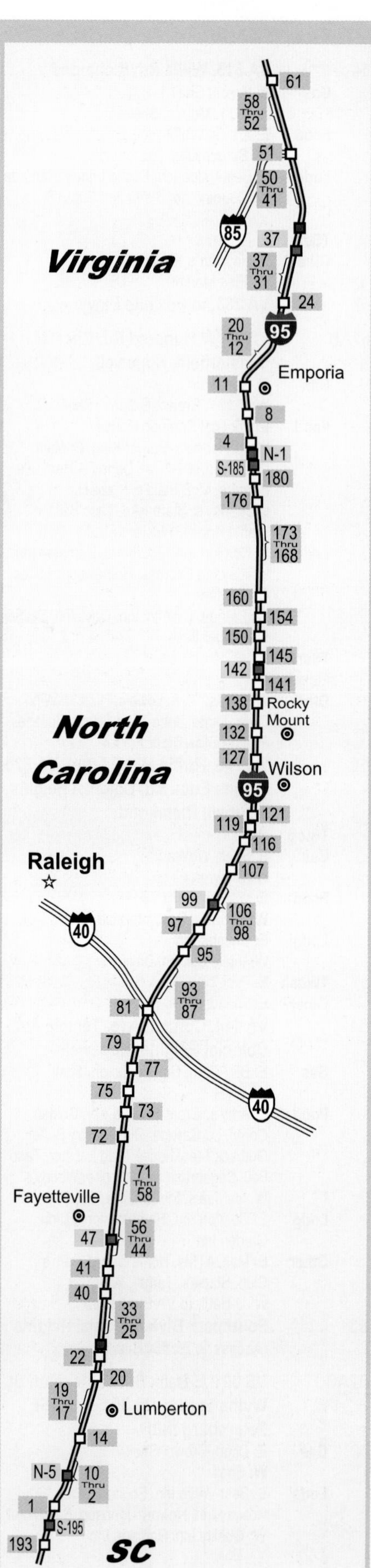

EXIT — NORTH CAROLINA

Food — E: Ralph's BBQ, Trigger's Steakhouse, Waffle House
W: Burger King, Cracker Barrel, Little Caesars, Hardee's, KFC, McDonald's, Pizza Hut, Ryan's Grill, Shoney's, Subway, Taco Bell, Wendy's
Lodg — E: Days Inn, Interstate Inn
W: Comfort Inn, Hampton Inn, Jameson Inn, Motel 6♥, Sleep Inn
Med — E: + Hospital
Other — E: **Interstate Inn Campground▲**
W: Auto Dealers, Auto Zone, ATMs, Dollar General, Firestone, Food Lion, **Walmart sc**

171 — NC 125, Roanoke Rapids
Lodg — W: Holiday Inn Express
Other — W: **NC State Hwy Patrol**

168 — NC 903, Roanoke Rapids, Halifax
Gas — E: Exxon◈, Shell◈
Food — E: Hardee's

160 — NC 561, Enfield, Louisburg
Gas — E: Exxon
W: Citgo◈
Food — W: Rest/Citgo

154 — NC 481, Enfield
Gas — E: Mobil
Other — W: **Enfield/Rocky Mt KOA▲**

(151) — Weigh Station (Both dir)

150 — NC 33, Whitakers
Gas — W: BP
Food — W: DQ/Stuckey's/BP

145 — NC 48, NC 4, to US 301, Battleboro
Gas — E: AmocoBP◈, Exxon, Shell◈
Food — E: Denny's, Hardee's, Shoney's, Waffle House, Wendy's, Rest/DI
Lodg — E: Comfort Inn, Days Inn, Deluxe Inn, Howard Johnson, Quality Inn, Super 8, Travelodge

(142) — Rest Area (Both dir)
(RR, Phone, Picnic, Vend)

141 — NC 43, Dortches Blvd, Main St, Rocky Mount, Red Oak
Gas — E: Exxon◈
W: BP◈
Food — W: Rest/Holiday Inn
Lodg — W: Econo Lodge, Holiday Inn

138 — US 64, Nashville, Rocky Mount
Food — E: Cracker Barrel
Med — E: + Hospital

132 — Mountain Rd, to NC 58, Nashville
Gas — E: Citgo◈

127 — NC 97, Bailey, Airport, Stanhope
Gas — E: BP◈
Food — E: **Cracker Barrel**, Denny's
Other — E: Rocky Mt Wilson Airport✈

121 — US 264 A, Wilson, Greenville
FStop — E: Kangaroo Express
Gas — E: BP, Citgo, Shell
Food — E: Blimpie, Bojangles, Hardee's, Long John Silver, KFC, McDonald's, Subway, Waffle House
W: Burger King, Cracker Barrel, McDonald's
Lodg — E: Comfort Inn
W: Hampton Inn, Holiday Inn, Jameson Inn, Microtel, Sleep Inn
Med — E: + Hospital
Other — E: ATMs, Lowe's, Staples, **Walmart sc**

119AB — US 264, to US 117, US 301

◈ = Regular Gas Stations with Diesel ▲ = RV Friendly Locations ♥ = Pet Friendly Locations
Red print shows large vehicle parking / access on site or nearby Brown Print = Campgrounds / RV PARKS

EXIT		NORTH CAROLINA
116		**NC 42, Wilson, Rock Ridge**
	Gas	E: Shell◈
		W: BP◈
	Other	W: Rock Ridge Campground▲
107		**US 301, Kenly**
	FStop	E: Kangaroo Express/BP
	TStop	E: Flying J Travel Plaza (Scales)
	Gas	E: Exxon◈, Shell
	Food	E: Rest/Flying J TP, Burger King, McDonald's, Pizza, Subway, Waffle House, Wendy's
	Lodg	E: Budget Inn, Deluxe Inn, Econo Lodge
	Other	E: Laundry/WiFi/Flying J TP, ATMs, Family Dollar, Food Lion
106		**Truck Stop Rd, Kenly**
	TStop	E: Flying J Travel Plaza (Scales)
		W: Travel Center of America (Scales), WilcoHess Travel Plaza #218 (Scales)
	Food	E: CountryMarket/FJ TP
		W: CountryPride/TA TC, Hardee's, Waffle House, FastFood/WilcoHess TP
	Lodg	W: Days Inn, Super 8
	TWash	W: Blue Beacon TW/TA TC, Speedco
	TServ	W: TA TC/Tires, Speedco
	Other	E: Laundry/WiFi/FJ TP
		W: Laundry/WiFi/TA TC
105		**Bagley Rd, Selma**
	TStop	E: Big Boy's Truck Stop/Citgo (Scales)
	Food	E: Bob's Big Boy/Big Boys TS
	TServ	E: Big Boy's TS/Tires
102		**Main St, Selma, Micro**
	Gas	E: BP
		W: Phillips 66
	Food	W: Wayne's Rest
101		**NC 2137, Pittman Rd, Selma**
(99)		**Rest Area (Both dir) (RR, Phone, Picnic, Vend)**
98		**Anderson St, Selma**
	Other	E: Rvacation Campground▲
97		**US 70, Selma, Pine Level**
	FStop	E: M&N Truck Stop/Citgo
	Gas	E: Discount Gas◈
		W: BP◈, Exxon, Shell
	Food	E: Denny's, Subway
		W: Bojangles, Denny's, Golden Corral, Hardee's, KFC, Pizza Hut, McDonald's, Shoney's, Waffle House
	Lodg	E: Holiday Inn Express
		W: Comfort Inn, Days Inn, Regency Inn, Masters Economy Inn
	TServ	W: I-95 Truck Center
	Med	W: + Hospital
	Other	E: ATMs, Food Lion, Pharmacy, J&R Outlets
95		**US 70 Bus, E Market St, Smithfield**
	FStop	W: Speedway
	Gas	W: Shell
	Food	E: Rest/HJ, Rest/Village Motor Lodge, Rest/Log Cabin Motel
		W: Bob Evans, Burger King, Waffle House Cracker Barrel, CiCi's, Outback Steakhouse, Ruby Tuesday, Smithfield BBQ, Zaxby's
	Lodg	E: Howard Johnson, Village Motor Lodge, Log Cabin Motel
		W: Jameson Inn, Super 8
	Other	W: Factory Outlet Stores

EXIT		NORTH CAROLINA
93		**Brogden Rd, Smithfield**
	Gas	W: BP◈, Shell
	TServ	E: Smithfield Diesel Repair
90		**US 701, NC 96, to US 301, Four Oaks**
	Gas	E: BP◈, Citgo◈
		W: Phillips 66
	Lodg	E: Travelers Inn
		W: Four Oaks Motel
	Other	E: Smithfield KOA▲, Holiday Trav-L-Park▲
		W: NC State Hwy Patrol Post
87		**Keen Rd (SB), Hockaday Rd, Main St, Brewer Rd (NB), Four Oaks**
(81AB)		**Jct I-40, W-Raleigh, E-Wilmington**
79		**NC 50, NC 242, Main St, Benson**
	Gas	E: Mobil, BP◈, Citgo, Phillips 66
		W: Coastal, Exxon
	Food	E: Benson's BBQ, Frank's Pizza, Waffle House
		W: Burger King, KFC, McDonald's, Pizza Hut, Subway
	Lodg	E: Dutch Inn
		W: Days Inn
	Other	E: Food Lion
		W: Grocery, Pharmacy
77		**Chapel Rd, Denning Rd, Parker Rd, Dunn, Hodges**
	TStop	E: Love's Travel Stop #412 (Scales)
	Food	E: Subway/Love's TS
	TServ	E: Rai Truck Repair Shop, Peterbilt
75		**Jonesboro Rd, Dunn**
	TStop	W: Sadler Travel Plaza/Shell (Scales)
	Food	W: Rest/Sadler TP, Milestone Diner, Quiznos
	TServ	W: Sadler TP/Tires, Peterbilt of Dunn
	Other	W: Sadler TP, ATMs
73		**US 421, NC 55, Dunn, Clinton**
	Gas	W: Exxon◈, Chevron
	Food	E: Cracker Barrel, Wendy's
		W: Bojangles, Burger King, KFC, Sagebrush Steakhouse, Triangle Waffle
	Lodg	W: Comfort Inn, Econo Lodge, Holiday Inn Express, Jameson Inn, Ramada Inn
	Med	W: + Hospital
	Other	E: Auto Dealers, ATMs, Grocery
		W: ATMs, Grocery, Campbell Univ
72		**Pope Rd, Poole Rd, Dunn**
	Gas	E: BP
		W: BP
	Food	E: Rest/Best Western
		W: Brass Lantern Steakhouse
	Lodg	E: Comfort Inn, Royal Inn
		W: Budget Inn, Express Inn
71		**Long Branch Rd, Dunn**
	TStop	E: Kangaroo/Citgo
	Food	E: Hardee's/Kangaroo
70		**NC 1811, Bud Hawkins Rd, Dunn**
	Lodg	E: Relax Inn
65		**NC 82, Godwin Falcon Rd, Godwin**
61		**Wade Stedman Rd, Wade**
	FStop	E: Citgo
		W: Lucky 7 Truck Stop/BP
	Food	E: Dixie Boy, DQ
		W: Subway/Lucky 7
	Other	E: Fayetteville/Wade KOA▲
58		**US 13, to US 401, Fayetteville, Newton Grove**
	Food	E: Rest/Days Inn
	Lodg	E: Days Inn

EXIT		NORTH CAROLINA
56		**I-95S Bus, to US 301, Fayetteville, Hope AFB, Fort Bragg (SB)**
55		**NC 1832, Murphy Rd, Fayetteville, Eastover**
	Gas	W: Apco, Kangaroo
	Lodg	W: Budget Inn
52AB		**NC 24, Fayetteville, Clinton**
49		**NC 53, NC 210, Fayetteville**
	Gas	E: BP◈, Exxon, Kangaroo, Shell
		W: Exxon◈, Shell◈
	Food	E: Burger King, Denny's, McDonald's, Pizza Hut, Waffle House
		W: Cracker Barrel, Ruby Tuesday, Shoney's
	Lodg	E: Days Inn, Deluxe Inn, Motel 6♥, Quality Inn
	Lodg	W: Best Western, Comfort Inn, Hampton Inn, Econo Lodge, Fairfield Inn, Holiday Inn, Innkeeper I-95, Red Roof Inn♥, Sheraton, Sleep Inn, Super 8
	TServ	W: Smith International Truck Center
(47)		**Rest Area (Both dir) (RR, Phone, Picnic, Vend)**
46AB		**NC 87, Fayetteville, Elizabethtown**
	Med	W: + Hospital
44		**NC 2341, Claude Lee Rd, Snow Hill Rd, Fayetteville**
	Other	W: Lazy Acres Campground▲, to Fayetteville Reg'l Airport✈
41		**NC 59, Chickenfoot Rd, Hope Mills, Fayetteville**
	Gas	E: Kangaroo
		W: BP◈
	Other	W: Spring Valley RV Park▲, Hawley's Camping Center
40		**Jct I-95 Bus, to US 301, Fayetteville, Fort Bragg, Hope AFB (NB)**
33		**US 301, to NC 71, St Pauls**
	Gas	E: BP◈
31		**NC 20, St Pauls, Raeford, Pinehurst**
	TStop	E: Poco Shop/Shell
	Gas	E: BP, Citgo, Mobil
		W: Exxon◈
	Food	E: Rest/Poco Shop, Burger King, Hardee's, Huddle House, McDonald's
	Lodg	E: Days Inn
	TServ	E: Central Carolina Trucks
25		**US 301, Lumberton**
	FStop	E: BP
(24)		**Weigh Station (Both dir)**
22		**US 301, Fayetteville Rd, Lumberton**
	FStop	W: Sun-Do
	TStop	W: Minuteman #24
	Gas	E: Exxon, Xpress Depot
		W: Mobil, Pure◈
	Food	E: Burger King, Denny's, Hardee's, Outback Steakhouse, Ryan's Grill, Smithfield BBQ, Waffle House, Rest/HI
		W: Rest/Minuteman
	Lodg	E: Best Western, Comfort Suites, Holiday Inn, Hampton Inn, Super 8
	Other	E: ATMs, Grocery, Goodyear, Lowe's, Office Depot, Walmart sc, NC State Hwy Patrol Post
20		**NC 211, Roberts Ave, to NC 41, Lumberton, Red Springs**
	Gas	E: Citgo, Exxon◈, Liberty◈

◈ = Regular Gas Stations with Diesel ▲ = RV Friendly Locations ♥ = Pet Friendly Locations
Red print shows large vehicle parking / access on site or nearby Brown Print = Campgrounds / RV PARKS

EXIT		NC / SC
	Gas	W: Exxon, Shell◈
	Food	E: Arby's, Bojangles, Burger King, CiCi's Pizza, Hardee's, KFC, Little Caesars Pizza, McDonald's, Shoney's, Subway, Taco Bell, Waffle House, Wendy's, Western Sizzlin, Rest/Ramada, Rest/Quality Inn W: Cracker Barrel
	Lodg	E: Deluxe Inn, Quality Inn, Ramada Ltd W: Comfort Inn, Country Suites, Days Inn, Econo Lodge
	Med	E: + Hospital
	Other	E: ATMs, CVS, Food Lion
19		**Carthage Rd, Lumberton**
	Gas	E: BP◈ W: Exxon◈, Texaco
	Food	E: Rest/Red Carpet Inn W: Sullivan's
	Lodg	E: Red Carpet Inn, Travelers Inn W: Knights Inn, Motel 6♥
17		**NC 72, NC 711, Caton Rd, Lumberton, Pembroke**
	Gas	E: BP◈, Citgo, Exxon, Mobil◈, Shell◈
	Food	E: Burger King, Hardee's, McDonald's, Waffle House, Huddle House/Exxon
	Lodg	E: Southern Inn, Budget Inn, Economy Inn, Super 8
	TServ	E: Smith International Truck Center
	Other	E: Auto Services, Food Lion, Pharmacy
(14)		**Jct I-74, US 74, Lumberton, to Maxton, Laurinburg**
	Gas	W: BP◈
	Food	W: Rest/Exit 14 Inn
	Lodg	W: Exit 14 Inn
	Other	**W: Sleepy Bear's Family Campground▲** **to** NC Battleship Memorial
10		**US 301S, Chicken Rd, Fairmont, Lumberton**
7		**Raynham Rd, Fairmont, McDonald, Raynham**
(5)		**NC Welcome Center (NB)** **(RR, Phone, Picnic, Vend)**
2		**NC 130, to NC 904, Rowland, Fairmont**
1AB		**US 301, US 501, Rowland, Dillon, South of the Border (SB)**
1		**US 301, US 501, Rowland, Dillon, Laurinburg, South of the Border**
	FStop	W: Border Shell
	Gas	E: Amoco, Exxon, Shell
	Food	E: Pedro's Diner, Sombrero Rest W: Waffle House
	Lodg	E: Budget Inn, South of the Border Motel W: Days Inn, Holiday Inn Express
	Other	**E: Camp Pedro▲**

EASTERN TIME ZONE

⬆NORTH CAROLINA
⬇SOUTH CAROLINA

NOTE: MM 198: North Carolina State Line

EASTERN TIME ZONE

EXIT		SOUTH CAROLINA
(195)		**SC Welcome Center (SB)** **(RR, Phone, Picnic, Vend, Info)**
193		**SC 9, SC 57, Dillon, Bennettsville, Little Rock, to N Myrtle Beach**
	Gas	E: BP, Mobil, Speedway◈, Sunoco W: BP◈
	Food	E: Burger King, Golden Corral, Huddle House, Shoney's, Waffle House, Wendy's
	Lodg	E: Best Value Inn♥, Comfort Inn, Days Inn♥, Hampton Inn, Knights Inn, Ramada Ltd W: Econo Lodge♥, Super 8♥
	TServ	W: Cottingham Trailer Service
	Med	E: + Mcleod Medical Center
	Other	W: Dillon Co Airport✈, **Bass Lake RV Campground▲**, Trailer Service
190		**SC 34, Dillon, Bingham**
	Tstop	W: Love's Travel Stop #371
	Gas	E: BP
	Food	E: Stuckey's/DQ W: Arby's/Love's TS
	Other	W: WiFi/Love's TS, ATMs,
181B		**SC 38W, SC 917, Bennettsville**
181A		**SC 38E, SC 917, Marion**
181		**SC 38, SC 917, Latta, Marion, to Myrtle Beach**
	TStop	E: Flying J Travel Plaza/Conoco (Scales) W: WilcoHess Travel Plaza #938 (Scales)
	Gas	E: BP, Shell W: Kangaroo
	Food	E: Cookery/FJ TP, McDonald's/Shell, Subway/BP W: Wendy's/WilcoHess TP
	Lodg	W: Best Western
	Other	E: Laundry/WiFi/**RVDump/LP**/FJ TP, Green's Tire Service W: Laundry/WiFi/WilcoHess TP, ATMs, Auto & Truck Repairs
(171)		**Pee Dee Rest Area (Both dir)** **(RR, Phones, Picnic, Vend)**
170		**SC 327, Florence, Marion, to Myrtle Beach**
	TStop	E: Pilot Travel Center #62 (Scales)
	Gas	E: BP
	Food	E: Wendy's/Pilot TC, Waffle & Egg, McDonald's
	Lodg	E: Holiday Inn Express
	Other	E: Laundry/WiFi/**RVDump**/Pilot TC, **Johnson's Trailer Park▲**, **to** Myrtle Beach
169		**TV Rd, Florence, Quinby**
	TStop	W: Petro Stopping Center #58/Exxon (Scales)
	Gas	W: BP
	Food	W: IronSkillet/PizzaHut/Petro SC
	Lodg	W: Best Value Inn♥, Rodeway Inn
	TWash	W: Blue Beacon TW/Petro SC
	TServ	E: Cummins, Peterbilt of Florence, Stone Truck Center W: Petro SC/Tires, K&L Chrome Shop
	Other	**E: Florence KOA▲** W: Laundry/WiFi/**RVDump**/Petro SC
164		**US 52, W Lucas St, Florence, Darlington, Darlington Int'l Raceway**
	TStop	W: Travel Center of America/BP (Scales), Pilot Travel Center #337 (Scales)
	Gas	E: Exxon◈, Raceway W: Hess◈
	Food	E: Cracker Barrel, Denny's, Hardee's, Kobe Japanese, McDonald's, Perkins, Ruby Tuesday, Waffle House, Wendy's W: Popeye's/TA TC, Subway/TacoBell/Pilot TC, Arby's, Bojangles, Burger King, KFC, McDonald's, Pizza Hut, Quincy's Steakhouse, Shoney's
	Lodg	E: Best Western, Comfort Inn, Hampton Inn, Holiday Inn♥, Motel 6♥, Super 8♥ W: Comfort Inn♥, Days Inn♥, Guest House Int'l, Microtel, Ramada Inn♥, Shoney's Inn, Sleep Inn, Suburban Hotel♥, Thunderbird Inn♥, Wingate Inn
	Med	W: + McLeod Reg'l Medical Center
	Other	E: Laundry/WiFi/TA TC, Auto Dealer, Auto Services, ATMs, Towing W: ATMs, Auto Services, Florence Darlington Tech College, Pee Dee Farmers Market, **to** Darlington Int'l Raceway
(160B)		**Jct I-20W, to Columbia**
(160A)		**Jct I-20 Bus E, US 76, to Florence**
	Gas	E: Shell◈, Scotchman
	Food	E: Arby's, Burger King, ChickFilA, Huddle House, IHOP, Pizza Hut, Outback Steakhouse, Red Lobster, Ruby Tuesday, Shoney's, Waffle House, Western Sizzlin
	Lodg	E: Courtyard, Fairfield Inn, Hampton Inn, Hilton Garden Inn, Red Roof Inn♥, Springhill Suites
	Other	E: Civic Center, Auto Services, Best Buy, CVS, Dollar Tree, Lowe's, Sam's Club, Target, **Walmart**, Mall
157		**US 76, Florence, Timmonsville**
	Gas	E: AmocoBP◈, Exxon◈, Kangaroo◈, Phillips 66 W: Sunoco
	Food	E: McDonald's, Las Palmas Family Mex Rest, Swamp Fox Diner, Waffle House W: Carol's, Magnolia Dining Room
	Lodg	E: Days Inn♥, Howard Johnson, Swamp Fox Inn, Travelodge W: Econo Lodge, Ramada at Young's Plantation
	Med	W: + Hospital
	Other	E: ATMs, Food Lion **W: Swamp Fox Campground▲**
153		**Honda Way, Timmonsville**
150		**SC 403, Timmonsville, Sardis**
	FStop	E: Sardis Auto Truck Plaza/BP
	Gas	W: Exxon◈
	Food	E: Rest/Sardis ATP
	Lodg	E: Budget Inn
	Other	**W: Lake Honeydew Campground▲**
146		**SC 341, Lynchburg Hwy, Lynchburg, Lake City, Olanta**
	Gas	E: Exxon◈
	Lodg	E: Relax Inn
141		**SC 53, SC 58, Lynchburg, Shiloh**
	FStop	E: Mary O's Exxon
	Gas	W: Shell
	Other	E: RV Center
(139)		**Shiloh Rest Area (Both dir)** **(RR, Phone, Picnic, Vend)**
135		**US 378, Clarence Coker Hwy, Lynchburg, Turbeville, Sumter**
	Gas	E: BP, Citgo◈ W: Exxon
	Food	E: Rest/Days Inn
	TServ	E: Truck Service Inc
	Lodg	E: Comfort Inn, Days Inn
	Other	W: **to** Dabbs Airport✈
132		**SC 527, Gable, Sardinia, Bishopville**

◈= Regular Gas Stations with Diesel ▲ = RV Friendly Locations ♥= Pet Friendly Locations
Red print shows large vehicle parking / access on site or nearby Brown Print = Campgrounds / RV PARKS

EXIT — SOUTH CAROLINA

122 — SC 521, Alcolu, Sumter, Manning
- Gas — W: Exxon◈

119 — SC 261, Paxville Hwy, Manning, Paxville
- TStop — E: Travel Center of America/BP (Scales)
- Gas — E: Shell; W: Exxon
- Food — E: Rest/FastFood/TA TC, Huddle House, Subway, Waffle House, Wendy's; W: Burger King
- Lodg — E: Best Western, Holiday Inn Express; W: Super 8
- TWash — E: Mid Eastern TW
- TServ — E: TA TC/Tires
- Med — E: + Hospital
- Other — E: Laundry/WiFi/CB/**RVDump**/TA TC, CVS, ATMs, Food Lion, Goodyear, **Walmart**, **Campers Paradise CG▲**

115 — US 301, Alex Harvin Hwy, Manning, Summerton
- FStop — W: Moore's Food Store/Shell
- Gas — E: Exxon◈
- Food — E: Rest/Travelers Inn; W: Rest/Days Inn
- Lodg — E: Carolina Inn, Travelers Inn; W: Days Inn, Econo Lodge, Sunset Inn

108 — SC 102, Buff Blvd, Summerton
- Gas — E: Citgo, Shell; W: BP
- Food — E: Stuckey's/DQ/Citgo; W: Summerton Motel, Family Folks
- Lodg — W: Knights Inn, Summerton Motel

102 — US 15, US 301N, Rd 400, N Santee, St Paul, Summerton
NOTE: US 15/US 301 exits NB, joins SB
- Gas — E: BP; W: Shell◈
- Food — E: Howard Johnson
- Lodg — E: Howard Johnson
- Other — E: **Santee Lakes Campground▲**; W: **Santee State Park**

**(99) — SC Welcome Center (SB)
Santee Rest Area (NB)**
(RR, Phone, Picnic, Vend, Info)

98 — SC 6, Santee, Eutawville
- Gas — E: BP, Chevron, Mobil; W: BP◈, Exxon, Hess◈, Horizon◈, Shell◈
- Food — E: Georgio's House of Pizza, Huddle House, Jake's Steaks, KFC, Shoney's, Subway, Western Steer; W: Burger King, **Cracker Barrel**, Denny's Hardee's, McDonald's, Waffle House
- Lodg — E: Best Western, Days Inn, Hampton Inn♥, Ramada Inn, Travelodge; W: Baymont Inn, Clark's Inn & Rest, Country Inn, Economy Inn, Holiday Inn, Quality Inn
- Other — E: Dollar General, Grocery, Golf Course, **Lake Marion Resort▲**; W: ATMs, Auto Services, CarQuest, Family Dollar, Food Lion, Grocery, NAPA, Pharmacy, Laundromat, US Post Office, Golf Course, **Santee State Park**

97 — US 301S, to Orangeburg
(SB exit, NB entr)
NOTE: US 301 joins NB, leaves SB

93 — US 15, Bass Dr, Holly Hill, Santee
NOTE: US 15 joins NB, leaves SB

90 — US 176, Old State Rd, Holly Hill

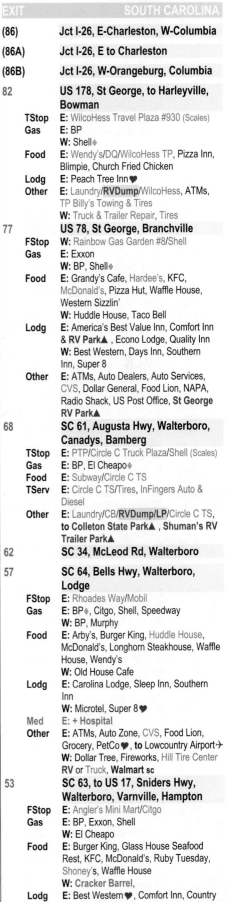

South Carolina
1, S-195, 193, 190, Dillon, 95, 181, 171, 170, 169, 164, 160, Florence, 20, 157, Sumter, 153, 150, 146, 141, Manning, 132 Thru 119, 139, 26, 115, 108, 102, 99, 98, 97, 93, 90, 86, 82, 77, St. George, 68, 62, 57, Walterboro, 53, 47, 42, 38, 33, 28, 22, 21, Beauford, 18, 8, 5, N-4.3, 16, 106 Thru 102, S-111, 99, Savannah, 94, 90, 87, Georgia, 76, 67, 58, 55, 49, 95, 42, S-40, 38

EXIT — SOUTH CAROLINA

(86) — Jct I-26, E-Charleston, W-Columbia

(86A) — Jct I-26, E to Charleston

(86B) — Jct I-26, W-Orangeburg, Columbia

82 — US 178, St George, to Harleyville, Bowman
- TStop — E: WilcoHess Travel Plaza #930 (Scales)
- Gas — E: BP; W: Shell◈
- Food — E: Wendy's/DQ/WilcoHess TP, Pizza Inn, Blimpie, Church Fried Chicken
- Lodg — E: Peach Tree Inn♥
- Other — E: Laundry/**RVDump**/WilcoHess, ATMs, TP Billy's Towing & Tires; W: Truck & Trailer Repair, Tires

77 — US 78, St George, Branchville
- FStop — W: Rainbow Gas Garden #8/Shell
- Gas — E: Exxon; W: BP, Shell◈
- Food — E: Grandy's Cafe, Hardee's, KFC, McDonald's, Pizza Hut, Waffle House, Western Sizzlin'; W: Huddle House, Taco Bell
- Lodg — E: America's Best Value Inn, Comfort Inn & **RV Park▲**, Econo Lodge, Quality Inn; W: Best Western, Days Inn, Southern Inn, Super 8
- Other — E: ATMs, Auto Dealers, Auto Services, CVS, Dollar General, Food Lion, NAPA, Radio Shack, US Post Office, **St George RV Park▲**

68 — SC 61, Augusta Hwy, Walterboro, Canadys, Bamberg
- TStop — E: PTP/Circle C Truck Plaza/Shell (Scales)
- Gas — E: BP, El Cheapo◈
- Food — E: Subway/Circle C TS
- TServ — E: Circle C TS/Tires, InFingers Auto & Diesel
- Other — E: Laundry/CB/**RVDump/LP**/Circle C TS, **to Colleton State Park▲**, **Shuman's RV Trailer Park▲**

62 — SC 34, McLeod Rd, Walterboro

57 — SC 64, Bells Hwy, Walterboro, Lodge
- FStop — E: Rhoades Way/Mobil
- Gas — E: BP◈, Citgo, Shell, Speedway; W: BP, Murphy
- Food — E: Arby's, Burger King, Huddle House, McDonald's, Longhorn Steakhouse, Waffle House, Wendy's; W: Old House Cafe
- Lodg — E: Carolina Lodge, Sleep Inn, Southern Inn; W: Microtel, Super 8♥
- Med — E: + Hospital
- Other — E: ATMs, Auto Zone, CVS, Food Lion, Grocery, PetCo♥, to Lowcountry Airport✈; W: Dollar Tree, Fireworks, Hill Tire Center RV or Truck, **Walmart sc**

53 — SC 63, to US 17, Sniders Hwy, Walterboro, Varnville, Hampton
- FStop — E: Angler's Mini Mart/Citgo
- Gas — E: BP, Exxon, Shell; W: El Cheapo
- Food — E: Burger King, Glass House Seafood Rest, KFC, McDonald's, Ruby Tuesday, Shoney's, Waffle House; W: **Cracker Barrel**,
- Lodg — E: Best Western♥, Comfort Inn, Country Hearth Inn, Econo Lodge, Howard

◈= Regular Gas Stations with Diesel ▲ = RV Friendly Locations ♥= Pet Friendly Locations
Red print shows large vehicle parking / access on site or nearby Brown Print = Campgrounds / RV PARKS

EXIT		SOUTH CAROLINA
	Lodg	E: Johnson Express♥, Ramada Inn♥ W: Days Inn, Deluxe Inn, Hampton Inn, Holiday Inn Express, Microtel
	Other	W: **New Green Acres RV Park▲**
(47)		**Hendersonville Rest Area** (Both dir) (RR, Phone, Picnic, Vend)
42		**US 21, Lowcountry Hwy, Walterboro, Orangeburg, Yemassee, Beaufort, Pt Royal**
38		**SC 68, Yemassee, Hampton, Beaufort, Port Royal**
	TStop	W: Simco Travel Plaza (Scales)
	Gas	E: Chevron W: BP, Exxon◈, Shell◈
	Food	W: Rest/Simco TP, J's Rest, Subway
	Lodg	W: Motel/Simco TP, Palmetto Lodge, Super 8♥
	TServ	W: Simco TP/Tires
33		**US 17N, Beaufort, Charleston, Point South** NOTE: US 17 exits NB, joins SB
	Gas	E: BP◈, Exxon, Marathon, Shell
	Food	E: Denny's, McDonald's, Waffle House
	Lodg	E: Best Western, Days Inn, Hampton Inn, Holiday Inn Express, Knights Inn
	Other	E: Visitor Info, **Point South KOA▲**, **The Oaks at Point South▲**
28		**SC 462, Coosawhatchie, Hilton Head Island**
	FStop	W: Tiger Express #11/Exxon
	Gas	W: Chevron
	Other	W: Auto & Truck Tires
22		**US 17S, Ridgeland** NOTE: US 17 exits SB, joins NB
	Gas	W: Sunoco
	Food	W: Duke's BBQ
	Lodg	W: Plantation Inn
21		**SC 336, Main St, Ridgeland, Hilton Head Island**
	Gas	W: BP◈, Chevron◈, Citgo, Exxon, Shell◈
	Food	W: Burger King, DQ/BP, Huddle House, KFC, Pizza, Subway, Waffle House
	Lodg	W: Comfort Inn♥, Carolina Lodge, Days Inn
	Other	E: RV Mega Store W: Family Dollar, Food Lion, RiteAid
18		**RD 13, Ridgeland, Switzerland**
(18)		**TRUCK Only Parking Area**
8		**US 278, Hardeeville, Hilton Head, Bluffton, Sun City**
	TStop	E: Joker Joe's Truck Stop/BP (Scales)
	Gas	E: Exxon, Kangaroo Express,
	Gas	W: Chevron◈, Kangaroo/Mobil
	Food	E: Huddle House/Wendy's/Joker Joe's TS, McDonald's/Shell W: KrispyKreme/NobleRomanPizza/ Subway/TCBY/Chevron, Pizza Hut, Waffle House
	Lodg	W: Holiday Inn Express, Motel 6♥
	Tires	E: Joker Joe's TS
	Med	E: + Coastal Carolina Hospital
	Other	E: Laundry/Joker Joe's TS, to **Hardeeville RV-Thomas Parks & Sites▲**, to Univ of SC/Beaufort W: Fireworks/GolfBallOutlet/Kangaroo
5		**US 17, US 321, Hardeeville, Savannah**
	FStop	W: Speedway, Sunoco #2656
	Gas	E: Exxon, Shell

EXIT		SC / GA
	Gas	W: BP◈, Citgo, Chevron, Exxon
	Food	E: KFC, Waffle House W: Burger King, Chinese Rest, KFC, McDonald's, Shoney's, Subway, Wendy's
	Lodg	E: Days Inn, Economy Inn♥, Sleep Inn♥ W: Clean Stay USA, Comfort Inn, Deluxe Inn, Econo Lodge, Knights Inn♥, Magnolia Motel, Quality Inn♥, Super 8♥
	Other	E: **Hardeeville RV-Thomas Parks & Sites▲** W: Auto Service/Exxon, Fireworks, Muni Stadium, Piggly Wiggly Grocery
(4.3)		**SC Welcome Center** (NB) (RR, Phone, Picnic, Vend, Info)
(3)		**Weigh Station** (Both dir)

SOUTH CAROLINA
GEORGIA

NOTE: MM 113: South Carolina State Line

EASTERN TIME ZONE

EXIT		SC / GA
(111)		**GA Welcome Center** (SB) (RR, Phone, Pic, Vend, Info, RVDump)
109		**GA 21, Augusta Rd, Port Wentworth, Savannah, Rincon** (Addt'l Serv E on GA 21)
	FStop	W: Circle K #5352/76
	TStop	E: Pilot Travel Center #71 (Scales)
	Gas	E: Enmark◈ W: Shell
	Food	E: McDonald's/Subway/Pilot TC, Waffle House W: Quiznos/Circle K, Sea Grill Rest, Wendy's, Zaxby's
	Lodg	E: Country Inn, Hampton Inn, Hilton Garden Inn, Inn at Mulberry Grove, Wingate Inn W: Comfort Suites♥, Days Inn, Holiday Inn Express, Quality Inn, Ramada Ltd♥, Savannah Inn♥, Sleep Inn♥, Super 8♥
	Tires	E: Pilot TC
	TServ	E: Kenworth of Savannah, Peterbilt of Savannah, Roberts WhiteGMC, Stuart's Alignment, Freightliner
	Other	E: Laundry/WiFi/Pilot TC W: to appr 3 mi **Whispering Pines RV Park▲**, appr 5mi **Greenpeace RV Park▲**
106		**Jimmy Deloach Pky, Pt Wentworth**
	Other	E: GA Tech/Savannah
104		**Airways Ave, Pooler Pky, Savannah Savannah Hilton Head Intl Airport**
	Gas	E: BP, Shell◈ W: Shell, Murphy
	Food	E: Starbucks, Waffle House, Rest/Fairfield Inn, Rest/Sheraton
	Food	W: Arby's, Cheddar's Cafe, ChickFilA, Ruby Tuesday, Zaxby's, Subway/Shell, McDonald's/WalMart
	Lodg	E: Cambria Suites, Candlewood Suites, Comfort Suites, Fairfield Inn, Four Points Sheraton, Hampton Inn, Hawthorn Suites♥ Hilton Garden Inn, Holiday Inn Express, Springhill Suites, Staybridge Suites♥, TownePlace Suites W: Embassy Suites, Red Roof Inn♥
	Other	E: Sav-HH Int'l Airport✈ W: ATMs, Home Depot, **Walmart sc**

EXIT		GEORGIA
102		**US 80, GA 26, Louisville Hwy, Pooler, Garden City, Tybee Beach, Ft Pulaski Nat'l Monument**
	FStop	E: Amit Food Mart #4/Shell W: Gate #209
	Gas	E: Enmark◈ W: BP
	Food	E: Cracker Barrel, Huddle House, Taco Bell, Krystal, McDonald's, Waffle House W: Burger King, El Potro Mex, Hardee's, Spanky's Pizza, Subway, Wendy's
	Lodg	E: Best Western, Jameson Inn, Microtel, Ramada Ltd, Travelodge W: Comfort Inn, Econo Lodge, Holiday Inn, Quality Inn, Sleep Inn
	Other	E: ATMs, Advance Auto Parts, Auto Zone, Family Fun Center, Food Lion, Museum, Tires, **Camping World, RV Center/ RVDump** W: ATMs, Auto Services, NAPA, Pooler Tire & Auto Center, Tires, U-Haul
(99)		**Jct I-16, E - Savannah, W - Macon**
(99A)		**Jct I-16, E to Savannah**
(99B)		**Jct I-16,W to Macon**
94		**GA 204, Bacon Hwy, Savannah, Pembroke**
	FStop	E: El Cheapo #41/Shell
	Gas	E: AmocoBP◈, Exxon, Murphy W: Chevron◈, Shell
	Food	E: Applebee's, Cracker Barrel, Denny's, Hardee's, Houlihan's, McDonald's, Perkins, Ruby Tuesday, Shellhouse Rest, Shoney's, Sonic, Waffle House W: El Potro Mex Rest, Hooters, Huddle House, Subway
	Lodg	E: America's Best Value Inn, Best Western, Clarion Inn, Comfort Suites, Country Inn, Days Inn, Fairfield Inn, Holiday Inn Express, Hampton Inn, Howard Johnson, La Quinta Inn♥, Quality Inn♥, Ramada Inn, Red Roof Inn♥, Sleep Inn, Springhill Suites, Super 8, Wingate Hotel W: Clean Stay, Econo Lodge, Knights Inn, Microtel, Travelodge
	Med	E: + Hospital
	Other	E: ATMs, **Walmart sc**, Bass Pro Shop, Car Wash, Keller's Flea Market/**RVParkg/ RVDump**, Savannah Festival Factory Outlet Stores, Savannah Mall **Biltmore Gardens RV Park▲**, to **Waterway RV Park▲** W: Savannah Harley Davidson, to appr 3mi **Savannah Oaks RV Resort▲**
90		**GA 144, Old Clyde Rd, Fort Stewart, Richmond Hill**
	TStop	W: Love's Travel Stop #338 (Scales)
	Gas	E: Chevron, Exxon, Shell◈ W: Shell
	Food	E: Little Caesars Pizza, Frank's BBQ W: McDonald's/Love's TS
	TServ	W: Roberts White/GMC, International
	Other	E: to **Waterway RV Park▲**, **Ft McAllister State Park**, Ft Stewart Military Res W: WiFi/**RVDump**/Love's TS, ATMs, **Dick Gores RV World**
87		**US 17, Coastal Hwy, GA 25, Richmond Hill**
	TStop	W: Travel Center of America (Scales), El Cheapo #4/Shell

◈= Regular Gas Stations with Diesel ▲ = RV Friendly Locations ♥= Pet Friendly Locations
Red print shows large vehicle parking / access on site or nearby Brown Print = Campgrounds / RV PARKS

EXIT		GEORGIA
	Gas	E: Chevron◈, Citgo, RaceTrac W: BP, Exxon◈, Speedway◈
	Food	E: Arby's, Denny's, Huddle House, McDonald's, Subway, Waffle House W: Rest/LongJohnSilver/PizzaHut/Popeyes/TA TC, McDonald's
	Lodg	E: Days Inn, Scottish Inn, Travelodge W: Best Western, Comfort Inn, Econo Lodge, Hampton Inn, Holiday Inn, Knights Inn, Motel 6
	TWash	W: TA TC
	TServ	W: TA TC/Tires
	Med	E: + Urgent Medical Care Center
	Other	W: Laundry/WiFi/TA TC, **Savannah South KOA▲**
76		**US 84, GA 38, Sunbury Rd, Midway, Hinesville, Sunbury, Fort Stewart**
	TStop	W: El Cheapo #50 (Scales)
	Gas	W: Parkers Travel Store/BP◈
	Food	W: Huddle House, Holton Seafood Rest
	Lodg	W: appr 10 mi
	Med	W: + Hospital
	Other	W: **Martin's Glebe Campground▲**
67		**US 17, Coastal Hwy, Riceboro, to South Newport**
	Gas	E: BP, Chevron◈, Citgo◈, El Cheapo W: BP
	Food	E: McDonald's, Subway/Chevron
	Other	W: **Riverfront RV Park▲**
58		**GA 57, GA 99, Ridge Rd, Wiregrass Trail, Townsend, Eulonia**
	Gas	E: BP◈, Citgo W: Chevron◈, Shell◈
	Food	W: Huddle House
	Lodg	W: Days Inn, Knights Inn, Ramada
	Other	W: **McIntosh Lake Campground▲**, **Lake Harmony RV Park▲**
(55)		Weigh Station (Both dir)
49		**GA 251, Bus I-95N, Briardam Rd, Darien**
	FStop	W: El Cheapo #54 (Scales)
	Gas	E: BP◈, Chevron◈ W: BP, Mobil◈, Shell◈
	Food	E: B & J's Steaks & Seafood, DQ, McDonald's, Skipper's Fish Camp, Waffle House W: Subs/El Cheapo, Burger King, Huddle House, Ruby Tuesday, Wendy's, Pizza Hut/Taco Bell, BBQ
	Lodg	E: Ft King George Motel, Open Gates B&B W: Clean Stay USA, Comfort Inn, Hampton Inn, Quality Inn♥, Super 8
	Other	E: Piggly Wiggly, **to appr 3 mi: Cathead Creek Ranch & RV Park▲**, **Tall Pines Campground▲**, **Darien Inland Harbor RV Park▲** W: Preferred Outlets at Darien, Interstate Truck Repair
42		**GA 99, Bus I-95S, Grant Ferry Rd, Darien**
(40)		Rest Area (SB) (RR, Ph, Pic, Vend, Info, WiFi, RVDump)
38		**to US 17, GA Spur 25, Brunswick, N Golden Isles Pkwy**
	Gas	E: Chevron◈, Conoco, RaceTrac W: BP, Shell◈
	Food	E: Applebee's, Captain D's Seafood, Millhouse Steak House, Ruby Tuesday W: China Town, Denny's,Huddle House, Mex Rest, Starbucks, Waffle House

EXIT		GEORGIA
	Lodg	E: Country Inn, Fairfield Inn, Holiday Inn, Jameson Inn, Microtel, St James Suites W: Baymont Inn, Courtyard, Econo Lodge, Quality Inn, Guest Cottage & Suites
	Med	E: + Applecare Minor Emergency Treatment Center, + Glynco Immed Care Center
	Other	E: ATMs, Glynco Jetport✈ W: ATMs, Grocery, Golden Isles Harley Davidson, Rainbow Car Wash, **Golden Isles Vacation Park▲**, **Blythe Island Regional Campground▲**
36		**US 25, US 341, Brunswick, Jesup**
	Gas	E: Chevron◈, Exxon◈, RaceWay W: BP, El Cheapo◈, Mobil◈, Sunoco
	Food	E: Burger King, Cracker Barrel, IHOP, KFC, Krystal, McDonald's, Pizza Hut, Quiznos, Shoney's, Starbucks, Subway/Chevron, Taco Bell, The GA Pig BBQ, Waffle House, Wendy's, W: Allen's BBQ, Beef O'Brady's, Capt Joe's Seafood, Denny's, Huddle House, Sonny's BBQ, Subway, Waffle House
	Lodg	E: Baymont Inn♥, Days Inn, Hampton Inn, Knights Inn, Red Roof Inn♥, Travelodge W: Best Western, Clarion Inn♥, Comfort Inn, Clean Stay USA, Motel 6♥, Ramada, Rodeway Inn, Sleep Inn, Super 8♥
	Other	E: **Newcastle RV Center** W: ATMs, Auto Services, Advance Auto Parts, Banks, CVS, Dollar General, Family Dollar, Fred's, Pharmacy, Winn Dixie, Express Lube & CarWash, Laundromat, **Police Dept, Suncoast RV Center, GA State Hwy Patrol Post**
36A		**US 25S, US 341S, Brunswick**
36B		**US 25N, US 341N, Jesup**
29		**US 17, US 82, GA 520, S Ga Pkwy, to GA 303, Brunswick**
	TStop	E: Love's Travel Stop #405 (Scales), El Cheapo #53/Shell (Scales) W: Flying J Travel Plaza/Conoco (Scales), GOASIS #702/TA TC,
	Gas	E: Citgo◈, Flash Foods/Exxon◈, P66 W: Citgo, Mobil◈, Sunoco
	Food	E: Steak'nShake/Subway/Love's TS, FastFood/El Cheapo, Church's Chicken, Huddle House, McDonald's, Krystal, Steak 'n Shake W: CountryMkt/FastFood/FJ TP, Burger King/PlanetSmoothie/SeattlesBestCoffee/Subway/GOASIS TC, Waffle House
	Lodg	E: Comfort Suites W: Days Inn, GuestHouse Inn, Microtel, Super 8
	TWash	E: Blue Beacon TW
	TServ	E: Speedco W: TA TC/Tires, Glenn Diesel & **RV** Service Angels CB & Chrome Shop
	Other	W: Laundry/WiFi/TA TC, Laundry/WiFi/RVDump/LP/FJ TP, Vet♥, **Golden Isles RV Park▲**, **to appr 3mi Blythe Island Reg'l Park▲**, **appr 12 mi** Golden Isles Speedway
26		**Dover Bluff Rd, CR 145, Waverly**
	Gas	E: Mobil◈
	Other	E: **Ocean Breeze Campground▲**
14		**GA 25 Spur, Woodbine**
	TStop	W: Sunshine Travel Center (Scales)
	Food	W: Rest/Sunshine TC
	Lodg	W: Stardust Motel

EXIT		GA / FL
	Other	W: Laundry/Sunshine TC
7		**Harrietts Bluff Rd, CR 141, Woodbine**
	FStop	E: Flash Foods #195/Exxon
	Gas	E: Shell W: BP◈
	Food	E: Huddle House, Jack's Famous BBQ, Subway
	Tires	E: A&D Tire Shop, Flash Foods
	Other	E: **Raintree RV Park▲**
6		**Colerain Rd, Kingsland, Laurel Island Pkwy, CR 90**
	TStop	E: AmBest/Cisco Travel Plaza #1/BP (Scales), Cone Auto Truck Plaza #201
	Food	E: Arby's/Cisco TP, FastFood/Cone ATP
	Other	E: Laurel Oaks Animal Hospital♥
3		**GA 40, Kingsland St, Mary's Rd, Kingsland, St Mary's**
	TStop	W: Petro 2 (Scales)
	Gas	E: BP◈, Chevron, El Cheapo, Mobil, Shell W: Citgo, Exxon◈, RaceWay
	Food	E: Applebee's, Bonzai Japanese Steak House, Burger King, ChickFilA, IHOP, McDonald's, KFC, New Hong Kong Buffet, Pizza Hut, Ponderosa, Ruby Tuesday, Shoney's, Sonny's BBQ, Subway, Taco Bell Waffle House, Wendy's, Zaxby's W: Church's/Quiznos/Petro 2, Cracker Barrel, IHOP, Shoney's, Waffle House
	Lodg	E: Comfort Suites, Country Inn, Fairfield Inn, Four Star Inn, Hampton Inn, Hawthorne Suites, Holiday Inn Express, Magnolia Inn♥, Microtel Inn, Sleep Inn, Super 8 W: Clean Stay USA♥, Days Inn♥, Econo Lodge, Jameson Inn, La Quinta Inn, Quality Inn, Ramada Inn, Red Roof Inn, Scottish Inn, Western Motel
	TServ	W: Petro 2/Tires
	Med	E: + Hospital
	Other	E: ATMs, Auto Dealers, Banks, CVS, Grocery, Publix, Vet♥, Winn Dixie, **to Walmart sc, to Crooked River State▲**, **Park A Big Wheel RV Park▲**, **to** St Mary's Airport✈ W: Laundry/RVDump/Petro2, **KiKi RV Park▲**, **Henry B's Mobile RV Repair,** Kingsland Welcome Center
1		**St Mary's Rd, CR 61, Kingsland, St Mary's**
		GA Welcome Center (NB) **(Next 116 mi)** E: (RR, Phone, Picnic, Vend, Info)
	TStop	W: WilcoHess Travel Plaza #3060 (Scales)
	Gas	E: Shell◈ W: BP◈, Chevron◈
	Food	W: Wendy's/WilcoHess TP, Jack's BBQ
	Lodg	W: Jameson Inn
	Other	W: **Jacksonville North/Kingsland KOA▲**, **Country Oaks RV Park & Campground▲**, **Good Sam Park▲**

↑ GEORGIA
↓ FLORIDA

NOTE:	**MM 382: Georgia State Line**
NOTE:	**Begin SB/End NB Motorist Call Boxes**
(381)	Inspection Station (Both dir)

◈= Regular Gas Stations with Diesel ▲ = RV Friendly Locations ♥= Pet Friendly Locations
Red print shows large vehicle parking / access on site or nearby **Brown Print = Campgrounds / RV PARKS**

EXIT	FLORIDA
380	**US 17, Yulee, Hilliard**
Gas	W: BP, Shell
Lodg	W: Americas Best Value Inn, Days Inn
Other	E: Hance's First in FL RV Park▲, Osprey RV Park▲, Crooked River State Park▲
	W: Bow & Arrow Campground▲
(378)	FL Welcome Center (SB) (RR/Fam, Ph, Pic, Pet, Vend, Sec247)
(376)	Weigh Station (Both dir)
373	**FL 200, FL A1A, Yulee, Callahan, Amelia, Amelia Island**
Gas	E: Flash Foods/Exxon
	W: BP, Citgo, Sunoco
Food	E: Burger King, KFC/PizzaHut, McDonald's, Subway Wendy's, Krystal/Flash Foods, on US 17: Jinwright Seafood Rest
	W: Waffle House, Subway/Citgo
Lodg	E: Comfort Inn, Country Inn, Holiday Inn Express
TServ	E: CAT Truck Service
Other	E: Lofton Creek Campground▲
366	**Pecan Park Rd, Jacksonville**
FStop	E: Baine Truck Stop (S on N Main St)
Other	W: Jacksonville Intl Airport✈, Pecan Park RV Resort▲, Pecan Park,Flea Market
363	**Duval Rd, Int'l Airport (SB)**
Gas	E: Chevron x2, Mobil◈, Sunoco
	W: BP, Flash Foods, Island Food Store, Kangaroo Express/Chevron, Shell◈, Sunoco
Food	E: Arby's, ChickFilA, Cracker Barrel, Chili's, Dunkin Donuts/Sunoco, Five Guys Famous Burgers, Green Papaya Rest, Olive Garden, Panda Express, Red Lobster, Starbucks, Wasabi Japanese Rest
	W: Denny's, Longhorn Steakhouse, Mill House Rest, Panera Bread, Ruby Tuesday, Subway, Waffle House, Wendy's, Zaxby's
Lodg	E: Red Roof Inn♥
	W: Best Western, Comfort Suites, Country Hearth Inn♥, Courtyard, Crowne Plaza, Days Inn, Econo Lodge♥, Hampton Inn♥, Hilton Garden Inn, Holiday Inn♥, Jacksonville Plaza Hotel & Suites, Ramada♥, Red Roof Inn, Travelodge♥, Wingate Inn
Other	E: ATMs, AT&T, Best Buy, Enterprise RAC, Gander Mountain, Lowe's, Office Max, PetSmart♥, Walmart sc
	W: Cinema, Mall, Jacksonville Int'l Airport✈ U-Haul, Dick Gore's RV World, Camping Time RV/Camping World
363A	**Duval Rd E, Jacksonville (NB)**
363B	**Duval Rd W, Airport (NB)**
Other	W: Jacksonville Int'l Airport✈
(362B)	**Jct I-295S, Jacksonville, Beaches**
(NEW)	**to FL 9A, Blount Island (SB)**
Other	E: Anheuser Busch Brewery
360	**FL 104, Dunn Ave, Busch Dr**
FStop	E: Gate #1143
Gas	W: BP, Chevron, Exxon, Hess, Shell
Food	E: Applebee's, Hardee's, Waffle House
	W: Arby's, Bono's BBQ, Burger King, CiCi's Pizza, KFC, Krystal, McDonald's, New Century Buffet, Popeye's Chicken,

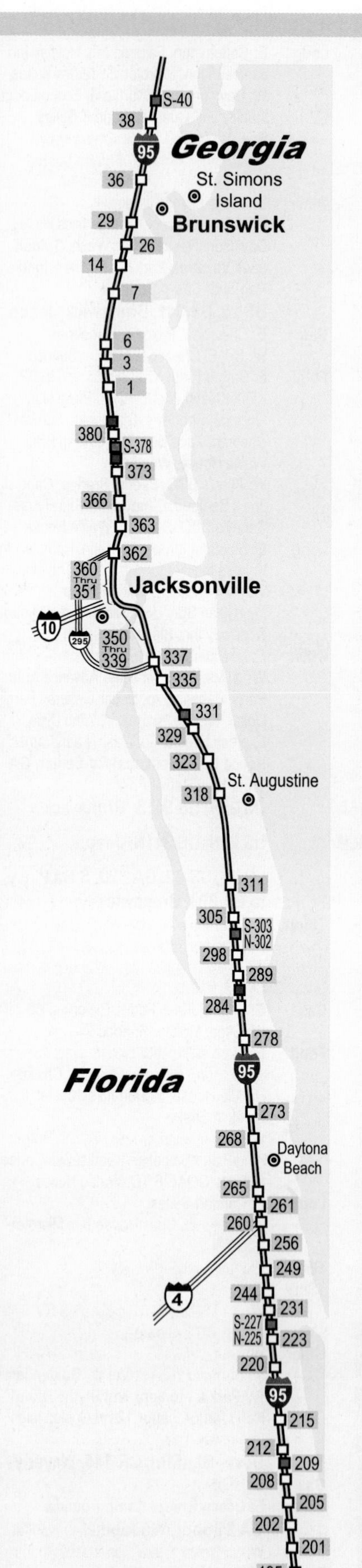

EXIT	FLORIDA
Food	W: Shoney's, Sonny's BBQ, Taco Bell, Wendy's
Lodg	E: Executive Inn, Value Place
	W: Best Western, Best Value Inn, La Quinta Inn♥, Motel 6♥
Med	W: + St Vincent's Family Med Center
Other	E: Sam's Club, Anheuser Busch Brewery, Bowling
	W: ATMs, Auto Services, Big Lots, Family Dollar, Jiffy Lube, Pep Boys, Publix, Radio Shack, Tires Plus, Walgreen's, Winn Dixie
358B	**Broward Rd, Jacksonville**
Lodg	W: Best USA Inn
358A	**FL 105, Zoo Pky, to US 17**
Other	E: Zoo, to Little Talbot Island St Park
357	**FL 111, Edgewood Ave**
Gas	E: BP, Shell
356B	**FL 115, Lem Turner Rd (NB)**
356A	**FL 117, Norwood Ave (NB)**
356	**FL 117 Norwood Ave, FL 115, Lem Turner Rd (SB)**
Gas	W: BP, Hess, Shell
Food	E: Hardee's
	W: Crab Hut, Krystal, Golden Egg Roll
Med	W: + St Vincent's Family Med Center
Other	W: Grocery, Walgreen's
355	**FL 122, Golfair Blvd, Jacksonville**
Gas	E: BP, Shell
	W: Chevron, RaceTrac
Lodg	W: Metro Inn
Other	E: ATMs, Publix, Greyhound Station
354B	**US 1N, MLK Jr Pky W, Amtrak**
354A	**US 1S, MLK Jr Pky E**
TServ	W: Cummins Southeastern
Med	E: + University Medical Center
353D	**FL 114, W 8th St**
Food	E: McDonald's
Med	E: + University Medical Center
Other	E: Walgreen's
353C	**US 23N, Kings Rd**
353B	**US 90 Alt, Union St, US 17N, US 23S FL 139S, Downtown**
Other	E: to Alltel Stadium
NOTE:	SB: Ongoing construction thru 2011
353A	**Church St, Monroe St, Forsyth St (SB)**
352C	**Monroe St (NB)**
352B	**Forsyth St (NB)**
352A	**Myrtle Ave**
351D	**Stockton St (SB)**
351C	**Margaret St (SB)**
(351B)	**Jct I-10W, to Lake City, Tallahassee (fr NB, Left Exit)**
NOTE:	NB: Ongoing construction thru 2011
351A	**Park St (NB exit, SB entr)**
350B	**FL 13, San Marco Blvd (SB ex, NB ent**
350A	**US 1N, Prudential Dr, Riverside Ave, FL 13, Main St, US 90W, FL 5N, FL 10W (NB)**
349	**US 90E, Jacksonville Beaches (SB exit, NB entr)**

◈= Regular Gas Stations with Diesel ▲ = RV Friendly Locations ♥= Pet Friendly Locations
Red print shows large vehicle parking / access on site or nearby Brown Print = Campgrounds / RV PARKS

348 US 1S, Philips Hwy (SB ex, NB ent)
Lodg W: City Center Hotel, Scottish Inn

347 US 1 Alt, FL 126, Emerson St
Gas E: Shell, Texaco
W: AmocoBP◈, Gate, Hess
Food E: Subway
W: McDonald's, Taco Bell
Lodg W: Emerson Inn, Howard Johnson♥, Villager Lodge
Other E: Auto Services, Family Dollar, Grocery, Walgreen's
W: Jacksonville Ice Rink

346AB FL 109, University Blvd (SB) (NB access via Exit #345)
Gas E: BP, Hess◈, Shell
W: RaceTrac, BP
Food E: Huddle House, Kosher Kitchen, DQ, Krystal, Subway, Hungry Howie's Pizza & Subs, Shoney's
W: Burger King, IHOP, Ryan's Grill, Taco Bell, Waffle House
Lodg W: Days Inn♥, Comfort Lodge, Red Carpet Inn, Ramada Inn♥, Super 8
TServ W: Detroit Diesel Truck Service
Med E: + Physician Care Center
W: + Jacksonville Gen'l Hospital
Other E: ATMs, CVS, Firestone, Firestone, Goodyear, Winn Dixie, Pharmacy
W: Auto Services, U-Haul, Vet♥

345 Bowden Rd, to FL 109, University Blvd (NB ex, SB entr)
Gas E: Chevron, Gate◈, Hess◈, Kangaroo Express
Food E: Bono Pit BBQ, Blimpie/Pizza/Hess. Larry's Giant Subs, Schnitzel House
Lodg E: Ramada
Other E: CVS, FedEx Office

344 FL 202, J Turner Butler Blvd, Jacksonville Beaches
Gas W: BP◈, Kwik Trip, Shell
Food E: Rest/Marriott, Dave & Busters
W: Applebee's, ChickFilA, Cracker Barrel, Hardee's, McDonald's, Sonic, Starbucks, Waffle House, Zaxby's
Lodg E: Best Western♥, Candlewood Suites, Econo Lodge♥, Hampton Inn, Holiday Inn Express, Howard Johnson, Marriott
W: Courtyard, Extended Stay America♥, Fairfield Inn, Jameson Inn, La Quinta Inn♥, Microtel♥, Red Roof Inn♥, Wingate Inn
Med E: + St Luke's Hospital, + Mayo Clinic
Other E: Pharmacy
W: ATMs, Budget Truck Rental, Tires

341 FL 152, Baymeadows Rd
Gas E: BP, Shell, Gate, Lil Champ
W: Exxon◈, Kangaroo, Shell
Food E: Applebee's, Arby's, Chili's, Hardee's, Quincy's Steak House, Roadhouse Grill, Subway, Waffle House
W: Bulls BBQ, Burger King, Denny's, Hardee's, IHOP, McDonald's, Pizza Hut, Red Lobster, Steak & Ale, Wendy's
Lodg E: AmeriSuites, Comfort Suites, Fairfield Inn, Embassy Suites, Holiday Inn♥, Homestead Inn♥
W: Best Inn♥, Comfort Inn, Homewood Suites♥, La Quinta Inn♥, Motel 6♥, Quality Inn♥, Residence Inn♥, Studio 6♥
Other E: FedEx Office, Food Lion, Publix, Tires
W: ATMs, Goodyear, Office Depot, Harley Davidson

340 FL 115, Southside Blvd (NB)
Gas E: Kangaroo Express
Food E: Five Guys Burgers, Longhorn Steakhouse, Sierra Grill
Lodg E: Marriott
Other E: ATMs, Best Buy, Borders, CompUSA, Home Depot, Target

339 US 1, FL 5, Phillips Hwy
Gas E: BP, Chevron, RaceTrac
W: BP◈
Food E: Arby's, Burger King, McDonald's, Olive Garden, Ruby Tuesday, Taco Bell, Waffle House
TServ E: Perkins Engine Parts & Service
Other E: ATMs, Auto Dealers, Best Buy, Tire Kingdom, Baywood Animal Hospital♥, WalMart, Mall

(337) Jct I-295N, Orange Park, Beaches

335 St Augustine Rd
Gas W: Gate, Shell
Food E: Applebee's,
W: Chili's, McDonald's, Panera Bread
Lodg E: Courtyard, Holiday Inn Express
W: Hampton Inn
Med E: + Baptist Medical Center
Other E: ATMs, Banks, Walgreen's
W: ATMs, Banks, UPS Store

(331) Rest Area (Both dir) (RR/Fam, Phone, Pic, Pet, Vend, Sec247)

329 CR 210, Jacksonville, Green Cove Springs
TStop E: Travel Center of America #126/Shell (Scales), Pilot Travel Center #91 (Scales)
Gas E: Speedway, Sunoco
W: BP◈, Mobil, Kangaroo Express
Food E: T&CRest/NobleRomansPizza/TA TC, McDonald's/Pilot TC, Waffle House
W: Subway/BP, Starbucks
TServ E: TA TC/Tires
Other E: Laundry/TA TC, Laundry/WiFi/Pilot TC, ATMs, **St Augustine KOA▲**
W: ATMs, CVS, Grocery

323 International Golf Pkwy, St Augustine
Gas E: BP◈, Shell◈
Food E: Subway/Shell, Sbarro
Lodg E: Comfort Suites
W: Renaissance Resort
Other W: Publix, PGA Tour, World Golf Hall of Fame, World Golf Imax Theatre

318 FL 16, St Augustine
Gas E: BP, Gate◈, Kangaroo, Shell
W: Exxon, RaceTrac
Food E: Burger King, DQ, McDonald's, Huddle House, Subway, Waffle House
W: Cracker Barrel, Denny's, KFC, IHOP, Ruby Tuesday, Shoney's, Sonny's BBQ, Taco Bell, Wendy's
Lodg E: America's Best Value Inn, Comfort Inn, Country Inn, Courtyard, Econo Lodge, Fairfield Inn, Holiday Inn Express, La Quinta Inn♥, Marriott, Quality Inn♥
W: Best Western♥, Days Inn, Hampton Inn, Ramada Inn♥, Super 8♥, Wingate Inn, Super 8
Other E: ATMs, Belz Outlet Mall, Prime Outlets, Budget Truck Rental, Gander Mountain, U-Haul, **Cooksey's RV Park▲**, **Camping World**

Other W: Ancient City Shooting Range, Harley Davidson, St Augustine Premium Outlet Center, **Stage Coach RV Park▲**

311 FL 207, St Augustine
Gas E: BP◈, Kangaroo Express/Chevron, Hess◈, Indian River Fruit
W: Mobil◈
Food E: Subway/Hess
Lodg W: Comfort Inn, Quality Inn, Sleep Inn, Super 8♥
Med E: + Hospital
Other E: **Indian Forest RV Park▲**, **St John's RV Park▲**, **St Augustine Beach KOA▲**, Flea Market & **RV Park▲**,

305 FL 206, St Augustine, to Hastings, Crescent Beach, Marineland
TStop E: Flying J Travel Plaza #5117 (Scales)
Gas E: Citgo
Food E: CountryMarket/FastFood/FJ TP
TServ W: Continental Truck Sales & Repair
Other E: Laundry/WiFi/**RVDump/LP**/FJ TP, **Gore RV Center**, **Ocean Grove RV Sales**

(303) Rest Area (SB) (RR, Phone, Picnic, Vend, Sec24/7)

(302) Rest Area (NB) (RR, Phone, Picnic, Vend, Sec24/7)

298 US 1, FL 5, St Augustine, Hastings
Gas E: BP◈, Citgo, Indian River Fruit/Sunoco, Shell
W: Mobil◈, Hess, Sunrise
Food W: DQ, Waffle House
Other W: John's Towing Service

289 Palm Coast Pkwy, to FL A1A (TOLL)
Gas E: Exxon◈, BP, RaceTrac, Shell
W: Shell, Kangaroo Express x2
Food E: Cracker Barrel, Denny's, McDonald's, KFC, Pizza Hut, Starbucks, Thai Rest, Wendy's
W: Bob Evans, China King, Dunkin Donuts, Firehouse Subs, Golden Corral, Outback Steakhouse, Papa John's Pizza, Perkins, Pizza Hut, Ruby Tuesday, Sonny's BBQ, Steak 'n Shake, Subway, Taco Bell
Lodg E: Best Western♥, Fairfield Inn♥, Microtel♥, Sleep Inn
W: Days Inn♥,
Med E: + Medi Quick Walk-in Clinic
Other E: ATMs, Advance Auto Parts, Auto Services, Banks, Bowling, CVS, Publix, Radio Shack, Staples, Walgreen's, **to A1A:** addt'l services and **Campgrounds/RV Parks▲**
W: ATMs, Advance Auto Parts, Banks, CVS Grocery, Home Depot, Lowe's, PetSmart♥ Pharmacy, Tire Kingdom, Tires Plus, US Post Office, Walgreen's,
Walmart sc,

(286) Weigh Station (Both dir)

284 FL 100, Moody Blvd, Palm Coast, Bunnell, Flagler Beach
Gas E: BP, Citgo, Chevron◈, Hess◈, Shell
W: BP◈
Food E: Burger King, Denny's, Domino's Pizza, KFC, McDonald's, Popeye's, Subway, Wendy's, Woody's BBQ
Food W: Hijacker's Rest
Lodg E: Hampton Inn, Holiday Inn Express
W: Hilton Garden Inn
Med W: + Hospital

◈ = Regular Gas Stations with Diesel ▲ = RV Friendly Locations ♥ = Pet Friendly Locations
Red print shows large vehicle parking / access on site or nearby **Brown Print = Campgrounds / RV PARKS**

EXIT **FLORIDA**

Other E: ATMs, Bowling, Car Wash, Dollar General, Winn Dixie, **Walmart sc, to A1A:** addt'l serv, **Campgrounds/RV Parks▲**
W: Auto Dealers, Flagler Co Airport✈

278 Old Dixie Hwy, Bunnell, Tomaka State Park
- **Gas** **E:** 7-11/Citgo
  W: BP◊
- **Lodg** **W:** Country Hearth Inn
- **Other** **E:** Publix, **Bulow Creek State Park, Bulow RV Resort Campground▲**
  W: Holiday Trav-L-Park Co-op▲

273 US 1, FL 5, Ormond Beach
- **TStop** **E:** Valero Truck Stop (Scales), Mobil #8
  W: Love's Travel Stop #316 (Scales)
- **Gas** **E:** Chevron/Kangaroo Express, RaceTrac, Sunoco
  W: Exxon
- **Food** **E:** Denny's, McDonald's, Waffle House
  W: Arby's/TJCinn/Love's TS, Burger King/Exxon, DQ, Houligan's, Pig Stand, Saddle Jack's Bar & Grill
- **Lodg** **E:** Comfort Inn♥, Econo Lodge
  W: Best Value Inn♥, Days Inn♥, Destination Daytona Hotel & Suites, Quality Inn, Super 8♥, Scottish Inn♥
- **TServ** **E:** Valero TS/Tires
  W: AA Accurate Truck & Tire Repair
- **Med** **E: + Ormond MemorialHospital**
- **Other** **E: RVDump**/Valero TS, **Giant Recreation World, Harris Village & RV Park▲**, to Ormond Beach Muni Airport✈
  W: WiFi/**RVDump**/Love's TS, Bruce Rossmeyer Harley Davidson, J & P Cycles, U-Haul, **RV Center, Encore Superpark RV Park▲**

268 FL 40, W Granada Blvd, Ormond Beach, Ocala, Silver Springs
- **Gas** **E:** Shell, Chevron◊
  W: 7-11, BP◊, Hess, Mobil◊, RaceTrac, Texaco
- **Food** **E:** Applebee's, Boston Market, Chili's, ChickFilA, Denny's, McDonald's, Steak 'n Shake, Starbucks, Subway, Waffle House, Wendy's
  W: Cracker Barrel, McDonald's, NY Pizza/BP
- **Lodg** **E:** America's Best Value Inn, Ivanhoe Beach Resort, Sleep Inn
  W: Hampton Inn, Jameson Inn♥
- **Med** **E: + Ormond Memorial Hospital**
- **Other** **E:** ATMs, Discount Tire, Lowe's, Love Whole Foods, Publix, Regal Cinemas, US Post Office, **Walmart sc, Tomaka State Park▲**
  W: Auto Repair, Walgreen's

265 LPGA Blvd, Holly Hill, Ormond Beach, Daytona Beach
- **Gas** **E:** 7-11, Shell◊
- **Food** **E:** Wendy's
- **Lodg** **W:** Holiday Inn

261B US 92W, DeLand (SB)

261A US 92E, Daytona Beach (SB)
- **Other** **E:** Daytona Int'l Speedway, Daytona Beach Int'l Airport✈

261 US 92, International Speedway Blvd, E-Daytona Beach, W-DeLand (NB)
- **Gas** **E:** 7-11◊, BP◊, Citgo, Chevron◊, Hess◊, Mobil, RaceWay, Shell◊
  W: BP◊, Exxon, Sunoco
- **Food** **E:** Bob Evans, Burger King, Carrabba's, ChickFilA, Chili's, Cracker Barrel, Hooters, Hops, KFC, Krystal, Longhorn Steakhouse, Logan's Roadhouse, Olive Garden, Red Lobster, Ruby Tuesday, Shoney's, Starbucks, Subway, Taco Bell, Waffle House, Wendy's
  W: Denny's, IHOP, McDonald's
- **Lodg** **E:** America's Best Value Inn, Castaways Beach Resort, Comfort Suites, Hampton Inn, Hilton Garden Inn, Holiday Inn Express, La Quinta Inn♥, Quality Inn, Ramada Inn♥, Travelodge
  W: Days Inn, Quality Inn, Super 8
- **Med** **E: + Hospital**
- **Other** **E:** AMC 8, Alamo RAC, Auto Dealers, Auto Services, BJ's, Barnes & Noble, Best Buy, Boaters World, Budget RAC, Firestone, Home Depot, IMAX, Office Depot, PetCo♥ Pep Boys, PetSmart♥, Sports Authority,
  E: Staples, Target, IMAX, Volusia Mall, Walgreen's, Daytona Beach Int'l Airport✈, Daytona Int'l Speedway, **International RV Park & Campground▲, Racetrack RV▲**
  W: Flea Market, Cycle World, **Town & Country RV Park▲, Crazy Horse Camping▲**

(260B) Jct I-4W, to Orlando, Tampa

260A FL 400E, to South Daytona
- **Gas** **E:** Chevron
- **Food** **E:** Red Carpet Inn

256 FL 421, Taylor Rd, Port Orange
- **Gas** **E:** Citgo◊, Kangaroo Exp/BP, Shell
  W: 7-11, Hess, Shell
- **Food** **E:** Bob Evans, ChickFilA, Denny's, Dustin's BBQ, Papa John's Pizza, Quiznos, Sonny's BBQ, Spruce Creek Pizza
  W: Subway, McDonald's, Wendy's
- **Lodg** **E:** Days Inn, Dream Inn of DB, Hampton Inn, Holiday Inn, La Quinta Inn
- **Med** **E: + Hospital**
- **Other** **E:** Carwash, Home Depot, Lowe's, Target, Walgreen's, **Walmart sc, Daytona Beach Campground▲, Nova Family Camp ground▲, Orange Isles Campground ▲**
  W: Publix

249B FL 44W, DeLand (SB)

249A FL 44E, New Smyrna Beach (SB)

249 FL 44, DeLand, New Smyrna Beach
- **Gas** **E:** Shell◊
  W: Chevron◊
- **Food** **E:** Burger King, Denny's, McDonald's
- **Med** **E: + Hospital**
- **Other** **E:** Publix, Harley Davidson, New Smyrna Beach Muni Airport✈

244 FL 442, Indian River Blvd, Edgewater, Oak Hill
- **Gas** **E:** BP◊
  W: Exxon◊
- **Other** **E:** FL Shores Truck Center, Massey Ranch Airpark✈, **Addtl Serv 3.5 mi to US 1**

231 CR 5A, Stuckway Rd, to US 1, Mims, Scottsmoor, Oak Hill
- **FStop** **E:** Sugar Creek Stuckey's/BP
- **Food** **E:** Stuckey's/BP
- **Other** **W: Crystal Lake RV Park▲**

(227) Rest Area Brevard Co (SB)
(RR/Fam, Phone, Pic, Pet, Vend, Sec247)

(225) Rest Area Brevard Co (NB)
(RR/Fam, Phone, Pic, Pet, Vend, Sec247)

223 FL 46, W Main St, Mims, Sanford
- **Gas** **W:** BP, Shell
- **Food** **E:** McDonald's
- **Other** **E: Willow Lakes Campground▲**
  W: Titusville/Kennedy Space Center KOA▲, Seasons RV Camp▲

220 FL 406, Garden St, Titusville
- **Gas** **E:** Shell◊, BP◊
  W: Chevron◊
- **Food** **E:** McDonald's, Subway, Wendy's
- **Lodg** **E:** Days Inn, Travelodge
- **Med** **E: + Hospital**
- **Other** **E:** Dollar General, Publix, Tires Plus, Walgreen's, Arthur Dunn Airpark✈

215 FL 50, Cheney Hwy, Titusville, to Orlando
- **FStop** **E:** Space Shuttle Fuel/Sunoco
- **Gas** **E:** BP◊, Circle K, Mobil◊, Shell◊, Murphy
- **Food** **E:** Burger King, Denny's, Durango's, KFC/Pizza Hut/BP, McDonald's, Sonny's BBQ, Waffle House, Wendy's
  W: Cracker Barrel, IHOP
- **Lodg** **E:** Best Western, Comfort Inn♥, Holiday Inn, Ramada♥
  W: Days Inn, Fairfield Inn, Hampton Inn
- **Other** **E:** Lowe's, Staples, **Walmart sc**, Space Coast Visitor's Center
  W: Great Outdoors RV Nature & Golf Resort▲, St John's National Wildlife Refuge

212 FL 407, Challenger Memorial Pkwy, to FL 528W (TOLL) (SB ex, NB entr)
- **Other** **E:** to Space Coast Reg'l Airport✈, John F Kennedy Space Center

(209) Parking Area (Both dir)

208 Port St John Rd, Cocoa

205 FL 528 (TOLL), Beachline Expy, to Cape Canaveral, City Point

202 FL 524, Cocoa
- **Gas** **E:** Shell◊
  W: BP◊
- **Lodg** **W:** Days Inn, Ramada Inn, Super 8

201 FL 520, Cocoa, Orlando
- **FStop** **E:** Sunshine Food Store/BP
- **TStop** **E:** Pilot Travel Center #88 (Scales)
- **Gas** **E:** Chevron
  W: Shell
- **Food** **E:** Subway/Pilot TC, IHOP, Olive Garden, Waffle House
  W: McDonald's
- **Med** **E: + Hospital**
- **Lodg** **E:** Best Western, Budget Inn
  W: Holiday Inn Express
- **Other** **E:** WiFi/Pilot TC
  W: Forest Village RV Park▲, Sun Coast RV Center

195 FL 519, Fiske Blvd, Rockledge
- **Gas** **E:** 7-11, Shell◊
- **Med** **E: + Hospital**
- **Other** **E:** Lowe's, Rockledge Airpark✈, **Space Coast RV Resort▲**

◊= Regular Gas Stations with Diesel ▲ = RV Friendly Locations ♥= Pet Friendly Locations
Red print shows large vehicle parking / access on site or nearby **Brown Print = Campgrounds / RV PARKS**

EXIT	FLORIDA
191	**FL 509, Wickham Rd, Melbourne, Satellite Beach, Patrick AFB**
Gas	**E:** 7-11, Hess◈ **W:** Chevron◈, Murphy
Food	**E:** Bob Evans, Denny's, McDonald's, Perkins, Wendy's **W:** Burger King, Chili's, Cracker Barrel, Longhorn Steakhouse, Mimi's Café, Starbucks, Subway
Lodg	**E:** Comfort Inn **W:** Baymont Inn, La Quinta Inn♥
Other	**E:** Pharmacy, **to** Patrick AFB **W:** ATMs, Petco♥, Target, **Walmart sc**
183	**FL 518, Eau Gallie Blvd, Melbourne, Indian Harbor Beach**
Gas	**E:** 7-11, BP, Chevron◈, RaceTrac
Other	**E: to** Melbourne Int'l Airport✈ **W:** Flea Market
180	**US 192, FL 500, W Melbourne**
Gas	**E:** 7-11, BP◈, Circle K, Mobil◈, Sam's **W:** Shell
Food	**E:** Denny's, IHOP, Shoney's, Steak 'n Shake, Waffle House
Lodg	**E:** Best Value Inn, Courtyard, Days Inn, Fairfield Inn, Holiday Inn, Hampton Inn, Howard Johnson, Super 8, Travelodge, York Inn
Med	**E:** + Hospital
Other	**E:** Sam's Club, Target, Melbourne Int'l Airport✈
176	**CR 516, Palm Bay Rd, Palm Bay**
Gas	**E:** 7-11, BP◈, Chevron, Murphy **W:** 7-11, Shell
Food	**E:** Applebee's, Bob Evans, Denny's, **Cracker Barrel**, Dunkin Donuts, Golden Corral, Starbucks, Taco Bell, Wendy's
Lodg	**E:** Jameson Inn, Ramada Inn
TServ	**E:** Ringhaver Power Systems
Other	**E:** Albertson's, BJ's, **Walmart sc** **W:** Walgreen's, Publix, USAF Annex
173	**FL 514, Palm Bay, Malabar**
FStop	**W:** Sunoco #2573
Gas	**E:** Shell◈ **W:** BP◈, Hess, Shell, Sunoco◈
Food	**W:** Arby's, Burger King, Dunkin Donuts, IHOP, McDonald's, Sonny's BBQ, Subway, Taco Bell, Texas Roadhouse, Waffle House, Wendy's, Woody's BBQ
Lodg	**W:** Motel 6♥
Med	**E:** + PCA Family Medical Center, + Palm Bay Community Hospital
Other	**E:** Firestone, Truck/**RV** Repair **W:** ATMs, Advance Auto Parts, Big Lots, CVS, Dollar General, Goodyear, Home Depot, Publix, Tires, Walgreen's, **Walmart sc**
(169)	**Rest Area (SB)** **(RR/Fam, Phone, Pic, Vend, Sec247)**
(168)	**Rest Area (NB)** **(RR/Fam, Phone, Pic, Vend, Sec247)**
NOTE:	**Begin NB / End SB Call Boxes**
156	**CR 512, Fellsmere Rd, 95th St**
Gas	**E:** BP◈, Chevron, Mobil◈
Food	**E:** McDonald's, Subway
Med	**E:** + Hospital
Other	**E: Encore RV Park▲**, Sebastian Muni Airport✈

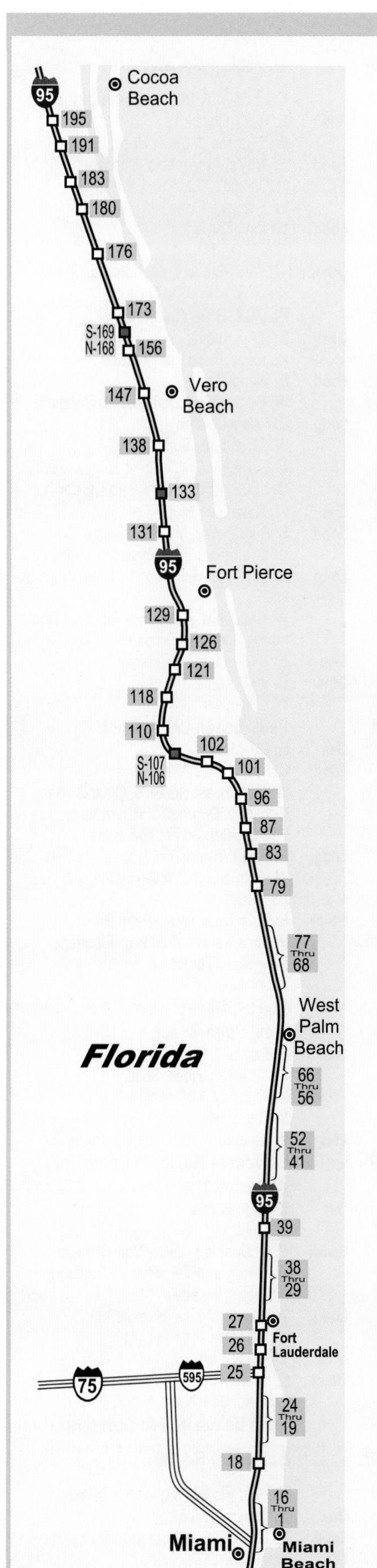

EXIT	FLORIDA
147	**FL 60, Osceola Blvd, Vero Beach, Lake Wales**
FStop	**E:** Hill Mart
TStop	**E:** Gator Truck Stop, Travel Center of America #197/Amoco (Scales)
Gas	**E:** 7-11, Hess, Mobil◈, Speedway **W:** Shell◈
Food	**E:** Rest/TA TC, Waffle House, Wendy's **W:** **Cracker Barrel**, McDonald's, Steak 'n Shake
Lodg	**E:** Howard Johnson, Best Western **W:** Country Inn, Hampton Inn, Holiday Inn Express,
TServ	**E:** TA TC/Tires
Med	**E:** + Hospital
Other	**E:** Laundry/WiFi/TA TC, NAPA, **to** Vero Beach Muni Airport✈ **W:** Prime Outlets
138	**FL 614, Indrio Rd, Fort Pierce**
Other	**E:** St Lucie Co Int'l Airport✈
(133)	**Rest Area St Lucie (Both dir)** **(RR, Phone, Pic, Pet, Vend, Sec24/7)**
131AB	**FL 68, Orange Ave, Ft Pierce**
TStop	**W:** Flying J Travel Plaza #5063 (Scales)
Gas	**E:** Valero
Food	**W:** Country Market/FastFood/FJ TP
TWash	**W:** Blue Beacon TW/FJ TP
Other	**W:** Laundry/BarbSh/WiFi/**RVDump/LP**/FJ TP
129	**FL 70, Okeechobee Rd, Ft Pierce**
FStop	**W:** Falcon Citgo Truck Stop
TStop	**W:** Pilot Travel Center #327 (Scales), Pilot Travel Center #90 (Scales)
Gas	**E:** Hess◈, RaceTrac, Sunoco◈, Murphy **W:** Chevron, Exxon, Shell◈
Food	**E:** Applebee's, Golden Corral, Waffle House **W:** McDonald's/Pilot TC, Arby's/Love's TS, Burger King, **Cracker Barrel**, Denny's, KFC, McDonald's, Red Lobster, Shoney's, Steak 'n Shake, Waffle House, Wendy's
Lodg	**W:** Crossroads Inn, Days Inn♥, Fairfield Inn, Hampton Inn, Holiday Inn Express, Motel 6♥, Quality Inn, Sleep Inn
Tires	**E:** Elpex Truck Tire Center
TWash	**W:** Wild Wash Truck Wash
TServ	**W:** Crossroads USA Truck Repair, K&R Truck, **RV & Bus Repair**
Med	**E:** + Hospital
Other	**E:** Orange Blossom Mall, Dollar Tree, Firestone, Goodyear, Home Depot, Radio Shack, **Walmart sc▲** **W:** Laundry/WiFi/Pilot TC, Laundry/WiFi/Love's TS, Grand Prix Amusement Park, **to** FL TPK
126	**CR 712, Midway Rd, Ft Pierce** **(All serv 3-5 mi E in Ft Pierce)**
121	**St Lucie West Blvd, Port St Lucie**
Gas	**E:** 7-11, Chevron, Shell◈, Murphy **W:** Mobil◈
Food	**E:** Bob Evans, Burger King, Chili's, McDonald's, Outback Steakhouse, Ruby Tuesday, Wendy's
Lodg	**E:** Hampton Inn, Spring Hill Suites
Other	**E:** Publix, Walgreen's, **Walmart sc**
118	**Gatlin Blvd, Port St Lucie**
FStop	**E:** BP
Gas	**E:** Chevron◈, Shell◈
Food	**E:** Burger King, Dunkin Donuts, Subway
Other	**E:** LP/BP

EXIT		FLORIDA
NOTE:		**SB: New In Motion Weigh Station Scheduled for Northern Martin Co**
110		**FL 714, Martin Hwy, Stuart, Palm City**
(107)		**Rest Area Martin Co (SB)** (RR/Fam, Ph, Pic, Pet, Vend, Sec247)
(106)		**Rest Area Martin Co (NB)** (RR/Fam, Ph, Pic, Pet, Vend, Sec247)
102		**CR 713, High Meadows Rd, Stuart, Palm City**
101		**FL 76, Kanner Hwy, Stuart**
	Gas	E: Chevron, Sunoco◈ W: Shell◈
	Food	E: Cracker Barrel, McDonald's, Wendy's W: Stuckey's/DQ
	Lodg	E: Best Western, Courtyard, Holiday Inn Express
	Med	E: + Hospital
	Other	E: Ronny's RV Ranch▲
96		**CR 708, SE Bridge Rd, Hobe Sound**
	Other	E: to Jonathan Dickinson State Park
(92)		**Weigh Station Hobe Sound (NB)**
87		**FL 706, Indiantown Rd, Jupiter, Okeechobee**
	FStop	E: Circle K Fuel Stop
	Gas	E: Chevron, Mobil, Hess, Shell, Mobil W: Mobil◈
	Food	E: Applebee's, Burger King, Dunkin Donuts, IHOP, KFC, Little Caesars Pizza, McDonald's, Subway, Taco Bell
	Lodg	E: Fairfield Inn, Wellesley Inn
	Med	E: + Hospital
	Other	E: ATMs, Advance Auto Parts, Auto Services, Home Depot, Laundromat, Publix, **Walmart**, Winn Dixie W: Tourist Info Center, **West Jupiter Camping Resort▲**
87B		**FL 706, Indiantown Rd, Jupiter, Okeechobee**
87A		**FL 706, Indiantown Rd, Jupiter, Okeechobee**
83		**Donald Ross Rd, Jupiter**
	Lodg	W: Donald Ross Inn
	Med	E: + Hospital
	Other	E: to Juno Beach RV Park▲
79C		**Military Trail S, FL 786, PGA Blvd (SB)**
79AB		**FL 786, PGA Blvd, Palm Beach (SB)**
	Gas	E: Sunoco W: Chevron, Hess, Shell◈
	Food	E: China Wok, Durango's Steak House W: Blvd Rest, Outback Steakhouse, Rest/Hol Inn
	Lodg	E: Marriott, Palm Beach Gardens W: Doubletree Hotel, Embassy Suites, Holiday Inn
	Med	E: + Hospital
	Other	E: Cinema 6, **Palm Beach Gardens RV Park▲** W: Publix
79B		**FL 786W, PGA Blvd (NB)**

EXIT		FLORIDA
79A		**FL 786E, PGA Blvd (NB)**
77		**CR 850, CR 809A, Northlake Blvd**
	Gas	E: Hess, Shell◈ W: Chevron, Mobil◈, Hess, Shell, Sunoco
	Food	E: Arby's, Applebee's, Checker's, McDonald's, Taco Bell, Wendy's W: Subway, Pizza Hut, Wendy's
	Lodg	W: Inn of America
	Med	E: + Hospital, + Northlake Medical
	Other	W: CVS, Grocery, Laundromat, Publix, Radio Shack, Winn Dixie
76		**FL 708, Blue Heron Blvd**
	Gas	E: BP◈, Shell◈ W: Mobil, RaceTrac, Texaco
	Food	E: Wendy's W: Burger King, Denny's, McDonald's
	Lodg	E: Villager Lodge W: Motel 6♥, Super 8
	TServ	E: Kenworth Truck Service, Mack Trucks
74		**CR 702, 45th St, W Palm Beach**
	Gas	W: RaceTrac, Mobil
	Food	E: Burger King, IHOP, Subway W: Cracker Barrel, Pizza Hut,Wendy's
	Lodg	E: Days Inn, Homewood Suites, Knights Inn W: Courtyard, Residence Inn, Red Roof Inn♥, Springhill Suites
	Med	E: + Glenbeigh Hospital
	Other	E: Walgreen's W: Goodyear
71		**Palm Beach Lakes Blvd**
	Gas	E: BP, Mobil
	Food	E: McDonald's, Wendy's W: Carrabbas, Hooter's, Olive Garden, Piccadilly, Durango's Steakhouse, Red Lobster, Sweet Tomatoes
	Lodg	E: Best Western W: Comfort Inn, Wellesley Inn
	Med	E: + Hospital
	Other	E: Palm Beach Mall, Palm Beach Co Visitor's Center, Best Buy, Firestone, Pharmacy, Target W: Walgreen's
70AB		**FL 704, Okeechobee Blvd, Downtwn West Palm Beach**
	Gas	E: Exxon W: Chevron, Hess, Shell
	Food	W: Subway, McDonald's, Waffle House
	Lodg	W: to appr 3 mi: La Quinta Inn♥
69		**Belvedere Rd, Palm Beach Int'l Airport (NB)**
	Gas	E: Fina, Exxon W: Shell
	Food	E: McDonald's, Lucky Star Chinese W: Denny's, IHOP, Phillip's Seafood, Shoney's, Wendy's
	Lodg	W: Crowne Plaza, Hampton Inn, Holiday Inn
	Med	E: + Hospital
	Other	E: Winn Dixie W: Palm Beach Int'l Airport✈
69B		**Palm Beach Int'l Airport (SB)**
69A		**Belvedere Rd (SB)**
68		**US 98, FL 80, Southern Blvd**
	Gas	E: Chevron, Mobill, Texaco
	Food	E: Grand China, Soprano's Pizza
	Lodg	W: Hilton
	Med	E: + Hospital

EXIT		FLORIDA
	Other	E: Publix, Pharmacy W: **W Palm Beach/Lion Country Safari KOA▲**
66		**FL 882, Forest Hill Blvd**
	Other	E: Palm Beach Zoo
64		**10th Ave N, Lake Worth**
	Gas	W: Citgo, Shell◈
63		**6th Ave S, Lake Worth**
	Med	W: + Hospital
61		**CR 812, Lantana Rd**
	Gas	E: Shell, Costco
	Food	E: Dunkin Donuts, KFC, McDonald's, Subway
	Lodg	E: Motel 6♥
	Med	W: + Hospital
	Other	E: ATMs, CVS, Costco, Dollar General, Laundromat, Publix, Pharmacy, **FL State Hwy Patrol Post** W: Palm Beach Co Park Airport✈
60		**Hypoluxo Rd, Lake Worth**
	FStop	W: High Ridge Marathon
	Gas	E: Mobil, Shell◈ W: Hess
	Food	E: Denny's, Shoney's, Taco Bell, Wendy's,
	Lodg	E: Best Western, Comfort Inn, Super 8,
	Other	E: ATMs, Sam's Club, Tires, U-Haul
59		**Gateway Blvd, NW 22nd Ave**
	Gas	E: Shell◈ W: Mobil◈
	Food	W: Carrabbas, Chili's, McDonald's
	Lodg	W: Hampton Inn
	Other	W: ATMs, Publix, Target
57		**FL 804, Boynton Beach Blvd**
	Gas	W: 7-11, Mobil, Shell◈
	Food	W: Wendy's, Waffle House, Subway, TGI Friday
	Lodg	E: Holiday Inn Express
	Other	W: ATMs, Auto Services, Publix, Office Depot, **Walmart sc**
56		**FL 792, Woolbright Rd**
	Gas	E: Shell W: RaceTrac
	Food	E: McDonald's W: Cracker Barrel, Subway
	Med	E: + Boynton Beach Medical Center
	Other	W: ATMs, Home Depot, Lowe's, Staples
52B		**FL 806W, Atlantic Ave (SB)**
52A		**FL 806E, Atlantic Ave (SB)**
52		**FL 806, Atlantic Ave, Delray Beach**
	Gas	E: BP W: Chevron, Shell, Mobil
	Food	W: Burger King, McDonald's, Sandwich Man, Moe's Seafood
	Lodg	W: Ramada
	Other	W: Amtrak, Publix, Walgreen's
51		**CR 782, Linton Blvd, Delray Beach**
	Gas	E: Exxon W: Chevron, Shell
	Food	E: Outback Steakhouse, McDonald's, DQ W: Palace, Grass Roots Café, The Grille
	Lodg	W: Hampton Inn, Springhill Suites
50		**Congress Ave, Boca Raton**
	Food	W: Denny's
	Lodg	W: Hilton, Homestead, Residence Inn, Studio Suites♥

◈= Regular Gas Stations with Diesel ▲ = RV Friendly Locations ♥= Pet Friendly Locations
Red print shows large vehicle parking / access on site or nearby **Brown Print = Campgrounds / RV PARKS**

EXIT FLORIDA

48B **FL 794W, Yamato Rd (NB)**

48A **FL 794E, Yamato Rd (NB)**

48 **FL 794, Yamato Rd (SB)**
- Gas: **E:** Chevron; **W:** Mobil
- Food: **W:** Café 777, BT Food, McDonald's, Park Place Food, Starbucks, Subway
- Lodg: **W:** Embassy, Hampton Inn, Springhill Suites

45 **FL 808, Glades Rd, Boca Raton**
- Gas: **E:** Shell; **W:** BP, DX Trading
- Food: **E:** PF Chang's; **W:** Chipolte Mex Grill, Houston Rest, Moe's SW Grill, Quiznos, Romano's Macaroni Grill, Starbucks
- Lodg: **E:** Fairfield Inn; **W:** Holiday Inn, Marriott, Residence Inn, Wyndham
- Med: **E:** + Hospital
- Other: **E:** Barnes & Noble, Town Center Mall, Whole Foods, Boca Raton Airport✈

44 **FL 798, Palmetto Park Rd**
- Gas: **E:** Exxon
- Food: **E:** BBQ, Denny's, Pizza Time, Subway
- Med: **E:** + Hospital
- Other: **E:** Publix

42 **FL 810E, Hillsboro Blvd (SB)**

42B **FL 810W, Hillsboro Blvd, Deerfield Beach (NB)**
- Gas: **W:** Chevron, Mobil◈
- Food: **W:** Boston Market, Pizza Hut, Denny's
- Lodg: **W:** Days Inn, Villager Inn, Wellesley Inn
- Other: **W:** CVS, Home Depot, Walgreen's,

42A **FL 810E, Hillsboro Blvd (NB)**
- Gas: **E:** BP, Shell◈
- Food: **E:** Pasta Cafe, Popeye's Chicken, McDonald's, Wendy's
- Lodg: **E:** Comfort Inn, Starwood Hotel, La Quinta Inn♥

41 **FL 869 (TOLL), SW 10th St, to I-75**
- Gas: **E:** Mobil◈
- Food: **E:** Cracker Barrel; **W:** Wok & Roll, Quiznos
- Lodg: **E:** Extended Stay America♥; **W:** Comfort Suites♥, Quality Inn

39 **FL 834, NW 36th, Sample Rd**
- Gas: **E:** BP, Hess, Mobil, Shell◈; **W:** Mobil◈
- Food: **E:** Port Hole, Four Corners, Hops Rest, **W:** Arby's, China Express, IHOP, McDonald's, Miami Subs, Subway
- Med: **E:** + Mini Medical Center, + North Broward Medical Center
- Other: **E:** **Highland Pines RV Resort Park▲**; **W:** CVS, Family Dollar, Winn Dixie, Harley Davidson

38B **Copans Rd W, Pompano Beach (SB)**

38A **Copans Rd W (SB)**

38 **Copans Rd, NW 24th (NB)**
- Gas: **E:** 7-11, BP
- Food: **E:** McDonald's

Personal Notes

EXIT FLORIDA

- Other: **E:** **Walmart**, Pompano Beach Airpark✈; **W:** Home Depot, Harley Davidson

36B **FL 814W, Atlantic Blvd (SB)**

36A **FL 814E, Atlantic Blvd (SB)**

36 **FL 814, Atlantic Blvd, Pompano Beach (NB)**
- FStop: **E:** Hardy Bros Marathon
- Gas: **E:** RaceTrac, Texaco; **W:** Mobil◈, Shell◈, Murphy
- Food: **E:** Burger King, Golden Corral, KFC, McDonald's, Taco Bell
- Med: **E:** + Hospital
- Other: **E:** CVS, Winn Dixie, Harness Racetrack; **W:** ATMs, Dollar Tree, Radio Shack, **Walmart sc**

33AB **FL 840, Cypress Creek Rd (NB)**

33 **FL 840, Cypress Creek Rd (SB)**
- Gas: **E:** BP, Hess; **W:** Hess, Shell
- Food: **E:** Duffy's Diner, Boston Bagel; **W:** Arby's, Burger King, Chili's, Hooters, Longhorn Steakhouse, McDonald's, Steak & Ale, Miami Subs, Wendy's
- Lodg: **E:** Extended Stay America, Hampton Inn, Westin; **W:** La Quinta Inn♥, Marriott, Sheraton
- Med: **E:** + North Ridge Gen'l Hospital
- Other: **W:** ATMs, Auto Services, Office Depot

EXIT FLORIDA

32 **FL 870, Commercial Blvd**
- Gas: **W:** BP, Circle K, Mobil, Coastal
- Food: **W:** Miami Subs, Sonny's BBQ, KFC, McDonald's, Waffle House
- Lodg: **W:** Best Western, Holiday Inn, Red Roof Inn♥, Travelodge
- Other: **W:** Ft Lauderdale Executive Airport✈

31B **FL 816W, Oakland Park Blvd (NB)**

31A **FL 816E, Oakland Park Blvd (NB)**

31 **FL 816, Oakland Park Blvd (SB) Fort Lauderdale**
- Gas: **E:** Chevron, Amoco, Mobil; **W:** BP◈, Hess, Shell
- Food: **E:** Checker's, Denny's, Miami Subs, Burger King, McDonald's, Wendy's; **W:** Burger King, Dunkin Donuts, IHOP
- Lodg: **E:** Roman Motel; **W:** Days Inn
- Med: **W:** + PCA Family Medical Center
- Other: **E:** ATMs, Laundromat, Lowe's; **W:** ATMs, Home Depot, US Post Office/Shell, Walgreen's, **RV Park▲**

29AB **FL 838, Sunrise Blvd (NB)**

29 **FL 838, Sunrise Blvd (SB)**
- Gas: **E:** Hess, Mobil; **W:** Exxon, Shell
- Food: **E:** Burger King, Popeye's Chicken; **W:** Church's Chicken, McDonald's
- Med: **W:** + Hospital
- Other: **W:** ATMs, Laundromat, Walgreen's

27 **FL 842, Broward Blvd, Downtown Fort Lauderdale**
- Gas: **E:** BP; **W:** Shell
- Lodg: **E:** Days Inn

(26D) **Jct I-595W (SB)**

(26C) **Jct I-595E, to Airport (SB)**
- Other: **E:** Ft Lauderdale/Hollywood Int'l Airport✈

26 **FL 736, Davie Blvd**
- Gas: **W:** BP, Hess, Mobil
- Food: **W:** Subway, Wendy's

25 **FL 84, SW 24th St, Marina Mile Rd**
- FStop: **E:** 84 Shell
- Gas: **E:** Texaco, Twin Mini Shop, Mobil
- Food: **E:** McDonald's, Barbell's Grill, Lil Red; **W:** Christopher's Ice Cream
- Lodg: **E:** Best Western, Hampton Inn, Motel 6♥, Sky Motel, Budget Inn; **W:** Red Carpet Inn, Ramada
- Other: **W:** **Yacht Heaven Park & Marina▲**

(24) **Jct I-595, FL 862, to Tpk, I-75, Fort Lauderdale Int'l Airport, Port Everglades (NB)**

23 **FL 818, Griffin Rd, Dania Beach**
- Gas: **W:** BP, Citgo◈
- Food: **E:** Garden Cafe, Rest/Sheraton; **W:** Rest/Bass Pro Shop
- Lodg: **E:** Hilton♥, Sheraton; **W:** Courtyard, Homewood Suites
- Other: **E:** Ft Lauderdale Int'l Airport✈; **W:** Bass Pro Shop, **North Coast RV Park & Marina▲**

EXIT		FLORIDA
22		**FL 848, Stirling Rd, Dania Beach**
	Gas	**E:** Mobil
		W: Circle K
	Food	**E:** Burger King, McDonald's, Taco Bell Sweet Tomatoes, TGI Friday, Wendy's
		W: Dunkin Donuts, Subway
	Lodg	**E:** Comfort Inn, Hampton Inn, Springhill Suites
	Other	**E:** ATMs, Barnes & Noble, Big Lots, BJ's, Home Depot, Boomers of Dania, RaceARama, Atlantis
	Other	**W:** ATMs, CVS, Walgreen's, Pep Boys, Tires, **to** Hollywood Indian Reservation
21		**FL 822, Sheridan St, Hollywood**
	Gas	**E:** BP, Cumberland Farms, Citgo, Mobil
		W: Shell
	Food	**E:** TGI Friday, Sweet Tomatoes
		W: Denny's
	Lodg	**E:** La Quinta Inn♥
		W: Days Inn, Holiday Inn
20		**FL 820, Hollywood Blvd**
	Gas	**E:** Gascom, Shell
		W: BP, Chevron, Mobil
	Food	**E:** Miami Subs, IHOP, McDonald's
		W: Boston Market, McDonald's, Subway Quizno's, Starbucks, Taco Bell
	Lodg	**E:** Howard Johnson Express
	Med	**W: + Hospital**
	Other	**W:** ATMs, Publix, Target, Walgreen's, Hollywood Mall, **Hollywood Police Dept**
19		**FL 824, Pembroke Rd, Hollywood**
	Gas	**E:** Shell, Mobil
		W: Sunoco◈
18		**FL 858, Hallandale Beach Blvd**
	Gas	**E:** 7-11, BP, Exxon
		W: BP, RaceTrac, Speedway
	Food	**E:** Burger King, Denny's, Dunkin Donuts, KFC, Little Caesars Pizza, Long John Silver, McDonald's, Smokehouse BBQ, Subway, Wendy's
		W: Park Food Court
	Lodg	**E:** Best Western, Ramada
	Med	**W: + PCA Family Medical Center**
	Other	**E:** Walgreen's, Winn Dixie, **Holiday RV Park▲**
16		**Ives Dairy Rd, NE 203rd St, Miami**
	Gas	**W:** 7-11, BP
	Food	**W:** Subway
	Med	**E: + Hospital**
	Other	**W: to** Dolphin Stadium
14		**FL 860, Miami Gardens Dr, North Miami Beach**
	Gas	**W:** BP, Chevron, Marathon◈
	Other	**W:** Walgreen's
12		**US 441S, FL 826, FL Tpk, FL 9N (SB exit, NB entr)**
12C		**US 441N, FL 7 (NB exit, SB entr)**
	Gas	**E:** Citgo, Hess, Valero
	Lodg	**E:** Days Inn, Holiday Inn
	Med	**E: + Hospital**
12B		**FL 826E, N Miami Beach (NB) (SB Access via Exit #12)**
12A		**FL 826W, FL Tpk (NB) (SB Access via Exit #12)**
11		**NW 151st St (NB exit, SB entr)**
	Gas	**W:** Twin Service Station, Sunoco
	Food	**W:** McDonald's

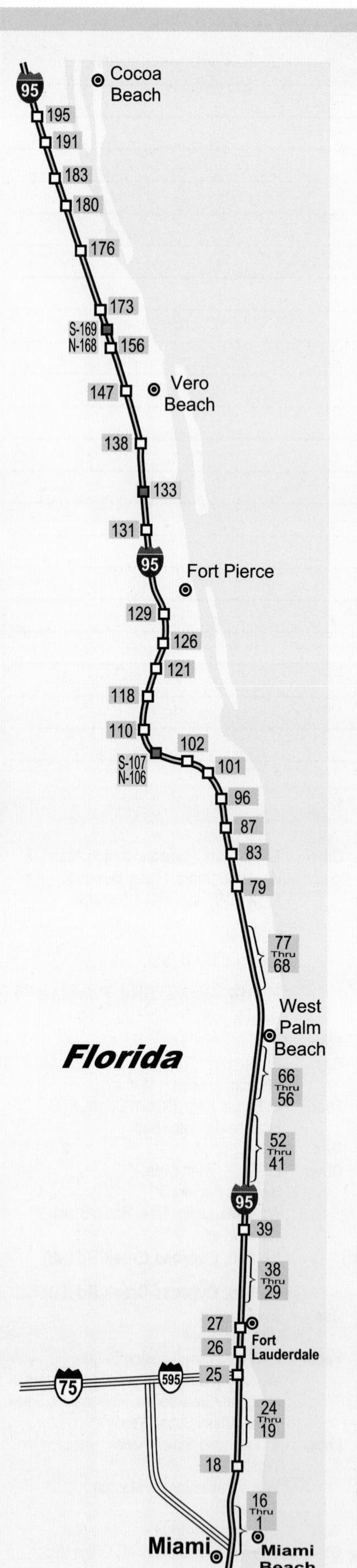

EXIT		FLORIDA
10B		**FL 916, Opa Locka Blvd**
	Gas	**W:** BP, Chevron, Liberty, Mobil
	Food	**W:** Subway, Pizza Hut
	Lodg	**W:** Motel 7, Uptown Arms Motel
10A		**NW 125th St, N Miami, Bal Harbour**
	Gas	**W:** Shell
	Food	**W:** Arnold's Castle, Wendy's
9		**FL 924, NW 119th St (NB ex, SB entr)**
	Gas	**E:** Mobil, BP
	Food	**W:** KFC, Sub Center, BBQ Barn
	Lodg	**W:** Bay Thrift Lodge
	Other	**W:** ATMs, Familly Dollar, Winn Dixie, Walgreen's
8B		**FL 932, NW 103rd St, Miami**
	Gas	**W:** Exxon, Shell, Chevron, Mobil
	Food	**W:** Carmen's, Dunkin Donuts
	Other	**W:** ATMs, Grocery
8A		**NW 95th St**
	Gas	BP, Mobil, Shell
	Food	**W:** Burger King, McDonald's
	Lodg	**W:** Days Inn
	Med	**W: + N Shore Medical Center**
	Other	**W:** ATMs, Walgreen's
7		**FL 934, NW 79th St, NW 81st St**
	Gas	**E:** Chevron◈
		W: Exxon, Shell
	Food	**W:** Ma's Rest
	Lodg	**W:** City Inn
6B		**NW 69th St (SB exit, NB entr)**
6A		**FL 944, NW 62nd St, NW 54th St, Dr Martin Luther King Jr Blvd**
	Gas	**W:** Shell
	Food	**W:** McDonald's, Subway
	Other	**W:** ATMs, Winn Dixie, Walgreen's
(4B)		**Jct I-195, FL 112W (TOLL) (NB)**
	Other	**W: to** Miami Int'l Airport✈
(4A)		**Jct I-195E, Miami Beach (NB)**
(4)		**Jct I-195E, FL 112 (TOLL), Miami Beach, Miami Int'l Airport (SB)**
3B		**NW 8th St, Port of Miami, Orange Bowl (SB exit, NB entr)**
3A		**FL 836W, Miami Int'l Airport (fr NB, LEFT exit)**
(2D)		**Jct I-395, NW 8th St, Orange Bowl (SB LEFT exit)**
	Other	**E: to** American Airlines Arena
2C		**Miami Ave (SB, LEFT exit)**
2B		**NW 2nd St (NB)**
	Other	**E:** Miami Art Museum
2A		**US 1, to S Miami Ave**
1B		**SW 8th St, SW 7th St**
1A		**SW 25th Rd, SW 26th Rd, Rickenbacker Causeway (SB)**

NOTE: I-95 begins/ends on US 1 in Miami, FL

EASTERN TIME ZONE

⬆ FLORIDA

Begin Northbound I-95 from Miami, FL to Maine/Canada border.

◈= Regular Gas Stations with Diesel ▲ = RV Friendly Locations ♥= Pet Friendly Locations
Red print shows large vehicle parking / access on site or nearby Brown Print = Campgrounds / RV PARKS

EXIT		MICHIGAN
		Begin Eastbound I-96 from Muskegon, MI to Detroit, MI.

MICHIGAN

EASTERN TIME ZONE

NOTE: I-96 Begins/Ends on US 31

1 **US 31 Bus N, Downtown Muskegon, to Ludington, Grand Haven**

1A **US 31S, Airline Rd, to Ludington, Grand Haven (EB) (WB access Hile Rd)**
- Other: S: Banks, Cinema, Muskegon Co Airport✈, Racetrack

1B **US 31N, to Ludington, Grand Haven**
- Gas: N: Citgo◊
- Food: N: Applebee's, Arby's, McDonald's, Old Country Buffet, Ruby Tuesday, Wendy's
- Lodg: N: Alpine Motel, Bel-Aire Motel, Comfort Inn
- Med: N: + Hospital
- Other: N: ATMs, Lowe's, Sam's Club, **Walmart sc**, **Quality RV**, **Seasons RV Center**

1C **E Hile Rd, Muskegon (EB only)**
- Gas: S: Exxon, Meijer
- Food: S: Bob Evans, Logan's Roadhouse, McDonald's, Olive Garden, Perkins, Red Lobster, Starbucks,
- Lodg: S: Baymont Inn, Fairfield Inn, Hampton Inn
- Other: S: AT&T, Banks, Barnes & Noble, Batteries Plus, Dick's Sporting Goods, Hobby Lobby, Meijer, Menard's, PetCo♥, Sprint, Target, TJ Maxx, The Lakes Mall, Racetrack, Vet♥

4 **Airline Rd (NB), 3rd Ave (SB)**
- Gas: N: Wesco◊
  S: Speedway◊, Shell, Wesco◊
- Food: S: McDonald's, Subway
- Lodg: S: Village Park B&B
- Other: S: Banks, Bowling, Fruitport Animal Hospital♥, US Post Office, to Pleasure Island Water Park

5 **Fruitport Rd, Fruitport (WB exit, EB entr)**

(8) **Rest Area Ottawa Co #502 (WB) (RR, Phone, Pic, Pet, Vend)**

9 **M 104, Spring Lake, Grand Haven, Spring Lake (WB exit, EB entr)**

10 **CR B 31, 112th Ave, Nunica**
- Gas: S: Nunica EZ Mart
- Other: S: **Dale's RV Sales & Service**, Cargo Trailers, Golf Course, **to Campers Paradise▲**, **Conestoga Grand River Campground▲**

16 **CR B 35, 68th Ave, Coopersville, Eastmanville**
- FStop: N: Speedway
- Gas: N: BP◊, Shell◊
- Food: N: Arby's, Burger King/Shell, Dunkin Donuts, Hardee's, McDonald's, Pizza Hut, Taco Bell
- Lodg: N: AmeriHost, Rodeway Inn
- Other: N: Banks, Grocery, Pharmacy, **Fun 'n Sun RV Center**, Tractor Supply
  S: to appr 21 mi: **Allendate/River Pines Campground▲**

19 **48th St, Coopersville, Lamont**
- Food: S: Sam's Joint
- Other: N: **Prime Time RV Sales & Service**

23 **16th Ave, Marne**
- Gas: N: Shell
- Other: N: Schneider's Tire Outlet
  S: Berlin Raceway, Fairgrounds

24 **M 11, 8th Ave, 4 Mile Rd, Grand Rapids, Walker, Grandville (EB)**
- Gas: S: Marathon◊
- Lodg: S: Wayside Motel

25 **8th Ave, 4 Mile Rd (WB) (Access to Exit #24 Serv)**

(25) **Rest Area Kent Co #503 (EB) (RR, Phone, Pic, Pet, Vend)**

26 **Fruit Ridge Ave, Grand Rapids**
- Gas: N: Citgo◊
  S: Citgo◊

28 **Walker Ave, Grand Rapids**
- Gas: S: Meijer◊
- Food: S: Blimpie, Bob Evans, McDonald's
- Lodg: S: Baymont Inn, Quality Inn
- Other: S: ATMs, Meijer

30B **M 37N, Alpine Ave, 3 Mile Rd,**
- Gas: N: 7-11, BP, Marathon, Shell, Sam's
- Food: N: Applebee's, Blimpie, Chuck E Cheese's Pizza, Cracker Barrel, Damon's, IHOP, Little Caesar's Pizza, Logan's Roadhouse, Olive Garden, Outback Steakhouse, Panera Bread, Perkins, Starbucks, Steak 'n Shake, Subway, Taco Bell, TGI Friday
- Lodg: N: Hampton Inn, Holiday Inn Express, Springhill Suites
- Other: N: AMC Theatres, Auto Services, Batteries Plus, Best Buy, CarQuest, Discount Tire, Dollar Tree, Enterprise RAC, Grocery, Hobby Lobby, Office Depot, Office Max, Pep Boys, PetCo♥, Radio Shack, RiteAid, Sam's Club, SavALot, Target, Walgreen's, **Walmart sc**,

30A **M 37S, Alpine Ave, 3 Mile Rd,**
- FStop: S: Speedway #8766
- Gas: S: Admiral◊, Meijer◊
- Food: S: Arby's, Burger King, KFC, Long John Silver, McDonald's, Papa John's Pizza, Ponderosa, Wendy's
- Lodg: S: Motel 6♥
- Other: S: Auto Services, Budget RAC, Goodyear, Home Depot, Tires, U-Haul, US Post Office, MI State Police

30AB **M 37N, Alpine Ave, 3 Mile Rd, Grand Rapids, Newaygo**

31AB **US 131, S-Kalamazoo, N-Cadillac**

33 **M 44 Connector, Plainfield Ave**
- Gas: N: Meijer◊, Speedway
  S: BP
- Food: N: Arby's, Burger King, KFC, McDonald's, Pizza Hut, Subway, Taco Bell, Wendy's
  S: Denny's
- Lodg: N: Grand Inn, Lazy T Motel
- Med: N: + Family Physicians Urgent Care
- Other: N: Auto Dealers, Auto Zone, Belle Tire, Big Lots, Discount Tire, Goodyear, Meijer, NAPA, NTB, Radio Shack, U-Haul, Walgreen's,

36 **Leonard St NE, Grand Rapids (Access to Ex #38 Serv)**

(37) **Jct I-196, Downtown Grand Rapids, Holland (WB, Left Exit)**
- TServ: S: Michigan CAT

38 **M 37S, M 44, E Beltline Ave, M 21, Grand Rapids, Flint**
- Lodg: S: Country inn
- Med: S: + Hospital
- Other: N: Cornerstone Univ

39 **M 21, E Fulton St, to Flint (EB)**

40A **Cascade Rd, Grand Rapids**
- Gas: S: Shell, Speedway◊
- Food: S: Jimmy's John's, Quiznos, Zoop
- Lodg: S: Harley Hotel

40B **Cascade Rd, Grand Rapids**
- Gas: N: 7-11, BP, Marathon◊
- Food: N: Subway

43A **M 11, 28th St, Kent Co Airport, Grand Rapids, Cascade**
- Gas: S: BP, Shell, Speedway
- Food: S: Arby's, Bob Evans, Chili's, Denny's, Dunkin Donuts, Hooters, IHOP, Olive Garden, McDonald's, Perkins, Rio Bravo, Red Lobster, Subway, Wendy's

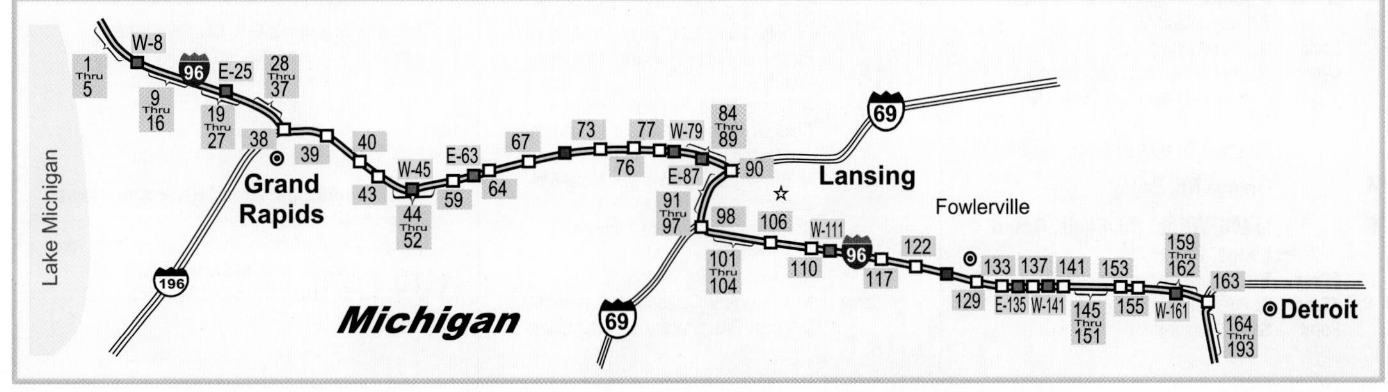

◊ = Regular Gas Stations with Diesel ▲ = RV Friendly Locations ♥ = Pet Friendly Locations
Red print shows large vehicle parking / access on site or nearby Brown Print = Campgrounds / RV PARKS

EXIT — MICHIGAN

Lodg — S: Clarion Inn, Comfort Inn, Extended Stay America, Exel Inn, Fairfield Inn, Hampton Inn, Hilton, Holiday Inn Select, Homewood Suites, Motel 6♥, Quality Inn, Ramada Inn Red Roof Inn♥, Residence Inn, Sleep Inn, Staybridge Suites, Super 8
Other — S: ATMs, Barnes & Noble, Best Buy, CarQuest, Centerpoint Mall, Costco, Gander Mountain, Hobby Lobby, Home Depot, PetSmart♥, Sam's Club, Staples, Target, U-Haul

43B — M 11, 28th St, Kent Co Airport, Grand Rapids, Cascade
Gas — N: Marathon◈, Meijer◈
Food — N: Akasaka Sushi, Brann's Steakhouse, Burger King, Pal's Diner, Panera Bread, Papa John's Pizza, Pizza Hut, Romano's Macaroni Grill, Shanghai Garden, Starbucks, Sundance Grill,
Lodg — N: Baymont Inn, Best Western, Country Inn, Crowne Plaza, Econo Lodge, Holiday Inn Express, Howard Johnson,
Other — N: ATMs, Auto Services, Banks, Carwash, Family Friends Veterinary Hospital♥, Grocery, Meier, RiteAid, Sprint, **Walmart**

44 — 36th St
Other — S: Gerald Ford Int'l Airport✈

46 — M 6, to Holland

52 — M 50, Alden Nash Ave, Lowell
Gas — N: Mobil◈
S: Marathon◈

59 — Nash Hwy, Clarksville

(63) — Rest Area (EB)
(RR, Phone, Pic, Pet, Vend, Info)

64 — Jordan Lake Rd, Lake Odessa
Other — N: **Ionia State Rec Area**
S: I-96 Speedway

67 — M 66, Ionia, Battle Creek
TStop — N: Pilot Travel Center #23 (Scales)
Gas — N: to Meijer◈
Food — N: Subway/Pilot TC
Lodg — N: Midway Motel, Super 8
Med — N: + Hospital
Other — N: Meijer, **to appr 4mi: Walmart sc**, Ionia Co Airport✈, **MI State Hwy Patrol**

(69) — Weigh Station (Both dir)

73 — Grand River Ave, Portland Rd, Portland, Lyons, Muir

76 — Kent Rd, Portland
Gas — N: Marathon◈

77 — I-196 Bus, Grand River Ave
TStop — N: Speedway #2319
Gas — N: BP, Marathon◈, Shell, Speedway◈
Food — N: Arby's, Burger King, McDonald's, Subway, Wendy's
Lodg — N: Best Western
Other — N: Banks, Family Dollar, Grocery, RiteAid,
S: Portland Veterinary Service♥,

(79) — Rest Area (WB)
(RR/Fam, Phone, Pic, Pet, Vend, Info)

84 — Grange Rd, Eagle

86 — M 100, Wright Rd, Eagle, Grand Ledge, Potterville
FStop — S: Speedway
TStop — S: Pohl Oil/Mobil
Food — S: McDonald's/Mobil, Subway/Speedway

EXIT — MICHIGAN

(87) — Rest Area Clinton Co #825 (EB)
(RR, Phone, Pic, Pet, Vend)

(89) — Jct I-69N, US 27N, to Flint (EB)

90 — I-196 Bus, Grand River Ave, Lansing
TStop — N: Flying J Travel Plaza #5126 (Scales)
Food — N: CountryMarket/FastFood/FJ TP
Other — N: Laundry/WiFi/**RVDump/LP**/FJ TP, Capital City Airport✈

(91) — Jct I-69N, US 27N, to Flint (WB)

93A — I-69 Bus, M 43, Saginaw Hwy, Lansing, Grand Ledge
Gas — S: BP
Food — S: Arby's, Bob Evans, Cracker Barrel, Steak 'n Shake, Subway
Lodg — S: Springhill Suites
Other — S: ATMs, Auto Dealers, Belle Tire, Discount Tire, Enterprise RAC, Gander Mountain, Lowe's, Michael's, PetSmart♥, Staples, Tractor Supply, **Walmart sc**,

93B — I-69 Bus, M 43, Saginaw Hwy, Lansing, Grand Ledge
Gas — N: Meijer◈, Shell, Speedway◈
Food — N: Burger King, Carrabba's, Denny's, McDonald's, Outback Steakhouse, Red Robin
Lodg — N: Best Western, Days Inn, Fairfield Inn, Hampton Inn, Holiday Inn, Motel 6♥, Quality Inn, Red Roof Inn♥, Residence Inn
Med — N: + Hospital
Other — N: Auto Dealers, Barnes & Noble, Best Buy, Big Lots, Burlington Coat Factory, Dollar Tree, Hobby Lobby, Kroger, Lansing Mall, Meijer, NAPA, Sprint, Target, UPS Store, Walgreen's

(95) — Jct I-496, Downtown Lansing

(97) — Jct I-69, US 27, S to Ft Wayne, N to Lansing

98AB — Lansing Rd, Lansing

101 — M 99, MLK Jr Blvd, Eaton Rapids Rd, Lansing, Eaton Rapids
FStop — S: Super Stop Express/Sunoco
Gas — S: Speedway◈
Food — S: McDonald's, Subway/Speedway, Wendy's
Other — S: CarQuest, Kroger, Lowe's, NAPA

104 — I-96 Bus, Cedar St, Pennsylvania Ave, Lansing, to Holt
Gas — N: Meijer◈, Shell x2, Speedway
S: Speedway, Kroger
Food — N: Applebee's, Arby's, Blimpie, Bob Evans, Burger King, CiCi's Pizza, Denny's, Dunkin Donuts, Long John Silver, Hooters, KFC, Pizza Hut, Steak 'n Shake, Taco Bell, Wendy's
S: Burger Kiing, Flapjack's Rest, LA Chicken & Ribs, McDonald's, Ponderosa, Tim Horton's
Lodg — N: Best Western, Days Inn, Motel 6♥, Super 8
S: Holiday Inn, Howard Johnson
Med — N: + Hospital
S: **+ Ready Care Walk-In Clinic**
Other — N: ATMs, Aldi, Celebration Cinema IMAX, Discount Tire, Grocery, Meijer, Menard's,

EXIT — MICHIGAN

Other — N: Pennsylvania Veterinary Care♥, Sam's Club, Target, Tires
S: ATMs, CVS, Kroger, Lowe's, NAPA, RiteAid, Tires

(106AB) — Jct I-496W, US 127, to Jackson, Lansing

110 — Okemos Rd, Okemos, Mason
Gas — N: 7-11, BP, Marathon, Mobil
Food — N: Applebee's, Arby's, Burger King, Big John Steak Onion, **Cracker Barrel**, Dunkin Donuts, McDonald's, Starbucks, Subway
Lodg — N: Comfort Inn, Fairfield Inn, Holiday Inn Express

(111) — Rest Area Okemos #811 (WB)
(RR, Phone, Pic, Pet, Vend, Info)

117A — N Williamston Rd, Williamston (EB)
FStop — S: Sunoco
Lodg — S: Wheatfield Inn B&B
Other — S: Cedar Creek Veterinary Clinic♥,

117B — N Williamston Rd, Williamston (EB)
Gas — N: Marathon◈

117 — N Williamston Rd, Williamston (WB)

122 — M 43W, M 52, Webberville, Stockbridge
FStop — N: Mobil
Food — N: West Side Deli, McDonald's

(126) — Weigh Station (Both dir)

129 — Fowlerville Rd, Grand Ave, Fowlerville
Gas — N: BP, Shell◈
S: Mobil
Food — N: Big Boy, Fowlerville Farms, McDonald's, Subway, Taco Bell, Wendy's
S: Quiznos, Subway
Lodg — N: Best Western
Med — N: **+ McAuley-McPherson Walk-in Clinic**
Other — S: Auto Dealers

133 — I-96 Bus, M 59, Highland Rd, Howell, Highland
Gas — N: 7-11, Sunoco◈
Food — N: Arby's, McDonald's/Sunoco
Lodg — N: AmeriHost, Baymont Inn, Holiday Inn Express
Other — N: Tanger Outlet Center, Livingston Co Spencer J Hardy Airport✈, **MI Sheriff**,

(135) — Rest Area Howell #812 (EB)
Livingston Co
(RR, Phone, Pic, Pet, Vend)

137 — CR D 19, Pinckney Rd, Howell
Gas — N: Mobil, Shell◈, Speedway◈, Sunoco
Food — N: Blimpie/BaskinRobbins/DunkinDonuts/ Sunoco, Five Star Pizza, Starbucks, Time Out Grill,
Food — S: Benny's Grill, Country Kitchen
Lodg — N: Kensington Inn, Quality Inn
S: Best Western
Med — N: + Hospital

(141) — Rest Area Lake Chemung #813 (WB)
(RR, Phone, Pic, Pet, Vend)

141 — I-96 Bus, Grand River Ave, Howell
Gas — N: Sunoco◈, Shell
Food — N: Applebee's, Bob Evans, Buffalo Wild Wings, KFC, McDonald's, Subway
S: Arby's, Taco Bell, Wendy's
Lodg — N: Grand View Inn

◈= Regular Gas Stations with Diesel ▲ = RV Friendly Locations ♥= Pet Friendly Locations
Red print shows large vehicle parking / access on site or nearby Brown Print = Campgrounds / RV PARKS

EXIT		MICHIGAN
	Other	N: AT&T, Auto Dealers, Discount Tire, Dollar Tree, Lowe's, Meijer/Pharmacy, O'Reilly Auto Parts, Staples, Tractor Supply, UPS Store, **Walmart SC**,
145		**Grand River Ave, Brighton**
	Gas	N: BP, Shell◈
		S: Clark◈, Meijer◈
	Food	N: Arby's, Cracker Barrel, Outback Steak House, Pizza Hut
		S: Border Cantina, Burger King, Chili's, Dunkin Donuts, KFC, McDonald's, Panera Bread, Ponderosa, Red Robin, Starbucks, Taco Bell
	Lodg	N: Courtyard
		S: Holiday Inn Express, Homewood Suites
	Med	S: + Walk-In Clinic
	Other	N: Auto Dealers, Convention Center
		S: ATMs, Best Buy, Bob's Tire & Auto, Borders, Brighton Mall, Cinema 16, Home Depot, Meijer, Michael's, Pharmacy, Radio Shack, RiteAid, Sprint, Staples, Target, Verizon, **to** Brighton Ski Area
147		**Spencer Rd, Brighton**
148AB		**US 23, N - Flint, S - Ann Arbor**
150		**Pleasant Valley Rd, Brighton (WB Exit, EB reaccess)**
	Other	S: **Island Lake State Rec Area**
151		**Kensington Rd, Brighton**
	Med	S: + Brighton Hospital
	Other	N: Kensington Metropark
		S: **Island Lake State Rec Area**
153		**Grand River Rd (EB), Kent Lake Rd, Huron River Pky, Milford**
	Gas	S: Mobil
	Other	N: Kensington Metropark
		S: **Island Lake State Rec Area**
155		**Milford Rd, Milford, Hudson (EB)**
155A		**Milford Rd, Milford, Hudson (WB)**
	Gas	S: BP, Mobil, Sunoco
	Food	S: Applebee's, Chili's, McDonald's, Starbucks, Subway, Tim Horton's, Wendy's
	Other	S: ATMs, Auto Dealers, Discount Tire, Lowe's, **Walmart sc**, **to** Oakland SW Airport✈,
155B		**Milford Rd N, Milford, Hudson (WB)**
159		**Wixom Rd, Wixom**
	Gas	S: Mobil, Shell, Valero, Meijer◈
	Food	S: Arby's, McDonald's, Taco Bell
	Lodg	N: Baymont Inn
		S: Comfort Suites
	Other	N: Ford Wixom Assembly Plant, **Proud Lake State Rec Area**
160		**12 Mile Rd, Beck Rd, Novi**
	Med	N: + Hospital
	Other	S: ATMs, Home Depot, Kroger, Staples
162		**Novi Rd, Novi, Walled Lake**
	Gas	N: BP
		S: Mobil, Sunoco
	Food	N: Buffalo Wild Wings, Carrabba's, Chuck E Cheese's Pizza, Denny's, Great Steak & Potato, Hooters, McDonald's, Pizza Hut, Red Lobster, Red Robin, Rojo Mex Rest
		S: Baja Fresh, BD's Mongolian BBQ, Bob Evans, Bonefish Grill, Famous Dave's, Hardee's, Mirchi Indian Cuisine, Olive Garden, Panera Bread, Pita Cafe, Red Robin, TGI Friday, Wendy's
	Lodg	N: Crowne Plaza, Hilton Garden Inn, Residence Inn
		S: Courtyard, Doubletree Hotel, Towneplace Suites, Wyndham
	Med	N: + Hospital
	Other	N: ATMs, Dick's Sporting Goods, Gander Mountain, Kroger, PetCo♥, Pharmacy, Radio Shack, Twelve Oaks Mall
		S: Animal Emergency Center♥, Borders, Cinema, Dan's Auto Repair, Discount Tire, NAPA, Shopping
	NOTE:	**I-96 runs below with I-275 for 10 mi. Exit #'s follow I-96.**
(163)		**Jct I-696, M 5, Grand River Ave (EB)**
164		**M 5N, 12 Mile Rd (EB)**
165		**M 5N, 12 Mile Rd (WB)**
167		**8 Mile Rd, Northville**
	Gas	S: Speedway, Meijer◈
	Food	S: Chili's, McDonald's, Kyoto Japanese Steakhouse, On the Border, Starbucks, Taco Bell
	Lodg	S: Country Inn, Extended Stay Delux, Hampton Inn, Holiday Inn Express, Sheraton
	Med	S: + Hospital
	Other	N: Farmington Hills Ice Arena, Golf Course, RiteAid,
		S: ATMs, Best Buy, CVS, Costco, Home Depot, Kroger/Pharmacy, Meijer/Pharmacy, Target/Pharmacy, Trader Joe's
169		**7 Mile Rd, Livonia (EB)**
169B		**7 Mile Rd, Livonia (WB)**
	Food	N: Lonestar Steakhouse
	Lodg	N: Embassy Suites
	Med	N: + Livonia Urgent Care
169A		**7 Mile Rd, Livonia (WB)**
	Food	S: Gaucho Steakhouse, J Alexander's, Romano's Macaroni Grill
	Lodg	S: AmeriSuites, Hyatt Place
	Med	S: + Hawthorn Center Hospital
	Other	S: AMC 30, Banks, Home Depot,
170		**6 Mile Rd, Livonia**
	Gas	S: AmocoBP, Mobil
	Food	N: Aksaka Japanese, Bob's Big Boy, Denison's, Indian Rest, Max & Erma's, Panera Bread, Red Robin, Thai Basil, The Ground Round
		S: Applebee's, Brann's Steakhouse, Fleming's Prime Steakhouse, McDonald's, Noodle & Co, PF Chang's, Papa Vino's Italian Kitchen, Tim Horton's
	Lodg	N: Best Western, Courtyard, Holiday Inn, Marriott, Quality Inn, Radisson
		S: Fairfield Inn, Residence Inn, Towneplace Suites
	Other	S: ATMs, Barnes & Noble, CVS, Kroger, Office Depot, PetSmart♥,
(172)		**Jct I-275S, to Toledo, M 14 W, Ann Arbor**
	NOTE:	**I-96 runs above with I-275 for 10 mi. Exit #'s follow I-96.**
173		**Newburgh Rd, Levan Rd (EB) Schoolcraft Rd**
	Other	S: GM Chassis Plant, Ford Livonia Plant
173A		**Newburgh Rd, Livonia (WB) Schoolcraft Rd**
173B		**Levan Rd (WB)**
	Med	N: + Hospital
174		**Farmington Rd, Livonia**
	Gas	N: Mobil◈
		S: Amoco
	Food	N: Looney Baker Café
		S: KFC, Mason's Grill
	Other	N: Ford Athletic Field
175		**Merriman Rd, Livonia**
	Gas	N: Mobil
		S: Sunoco
	Food	S: Mountain Jack's Steakhouse
	Other	S: Commerce Center
176		**Middlebelt Rd, Livonia**
	Gas	S: Meijer◈
	Food	N: Bob Evans, IHOP, Olive Garden
		S: Boss Hogg's BBQ, Mesquite Junction Steakhouse, Logan's Roadhouse
	Lodg	N: Comfort Inn, Super 8
	Other	S: ATMs, Costco, Home Depot, Meijer, **Walmart**, Ford Parts Depot, GM-Cadillac Div,. GM Inland Div

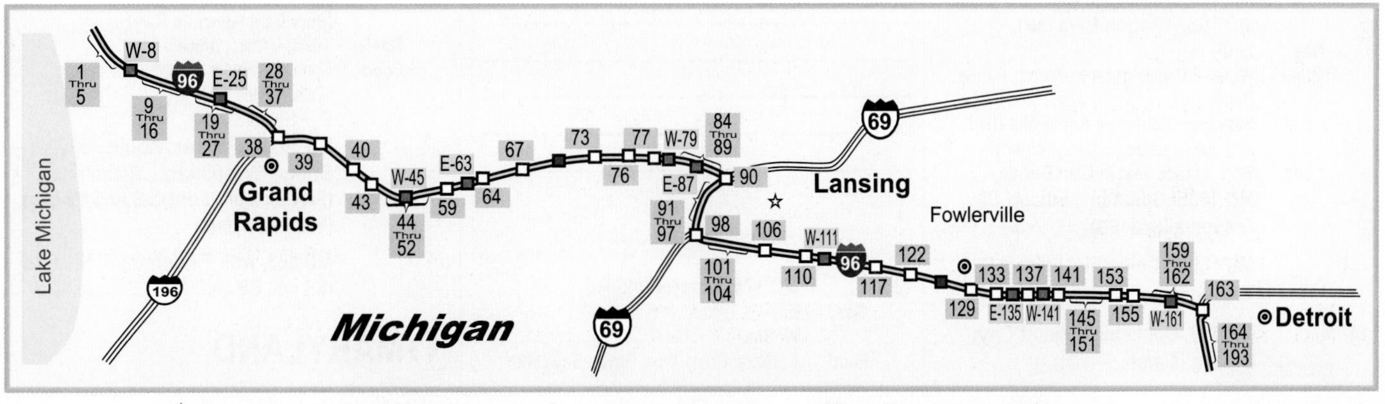

◈ = Regular Gas Stations with Diesel ▲ = RV Friendly Locations ♥ = Pet Friendly Locations
Red print shows large vehicle parking / access on site or nearby **Brown Print = Campgrounds / RV PARKS**

EXIT		MICHIGAN
177		**Inkster Rd, Livonia, Redford**
	Food	N: Panda Rest, Subway
	Other	N: 7-11
		S: Jerusalem Food Market
178		**Beech Daily Rd, Redford**
	Gas	N: Citgo
179		**US 24, Telegraph Rd, Redford, to Dearborn, Pontiac**
	Gas	S: BP, Marathon◊
	Food	N: Arby's, Taco Bell, White Castle
	Lodg	N: Tel 96 Inn
	Other	N: ATMs, Family Dollar, Goodyear
		S: Detroit Diesel
180		**Outer Dr West, I-96 Express**
	NOTE:	**EB: No exits til Exit #185**
182		**Evergreen Rd, Jeffries Rd, Glendale St (EB), Detroit**
183		**M 39, Southfield Freeway**
	NOTE:	**Begin/End I-96 Express Lanes**
184		**Greenfield Rd, Detroit**
185		**M 5, Grand River Ave, Schaefer Hwy, Detroit**
	Gas	N: BP, Mobil, Shell
		S: Sunoco
	Food	N: McDonald's
	Other	N: ATMs, CVS, Police Dept.
186A		**Wyoming St, Detroit**
186B		**M 8, Davison Ave, I-96 Express**
	NOTE:	**WB: no exits til Exit #182**
187		**M 5, Grand River Ave (EB)**
188		**Jeffries Frwy, Livernois Ave Joy Rd (access fr EB)**
	Gas	N: Mobil, Shell
	Food	N: Burger King, KFC, McDonald's, Wendy's, Young's BBQ
188A		**Jeffries Frwy, Livernois Ave Joy Rd (access fr EB)**
188B		**Joy Rd, Grand River Ave (WB)**
	Food	N: Famous Pizza, Popeye's Chicken
189		**W Grand Blvd, Tireman Ave**
	Gas	N: BP, Mobil
(190A)		**Jct I-94 (EB)**
190B		**Warren Ave, Detroit**
	Gas	N: Citgo
		S: Marathon
	Food	N: Green's BBQ
191		**MLK Blvd, to US 12, Michigan Ave**
(193)		**Jct I-75, N-Flint, S-Toledo, OH, to Porter St, Ambassador Br to Canada, to M 10, John C Lodge Frwy**
	Other	to Downtown Detroit, Civic Center

EASTERN TIME ZONE

MICHIGAN

Begin Westbound I-96 from Detroit, MI to Muskegon, MI.

EXIT		MARYLAND
		I-97 from Jct I-695 near Pumphrey, MD to Jct US 301/50 near Annapolis, MD

MARYLAND

EXIT		MARYLAND
(17)		**Jct I-895N, Harbor Tunnel**
(17B)		**Jct I-695E, Essex, Towson**
(17A)		**Jct I-695W, Baltimore**
(17)		**Jct I-695, Key Bridge, Baltimore, Towson, Dundalk (NB exit, SB entr)**
16		**MD 648, Baltimore Annapolis Rd, Glen Burnie, Ferndale (SB)**
	Gas	E: BP
		W: Mobil, Amoco
	Food	E: KFC, McDonald's, Wendy's, Deven's Deli, China King , Pizza Choice, Willie's, Heritage Rest
	Other	E: ATMs, Grocery, Banks
15A		**MD 176, Dorsey Rd (NB)**
15B		**MD 162, Aviation Blvd (NB)**
15		**MD 176, Dorsey Rd (SB) MD 162, Aviation Blvd (SB)**
	Gas	E: BP
	Other	W: to BWI Int'l Airport✈, Banks, Police Dept
	Food	Serv E on Baltimore Annapolis Blvd KFC, McDonald's, Subway, Wendy's
	Lodg	Serv 3 miles east in Glen Burnie
14A		**MD 100E, Columbia, Ellicott City, Gibson Island (SB)**
14B		**MD 100W, Columbia, Ellicott City, Gibson Island (SB)**
14		**MD 100, Columbia, Ellicott City, Gibson Island**

Personal Notes

EXIT		MARYLAND
13		**MD 174, Quarterfield Rd**
	Gas	E: 7-11, Exxon
		W: Shell◊
	Food	E: Pizza, China Wok, Bayou Bay Cafe
12		**MD 3 Bus N, Crain Hwy, New Cut Rd, Glen Burnie (Serv E on Veterans Hwy)**
	Gas	Amoco, Crown, Exxon, WaWa
	Food	Burger King, KFC, Taco Bell, Pizza Hut, Popeye's, Wendy'ssd
	Other	Banks, Goodyear, Target, **Walmart**, Walgreen's
10A		**Benfield Blvd E, Veterans Hwy (SB**
10B		**Benfield Blvd W, Veterans Hwy**
10		**Benfield Blvd, Veterans Hwy, Millersville, Severna Park**
	Gas	E: Exxon◊, Citco
	Food	E: Deli, Hella's Seafood
	Other	W: **Washington DC/Capitol KOA▲** **Police Dept**
7		**MD 32W, MD 3S, Laurel, Bowie, Columbia, Odenton**
	Food	Shoeless Joe, Bull's Eye Sport and Pub
	Lodg	Freestate Lodging
	Other	Elm Truck Maintenance
5		**MD 178, Generals Hwy, Crownsville (SB Exit, NB entr) (Serv E on Generals Hwy)**
	Gas	Texaco, Citco, Amoco
	Food	Sonny's Real Pit BBQ, SK Pizza And Subs, Trifles Rest
	Med	E: + Hospital
1		**US 301, US 50, Annapolis, Bay Bridge, Washington, Richmond (Serv E off of US 301)(SB exit, NB entr) (SB exit, NB entr)**
(0)		**MD 665, Aris T Allen Blvd, Riva Rd (SB exit, NB entr)**

MARYLAND

◊= Regular Gas Stations with Diesel ▲ = RV Friendly Locations ♥= Pet Friendly Locations
Red print shows large vehicle parking / access on site or nearby Brown Print = Campgrounds / RV PARKS

EXIT	PENNSYLVANIA

Begin Southbound I-99 from US 220 in Tyrone to Jct I-70/76 in Bedford

PENNSYLVANIA

EASTERN TIME ZONE

(EXIT) FUTURE **Jct I-80W**

83 **PA 550, Zion Rd, Zion, Bellafonte**
(Addtl Serv 2 mi west in Bellefonte)
Food Spectators Sport Bar

81 **PA 26S, to PA 64, Pleasant Gap**

80 **Harrison Rd, Bellafonte (NB, no reacc)**

NOTE: **Enter SB/Exit NB State Corr Institute at Rockview Property** EMER STOP ONLY

78B **PA 150N, Bellafonte**

78A **PA 150S**
Other Rockview State Corr Institution

NOTE: **Enter NB/Exit SB State Corr Institute at Rockview Property** EMER STOP ONLY

76 **Shiloh Rd**

74 **Park Ave, Innovation Park, Penn St Univ, State College (SB)**
Other W: University Park Airport✈

73 **US 322E, Penn State Univ, State College (NB), State College, Lewistown (SB)**
Gas Sheetz
Food DQ, Red Lobster
Other Grocery, **Walmart**

71 **Toftrees, Woodycrest**

70 **Valley Vista Dr, State College**

69 **US 322E Bus, Atherton St**
(exit only)

62 **US 322W, Phillipsburg**

61 **Port Matilda**

52 **PA 350, US 220S Bus, Bald Eagle**
Gas **W:** BP
Food **W:** Subway/BP

48 **PA 453, Tyrone, to PA 550**
Gas **W:** Sheetz◈, Amoco
Food **W:** Burger King, Mario's Pizza Palace, TCBY, Subway, Frozen Cow, Joybean, Italian Pizza
Med **W:** + Hospital
Other Grocery, Banks, RiteAid

45 **Tipton, Grazierville**
Gas **W:** Exxon
Food **W:** Pizza Hut
Med **W:** + Hospital
Other **W:** DelGrosso's Amusement Park, Auto Dealers

41 **PA 865N, Bellwood**
Gas **W:** Sheetz◈, Martin Gen'l Store◈
Other **W:** DelGrosso's Amusement Park

39 **PA 764S, Bellwood, Pinecroft**
Gas **W:** Choice, Sheetz
Lodg **W:** Cedar Grove Motel
Other **W:** Oak Spring Winery, Harley Davidson

33 **17th St, Altoona**
Gas **W:** Sheetz
Other **W:** ATMs, Lowe's, U-Haul, Penn State-Altoona, Central Business District, Museum

Personal Notes

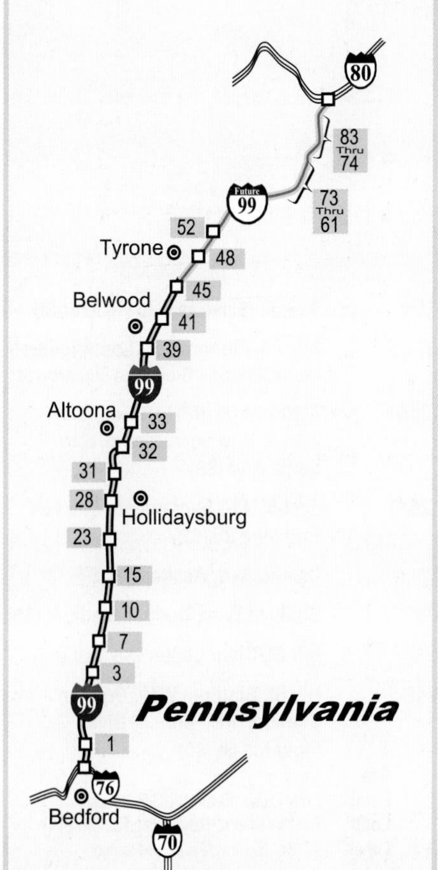

EXIT	PENNSYLVANIA

32 **to PA 36, Frankstown Rd, Altoona**
Gas **W:** Sheetz, Exxon, Rabit, GFF Oil
Food **W:** Dunkin Donuts, McDonald's, Olive Garden, Perkins, Pizza Hut, Red Lobster, Subway, Wendy's, Woody's
Lodg **W:** Days Inn, Econo Lodge, Holiday Inn, Super 8
Med **W:** + Hospital
Other **E: Canoe Creek State Park**
W: CVS, NAPA, Auto Zone, Radio Shack, Blair Co Stadium, Logan Valley Mall

31 **US 220 Bus, Plank Rd, Altoona**
Gas **W:** BP
Food **E:** Friendly's, Outback Steakhouse, Ruby Tuesday, TGI Friday
W: Applebee's, Arby's, Cracker Barrel, Denny's, KFC, Ponderosa, Ruby Tuesday, Taco Bell, TGI Friday, Subway/BP
Lodg **E:** Comfort Inn, Courtyard, Ramada Inn
Lodg **W:** Hampton Inn, Motel 6♥
Other **E:** ATMs, Firestone, Sam's Club, Target, **Walmart**, Blair Co Convention Center, **Wright's Orchard Station Campground▲**
W: ATMs, Advance Auto, Dollar General, Grocery, Pharmacy, Staples, Logan Valley Mall

28 **to US 22, Ebensburg,Hollidaysburg, PA 764, Duncansville**
Other **E: PA State Hwy Patrol Post**

23 **PA 36, PA 164, Roaring Spring, Portage, to US 22E**
Gas **E:** Exxon, Mobil◈, Sheetz
Food **E:** Pizza/Exxon, Blimpie/Mobil, Lynn's
Lodg **E:** Haven Rest Motel
Med **E:** + Hospital
Other **E:** Altoona-Blair Co Airport✈, **to Heritage Cove Resort▲**

15 **US 220N Bus, Claysburg, King**
Gas **W:** Sheetz
Food **W:** Burger King, Wendy's
Other **W:** Blue Knob Valley Airport✈

10 **Sarah Furnance Rd, Osterburg, Imler**
Other **W: Blue Knob State Park▲**

7 **PA 869, Osterburg, St Clairsville**

3 **PA 56, Quaker Valley Rd, US 220S Bus, Bedford, Johnstown, Cessna**
Gas RG's BP◈
Food Apple Bin Rest
Other **E:** Bedford Co Airport✈, **PA State Hwy Patrol Post**

(1) **Jct I-70/76, PA Tpk, US 220, Pittsburgh, Harrisburg**
Gas **E:** BP, Sheetz, Amoco, Sunoco
Food **E:** Denny's, Pizza Hut, Wendy's Long John Silver, China Inn, McDonald's, Ed's Steak House, Best Way Pizza, Donut Connections
Lodg **E:** Best Western, Hampton Inn, Super 8, Quality Inn, Travelodge, Econo Lodge, Janey's Lynn Motel, Jean Bonnet B & B
Other **E:** Bedford Airport✈, **Friendship Village Campground and RV Resort▲**

EASTERN TIME ZONE

PENNSYLVANIA

Begin I-99 Northbound from Jct I-70/76 in Bedford to US 220 in Tyrone

◈= Regular Gas Stations with Diesel ▲ = RV Friendly Locations ♥= Pet Friendly Locations
Red print shows large vehicle parking / access on site or nearby Brown Print = Campgrounds / RV PARKS

EXIT		CALIFORNIA
	Begin Eastbound I-105 near Imperial Hwy to I-605N.	

CALIFORNIA

1		**Imperial Hwy E, Inglewood (Addt'l Serv N on Century Blvd)**
	Food	Goody's Rest, Mexican Rest, Thai Rest, Cutting Board Snack Bar
	Lodg	Twin Towers Motel
	Other	LAX Int'l Airport
(2)		**Jct 405**
3		**Prairie Ave, Hawthorne Blvd**
	Gas	Shell, Arco, Chevron
	Food	Italian Rest, Jack in the Box
	Lodg	Howard Johnson, La Mirage Inn, Del Aire Inn, Jade Tree Motel, Holly Park Motel, Star Motel
	Other	Grocery, Casinos (N on Century Blvd)
5		**Crenshaw Blvd, Hawthorne**
	Gas	Mobil
	Food	China Spoon, China Express, New China Buffet, Subway, Thai Chinese Express
	Lodg	Marriott, Dream Inn, Palm Inn Motel, Kings Motel, Diamond Inn, Casa Belle Motel, Tourist Lodge
	Med	S: + Robert Kennedy Medical Center
	Other	ATMs, Auto Repair, Big Lots, Costco, Lowe's, Target, Hawthorne Muni Airport
7A		**Vermont Ave**
	Gas	Arco, Mobil, Shell, Mini Mart
	Food	Caesar Rest, LA Fried Chicken, Chinese & American Rest, Mom's BBQ
	Lodg	Vegas Motel, Magic Carpet Motor Inn, Paradise Inn, Western Motel
	Other	Auto Repairs
(7B)		**Jct I-110**
9		**Central Ave (Serv N on Imperial Hwy)**
	Gas	Shell
	Other	Magic Johnson Rec Center
10		**Wilington Ave, Los Angeles**
	Food	China Gate
	Lodg	Crown Motel
12		**Long Beach Blvd**
	Food	Chinese Rest, El Paraiso Rest
	Lodg	World Motel, Travelodge, Lynnwood Hotel, Mission Motel, Rainbow Inn, Rocky Motel, Flaming Motel
	Other	Lynnwood City Park
(13)		**Jct I-710**
14		**Garfield Ave, Paramont**
	Gas	Garfield Gas, Mobil, Shell
	Food	Dragon Lee Rest, Mexican Rest
16		**Lakewood Blvd**
	Gas	Mobil, Shell
	Food	Great China Rest, Little Caesar's Pizza
	Lodg	Colonial Motel, American Inn Motel
17		**Belleflower Blvd (Other Serv N on Imperial Hwy)**
	Other	Thompson Park, Boeing Defense & Space Group
(18AB)		**Jct I-605**

CALIFORNIA

Begin WB I-105 near I-605N to Imperial Hwy

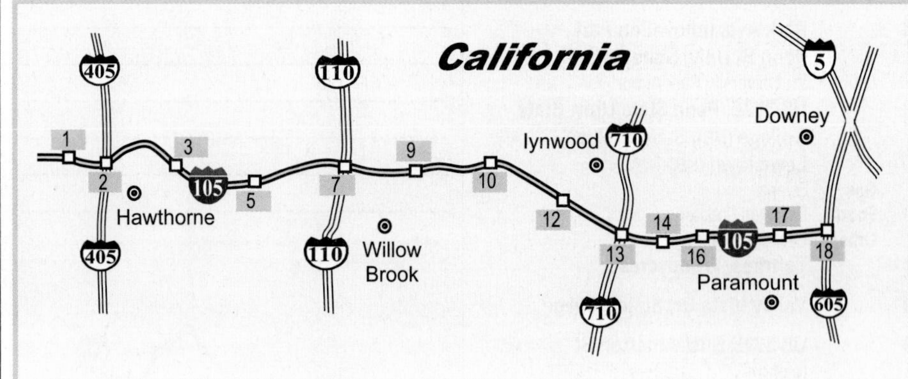

EXIT		CALIFORNIA
	Begin Southbound I-110 from Jct I-10 in Los Angeles to CA 47	

CALIFORNIA

(0)		**NB End / SB Begin CA 110 Fwy, California Blvd, to CA 134, I-210 (NB, Left Exit)**
31B		**Fair Oaks Ave, S Pasadena**
	Food	Baskin Robbins, El Pollo Loco, Starbucks
	Other	ATMs, Banks, Theatre
31A		**Orange Grove Ave**
	Gas	ArcoAmPm
30B		**Bridewell St (NB)**
30A		**York Blvd, Pasadena Ave (NB)**
30		**York Blvd, Pasadena Ave (SB)**
29		**Ave 60**
28B		**Via Marisol**
	Gas	Snack Shop
	Food	Big Burger, El Pollo Loco
28A		**Ave 52 (Services W to Figueroa St)**
27		**Ave 43, Figueroa St, Los Angeles (Auto Serv/Gas/Groc W to Figueroa St)**
(26B)		**Figueroa St (NB, Left Exit), Jct I-5, N to Sacramento, S to Santa Ana (SB)**
(26A)		**Jct I-5, N to Sacramento (NB, Left Exit), Ave 26 (SB)**
25		**Solano Ave, Academy Rd**
24D		**Stadium Way, Dodger Stadium (SB)**
24C		**Hill St, Civic Center (SB, Left exit)**
24B		**Hill St, Stadium Way, Dodger Stadium (NB), Sunset Blvd, Figueroa St (SB)**
	Gas	Chevron
	Food	Full House Seafood, Golden City
	Lodg	Best Western, Royal Pagoda Motel
	Other	ATMs, Banks, Grocery, Pavilion
24A		**US 101, N to Hollywood, S to I-5S, I-10E, Santa Ana, San Bernardino**
23C		**3rd St**
23B		**4th St, 3rd St, 6th St, Downtown**
	Other	ATMs, Auto Services, Banks, LA Chamber of Commerce, Museums, Theatres, Visitor & Conv Bureau, Wells Fargo Center I & II, World Trade Center LA
23A		**6th St (NB), Wilshire Blvd (SB)**
	Food	Pacific Grill, Starbucks, Cafe Wilshire
	Lodg	Wilshire Grand Hotel, City Center, Motel De Ville
	Med	W: + Good Samaritan Hospital
	Other	ATMs, Banks, LA Visitor & Conv Bureau
22B		**8th St, 9th St (SB)**
	Other	Avis RAC
22A		**Olympic Blvd (SB) (Rest/Lodging E to Figuaro St)**
	Other	ATMs, Banks, CarWash, Museum, LA Conv Center, Staples Center
22		**9th St, 6th St, Downtown (NB)**
	NOTE:	**NB continue as CA 110, SB start I-110**

◊ = Regular Gas Stations with Diesel ▲ = RV Friendly Locations ♥ = Pet Friendly Locations
Red print shows large vehicle parking / access on site or nearby Brown Print = Campgrounds / RV PARKS

EXIT	CALIFORNIA
(21)	**Jct I-10, W to Santa Monica, E to San Bernardino**
20C	**Adams Blvd**
Gas	Mobil
Food	Popeye's, Quiznos, Taco Bell, 2-4-1 Pizza
Other	Banks, Grocery, Midas
20B	**Exposition Blvd**
Gas	Chevron
Food	Sizzler
Lodg	Radisson
Other	LA Expo Park
20A	**MLK Jr Blvd**
Gas	Chevron
Food	La Pizza Loca, McDonald's, Subway
19B	**Vernon Ave (SB)**
Gas	Mobil, Shell
Food	Burger King, China Express, Jack in the Box
Other	Auto Services, Ralph's
19A	**51st St (SB)**
19	**Vernon Ave (NB)**
18B	**Slauson Ave, Los Angeles**
Gas	Mobil
18A	**Gage Ave**
Gas	ArcoAmPm, Valero
17	**Florence Ave**
Gas	Mobil, ArcoAmPm, Chevron, Shell
Food	Golden Ox, Jack in the Box, McDonald's
16	**Manchester Ave**
Gas	ArcoAmPm, Circle K
Food	El Pollo Loco, McDonald's, Church's Chicken, Chinatown Express, Jack in the Box, Popeye's Chicken
Other	Banks, Grocery, Pep Boys, Ralph's
15	**Century Blvd (SB)**
Gas	ArcoAmPm, Shell
(14B)	**Jct I-105W, Imperial Hwy, Century Blvd, to El Segundo**
(14A)	**Jct I-105E, to Norwalk**
13	**El Segundo Blvd, Gardena**
Food	Ceasars Rest, La Perla Tacos, Taco Bell
12	**Rosecrans Ave**
FStop	333 E Rosecrans: Gardena Truck Stop
Gas	ArcoAmPm, Chevron, Mobil, Valero
Food	Jack in the Box, Long John Silver, Subway

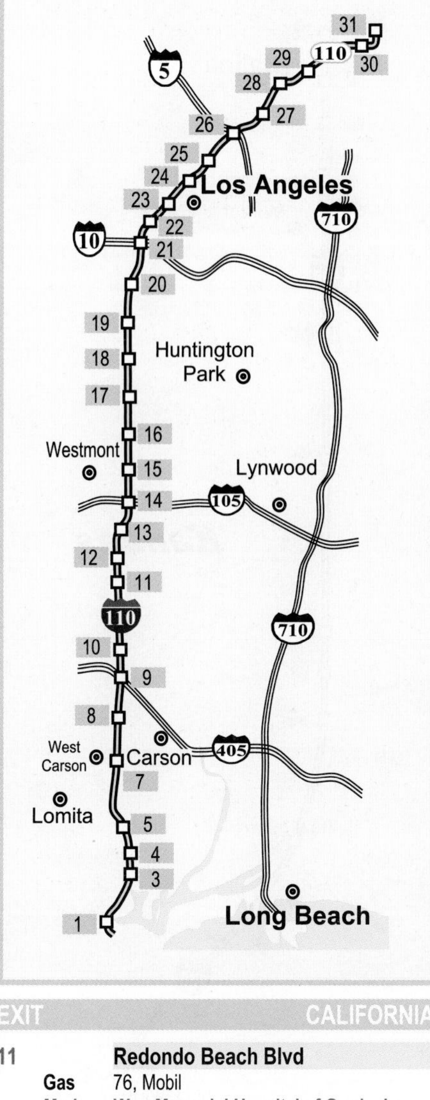

EXIT	CALIFORNIA
11	**Redondo Beach Blvd**
Gas	76, Mobil
Med	W: + Memorial Hospital of Gardenia
10B	**CA 91W, Artesia Blvd, Redondo Beach (NB)**
10A	**CA 91E, Anaheim, Riverside (NB)**

EXIT	CALIFORNIA
10	**CA 91, E - Anaheim, Riverside, W - Artesia Blvd, Redondo Bch (SB)**
Food	Jack in the Box, McDonald's, Taco Bell
Other	Albertson's, ATMs, Sam's Club
(9)	**Jct I-405, San Diego Fwy, N to Santa Monica, S to Long Beach, 190th St (SB)**
8	**Torrance Blvd, Del Amo Blvd**
Gas	Mobil, Shell◈
Food	Burger King, Starbucks
7B	**Carson St (SB)**
Gas	76, Mobil, Shell
Food	In 'n Out Burger, Jack in the Box, Starbucks
Med	W: + LA Co Harbor, UCLA Med Center
7A	**223rd St**
7	**Carson St (NB)**
5	**Sepulveda Blvd**
Gas	ArcoAmPm, Mobil
Food	Burger King, Carl's Jr, McDonald's, Popeye's Chicken, Starbucks, Taco Bell
Other	Albertson's, ATMs, Banks, Home Depot, RiteAid, Staples, Target, Von's Grocery
4	**CA 1, Pacific Coast Hwy**
Gas	Chevron, Mobil, Shell, PCH Quick Corner
Food	Alberta's Mex, Denny's, Jack in the Box
Lodg	Best Western, Islander Motel, W Coast Inn
Med	W: + Hospital
3B	**Anaheim St, Wilmington**
Gas	ArcoAmPm
Food	Boston Cream, Golden Kitchen
3A	**C St, Harry Bridges Blvd**
Gas	Shell◈
1B	**Channel St, John S Gibson Blvd, Gaffey St, San Pedro**
Gas	ArcoAmPm, Chevron
(1A)	**CA 47, Vincent Thomas Bridge, Terminal Island**

CALIFORNIA

Begin Northbound I-110 from CA 47 to Jct I-10 in Los Angeles

Begin Southbound I-135 from I-70 near Salina to Jct I-35, South of Wichita, KS.

KANSAS

NOTE: I-135 Begins/Ends on I-70, Ex #250, US 81 continues NB

EXIT	KANSAS
(95AB)	**Jct I-70, E-Kansas City, W-Denver, US 40, US 81, Topeka**
93	**KS 140, State Rd, Salina (Serv E to Broadway Blvd)**
Lodg	E: Ambassy Motel, Travelers Lodge
Other	E: ATMs, Ace Hardware, Museum
92	**Crawford St, Salina**
FStop	E: West Crawford 24-7/BP W: Salina West/Cenex
Gas	E: Citgo, Kwik Shop, Shell, Phillips 66◈
Food	E: Braum's, Gutierrez Mexican Rest, Hickory Hut BBQ, McDonald's, Quiznos, Russell's Rest, Spangles, Subway
Food	W: Rest/Quality Inn
Lodg	E: Best Western♥, Comfort Inn♥, Fairfield Inn, Ramada Inn♥, Rodeway Inn W: Quality Inn
TWash	E: Blue Beacon Truck Wash
TServ	E: Cross Midwest Tire Co, Thermo King
Med	E: + Salina Reg'l Health Center
Other	E: ATMs, Advance Auto Parts, Auto Repair Ace Hardware, Dillon's/Pharmacy, NAPA,
Other	E: Greyhound, Jiffy Lube, Radio Shack, Star Lumber, Tires, Walgreen's
90	**Magnolia Rd (Acc #89 E to 9th St)**
Gas	E: Phillips 66◈, Shell, Dillon's
Food	E: Burger King, Carlos O'Kelly's, Chili's, Golden Corral, Hong Kong Buffet, IHOP
Lodg	E: Americas Best Value Inn♥, Candlewood Suites, Country Inn
Other	E: ATMs, Advance Auto Parts, Carwash/ Shell & P66,Dillons/Pharmacy, Radio Shack Salina Veterinary Hospital♥, Central Mall W: Ks St Univ/Salina, Salina Muni Airport✈

◈= Regular Gas Stations with Diesel ▲ = RV Friendly Locations ♥= Pet Friendly Locations
Red print shows large vehicle parking / access on site or nearby Brown Print = Campgrounds / RV PARKS

EXIT		KANSAS
89		**Schilling Rd, Salina**
	Gas	E: Kwik Shop◈, Sam's
		W: Casey's General Store
	Food	E: Applebee's, Logan's Roadhouse, Los
	Gas	E: Phillips 66
	Food	E: Potrillos Mex Rest, McDonald's, Pizza Hut, Red Lobster, Tuscon's Steakhouse
	Lodg	E: Candlewood Suites, Country Inn, Courtyard, Hampton Inn
		W: Comfort Suites, Relax Inn♥, Super 8
	Other	E: ATMs, Aldi, Dollar General, Dollar Tree, Lowe's, Office Max, Radio Shack, Sam's Club, Target/Pharmacy, **Walmart sc**
88		**9th St, Schilling Rd**
86		**KS 141, Harrington, Smolan**
82		**KS 4, Falun Rd, Assaria**
	Other	E: Bank, US Post Office
78		**Bus 81, KS 4, Lindsborg, Roxbury**
	Gas	E: Shell
	Food	E: DQ/Stuckey's
	Med	W: + to Lindsborg Community Hospital
	Other	W: to appr 5 mi: Gas, Food, Lodging, Coronado Motel & RV Park▲, Movies 'n More RV Park▲, Old Mill Museum & Campground▲, Bethany College
72		**Bus 81, Smoky Valley Rd, Lindsborg, Roxbury (Acc to #78 W to 14th St - appr 4mi)**
(68)		Rest Area (Both dir, Left exit) (RR, Phone, Picnic, RVDump)
65		**Pawnee Rd**
60		**US 56, Bus 81, Kansas Ave, McPherson, Marion**
	FStop	W: Midway Oil
	Gas	W: BP, Kwik Shop
	Food	W: Applebee's, Arby's, Braum's, Golden Dragon Chinese, McDonald's, Montana Mike's, Nunan Chinese, Perkins, Pizza Hut
	Lodg	W: Americas Best Value Inn, Best Western, Days Inn, Holiday Inn Express, Red Coach Inn,

	Food	E: Potrillos Mex Rest, McDonald's, Pizza Hut, Red Lobster, Tuscon's Steakhouse
	Lodg	E: Candlewood Suites, Country Inn, Courtyard, Hampton Inn
		W: Comfort Suites, Relax Inn♥, Super 8
	Other	E: ATMs, Aldi, Dollar General, Dollar Tree, Lowe's, Office Max, Radio Shack, Sam's Club, Target/Pharmacy, **Walmart sc**
88		**9th St, Schilling Rd**
86		**KS 141, Harrington, Smolan**
82		**KS 4, Falun Rd, Assaria**
	Other	E: Bank, US Post Office
78		**Bus 81, KS 4, Lindsborg, Roxbury**
	Gas	E: Shell
	Food	E: DQ/Stuckey's
	Med	W: + to Lindsborg Community Hospital
	Other	W: to appr 5 mi: Gas, Food, Lodging, Coronado Motel & RV Park▲, Movies 'n More RV Park▲, Old Mill Museum & Campground▲, Bethany College
72		**Bus 81, Smoky Valley Rd, Lindsborg, Roxbury (Acc to #78 W to 14th St - appr 4mi)**
(68)		Rest Area (Both dir, Left exit) (RR, Phone, Picnic, RVDump)

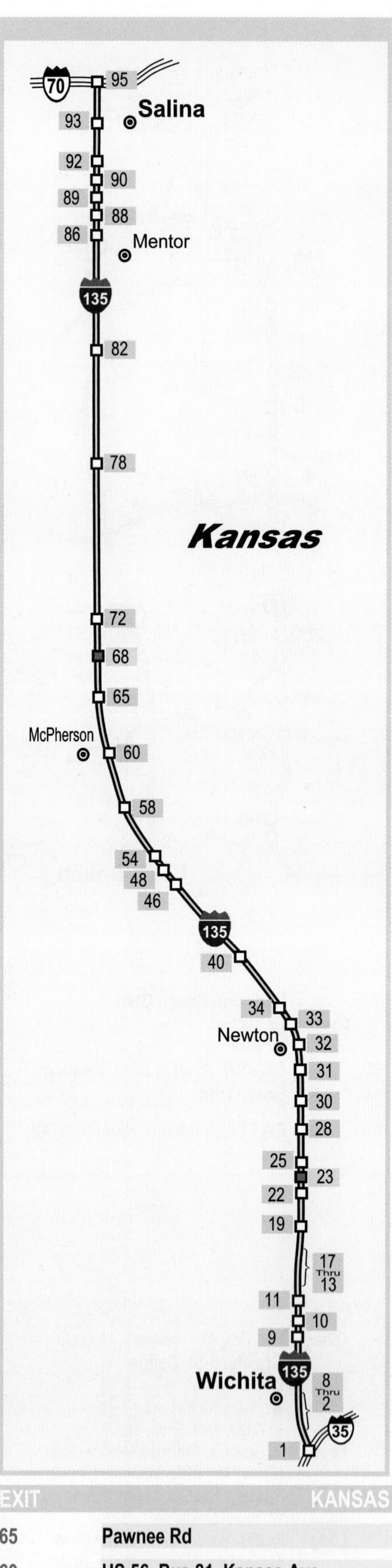

EXIT		KANSAS
65		**Pawnee Rd**
60		**US 56, Bus 81, Kansas Ave, McPherson, Marion**
	FStop	W: Midway Oil
	Gas	W: BP, Kwik Shop

EXIT		KANSAS
	Food	W: Applebee's, Arby's, Braum's, Golden Dragon Chinese, McDonald's, Montana Mike's, Nunan Chinese, Perkins, Pizza Hut
	Lodg	W: Americas Best Value Inn, Best Western, Days Inn, Holiday Inn Express, Red Coach Inn,
	Med	W: + Memorial Hospital
	Other	W: ATMs, Auto Zone, Auto Services, Dollar General, **Walmart sc**, McPherson College, Museum, Water Park, McPherson Airport✈ **Lacy RV, Mustang MH & RV Park▲**, **Shady Lane MH & RV Park▲**, to McPherson Fairgrounds/RVDump
58		**KS 61, to McPherson, Hutchinson**
54		**Comanche Rd, CR 445, Elyria**
48		**KS 260, 22nd Ave, Moundridge**
	Other	Spring Lake RV Resort▲
46		**KS 260, Arrowhead Rd, Moundridge**
	Gas	W: Food Mart/BP
	Med	W: + Mercy Hospital
	Other	W: Moundridge Muni Airport✈
40		**Lincoln Blvd, Hesston**
	FStop	W: Cenex
	Food	W: Pizza Hut, Sonic, Subway, Rest/ABVI
	Lodg	E: AmericInn
		W: Americas Best Value Inn, Hesston Inn
	TWash	W: Plaza Truck Wash
	Other	E: Cottonwood Grove RV Campground▲
		W: ATMs, Hesston College
34		**KS 15, Main St, Newton, Abilene**
	Food	W: Subway
	Other	E: Newton Golf Course
33		**US 50E, Peabody, Emporia (NB)**
	Other	W: Ks State Hwy Patrol Post
32		**Broadway Ave**
31		**1st St**
	FStop	E: AmBest/Newell Truck Plaza/Shamrock
	Gas	E: AmPride/Cenex, Conoco◈, Shell
	Food	E: Applebee's, Pancake House, KFC
	Lodg	E: Americas Best Value Inn, Days Inn
		W: Best Western
30		**US 50, KS 15, Newton, Hutchinson**
	Gas	W: Kwik Shop◈
	Med	W: + Hospital
	Other	W: Auto Zone, Grocery, **Walmart sc**, to Spring Lake RV Resort▲
28		**SE 36th St, Newton**
	Other	W: Newton Outlet Mall, Restaurants
25		**KS 196, White Water, El Dorado**
(23)		Rest Area (Both dir) (RR, Phone, Picnic, Vend, RVDump)
22		**125th St, Sedgewick**
19		**101st St**
	Other	Wagons HO RV Park▲
17		**KS Coliseum, Valley Ctr, 85th St**
16		**77th St, Wichita Greyhound Park**
14		**61st St, Kechi**
	Gas	E: QT◈, Coastal, W: Phillips 66◈
	Food	E: Applebee's, Cracker Barrel, Taco Bell
		W: KFC, McDonald's
	Lodg	Comfort Inn, W: Super 8
13		**53rd St**
	Gas	Phillips 66
	Food	Country Kitchen
	Lodg	Best Western, Days Inn
(11AB)		**Jct I-235W, KS 254, Hutchinson**

◈ = Regular Gas Stations with Diesel ▲ = RV Friendly Locations ♥ = Pet Friendly Locations
Red print shows large vehicle parking / access on site or nearby Brown Print = Campgrounds / RV PARKS

EXIT	KANSAS
10AB	KS 96E, 29th St
9	21st St, Wichita State Univ
8	13th St
7B	8th St, 9th St
7A	Central Ave
6C	1st St, 2nd St
6AB	US 54, US 400, Kellogg Ave
5B	US 54, US 400, Kellogg Ave
5A	Lincoln St, Wichita
Gas	W: QT
4	Harry St
Gas	QT, BP
Food	E: Denny's, McDonald's, Wendy's
3B	Pawnee St
3A	KS 15, SE Blvd
2	Hydraulic Ave
Gas	E: QT
Food	E: McDonald's, Subway
(1C)	Jct I-235N
1AB	47th St, US 81S
Gas	Coastal, Conoco, Phillips 66
Food	W: Applebee's, Burger King, KFC, Long John Silver, McDonald's, Subway
Lodg	E: Comfort Inn, Days Inn, Holiday Inn Express, W: Best Western, Red Carpet Inn
Other	W: ATMs, Grocery, O'Reilly Auto Parts

KANSAS

Begin NB I-135 from Jct I-35 near Wichita to Jct I-70 near Salina, KS.

EXIT	MICHIGAN

Begin I-196 on I-94 at Benton Harbor to I-96 in E Grand Rapids

MICHIGAN

NOTE: I-196 Begins/Ends on I-94, Ex #34

EXIT	MICHIGAN
(0)	Jct I-94, E - Detroit, W - Chicago
1	Red Arrow Hwy
Other	N: Ross Field Airport
4	Riverside, to Coloma
Gas	S: Marathon◈
Other	S: Coloma/St Joseph KOA▲
7	MI 63, to Benton Harbor
13	to Covert
Other	N: Van Buren State Park, CAMP▲
18	MI 140, MI 43, to Watervliet
Gas	N: Shell◈, Speedway, Xpress◈ S: Murphy
Food	N: Burger King,Ma's Coffeepot Rest, McDonald's, Pizza Hut
Lodg	N: Budget Lodge
Other	N: Auto Dealers
20	Rd A-2, Phoenix Rd
Gas	N: BP◈, Marathon◈ S: BP, Shell
Food	N: Arby's, Checkers, Taco Bell S: McDonald's, Wendy's
Lodg	N: Southaven Motel S: Hampton Inn, Holiday Inn Express
Med	N + Hospital
Other	N: ATMs, Auto Zone, Walgreen's, MI State Hwy Patrol Post S: Walmart sc
22	N Shore Dr
Other	N: to Kal Haven Trail State Park
(25)	Rest Area (EB) (RR, Phone, Picnic, Vend)
26	109th Ave, to Pullman
30	Rd A-2, Glenn, Ganges
34	MI 89, to Fennville
Gas	S: Shell
Other	S: Winery
36	Rd A-2, Ganges
Gas	N: Shell
Lodg	N: AmericInn

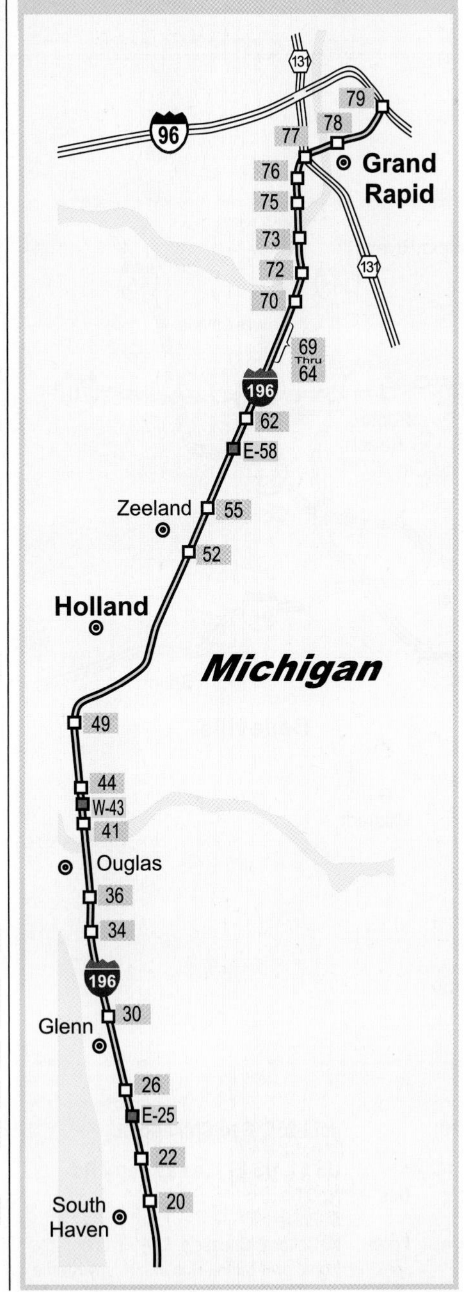

EXIT	MICHIGAN
41	Rd A-2, Douglas, Saugatuck
Gas	N: Marathon◈, Shell◈
Food	N: Burger King, Subway/Shell
Lodg	N: AmericInn, Holiday Inn Express
Other	N: ATMs, Dollar General, NAPA, Saugatuck RV Resort▲, Saugatuck State Park,
(43)	Rest Area (WB) (RR, Phone, Picnic, Vend)
44	US 31N, to Holland (EB)
Med	N: + Hospital
Other	N: to Oak Grove Campground▲ Resort▲, Drew's Country Camping
49	MI 40, to Allegan
TStop	S: Tulip City Marathon
Gas	N: BP◈
Food	N: McDonald's/BP
Lodg	N: Residence Inn
52	16th St, Adams St
Gas	N: Meijer◈, Speedway S: Mobil◈
Food	N: Wendy's S: Burger King, Subway/Mobil
Lodg	N: Best Inn, Econo Lodge
Med	N: + Hospital
Other	N: ATMs, Meijer
55	Byron Rd, Zeeland
Gas	N: 7-11
Food	N: McDonald's
Med	N: + Hospital
Other	N: Dutch Treat Camping & Rec▲
(58)	Rest Area (EB) (RR, Phone, Picnic, Vend)
62	32nd Ave, to Hudsonville
Gas	N: BP◈ S: Mobil◈
Food	N: Arby's, Burger King, McDonald's, Village Seafood & Grill S: Subway/Mobil
Lodg	N: Quality Inn, Super 8 S: AmeriHost Inn
64	MI 6E, to Lansing (fr WB, Left exit)
67	44th St
Gas	N: Mobil◈
Food	N: Burger King, Cracker Barrel, Panera Bread, Steak 'n Shake S: Famous Dave's BBQ, Logans, Starbucks
Lodg	N: Comfort Suites

◈= Regular Gas Stations with Diesel ▲ = RV Friendly Locations ♥= Pet Friendly Locations
Red print shows large vehicle parking / access on site or nearby Brown Print = Campgrounds / RV PARKS

EXIT	MICHIGAN
Other	**N:** ATMs, Auto Services, **Walmart**
	S: ATMs, Discount Tire, Gander Mountain, Lowes, PetSmart♥, World Market
69AB	**Chicago Dr**
Gas	**N:** Meijer◈
	S: BP, Speedway
Food	**N:** KFC, McDonald's, Perkins, Subway
	S: Arby's, Pizza Hut, Wendy's
Lodg	**S:** Best Western, Holiday Inn Express
Other	**N:** ATMs, Auto Zone, Big Lots, Dollar Tree, Dollar General, Radio Shack, Target
70AB	**MI 11, Grandville, Walker (WB, LEFT exit)**
Gas	**S:** BP◈, Shell, Speedway
Food	**S:** Arby's, Logan's Roadhouse, Subway/BP
Lodg	**S:** Days Inn, Lands Inn Hotel
72	**Jct I-196 Bus, Chicago Dr E (EB)**
Other	**E: to** GM Delphi Plant, Reynolds Metal Factory
73	**Market Ave, Grand Rapids**
Other	**N: to** Vanandel Arena

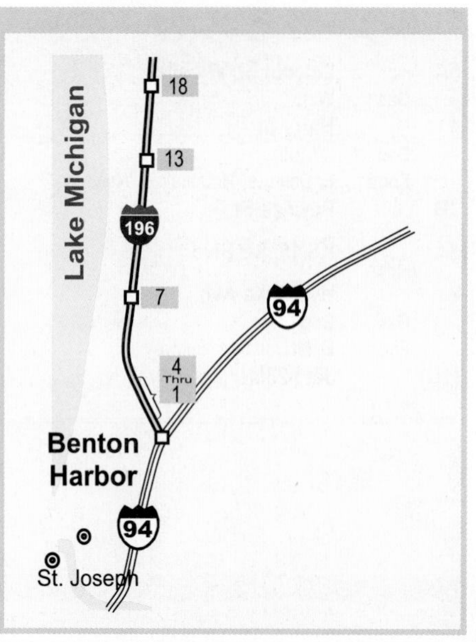

EXIT	MICHIGAN
75	**MI 45W, Lake Michigan Dr**
Other	**N: to** Grand Valley State Univ
76	**MI 45E, Lane Ave**
Gas	**S:** BP
Other	**S:** Gerald R Ford Museum, John Ball Park & Zoo
77AB	**US 131, S-Kalamazoo, N-Cadillac**
77C	**Ottawa Dr**
Other	**S:** Gerald Ford Museum, Zoo
78	**College Ave**
Gas	**S:** Dairy Mart, Marathon
Food	**S:** McDonald's
Med	**S:** + Hospital
79	**Fuller Ave**
Other	**N:** Sheriff's Dept

MICHIGAN

Begin I-196 on I-96 in E Grand Rapids to I-94, Ex #34 in Benton Harbor.

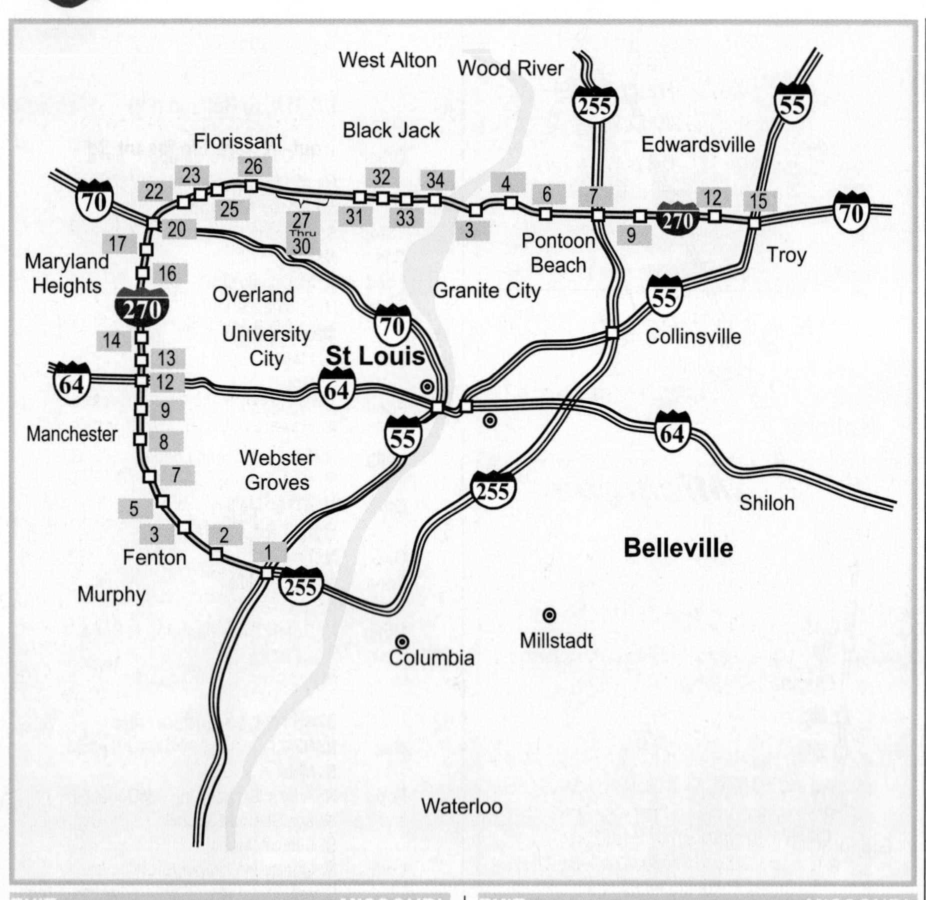

EXIT	MISSOURI
	Begin I-270 Western Loop at Jct I-55 around St Louis, Mo to Jct I-55/I-70 near Troy, IL.

MISSOURI

NOTE: Begins/Ends on I-55, Exit #196B

CENTRAL TIME ZONE

EXIT	MISSOURI
(0)	**Jct I-255, E to Chicago, IL**
1C	**US 61, US 67, Lemay Ferry Rd**
Gas	**N:** QT
	S: Phillips 66
Food	**N:** Chuck E Cheese's, El Pollo Loco, Hometown Buffet, Hooters, Krispy Kreme,

EXIT	MISSOURI
Food	**N:** JMcDonald's, Romano's Macaroni Grill, Subway
	S: CiCi's Pizza, Elecia's Pizza, Jack in the Box, McDonald's, Steak N Shake, White Castle
Lodg	**N:** Holiday Inn, Oak Grove Inn
Other	**N:** ATMs, Banks, Auto Dealers, Auto Services, Batteries Plus, Borders, Dobbs Tire & Auto Center, Enterprise RAC, Family Dollar, Gateway Harley Davidson, NTB, NAPA, New World Natural Health Foods, Office Max, South County Vet♥, U-Haul
	S: ATMs, Banks, Auto Services, Big Lots, Cinema, CompUSA, Dollar Tree, Firestone, Jiffy Lube, Kwik Kopy, PetSmart♥, Sam's Club, Vet♥, Walgreen's
(1B)	**Jct I-55, N to St Louis**
(1A)	**Jct I-55, S to Memphis**
2	**MO 21, Tesson Ferry Rd**
Gas	**N:** BP, Amoco
	S: Circle K/Shell◈, Phillips 66
Food	**N:** Jimmy's Johns, Pizza Hut, Shogun Japanese Steakhouse, Waffle House
	S: Dierbergs Bakery, Chevy's Fresh Mex, Jack in the Box, Starbucks
Med	**S:** + St Anthony's Medical Center
Other	**N:** ATMs, Banks, Auto Services, Auto Zone, Dobbs Tire & Auto Center, FedEx Office, Grocery, Tires, Concord Animal Hospital♥
	S: ATMs, Walgreen's
3	**MO 30, Gravois Rd (Most Serv N to Lindbergh Blvd)**
FStop	**N:** Alcorn Food Mart/ZX
Gas	**N:** BP, Phillips 66
Food	**N:** Bandana BBQ, Bella Sera Italian Grill
Other	**N:** ATMs, Banks, Auto Dealer, Auto Service Grocery, US Post Office, Walgreen's
(5A)	**Jct I-44, US 50, MO 366E, E to St Louis (Serv at 1st Exit)**

◈= Regular Gas Stations with Diesel ▲ = RV Friendly Locations ♥= Pet Friendly Locations
Red print shows large vehicle parking / access on site or nearby Brown Print = Campgrounds / RV PARKS

EXIT		MISSOURI
(5B)		**Jct I-44, US 50, W to Tulsa, OK** (Serv at 1st Exit)
7		**Big Bend Rd, Kirkwood** (SB exit, NB entr) (Most Serv N to Kirkwood Rd-2mi)
	Gas	**N:** Phillips 66
	Food	**N:** Arby's, Steak & Rice,
	Lodg	**N:** Best Western
	Med	**N:** + St Joseph Hospital
	Other	**N:** **to** ATMs, Banks, Car Wash, Doc's Harley Davidson, Lowe's, St Louis Comm College, Target, **Walmart**, Carwash/P66
8		**Dougherty Ferry Rd, St Louis**
	Food	**S:** Arby's, Fandango's
	Med	**S:** + Des Peres Hospital
	Other	**S:** Arch Animal Hospital♥
9		**MO 100, Manchester Rd, US 66**
	Gas	**W:** Shell
	Food	**E:** Chevy's Fresh Mex, CickFilA, Imo's Pizza, IHOP, McDonald's, Quiznos, Starbucks, Subway **W:** Applebee's, Arby's, Dickey's BBQ Pit, Imo's Pizza, McDonald's, Panera Bread, Qdoba Mex Grill, Red Robin, Starbucks, Surf & Sirloin, Taco Bell
	Med	**W:** + Hospital
	Other	**E:** ATMs, Banks, Ace Hardware, Apple Store, Barnes & Noble, FedEx Office, Grocery, US Post Office, Waldenbooks, Walgreen's, West Co Shopping Center **W:** ATMs, AT&T, Budget Truck Rental, Barrett Station Vet Clinic♥, Cinema, Golf Discount, Home Depot, Jiffy Lube, License Office, Midas, Petsmart♥, Sam's Club, Sports Authority, Trader Joe's, Walgreen's,
(12)		**Jct I-64, US 40E, US 61S, to Wentzville, St Louis** (NB)
	Med	**E/S:** + MO Baptist Hospital, + St John's Mercy Medical Center
(12B)		**Jct I-64, US 40W, US 61N, to Wentzville, St Louis** (SB)
13		**Route AB, Ladue Rd**
14		**MO 340, Olive Blvd, Creve Coeur**
	Gas	**E:** Phillips 66, Mobil **W:**
	Food	**E:** Applebee's, Denny's, Flavor of India, KFC, McDonald's, Pei Wei Asian Diner, Qdoba Mexican Grill, Starbucks **W:** Cold Stone Creamery, Gulf Shores, HuHot Mongolian Grill, Ichiban Sushi, Imo's Pizza, La Salsa Fresh Mexican Grill, Mayuri India Rest, Subway
	Lodg	**E:** Adams Mark Hotel, Courtyard, Drury Inn
	Med	**W:** + Barnes Jewish West County Hospital, + Medical Acute Care Center
	Other	**E:** ATMs, Banks, Auto Dealers, Auto Services, AT&T, Borders, Grocery, UPS Store, Spoede Animal Hospital♥, Vet♥, Walgreen's **W:** ATMs, Banks, AMC Theatres, Everything Pets Animal Hospital♥, Dierburg's Grocery, Office Depot, Pharmacy, Schnuck's Market, TJ Maxx, Vet♥, Walgreen's,
16A		**Route D East, Page Ave, St Louis**
	Gas	**E:** BP, QT, Shell, ZX/Sinclair
	Food	**E:** Casa Gallardo Mexican Rest, Dierdorf & Harts Steak House, Drunken Fish, Hardee's, Hooters, McDonald's, Ms Piggies BBQ, Panera Bread, Pujols, Starbucks, Steak N Shake,
	Lodg	**E:** Club House Inn, Comfort Inn♥, Courtyard, Extended Stay America, Homestead Suites, La Quinta Inn♥, Red Roof Inn, Residence Inn, Sheraton, Staybridge Suites, Studio Plus,
	Other	**E:** ATMs, Banks, Auto Services, Auto Zone, CarQuest, Enterprise RAC, Funny Bone Comedy Club, Home Depot, Page Animal Hospital♥, US Post Office, U-Haul,
16B		**MO 364W, Page Expwy**
	Other	**W:** **to** Creve Coeur Airport✈,
17		**Dorsett Rd, Hazelwood**
	Gas	**E:** BP, QT, Phillips 66 **W:** Mobil◈, Phillips 66, Shell
	Food	**E:** Bandana BBQ, Hardee's, Papa John's, Subway, Taco Bell, White Castle **W:** Arby's, Denny's, Domino's Pizza, Fuddruckers, Imo's Pizza, Indian Rest, McDonald's, Pasta House, Steak N Shake, Taco Bell, Thai Rest,
	Lodg	**E:** Drury Inn, Hampton Inn, Quality Inn♥ **W:** La Quinta Inn♥
	Other	**E:** ATMs, Auto Services, Advance Auto Parts, US Post Office **W:** ATMs, Carwash/Shell,Schnuck's Grocery, Walgreen's
20		**Jct I-70, to Kansas City, St Louis**
20A		**Jct I-70E, to St Louis**
20B		**Jct I-70W, to Kansas City**
20C		**MO 180, St Charles Rock Rd, Natural Bridge Rd, Bridgeton**
	Gas	**E:** BP, Mobil◈, Phillips 66 **W:** Citgo, QT
	Food	**E:** Casa Gallardo Mexican Rest, Domino's Pizza, HomeTown Buffet, Jack in the Box, KFC, McDonald's, Quiznos, Red Lobster, **W:** Bob Evans, Olive Garden, Waffle House
	Lodg	**E:** Economy Inn **W:** Americas Best Value Inn, Red Roof Inn, Super 8
	Med	**E:** + DePaul Hospital
	Other	**E:** ATMs, Banks, Animal Emergency Clinic♥, Auto Services, Best Buy,Bowling CarQuest, Carrollton Veterinary Clinic♥, CompUSA, Dollar Tree, Firestone, Garden Ridge, Lowe's, NTB, Office Depot, PetSmart♥, Target, US Post Office, Walgreen's, **to** Lambert-St Louis Intl Airport✈
22A		**Missouri Bottom Rd, Hazelwood** (EB exit, WB entr) (ReAcc via Campus Pky to Ex #23)
	Gas	**E:** Midwest Petro/Citgo
	Other	**E:** Budget Truck Rental, US Post Office
22AB		**MO 370W, St Charles County**
	Other	**W:** to St Louis Mills Shopping, Restaurants
23		**McDonnell Blvd, Hazelwood** (Acc to Ex #25-McDonnell, Lindbergh) (Dunn Rd/Frontage Rd thru Exit #34)
	Gas	**W:** QT, ZX, BP
	Food	**E:** Denny's, Quiznos **W:** Arby's, Jack in the Box, Lion's Choice, McDonald's, Starbucks, Steak N Shake
	Lodg	**E:** La Quinta Inn♥
	Other	**W:** Auto Dealer, Enterprise RAC, Carwash/BP
25		**US 67, Lindbergh Blvd, Hazelwood**
25A		**US 67S, Lindbergh Blvd**
	Gas	**S:** 7-11
	Lodg	**S:** Extended Stay America
	Other	**S:** ATMs, Auto Service, Carwash, US Post Office
25B		**US 67N, Lindbergh Blvd**
	Gas	**N:** BP, Phillips 66, QT,
	Food	**N:** Bandana's BBQ, IHOP, Jack in the Box, McDonald's, Outback Steakhouse, Pizza Hut, Pueblo Nuevo Mexican Rest, Rally's, Sonic, Starbucks, Waffle House, Wendy'
	Lodg	**N:** Comfort Inn, Extended Stay America, InTown Suites, La Quinta Inn♥, Ramada
	Other	**N:** ATMs, Auto Dealers, Auto Services, **Apache Village RV**, AT&T, Carwash Express, Community Animal Hospital♥, County Motorcyle Parts, Dierberg's, Enterprise RAC, Family Dollar, Goodyear, Jiffy Lube, Midas, NAPA, O'Reilly Auto Parts, SavALot, Schnucks/Pharmacy, UPS Store, Walgreen's, **Police Dept**
26A		**Jct I-170S, to Clayton**
26B		**Hanley Rd, Graham Rd, Florissant**
	Gas	**N:** 7-11
	Food	**N:** Arby's, Fazoli's, Long John Silver, Starbucks, Yacovelli's Rest **S:** McDonald's
	Lodg	**N:** Budget Host Inn, Hampton Inn, Red Roof Inn **S:** Days Inn
	Med	**N:** + Northwest Hospital
	Other	**S:** Dollar General, Hancock Fabrics,
27		**Route N, New Florissant Rd**
	Gas	**N:** BP, Shell
	Other	**N:** Carwash/BP & Shell
28		**Washington St, Elizabeth Ave**
	Gas	**N:** Sinclair **S:** BP
	Food	**N:** Jack in the Box, Taco Bell/Pizza Hut
	Other	**N:** ATMs, Auto Dealer, Bowling Center, Schnucks/Pharmacy, U-Haul, Walgreen's
29		**West Florissant Ave, Florissant**
	Food	**N:** Hometown Buffet, Jack in the Box, Pasta House **S:** Arby's, Burger King, Krispy Kreme, McDonald's, Wingstop
	Other	**N:** ATMs, Dierbergs, Dobbs Tire & Auto Center, Dollar General, Family Dollar, Firestone, Office Depot, Printing Etc, UPS Store, Verizon **S:** ATMs, Bank, AT&T, Auto Services, Auto Dealers, Big Lots, Dollar Tree, Gateway City Animal Clinic♥, Harbor Freight Tools, NTB, Sam's Club, Walgreen's, **WalMart**, **Addtl Serv 1-2 mi S**
30		**Route AC, New Halls Ferry Rd**
	Gas	**N:** Mobil◈, QT, ZX **S:** BP◈, Phillips 66
	Food	**N:** Applebee's, Captain D's, Lions Choice, Red Lobster, Wendy's, White Castle **S:** Church's Chicken, CiCi's Pizza, **Cracker Barrel**, IHOP, McDonald's, Steak N Shake
	Lodg	**N:** Knights Inn
	Other	**N:** ATMs, Auto Dealer, Auto Services, Car Wash, Enterprise RAC, Jiffy Lube, **S:** ATMs, Auto Dealer, Auto Zone, Carwash/BP, Enterprise RAC, Family Dollar, Home Depot, Meineke, O'Reilly Auto Parts,

◈= Regular Gas Stations with Diesel ▲ = RV Friendly Locations ♥= Pet Friendly Locations
Red print shows large vehicle parking / access on site or nearby Brown Print = Campgrounds / RV PARKS

EXIT		MISSOURI
30A		**Old Halls Ferry Rd (WB), St Louis**
	Gas	N: Phillips 66, ZX
		S: Conoco
	Food	S: Chop Suey
	Other	N: ATMs, Bank, U-Haul
		S: ATMs, Home Depot, Shop N Save
31A		**MO 367S, Lewis & Clark Blvd, St Louis, Alton**
31B		**MO 367N, Lewis & Clark Blvd, St Louis, Alton**
	Gas	N: QT
	Food	N: Jack in the Box
	Med	N: + Northeast Hospital
	Other	N: ATMs, Laundromat, Schnucks/ Pharmacy, Suburban Animal Hospital♥, Walgreen's
32		**Bellefontaine Rd, St Louis**
	FStop	N: Cheap Cheap
	Gas	N: Mobil◈, Shell
		S: BP
	Food	N: China King, Denny's, McDonald's, KFC, Papa John's Pizza, Pizza Hut, Steak 'N Shake, Subway
		S: Down Home Dining, White Castle
	Lodg	N: Economy Inn, Motel 6♥,
	Other	N: ATMs, Banks, Advance Auto Parts, Carwash/Shell, Firestone, Laundromat, Schnucks/Pharmacy,
		S: ATM, Aldi Grocery
33		**Lilac Ave, St Louis**
	FStop	S: QT Travel Center #605 (Scales), Westland Travel Center/P66
	Food	S: Hardee's
	Other	N: **North Country RV**, US Post Office
34		**Riverview Dr, to MO H (Dunn Rd / Frontage Rd thru Exit #23)**
		Welcome Center (Both dir)
		N: (RR, Phone, Picnic, Vend, Info)

CENTRAL TIME ZONE

NOTE: MM 35.5: Illinois State Line

⬆ MISSOURI

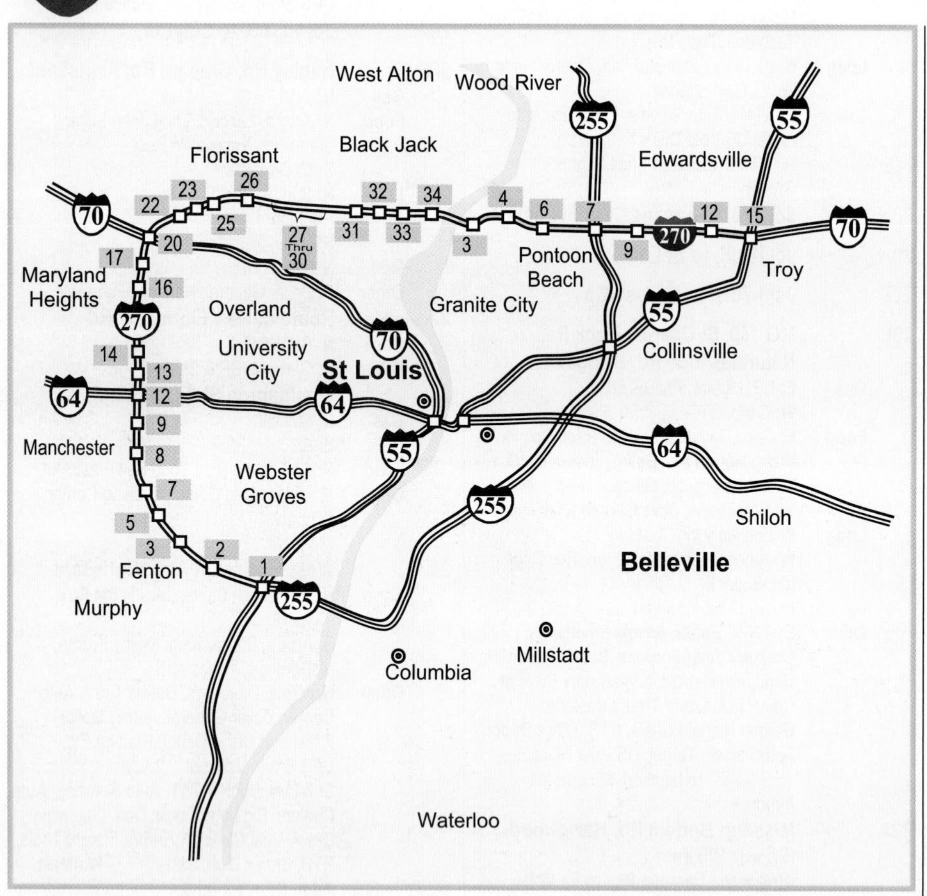

EXIT		ILLINOIS
		⬇ ILLINOIS
	NOTE:	**I-270 Begins/Ends on I-55/I-70, Ex #20**
3A		**IL 3S, Lewis & Clark Blvd, to W Chain of Rocks Rd, Granite City**
	Gas	S: Phillips 66
	Food	S: Hardee's, Waffle House
	Lodg	S: Budget Motel, Economy Inn, Econo Lodge
	Other	S: ATMs, Laundry/P66, **Trails End RV Park▲, Granite City KOA▲, MGM Lakeside Campground▲**
3B		**IL 3N, to Alton, Granite City**
	Other	N: to appr 4 mi: **Colman's Country Campers,**
4		**Old Alton Rd, W Chain of Rock Rd, Granite City (EB) IL 203, Nameoki Rd Chain of Rocks Rd (WB)**
	Other	S: Tri City Speedway
6		**IL 111, Wood River, Pontoon Beach**
	TStop	N: Flying J Travel Plaza #5070/Shell (Scales
	Gas	S: Mobil◈
	Food	N: CoutryMkt/FF/FJ TP, Hen House Rest,
		S: Denny's, La Mexicana Mexican Rest, McDonald's, Taco Bell
	Lodg	N: Apple Valley Motel♥, Best Western♥,
		S: Days Inn, Holiday Inn Express, Super 8
	TWash	N: Blue Beacon Truck Wash (Scales)
	TServ	N: Speedco
	Med	S: + Hospital
	Other	N: Laundry/WiFi/**RVDump/LP**/FJ TP, ATMs
		S: ATMs, Bank, Carwash/Mobil,
6A		**IL 111S, Wood River, Pontoon Beach**
6B		**IL 111N, Wood River, Pontoon Beach**
7		**I-255, IL 255, S to Memphis, W to Wood River (EB)**
7A		**I-255, S to Memphis (WB)**
7B		**IL 255, N to Wood River (WB)**
9		**IL 157, N Bluff Rd, Glen Carbon, Edwardsville**
	Gas	S: Phillips 66
	Lodg	N: Comfort Inn
		S: Hampton Inn
	Other	N: to Southern IL Univ
12		**IL 159, Troy Rd, Glen Carbon, to Collinsville, Centreville**
	Gas	N: Conoco◈, Phillips 66, QT
	Food	N: Applebee's, Denny's, China Rest, DQ, Hardee's, Jack in the Box, Quiznos, Steak N Shake
	Med	S: + Anderson Hospital
	Other	N: ATMs, Banks, Auto Dealers, Auto Services, Aldi Grocery, Car Wash, Dobbs Tire & Auto, Enterprise RAC, Hawthorne Animal Hospital♥, Home Depot, Lowe's, Office Max, PetSmart♥, Radio Shack, Schnucks, Target, UPS Store, Walgreen's, **Walmart**
15		**I-55, I-70W, to Chicago, St Louis (EB Exit, WB Entr)**
15A		**I-55S, I-70W, to St Louis**
15B		**I-55N, to Chicago**
(0)		**I-70E, to Indianapolis, IN**
	NOTE:	**I-270 Begins/Ends on I-55/I-70, Ex #20**

CENTRAL TIME ZONE

⬆ ILLINOIS

◈ = Regular Gas Stations with Diesel ▲ = RV Friendly Locations ♥ = Pet Friendly Locations

Red print shows large vehicle parking / access on site or nearby **Brown Print = Campgrounds / RV PARKS**

EXIT	OHIO

Begin I-270 Loop around Columbus, OH from Jct I-70/I-71 near Grove City to I-70

OHIO

NOTE: Begins/Ends on I-71, Ex #101

EASTERN TIME ZONE

2 — US 62, OH 3, Harrisburg Pike, Grove City

- **Gas** N: to BP, Swifty
  S: Certified, Speedway x2, Sunoco
- **Food** S: Big Boy, Burger King, Domino's Pizza, McDonald's, Quiznos, Subway, Tim Horton's, Wendy's, Waffle House
- **Lodg** S: Knights Inn♥
- **Other** N: Auto Services
  S: ATMs, Auto Services, Budget Truck Rental, Carwash & Lube, CVS, Enterprise RAC, Family Dollar, Firestone, Vet♥

5 — Georgesville Rd (WB chg to NB, SB chg to EB)

- **Gas** E: Marathon, Mobil, Sunoco
  W: Kroger
- **Food** E: Starbucks
  W: Applebee's, Arby's, Bob Evans, C Chipolte Mexican Grill, Fiesta Mariachi, Lone Star Steakhouse, Lotus Leaf Asian Rest, McDonald's, O'Charley's, Red Lobster, Steak N Shake, Subway, Wendy's, White Castle
- **Other** E: ATMs, Auto Services, Vet♥, **Walmart** sc, **Addtl Serv 1-2 mi** ATMs, Advance Auto Parts, Auto Dealers, Auto Services, Kroger/ Pharmacy, Lowe's, NTB, Regal Cinema, to Bolton Field Golf Course, Bolton Field Airport✈, Columbus SW Airport,

7 — US 40, Broad St, National Rd, (NB) (Acc to Ex #5 E to Georgesville Rd)

- **Gas** E: BP, Speedway◈, Sunoco◈
  W: GetGo, Speedway◈, Thornton's
- **Food** E: Bob Evans, Burger Kings, McDonald's, Popeye's Chicken, Wendy's, White Castle
  W: Arby's, KFC, Papa Johns, Waffle House
- **Lodg** E: Holiday Inn Express
  W: Holiday Inn, HomeTown Inn
- **Med** W: **+ Doctors Hospital**
- **Other** E: ATMs, Auto Dealers, Auto Services, Big Lots, Bowling Center, Family Dollar, Firestone, Goodyear, NTB, Sears Auto Center, Staples, Target, Vet♥, Walgreen's, Westland Mall, US Post Office, **to I-70**
  W: ATMs, CVS, FedEx Office, Giant Eagles, Goodyear, Grocery, Home Depot, Kroger, Mr Tire, **to appr 3 mi: Alton RV Park▲**, U-Haul

7A — US 40E, Broad St (SB)

7B — US 40W, Broad St (SB)

(8) — Jct I-70E, to Columbus, W to Dayton, Indianapolis (TS/All Serv E to Ex #94 / W to #91)

10 — Roberts Rd, Columbus

- **Gas** E: Thornton's◈
  W: Speedway, Kroger
- **Lodg** E: Value Place
  W: Courtyard, Quality Inn, Royal Inn Motel

EXIT	OHIO

- **Other** W: ATMs, Kroger, Penske Truck Rental

13 — Fishinger Rd, Upper Arlington Cemetery Rd, Hilliard (SB)

- **Gas** E: Exxon, Shell, Speedway
  W: UDF/Mobil, Speedway, Sunoco
- **Food** E: Burger King, Chili's, Chipolte Mexican Grill, Dave & Buster's, Panera Bread, Skyline Chili, Starbucks, Subway/Exxon, TGI Friday
  W: Bob Evan's, Max & Erma's, McDonald's, Wendy's
- **Lodg** E: Comfort Suites♥, Homewood Suites
  W: Hampton Inn, Motel 6♥
- **TServ** W: Columbus Kenworth, Cummins, Great Dane Trailers, Able Truck & Trailer Repair
- **Med** E: **+ Mount Carmel Urgent Care**
- **Other** E: ATMs, Auto Services, CVS, Carwash/ Shell, Carwash/Speedway, Discount Tire, Home Depot, Lowe's, Movies 12, Radio Shack, Staples, Target, Tire Discounters
  W: ATMs, Auto Dealer, Aquatic Adventures Batteries Plus, Enterprise RAC, Goodyear, Kroger, UPS Store, Avery Animal Hospital♥, Franklin Co Fairgrounds

13A — Fishinger Rd, Upper Arlington (NB)

13B — Cemetery Rd, Hilliard, Franklin Co Fairgrounds (NB)

- **Food** E: Tim Horton's, Wendy's
  W: Little Caesar's Pizza, Waffle House

15 — Tuttle Crossing Blvd, Dublin

- **Gas** E: BP, UDF/Mobil
  W: Exxon◈, Shell

EXIT	OHIO

- **Food** E: Chipolte Mexican Cafe, Longhorn Steakhouse, McDonald's, PF Chang's, Romano's Macaroni Grill, Starbucks, TGI Friday
  W: Quiznos, Steak 'n Shake
- **Lodg** E: Drury Inn, Homewood Suites, Hyatt, La Quinta Inn♥, Marriott
  W: Extended Stay Deluxe, Holiday Inn Express, Staybridge Suites
- **Other** E: ATMs, FedEx Office, Sears Auto Center, Verizon, Mall at Tuttle Crossing
  W: ATMs, Best Buy, Carwash/Shell, NTB, Office Max, US Post Office, **Walmart**, World Market

17A — US 33, OH 161, W Bridge St, Dublin Granville Rd, Dublin, Muirfield (NB chgs to EB, WB chgs to SB)

- **Gas** E: Marathon, Sunoco
- **Food** E: Bob Evans, Hyde Park Prime Steak House, Max & Erma's, McDonald's, Starbucks, Stoney River Rest, Subway
- **Lodg** E: America's Best Value Inn♥, Courtyard, Crowne Plaza, Embassy Suites, Hilton Garden Inn, Red Roof Inn♥, Residence Inn♥
- **Med** E: **+ Scioto Urgent Care**
- **Other** E: ATMs, Banks, Auto Dealers, Auto Services, CVS, Dublin Veterinarian Clinic♥, Kroger/Pharmacy, US Post Office

17B — US 33, OH 161, to Marysville, Plain City (Most Serv Avery Rd Area)

- **Gas** W: BP, Shell
- **Food** W: Buffalo Wild Wings, Cafe Ephesus, Caribou Coffee, Chipolte Mexican Grill,

◈= Regular Gas Stations with Diesel ▲ = RV Friendly Locations ♥= Pet Friendly Locations
Red print shows large vehicle parking / access on site or nearby Brown Print = Campgrounds / RV PARKS

EXIT		OHIO
	Food	W: Donato's Pizza, Panera Bread, Pizza Hut, Starbucks, Tim Horton's
	Med	W: + Dublin Methodist Hospital, + America's Urgent Care
	Other	W: ATMs, Auto Dealers, Auto Services, Banks, FedEx Office, Giant Eagle/ Pharmacy, Kroger/Pharmacy, Perimeter Veterinary Hospital♥, Tires, US Post Office, Walgreen's, Dublin Police Dept
20		**Sawmill Rd, Columbus, Zoo, (Acc to Ex #17A S to OH 161)**
	Gas	N: BP, Marathon◈, Kroger S: DM/Marathon, Shell, Speedway, Meijer
	Food	N: Burger King, McDonald's, Olive Garden, Papa John's Pizza, Subway, Taco Bell, Tim Horton's, Wendy's S: Applebee's, Arby's, Baja Fresh, Bob Evans, Burger King, Chili's, Cosi, Chipolte Mexican Grill, Golden Corral, Krisypy Kreme, KFC, McDonald's, Mongolian BBQ, Red Lobster, Ruby Tuesday, Steak 'n Shake, Ted's Montana Grill
	Lodg	S: Chase Suite Hotel, Extended Stay America, Hampton Inn, Marriott, Quality Inn
	Med	S: + OSU Medical Center
	Other	N: ATMs, Auto Dealers, CVS, Hertz RAC, Kroger, NTB, Tire Kingdom, Tires, Vet♥ S: ATMs, Banks, Auto Dealers, Barnes & Noble, Big Lots, Borders, Discount Tire, Dollar Tree, Firestone, Lowe's, Meijer, PetCo♥, Sam's Club, Staples, Target, Trader Joe's, Whole Foods Market, to OSU Airport✈, Walmart sc, Addtl Serv
22		**OH 315, Olentangy Fwy,**
	Gas	N: Marathon◈
	Food	N: Subway
	Other	N: ATMs, Bank
22A		**OH 315S, Columbus**
22B		**OH 315N, Columbus**
23		**US 23, N High St, Worthington, to Delaware, Toledo**
	Gas	N: to BP, Speedway S: BP, Speedway
	Food	N: Bob Evans, Bravo Italian Rest, Buffalo Wild Wings, Chipolte Mexican Grill, Hyde Park Steak House, J Alexander's, J Gilbert's, Panera Bread, Ruth's Chris Steak House, Starbucks S: Buca Di Beppo Italian Rest, Cosi, First Watch Rest, Jimmy's John's, McDonald's, Starbucks
	Lodg	N: AmeriSuites, Courtyard, Days Inn, Extended Stay America, Homewood Suites, Hyatt Place, Marriott, Motel 6♥, Red Roof Inn, Residence Inn, Sheraton, Towneplace Suites S: Econo Lodge, Holiday Inn
	Other	N: Cinema, Josephium College S: Auto Services, CVS, FedEx Office, Medical Center for Pets♥, NAPA
26		**Jct I-71, N to Cleveland, S to Columbus (All Serv at 1st Exits N/S)**
27		**OH 710, Cleveland Ave, Columbus (Many Serv S 1+ mi to OH 161)**
	Gas	N: Speedway S: Sunoco, Speedway
	Food	N: Subway, Tim Horton's, Wendy's S: Bob Evans, McDonald's, Steak 'n Shake, TGI Friday

EXIT		OHIO
	Lodg	N: Quality Inn, Ramada Inn, Signature Inn S: Embassy Suites
	Other	N: ATMs,CVS, NAPA S: Home Depot, Advance Auto Parts, Dollar Tree, Kroger/Pharmacy, Meijer, US Post Office
29		**OH 3, Westerville Rd, Westerville (EB chgs to SB, NB chgs to WB)**
	Gas	N: BP◈, Shell S: Speedway◈, Sunoco◈
	Food	N: Applebee's, Arby's, Chipolte Mexican Grill, McDonald's, KFC, Papa John's, Pizza Hut, Starbucks, Tim Horton's S: Domino's Pizza, Subway
	Lodg	N: Baymont Inn, Knights Inn
	Other	N: ATMs, Auto Dealers, Auto Services, Big Lots, CarQuest, Firestone, Goodyear, Kroger/Pharmacy, Office Max, Petland ♥, Radio Shack, S: ATMs, Auto Services, Aldi Grocery, Auto Zone, Budget RAC & Truck Rental, Family Dollar, Interstate Battery, Midas, U-Haul, Westerville Vet Clinic♥, US Post Office, to appr 3mi Post's Traveland RV Sales
30		**OH 161, E Dublin Granville Rd, to Worthington, New Albany**
	Gas	E: BP W: Swifty
	Food	E: Arby's, McDonald's W: Waffle House
	Other	E: ATMs, Car Wash, Goodyear, Kroger, Westerville East Animal Hospital♥ W: U-Haul
32		**Morse Rd, Gahanna, Columbus (Acc to #33 via Easton Lp, Morse Crsg)**
	Gas	E: Marathon, Speedway◈ W: BP, Mobil◈, Shell
	Food	E: Buffalo Wild Wings, Donato's Pizza, to Arby's, Chipolte Mex, CiCi's Pizza, First Watch, O'Charley's, Skyline Chili, Starbucks, W: Applebee's, Hometown Buffet, Kobe Japanese Steakhouse, McDonald's, On the Border, Pei Wei Asian Rest, Steak 'n Shake, Starbucks, Wendy's
	Lodg	W: Extended Stay America, Hampton Inn
	Other	E: Auto Dealer, CVS, to Cinema 16, Giant Eagle, Kroger, Asst'd Shops W: ATMs, Auto Dealers, Best Buy, Budget Truck Rental, Dick's Sporting Goods, Discount Tire, FedEx Office, Lowe's, NTB, Office Max, Sam's Club, Sports Authority, Staples, Target, Verizon, Walmart SC, Easton Town Center Mall
33		**Easton Way, Easton, Columbus (Acc to #32 via Easton Lp, Morse Crsg)**
	Food	W: Brio Tuscan Grill, Logan's Roadhouse, Panera Bread, Red Robin,
	Lodg	W: Hilton, Marriott, Residence Inn
	Other	W: ATMs, Apple Store, Barnes & Noble, PetSmart♥, Radio Shack, Trader Joe's, Ice Rink
35		**Jct I-670W, to Airport, US 62E, to Gahanna (NB)**
	Gas	E: Speedway◈
	Food	E: City BBQ, McDonald's, Tim Horton's
	Other	E: ATMs, Auto Services, CVS, Gahanna Animal Hospital♥, Kroger,

EXIT		OHIO
35A		**Jct I-670W, Airport (SB)**
35B		**US 62E, Gahanna (SB)**
37		**OH 317, Hamilton Rd, Gahanna**
	Gas	E: BP◈, Marathon, Speedway◈
	Food	E: Big Boy, Bob Evans, Burger King, KFC, Pizza Hut/Taco Bell, Starbucks W: to airport: McDonald's
	Lodg	E: Candlewood Suites, Holiday Inn Express, Springhill Suites, TownePlace Suites W: to Airport: Baymont Inn, Comfort Suites, Hampton Inn, Hilton Garden Inn
	Other	E: ATMs, Carwash/Marathon, Firestone, Kroger, Police Dept W: NAPA, Airport Golf Course, Rental Cars
39		**OH 16W, Broad St, to Whitehall**
	Gas	E: Speedway◈, Meijer◈ W: Shell
	Food	E: Arby's, Buffalo Wings, Chipolte Mexican Grill, Church's Chicken, Tim Horton's, Waffle House, White Castle W: Applebee's, McDonald's
	Lodg	E: Country Inn W: Ramada
	Med	E: + Mt Carmel East Hospital, + Urgent Care
	Other	E: ATMs, Auto & Tire Services, Giant Eagle, Walgreen's W: ATMs, Carwash/Shell, Kroger, Lowe's, Petland♥, Target, Town & Country Animal Clinic♥, Walgreen's, Vet♥
41A		**US 40W, Main St, to Whitehall**
	Gas	W: Mobil, Shell, Speedway
	Food	W: Don Pablo's, Fuddruckers, Golden Corral, Lone Star Steakhouse, Spageddies
	Lodg	W: Colonial Motel, Holiday Motel, Homestead Motel, Super Motor Lodge
	Other	W: ATMs, Banks, Aldi, Auto Dealer, Auto Services, Big Lots, Budget Truck Rental, Car Wash, Enterprise RAC, FedEx Office, Kroger, Laundromat, NAPA, Tires, Whitehall Animal Hospital♥
41B		**US 40E, Main St, to Reynoldsburg**
	Gas	E: BP, Shell
	Food	E: Bob Evans, Burger King, City BBQ, DQ, Hooters, McDonald's, Outback Steakhouse, Rally's, Starbucks, Steak 'n Shake, Texas Roadhouse, Tim Horton's, Wendy's
	Other	E: ATMs, Advance Auto Parts, Auto Zone, Auto Services, CVS, Grocery, Rosehill Veterinary Hospital♥, Walgreen's,
(43A)		**Jct I-70W, to Columbus**
(43B)		**Jct I-70E, to Zanesville, Wheeling**
46A		**US 33W, Southeast Expy, Bexley**
46B		**US 33E, Lancaster**
49		**Alum Creek Dr, Columbus, Obetz, Rickenbacker Int'l Airport (SB chgs to WB, EB chgs to NB)**
	Gas	N: Sunoco◈ S: AmPm◈
	Food	N: Donato's Pizza, KFC, Long John Silver, Subway S: Arby's, McDonald's, Taco Bell, Wendy's
	Lodg	S: Comfort Inn, Sleep Inn
	Other	N: ATMs, Car Wash, Penske Truck Rental
52A		**US 23N, High St, Columbus**
	Gas	N: Circle K, Exxon, Speedway, Kroger

◈= Regular Gas Stations with Diesel ▲ = RV Friendly Locations ♥= Pet Friendly Locations
Red print shows large vehicle parking / access on site or nearby Brown Print = Campgrounds / RV PARKS

EXIT — OHIO

Food — N: Arby's, Bob Evan's, China City Buffet, Golden Chinatown, McDonald's, Pizza Hut, Skyline Chili, Taco Bell, Tim Horton's, Waffle House, Wendy's, White Castle
Lodg — N: Kozy Inn

EXIT — OHIO

Other — N: ATMs, Advance Auto Parts, Auto Zone, Auto Services, Banks, Bowling, Dollar General, Family Dollar, Firestone, Kroger/Pharmacy, Lowe's, NAPA, Walgreen's, **Walmart**, U-Haul

52B — US 23S, Circleville
Gas — S: BP◈
Other — S: Scioto Downs

EXIT — OHIO

(55) — Jct I-71, to Columbus, Cincinnati
(All Serv S to Exit #100)

NOTE: **Begins/Ends on I-71, Ex #101**

OHIO

Begin I-270 Loop around Columbus, OH from Jct I-70/I-71 near Grove City to I-70

EXIT — FLORIDA

Begin I-275 on I-75 in Tampa to I-75 in St Petersburg

FLORIDA

53 — Bearss Ave
Gas — Citgo, BP, RaceTrac, Shell
Food — Burger King, McDonald's, Perkins, Subway, Wendy's
Lodg — Quality Inn
Other — Albertson's, ATMs, Pharmacy

52 — Fletcher Ave
Gas — RaceTrac, BP, Citgo
Lodg — Days Inn, Super 8

51 — FL 582, Fowler Ave
Gas — Citgo, Shell
Food — Burger King, Denny's, McDonald's, Ponderosa, Subway, Waffle House
Lodg — Howard Johnson, Quality Inn, Motel 6♥

50 — FL 580, Busch Blvd
Gas — Chevron, Exxon, Marathon, Shell
Food — Burger King, KFC, Wendy's
Lodg — Comfort Inn
Other — Busch Gardens, Home Depot, **Walmart**,

49 — Bird Ave (NB)
Gas — Shell
Food — KFC, Wendy's

48 — Sligh Ave
Gas — BP, Marathon
Other — Zoo

47AB — US 92, to US 41S, Hillsborough Ave
Gas — Citgo, Valero, BP
Food — Burger King, Wendy's

46B — FL 574, MLK Blvd
Gas — BP, Chevron, Marathon
Food — McDonald's
Med — W: + Hospital
Other — Grocery

46A — Floribraska Ave

(45B) — Jct I-4E, to Orlando, I-75

45A — Jefferson St

44 — Ashley Dr, Tampa St

42 — Howard Ave, Armenia Ave
Gas — Citgo, BP, Shell

41C — Himes Ave (SB)
Other — Raymond James Stadium

41AB — US 92, Dale Mabry Ave
Gas — BP, Exxon, Mobil, Shell
Food — Carrabba's, Krystal, Ruby Tuesday, Village Inn, Chili's, Denny's, Longhorn Steakhouse, KFC, Sweet Tomatos, Waffle House
Lodg — Courtyard, Days Inn, Westin Suites

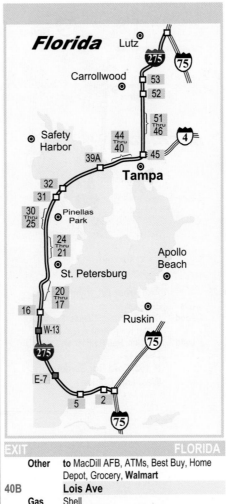

EXIT — FLORIDA

Other — to MacDill AFB, ATMs, Best Buy, Home Depot, Grocery, **Walmart**

40B — Lois Ave
Gas — Shell
Lodg — DoubleTree Hotel, Sheraton

40A — FL 587, Westshore Blvd
Gas — Citgo, Shell
Food — Steak & Ale, Waffle House, Durango
Lodg — Embassy Suites, Best Western, Marriott, SpringHill Suites

39AB — FL 60W, to Airport
Food — Outback Steakhouse
Lodg — Clarion Hotel

32 — FL 687S, 4th St N, to US 92

31B — FL 688W, Ulmerton Rd, to Largo, Seminole, Beaches, Airport
(Gas, Food, Lodg on FL 688W)

31A — 9th ST N, MLK St (SB, Left exit)

30 — FL 686, Roosevelt Blvd

EXIT — FLORIDA

28 — FL 694W, Gandy Blvd, Indian Shores
Other — Roberts M/H & RV Resort▲, Greyhound Racetrack

28AB — 54th Ave N, St Petersburg
Gas — Citgo, Racetrac
Food — Cracker Barrel, Waffle House
Lodg — Days Inn, Ramada Inn

25 — 38th Ave N, to Beaches
Gas — Citgo
Food — Burger King, McDonald's

24 — 22nd Ave N
Gas — 7-11, Racetrac
Other — Home Depot, Lowe's

23B — FL 595, 5th Ave N
Med — E: + Hospital

(23A) — Jct I-375, Downtown St Petersburg
Other — The Pier

(22) — Jct I-175E, to Tropicana Field, Downtown St Petersburg

21 — 28th St S, Downtown

20 — 31st Ave (NB)

19 — 22nd Ave S, Gulfport
Gas — Citgo

18 — 26th Ave S (NB)

17 — FL 682W, 54th Ave S, Pinellas Bayway, St Pete Beach
Gas — 7-11, Sunoco
Food — Bob Evans, Taco Bell, Wendy's
Lodg — Bayway Inn
Other — Pharmacy, Grocery, **to Beaches**

16 — Pinellas Pt Dr, Skyway Lane

(16) — TOLL Plaza (SB)

(13) — N Sunshine Skyway Fishing Pier
Rest Area (Both dir)
W: (RR, Phone, Picnic, Vend)

(7) — S Sunshine Skyway Fishing Pier
Rest Area (Both dir)
E: (RR, Phone, Picnic, Vend)

(6) — TOLL Plaza (NB)

5 — US 19, to Palmetto, Bradenton

2 — US 41, Palmetto, Bradenton

(0) — I-275 Begins / Ends on I-75

FLORIDA

Begin I-275 on I-75 in near Bradenton to I-75 in Tampa

EXIT	MICHIGAN

Begin I-275 on I-96 near Detroit to I-75, near Monroe, MI

MICHIGAN

NOTE: I-275 runs below with I-96 for 10 mi. Exit #'s follow I-96.

(163) **Jct I-696, M 5, Grand River Ave (EB)**

164 **M 5N, 12 Mile Rd (EB)**

165 **M 5N, 12 Mile Rd (WB)**

167 **8 Mile Rd, Baseline Rd, Northville**
- Gas S: Speedway, Meijer◈, Costco
- Food S: Big Boy, Chili's, McDonald's, Kyoto Japanese Steakhouse, On the Border, Taco Bell
- Lodg S: Hampton Inn, Hilton, Ramada, Sheraton
- Med S: + Hospital
- Other S: ATMs, Best Buy, Costco, Firestone, Grocery, Home Depot, Target

169A **7 Mile Rd West, Livonia**

169B **7 Mile Rd East, Livonia**

169AB **7 Mile Rd, Livonia**
- Food N: Lone Star Steakhouse, Rest/Embassy Suites
  S: Cooker, Romano's Macaroni Grill
- Lodg N: Embassy Suites
  S: AmeriSuites
- Other S: Home Depot

170 **6 Mile Rd, Livonia**
- Gas S: AmocoBP, Mobil
- Food N: Denison's, Max & Erma's, Red Robin, The Ground Round
  S: Applebee's, McDonald's, Italian Rest
- Lodg N: Best Western, Courtyard, Holiday Inn, Marriott, Quality Inn
  S: Fairfield Inn, Residence Inn
- Other N: Mall
  S: ATMs, CVS, Office Depot

(172/29) **Jct I-275S, to Toledo, M 14 W**
Jct I-96E, to Detroit, M 14W, to Ann Arbor

NOTE: I-275 above runs with I-96 for 10 mi. Exit #'s follow I-96.

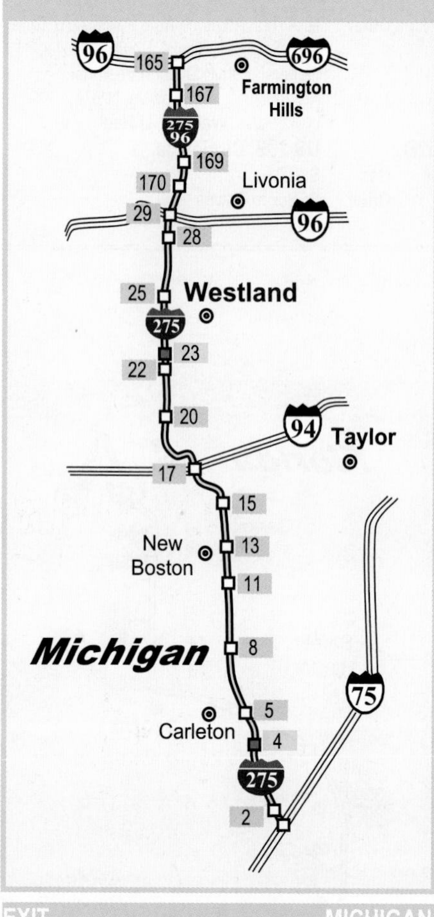

EXIT	MICHIGAN

28 **Ann Arbor Rd, Plymouth**
- Gas BP, Shell
- Food Denny's, Dunkin Donuts, Bennigan's Burger King, Steak & Ale
- Lodg Days Inn, Red Roof Inn♥, Quality Inn

25 **M 153, Ford Rd, Garden City, Westland, Canton**

EXIT	MICHIGAN

- Gas BP, Shell, Speedway, Sunoco◈
- Food Arby's, Bob Evans, Chili's, Chuck E Cheese's Pizza, Dunkin Donuts, KFC, Little Caesar's Pizza, Olive Garden, Outback Steakhouse, Tim Horton's, Wendy's, White Castle
- Lodg Baymont Inn, Extended Stay America, Fairfield Inn, Motel 6♥
- Other Discount Tire, Target

(23) **Rest Area (NB)**
(RR, Phone, Picnic, Info)

22 **US 12, Michigan Ave, to Wayne, Ypsilanti, Dearborn, Canton**
- Gas BP, Mobil◈, Shell, Speedway◈, Marathon◈
- Food McDonald's, Subway, Wendy's
- Lodg Days Inn, Holiday Inn Express, Super 8

20 **Ecorse Rd, to Romulus**
- Gas Mobil◈
- Food Burger King/Mobil
- Other Willow Run Airport

(17) **Jct I-94, E-Detroit, W-Ann Arbor, (W to Detroit Metro Airport)**

15 **Eureka Rd, to Detroit Metro Airport**

13 **Sibley Rd, New Boston**

11A **S Huron Rd East (SB)**

11B **S Huron Rd West (SB)**

11 **S Huron Rd**
- Gas Sunoco◈
- Food Burger King/Sunoco

8 **Will Carleton Rd, to Flat Rock**

5 **Carleton, S Rockwood**

(4) **Rest Area (SB)**
(RR, Phone, Picnic)

2 **US 24, to Telegraph Rd**
- Gas Marathon◈

(0/20) **Jct I-75, to Detroit, MI, Toledo, OH**

MICHIGAN

EXIT	PENNSYLVANIA

Begin Eastbound I-276 from Jct I-76 in Philadelphia, PA to NJ Tpk /NJ State Line

PENNSYLVANIA

EASTERN TIME ZONE

(326) **Jct I-76E, to US 202, Valley Forge, Philadelphia**

(328) **King of Prussia Service Plaza (WB)**
- FStop Sunoco
- Food Breyer's, Hot Dog City, McDonald's

(330) **PA State Hwy Patrol Post (EB)**

333 **Germantown Pike, to I-476S, Norristown**
- Gas N: Mobil
  S: Circle K
- Lodg N: Springhill Suites
- Med N: + Hospital
- Other N: Mall

(334) **Jct I-476N, Allentown (EB), Jct I-476, Philadelphia, Chester, Allentown (WB)**

339 **PA 309, Ft Washington, Philadelphia Ambler**
- Gas N: Circle K, Mobil
- Lodg N: Best Western, Holiday Inn
- Other N: Montgomery Mall, Ft Washington Expo Center, Temple Univ/Ambler Campus

340 **Virginia Dr, Ft Washington (WB)**
(EZ Pass only, NO Trucks)

343 **PA 611, Willow Grove, Doylestown, Jenkintown**
- Gas N: Mobil
  S: 7-11, Hess, Mobil, Shell
- Food S: Friendly's, McDonald's
- Lodg S: Hampton Inn
- Other S: ATMs, Auto Services, Best Buy, Staples, Peddlers Village, Penn's Purchase Factory Outlets, Penn State Univ/Abington Campus, Willow Grove Park

351 **US 1, to I-95, Philadelphia, Trenton**
- Gas S: AmocoBP, Exxon, Sunoco
- Food N: Bob Evans, Ruby Tuesday
- Lodg N: Hampton Inn, Holiday Inn
  S: Comfort Inn, Howard Johnson, Knights Inn

◈ = Regular Gas Stations with Diesel ▲ = RV Friendly Locations ♥ = Pet Friendly Locations
Red print shows large vehicle parking / access on site or nearby Brown Print = Campgrounds / RV PARKS

EXIT	PENNSYLVANIA
Other	S: ATMs, Banks, Target, Neshaminy Mall, Oxford Valley Mall, Franklin Mills, Sesame Place, Philadelphia Park Racetrack
(352)	**N Neshaminy Service Plaza (WB)**
FStop	Sunoco
Food	Burger King, Nathan's Express, Starbucks
(353)	**FUTURE: Phila Park Slip Ramp (EB) (E-Z Pass only)**
(355)	**FUTURE: PA TPK / I-95 / I-195 Interchange**
358	**US 13, Delaware Valley, Bristol, Levittown**
Fstop	S: Lukoil
Gas	N: WaWa S: Getty, Mobil
Food	S: Burger King, Italian Rest, McDonald's
Lodg	N: Days Inn, Ramada Inn
Other	S: LP/Lukoil
(359)	**Delaware River Bridge, NJ Tpk, to NY City, NY; Wilmington, DE**
NOTE:	**TOLL Plaza (End EB, Begin WB) (EB End, WB Begin Call Box for 34 mi)**

EASTERN TIME ZONE

PENNSYLVANIA

Begin Westbound I-276 from NJ / PA Border to Jct I-76 near King of Prussia, PA.

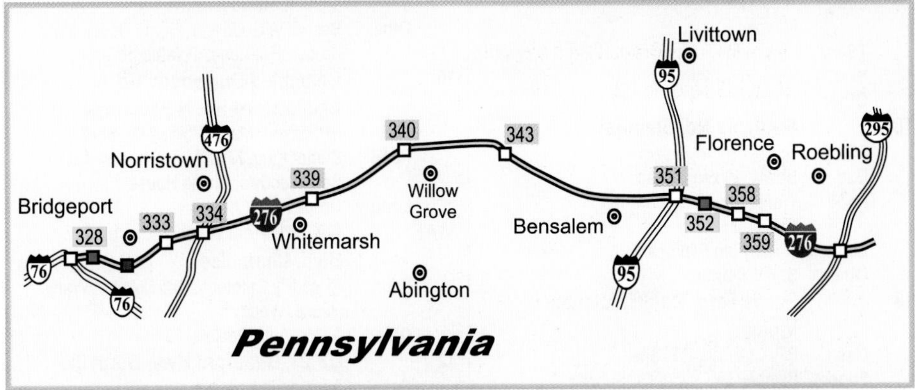

EXIT	GEORGIA
	Begin I-285 ByPass around Atlanta, GA from Jct I-85, South of Atlanta.

GEORGIA

EXIT	GEORGIA
1	**Washington Rd, Atlanta**
Gas	BP, Chevron, Texaco ◈
Food	Sunny Garden Family Buffet
Lodg	Mark Inn, Regency Inn
2	**Camp Creek Pkwy, Atlanta Airport**
Gas	BP, BP, Exxon, Shell, Texaco
Food	Checkers, McDonald's, Carino's, Chick-Fil-A, Jason's Deli, Longhorn Steak House, Panda Express, Red Lobster, Ruby Tuesday, Wendy's
Lodg	Clarion, Comfort Inn
Other	BJ's, Lowe's, PetSmart♥, Staples, Target, Walgreen's, Convention Center, Hartfield Jackson Atlanta Int'l Airport✈
5AB	**GA 166W, Lakewood Freeway, GA 154S, Campbellton Rd**
Gas	BP, Citgo◈, Conoco, Raceway, Shell ◈
Food	Burger King, Checkers, IHOP, KFC, Pizza Hut, Mrs Winner's, Starbucks, Taco Bell, Wendy's
Other	Greenbriar Mall, ATMs, CVS, Goodyear, Firestone, Family Dollar, Kroger, Auto Zone, Vet♥, to Fort McPherson
7	**Cascade Rd, Atlanta**
Gas	BP, Chevron, Marathon, Phillips 66, Shell
Food	Applebee's, KFC, McDonald's, Pizza Hut, Starbucks, Subway, Wendy's
Med	W: + Hospital
Other	Home Depot, Publix, Kroger, Tires Plus
9	**GA 139, ML King Jr Dr, Atlanta**
Gas	Amoco, Phillips 66, Chevron, Shell
Food	McDonald's, Mrs Winner's
Other	Grocery, to Fulton Co Airport Brown Field✈
(10A)	**Jct I-20, E-Atlanta (SB, Left exit)**
(10B)	**Jct I-20, W-Birmingham (NB, Left exit)**
Other	to Six Flags
12	**US 78, US 278, Bankhead Hwy**
TStop	E: Petro Stopping Center #22 (Scales)
Gas	BP, Citgo◈
Food	E: Rest/Petro SC, McDonald's, Mrs Winner's
TWash	E: Blue Beacon TW/Petro SC
TServ	E: Petro SC, Quick Fleet Tire Sales
Other	to Fulton Co Airport Brown Field✈
13	**GA 70, Bolton Rd (NB, No reacc)**

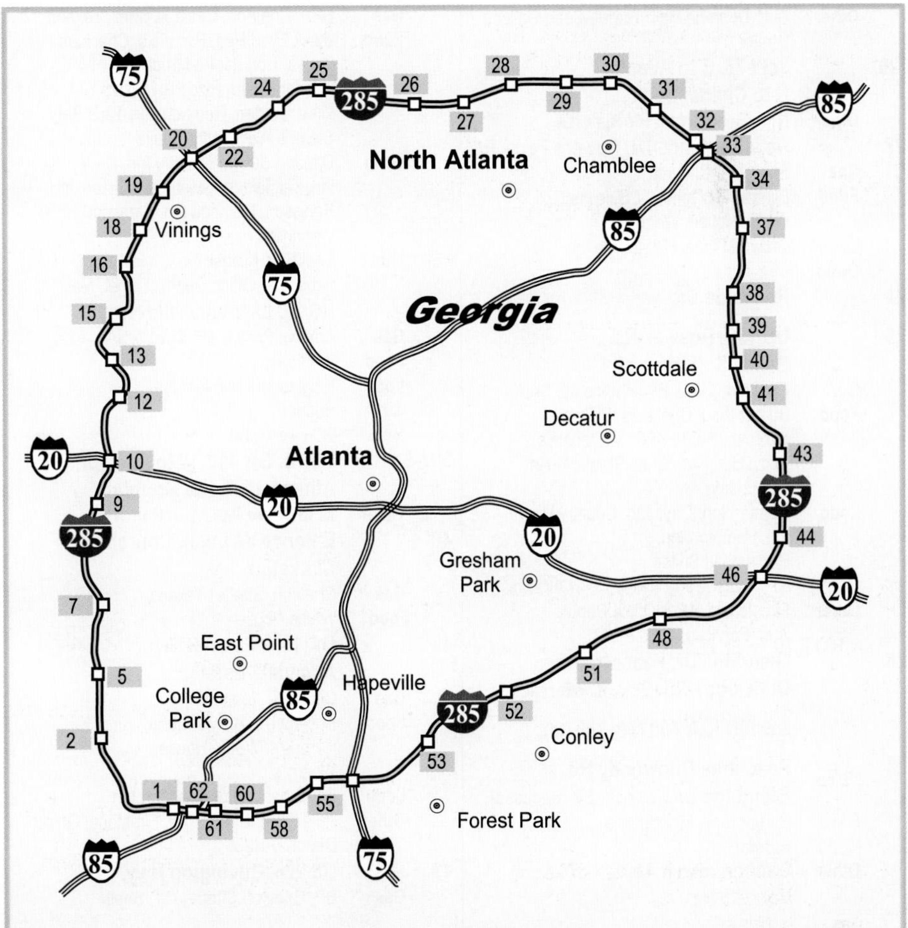

◈= Regular Gas Stations with Diesel ▲ = RV Friendly Locations ♥= Pet Friendly Locations
Red print shows large vehicle parking / access on site or nearby Brown Print = Campgrounds / RV PARKS

EXIT		GEORGIA
15		**GA 280, S Cobb Dr, Smyrna**
	Gas	BP◊, Exxon◊, RaceTrac, Shell
	Food	Arby's, IHOP, Krystal, Mrs Winner's, McDonald's, Subway, Taco Bell, Waffle House
	Lodg	AmeriHost, Comfort Inn, Knights Inn, Microtel
	TServ	Kenworth
	Med	W: + Hospital
	Other	U-Haul
16		**S Atlanta Rd, Smyrna**
	TStop	S: Pilot Travel Center #344 (Scales)
	Gas	Shell◊, Exxon, Texaco
	Food	Waffle House S: Wendy's/Pilot TC
	Lodg	Holiday Inn Express
	Other	S: RV Center
18		**Paces Ferry Rd SE, Atlanta, Vinings**
	Gas	BP, Chevron, QT, Shell
	Food	Blimpie, Mrs Winner's, Subway
	Lodg	Fairfield Inn, La Quinta Inn♥, Hampton Inn, Wyndham
	Other	Publix, Pharmacy, Home Depot, Goodyear
19		**US 41, GA 3, Cobb Pkwy SE, to Dobbins AFB**
	Gas	BP, Chevron, Citgo, Shell
	Food	Arby's, Carrabba's, Denny's, Hardee's, McDonald's, Olive Garden, Red Lobster, Steak 'n Shake, Waffle House
	Lodg	Hilton, Holiday Inn, Hampton Inn, Red Roof Inn♥, Sheraton, Wingate Inn
	Other	Auto Dealers, Mall, Target, Cobb Galleria Center
(20)		**Jct I-75, S to Atlanta, N to Chattanooga**
	Other	N: to Brookwood RV Resort▲
22		**New Northside Dr, Powers Ferry Rd**
	Gas	Shell, BP, Chevron
	Food	Blimpie, McDonald's, Sideline Grill, Waffle House, Wendy's
	Lodg	Crowne Plaza, Hawthorne Inn
	Other	CVS
24		**Riverside Dr**
25		**US 19S, Roswell Rd, Sandy Springs**
	Gas	Chevron, Citgo, BP, Phillips 66, Shell◊
	Food	Burger King, Checkers, El Toro Mexican, IHOP, KFC, McDonald's, Pizza Hut, Ruth Chris Steak House, TGI Friday
	Lodg	Comfort Inn, Days Inn, Country Hearth Inn, Hampton Inn, Homestead Suites
	Med	S: + St Joseph's Hospital of Atlanta
	Other	Firestone, NAPA, Office Depot, Auto Services, Tires Plus
26		**Glenridge Dr, Peachtree Dunwoody Rd (EB exit, WB reacc)**
27		**US 19N, GA 400 (SB, Toll Rd)**
28		**Peachtree-Dunwoody Rd, Glenridge Dr (WB exit, EB reaccess)**
	Food	Burger King, McDonald's
	Med	+ Hospital
	Other	Pharmacy, Publix, Mall

EXIT		GEORGIA
29		**Ashford-Dunwoody Rd**
	Gas	Amoco, Exxon, Chevron, Conoco
	Food	Applebee's, Burger King, Mrs Winner's, Subway
	Lodg	Fairfield Inn, Holiday Inn, Hilton Garden Marriott, Residence Inn
	Other	Best Buy, Goodyear, Home Depot, Mall, Kroger, Firestone, Oglethorpe Univ
30		**Chamblee-Dunwoody Rd, N Shallowford Rd, N Peachtree Rd**
	Gas	BP, Exxon, Mobil, Phillips 66, Shell
	Food	Burger King, KFC, Mrs Winner's, Taco Bell, Wendy's, Waffle House
	Lodg	Holiday Inn
31AB		**GA 141, Peachtree Industrial Blvd, Chamblee**
	Food	Piccadilly Cafeteria, Red Lobster, Waffle House, Wendy's
	Other	ATMs, Auto Dealers, CVS
32		**US 23, Beauford Hwy, Doraville**
	Gas	Amoco, Phillips 66◊
	Food	Arby's, Burger King, McDonald's, KFC, Mrs Winner's, Subway, Taco Bell
	Lodg	Comfort Inn
	Other	ATMs, Firestone, Goodyear, Target
(33)		**Jct I-85, N-Greenville, S-Atlanta**
34		**Chamblee-Tucker Rd**
	Gas	Chevron, Citgo, Phillips 66, Shell
	Food	Arby's, Mrs Winner's, KFC, Taco Bell Lone Star Steakhouse, Waffle House
	Lodg	Days Inn
	Other	Pharmacy, Big Lots, Dollar Tree, Kroger
37		**GA 236, LaVista Rd, Tucker**
	Gas	BP◊, Chevron, Circle K, Shell, Texaco
	Food	Black Eyed Pea, Blimpie's, Checkers Dunkin Donuts, Fuddrucker's, IHOP, Panera Bread, Piccadilly, Pizza Hut, Olive Garden, Red Lobster, Taco Bell, Steak & Ale, Waffle House
	Lodg	Comfort Suites, Country Inn, Days Inn, Fairfield Inn, Marriott, Masters Inn, Radisson, Ramada Inn, Starwood Hotel, Wyndham
	Other	Best Buy, Kroger, Pharmacy, Publix, Firestone, Office Depot, Target, Mall
38		**US 29, Lawrenceville Hwy**
	Gas	Amoco, Phillips 66, Shell, USA
	Food	Waffle House
	Lodg	Knights Inn, Masters Inn, Super 8
	Med	W: + Hospital
39AB		**US 78, GA 410, W to Decatur, E to Athens, to Stone Mountain**
	Other	E: to Stone Mountain Park▲
40		**E Ponce de Leon, Church St, Clarkston**
	Gas	Chevron, Shell◊, Texaco
	Food	Waffle House
41		**GA 10, Memorial Dr, Avondale Estates**
	Gas	Citgo, QT, Mobil, Shell◊
	Food	Applebee's, Arby's, Burger King, KFC, Hardee's, Waffle House, Wendy's
	Lodg	Savannah Suites, Comfort Inn
	Other	Auto Zone, Big 10 Tire, Firestone, Office Depot, U-Haul
43		**US 278, Covington Hwy.**
	Gas	BP, Chevron,Citgo◊, QT, Shell◊

EXIT		GEORGIA
	Food	Blimpie, Checkers, Hardee's, KFC, Mrs Winner's, Waffle House, Wendy's
	Lodg	Best Inn
44		**GA 260, Glenwood Rd, Decatur**
	Gas	Citgo, Shell
	Food	Burger King, Mrs Winner's
	Lodg	Glenwood Inn, Super 8
(46AB)		**Jct I-20, E-Atlanta, W-Augusta**
48		**GA 155, Flat Shoals Rd, Candler Rd.**
	Gas	Circle K, Marathon, QT, Shell◊
	Food	Arby's, Checkers, DQ, KFC, Pizza Hut, McDonald's, Taco Bell, Waffle King
	Lodg	Gulf American Inn, Econo Lodge, Ramada Inn
51		**Bouldercrest Rd, Atlanta**
	TStop	Pilot Travel Center #331 (Scales)
	Gas	Chevron◊
	Food	Wendy's/WiFi/Pilot TC, KFC
	Lodg	Knights Inn
(52)		**Jct I-675S, to Macon**
53		**US 23, GA 42, Conley, Ft Gillem**
	FStop	BP Food Shop Citgo Food Mart
	TStop	Conoco Fuel Stop Travel Center of America (Scales)
	Food	Rest/FastFood/TA TC, Popeye's, Wendy's
	Lodg	Econo Lodge
	TServ	TA TC /Tires
	Other	Laundry/WiFi/CB/TA TC, ATMs
55		**GA 54, Jonesboro Rd (EB) US 19, US 41, Forest Park (WB)**
	Gas	AmocoBP, Citgo◊, RaceTrac, Shell◊
	Food	Arby's, McDonald's, Waffle House
	Lodg	Super 8
	Other	Home Depot, Atlanta Expo Center
(58)		**Jct I-75, N to Atlanta, S to Macon to US 19, US 41, Forest Park (EB) (Serv on US 19S)**
	Gas	BP, Chevron
	Food	Subway, Waffle House, Wendy's
	Lodg	Home Lodge, Sunset Lodge
59		**Clark Howell Hwy**
	Other	Atlanta Int'l Airport✈, Air Cargo
60		**GA 139, Riverdale Rd, Atlanta**
	Gas	BP, Exxon, QT, Speedway, Shell◊
	Food	Burger King, Checker's, McDonald's, Waffle House, Wendy's
	Lodg	Best Western, Country Suites, Days Inn, Motel 6♥, Ramada, Microtel
	Other	Auto Services, Dollar General, Grocery, U-Haul
(61)		**Jct I-85, N-Atlanta, S-Montgomery (Access All Serv 1st I-85N, Exit #71)**
62		**GA 14, to GA 279, Old National Hwy**
	Gas	BP, Chevron, Exxon, Shell
	Food	Burger King, Checkers, KFC, Krystal, Longhorn Steakhouse, McDonald's, Mrs Winner's, Red Lobster, Taco Bell, Waffle House, Wendy's
	Lodg	Comfort Inn, Clarion, Days Inn, Fairfield Inn, La Quinta Inn♥, Howard Johnson Express, Motel 6, Radisson, Red Roof Inn♥
	Other	Auto Zone, Auto Repairs, ATMs, Family Dollar, NAPA, U-Haul

⬆ GEORGIA

Begin I-285 Bypass around Atlanta from near Jct I-85, South of Atlanta, GA.

◊ = Regular Gas Stations with Diesel ▲ = RV Friendly Locations ♥ = Pet Friendly Locations

Red print shows large vehicle parking / access on site or nearby **Brown Print = Campgrounds / RV PARKS**

EXIT ILLINOIS

Begin I-294 ByPass around Chicago.

ILLINOIS

NOTE: I-294 begins/ends on I-94, Ex #74.

NOTE: I-294 runs below with I-80 for 5 mi. Exit #'s follow I-80.

(160B) **Jct I-80E / I-94E, to Indiana**

NOTE: TOLL begins WB, Ends EB

(160A) **Jct I-94W, to Chicago, IL 394S, to Danville (SB ex, NB entr)**

(159) **Lincoln Oasis**
- FStop: Mobil
- Food: Burger King

157 **IL 1, Halsted St, 800W**

156 **Dixie Hwy** (SB ex, NB entr)

(155/5) **Jct I-80W, to I-57, to Iowa; Jct I-294N, Tri State Toll Plaza**

NOTE: I-294 runs above with I-80 for 5 mi. Exit #'s follow I-80

(6) **163rd St TOLL Plaza**

6 **US 6, 159th St, Harvey**
- Gas: BP, Mobil, Shell, Clark, Marathon
- Food: Burger King, Popeye's, Taco Bell
- Lodg: Holiday Inn Express
- Other: ATMs, Aldi, Auto Zone, Auto Services, Firestone, Grocery, Radio Shack, Walgreen's, U-Haul

12 **IL 50, Cicero Ave, IL 83, Islip**
- Gas: 7-11, Speedway, BP, Gas City◊
- Food: Boston Market, IHOP, Pizza Hut, Popeye's, Quiznos, Starbucks, Subway/ Gas City
- Lodg: Baymont Inn, Hampton Inn
- Other: ATMs, Best Buy, NTB, Pep Boys, Sears Auto Center

18 **US 12, US 20, 95th St, 76th Ave, Hickory Hill, Oaklawn**
- Gas: 7-11, Shell, Speedway◊
- Food: McDonald's, Papa John's Pizza, Arby's, Burger King, Denny's, Quiznos, Wendy's
- Lodg: Exel Inn
- Med: + Hospital
- Other: ATMs, Sears Auto Center, Mall, Walgreen's

(20) **83rd St TOLL Plaza** (NB) **82nd St TOLL Plaza** (SB)

21 **US 12, US 20, US 45, LaGrange Rd, Il 171, Archer Ave** (SB entr only)

22 **75th St, Willow Springs Rd, La Grange**

(23) **Jct I-55, to Chicago, St Louis**

24 **Wolf Rd** (NB ex, SB entr)

(25) **Hinsdale Oasis** (Both dir)
- Gas: Mobil◊
- Food: Baskin Robbins, Wendy's

28 **US 34, Ogden Ave**
- Gas: W: BP, Shell
- Food: W: Dunki Donuts, McDonald's, Starbucks
- Med: W: + Hospital
- Other: E: Zoo
  W: ATMs, Auto Dealers, Wild Oats Market

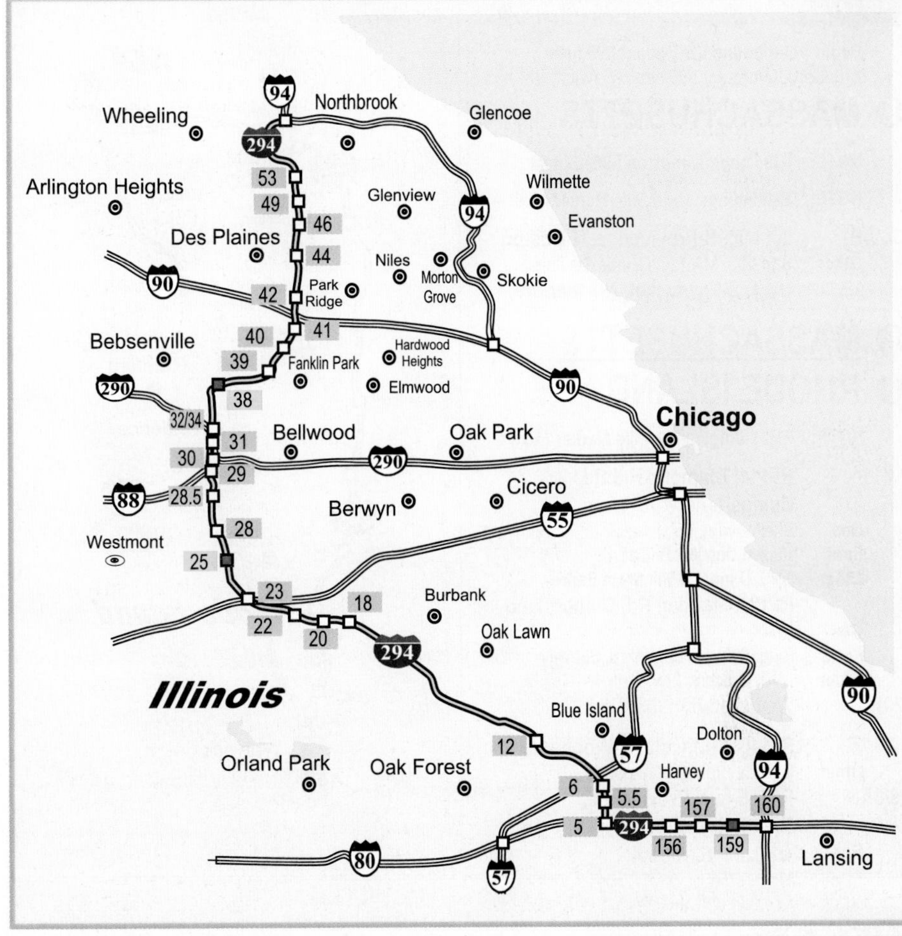

EXIT ILLINOIS

(29) **Jct I-88W, Ronald Reagan Memorial Tollway, to Aurora** (NB exit, SB entr)

29.5 **Cermak Rd, 22nd St** (SB, no reacc)

(30) **Cermak Rd TOLL Plaza**

31 **IL 38, Roosevelt Rd** (NB ex, SB entr) (diff NB reaccess)
- Gas: E: Citgo◊

(32) **Jct I-290E, to Chicago** (SB)

(34) **Jct I-290W, to US 20, IL 64,Rockford** (NB)

(38) **O'Hare Oasis** (Both dir)
- Gas: Mobil◊
- Food: Burger Kin, TCBY

39 **IL 19W, Irving Park Rd** (SB ex, NB ent)
- Gas: E: BP, Clark, Marathon◊
- Food: E: Dunkin Donuts, McDonald's, Subway, Wendy's
- Lodg: E: Comfort Suites
  W: Candlewood Suites, Days Inn, Hampton Inn, Howard Johnson, Sheraton
- Other: E: ATMs, Walgreen's

(39) **Irving Park TOLL Plaza** (SB)

EXIT ILLINOIS

(40) **Jct I-190W, River Rd, Des Plaines** (Gas/Food/Lodging on I-90)

(41) **Jct I-90, Rockford, Chicago**

(42) **Touhy Ave TOLL Plaza** (NB)

42 **Touhy Ave** (NB ex, SB entr)
- Gas: W: Mobil
- Lodg: W: Comfort Inn
- Other: W: ATM, Auto Services

44 **US 14, Dempster St** (NB, No reacc)
- Food: W: Dunkin Donuts, Subway
- Med: E: + Hospital

45 **IL 58, Golf Rd** (SB ex, NB entr)
- Gas: E: Citgo◊, Shell
- Other: E: ATMs, Auto Services, Best Buy, CVS, Target

49 **Willow Rd**
- Gas: BP
- Food: Burger King, Denny's, McDonald's, W: TGI Friday
- Lodg: W: Baymont Inn, Courtyard, DoubleTree Hotel, Fairfield Inn, Motel 6♥

(50.5-53) **Jct I-94E, Chicago**

54 **Lake Cook Rd** (NB, no reaccess)

NOTE: I-294 begins/ends on I-94

ILLINOIS

Begin I-294 ByPass around Chicago.

EXIT	MASSACHUSETTS

Begin Southbound I-295 at Jct I-95 near Attleboro, MA to Jct I-95 near Warwick, RI

MASSACHUSETTS

NOTE: I-295 begins/ends on I-95, Exit #4

NOTE: Exit listings show Mile Marker / Exit #

(3/2AB) **Jct I-95, S-Providence, N-Boston**
- Other: S to I-93, MA 128, Gillette Stadium

1.5/1AB **US 1, S-Pawtucket, N-Attleboro**

MASSACHUSETTS

RHODE ISLAND

NOTE: Exit listings show Mile Marker / Exit #

23/11 **RI 114, Diamond Hill Rd, Cumberland**
- Gas: Shell
- Food: Dunkin Donuts, J's Deli
- Other: CVS, **Diamond Hill State Park**

21/10 **RI 122, Mendon Rd, Cumberland**
- Gas: Gulf
- Food: Burger King, McDonald's, Subway
- Other: CVS, Grocery

(20) **Weigh Station** (Both dir)

19/9AB **RI 146, S-Lincoln, N-Woonsocket**
- Other: E: N Central State Airport✈

16/8AB **RI 7, S to N Providence, N to Smithfield**
- Gas: 7-11

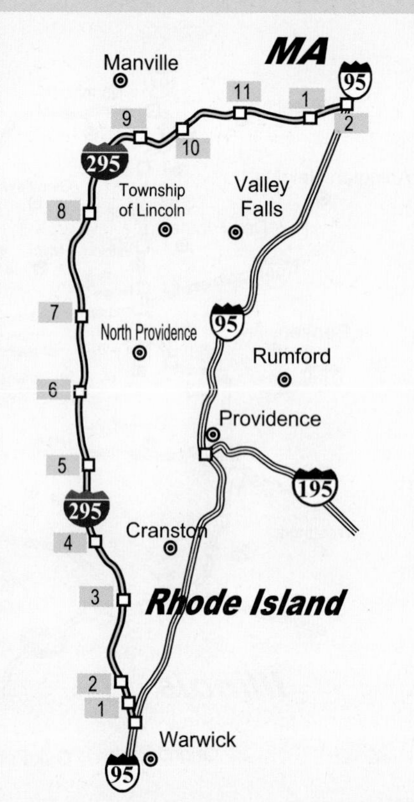

EXIT	RHODE ISLAND

- Other: E: N Central State Airport✈

13/7AB **US 44, E-Centerville, W-Greenville**
- Gas: Valero, Exxon, Mobil, Shell
- Food: Applebee's, Burger King, Chili's, KFC, McDonald's, Pizza Hut, Subway
- Med: E: + Hospital
- Other: NAPA, CVS, Home Depot, Target

10/6ABC **US 6, US 6A, Johnston, Providence**
- Gas: 7-11, Mobil, Shell
- Food: Burger King, KFC, Wendy's
- Lodg: HiWay Motel, Bel-Air Motor Inn
- Other: Auto Dealers, Auto Zone, ATMs, CVS

8/5 **RI Resource Recovery Indust Park**

7/4 **RI 14, Plainfield Pike, Johnston**

4/3B **RI 37W, to RI 51, Phenix Ave**

4/3A **RI 37E, to RI 2, Cranston**
- Other: E to TF Green State Airport✈, RI Nat'l Guard

1/2 **RI 2, Warwick, Cranston**
- Gas: Exxon, Mobil, Shell
- Food: Chili's, Chuck E Cheese's Pizza, Dunkin Donuts, Lone Star Steakhouse, McDonald's, Subway, Taco Bell, Wendy's
- Other: Mall, Sam's Club, **Walmart**, NAPA

0/1 **RI 113, East Ave, to I-95N**

NOTE: I-295 Begins/Ends on I-95, Exit #11

RHODE ISLAND

EXIT	DELAWARE

DELAWARE

NOTE: I-295 begins/ends on I-95

(14.5) **TOLL Plaza**

14 **DE 9, New Castle Ave, New Castle, to Wilmington**
- Gas: BP, Citgo
- Food: McDonald's
- Lodg: Days Inn, Motel 6♥
- Other: Grocery, Harley Davidson, Pharmacy

13 **Landers Lane (NB)**
US 13N, to Wilmington
US 13S, US 40W, US 301S, New Castle, Dover, Baltimore, Norfolk
- Gas: BP, Exxon, Hess, Shell
- Food: Burger King, Denny's, Dunkin Donuts, IHOP, McDonald's, Taco Bell
- Lodg: Quality Inn
- Other: Grocery, Pep Boys

(12) **Jct I-95, I-495, Port of Wilmington, Philadelphia**

NOTE: I-295 begins/ends on I-95

DELAWARE

EXIT	NEW JERSEY

Begin Southbound I-295 from Jct I-95 to Jct I-195.

NEW JERSEY

(1) **I-295N**

1A **NJ 49, Canal St, Pennsville (NB)**

1B **NJ 49, US 130, N Broadway (SB)**

1C **N Hook Rd, I-295**

2A **US 40W, to Delaware Bridge (NB)**

2B **US 40E, Hawks Bridge Rd, NJ 14 to NJ Tpk, Penns Grove (NB)**
- TStop: Pilot Travel Center (Scales), Turnpike Mobil, Route 40 Truck Stop
- Food: Subway/WiFi/Pilot TC
- Lodg: Comfort Inn, Econo Lodge, Holiday Inn Express, Quality Inn, Wellesley Inn

2C **Hawks Bridge Rd, NJ 140, to US 130, Penns Grove, Deepwater (SB)**
- TStop: Flying J Travel Plaza (Scales)
- Food: Rest/FastFood/Flying J TP
- Med: + Hospital
- Other: Laundry/WiFi/**RVDump/LP**/FJ TP

(3) **Rest Area (NB) (RR, Phones, Picnic, Vend)**

(4) **Weigh Station (NB)**

EXIT	NEW JERSEY

4 **NJ 48, Harding Hwy, Penns Grove, Woodstown**
- Other: **Four Seasons Campground▲**

7 **CR 643, Straughns Mill Rd, Pedricktown, Auburn**
- TStop: E: 295 Auto/Truck Plaza (Scales)

10 **CR 620, Center Square Rd, Swedesboro**
- Gas: Exxon
- Food: Applebee's, McDonald's, Subway
- Lodg: Hampton Inn, Holiday Inn
- Other: **Supplies/Service**

11 **US 322, Swedesboro, Mullica Hill, Bridgeport**

13 **US 130S, to US 322W, Bridgeport**

14 **CR 684, Repaupo Station Rd, Repaupo**

15 **CR 607, Gibbstown, Harrisonville**

16A **CR 653, Swedesboro, Paulsboro**

16B **CR 551, Gibbstown, Mickleton**

17 **CR 680, Gibbstown, Mickleton**
- Gas: Mobil
- Food: Burger King, Little Caesar's Pizza
- Lodg: Ramada Inn
- Other: Laundromat, Grocery, Pharmacy

◈= Regular Gas Stations with Diesel ▲ = RV Friendly Locations ♥= Pet Friendly Locations

Red print shows large vehicle parking / access on site or nearby **Brown Print = Campgrounds / RV PARKS**

EXIT		NEW JERSEY
18		**Timberlane Rd, Clarksboro (NB)**
	Other	Timberlane Campground▲
18AB		**CR 678, CR 667, Paulsboro, Mount Royal, Clarksboro**
	TStop	Travel Center of America /Exxon (Scales)
	Food	Rest/TA TC, Wendy's, McDonald's
	TServ	TA TC
	Other	Laundry/WiFi/TA TC, ATMs
19		**CR 656, Mantua Grove Rd, Mantua, Paulsboro**
20		**Mid Atlantic Pky, to CR 643, NJ 44, Thorofare, Nat'l Park**
21		**NJ 44, Crown Pt Rd (SB), CR 640, Delaware St, Thorofare (NB)**
	Lodg	Highway Motel, Red Bank Inn
22		**CR 644, Red Bank Ave, Thorofare, Redbank, Woodbury**
	Gas	Mobil
23		**US 130N, Academy Ave, Westville, Gloucester, Woodbury**
	Lodg	Budget Motel
24A		**NJ 45, Gateway Blvd, Westville (NB)**
24B		**CR 551, Broadway St, Westville (SB)**
25AB		**NJ 47, Delsea Dr, Westville (SB)**
(26)		**Jct I-76, NJ 42, to I-676, Bellmawr, Camden, Philadelphia**
8		**NJ 168, Black Horse Pike, to NJ Tpk, Bellmawr, Mt Ephraim**
	Gas	BP, Coastal, Exxon, Shell, Valero
	Food	Burger King, Dunkin Donuts, Wendy's, McDonald's, Subway, Taco Bell
	Lodg	Bellmawr Motel, Comfort Inn, Holiday Inn, Howard Johnson, Budget Inn
	Other	Walgreen's, CVS, Auto Zone, ATMs
29AB		**US 30, Copley Rd, Barrington, Berlin, Collingswood**
	Gas	BP, Exxon
	Food	Dunkin Donuts, KFC, Subway
	Med	E: + Hospital
	Other	ATMs, Auto Zone, Home Depot
30		**CR 669, Warwick Rd, Lawnside (SB)**
31		**Woodcrest Station**
32		**CR 561, Berlin Rd, Cherry Hill, Haddonfield, Voorhees**
	Gas	Shell
	Food	Burger King
	Med	E: + Hospital
34AB		**NJ 70, Marlton Pike, Cherry Hill**
	Gas	BP, Exxon, Mobil, Shell
	Food	Burger King, Denny's, Friendly's, Old Country Buffet, McDonald's, Steak & Ale
	Lodg	Clarion, Extended Stay America, Marriott, Residence Inn
	Med	W: + Hospital
36AB		**NJ 73, Mt Laurel, Berlin, Tacony Bridge, to NJ Tpk**
	Gas	E: Exxon, Mobil W: Citgo, Exxon, Shell
	Food	E: Bob Evans, Denny's, McDonald's W: Burger King, Dunkin Donuts, KFC, Pizza Hut, Ponderosa, Wendy's
	Lodg	E: Comfort Inn, Econo Lodge, Fairfield Inn, Radisson, Red Roof Inn♥, Super 8 W: Motel 6♥, Bel-Air Motel, Quality Inn, Rodeway Inn, Track & Turf Motel

EXIT		NEW JERSEY
	Other	ATMs, Firestone, Grocery, Home Depot, Pep Boys, Lowe's, Pharmacy, Mall
40AB		**NJ 38, Mt Holly, Moorestown**
	Gas	Exxon, Mobil
	Food	Dunkin Donuts
	Med	+ Hospital
	Other	ATMs, Target, U-Haul
43		**CR 636, Creek Rd, Mt Laurel, Rancocas Woods, Delran**
	Gas	Exxon
45AB		**CR 626, Rancocas Rd, Mt. Holly, Willingboro**
	Gas	Mobil
	Med	+ Hospital
	Other	E: Rancocas State Park
47AB		**CR 541, Burlington-Mt Holly Rd, Burlington, Mt Holly**
	Gas	Exxon, Mobil, Hess
	Food	Applebee's, Burger King, Chuck E Cheese's Pizza, Cracker Barrel, McDonald's, TGI Friday, Taco Bell, Wendy's
	Lodg	Best Western, Econo Lodge, Holiday Inn, Hampton Inn, Howard Johnson
	Med	W: + Hospital
	Other	Auto Zone, Grocery, Walmart, Mall
(50)		**Rest Area (Both dir) (RR, Phone, Picnic, Vend)**
52AB		**CR 656, Florence Columbus Rd, Bordentown, Columbus, Florence**
56		**Rising Sun Rd, to US 206, to NJ Tpk, Fort Dix, McGuire AFB (NB)**
	TStop	Petro Stopping Center (Scales)

EXIT		NEW JERSEY
	Food	IronSkillet/Petro SC
	Other	Tires/TServ/Twash/Petro SC, ATMs
57/AB		**US 130, US 206, Bordentown**
	TStop	SE: Love's Travel Stop #404
	Gas	Mobil, Shell
	Food	Wendy's/Love's TS, Chinese, McDonald's, Rosario's Pizza
	Lodg	Best Western, Comfort Inn, Days Inn, Ramada
	Other	E: Laundry/Love's TS, Grocery W: NJ State Hwy Patrol Post, UPS Store
(58)		**Scenic Overlook (Both dir)**
(60AB)		**Jct I-195, to I-95, W to Trenton, E to Neptune**
61AB		**CR 620, Arena Dr, Trenton**
62		**Olden Ave (fr SB, no reaccess)**
63AB		**NJ 33W, Rd 535, Mercerville, Trenton**
	Gas	Mobil, Exxon
	Food	Applebee's, McDonald's, Pizza Hut
64		**NJ 535N, to NJ 33E (SB)**
65AB		**CR 649, Sloan Ave, Trenton**
	Gas	Exxon
	Food	Burger King, Subway, Taco Bell
	Other	ATMs, CVS, Grocery
67AB		**US 1, Brunswick Pike, Trenton**

NOTE: **I-295 becomes I-95**

NEW JERSEY

Begin Southbound I-295 from Jct I-195 to Jct I-95.

◈= Regular Gas Stations with Diesel ▲ = RV Friendly Locations ♥ = Pet Friendly Locations
Red print shows large vehicle parking / access on site or nearby Brown Print = Campgrounds / RV PARKS

EXIT | MAINE

Begin Southbound I-295 at Jct I-95 near Gardiner, ME to Jct I-95 near Portland, ME

MAINE

EASTERN TIME ZONE

NOTE: Exit listings show Mile Marker/Exit #

51 **ME 9, ME 126, Gardiner, to ME Turnpike, to I-95S**

49 **US 201, Gardiner**
Other KOA▲

43 **ME 197, Richmond, Litchfield**

37 **ME 125, ME 138, Bowdoinham**
Other E: to Merrymeeting Field Airport✈

31AB **ME 196, New Lewiston Rd, Topsham S-Brunswick, N-Lisbon, Lewiston**
Gas Irving, J&S Oil Xpress Stop
Food Arby's, Pasta Conn, Subway, Wendy's

28 **to US 1, Coastal Rte, Brunswick, Bath (Serv E to US 1)**
Med + Hospital
Other to Brunswick Naval Air Station

24 **US 1, Freeport (NB)**

22 **ME 125, ME 136, Freeport, Durham (Serv E to US 1)**
Other W: Blueberry Pond Campground▲, Cedar Haven Campground▲, Freeport/ Durham KOA▲

20 **Desert Rd, Freeport, to US 1 (Serv E to US 1)**
Other E: to Recompence Shore Campground▲ Flying Point Campground▲ W: Desert of Maine▲

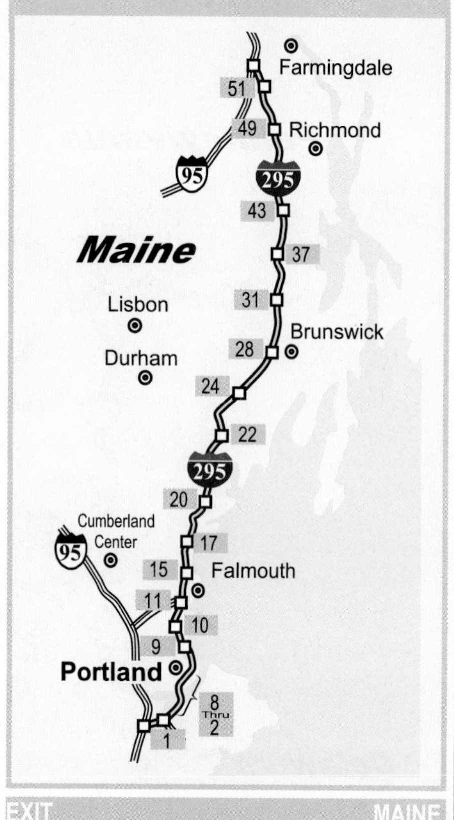

EXIT | MAINE

17 **US 1, Yarmouth, Freeport**
Visitor Info Center/Rest Area
(NB: next Rest Area 80 mi)
Gas Big Apple Food Store, Yarmouth Clipper Mart

EXIT | MAINE

15 **US 1, Yarmouth, Cumberland (SB) (Serv W to US 1)**

11 **US 1, Yarmouth, Cumberland (NB) Falmouth Spur (SB)**

10 **Bucknam Rd, Falmouth, Cumberland (Serv E to US 1)**

9 **US 1N (NB), US 1S, ME 26N, Baxter Blvd (SB), Portland**

8 **ME 26 N, Washington Ave (NB), ME 26 S, Washington Ave (SB)**
Other Andover College

7 **US 1A, Franklin Arterial, Portland**

6B **US 1N, US 302W, ME 100N**

6A **US 1, ME 100S, Univ of S ME**

5AB **ME 22, Congress St**

4 **US 1N, Portland, Waterfront (NB) US 1S, S Portland (SB)**

3 **ME 9, Westbrook St, Airport (SB)**
Other to Portland Int'l Jetport✈

2 **to US 1S, Scarborough (SB)**
Other to Portland Int'l Jetport✈

1 **to US 1, S Portland (NB), to ME Tpk, Maine Mall Rd (SB) (Serv W/N to Maine Mall Rd)**

(44) **Jct I-295N, Portland, Downtown**

NOTE: I-295 begins/ends on I-95, Exit #44

MAINE

EXIT | FLORIDA

Begin I-295 from Jct I-95, Exit #362AB around Jacksonville to Jct I-95, Exit #337

FLORIDA

NOTE: I-295 begins/ends on I-95, Exit #362B

(35AB) **Jct I-95, S to Jacksonville, N to Savannah**

33 **CR 110, Duval Rd, Jacksonville**
Other W: Jacksonville Int'l Airport✈

32 **FL 115, Lem Turner Rd**
Food E: McDonald's, Subway, Wendy's
Other E: ATMs, Home Depot, Walmart W: Flamingo Lake RV Resort▲

30 **FL 104, Dunn Ave**
Gas Gate, Shell
Food McDonald's
Other Big Tree RV Park▲

28AB **US 1, US 23, Jacksonville**
Gas BP, Chevron, Gate, RaceTrac
Other Amtrak

25 **Pritchard Rd**
Gas W: Kangaroo
Food W: Subway

22 **Commonwealth Ave**
Gas Kangaroo, Sprint
Food Burger King, Hardee's, Waffle House, Wendy's

EXIT | FLORIDA

Lodg Holiday Inn
TServ Kenworth, Freightliner, Cummins
Other ATMs, Grocery, Dogtrack

(21AB) **Jct I-10, W to Tallahassee, E to Jacksonville**

19 **FL 228, Normandy Blvd**
Gas BP, Shell, RaceTrac
Food Golden Corral, McDonald's, Pizza Hut, Popeye's, Subway, Wendy's
Other ATMs, Food Lion, Walgreen's, W: FL State Hwy Patrol Post

17 **FL 208, Wilson Blvd**
Gas BP, Hess

16 **FL 134, 103rd St, Cecil Field**
Gas BP, Exxon, Gate, Hess, Shell
Food Arby's, Burger King, IHOP, McDonald's, Pizza Hut, Popeye's, Wendy's,
Lodg Hospitality Inn
Other ATMs, Goodyear, Walgreen's, **Walmart**, U-Haul

12 **FL 21, Blanding Blvd**
Gas BP, Chevron, Kangaroo, RaceTrac
Food Burger King, Chili's, Denny's, Longhorn Steakhouse, McDonald's, Olive Garden, Steak & Ale, Taco Bell
Lodg Economy Inn, Hampton, Inn, La Quinta Inn♥, Motel 6♥, Red Roof Inn♥
Other ATMs, Home Depot, Publix, Target, Walgreen's,

EXIT | FLORIDA

10 **US 17, FL 15, Orange Park**
Gas BP, RaceTrac, Shell
Food Cracker Barrel, Krystal, Long John Silver, McDonald's, Pizza Hut, Waffle House
Lodg Comfort Inn, Days Inn, Econo Lodge, Holiday Inn, Quality Inn
Other E: Jacksonville Naval Air Station, MIL/Jay RV Park▲

5/AB **FL 13, San Jose Blvd**
Gas Exxon, Shell, BP
Food Applebee's, Arby's, Bob Evans, Chili's, Golden Corral, Hardee's, Pizza Hut
Lodg Baymont Inn, Ramada Inn
Other ATMs, Albertson's, NAPA, Publix, Target, Walgreen's, **Walmart**, U-Haul

3 **Old St Augustine Rd**
Gas BP, Gate, Shell, Kangaroo
Food Burger King, Denny's, McDonald's, Pizza Hut, Taco Bell
Lodg Holiday Inn
Other ATMs, Lowe's, Walgreen's, Publix, MIL/Pelican Roost RV Park▲

(0) **I-95, N to Jacksonville, S to St Augustine**

NOTE: I-295 begins/ends on I-95, Exit #337

FLORIDA

◊= Regular Gas Stations with Diesel ▲ = RV Friendly Locations ♥ = Pet Friendly Locations
Red print shows large vehicle parking / access on site or nearby Brown Print = Campgrounds / RV PARKS

EXIT VIRGINIA

Begin I-295 from Jct I-64 near Glen Allen to Jct I-95 near Petersburg, VA

VIRGINIA

NOTE: I-295 begins/ends on I-64, Exit #177

(53AB) **Jct I-64, E to Richmond, to US 250, W to Charlottesville**

51AB **Nuckols Rd, Glen Allen**
- Gas: BP, Exxon
- Other: ATMs, CVS

49AB **US 33, Glen Allen, Richmond**

45AB **Woodman Rd, Glen Allen**

(43) **US 1, Brook Rd, Glen Allen (EB) I-95, N-Washington, S-Richmond (WB) (All Serv on US 1)**

41AB **US 301, VA 2, Mechanicsville**
- Gas: BP, Exxon, Shell
- Food: McDonald's, Burger King, Subway

38AB **Meadowbridge Rd, Pole Green Rd, Mechanicsville**
- Gas: BP, Citgo

37AB **US 360, Mechanicsville**
- Gas: 7-11, BP, Crown, Shell
- Food: Applebee's, Arby's, Cracker Barrel, IHOP, McDonald's, Outback Steakhouse, Taco Bell, Waffle House, Wendy's
- Lodg: Hampton Inn, Holiday Inn
- Other: NAPA, BJ's, **Walmart**, Home Depot, Target, Grocery

34AB **VA 615, Creighton Rd, Mechanicsville**

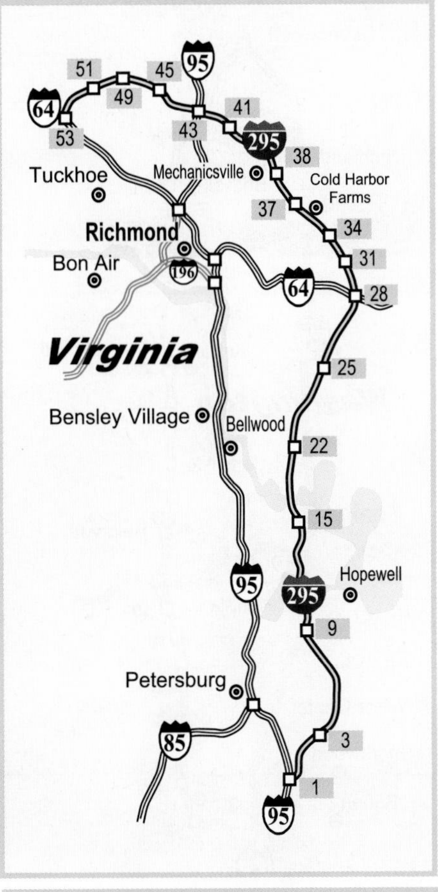

EXIT VIRGINIA

31AB **VA 156, N Airport Dr, Highland Springs**

(28AB) **Jct I-64, US 60, VA 156, Sandston (SB)**
- Other: W: Richmond Int'l Airport

EXIT VIRGINIA

28 **US 60, VA 156, Sandston (NB)**
- Other: W: Richmond Int'l Airport

25 **VA 895, (TOLL), to Richmond**

22AB **VA 5, New Market Rd, Richmond**
- Gas: BP, Exxon

15AB **VA 10, Chester, Hopewell**
- FStop: S: Mapco
- Gas: BP, Exxon, Citgo
- Food: Burger King, **Cracker Barrel**, Denny's, McDonald's, Waffle House, Wendy's
- Lodg: AmeriSuites, Hampton Inn, Holiday Inn
- Med: E: + Hospital

9AB **VA 36, Oaklawn Blvd, Hopewell**
- Gas: Chevron, BP, Shell, Exxon
- Food: Burger King, Denny's, McDonald's, Pizza Hut, Shoney's, Subway, Taco Bell, Waffle House, Wendy's, Western Sizzlin
- Lodg: Candlewood Suites, Econo Lodge, Fairfield Inn, Hampton Inn, Holiday Inn Express, InnKeeper
- Other: W: ATMs, Food Lion, U-Haul, Ft Lee Military Res

3AB **US 460, County Dr, Petersburg, to Norfolk**
- FStop: E: Mapco
- Gas: Exxon
- Food: Hardee's, McDonald's, Subway
- Other: W: Petersburg Nat'l Battlefield, Ft Lee Military Res

(1) **Jct I-95, N to Petersburg, S to Emporium**

NOTE: I-295 begins/ends on I-95, Exit #46

VIRGINIA

Begin I-295 from Jct I-95 near Petersburg to Jct I-64 near Glen Allen, VA

EXIT OREGON

Begin I-405 from Jct I-5, Exit #305B to Jct I-5, Exit #299B

OREGON

(3) **Jct I-5N, to Seattle** (NB ex, SB entr) **Kerby Ave** (NB exit, SB entr) **US 30E, The Dalles** (NB ex, SB entr) **US 30W, St Helens**

2B **Everett St**

2A **Burnside St, Couch St** (SB ex, NB ent) **Salmon St, PGE Park** (NB ex, SB ent)

1D **12th Ave** (NB ex, SB entr) **US 26W, Beaverton**

1C **US 26E, 6th Ave**

EXIT OREGON

1B **4th Ave** (NB exit, SB entr) **Jct I-5N, to I-84E, The Dalles, Seattle** (SB exit, NB entr)

1A **Naito Pkwy** (NB ex, SB entr)

EXIT OREGON

(0) **Jct I-5, S to Salem** (SB ex, NB entr)

OREGON

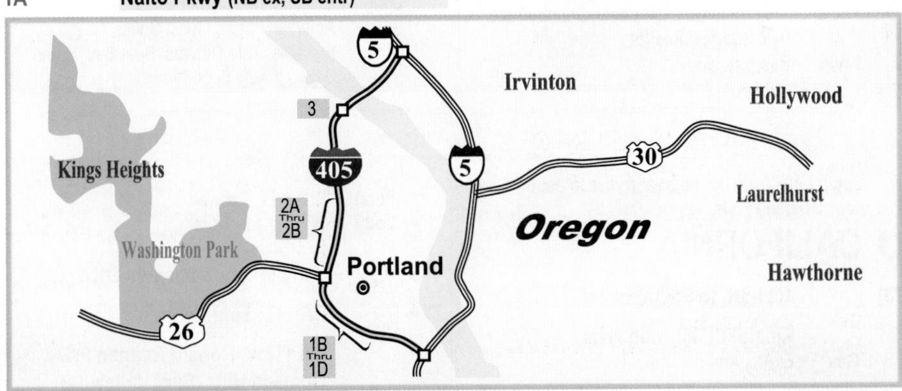

EXIT — WASHINGTON

Begin I-405 from Jct I-5 near Lynnwood to Jct I-5 near Seattle, WA

WASHINGTON

NOTE: I-405 begins/ends on I-5, Exit #177

(30) **Jct I-5, N to Canada, S to Seattle**

26 **WA 527, Bothel, Mill Creek**
- Gas W: 7-11, Chevron, Shell◈
- Food E: McDonald's
  W: Applebee's, Arby's, Bonefish Grill, Burger King, Denny's,Jack in the Box, Outback Steakhouse, Qdoba Mexican Rest, Starbucks, Taco Bell, Tully's Coffee
- Lodg E: Extended Stay America
  W: Comfort Inn,
- Other E: Lake Pleasant RV Park
  W: ATMs, Albertson's/Pharmacy, Grocery, RiteAid

24 **NE 195th St, Beardslee Blvd**
- Gas E: Shell◈
- Food E: Quiznos/Shell
- Lodg E: Country Inn, Residence Inn, Wyndham Garden Hotel

23B **WA 522W, Bothell**

23A **WA 522E, to WA 202, Woodinville, Monroe**

22 **NE 160th St, Bothell**
- Gas E: Chevron, Shell◈

21 **NE 132nd**

(NEW) **NE 128th**

20 **NE 124th St, Kirkland (SB)**
- Gas E: Kirkland Gas Mart/Arco, 76◈, Shell◈
  W: ArcoAmPm, Shell
- Food E: Denny's, Hunan Wok, Old Country Buffet, Pizza Hut, Subway
  W: Burger King, McDonald's, Starbucks, Taco Time, Wendy's
- Lodg E: Baymont Inn, Comfort Inn, Motel 6♥
  W: Courtyard
- Other E: ATMs, Auto Dealers, Auto Services, CompUSA, Discount Tire, Firestone, Grocery, RiteAid, Park & Ride,
  W: Auto Dealers, Grocery

20B **NE 124th St, Totem Lake Blvd (NB)**
- Gas E: 76, ArcoAmPm, Shell
- Food E: Cowboy Steakhouse, Denny's, Pizza Hut, Subway, Taco Bell
- Lodg E: Comfort Inn, Motel 6♥, Silver Cloud Inn
- Med E: + Hospital
- Other E: ATMs, Firestone, Grocery, Mall

20A **NE 116th St, Kirkland (NB ex, SB ent)**
- Food Jack in the Box, Little Italy, Shari's, Taco Bell, Subway, Rest/BI
- Lodg Baymont Inn

EXIT — WASHINGTON

18 **WA 908, Kirkland, Redmond**
- Gas E: Circle K, Chevron, Shell◈
  W: Chevron, Shell
- Food E: Burger King, Garlic Jim's, McDonald's, Outback Steakhouse, Starbucks, Subway,
  W: Subway, TGI Friday, Wendy's
- Other E: ATMs, Auto Dealers, Auto Services, Costco, PetCo♥, Tires, Walgreen's, U-Haul

17 **NE 70th Pl, NE 72nd Pl**

14AB **WA 520, Seattle, Redmond**

13B **NE 12th St, NE 8th St, NE 4th St, Main St, Bellevue**
- Gas E: ArcoAmPm, Chevron◈, Shell◈
- Food E: Burger King, Denny's, Hunan Garden,
  W: Starbucks
- Lodg E: DoubleTree Hotel, Extended Stay America, Pacific Guest Suites
- Other E: ATMs, Auto Dealers, Best Buy, Home Depot, Whole Food Market

EXIT — WASHINGTON

(NEW) **NE 6th St, HOV access only**

13A **NE 4th St, Main St**
- Lodg W: Best Western, Doubletree Hotel, Hilton, Hyatt, Sheraton

12 **SE 8th St, 116th Ave NE, Bellevue**

(11) **Jct I-90, E to Spokane, W to Seattle**

10 **Coal Creek Parkway, Bellevue, Factoria, Newport (Gas/Food/Lodg E to Factoria Blvd)**
- Other E: Mall, Grocery, RiteAid, Target

9 **112th Ave SE, Lake Washington Blvd Bellevue, Newcastle**

7 **NE 44th St, Renton**
- Food E: Denny's, Teriyaki Wok, McDonald's
- Lodg E: Econo Lodge,Travelers Inn

6 **NE 30th St, Renton**
- Gas E: ArcoAmPm
  W: 7-11, Shell

5 **WA 900E, NE Park Dr, Sunset Blvd**

4 **WA 900, Sunset Blvd NE (SB) WA 169S, WA 900W, Renton (NB)**

(NEW) **WA 515, Talbot Rd, Renton**

2B **WA 167N, Rainier Ave**

2A **WA 167S, Rainier Ave**

2 **WA 167, Rainier Ave, Renton, Kent, Auburn**
- Gas E: 76, ArcoAmPm, Chevron, Shell, USA
- Food W: Arby's, Applebee's, Burger King, Denny's, IHOP, Jack in the Box, King Buffet, McDonald's, Panda Express, Pizza Hut, Popeye's Chicken, Qdoba Mexican Grill, Taco Bell, Wendy's
- Lodg W: Holiday Inn
- Med E: + Hospital
- Other W: ATMs, Auto Dealers, Firestone, Les Schwab Tire, Radio Shack, Safeway, Walgreen's, **Walmart**,

1 **WA 181S, Seattle, Tukwila**
- Gas E: Chevron◈, Shell◈, 76◈
- Food E: Burger King, JackintheBox, McDonald's, Starbucks, Taco Bell, Wendy's
- Lodg E: Best Western, Comfort Inn, Courtyard, Embassy Suites, Hampton Inn, Harrah's Hotel & Casino
  W: Homewood Suites
- Other E: ATMs, Barnes & Noble, Firestone, Lowe's, Office Depot, Target, Mall

NOTE: I-405 begins/ends on I-5, Exit #154

WASHINGTON

Begin I-405 from Jct I-5 near Seattle to Jct I-5 near Lynnwood, WA.

EXIT — CALIFORNIA

Begin I-405 from Jct I-5 near Irvine to Jct I-5 near Granada Falls

CALIFORNIA

(73) **Jct I-5N, to Sacramento**

72 **Rinaldi St, Mission Hills**
- Gas E: ArcoAmPm

EXIT — CALIFORNIA

- W: Shell
- Food E: Arby's, Subway
- Lodg W: Granada Motel
- Med E: + Hospital

71B **San Fernando Mission Blvd**

71A **CA 118, Simi Valley**

71 **CA 118W, Ronald Reagan Frwy, Granada Hills, Simi Valley (SB)**

EXIT — CALIFORNIA

70 **Devonshire St, Granada Hills**
- Gas E: Mobil, Shell
- Food E: Holiday Burger
- Other E: ATMs, Grocery, Pharmacy

69 **Nordhoff St**
- Gas E: 7-11, Mobil
- Lodg E: Hillcrest Inn, Tahiti Inn, Vacation Inn

68 **Roscoe Blvd, to Panorama City**
- Gas E: 76, Exxon

◈= Regular Gas Stations with Diesel ▲ = RV Friendly Locations ♥= Pet Friendly Locations
Red print shows large vehicle parking / access on site or nearby Brown Print = Campgrounds / RV PARKS

EXIT		CALIFORNIA
	Gas	W: Shell
	Food	E: Burger King, Carl's, Denny's, Jack in the Box, McDonald's, Tyler Tx BBQ
	Lodg	E: Holiday Inn, Hiway Host Motor Inn, Panorama Motel, Travel Inn W: Motel 6♥
66B		**Sherman Way W (NB)**
66A		**Sherman Way E (NB)**
66		**Sherman Way, Van Nuys, Reseda**
	Gas	E: 76, Chevron, Mobil W: Mobil
	Food	E: Sizzling Wok
	Lodg	E: Hyland Motel
	Med	W: + Hospital
65		**Victory Blvd, Van Nuys**
	Gas	E: Mobil W: El Pollo Loco, Jack in the Box
64		**Burbank Blvd, Encino**
	Gas	E: Shell
	Food	E: Denny's
	Lodg	E: Best Western, Carriage Inn, Starlight Cottage
63B		**US 101, Ventura Frwy, Ventura, Sherman Oaks, Los Angeles**
63A		**Valley Vista Blvd, Ventura Blvd, Sepulveda Blvd**
	Gas	E: Mobil W: Chevron
	Food	E: Denny's W: McDonald's
	Lodg	W: Heritage Motel, Radisson
	Other	E: ATMs, Mall
61		**Mulholland Dr, Skirball Center Dr**
59		**Getty Center Dr**
57B		**Morago Dr (NB exit & entr)**
57A		**Sunset Blvd**
57		**Sunset Blvd (SB)**
	Gas	E: Chevron, Shell
	Other	E: to UCLA
56		**Waterford St (CLOSED), Montana Ave (NB exit only)**
55C		**Wilshire Blvd West (SB)**
55B		**Wilshire Blvd East (SB)**
55B		**Wilshire Blvd (NB)**
55A		**CA 2, Santa Monica Blvd**
	Gas	E: Exxon, Mobil W: 7-11, Shell
	Food	E: Jack in the Box
54		**Olympic Blvd, Pico Blvd (SB)**
	Gas	E: 7-11
	Food	E: Subway
(53)		**Jct I-10, Santa Monica Fwy (SB)**
(53B)		**Jct I-10, Santa Monica Freeway**
53A		**National Blvd (NB ex, SB entr)**
52		**Venice Blvd, Washington Blvd**
	Gas	E: Shell, Mobil
51		**Culver Blvd, Washington Blvd, Culver City**
50B		**CA 90W, Slauson Ave, Marina Del Ray**
	Gas	E: 76 W: ArcoAmPm

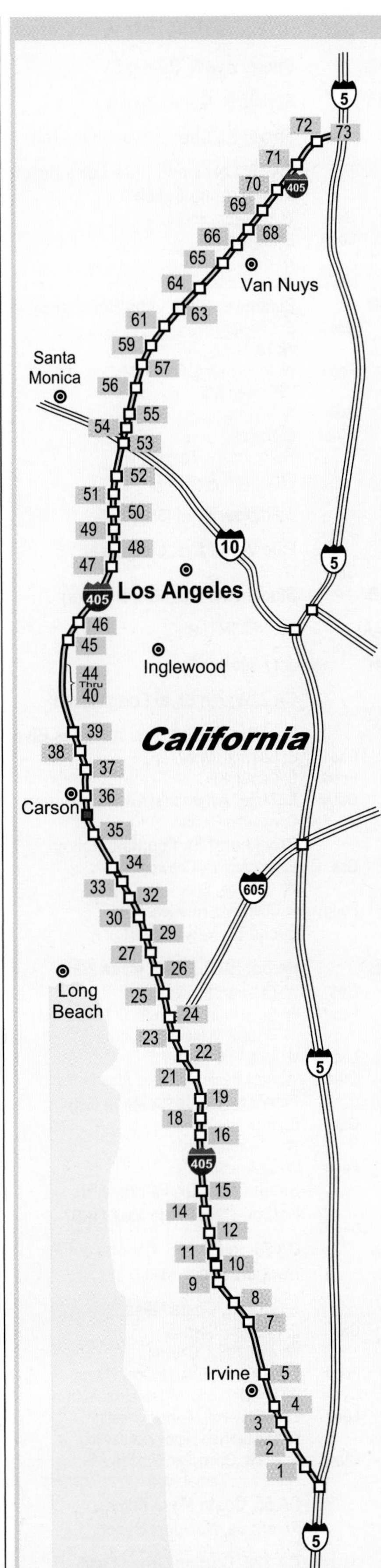

EXIT		CALIFORNIA
	Food	W: Denny's
	Other	W: ATMs, Albertson's
50A		**Jefferson Blvd (SB)**
	Other	W: to LAX Airport✈
49B		**Sepulveda Blvd, Slauson Ave**
49A		**Howard Hughes Pkwy, Sepulveda Blvd (NB)**
49		**Howard Hughes Pkwy, Centinela Ave, Speulveda Blvd (SB)**
	Gas	E: Mobil W: Chevron
	Lodg	E: Ramada Inn, Sheraton W: Extended Stay America
	Other	W: Pharmacy, Mall
48		**La Tijera Blvd**
	Gas	W: 76, Chevron
	Food	E: El Pollo Loco, McDonald's, KFC
47		**CA 42, Manchester Ave, Florence Ave, La Cienega Blvd, Inglewood**
	Gas	E: Chevron W: 76, Shell
	Food	E: Carl Jr's W: Arby's, Jack in the Box
	Lodg	E: Best Western W: Days Inn
46		**Century Blvd, LAX Airport, Imperial Hwy, Rental Car Return**
	Gas	E: 76 W: Chevron, Circle K
	Food	E: Burger King, Subway W: Carl Jr, Denny's, McDonald's
	Lodg	E: Best Western, Comfort Inn, Motel 6♥ W: Hampton Inn, Holiday Inn, Hilton, Travelodge, Westin
45B		**Imperial Hwy (NB)**
(45A)		**Jct I-105 (NB)**
(45)		**Jct I-105, El Segundo, Norwalk (SB)**
	Gas	E: Mobil, Shell
	Food	E: El Pollo Loco, Jack in the Box, McDonald's
44		**El Segundo Blvd, to El Segundo**
	Gas	E: ArcoAmPm, Chevron
	Food	E: Burger King, Jack in the Box W: Denny's
	Lodg	W: Ramada Inn
43B		**Rosecrans Ave W (SB)**
43A		**Rosecrans Ave E (SB)**
43		**Rosecrans Ave, Manhattan Beach**
	Gas	E: Mobil, Shell W: ArcoAmPm, Shell
	Food	E: El Pollo Loco, Pizza Hut, Subway W: McDonald's
	Other	E: Albertson's, Home Depot, Best Buy W: Costco
42B		**Inglewood Ave**
	Gas	E: ArcoAmPm W: Mobil, Shell
	Food	E: Denny's, Del Taco
42A		**CA 107, Hawthorne Blvd, Lawndale**
	Gas	W: Mobil, ArcoAmPm
	Food	E: Jack in the Box, McDonald's W: Subway, Taco Bell
	Lodg	E: Best Western, Days Inn
40B		**Redondo Beach Blvd, Hermosa Beach (SB ex, NB entr)**
	Gas	E: ArcoAmPm

EXIT		CALIFORNIA
	Food	E: Chuck E Cheese
		W: Boston Market
	Other	W: U-Haul, Grocery, Pharmacy
40A		**CA 91E, Artesia Blvd, to Torrance**
	Gas	E: 76, Chevron
40		**CA 91E, Artesia Blvd, Redondo Bch, Prairie Ave, Hermosa Beach (NB)**
39		**Crenshaw Blvd, to Torrance**
	Gas	E: Shell, Mobil, Chevron
		W: Mobil, Shell
	Food	E: Burger King, Denny's
		W: Subway
38B		**Western Ave, to Torrance**
	Gas	E: Chevron, Mobil
		W: Mobil
	Food	E: Denny's, Wendy's
	Lodg	W: Courtyard
38A		**Normandie Ave, to Gardena**
	Gas	W: Shell
	Food	W: Carl Jr, Subway, Taco Bell
	Lodg	W: Extended Stay America
37B		**Vermont Ave (SB ex, NB entr)**
	Lodg	W: Holiday Inn
	Other	W: CA State Hwy Patrol Post
(37A)		**Jct I-110, Harbor Freeway**
(37)		**Jct I-110, Harbor Fwy, S to San Pedro, N to Los Angeles (NB)**
36		**Main St (NB ex, SB entr)**
(36)		**Weigh Station (Both dir)**
35		**Avalon Blvd, to Carson**
	Gas	E: Chevron, Mobil, Shell
		W: Mobil, Shell
	Food	E: Denny's, Jack in the Box, Subway, McDonald's, Tony Roma
		W: IHOP
	Lodg	E: Quality Inn
	Other	E: Mall, Firestone
34		**Carson St, Avalon Blvd, to Carson**
	Gas	W: Mobil
	Food	W: Carl Jr, IHOP, Jack in the Box, Subway
	Lodg	E: Comfort Inn
		W: Hilton
33B		**Wilmington Ave**
	Gas	E: Chevron
		W: Shell
33A		**Alameda St, CA 47**
32D		**Santa Fe Ave, Hughes Way (SB)**
	Gas	W: Chevron, Shell
32C		**Hughes Way, Santa Fe Ave**
(32C)		**Jct I-710N, Long Beach Fwy (SB)**
(32B)		**Jct I-710S, to Long Beach (NB)**
(32A)		**Jct I-710N, to Pasadena (NB)**
(32)		**Jct I-710, Long Beach, Pasadena**
32A		**Pacific Ave (SB ex, NB entr)**
30B		**Long Beach Blvd**
	Gas	E: 76
		W: Mobil
	Med	W: + Hospital
30A		**Atlantic Ave, Long Beach**
	Gas	E: Chevron, Shell
	Food	E: Arby's, Denny's, Jack in the Box
	Med	W: + Hospital
29C		**Orange Ave**
	Gas	E: Mobil

EXIT		CALIFORNIA
29B		**Cherry Ave N, Spring St**
29A		**Spring St, Cherry Ave S**
29		**Spring St, Cherry Ave, Signal Hill**
27		**CA 19, Lakewood Blvd, Long Beach Airport, Long Beach**
	Gas	W: Chevron, Shell
	Lodg	E: Marriott
		W: Holiday Inn, Residence Inn
	Med	W: + Hospital
26B		**Bellflower Blvd, Long Beach (NB)**
	Gas	E: Chevron
		W: 76, Mobil
	Food	W: Burger King, Carl Jr, McDonald's, KFC, Wendy's
	Med	W: + Hospital
	Other	E: Lowe's
		W: Pharmacy, Target
26A		**Woodruff Ave (NB)**
26		**Bellflower Blvd (SB)**
25		**Palo Verde Ave, Long Beach**
	Gas	W: 76
24B		**Studebaker Rd (SB ex, NB entr)**
(24A)		**Jct I-605N (SB)**
(24)		**Jct I-605N (NB)**
23		**CA 22W, 7th St, to Long Beach**
22		**Seal Beach Blvd, Los Alamitos Blvd**
	Gas	E: Chevron, Mobil
	Food	E: Carl Jr, KFC
	Other	E: Target, Albertson's/Pharmacy, Grocery, Caribbean Casino
14		**Brookhurst St, Fountain Valley**
	Gas	E: ArcoAmPm, Chevron
		W: Chevron, Shell
	Lodg	E: Courtyard, Residence Inn
12		**Euclid St, Newhope St**
11B		**Harbor Blvd, Costa Mesa (SB)**
	Gas	W: Chevron, Mobil, Shell
	Food	W: Burger King, Denny's, El Pollo Loco, IHOP, Jack in the Box, Subway
	Lodg	W: Motel 6♥, Super 8
	Other	W: Auto Dealers, Target, Albertson's
11A		**Fairview Rd, Costa Mesa (SB)**
	Gas	E: Shell
		W: Chevron, Mobil
	Food	W: Jack in the Box
11		**South Coast Dr, Fairview Rd, Harbor Blvd, Costa Mesa (NB)**
10		**CA 73, to CA 55S, Corona del Mar, Newport Beach (SB)**
9B		**Bristol St, Costa Mesa**
	Gas	E: Chevron, Shell
		W: 7-11, Shell, Chevron
	Food	E: Jack in the Box, McDonald's
		W: El Pollo Loco, McDonald's, Subway
	Lodg	E: Holiday Inn, Marriott, Westin
		W: DoubleTree Hotel, Holiday Inn
	Other	E: ATMs, Goodyear, Grocery, Pharmacy, Target, Mall
9A		**CA 55, Costa Mesa Frwy, Riverside, Newport Beach**
21		**CA 22E, Garden Grove Fwy, Valley View St, Garden Grove**
	Gas	E: Mobil, Shell

EXIT		CALIFORNIA
	Other	E: Grocery, Pharmacy
19		**Westminster Ave, Springdale St**
	Gas	E: 76, ArcoAmPm, Chevron
		W: Chevron, Shell
	Food	E: Carl Jr, KFC, McDonald's
		W: Pizza Hut, Subway
	Lodg	E: Motel 6♥, Travelodge
		W: Best Western, Days Inn
	Other	E: ATMs, Albertson's, Home Depot
18		**Bolsa Ave, Golden West St**
	Gas	W: 76, Mobil, Shell
	Food	W: IHOP, Jack in the Box
	Other	W: Mall
16		**CA 39, Beach Blvd, Westminster, Huntington Beach**
	Gas	E: Shell
		W: 76, Mobil
	Food	E: Jack in the Box
		W: Arby's, Burger King, Jack in the Box, Popeye's
	Lodg	W: Holiday Inn
	Med	E: + Hospital
	Other	E: Kmart
		W: Target
15B		**Magnolia St, Warner Ave (SB)**
15A		**Warner Ave (SB ex, NB entr)**
15		**Magnolia St, Warner Ave (NB)**
	Gas	E: Shell
		W: Chevron, Mobil
	Lodg	W: Ramada Inn
	Other	W: Grocery, Pharmacy
8		**MacArthur Blvd**
	Gas	W: Chevron
	Food	E: Carl Jr, McDonald's
		W: IHOP
	Lodg	E: Embassy Suites, Holiday Inn
		W: Hilton, Marriott
	Other	W: John Wayne Airport✈
7		**Jamboree Rd, Irvine**
	Lodg	E: Courtyard, Residence Inn
		W: Marriott
5		**Culver Dr, Irvine**
	Gas	W: Chevron, Shell
	Food	W: Subway
4		**Jeffrey Rd, University Dr**
	Gas	E: Chevron
		W: Mobil
	Food	E: El Pollo Loco, McDonald's, Taco Bell
		W: IHOP
	Med	W: + Hospital
	Other	E: Grocery, Pharmacy, Irvine Valley College, Concordia Univ
3		**Sand Canyon Ave, Shady Canyon Dr**
	Med	E: + Hospital
2		**CA 133S, to Laguna Beach**
1C		**Irvine Center Dr, Irvine (SB)**
1B		**Baker Pkwy, Irvine**
1A		**Lake Forest Dr, Irvine**
1		**Irvine Center Dr, Irvine (NB)**

CALIFORNIA

Begin I-405 from I-5 near to Irvine, CA
I-5 near Granada Hills Irvine, CA.

◊ = Regular Gas Stations with Diesel ▲ = RV Friendly Locations ♥ = Pet Friendly Locations
Red print shows large vehicle parking / access on site or nearby **Brown Print = Campgrounds / RV PARKS**

EXIT ALABAMA

ALABAMA

NOTE: I-459 begins/ends on I-59, Exit #137

(33AB) **Jct I-59, N to Gadsden, S to Birmingham**

32 **US 11, Trussville**
- Gas E: Chevron, RaceTrac, Shell
  W: BP
- Food E: Arby's, Chili's, McDonald's, Waffle House
- Lodg E: Hampton Inn
- Other E: ATMs, Home Depot, Target

31 **Derby Parkway**

(29) **Jct I-20, E-Atlanta, W to Birmingham**

27 **Grants Mill Rd**

23 **Liberty Parkway**

19 **US 280, Mountain Brook, Childersburg**
- Gas N: Chevron
  S: Exxon
- Food S: Burger King, McDonald's
- Lodg S: Drury Inn, Fairfield Inn, Hilton, Hampton Inn, Holiday Inn Express

17 **Action Rd**
- Gas N: Shell
- Food N: Krystal, McDonald's

(15AB) **Jct I-65, N to Birmingham, S to Montgomery**

13AB **US 31, Galleria Rd, Hoover, Pelham**
- Gas N: Chevron, Shell
  S: Crown, Shell, Costco
- Food N: McDonald's, Shoney's, Subway
  S: Burger King, CiCi's Pizza, Grady's, Olive Garden, Piccadilly's, Taco Bell
- Lodg N: Comfort Inn, Days Inn, Hampton Inn, Holiday Inn
  S: AmeriSuites, Courtyard
- Other S: ATMs, Costco, Sam's Club, **Walmart**, Mall

10 **AL 150, Waverly, Hoover, Bessemer**
- Gas N: Chevron
  S: Crown, Exxon, Shell
- Other S: ATMs, Publix, Walgreen's

6 **AL 52, Morgan Rd, Bessemer, to Helena**
- Gas N: BP◈
  S: BP, Exxon, Shell, Texaco
- Food S: Arby's, Domino's Pizza, Johnny Ray's BBQ, McDonald's, Pizza Hut, Quiznos, Subway, Taco Bell/Texaco, Waffle House, Wendy's
- Lodg S: Sleep Inn
- Other N: ATMs, Auto Services, CVS, Tires, Vet♥, Ferrell Gas
  S: ATMs, CVS, Dollar General, True Value Hardware, UPS Store, Xpress Lube, Winn Dixie, Carwash/Shell, Carwash/Texaco, Hope Animal Clinic♥, to Bessemer Airport✈

1 **AL 18, Eastern Valley Rd, Bessemer, to McCalla**
- Gas N: Exxon, Shell◈
  S: BP◈
- Food N: Seafood Harbor, Subway
  S: McDonald's, Subway
- Other N: ATMs, JC Penny, Publix, Target,
  S: ATMs, Advance Auto Parts, CVS, Food World/Pharmacy, Vet♥, **to Tannehill State Park**

(0) **Jct I-459N, Jct I-20E, I-59N, to Birmingham, Meridian**

NOTE: I-459 begins/ends on I-20/59, Exit #106

ALABAMA

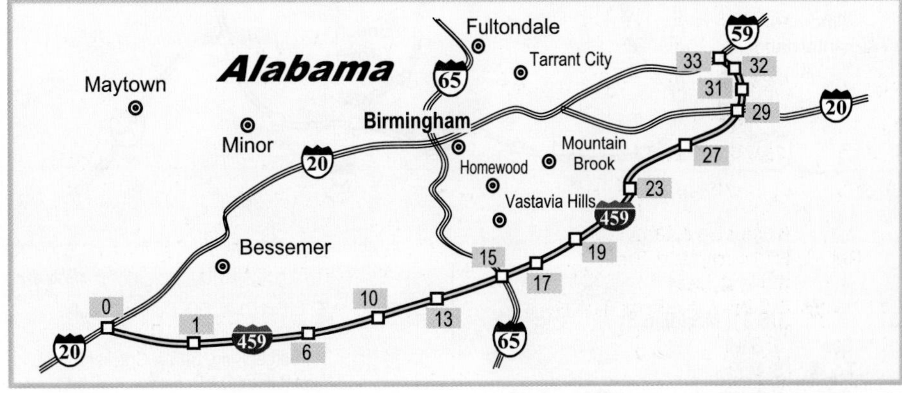

EXIT INDIANA

Begin I-465 ByPass around Indianapolis, IN from Jct I-65, Exit #108

INDIANA

(53AB) **Jct I-65, N to Indianapolis, S to Louisville, KY**

52 **Emerson Ave, Beech Grove**
- Gas N: Shell, Speedway
  S: Shell, Speedway
- Food N: Burger King, Domino's, KFC, Taco Bell, Subway, Wendy's
  S: Arby's, Hardee's, Hunan House, Pizza Hut, McDonald's, Ponderosa, Subway, Waffle House, White Castle
- Lodg N: Motel 6♥
  S: Holiday Inn, Red Roof Inn♥, Super 8
- Med N: + Hospital
- Other N: ATMs, CVS
  S: ATMs, Auto Zone, Walgreen's,

NOTE: I-465 runs below with I-74 for 20 mi. Exit #'s follow I-465

- Food W: Burger King, Fazoli's, McDonald's, Pizza Hut, Wendy's
- Lodg W: Signature Inn
- Other E: ATMs, Pharmacy, Target

(49AB) **Jct I-74E, US 421S, to Cincinnati**

48 **Shadeland Ave, to US 52 (NB)**

47 **US 52, Brooksville Rd, New Palestine**
- Gas E: Shell

46 **US 40, Washington St, Greenfield**
- Gas E: Marathon
  W: Thornton's
- Food E: Arby's, China Buffet, Olive Garden, Old Country Buffet, Perkins, Subway

(44) **Jct I-70, E to Columbus, W to Indianapolis**

42 **US 36E, IN 67N, Pendleton Pike**
- Gas W: Speedway, Thornton's
- Food E: Burger King, Hardee's, Pizza Hut
  W: Arby's, Denny's, Long John Silver's, McDonald's, Subway
- Lodg E: Days Inn, Sheraton
- Other W: ATMs, Grocery

40 **Shadeland Ave, 56th St**
- Gas E: Marathon

37A **IN 37S, Indianapolis**

37B **IN 37N, I-69, to Ft Wayne**

35 **Allisonville Rd**
- Gas Speedway, Shell
- Food E: Applebee's, Hardee's, McDonald's
  W: Bob Evans, Little Caesars Pizza, Perkins, Subway, White Castle
- Lodg E: Courtyard
  W: Signature Inn
- Other E: ATMs, Best Buy, Mall
  W: ATMs, Kroger

33 **IN 431, Keystone Ave**
- Gas N: BP, Shell
- Food N: Arby's, Bob Evans, Burger King, Steak & Ale, Subway
- Lodg N: Motel 6♥

◈ = Regular Gas Stations with Diesel ▲ = RV Friendly Locations ♥ = Pet Friendly Locations
Red print shows large vehicle parking / access on site or nearby **Brown Print = Campgrounds / RV PARKS**

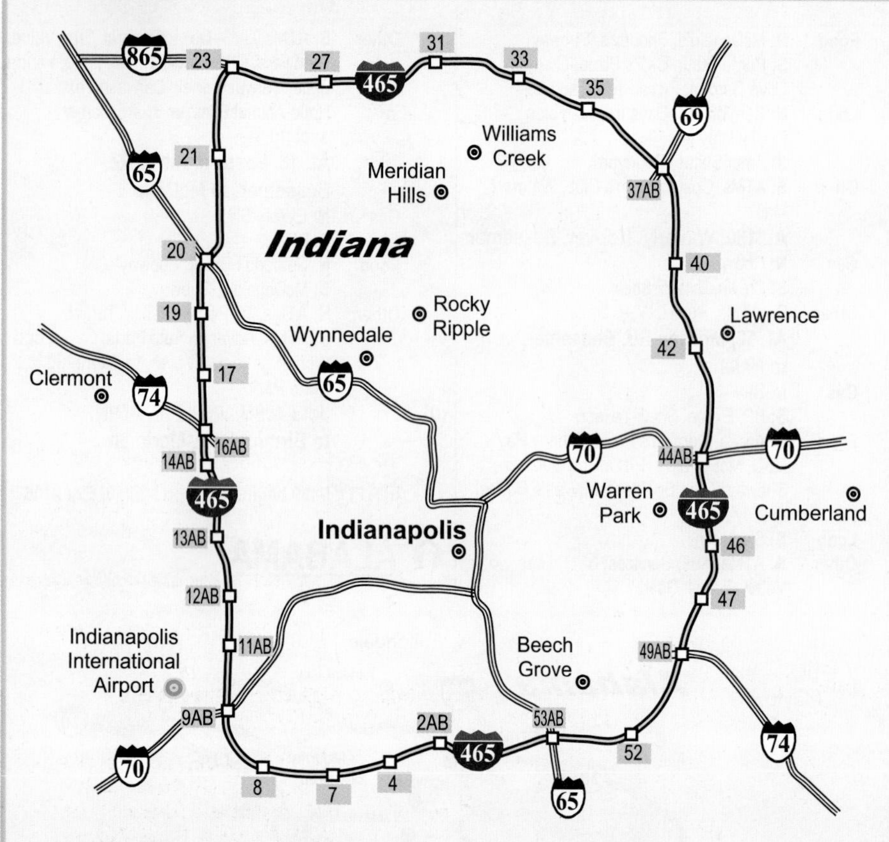

EXIT		INDIANA
31		**US 31, Meridian St**
	Gas	S: Shell
	Food	S: McDonald's
	Lodg	N: Residence Inn, Wyndham Garden Inn
27		**US 421N, Michigan Rd**
	Gas	S: BP, Shell, Sunoco
	Food	N: DQ, McDonald's
		S: Arby's, Black-Eyed Pea, Bob Evans, China Buffet, Cracker Barrel, Denny's, IHOP, Max & Erma's, Olive Garden, Outback Steakhouse, Red Lobster, Shoney's, Subway
	Lodg	S: Best Western, Comfort Inn, Drury Inn, Embassy Suites, Holiday Inn, Miicrotel, Quality Inn, Residence Inn
	Other	S: ATMs, CVS, Lowe's, Walmart
(25)		**Jct I-865W, to I-65N**
23		**86th St**
	Gas	E: Shell, Speedway
	Food	E: Arby's, Burger King
	Lodg	E: MainStay Suites
	Med	E: + Hospital
21		**71st St**
	Gas	E: Amoco, Marathon
	Food	E: Galahad's Café, McDonald's, Subway
	Lodg	E: Hampton Inn, Courtyard
(20)		**Jct I-65, N to Chicago, S to Indianapolis**
19		**56th St (NB)**
	Gas	E: Speedway
17		**38th St , Indianapolis**
	Gas	E: BP, Marathon, Shell

EXIT		INDIANA
	Food	E: China Chef, DQ, Dunkin Donuts, Pizza Hut, Subway
		W: Burger King, Chili's, Cracker Barrel, Don Pablo's, McDonald's, Taco Bell
	Lodg	E: Days Inn
		W: Signature Inn
	Other	E: ATMs, Home Depot, Kroger, Laundromat, Pharmacy
	NOTE:	**I-465 runs above with I-74 for 20 mi. Exit #'s follow I-465**
(16B)		**Jct I-74W, to Peoria, IL**
16A		**US 136, Crawfordsville Rd, Speedway, Clermont**
	Gas	N: Big Foot, Shell, Thornton's
	Food	N: Burger King, Denny's, Hardee's, KFC, Long John Silvers, Taco Bell, Wendy's, White Castle
	Lodg	N: Dollar Inn, Motel 6♥, Red Roof Inn♥, Super 8
	Other	N: ATMs,, Firestone, Goodyear, Kroger
		S: **Raceview Family Campground▲**
14AB		**10th St**
	Gas	N: Shell, Marathon
		S: BP, Shell, Speedway
	Food	N: Pizza Hut, Wendy's
		S: Arby's, Hardee's, McDonald's
	Other	S: ATMs, CVS, Grocery
13AB		**US 36E, Danville, Rockville Rd**
	Gas	N: Citgo
		S: Speedway

EXIT		INDIANA
	Food	N: Burger King
		S: Bob Evans
	Lodg	N: Comfort Inn, Wingate Inn
		S: Best Western
	Other	N: Sam's Club
12AB		**US 40E, Washington St, Plainfield**
	Gas	BP, Phillips 66, Shell, Thornton's
	Food	N: Burger King, McDonald's, Taco Bell, White Castle
	Food	S: Arby's, Burger King, Dunkin Donuts, Fazoli's, Hardee's, Long John Silvers,
	Food	S: Omelet Shop, Pizza Hut, Steak n Shake, Subway, Wendy's
	Lodg	S: Dollar Inn, Skylark Motel
	Other	N: ATMs, AutoZone, Kroger, U-Haul, Walgreen's,
		S: ATMs, Goodyear, Target
11AB		**Airport Expressway, Indianapolis Int'l Airport**
	Gas	S: BP
	Food	S: Burger King
	Lodg	N: Baymont Inn, Extended Stay America, Days Inn, Motel 6♥
		S: Holiday Inn, Hilton, Ramada Inn
(9AB)		**Jct I-70, E to Indianapolis, W to Terre Haute**
8		**IN 67S, Kentucky Ave, Mooresville Rd**
	Gas	S: BP, Speedway, Shell
	Food	S: Hardee's, KFC, Denny's
	Med	N: + Hospital
7		**Mann Rd**
	Med	N: + Hospital
4		**IN 37, Harding St, Martinsville, Bloomington**
	TStop	N: Mrr Fuel (Scales), Pilot Travel Center
		S: Flying J Travel Plaza (Scales)
	Gas	S: Marathon
	Food	N: Subway/Pilot TC, Omelet Shop
		S: Rest/FastFood/FJ TP, Hardee's, McDonald's, Waffle & Steak
	Lodg	N: Dollar Inn, Super 8
		S: Knights Inn
	TWash	S: FJ TP
	TServ	S: FJ TP, Stoop's Freightliner
	Other	S: Laundry/BarbSh/**RVDump/LP**/FJ TP, **to Indy Lakes Campground▲ , Lake Haven Retreat RV Campground▲**
2AB		**US 31, IN 37, Indianapolis, East St**
	Gas	BP, Shell, Sunoco
	Food	N: Arby's, Burger King, DQ, Dutch Oven, Golden Wok, Hardee's, KFC, Long John Silver, McDonald's, Old Country Buffet, Papa John's Pizza, Pizza Hut, Rally's, Steak 'n Shake, Steak & Ale, Taco Bell, White Castle
		S: Applebee's, Bob Evans, Denny's, Red Lobster, Wendy's
	Lodg	S: Comfort Inn, Days Inn, Holiday Inn Express, Quality Inn, Red Roof Inn♥
	Other	N: Auto Zone, Auto Werks, CVS, Firestone, Goodyear, Kroger, Target, U-Haul
(53AB)		**Jct I-65, N to Indianapolis, S to Louisville**

↑ INDIANA

Begin I-465 ByPass around Indianapolis, IN from Jct I-65, Exit #108

◈= Regular Gas Stations with Diesel ▲ = RV Friendly Locations ♥= Pet Friendly Locations
Red print shows large vehicle parking / access on site or nearby Brown Print = Campgrounds / RV PARKS

EXIT	PENNSYLVANIA
	Begin I-476 near Jct I-81 near Clarks Summit to Jct I-95 near Woodlyn, PA

PENNSYLVANIA

	NOTE:	**I-476 begins/ends on I-81, Exit #194**
131		**US 6, US 11, Clarks Summit**
	Lodg	W: Days Inn, Ramada, Summit Inn
122		**Keyser Ave, Old Forge, Taylor**
(121)		**TOLL Plaza**
115		**PA 315, to I-81, Pittston**
	TStop	W: Pilot Travel Center (Scales)
	Gas	W: Mobil
	Food	W: Wendy's/Pilot TC, Arby's, McDonald's, Perkins
	Lodg	W: Howard Johnson, Knights Inn
	Other	W: ATMs
(112)		**TOLL Plaza**
105		**PA 115, Bear Creek Bld, Wilkes Barre, Bear Creek**
	Gas	E: Mobil, Shell
(103)		**Parking Area (SB)**
(100)		**Parking Area (Both dir)**
(97)		**Parking Area (Both dir)**
95		**PA 940, to I-80, Lake Harmony, to Pocono, Hazelton**
	Gas	W: BP, Shell, WaWa
	Food	W: Arby's, McDonald's
	Lodg	W: Comfort Inn, Days Inn, Ramada
	Other	E: Hickory Run State Park
(90)		**Parking Area (SB)**
(86)		**Hickory Run Service Plaza (Both dir)**
	Gas	Sunoco
	Food	McDonald's
74		**US 209, Mahoning Valley**
	Gas	E: Shell
(71)		**Lehigh Tunnel**
56		**US 22, to I-78, Allentown**

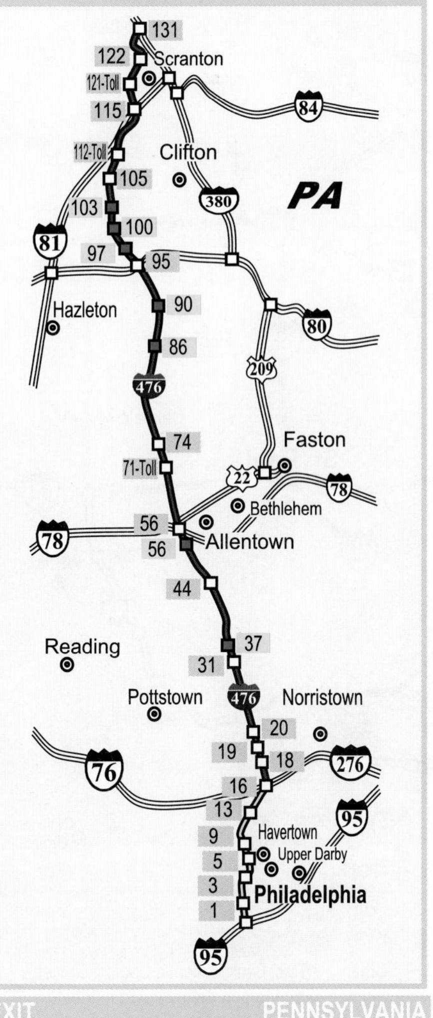

EXIT	PENNSYLVANIA
(56)	**Allentown Service Plaza (Both dir)**
Gas	Sunoco
Food	Nathan's, Pizza Hut, TCBY

EXIT		PENNSYLVANIA
44		**PA 663, Quakertown**
	Gas	E: BP, Mobil
	Lodg	E: Comfort Inn, Hampton Inn, Holiday Inn, Rodeway Inn
	Other	E: Tohickon Campground▲ , Quaker Woods Campground▲
(37)		**Parking Area (SB)**
31		**PA 63, Lansdale**
	Gas	E: BP, Mobil, WaWa
	NOTE:	**Begin NB/End SB Toll Rd / Motorist Call Box**
20		**Germantown Pike, to I-276W**
19		**Germantown Pike E**
18		**W Ridge Pike, Conshohocken (SB)**
	Gas	E: Lukoil, Sunoco
	Food	E: Burger King, Lone Star Steakhouse, McDonald's, Outback Steakhouse, Pizza, Starbucks
	Other	E: ATMs, Best Buy, Lowe's, Office Depot, PetSmart♥, Target W: BJ's, Home Depot, Harley Davidson
18AB		**W Ridge Pike, Connshohocken**
(16/AB)		**Jct I-76, to Philadelphia, Valley Forge**
13		**US 30, Saint Davids, Villanova**
	Other	Villanova Univ, Bryn Mawr College, Rosemont College, Haverford College
9		**PA 3, Broomall, Upper Derby**
	Med	E: + Hospital
5		**US 1, Lima, Springfield**
3		**Baltimore Pike, Media, Swarthmore**
	Med	E: + Hospital
	Other	E: Swarthmore College
1		**MacDade Blvd**
	Gas	E: Exxon
	Food	E: McDonald's, KFC

PENNSYLVANIA

EXIT	MINNESOTA
	Begin I-494 Loop around Southern/Western portion of metro Minneapolis-St Paul, MN.

MINNESOTA

CENTRAL TIME ZONE

(0)		**Jct I-94E, I-694 (Clockwise ex, counterclockwise entr)**
(27)		**Jct I-94W, to St Cloud (NB)**
26		**CR 10, Bass Lake Rd, Osseo**
	Gas	Freedom Value, Sinclair, BP
	Food	McDonald's, Subway
	Lodg	Extended Stay America, Hilton Garden Inn
23		**CR 9, Rockford Rd, Minneapolis**
	Gas	BP, Holiday Station Store, Freedom Value, PDQ
	Food	Chili's, Bakers Square, Caribou Coffee, DQ, Starbucksx2, Subway, TGI Friday
	Other	Auto Service, ATMs, Grocery, PetSmart♥, Radio Shack, Target, Walgreen's, Zylla Gallery, to Plymouth Creek Center
22		**TH 55, Minneapolis, to Buffalo, Rockford**
	Gas	Holiday Station Store◈ x2
	Food	McDonald's, Green Meal Rest, Starbucks, Arby's, Burger King, Chinese, Perkins, Rest/Comf Inn, Rest/Radisson
	Lodg	Best Western♥, Radisson Hotel, Red Roof Inn♥, Residence Inn♥, Comfort Inn, Days Inn, Holiday Inn
	Other	ATMs, Banks, Cinema 12, Goodyear, Tires Plus, Plymouth Ice Center
21		**CR 6, Plymouth, Orono**
	Gas	BP, Kwik Trip
	Other	ATMs, Discount Tire, Home Depot
20		**Carlson Pkwy, Plymouth**
	Gas	Holiday Station Store◈
	Food	Einstein Bros, Subway, Woody's Grill
	Lodg	Country Inn & Suites
(19)		**Jct I-394E, US 12, Minneapolis, Wayzata**
	Food	Applebee's, Bakers Square, Big Bowl, Origami West, Wendy's, Pizza
	Lodg	Country Inn, Radisson
	Other	ATMs, Best Buy, FedEx Office, Office Max, Pharmacy, Target, Tires Plus
(19A)		**Jct I-394E, US 12E, to Minneapolis**
(19B)		**Jct I-394E, US 12W, to Wayzata**

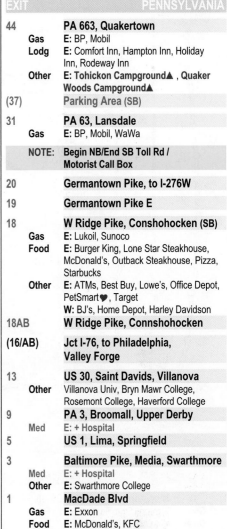

◈ = Regular Gas Stations with Diesel ▲ = RV Friendly Locations ♥ = Pet Friendly Locations
Red print shows large vehicle parking / access on site or nearby Brown Print = Campgrounds / RV PARKS

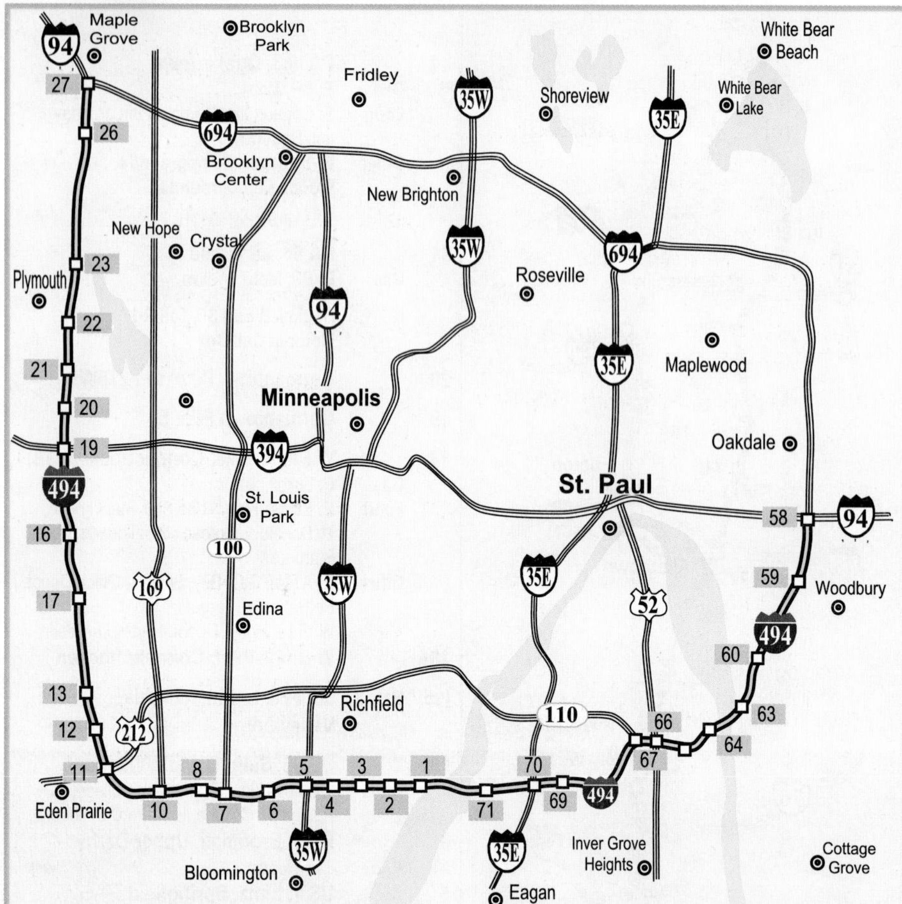

EXIT		MINNESOTA
17		**Minnetonka Blvd, CR 5, CR 16**
	Gas	Glenn's 1 Stop, Benny's Feed n Fuel
	Other	Minnetonka Police Dept
16		**TH 7, Minnetonka**
	Food	Famous Dave's BBQ, McDonald's, Perkins, General Store Cafe, Subway, Taco Bell
16A		**TH 7 East**
16B		**TH 7 West**
13		**TH 62, CR 62 (Services Avail E to Shady Oak Rd)**
12		**CR 39, Valley View Rd (SB) (Counterclockwise ex, clockwise entr)**
	Gas	Mobil
	Food	Outback Steakhouse
	Lodg	Extended Stay America
	Other	ATMs, Banks, Auto Services, Enterprise RAC, Home Depot, Tires
11C		**TH 5 West, Eden Prairie**
11		**US 212**
11A		**US 212W, Prairie Center Dr (WB)**
	Gas	Phillips 66, Mobil
	Food	Fuddrucker's, KFC, Subway Bakers Ribs, Starbucks, Caribou Cafe, Little Tokyo, Wendy's, McDonald's, Boston Market, Applebee's, Taco Bell, Cafe Oasis
	Lodg	Hampton Inn, Residence Inn, America's Suites, Courtyard, Fairfield Inn, Hyatt, Springhill Suites, TownePlace Suites, Best Western, Homestead Studio Suites
	Other	ATMs, Bank, Cinema, Costco, Grocery, Office Depot, **Walmart**, Eden Prairie Mall,
11B		**US 212 E, Flying Cloud Dr, N to I-35W, I-35E**
10		**US 169, N - Hopkins, S - Shakopee**
10A		**US 169 N, to Hopkins**
10B		**US 169 S, to Shakopee**
8		**CR 28, E Bush Lake Rd (Clockwise ex, counterclockwise entr) (Access to Exit #7B Services)**
7B		**CR 34, Normandale Blvd**
	Gas	Citgo, Langs 1 Stop◈, Holiday Station Store
	Food	Caribou Coffee, Burger King, Cafe in the Park, DQ, Subway, TGI Friday, Chili's, Moon Rise Cafe, Majors Sports Cafe, Tony Roma's, Classic Market, Olive Garden, Ryan's Grill
	Lodg	Country Inn, Crowne Plaza, Days Inn, La Quinta Inn♥, Hilton Garden Inn, Sheraton, Staybridge Suites
	Other	ATMs, Banks,Golf Course
7A		**TH 100, St Louis Park (Access to Exit #7B Services)**
6B		**CR 17, France Ave, Minneapolis**
	Gas	Bobby & Stevens Mobil, BP, Sinclair
	Food	McDonald's, Romano's Macaroni Grill, Fuddrucker's, Denny's, Joe Sensers Grill, Northland Cafe, Olive Garden
	Lodg	Residence Inn, Park Plaza, Le Bourget Suites, Hampton Inn, Embassy Suites
	Med	N: + Fairview Southdale Hospital
	Other	ATMs, CompUSA, Grocery, Office Depot, Southdale Shopping Center
6A		**CR 32, Penn Ave (diff EB reaccess)**
	Food	Applebee's, Starbucks, Steak & Ale, Atlantic Buffet, KFC, Red Lobster, Subway, Wendy's
	Other	Southtown Center, Best Buy, Grocery, Jiffy Lube, Pharmacy, Target, ATMs, Auto Dealers, Auto Services, Banks, Walgreen's, Cardinal Stritch Univ
(5)		**Jct I-35W, N to Minneapolis, S to Albert Lea**
(5A)		**Jct I-35W N, to Minneapolis**
(5B)		**Jct I-35W S, to Albert Lea**
4B		**Lyndale Ave**
	NOTE:	**Lyndale Ave Interchange closed for reconstruction-to be opened NOV 2009**
4A		**Nicollet Ave, CR 52**
	Gas	Super America◈, Holiday Station Store
	Food	Burger King, Johnny Angels, McDonald's
	Lodg	Candlewood Suites, Baymont Inn
	Other	Auto Services, Best Buy, Radio Shack, Home Depot, PetSmart♥, Sam's Club, Vet♥
3		**12th Ave, Portland Ave, CR 35**
	Gas	Sinclair, Phillips 66, BP
	Food	Arby's, Denny's, Hong Kong Rest, New Century Buffet, McDonald's, Outback Steakhouse, Subway, Shell's Cafe
	Lodg	AmericInn, Courtyard, Holiday Inn Express, Grand Lodge, Microtel, Quality Inn, Residence Inn, Travelodge
	Other	Walgreen's, **Walmart**
2CB		**TH 77, Cedar Ave, N to Minneapolis, E S to Eagan**
	Other	S: Mall of America
2B		**TH 77 N, to Minneapolis**
2C		**TH 77 S, to Eagan**
	Other	S: Mall of America
2A		**24th Ave, CR 1**
	Other	S: Mall of America
1B		**34th Ave, HHH Terminal (EB)**
	Lodg	Embassy Suites, Hilton, Holiday Inn
1A		**TH 5 E, Main Terminal, St Paul, Fort Snelling**
1AB		**TH 5E, Main Terminal, 34th Ave, HHH Terminal, St Paul (WB)**
		Crowne Plaza
71		**CR 31, Pilot Knob Rd**
	Lodg	Courtyard, Fairfield Inn, Best Western,
(70)		**Jct I-35E, N - St Paul, S - Albert Lea**
69		**TH 149, Dodd Rd, to TH 55**
	Food	Caribou Coffee, McDonald's, Subway
	Lodg	Budget Host Inn, Country Inn
67		**TH 110, to MN 3, Robert St (WB) MN 3, Robert St (EB)**
	Gas	BP, Mobil, Holiday Station Store
	Food	Arby's, Bakers Square, Burger King, Chuck E Cheese, Chipolte Mex Grill, KFC, Old Country Buffet, Pizza Hut, Taco Bell, Timber Lodge Steakhouse, White Castle

◈= Regular Gas Stations with Diesel ▲ = RV Friendly Locations ♥= Pet Friendly Locations

Red print shows large vehicle parking / access on site or nearby **Brown Print = Campgrounds / RV PARKS**

EXIT	MINNESOTA
Other	ATMs, Auto Services, Auto Dealers, Best Buy, Grocery, Target, Tires Plus, **Walmart**
66	**US 52, St Paul, Rochester**
Gas	Super America
Food	Applebee's, Major Sports Cafe, Old World Pizza, Outback Steakhouse, Quiznos
Lodg	Country Inn, Microtel
65	**5th Ave, 7th Ave**
NOTE:	**EB: Reconstruction/Upgrade Work on Exit #'s 64B - 60 thru 2010. Expect closures, delays, etc.**
64B	**TH 156, CR 56, Concord St**
Gas	Conoco◈
Lodg	Best Western, S St Paul Hotel
TServ	Peterbilt, Independent Diesel Repair
Other	Auto Services, Goodyear, **MN State Hwy Patrol Post**, Wakota Arena, S to South St Paul Muni Airport✈
64A	**Hardman Ave, Stockyard Rd**
TStop	Stockmen's Truck Stop (Scales)
Food	Rest/Stockmen's TS
Other	Laundry/WiFi/Stockmen's TS

EXIT	MINNESOTA
63C	**Maxwell Ave, CR 38**
63	**US 10, US 61, Bailey Rd, Hastings, Downtown St Paul**
Gas	BP, Super America
Food	Burger King, North Pole Rest, Pig in a Blanket, Subway
Lodg	Boyd's Motel, Extended Stay
Other	ATMs, Auto Services, Banks
63A	**US 10W, US 61N, Bailey Rd, Military Rd, St Paul, Hastings (SB)**
63B	**US 10E, US 61S, Bailey Rd, St Paul, Hastings (SB)**
60	**Lake Rd**
Gas	Super America◈
Lodg	Country Inn
Med	**W: + Health East Woodwinds Hospital**
NOTE:	**WB: Reconstruction/Upgrade work on Exit #'s 60 - 64B thru 2010. Expect closures, delays, etc.**
59	**Valley Creek Rd, CR 16**
Gas	BP, Super America◈, PDQ

EXIT	MINNESOTA
Food	Applebee's, Broadway Pizza, Chipolte Mex Grill, Cold Stone Creamery, DQ, Old Country Buffet, Perkins, Starbucks, Burger King, Pizza Hut, McDonald's, Subway
Lodg	Red Roof Inn, Hampton Inn
Other	ATMs, Banks, Best Buy, Goodyear, Grocery, Target, Walgreen's, Tires
58C	**Tamarack Rd (Services E 2mi to MN 13)**
(58)	**Jct I-94, W to St Paul, E to Madison**
(58A)	**Jct I-94W, to St Paul**
(58B)	**Jct I-94E, to Madison**
(0)	**Jct I-694 N, End I-494 (Counterclockwise ex, clockwise entr)**

CENTRAL TIME ZONE

MINNESOTA

Begin I-494 Loop around Southern / Western portion of metro Minneapolis-St Paul, MN.

EXIT	SOUTH CAROLINA

Begin I-526 Loop around Charleston South Carolina

SOUTH CAROLINA

EASTERN TIME ZONE

EXIT	SOUTH CAROLINA
(0)	**Jct US 17**
11AB	**Paul Cantrell Blvd, Ashley River Rd**
Gas	APlus, Jensen's Discount Gas, Hess
Food	Chick-Fil-A, McDonald's, Baskin Robbins
Lodg	Captain D's, O'Charley's, Burger King
Med	**W: + Hospital**
Other	Auto Service, Banks, ATM's, Grocery
14	**Leeds Ave**
15	**Dorchester Rd**
Gas	Citgo, Sunoco
Food	Burger King, Huddle House, Checkers
Lodg	Airport Inn
Other	Diesel Service
16AB	**International Blvd**
Gas	BP, Murphy
Food	Wendy's, Starbucks, Quiznos Sub, Palm Tree Grill, Sportz Cafe, Indigo
Lodg	Embassy Suites, Homeplace Suites, Holiday Inn, Hilton Garden Inn
Other	North Charleston Coliseum
(17AB)	**Jct I-26**
18AB	**US 52, US 78**
Gas	Hess, Kangaroo **X2**, Exxon
Food	Popeyes, McDonald's, KFC

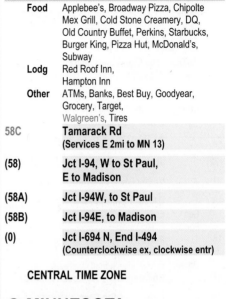

Personal Notes

EXIT	SOUTH CAROLINA
Lodg	Catalina Motel, Economy Inn, Extended Stay America
Other	Auto Service, Amtrak
19	**N Rhett Rd**
Gas	The Pantry
Food	Bagel Nation, Mcguiness Doe
20	**Virginia Ave**
Other	Banks, ATM's
23AB	**Clements Ferry Rd, Cainhoy Rd**
24	**Island Park Dr**
Gas	Citgo
Food	Soda Water Grill, Gourmet Ice Cream, Lana's Mexican Rest, Orlando Bros Pizza
Lodg	Hampton Inn
28	**Long Point Rd**
Gas	Blue Water, Rew's Run-In
Food	Starbucks, Wendy's, Brixx Wood Fired Pizza, Sunray's Dogs and Deli, Waffle House
29	**US 701, US 17**
Gas	Hess, The Loop Marts, Sunoco
Food	Applebee's, Subway, Dunkin' Donuts, Ye Olde Fashioned Ice Cream, Gullah Cuisine Lowcountry Rest
30	**Jct I-526 Bus, US 17 S**

SOUTH CAROLINA

Begin I-526 Loop around Charleston South Carolina

EXIT — CALIFORNIA

Begin I-605 ByPass around LA from Jct I-210 near Baldwin Park to Jct I-405, Seal Beach, CA

CALIFORNIA

NOTE: I-605 begins/ends on I-210

(28) **Jct I-210**

26 **Arrow Hwy, Live Oak Ave**
- Other — E: Santa Fe Dam Rec Area

24 **Lower Azusa Rd, LA St**

23 **Ramona Blvd, Baldwin Park**

(22) **Jct I-10, E - San Bernardino, W - LA**

21 **Valley Blvd, La Puente**

19 **CA 60, Pomona Fwy, Whittier**
- Gas — E: Chevron
- Food — E: McDonald's

18 **Peck Rd**
- Gas — E: Shell
- Other — E: Freightliner, Ford

17 **Beverley Blvd W, Rose Hills Rd**

16 **Beverley Blvd East**

15 **Whittier Blvd**
- Gas — E: 7-11, Shell
- Other — W: Auto Dealers

14B **Norwalk Blvd, Washington Blvd E**

14A **Washington Blvd W**

13 **Slauson Ave**
- Gas — E: ArcoAmPm, Mobil
- Food — E: Denny's
- Lodg — E: Motel 6♥
- Med — E: + Hospital

12 **Telegraph Rd**
- Other — E: CA State Hwy Patrol Post

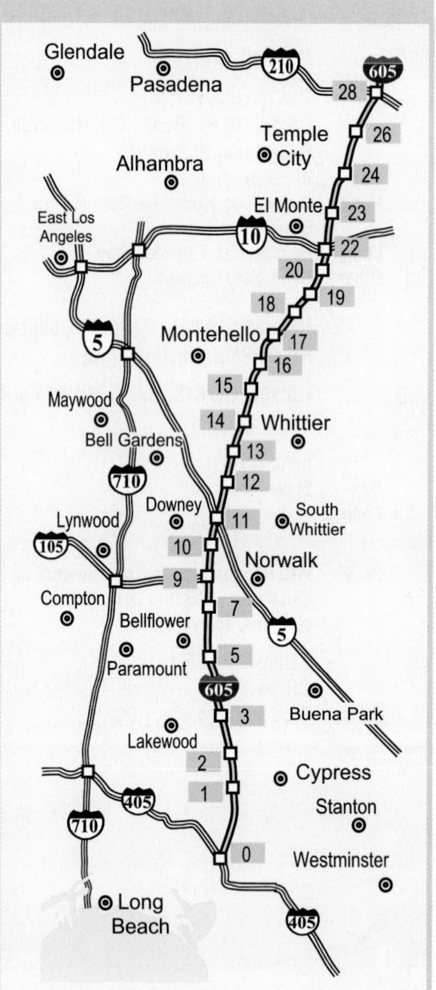

EXIT — CALIFORNIA

(11) **Jct I-5**

10 **Firestone Blvd**
- Gas — E: 76, Shell
- W: 76, Chevron
- Food — E: KFC, McDonald's, Taco Bell
- Lodg — E: Best Western

9A **Rosecrans Ave**

7B **Alondra Blvd**
- Gas — E: Chevron
- Lodg — E: Motel 6♥

5 **CA 91**

5B **South St, Cerritos**
- Gas — W: 76, Shell
- Other — E: Mall
- W: Auto Dealers

5A **Del Amo Blvd**

3 **Carson St**
- Gas — E: ArcoAmPm, Shell
- W: Chevron, Mobil
- Food — E: Jack in the Box, KFC, McDonald's
- W: Denny's, El Pollo Loco, TGI Friday
- Lodg — E: Lakewood Inn
- W: Tradewinds Motel
- Other — W: Lowe's, Sam's Club, **Walmart**

2B **Spring St**

2A **Willow St**

1D **Katella Ave, Los Alamitos**
- Med — E: + Hospital
- Other — E: Los Alamitos Armed Forces Res Center

(0) **Jct I-405**

NOTE: I-605 begins/ends on I-405

CALIFORNIA

Begin I-605 ByPass around LA from Jct I-405 near Seal Beach to Jct I-210, Baldwin Park, CA

EXIT — TENNESSEE

Begin I-640 ByPass around Knoxville

TENNESSEE

(0) **Jct I-40E, to Asheville, Jct 25W**

8 **Washington Pike, Millertown Pike, Mall Road North, Knoxville**
- Gas — N: Exxon, Conoco
- S: Shell
- Food — N: Applebee's, Burger King, **Cracker Barrel**, KFC, McDonald's, Taco Bell, Texas Roadhouse, Wendy's
- Other — N: ATMs, Sam's Club, **Walmart**, Mall
- S: ATMs, Food Lion, Home Depot, Lowe's

6 **US 441, Broadway**
- Gas — N: BP, Chevron, Phillips 66, Pilot
- Food — N: Arby's, CiCi's Pizza, Long John Silver, Subway, Taco Bell
- S: Buddy's BBQ, Shoney's
- Lodg — N: Best Western
- Other — N: Auto Zone, CVS, Kroger, Walgreen's
- S: ATMs, CVS, Walgreen's

(3) **Jct I-75N, to Lexington, KY**
Jct I-275S, to Knoxville

3A **US 25W N, Clinton Hwy (EB)**

3B **US 25W N, Gap Rd (WB)**

1AB **TN 62, Western Ave, Knoxville**
- Gas — N: Shell, RaceTrac
- S: BP
- Food — N: KFC, Long John Silver, Shoney's, McDonald's, Ruby Tuesday
- Other — N: CVS, Kroger

(0) **Jct I-40, E - Asheville, W - Nashville, Jct I-75S, to Chattanooga**

NOTE: I-640 begins/ends on I-40, Exit #385

TENNESSEE

Begin I-640 ByPass around Knoxville

Tennessee
75
Inskip
3A
3B
640
1AB
Loveland
Pleasant Hills
3
Lincoln Park
Plantation Hills
40
Chilhowee Hills
640
6
275
Park City
Third Creek
8
Knoxville
Island Home
40
Marble City

◊ = Regular Gas Stations with Diesel ▲ = RV Friendly Locations ♥ = Pet Friendly Locations
Red print shows large vehicle parking / access on site or nearby **Brown Print = Campgrounds / RV PARKS**

EXIT — **CALIFORNIA**

Begin Southbound I-680 from Jct I-80 near Cordelia to Jct I-280 in San Jose, CA.

CALIFORNIA

PACIFIC TIME ZONE

(71B) **Jct I-80W, to Oakland**

(71A) **Jct I-80E, to Sacramento**

70 **Green Valley Rd, Cordelia**
- Other: Costco, Long's, Safeway

68 **Gold Hill Rd, Fairfield**
- Gas: Tower Mart◈

65 **Marshview Rd**

63 **Parish Rd, Benicia**

61 **Lake Herman Rd**
- Gas: ArcoAmPm◈, Gas City, Shell◈
- Food: JackintheBox/Arco, Carl'sJr/Shell, Pot Belly Deli

60 **Industrial Park (SB)**
- Other: Auto Services

58B **Bayshore Rd, Industrial (NB)**

(58A) **Jct I-780, Benicia (NB, Left Exit)**

(58) **Jct I-780, Benicia (SB)**

56 **Marina Vista, Martinez**

54 **Pacheco Blvd (Both dir), Arthur Rd (SB)**
- Gas: 7-11, 76, Shell◈
- Food: Big Burger

53 **CA 4, E to Concord, W to Richmond**

52 **Concord Ave (Both dir), Burnett Ave (NB), Concord**
- Gas: 76, Chevron, Grand Gasoline, Shell
- Food: Burger King, McDonald's, Round Table Pizza, Starbucks, Taco Bell, Wendy's
- Lodg: Crowne Plaza, Holiday Inn
- Other: ATMs, Banks, Grocery, Jiffy Lube

51 **Willow Pass Rd, Taylor Blvd**
- Food: Baja Fresh, Benihana, Buffet City, Burger King, Cactus Cafe, Cinnabon, Denny's, Fuddruckers, Marie Callanders, McDonald Red Lobster, Sizzler, Starbucks, Subway
- Lodg: Hilton, Residence Inn
- Other: ATMs, Auto Services, Banks, CompUSA, Firestone, Office Depot, Trader Joe's, Sun Valley Mall, Willow Shopping Center

50 **CA 242, Concord (NB)**

49 **Monument Blvd, Gregory Ln, Pleasant Hill (SB)**
- Gas: Chevron, Valero
- Food: Boston Market, Fatburger, Jack in the Box, L & L Hawaiian BBQ, McDonald's, NY Pizza, Plaza Cafe, Starbucks, Taco Bell
- Lodg: Extended Stay America, Courtyard, Summerfield Suites, Sun Valley Inn
- Other: ATMs, Auto Services, Banks, Best Buy, Grocery

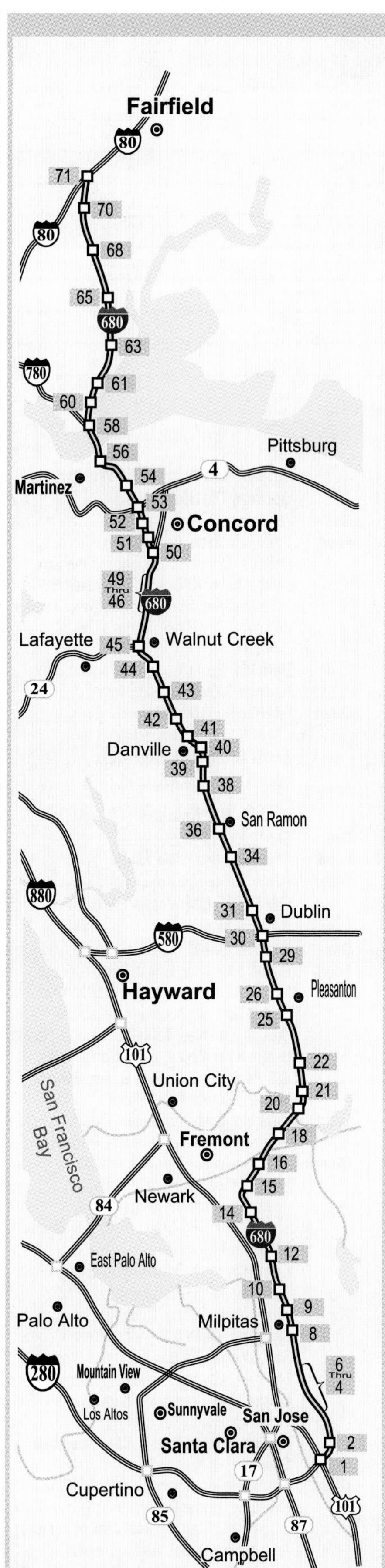

EXIT — **CALIFORNIA**

49B **Monument Blvd (NB)**

49A **Contra Costa Blvd (NB)**

48 **Treat Blvd, Geary Rd, Walnut Creek**
- Gas: 7-11, Chevron, Chevron, Shell◈
- Food: Subway, Black Angus Steakhouse, Burger King, Cactus Cafe, Curry House, Quiznos, Starbucks, Sweet Tomatoes, Wendy's
- Lodg: Embassy Suites, Extended Stay America, Courtyard, Holiday Inn, Renaissance
- Other: ATMs, Banks, Best Buy, Grocery, Staples, Walgreen's

47 **North Main St, Walnut Creek**
- Gas: Chevron, Shell, 76◈
- Food: Fuddrucker's, Foster Freeze, Jack in the Box, Plaza Deli, Starbucks, Taco Bell
- Lodg: Marriott, Motel 6, Walnut Creek Motel
- Other: Auto Dealers, Auto Services, ATM, Target

46B **Ygnacio Valley Rd**
- Gas: Chevron, USA

46A **CA 24W, to Lafayette, Oakland**
- Gas: USA

45 **South Main St, Walnut Creek (SB)**

45B **Olympic Blvd (NB)**

45A **South Main St (NB)**

44 **Rudgear Rd (NB)**

43 **Livorna Rd**

42B **Stone Valley Rd W, Alamo**
- Gas: Chevron, Shell◈
- Food: Asian House Rest, Bagel Street Cafe, High Tech Burrito, Round Table Pizza, Starbucks, Subway, Taco Bell
- Other: Safeway, Alamo Plaza Shopping Center

42A **Stone Valley Rd E, Alamo**

41 **El Pintado Rd, Danville (SB)**

40 **El Cerro Blvd**

39 **Diablo Rd, Danville**
- Gas: 76, Chevron, 76
- Food: Amber Bistro, Burger King, Christy's Donuts, Panda Express, Pizza Hut, Quiznos, Starbucks, Taco Bell, Uptown Cafe
- Other: ATMs, Albertson's, Banks, Jiffy Lube, Museum, Pharmacy

38 **Sycamore Valley Rd**
- Gas: Shell, 76, Valero, All Town Station
- Food: Bagel Street Cafe, Cold Stone Creamery, Denny's, High Tech Burrito, Luna Loca Mexican Rest, Patrick Davis Rest
- Lodg: Best Western
- Other: ATMs, Banks, Grocery

36 **Crow Canyon Rd, San Ramon**
- Gas: Shell, 76, Chevron, Shell, Valero
- Food: Burger King, Carl's Jr, Chili's, Boston Market, Chipolte Mex Grill, In 'n Out Burgers, McDonald's, NY Pizza, Rice Garden, Starbucks, Taco Bell, TGI Friday
- Lodg: Extended Stay America, Sierra Suites
- Other: Albertson's, ATMs, Auto Services, Pharmacy, RiteAid, Long's, Safeway

◈= Regular Gas Stations with Diesel ▲ = RV Friendly Locations ♥= Pet Friendly Locations

Red print shows large vehicle parking / access on site or nearby Brown Print = Campgrounds / RV PARKS

EXIT	CALIFORNIA
34	**Bollinger Canyon Rd**
Gas	Chevron, Valero
Food	Subway, Applebee's, Chevy's Mex Rest, Baja Fresh, Cactus Cafe, Rice Garden
Lodg	Marriott, Residence Inn, Courtyard, Homestead Studio Suites
Other	Banks, Grocery, Target, Whole Foods
31	**Alcosta Blvd, Dublin**
Gas	76, Chevron, Shell
Food	Chuck E Cheese, DQ, Lumpia House, McDonald's, Mountain Mike's Pizza, Pizza Palace, Starbucks, Subway, Taco Bell
Other	ATMs, Albertson's, Pharmacy, Walgreen's
(30B)	**Jct I-580W, to Oakland**
(30A)	**Jct I-580E, to Tracy**
29	**Stoneridge Dr, Pleasanton**
Food	Black Angus Steakhouse, Planet Fresh Burrito, Plaza Market & Deli, Starbucks, Taco Bell. Togos
Lodg	Crowne Plaza, Hilton, Wyndham
Other	ATMs, Banks, Stoneridge Shopping Center
26	**Bernal Ave, Pleasanton**
Gas	Shell
Food	Jack in the Box/Shell, Lindo's Mex Rest
25	**Sunol Blvd (Both dir), Castlewood Dr (SB)**
22	**Sunol (SB)**
21	**CA 84, Calaveras Rd, Dumbarton Bridge, Sunol**
21B	**CA 84E, Livermore (NB)**
21A	**CA 84W, Calaveras Rd, Sunol (NB)**
20	**Andrade Rd (Both dir), Sheridan Rd (SB), Sunol**
Gas	Sunol Super Stop
(18)	**Weigh Station (NB)**
18	**Vargas Rd (SB)**
18B	**Sheridan Rd (NB)**
18A	**Vargas Rd (NB)**
16	**CA 238N, Mission Blvd, Hayward**
Gas	Shell, Fig Tree Gas
Food	McDonald's
Lodg	Lord Bradley's Inn
15	**Washington Blvd (Both dir), Irvington District (NB)**
Gas	Quick Stop
Food	Chinese Rest, Covent Gardens, Mission Pizza
Other	Grocery
14	**Durham Rd, to Auto Mall Pkwy, Fremont**
Gas	76, Shell
Food	Subway, Jack in the Box/Shell, Starbucks
Other	Home Depot

Personal Notes

EXIT	CALIFORNIA
12	**Mission Blvd, to I-880, Warm Springs District**
Gas	76, Valero
Food	Baskin Robbins, Burger King, Carl's Jr, Denny's, Donut House, Jack in the Box, Jamba Juice, KFC, L & L Hawaiian BBQ, Little Caesars, Starbucks, Subway, Taco Bell, Wok City Diner, Zorba's Deli, Z Pizza
Lodg	Days Inn, Econo Lodge, Extended Stay America, Motel 6, Quality Inn
Other	Albertson's, ATMs, Banks, Long's, Pharmacy, Safeway, Walgreen's
10	**Scott Creek Rd (Both dir), Warm Springs District (NB)**
9	**Jacklin Rd, Milpitas**
Gas	Shell
Food	Chez Christina, Little Table
Other	ATMs, Grocery, Save Dollar Store
8	**CA 237W, Calaveras Blvd, Central Milpitas**
Gas	76, Shell, Shell
Food	El Torito Mexican Grill, Giorgio's, Pizza, McDonald's, Red Lobster, Sizzler, Subway, Sushi Maru, Sushi Lovers Japanese Cuisine, Luu New Tung Kee Noodle House, Burger King, Chili's, Lee's Sandwiches, 909 Restaurant, Flames Coffee Shop of Milpitas, Round Table Pizza
Lodg	Days Inn, Embassy Suites, Extended Stay America, Executive Inn, Park Inn
Other	Auto Services, ATMs, Albertson's, FedEx Office, Grocery, Library, Long's, Pharmacy, Staples, Target, Tires, Walgreen's, UPS Store, Vet♥, **El Monte RV Rentals & Sales**
6	**Landess Ave, Montague Expy**
Gas	76, ArcoAmPm, Chevron's
Food	Arby's, Burger King, Coconut Grove, Cinnabon, Dave & Buster's, Fresh Choice Rest, Jack in the Box, La Salsa Fresh Mexican Grill, McDonald's, Outback Steakhouse, Starbucks, Subway, Taco Bell, Togos
Lodg	Marriott, TownePlace Suites, Sleep Inn, Sheraton
Other	ATMs, Banks, Albertson's, Dollar Plus, Firestone, Home Depot, Pharmacy, RiteAid, Target, Walgreen's, Great Mall of the Bay Area, Home Depot, Radio Shack, Vet♥

EXIT	CALIFORNIA
5	**Capitol Ave, Hostetter Rd (SB)**
Gas	Shell, Valero
Food	Carl's Jr, KFC, Popeye's, Saiko Sushi Rest, Chinese Rest, Quiznos, Starbucks
Other	ATMs, Auto Services, Banks, Costco, Midas, **Walmart SC**
5B	**Capitol Ave (NB)**
5A	**Hostetter Rd (NB)**
4	**Bereyessa Rd**
Gas	ArcoAmPm, USA, Valero
Food	Bay Leaf Cuisine of India, Denny's, Jade China Chinese Rest, Lee's Sandwiches, McDonald's, Round Table Pizza, Rose Gardens Chinese Rest,Starbucks, Taco Bell
Other	Albertson's, Auto Zone, ATMs, Banks, Century Berryessa 10 Cinema, Home Depot, Long's, Pharmacy, Safeway, Target, UPS Store, San Jose Flea Market
2B	**McKee Rd, San Jose**
Gas	76, Chevron, Shell, World Gas
Food	Burger King, Pizza Hut, Quiznos, Sizzler, Starbucks, Togos, Baskin-Robbins, McDonald's, Winchells
Med	**W: + Regional Medical Center of San Jose**
Other	ATMs, Albertson's, Auto Services, Grocery, Pharmacy, Radio Shack, Target, Tires, Towing, U-Haul, Walgreen's
2A	**CA 130, Alum Rock Ave, San Jose**
Gas	Shell◊, 76, Exxon
Food	Carl's Jr, KFC, La Costa, Subway
Med	**W: + Santa Clara Valley Medical Center**
Other	ATMs, Auto Services, Banks, CarQuest Auto Parts, Calderon New & Used Tires, CarWash/Shell, Penske Truck Rental, Towing, US Post Office, Pharmacy, Vet♥, United Rentals/LP, **Cruise America Motor home Rental & Sales**
1D	**Capitol Expressway (SB)**
Other	**S to** Reid-Hillview Airport of Santa Clara County✈
1C	**King Rd (SB), Capitol Expy (NB)**
Gas	76, 7-11, Shell
Food	Jack in the Box, Taco Bell
Med	**E: + First Health Medical Clinic of San Jose/Urgent Care** **W: + Foothills Family Medical Clinic**
Other	Capital Car Wash, Golf Course, Radio Shack, Walgreen's
1B	**US 101, S - Los Angeles, N - San Francisco (SB), Jackson Ave (NB)**
(1A)	**Jct I-280 (SB, Left Exit), King Rd (NB)**
Other	**Calderon Gas/LP**, U-Haul, Towing

PACIFIC TIME ZONE

CALIFORNIA

Begin Southbound I-680 from Jct I-280 near San Jose to Jct I-80 near Cordelia, CA.

◊= Regular Gas Stations with Diesel ▲ = RV Friendly Locations ♥= Pet Friendly Locations
Red print shows large vehicle parking / access on site or nearby Brown Print = Campgrounds / RV PARKS

EXIT	MINNESOTA
	Begin I-694 Loop around Northern/Eastern portion of metro Minneapolis-St Paul, MN.

MINNESOTA

(0) **Jct I-494S, Eden Prairie (counterclockwise ex, clockwise entr)**

NOTE: **I-694 below runs with I-94 for 8 mi. Exit #'s follow I-694.**

(27) **Jct I-94W, to St Cloud**

28 **CR 61, Hemlock Lane**
- Gas: Citgo, BP
- Food: Arby's, Chuck E Cheese's Pizza, Famous Dave's BBQ, Hops Grill, Joe's Crab Shack, Old Country Buffet, Olive Garden, Perkins, Potbelly's, Qdoba Mex Rest, Red Lobster, Starbucks,
- Lodg: Courtyard, Hampton Inn, Holiday Inn, Staybridge Suites, Select Inn
- Other: ATMs, Best Buy, Grocery, Lowe's, Tires

29 **US 169, N - Osseo, S - Hopkins**

29A **US 169S, to Hopkins**

29B **US 169N, to Osseo**

30 **Boone Ave**
- Other: Discount Tire, Home Depot

31 **CR 81**
- Gas: Super America
- Food: Wendy's
- Lodg: Ramada Inn
- Other: S: to Crystal Airport✈

33 **CR 152, Brooklyn Blvd**
- Gas: Shell, Super America, BP
- Food: Subway, Arby's, Embers Rest, Taco Bell
- Other: ATMs, Grocery, Walgreen's

34 **to TH 100, Shingle Creek Pkwy**
- Food: Denny's, Olive Garden, TGI Friday, Perkin:
- Lodg: AmericInn, Comfort Inn, Country Inn, Days Inn, Extended Stay America, La Quinta Inn♥, Motel 6, Super 8
- Other: Best Buy, Target, Tires, Auto Services

35A **TH 100S, Brookdale (counterclockwise ex, clockwise entr)**

(35B) **Jct I-94E, Downtown Minneapolis**

NOTE: **I-694 above runs with I-94 for 8 mi. Exit #'s follow I-694.**

35C **TH 252N, to TH 610**
- Gas: Holiday Station Store, Super America

36 **East River Rd, CR 1**

37 **TH 47, University Ave, to Anoka, Coon Rapids**
- Gas: Holiday Station Store, SuperAmerica, Shel
- Food: Burger King, McDonald's, Pizza
- Other: ATMs, Auto Service, Grocery, Home Depo PetSmart♥, Walgreen's

38 **TH 65, Central Ave, NE Minneapolis Cambridge**
- Gas: Holiday Station Store◈, Super America
- Food: Applebee's, Arby's, Denny's, McDonald's, Papa John's Pizza, Subway, Wendy's
- Lodg: Starlite Motel
- Other: ATMs, Auto Services, Discount Tire,Target

39 **CR 44, Silver Lake Rd**
- Gas: BP, Sinclair
- Food: McDonald's, Culver's, Wendy's

40 **CR 45, Long Lake Rd, 10th St NW**

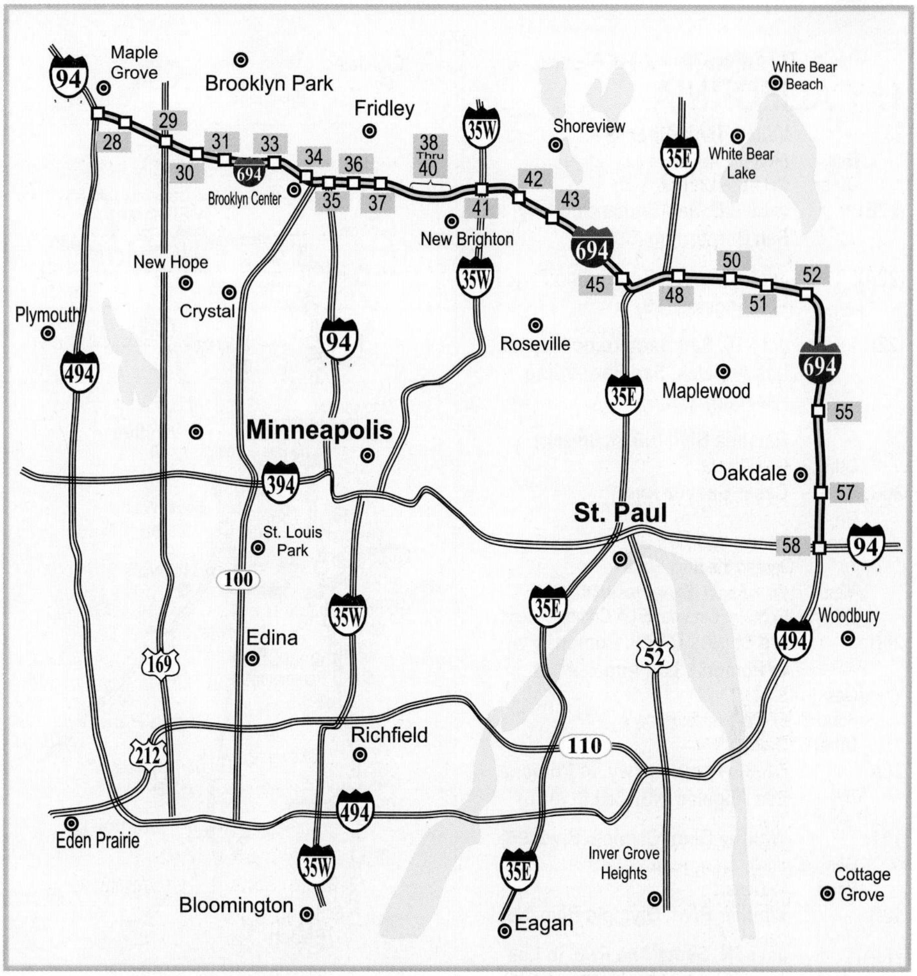

EXIT	MINNESOTA

(41) **Jct I-35W, N to Duluth, S to Downtown Minneapolis**

(41A) **Jct I-35W S, to Minneapolis**

(41B) **Jct I-35W N, to Duluth**

42B **US 10W, to Anoka (counterclockwise ex, clockwise entr)**

42A **TH 51, Snelling Ave, Hamline Ave (Left exit)**
- Gas: Shell
- Food: McDonald's
- Lodg: Country Inn, Holiday Inn

43A **CR 51, Lexington Ave**
- Gas: BP◈, Exxon, Sinclair
- Food: Burger King, Perkins, Subway, Wendy's
- Lodg: Hampton Inn, Hilton Garden Inn, Holiday Inn, Super 8
- Other: ATMs, Auto Services, Grocery, Target

43B **CR 52, Victoria St**

45 **TH 49, Rice St**
- Gas: Marathon◈x2, Phillips 66
- Food: Subway, Taco Bell, Burger King,

(46) **Jct I-35E S, US 10E, to St Paul**

(47) **Jct I-35E, N to Duluth**

48 **US 61, White Bear Lake**
- Food: Chili's, McDonald's, Olive Garden
- Lodg: Best Western

50 **CR 65, White Bear Ave**
- Gas: Gas4Less, Super America, BP, Shell

EXIT	MINNESOTA

- Food: Arby's, Applebee's, Bakers Square, Burger King, Caribou Coffee, Chili's, Denny's, IHOP, Old Country Buffet, Perkins, Red Lobster, TGI Friday, Taco Bell, Wendy's
- Lodg: Best Western
- Other: ATMs, Auto Services, Best Buy, Goodyear, Petco♥, Maplewood Mall

51 **TH 120, Century Ave**
- Gas: BP, Conoco, Super America◈, Kelly's
- Food: Starbucks, Taco Bell

52A **TH 36W, N St Paul, Stillwater**
- Gas: BP ◈
- Food: Burger King, DQ, Pizza,

52B **TH 36E, N St Paul, Stillwater**

55 **TH 5, 34th St N, Stillwater**
- Gas: Holiday Station Store◈

57 **10th St N, CR 10**
- Gas: Holiday Station Store
- Food: Burger King, KFC
- Other: ATMs, Grocery, Petco♥, Mall

(58) **Jct I-94, US 12, St Paul, Madison**

(58A) **Jct I-94W, US 12, to St Paul**

(58B) **Jct I-94E, US 12, to Madison**

(0) **Jct I-494S, End I-694 (clockwise ex, counterclockwise entr)**

MINNESOTA

Begin I-694 Loop around Northern/Eastern portion of metro Minneapolis-St Paul, MN.

◈= Regular Gas Stations with Diesel ▲ = RV Friendly Locations ♥= Pet Friendly Locations

Red print shows large vehicle parking / access on site or nearby Brown Print = Campgrounds / RV PARKS

EXIT — CALIFORNIA

Begin I-710 ByPass around Los Angeles

CALIFORNIA

23 **Valley Blvd, Alhambra**
- Gas: ArcoAmPm
- Other: Cal State Univ LA

(22B) **Jct I-10E, San Bernardino Fwy, to San Bernardino (SB)**

(22A) **Jct I-10W, San Bernardino Fwy, to Los Angeles (SB)**

(22) **Jct I-10, San Bernardino Fwy, to Los Angeles, San Bernardino, Pasadena (NB)**

21 **Ramona Blvd (NB ex, SB entr)**
- Other: Golf Course

20C **Cesar Chavez Ave**
- Gas: Star Mart, Shell
- Food: Domino's, Gallo's Grill, Channel Cafe, Jack in the Box, Pizza
- Med: W: + Santa Marta Hospital
- Other: Grocery, Cinema, E LA Comm College

20B **3rd St (NB), CA 60, Pomona Fwy, to Pomona, Los Angeles (SB)**
- Gas: Shell
- Food: El Pollo Loco, Porky's
- Other: Grocery

20A **CA 60, Pomona Fwy, to Pomona, Los Angeles (NB), 3rd St (SB)**

19 **Whittier Blvd, Olympic Blvd (SB)**
- Gas: Shell
- Food: McDonald's

18B **Whittier Blvd, Olympic Blvd (NB)**

(18A) **Jct I-5N, Santa Ana Fwy, to Los Angeles (NB Left exit, SB entr)**

(18) **Jct I-5S, to Santa Ana (SB Left exit, NB entr)**

17C **Washington Blvd, Commerce (NB)**

17B **Atlantic Blvd S (NB) Washington Blvd, Commerce (SB)**
- TStop: 4560 E Washington: CFN/Commerce Truck Stop (Scales)

17A **Atlantic Blvd N, Bandini Blvd E (NB) Atlantic Blvd, Bandini Blvd (SB)**
- FStop: 2mi W 3152 Bandini: CFN/Bandini Truck Terminal
- TStop: 2mi W 3308 Bandini: West Coast Petroleum
- Food: FastFood/WC Petro
- TWash: WC Petro
- TServ: WC Petro/Tires

15 **Florence Ave, CA 42, Bell Gardens**
- FStop: on Gage Ave: Webb Truck Service/Chevron
- Gas: Mobil
- Food: El Pollo Loco, IHOP, Jim's Grill, KFC, Little Caesars Pizza, Subway, Taco Bell
- Lodg: Ramada Inn
- Other: Grocery, RiteAid, Ralph's, Bicycle Club Casino, Florence Village MH & RV Park▲

13 **Firestone Blvd, Cudahy**
- FStop: CA 42W to 8330 Atlantic N: Cudahy Fuel Stop
- Gas: ArcoAmPm
- Food: Burger King, Denny's, McDonald's, Panda Express, Starbucks
- Lodg: GuestHouse Inn

EXIT — CALIFORNIA

- Med: E: + to Downey Reg'l Medical Center
- Other: ATMs, Auto Dealers, Grocery, Radio Shack, Sam's Club, Target

12 **Imperial Hwy, CA 90, Lynwood (NB)**
- Gas: Shell◈, Chevron◈, Shell, 76
- Food: Church's Chicken, Chinese Cook Rest, El Pollo Loco, McDonald's, Subway/Shell, Long John Silver, Panda Express, Subway Starbucks, Taco Bell/Pizza Hut
- Lodg: Cozy Motel
- Med: W: + to St Francis Medical Center
- Other: ATMs, Auto Repair, Auto Zone, Radio Shack, Tires, Walgreen's

12B **Imperial Hwy W, Lynwood (SB)**

12A **Imperial Hwy E, Lynwood (SB)**

11B **MLK Jr Blvd (SB exit & entr)**

(11A) **Jct I-105, Century Fwy, Norwalk, El Segundo (SB)**

(11) **Jct I-105, Century Fwy, Norwalk, El Segundo (NB)**

10 **Rosecrans Ave**
- FStop: E to 7201: PacPr/Cool Fuel Center
- Med: E: + to Kaiser Foundation Hospital

9B **Alondra Blvd W, Compton (SB)**

9A **Alondra Blvd E, Compton (SB)**
- Med: E: + to Suburban Medical Center

EXIT — CALIFORNIA

9 **Alondra Blvd, Compton (NB)**
- Other: Home Depot, Compton Comm College

8B **CA 91W (NB), CA 91E, Riverside (SB)**

8A **CA 91E, Riverside, Artesia Blvd (NB) CA 91W (SB)**

7B **Long Beach Blvd N (SB)**
- FStop: 6230 LB Blvd: Freeway Fuel

7A **Long Beach Blvd S (SB)**

7 **Long Beach Blvd (NB)**
- Gas: Mobil, ArcoAmPm
- Food: Jack in the Box, Taco Bell
- Lodg: Days Inn

6B **Del Amo Blvd West (NB)**

6A **Del Amo Blvd East (NB)**

6 **Del Amo Blvd (SB)**

(4) **Jct I-405, San Diego Fwy, N to Carson, S to CA 22, Seal Beach**

4 **Wardlow Rd (SB exit, NB entr)**
- Other: E to Long Beach Airport✈

3B **Willow St West**
- Gas: Chevron, Conoco
- Food: KFC, Popeye's
- Other: Auto Services, Ralph's

3A **Willow St East**
- Gas: Chevron
- Med: E: + Pacific Hospital of Long Beach, + Long Beach Memorial Medical Ctr
- Other: Walgreen's

2 **CA 1, Pacific Coast Hwy**
- FStop: 3 blks E to 1603 W PCH: Express C & T/ Chevron; 1mi W 2130 PCH: Harbor Truck Stop; 4 blks E 1670 W PCH: Long Beach Travel Center
- Gas: ArcoAmPm, Shell, Valero◈, 76, Mini Mart, Shell
- Food: Jack in the Box, McDonald's, Tom's Burgers, Winchells
- Lodg: Sea Breeze Motel

1D **Anaheim St (SB)**

1C **Shoreline Dr, Pico Ave, Downtown Long Beach, Aquarium, Piers B-E (SB Left exit, NB entr)**

1B **Pico Ave, Piers F thru J (SB)**
- FStop: Port Petroleum

1A **Harbor Scenic Dr (SB), Piers F - J, S & T, Queen Mary (SB exit, NB entr)**

1 **Anaheim St (NB)**
- FStop: E on Cowles: Speedy Fuel
- Gas: Valero, 76, Shell
- Food: Hong Kong Express, Golden Star, Jack in the Box, Larry's Pizza King, McDonald's
- Lodg: El Capitan Motor Inn, La Mirage Inn, Poolside Inn, Tower Motel, Travel King Motel, Eagle Motel, Highland Motel, Seabreeze Motel
- Med: E: + St Mary Medical Center

(0) **Port of Long Beach, Piers A - J**

CALIFORNIA

Begin I-710 ByPass around Los Angeles

◈= Regular Gas Stations with Diesel ▲ = RV Friendly Locations ♥= Pet Friendly Locations
Red print shows large vehicle parking / access on site or nearby Brown Print = Campgrounds / RV PARKS